2009

ESPN

SPORTS

ALMANAC

Gerry Brown
Michael Morrison
EDITORS

BALLANTINE BOOKS • NEW YORK

Editors

Gerry Brown

Michael Morrison

Featured Writers

Bill Simmons	Rick Reilly
Mike Greenberg	Mike Golic
Dick Vitale	Pat Forde
Tim Kurkjian	Peter Keating
Greg Garber	Ed Hinton
Ivan Maisel	Scott Burnside
Bonnie D. Ford	Dan Rafael

Published in the United States by ESPN Books, an imprint of ESPN, Inc., New York, and Ballantine Books, an imprint of The Random House Publishing Group, a division of Random House, Inc., New York.

BALLANTINE and colophon are registered trademarks of Random House, Inc.

The ESPN Books name and logo are registered trademarks of ESPN, Inc.

Comments and suggestions from readers are invited. The **ESPN Sports Almanac** does not rule on bets or wagers. Email: info@espnsportsalmanac.com

ISBN 978-0-345-51172-0

Printed in the United States of America

www.ballantinebooks.com

www.espnbooks.com

9 8 7 6 5 4 3 2 1

FIRST EDITION

2009 ESPN
SPORTS ALMANAC

With Year in Review Commentary from Analysts and Writers from ESPN The Magazine and ESPN.com:

Bill Simmons
on Pro Football
and Pro Basketball

Tim Kurkjian
on Baseball

Ivan Maisel
on College Football

Rick Reilly
on Golf

Pat Forde
on College Basketball,
Beijing Olympics, Golf
and Horse Racing

Dick Vitale
on College Basketball

Scott Burnside
on Hockey

Peter Keating
on Fantasy Sports

Mike Greenberg
on The Year in Review

Mike Golic
on The Year in Review

Graham Hays
on College Sports

Bonnie D. Ford
on International Sports

Greg Garber
on Tennis

Elizabeth Merrill
on Soccer

Mary Buckheit
on Action Sports

Ed Hinton
on Motor Sports

Dan Rafael
on Boxing

ALSO CONTRIBUTING

The Champions of 2008

Auto Racing
For all the statistics, see the Motor Sports section.

NASCAR Circuit
Daytona 500	Ryan Newman
Coca-Cola 600	Kasey Kahne
Allstate 400 at the Brickyard	Jimmie Johnson
Amp Energy 500	Tony Stewart
Chase For The Sprint Cup Leader	Jimmie Johnson
	(6248 pts. through Oct. 26)

Indy Racing League Circuit
Indianapolis 500	Scott Dixon
IndyCar Championship	Scott Dixon, 646 pts

Formula One Circuit
World Driving Leader	Lewis Hamilton
	(94 pts through Oct. 26)

Baseball
For all the statistics, see the Baseball section.

World Series	Philadelphia def. Tampa Bay, 4 games to 1
MVP	Cole Hamels, Philadelphia, P
ALCS	Tampa Bay def. Boston, 4 games to 3
NLCS	Philadelphia def. Los Angeles, 4 games to 1
All-Star Game	American League 4, National League 3 (15 innings)
MVP	J.D. Drew, AL (Boston), OF
Coll. World Series	Fresno St. def. Georgia, 2 games to 1

College Basketball
For all the statistics, see the College Basketball section.

Men's NCAA Tournament
Championship	Kansas 75, Memphis 68 (OT)
MVP	Mario Chalmers, Kansas, G

Women's NCAA Tournament
Championship	Tennessee 64, Stanford 48
MVP	Candace Parker, Tennessee, F

Pro Basketball
For all the statistics, see the Pro Basketball section.

NBA Finals	Boston def. LA Lakers, 4 games to 2
MVP	Paul Pierce, Boston, F
Eastern Final	Boston def. Detroit, 4 games to 2
Western Final	LA Lakers def. San Antonio, 4 games to 1
All-Star Game	East 134, West 128
MVP	LeBron James, East (Cleveland), F
Regular Season MVP	Kobe Bryant, LA Lakers, G
WNBA Finals	Detroit def. San Antonio, 3 games to 0
MVP	Katie Smith, Detroit, G
Regular Season MVP	Candace Parker, Los Angeles, F

College Football (2007)
For all the statistics, see the College Football section.

National Champions
AP	LSU (12-2)
USA Today Coaches'	LSU (12-2)

Major Bowls
BCS Title Game	LSU 38, Ohio St. 24
Rose	USC 49, Illinois 17
Orange	Kansas 24, Virginia Tech 21
Fiesta	West Virginia 48, Oklahoma 28
Sugar	Georgia 41, Hawaii 10
Heisman Trophy	Tim Tebow, Florida, QB

Pro Football (2007)
For all the statistics, see the Pro Football section.

Super Bowl XLII	NY Giants 17, New England 14
MVP	Eli Manning, NY Giants, QB
AFC Championship	New England 21, San Diego 12
NFC Championship	NY Giants 23, Green Bay 20 (OT)
Pro Bowl	NFC 42, AFC 30
MVP	Adrian Peterson, Minnesota, RB
ArenaBowl XXII ('08)	Philadelphia 59, San Jose 56
CFL Grey Cup	Saskatchewan 23, Winnipeg 19

Golf
For all the statistics, see the Golf section.

Men's Major Championships
Masters	Trevor Immelman
U.S. Open	Tiger Woods
British Open	Padraig Harrington
PGA Championship	Padraig Harrington

Champions (Seniors) Major Championships
The Tradition	Fred Funk
Senior PGA Championship	Jay Haas
U.S. Senior Open	Eduardo Romero
Senior Players Championship	D.A. Weibring
Senior British Open	Bruce Vaughan

Women's Major Championships
Kraft Nabisco Championship	Lorena Ochoa
LPGA Championship	Yani Tseng
U.S. Women's Open	Inbee Park
Women's British Open	Ji-Yai Shin

National Team Competition
Ryder Cup	United States 16½, Europe 11½

Hockey
For all the statistics, see the Hockey section.

Stanley Cup	Detroit def. Pittsburgh, 4 games to 2
MVP	Henrik Zetterberg, Detroit, LW
Eastern Final	Pittsburgh def. Philadelphia, 4 games to 1
Western Final	Detroit def. Dallas, 4 games to 2
All-Star Game	East 8, West 7
MVP	Eric Staal, East (Carolina), F

Horse Racing
For all the statistics, see the Horse Racing section.

Triple Crown Champions
Kentucky Derby	Big Brown (Kent Desormeaux)
Preakness Stakes	Big Brown (Kent Desormeaux)
Belmont Stakes	Da'Tara (Alan Garcia)

Harness Racing
Hambletonian	Deweycheatumnhowe (Ray Schnittker)
Little Brown Jug	Shadow Play (David Miller)

Olympics
For more, see the Beijing Olympics sections.

Most Golds (Individual)	Michael Phelps, USA, 8
Most Golds (Country)	China, 51
Most Overall Medals (Country)	USA, 110

Soccer
For all the statistics, see the Soccer section.

MLS Cup 2007	Houston 2, New England 1
MVP	Dwayne De Rosario, Houston, MF

Tennis
For all the statistics, see the Tennis section.

Men's Grand Slam Championships
Australian Open	Novak Djokovic
French Open	Rafael Nadal
Wimbledon	Rafael Nadal
U.S. Open	Roger Federer

Women's Grand Slam Championships
Australian Open	Maria Sharapova
French Open	Ana Ivanovic
Wimbledon	Venus Williams
U.S. Open	Serena Williams

Miscellaneous Champions
For more, see the Miscellaneous & Int'l Sports sections.

Little League World Series	Waipahu, Hawaii
Tour de France	Carlos Sastre (Spain)
Iditarod	Lance Mackey
Boston Marathon	Men's: Robert Cheruiyot (Kenya)
	Women's: Dire Tune (Ethiopia)
Bassmasters Classic	Alton Jones

CONTENTS

6

CONTENTS

EDITORS' NOTE

SPORTS HAS ALWAYS BEEN A RELIABLE DISTRACTION FROM LIFE'S TROUBLES.

And, boy, did we need it this year.

With an economic meltdown dominating the headlines, turning to the sports pages of the local newspaper has been even more pleasurable than usual — even a necessary mental health break, at times.

From many perspectives 2008 was one of the best sports years in history, and you'll find a complete recap of the year on the pages to follow. As much as it pains two New England Patriots fans to admit it (and it pains...a lot), the Super Bowl was truly an exciting game. And that was only the beginning. Other highlights included a fun NCAA tournament with an overtime finish, an old-school NBA Finals (where, for us, the Celtics made up somewhat for the Patriots' shortcomings), a one-legged Tiger doing what he does best, historic performances by Michael Phelps and Usain Bolt, among others, at the Summer Olympics, an unexpected rise by the Rays, and the first Phillies championship in almost three decades. It was all fun to watch...and it all came at just the right time.

We're not usually the kind of people who play favorites, but we need to single out a few of ours for their invaluable help this year: Chris Raymond, John Glenn, Sandy DeShong, Steve Wulf, John Hassan, Patrick Stiegman, Keith Jackson, Shannon Cross, Keith Hawkins, Liam Chapman and Howie Schwab at ESPN, Kevin O'Sullivan at AP Images, Barbara Zidovsky of Nielsen Media Research, Rick Sommers at Command Web and Rob Conte at SCI.

Founding Editor and boarding house operator Mike Meserole continues to support the cause. Also, we could never match their efforts on the home front and our wives Lisa and Lori have carried major water once again this year. We owe them our gratitude and an afternoon at the mall. Although maybe with what's been happening with the economy, we'd better make that the outlets.

Here's hoping for an even greater 2009...

Gerry Brown
Michael Morrison
October 30, 2008

Major League Cities & Teams

As of Oct. 31, 2008, there were 134 major league teams playing or scheduled to play baseball, men's basketball, NFL football, hockey and soccer in 54 cities in the United States and Canada. Listed below are the cities and the teams that play there.

Anaheim
AL   Los Angeles Angels of Anaheim
NHL   Ducks

Atlanta
NL   Braves   NFL   Falcons
NBA   Hawks   NHL   Thrashers

Baltimore
AL   Orioles   NFL   Ravens

Boston
AL   Red Sox
NBA   Celtics
NFL   N.E. Patriots (Foxboro)
NHL   Bruins
MLS   N.E. Revolution (Foxboro)

Buffalo
NFL   Bills (Orchard Park)
NHL   Sabres

Calgary
NHL   Flames

Charlotte
NBA   Bobcats
NFL   Carolina Panthers

Chicago
AL   White Sox
NL   Cubs
NBA   Bulls
NFL   Bears
NHL   Blackhawks
MLS   Fire (Bridgeview)

Cincinnati
NL   Reds   NFL   Bengals

Cleveland
AL   Indians   NBA   Cavaliers
NFL   Browns

Columbus
NHL   Blue Jackets
MLS   Crew

Dallas
AL   Texas Rangers (Arlington)
NBA   Mavericks
NFL   Cowboys (Irving)
NHL   Stars
MLS   FC Dallas (Frisco)

Denver
NL   Colorado Rockies
NBA   Nuggets
NFL   Broncos
NHL   Colorado Avalanche
MLS   Colo. Rapids (Commerce City)

Detroit
AL   Tigers
NBA   Pistons (Auburn Hills)
NFL   Lions
NHL   Red Wings

East Rutherford
NBA   New Jersey Nets
NFL   New York Giants
NFL   New York Jets
MLS   Red Bull New York

Edmonton
NHL   Oilers

Green Bay
NFL   Packers

Houston
NL   Astros
NBA   Rockets
NFL   Texans
MLS   Dynamo

Indianapolis
NBA   Indiana Pacers
NFL   Colts

Jacksonville
NFL   Jaguars

Kansas City
AL   Royals
NFL   Chiefs
MLS   Wizards

Los Angeles
NL   Dodgers
NBA   Clippers
NBA   Lakers
NHL   Kings
MLS   Galaxy (Carson)
MLS   Club Chivas USA (Carson)

Memphis
NBA   Grizzlies

Miami
NL   Florida Marlins
NBA   Heat
NFL   Dolphins
NHL   Florida Panthers (Sunrise)

Milwaukee
NL   Brewers
NBA   Bucks

Minneapolis
AL   Minnesota Twins
NBA   Minnesota Timberwolves
NFL   Minnesota Vikings

Montreal
NHL   Canadiens

Nashville
NFL   Tennessee Titans
NHL   Predators

New Orleans
NBA   New Orleans Hornets
NFL   New Orleans Saints

New York
AL   Yankees
NL   Mets (Flushing)
NBA   Knicks
NHL   Rangers
NHL   Islanders (Uniondale)

Newark
NHL   New Jersey Devils

Oakland
AL   Athletics
NBA   Golden St. Warriors
NFL   Raiders

Oklahoma City
NBA   Thunder

Orlando
NBA   Magic

Ottawa
NHL   Senators (Kanata)

Philadelphia
NL   Phillies
NBA   76ers
NFL   Eagles
NHL   Flyers

Phoenix
NL   Arizona Diamondbacks
NBA   Suns
NFL   Arizona Cardinals (Glendale)
NHL   Coyotes (Glendale)

Pittsburgh
NL   Pirates
NFL   Steelers
NHL   Penguins

Portland
NBA   Trail Blazers

Raleigh
NHL   Carolina Hurricanes

Sacramento
NBA   Kings

St. Louis
NL   Cardinals
NFL   Rams
NHL   Blues

St. Paul
NHL   Minnesota Wild

Salt Lake City
NBA   Utah Jazz
MLS   Real Salt Lake

San Antonio
NBA   Spurs
NFL   New Orleans Saints

San Diego
NL   Padres
NFL   Chargers

San Francisco
NL   Giants
NFL   49ers

San Jose
NHL   Sharks

Seattle
AL   Mariners
NFL   Seahawks

Tampa
AL   T.B. Rays (St. Petersburg)
NFL   T.B. Buccaneers
NHL   T.B. Lightning

Toronto
AL   Blue Jays
NBA   Raptors
NHL   Maple Leafs
MLS   Toronto FC

Vancouver
NHL   Canucks

Washington
NL   Nationals
NBA   Wizards
NFL   Redskins (Raljon, Md.)
NHL   Capitals
MLS   D.C. United

Sen. Barack Obama displays a customized Michigan State jersey he got on a campaign stop in 2008.

THE YEAR IN REVIEW

We sat down with ESPN Radio's Mike Golic & Mike Greenberg to get them to weigh in on some of the biggest stories and best performers of the year in sports.

Almanac: A year ago when we did this we were coming off a year that was kind of lackluster. We were dealing with the aftermaths of the Michael Vick dogfighting scandal and the cloud hovering over the NBA with the Tim Donaghy story. It seemed like in 2008 things were a lot more feel-good. We had some familiar faces, some surprises and of course that historic performance over in Beijing.

Golic

Greenie

Greenie: "If you are a sports fan, I don't know that you could have asked for much more than you got in 2008. Look at all the things that you got to see:

Maybe the best Super Bowl ever played, with an incredibly dramatic finish when the New York Giants shocked just about everyone and denied the New England Patriots an undefeated season. In the NBA you got your dream Finals with Los Angeles Lakers and Boston Celtics. In the NHL you got a marquee matchup with the Detroit Red Wings and the Sidney Crosby-led Pittsburgh Penguins. In tennis, you had the best Wimbledon final ever. In golf we had Tiger Woods winning the U.S. Open in perhaps the most dramatic fashion possible when he could barely walk the course at Torrey Pines but won a 19-hole playoff in probably

Mike Golic & Mike Greenberg can be heard weekday mornings from 6 A.M. to 10 A.M. ET on ESPN Radio's **Mike & Mike in the Morning.**

AP Images

Even **Michael Phelps** can hardly believe the sports year that was in 2008. It was almost too good to be true, especially for Phelps.

the most entertaining day of viewing all year long. In baseball, we had one of the great underdog stories of all-time unfold with the run the Tampa Bay Rays put together before the Phillies got their first World Series championship in nearly 30 seasons.

And this goes on and on...

In the Olympics, you had Michael Phelps do something that had never been done before when he broke Mark Spitz's record. In the NCAA men's basketball championship, Kansas beat Memphis in overtime.

So, frankly, if you are not satisfied with this year then we are never going to make you happy. It was, no doubt, the greatest year in sports that I can ever remember.

Golic: "Oh my God. It was one of the greatest years we've ever had. The old school NBA Finals was great. The Super Bowl. The Rays and all of it. But the cherry on top of it all for me was the Olympics. I was a competitive swimmer growing up and my daughter

Mike & MIKE in the morning

Legendary pitcher **Roger Clemens** showed that he's still a crafty right-hander.

ROGER CLEMENS JOINS THE RANKS OF PLAYERS TAINTED BY STEROID USE.

Greenie: "I have a hard time mustering up any sympathy for Roger Clemens. He goes on the list of players who were not who we thought they were. The reason we make heroes out of athletes is because we think we know that they are doing something special. And when it turns out that something else is going on, then we realize they really were never worthy of all the adulation in the first place."

Golic: "This was a tough story because I think everyone wanted to give Roger Clemens the benefit of the doubt. I always wondered after Barry Bonds, how people would react the next time a big name became tied to steroids. Everybody was ready to skewer Barry Bonds and say he was guilty, and everybody was ready to say Clemens was innocent. I think that's because most people just flat out don't like Bonds. And I think most of us liked Clemens. So I think it was unbelievably disheartening to see him get caught up in this mess — so that it seems now that he was a steroid user and we can lump him in with all the others that did it."

is a swimmer now. And so watching what went on with Michael Phelps and the U.S. swim team was just fantastic. It was appointment television in my house and so much fun to watch. That was the best thing about one of the best years in a long time."

Almanac: *All that being said, we did have to confront some unfortunate apparent truths about Roger Clemens...*

BIG BROWN FALLS SHORT IN HIS BID FOR THE TRIPLE CROWN

Almanac: *It seems like it happens quite a bit these days — a horse winning the first two legs of the Triple Crown before failing at the Belmont, but this year seemed different with Big Brown. It looked like it was really going to happen for the first time since 1978...*

Greenie: "I think the fact that Big Brown fell short of the Triple Crown isn't the worst thing in the world for horse racing. The Belmont and the sport as a whole drew the attention that Big Brown provided by winning the Derby and the Preakness. I think now that it has been 30 years makes it even more special — as long as a horse can challenge again for it sometime soon.

AP Images

Kent Desormeaux pulled up **Big Brown** (right) at the 2008 Belmont Stakes.

As a sports fan all of my life, but only a casual horse racing fan, I had never heard the sheer volume of discussion about exactly how humane horse racing is until the tragic death of filly Eight Belles took place at the Kentucky Derby. Honestly it had never really occurred to me. But for the first time that argument was made by people with legitimate credentials whom I respected, that changes could and should be made to the sport to improve the treatment of the horses — and I'm all in favor of that."

Golic: "What a stunner that was at the Belmont. It affirms just how hard it is to win a Triple Crown. Here was a horse that looked unbeatable, but once again couldn't get it done. Obviously with animals you can't ask them how they are feeling before a big race, but this seemed as automatic as you can get. But it was clearly otherwise.

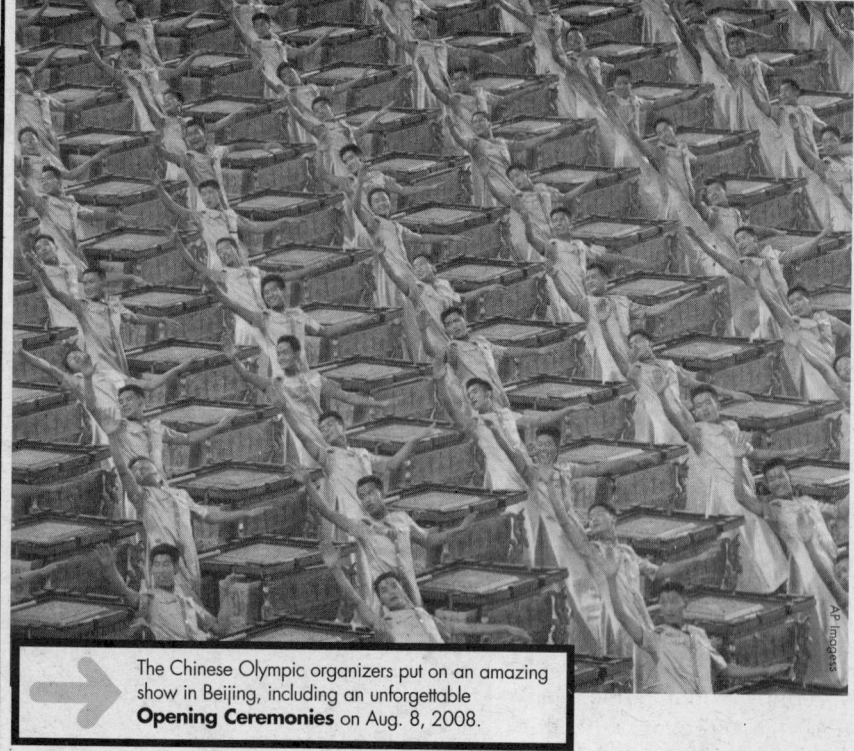

The Chinese Olympic organizers put on an amazing show in Beijing, including an unforgettable **Opening Ceremonies** on Aug. 8, 2008.

With Eight Belles, you can only ask that something good come from the bad situation. These horses are treated very well but the steroids can apparently cause them to break down and if they can get rid of the steroids in racing I think it would be a real positive to come from a real negative.

Almanac: *The Beijing Games were wrapped in controversy leading up to the Olympics between the fears of smog and the talk of human rights abuses?*

BEIJING OLYMPICS DELIVERED IN A BIG WAY

Golic: "What disheartened me early was people trying to use the athletes as pawns in bigger political statements. These athletes don't really have anything to do with politics. They are just busting their humps. The two big stars of the Games for me were Michael Phelps and Usain Bolt. What Phelps was chasing was so big and the races were so extraordinarily competitive. That finish of that 100 fly was amazing. I don't think any of us thought he could pull off that comeback. But obviously, electronic timing doesn't lie.

Bolt was beyond impressive. I remember hardly noticing the other runners during the introductions at each race because you knew they didn't have a chance. It was insane Usain. I was also a big fan of the beach volleyball. But I watch everything. I watch the synchronized diving. I am an Olympics freak."

Greenie: "I think it was a wonderful Olympics. The Games were as good as they've been in many, many years. Not only did we have the story of Michael Phelps, which was a once-in-a-lifetime story, but the men's basketball team did me proud for the first time since 1988, when a team of college kids went over and did the best they could, but got beat fair and square. Even in 1992 when the Dream Team won it with class in Barcelona, it wasn't that impressive to me. But after 2000 and especially 2004, both on the court and the team's general attitude — to see this team go to Beijing and take it seriously and genuinely put team and country ahead of personal glory made me proud in a way that I didn't think

AP Images

Jamaican sprinter **Usain Bolt** was only a blur to the competition on his way to three track and field gold medals at the Beijing Summer Games.

The **Boston Celtics** raised yet another banner to the rafters in 2008.

Pierce, Ray Allen and Kevin Garnett could so easily put aside their personal goals for the betterment of the team was special. And that it paid off with a championship was just great. I've always been a big fan of Garnett. I've just loved the way he plays so hard and at the same time so unselfishly.

That they were matched up against the Lakers and the best player in the game today — Kobe Bryant — was an added bonus. We all know his goal was to win a title without Shaq. He wants to be the Batman and maybe Pau Gasol can be the Robin this time around. But it was good to see the Celtics win with such a true team concept."

Greenie: "There is something that makes you feel that all is right in the world when the Celtics and Lakers are playing in the NBA Finals. For those of us old enough to remember the 1980's, we do so fondly because that was pro basketball at its very best. This year certainly brought back good memories of that. And to see such a classy group in Boston, including Kevin Garnett who has to be the most unselfish superstar in sports, get their rings was good to see. It was terrific. The Lakers had a great year and they are set up for a long run going forward."

was possible in the Olympics any more."

BOSTON CELTICS WIN THEIR 17TH NBA TITLE

Almanac: *The NBA Finals seemed to have a bit of a throw-back feel to them this year with a match-up of old foes in the Boston Celtics and Los Angeles Lakers...*

Golic: "There was a throwback element to be sure but it was the team concept of these Celtics that was so great to see. That Paul

ONE GIANT UPSET IN THE SUPER BOWL

Almanac: *The Patriots were on the way to 19-0 and the title of Best. Team. Ever. What happened in the Super Bowl?*

Greenie:

"Probably the best Super Bowl ever played and after Super Bowl III probably the most significant. I thought the Patriots were the best team I had ever seen and had they won that game, that's how they would have always been remembered, as the greatest team of all-time. To see them stopped by that team and in that fashion was incredibly dramatic. "

Golic: "Stunning. That was the best word for me to describe what happened there. If any, very few people picked the Giants to win this one. But the line 'any given Sunday' exists for a reason and it shows how difficult it is to go undefeated and finish it off. It's harder than we thought because we all assumed it was a done deal. It was about as automatic as Big Brown was at the Belmont."

AP Images

→ **Michael Strahan** and the Giants kept **Tom Brady** and the Patriots from history.

LSU WINS BCS

Almanac: *LSU won the BCS title but it seems like people keep wanting to talk about Ohio State's failure in big games...*

Greenie: "Like the Buffalo Bills run in the 90's, Ohio State's back-to-back appearances in the national championship game was impressive despite never taking the title. Every other team in America, but two (LSU and Florida), would have changed places with Ohio State in the blink of an eye.

Kansas was the best team in the tournament, but was there any doubt that Davidson's **Stephen Curry** was the best player?

which one are you taking?!? Everyone, be honest with yourself! You know you'd pick the two appearances and losses."

KANSAS WINS NATIONAL TITLE

Almanac: Kansas and Bill Self got over the top and won the national championship in 2008...

Greenie: "I felt good for Bill Self. He's been a good coach for many years and I think sometimes it can be unfair how we judge coaches in college basketball. You can have one bad night and you are viewed as a choker.

Certainly getting to the Final Four — and winning it— that puts you in a different category. The other story of the tournament was Stephen Curry, who was just unbelievable. It was the best performance in the tournament that I can remember for years and years."

And let's not forget about what LSU did this year either. Les Miles has built an impressive program in Baton Rouge. Any time an SEC team can survive and advance, it's an accomplishment."

Golic: "I always look at the other side of the coin. You send me to two straight national championships and I lose, yes, I'd be disappointed but I'd take it. If your resume says that you went to the national title game two of your four years in college and lost, or you didn't get to any title games,

Golic: "What Stephen Curry did this year is what the NCAA tournament is all about to me. When a team like George Mason a few years back or Valparaiso a few years before that steps up, or an individual that the nation has been largely unaware of like Curry can star in the national spotlight of the tournament, I think it's great. The Final Four is naturally about the best teams in the country but the rest of the tournament has room for fun stories. That's why I think it's greatest showcase in sports.

The Kansas-Memphis game was just amazing. It's so great too because after the entire season and tournament when you get to the national championship game you hope that it's not a clunker and obviously this year we had anything but that with the overtime thriller between Memphis and Kansas."

A HOBBLED TIGER WINS A U.S. OPEN PLAYOFF

Almanac: *Tiger had a gutsy performance at the U.S. Open, so did Rocco Mediate for that matter, who took him to his limits and maybe beyond...*

Golic: "What are you going to say? That was pure determination. You don't get off days in a golf tournament. You don't play one match on Sunday and then take the week off to rest if you are hurt. You have to go four days in a row, sometimes, five. So it's something you have to deal with over a period of time, even off the course. Yes. It hurts when he's playing but even when he's not, he needs to keep it from swelling if possible.

Tiger Woods was down but not out at Torrey Pines and won his third U.S. Open in 2008.

Does it calm down when he's not playing? He doesn't have a chance to practice. He may need to ice it.

A knee injury is not the typical injury you think of when you think of golf either. You tend to worry more about back issues but he gutted it out and got his 14th major championship. Wow."

Greenie: "If you asked me to pick the most memorable day of 2008 for me as a sports fan it would be that Monday at the U.S. Open. Here were had in Rocco

Spain's **Rafael Nadal** and Switzerland's Roger Federer put on a show for the ages in 2008.

Mediate, Rocky Balboa personified on a golf course slugging it out with the best player of all-time. The two of them going toe-to-toe. Seventy-two holes weren't enough. Ninety holes weren't enough! More than the Super Bowl or anything else, that Monday at Torrey Pines was the most fulfilling day of the year for me."

AN INSTANT CLASSIC AT WIMBLEDON

Almanac: *The Wimbledon men's singles final was so great* with that epic five-set win by Rafael Nadal. Has Nadal finally started to out-shine Roger Federer, who has been the dominant force in the sport for so many years?

Greenie: "What Roger Federer and Rafael Nadal did in the final at Wimbledon was — they elevated the sport to a level it had not reached in 30 years. I remember very vividly as a kid watching Bjorn Borg and John McEnroe battling it out at Wimbledon. I didn't think it would ever get back to that level of play or competition. It was right there with Borg and McEnroe. It was thrilling, and it was the best day tennis has had in a really long time."

Golic: "I, too, was a big fan of tennis back in the old days with not only guys like Borg and McEnroe but also Jimmy Connors and Ivan Lendl. But this was certainly a reminder of how great the sport can be. I don't watch tennis as much these days but that got me excited, for a little while anyway. When those guys (Nadal and Federer) face off, its must-see TV but the only problem is that it doesn't always happen and you have to go through all the preliminaries to get there. And if they don't both get there, it's a lot less watchable. It's kind of like the Tiger effect in golf."

TAMPA BAY RAYS

Almanac: How about those Tampa Bay Rays and the amazing season they put together...

Greenie: "The greatest accomplishment for the Tampa Bay Rays in 2008 was winning the American League East. The baseball season is a marathon and the fact that they, with an entire payroll less than the left-side of the Yankees infield, could beat the Yankees, the Blue Jays and the Red Sox is amazing. It was the greatest Cinderella story in baseball history."

Golic: "Everyone was saying this could have been the best story in team sports history. The only comparison for it would have been the U.S. 'Miracle on Ice' team from the 1980 Winter Olympics at Lake Placid. Obviously they fell a little short but you can't show me one person that called this one. You kept thinking they were going to drop off during the course of the regular season, but they never did. They are a young team. You just hope they can keep the team together for a while and get some more cracks at it.

Tampa Bay skipper **Joe Maddon** led the Rays all the way to the World Series.

It was refreshing to see, even if it poked holes in everyone's argument that you need a salary floor — if not a salary cap — in Major League Baseball. But it does show that if you build a team correctly, and make smart decisions from the top of the organization to the bottom, it is possible to compete with the big money clubs like the Yankees, Red Sox and Angels. Hopefully some other smaller-market teams will follow their lead."

Captain **Paul Azinger** (left), **Boo Weekley** and the rest of the U.S. Ryder Cup team had reason to celebrate after dethroning the Europeans in September at Valhalla.

RYDER CUP

Almanac: *Despite missing the best player in the world, the United States team was finally able to win back the Ryder Cup for the first time since they triumphed at Brookline in 1999. Is it possible that Tiger's absence actually spurred the Americans on to be better than they are?*

Greenie: "That's possible but I don't think you can ever say they were better without Tiger than they would be with him.

The glimpse of golf that we got with the loss of Tiger Woods was a chilling one. I am a golf fan but the only time I really got back into it after Tiger's departure with the knee injury was during the Ryder Cup."

Golic: "The Ryder Cup is interesting and the American team this year seemed relaxed and I think without Tiger the pressure was off in some way. Considering their recent history in the event and the fact that Tiger wasn't there, they certainly were not expected to win. But they did anyway. Good stuff."

EXTRA POINTS

2007 / 2008 YEAR IN REVIEW

Construction workers unearth the **David Ortiz jersey** that was buried underneath the new Yankee Stadium by another worker (and Red Sox fan) looking to jinx the Yankees.

EXTRA POINTS

A look back at some of the more offbeat sports moments, quotes and personalities from the past year.

Seems Like Old Times

Still-fiery John McEnroe got thrown out of his match against MaliVai Washington at the Hall of Fame Champions Cup for arguing a line call. McEnroe cursed, screamed at the chair umpire, and responded to increasing booing from the fans with an obscene gesture to the entire crowd.

Rose Goes In The Front

Growing a cheesy 70's mustache is one thing, but when the *Daily News* reported that Yankees first baseman Jason Giambi sometimes wears a gold thong under his uniform pants to help break out of a slump, many fans squirmed. "You've got to be pretty confident in yourself to let that one out," said former pitcher David Cone.

Orlovsky's Tough Start

Detroit Lions quarterback Dan Orlovsky had a memorable first NFL start, to say the least. On 3rd-and-10 from his own one-yard line in the first quarter against the Vikings, he took the snap, rolled right and did his best to avoid a sack by the pursuing Jared Allen. And then the whistle blew. Orlovsky had apparently lost his bearing, and run right out of the back of the endzone. Oops. The Vikings went up, 2-0, and ended up winning the game, 12-10.

"I just wasn't going to sit back there and try to hold the ball and be stupid and give them points. When they started blowing the whistle, I was like, 'Did we false start or something?' Then I looked and I was like, 'You are an idiot.'

AP Images

Cuba's **Angel Valodia Matos**, left, kicks match referee Chakir Chelbat of Sweden in the face during his bronze medal match against Kazakhstan's Arman Chilmanov in the men's taekwondo +80 kilogram class at the Beijing Olympics.

Hands As Soft As A Baby's...

Boxer Vitali Klitschko let everyone know his secret for helping his sore hands recover after a fight — he wraps them with his son's wet diapers. "Baby wee is good because it's pure, doesn't contain toxins and does-n't smell," the 37-year old boxer told Bild after winning the WBC title.

"I wrap nappies filled with my three-year-old son Max's wee around my fists. [They] hold the liquid and the swelling stays down."

Speed Freaks

"I was driving fast, that's it. It's got 200 on the dashboard. I was going 101." — LeBron James, who was stopped for speeding in his Mercedes in mid-January.

Formula One driver Lewis Hamilton had his license suspended in France after he was clocked driving 123 mph in his Mercedes in December, 2007.

AP/Wide World Photos

Justin Timberlake, center, hosted the 16th annual ESPY Awards at the Nokia Theater in Los Angeles on July 16. Here he salutes the Celtics' win over the Lakers in the NBA Finals.

Misplaced Swoosh

A brand new statue of former football star Ernie Davis was unveiled on the campus of Syracuse in late September. Davis was depicted with his familiar No. 44 jersey, a helmet (with a modern facemask)...and Nike cleats. The problem is, Nike wasn't around when Davis led Syracuse to the national title in 1959 and won the Heisman two years later. In October, changes to the helmet were made and the statue was de-cleated.

Junior Mint, Sort Of

Though no one would say why, Ken Griffey Jr. owed teammate Josh Fogg $1,500 and paid his debt — in pennies, 150,000 to be exact. Fogg arrived at the clubhouse on May 14 and was greeted with 60 boxes in his locker, each weighing 16 pounds and containing $25 in pennies. "Basically, it's like having 60 bowling balls in your locker, only with no holes to pick them up with," Griffey said.

There's ONLY An "I" In This Team

Bonnie Richardson of Rochelle (Texas) High School won the Class 1A Track & Field team championship — all by herself. On Day 1, she won the high jump (5 feet, 5 inches), placed second in the long jump (18-7) and was third in the discus (121-0). The next day, she won the 200 meters in 25.03 seconds and finished second (12.19) in the 100 meters. She earned a total of 42 team points to edge team runner-up Chilton (36).

Bonnie Richardson

AP Images

Packers Backer

Twelve-year-old Packers fan David Withhoft received a No. 4 Brett Favre jersey as a Christmas gift in 2003. And he wore it EVERY DAY, for 1,581 consecutive days until he finally retired it on April 23, 2008. It could have been worse. His mother washed it every other day and mended it whenever it was needed. She was thrilled, however, when he made the decision to take it off. "I'd like to see how he looks in red," she said.

On the flip side

Mathew Kowald was upset that his 7-year-old son wouldn't wear a Packers jersey during the team's playoff victory in January. So he took matters into his own hands, restraining the boy and taping the jersey onto him. He was cited for disorderly conduct and fined $186. He claimed it was all in good fun.

"The women are still coming out in flocks. My wife is not happy about it, but I still have it." – Oscar De La Hoya, discussing the large group of female admirers that show up to his fights...and his hotels.

Dog-Gone it!

Red Sox closer Jonathan Papelbon can't come up with the ball used for the final out of the 2007 World Series, given to him after the clinching game by catcher Jason Varitek. But he's got a good excuse: his dog ate it. "He plays with baseballs like they are his toys," Papelbon said. "He jumped up one day on the counter and snatched it...he tore that thing to pieces...I'll keep what's left of it."

Dog-Gone it! (Part Two)

Three suspicious packages left along the first-base side of Citizens Bank Park were detonated by a bomb squad before the Phillies-Braves game on September 24. The team later announced that "a commercial shoot was conducted at the park, during which hot dogs heavily wrapped in white packaging and duct tape were used as projectiles by the Phanatic's hot dog launcher. Three of those projectiles were inadvertently left behind on a light post at our First-Base gate."

> "God has gifted me with incredible hand speed. What else am I supposed to do but fight? There ain't no hand-racing competitions."
>
> — Roy Jones Jr., explaining one of his reasons for becoming a boxer.

Man vs. Hawk

Nationwide Tour golfer Tripp Isenhour reportedly became angry while filming an instructional video on Dec. 12 in Orlando, when a squawking red-shouldered hawk continued to interrupt his filming. He got about 300 yards away from the bird and started hitting balls at it to scare it away, but the bird didn't flinch. Minutes later, the hawk moved to within about 75 yards and Isenhour started firing away again. This time he was successful. The bird, which is protected as a migratory species, fell to the ground bleeding from both nostrils.

"As soon as this happened, I was mortified and extremely upset and continue to be upset," Isenhour said. "I want to let everyone know there was neither any malice nor deliberate intent whatsoever to hit or harm the hawk. I was trying to simply scare it into flying away."

Hawk vs. Girl

Eight-grader Alexa Rodriguez, 13, (yes, you read that right), was attacked by a red-tailed hawk while she toured Fenway Park in Boston with her school group.

She was taken to a local hospital and treated for scratches on her scalp, but was otherwise unharmed. The hawk had a nest with an egg in one of Fenway's many overhangs.

AP Images

Cincinnati Bengals wide receiver **Chad Ocho Cinco**, who recently had his name legally changed from Chad Johnson, warms up before the start of a game on September 7. The NFL issued a statement informing the Bengals that while the league recognized the legal name change, "certain issues remain to be resolved before Ocho Cinco will be permitted to wear his new name on his jersey.

Stanley Cup upside down!

The NHL procured British rockers Def Leppard to perform an opening-day show in Detroit to help celebrate the Red Wings' title and help kick off the 2008-09 season (apparently there are no good rock bands from Detroit to choose from). Frontman Joe Elliott held the Stanley Cup high over his head during the show, and placed it back down on a table – upside down. Fury ensued. And Elliott kind of, sort of apologized.

"I will, as always, take full responsibility for what happened because I have big pucks... the practice run the day before with a coffeemaker went swimmingly because it, like every other sporting cup I've ever seen, was wider at the top than the base... Like most of my fellow Brits, I'd never seen it (Stanley Cup) before until it was handed to me sideways, by which time I had a 50/50 chance of getting it right. Whoops."

2008 Heads Of The Class

Pot Head

Patriots running back Kevin Faulk missed the team's opening game against the Kansas City Chiefs for violating the league's substance abuse policy after being busted for possession of marijuana at a Li'l Wayne concert at the Cajundome in February. Some in New England believe that if Faulk had played in that game, he would have been blocking Chiefs' safety Bernard Pollard instead of teammate Sammy Morris. And Tom Brady never would have been hurt. As always, drugs are bad.

Waffle Head

In November 2007, with the New England Patriots well on their way to a 16-0 regular season, former Miami Dolphins coach Don Shula, who headed the perfect Dolphin team in 1972, claimed the Patriots' season should have an asterisk next to it, if the Patriots went undefeated.

"The Spygate thing has diminished what they've accomplished," he said. "You would hate to have that attached to your accomplishments. They've got it." Two months later, he changed his tune: "There shouldn't be an asterisk to it."

Knuckle Head

Mesa State's offensive lineman Trevor Wikre had a choice to make after being injured in practice in late September — give up a pinkie or give up the rest of your football season. For Wikre, the choice was easy. Pinkie gone. Game on. "I said, 'cut if off.' It wasn't a hard choice," he said. "A pinkie is not that bad in my mind."

Big Head

Stephon Marbury —

"Don't get me wrong, I love Jason Kidd, he is a great point guard. [But] how am I comparing myself to him when I think I'm the best point guard to play basketball? That makes no sense. I can't compare myself to somebody when I already think I'm the best. I'm telling you what it is. I know I'm the best point guard in the NBA.".

Air Heads

Players warming up before the start of the Duke-James Madison football game in late August were surprised to see two men parachuting into the stadium, holding a football. The parachuters made a clean landing...they just hit the wrong field. They were supposed to land at North Carolina's opening game eight miles away.

Dead Head

Elaine Fulps, 60, won a sweet prize at the Grand Prairie (Texas) AirHogs minor league baseball game in June, although it's one she hopes she won't be cashing in anytime soon. Fulps is the lucky recipient of a $10,000 paid funeral from Oak Grove Memorial Gardens. Fulps, who was wearing a neck brace, said she's had about 20 surgeries for a range of medical problems. "I almost croaked many times," she said.

Bone Heads

The high school baseball team from Stephens County, Georgia pulled a fast one on umpire Jeff Scott. In the fourth inning of a 13-1 loss, catcher Matt Hill appeared to miss a high fast ball from pitcher Cody Martin on purpose, letting the ball hit Scott in the mask. Scott had called out Martin's brother, Ethan, on strikes the inning before. The video became an instant YouTube hit.

Hot Head

Since breaking the record for all-time ejections by a major league manager in 2007, Atlanta Braves skipper Bobby Cox has steadily added to his total and now leads all managers with 143 times given the heave-ho.

"I See the" Head

Cynthia Rodriguez, wife of Alex Rodriguez divulged that the three-time Major League baseball MVP passed out during the birth of his first daughter. "The one nurse had a cold cloth on his head," she said on an episode of the YES Network's *YESterdays*.

"The other nurse had the blood pressure on his arm. And my mother was like rubbing his back. And he is passed out on a couch. And I am there, in the middle of labor…And he is there moaning. In between pushing, I am going, 'Honey, are you OK?' and 'Are you breathing? Are you OK?'"

Stephon Marbury   Alex Rodriguez

David Hayes holds his state record-breaking channel catfish while his three-year-old granddaughter **Alyssa** holds the Barbie rod and reel that Hayes used to reel in the 21-pound, 1-ounce fish in Elkin, N.C.

Blowouts of the year

1) The Slovakia women's hockey team set an international record with their 82-0 victory over Bulgaria. Bulgaria trailed 7-0 after 5 minutes, 19-0 after 10 and 31-0 at the end of the first period. They were outshot, 139-0. Slovakia scored an average of one goal per 44 seconds. "We took it as training," Slovakia coach Miroslav Karafiat said

2) The powerful Naples High School football team trounced Estero High, 91-0, in mid October, causing Estero defensive line coach Pat Hayes to quip, "I didn't even know 91 was a multiple of seven."

Manny Needing Money

Who says Manny Ramirez lives in his own world? When asked in the offseason whether he'll resign with the Dodgers, he answered, "I want to see who is the highest bidder. Gas is up and so am I."

Name of the Year

Former Formula One and current NASCAR driver

Scott Speed

Bengals See the Sign

Wide receiver Chris Henry has missed 10 games during the past two seasons for violating NFL conduct policies. But that didn't stop the team from inviting the talented but oft-troubled wide receiver back to the team in August. Bengals fans weren't exactly enamored with the decision, especially one, who paid to have an electronic billboard on I-75 just outside of Cincinnati read, "Chris Henry again? Are you serious?"

Michael Strahan shows off his fresh new wardrobe after the Giants' Super Bowl win over the Patriots on February 3.

November 2007

Sun	Mon	Tue	Wed	Thu	Fri	Sat
				1	2	3
4	5	6	7	8	9	10
11	12	13	14	15	16	17
18	19	20	21	22	23	24
25	26	27	28	29	30	

SportsNation ranks the greatest quarterbacks of all-time

		Points
1	Joe Montana	.881,869
2	Tom Brady	.710,001
3	Dan Marino	.707,835
4	Brett Favre	.693,007
5	John Elway	.689,924
6	Peyton Manning	.623,227
7	Johnny Unitas	.622,287
8	Terry Bradshaw	.534,428
9	Steve Young	.521,513
10	Troy Aikman	.466,060
11	Bart Starr	.423,153
12	Roger Staubach	.418,505
13	Joe Namath	.330,909
14	Otto Graham	.279,665
15	Fran Tarkenton	.266,895
16	Sammy Baugh	.266,792
17	Dan Fouts	.265,939
18	Warren Moon	.229,839
19	Phil Simms	.223,979
20	Bob Griese	.212,802

Total Votes: 49,153

1 **Joe Torre,** Brooklyn native and former Yankees manager, goes from one storied franchise to another as he signs a three-year, $13 million deal to manage the Los Angeles Dodgers.

Tennis star Martina Hingis announces her retirement after revealing that she had tested positive for cocaine. Hingis insists the positive test is in error, but opts to retire instead of fighting the accusations that she labels "horrendous" and "monstrous."

3 **Navy defeats Notre Dame,** 46-44, in triple overtime to end the Irish's 43-year winning streak over the Midshipmen. The last time Navy had beaten Notre Dame was 1963 when Roger Staubach was its quarterback.

4 **Vikings rookie Adrian Peterson** rushes for an NFL-record 296 yards to lead Minnesota to a 35-17 win over the San Diego Chargers. He snaps Jamal Lewis' previous mark of 295 set in 2003. It is just Peterson's eighth NFL game.

Paula Radcliffe and Martin Lel win the women's and men's divisions of the New York Marathon, each pulling away in the final mile.

7 **Gardner-Webb,** a program beginning just its sixth full season as a full Division I basketball member, takes down the No. 22-ranked Kentucky Wildcats, 84-68, at Rupp Arena. "A lot of people will think this is a misprint," Gardner-Webb coach Rick Scruggs said.

8 **Rays rid themselves of Devil.** In front of a crowd of roughly 7,000 people, the Tampa Bay Rays announce their new name, new team colors and new uniforms.

10 **Navy and North Texas** set a major-college football (FBS) record by combining for 136 points in a 74-62 Navy win. Just two weeks prior, FCS (formerly I-AA) schools Weber State and Portland State combined for 141 points in a 73-68 Weber State win.

11 **Justine Henin finishes** an amazing year with a win in the season-ending $1 million Sony Ericsson Championships. She comes from behind to defeat Maria Sharapova, 5-7, 7-5, 6-3.

Sebastien Bourdais ends his Champ Car career a winner, as he takes the Mexican Grand Prix and the overall Champ Car championship. Bourdais is leaving the circuit for Formula One beginning in 2008.

12 **Red Sox 2B Dustin Pedroia** and Milwaukee Brewers OF Ryan Braun are selected Major League Baseball's Rookies of the Year.

13 **Cleveland Indians' ace** CC Sabathia receives 19 of 28 first-place votes and wins the A.L. Cy Young Award.

AP Images

Los Angeles Dodgers owner **Frank McCourt** introduces his new manager, **Joe Torre**, at a news conference on November 5.

14 He's back! Running back Ricky Williams is reinstated — again — after an 18-month suspension for violating the league's substance abuse policy.

Bob Melvin of the Arizona Diamondbacks and Eric Wedge of the Cleveland Indians are named NL and AL Managers of the Year, respectively.

15 Barry Bonds is indicted on charges of perjury and obstruction of justice for telling a federal grand jury that he did not knowingly use performance-enhancing drugs.

San Diego Padres' flame-thrower Jake Peavy earns all 32 first-place votes, making him a unanimous selection for the NL Cy Young Award.

18 Jimmie Johnson plays it safe, finishing in seventh place in the season-ending Ford 400 near Miami. And that's enough to win him his second straight NASCAR Nextel Cup points championship. He wins the title over runner-up Jeff Gordon.

Roger Federer wins his fourth season-ending Masters Cup title in the last five years with a commanding 6-2, 6-3, 6-2 victory over David Ferrer.

19 Alex Rodriguez, slugging Yankees' third baseman, is the runaway winner of his third American League MVP award. The award comes just a few days after he agrees to an even more lucrative award — a 10-year, $275 million contract with the Bronx Bombers.

20 Phillies' shortstop Jimmy Rollins narrowly wins the National League MVP award over Rockies' outfielder Matt Holliday.

25 The Saskatchewan Roughriders defeat the Winnipeg Blue Bombers, 23-19, to win the CFL's Grey Cup. It is their first championship in 18 years.

27 Redskins safety Sean Taylor dies one day after being shot in the upper leg during a robbery at his home in Miami.

30 Daredevil Evel Knievel dies at the age of 69.

December 2007

Sun	Mon	Tue	Wed	Thu	Fri	Sat
						1
2	3	4	5	6	7	8
9	10	11	12	13	14	15
16	17	18	19	20	21	22
23/30	24/31	25	26	27	28	29

What do you think of the Mitchell report?

Will the Mitchell report have a big impact on Major League Baseball?

75.8% — Yes
24.2% — No

Were you surprised at the number of names in the report?

50.2% — No
49.8% — Yes

Who is more to blame for the steroid problem in baseball?

66.0% — The players
16.9% — The players' union
11.7% — Bud Selig
5.4% — The owners

Who would get your vote for the Baseball Hall of Fame?

37.8% — Neither
37.6% — Roger Clemens
22.2% — Both
2.4% — Barry Bonds

Total Votes: 159,236

1 **The BCS standings** are thrown for a loop as the top two ranked teams both lose. Top-ranked Missouri goes down to Oklahoma, 38-17, while West Virginia loses to Pittsburgh, 13-9. LSU beats Tennessee, 21-14, in the SEC Championship and throws itself back into the ever-changing title picture. A day later, the Tigers are announced as a participant in the BCS title game along with Ohio State.

3 **The New England Patriots** escape Baltimore with a fortunate, last-second 27-24 victory over the Ravens to move to 12-0 and keep their hopes of a perfect season alive.

4 **The Detroit Tigers** make a splash in the offseason, acquiring third baseman Miguel Cabrera and pitcher Dontrelle Willis from the Florida Marlins for pitcher Andrew Miller, outfielder Cameron Maybin and four other players.

8 **Florida Gators quarterback Tim Tebow** becomes the first sophomore to win the Heisman Trophy in the 73-year history of the award. He amasses 1,957 points to outdistance Arkansas running back Darren McFadden (1,703), Hawaii quarterback Colt Brennan (632) and Missouri quarterback Chase Daniel (425).

Floyd Mayweather Jr. stops Ricky Hatton in the 10th round of their welterweight title bout. Mayweather keeps his perfect record intact and improves to 39-0.

10 **Michael Vick is sentenced** to 23 months in prison for his role in an illegal dog-fighting ring. Judge Henry E. Hudson determined that the former Falcons quarterback hasn't "fully accepted" responsibility for his actions.

11 **In other "former Falcons" news,** head coach Bobby Petrino resigns from the Falcons after just 13 games to fill the coaching vacancy at Arkansas. Most Falcons players and fans are stunned and betrayed by the sudden departure, though not overly disappointed.

12 **Marion Jones' medals won** and marks set at the 2000 Sydney Olympics are officially erased from the record books by the International Olympic Committee. Jones had won three gold and two bronze medals.

13 **The long-awaited Mitchell Report** is released to the public. Eighty-six players are implicated in the report as having some connection to steroids and/or other performance-enhancing drugs. Most notable is pitcher Roger Clemens, who among the other nuggets, is reported to have been injected "four to six times with human growth hormone."

AP Images

> That's gonna leave a mark. **Floyd Mayweather Jr.** punches Ricky Hatton during their WBC welterweight title fight at the MGM Grand hotel-casino in Las Vegas on December 8.

14 Appalachian State, who kicked off its season with a 34-32 shocker over Michigan, wins its third straight FCS (I-AA) title with a 49-21 victory over Delaware.

15 Andy Pettitte, one of those players fingered in the Mitchell Report, admits to using HGH to help his elbow heal in 2002. He apologizes, sort of — "If what I did was an error in judgment on my part, I apologize...I accept responsibility for those two days."

16 Michigan hires West Virginia's Rich Rodriguez to replace the retiring Lloyd Carr as its head football coach.

The Miami Dolphins beat the Baltimore Ravens, 22-16, in overtime to lift their record to 1-13 and put a merciful end to what might have been the NFL's first winless season since the 0-14 Buccaneers in 1976.

18 Roger Clemens emphatically denies allegations by his former trainer Brian McNamee that he took performance-enhancing drugs.

19 The Big Tuna is now a Dolphin. Bill Parcells spurns the Atlanta Falcons' offer and agrees to come out of retirement and become the Vice President of Football Operations for the Miami Dolphins.

21 Patriots quarterback Tom Brady and LPGA golfer Lorena Ochoa are named The Associated Press Athletes of the Year for 2007.

23 Kobe Bryant scores 39 points in a 95-90 Lakers win over the Knicks to become the youngest player in NBA history to reach 20,000 points.

29 The New England Patriots come from behind to defeat the New York Giants, 38-35, to complete its perfect 16-0 regular season. Tom Brady throws his 50th touchdown pass and Randy Moss hauled in his 23rd touchdown reception to set new single-season marks in those categories. The Giants, hoping to play the role of the spoiler, led, 28-16, after three quarters.

January 2008

Sun	Mon	Tue	Wed	Thu	Fri	Sat
		1	2	3	4	5
6	7	8	9	10	11	12
13	14	15	16	17	18	19
20	21	22	23	24	25	26
27	28	29	30	31		

Rank the most memorable BCS moments

		Points
1	Vince Young runs to title	53,533
2	Ian Johnson pops question	42,078
3	Miami flagged for interference	41,842
4	Reggie Bush pitches to B. Walker	36,239
5	Bowden vs. Paterno	30,890

Total Votes: 6,411

Rank the most hated college football teams

Do shouts of "Roll Tide!" get your blood boiling? Do you hook your horns upside down? Does the thought of dotting your i's make you sick? If so, you've come to the right place.

	Team	Points
1	Notre Dame	910,978
2	Ohio State	909,894
3	USC	902,234
4	Florida	840,707
5	Miami	811,752
6	Michigan	779,824
7	Oklahoma	655,262
8	Texas	642,411
9	Alabama	611,321
10	Tennessee	606,764

Total Votes: 120,522

1 **USC trounces Illinois,** 42-17, in the Rose Bowl, amassing a Rose Bowl-record 633 yards of total offense in the process. In other major bowl action, Missouri routs Arkansas, 38-7, in the Cotton Bowl, Michigan takes down Florida and Heisman Trophy winner Tim Tebow, 41-35, in the Capital One Bowl and later in the evening, No. 4-ranked Georgia destroys Hawaii, 41-10, in the Sugar Bowl.

3 **To virtually no one's surprise,** Vice President Bill Parcells gives head coach Cam Cameron his walking papers after guiding the Miami Dolphins to a 1-15 record.

Bill Belichick is named NFL Coach of the Year after a regular season that saw him embroiled in the Spygate controversy, and still lead his team to a perfect 16-0 record.

Kansas defeats Virginia Tech, 24-21, in the Orange Bowl in Miami. The win gives the Jayhawks a school-record 12 wins for the season.

5 **The NFL playoffs kick off** as Seattle handles Washington, 35-14, and Jacksonville edges Pittsburgh, 31-29, in Wild Card action. A day later, the Giants and Chargers also advance.

Tom Brady is awarded the AP NFL MVP award after his record-breaking 50-touchdown season.

6 **Roger Clemens appears on** *60 Minutes* and tells Mike Wallace that the only substances former trainer Brian McNamee injected him with was vitamin B-12 and the painkiller lidocaine. "Swear?" asks Wallace. "Swear," responds Clemens.

7 **LSU storms to a 38-24** win over No. 1-ranked Ohio State in the BCS National Championship Game for its third national title overall and second in the last five years. The Buckeyes, who suffer a disappointing loss in the title game for the second year in a row, jump out to an early 10-0 lead, only to see the Tigers roar back with 31 unanswered points.

8 **Reliever Goose Gossage** is elected to the Baseball Hall of Fame on his ninth year on the ballot. He garners 85.8 percent of the vote and is the only player to reach the required 75 percent for the year. Former Red Sox slugger Jim Rice narrowly misses with 72.2 percent. Mark McGwire receives just 23.6 percent.

NFL Hall of Fame coach Joe Gibbs retires for the second time, with a year left on his contract. He cites the desire to spend more time with his family.

AP Images

→ **Maria Sharapova** smiles with her newest trophy on a boat on the Yarra river in downtown Melbourne after beating Ana Ivanovic to win the Australian Open on January 25.

Golf Channel anchor Kelly Tilghman is suspended for two weeks for joking that young players who want to challenge Tiger Woods should "lynch him in a back alley." Two weeks later, *Golfweek* adds fuel to the fire by running a cover with a noose on it. *Golfweek's* editor is subsequently fired.

10 Alex Ovechkin inks a 13-year, $124 million deal with the Washington Capitals.

Sir Edmund Hillary, the first person to climb Mount Everest (along with climbing companion Tenzing Norgay). dies at the age of 88.

11 Disgraced sprinter Marion Jones is sentenced to six months in prison for her role in a check fraud scam and lying to investigators about her use of performance-enhancing drugs.

13 The Indianapolis Colts and the Dallas Cowboys are dumped from the playoffs as the Colts go down to the Chargers, 28-24, and the Cowboys lose to the Giants, 21-17.

20 The Super Bowl matchups are set as the New England Patriots stay perfect with a 21-12 win over San Diego, and the New York Giants continue their amazing run with a 23-20 overtime win over Green Bay. Almost immediately, the boot on Tom Brady's right foot takes center stage.

21 Curlin captures the Eclipse Award as thoroughbred racing's horse of the year.

25 Maria Sharapova cruises to a straight-set, 7-5, 6-3 victory over Ana Ivanovic in the Australian Open women's singles final.

27 Novak Djokovic stops 38th-ranked Jo Wilfried Tsonga, 4-6, 6-4, 6-3, 7-6,in the Australian Open men's final for his first Grand Slam singles title.

The Eastern Conference wins the NHL All-Star Game in Atlanta, 8-7, on Marc Savard's goal with 20.9 seconds left.

Evan Lysacek and 14-year-old Mirai Nagasu win the men's and women's titles at the U.S. Figure Skating Championships.

February 2008

Sun	Mon	Tue	Wed	Thu	Fri	Sat
					1	2
3	4	5	6	7	8	9
10	11	12	13	14	15	16
17	18	19	20	21	22	23
24	25	26	27	28	29	

Was Super Bowl XLII the best ever?

The perfect escape ruined a shot at perfection, but where did Super Bowl XLII rank, SportsNation?

Where does this Giants victory rank among the greatest sports upsets?

65.3%	—	Top 5
20.5%	—	Top 10
9.4%	—	Top 20
4.8%	—	Not in the top 20

What — or whom — was most to blame for the loss for the Patriots?

50.4%	—	Pass protection
26.2%	—	Overconfidence
13.7%	—	Bill Belichick
7.6%	—	Tom Brady
1.5%	—	Josh McDaniels
0.6%	—	Randy Moss

Overall, how would you rank Super Bowl XLII?

50.3%	—	Among the top five
27.2%	—	The best ever
18.3%	—	Better than most
4.2%	—	Nothing special

Total Votes: 190,447

1 **The Mets' trade** for lefty hurler Johan Santana is completed when he agrees to a seven-year, $150 million deal, a record for a pitcher. The Twins receive four players in return.

The Los Angeles Lakers acquire forward Pau Gasol from the Memphis Grizzlies.

Russell Baze, the winningest jockey of all time, rides his 10,000th winner.

3 **The New York Giants** pull off one of the all-time stunners in NFL history with a thrilling 17-14 win over the New England Patriots in Super Bowl XLII. It is the Giants' first Super Bowl title since they defeated the Bills in 1991. The Patriots fall to 18-1 and see their quest for a perfect season unexpectedly squashed.

The Giants defense sacks Tom Brady five times and Eli Manning offers up the play of the game as he somehow spins out of a sack and heaves the ball to receiver David Tyree, who catches the ball by pinning it against his helmet to keep the winning drive alive. Manning is selected as the game's MVP.

Redskins legends Art Monk and Darrell Green highlight a class of six to be inducted into the Pro Football Hall of Fame.

4 **Bobby Knight,** the fiery coaching legend and all-time men's Division I coaching wins leader, resigns as head coach of Texas Tech and hands the reigns to his son — Red Raiders assistant Pat Knight.

6 **Center Shaquille O'Neal is traded** from the Miami Heat to the Phoenix Suns for forward Shawn Marion and guard Marcus Banks.

In a case that's getting stranger by the minute, Brian McNamee's lawyers claim to have turned over syringes and gauze pads with Roger Clemens' blood still on them. Two days later, McNamee tells congressional lawyers that he once injected Clemens' wife, Debbie, with HGH in the master bedroom of their Houston home.

10 **Florida Panthers' forward Richard Zednik** suffers a scary and gruesome injury in a 5-3 loss to Buffalo, when Olli Jokinen's skate accidentally kicks up and slices his neck. His carotid artery is partially severed, but surgery is successful. "Worst thing I've ever seen in hockey," teammate Stephen Weiss said.

The NFC defeats the AFC, 42-30, in the NFL Pro Bowl in Honolulu. Vikings rookie Adrian Peterson rushes for 129 yards and two touchdowns and is named the game's MVP.

11 **Boston College beats Harvard,** 6-5, in overtime to win the 56th Beanpot hockey tournament in Boston.

AP Images

If looks could kill. **Roger Clemens** listens to the testimony of his former personal trainer Brian McNamee on Capitol Hill in Washington, D.C. on February 13.

13 **Kelvin Sampson,** head basketball coach at Indiana, is in a familiar place — in hot water with the NCAA after he is accused of "major rules violations."

14 **Tennis legend Monica Seles** officially retires. She won nine Grand Slam singles titles and had her career famously interrupted when she was stabbed in the back during a match in Germany.

17 **Ryan Newman wins** the 50th running of the Daytona 500, thanks in part to a little push by his Penske teammate Kurt Busch. Busch places second, while Joe Gibbs Racing teammates Tony Stewart and Kyle Busch place third and fourth, respectively. Newman averages over 153 mph for the entire race.

LeBron James scores 27 points to lead the Eastern Conference to a 134-128 win over the West in the NBA All-Star Game. James is awarded the game's MVP award.

Point guard Jason Kidd is traded from the Nets to the Mavericks in a deal that involves six players and two picks.

18 **Shahar Peer becomes** the first Israeli to play tennis in one of the Persian Gulf states, as she defeats Slovenia's Andreja Klepac, 6-3, 6-4, in the first round of the Qatar Total Open in Doha.

22 **Champ Car and IRL** bury the hatchet and agree to unify beginning with the upcoming 2008-09 season. Champ Car will cease operations and essentially dissolve into the IRL's IndyCar Series.

23 **Longtime Dolphin linebacker Zach Thomas** signs a one-year, $3 million deal with the Dallas Cowboys.

24 **Tiger Woods wins** the WGC-Accenture Match Play Championship, 8&7, over Stewart Cink. It's his 63rd career victory as he passes Arnold Palmer for fourth on the PGA all-time wins list.

29 **Offseason NFL free agent signings** truly kick into gear as Patriots cornerback Asante Samuel bolts for the Philadelphia Eagles and huge defensive tackle Kris Jenkins signs with the New York Jets.

March 2008

Sun	Mon	Tue	Wed	Thu	Fri	Sat
						1
2	3	4	5	6	7	8
9	10	11	12	13	14	15
16	17	18	19	20	21	22
23/30	24/31	25	26	27	28	29

Do you agree with the Olympic torch protests?

What is your reaction to protesters attempting to extinguish the Olympic flame?

42.4%	—	The flame represents continuity; extinguishing it does nothing to further the cause behind the protest
31.8%	—	I have no problem with it; it sends a strong, non-violent message
25.8%	—	I can appreciate the meaning behind the action but it is dangerous and crosses the line

Have the protests inspired you to learn more about the issues at hand?

57.3%	—	No
42.7%	—	Yes

What would you do if the torch came through your city or town?

40.9%	—	I would stay at home
24.4%	—	I would show up in support
22.3%	—	I'd show up to watch the show
12.4%	—	I would protest

Total Votes: 7,493

2 **Ernie Els wins** the Honda Classic, snapping his four-year PGA Tour drought.

Yankees general partner Hank Steinbrenner does his part to ensure the Red Sox-Yankees rivalry continues with these comments to the *New York Times' Play Magazine*: "Red Sox Nation? What a bunch of $%@# that is...This is a Yankee country. We're going to put the Yankees back on top and restore the order to the universe."

4 **Speaking of rivalries,** Duke defeats North Carolina, 86-72, in Chapel Hill in a game that sees Tar Heels star Tyler Hansbrough leave the game early with 26 points, 17 rebounds and a broken nose, courtesy of an errant Gerald Henderson elbow.

6 **Green Bay Packers quarterback Brett Favre** announces his...ahem...retirement from the NFL, in a tearful press conference. "I don't think I've got anything left to give, and that's it. I know I can play, but I don't think I want to."

8 **American skier Lindsey Vonn** wins her 10th World Cup downhill event, breaking the all-time American record previously held by Picabo Street and Daron Rahlves.

11 **Troubled golfer John Daly** is dumped by his swing coach Butch Harmon for partying too much. "My whole goal for him was he's got to show me golf is the most important thing in his life," Harmon said. "And the most important thing in his life is getting drunk." a day later, he is kicked out of the Arnold palmer Invitational for missing the pro-am.

12 **The Houston Rockets** run their winning streak to 20 games with a 83-75 victory over the Atlanta Hawks. It ends at 22 games, six days later, with a 94-74 loss to Boston.

Tempers boil over in Florida as the Rays and Yankees engage in a bench-clearing brawl in the second inning of their preseason game.

Lance Mackey wins the Iditarod Trail Sled Dog Race for the second consecutive year, completing the trip from Anchorage to Nome in 9 days, 11 hours, 46 minutes and 48 seconds.

14 **Bode Miller and Lindsey Vonn** win the men's and women's overall World Cup alpine skiing titles, respectively, making it the first time since Phil Mahre and Tamara McKinney in 1983 that an American pair has swept the titles.

16 **On Selection Sunday,** North Carolina, Kansas, Memphis and UCLA are awarded the top seeds for the upcoming NCAA men's basketball tournament.

> Pro-Tibetan activists hold Tibetan flags during a protest at the **Beijing Olympic torch relay** in the village of Ancient Olympia, southern Greece, on March 24.

AP Images

17 It's Selection Monday for the women's tournament and the top seeds go to Connecticut, Maryland, North Carolina and of course, Tennessee.

19 Terrelle Pryor, the highly touted high school quarterback from Western Pennsylvania, finally makes his eagerly anticipated college choice — Ohio State.

20 The NCAA men's basketball tournament tips off with Duke squeaking by No. 15-seeded Belmont, 71-70, on a layup with just under 20 seconds to go (they're eventually ousted two days later by West Virginia). Last year's Cinderella George Mason is sent home with a 68-50 defeat to Notre Dame.

21 Lucky 13? Thirteen-seeded San Diego knocks off No. 4-seeded Connecticut, 70-69, while another 13-seed, Siena sends Vanderbilt home with a stunning 83-62 rout.

24 Geoff Ogilvy wins the CA Championship at Doral, snapping Tiger Woods' PGA winning streak at five tournaments. Woods finishes in fifth, two shots off the pace.

Numerous protesters disrupt the Beijing Olympics flame-lighting ceremony in Greece.

25 In Tokyo, Manny Ramirez launches a two-run double in the 10th inning to lift the Red Sox to a 6-5 win over the A's in Major League Baseball's first regular season game of the year.

28 Stephen Curry leads 10th-seeded Davidson to a surprisingly easy 73-56 win over Wisconsin and into the Elite Eight. it's the third straight game that Curry registers at least 30 points. He outscores the Badgers by himself, 22-20, in the second half.

30 The men's Final Four is set, and for the first time in history, all top seeds — Kansas, Memphis, North Carolina and UCLA — advance.

The Washington Nationals christen their brand new $611 million ballpark with a 3-2 win over the Atlanta Braves, on a walk-off home run by third baseman Ryan Zimmerman in the bottom of the ninth.

April 2008

Sun	Mon	Tue	Wed	Thu	Fri	Sat
		1	2	3	4	5
6	7	8	9	10	11	12
13	14	15	16	17	18	19
20	21	22	23	24	25	26
27	28	29	30			

Rank the biggest NCAA tournament shots

Where does Mario Chalmers' last-second three-point shot rank among the best shots in the history of the tournament?

		Points
1	Christian Laettner, Duke, '92	123,709
2	Mario Chalmers, Kansas, '08	123,241
3	Michael Jordan, UNC, '82	110,617
4	Lorenzo Charles, NC State, '83	98,494
5	Keith Smart, Indiana, '87	92,284
6	Tyus Edney, UCLA, '95	83,204
7	J. Whitehead, Marquette, '77	57,632
8	Tony Branch, Louisville, '80	51,824
9	Vic Rouse, Loyola-Chi., '63	51,636
10	Pete Brennan, UNC, '57	21,224

Total Votes: 16,078

Rank College Basketball's most prestigious teams

		Points
1	Kentucky	452,483
2	North Carolina	404,918
3	Kansas	395,383
4	Duke	387,152
5	UCLA	348,686

Total Votes: 23,702

2 **NFL owners install** a number of rule changes at their meeting in Palm Beach, Fla., most notably the elimination of the force-out rule on catches and interceptions. Beginning with the 2008-09 season, a player must get two feet in bounce for a catch to be legal, regardless of whether he is forced out by the opposition.

3 **Former Cubs leftfielder Moises Alou** absolves fan Steve Bartman of any blame for his not coming up with the infamous foul ball in Game 6 of the 2003 NLCS. "You know what the funny thing is," Alou says. "I wouldn't have caught it anyway."

5 **Kansas crushes** North Carolina and Memphis sprints past UCLA to reach the NCAA men's basketball championship game. The Jayhawks jump out to an insurmountable 40-12 first-half lead and coast to an 84-66 victory, while the Tigers beat the Bruins, 78-63, to move to 38-1 on the year, setting a new record for wins in a single season.

6 **Lorena Ochoa wins** the LPGA Kraft Nabisco Championship by five strokes in Rancho Mirage, Calif., for her second consecutive win in a major. Annika Sorenstam and Suzann Pettersen tie for second.

The NHL regular season comes to a close with Detroit (115 points) grabbing the top seed in the West and Montreal (140 points) finishing first in the East. Washington star Alex Ovechkin wins the Art Ross Trophy (for overall scoring) with 112 points, including 65 goals.

7 **Mario Chalmers knocks down** a clutch three-pointer with 2.1 seconds remaining to send the NCAA men's basketball championship game into overtime, where the Jayhawks pull away for a 75-68 win over Memphis. The Jayhawks trail by nine points with 2:12 remaining in regulation, when they begin fouling in earnest. The Tigers' horrendous foul shooting, their Achilles heel all year, eventually does them in. Chalmers is selected as the tournament's Most Outstanding Player. Derrick Rose scores 18 points and dishes out eight assists for the Tigers.

Centers Patrick Ewing and Hakeem Olajuwon are introduced as new inductees into the Basketball Hall of Fame along with Adrian Dantley, Pat Riley, Dick Vitale, women's pioneer Cathy Rush and Detroit Pistons owner Bill Davidson.

8 **Bill Buckner returns** to Fenway Park for the Red Sox opening day festivities and is treated to an extended standing ovation by the Boston fans.

AP Images

Former Boston first baseman **Bill Buckner** was welcomed back to Fenway Park with open arms, and a standing ovation, at the Red Sox' home opener on April 8.

Tennessee takes its second straight NCAA Division I women's basketball title and eighth overall with a 64-48 victory over Stanford. Candace Parker finishes with a game high 17 points and nine rebounds and is awarded the tournament's Most Outstanding Player award.

12 Boston College beats Notre Dame, 4-1, to win the NCAA Division I men's hockey championship. Nathan Gerbe scores twice and adds two assists to lead the Eagles.

13 Trevor Immelman cards a final-round 3-over-par 75 but hangs on to win the Masters by three strokes over runner-up Tiger Woods. It's his first major title and he becomes the first wire-to-wire winner of the Masters since 1976.

14 Rangers forward Sean Avery finds a new way to agitate Devils goalie Martin Brodeur, as he stands in front of him in the crease with his back to the play, waving his arms and stick in front of his face. One day later, a new rule is implemented, banning that behavior.

16 The NBA regular season ends, with LeBron James (30 ppg) becoming the Cavaliers' first league scoring champ.

19 Joe Calzaghe (45-0) overcomes a first-round knockdown and wins a split-decision over Bernard Hopkins.

20 Danica Patrick becomes the first woman to win a "major" racing event with her victory at the Indy Racing League's Japan Indy 300 in Motegi.

21 Kenya's Robert Cheruiyot and Ethiopia's Dire Tune win the men's and women's divisions of the Boston Marathon.

26 The Miami Dolphins select offensive tackle Jake Long of Michigan with the top overall pick in the NFL draft. Defensive end Chris Long goes second to St. Louis, while the Atlanta Falcons grab B.C. quarterback Matt Ryan third.

27 Ashley Force beats her father, John, to become the first female to win an NHRA Funny Car event. She reaches 320.36 miles per hour.

May 2008

Sun.	Mon	Tue	Wed	Thu	Fri	Sat
				1	2	3
4	5	6	7	8	9	10
11	12	13	14	15	16	17
18	19	20	21	22	23	24
25	26	27	28	29	30	31

SportsNation Does the Derby

Will you watch the Kentucky Derby?

87.5%	—	Yes
12.5%	—	No

Where would you most want to watch the Kentucky Derby?

44.2%	—	On Millionaire's Row
27.9%	—	On the infield
27.9	—	On my couch (watching TV)

Which is your favorite Kentucky Derby tradition?

41.1%	—	The playing of "My Old Kentucky Home"
29.8%	—	Mint juleps
29.0%	—	Extravagant hats

Which is your favorite leg of the Triple Crown?

78.9%	—	The Kentucky Derby
11.9%	—	The Belmont Stakes
9.2%	—	The Preakness Stakes

Total Votes: 13,280

2 Big Brown, ridden by Kent Desormeaux and trained by Rick Dutrow, wins the 134th Kentucky Derby at Churchill Downs by 4¾ lengths. Eight Belles places second while Denis of Cork rallies to come in third. Tragically, Eight Belles has to be euthanized after collapsing with two broken front ankles after the finish.

Julio Franco has finally had enough, and retires from Major League Baseball at the age of 49. He leaves the game with 2,586 hits in 23 major league seasons.

4 Brenden Morrow scores midway through the fourth overtime to lead the Dallas Stars to a 2-1 win over San Jose, a 4-2 series win and a berth in the Western Conference Finals where they have a daunting task in the Detroit Red Wings.

6 Lakers star Kobe Bryant wins his first NBA MVP award after leading his team to a No. 1 playoff seed in the Western Conference. Hornets' point guard Chris Paul finishes in second while Celtics forward Kevin Garnett places third.

7 The Cincinnati Reds hit seven home runs, three by rookie Joey Votto, in a 9-0 win over the Chicago Cubs.

10 Former Suns coach Mike D'Antoni signs a four-year, $24 million deal to become the new coach of the New York Knicks.

11 Kyle Busch wins the Sprint Cup race at Darlington Raceway, a week after wrecking fan-favorite Dale Earnhardt Jr., and is lustily booed by the crowd, as well as members of Junior's pit crew. Busch doesn't seem to mind, however. "If I win, it just makes 'em more upset and crying on their way home."

Reports surface that claim freshman USC college basketball star O.J. Mayo received thousands of dollars in cash and other gifts at USC and during his high school career.

12 Indians second baseman Asdrubal Cabrera becomes the 14th player in Major League Baseball history to turn an unassisted triple play. He then flips the ball into the crowd.

13 Golfing legend Annika Sorenstam announces her intentions to retire from the LPGA Tour at the end of the 2008 season — at the ripe old age of 37.

14 Belgian Justine Henin, the world's top-ranked women's tennis player for the last 118 weeks and counting, abruptly retires at the age of 25. She is the No. 1-ranked woman to retire in WTA history. She leaves with over $19 million in winnings and 41 titles including seven Grand Slam events.

Scott Dixon of New Zealand douses himself with milk after winning the Indianapolis 500 on May 25.

17 Big Brown makes is two-for-two in Triple Crown races as he romps to a 5¼-length win in the Preakness. 39-1 longshot Macho Again places second while 22-1 Icabad Crane finishes third.

Kasey Kahne wins the Sprint All-Star Race and its accompanying $1 million prize. Kahne, who failed to qualify for the event, earned his berth by way of a fan vote.

18 Paul Pierce and LeBron James wage a duel for the ages as the Celtics close out the Cavs, 97-92 in Game 7 of the Eastern Conference Semifinals. Pierce scores 41 points, while James finishes with 45 in a losing effort.

Russia defeats Canada, 5-4, in overtime to win the World Hockey Championship for the first time since 1993. Ilya Kovalchuk nets the game-winner.

19 Red Sox lefty Jon Lester throws Major League Baseball's first no-hitter of the season in a 7-0 Boston win. He allows just two baserunners. It is the fourth career no-hitter caught by catcher Jason Varitek.

20 The Chicago Bulls beat the odds in the NBA draft lottery and land the top overall pick in the upcoming NBA draft.

Mike Piazza, who hit more home runs than any other catcher in major league history, announces his retirement.

21 The L.A. Lakers rally from a 20-point deficit to beat the Spurs in Game 1 of the Western Conference Finals.

23 Diamondbacks pitcher Doug Davis returns from his battle with cancer and allows just one run in seven innings in an 11-1 win over the Atlanta Braves.

25 New Zealander Scott Dixon wins an accident-filled Indy 500. Feisty Danica Patrick is fighting mad after a pit-road accident with Ryan Briscoe.

Kasey Kahne wins the Coca-Cola 600 after race leader Tony Stewart suffers a flat tire with three laps to go.

30 It's a dream matchup for the NBA as the Celtics defeat the Pistons in six games to set up a Finals date with the Lakers.

June 2008

Sun	Mon	Tue	Wed	Thu	Fri	Sat
1	2	3	4	5	6	7
8	9	10	11	12	13	14
15	16	17	18	19	20	21
22	23	24	25	26	27	28
29	30					

Rank the best goalies of all time

After a 16-year career in the NHL, future Hall of Fame goaltender Dominik Hasek is calling it quits. Hasek's career is indisputably excellent, but where does he rank all-time?

		Points
1	Patrick Roy	261,513
2	Martin Brodeur	252,103
3	Dominik Hasek	201,165
4	Terry Sawchuk	201,149
5	Jacques Plante	162,320
6	Tony Esposito	148,142
7	Grant Fuhr	128,995
8	Ed Belfour	121,536
9	Glenn Hall	106,430
10	Curtis Joseph	89,686

Total Votes: 31,581

Rank the last 10 Stanley Cup winners

(Note: only the top five are listed)

		Points
1	Red Wings, '97-98	270,761
2	Red Wings, '01-02	254,698
3	Red Wings, '07-08	253,190
4	Avalanche, '00-01	194,477
5	Devils, '99-00	191,720

Total Votes: 33,656

3 **Detroit Pistons' coach Flip Saunders** is fired after he averaged 59 wins per season during his three-year tenure with the club, but was eliminated from the Eastern Conference Finals in all three years.

Randy Johnson records strikes out his 4,673rd batter to pass Roger Clemens and move into second place on the all-time list behind only Nolan Ryan (5,714).

4 **The Detroit Red Wings defeat** the Pittsburgh Penguins, 3-2, in Game 6 of the Stanley Cup Finals to win their fourth Cup in the last 11 years. Up 3-1 with less than two minutes left, the Wings had to survive a late goal by Marian Hossa, then a flurry around the net in the waning seconds. The win comes just two nights after a stunning Game 5 that saw the Pens tie the game with 34 seconds left, then win it in triple overtime to force Game 6. Henrik Zetterberg wins the Conn Smythe Trophy as playoff MVP.

5 **The Tampa Bay Rays** select Georgia high school shortstop Tim Beckham with the first overall pick in the Major League Baseball Draft. Pittsburgh follows with Vanderbilt third baseman Pedro Alvarez.

Paul Pierce returns to the court, after leaving in a wheelchair with an injured knee just minutes earlier, and leads the Celtics to a 98-88 win over the Lakers in Game 1 of the NBA Finals. Kevin Garnett and Kobe Bryant score 24, while Pierce adds 22.

7 **Da'Tara plays the role of spoiler** in the Belmont Stakes, thwarting Big Brown's bid to become thoroughbred racing's first Triple Crown winner since Affirmed in 1978. Denis of Cork places second and Ready's Echo comes in third, while Big Brown is eased and fails to finish.

Ana Ivanovic easily handles Dinara Safina, 6-4, 6-3, in the women's French Open final for the first major title of her career. With the win she becomes the top-ranked women's player in the world.

Legendary announcer Jim McKay dies of natural causes at the age of 86. McKay hosted ABC's *Wide World of Sports* for more than 40 years and covered multiple golfing majors and horse racing Triple Crown events. He also covered 12 Olympics, including the 1972 Games in Munich, where he famously guided watchers through the horrific massacre of 11 Israeli athletes.

8 **Rafael Nadal** crushes Roger Federer, 6-1, 6-3, 6-0, to win his fourth straight French Open singles title.

Sa-wing and a miss! Tampa Bay Rays pitcher **James Shields, right** (and right hook), takes exception to Red Sox outfielder **Coco Crisp** charging the mound on June 5.

9 Ken Griffey Jr. hits the 600th home run of his hall-of-fame career. The pitcher was Florida's Mark Hendrickson, the count was 3-and-1, and the ball sailed into the rightfield seats at Dolphin Stadium. He is the sixth player to join the 600-club.

Giants defensive end Michael Strahan retires from the NFL, while two-time MVP goalie Dominik Hasek of the Red Wings retires from the NHL.

12 The Celtics roar back from a 24-point deficit to beat the Lakers, 97-91, and take a commanding 3-1 NBA Finals lead.

Alex Ovechkin of the Washington Capitals wins the Hart Trophy as NHL MVP. Also, Red Wings defenseman Nicklas Lidstrom wins his sixth Norris Trophy and Devils goalie Martin Brodeur wins his fourth Vezina.

15 Tiger Woods, hobbled by a gimpy knee, and the loquacious Rocco Mediate wage a battle for the ages and wind up tied after 72 holes at the U.S. Open at Torrey Pines, setting up an 18-hole playoff the next day.

16 Woods and Mediate remained tied after 18 holes to force a sudden death playoff, where Woods wins with a par on the first hole. It's his 14th major title — and his last tournament of the season.

17 The Celtics trounce the Lakers, 131-92, to win the NBA Finals in 6 games. It is the 17th title for the franchise and first since 1986. Paul Pierce wins the Finals MVP award and an emotional Kevin Garnett pumps in 26 points and grabs 14 rebounds.

Willie Randolph is fired as manager of the underachieving New York Mets.

21 NHRA driver Scott Kalitta, 46, is killed in a fiery crash while qualifying for the Lucas Oil SuperNationals.

25 Fresno State, who lost 12 of its first 20 games this season, defeats Georgia, 6-1, to win the NCAA Division I baseball title.

26 The Chicago Bulls make Memphis point guard Derrick Rose the first pick in the NBA draft. Michael Beasley is chosen second (Miami), followed by O.J. Mayo (Minnesota).

July 2008

Sun	Mon	Tue	Wed	Thu	Fri	Sat
		1	2	3	4	5
6	7	8	9	10	11	12
13	14	15	16	17	18	19
20	21	22	23	24	25	26
27	28	29	30	31		

Manny and Griffey are traded

Manny Ramirez and Ken Griffey Jr. and their 1100-plus home runs were each traded at the trading deadline this year. Are they both headed for Cooperstown someday?

What is Ken Griffey Jr.'s Cooperstown fate?

49.3%	—	First-ballot lock
44.9%	—	Nice career but no chance
5.5%	—	In eventually but probably not first ballot
0.4%	—	Borderline material

What is Manny Ramirez's Cooperstown fate?

88.1%	—	First-ballot lock
9.8%	—	In eventually but probably not first ballot
1.4%	—	Borderline material
0.6%	—	Nice career but no chance

Rank MLB's Most Dangerous Hitters

		Points
1	Albert Pujols	489,186
2	Alex Rodriguez	456,988
3	Manny Ramirez	431,759
4	David Ortiz	383,317
5	Vladimir Guerrero	353,284

Total Votes: 60,227

2 **Quarterback Brett Favre** responds to an ESPN report that he's coming out of retirement — and dismisses it as "all rumor."

Seattle SuperSonics owner Clay Bennett says it best. "The NBA will be in Oklahoma City next season." He announces that the team has worked out a settlement of up to $75 million to break their lease with Seattle's KeyArena.

5 **Big sister Venus Williams** takes down Serena, 7-5, 6-4, in the women's Wimbledon singles final for her second straight Wimbledon title and fifth overall.

6 **Rafael Nadal scores** a epic five-set victory over Roger Federer at the men's Wimbledon final, 6-4, 6-4, 6-7, 6-7, 9-7. The match takes four hours, 48 minutes to complete and is considered by many to be the best final in the tournament's history. "This is my hardest loss by far," says Federer. It's Nadal's first Wimbledon win and puts an end to Federer's streak of five straight at the All England Club.

7 **Cy Young Award winner CC Sabathia** is traded from the Cleveland Indians to the Milwaukee Brewers in a deal that sends four prospects, including prized outfielder Matt LaPorta, to the Indians. A day later, the Cubs answer the Brewers' move by acquiring Rich Harden from the A's in a six-player deal.

9 **NASCAR driver Tony Stewart** announces his intentions to leave Joe Gibbs Racing after 12 successful years and two points championships.

11 **The Brett Favre saga** continues as he asks the Green Bay Packers for his release so he can come out of retirement and join another team. The Packers deny that request.

12 **Bobby Murcer,** five-time all-star and long-time member of the New York Yankees as a player, executive and broadcaster, dies after a battle with cancer at the age of 62.

Michael Chang is inducted into the Tennis Hall of Fame in Newport, Rhode Island.

14 **Justin Morneau defeats** Josh Hamilton, 5-3, in the Finals of the Home Run Derby at Yankee Stadium, but it's Hamilton's incredible 28 homers in the first round that truly has everyone buzzing. Hamilton's pair of 518-foot blasts are the longest of the night.

Much to David Stern's dismay, Tim Donaghy is back in the news when Fox News reports that the disgraced former referee made 134 calls to fellow official Scott Foster between October 2006 and April 2007 (a period that Donaghy was betting on NBA games).

Ron Jaworski, left, and musician **Jon Bon Jovi**, part of the ownership team of the Philadelphia Soul, celebrate their team's 59-56 win in ArenaBowl XXII.

AP Images

15 The American League makes it 11 in a row (not including the infamous tie in 2002) with a 4-3, 15-inning victory over the National League in the MLB All-Star Game at Yankee Stadium. The game takes four hours and 50 minutes and mercifully ends when Justin Morneau scores on Michael Young's sac fly. Boston's J.D. Drew is the game's MVP.

17 The Tour de France is again marred by doping as Italian rider Riccardo Ricco becomes the third positive test of the Tour, causing his entire Saunier Duval team to withdraw.

20 Padraig Harrington wins the British Open for the second straight year, by four strokes over Ian Poulter. 53-year-old newlywed Greg Norman heads into the final round with a surprising two-shot lead, but falls back to place fourth, six shots off the lead..

The WNBA's New York Liberty and Indiana Fever play the first outdoor game in professional basketball history. The Fever win, 71-55, in front of 19,393 fans at Arthur Ashe Stadium in New York.

22 After that "feel-good" moment for the WNBA comes a "feel-bad" moment as the L.A. Sparks and Detroit Shock engage in a nasty, final-minute fight that includes Shock assistant coach Rick Mahorn playing peacemaker, but also shoving Lisa Leslie to the floor.

27 Jimmie Johnson wins the Allstate 400 at the Brickyard for the second time in the last three years. Carl Edwards places second.

The Philadelphia Soul beat the defending champion San Jose SaberCats, 59-56, to win ArenaBowl XXII in New Orleans.

Spain's Carlos Sastre cruises down the Champs-Elysees and completes his victory in the 2008 Tour de France. Even the final stage is tainted, however, as yet another rider is busted after a positive drug test.

31 Enigmatic slugger Manny Ramirez is traded from the Red Sox to the Dodgers in a three-team, six-player deal that sends Jason Bay to the Red Sox. In other trading deadline news, Ken Griffey Jr. goes from the Reds to the White Sox.

August 2008

Sun	Mon	Tue	Wed	Thu	Fri	Sat
					1	2
3	4	5	6	7	8	9
10	11	12	13	14	15	16
17	18	19	20	21	22	23
24/31	25	26	27	28	29	30

Will Brett Favre be a big hit in the Big Apple?

Does the addition of Brett Favre make the Jets a Super Bowl contender?

58.1% — No
41.9% — Yes

Does the addition of Favre make the Jets a team you want to watch?

82.9% — Yes
17.1% — No

Has Brett Favre tarnished his legacy?

59.3% — The records outweigh the retirement mess
21.2% — This mess tarnished it no matter what
19.5% — Only if things go poorly in New York

How many more seasons will Favre play, including 2008?

49.6% — Two
31.6% — Three
18.8% — One

Total Votes: 75,882

6 **Brett Favre's career as a Green Bay Packer** is officially over as the future hall-of-famer is traded to the New York Jets for a conditional draft pick. Aaron Rodgers breathes a little easier as the new Packers quarterback, while Jets fans everywhere are elated. Long-time quarterback Chad Pennington is shipped off to Miami days later.

8 **The Summer Olympic Games** in Beijing are officially underway as the spectacular opening ceremony take place in the Beijing National Stadium. The event includes over 15,000 performers and takes place in front of over 100 heads of state/government. Yao Ming leads the Chinese delegation into the stadium next to 9-year-old Sichuan earthquake survivor Lin Hao.

Some of the ceremony's "spectacular-ness" is later called into question when it's learned that much of the fireworks video was digitally enhanced, and the song "Ode to the Motherland" was lip-synched by a 9-year-old girl because she was deemed "cuter" than the real singer.

9 **Michael Phelps starts** things off with a bang as he opens with his first gold medal and world record in the 400m IM.

Todd Bachman, father-in-law of U.S. volleyball coach Hugh McCutcheon, is stabbed to death in a seemingly random attack at the Drum Tower in Beijing. Bachman's wife Barbara is seriously wounded. The knife-wielding man commits suicide following the attacks.

10 **Jason Lezak comes from behind** and touches the wall just ahead of France's Alain Bernard to give the U.S. 4x100 freestyle relay team a gold medal — and Michael Phelps his second.

Padraig Harrington rallies to win his second straight major tournament, the PGA Championship at Oakland Hills (Mich.), by two strokes over Sergio Garcia and Ben Curtis.

12 **The Red Sox jump out** to a 10-0 first-inning lead, blow it, then come back to defeat the Texas Rangers, 19-17, at Fenway Park.

The U.S. women's gymnastics team wins the silver medal, while questions continue to be raised about the ages of the gold medal-winning Chinese squad.

15 **Michael Phelps edges** Serbia's Milorad Cavic by .01 seconds in the 100m butterfly for his seventh gold medal of the Games.

Americans Nastia Liukin and Shawn Johnson win the gold and silver, respectively, in the women's gymnastics all-around competition.

AP Images

> **President George W. Bush** practices his bumping skills with beach volleyball player **Misty May-Treanor** in Beijing on August 9.

16 Michael Phelps wins his eighth gold medal of the Beijing Games, breaking Mark Spitz's record that had stood for 26 years. The final win comes in the U.S. 4x100m medley relay team's world record breaking performance. "Without the help of my teammates, this isn't possible," he says.

Jamaica's Usain Bolt wins the gold in the 100m dash, running a 9.69 to smash his own world record of 9.72. He actually seems to slow down before the finish line, making his time even more incredible.

Dara Torres, 41, wins the silver medal in the women's 50m freestyle, narrowly missing the gold by .01 seconds.

20 Usain Bolt makes it two-for-two as he runs a 19.30 in the 200 meters to win his second gold medal and break Michael Johnson's mark of 19.32 (set in 1996).

Baseball umpires and management agree on a deal that will allow the sport to begin using instant replay to help determine close calls on the field.

21 The U.S. women's soccer team wins gold with a 1-0 victory over Brazil, but the U.S. softball team is stunned by Japan, 3-1, in their gold medal game.

Gene Upshaw, leader of the NFL Players Association and former hall-of-fame lineman for the Oakland Raiders, dies of pancreatic cancer at the age of 63.

24 The "Redeem Team" completes its mission as Dwyane Wade pours in 27 points to lead the Americans to a 118-107 win over Spain in the men's basketball gold medal game before the closing ceremonies in Beijing.

28 Defensive back Adam "Pacman" Jones has his 17-month suspension ended by NFL commissioner Roger Goodell, and suits up for the Dallas Cowboys.

30 The college football season is officially underway with a full slate of games that includes top-ranked Georgia winning, 45-21, over Georgia Southern and No. 9-ranked Clemson losing to Alabama, 34-10.

September 2008

Sun	Mon	Tue	Wed	Thu	Fri	Sat
	1	2	3	4	5	6
7	8	9	10	11	12	13
14	15	16	17	18	19	20
21	22	23	24	25	26	27
28	29	30				

ESPN SN sportsnation

Saying Goodbye to Yankee Stadium

What is the greatest baseball moment in Yankee Stadium history?

78.8%	—	Lou Gehrig's "Luckiest Man" speech, 1939
8.8%	—	Reggie Jackson hits 3 home runs in Game 6 to win the 1977 World Series
7.0%	—	Babe Ruth's final public appearance, 1948
4.6%	—	Aaron Boone's walk-off home run in Game 7 of the 2003 ALCS
0.8%	—	Jeffrey Maier gives Derek Jeter a key home run in the 1996 ALCS

What is the greatest non-baseball moment?

56.5%	—	Pope John Paul II visits the stadium, 1979
16.5%	—	9/11 Memorial tribute, 2001
11.0%	—	Colts over Giants, NFL championship game, 1958
8.3%	—	Army vs. Notre Dame, 'Game of the Century', 1946
7.7%	—	Joe Louis defeats Max Schmeling, 1938

Total Votes: 75,186

1 Cleveland's Cliff Lee blanks the Chicago White Sox, 5-0, to raise his record to 20-2, making him the Tribe's first 20-game winner since Gaylord Perry in 1974.

7 Tom Brady, Patriots starting quarterback and reigning NFL MVP, suffers a season-ending knee injury after being hit by Kansas City Chiefs safety Bernard Pollard in the first quarter of the Patriots season-opening 17-10 win. Brady had made 128 consecutive starts.

Speaking of consecutive starts, Brett Favre makes his regular season debut in a Jets uniform a successful one with a 20-14 win over Miami.

Hall-of-Fame coach Don Haskins dies at the age of 78. Haskins 1966 Texas Western team (now UTEP) features an all-black starting lineup when it defeated heavily favored Kentucky in the NCAA basketball title game.

Serena Williams beats Jelena Jankovic, 6-4, 7-5, for her third U.S. Open title and ninth overall Grand Slam singles win.

8 Aaron Rodgers makes his debut as a starting quarterback and looks sharp, completing 18 of 22 passes in a 24-19 Packers win over the Vikings on Monday Night Football.

Roger Federer wins his fifth straight U.S. Open tennis title with a 6-2, 7-5, 6-2 thrashing of Andy Murray. It is his 13th Grand Slam title, moving him just one behind Pete Sampras' all-time mark of 14.

9 Lance Armstrong announces his intention to return to competitive cycling and hopes to compete in — among other major races — the 2009 Tour de France.

13 USC races out to a 21-3 halftime lead and goes on to crush Ohio State, 35-3, in their highly anticipated college football showdown.

Francisco Rodriguez closes out the Angels' 5-2 win over the Seattle Mariners for his 58th save, breaking Bobby Thigpen's former mark of 57 set in 1990.

14 Carlos Zambrano throws Major League Baseball's second no-hitter of the season in a 5-0 Cubs win over the Milwaukee Brewers. The game is played at Miller Park in Milwaukee instead of Houston due to Hurricane Ike. It is the first Cubs no-hitter since Milt Pappas' in 1972.

Greg Biffle wins the Sylvania 300 in New Hampshire to kick off NASCAR's Chase for the Sprint Cup.

15 Longtime NFL referee Ed Hochuli is graded down after his botched call at the end of the San Diego-Denver game costs the Chargers an apparent victory.

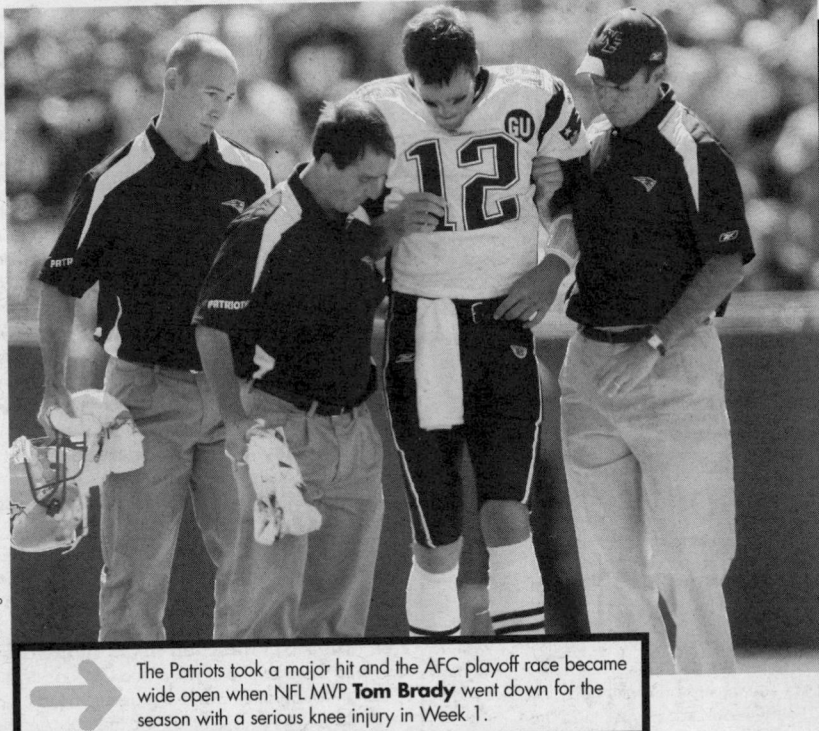

The Patriots took a major hit and the AFC playoff race became wide open when NFL MVP **Tom Brady** went down for the season with a serious knee injury in Week 1.

Ned Yost is fired as manager of the Milwaukee Brewers with just 12 games left in the season. The Brewers are tied for a wild card spot at the time of his firing, but have lost 11 of their last 14 games. Dale Sveum replaces him for the rest of the season.

16 **Derek Jeter goes 2-for-3** and breaks Lou Gehrig's all-time mark for hits at Yankee Stadium with his 1,270th.

18 **Shadow Play wins** harness racing's Little Brown Jug at the Delaware County Fairgrounds in Ohio, the second leg of the pacing Triple Crown.

21 **The United States squad** takes back the Ryder Cup, beating the Europeans, 16½-11½, at Valhalla Golf Club in Louisville. Jim Furyk's win over Miguel Angel Jimenez is the tournament clincher. It's the Americans' first Cup victory since 1999.

The Miami Dolphins pull off a stunner — beating the New England Patriots, 38-13, in Foxboro. Ronnie Brown scores four touchdowns and throws for another.

The New York Yankees play their final game at the "old" Yankee Stadium, a 7-3 win over Baltimore, and make way for their new $1.6 billion stadium starting in 2008.

24 **Matt Millen is fired** as president of the Detroit Lions after the team posted a horrible 31-84 mark since his tenure began in 2001.

25 **Classy Troy Brown** retires after 15 seasons with the Patriots.

27 **Alabama jumps** out to a 31-point lead and beats third-ranked Georgia, 41-30, two days after USC is upset, 27-21, by Oregon State. Oklahoma is now poised for the top spot.

Curlin becomes the first horse to top the $10 million mark in career earnings with a win in the Jockey Club Gold Cup.

28 **Uggh. Not again!** The Mets close out Shea Stadium on a sour note as they miss the playoffs again, thanks to a 4-2 loss to the Marlins. The Brewers advance instead.

30 **Jim Thome's homer** gives the White Sox a 1-0 win in their 163rd-game tiebreaker with the Twins, sending them to the playoffs.

October 2008

Sun	Mon	Tue	Wed	Thu	Fri	Sat
			1	2	3	4
5	6	7	8	9	10	11
12	13	14	15	16	17	18
19	20	21	22	23	24	25
26	27	28	29	30	31	

Where do these Phillies rank?

The Phillies provided Philadelphia with the city's first baseball championship in nearly three decades, but where does this team rank against the best teams to take the field since that title in 1980? **Note** that only the top 20 are listed.

	Year, Team	Points
1	2004 Red Sox	512,245
2	1998 Yankees	425,258
3	1999 Yankees	385,095
4	2007 Red Sox	369,820
5	2008 Phillies	364,716
6	2000 Yankees	343,511
7	1989 Athletics	341,007
8	1980 Phillies	325,480
9	1996 Yankees	324,570
10	2001 Diamondbacks	324,128
11	1995 Braves	319,184
12	1993 Blue Jays	299,686
13	1986 Mets	278.983
14	1988 Dodgers	268,634
15	2002 Angels	262,691
16	1984 Tigers	261,772
17	1991 Twins	252,943
18	1992 Blue Jays	244,233
19	1990 Reds	238,019
20	2003 Marlins	234,475

Total Votes: 28,383

1 **The International Gymnastics Federation** closes its investigation into the ages of the Chinese that competed at the Beijing Olympics, saying it now has sufficient proof that they were all at least 16.

2 **Helio Castroneves,** two-time Indy 500 champ and *Dancing With the Stars* winner, is indicted on charges of income tax evasion.

4 **Kimbo Slice,** MMA star and *YouTube* phenomenon, suffers an embarrassing loss on national television. He goes down in just 14 seconds to little-known Seth Petruzelli, who was merely serving as a fill-in for Ken Shamrock.

The Cubs drought reaches an even 100 years as the Dodgers complete their three-game sweep in the National League Divisional playoffs. They'll meet the Phillies in the NLCS, who get past the Brewers in four games.

5 **The New York Rangers** sweep both games of their NHL season-opening series in Prague, Czech Republic against the Tampa Bay Lightning.

The Detroit Shock win their third WNBA title in six seasons with a 76-60 Game 3 win over the San Antonio Silver Stars. Katie Smith is named Finals MVP.

6 **The ALCS matchup takes shape** as the Tampa Bay Rays take down the Chicago White Sox in four games, while the defending champion Boston Red Sox finish off the Los Angeles Angels in four on a Jed Lowrie walk-off single in the bottom of the ninth.

7 **Elgin Baylor resigns** as Vice President of Basketball Operations for the Los Angeles Clippers after 22 years as an executive with the club.

11 **Texas takes down** No. 1-ranked Oklahoma, 45-35, in a come-from behind thriller at the Cotton Bowl. "It was one of the greatest football games I've ever seen," said Longhorns coach Mack Brown. Elsewhere, third-ranked Missouri loses to Oklahoma State, 28-23, and the Florida Gators demolish the defending champion LSU Tigers, 51-21, in Gainesville.

12 **Kenya's Evans Cheruiyot** (2:06:25) and Russia's Lidiya Grigoryeva (2:27:17) win the men's and women's divisions of the Chicago Marathon.

13 **Kentucky Derby** and Preakness winner Big Brown's racing career comes to an end after he injures his right front foot during a workout.

New York Rangers budding prospect Alexei Cherepanov dies at the age of 19 after passing out on the bench just seconds after a shift with his Russian team, Avangard Omsk.

Texas running back **Chris Ogbonnaya** left multiple Sooners in his wake in the Longhorns' 45-35 thriller at the Cotton Bowl on October 11.

14 The Dallas Cowboys gain one player, lose another. They acquire wide receiver Roy Williams from the Detroit Lions at the trading deadline, while Pacman Jones is suspended for at least four games for his role in a disturbance at a Dallas hotel.

15 The Philadelphia Phillies beat the Dodgers, 5-1, and win the NLCS in five games. Cole Hamels is voted series MVP. It's the first pennant for the Phillies since 1993.

16 Denis Savard is fired as head coach of the Chicago Blackhawks, just four games into the season.

The Red Sox, down 7-0 and looking dead in the water in the seventh inning, stage an improbable comeback to beat the Rays, 8-7, in Game 5 of the ALCS.

18 Bernard Hopkins, 43, pummels middleweight champion and previously unbeaten Kelly Pavlik, easily winning by decision to improve his record to 49-5-1. "You're a great middleweight champion," he tells Pavlik. "Keep your head up."

19 The Tampa Bay Rays win Game 7 of the ALCS, 3-1, to reach their first World Series in team history. The Red Sox, who came back from a 3-1 series deficit, had no magic left — and no answer for ALCS MVP Matt Garza.

The first BCS standings of the season are released with Texas grabbing the top spot.

20 Mike Singletary is hired as head coach of the San Francisco 49ers when Mike Nolan is fired.

25 Raven's Pass upsets Curlin in the $5 million Breeders' Cup Classic at Santa Anita. Curlin finishes a disappointing fourth.

26 Jimmie Johnson's second-place finish in Atlanta all but assures him his third consecutive overall Sprint Cup points championship.

27 The skies open up in Philadelphia and Game 5 of the World Series is suspended with the Phillies and Rays tied, 2-2.

29 The Phillies win Game 5, 4-3, two days after it starts and capture their first World Series in 28 years, sending the entire city into a frenzy. Cole Hamels is the series MVP.

W2W4: What To Watch For in 2009

NFL Media

The Super Bowl returns to Tampa's Raymond James Stadium for the first time since 2001.

AP Images

The NHL's **Winter Classic** (shown here in Buffalo), heads to Wrigley Field on New Year's Day.

AP Images

Yankee Stadium and Citi Field open its doors in New York City for the 2009 MLB season.

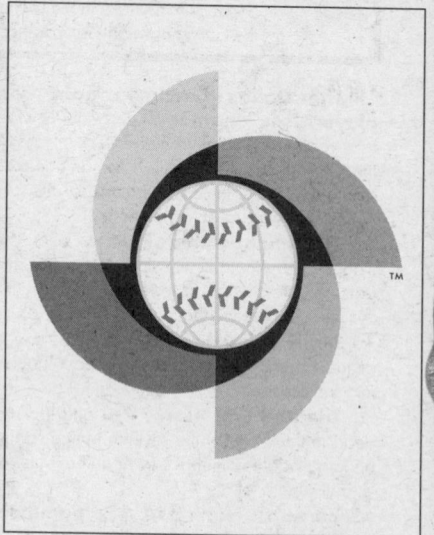

Major League Baseball

Japan looks to defend its title at the second installment of the **World Baseball Classic**, March 5-23.

BASEBALL

Josh Hamilton whipped the Yankee Stadium crowd into a frenzy at the Home Run Derby on July 14.

PHINALLIE PHILLIES

The Philadelphia Phillies beat the upstart Tampa Bay Rays in a rain-soaked World Series for their first title since 1980.

by Tim Kurkjian

IT WAS QUITE POSSIBLY THE STRANGEST WORLD SERIES OF ALL TIME.

It featured some of the worst hitting with runners in scoring position in postseason history, a 3-4 hitter combination that went hitless in its first 30 at-bats, multiple runs that scored without the benefit of a hit, some of the worst umpiring ever, miserable weather, a five-man infield, a game that ended on a bases-loaded swinging bunt, and another game — the clincher — that took three days to complete.

When it mercifully concluded, the Phillies were World Champions for the first time since 1980 and the second time in their 126-year history, beating the Tampa Bay Rays in five games, although it certainly seemed longer. It ended on a bitter cold night at Citizens Bank Park with closer Brad Lidge — who went 48-for-48 in save opportunities this year — striking out pinch-hitter Eric Hinske to protect a 4-3 lead that had been taken on an RBI single in the seventh by Pedro Feliz. The game had begun on a Monday night, but was suspended due to rain — the first suspended game in World Series history — for 46 hours until the rain stopped. But even that bizarre delay did not deter the delirious fans of the Phillies.

"I thought all year we'd win the World Series," said Phillies manager Charlie Manuel. "We did."

The loss in the World Series did nothing to diminish the marvelous story of the Rays, perhaps the best team story in baseball since the 1969 Mets. The team that had never won more than 70 games in any season, the team that had lost 972 games in its first 10 years (most by any team in

Tim Kurkjian is a senior baseball writer for ESPN.com and *ESPN The Magazine*.

Tampa Bay owner **Stuart Sternberg**, right, hugs manager **Joe Maddon** after the Rays' seven-game ALCS win over the Red Sox

AP Images

The eventual winning run in Game 1 scored on a groundout to the shortstop in the fourth inning. The Rays won Game 2, 4-2, behind 22-year-old David Price, who got the save, his second of the postseason — the first had come in Game 7 of the ALCS, making him the only rookie ever to save a postseason Game 7.

The Phillies went 1-for-28 with runners in scoring position the first two games, and weren't much better in Game 3. But they won, 5-4, in the ninth when Eric Bruntlett was hit by a pitch, stole second, went to third on a throwing error and scored on a 30-foot swinging bunt by Carlos Ruiz. Even the five-man infield deployed by Maddon couldn't prevent that odd ending. The Phillies hit four home runs — two by Ryan Howard — to win Game 4, 10-2, while the Rays' 3-4 hitters, Carlos Pena and Evan Longoria, ran their hitless streak to 0-for-29.

What happened from there defied belief, as did the entire World Series.

A World Series of this nature shouldn't have been surprising, however, following a regular season that also made little sense.

The Yankees' run of 13 consecutive playoff appearances ended — not exactly the send-off the Yankees were looking for in their final year at Yankee Stadium. The Mets became the first team in major league history to have a 3½ game lead in September two years in a row, but not make the playoffs in either year — not exactly the send-off the Mets were looking for in the final season at Shea

AP Images

Closer **Brad Lidge** and catcher **Carlos Ruiz** get the Phillies' celebration started after their rain-delayed victory in Game 5 of the World Series.

any 10-year period since the 1939-48 Phillies), won the powerful American League East and became the first team ever to win at least 95 games in a season after having posted the worst record in the major leagues.

The Rays dispatched the White Sox in the American League Division Series, then beat the defending champion Red Sox in seven games in the League Championship Series despite incredibly blowing a 7-0 lead in Game 5 — becoming the first team ever to lose a seven-run lead in a postseason elimination game.

The Rays were led by erudite manager Joe Maddon, who wears funny glasses and, in a three-week period in the postseason, used the words anticipatory, intuitive, incongruent, ameliorates and hyperbole in complete sentences. He was the perfect manager for a bunch of young, hungry kids who played on the biggest stage for the first time in their fledgling careers. But in the end, their magic, or whatever they had working, finally wore off.

"A mind once stretched," Maddon said after the game, waxing poetic about where this amazing season has taken the franchise, "has a difficult time going back to its original form."

The Rays lost the World Series opener, 3-2, to Phillies ace Cole Hamels, who won the World Series MVP with that win plus a solid six-inning effort in the clinching Game 5.

Stadium. The Brewers made the playoffs for the first time in 26 years, but at the expense of manager Ned Yost, who, in an unprecedented move in baseball history, was fired in the midst of a pennant race with only 12 games to go.

The Cubs and White Sox made the playoffs in the same season for the first time since 1906, but it didn't end well for either. The Cubs were swept out of the first round of the playoffs by the Dodgers, despite posting the best record in the league —not exactly the send-off they were looking for in the 100-year anniversary of their last World Championship.

"We were expecting more," said Cubs manager Lou Piniella.

The Tigers, who many picked to return to the World Series in 2008, finished last in the AL Central.

"We were expecting much more," said Tigers manager Jim Leyland.

The Mariners were supposed to contend in the AL West, but instead became the first team in history to lose 100 games with a payroll above $100 million. The Mariners were so bad, backup catcher Jamie Burke, was forced to pitch the 15th inning of a game against the Tigers, becoming the first positional player to take a loss in a game since Jeff Hamilton in 1989.

The Indians were supposed to contend, but didn't come close, so they traded the reigning Cy Young award winner, CC Sabathia, to Milwaukee. And yet the Indians produced another certain Cy Young winner, Cliff Lee, who spent the second half of 2007 in the minor leagues. Sabathia was the biggest (300 lbs.) Cy Young

winner in history in 2007, and maybe the smallest Cy Young will come this year from the NL in the Giants' Tim Lincecum, who weighs 165 lbs.

"The better he gets," said teammate Rich Aurilia, "the smaller he gets."

But Lincecum didn't do what Boston's Jon Lester and the Cubs' Carlos Zambrano did: throw a no-hitter. And they didn't do what Mike Mussina did: win 20 games, making him the oldest pitcher (39) to win 20 for the first time.

It was a season of change. After a spate of missed/controversial calls in a 10-day span in May, Major League Baseball adopted instant replay on home runs calls only (boundary calls, fair or foul).

For the first time since 1986, a season was played without Roger Clemens or Barry Bonds. Without Bonds, and maybe without rampant steroid use, home run totals dropped to their lowest point in 15 years. The AL home run leader didn't reach 40 for the first time since 1989.

But, it was still a great year for home runs. Manny Ramirez hit No. 500, (then soon after was traded to the Dodgers because he didn't want to play for the Red Sox anymore, and forced them to trade him).

Ken Griffey Jr. hit No. 600. The Rangers' Josh Hamilton put on one of the great power shows of all time in the All-Star Home Run Derby at Yankee Stadium. After the All-Star break, Hamilton was walked intentionally with the bases loaded by the Rays, only the second time that has happened since divisional play began in 1969.

Phillies ace **Cole Hamels** followed an impressive regular season with a 4-0 record in the postseason. He was MVP of the NLCS and the World Series.

AP Images

It was a season full of quirks, and firsts. Diamondbacks third baseman Mark Reynolds set the major league record for strikeouts in a season with 204 — more than the worst strikeout seasons of Babe Ruth, Ted Williams and Joe DiMaggio combined. Lumbering Brewers first baseman Prince Fielder hit the second inside-the-park home run of his career, giving him twice as many as Ichiro Suzuki and Rickey Henderson combined.

Seattle knuckleballer R.A. Dickey tied a major league record with four wild pitches in an inning — Mariano Rivera hasn't had four wild pitches in the last eight years. On June 22, the Rangers' Ian Kinsler and the Nationals' Willie Harris became the first players ever to hit a home run on their birthday in the same game. Greg Maddux became the oldest pitcher to steal a base, and, for the first time in his career, he threw a wild pitch, made a fielding error and hit a batter in one game.

And, in a 12-day stretch, Mets speedster Jose Reyes was thrown out trying to steal by the three Molina brothers — Bengie, Yadier and Jose.

It was that kind of year. And it was tremendous.

2008
Season in Review

SPORTS ALMANAC

Final Major League Standings

Division champions (*) and Wild Card (†) winners are noted. Number of seasons listed after each manager refers to current tenure with club.

American League
East Division

	W	L	Pct	GB	Home	Road
*Tampa Bay	97	65	.599	—	57-24	40-41
†Boston	95	67	.586	2	56-25	39-42
New York	89	73	.549	8	48-33	41-40
Toronto	86	76	.531	11	47-34	39-42
Baltimore	68	93	.422	28½	37-43	31-50

2008 Managers: TB–Joe Maddon (3rd season); **Bos**–Terry Francona (5th); **NY**–Joe Girardi (1st); **Tor**–John Gibbons (5th, 35-39) was fired on June 20 and replaced by Cito Gaston (51-37); **Bal**–Dave Trembley (2nd).
2007 Standings: 1. Boston (96-66); 2. New York (94-68); 3. Toronto (83-79); 4. Baltimore (69-93); 5. Tampa Bay (66-96).

Central Division

	W	L	Pct	GB	Home	Road
*Chicago	89	74	.546	—	54-28	35-46
Minnesota	88	75	.540	1	53-28	35-47
Cleveland	81	81	.500	7½	45-36	36-45
Kansas City	75	87	.463	13½	47-34	37-44
Detroit	74	88	.457	14½	40-41	34-47

2008 Managers: Chi–Ozzie Guillen (5th season); **Min**–Ron Gardenhire (7th); **Cle**–Eric Wedge (5th); **KC**–Trey Hillman (1st); **Det**–Jim Leyland (3rd).
2007 Standings: 1. Cleveland (96-66); 2. Detroit (88-74); 3. Minnesota (79-83); 4. Chicago (72-90); 5. Kansas City (69-93).
Note: Chicago won the division with a 1-0 victory over Minnesota in a one-game playoff.

West Division

	W	L	Pct	GB	Home	Road
*Los Angeles	100	62	.617	—	50-31	50-31
Texas	79	83	.488	21	40-41	39-42
Oakland	75	86	.466	24½	43-38	32-48
Seattle	61	101	.377	39	35-46	26-55

2008 Managers: LAA–Mike Scioscia (8th season); **Tex**–Ron Washington (2nd); **Oak**–Bob Geren (2nd); **Sea**–John McLaren (2nd, 25-47) was fired on June 19 and replaced by Jim Riggleman (36-54).
2007 Standings: 1. Los Angeles (94-68); 2. Seattle (88-74); 3. Oakland (76-86); 4. Texas (75-87).

National League
East Division

	W	L	Pct	GB	Home	Road
*Philadelphia	92	70	.568	—	48-33	44-37
New York	89	73	.549	3	48-33	41-40
Florida	84	77	.522	7½	45-36	39-41
Atlanta	72	90	.444	20	43-38	29-52
Washington	59	102	.366	32½	34-46	25-56

2008 Managers: Phi–Charlie Manuel (4th season); **NY**–Willie Randolph (4th, 34-35) was fired on June 17 and replaced by Jerry Manuel (55-38); **Fla**–Fredi Gonzalez (2nd); **Atl**–Bobby Cox (19th); **Wash**–Manny Acta (2nd).
2007 Standings: 1. Philadelphia (89-73); 2. New York (88-74); 3. Atlanta (84-78); 4. Washington (73-89); 5. Florida (71-91).

Central Division

	W	L	Pct	GB	Home	Road
*Chicago	97	64	.602	—	55-26	42-38
†Milwaukee	90	72	.556	7½	49-32	41-40
Houston	86	75	.534	11	47-33	39-42
St. Louis	86	76	.531	11½	46-35	40-41
Cincinnati	74	88	.457	23½	43-38	31-50
Pittsburgh	67	95	.414	30½	39-42	28-53

2008 Managers: Chi–Lou Piniella (2nd season); **Mil**–Ned Yost (6th, 83-67) was fired on Sept. 15 and replaced by Dale Sveum (7-5); **Hou**–Cecil Cooper (2nd); **St.L**–Tony La Russa (13th); **Cin**–Dusty Baker (1st); **Pit**–John Russell (1st).
2007 Standings: 1. Chicago (85-77); 2. Milwaukee (83-79); 3. St. Louis (78-84); 4. Houston (73-89); 5. Cincinnati (72-90); 6. Pittsburgh (68-94).

West Division

	W	L	Pct	GB	Home	Road
*Los Angeles	84	78	.519	—	48-33	36-45
Arizona	82	80	.506	2	48-33	34-47
Colorado	74	88	.457	10	43-38	31-50
San Francisco	72	90	.444	12	37-44	35-46
San Diego	63	99	.389	21	35-46	28-53

2008 Managers: LA–Joe Torre (1st season); **Ari**–Bob Melvin (4th); **Col**–Clint Hurdle (7th); **SF**–Bruce Bochy (2nd); **SD**–Bud Black (2nd).
2007 Standings: 1. Arizona (90-72); 2. Colorado (90-73); 3. San Diego (89-74); 4. Los Angeles (82-80); 5. San Francisco (71-91).

Interleague Play Standings

American League

	W-L	Pct		W-L	Pct
Minnesota	14-4	.778	Texas	10-8	.556
Kansas City	13-5	.722	Oakland	10-8	.556
Detroit	13-5	.722	Seattle	9-9	.500
Tampa Bay	12-6	.667	Toronto	8-10	.444
Chicago	12-6	.667	Cleveland	6-12	.333
Boston	11-7	.611	**Totals**	**149-103**	**.591**
Baltimore	11-7	.611			
New York	10-8	.556			
Los Angeles	10-8	.556			

National League

	W-L	Pct		W-L	Pct
New York	9-6	.600	Arizona	6-9	.400
Cincinnati	9-6	.600	Houston	7-11	.389
Atlanta	8-7	.533	San Francisco	6-12	.333
Milwaukee	7-8	.467	Florida	5-10	.333
St. Louis	7-8	.467	Los Angeles	5-10	.333
Colorado	7-8	.467	Philadelphia	4-11	.267
Washington	8-10	.444	San Diego	3-15	.167
Pittsburgh	6-9	.400	**Totals**	**103-149**	**.409**
Chicago	6-9	.400			

Minnesota Twins
Joe Mauer
Batting Avg.

Texas Rangers
Josh Hamilton
RBI, Total Bases

Cleveland Indians
Cliff Lee
ERA, Wins

Los Angeles Angels
Francisco Rodriguez
Saves, Appearances

American League Leaders

(*) indicates rookie.

Batting

	Bat	Gm	AB	R	H	Avg	TB	2B	3B	HR	RBI	BB	SO	SB	Slg Pct	OBP
Joe Mauer, Min	L	146	536	98	176	**.328**	242	31	4	9	85	84	50	1	.451	.413
Dustin Pedroia, Bos	R	157	653	118	213	**.326**	322	54	2	17	83	50.	52	20	.493	.376
Milton Bradley, Tex	S	126	414	78	133	**.321**	233	32	1	22	77	80	112	5	.563	.436
Ian Kinsler, Tex	R	121	518	102	165	**.319**	268	41	4	18	71	45	67	26	.517	.375
Magglio Ordonez, Det	R	146	561	72	178	**.317**	277	32	2	21	103	53	76	1	.494	.376
Kevin Youkilis, Bos	L	145	538	91	168	**.312**	306	43	4	29	115	62	108	3	.569	.390
Ichiro Suzuki, Sea	L	162	686	103	213	**.310**	265	20	7	6	42	51	65	43	.386	.361
David DeJesus, KC	L	135	518	70	159	**.307**	234	25	7	12	73	46	71	11	.452	.366
Placido Polanco, Det	R	141	580	90	178	**.307**	242	34	3	8	58	35	43	7	.417	.350
Nick Markakis, Bal	L	157	595	106	182	**.306**	292	48	1	20	87	99	113	10	.491	.406
Josh Hamilton, Tex	L	156	624	98	190	**.304**	331	35	5	32	130	64	126	9	.530	.371
Aubrey Huff, Bal	L	154	598	96	182	**.304**	330	48	2	32	108	53	89	4	.552	.360
Vladimir Guerrero, LA	R	143	541	85	164	**.303**	282	31	3	27	91	51	77	5	.521	.365
Johnny Damon, NY	L	143	555	95	168	**.303**	256	27	5	17	71	64	82	29	.461	.375
Alex Rodriguez, NY	R	138	510	104	154	**.302**	292	35	3	0	35	103	65	117	18	.573	.392

Note: Batters must have 3.1 plate appearances per their team's games played to qualify.

Home Runs

Cabrera, Det	37
Quentin, Chi	36
A. Rodriguez, NY.	35
Thome, Chi	34
Dye, Chi	34
Cust, Oak	33
Sizemore, Cle	33
Giambi, NY	32
Huff, Bal	32
Hamilton, Tex.	32

Triples

Granderson, Det	13
Crawford, TB	10
Iwamura, TB	9
Roberts, Bal	8
Rios, Tor	8
Seven tied with 7 each.	

On Base Pct.

Bradley, Tex.	.436
Mauer, Min	.413
Markakis, Bal	.406
Quentin, Chi	.394
A. Rodriguez, NY	.392
Youkilis, Bos.	.390
Upton, TB	.383
Roberts, Bal.	.378
Pena, TB	.377

Runs Batted In

Hamilton, Tx	130
Morneau, Min	129
Cabrera, Det	127
Youkilis, Bos.	115
Ibanez, Sea	110
Huff, Bal	108
Mora, Bal	104
A. Rodriguez, NY.	103
Ordonez, Det	103
Pena, TB	102

Doubles

Pedroia, Bos	54
Roberts, Bal.	51
Huff, Bal	48
Markakis, Bal.	48
Morneau, Min	47
Rios, Tor	47
Ibanez, Sea	43
Youkilis, Bos.	43

Slugging Pct.

A. Rodriguez, NY	.573
Quentin, Chi	.571
Youkilis, Bos.	.569
Bradley, Tex.	.563
Huff, Bal	.552
Dye, Chi	.541
Cabrera, Det	.537

Hits

Suzuki, Sea	213
Pedroia, Bos	213
Lopez, Sea	191
Hamilton, Tex.	190
Morneau, Min	187
Ibanez, Sea	186
Cabrera, Chi	186
Rios, Tor	185
Young, Tex.	183

Runs

Pedroia, Bos	118
Granderson, Det	112
Roberts, Bal.	107
Markakis, Bal.	106
A. Rodriguez, NY.	104
Peralta, Cle	104
Suzuki, Sea	103
Young, Tex.	102
Kinsler, Tex.	102

Walks

Cust, Oak	111
Markakis, Bal.	99
Sizemore, Cle	98
Upton, TB	97
Pena, TB	96
Thome, Chi	94
Mauer, Min	84

Stolen Bases

	SB	CS
Ellsbury*, Bos	50	11
Upton, TB	44	16
Suzuki, Sea	43	4
Roberts, Bal	40	10
Sizemore, Cle	38	5
Figgins, LA	34	13
Gomez, Min	33	11
Rios, Tor	32	8
Damon, NY	29	8

Total Bases

Hamilton, Tex.	331
Cabrera, Det	331
Huff, Bal	330
Pedroia, Bos	322
Dye, Chi	319
Sizemore, Cle	318
Morneau, Min	311
Youkilis, Bos.	306

Strikeouts

Cust, Oak	197
Pena, TB	166
Thome, Chi	147
Gomez, Min	142
Swisher, Chi	135
Upton, TB	134

Pitching

	Arm	W	L	ERA	Gm	GS	CG	ShO	Sv	IP	H	R	ER	HR	HB	BB	SO	WP
Cliff Lee, Cle	L	22	3	2.54	31	31	4	2	0	223.1	214	68	63	12	5	34	170	4
Roy Halladay, Tor	R	20	11	2.78	34	33	9	2	0	246.0	220	88	76	18	12	39	206	4
Daisuke Matsuzaka, Bos	R	18	3	2.90	29	29	0	0	0	167.2	128	58	54	12	7	94	154	5
Jon Lester, Bos	L	16	6	3.21	33	33	2	2	0	210.1	202	78	75	14	10	66	152	3
John Danks, Chi	L	12	9	3.32	33	33	0	0	0	195.0	182	74	72	15	4	57	159	7
Mike Mussina, NY	R	20	9	3.37	34	34	0	0	0	200.1	214	85	75	17	8	31	150	4
Joe Saunders, LA	L	17	7	3.41	31	31	1	0	0	198.0	187	82	75	21	6	53	103	3
Scott Baker, Min	R	11	4	3.45	28	28	0	0	0	172.1	161	66	66	20	3	42	141	6
Felix Hernandez, Sea	R	9	11	3.45	31	31	2	0	0	200.2	198	85	77	17	8	80	175	8
Zack Greinke, KC	R	13	10	3.47	32	32	1	0	0	202.1	202	87	78	21	4	56	183	4
Ervin Santana, LA	R	16	7	3.49	32	32	2	1	0	219.0	198	89	85	23	8	47	214	5
James Shields, TB	R	14	8	3.56	33	33	3	2	0	215.0	208	94	85	24	12	40	160	6
Jesse Litsch, Tor	R	13	9	3.58	29	28	2	2	0	176.0	178	79	70	20	8	39	99	4
Jeremy Guthrie, Bal	R	10	12	3.63	30	30	1	0	0	190.2	176	82	77	24	7	58	120	3
Matt Garza, TB	R	11	9	3.70	30	30	3	2	0	184.2	170	83	76	19	6	59	128	3

Note: Pitchers must have one inning pitched per their team's games played to qualify.

Wins

Lee, Cle	22-3
Mussina, NY	20-9
Halladay, Tor	20-11
Matsuzaka, Bos	18-3
Burnett, Tor	18-10
Saunders, LA	17-7
Floyd, Chi	17-8

Appearances

Rodriguez, LA	76
Guerrier, Min	76
Wright, Tex	75
Reyes, Min	75
Thornton, Chi	74
Delcarmen, Bos	73
Perez, Cle	73

Complete Games

Halladay, Tor	9
Lee, Cle	4
Millwood, Tex	3
Sabathia, Cle	3
Lackey, LA	3
Shields, TB	3
Garza, TB	3
Slowey, Min	3

Shutouts

Halladay, Tor	2
Sabathia, Cle	2
Lee, Cle	2
Shields, TB	2
Lester, Bos	2
Garza, TB	2
Slowey, Min	2
Litsch, Tor	2

Losses

Verlander, Det	11-17
Smith*, Oak	7-16
Bannister, KC	9-16
Vazquez, Chi	12-16
Silva, Sea	4-15
Batista, Sea	4-14
Washburn, Sea	5-14
Pettitte, NY	14-14

Innings

Halladay, Tor	246.0
Lee, Cle	223.1
Burnett, Tor	221.1
Santana, LA	219.0
Buehrle, Chi	218.2
Shields, TB	215.0
Meche, KC	210.1
Lester, Bos	210.1
Vazquez, Chi	208.1
Floyd, Chi	206.1
Pettitte, NY	204.0

Saves

	SV	BS
Rodriguez, LA	62	7
Soria, KC	42	3
Papelbon, Bos	41	5
Rivera, NY	39	1
Nathan, Min	39	6
Ryan, Tor	32	4
Sherrill, Bal	31	6
Jenks, Chi	30	4
Percival, TB	28	4
Wilson, Tex	24	4
Jones, Det	18	3
Street, Oak	18	7

Walks

Matsuzaka, Bos	94
Cabrera, Bal	90
Verlander, Det	87
Smith*, Oak	87
Burnett, Tor	86
Hernandez, Sea	80
Batista, Sea	79
Jackson, TB	77
Eveland, Oak	77
Meche, KC	73

HRs Allowed

Byrd, Cle-Bos	31
Floyd, Chi	30
Bannister, KC	29
Galarraga*, Det	28
Padilla, Tex	26
Lackey, LA	26
Robertson, Det	26

Wild Pitches

Cabrera, Bal	15
Wakefield, Bos	12
Padilla, Tex	12
Burnett, Tor	11
Dickey, Sea	11
Floyd, Chi	9

Hit Batters

Cabrera, Bal	18
Padilla, Tex	15
Verlander, Det	14
Wakefield, Bos	13
Halladay, Tor	12
Eveland, Oak	12
Shields, TB	12

Strikeouts

Burnett, Tor	231
Santana, LA	214
Halladay, Tor	206
Vazquez, Chi	200
Meche, KC	183
Greinke, KC	183
Hernandez, Sea	175
Beckett, Bos	172
Lee, Cle	170
Kazmir, TB	166

Opp. Batting Average

Matsuzaka, Bos	.211
Galarraga*, Det	.226
Wakefield, Bos	.228
Halladay, Tor	.237
Santana, LA	.237
Floyd, Chi	.241
Guthrie, Bal	.242
Smith*, Oak	.243
Garza, TB	.245
Danks, Chi	.246

WHIP
(Walks + Hits/IP)

Halladay, Tor	1.05
Lee, Cle	1.11
Santana, LA	1.12
Shields, TB	1.15
Baker, Min	1.18
Wakefield, Bos	1.18
Beckett, Bos	1.19
Galarraga*, Det	1.19
Saunders, LA	1.21
Mussina, NY	1.22

Fielding

Put Outs

Morneau, Min	1316
Overbay, Tor	1316
Cabrera, Det	1117
Millar, Bal	1099
Garko, Cle	1039
Barton*, Oak	1021
Konerko, Chi	1010
Pena, TB	991
Suzuki, Oak	927
Youkilis, Bos	923

Assists

Cano, NY	482
Cabrera, Chi	472
Young, Tex	465
Lopez, Sea	468
Pedroia, Bos	448
Roberts, Bal	441
Peralta, Cle	427
Betancourt, Sea	401
Iwamura, TB	397
Kinsler, Tex	390

OF Assists

Markakis, Bal	17
Upton, TB	16
Rios, Tor	14
Francisco*, Cle	12
Young, Min	11
Suzuki, Sea	11
Guillen, KC	10
Brown, Oak	10
Abreu, NY	10
Three tied with 9.	

Errors

Betancourt, Sea	21
Crede, Chi	20
Kinsler, Tex	18
Aybar, LA	18
Crosby, Oak	17
Gordon, KC	16
Cabrera, Chi	16
Renteria, Det	16
Bartlett, TB	16
Lugo, Bos	16

Atlanta Braves
Chipper Jones
Avg., OBP

Philadelphia Phillies
Ryan Howard
Home Runs, RBI

St. Louis Cardinals
Albert Pujols
SLG, Total Bases

New York Mets
Johan Santana
ERA, Innings

National League Leaders

(*) indicates rookie.

Batting

	Bat	Gm	AB	R	H	Avg	TB	2B	3B	HR	RBI	BB	SO	SB	Slg Pct	OBP
Chipper Jones, Atl	S	128	439	82	160	**.364**	252	24	1	22	75	90	61	4	.574	.470
Albert Pujols, St.L	R	148	524	100	187	**.357**	342	44	0	37	116	104	54	7	.653	.462
Matt Holliday, Col	R	139	539	107	173	**.321**	290	38	2	25	88	74	104	28	.538	.409
Cristian Guzman, Wash	S	138	579	77	183	**.316**	255	35	5	9	55	23	57	6	.440	.345
Lance Berkman, Hou	S	159	554	114	173	**.312**	314	46	4	29	106	99	108	18	.567	.420
Ryan Theriot, Chi	R	149	580	85	178	**.307**	208	19	4	1	38	73	58	22	.359	.387
Randy Winn, SF	S	155	598	84	183	**.306**	255	38	2	10	64	59	88	25	.426	.363
Brian Giles, SD	L	147	559	81	171	**.306**	255	40	4	12	63	87	52	2	.456	.398
Andre Ethier, LA	L	141	525	90	160	**.305**	268	38	5	20	77	59	88	6	.510	.375
David Wright, NY	R	160	626	115	189	**.302**	334	42	2	33	124	94	118	15	.534	.390
Skip Schumaker, St.L	L	153	540	87	163	**.302**	219	22	5	8	46	47	60	8	.406	.359
Brian McCann, Atl	L	145	509	68	153	**.301**	266	42	1	23	87	57	64	5	.523	.373
Hanley Ramirez, Fla	R	153	589	125	177	**.301**	318	34	4	33	67	92	122	35	.540	.400
Conor Jackson, Ari	R	144	540	87	162	**.300**	241	31	6	12	75	59	61	10	.446	.376
Ryan Ludwick, St.L	R	152	538	104	161	**.299**	318	40	3	37	113	62	146	4	.591	.375

Note: Batters must have 3.1 plate appearances per their team's games played to qualify.

Home Runs

Howard, Phi	48
Dunn, Cin-Ari	40
Delgado, NY	38
Pujols, St.L	37
Ludwick, St.L	37
Braun, Mil	37
A. Gonzalez, SD	36
Fielder, Mil	34
Four tied with 32 each.	

Runs Batted In

Howard, Phi	146
Wright, NY	124
A. Gonzalez, SD	119
Pujols, St.L	116
Delgado, NY	115
Ludwick, St.L	113
Beltran, NY	112
Ramirez, Chi	111
Berkman, Hou	106
Braun, Mil	106

Hits

Reyes, NY	204
Wright, NY	189
Pujols, St.L	187
Winn, SF	183
Guzman, Wash	183
Lee, Chi	181
Tejada, Hou	179
Drew, Ari	178
Theriot, Chi	178

Stolen Bases

	SB	CS
Taveras, Col	68	7
Reyes, NY	56	15
Rollins, Phi	47	3
Bourn, Hou	41	10
Pierre, LA	40	12
Victorino, Phi	36	11
Ramirez, Fla	35	12
Kemp, LA	35	11

Triples

Reyes, NY	19
Drew, Ari	11
Lewis, SF	11
Rollins, Phi	9
Victorino, Phi	8
Five tied with 7 each.	

Doubles

Berkman, Hou	46
McLouth, Pit	46
Hart, Mil	45
Ramirez, Chi	44
Pujols, St.L	44
Drew, Ari	44
Three tied with 42 each.	

Runs

Ramirez, Fla	125
Beltran, NY	116
Wright, NY	115
Berkman, Hou	114
Utley, Phi	113
Reyes, NY	113
McLouth, Pit	113
Holliday, Col	107

Total Bases

Pujols, St.L	342
Braun, Mil	338
Wright, NY	334
Howard, Phi	331
Reyes, NY	327
Utley, Phi	325
Ludwick, St.L	318
Ramirez, Fla	318

On Base Pct.

Jones, Atl	.470
Pujols, St.L	.462
Berkman, Hou	.420
Holliday, Col	.409
Ramirez, Fla	.400
Giles, SD	.398
Wright, NY	.390
Theriot, Chi	.387
Dunn, Cin-Ari	.386

Slugging Pct.

Pujols, St.L	.653
Ludwick, St.L	.591
Jones, Atl	.574
Berkman, Hou	.567
Braun, Mil	.553
Howard, Phi	.543
Ramirez, Fla	.540

Walks

Dunn, Cin-Ari	122
Pujols, St.L	104
Burrell, Phi	102
Berkman, Hou	99
Wright, NY	94
Beltran, NY	92
Ramirez, Fla	92

Strikeouts

Reynolds, Ari	204
Howard, Phi	199
Uggla, Fla	171
Young, Ari	165
Dunn, Cin-Ari	164
Kemp, LA	153
Ludwick, St.L	146

Pitching

	Arm	W	L	ERA	Gm	GS	CG	ShO	Sv	IP	H	R	ER	HR	HB	BB	SO	WP
Johan Santana, NY	L	16	7	2.53	34	34	3	2	0	234.1	206	74	66	23	4	63	206	9
Tim Lincecum, SF	R	18	5	2.62	34	33	2	1	0	227.0	182	72	66	11	6	84	265	17
Jake Peavy, SD	R	10	11	2.85	27	27	1	0	0	173.2	146	57	55	17	5	59	166	6
Ryan Dempster, Chi	R	17	6	2.96	33	33	1	0	0	206.2	174	75	68	14	7	76	187	5
Ben Sheets, Mil	R	13	9	3.09	31	31	5	3	0	198.1	181	74	68	17	1	47	158	8
Cole Hamels, Phi	L	14	10	3.09	33	33	2	2	0	227.1	193	89	78	28	1	53	196	0
Chad Billingsley, LA	R	16	10	3.14	35	32	1	1	0	200.2	188	76	70	14	8	80	201	10
Edinson Volquez, Cin	R	17	6	3.21	33	32	0	0	0	196.0	167	82	70	14	14	93	206	10
Derek Lowe, LA	R	14	11	3.24	34	34	1	0	0	211.0	194	84	76	14	1	45	147	2
Brandon Webb, Ari	R	22	7	3.30	34	34	3	1	0	226.2	206	95	83	13	12	65	183	8
Dan Haren, Ari	R	16	8	3.33	33	33	1	1	0	216.0	204	86	80	19	6	40	206	11
Ricky Nolasco, Fla	R	15	8	3.52	34	32	1	1	0	212.1	192	88	83	28	6	42	186	1
Roy Oswalt, Hou	R	17	10	3.54	32	32	3	2	0	208.2	199	89	82	23	10	47	165	1
Jair Jurrjens*, Atl	R	13	10	3.68	31	31	0	0	0	188.1	188	87	77	11	4	70	139	3
Paul Maholm, Pit	L	9	9	3.71	31	31	1	0	0	206.1	201	89	85	21	9	63	139	2

Note: Pitchers must have one inning pitched per their team's games played to qualify.

Wins
Webb, Ari 22-7
Lincecum, SF 18-5
Dempster, Chi 17-6
Volquez, Cin 17-6
Lilly, Chi 17-9
Oswalt, Hou 17-10
Moyer, Phi 16-7
Santana, NY 16-7
Haren, Ari 16-8
Cook, Col 16-9
Billingsley, LA 16-10

Appearances
Feliciano, NY 86
Ohman, Atl 83
Marmol, Chi 82
Smith, NY 82
Romero, Phi 81
Ayala, Wash-NY 81
Heilman, NY 78

Complete Games
Sabathia, Mil 7
Sheets, Mil 5
Santana, NY 3
Oswalt, Hou 3
Webb, Ari 3
Seven tied with 2 each.

Shutouts
Sabathia, Mil 3
Sheets, Mil 3
Santana, NY 2
Oswalt, Hou 2
Hamels, Phi 2
Kuroda*, LA 2

Losses
Harang, Cin 6-17
Zito, SF 10-17
Lannan*, Wash 9-15
Duke, Pit 5-14
Cain, SF 8-14
Cueto*, Cin 9-14
Backe, Hou 9-14
Looper, St.L 12-14

Innings
Santana, NY 234.1
Hamels, Phi 227.1
Lincecum, SF 227.0
Webb, Ari 226.2
Cain, SF 217.2
Haren, Ari 216.0
Nolasco, Fla 212.1
Cook, Col 211.1
Lowe, LA 211.0
Oswalt, Hou 208.2

Saves
	SV	BS
Valverde, Hou	44	7
Lidge, Phi	41	0
Wilson, SF	41	6
Wood, Chi	34	6
Cordero, Cin	34	6
Hoffman, SD	30	4
Fuentes, Col	30	4
Gregg, Fla	29	9
Torres, Mil	28	7
Wagner, NY	27	7
Lyon, Ari	26	5

Walks
Perez, NY 105
Jimenez, Col 103
Zito, SF 102
Volquez, Cin 93
Cain, SF 91
Snell, Pit 89
Lincecum, SF 84
Billingsley, LA 80
Backe, Hou 77

HR Allowed
Backe, Hou 36
Harang, Cin 35
Lilly, Chi 32
Suppan, Mil 30
Olsen, Fla 30
Four tied with 29 each.

Wild Pitches
Lincecum, SF 17
Parra, Mil 17
Jimenez, Col 16
De La Rosa, Col 14
Haren, Ari 11
Redding, Wash 10
Maine, NY 10
Volquez, Cin 10
Billingsley, LA 10

Hit Batters
Volquez, Cin 14
Kendrick, Phi 14
Cueto*, Cin 14
Pelfrey, NY 13

Strikeouts
Lincecum, SF 265
Santana, NY 206
Harén, Ari 206
Volquez, Cin 206
Billingsley, LA 201
Hamels, Phi 196
Dempster, Chi 187
Cain, SF 186
Nolasco, Fla 186

Opp. Batting Average
Lincecum, SF 221
Hamels, Phi 227
Dempster, Chi 227
Peavy, SD 229
Volquez, Cin 232
Santana, NY 232
Bush, Mil 234
Perez, NY 234
Nolasco, Fla 239
Lilly, Chi 239

WHIP
(Walks + Hits/IP)
Hamels, Phi 1.08
Nolasco, Fla 1.10
Haren, Ari 1.13
Lowe, LA 1.13
Bush, Mil 1.14
Santana, NY 1.15
Sheets, Mil 1.15
Lincecum, SF 1.17
Oswalt, Hou 1.18
Peavy, SD 1.18

Fielding

Put Outs
Howard, Phi 1408
Fielder, Mil 1369
Loney, LA 1364
Gonzalez, SD 1306
Pujols, St.L 1297
Berkman, Hou 1240
Delgado, NY 1237
Lee, Chi 1193
Ad. LaRoche, Pit . . . 1130
Votto*, Cin 1050

Assists
Utley, Phi 463
Tejada, Hou 442
Hardy, Mil 430
Johnson, Atl 425
Reyes, NY 422
Phillips, Cin 401
Ramirez, Fla 401
Escobar, Atl 396
Guzman, Wash 394
Rollins, Phi 393

OF Assists
Pence, Hou 16
Kemp, LA 16
Francouer, Atl 14
Ludwick, St.L 12
Burrell, Phi 12
Lewis, SF 11
Ethier, LA 11
Soriano, Chi 10
Schumaker, St.L 10
Nady, Pit 10

Errors
Reynolds, Ari 34
Encarnacion, Cin . . . 23
Ramirez, Fla 22
Cantu, Fla 20
Howard, Phi 19
Ramirez, Chi 18
Fielder, Mil 17
Hall, Mil 17
Reyes, NY 17
Guzman, Wash 17

Team Batting Statistics

American League

Team	Avg	AB	R	H	HR	RBI	SB
Texas	.283	5728	901	1619	194	867	81
Boston	.280	5596	845	1565	173	807	120
Minnesota	.279	5641	829	1572	111	791	102
New York	.271	5572	789	1512	180	758	118
Detroit	.271	5641	821	1529	200	780	63
Kansas City	.269	5608	691	1507	120	650	79
Los Angeles	.268	5540	765	1486	159	721	129
Baltimore	.267	5559	782	1486	172	750	81
Seattle	.265	5643	671	1498	124	631	90
Toronto	.264	5503	714	1453	126	681	80
Chicago	.263	5553	811	1458	235	785	67
Cleveland	.262	5543	805	1455	171	772	77
Tampa Bay	.260	5541	774	1443	180	735	142
Oakland	.242	5451	646	1318	125	610	88

National League

Team	Avg	AB	R	H	HR	RBI	SB
St. Louis	.281	5636	779	1585	174	744	73
Chicago	.278	5588	855	1552	184	811	87
Atlanta	.270	5604	753	1514	130	721	58
New York	.266	5606	799	1491	172	751	138
Los Angeles	.264	5506	700	1455	137	659	126
Colorado	.263	5557	747	1462	160	714	141
Houston	.263	5451	712	1432	167	684	114
San Francisco	.262	5543	640	1452	94	606	108
Pittsburgh	.258	5628	735	1454	153	705	57
Philadelphia	.255	5509	799	1407	214	762	136
Florida	.254	5499	770	1397	208	741	76
Milwaukee	.253	5535	750	1398	198	722	108
Washington	.251	5491	641	1376	117	608	81
Arizona	.251	5409	720	1355	159	683	58
San Diego	.250	5568	637	1390	154	615	36
Cincinnati	.247	5465	704	1351	187	677	85

Team Pitching Statistics

American League

Team	ERA	W	Sv	CG	ShO	HR	BB	SO
Toronto	3.49	86	44	15	13	134	467	1184
Tampa Bay	3.82	97	52	7	12	166	526	1143
Los Angeles	3.99	100	66	7	10	160	457	1106
Boston	4.01	95	47	5	16	147	548	1185
Oakland	4.01	75	33	4	7	135	576	1061
Chicago	4.06	89	34	4	10	156	460	1147
Minnesota	4.16	88	42	5	10	183	406	995
New York	4.28	89	42	1	11	143	489	1141
Cleveland	4.45	81	31	10	13	170	444	986
Kansas City	4.48	75	44	2	8	159	515	1085
Seattle	4.73	61	36	4	4	161	626	1016
Detroit	4.90	74	34	1	2	172	644	991
Baltimore	5.13	68	35	4	4	184	687	922
Texas	5.37	79	36	6	8	176	625	963

National League

Team	ERA	W	Sv	CG	ShO	HR	BB	SO
Los Angeles	3.68	84	35	5	11	123	480	1205
Milwaukee	3.85	90	45	12	10	175	528	1110
Chicago	3.87	97	44	2	8	160	548	1264
Philadelphia	3.88	92	47	4	11	160	533	1081
Arizona	3.98	82	39	6	9	147	451	1229
New York	4.07	89	43	5	12	163	590	1181
St. Louis	4.19	86	42	2	7	163	496	957
Houston	4.36	86	48	4	13	197	492	1095
San Francisco	4.38	72	41	4	12	147	652	1240
San Diego	4.41	63	30	3	6	165	561	1100
Florida	4.43	84	36	2	8	161	586	1127
Atlanta	4.46	72	26	2	7	156	586	1076
Cincinnati	4.55	74	34	2	6	201	557	1227
Washington	4.66	59	28	2	8	190	588	1063
Colorado	4.77	74	36	3	8	148	562	1041
Pittsburgh	5.08	67	34	3	7	176	657	963

Team Fielding Statistics

American League

Team	Pct	TC	E	PO	A	DP	TP
Toronto	.986	6123	84	4340	1699	137	0
New York	.986	5994	83	4325	1586	141	0
Boston	.986	6021	85	4339	1597	149	0
Los Angeles	.985	6091	91	4354	1646	159	0
Tampa Bay	.985	5958	90	4373	1495	153	0
Cleveland	.985	6094	94	4311	1689	182	1
Kansas City	.984	5981	96	4337	1548	159	0
Seattle	.984	6059	99	4306	1654	160	0
Oakland	.984	5976	98	4305	1573	169	0
Baltimore	.983	6027	100	4266	1661	163	0
Chicago	.983	6211	108	4373	1730	155	0
Minnesota	.982	6167	108	4377	1682	168	0
Detroit	.981	6082	113	4335	1634	172	0
Texas	.978	6134	132	4326	1676	191	0

National League

Team	Pct	TC	E	PO	A	DP	TP
Houston	.989	5939	67	4276	1596	142	0
St. Louis	.986	6264	85	4362	1817	156	0
New York	.986	6028	83	4393	1552	126	0
San Diego	.986	6086	85	4375	1626	149	0
Philadelphia	.985	6137	90	4349	1698	142	0
Colorado	.985	6250	96	4338	1816	176	0
Los Angeles	.984	6238	101	4342	1795	138	0
Milwaukee	.984	6166	101	4367	1698	160	0
San Francisco	.983	5815	96	4326	1393	129	1
Chicago	.983	5896	99	4352	1445	118	0
Pittsburgh	.983	6302	107	4365	1830	179	0
Atlanta	.983	6220	107	4322	1791	149	0
Arizona	.981	5982	113	4304	1565	137	0
Cincinnati	.981	6008	114	4327	1567	156	0
Florida	.980	5924	117	4306	1501	122	0
Washington	.980	6003	123	4302	1578	143	0

Pct—Fielding Percentage; **TC**—Total Chances; **E**—Errors; **PO**—Put Outs; **A**—Assists; **DP**—Double Plays; **TP**—Triple Plays.

2008 All-Star Game

79th Baseball All-Star Game. **Date:** July 15 at Yankee Stadium, New York, N.Y.; **Managers:** Clint Hurdle, Colorado (NL) and Terry Francona, Boston (AL); **Ted Williams MVP Award:** J.D. Drew (AL) 2-for-4 with a home run. **Note:** The league that wins the All-Star Game also secures home-field advantage for the World Series.

National League

	AB	R	H	BI	BB	SO	Avg
Hanley Ramirez, Fla, ss	3	1	2	0	0	1	.667
Miguel Tejada, Hou, ss	3	1	2	0	1	0	.667
Chase Utley, Phi, 2b	3	0	1	0	0	1	.333
Dan Uggla, Fla, 2b	4	0	0	0	0	3	.000
Lance Berkman, Hou, 1b	2	0	0	1	0	1	.000
Adrian Gonzalez, SD, 1b	3	0	1	1	0	1	.333
Albert Pujols, St.L, dh	3	0	2	0	0	0	.667
David Wright, NYM, ph-dh	3	0	1	0	1	2	.333
Chipper Jones, Atl, 3b	3	0	1	0	0	1	.333
Aramis Ramirez, Chi, 3b	0	0	0	0	1	0	—
Cristian Guzman, pr-3b	3	0	0	0	0	0	.000
Matt Holliday, Col, rf	3	1	1	0	0	1	.333
Corey Hart, Mil, rf	3	0	0	0	0	1	.000
Ryan Braun, Mil, lf	3	0	0	0	0	2	.000
Ryan Ludwick, St.L, lf	2	0	0	1	1	0	.000
Kosuke Fukudome, Chi, cf	2	0	0	1	0	1	.000
Nate McLouth, Pit, cf	4	0	1	0	0	1	.250
Geovany Soto, Chi, c	2	0	0	0	0	1	.000
Russell Martin, LA, c	3	0	1	0	0	0	.333
Brian McCann, Atl, c	0	0	0	0	0	0	—
TOTALS	52	3	13	3	4	17	.250

American League

	AB	R	H	BI	BB	SO	Avg
Ichiro Suzuki, Sea, rf	3	0	1	0	0	1	.333
J.D. Drew, Bos, rf	4	1	2	2	1	1	.500
Derek Jeter, NY, ss	3	0	1	0	0	0	.333
Michael Young, Tex, ss	4	0	1	1	0	2	.250
Josh Hamilton, Tex, cf-lf	3	0	1	0	0	1	.333
Carlos Quentin, Chi, lf	4	0	0	0	0	1	.000
Alex Rodriguez, NY, 3b	2	0	0	0	0	1	.000
Joe Crede, Chi, 3b	1	0	0	0	0	0	.000
Carlos Guillen, Det, ph-3b	3	0	1	0	1	1	.333
Manny Ramirez, Bos, lf	2	0	0	0	0	1	.000
Grady Sizemore, Cle, cf	5	1	1	0	0	2	.200
Milton Bradley, Tex, dh	2	0	0	0	1	0	.000
Evan Longoria, TB, ph-dh	4	0	1	1	0	2	.250
Kevin Youkilis, Bos, 1b	2	0	0	0	0	1	.000
Justin Morneau, Min, 1b	4	2	2	0	1	0	.500
Joe Mauer, Min, c	1	0	1	0	1	0	1.000
Ian Kinsler, Tex, pr-2b	5	0	1	0	0	1	.200
Dustin Pedroia, Bos, 2b	1	0	0	0	0	0	.000
Jason Varitek, Bos, c	0	0	0	0	0	0	—
Dioner Navarro, TB, ph-c	4	0	1	0	1	2	.250
TOTALS	57	4	14	4	7	17	.246

	1	2	3	4	5	6	7	8	9	10	11	12	13	14	15		R	H	E
National League	0	0	0	0	1	1	0	1	0	0	0	0	0	0	0	–	3	13	4
American League	0	0	0	0	0	0	0	0	0	0	0	0	0	0	1	–	4	14	1

E—Uggla 3, H. Ramirez (NL); Navarro (AL). **LOB**—National 11, American 17. **2B**—Morneau, Longoria, Guillen (AL). **HR**—Holliday (NL, 5th inning off Santana, 0 on); Drew (AL, 7th inning off Volquez, 1 on). **SB**—Tejada (NL); Drew, Sizemore, Jeter, Hamilton, Bradley, Kinsler (AL). **CS**—Guzman (NL); Kinsler (AL). **S**—Martin (NL). **SF**—Berkman, Gonzalez (NL); Young (AL). **GIDP**—Uggla (NL); Jeter (AL). **DP**—National 1; American 2.

NL Pitching	IP	H	R	ER	BB	SO
Ben Sheets, Mil	2.0	1	0	0	2	3
Carlos Zambrano, Chi	2.0	1	0	0	0	1
Dan Haren, Ari	2.0	2	0	0	1	2
Edinson Volquez, Cin	1.0	2	2	2	0	2
Brian Wilson, SF	0.2	0	0	0	0	1
Billy Wagner, NY	0.1	2	1	1	0	0
Ryan Dempster, Chi	1.0	0	0	0	0	3
Aaron Cook, Col	3.0	4	0	0	3	1
Carlos Marmol, Chi	1.0	0	0	0	0	2
Brandon Webb, Ari	1.0	0	0	0	0	2
Brad Lidge, Phi (L, 0-1)	0.2	2	1	1	1	0
TOTALS	14.2	14	4	4	7	17

AL Pitching	IP	H	R	ER	BB	SO
Cliff Lee, Cle	2.0	1	0	0	0	3
Joe Saunders, LA	1.0	1	0	0	0	0
Roy Halladay, Tor	1.0	0	0	0	0	1
Ervin Santana, LA	1.0	1	1	1	0	2
Justin Duchscherer, Oak	1.0	3	1	1	0	1
Joe Nathan, Min	1.0	0	0	0	0	1
Jonathan Papelbon, Bos	1.0	1	1	0	0	2
Francisco Rodriguez, LA	0.1	0	0	0	0	1
Mariano Rivera, NY	1.2	2	0	0	0	2
Joakim Soria, KC	1.2	2	0	0	0	2
George Sherrill, Bal	2.1	1	0	0	0	2
Scott Kazmir, TB (W, 1-0)	1.0	0	0	0	1	1
TOTALS	15.0	13	3	2	4	17

Umpires—Derryl Cousins (plate); Ed Rapuano (1b); Tom Hallion (2b); Mark Wegner (3b); Greg Gibson (lf); Phil Cuzzi (rf). **Attendance**—55,632 (56,936 capacity). **Time**—4:50. **TV Rating**—9.3/16 share (FOX) for first nine innings.

Home Run Derby

Results of the 2008 All-Star Home Run Derby held at Yankee Stadium in New York, N.Y. on July 14. Contest includes four sluggers from the American League and four from the National League.

Player	Round 1	Semis	Finals	Total	Long
Justin Morneau, Minnesota	8	9	5	22	453
Josh Hamilton, Texas	28	4	3	35	518
Lance Berkman, Houston	8	6	—	14	476
Ryan Braun, Milwaukee	7	7	—	14	439
Dan Uggla, Florida	6	—	—	6	437
Grady Sizemore, Cleveland	6	—	—	6	459
Chase Utley, Philadelphia	5	—	—	5	434
Evan Longoria, Tampa Bay	3	—	—	3	446

Top four from first round advance to semifinals. Top two from semis advance to finals. Homer total from Round 1 is carried over to the semis.

AL Team by Team Statistics

At least 135 at bats or 40 innings pitched during the regular season, unless otherwise indicated. Players who competed for more than one AL team are listed with their final club. Players traded from the NL are listed with AL team only if they have 135 AB or 40 IP. Note that (*) indicates rookie and PTBN indicates player to be named.

Baltimore Orioles

Batting (135 AB)	Avg	AB	R	H	HR	RBI	SB
Nick Markakis	.306	595	106	182	20	87	10
Aubrey Huff	.304	598	96	182	32	108	4
Brian Roberts	.296	611	107	181	9	57	40
Melvin Mora	.285	513	77	146	23	104	3
Adam Jones	.270	477	61	129	9	57	10
Ramon Hernandez . .	.257	463	49	119	15	65	0
Luke Scott	.257	475	67	122	23	65	2
Jay Payton	.243	338	41	82	7	41	8
Kevin Millar	.234	531	73	124	20	72	0
Juan Castro	.205	151	15	31	2	16	0
Guillermo Quiroz* . .	.187	134	12	25	2	14	0

Acquired: IF Castro from Col. for IF Mike McCoy (July 19); P Bass from Min. for PTBN (Sept. 5).

Pitching (50 IP)	ERA	W-L	Gm	IP	BB	SO
Jim Johnson*	2.23	2-4	54	68.2	28	38
Jeremy Guthrie	3.63	10-12	30	190.2	58	120
Lance Cormier	4.02	3-3	45	71.2	34	46
George Sherrill	4.73	3-5	57	53.1	33	58
Dennis Sarfate*	4.74	4-3	57	79.2	62	86
Brian Bass	4.84	4-4	49	89.1	31	45
Chris Waters*	5.01	3-5	11	64.2	29	32
Daniel Cabrera	5.25	8-10	30	180.0	90	95
Brian Burres	6.04	7-10	31	129.2	56	63
Garrett Olson*	6.65	9-10	26	132.2	62	83
Radhames Liz*	6.72	6-6	17	84.1	51	57

Saves: Sherrill (31); Johnson, Cormier, Bass, Rocky Cherry and Jim Miller (1). **Complete games:** Cabrera (2); Guthrie and Waters (1). **Shutouts:** Waters (1).

Boston Red Sox

Batting (150 AB)	Avg	AB	R	H	HR	RBI	SB
Dustin Pedroia	.326	653	118	213	17	83	20
Sean Casey	.322	199	14	64	0	17	1
Kevin Youkilis	.312	538	91	168	29	115	3
Manny Ramirez	.299	365	66	109	20	68	1
Jason Bay	.293	184	39	54	9	37	3
Coco Crisp	.283	361	55	102	7	41	20
J.D. Drew	.280	368	79	103	19	64	4
Jacoby Ellsbury* . . .	.280	554	98	155	9	47	50
Mike Lowell	.274	419	58	115	17	73	2
Alex Cora	.270	152	14	41	0	9	1
Julio Lugo	.268	261	27	70	1	22	12
David Ortiz	.264	416	74	110	23	89	1
Jed Lowrie*	.258	260	34	67	2	46	1
Jason Varitek	.220	423	37	93	13	43	0

Acquired: OF Bay in 3-team deal that sent OF Ramirez to LAD, OF Brandon Moss and P Craig Hansen from Bos. to Pit. and 3B Andy LaRoche and P Bryan Morris from LA-NL to Pit. (July 31); P Byrd from Cle. for PTBN (Aug. 12).

Pitching (50 IP)	ERA	W-L	Gm	IP	BB	SO
Jonathan Papelbon . .	2.34	5-4	67	69.1	8	77
Javier Lopez	2.43	2-0	70	59.1	27	38
Hideki Okajima	2.61	3-2	64	62.0	23	60
Daisuke Matsuzaka . .	2.90	18-3	29	167.2	94	154
Justin Masterson* . .	3.16	6-5	36	88.1	40	68
Jon Lester	3.21	16-6	33	210.1	66	152
Manny Delcarmen . .	3.27	1-2	73	74.1	28	72
Josh Beckett	4.03	12-10	27	174.1	34	172
Tim Wakefield	4.13	10-11	30	181.0	60	117
Paul Byrd	4.60	11-12	30	180.0	34	82
Clay Buchholz*	6.75	2-9	16	76.0	41	72

Saves: Papelbon (41); Delcarmen and Craig Hansen (2); Okajima and Timlin (1). **Complete games:** Lester (2); Beckett, Wakefield and Buchholz (1). **Shutouts:** Lester (2).

Chicago White Sox

Batting (130 AB)	Avg	AB	R	H	HR	RBI	SB
Jermaine Dye	.292	590	96	172	34	96	3
Alexei Ramirez*	.290	480	65	139	21	77	13
Carlos Quentin	.288	480	96	138	36	100	7
Orlando Cabrera . . .	.281	661	93	186	8	57	19
A.J. Pierzynski	.281	534	66	150	13	60	1
Ken Griffey Jr.	.260	131	16	34	3	18	0
Joe Crede	.248	335	41	83	17	55	0
Juan Uribe	.247	324	38	80	7	40	1
Jim Thome	.245	503	93	123	34	90	1
Paul Konerko	.240	438	59	105	22	62	2
Brian Anderson	.232	181	24	42	8	26	5
Nick Swisher	.219	497	86	109	24	69	3

Acquired: OF Griffey Jr. from Cin. for P Nick Masset and IF Danny Richar (July 31).

Pitching (45 IP)	ERA	W-L	Gm	IP	BB	SO
Bobby Jenks	2.63	3-1	57	61.2	17	38
Matt Thornton	2.67	5-3	74	67.1	19	77
John Danks	3.32	12-9	33	195.0	57	159
Scott Linebrink	3.69	2-2	50	46.1	9	40
Octavio Dotel	3.76	4-4	72	67.0	29	92
Mark Buehrle	3.79	15-12	34	218.2	52	140
Gavin Floyd	3.84	17-8	33	206.1	70	145
Jose Contreras	4.54	7-6	20	121.0	35	70
Javier Vazquez	4.67	12-16	33	208.1	61	200
Clayton Richard* . . .	6.04	2-5	13	47.2	13	29

Saves: Jenks (30); Dotel, Thornton, Linebrink and Nick Masset (1). **Complete games:** Buehrle, Floyd, Contreras and Vazquez (1). **Shutouts:** none.

Cleveland Indians

Batting (200 AB)	Avg	AB	R	H	HR	RBI	SB
Shin-Soo Choo	.309	317	68	98	14	66	4
Casey Blake	.289	325	46	94	11	58	2
Victor Martinez	.278	266	30	74	2	35	0
Jamey Carroll	.277	347	60	96	1	36	7
Jhonny Peralta	.276	605	104	167	23	89	3
Ryan Garko	.273	495	61	135	14	90	0
Grady Sizemore	.268	634	101	170	33	90	38
Ben Francisco*	.266	447	65	119	15	54	4
Kelly Shoppach	.261	352	67	92	21	55	0
Asdrubal Cabrera . . .	.259	352	48	91	6	47	4
Franklin Gutierrez . .	.248	399	54	99	8	41	9
David Dellucci	.238	336	41	80	11	47	3
Andy Marte*	.221	235	21	52	3	17	1

Acquired: P Jackson, P Rob Bryson, OF Matt LaPorta and OF Michael Brantley from Mil. for P Sabathia (July 7). **Traded:** IF Blake and cash to LA for P Jon Meloan and C Carlos Santana (July 26). **Signed:** P Rincon (June 24).

Pitching (40 IP)	ERA	W-L	Gm	IP	BB	SO
Cliff Lee	2.54	22-3	31	223.1	34	170
Rafael Perez	3.54	4-4	73	76.1	23	86
Jensen Lewis	3.82	0-4	51	66.0	27	52
CC Sabathia	3.83	6-8	18	122.1	34	123
Aaron Laffey*	4.23	5-7	16	93.2	31	43
Masa Kobayashi* . . .	4.53	4-5	57	55.2	14	35
Rafael Betancourt . . .	5.07	3-4	69	71.0	25	64
Fausto Carmona	5.44	8-7	22	120.2	70	58
Jeremy Sowers	5.58	4-9	22	121.0	39	64
Zach Jackson	5.60	2-3	9	54.2	14	33
Juan Rincon	5.86	3-3	47	55.1	24	39

Saves: Lewis (13); Kobayashi and Joe Borowski (6); Betancourt (4); Perez (2). **Complete games:** Lee (4); Sabathia (3); Byrd, Carmona and Jake Westbrook (1). **Shutouts:** Lee and Sabathia (2); Carmona (1).

Detroit Tigers

Batting (135 AB)	Avg	AB	R	H	HR	RBI	SB
Magglio Ordonez	.317	561	72	178	21	103	1
Placido Polanco	.307	580	90	178	8	58	7
Miguel Cabrera	.292	616	85	180	37	127	1
Carlos Guillen	.286	420	68	120	10	54	9
Curtis Granderson	.280	553	112	155	22	66	12
Edgar Renteria	.270	503	69	136	10	55	6
Matt Joyce*	.252	242	40	61	12	33	0
Marcus Thames	.241	316	50	76	25	56	0
Ryan Raburn	.236	182	26	43	4	20	3
Gary Sheffield	.225	418	52	94	19	57	9
Brandon Inge	.205	347	41	71	11	51	4

Acquired: P Farnsworth from NY-AL for C Ivan Rodriguez (July 31). Signed: P Glover (Aug. 17).

Pitching (40 IP)	ERA	W-L	Gm	IP	BB	SO
Aquilino Lopez	3.55	4-1	48	78.2	22	61
Armando Galarraga*	3.73	13-7	30	178.2	61	126
Freddy Dolsi*	3.97	1-5	42	47.2	28	29
Zach Miner	4.27	8-5	45	118.0	46	62
Jeremy Bonderman	4.29	3-4	12	71.1	36	44
Bobby Seay	4.47	1-2	60	56.1	25	58
Kyle Farnsworth	4.48	2-3	61	60.1	22	61
Justin Verlander	4.84	11-17	33	201.0	87	163
Fernando Rodney	4.91	0-6	38	40.1	30	49
Todd Jones	4.97	4-1	45	41.2	18	14
Gary Glover	5.30	2-3	47	54.1	22	37
Casey Fossum	5.66	3-1	31	41.1	18	28
Kenny Rogers	5.70	9-13	30	173.2	71	82
Nate Robertson	6.35	7-11	32	168.2	62	108

Saves: Jones (18); Rodney (13); Dolsi (2); Joel Zumaya (1). **Complete games:** Verlander (1). **Shutouts:** none.

Kansas City Royals

Batting (135 AB)	Avg	AB	R	H	HR	RBI	SB
Mike Aviles*	.325	419	68	136	10	51	8
David DeJesus	.307	518	70	159	12	73	11
Alberto Callaspo	.305	213	21	65	0	16	2
Mark Grudzielanek	.299	331	36	99	3	24	2
Billy Butler	.275	443	44	122	11	55	0
Ross Gload	.273	388	46	106	3	37	3
Jose Guillen	.264	598	66	158	20	97	2
Alex Gordon	.260	493	72	128	16	59	9
Mark Teahen	.255	572	66	146	15	59	4
Miguel Olivo	.255	306	29	78	12	41	7
Joey Gathright	.254	279	41	71	0	22	21
Esteban German	.245	216	30	53	0	22	7
John Buck	.224	370	48	83	9	48	0
Tony Pena Jr.	.169	225	22	38	1	14	3

Claimed: P Tejeda off waivers from Tex. (June 25). **Waived:** P Tomko (June 21).

Pitching (35 IP)	ERA	W-L	Gm	IP	BB	SO
Joakim Soria	1.60	2-3	63	67.1	19	66
Ramon Ramirez	2.64	3-2	71	71.2	31	70
Leo Nunez	2.98	4-1	45	48.1	15	26
Zack Greinke	3.47	13-10	32	202.1	56	183
Ron Mahay	3.48	5-0	57	64.2	29	49
Robinson Tejeda	3.97	2-2	29	45.1	24	45
Gil Meche	3.98	14-11	34	210.1	73	183
Kyle Davies	4.06	9-7	21	113.0	43	71
Brandon Duckworth	4.50	3-3	7	38.0	19	20
Yasuhiko Yabuta*	4.78	1-3	31	37.2	17	25
Luke Hochevar*	5.51	6-12	22	129.0	47	72
Brian Bannister	5.76	9-16	32	182.2	58	113
Joel Peralta	5.98	1-2	40	52.2	14	38
Brett Tomko	6.97	2-7	16	60.2	13	40

Saves: Soria (42); Ramirez and Jimmy Gobble (1). **Complete games:** Greinke and Bannister (1). **Shutouts:** none.

Los Angeles Angels

Batting (165 AB)	Avg	AB	R	H	HR	RBI	SB
Mark Texeira	.358	193	39	69	13	43	2
Howie Kendrick	.306	340	43	104	3	37	11
Vladimir Guerrero	.303	541	85	164	27	91	5
Garret Anderson	.293	557	66	163	15	84	7
Casey Kotchman	.287	373	47	107	12	54	2
Torii Hunter	.278	551	85	153	21	78	19
Erick Aybar	.277	346	53	96	3	39	7
Chone Figgins	.276	453	72	125	1	22	34
Mike Napoli	.273	227	39	62	20	49	7
Maicer Izturis	.269	290	44	78	3	37	11
Juan Rivera	.246	256	31	63	12	45	1
Gary Matthews Jr.	.242	426	53	103	8	46	8
Sean Rodriguez*	.204	167	18	34	3	10	3
Jeff Mathis	.194	283	35	55	9	42	2

Acquired: IF Texeira from Atl. for IF Kotchman and P Steve Marek (July 29).

Pitching (45 IP)	ERA	W-L	Gm	IP	BB	SO
Jose Arredondo*	1.62	10-2	52	61.0	22	55
Francisco Rodriguez	2.24	2-3	76	68.1	34	77
Scot Shields	2.70	6-4	64	63.1	29	64
Darren Oliver	2.88	7-1	54	72.0	16	48
Joe Saunders	3.41	17-7	31	198.0	53	103
Ervin Santana	3.49	16-7	32	219.0	47	214
John Lackey	3.75	12-5	24	163.1	40	130
Jered Weaver	4.33	11-10	30	176.2	54	152
Jon Garland	4.90	14-8	32	196.2	59	90
Justin Speier	5.03	2-8	61	68.0	27	56
Dustin Moseley	6.79	2-4	12	50.4	20	37

Saves: Rodriguez (62); Shields (4). **Complete games:** Lackey (3); Santana (2); Sauders and Garland (1). **Shutouts:** Santana (1).

Minnesota Twins

Batting (135 AB)	Avg	AB	R	H	HR	RBI	SB
Joe Mauer	.328	536	98	176	9	85	1
Justin Morneau	.300	623	97	187	23	129	0
Denard Span*	.294	347	70	102	6	47	18
Brian Buscher*	.294	218	29	64	4	47	0
Delmon Young	.290	575	80	167	10	69	14
Nick Punto	.284	338	43	96	2	28	15
Alexi Casilla	.281	385	58	108	7	50	7
Jason Kubel	.272	463	74	126	20	78	0
Brendan Harris	.265	434	57	115	7	49	1
Carlos Gomez	.258	577	79	149	7	59	33
Michael Cuddyer	.249	249	30	62	3	36	5
Mike Lamb	.233	236	20	55	1	32	0
Craig Monroe	.202	163	22	33	8	29	0

Acquired: P Guardado from Tex. for P Mark Hamburger (Aug. 25); **Claimed:** P Breslow off waivers from Cle. (May 29). **Waived:** P Hernandez (Aug. 1). **Released:** IF Lamb (Sept. 5)

Pitching (40 IP)	ERA	W-L	Gm	IP	BB	SO
Joe Nathan	1.33	1-2	68	67.2	18	74
Craig Breslow*	1.91	0-2	49	47.0	19	39
Dennys Reyes	2.33	3-0	75	46.1	15	39
Scott Baker	3.45	11-4	28	172.1	42	141
Jesse Crain	3.59	5-4	66	62.2	24	50
Francisco Liriano	3.91	6-4	14	76.0	32	67
Kevin Slowey	3.99	12-11	27	160.1	24	123
Nick Blackburn	4.05	11-11	33	193.1	39	96
Eddie Guardado	4.15	4-4	64	56.1	19	33
Glen Perkins*	4.41	12-4	26	151.0	39	74
Brian Bass	4.87	3-4	44	68.1	22	32
Matt Guerrier	5.19	6-9	76	76.1	37	59
Livan Hernandez	5.48	10-8	23	139.2	29	54
Boof Bonser	5.93	3-7	47	118.1	36	97

Saves: Nathan (39), Guardado (4); Guerrier, Bass and Craig Breslow (1). **Complete games:** Slowey (3); Hernandez (2). **Shutouts:** Slowey (2).

New York Yankees

Batting (135 AB)	Avg	AB	R	H	HR	RBI	SB
Johnny Damon	.303	555	95	168	17	71	29
Alex Rodriguez	.302	510	104	154	35	103	18
Derek Jeter.	.300	596	88	179	11	69	11
Bobby Abreu	.296	609	100	180	20	100	22
Hideki Matsui.	.294	337	43	99	9	45	0
Ivan Rodriguez	.276	398	44	110	7	35	10
Robinson Cano	.271	597	70	162	14	72	2
Jorge Posada	.268	168	18	45	3	22	0
Xavier Nady	.268	228	26	61	12	40	1
Wilson Betemit	.265	189	24	50	6	25	0
Melky Cabrera	.249	414	42	103	8	37	9
Jason Giambi	.247	458	68	113	32	96	2
Richie Sexson	.221	280	29	62	12	36	1
Jose Molina	.216	268	32	58	3	18	0

Acquired: OF Nady and P Damaso Marte from Pit. for OF Jose Tabata and P Ross Ohlendorf, Dan McCutchen and Jeff Karstens (July 26); C Rodriguez from Det. for P Kyle Farnsworth (July 31). **Signed:** P Ponson (June 19); IF Sexson (July 19).

Pitching (42 IP)	ERA	W-L	Gm	IP	BB	SO
Mariano Rivera	1.40	6-5	64	70.2	6	77
Joba Chamberlain* . .	2.60	4-3	42	100.1	39	118
Mike Mussina	3.37	20-9	34	200.1	31	150
Dan Giese*	3.53	1-3	20	43.1	14	29
Jose Veras*	3.59	5-3	60	57.2	29	63
Edwar Ramirez*	3.90	5-1	55	55.1	24	63
Chien-Ming Wang . . .	4.07	8-2	15	95.0	35	54
Andy Pettitte	4.54	14-14	33	204.0	55	158
Sidney Ponson	5.04	8-5	25	135.2	48	58
Darrell Rasner	5.40	5-10	24	113.1	39	67

Saves: Rivera (39), Ramirez, Farnsworth and Brian Bruney (1). **Complete games:** Wang and Ponson (1). **Shutouts:** none.

Oakland Athletics

Batting (135 AB)	Avg	AB	R	H	HR	RBI	SB
Ryan Sweeney*	.286	384	53	110	5	45	9
Kurt Suzuki	.279	530	54	148	7	42	2
Rajai Davis	.260	196	28	51	3	19	25
Emil Brown	.244	402	48	98	13	59	4
Carlos Gonzalez* . . .	.242	302	31	73	4	26	4
Frank Thomas	.240	246	27	59	8	30	0
Bobby Crosby	.237	556	66	132	7	61	7
Mark Ellis	.233	442	55	103	12	41	14
Jack Cust	.231	481	77	111	33	77	0
Daric Barton*	.226	446	59	101	9	47	2
Travis Buck	.226	155	16	35	7	25	1
Jack Hannahan	.218	436	48	95	9	47	2

Acquired: P Gallagher, OF Matt Murton, IF Eric Patterson and C Josh Donaldson from Chi-NL for P Harden and Gaudin (July 8). **Signed:** DH Thomas (April 24). **Claimed:** Davis off waivers from SF (April 23).

Pitching (40 IP)	ERA	W-L	Gm	IP	BB	SO
Joey Devine*	0.59	6-1	42	45.2	15	49
Brad Ziegler*	1.06	3-0	47	59.2	22	30
Rich Harden	2.34	5-1	13	77.0	31	92
Justin Duchscherer . .	2.54	10-8	22	141.2	34	95
Chad Gaudin	3.59	5-3	26	62.2	17	44
Huston Street	3.73	7-5	63	70.0	27	69
Santiago Casilla	3.93	2-1	51	50.1	20	43
Dallas Braden	4.14	5-4	19	71.2	25	41
Greg Smith*	4.16	7-16	32	190.1	87	111
Dana Eveland	4.34	9-9	29	168.0	77	118
Joe Blanton	4.96	5-12	20	127.0	35	62
Alan Embree	4.96	2-5	70	61.2	30	57
Sean Gallagher*	5.88	2-3	11	56.2	36	54

Saves: Street (18); Ziegler (11); Casilla (2); Devine and Keith Foulke (1). **Complete games:** Smith (2); Duchscherer and Eveland (1). **Shutouts:** Duchscherer (1).

Seattle Mariners

Batting (135 AB)	Avg	AB	R	H	HR	RBI	SB
Ichiro Suzuki	.310	686	103	213	6	42	43
Jose Lopez	.297	644	80	191	17	89	6
Raul Ibanez	.293	635	85	186	23	110	2
Yuniesky Betancourt . .	.279	559	66	156	7	51	4
Willie Bloomquist . . .	.279	165	32	46	0	9	14
Jeremy Reed	.269	286	30	77	2	31	2
Adrian Beltre	.266	556	74	148	25	77	8
Bryan LaHair*	.250	136	15	34	3	10	0
Miguel Cairo	.249	221	34	55	0	23	5
Jose Vidro	.234	308	28	72	7	45	2
Kenji Johjima	.227	379	29	86	7	39	2
Jeff Clement*	.227	203	17	46	5	23	0
Wladimir Balentien* . .	.202	243	23	49	7	24	0

Pitching (40 IP)	ERA	W-L	Gm	IP	BB	SO
Roy Corcoran	3.22	6-2	50	72.2	36	39
Brandon Morrow. . . .	3.34	3-4	45	64.2	34	75
Ryan Rowland-Smith .	3.42	5-3	47	118.1	48	77
Felix Hernandez	3.45	9-11	31	200.2	80	175
Erik Bedard	3.67	6-4	15	81.0	37	72
J.J. Putz	3.88	6-5	47	46.1	28	56
Sean Green	4.67	4-5	70	79.0	36	62
Jarrod Washburn . . .	4.69	5-14	28	153.2	50	87
R.A. Dickey	5.21	5-8	32	112.1	51	58
Mark Lowe	5.37	1-5	57	63.2	34	55
Miguel Batista	6.26	4-14	44	115.0	79	73
Carlos Silva	6.46	4-15	28	153.1	32	69

Saves: Putz (15); Morrow (10); Corcoran (3); Rowland-Smith (2); Washburn, Batista, Green, Lowe, Arthur Rhodes and Randy Messenger (1). **Complete games:** Hernandez (2); Washburn and Silva (1). **Shutouts:** none.

Tampa Bay Rays

Batting (135 AB)	Avg	AB	R	H	HR	RBI	SB
Dioner Navarro	.295	427	43	126	7	54	0
Jason Bartlett	.286	454	48	130	1	37	20
Akinori Iwamura	.274	627	91	172	6	48	8
Carl Crawford	.273	443	69	121	8	57	25
B.J. Upton	.273	531	85	145	9	67	44
Evan Longoria*	.272	448	67	122	27	85	7
Cliff Floyd	.268	246	32	66	11	39	1
Willy Aybar	.253	324	33	82	10	33	2
Ben Zobrist	.253	198	32	50	12	30	3
Carlos Pena	.247	490	76	121	31	102	1
Eric Hinske	.247	381	59	94	20	60	10
Gabe Gross	.242	302	40	73	13	38	2
Shawn Riggans*	.222	135	21	30	6	24	0
Jonny Gomes	.182	154	23	28	8	21	8

Acquired: OF Gross from Mil. for P Josh Butler (April 22); P Bradford from Bal. for PTBN (Aug. 7).

Pitching (40 IP)	ERA	W-L	Gm	IP	BB	SO
Grant Balfour	1.54	6-2	51	58.1	24	82
Chad Bradford	2.12	4-3	68	59.1	15	17
J.P. Howell	2.22	6-1	64	89.1	39	92
Dan Wheeler	3.12	5-6	70	66.1	22	53
Scott Kazmir	3.49	12-8	27	152.1	70	166
James Shields	3.56	14-8	33	215.0	40	160
Matt Garza	3.70	11-9	30	184.2	59	128
Trever Miller	4.15	2-0	68	43.1	20	44
Andy Sonnanstine . . .	4.38	13-9	32	193.1	37	124
Edwin Jackson	4.42	14-11	32	183.1	77	108
Troy Percival	4.53	2-1	50	45.2	27	38
Jason Hammel	4.60	4-4	40	78.1	35	44

Saves: Percival (28); Wheeler (3); Balfour (4); Howell (3); Miller and Hammel (1). **Complete games:** Shields and Garza (3); Sonnanstine (1). **Shutouts:** Shields and Garza (2); Sonnanstine (1).

Texas Rangers

Batting (110 AB)

	Avg	AB	R	H	HR	RBI	SB
Nelson Cruz	.330	115	19	38	7	26	3
Milton Bradley	.321	414	78	133	22	77	5
Ian Kinsler	.319	518	102	165	18	71	26
Josh Hamilton	.304	624	98	190	32	130	9
Marlon Byrd	.298	403	70	120	10	53	7
Joaquin Arias*	.291	110	15	32	0	9	4
Ramon Vazquez	.290	300	44	87	6	40	0
Hank Blalock	.287	258	37	74	12	38	1
Chris Davis*	.285	295	51	84	17	55	1
Michael Young	.284	645	102	183	12	82	10
Gerald Laird	.276	344	54	95	6	41	2
David Murphy*	.275	415	64	114	15	74	7
Frank Catalanotto	.274	248	28	68	2	21	1
Jarrod Saltalamacchia	.253	198	27	50	3	26	0
German Duran*	.231	143	22	33	3	16	1
Brandon Boggs*	.226	283	30	64	8	41	3

Pitching (30 IP)

	ERA	W-L	Gm	IP	BB	SO
Kameron Loe	3.23	1-0	14	30.2	8	20
Vicente Padilla	4.74	14-8	29	171.0	65	127
Warner Madrigal*	4.75	0-2	31	36.0	14	22
Kevin Millwood	5.07	9-10	29	168.2	49	125
Scott Feldman	5.29	6-8	28	151.1	56	74
Josh Rupe*	5.14	3-1	46	89.1	46	53
Jamey Wright	5.12	8-7	75	84.1	35	60
Matt Harrison*	5.49	9-3	15	83.2	31	42
Dustin Nippert	6.40	3-5	20	71.2	37	55
Frank Francisco	3.13	3-5	58	63.1	26	83
Luis Mendoza*	8.67	3-8	25	63.1	25	35
Kason Gabbard	4.82	2-3	12	56.0	39	33
C.J. Wilson	6.02	2-2	50	46.1	27	41
Joaquin Benoit	5.00	3-2	44	45.0	35	43

Saves: Wilson (24); Francisco (5); Benoit, Mendoza and Madrigal (1). **Complete games:** Millwood (3); Padilla and Harrison (1). **Shutouts:** Padilla and Harrison (1).

Toronto Blue Jays

Batting (135 AB)

	Avg	AB	R	H	HR	RBI	SB
Vernon Wells	.300	427	63	128	20	78	4
Joe Inglett	.297	344	45	102	3	39	9
Alex Rios	.291	635	91	185	15	79	32
Adam Lind	.282	326	48	92	9	40	2
David Eckstein	.277	260	27	72	1	23	2
Lyle Overbay	.270	544	74	147	15	69	1
Marco Scutaro	.267	517	76	138	7	60	7
Aaron Hill	.263	205	19	54	2	20	4
Scott Rolen	.262	408	58	107	11	50	5
Matt Stairs	.250	320	42	80	11	44	1
Rod Barajas	.249	349	44	87	11	49	0
Shannon Stewart	.240	175	14	42	1	14	3
Gregg Zaun	.237	245	29	58	6	30	2
Brad Wilkerson	.220	264	21	58	4	28	3
John McDonald	.210	186	21	39	1	18	3

Signed: OF Wilkerson (May 9). **Traded:** IF Stairs to Phi. for PTBN (Aug. 30); IF Eckstein to Ari. for P Chad Beck (Aug. 31).

Pitching (40 IP)

	ERA	W-L	Gm	IP	BB	SO
Scott Downs	1.78	0-3	66	70.2	27	57
Jesse Carlson*	2.25	7-2	69	60.0	21	55
Roy Halladay	2.78	20-11	34	246.0	39	206
Brian Tallet	2.88	1-2	51	56.1	22	47
B.J. Ryan	2.95	2-4	60	58.0	28	58
Shaun Marcum	3.39	9-7	25	151.1	50	123
Jesse Litsch	3.58	13-9	29	176.0	39	99
John Parrish	4.04	1-1	13	42.1	15	21
A.J. Burnett	4.07	18-10	35	221.1	86	231
Jason Frasor	4.18	1-2	49	47.1	32	42
Dustin McGowan	4.37	6-7	19	111.1	38	85
David Purcey*	5.54	3-6	12	65.0	29	58

Saves: Ryan (32); Downs (5); Jeremy Accardo (4); Carlson (2); Brandon League (1). **Complete games:** Halladay (9), Litsch (2); Burnett, McGowan, Purcey and Scott Richmond (1). **Shutouts:** Halladay and Litsch (2); Richmond (1).

Home Attendance

Overall 2008 Major League Baseball regular season attendance (based on tickets sold) was 78,614,880, the second-highest total ever but down 1.1 percent from 2007 totals. The average per game crowd was 32,539. Numbers in parentheses indicate ranking in 2007. HD indicates home dates.

American League

	Attendance	HD	Average
1 New York (1)	4,287,132	81	52,928
2 Los Angeles (2)	3,336,747	81	41,194
3 Detroit (3)	3,202,645	81	39,539
4 Boston (4)	3,048,250	81	37,633
5 Chicago (5)	2,500,648	81	30,872
6 Toronto (7)	2,399,786	81	29,627
7 Seattle (6)	2,329,788	81	28,763
8 Minnesota (9)	2,302,431	81	28,425
9 Cleveland (10)	2,169,760	80	27,122
10 Baltimore (11)	1,950,077	78	25,001
11 Texas (8)	1,945,857	80	24,323
12 Tampa Bay (14)	1,811,986	81	22,370
13 Oakland (12)	1,665,256	81	20,559
14 Kansas City (13)	1,578,922	79	19,986
TOTALS	34,529,285	1127	30,638

National League

	Attendance	HD	Average
1 New York (2)	4,042,045	79	51,165
2 Los Angeles (1)	3,730,750	81	46,059
3 St. Louis (3)	3,432,917	81	42,382
4 Philadelphia (6)	3,422,583	81	42,254
5 Chicago (4)	3,300,200	81	40,743
6 Milwaukee (8)	3,068,458	81	37,882
7 San Francisco (5)	2,863,847	81	35,356
8 Houston (7)	2,779,487	80	34,744
9 Colorado (11)	2,650,218	80	33,128
10 Atlanta (10)	2,532,834	81	31,270
11 Arizona (12)	2,509,946	81	30,987
12 San Diego (9)	2,427,535	81	29,970
13 Washington (14)	2,321,988	80	29,025
14 Cincinnati (13)	2,058,632	81	25,415
15 Pittsburgh (15)	1,609,076	80	20,113
16 Florida (16)	1,335,079	80	16,688
TOTALS	44,085,595	1289	34,201

NL Team by Team Statistics

At least 135 at bats or 40 innings pitched during the regular season unless otherwise indicated. Players who competed for more than one NL team are listed with their final club. Players traded from the AL are listed with NL team only if they have 135 AB or 40 IP. Note that (*) indicates rookie and PTBN indicates player to be named.

Arizona Diamondbacks

Batting (170 AB)	Avg	AB	R	H	HR	RBI	SB
Orlando Hudson	.305	407	54	124	8	41	4
Conor Jackson	.300	540	87	162	12	75	10
Stephen Drew	.291	611	91	178	21	67	3
Chad Tracy	.267	273	25	73	8	39	0
Miguel Montero	.255	184	24	47	5	18	0
Justin Upton	.250	356	52	89	15	42	1
Chris Young	.248	625	85	155	22	85	14
Adam Dunn	.236	517	79	122	40	100	2
Augie Ojeda	.242	231	27	56	0	17	0
Mark Reynolds	.239	539	87	129	28	97	11
Chris Snyder	.237	334	47	79	16	64	0
Eric Byrnes	.209	206	28	43	6	23	4

Acquired: P Rauch from Wash. for IF Emilio Bonifacio (July 22); OF Dunn from Cin. for P Dallas Buck, C Wilkin Castillo and PTBN (Aug. 11). **Claimed:** Ledezma off waivers from SD (Aug. 29).

Pitching (55 IP)	ERA	W-L	Gm	IP	BB	SO
Chad Qualls	2.81	4-8	77	73.2	18	71
Max Scherzer*	3.05	0-4	16	56.0	21	66
Brandon Webb	3.30	22-7	34	226.2	65	183
Dan Haren	3.33	16-8	33	216.0	40	206
Randy Johnson	3.91	11-10	30	184.0	44	173
Jon Rauch	4.14	4-8	74	71.2	16	66
Will Ledezma	4.17	0-2	28	58.1	41	53
Yusmeiro Petit	4.31	3-5	19	56.1	14	42
Doug Davis	4.32	6-8	26	146.0	64	112
Tony Pena	4.33	3-2	72	72.2	17	52
Brandon Lyon	4.70	3-5	61	59.1	13	44
Micah Owings	5.93	6-9	22	104.2	41	87

Saves: Lyon (26); Rauch (18); Qualls (9); Pena (3); Rauch (1). **Complete games:** Webb (3); Johnson (2); Haren (1). **Shutouts:** Webb and Haren (1).

Atlanta Braves

Batting (140 AB)	Avg	AB	R	H	HR	RBI	SB
Chipper Jones	.364	439	82	160	22	75	4
Martin Prado	.320	228	36	73	2	33	3
Brian McCann	.301	509	68	153	23	87	5
Omar Infante	.293	317	45	93	3	40	0
Mark Kotsay	.289	318	39	92	6	37	2
Yunel Escobar	.288	514	71	148	10	60	2
Kelly Johnson	.287	547	86	157	12	69	11
Mark Texeira	.283	381	63	108	20	78	0
Gregor Blanco*	.251	430	52	108	1	38	13
Greg Norton	.246	171	27	42	7	31	0
Jeff Francoeur	.239	599	70	143	11	71	0
Casey Kotchman	.237	152	18	36	2	20	0

Acquired: IF Norton from Sea. for PTBN (May 6); IF Kotchman and P Steve Marek from LA-AL for IF Texeira (July 29). **Traded:** OF Kotsay to Bos. for OF Luis Sumoza (Aug. 27).

Pitching (40 IP)	ERA	W-L	Gm	IP	BB	SO
Tim Hudson	3.17	11-7	23	142.0	40	85
Manny Acosta*	3.57	3-5	46	53.0	26	31
Buddy Carlyle	3.59	2-0	45	62.2	26	59
Jair Jurrjens*	3.68	13-10	31	188.1	70	139
Will Ohman	3.68	4-1	83	58.2	22	53
Jeff Bennett	3.70	3-7	72	97.1	47	68
Jorge Campillo*	3.91	8-7	39	158.2	38	107
Mike Hampton	4.85	3-4	13	78.0	28	38
Tom Glavine	5.54	2-4	13	63.1	37	37
Jo-Jo Reyes	5.81	3-11	23	113.0	52	78
Blaine Boyer	5.88	2-6	76	72.0	25	67
Charlie Morton	6.15	4-8	16	74.2	41	48

Saves: Gonzalez (14); Bennett, Acosta and Rafael Soriano (3); Boyer, Ohman and Peter Moylan (1). **Complete games:** Hudson and Campillo (1). **Shutouts:** Hudson (1).

Chicago Cubs

Batting (135 AB)	Avg	AB	R	H	HR	RBI	SB
Ryan Theriot	.307	580	85	178	1	38	22
Mike Fontenot	.305	243	42	74	9	40	2
Reed Johnson	.303	333	52	101	6	50	5
Derrek Lee	.291	623	93	181	20	90	8
Aramis Ramirez	.289	554	97	160	27	111	2
Mark DeRosa	.285	505	103	144	21	87	6
Geovany Soto*	.285	494	66	141	23	86	0
Alfonso Soriano	.280	453	76	127	29	75	19
Ronny Cedeno	.269	216	36	58	2	28	4
Kosuke Fukudome*	.257	501	79	129	10	58	12
Jim Edmonds	.235	340	53	80	20	55	2

Acquired: P Harden and P Chad Gaudin from Oak. for P Gallagher, OF Matt Murton, IF Eric Patterson and C Josh Donaldson (July 8). **Signed:** OF Edmonds (May 15).

Pitching (40 IP)	ERA	W-L	Gm	IP	BB	SO
Rich Harden	1.77	5-1	12	71.0	30	89
Carlos Marmol	2.68	2-4	82	87.1	41	114
Ryan Dempster	2.96	17-6	33	206.2	76	187
Kerry Wood	3.26	5-4	65	66.1	18	84
Michael Wuertz	3.63	1-1	45	44.2	20	30
Sean Marshall	3.86	3-5	34	65.1	23	58
Carlos Zambrano	3.91	14-6	30	188.2	72	130
Jon Lieber	4.05	2-3	26	46.2	6	27
Ted Lilly	4.09	17-9	34	204.2	64	184
Sean Gallagher*	4.45	3-4	12	58.2	22	49
Jason Marquis	4.53	11-9	29	167.0	70	91
Bob Howry	5.35	7-5	72	70.2	13	59

Saves: Wood (34); Marmol (7); Howry, Marshall and Jeff Samardzija (1). **Complete games:** Dempster and Zambrano (1). **Shutouts:** Zambrano (1).

Cincinnati Reds

Batting (130 AB)	Avg	AB	R	H	HR	RBI	SB
Jerry Hairston Jr.	.326	261	47	85	6	36	15
Ryan Freel	.298	131	17	39	0	10	6
Joey Votto*	.297	526	69	156	24	84	7
Jeff Keppinger	.266	459	45	122	3	43	3
Brandon Phillips	.261	559	80	146	21	78	23
Jay Bruce*	.254	413	63	105	21	52	4
Edwin Encarnacion	.251	506	75	127	26	68	1
Ken Griffey Jr.	.245	359	51	88	15	53	0
David Ross	.231	134	17	31	3	13	0
Paul Bako	.217	299	30	65	6	35	0
Corey Patterson	.205	366	46	75	10	34	14

Traded: OF Griffey Jr. to Chi-AL for P Nick Masset and IF Danny Richar (July 31). **Released:** C Ross (Aug. 19).

Pitching (40 IP)	ERA	W-L	Gm	IP	BB	SO
Bill Bray	2.87	2-2	63	47.0	24	54
Edinson Volquez	3.21	17-6	33	196.0	93	206
Jared Burton	3.22	5-1	54	58.2	25	58
David Weathers	3.25	4-6	72	69.1	30	46
Francisco Cordero	3.33	5-4	72	70.1	38	78
Jeremy Affeldt	3.33	1-1	74	78.1	25	80
Mike Lincoln	4.48	2-5	64	70.1	24	57
Bronson Arroyo	4.77	15-11	34	200.0	68	163
Aaron Harang	4.78	6-17	30	184.1	50	153
Johnny Cueto*	4.81	9-14	31	174.0	68	158
Gary Majewski	6.53	1-0	37	40.0	15	27
Josh Fogg	7.58	2-7	22	78.1	27	45

Saves: Cordero (34). **Complete games:** Arroyo and Harang (1). **Shutouts:** Harang (1).

Colorado Rockies

Batting (135 AB)

	Avg	AB	R	H	HR	RBI	SB
Matt Holliday	.321	539	107	173	25	88	28
Ryan Spilborghs	.313	233	38	73	6	36	7
Clint Barmes	.290	393	47	114	11	44	13
Garrett Atkins	.286	611	86	175	21	99	1
Brad Hawpe	.283	488	69	138	25	85	2
Jeff Baker	.268	299	55	80	12	48	4
Chris Iannetta	.264	333	50	88	18	65	0
Todd Helton	.264	299	39	79	7	29	0
Troy Tulowitzki	.263	377	48	99	8	46	1
Ian Stewart*	.259	266	33	69	10	41	1
Scott Podsednik	.253	162	22	41	1	15	12
Willy Taveras	.251	479	64	120	1	26	68
Yorvit Torrealba	.246	236	19	58	6	31	0
Omar Quintanilla	.238	210	28	50	2	15	0

Acquired: P Grilli from Det. for P Zach Simons (April 30). **Signed:** P Rusch (May 17).

Pitching (40 IP)

	ERA	W-L	Gm	IP	BB	SO
Taylor Buchholz	2.17	6-6	63	66.1	18	56
Brian Fuentes	2.73	1-5	67	62.2	22	82
Jason Grilli	2.93	3-2	51	61.1	31	59
Aaron Cook	3.96	16-9	32	211.1	48	96
Ubaldo Jimenez	3.99	12-12	34	198.2	103	172
Ryan Speier	4.06	2-1	43	51.0	18	33
Manuel Corpas	4.52	3-4	76	79.2	23	50
Jorge De La Rosa	4.92	10-8	28	130.0	62	128
Jeff Francis	5.01	4-10	24	143.2	49	94
Matt Herges	5.04	3-4	58	64.1	24	46
Luis Vizcaino	5.28	1-2	43	46.0	19	49
Glendon Rusch	5.16	5-5	35	83.2	25	55
Mark Redman	7.54	2-5	10	45.1	16	20
Greg Reynolds*	8.13	2-8	14	62.0	26	22

Saves: Fuentes (30); Corpas (4); Grilli and Buchholz (1). **Complete games:** Cook (2); Jimenez (1). **Shutouts:** Cook (1).

Florida Marlins

Batting (135 AB)

	Avg	AB	R	H	HR	RBI	SB
Hanley Ramirez	.301	589	125	177	33	67	35
John Baker*	.299	197	32	59	5	32	0
Jorge Cantu	.277	628	92	174	29	95	6
Alfredo Amezaga	.264	311	41	82	3	32	8
Luis Gonzalez	.261	341	30	89	8	47	1
Cody Ross	.260	461	59	120	22	73	6
Dan Uggla	.260	531	97	138	32	92	5
Josh Willingham	.254	351	54	89	15	51	3
Jeremy Hermida	.249	502	74	125	17	61	6
Mike Jacobs	.247	477	67	118	32	93	1
Wes Helms	.243	251	28	61	5	31	0
Paul Lo Duca	.243	173	16	42	0	15	1
Matt Treanor	.238	206	18	49	2	23	1

Signed: C Lo Duca (Aug. 9).

Pitching (47 IP)

	ERA	W-L	Gm	IP	BB	SO
Joe Nelson	2.00	3-1	59	54.0	22	60
Chris Volstad*	2.88	6-4	15	84.1	36	52
Matt Lindstrom	3.14	3-3	66	57.1	26	43
Kevin Gregg	3.41	7-8	72	68.2	37	58
Ricky Nolasco	3.52	15-8	34	212.1	42	186
Josh Johnson	3.61	7-1	14	87.1	27	77
Doug Waechter	3.69	4-2	48	63.1	21	46
Scott Olsen	4.20	8-11	33	201.2	69	113
Logan Kensing	4.23	3-1	48	55.1	33	55
Renyel Pinto	4.45	2-5	67	64.2	39	56
Mark Hendrickson	5.45	7-8	36	133.2	48	81
Anibal Sanchez	5.57	2-5	10	51.2	27	50
Andrew Miller	5.87	6-10	29	107.1	56	89
Burke Badenhop*	6.08	2-3	13	47.1	21	53

Saves: Gregg (29); Lindstrom (5); Nelson and Arthur Rhodes (1). **Complete games:** Nolasco and Johnson (1). **Shutouts:** Nolasco (1).

Houston Astros

Batting (150 AB)

	Avg	AB	R	H	HR	RBI	SB
Carlos Lee	.314	436	61	137	28	100	4
Lance Berkman	.312	554	114	173	29	106	18
Kazuo Matsui	.293	375	58	110	6	33	20
Ty Wigginton	.285	386	50	110	23	58	4
Miguel Tejada	.283	632	92	179	13	66	7
Mark Loretta	.280	261	27	73	4	38	0
Darin Erstad	.276	322	49	89	4	31	2
Hunter Pence	.269	595	78	160	25	83	11
Jose Castillo	.246	426	46	105	6	37	2
Geoff Blum	.240	325	36	78	14	53	1
Michael Bourn	.229	467	57	107	5	29	41
Humberto Quintero	.226	168	16	38	2	12	0
Brad Ausmus	.218	216	15	47	3	24	0

Acquired: P Wolf from SD for P Chad Reineke (July 23). **Claimed:** IF Castillo off waivers from SF (Aug. 21).

Pitchers (40 IP)

	ERA	W-L	Gm	IP	BB	SO
Geoff Geary	2.53	2-3	55	64.0	28	45
Jose Valverde	3.38	6-3	74	72.0	23	83
Roy Oswalt	3.54	17-10	32	208.2	47	165
Wandy Rodriguez	3.54	9-7	25	137.1	44	131
Tim Byrdak	3.90	2-1	59	55.1	29	47
Doug Brocail	3.93	7-5	72	68.2	21	64
Chris Sampson	4.22	6-4	54	117.1	23	61
Randy Wolf	4.30	12-12	33	190.1	71	162
Brian Moehler	4.56	11-8	31	150.0	36	82
Wesley Wright*	5.01	4-3	71	55.2	34	57
Shawn Chacon	5.04	2-3	15	85.2	41	53
Brandon Backe	6.05	9-14	31	166.2	77	127

Saves: Valverde (44); Brocail (2); Wright and LaTroy Hawkins (1). **Complete games:** Oswalt (3); Wolf (1). **Shutouts:** Oswalt (2); Wolf (1).

Los Angeles Dodgers

Batting (135 AB)

	Avg	AB	R	H	HR	RBI	SB
Manny Ramirez	.396	187	36	74	17	53	2
Rafael Furcal	.357	143	34	51	5	16	8
Andre Ethier	.305	525	90	160	20	77	6
Matt Kemp	.290	606	93	176	18	76	35
James Loney	.289	595	66	172	13	90	7
Juan Pierre	.283	375	44	106	1	28	40
Russell Martin	.280	553	87	155	13	69	18
Jeff Kent	.280	440	42	123	12	59	0
Nomar Garciaparra	.264	163	24	43	8	28	1
Blake DeWitt*	.264	368	45	97	9	52	3
Casey Blake	.251	211	25	53	10	23	1
Angel Berroa	.230	226	26	52	1	16	0
Andruw Jones	.158	209	21	33	3	14	0

Acquired: IF Blake and cash from Cle. for P Jon Meloan and C Carlos Santana (July 26); OF Ramirez from Bos. in 3-team deal that sent 3B Andy LaRoche and P Bryan Morris to Pit., OF Jason Bay from Pit. to Bos. and OF Brandon Moss and P Craig Hansen from Bos. to Pit. (July 31); P Maddux from SD for 2 PTBN (Aug. 20).

Pitching (40 IP)

	ERA	W-L	Gm	IP	BB	SO
Joe Beimel	2.02	5-1	71	49.0	21	32
Hong-Chih Kuo	2.14	5-3	42	80.0	21	96
Cory Wade	2.27	2-1	55	71.1	15	51
Takashi Saito	2.49	4-4	45	47.0	16	60
Jonathan Broxton	3.13	3-5	70	69.0	27	88
Chad Billingsley	3.14	16-10	35	200.2	80	201
Derek Lowe	3.24	14-11	34	211.0	45	147
Chan Ho Park	3.40	4-4	54	95.1	36	79
Hiroki Kuroda*	3.73	9-10	31	183.1	42	116
Greg Maddux	4.22	8-13	33	194.0	30	98
Clayton Kershaw*	4.26	5-5	22	107.2	52	100
Brad Penny	6.27	6-9	19	94.2	42	51

Saves: Saito (18); Broxton (14); Park (2); Kuo (1). **Complete games:** Kuroda (2); Billingsley, Lowe and Eric Stults (1). **Shutouts:** Kuroda (2); Billingsley and Stults (1).

Milwaukee Brewers

Batting (130 AB)	Avg	AB	R	H	HR	RBI	SB
Gabe Kapler	.301	229	36	69	8	38	3
Ray Durham	.289	370	64	107	6	45	8
Ryan Braun	.285	611	92	174	37	106	14
J.J. Hardy	.283	569	78	161	24	74	2
Prince Fielder	.276	588	86	162	34	102	3
Corey Hart	.268	612	76	164	20	91	23
Russell Branyan	.250	132	24	33	12	20	1
Jason Kendall	.246	516	46	127	2	49	8
Mike Cameron	.243	444	69	108	25	70	17
Rickie Weeks	.234	475	89	111	14	46	19
Craig Counsell	.226	248	31	56	1	14	3
Bill Hall	.225	404	50	91	15	55	5

Acquired: P Sabathia from Cle. for P Zach Jackson, P Rob Bryson, OF Matt LaPorta and OF Michael Brantley (July 7); IF Durham from SF for P Steve Hammond and OF Darren Ford (July 20).

Pitching (40 IP)	ERA	W-L	Gm	IP	BB	SO
CC Sabathia	1.65	11-2	17	130.2	25	128
Brian Shouse	2.81	5-1	69	51.1	14	33
Ben Sheets	3.09	13-9	31	198.1	47	158
Salomon Torres	3.49	7-5	71	80.0	33	51
Seth McClung	4.02	6-6	37	105.1	55	87
Carlos Villanueva	4.07	4-7	47	108.1	30	93
Guillermo Mota	4.11	5-6	58	57.0	28	50
Dave Bush	4.18	9-10	31	185.0	48	109
Manny Parra	4.39	10-8	32	166.0	75	147
Jeff Suppan	4.96	10-10	31	177.2	67	90
David Riske	5.31	1-2	45	42.1	25	27
Eric Gagne	5.44	4-3	50	46.1	22	38

Saves: Torres (28); Gagne (10); Shouse and Riske (2); Villanueva, Mota and Derrick Turnbow (1). **Complete games:** Sabathia (7); Sheets (5). **Shutouts:** Sabathia and Sheets (3).

New York Mets

Batting (135 AB)	Avg	AB	R	H	HR	RBI	SB
David Wright	.302	626	115	189	33	124	15
Fernando Tatis	.297	273	33	81	11	47	3
Jose Reyes	.297	688	113	204	16	68	56
Carlos Beltran	.284	606	116	172	27	112	25
Ryan Church	.276	319	54	88	12	49	2
Carlos Delgado	.271	598	96	162	38	115	1
Damion Easley	.269	316	33	85	6	44	0
Endy Chavez	.267	270	30	72	1	12	6
Brian Schneider	.257	335	30	86	9	38	0
Luis Castillo	.245	298	46	73	3	28	17
Ramon Castro	.245	143	15	35	7	24	0
Marlon Anderson	.210	138	16	29	1	10	2

Acquired: P Ayala from Wash. for PTBN (Aug. 17).

Pitching (40 IP)	ERA	W-L	Gm	IP	BB	SO
Billy Wagner	2.30	0-1	45	47.0	10	52
Johan Santana	2.53	16-7	34	234.1	63	206
Scott Schoeneweis	3.34	2-6	73	56.2	23	34
Joe Smith	3.55	6-3	82	63.1	31	52
Mike Pelfrey	3.72	13-11	32	200.2	64	110
Pedro Feliciano	4.05	3-4	86	53.1	26	50
John Maine	4.18	10-8	25	140.0	67	122
Oliver Perez	4.22	10-7	34	194.0	105	180
Duaner Sanchez	4.32	5-1	66	58.1	23	44
Nelson Figueroa	4.57	3-3	16	45.1	26	36
Aaron Heilman	5.21	3-8	78	76.0	46	80
Pedro Martinez	5.61	5-6	20	109.0	44	87
Luis Ayala	5.71	2-10	81	75.2	24	50

Saves: Wagner (27); Ayala (9); Heilman (3); Feliciano (2); Schoeneweis and Brian Stokes (1). **Complete games:** Santana (3); Pelfrey (2). **Shutouts:** Santana (2).

Philadelphia Phillies

Batting (135 AB)	Avg	AB	R	H	HR	RBI	SB
Greg Dobbs	.301	226	30	68	9	40	3
Shane Victorino	.293	570	102	167	14	58	36
Chase Utley	.292	607	113	177	33	104	14
Jimmy Rollins	.277	556	76	154	11	59	47
Jayson Werth	.273	418	73	114	24	67	20
Chris Coste	.263	274	28	72	9	36	0
Ryan Howard	.251	610	105	153	48	146	1
Pat Burrell	.250	536	74	134	33	86	0
Pedro Feliz	.249	425	43	106	14	58	0
Geoff Jenkins	.246	293	27	72	9	29	1
Tadahito Iguchi	.232	310	29	72	2	24	8
Carlos Ruiz	.219	320	47	70	4	31	1
Eric Bruntlett	.217	212	37	46	2	15	9

Acquired: P Blanton from Oak. for P Josh Outman, IF Adrian Cardenas and OF Matt Spencer (July 17). **Signed:** IF Iguchi (Sept. 5).

Pitchers (45 IP)	ERA	W-L	Gm	IP	BB	SO
Brad Lidge	1.95	2-0	72	69.1	35	92
J.C. Romero	2.75	4-4	81	59.0	38	52
Chad Durbin	2.87	5-4	71	87.2	35	63
Ryan Madson	3.05	4-2	76	82.2	23	67
Cole Hamels	3.09	14-10	33	227.1	53	196
Clay Condrey	3.26	3-4	56	69.0	19	34
Jamie Moyer	3.71	16-7	33	196.1	62	123
Joe Blanton	4.20	4-0	13	70.2	31	49
Brett Myers	4.55	10-13	30	190.0	65	163
Kyle Kendrick	5.49	11-9	31	155.2	57	68
Adam Eaton	5.80	4-8	21	107.0	44	57

Saves: Lidge (41); Tom Gordon (3); Madson, Durbin, Romero and Condrey (1). **Complete games:** Hamels and Myers (2). **Shutouts:** Hamels (2); Myers (1).

Pittsburgh Pirates

Batting (165 AB)	Avg	AB	R	H	HR	RBI	SB
Xavier Nady	.330	327	50	108	13	57	1
Ryan Doumit	.318	431	71	137	15	69	2
Jason Bay	.282	393	72	111	22	64	7
Doug Mientkiewicz	.277	285	37	79	2	30	0
Nate McLouth	.276	597	113	165	26	94	23
Chris Gomez	.273	183	26	50	1	20	0
Jack Wilson	.272	305	24	83	1	22	2
Freddy Sanchez	.271	569	75	154	9	52	0
Adam LaRoche	.270	492	66	133	25	85	1
Jose Bautista	.242	314	38	76	12	44	1
Jason Michaels	.228	228	25	52	8	44	1
Luis Rivas	.218	206	25	45	3	20	3
Andy LaRoche*	.166	223	17	37	5	18	2

Acquired: OF Michaels from Cle. for PTBN (May 8); P Karstens, P Dan McCutchen P Ross Ohlendorf and OF Jose Tabata from NY-AL for OF Nady and P Damaso Marte (July 26); LaRoche from LA-NL (for 3-way trade details, see Bos. or LA-NL notes). **Traded:** IF Bautista to Tor. for PTBN (Aug. 21).

Pitching (50 IP)	ERA	W-L	Gm	IP	BB	SO
John Grabow	2.84	6-3	74	76.0	37	62
Matt Capps	3.02	2-3	49	53.2	5	39
Paul Maholm	3.71	9-9	31	206.1	63	139
Jeff Karstens	4.66	2-6	9	51.1	13	23
Tyler Yates	4.66	6-3	72	73.1	41	63
Sean Burnett	4.76	1-1	58	56.2	34	42
Zach Duke	4.82	5-14	31	185.0	47	87
Phil Dumatrait*	5.26	3-4	21	78.2	42	52
Ian Snell	5.42	7-12	31	164.1	89	135
Franquelis Osoria	6.08	4-3	43	60.2	12	31
Tom Gorzelanny	6.66	6-9	21	105.1	70	64

Saves: Capps (21); Damaso Marte (5); Grabow (4); Yates, T.J. Beam, Craig Hansen and Romulo Sanchez (1). **Complete games:** Maholm, Karstens and Duke (1). **Shutouts:** Karstens and Duke (1).

St. Louis Cardinals

Batting (135 AB)	Avg	AB	R	H	HR	RBI	SB
Felipe Lopez	.385	156	30	60	4	21	4
Albert Pujols	.357	524	100	187	37	116	7
Aaron Miles	.317	379	49	120	4	31	3
Yadier Molina	.304	444	37	135	7	56	0
Skip Schumaker	.302	540	87	163	8	46	8
Ryan Ludwick	.299	538	104	161	37	113	4
Felipe Lopez	.283	481	64	136	6	46	8
Adam Kennedy	.280	339	42	95	2	36	7
Troy Glaus	.270	544	69	147	27	99	0
Brian Barton	.268	153	23	41	2	13	3
Rick Ankiel	.264	413	65	109	25	71	2
Cezar Izturis	.263	414	50	109	1	24	24
Chris Duncan	.248	222	26	55	6	27	2
Brendan Ryan	.244	197	30	48	0	10	7
Jason LaRue	.213	164	17	35	4	21	0

Signed: IF Lopez (Aug. 6).

Pitching (40 IP)	ERA	W-L	Gm	IP	BB	SO
Russ Springer	2.32	2-1	70	50.1	18	45
Adam Wainwright	3.20	11-3	20	132.0	34	91
Chris Perez*	3.46	3-3	41	41.2	22	42
Ryan Franklin	3.55	6-6	74	78.2	30	51
Todd Wellemeyer	3.71	13-9	32	191.2	62	134
Kyle Lohse	3.78	15-6	33	200.0	49	119
Kyle McClellan*	4.04	2-7	68	75.2	26	59
Braden Looper	4.16	12-14	33	199.0	45	108
Joel Pineiro	5.15	7-7	26	148.2	35	81
Brad Thompson	5.15	6-3	26	64.2	19	32
Ron Villone	4.68	1-2	74	50.0	37	50
Jason Isringhausen	5.70	1-5	42	42.2	22	36

Saves: Franklin (17); Isringhausen (12); Perez (7); Pineiro, McClellan, Villone, Randy Flores, Jason Motte and Anthony Reyes (1). **Complete games:** Wainwright and Looper (1). **Shutouts:** Looper (1).

San Diego Padres

Batting (140 AB)	Avg	AB	R	H	HR	RBI	SB
Brian Giles	.306	559	81	171	12	63	2
Jody Gerut	.296	328	46	97	14	43	6
Luis Rodriguez	.287	202	22	58	0	12	1
Adrian Gonzalez	.279	616	103	172	36	119	0
Edgar Gonzalez*	.274	325	38	89	7	33	1
Chase Headley*	.269	331	34	89	9	38	4
Kevin Kouzmanoff	.260	624	71	162	23	84	0
Scott Hairston	.248	326	42	81	17	31	3
Nick Hundley*	.237	198	21	47	5	24	0
Khalil Greene	.213	389	30	83	10	35	5
Paul McAnulty	.207	135	9	28	3	13	0
Josh Bard	.202	178	11	36	1	16	0

Acquired: P Baek from Sea. for P Jared Wells (May 29).

Pitching (40 IP)	ERA	W-L	Gm	IP	BB	SO
Mike Adams	2.48	2-3	54	65.1	19	74
Jake Peavy	2.85	10-11	27	173.2	59	166
Heath Bell	3.58	6-6	74	78.0	28	71
Trevor Hoffman	3.77	3-6	48	45.1	9	46
Chris Young	3.96	7-6	18	102.1	48	93
Cla Meredith	4.09	0-3	73	70.1	24	49
Cha Seung Baek	4.62	6-9	22	111.0	30	77
Shawn Estes	4.74	2-3	9	43.2	18	19
Josh Banks*	4.75	3-6	17	85.1	32	43
Justin Germano	5.98	0-3	12	43.2	13	17

Saves: Hoffman (30). **Complete games:** Peavy, Young and Banks (1). **Shutouts:** none.

San Francisco Giants

Batting (135 AB)	Avg	AB	R	H	HR	RBI	SB
Pablo Sandoval*	.345	145	24	50	3	24	0
Randy Winn	.306	598	84	183	10	64	25
Bengie Molina	.292	530	46	155	16	95	0
Emmanuel Burriss*	.283	240	37	68	1	18	13
Rich Aurilia	.283	407	33	115	10	52	1
Fred Lewis	.282	468	81	132	9	40	21
Aaron Rowand	.271	549	57	149	13	70	2
Eugenio Velez*	.262	275	32	72	1	30	15
John Bowker*	.255	326	31	83	10	43	1
Omar Vizquel	.222	266	24	59	0	23	5

Pitching (40 IP)	ERA	W-L	Gm	IP	BB	SO
Tim Lincecum	2.62	18-5	34	227.0	84	265
Keiichi Yabu	3.57	3-6	60	68.0	32	48
Matt Cain	3.76	8-14	34	217.2	91	186
Billy Sadler*	4.06	0-1	33	44.1	27	42
Tyler Walker	4.56	5-8	65	53.1	21	49
Brian Wilson	4.62	3-2	63	62.1	28	67
Jack Taschner	4.88	3-2	67	48.0	24	39
Jonathan Sanchez	5.01	9-12	29	158.0	75	157
Barry Zito	5.15	10-17	32	180.0	102	120
Pat Misch*	5.68	0-3	15	52.1	15	38
Kevin Correia	6.05	3-8	25	110.0	47	66
Brad Hennessey	7.81	1-2	17	40.1	15	21

Saves: Wilson (41). **Complete games:** Lincecum (2); Cain and Hennessey (1). **Shutouts:** Lincecum and Cain (1).

Washington Nationals

Batting (135 AB)	Avg	AB	R	H	HR	RBI	SB
Cristian Guzman	.316	579	77	183	9	55	6
Ronnie Belliard	.287	296	37	85	11	46	3
Ryan Zimmerman	.283	428	51	121	14	51	1
Dmitri Young	.280	150	15	42	4	10	0
Lastings Milledge	.268	523	65	140	14	61	24
Elijah Dukes	.264	276	48	73	13	44	13
Wil Nieves	.261	176	15	46	1	20	0
Jesus Flores	.256	301	23	77	8	59	0
Willie Harris	.251	367	58	92	13	43	13
Emilio Bonifacio*	.243	169	29	41	0	14	7
Aaron Boone	.241	232	23	56	6	28	0
Austin Kearns	.217	313	40	68	7	32	2
Kory Casto*	.215	163	15	35	2	16	1
Wily Mo Pena	.205	195	10	40	2	10	0

Acquired: IF Bonifacio from Ari. for P Jon Rauch (July 22).

Pitching (40 IP)	ERA	W-L	Gm	IP	BB	SO
Steven Shell*	2.16	2-2	39	50.0	20	41
John Lannan*	3.91	9-15	31	182.0	72	117
Joel Hanrahan	3.95	6-3	69	84.1	42	93
Saul Rivera	3.96	5-6	76	84.0	35	65
Garrett Mock*	4.17	1-3	26	41.0	23	46
Jesus Colome	4.31	2-2	61	71.0	39	55
Odalis Perez	4.34	7-12	30	159.2	55	119
Tim Redding	4.95	10-11	33	182.0	65	120
Jason Bergmann	5.09	2-11	30	139.2	47	96
Charlie Manning*	5.14	1-3	57	42.0	31	37
Collin Balester*	5.51	3-7	15	80.0	28	50
Shawn Hill	5.83	1-5	12	63.1	23	39
Matt Chico	6.19	0-6	11	48.0	17	31

Saves: Hanrahan (9); Shell (2). **Complete games:** Redding and Bergmann. **Shutouts:** none.

Players Who Played in Both Leagues in 2008

While all individual major league statistics count for career records, players cannot transfer their stats from one league to the other if they are traded during the regular season. Here are the combined stats for batters with at least 215 at bats and pitchers with at least 55 innings pitched, who played in both leagues in 2008. Players listed alphabetically.

Batters (215 AB)

	Avg	AB	R	H	HR	RBI	SB
Jose Bautista	.238	370	45	88	15	54	1
PIT	.242	314	38	76	12	44	1
TOR	.214	56	7	12	3	10	0
Jason Bay	.286	577	111	165	31	101	10
PIT	.282	393	72	111	22	64	7
BOS	.293	184	39	54	9	37	3
Casey Blake	.274	536	71	147	21	81	3
CLE	.289	325	46	94	11	58	2
LA-NL	.251	211	25	53	10	23	1
David Eckstein	.265	324	32	86	2	27	2
TOR	.277	260	27	72	1	23	2
ARI	.219	64	5	14	1	4	0
Ken Griffey Jr.	.249	490	67	122	18	71	0
CIN	.245	359	51	88	15	53	0
CHI-AL	.260	131	16	34	3	18	0
Gabe Gross	.238	345	46	82	13	40	4
MIL	.209	43	6	9	0	2	2
TB	.242	302	40	73	13	38	2
Casey Kotchman	.272	525	65	143	14	74	2
LA-AL	.287	373	47	107	12	54	2
ATL	.237	152	18	36	2	20	0
Mark Kotsay	.276	402	45	111	6	49	2
ATL	.289	318	39	92	6	37	2
BOS	.226	84	6	19	0	12	0
Mike Lamb	.235	247	22	58	1	32	0
MIN	.233	236	20	55	1	32	0
MIL	.273	11	2	3	0	0	0
Jason Michaels	.224	286	28	64	8	53	2
CLE	.207	58	3	12	0	9	1
PIT	.228	228	25	52	8	44	1
Brandon Moss	.246	236	19	58	8	34	1
BOS	.295	78	7	23	2	11	0
PIT	.222	158	12	35	6	23	0
Xavier Nady	.305	555	76	169	25	97	2
PIT	.330	327	50	108	13	57	1
NY-AL	.268	228	26	61	12	40	1
Manny Ramirez	.332	552	102	183	37	121	3
BOS	.299	365	66	109	20	68	1
LA-NL	.396	187	36	74	17	53	2
Matt Stairs	.252	337	46	85	13	49	1
TOR	.250	320	42	80	11	44	1
PHI	.294	17	4	5	2	5	0
Mark Texeira	.308	574	102	177	33	121	2
ATL	.283	381	63	108	20	78	0
LA-AL	.358	193	39	69	13	43	2

Pitchers (55 IP)

	ERA	W-L	Gm	IP	BB	SO
Cha Seung Baek	.4.79	6-10	32	141.0	43	92
SEA	.5.40	0-1	10	30.0	13	15
SD	.4.62	6-9	22	111.0	30	77
Denny Bautista	.5.22	4-4	51	60.1	42	44
DET	.3.32	0-1	16	19.0	14	10
PIT	.6.10	4-3	35	41.1	28	34
Joe Blanton	.4.69	9-12	33	197.2	66	111
OAK	.4.96	5-12	20	127.0	35	62
PHI	.4.20	4-0	13	70.2	31	49
Sean Gallagher	.5.15	5-7	23	115.1	58	103
CHI-NL	.4.45	3-4	12	58.2	22	49
OAK	.5.88	2-3	11	56.2	36	54
Chad Gaudin	.4.40	9-5	50	90.0	27	71
OAK	.3.59	5-3	26	62.2	17	44
CHI-NL	.6.26	4-2	24	27.1	10	27
Jason Grilli	.3.00	3-3	60	75.0	38	69
DET	.3.29	0-1	9	13.2	7	10
COL	.2.94	3-2	51	61.1	31	59
Rich Harden	.2.07	10-2	25	148.0	61	181
OAK	.2.34	5-1	13	77.0	31	92
CHI-NL	.1.78	5-1	12	71.0	30	89
LaTroy Hawkins	.3.92	3-1	57	62.0	22	48
NY-AL	.5.71	1-1	33	41.0	17	23
HOU	.0.43	2-0	24	21.0	5	25
Livan Hernandez	.6.05	13-11	31	180.0	43	67
MIN	.5.48	10-8	23	139.2	29	54
COL	.8.03	3-3	8	40.1	14	13
Zach Jackson	.5.55	2-3	11	58.1	16	31
MIL	.4.91	0-0	2	3.2	1	1
CLE	.5.60	2-3	9	54.2	14	30
Nick Masset	.3.92	2-0	42	62.0	26	43
CHI-AL	.4.63	1-0	32	44.2	21	32
CIN	.2.08	1-0	10	17.1	5	11
Damaso Marte	.4.02	5-3	72	65.0	26	71
PIT	.3.47	4-0	47	46.2	16	47
NY-AL	.5.40	1-3	25	18.1	10	24
Ross Ohlendorf	.6.13	1-4	30	62.2	31	49
NY-AL	.6.53	1-1	25	40.0	19	36
PIT	.6.35	0-3	5	22.2	12	13
CC Sabathia	.2.70	17-10	35	253.0	59	251
CLE	.3.83	6-8	18	122.1	34	123
MIL	.1.65	11-2	17	130.2	25	128
Brett Tomko	.6.30	2-7	22	70.0	18	49
KC	.6.97	2-7	16	60.2	13	40
SD	.1.93	0-0	6	9.1	5	9

Manny Ramirez
Red Sox to Dodgers

Ken Griffey Jr.
Reds to White Sox

CC Sabathia
Indians to Brewers

Rich Harden
A's to Cubs

BASEBALL PLAYOFFS

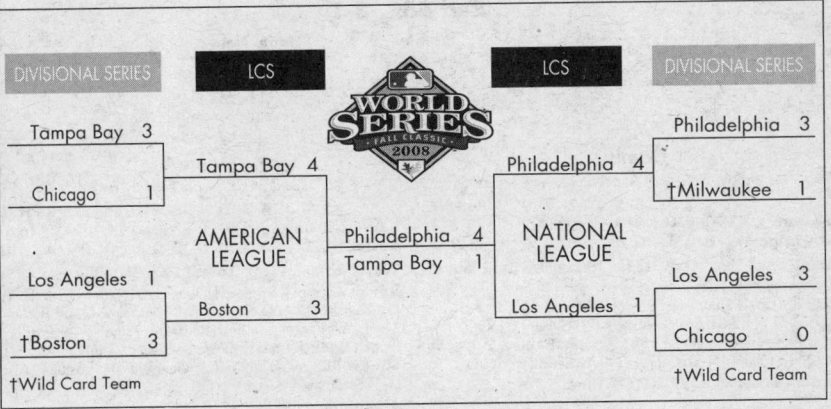

DIVISIONAL SERIES SUMMARIES
American League
Rays, 3-1

Date	Winner	Home Field
Oct. 2	Rays, 6-4	at Tampa Bay
Oct. 3	Rays, 6-2	at Tampa Bay
Oct. 5	White Sox, 5-3	at Chicago
Oct. 6	Rays, 6-2	at Chicago

Game 1
Thursday, Oct. 2, at Tropicana Field

	1 2 3	4 5 6	7 8 9		R	H	E
Chicago	0 0 3	0 0 0	0 0 1	-	4	7	0
Tampa Bay	0 1 3	0 2 0	0 0 x	-	6	11	0

Win: Shields, TB (1-0). **Loss:** Vazquez, Chi. (0-1). **Save:** Wheeler (1).

2B: Chicago—Dye (1); Tampa Bay—Navarro (1). **3B:** Tampa Bay—Iwamura (1). **HR:** Chicago—Wise (1, off Shields, 2 on), Konerko (1, off Wheeler, 0 on); Tampa Bay—Longoria 2 (2, off Vazquez, 0 on; off Vazquez, 0 on). **RBI:** Chicago—Wise 3 (3), Konerko (1); Tampa Bay—Longoria 3 (3), Iwamura (1), Aybar (1), Crawford (1). **CS:** Chicago—Pierzynski (1).
Attendance: 35,041 (36,048). **Time:** 3:10.

Game 2
Friday, Oct. 3, at Tropicana Field

	1 2 3	4 5 6	7 8 9		R	H	E
Chicago	2 0 0	0 0 0	0 0 0	-	2	12	1
Tampa Bay	0 1 0	0 2 0	0 3 x	-	6	12	0

Win: Kazmir, TB (1-0). **Loss:** Buehrle, Chi. (0-1).

2B: Tampa Bay—Aybar (1), Navarro (2). **3B:** Tampa Bay—Upton (1). **HR:** Tampa Bay—Iwamura (1, off Buehrle, 1 on). **RBI:** Chicago—Thome (1), Ramirez (1); Tampa Bay—Navarro 2 (2), Iwamura 2 (3), Crawford (2), Baldelli (1). **SB:** Tampa Bay—Crawford (1). **E:** Chicago—Ramirez (1).
Attendance: 35,257 (36,048). **Time:** 3:10.

Game 3
Sunday, Oct. 5, at U.S. Cellular Field

	1 2 3	4 5 6	7 8 9		R	H	E
Tampa Bay	0 1 0	0 0 0	2 0 0	-	3	8	0
Chicago	0 0 1	3 0 1	0 0 x	-	5	7	0

Win: Danks, Chi. (1-0). **Loss:** Garza, TB (0-1). **Save:** Jenks, Chi. (1).

2B: Tampa Bay—Navarro (3); Chicago—Thome (1), Wise (1), Pierzynski (1). **HR:** Tampa Bay—Upton (1, off Danks, 1 on). **RBI:** Tampa Bay—Iwamura (4), Upton 2 (2); Chicago—Pierzynski (1), Ramirez (2), Wise 2 (5), Uribe (1). **SB:** Chicago—Wise (1), Anderson (1), Uribe (1).
Attendance: 40,142 (40,615). **Time:** 3:07.

Game 4
Monday, Oct. 6, at U.S. Cellular Field

	1 2 3	4 5 6	7 8 9		R	H	E
Tampa Bay	1 0 1	2 1 0	1 0 0	-	6	10	0
Chicago	0 0 0	1 0 0	0 0 2	-	4	0	0

Win: Sonnanstine, TB (1-0). **Loss:** Floyd, Chi. (0-1).

2B: Tampa Bay—Floyd (1), Bartlett (1), Iwamura (1). **HR:** Tampa Bay—Upton 2 (3, off Floyd, 0 on; off Floyd, 0 on); Chicago—Konerko (2, off Sonnanstine, 0 on), Dye (1, off Sonnanstine, 0 on). **RBI:** Tampa Bay—Upton 2 (4), Floyd (1), Navarro (3), Pena 2 (2); Chicago—Konerko (2), Dye (1). **SB:** Tampa Bay—Pena 2 (2), Crawford (2). **CS:** Tampa Bay—Pena (1). **Pick:** Tampa Bay—Pena (1).
Attendance: 40,454 (40,615). **Time:** 3:13.

American League Divisional Series (Cont.)
Red Sox, 3-1

Date	Winner	Home Field
Oct. 1	Red Sox, 4-1	at Los Angeles
Oct. 3	Red Sox, 7-5	at Los Angeles
Oct. 5	Angels, 5-4 (12 inn.)	at Boston
Oct. 6	Red Sox, 3-2	at Boston

Game 1
Wednesday, Oct. 1, at Angel Stadium of Anaheim

	1 2 3	4 5 6	7 8 9	R H E
Boston	0 0 0	0 0 2	0 0 2	- 4 8 1
Los Angeles	0 0 1	0 0 0	0 0 0	- 1 9 1

Win: Lester, Bos. (1-0). **Loss:** Lackey, LA (0-1). **Save:** Papelbon, Bos. (1).

2B: Boston—Ellsbury (1), Bay (1). **HR:** Boston—Bay (1, off Lackey, 1 on). **RBI:** Boston—Bay 2 (2), Ellsbury (1), Ortiz (1); Los Angeles—Hunter (1). **SB:** Boston—Ellsbury 2 (2). **E:** Boston—Lowrie (1); Los Angeles—Matthews (1). **Attendance:** 44,996 (45,257). **Time:** 3:14.

Game 2
Friday, Oct. 3, at Angel Stadium of Anaheim

	1 2 3	4 5 6	7 8 9	R H E
Boston	4 0 0	1 0 0	0 0 2	- 7 14 0
Los Angeles	1 0 0	1 1 0	1 1 0	- 5 11 2

Win: Papelbon, Bos. (1-0). **Loss:** Rodriguez, LA (0-1).

2B: Boston—Drew (1), Cora (1), Ellsbury (2), Ortiz (1). **3B:** Los Angeles—Figgins (1). **HR:** Boston—Bay (2, off Santana, 2 on), Drew (1, off Rodriguez, 1 on). **RBI:** Boston—Drew 3 (3), Bay 3 (5), Ellsbury (2); Los Angeles—Hunter 2 (3), Figgins (1), Napoli (1), Teixeira (1). **SB:** Boston—Ellsbury (3). **E:** Los Angeles—Aybar (1), Hunter (1). **Attendance:** 45,354 (45,257). **Time:** 3:51.

Game 3
Sunday, Oct. 5, at Fenway Park

	1 2 3 4 5 6 7 8 9 10 11 12	R H E
L.A.	1 0 2 0 1 0 0 0 0 0 0 1	- 5 16 0
Boston	0 3 0 0 1 0 0 0 0 0 0 0	- 4 7 0

Win: Weaver, LA (1-0). **Loss:** Lopez, Bos. (0-1).

2B: Los Angeles—Figgins (1), Guerrero (1); Boston—Ellsbury (3), Youkilis (1). **HR:** Los Angeles—Napoli 2 (2, off Beckett, 1 on; off Beckett, 0 on). **RBI:** Los Angeles—Rivera (1), Napoli 3 (4), Aybar (1); Boston—Ellsbury 3 (5), Youkilis (1). **SB:** Los Angeles—Figgins (1), Guerrero (1); Boston—Crisp (1). **CS:** Boston—Ellsbury (1). **Attendance:** 39,067 (37,400). **Time:** 5:19.

Game 4
Monday, Oct. 6, at Fenway Park

	1 2 3	4 5 6	7 8 9	R H E
Los Angeles	0 0 0	0 0 0	0 2 0	- 2 6 1
Boston	0 0 0	0 2 0	0 0 1	- 3 9 0

Win: Delcarmen, Bos. (1-0). **Loss:** Shields, LA (0-1).

2B: Los Angeles—Morales (1); Boston—Pedroia (1), Bay (2). **RBI:** Los Angeles—Hunter 2 (5); Boston—Ellsbury (6), Pedroia (1), Lowrie (1). **CS:** Los Angeles—Willits (1). **E:** Los Angeles—Figgins (1). **Attendance:** 38,785 (37,400). **Time:** 2:50.

National League

Dodgers, 3-0

Date	Winner	Home Field
Oct. 1	Dodgers, 7-2	at Chicago
Oct. 2	Dodgers, 10-3	at Chicago
Oct. 4	Dodgers, 3-1	at Los Angeles

Game 1
Wednesday, Oct. 1, at Wrigley Field

	1 2 3	4 5 6	7 8 9	R H E
Los Angeles	0 0 0	0 4 0	1 1 1	- 7 8 1
Chicago	0 2 0	0 0 0	0 0 0	- 2 9 1

Win: Lowe, LA (1-0). **Loss:** Dempster, Chi. (0-1).

2B: Los Angeles—Kemp (1), DeWitt (1); Chicago—Ramirez (1). **HR:** Los Angeles—Loney (1, off Dempster, 3 on), Ramirez (1, off Marshall, 0 on), Martin (1, off Marquis, 0 on); Chicago—DeRosa (1, off Lowe, 1 on). **RBI:** Los Angeles—Loney 4 (4), Ramirez (1), Blake (1), Martin (1); Chicago—DeRosa 2 (2). **E:** Los Angeles—Blake (1); Chicago—Edmonds (1). **Attendance:** 42,099 (41,160). **Time:** 3:10.

Game 2
Thursday, Oct. 2, at Wrigley Field

	1 2 3	4 5 6	7 8 9	R H E
Los Angeles	0 5 0	0 1 0	1 2 1	- 10 12 0
Chicago	0 0 0	0 0 0	1 0 2	- 3 8 4

Win: Billingsley, LA (1-0). **Loss:** Zambrano, Chi. (0-1).

2B: Los Angeles—Martin (1), Kemp (2); Chicago—DeRosa 2 (2), Edmonds (1), Lee (1). **HR:** Los Angeles—Ramirez 2 (2, off Zambrano, 0 on). **RBI:** Los Angeles—DeWitt (1), Furcal 2 (2), Martin 3 (4), Ramirez 2 (3), Kemp (1), Blake (2); Chicago—Edmonds 2 (4), DeRosa 2 (4). **E:** Chicago—DeRosa (1), Lee (1), Ramirez (1), Theriot (1). **Attendance:** 42,136 (41,160). **Time:** 3:10.

Game 3
Saturday, Oct. 4, at Dodger Stadium

	1 2 3	4 5 6	7 8 9	R H E
Chicago	0 0 0	0 0 0	0 1 0	- 1 8 1
Los Angeles	2 0 0	0 1 0	0 0 x	- 3 6 0

Win: Kuroda, LA (1-0). **Loss:** Harden, Chi. (0-1). **Save:** Broxton, LA (1).

2B: Chicago—Lee 2 (3), Soto (1); Los Angeles—Martin 2 (3), Loney (1), DeWitt (2). **RBI:** Chicago—Ward (1); Los Angeles—Loney 2 (6), Martin (5). **SB:** Chicago—Cedeno (1). **E:** Chicago—Harden (1). **Attendance:** 56,000 (56,000). **Time:** 3:03.

Phillies, 3-1

Date	Winner	Home Field
Oct. 1	Phillies, 3-1	at Philadelphia
Oct. 2	Phillies, 5-2	at Philadelphia
Oct. 4	Brewers, 4-1	at Milwaukee
Oct. 5	Phillies, 6-2	at Milwaukee

Game 1
Wednesday, Oct. 1, at Citizens Bank Park

	1 2 3	4 5 6	7 8 9	R H E
Milwaukee	0 0 0	0 0 0	0 0 1 -	1 4 1
Philadelphia	0 0 3	0 0 0	0 0 x -	3 4 1

Win: Hamels, Phi. (1-0). **Loss:** Gallardo, Mil. (0-1). **Save:** Lidge, Phi. (1).

2B: Milwaukee—Braun (1); Philadelphia—Utley (1). **RBI:** Philadelphia—Utley 2 (2), Victorino (1). **SB:** Philadelphia—Victorino (1). **E:** Milwaukee—Weeks (1); Philadelphia—Utley (1).

Attendance: 45,929 (43,647). **Time:** 2:39.

Game 2
Thursday, Oct. 2, at Citizens Bank Park

	1 2 3	4 5 6	7 8 9	R H E
Milwaukee	1 0 0	0 0 0	1 0 0 -	2 3 0
Philadelphia	0 5 0	0 0 0	0 0 x -	5 9 1

Win: Myers, Phi. (1-0). **Loss:** Sabathia, Mil. (0-1). **Save:** Lidge, Phi. (2).

2B: Milwaukee—Braun (2), Hardy (1); Philadelphia—Victorino 2 (2), Werth 2 (2), Feliz (1), Rollins (1). **HR:** Milwaukee—Hardy (1), Counsell (1); Philadelphia—Feliz (1), Victorino 4 (5). **SB:** Philadelphia—Victorino 2 (3), Werth (1), Rollins (1). **CS:** Philadelphia—Rollins (1). **E:** Philadelphia—Rollins (1).

Attendance: 46,208 (43,647). **Time:** 3:00.

Game 3
Saturday, Oct. 4, at Miller Park

	1 2 3	4 5 6	7 8 9	R H E
Philadelphia	0 0 0	0 0 1	0 0 0 -	1 9 0
Milwaukee	2 0 0	0 1 0	1 0 x -	4 11 0

Win: Bush, Mil. (1-0). **Loss:** Moyer, Phi. (0-1). **Save:** Torres, Mil. (1).

2B: Philadelphia—Howard (1), Rollins (2), Werth (3). **3B:** Philadelphia—Werth (1). **RBI:** Philadelphia—Howard (1); Milwaukee—Fielder (1), Hardy (2), Braun (1), Kendall (1).

Attendance: 43,992 (41,900). **Time:** 3:31.

Game 4
Sunday, Oct. 5, at Miller Park

	1 2 3	4 5 6	7 8 9	R H E
Philadelphia	1 0 4	0 0 0	0 0 1 -	6 10 0
Milwaukee	0 0 0	0 0 0	1 1 0 -	2 8 0

Win: Blanton, Phi. (1-0). **Loss:** Suppan, Mil. (0-1).

2B: Philadelphia—Victorino (3). **HR:** Philadelphia—Rollins (1, off Suppan, 0 on), Burrell 2 (2, off Suppan, 2 on; off Mota, 0 on), Werth (1, off Suppan, 0 on); Milwaukee—Fielder (1, off Blanton, 0 on). **RBI:** Philadelphia—Rollins (1), Burrell 4 (4), Werth (1); Milwaukee—Fielder (2), Braun (2).

Attendance: 43,934 (41,900). **Time:** 2:53.

AMERICAN LEAGUE CHAMPIONSHIP SERIES

Rays, 4-3

Date	Winner	Home Field
Oct. 10	Red Sox, 2-0	at Tampa Bay
Oct. 11	Rays, 9-8 (11 inn.)	at Tampa Bay
Oct. 13	Rays, 9-1	at Boston
Oct. 14	Rays, 13-4	at Boston
Oct. 16	Red Sox, 8-7	at Boston
Oct. 18	Red Sox, 4-2	at Tampa Bay
Oct. 19	Rays, 3-1	at Tampa Bay

Game 1
Friday, Oct. 10, at Tropicana Field

	1 2 3	4 5 6	7 8 9	R H E
Boston	0 0 0	0 1 0	0 1 0 -	2 7 0
Tampa Bay	0 0 0	0 0 0	0 0 0 -	0 4 0

Win: Matsuzaka, Bos. (1-0). **Loss:** Shields, TB (0-1). **Save:** Papelbon, Bos. (1).

2B: Boston—Youkilis 2 (2), Kotsay (1). **RBI:** Boston—Lowrie (1), Youkilis (1). **SB:** Boston—Pedroia (1).

Attendance: 35,001 (36,048). **Time:** 3:25.

ALCS Most Valuable Player
Matt Garza, Tampa Bay, P

ERA	W-L	IP	H	ER	BB	K
1.38	2-0	13.0	8	2	6	14

Game 2
Saturday, Oct. 11, at Tropicana Field

	1 2 3	4 5 6	7 8 9 10 11	R H E
Boston	2 0 1	0 3 1	0 1 0 0 0 -	8 12 0
Tampa Bay	2 0 2	1 3 0	0 0 0 0 1 -	9 12 0

Win: Price, TB (1-0). **Loss:** Timlin, Bos. (0-1).

2B: Boston—Bay (1), Crisp 2 (2); Tampa Bay—Pena (1), Longoria 2 (2). **HR:** Boston—Pedroia 2 (2, off Kazmir, 0 on; off Kazmir, 0 on), Youkilis (1, off Kazmir, 0 on), Bay (1, off Balfour, 0 on); Tampa Bay—Longoria (1, off Beckett, 1 on), Upton (1, off Beckett, 0 on), Floyd (1, off Beckett, 0 on). **RBI:** Boston—Bay 4 (4), Pedroia 2 (2), Youkilis (2); Tampa Bay—Longoria 3 (3), Upton 2 (2), Crawford 2 (2), Floyd (1), Pena (1). **SB:** Tampa Bay—Upton (1). **Pick:** Tampa Bay—Crawford (1). **Attendance:** 34,904 (36,048). **Time:** 5:27.

Game 3
Monday, Oct. 13, at Fenway Park

	1 2 3	4 5 6	7 8 9	R H E
Tampa Bay	0 1 4	0 0 0	0 3 1 -	9 13 0
Boston	0 0 0	0 0 1	0 0 0 -	1 7 0

Win: Garza, TB (1-0). **Loss:** Lester, Bos. (0-1).

2B: Tampa Bay—Iwamura 2 (2); Boston—Pedroia (1), Kotsay (2). **HR:** Tampa Bay—Upton (2, off Lester, 2 on), Longoria (2, off Lester, 0 on), Baldelli (1, off Byrd, 2 on), Pena (1, off Byrd, 0 on). **RBI:** Tampa Bay—Navarro (1), Upton 3 (5), Longoria (4), Baldelli 3 (3), Pena (2); Boston—Ellsbury (1). **SB:** Tampa Bay—Pena (1).

Attendance: 38,031 (37,400). **Time:** 3:23.

American League Championship Series (Cont.)

Game 4
Tuesday, Oct. 14, at Fenway Park

	1 2 3	4 5 6	7 8 9	R H E
Tampa Bay	3 0 2	0 1 5	0 2 0	-13 14 3
Boston	0 0 1	0 0 0	1 2 0	- 4 7 0

Win: Sonnanstine, TB (1-0). **Loss:** Wakefield, Bos. (0-1).
2B: Tampa Bay—Crawford 2 (2); Boston—Youkilis (3). **3B:** Tampa Bay—Bartlett (1), Crawford (1); Boston—Ortiz (1). **HR:** Tampa Bay—Pena (2, off Wakefield, 1 on), Longoria (3, off Wakefield, 0 on), Aybar (1, off Wakefield, 1 on); Boston—Cash (1, off Sonnanstine, 0 on). **RBI:** Tampa Bay—Pena 2 (4), Longoria 2 (6), Aybar 5 (5), Upton (6), Crawford 2 (4), Navarro (2); Boston—Cash (1), Youkilis 2 (4), Pedroia (3). **SB:** Tampa Bay—Upton (2); Crawford 2 (2). **E:** Tampa Bay—Longoria 2 (2), Upton (1).
Attendance: 38,133 (37,400). **Time:** 3:07.

Game 5
Thursday, Oct. 16, at Fenway Park

	1 2 3	4 5 6	7 8 9	R H E
Tampa Bay	2 0 3	0 0 0	2 0 0	- 7 8 1
Boston	0 0 0	0 4 3 1	- 8 11 0

Win: Masterson, Bos. (1-0). **Loss:** Howell, TB (0-1).
2B: Tampa Bay—Upton (1); Boston—Lowrie (1), Kotsay (3). **HR:** Tampa Bay—Upton (3, off Matsuzaka, 1 on), Pena (3, off Matsuzaka, 1 on), Longoria (4, off Matsuzaka, 0 on); Boston—Ortiz (1, off Balfour, 2 on), Drew (1, off Wheeler, 1 on). **RBI:** Tampa Bay—Upton 4 (10), Pena 2 (6), Longoria (7); Boston—Pedroia (4), Ortiz 3 (3), Drew 3 (3), Crisp (1). **SB:** Tampa Bay—Gross (1), Iwamura 2 (2), Bartlett (1). **E:** Tampa Bay—Longoria (3).
Attendance: 38,437 (37,400). **Time:** 4:08.

Game 6
Saturday, Oct. 18, at Tropicana Field

	1 2 3	4 5 6	7 8 9	R H E
Boston	0 1 1	0 0 2	0 0 0	- 4 10 0
Tampa Bay	1 0 0	0 1 0	0 0 0	- 2 4 1

Win: Beckett, Bos. (1-0). **Loss:** Shields, TB (0-2). **Save:** Papelbon, Bos. (2).
2B: Boston—Ortiz (1), Drew (1). **HR:** Boston—Youkilis (4, off Shields, 0 on), Varitek (1, off Shields, 0 on); Tampa Bay—Upton (4, off Beckett, 0 on), Bartlett (1, off Beckett, 0 on). **RBI:** Boston—Youkilis 2 (6), Varitek (1), Ortiz (4); Tampa Bay—Upton (11), Bartlett (1). **SB:** Tampa Bay—Crawford (3). **CS:** Tampa Bay—Navarro (1). **Picked off:** Boston—Crisp. **E:** Tampa Bay—Bartlett (1).
Attendance: 40,947 (36,048). **Time:** 3:48.

Game 7
Sunday, Oct. 19, at Tropicana Field

	1 2 3	4 5 6	7 8 9	R H E
Boston	1 0 0	0 0 0	0 0 0	- 1 3 0
Tampa Bay	0 0 0	1 1 0	1 0 x	- 3 6 1

Win: Garza, TB (2-0). **Loss:** Lester, Bos. (0-2). **Save:** Price, TB (1).
2B: Tampa Bay—Longoria (3), Aybar (1). **HR:** Boston—Pedroia (3, off Garza, 0 on); Tampa Bay—Aybar (2, off Lester, 0 on). **RBI:** Boston—Pedroia (5); Tampa Bay—Longoria (8), Baldelli (4), Aybar (6). **SB:** Boston—Pedroia (2). **CS:** Boston—Pedroia (1). **E:** Tampa Bay—Bartlett (2).
Attendance: 40,473 (36,048). **Time:** 3:31.

ALCS Composite Box Score

Tampa Bay Rays

Batting	LCS vs. Boston							Overall AL Playoffs						
	Avg	AB	R	H	HR	RBI	BB	SO	Avg	AB	R	H	HR	RBI	BB	SO
Willy Aybar	.421	19	3	8	2	6	0	3	.367	30	5	11	2	7	0	5
Carl Crawford	.345	29	3	10	0	4	1	7	.302	43	5	13	0	6	3	9
Rocco Baldelli	.333	6	1	2	1	4	1	3	.214	14	3	3	1	5	2	3
B.J. Upton	.321	28	8	9	4	11	4	7	.304	46	13	14	7	15	5	12
Carlos Pena	.269	26	8	7	3	6	6	7	.333	36	8	12	3	8	7	11
Evan Longoria	.259	27	8	7	4	8	3	5	.262	42	10	11	6	11	5	11
Jason Bartlett	.217	23	4	5	1	1	1	5	.243	37	7	9	1	1	2	8
Akinori Iwamura	.207	29	4	6	0	0	5	5	.277	47	7	13	1	4	6	9
Cliff Floyd	.200	10	1	2	1	1	0	4	.200	15	2	3	1	2	0	7
Dioner Navarro	.192	26	1	5	0	2	2	4	.268	41	2	11	0	5	3	6
Gabe Gross	.000	10	0	0	0	0	1	5	.063	16	0	1	0	0	3	7
Ben Zobrist	.000	4	0	0	0	0	1	0	.000	4	0	0	0	0	-1	0
Fernando Perez	.000	0	0	0	0	0	0	2	.111	9	2	1	0	0	0	2
TOTALS	.252	242	43	61	16	43	25	57	.268	380	64	102	22	64	37	90

Pitching	ERA	W-L	Sv	Gm	IP	H	BB	SO	ERA	W-L	Sv	Gm	IP	H	BB	SO
Trever Miller	0.00	0-0	0	2	0.2	1	1	1	0.00	0-0	0	4	0.2	1	2	1
Edwin Jackson	0.00	0-0	0	2	2.1	0	2	4	0.00	0-0	0	2	2.1	0	2	4
David Price	0.00	0-0	1	3	2.1	0	2	4	0.00	1-0	1	3	2.1	0	2	4
Matt Garza	1.38	2-0	0	2	13.0	8	6	14	3.32	2-1	0	3	19.0	15	10	18
Chad Bradford	3.00	0-0	0	3	3.0	4	2	1	1.50	0-0	0	5	6.0	5	2	3
J.P. Howell	3.38	0-1	0	6	5.1	5	3	6	1.86	0-1	0	9	9.2	7	3	12
James Shields	3.46	0-2	0	2	13.0	15	5	9	3.72	1-2	0	3	19.1	21	6	13
Andy Sonnanstine	3.68	1-0	0	1	7.1	6	1	2	3.46	2-0	0	2	13.0	9	2	6
Scott Kazmir	4.35	0-0	0	2	10.1	8	6	9	4.02	1-0	0	3	15.2	16	8	13
Dan Wheeler	5.40	0-0	0	3	5.0	5	3	5	6.00	0-0	1	4	6.0	6	3	5
Grant Balfour	19.29	0-0	0	4	2.1	5	4	1	7.94	0-0	0	7	5.2	7	5	5
TOTALS	3.62	4-3	1	7	64.2	57	35	56	3.52	7-4	2	11	99.2	87	45	85

Boston Red Sox

Batting	Avg	AB	R	H	HR	RBI	BB	SO	Avg	AB	R	H	HR	RBI	BB	SO
				LCS vs. Tampa Bay								Overall AL Playoffs				
Coco Crisp	.450	20	2	9	0	1	4	3	.417	24	4	10	0	1	5	3
Dustin Pedroia	.346	26	9	9	3	5	5	3	.233	43	9	10	3	6	7	5
Kevin Cash	.333	3	1	1	1	1	0	1	.333	3	1	1	1	1	0	1
Kevin Youkilis	.333	30	4	10	2	6	2	4	.292	48	6	14	2	7	4	7
Jason Bay	.292	24	3	7	1	4	7	8	.341	41	6	14	3	9	9	12
J.D. Drew	.250	24	1	6	1	3	4	6	.263	38	3	10	2	6	4	10
Mark Kotsay	.233	30	1	7	0	0	0	6	.250	40	2	10	0	0	0	5
David Ortiz	.154	26	3	4	1	4	6	9	.186	43	4	8	1	5	9	13
Alex Cora	.143	7	0	1	0	0	0	1	.182	11	1	2	0	0	1	2
Jed Lowrie	.111	18	2	2	0	1	4	4	.207	29	4	6	0	2	5	7
Jason Varitek	.050	20	2	1	1	1	2	8	.118	34	4	4	1	1	2	9
Sean Casey	.000	2	0	0	0	0	0	2	.000	2	0	0	0	0	0	3
Jacoby Ellsbury	.000	14	0	0	0	0	1	3	.188	32	2	6	0	0	7	5
Mike Lowell	—	0	0	0	0	0	0	0	.000	8	0	0	0	0	0	3
David Ross	—	0	0	0	0	0	0	0	—	0	0	0	0	0	0	0
TOTALS	.234	244	28	57	10	27	35	56	.240	396	46	95	13	45	50	84

Pitching	ERA	W-L	Sv	Gm	IP	H	BB	SO	ERA	W-L	Sv	Gm	IP	H	BB	SO
Javier Lopez	0.00	0-0	0	2	1.2	3	0	0	3.38	0-1	0	3	2.2	6	0	1
Jonathan Papelbon	0.00	0-0	2	4	5.1	1	1	6	0.00	1-0	3	7	10.1	3	2	13
Hideki Okajima	0.00	0-0	0	5	7.1	1	1	5	1.80	0-0	0	8	10.0	4	2	5
Justin Masterson	1.59	1-0	0	5	5.2	4	2	6	1.86	1-0	0	9	9.2	10	5	9
Daisuke Matsuzaka	4.09	1-0	0	2	11.0	9	6	11	4.50	1-0	0	3	16.0	17	9	16
Jon Lester	4.97	0-2	0	2	12.2	14	2	15	2.36	1-2	0	4	26.2	24	5	26
Josh Beckett	9.64	1-0	0	2	9.1	13	2	8	8.79	1-0	0	3	14.1	22	6	14
Mike Timlin	10.13	0-1	0	2	2.2	4	0	0	10.13	0-1	0	2	2.2	4	0	0
Paul Byrd	10.80	0-0	0	1	3.1	5	0	2	10.80	0-0	0	1	3.1	5	0	2
Tim Wakefield	16.88	0-1	0	1	2.2	6	2	2	16.88	0-1	0	1	2.2	6	2	2
Manny Delcarmen	31.50	0-0	0	3	2.0	3	5	2	14.54	1-0	0	5	4.1	4	5	3
TOTALS	5.94	3-4	2	7	63.2	61	25	57	4.65	6-5	3	11	102.2	103	40	91

Score by Innings

	1	2	3	4	5	6	7	8	9	10	11		R	H	E
Boston	3	1	3	0	4	3	6	7	1	0	0	-	28	57	0
Tampa Bay	8	1	11	2	6	5	3	5	1	0	1	-	43	61	6

NATIONAL LEAGUE CHAMPIONSHIP SERIES

Phillies, 4-1

Date	Winner	Home Field
Oct. 9	Phillies, 3-2	at Philadelphia
Oct. 10	Phillies, 8-5	at Philadelphia
Oct. 12	Dodgers, 7-2	at Los Angeles
Oct. 13	Phillies, 7-5	at Los Angeles
Oct. 15	Phillies, 5-1	at Los Angeles

Game 1
Thursday, Oct. 9, at Citizens Bank Park

	1 2 3	4 5 6	7 8 9	R H E
Los Angeles	1 0 0	1 0 0	0 0 0	- 2 7 1
Philadelphia	0 0 0	0 0 3	0 0 x	- 3 7 0

Win: Hamels, Phi. (1-0). **Loss:** Lowe, LA (0-1). **Save:** Lidge, Phi. (1).

2B: Los Angeles—Ethier (1), Ramirez (1), Kemp (1). **HR:** Philadelphia—Utley (1, off Lowe, 1 on), Burrell (1, off Lowe, 0 on). **RBI:** Los Angeles—Ramirez (1), DeWitt (1); Philadelphia—Utley 2 (2), Burrell (1). **E:** Los Angeles—Furcal (1).

Attendance: 45,839 (43,647). **Time:** 2:36.

Game 2
Friday, Oct. 10, at Citizens Bank Park

	1 2 3	4 5 6	7 8 9	R H E
Los Angeles	0 1 1	3 0 0	0 0 0	- 5 8 1
Philadelphia	0 4 4	0 0 0	0 0 x	- 8 11 1

Win: Myers, Phi. (1-0). **Loss:** Billingsley, LA (0-1). **Save:** Lidge, Phi. (2).

2B: Los Angeles—Loney (1); Philadelphia—Ruiz (1), Werth (1). **3B:** Philadelphia—Victorino (1). **HR:** Los Angeles—Ramirez (1, off Myers, 2 on). **RBI:** Los Angeles—DeWitt (2), Loney (1), Ramirez 3 (4); Philadelphia—Ruiz (1), Myers 3 (3), Victorino 4 (4). **E:** Los Angeles—Kemp (1); Philadelphia—Dobbs (1).

Attendance: 45,883 (43,647). **Time:** 3:33.

Game 3
Sunday, Oct. 12, at Dodger Stadium

	1 2 3	4 5 6	7 8 9	R H E
Philadelphia	0 1 0	0 0 0	1 0 0	- 2 7 0
Los Angeles	5 1 0	1 0 0	0 0 x	- 7 10 0

Win: Kuroda, LA (1-0). **Loss:** Moyer, Phi. (0-1).

2B: Philadelphia—Howard (1), Utley (1). **3B:** Los Angeles—DeWitt (1). **HR:** Los Angeles—Furcal (1, off Moyer, 0 on). **RBI:** Philadelphia—Feliz (1), Burrell (2); Los Angeles—Ramirez (5), Blake (1), DeWitt 3 (5), Furcal (1), Garciaparra (1). **SB:** Los Angeles—Martin (1). **CS:** Philadelphia—Utley (1); Los Angeles—Kemp (1). **Picked off:** Los Angeles—Kemp (1).

Attendance: 56,800 (56,000). **Time:** 2:57.

National League Championship Series (Cont.)

Game 4
Monday, Oct. 13, at Dodger Stadium

	1 2 3	4 5 6	7 8 9	R	H	E
Philadelphia	. 2 0 0	0 0 1	0 4 0	- 7	12	1
Los Angeles	. .1 0 0	0 2 2	0 0 0	- 5	11	0

Win: Madson, Phi. (1-0). **Loss:** Wade, LA (0-1). **Save:** Lidge, Phi. (3).

2B: Philadelphia—Utley (2), Dobbs (1); Los Angeles—Loney (2), Pierre (1), Ramirez (2). **HR:** Philadelphia—Victorino (1, off Wade, 1 on), Stairs (1, off Broxton, 1 on); Los Angeles—Blake (1, off Durbin, 0 on). **RBI:** Philadelphia—Utley (3), Howard (1), Victorino 2 (6), Stairs 2 (2); Los Angeles—Loney (2), Ramirez (6), Martin (1), Blake (2). **SB:** Philadelphia—Rollins (1). **CS:** Philadelphia—Bruntlett (1); Los Angeles—Pierre (1). **E:** Philadelphia—Howard (1).

Attendance: 56,800 (56,000). **Time:** 3:44.

Game 5
Wednesday, Oct. 15, at Dodger Stadium

	1 2 3	4 5 6	7 8 9	R	H	E
Philadelphia	. 1 0 2	0 2 0	0 0 0	- 5	8	0
Los Angeles	. .0 0 0	0 0 1	0 0 0	- 1	7	3

Win: Hamels, Phi. (2-0). **Loss:** Billingsley, LA (0-2).

HR: Philadelphia—Rollins (1, off Billingsley, 0 on); Los Angeles—Ramirez (2, off Hamels, 0 on). **RBI:** Philadelphia—Rollins (1), Howard (2), Burrell (3); Los Angeles—Ramirez (7). **SB:** Philadelphia—Rollins (2). **E:** Los Angeles—Furcal 3 (4).

Attendance: 56,800 (56,000). **Time:** 3:14.

NLCS Most Valuable Player
Cole Hamels, Philadelphia, P

ERA	W-L	IP	H	ER	BB	K
1.93	2-0	14.0	11	3	5	13

NLCS Composite Box Score
Philadelphia Phillies

Batting	Avg	AB	R	H	HR	RBI	BB	SO	Avg	AB	R	H	HR	RBI	BB	SO
			LCS vs. Los Angeles								Overall NL Playoffs					
Matt Stairs	1.000	1	1	1	1	2	0	0	.333	3	1	1	1	2	0	0
Brett Myers	1.000	3	2	3	0	3	0	0	.800	5	3	4	0	3	1	0
Chris Coste	1.000	1	0	1	0	0	0	0	1.000	3	0	1	0	0	0	0
Greg Dobbs	.500	6	2	3	0	0	1	1	.545	11	2	6	0	1	1	2
Chase Utley	.353	17	4	6	1	3	6	5	.250	32	5	8	1	5	8	9
Pat Burrell	.333	18	1	6	1	3	0	7	.300	30	3	9	3	7	3	8
Carlos Ruiz	.313	16	3	5	0	1	1	0	.200	30	4	6	0	1	2	1
Ryan Howard	.300	20	4	6	0	2	3	2	.258	31	5	8	0	3	8	7
Shane Victorino	.222	18	4	4	1	6	2	1	.281	32	4	9	2	11	5	1
Cole Hamels	.200	5	0	1	0	0	0	2	.143	7	1	1	0	0	0	4
Jayson Werth	.190	21	2	4	0	0	1	7	.243	37	5	9	1	1	1	13
Pedro Feliz	.154	13	0	2	0	1	1	2	.192	26	1	5	0	2	1	3
Jimmy Rollins	.143	21	4	3	1	1	2	8	.243	37	6	9	2	2	3	10
Geoff Jenkins	.000	1	0	0	0	0	0	0	.000	1	0	0	0	0	0	0
So Taguchi	.000	4	0	0	0	0	0	0	.000	4	0	0	0	0	0	0
Eric Bruntlett	.000	2	0	0	0	1	0	0	.333	3	0	1	0	0	1	0
Joe Blanton	.000	2	0	0	0	0	0	2	.000	5	0	0	0	0	0	5
Jamie Moyer	—	0	0	0	0	0	0	0	.000	1	0	0	0	0	0	0
TOTALS	.266	169	25	45	5	22	19	37	.259	297	40	77	10	37	34	63

Pitching	ERA	W-L	Sv	Gm	IP	H	BB	SO	ERA	W-L	Sv	Gm	IP	H	BB	SO
Scott Eyre	0.00	0-0	0	2	1.1	0	1	0	3.86	0-0	0	3	2.1	3	1	1
J.C. Romero	0.00	0-0	0	3	2.1	0	3	3	0.00	0-0	0	4	2.2	0	3	3
Brad Lidge	0.00	0-0	3	4	4.1	2	2	6	1.23	0-0	5	7	7.1	5	3	10
Clay Condrey	0.00	0-0	0	1	0.2	0	1	0	5.40	0-0	0	2	1.2	1	3	1
Ryan Madson	0.00	1-0	0	4	5.0	4	1	4	1.00	1-0	0	7	9.0	7	1	6
Cole Hamels	1.93	2-0	0	2	14.0	11	5	13	1.23	3-0	0	3	22.0	13	6	22
J.A. Happ	3.00	0-0	0	1	3.0	4	2	2	3.00	0-0	0	1	3.0	4	2	2
Chad Durbin	4.50	0-0	0	3	2.0	2	3	2	3.38	0-0	0	4	2.2	2	3	3
Joe Blanton	5.40	0-0	0	1	5.0	7	4	4	3.27	1-0	0	2	11.0	12	4	11
Brett Myers	9.00	1-0	0	1	5.0	6	4	6	5.25	2-0	0	2	12.0	8	7	10
Jamie Moyer	40.50	0-1	0	1	1.1	6	0	2	13.50	0-2	0	2	5.1	10	3	5
TOTALS	3.89	4-1	3		44.0	43	25	42	3.19	7-2	5		79.0	69	35	74

Los Angeles Dodgers

Batting	LCS vs. Philadelphia								Overall NL Playoffs							
	Avg	AB	R	H	HR	RBI	BB	SO	Avg	AB	R	H	HR	RBI	BB	SO
Juan Pierre	.667	3	1	2	0	0	0	0	.500	4	2	2	0	0	0	0
Manny Ramirez	.533	15	4	8	2	7	7	1	.520	25	9	13	4	10	11	4
James Loney	.438	16	0	7	0	2	3	5	.333	30	2	10	1	8	3	7
Nomar Garciaparra	.429	7	0	3	0	1	1	2	.429	7	0	3	0	1	1	2
Matt Kemp	.333	15	1	5	0	0	4	4	.250	28	1	7	0	1	4	9
Casey Blake	.263	19	2	5	1	2	2	4	.267	30	4	8	1	4	2	5
Derek Lowe	.250	4	0	1	0	0	0	2	.200	5	0	1	0	0	2	2
Andre Ethier	.227	22	4	5	0	0	1	6	.188	32	6	6	0	0	5	10
Rafael Furcal	.211	19	5	4	1	1	3	2	.258	31	9	8	1	3	6	4
Russell Martin	.118	17	3	2	0	1	3	7	.200	30	5	6	1	6	4	10
Blake DeWitt	.077	13	0	1	0	5	1	4	.167	24	2	4	0	6	1	6
Jeff Kent	.000	8	0	0	0	0	0	0	.000	9	0	0	0	0	0	0
Pablo Ozuna	.000	1	0	0	0	0	0	0	.000	1	0	0	0	0	0	0
Angel Berroa	.000	1	0	0	0	0	0	0	.500	2	0	1	0	0	0	1
Chad Billingsley	.000	1	0	0	0	0	0	0	.000	4	0	0	0	0	0	1
Hiroki Kuroda	.000	3	0	0	0	0	0	1	.000	6	0	0	0	0	0	3
James McDonald	.000	1	0	0	0	0	0	0	.000	1	0	0	0	0	0	0
TOTALS	.261	165	20	43	4	19	25	42	.257	269	40	69	8	39	39	67

Pitching	ERA	W-L	Sv	Gm	IP	H	BB	SO	ERA	W-L	Sv	Gm	IP	H	BB	SO
Greg Maddux	0.00	0-0	0	2	3.0	3	1	3	0.00	0-0	0	4	4.0	4	1	3
Chan Ho Park	0.00	0-0	0	4	1.2	1	1	1	0.00	0-0	0	4	1.2	1	1	1
Joe Beimel	0.00	0-0	0	3	0.2	0	2	0	0.00	0-0	0	3	0.2	0	2	0
James McDonald	0.00	0-0	0	2	5.1	3	2	7	0.00	0-0	0	2	5.1	3	2	7
Hong-Chih Kuo	3.00	0-0	0	3	3.0	3	0	3	3.00	0-0	0	3	3.0	2	0	3
Hiroki Kuroda	3.00	1-0	0	1	6.0	5	1	3	1.46	2-0	0	2	12.1	11	3	7
Derek Lowe	3.48	0-1	0	2	10.1	12	2	6	3.31	1-1	0	3	16.1	19	3	12
Jonathan Broxton	3.86	0-0	0	2	2.1	3	1	2	1.59	0-0	0	5	5.2	3	2	7
Clayton Kershaw	4.50	0-0	0	2	2.0	1	2	1	4.50	0-0	0	2	2.0	1	2	1
Cory Wade	4.91	0-1	0	4	3.2	3	0	2	3.68	0-1	0	7	7.1	6	0	4
Chad Billingsley	18.00	0-2	0	2	5.0	12	7	9	8.49	1-2	0	3	11.2	17	8	16
Takashi Saito	—	0-0	0	0	0.0	0	0	0	—	0-0	0	1	0.0	3	0	0
TOTALS	4.40	1-4	0	5	43.0	45	19	37	3.47	4-4	1	8	70.0	70	25	61

Score by Innings

	1	2	3	4	5	6	7	8	9		R	H	E
Los Angeles	7	2	1	5	2	3	0	0	0	–	20	43	5
Philadelphia	3	5	6	0	2	4	1	4	0	–	25	45	2

WORLD SERIES

 vs.

Phillies, 4-1

Date	Winner	Home Field
Oct. 22	Phillies, 3-2	at Tampa Bay
Oct. 23	Rays, 4-2	at Tampa Bay
Oct. 25	Phillies, 5-4	at Philadelphia
Oct. 26	Phillies, 10-2	at Philadelphia
Oct. 27*	Phillies, 4-3	at Philadelphia

* Game ended on Oct. 29.

World Series (Cont.)

Game 1
Wednesday, Oct. 22, at Tropicana Field

Philadelphia	AB	R	H	RBI	Tampa Bay	AB	R	H	RBI
Rollins, ss	5	0	0	0	Iwamura, 2b	4	0	3	1
Werth, rf	4	1	2	0	Upton, cf	4	0	0	0
Utley, 2b	4	1	2	2	Pena, 1b	4	0	0	0
Howard, 1b	4	0	0	0	Longoria, 3b	4	0	0	0
Burrell, lf	3	0	0	0	Crawford, lf	4	1	1	1
Bruntlett, pr-lf	1	0	0	0	Aybar, dh	3	0	0	0
Victorino, cf	4	1	2	0	Navarro, c	3	0	0	0
Feliz, 3b	3	0	2	0	Zobrist, rf	3	0	1	0
Coste, dh	4	0	0	0	Bartlett, ss	1	1	0	0
Ruiz, c	3	0	0	1					
Totals	35	3	8	3	**Totals**	30	2	5	2

	R	H	E
Philadelphia . . . 200 100 000 —	3	8	1
Tampa Bay . . . . 000 110 000 —	2	5	1

E: Philadelphia—Howard (1); Tampa Bay—Pena (1). **2B:** Philadelphia—Werth 2 (2); Tampa Bay—Iwamura (1). **HR:** Philadelphia—Utley (1, off Kazmir, 1 on); Tampa Bay—Crawford (1, off Hamels, 0 on). **SB:** Philadelphia—Utley 2 (2), Werth (1); Tampa Bay—Bartlett (1). **CS:** Tampa Bay—Pena. **Pick:** Tampa Bay—Pena. **BB:** Philadelphia—Werth, Utley, Howard, Burrell, Feliz, Ruiz; Tampa Bay—Bartlett 2.

Philadelphia	IP	H	R	ER	BB	SO	P	ERA
Hamels (W, 1-0)	7	5	2	2	2	5	102	2.57
Madson	1	0	0	0	0	1	18	0.00
Lidge (S, 1)	1	0	0	0	0	2	15	0.00

Tampa Bay	IP	H	R	ER	BB	SO	P	ERA
Kazmir (L, 0-1)	6	6	3	3	4	4	110	4.50
Howell	⅔	1	0	0	1	2	19	0.00
Balfour	1⅔	1	0	0	1	2	27	0.00
Miller	⅓	0	0	0	0	1	4	0.00
Wheeler	⅓	0	0	0	0	0	5	0.00

IBB: by Balfour (Utley). **WP:** Howell.
Attendance: 40,783 (36,048). **Time:** 3:23.

Game 2
Thursday, Oct. 23, at Tropicana Field

Philadelphia	AB	R	H	RBI	Tampa Bay	AB	R	H	RBI
Rollins, ss	5	0	0	0	Iwamura, 2b	3	1	0	0
Werth, rf	5	0	1	0	Upton, cf	4	1	2	1
Utley, 2b	4	0	0	0	Pena, 1b	3	0	0	1
Howard, 1b	5	0	2	0	Longoria, 3b	4	0	1	1
Burrell, lf	3	0	0	0	Crawford, lf	4	0	0	0
Victorino, cf	4	0	2	0	Floyd, lf	3	1	1	0
Dobbs, dh	3	0	1	0	Navarro, c	3	1	2	0
Bruntlett, ph-dh	1	1	1	1	Baldelli, rf	2	0	0	0
Feliz, 3b	4	0	0	0	Bartlett, ss	2	0	2	1
Ruiz, c	2	1	2	0					
Totals	36	2	9	1	**Totals**	28	4	7	4

	R	H	E
Philadelphia . . . 000 000 011 —	2	9	2
Tampa Bay . . . . 210 100 00x —	4	7	1

E: Philadelphia—Werth (1), Ruiz (1); Tampa Bay—Longoria (1). **2B:** Philadelphia—Howard (1), Ruiz 2 (2). **HR:** Philadelphia—Bruntlett (1, off Price, 0 on). **SB:** Philadelphia—Ruiz (1); **S:** Tampa Bay—Bartlett. **BB:** Philadelphia—Utley, Burrell, Ruiz 2; Tampa Bay—Iwamura, Pena, Baldelli.

Philadelphia	IP	H	R	ER	BB	SO	P	ERA
Myers (W, 0-1)	7	7	4	3	3	2	85	3.86
Romero	1	0	0	0	0	1	9	0.00

Tampa Bay	IP	H	R	ER	BB	SO	P	ERA
Shields (W, 1-0)	5⅔	7	0	0	2	4	104	0.00
Wheeler	1	0	0	0	1	2	26	0.00
Price	2⅓	2	2	1	1	2	42	3.86

WP: Shields.
Attendance: 40,843 (36,048). **Time:** 3:05.

Game 3
Saturday, Oct. 25, at Citizens Bank Park

Tampa Bay	AB	R	H	RBI	Philadelphia	AB	R	H	RBI
Iwamura, 2b	4	0	0	0	Rollins, ss	4	1	2	0
Upton, cf	4	1	2	0	Werth, rf	2	0	1	0
Pena, 1b	3	0	0	0	Utley, 2b	4	1	1	2
Longoria, 3b	4	0	0	0	Howard, 1b	4	1	1	1
Crawford, lf	4	2	2	0	Burrell, lf	3	0	0	0
Navarro, c	4	1	2	0	Bruntlett, lf	0	1	0	0
Gross, rf	3	0	0	2	Victorino, cf	3	0	0	0
Bartlett, ss	4	0	0	1	Feliz, 3b	3	0	0	0
Garza, p	2	0	0	0	Dobbs, ph	0	0	0	0
Aybar, ph	0	0	0	0	Ruiz, c	3	1	2	2
					Moyer, p	2	0	0	0
					Jenkins, ph	1	0	0	0
Totals	32	4	6	3	**Totals**	29	5	7	5

	R	H	E
Tampa Bay . . . . 010 000 210 —	4	6	1
Philadelphia . . . 110 002 001 —	5	7	1

E: Tampa Bay—Navarro (1); Philadelphia—Ruiz (1). **2B:** Tampa Bay—Crawford (1), Navarro (1). **HR:** Philadelphia—Ruiz (1, off Garza, 0 on), Utley (2, off Garza, 0 on), Howard (1, off Garza, 0 on). **SB:** Tampa Bay—Crawford (1), Upton 3 (3); Philadelphia—Werth (2). **CS:** Philadelphia—Rollins (2). **Pick:** Philadelphia—Werth. **BB:** Tampa Bay—Pena, Aybar; Philadelphia—Werth 2, Victorino, Dobbs, Ruiz. **SF:** Tampa Bay—Gross.

Tampa Bay	IP	H	R	ER	BB	SO	P	ERA
Garza	6	6	4	4	2	7	102	6.00
Bradford	1	0	0	0	1	0	15	0.00
Howell (L, 0-1)	1	0	1	1	0	2	16	5.40
Balfour	0	1	0	0	2	0	15	0.00

Philadelphia	IP	H	R	ER	BB	SO	P	ERA
Moyer	6⅓	5	3	3	1	5	96	4.26
Durbin	⅓	0	0	0	1	0	6	0.00
Eyre	⅓	0	0	0	0	1	6	0.00
Madson	⅔	1	1	1	0	1	15	5.40
Romero (1-0)	1⅓	0	0	0	0	1	15	0.00

HBP: by Howell (Bruntlett). **IBB:** by Balfour (Victorino, Dobbs). **WP:** Garza, Balfour.
Attendance: 45,900 (43,647). **Time:** 3:41.

World Series MVP
Cole Hamels, Philadelphia, P

ERA	W-L	IP	H	ER	BB	K
2.77	1-0	13.0	10	4	3	8

Game 4
Sunday, Oct. 26, at Citizens Bank Park

Tampa Bay	AB	R	H	RBI	Philadelphia	AB	R	H	RBI
Iwamura, 2b	4	0	0	0	Rollins, ss	5	3	3	0
Upton, cf	4	0	0	0	Werth, rf	4	2	2	2
Pena, 1b	3	0	0	0	Utley, 2b	3	2	0	0
Longoria, 3b	4	0	0	0	Howard, 1b	4	2	3	5
Crawford, lf	3	1	1	1	Burrell, lf	3	0	0	1
Navarro, c	4	0	1	0	Bruntlett, lf	1	0	0	0
Zobrist, rf	3	0	0	0	Victorino, cf	5	0	0	0
Bartlett, ss	4	0	0	0	Feliz, 3b	4	0	2	1
Sonnanstine, p	1	0	1	0	Ruiz, c	4	0	1	0
Hinske, ph	1	1	1	1	Blanton, p	3	1	1	1
Aybar, ph	1	0	1	0	Stairs, ph	1	0	0	0
Baldelli, ph	1	0	0	0					
Totals	**33**	**2**	**5**	**2**	**Totals**	**37**	**10**	**12**	**10**

	R	H	E
Tampa Bay .... 000 110 000 —	2	5	2
Philadelphia ... 101 310 04x —	10	12	1

E: Tampa Bay—Iwamura 2 (2); Philadelphia—Romero (1). **2B:** Philadelphia—Rollins 2 (2), Werth (3). **HR:** Tampa Bay—Crawford (2, off Blanton, 0 on), Hinske (1, off Blanton, 0 on); Philadelphia—Howard 2 (3, off Sonnanstine, 2 on; off Miller, 1 on), Blanton (1, off Jackson, 0 on), Werth (1, off Wheeler, 1 on). **BB:** Tampa Bay—Pena, Zobrist; Philadelphia—Werth, Utley 2, Howard, Burrell.

Tampa Bay	IP	H	R	ER	BB	SO	P	ERA
Sonnanstine (L, 0-1)	4	6	5	3	3	2	89	6.75
Jackson	2	2	1	1	1	1	32	4.50
Wheeler	1⅓	3	2	2	0	1	22	6.75
Miller	⅔	1	2	2	1	0	10	18.00
Philadelphia	**IP**	**H**	**R**	**ER**	**BB**	**SO**	**P**	**ERA**
Blanton (W, 1-0)	6	4	2	2	2	7	99	3.00
Durbin	⅓	1	0	0	0	0	5	0.00
Eyre	⅓	0	0	0	0	0	5	0.00
Madson	1⅓	0	0	0	0	3	16	3.00
Romero	1	0	0	0	0	2	19	0.00

HBP: by Blanton (Crawford). **IBB:** by Jackson (Howard).
Attendance: 45,903 (43,647). **Time:** 3:08.

Game 5
Monday, Oct. 27*, at Citizens Bank Park

Tampa Bay	AB	R	H	RBI	Philadelphia	AB	R	H	RBI
Iwamura, 2b	4	0	2	0	Rollins, ss	3	0	0	0
Crawford, lf	4	0	1	0	Werth, rf	3	1	2	1
Upton, cf	4	1	1	0	Utley, 2b	3	1	0	0
Pena, 1b	4	1	2	1	Howard, 1b	4	0	0	0
Longoria, 3b	4	0	1	1	Burrell, lf	2	0	1	0
Navarro, c	3	0	0	0	Bruntlett, pr-lf	0	1	0	0
Perez, pr	0	0	0	0	Victorino, cf	4	0	1	2
Baldelli, rf	3	1	1	1	Feliz, 3b	4	0	2	1
Zobrist, ph	1	0	0	0	Ruiz, c	4	0	1	0
Bartlett, ss	3	0	1	0	Hamels, p	2	0	0	0
Hinske, ph	1	0	0	0	Jenkins, ph	1	1	1	0
Kazmir, p	2	0	0	0	Romero, p	1	0	0	0
Howell, p	0	0	0	0					
Totals	**33**	**3**	**10**	**3**	**Totals**	**31**	**4**	**8**	**4**

	R	H	E
Tampa Bay .... 000 101 100 —	3	10	0
Philadelphia ... 200 001 10x —	4	8	1

E: Philadelphia—Rollins (1). **2B:** Tampa Bay—Pena (1); Philadelphia—Jenkins (1), Burrell (1). **HR:** Tampa Bay—Baldelli (1, off Madson, 0 on). **SB:** Tampa Bay—Upton (4), Perez (1); Philadelphia—Werth (3), Utley (3). **S:** Tampa Bay—Howell; Philadelphia—Rollins. **BB:** Tampa Bay—Navarro; Philadelphia—Rollins, Werth 2, Utley, Howard, Burrell 2.

Tampa Bay	IP	H	R	ER	BB	SO	P	ERA
Kazmir	4	4	2	2	6	5	103	4.50
Balfour	1⅓	2	1	1	0	0	21	3.00
Howell (L, 0-2)	⅔	1	1	1	0	1	7	7.71
Bradford	1	1	0	0	0	0	10	0.00
Price	1	0	0	0	1	2	20	2.70
Philadelphia	**IP**	**H**	**R**	**ER**	**BB**	**SO**	**P**	**ERA**
Hamels	6	5	2	2	1	3	75	2.77
Madson	⅔	2	1	1	0	1	9	4.91
Romero (W, 1-0)	1⅓	2	0	0	0	0	14	0.00
Lidge (S, 2)	1	1	0	0	0	1	16	0.00

HBP: by Kazmir (Utley).
Attendance: 45,940 (43,647). **Time:** 3:28.

* Suspended due to rain in the middle of the sixth inning. The game was completed on Wednesday, October 29.

World Series Composite Box Score

Tampa Bay Rays

Batting	WS vs. Philadelphia								Overall Playoffs							
	Avg	AB	R	H	HR	RBI	BB	SO	Avg	AB	R	H	HR	RBI	BB	SO
Andy Sonnanstine	1.000	1	0	1	0	0	0	0	1.000	1	0	1	0	0	0	0
Eric Hinske	.500	2	1	1	1	1	0	1	.500	2	1	1	1	1	0	1
Dioner Navarro	.353	17	2	6	0	0	1	5	.293	58	4	17	0	5	4	11
Cliff Floyd	.333	3	1	1	0	0	0	0	.222	18	3	4	1	2	0	7
Carl Crawford	.263	19	4	5	2	2	0	1	.290	62	9	18	2	8	3	10
Akinori Iwamura	.263	19	1	5	0	1	1	3	.273	66	8	18	1	5	7	12
B.J. Upton	.250	20	3	5	0	1	0	4	.288	66	16	19	7	16	5	16
Willy Aybar	.250	4	0	1	0	0	1	1	.353	34	5	12	2	7	1	6
Jason Bartlett	.214	14	1	3	0	2	2	2	.235	51	8	12	1	3	4	10
Rocco Baldelli	.167	6	1	1	1	1	1	2	.200	20	4	4	2	6	3	5
Ben Zobrist	.143	7	0	1	0	0	2	1	.091	11	0	1	0	0	2	0
Carlos Pena	.118	17	1	2	0	2	3	6	.264	53	9	14	3	10	10	17
Evan Longoria	.050	20	1	1	0	0	0	9	.194	62	10	12	6	13	5	20
Gabe Gross	.000	2	0	0	0	2	0	0	.053	19	0	1	0	2	3	7
Scott Kazmir	.000	2	0	0	0	0	0	2	.000	2	0	0	0	0	0	2
Matt Garza	.000	2	0	0	0	0	0	2	.000	2	0	0	0	0	0	2
Fernando Perez	.000	0	0	0	0	0	0	0	.111	9	2	1	0	0	0	2
TOTALS	.212	156	15	33	4	14	10	36	.252	536	79	135	26	78	47	126

World Series Composite Box (Cont.)
Tampa Bay Rays (Cont.)

Pitching	WS vs. Philadelphia							Overall Playoffs						
	ERA	W-L	Sv	Gm	IP	H	BB	SO	ERA	W-L	Sv	Gm	IP	H	BB	SO
Chad Bradford	0.00	0-0	0	2	2.0	1	1	0	1.13	0-0	0	7	8.0	6	3	3
James Shields	0.00	1-0	0	1	5.2	7	2	4	2.88	2-2	0	4	25.0	28	8	17
David Price	2.70	0-0	0	2	3.1	2	2	4	1.59	1-0	1	5	5.2	2	4	8
Grant Balfour	3.00	0-0	0	3	3.0	4	3	2	6.23	0-0	0	10	8.2	11	8	7
Edwin Jackson	4.50	0-0	0	1	2.0	2	1	1	2.08	0-0	0	3	4.1	2	3	5
Scott Kazmir	4.50	0-1	0	2	10.0	10	10	9	4.21	1-1	0	5	25.2	26	18	22
Matt Garza	6.00	0-0	0	1	6.0	6	2	7	3.96	2-1	0	4	25.0	21	12	25
Dan Wheeler	6.75	0-0	0	3	2.2	3	1	3	6.23	0-0	1	7	8.2	9	4	9
Andy Sonnanstine	6.75	0-1	0	1	4.0	6	3	2	4.24	2-1	0	3	17.0	15	5	8
J.P. Howell	7.71	0-2	0	3	2.1	2	1	5	3.00	0-3	0	12	12.0	9	4	17
Trever Miller	18.00	0-0	0	2	1.0	1	1	1	10.80	0-0	0	6	1.2	2	3	2
TOTALS	4.50	1-4	0	5	42.0	44	27	38	3.81	8-8	2	16	141.2	131	72	123

Philadelphia Phillies

Batting	WS vs. Tampa Bay								Overall Playoffs							
	Avg	AB	R	H	HR	RBI	BB	SO	Avg	AB	R	H	HR	RBI	BB	SO
Geoff Jenkins	.500	2	1	1	0	0	0	0	.250	4	1	1	0	0	0	0
Jayson Werth	.444	18	4	8	1	3	6	4	.309	55	9	17	2	4	7	17
Carlos Ruiz	.375	16	2	6	1	3	4	0	.261	46	6	12	1	4	6	4
Pedro Feliz	.333	18	0	6	0	2	1	3	.250	44	1	11	0	4	2	6
Eric Bruntlett	.333	3	3	1	1	1	0	0	.333	6	3	2	1	1	1	0
Greg Dobbs	.333	3	0	1	0	0	1	2	.500	14	2	7	0	0	2	4
Joe Blanton	.333	3	1	1	1	1	0	1	.125	8	1	1	1	1	0	6
Ryan Howard	.286	21	3	6	3	6	3	9	.269	52	8	14	3	9	11	16
Shane Victorino	.250	20	1	5	0	2	1	3	.269	52	5	14	2	13	6	4
Jimmy Rollins	.227	22	4	5	0	1	3	3	.237	59	10	14	2	2	4	13
Chase Utley	.167	18	5	3	2	4	5	5	.220	50	10	11	3	9	13	14
Pat Burrell	.071	14	0	1	0	1	5	5	.227	44	3	10	3	8	8	13
Jamie Moyer	.000	2	0	0	0	0	0	1	.000	3	0	0	0	0	0	1
Matt Stairs	.000	1	0	0	0	0	0	0	.250	4	1	1	1	2	0	1
Scott Eyre	.000	0	0	0	0	0	0	0	.000	0	0	0	0	0	0	0
J.C. Romero	.000	1	0	0	0	0	0	0	.000	1	0	0	0	0	0	0
Chad Durbin	.000	0	0	0	0	0	0	0	.000	0	0	0	0	0	0	0
Brad Lidge	.000	0	0	0	0	0	0	0	.000	0	0	0	0	0	0	0
Ryan Madson	.000	0	0	0	0	0	0	0	.000	0	0	0	0	0	0	0
Cole Hamels	.000	2	0	0	0	0	0	0	.111	9	1	1	0	0	0	5
Chris Coste	.000	4	0	0	0	0	0	1	.200	5	0	1	0	0	0	1
Brett Myers	—	0	0	0	0	0	0	0	.800	5	3	4	0	3	1	0
Jamie Moyer	—	0	0	0	0	0	0	0	.000	3	0	0	0	0	0	0
So Taguchi	—	0	0	0	0	0	0	0	.000	4	0	0	0	0	0	0
TOTALS	.262	168	24	44	9	23	27	38	.260	465	64	121	19	60	61	101

Pitching	ERA	W-L	Sv	Gm	IP	H	BB	SO	ERA	W-L	Sv	Gm	IP	H	BB	SO
Scott Eyre	0.00	0-0	0	2	0.2	0	0	1	3.00	0-0	0	5	3.0	3	1	2
J.C. Romero	0.00	2-0	0	4	4.2	2	0	4	0.00	2-0	0	8	7.1	2	3	7
Chad Durbin	0.00	0-0	0	2	1.0	1	1	0	2.70	0-0	0	6	3.1	7	3	3
Brad Lidge	0.00	0-0	2	2	2.0	1	0	3	0.96	0-0	7	9	9.1	6	3	13
Cole Hamels	2.77	1-0	0	2	13.0	10	3	8	1.80	4-0	0	5	35.0	23	9	30
Joe Blanton	3.00	1-0	0	1	6.0	4	2	5	3.18	2-0	0	3	17.0	16	6	18
Brett Myers	3.86	0-1	0	1	7.0	7	3	2	4.74	2-1	0	3	19.0	15	10	12
Jamie Moyer	4.26	0-0	0	1	6.1	5	1	5	8.49	0-2	0	3	11.2	15	4	10
Ryan Madson	4.91	0-0	0	4	3.2	3	1	6	2.13	1-0	0	11	12.2	10	1	12
J.A. Happ	—	0-0	0	0	0.0	0	0	0	3.00	0-0	0	1	3.0	4	2	2
Clay Condrey	—	0-0	0	0	0.0	0	0	0	5.40	0-0	0	2	1.2	1	3	1
TOTALS	2.86	4-1	2	5	44.0	33	10	36	3.07	11-3	7	14	123.0	102	45	110

Score by Innings

	1	2	3	4	5	6	7	8	9		R	H	E
Tampa Bay	2	2	0	4	2	1	3	1	0	—	15	33	5
Philadelphia	6	1	1	4	1	3	1	5	2	—	24	44	5

E: Tampa Bay—Iwamura 2, Longoria, Navarro, Pena; Philadelphia—Ruiz, Howard, Rollins, Romero, Werth. **2B:** Tampa Bay—Navarro, Crawford, Iwamura, Pena; Philadelphia—Werth 3, Ruiz 2, Rollins 2, Jenkins, Howard, Burrell. **HR:** Tampa Bay—Crawford 2, Hinske, Baldelli; Philadelphia—Howard 3, Utley 2, Werth, Ruiz, Bruntlett, Blanton. **SB:** Tampa Bay—Upton 4, Bartlett, Crawford, Perez; Philadelphia—Utley 3, Werth 3, Ruiz. **CS:** Tampa Bay—Pena; Philadelphia—Rollins. **Pick:** Philadelphia—Werth. **S:** Tampa Bay—Bartlett, Howell; Philadelphia—Rollins. **SF:** Tampa Bay—Gross. **HBP:** by Blanton (Crawford), by Howell (Bruntlett), by Kazmir (Utley). **PB:** Philadelphia—Ruiz. **DP:** Tampa Bay—4; Philadelphia—6. **LOB:** Tampa Bay—23; Philadelphia—48.

COLLEGE

Final *Baseball America* Top 25

Final 2008 Division I Top 25, voted on by the editors of *Baseball America* and released after the NCAA College World Series. Given are final records (excluding ties) and winning percentage (including all postseason games); records in College World Series and team eliminated by; head coach (career years and four-year college record including 2008 postseason); preseason ranking and rank before start of CWS.

		Record	Pct	CWS Recap	Head Coach	Preseason Rank	Rank before CWS
1	Fresno St.	47-31	.603	5-2	Mike Batesole (13 yrs: 475-323-1)	18	8
2	Georgia	45-25	.643	4-2 (Fresno St.)	David Perno (7 yrs: 251-184-1)	—	7
3	North Carolina	54-15	.783	3-2 (Fresno St.)	Mike Fox (25 yrs: 991-332-5)	5	3
4	Miami-FL	53-11	.828	1-2 (Stanford)	Jim Morris (27 yrs: 1199-500-4)	10	1
5	Stanford	41-24	.631	2-2 (Georgia)	Mark Marquess (32 yrs: 1326-669-5)	—	6
6	LSU	49-19	.721	1-2 (UNC)	Paul Mainieri (26 yrs: 942-537-6)	—	4
7	Florida St.	54-14	.794	0-2 (Miami-FL)	Mike Martin (29 yrs: 1538-520-4)	—	2
8	Rice	47-15	.758	0-2 (LSU)	Wayne Graham (17 yrs: 787-299)	14	5
9	Arizona St.	49-13	.790		Pat Murphy (24 yrs: 949-443-4)	9	9
10	CS-Fullerton	41-22	.651		Dave Serrano (4 yrs: 155-88-1)	—	10
11	UC Irvine	42-18	.700		Mike Gillespie (21 yrs: 805-489-2)	—	11
12	Texas A&M	46-19	.708		Rob Childress (3 yrs: 119-69-1)	21	12
13	Wichita St.	48-17	.738		Gene Stephenson (31 yrs: 1653-550-3)	20	13
14	Arizona	42-19	.689		Andy Lopez (2 yrs: 939-577-7)	2	14
15	N.C. State	42-22	.656		Elliott Avent (20 yrs: 682-493)	—	15
16	Coastal Carolina	50-14	.781		Gary Gilmore (18 yrs: 717-357)	—	16
17	Oklahoma St.	44-18	.710		Frank Anderson (5 yrs: 198-109)	—	17
18	San Diego	44-17	.721		Rich Hill (21 yrs: 682-463-3)	11	18
19	Missouri	39-21	.650		Tim Jamieson (14 yrs: 491-335-3)	6	19
20	Nebraska	41-16	.719		Mike Anderson (6 yrs: 255-116)	—	20
21	Texas	39-22	.639		Augie Garrido (40 yrs: 1668-777-8)	16	21
22	Michigan	46-14	.767		Rich Maloney (13 yrs: 493-270-1)	8	22
23	TCU	45-19	.703		Jim Schlossnagle (7 yrs: 289-149)	—	23
24	Kentucky	44-19	.698		John Cohen (9 yrs: 321-196)	—	24
25	Long Beach St.	38-21	.644		Mike Weathers (18 yrs: 542-433-2)	13	25

College World Series

CWS participants: Florida St. (54-12); Fresno St. (42-29); Georgia (41-23); LSU (48-17); Miami-FL (52-9); North Carolina (51-13); Rice (47-13); Stanford (39-22).

Bracket One

June 14—Stanford 16 . . . . Florida St. 5
June 14—Georgia 7 . . . . Miami-FL 4
June 16—Miami-FL 7 . . . . Florida St. 5 (out)
June 16—Georgia 4 . . . . Stanford 3
June 18—Stanford 8 . . . . Miami-FL 3 (out)
June 21—Georgia 10 . . . . Stanford 8 (out)

Bracket Two

June 15—Fresno St. 17 . . . . Rice 5
June 15—North Carolina 8 . . . . LSU 4
June 17—LSU 6 . . . . Rice 5 (out)
June 17—Fresno St. 5 . . . . North Carolina 3
June 20—North Carolina 7 . . . . LSU 3 (out)
June 21—North Carolina 4 . . . . Fresno St. 3
June 22—Fresno St. 6 . . . . North Carolina 1 (out)

See page 458 for more coverage.

Championship Series

June 23—Georgia 7 . . . . Fresno St. 6
June 24—Fresno St. 19 . . . . Georgia 10
June 25—Fresno St. 6 . . . . Georgia 1 (out)

Most Outstanding Player

Tommy Mendonca, Fresno St., 3B

AB	R	H	HR	RBI	BB	AVG
13	2	3	2	4	1	.231

All-Tournament Team

C—Jason Castro, Stanford; **1B**—Dustin Ackley, North Carolina; **2B**—Erik Wetzel, Fresno St.; **3B**—Tommy Mendonca, Fresno St.; **SS**—Gordon Beckham, Georgia; **OF**—Tim Fedroff, North Carolina; Steve Susdorf, Fresno St. and Steve Detwiler, Fresno St.; **DH**—Ryan Peisel, Georgia; **P**—Alex White, North Carolina and Justin Wilson, Fresno St.

Annual Awards

Chosen by *Baseball America, Collegiate Baseball,* National Collegiate Baseball Writers Association, American Baseball Coaches Association and USA Baseball.

Player of the Year

Buster Posey, Florida St., C . . . . *BA,* ABCA, *CB*
Dick Howser (NCBWA)
& Golden Spikes
(USA Baseball)

Coaches of the Year

Mike Fox, North Carolina . . . . *BA*
Mike Batesole, Fresno St. . . . . .ABCA

Baseball America All-America Team

NCAA Division I All-Americans. Holdover from 2007 First Team in **bold**.

First Team

Pos		Cl	Avg	HR	RBI
C	Buster Posey, Florida St.	Jr.	.463	26	93
1B	Justin Smoak, South Carolina	Jr.	.383	23	72
2B	Josh Satin, California	Sr.	.379	18	52
3B	**Brett Wallace**, Arizona St.	Jr.	.410	22	83
SS	Gordon Beckham, Georgia	Jr.	.411	28	77
OF	Sawyer Carroll, Kentucky	Sr.	.419	18	83
OF	Blake Dean, LSU	So.	.353	20	73
OF	Chris Shehan, Ga. Southern	Jr.	.438	22	77
DH	Yonder Alonso, Miami-FL	Jr.	.370	24	72
UT	Ike Davis, Arizona St.	Jr.	.385	16	76

Pos		Cl	W-L	Sv	ERA
SP	Aaron Crow, Missouri	Jr.	13-0	0	2.35
SP	Brian Matusz, San Diego	Jr.	12-2	0	1.71
SP	Rob Musgrave, Wichita St.	Sr.	12-1	0	2.51
SP	Stephen Strasburg, SD St.	So.	8-3	0	1.57
RP	Scott Bittle, Mississippi	Jr.	7-1	8	1.78

Second Team

Pos		Cl	Avg	HR	RBI
C	Corey Kemp, East Carolina	Sr.	.341	18	72
1B	David Cooper, California	Jr.	.359	19	55
2B	Jemile Weeks, Miami-FL	Jr.	.363	13	62
3B	Conor Gillaspie, Wichita St.	Jr.	.419	11	82
SS	Reese Havens, South Carolina	Jr.	.359	18	57
OF	Tim Fedroff, North Carolina	So.	.404	12	71
OF	Blake Tekotte, Miami-FL	Jr.	.353	13	50
OF	Eric Thames, Pepperdine	Jr.	.407	13	59
DH	Nate Recknagel, Michigan	Sr.	.368	23	68
UT	Zach Putnam, Michigan	Jr.	.307	11	51

Pos		Cl	W-L	Sv	ERA
SP	Christian Friedrich, E. Kentucky	Jr.	5-1	0	1.43
SP	Scott Gorgen, UC Irvine	Jr.	11-3	0	2.26
SP	Chris Hernandez, Miami-FL	Fr.	11-0	0	2.72
SP	Mike Leake, Arizona St.	So.	11-3	1	3.49
RP	Andrew Cashner, TCU	Jr.	9-4	9	2.32

NCAA Division I Leaders

Batting

Average

(Min. 120 plate app. & 3.0/Gm)	Cl	Gm	AB	H	Avg
Buster Posey, Florida St.	Jr.	68	257	119	.463
Josh Phegley, Indiana	So.	61	224	98	.438
Chris Shehan, Ga. Southern	Jr.	58	224	98	.438
Jabari Graham, Alcorn St.	Jr.	42	151	66	.437
Tyron Childress, Alabama A&M	Sr.	39	125	54	.432
Clay Whittemore, Jacksonville St.	Sr.	57	226	96	.425
Spencer Lucian, Princeton	Sr.	42	146	62	.425
Tyler Kuhn, West Virginia	Sr.	56	238	101	.424
Ryan Keedy, UAB	Sr.	60	234	99	.423
Mike Sheridan, Wm. & Mary	Jr.	56	227	96	.423

Home Runs (per game)

(At least 15 HR)	Cl	Gm	HR	Avg
Michael Harrington, Col of Charleston	Sr.	58	26	0.45
Matt Clark, LSU	Jr.	65	28	0.43
Jeremie Tice, Col of Charleston	Jr.	59	25	0.42
Nate Recknagel, Michigan	Sr.	58	23	0.40
Gordon Beckham, Georgia	Jr.	71	28	0.39
Frank Pesanello, Northeastern	Jr.	51	20	0.39
Joseph Scaperotta, New Mexico St.	Sr.	59	23	0.39
Buster Posey, Florida St.	Jr.	68	26	0.39
Scott Krieger, George Mason	Jr.	55	21	0.38
Anthony Russell, East Tenn. St.	Jr.	55	21	0.38

Runs Batted In (per game)

(At least 50 RBI)	Cl	Gm	RBI	Avg
Ike Davis, Arizona St.	Jr.	52	76	1.46
Michael Harrington, Col of Charleston	Sr.	58	82	1.41
Jeremie Tice, Col of Charleston	Jr.	59	83	1.41
Joseph Scaperotta, New Mexico St.	Sr.	59	82	1.39
Brandon Sizemore, Col of Charleston	Jr.	59	82	1.39
Trent Lockwood, UTSA	So.	57	79	1.39
Mike Spina, Cincinnati	Jr.	57	79	1.39
Buster Posey, Florida St.	Jr.	68	93	1.37
Chad Cregar, Western Ky.	Jr.	60	82	1.37
Conor Gillaspie, Wichita St.	Jr.	60	82	1.37

Stolen Bases (per game)

(At least 24)	Cl	Gm	SB	CS	Avg
Roly Gonzalez, Texas Pan Am.	Sr.	56	46	9	0.82
Caleb Curry, Iowa	Sr.	55	45	7	0.82
Adam Yeager, Marshall	Jr.	61	47	9	0.77
Kyle Hudson, Illinois	Jr.	53	40	9	0.75
Tony Campana, Cincinnati	Sr.	59	44	11	0.75
Jimmy Miles, Old Dominion	Sr.	52	38	7	0.73
Rich Goulian, Fordham	Sr.	53	36	10	0.68
Ollie Linton, UC Irvine	Jr.	60	40	8	0.67
Scott Woodward, Coastal Carol.	Fr.	64	42	9	0.66
James Hayes, Rider	Jr.	57	37	7	0.65

Pitching

Earned Run Avg.

(At least 50 inn.)	Cl	Gm	IP	ERA
Matt Packer, Virginia	So.	25	71.1	1.14
Christian Friedrich, Eastern Ky.	Jr.	12	81.2	1.43
Stephen Strasburg, SD St.	So.	13	97.1	1.57
Hiram Burgos, Bethune-Cookman	Jr.	16	80.0	1.58
Boone Whiting, Centenary	Fr.	20	61.0	1.62
Brian Matusz, San Diego	Jr.	15	105.0	1.71
Alan Deratt, UNC Ashville	Sr.	16	98.0	1.74
Scott Bittle, Mississippi, Jr.	Jr.	27	70.2	1.78
Thomas Davis, Fordham	Sr.	13	90.0	1.90
Christian Bergman, UC Irvine	So.	25	60.1	1.94

Wins

	Cl	Gm	IP	W-L
Aaron Crow, Missouri	Jr.	15	107.1	13-0
Carlos Luna, Oral Roberts	Sr.	31	99.1	13-1
Alex White, North Carolina	So.	20	101.2	13-3
Tommy Rafferty, Arizona St.	Sr.	35	74.0	12-0
Shane Davis, Canisius	Fr.	13	89.1	12-1
Rob Musgrave, Wichita St.	Sr.	16	111.1	12-1
Bryan Cryer, New Orleans	Jr.	16	103.1	12-2
Matt Fairel, Florida St.	So.	18	111.2	12-2
Tyler Lyons, Oklahoma St.	So.	15	108.2	12-2
Brian Matusz, San Diego	Jr.	15	105.0	12-2
Cory Arbiso, CS Fullerton	Jr.	16	103.0	12-3
Scott Gorgen, UC Irvine	Jr.	17	115.2	12-3

Strikeouts (per 9 inn.)

(At least 55 inn.)	Cl	IP	SO	Avg
Scott Bittle, Mississippi	Jr.	70.2	130	16.6
Evan Fredrickson, San Francisco	Jr.	75.1	109	13.0
Stephen Strasburg, SD St.	So.	97.1	133	12.3
Christopher Manno, Duke	So.	58.2	80	12.4
Brian Matusz, San Diego	Jr.	105.0	141	12.1
Kyle Blair, San Diego	Fr.	74.2	99	11.9
Christian Friedrich, Eastern Ky.	Jr.	81.2	108	11.9
Bryan Morgado, Tennessee	Jr.	80.1	104	11.7
Sheldon McDonald, Northeastern	So.	56.2	72	11.4
Anthony Shawler, Old Dominion	Jr.	75.2	95	11.3

Saves

	Cl	Gm	IP	Sv
Tyler Conn, Southern Miss	Sr.	27	36.2	18
Joshua Fields, Georgia	Sr.	36	37.1	18
Eric Pettis, UC Irvine	So.	31	44.2	17
Justin Fitzgerald, UC Davis	Jr.	24	33.1	15
Nick Gaudi, Pepperdine	Sr.	29	43.2	15
Michael Schwimer, Virginia	Sr.	26	31.1	14
A.J. Griffin, San Diego	So.	29	46.0	14
Six tied with 13.				

Other College World Series

Participants' final records in parentheses.

NCAA Div. II
at Sauget, Ill. (May 24-31)

Participants: Ashland, Ohio (40-18); Central Missouri (47-17); Franklin Pierce, N.H. (43-15); Mount Olive, N.C. (58-6); Ouachita Baptist, Ark. (51-16); Shippensburg, Pa. (39-26); Sonoma St., Calif. (52-15); Tampa (42-11-1).

Championship: Mount Olive def. Ouachita Baptist, 6-2.

NCAA Div. III
at Grand Chute, Wis. (May 23-27)

Participants: Adrian, Mich. (36-13): Chapman, Calif. (40-5); Johns Hopkins (42-8); Kean, NJ (39-11); Linfield, Ore. (35-13); SUNY-Cortland (42-5); Trinity, Conn. (45-1); Wisconsin-Whitewater (42-10).

Championship: Trinity def. Johns Hopkins, 5-4.

2008 MLB First-Year Player Draft

First round selections at the 44th First-Year Player Draft held June 5-6, 2008 at Disney's Wide World of Sports complex in Orlando, Fla. Clubs select in reverse order of their standing from the preceding season. The Tampa Bay Rays chose 18-year-old Georgia prep school shortstop Tim Beckham with the top overall pick.

First Round

No		Pos
1	Tampa Bay .... Tim Beckham, Griffin (Ga.) HS	SS
2	Pittsburgh .... Pedro Alvarez, Vanderbilt	3B
3	Kansas City ..... Eric Hosmer, Plantation (Fla.) American Heritage HS	1B
4	Baltimore .... Brian Matusz, San Diego	LHP
5	San Francisco .... Buster Posey, Florida St.	C
6	Florida .... Kyle Shipworth, Riverside (Calif) Patriot HS	C
7	Cincinnati .... Yonder Alonso, Miami-FL	1B
8	Chicago-AL ...... Gordon Beckham, Georgia	SS
9	Washington .... Aaron Crow, Missouri	RHP
10	Houston .... Jason Castro, Stanford	C
11	Texas.......... Justin Smoak, South Carolina	1B
12	Oakland .... Jemile Weeks, Miami-FL	2B
13	St. Louis .... Brett Wallace, Arizona St.	3B
14	Minnesota.......... Aaron Hicks, Long Beach (Calif) Wilson HS	OF
15	Los Angeles-NL .... Ethan Martin, Toccoa (Ga.) Stephens County HS	RHP

No		Pos
16	Milwaukee .. Brett Lawrie, Langley (Brit. Colum.) Brookswood Secondary School	3B
17	Toronto .... David Cooper, California	1B
18	a-New York-NL.......... Ike Davis, Arizona St.	1B
19	Chicago-NL.......... Andrew Cashner, TCU	RHP
20	Seattle .... Josh Fields, Georgia	RHP
21	Detroit .... Ryan Perry, Arizona	RHP
22	New York-NL ...... Reese Havens, South Carolina	SS
23	San Diego...... Allan Dykstra, South Carolina	1B
24	Philadelphia .... Anthony Hewitt, Salisbury (Conn.) HS	SS
25	Colorado.......... Christian Friedrich, Eastern Ky.	LHP
26	Arizona .... Daniel Schlereth, Arizona	LHP
27	b-Minnesota ...... Carlos Gutierrez, Miami-FL	RHP
28	New York-AL.... Gerrit Cole, Orange (Calif.) Lutheran HS	RHP
29	Cleveland .... Lonnie Chisenhall, Pitt (N.C.) Community College	3B
30	Boston .... Casey Kelly, Sarasota (Fla.) HS	SS

a-from Atl. for signing Tom Glavine; **b**-from LA-AL for signing Torii Hunter.

Straight to the Majors

Since Major League baseball began its First-Year Player Draft in 1965, 20 selections have advanced directly to the major leagues without first playing in the minors

Draft		Pos	Team
1967	Mike Adamson, USC	P	Baltimore
1969	Steve Dunning, Stanford	P	Cleveland
1971	Pete Broberg, Dartmouth	P	Washington
	Rob Ellis, Michigan St.	OF	Milwaukee
	Burt Hooton, Texas	P	Chicago-NL
1972	Dave Roberts, Oregon	3B	San Diego
1973	Dick Ruthven, Fresno St.	P	Philadelphia
	David Clyde, Westchester HS (Tex.)	P	Texas
	Dave Winfield, Minnesota	OF	San Diego
	Eddie Bane, Arizona St.	P	Minnesota

Draft		Pos	Team
1978	Tim Conroy, Gateway HS (Pa.)	P	Oakland
	Bob Horner, Arizona St.	3B	Atlanta
	Brian Milner, Southwest HS (Tex.)	C	Toronto
	Mike Morgan, Valley HS (Nev.)	P	Oakland
1985	Pete Incaviglia, Oklahoma St.	OF	Montreal
1988	Jim Abbott, Michigan	P	California
1989	John Olerud, Washington St.	1B	Toronto
1993	Darren Dreifort, Wichita St.	P	LA Dodgers
1995	Ariel Prieto, Fajardo U (Cuba)	P	Oakland
2000	Xavier Nady, California	3B	San Diego

Minor League Triple-A Final Standings
Playoff qualifiers (*) are noted.

International League

North Division
	W	L	Pct	GB
*Scranton/Wilkes-Barre (Yankees)	88	56	.611	—
*Pawtucket (Red Sox)	85	58	.594	2½
Rochester (Twins)	74	70	.514	14
Syracuse (Blue Jays)	69	73	.486	18
Buffalo (Indians)	66	77	.462	21½
Lehigh Valley (Phillies)	55	89	.382	33

South Division
	W	L	Pct	GB
*Durham (Devil Rays)	74	70	.514	—
Norfolk (Orioles)	64	78	.451	9
Charlotte (White Sox)	63	78	.447	9½
Richmond (Braves)	63	78	.447	9½

West Division
	W	L	Pct	GB
*Louisville (Reds)	88	56	.611	—
Toledo (Tigers)	75	69	.521	13
Columbus (Nationals)	69	73	.486	18
Indianapolis (Pirates)	68	76	.472	20

Playoffs

First Round (Best-of-Five)
Scranton/Wilkes-Barre 3 . . . . Pawtucket 1
Durham 3 . . . . Louisville 1

Championship (Best-of-Five)
Scranton/Wilkes-Barre vs. Durham

Sept. 9	Scranton/Wilkes-Barre, 8-7	at Scranton/WB
Sept. 10	Scranton/Wilkes-Barre, 1-0 (13)	at Scranton/WB
Sept. 11	Durham, 3-2	at Richmond
Sept. 12	Scranton/Wilkes-Barre, 20-2	at Richmond

Scranton/Wilkes-Barre wins Governors' Cup, 3-1

Pacific Coast League

American Conference

Northern Division
	W	L	Pct	GB
*Iowa (Cubs)	83	59	.585	—
Memphis (Cardinals)	75	67	.528	8
Omaha (Royals)	63	81	.438	21
Nashville (Brewers)	59	81	.421	23

Southern Division
	W	L	Pct	GB
*Oklahoma City (Rangers)	76	68	.528	—
Albuquerque (Marlins)	68	75	.476	7½
New Orleans (Mets)	66	75	.468	8½
Round Rock (Astros)	64	79	.448	11½

Pacific Conference

Northern Division
	W	L	Pct	GB
*Salt Lake (Angels)	84	60	.583	—
Tacoma (Mariners)	80	64	.556	4
Colorado Springs (Rockies)	71	72	.497	12½
Portland (Padres)	70	74	.486	14

Southern Division
	W	L	Pct	GB
*Sacramento (A's)	83	61	.576	—
Las Vegas (Dodgers)	74	69	.517	8½
Fresno (Giants)	67	76	.469	15½
Tucson (Diamondbacks)	60	82	.423	22

Playoffs

Conference Finals (Best-of-Five)
Sacramento 3 . . . . Salt Lake 1
Oklahoma City 3 . . . . Iowa 2

Championship (Best-of-Five)
Sacramento vs. Oklahoma City

Sept. 9	Sacramento, 8-4	at Sacramento
Sept. 10	Oklahoma City, 11-2	at Sacramento
Sept. 12	Sacramento, 8-5	at Okla. City
Sept. 14	Sacramento, 4-2	at Okla. City

Sacramento wins PCL Championship, 3-1

The 2008 Bricktown Showdown
On Sept. 16, the Pacific Coast League champion Sacramento River Cats defeated the International League champion Scranton/Wilkes-Barre Yankees, 4-1, in the Triple-A championship game at Oklahoma City's AT&T Bricktown Ballpark.

2008 International League All-Star Team
As selected by IL managers, coaches and media.

Pos	Name/Team
C	Ryan Hanigan, Louisville
1B	Oscar Salazar, Norfolk
2B	Joe Thurston, Pawtucket
SS	Reid Brignac, Durham
3B	Mike Hessman, Toledo
DH	Brad Eldred, Charlotte
OF	Josh Anderson, Richmond
OF	Jeff Bailey, Pawtucket
OF	Chris Carter, Pawtucket
UT	Chris Getz, Charlotte
SP	Charlie Zink, Pawtucket
REL	Blaine Neal, Toledo

2008 Pacific Coast League All-Star Team
As selected by PCL managers and media representatives.

Pos	Name/Team
C	Rob Johnson, Tacoma
1B	Joe Koshansky, Colorado Springs
2B	Eric Patterson, Sacramento
SS	Brandon Wood, Salt Lake
3B	Matt Brown, Salt Lake
	Jamie D'Antona, Tucson
DH	Dallas McPherson, Albuquerque
OF	Nelson Cruz, Oklahoma
OF	Nick Stavinoha, Memphis
OF	Terry Tiffee, Las Vegas
P	Shane Loux, Salt Lake
P	Gio Gonzalez, Sacramento
P	Jason Bulger, Salt Lake

1876-2008
Through the Years

SPORTS ALMANAC

The World Series

The World Series began in 1903 when Pittsburgh of the older National League (founded in 1876) invited Boston of the American League (founded in 1901) to play a best-of-9 game series to determine which of the two league champions was the best. Boston was the surprise winner, 5 games to 3. The 1904 NL champion New York Giants refused to play Boston the following year, so there was no Series. Giants' owner John T. Brush and his manager John McGraw both despised AL president Ban Johnson and considered the junior circuit to be a minor league. By the following year, however, Brush and Johnson had smoothed out their differences and the Giants agreed to play Philadelphia in a best-of-7 game series. Since then the World Series has been a best-of-7 format, except from 1919-21 when it returned to best-of-9.

In the chart below, the National League teams are listed in CAPITAL letters. Also, each World Series champion's wins and losses are noted in parentheses after the Series score in games.

Multiple champions: New York Yankees (26); St. Louis Cardinals (10); Philadelphia-Oakland A's (9); Boston Red Sox (7); Brooklyn-Los Angeles Dodgers (6); Cincinnati Reds, New York-San Francisco Giants and Pittsburgh Pirates (5); Detroit Tigers (4); Baltimore Orioles, Boston-Milwaukee-Atlanta Braves, Chicago White Sox and Washington Senators-Minnesota Twins (3); Chicago Cubs, Cleveland Indians, Florida Marlins, New York Mets, Philadelphia Phillies and Toronto Blue Jays (2).

Year	Winner	Manager	Series	Loser	Manager
1903	Boston Red Sox	Jimmy Collins	5-3 (LWLLWWWW)	PITTSBURGH	Fred Clarke
1904	Not held				
1905	NY GIANTS	John McGraw	4-1 (WLWWW)	Philadelphia A's	Connie Mack
1906	Chicago White Sox	Fielder Jones	4-2 (WLWLWW)	CHICAGO CUBS	Frank Chance
1907	CHICAGO CUBS	Frank Chance	4-0-1 (TWWWW)	Detroit	Hughie Jennings
1908	CHICAGO CUBS	Frank Chance	4-1 (WWLWW)	Detroit	Hughie Jennings
1909	PITTSBURGH	Fred Clarke	4-3 (WLWLWLW)	Detroit	Hughie Jennings
1910	Philadelphia A's	Connie Mack	4-1 (WWWLW)	CHICAGO CUBS	Frank Chance
1911	Philadelphia A's	Connie Mack	4-2 (LWWWLW)	NY GIANTS	John McGraw
1912	Boston Red Sox	Jake Stahl	4-3-1 (WTLWWLLW)	NY GIANTS	John McGraw
1913	Philadelphia A's	Connie Mack	4-1 (WLWWW)	NY GIANTS	John McGraw
1914	BOSTON BRAVES	George Stallings	4-0	Philadelphia A's	Connie Mack
1915	Boston Red Sox	Bill Carrigan	4-1 (LWWWW)	PHILA. PHILLIES	Pat Moran
1916	Boston Red Sox	Bill Carrigan	4-1 (WWLWW)	BROOKLYN	Wilbert Robinson
1917	Chicago White Sox	Pants Rowland	4-2 (WWLLWW)	NY GIANTS	John McGraw
1918	Boston Red Sox	Ed Barrow	4-2 (WLWWLW)	CHICAGO CUBS	Fred Mitchell
1919	CINCINNATI	Pat Moran	5-3 (WWLWWLLW)	Chicago White Sox	Kid Gleason
1920	Cleveland	Tris Speaker	5-2 (WLLWWWW)	BROOKLYN	Wilbert Robinson
1921	NY GIANTS	John McGraw	5-3 (LLWWLWWW)	NY Yankees	Miller Huggins
1922	NY GIANTS	John McGraw	4-0-1 (WTWWW)	NY Yankees	Miller Huggins
1923	NY Yankees	Miller Huggins	4-2 (LWLWW)	NY GIANTS	John McGraw
1924	Washington	Bucky Harris	4-3 (LWLWLWW)	NY GIANTS	John McGraw
1925	PITTSBURGH	Bill McKechnie	4-3 (LWLLWWW)	Washington	Bucky Harris
1926	ST.L. CARDINALS	Rogers Hornsby	4-3 (LWWLLWW)	NY Yankees	Miller Huggins
1927	NY Yankees	Miller Huggins	4-0	PITTSBURGH	Donie Bush
1928	NY Yankees	Miller Huggins	4-0	ST.L. CARDINALS	Bill McKechnie
1929	Philadelphia A's	Connie Mack	4-1 (WWLWW)	CHICAGO CUBS	Joe McCarthy
1930	Philadelphia A's	Connie Mack	4-2 (WWLLWW)	ST.L. CARDINALS	Gabby Street
1931	ST.L. CARDINALS	Gabby Street	4-3 (LWWLWLW)	Philadelphia A's	Connie Mack
1932	NY GIANTS	Joe McCarthy	4-0	CHICAGO CUBS	Charlie Grimm
1933	NY GIANTS	Bill Terry	4-1 (WWLWW)	Washington	Joe Cronin
1934	ST.L. CARDINALS	Frankie Frisch	4-3 (WLWLLWW)	Detroit	Mickey Cochrane*
1935	Detroit	Mickey Cochrane	4-2 (LWWWLW)	CHICAGO CUBS	Charlie Grimm
1936	NY Yankees	Joe McCarthy	4-2 (WLWWLW)	NY GIANTS	Bill Terry
1937	NY Yankees	Joe McCarthy	4-1 (WWWLW)	NY GIANTS	Bill Terry
1938	NY Yankees	Joe McCarthy	4-0	CHICAGO CUBS	Gabby Hartnett
1939	NY Yankees	Joe McCarthy	4-0	CINCINNATI	Bill McKechnie
1940	CINCINNATI	Bill McKechnie	4-3 (LWLWLWW)	Detroit	Del Baker
1941	NY Yankees	Joe McCarthy	4-1 (WLWWW)	BKLN. DODGERS	Leo Durocher
1942	ST.L. CARDINALS	Billy Southworth	4-1 (LWWWW)	NY Yankees	Joe McCarthy
1943	NY Yankees	Joe McCarthy	4-1 (WLWWW)	ST.L. CARDINALS	Billy Southworth
1944	ST.L. CARDINALS	Billy Southworth	4-2 (LWWLWW)	St. Louis Browns	Luke Sewell
1945	Detroit	Steve O'Neill	4-3 (LWLWLWW)	CHICAGO CUBS	Charlie Grimm

The World Series (Cont.)

Year	Winner	Manager	Series	Loser	Manager
1946	ST.L. CARDINALS	Eddie Dyer	4-3 (LWLWLWW)	Boston Red Sox	Joe Cronin
1947	NY Yankees	Bucky Harris	4-3 (WWLLWLW)	BKLN. DODGERS	Burt Shotton
1948	Cleveland	Lou Boudreau	4-2 (LWWWLW)	BOSTON BRAVES	Billy Southworth
1949	NY Yankees	Casey Stengel	4-1 (WLWWW)	BKLN. DODGERS	Burt Shotton
1950	NY Yankees	Casey Stengel	4-0	PHILA. PHILLIES	Eddie Sawyer
1951	NY Yankees	Casey Stengel	4-2 (LWLWWW)	NY GIANTS	Leo Durocher
1952	NY Yankees	Casey Stengel	4-3 (LWLWLWW)	BKLN. DODGERS	Charlie Dressen
1953	NY Yankees	Casey Stengel	4-2 (WWLWWW)	BKLN. DODGERS	Charlie Dressen
1954	NY GIANTS	Leo Durocher	4-0	Cleveland	Al Lopez
1955	BKLN. DODGERS	Walter Alston	4-3 (LLWWWLW)	NY Yankees	Casey Stengel
1956	NY Yankees	Casey Stengel	4-3 (LLWWWLW)	BKLN. DODGERS	Walter Alston
1957	MILW. BRAVES	Fred Haney	4-3 (LWLWWW)	NY Yankees	Casey Stengel
1958	NY Yankees	Casey Stengel	4-3 (LLWLWWW)	MILW. BRAVES	Fred Haney
1959	LA DODGERS	Walter Alston	4-2 (LWWWLW)	Chicago White Sox	Al Lopez
1960	PITTSBURGH	Danny Murtaugh	4-3 (WLLWWLW)	NY Yankees	Casey Stengel
1961	NY Yankees	Ralph Houk	4-1 (WLWWW)	CINCINNATI	Fred Hutchinson
1962	NY Yankees	Ralph Houk	4-3 (WLWLWLW)	SF GIANTS	Alvin Dark
1963	LA DODGERS	Walter Alston	4-0	NY Yankees	Ralph Houk
1964	ST.L. CARDINALS	Johnny Keane	4-3 (WLLWWLW)	NY Yankees	Yogi Berra
1965	LA DODGERS	Walter Alston	4-3 (LLWWWLW)	Minnesota	Sam Mele
1966	Baltimore	Hank Bauer	4-0	LA DODGERS	Walter Alston
1967	ST.L. CARDINALS	Red Schoendienst	4-3 (LWWWLLW)	Boston Red Sox	Dick Williams
1968	Detroit	Mayo Smith	4-3 (LWLLWWW)	ST.L. CARDINALS	Red Schoendienst
1969	NY METS	Gil Hodges	4-1 (LWWWW)	Baltimore	Earl Weaver
1970	Baltimore	Earl Weaver	4-1 (WWWLW)	CINCINNATI	Sparky Anderson
1971	PITTSBURGH	Danny Murtaugh	4-3 (LLWWWLW)	Baltimore	Earl Weaver
1972	Oakland A's	Dick Williams	4-3 (WWLWLLW)	CINCINNATI	Sparky Anderson
1973	Oakland A's	Dick Williams	4-3 (WLWLWLW)	NY METS	Yogi Berra
1974	Oakland A's	Alvin Dark	4-1 (WLWWW)	LA DODGERS	Walter Alston
1975	CINCINNATI	Sparky Anderson	4-3 (LWWLWLW)	Boston Red Sox	Darrell Johnson
1976	CINCINNATI	Sparky Anderson	4-0	NY Yankees	Billy Martin
1977	NY Yankees	Billy Martin	4-2 (WLWWLW)	LA DODGERS	Tommy Lasorda
1978	NY Yankees	Bob Lemon	4-2 (LLWWWW)	LA DODGERS	Tommy Lasorda
1979	PITTSBURGH	Chuck Tanner	4-3 (LWLLWWW)	Baltimore	Earl Weaver
1980	PHILA. PHILLIES	Dallas Green	4-2 (WWLLWW)	Kansas City	Jim Frey
1981	LA DODGERS	Tommy Lasorda	4-2 (LLWWWW)	NY Yankees	Bob Lemon
1982	ST.L. CARDINALS	Whitey Herzog	4-3 (LWWLLWW)	Milwaukee Brewers	Harvey Kuenn
1983	Baltimore	Joe Altobelli	4-1 (LWWWW)	PHILA. PHILLIES	Paul Owens
1984	Detroit	Sparky Anderson	4-1 (WLWWW)	SAN DIEGO	Dick Williams
1985	Kansas City	Dick Howser	4-3 (LLWWLWW)	ST.L. CARDINALS	Whitey Herzog
1986	NY METS	Davey Johnson	4-3 (LLWWLWW)	Boston Red Sox	John McNamara
1987	Minnesota	Tom Kelly	4-3 (WWLLLWW)	ST.L. CARDINALS	Whitey Herzog
1988	LA DODGERS	Tommy Lasorda	4-1 (WWLWW)	Oakland A's	Tony La Russa
1989	Oakland A's	Tony La Russa	4-0	SF GIANTS	Roger Craig
1990	CINCINNATI	Lou Piniella	4-0	Oakland A's	Tony La Russa
1991	Minnesota	Tom Kelly	4-3 (WWLLLWW)	ATLANTA BRAVES	Bobby Cox
1992	Toronto	Cito Gaston	4-2 (LWWWLW)	ATLANTA BRAVES	Bobby Cox
1993	Toronto	Cito Gaston	4-2 (WLWWLW)	PHILA. PHILLIES	Jim Fregosi
1994	Not held				
1995	ATLANTA BRAVES	Bobby Cox	4-2 (WWLWLW)	Cleveland	Mike Hargrove
1996	NY Yankees	Joe Torre	4-2 (LLWWWW)	ATLANTA BRAVES	Bobby Cox
1997	FLORIDA	Jim Leyland	4-3 (WLWLWLW)	Cleveland	Mike Hargrove
1998	NY Yankees	Joe Torre	4-0	SAN DIEGO	Bruce Bochy
1999	NY Yankees	Joe Torre	4-0	ATLANTA BRAVES	Bobby Cox
2000	NY Yankees	Joe Torre	4-1 (WWLWW)	NY METS	Bobby Valentine
2001	ARIZONA	Bob Brenly	4-3 (WWLLLWW)	NY Yankees	Joe Torre
2002	Anaheim	Mike Scioscia	4-3 (LWWLLWW)	SF GIANTS	Dusty Baker
2003	FLORIDA	Jack McKeon	4-2 (WLLWWW)	NY Yankees	Joe Torre
2004	Boston	Terry Francona	4-0	ST. LOUIS	Tony La Russa
2005	Chicago White Sox	Ozzie Guillen	4-0	HOUSTON	Phil Garner
2006	ST. LOUIS	Tony La Russa	4-1 (WLWWW)	Detroit	Jim Leyland
2007	Boston	Terry Francona	4-0	COLORADO	Clint Hurdle
2008	PHILA. PHILLIES	Charlie Manuel	4-1 (WLWWW)	Tampa Bay	Joe Maddon

Most Valuable Players

Currently selected by media panel and World Series official scorers. Presented by *Sport* magazine from 1955-88 and by Major League Baseball since 1989. Winner who did not play for World Series champions is in **bold** type.

Multiple winners: Bob Gibson, Reggie Jackson and Sandy Koufax (2).

Year	Year	Year
1955 Johnny Podres, Bklyn, P	1974 Rollie Fingers, Oak., P	1991 Jack Morris, Min., P
1956 Don Larsen, NY, P	1975 Pete Rose, Cin., 3B	1992 Pat Borders, Tor., C
1957 Lew Burdette, Mil., P	1976 Johnny Bench, Cin., C	1993 Paul Molitor, Tor., DH/1B/3B
1958 Bob Turley, NY, P	1977 Reggie Jackson, NY, OF	1994 Series not held.
1959 Larry Sherry, LA, P	1978 Bucky Dent, NY, SS	1995 Tom Glavine, Atl., P
	1979 Willie Stargell, Pit., 1B	1996 John Wetteland, NY, P
1960 **Bobby Richardson**, NY, 2B		1997 Livan Hernandez, Fla., P
1961 Whitey Ford, NY, P	1980 Mike Schmidt, Phi., 3B	1998 Scott Brosius, NY, 3B
1962 Ralph Terry, NY, P	1981 Pedro Guerrero, LA, OF;	1999 Mariano Rivera, NY, P
1963 Sandy Koufax, LA, P	Ron Cey, LA, 3B;	
1964 Bob Gibson, St.L., P	& Steve Yeager, LA, C	2000 Derek Jeter, NY, SS
1965 Sandy Koufax, LA, P	1982 Darrell Porter, St.L., C	2001 Curt Schilling, Ari., P
1966 Frank Robinson, Bal., OF	1983 Rick Dempsey, Bal., C	& Randy Johnson, Ari., P
1967 Bob Gibson, St.L., P	1984 Alan Trammell, Det., SS	2002 Troy Glaus, Ana., 3B
1968 Mickey Lolich, Det., P	1985 Bret Saberhagen, KC, P	2003 Josh Beckett, Fla., P
1969 Donn Clendenon, NY, 1B	1986 Ray Knight, NY, 3B	2004 Manny Ramirez, Bos., OF
	1987 Frank Viola, Min., P	2005 Jermaine Dye, Chi., OF
1970 Brooks Robinson, Bal., 3B	1988 Orel Hershiser, LA, P	2006 David Eckstein, St.L, SS
1971 Roberto Clemente, Pit., OF	1989 Dave Stewart, Oak., P	2007 Mike Lowell, Bos., 3B
1972 Gene Tenace, Oak., C		2008 Cole Hamels, Phi., P
1973 Reggie Jackson, Oak., OF	1990 Jose Rijo, Cin., P	

All-Time World Series Leaders

CAREER

World Series leaders through 2008. Years listed indicate number of World Series appearances.

Hitting

Games

	Yrs	Gm
Yogi Berra, NY Yankees	14	75
Mickey Mantle, NY Yankees	12	65
Elston Howard, NY Yankees—Boston	10	54
Hank Bauer, NY Yankees	9	53
Gil McDougald, NY Yankees	8	53

At Bats

	Yrs	AB
Yogi Berra, NY Yankees	14	259
Mickey Mantle, NY Yankees	12	230
Joe DiMaggio, NY Yankees	10	199
Frankie Frisch, NY Giants-St.L.Cards	8	197
Gil McDougald, NY Yankees	8	190

Batting Avg. (minimum 50 AB)

	AB	H	Avg
Pepper Martin, St.L. Cards	55	23	.418
Paul Molitor, Mil. Brewers-Tor. Blue Jays	55	23	.418
Lou Brock, St. Louis	87	34	.391
Marquis Grissom, Atl-Cle	77	30	.390
Thurman Munson, NY Yankees	67	25	.373
George Brett, Kansas City	51	19	.373
Hank Aaron, Milw. Braves	55	20	.364

Hits

	AB	H	Avg
Yogi Berra, NY Yankees	259	71	.274
Mickey Mantle, NY Yankees	230	59	.257
Frankie Frisch, NYG-St.L. Cards	197	58	.294
Joe DiMaggio, NY Yankees	199	54	.271
Hank Bauer, NY Yankees	188	46	.245
Pee Wee Reese, Brooklyn	169	46	.272

Runs

	Gm	R
Mickey Mantle, NY Yankees	65	42
Yogi Berra, NY Yankees	75	41
Babe Ruth, Boston Red Sox-NY Yankees	41	37
Lou Gehrig, NY Yankees	34	30
Joe DiMaggio, NY Yankees	51	27
Derek Jeter, NY Yankees	32	27

Home Runs

	AB	HR
Mickey Mantle, NY Yankees	230	18
Babe Ruth, Boston Red Sox-NY Yankees	129	15
Yogi Berra, NY Yankees	259	12
Duke Snider, Brooklyn-LA	133	11
Lou Gehrig, NY Yankees	119	10
Reggie Jackson, Oakland-NY Yankees	98	10

Runs Batted In

	Gm	RBI
Mickey Mantle, NY Yankees	65	40
Yogi Berra, NY Yankees	75	39
Lou Gehrig, NY Yankees	34	35
Babe Ruth, Boston Red Sox-NY Yankees	41	33
Joe DiMaggio, NY Yankees	51	30

Stolen Bases

	Gm	SB
Lou Brock, St. Louis	21	14
Eddie Collins, Phi. A's-Chisox	34	14
Frank Chance, Chi. Cubs	20	10
Davey Lopes, Los Angeles	23	10
Phil Rizzuto, NY Yankees	52	10

All-Time World Series Leaders (Cont.)

Total Bases

	Gm	TB
Mickey Mantle, NY Yankees	.65	123
Yogi Berra, NY Yankees	.75	117
Babe Ruth, Boston Red Sox-NY Yankees	.41	96
Lou Gehrig, NY Yankees	.34	87
Joe DiMaggio, NY Yankees	.51	84

Games

	Yrs	Gm
Whitey Ford, NY Yankees	.11	22
Mike Stanton, Atlanta-NY Yankees	.6	20
Mariano Rivera, NY Yankees	.6	20
Rollie Fingers, Oakland	.3	16
Jeff Nelson, NY Yankees	.5	16
Allie Reynolds, NY Yankees	.6	15
Bob Turley, NY Yankees	.5	15

Wins

	Gm	W-L
Whitey Ford, NY Yankees	.22	10-8
Bob Gibson, St. Louis	.9	7-2
Allie Reynolds, NY Yankees	.15	7-2
Red Ruffing, NY Yankees	.10	7-2
Lefty Gomez, NY Yankees	.7	6-0
Chief Bender, Philadelphia A's	.10	6-4
Waite Hoyt, NY Yankees-Phi. A's	.12	6-4

ERA (minimum 25 IP)

	Gm	IP	ERA
Jack Billingham, Cincinnati	.7	25.1	0.36
Harry Brecheen, St. Louis	.7	32.2	0.83
Babe Ruth, Boston Red Sox	.3	31.0	0.87
Sherry Smith, Brooklyn	.3	30.1	0.89
Sandy Koufax, Los Angeles	.8	57.0	0.95

Saves

	Gm	IP	Sv
Mariano Rivera, NY Yankees	.20	22.0	9
Rollie Fingers, Oakland	.16	33.1	6
Allie Reynolds, NY Yankees	.15	77.1	4
Johnny Murphy, NY Yankees	.8	16.1	4
John Wetteland, NY Yankees	.5	4.1	4
Robb Nen, Florida-SF	.7	7.2	4

Ten pitchers tied with 3 each.

Slugging Pct. (minimum 50 AB)

	AB	Pct
Reggie Jackson, Oakland-NY Yankees	.98	.755
Babe Ruth, Boston Red Sox-NY Yankees	129	.744
Lou Gehrig, NY Yankees	119	.731
Al Simmons, Phi. A's-Cincinnati	.73	.658
Lou Brock, St. Louis	.87	.655

Pitching

Shutouts

	GS	CG	ShO
Christy Mathewson, NY Giants	.11	10	4
Three Finger Brown, Chi. Cubs	.7	5	3
Whitey Ford, NY Yankees	.22	7	3

Seven pitchers tied with 2 each.

Innings Pitched

	Gm	IP
Whitey Ford, NY Yankees	.22	146.0
Christy Mathewson, NY Giants	.11	101.2
Red Ruffing, NY Yankees	.10	85.2
Chief Bender, Philadelphia A's	.10	85.0
Waite Hoyt, NY Yankees-Phi. A's	.12	83.2

Complete Games

	GS	CG	W-L
Christy Mathewson, NY Giants	.11	10	5-5
Chief Bender, Philadelphia A's	.10	9	6-4
Bob Gibson, St. Louis	.9	8	7-2
Whitey Ford, NY Yankees	.22	7	10-8
Red Ruffing, NY Yankees	.10	7	7-2

Strikeouts

	Gm	IP	SO
Whitey Ford, NY Yankees	.22	146.0	94
Bob Gibson, St. Louis	.9	81.0	92
Allie Reynolds, NY Yankees	.15	77.1	62
Sandy Koufax, Los Angeles	.8	57.0	61
Red Ruffing, NY Yankees	.10	85.2	61

Losses

	Gm	W-L
Whitey Ford, NY Yankees	.22	10-8
Christy Mathewson, NY Giants	.11	5-5
Joe Bush, Phi. A's-Bosox-NY Yankees	.9	2-5
Rube Marquard, NY Giants-Brooklyn	.11	2-5
Eddie Plank, Philadelphia A's	.7	2-5
Schoolboy Rowe, Detroit	.8	2-5

World Series Appearances

In the 104 years that the World Series has been contested, American League teams have won 61 championships while National League teams have won 43. Note that the Brewers, now in the NL, were in the AL when they won their title. The following teams are ranked by number of appearances through the 2008 World Series; (*) indicates AL teams.

	App	W	L	Pct.	Last Series	Last Title
NY Yankees*	.39	26	13	.667	2003	2000
Bklyn/LA Dodgers	.18	6	12	.333	1988	1988
St.L. Cardinals	.17	10	7	.588	2006	2006
NY/SF Giants	.17	5	12	.294	2002	1954
Phi/KC/Oak.A's*	.14	9	5	.643	1990	1989
Boston Red Sox*	.11	7	4	.636	2007	2007
Detroit Tigers*	.10	4	6	.400	2006	1984
Chicago Cubs	.10	2	8	.200	1945	1908
Cincinnati Reds	.9	5	4	.556	1990	1990
Bos/Mil/Atl.Braves	.9	3	6	.333	1999	1995
Pittsburgh Pirates	.7	5	2	.714	1979	1979
St.L/Bal.Orioles*	.7	3	4	.429	1983	1983
Wash/Min.Twins*	.6	3	3	.500	1991	1991
Phi. Phillies	.6	2	4	.333	2008	2008
Chi. White Sox*	.5	3	2	.600	2005	2005
Cle. Indians*	.5	2	3	.400	1997	1948
NY Mets	.4	2	2	.500	2000	1986
Fla. Marlins	.2	2	0	1.000	2003	2003
Tor. Blue Jays*	.2	2	0	1.000	1993	1993
KC Royals*	.2	1	1	.500	1985	1985
SD Padres	.2	0	2	.000	1998	—
LA Angels of Anaheim*	1	1	0	1.000	2002	2002
Ari. Diamondbacks	.1	1	0	1.000	2001	2001
Colorado Rockies	.1	0	1	.000	2007	—
Sea/Mil.Brewers*	.1	0	1	.000	1982	—
Houston Astros	.1	0	1	.000	2005	—
Tampa Bay Rays	.1	0	1	.000	2008	—

League Championship Series

Division play came to the major leagues in 1969 when both the American and National Leagues expanded to 12 teams. With an East and West Division in each league, League Championship Series (LCS) became necessary to determine the NL and AL pennant winners. In 1994, teams were realigned into three divisions, the East, Central, and West with division winners and one wildcard team playing a best-of-5 League Divisional Series (see following pages for LDS results) to determine the LCS competitors.

In the tables below, the East Division champions are noted by the letter E, the Central division champions by C and the West Division champions by W. Wildcard winners are noted by WC. Also, each playoff winner's wins and losses are noted in parentheses after the series score. The LCS changed from best-of-5 to best-of-7 in 1985. Each league's LCS was canceled in 1994 due to the players' strike.

National League

Multiple champions: Atlanta, Cincinnati, LA Dodgers and St. Louis (5); NY Mets and Philadelphia (4); Florida, Pittsburgh, San Diego and San Francisco (2).

Year	Winner	Manager	Series	Loser	Manager
1969	E–New York	Gil Hodges	3-0	W–Atlanta	Lum Harris
1970	W–Cincinnati	Sparky Anderson	3-0	E–Pittsburgh	Danny Murtaugh
1971	E–Pittsburgh	Danny Murtaugh	3-1 (LWWW)	W–San Francisco	Charlie Fox
1972	W–Cincinnati	Sparky Anderson	3-2 (LWLWW)	E–Pittsburgh	Bill Virdon
1973	E–New York	Yogi Berra	3-2 (LWWLW)	W–Cincinnati	Sparky Anderson
1974	W–Los Angeles	Walter Alston	3-1 (WWLW)	E–Pittsburgh	Danny Murtaugh
1975	W–Cincinnati	Sparky Anderson	3-0	E–Pittsburgh	Danny Murtaugh
1976	W–Cincinnati	Sparky Anderson	3-0	E–Philadelphia	Danny Ozark
1977	W–Los Angeles	Tommy Lasorda	3-1 (LWWW)	E–Philadelphia	Danny Ozark
1978	W–Los Angeles	Tommy Lasorda	3-1 (WWLW)	E–Philadelphia	Danny Ozark
1979	E–Pittsburgh	Chuck Tanner	3-0	W–Cincinnati	John McNamara
1980	E–Philadelphia	Dallas Green	3-2 (WLLWW)	W–Houston	Bill Virdon
1981	W–Los Angeles	Tommy Lasorda	3-2 (WLLWW)	E–Montreal	Jim Fanning
1982	E–St. Louis	Whitey Herzog	3-0	W–Atlanta	Joe Torre
1983	E–Philadelphia	Paul Owens	3-1 (LWWW)	W–Los Angeles	Tommy Lasorda
1984	W–San Diego	Dick Williams	3-2 (LLWWW)	E–Chicago	Jim Frey
1985	E–St. Louis	Whitey Herzog	4-2 (LLWWWW)	W–Los Angeles	Tommy Lasorda
1986	E–New York	Davey Johnson	4-2 (LWWLWW)	W–Houston	Hal Lanier
1987	E–St. Louis	Whitey Herzog	4-3 (WLWLLWW)	W–San Francisco	Roger Craig
1988	W–Los Angeles	Tommy Lasorda	4-3 (LWLWLWW)	E–New York	Davey Johnson
1989	W–San Francisco	Roger Craig	4-1 (WLWWW)	E–Chicago	Don Zimmer
1990	W–Cincinnati	Lou Piniella	4-2 (LWWWLW)	E–Pittsburgh	Jim Leyland
1991	W–Atlanta	Bobby Cox	4-3 (LLWWLWW)	E–Pittsburgh	Jim Leyland
1992	W–Atlanta	Bobby Cox	4-3 (WWLWLLW)	E–Pittsburgh	Jim Leyland
1993	E–Philadelphia	Jim Fregosi	4-2 (WLLWWW)	W–Atlanta	Bobby Cox
1994	Not held				
1995	E–Atlanta	Bobby Cox	4-0	C–Cincinnati	Davey Johnson
1996	E–Atlanta	Bobby Cox	4-3 (WLLLWWWW)	C–St. Louis	Tony La Russa
1997	WC–Florida	Jim Leyland	4-2 (WLWWLW)	E–Atlanta	Bobby Cox
1998	W–San Diego	Bruce Bochy	4-2 (WWWLLW)	E–Atlanta	Bobby Cox
1999	E–Atlanta	Bobby Cox	4-2 (WWWWLLW)	WC–New York	Bobby Valentine
2000	WC–New York	Bobby Valentine	4-1 (WWLWW)	C–St. Louis	Tony La Russa
2001	W–Arizona	Bob Brenly	4-1 (WLWWW)	E–Atlanta	Bobby Cox
2002	WC–San Francisco	Dusty Baker	4-1 (WWLWW)	C–St. Louis	Tony La Russa
2003	WC–Florida	Jack McKeon	4-3 (WLLLWWWW)	C–Chicago	Dusty Baker
2004	C–St. Louis	Tony La Russa	4-3 (WWLLLWW)	WC–Houston	Phil Garner
2005	WC–Houston	Phil Garner	4-2 (LWWWLW)	C–St. Louis	Tony La Russa
2006	C–St. Louis	Tony La Russa	4-3 (LWWWLWLW)	E–New York	Willie Randolph
2007	WC–Colorado	Clint Hurdle	4-0	W–Arizona	Bob Melvin
2008	E–Philadelphia	Charlie Manuel	4-1 (WWLWW)	W–Los Angeles	Joe Torre

NLCS Most Valuable Players

Winners who did not play for NLCS champions are in **bold** type.

Multiple winner: Steve Garvey (2).

Year	Year	Year
1977 Dusty Baker, LA, OF	1988 Orel Hershiser, LA, P	1998 Sterling Hitchcock, SD, P
1978 Steve Garvey, LA, 1B	1989 Will Clark, SF, 1B	1999 Eddie Perez, Atl., C
1979 Willie Stargell, Pit., 1B	1990 Rob Dibble, Cin., P	2000 Mike Hampton, NY, P
1980 Manny Trillo, Phi., 2B	& Randy Myers, Cin., P	2001 Craig Counsell, Ari., 2B
1981 Burt Hooton, LA, P	1991 Steve Avery, Atl., P	2002 Benito Santiago, SF, C
1982 Darrell Porter, St.L., C	1992 John Smoltz, Atl., P	2003 Ivan Rodriguez, Fla., C
1983 Gary Matthews, Phi., OF	1993 Curt Schilling, Phi., P	2004 Albert Pujols, St.L, 1B
1984 Steve Garvey, SD, 1B	1994 LCS not held.	2005 Roy Oswalt, Hou., P
1985 Ozzie Smith, St.L., SS	1995 Mike Devereaux, Atl., OF	2006 Jeff Suppan, St.L, P
1986 **Mike Scott**, Hou., P	1996 Javy Lopez, Atl., C	2007 Matt Holliday, Col., OF
1987 **Jeff Leonard**, SF, OF	1997 Livan Hernandez, Fla., P	2008 Cole Hamels, Phi., P

League Championship Series (Cont.)
American League

Multiple champions: NY Yankees (10); Oakland (6); Baltimore (5); Boston (4); Cleveland, Detroit, Kansas City, Minnesota and Toronto (2).

Year	Winner	Manager	Series	Loser	Manager
1969	E–Baltimore	Earl Weaver	3-0	W–Minnesota	Billy Martin
1970	E–Baltimore	Earl Weaver	3-0	W–Minnesota	Bill Rigney
1971	E–Baltimore	Earl Weaver	3-0	W–Oakland	Dick Williams
1972	W–Oakland	Dick Williams	3-2 (WWLLW)	E–Detroit	Billy Martin
1973	W–Oakland	Dick Williams	3-2 (LWWLW)	E–Baltimore	Earl Weaver
1974	W–Oakland	Alvin Dark	3-1 (LWWW)	E–Baltimore	Earl Weaver
1975	E–Boston	Darrell Johnson	3-0	W–Oakland	Alvin Dark
1976	E–New York	Billy Martin	3-2 (WLWLW)	W–Kansas City	Whitey Herzog
1977	E–New York	Billy Martin	3-2 (LWLWW)	W–Kansas City	Whitey Herzog
1978	E–New York	Bob Lemon	3-1 (WWLW)	W–Kansas City	Whitey Herzog
1979	E–Baltimore	Earl Weaver	3-1 (WWLW)	W–California	Jim Fregosi
1980	W–Kansas City	Jim Frey	3-0	E–New York	Dick Howser
1981	E–New York	Bob Lemon	3-0	W–Oakland	Billy Martin
1982	E–Milwaukee	Harvey Kuenn	3-2 (LLWWW)	W–California	Gene Mauch
1983	E–Baltimore	Joe Altobelli	3-1 (LWWW)	W–Chicago	Tony La Russa
1984	E–Detroit	Sparky Anderson	3-0	W–Kansas City	Dick Howser
1985	W–Kansas City	Dick Howser	4-3 (LLWLWWW)	E–Toronto	Bobby Cox
1986	E–Boston	John McNamara	4-3 (LWLLWWW)	W–California	Gene Mauch
1987	W–Minnesota	Tom Kelly	4-1 (WWLWW)	E–Detroit	Sparky Anderson
1988	W–Oakland	Tony La Russa	4-0	E–Boston	Joe Morgan
1989	W–Oakland	Tony La Russa	4-1 (WWLWW)	E–Toronto	Cito Gaston
1990	W–Oakland	Tony La Russa	4-0	E–Boston	Joe Morgan
1991	W–Minnesota	Tom Kelly	4-1 (WLWWW)	E–Toronto	Cito Gaston
1992	E–Toronto	Cito Gaston	4-2 (LWWWLW)	W–Oakland	Tony La Russa
1993	E–Toronto	Cito Gaston	4-2 (WWLLWW)	W–Chicago	Gene Lamont
1994	Not held				
1995	C–Cleveland	Mike Hargrove	4-2 (LWLWWW)	W–Seattle	Lou Piniella
1996	E–New York	Joe Torre	4-1 (WLWWW)	WC–Baltimore	Davey Johnson
1997	C–Cleveland	Mike Hargrove	4-2 (LWWWLW)	E–Baltimore	Davey Johnson
1998	E–New York	Joe Torre	4-2 (WLLLWW)	C–Cleveland	Mike Hargrove
1999	E–New York	Joe Torre	4-1 (WWLWW)	WC–Boston	Jimy Williams
2000	E–New York	Joe Torre	4-2 (LWWWLW)	WC–Seattle	Lou Piniella
2001	E–New York	Joe Torre	4-1 (WWLWW)	W–Seattle	Lou Piniella
2002	WC–Anaheim	Mike Scioscia	4-1 (LWWWW)	C–Minnesota	Ron Gardenhire
2003	E–New York	Joe Torre	4-3 (LWWWLWL)	WC–Boston	Grady Little
2004	WC–Boston	Terry Francona	4-3 (LLLWWWW)	E–New York	Joe Torre
2005	C–Chicago	Ozzie Guillen	4-1 (LWWWW)	W–Los Angeles	Mike Scioscia
2006	WC–Detroit	Jim Leyland	4-0	W–Oakland	Ken Macha
2007	E–Boston	Terry Francona	4-3 (WLLLWWW)	C–Cleveland	Eric Wedge
2008	E–Tampa Bay	Joe Maddon	4-3 (LWWWLLW)	WC–Boston	Terry Francona

ALCS Most Valuable Players

Winner who did not play for ALCS champions is in **bold** type.

Multiple winner: Dave Stewart (2).

Year		Year		Year	
1980	Frank White, KC, 2B	1990	Dave Stewart, Oak., P	2000	Dave Justice, NY, OF
1981	Graig Nettles, NY, 3B	1991	Kirby Puckett, Min., OF	2001	Andy Pettitte, NY, P
1982	**Fred Lynn,** Cal., OF	1992	Roberto Alomar, Tor., 2B	2002	Adam Kennedy, Ana., 2B
1983	Mike Boddicker, Bal., P	1993	Dave Stewart, Tor., P	2003	Mariano Rivera, NY, P
1984	Kirk Gibson, Det., OF	1994	LCS not held.	2004	David Ortiz, Bos., DH
1985	George Brett, KC, 3B	1995	Orel Hershiser, Cle., P	2005	Paul Konerko, Chi., 1B
1986	Marty Barrett, Bos., 2B	1996	Bernie Williams, NY, OF	2006	Placido Polanco, Det., 2B
1987	Gary Gaetti, Min., 3B	1997	Marquis Grissom, Cle., OF	2007	Josh Beckett, Bos., P
1988	Dennis Eckersley, Oak., P	1998	David Wells, NY, P	2008	Matt Garza, TB, P
1989	Rickey Henderson, Oak., OF	1999	Orlando Hernandez, NY, P		

Walk-off HR to Win a Postseason Series

Year	Player	Team	Series, Game	Opponent	Final Score
2006	Magglio Ordonez	Detroit	ALCS, Game 4	Oakland	6-3
2005	Chris Burke	Houston	NLDS Game 4	Atlanta	7-6 (18 inn.)
2004	David Ortiz	Boston	ALDS Game 3	Anaheim	8-6 (10 inn.)
2003	Aaron Boone	NY Yankees	ALCS Game 7	Boston	6-5 (11 inn.)
1999	Todd Pratt	NY Mets	NLDS Game 4	Arizona	4-3 (10 inn.)
1993	Joe Carter	Toronto	WS, Game 6	Philadelphia	8-6
1976	Chris Chambliss	NY Yankees	ALCS, Game 5	Kansas City	7-6
1960	Bill Mazeroski	Pittsburgh	WS, Game 7	NY Yankees	10-9

League Divisional Series

In 1994, leagues were realigned into three divisions, the East, Central, and West with division winners and one wildcard team playing a best-of-5 League Divisional Series to determine the LCS competitors. In the tables below, the East Division champions are noted by the letter E, the Central division champions by C and the West Division champions by W. Wildcard winners are noted by WC. Also, each playoff winner's wins and losses are noted in parentheses after the series score. Each league's LDS was cancelled in 1994 due to the players' strike.

National League

Multiple champions: Atlanta and St. Louis (6); NY Mets (3); Arizona, Florida and Houston (2).

Year	Winner	Manager	Series		Loser	Manager
1995	E–Atlanta	Bobby Cox	3-1	(WWLW)	WC–Colorado	Don Baylor
	C–Cincinnati	Davey Johnson	3-0		W–Los Angeles	Tommy Lasorda
1996	E–Atlanta	Bobby Cox	3-0		WC–Los Angeles	Bill Russell
	C–St. Louis	Tony La Russa	3-0		W–San Diego	Bruce Bochy
1997	E–Atlanta	Bobby Cox	3-0		C–Houston	Larry Dierker
	WC–Florida	Jim Leyland	3-0		W–San Francisco	Dusty Baker
1998	E–Atlanta	Bobby Cox	3-0		WC–Chicago	Jim Riggleman
	W–San Diego	Bruce Bochy	3-1	(WLWW)	C–Houston	Larry Dierker
1999	E–Atlanta	Bobby Cox	3-1	(LWWW)	C–Houston	Larry Dierker
	WC–New York	Bobby Valentine	3-1	(WLWW)	W–Arizona	Buck Showalter
2000	C–St. Louis	Tony La Russa	3-0		E–Atlanta	Bobby Cox
	WC–New York	Bobby Valentine	3-1	(LWWW)	W–San Francisco	Dusty Baker
2001	E–Atlanta	Bobby Cox	3-0		C–Houston	Larry Dierker
	W–Arizona	Bob Brenly	3-2	(WLWLW)	WC–St. Louis	Tony La Russa
2002	WC–San Francisco	Dusty Baker	3-2	(WLLWW)	E–Atlanta	Bobby Cox
	C–St. Louis	Tony La Russa	3-0		W–Arizona	Bob Brenly
2003	C–Chicago	Dusty Baker	3-2	(WLWLW)	E–Atlanta	Bobby Cox
	WC–Florida	Jack McKeon	3-1	(LWWW)	W–San Francisco	Felipe Alou
2004	C–St. Louis	Tony La Russa	3-1	(WWLW)	W–Los Angeles	Jim Tracy
	WC–Houston	Phil Garner	3-2	(WLWLW)	E–Atlanta	Bobby Cox
2005	C–St. Louis	Tony La Russa	3-0		W–San Diego	Bruce Bochy
	WC–Houston	Phil Garner	3-1	(WLWW)	E–Atlanta	Bobby Cox
2006	C–St. Louis	Tony La Russa	3-1	(WWLW)	W–San Diego	Bruce Bochy
	E–New York	Willie Randolph	3-0		WC–Los Angeles	Grady Little
2007	W–Arizona	Bob Melvin	3-0		C–Chicago	Lou Piniella
	WC–Colorado	Clint Hurdle	3-0		E–Philadelphia	Charlie Manuel
2008	W–Los Angeles	Joe Torre	3-0		C–Chicago	Lou Piniella
	E–Philadelphia	Charlie Manuel	3-1	(WWLW)	WC–Milwaukee	Dale Sveum

American League

Multiple champions: NY Yankees (7); Boston (5); Cleveland (4); Seattle (3); Anaheim-Los Angeles Angels, Baltimore (2).

Year	Winner	Manager	Series		Loser	Manager
1995	C–Cleveland	Mike Hargrove	3-0		E–Boston	Kevin Kennedy
	W–Seattle	Lou Piniella	3-2	(LLWWW)	WC–New York	Buck Showalter
1996	E–New York	Joe Torre	3-1	(LWWW)	W–Texas	Johnny Oates
	WC–Baltimore	Davey Johnson	3-1	(WWLW)	C–Cleveland	Mike Hargrove
1997	E–Baltimore	Davey Johnson	3-1	(WWLW)	W–Seattle	Lou Piniella
	C–Cleveland	Mike Hargrove	3-2	(LWLWW)	WC–New York	Joe Torre
1998	E–New York	Joe Torre	3-0		W–Texas	Johnny Oates
	C–Cleveland	Mike Hargrove	3-1	(LWWW)	WC–Boston	Jimy Williams
1999	E–New York	Joe Torre	3-0		W–Texas	Johnny Oates
	WC–Boston	Jimy Williams	3-2	(LLWWW)	C–Cleveland	Mike Hargrove
2000	E–New York	Joe Torre	3-2	(LWWLW)	W–Oakland	Art Howe
	WC–Seattle	Lou Piniella	3-0		C–Chicago	Jerry Manuel
2001	E–New York	Joe Torre	3-2	(LLWWW)	WC–Oakland	Art Howe
	W–Seattle	Lou Piniella	3-2	(LWLWW)	C–Cleveland	Charlie Manuel
2002	WC–Anaheim	Mike Scioscia	3-1	(LWWW)	E–New York	Joe Torre
	C–Minnesota	Ron Gardenhire	3-2	(WLLWW)	W–Oakland	Art Howe
2003	E–New York	Joe Torre	3-1	(LWWW)	C–Minnesota	Ron Gardenhire
	WC–Boston	Grady Little	3-2	(LWLWW)	W–Oakland	Ken Macha
2004	E–New York	Joe Torre	3-1	(LWWW)	C–Minnesota	Ron Gardenhire
	WC–Boston	Terry Francona	3-0		W–Anaheim	Mike Scioscia
2005	W–Los Angeles	Mike Scioscia	3-2	(LWWLW)	E–New York	Joe Torre
	C–Chicago	Ozzie Guillen	3-0		WC–Boston	Terry Francona
2006	W–Oakland	Ken Macha	3-0		C–Minnesota	Ron Gardenhire
	WC–Detroit	Jim Leyland	3-1	(LWWW)	E–New York	Joe Torre
2007	E–Boston	Terry Francona	3-0		W–Los Angeles	Mike Scioscia
	C–Cleveland	Eric Wedge	3-1	(WWLW)	E–New York	Joe Torre
2008	E–Tampa Bay	Joe Maddon	3-1	(WWLW)	C–Chicago	Ozzie Guillen
	WC–Boston	Terry Francona	3-1	(WWLW)	W–Los Angeles	Mike Scioscia

Other Playoffs

Eleven times since 1946, playoffs have been necessary to decide league or division championships or wild card berths when two teams were tied at the end of the regular season. Additionally, in the strike year of 1981 there were playoffs between the first and second half-season champions in both leagues.

National League

Year	NL	W	L	Manager	Year	NL East	W	L	Manager
1946	Brooklyn	96	58	Leo Durocher	1981	(1st Half) Philadelphia	34	21	Dallas Green
	St. Louis	96	58	Eddie Dyer		(2nd Half) Montreal	30	23	Jim Fanning
	Playoff: (Best-of-3) St. Louis, 2-0					Playoff: (Best-of-5) Montreal, 3-2 (WWLLW)			

Year	NL	W	L	Manager	Year	NL West	W	L	Manager
1951	Brooklyn	96	58	Charlie Dressen	1981	(1st Half) Los Angeles	36	21	Tommy Lasorda
	New York	96	58	Leo Durocher		(2nd Half) Houston	33	20	Bill Virdon
	Playoff: (Best-of-3) New York, 2-1 (WLW)					Playoff: (Best-of-5) Los Angeles, 3-2 (LLWWW)			

Year	NL	W	L	Manager	Year	NL Wild Card	W	L	Manager
1959	Milwaukee	86	68	Fred Haney	1998	Chicago	89	73	Jim Riggleman
	Los Angeles	86	68	Walter Alston		San Francisco	89	73	Dusty Baker
	Playoff: (Best-of-3) Los Angeles, 2-0					Playoff: (1 game) Chicago, 5-3 (at Chicago)			

Year	NL	W	L	Manager	Year	NL Wild Card	W	L	Manager
1962	Los Angeles	101	61	Walter Alston	1999	Cincinnati	96	66	Jack McKeon
	San Francisco	101	61	Alvin Dark		New York	96	66	Bobby Valentine
	Playoff: (Best-of-3) San Francisco, 2-1 (WLW)					Playoff: (1 game) New York, 5-0 (at Cincinnati)			

Year	NL West	W	L	Manager	Year	NL Wild Card	W	L	Manager
1980	Houston	92	70	Bill Virdon	2007	Colorado	89	73	Clint Hurdle
	Los Angeles	92	70	Tommy Lasorda		San Diego	89	73	Bud Black
	Playoff: (1 game) Houston, 7-1 (at LA)					Playoff: (1 game) Colorado, 9-8 in 13 inn. (at Col.)			

American League

Year	AL	W	L	Manager	Year	AL West	W	L	Manager
1948	Boston	96	58	Joe McCarthy	1981	(1st Half) Oakland	37	23	Billy Martin
	Cleveland	96	58	Lou Boudreau		(2nd Half) Kan. City	30	23	Jim Frey
	Playoff: (1 game) Cleveland, 8-3 (at Boston)					Playoff: (Best-of-5), Oakland, 3-0			

Year	AL East	W	L	Manager	Year	AL West	W	L	Manager
1978	Boston	99	63	Don Zimmer	1995	Seattle	78	66	Lou Piniella
	New York	99	63	Bob Lemon		California	78	66	M. Lachemann
	Playoff: (1 game) New York, 5-4 (at Boston)					Playoff: (1 game) Seattle, 9-1 (at Seattle)			

Year	AL East	W	L	Manager	Year	AL Central	W	L	Manager
1981	(1st Half) N.Y.	34	22	Bob Lemon	2008	Chicago	88	74	Ozzie Guillen
	(2nd Half) Milw	31	22	Buck Rodgers		Minnesota	88	74	Ron Gardenhire
	Playoff: (Best-of-5) New York, 3-2 (WWLLW)					Playoff: (1 game) Chicago, 1-0 (at Chicago)			

Regular Season League & Division Winners

Regular season National and American League pennant winners from 1900-68, as well as West and East divisional champions from 1969-93. In 1994, both leagues went to three divisions, West, Central and East, and each league also sent a wild card (WC) team to the playoffs. Note that (*) indicates 1994 divisional champion is unofficial (due to the players' strike). Note that **GA** column indicates games ahead of the second place club.

National League

Year		W	L	Pct	GA	Year		W	L	Pct	GA
1900	Brooklyn	82	54	.603	4½	1922	New York	93	61	.604	7
1901	Pittsburgh	90	49	.647	7½	1923	New York	95	58	.621	4½
1902	Pittsburgh	103	36	.741	27½	1924	New York	93	60	.608	1½
1903	Pittsburgh	91	49	.650	6½	1925	Pittsburgh	95	58	.621	8½
1904	New York	106	47	.693	13	1926	St. Louis	89	65	.578	2
1905	New York	105	48	.686	9	1927	Pittsburgh	94	60	.610	1½
1906	Chicago	116	36	.763	20	1928	St. Louis	95	59	.617	2
1907	Chicago	107	45	.704	17	1929	Chicago	98	54	.645	10½
1908	Chicago	99	55	.643	1	1930	St. Louis	92	62	.597	2
1909	Pittsburgh	110	42	.724	6½	1931	St. Louis	101	53	.656	13
1910	Chicago	104	50	.675	13	1932	Chicago	90	64	.584	4
1911	New York	99	54	.647	7½	1933	New York	91	61	.599	5
1912	New York	103	48	.682	10	1934	St. Louis	95	58	.621	2
1913	New York	101	51	.664	12½	1935	Chicago	100	54	.649	4
1914	Boston	94	59	.614	10½	1936	New York	92	62	.597	5
1915	Philadelphia	90	62	.592	7	1937	New York	95	57	.625	3
1916	Brooklyn	94	60	.610	2½	1938	Chicago	89	63	.586	2
1917	New York	98	56	.636	10	1939	Cincinnati	97	57	.630	4½
1918	Chicago	84	45	.651	10½	1940	Cincinnati	100	53	.654	12
1919	Cincinnati	96	44	.686	9	1941	Brooklyn	100	54	.649	2½
1920	Brooklyn	93	61	.604	7	1942	St. Louis	106	48	.688	2
1921	New York	94	59	.614	4	1943	St. Louis	105	49	.682	18

Year	Team	W	L	Pct	GA
1944	St. Louis	105	49	.682	14½
1945	Chicago	98	56	.636	3
1946	St. Louis†	98	58	.628	2
1947	Brooklyn	94	60	.610	5
1948	Boston	91	62	.595	6½
1949	Brooklyn	97	57	.630	1
1950	Philadelphia	91	63	.591	2
1951	New York†	98	59	.624	1
1952	Brooklyn	96	57	.627	4½
1953	Brooklyn	105	49	.682	13
1954	New York	97	57	.630	5
1955	Brooklyn	98	55	.641	13½
1956	Brooklyn	93	61	.604	1
1957	Milwaukee	95	59	.617	8
1958	Milwaukee	92	62	.597	8
1959	Los Angeles†	88	68	.564	2
1960	Pittsburgh	95	59	.617	7
1961	Cincinnati	93	61	.604	4
1962	San Francisco†	103	62	.624	1
1963	Los Angeles	99	63	.611	6
1964	St. Louis	93	69	.574	1
1965	Los Angeles	97	65	.599	2
1966	Los Angeles	95	67	.586	1½
1967	St. Louis	101	60	.627	10½
1968	St. Louis	97	65	.599	9
1969	West—Atlanta	93	69	.574	3
	East—N.Y. Mets	100	62	.617	8
1970	West—Cincinnati	102	60	.630	14½
	East—Pittsburgh	89	73	.549	5
1971	West—San Francisco	90	72	.556	1
	East—Pittsburgh	97	65	.599	7
1972	West—Cincinnati	95	59	.617	10½
	East—Pittsburgh	96	59	.619	11
1973	West—Cincinnati	99	63	.611	3½
	East—N.Y. Mets	82	79	.509	1½
1974	West—Los Angeles	102	60	.630	4
	East—Pittsburgh	88	74	.543	1½
1975	West—Cincinnati	108	54	.667	20
	East—Pittsburgh	92	69	.571	6½
1976	West—Cincinnati	102	60	.630	10
	East—Philadelphia	101	61	.623	9
1977	West—Los Angeles	98	64	.605	10
	East—Philadelphia	101	61	.623	5
1978	West—Los Angeles	95	67	.586	2½
	East—Philadelphia	90	72	.556	1½
1979	West—Cincinnati	90	71	.559	1½
	East—Pittsburgh	98	64	.605	2
1980	West—Houston†	93	70	.571	1
	East—Philadelphia	91	71	.562	1
1981	West—Los Angeles$	63	47	.573	—
	East—Montreal$	60	48	.556	—
1982	West—Atlanta	89	73	.549	1
	East—St. Louis	92	70	.568	3
1983	West—Los Angeles	91	71	.562	3
	East—Philadelphia	90	72	.556	6
1984	West—San Diego	92	70	.568	12
	East—Chicago	96	65	.596	6½
1985	West—Los Angeles	95	67	.586	5½
	East—St. Louis	101	61	.623	3
1986	West—Houston	96	66	.593	10
	East—N.Y. Mets	108	54	.667	21½
1987	West—San Francisco	90	72	.556	6
	East—St. Louis	95	67	.586	3
1988	West—Los Angeles	94	67	.584	7
	East—N.Y. Mets	100	60	.625	15
1989	West—San Francisco	92	70	.568	3
	East—Chicago	93	69	.574	6
1990	West—Cincinnati	91	71	.562	5
	East—Pittsburgh	95	67	.586	4
1991	West—Atlanta	94	68	.580	1
	East—Pittsburgh	98	64	.605	14
1992	West—Atlanta	98	64	.605	8
	East—Pittsburgh	96	66	.593	9
1993	West—Atlanta	104	58	.642	1
	East—Philadelphia	97	65	.599	3
1994	West—Los Angeles*	58	56	.509	3½
	Central—Cincinnati*	66	48	.579	½
	East—Montreal*	74	40	.649	6
1995	West—Los Angeles	78	66	.542	1
	Central—Cincinnati	85	59	.590	9
	East—Atlanta	90	54	.625	21
	WC—Colorado	77	67	.535	—
1996	West—San Diego	91	71	.562	1
	Central—St. Louis	88	74	.543	6
	East—Atlanta	96	66	.593	8
	WC—Los Angeles	90	72	.556	—
1997	West—San Francisco	90	72	.556	2
	Central—Houston	84	78	.519	5
	East—Atlanta	101	61	.623	9
	WC—Florida	92	70	.568	—
1998	West—San Diego	98	64	.605	9½
	Central—Houston	102	60	.630	12½
	East—Atlanta	106	56	.654	18
	WC—Chicago†	90	73	.552	—
1999	West—Arizona	100	62	.617	14
	Central—Houston	97	65	.599	1½
	East—Atlanta	103	59	.636	6½
	WC—N.Y. Mets†	97	66	.595	—
2000	West—San Francisco	97	65	.599	11
	Central—St. Louis	95	67	.586	10
	East—Atlanta	95	67	.586	8
	WC—N.Y. Mets	94	68	.580	—
2001	West—Arizona	92	70	.568	2
	Central—Houston@	93	69	.574	—
	East—Atlanta	88	74	.543	2
	WC—St. Louis	93	69	.574	—
2002	West—Arizona	98	64	.605	2½
	Central—St. Louis	97	65	.599	13
	East—Atlanta	101	59	.631	19
	WC—San Francisco	95	66	.590	—
2003	West—San Francisco	100	61	.621	15½
	Central—Chicago	88	74	.543	1
	East—Atlanta	101	61	.623	10
	WC—Florida	91	71	.562	—
2004	West—Los Angeles	93	69	.574	2
	Central—St. Louis	105	57	.648	13
	East—Atlanta	96	66	.593	10
	WC—Houston	92	70	.568	—
2005	West—San Diego	82	80	.506	5
	Central—St. Louis	100	62	.617	11
	East—Atlanta	90	72	.556	2
	WC—Houston	89	73	.549	—
2006	West—San Diego@	88	74	.543	—
	Central—St. Louis	83	78	.516	1½
	East—N.Y. Mets	97	65	.599	12
	WC—Los Angeles	88	74	.543	—
2007	West—Arizona	90	72	.556	½
	Central—Chicago	85	77	.525	2
	East—Philadelphia	89	73	.549	1
	WC—Colorado†	90	73	.552	—
2008	West—Los Angeles	84	78	.519	2
	Central—Chicago	97	64	.602	7½
	East—Philadelphia	92	70	.568	3
	WC—Milwaukee	90	72	.556	—

†Regular season playoffs: See "Other Playoffs" on page 102 for details.

$Divisional playoffs: See "Other Playoffs" on page 102 for details.

@In 2001, Houston (93-69) won the Central over St. Louis (93-69) due to a better head-to-head record. In 2006, San Diego (88-74) won the West over Los Angeles (88-74) due to a better head-to-head record.

Regular Season League & Division Winners (Cont.)
American League

Year		W	L	Pct	GA
1901	Chicago	83	53	.610	4
1902	Philadelphia	83	53	.610	5
1903	Boston	91	47	.659	14½
1904	Boston	95	59	.617	1½
1905	Philadelphia	92	56	.622	2
1906	Chicago	93	58	.616	3
1907	Detroit	92	58	.613	1½
1908	Detroit	90	63	.588	½
1909	Detroit	98	54	.645	3½
1910	Philadelphia	102	48	.680	14½
1911	Philadelphia	101	50	.669	13½
1912	Boston	105	47	.691	14
1913	Philadelphia	96	57	.627	6½
1914	Philadelphia	99	53	.651	8½
1915	Boston	101	50	.669	2½
1916	Boston	91	63	.591	2
1917	Chicago	100	54	.649	9
1918	Boston	75	51	.595	2½
1919	Chicago	88	52	.629	3½
1920	Cleveland	98	56	.636	2
1921	New York	98	55	.641	4½
1922	New York	94	60	.610	1
1923	New York	98	54	.645	16
1924	Washington	92	62	.597	2
1925	Washington	96	55	.636	8½
1926	New York	91	63	.591	3
1927	New York	110	44	.714	19
1928	New York	101	53	.656	2½
1929	Philadelphia	104	46	.693	18
1930	Philadelphia	102	52	.662	8
1931	Philadelphia	107	45	.704	13½
1932	New York	107	47	.695	13
1933	Washington	99	53	.651	7
1934	Detroit	101	53	.656	7
1935	Detroit	93	58	.616	3
1936	New York	102	51	.667	19½
1937	New York	102	52	.662	13
1938	New York	99	53	.651	9½
1939	New York	106	45	.702	17
1940	Detroit	90	64	.584	1
1941	New York	101	53	.656	17
1942	New York	103	51	.669	9
1943	New York	98	56	.636	13½
1944	St. Louis	89	65	.578	1
1945	Detroit	88	65	.575	1½
1946	Boston	104	50	.675	12
1947	New York	97	57	.630	12
1948	Cleveland†	97	58	.626	1
1949	New York	97	57	.630	1
1950	New York	98	56	.636	3
1951	New York	98	56	.636	5
1952	New York	95	59	.617	2
1953	New York	99	52	.656	8½
1954	Cleveland	111	43	.721	8
1955	New York	96	58	.623	3
1956	New York	97	57	.630	9
1957	New York	98	56	.636	8
1958	New York	92	62	.597	10
1959	Chicago	94	60	.610	5
1960	New York	97	57	.630	8
1961	New York	109	53	.673	8
1962	New York	96	66	.593	5
1963	New York	104	57	.646	10½
1964	New York	99	63	.611	1
1965	Minnesota	102	60	.630	7
1966	Baltimore	97	63	.606	9
1967	Boston	92	70	.568	1
1968	Detroit	103	59	.636	12
1969	West—Minnesota	97	65	.599	9
	East—Baltimore	109	53	.673	19
1970	West—Minnesota	98	64	.605	9
	East—Baltimore	108	54	.667	15
1971	West—Oakland	101	60	.627	16
	East—Baltimore	101	57	.639	12
1972	West—Oakland	93	62	.600	5½
	East—Detroit	86	70	.551	½
1973	West—Oakland	94	68	.580	6
	East—Baltimore	97	65	.599	8
1974	West—Oakland	90	72	.556	5
	East—Baltimore	91	71	.562	2
1975	West—Oakland	98	64	.605	7
	East—Boston	95	65	.594	4½
1976	West—KansasCity	90	72	.556	2½
	East—New York	97	62	.610	10½
1977	West—Kansas City	102	60	.630	8
	East—New York	100	62	.617	2½
1978	West—Kansas City	92	70	.568	5
	East—New York†	100	63	.613	1
1979	West—California	88	74	.543	3
	East—Baltimore	102	57	.642	8
1980	West—Kansas City	97	65	.599	14
	East—New York	103	59	.636	3
1981	West—Oakland$	64	45	.587	—
	East—New York$	59	48	.551	—
1982	West—California	93	69	.574	3
	East—Milwaukee	95	67	.586	1
1983	West—Chicago	99	63	.611	20
	East—Baltimore	98	64	.605	6
1984	West—Kansas City	84	78	.519	3
	East—Detroit	104	58	.642	15
1985	West—Kansas City	91	71	.562	1
	East—Toronto	99	62	.615	2
1986	West—California	92	70	.568	5
	East—Boston	95	66	.590	5½
1987	West—Minnesota	85	77	.525	2
	East—Detroit	98	64	.605	2
1988	West—Oakland	104	58	.642	13
	East—Boston	89	73	.549	1
1989	West—Oakland	99	63	.611	7
	East—Toronto	89	73	.549	2
1990	West—Oakland	103	59	.636	9
	East—Boston	88	74	.543	2
1991	West—Minnesota	95	67	.586	8
	East—Toronto	91	71	.562	7
1992	West—Oakland	96	66	.593	6
	East—Toronto	96	66	.593	4
1993	West—Chicago	94	68	.580	8
	East—Toronto	95	67	.586	7
1994	West—Texas*	52	62	.456	1
	Central—Chicago*	67	46	.593	1
	East—New York*	70	43	.619	6½
1995	West—Seattle†	79	66	.545	1
	Central—Cleveland	100	44	.694	30
	East—Boston	86	58	.597	7
	WC—New York	79	65	.549	—
1996	West—Texas	90	72	.556	4½
	Central—Cleveland	99	62	.615	14½
	East—New York	92	70	.568	4
	WC—Baltimore	88	74	.543	—
1997	West—Seattle	90	72	.556	6
	Central—Cleveland	86	75	.534	6
	East—Baltimore	98	64	.605	2
	WC—New York	96	66	.593	—

Year		W	L	Pct	GA	Year		W	L	Pct	GA
1998	West—Texas	88	74	.543	3	2004	West—Anaheim	92	70	.568	1
	Central—Cleveland	89	73	.549	9		Central—Minnesota	92	70	.568	9
	East—New York	114	48	.704	22		East—New York	101	61	.623	3
	WC—Boston	92	70	.568	—		WC—Boston	98	64	.605	—
1999	West—Texas	95	67	.586	8	2005	West—Los Angeles	95	67	.586	7
	Central—Cleveland	97	65	.599	21½		Central—Chicago	99	63	.611	6
	East—New York	98	64	.605	4		East—New York@	95	67	.586	—
	WC—Boston	94	68	.580	—		WC—Boston	95	67	.586	—
2000	West—Oakland	91	70	.565	½	2006	West—Oakland	93	69	.574	4
	Central—Chicago	95	67	.586	5		Central—Minnesota	96	66	.593	1
	East—New York	87	74	.540	2½		East—New York	97	65	.599	10
	WC—Seattle	91	71	.562	—		WC—Detroit	95	67	.586	—
2001	West—Seattle	116	46	.716	14	2007	West—Los Angeles	94	68	.580	6
	Central—Cleveland	91	71	.562	6		Central—Cleveland	96	66	.593	8
	East—New York	95	65	.594	13½		East—Boston	96	66	.593	2
	WC—Oakland	102	60	.630	—		WC—New York	94	68	.580	—
2002	West—Oakland	103	59	.636	4	2008	West—Los Angeles	100	62	.617	21
	Central—Minnesota	94	67	.584	13½		Central—Chicago†	89	74	.546	1
	East—New York	103	58	.640	10½		East—Tampa Bay	97	65	.599	2
	WC—Anaheim	99	63	.611	—		WC—Boston	95	67	.586	—
2003	West—Oakland	96	66	.593	3						
	Central—Minnesota	90	72	.556	4						
	East—New York	101	61	.623	6						
	WC—Boston	95	67	.586	—						

†**Regular season playoffs:** See "Other Playoffs" on page 102 for details.
‡**Divisional playoffs:** See "Other Playoffs" on page 102 for details.
@In 2005, New York (95-67) won the East over Boston (95-67) due to a better head-to-head record.

The All-Star Game

Baseball's first All-Star Game was held on July 6, 1933, before 47,595 at Comiskey Park in Chicago. From that year on, the All-Star Game has matched the best players in the American League against the best in the National. From 1959-62, two All-Star Games were played. The only year an All-Star Game wasn't played was 1945, when World War II travel restrictions made it necessary to cancel the meeting. The NL leads the series, 40-37-2. In the chart below, the American League is listed in **bold** type.

Since 2002, the game's MVP award has been named the Ted Williams Award, after the Red Sox Hall of Famer. The actual trophy is the Arch Ward Trophy, named after the Chicago Tribune sports editor who founded the game in 1933. First given at the two All-Star Games in 1962, the name of the award was changed to the Commissioner's Trophy in 1970 and back to the Arch Ward Memorial Trophy in 1985.

Since 2003, the league that wins the All-Star Game receives home-field advantage in that season's World Series.

MVP Multiple winners: Gary Carter, Steve Garvey, Willie Mays and Cal Ripken Jr. (2).

Year		Host	AL Manager	NL Manager	MVP
1933	**American,** 4-2	Chicago (AL)	Connie Mack	John McGraw	No award
1934	**American,** 9-7	New York (NL)	Joe Cronin	Bill Terry	No award
1935	**American,** 4-1	Cleveland	Mickey Cochrane	Frankie Frisch	No award
1936	National, 4-3	Boston (NL)	Joe McCarthy	Charlie Grimm	No award
1937	**American,** 8-3	Washington	Joe McCarthy	Bill Terry	No award
1938	National, 4-1	Cincinnati	Joe McCarthy	Bill Terry	No award
1939	**American,** 3-1	New York (AL)	Joe McCarthy	Gabby Hartnett	No award
1940	National, 4-0	St. Louis (NL)	Joe Cronin	Bill McKechnie	No award
1941	**American,** 7-5	Detroit	Del Baker	Bill McKechnie	No award
1942	**American,** 3-1	New York (NL)	Joe McCarthy	Leo Durocher	No award
1943	**American,** 5-3	Philadelphia (AL)	Joe McCarthy	Billy Southworth	No award
1944	National, 7-1	Pittsburgh	Joe McCarthy	Billy Southworth	No award
1945	Not held				
1946	**American,** 12-0	Boston (AL)	Steve O'Neill	Charlie Grimm	No award
1947	**American,** 2-1	Chicago (NL)	Joe Cronin	Eddie Dyer	No award
1948	**American,** 5-2	St. Louis (AL)	Bucky Harris	Leo Durocher	No award
1949	**American,** 11-7	Brooklyn	Lou Boudreau	Billy Southworth	No award
1950	National, 4-3 (14)	Chicago (AL)	Casey Stengel	Burt Shotton	No award
1951	National, 8-3	Detroit	Casey Stengel	Eddie Sawyer	No award
1952	National, 3-2 (5, rain)	Philadelphia (NL)	Casey Stengel	Leo Durocher	No award
1953	National, 5-1	Cincinnati	Casey Stengel	Charlie Dressen	No award
1954	**American,** 11-9	Cleveland	Casey Stengel	Walter Alston	No award
1955	National, 6-5 (12)	Milwaukee	Al Lopez	Leo Durocher	No award
1956	National, 7-3	Washington	Casey Stengel	Walter Alston	No award
1957	**American,** 6-5	St. Louis	Casey Stengel	Walter Alston	No award
1958	**American,** 4-3	Baltimore	Casey Stengel	Fred Haney	No award
1959-a	National, 5-4	Pittsburgh	Casey Stengel	Fred Haney	No award
1959-b	**American,** 5-3	Los Angeles	Casey Stengel	Fred Haney	No award

The All-Star Game (Cont.)

Year		Host	AL Manager	NL Manager	MVP
1960-a	National, 5-3	Kansas City	Al Lopez	Walter Alston	No award
1960-b	National, 6-0	New York	Al Lopez	Walter Alston	No award
1961-a	National, 5-4 (10)	San Francisco	Paul Richards	Danny Murtaugh	No award
1961-b	TIE, 1-1 (9, rain)	Boston	Paul Richards	Danny Murtaugh	No award
1962-a	National, 3-1	Washington	Ralph Houk	Fred Hutchinson	Maury Wills, LA (NL), SS
1962-b	**American,** 9-4	Chicago (NL)	Ralph Houk	Fred Hutchinson	Leon Wagner, LA (AL), OF
1963	National, 5-3	Cleveland	Ralph Houk	Alvin Dark	Willie Mays, SF, OF
1964	National, 7-4	New York (NL)	Al Lopez	Walter Alston	Johnny Callison, Phi., OF
1965	National, 6-5	Minnesota	Al Lopez	Gene Mauch	Juan Marichal, SF, P
1966	National, 2-1 (10)	St. Louis	Sam Mele	Walter Alston	Brooks Robinson, Bal.,-3B
1967	National, 2-1 (15)	California	Hank Bauer	Walter Alston	Tony Perez, Cin., 3B
1968	National, 1-0	Houston	Dick Williams	Red Schoendienst	Willie Mays, SF, OF
1969	National, 9-3	Washington	Mayo Smith	Red Schoendienst	Willie McCovey, SF, 1B
1970	National, 5-4 (12)	Cincinnati	Earl Weaver	Gil Hodges	Carl Yastrzemski, Bos., OF-1B
1971	**American,** 6-4	Detroit	Earl Weaver	Sparky Anderson	Frank Robinson, Bal., OF
1972	National, 4-3 (10)	Atlanta	Earl Weaver	Danny Murtaugh	Joe Morgan, Cin., 2B
1973	National, 7-1	Kansas	Dick Williams	Sparky Anderson	Bobby Bonds, SF, OF
1974	National, 7-2	Pittsburgh	Dick Williams	Yogi Berra	Steve Garvey, LA, 1B
1975	National, 6-3	Milwaukee	Alvin Dark	Walter Alston	Bill Madlock, Chi. (NL), 3B & Jon Matlack, NY (NL), P
1976	National, 7-1	Philadelphia	Darrell Johnson	Sparky Anderson	George Foster, Cin., OF
1977	National, 7-5	New York (AL)	Billy Martin	Sparky Anderson	Don Sutton, LA, P
1978	National, 7-3	San Diego	Billy Martin	Tommy Lasorda	Steve Garvey, LA, 1B
1979	National, 7-6	Seattle	Bob Lemon	Tommy Lasorda	Dave Parker, Pit., OF
1980	National, 4-2	Los Angeles	Earl Weaver	Chuck Tanner	Ken Griffey, Cin., OF
1981	National, 5-4	Cleveland	Jim Frey	Dallas Green	Gary Carter, Mon., C
1982	National, 4-1	Montreal	Billy Martin	Tommy Lasorda	Dave Concepcion, Cin., SS
1983	**American,** 13-3	Chicago (AL)	Harvey Kuenn	Whitey Herzog	Fred Lynn, Cal., OF
1984	National, 3-1	San Francisco	Joe Altobelli	Paul Owens	Gary Carter, Mon., C
1985	National, 6-1	Minnesota	Sparky Anderson	Dick Williams	LaMarr Hoyt, SD, P
1986	**American,** 3-2	Houston	Dick Howser	Whitey Herzog	Roger Clemens, Bos., P
1987	National, 2-0 (13)	Oakland	John McNamara	Davey Johnson	Tim Raines, Mon., OF
1988	**American,** 2-1	Cincinnati	Tom Kelly	Whitey Herzog	Terry Steinbach, Oak., C
1989	**American,** 5-3	California	Tony La Russa	Tommy Lasorda	Bo Jackson, KC, OF
1990	**American,** 2-0	Chicago (NL)	Tony La Russa	Roger Craig	Julio Franco, Tex., 2B
1991	**American,** 4-2	Toronto	Tony La Russa	Lou Piniella	Cal Ripken Jr., Bal., SS
1992	**American,** 13-6	San Diego	Tom Kelly	Bobby Cox	Ken Griffey Jr., Sea., OF
1993	**American,** 9-3	Baltimore	Cito Gaston	Bobby Cox	Kirby Puckett, Min., OF
1994	National, 8-7 (10)	Pittsburgh	Cito Gaston	Jim Fregosi	Fred McGriff, Atl., 1B
1995	National, 3-2	Texas	Buck Showalter	Felipe Alou	Jeff Conine, Fla., PH
1996	National, 6-0	Philadelphia	Mike Hargrove	Bobby Cox	Mike Piazza, LA, C
1997	**American,** 3-1	Cleveland	Joe Torre	Bobby Cox	Sandy Alomar Jr., Cle., C
1998	**American,** 13-8	Colorado	Mike Hargrove	Jim Leyland	Roberto Alomar, Bal., 2B
1999	**American,** 4-1	Boston	Joe Torre	Bruce Bochy	Pedro Martinez, Bos., P
2000	**American,** 6-3	Atlanta	Joe Torre	Bobby Cox	Derek Jeter, NY (AL), SS
2001	**American,** 4-1	Seattle	Joe Torre	Bobby Valentine	Cal Ripken Jr., Bal., SS-3B
2002	TIE, 7-7 (11 inn.) *	Milwaukee	Joe Torre	Bob Brenly	No award
2003	**American,** 7-6	Chicago (AL)	Mike Scioscia	Dusty Baker	Garret Anderson, Ana., OF
2004	**American,** 9-4	Houston	Joe Torre	Jack McKeon	Alfonso Soriano, Tex., 2B
2005	**American,** 7-5	Detroit	Terry Francona	Tony La Russa	Miguel Tejada, Bal., SS
2006	**American,** 3-2	Pittsburgh	Ozzie Guillen	Phil Garner	Michael Young, Tex., 2B
2007	**American,** 5-4	San Francisco	Jim Leyland	Tony La Russa	Ichiro Suzuki, Sea., OF
2008	**American,** 4-2 (15)	New York (AL)	Terry Francona	Clint Hurdle	J.D. Drew, Bos., OF

* Due to the depletion of both the AL and NL rosters, the 2002 game was called a tie after 11 innings.

The 80th Major League Baseball All-Star Game will be held on July 14, 2009 at Busch Stadium in St. Louis.

Major League Franchise Origins

Here is what the current 30 teams in Major League Baseball have to show for the years they have put in as members of the National League (NL) and American League (AL). Pennants and World Series championships are since 1901.

National League

	1st Year	Pennants & World Series	Franchise Stops
Arizona Diamondbacks	..1998	1 NL (2001) 1 WS (2001)	• Phoenix (1998–)
Atlanta Braves	1876	9 NL (1914,48,57-58,91-92,95,96,99) 3 WS (1914,57,95)	• Boston (1876–1952) Milwaukee (1953–65) Atlanta (1966–)
Chicago Cubs	1876	10 NL (1906-08,10,18,29,32,35,38,45) 2 WS (1907-08)	• Chicago (1876–)
Cincinnati Reds	1876	9 NL (1919,39-40,61,70,72,75-76,90) 5 WS (1919,40,75-76,90)	• Cincinnati (1876–80) Cincinnati (1890–)
Colorado Rockies	1993	1 NL (2007)	• Denver (1993–)
Florida Marlins	1993	2 NL (1997, 2003) 2 WS (1997, 2003)	• Miami (1993–)
Houston Astros	1962	1 NL (2005)	• Houston (1962–)
Los Angeles Dodgers	1890	18 NL (1916,20,41,47,49,52-53,55-56, 59,63, 65-66,74,77-78, 81,88) 6 WS (1955,59,63,65,81,88)	• Brooklyn (1890-1957) Los Angeles (1958–)
Milwaukee Brewers	...1969	1 AL (1982)	• Seattle (1969) Milwaukee (1970–)
New York Mets	1962	4 NL (1969,73,86,00) 2 WS (1969,86)	• New York (1962–)
Philadelphia Phillies	1883	6 NL (1915,50,80,83,93, 2008) 2 WS (1980, 2008)	• Philadelphia (1883–)
Pittsburgh Pirates	1887	7 NL (1903,09,25,27,60,71,79) 5 WS (1909,25,60,71,79)	• Pittsburgh (1887–)
St. Louis Cardinals	1892	17 NL (1926,28,30-31,34,42-44,46,64, 67-68,82,85,87,2004,06) 10 WS (1926,31,34,42,44,46,64,67,82,2006)	• St. Louis (1892–)
San Diego Padres	1969	2 NL (1984,98)	• San Diego (1969–)
San Francisco Giants	1883	17 NL (1905,11-13,17,21-24,33,36-37,51, 54,62,89,2002) 5 WS (1905,21-22,33,54)	• New York (1883–1957) San Francisco (1958–)
Washington Nationals	...1969	None	• Montreal (1969–2004) Washington, DC (2005–)

American League

	1st Year	Pennants & World Series	Franchise Stops
Baltimore Orioles	1901	7 AL (1944,66,69-71,79,83) 3 WS (1966,70,83)	• Milwaukee (1901) St. Louis (1902–53) Baltimore (1954–)
Boston Red Sox	1901	11 AL (1903,12,15-16,18,46,67,75,86, 2004,07) 7 WS (1903,12,15-16,18,2004,07)	• Boston (1901–)
Chicago White Sox	1901	5 AL (1906,17,19,59,2005) 3 WS (1906,17,2005)	• Chicago (1901–)
Cleveland Indians	1901	5 AL (1920,48,54,95,97) 2 WS (1920,48)	• Cleveland (1901–)
Detroit Tigers	1901	10 AL (1907-09,34-35,40,45,68,84,2006) 4 WS (1935,45,68,84)	• Detroit (1901–)
Kansas City Royals	1969	2 AL (1980,85) 1 WS (1985)	• Kansas City (1969–)
Los Angeles Angels of Anaheim	1961	1 AL (2002) 1 WS (2002)	• Los Angeles (1961–65) Anaheim, CA (1966–)
Minnesota Twins	1901	6 AL (1924-25,33,65,87,91) 3 WS (1924,87,91)	• Washington, DC (1901–60) Bloomington, MN (1961–81) Minneapolis (1982–)
New York Yankees	1901	39 AL (1921-23,26-28,32,36-39,41-43,47, 49-53,55-58,60-64,76-78,81,96,98-01,03) 26 WS (1923,27-28,32,36-39,41,43,47, 49-53,56,58,61-62,77-78,96,98-00)	• Baltimore (1901–02) New York (1,903–)
Oakland Athletics	1901	14 AL (1905,10-11,13-14,29-31,72-74, 88-90) 9 WS (1910-11,13,29-30,72-74,89)	• Philadelphia (1901-54) Kansas City (1955–67) Oakland (1968–)
Seattle Mariners	1977	None	• Seattle (1977–)
Tampa Bay Rays	1998	1 AL (2008)	• Tampa Bay (1998–)
Texas Rangers	1961	None	• Washington, DC (1961–71) Arlington, TX (1972–)
Toronto Blue Jays	1977	2 AL (1992-93) 2 WS (1992-93)	• Toronto (1977–)

The Growth of Major League Baseball

The National League (founded in 1876) and the American League (founded in 1901) were both eight-team circuits at the turn of the century and remained that way until expansion finally came to Major League Baseball in the 1960s. The AL added two teams in 1961 and the NL did the same a year later. Both leagues went to 12 teams and split into two divisions in 1969. The AL then grew by two more teams to 14 in 1977, but the NL didn't follow suit until adding its 13th and 14th clubs in 1993. The NL added two teams (making it 16) in 1998 when the expansion Arizona Diamondbacks entered the league and the Milwaukee Brewers moved over from the AL. The Tampa Bay Devil Rays (now Rays) joined the AL in 1998, keeping the AL at 14 teams.

Expansion Timetable (Since 1901)

1961—Los Angeles Angels and Washington Senators (now Texas Rangers) join AL; **1962**—Houston Colt .45s (now Astros) and New York Mets join NL; **1969**—Kansas City Royals and Seattle Pilots (now Milwaukee Brewers) join AL, while Montreal Expos (now Washington Nationals) and San Diego Padres join NL; **1977**—Seattle Mariners and Toronto Blue Jays join AL; **1993**—Colorado Rockies and Florida Marlins join NL; **1998**—Arizona Diamondbacks join NL and Tampa Bay Devil Rays join AL.

City and Nickname Changes

National League

1953—Boston Braves move to Milwaukee; **1958**—Brooklyn Dodgers move to Los Angeles and New York Giants move to San Francisco; **1965**—Houston Colt .45s renamed Astros; **1966**—Milwaukee Braves move to Atlanta; **2004**—Montreal Expos move to Washington, D.C. and become Washington Nationals.

Other nicknames: Boston (Beaneaters and Doves through 1908, and Bees from 1936-40); **Brooklyn** (Superbas through 1926, then Robins from 1927-31; then Dodgers from 1932-57); **Cincinnati** (Red Legs from 1944-45, then Redlegs from 1954-60, then Reds since 1961); **Philadelphia** (Blue Jays from 1943-44).

American League

1902—Milwaukee Brewers move to St. Louis and become Browns; **1903**—Baltimore Orioles move to New York and become Highlanders; **1913**—NY Highlanders renamed Yankees; **1954**—St. Louis Browns move to Baltimore and become Orioles; **1955**—Philadelphia Athletics move to Kansas City; **1961**—Washington Senators move to Bloomington, Minn., and become Minnesota Twins; **1965**—LA Angels renamed California Angels; **1966**—California Angels move to Anaheim; **1968**—KC Athletics move to Oakland and become A's; **1970**—Seattle Pilots move to Milwaukee and become Brewers; **1972**—Washington Senators move to Arlington, Texas, and become Rangers; **1982**—Minnesota Twins move to Minneapolis; **1987**—Oakland A's renamed Athletics; **1997**—California Angels renamed Anaheim Angels; **2005**—Anaheim Angels renamed Los Angeles Angels of Anaheim; **2008**—Tampa Bay Devil Rays renamed Tampa Bay Rays.

Other nicknames: Boston (Pilgrims, Puritans, Plymouth Rocks and Somersets through 1906); **Cleveland** (Bronchos, Blues, Naps and Molly McGuires through 1914); **Washington** (Senators through 1904, then Nationals from 1905-44, then Senators again from 1945-60).

National League Pennant Winners from 1876-99

Founded in 1876, the National League played 24 seasons before the turn of the century and its eventual rivalry with the younger American League.

Multiple winners: Boston (8); Chicago (6); Baltimore (3); Brooklyn, New York and Providence (2).

Year		Year		Year		Year	
1876	Chicago	1882	Chicago	1888	New York	1894	Baltimore
1877	Boston	1883	Boston	1889	New York	1895	Baltimore
1878	Boston	1884	Providence	1890	Brooklyn	1896	Baltimore
1879	Providence	1885	Chicago	1891	Boston	1897	Boston
1880	Chicago	1886	Chicago	1892	Boston	1898	Boston
1881	Chicago	1887	Detroit	1893	Boston	1899	Brooklyn

Champions of Leagues That No Longer Exist

A Special Baseball Records Committee appointed by the commissioner found in 1968 that four extinct leagues qualified for major league status—the American Association (1882-91), the Union Association (1884), the Players' League (1890) and the Federal League (1914-15). The first years of the American League (1900) and Federal League (1913) were not recognized.

American Association

Year	Champion	Manager	Year	Champion	Manager	Year	Champion	Manager
1882	Cincinnati	Pop Snyder	1886	St. Louis	Charlie Comiskey	1890	Louisville	Jack Chapman
1883	Philadelphia	Lew Simmons	1887	St. Louis	Charlie Comiskey	1891	Boston	Arthur Irwin
1884	New York	Jim Mutrie	1888	St. Louis	Charlie Comiskey			
1885	St. Louis	Charlie Comiskey	1889	Brooklyn	Bill McGunnigle			

Union Association

Year	Champion	Manager
1884	St. Louis	Henry Lucas

Players' League

Year	Champion	Manager
1890	Boston	King Kelly

Federal League

Year	Champion	Manager
1914	Indianapolis	Bill Phillips
1915	Chicago	Joe Tinker

Annual Batting Leaders (since 1900)

Batting Average

National League

Multiple winners: Tony Gwynn and Honus Wagner (8); Rogers Hornsby and Stan Musial (7); Roberto Clemente and Bill Madlock (4); Pete Rose, Larry Walker and Paul Waner (3); Hank Aaron, Richie Ashburn, Barry Bonds, Jake Daubert, Tommy Davis, Ernie Lombardi, Willie McGee, Lefty O'Doul, Dave Parker and Edd Roush (2).

Year		Avg	Year		Avg	Year		Avg
1900	Honus Wagner, Pit	.381	1937	Joe Medwick, St.L	.374	1973	Pete Rose, Cin	.338
1901	Jesse Burkett, St.L	.382	1938	Ernie Lombardi, Cin	.342	1974	Ralph Garr, Atl	.353
1902	Ginger Beaumont, Pit	.357	1939	Johnny Mize, St.L	.349	1975	Bill Madlock, Chi	.354
1903	Honus Wagner, Pit	.355	1940	Debs Garms, Pit	.355	1976	Bill Madlock, Chi	.339
1904	Honus Wagner, Pit	.349	1941	Pete Reiser, Bklyn	.343	1977	Dave Parker, Pit	.338
1905	Cy Seymour, Cin	.377	1942	Ernie Lombardi, Bos	.330	1978	Dave Parker, Pit	.334
1906	Honus Wagner, Pit	.339	1943	Stan Musial, St.L	.357	1979	Keith Hernandez, St.L	.344
1907	Honus Wagner, Pit	.350	1944	Dixie Walker, Bklyn	.357	1980	Bill Buckner, Chi	.324
1908	Honus Wagner, Pit	.354	1945	Phil Cavarretta, Chi	.355	1981	Bill Madlock, Pit	.341
1909	Honus Wagner, Pit	.339	1946	Stan Musial, St.L	.365	1982	Al Oliver, Mon	.331
1910	Sherry Magee, Phi	.331	1947	Harry Walker, St.L-Phi	.363	1983	Bill Madlock, Pit	.323
1911	Honus Wagner, Pit	.334	1948	Stan Musial, St.L	.376	1984	Tony Gwynn, SD	.351
1912	Heinie Zimmerman, Chi.	.372	1949	Jackie Robinson, Bklyn	.342	1985	Willie McGee, St.L	.353
1913	Jake Daubert, Bklyn	.350	1950	Stan Musial, St.L	.346	1986	Tim Raines, Mon	.334
1914	Jake Daubert, Bklyn	.329	1951	Stan Musial, St.L	.355	1987	Tony Gwynn, SD	.370
1915	Larry Doyle, NY	.320	1952	Stan Musial, St.L	.336	1988	Tony Gwynn, SD	.313
1916	Hal Chase, Cin.	.339	1953	Carl Furillo, Bklyn	.344	1989	Tony Gwynn, SD	.336
1917	Edd Roush, Cin.	.341	1954	Willie Mays, NY	.345	1990	Willie McGee, St.L	.335
1918	Zack Wheat, Bklyn	.335	1955	Richie Ashburn, Phi	.338	1991	Terry Pendleton, Atl	.319
1919	Edd Roush, Cin.	.321	1956	Hank Aaron, Mil.	.328	1992	Gary Sheffield, SD	.330
1920	Rogers Hornsby, St.L.	.370	1957	Stan Musial, St.L	.351	1993	Andres Galarraga, Col	.370
1921	Rogers Hornsby, St.L	.397	1958	Richie Ashburn, Phi	.350	1994	Tony Gwynn, SD	.394
1922	Rogers Hornsby, St.L.	.401	1959	Hank Aaron, Mil.	.355	1995	Tony Gwynn, SD	.368
1923	Rogers Hornsby, St.L.	.384	1960	Dick Groat, Pit	.325	1996	Tony Gwynn, SD	.353
1924	Rogers Hornsby, St.L.	.424	1961	Roberto Clemente, Pit	.351	1997	Tony Gwynn, SD	.372
1925	Rogers Hornsby, St.L.	.403	1962	Tommy Davis, LA	.346	1998	Larry Walker, Col.	.363
1926	Bubbles Hargrave, Cin	.353	1963	Tommy Davis, LA	.326	1999	Larry Walker, Col.	.379
1927	Paul Waner, Pit.	.380	1964	Roberto Clemente, Pit	.339	2000	Todd Helton, Col.	.372
1928	Rogers Hornsby, Bos	.387	1965	Roberto Clemente, Pit	.329	2001	Larry Walker, Col.	.350
1929	Lefty O'Doul, Phi	.398	1966	Matty Alou, Pit	.342	2002	Barry Bonds, SF	.370
1930	Bill Terry, NY	.401	1967	Roberto Clemente, Pit	.357	2003	Albert Pujols, St.L	.359
1931	Chick Hafey, St.L	.349	1968	Pete Rose, Cin	.335	2004	Barry Bonds, SF	.362
1932	Lefty O'Doul, Bklyn	.368	1969	Pete Rose, Cin	.348	2005	Derrek Lee, Chi.	.335
1933	Chuck Klein, Phi	.368	1970	Rico Carty, Atl	.366	2006	Freddy Sanchez, Pit.	.344
1934	Paul Waner, Pit.	.362	1971	Joe Torre, St.L.	.363	2007	Matt Holliday, Col.	.340
1935	Arky Vaughan, Pit.	.385	1972	Billy Williams, Chi	.333	2008	Chipper Jones, Atl.	.364
1936	Paul Waner, Pit.	.373						

American League

Multiple winners: Ty Cobb (12); Rod Carew (7); Ted Williams (6); Wade Boggs (5); Harry Heilmann (4); George Brett, Nap Lajoie, Tony Oliva and Carl Yastrzemski (3); Luke Appling, Joe DiMaggio, Ferris Fain, Jimmie Foxx, Nomar Garciaparra, Edgar Martinez, Joe Mauer, Pete Runnels, Al Simmons, George Sisler, Ichiro Suzuki and Mickey Vernon (2).

Year		Avg	Year		Avg	Year		Avg
1901	Nap Lajoie, Phi.	.422	1926	Heinie Manush, Det	.378	1951	Ferris Fain, Phi	.344
1902	Ed Delahanty, Wash.	.376	1927	Harry Heilmann, Det	.398	1952	Ferris Fain, Phi	.327
1903	Nap Lajoie, Cle	.355	1928	Goose Goslin, Wash.	.379	1953	Mickey Vernon, Wash.	.337
1904	Nap Lajoie, Cle	.381	1929	Lew Fonseca, Cle	.369	1954	Bobby Avila, Clev.	.341
1905	Elmer Flick, Cle.	.306	1930	Al Simmons, Phi	.381	1955	Al Kaline, Det.	.340
1906	George Stone, St.L	.358	1931	Al Simmons, Phi	.390	1956	Mickey Mantle, NY	.353
1907	Ty Cobb, Det	.350	1932	Dale Alexander, Det-Bos	.367	1957	Ted Williams, Bos	.388
1908	Ty Cobb, Det	.324	1933	Jimmie Foxx, Phi	.356	1958	Ted Williams, Bos	.328
1909	Ty Cobb, Det	.377	1934	Lou Gehrig, NY	.363	1959	Harvey Kuenn, Det	.353
1910	Ty Cobb, Det	.383	1935	Buddy Myer, Wash.	.349	1960	Pete Runnels, Bos	.320
1911	Ty Cobb, Det	.420	1936	Luke Appling, Chi.	.388	1961	Norm Cash, Det	.361*
1912	Ty Cobb, Det	.409	1937	Charlie Gehringer, Det	.371	1962	Pete Runnels, Bos	.326
1913	Ty Cobb, Det	.390	1938	Jimmie Foxx, Bos.	.349	1963	Carl Yastrzemski, Bos.	.321
1914	Ty Cobb, Det	.368	1939	Joe DiMaggio, NY	.381	1964	Tony Oliva, Min	.323
1915	Ty Cobb, Det	.369	1940	Joe DiMaggio, NY	.352	1965	Tony Oliva, Min	.321
1916	Tris Speaker, Cle.	.386	1941	Ted Williams, Bos	.406	1966	Frank Robinson, Bal	.316
1917	Ty Cobb, Det	.383	1942	Ted Williams, Bos	.356	1967	Carl Yastrzemski, Bos.	.326
1918	Ty Cobb, Det	.382	1943	Luke Appling, Chi.	.328	1968	Carl Yastrzemski, Bos.	.301
1919	Ty Cobb, Det	.384	1944	Lou Boudreau, Clev.	.327	1969	Rod Carew, Min	.332
1920	George Sisler, St.L	.407	1945	Snuffy Stirnweiss, NY.	.309	1970	Alex Johnson, Cal.	.329
1921	Harry Heilmann, Det	.394	1946	Mickey Vernon, Wash.	.353	1971	Tony Oliva, Min	.337
1922	George Sisler, St.L	.420	1947	Ted Williams, Bos.	.343	1972	Rod Carew, Min	.318
1923	Harry Heilmann, Det	.403	1948	Ted Williams, Bos.	.369	1973	Rod Carew, Min	.350
1924	Babe Ruth, NY	.378	1949	George Kell, Det.	.343	1974	Rod Carew, Min	.364
1925	Harry Heilmann, Det	.393	1950	Billy Goodman, Bos	.354	1975	Rod Carew, Min	.359

Batting Average (Cont.)

Year		Avg	Year		Avg	Year		Avg
1976	George Brett, KC	.333	1987	Wade Boggs, Bos.	.363	1998	Bernie Williams, NY.	.339
1977	Rod Carew, Min	.388	1988	Wade Boggs, Bos.	.366	1999	Namar Garciaparra, Bos.	.357
1978	Rod Carew, Min.	.333	1989	Kirby Puckett, Min.	.339	2000	Nomar Garciaparra, Bos.	.372
1979	Fred Lynn, Bos	.333	1990	George Brett, KC	.329	2001	Ichiro Suzuki, Sea.	.350
1980	George Brett, KC	.390	1991	Julio Franco, Tex	.341	2002	Manny Ramirez, Bos.	.349
1981	Carney Lansford, Bos.	.336	1992	Edgar Martinez, Sea.	.343	2003	Bill Mueller, Bos.	.326
1982	Willie Wilson, KC.	.332	1993	John Olerud, Tor	.363	2004	Ichiro Suzuki, Sea.	.372
1983	Wade Boggs, Bos.	.361	1994	Paul O'Neill, NY	.359	2005	Michael Young, Tex.	.331
1984	Don Mattingly, NY	.343	1995	Edgar Martinez, Sea.	.356	2006	Joe Mauer, Min.	.347
1985	Wade Boggs, Bos.	.368	1996	Alex Rodriguez, Sea	.358	2007	Magglio Ordonez, Det.	.363
1986	Wade Boggs, Bos.	.357	1997	Frank Thomas, Chi	.347	2008	Joe Mauer, Min.	.328

*Norm Cash later admitted to using a corked bat the entire season. He played 16 other seasons and never hit better than .286.

Home Runs
National League

Multiple winners: Mike Schmidt (8); Ralph Kiner (7); Gavvy Cravath and Mel Ott (6); Hank Aaron, Chuck Klein, Willie Mays, Johnny Mize, Cy Williams and Hack Wilson (4); Willie McCovey (3); Ernie Banks, Johnny Bench, Barry Bonds, George Foster, Rogers Hornsby, Ryan Howard, Tim Jordan, Dave Kingman, Eddie Mathews, Mark McGwire, Dale Murphy, Bill Nicholson, Dave Robertson, Wildfire Schulte, Sammy Sosa and Willie Stargell (2).

Year		HR	Year		HR	Year		HR
1900	Herman Long, Bos	12	1935	Wally Berger, Bos.	34	1971	Willie Stargell, Pit.	48
1901	Sam Crawford, Cin.	16	1936	Mel Ott, NY.	33	1972	Johnny Bench, Cin	40
1902	Tommy Leach, Pit	6	1937	Joe Medwick, St.L.	31	1973	Willie Stargell, Pit.	44
1903	Jimmy Sheckard, Bklyn	9		& Mel Ott, NY.	31	1974	Mike Schmidt, Phi.	36
1904	Harry Lumley, Bklyn	9	1938	Mel Ott, NY.	36	1975	Mike Schmidt, Phi.	38
1905	Fred Odwell, Cin.	9	1939	Johnny Mize, St.L	28	1976	Mike Schmidt, Phi.	38
1906	Tim Jordan, Bklyn	12	1940	Johnny Mize, St.L	43	1977	George Foster, Cin	52
1907	Dave Brain, Bos	10	1941	Dolph Camilli, Bklyn.	34	1978	George Foster, Cin	40
1908	Tim Jordan, Bklyn	12	1942	Mel Ott, NY.	30	1979	Dave Kingman, Chi	48
1909	Red Murray, NY	7	1943	Bill Nicholson, Chi	29	1980	Mike Schmidt, Phi.	48
1910	Fred Beck, Bos.	10	1944	Bill Nicholson, Chi	33	1981	Mike Schmidt, Phi.	31
	& Wildfire Schulte, Chi	10	1945	Tommy Holmes, Bos	28	1982	Dave Kingman, NY.	37
1911	Wildfire Schulte, Chi.	21	1946	Ralph Kiner, Pit.	23	1983	Mike Schmidt, Phi.	40
1912	Heinie Zimmerman, Chi.	14	1947	Ralph Kiner, Pit.	51	1984	Dale Murphy, Atl.	36
1913	Gavvy Cravath, Phi.	19		& Johnny Mize, NY	51		& Mike Schmidt, Phi.	36
1914	Gavvy Cravath, Phi.	19	1948	Ralph Kiner, Pit.	40	1985	Dale Murphy, Atl.	37
1915	Gavvy Cravath, Phi.	24		& Johnny Mize, NY	40	1986	Mike Schmidt, Phi.	37
1916	Cy Williams, Chi	12	1949	Ralph Kiner, Pit.	54	1987	Andre Dawson, Chi	49
	& Dave Robertson, NY.	12	1950	Ralph Kiner, Pit.	47	1988	Darryl Strawberry, NY.	39
1917	Gavvy Cravath, Phi.	12	1951	Ralph Kiner, Pit.	42	1989	Kevin Mitchell, SF.	47
	& Dave Robertson, NY.	12	1952	Ralph Kiner, Pit.	37	1990	Ryne Sandberg, Chi	40
1918	Gavvy Cravath, Phi.	8		& Hank Sauer, Chi	37	1991	Howard Johnson, NY.	38
1919	Gavvy Cravath, Phi.	12	1953	Eddie Mathews, Mil	47	1992	Fred McGriff, SD	35
1920	Cy Williams, Phi.	15	1954	Ted Kluszewski, Cin	49	1993	Barry Bonds, SF.	46
1921	George Kelly, NY	23	1955	Willie Mays, NY.	51	1994	Matt Williams, SF.	43
1922	Rogers Hornsby, St.L.	42	1956	Duke Snider, Bklyn	43	1995	Dante Bichette, Col.	40
1923	Cy Williams, Phi.	41	1957	Hank Aaron, Mil.	44	1996	Andres Galarraga, Col	47
1924	Jack Fournier, Bklyn	27	1958	Ernie Banks, Chi.	47	1997	Larry Walker, Col	49
1925	Rogers Hornsby, St.L.	39	1959	Eddie Mathews, Mil	46	1998	Mark McGwire, St.L.	70
1926	Hack Wilson, Chi.	21	1960	Ernie Banks, Chi.	41	1999	Mark McGwire, St.L.	65
1927	Cy Williams, Phi.	30	1961	Orlando Cepeda, SF.	46	2000	Sammy Sosa, Chi.	50
	& Hack Wilson, Chi	30	1962	Willie Mays, SF	49	2001	Barry Bonds, SF.	73
1928	Jim Bottomley, St.L.	31	1963	Hank Aaron, Mil.	44	2002	Sammy Sosa, Chi.	49
	& Hack Wilson, Chi	31		& Willie McCovey, SF.	44	2003	Jim Thome, Phi	47
1929	Chuck Klein, Phi	43	1964	Willie Mays, SF.	47	2004	Adrian Beltre, LA	48
1930	Hack Wilson, Chi.	56	1965	Willie Mays, SF	52	2005	Andruw Jones, Atl.	51
1931	Chuck Klein, Phi	31	1966	Hank Aaron, Atl.	44	2006	Ryan Howard, Phi.	58
1932	Chuck Klein, Phi.	38	1967	Hank Aaron, Atl	39	2007	Prince Fielder, Mil.	50
	& Mel Ott, NY.	38	1968	Willie McCovey, SF	36	2008	Ryan Howard, Phi.	48
1933	Chuck Klein, Phi	28	1969	Willie McCovey, SF	45			
1934	Rip Collins, St.L	35	1970	Johnny Bench, Cin	45			
	& Mel Ott, NY.	35						

Note: In 1997 Mark McGwire hit 58 home runs — 34 in the AL, 24 in the NL.

American League

Multiple winners: Babe Ruth (12); Harmon Killebrew (6); Alex Rodriguez (5); Home Run Baker, Harry Davis, Jimmie Foxx, Hank Greenberg, Ken Griffey Jr., Reggie Jackson, Mickey Mantle and Ted Williams (4); Lou Gehrig and Jim Rice (3); Dick Allen, Tony Armas, Jose Canseco, Joe DiMaggio, Larry Doby, Cecil Fielder, Juan Gonzalez, Mark McGwire, Wally Pipp, Al Rosen and Gorman Thomas (2).

Year		HR	Year		HR	Year		HR
1901	Nap Lajoie, Phi	14	1905	Harry Davis, Phi.	8	1909	Ty Cobb, Det	9
1902	Socks Seybold, Phi	16	1906	Harry Davis, Phi.	12	1910	Jake Stahl, Bos.	10
1903	Buck Freeman, Bos	13	1907	Harry Davis, Phi.	8	1911	Home Run Baker, Phi.	11
1904	Harry Davis, Phi.	10	1908	Sam Crawford, Det.	7			

Year	HR	Year	HR	Year	HR
1912	Home Run Baker, Phi 10	1945	Vern Stephens, St.L 24	1979	Gorman Thomas, Mil 45
	& Tris Speaker, Bos. 10	1946	Hank Greenberg, Det.... 44	1980	Reggie Jackson, NY 41
1913	Home Run Baker, Phi.... 12	1947	Ted Williams, Bos 32		& Ben Oglivie, Mil 41
1914	Home Run Baker, Phi...... 9	1948	Joe DiMaggio, NY 39	1981	Tony Armas, Oak 22
1915	Braggo Roth, Chi-Cle 7	1949	Ted Williams, Bos 43		Dwight Evans, Bos 22
1916	Wally Pipp, NY..........12	1950	Al Rosen, Cle. 37		Bobby Grich, Cal 22
1917	Wally Pipp, NY......... 9	1951	Gus Zernial, Chi-Phi 33		& Eddie Murray, Bal. ... 22
1918	Babe Ruth, Bos 11	1952	Larry Doby, Cle.........32	1982	Reggie Jackson, Cal..... 39
	& Tilly Walker, Phi 11	1953	Al Rosen, Cle. 43		& Gorman Thomas, Mil... 39
1919	Babe Ruth, Bos......29	1954	Larry Doby, Cle.........32	1983	Jim Rice, Bos 39
1920	Babe Ruth, NY 54	1955	Mickey Mantle, NY...... 37	1984	Tony Armas, Bos......... 43
1921	Babe Ruth, NY 59	1956	Mickey Mantle, NY......52	1985	Darrell Evans, Det...... 40
1922	Ken Williams, St.L. ... 39	1957	Roy Sievers, Wash......42	1986	Jesse Barfield, Tor...... 40
1923	Babe Ruth, NY 41	1958	Mickey Mantle, NY......42	1987	Mark McGwire, Oak 49
1924	Babe Ruth, NY 46	1959	Rocky Colavito, Cle 42	1988	Jose Canseco, Oak...... 42
1925	Bob Meusel, NY 33		& Harmon Killebrew, Wash .42	1989	Fred McGriff, Tor 36
1926	Babe Ruth, NY 47	1960	Mickey Mantle, NY......40	1990	Cecil Fielder, Det 51
1927	Babe Ruth, NY 60	1961	Roger Maris, NY.......61	1991	Jose Canseco, Oak 44
1928	Babe Ruth, NY 54	1962	Harmon Killebrew, Min ...48		& Cecil Fielder, Det..... 44
1929	Babe Ruth, NY 46	1963	Harmon Killebrew, Min... 45	1992	Juan Gonzalez, Tex..... 43
1930	Babe Ruth, NY 49	1964	Harmon Killebrew, Min... 49	1993	Juan Gonzalez, Tex..... 46
1931	Lou Gehrig, NY.......46	1965	Tony Conigliaro, Bos.... 32	1994	Ken Griffey Jr., Sea..... 40
	& Babe Ruth, NY 46	1966	Frank Robinson, Bal 49	1995	Albert Belle, Cle 50
1932	Jimmie Foxx, Phi.......58	1967	Harmon Killebrew, Min... 44	1996	Mark McGwire, Oak 52
1933	Jimmie Foxx, Phi.......48		& Carl Yastrzemski, Bos... 44	1997	Ken Griffey Jr., Sea..... 56
1934	Lou Gehrig, NY.......49	1968	Frank Howard, Wash..... 44	1998	Ken Griffey Jr., Sea..... 56
1935	Jimmie Foxx, Phi.......36	1969	Harmon Killebrew, Min... 49	1999	Ken Griffey Jr., Sea..... 48
	& Hank Greenberg, Det... 36	1970	Frank Howard, Wash..... 44	2000	Troy Glaus, Ana....... 47
1936	Lou Gehrig, NY.......49	1971	Bill Melton, Chi 33	2001	Alex Rodriguez, Tex 52
1937	Joe DiMaggio, NY 46	1972	Dick Allen, Chi.........37	2002	Alex Rodriguez, Tex 57
1938	Hank Greenberg, Det.... 58	1973	Reggie Jackson, Oak ... 32	2003	Alex Rodriguez, Tex 47
1939	Jimmie Foxx, Bos.......35	1974	Dick Allen, Chi.........32	2004	Manny Ramirez, Bos.... 43
1940	Hank Greenberg, Det.... 41	1975	Reggie Jackson, Oak ... 36	2005	Alex Rodriguez, NY 48
1941	Ted Williams, Bos 37		& George Scott, Mil ... 36	2006	David Ortiz, Bos....... 54
1942	Ted Williams, Bos 36	1976	Graig Nettles, NY 32	2007	Alex Rodriguez, NY 54
1943	Rudy York, Det.........34	1977	Jim Rice, Bos 39	2008	Miguel Cabrera, Det..... 37
1944	Nick Etten, NY 22	1978	Jim Rice, Bos 46		

Runs Batted In
National League

Multiple winners: Hank Aaron, Rogers Hornsby, Sherry Magee, Mike Schmidt and Honus Wagner (4); Johnny Bench, George Foster, Joe Medwick, Johnny Mize and Heinie Zimmerman (3); Ernie Banks, Jim Bottomley, Orlando Cepeda, Gavvy Cravath, Andres Galarraga, Ryan Howard, George Kelly, Chuck Klein, Willie McCovey, Dale Murphy, Stan Musial, Bill Nicholson, Sammy Sosa and Hack Wilson (2).

Year	RBI	Year	RBI	Year	RBI
1900	Elmer Flick, Phi 110	1926	Jim Bottomley, St.L. 120	1954	Ted Kluszewski, Cin 141
1901	Honus Wagner, Pit 126	1927	Paul Waner, Pit.......131	1955	Duke Snider, Bklyn 136
1902	Honus Wagner, Pit 91	1928	Jim Bottomley, St.L. 136	1956	Stan Musial, St.L. 109
1903	Sam Mertes, NY 104	1929	Hack Wilson, Chi....... 159	1957	Hank Aaron, Mil 132
1904	Bill Dahlen, NY 80	1930	Hack Wilson, Chi....... 191	1958	Ernie Banks, Chi....... 129
1905	Cy Seymour, Cin 121	1931	Chuck Klein, Phi....... 121	1959	Ernie Banks, Chi....... 143
1906	Jim Nealon, Pit........ 83	1932	Don Hurst, Phi......... 143	1960	Hank Aaron, Mil 126
	& Harry Steinfeldt, Chi... 83	1933	Chuck Klein, Phi....... 120	1961	Orlando Cepeda, SF.... 142
1907	Sherry Magee, Phi 85	1934	Mel Ott, NY.......... 135	1962	Tommy Davis, LA 153
1908	Honus Wagner, Pit 109	1935	Wally Berger, Bos...... 130	1963	Hank Aaron, Mil 130
1909	Honus Wagner, Pit 100	1936	Joe Medwick, St.L. 138	1964	Ken Boyer, St.L....... 119
1910	Sherry Magee, Phi 123	1937	Joe Medwick, St.L. 154	1965	Deron Johnson, Cin..... 130
1911	Wildfire Schulte, Chi.... 121	1938	Joe Medwick, St.L. 122	1966	Hank Aaron, Atl....... 127
1912	Heinie Zimmerman, Chi. . 103	1939	Frank McCormick, Cin ... 128	1967	Orlando Cepeda, St.L. .. 111
1913	Gavvy Cravath, Phi..... 128	1940	Johnny Mize, St.L. 137	1968	Willie McCovey, SF 105
1914	Sherry Magee, Phi 103	1941	Dolph Camilli, Bklyn 120	1969	Willie McCovey, SF 126
1915	Gavvy Cravath, Phi..... 115	1942	Johnny Mize, NY 110	1970	Johnny Bench, Cin 148
1916	Heinie Zimmerman, Chi-NY .83	1943	Bill Nicholson, Chi 128	1971	Joe Torre, St.L......... 137
1917	Heinie Zimmerman, NY.. 102	1944	Bill Nicholson, Chi 122	1972	Johnny Bench, Cin 125
1918	Sherry Magee, Cin...... 76	1945	Dixie Walker, Bklyn..... 124	1973	Willie Stargell, Pit...... 119
1919	Hy Myers, Bklyn........ 73	1946	Enos Slaughter, St.L. 130	1974	Johnny Bench, Cin 129
1920	Rogers Hornsby, St.L 94	1947	Johnny Mize, NY 138	1975	Greg Luzinski, Phi...... 120
	& George Kelly, NY 94	1948	Stan Musial, St.L. 131	1976	George Foster, Cin. 121
1921	Rogers Hornsby, St.L.... 126	1949	Ralph Kiner, Pit........ 127	1977	George Foster, Cin. 149
1922	Rogers Hornsby, St.L.... 152	1950	Del Ennis, Phi......... 126	1978	George Foster, Cin. 120
1923	Irish Meusel, NY 125	1951	Monte Irvin, NY 121	1979	Dave Winfield, SD 118
1924	George Kelly, NY...... 136	1952	Hank Sauer, Chi....... 121	1980	Mike Schmidt, Phi. 121
1925	Rogers Hornsby, St.L 143	1953	Roy Campanella, Bklyn .. 142	1981	Mike Schmidt, Phi. 91

Runs Batted In (Cont.)

Year		RBI
1982	Dale Murphy, Atl	109
	& Al Oliver, Mon	109
1983	Dale Murphy, Atl	121
1984	Gary Carter, Mon	106
	& Mike Schmidt, Phi.	106
1985	Dave Parker, Cin	125
1986	Mike Schmidt, Phi.	119
1987	Andre Dawson, Chi	137
1988	Will Clark, SF	109
1989	Kevin Mitchell, SF.	125

Year		RBI
1990	Matt Williams, SF.	122
1991	Howard Johnson, NY	117
1992	Darren Daulton, Phi.	109
1993	Barry Bonds, SF	123
1994	Jeff Bagwell, Hou	116
1995	Dante Bichette, Col	128
1996	Andres Galarraga, Col	150
1997	Andres Galarraga, Col	140
1998	Sammy Sosa, Chi.	158
1999	Mark McGwire, St.L.	147

Year		RBI
2000	Todd Helton, Col	147
2001	Sammy Sosa, Chi.	160
2002	Lance Berkman, Hou	128
2003	Preston Wilson, Col	141
2004	Vinny Castilla, Col	131
2005	Andruw Jones, Atl.	128
2006	Ryan Howard, Phi	149
2007	Matt Holliday, Col.	137
2008	Ryan Howard, Phi.	146

Multiple winners: Babe Ruth (6); Lou Gehrig (5); Ty Cobb, Hank Greenberg and Ted Williams (4); Albert Belle, Sam Crawford, Cecil Fielder, Jimmie Foxx, Jackie Jensen, Harmon Killebrew, Vern Stephens and Bobby Veach (3); Home Run Baker, Cecil Cooper, Harry Davis, Joe DiMaggio, Buck Freeman, Nap Lajoie, Roger Maris, David Ortiz, Jim Rice, Alex Rodriguez, Al Rosen and Bobby Veach (2).

American League

Year		RBI
1901	Nap Lajoie, Phi.	125
1902	Buck Freeman, Bos.	121
1903	Buck Freeman, Bos.	104
1904	Nap Lajoie, Cle	102
1905	Harry Davis, Phi	83
1906	Harry Davis, Phi	96
1907	Ty Cobb, Det.	116
1908	Ty Cobb, Det.	108
1909	Ty Cobb, Det.	107
1910	Sam Crawford, Det.	120
1911	Ty Cobb, Det.	144
1912	Home Run Baker, Phi.	133
1913	Home Run Baker, Phi.	126
1914	Sam Crawford, Det.	104
1915	Sam Crawford, Det.	112
	& Bobby Veach, Det	112
1916	Del Pratt, St.L.	103
1917	Bobby Veach, Det.	103
1918	Bobby Veach, Det.	78
1919	Babe Ruth, Bos.	114
1920	Babe Ruth, NY	137
1921	Babe Ruth, NY	171
1922	Ken Williams, St.L.	155
1923	Babe Ruth, NY	131
1924	Goose Goslin, Wash.	129
1925	Bob Meusel, NY.	138
1926	Babe Ruth, NY	145
1927	Lou Gehrig, NY	175
1928	Lou Gehrig, NY	142
	& Babe Ruth, NY	142
1929	Al Simmons, Phi	157
1930	Lou Gehrig, NY	174
1931	Lou Gehrig, NY	184
1932	Jimmie Foxx, Phi.	169
1933	Jimmie Foxx, Phi.	163
1934	Lou Gehrig, NY	165
1935	Hank Greenberg, Det	170
1936	Hal Trosky, Cle.	162
1937	Hank Greenberg, Det	183

Year		RBI
1938	Jimmie Foxx, Bos	175
1939	Ted Williams, Bos.	145
1940	Hank Greenberg, Det	150
1941	Joe DiMaggio, NY.	125
1942	Ted Williams, Bos.	137
1943	Rudy York, Det	118
1944	Vern Stephens, St.L.	109
1945	Nick Etten, NY	111
1946	Hank Greenberg, Det	127
1947	Ted Williams, Bos.	114
1948	Joe DiMaggio, NY.	155
1949	Ted Williams, Bos.	159
	& Vern Stephens, Bos.	159
1950	Walt Dropo, Bos.	144
	& Vern Stephens, Bos.	144
1951	Gus Zernial, Chi-Phi.	129
1952	Al Rosen, Cle	105
1953	Al Rosen, Cle	145
1954	Larry Doby, Cle.	126
1955	Ray Boone, Det.	116
	& Jackie Jensen, Bos	116
1956	Mickey Mantle, NY.	130
1957	Roy Sievers, Wash	114
1958	Jackie Jensen, Bos.	122
1959	Jackie Jensen, Bos.	112
1960	Roger Maris, NY	112
1961	Roger Maris, NY	142
1962	Harmon Killebrew, Min	126
1963	Dick Stuart, Bos	118
1964	Brooks Robinson, Bal	118
1965	Rocky Colavito, Cle	108
1966	Frank Robinson, Bal	122
1967	Carl Yastrzemski, Bos	121
1968	Ken Harrelson, Bos	109
1969	Harmon Killebrew, Min	140
1970	Frank Howard, Wash	126
1971	Harmon Killebrew, Min	119
1972	Dick Allen, Chi	113
1973	Reggie Jackson, Oak.	117

Year		RBI
1974	Jeff Burroughs, Tex	118
1975	George Scott, Mil.	109
1976	Lee May, Bal	109
1977	Larry Hisle, Min	119
1978	Jim Rice, Bos	139
1979	Don Baylor, Cal	139
1980	Cecil Cooper, Mil.	122
1981	Eddie Murray, Bal.	78
1982	Hal McRae, KC.	133
1983	Cecil Cooper, Mil.	126
	& Jim Rice, Bos.	126
1984	Tony Armas, Bos.	123
1985	Don Mattingly, NY	145
1986	Joe Carter, Cle	121
1987	George Bell, Tor	134
1988	Jose Canseco, Oak.	124
1989	Ruben Sierra, Tex	119
1990	Cecil Fielder, Det	132
1991	Cecil Fielder, Det	133
1992	Cecil Fielder, Det	124
1993	Albert Belle, Cle	129
1994	Kirby Puckett, Min.	112
1995	Albert Belle, Cle	126
	& Mo Vaughn, Bos.	126
1996	Albert Belle, Cle	148
1997	Ken Griffey Jr., Sea.	147
1998	Juan Gonzalez, Tex.	157
1999	Manny Ramirez, Cle	165
2000	Edgar Martinez, Sea.	145
2001	Bret Boone, Sea	141
2002	Alex Rodriguez, Tex.	142
2003	Carlos Delgado, Tor	145
2004	Miguel Tejada, Bal	150
2005	David Ortiz, Bos.	148
2006	David Ortiz, Bos.	137
2007	Alex Rodriguez, NY	156
2008	Josh Hamilton, Tex.	130

Batting Triple Crown Winners

Players who led either league in Batting Average, Home Runs and Runs Batted In over a single season.

National League

	Year	Avg	HR	RBI
Paul Hines, Providence	1878	.358	4	50
Hugh Duffy, Boston	1894	.438	18	145
Heinie Zimmerman, Chicago	1912	.372	14	103
Rogers Hornsby, St. Louis	1922	.401	42	152
Rogers Hornsby, St. Louis	1925	.403	39	143
Chuck Klein, Philadelphia	1933	.368	28	120
Joe Medwick, St. Louis	1937	.374	31*	154

*Tied for league lead in HRs with Mel Ott, NY.

American League

	Year	Avg	HR	RBI
Nap Lajoie, Philadelphia	1901	.422	14	125
Ty Cobb, Detroit	1909	.377	9	115
Jimmie Foxx, Philadelphia	1933	.356	48	163
Lou Gehrig, New York	1934	.363	49	165
Ted Williams, Boston	1942	.356	36	137
Ted Williams, Boston	1947	.343	32	114
Mickey Mantle, New York	1956	.353	52	130
Frank Robinson, Baltimore	1966	.316	49	122
Carl Yastrzemski, Boston	1967	.326	44*	121

*Tied for league lead in HRs with Harmon Killebrew, Min.

Stolen Bases
National League

Multiple winners: Max Carey (10); Lou Brock (8); Vince Coleman and Maury Wills (6); Honus Wagner (5); Bob Bescher, Kiki Cuyler, Willie Mays and Tim Raines (4); Bill Bruton, Frankie Frisch, Pepper Martin, Jose Reyes and Tony Womack (3); George Burns, Luis Castillo, Frank Chance, Augie Galan, Marquis Grissom, Stan Hack, Sam Jethroe, Davey Lopes, Omar Moreno, Pete Reiser and Jackie Robinson (2).

Year		SB	Year		SB	Year		SB
1900	Patsy Donovan, St.L	45	1935	Augie Galan, Chi	22	1972	Lou Brock, St.L	63
	& George Van Haltren, NY.	45	1936	Pepper Martin, St.L	23	1973	Lou Brock, St.L	70
1901	Honus Wagner, Pit	49	1937	Augie Galan, Chi	23	1974	Lou Brock, St.L	118
1902	Honus Wagner, Pit	42	1938	Stan Hack, Chi	16	1975	Davey Lopes, LA	77
1903	Frank Chance, Chi	67	1939	Stan Hack, Chi	17	1976	Davey Lopes, LA	63
	& Jimmy Sheckard, Bklyn.	67		& Lee Handley, Pit	17	1977	Frank Taveras, Pit	70
1904	Honus Wagner, Pit	53	1940	Lonny Frey, Cin	22	1978	Omar Moreno, Pit	71
1905	Art Devlin, NY	59	1941	Danny Murtaugh, Phi	18	1979	Omar Moreno, Pit	77
	& Billy Maloney, Chi	59	1942	Pete Reiser, Bklyn	20	1980	Ron LeFlore, Mon	97
1906	Frank Chance, Chi	57	1943	Arky Vaughan, Bklyn	20	1981	Tim Raines, Mon	71
1907	Honus Wagner, Pit	61	1944	Johnny Barrett, Pit	28	1982	Tim Raines, Mon	78
1908	Honus Wagner, Pit	53	1945	Red Schoendienst, St.L	26	1983	Tim Raines, Mon	90
1909	Bob Bescher, Cin	54	1946	Pete Reiser, Bklyn	34	1984	Tim Raines, Mon	75
1910	Bob Bescher, Cin	70	1947	Jackie Robinson, Bklyn	29	1985	Vince Coleman, St.L	110
1911	Bob Bescher, Cin	81	1948	Richie Ashburn, Phi	32	1986	Vince Coleman, St.L	107
1912	Bob Bescher, Cin	67	1949	Jackie Robinson, Bklyn	37	1987	Vince Coleman, St.L	109
1913	Max Carey, Pit	61	1950	Sam Jethroe, Bos	35	1988	Vince Coleman, St.L	81
1914	George Burns, NY	62	1951	Sam Jethroe, Bos	35	1989	Vince Coleman, St.L	65
1915	Max Carey, Pit	36	1952	Pee Wee Reese, Bklyn	30	1990	Vince Coleman, St.L	77
1916	Max Carey, Pit	63	1953	Bill Bruton, Mil	26	1991	Marquis Grissom, Mon	76
1917	Max Carey, Pit	46	1954	Bill Bruton, Mil	34	1992	Marquis Grissom, Mon	78
1918	Max Carey, Pit	58	1955	Bill Bruton, Mil	25	1993	Chuck Carr, Fla	58
1919	George Burns, NY	40	1956	Willie Mays, NY	40	1994	Craig Biggio, Hou	39
1920	Max Carey, Pit	52	1957	Willie Mays, NY	38	1995	Quilvio Veras, Fla	56
1921	Frankie Frisch, NY	49	1958	Willie Mays, SF	31	1996	Eric Young, Col	53
1922	Max Carey, Pit	51	1959	Willie Mays, SF	27	1997	Tony Womack, Pit	60
1923	Max Carey, Pit	51	1960	Maury Wills, LA	50	1998	Tony Womack, Pit	58
1924	Max Carey, Pit	49	1961	Maury Wills, LA	35	1999	Tony Womack, Ari	72
1925	Max Carey, Pit	46	1962	Maury Wills, LA	104	2000	Luis Castillo, Fla	62
1926	Kiki Cuyler, Pit	35	1963	Maury Wills, LA	40	2001	Juan Pierre, Col	46
1927	Frankie Frisch, St.L	48	1964	Maury Wills, LA	53		& Jimmy Rollins, Phi	46
1928	Kiki Cuyler, Chi	37	1965	Maury Wills, LA	94	2002	Luis Castillo, Fla	48
1929	Kiki Cuyler, Chi	43	1966	Lou Brock, St.L	74	2003	Juan Pierre, Fla	65
1930	Kiki Cuyler, Chi	37	1967	Lou Brock, St.L	52	2004	Scott Podsednik, Mil	70
1931	Frankie Frisch, St.L	28	1968	Lou Brock, St.L	62	2005	Jose Reyes, NY	60
1932	Chuck Klein, Phi	20	1969	Lou Brock, St.L	53	2006	Jose Reyes, NY	64
1933	Pepper Martin, St.L	26	1970	Bobby Tolan, Cin	57	2007	Jose Reyes, NY	78
1934	Pepper Martin, St.L	23	1971	Lou Brock, St.L	64	2008	Willy Taveras, Col	68

30 Homers & 30 Stolen Bases in One Season

National League	Year	Gm	HR	SB		Year	Gm	HR	SB
Willie Mays, NY Giants	1956	152	36	40	Raul Mondesi, Los Angeles	1999	159	33	36
Willie Mays, NY Giants	1957	152	35	38	Preston Wilson, Florida	2000	161	31	36
Hank Aaron, Milwaukee	1963	161	44	31	Vladimir Guerrero, Montreal	2001	159	34	37
Bobby Bonds, San Francisco	1969	158	32	45	Bobby Abreu, Philadelphia	2001	162	31	36
Bobby Bonds, San Francisco	1973	160	39	43	Vladimir Guerrero, Montreal	2002	161	39	40
Dale Murphy, Atlanta	1983	162	36	30	Bobby Abreu, Philadelphia	2004	159	30	40
Eric Davis, Cincinnati	1987	129	37	50	Alfonso Soriano, Washington	2006	159	46	41
Howard Johnson, NY Mets	1987	157	36	32	Brandon Phillips, Cincinnati	2007	158	30	32
Darryl Strawberry, NY Mets	1987	154	39	36	David Wright, NY Mets	2007	160	30	34
Howard Johnson, NY Mets	1989	153	36	41	Jimmy Rollins, Philadelphia	2007	162	30	41
Ron Gant, Atlanta	1990	152	32	33	Hanley Ramirez, Florida	2008	153	33	35
Barry Bonds, Pittsburgh	1990	151	33	52	**American League**	**Year**	**Gm**	**HR**	**SB**
Ron Gant, Atlanta	1991	154	32	34	Kenny Williams, St. Louis	1922	153	39	37
Howard Johnson, NY Mets	1991	156	38	30	Tommy Harper, Milwaukee	1970	154	31	38
Barry Bonds, Pittsburgh	1992	140	34	39	Bobby Bonds, New York	1975	145	32	30
Sammy Sosa, Chicago	1993	159	33	36	Bobby Bonds, California	1977	158	37	41
Barry Bonds, San Francisco	1995	144	33	31	Bobby Bonds, Chicago-Texas	1978	156	31	43
Sammy Sosa, Chicago	1995	144	36	34	Joe Carter, Cleveland	1987	149	32	31
Barry Bonds, San Francisco	1996	158	42	40	Jose Canseco, Oakland	1988	158	42	40
Ellis Burks, Colorado	1996	156	40	32	Alex Rodriguez, Seattle	1998	161	42	46
Dante Bichette, Colorado	1996	159	31	31	Shawn Green, Toronto	1998	158	35	35
Barry Larkin, Cincinnati	1996	152	33	36	Jose Cruz Jr., Toronto	2001	146	34	32
Larry Walker, Colorado	1997	153	49	33	Alfonso Soriano, New York	2002	156	39	41
Barry Bonds, San Francisco	1997	159	40	37	Alfonso Soriano, New York	2003	156	38	35
Raul Mondesi, Los Angeles	1997	159	30	32	Alfonso Soriano, Texas	2005	156	36	30
Jeff Bagwell, Houston	1997	162	43	31	Grady Sizemore, Cleveland	2008	157	33	38
Jeff Bagwell, Houston	1999	162	42	30					

Note: In 2004, Carlos Beltran switched leagues mid-season. Combining his AL and NL totals, he hit 38 HR and stole 42 bases.

Stolen Bases (Cont.)
American League

Multiple winners: Rickey Henderson (12); Luis Aparicio (9); Bert Campaneris, George Case and Ty Cobb (6); Kenny Lofton (5); Ben Chapman, Eddie Collins, Carl Crawford and George Sisler (4); Bob Dillinger, Minnie Minoso and Bill Werber (3); Elmer Flick, Tommy Harper, Brian Hunter, Clyde Milan, Johnny Mostil, Bill North and Snuffy Stirnweiss (2).

Year		SB	Year		SB	Year		SB
1901	Frank Isbell, Chi	52	1937	Ben Chapman, Wash-Bos	35	1973	Tommy Harper, Bos	54
1902	Topsy Hartsel, Phi	47		& Bill Werber, Phi	35	1974	Bill North, Oak	54
1903	Harry Bay, Cle	45	1938	Frank Crosetti, NY	27	1975	Mickey Rivers, CA	70
1904	Elmer Flick, Cle	42	1939	George Case, Wash	51	1976	Bill North, Oak	75
1905	Danny Hoffman, Phi	46	1940	George Case, Wash	35	1977	Freddie Patek, KC	53
1906	John Anderson, Wash	39	1941	George Case, Wash	33	1978	Ron LeFlore, Det	68
	& Elmer Flick, Cle	39	1942	George Case, Wash	44	1979	Willie Wilson, KC	83
1907	Ty Cobb, Det	49	1943	George Case, Wash	61	1980	Rickey Henderson, Oak	100
1908	Patsy Dougherty, Chi	47	1944	Snuffy Stirnweiss, NY	55	1981	Rickey Henderson, Oak	56
1909	Ty Cobb, Det	76	1945	Snuffy Stirnweiss, NY	33	1982	Rickey Henderson, Oak	130
1910	Eddie Collins, Phi	81	1946	George Case, Cle	28	1983	Rickey Henderson, Oak	108
1911	Ty Cobb, Det	83	1947	Bob Dillinger, St.L	34	1984	Rickey Henderson, Oak	66
1912	Clyde Milan, Wash	88	1948	Bob Dillinger, St.L	28	1985	Rickey Henderson, NY	80
1913	Clyde Milan, Wash	75	1949	Bob Dillinger, St.L	20	1986	Rickey Henderson, NY	87
1914	Fritz Maisel, NY	74	1950	Dom DiMaggio, Bos	15	1987	Harold Reynolds, Sea	60
1915	Ty Cobb, Det	96	1951	Minnie Minoso, Cle-Chi	31	1988	Rickey Henderson, NY	93
1916	Ty Cobb, Det	68	1952	Minnie Minoso, Chi	22	1989	R. Henderson, NY-Oak	77
1917	Ty Cobb, Det	55	1953	Minnie Minoso, Chi	25	1990	Rickey Henderson, Oak	65
1918	George Sisler, St.L	45	1954	Jackie Jensen, Bos	22	1991	Rickey Henderson, Oak	58
1919	Eddie Collins, Chi	33	1955	Jim Rivera, Chi	25	1992	Kenny Lofton, Cle	66
1920	Sam Rice, Wash	63	1956	Luis Aparicio, Chi	21	1993	Kenny Lofton, Cle	70
1921	George Sisler, St.L	35	1957	Luis Aparicio, Chi	28	1994	Kenny Lofton, Cle	60
1922	George Sisler, St.L	51	1958	Luis Aparicio, Chi	29	1995	Kenny Lofton, Cle	54
1923	Eddie Collins, Chi	47	1959	Luis Aparicio, Chi	56	1996	Kenny Lofton, Cle	75
1924	Eddie Collins, Chi	42	1960	Luis Aparicio, Chi	51	1997	Brian Hunter, Det	74
1925	Johnny Mostil, Chi	43	1961	Luis Aparicio, Chi	53	1998	Rickey Henderson, Oak	66
1926	Johnny Mostil, Chi	35	1962	Luis Aparicio, Chi	31	1999	Brian Hunter, Det-Sea	44
1927	George Sisler, St.L	27	1963	Luis Aparicio, Bal	40	2000	Johnny Damon, KC	46
1928	Buddy Myer, Bos	30	1964	Luis Aparicio, Bal	57	2001	Ichiro Suzuki, Sea	56
1929	Charlie Gehringer, Det	28	1965	Bert Campaneris, KC	51	2002	Alfonso Soriano, NY	41
1930	Marty McManus, Det	23	1966	Bert Campaneris, KC	52	2003	Carl Crawford, TB	55
1931	Ben Chapman, NY	61	1967	Bert Campaneris, KC	55	2004	Carl Crawford, TB	59
1932	Ben Chapman, NY	38	1968	Bert Campaneris, Oak	62	2005	Chone Figgins, LAA	62
1933	Ben Chapman, NY	27	1969	Tommy Harper, Sea	73	2006	Carl Crawford, TB	58
1934	Bill Werber, Bos	40	1970	Bert Campaneris, Oak	42	2007	Carl Crawford, TB	50
1935	Bill Werber, Bos	29	1971	Amos Otis, KC	52		& Brian Roberts, Bal	50
1936	Lyn Lary, St.L	37	1972	Bert Campaneris, Oak	52	2008	Jacoby Ellsbury, Bos	50

Consecutive Game Streaks
(Regular season games through 2008)

Games Played

Gm		Dates of Streak
2632	Cal Ripken Jr., Bal	5/30/82 to 9/19/98
2130	Lou Gehrig, NY	6/1/25 to 4/30/39
1307	Everett Scott, Bos-NY	6/20/16 to 5/5/25
1207	Steve Garvey, LA-SD	9/3/75 to 7/29/83
1152	Miguel Tejada, Oak-Bal	6/1/00 to 6/21/07
1117	Billy Williams, Cubs	9/22/63 to 9/2/70
1103	Joe Sewell, Cle	9/13/22 to 4/30/30
895	Stan Musial, St.L	4/15/52 to 8/23/57
829	Eddie Yost, Wash	4/30/49 to 5/11/55
822	Gus Suhr, Pit	9/11/31 to 6/4/37
798	Nellie Fox, Chisox	8/8/55 to 9/3/60
745	Pete Rose, Cin-Phi	9/2/78 to 8/23/83
740	Dale Murphy, Atl	9/26/81 to 7/8/86
730	Richie Ashburn, Phi	6/7/50 to 4/13/55
717	Ernie Banks, Cubs	8/28/56 to 6/22/61
678	Pete Rose, Cin	9/28/73 to 5/7/78

Hitting

	Gm	Year
Joe DiMaggio, New York (AL)	56	1941
Willie Keeler, Baltimore (NL)	44	1897
Pete Rose, Cincinnati (NL)	44	1978
Bill Dahlen, Chicago (NL)	42	1894
George Sisler, St. Louis (AL)	41	1922
Ty Cobb, Detroit (AL)	40	1911
Paul Molitor, Milwaukee (AL)	39	1987
Jimmy Rollins, Philadelphia (NL)	38	2005-06
Tommy Holmes, Boston (NL)	37	1945
Billy Hamilton, Philadelphia (NL)	36	1894
Fred Clarke, Louisville (NL)	35	1895
Ty Cobb, Detroit (AL)	35	1917
Luis Castillo, Florida (NL)	35	2002
Chase Utley, Philadelphia (NL)	35	2006
Ty Cobb, Detroit (AL)	34	1912
George Sisler, St. Louis (AL)	34	1925
George McQuinn, St. Louis (AL)	34	1938
Dom DiMaggio, Boston (AL)	34	1949
Benito Santiago, San Diego (NL)	34	1987

Note: Rollins had a 36-game streak at the end of 2005.

Annual Pitching Leaders (since 1900)

Winning Percentage

At least 15 wins, except in strike years of 1981 and 1994 (when the minimum was 10).

National League

Multiple winners: Ed Reulbach and Tom Seaver (3); Larry Benton, Harry Brecheen, Jack Chesbro, Paul Derringer, Freddie Fitzsimmons, Don Gullett, Claude Hendrix, Carl Hubbell, Randy Johnson, Sandy Koufax, Bill Lee, Greg Maddux, Christy Mathewson, Don Newcombe, Preacher Roe and John Smoltz (2).

Year		W-L	Pct	Year		W-L	Pct
1900	Jesse Tannehill, Pittsburgh	.20-6	.769	1956	Don Newcombe, Brooklyn	.27-7	.794
1901	Jack Chesbro, Pittsburgh	.21-10	.677	1957	Bob Buhl, Milwaukee	.18-7	.720
1902	Jack Chesbro, Pittsburgh	.28-6	.824	1958	Warren Spahn, Milwaukee	.22-11	.667
1903	Sam Leever, Pittsburgh	.25-7	.781		& Lew Burdette, Milwaukee	.20-10	.667
1904	Joe McGinnity, New York	.35-8	.814	1959	Roy Face, Pittsburgh	.18-1	.947
1905	Christy Mathewson, New York	.31-8	.795	1960	Ernie Broglio, St. Louis	.21-9	.700
1906	Ed Reulbach, Chicago	.19-4	.826	1961	Johnny Podres, Los Angeles	.18-5	.783
1907	Ed Reulbach, Chicago	.17-4	.810	1962	Bob Purkey, Cincinnati	.23-5	.821
1908	Ed Reulbach, Chicago	.24-7	.774	1963	Ron Perranoski, Los Angeles	.16-3	.842
1909	Howie Camnitz, Pittsburgh	.25-6	.806	1964	Sandy Koufax, Los Angeles	.19-5	.792
	& Christy Mathewson, New York	.25-6	.806	1965	Sandy Koufax, Los Angeles	.26-8	.765
1910	King Cole, Chicago	.20-4	.833	1966	Juan Marichal, San Francisco	.25-6	.806
1911	Rube Marquard, New York	.24-7	.774	1967	Dick Hughes, St. Louis	.16-6	.727
1912	Claude Hendrix, Pittsburgh	.24-9	.727	1968	Steve Blass, Pittsburgh	.18-6	.750
1913	Bert Humphries, Chicago	.16-4	.800	1969	Tom Seaver, New York	.25-7	.781
1914	Bill James, Boston	.26-7	.788	1970	Bob Gibson, St. Louis	.23-7	.767
1915	Grover Alexander, Phila.	.31-10	.756	1971	Don Gullett, Cincinnati	.16-6	.727
1916	Tom Hughes, Boston	.16-3	.842	1972	Gary Nolan, Cincinnati	.15-5	.750
1917	Ferdie Schupp, New York	.21-7	.750	1973	Tommy John, Los Angeles	.16-7	.696
1918	Claude Hendrix, Chicago	.19-7	.731	1974	Andy Messersmith, Los Angeles	.20-6	.769
1919	Dutch Ruether, Cincinnati	.19-6	.760	1975	Don Gullett, Cincinnati	.15-4	.789
1920	Burleigh Grimes, Brooklyn	.23-11	.676	1976	Steve Carlton, Philadelphia	.20-7	.741
1921	Bill Doak, St. Louis	.15-6	.714	1977	John Candelaria, Pittsburgh	.20-5	.800
1922	Pete Donohue, Cincinnati	.18-9	.667	1978	Gaylord Perry, San Diego	.21-6	.778
1923	Dolf Luque, Cincinnati	.27-8	.771	1979	Tom Seaver, Cincinnati	.16-6	.727
1924	Emil Yde, Pittsburgh	.16-3	.842	1980	Jim Bibby, Pittsburgh	.19-6	.760
1925	Bill Sherdel, St. Louis	.15-6	.714	1981	Tom Seaver, Cincinnati	.14-2	.875
1926	Ray Kremer, Pittsburgh	.20-6	.769	1982	Phil Niekro, Atlanta	.17-4	.810
1927	Larry Benton, Boston-NY	.17-7	.708	1983	John Denny, Philadelphia	.19-6	.760
1928	Larry Benton, New York	.25-9	.735	1984	Rick Sutcliffe, Chicago	.16-1	.941
1929	Charlie Root, Chicago	.19-6	.760	1985	Orel Hershiser, Los Angeles	.19-3	.864
1930	Freddie Fitzsimmons, NY	.19-7	.731	1986	Bob Ojeda, New York	.18-5	.783
1931	Paul Derringer, St. Louis	.18-8	.692	1987	Dwight Gooden, New York	.15-7	.682
1932	Lon Warneke, Chicago	.22-6	.786	1988	David Cone, New York	.20-3	.870
1933	Ben Cantwell, Boston	.20-10	.667	1989	Mike Bielecki, Chicago	.18-7	.720
1934	Dizzy Dean, St. Louis	.30-7	.811	1990	Doug Drabek, Pittsburgh	.22-6	.786
1935	Bill Lee, Chicago	.20-6	.769	1991	John Smiley, Pittsburgh	.20-8	.714
1936	Carl Hubbell, New York	.26-6	.813		& Jose Rijo, Cincinnati	.15-6	.714
1937	Carl Hubbell, New York	.22-8	.733	1992	Bob Tewksbury, St. Louis	.16-5	.762
1938	Bill Lee, Chicago	.22-9	.710	1993	Mark Portugal, Houston	.18-4	.818
1939	Paul Derringer, Cincinnati	.25-7	.781	1994	Marvin Freeman, Colorado	.10-2	.833
1940	Freddie Fitzsimmons, Bklyn	.16-2	.889	1995	Greg Maddux, Atlanta	.19-2	.905
1941	Elmer Riddle, Cincinnati	.19-4	.826	1996	John Smoltz, Atlanta	.24-8	.750
1942	Larry French, Brooklyn	.15-4	.789	1997	Greg Maddux, Atlanta	.19-4	.826
1943	Mort Cooper, St. Louis	.21-8	.724	1998	John Smoltz, Atlanta	.17-3	.850
1944	Ted Wilks, St. Louis	.17-4	.810	1999	Mike Hampton, Houston	.22-4	.846
1945	Harry Brecheen, St. Louis	.14-4	.778	2000	Randy Johnson, Arizona	.19-7	.731
1946	Murray Dickson, St. Louis	.15-6	.714	2001	Curt Schilling, Arizona	.22-6	.786
1947	Larry Jansen, New York	.21-5	.808	2002	Randy Johnson, Arizona	.24-5	.828
1948	Harry Brecheen, St. Louis	.20-7	.741	2003	Jason Schmidt, San Francisco	.17-5	.773
1949	Preacher Roe, Brooklyn	.15-6	.714	2004	Roger Clemens, Houston	.18-4	.818
1950	Sal Maglie, New York	.18-4	.818	2005	Chris Carpenter, St. Louis	.21-5	.808
1951	Preacher Roe, Brooklyn	.22-3	.880	2006	Carlos Zambrano, Chicago	.16-7	.696
1952	Hoyt Wilhelm, New York	.15-3	.833	2007	Brad Penny, Los Angeles	.16-4	.800
1953	Carl Erskine, Brooklyn	.20-6	.769	2008	Tim Lincecum, San Francisco	.18-5	.783
1954	Johnny Antonelli, New York	.21-7	.750				
1955	Don Newcombe, Brooklyn	.20-5	.800				

Note: In 1984, Sutcliffe was also 4-5 with Cleveland for a combined AL-NL record of 20-6 (.769).

Winning Percentage (Cont.)

American League

Multiple winners: Lefty Grove (5); Chief Bender, Roger Clemens and Whitey Ford (3); Johnny Allen, Eddie Cicotte, Mike Cuellar, Lefty Gomez, Ron Guidry, Roy Halladay, Catfish Hunter, Randy Johnson, Walter Johnson, Pedro Martinez, Jim Palmer, Pete Vuckovich and Smokey Joe Wood (2).

Year		W-L	Pct	Year		W-L	Pct
1901	Clark Griffith, Chicago	24-7	.774	1958	Bob Turley, New York	21-7	.750
1902	Bill Bernhard, Phila-Cleve	18-5	.783	1959	Bob Shaw, Chicago	18-6	.750
1903	Cy Young, Boston	28-9	.757				
1904	Jack Chesbro, New York	41-12	.774	1960	Jim Perry, Cleveland	18-10	.643
1905	Andy Coakley, Philadelphia	20-7	.741	1961	Whitey Ford, New York	25-4	.862
1906	Eddie Plank, Philadelphia	19-6	.760	1962	Ray Herbert, Chicago	20-9	.690
1907	Wild Bill Donovan, Detroit	25-4	.862	1963	Whitey Ford, New York	24-7	.774
1908	Ed Walsh, Chicago	40-15	.727	1964	Wally Bunker, Baltimore	19-5	.792
1909	George Mullin, Detroit	29-8	.784	1965	Mudcat Grant, Minnesota	21-7	.750
				1966	Sonny Siebert, Cleveland	16-8	.667
1910	Chief Bender, Philadelphia	23-5	.821	1967	Joe Horlen, Chicago	19-7	.731
1911	Chief Bender, Philadelphia	17-5	.773	1968	Denny McLain, Detroit	31-6	.838
1912	Smokey Joe Wood, Boston	34-5	.872	1969	Jim Palmer, Baltimore	16-4	.800
1913	Walter Johnson, Washington	36-7	.837				
1914	Chief Bender, Philadelphia	17-3	.850	1970	Mike Cuellar, Baltimore	24-8	.750
1915	Smokey Joe Wood, Boston	15-5	.750	1971	Dave McNally, Baltimore	21-5	.808
1916	Eddie Cicotte, Chicago	15-7	.682	1972	Catfish Hunter, Oakland	21-7	.750
1917	Reb Russell, Chicago	15-5	.750	1973	Catfish Hunter, Oakland	21-5	.808
1918	Sad Sam Jones, Boston	16-5	.762	1974	Mike Cuellar, Baltimore	22-10	.688
1919	Eddie Cicotte, Chicago	29-7	.806	1975	Mike Torrez, Baltimore	20-9	.690
				1976	Bill Campbell, Minnesota	17-5	.773
1920	Jim Bagby, Cleveland	31-12	.721	1977	Paul Splittorff, Kansas City	16-6	.727
1921	Carl Mays, New York	27-9	.750	1978	Ron Guidry, New York	25-3	.893
1922	Joe Bush, New York	26-7	.788	1979	Mike Caldwell, Milwaukee	16-6	.727
1923	Herb Pennock, New York	19-6	.760				
1924	Walter Johnson, Washington	23-7	.767	1980	Steve Stone, Baltimore	25-7	.781
1925	Stan Coveleski, Washington	20-5	.800	1981	Pete Vuckovich, Milwaukee	14-4	.778
1926	George Uhle, Cleveland	27-11	.711	1982	Pete Vuckovich, Milwaukee	18-6	.750
1927	Waite Hoyt, New York	22-7	.759		& Jim Palmer, Baltimore	15-5	.750
1928	General Crowder, St. Louis	21-5	.808	1983	Rich Dotson, Chicago	22-7	.759
1929	Lefty Grove, Philadelphia	20-6	.769	1984	Doyle Alexander, Toronto	17-6	.739
				1985	Ron Guidry, New York	22-6	.786
1930	Lefty Grove, Philadelphia	28-5	.848	1986	Roger Clemens, Boston	24-4	.857
1931	Lefty Grove, Philadelphia	31-4	.886	1987	Roger Clemens, Boston	20-9	.690
1932	Johnny Allen, New York	17-4	.810	1988	Frank Viola, Minnesota	24-7	.774
1933	Lefty Grove, Philadelphia	24-8	.750	1989	Bret Saberhagen, Kansas City	23-6	.793
1934	Lefty Gomez, New York	26-5	.839				
1935	Eldon Auker, Detroit	18-7	.720	1990	Bob Welch, Oakland	27-6	.818
1936	Monte Pearson, New York	19-7	.731	1991	Scott Erickson, Minnesota	20-8	.714
1937	Johnny Allen, Cleveland	15-1	.938	1992	Mike Mussina, Baltimore	18-5	.783
1938	Red Ruffing, New York	21-7	.750	1993	Jimmy Key, New York	18-6	.750
1939	Lefty Grove, Boston	15-4	.789	1994	Jason Bere, Chicago	12-2	.857
				1995	Randy Johnson, Seattle	18-2	.900
1940	Schoolboy Rowe, Detroit	16-3	.842	1996	Charles Nagy, Cleveland	17-5	.773
1941	Lefty Gomez, New York	15-5	.750	1997	Randy Johnson, Seattle	20-4	.833
1942	Ernie Bonham, New York	21-5	.808	1998	David Wells, New York	18-4	.818
1943	Spud Chandler, New York	20-4	.833	1999	Pedro Martinez, Boston	23-4	.852
1944	Tex Hughson, Boston	18-5	.783				
1945	Hal Newhouser, Detroit	25-9	.735	2000	Tim Hudson, Oakland	20-6	.769
1946	Boo Ferriss, Boston	25-6	.806	2001	Roger Clemens, New York	20-3	.870
1947	Allie Reynolds, New York	19-8	.704	2002	Pedro Martinez, Boston	20-4	.833
1948	Jack Kramer, Boston	18-5	.783	2003	Roy Halladay, Toronto	22-7	.759
1949	Ellis Kinder, Boston	23-6	.793	2004	Curt Schilling, Boston	21-6	.778
				2005	Cliff Lee, Cleveland	18-5	.783
1950	Vic Raschi, New York	21-8	.724	2006	Roy Halladay, Toronto	16-5	.762
1951	Bob Feller, Cleveland	22-8	.733	2007	Justin Verlander, Detroit	18-6	.750
1952	Bobby Shantz, Philadelphia	24-7	.774	2008	Cliff Lee, Cleveland	22-3	.880
1953	Ed Lopat, New York	16-4	.800				
1954	Sandy Consuegra, Chicago	16-3	.842				
1955	Tommy Byrne, New York	16-5	.762				
1956	Whitey Ford, New York	19-6	.760				
1957	Dick Donovan, Chicago	16-6	.727				
	& Tom Sturdivant, New York	16-6	.727				

Earned Run Average

Earned Run Averages were based on at least 10 complete games pitched (1900-49), at least 154 innings pitched (1950-60), and at least 162 innings pitched since 1961 in the AL and 1962 in the NL. In the strike years of 1981, '94 and '95, qualifiers had to pitch at least as many innings as the total number of games their team played that season.

National League

Multiple winners: Grover Alexander, Sandy Koufax and Christy Mathewson (5); Greg Maddux (4); Carl Hubbell, Randy Johnson, Tom Seaver, Warren Spahn and Dazzy Vance (3); Kevin Brown, Bill Doak, Ray Kremer, Dolf Luque, Jake Peavy, Howie Pollet, Nolan Ryan, Bill Walker and Bucky Walters (2).

Year		ERA	Year		ERA	Year		ERA
1900	Rube Waddell, Pit	2.37	1937	Jim Turner, Bos	2.38	1973	Tom Seaver, NY	2.08
1901	Jesse Tannehill, Pit	2.18	1938	Bill Lee, Chi	2.66	1974	Buzz Capra, Atl	2.28
1902	Jack Taylor, Chi	1.33	1939	Bucky Walters, Cin	2.29	1975	Randy Jones, SD	2.24
1903	Sam Leever, Pit	2.06	1940	Bucky Walters, Cin	2.48	1976	John Denny, St.L	2.52
1904	Joe McGinnity, NY	1.61	1941	Elmer Riddle, Cin	2.24	1977	John Candelaria, Pit	2.34
1905	Christy Mathewson, NY	1.27	1942	Mort Cooper, St.L	1.78	1978	Craig Swan, NY	2.43
1906	Three Finger Brown, Chi	1.04	1943	Howie Pollet, St.L	1.75	1979	J.R. Richard, Hou	2.71
1907	Jack Pfiester, Chi	1.15	1944	Ed Heusser, Cin	2.38			
1908	Christy Mathewson, NY	1.43	1945	Hank Borowy, Chi	2.13	1980	Don Sutton, LA	2.21
1909	Christy Mathewson, NY	1.14	1946	Howie Pollet, St.L	2.10	1981	Nolan Ryan, Hou	1.69
			1947	Warren Spahn, Bos	2.33	1982	Steve Rogers, Mon	2.40
1910	George McQuillan, Phi	1.60	1948	Harry Brecheen, St.L	2.24	1983	Atlee Hammaker, SF	2.25
1911	Christy Mathewson, NY	1.99	1949	Dave Koslo, NY	2.50	1984	Alejandro Peña, LA	2.48
1912	Jeff Tesreau, NY	1.96				1985	Dwight Gooden, NY	1.53
1913	Christy Mathewson, NY	2.06	1950	Jim Hearn, St.L-NY	2.49	1986	Mike Scott, Hou	2.22
1914	Bill Doak, St.L	1.72	1951	Chet Nichols, Bos	2.88	1987	Nolan Ryan, Hou	2.76
1915	Grover Alexander, Phi	1.22	1952	Hoyt Wilhelm, NY	2.43	1988	Joe Magrane, St.L	2.18
1916	Grover Alexander, Phi	1.55	1953	Warren Spahn, Mil	2.10	1989	Scott Garrelts, SF	2.28
1917	Grover Alexander, Phi	1.86	1954	Johnny Antonelli, NY	2.30			
1918	Hippo Vaughn, Chi	1.74	1955	Bob Friend, Pit	2.83	1990	Danny Darwin, Hou	2.21
1919	Grover Alexander, Chi	1.72	1956	Lew Burdette, Mil	2.70	1991	Dennis Martinez, Mon	2.39
			1957	Johnny Podres, Bklyn	2.66	1992	Bill Swift, SF	2.08
1920	Grover Alexander, Chi	1.91	1958	Stu Miller, SF	2.47	1993	Greg Maddux, Atl	2.36
1921	Bill Doak, St.L	2.59	1959	Sam Jones, SF	2.83	1994	Greg Maddux, Atl	1.56
1922	Rosy Ryan, NY	3.01				1995	Greg Maddux, Atl	1.63
1923	Dolf Luque, Cin	1.93	1960	Mike McCormick, SF	2.70	1996	Kevin Brown, Fla.	1.89
1924	Dazzy Vance, Bklyn	2.16	1961	Warren Spahn, Mil	3.02	1997	Pedro Martinez, Mon	1.90
1925	Dolf Luque, Cin	2.63	1962	Sandy Koufax, LA	2.54	1998	Greg Maddux, Atl	2.22
1926	Ray Kremer, Pit	2.61	1963	Sandy Koufax, LA	1.88	1999	Randy Johnson, Ari.	2.48
1927	Ray Kremer, Pit	2.47	1964	Sandy Koufax, LA	1.74			
1928	Dazzy Vance, Bklyn	2.09	1965	Sandy Koufax, LA	2.04	2000	Kevin Brown, LA	2.58
1929	Bill Walker, NY	3.09	1966	Sandy Koufax, LA	1.73	2001	Randy Johnson, Ari.	2.49
			1967	Phil Niekro, Atl	1.87	2002	Randy Johnson, Ari.	2.32
1930	Dazzy Vance, Bklyn	2.61	1968	Bob Gibson, St.L	1.12	2003	Jason Schmidt, SF	2.34
1931	Bill Walker, NY	2.26	1969	Juan Marichal, SF	2.10	2004	Jake Peavy, SD	2.27
1932	Lon Warneke, Chi	2.37				2005	Roger Clemens, Hou	1.87
1933	Carl Hubbell, NY	1.66	1970	Tom Seaver, NY	2.81	2006	Roy Oswalt, Hou	2.98
1934	Carl Hubbell, NY	2.30	1971	Tom Seaver, NY	1.76	2007	Jake Peavy, SD	2.54
1935	Cy Blanton, Pit	2.58	1972	Steve Carlton, Phi	1.97	2008	Johan Santana, NY	2.53
1936	Carl Hubbell, NY	2.31						

Note: In 1945, Borowy had a 3.13 ERA in 18 games with New York (AL) for a combined ERA of 2.65.

American League

Multiple winners: Lefty Grove (9); Roger Clemens (6); Walter Johnson (5); Pedro Martinez (4); Spud Chandler, Stan Coveleski, Red Faber, Whitey Ford, Lefty Gomez, Ron Guidry, Addie Joss, Hal Newhouser, Jim Palmer, Gary Peters, Johan Santana, Luis Tiant and Ed Walsh (2).

Year		ERA	Year		ERA	Year		ERA
1901	Cy Young, Bos	1.62	1918	Walter Johnson, Wash	1.27	1934	Lefty Gomez, NY	2.33
1902	Ed Siever, Det	1.91	1919	Walter Johnson, Wash	1.49	1935	Lefty Grove, Bos	2.70
1903	Earl Moore, Cle	1.77				1936	Lefty Grove, Bos	2.81
1904	Addie Joss, Cle	1.59	1920	Bob Shawkey, NY	2.45	1937	Lefty Gomez, NY	2.33
1905	Rube Waddell, Phi	1.48	1921	Red Faber, Chi	2.48	1938	Lefty Grove, Bos	3.08
1906	Doc White, Chi	1.52	1922	Red Faber, Chi	2.80	1939	Lefty Grove, Bos	2.54
1907	Ed Walsh, Chi	1.60	1923	Stan Coveleski, Cle	2.76			
1908	Addie Joss, Cle	1.16	1924	Walter Johnson, Wash	2.72	1940	Ernie Bonham, NY	1.90
1909	Harry Krause, Phi	1.39	1925	Stan Coveleski, Wash	2.84	1941	Thornton Lee, Chi	2.37
			1926	Lefty Grove, Phi	2.51	1942	Ted Lyons, Chi	2.10
1910	Ed Walsh, Chi	1.27	1927	Wilcy Moore, NY	2.28	1943	Spud Chandler, NY	1.64
1911	Vean Gregg, Cle	1.81	1928	Garland Braxton, Wash	2.51	1944	Dizzy Trout, Det.	2.12
1912	Walter Johnson, Wash	1.39	1929	Lefty Grove, Phi	2.81	1945	Hal Newhouser, Det	1.81
1913	Walter Johnson, Wash	1.09	1930	Lefty Grove, Phi.	2.54	1946	Hal Newhouser, Det	1.94
1914	Dutch Leonard, Bos	1.01	1931	Lefty Grove, Phi.	2.06	1947	Spud Chandler, NY	2.46
1915	Smokey Joe Wood, Bos	1.49	1932	Lefty Grove, Phi.	2.84	1948	Gene Bearden, Cle	2.43
1916	Babe Ruth, Bos	1.75	1933	Monte Pearson, Cle	2.33	1949	Mel Parnell, Bos	2.77
1917	Eddie Cicotte, Chi	1.53						

Earned Run Average (Cont.)

Year		ERA	Year		ERA	Year		ERA
1950	Early Wynn, Cle	3.20	1970	Diego Segui, Oak.	2.56	1990	Roger Clemens, Bos	1.93
1951	Saul Rogovin, Det-Chi	2.78	1971	Vida Blue, Oak	1.82	1991	Roger Clemens, Bos	2.62
1952	Allie Reynolds, NY	2.06	1972	Luis Tiant, Bos	1.91	1992	Roger Clemens, Bos	2.41
1953	Ed Lopat, NY	2.42	1973	Jim Palmer, Bal	2.40	1993	Kevin Appier, KC	2.56
1954	Mike Garcia, Cle	2.64	1974	Catfish Hunter, Oak	2.49	1994	Steve Ontiveros, Oak	2.65
1955	Billy Pierce, Chi	1.97	1975	Jim Palmer, Bal	2.09	1995	Randy Johnson, Sea	2.48
1956	Whitey Ford, NY	2.47	1976	Mark Fidrych, Det.	2.34	1996	Juan Guzman, Tor.	2.93
1957	Bobby Shantz, NY	2.45	1977	Frank Tanana, Cal	2.54	1997	Roger Clemens, Tor	2.05
1958	Whitey Ford, NY	2.01	1978	Ron Guidry, NY	1.74	1998	Roger Clemens, Tor	2.65
1959	Hoyt Wilhelm, Bal.	2.19	1979	Ron Guidry, NY	2.78	1999	Pedro Martinez, Bos	2.07
1960	Frank Baumann, Chi	2.67	1980	Rudy May, NY	2.47	2000	Pedro Martinez, Bos	1.74
1961	Dick Donovan, Wash	2.40	1981	Steve McCatty, Oak	2.32	2001	Freddy Garcia, Sea	3.05
1962	Hank Aguirre, Det.	2.21	1982	Rick Sutcliffe, Cle	2.96	2002	Pedro Martinez, Bos	2.26
1963	Gary Peters, Chi	2.33	1983	Rick Honeycutt, Tex	2.42	2003	Pedro Martinez, Bos	2.22
1964	Dean Chance, LA	1.65	1984	Mike Boddicker, Bal	2.79	2004	Johan Santana, Min	2.61
1965	Sam McDowell, Cle	2.18	1985	Dave Stieb, Tor	2.48	2005	Kevin Millwood, Cle	2.86
1966	Gary Peters, Chi	1.98	1986	Roger Clemens, Bos	2.48	2006	Johan Santana, Min	2.77
1967	Joe Horlen, Chi	2.06	1987	Jimmy Key, Tor	2.76	2007	John Lackey, LA	3.01
1968	Luis Tiant, Cle	1.60	1988	Allan Anderson, Min	2.45	2008	Cliff Lee, Cle	2.54
1969	Dick Bosman, Wash	2.19	1989	Bret Saberhagen, KC	2.16			

Strikeouts

National League

Multiple winners: Dazzy Vance (7); Grover Alexander (6); Steve Carlton, Randy Johnson, Christy Mathewson and Tom Seaver (5); Dizzy Dean, Sandy Koufax and Warren Spahn (4); Don Drysdale, Sam Jones and Johnny Vander Meer (3); David Cone, Dwight Gooden, Bill Hallahan, Jake Peavy, J.R. Richard, Robin Roberts, Nolan Ryan, Curt Schilling, John Smoltz and Hippo Vaughn (2).

Year		SO	Year		SO	Year		SO
1900	Rube Waddell, Pit	130	1937	Carl Hubbell, NY	159	1972	Steve Carlton, Phi	310
1901	Noodles Hahn, Cin	239	1938	Clay Bryant, Chi	135	1973	Tom Seaver, NY	251
1902	Vic Willis, Bos	225	1939	Claude Passeau, Phi-Chi	137	1974	Steve Carlton, Phi	240
1903	Christy Mathewson, NY	267		& Bucky Walters, Cin	137	1975	Tom Seaver, NY	243
1904	Christy Mathewson, NY	212	1940	Kirby Higbe, Phi	137	1976	Tom Seaver, NY	235
1905	Christy Mathewson, NY	206	1941	John Vander Meer, Cin	202	1977	Phil Niekro, Atl	262
1906	Fred Beebe, Chi-St.L.	171	1942	John Vander Meer, Cin	186	1978	J.R. Richard, Hou	303
1907	Christy Mathewson, NY	178	1943	John Vander Meer, Cin	174	1979	J.R. Richard, Hou	313
1908	Christy Mathewson, NY	259	1944	Bill Voiselle, NY	161			
1909	Orval Overall, Chi	205	1945	Preacher Roe, Pit	148	1980	Steve Carlton, Phi	286
1910	Earl Moore, Phi	185	1946	Johnny Schmitz, Chi.	135	1981	F. Valenzuela, LA	180
1911	Rube Marquard, NY	237	1947	Ewell Blackwell, Cin.	193	1982	Steve Carlton, Phi	286
1912	Grover Alexander, Phi	195	1948	Harry Brecheen, St.L	149	1983	Steve Carlton, Phi	275
1913	Tom Seaton, Phi	168	1949	Warren Spahn, Bos	151	1984	Dwight Gooden, NY	276
1914	Grover Alexander, Phi	214	1950	Warren Spahn, Bos	191	1985	Dwight Gooden, NY	268
1915	Grover Alexander, Phi	241	1951	Don Newcombe, Bklyn	164	1986	Mike Scott, Hou	306
1916	Grover Alexander, Phi	167		& Warren Spahn, Bos	164	1987	Nolan Ryan, Hou	270
1917	Grover Alexander, Phi	201	1952	Warren Spahn, Bos	183	1988	Nolan Ryan, Hou	228
1918	Hippo Vaughn, Chi	148	1953	Robin Roberts, Phi	198	1989	Jose DeLeon, St.L	201
1919	Hippo Vaughn, Chi	141	1954	Robin Roberts, Phi	185			
1920	Grover Alexander, Chi	173	1955	Sam Jones, Chi	198	1990	David Cone, NY	233
1921	Burleigh Grimes, Bklyn	136	1956	Sam Jones, Chi	176	1991	David Cone, NY	241
1922	Dazzy Vance, Bklyn	134	1957	Jack Sanford, Phi	188	1992	John Smoltz, Atl.	215
1923	Dazzy Vance, Bklyn	197	1958	Sam Jones, St.L	225	1993	Jose Rijo, Cin	227
1924	Dazzy Vance, Bklyn	262	1959	Don Drysdale, LA	242	1994	Andy Benes, SD	189
1925	Dazzy Vance, Bklyn	221	1960	Don Drysdale, LA	246	1995	Hideo Nomo, LA	236
1926	Dazzy Vance, Bklyn	140	1961	Sandy Koufax, LA	269	1996	John Smoltz, Atl	276
1927	Dazzy Vance, Bklyn	184	1962	Don Drysdale, LA	232	1997	Curt Schilling, Phi	319
1928	Dazzy Vance, Bklyn	200	1963	Sandy Koufax, LA	306	1998	Curt Schilling, Phi	300
1929	Pat Malone, Chi	166	1964	Bob Veale, Pit	250	1999	Randy Johnson, Ari	364
1930	Bill Hallahan, St.L	177	1965	Sandy Koufax, LA	382	2000	Randy Johnson, Ari	347
1931	Bill Hallahan, St.L	159	1966	Sandy Koufax, LA	317	2001	Randy Johnson, Ari	372
1932	Dizzy Dean, St.L	191	1967	Jim Bunning, Phi	253	2002	Randy Johnson, Ari	334
1933	Dizzy Dean, St.L	199	1968	Bob Gibson, St.L	268	2003	Kerry Wood, Chi	266
1934	Dizzy Dean, St.L	195	1969	Ferguson Jenkins, Chi	273	2004	Randy Johnson, Ari	290
1935	Dizzy Dean, St.L	190	1970	Tom Seaver, NY	283	2005	Jake Peavy, SD	216
1936	Van Lingle Mungo, Bklyn	238	1971	Tom Seaver, NY	289	2006	Aaron Harang, Cin.	216
						2007	Jake Peavy, SD	240
						2008	Tim Lincecum, SF	265

Note: In 1998, Randy Johnson struck out 329 batters — 213 in the AL with Seattle, then 116 in the NL with Houston.

American League

Multiple winners: Walter Johnson (12); Nolan Ryan (9); Bob Feller and Lefty Grove (7); Rube Waddell (6); Roger Clemens and Sam McDowell (5); Randy Johnson (4); Lefty Gomez, Mark Langston, Pedro Martinez, Johan Santana and Camilo Pascual (3); Len Barker, Tommy Bridges, Jim Bunning, Hal Newhouser, Allie Reynolds, Herb Score, Ed Walsh and Early Wynn (2).

Year		SO	Year		SO	Year		SO
1901	Cy Young, Bos	158	1938	Bob Feller, Cle	240	1973	Nolan Ryan, Cal	383
1902	Rube Waddell, Phi	210	1939	Bob Feller, Cle	246	1974	Nolan Ryan, Cal	367
1903	Rube Waddell, Phi	302	1940	Bob Feller, Cle	261	1975	Frank Tanana, Cal	269
1904	Rube Waddell, Phi	349	1941	Bob Feller, Cle	260	1976	Nolan Ryan, Cal	327
1905	Rube Waddell, Phi	287	1942	Tex Hughson, Bos	113	1977	Nolan Ryan, Cal	341
1906	Rube Waddell, Phi	196		& Bobo Newsom, Wash	113	1978	Nolan Ryan, Cal	260
1907	Rube Waddell, Phi	232	1943	Allie Reynolds, Cle	151	1979	Nolan Ryan, Cal	223
1908	Ed Walsh, Chi	269	1944	Hal Newhouser, Det	187			
1909	Frank Smith, Chi.	177	1945	Hal Newhouser, Det	212	1980	Len Barker, Cle	187
			1946	Bob Feller, Cle	348	1981	Len Barker, Cle	127
1910	Walter Johnson, Wash	313	1947	Bob Feller, Cle	196	1982	Floyd Bannister, Sea	209
1911	Ed Walsh, Chi	255	1948	Bob Feller, Cle	164	1983	Jack Morris, Det	232
1912	Walter Johnson, Wash	303	1949	Virgil Trucks, Det	153	1984	Mark Langston, Sea	204
1913	Walter Johnson, Wash	243	1950	Bob Lemon, Cle	170	1985	Bert Blyleven, Cle-Min	206
1914	Walter Johnson, Wash	225	1951	Vic Raschi, NY	164	1986	Mark Langston, Sea	245
1915	Walter Johnson, Wash	203	1952	Allie Reynolds, NY	160	1987	Mark Langston, Sea	262
1916	Walter Johnson, Wash	228	1953	Billy Pierce, Chi	186	1988	Roger Clemens, Bos	291
1917	Walter Johnson, Wash	188	1954	Bob Turley, Bal	185	1989	Nolan Ryan, Tex	301
1918	Walter Johnson, Wash	162	1955	Herb Score, Cle	245			
1919	Walter Johnson, Wash	147	1956	Herb Score, Cle	263	1990	Nolan Ryan, Tex	232
			1957	Early Wynn, Cle.	184	1991	Roger Clemens, Bos	241
1920	Stan Coveleski, Cle	133	1958	Early Wynn, Chi.	179	1992	Randy Johnson, Sea	241
1921	Walter Johnson, Wash	143	1959	Jim Bunning, Det	201	1993	Randy Johnson, Sea	308
1922	Urban Shocker, St.L	149	1960	Jim Bunning, Det	201	1994	Randy Johnson, Sea	204
1923	Walter Johnson, Wash	130	1961	Camilo Pascual, Min	221	1995	Randy Johnson, Sea	294
1924	Walter Johnson, Wash	158	1962	Camilo Pascual, Min	206	1996	Roger Clemens, Bos	257
1925	Lefty Grove, Phi	116	1963	Camilo Pascual, Min	202	1997	Roger Clemens, Tor	292
1926	Lefty Grove, Phi	194	1964	Al Downing, NY	217	1998	Roger Clemens, Tor	271
1927	Lefty Grove, Phi	174	1965	Sam McDowell, Cle	325	1999	Pedro Martinez, Bos	313
1928	Lefty Grove, Phi	183	1966	Sam McDowell, Cle	225			
1929	Lefty Grove, Phi	170	1967	Jim Lonborg, Bos	246	2000	Pedro Martinez, Bos	284
1930	Lefty Grove, Phi	209	1968	Sam McDowell, Cle	283	2001	Hideo Nomo, Bos	220
1931	Lefty Grove, Phi	175	1969	Sam McDowell, Cle	279	2002	Pedro Martinez, Bos	239
1932	Red Ruffing, NY	190	1970	Sam McDowell, Cle	304	2003	Esteban Loaiza, Chi	207
1933	Lefty Gomez, NY	163	1971	Mickey Lolich, Det	308	2004	Johan Santana, Min	265
1934	Lefty Gomez, NY	158	1972	Nolan Ryan, Cal	329	2005	Johan Santana, Min	238
1935	Tommy Bridges, Det	163				2006	Johan Santana, Min	245
1936	Tommy Bridges, Det	175				2007	Scott Kazmir, TB	239
1937	Lefty Gomez, NY	194				2008	A.J. Burnett, Tor	231

Pitching Triple Crown Winners

Pitchers who led either league in Earned Run Average, Wins and Strikeouts over a single season.

National League

	Year	ERA	W-L	SO
Tommy Bond, Bos	1877	2.11	40-17	170
Hoss Radbourn, Prov	1884	1.38	60-12	441
Tim Keefe, NY	1888	1.74	35-12	333
John Clarkson, Bos	1889	2.73	49-19	284
Amos Rusie, NY.	1894	2.78	36-13	195
Christy Mathewson, NY	1905	1.27	31-8	206
Christy Mathewson, NY	1908	1.43	37-11	259
Grover Alexander, Phi	1915	1.22	31-10	241
Grover Alexander, Phi	1916	1.55	33-12	167
Grover Alexander, Phi	1917	1.86	30-13	201
Hippo Vaughn, Chi	1918	1.74	22-10	148
Grover Alexander, Chi	1920	1.91	27-14	173
Dazzy Vance, Bklyn	1924	2.16	28-6	262
Bucky Walters, Cin	1939	2.29	27-11	137
Sandy Koufax, LA	1963	1.88	25-5	306
Sandy Koufax, LA	1965	2.04	26-8	382
Sandy Koufax, LA	1966	1.73	27-9	317
Steve Carlton, Phi	1972	1.97	27-10	310
Dwight Gooden, NY	1985	1.53	24-4	268
Randy Johnson, Ari	2002	2.32	24-5	334
Jake Peavy, SD	2007	2.54	19-6	240

Ties: In 1894, Rusie tied for league lead in wins with Jouett Meekin, NY (36-10); in 1939, Walters tied for league lead in strikeouts with Claude Passeau, Phi-Chi; in 1963, Koufax tied for the league lead in wins with Juan Marichal, SF.

American League

	Year	ERA	W-L	SO
Cy Young, Bos	1901	1.62	33-10	158
Rube Waddell, Phi.	1905	1.48	26-11	287
Walter Johnson, Wash	1913	1.09	36-7	243
Walter Johnson, Wash	1918	1.27	23-13	162
Walter Johnson, Wash	1924	2.72	23-7	158
Lefty Grove, Phi	1930	2.54	28-5	209
Lefty Grove, Phi	1931	2.06	31-4	175
Lefty Gomez, NY	1934	2.33	26-5	158
Lefty Gomez, NY	1937	2.33	21-11	194
Hal Newhouser, Det	1945	1.81	25-9	212
Roger Clemens, Tor	1997	2.05	21-7	292
Roger Clemens, Tor	1998	2.65	20-6	271
Pedro Martinez, Bos	1999	2.07	23-4	313
Johan Santana, Min	2006	2.77	19-6	245

Ties: In 1998, Clemens tied for league lead in wins with David Cone, NY (20-7) and Rick Helling, Tex (20-7); in 2006, Santana tied for league lead in wins with Chien-Ming Wang, NY (19-6).

Saves

The "save" was created by Chicago baseball writer Jerome Holtzman in the 1960's and accepted as an official statistic by the Official Rules Committee of Major League Baseball in 1969. From 1969-72, a save was credited to a pitcher who finished a game his team won. From 1973-74, a save was credited to a pitcher who finished a game his team won with the tying or winning run on base or at bat. Since 1975 a pitcher has been credited with a save when he meets all three of the following conditions:

(1) He is the finishing pitcher in a game won by his club; (2) He is not the winning pitcher; (3) He qualifies under one of the following conditions: (a) He enters the game with a lead of no more than three runs and pitches for at least one inning; (b) He enters the game with the potential tying run either on base, or at bat, or on deck; (c) He pitches effectively for at least three innings.

National League

Multiple winners: Bruce Sutter (5); John Franco and Lee Smith (3); Rawly Eastwick, Rollie Fingers, Trevor Hoffman, Mike Marshall, Randy Myers, Jose Valverde and Todd Worrell (2).

Year		Svs	Year		Svs	Year		Svs
1969	Fred Gladding, Hou	.29	1983	Lee Smith, Chi	.29	1997	Jeff Shaw, Cin	.42
1970	Wayne Granger, Cin	.35	1984	Bruce Sutter, St.L	.45	1998	Trevor Hoffman, SD	.53
1971	Dave Giusti, Pit	.30	1985	Jeff Reardon, Mon	.41	1999	Ugueth Urbina, Mon	.41
1972	Clay Carroll, Cin	.37	1986	Todd Worrell, St.L	.36	2000	Antonio Alfonseca, Fla	.45
1973	Mike Marshall, Mon.	.31	1987	Steve Bedrosian, Phi.	.40	2001	Robb Nen, SF	.45
1974	Mike Marshall, LA	.21	1988	John Franco, Cin	.39	2002	John Smoltz, Atl	.55
1975	Rawly Eastwick, Cin	.22	1989	Mark Davis, SD.	.44	2003	Eric Gagne, LA	.55
	& Al Hrabosky, St.L	.22	1990	John Franco, NY	.33	2004	Armando Benitez, Fla	.47
1976	Rawly Eastwick, Cin	.26	1991	Lee Smith, St.L	.47		& Jason Isringhausen, St.L	.47
1977	Rollie Fingers, SD	.35	1992	Lee Smith, St.L	.43	2005	Chad Cordero, Wash	.47
1978	Rollie Fingers, SD	.37	1993	Randy Myers, Chi	.53	2006	Trevor Hoffman, SD	.46
1979	Bruce Sutter, Chi	.37	1994	John Franco, NY	.30	2007	Jose Valverde, Ari	.47
1980	Bruce Sutter, Chi	.28	1995	Randy Myers, Chi	.38	2008	Jose Valverde, Hou	.44
1981	Bruce Sutter, St.L	.25	1996	Jeff Brantley, Cin	.44			
1982	Bruce Sutter, St.L	.36		& Todd Worrell, LA	.44			

American League

Multiple winners: Dan Quisenberry (5); Rich Gossage, Mariano Rivera and Francisco Rodriguez (3); Dennis Eckersley, Sparky Lyle and Ron Perranoski (2).

Year		Svs	Year		Svs	Year		Svs
1969	Ron Perranoski, Min	.31	1983	Dan Quisenberry, KC	.45	1997	Randy Myers, Bal	.45
1970	Ron Perranoski, Min	.34	1984	Dan Quisenberry, KC	.44	1998	Tom Gordon, Bos	.46
1971	Ken Sanders, Mil.	.31	1985	Dan Quisenberry, KC	.37	1999	Mariano Rivera, NY	.45
1972	Sparky Lyle, NY.	.35	1986	Dave Righetti, NY	.46	2000	Todd Jones, Det.	.42
1973	John Hiller, Det	.38	1987	Tom Henke, Tor	.34		& Derek Lowe, Bos	.42
1974	Terry Forster, Chi	.24	1988	Dennis Eckersley, Oak	.45	2001	Mariano Rivera, NY.	.50
1975	Rich Gossage, Chi	.26	1989	Jeff Russell, Tex	.38	2002	Eddie Guardado, Min	.45
1976	Sparky Lyle, NY.	.23	1990	Bobby Thigpen, Chi	.57	2003	Keith Foulke, Oak	.43
1977	Bill Campbell, Bos	.31	1991	Bryan Harvey, Cal	.46	2004	Mariano Rivera, NY.	.53
1978	Rich Gossage, NY	.27	1992	Dennis Eckersley, Oak	.51	2005	Francisco Rodriguez, LA	.45
1979	Mike Marshall, Min	.32	1993	Jeff Montgomery, KC	.45		& Bob Wickman, Cle	.45
1980	Rich Gossage, NY	.33		& Duane Ward, Tor	.45	2006	Francisco Rodriguez, LA	.47
	& Dan Quisenberry, KC	.33	1994	Lee Smith, Bal	.33	2007	Joe Borowski, Cle	.45
1981	Rollie Fingers, Mil	.28	1995	Jose Mesa, Cle	.46	2008	Francisco Rodriguez, LA	.62
1982	Dan Quisenberry, KC	.35	1996	John Wetteland, NY	.43			

Perfect Games

Eighteen pitchers have thrown perfect games (27 up, 27 down) in major league history. However, the game pitched by Ernie Shore is not considered to be official.

National League

	Game	Date	Score
Lee Richmond	Wor. vs Cle.	6/12/1880	1-0
Monte Ward	Prov. vs Buf.	6/17/1880	5-0
Jim Bunning	Phi. at NY	6/21/1964	6-0
Sandy Koufax	LA vs Chi.	9/9/1965	1-0
Tom Browning	Cin. vs LA	9/16/1988	1-0
Dennis Martinez	Mon. at LA	7/28/1991	2-0
Randy Johnson	Ari. at Atl.	5/18/2004	2-0

Note: Pittsburgh's Harvey Haddix pitched 12 perfect innings against the Milwaukee Braves on May 26, 1959 before losing, 1-0, in the 13th. Braves' lead-off batter Felix Mantilla reached on a throwing error by Pirates 3B Don Hoak, Eddie Mathews sacrificed Mantilla to 2nd, Hank Aaron was walked intentionally, and Joe Adcock hit a 3-run HR. Adcock, however, passed Aaron on the bases and was only credited with a 1-run double.

Note: Montreal's Pedro Martinez pitched nine perfect innings against the San Diego Padres on June 3, 1995 before surrendering a leadoff double to Bip Roberts in the 10th. He was then relieved by Mel Rojas, who finished the game, which Montreal won, 1-0.

American League

	Game	Date	Score
Cy Young	Bos. vs Phi.	5/5/1904	3-0
Addie Joss	Cle. vs Chi.	10/2/1908	1-0
Ernie Shore	Bos. vs Wash.	6/23/1917	4-0*
Charlie Robertson	Chi. at Det.	4/30/1922	2-0
Catfish Hunter	Oak. vs Min.	5/8/1968	4-0
Len Barker	Cle. vs Tor.	5/15/1981	3-0
Mike Witt	Cal. at Tex.	9/30/1984	1-0
Kenny Rogers	Tex. vs Cal.	7/28/1994	4-0
David Wells	NY vs Min.	5/17/1998	4-0
David Cone	NY vs Mon.	7/18/1999	6-0

*Babe Ruth started for Boston, walking Senators' lead-off batter Ray Morgan, then was thrown out of game by umpire Brick Owens for arguing the call. Shore came on in relief. Morgan was caught stealing and Shore retired the next 26 batters in a row. While technically not a perfect game—since he didn't start—Shore gets credit anyway.

World Series

Pitcher	Game	Date	Score
Don Larsen	NY vs Bklyn	10/8/1956	2-0

No-Hit Games

Nine innings or more, including perfect games, since 1876. Losing pitchers in **bold** type. **Multiple no-hitters:** Nolan Ryan (7); Sandy Koufax (4); Larry Corcoran, Bob Feller and Cy Young (3); Jim Bunning, Steve Busby, Carl Erskine, Bob Forsch, Pud Galvin, Ken Holtzman, Randy Johnson, Addie Joss, Hub (Dutch) Leonard, Jim Maloney, Christy Mathewson, Hideo Nomo, Allie Reynolds, Warren Spahn, Bill Stoneman, Virgil Trucks, Johnny Vander Meer and Don Wilson (2).

National League

Year	Date	Pitcher	Result
1876	7/15	George Bradley	St.L vs Har, 2-0
1880	6/12	Lee Richmond	Wor vs Cle, 1-0
			(perfect game)
	6/17	Monte Ward	Prov vs Buf, 5-0
			(perfect game)
	8/19	Larry Corcoran	Chi vs Bos, 6-0
	8/20	Pud Galvin	Buf at Wor, 1-0
1882	9/20	Larry Corcoran	Chi vs Wor, 5-0
1883	7/25	Old Hoss Radbourn	Prov at Cle, 8-0
	9/13	Hugh Daily	Cle at Phi, 1-0
1884	6/27	Larry Corcoran	Chi vs Prov, 6-0
	8/4	Pud Galvin	Buf at Det, 18-0
1885	7/27	John Clarkson	Chi vs Prov, 6-0
	8/29	Charlie Ferguson	Phi vs Prov, 1-0
1891	6/22	Tom Lovett	Bklyn vs NY, 4-0
	7/31	Amos Rusie	NY vs Bklyn, 6-0
1892	8/6	John Stivetts	Bos vs Bklyn, 11-0
	8/22	Ben Sanders	Lou vs Bal, 6-2
	10/15	Bumpus Jones	Cin vs Pit, 7-1
			(1st major league game)
1893	8/16	Bill Hawke	Bal vs Wash, 5-0
1897	9/18	Cy Young	Cle vs Cin, 6-0
1898	4/22	Ted Breitenstein	Cin vs Pit, 11-0
	4/22	Jim Hughes	Bal vs Bos, 8-0
	7/8	Red Donahue	Phi vs Bos, 5-0
	8/21	Walter Thornton	Chi vs Bklyn, 2-0
1899	5/25	Deacon Phillippe	Lou vs NY, 7-0
1900	7/12	Noodles Hahn	Cin vs Phi, 4-0
1901	7/15	Christy Mathewson	NY at St.L, 5-0
1903	9/18	Chick Fraser	Phi at Chi, 10-0
1905	6/13	Christy Mathewson	NY at Chi, 1-0
1906	5/1	John Lush	Phi at Bklyn, 6-0
	7/20	Mal Eason	Bklyn at St.L, 2-0
1907	5/8	Frank Pfeffer	Bos vs Cin, 6-0
	9/20	Nick Maddox	Pit vs Bkn, 2-1
1908	7/4	Hooks Wiltse	NY vs Phi, 1-0 (10)
	9/5	Nap Rucker	Bklyn vs Bos, 6-0
1912	9/6	Jeff Tesreau	NY at Phi, 3-0
1914	9/9	George Davis	Bos vs Phi, 7-0
1915	4/15	Rube Marquard	NY vs Bklyn, 2-0
	8/31	Jimmy Lavender	Chi at N.Y, 2-0
1916	6/16	Tom Hughes	Bos vs. Pit, 2-0
1917	5/2	Fred Toney	Cin at Chi, 1-0 (10)
1919	5/11	Hod Eller	Cin at St.L, 6-0
1922	5/7	Jesse Barnes	NY vs Phi, 6-0
1924	7/17	Jesse Haines	St.L vs Bos, 5-0
1925	9/13	Dazzy Vance	Bklyn vs Phi, 10-1
1929	5/8	Carl Hubbell	NY vs Pif, 11-0
1934	9/21	Paul Dean	St.L at Bklyn, 3-0
1938	6/11	Johnny Vander Meer	Cin vs Bos, 3-0
	6/15	Johnny Vander Meer	Cin at Bklyn, 6-0
			(consecutive starts)
1940	4/30	Tex Carleton	Bklyn at Cin, 3-0
1941	8/30	Lon Warneke	St.L at Cin, 2-0
1944	4/27	Jim Tobin	Bos vs Bklyn, 2-0
	5/15	Clyde Shoun	Cin vs Bos, 1-0
1946	4/23	Ed Head	Bklyn vs Bos, 5-0
1947	6/18	Ewell Blackwell	Cin vs Bos, 6-0
1948	9/9	Rex Barney	Bklyn at NY, 2-0
1950	8/11	Vern Bickford	Bos vs Bklyn, 7-0
1951	5/6	Cliff Chambers	Pit at Bos, 3-0
1952	6/19	Carl Erskine	Bklyn vs Chi, 5-0
1954	6/12	Jim Wilson	Mil vs Phi, 2-0
1955	5/12	Sam Jones	Chi vs Pit, 4-0
1956	5/12	Carl Erskine	Bklyn vs NY, 3-0
	9/25	Sal Maglie	Bklyn vs Phi, 5-0
1960	5/15	Don Cardwell	Chi vs St.L, 4-0
	8/18	Lew Burdette	Mil vs Phi, 1-0
	9/16	Warren Spahn	Mil vs Phi, 4-0
1961	4/28	Warren Spahn	Mil vs SF, 1-0
1962	6/30	Sandy Koufax	LA vs NY, 5-0

Year	Date	Pitcher	Result
1963	5/11	Sandy Koufax	LA vs SF, 8-0
	5/17	Don Nottebart	Hou vs Phi, 4-1
	6/15	Juan Marichal	SF vs Hou, 1-0
1964	4/23	**Ken Johnson**	Hou vs Cin, 0-1
	6/4	Sandy Koufax	LA at Phi, 3-0
	6/21	Jim Bunning	Phi at NY, 6-0
			(perfect game)
1965	8/19	Jim Maloney	Cin at Chi, 1-0 (10)
	9/9	Sandy Koufax	LA vs Chi, 1-0
			(perfect game)
1967	6/18	Don Wilson	Hou vs Atl, 2-0
1968	7/29	George Culver	Cin at Phi, 6-1
	9/17	Gaylord Perry	SF vs St.L, 1-0
	9/18	Ray Washburn	St.L at SF, 2-0
			(next day, same park)
1969	4/17	Bill Stoneman	Mon at Phi, 7-0
	4/30	Jim Maloney	Cin vs Hou, 10-0
	5/1	Don Wilson	Hou at Cin, 4-0
	8/19	Ken Holtzman	Chi vs Atl, 3-0
	9/20	Bob Moose	Pit at NY, 4-0
1970	6/12	Dock Ellis	Pit at SD, 2-0
	7/20	Bill Singer	LA vs Phi, 5-0
1971	6/3	Ken Holtzman	Chi at Cin, 1-0
	6/23	Rick Wise	Phi at Cin, 4-0
	8/14	Bob Gibson	St.L at Pit, 11-0
1972	4/16	Burt Hooton	Chi vs Phi, 4-0
	9/2	Milt Pappas	Chi vs SD, 8-0
	10/2	Bill Stoneman	Mon vs NY, 7-0
1973	8/5	Phil Niekro	Atl vs SD, 9-0
1975	8/24	Ed Halicki	SF vs NY, 6-0
1976	7/9	Larry Dierker	Hou vs Mon, 6-0
	8/9	John Candelaria	Pit vs LA, 2-0
	9/29	John Montefusco	SF vs Atl, 9-0
1978	4/16	Bob Forsch	St.L vs Phi, 5-0
	6/16	Tom Seaver	Cin vs St.L, 4-0
1979	4/7	Ken Forsch	Hou vs Atl, 6-0
1980	6/27	Jerry Reuss	LA at SF, 8-0
1981	5/10	Charlie Lea	Mon vs SF, 4-0
	9/26	Nolan Ryan	Hou vs LA, 5-0
1983	9/26	Bob Forsch	St.L vs Mon, 3-0
1986	9/25	Mike Scott	Hou vs SF, 2-0
1988	9/16	Tom Browning	Cin vs LA, 1-0
			(perfect game)
1990	6/29	Fernando Valenzuela	LA vs St.L, 6-0
	8/15	Terry Mulholland	Phi vs SF, 6-0
1991	5/23	Tommy Greene	Phi at Mon, 2-0
	7/28	Dennis Martinez	Mon at LA, 2-0
			(perfect game)
	9/11	Mercker (6),	Atl vs SD, 1-0
		Wohlers (2) & Peña (1)	(combined no-hitter)
1992	8/17	Kevin Gross	LA vs SF, 2-0
1993	9/8	Darryl Kile	Hou vs NY, 7-1
1994	4/8	Kent Mercker	Atl at LA, 6-0
1995	7/14	Ramon Martinez	LA vs Fla, 7-0
1996	5/11	Al Leiter	Fla vs Col, 11-0
	9/17	Hideo Nomo	LA at.Col, 9-0
1997	6/10	Kevin Brown	Fla at SF, 9-0
	7/12	Francisco Cordova (9)	Pit vs. Hou, 3-0 (10 inn.)
		Ricardo Rincon (1)	(combined no-hitter)
1999	6/25	Jose Jimenez	St.L at Ari, 1-0
2001	5/12	A.J. Burnett	Fla at SD, 3-0
	9/3	Bud Smith	St.L at SD, 4-0
2003	4/27	Kevin Millwood	Phi vs SF, 1-0
	6/11	Oswalt (1), Munro (2.2)	Hou at NY-AL, 8-0
		Saarloos (1.1), Lidge (2),	(combined no-hitter)
		Dotel (1) & Wagner (1)	
2004	5/18	Randy Johnson	Ari at Atl, 2-0
			(perfect game)
2006	9/6	Anibal Sanchez	Ari at Fla, 2-0
2008	9/14	Carlos Zambrano	Chi at Hou, 5-0,

No-Hit Games (Cont.)
American League

Year	Date	Pitcher	Result
1902	9/20	Jimmy Callahan	Chi vs Det, 3-0
1904	5/5	Cy Young	Bos vs Phi, 3-0 (perfect game)
	8/17	Jesse Tannehill	Bos at Chi, 6-0
1905	7/22	Weldon Henley	Phi at St. L, 6-0
	9/6	Frank Smith	Chi at Det, 15-0
	9/27	Bill Dinneen	Bos vs Chi, 2-0
1908	6/30	Cy Young	Bos at NY, 8-0
	9/18	Dusty Rhoades	Cle vs Bos, 2-1
	9/20	Frank Smith	Chi vs Phi, 1-0
	10/2	Addie Joss	Cle vs Chi, 1-0 (perfect game)
1910	4/20	Addie Joss	Cle at Chi, 1-0
	5/12	Chief Bender	Phi vs Cle, 4-0
1911	7/29	Smokey Joe Wood	Bos vs St. L, 5-0
	8/27	Ed Walsh	Chi vs Bos, 5-0
1912	7/4	George Mullin	Det vs St. L, 7-0
	8/30	Earl Hamilton	St. L at Det, 5-1
1914	5/31	Joe Benz	Chi vs Cle, 6-1
1916	6/16	Rube Foster	Bos vs NY, 2-0
	8/26	Joe Bush	Phi vs Cle, 5-0
	8/30	Hub (Dutch) Leonard	Bos vs St. L, 4-0
1917	4/14	Ed Cicotte	Chi at St. L, 11-0
	4/24	George Mogridge	NY at Bos, 2-1
	5/5	Ernie Koob	St. L vs Chi, 1-0
	5/6	Bob Groom	St. L vs Chi, 3-0 (next day, same park)
	6/23	Babe Ruth (0) & Ernie Shore (9)	Bos vs Wash, 4-0 (combined no-hitter)
1918	6/3	Hub (Dutch) Leonard	Bos at Det, 5-0
1919	9/10	Ray Caldwell	Cle at NY, 3-0
1920	7/1	Walter Johnson	Wash at Bos, 1-0
1922	4/30	Charlie Robertson	Chi at Det, 2-0 (perfect game)
1923	9/4	Sam Jones	NY at Phi, 2-0
	9/7	Howard Ehmke	Bos at Phi, 4-0
1926	8/21	Ted Lyons	Chi at Bos, 6-0
1931	4/29	Wes Ferrell	Cle vs St. L, 9-0
	8/8	Bob Burke	Wash vs Bos, 5-0
1935	8/31	Vern Kennedy	Chi vs Cle, 5-0
1937	6/1	Bill Dietrich	Chi vs St. L, 8-0
1938	8/27	Monte Pearson	NY vs Cle, 13-0
1940	4/16	Bob Feller	Cle at Chi, 1-0 (Opening Day)
1945	9/9	Dick Fowler	Phi vs St. L, 1-0
1946	4/30	Bob Feller	Cle at NY, 1-0
1947	4/30	Don Black	Cle vs Phi, 3-0
	9/3	Bill McCahan	Phi vs Wash, 3-0
1948	6/30	Bob Lemon	Cle at Det, 2-0
1951	7/1	Bob Feller	Cle vs Det, 2-1
	7/12	Allie Reynolds	NY at Cle, 1-0
	9/28	Allie Reynolds	NY vs Bos, 8-0
1952	5/15	Virgil Trucks	Det vs Wash, 1-0
	8/25	Virgil Trucks	Det at NY, 1-0
1953	5/6	Bobo Holloman	St. L vs Phi, 6-0 (first major league start)
1956	7/14	Mel Parnell	Bos vs Chi, 4-0
	10/8	Don Larsen	NY vs Bklyn, 2-0 (perfect W. Series game)
1957	8/20	Bob Keegan	Chi vs Wash, 6-0
1958	7/20	Jim Bunning	Det at Bos, 3-0
	9/20	Hoyt Wilhelm	Bal vs NY, 1-0
1962	5/5	Bo Belinsky	LA vs Bal, 2-0
	6/26	Earl Wilson	Bos vs LA, 2-0
	8/1	Bill Monbouquette	Bos at Chi, 1-0
	8/26	Jack Kralick	Min vs KC, 1-0
1965	9/16	Dave Morehead	Bos vs Cle, 2-0
1966	6/10	Sonny Siebert	Cle vs Wash, 2-0
1967	4/30	Steve Barber (8⅔) & Stu Miller (⅓)	Bal vs Det, 1-2 (combined no-hitter)
	8/25	Dean Chance	Min at Cle, 2-1
	9/10	Joel Horlen	Chi vs Det, 6-0
1968	4/27	Tom Phoebus	Bal vs Bos, 6-0
	5/8	Catfish Hunter	Oak vs Min, 4-0 (perfect game)
1969	8/13	Jim Palmer	Bal vs Oak, 8-0
1970	7/3	Clyde Wright	Cal vs Oak, 4-0
	9/21	Vida Blue	Oak vs Min, 6-0
1973	4/27	Steve Busby	KC at Det, 3-0
	5/15	Nolan Ryan	Cal at KC, 3-0
	7/15	Nolan Ryan	Cal at Det, 6-0
	7/30	Jim Bibby	Tex at Oak, 6-0
1974	6/19	Steve Busby	KC at Mil, 2-0
	7/19	Dick Bosman	Cle vs Oak, 4-0
	9/28	Nolan Ryan	Cal vs Min, 4-0
1975	6/1	Nolan Ryan	Cal vs Bal, 1-0
	9/28	Vida Blue (5), Glenn Abbott (1), Paul Lindblad (1), & Rollie Fingers (2)	Oak vs Cal, 5-0 (combined no-hitter)
1976	7/28	John Odom (5) & Francisco Barrios (4)	Chi at Oak, 2-1 (combined no-hitter)
1977	5/14	Jim Colborn	KC vs Tex, 6-0
	5/30	Dennis Eckersley	Cle vs Cal, 1-0
	9/22	Bert Blyleven	Tex at Cal, 6-0
1981	5/15	Len Barker	Cle vs Tor, 3-0 (perfect game)
1983	7/4	Dave Righetti	NY vs Bos, 4-0
	9/29	Mike Warren	Oak vs Chi, 3-0
1984	4/7	Jack Morris	Det at Chi, 4-0
	9/30	Mike Witt	Cal at Tex, 1-0 (perfect game)
1986	9/19	Joe Cowley	Chi at Cal, 7-1
1987	4/15	Juan Nieves	Mil at Bal, 7-0
1990	4/11	Mark Langston (7) & Mike Witt (2)	Cal vs Sea, 1-0 (combined no-hitter)
	6/2	Randy Johnson	Sea vs Det, 2-0
	6/11	Nolan Ryan	Tex at Oak, 5-0
	6/29	Dave Stewart	Oak at Tor, 5-0
	9/2	Dave Stieb	Tor at Cle, 3-0
1991	5/1	Nolan Ryan	Tex vs Tor, 3-0
	7/13	Bob Milacki (6), Mike Flanagan (1), Mark Williamson (1) & Gregg Olson (1)	Bal at Oak, 2-0 (combined no-hitter)
	8/11	Wilson Alvarez	Chi at Bal, 7-0
	8/26	Bret Saberhagen	KC vs Chi, 7-0
1993	4/22	Chris Bosio	Sea vs Bos, 7-0
	9/4	Jim Abbott	NY vs Cle, 4-0
1994	4/27	Scott Erickson	Min vs Mil, 6-0
	7/28	Kenny Rogers	Tex vs Cal, 4-0 (perfect game)
1996	5/14	Dwight Gooden	NY vs Sea, 2-0
1998	5/17	David Wells	NY vs Min, 4-0 (perfect game)
1999	7/18	David Cone	NY vs Mon, 6-0 (perfect game)
	9/11	Eric Milton	Min vs Ana, 7-0
2001	4/4	Hideo Nomo	Bos at Bal, 3-0
2002	4/27	Derek Lowe	Bos vs TB, 10-0
2007	4/18	Mark Buehrle	Chi vs Tex, 6-0
	6/12	Justin Verlander	Det vs Mil, 4-0
	9/1	Clay Buchholz	Bos vs Bal, 10-0
2008	5/19	Jon Lester	Bos vs KC, 7-0

All-Time Major League Leaders

Through the 2008 regular season.

CAREER

Players active in 2008 in **bold** type.

Batting

Note that (*) indicates left-handed hitter and (†) indicates switch-hitter.

Batting Average
(Minimum 3,000 AB)

		Yrs	AB	H	Avg
1	Ty Cobb*	24	11,434	4189	.366
2	Rogers Hornsby	23	8,173	2930	.358
3	Joe Jackson*	13	4,981	1772	.356
4	Ed Delahanty	16	7,505	2596	.346
5	Tris Speaker*	22	10,195	3514	.345
6	Ted Williams*	19	7,706	2654	.344
7	Billy Hamilton*	14	6,269	2159	.344
8	Dan Brouthers*	19	6,711	2296	.342
9	Babe Ruth*	22	8,399	2873	.342
10	Harry Heilmann	17	7,787	2660	.342
11	Pete Browning	13	4,820	1646	.341
12	Willie Keeler*	19	8,591	2932	.341
13	Bill Terry*	14	6,428	2193	.341
14	George Sisler*	15	8,267	2812	.340
15	Lou Gehrig*	17	8,001	2721	.340
16	Jesse Burkett*	16	8,421	2850	.338
17	Tony Gwynn*	20	9,288	3141	.338
18	Nap Lajoie	21	9,589	3242	.338
19	Riggs Stephenson	14	4,508	1515	.336
20	**Albert Pujols**	8	4,578	1531	.334
21	Al Simmons	20	8,759	2927	.334
22	Paul Waner*	20	9,459	3152	.333
23	Eddie Collins*	25	9,949	3315	.333
24	Stan Musial*	22	10,972	3630	.331
25	Sam Thompson*	14	5,984	1979	.331

Hits

		Yrs	AB	H	Avg
1	Pete Rose†	24	14,053	**4256**	.303
2	Ty Cobb*	24	11,434	**4189**	.366
3	Hank Aaron	23	12,364	**3771**	.305
4	Stan Musial*	22	10,972	**3630**	.331
5	Tris Speaker*	22	10,195	**3514**	.345
6	Carl Yastrzemski*	23	11,988	**3419**	.285
7	Honus Wagner	21	10,430	**3415**	.327
8	Paul Molitor	21	10,835	**3319**	.306
9	Eddie Collins*	25	9,949	**3315**	.333
10	Willie Mays	22	10,881	**3283**	.302
11	Eddie Murray†	21	11,336	**3255**	.287
12	Nap Lajoie	21	9,589	**3242**	.338
13	Cal Ripken Jr.	21	11,551	**3184**	.276
14	George Brett*	21	10,349	**3154**	.305
15	Paul Waner*	20	9,459	**3152**	.333
16	Robin Yount	20	11,008	**3142**	.285
17	Tony Gwynn*	20	9,288	**3141**	.338
18	Dave Winfield	22	11,003	**3110**	.283
19	Craig Biggio	20	10,876	**3060**	.281
20	Rickey Henderson	25	10,961	**3055**	.279
21	Rod Carew*	19	9,315	**3053**	.328
22	Lou Brock*	19	10,332	**3023**	.293
23	Rafael Palmeiro*	20	10,472	**3020**	.288
24	Wade Boggs*	18	9,180	**3010**	.328
25	Al Kaline	22	10,116	**3007**	.297
26	Cap Anson	22	9,108	**3000**	.329
	Roberto Clemente	18	9,454	**3000**	.317

Players Active in 2008

		Yrs	AB	H	Avg
1	Albert Pujols	8	4,578	1531	.334
2	Ichiro Suzuki*	8	5,460	1805	.331
3	Todd Helton*	12	5,962	1957	.328
4	Vladimir Guerrero	13	6,617	2136	.323
5	Derek Jeter	14	8,025	2535	.316
6	Manny Ramirez	16	7,610	2392	.314
7	Nomar Garciaparra	13	5,426	1702	.314
8	Magglio Ordonez	12	5,861	1830	.312
9	Chipper Jones†	15	7,337	2277	.310
10	Miguel Cabrera	6	3,310	1022	.309

Players Active in 2008

		Yrs	AB	H	Avg
1	Ken Griffey Jr.*	20	9,316	**2680**	.288
2	Omar Vizquel†	20	9,745	**2657**	.273
3	Gary Sheffield	21	8,949	**2615**	.292
4	Ivan Rodriguez	18	8,645	**2605**	.301
5	Luis Gonzalez*	19	9,157	**2591**	.283
6	Derek Jeter	14	8,025	**2535**	.316
7	Frank Thomas	19	8,199	**2468**	.301
8	Jeff Kent	17	8,498	**2461**	.290
9	Alex Rodriguez	15	7,860	**2404**	.306
10	Manny Ramirez	16	7,610	**2392**	.314

Games Played

1	Pete Rose	3562
2	Carl Yastrzemski	3308
3	Hank Aaron	3298
4	Rickey Henderson	3081
5	Ty Cobb	3035
6	Stan Musial	3026
	Eddie Murray	3026
8	Cal Ripken Jr.	3001
9	Willie Mays	2992
10	Barry Bonds	2986
11	Dave Winfield	2973
12	Rusty Staub	2951
13	Brooks Robinson	2896
14	Robin Yount	2856
15	Craig Biggio	2850
16	Al Kaline	2834
17	Rafael Palmeiro	2831
18	Harold Baines	2830
19	Eddie Collins	2826
20	Reggie Jackson	2820

At Bats

1	Pete Rose	14,053
2	Hank Aaron	12,364
3	Carl Yastrzemski	11,988
4	Cal Ripken Jr.	11,551
5	Ty Cobb	11,434
6	Eddie Murray	11,336
7	Robin Yount	11,008
8	Dave Winfield	11,003
9	Stan Musial	10,972
10	Rickey Henderson	10,961
11	Willie Mays	10,881
12	Craig Biggio	10,876
13	Paul Molitor	10,835
14	Brooks Robinson	10,654
15	Rafael Palmeiro	10,472
16	Honus Wagner	10,430
17	George Brett	10,349
18	Lou Brock	10,332
19	Luis Aparicio	10,230
20	Tris Speaker	10,195

Total Bases

1	Hank Aaron	6856
2	Stan Musial	6134
3	Willie Mays	6066
4	Barry Bonds	5976
5	Ty Cobb	5854
6	Babe Ruth	5793
7	Pete Rose	5752
8	Carl Yastrzemski	5539
9	Eddie Murray	5397
10	Rafael Palmeiro	5388
11	Frank Robinson	5373
12	Dave Winfield	5221
13	Cal Ripken Jr.	5168
14	Tris Speaker	5101
15	**Ken Griffey Jr.**	5092
16	Lou Gehrig	5060
17	George Brett	5044
18	Mel Ott	5041
19	Jimmie Foxx	4956
20	Ted Williams	4884

Home Runs

		Yrs	AB	HR	AB/HR
1	Barry Bonds*	22	9,847	**762**	12.9
2	Hank Aaron	23	12,364	**755**	16.4
3	Babe Ruth*	22	8,399	**714**	11.8
4	Willie Mays	22	10,881	**660**	16.5
5	**Ken Griffey Jr.***	20	9,316	**611**	15.2
6	Sammy Sosa	18	8,813	**609**	14.5
7	Frank Robinson	21	10,006	**586**	17.1
8	Mark McGwire	16	6,187	**583**	10.6
9	Harmon Killebrew	22	8,147	**573**	14.2
10	Rafael Palmeiro*	20	10,472	**569**	18.4
11	Reggie Jackson*	21	9,864	**563**	17.5
12	**Alex Rodriguez**	15	7,860	**553**	14.2
13	Mike Schmidt	18	8,352	**548**	15.2
14	**Jim Thome***	18	7,344	**541**	13.6
15	Mickey Mantle†	18	8,102	**536**	15.1
16	Jimmie Foxx	20	8,134	**534**	15.2
17	**Manny Ramirez**	16	7,610	**527**	14.4
18	Ted Williams*	19	7,706	**521**	14.8
	Willie McCovey*	22	8,197	**521**	15.7
	Frank Thomas	19	8,199	**521**	15.7
21	Eddie Mathews*	17	8,537	**512**	16.7
	Ernie Banks	19	9,421	**512**	18.4
23	Mel Ott*	22	9,456	**511**	18.5
24	Eddie Murray†	21	11,336	**504**	22.5
25	**Gary Sheffield**	21	8,949	**499**	17.9

Runs Batted In

		Yrs	Gm	RBI	P/G
1	Hank Aaron	23	3298	**2297**	.70
2	Babe Ruth*	22	2503	**2213**	.88
3	Barry Bonds*	22	2986	**1996**	.67
4	Lou Gehrig*	17	2164	**1995**	.92
5	Stan Musial*	22	3026	**1951**	.64
6	Ty Cobb*	24	3034	**1938**	.64
7	Jimmie Foxx	20	2317	**1922**	.83
8	Eddie Murray†	21	2980	**1917**	.64
9	Willie Mays	22	2992	**1903**	.64
10	Mel Ott*	22	2730	**1860**	.68
11	Carl Yastrzemski*	23	3308	**1844**	.56
12	Ted Williams*	19	2292	**1839**	.80
13	Rafael Palmeiro*	20	2831	**1835**	.65
14	Dave Winfield	22	2973	**1833**	.62
15	Al Simmons	20	2215	**1827**	.82
16	Frank Robinson	21	2808	**1812**	.65
17	**Ken Griffey Jr.***	20	2521	**1772**	.70
18	Honus Wagner	21	2792	**1732**	.62
19	**Manny Ramirez**	16	2103	**1725**	.82
20	Cap Anson	22	2276	**1715**	.75
21	**Frank Thomas**	19	2322	**1704**	.73
22	Reggie Jackson*	21	2820	**1702**	.60
23	Cal Ripken Jr.	21	3001	**1695**	.56
24	Sammy Sosa	18	2354	**1667**	.71
25	Tony Perez	23	2777	**1652**	.59

Players Active in 2008

		Yrs	AB	HR	AB/HR
1	Ken Griffey Jr.*	20	9,316	**611**	15.2
2	Alex Rodriguez	15	7,860	**553**	14.2
3	Jim Thome*	18	7,344	**541**	13.6
4	Manny Ramirez	16	7,610	**527**	14.4
5	Frank Thomas	19	8,199	**521**	15.7
6	Gary Sheffield	21	8,949	**499**	17.9
7	Carlos Delgado*	16	7,189	**469**	15.3
8	Chipper Jones†	15	7,337	**408**	18.0
9	Jason Giambi*	14	6,332	**396**	16.0
10	Vladimir Guerrero	13	6,617	**392**	16.9
11	Jim Edmonds*	16	6,612	**382**	17.3
12	Jeff Kent	17	8,498	**377**	22.5
13	Andruw Jones	13	6,617	**371**	17.8
14	Luis Gonzalez*	19	9,157	**354**	25.9
15	Moises Alou	17	7,037	**332**	21.2

Players Active in 2008

		Yrs	Gm	RBI	P/G
1	Ken Griffey Jr.*	20	2521	**1772**	.70
2	Manny Ramirez	16	2103	**1725**	.82
3	Frank Thomas	19	2322	**1704**	.73
4	Gary Sheffield	21	2476	**1633**	.66
5	Alex Rodriguez	15	2042	**1606**	.79
6	Jeff Kent	18	2298	**1518**	.66
7	Carlos Delgado*	16	2009	**1489**	.74
8	Jim Thome*	18	2160	**1488**	.69
9	Luis Gonzalez*	19	2591	**1439**	.56
10	Chipper Jones†	15	2023	**1374**	.68
11	Garret Anderson*	15	2013	**1292**	.64
12	Moises Alou	17	1942	**1287**	.66
13	Jason Giambi*	14	1850	**1279**	.69
14	Vladimir Guerrero	13	1750	**1268**	.72
15	Ivan Rodriguez	18	2267	**1217**	.54

Runs

1	Rickey Henderson	2295
2	Ty Cobb	2246
3	Barry Bonds	2227
4	Babe Ruth	2174
	Hank Aaron	2174
6	Pete Rose	2165
7	Willie Mays	2062
8	Stan Musial	1949
9	Lou Gehrig	1888
10	Tris Speaker	1882
11	Mel Ott	1859
12	Craig Biggio	1844
13	Frank Robinson	1829
14	Eddie Collins	1821
15	Carl Yastrzemski	1816
16	Ted Williams	1798
17	Paul Molitor	1782
18	Charlie Gehringer	1774
19	Jimmie Foxx	1751
20	Honus Wagner	1736

Extra Base Hits

1	Hank Aaron	1477
2	Barry Bonds	1440
3	Stan Musial	1377
4	Babe Ruth	1356
5	Willie Mays	1323
6	Rafael Palmeiro	1192
7	Lou Gehrig	1190
8	Frank Robinson	1186
9	Carl Yastrzemski	1157
10	**Ken Griffey Jr.**	1152
11	Ty Cobb	1136
12	Tris Speaker	1131
13	George Brett	1119
14	Ted Williams	1117
	Jimmie Foxx	1117
16	Eddie Murray	1099
17	Dave Winfield	1093
18	Cal Ripken Jr.	1078
19	Reggie Jackson	1075
20	Mel Ott	1071

Slugging Percentage
(Minimum 3,000 AB)

1	Babe Ruth	.690
2	Ted Williams	.634
3	Lou Gehrig	.632
4	**Albert Pujols**	.624
5	Jimmie Foxx	.609
6	Barry Bonds	.607
7	Hank Greenberg	.605
8	**Manny Ramirez**	.593
9	Mark McGwire	.588
10	Joe DiMaggio	.579
11	**Alex Rodriguez**	.578
12	Rogers Hornsby	.577
13	**Vladimir Guerrero**	.575
14	**Todd Helton**	.574
15	Larry Walker	.565
16	Albert Belle	.564
17	Johnny Mize	.562
18	Juan Gonzalez	.561
19	**Jim Thome**	.560
20	**Lance Berkman**	.560

Stolen Bases

1	Rickey Henderson	1406
2	Lou Brock	938
3	Billy Hamilton	912
4	Ty Cobb	892
5	Tim Raines	808
6	Vince Coleman	752
7	Eddie Collins	745
8	Max Carey	738
9	Honus Wagner	722
10	Joe Morgan	689
11	Arlie Latham	679
12	Willie Wilson	668
13	Bert Campaneris	649
14	Tom Brown	627
15	Kenny Lofton	622
16	Otis Nixon	620
17	George Davis	616
18	Dummy Hoy	594
19	Maury Wills	586
20	George Van Haltren	583

Walks

1	Barry Bonds	2558
2	Rickey Henderson	2190
3	Babe Ruth	2062
4	Ted Williams	2019
5	Joe Morgan	1865
6	Carl Yastrzemski	1845
7	Mickey Mantle	1733
8	Mel Ott	1708
9	**Frank Thomas**	1667
10	Eddie Yost	1614
11	Darrell Evans	1605
12	Stan Musial	1599
13	Pete Rose	1566
14	Harmon Killebrew	1559
15	**Jim Thome**	1550
16	Lou Gehrig	1508
17	Mike Schmidt	1507
18	Eddie Collins	1499
19	Willie Mays	1464
20	Jimmie Foxx	1452

Strikeouts

1	Reggie Jackson	2597
2	Sammy Sosa	2306
3	**Jim Thome**	2190
4	Andres Galarraga	2003
5	Jose Canseco	1942
6	Willie Stargell	1936
7	Mike Schmidt	1883
8	Fred McGriff	1882
9	Tony Perez	1867
10	Dave Kingman	1816
11	Bobby Bonds	1757
12	Craig Biggio	1753
13	Dale Murphy	1748
14	Lou Brock	1730
15	**Carlos Delgado**	1725
16	Mickey Mantle	1710
17	Harmon Killebrew	1699
18	Chili Davis	1698
19	Dwight Evans	1697
20	Rickey Henderson	1694

Pitching

Note that (*) indicates left-handed pitcher. Active pitching leaders are listed for wins and strikeouts.

Wins

		Yrs	GS	W	L	Pct
1	Cy Young	22	815	511	316	.618
2	Walter Johnson	21	666	417	279	.599
3	Christy Mathewson	17	551	373	188	.665
	Grover Alexander	20	598	373	208	.642
5	Pud Galvin	15	688	365	310	.541
6	Warren Spahn*	21	665	363	245	.597
7	Kid Nichols	15	561	361	208	.634
8	**Greg Maddux**	23	740	355	227	.610
9	Roger Clemens	23	707	354	184	.658
10	Tim Keefe	14	594	342	225	.603
11	Steve Carlton*	24	709	329	244	.574
12	John Clarkson	12	518	328	178	.648
13	Eddie Plank*	17	529	326	194	.627
14	Don Sutton	23	756	324	256	.559
	Nolan Ryan	27	773	324	292	.526
16	Phil Niekro	24	716	318	274	.537
17	Gaylord Perry	22	690	314	265	.542
18	Tom Seaver	20	647	311	205	.603
19	Old Hoss Radbourn	12	503	309	195	.613
20	Mickey Welch	13	549	307	210	.594
21	**Tom Glavine***	22	682	305	203	.600
22	Lefty Grove*	17	456	300	141	.680
	Early Wynn	23	612	300	244	.551
24	Bobby Mathews	15	568	297	248	.545
25	**Randy Johnson***	21	586	295	160	.648
26	Tommy John*	26	700	288	231	.555
27	Bert Blyleven	22	685	287	250	.534
28	Robin Roberts	19	609	286	245	.539
29	Tony Mullane	13	504	284	220	.563
	Ferguson Jenkins	19	594	284	226	.557

Strikeouts

		Yrs	IP	SO	P/9
1	Nolan Ryan	27	5386.0	5714	9.55
2	**Randy Johnson***	21	4039.1	4789	10.67
3	Roger Clemens	24	4916.2	4672	8.55
4	Steve Carlton*	24	5217.1	4136	7.13
5	Bert Blyleven	22	4970.0	3701	6.70
6	Tom Seaver	20	4782.2	3640	6.85
7	Don Sutton	23	5282.1	3574	6.09
8	Gaylord Perry	22	5350.1	3534	5.94
9	Walter Johnson	21	5914.1	3508	5.34
10	**Greg Maddux**	23	5008.1	3371	6.06
11	Phil Niekro	24	5404.1	3342	5.57
12	Ferguson Jenkins	19	4500.2	3192	6.38
13	Bob Gibson	17	3884.1	3117	7.22
	Pedro Martinez	17	2782.2	3117	10.08
15	**Curt Schilling**	20	3261.0	3116	8.60
16	**John Smoltz**	21	3395.0	3011	7.98
17	Jim Bunning	17	3760.1	2855	6.83
18	Mickey Lolich*	16	3638.1	2832	7.01
19	**Mike Mussina**	18	3562.2	2813	7.11
20	Cy Young	22	7356.0	2803	3.43
21	Frank Tanana*	21	4186.2	2773	5.96
22	David Cone	17	2898.2	2668	8.28
23	Chuck Finley*	17	3197.1	2610	7.35
24	Tom Glavine*	22	4413.1	2607	5.32
25	Warren Spahn*	21	5243.2	2583	4.43
26	Bob Feller	18	3827.0	2581	6.07
27	Tim Keefe	14	5049.2	2564	4.57
28	Jerry Koosman*	19	3839.1	2556	5.99
29	Christy Mathewson	17	4781.0	2502	4.71
30	Don Drysdale	14	3432.0	2486	6.52

Pitchers Active in 2008

		Yrs	GS	W	L	Pct
1	Greg Maddux	23	740	355	227	.610
2	Tom Glavine*	22	682	305	203	.600
3	Randy Johnson*	21	586	295	160	.648
4	Mike Mussina	18	536	270	153	.638
5	Jamie Moyer*	22	584	246	185	.571
6	Kenny Rogers*	20	474	219	156	.584
7	Curt Schilling (DNP)	20	436	216	146	.597
8	Andy Pettitte*	14	426	215	127	.629
9	Pedro Martinez	17	400	214	99	.684
10	John Smoltz	20	466	210	147	.588

Pitchers Active in 2008

		Yrs	IP	SO	P/9
1	Randy Johnson*	21	4039.1	4789	10.67
2	Greg Maddux	23	5008.1	3371	6.06
3	Pedro Martinez	17	2782.2	3117	10.08
4	Curt Schilling (DNP)	20	3261.0	3116	8.60
5	John Smoltz	21	3395.0	3011	7.98
6	Mike Mussina	18	3562.2	2813	7.11
7	Tom Glavine*	22	4413.1	2607	5.32
8	Jamie Moyer*	22	3746.2	2248	5.40
9	Javier Vazquez	11	2270.2	2015	7.99
10	Andy Pettitte*	14	2731.2	2002	6.60

Winning Pct.

(Minimum 100 wins)

		Yrs	W-L	Pct
1	Al Spalding	7	252-65	.795
2	Spud Chandler	11	109-43	.717
3	Dave Foutz	11	147-66	.690
4	Whitey Ford*	16	236-106	.690
5	Bob Caruthers	9	218-99	.688
6	Don Gullett*	9	109-50	.686
7	**Pedro Martinez**	17	214-99	.684
8	**Johan Santana***	9	109-51	.681
9	Lefty Grove*	17	300-141	.680
10	Smokey Joe Wood	11	117-57	.672
11	**Roy Oswalt**	8	129-64	.668
12	Vic Raschi	10	132-66	.667
13	Larry Corcoran	8	177-89	.665
14	**Roy Halladay**	11	131-66	.665
15	Christy Mathewson	17	373-188	.665

Losses

		Yrs	GS	W	L	Pct
1	Cy Young	22	815	511	**316**	.618
2	Pud Galvin	15	688	365	**310**	.541
3	Nolan Ryan	27	773	324	**292**	.526
4	Walter Johnson	21	666	417	**279**	.599
5	Phil Niekro	24	716	318	**274**	.537
6	Gaylord Perry	22	690	314	**265**	.542
7	Don Sutton	23	756	324	**256**	.559
8	Jack Powell	16	516	245	**254**	.491
9	Eppa Rixey*	21	552	266	**251**	.515
10	Bert Blyleven	22	685	287	**250**	.534
11	Bobby Mathews	15	568	297	**248**	.545
12	Robin Roberts	19	609	286	**245**	.539
	Warren Spahn*	21	665	363	**245**	.597
14	Early Wynn	23	612	300	**244**	.551
	Steve Carlton*	24	709	329	**244**	.574

Appearances

1	Jesse Orosco	1252
2	Mike Stanton	1178
3	John Franco	1119
4	Dennis Eckersley	1071
5	Hoyt Wilhelm	1070
6	Dan Plesac	1064
7	**Mike Timlin**	1058
8	Kent Tekulve	1050
9	Lee Smith	1022
	Jose Mesa	1022
11	Roberto Hernandez	1010
12	Mike Jackson	1005
13	Rich Gossage	1002
14	Lindy McDaniel	987
15	Todd Jones	982

Innings Pitched

1	Cy Young	7356.0
2	Pud Galvin	6003.1
3	Walter Johnson	5914.1
4	Phil Niekro	5404.1
5	Nolan Ryan	5386.0
6	Gaylord Perry	5350.1
7	Don Sutton	5282.1
8	Warren Spahn	5243.2
9	Steve Carlton	5217.1
10	Grover Alexander	5190.0
11	Kid Nichols	5056.1
12	Tim Keefe	5049.2
13	**Greg Maddux**	5008.1
14	Bert Blyleven	4970.0
15	Bobby Mathews	4956.0

Earned Run Avg.

(Minimum 1500 IP)

1	Ed Walsh	1.82
2	Addie Joss	1.89
3	Al Spalding	2.04
4	Three Finger Brown	2.06
5	Monte Ward	2.10
6	Christy Mathewson	2.13
7	Rube Waddell	2.16
8	Walter Johnson	2.17
9	Orval Overall	2.23
10	Tommy Bond	2.25
11	Will White	2.28
12	Ed Reulbach	2.28
13	Jim Scott	2.30
14	Eddie Plank	2.35
15	Larry Corcoran	2.36

Shutouts

1	Walter Johnson	110
2	Grover Alexander	90
3	Christy Mathewson	79
4	Cy Young	76
5	Eddie Plank	69
6	Warren Spahn	63
7	Nolan Ryan	61
	Tom Seaver	61
9	Bert Blyleven	60
10	Don Sutton	58
11	Pud Galvin	57
	Ed Walsh	57
13	Bob Gibson	56
14	Three Finger Brown	55
	Steve Carlton	55

Walks Allowed

1	Nolan Ryan	2795
2	Steve Carlton	1833
3	Phil Niekro	1809
4	Early Wynn	1775
5	Bob Feller	1764
6	Bobo Newsom	1732
7	Amos Rusie	1704
8	Charlie Hough	1665
9	Roger Clemens	1580
10	Gus Weyhing	1566
11	Red Ruffing	1541
12	**Tom Glavine**	1500
13	**Randy Johnson**	1466
14	Bump Hadley	1442
15	Warren Spahn	1434

HRs Allowed

1	Robin Roberts	505
2	Ferguson Jenkins	484
3	Phil Niekro	482
4	Don Sutton	472
5	**Jamie Moyer**	464
6	Frank Tanana	448
7	Warren Spahn	434
8	Bert Blyleven	430
9	Steve Carlton	414
10	David Wells	407
11	Gaylord Perry	399
12	Jim Kaat	395
13	**Randy Johnson**	392
14	Jack Morris	389
15	Charlie Hough	383

Saves

1	**Trevor Hoffman**	554
2	**Mariano Rivera**	482
3	Lee Smith	478
4	John Franco	424
5	Dennis Eckersley	390
6	**Billy Wagner**	385
7	Jeff Reardon	367
8	**Troy Percival**	352
9	Randy Myers	347
10	Rollie Fingers	341
11	John Wetteland	330
12	Roberto Hernandez	326
13	Jose Mesa	321
14	**Todd Jones**	319
15	Rick Aguilera	318
16	Robb Nen	314
17	Tom Henke	311
18	Rich Gossage	310
19	Jeff Montgomery	304
20	Doug Jones	303
21	Bruce Sutter	300
22	**Jason Isringhausen**	293
23	Armando Benitez	289
24	Rod Beck	286
25	Bob Wickman	267
26	Todd Worrell	256
27	Dave Righetti	252
28	Dan Quisenberry	244
29	Sparky Lyle	238
30	Ugueth Urbina	237

SINGLE SEASON
Through 2008 regular season.
Batting

Home Runs

		Year	Gm	AB	HR
1	Barry Bonds, SF	2001	153	476	73
2	Mark McGwire, St.L	1998	155	509	70
3	Sammy Sosa, Chi-NL	1998	159	643	66
4	Mark McGwire, St.L	1999	153	521	65
5	Sammy Sosa, Chi-NL	2001	160	577	64
6	Sammy Sosa, Chi-NL	1999	162	625	63
7	Roger Maris, NY-AL	1961	162	590	61
8	Babe Ruth, NY-AL	1927	151	540	60
9	Babe Ruth, NY-AL	1921	152	540	59
10	Mark McGwire, Oak-St.L	1997	156	540	58
	Hank Greenberg, Det	1938	155	556	58
	Ryan Howard, Phi	2006	159	581	58
	Jimmie Foxx, Phi-AL	1932	154	585	58
14	Alex Rodriguez, Tex	2002	162	624	57
	Luis Gonzalez, Ari	2001	162	609	57
16	Hack Wilson, Chi-NL	1930	155	585	56
	Ken Griffey Jr., Sea	1997	157	608	56
	Ken Griffey Jr., Sea	1998	161	633	56
19	Six tied with 54 each.				

Hits

		Year	AB	H	Avg
1	Ichiro Suzuki, Sea.	2004	704	262	.372
2	George Sisler, StL-AL	1920	631	257	.407
3	Bill Terry, NY-NL	1930	633	254	.401
	Lefty O'Doul, Phi-NL	1929	638	254	.398
5	Al Simmons, Phi-AL	1925	658	253	.384
6	Rogers Hornsby, StL-NL	1922	623	250	.401
	Chuck Klein, Phi-NL	1930	648	250	.386
8	Ty Cobb, Det	1911	591	248	.420
9	George Sisler, StL-AL	1922	586	246	.420
10	Ichiro Suzuki, Sea	2001	692	242	.350
11	Babe Herman, Bklyn	1930	614	241	.393
	Heinie Manush, StL-AL	1928	638	241	.378
13	Wade Boggs, Bos	1985	653	240	.368
	Darin Erstad, Ana	2000	676	240	.355
15	Rod Carew, Min	1977	616	239	.388
16	Don Mattingly, NY-AL	1986	677	238	.352
	Ichiro Suzuki, Sea	2007	678	238	.351
18	Harry Heilmann, Det	1921	602	237	.394
	Paul Waner, Pit	1927	623	237	.380
	Joe Medwick, StL-NL	1937	633	237	.374

Batting Average

From 1900-49

		Year	AB	H	Avg
1	Rogers Hornsby, StL-NL	1924	536	227	.424
2	Nap Lajoie, Phi-AL	1901	543	229	.422
3	George Sisler, StL-AL	1922	586	246	.420
4	Ty Cobb, Det	1911	591	248	.420
5	Ty Cobb, Det	1912	553	227	.410
6	Joe Jackson, Cle	1911	571	233	.408
7	George Sisler, StL-AL	1920	631	257	.407
8	Ted Williams, Bos-AL	1941	456	185	.406
9	Rogers Hornsby, StL-NL	1925	504	203	.403
10	Harry Heilmann, Det	1923	524	211	.403

Since 1950

		Year	AB	H	Avg
1	Tony Gwynn, SD	1994	419	175	.394
2	George Brett, KC	1980	449	175	.390
3	Ted Williams, Bos	1957	420	163	.388
4	Rod Carew, Min	1977	616	239	.388
5	Larry Walker, Col	1999	438	166	.379
6	Todd Helton, Col	2000	580	216	.372
7	Nomar Garciaparra, Bos	2000	529	197	.372
8	Ichiro Suzuki, Sea	2004	704	262	.372
9	Tony Gwynn, SD	1997	592	220	.372
10	Andres Galarraga, Col	1993	470	174	.370

Total Bases

From 1900-49

		Year	TB
1	Babe Ruth, New York-AL	1921	457
2	Rogers Hornsby, St. Louis-NL	1922	450
3	Lou Gehrig, New York-AL	1927	447
4	Chuck Klein, Philadelphia-NL	1930	445
5	Jimmie Foxx, Philadelphia-AL	1932	438
6	Stan Musial, St. Louis-NL	1948	429
7	Hack Wilson, Chicago-NL	1930	423
8	Chuck Klein, Philadelphia-NL	1932	420
9	Lou Gehrig, New York-AL	1930	419
10	Joe DiMaggio, New York-AL	1937	418

Since 1950

		Year	TB
1	Sammy Sosa, Chicago-NL	2001	425
2	Luis Gonzalez, Arizona	2001	419
3	Sammy Sosa, Chicago-NL	1998	416
4	Barry Bonds, San Francisco	2001	411
5	Larry Walker, Colorado	1997	409
6	Jim Rice, Boston	1978	406
7	Todd Helton, Colorado	2000	405
8	Todd Helton, Colorado	2001	402
9	Hank Aaron, Milwaukee	1959	400
10	Albert Belle, Chicago-AL	1998	399

Runs Batted In

From 1900-49

		Year	Avg	HR	RBI
1	Hack Wilson, Chi-NL	1930	.356	56	191
2	Lou Gehrig, NY-AL	1931	.341	46	184
3	Hank Greenberg, Det	1937	.337	40	183
4	Lou Gehrig, NY-AL	1927	.373	47	175
	Jimmie Foxx, Bos-AL	1938	.349	50	175
6	Lou Gehrig, NY-AL	1930	.379	41	174
7	Babe Ruth, NY-AL	1921	.378	59	171
8	Chuck Klein, Phi-NL	1930	.386	40	170
	Hank Greenberg, Det	1935	.328	36	170
10	Jimmie Foxx, Phi-AL	1932	.364	58	169

Since 1950

		Year	Avg	HR	RBI
1	Manny Ramirez, Cle	1999	.333	44	165
2	Sammy Sosa, Chi-NL	2001	.328	64	160
3	Sammy Sosa, Chi-NL	1998	.308	66	158
4	Juan Gonzalez, Tex	1998	.318	45	157
5	Alex Rodriguez, NY-AL	2007	.314	54	156
6	Tommy Davis, LA-NL	1962	.346	27	153
7	Albert Belle, Chi-AL	1998	.328	49	152
8	Andres Galarraga, Col	1996	.304	47	150
	Miguel Tejada, Bal	2004	.311	34	150
10	George Foster, Cin	1977	.320	52	149
	Ryan Howard, Phi	2006	.313	58	149

Runs

		Year	Runs
1	Babe Ruth, New York-AL	1921	177
2	Lou Gehrig, New York-AL	1936	167
3	Babe Ruth, New York-AL	1928	163
	Lou Gehrig, New York-AL	1931	163
5	Babe Ruth, New York-AL	1920	158
	Babe Ruth, New York-AL	1927	158
	Chuck Klein, Philadelphia-NL	1930	158
8	Rogers Hornsby, Chicago-NL	1929	156
9	Kiki Cuyler, Chicago-NL	1930	155
10	Lefty O'Doul, Philadelphia-NL	1929	152
	Woody English, Chicago-NL	1930	152
	Al Simmons, Philadelphia-AL	1930	152
	Chuck Klein, Philadelphia-NL	1932	152
	Jeff Bagwell, Houston	2000	152
15	Babe Ruth, New York-AL	1923	151
	Jimmie Foxx, Philadelphia-AL	1932	151
	Joe DiMaggio, New York-AL	1937	151
18	Babe Ruth, New York-AL	1930	150
	Ted Williams, Boston-AL	1949	150
20	Lou Gehrig, New York-AL	1927	149
	Babe Ruth, New York-AL	1931	149

Walks

		Year	BB
1	Barry Bonds, San Francisco	2004	232
2	Barry Bonds, San Francisco	2002	198
3	Barry Bonds, San Francisco	2001	177
4	Babe Ruth, New York-AL	1923	170
5	Ted Williams, Boston-AL	1947	162
	Ted Williams, Boston-AL	1949	162
	Mark McGwire, St. Louis	1998	162
8	Ted Williams, Boston-AL	1946	156
9	Barry Bonds, San Francisco	1996	151
	Eddie Yost, Washington	1956	151

Extra Base Hits

		Year	EBH
1	Babe Ruth, New York-AL	1921	119
2	Lou Gehrig, New York-AL	1927	117
3	Chuck Klein, Philadelphia-NL	1930	107
	Barry Bonds, San Francisco	2001	107
5	Todd Helton, Colorado	2001	105
6	Chuck Klein, Philadelphia-NL	1932	103
	Hank Greenberg, Detroit	1937	103
	Stan Musial, St. Louis-NL	1948	103
	Albert Belle, Cleveland	1995	103
	Todd Helton, Colorado	2000	103
	Sammy Sosa, Chicago-NL	2001	103

Slugging Percentage
From 1900-49

		Year	Pct
1	Babe Ruth, New York-AL	1920	.847
2	Babe Ruth, New York-AL	1921	.846
3	Babe Ruth, New York-AL	1927	.772
4	Lou Gehrig, New York-AL	1927	.765
5	Babe Ruth, New York-AL	1923	.764
6	Rogers Hornsby, St. Louis-NL	1925	.756
7	Jimmie Foxx, Philadelphia-AL	1932	.749
8	Babe Ruth, New York-AL	1924	.739
9	Babe Ruth, New York-AL	1926	.737
10	Ted Williams, Boston-AL	1941	.735

Since 1950

		Year	Pct
1	Barry Bonds, San Francisco	2001	.863
2	Barry Bonds, San Francisco	2004	.812
3	Barry Bonds, San Francisco	2002	.799
4	Mark McGwire, St. Louis	1998	.752
5	Jeff Bagwell, Houston	1994	.750
6	Barry Bonds, San Francisco	2003	.749
7	Sammy Sosa, Chicago-NL	2001	.737
8	Ted Williams, Boston	1957	.731
9	Mark McGwire, Oakland	1996	.730
10	Frank Thomas, Chicago-AL	1994	.729

Doubles

		Year	2B
1	Earl Webb, Boston-AL	1931	67
2	George Burns, Cleveland	1926	64
	Joe Medwick, St. Louis-NL	1936	64
4	Hank Greenberg, Detroit	1934	63
5	Paul Waner, Pittsburgh	1932	62
6	Charlie Gehringer, Detroit	1936	60
7	Tris Speaker, Cleveland	1923	59
	Chuck Klein, Philadelphia-NL	1930	59
	Todd Helton, Colorado	2000	59
10	Three tied with 57 each.		

Triples
From 1900-49

		Year	3B
1	Chief Wilson, Pittsburgh	1912	36
2	Joe Jackson, Cleveland	1912	26
3	Sam Crawford, Detroit	1914	26
4	Kiki Cuyler, Pittsburgh	1925	26
5	Three tied with 25 each.		

Since 1950

		Year	3B
1	Curtis Granderson, Detroit	2007	23
2	Willie Wilson, Kansas City	1985	21
	Lance Johnson, New York-NL	1996	21
4	Willie Mays, New York-NL	1957	20
	George Brett, Kansas City	1979	20
	Cristian Guzman, Minnesota	2000	20
	Jimmy Rollins, Philadelphia	2007	20

Stolen Bases

		Year	SB
1	Rickey Henderson, Oakland	1982	130
2	Lou Brock, St. Louis	1974	118
3	Vince Coleman, St. Louis	1985	110
4	Vince Coleman, St. Louis	1987	109
5	Rickey Henderson, Oakland	1983	108
6	Vince Coleman, St. Louis	1986	107
7	Maury Wills, Los Angeles-NL	1962	104
8	Rickey Henderson, Oakland	1980	100
9	Ron LeFlore, Montreal	1980	97
10	Ty Cobb, Detroit	1915	96
	Omar Moreno, Pittsburgh	1980	96
12	Maury Wills, Los Angeles	1965	94
13	Rickey Henderson, New York-AL	1988	93
14	Tim Raines, Montreal	1983	90
15	Clyde Milan, Washington	1912	88

Strikeouts

		Year	SO
1	Mark Reynolds, Arizona	2008	204
2	Ryan Howard, Philadelphia	2007	199
	Ryan Howard, Philadelphia	2008	199
4	Jack Cust, Oakland	2008	197
5	Adam Dunn, Cincinnati	2004	195
6	Adam Dunn, Cincinnati	2006	194
7	Bobby Bonds, San Francisco	1970	189
8	Jose Hernandez, Milwaukee	2002	188
9	Bobby Bonds, San Francisco	1969	187
	Preston Wilson, Florida	2000	187

Pinch Hits
Career pinch hits in parentheses.

		Year	PH	
1	John Vander Wal, Colorado	1995	28	(129)
2	Lenny Harris, Col-Ari	1999	26	(212)
3	Jose Morales, Montreal	1976	25	(123)
4	Dave Philley, Baltimore	1961	24	(93)
	Vic Davalillo, St. Louis	1970	24	(95)
	Rusty Staub, New York-NL	1983	24	(100)
	Gerald Perry, St. Louis	1993	24	(95)

Pitching
Wins

From 1900-49

		Year	W	L	Pct
1	Jack Chesbro, NY-AL	1904	**41**	12	.774
2	Ed Walsh, Chi-AL	1908	**40**	15	.727
3	Christy Mathewson, NY-NL	1908	**37**	11	.771
4	Walter Johnson, Wash	1913	**36**	7	.837
5	Joe McGinnity, NY-NL	1904	**35**	8	.814
6	Smokey Joe Wood, Bos-AL	1912	**34**	5	.872
7	Cy Young, Bos-AL	1901	**33**	10	.767
	Grover Alexander, Phi-NL	1916	**33**	12	.733
	Christy Mathewson, NY-NL	1904	**33**	12	.733
10	Cy Young, Bos-AL	1902	**32**	11	.744

Since 1950

		Year	W	L	Pct
1	Denny McLain, Det	1968	**31**	6	.838
2	Robin Roberts, Phi-NL	1952	**28**	7	.800
3	Bob Welch, Oak	1990	**27**	6	.818
	Don Newcombe, Bklyn	1956	**27**	7	.794
	Sandy Koufax, LA	1966	**27**	9	.750
	Steve Carlton, Phi	1972	**27**	10	.730
7	Sandy Koufax, LA	1965	**26**	8	.765
	Juan Marichal, SF	1968	**26**	9	.743

Note: 11 pitchers tied with 25 wins, including Marichal twice.

Earned Run Average

From 1900-49

		Year	ShO	ERA
1	Dutch Leonard, Bos-AL	1914	7	1.01
2	Three Finger Brown, Chi-NL	1906	10	1.04
3	Walter Johnson, Wash	1913	11	1.09
4	Christy Mathewson, NY-NL	1909	8	1.14
5	Jack Pfiester, Chi-NL	1907	3	1.15
6	Addie Joss, Cle	1908	9	1.16
7	Carl Lundgren, Chi-NL	1907	7	1.17
8	Grover Alexander, Phi-NL	1915	12	1.22
9	Cy Young, Bos-AL	1908	3	1.26
10	Three pitchers tied at 1.27			

Since 1950

		Year	ShO	ERA
1	Bob Gibson, St.L	1968	13	1.12
2	Dwight Gooden, NY-NL	1985	8	1.53
3	Greg Maddux, Atl	1994	3	1.56
4	Luis Tiant, Cle	1968	9	1.60
5	Greg Maddux, Atl	1995	3	1.63
6	Dean Chance, LA-AL	1964	11	1.65
7	Nolan Ryan, Cal	1981	3	1.69
8	Sandy Koufax, LA	1966	5	1.73
9	Sandy Koufax, LA	1964	7	1.74
10	Pedro Martinez, Bos	2000	4	1.74

Note: Koufax's ERA in 1964 was 1.735. Martinez' ERA in 2000 was 1.742. The Yankees' Ron Guidry narrowly missed the top 10 list with an ERA of 1.743 in 1978.

Winning Pct.

		Year	W-L	Pct
1	Roy Face, Pit	1959	18-1	.947
2	Rick Sutcliffe, Chi-NL*	1984	16-1	.941
3	Johnny Allen, Cle	1937	15-1	.938
4	Greg Maddux, Atl	1995	19-2	.904
5	Randy Johnson, Sea	1995	18-2	.900
6	Ron Guidry, NY-AL	1978	25-3	.893
7	Freddie Fitzsimmons, Bklyn	1940	16-2	.889
8	Lefty Grove, Phi-AL	1931	31-4	.886
9	Bob Stanley, Bos	1978	15-2	.882
10	Preacher Roe, Bklyn	1951	22-3	.880
	Cliff Lee, Cle	2008	22-3	.880

*Sutcliffe began 1984 with Cleveland and was 4-5 before being traded to the Cubs; his overall winning pct. was .769 (20-6).

Strikeouts

		Year	SO	P/9
1	Nolan Ryan, Cal	1973	**383**	10.57
2	Sandy Koufax, LA	1965	**382**	10.24
3	Randy Johnson, Ari	2001	**372**	13.41
4	Nolan Ryan, Cal	1974	**367**	9.93
5	Randy Johnson, Ari	1999	**364**	12.06
6	Rube Waddell, Phi-AL	1904	**349**	8.20
7	Bob Feller, Cle	1946	**348**	8.43
8	Randy Johnson, Ari	2000	**347**	12.56
9	Nolan Ryan, Cal	1977	**341**	10.26
10	Randy Johnson, Ari	2002	**334**	11.56

Appearances

		Year	App	Sv
1	Mike Marshall, LA	1974	**106**	21
2	Kent Tekulve, Pit	1979	**94**	31
	Salomon Torres, Pit	2006	**94**	12
4	Mike Marshall, LA	1973	**92**	31
5	Kent Tekulve, Pit	1978	**91**	31
6	Wayne Granger, Cin	1969	**90**	27
	Mike Marshall, Min	1979	**90**	32
	Kent Tekulve, Phi	1987	**90**	3

Saves

		Year	App	Sv
1	Francisco Rodriguez, LA-AL	2008	76	62
2	Bobby Thigpen, Chi-AL	1990	77	57
3	John Smoltz, Atl	2002	75	55
	Eric Gagne, LA	2003	77	55
5	Randy Myers, Chi-NL	1993	73	53
	Trevor Hoffman, SD	1998	66	53
	Mariano Rivera, NY-AL	2004	74	53
8	Eric Gagne, LA	2002	77	52
9	Dennis Eckersley, Oak	1992	69	51
	Rod Beck, Chi-NL	1998	81	51

Innings Pitched (since 1920)

		Year	IP	W-L
1	Wilbur Wood, Chi-AL	1972	**376.2**	24-17
2	Mickey Lolich, Det	1971	**376.0**	25-14
3	Bob Feller, Cle	1946	**371.1**	26-15
4	Grover Alexander, Chi-NL	1920	**363.1**	27-14
5	Wilbur Wood, Chi-AL	1973	**359.1**	24-20

Shutouts

		Year	ShO	ERA
1	Grover Alexander, Phi-NL	1916	**16**	1.55
2	Jack Coombs, Phi-AL	1910	**13**	1.30
	Bob Gibson, St.L	1968	**13**	1.12
4	Christy Mathewson, NY-NL	1908	**12**	1.43
	Grover Alexander, Phi-NL	1915	**12**	1.22

Walks Allowed (since 1920)

		Year	BB	SO
1	Bob Feller, Cle	1938	**208**	240
2	Nolan Ryan, Cal	1977	**204**	341
3	Nolan Ryan, Cal	1974	**202**	367
4	Bob Feller, Cle	1941	**194**	260
5	Bobo Newsom, St.L-AL	1938	**192**	226

Home Runs Allowed

		Year	HRs
1	Bert Blyleven, Minnesota	1986	50
2	Jose Lima, Houston	2000	48
3	Robin Roberts, Philadelphia	1956	46
	Bert Blyleven, Minnesota	1987	46
5	Jamie Moyer, Seattle	2004	44

SINGLE GAME
Through 2008 regular season.

Batting

Home Runs

No		Date	Inn
4	Bobby Lowe, Boston-NL	5/30/1894	9
	Ed Delahanty, Philadelphia-NL	7/13/1896	9
	Lou Gehrig, New York-AL	6/3/1932	9
	Chuck Klein, Philadelphia-NL	7/10/1936	10
	Pat Seerey, Chicago-AL	7/18/1948	11
	Gil Hodges, Brooklyn	8/31/1950	9
	Joe Adcock, Milwaukee	7/31/1954	9
	Rocky Colavito, Cleveland	6/10/1959	9
	Willie Mays, San Francisco	4/30/1961	9
	Mike Schmidt, Philadelphia	4/17/1976	10
	Bob Horner, Atlanta	7/6/1986	9
	Mark Whiten, St. Louis	9/7/1993	9
	Mike Cameron, Seattle	5/2/2002	9
	Shawn Green, Los Angeles	5/23/2002	9
	Carlos Delgado, Toronto	9/25/2003	9

Runs

No		Date	Inn
7	Guy Hecker, Louisville	8/15/1886	9

Hits

No		Date	Inn
9	Johnny Burnett, Cleveland (9-for-11)	7/10/1932	18
7	Wilbert Robinson, Baltimore (7-for-7)	6/10/1892	9
	Rennie Stennett, Pittsburgh (7-for-7)	9/16/1975	9
	Cesar Gutierrez, Detroit (7-for-7)	6/21/1970	12
	Rocky Colavito, Detroit (7-for-10)	6/24/1962	22

Runs Batted In

No		Date	Inn
12	Jim Bottomley, St. Louis-NL	9/16/1924	9
	Mark Whiten, St. Louis	9/7/1993	9

Pitching

Strikeouts

No		Date	Inn
21	Tom Cheney, Washington	9/12/1962	16
20	Roger Clemens, Boston	4/29/1986	9
	Roger Clemens, Boston	9/18/1996	9
	Kerry Wood, Chicago-NL	5/6/1998	9
	Randy Johnson, Arizona	5/8/2001	9*

Innings Pitched

No		Date
26	Leon Cadore, Brooklyn (tie, 1-1)	5/1/1920
	Joe Oeschger, Boston-NL (tie, 1-1)	5/1/1920

*Johnson struck out 20 in nine innings and was removed with the game tied, 1-1. Arizona beat Cincinnati, 4-3, in 11 innings.

Unassisted Triple Plays

One of the rarest feats in baseball, the unassisted triple play has been accomplished only 14 times in major league history. Ironically, in what can only be described as a statistic anomaly, the trick was turned twice in two days in May of 1927.

Player, Position, Team	Date	Opponent
Paul Hines, OF, Providence	May 8, 1878	Boston-NL
Neal Ball, SS, Cleveland	July 19, 1909	Boston-AL
Bill Wambganss, 2B, Cleveland	Oct. 10, 1920	Brooklyn (World Series)
George Burns, 1B, Boston-AL	Sept. 14, 1923	Cleveland
Ernie Padgett, SS, Boston-NL	Oct. 6, 1923	Philadelphia
Glenn Wright, SS, Pittsburgh	May 7, 1925	St.Louis-NL
Jimmy Cooney, SS, Chicago-NL	May 30, 1927	Pittsburgh
Johnny Neun, 1B, Detroit	May 31, 1927	Cleveland
Ron Hansen, SS, Washington	July 30, 1968	Cleveland
Mickey Morandini, 2B, Philadelphia	Sept. 20, 1992	Pittsburgh
John Valentin, SS, Boston	July 8, 1994	Seattle
Randy Velarde, 2B, Oakland	May 29, 2000	NY Yankees
Rafael Furcal, SS, Atlanta	Aug. 10, 2003	St. Louis
Troy Tulowitzki, SS, Colorado	Apr. 29, 2007	Atlanta
Asdrubal Cabrera, 2B, Cleveland	May 12, 2008	Toronto

Most Gold Gloves (by position)

Gold Gloves have been awarded since the 1957 season by Rawlings Sporting Goods to superior major league fielders at each position in both leagues. Top 5 in each position are listed, through the 2007 season.

Pitchers	No
1 Greg Maddux	17
2 Jim Kaat	16
3 Bob Gibson	9
4 Bobby Shantz	8
5 Mark Langston	7

Catchers	No
1 Ivan Rodriguez	13
2 Johnny Bench	10
3 Bob Boone	7
4 Jim Sundberg	6
5 Bill Freehan	5

First Basemen	No
1 Keith Hernandez	11
2 Don Mattingly	9
3 George Scott	8
4 Vic Power	7
Bill White	7

Second Basemen	No
1 Roberto Alomar	10
2 Ryne Sandberg	9
3 Bill Mazeroski	8
Frank White	8
5 Joe Morgan	5
Bobby Richardson	5

Third Basemen	No
1 Brooks Robinson	16
2 Mike Schmidt	10
3 Scott Rolen	8
4 Three tied with 6 each.	

Shortstops	No
1 Ozzie Smith	13
2 Omar Vizquel	11
3 Luis Aparicio	9
4 Mark Belanger	8
5 Dave Concepcion	5

Outfielders	No
1 Roberto Clemente	12
Willie Mays	12
3 Ken Griffey Jr.	10
Al Kaline	10
Andruw Jones	10

All-Time Winningest Managers

Top 20 Major League career victories through the 2008 season. Career, regular season and postseason (playoffs and World Series) records are noted along with AL and NL pennants and World Series titles won. Managers active during 2008 season in **bold** type.

		Career			Regular Season			Postseason			
		Yrs	W	L	Pct	W	L	Pct	W	L	Pct	Titles
1	Connie Mack	53	**3755**	3967	.486	3731	3948	.486	24	19	.558	9 AL, 5 WS
2	John McGraw	33	**2866**	2012	.588	2840	1984	.589	26	28	.482	10 NL, 3 WS
3	**Tony La Russa**	30	**2520**	2194	.535	2461	2146	.534	59	48	.551	3 AL, 2 NL, 2 WS
4	**Bobby Cox**	27	**2393**	1920	.555	2327	1854	.557	66	66	.500	5 NL, 1 WS
5	**Joe Torre**	27	**2231**	1902	.540	2151	1848	.538	80	54	.597	6 AL, 4 WS
6	Sparky Anderson	26	**2228**	1855	.547	2194	1834	.545	34	21	.618	4 NL, 1 AL, 3 WS
7	Bucky Harris	29	**2168**	2228	.493	2157	2218	.493	11	10	.524	3 AL, 2 WS
8	Joe McCarthy	24	**2155**	1346	.616	2125	1333	.615	30	13	.698	1 NL, 8 AL, 7 WS
9	Walter Alston	23	**2063**	1634	.558	2040	1613	.558	23	21	.523	7 NL, 4 WS
10	Leo Durocher	24	**2015**	1717	.540	2008	1709	.540	7	8	.467	3 NL, 1 WS
11	Casey Stengel	25	**1942**	1868	.510	1905	1842	.508	37	26	.587	10 AL, 7 WS
12	Gene Mauch	26	**1907**	2044	.483	1902	2037	.483	5	7	.417	—None—
13	Bill McKechnie	25	**1904**	1737	.523	1896	1723	.524	8	14	.364	4 NL, 2 WS
14	**Lou Piniella**	21	**1724**	1588	.521	1701	1561	.521	23	27	.460	1 NL, 1 WS
15	Tommy Lasorda	21	**1630**	1469	.526	1599	1439	.526	31	30	.508	4 NL, 2 WS
16	Ralph Houk	20	**1627**	1539	.514	1619	1531	.514	8	8	.500	3 AL, 2 WS
17	Fred Clarke	19	**1609**	1189	.575	1602	1181	.576	7	8	.467	4 NL, 1 WS
18	Dick Williams	21	**1592**	1474	.519	1571	1451	.520	21	23	.477	3 AL, 1 NL, 2 WS
19	Earl Weaver	17	**1506**	1080	.582	1480	1060	.583	26	20	.565	4 AL, 1 WS
20	Clark Griffith	20	**1491**	1367	.522	1491	1367	.522	0	0	.000	1 AL (1901)

Notes: John McGraw's postseason record also includes two World Series tie games (1912,'22).

Where They Managed

Alston—Brooklyn/Los Angeles NL (1954-76); **Anderson**—Cincinnati NL (1970-78), Detroit AL (1979-95); **Clarke**— Louisville NL (1897-99), Pittsburgh NL (1900-15); **Cox**—Atlanta (1978-81, 1990–), Toronto (1982-85); **Durocher**—Brooklyn NL (1939-46,48), New York NL (1948-55), Chicago NL (1966-72), Houston NL (1972-73); **Griffith**—Chicago AL (1901-02), New York AL (1903-08), Cincinnati NL (1909-11), Washington AL (1912-20); **Harris**—Washington AL (1924- 28,35-42,50-54), Detroit AL (1929-33,55-56), Boston AL (1934), Philadelphia NL (1943), New York AL (1947-48); **Houk**—New York AL (1961-63,66-73), Detroit AL (1974-78), Boston AL (1981-84); **La Russa**—Chicago AL (1979-86), Oakland (1986-95); St. Louis (1996–) **Lasorda**—Los Angeles NL (1976-96); **Mack**—Pittsburgh NL (1894-96), Philadelphia AL (1901-50). **Mauch**—Philadelphia NL (1960-68), Montreal NL (1969-75), Minnesota AL (1976-80), California AL (1981-82,85-87); **McCarthy**—Chicago NL (1926-30), New York AL (1931-46), Boston AL (1948-50); **McGraw**—Baltimore NL (1899), Baltimore AL (1901-02), New York NL (1902-32); **McKechnie**—Newark FL (1915), Pittsburgh NL (1922-26), St. Louis (1928-29), Boston NL (1930-37), Cincinnati NL (1938-46); **Piniella**—New York AL (1986-88), Cincinnati (1990-92), Seattle (1993-2002), Tampa Bay (2003-05), Chicago NL (2007–); **Stengel**—Brooklyn NL (1934-36), Boston NL (1938-43), New York NL (1949-60), New York NL (1962-65); **Torre**—New York NL (1977-81), Atlanta (1982-84), St. Louis (1990-95), New York AL (1996-2007), Los Angeles NL (2008–); **Weaver**—Baltimore AL (1968-82,85-86); **Williams**—Boston AL (1967-69), Oakland AL (1971-73), California AL (1974-76), Montreal NL (1977-81), San Diego NL (1982-85), Seattle AL (1986-88).

Regular Season Winning Pct.

Minimum of 750 victories.

		Yrs	W	L	Pct	Pen
1	Joe McCarthy	24	2125	1333	**.615**	9
2	Charlie Comiskey	12	838	541	**.608**	4
3	Frank Selee	16	1284	862	**.598**	5
4	Billy Southworth	13	1044	704	**.597**	4
5	Frank Chance	11	946	648	**.593**	4
6	John McGraw	33	2840	1984	**.589**	10
7	Al Lopez	17	1410	1004	**.584**	2
8	Earl Weaver	17	1480	1060	**.583**	4
9	Cap Anson	20	1296	947	**.578**	5
10	Fred Clarke	19	1602	1181	**.576**	4
11	Davey Johnson	14	1148	888	**.564**	1
12	Steve O'Neill	14	1040	821	**.559**	1
13	Walter Alston	23	2040	1613	**.558**	7
14	**Bobby Cox**	27	2327	1854	**.557**	5
15	Bill Terry	10	823	661	**.555**	3
16	Miller Huggins	17	1413	1134	**.555**	6
17	Billy Martin	16	1253	1013	**.553**	2
18	**Mike Scioscia**	9	803	655	**.551**	1
19	Harry Wright	18	1000	825	**.548**	3
20	Charlie Grimm	19	1287	1067	**.547**	3

World Series Victories

		App	W	L	T	Pct	WS
1	Casey Stengel	10	37	26	0	.587	7
2	Joe McCarthy	9	30	13	0	.698	7
3	John McGraw	9	26	28	2	.482	3
4	Connie Mack	8	24	19	0	.558	5
5	**Joe Torre**	6	21	11	0	.656	4
6	Walter Alston	7	20	20	0	.500	4
7	Miller Huggins	6	18	15	1	.544	3
8	Sparky Anderson	5	16	12	0	.571	3
9	Tommy Lasorda	4	12	11	0	.522	2
	Dick Williams	4	12	14	0	.462	2
11	Frank Chance	4	11	9	1	.548	2
	Bucky Harris	3	11	10	0	.524	2
	Billy Southworth	4	11	10	0	.500	2
	Earl Weaver	4	11	13	0	.458	1
	Bobby Cox	5	11	18	0	.379	1
16	Whitey Herzog	3	11	10	0	.476	1
17	**Tony La Russa**	5	9	13	0	.409	2
18	Seven tied with eight wins each.						

Active Managers' Records
Regular season games only; through 2008 (updated as of Oct. 26).

National League

		Yrs	W	L	Pct
1	Tony La Russa, St.L	30	**2461**	2146	.534
2	Bobby Cox, Atl.	27	**2327**	1854	.557
3	Joe Torre, LA	27	**2151**	1848	.538
4	Lou Piniella, Chi	21	**1701**	1561	.521
5	Dusty Baker, Cin	15	**1236**	1129	.523
6	Bruce Bochy, SF	14	**1094**	1156	.486
7	Charlie Manuel, Phi	7	**579**	485	.544
8	Jerry Manuel, NY	7	**555**	509	.522
9	Clint Hurdle, Col	7	**516**	597	.464
10	Bob Melvin, Ari	6	**481**	491	.495
11	Fredi Gonzalez, Fla.	2	**155**	168	.480
12	Bud Black, SD	2	**152**	173	.468
13	Manny Acta, Wash.	2	**132**	191	.409
14	Cecil Cooper, Hou.	2	**101**	91	.526
15	John Russell, Pit. Milwaukee	1	**67**	95	.414

American League

		Yrs	W	L	Pct
1	Jim Leyland, Det.	17	**1326**	1360	.494
2	Mike Scioscia, Ana.	9	**803**	655	.551
3	Terry Francona, Bos.	9	**755**	703	.518
4	Cito Gaston, Tor.	10	**732**	672	.521
5	Ron Gardenhire, Min.	7	**622**	512	.549
6	Eric Wedge, Cle.	6	**496**	477	.510
7	Ozzie Guillen, Chi	5	**433**	378	.534
8	Joe Maddon, TB	5	**251**	286	.467
9	Joe Girardi, NY	2	**167**	157	.515
10	Ron Washington, Tex.	2	**154**	170	.475
11	Bob Geren, Oak.	2	**151**	172	.467
12	Dave Tremblay, Bal.	2	**108**	146	.425
13	Trey Hillman, KC Seattle	1	**75**	87	.463

Annual Awards

MOST VALUABLE PLAYER

There have been three different Most Valuable Player awards in baseball since 1911—the Chalmers Award (1911-14), presented by the Detroit-based automobile company; the League Award (1922-29), presented by the National and American Leagues; and the Baseball Writers' Award (since 1931), presented by the Baseball Writers' Association of America. Statistics for winning players are provided below. Stats for winning pitchers before advent of Cy Young Award are in MVP Pitchers' Statistics table.

Multiple winners: NL—Barry Bonds (7); Roy Campanella, Stan Musial and Mike Schmidt (3); Ernie Banks, Johnny Bench, Rogers Hornsby, Carl Hubbell, Willie Mays, Joe Morgan and Dale Murphy (2). **AL**—Yogi Berra, Joe DiMaggio, Jimmie Foxx, Mickey Mantle and Alex Rodriguez (3); Mickey Cochrane, Lou Gehrig, Juan Gonzalez, Hank Greenberg, Walter Johnson, Roger Maris, Hal Newhouser, Cal Ripken Jr., Frank Thomas, Ted Williams and Robin Yount (2). **NL & AL**—Frank Robinson (2, one in each).

Chalmers Award

National League

Year		Pos	HR	RBI	Avg
1911	Wildfire Schulte, Chi	OF	21	121	.300
1912	Larry Doyle, NY	2B	10	90	.330
1913	Jake Daubert, Bklyn	1B	2	52	.350
1914	Johnny Evers, Bos	2B	1	40	.279

American League

Year		Pos	HR	RBI	Avg
1911	Ty Cobb, Det	OF	8	144	.420
1912	Tris Speaker, Bos	OF	10	98	.383
1913	Walter Johnson, Wash	P	—	—	—
1914	Eddie Collins, Phi	2B	2	85	.344

League Award

National League

Year		Pos	HR	RBI	Avg
1922	No selection				
1923	No selection				
1924	Dazzy Vance, Bklyn	P	—	—	—
1925	Rogers Hornsby, St.L	2B-Mgr	39	143	.403
1926	Bob O'Farrell, St.L	C	7	68	.293
1927	Paul Waner, Pit	OF	9	131	.380
1928	Jim Bottomley, St.L	1B	31	136	.325
1929	Rogers Hornsby, Chi	2B	39	149	.380

American League

Year		Pos	HR	RBI	Avg
1922	George Sisler, St.L	1B	8	105	.420
1923	Babe Ruth, NY	OF	41	131	.393
1924	Walter Johnson, Wash	P	—	—	—
1925	Roger Peckinpaugh, Wash	SS	4	64	.294
1926	George Burns, Cle	1B	4	114	.358
1927	Lou Gehrig, NY	1B	47	175	.373
1928	Mickey Cochrane, Phi	C	10	57	.293
1929	No selection				

Most Valuable Player
National League

Year		Pos	HR	RBI	Avg
1931	Frankie Frisch, St.L	2B	4	82	.311
1932	Chuck Klein, Phi	OF	38	137	.348
1933	Carl Hubbell, NY	P	—	—	—
1934	Dizzy Dean, St.L	P	—	—	—
1935	Gabby Hartnett, Chi	C	13	91	.344
1936	Carl Hubbell, NY	P	—	—	—
1937	Joe Medwick, St.L	OF	31	154	.374
1938	Ernie Lombardi, Cin	C	19	95	.342
1939	Bucky Walters, Cin	P	—	—	—
1940	Frank McCormick, Cin	1B	19	127	.309
1941	Dolf Camilli, Bklyn	1B	34	120	.285
1942	Mort Cooper, St.L	P	—	—	—
1943	Stan Musial, St.L	OF	13	81	.357
1944	Marty Marion, St.L	SS	6	63	.267
1945	Phil Cavarretta, Chi	1B	6	97	.355
1946	Stan Musial, St.L	1B-OF	16	103	.365
1947	Bob Elliott, Bos	3B	22	113	.317
1948	Stan Musial, St.L	OF	39	131	.376
1949	Jackie Robinson, Bklyn	2B	16	124	.342
1950	Jim Konstanty, Phi	P	—	—	—
1951	Roy Campanella, Bklyn	C	33	108	.325
1952	Hank Sauer, Chi	OF	37	121	.270
1953	Roy Campanella, Bklyn	C	41	142	.312
1954	Willie Mays, NY	OF	41	110	.345
1955	Roy Campanella, Bklyn	C	32	107	.318
1956	Don Newcombe, Bklyn	P	—	—	—
1957	Hank Aaron, Mil	OF	44	132	.322
1958	Ernie Banks, Chi	SS	47	129	.313
1959	Ernie Banks, Chi	SS	45	143	.304
1960	Dick Groat, Pit	SS	2	50	.325
1961	Frank Robinson, Cin	OF	37	124	.323
1962	Maury Wills, LA	SS	6	48	.299
1963	Sandy Koufax, LA	P	—	—	—
1964	Ken Boyer, St.L	3B	24	119	.295
1965	Willie Mays, SF	OF	52	112	.317
1966	Roberto Clemente, Pit	OF	29	119	.317
1967	Orlando Cepeda, St.L	1B	25	111	.325
1968	Bob Gibson, St.L	P	—	—	—
1969	Willie McCovey, SF	1B	45	126	.320
1970	Johnny Bench, Cin	C	45	148	.293

Year		Pos	HR	RBI	Avg	Year		Pos	HR	RBI	Avg
1971	Joe Torre, St.L	3B	24	137	.363	1989	Kevin Mitchell, SF	OF	47	125	.291
1972	Johnny Bench, Cin	C	40	125	.270	1990	Barry Bonds, Pit	OF	33	114	.301
1973	Pete Rose, Cin	OF	5	64	.338	1991	Terry Pendleton, Atl	3B	22	86	.319
1974	Steve Garvey, LA	1B	21	111	.312	1992	Barry Bonds, Pit	OF	34	103	.311
1975	Joe Morgan, Cin	2B	17	94	.327	1993	Barry Bonds, SF	OF	46	123	.336
1976	Joe Morgan, Cin	2B	27	111	.320	1994	Jeff Bagwell, Hou	1B	39	116	.368
1977	George Foster, Cin	OF	52	149	.320	1995	Barry Larkin, Cin	SS	15	66	.319
1978	Dave Parker, Pit	OF	30	117	.334	1996	Ken Caminiti, SD	3B	40	130	.326
1979	Keith Hernandez, St.L	1B	11	105	.344	1997	Larry Walker, Col	OF	49	130	.366
	Willie Stargell, Pit	1B	32	82	.281	1998	Sammy Sosa, Chi	OF	66	158	.308
1980	Mike Schmidt, Phi	3B	48	121	.286	1999	Chipper Jones, Atl	3B	45	110	.319
1981	Mike Schmidt, Phi	3B	31	91	.316	2000	Jeff Kent, SF	2B	33	125	.334
1982	Dale Murphy, Atl	OF	36	109	.281	2001	Barry Bonds, SF	OF	73	137	.328
1983	Dale Murphy, Atl	OF	36	121	.302	2002	Barry Bonds, SF	OF	46	110	.370
1984	Ryne Sandberg, Chi	2B	19	84	.314	2003	Barry Bonds, SF	OF	45	90	.341
1985	Willie McGee, St.L	OF	10	82	.353	2004	Barry Bonds, SF	OF	45	101	.362
1986	Mike Schmidt, Phi	3B	37	119	.290	2005	Albert Pujols, St.L	1B	41	117	.330
1987	Andre Dawson, Chi	OF	49	137	.287	2006	Ryan Howard, Phi	1B	58	149	.313
1988	Kirk Gibson, LA	OF	25	76	.290	2007	Jimmy Rollins, Phi	SS	30	94	.296

American League

Year		Pos	HR	RBI	Avg	Year		Pos	HR	RBI	Avg
1931	Lefty Grove, Phi	P	—	—	—	1970	Boog Powell, Bal	1B	35	114	.297
1932	Jimmie Foxx, Phi	1B	58	169	.364	1971	Vida Blue, Oak	P	—	—	—
1933	Jimmie Foxx, Phi	1B	48	163	.356	1972	Dick Allen, Chi	1B	37	113	.308
1934	Mickey Cochrane, Det	C-Mgr	2	76	.320	1973	Reggie Jackson, Oak	OF	32	117	.293
1935	Hank Greenberg, Det	1B	36	170	.328	1974	Jeff Burroughs, Tex	OF	25	118	.301
1936	Lou Gehrig, NY	1B	49	152	.354	1975	Fred Lynn, Bos	OF	21	105	.331
1937	Charlie Gehringer, Det	2B	14	96	.371	1976	Thurman Munson, NY	C	17	105	.302
1938	Jimmie Foxx, Bos	1B	50	175	.349	1977	Rod Carew, Min	1B	14	100	.388
1939	Joe DiMaggio, NY	OF	30	126	.381	1978	Jim Rice, Bos	OF-DH	46	139	.315
1940	Hank Greenberg, Det	OF	41	150	.340	1979	Don Baylor, Cal	OF-DH	36	139	.296
1941	Joe DiMaggio, NY	OF	30	125	.357	1980	George Brett, KC	3B	24	118	.390
1942	Joe Gordon, NY	2B	18	103	.322	1981	Rollie Fingers, Mil	P	—	—	—
1943	Spud Chandler, NY	P	—	—	—	1982	Robin Yount, Mil	SS	29	114	.331
1944	Hal Newhouser, Det	P	—	—	—	1983	Cal Ripken Jr., Bal	SS	27	102	.318
1945	Hal Newhouser, Det	P	—	—	—	1984	Willie Hernandez, Det	P	—	—	—
1946	Ted Williams, Bos	OF	38	123	.342	1985	Don Mattingly, NY	1B	35	145	.324
1947	Joe DiMaggio, NY	OF	20	97	.315	1986	Roger Clemens, Bos	P	—	—	—
1948	Lou Boudreau, Cle	SS-Mgr	18	106	.355	1987	George Bell, Tor	OF	47	134	.308
1949	Ted Williams, Bos	OF	43	159	.343	1988	Jose Canseco, Oak	OF	42	124	.307
1950	Phil Rizzuto, NY	SS	7	66	.324	1989	Robin Yount, Mil	OF	21	103	.318
1951	Yogi Berra, NY	C	27	88	.294	1990	Rickey Henderson, Oak	OF	28	61	.325
1952	Bobby Shantz, Phi	P	—	—	—	1991	Cal Ripken Jr., Bal	SS	34	114	.323
1953	Al Rosen, Cle	3B	43	145	.336	1992	Dennis Eckersley, Oak	P	—	—	—
1954	Yogi Berra, NY	C	22	125	.307	1993	Frank Thomas, Chi	1B	41	128	.317
1955	Yogi Berra, NY	C	27	108	.272	1994	Frank Thomas, Chi	1B	38	101	.353
1956	Mickey Mantle, NY	OF	52	130	.353	1995	Mo Vaughn, Bos	1B	39	126	.300
1957	Mickey Mantle, NY	OF	34	94	.365	1996	Juan Gonzalez, Tex	OF-DH	47	144	.314
1958	Jackie Jensen, Bos	OF	35	122	.286	1997	Ken Griffey Jr., Sea	OF	56	147	.304
1959	Nellie Fox, Chi	2B	2	70	.306	1998	Juan Gonzalez, Tex	OF	45	157	.318
1960	Roger Maris, NY	OF	39	112	.283	1999	Ivan Rodriguez, Tex	C	35	113	.332
1961	Roger Maris, NY	OF	61	142	.269	2000	Jason Giambi, Oak	1B	43	137	.333
1962	Mickey Mantle, NY	OF	30	89	.321	2001	Ichiro Suzuki, Sea	OF	8	69	.350
1963	Elston Howard, NY	C	28	85	.287	2002	Miguel Tejada, Oak	SS	34	131	.308
1964	Brooks Robinson, Bal	3B	28	118	.317	2003	Alex Rodriguez, Tex	SS	47	118	.298
1965	Zoilo Versalles, Min	SS	19	77	.273	2004	Vladimir Guerrero, Ana	OF	39	126	.337
1966	Frank Robinson, Bal	OF	49	122	.316	2005	Alex Rodriguez, NY	3B	48	130	.321
1967	Carl Yastrzemski, Bos	OF	44	121	.326	2006	Justin Morneau, Min	1B	34	130	.321
1968	Denny McLain, Det	P	—	—	—	2007	Alex Rodriguez, NY	3B	54	156	.314
1969	Harmon Killebrew, Min	3B-1B	49	140	.276						

MVP Pitchers' Statistics

Pitchers have been named Most Valuable Player on 23 occasions, 10 times in the NL and 13 in the AL. For statistics of MVP pitchers since 1956, see Cy Young Award tables on following page.

National League

Year		Gm	W-L	SV	ERA
1924	Dazzy Vance, Bklyn	.35	28-6	0	2.16
1933	Carl Hubbell, NY	.45	23-12	5	1.66
1934	Dizzy Dean, St.L	.50	30-7	7	2.66
1936	Carl Hubbell, NY	.42	26-6	3	2.31
1939	Bucky Walters, Cin	.39	27-11	0	2.29
1942	Mort Cooper, St.L	.37	22-7	0	1.78
1950	Jim Konstanty, Phi	.74	16-7	22	2.66

American League

Year		Gm	W-L	SV	ERA
1913	Walter Johnson, Wash	.47	36-7	2	1.09
1924	Walter Johnson, Wash	.38	23-7	0	2.72
1931	Lefty Grove, Phi	.41	31-4	5	2.06
1943	Spud Chandler, NY	.30	20-4	0	1.64
1944	Hal Newhouser, Det	.47	29-9	2	2.22
1945	Hal Newhouser, Det	.40	25-9	0	1.81
1952	Bobby Shantz, Phi	.33	24-7	0	2.48

CY YOUNG AWARD

Voted on by the Baseball Writers Association of America. One award was presented from 1956-66, two since 1967. Pitchers who won the MVP and Cy Young awards in the same season are in **bold** type.

Multiple winners: NL—Steve Carlton, Greg Maddux and Randy Johnson (4); Sandy Koufax and Tom Seaver (3); Bob Gibson and Tom Glavine (2). **AL**—Roger Clemens (6); Jim Palmer (3); Pedro Martinez, Denny McLain and Johan Santana (2). **NL & AL**—Roger Clemens (7, six in AL, one in NL); Randy Johnson (5, four in NL, one in AL), Pedro Martinez (3, two in AL, one in NL) and Gaylord Perry (2, one in each).

NL and AL Combined

Year	National League	Gm	W-L	SV	ERA	Year	National League	Gm	W-L	SV	ERA
1956	**Don Newcombe**, Bklyn	38	27-7	0	3.06	1966	Sandy Koufax, LA	41	27-9	0	1.7
1957	Warren Spahn, Mil	39	21-11	3	2.69	**Year**	**American League**	**Gm**	**W-L**	**SV**	**ERA**
1960	Vernon Law, Pit	35	20-9	0	3.08	1958	Bob Turley, NY	33	21-7	1	2.9
1962	Don Drysdale, LA	43	25-9	1	2.83	1959	Early Wynn, Chi	37	22-10	0	3.1
1963	**Sandy Koufax**, LA	40	25-5	0	1.88	1961	Whitey Ford, NY	39	25-4	0	3.2
1965	Sandy Koufax, LA	43	26-8	2	2.04	1964	Dean Chance, LA	46	20-9	4	1.6

Separate League Awards

	National League						American League				
Year		**Gm**	**W-L**	**SV**	**ERA**	**Year**		**Gm**	**W-L**	**SV**	**ERA**
1967	Mike McCormick, SF	40	22-10	0	2.85	1967	Jim Lonborg, Bos	39	22-9	0	3.1
1968	**Bob Gibson**, St.L	34	22-9	0	1.12	1968	**Denny McLain**, Det	41	31-6	0	1.9
1969	Tom Seaver, NY	36	25-7	0	2.21	1969	Denny McLain, Det.	42	24-9	0	2.8
1970	Bob Gibson, St.L	34	23-7	0	3.12		Mike Cuellar, Bal	39	23-11	0	2.3
1971	Ferguson Jenkins, Chi	39	24-13	0	2.77	1970	Jim Perry, Min	40	24-12	0	3.0
1972	Steve Carlton, Phi	41	27-10	0	1.97	1971	**Vida Blue**, Oak	39	24-8	0	1.8
1973	Tom Seaver, NY	36	19-10	0	2.08	1972	Gaylord Perry, Cle	41	24-16	1	1.9
1974	Mike Marshall, LA	106	15-12	21	2.42	1973	Jim Palmer, Bal	38	22-9	1	2.40
1975	Tom Seaver, NY	36	22-9	0	2.38	1974	Catfish Hunter, Oak	41	25-12	0	2.4
1976	Randy Jones, SD	40	22-14	0	2.74	1975	Jim Palmer, Bal	39	23-11	1	2.09
1977	Steve Carlton, Phi	36	23-10	0	2.64	1976	Jim Palmer, Bal	40	22-13	0	2.5
1978	Gaylord Perry, SD	37	21-6	0	2.72	1977	Sparky Lyle, NY	72	13-5	26	2.1
1979	Bruce Sutter, Chi	62	6-6	37	2.23	1978	Ron Guidry, NY	35	25-3	0	1.7
1980	Steve Carlton, Phi	38	24-9	0	2.34	1979	Mike Flanagan, Bal	39	23-9	0	3.08
1981	Fernando Valenzuela, LA	25	13-7	0	2.48	1980	Steve Stone, Bal	37	25-7	0	3.23
1982	Steve Carlton, Phi	38	23-11	0	3.10	1981	**Rollie Fingers**, Mil	47	6-3	28	1.04
1983	John Denny, Phi	36	19-6	0	2.37	1982	Pete Vuckovich, Mil	30	18-6	0	3.34
1984	Rick Sutcliffe, Chi	20*	16-1	0	2.69	1983	LaMarr Hoyt, Chi.	36	24-10	0	3.66
1985	Dwight Gooden, NY	35	24-4	0	1.53	1984	**Willie Hernandez**, Det	80	9-3	32	1.92
1986	Mike Scott, Hou.	37	18-10	0	2.22	1985	Bret Saberhagen, KC	32	20-6	0	2.87
1987	Steve Bedrosian, Phi.	65	5-3	40	2.83	1986	**Roger Clemens**, Bos	33	24-4	0	2.48
1988	Orel Hershiser, LA	35	23-8	1	2.26	1987	Roger Clemens, Bos.	36	20-9	0	2.97
1989	Mark Davis, SD	70	4-3	44	1.85	1988	Frank Viola, Min	35	24-7	0	2.64
1990	Doug Drabek, Pit	33	22-6	0	2.76	1989	Bret Saberhagen, KC	36	23-6	0	2.16
1991	Tom Glavine, Atl	34	20-11	0	2.55	1990	Bob Welch, Oak	35	27-6	0	2.95
1992	Greg Maddux, Chi	35	20-11	0	2.18	1991	Roger Clemens, Bos.	35	18-10	0	2.62
1993	Greg Maddux, Atl	36	20-10	0	2.36	1992	**Dennis Eckersley**, Oak.	69	7-1	51	1.91
1994	Greg Maddux, Atl	25	16-6	0	1.56	1993	Jack McDowell, Chi	34	22-10	0	3.37
1995	Greg Maddux, Atl	28	19-2	0	1.63	1994	David Cone, KC	23	16-5	0	2.94
1996	John Smoltz, Atl.	35	24-8	0	2.94	1995	Randy Johnson, Sea.	30	18-2	0	2.48
1997	Pedro Martinez, Mon	31	17-8	0	1.90	1996	Pat Hentgen, Tor	35	20-10	0	3.22
1998	Tom Glavine, Atl	33	20-6	0	2.47	1997	Roger Clemens, Tor	34	21-7	0	2.05
1999	Randy Johnson, Ari	35	17-9	0	2.48	1998	Roger Clemens, Tor	33	20-6	0	2.65
2000	Randy Johnson, Ari	35	19-7	0	2.64	1999	Pedro Martinez, Bos.	31	23-4	0	2.07
2001	Randy Johnson, Ari	35	21-6	0	2.49	2000	Pedro Martinez, Bos.	29	18-6	0	1.74
2002	Randy Johnson, Ari	35	24-5	0	2.32	2001	Roger Clemens, NY	33	20-3	0	3.51
2003	Eric Gagne, LA	77	2-3	55	1.20	2002	Barry Zito, Oak	35	23-5	0	2.75
2004	Roger Clemens, Hou	33	18-4	0	2.98	2003	Roy Halladay, Tor	36	22-7	0	3.25
2005	Chris Carpenter, St.L	33	21-5	0	2.83	2004	Johan Santana, Min	34	20-6	0	2.61
2006	Brandon Webb, SD	33	16-8	0	3.10	2005	Bartolo Colon, LA	33	21-8	0	3.48
2007	Jake Peavy, SD	34	19-6	0	2.54	2006	Johan Santana, Min	34	19-6	0	2.77
						2007	C.C. Sabathia, Cle	34	19-7	0	3.21

*NL games only, Sutcliffe pitched 15 games with Cleveland before being traded to the Cubs.

ROOKIE OF THE YEAR

Voted on by the Baseball Writers Assn. of America. One award was presented from 1947-48. Two awards (one for each league) have been presented since 1949. Winners who were also named MVP in the same season are in **bold** type.

NL and AL Combined

Year		Pos	Year		Pos
1947	Jackie Robinson, Brooklyn	1B	1948	Alvin Dark, Boston-NL	SS

National League

Year		Pos	Year		Pos	Year		Pos
1949	Don Newcombe, Bklyn	P	1951	Willie Mays, NY	OF	1953	Jim Gilliam, Bklyn	2B
1950	Sam Jethroe, Bos	OF	1952	Joe Black, Bklyn	P	1954	Wally Moon, St.L	OF

Year		Pos	Year		Pos	Year		Pos
1955	Bill Virdon, St.L	OF	1973	Gary Matthews, SF	OF	1990	David Justice, Atl	OF
1956	Frank Robinson, Cin	OF	1974	Bake McBride, St.L	OF	1991	Jeff Bagwell, Hou	1B
1957	Jack Sanford, Phi	P	1975	John Montefusco, SF	P	1992	Eric Karros, LA	1B
1958	Orlando Cepeda, SF	1B	1976	Butch Metzger, SD	P	1993	Mike Piazza, LA	C
1959	Willie McCovey, SF	1B		& Pat Zachry, Cin	P	1994	Raul Mondesi, LA	OF
1960	Frank Howard, LA	OF	1977	Andre Dawson, Mon	OF	1995	Hideo Nomo, LA	P
1961	Billy Williams, Chi	OF	1978	Bob Horner, Atl	3B	1996	Todd Hollandsworth, LA	OF
1962	Ken Hubbs, Chi	2B	1979	Rick Sutcliffe, LA	P	1997	Scott Rolen, Phi	3B
1963	Pete Rose, Cin	2B	1980	Steve Howe, LA	P	1998	Kerry Wood, Chi	P
1964	Richie Allen, Phi	3B	1981	Fernando Valenzuela, LA	P	1999	Scott Williamson, Cin	P
1965	Jim Lefebvre, LA	2B	1982	Steve Sax, LA	2B	2000	Rafael Furcal, Atl	SS
1966	Tommy Helms, Cin	3B	1983	Darryl Strawberry, NY	OF	2001	Albert Pujols, St.L	OF-3B
1967	Tom Seaver, NY	P	1984	Dwight Gooden, NY	P	2002	Jason Jennings, Col	P
1968	Johnny Bench, Cin	C	1985	Vince Coleman, St.L	OF	2003	Dontrelle Willis, Fla	P
1969	Ted Sizemore, LA	2B	1986	Todd Worrell, St.L	P	2004	Jason Bay, Pit	OF
1970	Carl Morton, Mon	P	1987	Benito Santiago, SD	C	2005	Ryan Howard, Phi	1B
1971	Earl Williams, Atl	C	1988	Chris Sabo, Cin	3B	2006	Hanley Ramirez, Fla	SS
1972	Jon Matlack, NY	P	1989	Jerome Walton, Chi	OF	2007	Ryan Braun, Mil	OF

American League

Year		Pos	Year		Pos	Year		Pos
1949	Roy Sievers, St.L	OF	1969	Lou Piniella, KC	OF	1988	Walt Weiss, Oak	SS
1950	Walt Dropo, Bos	1B	1970	Thurman Munson, NY	C	1989	Gregg Olson, Bal	P
1951	Gil McDougald, NY	3B	1971	Chris Chambliss, Cle	1B	1990	Sandy Alomar Jr., Cle	C
1952	Harry Byrd, Phi	P	1972	Carlton Fisk, Bos	C	1991	Chuck Knoblauch, Min	2B
1953	Harvey Kuenn, Det	SS	1973	Al Bumbry, Bal	OF	1992	Pat Listach, Mil	SS
1954	Bob Grim, NY	P	1974	Mike Hargrove, Tex	1B	1993	Tim Salmon, Cal	OF
1955	Herb Score, Cle	P	1975	**Fred Lynn**, Bos	OF	1994	Bob Hamelin, KC	DH
1956	Luis Aparicio, Chi	SS	1976	Mark Fidrych, Det	P	1995	Marty Cordova, Min	OF
1957	Tony Kubek, NY	INF-OF	1977	Eddie Murray, Bal	DH-1B	1996	Derek Jeter, NY	SS
1958	Albie Pearson, Wash	OF	1978	Lou Whitaker, Det	2B	1997	Nomar Garciaparra, Bos	SS
1959	Bob Allison, Wash	OF	1979	John Castino, Min	3B	1998	Ben Grieve, Oak	OF
1960	Ron Hansen, Bal	SS		& Alfredo Griffin, Tor	SS	1999	Carlos Beltran, KC	OF
1961	Don Schwall, Bos	P	1980	Joe Charboneau, Cle	OF-DH	2000	Kazuhiro Sasaki, Sea	P
1962	Tom Tresh, NY	SS-OF	1981	Dave Righetti, NY	P	2001	**Ichiro Suzuki**, Sea	OF
1963	Gary Peters, Chi	P	1982	Cal Ripken Jr., Bal	SS-3B	2002	Eric Hinske, Tor	3B
1964	Tony Oliva, Min	OF	1983	Ron Kittle, Chi	OF	2003	Angel Berroa, KC	SS
1965	Curt Blefary, Bal	OF	1984	Alvin Davis, Sea	1B	2004	Bobby Crosby, Oak	SS
1966	Tommie Agee, Chi	OF	1985	Ozzie Guillen, Chi	SS	2005	Huston Street, Oak	P
1967	Rod Carew, Min	2B	1986	Jose Canseco, Oak	OF	2006	Justin Verlander, Det	P
1968	Stan Bahnsen, NY	P	1987	Mark McGwire, Oak	1B	2007	Dustin Pedroia, Bos	2B

MANAGER OF THE YEAR

Voted on by the Baseball Writers Association of America. Two awards (one for each league) presented since 1983. Note that (*) indicates manager's team won division and (†) indicates unofficial division won in 1994.

Multiple winners: Bobby Cox and Tony La Russa (4); Dusty Baker and Jim Leyland (3); Sparky Anderson, Tommy Lasorda, Jack McKeon, Lou Piniella, Buck Showalter and Joe Torre (2).

National League

Year		Diff. from previous year		
1983	Tommy Lasorda, LA	88-74	to	91-71*
1984	Jim Frey, Chi	71-91	to	96-75*
1985	Whitey Herzog, St. L	84-78	to	101-61*
1986	Hal Lanier, Hou	83-79	to	96-66*
1987	Buck Rodgers, Mon	78-83	to	91-71
1988	Tommy Lasorda, LA	73-89	to	94-67*
1989	Don Zimmer, Chi	77-85	to	93-69*
1990	Jim Leyland, Pit	74-88	to	95-67*
1991	Bobby Cox, Atl	65-97	to	94-68*
1992	Jim Leyland, Pit	98-64*	to	96-66*
1993	Dusty Baker, SF	72-90	to	103-59
1994	Felipe Alou, Mon	74-68	to	74-40†
1995	Don Baylor, Col	53-64	to	77-67
1996	Bruce Bochy, SD	70-74	to	91-71
1997	Dusty Baker, SF	68-94	to	90-72
1998	Larry Dierker, Hou	84-78	to	102-60*
1999	Jack McKeon, Cin	77-85	to	96-67
2000	Dusty Baker, SF	86-76	to	97-65*
2001	Larry Bowa, Phi	65-97	to	86-76
2002	Tony La Russa, St.L	93-69	to	97-65*
2003	Jack McKeon, Fla	79-83	to	91-71
2004	Bobby Cox, Atl	101-61	to	96-66*
2005	Bobby Cox, Atl	96-66*	to	90-72*
2006	Joe Girardi, Fla	83-79	to	78-84
2007	Bob Melvin, Ari	76-86	to	90-72*

American League

Year		Diff. from previous year		
1983	Tony La Russa, Chi	87-75	to	99-63*
1984	Sparky Anderson, Det	92-70	to	104-58*
1985	Bobby Cox, Tor	89-73	to	99-62*
1986	John McNamara, Bos	81-81	to	95-66*
1987	Sparky Anderson, Det	87-75	to	98-64*
1988	Tony La Russa, Oak	81-81	to	104-58*
1989	Frank Robinson, Bal	54-107	to	87-75
1990	Jeff Torborg, Chi	69-92	to	94-68
1991	Tom Kelly, Min	74-88	to	95-67*
1992	Tony La Russa, Oak	84-78	to	96-66*
1993	Gene Lamont, Chi	76-86	to	94-68*
1994	Buck Showalter, NY	88-74	to	70-43†
1995	Lou Piniella, Sea	49-63	to	79-66*
1996	Joe Torre, NY	79-65	to	92-70
	& Johnny Oates, Tex	74-70	to	90-72
1997	Davey Johnson, Bal	88-74	to	98-64
1998	Joe Torre, NY	96-66	to	114-48*
1999	Jimy Williams, Bos	92-70	to	94-68
2000	Jerry Manuel, Chi	75-86	to	95-67*
2001	Lou Piniella, Sea	91-71	to	116-46*
2002	Mike Scioscia, Ana	75-87	to	99-63
2003	Tony Pena, KC	62-100	to	83-79
2004	Buck Showalter, Tex	71-91	to	89-73
2005	Ozzie Guillen, Chi	83-79	to	99-63*
2006	Jim Leyland, Det	71-91	to	95-67
2007	Eric Wedge, Cle	78-84	to	96-66*

COLLEGE BASEBALL

College World Series

The NCAA Division I College World Series has been held in Kalamazoo, Mich. (1947-48), Wichita, Kan. (1949) and Omaha, Neb. (since 1950). Beginning in 2003, the championship series has been a best-of-three series.

Multiple winners: USC (12); Texas (6); Arizona St. and LSU (5); CS-Fullerton and Miami-FL (4); Arizona and Minnesota (3); California, Michigan, Oklahoma, Oregon St. and Stanford (2).

Year	Winner	Coach	Score	Runner-up
1947	California	Clint Evans	8-7	Yale
1948	USC	Sam Barry	9-2	Yale
1949	Texas	Bibb Falk	10-3	W. Forest
1950	Texas	Bibb Falk	3-0	Wash. St.
1951	Oklahoma	Jack Baer	3-2	Tennessee
1952	Holy Cross	Jack Barry	8-4	Missouri
1953	Michigan	Ray Fisher	7-5	Texas
1954	Missouri	Hi Simmons	4-1	Rollins
1955	Wake Forest	Taylor Sanford	7-6	W. Mich.
1956	Minnesota	Dick Siebert	12-1	Arizona
1957	California	Geo. Wolfman	1-0	Penn St.
1958	USC	Rod Dedeaux	8-7	Missouri
1959	Oklahoma St.	Toby Greene	5-3	Arizona
1960	Minnesota	Dick Siebert	2-1	USC
1961	USC	Rod Dedeaux	1-0	Okla. St.
1962	Michigan	Don Lund	5-4	S. Clara
1963	USC	Rod Dedeaux	5-2	Arizona
1964	Minnesota	Dick Siebert	5-1	Missouri
1965	Arizona St.	Bobby Winkles	2-1	Ohio St.
1966	Ohio St.	Marty Karow	8-2	Okla. St.
1967	Arizona St.	Bobby Winkles	11-2	Houston
1968	USC	Rod Dedeaux	4-3	So. Ill.
1969	Arizona St.	Bobby Winkles	10-1	Tulsa
1970	USC	Rod Dedeaux	2-1	Fla. St.
1971	USC	Rod Dedeaux	7-2	So. Ill.
1972	USC	Rod Dedeaux	1-0	Ariz. St.
1973	USC	Rod Dedeaux	4-3	Ariz. St.
1974	USC	Rod Dedeaux	7-3	Miami-FL
1975	Texas	Cliff Gustafson	5-1	S. Carolina
1976	Arizona	Jerry Kindall	7-1	E. Michigan
1977	Arizona St.	Jim Brock	2-1	S. Carolina
1978	USC	Rod Dedeaux	10-3	Ariz. St.
1979	CS-Fullerton	Augie Garrido	2-1	Arkansas
1980	Arizona	Jerry Kindall	5-3	Hawaii
1981	Arizona St.	Jim Brock	7-4	Okla. St.
1982	Miami-FL	Ron Fraser	9-3	Wichita St.
1983	Texas	Cliff Gustafson	4-3	Alabama
1984	CS-Fullerton	Augie Garrido	3-1	Texas
1985	Miami-FL	Ron Fraser	10-6	Texas
1986	Arizona	Jerry Kindall	10-2	Fla. St.
1987	Stanford	M. Marquess	9-5	Okla. St.
1988	Stanford	M. Marquess	9-4	Ariz. St.
1989	Wichita St.	G. Stephenson	5-3	Texas
1990	Georgia	Steve Webber	2-1	Okla. St.
1991	LSU	Skip Bertman	6-3	Wichita St.
1992	Pepperdine	Andy Lopez	3-2	CS-Fullerton
1993	LSU	Skip Bertman	8-0	Wichita St.
1994	Oklahoma	Larry Cochell	13-5	Ga. Tech
1995	CS-Fullerton	Augie Garrido	11-5	USC
1996	LSU	Skip Bertman	9-8	Miami-FL
1997	LSU	Skip Bertman	13-6	Alabama
1998	USC	Mike Gillespie	21-14	Arizona St.
1999	Miami-FL	Jim Morris	6-5	Fla. St.
2000	LSU	Skip Bertman	6-5	Stanford
2001	Miami-FL	Jim Morris	12-1	Stanford
2002	Texas	Augie Garrido	12-6	S. Carolina
2003	Rice	Wayne Graham	4-3 3-8 14-2	Stanford
2004	CS-Fullerton	George Horton	6-4 3-2	Texas
2005	Texas	Augie Garrido	4-2 6-2	Florida
2006	Oregon St.	Pat Casey	3-4 11-7 3-2	N. Carolina
2007	Oregon St.	Pat Casey	11-4 9-3	N. Carolina
2008	Fresno St.	Mike Batesole	6-7 19-10 6-1	Georgia

Most Outstanding Player

The Most Outstanding Player has been selected every year of the College World Series since 1949. Winners who did not play for the CWS champion are listed in **bold** type. No player has won the award more than once.

Year		Year		Year	
1949	**Charles Teague,** W. Forest, 2B	1970	**Gene Ammann,** Fla. St., P	1991	Gary Hymel, LSU, C
1950	**Ray VanCleef,** Rutgers, CF	1971	**Jerry Tabb,** Tulsa, 1B	1992	**Phil Nevin,** CS-Fullerton, 3B
1951	**Sidney Hatfield,** Tenn., P-1B	1972	Russ McQueen, USC, P	1993	Todd Walker, LSU, 2B
1952	James O'Neill, Holy Cross, P	1973	**Dave Winfield,** Minn., P-OF	1994	Chip Glass, Oklahoma, OF
1953	**J.L. Smith,** Texas, P	1974	George Milke, USC, P	1995	Mark Kotsay, CS-Fullerton, OF
1954	**Tom Yewcic,** Mich. St., C	1975	Mickey Reichenbach, Texas, 1B	1996	**Pat Burrell,** Miami-FL, 3B
1955	**Tom Borland,** Okla. St., P	1976	Steve Powers, Arizona, P-DH	1997	Brandon Larson, LSU, SS
1956	Jerry Thomas, Minn., P	1977	Bob Horner, Ariz. St., 3B	1998	Wes Rachels, USC, 2B
1957	**Cal Emery,** Penn St., P-1B	1978	Rod Boxberger, USC, P	1999	**Marshall McDougall,** Fla. St., 2B
1958	Bill Thom, USC, P	1979	Tony Hudson, CS-Fullerton, P		
1959	Jim Dobson, Okla. St., 3B	1980	Terry Francona, Arizona, LF	2000	Trey Hodges, LSU, P
1960	John Erickson, Minn., 2B	1981	Stan Holmes, Ariz. St., LF	2001	Charlton Jimerson, Miami-FL, CF
1961	**Littleton Fowler,** Okla. St., P	1982	Dan Smith, Miami-FL, P	2002	Huston Street, Texas, P
1962	**Bob Garibaldi,** Santa Clara, P	1983	Calvin Schiraldi, Texas, P	2003	**John Hudgins,** Stanford, P
1963	Bud Hollowell, USC, C	1984	John Fishel, CS-Fullerton, LF	2004	Jason Windsor, CS-Fullerton, P
1964	**Joe Ferris,** Maine, P	1985	Greg Ellena, Miami-FL, LF	2005	David Maroul, Texas, 3B
1965	Sal Bando, Ariz. St., 3B	1986	Mike Senne, Arizona, DH	2006	Jonah Nickerson, Oregon St., P
1966	Steve Arlin, Ohio St., P	1987	Paul Carey, Stanford, RF	2007	Jorge Reyes, Oregon St., P
1967	Ron Davini, Ariz. St., C	1988	Lee Plemel, Stanford, P	2008	Tommy Mendonca, Fresno St., 3B
1968	Bill Seinsoth, USC, 1B	1989	Greg Brummett, Wich. St., P		
1969	John Dolinsek, Ariz. St., LF	1990	Mike Rebhan, Georgia, P		

Annual Awards
Golden Spikes Award

First presented in 1978 by USA Baseball, honoring the nation's best amateur player; sponsored by the Major League Baseball Players Association. Alex Fernandez, the 1990 winner, has been the only junior college player chosen.

Year		Year		Year	
1978	Bob Horner, Ariz. St, 2B	1989	Ben McDonald, LSU, P	2000	Kip Bouknight, South Carolina, P
1979	Tim Wallach, CS-Fullerton, 1B	1990	Alex Fernandez, Miami-Dade, P	2001	Mark Prior, USC, P
1980	Terry Francona, Arizona, OF	1991	Mike Kelly, Ariz. St., OF	2002	Khalil Greene, Clemson, SS
1981	Mike Fuentes, Fla. St., OF	1992	Phil Nevin, CS-Fullerton, 3B	2003	Rickie Weeks, Southern, 2B
1982	Augie Schmidt, N. Orleans, SS	1993	Darren Dreifort, Wichita St., P	2004	Jered Weaver, Long Beach St., P
1983	Dave Magadan, Alabama, 1B	1994	Jason Varitek, Ga. Tech, C	2005	Alex Gordon, Nebraska, IF
1984	Oddibe McDowell, Ariz. St., OF	1995	Mark Kotsay, CS-Fullerton, OF	2006	Tim Lincecum, Washington, P
1985	Will Clark, Miss. St., 1B	1996	Travis Lee, San Diego St., 1B	2007	David Price, Vanderbilt, P
1986	Mike Loynd, Fla. St., P	1997	J.D. Drew, Florida St., OF	2008	Buster Posey, Florida St., C
1987	Jim Abbott, Michigan, P	1998	Pat Burrell, Miami-FL, 3B		
1988	Robin Ventura, Okla. St., 3B	1999	Jason Jennings, Baylor, DH/P		

Baseball America Player of the Year

Presented to the College Player of the Year since 1981 by *Baseball America*.

Year		Year		Year	
1981	Mike Sodders, Ariz. St., 3B	1991	David McCarty, Stanford, 1B	2001	Mark Prior, USC, P
1982	Jeff Ledbetter, Fla. St., OF/P	1992	Phil Nevin, CS-Fullerton, 3B	2002	Khalil Greene, Clemson, SS
1983	Dave Magadan, Alabama, 1B	1993	Brooks Kieschnick, Texas, DH/P	2003	Rickie Weeks, Southern, 2B
1984	Oddibe McDowell, Ariz. St., OF	1994	Jason Varitek, Ga. Tech, C	2004	Jered Weaver, Long Beach St., P
1985	Pete Incaviglia, Okla. St., OF	1995	Todd Helton, Tenn., 1B/P	2005	Alex Gordon, Nebraska, IF
1986	Casey Close, Michigan, OF	1996	Kris Benson, Clemson, P	2006	Andrew Miller, N. Carolina, P
1987	Robin Ventura, Okla. St., 3B	1997	J.D. Drew, Florida St., OF	2007	David Price, Vanderbilt, P
1988	John Olerud, Wash. St., 1B/P	1998	Jeff Austin, Stanford, P	2008	Buster Posey, Florida St., C
1989	Ben McDonald, LSU, P	1999	Jason Jennings, Baylor, DH/P		
1990	Mike Kelly, Ariz. St., OF	2000	Mark Teixeira, Ga. Tech, 3B		

Dick Howser Trophy

Presented to the College Player of the Year since 1987, by the American Baseball Coaches Association (ABCA) from 1987-98 and the National Collegiate Baseball Writers Association (NCBWA) beginning in 1999. Founded and owned by the St. Petersburg (Fla.) Area Chamber of Commerce. Named after the late two-time All-America shortstop and college coach at Florida State. Howser was also a major league manager with Kansas City and the New York Yankees.

Multiple winner: Brooks Kieschnick (2).

Year		Year		Year	
1987	Mike Fiore, Miami-FL, OF	1995	Todd Helton, Tenn., 1B/P	2003	Rickie Weeks, Southern, 2B
1988	Robin Ventura, Okla. St., 3B	1996	Kris Benson, Clemson, P	2004	Jered Weaver, Long Beach St., P
1989	Scott Bryant, Texas, DH	1997	J.D. Drew, Florida St., OF	2005	Alex Gordon, Nebraska, IF
1990	Paul Ellis, UCLA, C	1998	Eddie Furniss, LSU, 1B	2006	Brad Lincoln, Houston, P/UT
1991	Bobby Jones, Fresno St., P	1999	Jason Jennings, Baylor, DH/P	2007	David Price, Vanderbilt, P
1992	Brooks Kieschnick, Texas, DH/P	2000	Mark Teixeira, Ga. Tech, 3B	2008	Buster Posey, Florida St., C
1993	Brooks Kieschnick, Texas, DH/P	2001	Mark Prior, USC, P		
1994	Jason Varitek, Ga. Tech, C	2002	Khalil Greene, Clemson, SS		

Baseball America Coach of the Year

Presented to the College Coach of the Year since 1981 by *Baseball America*.

Multiple winners: Skip Bertman, Augie Garrido, Dave Snow and Gene Stephenson (2).

Year		Year		Year	
1981	Ron Fraser, Miami-FL	1990	Steve Webber, Georgia	2000	Ray Tanner, S. Carolina
1982	Gene Stephenson, Wichita St.	1991	Jim Hendry, Creighton	2001	Dave Van Horn, Nebraska
1983	Barry Shollenberger, Alabama	1992	Andy Lopez, Pepperdine	2002	Augie Garrido, Texas
1984	Augie Garrido, CS-Fullerton	1993	Gene Stephenson, Wichita St.	2003	George Horton, CS-Fullerton
1985	Ron Polk, Mississippi St.	1994	Jim Morris, Miami-FL	2004	Dave Perno, Georgia
1986	Skip Bertman, LSU	1995	Rod Delmonico, Tennessee	2005	Rick Jones, Tulane
	& Dave Snow, Loyola-CA	1996	Skip Bertman, LSU	2006	Pat Casey, Oregon St.
1987	Mark Marquess, Stanford	1997	Jim Wells, Alabama	2007	Dave Serrano, UC Irvine
1988	Jim Brock, Arizona St.	1998	Pat Murphy, Arizona St.	2008	Mike Fox, North Carolina
1989	Dave Snow, Long Beach St.	1999	Wayne Graham, Rice		

All-Time Winningest Division I Coaches

Coaches active in 2008 are in **bold** type. Records given are for four-year colleges only. Minimum 10 years in Division I required.

Top 10 Victories

		Yrs	W	L	T	Pct			Yrs	W	L	T	Pct
1	**Augie Garrido**	.40	**1668**	777	8	.682	6	Cliff Gustafson	.29	**1427**	373	2	.792
2	**Gene Stephenson**	.30	**1653**	550	3	.750	7	**Ron Polk**	.35	**1373**	702	2	.662
3	**Mike Martin**	.29	**1538**	520	4	.747	8	Rod Dedeaux	.44	**1342**	597	16	.691
4	**Larry Hays**	.38	**1508**	860	3	.637	9	Larry Cochell	.39	**1331**	813	3	.621
5	Chuck Hartman	.47	**1444**	816	8	.638	10	**Mark Marquess**	.32	**1326**	669	7	.665

Other NCAA Champions

Division II

Multiple winners: Florida Southern (9); Tampa (5); Cal Poly Pomona (3); Central Missouri St., CS-Chico, CS-Northridge, Jacksonville St., Troy St., UC-Irvine and UC-Riverside (2).

Year		Year		Year		Year	
1968	Chapman, CA	1979	Valdosta St., GA	1990	Jacksonville St., AL	2001	St. Mary's, TX
1969	Illinois St.	1980	Cal Poly Pomona	1991	Jacksonville St., AL	2002	Columbus St., GA
1970	CS-Northridge	1981	Florida Southern	1992	Tampa	2003	Central Missouri St.
1971	Florida Southern	1982	UC-Riverside	1993	Tampa	2004	Delta St., MS
1972	Florida Southern	1983	Cal Poly Pomona	1994	Central Missouri St.	2005	Florida Southern
1973	UC-Irvine	1984	CS-Northridge	1995	Florida Southern	2006	Tampa
1974	UC-Irvine	1985	Florida Southern	1996	Kennesaw St., GA	2007	Tampa
1975	Florida Southern	1986	Troy St., AL	1997	CS-Chico	2008	Mount Olive, NC
1976	Cal Poly Pomona	1987	Troy St., AL	1998	Tampa		
1977	UC-Riverside	1988	Florida Southern	1999	CS-Chico		
1978	Florida Southern	1989	Cal Poly SLO	2000	Southeastern Okla.		

Division III

Multiple winners: Eastern Conn. St. and Marietta (4); Montclair St. (3); CS-Stanislaus, Glassboro St., Ithaca, NC-Wesleyan, Southern Maine and Wm. Paterson, NJ (2).

Year		Year		Year		Year	
1976	CS-Stanislaus	1985	Wisconsin-Oshkosh	1994	Wisconsin-Oshkosh	2003	Chapman, CA
1977	CS-Stanislaus	1986	Marietta, OH	1995	La Verne, CA	2004	George Fox, OR
1978	Glassboro St., NJ	1987	Monclair St., NJ	1996	Wm. Paterson, NJ	2005	Wis.-Whitewater
1979	Glassboro St., NJ	1988	Ithaca, NY	1997	Southern Maine	2006	Marietta, OH
1980	Ithaca, NY	1989	NC-Wesleyan	1998	Eastern Conn. St.	2007	Kean, NJ
1981	Marietta, OH	1990	Eastern Conn. St.	1999	NC-Wesleyan	2008	Trinity, CT
1982	Eastern Conn. St.	1991	Southern Maine	2000	Montclair St., NJ		
1983	Marietta, OH	1992	Wm. Paterson, NJ	2001	St. Thomas, MN		
1984	Ramapo, NJ	1993	Montclair St., NJ	2002	Eastern Conn. St.		

Major League Number One Draft Picks

The Major League First-Year Player Draft has been held every year since 1965. Clubs select in reverse order of their won-loss records from the previous regular season. Until 2005, the National League and American League teams alternated, with AL teams selecting first in odd years and NL teams going first in even years. Now, league affiliation does not come into play.

Year		Pos	Team	Year		Pos	Team
1965	Rick Monday	OF	Kansas City Athletics	1987	Ken Griffey Jr.	OF	Seattle Mariners
1966	Steve Chilcott	C	New York Mets	1988	Andy Benes	P	San Diego Padres
1967	Ron Blomberg	1B	New York Yankees	1989	Ben McDonald	P	Baltimore Orioles
1968	Tim Foli	IF	New York Mets	1990	Chipper Jones	SS	Atlanta Braves
1969	Jeff Burroughs	OF	Washington Senators	1991	Brien Taylor	P	New York Yankees
1970	Mike Ivie	C	San Diego Padres	1992	Phil Nevin	3B	Houston Astros
1971	Danny Goodwin	C	Chicago White Sox	1993	Alex Rodriguez	SS	Seattle Mariners
1972	Dave Roberts	IF	San Diego Padres	1994	Paul Wilson	P	New York Mets
1973	David Clyde	P	Texas Rangers	1995	Darin Erstad	OF/P	California Angels
1974	Bill Almon	IF	San Diego Padres	1996	Kris Benson	P	Pittsburgh Pirates
1975	Danny Goodwin	C	California Angels	1997	Matt Anderson	P	Detroit Tigers
1976	Floyd Bannister	P	Houston Astros	1998	Pat Burrell	3B	Philadelphia Phillies
1977	Harold Baines	OF	Chicago White Sox	1999	Josh Hamilton	OF	T.B. Devil Rays
1978	Bob Horner	3B	Atlanta Braves	2000	Adrian Gonzalez	1B	Florida Marlins
1979	Al Chambers	OF	Seattle Mariners	2001	Joe Mauer	C	Minnesota Twins
1980	Darryl Strawberry	OF	New York Mets	2002	Bryan Bullington	P	Pittsburgh Pirates
1981	Mike Moore	P	Seattle Mariners	2003	Delmon Young	OF	T.B. Devil Rays
1982	Shawon Dunston	SS	Chicago Cubs	2004	Matt Bush	SS	San Diego Padres
1983	Tim Belcher	P	Minnesota Twins	2005	Justin Upton	SS	Ariz. Diamondbacks
1984	Shawn Abner	OF	New York Mets	2006	Luke Hochevar	P	Kansas City Royals
1985	B.J. Surhoff	C	Milwaukee Brewers	2007	David Price	P	T.B. Devil Rays
1986	Jeff King	IF	Pittsburgh Pirates	2008	Tim Beckham	SS	Tampa Bay Rays

COLLEGE FOOTBALL

2007 / 2008 YEAR IN REVIEW

Jerry Moore was carried off the field after his FCS Appalachian St. Mountaineers shocked Michigan and the rest of college football in 2007.

UPSETTING SEASON

LSU survived two losses and reigned supreme in one of the most "upsetting" years in recent memory.

by Ivan Maisel

THROUGH AN ENTIRE SEASON OF UPSETS AND UPHEAVAL, TEAMS MOVED IN AND OUT OF THE TOP OF THE POLLS AS IF IT WERE A FLEABAG MOTEL INSTEAD OF THE RITZ-CARLTON. NO ONE STAYED LONG, AND THE ONES THAT CLAIMED THEY BELONGED DIDN'T EXACTLY LOOK THE PART.

Until the last night of the season, that is. On the last night of the season, college football found an occupant for its penthouse.

The LSU Tigers are a dominant champion. They are a deserving champion. And as a fitting end to a season that never followed its script, college football has a two-loss champion.

LSU rolled over Ohio State, 38-24, in the Allstate BCS Championship Game, becoming not only the first two-loss champion in the modern era, but also the first two-time champion in the 10-year history of the BCS. That the Tigers managed to achieve both distinctions captures the uneven nature of their season, in which they lost two games in triple overtime and won three others in the final 90 seconds of regulation.

There would be no such thrills Monday night because LSU cut way down on its mistakes. The team that finished the season 118th in the nation in penalties per game (8.7) committed only four in the last, most important game. The Tigers (12-2) committed only one turnover. Ohio State (11-2), the team known for not beating itself, committed seven and three, respectively.

 Ivan Maisel is a senior writer at ESPN.com

AP Images

→ The two-loss **LSU Tigers** did some home-cooking and captured a national title with their win over Ohio State in the BCS Championship Game in New Orleans.

Give credit to LSU coach Les Miles, who has taken more shots in his three seasons at LSU than expected for a man with a 34-6 record.

Miles stuck with LSU even as his dream job at his alma mater, Michigan, opened and closed without him. Winning the national championship — and beating Michigan's archrival to do it — is some kind of consolation.

"This very special season," Miles labeled it, "this very special team."

These very special Tigers dominated with a physicality and a depth of talent on both sides of the ball that left the Buckeyes looking overmatched in the sport's biggest game for the second year in a row.

The speed issue, promulgated after Florida whipped Ohio State, 41-14, a year ago, was a canard, an easy way to explain the Buckeyes' awful performance. After Monday night, Ohio State has some more explaining to do.

"I just think they were more physical than us," said Ohio State All-American linebacker James Laurinaitis, the Butkus Award winner.

Ohio State had the game's leading rusher in sophomore Beanie Wells, who gained 146 yards on 20 carries and scored the first

Ohio State and coach **Jim Tressel** have had great success but are 0-for-2 in the last two BCS title games.

and the Tigers leveled him several times more.

Flynn, the senior quarterback who missed the SEC championship game with a shoulder injury, threw for four touchdowns. Two of them went to tight end Richard Dickson, but Flynn spread the ball to teammates one and all.

When he threw a 10-yard touchdown to Brandon LaFell with 7:25 left in the second quarter that put the Tigers ahead for good, 17-10, Flynn had thrown his first nine completions to six different receivers.

He won the Most Outstanding Player award on offense, completing 19-of-27 passes.

"What Flynn's meant to this team," Miles said, "is he's a great leader, an unbelievably competitive quarterback."

The three weeks before the Tigers began bowl practice allowed Flynn and All-American defensive tackle Glenn Dorsey to heal. Dorsey had played the second half of the season with a strained knee and bruised tailbone, but he looked like himself again.

"You saw a healthy LSU team," Dorsey said. "When we're healthy, we can come out and play with anybody."

The Tigers gave the 79,651 fans

touchdown of the game. Buckeyes quarterback Todd Boeckman threw for 208 yards, 34 more than his LSU counterpart, Matt Flynn. Not since Al Gore got 500,000 more votes than George Bush have the final statistics been so misleading.

For one thing, Wells gained 118 yards on his first seven carries, which leaves 28 yards to be spread over his final 13. For another, Boeckman got sacked five times

AP Images

and a national television audience two games for the price of one. In the first game, they fell behind, 10-0, before they even made a first down. The defense gave up a 65-yard touchdown run to Wells on the fourth play of the game. Hyped-up, All-American safety Craig Steltz overran the play in his rush to provide run support, and Wells sprinted right past him.

On LSU's first possession, center Brett Helms fired a shotgun snap past Flynn while the quarterback called an audible on third-and-7. Flynn sprinted back and fell on it at the LSU 6-yard-line.

The defense blew a coverage and let Boeckman complete a 44-yard pass to Brandon Saine that set up Ryan Pretorius' 25-yard field goal.

And then the Tigers, offense and defense, took a deep breath.

"Coach sat us down," said offensive tackle Ciron Black," and said, 'Hey, we been in big games before. We've been down before. Play like we know how to play.'"

The same message went to the defense.

"The stakes were high. The emotions were running high," said LSU defensive coordinator Bo Pelini, who, by the time he said it, was Nebraska head coach Bo Pelini. "...I just said, 'Hey, don't panic. We know what we have to do. Settle down and play football the way you know how.' We've been through it a million times."

It may have seemed like a million.

In fact, LSU fell behind by 10 points for the fourth time this season (Florida, Auburn, Alabama). There are two important things to know about that. One, LSU didn't let Ohio State get ahead by more. And two, LSU won all four of those games.

"We felt like they could not throw the football against us well enough to win the game, that they'd have to run it," Miles said. "And we felt like we'd eventually be able to turn that down, as well."

That pretty much describes the second game. LSU scored 31 unanswered points, controlling the line of scrimmage whether on offense or on defense, and forcing the Buckeyes to make the sort of crippling mistakes that the Tigers had inflicted on themselves so often this season.

There were the back-to-back nightmares for Ohio State in the second quarter with the score tied, 10-10. One play after Brian Robiskie dropped a 21-yard touchdown pass, LSU defensive tackle Ricky Jean-Francois, the Other Guy in the middle with Dorsey, blocked Ryan Pretorius' 38-yard field goal attempt. Jean-Francois, who also had 1 1/2 tackles for loss, became the game's Most Outstanding Player on defense.

Not only did Boeckman throw two interceptions and lose a fumble after a crushing hit by linebacker Ali Highsmith, but Ohio State committed five personal-foul penalties. The worst: a roughing-the-punter call on linebacker Austin Spitler on the first

Running-and-gunning Florida QB **Tim Tebow** became the first sophomore to win the Heisman.

possession of the second half. The Buckeyes, trailing 24-10, had stuffed the Tigers.

Spitler's penalty resuscitated LSU's drive at the Ohio State 45. After Jacob Hester's 2-yard gain, Buckeyes defensive end Cameron Heyward got busted for a dead-ball personal foul that moved the Tigers to the Ohio State 28. Three plays later, Flynn threw a 4-yard touchdown pass to Early Doucet for a 31-10 lead. Game. Set. Crystal football.

For the second consecutive season, college football's biggest night featured the champions of the Southeastern Conference and the Big Ten Conference, the two most politically powerful leagues in college football.

And for the second consecutive season, Ohio State got overwhelmed by its opponent. Throughout the second half, the three letters chanted by the purple-and-gold-clad fans in the dome were not "L-S-U!" but "S-E-C!"

After the game, just inside the locker-room door, there stood Dorsey, Sharpie in hand, signing the backs of LSU jerseys worn by his coaches' sons. Dorsey, towering over Omari Porter, the young son of assistant head coach Larry Porter, bellowed, "What's up, dawg? We champs, huh?"

For the second time in five seasons, the Tigers are champs.

2007-2008
Season in Review

SPORTS ALMANAC

Final AP Top 25 Poll

Voted on by panel of 65 sportswriters & broadcasters and released on Jan. 8, 2008, following the BCS Title Game: winning team receives the Bear Bryant Trophy, given since 1983; first place votes in parentheses, records, total points (based on 25 for 1st, 24 for 2nd, etc.) bowl game result, head coach and career record, preseason rank (released Aug. 19, 2007) and final regular season rank (released Dec. 2, 2007).

		Final Record	Points	Bowl Game	Head Coach	Aug. 19 Rank	Dec. 2 Rank
1	LSU (60)	12-2	1,620	won BCS	Les Miles (7 yrs: 62-27)	2	2
2	Georgia (3)	11-2	1,515	won Sugar	Mark Richt (7 yrs: 72-19)	13	4
3	USC	11-2	1,500	won Rose	Pete Carroll (7 yrs: 78-12)	1	6
4	Missouri	12-2	1,347	won Cotton	Gary Pinkel (17 yrs: 122-72-3)	-	7
5	Ohio St.	11-2	1,346	lost BCS	Jim Tressel (22 yrs: 208-73-1)	11	1
6	West Virginia	11-2	1,342	won Fiesta	Rich Rodriguez (14 yrs: 95-60-2) & Bill Stewart (4 yrs: 9-25)	3	11
7	Kansas (1)	12-1	1,303	won Orange	Mark Mangino (6 yrs: 37-36)	-	8
8	Oklahoma	11-3	1,139	lost Fiesta	Bob Stoops (9 yrs: 97-22*)	8	3
9	Virginia Tech	11-3	1,096	lost Orange	Frank Beamer (27 yrs: 209-108-4)	9	5
10	Texas	10-3	962	won Holiday	Mack Brown (24 yrs: 189-99-1)	4	17
	Boston College	11-3	962	won Champs Sports	Jeff Jagodzinski (1 yr: 11-3)	-	14
12	Tennessee	10-4	904	won Outback	Philip Fulmer (16 yrs: 147-45)	15	16
13	Florida	9-4	685	lost Capital	Urban Meyer (7 yrs: 70-16)	6	9
14	Brigham Young	11-2	654	won Las Vegas	Bronco Mendenhall (3 yrs: 28-10)	-	19
15	Auburn	9-4	648	won Chick-fil-A	Tommy Tuberville (12 yrs: 96-49)	18	22
16	Arizona St.	10-3	587	lost Holiday	Dennis Erickson (19 yrs: 158-68-1)	-	12
17	Cincinnati	10-3	566	won Papajohns.com	Brian Kelly (17 yrs: 147-54-2)	-	20
18	Michigan	9-4	508	won Capital One	Lloyd Carr (13 yrs: 122-40)	5	???
19	Hawaii	12-1	460	lost Sugar	June Jones (9 yrs: 75-41)	23	10
20	Illinois	9-4	443	lost Rose	Ron Zook (6 yrs: 36-37)	-	13
21	Clemson	9-4	353	lost Chick-fil-A	Tommy Bowden (11 yrs: 87-46)	-	15
22	Texas Tech	9-4	308	lost Gator	Mike Leach (8 yrs: 65-37)	-	-
23	Oregon	9-4	253	won Sun	Mike Bellotti (18 yrs: 129-77-2)	-	-
24	Wisconsin	9-4	202	lost Outback	Bret Bielema (2 yrs: 21-5)	7	18
25	Oregon St.	9-4	110	won Emerald	Mike Riley (7 yrs: 47-38)	-	-

Other teams receiving votes: 26. Virginia (66 pts); 27. **Penn St.** (61 pts); 28. **Kentucky** (57 pts); 29. **Wake Forest** (53 pts); 30. **Boise St.** (25 pts); 31. **Arkansas** (13 pts); 32. **Utah** (9 pts); 33. **Mississippi St.** (7 pts); 34. **Appalachian St.** (5 pts) and **South Florida** (5 pts); 36. **Tulsa** (4 pts); 37. **Connecticut** (3 pts); 36. **Air Force** (2 pts) and **Rutgers** (2 pts).

*The NCAA vacated Oklahoma's eight wins from the 2005 season. Bob Stoops' official career record is 89-22.

AP Preseason and Final Regular Season Polls

First place votes in parentheses.

Top 25
(Aug. 19, 2007)

		Pts
1	USC (62)	1,622
2	LSU (2)	1,511
3	West Va. (1)	1,396
4	Texas	1,375
5	Michigan	1,371
6	Florida	1,276
7	Wisconsin	1,192
8	Oklahoma	1,166
9	Virginia Tech	1,148
10	Louisville	1,031
11	Ohio St.	876
12	California	790
13	Georgia	782

		Pts
14	UCLA	605
15	Tennessee	571
16	Rutgers	560
17	Penn State	542
18	Auburn	519
19	Florida St.	392
20	Nebraska	377
21	Arkansas	376
22	TCU	283
23	Hawaii	256
24	Boise St.	187
25	Texas A&M	162

Top 25
(Dec. 2, 2007)

		Pts
1	Ohio St. (50)	1,578
2	LSU (11)	1,519
3	Oklahoma (1)	1,423
4	Georgia (1)	1,421
5	Virginia Tech (1)	1,380
6	USC	1,346
7	Missouri	1,195
8	Kansas	1,164
9	Florida	1,071
10	Hawaii	1,050
11	West Virginia	1,040
12	Arizona St.	939
13	Illinois	797

		Pts
14	Boston College	668
15	Clemson	614
16	Tennessee	554
17	Texas	517
18	Wisconsin	447
19	BYU	439
20	Cincinnati	394
21	Virginia	344
22	Auburn	264
23	South Florida	246
24	Boise St.	221
25	Arkansas	173

2007-2008 Bowl Games

Listed by bowls matching highest-ranked teams as of final regular season AP poll (released Dec. 2, 2007). Attendance figures indicate tickets sold.

Bowl		Winner	Final Record		Loser	Final Record	Score	Date	Attendance
BCS Title Game	#2	LSU	12-2	#1	Ohio St.	11-2	38-24	Jan. 7	79,651
Fiesta	#11	West Virginia	11-2	#3	Oklahoma	11-3	48-28	Jan. 2	70,016
Sugar	#4	Georgia	11-2	#10	Hawaii	12-1	41-10	Jan. 1	74,383
Orange	#8	Kansas	12-1	#5	Virginia Tech	11-3	24-21	Jan. 3	74,111
Rose	#6	USC	11-2	#13	Illinois	9-4	49-17	Jan. 1	93,923
Cotton	#7	Missouri	12-2	#25	Arkansas	8-5	38-7	Jan. 1	73,114
Capital One		Michigan	9-4	#9	Florida	9-4	41-35	Jan. 1	69,748
Holiday	#17	Texas	10-3	#12	Arizona St.	10-3	52-34	Dec. 27	64,020
Champs Sports	#14	Boston College	11-3		Michigan St.	7-6	24-21	Dec. 28	40,168
Chick-fil-A	#22	Auburn	9-4	#15	Clemson	9-4	23-20 OT	Dec. 31	74,413
Outback	#16	Tennessee	10-4	#18	Wisconsin	9-4	21-17	Jan. 1	60,121
Las Vegas	#19	BYU	11-2		UCLA	6-7	17-16	Dec. 22	40,712
Papajohns.com	#20	Cincinnati	10-3		Southern Miss	7-6	31-21	Dec. 22	35,258
Gator		Texas Tech	9-4	#21	Virginia	9-4	31-28	Jan. 1	60,243
Sun		Oregon	9-4	#23	South Florida	9-4	56-21	Dec. 31	49,867
Hawaii		East Carolina	8-5	#24	Boise St.	10-3	41-38	Dec. 23	30,467
Meineke Car Care		Wake Forest	9-4		Connecticut	9-4	24-10	Dec. 29	53,126
GMAC		Tulsa	10-4		Bowling Green	8-5	63-7	Jan. 6	36,932
International		Rutgers	8-5		Ball St.	7-6	52-30	Jan. 5	31,455
Poinsettia		Utah	9-4		Navy	8-5	35-32	Dec. 20	39,129
New Orleans		Florida Atlantic	8-5		Memphis	7-6	44-27	Dec. 21	25,146
New Mexico		New Mexico	9-4		Nevada	6-7	23-0	Dec. 22	30,223
Motor City		Purdue	8-5		C. Michigan	8-6	51-48	Dec. 26	60,624
Texas		TCU	8-5		Houston	8-5	20-13	Dec. 28	62,097
Emerald		Oregon St.	9-4		Maryland	6-7	21-14	Dec. 28	32,517
Liberty		Mississippi St.	8-5		C. Florida	10-4	10-3	Dec. 29	63,816
Independence		Alabama	7-6		Colorado	6-7	30-24	Dec. 30	47,043
Armed Forces		California	7-6		Air Force	9-4	42-36	Dec. 31	44,009
Humanitarian		Fresno St.	9-4		Georgia Tech	7-6	40-28	Dec. 31	27,062
Music City		Kentucky	8-5		Florida St.	7-6	35-28	Dec. 31	68,661
Insight		Oklahoma St.	7-6		Indiana	7-6	49-33	Dec. 31	48,892
Alamo		Penn St.	9-4		Texas A&M	7-6	24-17	Dec. 29	66,166

2007 Final BCS Standings

The Bowl Championship Series rankings were used for the first time during the 1998 season to determine BCS bowl match-ups and revised slightly for the 1999, 2001, 2002, 2004 and 2005 seasons. The final rankings were released Dec. 2, 2007.

		Polls						Computer Rankings							BCS
	Harris	Pts	%	USA	Pts	%	A&H	RB	CM	KM	JS	PW	%	Avg	BCS Avg
1 Ohio St.	1	2813	.9870	1	1469	.9793	25	25	21	23	22	21	.910	3	.9588
2 LSU	2	2630	.9228	2	1418	.9453	21	24	25	24	24	23	.950	2	.9394
3 Virginia Tech	6	2345	.8228	5	1242	.8280	22	22	24	25	25	25	.960	1	.8703
4 Oklahoma	3	2520	.8842	3	1331	.8873	18	21	18	18	23	24	.800	6	.8572
5 Georgia	4	2469	.8663	4	1277	.8513	20	17	23	22	19	19	.800	6	.8392
6 Missouri	7	2217	.7428	7	1104	.7360	24	16	22	21	20	22	.850	4	.7763
7 USC	5	2346	.8232	6	1227	.8180	17	23	14	14	17	17	.650	9	.7637
8 Kansas	8	2092	.7340	8	1099	.7327	23	20	16	20	21	20	.810	5	.7589
9 West Virginia	9	1924	.6751	9	1010	.6733	16	15	20	13	15	18	.640	10	.6628
10 Hawaii	10	1903	.6677	10	994	.6627	14	18	12	16	18	13	.610	12	.6468
11 Arizona St.	12	1628	.5712	11	900	.6000	19	19	17	17	13	16	.690	8	.6204
12 Florida	11	1786	.6267	12	890	.5933	15	14	19	19	14	14	.620	11	.6133
13 Illinois	13	1400	.4912	13	747	.4980	13	13	7	9	8	9	.390	16	.4597
14 Boston College	14	1124	.3944	14	617	.4113	12	12	15	15	16	15	.570	13	.4586
15 Clemson	16	1041	.3653	16	567	.3780	7	3	11	12	12	12	.410	15	.3844
16 Tennessee	18	870	.3053	18	480	.3200	11	6	9	11	9	5	.350	17	.3251
17 BYU	18	912	.3200	19	462	.3080	8	7	10	2	3	10	.280	19	.3027
18 Wisconsin	15	1079	.3786	15	594	.3960	3	11	0	5	0	0	.100	24	.2915
19 Texas	17	983	.3449	17	498	.3320	5	0	4	0	0	2	.080	25	.2523
20 Virginia	21	551	.1933	20	332	.2213	4	2	8	7	10	8	.290	18	.2349
21 South Florida	24	362	.1270	25	115	.0767	10	0	13	10	11	12	.430	14	.2112
22 Cincinnati	20	580	.2035	23	215	.1433	1	5	6	4	4	6	.190	20	.1789
23 Auburn	23	448	.1572	21	289	.1927	2	0	2	8	1	1	.120	23	.1566
24 Boise St.	22	541	.1898	22	246	.1640	0	10	0	0	0	0	.000	NR	.1179
25 UConn	29	52	.0182	28	23	.0153	0	8	3	3	6	7	.190	20	.0745

Note: Team percentages are derived by dividing a team's actual voting points by a maximum 2850 possible points in the Harris Interactive-Poll and 1550 in the USA Today Coaches Poll. Six computer rankings calculated in inverse points order (25 for #1, 24 for #2, etc.) are used to determine the overall computer component. The best and worst ranking for each team is dropped, and the remaining four are added and divided by 100 (the maximum possible points) to produce a Computer Rankings Percentage. Each computer ranking accounts for schedule strength and home/away performance in its formula. The BCS Average is calculated by averaging the percent totals of the Harris, USA Today Coaches, and computer polls. *Computer Rankings*—A&H = Anderson & Hester, RB = Richard Billingsley, CM = Colley Matrix, KM = Kenneth Massey, JS = Jeff Sagarin, PW = Peter Wolfe, Avg. refers to the teams average position in the computer rankings.

BCS Championship Game

Ohio State and LSU were ranked first and second, respectively, in the final Bowl Championship Series standings (as well as the AP and *USA Today* Coaches polls) and met at the Louisiana Superdome in the BCS championship game to decide Div. 1 college football's national title. Opponents' records and AP rank listed below are day of game. Final statistics listed below include the BCS title game.

LSU Tigers (12-2)

Date	AP Rank	Opponent	Result
Aug. 30	#2	at Mississippi St. (0-0)	W, 45-0
Sept. 8	#2	#9 Virginia Tech (1-0)	W, 48-7
Sept. 15	#2	at Middle Tennessee (0-2)	W, 44-0
Sept. 22	#2	#12 South Carolina (3-0)	W, 28-16
Sept. 29	#2	Tulane (1-2)	W, 34-9
Oct. 6	#1	#9 Florida (4-2)	W, 28-24
Oct. 13	#1	at #17 Kentucky (5-1)	L, 43-37
Oct. 20	#5	#17 Auburn (5-3)	W, 30-24
Nov. 3	#3	at #17 Alabama (5-3)	W, 41-34
Nov. 10	#2	Louisiana Tech (4-5)	W, 58-10
Nov. 17	#1	at Ole Miss (3-7)	W, 41-24
Nov. 23	#1	Arkansas (8-3)	L, 50-48 OT
Dec. 1	#5	#14 Tennessee* (9-3)	W, 21-14
Jan. 7	#2	#1 Ohio State† (11-1)	W, 38-24

*SEC Title Game in Atlanta.

†BCS Title Game at Louisiana Superdome.

Ohio State Buckeyes (11-2)

Date	AP Rank	Opponent	Result
Sept. 1	#11	Youngstown St. (0-0)	W, 38-6
Sept. 8	#12	Akron (1-0)	W, 20-2
Sept. 15	#10	at Washington (2-0)	W, 33-14
Sept. 22	#8	Northwestern (2-1)	W, 58-7
Sept. 29	#8	at Minnesota (1-3)	W, 30-7
Oct. 6	#4	at #23 Purdue (4-1)	W, 23-7
Oct. 13	#3	Kent St. (3-3)	W, 48-3
Oct. 20	#1	Michigan St. (5-2)	W, 24-17
Oct. 27	#1	at #25 Penn St. (6-2)	W, 37-17
Nov. 3	#1	at #25 Wisconsin (7-2)	W, 38-17
Nov. 10	#1	Illinois (8-2)	L, 28-21
Nov. 17	#7	at #21 Michigan	W, 14-3
Jan. 7	#1	#2 LSU† (11-2)	L, 38-24

†BCS Title Game at Louisiana Superdome.

Final Individual Statistics

Passing (5 Att)

	Att	Cmp	Pct.	Yds	TD	Rate
Matt Flynn	359	202	56.3	2407	21	125.8
Ryan Perriloux	75	51	68.0	694	8	175.6

Interceptions: Flynn 11, Perriloux 2.

Top Receivers

	No	Yds	Avg	Long	TD
Early Doucet	57	525	9.2	34	5
Brandon LaFell	50	656	13.1	56	4
Demetrius Byrd	35	621	17.7	62	7
Richard Dickson	32	375	11.7	35	5
Jacob Hester	14	106	7.6	28	1
Jared Mitchell	13	143	11.0	32	0

Top Rushers

	Car	Yds	Avg	Long	TD
Jacob Hester	225	1103	4.9	87	12
K. Williams	70	478	6.8	67	6
T. Holliday	53	364	6.9	33	2
Charles Scott	45	324	7.2	55	5
Richard Murphy	35	230	6.6	53	2
Matt Flynn	100	215	2.2	22	4

Most Touchdowns

	TD	Run	Rec	Ret	Pts
Jacob Hester	13	12	1	0	78
Charles Scott	7	5	2	0	42
K. Williams	7	6	1	0	42
Demetrius Byrd	7	0	7	0	42

Three tied at 5.

2-Pt. Conversions: Flynn 1, Perrilloux 1.

Kicking

	FG/Att	Lg	PAT/Att	Pts
Colt David	26/33	49	63/63	147

Punting

	No	Yds	Long	Blkd	Avg
Patrick Fisher	59	2627	62	0	44.5
Josh Hasper	1	40	40	0	40.0

Most Interceptions

Craig Steltz	6
Chevis Jackson	5
Jonathan Zenon	3
Curtis Taylor	3
Danny McCray	2

Most Sacks

Kirston Pittman	13.5
Glenn Dorsey	12.5
Ali Highsmith	9.0
Derry Beckwith	6.5
Craig Steltz	5.0
Tyson Jackson	4.5

Final Individual Statistics

Passing (5 Att)

	Att	Cmp	Pct.	Yds	TD	Rate
Todd Boeckman	299	191	63.9	2379	25	148.9
Rob Schoenhoft	25	17	68.0	129	0	111.3
Antonio Henton	6	3	50.0	57	1	184.8

Interceptions: Boeckman 14.

Top Receivers

	No	Yds	Avg	Long	TD
Brian Robiskie	55	935	17.0	68	11
Brian Hartline	52	694	13.3	65	6
Ray Small	20	267	13.4	60	2
Rory Nicol	16	84	5.2	11	0
Jake Ballard	13	149	11.5	22	2
Brandon Saine	12	160	13.3	44	1
Dane Sanzenbacher	12	89	7.4	15	1

Top Rushers

	Car	Yds	Avg	Long	TD
Chris Wells	274	1609	5.9	65	15
Maurice Wells	103	367	3.6	26	3
Brandon Saine	60	267	4.4	37	2
Todd Boeckman	56	63	1.1	35	0

Most Touchdowns

	TD	Run	Rec	Ret	Pts
Chris Wells	15	15	0	0	90
Brian Robiskie	11	0	11	0	66
Brian Hartline	7	0	6	1	42
Maurice Wells	4	3	1	0	24
Brandon Saine	3	2	1	0	18

2-Pt. Conversions: none.

Kicking

	FG/Att	Lg	PAT/Att	Pts
Ryan Pretorius	18/23	50	48/49	102

Punting

	No	Yds	Long	Blkd	Avg
A.J. Trapasso	53	2199	63	0	41.4
Jon Thoma	1	13	13	0	13.0

Most Interceptions

Malcolm Jenkins	4
James Laurinaitis	2

Most Sacks

Vernon Gholston	14.0
James Laurinaitis	5.0
Larry Grant	5.0
Anderson Russell	3.0

BCS Title Game Box Score

Monday, Jan. 7, 2008 at Louisiana Superdome, New Orleans, Louisiana.

LSU 38, Ohio St. 24

	1	2	3	4	F
#2 LSU (SEC)	3	21	7	7	38
#1 Ohio St. (Big Ten)	10	0	7	7	24

Favorite: LSU by 5½
Field: Turf
Time: 3:28
Off. MVP: Matt Flynn, LSU
Def. MVP: Ricky Jean-Francois, LSU

Attendance: 79,651
Weather: Indoors
TV Rating: 14.4/22 (FOX)

Scoring Summary

1st: 13:34; **OSU**—Chris Wells 65-yd run (Ryan Pretorius kick), 4 plays, 77 yards, 1:26.
9:12; **OSU**—Pretorius 25-yd field goal, 5 plays, 51 yards, 2:51.
02:21; **LSU**— Colt David 32-yd field goal, 14 plays, 65 yards, 6:51.

2nd: 13:00; **LSU**—Richard Dickson 13-yd pass from Matt Flynn (David kick), 7 plays, 84 yards, 2:07.
0:7:25; **LSU**—Brandon LaFell 10-yd pass from Flynn (David kick), 10 plays, 66 yards, 3:28.
04:16; **LSU**—Jacob Hester 1-yd run (David kick), 5 plays, 24 yards, 2:02.

3rd: 09:04; **LSU**—Early Doucet 4-yd pass from Flynn (David kick), 14 plays, 80 yards, 5:56.
01:38; **OSU**—Brian Robiskie 5-yd pass from Todd Boeckman (Pretorius kick), 4 plays, 11 yards, 2:06.

4th: 01:50; **LSU**—Richard Dickson 5-yd pass from Flynn (David kick), 9 plays, 54 yards, 3:53.
01:13; **OSU**—Brian Hartline, 15-yd pass from Boeckman (Pretorius kick), 4 plays, 54 yards, 0:37.

Team Statistics

	LSU	OSU
First downs	25	17
Total Plays	76	56
Total Net Yards	326	353
Carries/yards (includ. sacks)	49/152	30/145
Passing yards	174	208
Completions/attempts	19/27	15/26
Had intercepted	1	2
Fumbles/lost	2/0	3/1
Penalties/yards	4/36	7/83
Punts/average	3/56.7	3/50.0
3rd down conversions	11/18	3/13
4th down conversions	1/1	2/3
Red-Zone scores/chances	6/6	3/3
Sacks by/yards	5/36	1/15
Time of possession	33:56	26:04

Individual Statistics

LSU Tigers

Passing	Att	Cmp	Int	Yds	TD	Sack
Matt Flynn	27	18	1	174	4	1

Receivers	No	Yds	Avg	Long	TD
Early Doucet	7	51	7.3	16	1
Richard Dickson	4	44	11.0	15	2
Demetrius Byrd	2	28	14.0	20	0
Brandon LaFell	2	15	7.5	10	1
Keith Zinger	1	18	18.0	18	0
Charles Scott	1	16	16.0	16	0
Quinn Johnson	1	3	3.0	3	0
K. Williams	1	-1		0	0
TOTALS	19	174	9.2	20	4

Rushers	Car	Yds	Avg	Long	TD
Jacob Hester	21	86	4.1	20	1
Richard Murphy	2	33	16.5	24	0
K. Williams	2	20	10.0	10	0
T. Holliday	3	13	4.3	9	0
Matt Flynn	12	8	0.7	9	0
Early Doucet	2	7	3.4	4	0
Charles Scott	2	6	3.0	5	0
Ryan Perriloux	1	4	4.0	4	0
TOTALS	49	152	3.1	24	1

Field Goals	20-29	30-39	40-49	50-59	Total
Colt David	0-0	1-1	0-0	0-0	1-1

Punting	No	Yds	Long	Blkd	Avg
Patrick Fisher	3	170	62	0	56.7

Punt Returns	No	Yds	Long	Avg	TD
Chad Jones	1	8	8	8.0	0

Kickoff Returns	No	Yds	Long	Avg	TD
Charles Scott	1	-8	0	-	0
T. Holliday	1	30	30	30.0	0

Ohio State Buckeyes

Passing	Att	Cmp	Int	Yds	TD	Sack
Todd Boeckman	26	15	2	208	2	5

Receivers	No	Yds	Avg	Long	TD
Brian Hartline	6	75	12.5	17	1
Brian Robiskie	5	50	10.0	19	1
Brandon Saine	3	69	23.0	44	0
Ray Small	1	14	14.0	14	0
TOTALS	15	208	13.9	44	2

Rushers	Car	Yds	Avg	Long	TD
Chris Wells	20	146	7.3	65	1
Brian Hartline	1	6	6.0	6	0
Todd Boeckman	9	-7	-0.8	21	0
TOTALS	30	145	4.8	65	1

Field Goals	20-29	30-39	40-49	50-59	Total
Ryan Pretorius	1-1	0-1	0-0	0-0	1-2

Punting	No	Yds	Long	Blkd	Avg
A.J. Trapasso	3	150	63	0	50.0

Punt Returns	No	Yds	Long	Avg	TD
Brian Hartline	1	9	9	9.0	0

Kickoff Returns	No	Yds	Long	Avg	TD
Ray Small	5	95	35	19.0	0
Jamario O'Neal	1	10	10	10.0	0
Maurice Wells	1	19	19	19.0	0
TOTALS	7	124	35	17.7	0

USA Today Coaches Poll

Voted on by panel of 60 Division I-A head coaches; winning team receives the Sears Trophy (originally the McDonald's Trophy, 1991-93); first place votes in parentheses with total points (based on 25 for 1st, 24 for 2nd, etc.). Released Jan. 8, 2008.

Rank	Team	Rec	Pts	Pvs
1	LSU (60)	12-2	1,500	2
2	USC	11-2	1,380	6
3	Georgia	11-2	1,370	4
4	Ohio St.	11-2	1,287	1
5	Missouri	12-2	1,241	7
6	West Virginia	11-2	1,239	11
7	Kansas	12-1	1,217	8
8	Oklahoma	11-3	1,016	3
9	Virginia Tech	11-3	979	5
10	Texas	10-3	924	17
11	Boston College	11-3	898	14
12	Tennessee	10-4	826	16
13	Arizona St.	10-3	635	12
14	Auburn	9-4	624	22
15	BYU	11-2	624	19
16	Florida	9-4	567	9
17	Hawaii	12-1	427	10
18	Illinois	9-4	416	13
19	Michigan	9-4	413	NR
20	Cincinnati	10-3	376	20
21	Wisconsin	9-4	333	18
22	Clemson	9-4	319	15
23	Texas Tech	9-4	242	NR
24	Oregon	9-4	192	NR
25	Penn St.	9-4	127	NR

Other teams receiving votes: 26. Oregon St. (108 points); 27. Virginia (71); 28. Wake Forest (53); 29. Boise St. (33); 30. Fresno St. and Kentucky (11); 32. California and Connecticut (8); 34. Mississippi St. (7); 35. South Florida (6); 36. Tulsa (5); 37. UCF (4); 38. Utah (2); Arkansas (1).

AP Weekly Rankings

The Associated Press Top 25 college football polls on a weekly basis are listed below. The table starts with the preseason and progresses through the season.

Team	Pre	Sep 2	Sep 9	Sep 16	Sep 23	Sep 30	Oct 7	Oct 14	Oct 21	Oct 28	Nov 4	Nov 11	Nov 18	Nov 25	Dec 2	Jan 8
USC	1	1	1	1	1	2	10	13	9	13	12	11	11	8	6	3
LSU	2	2	2	2	1	1	1	5	3	3	2	1	1	5	2	1
West Virginia	3	3	4	5	5	13	8	9	6	7	6	5	4	2	11	6
Texas	4	7	6	7	8	19	23	19	17	14	15	12	13	17	17	10
Michigan	5	-	-	-	-	-	-	24	19	15	13	23	-	-	-	18
Florida	6	4	5	3	4	9	13	14	9	18	17	14	12	10	9	13
Wisconsin	7	5	7	9	9	5	19	-	-	-	-	24	22	19	18	24
Oklahoma	8	5	3	4	3	10	6	4	4	5	4	3	10	9	3	8
Virginia Tech	9	9	18	17	17	15	12	11	8	11	11	10	8	6	5	9
Louisville	10	8	9	18	-	-	-	-	-	-	-	-	-	-	-	-
Ohio St.	11	12	10	8	8	4	3	1	1	1	1	7	5	3	1	5
California	12	10	8	6	6	3	2	10	18	-	24	-	-	-	-	-
Georgia	13	11	23	22	15	12	24	21	20	10	10	8	6	4	4	2
UCLA	14	13	11	-	-	-	-	-	-	-	-	-	-	-	-	-
Tennessee	15	24	22	-	-	-	25	20	-	24	22	19	19	14	16	12
Rutgers	16	15	13	11	10	21	-	-	25	-	-	-	-	-	-	-
Penn St.	17	14	12	10	21	-	-	-	24	-	-	-	-	-	-	-
Auburn	18	17	-	-	-	-	22	18	23	19	18	-	25	23	22	15
Florida St.	19	-	-	-	-	-	21	-	-	-	-	-	-	-	-	-
Nebraska	20	16	14	24	25	25	-	-	-	-	-	-	-	-	-	-
Arkansas	21	18	16	-	-	-	-	-	-	-	-	-	-	-	-	-
TCU	22	19	-	-	-	-	-	-	-	-	-	-	-	-	-	-
Hawaii	23	20	24	19	19	16	16	17	16	12	14	13	14	11	10	19
Boise St.	24	22	-	-	-	-	-	-	21	19	17	17	24	24	-	-
Texas A&M	25	23	25	20	-	-	-	-	-	-	-	-	-	-	-	-
Georgia Tech	-	21	15	-	-	-	-	-	-	-	-	-	-	-	-	-
Clemson	-	25	20	15	13	22	-	-	-	25	20	15	21	16	15	21
South Carolina	-	17	12	16	11	7	6	15	23	-	-	-	-	-	-	-
Oregon	-	-	19	13	11	14	9	7	5	4	3	2	9	18	-	23
Boston College	-	-	21	14	12	7	4	3	2	2	8	18	15	12	14	11
Alabama	-	-	-	16	22	-	-	-	22	17	21	-	-	-	-	-
Kentucky	-	-	-	21	14	8	17	8	14	-	24	22	-	-	-	-
South Florida	-	-	-	23	18	6	5	2	11	20	-	-	-	25	23	-
Missouri	-	-	-	25	20	17	11	15	13	9	7	6	3	1	7	4
Arizona St.	-	-	-	-	23	18	14	12	7	6	9	9	7	13	12	16
Cincinnati	-	-	-	-	24	20	15	23	-	-	-	21	24	20	20	17
Purdue	-	-	-	-	-	23	-	-	-	-	-	-	-	-	-	-
Kansas St.	-	-	-	-	-	24	-	25	-	-	-	-	-	-	-	-
Illinois	-	-	-	-	-	-	18	-	-	-	-	20	18	15	13	20
Kansas	-	-	-	-	-	-	20	15	12	8	5	4	2	7	8	7
Texas Tech	-	-	-	-	-	-	22	-	-	-	-	-	-	-	-	22
Virginia	-	-	-	-	-	-	-	21	-	-	23	16	16	22	21	-
Connecticut	-	-	-	-	-	-	-	-	16	16	25	20	-	-	-	-
Wake Forest	-	-	-	-	-	-	-	-	-	21	-	-	-	-	-	-
BYU	-	-	-	-	-	-	-	-	-	-	-	-	23	21	19	14
Oregon St.	-	-	-	-	-	-	-	-	-	-	-	-	-	-	-	25

NCAA Division I-A Final Standings

Standings based on conference games only; overall records include postseason games.

Atlantic Coast Conference

Atlantic	Conference				Overall			
	W	L	PF	PA	W	L	PF	PA
*Boston College	.6	2	213	165	11	3	396	285
*Clemson	.5	3	230	149	9	4	430	243
*Wake Forest	.5	3	225	208	9	4	362	289
*Florida St.	.4	4	192	174	7	6	313	280
*Maryland	.3	5	194	180	6	7	313	280
N.C. State	.3	5	144	248	5	7	249	339

Coastal	Conference				Overall			
	W	L	PF	PA	W	L	PF	PA
*Virginia Tech	.7	1	255	120	11	3	402	225
*Virginia	.2	2	202	151	9	4	317	356
*Georgia Tech	.4	4	160	173	7	6	341	271
North Carolina	.3	5	161	188	4	8	254	294
Miami-FL	.2	6	146	232	5	7	247	312
Duke	.0	8	131	265	1	11	215	406

ACC championship game: Virginia Tech 30, Boston College 16 (Dec. 1, 2007).

*Bowls (2-6): Boston College (won Champs Sports); Maryland (lost Emerald); Wake Forest (won Meineke); Georgia Tech (lost Humanitarian); Florida St. (lost Music City); Clemson (lost Chick-fil-A); Virginia (lost Gator); Virginia Tech (lost Orange).

Big East Conference

	Conference				Overall			
	W	L	PF	PA	W	L	PF	PA
*West Virginia	.5	2	240	126	11	2	515	235
*Connecticut	.5	2	169	165	9	4	344	247
*Cincinnati	.4	3	209	170	10	3	472	244
*South Florida	.4	3	240	167	9	4	451	304
*Rutgers	.3	4	171	195	8	5	426	292
Louisville	.3	4	193	231	6	6	422	377
Pittsburgh	.3	4	141	169	5	7	274	291
Syracuse	.1	6	131	271	2	10	197	418

*Bowls (3-2): West Virginia (won Fiesta); Connecticut (lost Meineke); Cincinnati (won Papajohns.com); South Florda (lost Sun); Rutgers (won International).

Big Ten Conference

	Conference				Overall			
	W	L	PF	PA	W	L	PF	PA
*Ohio St.	.7	1	245	103	11	2	408	166
*Illinois	.6	2	221	157	9	4	362	283
*Michigan	.6	2	203	148	9	4	354	278
*Wisconsin	.5	3	215	212	9	4	383	301
*Penn St.	.4	4	204	177	9	4	394	228
Iowa	.4	4	139	179	6	6	222	225
*Indiana	.3	5	208	243	7	6	412	370
*Michigan St.	.3	5	278	260	7	6	430	346
*Purdue	.3	5	213	226	8	5	446	345
Northwestern	.3	5	207	307	6	6	310	372
Minnesota	.0	8	183	304	1	11	315	440

*Bowls (3-5): Ohio St. (lost BCS Championship Game); Illinois (lost Rose); Michigan (won Capital One); Wisconsin (lost Outback); Indiana (lost Insight); Penn St. (won Alamo); Michigan St. (lost Champs Sports); Purdue (won Motor City).

I-A Independents

	W	L	PF	PA
*Navy		.8	5	511	473
Western Kentucky		.7	5	398	250
Army		.3	9	203	364
Notre Dame		.3	9	197	345

*Bowl (0-1): Navy (lost Poinsettia).

Big 12 Conference

North	Conference				Overall			
	W	L	PF	PA	W	L	PF	PA
*Missouri	.7	1	335	181	12	2	558	326
*Kansas	.7	1	318	169	12	1	556	213
*Colorado	.4	4	238	276	6	7	355	383
Kansas St.	.3	5	285	278	5	7	422	370
Nebraska	.2	6	257	339	5	7	401	455
Iowa St.	.2	6	141	285	3	9	218	381

South	Conference				Overall			
	W	L	PF	PA	W	L	PF	PA
*Oklahoma	.6	2	280	172	11	3	592	284
*Texas	.5	3	284	223	10	3	484	329
*Texas Tech	.4	4	273	238	9	4	532	337
*Texas A&M	.4	4	190	213	7	6	363	337
*Oklahoma St.	.4	4	283	266	7	6	450	384
Baylor	.0	8	108	352	3	9	218	444

Big 12 championship game: Oklahoma 38, Missouri 17 (Dec. 1, 2007).

*Bowls (5-3): Kansas (won Orange); Oklahoma (lost Fiesta); Texas Tech (won Gator); Missouri (won Cotton); Oklahoma St. (won Insight); Colorado (lost Independence); Texas A&M (lost Alamo); Texas (won Holiday).

Conference USA

East	Conference				Overall			
	W	L	PF	PA	W	L	PF	PA
*UCF	.7	1	349	196	10	4	502	372
*East Carolina	.6	2	294	227	8	5	403	395
*Memphis	.6	2	259	282	7	6	380	419
*Southern Miss	.3	5	254	183	7	6	361	314
Marshall	.3	5	223	244	3	9	298	411
UAB	.1	7	158	302	2	10	235	421

West	Conference				Overall			
	W	L	PF	PA	W	L	PF	PA
*Tulsa	.6	2	328	251	10	4	576	467
*Houston	.6	2	288	248	8	5	449	379
Tulane	.3	5	215	256	4	8	293	375
Rice	.3	5	308	340	3	9	377	515
UTEP	.2	6	286	353	4	8	403	445
SMU	.0	8	251	331	1	11	340	477

Conference USA championship game: UCF 44, Tulsa 25 (Dec. 1, 2007).

*Bowls (2-4): Tulsa (won GMAC); UCF (lost Liberty); Houston (lost Texas); East Carolina (won Hawaii); Southern Miss. (lost Papajohns.com); Memphis (lost New Orleans).

Mid-American Conference

East	Conference				Overall			
	W	L	PF	PA	W	L	PF	PA
*Bowling Green	.6	2	271	219	8	5	392	417
Miami-OH	.5	2	165	130	6	7	250	333
Buffalo	.5	3	231	194	5	7	291	331
Ohio	.4	4	259	260	6	6	366	359
Temple	.4	4	140	195	4	8	197	315
Akron	.3	5	196	231	4	8	254	350
Kent St.	.1	7	175	225	3	9	259	350

West	Conference				Overall			
	W	L	PF	PA	W	L	PF	PA
*Central Michigan	.6	1	300	222	8	6	487	517
*Ball St.	.5	2	233	166	7	6	409	368
Western Michigan	.3	4	169	163	5	7	323	347
Eastern Michigan	.3	4	206	243	4	8	290	374
Toledo	.3	5	287	304	5	7	395	470
Northern Illinois	.1	6	126	206	2	10	229	370

MAC championship game: Central Michigan 35, Miami-OH 10 (Dec. 1, 2007).

*Bowls (0-3): Bowling Green (lost GMAC); Ball St. (lost International); Central Michigan (lost Motor City).

Mountain West Conference

	Conference				Overall		
	W	L	PF	PA	W	L	PF	PA
*BYU 8	0	248	129	11	2	391	241
*Air Force 6	2	228	164	9	4	389	274
*Utah 5	3	177	104	9	4	341	219
*New Mexico . . .5	3	161	176	9	4	321	247
*TCU 4	4	220	153	8	5	339	249
San Diego St. . . .3	5	196	265	4	8	301	413
Wyoming 2	6	130	233	5	7	233	311
Colorado State . .2	6	179	232	3	9	304	369
UNLV 1	7	148	231	2	10	218	343

Bowls (4-1): BYU (won Las Vegas); Air Force (lost Armed Forces); TCU (won Texas); Utah (won Poinsettia); New Mexico (won New Mexico).

Pacific-10 Conference

	Conference				Overall		
	W	L	PF	PA	W	L	PF	PA
*USC 7	2	250	150	11	2	424	208
*Arizona St. 7	2	274	211	10	3	420	293
*Oregon St. 6	3	253	229	9	4	362	294
*Oregon 5	4	301	231	9	4	496	307
*UCLA 5	4	236	192	6	7	291	290
Arizona 4	5	257	249	5	7	336	322
*California 3	6	218	241	7	6	381	348
Washington St. . .3	6	197	302	5	7	308	389
Stanford 3	6	148	280	4	8	235	339
Washington 2	7	272	321	4	9	380	411

Bowls (4-2): USC (won Rose); Arizona St. (lost Holiday); Oregon (won Sun); UCLA (lost Las Vegas); California (won Armed Forces); Oregon St. (won Emerald).

Sun Belt Conference

	Conference				Overall		
	W	L	PF	PA	W	L	PF	PA
*Florida Atlantic . .6	1	253	185	8	5	405	432
Troy 6	1	255	106	8	4	408	295
LA-Monroe 4	3	176	166	6	6	282	332
Middle Tenn. 4	3	207	187	5	7	308	339
Arkansas St. 3	4	161	187	5	7	291	331
LA-Lafayette 3	4	205	237	3	9	285	430
North Texas 1	6	161	251	2	10	298	541
Florida Int'l 1	6	149	248	1	11	181	469

Bowls (1-0): Florida Atlantic (won New Orleans).

Southeastern Conference

	Conference				Overall		
	W	L	PF	PA	W	L	PF	PA
*Tennessee 6	2	243	246	10	4	455	382
*Georgia 6	2	228	171	11	2	424	262
*Florida 5	3	305	224	9	4	552	331
South Carolina . .3	5	205	227	6	6	313	282
*Kentucky 3	5	249	276	8	5	475	385
Vanderbilt 2	6	198	203	5	7	260	271

Western								
	W	L	PF	PA	W	L	PF	PA
*LSU 6	2	298	215	12	2	541	279
*Auburn 5	3	156	138	9	4	315	220
*Arkansas 4	4	274	249	8	5	485	345
*Mississippi St. . . .4	4	157	215	8	5	279	301
*Alabama 4	4	212	190	7	6	352	286
Mississippi 0	8	131	252	3	9	241	342

SEC championship game: LSU 21, Tennessee 14 (Dec. 1, 2007).

Bowls (7-2): LSU (won BCS Title Game); Tennessee (won Outback); Georgia (won Sugar); Auburn (won Chick-fil-A); Florida (lost Capital One); Arkansas (lost Cotton); Mississippi St. (won Liberty); Alabama (won Independence); Kentucky (won Music City).

Western Athletic Conference

	Conference				Overall		
	W	L	PF	PA	W	L	PF	PA
*Hawaii 8	0	341	232	12	1	564	331
*Boise St. 7	1	385	179	10	3	551	281
*Fresno St. 6	2	252	192	9	4	427	351
*Nevada 4	4	315	270	6	7	435	418
La. Tech 4	4	199	237	5	7	249	368
San Jose St. 4	4	192	263	5	7	245	352
Utah St. 2	6	192	263	2	10	247	406
New Mexico St. . .1	7	174	317	4	9	312	471
Idaho 0	8	165	305	1	11	258	443

Bowls (1-3): Nevada (lost New Mexico); Boise St. (lost Hawaii); Fresno St. (won Humanitarian); Hawaii (lost Sugar).

NCAA Division I-A Individual Leaders

Total Offense

		Rushing				Passing		Total Offense			
	Cl	Car	Gain	Loss	Net	Att	Yds	Plays	Yds	YdsPP	YdsPG
Graham Harrell, Texas Tech . . . . . .Jr.	38	58	149	-91	713	5705	751	5614	7.48	431.8
Paul Smith, Tulsa . . . . .Sr.	105	344	225	119	544	5065	649	5184	7.99	370.3
Colt Brennan, Hawaii . . . . .Sr.	82	190	163	27	510	4343	592	4370	7.38	364.2
Dan LeFevour, Central Michigan . . .So.	188	1267	145	1122	543	3652	731	4774	6.53	341.0
Brian Brohm, Louisville . . . . .Sr.	57	117	163	-46	473	4024	530	3978	7.51	331.5
Chase Clement, Rice . . . . .Jr.	144	811	276	535	508	3377	652	3912	6.00	326.0
Chase Daniel, Missouri . . . . .Jr.	109	471	218	253	563	4306	672	4559	6.78	325.6
Chase Holbrook, N. Mexico St. . . .Jr.	55	148	143	5	543	3866	598	3871	6.47	322.6
Matt Ryan, Boston College . . . . . . .Sr.	68	231	229	2	654	4507	722	4509	6.25	322.1
Tim Tebow, Florida . . . . .So.	210	1002	107	895	350	3286	560	4181	7.47	321.6

All-Purpose Yards

	Cl	Gm	Rush	Rec	PR	KOR	Total Yds	YdsPG
Chris Johnson, East Carolina . . . . .Sr.	13	1423	528	0	1009	2960	227.69
Dante Love, Ball St. . . . . .Jr.	13	192	1398	9	1100	2690	206.92
Chad Hall, Air Force . . . . .Sr.	13	1478	524	176	505	2683	206.38
Matt Forte, Tulane . . . . .Sr.	12	2127	282	0	11	2420	201.67
Kevin Smith, UCF . . . . .Jr.	14	2567	242	0	0	2809	200.64
Devin Thomas, Michigan St. . . . . .Jr.	13	177	1260	18	1135	2590	199.23
Jeremy Maclin, Missouri . . . . .Fr.	14	375	1055	307	1039	2776	198.29
Kevin Robinson, Utah St. . . . . .Sr.	12	39	640	378	1260	2317	193.08
Jonathan Stewart, Oregon .Jr.	13	1722	145	0	614	2481	190.85

Passing Efficiency

(Minimum 15 attempts per game)

	Cl	Gm	Att	Cmp	Cmp Pct	Int	Int Pct	Yds	Yds/Att	TD	TD Pct	Rating Points
Sam Bradford, Oklahoma	Fr.	14	341	237	69.50	8	2.35	3121	9.15	36	10.56	176.5
Tim Tebow, Florida	So.	13	350	234	66.86	6	1.71	3286	9.39	32	9.14	172.5
Dennis Dixon, Oregon	Sr.	10	254	172	67.72	4	1.57	2136	8.41	20	7.87	161.2
Paul Smith, Tulsa	Sr.	14	544	327	60.11	19	3.49	5065	9.31	47	8.64	159.8
Colt Brennan, Hawaii	Sr.	12	510	359	70.39	17	3.33	4343	8.52	38	7.45	159.8
Graham Harrell, Texas Tech	Jr.	13	713	512	71.81	14	1.96	5705	8.00	48	6.73	157.3
Taylor Tharp, Boise St.	Sr.	11	423	289	68.32	11	2.60	3340	7.90	30	7.09	152.9
Brian Brohm, Louisville	Sr.	12	473	308	65.12	12	2.54	4024	8.51	30	6.34	152.4
Patrick White, West Virginia	Jr.	13	216	144	66.57	4	1.85	1724	7.98	14	6.48	151.4
Colin Kaepernick, Nevada	Fr.	11	247	133	53.85	3	1.21	2175	8.81	19	7.69	150.8
Ben Mauk, Cincinnati	Sr.	12	386	235	60.88	9	2.33	3121	8.09	31	8.03	150.6
Zac Robinson, Oklahoma St.	So.	13	333	201	60.36	9	2.70	2824	8.48	23	6.91	149.0
Todd Boeckman, Ohio St.	Jr.	13	298	190	63.76	14	4.70	2372	7.96	25	8.39	148.9
Todd Reesing, Kansas	Jr.	13	446	276	61.88	7	1.57	3486	7.82	33	7.40	148.8
Chase Daniel, Missouri	Jr.	14	563	384	68.21	11	1.95	4306	7.65	33	5.86	147.9

Rushing

	Cl	Car	Yds	TD	YdsPG
Kevin Smith, UCF	Jr.	450	2567	29	183.36
Matt Forte, Tulane	Sr.	361	2127	23	177.25
Ray Rice, Rutgers	Jr.	380	2012	24	154.77
Darren McFadden, Arkansas	Jr.	325	1830	16	140.77
Eugene Jarvis, Kent St.	So.	279	1669	10	139.08
Michael Hart, Michigan	Sr.	265	1361	14	136.10
Jonathan Stewart, Oregon	Jr.	280	1722	11	132.46
Rashard Mendenhall, Illinois	Jr.	262	1681	17	129.31
Jalen Parmele, Toledo	Jr.	179	1511	14	125.92
Jamaal Charles, Texas	Jr.	258	1619	18	124.54

Games: All played 13, except Smith (14), Forte, Jarvis and Parmele (12) and Hart (10).

Receptions

	Cl	No	Yds	TD	P/Gm
Michael Crabtree, Tex. Tech	Fr.	134	1962	22	10.31
Jordy Nelson, Kansas St.	Sr.	122	1606	11	10.17
Casey Fitzgerald, N. Texas	Jr.	111	1322	12	9.25
Danny Amendola, Tex. Tech	Sr.	109	1245	6	8.38
Davone Bess, Hawaii	Jr.	108	1266	12	8.31
Ryan Grice-Mullen, Hawaii	Jr.	106	1372	13	8.15
Dante Love, Ball St.	Jr.	100	1398	10	7.69
Jason Rivers, Hawaii	Sr.	92	1174	13	7.67
Kenneth Moore, Wake Forest	Sr.	98	1011	5	7.54
Antonio Brown, C. Mich.	Fr.	102	1003	6	7.29

Games: All played 13, except Nelson, Fitzgerald and Rivers (12) and Brown (14).

Interceptions

	Cl	No	Yds	TD	P/Gm
Elbert Mack, Troy	Sr.	8	48	1	0.67
DeAngelo Smith, Cincinnati	Jr.	8	82	1	0.62
Alphonso Smith, W. Forest	Jr.	8	166	3	0.62
Robert Vaughn, Connecticut	So.	7	112	0	0.58
P.J. Mahone, Bowling Green	So.	7	220	1	0.58
Reggie Corner, Akron	Sr.	7	142	1	0.58
William Moore, Missouri	Jr.	8	61	1	0.57
Jamie Silva, Boston College	Sr.	8	147	1	0.57
Tavious Polo, Fla. Atlantic	Fr.	7	17	0	0.54
Jairus Byrd, Oregon	Sr.	7	31	0	0.54
Shane Carter, Wisconsin	So.	7	92	0	0.54

Games: All played 13, except Mack, Vaughn, Mahone, Corner (12), Moore and Silva (14).

Scoring

Non-Kickers

	Cl	TD	Pts	P/Gm
Kevin Smith, UCF	Jr.	30	180	12.86
Matt Forte, Tulane	Sr.	23	140	11.67
Ray Rice, Rutgers	Jr.	25	150	11.54
Chris Johnson, East Carolina	Sr.	24	144	11.08
Tim Tebow, Florida	So.	23	138	10.62
Michael Crabtree, Tex. Tech	Fr.	22	132	10.15
Kalvin McRae, Ohio	Sr.	20	120	10.00
Marcus Thomas, UTEP	Sr.	18	108	9.82
Jehuu Caulcrick, Mich. St.	Sr.	21	126	9.69

Games: All played 13, except Smith (14), Thomas (11), McRae and Forte (12).

Kickers

	PAT/Att	FG/Att	Pts	P/Gm
Colt David, LSU	.63/63	26/33	147	10.50
John Sullivan, N. Mexico	.30/31	29/35	117	9.75
Jeff Wolfert, Missouri	.67/67	21/25	130	9.29
Jeremy Ito, Rutgers	.51/51	23/31	120	9.23
Scott Webb, Kansas	.66/67	18/26	120	9.23
Brooks Rossman, Kan. St.	.44/46	22/28	110	9.17
Thomas Weber, Ariz. St.	.46/48	24/25	118	9.08
Mark Bucholz, Clemson	.48/48	22/36	114	8.77
Kyle Brotzman, Boise St.	.66/66	16/18	114	8.77
Ryan Bailey, Texas	.58/59	18/22	112	8.62

Games: All played 13, except David and Wolfert (14), Sullivan and Rossman (12).

Field Goals

	Cl	FG/Att	Pct	P/Gm
John Sullivan, New Mexico	Sr.	29/35	.829	2.42
Gary Cismesia, Florida St.	Sr.	27/34	.794	2.08
Kai Forbath, UCLA	Fr.	25/30	.833	1.92
Leigh Tiffin, Alabama	So.	25/34	.735	1.92
Colt David, LSU	Jr.	26/33	.788	1.86
Thomas Weber, Arizona St.	Fr.	24/25	.960	1.85
Swayze Waters, UAB	Sr.	22/28	.786	1.83
Brooks Rossman, Kansas St.	Jr.	22/28	.786	1.83
Jeremy Ito, Rutgers	Sr.	23/31	.742	1.77
Travis Bell, Georgia Tech	Sr.	23/28	.821	1.77
Jason Bondzio, Arizona	Jr.	21/26	.808	1.75

Games: All played 13, except Sullivan, Waters and Rossman (12) and David (14).

Punting
(Minimum of 3.6 per game)

	Cl	No	Yds	Avg
Kevin Huber, Cincinnati	Jr.	57	2672	46.88
Brett Kern, Toledo	Sr.	52	2399	46.13
Chris Miller, Ball St.	Jr.	61	2772	45.44
Ryan Weigand, Virginia	Sr.	52	2352	45.23
Durant Brooks, Ga. Tech	Sr.	65	2929	45.06
Jacob Richardson, Miami-OH	Jr.	68	3063	45.04
Owen Tolson, Army	Sr.	73	3283	44.97
Thomas Morstead, SMU	Jr.	57	2545	44.65
Tim Reyer, Kansas St.	Sr.	58	2583	44.53
Patrick Fisher, LSU	Sr.	59	2627	44.53

Punt Returns
(Minimum of 1.2 per game)

	Cl	No	Yds	TD	Avg
Kevin Robinson, Utah St.	Sr.	20	378	1	18.90
Brandon James, Florida	So.	14	254	1	18.14
Deon Murphy, Kansas St.	Jr.	26	454	1	17.46
Leodis McKelvin, Troy	Sr.	25	436	3	17.44
Philip Beck, La. Tech	Jr.	18	313	0	17.39
Shiloh Keo, Idaho	So.	19	319	1	16.79
Javier Arenas, Alabama	So.	21	323	1	15.38
Jeremy Trimble, Army	Sr.	19	280	1	14.74
Derrek Richards, Utah	Sr.	29	426	1	14.69
Eddie Royal, Virginia Tech	Sr.	31	455	2	14.68

Kickoff Returns
(Minimum of 1.2 per game)

	Cl	No	Yds	TD	Avg
A.J. Jefferson, Fresno St.	So.	26	930	2	35.77
Bryan Williams, Akron	Jr.	21	670	1	31.90
Kevin Marion, Wake Forest	Sr.	28	876	1	31.29
Felix Jones, Arkansas	Jr.	22	652	2	29.64
Ryan Mouton, Hawaii	Jr.	14	414	1	29.57
Kevin Robinson, Utah St.	Sr.	43	1260	2	29.30
DeMarco Murray, Oklahoma	Fr.	15	439	2	29.27
Darius Marshall, Marshall	Fr.	19	556	1	29.26
Curtis Francis, UCF	Sr.	22	643	1	29.23
Malcolm Lane, Hawaii	So.	25	730	2	29.20

Sacks

	Cl	No	Yds	P/Gm
Greg Middleton, Indiana	So.	16	102	1.23
George Selvie, South Florida	So.	14½	87	1.12
Vernon Gholston, Ohio St.	Sr.	14	111	1.08
Chris Long, Virginia	Sr.	14	122	1.08
Jan Jorgensen, BYU	So.	13½	91	1.04

Games: All played 13.

NCAA Division I-A Team Leaders

Scoring Offense

	Gm	Record	Pts	Avg
Hawaii	13	12-1	564	43.38
Kansas	13	12-1	556	42.77
Florida	13	9-4	552	42.46
Boise St.	13	10-3	551	42.38
Oklahoma	14	11-3	592	42.29
Tulsa	14	10-4	576	41.14
Texas Tech	13	9-4	532	40.92
Missouri	14	12-2	558	39.86
West Virginia	13	11-2	515	39.62
Navy	13	8-5	511	39.31

Scoring Defense

	Gm	Record	Pts	Avg
Ohio St.	13	11-2	166	12.8
USC	13	11-2	208	16.0
Virginia Tech	14	11-3	225	16.1
Kansas	13	12-1	213	16.4
Utah	13	9-4	219	16.8
Auburn	13	9-4	220	16.9
Penn St.	13	9-4	228	17.5
West Virginia	13	11-2	235	18.1
BYU	12	11-2	241	18.5
TCU	13	8-5	243	18.7
Clemson	13	9-4	243	18.7

Total Offense

	Gm	Plays	Yds	Avg	TD	YdsPG
Tulsa	14	1126	7615	6.76	79	543.93
Texas Tech	13	1009	6885	6.82	70	529.62
Hawaii	13	942	6657	7.07	76	512.08
Houston	13	1036	6525	6.30	59	501.92
Missouri	14	1112	6864	6.17	70	490.29
Louisville	12	909	5856	6.44	55	488.00
Oklahoma St.	13	978	6322	6.46	60	486.31
Kansas	12	988	6237	6.31	72	479.77
Nebraska	12	898	5619	6.26	53	468.25
Oregon	13	1028	6078	5.91	62	467.54

Note: Touchdowns scored by rushing and passing only.

Total Defense

	Gm	Plays	Yds	Avg	TD	YdsPG
Ohio St.	13	832	3029	3.64	20	233.00
USC	13	875	3551	4.06	25	273.15
LSU	14	915	4043	4.42	35	288.79
Virginia Tech	14	960	4157	4.33	27	296.93
Pittsburgh	12	808	3572	4.42	35	297.67
Auburn	13	855	3873	4.53	25	297.92
West Virginia	13	871	3922	4.50	29	301.69
Oregon St.	13	891	3980	4.47	35	306.15
Clemson	13	877	3988	4.55	29	306.77
BYU	13	877	4002	4.56	27	307.85

Note: Opponents' TDs scored by rushing and passing only.

Underclassmen who declared for the 2008 draft

53 players forfeited the remainder of their college eligibility and declared for the 2008 NFL Draft held April 26-27. NFL teams drafted 40 underclassmen. Players listed in alphabetical order; first round selections in **bold** type.

	Pos	Drafted by	Overall Pick
Branden Albert, Virginia	.G	Kansas City	15
L.J. Anderson, Central Florida	.G	not drafted	–
Adrian Arrington, Michigan	.WR	N. Orleans	237
Earl Bennett, Vanderbilt	.WR	Chicago	70
Martellus Bennett, Tex. A&M	.TE	Dallas	61
Davone Bess, Hawaii	.WR	not drafted	–
Demario Bobo, Miss. St.	.DB	not drafted	–
Calais Campbell, Miami	.DE	Detroit	50
Jamaal Charles, Texas	.RB	Kansas City	73
Ryan Clady, Boise St.	.LT	Denver	12
Anthony Collins, Kansas	.LT	Cincinnati	112
Johnny Dingle, West Va.	.DE	not drafted	–
Franklin Dunbar, Mid. Tenn.	.OT	not drafted	–
Jermichael Finley, Texas	.TE	Green Bay	91
Brandon Flowers, Va. Tech	.CB	Kansas City	35
Jeremy Geathers, UNLV	.DE	not drafted	–
Vernon Gholston, Ohio St.	.DE	N.Y. Jets	6
Ryan Grice-Mullen, Hawaii	.WR	not drafted	–
Letroy Guion, Florida St.	.DT	Minnesota	152
James Hardy, Indiana	.WR	Buffalo	41
Derrick Harvey, Florida	.DE	Jacksonville	8
Geno Hayes, Florida St.	.LB	Tampa Bay	175
Erin Henderson, Maryland	.LB	not drafted	–
Jack Ikegwuonu, Wisconsin	.CB	Philadelphia	131
DeSean Jackson, California	.WR	Philadelphia	49
Josh Johnson, Marshall	.LB	Tampa Bay	160
Felix Jones, Arkansas	.RB	Dallas	22

	Pos	Drafted by	Overall Pick
Malcolm Kelly, Oklahoma	.WR	Washington	51
Justin King, Penn St.	.CB	St. Louis	101
Xavier Lee, Florida St.	.QB	not drafted	–
Curtis Lofton, Oklahoma	.LB	Atlanta	37
Selwyn Lymon, Purdue	.WR	not drafted	–
Mario Manningham, Michigan	WR	NY Giants	95
Jerod Mayo, Tennessee	.LB	N. England	10
Darren McFadden, Arkansas	RB	Oakland	4
Rashard Mendenhall, Illinois	RB	Pittsburgh	23
Phillip Merling, Clemson	.DE	Miami	32
DaJuan Morgan, N.C. State	.S	Kansas City	82
Lamar Myles, Louisville	.LB	not drafted	–
Sean Penix, Arkansas	.WR	not drafted	–
Kenny Phillips, Miami-FL	.S	NY Giants	31
Chilo Rachal, USC	.G	San Fran.	39
Darius Reynaud, West Va.	.WR	not drafted	–
Ray Rice, Rutgers	.RB	Baltimore	55
Orlando Scandrick, Boise St.	.CB	Dallas	143
Pat Sims, Auburn	.DT	Cincinnati	77
Steve Slaton, West Va.	.RB	Houston	89
Kevin Smith, C. Florida	.RB	Detroit	64
Reggie Smith, Oklahoma	.DB	San Fran.	75
Jonathan Stewart, Oregon	.RB	Carolina	13
Aqib Talib, Kansas	.CB	Tampa Bay	20
Devin Thomas, Michigan St.	.WR	Washington	34
Mario Urrutia, Louisville	.WR	Cincinnati	246

Annual Awards

Players of the Year

Tim Tebow, Florida, QB ....AP, Heisman, Maxwell
Darren McFadden, Arkansas, RB ....Camp

Payton Award (I-AA) .... Jayson Foster, Georgia Southern
Hill Trophy (Div. II) ....Danny Woodhead, Chadron St., RB
Gagliardi Trophy (Div. III) . Justin Beaver, Wisc-Whitewater

Position Players of the Year

O'Brien Award (Quarterback) ....Tim Tebow, Florida
Walker Award (Running Back) Darren McFadden, Arkansas
Biletnikoff Award (Receiver) ..Michael Crabtree, Tex. Tech
Outland Trophy (Int. Lineman) ....Glenn Dorsey, LSU
Lombardi Award (Lineman) ....Glenn Dorsey, LSU
Butkus Award (Linebacker) .... James Laurinaitis, Ohio St.
Thorpe Award (Def. Back) ......Antoine Cason, Arizona
Nagurski Award (Def. Player) ....Glenn Dorsey, LSU
Bednarik Award (Def. Player) ......Dan Connor, Penn St.
Groza Award (Kicker) ....Thomas Weber, Ariz. St.
Ray Guy Award (Punter) ....Durant Brooks, Ga. Tech
Mackey Award (Tight End) ....Fred Davis, USC

Coaches of the Year

Mark Mangino, Kansas ....AFCA, AP, Camp, FWAA
Lloyd Carr, Michigan ....Dodd

2007 Heisman Trophy Vote

Presented since 1935 by the Downtown Athletic Club of New York City and named after former college coach and DAC athletic director John W. Heisman. Voting done by national media and former Heisman winners. Each ballot allows for three names (points based on 3 for 1st, 2 for 2nd and 1 for 3rd).

Top 10 Vote-Getters

	Pos	1st	2nd	3rd	Pts
Tim Tebow, Florida	QB	462	229	113	1,957
Darren McFadden, Arkansas	RB	291	355	120	1,703
Colt Brennan, Hawaii	QB	54	114	242	632
Chase Daniel, Missouri	QB	25	84	182	425
Dennis Dixon, Oregon	QB	17	31	65	178
Patrick White, West Va.	QB	16	28	46	150
Matt Ryan, Boston College	QB	9	7	22	63
Kevin Smith, Central Fla.	RB	3	11	24	55
Glenn Dorsey, LSU	DT	3	6	9	30
Chris Long, Virginia	DE	1	2	10	17

Tim Tebow too good to wait

Florida quarterback Tim Tebow made history in 2007, becoming the first freshman or sophomore to win the Heisman Trophy in the 72-year history of the award. The sophomore passer did plenty of work on the ground, rushing for 23 touchdowns to break the season record by a quarterback, previously held by Air Force's Chase Harridge (22 in 2002). Tim Tebow is Florida's third Heisman Trophy winner, joining Steve Spurrier (1966) and Danny Wuerffel (1996).

Consensus All-America Team

NCAA Division I-A players cited most frequently by the following selectors: AFCA, AP, and Walter Camp Foundation. (*) indicates unanimous selection. Holdovers from the 2006 team is in **bold** type.

Offense

	Player	Class	Ht	Wt
WR	Jordy Nelson*, Kansas St.	Sr.	6-2	213
WR	Michael Crabtree*, Texas Tech	Fr.	6-3	208
TE	Martin Rucker, Missouri	Sr.	6-6	255
OL	**Jake Long***, Michigan	Sr.	6-7	313
OL	Martin O'Donnell, Illinois	Sr.	6-5	305
OL	Steve Justice, Wake Forest	Sr.	6-4	284
OL	Duke Robinson, Oklahoma	Jr.	6-5	330
OL	Anthony Collins, Kansas	Jr.	6-5	320
QB	Tim Tebow, Florida	So.	6-3	235
RB	**Darren McFadden***, Arkansas	Jr.	6-2	215
RB	Kevin Smith, C. Florida	Jr.	6-1	211
K	Thomas Weber, Arizona St.	Fr.	6-1	202

Defense

	Player	Class	Ht	Wt
DL	Chris Long*, Virginia	Sr.	6-4	280
DL	George Selvie*, So. Florida	So.	6-4	242
DL	Sedrick Ellis*, USC	Sr.	6-2	305
DL	**Glenn Dorsey***, LSU	Sr.	6-2	299
LB	Dan Connor, Penn St.	Sr.	6-3	233
LB	Jordan Dizon, Colorado	Sr.	6-0	220
LB	**James Laurinaitis***, Ohio St.	Jr.	6-3	240
DB	Aqib Talib*, Kansas	Jr.	6-2	195
DB	Antoine Cason, Arizona	Sr.	6-0	185
DB	Craig Steltz, LSU	Sr.	6-2	209
DB	Jamie Silva, Boston College	Sr.	5-11	210
P	Kevin Huber, Cincinnati	Jr.	6-1	210

NCAA Playoffs

Division I-AA

First Round (Nov. 24)

Delaware 44 . . . . .Delaware St. 7
Massachusetts 49 .Fordham 35
Appalachian St. 28 . . . . James Madison 27
Wofford 23 . . . . Montana 22
Southern Illinois 30 . . . . .Eastern Illinois 11
Richmond 31 . . . . .Eastern Kentucky 14
Northern Iowa 38 . . . . .New Hampshire 35
Eastern Washington 44 . . . . .McNeese St. 15

Quarterfinals (Dec. 1)

Appalachian St. 38 . . . . .Eastern Washington 35
Delaware 39 . . . . .Northern Iowa 27
Southern Illinois 34 . . . . .Massachusetts 27
Richmond 21 . . . . .Wofford 10

Semifinals (Dec. 7-8)

Appalachian St. 55 . . . . .Richmond 35
Delaware 20 . . . . .Southern Illinois 17

Championship Game

Dec. 14 at Chattanooga, Tenn. (Att: 23,010)
Appalachian St. 49 .Delaware 21
(11-4)   (13-2)

Division II

First Round (Nov. 17)

Indiana (PA) 45 . . . . .West Chester 35
So. Connecticut 45 .Bryant 28
Abilene Christian 56 . . . . .Mesa St. 12
Catawba 66 . . . . Albany St. (GA) 35
North Dakota 44 . . . . .Winona St. 2
Delta State 45 . . . . .Shaw 7
West Texas A&M 40 . . . . .Washburn 39
Central Washington 40 . . . . .Ashland 24

Second Round (Nov. 24)

California (PA) 43 . . . . .So. Connecticut 7
Shepherd 41 .Indiana (PA) 34
Grand Valley St. 21 . . . . .North Dakota 14
Valdosta St. 55 . . . . .Catawba 2
C. Washington 20 . . . . .Nebraska-Omaha 17
Chadron St. 76 . . . . .3 OT . .Abilene Christian 73
NW Missouri St. 56 . . . . .West Texas A&M 28
North Alabama 26 . . . . .Delta St. 17

Quarterfinals (Dec. 1)

California (PA) 58 .Shepherd 38
Grand Valley St. 41 . . . . .Central Washington 21
Valdosta St. 37 . . . . .North Alabama 23
NW Missouri St. 26 . . . . .Chadron St. 13

Semifinals (Dec. 8)

Valdosta St. 28 . . . . .California (PA) 24
NW Missouri St. 34 . . . . .Grand Valley St. 16

Championship Game

Dec. 15 at Florence, Ala.
Valdosta St. 25 . . . . .NW Missouri St. 20
(13-1)   (12-2)

Division III

First Round (Nov. 18)

Mount Union 42 . . . . .Ithaca 18
College of New Jersey 17 . . . . .Rensselaer 14
St. John Fisher 24 . . . . .Hobart 7
N.C. Wesleyan 35 . . . . .OT . . .Wash. and Jeff. 34
Muhlenberg 31 . . . . .Salisbury 21
North Central 44 . . . . .Franklin 42
Wabash 31 . . . . .Mount St. Joseph 21
Case Western Reserve 21 . . . . .Widener 20
Wesley 45 . . . . .Hampden-Sydney 17
Curry 42 . . . . .Hartwick 21
Central (IA) 38 . . . . .Olivet 17
St. John's (MN) 41 . . . . .Redlands 13
Wisc-Eau Claire 24 . . . . .St. Norbert 20
Bethel (MN) 28 . . . . .Concordia (WI) 0
Wisc-Whitewater 34 . . . . .Capital 14
Mary Hardin-Baylor 52 . . . . .Trinity (TX) 23

Second Round (Nov. 24)

Mount Union 59 . . . . .College of New Jersey 7
St. John Fisher 38 . . . . .Curry 7
Wesley 38 .Muhlenberg 21
Wabash 38 . . . . .Case Western Reserve 23
Central Iowa 37 . . . . .St. John's (MN) 7
Bethel (MN) 21 . . . . .Wisc-Eau Claire 12
Mary Hardin-Baylor 64 . . . . .N.C. Wesleyan 0
Wisc-Whitewater 59 . . . . .North Central 28

Quarterfinals (Dec. 1)

Mount Union 52 . . . . .St. John Fisher 10
Mary Hardin-Baylor 27 . . . . .Wesley 10
Bethel (MN) 27 . . . . .Central 13
Wisc-Whitewater 47 . . . . .Wabash 7

Semifinals (Dec. 8)

Mount Union 62 . . . . .Bethel (MN) 14
Wisc-Whitewater 16 . . . . .Mary Hardin-Baylor 7

Amos Alonzo Stagg Bowl

Dec. 15 at Salem, Va.
Wisc-Whitewater 31 . . . . .Mount Union 21
(14-1)   (14-1)

1869-2008
Through the Years

SPORTS ALMANAC

National Champions

Over the last 132 years, there have been 25 major selectors of national champions by way of polls (11), mathematical rating systems (10) and historical research (4). The best-known and most widely circulated of these surveys, the Associated Press poll of sportswriters and broadcasters, first appeared during the 1936 season. Champions prior to 1936 have been determined by retro polls, ratings and historical research.

The Early Years (1869-1935)

National champions based on the Dickinson mathematical system (DS) and three historical retro polls taken by the College Football Researchers Association (CFRA), the National Championship Foundation (NCF) and the Helms Athletic Foundation (HF). The CFRA and NCF polls start in 1869, college football's inaugural year, while the Helms poll begins in 1883, the first season the game adopted a point system for scoring. Frank Dickinson, an economics professor at Illinois, introduced his system in 1926 and retro-picked winners in 1924 and '25. Bowl game results were counted in the Helms selections, but not in the other three.

Multiple champions: Yale (18); Princeton (17); Harvard (9); Michigan (7); Notre Dame and Penn (4); Alabama, California, Cornell, Illinois, Pittsburgh and USC (3); Georgia Tech, Minnesota and Penn St. (2).

Year		Record	Year		Record	Year		Record
1869	**Princeton**	1-1-0	1880	**Yale** (CFRA)	4-0-1	1891	**Yale**	13-0-0
1870	**Princeton**	1-0-0		& **Princeton** (NCF)	4-0-1	1892	**Yale**	13-0-0
1871	No games played		1881	**Yale**	5-0-1	1893	**Princeton**	11-0-0
1872	**Princeton**	1-0-0	1882	**Yale**	8-0-0	1894	**Yale**	16-0-0
1873	**Princeton**	1-0-0	1883	**Yale**	8-0-0	1895	**Penn**	14-0-0
1874	**Yale**	3-0-0	1884	**Yale**	8-0-1	1896	**Princeton** (CFRA)	10-0-1
1875	**Princeton** (CFRA)	2-0-0	1885	**Princeton**	9-0-0		& **Lafayette** (NCF)	11-0-1
	& **Harvard** (NCF)	4-0-0	1886	**Yale**	9-0-1	1897	**Penn**	15-0-0
1876	**Yale**	3-0-0	1887	**Yale**	9-0-0	1898	**Harvard**	11-0-0
1877	**Yale**	3-0-1	1888	**Yale**	13-0-0	1899	**Princeton** (CFRA)	12-1-0
1878	**Princeton**	6-0-0	1889	**Princeton**	10-0-0		& **Harvard** (NCF, HF)	10-0-1
1879	**Princeton**	4-0-1	1890	**Harvard**	11-0-0			

Year		Record	Bowl Game	Head Coach	Outstanding Player
1900	**Yale**	12-0-0	No bowl	Malcolm McBride	Perry Hale, HB
1901	**Harvard** (CFRA)	12-0-0	No bowl	Bill Reid	Bob Kernan, HB
	& **Michigan** (NCF, HF)	11-0-0	Won Rose	Hurry Up Yost	Neil Snow, E
1902	**Michigan**	11-0-0	No bowl	Hurry Up Yost	Boss Weeks, QB
1903	**Princeton**	11-0-0	No bowl	Art Hillebrand	John DeWitt, G
1904	**Penn** (CFRA, HF)	12-0-0	No bowl	Carl Williams	Andy Smith, FB
	& **Michigan** (NCF)	10-0-0	No bowl	Hurry Up Yost	Willie Heston, HB
1905	**Chicago**	10-0-0	No bowl	Amos Alonzo Stagg	Walter Eckersall, QB
1906	**Princeton**	9-0-1	No bowl	Bill Roper	Cap Wister, E
1907	**Yale**	9-0-1	No bowl	Bill Knox	Tad Jones, HB
1908	**Penn** (CFRA, HF)	11-0-1	No bowl	Sol Metzger	Hunter Scarlett, E
	& **LSU** (NCF)	10-0-0	No bowl	Edgar Wingard	Doc Fenton, QB
1909	**Yale**	12-1-0	No bowl	Howard Jones	Ted Coy, FB
1910	**Harvard** (CFRA, HF)	8-0-1	No bowl	Percy Haughton	Percy Wendell, HB
	& **Pittsburgh** (NCF)	9-0-0	No bowl	Joe Thompson	Ralph Galvin, C
1911	**Princeton** (CFRA, HF)	8-0-2	No bowl	Bill Roper	Sam White, E
	& **Penn St.** (NCF)	8-0-1	No bowl	Bill Hollenback	Dexter Very, E
1912	**Harvard** (CFRA, HF)	9-0-0	No bowl	Percy Haughton	Charley Brickley, HB
	& **Penn St.** (NCF)	8-0-0	No bowl	Bill Hollenback	Dexter Very, E
1913	**Harvard**	9-0-0	No bowl	Percy Haughton	Eddie Mahan, FB
1914	**Army**	9-0-0	No bowl	Charley Daly	John McEwan, C
1915	**Cornell**	9-0-0	No bowl	Al Sharpe	Charley Barrett, QB
1916	**Pittsburgh**	8-0-0	No bowl	Pop Warner	Bob Peck, C
1917	**Georgia Tech**	9-0-0	No bowl	John Heisman	Ev Strupper, HB
1918	**Pittsburgh** (CFRA, HF)	4-1-0	No bowl	Pop Warner	Tom Davies, HB
	& **Michigan** (NCF)	5-0-0	No bowl	Hurry Up Yost	Frank Steketee, FB
1919	**Harvard** (CFRA-tie, HF)	9-0-1	Won Rose	Bob Fisher	Eddie Casey, HB
	Illinois (CFRA-tie)	6-1-0	No bowl	Bob Zuppke	Chuck Carney, E
	& **Notre Dame** (NCF)	9-0-0	No bowl	Knute Rockne	George Gipp, HB
1920	**California**	9-0-0	Won Rose	Andy Smith	Dan McMillan, T
1921	**California** (CFRA)	9-0-1	Tied Rose	Andy Smith	Brick Muller, E
	& **Cornell** (NCF, HF)	8-0-0	No bowl	Gil Dobie	Eddie Kaw, HB
1922	**Princeton** (CFRA)	8-0-0	No bowl	Bill Roper	Herb Treat, T
	California (NCF)	9-0-0	No bowl	Andy Smith	Brick Muller, E
	& **Cornell** (HF)	8-0-0	No bowl	Gil Dobie	Eddie Kaw, HB

Year		Record	Bowl Game	Head Coach	Outstanding Player
1923	Illinois (CFRA, HF)	8-0-0	No bowl	Bob Zuppke	Red Grange, HB
	& Michigan (NCF)	8-0-0	No bowl	Hurry Up Yost	Jack Blott, C
1924	Notre Dame	10-0-0	Won Rose	Knute Rockne	"The Four Horsemen"*
1925	Alabama (CFRA, HF)	10-0-0	Won Rose	Wallace Wade	Johnny Mack Brown, HB
	& Dartmouth (DS)	8-0-0	No bowl	Jesse Hawley	Swede Oberlander, HB
1926	Alabama (CFRA, HF)	9-0-1	Tied Rose	Wallace Wade	Hoyt Winslett, E
	& Stanford (DS)	10-0-1	Tied Rose	Pop Warner	Ted Shipkey, E
1927	Yale (CFRA)	7-1-0	No bowl	Tad Jones	Bill Webster, G
	& Illinois (NCF, HF, DS)	7-0-1	No bowl	Bob Zuppke	Bob Reitsch, C
1928	Georgia Tech (CFRA, NCF, HF)	10-0-0	Won Rose	Bill Alexander	Pete Pund, C
	& USC (DS)	9-0-1	No bowl	Howard Jones	Jesse Hibbs, T
1929	Notre Dame	9-0-0	No bowl	Knute Rockne	Frank Carideo, QB
1930	Alabama (CFRA)	10-0-0	Won Rose	Wallace Wade	Fred Sington, T
	& Notre Dame (NCF, HF, DS)	10-0-0	No bowl	Knute Rockne	Marchy Schwartz, HB
1931	USC	10-1-0	Won Rose	Howard Jones	John Baker, G
1932	USC (CFRA, NCF, HF)	10-0-0	Won Rose	Howard Jones	Ernie Smith, T
	& Michigan (DS)	8-0-0	No bowl	Harry Kipke	Harry Newman, QB
1933	Michigan	8-0-0	No bowl	Harry Kipke	Chuck Bernard, C
1934	Minnesota	8-0-0	No bowl	Bernie Bierman	Pug Lund, HB
1935	Minnesota (CFRA, NCF, HF)	8-0-0	No bowl	Bernie Bierman	Dick Smith, T
	& SMU (DS)	12-1-0	Lost Rose	Matty Bell	Bobby Wilson, HB

*Notre Dame's Four Horsemen were Harry Stuhldreher (QB), Jim Crowley (HB), Don Miller (HB-P) and Elmer Layden (FB).

The Media Poll Years (since 1936)

National champions according to seven media and coaches' polls: Associated Press (since 1936), United Press (1950-57), International News Service (1952-57), United Press International (1958-92), Football Writers Association of America (since 1954), National Football Foundation and Hall of Fame (since 1959) and USA Today/CNN (since 1991). In 1991, the American Football Coaches Association switched outlets for its poll from UPI to USA Today/CNN and then to USA Today/ESPN in 1997.

After 29 years of releasing its final Top 20 poll in early December, AP named its 1965 national champion following that season's bowl games. AP returned to a pre-bowls final vote in 1966 and '67, but has polled its writers and broadcasters after the bowl games since the 1968 season. The FWAA has selected its champion after the bowl games since the 1955 season, the NFF-Hall of Fame since 1971, UPI after 1974, USA Today/CNN 1991-96, and USA Today/ESPN since 1997.

The Associated Press changed the name of its final championship award from the AP trophy to the Bear Bryant Trophy after the legendary Alabama coach's death in 1983. The FootballWriters' trophy is called the Grantland Rice Award (after the celebrated sportswriter) and the NFF-Hall of Fame trophy is called the MacArthur Bowl (in honor of Gen. Douglas MacArthur).

Multiple champions: Notre Dame (9); Alabama, Ohio St., Oklahoma and USC (7); Miami-FL and Nebraska (5); Minnesota (4); LSU, Michigan St. and Texas (3); Army, Florida, Florida St., Georgia Tech, Michigan, Penn St., Pittsburgh and Tennessee (2).

Year		Record	Bowl Game	Head Coach	Outstanding Player
1936	Minnesota	7-1-0	No bowl	Bernie Bierman	Ed Widseth, T
1937	Pittsburgh	9-0-1	No bowl	Jock Sutherland	Marshall Goldberg, HB
1938	TCU	11-0-0	Won Sugar	Dutch Meyer	Davey O'Brien, QB
1939	Texas A&M	11-0-0	Won Sugar	Homer Norton	John Kimbrough, FB
1940	Minnesota	8-0-0	No Bowl	Bernie Bierman	George Franck, HB
1941	Minnesota	8-0-0	No bowl	Bernie Bierman	Bruce Smith, HB
1942	Ohio St.	9-1-0	No bowl	Paul Brown	Gene Fekete, FB
1943	Notre Dame	9-1-0	No bowl	Frank Leahy	Angelo Bertelli, QB
1944	Army	9-0-0	No bowl	Red Blaik	Glenn Davis, HB
1945	Army	9-0-0	No bowl	Red Blaik	Doc Blanchard, FB
1946	Notre Dame	8-0-1	No bowl	Frank Leahy	Johnny Lujack, QB
1947	Notre Dame	9-0-0	No bowl	Frank Leahy	Johnny Lujack, QB
1948	Michigan	9-0-0	No bowl	Bennie Oosterbaan	Dick Rifenburg, E
1949	Notre Dame	10-0-0	No bowl	Frank Leahy	Leon Hart, E
1950	Oklahoma	10-1-0	Lost Sugar	Bud Wilkinson	Leon Heath, FB
1951	Tennessee	10-0-0	Lost Sugar	Bob Neyland	Hank Lauricella, TB
1952	Michigan St. (AP, UP)	9-0-0	No bowl	Biggie Munn	Don McAuliffe, HB
	& Georgia Tech (INS)	12-0-0	Won Sugar	Bobby Dodd	Hal Miller, T
1953	Maryland	10-1-0	Lost Orange	Jim Tatum	Bernie Faloney, QB
1954	Ohio St. (AP, INS)	10-0-0	Won Rose	Woody Hayes	Howard Cassady, HB
	& UCLA (UP, FW)	9-0-0	No bowl	Red Sanders	Jack Ellena, T
1955	Oklahoma	11-0-0	Won Orange	Bud Wilkinson	Jerry Tubbs, C
1956	Oklahoma	10-0-0	No bowl	Bud Wilkinson	Tommy McDonald, HB
1957	Auburn (AP)	10-0-0	No bowl	Shug Jordan	Jimmy Phillips, E
	& Ohio St. (UP, FW, INS)	9-1-0	Won Rose	Woody Hayes	Bob White, FB
1958	LSU (AP, UPI)	11-0-0	Won Sugar	Paul Dietzel	Billy Cannon, HB
	& Iowa (FW)	8-1-0	Won Rose	Forest Evashevski	Randy Duncan, QB
1959	Syracuse	11-0-0	Won Cotton	Ben Schwartzwalder	Ernie Davis, HB
1960	Minnesota (AP, UPI, NFF)	8-2-0	Lost Rose	Murray Warmath	Tom Brown, G
	& Mississippi (FW)	10-0-1	Won Sugar	Johnny Vaught	Jake Gibbs, QB

National Champions (Cont.)

Year		Record	Bowl Game	Head Coach	Outstanding Player
1961	**Alabama** (AP, UPI, NFF)	11-0-0	Won Sugar	Bear Bryant	Billy Neighbors, T
	& **Ohio St.** (FW)	8-0-1	No bowl	Woody Hayes	Bob Ferguson, HB
1962	**USC**	11-0-0	Won Rose	John McKay	Hal Bedsole, E
1963	**Texas**	11-0-0	Won Cotton	Darrell Royal	Scott Appleton, T1964
	Alabama (AP, UPI),	10-1-0	Lost Orange	Bear Bryant	Joe Namath, QB
	Arkansas (FW)	11-0-0	Won Cotton	Frank Broyles	Ronnie Caveness, LB
	& **Notre Dame** (NFF)	9-1-0	No bowl	Ara Parseghian	John Huarte, QB
1965	**Alabama** (AP, FW-tie)	9-1-1	Won Orange	Bear Bryant	Paul.Crane, C
	& **Michigan St.** (UPI, NFF, FW-tie)	10-1-0	Lost Rose	Duffy Daugherty	George Webster, LB
1966	**Notre Dame** (AP, UPI, FW, NFF-tie)	9.0-0-1	No bowl	Ara Parseghian	Jim Lynch, LB
	& **Michigan St.** (NFF-tie)	9-0-1	No bowl	Duffy Daugherty	Bubba Smith, DE
1967	**USC**	10-1-0	Won Rose	John McKay	O.J. Simpson, HB
1968	**Ohio St.**	10-0-0	Won Rose	Woody Hayes	Rex Kern, QB
1969	**Texas**	11-0-0	Won Cotton	Darrell Royal	James Street, QB
1970	**Nebraska** (AP, FW)	11-0-1	Won Orange	Bob Devaney	Jerry Tagge, QB
	Texas (UPI, NFF-tie),	10-1-0	Lost Cotton	Darrell Royal	Steve Worster, RB
	& **Ohio St.** (NFF-tie)	9-1-0	Lost Rose	Woody Hayes	Jim Stillwagon, MG
1971	**Nebraska**	13-0-0	Won Orange	Bob Devaney	Johnny Rodgers, WR
1972	**USC**	12-0-0	Won Rose	John McKay	Charles Young, TE
1973	**Notre Dame** (AP, FW, NFF)	11-0-0	Won Sugar	Ara Parseghian	Mike Townsend, DB
	& **Alabama** (UPI)	11-1-0	Lost Sugar	Bear Bryant	Buddy Brown, OT
1974	**Oklahoma** (AP)	11-0-0	No bowl	Barry Switzer	Joe Washington, RB
	& **USC** (UPI, FW, NFF)	10-1-0	Won Rose	John McKay	Anthony Davis, RB
1975	**Oklahoma**	11-1-0	Won Orange	Barry Switzer	Lee Roy Selmon, DT
1976	**Pittsburgh**	12-0-0	Won Sugar	Johnny Majors	Tony Dorsett, RB
1977	**Notre Dame**	11-1-0	Won Cotton	Dan Devine	Ross Browner, DE
1978	**Alabama** (AP, FW, NFF)	11-1-0	Won Sugar	Bear Bryant	Marty Lyons, DT
	& **USC** (UPI)	12-1-0	Won Rose	John Robinson	Charles White, RB
1979	**Alabama**	12-0-0	Won Sugar	Bear Bryant	Jim Bunch, OT
1980	**Georgia**	12-0-0	Won Sugar	Vince Dooley	Herschel Walker, RB
1981	**Clemson**	12-0-0	Won Orange	Danny Ford	Jeff Davis, LB
1982	**Penn St.**	11-1-0	Won Sugar	Joe Paterno	Todd Blackledge, QB
1983	**Miami-FL**	11-1-0	Won Orange	H. Schnellenberger	Bernie Kosar, QB
1984	**BYU**	13-0-0	Won Holiday	LaVell Edwards	Robbie Bosco, QB
1985	**Oklahoma**	11-1-0	Won Orange	Barry Switzer	Brian Bosworth, LB
1986	**Penn St.**	12-0-0	Won Fiesta	Joe Paterno	D.J. Dozier, RB
1987	**Miami-FL**	12-0-0	Won Orange	Jimmy Johnson	Steve Walsh, QB
1988	**Notre Dame**	12-0-0	Won Fiesta	Lou Holtz	Tony Rice, QB
1989	**Miami-FL**	11-1-0	Won Sugar	Dennis Erickson	Craig Erickson, QB
1990	**Colorado** (AP, FW, NFF)	11-1-1	Won Orange	Bill McCartney	Eric Bieniemy, RB
	& **Georgia Tech** (UP)	11-0-1	Won Citrus	Bobby Ross	Shawn Jones, QB
1991	**Miami-FL** (AP)	12-0-0	Won Orange	Dennis Erickson	Gino Torretta, QB
	& **Washington** (USA, FW, NFF)	12-0-0	Won Rose	Don James	Steve Emtman, DT
1992	**Alabama**	13-0-0	Won Sugar	Gene Stallings	Eric Curry, DE
1993	**Florida St.**	12-1-0	Won Orange	Bobby Bowden	Charlie Ward, QB
1994	**Nebraska**	13-0-0	Won Orange	Tom Osborne	Zach Wiegert, OT
1995	**Nebraska**	12-0-0	Won Fiesta	Tom Osborne	Tommie Frazier, QB
1996	**Florida**	12-1*	Won Sugar	Steve Spurrier	Danny Wuerffel, QB
1997	**Michigan** (AP, FW, NFF)	12-0	Won Rose	Lloyd Carr	Charles Woodson, DB
	& **Nebraska** (ESPN/USA)	13-0	Won Orange	Tom Osborne	Ahman Green, RB
1998	**Tennessee**	13-0	Won Fiesta	Phillip Fulmer	Peerless Price, WR
1999	**Florida St.**	12-0	Won Sugar	Bobby Bowden	Peter Warrick, WR
2000	**Oklahoma**	13-0	Won Orange	Bob Stoops	Josh Heupel, QB
2001	**Miami-FL**	12-0	Won Rose	Larry Coker	Ken Dorsey, QB
2002	**Ohio St.**	14-0	Won Fiesta	Jim Tressel	Craig Krenzler, QB
2003	**USC** (AP)	12-1	Won Rose	Pete Carroll	Matt Leinart, QB
	& **LSU** (ESPN/USA)	13-1	Won Sugar	Nick Saban	Matt Mauck, QB
2004	**USC**	13-0	Won Orange	Pete Carroll	Matt Leinart, QB
2005	**Texas**	13-0	Won Rose	Mack Brown	Vince Young, QB
2006	**Florida**	13-1	Won BCS Game	Urban Meyer	Chris Leak, QB
2007	**LSU**	12-2	Won BCS Game	Les Miles	Matt Flynn, QB

*The NCAA instituted overtime for regular season games in 1996.

BCS Title Game

The Bowl Championship Series has staged a separate "national title" game outside of the traditional bowl system since the 2006 season.

Year	Winner	Loser	Score	Site	MVPs
2006	Florida	Ohio St.	41-14	Glendale, Ariz.	OFF-Chris Leak, DEF-Derrick Harvey, Fla.
2007	LSU	Ohio St.	38-24	New Orleans	OFF-Matt Flynn, DEF-Ricky Jean-Francois, LSU

Number 1 vs. Number 2

Since the Associated Press writers poll started keeping track of such things in 1936, the No. 1 and No. 2 ranked teams in the country have met 38 times; 20 during the regular season and 18 in bowl games. Since the first showdown in 1943, the No. 1 team has beaten the No. 2 team 22 times, lost 14 and there have been two ties. Each showdown is listed below with the date, the match-up, each team's record going into the game, the final score, the stadium and site.

Date		Match-up	Stadium
Oct. 9	#1	Notre Dame (2-0) 35	Michigan
1943	#2	Michigan (3-0) 12	(Ann Arbor)
Nov. 20	#1	Notre Dame (8-0) . . .14	Notre Dame
1943	#2	Iowa Pre-Flight (8-0) .13	(South Bend)
Dec. 2	#1	Army (8-0) 23	Municipal
1944	#2	Navy (6-2) 7	(Baltimore)
Nov. 10	#1	Army (6-0) 48	Yankee
1945	#2	Notre Dame (5-0-1) . .0	(New York)
Dec. 1	#1	Army (8-0) 32	Municipal
1945	#2	Navy (7-0-1) . . .13	(Philadelphia)
Nov. 9	#1	Army (7-0) 0	Yankee
1946	#2	Notre Dame (5-0) . . .0	(New York)
Jan. 1	#1	USC (10-0) 42	ROSE BOWL
1963	#2	Wisconsin (8-1) . . .37	(Pasadena)
Oct. 12	#2	Texas (3-0) 28	Cotton Bowl
1963	#1	Oklahoma (2-0) 7	(Dallas)
Jan. 1	#1	Texas (10-0) 28	COTTON BOWL
1964	#2	Navy (9-1) 6	(Dallas)
Nov. 19	#1	Notre Dame (8-0) . .10	Spartan
1966	#2	Michigan St. (9-0) . .10	(East Lansing)
Sept. 28	#1	Purdue (1-0) 37	Notre Dame
1968	#2	Notre Dame (1-0) . .22	(South Bend)
Jan. 1	#1	Ohio St. (9-0) 27	ROSE BOWL
1969	#2	USC (9-0-1) 16	(Pasadena)
Dec. 6	#1	Texas (9-0) 15	Razorback
1969	#2	Arkansas (9-0) 14	(Fayetteville)
Nov. 25	#1	Nebraska (10-0) . .35	Owen Field
1971	#2	Oklahoma (9-0) . . .31	(Norman)
Jan. 1	#1	Nebraska (12-0) . .38	ORANGE BOWL
1972	#2	Alabama (11-0) 6	(Miami)
Jan. 1	#2	Alabama (10-1) . . .14	SUGAR BOWL
1979	#1	Penn St. (11-0) 7	(New Orleans)
Sept. 26	#1	USC (2-0) 28	Coliseum
1981	#2	Oklahoma (1-0) . . .24	(Los Angeles)
Jan. 1	#2	Penn St. (10-1) . . .27	SUGAR BOWL
1983	#1	Georgia (11-0) 23	(New Orleans)
Oct. 19	#1	Iowa (5-0) 12	Kinnick
1985	#2	Michigan (5-0) 10	(Iowa City)
Sept. 27	#2	Miami-FL (3-0) 28	Orange Bowl
1986	#1	Oklahoma (2-0) . . .16	(Miami)
Jan. 2	#2	Penn St. (11-0) 14	FIESTA BOWL
1987	#1	Miami-FL (11-0) 10	(Tempe)
Nov. 21	#1	Oklahoma (10-0) . . .17	Memorial
1987	#1	Nebraska (10-0) 7	(Lincoln)
Jan. 1	#2	Miami-FL (11-0) 20	ORANGE BOWL
1988	#1	Oklahoma (11-0) . . .14	(Miami)
Nov. 26	#1	Notre Dame (10-0) . .27	Coliseum
1988	#2	USC (10-0) 10	(Los Angeles)
Sept. 16	#1	Notre Dame (1-0) . . .24	Michigan
1989	#2	Michigan (0-0) 19	(Ann Arbor)
Nov. 16	#1	Miami-FL (8-0) 17	Doak Campbell
1991	#2	Florida St. (10-0) . . .16	(Tallahassee)
Jan. 1	#2	Alabama (12-0) 34	SUGAR BOWL
1993	#1	Miami-FL (11-0) 13	(New Orleans)
Nov. 13	#2	Notre Dame (9-0) . . .31	Notre Dame
1993	#1	Florida St. (9-0) 24	(South Bend)
Jan. 1	#1	Florida St. (11-1) 18	ORANGE BOWL
1994	#2	Nebraska (11-0) 16	(Miami)
Jan. 2	#1	Nebraska (11-0) 62	FIESTA BOWL
1996	#2	Florida (12-0) 24	(Tempe)
Nov. 30	#2	Florida St. (10-0) 24	Doak Campbell
1996	#1	Florida (10-1) 21	(Tallahassee)
Jan. 4	#1	Tennessee (12-0) . . .23	FIESTA BOWL
1999	#2	Florida St. (11-1) . . .16	(Tempe)
Jan. 4	#1	Florida St. (11-0) . . .46	SUGAR BOWL
2000	#2	Virginia Tech (11-0) .29	(New Orleans)
Jan. 3	#2	Ohio St. (13-0) 31	FIESTA BOWL
2003	#1	Miami-FL (12-0) .2OT 24	(Tempe)
Jan. 4	#1	USC (12-0) 55	ORANGE BOWL
2005	#2	Oklahoma (12-0) . . .19	(Miami)
Jan. 4	#2	Texas (12-0) 41	ROSE BOWL
2006	#1	USC (12-0) 38	(Pasadena)
Jan. 8	#2	Florida (12-1) 41	BCS Title Game
2007	#1	Ohio St. (12-0) 14	(Glendale, AZ)
Jan. 7	#2	LSU (11-2) 38	BCS Title Game
2008	#1	Ohio St. (11-1) . . .24	(New Orleans)

Note: Bowl games are listed in CAPITAL letters.

Top 30 Rivalries

Top Division I-A and I-AA series records, including games through the 2007 season. All rivalries listed below are renewed annually with the following exception. **Nebraska-Oklahoma** now play only when matched up as part of the rotating Big 12 schedule.

	Gm	Series Leader		Gm	Series Leader
Alabama-Auburn	72	Alabama (38-33-1)	**Lafayette-Lehigh**	143	Lafayette (76-62-5)
Alabama-Tennessee	90	Alabama (45-38-7)	**LSU-Mississippi**	96	LSU (55-37-4)
Arizona-Arizona St.	81	Arizona (44-36-1)	**Michigan-Michigan St.**	100	Michigan (67-28-5)
Army-Navy	108	Navy (52-49-7)	**Michigan-Ohio St.**	104	Michigan (57-41-6)
Auburn-Georgia	111	Auburn (53-50-8)	**Minnesota-Wisconsin**	116	Minnesota (58-50-8)
California-Stanford	110	Stanford (55-44-11)	**Mississippi-Miss. St.**	104	Ole Miss (59-39-6)
Clemson-So. Carolina	105	Clemson (64-37-4)	**Missouri-Kansas**	116	Missouri (54-53-9)
Colorado-Nebraska	66	Nebraska (46-18-2)	**Nebraska-Oklahoma**	83	Oklahoma (42-38-3)
Florida-Florida St.	52	Florida (31-19-2)	**N. Mexico-N. Mexico St.**	97	New Mexico (64-28-5)
Florida-Georgia	86	Georgia (48-36-2)	**Notre Dame-USC**	79	Notre Dame (42-32-5)
Florida St.-Miami,FL	52	Miami (30-22-0)	**Oklahoma-Okla. St.**	102	Oklahoma (79-16-7)
Georgia-Georgia Tech	102	Georgia (59-38-5)*	**Oregon-Oregon St.**	111	Oregon (55-46-10)
Harvard-Yale	124	Yale (65-51-8)	**Texas-Oklahoma**	102	Texas (58-39-5)
Kansas-Kansas St.	105	Kansas (64-36-5)	**UCLA-USC**	77	USC (41-29-7)
Kentucky-Tennessee	103	Tennessee (71-23-9)	**Washington-Wash. St.**	100	Washington (65-29-6)

*Disputed series record: Georgia claims lead of 59-36-5

Associated Press Final Polls

The Associated Press introduced its weekly college football poll of sportswriters (later, sportswriters and broadcasters) in 1936. The final AP poll was released at the end of the regular season until 1965, when bowl results were included for one year. After a two-year return to regular season games only, the final poll has come out after the bowls since 1968. Starting in 1989, the AP Poll has ranked 25 teams.

1936

Final poll released Nov. 30. Top 20 regular season results after that: **Dec. 5**–#8 Notre Dame tied USC, 13-13; #17 Tennessee tied Ole Miss, 0-0; #18 Arkansas over Texas, 6-0. **Dec. 12**–#16 TCU over #6 Santa Clara, 9-0.

		As of Nov. 30	Head Coach	After Bowls
1	Minnesota	7-1-0	Bernie Bierman	same
2	LSU	9-0-1	Bernie Moore	9-1-1
3	Pittsburgh	7-1-1	Jock Sutherland	8-1-1
4	Alabama	8-0-1	Frank Thomas	same
5	Washington	7-1-1	Jimmy Phelan	7-2-1
6	Santa Clara	7-0-0	Buck Shaw	8-1-0
7	Northwestern	7-1-0	Pappy Waldorf	same
8	Notre Dame	6-2-0	Elmer Layden	6-2-1
9	Nebraska	7-2-0	Dana X. Bible	same
10	Penn	7-1-0	Harvey Harman	same
11	Duke	9-1-0	Wallace Wade	same
12	Yale	7-1-0	Ducky Pond	same
13	Dartmouth	7-1-1	Red Blaik	same
14	Duquesne	7-2-0	John Smith	8-2-0
15	Fordham	5-1-2	Jim Crowley	same
16	TCU	7-2-2	Dutch Meyer	9-2-2
17	Tennessee	6-2-1	Bob Neyland	6-2-2
18	Arkansas	6-3-0	Fred Thomsen	7-3-0
	Navy	6-3-0	Tom Hamilton	same
20	Marquette	7-1-0	Frank Murray	7-2-0

Key Bowl Games

Sugar–#6 Santa Clara over #2 LSU, 21-14; **Rose**–#3 Pitt over #5 Washington, 21-0; **Orange**–#14 Duquesne over Mississippi St., 13-12; **Cotton**–#16 TCU over #20 Marquette, 16-6.

1937

Final poll released Nov. 29. Top 20 regular season results after that: **Dec. 4**–#18 Rice over SMU, 15-7.

		As of Nov. 29	Head Coach	After Bowls
1	Pittsburgh	9-0-1	Jock Sutherland	same
2	California	9-0-1	Stub Allison	10-0-1
3	Fordham	7-0-1	Jim Crowley	same
4	Alabama	9-0-0	Frank Thomas	9-1-0
5	Minnesota	6-2-0	Bernie Bierman	same
6	Villanova	8-0-1	Clipper Smith	same
7	Dartmouth	7-0-2	Red Blaik	same
8	LSU	9-1-0	Bernie Moore	9-2-0
9	Notre Dame	6-2-1	Elmer Layden	same
	Santa Clara	8-0-0	Buck Shaw	9-0-0
11	Nebraska	6-1-2	Biff Jones	same
12	Yale	6-1-1	Ducky Pond	same
13	Ohio St.	6-2-0	Francis Schmidt	same
14	Holy Cross	8-0-2	Eddie Anderson	same
	Arkansas	6-2-2	Fred Thomsen	same
16	TCU	4-2-2	Dutch Meyer	same
17	Colorado	8-0-0	Bunnie Oakes	8-1-0
18	Rice	4-3-2	Jimmy Kitts	6-3-2
19	North Carolina	7-1-1	Ray Wolf	same
20	Duke	7-2-1	Wallace Wade	same

Key Bowl Games

Rose–#2 Cal over #4 Alabama, 13-0; **Sugar**–#9 Santa Clara over #8 LSU, 6-0; **Cotton**–#18 Rice over #17 Colorado, 28-14; **Orange**–Auburn over Michigan St., 6-0.

1938

Final poll released Dec. 5. Top 20 regular season results after that: **Dec. 26**–#14 Cal over Georgia Tech, 13-7.

		As of Dec. 5	Head Coach	After Bowls
1	TCU	10-0-0	Dutch Meyer	11-0-0
2	Tennessee	10-0-0	Bob Neyland	11-0-0
3	Duke	9-0-0	Wallace Wade	9-1-0
4	Oklahoma	10-0-0	Tom Stidham	10-1-0
5	Notre Dame	8-1-0	Elmer Layden	same
6	Carnegie Tech	7-1-0	Bill Kern	7-2-0
7	USC	8-2-0	Howard Jones	9-2-0
8	Pittsburgh	8-2-0	Jock Sutherland	same
9	Holy Cross	8-1-0	Eddie Anderson	same
10	Minnesota	6-2-0	Bernie Bierman	same
11	Texas Tech	10-0-0	Pete Cawthon	-10-1-0
12	Cornell	5-1-1	Carl Snavely	same
13	Alabama	7-1-1	Frank Thomas	same
14	California	9-1-0	Stub Allison	10-1-0
15	Fordham	6-1-2	Jim Crowley	same
16	Michigan	6-1-1	Fritz Crisler	same
17	Northwestern	4-2-2	Pappy Waldorf	same
18	Villanova	8-0-1	Clipper Smith	same
19	Tulane	7-2-1	Red Dawson	same
20	Dartmouth	7-2-0	Red Blaik	same

Key Bowl Games

Sugar–#1 TCU over #6 Carnegie Tech, 15-7; **Orange**–#2 Tennessee over #4 Oklahoma, 17-0; **Rose**–#7 USC over #3 Duke, 7-3; **Cotton**–St. Mary's over #11 Texas Tech 20-13.

1939

Final poll released Dec. 11. Top 20 regular season results after that: None.

		As of Dec. 11	Head Coach	After Bowls
1	Texas A&M	10-0-0	Homer Norton	11-0-0
2	Tennessee	10-0-0	Bob Neyland	10-1-0
3	USC	7-0-2	Howard Jones	8-0-2
4	Cornell	8-0-0	Carl Snavely	same
5	Tulane	8-0-1	Red Dawson	8-1-1
6	Missouri	8-1-0	Don Faurot	8-2-0
7	UCLA	6-0-4	Babe Horrell	same
8	Duke	8-1-0	Wallace Wade	same
9	Iowa	6-1-1	Eddie Anderson	same
10	Duquesne	8-0-1	Buff Donelli	same
11	Boston College	9-1-0	Frank Leahy	9-2-0
12	Clemson	8-1-0	Jess Neely	9-1-0
13	Notre Dame	7-2-0	Elmer Layden	same
14	Santa Clara	5-1-3	Buck Shaw	same
15	Ohio St.	6-2-0	Francis Schmidt	same
16	Georgia Tech	7-2-0	Bill Alexander	8-2-0
17	Fordham	6-2-0	Jim Crowley	same
18	Nebraska	7-1-1	Biff Jones	same
19	Oklahoma	6-2-1	Tom Stidham	same
20	Michigan	6-2-0	Fritz Crisler	same

Key Bowl Games

Sugar–#1 Texas A&M over #5 Tulane, 14-13; **Rose**–#3 USC over #2 Tennessee, 14-0; **Orange**–#16 Georgia Tech over #6 Missouri, 21-7; **Cotton**–#12 Clemson over #11 Boston College, 6-3.

1940

Final poll released Dec. 2. Top 20 regular season results after that: **Dec. 7**–#16 SMU over Rice, 7-6.

	As of Dec. 2	Head Coach	After Bowls
1 Minnesota	.8-0-0	Bernie Bierman	same
2 Stanford	.9-0-0	Clark Shaughnessy	10-0-0
3 Michigan	.7-1-0	Fritz Crisler	same
4 Tennessee	.10-0-0	Bob Neyland	10-1-0
5 Boston College	.10-0-0	Frank Leahy	11-0-0
6 Texas A&M	.8-1-0	Homer Norton	9-1-0
7 Nebraska	.8-1-0	Biff Jones	8-2-0
8 Northwestern	.6-2-0	Pappy Waldorf	same
9 Mississippi St.	.9-0-1	Allyn McKeen	10-0-1
10 Washington	.7-2-0	Jimmy Phelan	same
11 Santa Clara	.6-1-1	Buck Shaw	same
12 Fordham	.7-1-0	Jim Crowley	7-2-0
13 Georgetown	.8-1-0	Jack Hagerty	8-2-0
14 Penn	.6-1-1	George Munger	same
15 Cornell	.6-2-0	Carl Snavely	same
16 SMU	.7-1-1	Matty Bell	8-1-1
17 Hardin-Simmons	.9-0-0	Warren Woodson	same
18 Duke	.7-2-0	Wallace Wade	same
19 Lafayette	.9-0-0	Hooks Mylin	same
20 –			

Note: Only 19 teams ranked.

Key Bowl Games

Rose–#2 Stanford over #7 Nebraska, 21-13; **Sugar**– #5 Boston College over #4 Tennessee, 19-13; **Cotton**–#6 Texas A&M over #12 Fordham, 13-12; **Orange**–#9 Mississippi St. over #13 Georgetown, 14-7.

1941

Final poll released Dec. 1. Top 20 regular season results after that: **Dec. 6**–#4 Texas over Oregon, 71-7; #9 Texas A&M over #19 Washington St., 7-0; #16 Mississippi St. over San Francisco, 26-13.

	As of Dec. 1	Head Coach	After Bowls
1 Minnesota	.8-0-0	Bernie Bierman	same
2 Duke	.9-0-0	Wallace Wade	9-1-0
3 Notre Dame	.8-0-1	Frank Leahy	same
4 Texas	.7-1-1	Dana X. Bible	8-1-1
5 Michigan	.6-1-1	Fritz Crisler	same
6 Fordham	.7-1-0	Jim Crowley	8-1-0
7 Missouri	.8-1-0	Don Faurot	8-2-0
8 Duquesne	.8-0-0	Buff Donelli	same
9 Texas A&M	.8-1-0	Homer Norton	9-2-0
10 Navy	.7-1-1	Swede Larson	same
11 Northwestern	.5-3-0	Pappy Waldorf	same
12 Oregon St.	.7-2-0	Lon Stiner	8-2-0
13 Ohio St.	.6-1-1	Paul Brown	same
14 Georgia	.8-1-1	Wally Butts	9-1-1
15 Penn	.7-1-1	George Munger	same
16 Mississippi St.	.7-1-1	Allyn McKeen	8-1-1
17 Mississippi	.6-2-1	Harry Mehre	same
18 Tennessee	.8-2-0	John Barnhill	same
19 Washington St.	.6-3-0	Babe Hollingbery	6-4-0
20 Alabama	.8-2-0	Frank Thomas	9-2-0

Note: 1942 Rose Bowl moved to Durham, N.C., for one year after outbreak of World War II.

Key Bowl Games

Rose–#12 Oregon St. over #2 Duke, 20-16; **Sugar**–#6 Fordham over #7 Missouri, 2-0; **Cotton**–#20 Alabama over #9 Texas A&M, 29-21; **Orange**–#14 Georgia over TCU, 40-26.

1942

Final poll released Nov. 30. Top 20 regular season results after that: **Dec. 5**–#6 Notre Dame tied Great Lakes Naval Station, 13-13; #13 UCLA over Idaho, 40-13; #14 William & Mary over Oklahoma, 14-7; #17 Washington St. lost to Texas A&M, 21-0; #18 Mississippi St. over San Francisco, 19-7. **Dec. 12**–#13 UCLA over USC, 14-7.

	As of Nov. 30	Head Coach	After Bowls
1 Ohio St.	.9-1-0	Paul Brown	same
2 Georgia	.10-1-0	Wally Butts	11-1-0
3 Wisconsin	.8-1-1	Harry Stuhldreher	same
4 Tulsa	.10-0-0	Henry Frnka	10-1-0
5 Georgia Tech	.9-1-0	Bill Alexander	9-2-0
6 Notre Dame	.7-2-1	Frank Leahy	7-2-2
7 Tennessee	.8-1-1	John Barnhill	9-1-1
8 Boston College	.8-1-0	Denny Myers	8-2-0
9 Michigan	.7-3-0	Fritz Crisler	same
10 Alabama	.7-3-0	Frank Thomas	8-3-0
11 Texas	.8-2-0	Dana X. Bible	9-2-0
12 Stanford	.6-4-0	Marchy Schwartz	same
13 UCLA	.5-3-0	Babe Horrell	7-4-0
14 William & Mary	.8-1-1	Carl Voyles	9-1-1
15 Santa Clara	.7-2-0	Buck Shaw	same
16 Auburn	.6-4-1	Jack Meagher	same
17 Washington St.	.6-1-2	Babe Hollingbery	6-2-2
18 Mississippi St.	.7-2-0	Allyn McKeen	8-2-0
19 Minnesota	.5-4-0	George Hauser	same
Holy Cross	.5-4-1	Ank Scanlon	same
Penn St.	.6-1-1	Bob Higgins	same

Key Bowl Games

Rose–#2 Georgia over #13 UCLA, 9-0; **Sugar**–#7 Tennessee over #4 Tulsa, 14-7; **Cotton**–#11 Texas over #5 Georgia Tech, 14-7; **Orange**–#10 Alabama over #8 Boston College, 37-21.

1943

Final poll released Nov. 29. Top 20 regular season results after that: **Dec. 11**–#10 March Field over #19 Pacific, 19-0.

	As of Nov. 29	Head Coach	After Bowls
1 Notre Dame	.9-1-0	Frank Leahy	same
2 Iowa Pre-Flight	.9-1-0	Don Faurot	same
3 Michigan	.8-1-0	Fritz Crisler	same
4 Navy	.8-1-0	Billick Whelchel	same
5 Purdue	.9-0-0	Elmer Burnham	same
6 Great Lakes Naval Station	.10-2-0	Tony Hinkle	same
7 Duke	.8-1-0	Eddie Cameron	same
8 DelMonte Pre-Flight	7-1-0	Bill Kern	same
9 Northwestern	.6-2-0	Pappy Waldorf	same
10 March Field	.8-1-0	Paul Schissler	9-1-0
11 Army	.7-2-1	Red Blaik	same
12 Washington	.4-0-0	Ralph Welch	4-1-0
13 Georgia Tech	.7-3-0	Bill Alexander	8-3-0
14 Texas	.7-1-0	Dana X. Bible	7-1-1
15 Tulsa	.6-0-1	Henry Frnka	6-1-1
16 Dartmouth	.6-1-0	Earl Brown	same
17 Bainbridge Navy Training School	.7-0-0	Joe Maniaci	same
18 Colorado College	.7-0-0	Hal White	same
19 Pacific	.7-1-0	Amos A. Stagg	7-2-0
20 Penn	.6-2-1	George Munger	same

Key Bowl Games

Rose–USC over #12 Washington, 29-0; **Sugar**–#13 Georgia Tech over #15 Tulsa, 20-18; **Cotton**–#14 Texas tied Randolph Field, 7-7; **Orange**–LSU over Texas A&M, 19-14.

Associated Press Final Polls (Cont.)

1944

Final poll released Dec. 4. Top 20 regular season results after that: **Dec. 10**–#3 Randolph Field over #10 March Field, 20-7; #18 Fort Pierce over Kessler Field, 34-7; Morris Field over #20 Second Air Force, 14-7.

		As of Dec. 4	Head Coach	After Bowls
1	Army	.9-0-0	Red Blaik	same
2	Ohio St.	.9-0-0	Carroll Widdoes	same
3	Randolph Field	.10-0-0	Frank Tritico	12-0-0
4	Navy	.6-3-0	Oscar Hagberg	same
5	Bainbridge Navy Training School	.10-0-0	Joe Maniaci	same
6	Iowa Pre-Flight	.10-1-0	Jack Meagher	same
7	USC	.7-0-2	Jeff Cravath	8-0-2
8	Michigan	.8-2-0	Fritz Crisler	same
9	Notre Dame	.8-2-0	Ed McKeever	same
10	March Field	.7-0-2	Paul Schissler	7-1-2
11	Duke	.5-4-0	Eddie Cameron	6-4-0
12	Tennessee	.7-0-1	John Barnhill	7-1-1
13	Georgia Tech	.8-2-0	Bill Alexander	8-3-0
14	Norman Pre-Flight	.6-0-0	John Gregg	same
15	Illinois	.5-4-1	Ray Eliot	same
16	El Toro Marines	.8-1-0	Dick Hanley	same
17	Great Lakes Naval Station	.9-2-1	Paul Brown	same
18	Fort Pierce	.8-0-0	Hamp Pool	9-0-0
19	St. Mary's Pre-Flight	.4-4-0	Jules Sikes	same
20	Second Air Force	.10-2-1	Bill Reese	10-4-1

Key Bowl Games
Treasury–#3 Randolph Field over #20 Second Air Force, 13-6; **Rose**–#7 USC over #12 Tennessee, 25-0; **Sugar**–#11 Duke over Alabama, 29-26; **Orange**–Tulsa over #13 Georgia Tech, 26-12; **Cotton**–Oklahoma A&M over TCU, 34-0.

1945

Final poll released Dec. 3. Top 20 regular season results after that: None.

		As of Dec. 3	Head Coach	After Bowls
1	Army	.9-0-0	Red Blaik	same
2	Alabama	.9-0-0	Frank Thomas	10-0-0
3	Navy	.7-1-1	Oscar Hagberg	same
4	Indiana	.9-0-1	Bo McMillan	same
5	Oklahoma A&M	.8-0-0	Jim Lookabaugh	9-0-0
6	Michigan	.7-3-0	Fritz Crisler	same
7	St. Mary's-CA	.7-1-0	Jimmy Phelan	7-2-0
8	Penn	.6-2-0	George Munger	same
9	Notre Dame	.7-2-1	Hugh Devore	same
10	Texas	.9-1-0	Dana X. Bible	10-1-0
11	USC	.7-3-0	Jeff Cravath	7-4-0
12	Ohio St.	.7-2-0	Carroll Widdoes	same
13	Duke	.6-2-0	Eddie Cameron	same
14	Tennessee	.8-1-0	John Barnhill	same
15	LSU	.7-2-0	Bernie Moore	same
16	Holy Cross	.8-1-0	John DeGrosa	8-2-0
17	Tulsa	.8-2-0	Henry Frnka	8-3-0
18	Georgia	.8-2-0	Wally Butts	9-2-0
19	Wake Forest	.4-3-1	Peahead Walker	5-3-1
20	Columbia	.8-1-0	Lou Little	same

Key Bowl Games
Rose–#2 Alabama over #11 USC, 34-14; **Sugar**–#5 Oklahoma A&M over #7 St. Mary's, 33-13; **Cotton**–#10 Texas over Missouri, 40-27; **Orange**–Miami-FL over #16 Holy Cross, 13-6.

1946

Final poll released Dec. 2. Top 20 regular season results after that: None.

		As of Dec. 2	Head Coach	After Bowls
1	Notre Dame	.8-0-1	Frank Leahy	same
2	Army	.9-0-1	Red Blaik	same
3	Georgia	.10-0-0	Wally Butts	11-0-0
4	UCLA	.10-0-0	Bert LaBrucherie	10-1-0
5	Illinois	.7-2-0	Ray Eliot	8-2-0
6	Michigan	.6-2-1	Fritz Crisler	same
7	Tennessee	.9-1-0	Bob Neyland	9-2-0
8	LSU	.9-1-0	Bernie Moore	9-1-1
9	North Carolina	.8-1-1	Carl Snavely	8-2-1
10	Rice	.8-2-0	Jess Neely	9-2-0
11	Georgia Tech	.8-2-0	Bobby Dodd	9-2-0
12	Yale	.7-1-1	Howard Odell	same
13	Penn	.6-2-0	George Munger	same
14	Oklahoma	.7-3-0	Jim Tatum	8-3-0
15	Texas	.8-2-0	Dana X. Bible	same
16	Arkansas	.6-3-1	John Barnhill	6-3-2
17	Tulsa	.9-1-0	J.O. Brothers	same
18	N.C. State	.8-2-0	Beattie Feathers	8-3-0
19	Delaware	.9-0-0	Bill Murray	10-0-0
20	Indiana	.6-3-0	Bo McMillan	same

Key Bowl Games
Sugar–#3 Georgia over #9 N. Carolina, 20-10; **Rose**–#5 Illinois over #4 UCLA, 45-14; **Orange**–#10 Rice over #7 Tennessee, 8-0; **Cotton**–#8 LSU tied #16 Arkansas, 0-0.

1947

Final poll released Dec. 8. Top 20 regular season results after that: None.

		As of Dec. 8	Head Coach	After Bowls
1	Notre Dame	.9-0-0	Frank Leahy	same
2	Michigan	.9-0-0	Fritz Crisler	10-0-0
3	SMU	.9-0-1	Matty Bell	9-0-2
4	Penn St.	.9-0-0	Bob Higgins	9-0-1
5	Texas	.9-1-0	Blair Cherry	10-1-0
6	Alabama	.8-2-0	Red Drew	8-3-0
7	Penn	.7-0-1	George Munger	same
8	USC	.7-1-1	Jeff Cravath	7-2-1
9	North Carolina	.8-2-0	Carl Snavely	same
10	Georgia Tech	.9-1-0	Bobby Dodd	10-1-0
11	Army	.5-2-2	Red Blaik	same
12	Kansas	.8-0-2	George Sauer	8-1-2
13	Mississippi	.8-2-0	Johnny Vaught	9-2-0
14	William & Mary	.9-1-0	Rube McCray	9-2-0
15	California	.9-1-0	Pappy Waldorf	same
16	Oklahoma	.7-2-1	Bud Wilkinson	same
17	N.C. State	.5-3-1	Beattie Feathers	same
18	Rice	.6-3-1	Jess Neely	same
19	Duke	.4-3-2	Wallace Wade	same
20	Columbia	.7-2-0	Lou Little	same

Key Bowl Games
Rose–#2 Michigan over #8 USC, 49-0; **Cotton**–#3 SMU tied #4 Penn St., 13-13; **Sugar**–#5 Texas over #6 Alabama, 27-7; **Orange**–#10 Georgia Tech over #12 Kansas, 20-14.

Note: An unprecedented "Who's No. 1?" poll was conducted by AP after the Rose Bowl game, pitting Notre Dame against Michigan. The Wolverines won the vote, 226-119, but AP ruled that the Irish would be the No. 1 team of record.

1948

Final poll released Nov. 29. Top 20 regular season results after that: **Dec. 3**–#12 Vanderbilt over Miami-FL, 33-6. **Dec. 4**–#2 Notre Dame tied USC, 14-14; #11 Clemson over The Citadel, 20-0.

			As of Nov. 29	Head Coach	After Bowls
1	Michigan		9-0-0	Bennie Oosterbaan	same
2	Notre Dame		9-0-0	Frank Leahy	9-0-1
3	North Carolina		9-0-1	Carl Snavely	9-1-1
4	California		10-0-0	Pappy Waldorf	10-1-0
5	Oklahoma		9-1-0	Bud Wilkinson	10-1-0
6	Army		8-0-1	Red Blaik	same
7	Northwestern		7-2-0	Bob Voigts	8-2-0
8	Georgia		9-1-0	Wally Butts	9-2-0
9	Oregon		9-1-0	Jim Aiken	9-2-0
10	SMU		8-1-1	Matty Bell	9-1-1
11	Clemson		9-0-0	Frank Howard	11-0-0
12	Vanderbilt		7-2-1	Red Sanders	8-2-1
13	Tulane		9-1-0	Henry Frnka	same
14	Michigan St.		6-2-2	Biggie Munn	same
15	Mississippi		8-1-0	Johnny Vaught	same
16	Minnesota		7-2-0	Bernie Bierman	same
17	William & Mary		6-2-2	Rube McCray	7-2-2
18	Penn St.		7-1-1	Bob Higgins	same
19	Cornell		8-1-0	Lefty James	same
20	Wake Forest		6-3-0	Peahead Walker	6-4-0

Note: Big Nine "no-repeat" rule kept Michigan from Rose Bowl.

Key Bowl Games

Sugar–#5 Oklahoma over #3 North Carolina, 14-6; **Rose**–#7 Northwestern over #4 Cal, 20-14; **Orange**–Texas over #8 Georgia, 41-28; **Cotton**–#10 SMU over #9 Oregon, 21-13.

1949

Final poll released Nov. 28. Top 20 regular season results after that: **Dec. 2**–#14 Maryland over Miami-FL, 13-0. **Dec. 3**–#1 Notre Dame over SMU, 27-20; #10 Pacific over Hawaii, 75-0.

			As of Nov. 28	Head Coach	After Bowls
1	Notre Dame		9-0-0	Frank Leahy	10-0-0
2	Oklahoma		10-0-0	Bud Wilkinson	11-0-0
3	California		10-0-0	Pappy Waldorf	10-1-0
4	Army		9-0-0	Red Blaik	same
5	Rice		9-1-0	Jess Neely	10-1-0
6	Ohio St.		6-1-2	Wes Fesler	7-1-2
7	Michigan		6-2-1	Bennie Oosterbaan	same
8	Minnesota		7-2-0	Bernie Bierman	same
9	LSU		8-2-0	Gaynell Tinsley	8-3-0
10	Pacific		10-0-0	Larry Siemering	11-0-0
11	Kentucky		9-2-0	Bear Bryant	9-3-0
12	Cornell		8-1-0	Lefty James	same
13	Villanova		8-1-0	Jim Leonard	same
14	Maryland		7-1-0	Jim Tatum	9-1-0
15	Santa Clara		7-2-1	Len Casanova	8-2-1
16	North Carolina		7-3-0	Carl Snavely	7-4-0
17	Tennessee		7-2-1	Bob Neyland	same
18	Princeton		6-3-0	Charlie Caldwell	same
19	Michigan St.		6-3-0	Biggie Munn	same
20	Missouri		7-3-0	Don Faurot	7-4-0
	Baylor		8-2-0	Bob Woodruff	same

Key Bowl Games

Sugar–#2 Oklahoma over #9 LSU, 35-0; **Rose**–#6 Ohio St. over #3 Cal, 17-14; **Cotton**–#5 Rice over #16 North Carolina, 27-13; **Orange**–#15 Santa Clara over #11 Kentucky, 21-13.

1950

Final poll released Nov. 27. Top 20 regular season results after that: **Nov. 30**–#3 Texas over Texas A&M, 17-0. **Dec. 1**–#15 Miami-FL over Missouri, 27-9. **Dec. 2**–#1 Oklahoma over Okla. A&M, 41-14; Navy over #2 Army, 14-2; #4 Tennessee over Vanderbilt, 43-0; #16 Alabama over Auburn, 34-0; #19 Tulsa over Houston, 28-21; #20 Tulane tied LSU, 14-14. **Dec. 9**–#3 Texas over LSU, 21-6.

			As of Nov. 27	Head Coach	After Bowls
1	Oklahoma		9-0-0	Bud Wilkinson	10-1-0
2	Army		8-0-0	Red Blaik	8-1-0
3	Texas		7-1-0	Blair Cherry	9-2-0
4	Tennessee		9-1-0	Bob Neyland	11-1-0
5	California		9-0-1	Pappy Waldorf	9-1-1
6	Princeton		9-0-0	Charlie Caldwell	same
7	Kentucky		10-1-0	Bear Bryant	11-1-0
8	Michigan St.		8-1-0	Biggie Munn	same
9	Michigan		5-3-1	Bennie Oosterbaan	6-3-1
10	Clemson		8-0-1	Frank Howard	9-0-1
11	Washington		8-2-0	Howard Odell	same
12	Wyoming		9-0-0	Bowden Wyatt	10-0-0
13	Illinois		7-2-0	Ray Eliot	same
14	Ohio St.		6-3-0	Wes Fesler	same
15	Miami-FL		8-0-1	Andy Gustafson	9-1-1
16	Alabama		8-2-0	Red Drew	9-2-0
17	Nebraska		6-2-1	Bill Glassford	same
18	Wash. & Lee		8-2-0	George Barclay	8-3-0
19	Tulsa		8-1-1	J.O. Brothers	9-1-1
20	Tulane		6-2-0	Henry Frnka	6-2-1

Key Bowl Games

Sugar–#7 Kentucky over #1 Oklahoma, 13-7; **Cotton**–#4 Tennessee over #3 Texas, 20-14; **Rose**–#9 Michigan over #5 Cal, 14-6; **Orange**–#10 Clemson over #15 Miami-FL, 15-14.

1951

Final poll released Dec. 3. Top 20 regular season results after that: None.

			As of Dec. 3	Head Coach	After Bowls
1	Tennessee		10-0-0	Bob Neyland	10-1-0
2	Michigan St.		9-0-0	Biggie Munn	same
3	Maryland		9-0-0	Jim Tatum	10-0-0
4	Illinois		8-0-1	Ray Eliot	9-0-1
5	Georgia Tech		10-0-1	Bobby Dodd	11-0-1
6	Princeton		9-0-0	Charlie Caldwell	same
7	Stanford		9-1-0	Chuck Taylor	9-2-0
8	Wisconsin		7-1-1	Ivy Williamson	same
9	Baylor		8-1-1	George Sauer	8-2-1
10	Oklahoma		8-2-0	Bud Wilkinson	same
11	TCU		6-4-0	Dutch Meyer	6-5-0
12	California		8-2-0	Pappy Waldorf	same
13	Virginia		8-1-0	Art Guepe	same
14	San Francisco		9-0-0	Joe Kuharich	same
15	Kentucky		7-4-0	Bear Bryant	8-4-0
16	Boston Univ.		6-4-0	Buff Donelli	same
17	UCLA		5-3-1	Red Sanders	same
18	Washington St.		7-3-0	Forest Evashevski	same
19	Holy Cross		8-2-0	Eddie Anderson	same
20	Clemson		7-2-0	Frank Howard	7-3-0

Key Bowl Games

Sugar–#3 Maryland over #1 Tennessee, 28-13; **Rose**–#4 Illinois over #7 Stanford, 40-7; **Orange**–#5 Georgia Tech over #9 Baylor, 17-14; **Cotton**–#15 Kentucky over #11 TCU, 20-7.

Associated Press Final Polls (Cont.)

1952

Final poll released Dec. 1. Top 20 regular season results after that: **Dec. 6**–#15 Florida over #20 Kentucky, 27-20.

		As of Dec. 1	Head Coach	After Bowls
1	Michigan St.	.9-0-0	Biggie Munn	same
2	Georgia Tech	..11-0-0	Bobby Dodd	12-0-0
3	Notre Dame	7-2-1	Frank Leahy	same
4	Oklahoma	.8-1-1	Bud Wilkinson	same
5	USC	9-1-0	Jess Hill	10-1-0
6	UCLA	8-1-0	Red Sanders	same
7	Mississippi	.8-0-2	Johnny Vaught	8-1-2
8	Tennessee	8-1-1	Bob Neyland	8-2-1
9	Alabama	9-2-0	Red Drew	10-2-0
10	Texas	.8-2-0	Ed Price	9-2-0
11	Wisconsin	...6-2-1	Ivy Williamson	6-3-1
12	Tulsa	8-1-1	J.O. Brothers	8-2-1
13	Maryland	7-2-0	Jim Tatum	same
14	Syracuse	7-2-0	Ben Schwartzwalder	7-3-0
15	Florida	6-3-0	Bob Woodruff	8-3-0
16	Duke	8-2-0	Bill Murray	same
17	Ohio St.	6-3-0	Woody Hayes	same
18	Purdue	4-3-2	Stu Holcomb	same
19	Princeton	.8-1-0	Charlie Caldwell	same
20	Kentucky	5-3-2	Bear Bryant	5-4-2

Note: Michigan St. would officially join Big Ten in 1953.

Key Bowl Games

Sugar–#2 Georgia Tech over #7 Ole Miss, 24-7; **Rose**–#5 USC over #11 Wisconsin, 7-0; **Cotton**–#10 Texas over #8 Tennessee, 16-0; **Orange**–#9 Alabama over #14 Syracuse, 61-6.

1953

Final poll released Nov. 30. Top 20 regular season results after that: **Dec. 5**–#2 Notre Dame over SMU, 40-14.

		As of Nov. 30	Head Coach	After Bowls
1	Maryland	...10-0-0	Jim Tatum	10-1-0
2	Notre Dame	8-0-1	Frank Leahy	9-0-1
3	Michigan St.	8-1-0	Biggie Munn	9-1-0
4	Oklahoma	.8-1-1	Bud Wilkinson	9-1-1
5	UCLA	8-1-0	Red Sanders	8-2-0
6	Rice	8-2-0	Jess Neely	9-2-0
7	Illinois	7-1-1	Ray Eliot	same
8	Georgia Tech	..8-2-1	Bobby Dodd	9-2-1
9	Iowa	5-3-1	Forest Evashevski	same
10	West Virginia	..8-1-0	Art Lewis	8-2-0
11	Texas	7-3-0	Ed Price	same
12	Texas Tech	10-1-0	DeWitt Weaver	11-1-0
13	Alabama	6-2-3	Red Drew	6-3-3
14	Army	7-1-1	Red Blaik	same
15	Wisconsin	6-2-1	Ivy Williamson	same
16	Kentucky	7-2-1	Bear Bryant	same
17	Auburn	7-2-1	Shug Jordan	7-3-1
18	Duke	7-2-1	Bill Murray	same
19	Stanford	6-3-1	Chuck Taylor	same
20	Michigan	6-3-0	Bennie Oosterbaan	same

Key Bowl Games

Orange–#4 Oklahoma over #1 Maryland, 7-0; **Rose**–#3 Michigan St. over #5 UCLA, 28-20; **Cotton**–#6 Rice over #13 Alabama, 28-6; **Sugar**–#8 Georgia Tech over #10 West Virginia, 42-19.

1954

Final poll released Nov. 29. Top 20 regular season results after that: **Dec. 4**–#4 Notre Dame over SMU, 26-14.

		As of Nov. 29	Head Coach	After Bowls
1	Ohio St.	9-0-0	Woody Hayes	10-0-0
2	UCLA	9-0-0	Red Sanders	same
3	Oklahoma	10-0-0	Bud Wilkinson	same
4	Notre Dame	.8-1-0	Terry Brennan	9-1-0
5	Navy	7-2-0	Eddie Erdelatz	8-2-0
6	Mississippi	.9-1-0	Johnny Vaught	9-2-0
7	Army	7-2-0	Red Blaik	same
8	Maryland	7-2-1	Jim Tatum	same
9	Wisconsin	7-2-0	Ivy Williamson	same
10	Arkansas	8-2-0	Bowden Wyatt	8-3-0
11	Miami-FL	8-1-0	Andy Gustafson	same
12	West Virginia	..8-1-0	Art Lewis	same
13	Auburn	7-3-0	Shug Jordan	8-3-0
14	Duke	7-2-1	Bill Murray	8-2-1
15	Michigan	6-3-0	Bennie Oosterbaan	same
16	Virginia Tech	..8-0-1	Frank Moseley	same
17	USC	8-3-0	Jess Hill	8-4-0
18	Baylor	7-3-0	George Sauer	7-4-0
19	Rice	7-3-0	Jess Neely	same
20	Penn St.	7-2-0	Rip Engle	same

Note: PCC and Big Seven "no-repeat" rules kept UCLA and Oklahoma from Rose and Orange bowls, respectively.

Key Bowl Games

Rose–#1 Ohio St. over #17 USC, 20-7; **Sugar**–#5 Navy over #6 Ole Miss, 21-0; **Cotton**–Georgia Tech over #10 Arkansas, 14-6; **Orange**–#14 Duke over Nebraska, 34-7.

1955

Final poll released Nov. 28. Top 20 regular season results after that: None.

		As of Nov. 28	Head Coach	After Bowls
1	Oklahoma	...10-0-0	Bud Wilkinson	11-0-0
2	Michigan St.	8-1-0	Duffy Daugherty	9-1-0
3	Maryland	10-0-0	Jim Tatum	10-1-0
4	UCLA	9-1-0	Red Sanders	9-2-0
5	Ohio St.	7-2-0	Woody Hayes	same
6	TCU	9-1-0	Abe Martin	9-2-0
7	Georgia Tech	..8-1-1	Bobby Dodd	9-1-1
8	Auburn	8-1-1	Shug Jordan	8-2-1
9	Notre Dame	.8-2-0	Terry Brennan	same
10	Mississippi	.9-1-0	Johnny Vaught	10-1-0
11	Pittsburgh	7-3-0	John Michelosen	7-4-0
12	Michigan	7-2-0	Bennie Oosterbaan	same
13	USC	6-4-0	Jess Hill	same
14	Miami-FL	6-3-0	Andy Gustafson	same
15	Miami-OH	9-0-0	Ara Parseghian	same
16	Stanford	6-3-1	Chuck Taylor	same
17	Texas A&M	7-2-1	Bear Bryant	same
18	Navy	6-2-1	Eddie Erdelatz	same
19	West Virginia	..8-2-0	Art Lewis	same
20	Army	6-3-0	Red Blaik	same

Note: Big Ten "no-repeat" rule kept Ohio St. from Rose Bowl.

Key Bowl Games

Orange–#1 Oklahoma over #3 Maryland, 20-6; **Rose**–#2 Michigan St. over #4 UCLA, 17-14; **Cotton**–#10 Ole Miss over #6 TCU, 14-13; **Sugar**–#7 Georgia Tech over #11 Pitt, 7-0; **Gator**–Vanderbilt over #8 Auburn, 25-13.

1956

Final poll released Dec. 3. Top 20 regular season results after that: **Dec. 8**–#13 Pitt over #6 Miami-FL, 14-7.

	As of Dec. 3	Head Coach	After Bowls
1 Oklahoma	10-0-0	Bud Wilkinson	same
2 Tennessee	10-0-0	Bowden Wyatt	10-1-0
3 Iowa	8-1-0	Forest Evashevski	9-1-0
4 Georgia Tech	9-1-0	Bobby Dodd	10-1-0
5 Texas A&M	9-0-1	Bear Bryant	same
6 Miami-FL	8-0-1	Andy Gustafson	8-1-1
7 Michigan	7-2-0	Bennie Oosterbaan	same
8 Syracuse	7-1-0	Ben Schwartzwalder	7-2-0
9 Michigan St.	7-2-0	Duffy Daugherty	same
10 Oregon St.	7-2-1	Tommy Prothro	7-3-1
11 Baylor	8-2-0	Sam Boyd	9-2-0
12 Minnesota	6-1-2	Murray Warmath	same
13 Pittsburgh	6-2-1	John Michelosen	7-3-1
14 TCU	7-3-0	Abe Martin	8-3-0
15 Ohio St.	6-3-0	Woody Hayes	same
16 Navy	6-1-2	Eddie Erdelatz	same
17 G. Washington	7-1-1	Gene Sherman	8-1-1
18 USC	8-2-0	Jess Hill	same
19 Clemson	7-1-2	Frank Howard	7-2-2
20 Colorado	7-2-1	Dallas Ward	8-2-1

Note: Big Seven "no-repeat" rule kept Oklahoma from Orange Bowl and Texas A&M was on probation.

Key Bowl Games

Sugar–#11 Baylor over #2 Tennessee, 13-7; **Rose**–#3 Iowa over #10 Oregon St., 35-19; **Gator**–#4 Georgia Tech over #13 Pitt, 21-14; **Cotton**–#14 TCU over #8 Syracuse, 28-27; **Orange**–#20 Colorado over #19 Clemson, 27-21.

1957

Final poll released Dec. 2. Top 20 regular season results after that: **Dec. 7**–#10 Notre Dame over SMU, 54-21.

	As of Dec. 2	Head Coach	After Bowls
1 Auburn	10-0-0	Shug Jordan	same
2 Ohio St.	8-1-0	Woody Hayes	9-1-0
3 Michigan St.	8-1-0	Duffy Daugherty	9-1-0
4 Oklahoma	9-1-0	Bud Wilkinson	10-1-0
5 Navy	8-1-1	Eddie Erdelatz	9-1-1
6 Iowa	7-1-1	Forest Evashevski	same
7 Mississippi	8-1-1	Johnny Vaught	9-1-1
8 Rice	7-3-0	Jess Neely	7-4-0
9 Texas A&M	8-2-0	Bear Bryant	8-3-0
10 Notre Dame	6-3-0	Terry Brennan	7-3-0
11 Texas	6-3-1	Darrell Royal	6-4-1
12 Arizona St.	10-0-0	Dan Devine	same
13 Tennessee	7-3-0	Bowden Wyatt	8-3-0
14 Mississippi St.	6-2-1	Wade Walker	same
15 N.C. State	7-1-2	Earle Edwards	same
16 Duke	6-2-2	Bill Murray	6-3-2
17 Florida	6-2-1	Bob Woodruff	same
18 Army	7-2-0	Red Blaik	same
19 Wisconsin	6-3-0	Milt Bruhn	same
20 VMI	9-0-1	John McKenna	same

Note: Auburn on probation, ineligible for bowl game.

Key Bowl Games

Rose–#2 Ohio St. over Oregon, 10-7; **Orange**–#4 Oklahoma over #16 Duke, 48-21; **Cotton**–#5 Navy over #8 Rice, 20-7; **Sugar**–#7 Ole Miss over #11 Texas, 39-7; **Gator**–#13 Tennessee over #9 Texas A&M, 3-0.

1958

Final poll released Dec. 1. Top 20 regular season results after that: None.

	As of Dec. 1	Head Coach	After Bowls
1 LSU	10-0-0	Paul Dietzel	11-0-0
2 Iowa	7-1-1	Forest Evashevski	8-1-1
3 Army	8-0-1	Red Blaik	same
4 Auburn	9-0-1	Shug Jordan	same
5 Oklahoma	9-1-0	Bud Wilkinson	10-1-0
6 Air Force	9-0-1	Ben Martin	9-0-2
7 Wisconsin	7-1-1	Milt Bruhn	same
8 Ohio St.	6-1-2	Woody Hayes	same
9 Syracuse	8-1-0	Ben Schwartzwalder	8-2-0
10 TCU	8-2-0	Abe Martin	8-2-1
11 Mississippi	8-2-0	Johnny Vaught	9-2-0
12 Clemson	8-2-0	Frank Howard	8-3-0
13 Purdue	6-1-2	Jack Mollenkopf	same
14 Florida	6-3-1	Bob Woodruff	6-4-1
15 South Carolina	7-3-0	Warren Giese	same
16 California	7-3-0	Pete Elliott	7-4-0
17 Notre Dame	6-4-0	Terry Brennan	same
18 SMU	6-4-0	Bill Meek	same
19 Oklahoma St.	7-3-0	Cliff Speegle	8-3-0
20 Rutgers	8-1-0	John Stiegman	same

Key Bowl Games

Sugar–#1 LSU over #12 Clemson, 7-0; **Rose**–#2 Iowa over #16 Cal, 38-12; **Orange**–#5 Oklahoma over #9 Syracuse, 21-6; **Cotton**–#6 Air Force tied #10 TCU, 0-0.

1959

Final poll released Dec. 7. Top 20 regular season results after that: None.

	As of Dec. 7	Head Coach	After Bowls
1 Syracuse	10-0-0	Ben Schwartzwalder	11-0-0
2 Mississippi	9-1-0	Johnny Vaught	10-1-0
3 LSU	9-1-0	Paul Dietzel	9-2-0
4 Texas	9-1-0	Darrell Royal	9-2-0
5 Georgia	9-1-0	Wally Butts	10-1-0
6 Wisconsin	7-2-0	Milt Bruhn	7-3-0
7 TCU	8-2-0	Abe Martin	8-3-0
8 Washington	9-1-0	Jim Owens	10-1-0
9 Arkansas	8-2-0	Frank Broyles	9-2-0
10 Alabama	7-1-2	Bear Bryant	7-2-2
11 Clemson	8-2-0	Frank Howard	9-2-0
12 Penn St.	8-2-0	Rip Engle	9-2-0
13 Illinois	5-3-1	Ray Eliot	same
14 USC	8-2-0	Don Clark	same
15 Oklahoma	7-3-0	Bud Wilkinson	same
16 Wyoming	9-1-0	Bob Devaney	same
17 Notre Dame	5-5-0	Joe Kuharich	same
18 Missouri	6-4-0	Dan Devine	6-5-0
19 Florida	5-4-1	Bob Woodruff	same
20 Pittsburgh	6-4-0	John Michelosen	same

Note: Big Seven "no-repeat" rule kept Oklahoma from Orange Bowl.

Key Bowl Games

Cotton–#1 Syracuse over #4 Texas, 23-14; **Sugar**–#2 Ole Miss over #3 LSU, 21-0; **Orange**–#5 Georgia over #18 Missouri, 14-0; **Rose**–#8 Washington over #6 Wisconsin, 44-8; **Bluebonnet**–#11 Clemson over #7 TCU, 23-7; **Gator**–#9 Arkansas over Georgia Tech, 14-7; **Liberty**–#12 Penn St. over #10 Alabama, 7-0.

Associated Press Final Polls (Cont.)

1960

Final poll released Nov. 28. Top 20 regular season results after that: **Dec. 3**–UCLA over #10 Duke, 27-6.

		As of Nov. 28	Head Coach	After Bowls
1	Minnesota	8-1-0	Murray Warmath	8-2-0
2	Mississippi	9-0-1	Johnny Vaught	10-0-1
3	Iowa	8-1-0	Forest Evashevski	same
4	Navy	9-1-0	Wayne Hardin	9-2-0
5	Missouri	9-1-0	Dan Devine	10-1-0
6	Washington	9-1-0	Jim Owens	10-1-0
7	Arkansas	8-2-0	Frank Broyles	8-3-0
8	Ohio St.	7-2-0	Woody Hayes	same
9	Alabama	8-1-1	Bear Bryant	8-1-2
10	Duke	7-2-0	Bill Murray	8-3-0
11	Kansas	7-2-1	Jack Mitchell	same
12	Baylor	8-2-0	John Bridgers	8-3-0
13	Auburn	8-2-0	Shug Jordan	same
14	Yale	9-0-0	Jordan Olivar	same
15	Michigan St.	6-2-1	Duffy Daugherty	same
16	Penn St.	6-3-0	Rip Engle	7-3-0
17	New Mexico St.	10-0-0	Warren Woodson	11-0-0
18	Florida	8-2-0	Ray Graves	9-2-0
19	Syracuse	7-2-0	Ben Schwartzwalder	same
	Purdue	4-4-1	Jack Mollenkopf	same

Key Bowl Games

Rose–#6 Washington over #1 Minnesota, 17-7; **Sugar**–#2 Ole Miss over Rice, 14-6; **Orange**–#5 Missouri over #4 Navy, 21-14; **Cotton**–#10 Duke over #7 Arkansas, 7-6; **Bluebonnet**–#9 Alabama tied Texas, 3-3.

1961

Final poll released Dec. 4. Top 20 regular season results after that: None.

		As of Dec. 4	Head Coach	After Bowls
1	Alabama	10-0-0	Bear Bryant	11-0-0
2	Ohio St.	8-0-1	Woody Hayes	same
3	Texas	9-1-0	Darrell Royal	10-1-0
4	LSU	9-1-0	Paul Dietzel	10-1-0
5	Mississippi	9-1-0	Johnny Vaught	9-2-0
6	Minnesota	7-2-0	Murray Warmath	8-2-0
7	Colorado	9-1-0	Sonny Grandelius	9-2-0
8	Michigan St.	7-2-0	Duffy Daugherty	same
9	Arkansas	8-2-0	Frank Broyles	8-3-0
10	Utah St.	9-0-1	John Ralston	9-1-1
11	Missouri	7-2-1	Dan Devine	same
12	Purdue	6-3-0	Jack Mollenkopf	same
13	Georgia Tech	7-3-0	Bobby Dodd	7-4-0
14	Syracuse	7-3-0	Ben Schwartzwalder	8-3-0
15	Rutgers	9-0-0	John Bateman	same
16	UCLA	7-3-0	Bill Barnes	7-4-0
17	Rice	7-3-0	Jess Neely	7-4-0
	Penn St.	7-3-0	Rip Engle	8-3-0
	Arizona	8-1-1	Jim LaRue	same
20	Duke	7-3-0	Bill Murray	same

Note: Ohio St. faculty council turned down Rose Bowl invitation citing concern with OSU's overemphasis on sports.

Key Bowl Games

Sugar–#1 Alabama over #9 Arkansas, 10-3; **Cotton**–#3 Texas over #5 Ole Miss, 12-7; **Orange**–#4 LSU over #7 Colorado, 25-7; **Rose**–#6 Minnesota over #16 UCLA, 21-3; **Gotham**–Baylor over #10 Utah St., 24-9.

1962

Final poll released Dec. 3. Top 10 regular season results after that: None.

		As of Dec. 3	Head Coach	After Bowls
1	USC	10-0-0	John McKay	11-0-0
2	Wisconsin	8-1-0	Milt Bruhn	8-2-0
3	Mississippi	9-0-0	Johnny Vaught	10-0-0
4	Texas	9-0-1	Darrell Royal	9-1-1
5	Alabama	9-1-0	Bear Bryant	10-1-0
6	Arkansas	9-1-0	Frank Broyles	9-2-0
7	LSU	8-1-1	Charlie McClendon	9-1-1
8	Oklahoma	8-2-0	Bud Wilkinson	8-3-0
9	Penn St.	9-1-0	Rip Engle	9-2-0
10	Minnesota	6-2-1	Murray Warmath	same

Key Bowl Games

Rose–#1 USC over #2 Wisconsin, 42-37; **Sugar**–#3 Ole Miss over #6 Arkansas, 17-13; **Cotton**–#7 LSU over #4 Texas, 13-0; **Orange**–#5 Alabama over #8 Oklahoma, 17-0; **Gator**–Florida over #9 Penn St., 17-7.

1963

Final poll released Dec. 9. Top 10 regular season results after that: **Dec. 14**–#8 Alabama over Miami-FL, 17-12.

		As of Dec. 9	Head Coach	After Bowls
1	Texas	10-0-0	Darrell Royal	11-0-0
2	Navy	9-1-0	Wayne Hardin	9-2-0
3	Illinois	7-1-1	Pete Elliott	8-1-1
4	Pittsburgh	9-1-0	John Michelosen	same
5	Auburn	9-1-0	Shug Jordan	9-2-0
6	Nebraska	9-1-0	Bob Devaney	10-1-0
7	Mississippi	7-0-2	Johnny Vaught	7-1-2
8	Alabama	7-2-0	Bear Bryant	9-2-0
9	Michigan St.	6-2-1	Duffy Daugherty	same
10	Oklahoma	8-2-0	Bud Wilkinson	same

Key Bowl Games

Cotton–#1 Texas over #2 Navy, 28-6; **Rose**–#3 Illinois over Washington, 17-7; **Orange**–#6 Nebraska over #5 Auburn, 13-7; **Sugar**–#8 Alabama over #7 Ole Miss, 12-7.

1964

Final poll released Nov. 30. Top 10 regular season results after that: **Dec. 5**–Florida over #7 LSU, 20-6.

		As of Nov. 30	Head Coach	After Bowls
1	Alabama	10-0-0	Bear Bryant	10-1-0
2	Arkansas	10-0-0	Frank Broyles	11-0-0
3	Notre Dame	9-1-0	Ara Parseghian	same
4	Michigan	8-1-0	Bump Elliott	9-1-0
5	Texas	9-1-0	Darrell Royal	10-1-0
6	Nebraska	9-1-0	Bob Devaney	9-2-0
7	LSU	7-1-1	Charlie McClendon	8-2-1
8	Oregon St.	8-2-0	Tommy Prothro	8-3-0
9	Ohio St.	7-2-0	Woody Hayes	same
10	USC	7-3-0	John McKay	same

Key Bowl Games

Orange–#5 Texas over #1 Alabama, 21-17; **Cotton**–#2 Arkansas over #6 Nebraska, 10-7; **Rose**–#4 Michigan over #8 Oregon St., 34-7; **Sugar**–#7 LSU over Syracuse, 13-10.

1965

Final poll taken after bowl games for the first time.

		After Bowls	Head Coach	Regular Season
1	Alabama	9-1-1	Bear Bryant	8-1-1
2	Michigan St	10-1-0	Duffy Daugherty	10-0-0
3	Arkansas	10-1-0	Frank Broyles	10-0-0
4	UCLA	8-2-1	Tommy Prothro	7-1-1
5	Nebraska	10-1-0	Bob Devaney	10-0-0
6	Missouri	8-2-1	Dan Devine	7-2-1
7	Tennessee	8-1-2	Doug Dickey	6-1-2
8	LSU	8-3-0	Charlie McClendon	7-3-0
9	Notre Dame	7-2-1	Ara Parseghian	same
10	USC	7-2-1	John McKay	same

Key Bowl Games

Rankings below reflect final regular season poll, released Nov. 29. No bowls for then #8 USC or #9 Notre Dame. **Rose**–#5 UCLA over #1 Michigan St., 14-12; **Cotton**–LSU over #2 Arkansas, 14-7; **Orange**–#4 Alabama over #3 Nebraska, 39-28; **Sugar**–#6 Missouri over Florida, 20-18; **Bluebonnet**–#7 Tennessee over Tulsa, 27-6; **Gator**–Georgia Tech over #10 Texas Tech, 31-21.

1966

Final poll released Dec. 5, returning to pre-bowl status. Top 10 regular season results after that: None.

		As of Dec. 5	Head Coach	After Bowls
1	Notre Dame	9-0-1	Ara Parseghian	same
2	Michigan St	9-0-1	Duffy Daugherty	same
3	Alabama	10-0-0	Bear Bryant	11-0-0
4	Georgia	9-1-0	Vince Dooley	10-1-0
5	UCLA	9-1-0	Tommy Prothro	same
6	Nebraska	9-1-0	Bob Devaney	9-2-0
7	Purdue	8-2-0	Jack Mollenkopf	9-2-0
8	Georgia Tech	9-1-0	Bobby Dodd	9-2-0
9	Miami-FL	7-2-1	Charlie Tate	8-2-1
10	SMU	8-2-0	Hayden Fry	8-3-0

Key Bowl Games

Sugar–#3 Alabama over #6 Nebraska, 34-7; **Cotton**–#4 Georgia over #10 SMU, 24-9; **Rose**–#7 Purdue over USC, 14-13; **Orange**–Florida over #8 Georgia Tech, 27-12; **Liberty**–#9 Miami-FL over Virginia Tech, 14-7.

1967

Final poll released Nov. 27. Top 10 regular season results after that: **Dec. 2**–#2 Tennessee over Vanderbilt, 41-14; #3 Oklahoma over Oklahoma St., 38-14; #8 Alabama over Auburn, 7-3.

		As of Nov. 27	Head Coach	After Bowls
1	USC	9-1-0	John McKay	10-1-0
2	Tennessee	8-1-0	Doug Dickey	9-2-0
3	Oklahoma	8-1-0	Chuck Fairbanks	10-1-0
4	Indiana	9-1-0	John Pont	9-2-0
5	Notre Dame	8-2-0	Ara Parseghian	same
6	Wyoming	10-0-0	Lloyd Eaton	10-1-0
7	Oregon St.	7-2-1	Dee Andros	same
8	Alabama	7-1-1	Bear Bryant	8-2-1
9	Purdue	8-2-0	Jack Mollenkopf	same
10	Penn St.	8-2-0	Joe Paterno	8-2-1

Key Bowl Games

Rose–#1 USC over #4 Indiana, 14-3; **Orange**–#3 Oklahoma over #2 Tennessee, 26-24; **Sugar**–LSU over #6 Wyoming, 20-13; **Cotton**–Texas A&M over #8 Alabama, 20-16; **Gator**–#10 Penn St. tied Florida St. 17-17.

1968

Final poll taken after bowl games for first time since close of 1965 season.

		After Bowls	Head Coach	Regular Season
1	Ohio St.	10-0-0	Woody Hayes	9-0-0
2	Penn St.	11-0-0	Joe Paterno	10-0-0
3	Texas	9-1-1	Darrell Royal	8-1-1
4	USC	9-1-1	John McKay	9-0-1
5	Notre Dame	7-2-1	Ara Parseghian	same
6	Arkansas	10-1-0	Frank Broyles	9-1-0
7	Kansas	9-2-0	Pepper Rodgers	9-1-0
8	Georgia	8-1-2	Vince Dooley	8-0-2
9	Missouri	8-3-0	Dan Devine	7-3-0
10	Purdue	8-2-0	Jack Mollenkopf	same
11	Oklahoma	7-4-0	Chuck Fairbanks	7-3-0
12	Michigan	8-2-0	Bump Elliott	same
13	Tennessee	8-2-1	Doug Dickey	8-1-1
14	SMU	8-3-0	Hayden Fry	7-3-0
15	Oregon St.	7-3-0	Dee Andros	same
16	Auburn	7-4-0	Shug Jordan	6-4-0
17	Alabama	8-3-0	Bear Bryant	8-2-0
18	Houston	6-2-2	Bill Yeoman	same
19	LSU	8-3-0	Charlie McClendon	7-3-0
20	Ohio Univ	10-1-0	Bill Hess	10-0-0

Key Bowl Games

Rankings below reflect final regular season poll, released Dec. 2. No bowls for then #7 Notre Dame and #11 Pudue. **Rose**–#1 Ohio St. over #2 USC, 27-16; **Orange**–#3 Penn St. over #6 Kansas, 15-14; **Sugar**–#9 Arkansas over #4 Georgia, 16-2; **Cotton**–#5 Texas over #8 Tennessee, 36-13; **Bluebonnet**–#20 SMU over #10 Oklahoma, 28-27; **Gator**–#16 Missouri over #12 Alabama, 35-10.

1969

Final poll taken after bowl games.

		After Bowls	Head Coach	Regular Season
1	Texas	11-0-0	Darrell Royal	10-0-0
2	Penn St	11-0-0	Joe Paterno	10-0-0
3	USC	10-0-1	John McKay	9-0-1
4	Ohio St.	8-1-0	Woody Hayes	same
5	Notre Dame	8-2-1	Ara Parseghian	8-1-1
6	Missouri	9-2-0	Dan Devine	9-1-0
7	Arkansas	9-2-0	Frank Broyles	9-1-0
8	Mississippi	8-3-0	Johnny Vaught	7-3-0
9	Michigan	8-3-0	Bo Schembechler	8-2-0
10	LSU	9-1-0	Charlie McClendon	same
11	Nebraska	9-2-0	Bob Devaney	8-2-0
12	Houston	9-2-0	Bill Yeoman	8-2-0
13	UCLA	8-1-1	Tommy Prothro	same
14	Florida	9-1-1	Ray Graves	8-1-1
15	Tennessee	9-2-0	Doug Dickey	9-1-0
16	Colorado	8-3-0	Eddie Crowder	7-3-0
17	West Virginia	10-1-0	Jim Carlen	9-1-0
18	Purdue	8-2-0	Jack Mollenkopf	same
19	Stanford	7-2-1	John Ralston	same
20	Auburn	8-3-0	Shug Jordan	8-2-0

Key Bowl Games

Rankings below reflect final regular season poll, released Dec. 8. No bowls for then #4 Ohio St., #8 LSU and #10 UCLA.

Cotton–#1 Texas over #9 Notre Dame, 21-17; **Orange**–#2 Penn St. over #6 Missouri, 10-3; **Sugar**–#13 Ole Miss over #3 Arkansas, 27-22; **Rose**–#5 USC over #7 Michigan, 10-3.

Associated Press Final Polls (Cont.)

1970

		After Bowls	Head Coach	Regular Season
1	Nebraska	11-0-1	Bob Devaney	10-0-1
2	Notre Dame	10-1-0	Ara Parseghian	9-0-1
3	Texas	10-1-0	Darrell Royal	10-0-0
4	Tennessee	11-1-0	Bill Battle	10-1-0
5	Ohio St.	9-1-0	Woody Hayes	9-0-0
6	Arizona St.	11-0-0	Frank Kush	10-0-0
7	LSU	9-3-0	Charlie McClendon	9-2-0
8	Stanford	9-3-0	John Ralston	8-3-0
9	Michigan	9-1-0	Bo Schembechler	same
10	Auburn	9-2-0	Shug Jordan	8-2-0
11	Arkansas	9-2-0	Frank Broyles	same
12	Toledo	12-0-0	Frank Lauterbur	11-0-0
13	Georgia Tech	9-3-0	Bud Carson	8-3-0
14	Dartmouth	9-0-0	Bob Blackman	same
15	USC	6-4-1	John McKay	same
16	Air Force	9-3-0	Ben Martin	9-2-0
17	Tulane	8-4-0	Jim Pittman	7-4-0
18	Penn St.	7-3-0	Joe Paterno	same
19	Houston	8-3-0	Bill Yeoman	same
20	Oklahoma	7-4-1	Chuck Fairbanks	7-4-0
	Mississippi	7-4-0	Johnny Vaught	7-3-0

Key Bowl Games

Rankings below reflect final regular season poll, released Dec. 7. No bowls for then #4 Arkansas and #7 Michigan. **Cotton**–#6 Notre Dame over #1 Texas, 24-11; **Rose**–#12 Stanford over #2 Ohio St., 27-17; **Orange**–#3 Nebraska over #8 LSU, 17-12; **Sugar**–#5 Tennessee over #11 Air Force, 34-13; **Peach**–#9 Ariz. St. over N. Carolina, 48-26.

1972

		After Bowls	Head Coach	Regular Season
1	USC	12-0-0	John McKay	11-0-0
2	Oklahoma	11-1-0	Chuck Fairbanks	10-1-0
3	Texas	10-1-0	Darrell Royal	9-1-0
4	Nebraska	9-2-1	Bob Devaney	8-2-1
5	Auburn	10-1-0	Shug Jordan	9-1-0
6	Michigan	10-1-0	Bo Schembechler	same
7	Alabama	10-2-0	Bear Bryant	10-1-0
8	Tennessee	10-2-0	Bill Battle	9-2-0
9	Ohio St.	9-2-0	Woody Hayes	9-1-0
10	Penn St.	10-2-0	Joe Paterno	10-1-0
11	LSU	9-2-1	Charlie McClendon	9-1-1
12	North Carolina	11-1-0	Bill Dooley	10-1-0
13	Arizona St.	10-2-0	Frank Kush	9-2-0
14	Notre Dame	8-3-0	Ara Parseghian	8-2-0
15	UCLA	8-3-0	Pepper Rodgers	same
16	Colorado	8-4-0	Eddie Crowder	8-3-0
17	N.C. State	8-3-1	Lou Holtz	7-3-1
18	Louisville	9-1-0	Lee Corso	same
19	Washington St.	7-4-0	Jim Sweeney	same
20	Georgia Tech	7-4-1	Bill Fulcher	6-4-1

Key Bowl Games

Rankings below reflect final regular season poll, released Dec. 4. No bowl for then #8 Michigan. **Rose**–#1 USC over #3 Ohio St., 42-17; **Sugar**–#2 Oklahoma over #5 Penn St., 14-0; **Cotton**–#7 Texas over #4 Alabama, 17-13; **Orange**–#9 Nebraska over #12 Notre Dame, 40-6; **Gator**–#6 Auburn over #13 Colorado, 24-3; **Bluebonnet**–#11 Tennessee over #10 LSU, 24-17.

1971

		After Bowls	Head Coach	Regular Season
1	Nebraska	13-0-0	Bob Devaney	12-0-0
2	Oklahoma	11-1-0	Chuck Fairbanks	10-1-0
3	Colorado	10-2-0	Eddie Crowder	9-2-0
4	Alabama	11-1-0	Bear Bryant	11-0-0
5	Penn St.	11-1-0	Joe Paterno	10-1-0
6	Michigan	11-1-0	Bo Schembechler	11-0-0
7	Georgia	11-1-0	Vince Dooley	10-1-0
8	Arizona St.	11-1-0	Frank Kush	10-1-0
9	Tennessee	10-2-0	Bill Battle	9-2-0
10	Stanford	9-3-0	John Ralston	8-3-0
11	LSU	9-3-0	Charlie McClendon	8-3-0
12	Auburn	9-2-0	Shug Jordan	9-1-0
13	Notre Dame	8-2-0	Ara Parseghian	same
14	Toledo	12-0-0	John Murphy	11-0-0
15	Mississippi	10-2-0	Billy Kinard	9-2-0
16	Arkansas	8-3-1	Frank Broyles	8-2-1
17	Houston	9-3-0	Bill Yeoman	9-2-0
18	Texas	8-3-0	Darrell Royal	8-2-0
19	Washington	8-3-0	Jim Owens	same
20	USC	6-4-1	John McKay	same

Key Bowl Games

Rankings below reflect final regular season poll, released Dec. 6. **Orange**–#1 Nebraska over #2 Alabama, 38-6; **Sugar**–#3 Oklahoma over #5 Auburn, 40-22; **Rose**–#16 Stanford over #4 Michigan, 13-12; **Gator**–#6 Georgia over N. Carolina, 7-3; **Bluebonnet**–#7 Colorado over #15 Houston, 29-17; **Fiesta**–#8 Ariz. St. over Florida St., 45-38; **Cotton**–#10 Penn St. over #12 Texas, 30-6.

1973

		After Bowls	Head Coach	Regular Season
1	Notre Dame	11-0-0	Ara Parseghian	10-0-0
2	Ohio St.	10-0-1	Woody Hayes	9-0-1
3	Oklahoma	10-0-1	Barry Switzer	same
4	Alabama	11-1-0	Bear Bryant	11-0-0
5	Penn St.	12-0-0	Joe Paterno	11-0-0
6	Michigan	10-0-1	Bo Schembechler	same
7	Nebraska	9-2-1	Tom Osborne	8-2-1
8	USC	9-2-1	John McKay	9-1-1
9	Arizona St.	11-1-0	Frank Kush	10-1-0
	Houston	11-1-0	Bill Yeoman	10-1-0
11	Texas Tech	11-1-0	Jim Carlen	10-1-0
12	UCLA	9-2-0	Pepper Rodgers	same
13	LSU	9-3-0	Charlie McClendon	9-2-0
14	Texas	8-3-0	Darrell Royal	8-2-0
15	Miami-OH	11-0-0	Bill Mallory	10-0-0
16	N.C. State	9-3-0	Lou Holtz	8-3-0
17	Missouri	8-4-0	Al Onofrio	7-4-0
18	Kansas	7-4-1	Don Fambrough	7-3-1
19	Tennessee	8-4-0	Bill Battle	8-3-0
20	Maryland	8-4-0	Jerry Claiborne	8-3-0
	Tulane	9-3-0	Bennie Ellender	9-2-0

Key Bowl Games

Rankings below reflect final regular season poll, released Dec. 3. No bowls for then #2 Oklahoma (probation), #5 Michigan and #9 UCLA. **Sugar**–#3 Notre Dame over #1 Alabama, 24-23; **Rose**–#4 Ohio St. over #7 USC, 42-21; **Orange**–#6 Penn St. over #13 LSU, 16-9; **Cotton**–#12 Nebraska over #8 Texas, 19-3; **Fiesta**–#10 Ariz. St. over Pitt, 28-7; **Bluebonnet**–#14 Houston over #17 Tulane, 47-7.

1974

	After Bowls	Head Coach	Regular Season
1 Oklahoma	11-0-0	Barry Switzer	same
2 USC	10-1-1	John McKay	9-1-1
3 Michigan	10-1-0	Bo Schembechler	same
4 Ohio St.	10-2-0	Woody Hayes	10-1-0
5 Alabama	11-1-0	Bear Bryant	11-0-0
6 Notre Dame	10-2-0	Ara Parseghian	9-2-0
7 Penn St.	10-2-0	Joe Paterno	9-2-0
8 Auburn	10-2-0	Shug Jordan	9-2-0
9 Nebraska	9-3-0	Tom Osborne	8-3-0
10 Miami-OH	10-0-1	Dick Crum	9-0-1
11 N.C. State	9-2-1	Lou Holtz	9-2-0
12 Michigan St.	7-3-1	Denny Stolz	same
13 Maryland	8-4-0	Jerry Claiborne	8-3-0
14 Baylor	8-4-0	Grant Teaff	8-3-0
15 Florida	8-4-0	Doug Dickey	8-3-0
16 Texas A&M	8-3-0	Emory Ballard	same
17 Mississippi St.	9-3-0	Bob Tyler	8-3-0
Texas	8-4-0	Darrell Royal	8-3-0
19 Houston	8-3-1	Bill Yeoman	8-3-0
20 Tennessee	7-3-2	Bill Battle	6-3-2

Key Bowl Games

Rankings below reflect final regular season poll, released Dec. 2. No bowls for #1 Oklahoma (probation) and then #4 Michigan.

Orange—#9 Notre Dame over #2 Alabama, 13-11; **Rose**—#5 USC over #3 Ohio St., 18-17; **Gator**—#6 Auburn over #11 Texas, 27-3; **Cotton**—#7 Penn St. over #12 Baylor, 41-20; **Sugar**—#8 Nebraska over #18 Florida, 13-10; **Liberty**—Tennessee over #10 Maryland, 7-3.

1975

	After Bowls	Head Coach	Regular Season
1 Oklahoma	11-1-0	Barry Switzer	10-1-0
2 Arizona St.	12-0-0	Frank Kush	11-0-0
3 Alabama	11-1-0	Bear Bryant	10-1-0
4 Ohio St.	11-1-0	Woody Hayes	11-0-0
5 UCLA	9-2-1	Dick Vermeil	8-2-1
6 Texas	10-2-0	Darrell Royal	9-2-0
7 Arkansas	10-2-0	Frank Broyles	9-2-0
8 Michigan	8-2-2	Bo Schembechler	8-1-2
9 Nebraska	10-2-0	Tom Osborne	10-1-0
10 Penn St.	9-3-0	Joe Paterno	9-2-0
11 Texas A&M	10-2-0	Emory Bellard	10-1-0
12 Miami-OH	11-1-0	Dick Crum	10-1-0
13 Maryland	9-2-1	Jerry Claiborne	8-2-1
14 California	8-3-0	Mike White	same
15 Pittsburgh	8-4-0	Johnny Majors	7-4-0
16 Colorado	9-3-0	Bill Mallory	9-2-0
17 USC	8-4-0	John McKay	7-4-0
18 Arizona	9-2-0	Jim Young	same
19 Georgia	9-3-0	Vince Dooley	9-2-0
20 West Virginia	9-3-0	Bobby Bowden	8-3-0

Key Bowl Games

Rankings below reflect final regular season poll, released Dec. 1. Texas A&M was unbeaten and ranked 2nd in that poll, but lost to #18 Arkansas, 31-6, in its final regular season game on Dec.6.

Rose—#11 UCLA over #1 Ohio St., 23-10; **Liberty**—#17 USC over #2 Texas A&M, 20-0; **Orange**—#3 Oklahoma over #5 Michigan, 14-6; **Sugar**—#4 Alabama over #8 Penn St., 13-6; **Fiesta**—#7 Ariz. St. over #6 Nebraska, 17-14; **Bluebonnet**—#9 Texas over #10 Colorado, 38-21; **Cotton**—#18 Arkansas over #12 Georgia, 31-10.

1976

	After Bowls	Head Coach	Regular Season
1 Pittsburgh	12-0-0	Johnny Majors	11-0-0
2 USC	11-1-0	John Robinson	10-1-0
3 Michigan	10-2-0	Bo Schembechler	10-1-0
4 Houston	10-2-0	Bill Yeoman	9-2-0
5 Oklahoma	9-2-1	Barry Switzer	8-2-1
6 Ohio St.	9-2-1	Woody Hayes	8-2-1
7 Texas A&M	10-2-0	Emory Bellard	9-2-0
8 Maryland	11-1-0	Jerry Claiborne	11-0-0
9 Nebraska	9-3-1	Tom Osborne	8-3-1
10 Georgia	10-2-0	Vince Dooley	10-1-0
11 Alabama	9-3-0	Bear Bryant	8-3-0
12 Notre Dame	9-3-0	Dan Devine	8-3-0
13 Texas Tech	10-2-0	Steve Sloan	10-1-0
14 Oklahoma St.	9-3-0	Jim Stanley	8-3-0
15 UCLA	9-2-1	Terry Donahue	9-1-1
16 Colorado	8-4-0	Bill Mallory	8-3-0
17 Rutgers	11-0-0	Frank Burns	same
18 Kentucky	8-4-0	Fran Curci	7-4-0
19 Iowa St.	8-3-0	Earle Bruce	same
20 Mississippi St.	9-3-0	Bob Tyler	same

Key Bowl Games

Rankings below reflect final regular season poll, released Nov. 29. No bowl for then #20 Miss. St. (probation).

Sugar—#1 Pitt over #5 Georgia, 27-3; **Rose**—#3 USC over #2 Michigan, 14-6; **Cotton**—#6 Houston over #4 Maryland, 30-21; **Liberty**—#16 Alabama over #7 UCLA, 36-6; **Fiesta**—#8 Oklahoma over Wyoming, 41-7; **Bluebonnet**—#13 Nebraska over #9 Texas Tech, 27-24; **Sun**—#10 Texas A&M over Florida, 37-14; **Orange**—#11 Ohio St. over #12 Colorado, 27-10.

1977

	After Bowls	Head Coach	Regular Season
1 Notre Dame	11-1-0	Dan Devine	10-1-0
2 Alabama	11-1-0	Bear Bryant	10-1-0
3 Arkansas	11-1-0	Lou Holtz	10-1-0
4 Texas	11-1-0	Fred Akers	11-0-0
5 Penn St.	11-1-0	Joe Paterno	10-1-0
6 Kentucky	10-1-0	Fran Curci	same
7 Oklahoma	10-2-0	Barry Switzer	10-1-0
8 Pittsburgh	9-2-1	Jackie Sherrill	8-2-1
9 Michigan	10-2-0	Bo Schembechler	10-1-0
10 Washington	8-4-0	Don James	7-4-0
11 Ohio St.	9-3-0	Woody Hayes	9-2-0
12 Nebraska	9-3-0	Tom Osborne	8-3-0
13 USC	8-4-0	John Robinson	7-4-0
14 Florida St.	10-2-0	Bobby Bowden	9-2-0
15 Stanford	9-3-0	Bill Walsh	8-3-0
16 San Diego St.	10-1-0	Claude Gilbert	same
17 North Carolina	8-3-1	Bill Dooley	8-2-1
18 Arizona St.	9-3-0	Frank Kush	9-2-0
19 Clemson	8-3-1	Charley Pell	8-2-1
20 BYU	9-2-0	LaVell Edwards	same

Key Bowl Games

Rankings below reflect final regular season poll, released Nov. 28. No bowl for then #7 Kentucky (probation).

Cotton—#5 Notre Dame over #1 Texas, 38-10; **Orange**—#6 Arkansas over #2 Oklahoma, 31-6; **Sugar**—#3 Alabama over #9 Ohio St., 35-6; **Rose**—#13 Washington over #4 Michigan, 27-20; **Fiesta**—#8 Penn St. over #15 Ariz. St., 42-30; **Gator**—#10 Pitt over #11 Clemson, 34-3.

Associated Press Final Polls (Cont.)

1978

		After Bowls	Head Coach	Regular Season
1	Alabama	11-1-0	Bear Bryant	10-1-0
2	USC	12-1-0	John Robinson	11-1-0
3	Oklahoma	11-1-0	Barry Switzer	10-1-0
4	Penn St.	11-1-0	Joe Paterno	11-0-0
5	Michigan	10-2-0	Bo Schembechler	10-1-0
6	Clemson	11-1-0	Charley Pell	10-1-0
7	Notre Dame	9-3-0	Dan Devine	8-3-0
8	Nebraska	9-3-0	Tom Osborne	9-2-0
9	Texas	9-3-0	Fred Akers	8-3-0
10	Houston	9-3-0	Bill Yeoman	9-2-0
11	Arkansas	9-2-1	Lou Holtz	9-2-0
12	Michigan St.	8-3-0	Darryl Rogers	same
13	Purdue	9-2-1	Jim Young	8-2-1
14	UCLA	8-3-1	Terry Donahue	8-3-0
15	Missouri	8-4-0	Warren Powers	7-4-0
16	Georgia	9-2-1	Vince Dooley	9-1-1
17	Stanford	8-4-0	Bill Walsh	7-4-0
18	N.C. State	9-3-0	Bo Rein	8-3-0
19	Texas A&M	8-4-0	Emory Bellard (4-2) & Tom Wilson (4-2)	7-4-0
20	Maryland	9-3-0	Jerry Claiborne	9-2-0

Key Bowl Games

Rankings below reflect final regular season poll, released Dec. 4. No bowl for then #12 Michigan St. (probation).

Sugar–#2 Alabama over #1 Penn St., 14-7; **Rose**–#3 USC over #5 Michigan, 17-10; **Orange**–#4 Oklahoma over #6 Nebraska, 31-24; **Gator**–#7 Clemson over #20 Ohio St., 17-15; **Fiesta**–#8 Arkansas tied #15 UCLA, 10-10; **Cotton**–#10 Notre Dame over #9 Houston, 35-34.

1979

		After Bowls	Head Coach	Regular Season
1	Alabama	12-0-0	Bear Bryant	11-0-0
2	USC	11-0-1	John Robinson	10-0-1
3	Oklahoma	11-1-0	Barry Switzer	10-1-0
4	Ohio St.	11-1-0	Earle Bruce	11-0-0
5	Houston	11-1-0	Bill Yeoman	10-1-0
6	Florida St.	11-1-0	Bobby Bowden	11-0-0
7	Pittsburgh	11-1-0	Jackie Sherrill	10-1-0
8	Arkansas	10-2-0	Lou Holtz	10-1-0
9	Nebraska	10-2-0	Tom Osborne	10-1-0
10	Purdue	10-2-0	Jim Young	9-2-0
11	Washington	9-3-0	Don James	8-3-0
12	Texas	9-3-0	Fred Akers	9-2-0
13	BYU	11-1-0	LaVell Edwards	11-0-0
14	Baylor	8-4-0	Grant Teaff	7-4-0
15	North Carolina	8-3-1	Dick Crum	7-3-1
16	Auburn	8-3-0	Doug Barfield	same
17	Temple	10-2-0	Wayne Hardin	9-2-0
18	Michigan	8-4-0	Bo Schembechler	8-3-0
19	Indiana	8-4-0	Lee Corso	7-4-0
20	Penn St.	8-4-0	Joe Paterno	7-4-0

Key Bowl Games

Rankings below reflect final regular season poll, released Dec. 3. No bowl for then #17 Auburn (probation).

Sugar–#2 Alabama over #6 Arkansas, 24-9; **Rose**–#3 USC over #1 Ohio St., 17-16; **Orange**–#5 Oklahoma over #4 Florida St., 24-7; **Sun**–#13 Washington over #11 Texas, 14-7; **Cotton**–#8 Houston over #7 Nebraska, 17-14; **Fiesta**–#10 Pitt over Arizona, 16-10.

1980

		After Bowls	Head Coach	Regular Season
1	Georgia	12-0-0	Vince Dooley	11-0-0
2	Pittsburgh	11-1-0	Jackie Sherrill	10-1-0
3	Oklahoma	10-2-0	Barry Switzer	9-2-0
4	Michigan	10-2-0	Bo Schembechler	9-2-0
5	Florida St.	10-2-0	Bobby Bowden	10-1-0
6	Alabama	10-2-0	Bear Bryant	9-2-0
7	Nebraska	10-2-0	Tom Osborne	9-2-0
8	Penn St.	10-2-0	Joe Paterno	9-2-0
9	Notre Dame	9-2-1	Dan Devine	9-1-1
10	North Carolina	11-1-0	Dick Crum	10-1-0
11	USC	8-2-1	John Robinson	same
12	BYU	12-1-0	LaVell Edwards	11-1-0
13	UCLA	9-2-0	Terry Donahue	same
14	Baylor	10-2-0	Grant Teaff	10-1-0
15	Ohio St.	9-3-0	Earle Bruce	9-2-0
16	Washington	9-3-0	Don James	9-2-0
17	Purdue	9-3-0	Jim Young	8-3-0
18	Miami-FL	9-3-0	H. Schnellenberger	8-3-0
19	Mississippi St.	9-3-0	Emory Bellard	9-2-0
20	SMU	8-4-0	Ron Meyer	8-3-0

Key Bowl Games

Rankings below reflect final regular season poll, released Dec. 8.

Sugar–#1 Georgia over #7 Notre Dame, 17-10; **Orange**–#4 Oklahoma over #2 Florida St., 18-17; **Gator**–#3 Pitt over #18 S. Carolina, 37-9; **Rose**–#5 Michigan over #16 Washington, 23-6; **Cotton**–#9 Alabama over #6 Baylor, 30-2; **Sun**–#8 Nebraska over #17 Miss. St., 31-17; **Fiesta**–#10 Penn St. over #11 Ohio St., 31-19; **Bluebonnet**–#13 N. Carolina over Texas, 16-7.

1981

		After Bowls	Head Coach	Regular Season
1	Clemson	12-0-0	Danny Ford	11-0-0
2	Texas	10-1-1	Fred Akers	9-1-1
3	Penn St.	10-2-0	Joe Paterno	9-2-0
4	Pittsburgh	11-1-0	Jackie Sherrill	10-1-0
5	SMU	10-1-0	Ron Meyer	same
6	Georgia	10-2-0	Vince Dooley	10-1-0
7	Alabama	9-2-1	Bear Bryant	9-1-1
8	Miami-FL	9-2-0	H. Schnellenberger	same
9	North Carolina	10-2-0	Dick Crum	9-2-0
10	Washington	10-2-0	Don James	9-2-0
11	Nebraska	9-3-0	Tom Osborne	9-2-0
12	Michigan	9-3-0	Bo Schembechler	8-3-0
13	BYU	11-2-0	LaVell Edwards	10-2-0
14	USC	9-3-0	John Robinson	9-2-0
15	Ohio St.	9-3-0	Earle Bruce	8-3-0
16	Arizona St.	9-2-0	Darryl Rogers	same
17	West Virginia	9-3-0	Don Nehlen	8-3-0
18	Iowa	8-4-0	Hayden Fry	8-3-0
19	Missouri	8-4-0	Warren Powers	7-4-0
20	Oklahoma	7-4-1	Barry Switzer	6-4-1

Key Bowl Games

Rankings below reflect final regular season poll, released Nov. 30. No bowl for then #5 SMU (probation), #9 Miami-FL (probation), and #17 Ariz. St. (probation).

Orange–#1 Clemson over #4 Nebraska, 22-15; **Sugar**–#10 Pitt over #2 Georgia, 24-20; **Cotton**–#6 Texas over #3 Alabama, 14-12; **Fiesta**–#7 Penn St. over #8 USC, 26-10; **Gator**–#11 N. Carolina over Arkansas, 31-27; **Rose**–#12 Washington over #13 Iowa, 28-0.

1982

	After Bowls	Head Coach	Regular Season
1	Penn St. 11-1-0	Joe Paterno	10-1-0
2	SMU 11-0-1	Bobby Collins	10-0-1
3	Nebraska 12-1-0	Tom Osborne	11-1-0
4	Georgia 11-1-0	Vince Dooley	11-0-0
5	UCLA 10-1-1	Terry Donahue	9-1-1
6	Arizona St. 10-2-0	Darryl Rogers	9-2-0
7	Washington 10-2-0	Don James	9-2-0
8	Clemson 9-1-1	Danny Ford	same
9	Arkansas 9-2-1	Lou Holtz	8-2-1
10	Pittsburgh 9-3-0	Foge Fazio	9-2-0
11	LSU 8-3-1	Jerry Stovall	8-2-1
12	Ohio St. 9-3-0	Earle Bruce	8-3-0
13	Florida St. 9-3-0	Bobby Bowden	8-3-0
14	Auburn 9-3-0	Pat Dye	8-3-0
15	USC 8-3-0	John Robinson	same
16	Oklahoma 8-4-0	Barry Switzer	8-3-0
17	Texas 9-3-0	Fred Akers	9-2-0
18	North Carolina . .8-4-0	Dick Crum	7-4-0
19	West Virginia . . .9-3-0	Don Nehlen	9-2-0
20	Maryland 8-4-0	Bobby Ross	8-3-0

Key Bowl Games

Rankings below reflect final regular season poll, released Dec. 6. No bowl for then #7 Clemson (probation) and #15 USC (probation).

Sugar–#2 Penn St. over #1 Georgia, 27-23; **Orange**–#3 Nebraska over #13 LSU, 21-20; **Cotton**–#4 SMU over #6 Pitt, 7-3; **Rose**–#5 UCLA over #19 Michigan, 24-14; **Aloha**–#9 Washington over #16 Maryland, 21-20; **Fiesta**–#11 Ariz. St. over #12 Oklahoma, 32-21; **Bluebonnet**–#14 Arkansas over Florida, 28-24.

1983

	After Bowls	Head Coach	Regular Season
1	Miami-FL 11-1-0	H. Schnellenberger	10-1-0
2	Nebraska 12-1-0	Tom Osborne	12-0-0
3	Auburn 11-1-0	Pat Dye	10-1-0
4	Georgia 10-1-1	Vince Dooley	9-1-1
5	Texas 11-1-0	Fred Akers	11-0-0
6	Florida 9-2-1	Charley Pell	8-2-1
7	BYU 11-1-0	LaVell Edwards	10-1-0
8	Michigan 9-3-0	Bo Schembechler	9-2-0
9	Ohio St. 9-3-0	Earle Bruce	8-3-0
10	Illinois 10-2-0	Mike White	10-1-0
11	Clemson 9-1-1	Danny Ford	same
12	SMU 10-2-0	Bobby Collins	10-1-0
13	Air Force 10-2-0	Ken Hatfield	9-2-0
14	Iowa 9-3-0	Hayden Fry	9-2-0
15	Alabama 8-4-0	Ray Perkins	7-4-0
16	West Virginia . . .9-3-0	Don Nehlen	8-3-0
17	UCLA 7-4-1	Terry Donahue	6-4-1
18	Pittsburgh 8-3-1	Foge Fazio	8-2-1
19	Boston College . .9-3-0	Jack Bicknell	9-2-0
20	East Carolina . . .8-3-0	Ed Emory	same

Key Bowl Games

Rankings below reflect final regular season poll, released Dec. 5. No bowl for then #12 Clemson (probation).

Orange–#5 Miami-FL over #1 Nebraska, 31-30; **Cotton**–#7 Georgia over #2 Texas, 10-9; **Sugar**–#3 Auburn over #8 Michigan, 9-7; **Rose**–UCLA over #4 Illinois, 45-9; **Holiday**–#9 BYU over Missouri, 21-17; **Gator**–#11 Florida over #10 Iowa, 14-6; **Fiesta**–#14 Ohio St. over #15 Pitt, 28-23.

1984

	After Bowls	Head Coach	Regular Season
1	BYU 13-0-0	LaVell Edwards	12-0-0
2	Washington 11-1-0	Don James	10-1-0
3	Florida 9-1-1	Charley Pell (0-1-1) & Galen Hall (9-0)	same
4	Nebraska 10-2-0	Tom Osborne	9-2-0
5	Boston College .10-2-0	Jack Bicknell	9-2-0
6	Oklahoma 9-2-1	Barry Switzer	9-1-1
7	Oklahoma St. . .10-2-0	Pat Jones	9-2-0
8	SMU 10-2-0	Bobby Collins	9-2-0
9	UCLA 9-3-0	Terry Donahue	8-3-0
10	USC 9-3-0	Ted Tollner	8-3-0
11	South Carolina .10-2-0	Joe Morrison	10-1-0
12	Maryland 9-3-0	Bobby Ross	8-3-0
13	Ohio St. 9-3-0	Earle Bruce	9-2-0
14	Auburn 9-4-0	Pat Dye	8-4-0
15	LSU 8-3-1	Bill Arnsparger	8-2-1
16	Iowa 8-4-1	Hayden Fry	7-4-1
17	Florida St. 7-3-2	Bobby Bowden	7-3-1
18	Miami-FL 8-5-0	Jimmy Johnson	8-4-0
19	Kentucky 9-3-0	Jerry Claiborne	8-3-0
20	Virginia 8-2-2	George Welsh	7-2-2

Key Bowl Games

Rankings below reflect final regular season poll, released Dec. 3. No bowl for then #3 Florida (probation).

Holiday–#1 BYU over Michigan, 24-17; **Orange**–#4 Washington over #2 Oklahoma, 28-17; **Sugar**–#5 Nebraska over #11 LSU, 28-10; **Rose**–#18 USC over #6 Ohio St., 20-17; **Gator**–#9 Okla. St. over #7 S. Carolina, 21-14; **Cotton**–#8 BC over Houston, 45-28; **Aloha**–#10 SMU over #17 Notre Dame, 27-20.

1985

	After Bowls	Head Coach	Regular Season
1	Oklahoma 11-1-0	Barry Switzer	10-1-0
2	Michigan 10-1-1	Bo Schembechler	9-1-1
3	Penn St. 11-1-0	Joe Paterno	11-0-0
4	Tennessee 9-1-2	Johnny Majors	8-1-2
5	Florida 9-1-1	Galen Hall	same
6	Texas A&M 10-2-0	Jackie Sherrill	9-2-0
7	UCLA 9-2-1	Terry Donahue	8-2-1
8	Air Force 12-1-0	Fisher DeBerry	11-1-0
9	Miami-FL 10-2-0	Jimmy Johnson	10-1-0
10	Iowa 10-2-0	Hayden Fry	10-1-0
11	Nebraska 9-3-0	Tom Osborne	9-2-0
12	Arkansas 10-2-0	Ken Hatfield	9-2-0
13	Alabama 9-2-1	Ray Perkins	8-2-1
14	Ohio St. 9-3-0	Earle Bruce	8-3-0
15	Florida St. 9-3-0	Bobby Bowden	8-3-0
16	BYU 11-3-0	LaVell Edwards	11-2-0
17	Baylor 9-3-0	Grant Teaff	8-3-0
18	Maryland 9-3-0	Bobby Ross	8-3-0
19	Georgia Tech . . .9-2-1	Bill Curry	8-2-1
20	LSU 9-2-1	Bill Arnsparger	9-1-1

Key Bowl Games

Rankings below reflect final regular season poll, released Dec. 9. No bowl for then #6 Florida (probation).

Orange–#3 Oklahoma over #1 Penn St., 25-10; **Sugar**–#8 Tennessee over #2 Miami-FL, 35-7; **Rose**–#13 UCLA over #4 Iowa, 45-28; **Fiesta**–#5 Michigan over #7 Nebraska, 27-23; **Bluebonnet**–#10 Air Force over Texas, 24-16; **Cotton**–#11 Texas A&M over #16 Auburn, 36-16.

Associated Press Final Polls (Cont.)

1986

	After Bowls	Head Coach	Regular Season
1	Penn St. 12-0-0	Joe Paterno	11-0-0
2	Miami-FL 11-1-0	Jimmy Johnson	11-0-0
3	Oklahoma 11-1-0	Barry Switzer	10-1-0
4	Arizona St. 10-1-1	John Cooper	9-1-1
5	Nebraska 10-2-0	Tom Osborne	9-2-0
6	Auburn 10-2-0	Pat Dye	9-2-0
7	Ohio St. 10-3-0	Earle Bruce	9-3-0
8	Michigan 11-2-0	Bo Schembechler	11-1-0
9	Alabama 10-3-0	Ray Perkins	9-3-0
10	LSU 9-3-0	Bill Arnsparger	9-2-0
11	Arizona 9-3-0	Larry Smith	8-3-0
12	Baylor 9-3-0	Grant Teaff	8-3-0
13	Texas A&M ...9-3-0	Jackie Sherrill	9-2-0
14	UCLA 8-3-1	Terry Donahue	7-3-1
15	Arkansas 9-3-0	Ken Hatfield	9-2-0
16	Iowa 9-3-0	Hayden Fry	8-3-0
17	Clemson 8-2-2	Danny Ford	7-2-2
18	Washington ...8-3-1	Don James	8-2-1
19	Boston College .9-3-0	Jack Bicknell	8-3-0
20	Virginia Tech 9-2-1	Bill Dooley	8-2-1

Key Bowl Games

Rankings below reflect final regular season poll, released Dec. 1.

Fiesta–#2 Penn St. over #1 Miami-FL, 14-10; **Orange**–#3 Oklahoma over #9 Arkansas, 42-8; **Rose**–#7 Ariz. St. over #4 Michigan, 22-15; **Sugar**–#6 Nebraska over #5 LSU, 30-15; **Cotton**–#11 Ohio St. over #8 Texas A&M, 28-12; **Citrus**–#10 Auburn over USC, 16-7; **Sun**–#13 Alabama over #12 Washington, 28-6.

1987

	After Bowls	Head Coach	Regular Season
1	Miami-FL 12-0-0	Jimmy Johnson	11-0-0
2	Florida St. 11-1-0	Bobby Bowden	10-1-0
3	Oklahoma 11-1-0	Barry Switzer	11-0-0
4	Syracuse 11-0-1	Dick MacPherson	11-0-0
5	LSU 10-1-1	Mike Archer	9-1-1
6	Nebraska 10-2-0	Tom Osborne	10-1-0
7	Auburn 9-1-2	Pat Dye	9-1-1
8	Michigan St. ...9-2-1	George Perles	8-2-1
9	UCLA 10-2-0	Terry Donahue	9-2-0
10	Texas A&M 10-2-0	Jackie Sherrill	9-2-0
11	Oklahoma St. ..10-2-0	Pat Jones	9-2-0
12	Clemson 10-2-0	Danny Ford	9-2-0
13	Georgia 9-3-0	Vince Dooley	8-3-0
14	Tennessee 10-2-1	Johnny Majors	9-2-1
15	South Carolina ..8-4-0	Joe Morrison	8-3-0
16	Iowa 10-3-0	Hayden Fry	9-3-0
17	Notre Dame ...8-4-0	Lou Holtz	8-3-0
18	USC 8-4-0	Larry Smith	8-3-0
19	Michigan 8-4-0	Bo Schembechler	7-4-0
20	Arizona St. 7-4-1	John Cooper	6-4-1

Key Bowl Games

Rankings below reflect final regular season poll, released Dec. 7.

Orange–#2 Miami-FL over #1 Oklahoma, 20-14; **Fiesta**–#3 Florida St. over #5 Nebraska, 31-28; **Sugar**–#4 Syracuse tied #6 Auburn, 16-16; **Gator**–#7 LSU over #9 S. Carolina, 30-13; **Rose**–#8 Mich. St. over #16 USC, 20-17; **Aloha**–#10 UCLA over Florida, 20-16; **Cotton**–#13 Texas A&M over #12 Notre Dame, 35-10.

1988

	After Bowls	Head Coach	Regular Season
1	Notre Dame ...12-0-0	Lou Holtz	11-0-0
2	Miami-FL 11-1-0	Jimmy Johnson	10-1-0
3	Florida St. 11-1-0	Bobby Bowden	10-1-0
4	Michigan 9-2-1	Bo Schembechler	8-2-1
5	West Virginia ..11-1-0	Don Nehlen	11-0-0
6	UCLA 10-2-0	Terry Donahue	9-2-0
7	USC 10-2-0	Larry Smith	10-1-0
8	Auburn 10-2-0	Pat Dye	10-1-0
9	Clemson 10-2-0	Danny Ford	9-2-0
10	Nebraska 11-2-0	Tom Osborne	11-1-0
11	Oklahoma St. ..10-2-0	Pat Jones	9-2-0
12	Arkansas 10-2-0	Ken Hatfield	10-1-0
13	Syracuse 10-2-0	Dick MacPherson	9-2-0
14	Oklahoma 9-3-0	Barry Switzer	9-2-0
15	Georgia 9-3-0	Vince Donahue	8-3-0
16	Washington St. ..9-3-0	Dennis Erickson	8-3-0
17	Alabama 9-3-0	Bill Curry	8-3-0
18	Houston 9-3-0	Jack Pardee	9-2-0
19	LSU 8-4-0	Mike Archer	8-3-0
20	Indiana 8-3-1	Bill Mallory	7-3-1

Key Bowl Games

Rankings below reflect final regular season poll, released Dec. 5.

Fiesta–#1 Notre Dame over #3 West Va., 34-21; **Orange**–#2 Miami-FL over #6 Nebraska, 23-3; **Sugar**–#4 Florida St. over #7 Auburn, 13-7; **Rose**–#11 Michigan over #5 USC, 22-14; **Cotton**–#9 UCLA over #8 Arkansas, 17-3; **Citrus**–#13 Clemson over #10 Oklahoma, 13-6.

1989

	After Bowls	Head Coach	Regular Season
1	Miami-FL 11-1-0	Dennis Erickson	10-1-0
2	Notre Dame ...12-1-0	Lou Holtz	11-1-0
3	Florida St. 10-2-0	Bobby Bowden	9-2-0
4	Colorado 11-1-0	Bill McCartney	11-0-0
5	Tennessee 11-1-0	Johnny Majors	10-1-0
6	Auburn 10-2-0	Pat Dye	9-2-0
7	Michigan 10-2-0	Bo Schembechler	10-1-0
8	USC 9-2-1	Larry Smith	8-2-1
9	Alabama 10-2-0	Bill Curry	10-1-0
10	Illinois 10-2-0	John Mackovic	9-2-0
11	Nebraska 10-2-0	Tom Osborne	10-1-0
12	Clemson 10-2-0	Danny Ford	9-2-0
13	Arkansas 10-2-0	Ken Hatfield	10-1-0
14	Houston 9-2-0	Jack Pardee	same
15	Penn St. 8-3-1	Joe Paterno	7-3-1
16	Michigan St. ...8-4-0	George Perles	7-4-0
17	Pittsburgh 8-3-1	Mike Gottfried (7-3-1) & Paul Hackett (1-0)	7-3-1
18	Virginia 10-3-0	George Welsh	10-2-0
19	Texas Tech 9-3-0	Spike Dykes	8-3-0
20	Texas A&M 8-4-0	R.C. Slocum	8-3-0
21	West Virginia ..8-3-1	Don Nehlen	8-2-1
22	BYU 10-3-0	LaVell Edwards	10-2-0
23	Washington 8-4-0	Don James	7-4-0
24	Ohio St. 8-4-0	John Cooper	8-3-0
25	Arizona 8-4-0	Dick Tomey	7-4-0

Key Bowl Games

Rankings below reflect final regular season poll, released Dec. 11. No bowl for then #13 Houston (probation).

Orange–#4 Notre Dame over #1 Colorado, 21-6; **Sugar**–#2 Miami-FL over #7 Alabama, 33-25; **Rose**–#12 USC over #3 Michigan, 17-10; **Fiesta**–#5 Florida St. over #6 Nebraska, 41-17; **Cotton**–#8 Tennessee over #10 Arkansas, 31-27; **Hall of Fame**–#9 Auburn over #21 Ohio St., 31-14; **Citrus**–#11 Illinois over #15 Virginia, 31-21.

1990

	After Bowls	Head Coach	Regular Season
1 Colorado	11-1-1	Bill McCartney	10-1-1
2 Georgia Tech	11-0-1	Bobby Ross	10-0-1
3 Miami-FL	10-2-0	Dennis Erickson	9-2-0
4 Florida St.	10-2-0	Bobby Bowden	9-2-0
5 Washington	10-2-0	Don James	9-2-0
6 Notre Dame	9-3-0	Lou Holtz	9-2-0
7 Michigan	9-3-0	Gary Moeller	8-3-0
8 Tennessee	9-2-2	Johnny Majors	8-2-2
9 Clemson	10-2-0	Ken Hatfield	9-2-0
10 Houston	10-1-0	John Jenkins	same
11 Penn St.	9-3-0	Joe Paterno	9-2-0
12 Texas	10-2-0	David McWilliams	10-1-0
13 Florida	9-2-0	Steve Spurrier	same
14 Louisville	10-1-1	H. Schnellenberger	9-1-1
15 Texas A&M	9-3-1	R.C. Slocum	8-3-1
16 Michigan St.	8-3-1	George Perles	7-3-1
17 Oklahoma	8-3-0	Gary Gibbs	same
18 Iowa	8-4-0	Hayden Fry	8-3-0
19 Auburn	8-3-1	Pat Dye	7-3-1
20 USC	8-4-1	Larry Smith	8-3-1
21 Mississippi	9-3-0	Billy Brewer	9-2-0
22 BYU	10-3-0	LaVell Edwards	10-2-0
23 Virginia	8-4-0	George Welsh	8-3-0
24 Nebraska	9-3-0	Tom Osborne	9-2-0
25 Illinois	8-4-0	John Mackovic	8-3-0

Key Bowl Games

Rankings below reflect final regular season poll, released Dec. 3. No bowl for then #9 Houston (probation), #11 Florida (probation) and #20 Oklahoma (probation).
Orange—#1 Colorado over #5 Notre Dame, 10-9; **Citrus**—#2 Ga. Tech over #19 Nebraska, 45-21; **Cotton**—#4 Miami-FL over #3 Texas, 46-3; **Blockbuster**—#6 Florida St. over #7 Penn St., 24-17; **Rose**—#8 Washington over #17 Iowa, 46-34; **Sugar**—#10 Tennessee over Virginia, 23-22; **Gator**—#12 Michigan over #15 Ole Miss, 35-3.

1991

	After Bowls	Head Coach	Regular Season
1 Miami-FL	12-0-0	Dennis Erickson	11-0-0
2 Washington	12-0-0	Don James	11-0-0
3 Penn St.	11-2-0	Joe Paterno	10-2-0
4 Florida St.	11-2-0	Bobby Bowden	10-2-0
5 Alabama	11-1-0	Gene Stallings	10-1-0
6 Michigan	10-2-0	Gary Moeller	10-1-0
7 Florida	10-2-0	Steve Spurrier	10-1-0
8 California	10-2-0	Bruce Snyder	9-2-0
9 East Carolina	11-1-0	Bill Lewis	10-1-0
10 Iowa	10-1-1	Hayden Fry	10-1-0
11 Syracuse	10-2-0	Paul Pasqualoni	9-2-0
12 Texas A&M	10-2-0	R.C. Slocum	10-1-0
13 Notre Dame	10-3-0	Lou Holtz	9-3-0
14 Tennessee	9-3-0	Johnny Majors	9-2-0
15 Nebraska	9-2-1	Tom Osborne	9-1-1
16 Oklahoma	9-3-0	Gary Gibbs	8-3-0
17 Georgia	9-3-0	Ray Goff	8-3-0
18 Clemson	9-2-1	Ken Hatfield	9-1-1
19 UCLA	9-3-0	Terry Donahue	8-3-0
20 Colorado	8-3-1	Bill McCartney	8-2-1
21 Tulsa	10-2-0	David Rader	8-3-0
22 Stanford	8-4-0	Dennis Green	8-3-0
23 BYU	8-3-2	LaVell Edwards	8-3-1
24 N.C. State	9-3-0	Dick Sheridan	9-2-0
25 Air Force	10-3-0	Fisher DeBerry	9-3-0

Key Bowl Games

Rankings below reflect final regular season poll, taken Dec. 2.
Orange—#1 Miami-FL over #11 Nebraska, 22-0; **Rose**—#2 Washington over #4 Michigan, 34-14; **Sugar**—#18 Notre Dame over #3 Florida, 39-28; **Cotton**—#5 Florida St. over #9 Texas A&M, 10-2; **Fiesta**—#6 Penn St. over #10 Tennessee, 42-17; **Holiday**—#7 Iowa tied BYU, 13-13; **Blockbuster**—#8 Alabama over #15 Colorado, 30-25; **Citrus**—#14 California over #13 Clemson, 37-13.

1992

	After Bowls	Head Coach	Regular Season
1 Alabama	13-0-0	Gene Stallings	12-0-0
2 Florida St.	11-1-0	Bobby Bowden	10-1-0
3 Miami-FL	11-1-0	Dennis Erickson	11-0-0
4 Notre Dame	10-1-1	Lou Holtz	9-1-1
5 Michigan	9-0-3	Gary Moeller	8-0-3
6 Syracuse	10-2-0	Paul Pasqualoni	9-2-0
7 Texas A&M	12-1-0	R.C. Slocum	12-0-0
8 Georgia	10-2-0	Ray Goff	9-2-0
9 Stanford	10-3-0	Bill Walsh	9-3-0
10 Florida	9-4-0	Steve Spurrier	8-4-0
11 Washington	9-3-0	Don James	9-2-0
12 Tennessee	9-3-0	Johnny Majors (5-3) & Phillip Fulmer (4-0)	8-3-0
13 Colorado	9-2-1	Bill McCartney	9-1-1
14 Nebraska	9-3-0	Tom Osborne	9-2-0
15 Washington St.	9-3-0	Mike Price	8-3-0
16 Mississippi	9-3-0	Billy Brewer	8-3-0
17 N.C. State	9-3-1	Dick Sheridan	9-2-1
18 Ohio St.	8-3-1	John Cooper	8-2-1
19 North Carolina	9-3-0	Mack Brown	8-3-0
20 Hawaii	11-2-0	Bob Wagner	10-2-0
21 Boston College	8-3-1	Tom Coughlin	8-2-1
22 Kansas	8-4-0	Glen Mason	7-4-0
23 Mississippi St.	7-5-0	Jackie Sherrill	7-4-0
24 Fresno St.	9-4-0	Jim Sweeney	9-3-0
25 Wake Forest	8-4-0	Bill Dooley	7-4-0

Key Bowl Games

Rankings below reflect final regular season poll, taken Dec. 5.
Sugar—#2 Alabama over #1 Miami-FL, 34-13; **Orange**—#3 Florida St. over #11 Nebraska, 27-14; **Cotton**—#5 Notre Dame over #4 Texas A&M, 28-3; **Fiesta**—#6 Syracuse over #10 Colorado, 26-22; **Rose**—#7 Michigan over #9 Washington, 38-31; **Citrus**—#8 Georgia over #15 Ohio St., 21-14.

1993

	After Bowls	Head Coach	Regular Season
1 Florida St	12-1-0	Bobby Bowden	11-1-0
2 Notre Dame	11-1-0	Lou Holtz	10-1-0
3 Nebraska	11-1-0	Tom Osborne	11-0-0
4 Auburn	11-0-0	Terry Bowden	11-0-0
5 Florida	11-2-0	Steve Spurrier	10-2-0
6 Wisconsin	10-1-1	Barry Alvarez	9-1-1
7 West Virginia	11-1-0	Don Nehlen	11-0-0
8 Penn St.	10-2-0	Joe Paterno	9-2-0
9 Texas A&M	10-2-0	R.C. Slocum	10-1-0
10 Arizona	10-2-0	Dick Tomey	9-2-0
11 Ohio St	10-1-1	John Cooper	9-1-1
12 Tennessee	9-2-1	Phillip Fulmer	9-1-1
13 Boston College	9-3-0	Tom Coughlin	8-3-0
14 Alabama	9-3-1	Gene Stallings	8-3-1
15 Miami-FL	9-3-0	Dennis Erickson	9-2-0
16 Colorado	8-3-1	Bill McCartney	7-3-1
17 Oklahoma	9-3-0	Gary Gibbs	8-3-0
18 UCLA	8-4-0	Terry Donahue	8-3-0
19 North Carolina	10-3-0	Mack Brown	10-2-0
20 Kansas St	9-2-1	Bill Snyder	8-2-1
21 Michigan	8-4-0	Gary Moeller	7-4-0
22 Va. Tech	9-3-0	Frank Beamer	9-2-0
23 Clemson	9-3-0	Ken Hatfield (8-3) & Tommy West (1-0)	8-3-0
24 Louisville	9-3-0	H. Schnellenberger	8-3-0
25 California	9-4-0	Keith Gilbertson	8-4-0

Key Bowl Games

Rankings below reflect final regular season poll, taken Dec. 5. No bowl for then #5 Auburn (probation). **Orange**—#1 Florida St. over #2 Nebraska, 18-16; **Sugar**—#8 Florida over #3 West Virginia, 41-7; **Cotton**—#4 Notre Dame over #7 Texas A&M, 24-21; **Citrus**—#13 Penn St. over #6 Tennessee, 31-13; **Rose**—#9 Wisconsin over #14 UCLA, 21-16; **Fiesta**—#16 Arizona over #10 Miami-FL, 29-0;

Associated Press Final Polls (Cont.)

1994

	After Bowls	Head Coach	Regular Season
1 Nebraska	13-0-0	Tom Osborne	12-0-0
2 Penn St	12-0-0	Joe Paterno	11-0-0
3 Colorado	11-1-0	Bill McCartney	10-1-0
4 Florida St	10-1-1	Bobby Bowden	9-1-1
5 Alabama	12-1-0	Gene Stallings	11-1-0
6 Miami-FL	10-2-0	Dennis Erickson	10-1-0
7 Florida	10-2-1	Steve Spurrier	10-1-1
8 Texas A&M	10-0-1	R.C. Slocum	same
9 Auburn	9-1-1	Terry Bowden	same
10 Utah	10-2-0	Ron McBride	9-2-0
11 Oregon	9-4-0	Rich Brooks	9-3-0
12 Michigan	8-4-0	Gary Moeller	7-4-0
13 USC	8-3-1	John Robinson	7-3-1
14 Ohio St	9-4-0	John Cooper	9-3-0
15 Virginia	9-3-0	George Welsh	8-3-0
16 Colorado St	10-2-0	Sonny Lubick	10-1-0
17 N.C. State	9-3-0	Mike O'Cain	8-3-0
18 BYU	10-3-0	LaVell Edwards	9-3-0
19 Kansas St	9-3-0	Bill Snyder	9-2-0
20 Arizona	8-4-0	Dick Tomey	8-3-0
21 Washington St	8-4-0	Mike Price	7-4-0
22 Tennessee	8-4-0	Phillip Fulmer	7-4-0
23 Boston College	7-4-1	Dan Henning	6-4-1
24 Mississippi St	8-4-0	Jackie Sherrill	8-3-0
25 Texas	8-4-0	John Mackovic	7-4-0

Key Bowl Games

Rankings below reflect final regular season poll, taken Dec. 4. No bowls for then #8 Texas A&M (probation) and #9 Auburn (probation). **Orange**—#1 Nebraska over #3 Miami-FL, 24-17; **Rose**—#2 Penn St. over #12 Oregon, 38-20; **Fiesta**—#4 Colorado over Notre Dame, 41-24; **Sugar**—#7 Florida St. over #5 Florida, 23-17; **Citrus**—#6 Alabama over #13 Ohio St., 24-17; **Freedom**—#14 Utah over #15 Arizona, 16-13.

1996

	After Bowls	Head Coach	Regular Season
1 Florida	12-1	Steve Spurrier	11-1
2 Ohio St.	11-1	John Cooper	10-1
3 Florida St.	11-1	Bobby Bowden	11-0
4 Arizona St	11-1	Bruce Snyder	11-0
5 BYU	14-1	LaVell Edwards	13-1
6 Nebraska	11-2	Tom Osborne	10-2
7 Penn St.	11-2	Joe Paterno	10-2
8 Colorado	10-2	Rick Neuheisel	9-2
9 Tennessee	10-2	Phillip Fulmer	9-2
10 North Carolina	10-2	Mack Brown	9-2
11 Alabama	10-3	Gene Stallings	9-3
12 LSU	10-2	Gerry DiNardo	9-2
13 Virginia Tech	10-2	Frank Beamer	10-1
14 Miami-FL	9-3	Butch Davis	8-3
15 Northwestern	9-3	Gary Barnett	9-2
16 Washington	9-3	Jim Lambright	9-2
17 Kansas St.	9-3	Bill Snyder	9-2
18 Iowa	9-3	Hayden Fry	8-3
19 Notre Dame	8-3	Lou Holtz	same
20 Michigan	8-4	Lloyd Carr	8-3
21 Syracuse	9-3	Paul Pasqualoni	8-3
22 Wyoming	10-2	Joe Tiller	same
23 Texas	8-5	John Mackovic	8-4
24 Auburn	8-4	Terry Bowden	7-4
25 Army	10-2	Bob Sutton	10-1

Key Bowl Games

Rankings below reflect final regular season poll, taken Dec. 8. No bowl for then #18 N. Dame and #22 Wyoming. **Sugar**—#3 Fla. over #1 Fla. St., 52-20; **Rose**—#4 Ohio St. over #2 Ariz. St., 20-17; **Fiesta**—#7 Penn St. over #20 Texas, 38-15; **Cotton**—#5 BYU over #14 Kansas St., 19-15; **Citrus**—#9 Tenn. over #11 Northwestern, 48-28; **Orange**—#6 Neb. over #10 Va. Tech, 41-21.

1995

	After Bowls	Head Coach	Regular Season
1 Nebraska	12-0-0	Tom Osborne	11-0-0
2 Florida	12-1-0	Steve Spurrier	12-0-0
3 Tennessee	11-1-0	Phillip Fulmer	10-1-0
4 Florida St	10-2-0	Bobby Bowden	9-2-0
5 Colorado	10-2-0	Rick Neuheisel	9-2-0
6 Ohio St	11-2-0	John Cooper	11-1-0
7 Kansas St	10-2-0	Bill Snyder	9-2-0
8 Northwestern	10-2-0	Gary Barnett	10-1-0
9 Kansas	10-2-0	Glen Mason	9-2-0
10 Virginia Tech	10-2-0	Frank Beamer	9-2-0
11 Notre Dame	9-3-0	Lou Holtz	9-2-0
12 USC	9-2-1	John Robinson	8-2-1
13 Penn St	9-3-0	Joe Paterno	8-3-0
14 Texas	10-2-1	John Mackovic	10-1-1
15 Texas A&M	9-3-0	R.C. Slocum	8-3-0
16 Virginia	9-4-0	George Welsh	8-4-0
17 Michigan	9-4-0	Lloyd Carr	9-3-0
18 Oregon	9-3-0	Mike Bellotti	9-2-0
19 Syracuse	9-3-0	Paul Pasqualoni	8-3-0
20 Miami-FL	8-3-0	Butch Davis	same
21 Alabama	8-3-0	Gene Stallings	same
22 Auburn	8-4-0	Terry Bowden	8-3-0
23 Texas Tech	9-3-0	Spike Dykes	8-3-0
24 Toledo	11-0-1	Gary Pinkel	10-0-1
25 Iowa	8-4-0	Hayden Fry	7-4-0

Key Bowl Games

Rankings below reflect final regular season poll, taken Dec. 3. No bowl for then #21 Ala. (probation) and #22 Miami-FL (probation). **Fiesta**—#1 Neb. over #2 Fla., 62-24; **Rose**—#17 USC over #3 Northwestern, 41-32; **Citrus**—#4t Tenn. over #4t Ohio St., 20-14; **Orange**—#8 Fla. St. over N. Dame, 31-26; **Cotton**—#7 Colo. over #12 Oregon, 38-6; **Sugar**—#13 Va. Tech over #9 Texas, 28-10.

1997

	After Bowls	Head Coach	Regular Season
1 Michigan	12-0	Lloyd Carr	11-0
2 Nebraska	13-0	Tom Osborne	12-0
3 Florida St	11-1	Bobby Bowden	10-1
4 Florida	10-2	Steve Spurrier	9-2
5 UCLA	10-2	Bob Toledo	9-2
6 North Carolina	11-1	Mack Brown (10-1) & Carl Torbush	10-1 (1-0)
7 Tennessee	11-2	Phillip Fulmer	11-1
8 Kansas St	11-1	Bill Snyder	10-1
9 Washington St.	10-2	Mike Price	10-1
10 Georgia	10-2	Jim Donnan	9-2
11 Auburn	10-3	Terry Bowden	9-3
12 Ohio St.	10-3	John Cooper	10-2
13 LSU	9-3	Gerry DiNardo	8-3
14 Arizona St.	8-3	Bruce Snyder	7-3
15 Purdue	9-3	Joe Tiller	8-3
16 Penn St.	9-3	Joe Paterno	9-2
17 Colorado St.	11-2	Sonny Lubick	10-2
18 Washington	8-4	Jim Lambright	7-4
19 So. Mississippi	9-3	Jeff Bower	8-3
20 Texas A&M	9-4	R.C. Slocum	9-3
21 Syracuse	9-4	Paul Pasqualoni	9-3
22 Mississippi	8-4	Tommy Tuberville	7-4
23 Missouri	7-5	Larry Smith	6-5
24 Oklahoma St.	8-4	Bobby Simmons	8-3
25 Georgia Tech	7-5	George O'Leary	6-5

Key Bowl Games

Rankings below reflect final regular season poll, taken Dec. 7. **Rose**—#1 Michigan over #7 Washington St., 21-16; **Orange**—#2 Nebraska over #3 Tennessee, 42-17; **Sugar**—#4 Florida St. over #10 Ohio St., 31-14; **Gator**—#5 North Carolina over Virginia Tech, 42-3; **Cotton**—#6 UCLA over #19 Texas A&M, 29-23; **Citrus**—#8 Florida over #12 Penn St., 21-6; **Fiesta**—#9 Kansas St. over #14 Syracuse, 35-18.

1998

		After Bowls	Head Coach	Regular Season
1	Tennessee	13-0	Phillip Fulmer	12-0
2	Ohio St.	11-1	John Cooper	10-1
3	Florida St.	11-2	Bobby Bowden	11-1
4	Arizona	12-1	Dick Tomey	11-1
5	Florida	10-2	Steve Spurrier	9-2
6	Wisconsin	11-1	Barry Alvarez	10-1
7	Tulane	12-0	Tommy Bowden	11-0
8	UCLA	10-2	Bob Toledo	10-1
9	Georgia Tech	10-2	George O'Leary	9-2
10	Kansas St.	11-2	Bill Snyder	11-1
11	Texas A&M	11-3	R.C. Slocum	11-2
12	Michigan	10-3	Lloyd Carr	9-3
13	Air Force	12-1	Fisher DeBerry	11-1
14	Georgia	9-3	Jim Donnan	8-3
15	Texas	9-3	Mack Brown	8-3
16	Arkansas	9-3	Houston Nutt	9-2
17	Penn St.	9-3	Joe Paterno	8-3
18	Virginia	9-3	George Welsh	9-2
19	Nebraska	9-4	Frank Solich	9-3
20	Miami-FL	9-3	Butch Davis	8-3
21	Missouri	8-4	Larry Smith	7-4
22	Notre Dame	9-3	Bob Davie	9-2
23	Va. Tech	9-3	Frank Beamer	8-3
24	Purdue	9-4	Joe Tiller	8-4
25	Syracuse	8-4	Paul Pasqualoni	8-3

Key Bowl Games
Rankings below reflect final regular season poll, taken Dec. 6. **Fiesta**–#1 Tennessee over #2 Florida St., 23-16; **Sugar**–#3 Ohio St. over #8 Texas A&M, 24-14; **Orange**–#7 Florida over #18 Syracuse, 31-10; **Rose**–#9 Wisconsin over #6 UCLA, 38-31; **Holiday**–#5 Arizona over #14 Nebraska, 23-20; **Alamo**–Purdue over #4 Kansas St., 37-34.

1999

		After Bowls	Head Coach	Regular Season
1	Florida St.	12-0	Bobby Bowden	11-0
2	Va. Tech	11-1	Frank Beamer	11-0
3	Nebraska	12-1	Frank Solich	11-1
4	Wisconsin	10-2	Barry Alvarez	9-2
5	Michigan	10-2	Lloyd Carr	9-2
6	Kansas St.	11-1	Bill Snyder	10-1
7	Michigan St.	10-2	Nick Saban (9-2) & B. Williams (1-0)	9-2
8	Alabama	10-3	Mike DuBose	10-2
9	Tennessee	9-3	Phillip Fulmer	8-3
10	Marshall	13-0	Bob Pruett	12-0
11	Penn St.	10-3	Joe Paterno	9-3
12	Florida	9-4	Steve Spurrier	9-3
13	Mississippi St.	10-2	Jackie Sherrill	9-2
14	Southern Miss.	9-3	Jeff Bower	8-3
15	Miami-FL	9-4	Butch Davis	8-4
16	Georgia	8-4	Jim Donnan	7-4
17	Arkansas	8-4	Houston Nutt	7-4
18	Minnesota	8-4	Glen Mason	8-3
19	Oregon	9-3	Mike Bellotti	8-3
20	Georgia Tech	8-4	George O'Leary	8-3
21	Texas	9-5	Mack Brown	9-4
22	Mississippi	8-4	David Cutcliffe	7-4
23	Texas A&M	8-4	R.C. Slocum	8-3
24	Illinois	8-4	Ron Turner	7-4
25	Purdue	7-5	Joe Tiller	7-4

Key Bowl Games
Rankings below reflect final regular season poll, taken Dec. 5. **Sugar**–#1 Florida St. over #2 Va. Tech, 46-29; **Fiesta**–#3 Nebraska over #6 Tennessee, 31-21; **Rose**–#4 Wisconsin over #22 Stanford, 17-9; **Orange**–#8 Michigan over #5 Alabama, 35-34; **Holiday**–#7 Kansas St. over Washington, 24-20; **Citrus**–#9 Michigan St. over #10 Florida, 37-34.

2000

		After Bowls	Head Coach	Regular Season
1	Oklahoma	13-0	Bob Stoops	12-0
2	Miami-FL	11-1	Butch Davis	10-1
3	Washington	11-1	Rick Neuheisel	10-1
4	Oregon St.	11-1	Dennis Erickson	10-1
5	Florida St.	11-2	Bobby Bowden	11-1
6	Va. Tech	11-1	Frank Beamer	10-1
7	Oregon	10-2	Mike Bellotti	9-2
8	Nebraska	10-2	Frank Solich	9-2
9	Kansas St.	11-3	Bill Snyder	10-3
10	Florida	10-3	Steve Spurrier	10-2
11	Michigan	9-3	Lloyd Carr	8-3
12	Texas	9-3	Mack Brown	9-2
13	Purdue	8-4	Joe Tiller	8-3
14	Colorado St.	10-2	Sonny Lubick	9-2
15	Notre Dame	9-3	Bob Davie	9-2
16	Clemson	9-3	Tommy Bowden	9-2
17	Georgia Tech	9-3	George O'Leary	9-2
18	Auburn	9-4	Tommy Tuberville	9-3
19	South Carolina	8-4	Lou Holtz	7-4
20	Georgia	8-4	Jim Donnan	7-4
21	TCU	10-2	D. Franchione (10-1) & G. Patterson (0-1)	10-1
22	LSU	8-4	Nick Saban	7-4
23	Wisconsin	9-4	Barry Alvarez	8-4
24	Mississippi St.	8-4	Jackie Sherrill	7-4
25	Iowa St.	9-3	Dan McCarney	8-3

Key Bowl Games
Rankings below reflect final regular season poll, taken Dec. 4. **Orange**–#1 Oklahoma over #3 Florida St., 13-2; **Sugar**–#2 Miami-FL over #7 Florida, 37-20; **Rose**–#4 Washington over #14 Purdue, 34-24; **Fiesta**–#5 Oregon St. over #10 Notre Dame, 41-9; **Gator**–#6 Virginia Tech over #16 Clemson, 41-20; **Holiday**–#8 Oregon over #12 Texas, 35-30; **Alamo**–#9 Nebraska over #18 Northwestern, 66-17.

2001

		After Bowls	Head Coach	Regular Season
1	Miami-FL	12-0	Larry Coker	11-0
2	Oregon	11-1	Mike Bellotti	10-1
3	Florida	10-2	Steve Spurrier	9-2
4	Tennessee	11-2	Phillip Fulmer	10-2
5	Texas	11-2	Mack Brown	10-2
6	Oklahoma	11-2	Bob Stoops	10-2
7	LSU	10-3	Nick Saban	9-3
8	Nebraska	11-2	Frank Solich	11-1
9	Colorado	10-3	Gary Barnett	10-2
10	Washington St.	10-2	Mike Price	9-2
11	Maryland	10-2	Ralph Friedgen	10-1
12	Illinois	10-2	Ron Turner	10-1
13	South Carolina	9-3	Lou Holtz	8-3
14	Syracuse	10-3	Paul Pasqualoni	9-3
15	Florida St.	8-4	Bobby Bowden	7-4
16	Stanford	9-3	Tyrone Willingham	9-2
17	Louisville	11-2	John L. Smith	10-2
18	Va. Tech	8-4	Frank Beamer	8-3
19	Washington	8-4	Rick Neuheisel	8-3
20	Michigan	8-4	Lloyd Carr	8-3
21	Boston College	8-4	Tom O'Brien	7-4
22	Georgia	8-4	Mark Richt	8-3
23	Toledo	10-2	Tom Amstutz	9-2
24	Georgia Tech	8-5	George O'Leary (7-5) & Mac McWhorter (1-0)	7-5
25	BYU	12-2	Gary Crowton	12-1

Key Bowl Games
Rankings below reflect final regular season poll, taken Dec. 9. **Rose**–#1 Miami-FL over #4 Nebraska, 37-14; **Fiesta**–#2 Oregon over #3 Colorado, 38-16; **Orange**–#5 Florida over #6 Maryland, 56-23; **Sugar**–#12 LSU over #7 Illinois 47-34; **Citrus**–#8 Tennessee over #17 Michigan, 45-17; **Holiday**–#9 Texas over #21 Washington, 47-43; **Cotton**–#10 Oklahoma over Arkansas, 10-3;

Associated Press Final Polls (Cont.)

2002

		After Bowls	Head Coach	Regular Season
1	Ohio St.	14-0	Jim Tressel	13-0
2	Miami-FL	12-1	Larry Coker	12-0
3	Georgia	13-1	Mark Richt	12-1
4	USC	11-2	Pete Carroll	10-2
5	Oklahoma	12-2	Bob Stoops	11-2
6	Texas	11-2	Mack Brown	10-2
7	Kansas St.	11-2	Bill Snyder	10-2
8	Iowa	11-2	Kirk Ferentz	11-1
9	Michigan	10-3	Lloyd Carr	9-3
10	Washington St.	10-3	Mike Price	10-2
11	Alabama	10-3	Dennis Franchione	10-3
12	N.C. State	11-3	Chuck Amato	10-3
13	Maryland	11-3	Ralph Friedgen	10-3
14	Auburn	9-4	Tommy Tuberville	8-4
15	Boise St.	12-1	Dan Hawkins	11-1
16	Penn St.	9-4	Joe Paterno	9-2
17	Notre Dame	10-3	Tyrone Willingham	10-2
18	Va. Tech	10-4	Frank Beamer	9-4
19	Pittsburgh	9-4	Walt Harris	8-4
20	Colorado	9-5	Gary Barnett	9-4
21	Florida St.	9-5	Bobby Bowden	9-4
22	Virginia	9-5	Al Groh	8-5
23	TCU	10-2	Gary Patterson	9-2
24	Marshall	11-2	Bob Pruett	10-2
25	West Virginia	9-4	Rich Rodriguez	9-3

Key Bowl Games

Rankings below reflect final regular season poll, taken Dec. 8. No bowl for then #13 Alabama (probation).
Fiesta–#2 Ohio St. over #1 Miami-FL, 31-24 (2OT); **Orange**–#5 USC over #3 Iowa, 38-17; **Sugar**–#4 Georgia over #16 Florida St. 26-13; **Holiday**–#6 Kansas St. over Arizona St., 34-27; **Rose**–#8 Oklahoma over #7 Washington St., 34-14; **Cotton**–#9 Texas over LSU, 35-20; **Capital One**–#19 Auburn over #10 Penn St., 13-9;

2003

		After Bowls	Head Coach	Regular Season
1	USC	12-1	Pete Carroll	11-1
2	LSU	13-1	Nick Saban	12-1
3	Oklahoma	12-2	Bob Stoops	12-1
4	Ohio State	11-2	Jim Tressel	10-2
5	Miami-FL	11-2	Larry Coker	10-2
6	Michigan	11-2	Lloyd Carr	11-1
7	Georiga	11-3	Mark Richt	10-3
8	Iowa	10-3	Kirk Ferentz	9-3
9	Washington St.	10-3	Bill Doba	9-3
10	Miami-OH	13-1	Terry Hoeppner	12-1
11	Florida St.	10-3	Bobby Bowden	9-3
12	Texas	10-3	Mack Brown	10-2
13	Mississippi	10-3	David Cutliffe	9-3
14	Kansas St.	11-4	Bill Snyder	11-3
15	Tennessee	10-3	Phillip Fulmer	10-2
16	Boise St.	13-1	Dan Hawkins	12-1
17	Maryland	10-3	Ralph Friedgen	9-3
18	Purdue	9-4	Joe Tiller	9-3
19	Nebraska	10-3	Frank Solich (9-3) & Bo Pelini (1-0)	9-3
20	Minnesota	10-3	Glen Mason	9-3
21	Utah	10-2	Urban Meyer	9-2
22	Clemson	9-4	Tommy Bowden	8-4
23	Bowling Green	11-3	Gregg Brandon	10-3
24	Florida	8-5	Ron Zook	8-4
25	TCU	11-2	Gary Patterson	11-1

Key Bowl Games

Rankings below reflect final regular season poll, taken Dec. 7. **Rose**–#1 USC over #4 Michigan, 28-14; **Sugar**–#2 LSU over #3 Oklahoma, 21-14; **Holiday**–#14 Washington St. over #5 Texas, 28-20; **Fiesta**–#6 Ohio St. over #10 Kansas St., 35-28; **Peach**–Clemson over #7 Tennessee, 27-14; **Orange**–#9 Miami-FL over #8 Florida St., 16-14.

2004

		After Bowls	Head Coach	Regular Season
1	USC	13-0	Pete Carroll	12-0
2	Auburn	13-0	Tommy Tuberville	12-0
3	Oklahoma	12-1	Bob Stoops	12-0
4	Utah	12-0	Urban Meyer	11-0
5	Texas	11-1	Mack Brown	10-1
6	Louisville	11-1	Bobby Petrino	10-1
7	Georgia	10-2	Mark Richt	9-2
8	Iowa	10-2	Kirk Ferentz	9-2
9	California	10-2	Jeff Tedford	10-1
10	Virginia Tech	10-3	Frank Beamer	12-1
11	Miami-FL	9-3	Larry Coker	8-3
12	Boise St.	11-1	Dan Hawkins	11-0
13	Tennessee	10-3	Philip Fullmer	9-3
14	Michigan	9-3	Lloyd Carr	8-3
15	Florida St.	9-3	Bobby Bowden	8-3
16	LSU	9-3	Nick Saban	9-2
17	Wisconsin	9-3	Barry Alvarez	9-2
18	Texas Tech	8-4	Mike Leach	7-4
19	Arizona St.	9-3	Dirk Koetter	8-3
20	Ohio St.	8-4	Jim Tressel	7-4
21	Boston College	9-3	Tom O'Brien	8-3
22	Fresno St.	9-3	Pat Hill	8-3
23	Virginia	8-4	Al Groh	8-3
24	Navy	10-2	Paul Johnson	9-2
25	Pittsburgh	8-4	Walt Harris	8-3

Key Bowl Games

Rankings below reflect final regular season poll, taken Dec. 5. **Orange**–#1 USC over #2 Oklahoma, 55-19; **Sugar**–#3 Auburn over #9 Virginia Tech, 16-13; **Holiday**–#23 Texas Tech over #4 California, 45-31; **Fiesta**–#5 Utah. over #19 Pittsburgh, 35-7; **Rose**–#6 Texas over #13 Michigan, 38-37; **Liberty**–#7 Louisville over #10 Boise St., 44-40; **Outback**–#8 Georgia over #16 Wisconsin, 24-21.

All-Time AP Top 20

The composite AP Top 20 from the 1936 season through the 2007 season, based on the final rankings of each year. The final AP poll has been taken after the bowl games in 1965 and since 1968. Team point totals are based on 20 points for all 1st place finishes, 19 for each 2nd, etc. Also listed are the number of times each team has been named national champion by AP and times ranked in the final Top 10 and Top 20.

		Pts	No.1	Top 10	Top 20
1	Oklahoma	.668	7	35	48
2	Notre Dame	.652	8	35	48
	Michigan	.652	2	37	54
4	Ohio St	.592	4	28	46
5	Alabama	.587	6	32	44
6	Nebraska	.548	4	29	42
7	USC	.525	5	26	42
8	Texas	.510	3	24	40
9	Tennessee	.473	2	22	40
10	Penn St	.426	2	22	37
11	LSU	.368	2	19	31
12	Miami-FL	.359	5	17	29
13	Georgia	.338	1	19	29
14	Florida St	.336	2	16	23
15	Auburn	.335	1	16	32
16	UCLA	.327	0	16	30
17	Florida	.294	2	14	25
18	Arkansas	.273	0	13	26
19	Michigan St	.252	1	13	20
20	Washington	.222	0	11	21

2005

		After Bowls	Head Coach	Regular Season
1	Texas	13-0	Mack Brown	12-0
2	USC	12-1	Pete Carroll	12-0
3	Penn St.	11-1	Joe Paterno	10-1
4	Ohio St.	10-2	Jim Tressel	9-2
5	West Virginia	11-1	Rich Rodriguez	10-1
6	LSU	11-2	Les Miles	10-2
7	Virginia Tech	11-2	Frank Beamer	10-2
8	Alabama	10-2	Mike Shula	9-2
9	Notre Dame	9-3	Charlie Weis	9-2
10	Georgia	10-3	Mark Richt	9-3
11	TCU	11-1	Gary Patterson	10-1
12	Florida	9-3	Urban Meyer	8-3
	Oregon	10-2	Mike Bellotti	10-1
14	Auburn	9-3	Tommy Tuberville	9-2
15	Wisconsin	10-3	Barry Alvarez	9-3
16	UCLA	10-2	Karl Dorrell	9-2
17	Miami-FL	9-3	Larry Coker	9-2
18	Boston College	9-3	Tom O'Brien	8-3
19	Louisville	9-3	Bobby Petrino	9-2
20	Texas Tech	9-3	Mike Leach	9-2
21	Clemson	8-4	Tommy Bowden	7-4
22	Oklahoma	8-4	Bob Stoops	7-4
23	Florida St.	8-5	Bobby Bowden	8-4
24	Nebraska	8-4	Bill Callahan	7-4
25	California	8-4	Jeff Tedford	7-4

Key Bowl Games

Rankings below reflect final regular season poll, taken Dec. 6. **Rose**–#2 Texas over #1 USC over 41-38; **Orange**–#3 Penn St. over #22 Florida St., 26-23 3OT; **Fiesta**–#4 Ohio St. over #5 Notre Dame, 34-20; **Holiday**– Oklahoma over #6 Oregon, 17-14; **Capital One**–#21 Wisconsin over #7 Auburn, 24-10; **Sugar**–#11 West Virginia over #8 Georgia, 38-35; **Peach**–#10 LSU over #9 Miami-FL, 40-3.

2006

		After Bowls	Head Coach	Regular Season
1	Florida	13-1	Urban Meyer	12-1
2	Ohio St.	12-1	Jim Tressel	12-0
3	LSU	11-2	Les Miles	10-2
4	USC	12-1	Pete Carroll	11-1
5	Boise St.	13-0	Chris Petersen	12-0
6	Louisville	12-1	Bobby Petrino	11-1
7	Wisconsin	12-1	Barry Alvarez	11-1
8	Michigan	11-2	Lloyd Carr	11-1
9	Auburn	11-2	Tommy Tuberville	10-2
10	West Virginia	11-2	Rich Rodriguez	10-2
11	Oklahoma	11-3	Bob Stoops	11-2
12	Rutgers	11-2	Greg Schiano	10-2
13	Texas	10-3	Mack Brown	9-3
14	California	10-3	Jeff Tedford	9-3
15	Arkansas	10-4	Houston Nutt	10-3
16	Brigham Young	11-2	Bronco Mendenhall	10-2
17	Notre Dame	10-3	Charlie Weis	10-2
18	Wake Forest	11-3	Jim Grobe	11-2
19	Virginia Tech	10-3	Frank Beamer	10-2
20	Boston College	10-3	Tom O'Brien	9-3
21	Oregon St.	10-4	Mike Riley	9-4
22	TCU	11-2	Gary Patterson	10-2
23	Georgia	9-4	Mark Richt	8-4
24	Penn St.	9-4	Joe Paterno	8-4
25	Tennessee	9-4	Philip Fulmer	9-3

Key Bowl Games

Rankings below reflect final regular season poll, taken Dec. 3. **BCS**–#2 Florida over #1 Ohio St., 41-14; **Sugar**–#4 LSU over #11 Notre Dame, 41-14; **Fiesta**–#9 Boise St. over #7 Oklahoma, 43-42 OT; **Orange**– #5 Louisville over #15 Wake Forest, 24-13; **Rose**–#8 USC over #3 Michigan, 32-18; **Capital One**–#6 Wisconsin over #12 Arkansas, 17-14.

2007

		After Bowls	Head Coach	Regular Season
1	LSU	12-2	Les Miles	11-2
2	Georgia	11-2	Mark Richt	10-2
3	USC	11-2	Pete Carroll	10-2
4	Missouri	12-2	Gary Pinkel	11-2
5	Ohio St.	11-2	Jim Tressel	11-1
6	West Virginia	11-2	Rich Rodriguez (10-2) & Bill Stewart (1-0)	10-2
7	Kansas	12-1	Mark Mangino	11-1
8	Oklahoma	11-3	Bob Stoops	10-3
9	Virginia Tech	11-3	Frank Beamer	11-3
10	Texas	10-3	Mack Brown	9-3
	Boston College	11-3	Jeff Jagodzinski	10-3
12	Tennessee	10-4	Philip Fulmer	9-4
13	Florida	9-4	Urban Meyer	9-3
14	Brigham Young	11-2	Bronco Mendenhall	10-2
15	Auburn	9-4	Tommy Tuberville	8-4
16	Arizona St.	10-3	Dennis Erickson	10-2
17	Cincinnati	10-3	Brian Kelly	9-2
18	Michigan	9-4	Lloyd Carr	8-4
19	Hawaii	12-1	June Jones	12-0
20	Illinois	9-4	Ron Zook	9-3
21	Clemson	9-4	Tommy Bowden	8-4
22	Texas Tech	9-4	Mike Leach	9-3
23	Oregon	9-4	Mike Bellotti	8-4
24	Wisconsin	9-4	Bret Bielema	9-3
25	Oregon St.	9-4	Mike Riley	8-4

Key Bowl Games

Rankings below reflect final regular season poll, taken Dec. 3. **BCS**–#2 LSU over #1 Ohio St., 38-24; **Fiesta**–#11 West Va. over #3 Oklahoma, 48-28; **Sugar**–#4 Georgia over #10 Hawaii, 41-10; **Orange**– #8 Kansas over #5 Va. Tech, 24-21; **Rose**–#6 USC over #13 Illinois, 49-17; **Capital One**– Michigan over #9 Florida, 41-35.

All-Time BCS Top 20

The composite BCS Top 20 from the 1998 season through the 2007 season, based on the final rankings of each year. The original BCS rankings listed 15 teams from 1998-2002 before expanding the rankings to a Top 25 in 2003. Team point totals are based on 20 points for all 1st place finishes, 19 for each 2nd, etc. Also listed are the number of times each team has been ranked first, in the final Top 10 and Top 20.

		Pts	No.1	Top 10	Top 20
1	Oklahoma	111	2	6	7
2	Ohio St	109	1	5	5
3	USC	105	2	6	6
4	Texas	95	0	5	9
5	Florida	92	2	5	8
6	Miami-FL	90	2	5	6
7	Florida St	84	1	4	6
8	Virginia Tech	83	0	5	6
9	LSU	82	0	2	6
10	Tennessee	74	1	4	6
11	Georgia	71	0	4	5
12	Kansas St.	69	0	5	5
13	Nebraska	61	0	3	5
14	Wisconsin	50	0	3	6
15	Michigan	49	0	2	5
16	Notre Dame	47	0	2	4
17	Oregon	44	0	3	3
18	Auburn	42	0	3	3
19	Penn St	37	0	1	3
20	Iowa	33	0	1	3

Bowl Games

From Jan. 1, 1902 through Jan. 7, 2008. Please note that the Bowl selection process is now dominated by the Bowl Championship Series (which includes the Fiesta, Orange, Rose and Sugar bowls) and the following non-BCS bowls' so called "automatic berths" are contingent upon several factors, including the leftovers from the BCS, Notre Dame's record and the record of their designated choices.

Rose Bowl

City: Pasadena, Calif. **Stadium:** Rose Bowl. **Capacity:** 102,083. **Playing surface:** Grass. **First game:** Jan. 1, 1902. **Playing sites:** Tournament Park (1902, 1916-22), Rose Bowl (1923-41 and since 1943) and Duke Stadium in Durham, N.C. (1942, due to wartime restrictions following Japan's attack at Pearl Harbor on Dec. 7, 1941). **Corporate sponsors:** AT&T (1998-2002), Sony Playstation 2 (2003) and Citi (2004).

Automatic berths: Pacific Coast Conference champion vs. opponent selected by PCC (1924-45 seasons); Big Ten champion vs. Pac-10 champion (1946-97); Bowl Championship Series: Big Ten champion vs. Pac-10 champion, if available (1998-2000, 2002-05 seasons) and #1 vs. #2 in Jan. 2002 and Jan. 2006.

Multiple wins: USC (23); Michigan (8); Washington (7); Ohio St. (6); Stanford and UCLA (5); Alabama (4); Illinois, Michigan St. and Wisconsin (3); California, Iowa and Texas (2).

Year		Year		Year	
1902*	Michigan 49, Stanford 0	1947	Illinois 45, UCLA 14	1979	USC 17, Michigan 10
1916	Washington St. 14, Brown 0	1948	Michigan 49, USC 0	1980	USC 17, Ohio St. 16
1917	Oregon 14, Penn 0	1949	Northwestern 20, California 14	1981	Michigan 23, Washington 6
1918	Mare Island 19, Camp Lewis 7	1950	Ohio St. 17, California 14	1982	Washington 28, Iowa 0
1919	Great Lakes 17, Mare Island 0	1951	Michigan 14, California 6	1983	UCLA 24, Michigan 14
1920	Harvard 7, Oregon 6	1952	Illinois 40, Stanford 7	1984	UCLA 45, Illinois 9
1921	California 28, Ohio St. 0	1953	USC 7, Wisconsin 0	1985	USC 20, Ohio St. 17
1922	0-0, California vs Wash. & Jeff.	1954	Michigan St. 28, UCLA 20	1986	UCLA 45, Iowa 28
1923	USC 14, Penn St. 3	1955	Ohio St. 20, USC 7	1987	Arizona St. 22, Michigan 15
1924	14-14, Navy vs Washington	1956	Michigan St. 17, UCLA 14	1988	Michigan St. 20, USC 17
1925	Notre Dame 27, Stanford 10	1957	Iowa 35, Oregon St. 19	1989	Michigan 22, USC 14
1926	Alabama 20, Washington 19	1958	Ohio St. 10, Oregon 7	1990	USC 17, Michigan 10
1927	7-7, Alabama vs Stanford	1959	Iowa 38, California 12	1991	Washington 46, Iowa 34
1928	Stanford 7, Pittsburgh 6	1960	Washington 44, Wisconsin 8	1992	Washington 34, Michigan 14
1929	Georgia Tech 8, California 7	1961	Washington 17, Minnesota 7	1993	Michigan 38, Washington 31
1930	USC 47, Pittsburgh 14	1962	Minnesota 21, UCLA 3	1994	Wisconsin 21, UCLA 16
1931	Alabama 24, Washington St. 0	1963	USC 42, Wisconsin 37	1995	Penn St. 38, Oregon 20
1932	USC 21, Tulane 12	1964	Illinois 17, Washington 7	1996	USC 41, Northwestern 32
1933	USC 35, Pittsburgh 0	1965	Michigan 34, Oregon St. 7	1997	Ohio St. 20, Arizona St. 17
1934	Columbia 7, Stanford 0	1966	UCLA 14, Michigan St. 12	1998	Michigan 21, Washington St. 16
1935	Alabama 29, Stanford 13	1967	Purdue 14, USC 13	1999	Wisconsin 38, UCLA 31
1936	Stanford 7, SMU 0	1968	USC 14, Indiana 3	2000	Wisconsin 17, Stanford 9
1937	Pittsburgh 21, Washington 0	1969	Ohio St. 27, USC 16	2001	Washington 34, Purdue 24
1938	California 13, Alabama 0	1970	USC 10, Michigan 3	2002	Miami-FL 37, Nebraska 14
1939	USC 7, Duke 3	1971	Stanford 27, Ohio St. 17	2003	Oklahoma 34, Washington St. 14
1940	USC 14, Tennessee 0	1972	Stanford 13, Michigan 12	2004	USC 28, Michigan 14
1941	Stanford 21, Nebraska 13	1973	USC 42, Ohio St. 17	2005	Texas 38, Michigan 37
1942	Oregon St. 20, Duke 16	1974	Ohio St. 42, USC 21	2006	Texas 41, USC 38
1943	Georgia 9, UCLA 0	1975	USC 18, Ohio St. 17	2007	USC 32, Michigan 18
1944	USC 29, Washington 0	1976	UCLA 23, Ohio St. 10	2008	USC 49, Illinois 17
1945	USC 25, Tennessee 0	1977	USC 14, Michigan 6		* January game since 1902.
1946	Alabama 34, USC 14	1978	Washington 27, Michigan 20		

Fiesta Bowl

City: Glendale, Ariz. **Stadium:** University of Phoenix. **Capacity:** 73,000. **Playing surface:** Grass. **First game:** Dec. 27, 1971. **Playing site:** Sun Devil Stadium (since 1971). **Corporate title sponsors:** Sunkist Citrus Growers (1986-91), IBM OS/2 (1993-95) and Frito-Lay Tostitos chips (since 1996).

Automatic berths: Western Athletic Conference champion vs. at-large opponent (1971-79 seasons); Two of first five picks from 8-team Bowl Coalition pool (1992-94). Bowl Alliance (#1 vs. #2 on Jan. 2, 1996; #3 vs. #5 on Jan. 1, 1997; and #4 vs. #6 on Dec. 31, 1997); Big 12 champion vs. next best team in pool (New Bowl Alliance 1995-1997 seasons); Bowl Championship Series: #1 vs. #2 on Jan. 4, 1999, Jan., 2003 and Jan. 2007 and Big 12 champion, if available, vs. at-large (1999-2001 and 2003-05 seasons).

Multiple wins: Penn St. (6); Arizona St. (5); Ohio St. (4); Florida St. and Nebraska (2).

Year		Year		Year	
1971†	Arizona St. 45, Florida St. 38	1985	UCLA 39, Miami-FL 37	1997†	Kansas St. 35, Syracuse 18
1972	Arizona St. 49, Missouri 35	1986	Michigan 27, Nebraska 23	1999	Tennessee 23, Florida St. 16
1973	Arizona St. 28, Pittsburgh 7	1987	Penn St. 14, Miami-FL 10	2000	Nebraska 31, Tennessee 21
1974	Oklahoma 16, BYU 6	1988	Florida St. 31, Nebraska 28	2001	Oregon St. 41, Notre Dame 9
1975	Arizona St. 17, Nebraska 14	1989	Notre Dame 34, West Va. 21	2002	Oregon 38, Colorado 16
1976	Oklahoma 41, Wyoming 7	1990	Florida St. 41, Nebraska 17	2003	Ohio St. 31, Miami-FL 24 (2OT)
1977	Penn St. 42, Arizona St. 30	1991	Louisville 34, Alabama 7	2004	Ohio St. 35, Kansas St. 28
1978	10-10, Arkansas vs UCLA	1992	Penn St. 42, Tennessee 17	2005	Utah 35, Pittsburgh 7
1979	Pittsburgh 16, Arizona 10	1993	Syracuse 26, Colorado 22	2006	Ohio St. 34, Notre Dame 20
1980	Penn St. 31, Ohio St. 19	1994	Arizona 29, Miami-FL 0	2007	Boise St. 43, Oklahoma 42 (OT)
1982*	Penn St. 26, USC 10	1995	Colorado 41, Notre Dame 24	2008	West Va. 48, Oklahoma 28
1983	Arizona St. 32, Oklahoma 21	1996	Nebraska 62, Florida 24	†December game from 1971-80 and in
1984	Ohio St. 28, Pittsburgh 23	1997	Penn St. 38, Texas 15	'97. *January game since 1982.

Sugar Bowl

City: Atlanta, Ga. **Stadium:** Georgia Dome. **Capacity:** 71,228. **Playing surface:** Turf. **First game:** Jan. 1, 1935. **Playing sites:** Tulane Stadium (1935-74), Louisiana Superdome (1975-2005), Georgia Dome (2006). **Corporate title sponsors:** USF&G Financial Services (1987-95), Nokia (1995-2006) and Allstate (since 2006).

Automatic berths: SEC champion vs. at-large opponent (1976-91 seasons); SEC champion vs. one of first five picks from 8-team Bowl Coalition pool (1992-94 seasons); #4 vs. #6 on Dec. 31, 1995; #1 vs. #2 on Jan. 2, 1997; and #3 vs. #5 on Jan. 1, 1998; Bowl Championship Series: SEC champion, if available, vs. at-large (1998-99, 2000-02, 2004-05 seasons) and #1 vs. #2 on Jan. 4, 2000 and Jan. 2004.

Multiple wins: Alabama (8); LSU (6); Mississippi (5); Florida St., Georgia, Georgia Tech, Oklahoma and Tennessee (4); Nebraska (3); Auburn, Florida, Miami-FL, Notre Dame, Pittsburgh, Santa Clara and TCU (2).

Year		Year		Year	
1935*	Tulane 20, Temple 14	1961	Mississippi 14, Rice 6	1987	Nebraska 30, LSU 15
1936	TCU 3, LSU 2	1962	Alabama 10, Arkansas 3	1988	16-16, Syracuse vs Auburn
1937	Santa Clara 21, LSU 14	1963	Mississippi 17, Arkansas 13	1989	Florida St. 13, Auburn 7
1938	Santa Clara 6, LSU 0	1964	Alabama 12, Mississippi 7	1990	Miami-FL 33, Alabama 25
1939	TCU 15, Carnegie Tech 7	1965	LSU 13, Syracuse 10	1991	Tennessee 23, Virginia 22
1940	Texas A&M 14, Tulane 13	1966	Missouri 20, Florida 18	1992	Notre Dame 39, Florida 28
1941	Boston College 19, Tennessee 13	1967	Alabama 34, Nebraska 7	1993	Alabama 34, Miami-FL 13
1942	Fordham 2, Missouri 0	1968	LSU 20, Wyoming 13	1994	Florida 41, West Va. 7
1943	Tennessee 14, Tulsa 7	1969	Arkansas 16, Georgia 2	1995	Florida St. 23, Florida 17
1944	Georgia Tech 20, Tulsa 18	1970	Mississippi 27, Arkansas 22	1995†	Va. Tech 28, Texas 10
1945	Duke 29, Alabama 26	1971	Tennessee 34, Air Force 13	1997	Florida 52, Florida St. 20
1946	Okla. A&M 33, St. Mary's 13	1972	Oklahoma 40, Auburn 22	1998	Florida St. 31, Ohio St. 14
1947	Georgia 20, N. Carolina 10	1972†	Oklahoma 14, Penn St. 0	1999	Ohio St. 24, Texas A&M 14
1948	Texas 27, Alabama 7	1973	Notre Dame 24, Alabama 23	2000	Florida St. 46, Va. Tech 29
1949	Oklahoma 14, N. Carolina 6	1974	Nebraska 13, Florida 10	2001	Miami-FL 37, Florida 20
1950	Oklahoma 35, LSU 0	1975	Alabama 13, Penn St. 6	2002	LSU 47, Illinois 34
1951	Kentucky 13, Oklahoma 7	1977*	Pittsburgh 27, Georgia 3	2003	Georgia 26, Florida St. 13
1952	Maryland 28, Tennessee 13	1978	Alabama 35, Ohio St. 6	2004	LSU 21, Oklahoma 14
1953	Georgia Tech 24, Mississippi 7	1979	Alabama 14, Penn St. 7	2005	Auburn 16, Va. Tech 13
1954	Georgia Tech 42, West Va. 19	1980	Alabama 24, Arkansas 9	2006	West Virginia 38, Georgia 35
1955	Navy 21, Mississippi 0	1981	Georgia 17, Notre Dame 10	2007	LSU 41, Notre Dame 14
1956	Georgia Tech 7, Pittsburgh 0	1982	Pittsburgh 24, Georgia 20	2008	Georgia 41, Hawaii 10
1957	Baylor 13, Tennessee 7	1983	Penn St. 27, Georgia 23		
1958	Mississippi 39, Texas 7	1984	Auburn 9, Michigan 7		* January game from 1935-72 and
1959	LSU 7, Clemson 0	1985	Nebraska 28, LSU 10		since 1977 (except in 1995).
1960	Mississippi 21, LSU 0	1986	Tennessee 35, Miami-FL 7		† Game played on Dec. 31 from
					1972-75 and in 1995.

Orange Bowl

City: Miami, Fla. **Stadium:** Dolphin. **Capacity:** 74,916. **Playing surface:** Grass. **First game:** Jan. 1, 1935. **Playing sites:** Orange Bowl (1935-95); Dolphin Stadium (since 1996). Dolphin Stadium was originally named Joe Robbie Stadium then was named Pro Player Stadium (1996-2004). **Corporate title sponsor:** Federal Express (since 1989).

Automatic berths: Big 8 champion vs. Atlantic Coast Conference champion (1953-57 seasons); Big 8 champion vs. at-large opponent (1958-63 seasons and 1975-91 seasons); Big 8 champion vs. one of first five picks from 8-team Bowl Coalition pool (1992-94 seasons); #3 vs. #5 on Jan. 1, 1996; #4 vs. #6 on Dec. 31, 1996; and #1 vs. #2 on Jan. 2, 1998 (New Bowl Alliance 1995-97 seasons); Bowl Championship Series: Big East or ACC champion, if available, vs. at-large (1998-99, 2001-03, 2005 seasons) and #1 vs. #2 Jan. 3, 2001 and Jan. 2005.

Multiple wins: Oklahoma (12); Nebraska (8); Miami-FL (6); Alabama and Penn St. (4); Florida, Florida State and Georgia Tech (3); Clemson, Colorado, Georgia, LSU, Notre Dame, Texas and USC (2).

Year		Year		Year	
1935*	Bucknell 26, Miami-FL 0	1955	Duke 34, Nebraska 7	1975	Notre Dame 13, Alabama 11
1936	Catholic U. 20, Mississippi 19	1956	Oklahoma 20, Maryland 6	1976	Oklahoma 14, Michigan 6
1937	Duquesne 13, Mississippi St. 12	1957	Colorado 27, Clemson 21	1977	Ohio St. 27, Colorado 10
1938	Auburn 6, Michigan St. 0	1958	Oklahoma 48, Duke 21	1978	Arkansas 31, Oklahoma 6
1939	Tennessee 17, Oklahoma 0	1959	Oklahoma 21, Syracuse 6	1979	Oklahoma 31, Nebraska 24
1940	Georgia Tech 21, Missouri 7	1960	Georgia 14, Missouri 0	1980	Oklahoma 24, Florida St. 7
1941	Mississippi St. 14, Georgetown 7	1961	Missouri 21, Navy 14	1981	Oklahoma 18, Florida St. 17
1942	Georgia 40, TCU 26	1962	LSU 25, Colorado 7	1982	Clemson 22, Nebraska 15
1943	Alabama 37, Boston College 21	1963	Alabama 17, Oklahoma 0	1983	Nebraska 21, LSU 20
1944	LSU 19, Texas A&M 14	1964	Nebraska 13, Auburn 7	1984	Miami-FL 31, Nebraska 30
1945	Tulsa 26, Georgia Tech 12	1965†	Texas 21, Alabama 17	1985	Washington 28, Oklahoma 17
1946	Miami-FL 13, Holy Cross 6	1966	Alabama 39, Nebraska 28	1986	Oklahoma 25, Penn St. 10
1947	Rice 8, Tennessee 0	1967	Florida 27, Georgia Tech 12	1987	Oklahoma 42, Arkansas 8
1948	Georgia Tech 20, Kansas 14	1968	Oklahoma 26, Tennessee 24	1988	Miami-FL 20, Oklahoma 14
1949	Texas 41, Georgia 28	1969	Penn St. 15, Kansas 14	1989	Miami-FL 23, Nebraska 3
1950	Santa Clara 21, Kentucky 13	1970	Penn St. 10, Missouri 3	1990	Notre Dame, 21, Colorado 6
1951	Clemson 15, Miami-FL 14	1971	Nebraska 17, LSU 12	1991	Colorado 10, Notre Dame 9
1952	Georgia Tech 17, Baylor 14	1972	Nebraska 38, Alabama 6	1992	Miami-FL 22, Nebraska 0
1953	Alabama 61, Syracuse 6	1973	Nebraska 40, Notre Dame 6	1993	Florida St. 27, Nebraska 14
1954	Oklahoma 7, Maryland 0	1974	Penn St. 16, LSU 9	1994	Florida St. 18, Nebraska 16

Bowl Games (Cont.)
Orange Bowl (Cont.)

Year		Year		Year	
1995	Nebraska 24, Miami-FL 17	2001	Oklahoma 13, Florida St. 2	2007	Louisville 24, Wake Forest 13
1996	Florida St. 31, Notre Dame 26	2002	Florida 56, Maryland 23	2008	Kansas 24, Virginia Tech 21
1996**	Nebraska 41, Virginia Tech 21	2003	USC 38, Iowa 17	*	January game 1935-1996 and since
1998*	Nebraska 42, Tennessee 17	2004	Miami-FL 16, Florida St. 14		'98.
1999	Florida 31, Syracuse 10	2005	USC 55, Oklahoma 19	**	December game in 1996
2000	Michigan 35, Alabama 34	2006	Penn St. 26, Florida St. 23 3OT	†	Night game since 1965.

Cotton Bowl

City: Dallas, Tex. **Stadium:** Cotton Bowl. **Capacity:** 71,252. **Playing surface:** Grass. **First game:** Jan 1, 1937. **Playing sites:** Fair Park Stadium (1937) and Cotton Bowl (since 1938). **Corporate title sponsor:** Mobil Corporation (1988-95), AT&T Communications, previously Southwestern Bell and SBC Communications (since 1997).

Automatic berths: SWC champion vs. at-large opponent (1941-91 seasons); SWC champion vs. one of first five picks from 8-team Bowl Coalition pool (1992-1994 seasons); second pick from Big 12 vs. first choice of WAC champion or second pick from Pac-10 (1995-97 seasons); Big 12 vs. SEC (since 1998).

Multiple wins: Texas (11); Notre Dame (5); Texas A&M (4); Alabama, Arkansas, Rice and Tennessee (3); Georgia, Houston, LSU, Mississippi, Penn St., SMU, TCU and UCLA (2).

Year		Year		Year	
1937*	TCU 16, Marquette 6	1962	Texas 12, Mississippi 7	1987	Ohio St. 28, Texas A&M 12
1938	Rice 28, Colorado 14	1963	LSU 13, Texas 0	1988	Texas A&M 35, Notre Dame 10
1939	St. Mary's 20, Texas Tech 13	1964	Texas 28, Navy 6	1989	UCLA 17, Arkansas 3
1940	Clemson 6, Boston College 3	1965	Arkansas 10, Nebraska 7	1990	Tennessee 31, Arkansas 27
1941	Texas A&M 13, Fordham 12	1966	LSU 14, Arkansas 7	1991	Miami-FL 46, Texas 3
1942	Alabama 29, Texas A&M 21	1966†	Georgia 24, SMU 9	1992	Florida St. 10, Texas A&M 2
1943	Texas 14, Georgia Tech 7	1968*	Texas A&M 20, Alabama 16	1993	Notre Dame 28, Texas A&M 3
1944	7-7, Texas vs Randolph Field	1969	Texas 36, Tennessee 13	1994	Notre Dame 24, Texas A&M 21
1945	Oklahoma A&M 34, TCU 0	1970	Texas 21, Notre Dame 17	1995	USC 55, Texas Tech 14
1946	Texas 40, Missouri 27	1971	Notre Dame 24, Texas 11	1996	Colorado 38, Oregon 6
1947	0-0, Arkansas vs LSU	1972	Penn St. 30, Texas 6	1997	BYU 19, Kansas St. 15
1948	13-13, SMU vs Penn St.	1973	Texas 17, Alabama 13	1998	UCLA 29, Texas A&M 23
1949	SMU 21, Oregon 13	1974	Nebraska 19, Texas 3	1999	Texas 38, Mississippi St. 11
1950	Rice 27, N. Carolina 13	1975	Penn St. 41, Baylor 20	2000	Arkansas 27, Texas 6
1951	Tennessee 20, Texas 14	1976	Arkansas 31, Georgia 10	2001	Kansas St. 35, Tennessee 21
1952	Kentucky 20, TCU 7	1977	Houston 30, Maryland 21	2002	Oklahoma 10, Arkansas 3
1953	Texas 16, Tennessee 0	1978	Notre Dame 38, Texas 10	2003	Texas 35, LSU 20
1954	Rice 28, Alabama 6	1979	Notre Dame 35, Houston 34	2004	Mississippi 31, Oklahoma St. 28
1955	Georgia Tech 14, Arkansas 6	1980	Houston 17, Nebraska 14	2005	Tennessee 38, Texas A&M 7
1956	Mississippi 14, TCU 13	1981	Alabama 30, Baylor 2	2006	Alabama 13, Texas Tech 10
1957	TCU 28, Syracuse 27	1982	Texas 14, Alabama 12	2007	Auburn 17, Nebraska 14
1958	Navy 20, Rice 7	1983	SMU 7, Pittsburgh 3	2008	Missouri 38, Arkansas 7
1959	0-0, TCU vs Air Force	1984	Georgia 10, Texas 9		
1960	Syracuse 23, Texas 14	1985	Boston College 45, Houston 28	*	January game from 1937-66 and
1961	Duke 7, Arkansas 6	1986	Texas A&M 36, Auburn 16		since 1968.
				†	Game played on Dec. 31, 1966.

Capital One Bowl

City: Orlando, Fla. **Stadium:** Florida Citrus Bowl. **Capacity:** 70,188. **Playing surface:** Grass. **First game:** Jan. 1, 1947. **Name change:** Tangerine Bowl (1947-82), Florida Citrus Bowl (1983-2002) and Capital One Bowl (since 2003). **Playing sites:** Tangerine Bowl (1947-72, 1974-82), Florida Field in Gainesville (1973), Orlando Stadium (1983-85) and Florida Citrus Bowl (since 1986). The Tangerine Bowl, Orlando Stadium and Florida Citrus Bowl are all the same stadium. **Corporate title sponsors:** Florida Department of Citrus (1983-2002), CompUSA (1992-99), Ourhouse.com (2000) and Capital One (since 2001).

Automatic berths: Championship game of Atlantic Coast Regional Conference (1964-67 seasons); Mid-American Conference champion vs. Southern Conference champion (1968-71 seasons); ACC champion vs. at-large opponent (1988-91 seasons); second pick from SEC, if available, vs. second pick from Big 10, if available (since 1992 season).

Multiple wins: Tennessee (4); Auburn, East Texas St., Miami-OH, Michigan and Toledo (3); Catawba, Clemson, East Carolina, Florida, Georgia and Wisconsin (2).

Year		Year		Year	
1947*	Catawba 31, Maryville 6	1958†	E. Texas St. 26, Mo. Valley 7	1970	Toledo 40, Wm. & Mary 12
1948	Catawba 7, Marshall 0	1960*	Mid. Tenn. 21, Presbyterian 12	1971	Toledo 28, Richmond 3
1949	21-21, Murray St. vs Sul Ross St.	1960†	Citadel 27, Tenn. Tech 0	1972	Tampa 21, Kent St. 18
1950	St. Vincent 7, Emory & Henry 6	1961	Lamar 21, Middle Tenn. 14	1973	Miami-OH 16, Florida 7
1951	M. Harvey 35, Emory & Henry 14	1962	Houston 49, Miami-OH 21	1974	Miami-OH 21, Georgia 10
1952	Stetson 35, Arkansas St. 20	1963	Western Ky. 27, Coast Guard 0	1975	Miami-OH 20, S. Carolina 7
1953	E. Texas St. 33, Tenn. Tech 0	1964	E. Carolina 14, Massachusetts 13	1976	Oklahoma 49, BYU 21
1954	7-7, E. Texas St. vs Arkansas St.	1965	E. Carolina 31, Maine 0	1977	Florida St. 40, Texas Tech 17
1955	Neb.-Omaha 7, Eastern Ky. 6	1966	Morgan St. 14, West Chester 6	1978	N.C. State 30, Pittsburgh 17
1956	6-6, Juniata vs Missouri Valley	1967	Tenn-Martin 25, West Chester 8	1979	LSU 34, Wake Forest 17
1957	W. Texas St. 20, So. Miss. 13	1968	Richmond 49, Ohio U. 42	1980	Florida 35, Maryland 20
1958	E. Texas St. 10, So. Miss. 9	1969	Toledo 56, Davidson 33	1981	Missouri 19, Southern Miss. 17

Year		Year		Year	
1982	Auburn 33, Boston College 26	1993	Georgia 21, Ohio St. 14	2003	Auburn 13, Penn St. 9
1983	Tennessee 30, Maryland 23	1994	Penn St. 31, Tennessee 13	2004	Georgia 34, Purdue 27 OT
1984	17-17, Florida St. vs Georgia	1995	Alabama 24, Ohio St. 17	2005	Iowa 30, LSU 25
1985	Ohio St. 10, BYU 7	1996	Tennessee 20, Ohio St. 14	2006	Wisconsin 24, Auburn 10
1987*	Auburn 16, USC 7	1997	Tennessee 48, Northwestern 28	2007	Wisconsin 17, Arkansas 14
1988	Clemson 35, Penn St. 10	1998	Florida 21, Penn St. 6	2008	Michigan 41, Florida 35
1989	Clemson 13, Oklahoma 6	1999	Michigan 45, Arkansas 31		
1990	Illinois 31, Virginia 21	2000	Michigan St. 37, Florida 34	*January game from 1947-58, in	
1991	Georgia Tech 45, Nebraska 21	2001	Michigan 31, Auburn 28	1960 and since 1987.	
1992	California 37, Clemson 13	2002	Tennessee 45, Michigan 17	†December game in 1958, 1960-85.	

Gator Bowl

City: Jacksonville, Fla. **Stadium:** Jacksonville Municipal. **Capacity:** 73,000. **Playing surface:** Grass. **First game:** Jan. 1, 1946. **Playing sites:** Gator Bowl (1946-93), Florida Field in Gainesville (1994) and Jacksonville Municipal Stadium (since 1995). Jacksonville Municipal Stadium was formerly named ALLTEL Stadium (1997-2006). **Corporate title sponsors:** Mazda Motors of America, Inc. (1986-91), Outback Steakhouse, Inc. (1992-94) and Toyota Motor Co. (since 1995).

   Automatic berths: Third pick from SEC vs. sixth pick from 8-team Bowl Coalition pool (1992-94 seasons); second pick from ACC, if available, vs. second pick from Big East or Notre Dame, if available (since 1995 season).

   Multiple wins: Florida (6); Florida St. and North Carolina (5); Auburn, Clemson (4); Georgia Tech, Maryland, Tennessee and Texas Tech (3); Georgia, Miami-FL, Oklahoma, Pittsburgh and Virginia Tech (2).

Year		Year		Year	
1946*	Wake Forest 26, S. Carolina 14	1968	Missouri 35, Alabama 10	1991†	Oklahoma 48, Virginia 14
1947	Oklahoma 34, N.C. State 13	1969	Florida 14, Tennessee 13	1992	Florida 27, N.C. State 10
1948	20-20, Maryland vs Georgia	1971*	Auburn 35, Mississippi 28	1993	Alabama 24, N. Carolina 10
1949	Clemson 24, Missouri 23	1971†	Georgia 7, N. Carolina 3	1994	Tennessee 45, Va. Tech 23
1950	Maryland 20, Missouri 7	1972	Auburn 24, Colorado 3	1996*	Syracuse 41, Clemson 0
1951	Wyoming 20, Wash. & Lee 7	1973	Texas Tech 28, Tennessee 19	1997	N. Carolina 20, West Va. 13
1952	Miami-FL 14, Clemson 0	1974	Auburn 27, Texas 3	1998	N. Carolina 42, Va. Tech 3
1953	Florida 14, Tulsa 13	1975	Maryland 13, Florida 0	1999	Ga. Tech 35, Notre Dame 28
1954	Texas Tech 35, Auburn 13	1976	Notre Dame 20, Penn St. 9	2000	Miami-FL 28, Ga. Tech 13
1954†	Auburn 33, Baylor 13	1977	Pittsburgh 34, Clemson 3	2001	Va. Tech 41, Clemson 20
1955	Vanderbilt 25, Auburn 13	1978	Clemson 17, Ohio St. 15	2002	Florida St. 30, Va. Tech 17
1956	Georgia Tech 21, Pittsburgh 14	1979	N. Carolina 17, Michigan 15	2003	N.C. State 28, Notre Dame 6
1957	Tennessee 3, Texas A&M 0	1980	Pittsburgh 37, S. Carolina 9	2004	Maryland 41, West Va. 7
1958	Mississippi 7, Florida 3	1981	N. Carolina 31, Arkansas 27	2005	Florida St. 30, West Va. 18
1960*	Arkansas 14, Georgia Tech 7	1982	Florida St. 31, West Va. 12	2006	Va. Tech 35, Louisville 24
1960†	Florida 13, Baylor 12	1983	Florida 14, Iowa 6	2007	West Virginia 38, Ga. Tech 35
1961	Penn St. 30, Georgia Tech 15	1984	Oklahoma St. 21, S. Carolina 14	2008	Texas Tech 31, Virginia 28
1962	Florida 17, Penn St. 7	1985	Florida St. 34, Oklahoma St. 23	* January game from 1946-54, 1960,	
1963	N. Carolina 35, Air Force 0	1986	Clemson 27, Stanford 21	1965, 1971, 1989, 1991 and since	
1965*	Florida St. 36, Oklahoma 19	1987	LSU 30, S. Carolina 13	1996.	
1965†	Georgia Tech 31, Texas Tech 21	1989*	Georgia 34, Michigan St. 27	† December game from 1954-58, 1960-	
1966	Tennessee 18, Syracuse 12	1989†	Clemson 27, West Va. 7	63, 1965-69, 1971-87, 1989 and	
1967	17-17, Florida St. vs Penn St.	1991*	Michigan 35, Mississippi 3	1991-94.	

Holiday Bowl

City: San Diego, Calif. **Stadium:** Qualcomm. **Capacity:** 71,000. **Playing surface:** Grass. **First game:** Dec. 22, 1978. **Playing site:** San Diego/Jack Murphy Stadium (since 1978). Name changed to Qualcomm Stadium in 1997. **Corporate title sponsors:** SeaWorld (1986-90), Thrifty Car Rental (1991-94), Chrysler-Plymouth Division of Chrysler Corp. (1995-97), U.S. Filter/Culligan Water Tech. (1998-2001) and Pacific Life Insurance Co. (since 2002).

   Automatic berths: WAC champion vs. at-large opponent (1978-84, 1986-90 seasons); WAC champ vs. second pick from Big 10 (1991 season); WAC champ vs. third pick from Big 10 (1992-94 seasons); choice of WAC champion, if available, or second pick from Pac-10, if available vs. third pick from Big 12, if available (1995-99); second pick from Pac-10 vs. third pick from Big 12 (since 2000).

   Multiple wins: BYU (4); Kansas St. (3) Iowa, Ohio St. and Texas (2).

Year		Year		Year	
1978†	Navy 23, BYU 16	1989	Penn St. 50, BYU 39	2000	Oregon 35, Texas 30
1979	Indiana 38, BYU 37	1990	Texas A&M 65, BYU 14	2001	Texas 47, Washington 43
1980	BYU 46, SMU 45	1991	13-13, Iowa vs BYU	2002	Kansas St. 34, Arizona St. 27
1981	BYU 38, Washington St. 36	1992	Hawaii 27, Illinois 17	2003	Washington St. 28, Texas 20
1982	Ohio St. 47, BYU 17	1993	Ohio St. 28, BYU 21	2004	Texas Tech 45, California 31
1983	BYU 21, Missouri 17	1994	Michigan 24, Colo. St. 14	2005	Oklahoma 17, Oregon 14
1984	BYU 24, Michigan 17	1995	Kansas St. 54, Colorado St. 21	2006	California 45, Texas A&M 10
1985	Arkansas 18, Arizona St. 17	1996	Colorado 33, Washington 21	2007	Texas 52, Arizona St. 34
1986	Iowa 39, San Diego St. 38	1997	Colorado St. 35, Missouri 24		
1987	Iowa 20, Wyoming 19	1998	Arizona 23, Nebraska 20	†December game since 1978.	
1988	Oklahoma St. 62, Wyoming 14	1999	Kansas St. 24, Washington 20		

Bowl Games (Cont.)
Chick-fil-A Bowl

City: Atlanta, Ga. **Stadium:** Georgia Dome. **Capacity:** 71,228. **Playing surface:** Turf. **First game:** Dec. 30, 1968
Playing sites: Grant Field (1968-70), Atlanta-Fulton County Stadium (1971-92) and Georgia Dome (since 1993). **Name change:** Peach Bowl (1968-2005), Chick-fil-A Bowl (since 2006); **Corporate title sponsor:** Chick-fil-A (since 1998).
    Automatic berths: Third pick from ACC vs. at-large opponent (1992 season); third pick from ACC vs. fourth pick from SEC (1993-94 seasons); third pick from ACC, if available, vs. fourth pick from SEC, if available (since 1995 season).
    Multiple wins: N.C. State (4); LSU, Georgia and West Virginia (3); Auburn, Miami-FL, North Carolina and Virginia (2)

Year		Year		Year	
1968†	LSU 31, Florida St. 27	1984	Virginia 27, Purdue 24	2000	LSU 28, Ga. Tech 14
1969	West Va. 14, S. Carolina 3	1985	Army 31, Illinois 29	2001	N. Carolina 16, Auburn 10
1970	Arizona St. 48, N. Carolina 26	1986	Va. Tech 25, N.C. State 24	2002	Maryland 30, Tennessee 3
1971	Mississippi 41, Georgia Tech 18	1988*	Tennessee 27, Indiana 22	2004*	Clemson 27, Tennessee 14
1972	N.C. State 49, West Va. 13	1988†	N.C. State 28, Iowa 23	2004†	Miami-FL 27, Florida 10
1973	Georgia 17, Maryland 16	1989	Syracuse 19, Georgia 18	2005	LSU 40, Miami-FL 3
1974	6-6, Vanderbilt vs Texas Tech	1990	Auburn 27, Indiana 23	2006	Georgia 31, Va. Tech 24
1975	West Va. 13, N.C. State 10	1992*	E. Carolina 37, N.C. State 34	2007	Auburn 23, Clemson 20 OT
1976	Kentucky 21, N. Carolina 0	1993	N. Carolina 21, Miss. St. 17	
1977	N.C. State 24, Iowa St. 14	1993†	Clemson 14, Kentucky 13	†December game from 1968-79,
1978	Purdue 41, Georgia Tech 21	1995*	N.C. State 28, Miss. St. 24	1981-86, 1988-90, 1993, 1995,
1979	Baylor 24, Clemson 18	1995†	Virginia 34, Georgia 27	1996, 1998, 1999-2002 and 2004.
1981*	Miami-FL 20, Va. Tech 10	1996	LSU 10, Clemson 7	*January game in 1981, 1988, 1992-
1981†	West Va. 26, Florida 6	1998*	Auburn 21, Clemson 17	93, 1995 and 1998 and 2004.
1982	Iowa 28, Tennessee 22	1998†	Georgia 35, Virginia 33	
1983	Florida St. 28, N. Carolina 3	1999	Mississippi St. 17, Clemson 7	

Sun Bowl

City: El Paso, Tex. **Stadium:** Sun Bowl. **Capacity:** 52,000. **Playing surface:** Turf. **First game:** Jan. 1, 1936. **Name changes:** Sun Bowl (1936-85), John Hancock Sun Bowl (1986-88), John Hancock Bowl (1989-93), Sun Bowl (1994) Norwest Sun Bowl (1996-98), Wells Fargo Sun Bowl (1999-2003), Vitalis Sun Bowl (2004-05) and Brut Sun Bowl (since 2006). **Playing sites:** Kidd Field (1936-62) and Sun Bowl (since 1963). **Corporate title sponsors:** John Hancock Financial Services (1986-93), Norwest Bank (1996-98), Wells Fargo (1999-2003), Helen of Troy Limited (since 2004).
    Automatic berths: Eighth pick from 8-team Bowl Coalition pool vs. at-large opponent (1992); Seventh and eighth picks from 8-team Bowl Coalition pool (1993-94 seasons); third pick from Pac-10, if available, vs. fifth pick from Big 10, if available (1995-2005); Pac-10 vs. Big 12/Big East/Notre Dame (2006-09).
    Multiple wins: Texas Western/UTEP (5); Alabama, Oregon and Wyoming (3); Arizona St., Nebraska, New Mexico St., North Carolina, Oklahoma, Pittsburgh, Southwestern, Stanford, Texas, UCLA, West Texas St. and West Virginia (2).

Year		Year		Year	
1936*	14-14, Hardin-Simmons vs New Mexico St.	1960	New Mexico St. 20, Utah St. 13	1987	Oklahoma St. 35, West Va. 33
1937	Hardin-Simmons 34, Texas Mines 6	1961	Villanova 17, Wichita St. 9	1988	Alabama 29, Army 28
1938	West Va. 7, Texas Tech 6	1962	West Texas 15, Ohio U. 14	1989	Pittsburgh 31, Texas A&M 28
1939	Utah 26, New Mexico 0	1963	Oregon 21, SMU 14	1990	Michigan St. 17, USC 16
1940	0-0, Catholic U. vs Arizoha St.	1964	Georgia 7, Texas Tech 0	1991	UCLA 6, Illinois 3
1941	W. Reserve 26, Arizona St. 13	1965	Texas Western 13, TCU 12	1992	Baylor 20, Arizona 15
1942	Tulsa 6, Texas Tech 0	1966	Wyoming 28, Florida St. 20	1993	Oklahoma 41, Texas Tech 10
1943	Second Air Force 13, Hardin-Simmons 7	1967	UTEP 14, Mississippi 7	1994	Texas 35, N. Carolina 31
1944	Southwestern 7, New Mexico 0	1968	Auburn 34, Arizona 10	1995	Iowa 38, Washington 18
1945	Southwestern 35, U. of Mexico 0	1969	Nebraska 45, Georgia 6	1996	Stanford 38, Michigan St. 0
1946	New Mexico 34, Denver 24	1970	Georgia Tech 17, Texas Tech 9	1997	Arizona St. 17, Iowa 7
1947	Cincinnati 18, Va. Tech 6	1971	LSU 33, Iowa St. 15	1998	TCU 28, USC 19
1948	Miami-OH 13, Texas Tech 12	1972	N. Carolina 32, Texas Tech 28	1999	Oregon 24, Minnesota 20
1949	West Va. 21, Texas Mines 12	1973	Missouri 34, Auburn 17	2000	Wisconsin 21, UCLA 20
1950	Tex. Western 33, Georgetown 20	1974	Miss. St. 26, N. Carolina 24	2001	Washington St. 33, Purdue 27
1951	West Texas 14, Cincinnati 13	1975	Pittsburgh 33, Kansas 19	2002	Purdue 34, Washington 24
1952	Texas Tech 25, Pacific 14	1977*	Texas A&M 37, Florida 14	2003	Minnesota 31, Oregon 30
1953	Pacific 26, Southern Miss. 7	1977†	Stanford 24, LSU 14	2004	Arizona St. 27, Purdue 23
1954	Tex. Western 37, So. Miss. 14	1978	Texas 42, Maryland 0	2005	UCLA 50, Northwestern 38
1955	Tex. Western 47, Florida St. 20	1979	Washington 14, Texas 7	2006	Oregon St. 39, Missouri 38
1956	Wyoming 21, Texas Tech 14	1980	Nebraska 31, Miss. St. 17	2007	Oregon 56, South Florida 21
1957	Geo. Wash. 13, Tex. Western 0	1981	Oklahoma 40, Houston 14	*January game from 1936-58 and in
1958*	Louisville 34, Drake 20	1982	N. Carolina 26, Texas 10	1977.
1958†	Wyoming 14, Hardin-Simmons 6	1983	Alabama 28, SMU 7	†December game from 1958-75 and
1959	New Mexico St. 28, N. Texas 8	1984	Maryland 28, Tennessee 27	since 1977.
		1985	13-13, Georgia vs Arizona	
		1986	Alabama 28, Washington 6	

Outback Bowl

City: Tampa, Fla. **Stadium:** Raymond James. **Capacity:** 66,005. **Playing surface:** Grass. **First game:** Dec. 23, 1986. **Name change:** Hall of Fame Bowl (1986-95) and Outback Bowl (since 1995). **Playing sites:** Tampa/Houlihan's Stadium (1986-98) and Raymond James Stadium (since 1999). **Corporate title sponsor:** Outback Steakhouse, Inc. (since 1995).

Automatic berths: Fourth pick from ACC vs. fourth pick from Big 10 (1993-94 seasons); third pick from Big 10, if available, vs. third pick from SEC, if available (1995-99); fourth pick from Big 10 vs. third pick from SEC (2000 season).

Multiple wins: Georgia, Michigan and Penn St. (3); South Carolina, Syracuse and Tennessee (2).

Year		Year		Year	
1986†	Boston College 27, Georgia 24	1995	Wisconsin 34, Duke 20	2003	Michigan 38, Florida 30
1988*	Michigan 28, Alabama 24	1996	Penn St. 43, Auburn 14	2004	Iowa 37, Florida 17
1989	Syracuse 23, LSU 10	1997	Alabama 17, Michigan 14	2005	Georgia 24, Wisconsin 21
1990	Auburn 31, Ohio St. 14	1998	Georgia 33, Wisconsin 6	2006	Florida 31, Iowa 24
1991	Clemson 30, Illinois 0	1999	Penn St. 26, Kentucky 14	2007	Penn St. 20, Tennessee 10
1992	Syracuse 24, Ohio St. 17	2000	Georgia 28, Purdue 25 OT	2008	Tennessee 21, Wisconsin 17
1993	Tennessee 38, Boston Col. 23	2001	S. Carolina 24, Ohio St. 7		†December game in 1986.
1994	Michigan 42, N.C. State 7	2002	S. Carolina 31, Ohio St. 28		*January game since 1988.

Liberty Bowl

City: Memphis, Tenn. **Stadium:** Liberty Bowl Memorial. **Capacity:** 62,338. **Playing surface:** Grass. **First game:** Dec. 19, 1959. **Playing sites:** Municipal Stadium in Philadelphia (1959-63), Convention Hall in Atlantic City, N.J. (1964), Memphis Memorial Stadium (1965-75) and Liberty Bowl Memorial Stadium (since 1976). Memphis Memorial Stadium renamed Liberty Bowl Memorial in 1976. **Corporate title sponsors:** St. Jude's Hospital (since 1993), AXA/Equitable (1997-2003), AutoZone (since 2004).

Automatic berths: Commander-in-Chief's Trophy winner (Army, Navy or Air Force) vs. at-large opponent (1989-92 seasons); none (1993 season); first pick from independent group of Cincinnati, East Carolina, Memphis, Southern Miss. and Tulane vs. at-large opponent (for 1994 and '95 seasons); Conference USA champion vs. fourth pick from the Big East (1996-97 seasons); Conference USA champion, if available, vs. fifth, sixth or seventh pick or at-large from SEC (1998-99 seasons); Mountain West champion vs. Conference USA champion, if available (2000-05); SEC vs. Conference USA champ (since 2006).

Multiple wins: Mississippi (4); Penn St. and Tennessee (3); Air Force, Alabama, Louisville, Mississippi St., N.C. State, Southern Miss., Syracuse and Tulane (2).

Year		Year		Year	
1959†	Penn St. 7, Alabama 0	1976	Alabama 36, UCLA 6	1993	Louisville 18, Michigan St. 7
1960	Penn St. 41, Oregon 12	1977	Nebraska 21, N. Carolina 17	1994	Illinois 30, E. Carolina 0
1961	Syracuse 15, Miami-FL 14	1978	Missouri 20, LSU 15	1995	E. Carolina 19, Stanford 13
1962	Oregon St. 6, Villanova 0	1979	Penn St. 9, Tulane 6	1996	Syracuse 30, Houston 17
1963	Mississippi St. 16, N.C. State 12	1980	Purdue 28, Missouri 25	1997	Southern Miss. 41, Pittsburgh 7
1964	Utah 32, West Virginia 6	1981	Ohio St. 31, Navy 28	1998	Tulane 41, BYU 27
1965	Mississippi 13, Auburn 7	1982	Alabama 21, Illinois 15	1999	Southern Miss. 23, Colorado St. 17
1966	Miami-FL 14, Virginia Tech 7	1983	Notre Dame 19, Boston Col. 18	2000	Colorado St. 22, Louisville 17
1967	N.C. State 14, Georgia 7	1984	Auburn 21, Arkansas 15	2001	Louisville 28, BYU 10
1968	Mississippi 34, Virginia Tech 17	1985	Baylor 21, LSU 7	2002	TCU 17, Colorado St. 3
1969	Colorado 47, Alabama 33	1986	Tennessee 21, Minnesota 14	2003	Utah 17, Southern Miss. 0
1970	Tulane 17, Colorado 3	1987	Georgia 20, Arkansas 17	2004	Louisville 44, Boise St. 40
1971	Tennessee 14, Arkansas 13	1988	Indiana 34, S. Carolina 10	2005	Tulsa 31, Fresno St. 24
1972	Georgia Tech 31, Iowa St. 30	1989	Mississippi 42, Air Force 29	2006	South Carolina 44, Houston 36
1973	N.C. State 31, Kansas 18	1990	Air Force 23, Ohio St. 11	2007	Mississippi St. 10, C. Florida 3
1974	Tennessee 7, Maryland 3	1991	Air Force 38, Mississippi St. 15		† December game since 1959.
1975	USC 20, Texas A&M 0	1992	Mississippi 13, Air Force 0		

Champs Sports Bowl

City: Orlando, Fla. **Stadium:** Florida Citrus Bowl. **Capacity:** 70,188. **Playing surface:** Grass. **First game:** Dec. 28, 1990. **Name change:** Blockbuster Bowl (1990-93), Carquest Bowl (1994-97), Micron PC Bowl (1998), Micron-PC.com Bowl (1999-2000), Visit Florida Tangerine Bowl (2001) and Mazda Tangerine Bowl (2002-03). The game was called the Sunshine Football Classic for a short time in the offseason after Carquest Auto Parts dropped its sponsorship and before Micron signed on. Also, this game should not be confused with the Tangerine Bowl that became the Citrus Bowl in 1982. **Playing sites:** Joe Robbie Stadium (1990-2000). Name changed to Pro Player Stadium in 1996; Florida Citrus Bowl (since 2001). **Corporate title sponsors:** Blockbuster Video (1990-93), Carquest Auto Parts (1993-97), Micron Electronics (1998-2000), Mazda (2002-04) and Champs Sports (since 2005).

Automatic berths: Penn St. vs. seventh pick from 8-team Bowl Coalition pool (1992 season); third pick from Big East vs. fifth pick from SEC (1993-94 seasons); third pick from Big East vs. fifth pick from SEC (1995 season); third pick from Big East vs. fourth pick from ACC (1996-97 seasons); sixth pick from Big Ten, if available, vs. fourth pick from ACC, if available (1998-2000 seasons); fifth pick from ACC vs. fifth pick from Big East (2001-2005); ACC vs. Big Ten (since 2006).

Multiple wins: Boston College, Georgia Tech, Miami-FL and N.C. State (2).

Year		Year		Year	
1990†	Florida St. 24, Penn St. 17	1997	Ga. Tech 35, W. Virginia 30	2004	Ga. Tech 51, Syracuse 14
1991	Alabama 30, Colorado 25	1998	Miami-FL 46, N.C. State 23	2005	Clemson 19, Colorado 10
1993*	Stanford 24, Penn St. 3	1999	Illinois 63, Virginia 21	2006	Maryland 24, Purdue 7
1994	Boston College 31, Virginia 13	2000	N.C. State 38, Minnesota 30	2007	Boston Coll. 24, Mich. St. 21
1995	S. Carolina 24, West Va. 21	2001	Pittsburgh 34, N.C. State 19		†December game from 1990-91 and
1995†	N. Carolina 20, Arkansas 10	2002	Texas Tech 55, Clemson 15		since 1995.
1996	Miami-FL 31, Virginia 21	2003	N.C. State 56, Kansas 26		*January game 1993-95.

Bowl Games (Cont.)
Insight Bowl

City: Tempe, Ariz. **Stadium:** Sun Devil. **Capacity:** 73,379. **Playing surface:** Grass. **First game:** Dec. 31, 1989. **Name changes:** Copper Bowl (1989-1996), Insight.com Bowl (1997-2001) and Insight Bowl (since 2002). **Playing sites:** Arizona Stadium (1989-2000), Chase Field, previously Bank One Ballpark (2000-05) and Sun Devil Stadium (2006–). **Corporate title sponsors:** Domino's Pizza (1990-91), Weiser Lock (1992-1996) and Insight Enterprises (since 1997).

Automatic berths: Third pick from WAC vs. at-large opponent (1992 season); third pick from WAC vs. fourth pick from Big Eight (1993-94 seasons); second pick from WAC vs. sixth pick from Big 12 (1995-97); third pick from Big East or Notre Dame, if available vs. fifth pick from Big 12, if available (1998-2001); third pick from Big East or Notre Dame, if available vs. fourth pick from Big East (2002); Big East vs. Pac-10 (2003-05); Big Ten vs. Big 12 (since 2006).

Multiple wins: Arizona and California (2).

Year		Year		Year	
1989†	Arizona 17, N.C. State 10	1996	Wisconsin 38, Utah 10	2003	California 52, Virginia Tech 49
1990	California 17, Wyoming 15	1997	Arizona 20, New Mexico 14	2004	Oregon St. 38, Notre Dame 21
1991	Indiana 24, Baylor 0	1998	Missouri 34, West Virginia 31	2005	Arizona St. 45, Rutgers 40
1992	Washington St. 31, Utah 28	1999	Colorado 62, Boston College 28	2006	Texas Tech 44, Minnesota 41 OT
1993	Kansas St. 52, Wyoming 17	2000	Iowa St. 37, Pittsburgh 29	2007	Oklahoma St. 49, Indiana 33
1994	BYU 31, Oklahoma 6	2001	Syracuse 26, Kansas St. 3		†December game since 1989.
1995	Texas Tech 55, Air Force 41	2002	Pittsburgh 38, Oregon St. 13		

Humanitarian Bowl

City: Boise, Idaho. **Stadium:** Bronco. **Capacity:** 30,000. **Playing surface:** Turf. **First game:** Dec. 29, 1997. **Name change:** Humanitarian Bowl (1997-98, 2004), Crucial.com Humanitarian Bowl (1999-2002), MPC Computers Bowl (2000-2006), Roady's Humanitarian Bowl (since 2007). **Playing site:** Bronco Stadium (since 1997). **Corporate title sponsors:** World Sports Humanitarian Hall of Fame (1997-98), Crucial.com (1999-2002), MPC Computers (2004-06); Roady's Truck Stops (since 2007). **Automatic berths:** Big West champion, if available, vs. at-large (1997-2002) WAC vs. ACC (since 2004). **Multiple wins:** Boise St. and Fresno St. (3).

Year		Year		Year	
1997†	Cincinnati 35, Utah St. 19	2002	Boise St. 34, Iowa St. 16	2007	Fresno St. 40, Ga. Tech 28
1998	Idaho 42, Southern Miss. 35	2004*	Georgia Tech 52, Tulsa 10		†Dec. game 1997-2002 and since '04
1999	Boise St. 34, Louisville 31	2004†	Fresno St. 37, Virginia 34 OT		*January game in 2004
2000	Boise St. 38, UTEP 23	2005	Boston College 27, Boise St. 21		
2001	Clemson 49, La. Tech 24	2006	Miami-FL 21, Nevada 20		

Las Vegas Bowl

City: Las Vegas, Nev. **Stadium:** Sam Boyd. **Capacity:** 40,000. **Playing surface:** Turf. **First game:** Dec. 18, 1992. **Playing site:** Sam Boyd Stadium (since 1992). **Corporate title sponsors:** EA Sports (1999-2000) Sega Sports (2001-02).

Automatic berths: Mid-American champion vs. Big West champion (1992-96 season); none (1997 season); second or third pick from WAC, if available vs. at-large (1998-2000), second pick from Mountain West vs. fifth pick from Pac-10 (since 2001).

Multiple wins: Fresno St. (4); UNLV (3); Bowling Green, BYU, San Jose St., Toledo and Utah (2).

Year		Year		Year	
1981†	Toledo 27, San Jose St. 25	1991	Bowling Green 28, Fresno St. 21	2001	Utah 10, USC 6
1982	Fresno St. 29, Bowling Green 28	1992	Bowling Green 35, Nevada 34	2002	UCLA 27, New Mexico 13
1983	Northern Ill. 20, CS-Fullerton 13	1993	Utah St. 42, Ball St. 33	2003	Oregon St. 55, New Mexico 14
1984*	UNLV 30, Toledo 13	1994	UNLV 52, C. Michigan 24	2004	Wyoming 24, UCLA 21
1985	Fresno St. 51, Bowling Green 7	1995	Toledo 40, Nevada 37 (OT)	2005	California 35, BYU 28
1986	San Jose St. 37, Miami-OH 7	1996	Nevada 18, Ball St. 15	2006	BYU 38, Oregon 8
1987	E. Michigan 30, San Jose St. 27	1997	Oregon 41, Air Force 13	2007	BYU 17, UCLA 16
1988	Fresno St. 35, W. Michigan 30	1998	N. Carolina 20, San Diego St. 13		†December game since 1981.
1989	Fresno St. 27, Ball St. 6	1999	Utah 17, Fresno St. 16		*Toledo later ruled winner of '84 game
1990	San Jose St. 48, C. Michigan 24	2000	UNLV 31, Arkansas 14		because UNLV used ineligible players.

Note: The MAC and Big West champs met in a bowl game from 1981 to 1996, originally in Fresno at the California Bowl (1981-88, 1992) and California Raisin Bowl (1989-91). The results from 1981-91 are included above.

Independence Bowl

City: Shreveport, La. **Stadium:** Independence. **Capacity:** 50,832. **Playing surface:** Grass. **First game:** Dec. 13, 1976. **Playing site:** Independence Stadium (since 1976). **Corporate title sponsors:** Poulan/Weed Eater (1990-97), Sanford (1998-2000) and MainStay (since 2001). **Automatic berths:** Southland Conference champion vs. at-large opponent (1976-81 seasons); none (1982-95 seasons); fifth pick from SEC, if available, vs. at-large (1995-97 season); fifth, sixth or seventh pick from SEC, if available, vs. at-large (1998-99 season); sixth pick from Big 12 vs. SEC (since 2000 season).

Multiple wins: Mississippi (4); Alabama, Air Force, LSU and Southern Miss (2).

Year		Year		Year	
1976†	McNeese St. 20, Tulsa 16	1987	Washington 24, Tulane 12	1998	Mississippi 35, Texas Tech 18
1977	La. Tech 24, Louisville 14	1988	Southern Miss 38, UTEP 18	1999	Mississippi 27, Oklahoma 25
1978	E. Carolina 35, La. Tech 13	1989	Oregon 27, Tulsa 24	2000	Mississippi St. 43, Texas A&M 41
1979	Syracuse 31, McNeese St. 7	1990	34-34, La. Tech vs Maryland	2001	Alabama 14, Iowa St. 13
1980	Southern Miss 16, McNeese St. 14	1991	Georgia 24, Arkansas 15	2002	Mississippi 27, Nebraska 23
1981	Texas A&M 33, Oklahoma St. 16	1992	Wake Forest 39, Oregon 35	2003	Arkansas 27, Missouri 14
1982	Wisconsin 14, Kansas St. 3	1993	Va. Tech 45, Indiana 20	2004	Iowa St. 17, Miami-OH 13
1983	Air Force 9, Mississippi 3	1994	Virginia 20, TCU 10	2005	Missouri 38, South Carolina 31
1984	Air Force 23, Va. Tech 7	1995	LSU 45, Michigan St. 26	2006	Oklahoma St. 34, Alabama 31
1985	Minnesota 20, Clemson 13	1996	Auburn 32, Army 29	2007	Alabama 30, Colorado 24
1986	Mississippi 20, Texas Tech 17	1997	LSU 27, Notre Dame 9		†December game since 1976.

Alamo Bowl

City: San Antonio, Tex. **Stadium:** Alamodome. **Capacity:** 65,000. **Playing surface:** Turf. **First game:** Dec. 31, 1993. **Playing site:** Alamodome (since 1993). **Corporate title sponsor:** Builders Square (1993-98), Sylvania (1999-2001) and Mastercard (2004).

Automatic berths: third pick from SWC vs. fourth pick from Pac-10 (1993-94 seasons); fourth pick from Big 10, if available vs. fourth pick from Big 12, if available (1995-99 seasons); fourth pick from Big 12 vs. third pick from Big 10 (2000 season).

Multiple wins: Nebraska (3), Iowa, Penn St. and Purdue (2).

Year		Year		Year	
1993†	California 37, Iowa 3	1999	Penn St. 24, Texas A&M 0	2005	Nebraska 32, Michigan 28
1994	Washington St. 10, Baylor 3	2000	Nebraska 66, Northwestern 17	2006	Texas 26, Iowa 24
1995	Texas A&M 22, Michigan 20	2001	Iowa 19, Texas Tech 16	2007	Penn St. 24, Texas A&M 17
1996	Iowa 27, Texas Tech 0	2002	Wisconsin 31, Colorado 28 (OT)	†December game since 1993.	
1997	Purdue 33, Oklahoma St. 20	2003	Nebraska 17, Michigan St. 3		
1998	Purdue 37, Kansas St. 34	2004	Ohio St. 33, Oklahoma St. 7		

Motor City Bowl

City: Detroit, Mich. **Stadium:** Ford Field. **Capacity:** 65,000. **Playing surface:** Turf. **First game:** Dec. 26, 1997. **Playing site:** Pontiac Silverdome (1997-2001) and Ford Field (since 2002). **Corporate title sponsor:** Ford Division of Ford Motor Company (since 1997), Daimler Chrysler and General Motors (since 2002). **Automatic berths:** Mid-American champions vs at-large (1997-99 season); Mid-American champions vs. fourth pick from Conference USA (2000 season).

Multiple wins: Marshall (3).

Year		Year		Year	
1997†	Mississippi 34, Marshall 31	2001	Toledo 23, Cincinnati 16	2005	Memphis 38, Akron 31
1998	Marshall 48, Louisville 29	2002	Boston College 51, Toledo 25	2006	C. Mich. 31, Mid Tenn. St. 14
1999	Marshall 21, BYU 3	2003	Bowling Green 28, N'western 24	2007	Purdue 51, C. Michigan 48
2000	Marshall 25, Cincinnati 14	2004	Connecticut 39, Toledo 10	†December game since 1997.	

Music City Bowl

City: Nashville, Tenn. **Stadium:** LP Field. **Capacity:** 67,000. **Playing surface:** Grass. **First game:** Dec. 29, 1998. **Playing sites:** Vanderbilt Stadium (1998) and Adelphia Coliseum (since 1999). **Corporate title sponsors:** American General (1998), HomePoint.com (1999-2000) and Gaylord Hotels (since 2002). **Automatic berths:** sixth choice from the SEC, if available, vs. at-large (1998-99 season); fourth pick from Big East, if available vs. SEC (2000-01); Big Ten vs. SEC (2002-05); ACC vs. SEC (since 2006).

Multiple wins: Kentucky and Minnesota (2).

Year		Year		Year	
1998†	Va. Tech 38, Alabama 7	2002	Minnesota 29, Arkansas 14	2006	Kentucky 28, Clemson 20
1999	Syracuse 20, Kentucky 13	2003	Auburn 28, Wisconsin 14	2007	Kentucky 35, Florida St. 28
2000	West Va. 49, Mississippi 38	2004	Minnesota 20, Alabama 16	†December game since 1998.	
2001	Boston College 20, Georgia 16	2005	Virginia 34, Minnesota 31		

GMAC Bowl

City: Mobile, Ala. **Stadium:** Ladd-Peebles. **Capacity:** 40,646. **Playing surface:** Grass. **First game:** Dec. 22, 1999. **Name change:** Mobile Bowl (1999-2000), GMAC Bowl (since 2001). **Playing sites:** Ladd-Peebles Stadium (since 1999). **Corporate title sponsors:** GMAC Financial Services (since 2001). **Automatic berths:** WAC champions (if team is from the east) or second pick from WAC vs. second pick from Conference USA, if available (2000), Mid-American vs. Conference USA (2001), Conference USA vs. Mid-American/WAC (2002-2006).

Multiple wins: Marshall and Southern Miss. (2).

Year		Year		Year	
1999†	TCU 28, E. Carolina 14	2002	Marshall 38, Louisville 15	2005	Toledo 45, UTEP 13
2000	So. Miss 28, TCU 21	2003	Miami-OH 49, Louisville 28	2006	So. Miss. 28, Ohio 7
2001	Marshall 64, E. Caro. 61 (2OT)	2004	Bowling Green 52, Memphis 35	2007	Tulsa 63, Bowling Green 7
				†December game since 1999.	

New Orleans Bowl

City: Lafayette, La. **Stadium:** Cajun Field. **Capacity:** 31,000. **Playing surface:** Grass. **First game:** Dec. 18, 2001. **Playing sites:** Louisiana Superdome (2001-04), Cajun Field (2005). **Corporate title sponsors:** Wyndam Hotels (since 2004). **Automatic berths:** Sun Belt champion vs. Conference USA (since 2002).

Multiple wins: Southern Mississippi (2).

Year		Year		Year	
2001†	Colorado St. 45, North Texas 20	2004	So. Miss. 31, North Texas 10	2007	Fla. Atlantic 44, Memphis 27
2002	North Texas 24, Cincinnati 19	2005	So. Miss. 31, Arkansas St. 19	†December game since 2001.	
2003	Memphis 27, North Texas 17	2006	Troy 41, Rice 17		

Emerald Bowl

City: San Francisco, Calif. **Stadium:** AT&T Park. **Capacity:** 37,000. **Playing surface:** Grass. **First game:** Dec. 31, 2002. **Name change:** Diamond Walnut San Francisco Bowl (2002-03), Emerald Bowl (since 2004). **Playing sites:** AT&T (formerly known as Pacific Bell then SBC) Park (since 2002). **Corporate title sponsors:** Diamond Walnut (2002-03), Emerald Nuts (since 2004). **Automatic berths:** Mountain West vs. Big East or Notre Dame (2002-03).

Year		Year		Year	
2002†	Virginia Tech 20, Air Force 13	2004	Navy 34, New Mexico 19	2006	Florida St. 44, UCLA 27
2003	Boston Col. 35, Colorado St. 21	2005	Utah 38, Georgia Tech 10	2007	Oregon St 21, Maryland 14
				†December game since 2002.	

Bowl Games (Cont.)
Meineke Car Care Bowl

City: Charlotte, N.C. **Stadium:** Bank of America. **Capacity:** 73,367. **Playing surface:** Grass. **First game:** Dec. 28, 2002. **Name change:** Continental Tire Bowl (2002-04), Meineke Car Care Bowl (starting in Dec. 2005). **Playing sites:** Bank of America (formerly known as Ericsson) Stadium (since 2002). **Corporate title sponsors:** Continental Tire North America (2002-04), Meineke Car Care (since 2005). **Automatic berths:** ACC vs. Big East or Notre Dame (since 2002). **Multiple wins:** Boston College and Virginia (2).

Year		Year		Year	
2002†	Virginia 48, West Va. 22	2005	N.C. State 14, So. Florida 0	2007	Wake Forest 24, UConn 10
2003	Virginia 23, Pittsburgh 16	2006	Boston Col. 25, Navy 24		†December game since 2002.
2004	Boston Col. 37, N. Carolina 24				

Hawaii Bowl

City: Honolulu, Hi. **Stadium:** Aloha Bowl. **Capacity:** 50,000. **Playing surface:** Turf. **First game:** Dec. 25, 2002. **Playing sites:** Aloha Bowl (since 2002). **Corporate title sponsors:** ConAgra Foods (2002) and Sheraton Hotels & Resorts (since 2003). **Automatic berths:** Hawaii (if bowl eligible) otherwise another WAC school vs. Conference USA (since 2002). **Multiple wins:** Hawaii (3).

Year		Year		Year	
2002†	Tulane 36, Hawaii 28	2005	Nevada 49, C. Florida 48 OT	2007	E. Carolina 41, Boise St. 38
2003	Hawaii 54, Houston 48 (3OT)	2006	Hawaii 41, Arizona St. 24		†December game since 2002.
2004	Hawaii 59, UAB 40				

Armed Forces Bowl

City: Fort Worth, Tex. **Stadium:** Amon Carter. **Capacity:** 46,000. **Playing surface:** Grass. **First game:** Dec. 23, 2003. **Playing sites:** Amon Carter Stadium (since 2003). **Corporate title sponsors:** PlainsCapital Corp. (2003-04) Bell Helicopter (since 2006) There was no title sponsor in 2005. **Name change:** Fort Worth Bowl (2003-2005), Bell Helicopter Armed Forces Bowl (since 2006); **Automatic berths:** Big 12 vs. Conference USA (2003-05), Mountain West vs. Conference USA (2006 and 2008), Pac-10 vs. Mountain West (2007 and 2009).

Year		Year		Year	
2003†	Bosie St. 34, TCU 31	2005	Kansas 42, Houston 13	2007	California 42, Air Force 36
2004	Cincinnati 32, Marshall 14	2006	Utah 25, Tulsa 13		†December game since 2003.

Poinsettia Bowl

City: San Diego, Calif. **Stadium:** Qualcomm Stadium. **Capacity:** 71,500. **Playing surface:** Grass. **First game:** Dec. 22, 2005. **Playing sites:** Qualcomm Stadium (since 2005). **Corporate title sponsors:** San Diego County Credit Union. (since 2005). **Automatic berths:** Mountain West vs. at-large (since 2005).

Year		Year		Year	
2005†	Navy 51, Colorado St. 30	2006	TCU 37, No. Illinois 7	2007	Utah 35, Navy 32
					†December game since 2005.

Papajohns.com Bowl

City: Birmingham, Ala. **Stadium:** Legion Field. **Capacity:** 71,594. **Playing surface:** Grass. **First game:** Dec. 23, 2006. **Playing sites:** Legion Field (since 2006). **Corporate title sponsors:** Papajohns.com (since 2006). **Automatic berths:** Big East vs. Conference USA (since 2006).

Year		Year			
2006†	So. Florida 24, E. Carolina 7	2007	Cincinnati 31, So. Miss. 21		†December game since 2006.

New Mexico Bowl

City: Albuquerque, N.M. **Stadium:** University Stadium. **Capacity:** 37,000. **Playing surface:** Turf. **First game:** Dec. 23, 2006. **Playing sites:** University Stadium (since 2006). **Automatic berths:** Mountain West vs. WAC (since 2006).

Year		Year			
2006†	San Jose St. 20, N. Mexico 12	2007	New Mexico 23, Nevada 0		†December game since 2006.

International Bowl

City: Toronto, Ontario. **Stadium:** Rogers Centre. **Capacity:** 53,506. **Playing surface:** Turf. **First game:** Jan. 6, 2007. **Playing sites:** Rogers Centre (since 2007). **Automatic berths:** Mid-American vs. Big East (since 2007).

Year		Year			
2007†	Cincinnati 27, W. Michigan 24	2008	Rutgers 52, Ball St. 30		†January game since 2007.

Division I-A Teams

Schools classified as FBS (Division I-A) for at least 10 years; through 2007 season (including bowl games).

Top 25 Winning Percentage

		Yrs	Gm	W	L	T	Pct	Bowls App	Bowls Record	2007 Season Bowl	Record
1	Michigan	128	1191	869	286	36	.745	39	19-20-0	won Capital One	9-4
2	Notre Dame	119	1144	824	278	42	.739	28	13-15-0	none	3-9
3	Texas	115	1169	820	316	33	.716	47	24-21-2	won Holiday	10-3
4	Oklahoma	113	1127	779	295	53	.715	41	24-16-1	lost Fiesta	11-3
5	Ohio St.	118	1155	798	304	53	.714	39	18-21-0	lost BCS Title Game	11-2
6	Alabama	113	1144	787	314	43	.707	55	31-21-3	won Independence	7-6
7	USC	115	1110	754	302	54	.704	46	30-16-0	won Rose	11-2
8	Nebraska	118	1181	808	333	40	.701	44	22-22-0	none	5-7
9	Tennessee	111	1143	770	320	53	.697	47	25-22-0	won Outback	10-4
10	Boise St.	40	472	327	143	2	.695	8	5-3-0	lost Hawaii	10-3
11	Penn St.	121	1177	789	347	41	.688	40	26-12-2	won Alamo	9-4
12	Florida St.	61	684	450	217	17	.670	36	20-14-2	lost Music City	7-6
13	Georgia	114	1148	713	381	54	.645	43	24-16-3	won Sugar	11-2
14	LSU	114	1117	692	378	47	.641	39	20-18-1	won BCS Title Game	12-2
15	Miami-FL	81	860	537	304	19	.635	31	18-13-0	none	5-7
16	Miami-OH	119	1060	647	369	44	.631	9	6-3-0	none	6-7
17	Auburn	115	1111	676	388	47	.630	34	19-13-2	won Chick-fil-A	9-4
18	Florida	101	1040	628	327	40	.623	35	16-19-0	lost Capital One	9-4
19	Washington	118	1088	650	388	50	.620	29	14-14-1	none	4-9
20	Arizona St.	95	891	540	327	24	.620	28	12-11-1	lost Holiday	10-3
21	Central Michigan	107	934	550	348	36	.608	4	1-3-0	lost Motor City	8-6
22	Colorado	118	1113	658	419	36	.607	28	12-16-0	lost Independence	6-7
23	Texas A&M	113	1128	655	425	48	.602	30	13-17-0	lost Alamo	7-6
24	Virginia Tech	114	1114	647	421	46	.601	20	7-13-0	lost Orange	11-3
25	UCLA	89	922	534	351	37	.599	29	13-15-1	lost Las Vegas	7-6

Top 50 Victories

		Wins			Wins			Wins
1	Michigan	869	18	Georgia Tech	653	35	Wisconsin	596
2	Notre Dame	824	19	Washington	650	36	Maryland	591
3	Texas	820	20	Miami-OH	647	37	Missouri	589
4	Nebraska	808		Virginia Tech	647	38	Rutgers	588
5	Ohio St	798	22	Arkansas	646	39	Utah	581
6	Penn St	789	23	Pittsburgh	644	40	Purdue	566
7	Alabama	787	24	Army	634	41	Illinois	558
8	Oklahoma	779	25	North Carolina	631		Iowa	558
9	Tennessee	770	26	Minnesota	630	43	Kansas	554
10	USC	754	27	Florida	628	44	Kentucky	553
11	Georgia	713	28	Clemson	625	45	Central Michigan	550
12	LSU	692	29	Navy	624	46	Oregon	548
13	Auburn	676	30	Virginia	606	47	Stanford	547
14	Syracuse	671	31	California	605		Vanderbilt	547
15	West Virginia	664	32	Michigan St	601	49	TCU	545
16	Colorado	658	33	Boston College	600	50	Arizona St	540
17	Texas A&M	655	34	Mississippi	597			

Top 40 Bowl Appearances

		App	Record			App	Record			App	Record
1	Alabama	55	31-21-3	15	Florida	35	16-19-0		Missouri	25	11-14-0
2	Tennessee	47	25-22-0	16	Auburn	34	19-13-2	30	Pittsburgh	24	10-14-0
	Texas	47	24-21-2	17	Mississippi	31	19-12-0		Arizona St.	24	12-11-1
4	USC	46	30-16-0		Miami-FL	31	18-13-0	32	N.C. State	23	12-10-1
5	Nebraska	44	22-22-0		Texas Tech	31	9-21-1		TCU	23	9-13-1
6	Georgia	43	24-16-3	20	Texas A&M	30	13-17-0	34	Syracuse	22	12-9-1
7	Oklahoma	41	24-16-1		Clemson	30	15-15-0		Iowa	22	11-10-1
8	Penn St	40	26-12-2	22	Washington	29	14-14-1	36	Maryland	21	9-10-2
9	LSU	39	20-18-1		UCLA	29	13-15-1	37	Stanford	20	9-10-1
	Ohio St	39	18-21-0	24	Notre Dame	28	13-15-0	38	Oregon	20	8-12-0
	Michigan	39	19-20-0		Colorado	28	12-16-0		Virginia Tech	20	7-13-0
12	Arkansas	36	11-22-3	26	West Virginia	27	12-15-0	40	Boston College	19	13-6-0
	Georgia Tech	36	22-14-0	27	BYU	26	9-16-1		Wisconsin	19	10-9-0
	Florida St	36	20-14-2	28	North Carolina	25	12-13-0				

Major Conference Champions
Atlantic Coast Conference

Founded in 1953 when charter members all left Southern Conference to form ACC. **Charter members** (7): Clemson, Duke, Maryland, North Carolina, N.C. State, South Carolina and Wake Forest. **Admitted later** (6): Virginia in 1953 (began play in '54), Georgia Tech in 1979 (began play in '83), Florida St. in 1990 (began play in '92), Boston College, Virginia Tech and Miami-FL in 2003 (Virginia Tech and Miami began play in '04, Boston College in '05). **Withdrew later** (1): South Carolina in 1971 (became an independent after '70 season). **2007 playing membership** (12): ATLANTIC— Boston College, Clemson, Florida St., Maryland, N.C. State and Wake Forest; COASTAL—Duke, Georgia Tech, Miami-FL, North Carolina, Virginia and Virginia Tech.

    Multiple titles: Clemson (13); Florida St. (12); Maryland (9); Duke and N.C. State (7); North Carolina (5); Georgia Tech, Virginia, Virginia Tech and Wake Forest (2).

Year		Year		Year		Year	
1953	Duke (4-0)	1965	Clemson (5-2)	1980	North Carolina (6-0)	1994	Florida St. (8-0)
	& Maryland (3-0)		& N.C. State (5-2)	1981	Clemson (6-0)	1995	Virginia (7-1)
1954	Duke (4-0)	1966	Clemson (6-1)	1982	Clemson (6-0)		& Florida St. (7-1)
1955	Maryland (4-0)	1967	Clemson (6-0)	1983	Clemson (7-0) †	1996	Florida St. (8-0)
	& Duke (4-0)	1968	N.C. State (6-1)		& Maryland (5-0)	1997	Florida St. (8-0)
1956	Clemson (4-0-1)	1969	South Carolina (6-0)	1984	Maryland (5-0)	1998	Florida St. (7-1)
1957	N.C. State (5-0-1)	1970	Wake Forest (5-1)	1985	Maryland (6-0)		& Georgia Tech (7-1)
1958	Clemson (5-1)	1971	North Carolina (6-0)	1986	Clemson (5-1-1)	1999	Florida St. (8-0)
1959	Clemson (6-1)	1972	North Carolina (6-0)	1987	Clemson (6-1)	2000	Florida St. (8-0)
1960	Duke (5-1)	1973	N.C. State (6-0)	1988	Clemson (6-1)	2001	Maryland (7-1)
1961	Duke (5-1)	1974	Maryland (6-0)	1989	Virginia (6-1)	2002	Florida St. (7-1)
1962	Duke (6-0)	1975	Maryland (5-0)		& Duke (6-1)	2003	Florida St. (7-1)
1963	North Carolina (6-1)	1976	Maryland (5-0)	1990	Georgia Tech (6-0-1)	2004	Virginia Tech (7-1)
	& N.C. State (6-1)	1977	North Carolina (5-0-1)	1991	Clemson (6-0-1)		†On probation, ineligible
1964	N.C. State (5-2)	1978	Clemson (6-0)	1992	Florida St. (8-0)		for championship.
		1979	N.C. State (5-1)	1993	Florida St. (8-0)		

ACC Championship Game

After expanding to 12 teams and splitting into two divisions in 2005, the ACC began staging a conference championship game between the two division winners on the first Saturday in December. **Site:** Jacksonville Municipal Stadium (formerly Alltel Stadium) in Jacksonville, Fla. since 2005.

Year		Year		Year	
2005	Florida St. 27, Va. Tech 22	2006	Wake Forest 9, Ga. Tech 6	2007	Va. Tech 30, Boston Col. 16

Big East Conference

Founded in 1991 when charter members gave up independent football status to form Big East. **Charter members** (8): Boston College, Miami-FL, Pittsburgh, Rutgers, Syracuse, Temple, Virginia Tech and West Virginia. **Admitted later** (4): Connecticut (a charter member in all other sports) in 2004; Cincinnati, Louisville and South Florida in 2003 (to begin play in '05). **Withdrew later** (4): Temple in 2004 (began play in '05); Miami-FL and Virginia Tech in 2003 (Miami and Va. Tech joined ACC for 2004 season, Boston College joined ACC in 2005). Temple became an independent following 2004 season.

2007 playing membership (8): Cincinnati, Connecticut, Louisville, Pittsburgh, Rutgers, South Florida, Syracuse and West Virginia. **Conference champion:** Member schools needed two years to adjust their regular season schedules in order to begin round-robin conference play in 1993. In the meantime, the 1991 and '92 Big East titles went to the highest-ranked member in the final regular season *USA Today*/CNN coaches' poll.

    Multiple titles: Miami-FL (9); Syracuse (5); West Virginia (4); Virginia Tech (3).

Year		Year		Year		Year	
1991	Miami-FL (2-0, #1)	1996	Virginia Tech,	2001	Miami-FL (7-0)	2005	West Virginia (7-0)
	& Syracuse (5-0, #16)		Miami-FL	2002	Miami-FL (7-0)	2006	Louisville (6-1)
1992	Miami-FL (4-0, #1)		& Syracuse (6-1)	2003	Miami-FL	2007	West Virginia
1993	West Virginia (7-0)	1997	Syracuse (6-1)		& West Virginia (6-1)		& Connecticut (5-2)
1994	Miami-FL (7-0)	1998	Syracuse (6-1)	2004	Boston College,		
1995	Virginia Tech (6-1)	1999	Virginia Tech (7-0)		Pittsburgh, Syracuse		
	& Miami-FL (6-1)	2000	Miami-FL (7-0)		& WVU (4-2)		

Big Ten Conference

Originally founded in 1895 as the Intercollegiate Conference of Faculty Representatives, better known as the Western Conference. **Charter members** (7): Chicago, Illinois, Michigan, Minnesota, Northwestern, Purdue and Wisconsin. **Admitted later** (5): Indiana and Iowa in 1899; Ohio St. in 1912; Michigan St. in 1950 (began play in '53); Penn St. in 1990 (began play in '93). **Withdrew later** (2): Michigan in 1907 (rejoined in '17); Chicago in 1940 (dropped football after '39 season). **Note:** Iowa belonged to both the Western and Missouri Valley conferences from 1907-10.

    Unofficially called the **Big Ten** from 1912 until Chicago's withdrawal in 1939, then the **Big Nine** from 1940 until Michigan St. began conference play in 1953. Formally named the **Big Ten** in 1984 and has kept the name even after adding Penn St. as its 11th member in 1990.

    2007 playing membership (11): Illinois, Indiana, Iowa, Michigan, Michigan St., Minnesota, Northwestern, Ohio St., Penn St., Purdue and Wisconsin.

    Multiple titles: Michigan (42); Ohio St. (32); Minnesota (18); Illinois (15); Iowa and Wisconsin (11); Purdue and Northwestern (8); Chicago and Michigan St. (6); Indiana and Penn St. (2).

Year		Year		Year		Year	
1896	Wisconsin (2-0-1)	1901	Michigan (4-0)	1904	Minnesota (3-0)	1907	Chicago (4-0)
1897	Wisconsin (3-0)		& Wisconsin (2-0)		& Michigan (2-0)	1908	Chicago (5-0)
1898	Michigan (3-0)	1902	Michigan (5-0)	1905	Chicago (7-0)	1909	Minnesota (3-0)
1899	Chicago (4-0)	1903	Michigan (3-0-1),	1906	Wisconsin (3-0),	1910	Illinois (4-0)
1900	Iowa (3-0-1)		Minnesota (3-0-1)		Minnesota (2-0)		& Minnesota (2-0)
	& Minnesota (3-0-1)		& Northwestern (1-0-2)		& Michigan (1-0)	1911	Minnesota (3-0-1)

Year		Year		Year		Year	
1912	Wisconsin (6-0)	1935	Minnesota (5-0)	1964	Michigan (6-1)	1987	Michigan St. (7-0-1)
1913	Chicago (7-0)		& Ohio St. (5-0)	1965	Michigan St. (7-0)	1988	Michigan (7-0-1)
1914	Illinois (6-0)	1936	Northwestern (6-0)	1966	Michigan St. (7-0)	1989	Michigan (8-0)
1915	Minnesota (3-0-1)	1937	Minnesota (5-0)	1967	Indiana (6-1),	1990	Iowa (6-2),
	& Illinois (3-0-2)	1938	Minnesota (4-1)		Purdue (6-1)		Michigan (6-2),
1916	Ohio St. (4-0)	1939	Ohio St. (5-1)		& Minnesota (6-1)		Michigan St. (6-2)
1917	Ohio St. (4-0)	1940	Minnesota (6-0)	1968	Ohio St. (7-0)		& Illinois (6-2)
1918	Illinois (4-0),	1941	Minnesota (5-0)	1969	Ohio St. (6-1)	1991	Michigan (8-0)
	Michigan (2-0)	1942	Ohio St. (5-1)		& Michigan (6-1)	1992	Michigan (6-0-2)
	& Purdue (1-0)	1943	Purdue (6-0)			1993	Wisconsin (6-1-1)
1919	Illinois (6-1)		& Michigan (6-0)	1970	Ohio St. (7-0)		& Ohio St. (6-1-1)
1920	Ohio St. (5-0)	1944	Ohio St. (6-0)	1971	Michigan (8-0)	1994	Penn St. (8-0)
1921	Iowa (5-0)	1945	Indiana (5-0-1)	1972	Ohio St. (7-1)	1995	Northwestern (8-0)
1922	Iowa (5-0)	1946	Illinois (6-1)		& Michigan (7-1)	1996	Ohio St. (7-1)
	& Michigan (4-0)	1947	Michigan (6-0)	1973	Ohio St. (7-0-1)		& Northwestern (7-1)
1923	Illinois (5-0)	1948	Michigan (6-0)		& Michigan (7-0-1)	1997	Michigan (8-0)
	& Michigan (4-0)	1949	Ohio St. (4-1-1)	1974	Ohio St. (7-1)	1998	Ohio St. (7-1),
1924	Chicago (3-0-3)		& Michigan (4-1-1)		& Michigan (7-1)		Wisconsin (7-1)
1925	Michigan (5-1)	1950	Michigan (4-1-1)	1975	Ohio St. (8-0)		& Michigan (7-1)
1926	Michigan (5-0)	1951	Illinois (5-0-1)	1976	Michigan (7-1)	1999	Wisconsin (7-1)
	& Northwestern (5-0)	1952	Wisconsin (4-1-1)		& Ohio St. (7-1)	2000	Purdue (6-2),
1927	Illinois (5-0)		& Purdue (4-1-1)	1977	Michigan (7-1)		Michigan (6-2)
	& Minnesota (3-0-1)	1953	Michigan St. (5-1)		& Ohio St. (7-1)		& Northwestern (6-2)
1928	Illinois (4-1)		& Illinois (5-1)	1978	Michigan (7-1)	2001	Illinois (7-1)
1929	Purdue (5-0)	1954	Ohio St. (7-0)		& Michigan St. (7-1)	2002	Ohio St. (8-0)
1930	Michigan (5-0)	1955	Ohio St. (6-0)	1979	Ohio St. (8-0)		& Iowa (8-0)
	& Northwestern (5-0)	1956	Iowa (5-1)	1980	Michigan (8-0)	2003	Michigan (7-1)
1931	Purdue (5-1),	1957	Ohio St. (7-0)	1981	Iowa (6-2)	2004	Iowa (7-1)
	Michigan (5-1)	1958	Iowa (5-1)		& Ohio St. (6-2)		& Michigan (7-1)
	& Northwestern (5-1)	1959	Wisconsin (5-2)	1982	Michigan (8-1)	2005	Ohio St. (7-1)
1932	Michigan (6-0)	1960	Minnesota (5-1)	1983	Illinois (9-0)		& Penn St. (7-1)
	& Purdue (5-0-1)		& Iowa (5-1)	1984	Ohio St. (7-2)	2006	Ohio St. (8-0)
1933	Michigan (5-0-1)	1961	Ohio St. (6-0)	1985	Iowa (7-1)	2007	Ohio St. (7-1)
	& Minnesota (2-0-4)	1962	Wisconsin (6-1)	1986	Michigan (7-1)		
1934	Minnesota (5-0)	1963	Illinois (5-1-1)		& Ohio St. (7-1)		

Big 12 Conference

Originally founded in 1996 by the former teams of the Big Eight and four schools from the Southwest Conference. The league stages a conference championship game between the two division winners on the first Saturday in December. **Playing sites:** Trans World Dome in St. Louis (1996, 1998), the Alamodome in San Antonio (1997, 1999), Arrowhead Stadium in Kansas City, Mo. (2000, 2003, 2004 and 2006), Texas Stadium in Irving, Texas (2001) and Reliant Stadium in Houston (2002, 2005). **2007 playing membership:** (12) NORTH—Colorado, Iowa St., Kansas, Kansas St., Missouri and Nebraska; SOUTH—Baylor, Oklahoma, Oklahoma St., Texas, Texas A&M and Texas Tech.
   Multiple titles: Oklahoma (5), Nebraska and Texas (2).

Year		Year		Year	
1996	Texas 37, Nebraska 27	2000	Oklahoma 27, Kansas St. 24	2004	Oklahoma 42, Colorado 3
1997	Nebraska 54, Texas A&M 15	2001	Colorado 39, Texas 37	2005	Texas 70, Colorado 3
1998	Texas A&M 36, Kansas St. 33	2002	Oklahoma 29, Colorado 7	2006	Oklahoma 21, Nebraska 7
1999	Nebraska 22, Texas 6	2003	Kansas St. 35, Oklahoma 7	2007	Oklahoma 38, Missouri 17

Big West Conference (1969-2000)

Originally founded in 1969 as Pacific Coast Athletic Assn. **Charter members** (7): CS-Los Angeles, Fresno St., Long Beach St., Pacific, San Diego St., San Jose St. and UC-Santa Barbara. **Admitted later** (12): CS-Fullerton in 1974; Utah St. in 1977 (began play in '78); UNLV in 1982; New Mexico St. in 1983 (began play in '84); Nevada in 1991 (began play in '92); Arkansas St., Louisiana Tech, Northern Illinois and SW Louisiana in 1992 (all four began play in football only in '93); Boise St., Idaho and North Texas in 1994 (all three began play in '96); Arkansas St. rejoined in 1999 (in football only). **Withdrew later** (14): CS-Los Angeles and UC-Santa Barbara in 1972 (both dropped football after '71 season); San Diego St. in 1975 (became an independent after '75 season); Fresno St. in 1991 (left for WAC after '91 season); Long Beach St. in 1991 (dropped football after '91 season); CS-Fullerton in 1992 (dropped football after '92 season); San Jose St. and UNLV in 1994 (left for WAC after '95 season); Pacific in 1995 (dropped football after '95 season); Arkansas St., Louisiana Tech, Northern Illinois and SW Louisiana in 1995 (all four returned to independent football status after '95 season); Nevada in 2000 (left for WAC after '99 season). **Conference renamed** Big West in 1988.
   Multiple titles: San Jose St. (8); Fresno St. (6); Nevada, San Diego St. and Utah St. (5); Long Beach St. (3); Boise St., CS-Fullerton and SW Louisiana (2).

Year		Year		Year		Year	
1969	San Diego St. (6-0)	1979	Utah St. (4-0-1)*	1991	Fresno St. (6-1)	1997	Utah St. (4-1)
1970	Long Beach St. (5-1)	1980	Long Beach St. (5-0)		& San Jose St. (6-1)		& Nevada (4-1)
	& San Diego St. (5-1)	1981	San Jose St. (5-0)	1992	Nevada (5-1)	1998	Idaho (4-1)
1971	Long Beach St. (5-1)	1982	Fresno St. (6-0)	1993	Utah St. (5-1)	1999	Boise St. (5-1)
1972	San Diego St. (4-0)	1983	CS-Fullerton (5-1)		& SW Louisiana (5-1)	2000	Boise St. (5-0)
1973	San Diego St. (3-0-1)	1984	CS-Fullerton (6-1)†	1994	UNLV (5-1),		
1974	San Diego St. (4-0)	1985	Fresno St. (7-0)		Nevada (5-1),	*San Jose St. (4-0-1) forfeit-
1975	San Jose St. (5-0)	1986	San Jose St. (7-0)		& SW Louisiana (5-1)	ed share of 1979 title for
1976	San Jose St. (4-0)	1987	San Jose St. (7-0)	1995	Nevada (6-0)	using ineligible player.
1977	Fresno St. (4-0)	1988	Fresno St. (7-0)	1996	Nevada (4-1)	†UNLV (7-0) forfeited title in
1978	San Jose St. (4-1)	1989	Fresno St. (7-0)		& Utah St. (4-1)	1984 for use of ineligible
	& Utah St. (4-1)	1990	San Jose St. (7-0)			players.

Big Eight Conference (1907-1996)

Originally founded in 1907 as the Missouri Valley Intercollegiate Athletic Assn. **Charter members** (5): Iowa, Kansas, Missouri, Nebraska and Washington University of St. Louis. **Admitted later** (11): Drake and Iowa St. (then Ames College) in 1908; Kansas St. (then Kansas College of Applied Science and Agriculture) in 1913; Grinnell (Iowa) College in 1919; Oklahoma in 1920; Oklahoma A&M (now Oklahoma St.) in 1925; Colorado in 1947 (began play in '48).
Withdrew later (9): Iowa in 1911 (left for Big Ten after 1910 season), Colorado, Iowa St., Kansas, Kansas St. Missouri, Nebraska, Oklahoma and Oklahoma St. in 1996 (left for Big 12 after 1995 season); **Excluded later** (4): Drake, Grinnell, Oklahoma A&M and Washington-MO (left out when MVIAA cut membership to six teams in 1928).
Streamlined MVIAA unofficially called **Big Six** from 1928-47 with surviving members Iowa St., Kansas, Kansas St., Missouri, Nebraska and Oklahoma. Became the **Big Seven** after 1947 season when Colorado came over from the Skyline Conference, and then the **Big Eight** with the return of Oklahoma A&M in 1957. A&M, which resumed conference play in '60, became Oklahoma St. on July 10, 1957. The MVIAA was officially renamed the Big Eight in 1964. The league folded in 1996 when the existing members formed the newly created Big 12 along with four schools from the Southwest Conference.

Multiple titles: Nebraska (43); Oklahoma (34); Missouri (12); Colorado and Kansas (5); Iowa St. and Oklahoma St. (2).

Year		Year		Year		Year	
1907	Iowa (1-0) & Nebraska (1-0)	1928	Nebraska (4-0)	1952	Oklahoma (5-0-1)	1976	Colorado (5-2), Oklahoma (5-2) & Oklahoma St. (5-2)
1908	Kansas (4-0)	1929	Nebraska (3-0-2)	1953	Oklahoma (6-0)		
1909	Missouri (4-0-1)	1930	Kansas (4-1)	1954	Oklahoma (6-0)		
1910	Nebraska (2-0)	1931	Nebraska (5-0)	1955	Oklahoma (6-0)	1977	Oklahoma (7-0)
1911	Iowa St. (2-0-1) & Nebraska (2-0-1)	1932	Nebraska (5-0)	1956	Oklahoma (6-0)	1978	Nebraska (6-1) & Oklahoma (6-1)
1912	Iowa St. (2-0) & Nebraska (2-0)	1933	Nebraska (5-0)	1957	Oklahoma (6-0)	1979	Oklahoma (7-0)
		1934	Kansas St. (5-0)	1958	Oklahoma (6-0)	1980	Oklahoma (7-0)
1913	Missouri (4-0) & Nebraska (3-0)	1935	Nebraska (4-0-1)	1959	Oklahoma (5-1)	1981	Nebraska (7-0)
1914	Nebraska (3-0)	1936	Nebraska (5-0)	1960	Missouri (7-0)	1982	Nebraska (7-0)
1915	Nebraska (4-0)	1937	Nebraska (3-0-2)	1961	Colorado (7-0)	1983	Nebraska (7-0)
1916	Nebraska (3-1)	1938	Oklahoma (5-0)	1962	Oklahoma (7-0)	1984	Oklahoma (6-1) & Nebraska (6-1)
1917	Nebraska (2-0)	1939	Missouri (5-0)	1963	Nebraska (7-0)		
1918	Vacant (WW I)	1940	Nebraska (5-0)	1964	Nebraska (6-1)	1985	Oklahoma (7-0)
1919	Missouri (4-0-1)	1941	Missouri (5-0)	1965	Nebraska (7-0)	1986	Oklahoma (7-0)
1920	Oklahoma (4-0-1)	1942	Missouri (4-0-1)	1966	Nebraska (6-1)	1987	Oklahoma (7-0)
1921	Nebraska (3-0)	1943	Oklahoma (5-0)	1967	Oklahoma (5-1)	1988	Nebraska (7-0)
1922	Nebraska (5-0)	1944	Oklahoma (4-0-1)	1968	Kansas (6-1) & Oklahoma (6-1)	1989	Colorado (7-0)
1923	Nebraska (3-0-2) & Kansas (3-0-3)	1945	Missouri (5-0)	1969	Missouri (6-1) & Nebraska (6-1)	1990	Colorado (7-0)
		1946	Oklahoma (4-1) & Kansas (4-1)			1991	Nebraska (6-0-1) & Colorado (6-0-1)
1924	Missouri (5-1)	1947	Kansas (4-0-1) & Oklahoma (4-0-1)	1970	Nebraska (7-0)		
1925	Missouri (5-1)	1948	Oklahoma (5-0)	1971	Nebraska (7-0)	1992	Nebraska (7-0)
1926	Okla. A&M (3-0-1)	1949	Oklahoma (5-0)	1972	Nebraska (5-1-1)*	1993	Nebraska (7-0)
1927	Missouri (5-1)	1950	Oklahoma (6-0)	1973	Oklahoma (7-0)	1994	Nebraska (7-0)
		1951	Oklahoma (6-0)	1974	Oklahoma (7-0)	1995	Nebraska (7-0)
				1975	Nebraska (6-1) & Oklahoma (6-1)		

*Oklahoma (6-1) forfeited title in 1972 after a player was ruled ineligible.

Conference USA

Founded in 1994 by six independent football schools which began play as a conference in 1996. **Charter members** (6): Cincinnati, Houston, Louisville, Memphis, Southern Mississippi and Tulane. **Admitted later** (11): East Carolina in 1997, Univ. of Alabama-Birmingham in 1999, Texas Christian Univ. in 2001, South Florida in 2003, Central Florida, Marshall, Rice, SMU, Tulsa and UTEP in 2005. **Withdrew later** (5): Cincinnati, Louisville and South Florida are set to leave for the Big East in 2005; Army is going back to independent and TCU is going to the Mountain West in 2005.
2007 playing members (12): EAST—Alabama-Birmingham, Central Florida, East Carolina, Marshall, Memphis and Southern Mississippi, WEST—Houston, Rice, SMU, Tulane, Tulsa and UTEP.

Multiple titles: Southern Mississippi (4), Louisville (3).

Year		Year		Year	
1996	Southern Mississippi (4-1) & Houston (4-1)	1999	Southern Mississippi (6-0)	2002	TCU (6-2) & Cincinnati (6-2)
1997	Southern Mississippi (6-0)	2000	Louisville (6-1)	2003	Southern Mississippi (8-0)
1998	Tulane (6-0)	2001	Louisville (6-1)	2004	Louisville (8-0)

Conference USA Championship Game

After expanding to 12 teams and splitting into two divisions in 2005, Conference USA began staging a conference championship game between the two division winners on the first Saturday in December. The inaugural game was held Dec. 3, 2005 at the Florida Citrus Bowl in Orlando, Fla.

Year		Year		Year	
2005	Tulsa 44, Cen. Florida 27	2006	Houston 34, Southern Miss. 20	2007	Cen. Florida 44, Tulsa 25

Mid-American Conference

Founded in 1946. **Charter members** (6): Butler, Cincinnati, Miami-OH, Ohio University, Western Michigan and Western Reserve (Miami and WMU began play in '48). **Admitted later** (14): Kent St. (now Kent) and Toledo in 1951 (Toledo began play in '52); Bowling Green in 1952; Marshall in 1954; Central Michigan and Eastern Michigan in 1972 (CMU began play in '75 and EMU in '76); Ball St. and Northern Illinois in 1973 (both began play in '75); Akron in 1991 (began play in '92); Marshall and Northern Illinois in 1995 (both resumed play in '97); Buffalo in 1995 (resumed play in '99); Central Florida in 2002; Temple in 2007.

Withdrew later (6): Butler in 1950 (left for the Indiana Collegiate Conference); Cincinnati in 1953 (went independent); Western Reserve (now Case Western) in 1955 (left for President's Athletic Conference; Marshall in 1969 (went independent) and again in 2005 (left for Conference USA); Northern Illinois in 1986 (went independent); Central Florida in 2005 (left. for Conference USA). **2007 playing membership** (13): EAST–Akron, Bowling Green, Buffalo, Kent St., Miami-OH, Ohio University and Temple; WEST–Ball St., Central Michigan, Eastern Michigan, Northern Illinois, Toledo and Western Michigan.

  Multiple titles: Miami-OH (14); Bowling Green (10); Toledo (9); Central Michigan (6); Ball St., Marshall and Ohio University (5); Cincinnati (4); Western Michigan (2).

Year		Year		Year		Year	
1947	Cincinnati (3-1)	1959	Bowling Green (6-0)	1970	Toledo (5-0)	1984	Toledo (7-1-1)
1948	Miami-OH (4-0)	1960	Ohio Univ. (6-0)	1971	Toledo (5-0)	1985	Bowling Green (9-0)
1949	Cincinnati (4-0)	1961	Bowling Green (5-1)	1972	Kent St. (4-1)	1986	Miami-OH (6-2)
1950	Miami-OH (4-0)	1962	Bowling Green (5-0-1)	1973	Miami-OH (5-0)	1987	Eastern Mich. (7-1)
1951	Cincinnati (3-0)	1963	Ohio Univ. (5-1)	1974	Miami-OH (5-0)	1988	Western Mich. (7-1)
1952	Cincinnati (3-0)	1964	Bowling Green (5-1)	1975	Miami-OH (6-0)	1989	Ball St. (6-1-1)
1953	Ohio Univ. (5-0-1)	1965	Bowling Green (5-1)	1976	Ball St. (4-1)	1990	Central Mich. (7-1)
	& Miami-OH (3-0-1)		& Miami-OH (5-1)	1977	Miami-OH (5-0)		& Toledo (7-1)
1954	Miami-OH (4-0)	1966	Miami-OH (5-1)	1978	Ball St. (8-0)	1991	Bowling Green (8-0)
1955	Miami-OH (5-0)		& Western Mich. (5-1)	1979	Central Mich. (8-0-1)	1992	Bowling Green (8-0)
1956	Bowling Green (5-0-1)	1967	Toledo (5-1)	1980	Central Mich. (7-2)	1993	Ball St. (7-0-1)
	& Miami-OH (4-0-1)		& Ohio Univ. (5-1)	1981	Toledo (8-1)	1994	Central Mich. (8-1)
1957	Miami-OH (5-0)	1968	Ohio Univ. (6-0)	1982	Bowling Green (7-2)	1995	Toledo (7-0-1)
1958	Miami-OH (5-0)	1969	Toledo (5-0)	1983	Northern Ill. (8-1)	1996	Ball St. (7-1)

MAC Championship Game

After expanding to 12 teams and splitting into two divisions in 1997, the MAC began staging a conference championship game between the two division winners on the first Saturday in December. The game has been played at Marshall Stadium in Huntington, W.V. (1997-2000, 2002), Glass Bowl Stadium in Toledo, Ohio (2001), Doyt Perry Stadium in Bowling Green, Ohio (2003) and Ford Field in Detroit (2004-07).

Year		Year		Year	
1997	Marshall 34, Toledo 13	2001	Toledo 41, Marshall 36	2005	Akron 31, Northern Illinois 30
1998	Marshall 23, Toledo 17	2002	Marshall 49, Toledo 45	2006	C. Mich. 31, Ohio 10
1999	Marshall 34, W. Michigan 30	2003	Miami-OH 49, Bowl. Green 27	2007	C. Mich. 35, Miami-OH 10
2000	Marshall 19, W. Michigan 14	2004	Toledo 35, Miami-OH 27		

Mountain West Conference

Founded in 1999. **Charter members** (8): Air Force, Brigham Young, Colorado St., New Mexico, Nevada-Las Vegas, San Diego St., Utah and Wyoming. **Admitted later** (1): TCU (from Conference USA) in 2005.

  2007 playing membership (9): Air Force, Brigham Young, Colorado St., New Mexico, Nevada-Las Vegas, San Diego St., TCU, Utah and Wyoming.

  Multiple titles: BYU (4); Colorado St. and Utah (3).

Year		Year		Year		Year	
1999	BYU (5-2),	2000	Colorado St. (6-1)	2003	Utah (6-1)	2006	BYU (8-0)
	Colorado St. (5-2)	2001	BYU (7-0)	2004	Utah (7-0)	2007	BYU (8-0)
	& Utah (5-2)	2002	Colorado St. (6-1)	2005	TCU (8-0)		

Pacific-10 Conference

Originally founded in 1915 as Pacific Coast Conference. **Charter members** (4): California, Oregon, Oregon St. and Washington. **Admitted later** (6): Washington St. in 1917; Stanford in 1918; Idaho and USC (Southern Cal) in 1922; Montana in 1924; and UCLA in 1928. **Withdrew later** (1): Montana in 1950 (left for the Mountain States Conf.).

  The **PCC** dissolved in 1959 and the **AAWU** (Athletic Assn. of Western Universities) was founded. **Charter members** (5): California, Stanford, UCLA, USC and Washington. **Admitted later** (5):Washington St. in 1962; Oregon and Oregon St. in 1964; Arizona and Arizona St. in 1978. **Conference renamed** Pacific-8 in 1968 and Pacific-10 in 1978.

  2007 playing membership (10): Arizona, Arizona St., California, Oregon, Oregon St., Stanford, UCLA, USC, Washington and Washington St.

  Multiple titles: USC (37); UCLA (17); Washington (15); California (14); Stanford (12); Oregon (7); Oregon St. (5); Washington St. (4); Arizona St. (3).

Year		Year		Year		Year	
1916	Washington (3-0-1)	1933	Oregon (4-1)	1947	USC (6-0)	1962	USC (4-0)
1917	Washington St. (3-0)		& Stanford (4-1)	1948	California (6-0)	1963	Washington (4-1)
1918	California (3-0)	1934	Stanford (5-0)		& Oregon (6-0)	1964	Oregon St. (3-1)
1919	Oregon (2-1)	1935	California (4-1),	1949	California (7-0)		& USC (3-1)
	& Washington (2-1)		Stanford (4-1)	1950	California (5-0-1)	1965	UCLA (4-0)
1920	California (3-0)		& UCLA (4-1)	1951	Stanford (6-1)	1966	USC (4-1)
1921	California (5-0)	1936	Washington (6-0-1)	1952	USC (6-0)	1967	USC (6-1)
1922	California (3-0)	1937	California (6-0-1)	1953	UCLA (6-1)	1968	USC (6-0)
1923	California (5-0)	1938	USC (6-1)	1954	UCLA (6-0)	1969	USC (6-0)
1924	Stanford (3-0-1)		& California (6-1)	1955	UCLA (6-0)	1970	Stanford (6-1)
1925	Washington (5-0)	1939	USC (5-0-2)	1956	Oregon St. (6-1-1)	1971	Stanford (6-1)
1926	Stanford (4-0)		& UCLA (5-0-3)	1957	Oregon (6-2)	1972	USC (7-0)
1927	USC (4-0-1)	1940	Stanford (7-0)		& Oregon St. (6-2)	1973	USC (7-0)
	& Stanford (4-0-1)	1941	Oregon St. (7-2)	1958	California (6-1)	1974	USC (6-0-1)
1928	USC (4-0-1)	1942	UCLA (6-1)	1959	Washington (3-1),	1975	UCLA (6-1)
1929	USC (6-1)	1943	USC (4-0)		USC (3-1)		& California (6-1)
1930	Washington St. (6-0)	1944	USC (3-0-2)		& UCLA (3-1)	1976	USC (7-0)
1931	USC (7-0)	1945	USC (5-1)	1960	Washington (4-0)	1977	Washington (6-1)
1932	USC (6-0)	1946	UCLA (7-0)	1961	UCLA (3-1)	1978	USC (6-1)

Major Conference Champions (Cont.)
Pacific-10 Conference (Cont.)

Year		Year		Year		Year	
1979	USC (6-0-1)	1988	USC (8-0)	1995	USC (6-1-1)	2001	Oregon (7-1)
1980	Washington (6-1)	1989	USC (6-0-1)		& Washington (6-1-1)	2002	Washington St. (7-1)
1981	Washington (6-2)	1990	Washington (7-1)	1996	Arizona St. (8-0)		& USC (7-1)
1982	UCLA (5-1-1)	1991	Washington (8-0)	1997	Washington St. (7-1)	2003	USC (7-1)
1983	UCLA (6-1-1)	1992	Washington (6-2)		& UCLA (7-1)	2004	USC (8-0)
1984	USC (7-1)		& Stanford (6-2)	1998	UCLA (8-0)	2005	USC (8-0)
1985	UCLA (6-2)	1993	UCLA (6-2),	1999	Stanford (7-1)	2006	USC (7-2)
1986	Arizona St. (5-1-1)		Arizona (6-2)	2000	Washington (7-1),		& California (7-2)
1987	USC (7-1)		& USC (6-2)		Oregon St. (7-1)	2007	USC (7-2)
	& UCLA (7-1)	1994	Oregon (7-1)		& Oregon (7-1)		& Arizona St. (7-2)

Southwest Conference (1914-95)

Founded in 1914 as Southwest Intercollegiate Athletic Conference. **Charter members** (8): Arkansas, Baylor, Oklahoma, Oklahoma A&M (now Oklahoma St.), Rice, Southwestern, Texas and Texas A&M. **Admitted later** (5): SMU (Southern Methodist) in 1918; Phillips University in 1920; TCU (Texas Christian) in 1923; Texas Tech in 1956 (began play in '60); Houston in 1971 (began play in '76). **Withdrew later** (13): Southwestern in 1917 (went independent); Oklahoma in 1920 (left for Missouri Valley after '19 season); Phillips in 1921; Oklahoma A&M (now Oklahoma St.) in 1925 (left for Big Six); Arkansas in 1990 (left for SEC after '91 season); Baylor, Texas, Texas A&M and Texas Tech in 1994 (all four left for Big 12 after '95 season); Rice, SMU and TCU in 1994 (all three left for WAC after '95 season); Houston in 1994 (left for Conference USA after '95 season). Conference folded on June 30, 1996.

Multiple titles: Texas (25); Texas A&M (17); Arkansas (13); SMU (9); TCU (9); Rice (7); Baylor (5); Houston (4); Texas Tech (2).

Year		Year		Year		Year	
1914	No champion	1940	Texas A&M (5-1)	1961	Texas (6-1)	1981	SMU (7-1)
1915	Oklahoma (3-0)	1941	Texas A&M (5-1)		& Arkansas (6-1)	1982	SMU (7-0-1)
1916	No champion	1942	Texas (5-1)	1962	Texas (6-0-1)	1983	SMU (8-0)
1917	Texas A&M (2-0)	1943	Texas (5-0)	1963	Texas (7-0)	1984	SMU (6-2)
1918	No champion	1944	TCU (3-1-1)	1964	Arkansas (7-0)		& Houston (6-2)
1919	Texas A&M (4-0)	1945	Texas (5-1)	1965	Arkansas (7-0)	1985	Texas A&M (6-1)
1920	Texas (5-0)	1946	Rice (5-1)	1966	SMU (6-1)	1986	Texas A&M (7-1)
1921	Texas A&M (3-0-2)		& Arkansas (5-1)	1967	Texas A&M (6-1)	1987	Texas A&M (6-1)
1922	Baylor (5-0)	1947	SMU (5-0-1)	1968	Arkansas (6-1)	1988	Arkansas (7-0)
1923	SMU (5-0)	1948	SMU (5-0-1)		& Texas (6-1)	1989	Arkansas (7-1)
1924	Baylor (4-0-1)	1949	Rice (6-0)	1969	Texas (7-0)	1990	Texas (8-0)
1925	Texas A&M (4-1)	1950	Texas (6-0)	1970	Texas (7-0)	1991	Texas A&M (8-0)
1926	SMU (5-0)	1951	TCU (5-1)	1971	Texas (6-1)	1992	Texas A&M (7-0)
1927	Texas A&M (4-0-1)	1952	Texas (6-0)	1972	Texas (7-0)	1993	Texas A&M (7-0)
1928	Texas (5-1)	1953	Rice (5-1)	1973	Texas (7-0)	1994	Baylor, Rice, TCU,
1929	TCU (4-0-1)		& Texas (5-1)	1974	Baylor (6-1)		Texas and Texas Tech†
1930	Texas (4-1)	1954	Arkansas (5-1)	1975	Arkansas (6-1),		(4-3)
1931	SMU (5-0-1)	1955	TCU (5-1)		Texas (6-1)	1995	Texas (7-0)
1932	TCU (6-0)	1956	Texas A&M (6-0)		& Texas A&M (6-1)		
1933	Arkansas (4-1)*	1957	Rice (5-1)	1976	Houston (7-1)	*Arkansas (4-1) forced to
1934	Rice (5-1)	1958	TCU (5-1)		& Texas Tech (7-1)	vacate 1933 title for use of
1935	SMU (6-0)	1959	Texas (5-1),	1977	Texas (8-0)	ineligible player.
1936	Arkansas (5-1)		TCU (5-1)	1978	Houston (7-1)	†Texas A&M had the best
1937	Rice (4-1-1)		& Arkansas (5-1)	1979	Houston (7-1)	record (6-0-1) in 1994 but
1938	TCU (6-0)	1960	Arkansas (6-1)		& Arkansas (7-1)	was on probation and
1939	Texas A&M (6-0)			1980	Baylor (8-0)	therefore ineligible for the
						Southwest championship.

Southeastern Conference

Founded in 1933 when charter members all left Southern Conference to form SEC. **Charter members** (13): Alabama, Auburn, Florida, Georgia, Georgia Tech, Kentucky, LSU (Louisiana St.), Mississippi, Mississippi St., Sewanee, Tennessee, Tulane and Vanderbilt. **Admitted later** (2): Arkansas and South Carolina in 1990 (both began play in '92). **Withdrew later** (3): Sewanee in 1940; Georgia Tech in 1964; and Tulane in 1966.

2007 playing membership (12): Alabama, Arkansas, Auburn, Florida, Georgia, Kentucky, LSU, Mississippi, Mississippi St., South Carolina, Tennessee and Vanderbilt. **Note:** Conference title decided by championship game between Western and Eastern division winners since 1992.

Multiple titles: Alabama (21); Tennessee (13); Georgia (12); Florida and LSU (10); Auburn and Mississippi (6); Georgia Tech (5); Kentucky and Tulane (3).

Year		Year		Year		Year	
1933	Alabama (5-0-1)	1940	Tennessee (5-0)	1948	Georgia (6-0)	1957	Auburn (7-0)
1934	Tulane (8-0)	1941	Mississippi St. (4-0-1)	1949	Tulane (5-1)	1958	LSU (6-0)
	& Alabama (7-0)	1942	Georgia (6-1)	1950	Kentucky (5-1)	1959	Georgia (7-0)
1935	LSU (5-0)	1943	Georgia Tech (3-0)	1951	Georgia Tech (7-0)	1960	Mississippi (5-0-1)
1936	LSU (6-0)	1944	Georgia Tech (4-0)		& Tennessee (5-0)	1961	Alabama (7-0)
1937	Alabama (6-0)	1945	Alabama (6-0)	1952	Georgia Tech (6-0)		& LSU (6-0)
1938	Tennessee (7-0)	1946	Georgia (5-0)	1953	Alabama (4-0-3)	1962	Mississippi (6-0)
1939	Tennessee (6-0),		& Tennessee (5-0)	1954	Mississippi (5-1)	1963	Mississippi (5-0-1)
	Georgia Tech (6-0)	1947	Mississippi (6-1)	1955	Mississippi (5-1)	1964	Alabama (8-0)
	& Tulane (5-0)			1956	Tennessee (6-0)		

Year		Year		Year		Year	
1965	Alabama (6-1-1)	1974	Alabama (6-0)	1981	Georgia (6-0)	1988	Auburn (6-1)
1966	Alabama (6-0)	1975	Alabama (6-0)		& Alabama (6-0)		& LSU (6-1)
	& Georgia (6-0)	1976	Georgia (5-1)	1982	Georgia (6-0)	1989	Alabama (6-1),
1967	Tennessee (6-0)		& Kentucky (5-1)	1983	Auburn (6-0)		Tennessee (6-1)
1968	Georgia (5-0-1)	1977	Alabama (7-0)	1984	Florida (5-0-1)*		& Auburn (6-1)
1969	Tennessee (5-1)		& Kentucky (6-0)	1985	Florida (5-1)†	1990	Florida (6-1)†
1970	LSU (5-0)	1978	Alabama (6-0)		& Tennessee (5-1)		& Tennessee (5-1-1)
1971	Alabama (7-0)	1979	Alabama (6-0)	1986	LSU (5-1)	1991	Florida (7-0)
1972	Alabama (7-1)	1980	Georgia (6-0)	1987	Auburn (5-0-1)		*Title vacated.
1973	Alabama (8-0)						†On probation, ineligible
							for championship.

SEC Championship Game

Since expanding to 12 teams and splitting into two divisions in 1992, the SEC has staged a conference championship game between the two division winners on the first Saturday in December. The game has been played at Legion Field in Birmingham, Ala., (1992-93) and the Georgia Dome in Atlanta (since 1994). The divisions: EAST— Florida, Georgia, Kentucky, South Carolina, Tennessee and Vanderbilt; WEST— Alabama, Arkansas, Auburn, LSU, Mississippi and Mississippi St.

Year		Year		Year	
1992	Alabama 28, Florida 21	1998	Tennessee 24, Miss. St. 14	2004	Auburn 38, Tennessee 28
1993	Florida 28, Alabama 23	1999	Alabama 34, Florida 7	2005	Georgia 34, LSU 14
1994	Florida 24, Alabama 23	2000	Florida 28, Auburn 6	2006	Florida 38, Arkansas 28
1995	Florida 34, Arkansas 3	2001	LSU 31, Tennessee 20	2007	LSU 21, Tennessee 14
1996	Florida 45, Alabama 30	2002	Georgia 30, Arkansas 3		
1997	Tennessee 30, Auburn 29	2003	LSU 34, Georgia 13		

Sun Belt Conference

Founded in 2001 when the Sun Belt Conference sponsored football for the first time. **Charter members** (7): Arkansas State, Idaho, Louisiana-Lafayette, Louisiana-Monroe, Middle Tennessee State, New Mexico State and North Texas. **Admitted later** (4): Utah St. in 2003, Troy St. (now Troy) in 2004, Florida Atlantic and Florida International in 2005. **Withdrew later** (3): Idaho, New Mexico St. and Utah St. in 2005 (left for WAC). **2007 playing membership** (8): Arkansas State, Florida Atlantic, Florida International, Louisiana-Lafayette, Louisiana-Monroe, Middle Tennessee, North Texas and Troy

   Multiple titles: North Texas (4); Middle Tennessee St. and Troy (2)

Year		Year		Year	
2001	North Texas (5-1)	2004	North Texas (7-0)	2006	Troy (6-1)
	& Mid. Tenn. St. (5-1)	2005	Arkansas St. (5-2),		& Mid. Tenn. St. (6-1)
2002	North Texas (6-0)		LA-Lafayette (5-2)	2007	Florida Atlantic (6-1)
2003	North Texas (7-0)		& LA-Monroe (5-2)		& Troy (6-1)

Western Athletic Conference

Founded in 1962 when charter members left the Skyline and Border conferences to form the WAC. **Charter members** (6): Arizona and Arizona St. from Border; BYU (Brigham Young), New Mexico, Utah and Wyoming from Skyline. **Admitted later** (18): Colorado St. and UTEP (Texas-El Paso) in 1967 (both began play in '68); San Diego St. in 1978; Hawaii in 1979; Air Force in 1980; Fresno St. in 1991 (began play in '92); Rice, San Jose St., SMU , TCU , Tulsa and UNLV in 1994 (all began play in '96); Nevada in 2000; Boise St. and Louisiana Tech in 2001; Idaho, New Mexico St. and Utah St. in 2005. **Withdrew later** (13): Arizona and Arizona St. in 1978 (left for Pac-10 after '77 season); Air Force, BYU, Colorado St., New Mexico, San Diego St., UNLV, Utah and Wyoming (left to form Mountain West conference in '99); TCU in 2000 (left for Conference USA after 2000 season); Rice, SMU, Tulsa and UTEP in 2005 (left for Conference USA). **2007 playing membership** (9): Boise St., Fresno St., Hawaii, Idaho, Louisiana Tech, Nevada, New Mexico St., San Jose St., and Utah St.

   Multiple titles: BYU (19); Arizona St. and Wyoming (7); Boise St. (5); Air Force, Fresno St., Hawaii, New Mexico and Colorado St. (3); Arizona, TCU and Utah (2).

Year		Year		Year		Year	
1962	New Mexico (2-1-1)	1974	BYU (6-0-1)	1986	San Diego St. (7-1)		BYU (6-2)
1963	New Mexico (3-1)	1975	Arizona St. (7-0)	1987	Wyoming (8-0)		& Utah (6-2)
1964	Utah (3-1),	1976	BYU (6-1)	1988	Wyoming (8-0)	1996-98	See below
	New Mexico (3-1)		& Wyoming (6-1)	1989	BYU (7-1)	1999	Fresno St. (5-2),
	& Arizona (3-1)	1977	Arizona St. (6-1)	1990	BYU (7-1)		Hawaii (7-2)
1965	BYU (4-1)		& BYU (6-1)	1991	BYU (7-0-1)		& TCU (7-2)
1966	Wyoming (5-0)	1978	BYU (5-1)	1992	Hawaii (6-2),	2000	TCU (7-1)
1967	Wyoming (5-0)	1979	BYU (7-0)		BYU (6-2)		& UTEP (7-1)
1968	Wyoming (6-1)	1980	BYU (6-1)		& Fresno St. (6-2)	2001	La. Tech (7-1)
1969	Arizona St. (6-1)	1981	BYU (7-1)	1993	BYU (6-2),	2002	Boise St. (8-0)
1970	Arizona St. (7-0)	1982	BYU (7-1		Fresno St. (6-2)	2003	Boise St. (8-0)
1971	Arizona St. (7-0)	1983	BYU (7-0)		& Wyoming (6-2)	2004	Boise St. (8-0)
1972	Arizona St. (5-1)	1984	BYU (8-0)	1994	Colorado St. (7-1)	2005	Nevada (7-1)
1973	Arizona St. (6-1)	1985	Air Force (7-1)	1995	Colorado St. (6-2),		& Boise St. (7-1)
	& Arizona (6-1)		& BYU (7-1)		Air Force (6-2),	2006	Boise St. (8-0)
						2007	Hawaii (8-0)

WAC Championship Game (1996-98)

In addition to expanding to 16 teams and splitting into two divisions in 1996, the WAC staged a conference championship game between the two division winners on the first Saturday in December at Sam Boyd Stadium in Las Vegas until eight teams split off and formed the Mountain West Conference in 1999. The divisions: PACIFIC—BYU, Fresno St., Hawaii, New Mexico, San Diego St., San Jose St., UTEP, Utah; MOUNTAIN—Air Force, Colorado St., Rice, SMU, TCU, Tulsa, UNLV, Wyoming.

Year		Year		Year	
1996	BYU 28, Wyoming 25 (OT)	1997	Colorado St. 41, New Mexico 13	1998	Air Force 20, BYU 13

Annual NCAA Division I-A Leaders

Note that Oklahoma A&M is now Oklahoma St. and Texas Mines is now UTEP.

Rushing

Individual championship decided on Rushing Yards (1937-69), and on Yards Per Game (since 1970).

Multiple winners: Troy Davis, Marshall Faulk, Art Luppino, Ed Marinaro, Rudy Mobley, Jim Pilot, O.J. Simpson, LaDainian Tomlinson and Ricky Williams (2).

Year		Car	Yards		Year		Car	Yards	P/Gm
1937	Byron (Whizzer) White, Colorado	181	1121		1973	Mark Kellar, Northern Ill	291	1719	156.3
1938	Len Eshmont, Fordham	132	831		1974	Louie Giammona, Utah St.	329	1534	153.4
1939	John Polanski, Wake Forest	137	882		1975	Ricky Bell, USC	357	1875	170.5
1940	Al Ghesquiere, Detroit	146	957		1976	Tony Dorsett, Pittsburgh	338	1948	177.1
1941	Frank Sinkwich, Georgia	209	1103		1977	Earl Campbell, Texas	267	1744	158.5
1942	Rudy Mobley, Hardin-Simmons	187	1281		1978	Billy Sims, Oklahoma	231	1762	160.2
1943	Creighton Miller, Notre Dame	151	911		1979	Charles White, USC.	293	1803	180.3
1944	Red Williams, Minnesota	136	911		1980	George Rogers, S. Carolina	297	1781	161.9
1945	Bob Fenimore, Oklahoma A&M	142	1048		1981	Marcus Allen, USC.	403	2342	212.9
1946	Rudy Mobley, Hardin-Simmons	227	1262		1982	Ernest Anderson, Okla. St.	353	1877	170.6
1947	Wilton Davis, Hardin-Simmons.	193	1173		1983	Mike Rozier, Nebraska	275	2148	179.0
1948	Fred Wendt, Texas Mines	184	1570		1984	Keith Byars, Ohio St.	313	1655	150.5
1949	John Dottley, Ole Miss	208	1312		1985	Lorenzo White, Mich. St.	386	1908	173.5
1950	Wilford White, Arizona St	199	1502		1986	Paul Palmer, Temple	346	1866	169.6
1951	Ollie Matson, San Francisco	245	1566		1987	Ickey Woods, UNLV	259	1658	150.7
1952	Howie Waugh, Tulsa	164	1372		1988	Barry Sanders, Okla. St.	344	2628	238.9
1953	J.C. Caroline, Illinois	194	1256		1989	Anthony Thompson, Ind	358	1793	163.0
1954	Art Luppino, Arizona	179	1359		1990	Gerald Hudson, Okla. St	279	1642	149.3
1955	Art Luppino, Arizona	209	1313		1991	Marshall Faulk, S. Diego St.	201	1429	158.8
1956	Jim Crawford, Wyoming	200	1104		1992	Marshall Faulk, S. Diego St.	265	1630	163.0
1957	Leon Burton, Arizona St	117	1126		1993	LeShon Johnson, No. Ill.	327	1976	179.6
1958	Dick Bass, Pacific	205	1361		1994	Rashaan Salaam, Colorado	298	2055	186.8
1959	Pervis Atkins, New Mexico St	130	971		1995	Troy Davis, Iowa St.	345	2010	182.7
1960	Bob Gaiters, New Mexico St	197	1338		1996	Troy Davis, Iowa St.	402	2185	198.6
1961	Jim Pilot, New Mexico St	191	1278		1997	Ricky Williams, Texas.	279	1893	172.1
1962	Jim Pilot, New Mexico St	208	1247		1998	Ricky Williams, Texas.	361	2124	193.1
1963	Dave Casinelli, Memphis St	219	1016		1999	LaDainian Tomlinson, TCU	268	1850	168.2
1964	Brian Piccolo, Wake Forest	252	1044		2000	LaDainian Tomlinson, TCU	369	2158	196.2
1965	Mike Garrett, USC	267	1440		2001	Chance Kretschmer, Nevada	302	1732	157.5
1966	Ray McDonald, Idaho	259	1329		2002	Larry Johnson, Penn St.	271	2087	160.5
1967	O.J. Simpson, USC.	266	1415		2003	Patrick Cobbs, No. Texas	307	1680	152.7
1968	O.J. Simpson, USC.	355	1709		2004	Jamario Thomas, No. Texas	285	1801	180.1
1969	Steve Owens, Oklahoma	358	1523		2005	DeAngelo Williams, Memphis	310	1964	178.6

Year		Car	Yards	P/Gm
1970	Ed Marinaro, Cornell	285	1425	158.3
1971	Ed Marinaro, Cornell	356	1881	209.0
1972	Pete VanValkenburg, BYU	232	1386	138.6.

(2006) Garrett Wolfe, Northern Ill. | 309 | 1928 | 148.3
(2007) Kevin Smith, UCF | 450 | 2567 | 183.36

All-Purpose Yardage

Multiple winners: Marcus Allen, Pervis Atkins, Ryan Benjamin, Troy Davis, Troy Edwards, Louie Giammona, Tom Harmon, Art Luppino, Napolean McCallum, O.J. Simpson, Charles White and Gary Wood (2).

Year		Yards	P/Gm		Year		Yards	P/Gm
1937	Byron (Whizzer) White, Colorado	1970	246.3		1957	Overton Curtis, Utah St	1608	160.8
1938	Parker Hall, Ole Miss	1420	129.1		1958	Dick Bass, Pacific	1878	187.8.
1939	Tom Harmon, Michigan.	1208	151.0		1959	Pervis Atkins, New Mexico St	1800	180.0
1940	Tom Harmon, Michigan.	1312	164.0		1960	Pervis Atkins, New Mexico St	1613	161.3
1941	Bill Dudley, Virginia	1674	186.0		1961	Jim Pilot, New Mexico St	1606	160.6
1942	Complete records not available				1962	Gary Wood, Cornell	1395	155.0
1943	Stan Koslowski, Holy Cross	1411	176.4		1963	Gary Wood, Cornell	1508	167.6
1944	Red Williams, Minnesota	1467	163.0		1964	Donny Anderson, Texas Tech	1710	171.0
1945	Bob Fenimore, Oklahoma A&M	1577	197.1		1965	Floyd Little, Syracuse	1990	199.0
1946	Rudy Mobley, Hardin-Simmons	1765	176.5		1966	Frank Quayle, Virginia	1616	161.6
1947	Wilton Davis, Hardin-Simmons	1798	179.8		1967	O.J. Simpson, USC	1700	188.9
1948	Lou Kusserow, Columbia	1737	193.0		1968	O.J. Simpson, USC.	1966	196.6
1949	Johnny Papit, Virginia	1611	179.0		1969	Lynn Moore, Army	1795	179.5
1950	Wilford White, Arizona St.	2065	206.5		1970	Don McCauley, North Carolina	2021	183.7
1951	Ollie Matson, San Francisco	2037	226.3		1971	Ed Marinaro, Cornell	1932	214.7
1952	Billy Vessels, Oklahoma	1512	151.2		1972	Howard Stevens, Louisville	2132	213.2
1953	J.C. Caroline, Illinois	1470	163.3		1973	Willard Harrell, Pacific	1777	177.7
1954	Art Luppino, Arizona	2193	219.3		1974	Louie Giammona, Utah St	1984	198.4
1955	Jim Swink, TCU	1702	170.2		1975	Louie Giammona, Utah St	2045	185.9
	& Art Luppino, Arizona	1702	170.2		1976	Tony Dorsett, Pittsburgh	2021	183.7
1956	Jack Hill, Utah St	1691	169.1		1977	Earl Campbell, Texas	1855	168.6
					1978	Charles White, USC.	2096	174.7

Year		Yards	P/Gm
1979	Charles White, USC	1941	194.1
1980	Marcus Allen, USC	1794	179.4
1981	Marcus Allen, USC	2559	232.6
1982	Carl Monroe, Utah	2036	185.1
1983	Napoleon McCallum, Navy	2385	216.8
1984	Keith Byars, Ohio St	2284	207.6
1985	Napoleon McCallum, Navy	2330	211.8
1986	Paul Palmer, Temple	2633	239.4
1987	Eric Wilkerson, Kent St.	2074	188.6
1988	Barry Sanders, Oklahoma St.	3250	295.5
1989	Mike Pringle, CS-Fullerton	2690	244.6
1990	Glyn Milburn, Stanford	2222	202.0
1991	Ryan Benjamin, Pacific	2995	249.6
1992	Ryan Benjamin, Pacific	2597	236.1
1993	LeShon Johnson, Northern Ill.	2082	189.3

Year		Yards	P/Gm
1994	Rashaan Salaam, Colorado	2349	213.5
1995	Troy Davis, Iowa St.	2466	224.2
1996	Troy Davis, Iowa St.	2364	214.9
1997	Troy Edwards, La. Tech	2144	194.9
1998	Troy Edwards, La. Tech	2784	232.0
1999	Trevor Insley, Nevada	2176	197.8
2000	Emmett White, Utah St.	2628	238.9
2001	Levron Williams, Indiana	2201	200.1
2002	Larry Johnson, Penn St.	2655	204.2
2003	DeAngelo Williams, Memphis	2113	192.1
2004	Darren Sproles, Kansas St.	2067	187.9
2005	Reggie Bush, USC	2890	223.3
2006	Garrett Wolfe, Northern Ill.	2177	167.5
2007	Chris Johnson, East Carolina	2960	227.7

Total Offense

Individual championship decided on Total Yards (1937-69) and on Yards Per Game (since 1970).

Multiple winners: Tim Rattay (3); Colt Brennan, Johnny Bright, Bob Fenimore, Mike Maxwell and Jim McMahon (2).

Year		Plays	Yards
1937	Byron (Whizzer) White, Colorado	224	1596
1938	Davey O'Brien, TCU	291	1847
1939	Kenny Washington, UCLA	259	1370
1940	Johnny Knolla, Creighton	298	1420
1941	Bud Schwenk, Washington-MO	354	1928
1942	Frank Sinkwich, Georgia	341	2187
1943	Bob Hoernschemeyer, Indiana	355	1648
1944	Bob Fenimore, Oklahoma A&M	241	1758
1945	Bob Fenimore, Oklahoma A&M	203	1641
1946	Travis Tidwell, Auburn	339	1715
1947	Fred Enke, Arizona	329	1941
1948	Stan Heath, Nevada-Reno	233	1992
1949	Johnny Bright, Drake	275	1950
1950	Johnny Bright, Drake	320	2400
1951	Dick Kazmaier, Princeton	272	1827
1952	Ted Marchibroda, Detroit	305	1813
1953	Paul Larson, California	262	1572
1954	George Shaw, Oregon	276	1536
1955	George Welsh, Navy	203	1348
1956	John Brodie, Stanford	295	1642
1957	Bob Newman, Washington St	263	1444
1958	Dick Bass, Pacific	218	1440
1959	Dick Norman, Stanford	319	2018
1960	Billy Kilmer, UCLA	292	1889
1961	Dave Hoppmann, Iowa St.	320	1638
1962	Terry Baker, Oregon St	318	2276
1963	George Mira, Miami-FL	394	2318
1964	Jerry Rhome, Tulsa	470	3128
1965	Bill Anderson, Tulsa	580	3343
1966	Virgil Carter, BYU	388	2545
1967	Sal Olivas, New Mexico St.	368	2184
1968	Greg Cook, Cincinnati	507	3210
1969	Dennis Shaw, San Diego St	388	3197

Year		Plays	Yards	P/Gm
1970	Pat Sullivan, Auburn	333	2856	285.6
1971	Gary Huff, Florida St.	386	2653	241.2
1972	Don Strock, Va. Tech	480	3170	288.2
1973	Jesse Freitas, San Diego St.	410	2901	263.7
1974	Steve Joachim, Temple	331	2227	222.7
1975	Gene Swick, Toledo	490	2706	246.0
1976	Tommy Kramer, Rice	562	3272	297.5
1977	Doug Williams, Grambling	377	3229	293.5
1978	Mike Ford, SMU	459	2957	268.8
1979	Marc Wilson, BYU	488	3580	325.5
1980	Jim McMahon, BYU	540	4627	385.6
1981	Jim McMahon, BYU	487	3458	345.8
1982	Todd Dillon, Long Beach St	585	3587	326.1
1983	Steve Young, BYU	531	4346	395.1
1984	Robbie Bosco, BYU	543	3932	327.7
1985	Jim Everett, Purdue	518	3589	326.3
1986	Mike Perez, San Jose St.	425	2969	329.9
1987	Todd Santos, San Diego St.	562	3688	307.3
1988	Scott Mitchell, Utah	589	4299	390.8
1989	Andre Ware, Houston	628	4661	423.7
1990	David Klingler, Houston	704	5221	474.6
1991	Ty Detmer, BYU	478	4001	333.4
1992	Jimmy Klingler, Houston	544	3768	342.6
1993	Chris Vargas, Nevada	535	4332	393.8
1994	Mike Maxwell, Nevada	477	3498	318.0
1995	Mike Maxwell, Nevada	443	3623	402.6
1996	Josh Wallwork, Wyoming	525	4209	350.8
1997	Tim Rattay, La. Tech	541	3968	360.7
1998	Tim Rattay, La. Tech	602	4840	403.3
1999	Tim Rattay, La. Tech	562	3810	381.0
2000	Drew Brees, Purdue	564	3939	358.1
2001	Rex Grossman, Florida	429	3904	354.9
2002	Byron Leftwich, Marshall	528	4267	355.6
2003	B.J. Symons, Texas Tech	798	5976	459.7
2004	Sonny Cumbie, Texas Tech	694	4575	381.3
2005	Colt Brennan, Hawaii	614	4455	371.3
2006	Colt Brennan, Hawaii	645	5915	422.5
2007	Graham Harrell, Texas Tech	751	5614	431.8

Sacks

Pass sacks have only been compiled by the NCAA since the 2000 season.

Year		Gms	Total
2000	Michael Josiah, Louisville	91	12½
2001	Dwight Freeney, Syracuse	12	17½
2002	Terrell Suggs, Arizona St.	14	24
2003	Dave Ball, UCLA	13	16½
	Kenechi Udeze, USC	13	16½
	& D.D. Acholonu, Wash. St.	13	16½

Year		Gms	Total
2004	Jonathan Goddard, Marshall	12	16
2005	Elvis Dumervil, Louisville	12	20
2006	Ameer Ismail, Western Mich.	13	17
2007	Greg Middleton, Indiana	13	16

Annual NCAA Division I-A Leaders (Cont.)

Passing

Individual championship decided on Completions (1937-69), on Completions Per Game (1970-78) and on Passing Efficiency rating points (since 1979).

Multiple winners: Elvis Grbac, Don Heinrich, Jim McMahon, Davey O'Brien and Don Trull (2).

Year		Cmp	Pct	TD	Yds
1937	Davey O'Brien, TCU	94	.402	–	969
1938	Davey O'Brien, TCU	93	.557	–	1457
1939	Kay Eakin, Arkansas	78	.404	–	962
1940	Billy Sewell, Wash. St	86	.494	–	1023
1941	Bud Schwenk, Wash.-MO	114	.487	–	1457
1942	Ray Evans, Kansas	101	.505	–	1117
1943	Johnny Cook, Georgia	73	.465	–	1007
1944	Paul Rickards, Pittsburgh	84	.472	–	997
1945	Al Dekdebrun, Cornell	90	.464	–	1227
1946	Travis Tidwell, Auburn	79	.500	5	943
1947	Charlie Conerly, Ole Miss	133	.571	18	1367
1948	Stan Heath, Nev-Reno	126	.568	22	2005
1949	Adrian Burk, Baylor	110	.576	14	1428
1950	Don Heinrich, Washington	134	.606	14	1846
1951	Don Klosterman, Loyola-CA	159	.505	9	1843
1952	Don Heinrich, Washington	137	.507	13	1647
1953	Bob Garrett, Stanford	118	.576	17	1637
1954	Paul Larson, California	125	.641	10	1537
1955	George Welsh, Navy	94	.627	8	1319
1956	John Brodie, Stanford	139	.579	12	1633
1957	Ken Ford, H-Simmons	115	.561	14	1254
1958	Buddy Humphrey, Baylor	112	.574	7	1316
1959	Dick Norman, Stanford	152	.578	11	1963
1960	Harold Stephens, H-Simm	145	.566	3	1254
1961	Chon Gallegos, S. Jose St	117	.594	14	1480
1962	Don Trull, Baylor	125	.546	11	1627
1963	Don Trull, Baylor	174	.565	12	2157
1964	Jerry Rhome, Tulsa	224	.687	32	2870
1965	Bill Anderson, Tulsa	296	.582	30	3464
1966	John Eckman, Wichita St	195	.426	7	2339
1967	Terry Stone, N. Mexico	160	.476	9	1946
1968	Chuck Hixson, SMU	265	.566	21	3103
1969	John Reaves, Florida	222	.561	24	2896

Year		Cmp	P/Gm	TD	Yds
1970	Sonny Sixkiller, Wash	186	18.6	15	2303
1971	Brian Sipe, S. Diego St	196	17.8	17	2532
1972	Don Strock, Va. Tech	228	20.7	16	3243
1973	Jesse Freitas, S. Diego St.	227	20.6	21	2993

Year		Cmp	P/Gm	TD	Yds
1974	Steve Bartkowski, Cal	182	16.5	12	2580
1975	Craig Penrose, S. Diego St.	198	18.0	15	2660
1976	Tommy Kramer, Rice	269	24.5	21	3317
1977	Guy Benjamin, Stanford	208	20.8	19	2521
1978	Steve Dils, Stanford	247	22.5	22	2943

Year		Cmp	TD	Yds	Rating
1979	Turk Schonert, Stanford	148	19	1922	163.0
1980	Jim McMahon, BYU	284	47	4571	176.9
1981	Jim McMahon, BYU	272	30	3555	155.0
1982	Tom Ramsey, UCLA	191	21	2824	153.5
1983	Steve Young, BYU	306	33	3902	168.5
1984	Doug Flutie, BC	233	27	3454	152.9
1985	Jim Harbaugh, Michigan	139	18	1913	163.7
1986	Vinny Testaverde, Miami-FL	175	26	2557	165.8
1987	Don McPherson, Syracuse	129	22	2341	164.3
1988	Timm Rosenbach, Wash. St.	199	23	2791	162.0
1989	Ty Detmer, BYU	265	32	4560	175.6
1990	Shawn Moore, Virginia	144	21	2262	160.7
1991	Elvis Grbac, Michigan	152	24	1955	169.0
1992	Elvis Grbac, Michigan	112	15	1465	154.2
1993	Trent Dilfer, Fresno St.	217	28	3276	173.1
1994	Kerry Collins, Penn St.	176	21	2679	172.9
1995	Danny Wuerffel, Florida	210	35	3266	178.4
1996	Steve Sarkisian, BYU	278	33	4027	173.6
1997	Cade McNown, UCLA	173	22	2877	168.6
1998	Shaun King, Tulane	223	36	3232	183.3
1999	Michael Vick, Va. Tech.	90	12	1840	180.4
2000	Bart Hendricks, Boise St.	210	35	3364	170.6
2001	Rex Grossman, Florida	259	34	3896	170.8
2002	Brad Banks, Iowa	170	26	2573	157.1
2003	Philip Rivers, N.C. State	348	34	4491	170.5
2004	Stefan Lefors, Louisville	189	20	2596	181.7
2005	Rudy Carpenter, Arizona St.	156	17	2273	175.0
2006	Colt Brennan, Hawaii	406	58	5549	186.0
2007	Sam Bradford, Oklahoma	341	36	3121	176.5

Receptions

Championship decided on Passes Caught (1937-69) and on Catches Per Game (since 1970). Touchdown totals unavailable in 1939 and 1941-45.

Multiple winners: Neil Armstrong, Hugh Campbell, Manny Hazard, Reid Moseley, Jason Phillips, Howard Twilley and Alex Van Dyke (2).

Year		No	TD	Yds
1937	Jim Benton, Arkansas	47	7	754
1938	Sam Boyd, Baylor	32	5	537
1939	Ken Kavanaugh, LSU	30	–	467
1940	Eddie Bryant, Virginia	30	2	222
1941	Hank Stanton, Arizona	50	–	820
1942	Bill Rogers, Texas A&M	39	–	432
1943	Neil Armstrong, Okla. A&M	39	–	317
1944	Reid Moseley, Georgia	32	–	506
1945	Reid Moseley, Georgia	31	–	662
1946	Neil Armstrong, Okla. A&M	32	1	479
1947	Barney Poole, Ole Miss	52	8	513
1948	Red O'Quinn, Wake Forest	39	7	605
1949	Art Weiner, N. Carolina	52	7	762
1950	Gordon Cooper, Denver	46	8	569
1951	Dewey McConnell, Wyoming	47	9	725
1952	Ed Brown, Fordham	57	6	774
1953	John Carson, Georgia	45	4	663
1954	Jim Hanifan, California	44	7	569
1955	Hank Burnine, Missouri	44	2	594
1956	Art Powell, San Jose St	40	5	583
1957	Stuart Vaughan, Utah	53	5	756

Year		No	TD	Yds
1958	Dave Hibbert, Arizona	61	4	606
1959	Chris Burford, Stanford	61	6	756
1960	Hugh Campbell, Wash. St	66	10	881
1961	Hugh Campbell, Wash. St	53	5	723
1962	Vern Burke, Oregon St	69	10	1007
1963	Lawrence Elkins, Baylor	70	8	873
1964	Howard Twilley, Tulsa	95	13	1178
1965	Howard Twilley, Tulsa	134	16	1779
1966	Glenn Meltzer, Wichita St	91	4	1115
1967	Bob Goodridge, Vanderbilt	79	6	1114
1968	Ron Sellers, Florida St	86	12	1496
1969	Jerry Hendren, Idaho	95	12	1452

Year		No	P/Gm	TD	Yds
1970	Mike Mikolayunas, Davidson	87	8.7	8	1128
1971	Tom Reynolds, San Diego St	67	6.7	7	1070
1972	Tom Forzani, Utah St	85	7.7	8	1169
1973	Jay Miller, BYU	100	9.1	8	1181
1974	D. McDonald, San Diego St	86	7.8	7	1157
1975	Bob Farnham, Brown	56	6.2	2	701
1976	Billy Ryckman, La. Tech	77	7.0	10	1382
1977	W. Tolleson, W. Carolina	73	6.6	7	1101

Year		No	P/Gm	TD	Yds	Year		No	P/Gm	TD	Yds
1978	Dave Petzke, Northern Ill	.91	8.3	11	1217	1994	Alex Van Dyke, Nevada	.98	8.9	10	1246
1979	Rick Beasley, Appalach. St	.74	6.7	12	1205	1995	Alex Van Dyke, Nevada	.129	11.7	16	1854
1980	Dave Young, Purdue	.67	6.1	8	917	1996	Damond Wilkins, Nevada	.114	10.4	4	1121
1981	Pete Harvey, N. Texas St	.57	6.3	3	743	1997	Eugene Baker, Kent	.103	9.4	18	1549
1982	Vincent White, Stanford.	.68	6.8	8	677	1998	Troy Edwards, La. Tech	.140	11.7	27	1996
1983	Keith Edwards, Vanderbilt	.97	8.8	8	909	1999	Trevor Insley, Nevada	.134	12.2	13	2060
1984	David Williams, Illinois	.101	9.2	8	1278	2000	James Jordan, La. Tech	.109	9.1	4	1003
1985	Rodney Carter, Purdue	.98	8.9	4	1099	2001	Kevin Curtis, Utah St.	.100	9.1	10	1531
1986	Mark Templeton, L. Beach St	.99	9.0	2	688	2002	Nate Burleson, Nevada	.138	11.5	12	1629
1987	Jason Phillips, Houston	.99	9.0	3	875	2003	Lance Moore, Toledo	.103	8.6	9	1194
1988	Jason Phillips, Houston.	.108	9.8	15	1444	2004	Dante Ridgeway, Ball St.	.105	9.6	8	1399
1989	Manny Hazard, Houston	.142	12.9	22	1689	2005	Greg Jennings, W. Mich.	.98	8.9	14	1259
1990	Manny Hazard, Houston	.78	7.8	9	946	2006	Chris Williams, N. Mex. St.	.92	7.7	12	1415
1991	Fred Gilbert, Houston.	.106	9.6	7	957	2007	Michael Crabtree, Tex. Tech	134	10.3	22	1962
1992	Sherman Smith, Houston	.103	9.4	6	923						
1993	Chris Penn, Tulsa	.105	9.6	12	1578						

Scoring

Championship decided on Total Points (1937-69) and on Points Per Game (since 1970).

Multiple winners: Tom Harmon and Billy Sims (2).

Year		TD	XP	FG	Pts	Year		TD	XP	FG	Pts	P/Gm
1937	Byron (Whizzer) White, Colo	16	23	1	122	1972	Harold Henson, Ohio St.	20	0	0	120	12.0
1938	Parker Hall, Ole Miss	11	7	0	73	1973	Jim Jennings, Rutgers	21	2	0	128	11.6
1939	Tom Harmon, Michigan	14	15	1	102	1974	Bill Marek, Wisconsin	19	0	0	114	12.7
1940	Tom Harmon, Michigan	16	18	1	117	1975	Pete Johnson, Ohio St.	25	0	0	150	13.6
1941	Bill Dudley, Virginia	18	23	1	134	1976	Tony Dorsett, Pitt	22	2	0	134	12.2
1942	Bob Steuber, Missouri	18	13	0	121	1977	Earl Campbell, Texas	19	0	0	114	10.4
1943	Steve Van Buren, LSU	14	14	0	98	1978	Billy Sims, Oklahoma	20	0	0	120	10.9
1944	Glenn Davis, Army	20	0	0	120	1979	Billy Sims, Oklahoma	22	0	0	132	12.0
1945	Doc Blanchard, Army	19	1	0	115	1980	Sammy Winder, So. Miss	20	0	0	120	10.9
1946	Gene Roberts, Tenn-Chatt.	18	9	0	117	1981	Marcus Allen, USC	23	0	0	138	12.5
1947	Lou Gambino, Maryland	16	0	0	96	1982	Greg Allen, Fla. St	21	0	0	126	11.5
1948	Fred Wendt, Texas Mines	20	32	0	152	1983	Mike Rozier, Nebraska	29	0	0	174	14.5
1949	George Thomas, Oklahoma	19	3	0	117	1984	Keith Byars, Ohio St	24	0	0	144	13.1
1950	Bobby Reynolds, Nebraska	22	25	0	157	1985	Bernard White, B. Green.	19	0	0	114	10.4
1951	Ollie Matson, San Francisco	21	0	0	126	1986	Steve Bartalo, Colo. St.	19	0	0	114	10.4
1952	Jackie Parker, Miss. St.	16	24	0	120	1987	Paul Hewitt, S. Diego St.	24	0	0	144	12.0
1953	Earl Lindley, Utah St.	13	3	0	81	1988	Barry Sanders, Okla.St.	39	0	0	234	21.3
1954	Art Luppino, Arizona	24	22	0	166	1989	Anthony Thompson, Ind	25	4	0	154	14.0
1955	Jim Swink, TCU	20	5	0	125	1990	Stacey Robinson, No. Ill.	19	6	0	120	10.9
1956	Clendon Thomas, Oklahoma	18	0	0	108	1991	Marshall Faulk, S.D. St.	23	2	0	140	15.6
1957	Leon Burton, Ariz. St.	16	0	0	96	1992	Garrison Hearst, Georgia	21	0	0	126	11.5
1958	Dick Bass, Pacific	18	8	0	116	1993	Bam Morris, Texas Tech	22	2	0	134	12.2
1959	Pervis Atkins, N. Mexico St.	17	5	0	107	1994	Rashaan Salaam, Colo	24	0	0	144	13.1
1960	Bob Gaiters, N. Mexico St.	23	7	0	145	1995	Eddie George, Ohio St.	24	0	0	144	12.0
1961	Jim Pilot, N. Mexico St.	21	12	0	138	1996	Corey Dillon, Washington	23	0	0	138	12.6
1962	Jerry Logan, W. Texas St.	13	32	0	110	1997	Ricky Williams, Texas	25	2	0	152	13.8
1963	Cosmo Iacavazzi, Princeton	14	0	0	84	1998	Troy Edwards, La. Tech	31	2	0	188	15.7
	& Dave Casinelli, Memphis St.	14	0	0	84	1999	Shaun Alexander, Alabama	24	0	0	144	13.1
1964	Brian Piccolo, Wake Forest	17	9	0	111	2000	Lee Suggs, Va. Tech	28	0	0	168	15.3
1965	Howard Twilley, Tulsa	16	31	0	127	2001	Luke Staley, BYU	28	0	0	170	15.5
1966	Ken Hebert, Houston	11	41	2	113	2002	Brock Forsey, Boise St.	32	0	0	192	14.8
1967	Leroy Keyes, Purdue	19	0	0	114	2003	Patrick Cobbs, No. Texas	21	0	0	126	11.5
1968	Jim O'Brien, Cincinnati	12	31	13	142	2004	Tyler Jones, Boise St.	0	69	24	141	11.8
1969	Steve Owens, Oklahoma	23	0	0	138	2005	Michael Bush, Louisville	24	0	0	144	14.4

Year		TD	XP	FG	Pts	P/Gm							
1970	Brian Bream, Air Force	20	0	0	120	12.0	2006	Ian Johnson, Boise St.	25	0	0	152	12.7
	& Gary Kosins, Dayton	18	0	0	108	12.0	2007	Kevin Smith, UCF	30	0	0	180	12.9
1971	Ed Marinaro, Cornell	24	4	0	148	16.4							

All-Time Best Records by a Starting Quarterback

(Minimum 25 starts) Source: NCAA Record Book

	Years	W-L-T	Win Pct.
Chuck Ealey, Toledo	1969-71	35-0-0	1.000
Jimmy Harris, Oklahoma	1954-56	25-0-0	1.000
Steve Davis, Oklahoma	1973-75	32-1-1	.956
Ken Dorsey, Miami-FL	1999-2002	38-2-0	.950
Matt Leinart, USC	2002-05	37-2-0	.949
Jerry Tagge, Nebraska	1969-71	24-1-1	.942

All-Time NCAA Division I-A Leaders

Through the 2007 season. The NCAA does not recognize active players among career Per Game leaders.

CAREER

Passing

(Minimum 500 Completions)

Passing Efficiency	Years	Rating
1 Ryan Dinwiddie, Boise St.	2000-03	168.9
2 Colt Brennan, Hawaii	2005-07	167.7
3 Danny Wuerffel, Florida	1993-96	163.6
4 Omar Jacobs, Bowling Green	2003-05	163.5
5 Ty Detmer, BYU	1988-91	162.7

Yards Gained	Years	Yards
1 Timmy Chang, Hawaii	2000-04	17,072
2 Ty Detmer, BYU	1988-91	15,031
3 Colt Brennan, Hawaii	2005-07	14,193
4 Philip Rivers, N.C. State	2000-03	13,484
5 Kevin Kolb, Houston	2003-06	12,964

Completions	Years	No
1 Timmy Chang, Hawaii	2000-04	1388
2 Kliff Kingsbury, Texas Tech	1999-02	1231
3 Philip Rivers, N.C. State	2000-03	1147
4 Colt Brennan, Hawaii	2005-07	1115
5 Luke McCown, La. Tech	2000-03	1063

Receptions

Catches	Years	No
1 Taylor Stubblefield, Purdue	2001-04	316
2 Josh Davis, Marshall	2001-04	306
3 Taurean Henderson, Texas Tech	2002-05	303
4 Arnold Jackson, Louisville	1997-00	300
5 Trevor Insley, Nevada	1996-99	298

Catches Per Game	Years	No	P/Gm
1 Manny Hazard, Houston	1989-90	220	10.5
2 Alex Van Dyke, Nevada	1994-95	227	10.3
3 Howard Twilley, Tulsa	1963-65	261	10.0
4 Jason Phillips, Houston	1987-88	207	9.4
5 Troy Edwards, La. Tech	1996-98	280	8.2

Yards Gained	Years	No	Yards
1 Trevor Insley, Nevada	1996-99	298	5005
2 Marcus Harris, Wyoming	1993-96	259	4518
3 Rashaun Woods, Oklahoma St.	2000-03	293	4412
4 Ryan Yarborough, Wyoming	1990-93	229	4357
5 Troy Edwards, La. Tech	1996-98	280	4352

Rushing

Yards Gained	Years	Yards
1 Ron Dayne, Wisconsin	1996-99	6397
2 Ricky Williams, Texas	1995-98	6279
3 Tony Dorsett, Pittsburgh	1973-76	6082
4 DeAngelo Williams, Memphis	2002-05	6026
5 Charles White, USC	1976-79	5598

Yards Per Game	Years	Yards	P/Gm
1 Ed Marinaro, Cornell	1969-71	4715	174.6
2 O.J. Simpson, USC	1967-68	3124	164.4
3 Herschel Walker, Georgia	1980-82	5259	159.4
4 Garrett Wolfe, No. Ill	2003-06	5164	156.5
5 LeShon Johnson, No. Ill.	1992-93	3314	150.6

Total Offense

Yards Gained	Years	Yards
1 Timmy Chang, Hawaii	2000-04	16,910
2 Colt Brennan, Hawaii	2005-07	14,740
3 Ty Detmer, BYU	1988-91	14,665
4 Kevin Kolb, Houston	2003-06	13,715
5 Philip Rivers, N.C. State	2000-03	13,582
6 Brad Smith, Missouri	2002-05	13,088

Yards Per Game	Years	Yards	P/Gm
1 Colt Brennan, Hawaii	2005-07	14,740	387.9
2 Tim Rattay, La. Tech	1997-99	12,689	382.4
3 Chris Vargas, Nevada	1992-93	6,417	320.9
4 Timmy Chang, Hawaii	2000-04	16,910	319.1
5 Ty Detmer, BYU	1988-91	14,665	318.8

All-Purpose Yardage

Yards Gained	Years	Yards
1 DeAngelo Williams, Memphis	2002-05	7573
2 Ricky Williams, Texas	1995-98	7206
3 Napoleon McCallum, Navy	1981-85	7172
4 Chris Johnson, East Carolina	2004-07	6993
5 Darrin Nelson, Stanford	1977-78, 80-81	6885

Yards Per Game	Years	Yards	P/Gm
1 Ryan Benjamin, Pacific	1990-92	5706	237.8
2 Sheldon Canley, S. Jose St.	1988-90	5146	205.8
3 Howard Stevens, Louisville	1971-72	3873	193.7
4 O.J. Simpson, USC	1967-68	3666	192.9
5 Alex Van Dyke, Nevada	1994-95	4146	188.5

Miscellaneous

Punting Average*	Years	Avg
1 Daniel Sepulveda, Baylor	2003-06	45.2
2 Shane Lechler, Texas A&M	1996-99	44.7
3 Bill Smith, Mississippi	1983-86	44.3
4 Jim Arnold, Vanderbilt	1979-82	43.9
5 Ralf Mojsiejenko, Michigan St.	1981-84	43.6

*Minimum 250 punts.

Punting Return Average*	Years	Avg
1 Jack Mitchell, Oklahoma	1946-48	23.6
2 Gene Gibson, Cincinnati	1949-50	20.5
3 Eddie Macon, Pacific	1949-51	18.9
4 Jackie Robinson, UCLA	1939-40	18.8
5 Dan Shelton, N. Illinois	2001-04	17.9

*Minimum 1.2 punt returns per game and 30 career returns.

Kickoff Return Average*	Years	Avg
1 Anthony Davis, USC	1972-74	35.1
2 Eric Booth, So. Miss.	1994-97	32.4
3 Overton Curtis, Utah St	1957-58	31.0
4 Fred Montgomery, New Mexico St.	1991-92	30.5
5 Altie Taylor, Utah St.	1966-68	29.3

*Minimum 1.2 kickoff returns per game and 30 career returns.

Interceptions	Years	No
1 Al Brosky, Illinois	1950-52	29
2 John Provost, Holy Cross	1972-74	27
Martin Bayless, Bowling Green	1980-83	27
4 Tom Curtis, Michigan	1967-69	25
Tony Thurman, Boston College	1981-84	25
Tracy Saul, Texas Tech.	1989-92	25

Blocked Kicks	Years	FG	XP	P	Tot
1 James Ferebee, N. Mexico St.	1978-81	8	6	5	19
2 Max McGeary, Baylor	1977-80	6	4	6	16
3 James King, C. Michigan	2001-04	1	2	10	13
4 Terrence Holt, N.C. State	1999-02	8	0	4	12
Matt Harding, Hawaii	1992-95	5	1	6	12

Note: The blocked kicks category is a combined total of blocked field goals (FG), extra points (XP) and punts (P).

> **Editor's Note:** The keeping of complete defensive statistics, except for blocked kicks (see above), had been inconsistent until recently. As a result the NCAA only tracks most defensive stats back to 2000 and due to the lack of historical context, those records have been omitted here.

Scoring
Non-kickers

Points	Years	TD	Xpt	FG	Pts
1 Travis Prentice, Miami-OH	1996-99	78	0	0	468
2 Ricky Williams, Texas	1995-98	75	2	0	452
3 Taurean Henderson, Tex. Tech	2002-05	69	0	0	414
4 Brock Forsey, Boise St.	1999-02	68	0	0	408
5 Cedric Benson, Texas	2001-04	67	1	0	404

Points Per Game	Years	Pts	P/Gm
1 Marshall Faulk, S. Diego St.	1991-93	376	12.1
2 Ed Marinaro, Cornell.	1969-71	318	11.8
3 Bill Burnett, Arkansas	1968-70	294	11.3
4 Steve Owens, Oklahoma	1967-69	336	11.2
5 Eddie Talboom, Wyoming	1948-50	303	10.8

Touchdowns Rushing	Years	No
1 Travis Prentice, Miami-OH	1996-99	73
2 Ricky Williams, Texas	1995-98	72
3 Anthony Thompson, Indiana.	1986-89	64
Cedric Benson, Texas	2001-04	64
5 Ron Dayne, Wisconsin	1996-99	63

Touchdowns Passing	Years	No
1 Colt Brennan, Hawaii	2005-07	131
2 Ty Detmer, BYU.	1988-91	121
3 Timmy Chang, Hawaii	2000-04	117
4 Tim Rattay, La. Tech	1997-99	115
5 Danny Wuerffel, Florida	1993-96	114
6 Chad Pennington, Marshall	1997-99	100

Touchdowns Catches	Years	No
1 Troy Edwards, La. Tech	1996-98	50
2 Darius Watts, Marshall	2000-03	47
3 Aaron Turner, Pacific	1989-92	43
4 Ryan Yarborough, Wyoming	1990-93	42
Rashaun Woods, Oklahoma St.	2000-03	42

Kickers

Points	Years	FG	XP	Pts
1 Art Carmody, Louisville	2004-07	60	253	433
2 Roman Anderson, Hou	1988-91	70	213	423
3 Billy Bennett, Georgia	2000-03	87	110	409
4 Jeremy Ito, Rutgers	2004-07	80	160	400
5 Carlos Huerta, Mia-FL	1988-91	73	178	397

Field Goals	Years	No
1 Billy Bennett, Georgia	2000-03	87
2 Jeff Jaeger, Washington	1983-86	80
Nick Novak, Maryland	2001-04	80
Jeremy Ito, Rutgers	2004-07	80
Alexis Serna, Oregon St.	2004-07	80
6 John Lee, UCLA	1982-85	79
Jason Elam, Hawaii	1988-89, 91-92	79

SINGLE SEASON

Note that starting with the 2002 season, postseason and bowl games are included in single season records.

Rushing

Yards Gained	Year	Gm	Car	Yards
Barry Sanders, Okla. St	1988	11	344	2628
Kevin Smith, UCF	2007	14	450	2567
Marcus Allen, USC	1981	11	403	2342
Troy Davis, Iowa St.	1996	11	402	2185
LaDainian Tomlinson, TCU	2000	11	369	2158

Yards Per Game	Year	Gm	Yards	P/Gm
Barry Sanders, Okla. St	1988	11	2628	238.9
Marcus Allen, USC	1981	11	2342	212.9
Ed Marinaro, Cornell.	1971	9	1881	209.0
Troy Davis, Iowa St.	1996	11	2185	198.6
LaDainian Tomlinson, TCU	2000	11	2158	196.2

Passing
(Minimum 15 Attempts Per Game)

Passing Efficiency	Year	Rating
Colt Brennan, Hawaii	2006	186.0
Shaun King, Tulane	1998	183.3
Stefan Lefors, Louisville	2004	181.7
Michael Vick, Va. Tech	1999	180.4
Danny Wuerffel, Florida	1995	178.4

Yards Gained	Year	Yards
B.J. Symons, Texas Tech	2003	5833
Graham Harrell, Texas Tech	2007	5705
Colt Brennan, Hawaii	2006	5549
Ty Detmer, BYU.	1990	5188
David Klingler, Houston.	1990	5140

Completions	Year	Att	No
Graham Harrell, Texas Tech	2007	713	512
Kliff Kingsbury, Texas Tech	2002	712	479
B.J. Symons, Texas Tech	2003	719	470
Colt Brennan, Hawaii	2006	559	406
Chase Holbrook, N. Mexico St.	2006	567	397

Receptions

Catches	Year	Gm	No
Manny Hazard, Houston	1989	11	142
Troy Edwards, La. Tech	1998	12	140
Nate Burleson, Nevada	2002	12	138
Howard Twilley, Tulsa	1965	10	134
Trevor Insley, Nevada	1999	11	134
Michael Crabtree, Texas Tech	2007	13	134

Catches Per Game	Year	No	P/Gm
Howard Twilley, Tulsa	1965	134	13.4
Manny Hazard, Houston	1989	142	12.9
Trevor Insley, Nevada	1999	134	12.2
Alex Van Dyke, Nevada	1995	129	11.7
Troy Edwards, La. Tech	1998	140	11.7

Yards Gained	Year	No	Yards
Trevor Insley, Nevada	1999	134	2060
Troy Edwards, La. Tech	1998	140	1996
Michael Crabtree, Texas Tech	2007	134	1962
Alex Van Dyke, Nevada	1995	129	1854
J.R. Tolver, San Diego St.	2002	128	1785

Total Offense

Yards Gained	Year	Gm	Plays	Yards
B.J. Symons, Texas Tech	2003	13	798	5976
Colt Brennan, Hawaii	2006	14	645	5915
Graham Harrell, Texas Tech	2007	13	751	5614
David Klingler, Houston.	1990	11	704	5221
Paul Smith, Tulsa	2007	14	649	5184

Yards Per Game	Year	Gm	Yards	P/Gm
David Klingler, Houston.	1990	11	5221	474.6
B.J. Symons, Texas Tech	2003	13	5976	459.7
Graham Harrell, Texas Tech	2007	13	5614	431.8
Andre Ware, Houston	1989	11	4661	423.7
Colt Brennan, Hawaii	2006	14	5915	422.5

All-Purpose Yardage

Yards Gained	Year	Yards
Barry Sanders, Okla. St	1988	3250
Ryan Benjamin, Pacific	1991	2995
Chris Johnson, East Carolina	2007	2960
Reggie Bush, USC	2005	2890
Kevin Smith, UCF	2007	2809

Yards Per Game	Year	Yards	P/Gm
Barry Sanders, Okla. St	1988	3250	295.5
Ryan Benjamin, Pacific	1991	2995	249.6
Byron (Whizzer) White, Colo	1937	1970	246.3
Mike Pringle, CS-Fullerton	1989	2690	244.6
Paul Palmer, Temple	1986	2633	239.4

All-Time NCAA Division I-A Leaders (Cont.)
SINGLE SEASON
Scoring

Points	Year	TD	Xpt	FG	Pts
Barry Sanders, Okla. St	1988	39	0	0	234
Brock Forsey, Boise St.	2002	32	0	0	192
Troy Edwards, La. Tech	1998	31	2	0	188
Kevin Smith, UCF	2007	30	0	0	180
Mike Rozier, Nebraska	1983	29	0	0	174
Lydell Mitchell, Penn St	1971	29	0	0	174

Touchdowns Passing	Year	No
Colt Brennan, Hawaii	2006	58
David Klingler, Houston	1990	54
B.J. Symons, Texas Tech	2003	52
Graham Harrell, Texas Tech	2007	48
Jim McMahon, BYU	1980	47
Paul Smith, Tulsa	2007	47

Points Per Game	Year	Pts	P/Gm
Barry Sanders, Okla. St	1988	234	21.3
Bobby Reynolds, Nebraska	1950	157	17.4
Art Luppino, Arizona	1954	166	16.6
Ed Marinaro, Cornell	1971	148	16.4
Lydell Mitchell, Penn St	1971	174	15.8

Touchdown Catches	Year	No
Troy Edwards, La. Tech	1998	27
Randy Moss, Marshall	1997	25
Manny Hazard, Houston	1989	22
Larry Fitzgerald, Pittsburgh	2003	22
Michael Crabtree, Texas Tech	2007	22

Touchdowns Rushing	Year	No
Barry Sanders, Okla. St	1988	37
Mike Rozier, Nebraska	1983	29
Kevin Smith, UCF	2007	29
Willis McGahee, Miami-FL	2002	28
Ricky Williams, Texas	1998	27
Lee Suggs, Va. Tech	2000	27

Field Goals	Year	No
Billy Bennett, Georgia	2003	31
John Lee, UCLA	1984	29
John Sullivan, New Mexico	2007	29
Paul Woodside, West Virginia	1982	28
Luis Zendejas, Arizona St	1983	28
Nick Browne, TCU	2003	28

Miscellaneous

Interceptions	Year	No
Al Worley, Washington	1968	14
George Shaw, Oregon	1951	13
Eight tied with 12 each.		

Punt Return Average*	Year	Avg
Maurice Drew, UCLA	2005	28.5
Bill Blackstock, Tennessee	1951	25.9
Ted Ginn Jr., Ohio St.	2004	25.6
George Sims, Baylor	1948	25.0
*At least 1.2 punt returns per game.		

Punting Average*	Year	Avg
Chad Kessler, LSU	1997	50.3
Reggie Roby, Iowa	1981	49.8
Kirk Wilson, UCLA	1956	49.3
Todd Sauerbrun, West Virginia	1994	48.4
Travis Dorsch, Purdue	2001	48.4
*Qualifiers for championship.		

Kickoff Return Average*	Year	Avg
Paul Allen, BYU	1961	40.1
Tremain Mack, Miami-FL	1996	39.5
Leeland McElroy, Texas A&M.	1993	39.3
Forrest Hall, San Francisco	1946	38.2
*At least 1.2 kickoff returns per game.		

SINGLE GAME

Rushing

Yards Gained	Opponent	Year	Yds
LaDainian Tomlinson, TCU	UTEP	1999	406
Tony Sands, Kansas	Missouri	1991	396
Marshall Faulk, San Diego St	Pacific	1991	386
Troy Davis, Iowa St.	Missouri	1996	378
Anthony Thompson, Indiana	Wisconsin	1989	377
Robbie Mixon, C. Michigan	E. Michigan	2002	377
Travis Prentice, Miami-OH	Akron	1999	376
Astron Whatley, Kent St.	E. Mich	1997	373
Rueben Mayes, Wash. St.	Oregon	1984	357
Mike Pringle, CS-Fullerton	N. Mexico St.	1989	357

Total Offense

Yards Gained	Opponent	Year	Yds
David Klingler, Houston	Arizona St.	1990	732
Matt Vogler, TCU	Houston	1990	696
B.J. Symons, Texas Tech	Mississippi	2003	681
Brian Lindgren, Idaho	Mid. Tenn. St.	2001	657
Graham Harrell, Texas Tech	Okla. St.	2007	643

Passing

Yards Gained	Opponent	Year	Yds
David Klingler, Houston	Arizona St.	1990	716
Matt Vogler, TCU	Houston	1990	690
B.J. Symons, Texas Tech	Mississippi	2003	661
Graham Harrell, Texas Tech	Okla. St.	2007	646
Cody Hodges, Texas Tech	Kansas St.	2005	643

Receiving

Catches	Opponent	Year	No
Randy Gatewood, UNLV.	Idaho	1994	23
Jay Miller, BYU	New Mexico	1973	22
Troy Edwards, La. Tech	Nebraska	1998	21
Chris Daniels, Purdue	Mich. St.	1999	21
Rick Eber, Tulsa	Idaho St.	1967	20
Kenny Christian, E. Mich	Temple	2000	20

Attempts	Opponent	Year	No
Drew Brees, Purdeu	Wisconsin	1998	83
Matt Vogler, TCU	Houston	1990	79
Rusty LaRue, Wake Fores	Duke	1995	78
David Klingler, Houston	SMU	1990	76

Yards Gained	Opponent	Year	Yds
Troy Edwards, La. Tech	Nebraska	1998	405
Randy Gatewood, UNLV.	Idaho	1994	363
Chuck Hughes, UTEP*	N. Texas St.	1965	349
Donnie Avery, Houston	Rice	2007	346
Casey Fitzgerald, N. Texas	SMU	2007	327
*UTEP was Texas Western in 1965.			

Completions	Opponent	Year	No
Drew Brees, Purdue	Wisconsin	1998	55
Rusty LaRue, Wake Forest.	Duke	1995	55
Rusty LaRue, Wake Forest.	N.C. St.	1995	50
Five tied with 49 each (including twice by Kliff Kingsbury).			

All-Purpose Yards

Catches	Opponent	Year	No
Emmett White, Utah St.	N. Mex. St.	2000	578
Reggie Bush, USC	Fresno St.	2005	513
Brian Pruitt, C. Michigan	Toledo	1994	435
Moe Williams, Kentucky	South Carolina	1995	429

Scoring

Points	Opponent	Year	Pts
Howard Griffith, Illinois	So. Ill.	1990	48
Marshall Faulk, S. Diego St	Pacific	1991	44
Jim Brown, Syracuse	Colgate	1956	43
Showboat Boykin, Ole Miss	Miss. St.	1951	42
Fred Wendt, UTEP*	N. Mex. St.	1948	42
Rashaun Woods, Oklahoma St.	SMU	2003	42

*UTEP was Texas Mines in 1948.

Touchdowns Rushing	Opponent	Year	No
Howard Griffith, Illinois	So. Ill	1990	8
Showboat Boykin, Ole Miss	Miss. St.	1951	7

Note: Griffith's TD runs (5-51-7-41-5-18-5-3).

Touchdown Catches	Opponent	Year	No
Rashaun Woods, Oklahoma St.	SMU	2003	7
Tim Delaney, S. Diego St	N. Mex. St.	1969	6

Note: Woods' TD catches (2-10-34-32-25-5-11).

Touchdowns Passing	Opponent	Year	No
David Klingler, Houston	E.Wash.	1990	11
Dennis Shaw, San Diego St	N. Mex. St.	1969	9

Note: Klingler's TD passes (5-48-29-7-3-7-40-8-7-8-51).

Field Goals	Opponent	Year	No
Dale Klein, Nebraska	Missouri	1985	7
Mike Prindle, W. Michigan	Marshall	1984	7

Note: Klein's FGs (32-22-43-44-29-43-43); Prindle's FGs (32-44-42-23-48-41-27).

Extra Points (Kick)	Opponent	Year	No
Terry Leiweke, Houston	Tulsa	1968	13
Derek Mahoney, Fresno St	New Mexico	1991	13

Longest Plays (since 1941)

Rushing	Opponent	Year	Yds
Gale Sayers, Kansas	Nebraska	1963	99
Max Anderson, Ariz. St	Wyoming	1967	99
Ralph Thompson, W. Texas St	Wich. St.	1970	99
Kelsey Finch, Tennessee	Florida	1977	99
Eric Vann, Kansas	Oklahoma	1997	99
Terry Caulley, Connecticut	Army	2006	99

Eleven tied at 98 each.

Passing	Opponent	Year	Yds
Fred Owens to Jack Ford, Portland	St. Mary's	1947	99
Bo Burris to Warren McVea, Houston	Wash. St.	1966	99
Colin Clapton to Eddie Jenkins, Holy Cross	Boston U.	1970	99
Terry Peel to Robert Ford, Houston	Syracuse	1970	99
Terry Peel to Robert Ford, Houston	S. Diego St.	1972	99
Cris Collinsworth to Derrick Gaffney, Florida	Rice	1977	99
Scott Ankrom to James Maness, TCU	Rice	1984	99
Gino Torretta to Horace Copeland, Miami-FL	Ark.	1991	99

Passing (cont.)	Opponent	Year	Yds
John Paci to Thomas Lewis, Indiana	Penn St.	1993	99
Troy DeGar to Wes Caswell, Tulsa	Oklahoma	1996	99
Drew Brees to Vinny Sutherland, Purdue	N'western	1999	99
Dan Urban to Justin McCariens, N. Ill	Ball St.	2000	99
Jason Johnson to Brandon Marshall, Ariz.	Idaho	2001	99
Jim Sorgi to Lee Evans, Wisconsin	Akron	2003	99
Dondrial Pinkins to Troy Williamson, South Carolina	Virginia	2003	99
Giovanni Vizza to Casey Fitzgerald, N. Texas	LA-Monroe	2007	99

Field Goals	Opponent	Year	Yds
Steve Little, Arkansas	Texas	1977	67
Russell Erxleben, Texas	Rice	1977	67
Joe Williams, Wichita St	So. Ill.	1978	67
Tony Franklin, Tex. A&M	Baylor	1976	65
Martin Gramatica, Kan. St.	No. Ill.	1998	65

Note: Gramatica's FG is the only one listed above that was not off a tee and through the narrower (18'6") goal posts.

Longest Streaks

Winning Streaks
(Including bowl games)

No	Seasons	Spoiler	Score
47	Oklahoma 1953-57	Notre Dame	7-0
39	Washington 1908-14	Oregon St.	0-0
37	Yale 1890-93	Princeton	6-0
37	Yale 1887-89	Princeton	10-0
35	Toledo 1969-71	Tampa	21-0
34	USC 2003-05	Texas	41-38*
34	Miami-FL 2000-02	Ohio St.	31-24*
34	Penn 1894-96	Lafayette	6-4
31	Oklahoma 1948-50	Kentucky	13-7*
31	Pittsburgh 1914-18	Cleve. Naval	10-9
31	Penn 1896-98	Harvard	10-0
30	Texas 1968-70	Notre Dame	24-11*
29	Miami-FL 1990-93	Alabama	34-13
29	Michigan 1901-03	Minnesota	6-6

*Texas beat USC in 2006 Rose Bowl; Ohio St. beat Miami in 2003 Fiesta Bowl in double overtime; Kentucky beat Oklahoma in 1951 Sugar Bowl and Notre Dame beat Texas in 1971 Cotton Bowl.

Unbeaten Streaks
(Including bowl games)

No	W-T	Seasons	Spoiler	Score
63	59-4	Washington 1907-17	California	27-0
56	55-1	Michigan 1901-05	Chicago	2-0
50	46-4	California 1920-25	Olympic Club	15-0
48	47-1	Oklahoma 1953-57	N. Dame	7-0
48	47-1	Yale 1885-89	Princeton	10-0
47	42-5	Yale 1879-85	Princeton	6-5
44	42-2	Yale 1894-96	Princeton	24-6
42	39-3	Yale 1904-08	Harvard	4-0
39	37-2	N. Dame 1946-50	Purdue	28-14

Losing Streaks

No	Seasons	Victim	Score
34	Northwestern 1979-82	No. Illinois	31-6
28	Virginia 1958-60	Wm. & Mary	21-6
28	Kansas St 1944-48	Arkansas St.	37-6

Note: Virginia ended its losing streak in the opening game of the 1961 season. Div. I-AA Prairie View A&M lost 80 straight games from 1989-98.

Annual Awards
Heisman Trophy

Originally presented in 1935 as the DAC Trophy by the Downtown Athletic Club of New York City to the best college football player east of the Mississippi. In 1936, players across the country were eligible and the award was renamed the Heisman Trophy following the death of former college coach and DAC athletic director John W. Heisman.

Multiple winner: Archie Griffin (2).

Winner in sophomore year (1): Tim Tebow (2007); **Winners in junior year** (16): Doc Blanchard (1945), Reggie Bush (2005), Ty Detmer (1990); Archie Griffin (1974), Desmond Howard (1991), Vic Janowicz (1950), Matt Leinart (2004), Rashaan Salaam (1994), Barry Sanders (1988), Billy Sims (1978), Roger Staubach (1963), Doak Walker (1948), Herschel Walker (1982), Andre Ware (1989), Jason White (2003) and Charles Woodson (1997).

Winners on AP national champions (11): Angelo Bertelli (Notre Dame, 1943); Doc Blanchard (Army, 1945); Tony Dorsett (Pittsburgh, 1976); Leon Hart (Notre Dame, 1949); Matt Leinart (USC, 2004); Johnny Lujack (Notre Dame, 1947); Davey O'Brien (TCU, 1938); Bruce Smith (Minnesota, 1941); Charlie Ward (Florida St., 1993); Danny Wuerffel (Florida, 1996); Charles Woodson (Michigan, 1997).

Year		Points
1935	**Jay Berwanger,** Chicago, HB	.84
	2nd–Monk Meyer, Army, HB	.29
	3rd–Bill Shakespeare, Notre Dame, HB	.23
	4th–Pepper Constable, Princeton, FB	.20
1936	**Larry Kelley,** Yale, E	.219
	2nd–Sam Francis, Nebraska, FB	.47
	3rd–Ray Buivid, Marquette, HB	.43
	4th–Sammy Baugh, TCU, HB	.39
1937	**Clint Frank,** Yale, HB	.524
	2nd–Byron (Whizzer) White, Colo., HB	.264
	3rd–Marshall Goldberg, Pitt, HB	.211
	4th–Alex Wojciechowicz, Fordham, C	.85
1938	**Davey O'Brien,** TCU, QB	.519
	2nd–Marshall Goldberg, Pitt, HB	.294
	3rd–Sid Luckman, Columbia, QB	.154
	4th–Bob MacLeod, Dartmouth, HB	.78
1939	**Nile Kinnick,** Iowa, HB	.651
	2nd–Tom Harmon, Michigan, HB	.405
	3rd–Paul Christman, Missouri, QB	.391
	4th–George Cafego, Tennessee, QB	.296
1940	**Tom Harmon,** Michigan, HB	.1303
	2nd–John Kimbrough, Texas A&M, FB	.841
	3rd–George Franck, Minnesota, HB	.102
	4th–Frankie Albert, Stanford, QB	.90
1941	**Bruce Smith,** Minnesota, HB	.554
	2nd–Angelo Bertelli, Notre Dame, QB	.345
	3rd–Frankie Albert, Stanford, QB	.336
	4th–Frank Sinkwich, Georgia, HB	.249
1942	**Frank Sinkwich,** Georgia, TB	.1059
	2nd–Paul Governali, Columbia, QB	.218
	3rd–Clint Castleberry, Ga. Tech, HB	.99
	4th–Mike Holovak, Boston College, FB	.95
1943	**Angelo Bertelli,** Notre Dame, QB	.648
	2nd–Bob Odell, Penn, HB	.177
	3rd–Otto Graham, Northwestern, QB	.140
	4th–Creighton Miller, Notre Dame, HB	.134
1944	**Les Horvath,** Ohio St., TB-QB	.412
	2nd–Glenn Davis, Army, HB	.287
	3rd–Doc Blanchard, Army, FB	.237
	4th–Don Whitmire, Navy, T	.115
1945	**Doc Blanchard,** Army, HB	.860
	2nd–Glenn Davis, Army, HB	.638
	3rd–Bob Fenimore, Oklahoma A&M, HB	.187
	4th–Herman Wedemeyer, St. Mary's, HB	.152
1946	**Glenn Davis,** Army, HB	.792
	2nd–Charlie Trippi, Georgia, HB	.435
	3rd–Johnny Lujack, Notre Dame, QB	.379
	4th–Doc Blanchard, Army, FB	.267
1947	**Johnny Lujack,** Notre Dame, QB	.742
	2nd–Bob Chappuis, Michigan, HB	.555
	3rd–Doak Walker, SMU, HB	.196
	4th–Charlie Conerly, Mississippi, QB	.186
1948	**Doak Walker,** SMU, HB	.778
	2nd–Charlie Justice, N. Carolina, HB	.443
	3rd–Chuck Bednarik, Penn, C	.336
	4th–Jackie Jensen, California, HB	.143
1949	**Leon Hart,** Notre Dame, E	.995
	2nd–Charlie Justice, N. Carolina, HB	.272
	3rd–Doak Walker, SMU, HB	.229
	4th–Arnold Galiffa, Army QB	.196

Year		Points
1950	**Vic Janowicz,** Ohio St., HB	.633
	2nd–Kyle Rote, SMU, HB	.280
	3rd–Reds Bagnell, Penn, HB	.231
	4th–Babe Parilli, Kentucky, QB	.214
1951	**Dick Kazmaier,** Princeton, TB	.1777
	2nd–Hank Lauricella, Tennessee, HB	.424
	3rd–Babe Parilli, Kentucky, QB	.344
	4th–Bill McColl, Stanford, E	.313
1952	**Billy Vessels,** Oklahoma, HB	.525
	2nd–Jack Scarbath, Maryland, QB	.367
	3rd–Paul Giel, Minnesota, HB	.329
	4th–Donn Moomaw, UCLA, C	.257
1953	**Johnny Lattner,** Notre Dame, HB	.1850
	2nd–Paul Giel, Minnesota, HB	.1794
	3rd–Paul Cameron, UCLA, HB	.444
	4th–Bernie Faloney, Maryland, QB	.258
1954	**Alan Ameche,** Wisconsin, FB	.1068
	2nd–Kurt Burris, Oklahoma, C	.838
	3rd–Howard Cassady, Ohio St., HB	.810
	4th–Ralph Guglielmi, Notre Dame, QB	.691
1955	**Howard Cassady,** Ohio St., HB	.2219
	2nd–Jim Swink, TCU, HB	.742
	3rd–George Welsh, Navy, QB	.383
	4th–Earl Morrall, Michigan St., QB	.323
1956	**Paul Hornung,** Notre Dame, QB	.1066
	2nd–Johnny Majors, Tennessee, HB	.994
	3rd–Tommy McDonald, Oklahoma, HB	.973
	4th–Jerry Tubbs, Oklahoma, C	.724
1957	**John David Crow,** Texas A&M, HB	.1183
	2nd–Alex Karras, Iowa, T	.693
	3rd–Walt Kowalczyk, Mich. St., HB	.630
	4th–Lou Michaels, Kentucky, T	.330
1958	**Pete Dawkins,** Army, HB	.1394
	2nd–Randy Duncan, Iowa, QB	.1021
	3rd–Billy Cannon, LSU, HB	.975
	4th–Bob White, Ohio St., FB	.365
1959	**Billy Cannon,** LSU, HB	.1929
	2nd–Richie Lucas, Penn St., QB	.613
	3rd–Don Meredith, SMU, QB	.286
	4th–Bill Burrell, Illinois, G	.196
1960	**Joe Bellino,** Navy, HB	.1793
	2nd–Tom Brown, Minnesota, G	.731
	3rd–Jake Gibbs, Mississippi, QB	.453
	4th–Ed Dyas, Auburn, HB	.319
1961	**Ernie Davis,** Syracuse, HB	.824
	2nd–Bob Ferguson, Ohio St., HB	.771
	3rd–Jimmy Saxton, Texas, HB	.551
	4th–Sandy Stephens, Minnesota, QB	.543
1962	**Terry Baker,** Oregon St., QB	.707
	2nd–Jerry Stovall, LSU, HB	.618
	3rd–Bobby Bell, Minnesota, T	.429
	4th–Lee Roy Jordan, Alabama, C	.321
1963	**Roger Staubach,** Navy, QB	.1860
	2nd–Billy Lothridge, Ga. Tech, QB	.504
	3rd–Sherman Lewis, Mich. St., HB	.369
	4th–Don Trull, Baylor, QB	.253
1964	**John Huarte,** Notre Dame, QB	.1026
	2nd–Jerry Rhome, Tulsa, QB	.952
	3rd–Dick Butkus, Illinois, C	.505
	4th–Bob Timberlake, Michigan, QB	.361

Year		Points
1965	**Mike Garrett,** USC, HB	926
	2nd–Howard Twilley, Tulsa, E	528
	3rd–Jim Grabowski, Illinois, FB	481
	4th–Donny Anderson, Texas Tech, HB	408
1966	**Steve Spurrier,** Florida, QB	1679
	2nd–Bob Griese, Purdue, QB	816
	3rd–Nick Eddy, Notre Dame, HB	456
	4th–Gary Beban, UCLA, QB	318
1967	**Gary Beban,** UCLA, QB	1968
	2nd–O.J. Simpson, USC, HB	1722
	3rd–Leroy Keyes, Purdue, HB	1366
	4th–Larry Csonka, Syracuse, FB	136
1968	**O.J. Simpson,** USC, HB	2853
	2nd–Leroy Keyes, Purdue, HB	1103
	3rd–Terry Hanratty, Notre Dame, QB	387
	4th–Ted Kwalick, Penn St., TE	254
1969	**Steve Owens,** Oklahoma, HB	1488
	2nd–Mike Phipps, Purdue, QB	1344
	3rd–Rex Kern, Ohio St., QB	856
	4th–Archie Manning, Mississippi, QB.	582
1970	**Jim Plunkett,** Stanford, QB	2229
	2nd–Joe Theismann, Notre Dame, QB	1410
	3rd–Archie Manning, Mississippi, QB	849
	4th–Steve Worster, Texas, RB	398
1971	**Pat Sullivan,** Auburn, QB	1597
	2nd–Ed Marinaro, Cornell, RB	1445
	3rd–Greg Pruitt, Oklahoma, RB	586
	4th–Johnny Musso, Alabama, RB	365
1972	**Johnny Rodgers,** Nebraska, FL	1310
	2nd–Greg Pruitt, Oklahoma, RB.	966
	3rd–Rich Glover, Nebraska, MG.	652
	4th–Bert Jones, LSU, QB	351
1973	**John Cappelletti,** Penn St., RB.	1057
	2nd–John Hicks, Ohio St., OT	524
	3rd–Roosevelt Leaks, Texas, RB	482
	4th–David Jaynes, Kansas, QB.	394
1974	**Archie Griffin,** Ohio St., RB	1920
	2nd–Anthony Davis, USC, RB.	819
	3rd–Joe Washington, Oklahoma, RB.	661
	4th–Tom Clements, Notre Dame, QB.	244
1975	**Archie Griffin,** Ohio St., RB	1800
	2nd–Chuck Muncie, California, RB	730
	3rd–Ricky Bell, USC, RB	708
	4th–Tony Dorsett, Pitt, RB	616
1976	**Tony Dorsett,** Pittsburgh, RB	2357
	2nd–Ricky Bell, USC, RB	1346
	3rd–Rob Lytle, Michigan, RB.	413
	4th–Terry Miller, Oklahoma St., RB	197
1977	**Earl Campbell,** Texas, RB	1547
	2nd–Terry Miller, Oklahoma St., RB.	812
	3rd–Ken MacAfee, Notre Dame, TE	343
	4th–Doug Williams, Grambling, QB.	266
1978	**Billy Sims,** Oklahoma, RB	827
	2nd–Chuck Fusina, Penn St., QB	750
	3rd–Rick Leach, Michigan, QB.	435
	4th–Charles White, USC, RB	354
1979	**Charles White,** USC, RB	1695
	2nd–Billy Sims, Oklahoma, RB	773
	3rd–Marc Wilson, BYU, QB	589
	4th–Art Schlichter, Ohio St., QB.	251
1980	**George Rogers,** South Carolina, RB	1128
	2nd–Hugh Green, Pittsburgh, DE	861
	3rd–Herschel Walker, Georgia, RB	683
	4th–Mark Herrmann, Purdue, QB.	405
1981	**Marcus Allen,** USC, RB	1797
	2nd–Herschel Walker, Georgia, RB	1199
	3rd–Jim McMahon, BYU, QB	706
	4th–Dan Marino, Pitt, QB	256
1982	**Herschel Walker,** Georgia, RB	1926
	2nd–John Elway, Stanford, QB	1231
	3rd–Eric Dickerson, SMU, RB	465
	4th–Anthony Carter, Michigan, WR	142
1983	**Mike Rozier,** Nebraska, RB.	1801
	2nd–Steve Young, BYU, QB	1172
	3rd–Doug Flutie, Boston College, QB	253
	4th–Turner Gill, Nebraska, QB.	190

Year		Points
1984	**Doug Flutie,** Boston College, QB	2240
	2nd–Keith Byars, Ohio St., RB	1251
	3rd–Robbie Bosco, BYU, QB	443
	4th–Bernie Kosar, Miami-FL, QB.	320
1985	**Bo Jackson,** Auburn, RB	1509
	2nd–Chuck Long, Iowa, QB.	1464
	3rd–Robbie Bosco, BYU, QB	459
	4th–Lorenzo White, Michigan St., RB	391
1986	**Vinny Testaverde,** Miami-FL, QB	2213
	2nd–Paul Palmer, Temple, RB	672
	3rd–Jim Harbaugh, Michigan, QB.	458
	4th–Brian Bosworth, Oklahoma, LB	395
1987	**Tim Brown,** Notre Dame, WR.	1442
	2nd–Don McPherson, Syracuse, QB	831
	3rd–Gordie Lockbaum, Holy Cross, WR-DB.	657
	4th–Lorenzo White, Michigan St., RB	632
1988	**Barry Sanders,** Oklahoma St., RB	1878
	2nd–Rodney Peete, USC, QB	912
	3rd–Troy Aikman, UCLA, QB	582
	4th–Steve Walsh, Miami-FL, QB	341
1989	**Andre Ware,** Houston, QB	1073
	2nd–Anthony Thompson, Ind., RB	1003
	3rd–Major Harris, West Va., QB	709
	4th–Tony Rice, Notre Dame, QB	523
1990	**Ty Detmer,** BYU, QB.	1482
	2nd–Rocket Ismail, Notre Dame, FL.	1177
	3rd–Eric Bieniemy, Colorado, RB	798
	4th–Shawn Moore, Virginia, QB	465
1991	**Desmond Howard,** Michigan, WR	2077
	2nd–Casey Weldon, Florida St., QB.	503
	3rd–Ty Detmer, BYU, QB.	445
	4th–Steve Emtman, Washington, DT	357
1992	**Gino Torretta,** Miami-FL, QB	1400
	2nd–Marshall Faulk, San Diego St., RB	1080
	3rd–Garrison Hearst, Georgia, RB	982
	4th–Marvin Jones, Florida St., LB	392
1993	**Charlie Ward,** Florida St., QB	2310
	2nd–Heath Shuler, Tennessee, QB	688
	3rd–David Palmer, Alabama, RB	292
	4th–Marshall Faulk, S. Diego St., RB	250
1994	**Rashaan Salaam,** Colorado, RB	1743
	2nd–Ki-Jana Carter, Penn St., RB	901
	3rd–Steve McNair, Alcorn St., QB.	655
	4th–Kerry Collins, Penn St., QB	639
1995	**Eddie George,** Ohio St., RB	1460
	2nd–Tommie Frazier, Nebraska, QB	1196
	3rd–Danny Wuerffel, Florida, QB	987
	4th–Darnell Autry, Northwestern, RB	535
1996	**Danny Wuerffel,** Florida, QB	1363
	2nd–Troy Davis, Iowa St., RB	1174
	3rd–Jake Plummer, Arizona St., QB.	685
	4th–Orlando Pace, Ohio St., OT	599
1997	**Charles Woodson,** Michigan, DB-WR	1815
	2nd–Peyton Manning, Tennessee, QB	1543
	3rd–Ryan Leaf, Washington St., QB	861
	4th–Randy Moss, Marshall, WR.	253
1998	**Ricky Williams,** Texas, RB	2355
	2nd–Michael Bishop, Kansas St., QB	792
	3rd–Cade McNown, UCLA, QB	696
	4th–Tim Couch, Kentucky, QB.	527
1999	**Ron Dayne,** Wisconsin, RB	2042
	2nd–Joe Hamilton, Ga. Tech, QB.	994
	3rd–Michael Vick, Va. Tech, QB	319
	4th–Drew Brees, Purdue, QB.	308
2000	**Chris Weinke,** Florida St., QB	1628
	2nd–Josh Heupel, Oklahoma, QB	1552
	3rd–Drew Brees, Purdue, QB	619
	4th–LaDainian Tomlinson, TCU, RB	566
2001	**Eric Crouch,** Nebraska, QB	770
	2nd–Rex Grossman, Florida, QB	708
	3rd–Ken Dorsey, Miami-FL, QB.	638
	4th–Joey Harrington, Oregon, QB.	364
2002	**Carson Palmer,** USC, QB	1328
	2nd–Brad Banks, Iowa, QB	1095
	3rd–Larry Johnson, Penn St., RB	726
	4th–Willis McGahee, Miami-FL, RB	660

Annual Awards (Cont.)

2003 **Jason White**, Oklahoma, QB 1481
    2nd–Larry Fitzgerald, Pittsburgh, WR 1353
    3rd–Eli Manning, Mississippi, QB 710
    4th–Chris Perry, Michigan, RB 341
2004 **Matt Leinart**, USC, QB 1325
    2nd–Adrian Peterson, Oklahoma, RB 997
    3rd–Jason White, Oklahoma, QB 957
    4th–Alex Smith, Utah, QB 635
2005 **Reggie Bush**, USC, RB 2541
    2nd–Vince Young, Texas, QB 1608

    3rd–Matt Leinart, USC, QB 797
    4th–Brady Quinn, Notre Dame, QB 191
2006 **Troy Smith**, Ohio St., QB 2540
    2nd–Darren McFadden, Arkansas, RB 878
    3rd–Brady Quinn, Notre Dame, QB 782
    4th–Steve Slaton, West Virginia, RB 214
2007 **Tim Tebow**, Florida, QB 1957
    2nd–Darren McFadden, Arkansas, RB 1703
    3rd–Colt Brennan, Hawaii, QB 632
    4th–Chase Daniel, Missouri, QB 425

Maxwell Award

First presented in 1937 by the Maxwell Memorial Football Club of Philadelphia, the award is named after Robert (Tiny) Maxwell, a Philadelphia native who was a standout lineman at the University of Chicago at the turn of the century. Like the Heisman, the Maxwell is given to the outstanding college player in the nation. Both awards have gone to the same player in the same season 35 times. Those players are preceded by (#). Glenn Davis of Army and Doak Walker of SMU won both but in different years. **Multiple winner:** Johnny Lattner (2).

Year		Year		Year	
1937	#Clint Frank, Yale, HB	1961	Bob Ferguson, Ohio St., HB	1985	Chuck Long, Iowa, QB
1938	#Davey O'Brien, TCU, QB	1962	#Terry Baker, Oregon St., QB	1986	#V. Testaverde, Miami-FL, QB
1939	#Nile Kinnick, Iowa, HB	1963	#Roger Staubach, Navy, QB	1987	Don McPherson, Syracuse, QB
1940	#Tom Harmon, Michigan, HB	1964	Glenn Ressler, Penn St., G	1988	#Barry Sanders, Okla. St., RB
1941	Bill Dudley, Virginia, HB	1965	Tommy Nobis, Texas, LB	1989	Anthony Thompson, Indiana, RB
1942	Paul Governali, Columbia, QB	1966	Jim Lynch, Notre Dame, LB	1990	#Ty Detmer, BYU, QB
1943	Bob Odell, Penn, HB	1967	#Gary Beban, UCLA, QB	1991	#Desmond Howard, Mich., WR
1944	Glenn Davis, Army, HB	1968	#O.J. Simpson, USC, HB	1992	#Gino Torretta, Miami-FL, QB
1945	#Doc Blanchard, Army, FB	1969	Mike Reid, Penn St., DT	1993	#Charlie Ward, Florida St., QB
1946	Charley Trippi, Georgia, HB	1970	#Jim Plunkett, Stanford, QB	1994	Kerry Collins, Penn St., QB
1947	Doak Walker, SMU, HB	1971	Ed Marinaro, Cornell, RB	1995	#Eddie George, Ohio St., RB
1948	Chuck Bednarik, Penn, C	1972	Brad Van Pelt, Michigan St., DB	1996	#Danny Wuerffel, Florida, QB
1949	#Leon Hart, Notre Dame, E	1973	#John Cappelletti, Penn St., RB	1997	Peyton Manning, Tennessee, QB
1950	Reds Bagnell, Penn, HB	1974	Steve Joachim, Temple, QB	1998	#Ricky Williams, Texas, RB
1951	#Dick Kazmaier, Princeton, TB	1975	#Archie Griffin, Ohio St., HB	1999	#Ron Dayne, Wisconsin, RB
1952	Johnny Lattner, Notre Dame, HB	1976	#Tony Dorsett, Pitt, RB	2000	Drew Brees, Purdue, QB
1953	#Johnny Lattner, N. Dame, HB	1977	Ross Browner, Notre Dame, DE	2001	Ken Dorsey, Miami-FL, QB
1954	Ron Beagle, Navy, E	1978	Chuck Fusina, Penn St., QB	2002	Larry Johnson, Penn St., RB
1955	#Howard Cassady, Ohio St., HB	1979	#Charles White, USC, RB	2003	Eli Manning, Mississippi, QB
1956	Tommy McDonald, Okla., HB	1980	Hugh Green, Pitt, DE	2004	Jason White, Oklahoma, QB
1957	Bob Reifsnyder, Navy, T	1981	#Marcus Allen, USC, RB	2005	Vince Young, Texas, QB
1958	#Pete Dawkins, Army, HB	1982	#Herschel Walker, Georgia, RB	2006	Brady Quinn, Notre Dame, QB
1959	Rich Lucas, Penn St., QB	1983	#Mike Rozier, Nebraska, RB	2007	#Tim Tebow, Florida, QB
1960	#Joe Bellino, Navy, HB	1984	#Doug Flutie, Boston Col., QB		

Outland Trophy

First presented in 1946 by the Football Writers Association of America, honoring the nation's outstanding interior lineman. The award is named after its benefactor, Dr. John H. Outland (Kansas, Class of 1898). Players listed in **bold** type helped lead their team to a national championship (according to AP).

    Multiple winner: Dave Rimington (2). **Winners in junior year:** Ross Browner (1976), Steve Emtman (1991), Rien Long (2002), Orlando Pace (1996) and Rimington (1981).

Year		Year		Year	
1946	**George Connor**, N. Dame, T	1967	**Ron Yary**, USC, T	1988	Tracy Rocker, Auburn, DT
1947	Joe Steffy, Army, G	1968	Bill Stanfill, Georgia, T	1989	Mohammed Elewonibi, BYU, G
1948	Bill Fischer, Notre Dame, G	1969	Mike Reid, Penn St., DT	1990	Russell Maryland, Miami-FL, NT
1949	Ed Bagdon, Michigan St., G	1970	Jim Stillwagon, Ohio St., MG	1991	Steve Emtman, Washington, DT
1950	Bob Gain, Kentucky, T	1971	**Larry Jacobson**, Neb., DT	1992	Will Shields, Nebraska, G
1951	Jim Weatherall, Oklahoma, T	1972	Rich Glover, Nebraska, MG	1993	Rob Waldrop, Arizona, NG
1952	Dick Modzelewski, Maryland, T	1973	John Hicks, Ohio St., OT	1994	**Zach Wiegert,** Nebraska, OT
1953	J.D. Roberts, Oklahoma, G	1974	Randy White, Maryland, DT	1995	Jonathan Ogden, UCLA, OT
1954	Bill Brooks, Arkansas, G	1975	**Lee Roy Selmon**, Okla., DT	1996	Orlando Pace, Ohio St., OT
1955	Calvin Jones, Iowa, G	1976	Ross Browner, Notre Dame, DE	1997	Aaron Taylor, Nebraska, G
1956	Jim Parker, Ohio St., G	1977	Brad Shearer, Texas, DT	1998	Kris Farris, UCLA, OT
1957	Alex Karras, Iowa, T	1978	Greg Roberts, Oklahoma, G	1999	Chris Samuels, Alabama, OT
1958	Zeke Smith, Auburn, G	1979	Jim Richter, N.C. State, C	2000	John Henderson, Tennessee, DT
1959	Mike McGee, Duke, T	1980	Mark May, Pittsburgh, OT	2001	**Bryant McKinnie,** Miami-FL, OT
1960	**Tom Brown,** Minnesota, G	1981	Dave Rimington, Nebraska, C	2002	Rien Long, Washington St., DT
1961	Merlin Olsen, Utah St., T	1982	Dave Rimington, Nebraska, C	2003	Robert Gallery, Iowa, OT
1962	Bobby Bell, Minnesota, T	1983	Dean Steinkuhler, Nebraska, G	2004	Jammal Brown, Oklahoma, OT
1963	**Scott Appleton,** Texas, T	1984	Bruce Smith, Virginia Tech, DT	2005	Greg Eslinger, Minnesota, C
1964	Steve DeLong, Tennessee, T	1985	Mike Ruth, Boston College, NG	2006	Joe Thomas, Wisconsin, OT
1965	Tommy Nobis, Texas, G	1986	Jason Buck, BYU, DT	2007	**Glenn Dorsey**, LSU, DT
1966	Loyd Phillips, Arkansas, T	1987	Chad Hennings, Air Force, DT		

Butkus Award

First presented in 1985 by the Downtown Athletic Club of Orlando, Fla., to honor the nation's outstanding linebacker. The award is named after Dick Butkus, two-time consensus All-America at Illinois and six-time All-Pro with the Chicago Bears.

Multiple winner: Brian Bosworth (2).

Year		Year		Year	
1985	Brian Bosworth, Oklahoma	1993	Trev Alberts, Nebraska	2001	Rocky Calmus, Oklahoma
1986	Brian Bosworth, Oklahoma	1994	Dana Howard, Illinois	2002	E.J. Henderson, Maryland
1987	Paul McGowan, Florida St.	1995	Kevin Hardy, Illinois	2003	Teddy Lehman, Oklahoma
1988	Derrick Thomas, Alabama	1996	Matt Russell, Colorado	2004	Derrick Johnson, Texas
1989	Percy Snow, Michigan St.	1997	Andy Katzenmoyer, Ohio St.	2005	Paul Posluszny, Penn St.
1990	Alfred Williams, Colorado	1998	Chris Claiborne, USC	2006	Patrick Willis, Mississippi
1991	Erick Anderson, Michigan	1999	LaVar Arrington, Penn St.	2007	James Laurinaitis, Ohio St.
1992	Marvin Jones, Florida St.	2000	Dan Morgan, Miami-FL		

Lombardi Award

First presented in 1970 by the Rotary Club of Houston, honoring the nation's best lineman. The award is named after pro football coach Vince Lombardi, who, as a guard, was a member of the famous "Seven Blocks of Granite" at Fordham in the 1930s. The Lombardi and Outland awards have gone to the same player in the same year 11 times. Those players are preceded by (#). Ross Browner of Notre Dame won both, but in different years.

Multiple winner: Orlando Pace (2).

Year		Year		Year	
1970	#Jim Stillwagon, Ohio St., MG	1983	#Dean Steinkuhler, Neb., G	1996	#Orlando Pace, Ohio St., OT
1971	Walt Patulski, Notre Dame, DE	1984	Tony Degrate, Texas, DT	1997	Grant Wistrom, Nebraska, DE
1972	#Rich Glover, Nebraska, MG	1985	Tony Casillas, Oklahoma, NG	1998	Dat Nguyen, Tex. A&M, LB
1973	#John Hicks, Ohio St., OT	1986	Cornelius Bennett, Alabama, LB	1999	Corey Moore, Va. Tech, DE
1974	#Randy White, Maryland, DT	1987	Chris Spielman, Ohio St., LB	2000	Jamal Reynolds, Florida St., DE
1975	#Lee Roy Selmon, Okla., DT	1988	#Tracy Rocker, Auburn, DT	2001	Julius Peppers, N. Carolina, DE
1976	Wilson Whitley, Houston, DT	1989	Percy Snow, Michigan St., LB	2002	Terrell Suggs, Arizona St., DE
1977	Ross Browner, Notre Dame, DE	1990	Chris Zorich, Notre Dame, NT	2003	Tommie Harris, Oklahoma, DE
1978	Bruce Clark, Penn St., DT	1991	#Steve Emtman, Wash., DT	2004	David Pollack, Georgia, DE
1979	Brad Budde, USC, G	1992	Marvin Jones, Florida St., LB	2005	A.J. Hawk, Ohio St., LB
1980	Hugh Green, Pitt, DE	1993	Aaron Taylor, Notre Dame, OT	2006	LaMarr Woodley, Michigan, DE
1981	Kenneth Sims, Texas, DT	1994	Warren Sapp, Miami-FL, DT	2007	#Glenn Dorsey, LSU, DT
1982	#Dave Rimington, Neb., C	1995	Orlando Pace, Ohio St., OT		

O'Brien Quarterback Award

First presented in 1977 as the O'Brien Memorial Trophy, the award went to the outstanding player in the Southwest. In 1981, however, the Davey O'Brien Educational and Charitable Trust of Ft. Worth renamed the prize the O'Brien National Quarterback Award and now honors the nation's best quarterback. The award is named after 1938 Heisman Trophy-winning QB Davey O'Brien of Texas Christian.

Multiple winners: Ty Detmer, Mike Singletary, Jason White and Danny Wuerffel (2).

Memorial Trophy

Year		Year		Year	
1977	Earl Campbell, Texas, RB	1979	Mike Singletary, Baylor, LB	1980	Mike Singletary, Baylor, LB
1978	Billy Sims, Oklahoma, RB				

National QB Award

Year		Year		Year	
1981	Jim McMahon, BYU	1990	Ty Detmer, BYU	1999	Joe Hamilton, Ga. Tech
1982	Todd Blackledge, Penn St.	1991	Ty Detmer, BYU	2000	Chris Weinke, Florida St.
1983	Steve Young, BYU	1992	Gino Torretta, Miami-FL	2001	Eric Crouch, Nebraska
1984	Doug Flutie, Boston College	1993	Charlie Ward, Florida St.	2002	Brad Banks, Iowa
1985	Chuck Long, Iowa	1994	Kerry Collins, Penn St.	2003	Jason White, Oklahoma
1986	Vinny Testaverde, Miami, FL	1995	Danny Wuerffel, Florida	2004	Jason White, Oklahoma
1987	Don McPherson, Syracuse	1996	Danny Wuerffel, Florida	2005	Vince Young, Texas
1988	Troy Aikman, UCLA	1997	Peyton Manning, Tennessee	2006	Troy Smith, Ohio St.
1989	Andre Ware, Houston	1998	Michael Bishop, Kansas St.	2007	Tim Tebow, Florida

Thorpe Award

First presented in 1986 by the Jim Thorpe Athletic Club of Oklahoma City to honor the nation's outstanding defensive back. The award is named after Jim Thorpe–Olympic champion and two-time consensus All-America halfback at Carlisle.

Year		Year		Year	
1986	Thomas Everett, Baylor	1993	Antonio Langham, Alabama	2001	Roy Williams, Oklahoma
1987	Bennie Blades, Miami-FL & Rickey Dixon, Oklahoma	1994	Chris Hudson, Colorado	2002	Terence Newman, Kansas St.
		1995	Greg Myers, Colorado St.	2003	Derrick Strait, Oklahoma
1988	Deion Sanders, Florida St.	1996	Lawrence Wright, Florida	2004	Carlos Rogers, Auburn
1989	Mike Carrier, USC	1997	Charles Woodson, Michigan	2005	Michael Huff, Texas
1990	Darryl Lewis, Arizona	1998	Antoine Winfield, Ohio St.	2006	Aaron Ross, Texas
1991	Terrell Buckley, Florida St.	1999	Tyrone Carter, Minnesota	2007	Antoine Cason, Arizona
1992	Deon Figures, Colorado	2000	Jamar Fletcher, Wisconsin		

All-Time Winningest Division I-A Coaches

Minimum of 10 years in Division I-A through 2007 season. Regular season and bowl games included. Coaches active in 2007 in **bold** type.

Top 25 Winning Percentage

		Yrs	W	L	T	Pct
1	Knute Rockne	13	105	12	5	.881
2	Frank Leahy	13	107	13	9	.864
3	George Woodruff	12	142	25	2	.846
4	Barry Switzer	16	157	29	4	.837
5	Tom Osborne	25	255	49	3	.836
6	Percy Haughton	13	96	17	6	.832
7	Bob Neyland	21	173	31	12	.829
8	Hurry Up Yost	29	196	36	12	.828
9	Bud Wilkinson	17	145	29	4	.826
10	Jock Sutherland	20	144	28	14	.812
11	Bob Devaney	16	136	30	7	.806
12	Frank Thomas	19	141	33	9	.795
13	Henry Williams	23	141	34	12	.786
14	Gil Dobie	33	180	45	15	.781
15	Bear Bryant	38	323	85	17	.780
16	Fred Folsom	19	106	28	6	.779
17	Bo Schembechler	27	234	65	8	.775
18	Fritz Crisler	18	116	32	9	.768
19	**Phillip Fulmer**	16	147	45	0	.766
20	Wallace Wade	24	171	49	10	.765
21	Frank Kush	22	176	54	1	.764
22	Dan McGugin	30	197	55	19	.762
23	Jimmy Crowley	13	78	21	10	.761
24	Andy Smith	17	116	32	13	.761
25	Woody Hayes	33	238	72	10	.759

Top 25 Victories

		Yrs	W	L	T	Pct
1	**Bobby Bowden**	42	373	119	4	.756
2	**Joe Paterno**	42	372	125	3	.747
3	Bear Bryant	38	323	85	17	.780
4	Pop Warner	44	319	106	32	.733
5	Amos Alonzo Stagg	57	314	199	35	.605
6	LaVell Edwards	29	257	101	3	.722
7	Tom Osborne	25	255	49	3	.836
8	Lou Holtz	33	249	132	7	.651
9	Woody Hayes	33	238	72	10	.759
10	Bo Schembechler	27	234	65	8	.775
11	Hayden Fry	37	232	178	10	.564
12	**Frank Beamer**	27	209	108	4	.657
13	Jess Neely	40	207	176	19	.539
14	Warren Woodson	31	203	95	14	.673
15	Don Nehlen	30	202	128	8	.609
16	Vince Dooley	25	201	77	10	.715
	Eddie Anderson	39	201	128	15	.606
18	Jim Sweeney	32	200	154	4	.564
19	Dana X. Bible	33	198	72	23	.715
20	Dan McGugin	30	197	55	19	.762
21	Hurry Up Yost	29	196	36	12	.828
22	Howard Jones	29	194	64	21	.733
23	John Cooper	24	192	84	6	.691
24	Johnny Vaught	25	190	61	12	.745
25	**Mack Brown**	24	189	99	1	.656

Note: John Gagliardi of Division III St. John's (Minn.) became the all-time leader in college football coaching wins in 2003 (passing Grambling's Eddie Robinson at 408 wins), and currently boasts a career record of 453-122-11 over 56 seasons at St. John's and three seasons at Montana's Carroll College.

Where They Coached

Anderson–Loras (1922-24), DePaul (1925-31), Holy Cross (1933-38), Iowa (1939-42), Holy Cross (1950-64); **Beamer**–Murray St. (1981-86), Virginia Tech (1987—); **Bible**– Mississippi College (1913-15), LSU (1916), Texas A&M (1917,1919-28), Nebraska (1929-36), Texas (1937-46); **Bowden**– Samford (1959-62), West Virginia (1970-75), Florida St. (1976–); **Brown**–Appalachian St. (1983), Tulane (1985-87), North Carolina (1988-97), Texas (1998—); **Bryant**–Maryland (1945), Kentucky (1946-53), Texas A&M (1954-57), Alabama (1958-82); **Cooper**– Tulsa (1977-84), Arizona St. (1985-87), Ohio St. (1988-2000); **Crisler**– Minnesota (1930-31), Princeton (1932-37), Michigan (1938-47); **Crowley**– Michigan St. (1929-32), Fordham (1933-41); **Devaney**–Wyoming (1957-61), Nebraska (1962-72); **Dobie**–North Dakota St. (1906-07), Washington (1908-16), Navy (1917-19), Cornell (1920-35), Boston College (1936- 38); **V. Dooley**–Georgia (1964-88); **Edwards**–BYU (1972-2000); **Folsom**–Colorado (1895-99, 1901-02), Dartmouth (1903-06), Colorado (1908-15); **Fry**–SMU (1962-72), North Texas (1973-78), Iowa (1979-98); **Fulmer**–Tennessee (1992–).

Haughton–Cornell (1899-1900), Harvard (1908-16), Columbia (1923-24); **Hayes**–Denison (1946-48), Miami-OH (1949-51), Ohio St. (1951-78); **Holtz**–William & Mary (1969-71), N.C. State (1972-75), Arkansas (1977-83), Minnesota (1984-85), Notre Dame (1986-96), South Carolina (1999-2004); **Jones**–Syracuse (1908), Yale (1909), Ohio St. (1910), Yale (1913), Iowa (1916-23), Duke (1924), USC (1925- 40); **Kush**–Arizona St. (1958-79); **Leahy**–Boston College (1939-40), Notre Dame (1941-43, 1946-53).

Neely–Rhodes (1924-27), Clemson (1931-39), Rice (1940-66); **Nehlen**–Bowling Green (1968-76), West Virginia (1980-2000); **Neyland**–Tennessee (1926-34, 1936-40, 1946-52); **Osborne**–Nebraska (1973-97); **Paterno**–Penn St. (1966–); **Rockne**–Notre Dame (1918-30); **Schembechler**–Miami-OH (1963-68), Michigan (1969-89); **Smith**–Penn (1905, 1909-12), Purdue (1913-15), California (1916-25); **Stagg**–Springfield College (1890-91), Chicago (1892-1932), Pacific (1933-46); **Sutherland**– Lafayette (1919-23), Pittsburgh (1924-38); **Sweeney**–Montana St. (1963-67), Washington St. (1968-75), Fresno St. (1976- 96); **Switzer**–Oklahoma (1973-88).

Thomas–Chattanooga (1925-28), Alabama (1931-42, 1944-46); **Vaught**–Mississippi (1947-70); **Wade**–Alabama (1923-30), Duke (1931-41, 1946-50); **Warner**–Georgia (1895-96), Cornell (1897-98), Carlisle (1899-1903), Cornell (1904-06), Carlisle (1907-13), Pittsburgh (1915-23), Stanford (1924-32), Temple (1933-38); **Wilkinson**–Oklahoma (1947-63); **Williams**–Army (1891), Minnesota (1900-21); **Woodruff**–Penn (1892-1901), Illinois (1903), Carlisle (1905); **Woodson**–Central Arkansas (1935-39), Hardin-Simmons (1941-42, 1946-51), Arizona (1952-56), New Mexico St. (1958-67), Trinity-TX (1972-73); **Yost**–Ohio Wesleyan (1897), Nebraska (1898), Kansas (1899), Stanford (1900), Michigan (1901-23, 1925-26).

All-Time Bowl Appearances

Coaches active in 2007 in **bold** type.

		App	W	L	T
1	**Joe Paterno**	34	23	10	1
2	**Bobby Bowden**	31	20	10	1
3	Bear Bryant	29	15	12	2
4	Tom Osborne	25	12	13	0
5	LaVell Edwards	22	7	14	1
	Lou Holtz	22	12	8	2
7	Vince Dooley	20	8	10	2
	Johnny Vaught	18	10	8	0
9	Hayden Fry	17	7	9	1
	Bo Schembechler	17	5	12	0
11	Johnny Majors	16	9	7	0
	Darrell Royal	16	8	7	1
	Mack Brown	16	10	6	0
14	Don James	15	10	5	0
	George Welsh	15	5	10	0
	Phillip Fulmer	15	8	7	0
	Frank Beamer	15	6	9	0
18	Jackie Sherrill	14	8	6	0
	Steve Spurrier	14	7	7	0
	John Cooper	14	5	9	0

Active Coaches' Victories

(Minimum 5 years in Division I-A.)

		Yrs	W	L	T	Pct
1	Bobby Bowden, Fla. St	42	**373**	119	4	.756
2	Joe Paterno, Penn St	42	**372**	125	3	.747
3	Frank Beamer, Va. Tech	27	**209**	108	4	.657
4	Jim Tressel, Ohio St.	22	**208**	73	2	.739
5	Chris Ault, Nevada	23	**191**	85	1	.691
6	Mack Brown, Texas	24	**189**	99	1	.656
7	Joe Glenn, Wyoming	23	**183**	93	1	.662
8	Dick Tomey, San Jose St.	27	**175**	129	7	.574
9	Steve Spurrier, So. Carolina	18	**163**	56	2	.742
10	Dennis Erickson, Ariz. St.	19	**158**	68	1	.698
11	Mike Price, UTEP	26	**154**	145	0	.515
12	Brian Kelly, Cincinnati	18	**148**	54	2	.730
13	Phillip Fulmer, Tennessee	16	**147**	45	0	.766
14	Howard Schnellenberger, FAU	23	**141**	119	3	.542
15	Larry Blakeney, Troy	17	**135**	69	1	.661
16	Mike Bellotti, Oregon	18	**127**	77	2	.621
17	Gary Pinkel, Missouri	17	**122**	74	3	.621
	Joe Tiller, Purdue	17	**122**	84	1	.592
19	Rich Brooks, Kentucky	23	**116**	144	4	.447
20	Houston Nutt, Mississippi	15	**110**	71	0	.608

AFCA Coach of the Year

First presented in 1935 by the American Football Coaches Association.

Multiple winners: Joe Paterno (5), Bear Bryant (3), John McKay and Darrell Royal (2).

Year

1935	Pappy Waldorf, Northwestern
1936	Dick Harlow, Harvard
1937	Hooks Mylin, Lafayette
1938	Bill Kern, Carnegie Tech
1939	Eddie Anderson, Iowa
1940	Clark Shaughnessy, Stanford
1941	Frank Leahy, Notre Dame
1942	Bill Alexander, Georgia Tech
1943	Amos Alonzo Stagg, Pacific
1944	Carroll Widdoes, Ohio St.
1945	Bo McMillin, Indiana
1946	Red Blaik, Army
1947	Fritz Crisler, Michigan
1948	Bennie Oosterbaan, Michigan
1949	Bud Wilkinson, Oklahoma
1950	Charlie Caldwell, Princeton
1951	Chuck Taylor, Stanford
1952	Biggie Munn, Michigan St.
1953	Jim Tatum, Maryland
1954	Red Sanders, UCLA
1955	Duffy Daugherty, Michigan St.
1956	Bowden Wyatt, Tennessee
1957	Woody Hayes, Ohio St.
1958	Paul Dietzel, LSU
1959	Ben Schwartzwalder, Syracuse
1960	Murray Warmath, Minnesota

Year

1961	Bear Bryant, Alabama
1962	John McKay, USC
1963	Darrell Royal, Texas
1964	Frank Broyles, Arkansas & Ara Parseghian, Notre Dame
1965	Tommy Prothro, UCLA
1966	Tom Cahill, Army
1967	John Pont, Indiana
1968	Joe Paterno, Penn St.
1969	Bo Schembechler, Michigan
1970	Charlie McClendon, LSU & Darrell Royal, Texas
1971	Bear Bryant, Alabama
1972	John McKay, USC
1973	Bear Bryant, Alabama
1974	Grant Teaff, Baylor
1975	Frank Kush, Arizona St.
1976	Johnny Majors, Pittsburgh
1977	Don James, Washington
1978	Joe Paterno, Penn St.
1979	Earle Bruce, Ohio St.
1980	Vince Dooley, Georgia
1981	Danny Ford, Clemson
1982	Joe Paterno, Penn St.
1983	Ken Hatfield, Air Force
1984	LaVell Edwards, BYU

Year

1985	Fisher DeBerry, Air Force
1986	Joe Paterno, Penn St.
1987	Dick MacPherson, Syracuse
1988	Don Nehlen, West Virginia
1989	Bill McCartney, Colorado
1990	Bobby Ross, Georgia Tech
1991	Bill Lewis, East Carolina
1992	Gene Stallings, Alabama
1993	Barry Alvarez, Wisconsin
1994	Tom Osborne, Nebraska
1995	Gary Barnett, Northwestern
1996	Bruce Snyder, Arizona St.
1997	Lloyd Carr, Michigan
1998	Phillip Fulmer, Tennessee
1999	Frank Beamer, Va. Tech
2000	Bob Stoops, Oklahoma
2001	Ralph Friedgen, Maryland & Larry Coker, Miami-FL
2002	Jim Tressel, Ohio St.
2003	Pete Carrol, USC
2004	Tommy Tuberville, Auburn
2005	Joe Paterno, Penn St.
2006	Jim Grobe, Wake Forest
2007	Mark Mangino, Kansas

FWAA Coach of the Year

First presented in 1957 by the Football Writers Association of America. The FWAA and AFCA awards have both gone to the same coach in the same season 33 times. Those double winners are preceded by (#).

Multiple winners: Woody Hayes and Joe Paterno (3); Lou Holtz, Johnny Majors and John McKay (2).

Year

1957	#Woody Hayes, Ohio St.
1958	#Paul Dietzel, LSU
1959	#Ben Schwartzwalder, Syracuse
1960	#Murray Warmath, Minnesota
1961	Darrell Royal, Texas
1962	#John McKay, USC
1963	#Darrell Royal, Texas
1964	#Ara Parseghian, Notre Dame
1965	Duffy Daugherty, Michigan St.
1966	#Tom Cahill, Army
1967	#John Pont, Indiana
1968	Woody Hayes, Ohio St.

Year

1969	#Bo Schembechler, Michigan
1970	Alex Agase, Northwestern
1971	Bob Devaney, Nebraska
1972	#John McKay, USC
1973	Johnny Majors, Pitt
1974	#Grant Teaff, Baylor
1975	Woody Hayes, Ohio St.
1976	#Johnny Majors, Pitt
1977	Lou Holtz, Arkansas
1978	#Joe Paterno, Penn St.
1979	#Earle Bruce, Ohio St.
1980	#Vince Dooley, Georgia

Year

1981	#Danny Ford, Clemson
1982	#Joe Paterno, Penn St.
1983	Howard Schnellenberger, Miami-FL
1984	#LaVell Edwards, BYU
1985	#Fisher DeBerry, Air Force
1986	#Joe Paterno, Penn St.
1987	#Dick MacPherson, Syracuse
1988	Lou Holtz, Notre Dame
1989	#Bill McCartney, Colorado
1990	#Bobby Ross, Georgia Tech
1991	Don James, Washington
1992	#Gene Stallings, Alabama

FWAA Coach of the Year (Cont.)

Year		Year		Year	
1993	Terry Bowden, Auburn	1998	#Phillip Fulmer, Tennessee	2003	Nick Saban, LSU
1994	Rich Brooks, Oregon	1999	#Frank Beamer, Va. Tech	2004	Urban Meyer, Utah
1995	#Gary Barnett, Northwestern	2000	#Bob Stoops, Oklahoma	2005	Charlie Weis, Notre Dame
1996	#Bruce Snyder, Arizona St.	2001	#Ralph Friedgen, Maryland	2006	Greg Schiano, Rutgers
1997	Mike Price, Washington St.	2002	#Jim Tressel, Ohio St.	2007	#Mark Mangino, Kansas

All-Time NCAA Division I-AA Leaders
CAREER

Total Offense

Yards Gained

		Years	Yards
1	Steve McNair, Alcorn St.	1991-94	16,823
2	Ricky Santos, New Hampshire	2004-07	14,615
3	Bruce Eugene, Grambling	2001-05	14,720
4	Marcus Brady, CS-Northridge	1998-01	13,095
5	Willie Totten, Miss. Valley	1982-85	13,007

Yards per Game

		Years	Yards	P/Gm
1	Steve McNair, Alcorn St.	1991-94	16,823	400.5
2	Neil Lomax, Portland St.	1978-80	11,647	352.9
3	Aaron Flowers, CS-N'ridge	1996-97	6,754	337.7
4	David Macchi, Valparaiso	2002-03	7,628	331.7
5	Chris Sanders, Chattanooga	1999-00	7,247	329.4

Passing
(Minimum 425 Completions)

Passing Efficiency

		Years	Rating
1	Josh Johnson, San Diego	2004-07	176.7
2	Erik Meyer, E. Washington	2002-05	166.5
3	Dave Dickenson, Montana	1992-95	166.3
4	Eric Sanders, UNI	2004-07	161.4
5	Drew Miller, Montana	1999-00	160.5

Yards Gained

		Years	Yards
1	Steve McNair, Alcorn St.	1991-94	14,496
2	Bruce Eugene, Grambling	2002-05	13,513
3	Ricky Santos, New Hampshire	2004-07	13,212
4	Willie Totten, Miss. Valley	1982-85	12,711
5	Marcus Brady, CS-Northridge	1998-01	12,479

Receiving

Catches

		Years	No
1	Jacquay Nunnally, Fla. A&M	1997-00	317
2	Stephen Campbell, Brown	1997-00	305
3	David Ball, New Hampshire	2003-06	304
4	Jerry Rice, Miss. Valley.	1981-84	301
5	Javarus Dudley, Fordham	2000-03	295

Yards Gained

		Years	No	Yards
1	Jerry Rice, Miss. Valley.	1981-84	301	4693
2	David Ball, New Hampshire	2003-06	304	4655
3	Jacquay Nunnally, Fla. A&M	1997-00	317	4239
4	Javarus Dudley, Fordham	2000-03	295	4197
5	Eric Kimble, E. Washington	2002-05	253	4140

All-Purpose Yardage

Yards per Game

		Years	Yards	P/Gm
1	B. Westbrook, Villanova	1997-98,00-01	9512	216.2
2	Jerry Azumah, N. Hampshire	1995-98	9376	204.3
3	Arnold Mickens, Butler	1994-95	3947	197.4
4	Tim Hall , Robert Morris	1994-95	3701	194.8
5	Reggie Greene, Siena	1994-97	6959	193.3

Scoring
Non-Kickers

Points

		Years	TD	XP	Pts
1	B. Westbrook, Villanova	1997-98,00-01	89	10	544
2	Adrian Peterson, Ga. Southern	1998-01	87	2	524
3	Kevin Richardson, App. St.	2004-07	74	0	444
4	Omar Cuff, Delaware	2004-07	73	2	440
5	Matt Cannon, S. Utah	1997-00	69	6	420

Touchdowns Passing

		Years	No
1	Bruce Eugene, Grambling	2001-05	140
2	Willie Totten, Miss. Valley	1982-85	139
3	Ricky Santos, New Hampshire	2004-07	123
4	Steve McNair, Alcorn St.	1991-94	119
5	Josh Johnson, San Diego	2004-07	113

Rushing

Yards Gained

		Years	Yards
1	Adrian Peterson, Ga. Southern	1998-01	6559
2	Charles Roberts, CS-Sac.	1997-00	6553
3	Jerry Azumah, N. Hampshire.	1995-98	6193
4	Scott Phaydavong, Drake	2004-07	5830
5	Matt Cannon, S. Utah	1997-00	5489

Yards per Game

		Years	Yards	P/Gm
1	Arnold Mickens, Butler	1994-95	3813	190.7
2	Adrian Peterson, Ga. So.	1998-01	6559	156.2
3	Aaron Stecker, W. Ill.	1997-98	3081	154.1
4	Tim Hall, Robert Morris	1994-95	2908	153.1
5	Jerry Azumah, N. Hampshire .	1995-98	6193	151.0

Miscellaneous

Interceptions

		Years	No
1	Rashean Mathis, Bethune-Cookman	1999-02	31
2	Dave Murphy, Holy Cross	1986-89	28
	Leigh Bodde, Duquesne	1999-02	28
4	Cedric Walker, S.F. Austin	1990-93	25
5	Four tied at 24.		

Punting Average (min. 150 punts)

		Years	Avg
1	Mark Gould, Northern Ariz.	2000-03	44.8
2	Pumpy Tudors, Tenn.-Chatt.	1989-91	44.4
3	Case de Brujin, Idaho St.	1978-81	43.7
4	Mike Scifres, Western Illinois	1999-02	43.6
5	Terry Belden, Northern Ariz.	1990-93	43.4

Note: Northeastern's Tyler Grogan holds the 1-AA record for longest punt with a 93-yarder against Villanova in 2001.

Punt Return Average*

		Years	Avg
1	Terrence McGee, Northweseern St.	1999-02	17.4
2	Willie Ware, Miss. Valley	1982-85	16.4
3	Buck Phillips, Western Ill.	1994-95	16.4
4	Tim Egerton, Delaware St.	1986-89	16.1
5	Mark Orlando, Towson St.	1991-94	15.7

Kickoff Return Average*

		Years	Avg
1	Lamont Brightful, E. Wash.	1998-01	30.0
2	Troy Brown, Marshall	1991-92	29.7
3	Cedric Bowen, Ark-Pine Bluff	2001-04	29.6
4	Charles Swann, Indiana St.	1989-91	29.3
5	Craig Richardson, Eastern Wash.	1983-86	28.5

*(Minimum 1.2 returns per game)

Blocked Kicks

		Years	FG	XP	P	Tot
1	Leonard Smith, McNeese St.	1980-82	10	4	3	17
2	Trey Woods, Sam Houston St.	1992-95	2	2	8	12
	Ryan Crawford, Davidson	1997-00	5	0	7	12
4	Mark Weivoda, Idaho St.	200-03	8	3	0	11
5	Bryan Cox, W. Illinois	1987-90	4	5	1	10

Note: The blocked kicks category is a combined total of blocked field goals (FG), extra points (XP) and punts (P).

Touchdowns Rushing

		Years	No
1	Adrian Peterson, Ga. Southern	1998-01	84
2	Matt Cannon, S. Utah	1997-00	69
3	Kevin Richardson, Appalachian St.	2004-07	66
4	Omar Cuff, Delaware	2004-07	65
5	David Dinkins, Morehead St.	1997-00	63

Touchdown Catches

		Years	No
1	David Ball, New Hampshire	2003-06	58
2	Jerry Rice, Miss. Valley	1981-84	50
3	Eric Kimble, Eastern Wash.	2002-05	46
4	Rennie Benn, Lehigh	1982-85	44
5	Jerome Simpson, Coastal Carolina	2004-07	44

Kickers

Points	Years	FG	XP	Pts		Field Goals	Years	FG	Att
1 Dan Carpenter, Montana	2004-07	75	182	413		1 Dan Carpenter, Montana	2004-07	.75	103
2 Chris Snyder, Montana	2000-03	70	182	394		2 Marty Zendejas, Nevada	1984-87	.72	90
3 Marty Zendejas, Nevada	1984-87	72	169	385		3 Kirk Roach, Western Carolina	1984-87	.71	102
4 Craig Coffin, Southern Ill.	2002-06	50	229	379		4 Tony Zendejas, Nevada	1981-83	.70	86
5 Julian Rauch, App. St.	2004-07	42	247	373		Chris Snyder, Montana	2000-03	.70	105

Note: Carpenter's point total includes 1 TD; Snyder's point total includes one two-point conversion.

Note: South Florida's Bill Gramatica, Arkansas State's Scott Roper and Georgia Southern's Tim Foley share the 1-AA record for longest field goal at 63 yards.

Payton Award

First presented in 1987 by the Sports Network and Division I-AA sports information directors to honor the nation's outstanding Division I-AA player. The award is named after Walter Payton, the NFL's all-time leading rusher who was an All-America running back at Jackson St.

Year		Year		Year	
1987	Kenny Gamble, Colgate, RB	1995	Dave Dickenson, Montana, QB	2002	Tony Romo, Eastern Illinois, QB
1988	Dave Meggett, Towson St., RB	1996	Archie Amerson, N. Arizona, RB	2003	Jamaal Branch, Colgate, RB
1989	John Friesz, Idaho, QB	1997	Brian Finneran, Villanova, WR	2004	Lang Campbell,
1990	Walter Dean, Grambling, RB	1998	Jerry Azumah, N. Hampshire, RB		Wm & Mary, QB
1991	Jamie Martin, Weber St., QB	1999	Adrian Peterson,	2005	Erik Meyer, E. Washington, QB
1992	Michael Payton, Marshall, QB		Ga. Southern, RB	2006	Ricky Santos, N. Hampshire, QB
1993	Doug Nussmeier, Idaho, QB	2000	Louis Ivory, Furman, RB	2007	Jayson Foster, Ga. Southern, QB
1994	Steve McNair, Alcorn St., QB	2001	Brian Westbrook, Villanova, RB		

All-Time NCAA Division I-AA Winningest Programs

Includes record at a senior college only, minimum of 20 seasons of competition. Bowl and playoff games are included in the overall records but only 1-AA playoff games (since they began in 1978) are included in the W-L column under 1-AA playoffs.

Top 20 Winning Percentage

		Yrs	Gm	W	L	T	Pct.	1-AA Playoffs W-L	Titles
1	Georgia Southern	.26	334	245	88	1	.735	38-11	6
2	Yale	.135	1231	847	329	55	.710	0-0	0
3	Grambling St.	.65	704	488	201	15	.704	9-7	0
4	Florida A&M	.75	771	522	231	18	.689	5-6	1
5	Princeton	.138	1183	776	357	50	.677	0-0	0
6	Harvard	.133	1212	789	373	50	.672	0-0	0
7	Tennessee St.	.80	762	495	237	30	.669	2-5	0
8	Dayton	.100	957	594	337	26	.634	0-0	0
9	Appalachian St.	.78	840	517	294	29	.633	16-12	2
10	Southern	.86	849	525	299	25	.633	0-0	0
11	Pennsylvania	.131	1283	790	451	42	.632	0-0	0
12	Eastern Kentucky	.84	846	521	298	27	.632	16-15	2
13	McNeese St.	.57	624	384	226	14	.627	11-10	0
14	Jackson St.	.62	644	397	234	13	.627	0-12	0
15	Fordham	.109	1218	733	432	53	.624	1-1	0
16	S. Carolina St.	.80	756	454	275	27	.618	2-2	0
17	Delaware	.116	1072	629	399	44	.607	16-12	1
18	UNI	.109	999	583	369	47	.607	16-13	0
19	Albany	.35	356	216	140	0	.607	0-0	0
20	Hofstra	.67	659	394	254	11	.606	2-5	0

Top 50 Victories

		Wins			Wins			Wins
1	Yale	847	17	Drake	543	34	Western Ill.	474
2	Pennsylvania	790		Furman	543	35	Maine	473
3	Harvard	789	19	Villanova	538	36	Chattanooga	469
4	Princeton	776	20	Massachusetts	532	37	UC-Davis	466
5	Fordham	733	21	Southern	525		Richmond	466
6	Dartmouth	643	22	Florida A&M	522	39	Texas St.	462
7	Lafayette	633	23	Butler	521		Howard	462
8	Delaware	629		E. Kentucky	521	41	Georgetown	460
9	Lehigh	620	25	Appalachian St.	517	42	Eastern Ill.	455
10	Cornell	612	26	William & Mary	516	43	S. Carolina St.	454
11	North Dakota St.	595	27	South Dakota St.	513	44	Elon	453
12	Dayton	594	28	Hampton	512	45	Wofford	451
13	N. Iowa	583	29	Montana	502	46	VMI	449
14	Colgate	578	30	Tennessee St.	495	47	The Citadel	447
14	Holy Cross	576		New Hampshire	495	48	E. Washington	445
15	Brown	558	32	Grambling St.	488	49	Idaho St.	441
16	Bucknell	554	33	Northwestern St.	485	50	Alabama St.	434

Top 10 Playoff Game Appearances

Ranked by NCAA Division 1-AA playoff games played from 1978-2006. CH refers to championships won.

		Years	Games	Record	CH			Years	Games	Record	CH
1	Georgia Southern	16	48	38-10	6	6	Marshall*	8	29	23-6	2
2	Montana	17	39	24-15	2	7	Delaware	13	28	16-12	1
√3	Youngstown St.	11	32	25-7	4		Appalachian St.	14	28	16-12	2
4	Furman	15	31	17-14	1	9	Northern Iowa	12	27	15-12	0
	Eastern Ky.	17	31	16-15	2	10	McNeese St.	12	23	11-12	0

*Marshall moved up to 1-A in 1997.

All-Time Winningest Division I-AA Coaches

Minimum of 10 years as a Division I-A and/or Division I-AA through 2007 season. Coaches active in 1-AA in 2007 in **bold** type. Active coaches and former 1-AA coaches who coached at only one school are listed with current/sole school.

Top 15 Winning Percentage

		Yrs	W	L	T	Pct
1	**Mike Kelly**, Dayton	27	246	54	1	.819
2	Greg Gattuso, Duquesne	12	97	32	0	.752
3	**Al Bagnoli**, Penn	26	194	69	0	.738
4	**Joe Taylor**, Hampton	25	197	76	4	.718
5	Chris Ault*, Nevada	16	138	53	1	.721
6	Tubby Raymond, Delaware	36	300	119	3	.714
7	Roy Kidd, Eastern Ky.	39	314	124	8	.713
8	W.C. Gorden, Jackson St.	16	119	47	5	.711
9	**Pete Richardson**, Southern	19	155	63	1	.710
10	Eddie Robinson, Grambling	55	408	165	15	.707
11	Jim Tressel*, Youngstown St.	15	135	57	2	.701
12	**Don Brown**, Massachusetts	11	88	40	0	.688
13	Billy Joe	31	237	108	4	.685
14	**Dick Biddle**, Colgate	12	95	46	0	.674
15	Mark Whipple	16	120	60	0	.667

Top 15 Victories

		Yrs	W	L	T	Pct
1	Eddie Robinson, Grambling	55	408	165	15	.707
2	Roy Kidd, Eastern Ky.	39	313	124	8	.712
3	Tubby Raymond, Delaware	36	300	119	3	.714
4	**Mike Kelly**, Dayton	27	246	54	1	.819
5	Billy Joe	31	237	108	4	.685
6	Ron Randleman	36	218	167	6	.565
7	**Joe Taylor**, Hampton	25	197	76	4	.718
8	Bill Hayes	27	196	103	2	.654
9	**Al Bagnoli**, Penn	26	194	69	0	.738
	Jerry Moore, Appalachian St.	26	194	118	1	.621
11	**Walt Hameline**, Wagner	27	186	97	2	.656
12	**Jimmye Laycock**, Wm. & Mary	28	182	134	2	.575
	Rob Ash, Drake	28	182	104	5	.634
	Andy Talley, Villanova	28	182	116	2	.610
15	Carmen Cozza, Yale	32	179	119	5	.599

*Chris Ault (Nevada) and Jim Tressel (Ohio St.) are still active in 1-A. Only their 1-AA numbers are included above.

Division I-AA Coach of the Year

First presented in 1983 by the American Football Coaches Association.

Multiple winners: Jerry Moore (3); Mark Duffner, Paul Johnson and Erk Russell (2).

Year		Year		Year	
1983	Rey Dempsey, Southern Ill.	1992	Charlie Taaffe, Citadel	2001	Bobby Johnson, Furman
1984	Dave Arnold, Montana St.	1993	Dan Allen, Boston Univ.	2002	Jack Harbaugh, E. Kentucky
1985	Dick Sheridan, Furman	1994	Jim Tressel, Youngstown St.	2003	Dick Biddle, Colgate
1986	Erk Russell, Ga. Southern	1995	Don Read, Montana	2004	Mickey Matthews, James Madison
1987	Mark Duffner, Holy Cross	1996	Ray Tellier, Columbia	2005	Jerry Moore, Appalachian St.
1988	Jimmy Satterfield, Furman	1997	Andy Talley, Villanova	2006	Jerry Moore, Appalachian St.
1989	Erk Russell, Ga. Southern	1998	Mark Whipple, Massachusetts	2007	Jerry Moore, Appalachian St.
1990	Tim Stowers, Ga. Southern	1999	Paul Johnson, Ga. Southern		
1991	Mark Duffner, Holy Cross	2000	Paul Johnson, Ga. Southern		

NCAA Playoffs

Division I-AA

Established in 1978 as a four-team playoff. Tournament field increased to eight teams in 1981, 12 teams in 1982 and 16 teams in 1986. Automatic berths are awarded to champions of the Big Sky, Gateway, Mid-Eastern Athletic, Ohio Valley, Patriot, Southern, Southland and Atlantic 10 conferences.

Multiple winners: Georgia Southern (6); Youngstown St. (4); Appalachian St. (3); Eastern Kentucky, Marshall and Montana (2).

Year	Winner	Score	Loser	Year	Winner	Score	Loser
1978	Florida A&M	35-28	Massachusetts	1993	Youngstown St.	17-5	Marshall
1979	Eastern Kentucky	30-7	Lehigh, PA	1994	Youngstown St.	28-14	Boise St.
1980	Boise St., ID	31-29	Eastern Kentucky	1995	Montana	22-20	Marshall
1981	Idaho St.	34-23	Eastern Kentucky	1996	Marshall	49-29	Montana
1982	Eastern Kentucky	17-14	Delaware	1997	Youngstown St.	10-9	McNeese St.
1983	Southern Illinois	43-7	Western Carolina	1998	Massachusetts	55-43	Georgia Southern
1984	Montana St.	19-6	Louisiana Tech	1999	Georgia Southern	59-24	Youngstown St.
1985	Georgia Southern	44-42	Furman, SC	2000	Georgia Southern	27-25	Montana
1986	Georgia Southern	48-21	Arkansas St.	2001	Montana	13-6	Furman
1987	NE Louisiana	43-42	Marshall, WV	2002	Western Kentucky	34-14	McNeese St.
1988	Furman, SC	17-12	Georgia Southern	2003	Delaware	40-0	Colgate
1989	Georgia Southern	37-34	S.F. Austin St.	2004	James Madison	31-21	Montana
1990	Georgia Southern	36-13	Nevada-Reno	2005	Appalachian St.	21-16	Northern Iowa
1991	Youngstown St., OH	25-17	Marshall	2006	Appalachian St.	28-17	Massachusetts
1992	Marshall	31-28	Youngstown St.	2007	Appalachian St.	49-21	Delaware

Division II

Established in 1973 as an eight-team playoff. Tournament field increased to 16 teams in 1988. From 1964-72, eight qualifying NCAA College Division member institutions competed in four regional bowl games, but there was no tournament and no national championship until 1973.

Multiple winners: North Dakota St. (5); Grand Valley St. (4); North Alabama (3); Northern Colorado, Northwest Missouri St., Southwest Texas St. and Troy St. (2).

Year	Winner	Score	Loser	Year	Winner	Score	Loser
1973	Louisiana Tech	.34-0	Western Kentucky	1991	Pittsburg St., KS	.23-6	Jacksonville St., AL
1974	Central Michigan	.54-14	Delaware	1992	Jacksonville St., AL	.17-13	Pittsburg St., KS
1975	Northern Michigan	.16-14	Western Kentucky	1993	North Alabama	.41-34	Indiana, PA
1976	Montana St.	.24-13	Akron, OH	1994	North Alabama	.16-10	Tex. A&M (Kings.)
1977	Lehigh, PA.	.33-0	Jacksonville St., AL	1995	North Alabama	.27-7	Pittsburg St., KS
1978	Eastern Illinois	.10-9	Delaware	1996	Northern Colorado	.23-14	Carson-Newman
1979	Delaware	.38-21	Youngstown St., OH	1997	Northern Colorado	.51-0	New Haven
1980	Cal Poly-SLO	.21-13	Eastern Illinois	1998	NW Missouri St.	.24-6	Carson-Newman
1981	SW Texas St.	.42-13	North Dakota St.	1999	NW Missouri St.	.58-52*	Carson-Newman
1982	SW Texas St.	.34-9	UC-Davis	2000	Delta St., MS	.63-34	Bloomsburg, PA
1983	North Dakota St.	.41-21	Central St., OH	2001	North Dakota	.17-14	Grand Valley St.
1984	Troy St., AL	.18-17	North Dakota St.	2002	Grand Valley St., MI	.31-24	Valdosta St., GA
1985	North Dakota St.	.35-7	North Alabama	2003	Grand Valley St., MI	.10-3	North Dakota
1986	North Dakota St.	.27-7	South Dakota	2004	Valdosta St., GA	.36-31	Pittsburg St., KS
1987	Troy St., AL	.31-17	Portland St., OR	2005	Grand Valley St., MI	.21-17	NW Missouri St.
1988	North Dakota St.	.35-21	Portland St., OR	2006	Grand Valley St., MI	.17-14	NW Missouri St.
1989	Mississippi Col.	.3-0	Jacksonville St., AL	2007	Valdosta St., GA	.25-20	NW Missouri St.
1990	North Dakota St.	.51-11	Indiana, PA		*Four overtimes		

Hill Trophy

First presented in 1986 by the Harlon Hill Awards Committee in Florence, Ala., to honor the nation's outstanding Division II player. The award is named after three-time NFL All-Pro Harlon Hill, who played college ball at North Alabama.

Multiple winners: Johnny Bailey (3), Dusty Bonner and Danny Woodhead (2).

Year		Year		Year	
1986	Jeff Bentrim, N. Dakota St., QB	1994	Chris Hatcher, Valdosta St., QB	2002	Curt Anes, Grand Valley St., QB
1987	Johnny Bailey, Texas A&I, RB	1995	Ronald McKinnon, N. Ala., LB	2003	Will Hall, N. Alabama, QB
1988	Johnny Bailey, Texas A&I, RB	1996	Jarrett Anderson, Truman St., RB	2004	Chad Friehauf, Colo-Mines, QB
1989	Johnny Bailey, Texas A&I, RB	1997	Irv Sigler, Bloomsburg, RB	2005	Jimmy Terwilliger,
1990	Chris Simdorn, N. Dakota St., QB	1998	Brian Shay, Emporia St., RB		E. Stroudsburg, QB
1991	Ronnie West, Pittsburg St., WR	1999	Corte McGuffet, N. Colo., QB	2006	Danny Woodhead,
1992	Ronald Moore, Pittsburg St., RB	2000	Dusty Bonner, Valdosta St., QB		Chadron St., RB
1993	Roger Graham, New Haven, RB	2001	Dusty Bonner, Valdosta St., QB	2007	Danny Woodhead,
					Chadron St., RB

Division III

Established in 1973 as a four-team playoff. Tournament field increased to eight teams in 1975, 16 teams in 1985 and 28 teams in 1999. From 1969-72, four qualifying NCAA College Division member institutions competed in two regional bowl games, but there was no tournament and no national championship until 1973. (*) denotes overtime.

Multiple winners: Mt. Union (9); Augustana (4); Ithaca (3); Dayton, St. John's, Widener, WI-La Crosse and Wittenberg (2).

Year	Winner	Score	Loser	Year	Winner	Score	Loser
1973	Wittenberg, OH	.41-0	Juniata, PA	1991	Ithaca, NY	.34-20	Dayton, OH
1974	Central, IA	.10-8	Ithaca, NY	1992	WI-La Crosse	.16-12	Wash. & Jeff., PA
1975	Wittenberg, OH	.28-0	Ithaca, NY	1993	Mt. Union, OH	.34-24	Rowan, NJ
1976	St. John's, MN	.31-28	Towson St., MD	1994	Albion, MI	.38-15	Wash. & Jeff.
1977	Widener, PA	.39-36	Wabash, IN	1995	WI-La Crosse	.36-7	Rowan, NJ
1978	Baldwin-Wallace	.24-10	Wittenberg, OH	1996	Mt. Union, OH	.56-24	Rowan, NJ
1979	Ithaca, NY	.14-10	Wittenberg, OH	1997	Mt. Union, OH	.61-12	Lycoming
1980	Dayton, OH	.63-0	Ithaca, NY	1998	Mt. Union, OH	.44-24	Rowan, NJ
1981	Widener, PA	.17-10	Dayton, OH	1999	Pacific Lutheran	.42-13	Rowan, NJ
1982	West Georgia	.14-0	Augustana, IL	2000	Mt. Union, OH	.10-7	St. John's, MN
1983	Augustana, IL	.21-17	Union, NY	2001	Mt. Union, OH	.30-27	Bridgewater, VA
1984	Augustana, IL	.21-12	Central, IA	2002	Mt. Union, OH	.48-7	Trinity, TX
1985	Augustana, IL	.20-7	Ithaca	2003	St. John's, MN	.24-6	Mt. Union, OH
1986	Augustana, IL	.31-3	Salisbury St., MD	2004	Linfield	.28-21	Mary Hardin-Baylor
1987	Wagner, NY	.19-3	Dayton, OH	2005	Mt. Union, OH	.35-28	WI-Whitewater
1988	Ithaca, NY	.39-24	Central, IA	2006	Mt. Union, OH	.35-16	WI-Whitewater
1989	Dayton, OH	.17-7	Union, NY	2007	WI-Whitewater	.31-21	Mt. Union, OH
1990	Allegheny, PA	.21-14*	Lycoming, PA				

Gagliardi Trophy

First presented in 1993 by the St. John's (Minn.) University J-Club, to honor the nation's outstanding Division III player. The award is named after John Gagliardi, St. John's legendary head coach, one of only two (Ediie Robinson) coaches in college football history with 400 wins.

Year		Year		Year	
1993	Jim Ballard, Mt. Union, QB	1999	Danny Ragsdale, Redlands, QB	2004	Rocky Myers, Wesley, S
1994	Carey Bender, Coe, RB	2000	Chad Johnson, Pac. Luth., QB	2005	Brett Elliott, Linfield, QB
1995	Chris Palmer, St. John's, WR	2001	Chuck Moore, Mt. Union, RB	2006	Josh Brehm, Alma, QB
1996	Lon Erickson, Ill. Wesleyan, QB	2002	Dan Pugh, Mt. Union, RB	2007	Justin Beaver, WI-Whitewater, RB
1997	Bill Borchert, Mt. Union, QB	2003	Blake Ellitott, St. John's, WR		
1998	Scott Hvistendahl, Augsburg, WR/P				

NAIA Playoffs

Division I

Established in 1956 as two-team playoff. Tournament field increased to four teams in 1958, eight teams in 1978 and 16 teams in 1987 before cutting back to eight teams in 1989. NAIA went back to a single division 16-team playoff in 1997. The title game has ended in a tie four times (1956, '64, '84 and '85). Note that Northeastern St., OK was called NE Oklahoma in 1958.

Multiple winners: Texas A&I (7); Carroll-MT and Carson-Newman (5); Central Arkansas and Central St-OH (3); Abilene Christian, Central St-OK, Elon, Georgetown-KY, Northeastern St-OK, Pittsburg St. and St. John's-MN (2).

Year	Winner	Score	Loser	Year	Winner	Score	Loser
1956	Montana St.	0-0	St. Joseph's, IN	1982	Central St., OK	14-11	Mesa, CO
1957	Pittsburg St., KS	27-26	Hillsdale, MI	1983	Car-Newman, TN	36-28	Mesa, CO
1958	NE Oklahoma	19-13	Northern Arizona	1984	Car-Newman, TN	19-19	Central Arkansas
1959	Texas A&I	20-7	Lenoir-Rhyne, NC	1985	Hillsdale, MI	10-10	Central Arkansas
1960	Lenoir-Rhyne, NC	15-14	Humboldt St., CA	1986	Car-Newman, TN	17-0	Cameron, OK
1961	Pittsburg St., KS	12-7	Linfield, OR	1987	Cameron, OK	30-2	Car-Newman, TN
1962	Central St., OK	28-13	Lenoir-Rhyne, NC	1988	Car-Newman, TN	56-21	Adams St., CO
1963	St. John's, MN	33-27	Prairie View A&M, TX	1989	Car-Newman, TN	34-20	Emporia St., KS
1964	Concordia, MN	7-7	Sam Houston St., TX	1990	Central St., OH	38-16	Mesa, CO
1965	St. John's, MN	33-0	Linfield, OR	1991	Central Arkansas	19-16	Central St., OH
1966	Waynesburg, PA	42-21	WI-Whitewater	1992	Central St., OH	19-16	Gardner-Webb, NC
1967	Fairmont St., WV	28-21	Eastern Wash.	1993	E. Central, OK	49-35	Glenville St., WV
1968	Troy St., AL.	43-35	Texas A&I	1994	N'eastern St., OK	13-12	Ark-Pine Bluff
1969	Texas A&I	32-7	Concordia, MN	1995	Central St., OH	37-7	N'eastern St., OK
1970	Texas A&I	48-7	Wofford, SC	1996	SW Oklahoma St.	33-31	Montana Tech
1971	Livingston, AL	14-12	Arkansas Tech	1997	Findlay, OH	14-7	Willamette, OR
1972	East Texas St.	21-18	Car-Newman, TN	1998	Azusa Pacific, CA	17-14	Olivet Nazarene, IL
1973	Abilene Christian.	42-14	Elon, NC	1999	NW Oklahoma St.	34-26	Georgetown, KY
1974	Texas A&I	34-23	Henderson St., AR	2000	Georgetown, KY	20-0	NW Oklahoma St.
1975	Texas A&I	37-0	Salem, WV	2001	Georgetown, KY	49-27	Sioux Falls, S.D.
1976	Texas A&I	26-0	Central Arkansas	2002	Carroll, MT	28-7	Georgetown, KY
1977	Abilene Christian	24-7	SW Oklahoma	2003	Carroll, MT	41-28	NW Oklahoma St.
1978	Angelo St., TX	34-14	Elon, NC	2004	Carroll, MT	15-13	St. Francis, IN
1979	Texas A&I	20-14	Central St., OK	2005	Carroll, MT	27-10	St. Francis, IN
1980	Elon, NC	17-10	NE Oklahoma	2006	Sioux Falls, SD	23-19	St. Francis, IN
1981	Elon, NC	3-0	Pittsburg St., KS	2007	Carroll, MT	17-9	Sioux Falls, SD

Division II

Established in 1970 as four-team playoff. Tournament field increased to eight teams in 1978 and 16 teams in 1987. NAIA went back to a single division playoff in 1997. The title game has ended in a tie twice (1981 and '87).

Multiple winners: Westminster (6); Findlay, Linfield and Pacific Lutheran (3); Concordia-MN, Northwestern-IA and Texas Lutheran (2).

Year	Winner	Score	Loser	Year	Winner	Score	Loser
1970	Westminster, PA	21-16	Anderson, IN	1984	Linfield, OR	33-22	Northwestern, IA
1971	Calif. Lutheran	30-14	Westminster, PA	1985	WI-La Crosse	24-7	Pacific Lutheran
1972	Missouri Southern	21-14	Northwestern, IA	1986	Linfield, OR	17-0	Baker, KS
1973	Northwestern, IA	10-3	Glenville St., WV	1987	Pacific Lutheran	16-16	WI-Stevens Pt.*
1974	Texas Lutheran	42-0	Missouri Valley	1988	Westminster, PA	21-14	WI-La Crosse
1975	Texas Lutheran	34-8	Calif. Lutheran	1989	Westminster, PA	51-30	WI-La Crosse
1976	Westminster, PA	20-13	Redlands, CA	1990	Peru St., NE	17-7	Westminster, PA
1977	Westminster, PA	17-9	Calif. Lutheran	1991	Georgetown, KY	28-20	Pacific Lutheran
1978	Concordia, MN	7-0	Findlay, OH	1992	Findlay, OH	26-13	Linfield, OR
1979	Findlay, OH	51-6	Northwestern, IA	1993	Pacific Lutheran	50-20	Westminster, PA
1980	Pacific Lutheran	38-10	Wilmington, OH	1994	Westminster, PA	27-7	Pacific Lutheran
1981	Austin College, TX	24-24	Concordia, MN	1995	Findlay, OH	21-21	Central Wash.
1982	Linfield, OR	33-15	Wm. Jewell, MO	1996	Sioux Falls, S.D.	47-25	W. Washington
1983	Northwestern, IA	25-21	Pacific Lutheran				

*Wisconsin-Stevens Point forfeited its entire 1987 schedule due to its use of an ineligible player.

PRO FOOTBALL

2007 / 2008 YEAR IN REVIEW

Giants quarterback **Eli Manning** and coach **Tom Coughlin** celebrate their unlikely Super Bowl victory.

FREE FALLIN'
OUT INTO NOTHING

The Patriots recorded 16 wins in the regular season, two more in the postseason...and then one Giant loss in Super Bowl XLII.

by Bill Simmons

NOW IT ALL MAKES SENSE.

You bleed for your team, you follow them through thick and thin, you monitor every free-agent signing, you immerse yourself in draft day, you purchase the jerseys and caps, you plan your Sundays around the games...and there's a little rainbow waiting at the end. You can't see it, but you know it's there. It's there. It has to be there. So you believe.

Of course, there's one catch: You might never get there. Every fan's worst fear. All that energy over the years just getting displaced, no release, no satisfaction, nothing. Season after season, no championship... and then you die. I mean, isn't that what this is all about? Isn't that the nagging fear? That those little moral victories over the years won't make up for the lack of a big payoff at the end — that one moment when everything comes together, when your team keeps winning, when you keep getting the breaks and you just can't lose.

And if none of this makes sense, well... it does to me. I just watched somebody else's team win the Super Bowl. Giants 17, Patriots 14.

If you're wondering why this column feels familiar, it's because I pulled the previous three-and-a-half paragraphs from my postgame column after the Patriots stunned the Rams in Super Bowl XXXVI. This time around, we were the Rams. We were rooting for the unlikable double-digit favorites with an unstoppable offense. We were the arrogant fans who dismissed the chances of the other team. We had the Super Bowl postgame party looming that had been a hot ticket all week. Then the game started, and everything went right to hell. We looked flat from the first minute. Our underdog opponent gained confidence, punched us in the mouth a few times, kept punching and punching, caught a few breaks, threw a few more punches, ran out of gas near the end, looked to be done...and out of nowhere, rallied for a miracle drive to steal the championship. We stood there slack-jawed while the other fans celebrated; we

 Bill Simmons is a columnist for ESPN.com and *ESPN The Magazine.*

When defensive end **Michael Strahan** eventually landed, it was on top of Patriots quarterback Tom Brady for one of the Giants' five sacks on the day.

AP Images

were unable to breathe and wondered what the heck just happened. And then we hustled out of the stadium like we were fleeing a crime scene.

The symmetry was incredible. It was staggering. It was epic. During the two weeks leading up to the game, I heard and read different media members make the case there were potential similarities between Super Bowl XXXVI and Super Bowl XLII, never believing the comparison had merit because the 2008 Giants were so different than the 2002 Patriots. The Giants had a deep threat. They had a monster defensive line. They had a semi-experienced quarterback and a good running game. Unlike in 2002, some people were giving this underdog a chance. I just didn't see it.

But standing there in Section 129 and surrounded by delirious Giants fans who were hugging and screaming and crying and acting like stranded castaways who just noticed a rescue boat? I saw it.

Truth be told, I started seeing it during the halftime show, immediately after the Patriots headed into the locker room with a deceiving 7-3 lead. Their lack of energy was alarming and almost inexplicable — not just during the first half, but when they were warming up beforehand and getting "fired up" during the pregame introductions. (Remember that bizarre NFL Films clip before Super Bowl XXXVI, when a psyched-up Brady momentarily freaked out in the tunnel, jumped toward Drew Bledsoe, grabbed Bledsoe's helmet with both hands and started head-butting him and screaming like a lunatic? Those days were long gone.) There were red flags everywhere. New England's offensive line was getting overwhelmed by

David Tyree's miracle catch after Eli Manning's great escape continued the Giants' game-winning drive.

AP Images

New York's front four. An uncharacteristically sloppy Brady had me telling everyone within earshot, "You know, I really think his ankle is bothering him," at least 73 times in 90 minutes. Even worse, the game had no discernible flow because of New York's 10-minute opening drive, followed by an endless slew of commercial breaks so Fox could catch up.

One moment in the second quarter stood out: when the Pats blew an easy third-and-1 from their own 42. For the first three months of the season, back when they were the Big, Bad, Invincible Pats, that would have been two-down territory for them — they would have thrown on third down and maybe even tried to make a big play. If they didn't

get it, they would have banged it past the chain on the next play. This time? They played it safe, ran Maroney to the left side, lost two yards and quickly sent out the punt team while every Pats fan turned into the confused wife from "Airplane" who couldn't understand why her husband had ordered the second cup of coffee.

Who were these guys? Where was the team I watched for the past few months? Why aren't we attacking these guys? Why did we stick with our January cold-weather offense when we're playing indoors?

And right as I was wondering about all this stuff, Tom Petty started playing "Free Fallin'."

Now...

Right after the 2002 Pats roared into the locker room with a 14-3 lead and had the Superdome buzzing, U2 roared out and sang "Beautiful Day." It was a seminal moment for every Patriots fan in the building. If you could have picked anything to happen at that specific moment to capture what everyone was feeling, you would have brought U2 out to sing "Beautiful Day." I remember thinking to myself, "Every time I hear this song for the rest of my life, I'm going to think about this game."

Six years later, I was standing there watching Petty sing "Free Fallin'" and thinking, "Good God, is this the Bizarro Beautiful Day?"

My feet started to go numb. My stomach started to churn. Supremely confident for the entire week, I had been quietly worrying even before the opening kickoff when we walked into the stadium and noticed the staggering number of Giants and Patriots fans. It's a dirty little secret, but Super Bowl crowds stink for the same reason that All-Star crowds stink — more than half of the tickets get chewed up by sports executives, corporate sponsors, people working for the league or the advertising companies that support the league, celebrities and pseudo-celebrities, rich people and neutral fans who just want to be there because it's something to do. Arizona wasn't *anything* like that. Super Bowl XLII broke the record for "most fans of one team or the other" as well as "most fans wearing jerseys" and "most dead-even split of fans representing both franchises."

Because of the unique makeup of the crowd, I became convinced we were headed for something special, even texting a few friends to predict a close and special game. Soaking in the atmosphere, seeing the sea of jerseys, hearing the sounds that genuine fans make, suddenly a blowout seemed impossible. This was too good. This was what sports was all about, right? Stupidly, I thought the atmosphere could potentially resemble a World Cup match, with fans loudly supporting both teams and cheering on every play, forgetting that the NFL would kill any chance of this happening by over-powering us with rock music and the Jumbotron. But the possibility of an unforgettable game remained. You could feel it before the game, and you could definitely feel it heading into the second half.

With that said, I never thought the Patriots would lose. I thought they'd be tested, I thought the game would be great...but lose??? You could point out 10 different instances when the Pats blew a chance to make a monster play or put the game away, and you could point out all the different times the Giants caught a break or had a ball bounce their way, but really, everything you need to know about Super Bowl XLII happened on the Miracle Play To Be Named Later — you know, the third down on the do-or-die drive when Eli Manning ripped himself away from the entire Patriots defensive line (THEY HAD HIS JERSEY!!!!!!) and threw a pass that hung in the air forever like one of those sports movie passes, and even though David Tyree and Rodney Harrison had an equal chance of getting it, Tyree jumped a little bit higher, hauled in the football, trapped it against his helmet and somehow held on while Harrison was doing everything but performing a figure-four leg lock on him.

Seriously, what else do you need to know about this game beyond that play and the 30-second loop of Brady getting pounded by various defensive linemen? The Giants played well enough to win, they were tougher, they were luckier and they wanted it just a little bit more. Now we live in a world that Tom Coughlin outcoached Bill Belichick in a Super Bowl, that Eli Manning outplayed Tom Brady in a Super Bowl, that a Belichick-era Patriots team lost a Super Bowl because they weren't tough enough, that the Ewing Theory has been replaced by the Tiki Theory. The Giants deserved to win. They were better. They peaked at the right time. And watching their fans celebrate afterward, a small part of me actually felt happy for them. Envious, even. It's one thing to win a championship...it's another to win a championship *like that*. You can't possibly understand unless it happens to you.

Other than that "Free Fallin'" moment and the Miracle Play To Be Named Later, I will forever remember eight things about Super Bowl XLII:

1. Before the pregame introductions, the Patriots were jogging off the field and the Jumbotron caught Brady briefly break stride to shake hands with Pat O'Brien. This bothered me for some reason — somewhere along the line, the team and the quarterback almost became *too* famous, as symbolized by that handshake and the fact Brady would have run right by O'Brien six years ago because he would have wanted to flip out in the tunnel and inexplicably head-butt Bledsoe over and over again. Look, I'm not blaming Brady for the handshake. This was the season when his fame transcended sports and morphed into something else, and part of that "something else" involves the occasional random pregame handshake with the likes of Pat O'Brien. You have to do things like this when you're famous, even if you don't really want to do them. At the same time, I thought this was a terrible omen and a defining moment of the season. In the Super Bowl, you'd much rather be the "Nobody believes in us!" team than the "Not only does everybody believe in us, but our QB shakes hands before games with Pat O'Brien" team. You just would.

2. Speaking of Brady, if the Patriots had finished 19-0, I planned to start my column with a scene from the Patriots' postgame party. Through some mutual friends, I had arranged to hang out with Brady's crew for what promised to be a laid-back celebration in somebody's hotel room, probably no more than 15-20 people since Brady's circle is surprisingly and refreshingly small. Because it was a rare chance to catch Brady in an unguarded moment — and an important moment at that — I spent most of Friday and Saturday thinking about that first paragraph and all the different ways it could start. I kept seeing Brady sitting in a chair with his right ankle encased in ice, quietly sipping a bottle of champagne with a satisfied smile on his face, and Gisele would be there, and everyone would be recapping 19-0 and remembering the incredible season. I liked the thought of a famous person celebrating a historic night in such a totally normal and relatable way.

And that's what it will remain. A thought and only a thought. It never happened.

3. First entry in my notebook right after the game ended: "Eli Manning just gave me the Eli Manning Face." And he did.

4. For the rest of eternity, I will never understand why the Patriots — a team that broke all kinds of offensive records by attacking teams with an aggressive, run-and-shoot offense that thrived on audibles, checks and the intelligence of the quarterback and his receivers — became passive in the single biggest game of the season. It's one thing to change styles because it's 20 degrees and windy outside and you're worried about throwing the ball. But indoors? Only on the last drive did the Patriots look like the Patriots. I will never understand what took so long. Ever. I will never understand it. I wasn't even that depressed after the game, just confused. What happened to the remarkable offensive juggernaut from the first three months of the season? Where did their arrogance go? What happened to their swagger? Did the never-ending attention and nonstop pressure eventually get to them? For most of Sunday's game, it seemed the Patriots were playing not to lose. And maybe they were.

I will say this: Even though Friday's column will probably earn the No. 1 spot on the "Columns I Wish Weren't In My Archives" list before everything's said and done, Super Bowl XLII inadvertently proved my point. To finish 19-0, you really need a perfect storm of things to fall your way — not just off the field when you're building the team, but for 19 straight games over the span of five months, and on top of that, the pressure builds every week because of the streak, so it's inevitable you'll wear down in the final two months. I don't think we'll ever see a 19-0 team. If this particular Patriots team couldn't pull it off, nobody's doing it.

Patriots' cornerback **Ellis Hobbs** is a couple of steps behind as he watches Eli Manning's game-winning touchdown pass settle into the awaiting arms of **Plaxico Burress**.

5. Much like the Patriots, I choked heading into the weekend: Somehow, I forgot to pack my good-luck Wes Welker jersey and headed to the game without any Pats gear. Originally intent on buying a Pats hat at the game, once I saw all the jerseys in the stands and in my section, I made the executive decision to fine myself $85 dollars (the price of a white No. 81 Moss jersey at one of those merchandise booths). You can currently find that jersey at the bottom of the garbage can in my hotel room. I might take it home and burn it. I haven't decided yet.

6. Over the weekend, I was arguing with a friend about the unthinkable scenario of a Patriots defeat and whether it would become the most famous loss in the history of team sports. You can have famous wins and famous losses — for instance, when an undefeated UNLV team lost to Duke, that was a famous loss. When Villanova beat Georgetown in '85, that was a famous win. When the Mets beat the Red Sox in the '86 World Series, that was a famous win and a

famous loss, although it was definitely more famous for the "loss" part. When the '80 USA hockey team beat the Russians, it was a famous win here and a famous loss in Russia. You get the idea.

Eventually, we decided that an upset of the Pats would be like the '86 World Series — more of a famous loss than a famous win, but something that would definitely get major play as a win because of the New York media. (By contrast, if Tampa Bay or Seattle had toppled the 18-0 Patriots, it would have been remembered as a famous loss and that's it.) Now it's playing out exactly like we predicted, and I guess what I'm trying to say here is that I spent most of the second half hating myself for ever having the conversation in the first place.

(Along those same lines, has there ever been a better performance by the Karma Gods than Super Bowl XLII? On one side, you have the Patriots cheating in Week 1, going into "Eff-You" mode and running up scores for the next two months...and just when it seemed like there wouldn't be any real repercussions, they suffered the double-whammy of Brady's ankle sprain and Spygate blowing up again days before the final game. On the other side, you have the G-Men nobly playing their starters in Week 17 and giving everyone such a wonderful and unexpected sporting event...and they're rewarded with four straight wins, a Super Bowl title and one of the most famous upset victories in the history of professional sports. Hmmmmmmm.)

7. From the "Now It Can Be Told" department: Everyone blamed me for "jinxing" the Patriots two weeks ago after I posted my Dr. Jack Breakdown of the '86 Celtics and the '07 Pats. (And by the way, I think we have a final verdict. And then some.) Well, a significantly more blatant jinx had already happened: For my father's 60th birthday present at the end of November, I bought him a flight from Boston to Arizona and got him a hotel room and a ticket for Super Bowl XLII, although we took great pains to say "Going to the Super Bowl" instead of "Seeing the Pats in the Super Bowl" on every level. One week later? The Baltimore game happened. Yeah. Exactly. I didn't even write about this because I didn't want to get murdered by a deranged Patriots fan.

Anyway, the Patriots won their two playoff games and set the stage for another great father-son sports moment in a lifetime of great father-son sports moments. We went to the triple-OT Suns-Celts game together in 1976. We went to Games 5 and 7 of the Sixers-Celtics series in '81. We saw the Celtics clinch titles in '84 and '86, and we saw the game when Bird stole the ball from Isiah. Best of all, we were in Fenway for Games 4 and 5 of the 2004 ALCS at Fenway. But we had never seen the Patriots win the Super Bowl together; now, we had the chance to see them make history. As it turned out, the only history made was Dad

breaking the record for "Most pee breaks during a single football game." This definitely turned out to be a bonding moment, but for different reasons — I haven't seen him this decimated by a sporting event since Magic made the baby sky hook in '87.

After the game, we reacted in different ways: I took the approach of "we didn't deserve to win, we sucked, we choked and I'm not getting distraught over this when the city of Boston has won five titles since 2002" (note: I didn't fully believe this but desperately tried to talk myself into it), while my father went with the approach of "I look like a doctor just gave me horrible news, and I can't speak." He was totally blindsided by what happened; in his defense, he wasn't picking up on all the bad omens during the game, and he missed the Brady-O'Brien handshake. But we didn't say much after the game, and he didn't even laugh when I asked if he wanted to flip a coin with the winner getting to FedEx a turd sandwich to Josh McDaniels this week. In fact, I never thought he'd get his sense of humor back until we had this exchange:

Me: "Dad, are you gonna be all right? I'm starting to get worried."

Dad doesn't say anything. There's a long pause.

Me: "Dad?"

Dad: "I don't think I want to go to the Patriots' postgame party."

8. Finally, can you guess the last thing we heard as we were walking (OK, hustling) out of the stadium right after the final play? That's right, it was the sound of euphoric Giants fans chanting, "Eighteen and one! Eighteen and one! Eighteen and one!" Yes, it's safe to say the Boston-New York rivalry has been taken to new heights. As a tennis umpire would say, "Advantage, New York."

Eighteen and one! Eighteen and one!

I can still hear them. I will always hear them.

2007-2008 Season in Review

ESPN SPORTS ALMANAC

Final NFL Standings

Division champions (*) and wild card playoff qualifiers (†) are noted; division champions with two best records received first round byes. Number of seasons listed after each head coach refers to latest tenure with club through 2007 season.

American Football Conference

East Division

	W	L	T	PF	PA	vs Div	vs AFC
*New England	16	0	0	589	274	6-0	12-0
Buffalo	7	9	0	252	354	4-2	6-6
NY Jets	4	12	0	268	355	2-4	4-8
Miami	1	15	0	267	437	0-6	1-11

2007 Head Coaches: NE—Bill Belichick (8th season); **Buf**—Dick Jauron (2nd); **NY**—Eric Mangini (2nd); **Mia**—Cam Cameron (1st).
2006 Standings: 1. New England (12-4); 2. NY Jets (10-6); 3. Buffalo (7-9); 4. Miami (6-10).

North Division

	W	L	T	PF	PA	vs Div	vs AFC
*Pittsburgh	10	6	0	393	269	5-1	7-5
Cleveland	10	6	0	402	382	3-3	7-5
Cincinnati	7	9	0	380	385	3-3	6-6
Baltimore	5	11	0	275	384	1-5	2-12

2007 Head Coaches: Pit—Mike Tomlin (1st season); **Cle**—Romeo Crennel (3rd); **Cin**—Marvin Lewis (5th); **Bal**—Brian Billick (9th).
2006 Standings: 1. Baltimore (13-3); 2. Cincinnati (8-8); 3. Pittsburgh (8-8); 4. Cleveland (4-12).

South Division

	W	L	T	PF	PA	vs Div	vs AFC
*Indianapolis	13	3	0	450	262	5-1	9-3
†Jacksonville	11	5	0	411	304	2-4	8-4
†Tennessee	10	6	0	301	297	4-2	7-5
Houston	8	8	0	379	384	1-5	5-7

2007 Head Coaches: Ind—Tony Dungy (6th season); **Jax**—Jack Del Rio (5th); **Ten**—Jeff Fisher (14th); **Hou**—Gary Kubiak (2nd).
2006 Standings: 1. Indianapolis (12-4); 2. Tennessee (8-8); 3. Jacksonville (8-8); 4. Houston (6-10).

West Division

	W	L	T	PF	PA	vs Div	vs AFC
*San Diego	11	5	0	412	284	5-1	9-3
Denver	7	9	0	320	409	3-3	6-6
Kansas City	4	12	0	226	335	2-4	3-9
Oakland	4	12	0	283	398	2-4	4-8

2007 Head Coaches: SD—Norv Turner (1st season); **Den**—Mike Shanahan (13th); **KC**—Herman Edwards (2nd); **Oak**—Lane Kiffin (1st).
2006 Standings: 1. San Diego (14-2); 2. Kansas City (9-7); 3. Denver (9-7); 4. Oakland (2-14).

AFC Tiebreakers: Pittsburgh won the AFC North over Cleveland based on a head-to-head sweep (2-0). Tennessee won the AFC wildcard berth over Cleveland based on a better record in common games (4-1 to Browns' 3-2).

National Football Conference

East Division

	W	L	T	PF	PA	vs Div	vs NFC
*Dallas	13	3	0	455	325	4-2	10-2
†NY Giants	10	6	0	373	351	3-3	7-5
†Washington	9	7	0	334	310	3-3	7-5
Philadelphia	8	8	0	336	300	2-4	5-7

2007 Head Coaches: Dal—Wade Phillips (1st); **NY**—Tom Coughlin (4th); **Wash**—Joe Gibbs (4th); **Phi**—Andy Reid (8th).
2006 Standings: 1. Philadelphia (10-6); 2. Dallas (9-7); 3. NY Giants (8-8); 4. Washington (5-11).

North Division

	W	L	T	PF	PA	vs Div	vs NFC
*Green Bay	13	3	0	435	291	4-2	9-3
Minnesota	8	8	0	365	311	3-3	6-6
Detroit	7	9	0	346	444	3-3	4-8
Chicago	7	9	0	334	348	2-4	4-8

2007 Head Coaches: GB—Mike McCarthy (2nd season); **Min**—Brad Childress (2nd); **Det**—Rod Marinelli (2nd); **Chi**—Lovie Smith (4th).
2006 Standings: 1. Chicago (13-3); 2. Green Bay (8-8); 3. Minnesota (6-10); 4. Detroit (3-13).

South Division

	W	L	T	PF	PA	vs Div	vs NFC
*Tampa Bay	9	7	0	334	270	5-1	8-4
Carolina	7	9	0	267	347	3-3	7-5
New Orleans	7	9	0	379	388	3-3	6-6
Atlanta	4	12	0	259	414	1-5	3-9

2007 Head Coaches: TB—Jon Gruden (6th season); **Car**—John Fox (6th); **NO**—Sean Payton (2nd); **Atl**—Bobby Petrino (1st, 3-10) resigned on Dec. 11 and was replaced for the remainder of the season by asst. coach Emmitt Thomas (1-2).
2006 Standings: 1. New Orleans (10-6); 2. Carolina (8-8); 3. Atlanta (7-9); 4. Tampa Bay (4-12).

West Division

	W	L	T	PF	PA	vs Div	vs NFC
*Seattle	10	6	0	393	291	5-1	8-4
Arizona	8	8	0	404	399	3-3	5-7
San Francisco	5	11	0	219	364	3-3	4-8
St. Louis	3	13	0	263	438	1-5	3-9

2007 Head Coaches: Sea—Mike Holmgren (9th season); **Ariz**—Ken Whisenhunt (1st); **SF**—Mike Nolan (3rd); **St.L**—Scott Linehan (2nd).
2006 Standings: 1. Seattle (9-7); 2. St. Louis (8-8); 3. San Francisco (7-9); 4. Arizona (5-11).

NFC Tiebreaker: Dallas finished ahead of Green Bay based on its head-to-head victory.

NFL Regular Season Individual Leaders
(* indicates rookies)

Passing Efficiency
(Minimum of 224 attempts)

AFC	Att	Cmp	Cmp Pct	Yds	Yds/ Att	TD	Long	Int	Sack/Lost	Rating Points
Tom Brady, NE	578	398	68.9	4806	8.31	50	69-td	8	21/128	117.2
Ben Roethlisberger, Pit	404	264	65.3	3154	7.81	32	83	11	47/347	104.1
David Garrard, Jax	325	208	64.0	2509	7.72	18	59-td	3	21/99	102.2
Peyton Manning, Ind	515	337	65.4	4040	7.84	31	73-td	14	21/124	98.0
Jay Cutler, Den	467	297	63.6	3497	7.49	20	68-td	14	27/153	88.1
Matt Schaub, Hou	289	192	66.4	2241	7.75	9	77-td	9	16/126	87.2
Carson Palmer, Cin	575	373	64.9	4131	7.18	26	70-td	20	17/119	86.7
Chad Pennington, NYJ	260	179	68.8	1765	6.79	10	57-td	9	26/178	86.1
Sage Rosenfels, Hou	240	154	64.2	1684	7.02	15	53-td	12	6/48	84.8
Derek Anderson, Cle	527	298	56.5	3787	7.19	29	78-td	19	14/109	82.5
Philip Rivers, SD	460	277	60.2	3152	6.85	21	49-td	15	22/163	82.4
Damon Huard, KC	332	206	62.0	2257	6.80	11	58	13	36/234	76.8
Kyle Boller, Bal	275	168	61.1	1743	6.34	9	53	10	24/159	75.2
Vince Young, Ten	382	238	62.3	2546	6.66	9	73	17	25/157	71.1
Cleo Lemon, Mia	309	173	56.0	1773	5.74	6	64-td	6	25/166	71.0

NFC	Att	Cmp	Cmp Pct	Yds	Yds/ Att	TD	Long	Int	Sack/Lost	Rating Points
Tony Romo, Dal	520	335	64.4	4211	8.10	36	59-td	19	24/176	97.4
Brett Favre, GB	535	356	66.5	4155	7.77	28	82-td	15	15/93	95.7
Jeff Garcia, TB	327	209	63.9	2440	7.46	13	69-td	4	19/104	94.6
Matt Hasselbeck, Sea	562	352	62.6	3966	7.06	28	65	12	33/204	91.4
Donovan McNabb, Phi	473	291	61.5	3324	7.03	19	75-td	7	44/227	89.9
Kurt Warner, Ari	451	281	62.3	3417	7.58	27	62	17	20/140	89.8
Drew Brees, NO	652	440	67.5	4423	6.78	28	58	18	16/109	89.4
Jon Kitna, Det	561	355	63.3	4068	7.25	18	91-td	20	51/320	80.9
Jason Campbell, Wash	417	250	60.0	2700	6.47	12	54	11	21/110	77.6
Joey Harrington, Atl	348	215	61.8	2215	6.36	7	69-td	8	32/192	77.2
Brian Griese, Chi	262	161	61.5	1803	6.88	10	81-td	12	15/114	75.6
Eli Manning, NYG	529	297	56.1	3336	6.31	23	60-td	20	27/217	73.9
Tavaris Jackson, Min	294	171	58.2	1911	6.50	9	71	12	19/70	70.8
Marc Bulger, St.L	378	221	58.5	2392	6.33	11	40	15	37/269	70.3
Rex Grossman, Chi	225	122	54.2	1411	6.27	4	59-td	7	25/198	66.4

Receptions

AFC	No	Yds	Avg	Long	TD
Wes Welker, NE	112	1175	10.5	42	8
T.J. Houshmandzadeh, Cin	112	1143	10.2	42-td	12
Reggie Wayne, Ind	104	1510	14.5	64	10
Derrick Mason, Bal	103	1087	10.6	79-td	5
Brandon Marshall, Den.	102	1325	13.0	68-td	7
Tony Gonzalez, KC	99	1172	11.8	31	5
Randy Moss, NE	98	1493	15.2	65-td	23
Chad Johnson, Cin	93	1440	15.5	70-td	8
Jericho Cotchery, NYJ	82	1130	13.8	50	2
Kellen Winslow, Cle	82	1106	13.5	49	5
Braylon Edwards, Cle.	80	1289	16.1	78-td	16
Antonio Gates, SD	75	984	13.1	49-td	9
Hines Ward, Pit	71	732	10.3	25	7

NFC	No	Yds	Avg	Long	TD
Larry Fitzgerald, Ari	100	1409	14.1	48-td	10
Marques Colston, NO	98	1202	12.3	45	11
Jason Witten, Dal	96	1145	11.9	53	7
Bobby Engram, Sea	94	1147	12.2	49	6
Torry Holt, St.L	93	1189	12.8	40	7
Brian Westbrook, Phi	90	771	8.6	57-td	5
Steve Smith, Car	87	1002	11.5	74-td	7
Roddy White, Atl	83	1202	14.5	69-td	6
Donald Driver, GB	82	1048	12.8	47	2
Terrell Owens, Dal	81	1355	16.7	52-td	15
Shaun McDonald, St.L	79	943	11.9	49-td	6
Kevin Curtis, Phi	77	1110	14.4	75-td	6
Reggie Bush, NO	73	417	5.7	25	2
Bernard Berrian, Chi	71	951	13.4	59-td	5
Anquan Boldin, Ari	71	853	12.0	44-td	9

Rushing Yards

AFC	Att	Yds	Avg	Long	TD
LaDainian Tomlinson, SD	315	1474	4.7	49	15
Willie Parker, Pit	321	1316	4.1	32	2
Jamal Lewis, Cle	298	1304	4.4	66-td	9
Willis McGahee, Bal	294	1207	4.1	46-td	7
Fred Taylor, Jax	223	1202	5.4	80-td	5
Thomas Jones, NYJ	310	1119	3.6	36	1
Marshawn Lynch*, Buf	280	1115	4.0	56-td	7
LenDale White, Ten	303	1110	3.7	28	7
Joseph Addai, Ind	261	1072	4.1	23	12
Justin Fargas, Oak	222	1009	4.5	48	4
Laurence Maroney, NE	185	835	4.5	59-td	6
Ron Dayne, Hou	194	773	4.0	39	6
Maurice Jones-Drew, Jax	167	768	4.6	57-td	7
Kenny Watson, Cin	178	763	4.3	24	7

NFC	Att	Yds	Avg	Long	TD
Adrian Peterson*, Min	238	1341	5.6	73-td	12
Brian Westbrook, Phi	278	1333	4.8	36	7
Clinton Portis, Wash.	325	1262	3.9	32	11
Edgerrin James, Ari	324	1222	3.8	27	7
Frank Gore, SF	260	1102	4.2	43-td	5
Brandon Jacobs, NYG	202	1009	5.0	43-td	4
Steven Jackson, St.L	237	1002	4.2	54	5
Marion Barber, Dal	204	975	4.8	54	10
Ryan Grant, GB	188	956	5.1	66-td	8
Earnest Graham, TB	222	898	4.0	28-td	10
DeShaun Foster, Car	247	876	3.5	20	3
Chester Taylor, Min	157	844	5.4	84-td	7
Warrick Dunn, Atl	227	720	3.2	38	4
DeAngelo Williams, Car.	144	717	5.0	75	4

New England Patriots
Tom Brady
Passing Efficiency

New England Patriots
Randy Moss
Touchdowns

San Diego Chargers
LaDainian Tomlinson
Rushing

Kansas City Chiefs
Jared Allen
Sacks

All-Purpose Yardage

AFC	Rush	Rec	Ret	Total	NFC	Rush	Rec	Ret	Total
Joshua Cribbs, Cle	61	37	2214	2312	Jerious Norwood, Atl	613	277	1317	2207
Ted Ginn Jr.*, Mia	3	420	1663	2086	Brian Westbrook, Phi	1333	771	79	2183
Leon Washington, NYJ	353	213	1474	2040	Adrian Peterson*, Min	1341	268	412	2021
Maurice Jones-Drew, Jax	768	407	839	2014	Nate Burleson, Sea	4	694	1248	1946
LaDainian Tomlinson, SD	1474	475	0	1949	Steve Breaston*, Ari	8	92	1786	1886
Wes Welker, NE	34	1175	425	1634	Devin Hester, Chi	-10	299	1585	1874
Glenn Holt, Cin	2	143	1432	1577	Maurice Hicks, SF	117	86	1502	1705
Jamal Lewis, Cle	1304	248	0	1552	Clinton Portis, Wash	1262	389	0	1651
Andre Davis, Hou	0	583	968	1551	Frank Gore, SF	1102	436	0	1538
Reggie Wayne, Ind	4	1510	0	1514	Edgerrin James, Ari	1222	204	0	1426
Randy Moss, NE	0	1493	0	1493	Larry Fitzgerald, Ari	0	1409	0	1409
Chad Johnson, Cin	47	1440	0	1487	Terrell Owens, Dal	5	1355	0	1360
Willie Parker, Pit	1316	164	0	1480	Rock Cartwright, Wash	0	0	1339	1339
Willis McGahee, Bal	1207	231	0	1438	Earnest Graham, TB	898	324	90	1312
Joseph Addai, Ind	1072	364	0	1436	Steven Jackson, St.L	1002	271	0	1273

Ret column indicates all kickoff, punt, fumble and interception returns.

Scoring

Touchdowns

AFC	TD	Rush	Rec	Ret	Pts
Randy Moss, NE	23	0	23	0	138
LaDainian Tomlinson, SD	18	15	3	0	108
Braylon Edwards, Cle	16	0	16	0	96
Joseph Addai, Ind	15	12	3	0	92†
T.J. Houshmandzadeh, Cin	12	0	12	0	72
Dallas Clark, Ind	11	0	11	0	66
Jamal Lewis, Cle	11	9	2	0	66
Maurice Jones-Drew, Jax	10	9	0	1	60
Reggie Wayne, Ind	10	0	10	0	60
Reggie Williams, Jax	10	0	10	0	60
Antonio Gates, SD	9	0	9	0	54
Santonio Holmes, Pit	8	0	8	0	50†

Four tied with 8 TD for 48 pts.
† Two-point conversions: Addai, Holmes (1).

NFC	TD	Rush	Rec	Ret	Pts
Terrell Owens, Dal	15	0	15	0	90
Adrian Peterson*, Min	13	12	1	0	78
Marion Barber, Dal	12	10	2	0	72
Plaxico Burress, NYG	12	0	12	0	72
Greg Jennings, GB	12	0	12	0	72
Brian Westbrook, Phi	12	7	5	0	72
Nate Burleson, Sea	11	0	9	2	66
Marques Colston, NO	11	0	11	0	66
Clinton Portis, Wash	11	11	0	0	66
Larry Fitzgerald, Ari	10	0	10	0	60
Earnest Graham, TB	10	10	0	0	60
Anquan Boldin, Ari	9	0	9	0	54
Chris Cooley, Wash	8	0	8	0	50†

† Two-point conversions: Cooley (1).

Kickers

AFC	PAT	FG	Long	Pts
Stephen Gostkowski, NE	74/74	21/24	45	137
Rob Bironas, Ten	28/28	35/39	56	133
Shayne Graham, Cin	37/37	31/34	48	130
Phil Dawson, Cle	42/43	26/30	51	120
Nate Kaeding, SD	46/46	24/27	51	118
Adam Vinatieri, Ind	49/51	23/29	39	118
Kris Brown, Hou	40/40	25/29	57	115
Jason Elam, Den	33/33	27/31	50	114
Jeff Reed, Pit	44/44	23/25	49	113
Mike Nugent, NYJ	23/24	29/36	50	110
Matt Stover, Bal	26/26	27/32	49	107
Sebastian Janikowski, Oak.	28/28	23/32	54	97
Rian Lindell, Buf	24/24	24/27	52	96
Jay Feely, Mia	26/26	21/23	53	89

NFC	PAT	FG	Long	Pts
Mason Crosby*, GB	48/48	31/39	53	141
Nick Folk*, Dal	53/53	26/31	53	131
Josh Brown, Sea	43/43	28/34	54	127
Robbie Gould, Chi	33/33	31/36	49	126
Jason Hanson, Det	35/36	29/35	53	122
Matt Bryant, TB	34/34	28/33	49	118
Shaun Suisham, Wash	29/30	29/35	50	116
Neil Rackers, Ari	47/48	21/30	52	110
Lawrence Tynes, NYG	40/42	23/27	48	109
David Akers, Phi	36/36	24/32	53	108
Morten Andersen, Atl	24/24	25/28	47	99
John Kasay, Car	27/27	24/28	53	99
Ryan Longwell, Min	39/40	20/24	55	99
Jeff Wilkins, St.L	25/25	24/32	53	97

NFL Regular Season Individual Leaders (Cont.)

Sacks

AFC	No
Jared Allen, KC	15.5
Mario Williams, Hou	14.0
Elvis Dumervil, Den	12.5
Shawne Merriman, SD	12.5
Mike Vrabel, NE	12.5

NFC	No
Patrick Kerney, Sea	14.5
DeMarcus Ware, Dal	14.0
Osi Umenyiora, NYG	13.0
Trent Cole, Phi	12.5
Greg Ellis, Dal	12.5

Interceptions

AFC	No	Yds	Long	TD
Antonio Cromartie, SD	10	144	70-td	1
Ed Reed, Bal	7	130	32	0
Thomas Howard, Oak	6	172	66-td	2
Asante Samuel, NE	6	89	42	1
Leigh Bodden, Cle	6	75	26	0
Seven tied with 5 each.				

NFC	No	Yds	Long	TD
O.J. Atogwe, St.L	8	125	52-td	1
Marcus Trufant, Sea	7	150	84-td	1
Anthony Henry, Dal	6	81	28-td	1
Seven tied with 5 each.				

Punting

AFC	No	Yds	Lg	Avg	In20
Shane Lechler, Oak	73	3585	70	49.1	25
Todd Sauerbrun, Den	47	2200	65	46.8	14
Mike Scifres, SD	81	3735	70	46.1	36
Dustin Colquitt, KC	95	4322	81	45.5	20
Sam Koch, Bal	78	3397	64	43.6	20

NFC	No	Yds	Lg	Avg	In20
Andy Lee, SF	105	4968	74	47.3	42
Donnie Jones, St.L	78	3684	80	47.2	18
Mat McBriar, Dal	63	2970	64	47.1	17
Chris Kluwe, Min	81	3621	70	44.7	34
Jon Ryan, GB	60	2664	72	44.4	18

Punt Returns

(Minimum of 20 returns)

AFC	No	Yds	Avg	Long	TD
Roscoe Parrish, Buf	27	440	16.3	74-td	1
Josh Cribbs, Cle	30	405	13.5	76-td	1
Wes Welker, NE	25	249	10.0	35	0
Ted Ginn Jr.*, Mia	24	230	9.6	87-td	1
Darren Sproles, SD	24	229	9.5	45-td	1

NFC	No	Yds	Avg	Long	TD
Devin Hester, Chi	42	651	15.5	89-td	4
Nate Burleson, Sea	58	658	11.3	94-td	1
Steve Breaston*, Ari	42	395	9.4	73-td	1
Lance Moore, NO	20	185	9.3	48	0
Patrick Crayton, Dal	22	201	9.1	49	0

Kickoff Returns

(Minimum of 20 returns)

AFC	No	Yds	Avg	Long	TD
Josh Cribbs, Cle	59	1809	30.7	100-td	2
Andre Davis, Hou	32	968	30.3	104-td	3
Leon Washington, NYJ	47	1291	27.5	98-td	3
Darren Sproles, SD	37	1008	27.2	89-td	1
Maurice Jones-Drew, Jax	31	811	26.2	100-td	1

NFC	No	Yds	Avg	Long	TD
Aundrae Allison*, Min	20	574	28.7	104-td	1
Rock Cartwright, Wash	52	1339	25.8	80	0
Miles Austin, Dal	24	612	25.5	60	0
Derek Stanley*, St.L	20	509	25.5	49	0
Jerious Norwood, Atl	52	1317	25.3	76	0

Single Game Highs

Passing Yards

AFC	Cmp/Att	Yds	TD
Carson Palmer, Cin vs Cle (9/16)	33/50	401	6
Tom Brady, NE vs Pit (12/9)	32/46	399	4
Tom Brady, NE vs Dal (10/14)	31/46	388	5
Tom Brady, NE vs Phi (11/25)	34/54	380	5
Tom Brady, NE vs Buf (11/18)	31/39	373	5

NFC	Cmp/Att	Yds	TD
Kurt Warner, Ari vs SF (11/25)	34/48	484	2
Jon Kitna, Det vs Phi (9/23)	29/46	446	2
Drew Brees, NO vs Jax (11/4)	35/49	445	3
Donovan McNabb, Phi vs Det (9/23)	21/26	381	4
Brian Griese, Chi vs Min (10/14)	26/45	381	3
Brett Favre, GB vs Det (11/22)	31/41	381	3

Rushing Yards

AFC	Car	Yds	TD
Jamal Lewis, Cle vs Cin (9/16)	27	216	1
LaDainian Tomlinson, SD vs Oak (10/14)	24	198	4
Justin Fargas, Oak vs Mia (9/30)	22	178	0
LaDainian Tomlinson, SD vs KC (12/2)	23	177	2
Chris Brown, Ten vs Jax (9/9)	19	175	0

NFC	Car	Yds	TD
Adrian Peterson, Min vs SD (11/4)	30	296	3
Adrian Peterson, Min vs Chi (10/14)	20	224	3
Clinton Portis, Wash vs NYJ (11/4)	36	196	1
Chester Taylor, Min vs Oak (11/18)	22	164	3
Ryan Grant, GB vs Oak (12/9)	29	156	1

Receiving Yards

AFC	Ct	Yds	TD
Chad Johnson, Cin vs Cle (9/16)	11	209	2
Randy Moss, NE vs NYJ (9/9)	9	183	1
Reggie Wayne, Ind vs Car (10/28)	7	168	1
Lee Evans, Buf vs Cin (11/4)	9	165	1
Jerricho Cotchery, NYJ vs Bal (9/16)	7	165	0

NFC	Ct	Yds	TD
Kevin Curtis, Phi vs Det (9/23)	11	221	3
Roy Williams, Det vs Phi (9/23)	9	204	1
Patrick Crayton, Dal (9/30)	7	184	2
Anquan Boldin, Ari vs Bal (9/23)	14	181	2
Terrell Owens, Dal vs Phi (11/4)	10	174	1

NFL Bests

Longest Field Goal
57 yds . . . . Kris Brown, Hou vs Mia (10/7)

Longest Run from Scrimmage
88 yds . . . Ahmad Bradshaw, NYG vs Buf (10/23) TD

Longest Pass Play
91 yds . . Jon Kitna to Roy Williams, Det vs Phi (9/23) TD

Longest Interception Return
100 yds . . . . Brodney Pool, Cle vs Bal (11/18) TD

Longest Punt Return
94 yds . . . . by two players

Longest Kickoff Return
108 yds . . . . Ellis Hobbs, NE vs NYJ (9/9) TD

Note: On 11/4 San Diego's Antonio Cromartie returned a missed FG 109 yards for the longest play in NFL history.

NFL Regular Season Team Leaders

Offense

AFC	Points For	Avg	Yardage Rush	Pass	Total
New England	589	36.8	115.6	295.7	411.3
Indianapolis	450	28.1	106.6	252.1	358.7
Jacksonville	411	25.7	149.4	208.0	357.4
Cleveland	402	25.1	118.4	232.9	351.3
Cincinnati	380	23.8	97.3	250.8	348.0
Denver	320	20.0	122.3	224.0	346.3
Houston	379	23.7	99.1	234.4	333.6
Pittsburgh	393	24.6	135.5	191.9	327.4
San Diego	412	25.8	127.4	187.8	315.3
Tennessee	301	18.8	131.8	179.9	311.7
Baltimore	275	17.2	112.3	189.7	302.0
Oakland	283	17.7	130.4	164.4	294.8
NY Jets	268	16.8	106.3	188.4	294.7
Miami	267	16.7	98.1	189.4	287.5
Buffalo	252	15.8	112.5	164.6	277.1
Kansas City	226	14.1	78.0	198.8	276.8

Defense

AFC	Points For	Avg	Yardage Rush	Pass	Total
Pittsburgh	269	16.8	89.9	176.5	266.4
Indianapolis	262	16.4	106.9	172.8	279.7
New England	274	17.1	98.3	190.1	288.3
Tennessee	297	18.6	92.4	199.2	291.6
Baltimore	384	24.0	79.3	222.3	301.6
Jacksonville	304	19.0	100.3	213.5	313.8
Kansas City	335	20.9	130.6	188.9	319.4
San Diego	284	17.8	107.0	213.3	320.3
NY Jets	355	22.2	134.8	197.1	331.9
Denver	409	25.6	142.6	193.4	336.0
Oakland	398	24.9	145.9	195.8	341.6
Miami	437	27.3	153.5	188.7	342.2
Houston	384	24.0	114.1	230.1	344.2
Cincinnati	385	24.1	118.3	230.4	348.8
Cleveland	382	23.9	129.5	230.1	359.6
Buffalo	354	22.1	124.6	238.4	362.9

NFC	Points For	Avg	Yardage Rush	Pass	Total
Green Bay	435	27.2	99.8	270.9	370.7
Dallas	455	28.4	109.1	256.6	365.7
New Orleans	379	23.7	91.6	269.6	361.3
Philadelphia	336	21.0	123.4	234.7	358.1
Seattle	393	24.6	101.2	247.8	348.9
Arizona	404	25.3	90.0	254.1	344.1
Minnesota	365	22.8	164.6	171.6	336.2
Washington	334	20.9	116.9	216.4	333.4
NY Giants	373	23.3	134.3	197.1	331.4
Tampa Bay	334	20.9	117.0	209.8	326.8
Detroit	346	21.6	80.5	242.4	322.9
Atlanta	259	16.2	95.0	206.0	301.0
St. Louis	263	16.4	95.4	202.1	297.5
Chicago	334	20.9	83.1	210.1	293.3
Carolina	267	16.7	114.0	170.9	284.9
San Francisco	219	13.7	92.3	145.0	237.3

NFC	Points For	Avg	Yardage Rush	Pass	Total
Tampa Bay	270	16.9	107.9	170.5	278.4
NY Giants	351	21.9	97.7	207.3	305.0
Washington	310	19.4	91.3	214.0	305.3
Dallas	325	20.3	94.6	213.1	307.6
Philadelphia	300	18.8	95.8	215.6	311.4
Green Bay	291	18.2	102.9	210.4	313.3
Seattle	291	18.2	102.8	219.1	321.8
Carolina	347	21.7	110.7	214.1	324.8
Arizona	399	24.9	97.9	232.3	330.2
Minnesota	311	19.4	74.1	264.1	338.1
St. Louis	438	27.4	115.3	225.8	341.1
San Francisco	364	22.8	118.5	227.7	346.2
New Orleans	388	24.3	102.9	245.3	348.1
Chicago	348	21.8	122.9	231.8	354.7
Atlanta	414	25.9	127.1	228.4	355.5
Detroit	444	27.8	119.4	258.2	377.6

Overall Club Rankings

Combined AFC and NFC rankings by yards gained on offense and yards given up on defense. Teams are ranked alphabetically, with AFC teams in *italics*. (†) indicates tied for position.

	Offense Rush	Pass	Rank	Defense Rush	Pass	Rank
Arizona	29	5	12	9	28	17
Atlanta	26	18	23	26	23	29
Baltimore	16	23	22	2	20	6
Buffalo	15	30	30	25	29	31
Carolina	14	29	29	18	17	16
Chicago	30	15	27	24	27	28
Cincinnati	24	7	10	21	26	27
Cleveland	10	12	8	27	24	30
Dallas	17	4	3	6	13	9
Denver	9	13	11	30	7	19
Detroit	31	9	19	23	31	32
Green Bay	21	2	2	14	12	11
Houston	22	11	14	19	25	24
Indianapolis	18	6	6	15	-2	3
Jacksonville	2	17	7	11	15	12
Kansas City	32	20	31	28	5	13
Miami	23	24	28	32	4	23
Minnesota	1	28	13	1	32	20
New England	13	1	1	10	6	4
New Orleans	28	3	4	13	30	26
NY Giants	4	21	16	8	11	7
NY Jets	19	25	26	29	9	18
Oakland	6	31	25	31	8	22
Philadelphia	8	10	6	7	18	10
Pittsburgh	3	22	17	3	3	1
St. Louis	25	19	24	20	21	21
San Diego	7	26	20	16	14	14
San Francisco	27	32	32	22	22	25
Seattle	20	8	9	12	19	15
Tampa Bay	11	16	18	17	1	2
Tennessee	5	27	21	5	10	5
Washington	12	14	15	4	16	8

AFC Team by Team Results
(*) indicates overtime game.

Baltimore Ravens (5-11)

at Cincinnati	L, 20-27
NY Jets	W, 20-13
Arizona	W, 26-23
at Cleveland	L, 13-27
at San Francisco	W, 9-7
St. Louis	W, 22-3
at Buffalo	L, 14-19
BYE	—
at Pittsburgh	L, 7-38
Cincinnati	L, 7-21
Cleveland	L, 30-33*
at San Diego	L, 14-32
New England	L, 24-27
Indianapolis	L, 20-44
at Miami	L, 16-22*
at Seattle	L, 6-27
Pittsburgh	W, 27-21

Buffalo Bills (7-9)

Denver	L, 14-15
at Pittsburgh	L, 3-26
at New England	L, 7-38
NY Jets	W, 17-14
Dallas	L, 24-25
BYE	—
Baltimore	W, 19-14
at NY Jets	W, 13-3
Cincinnati	W, 33-21
at Miami	W, 13-10
New England	L, 10-56
at Jacksonville	L, 14-36
at Washington	W, 17-16
Miami	W, 38-17
at Cleveland	L, 0-8
NY Giants	L, 21-38
at Philadelphia	L, 9-17

Cincinnati Bengals (7-9)

Baltimore	W, 27-20
at Cleveland	L, 45-51
at Seattle	L, 21-24
New England	L, 13-34
BYE	—
at Kansas City	L, 20-27
NY Jets	W, 38-31
Pittsburgh	L, 13-24
at Buffalo	L, 21-33
at Baltimore	W, 21-7
Arizona	L, 27-35
Tennessee	W, 35-6
at Pittsburgh	L, 10-24
St. Louis	W, 19-10
at San Francisco	L, 13-20
Cleveland	W, 19-14
at Miami	W, 38-25

Cleveland Browns (10-6)

Pittsburgh	L, 7-34
Cincinnati	W, 54-45
at Oakland	L, 24-26
Baltimore	W, 27-13
at New England	L, 17-34
Miami	W, 41-31
BYE	—
at St. Louis	W, 27-20
Seattle	W, 33-30*
at Pittsburgh	L, 28-31
at Baltimore	W, 33-30*
Houston	W, 27-17
at Arizona	L, 21-27
at NY Jets	W, 24-18
Buffalo	W, 8-0
at Cincinnati	L, 14-19
San Francisco	W, 20-7

Denver Broncos (7-9)

at Buffalo	W, 15-14
Oakland	W, 23-20*
Jacksonville	L, 14-23
at Indianapolis	L, 20-38
San Diego	L, 3-41
BYE	—
Pittsburgh	W, 31-28
Green Bay	L, 13-19*
at Detroit	L, 7-44
at Kansas City	W, 27-11
Tennessee	W, 34-20
at Chicago	L, 34-37*
at Oakland	L, 20-34
Kansas City	W, 41-7
at Houston	L, 13-31
at San Diego	L, 3-23
Minnesota	W, 22-19*

Houston Texans (8-8)

Kansas City	W, 20-3
at Carolina	W, 34-21
Indianapolis	L, 24-30
at Atlanta	L, 16-26
Miami	W, 22-19
at Jacksonville	L, 17-37
Tennessee	L, 36-38
at San Diego	L, 10-35
at Oakland	W, 24-17
BYE	—
New Orleans	W, 23-10
at Cleveland	L, 17-27
at Tennessee	L, 20-28
Tampa Bay	W, 28-14
Denver	W, 31-13
at Indianapolis	L, 15-38
Jacksonville	W, 42-28

Indianapolis Colts (13-3)

New Orleans	W, 41-10
at Tennessee	W, 22-20
at Houston	W, 30-24
Denver	W, 38-20
Tampa Bay	W, 33-14
BYE	—
at Jacksonville	W, 29-7
at Carolina	W, 31-7
New England	L, 20-24
at San Diego	L, 21-23
Kansas City	W, 13-10
at Atlanta	W, 31-13
Jacksonville	W, 28-25
at Baltimore	W, 44-20
at Oakland	W, 21-14
Houston	W, 38-15
Tennessee	L, 10-16

Jacksonville Jaguars (11-5)

Tennessee	L, 10-13
Atlanta	W, 13-7
at Denver	W, 23-14
BYE	—
at Kansas City	W, 17-7
Houston	W, 37-17
Indianapolis	L, 7-29
at Tampa Bay	W, 24-23
at New Orleans	L, 24-41
at Tennessee	W, 28-13
San Diego	W, 24-17
Buffalo	W, 36-14
at Indianapolis	L, 25-28
Carolina	W, 37-6
at Pittsburgh	W, 29-22
Oakland	W, 49-11
at Houston	L, 28-42

Kansas City Chiefs (4-12)

at Houston	L, 3-20
at Chicago	L, 10-20
Minnesota	W, 13-10
at San Diego	W, 30-16
Jacksonville	L, 7-17
Cincinnati	W, 27-20
at Oakland	W, 12-10
BYE	—
Green Bay	L, 22-33
Denver	L, 11-27
at Indianapolis	L, 10-13
Oakland	L, 17-20
San Diego	L, 10-24
at Denver	L, 7-41
Tennessee	L, 17-26
at Detroit	L, 20-25
at NY Jets	L, 10-13*

Miami Dolphins (1-15)

at Washington	L, 13-16*
Dallas	L, 20-37
at NY Jets	L, 28-31
Oakland	L, 17-35
at Houston	L, 19-22
at Cleveland	L, 31-41
New England	L, 28-49
NY Giants	L, 10-13
BYE	—
Buffalo	L, 10-13
at Philadelphia	L, 7-17
at Pittsburgh	L, 0-3
NY Jets	L, 13-40
at Buffalo	L, 17-38
Baltimore	W, 22-16*
at New England	L, 7-28
Cincinnati	L, 25-38

New England Patriots (16-0)

at NY Jets	W, 38-14
San Diego	W, 38-14
Buffalo	W, 38-7
at Cincinnati	W, 34-13
Cleveland	W, 34-17
at Dallas	W, 48-27
at Miami	W, 49-28
Washington	W, 52-7
at Indianapolis	W, 24-20
BYE	—
at Buffalo	W, 56-10
Philadelphia	W, 31-28
at Baltimore	W, 27-24
Pittsburgh	W, 34-13
NY Jets	W, 20-10
Miami	W, 28-7
at NY Giants	W, 38-35

New York Jets (4-12)

New England	L, 14-38
at Baltimore	L, 13-20
Miami	W, 31-28
at Buffalo	L, 14-17
at NY Giants	L, 24-35
Philadelphia	L, 9-16
at Cincinnati	L, 31-38
Buffalo	L, 3-13
Washington	L, 20-23*
BYE	—
Pittsburgh	W, 19-16*
at Dallas	L, 3-34
at Miami	W, 40-13
Cleveland	L, 18-24
at New England	L, 10-20
at Tennessee	L, 6-10
Kansas City	W, 13-10*

Oakland Raiders (4-12)

Detroit	L, 21-36
at Denver	L, 20-23*
Cleveland	W, 26-24
at Miami	W, 35-17
BYE	—
at San Diego	L, 14-28
Kansas City	L, 10-12
at Tennessee	L, 9-13
Houston	L, 17-24
Chicago	L, 6-17
at Minnesota	L, 22-29
at Kansas City	W, 20-17
Denver	W, 34-20
at Green Bay	L, 7-38
Indianapolis	L, 14-21
at Jacksonville	L, 11-49
San Diego	L, 17-30

Pittsburgh Steelers (10-6)

at Cleveland	W, 34-7
Buffalo	W, 26-3
San Francisco	W, 37-16
at Arizona	L, 14-21
Seattle	W, 21-0
BYE	—
at Denver	L, 28-31
at Cincinnati	W, 24-13
Baltimore	W, 38-7
Cleveland	W, 31-28
at NY Jets	L, 16-19*
Miami	W, 3-0
Cincinnati	W, 24-10
at New England	L, 13-34
Jacksonville	L, 22-29
at St. Louis	W, 41-24
at Baltimore	L, 21-27

San Diego Chargers (11-5)

Chicago	W, 14-3
at New England	L, 14-38
at Green Bay	L, 24-31
Kansas City	L, 16-30
at Denver	W, 41-3
Oakland	W, 28-14
BYE	—
Houston	W, 35-10
at Minneapolis	L, 17-35
Indianapolis	W, 23-21
at Jacksonville	L, 17-24
Baltimore	W, 32-14
at Kansas City	W, 24-10
at Tennessee	W, 23-17*
Detroit	W, 51-14
Denver	W, 23-3
at Oakland	W, 30-17

Tennessee Titans (10-6)

at Jacksonville	W, 13-10
Indianapolis	L, 20-22
at New Orleans	W, 31-14
BYE	—
Atlanta	W, 20-13
at Tampa Bay	W, 10-13
at Houston	W, 38-36
Oakland	W, 13-9
Carolina	W, 20-7
Jacksonville	L, 13-28
at Denver	L, 20-34
at Cincinnati	L, 6-35
Houston	W, 28-20
San Diego	L, 17-23*
at Kansas City	W, 26-17
NY Jets	W, 10-6
at Indianapolis	W, 16-10

NFC Team by Team Results
(*) indicates overtime game

Arizona Cardinals (8-8)

at San Francisco	L, 17-20
Seattle	W, 23-20
at Baltimore	L, 23-26
Pittsburgh	W, 21-14
at St. Louis	W, 34-31
Carolina	L, 10-25
at Washington	L, 19-21
BYE	—
at Tampa Bay	L, 10-17
Detroit	W, 31-21
at Cincinnati	W, 35-27
San Francisco	L, 31-37*
Cleveland	W, 27-21
at Seattle	L, 21-42
at New Orleans	L, 24-31
Atlanta	W, 30-27*
St. Louis	W, 48-19

Atlanta Falcons (4-12)

at Minnesota	L, 3-24
at Jacksonville	L, 7-13
Carolina	L, 20-27
Houston	W, 26-16
at Tennessee	L, 13-20
NY Giants	L, 10-31
at New Orleans	L, 16-22
BYE	—
San Francisco	W, 20-16
at Carolina	W, 20-13
Tampa Bay	L, 7-31
Indianapolis	L, 13-31
at St. Louis	L, 16-28
New Orleans	L, 14-34
at Tampa Bay	L, 3-37
at Arizona	L, 27-30*
Seattle	W, 44-41

Carolina Panthers (7-9)

at St. Louis	W, 27-13
Houston	L, 21-34
at Atlanta	W, 27-20
Tampa Bay	L, 7-20
at New Orleans	W, 16-13
at Arizona	W, 25-10
BYE	—
Indianapolis	L, 7-31
at Tennessee	L, 7-20
Atlanta	L, 13-20
at Green Bay	L, 17-31
New Orleans	L, 6-31
San Francisco	W, 31-14
at Jacksonville	L, 6-37
Seattle	W, 13-10
Dallas	L, 13-20
at Tampa Bay	W, 31-23

Chicago Bears (7-9)

at San Diego	L, 3-14
Kansas City	W, 20-10
Dallas	L, 10-34
at Detroit	L, 27-37
at Green Bay	W, 27-20
Minnesota	L, 31-34
at Philadelphia	W, 19-16
Detroit	L, 7-16
BYE	—
at Oakland	W, 17-6
at Seattle	L, 23-30
Denver	W, 37-34*
NY Giants	L, 16-21
at Washington	L, 16-24
at Minnesota	L, 13-20
Green Bay	W, 35-7
New Orleans	W, 33-25

Dallas Cowboys (13-3)

NY Giants	W, 45-35
at Miami	W, 37-20
at Chicago	W, 34-10
St. Louis	W, 35-7
at Buffalo	W, 25-24
New England	L, 27-48
Minnesota	W, 24-14
BYE	—
at Philadelphia	W, 38-17
at NY Giants	W, 31-20
Washington	W, 28-23
NY Jets	W, 34-3
Green Bay	W, 37-27
at Detroit	W, 28-27
Philadelphia	L, 6-10
at Carolina	W, 20-13
at Washington	L, 6-27

Detroit Lions (7-9)

at Oakland	W, 36-21
Minnesota	W, 20-17*
at Philadelphia	L, 21-56
Chicago	W, 37-27
at Washington	L, 3-34
BYE	—
Tampa Bay	W, 23-16
at Chicago	W, 16-7
Denver	W, 44-7
at Arizona	L, 21-31
NY Giants	L, 10-16
Green Bay	L, 26-37
at Minnesota	L, 10-42
Dallas	L, 27-28
at San Diego	L, 14-51
Kansas City	W, 25-20
at Green Bay	L, 13-34

Green Bay Packers (13-3)

Philadelphia	W, 16-13
at NY Giants	W, 35-13
San Diego	W, 31-24
at Minnesota	W, 23-16
Chicago	L, 20-27
Washington	W, 17-14
BYE	—
at Denver	W, 19-13*
at Kansas City	W, 33-22
Minnesota	W, 34-0
Carolina	W, 31-17
at Detroit	W, 37-26
at Dallas	L, 27-37
Oakland	W, 38-7
at St. Louis	W, 33-14
at Chicago	L, 7-35
Detroit	W, 34-13

Minnesota Vikings (8-8)

Atlanta	W, 24-3
at Detroit	L, 17-20*
at Kansas City	L, 10-13
Green Bay	L, 16-23
BYE	—
at Chicago	W, 34-31
at Dallas	L, 14-24
Philadelphia	L, 16-23
San Diego	W, 35-17
at Green Bay	L, 0-34
Oakland	W, 29-22
at NY Giants	W, 41-17
Detroit	W, 42-10
at San Francisco	W, 27-7
Chicago	W, 20-13
Washington	L, 21-32
at Denver	L, 19-22*

NFC Team by Team Results (Cont.)

New Orleans Saints (7-9)

at Indianapolis	L, 10-41
at Tampa Bay	L, 14-31
Tennessee	L, 14-31
BYE	—
Carolina	L, 13-16
at Seattle	W, 28-17
Atlanta	W, 22-16
at San Fran.	W, 31-10
Jacksonville	W, 41-24
St. Louis	L, 29-37
at Houston	L, 10-23
at Carolina	W, 31-6
Tampa Bay	L, 23-27
at Atlanta	W, 34-14
Arizona	W, 31-24
Philadelphia	L, 23-38
at Chicago	L, 25-33

New York Giants (10-6)

at Dallas	L, 35-45
Green Bay	L, 13-35
at Washington	W, 24-17
Philadelphia	W, 16-3
NY Jets	W, 35-24
at Atlanta	W, 31-10
San Francisco	W, 33-15
at Miami	W, 13-10
BYE	—
Dallas	L, 20-31
at Detroit	W, 16-10
Minnesota	L, 17-41
at Chicago	W, 21-16
at Philadelphia	W, 16-13
Washington	L, 10-22
at Buffalo	W, 38-21
New England	L, 35-38

Philadelphia Eagles (8-8)

at Green Bay	L, 13-16
Washington	L, 12-20
Detroit	W, 56-21
at NY Giants	L, 3-16
BYE	—
at NY Jets	W, 16-9
Chicago	L, 16-19
at Minnesota	W, 23-16
Dallas	L, 17-38
at Washington	W, 33-25
Miami	W, 17-7
at New England	L, 28-31
Seattle	L, 24-28
NY Giants	L, 13-16
at Dallas	W, 10-6
at New Orleans	W, 38-23
Buffalo	W, 17-9

St. Louis Rams (3-13)

Carolina	L, 13-27
San Francisco	L, 16-17
at Tampa Bay	L, 3-24
at Dallas	L, 7-35
Arizona	L, 31-34
at Baltimore	L, 3-22
at Seattle	L, 6-33
Cleveland	L, 20-27
BYE	—
at New Orleans	W, 37-29
at San Francisco	W, 13-9
Seattle	L, 19-24
Atlanta	W, 28-16
at Cincinnati	L, 10-19
Green Bay	L, 14-33
Pittsburgh	L, 24-41
at Arizona	L, 19-48

San Francisco 49ers (5-11)

Arizona	W, 20-17
at St. Louis	W, 17-16
at Pittsburgh	L, 16-37
Seattle	L, 3-23
Baltimore	L, 7-9
BYE	—
at NY Giants	L, 15-33
New Orleans	L, 10-31
at Atlanta	L, 16-20
at Seattle	L, 0-24
St. Louis	L, 9-13
at Arizona	W, 37-31*
at Carolina	L, 14-31
Minnesota	L, 7-27
Cincinnati	W, 20-13
Tampa Bay	W, 21-19
at Cleveland	L, 7-20

Seattle Seahawks (10-6)

Tampa Bay	W, 20-6
at Arizona	L, 20-23
Cincinnati	W, 24-21
at San Francisco	W, 23-3
at Pittsburgh	L, 0-21
New Orleans	L, 17-28
St. Louis	W, 33-6
BYE	—
at Cleveland	L, 30-33*
San Francisco	W, 24-0
Chicago	W, 30-23
at St. Louis	W, 24-19
at Philadelphia	W, 28-24
Arizona	W, 42-21
at Carolina	L, 10-13
Baltimore	W, 27-6
at Atlanta	L, 41-44

Tampa Bay Buccaneers (9-7)

at Seattle	L, 6-20
New Orleans	W, 31-14
St. Louis	W, 24-3
at Carolina	W, 20-7
at Indianapolis	L, 14-33
Tennessee	W, 13-10
at Detroit	L, 16-23
Jacksonville	L, 23-24
Arizona	W, 17-10
BYE	—
at Atlanta	W, 31-7
Washington	W, 19-13
at New Orleans	W, 27-23
at Houston	L, 14-28
Atlanta	W, 37-3
at San Francisco	L, 19-21
Carolina	L, 23-31

Washington Redskins (9-7)

Miami	W, 16-13*
at Philadelphia	W, 20-12
NY Giants	L, 17-24
BYE	—
Detroit	W, 34-3
at Green Bay	L, 14-17
Arizona	W, 21-19
at New England	L, 7-52
at NY Jets	W, 23-20*
Philadelphia	L, 25-33
at Dallas	L, 23-28
at Tampa Bay	L, 13-19
Buffalo	L, 16-17
Chicago	W, 24-16
at NY Giants	W, 22-10
at Minnesota	W, 32-21
Dallas	W, 27-6

Takeaways/Giveaways

AFC	Takeaways Int	Fum	Total	Giveaways Int	Fum	Total	Net Diff
San Diego	30	18	48	16	8	24	+24
Indianapolis	22	15	37	14	5	19	+18
New England	19	12	31	9	6	15	+16
Buffalo	18	12	30	14	7	21	+9
Jacksonville	20	10	30	8	13	21	+9
Cincinnati	19	16	35	20	10	30	+5
Pittsburgh	11	14	25	14	8	22	+3
Denver	14	16	30	15	14	29	+1
Tennessee	22	12	34	17	17	34	0
Cleveland	17	10	27	20	9	29	-2
NY Jets	15	6	21	19	6	25	-4
Miami	14	8	22	16	13	29	-7
Kansas City	14	8	22	20	13	33	-11
Oakland	18	8	26	20	17	37	-11
Houston	11	14	25	21	17	38	-13
Baltimore	17	6	23	14	26	40	-17
TOTALS	281	185	466	257	189	446	+20

NFC	Takeaways Int	Fum	Total	Giveaways Int	Fum	Total	Net Diff
Tampa Bay	16	19	35	8	12	20	+15
Seattle	20	14	34	13	11	24	+10
Dallas	19	10	29	19	5	24	+5
Atlanta	16	12	28	15	9	24	+4
Green Bay	19	9	28	15	9	24	+4
Carolina	14	16	30	17	12	29	+1
Minnesota	15	16	31	14	16	30	+1
Chicago	16	17	33	21	13	34	-1
Detroit	17	18	35	22	14	36	-1
Washington	14	10	24	11	18	29	-5
Arizona	18	11	29	24	12	36	-7
New Orleans	13	10	23	18	12	30	-7
Philadelphia	11	8	19	15	12	27	-8
NY Giants	15	10	25	20	14	34	-9
St. Louis	18	9	27	28	9	37	-10
San Francisco	12	10	22	17	17	34	-12
TOTALS	253	199	452	277	195	472	-20

AFC Team by Team Statistics

Players with more than one team during the regular season are listed with club they ended season with; (*) indicates rookies.

Baltimore Ravens

Passing (5 Att)	Att	Cmp	Pct	Yds	TD	Rate
Kyle Boller	.275	168	61.1	1743	9	75.2
Steve McNair	.205	133	64.9	1113	2	73.9
Troy Smith*	.76	40	52.6	452	2	79.5

Interceptions: Boller 10, McNair 4.

Top Receivers	No	Yds	Avg	Long	TD
Derrick Mason	.103	1087	10.6	79-td	5
Mark Clayton	.48	531	11.1	52	0
Willis McGahee	.43	231	5.4	30	1
Quinn Sypniewski	.34	246	7.2	13	1
Musa Smith	.27	192	7.1	29	0
Todd Heap	.23	239	10.4	37	1
Demetrius Williams	.20	290	14.5	34	0

Top Rushers	Car	Yds	Avg	Long	TD
Willis McGahee	.294	1207	4.1	46-td	7
Musa Smith	.75	264	3.5	24	2
Kyle Boller	.19	89	4.7	15	0
Cory Ross*	.12	72	6.0	32-td	1

Most Touchdowns	TD	Run	Rec	Ret	Pts
Willis McGahee	.8	7	1	0	48
Derrick Mason	.5	0	5	0	30
Devard Darling	.3	0	3	0	18
Yamon Figurs*	.2	0	0	2	12
Musa Smith	.2	2	0	0	12

2-Pt. Conversions: (0-2).

Kicking	PAT/Att	FG/Att	Lg	Pts
Matt Stover	.26/26	27/32	49	107

Punts (10 or more)	No	Yds	Long	Avg	In20
Sam Koch	.78	3397	64	43.6	20

Most Interceptions		Most Sacks	
Ed Reed	.7	Terrell Suggs	5.0

Buffalo Bills

Passing (5 Att)	Att	Cmp	Pct	Yds	TD	Rate
Trent Edwards*	.269	151	56.1	1630	7	70.4
J.P. Losman	.175	111	63.4	1204	4	76.9

Interceptions: Edwards 8, Losman 6.

Top Receivers	No	Yds	Avg	Long	TD
Lee Evans	.55	849	15.4	85-td	5
Josh Reed	.51	578	11.3	30	0
Roscoe Parrish	.35	352	10.1	47-td	1
Robert Royal	.25	248	9.9	28-td	3
Michael Gaines	.25	215	8.6	20	2
Fred Jackson	.22	190	8.6	54	0
Marshawn Lynch*	.18	184	10.2	30	0

Top Rushers	Car	Yds	Avg	Long	TD
Marshawn Lynch*	.280	1115	4.0	56-td	7
Fred Jackson	.58	300	5.2	27	0
J.P. Losman	.20	110	5.5	17	0

Most Touchdowns	TD	Run	Rec	Ret	Pts
Marshawn Lynch*	.7	7	0	0	44
Lee Evans	.5	0	5	0	30
Roscoe Parrish	.3	1	1	1	18
Robert Royal	.3	0	3	0	18

Two tied with 2 TD for 12 pts.

2-Pt. Conversions: (1-1) Lynch.

Kicking	PAT/Att	FG/Att	Lg	Pts
Rian Lindell	.24/24	24/27	52	96

Punts (10 or more)	No	Yds	Long	Avg	In20
Brian Moorman	.81	3302	75	40.8	30

Most Interceptions		Most Sacks	
Terrence McGee	4	Aaron Schobel	6.5

Cincinnati Bengals

Passing (5 Att)	Att	Cmp	Pct	Yds	TD	Rate
Carson Palmer	.575	373	64.9	4131	26	86.7

Interceptions: Palmer 20.

Top Receivers	No	Yds	Avg	Long	TD
T.J. Houshmandzadeh	112	1143	10.2	42-td	12
Chad Johnson	.93	1440	15.5	70-td	8
Kenny Watson	.52	374	7.2	43	0
Chris Henry	.21	343	16.3	52-td	2
Reggie Kelly	.20	211	10.6	26	0
Antonio Chatman	.19	149	7.8	15	1

Top Rushers	Car	Yds	Avg	Long	TD
Kenny Watson	.178	763	4.3	24	7
Rudi Johnson	.170	497	2.9	22	3
DeDe Dorsey	.21	183	8.7	45	0

Most Touchdowns	TD	Run	Rec	Ret	Pts
T.J. Houshmandzadeh	.12	0	12	0	72
Chad Johnson	.8	0	8	0	48
Kenny Watson	.7	7	0	0	42
Rudi Johnson	.4	3	1	0	26
Chris Henry	.2	0	2	0	12
Glenn Holt	.2	0	1	1	12

2-Pt. Conversions: (1-3) R. Johnson.

Kicking	PAT/Att	FG/Att	Lg	Pts
Shayne Graham	.37/37	31/34	48	130
Kyle Larson	.0/1	0/0	—	0

Punts (10 or more)	No	Yds	Long	Avg	In20
Kyle Larson	.59	2437	55	41.3	21

Most Interceptions		Most Sacks	
Leon Hall*	.5	Robert Geathers	.3.5

Cleveland Browns

Passing (5 Att)	Att	Cmp	Pct	Yds	TD	Rate
Derek Anderson	.527	298	56.5	3787	29	82.5
Brady Quinn*	.8	3	37.5	45	0	56.8

Interceptions: Anderson 19.

Top Receivers	No	Yds	Avg	Long	TD
Kellen Winslow	.82	1106	13.5	49	5
Braylon Edwards	.80	1289	16.1	78-td	16
Joe Jurevicius	.50	614	12.3	50	3
Jamal Lewis	.30	248	8.3	34	2
Jason Wright	.24	233	9.7	23	0
Lawrence Vickers	.13	91	7.0	25	2

Top Rushers	Car	Yds	Avg	Long	TD
Jamal Lewis	.298	1304	4.4	66-td	9
Jason Wright	.60	277	4.6	18	1
Jerome Harrison	.23	142	6.2	17	0
Derek Anderson	.32	70	2.2	11	3

Most Touchdowns	TD	Run	Rec	Ret	Pts
Braylon Edwards	.16	0	16	0	96
Jamal Lewis	.11	9	2	0	66
Kellen Winslow	.5	0	5	0	32
Joe Jurevicius	.3	0	3	0	20
Derek Anderson	.3	3	0	0	18
Josh Cribbs	.3	0	0	3	18

2-Pt. Conversions: (2-3) Jurevicius, Winslow.

Kicking	PAT/Att	FG/Att	Lg	Pts
Phil Dawson	.42/43	26/30	51	120

Punts (10 or more)	No	Yds	Long	Avg	In20
Dave Zastudil	.49	2046	64	41.8	14
Scott Player	.13	593	57	45.6	6

Most Interceptions		Most Sacks	
Leigh Bodden	.6	Kamerion Wimbley	.5.0

Denver Broncos

Passing (5 Att)

	Att	Cmp	Pct	Yds	TD	Rate
Jay Cutler	.467	297	63.6	3497	20	88.1
Patrick Ramsey	.48	29	60.4	262	1	73.4

Interceptions: Cutler 14, Ramsey 1.

Top Receivers

	No	Yds	Avg	Long	TD
Brandon Marshall	.102	1325	13.0	68-td	7
Tony Scheffler	.49	549	11.2	41	5
Brandon Stokley	.40	635	15.9	58	5
Selvin Young*	.35	231	6.6	24	0
Javon Walker	.26	287	11.0	24	0
Daniel Graham	.24	246	10.3	28	2

Top Rushers

	Car	Yds	Avg	Long	TD
Selvin Young*	.140	729	5.2	50	1
Travis Henry	.167	691	4.1	33	4
Andre Hall*	.44	216	4.9	62-td	3
Jay Cutler	.44	205	4.7	31	1
Cecil Sapp	.18	59	3.3	12	2

Most Touchdowns

	TD	Run	Rec	Ret	Pts
Brandon Marshall	.7	0	7	0	42
Tony Scheffler	.5	0	5	0	30
Brandon Stokley	.5	0	5	0	30
Travis Henry	.4	4	0	0	24
Cecil Sapp	.3	2	1	0	18

Two tied with 2 TD each for 12 pts.

2-Pt. Conversions: (0-1).

Kicking

	PAT/Att	FG/Att	Lg	Pts
Jason Elam	.33/33	27/31	50	114

Punts (15 or more)

	No	Yds	Long	Avg	In20
Todd Sauerbrun	.47	2200	65	46.8	14

Most Interceptions
Dre' Bly 5

Most Sacks
Elvis Dumervil 12.5

Houston Texans

Passing (5 Att)

	Att	Cmp	Pct	Yds	TD	Rate
Matt Schaub	.289	192	66.4	2241	9	87.2
Sage Rosenfels	.240	154	64.2	1684	15	84.8

Interceptions: Schaub 9, Rosenfels 12.

Top Receivers

	No	Yds	Avg	Long	TD
Kevin Walter	.65	800	12.3	46	4
Owen Daniels	.63	768	12.2	29	3
Andre Johnson	.60	851	14.2	77-td	8
Andre Davis	.33	583	17.7	53-td	3
Vonta Leach	.25	108	4.3	15	2
Ron Dayne	.17	112	6.6	17	0

Top Rushers

	Car	Yds	Avg	Long	TD
Ron Dayne	.194	773	4.0	39	6
Darius Walker	.58	264	4.6	41	1
Ahman Green	.70	260	3.7	18	2
A. Echemandu	.20	85	4.3	20	0
Matt Schaub	.17	52	3.1	12	0

Signed: Echemandu (Oct. 10).

Most Touchdowns

	TD	Run	Rec	Ret	Pts
Andre Johnson	.8	0	8	0	48
Andre Davis	.6	0	3	3	38
Ron Dayne	.6	6	0	0	36
Kevin Walter	.5	0	4	1	30
Owen Daniels	.3	0	3	0	18
Vonta Leach	.3	1	2	0	18

2-Pt. Conversions: (3-3) Davis, Walker, Samkon Gado.

Kicking

	PAT/Att	FG/Att	Lg	Pts
Kris Brown	.40/40	25/29	57	115

Punts (10 or more)

	No	Yds	Long	Avg	In20
Matt Turk	.55	2296	59	41.7	24

Most Interceptions
Fred Bennett* .3

Most Sacks
Mario Williams 14.0

Indianapolis Colts

Passing (5 Att)

	Att	Cmp	Pct	Yds	TD	Rat
Peyton Manning	.515	337	65.4	4040	31	98.
Jim Sorgi	.36	18	50.0	132	1	68.

Interceptions: Manning 14.

Top Receivers

	No	Yds	Avg	Long	TD
Reggie Wayne	.105	1510	14.5	64	1
Dallas Clark	.58	616	10.6	39	1
Joseph Addai	.41	364	8.9	73-td	
Anthony Gonzalez*	.37	576	15.6	57-td	
Ben Utecht	.31	364	11.7	30	
Marvin Harrison	.20	247	12.4	42	

Top Rushers

	Car	Yds	Avg	Long	TD
Joseph Addai	.261	1072	4.1	23	
Kenton Keith*	.121	533	4.4	22	
Clifton Dawson	.30	64	2.1	12	

Signed: Dawson on Sept. 28.

Most Touchdowns

	TD	Run	Rec	Ret	Pts
Joseph Addai	.15	12	3	0	92
Dallas Clark	.11	0	11	0	66
Reggie Wayne	.10	0	10	0	60
Kenton Keith*	.4	3	1	0	24
Anthony Gonzalez*	.3	0	3	0	18
Peyton Manning	.3	3	0	0	18

2-Pt. Conversions: (2-3) Addai, Bryan Fletcher.

Kicking

	PAT/Att	FG/Att	Lg	Pts
Adam Vinatieri	.49/51	23/29	39	118

Punts (10 or more)

	No	Yds	Long	Avg	In20
Hunter Smith	.52	2181	63	41.9	18

Most Interceptions
Gary Brackett 4
Antoine Bethea 4

Most Sacks
Robert Mathis 7.0

Jacksonville Jaguars

Passing (5 Att)

	Att	Cmp	Pct	Yds	TD	Rate
David Garrard	.325	208	64.0	2509	18	102.2
Quinn Gray	.144	80	55.6	986	10	85.4

Interceptions: Gray 5; Garrard 3.

Top Receivers

	No	Yds	Avg	Long	TD
Ernest Wilford	.45	518	11.5	35	3
Dennis Northcutt	.44	601	13.7	55-td	4
Maurice Jones-Drew	.40	407	10.2	43	0
Reggie Williams	.38	629	16.6	80-td	10
Marcedes Lewis	.37	391	10.6	25	2
Matt Jones	.24	317	13.2	48	4

Top Rushers

	Car	Yds	Avg	Long	TD
Fred Taylor	.223	1202	5.4	80-td	5
Maurice Jones-Drew	.167	768	4.6	57-td	9
David Garrard	.49	185	3.8	19	1
Greg Jones	.42	119	2.8	11	2

Most Touchdowns

	TD	Run	Rec	Ret	Pts
Maurice Jones-Drew	.10	9	1	0	60
Reggie Williams	.10	0	10	0	60
Fred Taylor	.5	5	0	0	30
Greg Jones	.4	2	2	0	24
Matt Jones	.4	0	4	0	24
Dennis Northcutt	.4	0	4	0	24

2-Pt. Conversions: (1-2) Garrard.

Kicking

	PAT/Att	FG/Att	Lg	Pts
Josh Scobee	.26/27	12/13	48	62

Signed: John Carney on Sept. 11. **Released:** Carney on Nov. 19 (see KC).

Punts (10 or more)

	No	Yds	Long	Avg	In20
Adam Podlesh*	.54	2249	76	41.6	14

Most Interceptions
Reggie Nelson* 5

Most Sacks
Paul Spicer 7.5

Kansas City Chiefs

Passing (10 Att)

	Att	Cmp	Pct	Yds	TD	Rate
Damon Huard	.332	206	62.0	2257	11	76.8
Brodie Croyle	.224	127	56.7	1227	6	69.9

Interceptions: Huard 13, Croyle 6, Tyler Thigpen 1.

Top Receivers

	No	Yds	Avg	Long	TD
Tony Gonzalez	.99	1172	11.8	31	5
Dwayne Bowe*	.70	995	14.2	58	5
Larry Johnson	.30	186	6.2	30-td	1
Jeff Webb	.28	313	11.2	32	1
Samie Parker	.24	298	12.4	24	2
Kris Wilson	.24	180	7.5	31	1

Top Rushers

	Car	Yds	Avg	Long	TD
Larry Johnson	.158	559	3.5	54	3
Kolby Smith*	.112	407	3.6	19	2
Priest Holmes	.46	137	3.0	11	0

Most Touchdowns

	TD	Run	Rec	Ret	Pts
Dwayne Bowe*	.5	0	5	0	30
Tony Gonzalez	.5	0	5	0	30
Larry Johnson	.4	3	1	0	24

2-Pt. Conversions: (1-3) Priest Holmes

Kicking (5 pts)

	PAT/Att	FG/Att	Lg	Pts
John Carney	.27/28	12/14	41	63
JAX	.20/21	9/11	41	47
KC	.7/7	3/3	40	16
Dave Rayner	.14/14	15/22	49	59

Signed: Carney on 11/27. **Released:** Justin Medlock on 9/11; Rayner on 11/27.

Punts (10 or more)

	No	Yds	Long	Avg	In20
Dustin Colquitt	.95	4322	81	45.5	27

Most Interceptions
Jarrad Page 3

Most Sacks
Jared Allen 15.5

Miami Dolphins

Passing (5 Att)

	Att	Cmp	Pct	Yds	TD	Rate
Cleo Lemon	.309	173	56.0	1773	6	71.0
Trent Green	.141	85	60.3	987	5	72.6
John Beck*	.107	60	56.1	559	1	62.0

Interceptions: Green 7, Lemon 6, Beck 3.

Top Receivers

	No	Yds	Avg	Long	TD
Marty Booker	.50	556	11.1	26	1
Ronnie Brown	.39	389	10.0	43	1
Ted Ginn Jr.*	.34	420	12.4	54	2
David Martin	.34	303	8.9	28	2
Derek Hagan	.29	373	12.9	22-td	2
Justin Peelle	.29	228	7.9	35	2

Top Rushers

	Car	Yds	Avg	Long	TD
Ronnie Brown	.119	602	5.1	60	4
Jesse Chatman	.128	515	4.0	30	1
Samkon Gado	.53	150	2.8	20-td	4
HOU	.18	46	2.6	7	1
MIA	.35	104	3.0	20-td	3

Claimed: Gado off waivers from HOU (10/24).

Most Touchdowns

	TD	Run	Rec	Ret	Pts
Ronnie Brown	.5	4	1	0	32
Samkon Gado	.4	4	0	0	26
HOU	.1	1	0	0	8
MIA	.3	3	0	0	18
Cleo Lemon	.	4	0	0	24

2-Pt. Conversions: (2-2) Brown, Hagan, Gado (w/Hou.)

Kicking

	PAT/Att	FG/Att	Lg	Pts
Jay Feely	.26/26	21/23	53	89

Punts (10 or more)

	No	Yds	Long	Avg	In20
Brandon Fields*	.77	3327	61	43.2	10

Most Interceptions
Jason Allen 3

Most Sacks
Jason Taylor 11.0

New England Patriots

Passing (5 Att)

	Att	Cmp	Pct	Yds	TD	Rate
Tom Brady	.578	398	68.9	4806	50	117.2
Matt Cassel	.7	4	57.1	38	0	32.7

Interceptions: Brady 8, Cassel 1.

Top Receivers

	No	Yds	Avg	Long	TD
Wes Welker	.112	1175	10.5	42	8
Randy Moss	.98	1493	15.2	65-td	23
Kevin Faulk	.47	383	8.1	23	1
Donte' Stallworth	.46	697	15.2	69-td	3
Jabar Gaffney	.36	449	12.5	56-td	5
Ben Watson	.36	389	10.8	35	6

Top Rushers

	Car	Yds	Avg	Long	TD
Laurence Maroney	.185	835	4.5	59-td	6
Sammy Morris	.85	384	4.5	49	3
Kevin Faulk	.62	265	4.3	14	0
Heath Evans	.34	121	3.6	11	3
Tom Brady	.37	98	2.6	19	2

Most Touchdowns

	TD	Run	Rec	Ret	Pts
Randy Moss	.23	0	23	0	138
Wes Welker	.8	0	8	0	48
Laurence Maroney	.6	6	0	0	38
Ben Watson	.6	0	6	0	36
Jabar Gaffney	.5	0	5	0	30

Three tied with 3 TD for 18 pts.

2-Pt. Conversions: (1-1) Maroney.

Kicking

	PAT/Att	FG/Att	Lg	Pts
Stephen Gostkowski	.74/74	21/24	45	137

Punts (10 or more)

	No	Yds	Long	Avg	In20
Chris Hanson	.44	1821	64	41.4	13

Most Interceptions
Asante Samuel 6

Most Sacks
Mike Vrabel 12.5

New York Jets

Passing (5 Att)

	Att	Cmp	Pct	Yds	TD	Rate
Chad Pennington	.260	179	68.8	1765	10	86.1
Kellen Clemens	.250	130	52.0	1529	5	60.9

Interceptions: Clemens 10, Pennington 9.

Top Receivers

	No	Yds	Avg	Long	TD
Jerricho Cotchery	.82	1130	13.8	50	2
Laveranues Coles	.55	646	11.7	57-td	6
Chris Baker	.41	409	10.0	22	3
Leon Washington	.36	213	5.9	18	0
Brad Smith	.32	325	10.2	29	2
Thomas Jones	.28	217	7.8	25	1
Justin McCareins	.19	232	12.2	51	0

Top Rushers

	No	Yds	Avg	Long	TD
Thomas Jones	.310	1119	3.6	36	1
Leon Washington	.71	353	5.0	49	3
Kellen Clemens	.27	111	4.1	18	1
Brad Smith	.12	45	3.8	11	0

Most Touchdowns

	TD	Run	Rec	Ret	Pts
Leon Washington	.6	3	0	3	38
Laveranues Coles	.6	0	6	0	36
Chris Baker	.3	0	3	0	18
Jerricho Cotchery	.2	0	2	0	12
Thomas Jones	.2	1	1	0	12
Brad Smith	.2	0	2	0	12

2-Pt. Conversions: (1-2) Washington.

Kicking

	PAT/Att	FG/Att	Lg	Pts
Mike Nugent	.23/24	29/36	50	110

Punts (10 or more)

	No	Yds	Long	Avg	In20
Ben Graham	.66	2855	62	43.3	23

Most Interceptions
Kerry Rhodes 5

Most Sacks
David Harris 5.0
Shaun Ellis 5.0

Oakland Raiders

Passing (10 Att)

	Att	Cmp	Pct	Yds	TD	Rate
Josh McCown	.190	111	58.4	1151	10	69.4
Daunte Culpepper	.186	108	58.1	1331	5	78.0
JaMarcus Russell*	.66	36	54.5	373	2	55.9

Interceptions: McCown 11, Culpepper 5, Russell 4.

Top Receivers

	No	Yds	Avg	Long	TD
Ronald Curry	.55	717	13.0	49	4
Jerry Porter	.44	705	16.0	59	6
Zach Miller*	.44	444	10.1	28	3
LaMont Jordan	.28	247	8.8	27	0
Justin Griffith	.26	165	6.3	29	1
Justin Fargas	.23	188	8.2	17	0

Top Rushers

	Car	Yds	Avg	Long	TD
Justin Fargas	.222	1009	4.5	48	4
LaMont Jordan	.144	549	3.8	33	3
Dominic Rhodes	.75	302	4.0	25	1
Josh McCown	.29	143	4.9	24	0
Daunte Culpepper	.20	40	2.0	9	3

Most Touchdowns

	TD	Run	Rec	Ret	Pts
Jerry Porter	.6	0	6	0	36
Ronald Curry	.4	0	4	0	28
Justin Fargas	.4	4	0	0	24
Daunte Culpepper	.3	3	0	0	18
LaMont Jordan	.3	3	0	0	18
Zach Miller*	.3	0	3	0	18

2-Pt. Conversions: (2-2) Curry 2.

Kicking

	PAT/Att	FG/Att	Lg	Pts
Sebastian Janikowski	.28/28	23/32	54	97

Punts (10 or more)

	No	Yds	Long	Avg	In20
Shane Lechler	.73	3585	62	49.1	25

Most Interceptions
Thomas Howard 6

Most Sacks
Derrick Burgess 8.0
Chris Clemons 8.0

Pittsburgh Steelers

Passing (5 Att)

	Att	Cmp	Pct	Yds	TD	Rate
Ben Roethlisberger	.404	264	65.3	3154	32	104.1
Charlie Batch	.36	17	47.2	232	2	52.1

Interceptions: Roethlisberger 11, Batch 3.

Top Receivers

	No	Yds	Avg	Long	TD
Hines Ward	.71	732	10.3	25	7
Santonio Holmes	.52	942	18.1	83	8
Heath Miller	.47	566	12.0	29	7
Nate Washington	.29	450	15.5	40	5
Willie Parker	.23	164	7.1	22	0
Cedrick Wilson	.18	207	11.5	18	1
Najeh Davenport	.18	184	10.2	32-td	2

Top Rushers

	Car	Yds	Avg	Long	TD
Willie Parker	.321	1316	4.1	32	2
Najeh Davenport	.107	499	4.7	45	5
Ben Roethlisberger	.35	204	5.8	30-td	2
Carey Davis	.17	68	4.0	12	0

Most Touchdowns

	TD	Run	Rec	Ret	Pts
Santonio Holmes	.8	0	8	0	50
Hines Ward	.7	0	7	0	44
Najeh Davenport	.7	5	2	0	42
Heath Miller	.7	0	7	0	42
Nate Washington	.5	0	5	0	30

2-Pt. Conversions: (2-2) Holmes, Ward.

Kicking

	PAT/Att	FG/Att	Lg	Pts
Jeff Reed	.44/44	23/25	49	113

Punts (10 or more)

	No	Yds	Long	Avg	In20
Daniel Sepulveda*	.68	2880	59	42.4	28

Most Interceptions
Ike Taylor 3

Most Sacks
James Harrison 8.5

San Diego Chargers

Passing (5 Att)

	Att	Cmp	Pct	Yds	TD	Rate
Philip Rivers	.460	277	60.2	3152	21	82.4
Billy Volek	.10	3	30.0	6	0	0.0

Interceptions: Rivers 15, Volek 1.

Top Receivers

	No	Yds	Avg	Long	TD
Antonio Gates	.75	984	13.1	49-td	9
Chris Chambers	.66	970	14.7	44	4
MIA	.31	415	13.4	28	0
SD	.35	555	15.9	44	4
LaDainian Tomlinson	.60	475	7.9	36	3
Vincent Jackson	.41	623	15.2	45	3
Craig Davis*	.20	188	9.4	18	1

Acquired: Chambers from Mia. for an '08 2nd-round pick (Oct. 16).

Top Rushers

	No	Yds	Avg	Long	TD
LaDainian Tomlinson	.315	1474	4.7	49	15
Michael Turner	.71	316	4.5	74-td	1
Darren Sproles	.37	164	4.4	34	2
Philip Rivers	.29	33	1.1	10	1

Most Touchdowns

	TD	Run	Rec	Ret	Pts
LaDainian Tomlinson	.18	15	3	0	108
Antonio Gates	.9	0	9	0	54
Chris Chambers	.4	0	4	0	24
Darren Sproles	.4	2	0	2	24

Two tied with 3 TD each for 18 pts.

2-Pt. Conversions: (0-2)

Kicking

	PAT/Att	FG/Att	Lg	Pts
Nate Kaeding	.46/46	24/27	51	118

Punts (10 or more)

	No	Yds	Long	Avg	In20
Mike Scifres	.82	3735	70	46.1	36

Most Interceptions
Antonio Cromartie . . .10

Most Sacks
Shawne Merriman . . .12.5

Tennessee Titans

Passing (5 Att)

	Att	Cmp	Pct	Yds	TD	Rate
Vince Young	.382	238	62.3	2546	9	71.1
Kerry Collins	.82	50	61.0	531	0	79.9

Interceptions: Young 17.

Top Receivers

	No	Yds	Avg	Long	TD
Justin Gage	.55	750	13.6	73	2
Roydell Williams	.55	719	13.1	48	4
Bo Scaife	.46	421	9.2	26	1
Eric Moulds	.32	342	10.7	46	0
Brandon Jones	.21	248	11.8	35-td	2
LenDale White	.20	114	5.7	15	0
Chris Brown	.19	128	6.7	16	0

Top Rushers

	Car	Yds	Avg	Long	TD
LenDale White	.303	1110	3.7	28	7
Chris Brown	.102	462	4.5	42	1
Vince Young	.93	395	4.2	21	3
Chris Henry*	.31	119	3.8	24-td	2

Most Touchdowns

	TD	Run	Rec	Ret	Pts
LenDale White	.7	7	0	0	42
Chris Brown	.5	3	1	0	30
Roydell Williams	.4	0	4	0	24
Vince Young	.3	3	0	0	18

Four tied with 2 TD for 12 pts.

2-Pt. Conversions: (0-0)

Kicking

	PAT/Att	FG/Att	Lg	Pts
Rob Bironas	.28/28	35/39	56	133

Punts (10 or more)

	No	Yds	Long	Avg	In20
Craig Hentrich	.70	2939	66	42.0	24

Most Interceptions
Keith Bulluck 5

Most Sacks
Kyle Vanden Bosch . . .12.0

NFC Team by Team Statistics

Players with more than one team during the regular season are listed with club they ended season with; (*) indicates rookies.

Arizona Cardinals

Passing (5 Att)	Att	Cmp	Pct	Yds	TD	Rate
Kurt Warner	.451	281	62.3	3417	27	89.8
Matt Leinart	.112	60	53.6	647	2	61.9
Tim Rattay	.27	15	55.6	164	3	71.1

Interceptions: Warner 17, Leinart 4, Rattay 3.

Top Receivers	No	Yds	Avg	Long	TD
Larry Fitzgerald	.100	1409	14.1	48-td	10
Anquan Boldin	.71	853	12.0	44-td	9
Bryant Johnson	.46	528	11.5	30	2
J.J. Arrington	.29	241	8.3	32	1
Edgerrin James	.24	204	8.5	26	0
Leonard Pope	.23	238	10.3	31	5

Top Rushers	Car	Yds	Avg	Long	TD
Edgerrin James	.324	1222	3.8	27	7
J.J. Arrington	.26	78	3.0	12	0
Matt Leinart	.11	42	3.8	20	0

Most Touchdowns	TD	Run	Rec	Ret	Pts
Larry Fitzgerald	.10	0	10	0	60
Anquan Boldin	.9	0	9	0	54
Edgerrin James	.7	7	0	0	42
Leonard Pope	.5	0	5	0	30
Antrel Rolle	.3	0	0	3	18

2-Pt. Conversions: (0-1).

Kicking	PAT/Att	FG/Att	Lg	Pts
Neil Rackers	.47/47	21/30	52	110

Punts (10 or more)	No	Yds	Long	Avg	In20
Mike Barr*	.59	2385	61	40.4	15
Mitch Berger	.20	813	56	40.7	6

Most Interceptions		Most Sacks	
Antrel Rolle	.5	Darnell Dockett	.9.0
Roderick Hood	.5		

Atlanta Falcons

Passing (5 Att)	Att	Cmp	Pct	Yds	TD	Rate
Joey Harrington	.348	215	61.8	2215	7	77.2
Chris Redman	.149	89	59.7	1079	10	90.4
Byron Lefwich	.58	32	55.2	279	1	59.5

Interceptions: Harrington 8, Redman 5, Leftwich 2.

Top Receivers	No	Yds	Avg	Long	TD
Roddy White	.83	1202	14.5	69-td	6
Michael Jenkins	.53	532	10.0	29	4
Alge Crumpler	.42	444	10.6	55-td	5
Laurent Robinson*	.37	437	11.8	74-td	1
Warrick Dunn	.37	238	6.4	35	0
Jerious Norwood	.28	277	9.9	46	0

Top Rushers	Car	Yds	Avg	Long	TD
Warrick Dunn	.227	720	3.2	38	4
Jerious Norwood	.103	613	6.0	67-td	1

Most Touchdowns	TD	Run	Rec	Ret	Pts
Roddy White	.6	0	6	0	36
Alge Crumpler	.5	0	5	0	30
Warrick Dunn	.4	4	0	0	24
Michael Jenkins	.4	0	4	0	24

2-Pt. Conversions: (0-1).

Kicking	PAT/Att	FG/Att	Lg	Pts
Morten Andersen	.24/24	25/28	47	99
Matt Prater*	.1/1	1/4	45	4
Michael Koenen	.0/0	0/2	—	0

Signed: Anderson (9/17). **Waived:** Prater (9/17).

Punts (10 or more)	No	Yds	Long	Avg	In20
Michael Koenen	.88	3824	63	43.5	30

Most Interceptions		Most Sacks	
DeAngelo Hall	.5	John Abraham	.10.0

Carolina Panthers

Passing (5 Att)	Att	Cmp	Pct	Yds	TD	Rate
Vinny Testaverde	..172	94	54.7	952	5	65.8
David Carr	.136	73	53.7	635	3	58.3
Matt Moore*	.111	63	56.8	730	3	67.0
Jake Delhomme	..86	55	64.0	624	8	111.8

Interceptions: Testaverde 6, Carr and Moore 5, Delhomme 1.

Top Receivers	No	Yds	Avg	Long	TD
Steve Smith	.87	1002	11.5	74-td	7
Jeff King	.46	406	8.8	29	2
Drew Carter	.38	517	13.6	49	4
Keary Colbert	.32	332	10.4	43	0
DeShaun Foster	.25	182	7.3	23	1
DeAngelo Williams	...23	175	7.6	30	1

Top Rushers	Car	Yds	Avg	Long	TD
DeShaun Foster	.247	876	3.5	20	3
DeAngelo Williams	..144	717	5.0	75	4
Steve Smith	.9	66	7.3	22	0

Most Touchdowns	TD	Run	Rec	Ret	Pts
Steve Smith	.7	0	7	0	42
DeAngelo Williams	.5	4	1	0	30
Drew Carter	.4	0	4	0	24
DeShaun Foster	.4	3	1	0	24

2-Pt. Conversions: (0-0).

Kicking	PAT/Att	FG/Att	Lg	Pts
John Kasay	.27/27	24/28	53	99

Punts (10 or more)	No	Yds	Long	Avg	In20
Jason Baker	.90	3978	64	44.2	22

Most Interceptions		Most Sacks	
Richard Marshall	.3	Na'il Diggs	.3.5
Deke Cooper	.3	Damione Lewis	.3.5

Chicago Bears

Passing (5 Att)	Att	Cmp	Pct	Yds	TD	Rate
Brian Griese	.262	161	61.5	1803	10	75.6
Rex Grossman	.225	122	54.2	1411	4	66.4
Kyle Orton	.80	43	53.8	478	3	73.9

Interceptions: Griese 12, Grossman 7, Orton 2.

Top Receivers	No	Yds	Avg	Long	TD
Bernard Berrian	.71	951	13.4	59-td	5
Adrian Peterson	.51	420	8.2	30	0
Desmond Clark	.44	545	12.4	52	4
Muhsin Muhammad	.40	570	14.3	44	3
Greg Olsen*	.39	391	10.0	31	2
Devin Hester	.20	299	15.0	81-td	2

Top Rushers	Car	Yds	Avg	Long	TD
Cedric Benson	.196	674	3.4	43-td	4
Adrian Peterson	.151	510	3.4	21	3
Garrett Wolfe*	.31	85	2.7	25	0

Most Touchdowns	TD	Run	Rec	Ret	Pts
Devin Hester	.8	0	2	6	48
Bernard Berrian	.5	0	5	0	30
Cedric Benson	.4	4	0	0	24
Desmond Clark	.4	0	4	0	24
Muhsin Muhammad	.3	0	3	0	18
Adrian Peterson	.3	3	0	0	18

2-Pt. Conversions: (1-1) Greg Olsen.

Kicking	PAT/Att	FG/Att	Lg	Pts
Robbie Gould	.33/33	31/36	49	126

Punts (10 or more)	No	Yds	Long	Avg	In20
Brad Maynard	.88	3682	56	41.8	27

Most Interceptions		Most Sacks	
Brian Urlacher	.5	Adewale Ogunleye	.9.0

Dallas Cowboys

Passing (5 Att)	Att	Cmp	Pct	Yds	TD	Rate
Tony Romo	520	335	64.4	4211	36	97.4
Brad Johnson	11	7	63.6	79	0	85.0

Interceptions: Romo 19.

Top Receivers	No	Yds	Avg	Long	TD
Jason Witten	96	1145	11.9	53	7
Terrell Owens	81	1355	16.7	52-td	15
Patrick Crayton	50	697	13.9	59-td	7
Marion Barber	44	282	6.4	29	2
Julius Jones	23	203	8.8	24	0
Sam Hurd	19	314	16.5	51-td	1
Anthony Fasano	14	143	10.2	26-td	1

Top Rushers	Car	Yds	Avg	Long	TD
Marion Barber	204	975	4.8	54	10
Julius Jones	164	588	3.6	25	2
Tony Romo	31	129	4.2	17	2
Tyson Thompson	14	54	3.9	23	0

Most Touchdowns	TD	Run	Rec	Ret	Pts
Terrell Owens	15	0	15	0	90
Marion Barber	12	10	2	0	72
Patrick Crayton	7	0	7	0	42
Jason Witten	7	0	7	0	42
Tony Curtis	3	0	3	0	18
Julius Jones	2	2	0	0	12
Tony Romo	2	2	0	0	12

2-Pt. Conversions: (0-1).

Kicking	PAT/Att	FG/Att	Lg	Pts
Nick Folk*	53/53	26/31	53	131

Punts (10 or more)	No	Yds	Long	Avg	In20
Mat McBriar	63	2970	64	47.1	17

Most Interceptions
Anthony Henry 6

Most Sacks
DeMarcus Ware 14.0

Green Bay Packers

Passing (5 Att)	Att	Cmp	Pct	Yds	TD	Rate
Brett Favre	535	356	66.5	4155	28	95.7
Aaron Rodgers	28	20	71.4	218	1	106.0
Craig Nall	15	7	46.7	88	1	87.6

Interceptions: Favre 15.
Signed: Free agent Nall on Dec. 1.

Top Receivers	No	Yds	Avg	Long	TD
Donald Driver	82	1048	12.8	47	2
Greg Jennings	53	920	17.4	82-td	12
Donald Lee	48	575	12.0	60	6
James Jones*	47	676	14.4	79-td	2
Vernand Morency	30	199	6.6	18	0
Ryan Grant	30	145	4.8	21	0

Top Rushers	Car	Yds	Avg	Long	TD
Ryan Grant	188	956	5.1	66-td	8
Brandon Jackson*	75	267	3.6	46	1
DeShawn Wynn*	50	203	4.1	44	4
Vernand Morency	29	108	3.7	15	0

Most Touchdowns	TD	Run	Rec	Ret	Pts
Greg Jennings	12	0	12	0	72
Ryan Grant	8	8	0	0	48
Donald Lee	6	0	6	0	36
Ruvell Martin	4	0	4	0	24
DeShawn Wynn*	4	4	0	0	24
Bubba Franks	3	0	3	0	18

2-Pt. Conversions: (0-0).

Kicking	PAT/Att	FG/Att	Lg	Pts
Mason Crosby*	48/48	31/39	53	141

Punts (10 or more)	No	Yds	Long	Avg	In20
Jon Ryan	60	2664	72	44.4	18

Most Interceptions
Atari Bigby 5

Most Sacks
Aaron Kampman 12.0

Detroit Lions

Passing (5 Att)	Att	Cmp	Pct	Yds	TD	Rate
Jon Kitna	561	355	63.3	4068	18	80.9
J.T. O'Sullivan	26	13	50.0	148	1	48.2

Interceptions: Kitna 22.

Top Receivers	No	Yds	Avg	Long	TD
Shaun McDonald	79	943	11.9	49-td	6
Roy Williams	64	838	13.1	91-td	5
Mike Furrey	61	664	10.9	49	1
Calvin Johnson*	48	756	15.8	49	4
Kevin Jones	32	197	6.2	16	0
Sean McHugh	17	252	14.8	46	0

Top Rushers	Car	Yds	Avg	Long	TD
Kevin Jones	153	581	3.8	34	8
T.J. Duckett	65	335	5.2	53	3
Tatum Bell	44	182	4.1	24	1
Jon Kitna	25	63	2.5	11	0

Most Touchdowns	TD	Run	Rec	Ret	Pts
Kevin Jones	8	8	0	0	48
Shaun McDonald	6	0	6	0	36
Calvin Johnson*	5	1	4	0	30
Roy Williams	5	0	5	0	30
T.J. Duckett	3	3	0	0	18
Casey Fitzsimmons	2	0	1	1	14

2-Pt. Conversions: (0-1).

Kicking	PAT/Att	FG/Att	Lg	Pts
Jason Hanson	35/36	29/35	53	122

Punts (10 or more)	No	Yds	Long	Avg	In20
Nick Harris	68	3010	58	44.3	26

Most Interceptions
Keith Smith 3

Most Sacks
Shaun Rogers 7.0

Minnesota Vikings

Passing (5 Att)	Att	Cmp	Pct	Yds	TD	Rate
Tavaris Jackson	294	171	58.2	1911	9	70.8
Kelly Holcomb	83	42	50.6	515	2	73.1
Brooks Bollinger	50	33	66.0	311	1	88.0

Interceptions: Jackson 12, Holcomb 1, Bollinger 1.

Top Receivers	No	Yds	Avg	Long	TD
Bobby Wade	54	647	12.0	40	3
Robert Ferguson	32	391	12.2	71	1
Sidney Rice*	31	396	12.8	60-td	4
Chester Taylor	29	281	9.7	50	0
Visanthe Shiancoe	27	323	12.0	79	1
Adrian Peterson*	19	268	14.1	60-td	1

Top Rushers	Car	Yds	Avg	Long	TD
Adrian Peterson*	238	1341	5.6	73-td	12
Chester Taylor	157	844	5.4	84-td	7
Tavaris Jackson	54	260	4.8	32	3
Mewelde Moore	20	113	5.7	17	0

Most Touchdowns	TD	Run	Rec	Ret	Pts
Adrian Peterson*	13	12	1	0	78
Chester Taylor	7	7	0	0	42
Sidney Rice*	4	0	4	0	24
Tavaris Jackson	3	3	0	0	22
Bobby Wade	3	0	3	0	18

2-Pt. Conversions: (3-3) Jackson 2, Brooks Bollinger 1.

Kicking	PAT/Att	FG/Att	Lg	Pts
Ryan Longwell	39/40	20/24	55	99

Punts (10 or more)	No	Yds	Long	Avg	In20
Chris Kluwe	81	3621	70	44.7	34

Most Interceptions
Dwight Smith 4
Darren Sharper 4

Most Sacks
Three tied with 5 each.

New Orleans Saints

Passing (5 Att)	Att	Cmp	Pct	Yds	TD	Rate
Drew Brees	652	440	67.5	4423	28	89.4

Interceptions: Brees 18.

Top Receivers	No	Yds	Avg	Long	TD
Marques Colston	98	1202	12.3	45	11
Reggie Bush	73	417	5.7	25	2
David Patten	54	792	14.7	58	3
Eric Johnson	48	378	7.9	22	2
Aaron Stecker	36	211	5.9	26	0
Lance Moore	32	302	9.4	22	2
Billy Miller	27	328	12.1	57	1

Top Rushers	Car	Yds	Avg	Long	TD
Reggie Bush	157	581	3.7	22	4
Aaron Stecker	115	448	3.9	26	5
Pierre Thomas*	52	252	4.8	24-td	3
Deuce McAllister	24	92	3.8	15	0

Most Touchdowns	TD	Run	Rec	Ret	Pts
Marques Colston	11	0	11	0	66
Reggie Bush	6	4	2	0	42
Aaron Stecker	5	5	0	0	30
Pierre Thomas*	3	1	1	1	20

Three tied with 3 TD for 18 pts.

2-Pt. Conversions: (4-5) Bush 3, Thomas 1.

Kicking	PAT/Att	FG/Att	Lg	Pts
Olindo Mare	34/34	10/17	52	66
Martin Gramatica	8/8	5/5	55	23

Signed: Gramatica on Dec. 12.

Punts (10 or more)	No	Yds	Long	Avg	In20
Steven Weatherford	63	2757	61	43.8	20

Most Interceptions
Three tied with 3 each.

Most Sacks
Will Smith 7.0

New York Giants

Passing (5 Att)	Att	Cmp	Pct	Yds	TD	Rate
Eli Manning	529	297	56.1	3336	23	73.9
Jared Lorenzen	8	4	50.0	28	0	58.3
Anthony Wright	7	1	14.3	12	0	39.6

Interceptions: Manning 20.

Top Receivers	No	Yds	Avg	Long	TD
Plaxico Burress	70	1025	14.6	60-td	12
Amani Toomer	59	760	12.9	40	3
Jeremy Shockey	57	619	10.9	29	3
Derrick Ward	26	179	6.9	17	1
Brandon Jacobs	23	174	7.6	34	2
Sinorice Moss	21	225	10.7	20	0

Top Rushers	Car	Yds	Avg	Long	TD
Brandon Jacobs	202	1009	5.0	43-td	4
Derrick Ward	125	602	4.8	44	3
Reuben Droughns	85	275	3.2	45	6
Ahmad Bradshaw	23	190	8.3	88-td	1

Most Touchdowns	TD	Run	Rec	Ret	Pts
Plaxico Burress	12	0	12	0	72
Reuben Droughns	6	6	0	0	36
Brandon Jacobs	6	4	2	0	36
Derrick Ward	4	3	1	0	24
Jeremy Shockey	3	0	3	0	18
Amani Toomer	3	0	3	0	18

2-Pt. Conversions: (0-2).

Kicking	PAT/Att	FG/Att	Lg	Pts
Lawrence Tynes	40/42	23/27	48	109

Punts (10 or more)	No	Yds	Long	Avg	In20
Jeff Feagles	71	2865	60	40.4	25

Most Interceptions
Sam Madison 4
Gibril Wilson 4

Most Sacks
Osi Umenyiora 13.0

Philadelphia Eagles

Passing (5 Att)	Att	Cmp	Pct	Yds	TD	Rate
Donovan McNabb	473	291	61.5	3324	19	89.9
A.J. Feeley	103	59	57.3	681	5	61.2

Interceptions: McNabb 7, Feeley 8.

Top Receivers	No	Yds	Avg	Long	TD
Brian Westbrook	90	771	8.6	57-td	5
Kevin Curtis	77	1110	14.4	75-td	6
Reggie Brown	61	780	12.8	45-td	4
Jason Avant	23	267	11.6	31	2
L.J. Smith	22	236	10.7	26	1
Brent Celek*	16	178	11.1	29	1
Hank Baskett	16	142	8.9	25	1
Greg Lewis	13	265	20.4	50	3

Top Rushers	Car	Yds	Avg	Long	TD
Brian Westbrook	278	1333	4.8	36	7
Correll Buckhalter	62	313	5.0	30-td	4
Donovan McNabb	50	236	4.7	40	0

Most Touchdowns	TD	Run	Rec	Ret	Pts
Brian Westbrook	12	7	5	0	72
Kevin Curtis	8	0	6	2	48
Reggie Brown	4	0	4	0	24
Correll Buckhalter	4	4	0	0	24
Greg Lewis	3	0	3	0	18
Jason Avant	2	0	2	0	12

2-Pt. Conversions: (0-2).

Kicking	PAT/Att	FG/Att	Lg	Pts
David Akers	36/36	24/32	53	108

Punts (10 or more)	No	Yds	Long	Avg	In20
Save Rocca*	73	3066	65	42.0	24

Most Interceptions
Sheldon Brown 3

Most Sacks
Trent Cole 12.5

St. Louis Rams

Passing (5 Att)	Att	Cmp	Pct	Yds	TD	Rate
Marc Bulger	378	221	58.5	2392	11	70.3
Gus Frerotte	167	94	56.3	1014	7	58.3
Brock Berlin	28	17	60.7	153	0	60.6

Interceptions: Bulger 15, Frerotte 12, Berlin 1.

Top Receivers	No	Yds	Avg	Long	TD
Torry Holt	93	1189	12.8	40	7
Isaac Bruce	55	733	13.3	37	4
Randy McMichael	39	429	11.0	29-td	3
Steven Jackson	38	271	7.1	37	1
Drew Bennett	33	375	11.4	24	3
Brian Leonard	30	183	6.1	16	0
Travis Minor	12	86	7.2	20	0

Top Rushers	Car	Yds	Avg	Long	TD
Steven Jackson	237	1002	4.2	54	5
Brian Leonard*	86	303	3.5	31	0
Antonio Pittman*	38	139	3.7	43	0
Travis Minor	17	68	4.0	13	0

Most Touchdowns	TD	Run	Rec	Ret	Pts
Torry Holt	7	0	7	0	44
Steven Jackson	6	5	1	0	36
Isaac Bruce	4	0	4	0	24
Drew Bennett	3	0	3	0	18
Randy McMichael	3	0	3	0	18

2-Pt. Conversions: (1-2) Holt.

Kicking	PAT/Att	FG/Att	Lg	Pts
Jeff Wilkins	25/25	24/32	53	97

Punts (10 or more)	No	Yds	Long	Avg	In20
Donnie Jones	78	3684	80	47.2	18

Most Interceptions
O.J. Atogwe 8

Most Sacks
Will Witherspoon 7.0

San Francisco 49ers

Passing (5 Att)

	Att	Cmp	Pct	Yds	TD	Rate
Trent Dilfer	.219	113	51.6	1166	7	55.1
Alex Smith	.193	94	48.7	914	2	57.2
Shaun Hill	.79	54	68.4	501	5	101.3
Chris Weinke	.22	13	59.1	104	1	86.2

Interceptions: Dilfer 12, Smith 4, Hill 1.

Top Receivers

	No	Yds	Avg	Long	TD
Frank Gore	.53	436	8.2	23-td	1
Vernon Davis	.52	509	9.8	31	4
Arnaz Battle	.50	600	12.0	57-td	5
Darrell Jackson	.46	497	10.8	34	3
Delanie Walker	.21	174	8.3	26	1

Top Rushers

	Car	Yds	Avg	Long	TD
Frank Gore	.260	1102	4.2	43-td	5
Michael Robinson	.26	121	4.7	28	0
Maurice Hicks	.21	117	5.6	18	1
Alex Smith	.13	89	6.8	25	0

Most Touchdowns

	TD	Run	Rec	Ret	Pts
Arnaz Battle	.6	1	5	0	36
Frank Gore	.6	5	1	0	36
Vernon Davis	.4	0	4	0	24
Darrell Jackson	.3	0	3	0	18

Five tied with 1 TD for 6 pts.

2-Pt. Conversions: (0-1).

Kicking

	PAT/Att	FG/Att	Lg	Pts
Joe Nedney	.22/22	17/19	50	73

Punts (10 or more)

	No	Yds	Long	Avg	In20
Andy Lee	.105	4698	74	47.3	42

Most Interceptions
Nate Clements 4
Walt Harris 4

Most Sacks
Bryant Young 6.5

Seattle Seahawks

Passing (5 Att)

	Att	Cmp	Pct	Yds	TD	Rate
Matt Hasselbeck	.562	352	62.6	3966	28	91.4
Seneca Wallace	.28	19	67.9	215	2	99.6

Interceptions: Hasselbeck 12, Wallace 1.

Top Receivers

	No	Yds	Avg	Long	TD
Bobby Engram	.94	1147	12.2	49	6
Nate Burleson	.50	694	13.9	45-td	9
Deion Branch	.49	661	13.5	65	4
Leonard Weaver	.39	313	8.0	46	0
D.J. Hackett	.32	384	12.0	59	3
Marcus Pollard	.28	273	9.8	22	2
Maurice Morris	.23	213	9.3	34-td	1

Top Rushers

	Car	Yds	Avg	Long	TD
Shaun Alexander	.207	716	3.5	25	4
Maurice Morris	.140	628	4.5	46	4
Leonard Weaver	.33	146	4.4	37	1
Matt Hasselbeck	.39	89	2.3	12	0

Most Touchdowns

	TD	Run	Rec	Ret	Pts
Nate Burleson	.11	0	9	2	66
Bobby Engram	.6	0	6	0	36
Shaun Alexander	.5	4	1	0	30
Maurice Morris	.5	4	1	0	30
Deion Branch	.4	0	4	0	24
D.J. Hackett	.3	0	3	0	18
Will Heller	.3	0	3	0	18

2-Pt. Conversions: (0-1).

Kicking

	PAT/Att	FG/Att	Lg	Pts
Josh Brown	.43/43	28/34	54	127

Punts (10 or more)

	No	Yds	Long	Avg	In20
Ryan Plackemeier	.86	3436	62	40.0	30

Most Interceptions
Marcus Trufant 7

Most Sacks
Patrick Kerney 14.5

Tampa Bay Buccaneers

Passing (5 Att)

	Att	Cmp	Pct	Yds	TD	Rate
Jeff Garcia	.327	209	63.9	2440	13	94.6
Luke McCown	.139	94	67.6	1009	5	91.7
Bruce Gradkowski	.24	13	54.2	130	0	52.4

Interceptions: Garcia 4, McCown 3, Gradkowski 1.

Top Receivers

	No	Yds	Avg	Long	TD
Ike Hilliard	.62	722	11.6	56	1
Joey Galloway	.57	1014	17.8	69-td	6
Earnest Graham	.49	324	6.6	21	0
Alex Smith	.32	385	12.0	33	3
Michael Pittman	.26	191	7.3	16	0

Top Rushers

	Car	Yds	Avg	Long	TD
Earnest Graham	.222	898	4.0	28-td	10
Michael Pittman	.68	286	4.2	29	0
Michael Bennett	.61	241	4.0	28	1
KC	.20	52	2.6	12	0
TB	.41	189	4.6	28	1
Cadillac Williams	.54	208	3.9	20	3

Acquired: Bennett from KC for '08 and '09 conditional picks (Oct. 16)

Most Touchdowns

	TD	Run	Rec	Ret	Pts
Earnest Graham	.10	10	0	0	60
Joey Galloway	.6	0	6	0	36
Jerramy Stevens	.4	0	4	0	24
Alex Smith	.3	0	3	0	18
Cadillac Williams	.3	3	0	0	18

2-Pt. Conversions: (0-2).

Kicking

	PAT/Att	FG/Att	Lg	Pts
Matt Bryant	.34/34	28/33	49	118

Punts (10 or more)

	No	Yds	Long	Avg	In20
Josh Bidwell	.77	3382	61	43.9	30

Most Interceptions
Jermaine Phillips 4

Most Sacks
Greg White 8.0

Washington Redskins

Passing (5 Att)

	Att	Cmp	Pct	Yds	TD	Rate
Jason Campbell	.417	250	60.0	2700	12	77.6
Todd Collins	.105	67	63.8	888	5	106.4

Interceptions: Campbell 11.

Top Receivers

	No	Yds	Avg	Long	TD
Chris Cooley	.66	786	11.9	39-td	8
Santana Moss	.61	808	13.2	49	3
Antwaan Randle El	.51	728	14.3	54	1
Clinton Portis	.47	389	8.3	54	0
Keenan McCardell	.22	256	11.6	32	1
Ladell Betts	.21	174	8.3	28	1

Top Rushers

	Car	Yds	Avg	Long	TD
Clinton Portis	.325	1262	3.9	32	11
Ladell Betts	.93	335	3.6	20	1
Jason Campbell	.36	185	5.1	29	1
Mike Sellers	.26	78	3.0	15	2

Most Touchdowns

	TD	Run	Rec	Ret	Pts
Clinton Portis	.11	11	0	0	66
Chris Cooley	.8	0	8	0	50
Santana Moss	.3	0	3	0	18
Mike Sellers	.3	2	1	0	18
Ladell Betts	.2	1	1	0	12
James Thrash	.2	0	2	0	12

2-Pt. Conversions: (2-5) Cooley, Randle El.

Kicking

	PAT/Att	FG/Att	Lg	Pts
Shaun Suisham	.29/30	29/35	50	116

Punts (10 or more)

	No	Yds	Long	Avg	In20
Derrick Frost	.75	3072	64	41.0	23

Most Interceptions
Sean Taylor 5

Most Sacks
Andre Carter 10.5

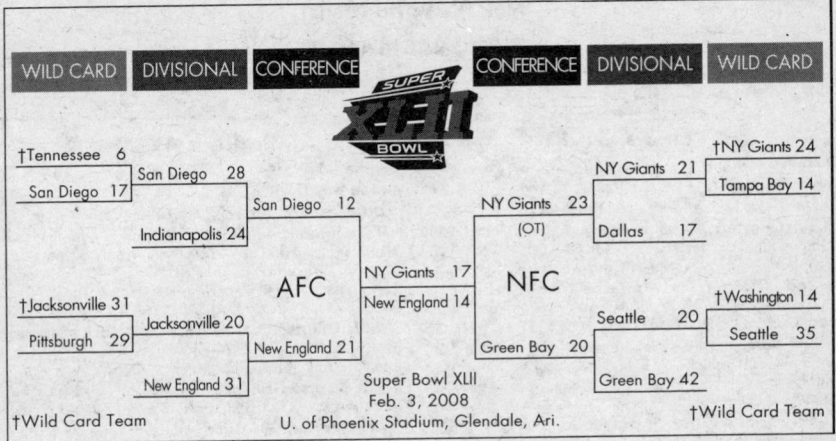

WILD CARD   DIVISIONAL   CONFERENCE   SUPER BOWL XLII   CONFERENCE   DIVISIONAL   WILD CARD

†Tennessee 6
San Diego 17
San Diego 28
Indianapolis 24
San Diego 12

NY Giants 17
New England 14

†Jacksonville 31
Pittsburgh 29
Jacksonville 20
New England 21
New England 31

AFC

Super Bowl XLII
Feb. 3, 2008
U. of Phoenix Stadium, Glendale, Ari.

†Wild Card Team

NFC

NY Giants 23
(OT)

Green Bay 20

†NY Giants 24
Tampa Bay 14
NY Giants 21
Dallas 17

†Washington 14
Seattle 35
Seattle 20
Green Bay 42

†Wild Card Team

Playoff Game Summaries

Team records listed in parentheses indicate records before game.

WILD CARD ROUND

AFC

Jaguars, 31-29

Jacksonville (11-5)	7	14	7	3—	**31**
Pittsburgh (10-6)	7	0	3	19—	**29**

Date—Jan. 5. **Att**—63,629. **Time**—3:24.

1st Quarter: PIT—Najeh Davenport 1-yd run (Jeff Reed kick), 10:03; JAX—Fred Taylor 1-yd run (Josh Scobee kick), 9:39.

2nd Quarter: JAX—Rashean Mathis 63-yd interception return (Scobee kick), 10:19; JAX—Maurice Jones-Drew 43-yd pass from David Garrard (Scobee kick), 8:34.

3rd Quarter: PIT—Reed 28-yd FG, 9:24; JAX—Jones-Drew 10-yd run (Scobee kick), 4:39.

4th Quarter: PIT—Santonio Holmes 37-yd pass from Ben Roethlisberger (Reed kick), 14:53; PIT—Heath Miller 14-yd pass from Roethlisberger (run failed), 10:25; PIT—Davenport 1-yd run (pass failed), 6:21; JAX—Scobee 25-yd FG, 0:37.

Chargers, 17-6

Tennessee (10-6)	3	3	0	0—	**6**
San Diego (11-5)	0	0	10	7—	**17**

Date—Jan. 6. **Att**—65,540. **Time**—3:04.

1st Quarter: TEN—Rob Bironas 30-yd FG, 9:37.

2nd Quarter: TEN—Bironas 44-yd FG, 0:00.

3rd Quarter: SD—Nate Kaeding 20-yd FG, 9:41; SD—Vincent Jackson 25-yd pass from Philip Rivers (Kaeding kick), 2:35.

4th Quarter: SD—LaDainian Tomlinson 1-yd run (Kaeding kick), 8:45.

NFC

Seahawks, 35-14

Washington (9-7)	0	0	0	14—	**14**
Seattle (10-6)	7	3	3	22—	**35**

Date—Jan. 5. **Att**—68,297. **Time**—3:18.

1st Quarter: SEA—Leonard Weaver 17-yd run (Josh Brown kick), 3:45.

2nd Quarter: SEA—Brown 50-yd FG, 8:58.

3rd Quarter: SEA—Brown 33-yd FG, 4:30.

4th Quarter: WAS—Antwaan Randle El 7-yd pass from Todd Collins (Shaun Suisham kick), 14:53; WAS—Santana Moss 30-yd pass from Collins (Suisham kick), 12:38; SEA—D.J. Hackett 20-yd pass from Matt Hasselbeck (Marcus Pollard pass from Hasselbeck), 6:06; SEA—Marcus Trufant 78-yd interception return (Brown kick), 5:38; SEA—Jordan Babineaux 57-yd interception return (Brown kick), 0:27.

Giants, 24-14

NY Giants (10-6)	0	14	3	7—	**24**
Buccaneers (9-7)	7	0	0	7—	**14**

Date—Jan. 6. **Att**—65,621. **Time**—2:53.

1st Quarter: TB—Earnest Graham 1-yd run (Matt Bryant kick), 1:49.

2nd Quarter: NYG—Brandon Jacobs 5-yd pass from Eli Manning (Lawrence Tynes kick), 10:02; NYG—Jacobs 8-yd run (Tynes kick), 4:06.

3rd Quarter: NYG—Tynes 25-yd FG, 9:56.

4th Quarter: NYG—Amani Toomer 4-yd pass from Manning (Tynes kick), 8:03; TB—Alex Smith 6-yd pass from Jeff Garcia (Bryant kick), 3:25.

NFL Playoffs (Cont.)
DIVISIONAL PLAYOFFS

AFC

Patriots, 31-20

Jacksonville (12-5)	7	7	3	3—	**20**
New England (16-0)	7	7	14	3—	**31**

Date—Jan. 12. **Att**—68,756. **Time**—2:48.

1st Quarter: JAX—Matt Jones 8-yd pass from David Garrard (Josh Scobee kick), 10:50; NE—Ben Watson 3-yd pass from Tom Brady (Stephen Gostkowski kick), 5:01.

2nd Quarter: NE—Laurence Maroney 1-yd run (Gostkowski kick), 14:57; JAX—Ernest Wilford 6-yd pass from Garrard (Scobee kick), 7:46.

3rd Quarter: NE—Wes Welker 6-yd pass from Tom Brady (Gostkowski kick), 8:49; JAX—Scobee 39-yd FG, 4:04; NE—Watson 9-yd pass from Brady (Gostkowski kick), 0:49.

4th Quarter: JAX—Scobee 25-yd FG, 9:44; NE—Gostkowski 35-yd FG, 6:39.

Chargers, 28-24

San Diego (12-5)	0	7	14	7—	**28**
Indianapolis (13-3)	7	3	7	7—	**24**

Date—Jan. 13. **Att**—56,950. **Time**—3:12.

1st Quarter: IND—Dallas Clark 25-yd pass from Peyton Manning (Adam Vinatieri kick), 9:13.

2nd Quarter: SD—Vincent Jackson 14-yd pass from Philip Rivers (Nate Kaeding kick), 8:38; IND—Vinatieri 46-yd FG, 5:10.

3rd Quarter: SD—Chris Chambers 30-yd pass from Rivers (Kaeding kick), 11:33; IND—Reggie Wayne 9-yd pass from Manning (Vinatieri kick), 2:53; SD—Darren Sproles 56-yd pass from Rivers (Kaeding kick), 0:00.

4th Quarter: IND—Anthony Gonzalez 55-yd pass from Manning (Vinatieri kick), 10:07; SD—Billy Volek 1-yd run (Kaeding kick), 4:50.

NFC

Packers, 42-20

Seattle (11-6)	14	3	3	0—	**20**
Green Bay (13-3)	14	14	7	7—	**42**

Date—Jan. 12. **Att**—72,168. **Time**—2:58.

1st Quarter: SEA—Shaun Alexander 1-yd run (Josh Brown kick), 14:40; SEA—Bobby Engram 11-yd pass from Matt Hasselbeck (Brown kick), 10:59; GB—Greg Jennings 15-yd pass from Brett Favre (Mason Crosby kick); GB—Ryan Grant 1-yd run (Crosby kick), 1:02.

2nd Quarter: GB—Jennings 2-yd pass from Favre (Crosby kick), 13:22; SEA—Brown 29-yd FG, 7:18; GB—Grant 3-yd run (Crosby kick), 0:26.

3rd Quarter: GB—Brandon Jackson 13-yd pass from Favre (Crosby kick), 10:25; SEA—Brown 27-yd FG, 2:46.

4th Quarter: GB—Grant 1-yd run (Crosby kick), 13:26.

Giants, 21-17

NY Giants (11-6)	7	7	0	7—	**21**
Dallas (13-3)	0	14	3	0—	**17**

Date—Jan. 13. **Att**—63,660. **Time**—3:05.

1st Quarter: NYG—Amani Toomer 52-yd pass from Eli Manning (Lawrence Tynes kick), 11:50.

2nd Quarter: DAL—Terrell Owens 5-yd pass from Tony Romo (Nick Folk kick), 14:56; DAL—Marion Barber 1-yd run (Folk kick), 0:53; NYG—Toomer 4-yd pass from Manning (Tynes kick), 0:07.

3rd Quarter: DAL—Folk 34-yd FG, 6:53.

4th Quarter: NYG—Brandon Jacobs 1-yd run (Tynes kick), 13:29.

CONFERENCE CHAMPIONSHIPS

AFC

Patriots, 21-12

San Diego (13-5)	3	6	3	0—	**12**
New England (17-0)	0	14	0	7—	**21**

Date—Jan. 20. **Att**—68,756. **Time**—2:55.

1st Quarter: SD—Nate Kaeding 26-yd FG, 2:55.

2nd Quarter: NE—Laurence Maroney 1-yd run (Stephen Gostkowski kick), 13:48; SD—Kaeding 23-yd FG, 9:14; NE—Jabar Gaffney 12-yd pass from Tom Brady (Gostkowski kick), 3:51; SD—Kaeding 40-yd FG, 0:08.

3rd Quarter: SD—Kaeding 24-yd FG, 8:36.

4th Quarter: NE—Wes Welker 6-yd pass from Brady (Gostkowski kick), 12:15.

Giants, 23-20 (OT)

NY Giants (12-6)	3	3	14	0	3—	**23**
Green Bay (14-3)	0	10	7	3	0—	**20**

Date—Jan. 20. **Att**—72,740. **Time**—3:33.

1st Quarter: NYG—Lawrence Tynes 29-yd FG, 4:50.

2nd Quarter: NYG—Tynes 37-yd FG, 11:41; GB—Donald Driver 90-yd pass from Brett Favre (Mason Crosby kick), 11:18; GB—Crosby 36-yd FG, 1:30.

3rd Quarter: NYG—Brandon Jacobs 1-yd run (Tynes kick), 7:56; GB—Donald Lee 12-yd pass from Favre (Crosby kick), 5:00; NYG—Ahmad Bradshaw 4-yd run (Tynes kick), 2:12.

4th Quarter: GB—Crosby 37-yd FG, 11:46.

Overtime: NYG—Tynes 47-yd FG, 12:25.

Super Bowl XLII

Sunday, Feb. 3, 2008 at University of Phoenix Stadium in Glendale, Arizona

NY Giants (13-6)	.3	0	0	14—	**17**
New England (18-0)	.0	7	0	7—	**14**

1st Quarter

NYG—Lawrence Tynes 32-yd FG, 5:01. Drive: 63 yards in 16 plays. Key play: Plaxico Burress 14-yd pass from Eli Manning to NYG 42.

2nd Quarter

NE—Laurence Maroney 1-yd run (Stephen Gostkowski kick), 14:57. Drive: 56 yards in 12 plays. Key play: NYG pass interference on Antonio Pierce on 3rd and 10 to NYG 1.

4th Quarter

NYG—David Tyree 5-yd pass from Manning (Tynes kick), 11:05. Drive: 80 yards in 6 plays. Key play: Kevin Boss 45-yd pass from Manning to NE 35.

NE—Randy Moss 6-yd pass from Tom Brady (Gostkowski kick), 2:42. Drive: 80 yards in 12 plays. Key play: Kevin Faulk 12-yd pass from Brady to NYG 6.

NYG—Burress 13-yd pass from Manning (Tynes kick), 0:35. Drive: 83 yards in 12 plays. Key play: Tyree 32-yd pass from Manning on 3rd and 5 to NE 24.

Favorite: Patriots by 12 **Attendance:** 71,101
Field: Grass **Time:** 3:35
Weather: Roof closed **TV Rating:** 43.3/65 share (FOX)

Most Valuable Player
Eli Manning, NY Giants, QB
19-34 for 255 yards, 2 TD, 1 int

Team Statistics

	Giants	Patriots
First downs	.17	22
Rushing	.4	3
Passing	.13	17
Penalty	.0	2
3rd down efficiency	.8/16	7/14
4th down efficiency	.1/1	0/2
Total offense (net yards)	.338	274
Plays	.63	69
Average gain	.5.4	4.0
Rushes/yards	.26/91	16/45
Yards per rush	.3.5	2.8
Passing yards (net)	.247	229
Times sacked/yards lost	.3/8	5/37
Passing yards (gross)	.255	266
Completions/attempts	.19/34	29/48
Yards per pass play	.6.7	4.3
Times intercepted	.1	0
Return yardage	.64	132
Punt returns/yards	.3/25	1/15
Kickoff returns/yards	.2/39	4/94
Interceptions/yards	.0/0	1/23
Fumbles/lost	.2/0	1/1
Penalties/yards	.4/36	5/35
Punts/average	.4/39.0	4/43.8
Punts blocked	.0	0
Field Goals made/attempted	.1/1	0/0
Time of possession	.30:27	29:33

Individual Statistics

New York Giants

Passing
	Att	Cmp	Pct.	Yds	TD	Int	Rate
Eli Manning	.34	19	55.9	255	2	1	87.3

Receiving
	No	Yds	Avg	Long	TD
Amani Toomer	.6	84	14.0	38	0
Steve Smith	.5	50	10.0	17	0
David Tyree	.3	43	14.3	32	1
Plaxico Burress	.2	27	13.5	14	1
Kevin Boss	.1	45	45.0	45	0
Madison Hedgecock	.1	3	3.0	3	0
Ahmad Bradshaw	.1	3	3.0	3	0
TOTAL	.19	255	13.4	45	2

Rushing
	Car	Yds	Avg	Long	TD
Ahmad Bradshaw	.9	45	5.0	13	0
Brandon Jacobs	.14	42	3.0	7	0
Eli Manning	.3	4	1.3	5	0
TOTAL	.26	91	3.5	13	0

Field Goals
	20-29	30-39	40-49	50-59	Total
Lawrence Tynes	.0-0	1-1	0-0	0-0	1-1

Punting
	No	Yds	Avg	Long	In20	Blk
Jeff Feagles	.4	156	39.0	55	2	0

Punt Returns
	Ret	Yds	Avg	Long	FC	TD
R.W. McQuarters	.3	25	8.3	16	0	0

Kickoff Returns
	Ret	Yds	Avg	Long	FC	TD
Domenik Hixon	.2	39	19.5	25	0	0

Interceptions
none

Sacks
Justin Tuck	.2.0
Kawika Mitchell	.1.0
Michael Strahan	.1.0
Jay Alford	.1.0

Most Tackles (solo + asst)
James Butler	.10
Antonio Pierce	.10

New England Patriots

Passing
	Att	Cmp	Pct.	Yds	TD	Int	Rate
Tom Brady	.48	29	60.4	266	1	0	82.5

Receiving
	No	Yds	Avg	Long	TD
Wes Welker	.11	103	9.4	19	0
Kevin Faulk	.7	52	7.4	14	0
Randy Moss	.5	64	12.4	18	1
Donte' Stallworth	.3	34	11.3	18	0
Laurence Maroney	.2	12	6.0	8	0
Kyle Brady	.1	3	3.0	3	0
TOTAL	.29	266	9.2	19	1

Rushing
	Car	Yds	Avg	Long	TD
Laurence Maroney	.14	36	2.6	9	1
Kevin Faulk	.1	7	7.0	7	0
Heath Evans	.1	2	2.0	2	0
TOTAL	.16	45	2.8	9	1

Field Goals
none

Punting
	No	Yds	Avg	Long	In20	Blk
Chris Hanson	.4	175	43.8	49	0	0

Punt Returns
	Ret	Yds	Avg	Long	FC	TD
Wes Welker	.1	15	15.0	15	1	0
Kevin Faulk	.0	0	0.0	—	1	0

Kickoff Returns
	Ret	Yds	Avg	Long	FC	TD
Laurence Maroney	.4	94	23.5	43	0	0

Interceptions
	No	Yds	Avg	Long	TD
Ellis Hobbs	.1	23	23.0	23	0

Sacks
Adalius Thomas	.2.0
Jarvis Green	.1.0

Most Tackles (solo + asst)
Rodney Harrison	.12

Super Bowl Finalists' Playoff Statistics

New York Giants (4-0)

Passing (5 att)

	Att	Cmp	Pct.	Yds	TD	Rating
Eli Manning	119	72	60.5	854	6	95.7

Interceptions: Manning 1.

Top Receivers

	No	Yds	Avg	Long	TD
Amani Toomer	21	280	13.3	52-td	3
Plaxico Burress	18	221	12.3	32	1
Steve Smith	14	152	10.9	22	0
Kevin Boss	5	90	18.0	45	0
David Tyree	4	47	11.8	32	1
Brandon Jacobs	4	29	7.3	11	1
Ahmad Bradshaw	4	27	6.8	9	0

Top Rushers

	Car	Yds	Avg	Long	TD
Ahmad Bradshaw	48	208	4.3	13	1
Brandon Jacobs	62	197	3.2	12	3

Most Touchdowns

	TD	Run	Rec	Ret	Pts
Brandon Jacobs	4	3	1	0	24
Amani Toomer	3	0	3	0	18

Three tied with 1 TD each for 6 pts.
2-Pt. Conversions: (0-0).

Kicking

	PAT/Att	FG/Att	Lg	Pts
Lawrence Tynes	10/10	5/7	47	25

Punts (5 or more)

	No	Yds	Avg	Long	In20
Jeff Feagles	19	767	40.4	55	5

Interceptions

R.W. McQuarters	3
Corey Webster	2

Most Sacks

Michael Strahan	2.0
Justin Tuck	2.0
Kawika Mitchell	2.0

New England Patriots (2-1)

Passing (5 att)

	Att	Cmp	Pct.	Yds	TD	Rating
Tom Brady	109	77	70.6	737	6	96.0

Interceptions: Brady 3.

Top Receivers

	No	Yds	Avg	Long	TD
Wes Welker	27	213	7.9	19	2
Kevin Faulk	20	170	8.5	14	0
Donte' Stallworth	8	113	14.1	53	0
Randy Moss	7	94	13.4	18	1
Laurence Maroney	5	61	12.2	33	0
Jabar Gaffney	4	38	9.5	13	1
Ben Watson	3	20	6.7	9	2

Top Rushers

	Car	Yds	Avg	Long	TD
Laurence Maroney	61	280	4.6	29	3
Kevin Faulk	6	24	4.0	8	0

Most Touchdowns

	TD	Run	Rec	Ret	Pts
Laurence Maroney	3	3	0	0	18
Ben Watson	2	0	2	0	12
Wes Welker	2	0	2	0	12

2-Pt. Conversions: (0-0).

Kicking

	PAT/Att	FG/Att	Lg	Pts
Stephen Gostkowski	9/9	1/2	35	12

Punts (5 or more)

	No	Yds	Avg	Long	In20
Chris Hanson	9	365	40.6	49	1

Interceptions

Ellis Hobbs	2
Asante Samuel	1
Rodney Harrison	1

Most Sacks

Adalius Thomas	2.0

Three tied with 1 each.

NFL Playoff Leaders

Passing Efficiency
(Minimum of 25 attempts)

	Gm	Att	Cmp	Cmp%	Yards	Avg Gain	TD	TD%	Int	Int%	Rating
Brett Favre, GB	2	58	37	63.8	409	7.1	5	8.6	2	3.4	99.0
Peyton Manning, Ind	1	48	33	68.8	402	8.4	3	6.3	2	4.2	97.7
Tom Brady, NE	3	109	77	70.6	737	6.8	6	5.5	3	2.8	96.0
Eli Manning, NYG	4	119	72	60.5	854	7.2	6	5.0	1	0.8	95.7
Philip Rivers, SD	3	86	52	60.5	767	8.9	4	4.7	4	4.7	85.8

Receptions

	No	Yds	Avg	Long	TD
Wes Welker, NE	27	213	7.9	19	2
Amani Toomer, NYG	21	280	13.3	52-td	3
Kevin Faulk, NE	20	170	8.5	14	0
Vincent Jackson, SD	18	300	16.7	34	2
Plaxico Burress, NYG	18	221	12.3	32	1

Kicking

	PAT	FG	Long	Pts
Lawrence Tynes, NYG	10/10	5/7	47	25
Nate Kaeding, SD	6/6	5/7	40	21
Josh Brown, Sea	5/5	4/4	50	17
Josh Scobee, Jax	6/6	3/4	39	15
Mason Crosby, GB	8/8	2/2	37	14

Rushing

	No	Yds	Avg	Long	TD
Laurence Maroney, NE	61	280	4.6	29	3
Ryan Grant, GB	40	230	5.8	43	3
Ahmad Bradshaw, NYG	48	208	4.3	13	1
Brandon Jacobs, NYG	62	197	3.2	12	3
Michael Turner, SD	43	164	3.8	19	0

Interceptions

	No	Yds	Long	TD
R.W. McQuarters, NYG	3	11	11	0
Antonio Cromartie, SD	2	37	30	0
Drayton Florence, SD	2	17	10	0
Ellis Hobbs, NE	2	20	23	0
LaRon Landry, Wash	2	2	2	0
Rashean Mathis, Jax	2	64	63-td	1
Corey Webster, NYG	2	9	9	0

Touchdowns

	TD	Rush	Rec	Ret	Pts
Brandon Jacobs, NYG	4	3	1	0	24
Amani Toomer, NYG	3	0	3	0	18
Ryan Grant, GB	3	3	0	0	18
Laurence Maroney, NE	3	3	0	0	18

Six tied with 2 TD for 12 pts.

Sacks

Eight tied with 2.0 each.

NFL Pro Bowl

58th NFL Pro Bowl Game and 38th AFC-NFC contest (series is tied,19-19). **Date:** Feb. 10, 2008 at Aloha Stadium in Honolulu. **Coaches:** Norv Turner, SD (AFC) and Mike McCarthy, GB (NFC). **Most Valuable Player:** RB Adrian Peterson, Min. (16 rushes for 129 yards and 2 TD). **Attendance:** 50,044. **TV Rating:** 6.3/12 (FOX). **Time:** 3:03.

AFC	17	10	3—	30
NFC	7	14	7	14—	42

1st Quarter: AFC—Lorenzo Neal 1-yd run (Rob Bironas kick), 10:59; **NFC**—Larry Fitzgerald 6-yd pass from Tony Romo (Nick Folk kick), 7:08; **AFC**—T.J. Houshmandzadeh 16-yd pass from Peyton Manning (Bironas kick), 2:42; **AFC**—Bironas 33-yd FG, 0:48.

2nd Quarter: AFC—Houshmandzadeh 1-yd pass from Ben Roethlisberger (Bironas kick), 12:08; **NFC**—Terrell Owens 6-yd pass from Romo (Folk kick), 7:58; **AFC**—Bironas 48-yd FG, 3:30; **NFC**—Chris Cooley 17-yd pass from Matt Hasselbeck (Folk kick), 0:28.

3rd Quarter: NFC—Adrian Peterson 17-yd run (Folk kick), 9:49; **AFC**—Bironas 28-yd FG, 6:58.

4th Quarter: NFC—Owens 6-yd pass from Jeff Garcia (Folk kick), 12:47; **NFC**—Peterson 6-yd run (Folk kick), 2:43.

Individual Statistics

AFC

Passing	Att	Cmp	Pct.	Yds	TD	Int	Rate
Derek Anderson	.26	10	38.5	103	0	1	34.6
Peyton Manning	.16	11	68.8	147	1	0	118.5
Ben Roethlisberger	9	5	55.6	42	1	0	104.9

Receiving Leaders	No	Yds	Avg	Long	TD
Reggie Wayne	.5	55	11.0	17	0
Tony Gonzalez	.4	79	19.8	29	0
T.J. Houshmandzadeh	.4	44	11.0	16-td	2
Joseph Addai	.3	16	5.3	12	0
Lorenzo Neal	.3	8	2.7	5	0
Braylon Edwards	.2	40	20.0	31	0
Chad Johnson	.2	30	15.0	18	0
Willis McGahee	.2	9	4.5	7	0

Rushing Leaders	Car	Yds	Avg	Long	TD
Ben Roethlisberger	.1	18	18.0	18	0
Fred Taylor	.3	15	5.0	11	0
Willis McGahee	.2	6	3.0	3	0

Interceptions	No	Yds	Avg	Long	TD
Antonio Cromartie	.2	77	38.5	56	0

Sacks		Most Tackles	
Kyle Vanden Bosch	.1.0	Antoine Bethea	.9

NFC

Passing	Att	Cmp	Pct.	Yds	TD	Int	Rate
Tony Romo	.16	9	56.3	87	2	1	85.2
Jeff Garcia	.10	8	80.0	117	1	1	109.2
Matt Hasselbeck	.9	7	77.8	78	1	0	139.8
Andy Lee	.1	1	100.0	11	0	0	112.5

Receiving Leaders	No	Yds	Avg	Long	TD
Terrell Owens	.8	101	12.6	34	2
Chris Cooley	.3	41	13.7	17-yd	1
Jason Witten	.3	38	12.7	24	0
Larry Fitzgerald	.3	25	8.3	11	1
Donald Driver	.2	31	15.5	16	0
Torry Holt	.2	29	14.5	17	0
Brian Westbrook	.2	8	4.0	8	0

Rushing Leaders	Car	Yds	Avg	Long	TD
Adrian Peterson	.16	129	8.1	39	2
Marion Barber	.6	37	6.2	15	0
Brian Westbrook	.1	4	4.0	4	0

Interceptions	No	Yds	Avg	Long	TD
Darren Sharper	.1	0	0.0	0	0

Sacks		Most Tackles	
Aaron Kampman	.1.0	Marcus Trufant	.5
Osi Umenyiora	.1.0	Al Harris	.5

2007 All-NFL Team

The 2007 All-NFL team combining the All-Pro selections of the Associated Press, *The Sporting News (TSN)* and the Pro Football Writers of America/*Pro Football Weekly* (PFWA). Holdovers from the 2006 All-NFL Team in **bold** type.

Offense

Pos		Selectors
WR—	Randy Moss, New England	AP, TSN, PFWA
WR—	Terrell Owens, Dallas	AP, PFWA
WR—	Braylon Edwards, Cleveland	TSN
TE—	Jason Witten, Dallas	AP, TSN, PFWA
T—	Matt Light, New England	AP, PFWA
T—	**Walter Jones**, Seattle	AP, TSN, PFWA
T—	Jason Peters, Buffalo	TSN
G—	**Steve Hutchinson**, Minnesota	AP, TSN, PFWA
G—	**Alan Faneca**, Pittsburgh	AP
G—	Logan Mankins, New England	TSN, PFWA
C—	Jeff Saturday, Indianapolis	AP, PFWA
C—	Andre Gurode, Dallas	TSN
QB—	Tom Brady, New England	AP, TSN, PFWA
RB—	**LaDainian Tomlinson**, SD	AP, TSN, PFWA
RB—	Brian Westbrook, Philadelphia	AP, PFWA
RB—	Adrian Peterson, Minnesota	TSN
FB—	**Lorenzo Neal**, San Diego	AP

Defense

Pos		Selectors
DE—	Patrick Kerney, Seattle	AP, PFWA
DE—	Jared Allen, Kansas City	AP, TSN, PFWA
DE—	Mario Williams, Houston	TSN
DT—	**Kevin Williams**, Minnesota	AP, TSN, PFWA
DT—	Albert Haynesworth, Tennessee	AP, TSN, PFWA
LB—	Mike Vrabel, New England	AP, PFWA
LB—	DeMarcus Ware, Dallas	AP, TSN, PFWA
LB—	Lofa Tatupu, Seattle	AP
LB—	Patrick Willis, San Francisco	AP, TSN, PFWA
LB—	DeMeco Ryans, Houston	TSN
CB—	Antonio Cromartie, San Diego	AP, PFWA
CB—	Asante Samuel, New England	AP, TSN, PFWA
CB—	Marcus Trufant, Seattle	TSN
S—	Bob Sanders, Indianapolis	AP, TSN, PFWA
S—	**Ed Reed**, Baltimore	AP, TSN, PFWA

Specialists

Pos		Selectors
K—	Rob Bironas, Tennessee	AP, TSN, PFWA
P—	Andy Lee, San Francisco	AP, PFWA
P—	Shane Lechler, Oakland	TSN
ST—	Kassim Osgood, San Diego	PFWA

Pos		Selectors
KR—	**Devin Hester**, Chicago	AP
KR—	Josh Cribbs, Cleveland	TSN, PFWA
PR—	**Devin Hester**, Chicago	TSN, PFWA

Annual Awards

The NFL does not sanction any of the major postseason awards for players and coaches, but many are given out. Among the presenters for the 2007 regular season were AP, The Maxwell Football Club of Philadelphia (Bert Bell Award for player; Greasy Neale Award for coach), *The Sporting News* and the Pro Football Writers of America/Pro Football Weekly.

Most Valuable Player

Tom Brady, New England, QB . . . . . AP, *TSN*, Bell, PFWA

Offensive Player of the Year

Tom Brady, New England, QB . . . . AP, PFWA

Defensive Player of the Year

Bob Sanders, Indianapolis, S . . . . AP, PFWA

Coach of the Year

Bill Belichick, New England . . . . . . AP, *TSN*, PFWA, Neale

Rookies of the Year

NFL	Adrian Peterson, Minnesota	. . . . *TSN*
Offense	Adrian Peterson, Minnesota	. . . . . . AP, PFWA
Defense	Patrick Willis, San Francisco	. . . . . AP, PFWA

Comeback Players of the Year

Greg Ellis, Dallas . . . . .AP
Randy Moss, New England . . . . .PFWA

2008 NFL Draft

First and second round selections at the 73rd annual NFL Draft held April 26-27, 2008, at Radio City Music Hall in New York City. Twenty-two underclassmen were among the first 63 players chosen and are listed in capital LETTERS.

First Round

No	Team		Pos
1	Miami	Jake Long, Michigan	T
2	St. Louis	Chris Long, Virginia	DE
3	Atlanta	Matt Ryan, Boston College	QB
4	Oakland	DARREN McFADDEN, Arkansas	RB
5	Kansas City	Glenn Dorsey, LSU	DT
6	NY Jets	VERNON GHOLSTON, Ohio St.	LB
7	a-New Orleans	Sedrick Ellis, USC	DT
8	b-Jacksonville	DERRICK HARVEY, Florida	DE
9	Cincinnati	Keith Rivers, USC	LB
10	c-New England	JEROD MAYO, Tennessee	LB
11	Buffalo	Leodis McKelvin, Troy	DB
12	Denver	RYAN CLADY, Boise St.	T
13	Carolina	JONATHAN STEWART, Oregon	RB
14	Chicago	Chris Williams, Vanderbilt	T
15	d-Kansas City	BRANDEN ALBERT, Virginia	T
16	Arizona	D. Rodgers-Cromartie, Tenn. St.	DB
17	e-Detroit	Gosder Cherilus, Boston College	T
18	f-Baltimore	Joe Flacco, Delaware	QB
19	g-Carolina	Jeff Otah, Pittsburgh	T
20	Tampa Bay	AQIB TALIB, Kansas	DB
21	h-Atlanta	Sam Baker, USC	T
22	i-Dallas	FELIX JONES, Arkansas	RB
23	Pittsburgh . . .	RASHARD MENDENHALL, Illinois	RB
24	Tennessee	Chris Johnson, East Carolina	RB
25	j-Dallas	Mike Jenkins, South Florida	DB
26	k-Houston	Duane Brown, Virginia Tech	T
27	San Diego	Antoine Cason, Arizona	DB
28	l-Seattle	Lawrence Jackson, USC	DE
29	m-San Francisco . . .	Kentwan Balmer, N. Carolina	DT
30	n-NY Jets	Dustin Keller, Purdue	TE
31	New England	pick forfeited	
32	NY Giants	KENNY PHILLIPS, Miami	DB

Second Round

No	Team		Pos
33	Miami	PHILLIP MERLING, Clemson	DE
34	St. Louis	Donnie Avery, Houston	WR
35	o-Washington . .	DEVIN THOMAS, Michigan St.	WR
36	Kansas City . .	BRANDON FLOWERS, Va. Tech	DB
37	p-Green Bay	Jordy Nelson, Kansas St.	WR
38	Atlanta	CURTIS LOFTON, Oklahoma	LB
39	q-Seattle	John Carlson, Notre Dame	TE
40	San Francisco	CHILO RACHAL, USC	G
41	New Orleans	Tracy Porter, Indiana	DB
42	Buffalo	JAMES HARDY, Indiana	WR
43	Denver	Eddie Royal, Virginia Tech	WR
44	r-Minnesota	Tyrell Johnson, Arkansas St.	DB
45	Chicago	Matt Forte, Tulane	RB
46	Detroit	Jordon Dizon, Colorado	LB
47	Cincinnati .	Jerome Simpson, Coastal Carolina	WR
48	s-Philadelphia	Trevor Laws, Notre Dame	DT
49	t-Washington	Fred Davis, USC	TE
50	Philadelphia . .	DeSEAN JACKSON, California	WR
51	Arizona	CALAIS CAMPBELL, Miami-FL	DE
52	Washington	MALCOLM KELLY, Oklahoma	WR
53	u-Jacksonville	Quentin Groves, Auburn	DE
54	Pittsburgh	Limas Sweed, Texas	WR
55	Tennessee	Jason Jones, Eastern Mich.	DT
56	v-Baltimore	RAY RICE, Rutgers	RB
57	w-Green Bay	Brian Brohm, Louisville	QB
58	x-Miami	Chad Henne, Michigan	QB
59	y-Tampa Bay .	Dexter Jackson, Appalachian St.	WR
60	Indianapolis	Mike Pollak, Arizona St.	G
61	Green Bay	Patrick Lee, Auburn	DB
62	Dallas	MARTELLUS BENNETT, Texas A&M	TE
63	New England . . .	Terrence Wheatley, Colorado	DB
64	NY Giants	Terrell Thomas, USC	DB

a-from SF via NE; **b**-from Bal.; **c**-from NO; **d**-from Det.; **e**-from Min. via KC; **f**-from Hou.; **g**-from Phi.; **h**-from Wash.; **i**-from Cle.; **j**-from Sea.; **k**-from Jax. via Bal.; **l**-from Dal.; **m**-from Ind.; **n**-from GB; **o**-from Oak. via Atl.; **p**-from NYJ; **q**-from Bal.; **r**-from Car. via Phi.; **s**-from Min.; **t**-from Hou. via Atl.; **u**-from TB; **v**-from Sea.; **w**-from Cle.; **x**-from SD; **y**-from Jax.

2008 Draft By The Numbers

Through all seven rounds of the 2008 draft (252 players total).

By Position — Top 5		By School — Top 5		By Conference — Top 5	
1 Defensive Back 45		1 USC 10		1 SEC 35	
2 Wide Receiver 35		2 Virginia Tech 8		2 Pacific-10 34	
3 Linebacker 30		3 LSU 7		3 ACC 33	
4 Running Back 27		4 Three tied with 6 each.		4 Big 12 29	
5 OT & DE (tie) 23				5 Big Ten 28	

Arena Football
Final 2008 Standings

Division champions (*) and playoff qualifiers (†) are noted; top six teams from each conference advance to the playoffs.

American Conference
Central Division

	W	L	T	Pct.	PF	PA
*Chicago	11	5	0	.688	926	765
†Grand Rapids	6	10	0	.375	952	968
†Colorado	6	10	0	.375	847	909
Kansas City	3	13	0	.188	752	923

Western Division

	W	L	T	Pct.	PF	PA
*San Jose	11	5	0	.688	945	875
†Arizona	8	8	0	.500	842	906
†Utah	6	10	0	.375	940	959
Los Angeles	5	11	0	.313	847	1004

National Conference
Eastern Division

	W	L	T	Pct.	PF	PA
*Philadelphia	13	3	0	.813	992	810
†Dallas	12	4	0	.750	861	798
†Cleveland	9	7	0	.563	901	895
†New York	8	8	0	.500	822	819
Columbus	3	13	0	.188	750	893

Southern Division

	W	L	T	Pct.	PF	PA
*Georgia	10	6	0	.625	927	848
†Orlando	9	7	0	.563	881	898
Tampa Bay	8	8	0	.500	903	876
New Orleans	8	8	0	.500	893	835

Playoffs

Wild Card Round

American: Colorado 49 . . . . .at Utah 44
Grand Rapids 48 . . . . .at Arizona 41
National: New York 77 . . . . .at Dallas 63
at Cleveland 69 . . . . .Orlando 66

Division Round

American: at San Jose 64 . . . . .Colorado 51
Grand Rapids 58 . . . . .at Chicago 41
National: at Philadelphia 49 . . . . .New York 48
Cleveland 73 . . . . .at Georgia 70

Conference Championships

American: at San Jose 81 . . . . .Grand Rapids 55
National: at Philadelphia 70 . . . . .Cleveland 35

2008 All-Arena First Team

Holdovers from the 2007 All-Arena First Team in **bold**.

Offense		**Defense**	
QB	Matt D'Orazio, Phi.	DL	Aaron McConnell, Col.
FB	Marlion Jackson, Cle.	DL	**C. Weatherington**, Dal.
WR	**Chris Jackson**, Phi.	DL	Henry Taylor, NY
WR	Huey Whittaker, Utah	LB	Steve Watson, SJ
WR	T.T. Toliver, Orl.	LB	**DeJuan Alfonzo**, Chi.
OL	**Phil Bogle**, Phi.	DB	Dennison Robinson, Chi.
OL	Martin Bibla, Phi.	DB	Marquis Floyd, SJ
C	Will Rabatin, Clb.	DB	Billy Parker, NY
K	A.J. Haglund, SJ		

Annual Awards

Ironman of the Year . . . . .Will Pettis, Dallas, WR/DB
Offensive Player of the Year . . . . .Chris Jackson, Phi., WR
Defensive Player of the Year . .Dennison Robinson, Chi., DB
Lineman of the Year . . . .Colston Weatherington, Dallas, DL
Rookies of the Year . . . . . .Donovan Morgan, Chicago, WR
Coach of the Year . . . . .Mike Wilpolt, Cleveland
Al Lucas Hero Award . . . . . .Mike Brown, Philadelphia, DB

ArenaBowl XXII

July 27, 2008 at New Orleans Arena, New Orleans, LA

	1	2	3	4—	F
San Jose SaberCats (13-5)	14	13	7	22—	56
Philadelphia Soul (15-3)	14	23	9	13—	59

1st Quarter: SJ—Rodney Wright 8-yd pass from Mark Grieb (AJ Haglund kick), 11:21; **PHI**—Brent Holmes 34-yd pass from Matt D'Orazio (Connor Hughes kick), 9:30; **SJ**—Jason Geathers 5-yd pass from Grieb (Haglund kick), 5:30; **PHI**—Chris Jackson 34-yd pass from D'Orazio (Hughes kick), 2:59.

2nd Quarter: SJ—Geathers 22-yd pass from Grieb (kick failed), 14:54; **PHI**—Jackson 13-yd pass from D'Orazio (kick failed), 8:59; **PHI**—Larry Brackins 2-yd pass from D'Orazio (Hughes kick), 5:31; **PHI**—D'Orazio 8-yd run (Hughes kick), 0:54; **SJ**—Geathers 23-yd pass from Grieb (Haglund kick), 0:29; **PHI**—Hughes 20-yd FG, 0:00.

3rd Quarter: PHI—Jackson 32-yd pass from D'Orazio (Hughes kick), 7:56; **PHI**—Raheem Orr safety; **SJ**—Geathers 12-yd pass from Grieb (Haglund kick).

4th Quarter: PHI—Brackins 7-yd pass from D'Orazio (kick failed), 6:49; **SJ**—Brian Johnson 3-yd pass from Grieb (Cleannord Saintil pass from Grieb), 2:13; **PHI**—Phil Bogle 2-yd pass from D'Orazio (Hughes kick); **SJ**—Wright 26-yd pass from Grieb (rush failed), 0:28; **SJ**—Geathers 14-yd pass from Grieb (Geathers rush), 0:17.

Attendance: 17,244. **Time:** 3:05.

Most Valuable Player

Matt D'Orazio, Philadelphia, QB
26-43 for 302 yards, 7 TD, 1 int

Arena Football (Cont.)
Regular Season Individual Leaders
Passing Yards

	Att	Cmp	Cmp Pct	Yds	Yds/ Att	TD	TD Pct	Int	Int Pct	Rating
Matt D'Orazio, Phi	.416	301	72.4	3331	8.01	72	17.3	4	1.0	131.3
Raymond Philyaw, Cle	.525	358	68.2	4287	8.17	83	15.8	10	1.9	124.5
Joe Germaine, Utah	.603	411	68.2	4859	8.06	97	16.1	13	2.2	123.1
Russ Michna, Chi	.349	239	68.5	2721	7.80	57	16.3	7	2.0	122.9
Chris Greisen, Geo	.584	398	68.2	4946	8.47	97	16.6	17	2.9	121.6

Receptions

	No	Yards	Avg	TD
Derek Lee, Clb	141	1755	12.4	31
Chris Jackson, Phi	140	1719	12.3	49
Jason Willis, NY	135	1544	11.4	30
Aaron Boone, Utah	135	1527	11.3	23
Rodney Wright, SJ	134	1457	10.9	24
Jerel Myers, KC	134	1304	9.7	19

Rushing

	Car	Yards	Avg	TD
Marlion Jackson, Cle	108	356	3.3	23
Josh White, Dal	88	259	2.9	8
Dan Alexander, Chi	73	252	3.5	12
Dawan Moss, KC	86	242	2.8	10
Matt D'Orazio, Phi	54	227	4.2	11

Touchdowns

	TD	Rus	Rec	Ret	Pts
Otis Amey, Cle	50	1	48	1	302
Chris Jackson, Phi	49	0	49	0	294
Huey Whittaker, Utah	40	8	32	0	244
Kenny Higgins, GR	39	5	34	0	248
J.J. McKelvey, Utah	38	0	38	0	228

Kicking

	PAT	FG	Long	Pts
A.J. Haglund, SJ	116/124	21/25	47	179
Brian Gowins, GR	119/126	10/17	50	149
Jason Balt, Cle	99/118	16/21	46	147
Seth Marler, TB	112/125	11/19	41	145
Connor Hughes, Phi	123/136	5/14	34	138

Canadian Football League
Final 2007 Standings

Division champions (*) and playoff qualifiers (†) are noted. Wins are worth two points in the standings, ties are worth one point.

East Division

	W	L	T	Pts	PF	PA
*Toronto	11	7	0	22	440	336
†Winnipeg	10	7	1	21	439	404
†Montreal	8	10	0	16	398	433
Hamilton	3	15	0	6	315	514

West Division

	W	L	T	Pts	PF	PA
*British Columbia	14	3	1	29	542	379
†Saskatchewan	12	6	0	24	530	434
†Calgary	7	10	1	15	473	527
Edmonton	5	12	1	11	399	509

Playoffs

Division Semifinals (Nov. 11)

East:	at Winnipeg 24	Montreal 22
West:	at Saskatchewan 26	Calgary 24

Division Championships (Nov. 18)

East:	Winnipeg 19	at Toronto 9
West:	Saskatchewan 26	at British Columbia 17

2007 CFL All-Star Team

Holdovers from the 2006 All-Star Team in **bold**.

Offense

QB	Kerry Joseph, Sask.	
R	Derick Armstrong, Win.	
R	Jason Clermont, BC	
R	Terrence Edwards, Win.	
R	**Geroy Simon**, BC	
RB	Charles Roberts, Win.	
RB	Joe Smith, BC	
T	Dan Goodspeed, Win.	
T	**Rob Murphy**, BC	
G	Kelly Bates, BC	
G	**Scott Flory**, Mon.	
C	**Jeremy O'Day**, Sask.	

Special Teams

K	Nick Setta, Ham.	
ST	Ian Smart, BC	

Defense

DE	Jonathan Brown, Tor.
DE	Cameraon Wake, BC
DT	**Doug Brown**, Win.
DT	**Tyrone Williams**, BC
LB	Kevin Eiben, Tor.
LB	Zeke Moreno, Ham.
LB	**Barrin Simpson**, Win.
DB	Ryan Phillips, BC
DB	Kenny Wheaton, Tor.
CB	**Byron Parker**, Tor.
CB	Jordan Younger, Tor.
S	Orlondo Steinauer, Tor.

P   Damon Duval, Mon.

95th Grey Cup Championship
November 25, 2007
at Rogers Centre in Toronto, Ontario
(Att: 52,230)

Saskatchewan	0	10	6	7—	23
Winnipeg	3	4	7	5—	19

MVP: James Johnson, Saskatchewan, DB
(5 tackles, 3 interceptions, 1 touchdown)

Most Outstanding Awards

Player	Kerry Joseph, Saskatchewan, QB
Canadian	Jason Clermont, British Columbia, SB
Lineman	Rob Murphy, British Columbia, OG
Defensive Player	Cameron Wake, British Columbia, DE
Rookie	Cameron Wake, British Columbia, DE
Special Teams	Ian Smart, British Columbia, RB
Coach (Annis Stukus award)	Kent Austin, Saskatchewan
Tom Pate Award (Sportsmanship)	Milt Stegall, Winnipeg, SB

1920-2008
Through the Years

SPORTS ALMANAC

The Super Bowl

The first AFL-NFL World Championship Game, as it was originally called, was played seven months after the two leagues agreed to merge in June of 1966. It became the Super Bowl (complete with roman numerals) by the third game in 1969. The Super Bowl winner has been presented the Vince Lombardi Trophy since 1971. Lombardi, whose Green Bay teams won the first two title games, died in 1970. NFL champions (1966-69) and NFC champions (since 1970) are listed in CAPITAL letters.

Multiple winners: Dallas, Pittsburgh and San Francisco (5); Green Bay, New England, NY Giants, Oakland-LA Raiders and Washington (3); Baltimore-Indianapolis Colts, Denver and Miami (2).

Bowl	Date	Winner	Head Coach	Score	Loser	Head Coach	Site
I	1/15/67	GREEN BAY	Vince Lombardi	35-10	Kansas City	Hank Stram	Los Angeles
II	1/14/68	GREEN BAY	Vince Lombardi	33-14	Oakland	John Rauch	Miami
III	1/12/69	NY Jets	Weeb Ewbank	16-7	BALT. COLTS	Don Shula	Miami
IV	1/11/70	Kansas City	Hank Stram	23-7	MINNESOTA	Bud Grant	New Orleans
V	1/17/71	Balt. Colts	Don McCafferty	16-13	DALLAS	Tom Landry	Miami
VI	1/16/72	DALLAS	Tom Landry	24-3	Miami	Don Shula	New Orleans
VII	1/14/73	Miami	Don Shula	14-7	WASHINGTON	George Allen	Los Angeles
VIII	1/13/74	Miami	Don Shula	24-7	MINNESOTA	Bud Grant	Houston
IX	1/12/75	Pittsburgh	Chuck Noll	16-6	MINNESOTA	Bud Grant	New Orleans
X	1/18/76	Pittsburgh	Chuck Noll	21-17	DALLAS	Tom Landry	Miami
XI	1/9/77	Oakland	John Madden	32-14	MINNESOTA	Bud Grant	Pasadena
XII	1/15/78	DALLAS	Tom Landry	27-10	Denver	Red Miller	New Orleans
XIII	1/21/79	Pittsburgh	Chuck Noll	35-31	DALLAS	Tom Landry	Miami
XIV	1/20/80	Pittsburgh	Chuck Noll	31-19	LA RAMS	Ray Malavasi	Pasadena
XV	1/25/81	Oakland	Tom Flores	27-10	PHILADELPHIA	Dick Vermeil	New Orleans
XVI	1/24/82	SAN FRANCISCO	Bill Walsh	26-21	Cincinnati	Forrest Gregg	Pontiac, MI
XVII	1/30/83	WASHINGTON	Joe Gibbs	27-17	Miami	Don Shula	Pasadena
XVIII	1/22/84	LA Raiders	Tom Flores	38-9	WASHINGTON	Joe Gibbs	Tampa
XIX	1/20/85	SAN FRANCISCO	Bill Walsh	38-16	Miami	Don Shula	Stanford
XX	1/26/86	CHICAGO	Mike Ditka	46-10	New England	Raymond Berry	New Orleans
XXI	1/25/87	NY GIANTS	Bill Parcells	39-20	Denver	Dan Reeves	Pasadena
XXII	1/31/88	WASHINGTON	Joe Gibbs	42-10	Denver	Dan Reeves	San Diego
XXIII	1/22/89	SAN FRANCISCO	Bill Walsh	20-16	Cincinnati	Sam Wyche	Miami
XXIV	1/28/90	SAN FRANCISCO	George Seifert	55-10	Denver	Dan Reeves	New Orleans
XXV	1/27/91	NY GIANTS	Bill Parcells	20-19	Buffalo	Marv Levy	Tampa
XXVI	1/26/92	WASHINGTON	Joe Gibbs	37-24	Buffalo	Marv Levy	Minneapolis
XXVII	1/31/93	DALLAS	Jimmy Johnson	52-17	Buffalo	Marv Levy	Pasadena
XXVIII	1/30/94	DALLAS	Jimmy Johnson	30-13	Buffalo	Marv Levy	Atlanta
XXIX	1/29/95	SAN FRANCISCO	George Seifert	49-26	San Diego	Bobby Ross	Miami
XXX	1/28/96	DALLAS	Barry Switzer	27-17	Pittsburgh	Bill Cowher	Tempe, AZ
XXXI	1/26/97	GREEN BAY	Mike Holmgren	35-21	New England	Bill Parcells	New Orleans
XXXII	1/25/98	Denver	Mike Shanahan	31-24	GREEN BAY	Mike Holmgren	San Diego
XXXIII	1/31/99	Denver	Mike Shanahan	34-19	ATLANTA	Dan Reeves	Miami
XXXIV	1/30/00	ST.L RAMS	Dick Vermeil	23-16	Tennessee	Jeff Fisher	Atlanta
XXXV	1/28/01	Balt. Ravens	Brian Billick	34-7	NY GIANTS	Jim Fassel	Tampa
XXXVI	2/3/02	New England	Bill Belichick	20-17	ST.L RAMS	Mike Martz	New Orleans
XXXVII	1/26/03	TAMPA BAY	Jon Gruden	48-21	Oakland	Bill Callahan	San Diego
XXXVIII	2/1/04	New England	Bill Belichick	32-29	CAROLINA	John Fox	Houston
XXXIX	2/6/05	New England	Bill Belichick	24-21	PHILADELPHIA	Andy Reid	Jacksonville
XL	2/5/06	Pittsburgh	Bill Cowher	21-10	SEATTLE	Mike Holmgren	Detroit
XLI	2/4/07	Indianapolis	Tony Dungy	29-17	CHICAGO	Lovie Smith	Miami
XLII	2/3/08	NY GIANTS	Tom Coughlin	17-14	New England	Bill Belichick	Glendale, AZ

Future Super Bowl Sites

Game	Date	Stadium	Location
Super Bowl XLIII	February 1, 2009	Raymond James Stadium	Tampa, Florida
Super Bowl XLIV	February 7, 2010	Dolphin Stadium	Miami, Florida
Super Bowl XLV	February 6, 2011	Dallas Cowboys new stadium	Arlington, Texas
Super Bowl XLVI	February 5, 2012	Lucas Oil Stadium	Indianapolis, Indiana

Super Bowl Appearances

App		W	L	Pct	PF	PA	App		W	L	Pct	PF	PA
8	Dallas	.5	3	.625	221	132	3	LA/St.L Rams	.1	2	.333	59	67
6	Pittsburgh	.5	1	.833	141	110	2	Chicago	.1	1	.500	63	39
6	New England	.3	3	.500	121	165	2	Kansas City	.1	1	.500	33	42
6	Denver	.2	4	.333	115	206	2	Cincinnati	.0	2	.000	37	46
5	San Francisco	.5	0	1.000	188	89	2	Philadelphia	.0	2	.000	31	51
5	Oak./LA Raiders	.3	2	.600	132	114	1	Baltimore Ravens	.1	0	1.000	34	7
5	Washington	.3	2	.600	122	103	1	NY Jets	.1	0	1.000	16	7
5	Miami	.2	3	.400	74	103	1	Tampa Bay	.1	0	1.000	48	21
4	Green Bay	.3	1	.750	127	76	1	Atlanta	.0	1	.000	19	34
4	NY Giants	.3	1	.750	83	87	1	Carolina	.0	1	.000	29	32
4	Buffalo	.0	4	.000	73	139	1	San Diego	.0	1	.000	26	49
4	Minnesota	.0	4	.000	34	95	1	Seattle	.0	1	.000	10	21
3	Bal./Ind. Colts	.2	1	.667	52	46	1	Tennessee	.0	1	.000	16	23

Pete Rozelle Award (MVP)

The Most Valuable Player in the Super Bowl. Currently selected by a panel made up of national pro football writers and broadcasters chosen by the NFL (80 percent) and fans voting via the internet and text message (20 percent). Presented by *Sport* magazine from 1967-89 and by the NFL since 1990. Named after former NFL commissioner Pete Rozelle in 1990. Winner who did not play for Super Bowl champion is in **bold** type.

Multiple winners: Joe Montana (3); Terry Bradshaw, Tom Brady and Bart Starr (2).

Bowl		Bowl		Bowl	
I	Bart Starr, Green Bay, QB	XV	Jim Plunkett, Oakland, QB	XXX	Larry Brown, Dallas, CB
II	Bart Starr, Green Bay, QB	XVI	Joe Montana, San Francisco, QB	XXXI	Desmond Howard, Gr. Bay, KR
III	Joe Namath, NY Jets, QB	XVII	John Riggins, Washington, RB	XXXII	Terrell Davis, Denver, RB
IV	Len Dawson, Kansas City, QB	XVIII	Marcus Allen, LA Raiders, RB	XXXIII	John Elway, Denver, QB
V	**Chuck Howley, Dallas, LB**	XIX	Joe Montana, San Francisco, QB	XXXIV	Kurt Warner, St. Louis, QB
VI	Roger Staubach, Dallas, QB	XX	Richard Dent, Chicago, DE	XXXV	Ray Lewis, Baltimore, LB
VII	Jake Scott, Miami, S	XXI	Phil Simms, NY Giants, QB	XXXVI	Tom Brady, New England, QB
VIII	Larry Csonka, Miami, RB	XXII	Doug Williams, Washington, QB	XXXVII	Dexter Jackson, Tampa Bay, S
IX	Franco Harris, Pittsburgh, RB	XXIII	Jerry Rice, San Francisco, WR	XXXVIII	Tom Brady, New England, QB
X	Lynn Swann, Pittsburgh, WR	XXIV	Joe Montana, San Francisco, QB	XXXIX	Deion Branch, New England, WR
XI	Fred Biletnikoff, Oakland, WR	XXV	Ottis Anderson, NY Giants, RB	XL	Hines Ward, Pittsburgh, WR
XII	Harvey Martin, Dallas, DE & Randy White, Dallas, DT	XXVI	Mark Rypien, Washington, QB	XLI	Peyton Manning, Ind., QB
XIII	Terry Bradshaw, Pittsburgh, QB	XXVII	Troy Aikman, Dallas, QB	XLII	Eli Manning, NY Giants, QB
XIV	Terry Bradshaw, Pittsburgh, QB	XXVIII	Emmitt Smith, Dallas, RB		
		XXIX	Steve Young, San Fran., QB		

Five Super Bowl Wins
Dallas Cowboys

Year	Bowl	Head Coach	Quarterback	MVP	Opponent	Score	Site
1972	VI	Tom Landry	Roger Staubach	Staubach	Miami	24-3	New Orleans
1978	XII	Tom Landry	Roger Staubach	Martin/White	Denver	27-10	New Orleans
1993	XXVII	Jimmy Johnson	Troy Aikman	Aikman	Buffalo	52-17	Pasadena
1994	XXVIII	Jimmy Johnson	Troy Aikman	Emmitt Smith	Buffalo	30-13	Atlanta
1996	XXX	Barry Switzer	Troy Aikman	Larry Brown	Pittsburgh	27-17	Tempe

Pittsburgh Steelers

Year	Bowl	Head Coach	Quarterback	MVP	Opponent	Score	Site
1975	IX	Chuck Noll	Terry Bradshaw	Franco Harris	Minnesota	16-6	New Orleans
1976	X	Chuck Noll	Terry Bradshaw	Lynn Swann	Dallas	21-17	Miami
1979	XIII	Chuck Noll	Terry Bradshaw	Bradshaw	Dallas	35-31	Miami
1980	XIV	Chuck Noll	Terry Bradshaw	Bradshaw	LA Rams	31-19	Pasadena
2006	XL	Bill Cowher	Ben Roethlisberger	Hines Ward	Seattle	21-10	Detroit

San Francisco 49ers

Year	Bowl	Head Coach	Quarterback	MVP	Opponent	Score	Site
1982	XVI	Bill Walsh	Joe Montana	Montana	Cincinnati	26-21	Pontiac
1985	XIX	Bill Walsh	Joe Montana	Montana	Miami	38-16	Stanford
1989	XXIII	Bill Walsh	Joe Montana	Jerry Rice	Cincinnati	20-16	Miami
1990	XXIV	George Seifert	Joe Montana	Montana	Denver	55-10	New Orleans
1995	XXIX	George Seifert	Steve Young	Young	San Diego	49-26	Miami

All-Time Super Bowl Leaders

Through 2008; participants in Super Bowl XLII in **bold** type.

CAREER

Passing Efficiency

	(Minimum 25 passing attempts)	Gm	Att	Cmp	Cmp%	Yards	Avg Gain	TD	TD%	Int	Int%	Rating
1	Phil Simms, NYG	1	25	22	88.0	268	10.72	3	12.0	0	0.0	150.9
2	Steve Young, SF	2	39	26	66.7	345	8.85	6	15.4	0	0.0	134.1
3	Doug Williams, Wash.	1	29	18	62.1	340	11.72	4	13.8	1	3.4	128.1
4	Joe Montana, SF	4	122	83	68.0	1142	9.36	11	9.0	0	0.0	127.8
5	Jim Plunkett, Raiders	2	46	29	63.0	433	9.41	4	8.7	0	0.0	122.8
6	Jake Delhomme, Car.	1	33	16	48.5	323	9.79	3	9.1	0	0.0	113.6
7	Terry Bradshaw, Pit.	4	84	49	58.3	932	11.10	9	10.7	4	4.8	112.8
8	Troy Aikman, Dal	3	80	56	70.0	689	8.61	5	6.3	1	1.3	111.9
9	Bart Starr, GB	2	47	29	61.7	452	9.62	3	6.4	1	2.1	106.0
10	Brett Favre, GB	2	69	39	56.5	502	7.28	5	7.2	1	1.4	97.6

Ratings based on performance standards established for completion percentage, average gain, touchdown percentage and interception percentage. Quarterbacks are allocated points according to how their statistics measure up to those standards.

Passing Yards

		Gm	Att	Cmp	Pct	Yds
1	Joe Montana, SF	4	122	83	68.0	1142
2	John Elway, Den	5	152	76	50.0	1128
3	**Tom Brady**, NE	4	156	100	64.1	1001
4	Terry Bradshaw, Pit	4	84	49	58.3	932
5	Jim Kelly, Buf	4	145	81	55.9	829
6	Kurt Warner, St.L	2	89	52	58.4	779
7	Roger Staubach, Dal	4	98	61	62.2	734
8	Troy Aikman, Dal	3	80	56	70.0	689
9	Brett Favre, GB	2	69	39	56.5	502
10	Fran Tarkenton, Min	3	89	46	51.7	489

Receptions

		Gm	No	Yds	Avg	TD
1	Jerry Rice, SF-Oak	4	33	589	17.8	8
2	Andre Reed, Buf	4	27	323	12.0	0
3	Deion Branch, NE	2	21	276	13.1	1
4	Roger Craig, SF	3	20	212	10.6	2
	Thurman Thomas, Buf	4	20	144	7.2	0
6	Jay Novacek, Dal	3	17	148	8.7	2
7	Lynn Swann, Pit	4	16	364	22.8	3
	Michael Irvin, Dal	3	16	256	16.0	2
	Troy Brown, NE	3	16	182	11.4	0
10	Chuck Foreman, Min	3	15	139	9.3	0

Rushing

		Gm	Car	Yds	Avg	TD
1	Franco Harris, Pit	4	101	354	3.5	4
2	Larry Csonka, Mia	3	57	297	5.2	2
3	Emmitt Smith, Dal	3	70	289	4.1	5
4	Terrell Davis, Den	2	55	259	4.7	3
5	John Riggins, Wash	2	64	230	3.6	2
6	Timmy Smith, Wash	1	22	204	9.3	2
	Thurman Thomas, Buf	4	52	204	3.9	4
8	Roger Craig, SF	3	52	201	3.9	2
9	Marcus Allen, Raiders	1	20	191	9.5	2
10	Antowain Smith, NE	2	44	175	4.0	1

All-Purpose Yards

		Gm	Rush	Rec	Ret	Total
1	Jerry Rice, SF-Oak	4	15	589	0	604
2	Franco Harris, Pit	4	354	114	0	468
3	Roger Craig, SF	3	201	212	0	413
4	Lynn Swann, Pit	4	-7	364	34	391
5	Thurman Thomas, Buf	4	204	144	0	348

Scoring

Points

		Gm	TD	FG	PAT	Pts
1	Jerry Rice, SF-Oak	4	8	0	0	48
2	Adam Vinatieri, NE-Ind	5	0	7	13	34
3	Emmitt Smith, Dal	3	5	0	0	30
4	Roger Craig, SF	3	4	0	0	24
	Franco Harris, Pit	4	4	0	0	24
	Thurman Thomas, Buf	4	4	0	0	24
	John Elway, Den	5	4	0	0	24
8	Ray Wersching, SF	2	0	5	7	22
9	Don Chandler, GB	2	0	4	8	20

10 Six tied with 18 pts. each.

Interceptions

		Gm	No	Yds	TD
1	Larry Brown, Dal	3	3	77	0
	Chuck Howley, Dal	2	3	63	0
	Rod Martin, Raiders	2	3	44	0

4 Thirteen tied with 2 each.

Sacks

		Gm	No
1	Charles Haley, SF-Dal	5	4.5
2	Reggie White, GB	2	3.0
	Leonard Marshall, NYG	2	3.0
	Danny Stubbs, SF	2	3.0
	Mike Vrabel, NE	3	3.0
	Jeff Wright, Buf	4	3.0
	Tedy Bruschi, NE	4	3.0
	Willie McGinest, NE	4	3.0

Note: The NFL did not begin officially compiling sacks until 1982.

Touchdowns

		Gm	Rush	Rec	Ret	TD
1	Jerry Rice, SF-Oak	4	0	8	0	8
2	Emmitt Smith, Dal	3	5	0	0	5
3	Roger Craig, SF	3	2	2	0	4
	Franco Harris, Pit	4	4	0	0	4
	John Elway, Den	5	4	0	0	4
	Thurman Thomas, Buf	4	4	0	0	4

7 Six tied with 3 TD each.

Punting

	(Minimum 10 Punts)	Gm	No	Yds	Avg.
1	Jerrel Wilson, KC	2	11	511	46.5
2	Tom Rouen, Den-Sea	3	11	482	43.8
3	Tom Tupa, NE-TB	2	12	516	43.0
	Kyle Richardson, Bal	1	10	430	43.0
5	Ray Guy, Raiders	3	14	587	41.9

All-Time Super Bowl Leaders (Cont.)

Punt Returns

(Minimum 4 Returns)	Gm	No	Yds	Avg.	TD
1 John Taylor, SF	3	6	94	15.7	0
2 Desmond Howard, GB	1	6	90	15.0	0
3 Dave Meggett, NYG-NE	2	6	67	11.2	0
4 Neal Colzie, Raiders	1	4	43	10.8	0
5 Dana McLemore, SF	1	5	51	10.2	0

Kickoff Returns

(Minimum 4 Returns)	Gm	No	Yds	Avg.	TD
1 Tim Dwight, Atl	1	5	210	42.0	1
2 Desmond Howard, GB	1	4	154	38.5	1
3 Fulton Walker, Mia	2	8	283	35.4	1
4 Andre Coleman, SD	1	8	242	30.3	1
5 Larry Anderson, Pit	2	8	207	25.9	0

SINGLE GAME

Passing

Yards Gained	Year	Att/Cmp	Yds
1 Kurt Warner, St.L vs Ten	2000	45/24	414
2 Kurt Warner, St.L vs NE	2002	44/28	365
3 Joe Montana, SF vs Cin	1989	36/23	357
Donovan McNabb, Phi vs NE	2005	51/30	357
5 Tom Brady, NE vs Car	2004	48/32	354

Touchdown Passes	Year	TD	Int
1 Steve Young, SF vs SD	1995	6	0
2 Joe Montana, SF vs Den	1990	5	0
3 Terry Bradshaw, Pit vs Dal	1979	4	1
Doug Williams, Wash vs Den	1988	4	1
Troy Aikman, Dal vs Buf	1993	4	0

Receiving

Catches	Year	No	Yds	TD
1 Dan Ross, Cin vs SF	1982	11	104	2
Jerry Rice, SF vs Cin	1989	11	215	1
Deion Branch, NE vs Phi	2005	11	133	0
Wes Welker, NE vs NYG	2008	11	103	0
5 Tony Nathan, Mia vs SF	1985	10	83	0
Jerry Rice, SF vs SD	1995	10	149	3
Andre Hastings, Pit vs Dal	1996	10	98	0
Deion Branch, NE vs Car	2004	10	143	1
Joseph Addai, Ind vs Chi	2007	10	66	0

Yards Gained	Year	No	Yds	TD
1 Jerry Rice, SF vs Cin	1989	11	215	1
2 Ricky Sanders, Wash vs Den	1988	9	193	2
3 Isaac Bruce, St.L vs Ten	2000	6	162	1
4 Lynn Swann, Pit vs Dal	1976	4	161	1
5 Andre Reed, Buf vs Dal	1993	8	152	0
Rod Smith, Den vs Atl	1999	5	152	1

Rushing

Yards Gained	Year	Car	Yds	TD
1 Timmy Smith, Wash vs Den	1988	22	204	2
2 Marcus Allen, Raiders vs Wash	1984	20	191	2
3 John Riggins, Wash vs Mia	1983	38	166	1
4 Franco Harris, Pit vs Min	1975	34	158	1
5 Terrell Davis, Den vs GB	1998	30	157	3

All-Purpose Yards

Yards Gained	Year	Run	Rec	Tot
1 Desmond Howard, GB vs NE	1997	0	0	244
2 Andre Coleman, SD vs SF	1995	0	0	242
3 Ricky Sanders, Wash vs Den	1988	193	-4	235
4 Antonio Freeman, GB vs Den	1998	0	126	230
5 Jerry Rice, SF vs Cin	1989	5	215	220

Return Yardage: Howard 244, Coleman 242, Sanders 46, Freeman 104.

Scoring

Points	Year	TD	FG	PAT	Pts
1 Roger Craig, SF vs Mia	1985	3	0	0	18
Jerry Rice, SF vs Den	1990	3	0	0	18
Jerry Rice, SF vs SD	1995	3	0	0	18
Ricky Watters, SF vs SD	1995	3	0	0	18
Terrell Davis, Den vs GB	1998	3	0	0	18

Touchdowns	Year	TD	Rush	Rec
1 Roger Craig, SF vs Mia	1985	3	1	2
Jerry Rice, SF vs Den	1990	3	0	3
Jerry Rice, SF vs SD	1995	3	0	3
Ricky Watters, SF vs SD	1995	3	1	2
Terrell Davis, Den vs GB	1998	3	3	0

Punt Returns

(Minimum 3 returns)	Year	No	Yds	Avg
1 John Taylor, SF vs Cin	1989	3	56	18.7
2 Desmond Howard, GB vs NE	1997	6	90	15.0
3 **Terrence Wilkins**, Ind vs Chi	2007	3	42	14.0
4 John Taylor, SF vs Den	1990	3	38	12.7
5 Kelvin Martin, Dal vs Buf	1993	3	35	11.7

Punting

(Minimum 4 punts)	Year	No	Yds	Avg
1 Tom Rouen, Sea vs Pit	2006	6	301	50.2
2 Bryan Wagner, SD vs SF	1995	4	195	48.8
3 Chris Gardocki, Pit vs Sea	2006	6	292	48.7
4 Jerrel Wilson, KC vs Min	1970	4	194	48.5
5 Jim Miller, SF vs Cin	1982	4	185	46.3

Kickoff Returns

(Minimum 3 returns)	Year	No	Yds	Avg
1 Fulton Walker, Mia vs Wash	1983	4	190	47.5
2 Tim Dwight, Atl vs Den	1999	5	210	42.0
3 Desmond Howard, GB vs NE	1997	4	154	38.5
4 Larry Anderson, Pit vs Rams	1980	5	162	32.4
5 Rick Upchurch, Den vs Dal	1978	3	94	31.3

Interceptions

	Year	No	Yds	TD
1 Rod Martin, Raiders vs Phi	1981	3	44	0

Eleven tied with 2 each.

*Kicker **Adam Vinatieri** played in his fifth Super Bowl in 2007, tying him with 12 other players for the second most in NFL history. Only one player has played in six Super Bowls — defensive lineman **Mike Lodish**, who lost four with the Bills (1991-94) before winning two with the Broncos (1998-99).*

Super Bowl Playoffs

The Super Bowl forced the NFL to set up pro football's first guaranteed multiple-game playoff format. Over the years, the NFL-AFL merger, the creation of two conferences comprised of four divisions each and the proliferation of wild card entries has seen the postseason field grow from four teams (1966), to six (1967-68), to eight (1969-77), to 10 (1978-81, 1983-89), to the present 12 (since1990). In 1968, there was a special playoff between Oakland and Kansas City which were both 12-2 and tied for first in the AFL's Western Division. In 1982, when a 57-day players' strike shortened the regular season to just nine games, playoff berths were extended to 16 teams (eight from each conference) and a 15-game tournament was played.

Note that in the following year-by-year summary, records of finalists include all games leading up to the Super Bowl; (*) indicates non-division winners or wild card teams.

1966 SEASON

AFL Playoffs

Championship . . . . .Kansas City 31, at Buffalo 7

NFL Playoffs

Championship . . . . .Green Bay 34, at Dallas 27

Super Bowl I

Jan. 15, 1967
Memorial Coliseum, Los Angeles
Favorite: Packers by 14—Attendance: 61,946

Kansas City (12-2-1) . . . . .0 10 0 0 —**10**
Green Bay (13-2) . . . . .7 7 14 7 —**35**
MVP: Green Bay QB Bart Starr (16 for 23, 250 yds, 2 TD)

1967 SEASON

AFL Playoffs

Championship . . . . .at Oakland 40, Houston 7

NFL Playoffs

Eastern Conference . . . . .at Dallas 52, Cleveland 14
Western Conference . . . . . . .at Green Bay 28, LA Rams 7
Championship . . . . .at Green Bay 21, Dallas 17

Super Bowl II

Jan. 14, 1968
Orange Bowl, Miami
Favorite: Packers by 13½—Attendance: 75,546

Green Bay (11-4-1) . . . . .3 13 10 7 —**33**
Oakland (14-1) . . . . .0 7 0 7 —**14**
MVP: Green Bay QB Bart Starr (13 for 24, 202 yds,1 TD)

1968 SEASON

AFL Playoffs

Western Div. Playoff . . . . . .at Oakland 41, Kansas City 6
AFL Championship . . . . .at NY Jets 27, Oakland 23

NFL Playoffs

Eastern Conference . . . . .at Cleveland 31, Dallas 20
Western Conference . . . . .at Baltimore 24, Minnesota 14
NFL Championship . . . . . . .Baltimore 34, at Cleveland 0

Super Bowl III

Jan. 12, 1969
Orange Bowl, Miami
Favorite: Colts by 18—Attendance: 75,389

NY Jets (12-3) . . . . .0 7 6 3 —**16**
Baltimore (15-1) . . . . .0 0 0 7 — **7**
MVP: NY Jets QB Joe Namath (17 for 28, 206 yds)

1969 SEASON

AFL Playoffs

Inter-Division . . . .*Kansas City 13, at NY Jets 6
at Oakland 56, *Houston 7
AFL Championship . . . . . .Kansas City 17, at Oakland 7

NFL Playoffs

Eastern Conference . . . . .Cleveland 38, at Dallas 14
Western Conference . . . . . .at Minnesota 23, LA Rams 20
NFL Championship . . . . . . .at Minnesota 27, Cleveland 7

Super Bowl IV

Jan. 11, 1970   Tulane Stadium, New Orleans
Favorite: Vikings by 12—Attendance: 80,562

Minnesota (14-2) . . . . .0 0 7 .0 — **7**
Kansas City (13-3) . . . . .3 13 7 0 — **23**
MVP: KC QB Len Dawson (12 for 17, 142 yds, 1 TD, 1Int)

1970 SEASON

AFC Playoffs

First Round . . . . .at Baltimore 17, Cincinnati 0
at Oakland 21,*Miami 14
Championship . . . . .at Baltimore 27, Oakland 17

NFC Playoffs

First Round. . : . . . . .at Dallas 5, *Detroit 0
San Francisco 17, at Minnesota 14
Championship . . . . .Dallas 17, at San Francisco 10

Super Bowl V

Jan. 17, 1971   Orange Bowl, Miami
Favorite: Cowboys by 2½—Attendance: 79,204

Baltimore (13-2-1) . . . . .0 6 0 10 — **16**
Dallas (12-4) . . . . .3 10 0 0 — **13**
MVP: Dallas LB Chuck Howley (2 interceptions for 22 yds)

1971 SEASON

AFC Playoffs

First Round . . . . .Miami 27, at Kansas City 24 (OT)
*Baltimore 20, at Cleveland 3
Championship . . . . .at Miami 21, Baltimore 0

NFC Playoffs

First Round . . . . .Dallas 20, at Minnesota 12
at San Francisco 24,*Washington 20
Championship . . . . .at Dallas 14, San Francisco 3

Super Bowl VI

Jan. 16, 1972   Tulane Stadium, New Orleans
Favorite: Cowboys by 6—Attendance: 81,023

Dallas (13-3) . . . . .3 7 7 7 — **24**
Miami (12-3-1) . . . . .0 3 0 0 — **3**
MVP: Dallas QB Roger Staubach (12 for 19, 119 yds, 2 TD)

1972 SEASON

AFC Playoffs

First Round . . . . .at Pittsburgh 13, Oakland 7
at Miami 20, *Cleveland 14
Championship . . . . .Miami 21, at Pittsburgh 17

NFC Playoffs

First Round . . . .*Dallas 30, at San Francisco 28
at Washington 16, Green Bay 3
Championship . . . . .at Washington 26, Dallas 3

Super Bowl VII

Jan. 14, 1973
Memorial Coliseum, Los Angeles
Favorite: Redskins by 1½—Attendance: 90,182

Miami (16-0) . . . . .7 7 0 0 — **14**
Washington (13-3) . . . . .0 0 0 7 — **7**
MVP: Miami safety Jake Scott (2 interceptions for 63 yds)

1973 SEASON

AFC Playoffs

First Round . . . . .at Oakland 33, *Pittsburgh 14
at Miami 34, Cincinnati 16
Championship . . . . .at Miami 27, Oakland 10

NFC Playoffs

First Round . . . . .at Minnesota 27, *Washington 20
at Dallas 27, LA Rams 16
Championship . . . . .Minnesota 27, at Dallas 10

Super Bowl VIII

Jan. 13, 1974
Rice Stadium, Houston
Favorite: Dolphins by 6½—Attendance: 71,882

Minnesota (14-2) . . . . .0 0 0 7 — **7**
Miami (12-4) . . . . .14 3 7 0 — **24**
MVP: Miami FB Larry Csonka (33 carries, 145 yds, 2 TD)

1974 SEASON

AFC Playoffs

First Round . . . . .at Oakland 28, Miami 26
at Pittsburgh 32, *Buffalo 14
Championship . . . . .Pittsburgh 24, at Oakland 13

NFC Playoffs

First Round . . . . .at Minnesota 30, St. Louis 14
at LA Rams 19, *Washington 10
Championship . . . . .at Minnesota 14, LA Rams 10

Super Bowl IX

Jan. 12, 1975
Tulane Stadium, New Orleans
Favorite: Steelers by 3—Attendance: 80,997

Pittsburgh (12-3-1) . . . . .0 2 7 7 — **16**
Minnesota (12-4) . . . . .0 0 0 6 — **6**
MVP: Pittsburgh RB Franco Harris (34 carries, 158 yds, 1 TD)

1975 SEASON

AFC Playoffs

First Round . . . . .at Pittsburgh 28, Baltimore 10
at Oakland 31, *Cincinnati 28
Championship . . . . .at Pittsburgh 16, Oakland 10

NFC Playoffs

First Round . . . . .at LA Rams 35, St. Louis 23
*Dallas 17, at Minnesota 14
Championship . . . . .Dallas 37, at LA Rams 7

Super Bowl X

Jan. 18, 1976
Orange Bowl, Miami
Favorite: Steelers by 6½—Attendance: 80,187

Dallas (12-4) . . . . .7 3 0 7 — **17**
Pittsburgh (14-2) . . . . .7 0 0 14 — **21**
MVP: Pittsburgh WR Lynn Swann (4 catches, 161 yds, 1 TD)

1976 SEASON

AFC Playoffs

First Round . . . . .at Oakland 24, *New England 21
Pittsburgh 40, Baltimore 14
Championship . . . . .at Oakland 24, Pittsburgh 7

NFC Playoffs

First Round . . . . .at Minnesota 35, *Washington 20
LA Rams 14, at Dallas 12
Championship . . . . .at Minnesota 24, LA Rams 13

Super Bowl XI

Jan. 9, 1977   Rose Bowl, Pasadena
Favorite: Raiders by 4½—Attendance: 103,438

Oakland (15-1) . . . . .0 16 3 13 — **32**
Minnesota (13-2-1) . . . . .0 0 7 7 — **14**
MVP: Oakland WR Fred Biletnikoff (4 catches, 79 yds)

1977 SEASON

AFC Playoffs

First Round . . . . .at Denver 34, Pittsburgh 21
*Oakland 37, at Baltimore 31 (OT)
Championship . . . . .at Denver 20, Oakland 17

NFC Playoffs

First Round . . . . .at Dallas 37, *Chicago 7
Minnesota 14, at LA Rams 7
Championship . . . . .at Dallas 23, Minnesota 6

Super Bowl XII

Jan. 15, 1978
Louisiana Superdome, New Orleans
Favorite: Cowboys by 6—Attendance: 75,583

Dallas (14-2) . . . . .10 3 7 7 — **27**
Denver (14-2) . . . . .0 0 10 0 — **10**
MVPs: Dallas DE Harvey Martin and DT Randy White (Cowboys' defense forced 8 turnovers)

Most Popular Playing Sites
Stadiums hosting more than one Super Bowl.

No		Years	No		Years
6	Superdome (N. Orleans)	1978, 81, 86, 90, 97, 2002	3	Tulane Stadium (N. Orleans)	1970, 72, 75
5	Orange Bowl (Miami)	1968-69, 71, 76, 79	3	Jack Murphy/Qualcomm Stadium (San Diego)	1988, 98, 2003
5	Rose Bowl (Pasadena)	1977, 80, 83, 87, 93	2	LA Memorial Coliseum	1967, 73
4	Joe Robbie/Pro Player/ Dolphin Stadium (Miami)	1989, 95, 99, 2007	2	Tampa Stadium	1984, 91
			2	Georgia Dome (Atlanta)	1994, 2000

1978 SEASON

AFC Playoffs

First Round . . . .*Houston 17, at *Miami 9
Second Round . . . . .Houston 31, at New England 14
at Pittsburgh 33, Denver 10
Championship . . . . .at Pittsburgh 34, Houston 5

NFC Playoffs

First Round . . . . .at *Atlanta 14, *Philadelphia 13
Second Round . . . . .at Dallas 27, Atlanta 20
at LA Rams 34, Minnesota 10
Championship . . . . .Dallas 28, at LA Rams 0

Super Bowl XIII

Jan. 21, 1979   Orange Bowl, Miami
Favorite: Steelers by 4—Attendance: 79,484

Pittsburgh (16-2) 7   14   0   14 — **35**
Dallas (14-4) 7   7   3   14 — **31**
MVP: Pit. QB Terry Bradshaw (17 for 30, 318 yds, 4 TD)

1979 SEASON

AFC Playoffs

First Round . . . . .at *Houston 13, *Denver 7
Second Round . . . . .Houston 17, at San Diego 14
at Pittsburgh 34, Miami 14
Championship . . . . .at Pittsburgh 27, Houston 13

NFC Playoffs

First Round . . . . .at *Philadelphia 27, *Chicago 17
Second Round . . . . . . .at Tampa Bay 24, Philadelphia 17
LA Rams 21, at Dallas 19
Championship . . . . .LA Rams 9,at Tampa Bay 0

Super Bowl XIV

Jan. 20, 1980   Rose Bowl, Pasadena
Favorite: Steelers by 10½—Attendance: 103,985

LA Rams (11-7) 7   6   6   0 — **19**
Pittsburgh (14-4) 3   7   7   14 — **31**
MVP: Pit. QB Terry Bradshaw (14 for 21, 309 yds, 2 TD)

1980 SEASON

AFC Playoffs

First Round . . . . .at *Oakland 27, *Houston 7
Second Round . . .. .at San Diego 20, Buffalo 14
Oakland 14, at Cleveland 12
Championship . . . . .Oakland 34, at San Diego 27

NFC Playoffs

First Round . . . . .at *Dallas 34, *LA Rams 13
Second Round . . . .at Philadelphia 31, Minnesota 16
Dallas 30, at Atlanta 27
Championship . . . . . . .at Philadelphia 20, Dallas 7

Super Bowl XV

Jan. 25, 1981   Louisiana Superdome, New Orleans
Favorite: Eagles by 3—Attendance: 76,135

Oakland (14-5) 14   0   10   3 — **27**
Philadelphia (14-4) 0   3   0   7 — **10**
MVP: Oakland QB Jim Plunkett (13 for 21, 261 yds, 3 TD)

1981 SEASON

AFC Playoffs

First Round . . . .*Buffalo 31, at *NY Jets 27
Second Round . . . . . . .San Diego 41, at Miami 38 (OT)
at Cincinnati 28, Buffalo 21
Championship . . . . .at Cincinnati 27, San Diego 7

NFC Playoffs

First Round . . . .*NY Giants 27, at *Philadelphia 21
Second Round . . . . .at Dallas 38, Tampa Bay 0
at San Francisco 38, NY Giants 24
Championship . . . . .at San Francisco 28, Dallas 27

Super Bowl XVI

Jan. 24, 1982
Pontiac Silverdome, Pontiac, Mich.
Favorite: Pick'em—Attendance: 81,270

San Francisco (15-3) 7   13   0   6 — **26**
Cincinnati (14-4) 0   0   7   14 — **21**
MVP: San Francisco QB Joe Montana (14 for 22, 157 yds, 1 TD; 6 carries, 18 yds, 1 TD)

1982 SEASON

A 57-day players' strike shortened the regular season from 16 games to nine. The playoff format was changed to a 16-team tournament open to the top eight teams in each conference.

AFC Playoffs

First Round . . . . .at LA Raiders 27, Cleveland 10
at Miami 28, New England 3
NY Jets 44, at Cincinnati 17
San Diego 31, at Pittsburgh 28
Second Round . . . . .NY Jets 17, at LA Raiders 14
at Miami 34, San Diego 13
Championship . . . . .at Miami 14, NY Jets 0

NFC Playoffs

First Round . . . . .at Washington 31, Detroit 7
at Dallas 30, Tampa Bay 17
at Green Bay 41, St. Louis 16
at Minnesota 30, Atlanta 24
Second Round . . . . .at Washington 21, Minnesota 7
at Dallas 37, Green Bay 26
Championship . . . . .at Washington 31, Dallas 17

Super Bowl XVII

Jan. 30, 1983
Rose Bowl, Pasadena
Favorite: Dolphins by 3—Attendance: 103,667

Miami (10-2) 7   10   0   0 —**17**
Washington (11-1) 0   0   10   3   14 —**27**
MVP: Washington RB John Riggins (38 carries, 166 yds, 1 TD; 1 catch, 15 yds)

1983 SEASON

AFC Playoffs

First Round . . . . .at *Seattle 31, *Denver 7
Second Round . . . . .Seattle 27, at Miami 20
at LA Raiders 38, Pittsburgh 10
Championship . . . . .at LA Raiders 30, Seattle 14

NFC Playoffs

First Round . . . .*LA Rams 24, at *Dallas 17
Second Round . . . . .at San Francisco 24, Detroit 23
at Washington 51, LA Rams 7
Championship . . . . . .at Washington 24, San Francisco 21

Super Bowl XVIII

Jan. 22, 1984
Tampa Stadium, Tampa
Favorite: Redskins by 3—Attendance: 72,920

Washington (16-2) 0   3   6   0 — **9**
LA Raiders (14-4) 7   14 14   3 — **38**
MVP: LA Raiders RB Marcus Allen (20 carries, 191 yds, 2 TD; 2 catches, 18 yds)

1984 SEASON

AFC Playoffs

First Round . . . . .at *Seattle 13, *LA Raiders 7
Second Round . . . . .at Miami 31, Seattle 10
                     Pittsburgh 24, at Denver 17
Championship . . . . .at Miami 45, Pittsburgh 28

NFC Playoffs

First Round . . . .*NY Giants 16, at *LA Rams 13
Second Round . . . . . . .at San Francisco 21, NY Giants 10
                    Chicago 23, at Washington 19
Championship . . . . .at San Francisco 23, Chicago 0

Super Bowl XIX

Jan. 20, 1985
Stanford Stadium, Stanford, Calif.
Favorite: 49ers by 3—Attendance: 84,059

Miami (16-2) 10   6   0   0 — **16**
San Francisco (17-1) . . . . .7 21 10   0 — **38**
MVP: San Francisco QB Joe Montana (24 for 35, 331 yds, 2 TD; 5 carries, 59 yards, 1 TD)

1985 SEASON

AFC Playoffs

First Round . . . .*New England 26, at *NY Jets 14
Second Round . . . . .at Miami 24, Cleveland 21
               New England 27, at LA Raiders 20
Championship . . . . .New England 31, at Miami 14

NFC Playoffs

First Round . . . . . . .at *NY Giants 17, *San Francisco 3
Second Round . . . . .at LA Rams 20, Dallas 0
                at Chicago 21, NY Giants 0
Championship . . . . .at Chicago 24, LA Rams 0

Super Bowl XX

Jan. 26, 1986
Louisiana Superdome, New Orleans
Favorite: Bears by 10—Attendance: 73,818

Chicago Bears (17-1) . . . . .13 10 21   2 — **46**
New England (14-5) 3   0   0   7 — **10**
MVP: Chicago DE Richard Dent (Bears defense: 7 sacks, 6 turnovers, 1 safety and gave up just 123 total yards)

1986 SEASON

AFC Playoffs

First Round . . . . .at *NY Jets 35, *Kansas City 15
Second Round . . . . . . .at Cleveland 23, NY Jets 20 (OT)
               at Denver 22, New England 17
Championship . . . . .Denver 23, at Cleveland 20 (OT)

NFC Playoffs

First Round . . . . .at *Washington 19, *LA Rams 7
Second Round . . . . .Washington 27, at Chicago 13
               at NY Giants 49, San Francisco 3
Championship . . . . .at NY Giants 17, Washington 0

Super Bowl XXI

Jan. 25, 1987
Rose Bowl, Pasadena
Favorite: Giants by 9½—Attendance: 101,063

Denver (13-5) 10   0   0 10 — **20**
NY Giants (16-2) 7   2 17 13 — **39**
MVP: NY Giants QB Phil Simms (22 for 25, 268 yds, 3 TD; 3 carries, 25 yds)

1987 SEASON

A 24-day players' strike shortened the regular season to 15 games with replacement teams playing for three weeks.

AFC Playoffs

First Round . . . . .at *Houston 23, *Seattle 20 (OT)
Second Round . . . . .at Cleveland 38, Indianapolis 21
                 at Denver 34, Houston 10
Championship . . . . .at Denver 38, Cleveland 33

NFC Playoffs

First Round . . . .*Minnesota 44, at *New Orleans 10
Second Round . . . . . .Minnesota 36, at San Francisco 24
               Washington 21, at Chicago 17
Championship . . . . .at Washington 17, Minnesota 10

Super Bowl XXII

Jan. 31, 1988
San Diego/Jack Murphy Stadium
Favorite: Broncos by 3½—Attendance: 73,302

Washington (13-4) . . . . .0 35   0   7 — **42**
Denver (12-4-1) 10   0   0   0 — **10**
MVP: Washington QB Doug Williams (18 for 29, 340 yds, 4 TD, 1 Int)

1988 SEASON

AFC Playoffs

First Round . . . .*Houston 24, at *Cleveland 23
Second Round . . . . .at Buffalo 17, Houston 10
               at Cincinnati 21, Seattle 13
Championship . . . . .at Cincinnati 21, Buffalo 10

NFC Playoffs

First Round . . . . .at *Minnesota 28, *LA Rams 17
Second Round . . . . .at San Francisco 34, Minnesota 9
               at Chicago 20, Philadelphia 12
Championship . . . . .San Francisco 28, at Chicago 3

Super Bowl XXIII

Jan. 22, 1989
Joe Robbie Stadium, Miami
Favorite: 49ers by 7—Attendance: 75,129

Cincinnati (14-4) 0   3 10   3 — **16**
San Francisco (12-6) 3   0   3 14 — **20**
MVP: San Francisco WR Jerry Rice (11 catches, 215 yds, 1 TD; 1 carry, 5 yds)

1989 SEASON

AFC Playoffs

First Round . . . .*Pittsburgh 26, at *Houston 23
Second Round . . . . .at Cleveland 34, Buffalo 30
               at Denver 24, Pittsburgh 23
Championship . . . . .at Denver 37, Cleveland 21

NFC Playoffs

First Round . . . .*LA Rams 21, at *Philadelphia 7
Second Round . . . . .LA Rams 19, NY Giants 13 (OT)
              at San Francisco 41, Minnesota 13
Championship . . . . .at San Francisco 30, LA Rams 3

Super Bowl XXIV

Jan. 28, 1990
Louisiana Superdome, New Orleans
Favorite: 49ers by 12½—Attendance: 72,919

San Francisco (17-2) . . . . .13 14 14 14 — **55**
Denver (13-6) 3   0   7   0 — **10**
MVP: San Francisco QB Joe Montana (22 for 29, 297 yds, 5 TD)

1990 SEASON

AFC Playoffs

First Round . . . . .at *Miami 17, *Kansas City 16
at Cincinnati 41, *Houston 14
Second Round . . . . .at Buffalo 44, Miami 34
at LA Raiders 20, Cincinnati 10
Championship . . . . .at Buffalo 51, LA Raiders 3

NFC Playoffs

First Round . . . .*Washington 20, at *Philadelphia 6
at Chicago 16, *New Orleans 6
Second Round . . . . . .at San Francisco 28, Washington 10
at NY Giants 31, Chicago 3
Championship . . . . . . .NY Giants 15, at San Francisco 13

Super Bowl XXV
Jan. 27, 1991
Tampa Stadium, Tampa
Favorite: Bills by 7—Attendance: 73,813

Buffalo (15-4) . . . . .3 9 0 7 **—19**
NY Giants (16-3) . . . . .3 7 7 3 **—20**
MVP: NY Giants RB Ottis Anderson (21 carries, 102 yds, 1 TD; 1 catch, 7 yds)

1991 SEASON

AFC Playoffs

First Round . . . . .at *Kansas City 10, *LA Raiders 6
at Houston 17, *NY Jets 10
Second Round . . . . .at Denver 26, Houston 24
at Buffalo 37, Kansas City 14
Championship . . . . .at Buffalo 10, Denver 7

NFC Playoffs

First Round . . . .*Atlanta 27, at New Orleans 20
*Dallas 17, at *Chicago 13
Second Round . . . . . .at Washington 24, Atlanta 7
at Detroit 38, Dallas 6
Championship . . . . .at Washington 41, Detroit 10

Super Bowl XXVI
Jan. 26, 1992
Hubert Humphrey Metrodome, Minneapolis
Favorite: Redskins by 7—Attendance: 63,130

Washington (16-2) . . . . .0 17 14 6 **— 37**
Buffalo (15-3) . . . . .0 0 10 14 **— 24**
MVP: Washington QB Mark Rypien (18 for 33, 292 yds, 2 TD, 1 Int)

1992 SEASON

AFC Playoffs

First Round . . . . .at *Buffalo 41, *Houston 38 (OT)
at San Diego 17, *Kansas City 0
Second Round . . . . .Buffalo 24, at Pittsburgh 3
at Miami 31, San Diego 0
Championship . . . . .Buffalo 29, at Miami 10

NFC Playoffs

First Round . . . .*Washington 24, at Minnesota 7
*Philadelphia 36, at *New Orleans 20
Second Round . . . . . .at San Francisco 20, Washington 13
at Dallas 34, Philadelphia 10
Championship . . . . . . .Dallas 30, at San Francisco 20

Super Bowl XXVII
Jan. 31, 1993
Rose Bowl, Pasadena
Favorite: Cowboys by 7—Attendance: 98,374

Buffalo (14-5) . . . . .7 3 7 0 **— 17**
Dallas (15-3) . . . . .14 14 3 21 **— 52**
MVP: Dallas QB Troy Aikman (22 for 30, 273 yds, 4 TD)

1993 SEASON

AFC Playoffs

First Round . . . . . .at Kansas City 27, *Pittsburgh 24 (OT)
at *LA Raiders 42, *Denver 24
Second Round . . . . .at Buffalo 29, LA Raiders 23
Kansas City 28, at Houston 20
Championship . . . . .at Buffalo 30, Kansas City 13

NFC Playoffs

First Round . . . .*Green Bay 28, at Detroit 24
at *NY Giants 17, *Minnesota 10
Second Round . . . . .at San Francisco 44, NY Giants 3
at Dallas 27, Green Bay 17
Championship . . . . .at Dallas 38, San Francisco 21

Super Bowl XXVIII
Jan. 30, 1994
Georgia Dome, Atlanta
Favorite: Cowboys by 10½—Attendance: 72,817

Dallas (15-4) . . . . .6 0 14 10 **— 30**
Buffalo (14-5) . . . . .3 10 0 0 **— 13**
MVP: Dallas RB Emmitt Smith (30 carries, 132 yds, 2 TDs; 4 catches, 26 yds)

1994 SEASON

AFC Playoffs

First Round . . . . .at Miami 27, *Kansas City 17
at *Cleveland 20, *New England 13
Second Round . . . . .at Pittsburgh 29, Cleveland 9
at San Diego 22, Miami 21
Championship . . . . .San Diego 17, at Pittsburgh 13

NFC Playoffs

First Round . . . . .at *Green Bay 16, *Detroit 12
*Chicago 25, at Minnesota 18
Second Round . . . . .at San Francisco 44, Chicago 15
at Dallas 35, Green Bay 9
Championship . . . . .at San Francisco 38, Dallas 28

Super Bowl XXIX
Jan. 29, 1995
Joe Robbie Stadium, Miami
Favorite: 49ers by 18 —Attendance: 74,107

San Diego (13-5) . . . . .7 3 8 8 **—26**
San Francisco (15-3) . . . . .14 14 14 7 **—49**
MVP: San Francisco QB Steve Young (24 for 36, 325 yds, 6 TD)

1995 SEASON

AFC Playoffs

First Round . . . . .at Buffalo 37, *Miami 22
*Indianapolis 35, at *San Diego 20
Second Round . . . . .at Pittsburgh 40, Buffalo 21
Indianapolis 10, at Kansas City 7
Championship . . . . .at Pittsburgh 20, Indianapolis 16

NFC Playoffs

First Round . . . . .at *Philadelphia 58, *Detroit 37
at Green Bay 37, *Atlanta 20
Second Round . . . . . .Green Bay 27, at San Francisco 17
at Dallas 30, Philadelphia 11
Championship . . . . .at Dallas 38, Green Bay 27

Super Bowl XXX
Jan. 28, 1996
Sun Devil Stadium, Tempe, Ariz.
Favorite: Cowboys by 13½—Attendance: 76,347

Dallas (14-4) . . . . .10 3 7 7 **— 27**
Pittsburgh (13-5) . . . . .0 7 0 10 **— 17**
MVP: Dallas CB Larry Brown (2 interceptions for 77 yds)

1996 SEASON

AFC Playoffs

First Round . . . .*Jacksonville 30, at *Buffalo 27
at Pittsburgh 42, *Indianapolis 14
Second Round . . . . Jacksonville 30, at Denver 27
at New England 28, Pittsburgh 3
Championship . . . . . . .at New England 20, Jacksonville 6

NFC Playoffs

First Round . . . . at Dallas 40, *Minnesota 15
at *San Francisco 14, *Philadelphia 0
Second Round . . . . . . at Green Bay 35, San Francisco 14
at Carolina 26, Dallas 17
Championship . . . . at Green Bay 30, Carolina 13

Super Bowl XXXI

Jan. 26, 1997
Louisiana Superdome, New Orleans
Favorite: Packers by 14—Attendance: 72,301

New England (13-5) 14	0	7	0	—	**21**
Green Bay (15-3) 10	17	8	0	—	**35**

MVP: Green Bay KR Desmond Howard (4 kickoff returns for 154 yds and 1 TD, also 6 punt returns for 90 yds)

1997 SEASON

AFC Playoffs

First Round . . . . .at *Denver 42, *Jacksonville 17
at New England 17, *Miami 3
Second Round . . . . .at Pittsburgh 7, New England 6
Denver 14, at Kansas City 10
Championship . . . . Denver 24, at Pittsburgh 21

NFC Playoffs

First Round . . . .*Minnesota 23, at NY Giants 22
at *Tampa Bay 20, *Detroit 10
Second Round . . . . . . .at San Francisco 38, Minnesota 22
at Green Bay 21, Tampa Bay 7
Championship . . . . . . .Green Bay 23, at San Francisco 10

Super Bowl XXXII

Jan. 25, 1998
Qualcomm Stadium, San Diego
Favorite: Packers by 11½—Attendance: 68,912

Green Bay (15-3) 7	7	3	7	—	**24**
Denver (15-4) 7	10	7	7	—	**31**

MVP: Denver RB Terrell Davis (30 carries, 157 yds, 3 TD)

1998 SEASON

AFC Playoffs

First Round . . . . .at *Miami 24, *Buffalo 17
at Jacksonville 25, *New England 10
Second Round . . . . .at NY Jets 34, Jacksonville 24
at Denver 38, Miami 3
Championship . . . . at Denver 23, NY Jets 10

NFC Playoffs

First Round . . . . . . .at *San Francisco 30, *Green Bay 27
*Arizona 20, at Dallas 7
Second Round . . . . .at Atlanta 20, San Francisco 18
at Minnesota 41, Arizona 21
Championship . . . . .Atlanta 30, at Minnesota 27 (OT)

Super Bowl XXXIII

Jan. 31, 1999
Pro Player Stadium, Miami
Favorite: Broncos by 7½—Attendance: 74,803

Denver (16-2) 7	10	0	17	—	**34**
Atlanta (16-2) 3	3	0	13	—	**19**

MVP: Denver QB John Elway (18 for 29, 336 yds, 1 TD, 1 Int and 1 rushing TD)

1999 SEASON

AFC Playoffs

First Round . . . . .at *Tennessee 22, *Buffalo 16
*Miami 20, at Seattle 17
Second Round . . . . .at Jacksonville 62, Miami 7
Tennessee 19, at Indianapolis 16
Championship . . . . . . .Tennessee 33, at Jacksonville 14

NFC Playoffs

First Round . . . . .at Washington 27, *Detroit 13
at *Minnesota 27, *Dallas 10
Second Round . . . . . . .at Tampa Bay 14, Washington 13
at St. Louis 49, Minnesota 37
Championship . . . . .at St. Louis 11, Tampa Bay 6

Super Bowl XXXIV

Jan. 30, 2000
Georgia Dome, Atlanta
Favorite: Rams by 7—Attendance: 72,625

St. Louis (13-3) 3	6	7	7	—	**23**
Tennessee (16-3) 0	0	6	10	—	**16**

MVP: St. Louis QB Kurt Warner (24 for 45, 414 yds, 2 TD)

2000 SEASON

AFC Playoffs

First Round . . . . .at Miami 23, *Indianapolis 17 (OT)
at *Baltimore 21, *Denver 3
Second Round . . . . .at Oakland 27, Miami 0
Baltimore 24, at Tennessee 10
Championship . . . . .Baltimore 16, at Oakland 3

NFC Playoffs

First Round . . . . .at New Orleans 31, *St. Louis 28
at *Philadelphia 21, *Tampa Bay 3
Second Round . . . . . . .at Minnesota 34, New Orleans 16
at NY Giants 20, Philadelphia 10
Championship . . . . .at NY Giants 41, Minnesota 0

Super Bowl XXXV

Jan. 28, 2001
Raymond James Stadium, Tampa
Favorite: Ravens by 3—Attendance: 71,921

Baltimore (15-4) 7	3	14	10	—	**34**
NY Giants (14-4) 0	0	7	0	—	**7**

MVP: Baltimore LB Ray Lewis (5 tackles, 4 passes defended)

2001 SEASON

AFC Playoffs

First Round . . . . .at Oakland 38, *NY Jets 24
*Baltimore 20, at *Miami 3
Second Round . . .at New England 16, Oakland 13 (OT)
at Pittsburgh 27, Baltimore 10
Championship . . . . New England 24, at Pittsburgh 17

NFC Playoffs

First Round . . . . .at Philadelphia 31, *Tampa Bay 9
at *Green Bay 25, *San Francisco 15
Second Round . . . . .Philadelphia 33, at Chicago 19
at St. Louis 45, Green Bay 17
Championship . . . . .at St. Louis 29, Philadelphia 24

Super Bowl XXXVI

Feb. 3, 2002
Louisiana Superdome, New Orleans
Favorite: Rams by 14—Attendance: 72,922

St. Louis (16-2) 3	0	0	14	—	**17**
New England (13-5) 0	14	3	3	—	**20**

MVP: New England QB Tom Brady (16 for 27, 145 yds, 1 TD)

2002 SEASON

AFC Playoffs

First Round . . . . .at NY Jets 41, *Indianapolis 0
at Pittsburgh 36, *Cleveland 33
Second Round . . . . .at Tennessee 34, Pittsburgh 31 (OT)
at Oakland 30, NY Jets 10
Championship . . . . at Oakland 41, Tennessee 24

NFC Playoffs

First Round . . . .*Atlanta 27, at Green Bay 7
at San Francisco 39, *NY Giants 38
Second Round . . . . .at Philadelphia 20, Atlanta 6
at Tampa Bay 31, San Francisco 6
Championship . . . . . . Tampa Bay 27, at Philadelphia 10

Super Bowl XXXVII

Jan. 26, 2003
Qualcomm Stadium, San Diego
Favorite: Raiders by 3½—Attendance: 67,603

Oakland (13-5) 3   0   6   12—**21**
Tampa Bay (14-4) 3   17   14   14—**48**
MVP: Tampa Bay S Dexter Jackson (2 interceptions for 34 yards)

2003 SEASON

AFC Playoffs

First Round . . . .*Tennessee 20, at Baltimore 17
at Indianapolis 41, *Denver 10
Second Round . . . . . .at New England 17, Tennessee 14
Indianapolis 38, at Kansas City 31
Championship . . . . at New England 24, Indianapolis 14

NFC Playoffs

First Round . . . . .at Carolina 29, *Dallas 10
at Green Bay 33, Seattle 27 (OT)
Second Round . . . . . .Carolina 29, at St. Louis 23 (2OT)
at Philadelphia 20, Green Bay 17 (OT)
Championship . . . . Carolina 14, at Philadelphia 3

Super Bowl XXXVIII

Feb. 1, 2004
Reliant Stadium, Houston
Favorite: Patriots by 7—Attendance: 71,525

Carolina (14-5) 0   10   0   19—**29**
New England (16-2) 0   14   0   18—**32**
MVP: New England QB Tom Brady (32 for 48, 354 yds, 3 TD, 1 Int)

2004 SEASON

AFC Playoffs

First Round . . . .*NY Jets 20, at San Diego 17 (OT)
at Indianapolis 49, *Denver 24
Second Round . . . . . .at Pittsburgh 20, NY Jets 17 (OT)
at New England 20, Indianapolis 3
Championship . . . . . . New England 41, at Pittsburgh 27

NFC Playoffs

First Round . . . .*St. Louis 27, at Seattle 20
*Minnesota 31, at Green Bay 17
Second Round . . . . .at Atlanta 47, St. Louis 17
at Philadelphia 27, Minnesota 14
Championship . . . . at Philadelphia 27, Atlanta 10

Super Bowl XXXIX

Feb. 6, 2005
ALLTEL Stadium, Jacksonville
Favorite: Patriots by 7—Attendance: 78,125

New England (16-2) 0   7   7   10—**24**
Philadelphia (15-3) 0   7   7   7—**21**
MVP: New England WR Deion Branch (11 catches, 133 yds)

2005 SEASON

AFC Playoffs

First Round . . . . .at New England 28, *Jacksonville 3
*Pittsburgh 31, at Cincinnati 17
Second Round . . . . .at Denver 27, New England 13
Pittsburgh 21, at Indianapolis 18
Championship . . . . Pittsburgh 34, at Denver 17

NFC Playoffs

First Round . . . .*Washington 17, at Tampa Bay 10
*Carolina 23, at NY Giants 0
Second Round . . . . .at Seattle 20, Washington 10
Carolina 29, at Chicago 21
Championship . . . . at Seattle 34, Carolina 14

Super Bowl XL

Feb. 5, 2006
Ford Field, Detroit
Favorite: Steelers by 3½—Attendance: 68,206

Seattle (15-3) 3   0   7   0—**10**
Pittsburgh (14-5) 0   7   7—**21**
MVP: Pittsburgh WR Hines Ward (5 catches, 123 yds, 1 TD)

2006 SEASON

AFC Playoffs

First Round . . . . .at Indianapolis 23, *Kansas City 8
at New England 37, *NY Jets 16
Second Round . . . . .Indianapolis 15, at Baltimore 6
New England 24, at San Diego 21
Championship . . . . . at Indianapolis 38, New England 34

NFC Playoffs

First Round . . . . .at Seattle 21, *Dallas 20
at Philadelphia 23, *NY Giants 20
Second Round . . . .at New Orleans 27, Philadelphia 24
at Chicago 27, Seattle 24 (OT)
Championship . . . . . . .at Chicago 39, New Orleans 14

Super Bowl XLI

Feb. 4, 2007
Dolphin Stadium, Miami
Favorite: Colts by 7—Attendance: 74,512

Indianapolis (15-4) 6   10   6   7—**29**
Chicago (15-3) 14   0   3   0—**17**
MVP: Indianapolis QB Peyton Manning (25 for 38, 247 yds, 1 TD, 1 Int)

2007 SEASON

AFC Playoffs

First Round . . . .*Jacksonville 31, at Pittsburgh 29
at San Diego 17, *Tennessee 6
Second Round . . . . .at New England 31, Jacksonville 20
San Diego 28, at Indianapolis 24
Championship . . . . . at New England 21, San Diego 12

NFC Playoffs

First Round . . . . .at Seattle 35, *Washington 14
*NY Giants 24, at Tampa Bay 14
Second Round . . . . .at Green Bay 42, Seattle 20
NY Giants 21, at Dallas 17
Championship . . . . NY Giants 23, at Green Bay 20 (OT)

Super Bowl XLII

Feb. 3, 2008
University of Phoenix Stadium, Glendale, AZ
Favorite: Patriots by 12—Attendance: 71,101

NY Giants (13-6) 3   0   0   14—**17**
New England (18-0) 0   7   0   7—**14**
MVP: NY Giants QB Eli Manning (19 for 34, 255 yds, 2 TD, 1 Int)

Before the Super Bowl

The first NFL champion was the Akron Pros in 1920, when the league was called the American Professional Football Association (APFA) and the title went to the team with the best regular season record. The APFA changed its name to the National Football League in 1922.

The first playoff game with the championship at stake came in 1932, when the Chicago Bears (6-1-6) and Portsmouth (Ohio) Spartans (6-1-4) ended the regular season tied for first place. The Bears won the subsequent playoff, 9-0. Due to a snowstorm and cold weather, the game was moved from Wrigley Field to an improvised 80-yard dirt field at Chicago Stadium, making it the first indoor title game as well.

The NFL Championship Game decided the league title until the NFL merged with the AFL and the first Super Bowl was played following the 1966 season.

NFL Champions, 1920-32

Winning player-coaches noted by position.
Multiple winners: Canton-Cleveland Bulldogs and Green Bay (3); Chicago Staleys/Bears (2).

Year	Champion	Head Coach	Year	Champion	Head Coach
1920	Akron Pros	Fritz Pollard, HB & Elgie Tobin, QB	1927	New York Giants	Earl Potteiger, QB
			1928	Providence Steam Roller	Jimmy Conzelman, HB
1921	Chicago Staleys	George Halas, E	1929	Green Bay Packers	Curly Lambeau, QB
1922	Canton Bulldogs	Guy Chamberlin, E	1930	Green Bay Packers	Curly Lambeau
1923	Canton Bulldogs	Guy Chamberlin, E	1931	Green Bay Packers	Curly Lambeau
1924	Cleveland Bulldogs	Guy Chamberlin, E	1932	Chicago Bears	Ralph Jones
1925	Chicago Cardinals	Norm Barry	(Bears beat Portsmouth-OH in playoff, 9-0)		
1926	Frankford Yellow Jackets	Guy Chamberlin, E			

NFL-NFC Championship Game

NFL Championship games from 1933-69 and NFC Championship games since the completion of the NFL-AFL merger following the 1969 season.

Multiple winners: Green Bay (10); Chicago Bears and Dallas (8); NY Giants and Washington (7); San Francisco, Cle-LA-St.L Rams and Philadelphia (5); Cleveland Browns, Detroit and Minnesota (4); Baltimore Colts (3).

Season	Winner	Head Coach	Score	Loser	Head Coach	Site
1933	Chicago Bears	George Halas	23-21	New York	Steve Owen	Chicago
1934	New York	Steve Owen	30-13	Chicago Bears	George Halas	New York
1935	Detroit	Potsy Clark	26-7	New York	Steve Owen	Detroit
1936	Green Bay	Curly Lambeau	21-6	Boston Redskins	Ray Flaherty	New York
1937	Washington Redskins	Ray Flaherty	28-21	Chicago Bears	George Halas	Chicago
1938	New York	Steve Owen	23-17	Green Bay	Curly Lambeau	New York
1939	Green Bay	Curly Lambeau	27-0	New York	Steve Owen	Milwaukee
1940	Chicago Bears	George Halas	73-0	Washington	Ray Flaherty	Washington
1941	Chicago Bears	George Halas	37-9	New York	Steve Owen	Chicago
1942	Washington	Ray Flaherty	14-6	Chicago Bears	Hunk Anderson & Luke Johnsos	Washington
1943	Chicago Bears	Hunk Anderson & Luke Johnsos	41-21	Washington	Arthur Bergman	Chicago
1944	Green Bay	Curly Lambeau	14-7	New York	Steve Owen	New York
1945	Cleveland Rams	Adam Walsh	15-14	Washington	Dudley DeGroot	Cleveland
1946	Chicago Bears	George Halas	24-14	New York	Steve Owen	New York
1947	Chicago Cardinals	Jimmy Conzelman	28-21	Philadelphia	Greasy Neale	Chicago
1948	Philadelphia	Greasy Neale	7-0	Chicago Cardinals	Jimmy Conzelman	Philadelphia
1949	Philadelphia	Greasy Neale	14-0	Los Angeles Rams	Clark Shaughnessy	Los Angeles
1950	Cleveland Browns	Paul Brown	30-28	Los Angeles	Joe Stydahar	Cleveland
1951	Los Angeles	Joe Stydahar	24-17	Cleveland	Paul Brown	Los Angeles
1952	Detroit	Buddy Parker	17-7	Cleveland	Paul Brown	Cleveland
1953	Detroit	Buddy Parker	17-16	Cleveland	Paul Brown	Detroit
1954	Cleveland	Paul Brown	56-10	Detroit	Buddy Parker	Cleveland
1955	Cleveland	Paul Brown	38-14	Los Angeles	Sid Gillman	Los Angeles
1956	New York	Jim Lee Howell	47-7	Chicago Bears	Paddy Driscoll	New York
1957	Detroit	George Wilson	59-14	Cleveland	Paul Brown	Detroit
1958	Balt. Colts	Weeb Ewbank	23-17*	New York	Jim Lee Howell	New York
1959	Balt. Colts	Weeb Ewbank	31-16	New York	Jim Lee Howell	Baltimore
1960	Philadelphia	Buck Shaw	17-13	Green Bay	Vince Lombardi	Philadelphia
1961	Green Bay	Vince Lombardi	37-0	New York	Allie Sherman	Green Bay
1962	Green Bay	Vince Lombardi	16-7	New York	Allie Sherman	New York
1963	Chicago	George Halas	14-10	New York	Allie Sherman	Chicago
1964	Cleveland	Blanton Collier	27-0	Balt. Colts	Don Shula	Cleveland
1965	Green Bay	Vince Lombardi	23-12	Cleveland	Blanton Collier	Green Bay
1966	Green Bay	Vince Lombardi	34-27	Dallas	Tom Landry	Dallas
1967	Green Bay	Vince Lombardi	21-17	Dallas	Tom Landry	Green Bay
1968	Balt. Colts	Don Shula	34-0	Cleveland	Blanton Collier	Cleveland
1969	Minnesota	Bud Grant	27-7	Cleveland	Blanton Collier	Minnesota
1970	Dallas	Tom Landry	17-10	San Francisco	Dick Nolan	San Francisco

Season	Winner	Head Coach	Score	Loser	Head Coach	Site
1971	Dallas	Tom Landry	14-3	San Francisco	Dick Nolan	Dallas
1972	Washington	George Allen	26-3	Dallas	Tom Landry	Washington
1973	Minnesota	Bud Grant	27-10	Dallas	Tom Landry	Dallas
1974	Minnesota	Bud Grant	14-10	Los Angeles	Chuck Knox	Minnesota
1975	Dallas	Tom Landry	37-7	Los Angeles	Chuck Knox	Los Angeles
1976	Minnesota	Bud Grant	24-13	Los Angeles	Chuck Knox	Minnesota
1977	Dallas	Tom Landry	23-6	Minnesota	Bud Grant	Dallas
1978	Dallas	Tom Landry	28-0	Los Angeles	Ray Malavasi	Los Angele
1979	Los Angeles	Ray Malavasi	9-0	Tampa Bay	John McKay	Tampa Bay
1980	Philadelphia	Dick Vermeil	20-7	Dallas	Tom Landry	Philadelphia
1981	San Francisco	Bill Walsh	28-27	Dallas	Tom Landry	San Francisco
1982	Washington	Joe Gibbs	31-17	Dallas	Tom Landry	Washington
1983	Washington	Joe Gibbs	24-21	San Francisco	Bill Walsh	Washington
1984	San Francisco	Bill Walsh	23-0	Chicago	Mike Ditka	San Francisco
1985	Chicago	Mike Ditka	24-0	Los Angeles	John Robinson	Chicago
1986	New York	Bill Parcells	17-0	Washington	Joe Gibbs	New York
1987	Washington	Joe Gibbs	17-10	Minnesota	Jerry Burns	Washington
1988	San Francisco	Bill Walsh	28-3	Chicago	Mike Ditka	Chicago
1989	San Francisco	George Seifert	30-3	Los Angeles	John Robinson	San Francisco
1990	New York	Bill Parcells	15-13	San Francisco	George Seifert	San Francisco
1991	Washington	Joe Gibbs	41-10	Detroit	Wayne Fontes	Washington
1992	Dallas	Jimmy Johnson	30-20	San Francisco	George Seifert	San Francisco
1993	Dallas	Jimmy Johnson	38-21	San Francisco	George Seifert	Dallas
1994	San Francisco	George Seifert	38-28	Dallas	Barry Switzer	San Francisco
1995	Dallas	Barry Switzer	38-27	Green Bay	Mike Holmgren	Dallas
1996	Green Bay	Mike Holmgren	30-13	Carolina	Dom Capers	Green Bay
1997	Green Bay	Mike Holmgren	23-10	San Francisco	Steve Mariucci	San Francisco
1998	Atlanta	Dan Reeves	30-27*	Minnesota	Dennis Green	Minnesota
1999	St. Louis	Dick Vermeil	11-6	Tampa Bay	Tony Dungy	St. Louis
2000	New York	Jim Fassel	41-0	Minnesota	Dennis Green	New York
2001	St. Louis	Mike Martz	29-24	Philadelphia	Andy Reid	St. Louis
2002	Tampa Bay	Jon Gruden	27-10	Philadelphia	Andy Reid	Philadelphia
2003	Carolina	John Fox	14-3	Philadelphia	Andy Reid	Philadelphia
2004	Philadelphia	Andy Reid	27-10	Atlanta	Jim Mora Jr.	Philadelphia
2005	Seattle	Mike Holmgren	34-14	Carolina	John Fox	Seattle
2006	Chicago	Lovie Smith	39-14	New Orleans	Sean Payton	Chicago
2007	New York	Tom Coughlin	23-20*	Green Bay	Mike McCarthy	Green Bay

*Sudden death overtime

NFL-NFC Championship Game Appearances

App		W	L	Pct	PF	PA	App		W	L	Pct	PF	PA
18	NY Giants	7	11	.389	304	342	8	Minnesota	4	4	.500	151	151
16	Dallas Cowboys	8	8	.500	361	319	6	Detroit	4	2	.667	139	141
14	Green Bay Packers	10	4	.714	323	200	4	Baltimore Colts	3	1	.750	88	60
14	Chicago Bears	8	6	.571	325	259	3	Tampa Bay	1	2	.333	30	30
14	Cle-LA-St.L Rams	5	9	.357	163	300	3	Carolina	1	2	.333	41	67
12	Boston-Wash. Redskins	7	5	.583	222	255	2	Chicago Cardinals	1	1	.500	28	28
12	San Francisco	5	7	.417	245	222	2	Atlanta	1	1	.500	40	54
11	Cleveland Browns	7	4	.364	224	253	1	Seattle	1	0	1.000	34	14
9	Philadelphia	5	4	.556	143	128	1	New Orleans	0	1	.000	14	39

AFL-AFC Championship Game

AFL Championship games from 1960-69 and AFC Championship games since the completion of the NFL-AFL merger following the 1969 season.

Multiple winners: Buffalo, Denver, New England and Pittsburgh (6); Miami and Oakland-LA Raiders (5); Dallas Texans-KC Chiefs and Houston Oilers-Tennessee Titans (3); Cincinnati and San Diego (2).

Season	Winner	Head Coach	Score	Loser	Head Coach	Site
1960	Houston	Lou Rymkus	24-16	LA Chargers	Sid Gillman	Houston
1961	Houston	Wally Lemm	10-3	SD Chargers	Sid Gillman	San Diego
1962	Dallas	Hank Stram	20-17*	Houston	Pop Ivy	Houston
1963	San Diego	Sid Gillman	51-10	Boston Patriots	Mike Holovak	San Diego
1964	Buffalo	Lou Saban	20-7	SanDiego	Sid Gillman	Buffalo
1965	Buffalo	Lou Saban	23-0	San Diego	Sid Gillman	San Diego
1966	Kansas City	Hank Stram	31-7	Buffalo	Joe Collier	Buffalo
1967	Oakland	John Rauch	40-7	Houston	Wally Lemm	Oakland
1968	NY Jets	Weeb Ewbank	27-23	Oakland	John Rauch	New York
1969	Kansas City	Hank Stram	17-7	Oakland	John Madden	Oakland
1970	Balt. Colts	Don McCafferty	27-17	Oakland	John Madden	Baltimore
1971	Miami	Don Shula	21-0	Balt. Colts	Don McCafferty	Miami
1972	Miami	Don Shula	21-17	Pittsburgh	Chuck Noll	Pittsburgh
1973	Miami	Don Shula	27-10	Oakland	John Madden	Miami

AFL-AFC Championship Game (Cont.)

Season	Winner	Head Coach	Score	Loser	Head Coach	Site
1974	Pittsburgh	Chuck Noll	24-13	Oakland	John Madden	Oakland
1975	Pittsburgh	Chuck Noll	16-10	Oakland	John Madden	Pittsburgh
1976	Oakland	John Madden	24-7	Pittsburgh	Chuck Noll	Oakland
1977	Denver	Red Miller	20-17	Oakland	John Madden	Denver
1978	Pittsburgh	Chuck Noll	34-5	Houston	Bum Phillips	Pittsburgh
1979	Pittsburgh	Chuck Noll	27-13	Houston	Bum Phillips	Pittsburgh
1980	Oakland	Tom Flores	34-27	San Diego	Don Coryell	San Diego
1981	Cincinnati	Forrest Gregg	27-7	San Diego	Don Coryell	Cincinnati
1982	Miami	Don Shula	14-0	NY Jets	Walt Michaels	Miami
1983	LA Raiders	Tom Flores	30-14	Seattle	Chuck Knox	Los Angeles
1984	Miami	Don Shula	45-28	Pittsburgh	Chuck Noll	Miami
1985	New England	Raymond Berry	31-14	Miami	Don Shula	Miami
1986	Denver	Dan Reeves	23-20*	Cleveland	Marty Schottenheimer	Cleveland
1987	Denver	Dan Reeves	38-33	Cleveland	Marty Schottenheimer	Denver
1988	Cincinnati	Sam Wyche	21-10	Buffalo	Marv Levy	Cincinnati
1989	Denver	Dan Reeves	37-21	Cleveland	Bud Carson	Denver
1990	Buffalo	Marv Levy	51-3	LA Raiders	Art Shell	Buffalo
1991	Buffalo	Marv Levy	10-7	Denver	Dan Reeves	Buffalo
1992	Buffalo	Marv Levy	29-10	Miami	Don Shula	Miami
1993	Buffalo	Marv Levy	30-13	Kansas City	Marty Schottenheimer	Buffalo
1994	San Diego	Bobby Ross	17-13	Pittsburgh	Bill Cowher	Pittsburgh
1995	Pittsburgh	Bill Cowher	20-16	Indianapolis	Ted Marchibroda	Pittsburgh
1996	New England	Bill Parcells	20-6	Jacksonville	Tom Coughlin	New England
1997	Denver	Mike Shanahan	24-21	Pittsburgh	Bill Cowher	Pittsburgh
1998	Denver	Mike Shanahan	23-10	NY Jets	Bill Parcells	Denver
1999	Tennessee	Jeff Fisher	33-14	Jacksonville	Tom Coughlin	Jacksonville
2000	Balt. Ravens	Brian Billick	16-3	Oakland	Jon Gruden	Oakland
2001	New England	Bill Belichick	24-17	Pittsburgh	Bill Cowher	Pittsburgh
2002	Oakland	Bill Callahan	41-24	Tennessee	Jeff Fisher	Oakland
2003	New England	Bill Belichick	24-14	Indianapolis	Tony Dungy	New England
2004	New England	Bill Belichick	41-27	Pittsburgh	Bill Cowher	Pittsburgh
2005	Pittsburgh	Bill Cowher	34-17	Denver	Mike Shanahan	Denver
2006	Indianapolis	Tony Dungy	38-34	New England	Bill Belichick	Indianapolis
2007	New England	Bill Belichick	21-12	San Diego	Norv Turner	New England

*Sudden death overtime

AFL-AFC Championship Game Appearances

App		W	L	Pct	PF	PA
14	Oakland-LA Raiders	5	9	.357	272	304
12	Pittsburgh	6	6	.500	258	229
9	LA-San Diego Chargers	2	7	.222	140	182
8	Buffalo	6	2	.750	180	92
8	Denver	6	2	.750	189	166
8	Boston-NE Patriots	6	2	.750	205	179
8	Houston Oilers/Ten. Titans	3	5	.375	133	195
7	Miami	5	2	.714	152	115
5	Baltimore-Indy Colts	2	3	.400	95	116
4	Dallas Texans/KC Chiefs	3	1	.750	81	61
3	NY Jets	1	2	.333	37	60
3	Cleveland	0	3	.000	74	98
2	Cincinnati	2	0	1.000	48	17
2	Jacksonville	0	2	.000	20	53
1	Baltimore Ravens	1	0	1.000	16	3
1	Seattle	0	1	.000	14	30

Overall Postseason Games

The postseason records of all NFL teams, ranked by number of playoff games participated in from 1933 through the 2007-08 postseason.

Gm		W	L	Pct	PF	PA
56	Dallas Cowboys	32	24	.571	1318	1050
47	Pittsburgh Steelers	28	19	.596	1095	959
43	Oakland-LA Raiders	25	18	.581	1028	797
43	New York Giants	20	23	.465	752	810
43	Cle-LA-St.L Rams	19	24	.442	770	944
42	San Francisco 49ers	25	17	.595	1044	853
42	Minnesota Vikings	18	24	.429	824	957
40	Green Bay Packers	25	15	.625	950	766
40	Boston-Wash. Redskins	23	17	.575	819	707
39	Miami Dolphins	20	19	.513	780	848
34	Boston-NE Patriots	21	13	.618	730	666
34	Balt-Indianapolis Colts	17	17	.500	685	695
34	Philadelphia Eagles	17	17	.500	653	608
33	Chicago Bears	16	17	.485	702	681
32	Denver Broncos	17	15	.531	694	794
32	Houston Oilers/Ten. Titans	14	18	.438	569	749
31	Cleveland Browns	11	20	.355	629	728
29	Buffalo Bills	14	15	.483	681	658
23	LA-San Diego Chargers	9	14	.391	427	523
21	Dallas Texans/KC Chiefs	8	13	.381	340	445
19	New York Jets	8	11	.421	388	389
17	Detroit Lions	7	10	.412	365	404
17	Seattle Seahawks	7	10	.412	356	367
15	Tampa Bay Buccaneers	6	9	.400	230	279
14	Atlanta Falcons	6	8	.429	298	331
13	Cincinnati Bengals	5	8	.385	263	288
11	Jacksonville Jaguars	5	6	.455	262	288
9	Carolina Panthers	6	3	.667	206	170
8	Baltimore Ravens	5	3	.625	148	88
8	New Orleans Saints	2	6	.250	144	248
7	Chi-St.L.-Ari. Cardinals	2	5	.286	122	182

NFL Divisional Champions

The NFL adopted divisional play for the first time in 1967, splitting both conferences into two four-team divisions—the Capitol and Century divisions in the East and the Central and Coastal divisions in the West. A merger with the AFL in 1970 increased NFL membership to 26 teams and made it necessary for realignment. Two 13-team conferences—the AFC and NFC—were formed by moving established NFL clubs in Baltimore, Cleveland and Pittsburgh to the AFC and rearranging both conferences into Eastern, Central and Western divisions. Expansion has since increased the league to 32 teams (beginning in 2002) with four NFC divisions and four AFC divisions, all with four teams each.

Division champions are listed below; teams that went on to win the Super Bowl are in **bold** type. Note that in the 1980 season, Oakland won the Super Bowl as a wild card team, as did Denver in 1997, Baltimore in 2000, Pittsburgh in 2005 and the NY Giants in 2007; and in 1982, the players' strike shortened the regular season to nine games and eliminated divisional play for one season.

Multiple champions (since 1970): AFC–Pittsburgh (18); Miami and Oakland-LA Raiders (12); Baltimore-Indianapolis Colts (11); Denver and New England (10); San Diego (8); Buffalo (7); Cincinnati and Cleveland (6); Kansas City (5); Houston Oilers-Tennessee Titans (4); Baltimore Ravens, Jacksonville, NY Jets and Seattle (2). NFC–San Francisco (17); Dallas (16); Minnesota (14); LA-St. Louis Rams (11); Chicago (9); Green Bay (8); Philadelphia (7); NY Giants, Tampa Bay and Washington (6); Seattle (4); Atlanta, Detroit and New Orleans (3); Carolina and St. Louis Cardinals (2).

American Football League

Season	East	West
1966	Buffalo	Kansas City

Season	East	West
1967	Houston	Oakland
1968	**NY Jets**	Oakland
1969	NY Jets	Oakland

National Football League

Season	East	West
1966	Dallas	**Green Bay**

Season	Capitol	Century	Central	Coastal
1967	Dallas	Cleveland	**Green Bay**	LA Rams
1968	Dallas	Cleveland	Minnesota	Baltimore
1969	Dallas	Cleveland	Minnesota	LA Rams

Note: Kansas City, an AFL second-place team, won the Super Bowl in the 1969 season.

American Football Conference

Season	East	Central	West
1970	**Balt. Colts**	Cincinnati	Oakland
1971	Miami	Cleveland	Kansas City
1972	**Miami**	Pittsburgh	Oakland
1973	**Miami**	Cincinnati	Oakland
1974	Miami	**Pittsburgh**	Oakland
1975	Balt.Colts	**Pittsburgh**	Oakland
1976	Balt.Colts	Pittsburgh	**Oakland**
1977	Balt.Colts	Pittsburgh	Denver
1978	New England	**Pittsburgh**	Denver
1979	Miami	**Pittsburgh**	San Diego
1980	Buffalo	Cleveland	San Diego
1981	Miami	Cincinnati	San Diego
1982	—	—	—
1983	Miami	Pittsburgh	**LA Raiders**
1984	Miami	Pittsburgh	Denver
1985	Miami	Cleveland	LA Raiders
1986	New England	Cleveland	Denver
1987	Indianapolis	Cleveland	Denver
1988	Buffalo	Cincinnati	Seattle
1989	Buffalo	Cleveland	Denver
1990	Buffalo	Cincinnati	LA Raiders
1991	Buffalo	Houston	Denver
1992	Miami	Pittsburgh	San Diego
1993	Buffalo	Houston	Kansas City
1994	Miami	Pittsburgh	San Diego
1995	Buffalo	Pittsburgh	Kansas City
1996	New England	Pittsburgh	Denver
1997	New England	Pittsburgh	Kansas City
1998	NY Jets	Jacksonville	**Denver**
1999	Indianapolis	Jacksonville	Seattle
2000	Miami	Tennessee	Oakland
2001	**New England**	Pittsburgh	Oakland

Season	East	North	South	West
2002	NY Jets	Pittsburgh	Tennessee	Oakland
2003	**New Eng.**	Baltimore	Indianapolis	Kansas City
2004	**New Eng.**	Pittsburgh	Indianapolis	San Diego
2005	New Eng.	Cincinnati	Indianapolis	Denver
2006	New Eng.	Baltimore	**Indianap.**	San Diego
2007	New Eng.	Pittsburgh	Indianapolis	San Diego

National Football Conference

Season	East	Central	West
1970	Dallas	Minnesota	San Francisco
1971	**Dallas**	Minnesota	San Francisco
1972	Washington	Green Bay	San Francisco
1973	Dallas	Minnesota	LA Rams
1974	St. Louis	Minnesota	LA Rams
1975	St. Louis	Minnesota	LA Rams
1976	Dallas	Minnesota	LA Rams
1977	**Dallas**	Minnesota	LA Rams
1978	Dallas	Minnesota	LA Rams
1979	Dallas	Tampa Bay	LA Rams
1980	Philadelphia	Minnesota	Atlanta
1981	Dallas	Tampa Bay	**San Francisco**
1982	—	—	—
1983	Washington	Detroit	San Francisco
1984	Washington	Chicago	**San Francisco**
1985	Dallas	**Chicago**	LA Rams
1986	**NY Giants**	Chicago	San Francisco
1987	**Washington**	Chicago	San Francisco
1988	Philadelphia	Chicago	**San Francisco**
1989	NY Giants	Minnesota	**San Francisco**
1990	**NY Giants**	Chicago	San Francisco
1991	**Washington**	Detroit	New Orleans
1992	**Dallas**	Minnesota	San Francisco
1993	**Dallas**	Detroit	San Francisco
1994	Dallas	Minnesota	**San Francisco**
1995	**Dallas**	Green Bay	San Francisco
1996	Dallas	**Green Bay**	Carolina
1997	NY Giants	Green Bay	San Francisco
1998	Dallas	Minnesota	Atlanta
1999	Washington	Tampa Bay	**St. Louis**
2000	NY Giants	Minnesota	New Orleans
2001	Philadelphia	Chicago	St. Louis

Season	East	North	South	West
2002	Philadelphia	Green Bay	**Tampa Bay**	San Fran.
2003	Philadelphia	Green Bay	Carolina	St. Louis
2004	Philadelphia	Green Bay	Atlanta	Seattle
2005	NY Giants	Chicago	Tampa Bay	Seattle
2006	Philadelphia	Chicago	New Orleans	Seattle
2007	Dallas	Green Bay	Tampa Bay	Seattle

Champions of Leagues That No Longer Exist

No professional league in American sports has had to contend with more pretenders to the throne than the NFL. Eight times in nine decades, a rival league has risen up to challenge the NFL and seven of them went under in less than five seasons. Only the fourth American Football League (1960-69) succeeded, forcing the older league to sue for peace and a full partnership in 1966.

Of the seven leagues that didn't make it, only the All-America Football Conference (1946-49) lives on—the Cleveland Browns and San Francisco 49ers joined the NFL after the AAFC folded in 1949. The champions of leagues past are listed below.

American Football League I

Year		Head Coach
1926	Philadelphia Quakers (8-2)	Bob Folwell

Note: Philadelphia was challenged to a postseason game by the 7th place New York Giants (8-4-1) of the NFL. The Giants won, 31-0, in a snowstorm.

American Football League II

Year		Head Coach
1936	Boston Shamrocks (8-3)	George Kenneally
1937	Los Angeles Bulldogs (9-0)	Gus Henderson

Note: Boston was scheduled to play 2nd place Cleveland (5-2-2) in the '36 championship game, but the Shamrock players refused to participate because they were owed pay for past games.

American Football League III

Year		Head Coach
1940	Columbus Bullies (8-1-1)	Phil Bucklew
1941	Columbus Bullies (5-1-2)	Phil Bucklew

All-America Football Conference

Year	Winner	Head Coach	Score	Loser	Head Coach	Site
1946	Cleveland Browns	Paul Brown	14-9	NY Yankees	Ray Flaherty	Cleveland
1947	Cleveland Browns	Paul Brown	14-3	NY Yankees	Ray Flaherty	New York
1948	Cleveland Browns	Paul Brown	49-7	Buffalo Bills	Red Dawson	Cleveland
1949	Cleveland Browns	Paul Brown	21-7	S.F. 49ers	Buck Shaw	Cleveland

World Football League

Year	Winner	Head Coach	Score	Loser	Head Coach	Site
1974	Birmingham Americans	Jack Gotta	22-21	Florida Blazers	Jack Pardee	Birmingham

United States Football League

Year	Winner	Head Coach	Score	Loser	Head Coach	Site
1983	Michigan Panthers	Jim Stanley	24-22	Philadelphia Stars	Jim Mora	Denver
1984	Philadelphia Stars	Jim Mora	23-3	Arizona Wranglers	George Allen	Tampa
1985	Baltimore Stars	Jim Mora	28-24	Oakland Invaders	Charlie Sumner	E. Rutherford

XFL

Year	Winner	Head Coach	Score	Loser	Head Coach	Site
2001	Los Angeles Xtreme	Al Luginbill	38-6	San Fran. Demons	Jim Skipper	Los Angeles

Defunct Leagues

AFL I (1926): Boston Bulldogs, Brooklyn Horseman, Chicago Bulls, Cleveland Panthers, Los Angeles Wildcats, New York Yankees, Newark Bears, Philadelphia Quakers, Rock Island Independents.

AFL II (1936-37): Boston Shamrocks (1936-37); Brooklyn Tigers (1936); Cincinnati Bengals (1937); Cleveland Rams (1936); Los Angeles Bulldogs (1937); New York Yankees (1936-37); Pittsburgh Americans (1936-37); Rochester Tigers (1936-37).

AFL III (1940-41): Boston Bears (1940); Buffalo Indians (1940-41); Cincinnati Bengals (1940-41); Columbus Bullies (1940-41); Milwaukee Chiefs (1940-41); New York Yankees (1940) renamed Americans (1941).

AAFC (1946-49): Brooklyn Dodgers (1946-48) merged to become Brooklyn-New York Yankees (1949); Buffalo Bisons (1946) renamed Bills (1947-49); Chicago Rockets (1946-48) renamed Hornets (1949); Cleveland Browns (1946-49); Los Angeles Dons (1946-49); Miami Seahawks (1946) became Baltimore Colts (1947-49); New York Yankees (1946-48) merged to become Brooklyn-New York Yankees (1949); San Francisco 49ers (1946-49).

WFL (1974-75): Birmingham Americans (1974) renamed Vulcans (1975); Chicago Fire (1974) renamed Winds (1975); Detroit Wheels (1974); Florida Blazers (1974) became San Antonio Wings (1975); The Hawaiians (1974-75); Houston Texans (1974) became Shreveport (La.) Steamer (1974-75); Jacksonville Sharks (1974) renamed Express (1975); Memphis Southmen (1974) also known as Grizzlies (1975); New York Stars (1974) became Charlotte Hornets (1974-75); Philadelphia Bell (1974-75); Portland Storm (1974) renamed Thunder (1975); Southern California Sun (1974-75).

USFL (1983-85): Arizona Wranglers (1983-84) merged with Oklahoma to become Arizona Outlaws (1985); Birmingham Stallions (1983-85); Boston Breakers (1983) became New Orleans Breakers (1984) and then Portland Breakers (1985); Chicago Blitz (1983-84); Denver Gold (1983-85); Houston Gamblers (1984-85); Jacksonville Bulls (1984-85); Los Angeles Express (1983-85); Memphis Showboats (1984-85).

Michigan Panthers (1983-84) merged with Oakland (1985); New Jersey Generals (1983-85); Oakland Invaders (1983-85); Oklahoma Outlaws (1984) merged with Arizona to become Arizona Outlaws (1985); Philadelphia Stars (1983-84) became Baltimore Stars (1985); Pittsburgh Maulers (1984); San Antonio Gunslingers (1984-85); Tampa Bay Bandits (1983-85); Washington Federals (1983-84) became Orlando Renegades (1985).

XFL (2001): Birmingham Thunderbolts, Chicago Enforcers, Las Vegas Outlaws, Los Angeles Xtreme, Memphis Maniax, New York New Jersey Hitmen, Orlando Rage, San Francisco Demons.

NFL Pro Bowl

A postseason All-Star game between the new league champion and a team of professional all-stars was added to the NFL schedule in 1939. In the first game at Wrigley Field in Los Angeles, the NY Giants beat a team made up of players from NFL teams and two independent clubs in Los Angeles (the LA Bulldogs and Hollywood Stars). An all-NFL All-Star team provided the opposition over the next four seasons, but the game was cancelled in 1943.

The Pro Bowl was revived in 1951 as a contest between conference all-star teams: American vs National (1951-53), Eastern vs Western (1954-70), and AFC vs NFC (since 1971). The current AFC-NFC series is tied, 19-19.

The MVP trophy was named the Dan McGuire Award in 1984 after the late SF 49ers publicist and *Honolulu Advertiser* sports columnist.

Year	Winner	Score	Loser
1939	NY Giants	13-10	All-Stars
1940	Green Bay	16-7	All-Stars
1940	Chicago Bears	28-14	All-Stars
1942	Chicago Bears	35-24	All-Stars
1942	All-Stars	17-14	Washington
1943-50	No game		

Year	Winner	MVP
1951	American, 28-27	Otto Graham, Cle., QB
1952	National, 30-13	Dan Towler, LA Rams, HB
1953	National, 27-7	Don Doll, Det., DB
1954	East, 20-9	Chuck Bednarik, Phi., LB
1955	West, 26-19	Billy Wilson, SF, E
1956	East, 31-30	Ollie Matson, Cards, HB
1957	West, 19-10	Back–Bert Rechichar, Bal.
		Line–Ernie Stautner, Pit.
1958	West, 26-7	Back–Hugh McElhenny, SF
		Line–Gene Brito, Wash.
1959	East, 28-21	Back–Frank Gifford, NY
		Line–Doug Atkins, Chi.
1960	West, 38-21	Back–Johnny Unitas, Bal.
		Line–Big Daddy Lipscomb, Pit.
1961	West, 35-31	Back–Johnny Unitas, Bal.
		Line–Sam Huff, NY
1962	West, 31-30	Back–Jim Brown, Cle.
		Line–Henry Jordan, GB
1963	East, 30-20	Back–Jim Brown, Cle.
		Line–Big Daddy Lipscomb, Pit.
1964	West, 31-17	Back–Johnny Unitas, Bal.
		Line–Gino Marchetti, Bal.
1965	West, 34-14	Back–Fran Tarkenton, Min.
		Line–Terry Barr, Det.
1966	East, 36-7	Back–Jim Brown, Cle.
		Line–Dale Meinhart, St. L.
1967	East, 20-10	Back–Gale Sayers, Chi.
		Line–Floyd Peters, Phi.
1968	West, 38-20	Back–Gale Sayers, Chi.
		Line–Dave Robinson, GB
1969	West, 10-7	Back–Roman Gabriel, LA Rams
		Line–Merlin Olsen, LA Rams
1970	West, 16-13	Back–Gale Sayers, Chi.
		Line–George Andrie, Dal.

Year	Winner	MVP
1971	NFC, 27-6	Back–Mel Renfro, Dal.
		Line–Fred Carr, GB
1972	AFC, 26-13	Off–Jan Stenerud, KC
		Def–Willie Lanier, KC
1973	AFC, 33-28	O.J. Simpson, Buf., RB
1974	AFC, 15-13	Garo Yepremian, Mia., PK
1975	NFC, 17-10	James Harris, LA Rams, QB
1976	NFC, 23-20	Billy Johnson, Hou., KR
1977	AFC, 24-14	Mel Blount, Pit., CB
1978	NFC, 14-13	Walter Payton, Chi., RB
1979	NFC, 13-7	Ahmad Rashad, Min., WR
1980	NFC, 37-27	Chuck Muncie, NO, RB
1981	NFC, 21-7	Eddie Murray, Det., PK
1982	AFC, 16-13	Kellen Winslow, SD, WR
		& Lee Roy Selmon, TB, DE
1983	NFC, 20-19	Dan Fouts, SD, QB
		& John Jefferson, GB, WR
1984	NFC, 45-3	Joe Theismann, Wash., QB
1985	AFC, 22-14	Mark Gastineau, NYJ, DE
1986	NFC, 28-24	Phil Simms, NYG, QB
1987	AFC, 10-6	Reggie White, Phi., DE
1988	AFC, 15-6	Bruce Smith, Buf., DE
1989	NFC, 34-3	Randall Cunningham, Phi., QB
1990	NFC, 27-21	Jerry Gray, LA Rams, CB
1991	AFC, 23-21	Jim Kelly, Buf., QB
1992	NFC, 21-15	Michael Irvin, Dal., WR
1993	AFC, 23-20 (OT)	Steve Tasker, Buf., Sp. Teams
1994	NFC, 17-3	Andre Rison, Atl., WR
1995	AFC, 41-13	Marshall Faulk, Ind., RB
1996	NFC, 20-13	Jerry Rice, SF, WR
1997	AFC, 26-23 (OT)	Mark Brunell, Jax, QB
1998	AFC, 29-24	Warren Moon, Sea., QB
1999	AFC, 23-10	Ty Law, NE, CB
		& Keyshawn Johnson, NYJ, WR
2000	NFC, 51-31	Randy Moss, Min., WR
2001	AFC, 38-17	Rich Gannon, Oak., QB
2002	AFC, 38-30	Rich Gannon, Oak., QB
2003	AFC, 45-20	Ricky Williams, Mia., RB
2004	NFC, 55-52	Marc Bulger, St.L, QB
2005	AFC, 38-27	Peyton Manning, Ind., QB
2006	NFC, 23-17	Derrick Brooks, TB, LB
2007	AFC, 31-28	Carson Palmer, Cin., QB
2008	NFC, 42-30	Adrian Peterson, Min., RB

Playing sites: Wrigley Field in Los Angeles (1939); Gilmore Stadium in Los Angeles (1940–both games); Polo Grounds in New York (Jan., 1942); Shibe Park in Philadelphia (Dec., 1942); Memorial Coliseum in Los Angeles (1951-72 and 1979); Texas Stadium in Irving, TX (1973); Arrowhead Stadium in Kansas City (1974); Orange Bowl in Miami (1975); Superdome in New Orleans (1976); Kingdome in Seattle (1977); Tampa Stadium in Tampa (1978) and Aloha Stadium in Honolulu (since 1980).

AFL All-Star Game

The AFL did not play an All-Star game after its first season in 1960 but did stage All-Star games from 1962-70. All-Star teams from the Eastern and Western divisions played each other every year except 1966 with the West winning the series, 6-2. In 1966, the league champion Buffalo Bills met an elite squad made up of the best players from the league's other eight clubs and lost, 30-19.

Year	Winner	MVP
1962	West, 47-27	Cotton Davidson, Oak., QB
1963	West, 21-14	Off–Curtis McClinton, Dal.
		Def–Earl Faison, SD
1964	West, 27-24	Off–Keith Lincoln, SD
		Def–Archie Matsos, Oak.
1965	West, 38-14	Off–Keith Lincoln, SD
		Def–Willie Brown, Den.
1966	All-Stars 30	Off–Joe Namath, NY
	Buffalo 19	Def–Frank Buncom, SD

Year	Winner	MVP
1967	East, 30-23	Off–Babe Parilli, Bos.
		Def–Verlon Biggs, NY
1968	East, 25-24	Off–Joe Namath, NY
		& Don Maynard, NY
		Def–Speedy Duncan, SD
1969	West, 38-25	Off–Len Dawson, KC
		Def–George Webster, Hou.
1970	West, 26-3	John Hadl, SD, QB

Playing sites: Balboa Stadium in San Diego (1962-64); Jeppesen Stadium in Houston (1965); Rice Stadium in Houston (1966); Oakland Coliseum (1967); Gator Bowl in Jacksonville (1968-69) and Astrodome in Houston (1970).

NFL Franchise Origins

Here is what the current 32 teams in the National Football League have to show for the years they have put in as members of the American Professional Football Association (APFA), the NFL, the All-America Football Conference (AAFC) and the American Football League (AFL). Years given for league titles indicate seasons championships were won.

American Football Conference

	First Season	League Titles	Franchise Stops
Baltimore Ravens	1996 (NFL)	1 Super Bowl (2000)	• Baltimore (1996—)
Buffalo Bills	1960 (AFL)	2 AFL (1964-65)	• Buffalo (1960-72) Orchard Park, NY (1973—)
Cincinnati Bengals	1968 (AFL)	None	• Cincinnati (1968—)
Cleveland Browns	1946 (AAFC)	4 AAFC (1946-49) 4 NFL (1950,54-55,64)	• Cleveland (1946-95, 99—)
Denver Broncos	1960 (AFL)	2 Super Bowls (1997-98)	• Denver (1960—)
Houston Texans	2002 (NFL)	None	• Houston (2002—)
Indianapolis Colts	1953 (NFL)	3 NFL (1958-59,68) 2 Super Bowls (1970,2006)	• Baltimore (1953-83) Indianapolis (1984—)
Jacksonville Jaguars	1995 (NFL)	None	• Jacksonville, FL (1995—)
Kansas City Chiefs	1960 (AFL)	3 AFL (1962,66,69) 1 Super Bowl (1969)	• Dallas (1960-62) Kansas City (1963—)
Miami Dolphins	1966 (AFL)	2 Super Bowls (1972-73)	• Miami (1966—)
New England Patriots	1960 (AFL)	3 Super Bowls (2001,03-04)	• Boston (1960-70) Foxboro, MA (1971—)
New York Jets	1960 (AFL)	1 AFL (1968) 1 Super Bowl (1968)	• New York (1960-83) E. Rutherford, NJ (1984—)
Oakland Raiders	1960 (AFL)	1 AFL (1967) 3 Super Bowls (1976,80,83)	• Oakland (1960-81, 1995—) Los Angeles (1982-94)
Pittsburgh Steelers	1933 (NFL)	5 Super Bowls (1974-75,78-79, 2005)	• Pittsburgh (1933—)
San Diego Chargers	1960 (AFL)	1 AFL (1963)	• Los Angeles (1960) San Diego (1961—)
Tennessee Titans	1960 (AFL)	2 AFL (1960-61)	• Houston (1960-96) Memphis (1997) Nashville (1998—)

National Football Conference

	First Season	League Titles	Franchise Stops
Arizona Cardinals	1920 (APFA)	2 NFL (1925,47)	• Chicago (1920-59) St. Louis (1960-87) Tempe, AZ (1988-2005) Glendale, AZ (2006—)
Atlanta Falcons	1966 (NFL)	None	• Atlanta (1966—)
Carolina Panthers	1995 (NFL)	None	• Clemson, SC (1995) Charlotte, NC (1996—)
Chicago Bears	1920 (APFA)	8 NFL (1921, 32-33,40-41,43,46,63) 1 Super Bowl (1985)	• Decatur, IL (1920) Chicago (1921—)
Dallas Cowboys	1960 (NFL)	5 Super Bowls (1971,77,92-93,95)	• Dallas (1960-70) Irving, TX (1971—)
Detroit Lions	1930 (NFL)	4 NFL (1935,52-53,57)	• Portsmouth, OH (1930-33) Detroit (1934-74, 2002—) Pontiac, MI (1975-2001)
Green Bay Packers	1921 (APFA)	11 NFL (1929-31,36,39,44,61-62,65-67) 3 Super Bowls (1966-67,96)	• Green Bay (1921—)
Minnesota Vikings	1961 (NFL)	1 NFL (1969)	• Bloomington, MN (1961-81) Minneapolis, MN (1982—)
New Orleans Saints	1967 (NFL)	None	• New Orleans (1967—)
New York Giants	1925 (NFL)	4 NFL (1927,34,38,56) 3 Super Bowls (1986,90,2007)	• New York (1925-73,75) New Haven, CT (1973-74) E. Rutherford, NJ (1976—)
Philadelphia Eagles	1933 (NFL)	3 NFL (1948-49,60)	• Philadelphia (1933—)
St. Louis Rams	1937 (NFL)	2 NFL (1945,51) 1 Super Bowl (1999)	• Cleveland (1937-45) Los Angeles (1946-79) Anaheim (1980-94) St. Louis (1995—)
San Francisco 49ers	1946 (AAFC)	5 Super Bowls (1981,84,88-89,94)	• San Francisco (1946—)
Seattle Seahawks	1976 (NFL)	None	• Seattle (1976—)
Tampa Bay Buccaneers	1976 (NFL)	1 Super Bowl (2002)	• Tampa, FL (1976—)
Washington Redskins	1932 (NFL)	2 NFL (1937,42) 3 Super Bowls (1982,87,91)	• Boston (1932-36) Washington, DC (1937-96) Raljon, MD (1997—)

The Growth of the NFL

Of the 14 franchises that comprised the American Professional Football Association in 1920, only two remain—the Arizona Cardinals (then the Chicago Cardinals) and the Chicago Bears (originally the Decatur-IL Staleys). Green Bay joined the APFC in 1921 and the league changed its name to the NFL in 1922. Since then, 54 NFL clubs have come and gone, six rival leagues have expired and two other leagues have been swallowed up.

The NFL merged with the **All-America Football Conference** (1946-49) following the 1949 season and adopted three of its seven clubs—the Baltimore Colts, Cleveland Browns and San Francisco 49ers. The four remaining AAFC teams—the Brooklyn/NY Yankees, Buffalo Bills, Chicago Hornets and Los Angeles Dons—did not survive. After the 1950 season, the financially troubled Colts were sold back to the NFL. The league folded the team and added its players to the 1951 college draft pool. A new Baltimore franchise, also named the Colts, joined the NFL in 1953.

The formation of the **American Football League** (1960-69) was announced in 1959 with ownership lined up in eight cities—Boston, Buffalo, Dallas, Denver, Houston, Los Angeles, Minneapolis and New York. Set to begin play in the autumn of 1960, the AFL was stunned early that year when Minneapolis withdrew to accept an offer to join the NFL as an expansion team in 1961. The new league responded by choosing Oakland to replace Minneapolis and inherit the departed team's draft picks. Since no AFL team actually played in Minneapolis, it is not considered the original home of the Oakland Raiders.

In 1966, the NFL and AFL agreed to a merger that resulted in the first Super Bowl (originally called the AFL-NFL World Championship Game) following the '66 league playoffs. In 1970, the now 10-member AFL officially joined the NFL, forming a 26-team league made up of two conferences of three divisions each. In 2002, the 32-team league was realigned into two conferences of four divisions each.

Expansion/Merger Timetable

For teams currently in NFL.

1921–Green Bay Packers; **1925**–New York Giants; **1930**–Portsmouth-OH Spartans (now Detroit Lions); **1932**–Boston Braves (now Washington Redskins); **1933**–Philadelphia Eagles and Pittsburgh Pirates (now Steelers); **1937**–Cleveland Rams (now St. Louis); **1950**–added AAFC's Cleveland Browns and San Francisco 49ers; **1953**–Baltimore Colts (now Indianapolis). **1960**–Dallas Cowboys; **1961**–Minnesota Vikings; **1966**–Atlanta Falcons; **1967**–New Orleans Saints; **1970**–added AFL's Boston Patriots (now New England), Buffalo Bills, Cincinnati Bengals (1968 expansion team), Denver Broncos, Houston Oilers (now Tennessee Titans), Kansas City Chiefs, Miami Dolphins (1966 expansion team), New York Jets, Oakland Raiders and San Diego Chargers (the AFL-NFL merger divided the league into two 13-team conferences with old-line NFL clubs Baltimore, Cleveland and Pittsburgh moving to the AFC); **1976**–Seattle Seahawks and Tampa Bay Buccaneers (Seattle was originally in the NFC West and Tampa Bay in the AFC West, but were switched to AFC West and NFC Central, respectively, in 1977); **1995**–Carolina Panthers and Jacksonville Jaguars; **1996**—Cleveland Browns move to Baltimore and become Ravens. City of Cleveland retains rights to team name, colors and all memorabilia; **1999**–Cleveland Browns return to the NFL. **2002**–Houston Texans. Seattle moves back to the NFC West.

City and Nickname Changes

1921—Decatur Staleys move to Chicago; **1922**—Chicago Staleys renamed Bears; **1933**—Boston Braves renamed Redskins; **1937**—Boston Redskins move to Washington; **1934**—Portsmouth (Ohio) Spartans move to Detroit and become Lions; **1941**—Pittsburgh Pirates renamed Steelers; **1943**—Philadelphia and Pittsburgh merge for one season and become Phil-Pitt, or the "Steagles"; **1944**—Chicago Cardinals and Pittsburgh merge for one season and become Card-Pitt; **1946**—Cleveland Rams move to Los Angeles.

1960—Chicago Cardinals move to St. Louis; **1961**—Los Angeles Chargers (AFL) move to San Diego; **1963**—New York Titans (AFL) renamed Jets and Dallas Texans (AFL) move to Kansas City and become Chiefs; **1971**—Boston Patriots become New England Patriots; **1982**—Oakland Raiders move to Los Angeles; **1984**—Baltimore Colts move to Indianapolis; **1988**—St. Louis Cardinals move to Phoenix; **1994**—Phoenix Cardinals become Arizona Cardinals; **1995**—L.A. Rams move to St. Louis and L.A. Raiders move back to Oakland; **1996**—Cleveland Browns move to Baltimore and become Ravens. City of Cleveland retains rights to team name, colors and all memorabilia; **1997**—Houston Oilers move to Memphis and become Tennessee Oilers; **1998**—Tennessee Oilers move to Nashville; **1999**—Tennessee Oilers renamed Titans.

Defunct NFL Teams

Teams that once played in the APFA and NFL, but no longer exist.

Akron-OH–Pros (1920-25) and Indians (1926); **Baltimore**–Colts (1950); **Boston**–Bulldogs (1926) and Yanks (1944-48); **Brooklyn**–Lions (1926), Dodgers (1930-43) and Tigers (1944); **Buffalo**–All-Americans (1920-23), Bisons (1924-25), Rangers (1926), Bisons (1927,1929); **Canton-OH**–Bulldogs (1920-23,1925-26); **Chicago**–Tigers (1920); **Cincinnati**–Celts (1921) and Reds (1933-34); **Cleveland**–Tigers (1920), Indians (1921), Indians (1923), Bulldogs (1924-25,1927) and Indians (1931); **Columbus-OH**–Panhandles (1920-22) and Tigers (1923-26); **Dallas**–Texans (1952); **Dayton-OH**–Triangles (1920-29). **Detroit**–Heralds (1920-21), Panthers (1925-26) and Wolverines (1928); **Duluth-MN**–Kelleys (1923-25) and Eskimos (1926-27); **Evansville-IN**–Crimson Giants (1921-22); **Frankford-PA**–Yellow Jackets (1924-31); **Hammond-IN**–Pros (1920-26); **Hartford**–Blues (1926); **Kansas City**–Blues (1924) and Cowboys (1925-26); **Kenosha-WI**–Maroons (1924); **Los Angeles**–Buccaneers (1926); **Louisville**–Brecks (1921-23) and Colonels (1926); **Marion-OH**–Oorang Indians (1922-23); **Milwaukee**–Badgers (1922-26); **Minneapolis**–Marines (1922-24) and Red Jackets (1929-30); **Muncie-IN**–Flyers (1920-21). **New York**–Giants (1921), Yankees (1927-28), Bulldogs (1949) and Yankees (1950-51); **Newark-NJ**–Tornadoes (1930); **Orange-NJ**–Tornadoes (1929); **Pottsville-PA**–Maroons (1925-28); **Providence-RI**–Steam Roller (1925-31); **Racine-WI**–Legion (1922-24) and Tornadoes (1926); **Rochester-NY**–Jeffersons (1920-25); **Rock Island-IL**– Independents (1920-26); **Staten Island-NY**–Stapletons (1929-32); **St. Louis**–All-Stars (1923) and Gunners (1934); **Toledo-OH**–Maroons (1922-23); **Tonawanda-NY**–Kardex (1921), also called Lumbermen; **Washington**–Senators (1921).

Annual NFL Leaders

Individual leaders in NFL (1932-69), NFC (since 1970), AFL (1960-69) and AFC (since 1970).

Passing

Since 1932, the NFL has used several formulas to determine passing leadership, from Total Yards alone (1932-37), to the current passer rating system adopted in 1973. The quarterbacks listed below all led the league according to the system in use at the time.

NFL-NFC

Multiple winners: Sammy Baugh and Steve Young (6); Joe Montana and Roger Staubach (5); Arnie Herber, Sonny Jurgensen, Bart Starr and Norm Van Brocklin (3); Daunte Culpepper, Ed Danowski, Otto Graham, Cecil Isbell, Milt Plum, Kurt Warner and Bob Waterfield (2).

Year	Player	Att	Cmp	Yds	TD	Year	Player	Att	Cmp	Yds	TD
1932	Arnie Herber, GB	101	37	639	9	1970	John Brodie, SF	378	223	2941	24
1933	Harry Newman, NY	136	53	973	11	1971	Roger Staubach, Dal	211	126	1882	15
1934	Arnie Herber, GB	115	42	799	8	1972	Norm Snead, NY	325	196	2307	17
1935	Ed Danowski, NY	113	57	794	10	1973	Roger Staubach, Dal	286	179	2428	23
1936	Arnie Herber, GB	173	77	1239	11	1974	Sonny Jurgensen, Wash	167	107	1185	11
1937	Sammy Baugh, Wash	171	81	1127	8	1975	Fran Tarkenton, Min	425	273	2994	25
1938	Ed Danowski, NY	129	70	848	7	1976	James Harris, LA	158	91	1460	8
1939	Parker Hall, Cle. Rams	208	106	1227	9	1977	Roger Staubach, Dal	361	210	2620	18
1940	Sammy Baugh, Wash	177	111	1367	12	1978	Roger Staubach, Dal	413	231	3190	25
1941	Cecil Isbell, GB	206	117	1479	15	1979	Roger Staubach, Dal	461	267	3586	27
1942	Cecil Isbell, GB	268	146	2021	24	1980	Ron Jaworski, Phi	451	257	3529	27
1943	Sammy Baugh, Wash	239	133	1754	23	1981	Joe Montana, SF	488	311	3565	19
1944	Frank Filchock, Wash	147	84	1139	13	1982	Joe Theismann, Wash	252	161	2033	13
1945	Sammy Baugh, Wash	182	128	1669	11	1983	Steve Bartkowski, Atl	432	274	3167	22
	& Sid Luckman, Chi. Bears	217	117	1725	14	1984	Joe Montana, SF	432	279	3630	28
1946	Bob Waterfield, LA	251	127	1747	18	1985	Joe Montana, SF	494	303	3653	27
1947	Sammy Baugh, Wash	354	210	2938	25	1986	Tommy Kramer, Min	372	208	3000	24
1948	Tommy Thompson, Phi	246	141	1965	25	1987	Joe Montana, SF	398	266	3054	31
1949	Sammy Baugh, Wash	255	145	1903	18	1988	Wade Wilson, Min	332	204	2746	15
1950	Norm Van Brocklin, LA	233	127	2061	18	1989	Don Majkowski, GB	599	353	4318	27
1951	Bob Waterfield, LA	176	88	1566	13	1990	Joe Montana, SF	520	321	3944	26
1952	Norm Van Brocklin, LA	205	113	1736	14	1991	Steve Young, SF	279	180	2517	17
1953	Otto Graham, Cle	258	167	2722	11	1992	Steve Young, SF	402	268	3465	25
1954	Norm Van Brocklin, LA	260	139	2637	13	1993	Steve Young, SF	462	314	4023	29
1955	Otto Graham, Cle	185	98	1721	15	1994	Steve Young, SF	461	324	3969	35
1956	Ed Brown, Chi. Bears	168	96	1667	11	1995	Brett Favre, GB	570	359	4413	38
1957	Tommy O'Connell, Cle	110	63	1229	9	1996	Steve Young, SF	316	214	2410	14
1958	Eddie LeBaron, Wash	145	79	1365	11	1997	Steve Young, SF	356	241	3029	19
1959	Charlie Conerly, NY	194	113	1706	14	1998	Randall Cunningham, Min	425	259	3704	34
1960	Milt Plum, Cle	250	151	2297	21	1999	Kurt Warner, St.L	499	325	4353	41
1961	Milt Plum, Cle	302	177	2416	16	2000	Trent Green, St.L	240	145	2063	16
1962	Bart Starr, GB	285	178	2438	12	2001	Kurt Warner, St.L	546	375	4830	36
1963	Y.A. Tittle, NY	367	221	3145	36	2002	Brad Johnson, TB	451	281	3049	22
1964	Bart Starr, GB	272	163	2144	15	2003	Daunte Culpepper, Min	454	295	3479	25
1965	Rudy Bukich, Chi	312	176	2641	20	2004	Daunte Culpepper, Min	548	379	4717	39
1966	Bart Starr, GB	251	156	2257	14	2005	Matt Hasselbeck, Sea	449	294	3459	24
1967	Sonny Jurgensen, Wash	508	288	3747	31	2006	Drew Brees, NO	554	356	4418	26
1968	Earl Morrall, Bal	317	182	2909	26	2007	Tony Romo, Dal	520	335	4211	36
1969	Sonny Jurgensen, Wash	442	274	3102	22						

AFL-AFC

Multiple winners: Dan Marino (5); Ken Anderson, Len Dawson and Peyton Manning (4); Bob Griese, Daryle Lamonica, Warren Moon and Ken Stabler (2).

Year	Player	Att	Cmp	Yds	TD	Year	Player	Att	Cmp	Yds	TD
1960	Jack Kemp, LA	406	211	3018	20	1984	Dan Marino, Mia	564	362	5084	48
1961	George Blanda, Hou	362	187	3330	36	1985	Ken O'Brien, NY	488	297	3888	25
1962	Len Dawson, Dal	310	189	2759	29	1986	Dan Marino, Mia	623	378	4746	44
1963	Tobin Rote, SD	286	170	2510	20	1987	Bernie Kosar, Cle	389	241	3033	22
1964	Len Dawson, KC	354	199	2879	30	1988	Boomer Esiason, Cin	388	223	3572	28
1965	John Hadl, SD	348	174	2798	20	1989	Dan Marino, Mia	550	308	3997	24
1966	Len Dawson, KC	284	159	2527	26	1990	Warren Moon, Hou	584	362	4689	33
1967	Daryle Lamonica, Oak	425	220	3228	30	1991	Jim Kelly, Buf	474	304	3844	33
1968	Len Dawson, KC	224	131	2109	17	1992	Warren Moon, Hou	346	224	2521	18
1969	Greg Cook, Cin	197	106	1854	15	1993	John Elway, Den	551	348	4030	25
1970	Daryle Lamonica, Oak	356	179	2516	22	1994	Dan Marino, Mia	615	385	4453	30
1971	Bob Griese, Mia	263	145	2089	19	1995	Jim Harbaugh, Ind	314	200	2575	17
1972	Earl Morrall, Mia	150	83	1360	11	1996	John Elway, Den	466	287	3328	26
1973	Ken Stabler, Oak	260	163	1997	14	1997	Mark Brunell, Jax	435	264	3281	18
1974	Ken Anderson, Cin	328	213	2667	18	1998	Vinny Testaverde, NYJ	421	259	3256	29
1975	Ken Anderson, Cin	377	228	3169	21	1999	Peyton Manning, Ind	533	331	4135	26
1976	Ken Stabler, Oak	291	194	2737	27	2000	Brian Griese, Den	336	216	2688	19
1977	Bob Griese, Mia	307	180	2252	22	2001	Rich Gannon, Oak	549	361	3828	27
1978	Terry Bradshaw, Pit	368	207	2915	28	2002	Chad Pennington, NYJ	399	275	3120	22
1979	Dan Fouts, SD	530	332	4082	24	2003	Steve McNair, Ten	400	250	3215	24
1980	Brian Sipe, Cle	554	337	4132	30	2004	Peyton Manning, Ind	497	336	4557	49
1981	Ken Anderson, Cin	479	300	3753	29	2005	Peyton Manning, Ind	453	305	3747	28
1982	Ken Anderson, Cin	309	218	2495	12	2006	Peyton Manning, Ind	557	362	4397	31
1983	Dan Marino, Mia	296	173	2210	20	2007	Tom Brady, NE	578	398	4806	50

Receptions

NFL-NFC

Multiple winners: Don Hutson (8); Raymond Berry, Tom Fears, Pete Pihos, Jerry Rice, Sterling Sharpe and Billy Wilson (3); Dwight Clark, Larry Fitzgerald, Torry Holt, Herman Moore, Muhsin Muhammad, Ahmad Rashad and Charley Taylor (2).

Year	Player	No	Yds	Avg	TD
1932	Ray Flaherty, NY	21	350	16.7	3
1933	Shipwreck Kelly, Bklyn	22	246	11.2	3
1934	Joe Carter, Phi	16	238	14.9	4
	& Red Badgro, NY	16	206	12.9	1
1935	Tod Goodwin, NY	26	432	16.6	4
1936	Don Hutson, GB	34	536	15.8	8
1937	Don Hutson, GB	41	552	13.5	7
1938	Gaynell Tinsley, Chi. Cards	41	516	12.6	1
1939	Don Hutson, GB	34	846	24.9	6
1940	Don Looney, Phi	58	707	12.2	4
1941	Don Hutson, GB	58	739	12.7	10
1942	Don Hutson, GB	74	1211	16.4	17
1943	Don Hutson, GB	47	776	16.5	11
1944	Don Hutson, GB	58	866	14.9	9
1945	Don Hutson, GB	47	834	17.7	9
1946	Jim Benton, LA	63	981	15.6	6
1947	Jim Keane, Chi. Bears	64	910	14.2	10
1948	Tom Fears, LA	51	698	13.7	4
1949	Tom Fears, LA	77	1013	13.2	9
1950	Tom Fears, LA	84	1116	13.3	7
1951	Elroy Hirsch, LA	66	1495	22.7	17
1952	Mac Speedie, Cle	62	911	14.7	5
1953	Pete Pihos, Phi	63	1049	16.7	10
1954	Pete Pihos, Phi	60	872	14.5	10
	& Billy Wilson, SF	60	830	13.8	5
1955	Pete Pihos, Phi	62	864	13.9	7
1956	Billy Wilson, SF	60	889	14.8	5
1957	Billy Wilson, SF	52	757	14.6	6
1958	Raymond Berry, Bal	56	794	14.2	9
	& Pete Retzlaff, Phi	56	766	13.7	2
1959	Raymond Berry, Bal	66	959	14.5	14
1960	Raymond Berry, Bal	74	1298	17.5	10
1961	Red Phillips, LA	78	1092	14.0	5
1962	Bobby Mitchell, Wash	72	1384	19.2	11
1963	Bobby Joe Conrad, St.L	73	967	13.2	10
1964	Johnny Morris, Chi. Bears	93	1200	12.9	10
1965	Dave Parks, SF	80	1344	16.8	12
1966	Charley Taylor, Wash	72	1119	15.5	12
1967	Charley Taylor, Wash	70	990	14.1	9
1968	Clifton McNeil, SF	71	994	14.0	7
1969	Dan Abramowicz, NO	73	1015	13.9	7
1970	Dick Gordon, Chi	71	1026	14.5	13
1971	Bob Tucker, NY	59	791	13.4	4
1972	Harold Jackson, Phi	62	1048	16.9	4
1973	Harold Carmichael, Phi	67	1116	16.7	9
1974	Charles Young, Phi	63	696	11.0	3
1975	Chuck Foreman, Min	73	691	9.5	9
1976	Drew Pearson, Dal	58	806	13.9	6
1977	Ahmad Rashad, Min	51	681	13.4	2
1978	Rickey Young, Min	88	704	8.0	5
1979	Ahmad Rashad, Min	80	1156	14.5	9
1980	Earl Cooper, SF	83	567	6.8	4
1981	Dwight Clark, SF	85	1105	13.0	4
1982	Dwight Clark, SF	60	913	12.2	5
1983	Roy Green, St.L	78	1227	15.7	14
	Charlie Brown, Wash	78	1225	15.7	8
	& Earnest Gray, NY	78	1139	14.6	5
1984	Art Monk, Wash	106	1372	12.9	7
1985	Roger Craig, SF	92	1016	11.0	6
1986	Jerry Rice, SF	86	1570	18.3	15
1987	J.T. Smith, St.L	91	1117	12.3	8
1988	Henry Ellard, LA	86	1414	16.4	10
1989	Sterling Sharpe, GB	90	1423	15.8	12
1990	Jerry Rice, SF	100	1502	15.0	13
1991	Michael Irvin, Dal	93	1523	16.4	8
1992	Sterling Sharpe, GB	108	1461	13.5	13
1993	Sterling Sharpe, GB	112	1274	11.4	11
1994	Cris Carter, Min	122	1256	10.3	7
1995	Herman Moore, Det	123	1686	13.7	14
1996	Jerry Rice, SF	108	1254	11.6	8
1997	Herman Moore, Det	104	1293	12.4	8
1998	Frank Sanders, Ari	89	1145	12.9	3
1999	Muhsin Muhammad, Car	96	1253	13.1	8
2000	Muhsin Muhammad, Car	102	1183	11.6	6
2001	Keyshawn Johnson, TB	106	1266	11.9	1
2002	Randy Moss, Min	106	1347	12.7	7
2003	Torry Holt, St.L	117	1696	14.5	12
2004	Joe Horn, NO	94	1399	14.9	11
	& Torry Holt, St.L	94	1372	14.6	10
2005	Steve Smith, Car	103	1563	15.2	12
	& Larry Fitzgerald, Ari	103	1409	13.7	10
2006	Mike Furrey, Det	98	1086	11.1	6
2007	Larry Fitzgerald, Ari	100	1409	14.1	10

AFL-AFC

Multiple winners: Lionel Taylor (5); Lance Alworth, Haywood Jeffires, Lydell Mitchell and Kellen Winslow (3); Fred Biletnikoff, Todd Christensen, Marvin Harrison, Carl Pickens and Al Toon (2).

Year	Player	No	Yds	Avg	TD
1960	Lionel Taylor, Den	92	1235	13.4	12
1961	Lionel Taylor, Den	100	1176	11.8	4
1962	Lionel Taylor, Den	77	908	11.8	4
1963	Lionel Taylor, Den	78	1101	14.1	10
1964	Charley Hennigan, Hou	101	1546	15.3	8
1965	Lionel Taylor, Den	85	1131	13.3	6
1966	Lance Alworth, SD	73	1383	18.9	13
1967	George Sauer, NY	75	1189	15.9	6
1968	Lance Alworth, SD	68	1312	19.3	10
1969	Lance Alworth, SD	64	1003	15.7	4
1970	Marlin Briscoe, Buf	57	1036	18.2	8
1971	Fred Biletnikoff, Oak	61	929	15.2	9
1972	Fred Biletnikoff, Oak	58	802	13.8	7
1973	Fred Willis, Hou	57	371	6.5	1
1974	Lydell Mitchell, Bal	72	544	7.6	2
1975	Reggie Rucker, Cle	60	770	12.8	3
	& Lydell Mitchell, Bal	60	544	9.1	4
1976	MacArthur Lane, KC	66	686	10.4	1
1977	Lydell Mitchell, Bal	71	620	8.7	4
1978	Steve Largent, Sea	71	1168	16.5	8
1979	Joe Washington, Bal	82	750	9.1	3
1980	Kellen Winslow, SD	89	1290	14.5	9
1981	Kellen Winslow, SD	88	1075	12.2	10
1982	Kellen Winslow, SD	54	721	13.4	6
1983	Todd Christensen, LA	92	1247	13.6	12
1984	Ozzie Newsome, Cle	89	1001	11.2	5
1985	Lionel James, SD	86	1027	11.9	6
1986	Todd Christensen, LA	95	1153	12.1	8
1987	Al Toon, NY	68	976	14.4	5
1988	Al Toon, NY	93	1067	11.5	5
1989	Andre Reed, Buf	88	1312	14.9	9
1990	Haywood Jeffires, Hou	74	1048	14.2	8
	& Drew Hill, Hou	74	1019	13.8	5
1991	Haywood Jeffires, Hou	100	1181	11.8	7
1992	Haywood Jeffires, Hou	90	913	10.1	9
1993	Reggie Langhorne, Ind	85	1038	12.2	3
1994	Ben Coates, NE	96	1174	12.2	7
1995	Carl Pickens, Cin	99	1234	12.5	17
1996	Carl Pickens, Cin	100	1180	11.8	12
1997	Tim Brown, Oak	104	1408	13.5	5
1998	O.J. McDuffie, Mia	90	1050	11.7	7
1999	Jimmy Smith, Jax	116	1636	14.1	6
2000	Marvin Harrison, Ind	102	1413	13.9	14
2001	Rod Smith, Den	113	1343	11.9	11
2002	Marvin Harrison, Ind	143	1722	12.0	11
2003	LaDainian Tomlinson, SD	100	725	7.3	4
2004	Tony Gonzalez, KC	102	1258	12.3	7
2005	Chad Johnson, Cin	97	1432	14.8	9
2006	Andre Johnson, Hou	103	1147	11.1	5
2007	Wes Welker, NE	112	1175	10.5	8
	& T.J. Houshmandzadeh, Cin	112	1143	10.2	12

Rushing
NFL-NFC

Multiple winners: Jim Brown (8); Walter Payton and Barry Sanders (5); Emmitt Smith and Steve Van Buren (4); Eric Dickerson (3); Shaun Alexander, Cliff Battles, John Brockington, Larry Brown, Bill Dudley, Leroy Kelly, Bill Paschal, Joe Perry, Gale Sayers, Stephen Davis and Whizzer White (2).

Year		Car	Yds	Avg	TD	Year		Car	Yds	Avg	TD
1932	Cliff Battles, Bos	148	576	3.9	3	1970	Larry Brown, Wash	237	1125	4.7	5
1933	Jim Musick, Bos	173	809	4.7	5	1971	John Brockington, GB	216	1105	5.1	4
1934	Beattie Feathers, Chi. Bears	119	1004	8.4	8	1972	Larry Brown, Wash	285	1216	4.3	8
1935	Doug Russell, Chi. Cards	140	499	3.6	0	1973	John Brockington, GB	265	1144	4.3	3
1936	Tuffy Leemans, NY	206	830	4.0	2	1974	Lawrence McCutcheon, LA	236	1109	4.7	3
1937	Cliff Battles, Wash	216	874	4.0	5	1975	Jim Otis, St.L	269	1076	4.0	5
1938	Whizzer White, Pit	152	567	3.7	4	1976	Walter Payton, Chi	311	1390	4.5	13
1939	Bill Osmanski, Chi. Bears	121	699	5.8	7	1977	Walter Payton, Chi	339	1852	5.5	14
1940	Whizzer White, Det	146	514	3.5	5	1978	Walter Payton, Chi	333	1395	4.2	11
1941	Pug Manders, Bklyn	111	486	4.4	5	1979	Walter Payton, Chi	369	1610	4.4	14
1942	Bill Dudley, Pit	162	696	4.3	5	1980	Walter Payton, Chi	317	1460	4.6	6
1943	Bill Paschal, NY	147	572	3.9	10	1981	George Rogers, NO	378	1674	4.4	13
1944	Bill Paschal, NY	196	737	3.8	9	1982	Tony Dorsett, Dal	177	745	4.2	5
1945	Steve Van Buren, Phi	143	832	5.8	15	1983	Eric Dickerson, LA	390	1808	4.6	18
1946	Bill Dudley, Pit	146	604	4.1	3	1984	Eric Dickerson, LA	379	2105	5.6	14
1947	Steve Van Buren, Phi	217	1008	4.6	13	1985	Gerald Riggs, Atl	397	1719	4.3	10
1948	Steve Van Buren, Phi	201	945.	4.7	10	1986	Eric Dickerson, LA	404	1821	4.5	11
1949	Steve Van Buren, Phi	263	1146	4.4	11	1987	Charles White, LA	324	1374	4.2	11
1950	Marion Motley, Cle	140	810	5.8	3	1988	Herschel Walker, Dal	361	1514	4.2	5
1951	Eddie Price, NY Giants	271	971	3.6	7	1989	Barry Sanders, Det	280	1470	5.3	14
1952	Dan Towler, LA	156	894	5.7	10	1990	Barry Sanders, Det	255	1304	5.1	13
1953	Joe Perry, SF	192	1018	5.3	10	1991	Emmitt Smith, Dal	365	1563	4.3	12
1954	Joe Perry, SF	173	1049	6.1	8	1992	Emmitt Smith, Dal	373	1713	4.6	18
1955	Alan Ameche, Bal	213	961	4.5	9	1993	Emmitt Smith, Dal	283	1486	5.3	9
1956	Rick Casares, Chi. Bears	234	1126	4.8	12	1994	Barry Sanders, Det	331	1883	5.7	7
1957	Jim Brown, Cle	202	942	4.7	9	1995	Emmitt Smith, Dal	377	1773	4.7	25
1958	Jim Brown, Cle	257	1527	5.9	17	1996	Barry Sanders, Det	307	1553	5.1	11
1959	Jim Brown, Cle	290	1329	4.6	14	1997	Barry Sanders, Det	335	2053	6.1	11
1960	Jim Brown, Cle	215	1257	5.8	9	1998	Jamal Anderson, Atl	410	1846	4.5	14
1961	Jim Brown, Cle	305	1408	4.6	8	1999	Stephen Davis, Wash	290	1405	4.8	17
1962	Jim Taylor, GB	272	1474	5.4	19	2000	Robert Smith, Min	295	1521	5.2	7
1963	Jim Brown, Cle	291	1863	6.4	12	2001	Stephen Davis, Wash	356	1432	4.0	5
1964	Jim Brown, Cle	280	1446	5.2	7	2002	Deuce McAllister, NO	325	1388	4.3	13
1965	Jim Brown, Cle	289	1544	5.3	17	2003	Ahman Green, GB	355	1883	5.3	15
1966	Gale Sayers, Chi	229	1231	5.4	8	2004	Shaun Alexander, Sea	353	1696	4.8	16
1967	Leroy Kelly, Cle	235	1205	5.1	11	2005	Shaun Alexander, Sea	370	1880	5.1	27
1968	Leroy Kelly, Cle	248	1239	5.0	16	2006	Frank Gore, SF	312	1695	5.4	8
1969	Gale Sayers, Chi	236	1032	4.4	8	2007	Adrian Peterson, Min	238	1341	5.6	12

AFL-AFC

Multiple winners: Earl Campbell and O.J. Simpson (4); Terrell Davis and Thurman Thomas (3); Eric Dickerson, Cookie Gilchrist, Edgerrin James, Floyd Little, Curtis Martin, Jim Nance, LaDainian Tomlinson and Curt Warner (2).

Year		Car	Yds	Avg	TD	Year		Car	Yds	Avg	TD
1960	Abner Haynes, Dal	157	875	5.6	9	1984	Earnest Jackson, SD	296	1179	4.0	8
1961	Billy Cannon, Hou	200	948	4.7	6	1985	Marcus Allen, LA	380	1759	4.6	11
1962	Cookie Gilchrist, Buf	214	1096	5.1	13	1986	Curt Warner, Sea	319	1481	4.6	13
1963	Clem Daniels, Oak	215	1099	5.1	3	1987	Eric Dickerson, Ind	223	1011	4.5	5
1964	Cookie Gilchrist, Buf	230	981	4.3	6	1988	Eric Dickerson, Ind	388	1659	4.3	14
1965	Paul Lowe, SD	222	1121	5.0	7	1989	Christian Okoye, KC	370	1480	4.0	12
1966	Jim Nance, Bos	299	1458	4.9	11	1990	Thurman Thomas, Buf	271	1297	4.8	11
1967	Jim Nance, Bos	269	1216	4.5	7	1991	Thurman Thomas, Buf	288	1407	4.9	7
1968	Paul Robinson, Cin	238	1023	4.3	8	1992	Barry Foster, Pit	390	1690	4.3	11
1969	Dickie Post, SD	182	873	4.8	6	1993	Thurman Thomas, Buf	355	1315	3.7	6
1970	Floyd Little, Den	209	901	4.3	3	1994	Chris Warren, Sea	333	1545	4.6	9
1971	Floyd Little, Den	284	1133	4.0	6	1995	Curtis Martin, NE	368	1487	4.0	14
1972	O.J. Simpson, Buf	292	1251	4.3	6	1996	Terrell Davis, Den	345	1538	4.5	13
1973	O.J. Simpson, Buf	332	2003	6.0	12	1997	Terrell Davis, Den	369	1750	4.7	15
1974	Otis Armstrong, Den	263	1407	5.3	9	1998	Terrell Davis, Den	392	2008	5.1	21
1975	O.J. Simpson, Buf	329	1817	5.5	16	1999	Edgerrin James, Ind	369	1553	4.2	13
1976	O.J. Simpson, Buf	290	1503	5.2	8	2000	Edgerrin James, Ind	387	1709	4.4	13
1977	Mark van Eeghen, Oak	324	1273	3.9	7	2001	Priest Holmes, KC	327	1555	4.8	8
1978	Earl Campbell, Hou	302	1450	4.8	13	2002	Ricky Williams, Mia	383	1853	4.8	16
1979	Earl Campbell, Hou	368	1697	4.6	19	2003	Jamal Lewis, Bal	387	2066	5.3	14
1980	Earl Campbell, Hou	373	1934	5.2	13	2004	Curtis Martin, NYJ	371	1697	4.6	12
1981	Earl Campbell, Hou	361	1376	3.8	10	2005	Larry Johnson, KC	336	1750	5.2	20
1982	Freeman McNeil, NY	151	786	5.2	6	2006	LaDainian Tomlinson, SD	348	1815	5.2	28
1983	Curt Warner, Sea	335	1449	4.3	13	2007	LaDainian Tomlinson, SD	315	1474	4.7	15

Note: Eric Dickerson was traded to Indianapolis from the NFC's LA Rams during the 1987 season. In three games with the Rams, he carried the ball 60 times for 277 yds, a 4.6 avg and 1 TD. His official AFC statistics above came in nine games with the Colts.

Scoring
NFL-NFC

Multiple winners: Don Hutson (5); Dutch Clark, Pat Harder, Paul Hornung, Chip Lohmiller and Mark Moseley (3); Kevin Butler, Mike Cofer, Fred Cox, Marshall Faulk, Jack Manders, Chester Marcol, Eddie Murray, Emmitt Smith, Gordy Soltau, Jeff Wilkins and Doak Walker (2).

Year		TD	FG	PAT	Pts
1932	Dutch Clark, Portsmouth	6	3	10	55
1933	Glenn Presnell, Portsmouth	6	6	10	64
	& Ken Strong, NY	6	5	13	64
1934	Jack Manders, Chi. Bears	3	10	31	79
1935	Dutch Clark, Det	6	1	16	55
1936	Dutch Clark, Det	7	4	19	73
1937	Jack Manders, Chi. Bears	5	8	15	69
1938	Clarke Hinkle, GB	7	3	7	58
1939	Andy Farkas, Wash	11	0	2	68
1940	Don Hutson, GB	7	0	15	57
1941	Don Hutson, GB	12	1	20	95
1942	Don Hutson, GB	17	1	33	138
1943	Don Hutson, GB	12	3	26	117
1944	Don Hutson, GB	9	0	31	85
1945	Steve Van Buren, Phi	18	0	2	110
1946	Ted Fritsch, GB	10	9	13	100
1947	Pat Harder, Chi. Cards	7	7	39	102
1948	Pat Harder, Chi. Cards	6	7	53	110
1949	Gene Roberts, NY Giants	17	0	0	102
	& Pat Harder, Chi. Cards	8	3	45	102
1950	Doak Walker, Det	11	8	38	128
1951	Elroy Hirsch, LA	17	0	0	102
1952	Gordy Soltau, SF	7	6	34	94
1953	Gordy Soltau, SF	6	10	48	114
1954	Bobby Walston, Phi	11	4	36	114
1955	Doak Walker, Det	7	9	27	96
1956	Bobby Layne, Det	5	12	33	99
1957	Sam Baker, Wash	1	14	29	77
	& Lou Groza, Cle	0	15	32	77
1958	Jim Brown, Cle	18	0	0	108
1959	Paul Hornung, GB	7	7	31	94
1960	Paul Hornung, GB	15	15	41	176
1961	Paul Hornung, GB	10	15	41	146
1962	Jim Taylor, GB	19	0	0	114
1963	Don Chandler, NY	0	18	52	106
1964	Lenny Moore, Bal	20	0	0	120
1965	Gale Sayers, Chi	22	0	0	132
1966	Bruce Gossett, LA	0	28	29	113
1967	Jim Bakken, St.L	0	27	36	117
1968	Leroy Kelly, Cle	20	0	0	120
1969	Fred Cox, Min	0	26	43	121
1970	Fred Cox, Min	0	30	35	125
1971	Curt Knight, Wash	0	29	27	114
1972	Chester Marcol, GB	0	33	29	128
1973	David Ray, LA	0	30	40	130
1974	Chester Marcol, GB	0	25	19	94
1975	Chuck Foreman, Min	22	0	0	132
1976	Mark Moseley, Wash	0	22	31	97
1977	Walter Payton, Chi	16	0	0	96
1978	Frank Corral, LA	0	29	31	118
1979	Mark Moseley, Wash	0	25	39	114
1980	Eddie Murray, Det	0	27	35	116
1981	Rafael Septien, Dal	0	27	40	121
	& Eddie Murray, Det	0	25	46	121
1982	Wendell Tyler, LA	13	0	0	78
1983	Mark Moseley, Wash	0	33	62	161
1984	Ray Wersching, SF	0	25	56	131
1985	Kevin Butler, Chi	0	31	51	144
1986	Kevin Butler, Chi	0	28	36	120
1987	Jerry Rice, SF	23	0	0	138
1988	Mike Cofer, SF	0	27	40	121
1989	Mike Cofer, SF	0	29	49	136
1990	Chip Lohmiller, Wash	0	30	41	131
1991	Chip Lohmiller, Wash	0	31	56	149
1992	Chip Lohmiller, Wash	0	30	30	120
	& Morten Andersen, NO	0	29	33	120
1993	Jason Hanson, Det	0	34	28	130
1994	Emmitt Smith, Dal	22	0	0	132
	& Fuad Reveiz, Min	0	34	30	132
1995	Emmitt Smith, Dal	25	0	0	150
1996	John Kasay, Car.	0	37	34	145
1997	Richie Cunningham, Dal	0	34	24	126
1998	Gary Anderson, Min	0	35	59	164
1999	Jeff Wilkins, St.L	0	20	64	124
2000	Marshall Faulk, St.L	26	0	4	160
2001	Marshall Faulk, St.L	21	0	2	128
2002	Jay Feely, Atl	0	32	42	138
2003	Jeff Wilkins, St.L	0	39	46	163
2004	David Akers, Phi	0	27	41	122
2005	Shaun Alexander, Sea	28	0	0	168
2006	Robbie Gould, Chi	0	32	47	143
2007	Mason Crosby, GB	0	31	48	141

AFL-AFC

Multiple winners: Gino Cappelletti (5); Gary Anderson (3); Jim Breech, Roy Gerela, Priest Holmes, Gene Mingo, Nick Lowery, John Smith, Pete Stoyanovich, Jim Turner and Mike Vanderjagt (2).

Year		TD	FG	PAT	Pts
1960	Gene Mingo, Den	6	18	33	123
1961	Gino Cappelletti, Bos	8	17	48	147
1962	Gene Mingo, Den	4	27	32	137
1963	Gino Cappelletti, Bos	2	22	35	113
1964	Gino Cappelletti, Bos	7	25	36	155
1965	Gino Cappelletti, Bos	9	17	27	132
1966	Gino Cappelletti, Bos	6	16	35	119
1967	George Blanda, Oak	0	20	56	116
1968	Jim Turner, NY	0	34	43	145
1969	Jim Turner, NY	0	32	33	129
1970	Jan Stenerud, KC	0	30	26	116
1971	Garo Yepremian, Mia	0	28	33	117
1972	Bobby Howfield, NY	0	27	40	121
1973	Roy Gerela, Pit	0	29	36	123
1974	Roy Gerela, Pit	0	20	33	93
1975	O.J. Simpson, Buf	23	0	0	138
1976	Toni Linhart, Bal	0	20	49	109
1977	Errol Mann, Oak	0	20	39	99
1978	Pat Leahy, NY	0	22	41	107
1979	John Smith, NE	0	23	46	115
1980	John Smith, NE	0	26	51	129
1981	Nick Lowery, KC	0	26	37	115
	& Jim Breech, Cin	0	22	49	115
1982	Marcus Allen, LA	14	0	0	84
1983	Gary Anderson, Pit	0	27	38	119
1984	Gary Anderson, Pit	0	24	45	117
1985	Gary Anderson, Pit	0	33	40	139
1986	Tony Franklin, NE	0	32	44	140
1987	Jim Breech, Cin	0	24	25	97
1988	Scott Norwood, Buf	0	32	33	129
1989	David Treadwell, Den	0	27	39	120
1990	Nick Lowery, KC	0	34	37	139
1991	Pete Stoyanovich, Mia	0	31	28	121
1992	Pete Stoyanovich, Mia	0	30	34	124
1993	Jeff Jaeger, LA	0	35	27	132
1994	John Carney, SD	0	34	33	135
1995	Norm Johnson, Pit	0	34	39	141
1996	Cary Blanchard, Ind	0	36	27	135
1997	Mike Hollis, Jax	0	31	41	134
1998	Steve Christie, Buf	0	33	41	140
1999	Mike Vanderjagt, Ind	0	34	43	145
2000	Matt Stover, Bal	0	35	30	135
2001	Mike Vanderjagt, Ind	0	28	41	125
2002	Priest Holmes, KC	24	0	0	144
2003	Priest Holmes, KC	27	0	0	162
2004	Adam Vinatieri, NE	0	31	48	141
2005	Shayne Graham, Cin	0	28	47	131
2006	LaDainian Tomlinson, SD	31	0	0	186
2007	Randy Moss, NE	23	0	0	138

All-Time NFL Leaders

Through 2007 regular season.

CAREER

Players active in 2007 in **bold** type.

Passing Efficiency

Ratings based on performance standards established for completion percentage, average gain, touchdown percentage and interception percentage. Quarterbacks are allocated points according to how their statistics measure up to those standards. Minimum 1500 passing attempts.

		Yrs	Att	Cmp	Cmp%	Yards	Avg Gain	TD	TD%	Int	Int%	Rating
1	Steve Young	15	4149	2667	64.3	33,124	7.98	232	5.6	107	2.6	96.8
2	**Peyton Manning**	10	5405	3468	64.2	41,626	7.70	306	5.7	153	2.8	94.7
3	**Kurt Warner**	10	2959	1926	65.1	24,008	8.11	152	5.1	100	3.4	93.2
4	**Tom Brady**	8	3642	2294	63.0	26,370	7.24	197	5.4	86	2.4	92.9
5	Joe Montana	15	5391	3409	63.2	40,551	7.52	273	5.1	139	2.6	92.3
6	**Carson Palmer**	4	2036	1305	64.1	14,899	7.32	104	5.1	63	3.1	90.1
7	**Daunte Culpepper**	9	2927	1867	63.8	22,422	7.66	142	4.9	94	3.2	89.9
8	**Chad Pennington**	8	1919	1259	65.6	13,738	7.16	82	4.3	55	2.9	88.9
9	**Marc Bulger**	6	2484	1578	63.5	18,625	7.50	106	4.3	74	3.0	88.1
10	**Drew Brees**	7	3015	1921	63.7	21,189	7.03	134	4.4	82	2.7	87.9
11	Jeff Garcia	9	3300	2020	61.2	22,885	6.92	149	4.5	77	2.3	87.2
12	**Trent Green**	10	3668	2228	60.7	27,950	7.62	162	4.4	108	2.9	86.9
13	Dan Marino	17	8358	4967	59.4	61,361	7.34	420	5.0	252	3.0	86.4
14	**Matt Hasselbeck**	9	3138	1904	60.7	22,333	7.12	142	4.5	84	2.7	86.2
15	**Donovan McNabb**	9	3732	2189	58.7	25,404	6.81	171	4.6	79	2.1	85.8
16	**Brett Favre**	17	8758	5377	61.4	61,655	7.04	442	5.0	288	3.3	85.7
17	**Jake Delhomme**	7	2020	1206	59.7	14,589	7.22	100	5.0	64	3.2	85.2
18	Rich Gannon	16	4206	2533	60.2	28,743	6.83	180	4.3	104	2.5	84.7
19	Jim Kelly	11	4779	2874	60.1	35,467	7.42	237	5.0	175	3.7	84.4
20	**Mark Brunell**	14	4594	2738	59.6	31,826	6.93	182	4.0	106	2.3	84.2
21	**Brian Griese**	10	2612	1642	62.9	18,367	7.03	114	4.4	92	3.5	83.6
22	Roger Staubach	11	2958	1685	57.0	22,700	7.67	153	5.2	109	3.7	83.4
23	**Brad Johnson**	14	4248	2627	61.8	28,627	6.74	164	3.9	117	2.8	83.1
24	**Steve McNair**	13	4544	2733	60.1	31,304	6.89	174	3.8	119	2.6	82.8
25	Neil Lomax	8	3153	1817	57.6	22,771	7.22	136	4.3	90	2.9	82.7

Note: The NFL does not recognize records from the All-American Football Conference (1946-49). If it did, **Otto Graham** would rank 13th (after Green) with the following stats: 10 Yrs; 2,626 Att; 1,464 Comp; 55.8 Comp Pct; 23,584 Yards; 8.98 Avg Gain; 174 TD; 6.6 TD Pct; 135 Int; 5.1 Int Pct; and 86.6 Rating Pts.

Touchdown Passes

		No			No			No
1	**Brett Favre**	442	17	Jim Kelly	237		Steve DeBerg	196
2	Dan Marino	420	18	George Blanda	236	34	Ken Stabler	194
3	Fran Tarkenton	342	19	Steve Young	232	35	Bob Griese	192
4	**Peyton Manning**	306	20	John Brodie	214	36	Sammy Baugh	187
5	John Elway	300	21	Terry Bradshaw	212	37	Craig Morton	183
6	Warren Moon	291		Y.A. Tittle	212	38	Steve Grogan	182
7	Johnny Unitas	290	23	Jim Hart	209		**Mark Brunell**	182
8	**Vinny Testaverde**	275	24	Randall Cunningham	207	40	Rich Gannon	180
9	Joe Montana	273	25	Jim Everett	203	41	Ron Jaworski	179
10	Dave Krieg	261	26	Roman Gabriel	201	42	Babe Parilli	178
11	Sonny Jurgensen	255	27	Phil Simms	199	43	**Kerry Collins**	174
12	Dan Fouts	254	28	Ken Anderson	197		**Steve McNair**	174
13	Drew Bledsoe	251		**Tom Brady**	197	45	Charlie Conerly	173
14	Boomer Esiason	247	30	Joe Ferguson	196		Joe Namath	173
15	John Hadl	244		Bobby Layne	196		Norm Van Brocklin	173
16	Len Dawson	239		Norm Snead	196			

Note: The NFL does not recognize records from the All-American Football Conference (1946-49). If it did, **Y.A. Tittle** would move up from 21st to 16th (after Hadl) with 242 TDs and **Otto Graham** would be tied for 43rd with 174 TDs.

Passes Intercepted

		No			No			No
1	**Brett Favre**	288	10	Bobby Layne	245	19	Terry Bradshaw	210
2	George Blanda	277	11	Dan Fouts	242	20	Joe Ferguson	209
3	John Hadl	268	12	Warren Moon	233	21	Steve Grogan	208
4	**Vinny Testaverde**	267	13	John Elway	226	22	Drew Bledsoe	206
5	Fran Tarkenton	266	14	John Brodie	224	23	Steve DeBerg	204
6	Norm Snead	257	15	Ken Stabler	222	24	Sammy Baugh	203
7	Johnny Unitas	253	16	Y.A. Tittle	221	25	Dave Krieg	199
8	Dan Marino	252	17	Joe Namath	220			
9	Jim Hart	247		Babe Parilli	220			

Passing Yards

		Yrs	Att	Comp	Pct	Yards
1	**Brett Favre**	17	8758	5377	61.4	61,655
2	Dan Marino	17	8358	4967	59.4	61,361
3	John Elway	16	7250	4123	56.9	51,475
4	Warren Moon	17	6823	3988	58.5	49,325
5	Fran Tarkenton	18	6467	3686	57.0	47,003
6	**Vinny Testaverde**	21	6701	3787	56.5	46,233
7	Drew Bledsoe	14	6717	3839	57.2	44,611
8	Dan Fouts	15	5604	3297	58.8	43,040
9	**Peyton Manning**	10	5405	3468	64.2	41,626
10	Joe Montana	15	5391	3409	63.2	40,551
11	Johnny Unitas	18	5186	2830	54.6	40,239
12	Dave Krieg	19	5311	3105	58.5	38,147
13	Boomer Esiason	14	5205	2969	57.0	37,920
14	Jim Kelly	11	4779	2874	60.1	35,467
15	Jim Everett	12	4923	2841	57.7	34,837
16	**Kerry Collins**	13	5254	2918	55.5	34,717
17	Jim Hart	19	5076	2593	51.1	34,665
18	Steve DeBerg	17	5024	2874	57.2	34,241
19	John Hadl	16	4687	2363	50.4	33,503
20	Phil Simms	14	4647	2576	55.4	33,462
21	Steve Young	15	4149	2667	64.3	33,124
22	Troy Aikman	12	4715	2898	61.5	32,942
23	Ken Anderson	16	4475	2654	59.3	32,838
24	Sonny Jurgensen	18	4262	2433	57.1	32,224
25	**Mark Brunell**	14	4594	2738	59.6	31,826

Note: The NFL does not recognize records from the All-American Football Conference (1946-49). If it did, **Y.A. Tittle** would rank 22nd (after Young) with the following stats: 17 Yrs; 4,395 Att; 2,427 Comp; 55.2 Pct; and 33,070 Yards.

Receptions

		Yrs	No	Yards	Avg	TD
1	Jerry Rice	20	1549	22,895	14.8	197
2	Cris Carter	16	1101	13,899	12.6	130
3	Tim Brown	17	1094	14,934	13.7	100
4	**Marvin Harrison**	12	1042	13,944	13.4	123
5	Andre Reed	16	951	13,198	13.9	87
6	**Isaac Bruce**	14	942	14,109	15.0	84
7	Art Monk	16	940	12,721	13.5	68
8	**Keenan McCardell**	16	883	11,373	12.9	63
9	**Terrell Owens**	12	882	13,070	14.8	129
10	Jimmy Smith	12	862	12,287	14.3	67
11	Irving Fryar	17	851	12,785	15.0	84
12	Rod Smith	12	849	11,389	13.4	68
13	Larry Centers	14	827	6,797	8.2	28
14	**Tony Gonzalez**	11	820	9,882	12.1	66
15	Steve Largent	14	819	13,089	16.0	100
16	Shannon Sharpe	14	815	10,060	12.3	62
17	Henry Ellard	16	814	13,777	16.9	65
	Keyshawn Johnson	11	814	10,571	13.0	64
19	**Torry Holt**	9	805	11,864	14.7	71
20	**Randy Moss**	10	774	12,193	15.8	124
21	Marshall Faulk	12	767	6,875	9.0	36
22	James Lofton	16	764	14,004	18.3	75
	Eric Moulds	11	764	9,995	13.1	49
24	Charlie Joiner	18	750	12,146	16.2	65
	Michael Irvin	12	750	11,904	15.9	65

Rushing Yards

		Yrs	Car	Yards	Avg	TD
1	Emmitt Smith	15	4409	18,355	4.2	164
2	Walter Payton	13	3838	16,726	4.4	110
3	Barry Sanders	10	3062	15,269	5.0	99
4	Curtis Martin	11	3518	14,101	4.0	90
5	Jerome Bettis	13	3479	13,662	3.9	91
6	Eric Dickerson	11	2996	13,259	4.4	90
7	Tony Dorsett	12	2936	12,739	4.3	77
8	Jim Brown	9	2359	12,312	5.2	106
9	Marshall Faulk	12	2836	12,279	4.3	100
10	Marcus Allen	16	3022	12,243	4.1	123
11	Franco Harris	13	2949	12,120	4.1	91
12	Thurman Thomas	13	2877	12,074	4.2	65
13	**Edgerrin James**	9	2849	11,607	4.1	77
14	John Riggins	14	2916	11,352	3.9	104
15	Corey Dillon	10	2618	11,241	4.3	82
16	O.J. Simpson	11	2404	11,236	4.7	61
17	**Fred Taylor**	10	2285	10,715	4.7	61
18	**LaDainian Tomlinson**	7	2365	10,650	4.5	115
19	Ricky Watters	10	2622	10,643	4.1	78
20	Tiki Barber	10	2217	10,449	4.7	55
21	Eddie George	9	2865	10,441	3.6	68
22	Ottis Anderson	14	2562	10,273	4.0	81
23	**Warrick Dunn**	11	2483	10,181	4.1	47
24	**Shaun Alexander**	8	2176	9,429	4.3	100
25	Earl Campbell	8	2187	9,407	4.3	74

Note: The NFL does not recognize records from the All-American Football Conference (1946-49). If it did, **Joe Perry** would rank 24th (after Dunn) with the following stats: 16 Yrs; 1,929 Att; 9,723 Yards; 5.0 Avg; and 71 TD.

All-Purpose Yards

		Rush	Rec	Ret	Total
1	Jerry Rice	645	22,895	6	23,546
2	Brian Mitchell	1,967	2,336	19,027	23,330
3	Walter Payton	16,726	4,538	539	21,803
4	Emmitt Smith	18,355	3,224	-15	21,564
5	Tim Brown	190	14,934	4,558	19,682
6	Marshall Faulk	12,279	6,875	36	19,190
7	Barry Sanders	15,269	2,921	118	18,308
8	Herschel Walker	8,225	4,859	5,084	18,168
9	Marcus Allen	12,243	5,411	-6	17,648
10	Curtis Martin	14,101	3,329	-9	17,421
11	Tiki Barber	10,449	5,183	1,727	17,359
12	Eric Metcalf	2,392	5,572	9,266	17,230
13	Thurman Thomas	12,074	4,458	0	16,532
14	Tony Dorsett	12,739	3,554	33	16,326
15	Henry Ellard	50	13,777	1,891	15,718
16	Irving Fryar	242	12,785	2,567	15,594
17	Jim Brown	12,312	2,499	648	15,459
18	Eric Dickerson	13,259	2,137	15	15,411
19	Jerome Bettis	13,662	1,449	2	15,113
20	Glyn Milburn	817	1,322	12,772	14,911
21	James Brooks	7,962	3,621	3,327	14,910
22	Ricky Watters	10,643	4,248	0	14,891
23	**Edgerrin James**	11,607	3,260	0	14,867
24	Franco Harris	12,120	2,287	215	14,622
25	**Warrick Dunn**	10,181	4,009	358	14,548

Years played: Allen (16), Barber (10), Bettis (12), Brooks (12), J. Brown (9), T. Brown (17), Dickerson (11), Dorsett (12), Dunn (11), Ellard (16), Faulk (11), Fryar (17), Harris (13), James (9), Martin (10), Metcalf (13), Milburn (9), Mitchell (14), Payton (13), Rice (20), Sanders (10), Smith (15), Thomas (13), Walker (12) and Watters (10).

Scoring

Points

		Yrs	TD	FG	PAT	Total
1	**Morten Andersen**	.25	0	565	849	2544
2	Gary Anderson	.23	0	538	820	2434
3	George Blanda	.26	9	335	943	2002
4	**Matt Stover**	.17	0	435	517	1822
5	John Carney	.20	0	425	537	1812
6	**Jason Elam**	.15	0	395	601	1786
7	Norm Johnson	.18	0	366	638	1736
8	Nick Lowery	.18	0	383	562	1711
9	Jan Stenerud	.19	0	373	580	1699
10	**Jason Hanson**	.16	0	385	504	1659†
11	Eddie Murray	.19	0	352	538	1594
12	Al Del Greco	.17	0	347	543	1584
13	**John Kasay**	.16	0	358	430	1504
14	Steve Christie	.15	0	336	468	1476
15	Pat Leahy	.18	0	304	558	1470
16	Jim Turner	.16	1	304	521	1439
17	Matt Bahr	.17	0	300	522	1422
18	**Jeff Wilkins**	.14	0	307	495	1416
19	**Adam Vinatieri**	.12	0	311	454	1389†
20	Mark Moseley	.16	0	300	482	1382
21	Jim Bakken	.17	0	282	534	1380
22	Fred Cox	.15	0	282	519	1365
23	Lou Groza	.17	1	234	641	1349
24	Jerry Rice	.20	208	0	0	1256†
25	Jim Breech	.14	0	243	517	1246

†Vinatieri's total includes one 2-point conversion. Rice's total includes four 2-point conversions.
Note: The NFL does not recognize records from the All-American Football Conference (1946-49). If it did, **Lou Groza** would move up from 23rd to 11th (after Hanson) with the following stats: 21 Yrs; 1 TD; 264 FG, 810 PAT; 1,608 Pts.

Interceptions

		Yrs	No	Yards	TD
1	Paul Krause	.16	81	1185	3
2	Emlen Tunnell	.14	79	1282	4
3	Rod Woodson	.17	71	1483	12
4	Dick (Night Train) Lane	.14	68	1207	5
5	Ken Riley	.15	65	596	5

Sacks

		Yrs	No
1	Bruce Smith	.19	200.0
2	Reggie White	.15	198.0
3	Kevin Greene	.15	160.0
4	Chris Doleman	.15	150.5
5	**Michael Strahan**	.15	141.5

Note: The NFL did not begin officially compiling sacks until 1982. Deacon Jones, who played with the Rams, Chargers and Redskins from 1961-74, is often credited with 173.5 sacks. Jack Youngblood and Alan Page are unofficially credited with 150.5 and 148, respectively. Also, Lawrence Taylor has 142 career sacks if you count his rookie year of 1981, the year before sacks became an official stat.

Safeties

		Yrs	No
1	Ted Hendricks	.15	4
	Doug English	.10	4
3	Seventeen players tied with 3 each.		

Touchdowns

		Yrs	Rush	Rec	Ret	Total
1	Jerry Rice	.20	10	197	1	208
2	Emmitt Smith	.15	164	11	0	175
3	Marcus Allen	.16	123	21	1	145
4	Marshall Faulk	.12	100	36	0	136
5	**Terrell Owens**	.12	2	129	0	131
	Cris Carter	.16	0	130	1	131
7	**LaDainian Tomlinson**	7	115	14	0	129
8	Jim Brown	.9	106	20	0	126
9	**Randy Moss**	.10	0	124	1	125
	Walter Payton	.13	110	15	0	125
11	**Marvin Harrison**	.12	0	123	0	123
12	John Riggins	.14	104	12	0	116
13	Lenny Moore	.12	63	48	2	113
14	**Shaun Alexander**	.8	100	12	0	112
15	Barry Sanders	.10	99	10	0	109
16	Don Hutson	.11	3	99	3	105
	Tim Brown	.17	1	100	4	105
18	Steve Largent	.14	1	100	0	101
19	Franco Harris	.13	91	9	0	100
	Curtis Martin	.11	90	10	0	100
21	Eric Dickerson	.11	90	6	0	96
22	Jerome Bettis	.13	91	3	0	94
	Priest Holmes	.9	86	8	0	94
24	Jim Taylor	.10	83	10	0	93
25	Tony Dorsett	.12	77	13	1	91
	Bobby Mitchell	.11	18	65	8	91
	Ricky Watters	.10	78	13	0	91

Kickoff Returns

Minimum 75 returns.

		Yrs	No	Yards	Avg	TD
1	Gale Sayers	.7	91	2781	30.6	6
2	Lynn Chandnois	.7	92	2720	29.6	3
3	Abe Woodson	.9	193	5538	28.7	5
4	Buddy Young	.6	90	2514	27.9	2
5	Travis Williams	.5	102	2801	27.5	6

Punting

Minimum 300 punts.

		Yrs	No	Yards	Avg
1	**Shane Lechler**	.8	592	27,511	46.5
2	Sammy Baugh	.16	338	15,245	45.1
3	Tommy Davis	.11	511	22,833	44.7
4	Yale Lary	.11	503	22,279	44.3
5	**Todd Sauerbrun**	.13	889	39,208	44.1

Punt Returns

Minimum 75 returns.

		Yrs	No	Yards	Avg	TD
1	**Devin Hester**	.2	89	1251	14.1	7
2	George McAfee	.8	112	1431	12.8	2
3	Jack Christiansen	.8	85	1084	12.8	8
4	Claude Gibson	.5	110	1381	12.6	3
5	Bill Dudley	.9	124	1515	12.2	3

Long-Playing Records

Seasons

		No
1	George Blanda, QB-K	.26
2	**Morten Andersen**, K	.25
3	Gary Anderson, K	.23

Games

		No
1	**Morten Andersen**, K	.382
2	Gary Anderson, K	.353
3	George Blanda, QB-K	.340

Consecutive Games

		No
1	**Jeff Feagles**, P	.320
2	Jim Marshall, DE	.282
3	**Brett Favre**, QB	.253

SINGLE SEASON
Passing

Yards Gained	Year	Att	Cmp	Pct	Yds		Efficiency	Year	Att/Cmp	TD	Rtg
Dan Marino, Mia	1984	564	362	64.2	5084		Peyton Manning, Ind	2004	497/336	49	121.1
Kurt Warner, St.L	2001	546	375	68.7	4830		**Tom Brady**, NE	2007	398/578	50	117.2
Tom Brady, NE	2007	578	398	68.9	4806		Steve Young, SF	1994	461/324	35	112.8
Dan Fouts, SD	1981	609	360	59.1	4802		Joe Montana, SF	1989	386/271	26	112.4
Dan Marino, Mia	1986	623	378	60.7	4746		Daunte Culpepper, Min	2004	548/379	39	110.9
Daunte Culpepper, Min	2004	548	379	69.2	4717		Milt Plum, Cle	1960	250/151	21	110.4
Dan Fouts, SD	1980	589	348	59.1	4715		Sammy Baugh, Wash	1945	182/128	11	109.9
Warren Moon, Hou	1991	655	404	61.7	4690		Kurt Warner, St.L	1999	499/325	41	109.2
Rich Gannon, Oak	2002	618	418	67.6	4689		Dan Marino, Mia	1984	564/362	48	108.9
Warren Moon, Hou	1990	584	362	62.0	4689		Sid Luckman, Chi. Bears	1943	202/110	28	107.5

Receptions

Catches	Year	No	Yds
Marvin Harrison, Ind	2002	143	1722
Herman Moore, Det	1995	123	1686
Jerry Rice, SF	1995	122	1848
Cris Carter, Min	1995	122	1371
Cris Carter, Min	1994	122	1256
Isaac Bruce, St.L	1995	119	1781
Torry Holt, St.L	2003	117	1696
Jimmy Smith, Jax	1999	116	1636
Marvin Harrison, Ind	1999	115	1663
Rod Smith, Den	2001	113	1343

Six tied with 112 receptions each.

Rushing

Yards Gained	Year	Car	Yds	Avg
Eric Dickerson, LA Rams	1984	379	2105	5.6
Jamal Lewis, Bal.	2003	387	2066	5.3
Barry Sanders, Det	1997	335	2053	6.1
Terrell Davis, Den	1998	392	2008	5.1
O.J. Simpson, Buf	1973	332	2003	6.0
Earl Campbell, Hou	1980	373	1934	5.2
Barry Sanders, Det	1994	331	1883	5.7
Ahman Green, GB	2003	355	1883	5.3
Shaun Alexander, Sea	2005	370	1880	5.1
Jim Brown, Cle	1963	291	1863	6.4
Tiki Barber, NYG	2005	357	1860	5.2
Ricky Williams, Mia	2002	383	1853	4.8
Walter Payton, Chi	1977	339	1852	5.5
Jamal Anderson, Atl	1998	410	1846	4.5

Scoring
Points

	Year	TD	PAT	FG	Pts
LaDainian Tomlinson, SD	2006	31	0	0	186
Paul Hornung, GB	1960	15	41	15	176
Shaun Alexander, Sea	2005	28	0	0	168
Gary Anderson, Min	1998	0	59	35	164
Jeff Wilkins, St.L	2003	0	46	39	163
Priest Holmes, KC	2003	27	0	0	162
Mark Moseley, Wash	1983	0	62	33	161
Marshall Faulk, St.L	2000	26	4	0	160
Mike Vanderjagt, Ind	2003	0	46	37	157
Gino Cappelletti, Bos	1964	7	38	25	155
Emmitt Smith, Dal	1995	25	0	0	150
Chip Lohmiller, Wash	1991	0	56	31	149

Touchdowns

	Year	Rush	Rec	Ret	Total
LaDainian Tomlinson, SD	2006	28	3	0	31
Shaun Alexander, Sea	2005	27	1	0	28
Priest Holmes, KC	2003	27	0	0	27
Marshall Faulk, St.L	2000	18	8	0	26
Emmitt Smith, Dal	1995	25	0	0	25
John Riggins, Wash	1983	24	0	0	24
Priest Holmes, KC	2002	21	3	0	24
Terrell Davis, Den	1998	21	2	0	23
O.J. Simpson, Buf	1975	16	7	0	23
Jerry Rice, SF	1987	1	22	0	23
Randy Moss, NE	2007	0	23	0	23

Three tied with 22 TD each.

Note: The NFL regular season schedule grew from 12 games (1947-60) to 14 (1961-77) to 16 (1978-present). The AFL regular season schedule was always 14 games (1960-69).

Touchdowns Passing

	Year	No
Tom Brady, New England	2007	50
Peyton Manning, Indianapolis	2004	49
Dan Marino, Miami	1984	48
Dan Marino, Miami	1986	44
Kurt Warner, St. Louis	1999	41
Brett Favre, Green Bay	1996	39
Daunte Culpepper, Minnesota	2004	39
Brett Favre, Green Bay	1995	38
George Blanda, Houston	1961	36
Y.A. Tittle, NY Giants	1963	36
Steve Young, San Francisco	1998	36
Steve Beuerlein, Carolina	1999	36
Kurt Warner, St. Louis	2001	36
Tony Romo, Dallas	2007	36

Touchdowns Receiving

	Year	No
Randy Moss, New England	2007	23
Jerry Rice, San Francisco	1987	22
Mark Clayton, Miami	1984	18
Sterling Sharpe, Green Bay	1994	18
Don Hutson, Green Bay	1942	17
Elroy (Crazylegs) Hirsch, LA Rams	1951	17
Bill Groman, Houston	1961	17
Jerry Rice, San Francisco	1989	17
Cris Carter, Minnesota	1995	17
Carl Pickens, Cincinnati	1995	17
Randy Moss, Minnesota	1998	17
Randy Moss, Minnesota	2003	17
Art Powell, Oakland	1963	16
Terrell Owens, SF	2001	16
Muhsin Muhammad, Carolina	2004	16
Braylon Edwards, Cleveland	2007	16

Touchdowns Rushing

	Year	No
LaDainian Tomlinson, San Diego	2006	28
Priest Holmes, Kansas City	2003	27
Shaun Alexander, Seattle	2005	27
Emmitt Smith, Dallas	1995	25
John Riggins, Washington	1983	24
Joe Morris, NY Giants	1985	21
Emmitt Smith, Dallas	1994	21
Terry Allen, Washington	1996	21
Terrell Davis, Denver	1998	21
Priest Holmes, Kansas City	2002	21
Larry Johnson, Kansas City	2005	20
Jim Taylor, Green Bay	1962	19
Earl Campbell, Houston	1979	19
Chuck Muncie, San Diego	1981	19

Field Goals

	Year	Att	No
Neil Rackers, Arizona	2005	42	40
Jeff Wilkins, St. Louis	2003	42	39
Olindo Mare, Miami	1999	46	39
Mike Vanderjagt, Indianapolis	2003	37	37
John Kasay, Carolina	1996	45	37
Cary Blanchard, Indianapolis	1996	40	36
Al Del Greco, Tennessee	1998	39	36
Ali Haji-Sheikh, NY Giants	1983	42	35
Jeff Jaeger, LA Raiders	1993	44	35
Gary Anderson, Minnesota	1998	35	35
Matt Stover, Baltimore	2000	39	35
Jay Feely, NY Giants	2005	42	35
Rob Bironas, Tennessee	2007	39	35
Ten tied with 34 FG each.			

Interceptions

	Year	No
Dick (Night Train) Lane, Detroit	1952	14
Dan Sandifer, Washington	1948	13
Spec Sanders, NY Yanks	1950	13
Lester Hayes, Oakland	1980	13
Nine tied with 12 each.		

Punting

Qualifiers	Year	Avg
Sammy Baugh, Washington	1940	51.4
Shane Lechler, Oakland	2007	49.1
Yale Lary, Detroit	1963	48.9
Sammy Baugh, Washington	1941	48.7
Yale Lary, Detroit	1961	48.4

Kickoff Returns

	Year	Avg
Travis Williams, Green Bay	1967	41.1
Gale Sayers, Chicago Bears	1967	37.7
Ollie Matson, Chicago Cards	1958	35.5
Jim Duncan, Baltimore Colts	1970	35.4
Lynn Chandnois, Pittsburgh	1952	35.2

Punt Returns

	Year	Avg
Herb Rich, Baltimore	1950	23.0
Jack Christiansen, Detroit	1952	21.5
Dick Christy, NY Titans	1961	21.3
Bob Hayes, Dallas	1968	20.8
Claude Young, NY Yanks	1951	19.3

Sacks

	Year	No
Michael Strahan, NY Giants	2001	22.5
Mark Gastineau, NY Jets	1984	22
Reggie White, Philadelphia	1987	21

	Year	No
Chris Doleman, Minnesota	1989	21
Lawrence Taylor, NY Giants	1986	20.5
Derrick Thomas, Kansas City	1990	20

Note: The NFL did not begin officially compiling sacks until 1982. Cincinnati's Coy Bacon is widely, although not officially, credited with 26 sacks during the 1976 season.

SINGLE GAME

Passing

Yards Gained	Date	Yds
Norm Van Brocklin, LA vs NY Yanks	9/28/51	554
Warren Moon, Hou vs KC	12/16/90	527
Boomer Esiason, Ariz vs Wash.	11/10/96	522
Dan Marino, Mia vs NYJ	10/23/88	521
Phil Simms, NYG vs Cin	10/13/85	513

Completions	Date	No
Drew Bledsoe, NE vs Min	11/13/94	45
Rich Gannon, Oak vs Pit	9/15/02	43
Richard Todd, NYJ vs SF	9/21/80	42
Vinny Testaverde, NYJ vs Sea	12/6/98	42
Warren Moon, Hou vs Dal	11/10/91	41
Five tied with 40 each.		

Receiving

Catches	Date	No
Terrell Owens, SF vs Chi	12/17/00	20
Tom Fears, LA vs GB	12/3/50	18
Clark Gaines, NYJ vs SF	9/21/80	17
Four tied with 16 each.		

Yards Gained	Date	Yds
Flipper Anderson, LA Rams vs NO	11/26/89	336
Stephone Paige, KC vs SD	12/22/85	309
Jim Benton, Cle vs Det	11/22/45	303
Cloyce Box, Det vs Bal	12/3/50	302
Jimmy Smith, Jax vs Bal	9/10/00	291
Jerry Rice, SF vs Det	9/25/95	289

Rushing

Yards Gained	Date	Yds
Adrian Peterson, Min vs SD	11/4/07	296
Jamal Lewis, Bal vs Cle	9/14/03	295
Corey Dillon, Cin vs Den	10/22/00	278
Walter Payton, Chi vs Min	11/20/77	275
O.J. Simpson, Buf vs Det	11/25/76	273
Shaun Alexander, Sea vs Oak	11/11/01	266
Mike Anderson, Den vs NO	12/3/00	251
O.J. Simpson, Buf vs NE	9/16/73	250

All-Purpose Yards

	Date	Yds
Glyn Milburn, Den vs Sea	12/10/95	404
Billy Cannon, Hou vs NY Titans	12/10/61	373
Adrian Peterson, Min vs Chi	10/14/07	361
Michael Lewis, NO vs Wash	10/13/02	356
Tyrone Hughes, NO vs LA Rams	10/23/94	347
Lionel James, SD vs Raiders	11/10/85	345
Timmy Brown, Phi vs St.L	12/16/62	341
Gale Sayers, Chi vs Min	12/18/66	339
Gale Sayers, Chi vs SF	12/12/65	336
Flipper Anderson, LA Rams vs NO	11/26/89	336

Scoring

Points

	Date	Pts
Ernie Nevers, Chi. Cards vs Chi. Bears	11/28/29	40
Dub Jones, Cle vs Chi. Bears	11/25/51	36
Gale Sayers, Chi vs SF	12/12/65	36
Paul Hornung, GB vs Bal	10/8/61	33
Bob Shaw, Chi. Cards vs Bal	10/2/50	30
Jim Brown, Cle vs Bal	11/1/59	30
Abner Haynes, Dal. Texans vs Oak	11/26/61	30
Billy Cannon, Hou vs NY Titans	12/10/61	30
Cookie Gilchrist, Buf vs NY Jets	12/8/63	30
Kellen Winslow, SD vs Oak	11/22/81	30
Jerry Rice, SF vs Atl	10/14/90	30
James Stewart, Jax vs Phi	10/12/97	30
Shaun Alexander, Sea vs Min	9/29/02	30
Clinton Portis, Den vs KC	12/7/03	30

Note: Nevers celebrated Thanksgiving, 1929, by scoring all of the Chicago Cardinals' points on six rushing TDs and four PATs. The Cards beat Red Grange and the Chicago Bears, 40-6.

Touchdowns Passing

	Date	No
Sid Luckman, Chi. Bears vs NYG	11/14/43	7
Adrian Burk, Phi vs Wash	10/17/54	7
George Blanda, Hou vs NY Titans	11/19/61	7
Y.A. Tittle, NYG vs Wash	10/28/62	7
Joe Kapp, Min vs Bal	9/28/69	7

Touchdowns Receiving

	Date	No
Bob Shaw, Chi. Cards vs Bal	10/2/50	5
Kellen Winslow, SD vs Oak	11/22/81	5
Jerry Rice, SF vs Atl	10/14/90	5

Touchdowns Rushing

	Date	No
Ernie Nevers, Chi. Cards vs Chi. Bears	11/28/29	6
Jim Brown, Cle vs Bal	11/1/59	5
Cookie Gilchrist, Buf vs NY Jets	12/8/63	5
James Stewart, Jax vs Phi	10/12/97	5
Clinton Portis, Den vs KC	12/7/03	5

Field Goals

	Date	No (Att)
Rob Bironas, Ten vs Hou	10/21/07	8 (8)
Jim Bakken, St.L vs Pit	9/24/67	7 (9)
Rich Karlis, Min vs LA Rams	11/5/89	7 (7)
Chris Boniol, Dal vs GB	11/18/96	7 (7)
Billy Cundiff, Dal vs NYG	9/15/03	7 (8)
Shayne Graham, Cin vs Bal	11/11/07	7 (7)

Extra Point Kicks

	Date	No
Pat Harder, Cards vs NYG	10/17/48	9
Bob Waterfield, LA Rams vs Bal	10/22/50	9
Charlie Gogolak, Wash vs NYG	11/27/66	9

Interceptions

	No
By 18 players	4

Sacks

	Date	No
Derrick Thomas, KC vs Sea	11/11/90	7.0
Fred Dean, SF vs NO	11/13/83	6.0
Derrick Thomas, KC vs Oak	9/6/98	6.0
Osi Umenyiora, NYG vs Phi	9/30/07	6.0

Longest Plays

Passing (all for TDs)

	Date	Yds
Frank Filchock to Andy Farkas, Wash vs Pit	10/15/39	99
George Izo to Bobby Mitchell, Wash vs Cle	9/15/63	99
Karl Sweetan to Pat Studstill, Det vs Bal	10/16/66	99
Sonny Jurgensen to Gerry Allen, Wash vs Chi	9/15/68	99
Jim Plunkett to Cliff Branch, LA Raiders vs Wash	10/2/83	99
Ron Jaworski to Mike Quick, Phi vs Atl	11/10/85	99
Stan Humphries to Tony Martin, SD vs Sea	9/18/94	99
Brett Favre to Robert Brooks, GB vs Chi	9/11/95	99
Trent Green to Marc Boerigter, KC vs SD	12/22/02	99
Jeff Garcia to Andre Davis, Cle vs Cin	10/17/04	99

Runs from Scrimmage (all for TDs)

	Date	Yds
Tony Dorsett, Dal vs Min	1/3/83	99
Ahman Green, GB vs Den	12/28/03	98
Andy Uram, GB vs Chi. Cards	10/8/39	97
Bob Gage, Pit vs Bears	12/4/49	97

Four players tied with 96-yd rushes.

Punts

	Date	Yds
Steve O'Neal, NYJ vs Den	9/21/69	98
Joe Lintzenich, Chi. Bears vs NYG	11/15/31	94
Shawn McCarthy, NE vs Buf	11/3/91	93

Field Goals

	Date	Yds
Tom Dempsey, NO vs Det	11/8/70	63
Jason Elam, Den vs Jax	10/25/98	63
Matt Bryant, TB vs Phi	10/22/06	62
Steve Cox, Cle vs Cin	10/21/84	60
Morten Andersen, NO vs Chi	10/27/91	60
Rob Bironas, Ten vs Ind	12/3/06	60

Punt Returns (all for TDs)

	Date	Yds
Robert Bailey, Rams vs NO	10/23/94	103
Gil LeFebvre, Cin vs Bklyn	12/3/33	98
Charlie West, Min vs Wash	11/3/68	98
Dennis Morgan, Dal vs St.L	10/13/74	98
Terance Mathis, NYJ vs Dal	11/4/90	98

Kickoff Returns (all for TDs)

	Date	Yds
Ellis Hobbs, NE vs NYJ	9/9/07	108
Al Carmichael, GB vs Chi. Bears	10/7/56	106
Noland Smith, KC vs Den	12/17/67	106
Roy Green, St.L vs Dal	10/21/79	106

Interception Returns (all for TDs)

	Date	Yds
Ed Reed, Bal vs Cle	11/17/04	106
James Willis (14 yds) lateral to Troy Vincent (90 yds), Phi vs Dal	11/3/96	104
Vencie Glenn, SD vs Den	11/29/87	103
Louis Oliver, Mia vs Buf	10/4/92	103

Nine players tied with 102-yd returns.

Returns of Missed FG (all for TDs)

	Date	Yds
Antonio Cromartie, SD vs Min	11/4/07	109
Nathan Vasher, Chi vs SF	11/13/05	108
Devin Hester, Chi vs NYG	11/12/06	108

Monday Night Football All-Time Leaders

The first episode of *Monday Night Football* aired on ABC on September 21, 1970 with the Cleveland Browns defeating the New York Jets, 31-21, at Municipal Stadium in Cleveland. The series continued on ABC for 36 seasons, until ESPN bought the rights to Monday Night games beginning with the 2006 season. Listed are all-time *Monday Night Football* records, through 2007 regular season.

Passing

Yards
Dan Marino	9654
Brett Favre	7878
Joe Montana	5148

Touchdowns
Dan Marino	74
Brett Favre	57
Steve Young	42

300-yd Games
Dan Marino	8
Brett Favre	8
Joe Montana	6
Randall Cunningham	6

Rushing

Yards
Emmitt Smith	2434
Tony Dorsett	1897
Thurman Thomas	1769

Touchdowns
Emmitt Smith	23
Marcus Allen	17
Eric Dickerson	14

100-yd Games
Emmitt Smith	12
Jerome Bettis	8
Franco Harris	7
Eric Dickerson	7

Receiving

Receptions
Jerry Rice	254
Andre Reed	124
Cris Carter	123

Yards
Jerry Rice	4029
Andre Reed	1783
Art Monk	1537

Touchdowns
Jerry Rice	34
Terrell Owens	16
Mark Clayton	15

Scoring

Touchdowns
Jerry Rice	36
Emmitt Smith	24
Marcus Allen	19

Field Goals
Gary Anderson	51
Jason Elam	48
Morten Andersen	36
Ryan Longwell	36

Interceptions
Everson Walls	11
Merton Hanks	9
Emmitt Thomas	8

Sacks
Bruce Smith	24.5
Richard Dent	20.0
Kevin Greene	18.0

Coaching Wins
Don Shula	31
Tom Landry	19
George Seifert	18
Bill Cowher	18

In The Booth

A look at Monday Night Football announcers through the years.

Years	Announcer Combination
1970	Keith Jackson, Howard Cosell, Don Meredith
1971-73	Frank Gifford, Howard Cosell, Don Meredith
1974	Frank Gifford, Howard Cosell, Alex Karras, Fred Williamson
1975-76	Frank Gifford, Howard Cosell, Alex Karras
1977-78	Frank Gifford, Howard Cosell, Don Meredith
1979-82	Frank Gifford, Howard Cosell, Don Meredith, Fran Tarkenton
1983	Frank Gifford, Howard Cosell, Don Meredith, O.J. Simpson
1984	Frank Gifford, Don Meredith, O.J. Simpson
1985	Frank Gifford, O.J. Simpson, Joe Namath
1986	Al Michaels, Frank Gifford
1987-97	Al Michaels, Frank Gifford, Dan Dierdorf
1998	Al Michaels, Dan Dierdorf, Boomer Esiason
1999	Al Michaels, Boomer Esiason
2000-01	Al Michaels, Dan Fouts, Dennis Miller
2002-05	Al Michaels, John Madden
2006	Mike Tirico, Joe Theisman, Tony Kornheiser
2007—	Mike Tirico, Ron Jaworski, Tony Kornheiser

Source: *The ESPN Pro Football Encyclopedia*, The NFL and Elias Sports Bureau

Chicago College All-Star Game

On Aug. 31, 1934, a year after sponsoring Major League Baseball's first All-Star Game, *Chicago Tribune* sports editor Arch Ward presented the first Chicago College All-Star Game at Soldier Field. A crowd of 79,432 turned out to see an all-star team of graduated college seniors battle the 1933 NFL champion Chicago Bears to a scoreless tie. The preseason game was played at Soldier Field and pitted the College All-Stars against the defending NFL champions (1933-1966) or Super Bowl champions (1967-75) every year except 1935 until it was cancelled in 1977. The NFL champs won the series, 31-9-1.

Year
1934 Chi. Bears 0, All-Stars 0
1935 Chi. Bears 5, All-Stars 0
1936 Detroit 7, All-Stars 0
1937 All-Stars 6, Green Bay 0
1938 All-Stars 28, Washington 16
1939 NY Giants 9, All-Stars 0

1940 Green Bay 45, All-Stars 28
1941 Chi. Bears 37, All-Stars 13
1942 Chi. Bears 21, All-Stars 0
1943 All-Stars 27, Washington 7
1944 Chi. Bears 24, All-Stars 21
1945 Green Bay 19, All-Stars 7
1946 All-Stars 16, LA Rams 0
1947 All-Stars 16, Chi. Bears 0
1948 Chi. Cards 28, All-Stars 0

Year
1949 Philadelphia 38, All-Stars 0

1950 All-Stars 17, Philadelphia 7
1951 Cleveland 33, All-Stars 0
1952 LA Rams 10, All-Stars 7
1953 Detroit 24, All-Stars 10
1954 Detroit 31, All-Stars 6
1955 All-Stars 30, Cleveland 27
1956 Cleveland 26, All-Stars 0
1957 NY Giants 22, All-Stars 12
1958 All-Stars 35, Detroit 19
1959 Baltimore 29, All-Stars 0

1960 Baltimore 32, All-Stars 7
1961 Philadelphia 28, All-Stars 14
1962 Green Bay 42, All-Stars 20
1963 All-Stars 20, Green Bay 17

Year
1964 Chi. Bears 28, All-Stars 17
1965 Cleveland 24, All-Stars 16
1966 Green Bay 38, All-Stars 0
1967 Green Bay 27, All-Stars 0
1968 Green Bay 34, All-Stars 17
1969 NY Jets 26, All-Stars 24

1970 Kansas City 24, All-Stars 3
1971 Baltimore 24, All-Stars 17
1972 Dallas 20, All-Stars 7
1973 Miami 14, All-Stars 3
1974 No Game (NFLPA Strike)
1975 Pittsburgh 21, All-Stars 14
1976 Pittsburgh 24, All-Stars 0*

*Downpour flooded field, game called with 1:22 left in 3rd quarter.

Number One Draft Choices

In an effort to blunt the dominance of the Chicago Bears and New York Giants in the 1930s and distribute talent more evenly throughout the league, the NFL established the college draft in 1936. The first player chosen in the first draft was Jay Berwanger, who was also college football's first Heisman Trophy winner. In all, 17 Heisman winners have also been the NFL's No. 1 draft choice. They are noted in **bold** type. The American Football League (formed in 1960) held its own draft for six years before agreeing to merge with the NFL and select players in a common draft starting in 1967.

Year	Team	
1936	Philadelphia	**Jay Berwanger**, HB, Chicago
1937	Philadelphia	Sam Francis, FB, Nebraska
1938	Cleveland Rams	Corbett Davis, FB, Indiana
1939	Chicago Cards	Ki Aldrich, C, TCU
1940	Chicago Cards	George Cafego, HB, Tennessee
1941	Chicago Bears	**Tom Harmon**, HB, Michigan
1942	Pittsburgh	Bill Dudley, HB, Virginia
1943	Detroit	**Frank Sinkwich**, HB, Georgia
1944	Boston Yanks	**Angelo Bertelli**, QB, N. Dame
1945	Chicago Cards	Charley Trippi, HB, Georgia
1946	Boston Yanks	Frank Dancewicz, QB, N. Dame
1947	Chicago Bears	Bob Fenimore, HB, Okla. A&M
1948	Washington	Harry Gilmer, QB, Alabama
1949	Philadelphia	Chuck Bednarik, C, Penn
1950	Detroit	**Leon Hart**, E, Notre Dame
1951	NY Giants	Kyle Rote, HB, SMU
1952	LA Rams	Bill Wade, QB, Vanderbilt
1953	San Francisco	Harry Babcock, E, Georgia
1954	Cleveland	Bobby Garrett, QB, Stanford
1955	Baltimore	George Shaw, QB, Oregon
1956	Pittsburgh	Gary Glick, DB, Colo. A&M
1957	Green Bay	**Paul Hornung**, QB, N. Dame
1958	Chicago Cards	King Hill, QB, Rice
1959	Green Bay	Randy Duncan, QB, Iowa
1960	NFL–LA Rams	**Billy Cannon**, HB, LSU
	AFL–No choice	
1961	NFL–Minnesota	Tommy Mason, HB, Tulane
	AFL–Buffalo	Ken Rice, G, Auburn
1962	NFL–Washington	**Ernie Davis**, HB, Syracuse
	AFL–Oakland	Roman Gabriel, QB, N.C. State
1963	NFL–LA Rams	**Terry Baker**, QB, Oregon St.
	AFL–Kan.City	Buck Buchanan, DT, Grambling
1964	NFL–San Fran	Dave Parks, E, Texas Tech
	AFL–Boston	Jack Concannon, QB, Boston Col.
1965	NFL–NY Giants	Tucker Frederickson, FB, Auburn
	AFL–Houston	Lawrence Elkins, E, Baylor
1966	NFL–Atlanta	Tommy Nobis, LB, Texas
	AFL–Miami	Jim Grabowski, FB, Illinois
1967	Baltimore	Bubba Smith, DT, Michigan St.
1968	Minnesota	Ron Yary, T, USC

Year	Team	
1969	Buffalo	**O.J. Simpson**, RB, USC
1970	Pittsburgh	Terry Bradshaw, QB, La.Tech
1971	New England	**Jim Plunkett**, QB, Stanford
1972	Buffalo	Walt Patulski, DE, Notre Dame
1973	Houston	John Matuszak, DE, Tampa
1974	Dallas	Ed (Too Tall) Jones, DE, Tenn. St.
1975	Atlanta	Steve Bartkowski, QB, Calif.
1976	Tampa Bay	Lee Roy Selmon, DE, Oklahoma
1977	Tampa Bay	Ricky Bell, RB, USC
1978	Houston	**Earl Campbell**, RB, Texas
1979	Buffalo	Tom Cousineau, LB, Ohio St.
1980	Detroit	**Billy Sims**, RB, Oklahoma
1981	New Orleans	**George Rogers**, RB, S. Carolina
1982	New England	Kenneth Sims, DT, Texas
1983	Baltimore	John Elway, QB, Stanford
1984	New England	Irving Fryar, WR, Nebraska
1985	Buffalo	Bruce Smith, DE, Va. Tech
1986	Tampa Bay	**Bo Jackson**, RB, Auburn
1987	Tampa Bay	**V. Testaverde**, QB, Miami-FL
1988	Atlanta	Aundray Bruce, LB, Auburn
1989	Dallas	Troy Aikman, QB, UCLA
1990	Indianapolis	Jeff George, QB, Illinois
1991	Dallas	Russell Maryland, DT, Miami-FL
1992	Indianapolis	Steve Emtman, DT, Washington
1993	New England	Drew Bledsoe, QB, Washington St.
1994	Cincinnati	Dan Wilkinson, DT, Ohio St.
1995	Cincinnati	Ki-Jana Carter, RB, Penn St.
1996	NY Jets	Keyshawn Johnson, WR, USC
1997	St. Louis	Orlando Pace, OT, Ohio St.
1998	Indianapolis	Peyton Manning, QB, Tennessee
1999	Cleveland	Tim Couch, QB, Kentucky
2000	Cleveland	Courtney Brown, DE, Penn St.
2001	Atlanta	Michael Vick, QB, Va. Tech
2002	Houston	David Carr, QB, Fresno St.
2003	Cincinnati	**Carson Palmer**, QB, USC
2004	San Diego	Eli Manning, QB, Mississippi
2005	San Francisco	Alex Smith, QB, Utah
2006	Houston	Mario Williams, DE, NC State
2007	Oakland	JaMarcus Russell, QB, LSU
2008	Miami	Jake Long, OT, Michigan

AP/Wide World Photos
Don Shula

NFL Media
Marv Levy

NFL Media
Bill Belichick

NFL Media
Tony Dungy

All-Time Winningest NFL Coaches

NFL career victories through the 2007 season. Career, regular season and playoff records are noted along with NFL, AFL and Super Bowl titles won. Coaches active during 2007 season in **bold** type.

		Career				Regular Season				Playoffs			
		Yrs	W	L	T	Pct	W	L	T	Pct	W	L	Pct.	League Titles
1	Don Shula	33	**347**	173	6	.665	328	156	6	.676	19	17	.528	2 Super Bowls and 1 NFL
2	George Halas	40	**324**	151	31	.671	318	148	31	.671	6	3	.667	5 NFL
3	Tom Landry	29	**270**	178	6	.601	250	162	6	.605	20	16	.556	2 Super Bowls
4	Curly Lambeau	33	**229**	134	22	.623	226	132	22	.624	3	2	.600	6 NFL
5	Chuck Noll	23	**209**	156	1	.572	193	148	1	.566	16	8	.667	4 Super Bowls
6	Marty Schottenheimer	21	**205**	139	1	.596	200	126	1	.613	5	13	.278	—None—
7	Dan Reeves	23	**201**	174	2	.536	190	165	2	.535	11	9	.550	—None—
8	Chuck Knox	22	**193**	158	1	.550	186	147	1	.558	7	11	.389	—None—
9	Bill Parcells	19	**183**	138	1	.570	172	130	1	.569	11	8	.579	2 Super Bowls
10	**Joe Gibbs**	16	**171**	101	0	.629	154	94	0	.621	17	7	.708	3 Super Bowls
11	Paul Brown	21	**170**	108	6	.609	166	100	6	.621	4.	8	.333	3 NFL
	Mike Holmgren	16	**170**	110	0	.607	157	99	0	.613	13	11	.542	1 Super Bowl
13	Bud Grant	18	**168**	108	5	.607	158	96	5	.620	10	12	.455	1 NFL
14	Bill Cowher	15	**161**	99	1	.619	149	90	1	.598	12	9	.571	1 Super Bowl
15	Marv Levy	17	**154**	120	0	.562	143	112	0	.561	11	8	.579	—None—
16	Steve Owen	23	**153**	108	17	.581	151	100	17	.595	2	8	.200	2 NFL
17	**Mike Shanahan**	15	**146**	95	0	.606	138	90	0	.605	8	5	.615	2 Super Bowls
18	**Bill Belichick**	13	**142**	85	0	.626	127	81	0	.611	15	4	.789	3 Super Bowls
19	**Tony Dungy**	12	**136**	74	0	.648	127	65	0	.661	9	9	.500	1 Super Bowl
	Hank Stram	17	**136**	100	10	.573	131	97	10	.571	5	3	.625	1 Super Bowl and 3 AFL
21	Weeb Ewbank	20	**134**	130	7	.507	130	129	7	.502	4	1	.800	1 Super Bowl, 2 NFL, and 1 AFL
22	Mike Ditka	14	**127**	101	0	.557	121	95	0	.560	6	6	.500	1 Super Bowl
23	Dick Vermeil	15	**126**	114	0	.525	120	109	0	.524	6	5	.545	1 Super Bowl
24	Jim Mora	15	**125**	112	0	.527	125	106	0	.541	0	6	.000	—None—
25	George Seifert	11	**124**	67	0	.649	114	62	0	.648	10	5	.667	2 Super Bowls

Notes: The NFL does not recognize records from the All-American Football Conference (1946-49). If it did, **Paul Brown** (52-4-3 in four AAFC seasons) would move up from 11th to 5th on the all-time list with the following career stats— 25 Yrs; 222 Wins; 112 Losses; 9 Ties; .660 Pct; 9-8 playoff record; and 4 AAFC titles.
The NFL also considers the Playoff Bowl or "Runner-up Bowl" (officially: the Bert Bell Benefit Bowl) as a postseason exhibition game. The Playoff Bowl was contested every year from 1960-69 in Miami between Eastern and Western Conference second place teams. While the games did not count, four of the coaches above went to the Playoff Bowl at least once and came away with the following records— Brown (0-1), Grant (0-1), Landry (1-2) and Shula (2-0).

Where They Coached

Belichick—Cleveland (1991-95), New England (2000—); **Brown**—Cleveland (1950-62), Cincinnati (1968-75); **Cowher**—Pittsburgh (1992-2006); **Ditka**—Chicago (1982-92), New Orleans (1997-99); **Dungy**—Tampa Bay (1996-2001), Indianapolis (2002—); **Ewbank**—Baltimore (1954-62), NY Jets (1963-73); **Gibbs**—Washington (1981-92, 2004-08); **Grant**—Minnesota (1967-83,1985); **Halas**—Chicago Bears (1920-29,33-42,46-55,58-67); **Holmgren**—Green Bay (1992-98), Seattle (1999—); **Knox**— LA Rams (1973-77, 1992-94), Buffalo (1978-82), Seattle (1983-91); **Lambeau**—Green Bay (1921-49), Chicago Cards (1950-51), Washington (1952-53); **Landry**—Dallas (1960-88); **Levy**— Kansas City (1978-82), Buffalo (1986-97); **Mora**—New Orleans (1986-1995), Indianapolis (1998-2001); **Noll**—Pittsburgh (1969-91). **Owen**—NY Giants (1931-53); **Parcells**— NY Giants (1983-90), New England (1993-97), NY Jets (1997-99), Dallas (2003-06); **Reeves**— Denver (1981-92), NY Giants (1993-96), Atlanta (1997-2003); **Schottenheimer**—Cleveland (1984-88), Kansas City (1989-98), Washington (2001), San Diego (2002-06); **Seifert**—San Francisco (1989-96), Carolina (1999-2001); **Shanahan**—LA Raiders (1988-89), Denver (1995—); **Shula**—Baltimore (1963-69), Miami (1970-95); **Stram**—Dallas-Kansas City (1960-74), New Orleans (1976-77), Kansas City (2001-05).

Top Winning Percentages
Minimum of 85 NFL victories, including playoffs.

		Yrs	W	L	T	Pct
1	Vince Lombardi	10	105	35	6	.740
2	John Madden	10	112	39	7	.731
3	George Allen	12	118	54	5	.681
4	George Halas	40	324	151	31	.671
5	Don Shula	33	347	173	6	.665
6	George Seifert	11	124	67	0	.649
7	**Tony Dungy**	12	136	74	0	.648
8	Joe Gibbs	16	171	101	0	.629
9	**Bill Belichick**	13	142	85	0	.626
10	Curly Lambeau	33	229	134	22	.623
11	Bill Cowher	15	161	99	1	.619
12	Bill Walsh	10	102	63	1	.617
13	Paul Brown	21	170	108	6	.609
14	**Andy Reid**	9	96	62	0	.608
15	**Mike Holmgren**	16	170	110	0	.607
16	Bud Grant	18	168	108	5	.607
17	**Mike Shanahan**	15	146	95	0	.606
18	Tom Landry	29	270	178	6	.601
19	Marty Schottenheimer	21	205	139	1	.596
20	Steve Owen	23	153	108	17	.581
21	Buddy Parker	15	107	76	9	.581
22	Hank Stram	17	136	100	10	.573
23	Chuck Noll	23	209	156	1	.572
24	Bill Parcells	19	183	138	1	.570
25	Jimmy Johnson	9	89	68	0	.567

Note: If AAFC records are included, **Paul Brown** moves from 13th to 6th with a percentage of .660 (25 yrs, 222-112-9) and **Buck Shaw** would be 12th at .619 (8 yrs, 91-55-5).

Active Coaches' Victories
Through 2007 season, including playoffs.

		Yrs	W	L	T	Pct
1	Mike Holmgren, Seattle	16	'170	110	0	.607
2	Mike Shanahan, Denver	15	146	95	0	.606
3	Bill Belichick, New England	13	142	85	0	.626
4	Tony Dungy, Indianapolis	12	136	74	0	.648
5	Jeff Fisher, Tennessee	13	120	104	0	.536
6	Tom Coughlin, NY Giants	12	111	95	0	.539
7	Andy Reid, Philadelphia	9	96	62	0	.608
8	Jon Gruden, Tampa Bay	10	91	78	0	.538
9	Norv Turner, SD	10	72	89	1	.448
10	Wade Phillips, Dallas	8	61	46	0	.570
11	John Fox, Carolina	6	56	47	0	.544
12	Herman Edwards, KC	7	54	64	0	.458
13	Dick Jauron, Buffalo	8	50	68	0	.424
14	Jack Del Rio, Jacksonville	5	46	37	0	.554
15	Marvin Lewis, Cincinnati	5	42	39	0	.519
16	Lovie Smith, Chicago	4	38	30	0	.559
17	Mike McCarthy, Green Bay	2	22	12	0	.647
18	Romeo Crennel, Cleveland	3	20	28	0	.417
19	Sean Payton, New Orleans	2	18	16	0	.529
20	Mike Nolan, San Fran.	3	16	32	0	.333
21	Brad Childress, Minnesota	2	14	18	0	.438
	Eric Mangini, NY Jets	2	14	19	0	.424
	Gary Kubiak, Houston	2	14	18	0	.438
24	Scott Linehan, St. Louis	2	11	21	0	.344
25	Mike Tomlin, Pittsburgh	1	10	7	0	.588
	Rod Marinelli, Detroit	2	10	22	0	.313
27	Ken Whisenhunt, Arizona	1	8	8	0	.500
28	Lane Kiffin, Oakland	1	4	12	0	.250
29	John Harbaugh, Baltimore	0	0	0	0	—
	Mike Smith, Atlanta	0	0	0	0	—
	Tony Sparano, Miami	0	0	0	0	—
	Jim Zorn, Washington	0	0	0	0	—

Annual Awards
Most Valuable Player

Currently, the NFL does not sanction an official MVP award. It awarded the Joe F. Carr Trophy (Carr was NFL president from 1921-39) to the league MVP from 1938 to 1946. Since then, four principal MVP awards have been given out throughout the years and are noted below: UPI (1953-69), AP (since 1957), the Maxwell Club of Philadelphia's Bert Bell Trophy (since 1959) and the Pro Football Writers Assn. (since 1976). UPI switched to AFC and NFC Player of the Year awards in 1970 and then discontinued its awards in 1997.

Multiple winners (more than one season): Jim Brown (4); Randall Cunningham, Brett Favre, Johnny Unitas and Y.A. Tittle (3); Earl Campbell, Marshall Faulk, Rich Gannon, Otto Graham, Don Hutson, Peyton Manning, Joe Montana, Walter Payton, Barry Sanders, Ken Stabler, Joe Theismann, Kurt Warner and Steve Young (2).

Year	Awards
1938 Mel Hein, NY Giants, C	Carr
1939 Parker Hall, Cleveland Rams, HB	Carr
1940 Ace Parker, Brooklyn, HB	Carr
1941 Don Hutson, Green Bay, E	Carr
1942 Don Hutson, Green Bay, E	Carr
1943 Sid Luckman, Chicago Bears, QB	Carr
1944 Frank Sinkwich, Detroit, HB	Carr
1945 Bob Waterfield, Cleveland Rams, QB	Carr
1946 Bill Dudley, Pittsburgh, HB	Carr
1947-52 No award	
1953 Otto Graham, Cleveland Browns, QB	UPI
1954 Joe Perry, San Francisco, FB	UPI
1955 Otto Graham, Cleveland, QB	UPI
1956 Frank Gifford, NY Giants, HB	UPI
1957 Y.A. Tittle, San Francisco, QB	UPI
& Jim Brown, Cleveland, FB	AP
1958 Jim Brown, Cleveland, FB	UPI
& Gino Marchetti, Baltimore, DE	AP
1959 Johnny Unitas, Baltimore, QB	UPI, Bell
& Charley Conerly, NY Giants, QB	AP
1960 Norm Van Brocklin, Phi., QB	UPI, AP (tie)
& Joe Schmidt, Detroit, LB	AP (tie)
1961 Paul Hornung, Green Bay, HB	UPI, AP, Bell
1962 Y.A. Tittle, NY Giants, QB	UPI
Jim Taylor, Green Bay, FB	AP
& Andy Robustelli, NY Giants, DE	Bell
1963 Jim Brown, Cleveland, FB	UPI, Bell
& Y.A. Tittle, NY Giants, QB	AP

Year	Awards
1964 Johnny Unitas, Baltimore, QB	UPI, AP, Bell
1965 Jim Brown, Cleveland, FB	UPI, AP
& Pete Retzlaff, Philadelphia, TE	Bell
1966 Bart Starr, Green Bay, QB	UPI, AP
& Don Meredith, Dallas, QB	Bell
1967 Johnny Unitas, Baltimore, QB	UPI, AP, Bell
& Leroy Kelly, Cleveland, RB	Bell
1968 Earl Morrall, Baltimore, QB	UPI, AP
& Leroy Kelly, Cleveland, RB	Bell
1969 Roman Gabriel, LA Rams, QB	UPI, AP, Bell
1970 John Brodie, San Francisco, QB	AP
& George Blanda, Oakland, QB-PK	Bell
1971 Alan Page, Minnesota, DT	AP
& Roger Staubach, Dallas, QB	Bell
1972 Larry Brown, Washington, RB	AP, Bell
1973 O.J. Simpson, Buffalo, RB	AP, Bell
1974 Ken Stabler, Oakland, QB	AP, Bell
& Merlin Olsen, LA Rams, DT	Bell
1975 Fran Tarkenton, Minnesota, QB	AP, Bell
1976 Bert Jones, Baltimore, QB	AP, PFWA
& Ken Stabler, Oakland, QB	Bell
1977 Walter Payton, Chicago, RB	AP, PFWA
& Bob Griese, Miami, QB	Bell
1978 Terry Bradshaw, Pittsburgh, QB	AP, Bell
& Earl Campbell, Houston, RB	PFWA
1979 Earl Campbell, Houston, RB	AP, Bell, PFWA
1980 Brian Sipe, Cleveland, QB	AP, PFWA
& Ron Jaworski, Philadelphia, QB	Bell
1981 Ken Anderson, Cincinnati, QB	AP, Bell, PFWA

Year	Awards	Year	Award
1982 Mark Moseley, Washington, PK	AP	1994 Steve Young, San Francisco, QB	AP, Bell, PFWA
Joe Theismann, Washington, QB	Bell	1995 Brett Favre, Green Bay, QB	AP, Bell, PFWA
& Dan Fouts, San Diego, QB	PFWA	1996 Brett Favre, Green Bay, QB	AP, Bell, PFWA
1983 Joe Theismann, Washington, QB	AP, PFWA	1997 Barry Sanders, Detroit, RB	AP (tie), Bell, PFWA
& John Riggins, Washington, RB	Bell	& Brett Favre, Green Bay, QB	AP (tie)
1984 Dan Marino, Miami, QB	AP, Bell, PFWA	1998 Terrell Davis, Denver, RB	AP, PFWA
1985 Marcus Allen, LA Raiders, RB	AP, PFWA	& Randall Cunningham, Minnesota, QB	Be
& Walter Payton, Chicago, RB	Bell	1999 Kurt Warner, St. Louis, QB	AP, Bell, PFWA
1986 Lawrence Taylor, NY Giants, LB	AP, Bell, PFWA	2000 Marshall Faulk, St. Louis, RB	AP, PFWA
1987 Jerry Rice, San Francisco, WR	Bell, PFWA	& Rich Gannon, Oakland, QB	Be
& John Elway, Denver, QB	AP	2001 Kurt Warner, St. Louis, QB	A
1988 Boomer Esiason, Cincinnati, QB	AP, PFWA &	& Marshall Faulk, St. Louis, RB	Bell, PFWA
Randall Cunningham, Phila., QB	Bell	2002 Rich Gannon, Oakland, QB	AP, Bell, PFWA
1989 Joe Montana, San Francisco, QB	AP, Bell, PFWA	2003 Peyton Manning, Indianapolis, QB	AP (tie), Bell
1990 Randall Cunningham, Phila., QB	Bell, PFWA	Steve McNair, Tennessee, QB	AP (tie)
& Joe Montana, San Francisco, QB	AP	& Jamal Lewis, Baltimore, RB	PFWA
1991 Thurman Thomas, Buffalo, RB	AP, PFWA	2004 Peyton Manning, Indianapolis, QB	AP, Bell, PFWA
& Barry Sanders, Detroit, RB	Bell	2005 Shaun Alexander, Seattle, RB	AP, Bell, PFWA
1992 Steve Young, San Francisco, QB	AP, Bell, PFWA	2006 LaDainian Tomlinson, San Diego, RB	AP, Bell, PFWA
1993 Emmitt Smith, Dallas, RB	AP, Bell, PFWA	2007 Tom Brady, New England, QB	AP, Bell, PFWA

AP Offensive Player of the Year

Selected by The Associated Press in balloting by a nationwide media panel. Given out since 1972. Rookie winners are in **bold** type.
Multiple winners: Earl Campbell and Marshall Faulk (3); Terrell Davis, Jerry Rice and Barry Sanders (2).

Year	Pos	Year	Pos	Year	Pos
1972 Larry Brown, Was	RB	1984 Dan Marino, Mia	QB	1996 Terrell Davis, Den	RB
1973 O.J. Simpson, Buf	RB	1985 Marcus Allen, Raiders	RB	1997 Barry Sanders, Det	RB
1974 Ken Stabler, Oak	QB	1986 Eric Dickerson, Rams	RB	1998 Terrell Davis, Den	RB
1975 Fran Tarkenton, Min	QB	1987 Jerry Rice, SF	WR	1999 Marshall Faulk, St.L	RB
1976 Bert Jones, Bal	QB	1988 Roger Craig, SF	RB	2000 Marshall Faulk, St.L	RB
1977 Walter Payton, Chi	RB	1989 Joe Montana, SF	QB	2001 Marshall Faulk, St.L	RB
1978 **Earl Campbell**, Hou	RB	1990 Warren Moon, Hou	QB	2002 Priest Holmes, KC	RB
1979 Earl Campbell, Hou	RB	1991 Thurman Thomas, Buf	RB	2003 Jamal Lewis, Bal	RB
1980 Earl Campbell, Hou	RB	1992 Steve Young, SF	QB	2004 Peyton Manning, Ind	QB
1981 Ken Anderson, Cin	QB	1993 Jerry Rice, SF	WR	2005 Shaun Alexander, Sea	RB
1982 Dan Fouts, SD	QB	1994 Barry Sanders, Det	RB	2006 LaDainian Tomlinson, SD	RB
1983 Joe Theismann, Was	QB	1995 Brett Favre, GB	QB	2007 Tom Brady, NE	QB

AP Defensive Player of the Year

Selected by The Associated Press in balloting by a nationwide media panel. Given out since 1971. Rookie winners are in **bold** type.
Multiple winners: Lawrence Taylor (3); Joe Greene, Ray Lewis, Mike Singletary, Bruce Smith and Reggie White (2).

Year	Pos	Year	Pos	Year	Pos
1971 Alan Page, Min	DT	1984 Kenny Easley, Sea	S	1996 Bruce Smith, Buf	DE
1972 Joe Greene, Pit	DT	1985 Mike Singletary, Chi	LB	1997 Dana Stubblefield, SF	DT
1973 Dick Anderson, Mia	S	1986 Lawrence Taylor, NYG	LB	1998 Reggie White, GB	DE
1974 Joe Greene, Pit	DT	1987 Reggie White, Phi	DE	1999 Warren Sapp, TB	DT
1975 Mel Blount, Pit	CB	1988 Mike Singletary, Chi	LB	2000 Ray Lewis, Bal	LB
1976 Jack Lambert, Pit	LB	1989 Keith Millard, Min	DT	2001 Michael Strahan, NYG	DE
1977 Harvey Martin, Dal	DE	1990 Bruce Smith, Buf	DE	2002 Derrick Brooks, TB	LB
1978 Randy Gradishar, Den	LB	1991 Pat Swilling, NO	LB	2003 Ray Lewis, Bal	LB
1979 Lee Roy Selmon, TB	DE	1992 Cortez Kennedy, Sea	DT	2004 Ed Reed, Bal	CB
1980 Lester Hayes, Oak	CB	1993 Rod Woodson, Pit	CB	2005 Brian Urlacher, Chi	LB
1981 **Lawrence Taylor**, NYG	LB	1994 Deion Sanders, SF	CB	2006 Jason Taylor, Mia	DE
1982 Lawrence Taylor, NYG	LB	1995 Bryce Paup, Buf	LB	2007 Bob Sanders, Ind	S
1983 Doug Betters, Mia	DE				

UPI NFC Player of the Year

Given out by UPI from 1970-96. Offensive and defensive players honored since 1983. Rookie winners are in **bold** type.
Multiple winners: Eric Dickerson, Reggie White and Mike Singletary (3); Brett Favre, Charles Haley, Walter Payton, Lawrence Taylor and Steve Young (2).

Year	Pos	Year	Pos	Year	Pos
1970 John Brodie, SF	QB	1984 Off–Eric Dickerson, Rams	RB	1991 Off–Mark Rypien, Was	QB
1971 Alan Page, Min	DT	Def–Mike Singletary, Chi	LB	Def–Reggie White, Phi	DE
1972 Larry Brown, Was	RB	1985 Off–Walter Payton, Chi	RB	1992 Off–Steve Young, SF	QB
1973 John Hadl, Rams	QB	Def–Mike Singletary, Chi	LB	Def–Chris Doleman, Min	DE
1974 Jim Hart, St.L	QB	1986 Off–Eric Dickerson, Rams	RB	1993 Off–Emmitt Smith, Dal	RB
1975 Fran Tarkenton, Min	QB	Def–Lawrence Taylor, NYG	LB	Def–Eric Allen, Phi	CB
1976 Chuck Foreman, Min	RB	1987 Off–Jerry Rice, SF	WR	1994 Off–Steve Young, SF	QB
1977 Walter Payton, Chi	RB	Def–Reggie White, Phi	DE	Def–Charles Haley, Dal	DE
1978 Archie Manning, NO	QB	1988 Off–Roger Craig, SF	RB	1995 Off–Brett Favre, GB	QB
1979 Ottis Anderson, St.L	RB	Def–Mike Singletary, Chi	LB	Def–Reggie White, GB	DE
1980 Ron Jaworski, Phi	QB	1989 Off–Joe Montana, SF	QB	1996 Off–Brett Favre, GB	QB
1981 Tony Dorsett, Dal	RB	Def–Keith Millard, Min	DT	Def–Kevin Greene, Car	LB
1982 Mark Moseley, Was	PK	1990 Off–Randall Cunningham, Phi.	QB	1997 Award discontinued.	
1983 Off–Eric Dickerson, Rams	RB	Def–Charles Haley, SF	LB		
Def–Lawrence Taylor, NYG	LB				

UPI AFL-AFC Player of the Year

Presented by UPI to the top player in the AFL (1960-69) and AFC (1970-96). Offensive and defensive players have been honored since 1983. Rookie winners are in **bold** type.

Multiple winners: Bruce Smith (4); O.J. Simpson (3); Cornelius Bennett, George Blanda, John Elway, Dan Fouts, Daryle Lamonica, Dan Marino and Curt Warner (2).

Year		Pos	Year		Pos	Year		Pos
1960	**Abner Haynes**, Dal	HB	1978	**Earl Campbell**, Hou	RB	1989	Off–Christian Okoye, KC	RB
1961	George Blanda, Hou	QB	1979	Dan Fouts, SD	QB		Def–Michael Dean Perry,Cle	NT
1962	Cookie Gilchrist, Buf	FB	1980	Brian Sipe, Cle	QB	1990	Off–Warren Moon, Hou	QB
1963	Lance Alworth, SD	FL	1981	Ken Anderson, Cin	QB		Def–Bruce Smith,Buf	DE
1964	Gino Cappelletti, Bos	FL-PK	1982	Dan Fouts, SD	QB	1991	Off–Thurman Thomas, Buf	RB
1965	Paul Lowe, SD	HB	1983	Off–**Curt Warner**, Sea	RB		Def–Cornelius Bennett, Buf	LB
1966	Jim Nance, Bos	FB		Def–Rod Martin, Raiders	LB	1992	Off–Barry Foster, Pit	RB
1967	Daryle Lamonica, Raiders	QB	1984	Off–Dan Marino, Mia	QB		Def–Junior Seau, SD	LB
1968	Joe Namath, NYJ	QB		Def–Mark Gastineau, NYJ	DE	1993	Off–John Elway, Den	QB
1969	Daryle Lamonica, Raiders	QB	1985	Off–Marcus Allen, Raiders	RB		Def–Rod Woodson, Pit	CB
1970	George Blanda, Raiders	QB-PK		Def–Andre Tippett, NE	LB	1994	Off–Dan Marino, Mia	QB
1971	Otis Taylor, KC	WR	1986	Off–Curt Warner, Sea	RB		Def–Greg Lloyd, Pit	LB
1972	O.J. Simpson, Buf	RB		Def–Rulon Jones, Den	DE	1995	Off–Jim Harbaugh, Ind	QB
1973	O.J. Simpson, Buf	RB	1987	Off–John Elway, Den	QB		Def–Bryce Paup, Buf	LB
1974	Ken Stabler, Raiders	QB		Def–Bruce Smith, Buf	DE	1996	Off–Terrell Davis, Den	RB
1975	O.J. Simpson, Buf	RB	1988	Off–Boomer Esiason, Cin	QB		Def–Bruce Smith, Buf	DE
1976	Bert Jones, Bal	QB		Def–Bruce Smith, Buf	DE	1997	Award discontinued.	
1977	Craig Morton, Den	QB		& Cornelius Bennett, Buf	LB			

UPI NFL-NFC Rookie of the Year

Presented by UPI to the top rookie in the NFL (1955-69) and NFC (1970-96). Players who were the overall first pick in the NFL draft are in **bold** type.

Year		Pos	Year		Pos	Year		Pos
1955	Alan Ameche, Bal	FB	1970	Bruce Taylor, SF	DB	1985	Jerry Rice, SF	WR
1956	Lenny Moore, Bal	HB	1971	John Brockington, GB	RB	1986	Reuben Mayes, NO	RB
1957	Jim Brown, Cle	FB	1972	Chester Marcol, GB	PK	1987	Robert Awalt, St.L	TE
1958	Jimmy Orr, Pit	FL	1973	Charle Young, Phi	TE	1988	Keith Jackson, Phi	TE
1959	Boyd Dowler, GB	FL	1974	Jim Hicks, NY	G	1989	Barry Sanders, Det	RB
1960	Gail Cogdill, Det	FL	1975	Mike Thomas, Wash	RB	1990	Mark Carrier, Chi	S
1961	Mike Ditka, Chi	TE	1976	Sammy White, Min	WR	1991	Lawrence Dawsey, TB	WR
1962	Ronnie Bull, Chi	FB	1977	Tony Dorsett, Dal	RB	1992	Robert Jones, Dal	LB
1963	Paul Flatley, Min	FL	1978	Bubba Baker, Det	DE	1993	Jerome Bettis, LA	RB
1964	Charley Taylor, Wash	HB	1979	Ottis Anderson, St.L	RB	1994	Bryant Young, SF	DT
1965	Gale Sayers, Chi	HB	1980	**Billy Sims**, Det	RB	1995	Rashaan Salaam, Chi	RB
1966	Johnny Roland, St.L	HB	1981	**George Rogers**, NO	RB	1996	Simeon Rice, Ari.	DE
1967	Mel Farr, Det	RB	1982	Jim McMahon, Chi	QB	1997	Award discontinued.	
1968	Earl McCullough, Det	FL	1983	Eric Dickerson, LA	RB			
1969	Calvin Hill, Dal	RB	1984	Paul McFadden, Phi	PK			

UPI AFL-AFC Rookie of the Year

Presented by UPI to the top rookie in the AFL (1960-69) and AFC (1970-96). Players who were the overall first pick in the AFL or NFL draft are in **bold** type.

Year		Pos	Year		Pos	Year		Pos
1960	Abner Haynes, Dal	HB	1973	Bobbie Clark, Cin	RB	1986	Leslie O'Neal, SD	DE
1961	Earl Faison, SD	DE	1974	Don Woods, SD	RB	1987	Shane Conlan, Buf	LB
1962	Curtis McClinton, Dal	FB	1975	Robert Brazile, Hou	LB	1988	John Stephens, NE	RB
1963	Billy Joe, Den	FB	1976	Mike Haynes, NE	DB	1989	Derrick Thomas, KC	LB
1964	Matt Snell, NY	FB	1977	A.J. Duhe, Mia	DE	1990	Richmond Webb, Mia	OT
1965	Joe Namath, NY	QB	1978	**Earl Campbell**, Hou	RB	1991	Mike Croel, Den	LB
1966	Bobby Burnett, Buf	HB	1979	Jerry Butler, Buf	WR	1992	Dale Carter, KC	CB
1967	George Webster, Hou	LB	1980	Joe Cribbs, Buf	RB	1993	Rick Mirer, Sea	QB
1968	Paul Robinson, Cin	RB	1981	Joe Delaney, KC	RB	1994	Marshall Faulk, Ind	RB
1969	Greg Cook, Cin	QB	1982	Marcus Allen, LA	RB	1995	Curtis Martin, NE	RB
1970	Dennis Shaw, Buf	QB	1983	Curt Warner, Sea	RB	1996	Terry Glenn, NE	WR
1971	**Jim Plunkett**, NE	QB	1984	Louis Lipps, Pit	WR	1997	Award discontinued.	
1972	Franco Harris, Pit	RB	1985	Kevin Mack, Cle	RB			

Annual Awards (Cont.)
AP Offensive Rookie of the Year

Selected by The Associated Press in balloting by a nationwide media panel. Given out since 1967.

Year		Pos	Year		Pos	Year		Pos
1967	Mel Farr, Det	RB	1981	George Rogers, NO	RB	1995	Curtis Martin, NE	RB
1968	Earl McCullouch, Det	OE	1982	Marcus Allen, Raiders	RB	1996	Eddie George, Hou	RB
1969	Calvin Hill, Dal	RB	1983	Eric Dickerson, Rams	RB	1997	Warrick Dunn, TB	RB
1970	Dennis Shaw, Buf	QB	1984	Louis Lipps, Pit	WR	1998	Randy Moss, Min	WR
1971	John Brockington, GB	RB	1985	Eddie Brown, Cin	WR	1999	Edgerrin James, Ind	RB
1972	Franco Harris, Pit	RB	1986	Reuben Mayes, NO	RB	2000	Mike Anderson, Den	RB
1973	Chuck Foreman, Min	RB	1987	Troy Stradford, Mia	RB	2001	Anthony Thomas, Chi	RB
1974	Don Woods, SD	RB	1988	John Stephens, NE	RB	2002	Clinton Portis, Den	RB
1975	Mike Thomas, Was	RB	1989	Barry Sanders, Det	RB	2003	Anquan Boldin, Ari	WR
1976	Sammy White, Min	WR	1990	Emmitt Smith, Dal	RB	2004	Ben Roethlisberger, Pit	QB
1977	Tony Dorsett, Dal	RB	1991	Leonard Russell, NE	RB	2005	Carnell Williams, TB	RB
1978	Earl Campbell, Hou	RB	1992	Carl Pickens, Cin	WR	2006	Vince Young, Ten	QB
1979	Ottis Anderson, St.L	RB	1993	Jerome Bettis, Rams	RB	2007	Adrian Peterson, Min	RB
1980	Billy Sims, Det	RB	1994	Marshall Faulk, Ind	RB			

AP Defensive Rookie of the Year

Selected by The Associated Press in balloting by a nationwide media panel. Given out since 1967.

Year		Pos	Year		Pos	Year		Pos
1967	Lem Barney, Det	CB	1981	Lawrence Taylor, NYG	LB	1996	Simeon Rice, Ari	DE
1968	Claude Humphrey, Atl	DE	1982	Chip Banks, Cle	LB	1997	Peter Boulware, Bal	LB
1969	Joe Greene, Pit	DT	1983	Vernon Maxwell, Bal	LB	1998	Charles Woodson, Raiders	CB
1970	Bruce Taylor, SF	CB	1984	Bill Maas, KC	DT	1999	Jevon Kearse, Ten	DE
1971	Isiah Robertson, Rams	LB	1985	Duane Bickett, Ind	LB	2000	Brian Urlacher, Chi	LB
1972	Willie Buchanon, GB	CB	1986	Leslie O'Neal, SD	DE	2001	Kendrell Bell, Pit	LB
1973	Wally Chambers, Chi	DT	1987	Shane Conlan, Buf	LB	2002	Julius Peppers, Car	DE
1974	Jack Lambert, Pit	LB	1988	Erik McMillan, NYJ	S	2003	Terrell Suggs, Bal	LB
1975	Robert Brazile, Hou	LB	1989	Derrick Thomas, KC	LB	2004	Jonathan Vilma, NYJ	LB
1976	Mike Haynes, NE	CB	1990	Mark Carrier, Chi	S	2005	Shawne Merriman, SD	LB
1977	A.J. Duhe, Mia	DE	1991	Mike Croel, Den	LB	2006	DeMeco Ryans, Hou	LB
1978	Al Baker, Det	DE	1992	Dale Carter, KC	CB	2007	Patrick Willis, SF	LB
1979	Jim Haslett, Buf	LB	1993	Dana Stubblefield, SF	DT			
1980	Buddy Curry, Atl	LB	1994	Tim Bowens, Mia	DT			
	& Al Richardson, Atl	LB	1995	Hugh Douglas, NYJ	DE			

Coach of the Year

Presented by UPI to the top coach in the AFL-NFL (1955-69) and AFC-NFC (1970-96). In 1997, the UPI awards were discontinued. Awards beginning in 1997 are the consensus selections from presenters such as AP, The Maxwell Football Club of Philadelphia, *The Sporting News* and the Pro Football Writers Association. Records indicate the team's change in record from the previous season.

Multiple winners: Dan Reeves (4); Paul Brown, Chuck Knox, Marty Schottenheimer and Don Shula (3); George Allen, Leeman Bennett, Bill Belichick, Mike Ditka, George Halas, Tom Landry, Marv Levy, Bill Parcells, Jack Pardee, Sam Rutigliano, Lou Saban, Allie Sherman, Dick Vermeil and Bill Walsh (2).

Year		Improvement	Year		Improvement
1955	NFL–Joe Kuharich, Washington	3-9 to 8-4	1969	NFL–Bud Grant, Minnesota	8-6 to 12-2
1956	NFL–Buddy Parker, Detroit	3-9 to 9-3		AFL–Paul Brown, Cincinnati	3-11 to 4-9-1
1957	NFL–Paul Brown, Cleveland	5-7 to 9-2-1	1970	NFC–Alex Webster, New York	6-8 to 9-5
1958	NFL–Weeb Ewbank, Baltimore	7-5 to 9-3		AFC–Paul Brown, Cincinnati	4-9-1 to 8-6
1959	NFL–Vince Lombardi, Green Bay	1-10-1 to 7-5	1971	NFC–George Allen, Washington	6-8 to 9-4-1
1960	NFL–Buck Shaw, Philadelphia	7-5 to 10-2		AFC–Don Shula, Miami	10-4 to 10-3-1
	AFL–Lou Rymkus, Houston	10-4	1972	NFC–Dan Devine, Green Bay	4-8-2 to 10-4
1961	NFL–Allie Sherman, New York	6-4-2 to 10-3-1		AFC–Chuck Noll, Pittsburgh	6-8 to 11-3
	AFL–Wally Lemm, Houston	10-4 to 10-3-1	1973	NFC–Chuck Knox, Los Angeles	6-7-1 to 12-2
1962	NFL–Allie Sherman, New York	10-3-1 to 12-2		AFC–John Ralston, Denver	5-9 to 7-5-2
	AFL–Jack Faulkner, Denver	3-11 to 7-7	1974	NFC–Don Coryell, St. Louis	4-9-1 to 10-4
1963	NFL–George Halas, Chicago	9-5 to 11-1-2		AFC–Sid Gillman, Houston	1-13 to 7-7
	AFL–Al Davis, Oakland	1-13 to 10-4	1975	NFC–Tom Landry, Dallas	8-6 to 10-4
1964	NFL–Don Shula, Baltimore	8-6 to 12-2		AFC–Ted Marchibroda, Baltimore	2-12 to 10-4
	AFL–Lou Saban, Buffalo	7-6-1 to 12-2	1976	NFC–Jack Pardee, Chicago	4-10 to 7-7
1965	NFL–George Halas, Chicago	5-9 to 9-5		AFC–Chuck Fairbanks, New England	3-11 to 11 3
	AFL–Lou Saban, Buffalo	12-2 to 10-3-1	1977	NFC–Leeman Bennett, Atlanta	4-10 to 7-7
1966	NFL–Tom Landry, Dallas	7-7 to 10-3-1		AFC–Red Miller, Denver	9-5 to 12-2
	AFL–Mike Holovak, Boston	4-8-2 to 8-4-2	1978	NFC–Dick Vermeil, Philadelphia	5-9 to 9-7
1967	NFL–George Allen, Los Angeles	8-6 to 11-1-2		AFC–Walt Michaels, New York	3-11 to 8-8
	AFL–John Rauch, Oakland	8-5-1 to 13-1	1979	NFC–Jack Pardee, Washington	8-8 to 10-6
1968	NFL–Don Shula, Baltimore	11-1-2 to 13-1		AFC–Sam Rutigliano, Cleveland	8-8 to 9-7
	AFL–Hank Stram, Kansas City	9-5 to 12-2			

Year		Improvement
1980	NFC–Leeman Bennett, Atlanta	6-10 to 12-4
	AFC–Sam Rutigliano, Cleveland	9-7 to 11-5
1981	NFC–Bill Walsh, San Francisco	6-10 to 13-3
	AFC–Forrest Gregg, Cincinnati	6-10 to 12-4
1982	NFC–Joe Gibbs, Washington	8-8 to 8-1
	AFC–Tom Flores, Los Angeles	7-9 to 8-1
1983	NFC–John Robinson, Los Angeles	2-7 to 9-7
	AFC–Chuck Knox, Seattle	4-5 to 9-7
1984	NFC–Bill Walsh, San Francisco	10-6 to 15-1
	AFC–Chuck Knox, Seattle	9-7 to 12-4
1985	NFC–Mike Ditka, Chicago	10-6 to 15-1
	AFC–Raymond Berry, New England	9-7 to 11-5
1986	NFC–Bill Parcells, New York	10-6 to 14-2
	AFC–Marty Schottenheimer, Cleveland	8-8 to 12-4
1987	NFC–Jim Mora, New Orleans	7-9 to 12-3
	AFC–Ron Meyer, Indianapolis	3-13 to 9-6
1988	NFC–Mike Ditka, Chicago	11-4 to 12-4
	AFC–Marv Levy, Buffalo	7-8 to 12-4
1989	NFC–Lindy Infante, Green Bay	4-12 to 10-6
	AFC–Dan Reeves, Denver	8-8 to 11-5
1990	NFC–Jimmy Johnson, Dallas	1-15 to 7-9
	AFC–Art Shell, Los Angeles	8-8 to 12-4

Year		Improvement
1991	NFC–Wayne Fontes, Detroit	6-10 to 12-4
	AFC–Dan Reeves, Denver	5-11 to 12-4
1992	NFC–Dennis Green, Minnesota	8-8 to 11-5
	AFC–Bobby Ross, San Diego	4-12 to 11-5
1993	NFC–Dan Reeves, New York	6-10 to 11-5
	AFC–Marv Levy, Buffalo	11-5 to 12-4
1994	NFC–Dave Wannstedt, Chicago	7-9 to 9-7
	AFC–Bill Parcells, New England	5-11 to 10-6
1995	NFC–Ray Rhodes, Philadelphia	7-9 to 10-6
	AFC–Marty Schottenheimer, Kansas City	9-7 to 13-3
1996	NFC–Dom Capers, Carolina	7-9 to 12-4
	AFC–Tom Coughlin, Jacksonville	4-12 to 9-7
1997	NFL–Jim Fassel, NY Giants	6-10 to 10-5-1
1998	NFL–Dan Reeves, Atlanta	7-9 to 14-2
1999	NFL–Dick Vermeil, St. Louis	4-12 to 13-3
2000	NFL–Jim Haslett, New Orleans	3-13 to 10-6
2001	NFL–Dick Jauron, Chicago	5-11 to 13-3
2002	NFL–Andy Reid, Philadelphia	11-5 to 12-4
2003	NFL–Bill Belichick, New England	9-7 to 14-2
2004	NFL–Marty Schottenheimer, San Diego	4-12 to 12-4
2005	NFL–Lovie Smith, Chicago	5-11 to 11-5
2006	NFL–Sean Payton, New Orleans	3-13 to 10-6
2007	NFL–Bill Belichick, New England	12-4 to 16-0

ARENA FOOTBALL

The Arena Football League debuted in June of 1987 with four teams in Chicago, Denver, Pittsburgh and Washington D.C. Currently there are 19 teams in the league (including the New Orleans VooDoo, who returned in 2007 after a Hurricane Katrina-related absence in 2006), divided into two conferences and four divisions.

ArenaBowl

Multiple Winners: Tampa Bay (5); Detroit (4); San Jose (3); Arizona and Orlando (2).

Bowl	Year	Winner	Head Coach	Score	Loser	Head Coach	Site
I	1987	Denver	Tim Marcum	45-16	Pittsburgh	Joe Haering	Pittsburgh
II	1988	Detroit	Tim Marcum	24-13	Chicago	Perry Moss	Chicago
III	1989	Detroit	Tim Marcum	39-26	Pittsburgh	Joe Haering	Detroit
IV	1990	Detroit	Perry Moss	51-27	Dallas	Ernie Stautner	Detroit
V	1991	Tampa Bay	Fran Curci	48-42	Detroit	Tim Marcum	Detroit
VI	1992	Detroit	Tim Marcum	56-38	Orlando	Perry Moss	Orlando
VII	1993	Tampa Bay	Lary Kuharich	51-31	Detroit	Tim Marcum	Detroit
VIII	1994	Arizona	Danny White	36-31	Orlando	Perry Moss	Orlando
IX	1995	Tampa Bay	Tim Marcum	48-35	Orlando	Perry Moss	St. Petersburg
X	1996	Tampa Bay	Tim Marcum	42-38	Iowa	John Gregory	Des Moines
XI	1997	Arizona	Danny White	55-33	Iowa	John Gregory	Phoenix
XII	1998	Orlando	Jay Gruden	62-31	Tampa Bay	Tim Marcum	Tampa
XIII	1999	Albany	Mike Dailey	59-48	Orlando	Jay Gruden	Albany
XIV	2000	Orlando	Jay Gruden	41-38	Nashville	Pat Sperduto	Orlando
XV	2001	Grand Rapids	Michael Trigg	64-42	Nashville	Pat Sperduto	Grand Rapids
XVI	2002	San Jose	Darren Arbet	52-14	Arizona	Danny White	San Jose
XVII	2003	Tampa Bay	Tim Marcum	43-29	Arizona	Danny White	Tampa
XVIII	2004	San Jose	Darren Arbet	69-62	Arizona	Danny White	Phoenix
XIX	2005	Colorado	Mike Dailey	51-48	Georgia	Doug Plank	Las Vegas
XX	2006	Chicago	Mike Hohensee	69-61	Orlando	Jay Gruden	Las Vegas
XXI	2007	San Jose	Darren Arbet	55-33	Columbus	Doug Kay	New Orleans
XXII	2008	Philadelphia	Bret Munsey	59-56	San Jose	Darren Arbet	New Orleans

ArenaBowl MVP

Multiple Winners: George LaFrance (3); Mark Grieb and Stevie Thomas (2).

Year		Year		Year	
1987	Gary Mullen, Denver, WR	1996	Stevie Thomas, TB, WR/LB	2004	Off–Mark Grieb, San Jose, QB
1988	Steve Griffin, Detroit, WR/DB	1997	Donnie Davis, Arizona, QB		Def–Ricky Parker, Arizona, DS
1989	George LaFrance, Det., WR/DB	1998	Rick Hamilton, Orlando, FB/LB	2005	Off–Willis Marshall, Col., WR
1990	Art Schlichter, Detroit, QB	1999	Eddie Brown, Albany, OS		Def–Ahmad Hawkins, Col., DB
1991	Stevie Thomas, TB, WR/LB	2000	Connell Maynor, Orlando, QB	2006	Off–Matt D'Orazio, Chi. QB
1992	George LaFrance, Detroit, OS	2001	Terrill Shaw, Grand Rapids, OS		Def–Dennison Robinson, Chi., DB
1993	Jay Gruden, Tampa Bay, QB	2002	John Dutton, San Jose, QB	2007	Off–Mark Grieb, San Jose, QB
1994	Sherdrick Bonner, Arizona, QB	2003	Lawrence Samuels, TB, WR/LB		Def–Omarr Smith, San Jose, DB
1995	George LaFrance, Tampa Bay, OS			2008	Matt D'Orazio, Philadelphia, QB

Arena Football (Cont.)

Offensive Player Of The Year

Regular Season Offensive Player of the Year as voted on by AFL head coaches, fans, players and the Arena Football League Writers Association (AFLWA). The award was known as the Most Valuable Player Award from 1987-95.

Multiple Winners: Eddie Brown (3); Damian Harrell, Chris Jackson, George LaFrance and Barry Wagner (2).

Year	Year	Year
1987 Russell Hairston, Pittsburgh	1995 Barry Wagner, Orlando	2003 Chris Jackson, Los Angeles
1988 Ben Bennett, Chicago	1996 Eddie Brown, Albany	2004 Marcus Nash, Las Vegas
1989 George LaFrance, Detroit	1997 Barry Wagner, Orlando	2005 Damian Harrell, Colorado
1990 Art Schlichter, Detroit	1998 Calvin Schexnayder, Arizona	2006 Damian Harrell, Colorado
1991 George LaFrance, Detroit	1999 Eddie Brown, Albany	2007 Siaha Burley, Utah
1992 Jay Gruden, Tampa Bay	2000 Mike Horacek, Iowa	2008 Chris Jackson, Philadelphia
1993 Hunkie Cooper, Arizona	2001 Aaron Garcia, New York	
1994 Eddie Brown, Albany	2002 Mark Grieb, San Jose	

Defensive Player Of The Year

Regular Season Offensive Player of the Year as voted on by AFL head coaches, fans, players and the Arena Football League Writers Association (AFLWA).

Multiple Winners: Kenny McEntyre (3); Clevan Thomas (2).

Year	Year	Year
1996 David McLeod, Albany	2001 Kenny McEntyre, Orlando	2006 Jerald Brown, Columbus
1997 Tracey Perkins, Tampa Bay	2002 Clevan Thomas, San Jose	2007 Greg White, Orlando
1998 Johnnie Harris, Tamp Bay	2003 Clevan Thomas, San Jose	2008 Dennison Robinson, Chicago
1999 James Baron, Nashville	2004 Kenny McEntyre, Orlando	
2000 Kenny McEntyre, Orlando	2005 Silas Demary, Los Angeles	

Arena Football 101

The Field

- Indoor padded surface, 85 feet wide (size of an NHL rink) and 50 yards long with eight-yard end zones.
- Goal posts are nine feet wide with a crossbar height of 15 feet (NFL goal posts are 18 1/2 feet wide with the crossbar at 10 feet).
- The goal-side rebound nets are 30 feet wide by 32 feet high. The bottoms of the nets are eight feet above the ground.

The Ball

- Same size and weight as an NFL ball.

Cool Rules

- Punting is illegal. On fourth down, a team may go for a first down, touchdown or field goal.
- The receiving team may field any kickoff or missed field goal that rebounds off the net.
- A forward pass that rebounds off of the end zone net is a live ball and is in play until it touches the playing surface.
- One receiver may go in forward motion before the snap.
- Each team has eight players on the field at all times (as opposed to the NFL, which is 11 a side.
- Teams get three points for a field goal by placement...or four points for a field goal by drop kick.

Source: *Arena Football League*

CANADIAN FOOTBALL

The Grey Cup

Earl Grey, the Governor-General of Canada (1904-11), donated a trophy in 1909 for the Rugby Football Championship of Canada. The trophy, which later became known as the Grey Cup, was originally open to competition for teams registered with the Canada Rugby Union. Since 1954, the Cup has gone to the champion of the Canadian Football League (CFL).

Overall multiple winners: Toronto Argonauts (15); Edmonton Eskimos (13); Winnipeg Blue Bombers (9); Hamilton Tiger-Cats (8); Ottawa Rough Riders (7); B.C. Lions, Calgary Stampeders, Hamilton Tigers and Montreal Alouettes (5); University of Toronto (4); Queen's University and Saskatchewan Roughriders (3); Ottawa Senators, Sarnia Imperials and Toronto Balmy Beach (2).

CFL multiple winners (since 1954): Edmonton (13); Hamilton and Winnipeg (7); B.C. Lions, Ottawa and Toronto (5); Calgary and Montreal (4); Saskatchewan (3).

Year Cup Final	Year Cup Final
1909 Univ. of Toronto 26, Toronto Parkdale 6	1921 Toronto Argonauts 23, Edmonton Eskimos 0
1910 Univ. of Toronto 16, Hamilton Tigers 7	1922 Queens Univ. 13, Edmonton Elks 1
1911 Univ. of Toronto 14, Toronto Argonauts 7	1923 Queens Univ. 54, Regina Roughriders 0
1912 Hamilton Alerts 11, Toronto Argonauts 4	1924 Queens Univ. 11, Toronto Balmy Beach 3
1913 Hamilton Tigers 44, Toronto Parkdale 2	1925 Ottawa Senators 24, Winnipeg Tigers 1
1914 Toronto Argonauts 14, Univ. of Toronto 2	1926 Ottawa Senators 10, Univ. of Toronto 7
1915 Hamilton Tigers 13, Toronto Rowing 7	1927 Toronto Balmy Beach 9, Hamilton Tigers 6
1916-19 Not held (WWI)	1928 Hamilton Tigers 30, Regina Roughriders 0
1920 Univ. of Toronto 16, Toronto Argonauts 3	1929 Hamilton Tigers 14, Regina Roughriders 3

Year Cup Final
1930 Toronto Balmy Beach 11, Regina Roughriders 6
1931 Montreal AAA 22, Regina Roughriders 0
1932 Hamilton Tigers 25, Regina Roughriders 6
1933 Toronto Argonauts 4, Sarnia Imperials 3
1934 Sarnia Imperials 20, Regina Roughriders 12
1935 Winnipeg 'Pegs 18, Hamilton Tigers 12
1936 Sarnia Imperials 26, Ottawa Rough Riders 20
1937 Toronto Argonauts 4, Winnipeg Blue Bombers 3
1938 Toronto Argonauts 30, Winnipeg Blue Bombers 7
1939 Winnipeg Blue Bombers 8, Ottawa Rough Riders 7

1940 Gm 1: Ottawa Rough Riders 8, Toronto B-Beach 2
     Gm 2: Toronto Rough Riders 12, Toronto B-Beach 5
1941 Winnipeg Blue Bombers 18, Ottawa Rough Riders 16

Year Cup Final
1942 Toronto RACF 8, Winnipeg RACF 5
1943 Hamilton Wildcats 23, Winnipeg RACF 14
1944 Montreal HMCS 7, Hamilton Wildcats 6
1945 Toronto Argonauts 35, Winnipeg Blue Bombers 0
1946 Toronto Argonauts 28, Winnipeg Blue Bombers 6
1947 Toronto Argonauts 10, Winnipeg Blue Bombers 9
1948 Calgary Stampeders 12, Ottawa Rough Riders 7
1949 Montreal Alouettes 28, Calgary Stampeders 15

1950 Toronto Argonauts 13, Winnipeg Blue Bombers 0
1951 Ottawa Rough Riders 21, Saskatch. Roughriders 14
1952 Toronto Argonauts 21, Edmonton Eskimos 11
1953 Hamilton Tiger-Cats 12, Winnipeg Blue Bombers 6

Year	Winner	Head Coach	Score	Loser	Head Coach	Site
1954	Edmonton	Frank (Pop) Ivy	26-25	Montreal	Doug Walker	Toronto
1955	Edmonton	Frank (Pop) Ivy	34-19	Montreal	Doug Walker	Vancouver
1956	Edmonton	Frank (Pop) Ivy	50-27	Montreal	Doug Walker	Toronto
1957	Hamilton	Jim Trimble	32-7	Winnipeg	Bud Grant	Toronto
1958	Winnipeg	Bud Grant	35-28	Hamilton	Jim Trimble	Vancouver
1959	Winnipeg	Bud Grant	21-7	Hamilton	Jim Trimble	Toronto
1960	Ottawa	Frank Clair	16-6	Edmonton	Eagle Keys	Vancouver
1961	Winnipeg	Bud Grant	21-14 (OT)	Hamilton	Jim Trimble	Toronto
1962	Winnipeg	Bud Grant	28-27*	Hamilton	Jim Trimble	Toronto
1963	Hamilton	Ralph Sazio	21-10	B.C. Lions	Dave Skrien	Vancouver
1964	B.C. Lions	Dave Skrien	34-24	Hamilton	Ralph Sazio	Toronto
1965	Hamilton	Ralph Sazio	22-16	Winnipeg	Bud Grant	Toronto
1966	Saskatchewan	Eagle Keys	29-14	Ottawa	Frank Clair	Vancouver
1967	Hamilton	Ralph Sazio	24-1	Saskatchewan	Eagle Keys	Ottawa
1968	Ottawa	Frank Clair	24-21	Calgary	Jerry Williams	Toronto
1969	Ottawa	Frank Clair	29-11	Saskatchewan	Eagle Keys	Montreal
1970	Montreal	Sam Etcheverry	23-10	Calgary	Jim Duncan	Toronto
1971	Calgary	Jim Duncan	14-11	Toronto	Leo Cahill	Vancouver
1972	Hamilton	Jerry Williams	13-10	Saskatchewan	Dave Skrien	Hamilton
1973	Ottawa	Jack Gotta	22-18	Edmonton	Ray Jauch	Toronto
1974	Montreal	Marv Levy	20-7	Edmonton	Ray Jauch	Vancouver
1975	Edmonton	Ray Jauch	9-8	Montreal	Marv Levy	Calgary
1976	Ottawa	George Brancato	23-20	Saskatchewan	John Payne	Toronto
1977	Montreal	Marv Levy	41-6	Edmonton	Hugh Campbell	Montreal
1978	Edmonton	Hugh Campbell	20-13	Montreal	Joe Scannella	Toronto
1979	Edmonton	Hugh Campbell	17-9	Montreal	Joe Scannella	Montreal
1980	Edmonton	Hugh Campbell	48-10	Hamilton	John Payne	Toronto
1981	Edmonton	Hugh Campbell	26-23	Ottawa	George Brancato	Montreal
1982	Edmonton	Hugh Campbell	32-16	Toronto	Bob O'Billovich	Toronto
1983	Toronto	Bob O'Billovich	18-17	B.C. Lions	Don Matthews	Vancouver
1984	Winnipeg	Cal Murphy	47-17	Hamilton	Al Bruno	Edmonton
1985	B.C. Lions	Don Matthews	37-24	Hamilton	Al Bruno	Montreal
1986	Hamilton	Al Bruno	39-15	Edmonton	Jack Parker	Vancouver
1987	Edmonton	Joe Faragalli	38-36	Toronto	Bob O'Billovich	Vancouver
1988	Winnipeg	Mike Riley	22-21	B.C. Lions	Larry Donovan	Ottawa
1989	Saskatchewan	John Gregory	43-40	Hamilton	Al Bruno	Toronto
1990	Winnipeg	Mike Riley	50-11	Edmonton	Joe Faragalli	Vancouver
1991	Toronto	Adam Rita	36-21	Calgary	Wally Buono	Winnipeg
1992	Calgary	Wally Buono	24-10	Winnipeg	Urban Bowman	Toronto
1993	Edmonton	Ron Lancaster	33-23	Winnipeg	Cal Murphy	Calgary
1994	B.C. Lions	Dave Ritchie	26-23	Baltimore	Don Matthews	Vancouver
1995	Baltimore	Don Matthews	37-20	Calgary	Wally Buono	Regina
1996	Toronto	Don Matthews	43-37	Edmonton	Ron Lancaster	Hamilton
1997	Toronto	Don Matthews	47-23	Saskatchewan	Jim Daley	Edmonton
1998	Calgary	Wally Buono	26-24	Hamilton	Ron Lancaster	Winnipeg
1999	Hamilton	Ron Lancaster	32-21	Calgary	Wally Buono	Vancouver
2000	B.C. Lions	Steve Buratto	28-26	Montreal	Charlie Taaffe	Calgary
2001	Calgary	Wally Buono	27-19	Winnipeg	Dave Ritchie	Montreal
2002	Montreal	Don Matthews	25-16	Edmonton	Tom Higgins	Edmonton
2003	Edmonton	Tom Higgins	34-22	Montreal	Don Matthews	Regina
2004	Toronto	Mike Clemons	27-19	B.C. Lions	Wally Buono	Ottawa
2005	Edmonton	Danny Maciocia	38-35 (OT)	Montreal	Don Matthews	Vancouver
2006	B.C. Lions	Wally Buono	25-14	Montreal	Jim Popp	Winnipeg
2007	Saskatchewan	Kent Austin	23-19	Winnipeg	Doug Berry	Toronto

*Halted by fog in 4th quarter, final 9:29 played the following day.

CFL Most Outstanding Player

Regular season Player of the Year as selected by The Football Reporters of Canada since 1953.
Multiple winners: Doug Flutie (6); Russ Jackson and Jackie Parker (3); Dieter Brock, Ron Lancaster and Mike Pringle (2).

Year	Year	Year
1953 Billy Vessels, Edmonton, RB	1972 Garney Henley, Hamilton, WR	1991 Doug Flutie, B.C. Lions, QB
1954 Sam Etcheverry, Montreal, QB	1973 Geo. McGowan, Edmonton, WR	1992 Doug Flutie, Calgary, QB
1955 Pat Abbruzzi, Montreal, RB	1974 Tom Wilkinson, Edmonton, QB	1993 Doug Flutie, Calgary, QB
1956 Hal Patterson, Montreal, E-DB	1975 Willie Burden, Calgary, RB	1994 Doug Flutie, Calgary, QB
1957 Jackie Parker, Edmonton, RB	1976 Ron Lancaster, Saskatch., QB	1995 Mike Pringle, Baltimore, RB
1958 Jackie Parker, Edmonton, QB	1977 Jimmy Edwards, Hamilton, RB	1996 Doug Flutie, Toronto, QB
1959 Johnny Bright, Edmonton, RB	1978 Tony Gabriel, Ottawa, TE	1997 Doug Flutie, Toronto, QB
1960 Jackie Parker, Edmonton, QB	1979 David Green, Montreal, RB	1998 Mike Pringle, Montreal, RB
1961 Bernie Faloney, Hamilton, QB	1980 Dieter Brock, Winnipeg, QB	1999 Danny McManus, Hamilton, QB
1962 George Dixon, Montreal, RB	1981 Dieter Brock, Winnipeg, QB	2000 Dave Dickenson, Calgary, QB
1963 Russ Jackson, Ottawa, QB	1982 Condredge Holloway, Tor., QB	2001 Khari Jones, Winnipeg, QB
1964 Lovell Coleman, Calgary, RB	1983 Warren Moon, Edmonton, QB	2002 Milt Stegall, Winnipeg, SB
1965 George Reed, Saskatchewan, RB	1984 Willard Reaves, Winnipeg, RB	2003 Anthony Calvillo, Montreal, QB
1966 Russ Jackson, Ottawa, QB	1985 Merv Fernandez, B.C. Lions, WR	2004 Casey Printers, B.C. Lions, QB
1967 Peter Liske, Calgary, QB	1986 James Murphy, Winnipeg, WR	2005 Ricky Ray, Edmonton, QB
1968 Bill Symons, Toronto, RB	1987 Tom Clements, Winnipeg, QB	2006 Geroy Simon, B.C. Lions, SB
1969 Russ Jackson, Ottawa, QB	1988 David Williams, B.C. Lions, WR	2007 Kerry Joseph, Saskatchewan, QB
1970 Ron Lancaster, Saskatch., QB	1989 Tracy Ham, Edmonton, QB	
1971 Don Jonas, Winnipeg, QB	1990 Mike Clemons, Toronto, RB	

Top 20 All-Time CFL Players

In 2006, *TSN* assembled an independent voting panel of 60 past and present CFL executives, players and media to rank the top 50 players, in order, from the post-WWII history of the CFL. Listed are the top 20.

1 Doug Flutie, QB, 1990-97	8 Russ Jackson, QB, 1958-69	15 Milt Stegall, WR, 1995–
2 George Reed, RB, 1963-75	9 Wayne Harris Sr., LB, 1961-72	16 Willie Pless, LB, 1986-99
3 Jackie Parker, QB, 1954-68	10 Allen Pitts, WR, 1990-2000	17 John Barrow, DL/OL, 1957-70
4 Mike Pringle, RB, 1992-2004	11 Dan Kepley, LB, 1975-84	18 Tony Gabriel, WR, 1971-81
5 Warren Moon, QB, 1978-83	12 John Helton, DL, 1969-82	19 Johnny Bright, RB, 1952-64
6 Garney Henley, DB, 1960-75	13 Hal Patterson, WR/DB, 1954-67	20 Brian Kelly, WR, 1979-87
7 Ron Lancaster, QB, 1960-78	14 Damon Allen, QB, 1985-2007	

NFL EUROPA

The World League of American Football was formed in 1991 and consisted of three European teams (London, Barcelona and Frankfurt), and seven North American teams (New York/New Jersey, Orlando, Montreal, Raleigh-Durham, Birmingham, Sacramento and San Antonio). In the fall of 1992, the NFL and WLAF Board of Directors voted to restructure the league to include more European teams. Play was subsequently suspended. In 1993, NFL clubs approved a six-team European-only league to resume play in 1995. In January 1998, the name of the league was changed to NFL Europa. In August, 2007, the NFL discontinued NFL Europa, choosing instead to direct its focus on playing regular season NFL games overseas.

The World Bowl

Multiple Winners: Frankfurt (4); Berlin and Rhein (2).

Bowl	Year	Winner	Head Coach	Score	Loser	Head Coach	Site
I	1991	London	Larry Kennan	21-0	Barcelona	Jack Bicknell	London
II	1992	Sacramento	Kay Stephenson	21-17	Orlando	Galen Hall	Montreal
III	1995	Frankfurt	Ernie Stautner	26-22	Amsterdam	Al Luginbill	Amsterdam
IV	1996	Scotland	Jim Criner	32-27	Frankfurt	Ernie Stautner	Edinburgh, Scot.
V	1997	Barcelona	Jack Bicknell	38-24	Rhein	Galen Hall	Barcelona
VI	1998	Rhein	Galen Hall	34-10	Frankfurt	Dick Curl	Frankfurt
VII	1999	Frankfurt	Dick Curl	38-24	Barcelona	Jack Bicknell	Dusseldorf
VIII	2000	Rhein	Galen Hall	13-10	Scotland	Jim Criner	Frankfurt
IX	2001	Berlin	Peter Vaas	24-17	Barcelona	Jack Bicknell	Amsterdam
X	2002	Berlin	Peter Vaas	26-20	Rhein	Pete Kuharchek	Glasgow
XI	2003	Frankfurt	Doug Graber	35-16	Rhein	Pete Kuharchek	Glasgow
XII	2004	Berlin	Rick Lantz	30-24	Frankfurt	Mike Jones	Gelsenkirchen, Ger.
XIII	2005	Amsterdam	Bart Andrus	27-21	Berlin	Rick Lantz	Dusseldorf
XIV	2006	Frankfurt	Mike Jones	22-7	Amsterdam	Bart Andrus	Dusseldorf
XV	2007	Hamburg	Vince Martino	37-28	Frankfurt	Mike Jones	Frankfurt

World Bowl MVP

Year	Year	Year
1991 Dan Crossman, London, S	1998 Jim Arellanes, Rhein, QB	2003 Jonas Lewis, Frankfurt, RB
1992 Davis Archer, Sacramento, QB	1999 Andy McCullough, Frankfurt, WR	2004 Eric McCoo, Berlin, RB
1995 Paul Justin, Frankfurt, QB	2000 Aaron Stecker, Scotland, RB	2005 Kurt Kittner, Amsterdam, QB
1996 Yo Murphy, Scotland, WR	2001 Jonathan Quinn, Berlin, QB	2006 Butchie Wallace, Frankfurt, RB
1997 Jon Kitna, Barcelona, QB	2002 Dane Looker, Berlin, WR	2007 Casey Bramlet, Hamburg, QB

COLLEGE BASKETBALL

2007 / 2008 YEAR IN REVIEW

After a long time on the coaching trail Kansas coach **Bill Self** cut down the nets at the Final Four in San Antonio.

ROCK CHALK JAYHAWK

Bill Self, Mario Chalmers and Kansas made the most of their big moment to beat a talent-packed Memphis squad.

By Pat Forde

The shot that saved a season took just a moment — a Shining Moment, you could say.

The hug lasted for minutes.

After hitting the biggest Final Four jumper since Keith Smart's in 1987, Mario Chalmers summoned his mother, Almarie, down from the Alamodome stands to courtside. The unflappable Kansas Jayhawk wrapped both arms around her, laid his head on her shoulder and bawled like a baby.

She pumped her left arm. He wouldn't let go.

"We did it, Mom," Chalmers said between sobs.

"A dream come true," Almarie said later, her own eyes glistening. "A prayer answered. We've been waiting on this moment since he was 2."

This moment—this Shining Moment — was almost preordained four years earlier, when Mario went to the Final Four in this same building with his dad, current Kansas director of basketball operations Ronnie Chalmers. They watched Connecticut beat Georgia Tech for the title, and Ronnie remembers one spectacular play from that game when he jumped to his feet but

Mario remained in his chair.

"What's wrong?" Ronnie asked his son.

"I'm thinking," Mario said.

"What are you thinking about?"

"One day," Mario said, "I'm going to be out there winning the national championship."

That goal guided the Chalmers family from Alaska to Kansas three years ago. It guided them to this game and ultimately to this moment—this Shining Moment—that rescued Kansas from near-certain defeat and gave the 2008 NCAA tournament its signature.

Chalmers' shot capped the Jayhawks' steely nine-point comeback in the final 2:12 of regulation on their way to a 75-68 overtime triumph. It was the blow that broke an excellent Tigers squad—a Tigers squad that turned the school's first championship into a stunning championship choke.

"You have a lead like that," coach John Calipari said, "you're supposed to win the game."

The emotional whiplash that fol-

 Pat Forde is a senior writer at ESPN.com

AP Images

➜ Kansas guard **Mario Chalmers** knocked down a huge three-pointer to send the national championship game to overtime, where the Jayhawks eventually triumphed.

lowed Chalmers' 3-pointer with 2.1 seconds remaining will be felt for years on both campuses. Memphis will always love a team that finished 38-2 – but always wince at the way it unraveled at the very end. And giddy Kansas now has another name to add to its list of all-time heroes: Clyde Lovellette, Wilt Chamberlain, Danny Manning …

Mario Chalmers.

On the 20th anniversary of Danny and the Miracles' winning Kansas' last championship, give a Rock Chalk salute to Miracle Mario.

"It will probably be the biggest shot in Kansas history," coach Bill Self said.

The kid scored 18 on the night, earning Most Outstanding Player honors. But the replay that will live forever in Lawrence will focus on a single shot.

For years to come, kids all over Kansas will go into the driveway or the backyard or the gym and pretend to be Mario Chalmers swishing that jumper.

With 10.8 seconds left, Self diagrammed the play. It called for the potential tying shot to be in Chalmers' calm hands – a pass from penetrating Sherron Collins for a 3.

Of course Chalmers was the choice: He has home-state ice water in his veins. He's been good in the clutch his entire career.

"In YMCA and AAU and high school, he was always the go-to guy," Ronnie Chalmers said.

For the go-to guy's shot to matter, though, Kansas needed at least one more in a nightmarish series of missed free throws from Memphis.

Awful foul shooting was the endless-

Sophomore shooting guard **Stephen Curry** carried the surprising Davidson Wildcats all the way to the Elite Eight

Collins dribbled upcourt and veered to his right – almost losing the ball as Memphis players hacked at him, trying to foul and prevent a 3 from being hoisted. Collins' strength probably prevented a whistle, though, and he shoved a pass to Chalmers as he came curling off the wing.

The ball came up into Chalmers' chest. He took one rushed dribble to his left and elevated. Rose jumped with him, arm outstretched. Chalmers arched the shot over Rose's fingers and into the tension-drenched Texas air.

"I thought it was going in when it left my hands," Chalmers said.

Teammate Brandon Rush, who was directly underneath the basket, concurred.

"I could see it splash right in there," Rush said. "Pretty cool."

Blessed with a good sight line in the stands behind the play, Almarie Chalmers knew, too.

"I saw it going straight in," she said. "When it hit the bottom of the net, I breathed."

Everyone else screamed. Kansas fans in ecstasy. Memphis fans in agony.

The Tigers had nothing left in overtime. No momentum. No Joey Dorsey, who had fouled out. No legs for tired Douglas-Roberts and cramping Rose. Kansas scored the first six in OT to take command of a game it had come amazingly close to losing.

ly discussed weakness of these Tigers, but they had made it a moot point in three straight rampaging NCAA tournament victories over Michigan State, Texas and UCLA. Now, with the title right there for the taking, star junior Chris Douglas-Roberts missed three straight, leaving the door open for Kansas.

Then, with 10.8 seconds on the clock, sensational freshman Derrick Rose stood on the line with Memphis up two, trying to ice it. His first shot hit the rim and fell off. He made the second, but the one miss gave Kansas its opportunity to tie.

Continued on page 290

AP Images

DICK VITALE'S

Biggest Stories of the Year in **College Basketball**

10 **Tennessee captures** its eighth national title under Pat Summitt's tutelage, defeating Stanford 64-48. Candace Parker scores 17 points and grabs nine rebounds to help the Lady Vols capture their second straight championship.

09 **Lute Olson steps aside.** The Arizona coach takes time off, leaving Kevin O'Neill in charge for the season. Olson decides to return for the 2008-09 campaign.

08 **Drake dominates MVC.** A program picked ninth in the league's preseason poll, one whose last NCAA tournament appearance came in 1971, stunned a lot of folks. Keno Davis did a terrific coaching job, then left for Providence.

07 **Tar Heels return.** After the 2007-08 season, there was a lot of speculation over the futures of Tyler Hansbrough, Ty Lawson, Wayne Ellington and Danny Green. The foursome made coach Roy Williams happy by returning to Chapel Hill for the 2008-09 campaign.

06 **Early Season Upsets.** None was bigger than Gardner-Webb's win in Lexington. Rick Scruggs' squad jumped out to a 14-0 lead en route to a stunner over Kentucky. Mercer also ruined the debut of O.J. Mayo by stunning USC.

05 **Milestone Wins for Coaching Legends.** The General, Robert Montgomery Knight, earned his 900th W when Texas Tech beat Texas A&M, 68-53 in January 2008. Eddie Sutton earned his 800th career victory while coaching at San Francisco.

04 **Davidson Makes Elite 8.** Led by Stephen Curry, Bob McKillop's team was the Cinderella story of the NCAA, beating Gonzaga, Georgetown and Wisconsin before falling in a nailbiter against Kansas, just one step from the Final Four.

03 **Fearsome Foursome.** For the first time since the tournament started seeding teams in 1979, all number one seeds made it to the Final Four.

02 **Super Mario.** Kansas guard Mario Chalmers hit a dramatic game-tying three-pointer to send the national title game vs. Memphis into overtime. It was rock, chalk, Jayhawk as Bill Self got his first national championship.

01 **Year of the Freshmen.** So many diaper dandies had a major impact on the sport. Many were one-and-done, off to the NBA after just one season in college.

➜ *Continued from page 288*

Earlier in the second half, as the game began slipping away from the Jayhawks, Self was telling his players, "You've got to believe." But the situation was dire enough that when Memphis' Robert Dozier went to the foul line with 2:12 left and the Tigers up seven, Ronnie Chalmers reached into his pocket for some divine guidance.

On a piece of paper, he'd written two verses from Psalms: 46:10 and 46:1. He pulled them out and read them to himself.

"Be still, and know that I am God," reads 46:10.

"God is a refuge and strength. A very present help in trouble," reads 46:1.

"We were in trouble at that time," Ronnie said.

Ya think?

The trouble deepened when Dozier swished both free throws. The lead was 60-51 as the clock slipped inside two minutes. This was desperate.

But Chalmers and Collins — two guards who had taken some very bad shots as Memphis asserted itself — rode to the rescue.

Chalmers passed to Darrell Arthur for a jump shot that made it 60-53. Then, after a timeout, Collins made the two plays that really made it a ballgame— he stole the ball from Antonio Anderson and, after a couple of quick passes, got it back in the corner for a 3-pointer.

Until then, Kansas was 1-for-9 from 3-point range. Collins swished it.

After a pair of Douglas-Roberts free throws, Chalmers made a pair of his own. That set the stage for Memphis'

Memphis point guard **Derrick Rose** keyed a deep tourney run and made enough of a splash to get the NBA's attention.

foul-line debacle, which was augmented by a bad decision to attack the basket with 20 seconds left instead of pulling the ball out and killing the clock while clinging to a two-point lead.

But all the Memphis foibles down the stretch could have been survived if Chalmers hadn't hit the shot of a lifetime.

"First, I'm happy for Mario," Ronnie Chalmers said. "Then I'm happy for Coach Self—he was long overdue for this. Then I'm happy for the team.

"It's great for a parent to see their son's dream come true. ... You've got to think about it every day the rest of your life. This is *the* moment."

One Shining Moment.

2007-2008
Season in Review

ESPN
SPORTS ALMANAC

Final Regular Season AP Men's Top 25 Poll
Taken **before** start of NCAA tournament.

The sportswriters & broadcasters poll: first place votes in parentheses; records through Tuesday, March 18, 2008; total points (based on 25 for 1st, 24 for 2nd, etc.); record in NCAA tourney and team lost to; head coach (career years and record including 2007 postseason), and preseason ranking. Teams in **bold** type went on to reach NCAA Final Four.

		Mar. 18 Record	Points	NCAA Recap	Head Coach	Preseason Rank
1	**North Carolina** (53)	32-2	1779	4-1 (Kansas)	Roy Williams (20 yrs: 560-134)	1
2	**Memphis** (13)	33-1	1710	5-1 (Kansas)	John Calipari (16 yrs: 408-135)	3
3	UCLA (5)	31-3	1674	4-1 (Memphis)	Ben Howland (14 yrs: 263-140)	2
4	**Kansas** (1)	31-3	1706	6-0	Bill Self (15 yrs: 345-138)	4
5	Tennessee	29-4	1449	2-1 (Tennessee)	Bruce Pearl (16 yrs: 394-108)	7
6	Wisconsin	29-4	1412	2-1 (Davidson)	Bo Ryan (24 yrs: 556-163)	
7	Texas	28-6	1390	3-1 (Memphis)	Rick Barnes (21 yrs: 449-227)	15
8	Georgetown	27-5	1271	1-1 (Davidson)	John Thompson III (8 yrs: 168-78)	5
9	Duke	27-5	1223	1-1 (West Virginia)	Mike Krzyzewski (33 yrs: 803-267)	13
10	Stanford	26-7	1122	2-1 (Texas)	Trent Johnson (9 yrs: 159-122)	23
11	Butler	29-3	1004	1-1 (Tennessee)	Todd Lickliter (7 yrs: 161-65)	-
12	Xavier	27-6	957	3-1 (UCLA)	Sean Miller (4 yrs: 93-39)	-
13	Louisville	24-8	894	3-1 (N. Carolina)	Rick Pitino (22 yrs: 521-191)	6
14	Drake	28-4	794	0-1 (Western Ky.)	Keno Davis (1 yr: 28-5)	-
15	Notre Dame	24-7	672	1-1 (Washington St.)	Mike Brey (13 yrs: 266-138)	-
16	Connecticut	24-8	670	0-1 (San Diego)	Jim Calhoun (36 yrs: 773-337)	-
17	Pittsburgh	26-9	586	1-1 (Michigan St.)	Jamie Dixon (5 yrs: 130-39)	22
18	Michigan St.	25-8	523	2-1 (Memphis)	Tom Izzo (13 yrs: 305-130)	8
19	Vanderbilt	26-7	493	0-1 (Siena)	Kevin Stallings (15 yrs: 293-179)	-
20	Purdue	24-8	418	1-1 (Xavier)	Matt Painter (4 yrs: 81-45)	-
21	Washington St.	24-8	377	2-1 (N. Carolina)	Tony Bennett (2 yrs: 52-17)	10
22	Clemson	24-9	364	0-1 (Villanova)	Oliver Purnell (20 yrs: 326-249)	-
23	Davidson	26-6	253	3-1 (Kansas)	Bob McKillop (19 yrs: 338-224)	-
24	Gonzaga	25-7	232	0-1 (Davidson)	Mark Few (10 yrs: 236-60)	14
25	Marquette	24-9	174	1-1 (Stanford)	Tom Crean (9 yrs: 190-96)	11

Others receiving votes: 26. **Indiana** 135 points; 27. **USC** 70; 28. **BYU** 49; 29. **UNLV** 37; 30. **Kent St.** 26; 31. **Arkansas** 11; 32. **West Virginia** 7; 33. **Cornell** 6; 34. **Mississippi St., Texas A&M** and **W. Kentucky** 4; 37. **St. Mary's-CA** 3; 38. **Georgia** and **Saint Joseph's** 2; 40. **Boise St., South Alabama** and **UMBC** 1.

NCAA Men's Division I Tournament Seeds

	WEST	MIDWEST	SOUTH	EAST
1	UCLA (31-3)	Kansas (31-3)	Memphis (33-1)	North Carolina (32-2)
2	Duke (27-5)	Georgetown (27-5)	Texas (28-6)	Tennessee (29-4)
3	Xavier (27-6)	Wisconsin (29-4)	Stanford (26-7)	Louisville (24-8)
4	Connecticut (24-8)	Vanderbilt (26-7)	Pittsburgh (26-9)	Washington St. (24-8)
5	Drake (28-4)	Clemson (24-9)	Michigan St. (22-10)	Notre Dame (24-7)
6	Purdue (24-8)	USC (21-11)	Marquette (24-9)	Oklahoma (22-11)
7	West Virginia (24-10)	Gonzaga (25-7)	Miami (22-10)	Butler (29-3)
8	BYU (27-7)	UNLV (26-7)	Mississippi St. (22-10)	Indiana (25-7)
9	Texas A&M (24-10)	Kent St. (28-6)	Oregon (18-13)	Arkansas (22-11)
10	Arizona (19-14)	Davidson (26-6)	St. Mary's-CA (25-6)	South Alabama (26-6)
11	Baylor (21-10)	Kansas St. (20-11)	Kentucky (18-12)	St. Joseph's (21-12)
12	Western Ky. (27-6)	Villanova (20-12)	Temple (21-12)	George Mason (23-10)
13	San Diego (21-13)	Siena (22-10)	Oral Roberts (24-8)	Winthrop (22-11)
14	Georgia (17-16)	CS-Fullerton (24-8)	Cornell (22-5)	Boise St. (25-8)
15	Belmont (25-8)	UMBC (24-8)	Austin Peay (24-10)	American (21-11)
16	Miss. Valley St. (17-15)	Portland St. (23-9)	Texas-Arlington (21-11)	Mt. St. Mary's* (19-14)

*Mt. St. Mary's defeated Coppin St., 69-60, in the NCAA Tournament "opening-round" play-in game at Dayton, Ohio for a berth in the field of 64.

2008 NCAA Tournament Men's Division

NCAA Men's Championship Game

70th NCAA Division I Championship Game. **Date:** Monday, April 7, at the Alamodome in San Antonio, Texas. **Coaches:** Bill Self of Kansas and John Calipari of Memphis. **Favorite:** Memphis by 2.
Attendance: 43,257; **Officials:** John Cahill, Ed Hightower and Edward Corbett. **TV Rating:** 12.1/20 share (CBS).

Kansas 75

	Min	FG M-A	FT M-A	Pts	Reb O-T	A	PF
Darrell Arthur	35	9-13	2-2	20	5-10	1	3
Darnell Jackson	29	3-4	2-2	8	1-8	1	1
Russell Robinson	20	1-1	0-0	2	0-4	1	3
Mario Chalmers	40	5-13	6-6	18	1-3	3	3
Brandon Rush	42	5-9	2-3	12	1-6	2	3
Sherron Collins	34	4-10	2-2	11	0-4	6	3
Sasha Kaun	21	2-5	0-0	4	1-2	0	2
Cole Aldrich	4	0-0	0-0	0	0-0	0	0
TOTALS	200	29-55	14-15	75	9-37	14	18

Three-point FG: 3-12 (Rush 0-2, Chalmers 2-6, Collins 1-4); **Blocked Shots:** 1 (Rush); **Turnovers:** 17 (Rush 3, Chalmers 3, Robinson 3, Kaun, Collins 4, Arthur 3); **Steals:** 11 (Rush, Chalmers 4, Jackson, Robinson, Collins 3, Arthur); **Percentages:** 3-Pt FG (.250), Total FG (.527), Free Throws (.933).

Memphis 68

	Min	FG M-A	FT M-A	Pts	Reb O-T	A	PF
Robert Dozier	39	4-11	2-3	11	5-10	3	2
Joey Dorsey	26	3-3	0-0	6	1-2	1	5
Antonio Anderson	42	3-9	1-3	9	1-5	1	3
C. Douglas-Roberts	42	7-16	6-9	22	0-1	1	4
Derrick Rose	45	7-17	3-4	18	2-6	8	1
Shawn Taggart	24	1-5	0-0	2	2-3	0	2
Willie Kemp	4	0-0	0-0	0	0-0	0	0
Pierre Niles	1	0-0	0-0	0	0-0	0	0
Doneal Mack	2	0-1	0-0	0	0-0	0	0
TOTALS	200	25-62	12-19	68	11-27	14	17

Three-point FGs: 6-22 (Rose 1-6, Anderson 2-7, Taggart 0-1, Douglas-Roberts 2-5, Dozier 1-2, Mack 0-1); **Blocked Shots:** 3 (Dorsey 2, Dozier); **Turnovers:** 13 (Rose 5, Anderson 2, Taggart, Dorsey, Douglas-Roberts 2, Dozier, Kemp); **Steals:** 11 (Rose 2, Anderson 4, Taggart, Dorsey, Douglas-Roberts, Dozier, Kemp). **Percentages:** 3-Pt FG (.273), Total FG (.403), Free Throws (.632).

	1	2	OT	F
Kansas (Big 12)	33	30	12—	75
Memphis (C-USA)	28	35	5—	68

Final ESPN/USA Today Coaches' Poll

Taken **after** NCAA Tournament.
Voted on by a panel of 31 Division I head coaches following the NCAA tournament: first place votes in parentheses with total points (based on 25 for 1st, 24 for 2nd, etc.). Schools on major probation are ineligible to be ranked.

		W-L	Pts	Before NCAAs W-L	Rank
1	Kansas (31)	37-3	775	31-3	4
2	Memphis	38-2	744	33-1	3
3	North Carolina	36-3	708	32-2	1
4	UCLA	35-4	687	31-3	2
5	Texas	31-7	631	28-6	7
6	Louisville	27-9	602	24-8	13
7	Tennessee	31-5	554	29-4	6
8	Xavier	30-7	543	27-6	12
9	Davidson	29-7	512	26-6	23
10	Wisconsin	31-5	499	29-4	5
11	Stanford	28-8	474	26-7	11
12	Georgetown	28-6	395	27-5	8
13	Michigan St.	27-9	359	25-8	20
14	Butler	30-4	339	29-3	10
15	Washington St.	26-9	328	24-8	21
16	Duke	28-6	312	27-5	9
17	West Virginia	26-11	197	24-10	-
18	Pittsburgh	27-10	194	26-9	19
19	Notre Dame	25-8	180	24-7	15
20	Purdue	25-9	164	24-8	18
21	Marquette	25-10	153	24-9	24
22	Western Ky.	29-7	139	27-6	-
23	Drake	28-5	117	28-4	14
24	Villanova	22-13	110	20-12	-
25	Vanderbilt	26-8	70	26-7	16

Others receiving votes: 26. **Connecticut** (64 pts); 27. **Texas A&M** (51); 28. **Mississippi St.** (43); 29. **Clemson** (41); 30. **Kansas St.** (28); 31. **Gonzaga** (17); 32. **Arkansas** (11); 33. **Indiana** (10); 34. **UNLV** (9); 35. **BYU** and **Ohio St.** (5); 37. **Miami-FL** (3); 38. **USC** and **Tulsa** (1).

THE FINAL FOUR

at the Alamodome in San Antonio.
(Apr. 5-7, 2008).

Semifinal — Game One

West Regional champ UCLA vs. South Regional champ Memphis; Saturday, Apr. 5 (6:07 p.m. tipoff). **Coaches:** Ben Howland, UCLA and John Calipari, Memphis.

UCLA (Pac-10)	35	28—	63
Memphis (C-USA)	38	40—	78

High scorers— Russell Westbrook, UCLA (22) and Chris Douglas-Roberts, Memphis (28); **Att**— 43,178.

Semifinal — Game Two

Midwest Regional champ Kansas vs. East Regional champ North Carolina; Saturday, Apr. 5 (8:47 p.m. tipoff). **Coaches:** Roy Williams of UNC and Bill Self of Kansas.

Kansas (Big 12)	44	40—	84
North Carolina (ACC)	27	39—	66

High scorers— Wayne Ellington, North Carolina (18) and Brandon Rush, Kansas (25); **Att**— 43,178.

Most Outstanding Player

Mario Chalmers, Kansas, junior guard
SEMIFINAL—31 minutes, 11 points, 4 rebounds, 3 assists; FINAL—40 minutes, 18 points, 3 rebounds, 3 assists.

All-Final Four Team

Chalmers, Brandon Rush and Sherron Collins of Kansas and Chris Douglas-Roberts and Derrick Rose of Memphis.

NCAA Finalists' Tournament and Season Statistics

At least 13 games played during the overall season.

Kansas (37-3)

| | NCAA Tournament | | | | | | Overall Season | | | | | |
| | | | —Per Game— | | | | | | | —Per Game— | | |
	Gm	FG %	TPts	Pts	Reb	Ast	Gm	FG %	TPts	Pts	Reb	Ast
Brandon Rush	6	.481	95	15.8	6.0	2.0	38	.435	507	13.3	5.1	2.1
Mario Chalmers	6	.492	89	14.8	3.2	3.0	39	.516	498	12.8	3.1	4.3
Darrell Arthur	6	.612	66	11.0	6.5	1.0	40	.543	510	12.8	6.3	0.8
Darnell Jackson	6	.576	51	8.5	6.3	1.5	40	.626	447	11.2	6.7	1.1
Sherron Collins	6	.432	50	8.3	3.0	3.8	34	.462	315	9.3	2.2	3.1
Russell Robinson	6	.500	42	7.0	2.7	2.8	40	.424	291	7.3	2.8	4.1
Sasha Kaun	6	.667	37	6.2	4.0	0.0	40	.619	284	7.1	3.9	0.3
Cole Aldrich	6	.571	12	2.0	1.8	0.3	40	.518	112	2.8	3.0	0.1
Jeremy Case	5	.667	6	1.2	0.2	0.2	17	.378	47	1.6	0.3	0.9
Rodrick Stewart	2	1.000	2	1.0	1.0	0.0	33	.493	92	2.8	2.2	1.4
Tyrel Reed	4	.000	0	0.0	0.0	0.3	23	.514	47	2.0	0.4	0.9
Matt Kleinmann	4	.000	0	0.0	0.5	0.0	20	.429	7	0.4	0.7	0.1
Conner Teahan	4	.000	0	0.0	0.0	0.0	21	.593	46	2.2	0.4	0.3
Chase Buford	0	—	0	0.0	0.0	0.0	13	.111	2	0.2	0.4	0.1
KANSAS	6	.526	450	75.0	37.7	14.8	40	.508	3221	80.5	38.7	18.0
OPPONENTS	6	.362	365	60.8	29.7	10.0	40	.379	2460	61.5	30.8	11.3

Three-pointers: NCAA TOURNAMENT—Chalmers (13-31), Rush (11-32), Collins (6-15), Robinson (6-17), Case (2-3) Overall (38-98 for .388 pct.); OVERALL— Rush (80-191), Chalmers (73-156), Collins (38-105), Robinson (35-110), Teahan (12-20), Reed (11-24), Case (11-29), Stewart (5-16), Arthur (2-12), Jackson (2-6), Bechard (2-5), Witherspoon (0-3), Buford (0-6), Team (271-683 for .397 pct.).

Memphis (38-2)

| | NCAA Tournament | | | | | | Overall Season | | | | | |
| | | | —Per Game— | | | | | | | —Per Game— | | |
	Gm	FG %	TPts	Pts	Reb	Ast	Gm	FG %	TPts	Pts	Reb	Ast
Chris Douglas-Roberts	6	.494	140	23.3	4.2	2.3	40	.541	724	18.1	4.1	1.8
Derrick Rose	6	.518	125	20.8	6.5	6.0	40	.477	597	14.9	4.5	4.7
Robert Dozier	6	.383	49	8.2	6.5	0.8	37	.440	339	9.2	6.8	1.0
Antonio Anderson	6	.388	61	10.2	4.2	3.5	40	.408	342	8.6	3.7	3.4
Doneal Mack	6	.455	13	2.2	0.3	0.2	39	.389	268	6.9	1.6	0.5
Joey Dorsey	6	.621	39	6.5	9.0	0.8	38	.647	261	6.9	9.5	0.5
Shawn Taggart	6	.379	28	4.7	0.3	0.3	39	.500	230	5.9	4.2	0.4
Willie Kemp	6	.538	25	4.2	0.2	0.3	40	.383	201	5.0	1.0	1.5
Andre Allen	4	.143	5	1.3	0.3	1.2	37	.311	122	3.3	1.2	2.1
Jeff Robinson	2	.000	0	0.0	0.0	0.0	28	.446	84	3.0	2.3	0.1
Pierre Niles	5	1.000	2	0.4	0.0	0.0	26	.400	17	0.7	0.8	0.1
Chance McGrady	1	.000	0	0.0	0.0	0.0	14	.571	9	0.6	0.7	0.4
MEMPHIS	6	.466	487	81.2	38.8	15.3	40	.466	3196	79.9	40.5	15.9
OPPONENTS	6	.434	416	69.3	34.2	13.0	40	.391	2477	61.9	34.3	11.0

Three-pointers: NCAA TOURNAMENT— Anderson (10-27), Kemp (7-13), Rose (5-15), Douglas-Roberts (5-20), Mack (3-8), Taggart (1-6), Dozier (1-2), Team (32-94 for .340 pct.); OVERALL— Mack (66-182), Kemp (51-139), Anderson (51-153), Douglas-Roberts (45-109), Rose (35-104), Allen (24-82), Dozier (10-33), Taggart (10-28), Robinson (10-34) Team (302-865 for .349 pct.).

Kansas' Schedule

Reg. Season (28-3)

W	LA-Monroe	107-78
W	UMKC	85-62
W	Washburn	92-60
W	Northern Ariz	87-46
W	Arizona	76-72
W	Florida Atlantic	87-49
W	at USC	59-55
W	Eastern Wash	85-47
W	DePaul	84-66
W	Ohio	88-51
W	at Georgia Tech	71-66
W	Miami	78-54
W	Yale	86-53
W	at Boston College	85-60
W	at Loyola	90-60
W	at Nebraska	79-58
W	Oklahoma	85-55
W	at Missouri	76-70
W	Iowa St.	83-59
W	Nebraska	84-49
L	at Kansas St.	75-84
W	at Colorado	72-59
W	Missouri	90-71
W	Baylor	100-90
L	at Texas	69-72
W	Colorado	69-45
L	at Oklahoma St.	60-61
W	at Iowa St.	75-64
W	Kansas St.	88-74
W	Texas Tech	109-51
W	at Texas A&M	72-55

Big 12 Tourney (3-0)

W	Nebraska	64-54
W	Texas A&M	77-71
W	Texas	84-74

NCAA Tourney (6-0)

W	Portland St.	85-61
W	UNLV	75-56
W	Villanova	72-57
W	Davidson	59-57
W	North Carolina	84-66
W	Memphis	75-68

Memphis' Schedule

Reg. Season (30-1)

W	Tenn-Martin	102-71
W	Richmond	80-63
W	Oklahoma	63-53
W	Connecticut	81-70
W	Arkansas St.	84-63
W	Austin Peay	104-82
W	USC	62-58
W	at Mid Tenn	65-41
W	at Cincinnati	79-69
W	Georgetown	85-71
W	Arizona	76-63
W	Siena	102-58
W	Pepperdine	90-53
W	East Carolina	99-58
W	at Marshall	68-45
W	at Rice	77-50
W	Southern Miss	83-47
W	at Tulsa	56-41
W	Gonzaga	81-73
W	at Houston	89-77
W	UTEP	70-64
W	SMU	77-48
W	UCF	85-64
W	Houston	68-59
W	at UAB	79-78
W	at Tulane	97-71
L	Tennessee	62-66
W	Tulsa	82-67
W	at So. Miss.	76-67
W	at SMU	72-55
W	UAB	77-51

C-USA Tourney (3-0)

W	Tulane	75-56
W	Southern Miss	69-53
W	Tulsa	77-51

NCAA Tourney (5-1)

W	UT-Arlington	87-63
W	Mississippi St.	77-74
W	Michigan St.	92-74
W	Texas	85-67
W	UCLA	78-63
L	Kansas	68-75

Final NCAA Men's Division I Standings

Conference records include regular season games only. Overall records include all postseason tournament games.

America East Conference

Team	Conference			Overall		
	W	L	Pct	W	L	Pct
*UMBC	13	3	.813	24	9	.727
Hartford	10	6	.625	18	16	.529
Albany	10	6	.625	15	15	.500
Vermont	9	7	.563	16	15	.516
Binghamton	9	7	.563	14	16	.467
Boston University	9	7	.563	14	17	.452
New Hampshire	6	10	.375	9	20	.310
Maine	3	13	.188	7	23	.233
Stony Brook	3	13	.188	7	23	.233

Conf. Tourney Final: UMBC 82, Hartford 65.
***NCAA Tourney (0-1):** Albany (0-1).

Atlantic Coast Conference

Team	Conference			Overall		
	W	L	Pct	W	L	Pct
*North Carolina	14	2	.875	36	3	.923
*Duke	13	3	.813	28	6	.824
*Clemson	10	6	.625	24	10	.706
†Virginia Tech	9	7	.563	21	14	.600
†Miami-FL	8	8	.500	23	11	.676
†Maryland	8	8	.500	19	15	.559
Georgia Tech	7	9	.438	15	17	.469
Wake Forest	7	9	.438	17	13	.567
†Florida St	7	9	.438	19	15	.559
Virginia	5	11	.313	17	16	.515
Boston College	4	12	.250	14	17	.452
N.C. State	4	12	.250	15	16	.484

Conf. Tourney Final: North Carolina 86, Clemson 81.
***NCAA Tourney (6-4):** North Carolina (4-1), Duke (1-1), Miami-FL (1-1), Clemson (0-1).
†NIT (3-3): Virginia Tech (2-1), Maryland (1-1), Florida St. (0-1).

Atlantic 10 Conference

Team	Conference			Overall		
	W	L	Pct	W	L	Pct
*Xavier	14	2	.875	30	7	.811
*Temple	11	5	.688	21	13	.618
†Massachusetts	10	6	.625	25	11	.694
Richmond	9	7	.563	16	15	.516
*Saint Joseph's	9	7	.563	21	13	.618
Charlotte	9	7	.563	20	14	.588
La Salle	8	8	.500	15	17	.469
†Dayton	8	8	.500	23	11	.676
Saint Louis	7	9	.438	16	15	.516
Duquesne	7	9	.438	17	13	.567
Rhode Island	7	9	.438	21	12	.636
Fordham	6	10	.375	12	17	.414
George Washington	5	11	.313	9	17	.346
St. Bonaventure	2	17	.125	8	22	.267

Conf. Tourney Final: Temple 69, Saint Joseph's 64.
***NCAA Tourney (3-3):** Xavier (3-1), Temple (0-1), Saint Joseph's (0-1).
†NIT (4-2): Massachusetts (3-1), Dayton (1-1).

2007-08 NCAA Attendance Leaders		
Team (2006-07 rank)	**Gms**	**Average**
1 Kentucky (1)	18	22,554
2 North Carolina (3)	16	20,497
3 Syracuse (2)	22	20,345
4 Tennessee (4)	16	20,267
5 Louisville (5)	17	19,481
6 Maryland (8)	19	17,950
7 Wisconsin (7)	18	17,190

Atlantic Sun Conference

Team	Conference			Overall		
	W	L	Pct	W	L	Pct
*Belmont	14	2	.875	25	9	.735
Jacksonville	12	4	.750	18	13	.581
†East Tennessee St.	11	5	.688	19	13	.594
Stetson	11	5	.688	16	16	.500
Gardner-Webb	9	7	.563	16	16	.500
Lipscomb	9	7	.563	15	16	.484
Kennesaw St.	7	9	.438	10	20	.333
Mercer	6	10	.375	11	19	.367
Florida Gulf Coast	6	10	.375	10	21	.323
Campbell	5	11	.313	10	20	.333
USC Upstate	5	11	.313	7	23	.233
UNF	1	15	.063	3	26	.103

Conf. Tourney Final: Belmont 94, East Tenn. St. 67.
***NCAAs (0-1):** Belmont (0-1). **†NIT (0-1):** E. Tenn. St. (0-1).

Big East Conference

Team	Conference			Overall		
	W	L	Pct	W	L	Pct
*Georgetown	15	3	.833	28	6	.824
*Louisville	14	4	.778	27	9	.750
*Notre Dame	14	4	.778	25	8	.758
*Connecticut	13	5	.722	24	9	.727
*West Virginia	11	7	.611	26	11	.702
*Marquette	11	7	.611	25	10	.714
*Pittsburgh	10	8	.556	27	10	.730
*Villanova	9	9	.500	22	13	.629
†Syracuse	9	9	.500	21	14	.600
Cincinnati	8	10	.444	13	18	.419
Seton Hall	7	11	.389	17	15	.531
Providence	6	12	.333	15	16	.484
DePaul	6	12	.333	11	19	.367
St. John's	5	13	.278	11	19	.367
USF	3	15	.167	12	19	.387
Rutgers	3	15	.167	11	20	.355

Conf. Tourney Final: Pittsburgh 74, Georgetown 65.
***NCAA Tourney (10-8):** Georgetown (1-1), Louisville (3-1), Notre Dame (1-1), Villanova (2-1), Pittsburgh (1-1), Connecticut (0-1), Marquette (1-1), West Virginia (1-1).
†NIT (2-1): Syracuse (2-1).

Big Sky Conference

Team	Conference			Overall		
	W	L	Pct	W	L	Pct
*Portland St.	14	2	.875	23	10	.697
Northern Arizona	11	5	.688	21	11	.656
Weber St	10	6	.625	16	14	.533
Idaho St	8	8	.500	12	19	.387
Montana	8	8	.500	14	15	.482
Montana St	7	9	.438	13	15	.500
Northern Colorado	6	10	.375	13	16	.448
Eastern Washington	6	10	.375	19	19	.367
Sacramento St.	2	14	.125	4	24	.143

Conf. Tourney Final: Portland St. 67, Northern Ariz. 51.
***NCAA Tourney (0-1):** Portland St. (0-1).

Big South Conference

Team	Conference			Overall		
	W	L	Pct	W	L	Pct
†NC-Asheville	10	4	.714	23	10	.697
*Winthrop	10	4	.714	22	12	.647
High Point	8	6	.571	17	14	.548
Liberty	7	7	.500	16	16	.500
VMI	6	8	.429	14	15	.483
Coastal Carolina	6	8	.429	13	15	.464
Radford	5	9	.357	10	20	.333
Charleston Southern	4	10	.286	10	20	.333

Conf. Tourney Final: Winthrop 66, NC-Asheville 48.
***NCAA Tourney (0-1):** Winthrop (0-1). **†NIT (0-1):** NC-Ash (0-1).

Final NCAA Men's Division I Standings (Cont.)

Big Ten Conference

Team	Conference			Overall		
	W	L	Pct	W	L	Pct
*Wisconsin	16	2	.889	31	5	.861
*Purdue	15	3	.833	25	9	.735
*Indiana	14	4	.778	25	8	.758
*Michigan St	12	6	.667	27	9	.750
†Ohio St	10	8	.556	24	13	.649
†Minnesota	8	10	.444	20	14	.588
Penn St	7	11	.389	15	16	.484
Iowa	6	12	.333	13	19	.406
Illinois	5	13	.278	16	19	.457
Michigan	5	13	.278	8	22	.267
Northwestern	1	17	.056	8	22	.267

Conf. Tourney Final: Wisconsin 61, Illinois 48.
***NCAA Tourney (5-4):** Michigan St. (2-1), Wisconsin (2-1), Purdue (1-1), Indiana (0-1).
†NIT (5-1): Ohio St. (5-0), Minnesota (0-1).

Big 12 Conference

Team	Conference			Overall		
	W	L	Pct	W	L	Pct
*Texas	13	3	.813	31	7	.816
*Kansas	13	3	.813	37	3	.925
*Kansas St	10	6	.625	21	12	.636
*Oklahoma	9	7	.563	23	12	.657
*Baylor	9	7	.563	23	12	.657
*Texas A&M	8	8	.500	25	11	.694
†Nebraska	7	9	.438	20	13	.606
Texas Tech	7	9	.438	16	15	.516
Missouri	6	10	.375	16	16	.500
†Oklahoma St.	7	9	.438	17	16	.515
Iowa St.	4	12	.250	14	18	.438
Colorado	3	13	.188	12	20	.375

Conf. Tourney Final: Kansas 84, Texas 74.
***NCAA Tourney (12-5):** Kansas (6-0), Texas (3-1), Kansas St. (1-1); Texas A&M (1-1), Baylor (0-1), Oklahoma (1-1).
†NIT (1-2): Nebraska (1-1), Oklahoma St. (0-1).

Big West Conference

Team	Conference			Overall		
	W	L	Pct	W	L	Pct
†UC-Santa Barbara	12	4	.750	23	9	.719
Cal St.-Northridge	12	4	.750	20	10	.667
*Cal St.-Fullerton	12	4	.750	24	9	.727
Pacific	11	5	.688	21	10	.677
UC-Irvine	9	7	.563	18	16	.529
Cal Poly	7	9	.438	12	18	.400
UC-Riverside	4	12	.250	9	21	.300
Long Beach St	3	13	.188	6	25	.194
UC-Davis	2	14	.125	9	22	.290

Conf. Tourney Final: Cal St.-Fullerton 81, UC Irvine 66.
***NCAA Tourney (0-1):** Cal St.-Fullerton (0-1).
†NIT (0-1): UC-Santa Barbara (0-1).

Conference USA

Team	Conference			Overall		
	W	L	Pct	W	L	Pct
*Memphis	16	0	1.000	38	2	.950
Ala-Birmingham	12	4	.750	23	11	.676
Houston	11	5	.688	24	10	.706
So. Mississippi	9	7	.563	19	14	.576
UCF	9	7	.563	16	15	.516
Tulsa	8	8	.500	25	14	.641
UTEP	8	8	.500	19	14	.576
Marshall	8	8	.500	16	14	.533
Tulane	6	10	.375	17	15	.531
East Carolina	5	11	.312	11	19	.367
SMU	4	12	.250	10	20	.333
Rice	0	16	.000	3	27	.100

Conf. Tourney Final: Memphis 71, Tulsa 51.
***NCAA Tourney (5-1):** Memphis (5-1).

Colonial Athletic Association

Team	Conference			Overall		
	W	L	Pct	W	L	Pct
†Va. Commonwealth	15	3	.833	24	8	.750
*George Mason	12	6	.667	23	11	.676
NC-Wilmington	12	6	.667	20	13	.606
Old Dominion	11	7	.611	18	16	.529
William & Mary	10	8	.556	17	16	.515
Delaware	9	9	.500	14	17	.452
Northeastern	9	9	.500	14	17	.452
Hofstra	8	10	.444	12	18	.400
Towson	7	11	.389	13	18	.419
James Madison	5	13	.278	13	17	.433
Drexel	5	13	.278	12	20	.375
Georgia St.	5	13	.278	9	21	.300

Conf. Tourney Final: Geo. Mason 68, Wm. & Mary 59.
***NCAA Tourney (0-1):** George Mason (0-1).
†NIT (0-1): VCU (0-1).

Horizon League

Team	Conference			Overall		
	W	L	Pct	W	L	Pct
*Butler	16	2	.889	30	4	.882
†Cleveland St.	12	6	.667	21	13	.618
Wright St	12	6	.667	21	10	.677
Illinois-Chicago	9	9	.500	18	15	.545
WI-Milwaukee	9	9	.500	14	16	.467
Valparaiso	9	9	.500	22	14	.611
WI-Green Bay	9	9	.500	15	15	.500
Loyola-IL	6	12	.333	12	19	.387
Youngstown St.	5	13	.278	9	21	.300
Detroit	3	15	.167	7	23	.233

Conf. Tourney Final: Butler 70, Cleveland 55.
***NCAA Tourney (1-1):** Butler (1-1).
†NIT (0-1): Cleveland St. (0-1).

Ivy League

Team	Conference			Overall		
	W	L	Pct	W	L	Pct
*Cornell	14	0	1.000	22	6	.786
Brown	11	3	.785	19	10	.655
Pennsylvania	8	6	.571	13	18	.419
Columbia	7	7	.500	14	15	.483
Yale	7	7	.500	13	15	.464
Dartmouth	3	11	.214	10	18	.357
Harvard	3	11	.214	8	22	.267
Princeton	3	11	.214	6	23	.207

Conf. Tourney Final: Ivy League has no tournament.
***NCAA Tourney (0-1):** Cornell (0-1).

Metro Atlantic Athletic Conference

Team	Conference			Overall		
	W	L	Pct	W	L	Pct
*Siena	13	5	.722	23	11	.676
Rider	13	5	.722	23	11	.676
Niagara	12	6	.667	19	10	.655
Loyola	12	6	.667	19	14	.576
Marist	11	7	.611	18	14	.563
Fairfield	11	7	.611	14	16	.467
Iona	8	10	.444	12	20	.375
Manhattan	5	13	.278	12	19	.387
Saint Peter's	3	15	.167	6	24	.200
Canisius	2	16	.111	6	25	.194

Conf. Tourney Final: Siena 74, Rider 53.
***NCAA Tourney (1-1):** Siena (1-1).

Mid-American Conference

East	Conference			Overall		
	W	L	Pct	W	L	Pct
*Kent St.	13	3	.812	28	7	.800
†Akron	11	5	.688	24	11	.686
Ohio	9	7	.562	20	13	.606
Miami-OH	9	7	.562	17	16	.515
Bowling Green	7	9	.438	13	17	.433
Buffalo	3	13	.188	10	20	.333
West	W	L	Pct	W	L	Pct
Western Mich	12	4	.750	20	12	.625
Central Mich	8	8	.500	14	17	.452
Eastern Mich	8	8	.500	14	17	.452
Toledo	7	8	.467	11	19	.367
Ball St.	5	11	.312	6	24	.200
N. Illinois	3	13	.200	6	22	.214

Conf. Tourney Final: Kent St. 74, Akron 55.
***NCAA Tourney (0-1):** Kent St. (0-1).
†**NIT (1-1):** Akron (1-1).

Mid-Eastern Athletic Conference

Team	Conference			Overall		
	W	L	Pct	W	L	Pct
Morgan St.	14	2	.875	22	10	.688
Hampton	11	5	.688	18	12	.600
Norfolk St.	11	5	.688	16	15	.516
Delaware St.	10	6	.625	14	16	.467
N. Carolina A&T	9	7	.563	15	16	.484
Florida A&M	9	7	.563	15	17	.469
*Coppin St.	7	9	.438	16	20	.444
S.C. State	7	9	.438	13	20	.394
Bethune-Cookman	5	11	.313	11	21	.344
Howard	3	13	.188	6	26	.188
MD-Eastern Shore	2	14	.125	4	28	.125

Conf. Tourney Final: Coppin St. 62, Morgan St. 60.
***NCAA Tourney (0-1):** Coppin St. (0-1).

Missouri Valley Conference

Team	Conference			Overall		
	W	L	Pct	W	L	Pct
*Drake	15	3	.833	28	5	.848
†Illinois St.	13	5	.722	25	10	.714
†Southern Illinois	11	7	.611	18	15	.545
†Creighton	10	8	.556	22	11	.667
Northern Iowa	9	9	.500	18	14	.563
Bradley	9	9	.500	21	17	.553
Missouri St.	8	10	.444	17	16	.515
Indiana St.	8	10	.444	15	16	.484
Wichita St.	4	14	.222	11	20	.355
Evansville	3	15	.167	9	21	.300

Conf. Tourney Final: Drake 79, Illinois St. 49.
***NCAA Tourney (0-1):** Drake (0-1).
†**NIT (2-3):** Creighton (1-1), Illinois St. (1-1), Southern Ill. (0-1).

Mountain West Conference

Team	Conference			Overall		
	W	L	Pct	W	L	Pct
*BYU	14	2	.875	27	8	.771
*UNLV	12	4	.750	27	8	.771
†New Mexico	11	5	.688	24	9	.727
†San Diego St.	9	7	.563	20	13	.606
Air Force	8	8	.500	16	14	.533
Utah	7	9	.438	18	15	.545
TCU	6	10	.375	14	16	.467
Wyoming	5	11	.313	12	18	.400
Colorado St.	0	16	.000	7	25	.219

Conf. Tourney Final: UNLV 76, BYU 61.
***NCAA Tourney (1-2):** UNLV (1-1), BYU (0-1).
†**NIT (0-2):** New Mexico (0-1), San Diego St. (0-1).

Northeast Conference

Team	Conference			Overall		
	W	L	Pct	W	L	Pct
†Robert Morris	16	2	.889	26	8	.765
Wagner	15	3	.833	23	8	.742
Sacred Heart	13	5	.722	18	14	.562
*Mt. St. Mary's	11	7	.611	19	15	.559
Quinnipiac	11	7	.611	15	15	.500
Central Connecticut St.	10	8	.556	14	16	.467
LIU Brooklyn	7	11	.389	15	15	.500
Fairleigh Dickinson	4	14	.222	8	20	.286
St. Francis-NY	4	14	.222	7	22	.241
Monmouth	4	14	.222	7	24	.226
St. Francis-PA	4	14	.222	6	23	.207

Conf. Tourney Final: Mt. St. Mary's 68, Sacred Heart 55.
***NCAA Tourney (1-1):** Mt. St. Mary's (1-1).
†**NIT (0-1):** Robert Morris (0-1).

Ohio Valley Conference

Team	Conference			Overall		
	W	L	Pct	W	L	Pct
*Austin Peay	16	4	.800	24	11	.686
Murray St.	13	7	.650	18	13	.581
Morehead St.	12	8	.600	15	15	.500
Tennessee-Martin	11	9	.550	17	16	.515
Samford	10	10	.500	14	16	.467
Tennessee St.	10	10	.500	15	17	.469
Tennessee Tech	10	10	.500	13	19	.406
Eastern Kentucky	10	10	.500	14	16	.467
SE Missouri St	7	13	.350	12	19	.387
Eastern Illinois	6	14	.300	7	22	.241
Jacksonville St.	5	15	.250	7	22	.241

Conf. Tourney Final: Austin Peay 82, Tennessee St. 64.
***NCAA Tourney (0-1):** Austin Peay (0-1).

Pacific-10 Conference

Team	Conference			Overall		
	W	L	Pct	W	L	Pct
*UCLA	16	2	.889	35	4	.897
*Stanford	13	5	.722	28	8	.778
*Washington St.	11	7	.600	26	9	.743
*USC	11	7	.600	21	12	.636
†Arizona St.	9	9	.500	21	13	.618
*Oregon	9	9	.500	18	14	.563
*Arizona	8	10	.444	19	15	.559
Washington	7	11	.389	16	17	.484
†California	6	12	.333	17	16	.515
Oregon St.	0	18	.000	6	25	.194

Conf. Tourney Final: UCLA 67, Stanford 64.
***NCAA Tourney (8-6):** UCLA (4-1), Stanford (2-1), Washington St. (2-1), Oregon (0-1), USC (0-1), Arizona (0-1).
†**NIT (3-2):** Arizona St. (2-1), California (1-1)

Patriot League

Team	Conference			Overall		
	W	L	Pct	W	L	Pct
*American	10	4	.714	21	12	.636
Navy	9	5	.643	16	14	.533
Colgate	7	7	.500	18	14	.563
Lehigh	7	7	.500	14	15	.483
Army	6	8	.429	14	16	.467
Lafayette	6	8	.429	15	15	.500
Bucknell	6	8	.429	12	19	.327
Holy Cross	9	5	.357	15	14	.517

Conf. Tourney Final: American 52, Colgate 46.
***NCAA Tourney (0-1):** American (0-1).

Final NCAA Men's Division I Standings (Cont.)

Southeastern Conference

Eastern Div.	Conference			Overall		
	W	L	Pct	W	L	Pct
*Tennessee	14	2	.875	31	5	.861
*Kentucky	12	4	.750	18	13	.581
*Vanderbilt	10	6	.625	26	8	.765
†Florida	8	8	.500	24	12	.667
South Carolina	5	11	.313	14	18	.438
*Georgia	4	12	.250	17	17	.500

Western Div.	Conference			Overall		
	W	L	Pct	W	L	Pct
*Mississippi St	12	4	.750	23	11	.676
*Arkansas	9	7	.563	23	12	.657
†Mississippi	7	9	.438	24	11	.686
LSU	6	10	.375	13	18	.419
Alabama	5	11	.313	17	16	.515
Auburn	4	12	.250	14	16	.467

Conf. Tourney Final: Georgia 66, Arkansas 57.

*NCAA Tourney (4-6): Tennessee (2-1), Mississippi St. (1-1), Arkansas (1-1), Vanderbilt (0-1), Georgia (0-1), Kentucky (0-1).

†NIT (6-3): Florida (3-1), Mississippi (3-1).

Southern Conference

North Div.	Conference			Overall		
	W	L	Pct	W	L	Pct
Appalachian St.	13	7	.650	18	13	.581
Chattanooga	13	7	.650	18	13	.581
NC-Greensboro	12	8	.600	19	12	.613
Elon	9	11	.450	14	19	.424
W. Carolina	6	14	.300	10	21	.323

South Div.	Conference			Overall		
	W	L	Pct	W	L	Pct
*Davidson	20	0	1.000	29	7	.806
Georgia Southern	13	7	.650	20	12	.625
College of Charleston	9	11	.450	16	17	.485
Wofford	8	12	.400	16	16	.500
Furman	6	14	.300	7	23	.233
The Citadel	1	19	.050	6	24	.200

Conf. Tourney Final: Davidson 65, Elon 49.

*NCAA Tourney (3-1): Davidson (3-1).

Southland Conference

East Div.	Conference			Overall		
	W	L	Pct	W	L	Pct
Lamar	13	3	.813	19	11	.633
SE Louisiana	9	7	.563	17	13	.567
Northwestern St.	9	7	.563	15	18	.455
McNeese St.	7	9	.438	13	16	.448
Nicholls St.	5	11	.313	10	21	.323
Central Arkansas	4	12	.250	14	16	.467

West Div.	Conference			Overall		
	W	L	Pct	W	L	Pct
†Stephen F. Austin	13	3	.813	26	6	.813
Sam Houston St.	10	6	.625	23	8	.742
*Texas-Arlington	7	9	.438	21	12	.636
UTSA	7	9	.438	13	17	.433
Texas St.	6	10	.375	13	16	.448
Texas A&M-Corpus Christi	6	10	.375	9	20	.310

Conf. Tourney Final: Texas-Arlington 82, Northwestern St. 79.

*NCAA Tourney (0-1): Texas-Arlington (0-1).

†NIT (0-1): Stephen F. Austin (0-1).

Southwestern Athletic Conference

Team	Conference			Overall		
	W	L	Pct	W	L	Pct
†Alabama St.	15	3	.833	20	11	.645
†Miss. Valley St	12	6	.667	17	16	.515
Alabama A&M	11	7	.611	14	15	.483
Jackson St	10	8	.556	14	20	.412
Southern	9	9	.500	11	19	.367
Ark-Pine Bluff	8	10	.444	13	18	.419
Grambling St.	7	11	.389	7	19	.269
Prairie View A&M	6	12	.333	8	22	.267
Alcorn St.	6	12	.333	7	24	.226
Texas Southern	6	12	.333	7	25	.219

Conf. Tourney Final: Miss. Valley St. 59, Jackson St. 58.

*NCAA Tourney (0-1): Miss. Valley St. (0-1).

†NIT (0-1): Alabama St. (0-1).

The Summit League

Team	Conference			Overall		
	W	L	Pct	W	L	Pct
*Oral Roberts	16	2	.889	24	9	.727
IUPUI	15	3	.833	26	7	.788
Oakland	11	7	.611	17	14	.548
North Dakota St.	10	8	.556	16	13	.552
IPFW	9	9	.500	13	18	.419
Southern Utah	9	9	.500	11	19	.367
Western Illinois	7	11	.389	12	18	.400
Missouri-KC	6	12	.333	12	18	.400
Centenary	4	14	.222	10	21	.323
Valparaiso	3	15	.167	8	21	.276

Conf. Tourney Final: Oral Roberts 71, IUPUI 64.

*NCAA Tourney (0-1): Oral Roberts (0-1).

Sun Belt Conference

East Div.	Conference			Overall		
	W	L	Pct	W	L	Pct
*Western Kentucky	16	2	.889	29	7	.806
*South Alabama	16	2	.889	26	7	.788
Middle Tennessee	11	7	.611	17	15	.531
Florida Atlantic	8	10	.444	15	18	.455
Florida International	6	12	.333	9	20	.310
Troy	4	14	.222	12	19	.387

West Div.	Conference			Overall		
	W	L	Pct	W	L	Pct
Arkansas-Little Rock	11	7	.611	20	11	.645
Louisiana-Lafayette	11	7	.611	15	15	.500
North Texas	10	8	.556	20	11	.645
New Orleans	8	10	.444	19	13	.594
Denver	7	11	.389	11	19	.367
Arkansas St	5	13	.278	10	20	.333
Louisiana-Monroe	4	14	.222	10	21	.323

Conf. Tourney Final: Western Kentucky 67, Middle Tennessee 57.

*NCAA Tourney (2-2): Western Kentucky (2-1), South Alabama (0-1).

West Coast Conference

Team	Conference			Overall		
	W	L	Pct	W	L	Pct
*Gonzaga	13	1	.929	25	8	.758
*St. Mary's	12	2	.857	25	7	.781
*San Diego	11	3	.786	21	14	.611
Santa Clara	6	8	.429	15	16	.484
San Francisco	5	9	.357	10	21	.323
Pepperdine	4	10	.286	11	21	.344
Portland	3	11	.214	9	22	.290
Loyola Marymount	2	12	.143	5	26	.161

Conf. Tourney Final: San Diego 69, Gonzaga 62.

*NCAA Tourney (0-3): Gonzaga (0-1), St. Mary's (0-1), San Diego (0-1).

Western Athletic Conference

Team	Conference			Overall		
	W	L	Pct	W	L	Pct
Boise St.	12	4	.750	25	9	.735
†Utah St.	12	4	.750	24	11	.686
Nevada	12	4	.750	21	12	.636
New Mexico St.	12	4	.750	21	14	.600
Hawaii	7	9	.438	11	19	.367
Fresno St.	5	11	.313	13	19	.406
Idaho	5	11	.313	8	21	.276
San Jose St	4	12	.250	13	19	.406
Louisiana Tech	3	13	.188	6	24	.200

Conf. Tourney Final: Boise St. 107, New Mexico St. 102 3 OT.

*NCAA Tourney (0-1): Boise St. (0-1)

†NIT (0-1): Utah St. (0-1).

Division I Independents

Team	Overall		
	W	L	Pct
Texas-Pan American	18	13	.581
Utah Valley St.	15	14	.517
Savannah St.	13	18	.419
Winston-Salem	12	18	.400
Chicago St.	11	17	.393
Longwood	9	22	.290
Cal St. Bakersfield	8	21	.276
Presbyterian	5	25	.167
North Carolina Central	4	26	.133
New Jersey Tech	0	29	.000

Annual Awards

Player of the Year

Tyler Hansbrough, N. Carolina . . .AP, Wooden, Naismith, NABC, Rupp, USBWA

Wooden Award Voting

Presented since 1977 by the Los Angeles Athletic Club and named after the former Purdue All-America and UCLA coach John Wooden. Voting done by panel of over 1,000 members of the national media; candidates must have a cumulative college grade point average of 2.0 (out of 4.0) and be making progress toward graduation.

		Cl	Pos	Pts
1	Tyler Hansbrough, North Carolina	Jr.	F	4653
2	Michael Beasley, Kansas St.	Fr.	F	4042
3	Kevin Love, UCLA	Fr.	C	3021
4	D.J. Augustin, Texas	So	G	2266
5	Stephen Curry, Davidson	So.	G	1936
6	Chris Douglas-Roberts, Memphis	Jr.	G	1891
7	Brandon Rush, Kansas	Jr.	G	1367
8	Luke Harangody, Notre Dame	So.	F	1248
9	Derrick Rose, Memphis	Fr.	G	1090
10	Chris Lofton, Tennessee	Sr.	G	1034

Defensive Player of the Year

Formerly the Henry Iba Award, for defensive skills, sportsmanship and dedication; first presented by the Rotary Club of River Oaks in Houston in 1987 and named after the late Oklahoma State and U.S. Olympic team coach. Voting done by the National Association of Basketball Coaches.

Hasheem Thabeet, Connecticut

Div. II and III Awards

Awarded by the National Association of Basketball Coaches.

Players of the Year
Div. II . . . . John Smith, Winona St.
Div. III . . . . .Andrew Olson, Amherst

Coaches of the Year
Div. II . . . . .Mike Leaf, Winona St.
Div. III . . . . Mark Edwards, Washington U. (Mo.)

Coaches of the Year

Keno Davis, Drake . . . . .AP, USBWA
John Calipari, Memphis . . . . .Naismith
Bruce Pearl, Tennessee . . . . .Rupp
Bob McKillop, Davidson . . . . .NABC

Consensus All-America Teams

The NCAA Division I players cited most frequently by the following All-America selectors: Associated Press, U.S. Basketball Writers, National Association of Basketball Coaches and Wooden Award Committee. (*) indicates unanimous first team selection. Holdover from the 2006-07 first team in **bold** type.

First Team

	Class	Hgt	Pos
Tyler Hansbrough, North Carolina	Jr.	6-9	F
Michael Beasely, Kansas St.	Fr.	6-10	F
D.J. Augustin, Texas	So.	6-0	G
Kevin Love, UCLA	Fr.	6-10	C
Chris Douglas-Roberts, Memphis	Jr.	6-7	G

Second Team

	Class	Hgt	Pos
Shan Foster, Vanderbilt	Sr.	6-6	G/F
Luke Harangody, Notre Dame	So.	6-8	F
Chris Lofton, Tennessee	Sr.	6-2	G
D.J. White, Indiana	Sr.	6-9	F
Stephen Curry, Davidson	So.	6-2	G

Third Team

	Class	Hgt	Pos
Derrick Rose, Memphis	Fr.	6-3	G
Darren Collison, UCLA	Jr.	6-1	G
A.J. Price, Connecticut	Jr.	6-2	G
Eric Gordon, Indiana	Fr.	6-4	G
Brook Lopez, Stanford	So.	7-0	C

The AP started choosing All-America teams after the 1947-48 season and for 60 years there was at least one senior on every first team. Finally in 2008 no senior was chosen. The AP Team was comprised of two juniors, two freshmen and one sophomore: Tyler Hansbrough, Michael Beasley, Kevin Love, D.J. Augustin and Chris Douglas-Roberts.

DID YOU KNOW?

NCAA Men's Division I Leaders

Includes games through NCAA and NIT tourneys.

INDIVIDUAL

Scoring

	Cl	Gm	FG%	3FG/Att	FT%	Reb	Ast	Stl	Blk	Pts	Avg	Hi
Reggie Williams, VMI	Sr.	25	.528	43/154	.671	242	97	55	17	695	27.8	43
Charron Fisher, Niagara	Sr.	29	.397	69/217	.771	275	34	49	18	800	27.6	45
Michael Beasley, Kansas St.	Fr.	33	.532	36/95	.774	408	38	42	54	866	26.2	44
Stephen Curry, Davidson	So.	36	.483	162/369	.894	165	104	73	14	931	25.9	41
Lester Hudson, Tenn-Martin	Jr.	33	.464	124/320	.834	259	148	94	22	847	25.7	38
Arizona Reid, High Point	Sr.	31	.532	34/90	.746	342	75	54	16	742	23.9	42
Stefon Jackson, UTEP	Jr.	33	.464	35/105	.729	188	57	39	3	778	23.6	41
Robert McKiver, Houston	Sr.	34	.396	145/376	.884	131	99	56	2	801	23.6	52
Bo McCalebb, New Orleans	Sr.	32	.506	47/116	.772	143	99	76	3	742	23.2	33
David Holston, Chicago St.	Jr.	28	.430	130/322	.848	86	142	58	2	646	23.1	39
Antoine Agudio, Hofstra	Sr.	27	.431	84/205	.776	106	77	31	0	612	22.7	36
Tyler Hansbrough, N. Carolina	Jr.	39	.540	0/7	.806	399	35	59	14	882	22.6	39
Jaycee Carroll, Utah St.	Sr.	35	.526	114/229	.919	209	76	33	7	785	22.4	33
Greg Sprink, Navy	Sr.	30	.361	76/254	.858	190	86	39	5	653	21.8	37
DeMario Anderson, Quinnipiac	Sr.	28	.447	35/94	.805	181	91	43	12	607	21.7	30
George Hill, IUPUI	Jr.	32	.545	49/109	.812	216	137	57	13	688	21.5	34
Donovan Morris, Long Beach St.	Jr.	31	.461	75/180	.847	161	72	26	10	656	21.2	33
Ryan Anderson, California	So.	33	.490	64/156	.869	328	47	12	18	697	21.1	36
Robert Vaden, UAB	Jr.	33	.408	142/355	.863	116	85	32	7	695	21.1	41
Tyrese Rice, Boston College	Jr.	30	.433	64/179	.846	98	149	48	6	629	21.0	46

Rebounding

	Cl	Gm	No	Avg
Michael Beasley, Kansas St.	Fr.	33	408	12.4
Jason Thompson, Rider	Sr.	34	412	12.1
Jon Brockman, Washington	Jr.	32	370	11.6
Durrell Vinson, Wagner	Sr.	31	358	11.5
Marqus Blakely, Vermont	So.	29	320	11.0
Arizona Reid, High Point	Sr.	31	342	11.0
Boubacar Coly, Morgan St.	Sr.	33	361	10.9
Ryan Bright, Sam Houston St.	Sr.	31	337	10.9
Kentrell Gransberry, South Florida	Sr.	30	325	10.8
Thomas Sanders, Gardner-Webb	Sr.	32	346	10.8
Kevin Love, UCLA	Fr.	39	415	10.6
Luke Harangody, Notre Dame	So.	33	351	10.6
Todd Sowell, St. Peter's	Sr.	30	312	10.4
Will Thomas, George Mason	Sr.	34	353	10.4
Damion James, Texas	So.	38	393	10.3
D.J. White, Indiana	Sr.	33	341	10.3
Tyler Hansbrough, North Carolina	Jr.	39	399	10.2
Arturas Valeika, Weber St.	Sr.	30	305	10.2
Aleks Maric, Nebraska	Sr.	33	335	10.2
Jonathan Rodriguez, Campbell	So.	30	304	10.1

Assists

	Cl	Gm	No	Avg
Jason Richards, Davidson	Sr.	36	293	8.1
TeeJay Bannister, Liberty	Sr.	31	224	7.2
Paul Stoll, TX-Pan American	Sr.	31	224	7.2
Jay Greene, UMBC	Jr.	33	236	7.2
Mike Jefferson, High Point	Sr.	31	216	7.0
Nikola Stojakovic, Morehead St.	Sr.	30	204	6.8
Greivis Vasquez, Maryland	So.	34	231	6.8
Adam Emmenecker, Drake	Sr.	33	213	6.5
Kris Clark, Utah St.	Sr.	35	224	6.4
Tony Lee, Robert Morris	Sr.	34	217	6.4
DeAndre Bray, Jacksonville St.	Jr.	29	185	6.4
Josh Jenkins, CS-Northridge	Jr.	30	191	6.4
Chris Lowe, Massachusetts	Jr.	34	214	6.3
Jonathan Han, Fairfield	Jr.	30	186	6.2
Nick Calathes, Florida	Fr.	36	221	6.1
Brandon Brooks, Alabama St.	Jr.	31	190	6.1
Sean Singletary, Virginia	Sr.	33	202	6.1
Darrell Jenkins, East Carolina	Sr.	30	181	6.0
Dwayne Foreman, Ga. Southern	Sr.	32	193	6.0
Jeremy Pargo, Gonzaga	Jr.	33	199	6.0

Field Goal Percentage

Minimum 5 Field Goals made per game.

	Cl	Gm	FG	FGA	Pct
Kenny George, NC-Asheville	Sr.	28	151	217	69.6
Vladimir Kuljanin, NC-Wilmington	Sr.	33	188	282	66.7
Matt Nelson, Boise St.	Sr.	33	202	312	64.7
Ahmad Nivins, St. Joseph's	Jr.	33	165	255	64.7
Will Thomas, George Mason	Sr.	34	208	324	64.2
Andrew Strait, Montana	Sr.	30	166	260	63.8
Dwayne Curtis, Mississippi	Sr.	35	212	335	63.3
Arinze Onuaku, Syracuse	Jr.	35	186	296	62.8
Marreese Speights, Florida	So.	36	216	346	62.4
Jordan Hill, Arizona	So.	34	184	297	62.0
Leon Williams, Ohio	Sr.	33	180	293	61.4
Roy Hibbert, Georgetown	Sr.	34	179	294	60.9
D.J. White, Indiana	Sr.	33	216	357	60.5
Jaraun Burrows, IPFW	Sr.	31	155	257	60.3
Richard Hendrix, Alabama	Jr.	32	229	383	59.8
Donte Minter, Appalachian St.	Sr.	30	164	276	59.4

Free Throw Percentage

Minimum 2.5 Free Throws made per game.

	Cl	Gm	FT	FTA	Pct
Tyler Relph, St. Bonaventure	Sr.	29	75	80	93.8
Jaycee Carroll, Utah St.	Sr.	35	137	149	91.9
Jack McClinton, Miami-FL	Jr.	32	114	124	91.9
Justin Hare, Belmont	Sr.	33	112	122	91.8
Julio Anthony, Eastern Ill.	Sr.	27	75	82	91.5
Mike Schachtner, Green Bay	Jr.	30	104	115	90.4
Josh Akognon, CS-Fullerton	Jr.	32	107	119	89.9
Louis Dale, Cornell	So.	28	96	107	89.7
Stephen Curry, Davidson	So.	36	135	151	89.4
Deven Mitchell, Missouri St.	Jr.	33	159	178	89.3
Garrison Carr, American	Jr.	33	91	102	89.2
Jon Scheyer, Duke	So.	34	120	135	88.9
Domonic Tilford, So. Alabama	Jr.	33	84	95	88.4
Robert McKiver, Houston	Sr.	34	190	215	88.4
Austin Daye, Gonzaga	Fr.	33	89	101	88.2
Bobby Nash, Hawaii	Sr.	30	80	91	87.9

VMI
Reggie Williams
Scoring

Davidson
Jason Richards
Assists

NC-Asheville
Kenny George
FG Percentage

UTSA
Devin Gibson
Steals

3-Pt Field Goal Percentage
Minimum 2.5 Three-Point FGs made per game.

	Cl	Gm	FG	FGA	Pct
Jaycee Carroll, Utah St.	Sr.	35	114	229	49.8
Chad Toppert, New Mexico	Jr.	33	85	177	48.0
Shawn Huff, Valparaiso	Sr.	36	91	190	47.9
Darnell Harris, La Salle	Sr.	32	123	257	47.9
Henry Salter, TCU	Jr.	24	62	130	47.7
Paul Stoll, TX-Pan American	Sr.	31	86	181	47.5
Josh Mayo, Ill-Chicago	Jr.	33	94	200	47.0
Shan Foster, Vanderbilt	Sr.	34	134	286	46.9
Ryan Wittman, Cornell	So.	28	78	170	45.9
Pete Campbell, Butler	Sr.	31	102	223	45.7
Brian Roberts, Dayton	Sr.	34	100	220	45.5
Mikko Koivisto, NC-Greensboro	So.	30	80	176	45.5

3-Pt Field Goals Per Game

	Cl	Gm	No	Avg
David Holston, Chicago St.	Jr.	28	130	4.6
Stephen Curry, Davidson	So.	36	162	4.5
Robert Vaden, UAB	Jr.	33	142	4.3
Robert McKiver, Houston	Sr.	34	145	4.3
Garrison Carr, American	Jr.	33	135	4.1
Jack Leasure, Coastal Carolina	Sr.	28	111	4.0
Shan Foster, Vanderbilt	Sr.	34	134	3.9
Darnell Harris, La Salle	Sr.	32	123	3.8
Leemire Goldwire, Charlotte	Sr.	34	128	3.8
Lester Hudson, Tenn-Martin	Jr.	33	124	3.8
Josh Akognon, CS-Fullerton	Jr.	32	116	3.6

Blocked Shots

	Cl	Gm	No	Avg
Jarvis Varnado, Mississippi St.	So.	34	157	4.6
Mickell Gladness, Alabama A&M	Sr.	29	131	4.5
Haseem Thabeet, Connecticut	So.	33	147	4.5
Kleon Penn, McNeese St.	Sr.	29	117	4.0
Shawn James, Duquesne	Jr.	28	111	4.0
Jerome Jordan, Tulsa	So.	39	143	3.7
Tyrelle Blair, Boston College	Sr.	31	105	3.4
Kenny George, NC-Asheville	Jr.	28	93	3.3
Kyle Hines, NC-Greensboro	Sr.	31	95	3.1
Hamady N'Diaye, Rutgers	So.	31	93	3.0
Larry Sanders, VCU	Fr.	32	95	3.0
Ekpe Udoh, Michigan	So.	32	92	2.9
Daniel Northern, Tennessee Tech	Jr.	32	90	2.8

Steals

	Cl	Gm	No	Avg
Devin Gibson, UTSA	Fr.	28	93	3.3
Devan Downey, South Carolina	Jr.	32	103	3.2
Chris Gaynor, Winthrop	Sr.	34	97	2.9
Lester Hudson, Tenn-Martin	Jr.	33	94	2.8
Tony Lee, Robert Morris	Sr.	34	95	2.8
Brandon Johnson, Old Dominion	Sr.	34	91	2.7
Toney Douglas, Florida St.	Jr.	34	90	2.6
Jonathan Amos, Toledo	Jr.	30	78	2.6
Cedric Jackson, Cleveland St.	Jr.	34	88	2.6
Paul Stoll, Texas-Pan American	Sr.	31	79	2.5
Derek Wright, Austin Peay	Sr.	35	89	2.5

Single Game Highs

Points

No		Opponent	Date
52	Robert McKiver, Houston	So. Miss.	Feb. 27
46	Tyrese Rice, Boston College	UNC	Mar. 1
45	Charron Fisher, Niagara	Loyola-MD	Feb. 10
44	Michael Beasley, Kansas St.	Baylor	Feb. 23
44	Justin Jonas, Troy	Paul Quinn	Nov. 14

Rebounds

No		Opponent	Date
24	Jason Thompson, Rider	Siena	Feb. 10
24	Michael Beasley, Kansas St.	Sac. St.	Nov. 9
23	J.J. Hickson, N.C. State	Clemson	Feb. 16
23	Richard Hendrix, Alabama	Troy	Nov. 9

Assists

No		Opponent	Date
20	Brandon Brooks, Ala. St.	Jackson St.	Mar. 8
16	Mitch Johnson, Stanford	Marquette	Mar. 22
15	Three tied.		

Blocks

No		Opponent	Date
12	Shawn James, Duquesne	Oakland	Nov. 20
11	Tyrelle Blair, Boston College	Maryland	Dec. 9
10	Eight tied.		

Steals

No		Opponent	Date
10	Lester Hudson, Tenn-Martin	Cen. Bptst.	Nov. 13
9	Jerome Dyson, UConn	St. John's	Jan. 8
8	Nine tied.		

3-point FGs

No		Opponent	Date
11	Gary Patterson, IUPUI	So. Utah	Jan. 31
10	Justin Jonas, Troy	So. Alabama	Feb. 10
10	Andre Smith, George Mason	JMU	Jan. 19
10	Samuel Haanpaa, Valparaiso	Chi. St.	Dec. 15
10	Steven Rush, N.C. A&T	DePaul	Nov. 24

NCAA Men's Division I Leaders (Cont.)
TEAM

Scoring Offense

	Gm	W-L	Pts	Avg
VMI	29	14-15	2649	91.3
North Carolina	39	36-3	3454	88.6
Texas St.	29	13-16	2423	83.6
Duke	34	28-6	2830	83.2
Duquesne	30	17-13	2470	82.3
Tennessee	36	31-5	2946	81.8
CS-Fullerton	33	24-9	2700	81.8
Massachusetts	36	25-11	2934	81.5
Lamar	30	19-11	2445	81.5
Boise St.	34	25-9	2767	81.4

Scoring Defense

	Gm	W-L	Pts	Avg
Wisconsin	36	31-5	1958	54.4
Stephen F. Austin	32	26-6	1805	56.4
Washington St.	35	26-9	1975	56.4
Air Force	30	16-14	1715	57.2
Iowa	32	13-19	1857	58.0
Georgetown	34	28-6	1976	58.1
Butler	34	30-4	1985	58.4
Winthrop	34	22-12	1990	58.5
VCU	32	24-8	1881	58.8
UCLA	39	35-4	2300	59.0

Scoring Margin

	Off	Def	Mar
Kansas	80.5	61.5	19.0
Memphis	79.9	61.9	18.0
North Carolina	88.6	72.5	16.1
Davidson	77.9	63.2	14.7
UCLA	73.5	59.0	14.5
Duke	83.2	69.4	13.8
Wisconsin	67.3	54.4	12.9
Gonzaga	76.5	63.8	12.7
St. Mary's	75.7	63.7	12.0
Tennessee	81.8	70.0	11.9

Won-Lost Percentage

	W	L	Pct
Memphis	38	2	95.0
Kansas	37	3	92.5
North Carolina	36	3	92.3
UCLA	36	3	89.7
Butler	30	4	88.2
Wisconsin	31	5	86.1
Tennessee	31	5	86.1
Drake	28	5	84.8
Georgetown	28	6	82.4
Duke	28	6	82.4

Field Goal Percentage

	FG	FGA	Pct
Utah St.	923	1797	51.4
Kansas	1176	2314	50.8
Boise St.	994	1956	80.8
IUPUI	883	1754	50.3
Pacific	772	1569	49.2
Georgetown	855	1744	49.0
Murray St.	812	1659	48.9
Florida	1029	2108	48.8
NC-Asheville	901	1846	48.8
North Carolina	1250	2564	48.8

Field Goal Percentage Defense

	FG	FGA	Pct
Georgetown	669	1827	36.6
Mississippi St.	790	2137	37.0
Kansas	853	2249	37.9
VCU	647	1698	38.1
Wisconsin	719	1879	38.3
Connecticut	839	2170	38.7
Sam Houston St.	668	1727	38.7
Louisville	774	1997	38.8
Texas	861	2214	38.9
Ohio St.	846	2175	38.9

Rebound Margin

	Off	Def	Mar
North Carolina	43.5	32.5	11.0
New Mexico St.	41.7	32.8	8.9
Kansas St.	41.3	32.9	8.4
UCLA	36.7	28.5	8.2
Kansas	38.7	30.8	7.9
Stanford	39.1	31.4	7.8
Albany	37.5	30.2	7.3
Texas A&M	38.9	31.9	7.1
Michigan St.	36.9	30.2	6.8
Sam Houston St.	41.2	34.5	6.7

Free Throw Percentage

	FT	FTA	Pct
Utah St.	532	672	79.2
UC-Davis	401	515	77.9
California	533	687	77.6
IUPUI	498	642	77.6
Florida St.	529	684	77.3
Houston	552	717	77.0
Loyola-MD	541	704	76.8
Denver	373	489	76.3
Cornell	392	515	76.1
Indiana	577	760	75.9

3-point FG Percentage

	3PT	3PTA	Pct
IUPUI	246	582	42.3
New Mexico	271	646	42.0
UC-Santa Barbara	242	590	41.0
Cornell	228	558	40.9
Brown	227	556	40.8
American	260	638	40.8
Notre Dame	274	677	40.8
Pacific	234	580	40.3
Utah St.	207	516	40.1
Vanderbilt	303	760	39.9

3-point FG Made Per Game

	Gm	No	Avg
VMI	29	336	11.6
Houston	34	375	11.0
Troy	31	335	10.8
Belmont	34	357	10.5
Lafayette	30	299	10.0
Navy	30	288	9.6
New Hampshire	29	275	9.5
Citadel	30	283	9.4
Drake	33	310	9.4
Butler	34	319	9.4

Other 2008 Men's Tournaments

NIT Tournament

The 71st annual National Invitation Tournament had a 32-team field, down from 40 teams in recent years. First three rounds played on home courts of higher seeded teams. Semifinal and Championship games played April 1-3 at Madison Square Garden in New York City.

1st Round

Massachusetts 80	Stephen F. Austin 60
Ohio St. 84	NC-Asheville 66
Syracuse 87	Robert Morris 81
Akron 65 OT	Florida St. 60
Southern Illinois 69	Oklahoma St. 53
Maryland 68	Minnesota 58
Creighton 74	Rhode Island 73
Arizona St. 64	Alabama St. 53
Dayton 66	Cleveland St. 57
Virginia Tech 94	Morgan St. 62
UAB 80	Va. Commonwealth 77
Mississippi 83	UC Santa Barbara 68
Nebraska 67	Charlotte 48
Florida 73	San Diego St. 49
Illinois St. 61	Utah St. 57
California 68	New Mexico 66

2nd Round

Syracuse 88	Maryland 72
Arizona St. 65	Southern Illinois 51
Florida 82	Creighton 54
Massachusetts 68	Akron 63
Ohio St. 73	California 56
Dayton 55	Illinois St. 48
Virginia Tech 75	UAB 49
Mississippi 85 OT	Nebraska 75

Quarterfinals

Massachusetts 81	Syracuse 77
Florida 70	Arizona St. 57
Mississippi 81	Virginia Tech 72
Ohio St. 74	Dayton 63

Semifinals

Massachusetts 78	Florida 66
Ohio St. 81	Mississippi 69

Championship

Ohio St. 92	Massachusetts 85

Tournament MVPs

NIT

Kosta Koufos
Ohio St. freshman center

NCAA Division II

Jonte Flowers
Winona St. senior guard

NCAA Division III

Troy Ruths
Washington U. forward

CBI Tournament

The inaugural College Basketball Invitational had a 16-team field. The championship was decided by a best-of-three series.

1st Round

Virginia 66	Richmond 64
Old Dominion 68	Rider 65
Bradley 70	Cincinnati 67
Ohio 80	Brown 74
Utah 81	UTEP 69
Tulsa 61	Miami-OH 45
Valparaiso 72	Washington 71
Houston 80	Nevada 79

Quarterfinals

Virginia 80	Old Dominion 76
Bradley 79	Ohio 73
Tulsa 69	Utah 60
Houston 91	Valparaiso 67

Semifinals

Bradley 96	Virginia 85
Tulsa 73	Houston 69

Championship

Tulsa 73	Bradley 68
Bradley 83	Tulsa 74
Tulsa 70	Bradley 64

NCAA Division II

The eight regional winners of the 64-team field: NORTHEAST—Bentley; EAST—California-PA; SOUTH ATLANTIC—Augusta St.; SOUTH—North Alabama; SOUTH CENTRAL—Central Oklahoma; GREAT LAKES—Grand Valley St.; NORTH CENTRAL—Winona St.; WEST—Alaska-Anchorage.

The Elite Eight was played March 26-29, at Springfield, Massachusetts. There was no Third Place game.

Quarterfinals

Augusta St. 106 2OT	Central Okla 104
Alaska-Anchorage 55	California-PA 52
Winona St. 67	Grand Valley St. 54
Bentley 102	North Alabama 92

Semifinals

Augusta St. 56	Alaska-Anchorage 50
Winona St. 86	Bentley 75

Championship

Winona St. 87	Augusta St. 76

NCAA Division III

The four sectional winners of the 48-team field: Hope (69-3), Ursinius (28-2), Amherst (25-3), Washington U.-St. Louis (22-6).

The Final Four was played March 21-22, at Salem Civic Center in Salem, Va.

Semifinals

Amherst 84	Ursinius 58
Washington U. 89	Hope 74

Championship

Washington U 90	Amherst 68

Women

Final Regular Season AP Top 25 Poll

Taken **before** start of NCAA tournament.

The sportswriters & broadcasters poll: first place votes in parentheses; records through Tuesday, March 18, 2008; total points and preseason ranking.

		Record	Points	Preseason Rank
1	Connecticut (49)	32-1	1249	2
2	North Carolina (1)	30-2	1188	8
3	Tennessee	30-2	1158	1
4	Stanford	30-3	1091	7
5	Maryland	30-3	1027	4
6	LSU	27-5	1014	5
7	Rutgers	24-6	952	3
8	Texas A&M	26-7	858	11
9	Duke	23-9	817	10
10	California	26-6	788	13
11	Old Dominion	29-4	711	-
12	Baylor	24-6	705	15
13	Oklahoma St.	25-7	552	-
14	Oklahoma	21-8	535	6
15	Notre Dame	23-8	477	24
16	Kansas St.	21-9	436	-
17	West Virginia	24-7	434	18
18	Utah	27-4	426	-
19	Louisville	24-9	371	21
20	George Washington	25-6	352	14
21	Vanderbilt	23-8	263	23
22	Marist	31-2	222	-
23	UTEP	27-3	218	-
24	Virginia	23-9	113	-
25	Ohio St.	22-8	86	16

Others receiving votes: 26. **Georgia** (34 points); 27. **Pittsburgh** (31); 28. **Texas** (24); 29. **Xavier** (18); 30. **Hartford** (16); 31. **Chattanooga** (15); 32. **Wyoming** (13); 33. **Purdue** (12); 34. **Arizona St.** (11); 35. **SMU** (8); 36. **Illinois St.** (7); 37. **DePaul** and **Liberty** (5); 39. **Iowa** (3); 40. **TCU** and **Western Kentucky** (2); 42. **Syracuse** (1).

Final *ESPN/USA Today* Coaches' Poll

Taken **after** NCAA tournament.

Voted on by a panel of 31 women's coaches and media following the NCAA tournament: first place votes in parentheses.

		Record	Points	Preseason Rank
1	Tennessee (31)	36-2	775	1
2	Stanford	35-4	740	8
3	Connecticut	36-2	704	2
4	LSU	31-6	694	5
5	North Carolina	33-3	623	7
6	Rutgers	27-7	617	3
7	Maryland	33-4	594	4
8	Texas A&M	29-8	585	11
9	Duke	25-10	451	9
10	Old Dominion	31-5	438	-
11	Oklahoma St.	27-8	428	-
12	Louisville	26-10	422	23
13	Notre Dame	25-9	415	-
14	George Washington	27-7	372	13
15	Vanderbilt	25-9	331	17
16	Pittsburgh	24-11	284	21
17	Baylor	25-7	277	15
18	California	27-7	259	14
19	Oklahoma	22-9	188	-
20	West Virginia	25-8	167	22
21	Kansas St.	22-10	150	-
22	Virginia	24-10	118	-
23	Marist	32-3	102	-
24	Georgia	23-10	81	10
25	UTEP	28-4	63	-

Others receiving votes: 26. **Arizona St.** (43 points); 27. **Utah** (32); 28. **Florida St.** (29); 29. **Iowa St.** (21); 30. **Nebraska** (20); 31. **Texas** (16); 32. **Hartford** (15); 33. **Marquette** (6); 34. **DePaul** and **Georgia Tech** (5); 36. **Ohio St.** (3) and 37. **Purdue** (2).

NCAA Women's Division I Leaders

Includes games through NCAA and WNIT tourneys.

INDIVIDUAL

Scoring

	Cl	Gm	Pts	Avg
Amber Holt, Middle Tenn.	Sr.	34	930	27.4
Natalie Doma, Idaho St.	Sr.	30	742	24.7
Sade Logan, Robert Morris	Jr.	33	815	24.7
Angel McCoughtry, Louisville	Jr.	36	858	23.8
Andrea Riley, Oklahoma St.	So.	35	807	23.1
Crystal Kelly, Western Ky.	Sr.	34	767	22.6
Amanda Jackson, Miami-OH	Sr.	33	712	21.6
Candace Parker, Tennessee	Sr.	38	809	21.3
Traci Edwards, Milwaukee	Jr.	31	639	20.6
Valerie Nainima, Long Island	So.	32	653	20.4

Assists

	Cl	Gm	No	Avg
Claire Fischer, Portland St.	So.	31	274	8.8
Amanda Rego, San Diego	Sr.	32	272	8.5
Tiera DeLaHoussaye, Western Mich.	Jr.	32	251	7.8
Leilani Mitchell, Utah	Sr.	32	240	7.5
Kristi Toliver, Maryland	Jr.	37	275	7.4
Patrika Barlow, Louisville	Sr.	36	251	7.0
Kate Archer, Bowling Green	Sr.	34	234	6.9
Christine Kinneary, Boston Univ.	Jr.	32	214	6.7

Rebounding

	Cl	Gm	No	Avg
Courtney Paris, Oklahoma	Jr.	31	466	15.0
Natalie Doma, Idaho St.	Sr.	30	371	12.4
Tanya Smith, Hawaii	Sr.	30	353	11.8
Khadijah Washington, N.C. State	Sr.	34	398	11.7
Tia Lewis, UCF	Fr.	30	345	11.5
Ta'Shia Phillips, Xavier	Fr.	33	371	11.2
Laura Markwood, Miami-OH	Sr.	34	359	10.6
Crystal Kelly, Western Ky.	Sr.	34	357	10.5
Noteisha Womack, Seton Hall	Jr.	21	220	10.5
Tamera Young, James Madison	Sr.	34	352	10.4

Blocked Shots

	Cl	Gm	No	Avg
Louelia Tomlinson, St. Mary's	Fr.	32	156	4.9
Brittany Pittman, Morehead St.	So.	30	123	4.1
Allyssa DeHaan, Michigan St.	So.	37	150	4.1

Steals

	Cl	Gm	No	Avg
Kyle DeHaven, Delaware	Sr.	29	133	4.6
Angel McCoughtry, Louisville	Jr.	36	148	4.1
Corin Adams, Morgan St.	So.	31	123	4.0

2008 NCAA Tournament Women's Division

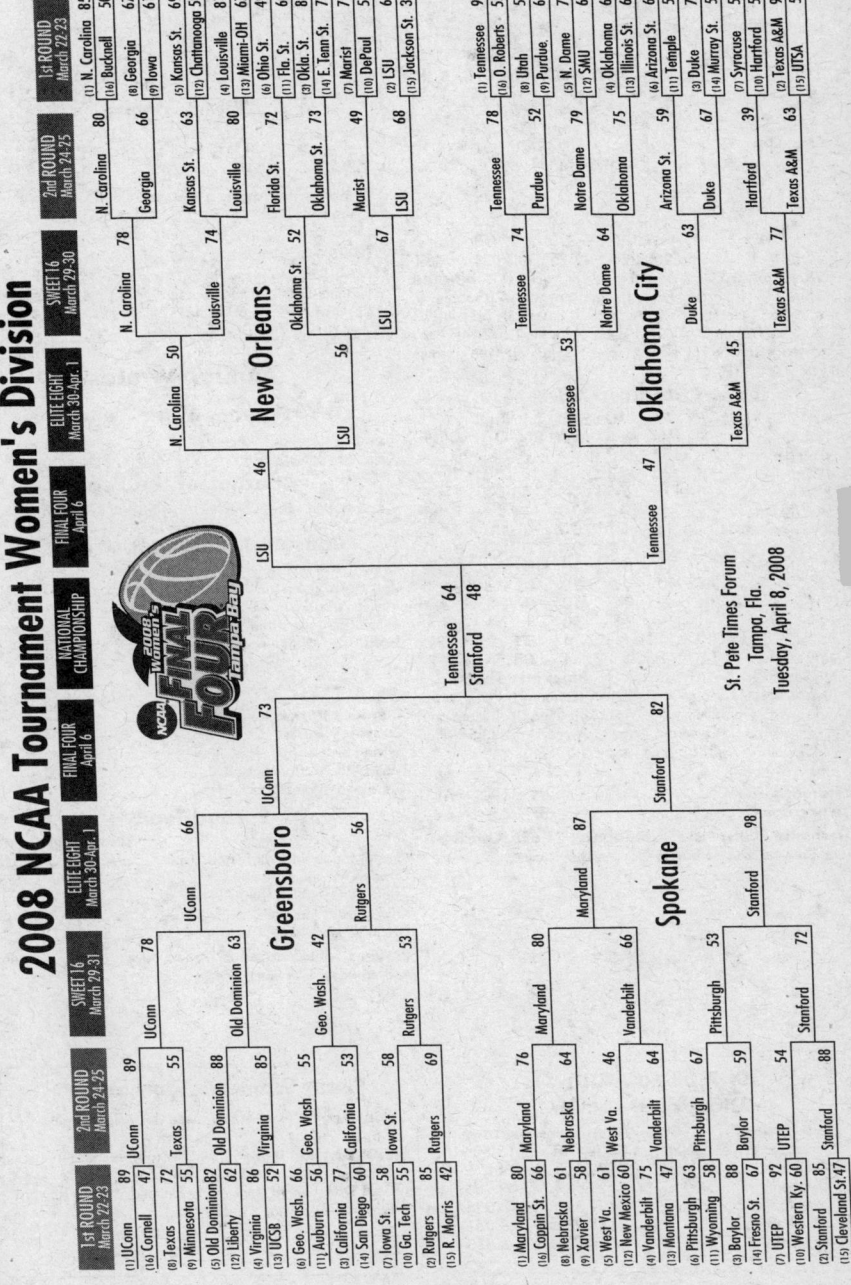

Greensboro

1st ROUND March 22-23	2nd ROUND March 24-25	SWEET 16 March 29-31	ELITE EIGHT March 30-Apr. 1
(1) UConn 89	UConn 89		
(16) Cornell 47		UConn 78	
(8) Texas 72	Texas 55		UConn 66
(9) Minnesota 55			
(5) Old Dominion 82	Old Dominion 88		
(12) Liberty 62		Old Dominion 63	
(4) Virginia 86	Virginia 85		
(13) UCSB 52			
(6) Geo. Wash. 66	Geo. Wash. 55		
(11) Auburn 56		Geo. Wash. 42	
(3) California 77	California 53		Rutgers 56
(14) San Diego 60			
(7) Iowa St. 58	Iowa St. 58		
(10) Ga. Tech 55		Rutgers 53	
(2) Rutgers 85	Rutgers 69		
(15) R. Morris 42			

Spokane

1st ROUND March 22-23	2nd ROUND March 24-25	SWEET 16 March 29-31	ELITE EIGHT March 30-Apr. 1
(1) Maryland 80	Maryland 76		
(16) Coppin St. 66		Maryland 80	
(8) Nebraska 61	Nebraska 64		Maryland 87
(9) Xavier 58			
(5) West Va. 58	West Va. 46		
(12) New Mexico 60		Vanderbilt 66	
(4) Vanderbilt 75	Vanderbilt 64		
(13) Montana 47			
(6) Pittsburgh 63	Pittsburgh 67		
(11) Wyoming 58		Pittsburgh 53	
(3) Baylor 88	Baylor 59		Stanford 98
(14) Fresno St. 67			
(7) UTEP 92	UTEP 54		
(10) Western Ky. 60		Stanford 72	
(2) Stanford 85	Stanford 88		
(15) Cleveland St. 47			

New Orleans

1st ROUND March 22-23	2nd ROUND March 24-25	SWEET 16 March 29-30	ELITE EIGHT March 30-Apr. 1
(1) N. Carolina 85	N. Carolina 80		
(16) Bucknell 50		N. Carolina 78	
(8) Georgia 67	Georgia 66		N. Carolina 50
(9) Iowa 61			
(5) Kansas St. 69	Kansas St. 63		
(12) Chattanooga 59		Louisville 74	
(4) Louisville 81	Louisville 80		
(13) Miami-OH 67			
(6) Ohio St. 49	Florida St. 72		
(11) Fla. St. 60		Oklahoma St. 52	
(14) Okla. St. 85	Oklahoma St. 73		LSU 56
(14) E. Tenn St. 73			
(7) Marist 76	Marist 49		
(10) DePaul 57		LSU 67	
(2) LSU 66	LSU 68		
(15) Jackson St. 32			

Oklahoma City

1st ROUND March 22-23	2nd ROUND March 24-25	SWEET 16 March 29-30	ELITE EIGHT March 30-Apr. 1
(1) Tennessee 94	Tennessee 78		
(16) O. Roberts 55		Tennessee 74	
(8) Utah 59	Purdue 52		Tennessee 53
(9) Purdue 66			
(5) N. Dame 75	Notre Dame 79		
(12) SMU 62		Notre Dame 64	
(4) Oklahoma 69	Oklahoma 75		
(13) Illinois St. 61			
(6) Arizona St. 61	Arizona St. 59		
(11) Temple 54		Duke 63	
(3) Duke 78	Duke 67		Texas A&M 45
(14) Murray St. 57			
(7) Syracuse 55	Hartford 39		
(10) Hartford 59		Texas A&M 77	
(2) Texas A&M 91	Texas A&M 63		
(15) UTSA 52			

FINAL FOUR April 6

N. Carolina 46
LSU 46

Tennessee 47

FINAL FOUR April 6

UConn 73
Stanford 82

Maryland ...
Stanford ...

NATIONAL CHAMPIONSHIP

Tennessee 64
Stanford 48

St. Pete Times Forum
Tampa, Fla.
Tuesday, April 8, 2008

NCAA Championship Game

Apr. 8, 2008 at St. Pete Times Forum in Tampa, Fla.

Tennessee 64

	Min	FG M-A	FT M-A	Pts	Reb O-T	A	PF
C. Parker	37	5-10	7-11	17	1-9	1	2
A. Auguste	39	3-7	1-2	7	3-7	2	4
N. Anosike	28	6-11	0-1	12	3-8	0	3
S. Bobbitt	37	4-12	2-2	13	0-0	0	0
A. Hornbuckle	28	1-7	4-5	6	0-1	3	3
A. Bjorkland	15	0-5	0-0	0	1-1	0	0
S. Smallbone	1	0-0	0-0	0	1-1	0	0
V. Baugh	13	3-4	2-2	8	3-4	0	2
A. Fuller	1	0-0	0-0	0	0-0	0	0
TOTALS	200	22-56	17-25	64	11-31	6	14

Three-point FG: 3-9 (Bobbitt 3-8, Bjorklund 0-1); **Blocked Shots:** 2 (Anosike, Parker); **Turnovers:** 14 (Bobbitt 3, Anosike 2, Hornbuckle 2, Auguste 3, Parker 4); **Steals:** 13 (Anosike 6, Hornbuckle, Bjorklund, Auguste, Parker 4); **Percentages:** 3-Pt FG (.333); Total FG (.393); Free Throws (.680).

Stanford 48

	Min	FG M-A	FT M-A	Pts	Reb O-T	A	PF
K. Pedersen	37	2-7	3-4	7	2-10	0	4
J. Appel	36	6-13	4-10	16	3-5	3	5
J. Hones	34	2-5	0-0	5	0-2	3	2
C. Wiggins	39	6-16	0-0	14	1-4	1	3
R. Gold-Onwude	16	1-2	0-0	2	0-3	0	2
C. Pierce	1	0-0	0-0	0	0-0	0	0
H. Donaghe	1	0-0	0-0	0	0-0	0	0
J. Pohlen	10	0-2	0-0	0	0-1	0	1
A. Cimino	1	0-0	0-0	0	0-0	0	0
J. Harmon	24	2-3	0-0	4	2-4	1	4
TOTALS	220	19-49	7-14	48	8-29	8	21

Three-point FG: 3-11 (Hones 1-2, Pohlen 0-1, Wiggins 2-5, Pedersen 0-2, Clyburn 0-1); **Blocked Shots:** 0; **Turnovers:** 24 (Hones 4, Pohlen 1, Harmon 3, Wiggins 6, Pedersen 2, Gold-Onwude 4, Appel 4); **Steals:** 7 (Harmon, Wiggins 4, Gold-Onwude, Appel); **Percentages:** 3-Pt FG (.273); Total FG (.388); Free Throws (.500).

	1	2	F
Stanford (Pac-10)	29	19	48
Tennessee (SEC)	37	27	64

Technical Fouls: None. **Attendance:** 21,655. **Officials:** Eric Brewton, Denise Brooks-Clauser, Dee Kantner

---

WOMEN'S FINAL FOUR

at Tampa, Fla. (April 6-8).

Semifinals

Stanford 82 . . . . Connecticut 73
Tennessee 47 . . . . LSU 46

Championship

Tennessee 64 . . . . Stanford 48

Final Records: Connecticut (36-2), LSU (31-6), Tennessee (36-2), Stanford (35-4).

Most Outstanding Player: Candace Parker, Tennessee. SEMIFINAL—36 minutes, 13 points, 15 rebounds, 1 assist; FINAL—37 minutes, 17 points, 9 rebounds, 1 assist.

All-Tournament Team: Parker, Nicky Anosike and Shannon Bobbitt of Tennessee; Sylvia Fowles of LSU and Candice Wiggins of Stanford.

Annual Awards

Players of the Year

Candice Wiggins, Stanford . . . . Wade
Candace Parker, Tenn . . . AP, Wooden, Broderick, USBWA

Coaches of the Year

Geno Auriemma, UConn . . AP, USBWA, Naismith, WBCA

Consensus All-America Team

The NCAA Division I players cited most frequently by the Associated Press, US Basketball Writers Association, the Women's Basketball Coaches Association and Wooden Committee. Holdovers from 2006-07 All-America first team are in **bold** type; (*) indicates unanimous first team selection.

First Team

	Class	Hgt	Pos
Candace Parker*, Tennessee	Jr.	6-4	F
Courtney Paris*, Oklahoma	Jr	6-4	C
Sylvia Fowles, LSU	Sr.	6-6	C
Maya Moore, Connecticut	Fr.	6-0	F
Candice Wiggins, Stanford	Sr.	5-11	G

Second Team

	Class	Hgt	Pos
Crystal Langhorne, Maryland	Sr.	6-2	C/F
Candice Wiggins, Stanford	Jr.	5-11	G
Angel McCoughtry, Louisville	Jr.	6-2	F
Kristi Toliver, Maryland	Jr.	5-7	G
Erlana Larkins, North Carolina	Sr.	6-1	F

Players also named: Renee Montgomery, UConn; Andrea Riley, Oklahoma St.

2007-08 NCAA Div. I Attendance Leaders

Team (2006-07)	Gms	Attendance	Average
1 Tennessee (1)	15	236,940	15,796
2 Connecticut (2)	19	199,103	10,479
3 Oklahoma (4)	13	129,527	9,964
4 Iowa St. (7)	17	159,592	9,388
5 Purdue (8)	16	141,931	8,871
6 New Mexico (5)	19	164,124	8,638

Other Women's Tournaments

WNIT (Apr. 5): Final— Marquette def. Michigan St., 81-66.
NCAA Division II (Mar. 29 at Kearney, Neb.): Northern Kentucky def. South Dakota, 63-58.
NCAA Division III (Mar. 22 at Holland, Mich.): Howard Payne def. Messiah, 68-54.

1901-2008
Through the Years

SPORTS ALMANAC

National Champions and NCAA Final Four

The Helms Foundation of Los Angeles, under the direction of founder Bill Schroeder, selected national college basketball champions from 1942-82 and researched retroactive picks from 1901-41. The first NIT tournament and then the NCAA tournament have settled the national championship since 1938, but there are four years (1939, '40, '44 and '54) where the Helms selections differ. In 1939, Helms picked undefeated LIU-Brooklyn (24-0), winners of the NIT. In 1940, Helms picked USC (20-3) although they were beaten by Kansas in the West Regionals of the NCAA tourney. In 1944, Helms picked unbeaten Army (15-0). Army did not lift its policy barring postseason play until the 1961 NIT. In 1954, Helms chose unbeaten Kentucky (25-0), even though Kentucky refused its NCAA bid after seniors Cliff Hagan, Frank Ramsey and Lou Tsioropoulos were declared ineligible.

Multiple champions (1901-37): Chicago, Columbia and Wisconsin (3); Kansas, Minnesota, Notre Dame, Penn, Pittsburgh, Syracuse and Yale (2).

Multiple champions (since 1938): UCLA (11); Kentucky (7); Indiana (5); North Carolina (4); Duke and Kansas (3); Cincinnati, Connecticut, Florida, Louisville, Michigan St., N.C. State, Oklahoma A&M (now Oklahoma St.) and San Francisco (2).

Year	Champion	Record	Head Coach	Outstanding Player
1901	Yale	10-4	No coach	G.M. Clark, F
1902	Minnesota	11-0	Louis Cooke	W.C. Deering, F
1903	Yale	15-1	W.H. Murphy	R.B. Hyatt, F
1904	Columbia	17-1	No coach	Harry Fisher, F
1905	Columbia	19-1	No coach	Harry Fisher, F
1906	Dartmouth	16-2	No coach	George Grebenstein, F
1907	Chicago	22-2	Joseph Raycroft	John Schommer, C
1908	Chicago	21-2	Joseph Raycroft	John Schommer, C
1909	Chicago	12-0	Joseph Raycroft	John Schommer, C
1910	Columbia	11-1	Harry Fisher	Ted Kiendl, F
1911	St. John's-NY	14-0	Claude Allen	John Keenan, F/C
1912	Wisconsin	15-0	Doc Meanwell	Otto Stangel, F
1913	Navy	9-0	Louis Wenzell	Laurence Wild, F
1914	Wisconsin	15-0	Doc Meanwell	Gene Van Gent, C
1915	Illinois	16-0	Ralph Jones	Ray Woods, G
1916	Wisconsin	20-1	Doc Meanwell	George Levis, F
1917	Washington St	25-1	Doc Bohler	Roy Bohler, G
1918	Syracuse	16-1	Edmund Dollard	Joe Schwarzer, G
1919	Minnesota	13-0	Louis Cooke	Arnold Oss, F
1920	Penn	22-1	Lon Jourdet	George Sweeney, F
1921	Penn	21-2	Edward McNichol	Danny McNichol, G
1922	Kansas	16-2	Phog Allen	Paul Endacott, G
1923	Kansas	17-1	Phog Allen	Paul Endacott, G
1924	North Carolina	25-0	Bo Shepard	Jack Cobb, F
1925	Princeton	21-2	Al Wittmer	Art Loeb, G
1926	Syracuse	19-1	Lew Andreas	Vic Hanson, F
1927	Notre Dame	19-1	George Keogan	John Nyikos, C
1928	Pittsburgh	21-0	Doc Carlson	Chuck Hyatt, F
1929	Montana St.	36-2	Schubert Dyche	John (Cat) Thompson, F
1930	Pittsburgh	23-2	Doc Carlson	Chuck Hyatt, F
1931	Northwestern	16-1	Dutch Lonborg	Joe Reiff, C
1932	Purdue	17-1	Piggy Lambert	John Wooden, G
1933	Kentucky	20-3	Adolph Rupp	Forest Sale, F
1934	Wyoming	26-3	Willard Witte	Les Witte, G
1935	NYU	19-1	Howard Cann	Sid Gross, F
1936	Notre Dame	22-2-1	George Keogan	John Moir, F
1937	Stanford	25-2	John Bunn	Hank Luisetti, F

Year		Record	Winner	Head Coach	Outstanding Player
1938	Temple	23-2	NIT	James Usilton	Meyer Bloom, G

Year	Champion	Runner-up	Score	Final Two	— Third Place —	
1939	Oregon	Ohio St.	46-33	@ Evanston, IL	Oklahoma	Villanova
1940	Indiana	Kansas	60-42	@ Kansas City	Duquesne	USC
1941	Wisconsin	Washington St.	39-34	@ Kansas City	Arkansas	Pittsburgh
1942	Stanford	Dartmouth	53-38	@ Kansas City	Colorado	Kentucky
1943	Wyoming	Georgetown	46-34	@ New York	DePaul	Texas
1944	Utah	Dartmouth	42-40 (OT)	@ New York	Iowa St.	Ohio St.
1945	Oklahoma A&M	NYU	49-45	@ New York	Arkansas	Ohio St.

NCAA Final Four (Cont.)

Year	Champion	Runner-up	Score	Final Two	Third Place	Fourth Place
1946	Oklahoma A&M	North Carolina	43-40	@ New York	Ohio St.	California
1947	Holy Cross	Oklahoma	58-47	@ New York	Texas	CCNY
1948	Kentucky	Baylor	58-42	@ New York	Holy Cross	Kansas St.
1949	Kentucky	Oklahoma A&M	46-36	@ Seattle	Illinois	Oregon St.
1950	CCNY	Bradley	71-68	@ New York	N.C. State	Baylor
1951	Kentucky	Kansas St.	68-58	@ Minneapolis	Illinois	Oklahoma A&M

Year	Champion	Runner-up	Score	Third Place	Fourth Place	Final Four
1952	Kansas	St. John's	80-63	Illinois	Santa Clara	@ Seattle
1953	Indiana	Kansas	69-68	Washington	LSU	@ Kansas City
1954	La Salle	Bradley	92-76	Penn St.	USC	@ Kansas City
1955	San Francisco	La Salle	77-63	Colorado	Iowa	@ Kansas City
1956	San Francisco	Iowa	83-71	Temple	SMU	@ Evanston, IL
1957	North Carolina	Kansas	54-53 (3OT)	San Francisco	Michigan St.	@ Kansas City
1958	Kentucky	Seattle	84-72	Temple	Kansas St.	@ Louisville
1959	California	West Virginia	71-70	Cincinnati	Louisville	@ Louisville
1960	Ohio St.	California	75-55	Cincinnati	NYU	@ San Francisco
1961	Cincinnati	Ohio St.	70-65 (OT)	St. Joseph's-PA	Utah	@ Kansas City
1962	Cincinnati	Ohio St.	71-59	Wake Forest	UCLA	@ Louisville
1963	Loyola-IL	Cincinnati	60-58 (OT)	Duke	Oregon St.	@ Louisville
1964	UCLA	Duke	98-83	Michigan	Kansas St.	@ Kansas City
1965	UCLA	Michigan	91-80	Princeton	Wichita St.	@ Portland, OR
1966	Texas Western	Kentucky	72-65	Duke	Utah	@ College Park, MD
1967	UCLA	Dayton	79-64	Houston	North Carolina	@ Louisville
1968	UCLA	North Carolina	78-55	Ohio St.	Houston	@ Los Angeles
1969	UCLA	Purdue	92-72	Drake	North Carolina	@ Louisville
1970	UCLA	Jacksonville	80-69	New Mexico St.	St. Bonaventure	@ College Park, MD
1971	UCLA	Villanova	68-62	Western Ky.	Kansas	@ Houston
1972	UCLA	Florida St.	81-76	North Carolina	Louisville	@ Los Angeles
1973	UCLA	Memphis St.	87-66	Indiana	Providence	@ St. Louis
1974	N.C. State	Marquette	76-64	UCLA	Kansas	@ Greensboro, NC
1975	UCLA	Kentucky	92-85	Louisville	Syracuse	@ San Diego
1976	Indiana	Michigan	86-68	UCLA	Rutgers	@ Philadelphia
1977	Marquette	North Carolina	67-59	UNLV	NC-Charlotte	@ Atlanta
1978	Kentucky	Duke	94-88	Arkansas	Notre Dame	@ St. Louis
1979	Michigan St.	Indiana St.	75-64	DePaul	Penn	@ Salt Lake City
1980	Louisville	UCLA	59-54	Purdue	Iowa	@ Indianapolis
1981	Indiana	North Carolina	63-50	Virginia	LSU	@ Philadelphia

Year	Champion	Runner-up	Score	Third Place		Final Four
1982	North Carolina	Georgetown	63-62	Houston	Louisville	@ New Orleans
1983	N.C. State	Houston	54-52	Georgia	Louisville	@ Albuquerque
1984	Georgetown	Houston	84-75	Kentucky	Virginia	@ Seattle
1985	Villanova	Georgetown	66-64	Memphis St.	St. John's	@ Lexington
1986	Louisville	Duke	72-69	Kansas	LSU	@ Dallas
1987	Indiana	Syracuse	74-73	Providence	UNLV	@ New Orleans
1988	Kansas	Oklahoma	83-79	Arizona	Duke	@ Kansas City
1989	Michigan	Seton Hall	80-79 (OT)	Duke	Illinois	@ Seattle
1990	UNLV	Duke	103-73	Arkansas	Georgia Tech	@ Denver
1991	Duke	Kansas	72-65	North Carolina	UNLV	@ Indianapolis
1992	Duke	Michigan	71-51	Cincinnati	Indiana	@ Minneapolis
1993	North Carolina	Michigan	77-71	Kansas	Kentucky	@ New Orleans
1994	Arkansas	Duke	76-72	Arizona	Florida	@ Charlotte
1995	UCLA	Arkansas	89-78	North Carolina	Oklahoma St.	@ Seattle
1996	Kentucky	Syracuse	76-67	UMass	Mississippi St.	@ E. Rutherford, NJ
1997	Arizona	Kentucky	84-79 (OT)	Minnesota	North Carolina	@ Indianapolis
1998	Kentucky	Utah	78-69	Stanford	North Carolina	@ San Antonio
1999	Connecticut	Duke	77-74	Michigan St.	Ohio St.	@ St. Petersburg, FL
2000	Michigan St.	Florida	89-76	Wisconsin	North Carolina	@ Indianapolis
2001	Duke	Arizona	82-72	Michigan St.	Maryland	@ Minneapolis
2002	Maryland	Indiana	64-52	Oklahoma	Kansas	@ Atlanta
2003	Syracuse	Kansas	81-78	Marquette	Texas	@ New Orleans
2004	Connecticut	Georgia Tech	82-73	Duke	Oklahoma St.	@ San Antonio
2005	North Carolina	Illinois	75-70	Michigan St.	Louisville	@ St. Louis
2006	Florida	UCLA	73-57	George Mason	LSU	@ Indianapolis
2007	Florida	Ohio St.	84-75	Georgetown	UCLA	@ Atlanta
2008	Kansas	Memphis	75-68	North Carolina	UCLA	@ San Antonio

Note: Six teams have had their standing in the Final Four vacated for using ineligible players: 1961–St. Joseph's-PA (3rd place); 1971–Villanova (Runner-up) and Western Kentucky (3rd); 1980–UCLA (Runner-up); 1985–Memphis St. (3rd); 1996–UMass (3rd).

Most Outstanding Player

A Most Outstanding Player has been selected every year of the NCAA tournament. Winners who did not play for the tournament champion are listed in **bold** type. The 1939 and 1951 winners are unofficial and not recognized by the NCAA. Statistics listed are for Final Four games only.

Multiple winners: Lew Alcindor (3); Alex Groza, Bob Kurland, Jerry Lucas and Bill Walton (2).

Year		Gm	FGM	Pct	3PTM	3PTA	FTM	Pct	Reb	Ast	Blk	Stl	PPG
1939	**Jimmy Hull**, Ohio St.	2	15	—	—	—	10	.833	—	—	—	—	20.0
1940	Marv Huffman, Indiana	2	7	—	—	—	4	—	—	—	—	—	9.0
1941	John Kotz, Wisconsin	2	8	—	—	—	6	—	—	—	—	—	11.0
1942	Howie Dallmar, Stanford	2	8	—	—	—	4	.667	—	—	—	—	10.0
1943	Kenny Sailors, Wyoming	2	10	—	—	—	8	.727	—	—	—	—	14.0
1944	Arnie Ferrin, Utah	2	11	—	—	—	6	—	—	—	—	—	14.0
1945	Bob Kurland, Okla. A&M	2	16	—	—	—	5	—	—	—	—	—	18.5
1946	Bob Kurland, Okla. A&M	2	21	—	—	—	10	.667	—	—	—	—	26.0
1947	George Kaftan, Holy Cross	2	18	—	—	—	12	.706	—	—	—	—	24.0
1948	Alex Groza, Kentucky	2	16	—	—	—	5	—	—	—	—	—	18.5
1949	Alex Groza, Kentucky	2	19	—	—	—	14	—	—	—	—	—	26.0
1950	Irwin Dambrot, CCNY	2	12	.429	—	—	4	.500	—	—	—	—	14.0
1951	Bill Spivey, Kentucky	2	20	.400	—	—	10	.625	37	—	—	—	25.0
1952	Clyde Lovellette, Kansas	2	24	—	—	—	18	—	—	—	—	—	33.0
1953	**B.H. Born**, Kansas	2	17	—	—	—	17	—	—	—	—	—	25.5
1954	Tom Gola, La Salle	2	12	—	—	—	14	—	—	—	—	—	19.0
1955	Bill Russell, San Francisco	2	19	—	—	—	9	—	—	—	—	—	23.5
1956	**Hal Lear**, Temple	2	32	—	—	—	16	—	—	—	—	—	40.0
1957	**Wilt Chamberlain**, Kansas	2	18	.514	—	—	19	.704	25	—	—	—	32.5
1958	**Elgin Baylor**, Seattle	2	18	.340	—	—	12	.750	41	—	—	—	24.0
1959	**Jerry West**, West Virginia	2	22	.667	—	—	22	.688	25	—	—	—	33.0
1960	Jerry Lucas, Ohio St.	2	16	.667	—	—	3	1.000	23	—	—	—	17.5
1961	**Jerry Lucas**, Ohio St.	2	20	.714	—	—	16	.941	25	—	—	—	28.0
1962	Paul Hogue, Cincinnati	2	23	.639	—	—	12	.632	38	—	—	—	29.0
1963	**Art Heyman**, Duke	2	18	.409	—	—	15	.682	19	—	—	—	25.5
1964	Walt Hazzard, UCLA	2	11	.550	—	—	8	.667	10	—	—	—	15.0
1965	**Bill Bradley**, Princeton	2	34	.630	—	—	19	.950	24	—	—	—	43.5
1966	**Jerry Chambers**, Utah	2	25	.532	—	—	20	.833	35	—	—	—	35.0
1967	Lew Alcindor, UCLA	2	14	.609	—	—	11	.458	38	—	—	—	19.5
1968	Lew Alcindor, UCLA	2	22	.629	—	—	9	.900	34	—	—	—	26.5
1969	Lew Alcindor, UCLA	2	23	.676	—	—	16	.640	41	—	—	—	31.0
1970	Sidney Wicks, UCLA	2	15	.714	—	—	9	.600	34	—	—	—	19.5
1971	**Howard Porter**, Villanova	2	20	.488	—	—	7	.778	24	—	—	—	23.5
1972	Bill Walton, UCLA	2	20	.690	—	—	17	.739	41	—	—	—	28.5
1973	Bill Walton, UCLA	2	28	.824	—	—	2	.400	30	—	—	—	29.0
1974	David Thompson, N.C. State	2	19	.514	—	—	11	.786	17	—	—	—	24.5
1975	Richard Washington, UCLA	2	23	.548	—	—	8	.727	20	—	—	—	27.0
1976	Kent Benson, Indiana	2	17	.500	—	—	7	.636	18	—	—	—	20.5
1977	Butch Lee, Marquette	2	11	.344	—	—	8	1.000	6	2	1	1	15.0
1978	Jack Givens, Kentucky	2	28	.651	—	—	8	.667	17	4	1	3	32.0
1979	Magic Johnson, Michigan St.	2	17	.680	—	—	19	.864	17	3	0	2	26.5
1980	Darrell Griffith, Louisville	2	23	.622	—	—	11	.688	7	15	0	2	28.5
1981	Isiah Thomas, Indiana	2	14	.560	—	—	9	.818	4	9	3	4	18.5
1982	James Worthy, N. Carolina	2	20	.741	—	—	2	.286	8	9	0	4	21.0
1983	**Akeem Olajuwon**, Houston	2	16	.552	—	—	9	.643	40	3	2	5	20.5
1984	Patrick Ewing, Georgetown	2	8	.571	—	—	2	1.000	18	1	15	1	9.0
1985	Ed Pinckney, Villanova	2	8	.571	—	—	12	.750	15	6	3	0	14.0
1986	Pervis Ellison, Louisville	2	15	.600	—	—	6	.750	24	2	3	1	18.0
1987	Keith Smart, Indiana	2	14	.636	0	1	7	.778	7	7	0	2	17.5
1988	Danny Manning, Kansas	2	25	.556	0	1	6	.667	17	4	8	9	28.0
1989	Glen Rice, Michigan	2	24	.490	7	16	4	1.000	16	1	0	3	29.5
1990	Anderson Hunt, UNLV	2	19	.613	9	16	2	.500	4	9	1	1	24.5
1991	Christian Laettner, Duke	2	12	.545	1	1	21	.913	17	2	1	2	23.0
1992	Bobby Hurley, Duke	2	10	.417	7	12	8	.800	3	11	0	3	17.5
1993	Donald Williams, N. Carolina	2	15	.652	10	14	10	1.000	4	1	0	2	25.0
1994	Corliss Williamson, Arkansas	2	21	.500	0	0	10	.714	21	8	3	4	26.0
1995	Ed O'Bannon, UCLA	2	16	.457	3	8	10	.769	25	3	1	7	22.5
1996	Tony Delk, Kentucky	2	15	.417	8	16	6	.546	9	2	3	2	22.0
1997	Miles Simon, Arizona	2	17	.459	3	10	17	.773	8	6	0	1	27.0
1998	Jeff Sheppard, Kentucky	2	16	.552	4	10	7	.778	10	7	0	4	21.5
1999	Richard Hamilton, Connecticut	2	20	.513	3	7	8	.727	12	4	1	2	25.5

Most Outstanding Player (Cont.)

Year		Gm	FGM	Pct	3PTM	3PTA	FTM	Pct	Reb	Ast	Blk	Stl	PPG
2000	Mateen Cleaves, Michigan St.	2	8	.444	3	4	10	.833	6	5	0	2	14.5
2001	Shane Battier, Duke	2	13	.464	5	12	12	.706	19	8	6	2	21.5
2002	Juan Dixon, Maryland	2	16	.593	7	15	12	.800	8	5	0	7	25.5
2003	Carmelo Anthony, Syracuse	2	19	.543	6	9	9	.818	24	8	0	4	26.5
2004	Emeka Okafor, Connecticut	2	17	.654	0	0	8	.533	22	2	4	1	21.0
2005	Sean May, North Carolina	2	19	.655	0	0	10	.714	17	5	2	1	24.0
2006	Joakim Noah, Florida	2	12	.600	0	1	4	1.000	17	5	10	2	14.0
2007	Corey Brewer, Florida	2	9	.474	7	13	7	.875	10	2	3	3	16.0
2008	Mario Chalmers, Kansas	2	10	.385	3	9	6	.750	7	9	0	7	14.5

All-Time Seeds Records

All-time records of NCAA tournament seeds since tourney began seeding teams in 1979. Records are through the 2008 NCAA Tournament. Note that 1st refers to championships. 2nd refers to runners-up and FF refers to Final Four appearances not including 1st and 2nd place finishes.

Seed	W	L	Pct.	1st	2nd	FF
1	377	105	.782	16	12	23
2	268	114	.702	6	7	13
3	199	116	.632	4	5	5
4	164	119	.580	1	1	8
5	141	121	.538	0	2	3
6	154	118	.566	2	1	3
7	104	120	.463	0	0	1
8	88	119	.425	1	1	2
9	69	121	.363	0	0	1
10	77	120	.390	0	0	0
11	52	116	.310	0	0	2
12	51	116	.305	0	0	0
13	24	96	.200	0	0	0
14	17	96	.150	0	0	0
15	4	96	.040	0	0	0
16	0	96	.000	0	0	0

Note: Although a 16 seed has never won an NCAA tournament game (not including the recently added play-in round), four 15 seeds have pulled off the first round upset. They are, as follows: **2001**-Hampton over Iowa State, 58-57; **1997**-Coppin State over South Carolina, 78-65; **1993**-Santa Clara over Arizona, 64-61; **1991**-Richmond over Syracuse, 73-69. All four teams lost their second round games.

Fifteen 14 seeds have won first round games (most recently Northwestern St. in 2006). Two of those teams won their second-round game as well (Chattanooga in 1997 and Cleveland St. in 1986) before ultimately losing in the Sweet 16.

Teams in Both NCAA and NIT

Fourteen teams played in both the NCAA and NIT tournaments from 1940-52. Colorado (1940), Utah (1944), Kentucky (1949) and BYU (1951) won one of the titles, while CCNY won two in 1950, beating Bradley in both championship games.

Year		NIT	NCAA
1940	Colorado	**Won Final**	Lost 1st Rd
	Duquesne	Lost Final	Lost 2nd Rd
1944	Utah	Lost 1st Rd	**Won Final**
1949	Kentucky	Lost 2nd Rd	**Won Final**
1950	CCNY	**Won Final**	**Won Final**
	Bradley	Lost Final	Lost Final
1951	BYU	**Won Final**	Lost 2nd Rd
	St. John's	Lost 3rd Rd	Lost 2nd Rd
	N.C. State	Lost 2nd Rd	Lost 2nd Rd
	Arizona	Lost 2nd Rd	Lost 1st Rd
1952	St. John's	Lost 2nd Rd	Lost Final
	Dayton	Lost Final	Lost 1st Rd
	Duquesne	Lost 3rd Rd	Lost 2nd Rd

Seeds at the Final Four

NCAA champions in **bold** type.

Year	Seeds (Total)	Teams
1979	1,2,2,9 (14)	Indiana St., **Michigan St.**, DePaul, Pennsylvania
1980	2,5,6,8 (21)	**Louisville**, Iowa, Purdue, UCLA
1981	1,1,2,3 (7)	Virginia, LSU, No. Carolina, **Indiana**
1982	1,1,3,6 (11)	**North Carolina**, Georgetown, Louisville, Houston
1983	1,1,4,6 (12)	Houston, Louisville, Georgia, **N.C. State**
1984	1,1,2,7 (11)	Kentucky, **Georgetown**, Houston, Virginia
1985	1,1,2,8 (12)	St. John's, Georgetown, Memphis, **Villanova**
1986	1,1,2,11 (15)	Duke, Kansas, **Louisville**, LSU
1987	1,1,2,6 (10)	UNLV, **Indiana**, Syracuse, Providence
1988	1,1,2,6 (10)	Arizona, Oklahoma, Duke, **Kansas**
1989	1,2,3,3 (9)	Illinois, Duke, Seton Hall, **Michigan**
1990	1,3,4,4 (12)	**UNLV**, Duke, Georgia Tech, Arkansas
1991	1,1,2,3 (7)	UNLV, North Carolina, **Duke**, Kansas
1992	1,2,4,6 (13)	**Duke**, Indiana, Cincinnati, Michigan
1993	1,1,1,2 (5)	**No. Carolina**, Kentucky, Michigan, Kansas
1994	1,2,2,3 (8)	**Arkansas**, Arizona, Duke, Florida
1995	1,2,2,4 (9)	**UCLA**, Arkansas, North Carolina, Oklahoma St.
1996	1,1,4,5 (11)	**Kentucky**, Massachusetts, Syracuse, Mississippi St.
1997	1,1,1,4 (7)	Kentucky, North Carolina, Minnesota, **Arizona**
1998	1,2,3,3 (9)	North Carolina, **Kentucky**, Stanford, Utah
1999	1,1,1,4 (7)	**Connecticut**, Duke, Michigan St., Ohio St.
2000	1,5,8,8 (22)	**Michigan St.**, Florida, Wisconsin, North Carolina
2001	1,1,2,3 (7)	**Duke**, Michigan St., Arizona, Maryland
2002	1,1,2,5 (9)	**Maryland**, Kansas, Oklahoma, Indiana
2003	1,2,3,3 (9)	Texas, Kansas, **Syracuse**, Marquette
2004	1,2,2,3 (8)	Duke, **Connecticut**, Oklahoma St., Georgia Tech
2005	1,1,4,5 (11)	**North Carolina**, Illinois, Louisville, Michigan St.
2006	2,3,4,11 (20)	UCLA, **Florida**, LSU, George Mason
2007	1,1,2,2 (6)	**Florida**, Ohio St., UCLA, Georgetown
2008	1,1,1,1 (4)	**Kansas**, Memphis, UCLA, North Carolina

Note: teams were not seeded before 1979.

NCAA Tournament Appearances

App		W-L	F4	Championships
50	Kentucky	100-45	13	7 (1948-49, 51, 58, 78, 96, 98)
42	UCLA	98-35	18	11 (1964-65,67-73,75,95)
40	N. Carolina	96-39	17	4 (1957, 82, 93, 2005)
36	Kansas	82-36	12	3 (1952, 88, 2008)
35	Indiana	60-30	8	5 (1940,53,76,81,87)
34	Louisville	57-36	8	2 (1980,86)
32	Duke	86-29	14	3 (1991-92, 2001)
31	Syracuse	48-31	4	1 (2003)
29	Notre Dame	30-33	1	None
29	Arkansas	40-29	6	1 (1994)
29	Villanova	44-29	3	1 (1985)
28	Connecticut	42-27	2	2 (1999, 2004)
27	St. John's	27-29	2	None
27	Illinois	38-28	5	None
27	Arizona	41-26	3	1 (1997)
26	Utah	35-29	4	1 (1944)
26	Marquette	33-27	3	1 (1977)
26	Texas	32-29	3	None
25	Oklahoma	32-25	4	None
25	Temple	31-25	2	None
25	Georgetown	45-24	5	1 (1984)
24	Ohio St.	43-23	10	1 (1960)
24	Cincinnati	40-23	6	2 (1961-62)
23	Princeton	13-27	1	None
23	Pennsylvania	13-25	1	None
23	Kansas St.	28-27	4	None
23	BYU	11-26	0	None
22	DePaul	21-25	2	None
22	Oklahoma St.	37-21	6	2 (1945-46)
22	Iowa	27-24	3	None
22	N.C. State	32-21	3	2 (1974,83)
22	Maryland	36-21	2	1 (2002)
22	Michigan St.	43-21	7	1 (1989)
22	Purdue	28-21	2	None

Note: Although all NCAA tournament appearances are included above, the NCAA has officially voided the records of Villanova (4-1) and Western Ky. (4-1) in 1971; UCLA (5-1) in 1980 and again (0-1) in 1999; Oregon St. (2-3) from 1980-82; DePaul (6-4) from 1986-89; N.C. State (0-2) from 1987-88; Kentucky (2-1) and Maryland (1-1) in 1988; Missouri (3-1) in 1994; Connecticut (2-1) and Purdue (1-1) in 1996; Arizona (0-1) in 1999.

All-Time NCAA Division I Tournament Leaders

Through 2008; minimum of six games; **Last** column indicates final year played.

CAREER

Scoring

	Points	Yrs	Last	Gm	Pts
1	Christian Laettner, Duke	4	1992	23	407
2	Elvin Hayes, Houston	3	1968	13	358
3	Danny Manning, Kansas	4	1988	16	328
4	Oscar Robertson, Cincinnati	3	1960	10	324
5	Glen Rice, Michigan	4	1989	13	308
6	Lew Alcindor, UCLA	3	1969	12	304
7	Bill Bradley, Princeton	3	1965	9	303
	Corliss Williamson, Arkansas	3	1995	15	303
9	Juan Dixon, Maryland	4	2002	16	294
10	Austin Carr, Notre Dame	3	1971	7	289

	Average	Yrs	Last	Pts	Avg
1	Austin Carr, Notre Dame	3	1971	289	41.3
2	Bill Bradley, Princeton	3	1965	303	33.7
3	Oscar Robertson, Cincinnati	3	1960	324	32.4
4	Jerry West, West Virginia	3	1960	275	30.6
5	Bob Pettit, LSU	2	1954	183	30.5
6	Dan Issel, Kentucky	3	1970	176	29.3
	Jim McDaniels, Western Ky	2	1971	176	29.3
8	Dwight Lamar, SW Louisiana	2	1973	175	29.2
9	Bo Kimble, Loyola-CA	3	1990	204	29.1
10	David Robinson, Navy	3	1987	200	28.6

Rebounds

	Total	Yrs	Last	Gm	No
1	Elvin Hayes, Houston	3	1968	13	222
2	Lew Alcindor, UCLA	3	1969	12	201
3	Jerry Lucas, Ohio St.	3	1962	12	197
4	Nick Collison, Kansas	4	2003	16	181
5	Bill Walton, UCLA	3	1974	12	176
6	Christian Laettner, Duke	4	1992	23	169
7	Tim Duncan, Wake Forest	4	1997	11	165
8	Paul Hogue, Cincinnati	3	1962	12	160
9	Sam Lacey, New Mexico St.	3	1970	11	157
10	Derrick Coleman, Syracuse	4	1990	14	155

	Average	Yrs	Last	Reb	Avg
1	Johnny Green, Michigan St.	2	1959	118	19.7
2	Artis Gilmore, Jacksonville	2	1971	115	19.2
3	Paul Silas, Creighton	3	1964	111	18.5
4	Len Chappell, Wake Forest	2	1962	137	17.1
5	Elvin Hayes, Houston	3	1968	222	17.1
6	Lew Alcindor, UCLA	3	1969	201	16.8
7	Jerry Lucas, Ohio St.	3	1962	197	16.4
8	Tim Duncan, Wake Forest	4	1997	165	15.0
9	Bill Walton, UCLA	3	1974	176	14.7
10	Sam Lacey, New Mexico St.	3	1970	157	14.3

3-Pt Field Goals

	Total	Yrs	Last	Gm	No
1	Lee Humphrey, Florida	4	2007	14	47
2	Bobby Hurley, Duke	4	1993	20	42
3	Tony Delk, Kentucky	4	1996	17	40
4	Jeff Fryer, Loyola-CA	3	1990	7	38
	Donald Williams, North Carolina	4	1995	15	38
	Juan Dixon, Maryland	4	2002	16	38

Assists

	Total	Yrs	Last	Gm	No
1	Bobby Hurley, Duke	4	1993	20	145
2	Ed Cota, N. Carolina	4	2000	16	118
3	Sherman Douglas, Syracuse	4	1989	14	106
4	Greg Anthony, UNLV	3	1991	15	100
	Aaron Miles, Kansas	3	2004	15	100

SINGLE TOURNAMENT

Scoring

	Points	Year	Gm	Pts
1	Glen Rice, Michigan	1989	6	184
2	Bill Bradley, Princeton	1965	5	177
3	Elvin Hayes, Houston	1968	5	167
4	Danny Manning, Kansas	1988	6	163
5	Hal Lear, Temple	1956	5	160
	Jerry West, West Virginia	1959	5	160

	Average	Year	Gm	Pts	Avg
1	Austin Carr, Notre Dame	1970	3	158	52.7
2	Austin Carr, Notre Dame	1971	3	125	41.7
3	Jerry Chambers, Utah	1966	4	143	35.8
	Bo Kimble, Loyola-CA	1990	4	143	35.8
5	Bill Bradley, Princeton	1965	5	177	35.4
6	Clyde Lovellette, Kansas	1952	4	141	35.3

Rebounds

	Total	Year	Gm	No	Avg
1	Elvin Hayes, Houston	1968	5	97	19.4
2	Artis Gilmore, Jacksonville	1970	5	93	18.6
3	Elgin Baylor, Seattle	1958	5	91	18.2
4	Sam Lacey, New Mexico St.	1970	5	90	18.0
5	Clarence Glover, Western Ky	1971	5	89	17.8
6	Len Chappell, Wake Forest	1962	5	86	17.2

Assists

	Total	Year	Gm	No	Avg
1	Mark Wade, UNLV	1987	5	61	12.2
2	Rumeal Robinson, Michigan	1989	6	56	9.3
3	T.J. Ford, Texas	2003	5	51	10.2
4	Sherman Douglas, Syracuse	1987	6	49	8.2
5	Bobby Hurley, Duke	1992	6	47	7.8
6	Lazarus Sims, Syracuse	1996	6	46	7.7

SINGLE GAME

Scoring

	Points	Year	Pts
1	Austin Carr, Notre Dame vs Ohio Univ	1970	61
2	Bill Bradley, Princeton vs Wichita St.	1965	58
3	Oscar Robertson, Cincinnati vs Arkansas	1958	56
4	Austin Carr, Notre Dame vs Kentucky	1970	52
	Austin Carr, Notre Dame vs TCU	1971	52
6	David Robinson, Navy vs Michigan	1987	50
7	Elvin Hayes, Houston vs Loyola-IL	1968	49
8	Hal Lear, Temple vs SMU	1956	48
9	Austin Carr, Notre Dame vs Houston	1971	47
10	Dave Corzine, DePaul vs Louisville	1978	46
11	Bob Houbregs, Washington vs Seattle	1953	45
	Austin Carr, Notre Dame vs Iowa	1970	45
	Bo Kimble, Loyola-CA vs New Mexico St.	1990	45
14	Seven players tied with 44 each.		

Rebounds

	Total	Year	No
1	Fred Cohen, Temple vs UConn	1956	34
2	Nate Thurmond, Bowl. Green vs Miss. St.	1963	31
3	Jerry Lucas, Ohio St. vs Kentucky	1961	30
4	Toby Kimball, UConn vs St. Joseph's-PA	1965	29
5	Elvin Hayes, Houston vs Pacific	1966	28
6	Four players tied with 27 each.		

Assists

	Total	Year	No
1	Mark Wade, UNLV vs Indiana	1987	18
2	Sam Crawford, N. Mexico St. vs Nebraska	1993	16
3	Kenny Patterson, DePaul vs Syracuse	1985	15
	Keith Smart, Indiana vs Auburn	1987	15
	Pepe Sanchez, Temple vs. Lafayette	2000	15

SINGLE FINAL FOUR GAME

Letters in the **Year** column indicate the following: C for Consolation Game, F for Final and S for Semifinal.

Scoring

	Points	Year	Pts
1	Bill Bradley, Princeton vs Wichita St	1965-C	58
2	Hal Lear, Temple vs SMU	1956-C	48
3	Bill Walton, UCLA vs Memphis St	1973-F	44
4	Bob Houbregs, Washington vs LSU	1953-C	42
	Jack Egan, St. Joseph's-PA vs Utah	1961-C	42*
	Gail Goodrich, UCLA vs Michigan	1965-C	42
7	Jack Givens, Kentucky vs Duke	1978-F	41
8	Oscar Robertson, Cincinnati vs L'ville	1959-C	39
	Al Wood, N. Carolina vs Virginia	1981-S	39
10	Jerry West, West Va. vs Louisville	1959-S	38
	Jerry Chambers, Utah vs Texas Western	1966-S	38
	Freddie Banks, UNLV vs Indiana	1987-S	38

*Four overtimes.

3-Pt Field Goals

	Total	Year	No
1	Freddie Banks, UNLV vs. Indiana	1987-S	10
2	Four players tied with 7 each.		

Rebounds

	Total	Year	No
1	Bill Russell, San Francisco vs Iowa	1956-F	27
2	Elvin Hayes, Houston vs UCLA	1967-S	24
3	Bill Russell, San Francisco vs SMU	1956-S	23
4	Elgin Baylor, Seattle vs Kansas St.	1958-S	22
	Tom Sanders, NYU vs Ohio St.	1960-S	22
	Larry Kenon, Memphis vs Providence	1973-S	22
	Akeem Olajuwon, Houston vs Louisville	1983-S	22
8	Bill Spivey, Kentucky vs Kansas St.	1951-C	21
	Lew Alcindor, UCLA vs Drake	1969-C	21
	Artis Gilmore, Jacksonville vs. St. Bonav.	1970-S	21
	Bill Walton, UCLA vs Louisville	1972-S	21
	Nick Collison, Kansas vs Syracuse	2003-C	21

Assists

	Total	Year	No
1	Mark Wade, UNLV vs Indiana	1987-S	18
2	T.J. Ford, Texas vs. Syracuse	2003-C	13
3	Rumeal Robinson, Michigan vs Illinois	1989-S	12
	Edgar Padilla, UMass vs Ky.	1996-S	12
5	Michael Jackson, G'town vs St. John's	1985-S	11
	Milt Wagner, Louisville vs LSU	1986-S	11
	Rumeal Robinson, Mich. vs Seton Hall	1989-F	11*
	Steve Blake, Maryland vs Kansas	2002-S	11

*Overtime.

Blocked Shots

	Total	Year	No
1	Danny Manning, Kansas vs Duke	1988-S	6
	Marcus Camby, UMass vs Kentucky	1996-S	6
	Joakim Noah, Florida vs UCLA	2006-C	6

Steals

	Total	Year	No
1	Tommy Amaker, Duke vs. Louisville	1986-C	7
	Mookie Blaylock, Oklahoma vs. Kansas	1988-C	7
3	Gilbert Arenas, Arizona vs Michigan St.	2001-S	6

Triple Doubles

	Total	Year	No
1	Oscar Robertson, Cincinnati vs. Louisville	1959-C	1
	Magic Johnson, Mich. St. vs. Penn	1979-S	1

Note: Robertson had 39 pts, 17 rebs and 10 asts; Johnson had 29 pts, 10 rebs, 10 asts

Most Popular Final Four Sites

The NCAA has staged its Men's Division I championship—the Final Two (1939-51) and Final Four (since 1952)—at 33 different arenas and indoor stadiums in 27 different cities. The following facilities have all hosted the event more than twice.

No	Arena	Years
9	Municipal Auditorium (KC)	1940-42, 53-55, 57, 61, 64
7	Madison Sq. Garden (NYC)	1943-48, 50
6	Freedom Hall (Louisville)	1958-59, 62-63, 67, 69
4	Superdome (New Orleans)	1982, 87, 93, 2003
	RCA Dome (Indianapolis)	1991, 97, 2000, 2006
3	Kingdome (Seattle)	1984, 89, 95
3	Alamodome (San Antonio)	1998, 2004, 2008

NIT Championship

The National Invitation Tournament began under the sponsorship of the Metropolitan New York Basketball Writers Association in 1938. The NIT is now administered by the Metropolitan Intercollegiate Basketball Association. All championship games have been played at Madison Square Garden. **Multiple winners:** St. John's (6); Bradley (4); Michigan (3); BYU, Dayton, Kentucky, LIU-Brooklyn, Minnesota, Ohio St., Providence, South Carolina, Temple, Tulsa, Virginia and Virginia Tech (2).

Year	Winner	Score	Loser	Year	Winner	Score	Loser
1938	Temple	60-36	Colorado	1974	Purdue	97-81	Utah
1939	LIU-Brooklyn	44-32	Loyola-IL	1975	Princeton	80-69	Providence
1940	Colorado	51-40	Duquesne	1976	Kentucky	71-67	NC-Charlotte
1941	LIU-Brooklyn	56-42	Ohio Univ.	1977	St. Bonaventure	94-91	Houston
1942	West Virginia	47-45	Western Ky.	1978	Texas	101-93	N.C. State
1943	St. John's	48-27	Toledo	1979	Indiana	53-52	Purdue
1944	St. John's	47-39	DePaul	1980	Virginia	58-55	Minnesota
1945	DePaul	71-54	Bowling Green	1981	Tulsa	86-84 (OT)	Syracuse
1946	Kentucky	46-45	Rhode Island	1982	Bradley	67-58	Purdue
1947	Utah	49-45	Kentucky	1983	Fresno St.	69-60	DePaul
1948	Saint Louis	65-52	NYU	1984	Michigan	83-63	Notre Dame
1949	San Francisco	48-47	Loyola-IL	1985	UCLA	65-62	Indiana
1950	CCNY	69-61	Bradley	1986	Ohio St.	73-63	Wyoming
1951	BYU	62-43	Dayton	1987	Southern Miss.	84-80	La Salle
1952	La Salle	75-64	Dayton	1988	Connecticut	72-67	Ohio St.
1953	Seton Hall	58-46	St. John's	1989	St. John's	73-65	Saint Louis
1954	Holy Cross	71-62	Duquesne	1990	Vanderbilt	74-72	Saint Louis
1955	Duquesne	70-58	Dayton	1991	Stanford	78-72	Oklahoma
1956	Louisville	93-80	Dayton	1992	Virginia	81-76 (OT)	Notre Dame
1957	Bradley	84-83	Memphis St.	1993	Minnesota	62-61	Georgetown
1958	Xavier-OH	78-74 (OT)	Dayton	1994	Villanova	80-73	Vanderbilt
1959	St. John's	76-71 (OT)	Bradley	1995	Virginia Tech	65-64 (OT)	Marquette
1960	Bradley	88-72	Providence	1996	Nebraska	60-56	St. Joseph's
1961	Providence	62-59	Saint Louis	1997	Michigan	82-72	Florida St.
1962	Dayton	73-67	St. John's	1998	Minnesota	79-72	Penn St.
1963	Providence	81-66	Canisius	1999	California	61-60	Clemson
1964	Bradley	86-54	New Mexico	2000	Wake Forest	71-61	Notre Dame
1965	St. John's	55-51	Villanova	2001	Tulsa	79-60	Alabama
1966	BYU	97-84	NYU	2002	Memphis	72-62	South Carolina
1967	Southern Illinois	71-56	Marquette	2003	St. John's	70-67	Georgetown
1968	Dayton	61-48	Kansas	2004	Michigan	62-55	Rutgers
1969	Temple	89-76	Boston Coll.	2005	South Carolina	60-57	St. Joseph's
1970	Marquette	65-53	St. John's	2006	South Carolina	76-64	Michigan
1971	North Carolina	84-66	Georgia Tech	2007	West Virginia	78-73	Clemson
1972	Maryland	100-69	Niagara	2008	Ohio St.	92-85	Massachusetts
1973	Virginia Tech	92-91 (OT)	Notre Dame				

Most Valuable Player

A Most Valuable Player has been selected every year of the NIT tournament. Winners who did not play for the tournament champion are listed in **bold** type. Note the all-time team listed below was selected by a media panel on Mar. 15, 1997.
   Multiple winners: None. However, Tom Gola of La Salle is the only player to be named MVP in the NIT (1952) and Most Outstanding Player of the NCAA tournament (1954).

Year
1938 Don Shields, Temple
1939 **Bill Lloyd**, St. John's
1940 Bob Doll, Colorado
1941 **Frank Baumholtz**, Ohio U.
1942 Rudy Baric, West Virginia
1943 Harry Boykoff, St. John's
1944 Bill Kotsores, St. John's
1945 George Mikan, DePaul
1946 Ernie Calverley, Rhode Island
1947 Vern Gardner, Utah
1948 Ed Macauley, Saint Louis
1949 Don Lofgan, San Francisco
1950 Ed Warner, CCNY
1951 Roland Minson, BYU
1952 Tom Gola, La Salle
   & Norm Grekin, La Salle
1953 Walter Dukes, Seton Hall
1954 Togo Palazzi, Holy Cross
1955 **Maurice Stokes**, St. Francis-PA
1956 Charlie Tyra, Louisville
1957 **Win Wilfong**, Memphis St.
1958 Hank Stein, Xavier-OH
1959 Tony Jackson, St. John's
1960 **Lenny Wilkens**, Providence
1961 Vinny Ernst, Providence

Year
1962 Bill Chmielewski, Dayton
1963 Ray Flynn, Providence
1964 Lavern Tart, Bradley
1965 Ken McIntyre, St. John's
1966 **Bill Melchionni**, Villanova
1967 Walt Frazier, So. Illinois
1968 Don May, Dayton
1969 **Terry Driscoll**, Boston College
1970 Dean Meminger, Marquette
1971 Bill Chamberlain, N. Carolina
1972 Tom McMillen, Maryland
1973 **John Shumate**, Notre Dame
1974 **Mike Sojourner**, Utah
1975 **Ron Lee**, Oregon
1976 **Cedric Maxwell**, NC-Charlotte
1977 Greg Sanders, St. Bonaventure
1978 Ron Baxter, Texas
   & Jim Krivacs, Texas
1979 Clarence Carter, Indiana
   & Ray Tolbert, Indiana
1980 Ralph Sampson, Virginia
1981 Greg Stewart, Tulsa
1982 Mitchell Anderson, Bradley
1983 Ron Anderson, Fresno St.
1984 Tim McCormick, Michigan

Year
1985 Reggie Miller, UCLA
1986 Brad Sellers, Ohio St.
1987 Randolph Keys, So. Miss.
1988 Phil Gamble, Connecticut
1989 Jayson Williams, St. John's
1990 Scott Draud, Vanderbilt
1991 Adam Keefe, Stanford
1992 Bryant Stith, Virginia
1993 Voshon Lenard, Minnesota
1994 **Doremus Bennerman**, Siena
1995 Shawn Smith, Va. Tech
1996 Erick Strickland, Nebraska
1997 Robert Traylor, Michigan
1998 Kevin Clark, Minnesota
1999 Sean Lampley, California
2000 Robert O'Kelley, Wake Forest
2001 Marcus Hill, Tulsa
2002 Dajuan Wagner, Memphis
2003 Marcus Hatten, St. John's
2004 Daniel Horton, Michigan
2005 Carlos Powell, South Carolina
2006 Renaldo Balkman, South Carolina
2007 Frank Young, West Virginia
2008 Kosta Koufos, Ohio St.

All-Time Winningest Division I Teams
Top 25 Winning Percentage

Division I schools with best winning percentages through 2007-08 season (including tournament games). Years in Division I only; minimum 20 years. NCAA tournament columns indicate years in tournament, record and number of championships.

		First Year	Yrs	Games	Won	Lost	Tied	Pct	NCAA Tourney Yrs	W-L	Titles
1	Kentucky	1903	105	2598	1966	631	1	.757	50	100-45	7
2	North Carolina	1911	98	2649	1950	699	0	.736	40	96-39	4
3	UNLV	1959	50	1455	1037	418	0	.713	16	33-15	1
4	Kansas	1899	110	2728	1943	785	0	.712	36	82-36	3
5	Duke	1906	103	2652	1846	806	0	.696	32	86-29	3
6	UCLA	1920	89	2363	1646	717	0	.697	42	98-35	11
7	Syracuse	1901	107	2516	1725	796	0	.686	31	15-20	1
8	Western Kentucky	1915	89	2348	1577	771	0	.672	19	15-20	0
9	St. John's	1908	101	2520	1670	850	0	.663	27	27-29	0
10	Utah	1909	100	2461	1613	848	0	.655	26	35-29	1
11	Louisville	1912	94	2381	1556	825	0	.654	34	57-36	2
12	Illinois	1906	103	2428	1585	843	0	.653	27	38-28	0
13	Indiana	1901	108	2519	1635	884	0	.649	35	60-30	5
14	Arizona	1905	103	2392	1547	844	1	.647	27	41-26	1
15	Missouri St.	1909	96	2300	1484	813	0	.647	6	3-6	0
16	Arkansas	1924	85	2279	1473	806	0	.646	29	40-29	1
17	Notre Dame	1898	103	2524	1630	893	1	.646	29	30-33	0
18	Temple	1895	112	2637	1689	948	0	.641	25	31-25	0
19	Pennsylvania	1897	108	2580	1647	931	2	.639	23	13-25	0
20	Connecticut	1901	105	2302	1468	834	0	.638	28	42-27	2
21	Villanova	1921	88	2317	1475	842	0	.637	29	44-29	1
22	Murray St.	1926	83	2172	1378	794	0	.634	13	1-13	0
23	DePaul	1924	85	2128	1343	785	0	.631	22	21-25	0
24	Weber St.	1963	46	1317	831	486	0	.631	14	6-15	0
25	Cincinnati	1902	107	2435	1535	900	0	.630	24	40-23	2

Top 35 All-Time Victories

Division I schools with most victories through 2007-08 (including postseason tournaments). Minimum 20 years in Division I.

		Wins			Wins			Wins			Wins
1	Kentucky	1966	10	Indiana	1635	19	BYU	1553	28	Villanova	1475
2	North Carolina	1950	11	Notre Dame	1630	20	Arizona	1547	29	Arkansas	1473
3	Kansas	1943	12	Utah	1613	21	Princeton	1539	30	Oklahoma	1469
4	Duke	1846	13	Illinois	1585	22	Purdue	1538	31	Connecticut	1468
5	Syracuse	1725	14	Western Ky.	1577	23	Cincinnati	1535	32	Alabama	1464
6	Temple	1689	15	Oregon St.	1576	24	West Virginia	1527	33	St. Joseph's	1460
7	St. John's	1670	16	Washington	1564	25	N.C. State	1518		Georgetown	1460
8	Penn	1647	17	Texas	1563	26	Bradley	1516	35	Oklahoma St.	1458
9	UCLA	1646	18	Louisville	1556	27	Missouri St.	1484			

Top 25 Single-Season Victories

Division I schools with most victories in a season through 2007-08 (including postseason tournaments). NCAA champions in **bold** type.

		Year	W-L		Year	W-L
1	Memphis	2008	38-2	Ohio St.	2007	35-4
2	UNLV	1987	37-2	UCLA	2008	35-4
	Duke	1999	37-2	**Florida**	2007	35-5
	Illinois	2005	37-2	**UNLV**	1990	35-5
	Duke	1986	37-3	Kentucky	1997	35-5
	Kansas	2008	37-3	22 UNLV	1991	34-1
7	**Kentucky**	1948	36-3	**Connecticut**	1999	34-2
	N. Carolina	2008	36-3	Duke	1992	34-2
9	Massachusetts*	1996	35-2	**Kentucky**	1996	34-2
	Georgetown	1985	35-3	Kansas	1997	34-2
	Arizona	1988	35-3	Kentucky	1947	34-3
	Duke	2001	35-4	**Georgetown**	1984	34-3
	Kansas	1986	35-4	Arkansas	1991	34-4
	Kansas	1998	35-4	**N. Carolina**	1993	34-4
	Kentucky	1998	35-4	N. Carolina	1998	34-4
	Oklahoma	1988	35-4			

*NCAA later stripped Massachusetts of its four 1996 tournament victories after learning that center Marcus Camby accepted gifts from an agent.

Division I Winning Streaks
Full Season
(including tournaments)

No		Seasons	Broken by	Score
88	UCLA	1971-74	Notre Dame	71-70
60	San Francisco	1955-57	Illinois	62-33
47	UCLA	1966-68	Houston	71-69
45	UNLV	1990-91	Duke	79-77
44	Texas	1913-17	Rice	24-18
43	Seton Hall	1939-41	LIU-Bklyn	49-26
43	LIU-Brooklyn	1935-37	Stanford	45-31
41	UCLA	1968-69	USC	46-44
39	Marquette	1970-71	Ohio St.	60-59
37	Cincinnati	1962-63	Wichita St.	65-64
37	North Carolina	1957-58	West Virginia	75-64

Home Court

No		Seasons	Broken By	Score
129	Kentucky	1943-55	Georgia Tech	59-58
99	St. Bonaventure	1948-61	Detroit	77-70
98	UCLA	1970-76	Oregon	65-45
86	Cincinnati	1957-64	Kansas	51-47
81	Arizona	1945-51	Kansas St.	76-57
81	Marquette	1967-73	Notre Dame	71-69
80	Lamar	1978-84	Louisiana Tech	68-65

Associated Press Final Polls

Taken before NCAA, NIT and Collegiate Commissioner's Association (1974-75) tournaments.

The Associated Press introduced its weekly college basketball poll of sportswriters (later, sportswriters and broadcasters) during the 1948-49 season.

Since the NCAA Division I tournament has determined the national champion since 1939, the final AP poll ranks the nation's best teams through the regular season and conference tournaments.

Except for four seasons (see AP Post-Tournament Final Polls), the final AP poll has been released prior to the NCAA and NIT tournaments and has gone from a Top 10 (1949 and 1963-67) to a Top 20 (1950-62 and 1968-89) to a Top 25 (since 1990). Tournament champions are in **bold** type.

1949

		Before Tourns	Head Coach	Final Record
1	**Kentucky**	.29-1	Adolph Rupp	32-2
2	Oklahoma A&M	.21-4	Hank Iba	23-5
3	Saint Louis	.22-3	Eddie Hickey	22-4
4	Illinois	.19-3	Harry Combes	21-4
5	Western Ky.	.25-3	Ed Diddle	25-4
6	Minnesota	.18-3	Ozzie Cowles	same
7	Bradley	.25-6	Forddy Anderson	27-8
8	**San Francisco**	.21-5	Pete Newell	25-5
9	Tulane	.24-4	Cliff Wells	same
10	Bowling Green	.21-6	Harold Anderson	24-7

NCAA Final Four (at Edmundson Pavilion, Seattle): **Third Place**—Illinois 57, Oregon St. 53. **Championship** —Kentucky 46, Oklahoma A&M 36.

NIT Final Four (at Madison Square Garden): **Semifinals**—San Francisco 49, Bowling Green 39; Loyola-IL 55, Bradley 50. **Third Place**—Bowling Green 82, Bradley 77. **Championship**—San Francisco 48, Loyola-IL 47.

1951

		Before Tourns	Head Coach	Final Record
1	**Kentucky**	.28-2	Adolph Rupp	32-2
2	Oklahoma A&M	.27-4	Hank Iba	29-6
3	Columbia	.22-0	Lou Rossini	22-1
4	Kansas St.	.22-3	Jack Gardner	25-4
5	Illinois	.19-4	Harry Combes	22-5
6	Bradley	.32-6	Forddy Anderson	same
7	Indiana	.19-3	Branch McCracken	same
8	N.C. State	.29-4	Everett Case	30-7
9	St. John's	.22-3	Frank McGuire	26-5
10	Saint Louis	.21-7	Eddie Hickey	22-8
11	**BYU**	.22-8	Stan Watts	26-10
12	Arizona	.24-4	Fred Enke	24-6
13	Dayton	.24-4	Tom Blackburn	27-5
14	Toledo	.23-8	Jerry Bush	same
15	Washington	.22-5	Tippy Dye	24-6
16	Murray St.	.21-6	Harlan Hodges	same
17	Cincinnati	.18-3	John Wiethe	18-4
18	Siena	.19-8	Dan Cunha	same
19	USC	.21-6	Forrest Twogood	same
20	Villanova	.25-6	Al Severance	25-7

NCAA Final Four (at Williams Arena, Minneapolis): **Third Place**—Illinois 61, Oklahoma St. 46. **Championship**—Kentucky 68, Kansas St. 58.

NIT Final Four (at Madison Sq. Garden): **Semifinals**—Dayton 69, St. John's 62 (OT); BYU 69, Seton Hall 59. **Third Place**—St. John's 70, Seton Hall 68 (2 OT). **Championship**—BYU 62, Dayton 43.

1950

		Before Tourns	Head Coach	Final Record
1	Bradley	.28-3	Forddy Anderson	32-5
2	Ohio St.	.21-3	Tippy Dye	22-4
3	Kentucky	.25-4	Adolph Rupp	25-5
4	Holy Cross	.27-2	Buster Sheary	27-4
5	N.C. State	.25-5	Everett Case	27-6
6	Duquesne	.22-5	Dudey Moore	23-6
7	UCLA	.24-5	John Wooden	24-7
8	Western Ky.	.24-5	Ed Diddle	25-6
9	St. John's	.23-4	Frank McGuire	24-5
10	La Salle	.20-3	Ken Loeffler	21-4
11	Villanova	.25-4	Al Severance	same
12	San Francisco	.19-6	Pete Newell	19-7
13	LIU-Brooklyn	.20-4	Clair Bee	20-5
14	Kansas St.	.17-7	Jack Gardner	same
15	Arizona	.26-4	Fred Enke	26-5
16	Wisconsin	.17-5	Bud Foster	same
17	San Jose St.	.21-7	Walter McPherson	same
18	Washington St.	.19-13	Jack Friel	same
19	Kansas	.14-11	Phog Allen	same
20	Indiana	.17-5	Branch McCracken	same

Note: Unranked **CCNY**, coached by Nat Holman, won both the NCAAs and NIT. The Beavers entered the postseason at 17-5 and had a final record of 24-5.

NCAA Final Four (at Madison Square Garden): **Third Place**—N. Carolina St. 53, Baylor 41. **Championship**— CCNY 71, Bradley 68.

NIT Final Four (at Madison Square Garden): **Semifinals**—Bradley 83, St. John's 72; CCNY 62, Duquesne 52. **Third Place**—St. John's 69, Duquesne 67 (OT). **Championship**—CCNY 69, Bradley 61.

1952

		Before Tourns	Head Coach	Final Record
1	Kentucky	.28-2	Adolph Rupp	29-3
2	Illinois	.19-3	Harry Combes	22-4
3	Kansas St.	.19-5	Jack Gardner	same
4	Duquesne	.21-1	Dudey Moore	23-4
5	Saint Louis	.22-6	Eddie Hickey	23-8
6	Washington	.25-6	Tippy Dye	same
7	Iowa	.19-3	Bucky O'Connor	same
8	**Kansas**	.24-3	Phog Allen	28-3
9	West Virginia	.23-4	Red Brown	same
10	St. John's	.22-3	Frank McGuire	25-5
11	Dayton	.24-3	Tom Blackburn	28-5
12	Duke	.24-6	Harold Bradley	same
13	Holy Cross	.23-3	Buster Sheary	24-4
14	Seton Hall	.25-2	Honey Russell	25-3
15	St. Bonaventure	.19-5	Ed Melvin	21-6
16	Wyoming	.27-6	Everett Shelton	28-7
17	Louisville	.20-5	Peck Hickman	20-6
18	Seattle	.29-7	Al Brightman	29-8
19	UCLA	.19-10	John Wooden	19-12
20	SW Texas St.	.30-1	Milton Jowers	same

Note: Unranked La Salle, coached by Ken Loeffler, won the NIT. The Explorers entered the postseason at 21-7 and had a final record of 25-7.

NCAA Final Four (at Edmundson Pavillion, Seattle): **Semifinals**—St. John's 61, Illinois 59; Kansas 74, Santa Clara 59. **Third Place**—Illinois 67, Santa Clara 64. **Championship**—Kansas 80, St. John's 63.

NIT Final Four (at Madison Sq. Garden): **Semifinals**—La Salle 59, Duquesne 46; Dayton 69, St. Bonaventure 62. **Third Place**—St. Bonaventure 48, Duquesne 34. **Championship**—La Salle 75, Dayton 64.

Associated Press Final Polls (Cont.)

1953

		Before Tourns	Head Coach	Final Record
1	Indiana	.18-3	Branch McCracken	23-3
2	La Salle	.25-2	Ken Loeffler	25-3
3	Seton Hall	.28-2	Honey Russell	31-2
4	Washington	.27-2	Tippy Dye	30-3
5	LSU	.22-1	Harry Rabenhorst	24-3
6	Kansas	.16-5	Phog Allen	19-6
7	Oklahoma A&M	.22-6	Hank Iba	23-7
	Kansas St.	.17-4	Jack Gardner	same
9	Western Ky.	.25-5	Ed Diddle	25-6
10	Illinois	.18-4	Harry Combes	same
11	Oklahoma City	.18-4	Doyle Parrick	18-6
12	N.C. State	.26-6	Everett Case	same
13	Notre Dame	.17-4	John Jordan	19-5
14	Louisville	.21-5	Peck Hickman	22-6
	Seattle	.27-3	Al Brightman	29-4
16	Miami-OH	.17-5	Bill Rohr	17-6
17	Eastern Ky.	.16-8	Paul McBrayer	16-9
18	Duquesne	.18-7	Dudey Moore	21-8
	Navy	.16-4	Ben Carnevale	16-5
20	Holy Cross	.18-5	Buster Sheary	20-6

NCAA Final Four (at Municipal Auditorium, Kansas City): **Semifinals**—Indiana 80, LSU 67; Kansas 79, Washington 53. **Third Place**—Washington 88, LSU 69. **Championship**—Indiana 69, Kansas 68.
NIT Final Four (at Madison Sq. Garden): **Semifinals**—Seton Hall 74, Manhattan 56; St. John's 64, Duquesne 55. **Third Place**—Duquesne 81, Manhattan 67. **Championship**—Seton Hall 58, St. John's 46.

1955

		Before Tourns	Head Coach	Final Record
1	San Francisco	.23-1	Phil Woolpert	28-1
2	Kentucky	.22-2	Adolph Rupp	23-3
3	La Salle	.22-4	Ken Loeffler	26-5
4	N.C. State	.28-4	Everett Case	same
5	Iowa	.17-5	Bucky O'Connor	19-7
6	Duquesne	.19-4	Dudey Moore	22-4
7	Utah	.23-3	Jack Gardner	24-4
8	Marquette	.22-2	Jack Nagle	24-3
9	Dayton	.23-3	Tom Blackburn	25-4
10	Oregon St.	.21-7	Slats Gill	22-8
11	Minnesota	.15-7	Ozzie Cowles	same
12	Alabama	.19-5	Johnny Dee	same
13	UCLA	.21-5	John Wooden	same
14	G. Washington	.24-6	Bill Reinhart	same
15	Colorado	.16-5	Bebe Lee	19-6
16	Tulsa	.20-6	Clarence Iba	21-7
17	Vanderbilt	.16-6	Bob Polk	same
18	Illinois	.17-5	Harry Combes	same
19	West Virginia	.19-10	Fred Schaus	19-11
20	Saint Louis	.19-7	Eddie Hickey	20-8

NCAA Final Four (at Municipal Auditorium, Kansas City): **Semifinals**—La Salle 76, Iowa 73; San Francisco 62, Colorado 50. **Third Place**—Colorado 75, Iowa 74. **Championship**—San Francisco 77, La Salle 63.
NIT Final Four (at Madison Square Garden): **Semifinals**—Dayton 79, St. Francis-PA 73 (OT); Duquesne 65, Cincinnati 51. **Third Place**—Cincinnati 96, St. Francis-PA 91 (OT). **Championship**—Duquesne 70, Dayton 58.

1954

		Before Tourns	Head Coach	Final Record
1	Kentucky	.25-0	Adolph Rupp	same*
2	Indiana	.19-3	Branch McCracken	20-4
3	Duquesne	.24-2	Dudey Moore	26-3
4	Western Ky.	.28-1	Ed Diddle	29-3
5	Oklahoma A&M	.23-4	Hank Iba	24-5
6	Notre Dame	.20-2	John Jordan	22-3
7	Kansas	.16-5	Phog Allen	same
8	Holy Cross	.23-2	Buster Sheary	26-2
9	LSU	.21-3	Harry Rabenhorst	21-5
10	La Salle	.21-4	Ken Loeffler	26-4
11	Iowa	.17-5	Bucky O'Connor	same
12	Duke	.22-6	Harold Bradley	same
13	Colorado A&M	.22-5	Bill Strannigan	22-7
14	Illinois	.17-5	Harry Combes	same
15	Wichita	.27-3	Ralph Miller	27-4
16	Seattle	.26-1	Al Brightman	26-2
17	N.C. State	.26-6	Everett Case	28-7
18	Dayton	.24-6	Tom Blackburn	25-7
	Minnesota	.17-5	Ozzie Cowles	same
20	Oregon St.	.19-10	Slats Gill	same
	UCLA	.18-7	John Wooden	same
	USC	.17-12	Forrest Twogood	19-14

*Kentucky turned down invitation to NCAA tournament after NCAA declared seniors Cliff Hagan, Frank Ramsey and Lou Tsioropoulos ineligible for postseason play.
NCAA Final Four (at Municipal Auditorium, Kansas City): **Semifinals**—La Salle 69, Penn St. 54; Bradley 74, USC 72. **Third Place**—Penn St. 70, USC 61. **Championship**—La Salle 92, Bradley 76.
NIT Final Four (at Madison Square Garden): **Semifinals**—Duquesne 66, Niagara 51; Holy Cross 75, Western Ky. 69. **Third Place**—Niagara 71, Western Ky. 65. **Championship**—Holy Cross 71, Duquesne 62.

1956

		Before Tourns	Head Coach	Final Record
1	San Francisco	.25-0	Phil Woolpert	29-0
2	N.C. State	.24-3	Everett Case	24-4
3	Dayton	.23-3	Tom Blackburn	25-4
4	Iowa	.17-5	Bucky O'Connor	20-6
5	Alabama	.21-3	Johnny Dee	same
6	Louisville	.23-3	Peck Hickman	26-3
7	SMU	.22-2	Doc Hayes	25-4
8	UCLA	.21-5	John Wooden	22-6
9	Kentucky	.19-5	Adolph Rupp	20-6
10	Illinois	.18-4	Harry Combes	same
11	Oklahoma City	.18-6	Abe Lemons	20-7
12	Vanderbilt	.19-4	Bob Polk	same
13	North Carolina	.18-5	Frank McGuire	same
14	Holy Cross	.22-4	Roy Leenig	22-5
15	Temple	.23-3	Harry Litwack	27-4
16	Wake Forest	.19-9	Murray Greason	same
17	Duke	.19-7	Harold Bradley	same
18	Utah	.21-5	Jack Gardner	22-6
19	Oklahoma A&M	.18-8	Hank Iba	18-9
20	West Virginia	.21-8	Fred Schaus	21-9

NCAA Final Four (at McGaw Hall, Evanston, IL): **Semifinals**—Iowa 83, Temple 76; San Francisco 76, SMU 68. **Third Place**—Temple 90, SMU 81. **Championship**—San Francisco 83, Iowa 71.
NIT Final Four (at Madison Square Garden): **Semifinals**—Dayton 89, St. Francis-NY 58; Louisville 89, St. Joseph's-PA 79. **Third Place**—St. Joseph's-PA 93, St. Francis-NY 82. **Championship**—Louisville 93, Dayton 80.

1957

		Before Tourns	Head Coach	Final Record
1	**N. Carolina**	.27-0	Frank McGuire	32-0
2	Kansas	.21-2	Dick Harp	24-3
3	Kentucky	.22-4	Adolph Rupp	23-5
4	SMU	.21-3	Doc Hayes	22-4
5	Seattle	.24-2	John Castellani	24-3
6	Louisville	.21-5	Peck Hickman	same
7	West Va.	.25-4	Fred Schaus	25-5
8	Vanderbilt	.17-5	Bob Polk	same
9	Oklahoma City	.17-8	Abe Lemons	19-9
10	Saint Louis	.19-7	Eddie Hickey	19-9
11	Michigan St.	.14-8	Forddy Anderson	16-10
12	Memphis St.	.21-5	Bob Vanatta	24-6
13	California	.20-4	Pete Newell	21-5
14	UCLA	.22-4	John Wooden	same
15	Mississippi St.	.17-8	Babe McCarthy	same
16	Idaho St.	.24-2	John Grayson	25-4
17	Notre Dame	.18-7	John Jordan	20-8
18	Wake Forest	.19-9	Murray Greason	same
19	Canisius	.20-5	Joe Curran	22-6
20	Oklahoma A&M	.17-9	Hank Iba	same

Note: Unranked **Bradley**, coached by Chuck Orsborn, won the NIT. The Braves entered the tourney at 19-7 and had a final record of 22-7.

NCAA Final Four (at Municipal Auditorium, Kansas City): **Semifinals**–North Carolina 74, Michigan St. 70 (3 OT); Kansas 80, San Francisco 56. **Third Place**–San Francisco 67, Michigan St. 60. **Championship**–North Carolina 54, Kansas 53 (3 OT).

NIT Final Four (at Madison Square Garden): **Semifinals**–Memphis St. 80, St. Bonaventure 78; Bradley 78, Temple 66. **Third Place**–Temple 67, St. Bonaventure 50. **Championship**–Bradley 84, Memphis St. 83.

1959

		Before Tourns	Head Coach	Final Record
1	Kansas St.	.24-1	Tex Winter	25-2
2	Kentucky	.23-2	Adolph Rupp	24-3
3	Mississippi St.	.24-1	Babe McCarthy	same*
4	Bradley	.23-3	Chuck Orsborn	25-4
5	Cincinnati	.23-3	George Smith	26-4
6	N.C. State	.22-4	Everett Case	same
7	Michigan St.	.18-3	Forddy Anderson	19-4
8	Auburn	.20-2	Joel Eaves	same
9	North Carolina	.20-4	Frank McGuire	20-5
10	West Virginia	.25-4	Fred Schaus	29-5
11	**California**	.21-4	Pete Newell	25-4
12	Saint Louis	.20-5	John Benington	20-6
13	Seattle	.23-6	Vince Cazzetta	same
14	St. Joseph's-PA	.22-3	Jack Ramsay	22-5
15	St. Mary's-CA	.18-5	Jim Weaver	19-6
16	TCU	.19-5	Buster Brannon	20-6
17	Oklahoma City	.20-6	Abe Lemons	20-7
18	Utah	.21-5	Jack Gardner	21-7
19	St. Bonaventure	.20-2	Eddie Donovan	20-3
20	Marquette	.22-4	Eddie Hickey	23-6

*Mississippi St. turned down invitation to NCAA tournament because it was an integrated event.
Note: Unranked **St. John's**, coached by Joe Lapchick, won the NIT. The Redmen entered the tourney at 16-6 and had a final record of 20-6.

NCAA Final Four (at Freedom Hall, Louisville): **Semifinals**–West Virginia 94, Louisville 79; California 64, Cincinnati 58. **Third Place**–Cincinnati 98, Louisville 85. **Championship**–California 71, West Virginia 70.

NIT Final Four (at Madison Square Garden): **Semifinals**–Bradley 59, NYU 57; St. John's 76, Providence 55. **Third Place**–NYU 71, Providence 57. **Championship**–St. John's 76, Bradley 71 (OT).

1958

		Before Tourns	Head Coach	Final Record
1	West Virginia	.26-1	Fred Schaus	26-2
2	Cincinnati	.24-2	George Smith	25-3
3	Kansas St.	.20-3	Tex Winter	22-5
4	San Francisco	.24-1	Phil Woolpert	25-2
5	Temple	.24-2	Harry Litwack	27-3
6	Maryland	.20-6	Bud Millikan	22-7
7	Kansas	.18-5	Dick Harp	same
8	Notre Dame	.22-4	John Jordan	24-5
9	**Kentucky**	.19-6	Adolph Rupp	23-6
10	Duke	.18-7	Harold Bradley	same
11	Dayton	.23-3	Tom Blackburn	25-4
12	Indiana	.12-10	Branch McCracken	13-11
13	North Carolina	.19-7	Frank McGuire	same
14	Bradley	.20-6	Chuck Orsborn	20-7
15	Mississippi St.	.20-5	Babe McCarthy	same
16	Auburn	.16-6	Joel Eaves	same
17	Michigan St.	.16-6	Forddy Anderson	same
18	Seattle	.20-6	John Castellani	24-7
19	Oklahoma St.	.19-7	Hank Iba	21-8
20	N.C. State	.18-6	Everett Case	same

Note: Unranked **Xavier-OH**, coached by Jim McCafferty, won the NIT. The Musketeers entered the tourney at 15-11 and had a final record of 19-11.

NCAA Final Four (at Freedom Hall, Louisville): **Semifinals**–Kentucky 61, Temple 60; Seattle 73, Kansas St. 51. **Third Place**–Temple 67, Kansas St. 57. **Championship**–Kentucky 84, Seattle 72.

NIT Final Four (at Madison Square Garden): **Semifinals**–Dayton 80, St. John's 56; Xavier-OH 72, St. Bonaventure 53. **Third Place**–St. Bonaventure 84, St. John's 69. **Championship**–Xavier-OH 78, Dayton 74 (OT).

1960

		Before Tourns	Head Coach	Final Record
1	Cincinnati	.25-1	George Smith	28-2
2	California	.24-1	Pete Newell	28-2
3	**Ohio St.**	.21-3	Fred Taylor	25-3
4	**Bradley**	.24-2	Chuck Orsborn	27-2
5	West Virginia	.24-4	Fred Schaus	26-5
6	Utah	.24-2	Jack Gardner	26-3
7	Indiana	.20-4	Branch McCracken	same
8	Utah St.	.22-4	Cecil Baker	24-5
9	St. Bonaventure	.19-3	Eddie Donovan	21-5
10	Miami-FL	.23-3	Bruce Hale	23-4
11	Auburn	.19-3	Joel Eaves	same
12	NYU	.19-4	Lou Rossini	22-5
13	Georgia Tech	.21-5	Whack Hyder	22-6
14	Providence	.21-4	Joe Mullaney	24-5
15	Saint Louis	.19-7	John Benington	19-8
16	Holy Cross	.20-5	Roy Leenig	20-6
17	Villanova	.19-5	Al Severance	20-6
18	Duke	.15-10	Vic Bubas	17-11
19	Wake Forest	.21-7	Bones McKinney	same
20	St. John's	.17-7	Joe Lapchick	17-8

NCAA Final Four (at the Cow Palace, San Fran.): **Semifinals**–Ohio St. 76, NYU 54; California 77, Cincinnati 69. **Third Place**–Cincinnati 95, NYU 71. **Championship**–Ohio St. 75, California 55.

NIT Final Four (at Madison Square Garden): **Semifinals**–Bradley 82, St. Bonaventure 71; Providence 68, Utah St. 62. **Third Place**–Utah St. 99, St. Bonaventure 93. **Championship**–Bradley 88, Providence 72.

Associated Press Final Polls (Cont.)

1961

		Before Tourns	Head Coach	Final Record
1	Ohio St.	.24-0	Fred Taylor	27-1
2	**Cincinnati**	.23-3	Ed Jucker	27-3
3	St. Bonaventure	.22-3	Eddie Donovan	24-4
4	Kansas St.	.22-3	Tex Winter	23-4
5	North Carolina	.19-4	Frank McGuire	same
6	Bradley	.21-5	Chuck Orsborn	same
7	USC	.20-6	Forrest Twogood	21-8
8	Iowa	.18-6	S. Scheuerman	same
9	West Virginia	.23-4	George King	same
10	Duke	.22-6	Vic Bubas	same
11	Utah	.21-6	Jack Gardner	23-8
12	Texas Tech	.14-9	Polk Robison	15-10
13	Niagara	.16-4	Taps Gallagher	16-5
14	Memphis St.	.20-2	Bob Vanatta	20-3
15	Wake Forest	.17-10	Bones McKinney	19-11
16	St. John's	.20-4	Joe Lapchick	20-5
17	St. Joseph's-PA	.22-4	Jack Ramsay	25-5
18	Drake	.19-7	Maury John	same
19	Holy Cross	.19-4	Roy Leenig	22-5
20	Kentucky	.18-8	Adolph Rupp	19-9

Note: Unranked **Providence**, coached by Joe Mullaney, won the NIT. The Friars entered the tourney at 20-5 and had a final record of 24-5.

NCAA Final Four (at Municipal Auditorium, Kansas City): **Semifinals**—Ohio St. 95, St. Joseph's-PA 69; Cincinnati 82, Utah 67. **Third Place**—St. Joseph's-PA 127, Utah 120 (4 OT). **Championship**—Cincinnati 70, Ohio St. 65 (OT).

NIT Final Four (at Madison Square Garden) **Semifinals**—St. Louis 67, Dayton 60; Providence 90, Holy Cross 83 (OT). **Third Place**—Holy Cross 85, Dayton 67. **Championship**—Providence 62, St. Louis 59.

1962

		Before Tourns	Head Coach	Final Record
1	Ohio St.	.23-1	Fred Taylor	26-2
2	**Cincinnati**	.25-2	Ed Jucker	29-2
3	Kentucky	.22-2	Adolph Rupp	23-3
4	Mississippi St.	.19-6	Babe McCarthy	same
5	Bradley	.21-6	Chuck Orsborn	21-7
6	Kansas St.	.22-3	Tex Winter	same
7	Utah	.22-3	Jack Gardner	same
8	Bowling Green	.21-3	Harold Anderson	same
9	Colorado	.18-6	Sox Walseth	19-7
10	Duke	.20-5	Vic Bubas	same
11	Loyola-IL	.21-3	George Ireland	23-4
12	St. John's	.19-4	Joe Lapchick	21-5
13	Wake Forest	.18-8	Bones McKinney	22-9
14	Oregon St.	.22-4	Slats Gill	24-5
15	West Virginia	.24-5	George King	24-6
16	Arizona St.	.23-3	Ned Wulk	23-4
17	Duquesne	.20-5	Red Manning	22-7
18	Utah St.	.21-5	Ladell Andersen	22-7
19	UCLA	.16-9	John Wooden	18-11
20	Villanova	.19-6	Jack Kraft	21-7

Note: Unranked **Dayton**, coached by Tom Blackburn, won the NIT. The Flyers entered the tourney at 20-6 and had a final record of 24-6.

NCAA Final Four (at Freedom Hall, Louisville): **Semifinals**—Ohio St. 84, Wake Forest 68; Cincinnati 72, UCLA 70. **Third Place**—Wake Forest 82, UCLA 80. **Championship**—Cincinnati 71, Ohio St. 59.

NIT Final Four (at Madison Square Garden): **Semifinals**—Dayton 98, Loyola-IL 82; St. John's 76, Duquesne 65. **Third Place**—Loyola-IL 95, Duquesne 84. **Championship**—Dayton 73, St. John's 67.

1963

AP ranked only 10 teams from the 1962-63 season through 1967-68.

		Before Tourns	Head Coach	Final Record
1	Cincinnati	.23-1	Ed Jucker	26-2
2	Duke	.24-2	Vic Bubas	27-3
3	**Loyola-IL**	.24-2	George Ireland	29-2
4	Arizona St.	.24-2	Ned Wulk	26-3
5	Wichita	.19-7	Ralph Miller	19-8
6	Mississippi St.	.21-5	Babe McCarthy	22-6
7	Ohio St.	.20-4	Fred Taylor	same
8	Illinois	.19-5	Harry Combes	20-6
9	NYU	.17-3	Lou Rossini	18-5
10	Colorado	.18-6	Sox Walseth	19-7

Note: Unranked **Providence**, coached by Joe Mullaney, won the NIT. The Friars entered the tourney at 21-4 and had a final record of 24-4.

NCAA Final Four (at Freedom Hall, Louisville): **Semifinals**—Loyola-IL 94, Duke 75; Cincinnati 80, Oregon St. 46. **Third Place**—Duke 85, Oregon St. 63. **Championship**—Loyola-IL 60, Cincinnati 58 (OT).

NIT Final Four (at Madison Square Garden): **Semifinals**—Providence 70, Marquette 64; Canisius 61, Villanova 46. **Third Place**—Marquette 66, Villanova 58. **Championship**—Providence 81, Canisius 66.

1964

AP ranked only 10 teams from the 1962-63 season through 1967-68.

		Before Tourns	Head Coach	Final Record
1	UCLA	.26-0	John Wooden	30-0
2	Michigan	.20-4	Dave Strack	23-5
3	Duke	.23-4	Vic Bubas	26-5
4	Kentucky	.21-4	Adolph Rupp	21-6
5	Wichita St.	.22-5	Ralph Miller	23-6
6	Oregon St.	.25-3	Slats Gill	25-4
7	Villanova	.22-3	Jack Kraft	24-4
8	Loyola-IL	.20-5	George Ireland	22-6
9	DePaul	.21-3	Ray Meyer	21-4
10	Davidson	.22-4	Lefty Driesell	same

Note: Unranked **Bradley**, coached by Chuck Orsborn, won the NIT. The Braves entered the tourney at 20-6 and finished with a record of 23-6.

NCAA Final Four (at Municipal Auditorium, Kansas City): **Semifinals**—Duke 91, Michigan 80; UCLA 90, Kansas St. 84. **Third Place**—Michigan 100, Kansas St. 90. **Championship**—UCLA 98, Duke 83.

NIT Final Four (at Madison Square Garden): **Semifinals**—New Mexico 72, NYU 65; Bradley 67, Army 52. **Third Place**—Army 60, NYU 59. **Championship**—Bradley 86, New Mexico 54.

Undefeated National Champions

Seven NCAA seasons have ended with an undefeated national champion. UCLA has accomplished the feat four times.

Year		W-L
1956	San Francisco	.29-0
1957	North Carolina	.32-0
1964	UCLA	.30-0
1967	UCLA	.30-0
1972	UCLA	.30-0
1973	UCLA	.30-0
1976	Indiana	.32-0

1965

AP ranked only 10 teams from the 1962-63 season through 1967-68.

		Before Tourns	Head Coach	Final Record
1	Michigan	21-3	Dave Strack	24-4
2	**UCLA**	24-2	John Wooden	28-2
3	St. Joseph's-PA	25-1	Jack Ramsay	26-3
4	Providence	22-1	Joe Mullaney	24-2
5	Vanderbilt	23-3	Roy Skinner	24-4
6	Davidson	24-2	Lefty Driesell	same
7	Minnesota	19-5	John Kundla	same
8	Villanova	21-4	Jack Kraft	23-5
9	BYU	21-5	Stan Watts	21-7
10	Duke	20-5	Vic Bubas	same

Note: Unranked **St. John's**, coached by Joe Lapchick, won the NIT. The Redmen entered the tourney at 17-8 and finished with a record of 21-8.

NCAA Final Four (at Memorial Coliseum, Portland, OR): **Semifinals**—Michigan 93, Princeton 76; UCLA 108, Wichita St. 89. **Third Place**—Princeton 118, Wichita St. 82. **Championship**—UCLA 91, Michigan 80.

NIT Final Four (at Madison Square Garden): **Semifinals**—Villanova 91, NYU 69; St. John's 67, Army 60. **Third Place**—Army 75, NYU 74. **Championship**—St. John's 55, Villanova 51.

1966

AP ranked only 10 teams from the 1962-63 season through 1967-68.

		Before Tourns	Head Coach	Final Record
1	Kentucky	24-1	Adolph Rupp	27-2
2	Duke	23-3	Vic Bubas	26-4
3	**Texas Western**	23-1	Don Haskins	28-1
4	Kansas	22-3	Ted Owens	23-4
5	St. Joseph's-PA	22-4	Jack Ramsay	24-5
6	Loyola-IL	22-2	George Ireland	22-3
7	Cincinnati	21-5	Tay Baker	21-7
8	Vanderbilt	22-4	Roy Skinner	same
9	Michigan	17-7	Dave Strack	18-8
10	Western Ky.	23-2	Johnny Oldham	25-3

Note: Unranked **BYU**, coached by Stan Watts, won the NIT. The Cougars entered the tourney at 17-5 and had a final record of 20-5.

NCAA Final Four (at Cole Fieldhouse, College Park, MD): **Semifinals**—Kentucky 83, Duke 79; Texas Western 85, Utah 78. **Third Place**—Duke 79, Utah 77. **Championship**—Texas Western 72, Kentucky 65.

NIT Final Four (at Madison Square Garden): **Semifinals**—BYU 66, Army 60; NYU 69, Villanova 63. **Third Place**—Villanova 76, Army 65. **Championship**—BYU 97, NYU 84.

1967

AP ranked only 10 teams from the 1962-63 season through 1967-68.

		Before Tourns	Head Coach	Final Record
1	UCLA	26-0	John Wooden	30-0
2	Louisville	23-3	Peck Hickman	23-5
3	Kansas	22-3	Ted Owens	23-4
4	North Carolina	24-4	Dean Smith	26-6
5	Princeton	23-2	B. van Breda Kolff	25-3
6	Western Ky.	23-2	Johnny Oldham	23-3
7	Houston	23-3	Guy Lewis	27-4
8	Tennessee	21-5	Ray Mears	21-7
9	Boston College	19-2	Bob Cousy	21-3
10	Texas Western	20-5	Don Haskins	22-6

Note: Unranked **Southern Illinois**, coached by Jack Hartman, won the NIT. The Salukis entered the tourney at 20-2 and had a final record of 24-2.

NCAA Final Four (at Freedom Hall, Louisville): **Semifinals**—Dayton 76, N. Carolina 62; UCLA 73, Houston 58. **Third Place**—Houston 84, N. Carolina 62. **Championship**—UCLA 79, Dayton 64.

NIT Final Four (at Madison Square Garden): **Semifinals**—Marquette 83, Marshall 78; Southern Ill. 79, Rutgers 70. **Third Place**—Rutgers 93, Marshall 76. **Championship**—Southern Ill. 71, Marquette 56.

1968

AP ranked only 10 teams from the 1962-63 season through 1967-68.

		Before Tourns	Head Coach	Final Record
1	Houston	28-0	Guy Lewis	31-2
2	**UCLA**	25-1	John Wooden	29-1
3	St. Bonaventure	22-0	Larry Weise	23-2
4	North Carolina	25-3	Dean Smith	28-4
5	Kentucky	21-4	Adolph Rupp	22-5
6	New Mexico	23-3	Bob King	23-5
7	Columbia	21-4	Jack Rohan	23-5
8	Davidson	22-4	Lefty Driesell	24-5
9	Louisville	20-6	John Dromo	21-7
10	Duke	21-5	Vic Bubas	22-6

Note: Unranked **Dayton**, coached by Don Donoher, won the NIT. The Flyers entered the tourney at 17-9 and had a final record of 21-9.

NCAA Final Four (at the Sports Arena, Los Angeles): **Semifinals**—North Carolina 80, Ohio St. 66; UCLA 101, Houston 69. **Third Place**—Ohio St. 89, Houston 85. **Championship**—UCLA 78, North Carolina 55.

NIT Final Four (at Madison Square Garden): **Semifinals**—Dayton 76, Notre Dame 74 (OT); Kansas 58, St. Peter's 46. **Third Place**—Notre Dame 81, St.Peter's 78. **Championship**—Dayton 61, Kansas 48.

All-Time AP Top 20

The composite AP Top 20 from the 1948-49 season through 2007-08, based on the final regular season rankings of each year. The final AP poll has been taken before the NCAA and NIT tournaments each season since 1949 except in 1953 and '54 and again in 1974 and '75 when the final poll came out after the postseason. Team point totals are based on 20 points for all 1st place finishes, 19 for each 2nd, etc. Also listed are the number of times ranked No.1 by AP going into the tournaments, and times ranked in the pre-tournament Top 10 and Top 20.

		Pts	No.1	Top 10	Top 20			Pts	No.1	Top 10	Top 20
1	Kentucky	672	8	38	45	11	Ohio St	211	3	12	15
2	North Carolina	575	6	32	41	12	Michigan	200	2	10	15
3	Duke	494	7	28	37	13	Notre Dame	197	0	12	20
4	UCLA	498	7	25	38	14	Marquette	187	0	12	17
5	Kansas	414	1	21	32	15	N.C. State	182	1	9	17
6	Indiana	293	4	16	24	16	Syracuse	179	0	9	20
7	Louisville	274	0	12	26	17	UNLV	173	2	8	13
8	Cincinnati	259	2	13	19	18	Arkansas	166	0	9	15
9	Arizona	245	1	12	20	19	Maryland	164	0	8	18
10	Illinois	235	1	10	24	20	Oklahoma	157	1	7	13

Associated Press Final Polls (Cont.)

1969

		Before Tourns	Head Coach	Final Record
1	**UCLA**	25-1	John Wooden	29-1
2	La Salle	23-1	Tom Gola	same*
3	Santa Clara	26-1	Dick Garibaldi	27-2
4	North Carolina	25-3	Dean Smith	27-5
5	Davidson	24-2	Lefty Driesell	26-3
6	Purdue	20-4	George King	23-5
7	Kentucky	22-4	Adolph Rupp	23-5
8	St. John's	22-4	Lou Carnesecca	23-6
9	Duquesne	19-4	Red Manning	21-5
10	Villanova	21-4	Jack Kraft	21-5
11	Drake	23-4	Maury John	26-5
12	New Mexico St.	23-3	Lou Henson	24-5
13	South Carolina	20-6	Frank McGuire	21-7
14	Marquette	22-4	Al McGuire	24-5
15	Louisville	20-5	John Dromo	21-6
16	Boston College	21-3	Bob Cousy	24-4
17	Notre Dame	20-6	Johnny Dee	20-7
18	Colorado	20-6	Sox Walseth	21-7
19	Kansas	20-6	Ted Owens	20-7
20	Illinois	19-5	Harvey Schmidt	same

*On probation

Note: Unranked **Temple**, coached by Harry Litwack, won the NIT. The Owls entered the tourney at 18-8 and finished with a record of 22-8.

NCAA Final Four (at Freedom Hall, Louisville): **Semifinals**—Purdue 92, N. Carolina 65; UCLA 85, Drake 82. **Third Place**—Drake 104, N. Carolina 84. **Championship**—UCLA 92, Purdue 72.

NIT Final Four (at Madison Square Garden): **Semifinals**—Temple 63, Tennessee 58; Boston College 73, Army 61. **Third Place**—Tennessee 64, Army 52. **Championship**—Temple 89, Boston College 76.

1971

		Before Tourns	Head Coach	Final Record
1	UCLA	25-1	John Wooden	29-1
2	Marquette	26-0	Al McGuire	28-1
3	Penn	26-0	Dick Harter	28-1
4	Kansas	25-1	Ted Owens	27-3
5	USC	24-2	Bob Boyd	24-2
6	South Carolina	23-4	Frank McGuire	23-6
7	Western Ky.	20-5	John Oldham	24-6
8	Kentucky	22-4	Adolph Rupp	22-6
9	Fordham	25-1	Digger Phelps	26-3
10	Ohio St.	19-5	Fred Taylor	20-6
11	Jacksonville	22-3	Tom Wasdin	22-4
12	Notre Dame	19-7	Johnny Dee	20-9
13	**N. Carolina**	22-6	Dean Smith	26-6
14	Houston	20-6	Guy Lewis	22-7
15	Duquesne	21-3	Red Manning	21-4
16	Long Beach St.	21-4	Jerry Tarkanian	23-5
17	Tennessee	20-6	Ray Mears	21-7
18	Villanova	19-5	Jack Kraft	23-6
19	Drake	20-7	Maury John	21-8
20	BYU	18-9	Stan Watts	18-11

NCAA Final Four (at the Astrodome, Houston): **Semifinals**—Villanova 92, Western Ky. 89 (2 OT); UCLA 68, Kansas 60. **Third Place**—Western Ky. 77, Kansas 75. **Championship**—UCLA 68, Villanova 62.

NIT Final Four (at Madison Square Garden): **Semifinals**—N. Carolina 73, Duke 69; Ga.Tech 76, St. Bonaventure 71 (2 OT). **Third Place**—St. Bonaventure 92, Duke 88 (OT). **Championship**—N. Carolina 84, Ga. Tech 66.

1970

		Before Tourns	Head Coach	Final Record
1	Kentucky	25-1	Adolph Rupp	26-2
2	UCLA	24-2	John Wooden	28-2
3	St. Bonaventure	22-1	Larry Weise	25-3
4	Jacksonville	23-1	Joe Williams	27-2
5	New Mexico St.	23-2	Lou Henson	27-3
6	South Carolina	25-3	Frank McGuire	25-3
7	Iowa	19-4	Ralph Miller	20-5
8	**Marquette**	22-3	Al McGuire	26-3
9	Notre Dame	20-6	Johnny Dee	21-8
10	N.C. State	22-6	Norm Sloan	23-7
11	Florida St.	23-3	Hugh Durham	23-3
12	Houston	24-3	Guy Lewis	25-5
13	Penn	25-1	Dick Harter	25-2
14	Drake	21-6	Maury John	22-7
15	Davidson	22-4	Terry Holland	22-5
16	Utah St.	20-6	Ladell Andersen	22-7
17	Niagara	21-5	Frank Layden	22-7
18	Western Ky.	22-2	John Oldham	22-3
19	Long Beach St.	23-3	Jerry Tarkanian	24-5
20	USC	18-8	Bob Boyd	18-8

NCAA Final Four (at Cole Fieldhouse, College Park, MD): **Semifinals**—Jacksonville 91, St. Bonaventure 83; UCLA 93, New Mexico St. 77. **Third Place**—N. Mexico St. 79, St. Bonaventure 73. **Championship**—UCLA 80, Jacksonville 69.

NIT Final Four (at Madison Square Garden): **Semifinals**—St. John's 60, Army 59; Marquette 101, LSU 79. **Third Place**—Army 75, LSU 68. **Championship**—Marquette 65, St. John's 53.

1972

		Before Tourns	Head Coach	Final Record
1	**UCLA**	26-0	John Wooden	30-0
2	North Carolina	23-4	Dean Smith	26-5
3	Penn	23-2	Chuck Daly	25-3
4	Louisville	23-4	Denny Crum	26-5
5	Long Beach St.	23-3	Jerry Tarkanian	25-4
6	South Carolina	22-4	Frank McGuire	24-5
7	Marquette	24-2	Al McGuire	25-4
8	SW Louisiana	23-3	Beryl Shipley	25-4
9	BYU	21-4	Stan Watts	21-5
10	Florida St.	23-5	Hugh Durham	27-6
11	Minnesota	17-6	Bill Musselman	18-7
12	Marshall	23-3	Carl Tacy	23-4
13	Memphis St.	21-6	Gene Bartow	21-7
14	**Maryland**	23-5	Lefty Driesell	27-5
15	Villanova	19-6	Jack Kraft	20-8
16	Oral Roberts	25-1	Ken Trickey	26-2
17	Indiana	17-7	Bob Knight	17-8
18	Kentucky	20-6	Adolph Rupp	21-7
19	Ohio St.	18-6	Fred Taylor	same
20	Virginia	21-6	Bill Gibson	21-7

NCAA Final Four (at the Sports Arena, Los Angeles): **Semifinals**—Florida St. 79, N. Carolina 75; UCLA 96, Louisville 77. **Third Place**—N. Carolina 105, Louisville 91. **Championship**—UCLA 81, Florida St. 76.

NIT Final Four (at Madison Square Garden): **Semifinals**—Maryland 71, Jacksonville 77; Niagara 69, St. John's 67. **Third Place**—Jacksonville 83, St. John's 80. **Championship**—Maryland 100, Niagara 69.

1973

		Before Tours	Head Coach	Final Record
1	**UCLA**	26-0	John Wooden	30-0
2	N.C. State	27-0	Norm Sloan	same*
3	Long Beach St.	..24-2	Jerry Tarkanian	26-3
4	Providence	24-2	Dave Gavitt	27-4
5	Marquette	23-3	Al McGuire	25-4
6	Indiana	19-5	Bob Knight	22-6
7	SW Louisiana	...23-2	Beryl Shipley	24-5
8	Maryland	22-6	Lefty Driesell	23-7
9	Kansas St.	22-4	Jack Hartman	23-5
10	Minnesota	...20-4	Bill Musselman	21-5
11	North Carolina	..22-7	Dean Smith	25-8
12	Memphis St.	...21-5	Gene Bartow	24-6
13	Houston	23-3	Guy Lewis	23-4
14	Syracuse	22-4	Roy Danforth	24-5
15	Missouri	21-5	Norm Stewart	21-6
16	Arizona St.	18-7	Ned Wulk	19-9
17	Kentucky	19-7	Joe B. Hall	20-8
18	Penn	20-5	Chuck Daly	21-7
19	Austin Peay	...21-5	Lake Kelly	22-7
20	San Francisco	..22-4	Bob Gaillard	23-5

*N.C. State was ineligible for NCAA tournament for using improper methods to recruit David Thompson.
Note: Unranked **Virginia Tech**, coached by Don DeVoe, won the NIT. The Hokies entered the tourney at 18-5 and finished with a record of 22-5.
NCAA Final Four (at The Arena, St. Louis): **Semifinals**—Memphis St. 98, Providence 85; UCLA 70, Indiana 59. **Third Place**—Indiana 97, Providence 59. **Championship**—UCLA 87, Memphis St. 66.
NIT Final Four (at Madison Square Garden): **Semifinals**—Va. Tech 74, Alabama 73; Notre Dame 78, N. Carolina 71. **Third Place**—N. Carolina 88, Alabama 69. **Championship**—Va. Tech 92, Notre Dame 91 (OT).

1974

		Before Tours	Head Coach	Final Record
1	**N.C. State**	26-1	Norm Sloan	30-1
2	UCLA	23-3	John Wooden	26-4
3	Notre Dame	...24-2	Digger Phelps	26-3
4	Maryland	23-5	Lefty Driesell	same
5	Providence	...26-3	Dave Gavitt	28-4
6	Vanderbilt	...23-3	Roy Skinner	23-5
7	Marquette	...22-4	Al McGuire	26-5
8	North Carolina	..22-5	Dean Smith	22-6
9	Long Beach St.	..24-2	Lute Olson	same
10	**Indiana**	20-5	Bob Knight	23-5
11	Alabama	22-4	C.M. Newton	same
12	Michigan	...21-4	Johnny Orr	22-5
13	Pittsburgh	23-3	Buzz Ridl	25-4
14	Kansas	21-5	Ted Owens	23-7
15	USC	22-4	Bob Boyd	24-5
16	Louisville	21-6	Denny Crum	21-7
17	New Mexico	...21-6	Norm Ellenberger	22-7
18	South Carolina	..22-4	Frank McGuire	22-5
19	Creighton	22-6	Eddie Sutton	23-7
20	Dayton	19-7	Don Donoher	20-9

NCAA Final Four (at Greensboro, NC, Coliseum): **Semifinals**—N.C. State 80, UCLA 77 (2 OT); Marquette 64, Kansas 51. **Third Place**—UCLA 78, Kansas 61. **Championship**—N.C. State 76, Marquette 64.
NIT Final Four (at Madison Square Garden): **Semifinals**—Purdue 78, Jacksonville 63; Utah 117, Boston Col. 93. **Third Place**—Boston Col. 87, Jacksonville 77. **Championship**—Purdue 87, Utah 81.
CCA Final Four (at The Arena, St. Louis): **Semifinals**—Indiana 73, Toledo 72; USC 74, Bradley 73. **Championship**—Indiana 85, USC 60.

1975

		Before Tours	Head Coach	Final Record
1	Indiana	29-0	Bob Knight	31-1
2	**UCLA**	23-3	John Wooden	28-3
3	Louisville	24-2	Denny Crum	28-3
4	Maryland	22-4	Lefty Driesell	24-5
5	Kentucky	22-4	Joe B. Hall	26-5
6	North Carolina	..21-7	Dean Smith	23-8
7	Arizona St.	23-3	Ned Wulk	25-4
8	N.C.State	22-6	Norm Sloan	22-6
9	Notre Dame	...18-8	Digger Phelps	19-10
10	Marquette	23-3	Al McGuire	23-4
11	Alabama	22-4	C.M. Newton	22-5
12	Cincinnati	21-5	Gale Catlett	23-6
13	Oregon St.	18-10	Ralph Miller	19-12
14	**Drake**	16-10	Bob Ortegel	19-10
15	Penn	23-4	Chuck Daly	23-5
16	UNLV	22-4	Jerry Tarkanian	24-5
17	Kansas St.	18-8	Jack Hartman	20-9
18	USC	18-7	Bob Boyd	18-8
19	Centenary	...25-4	Larry Little	same
20	Syracuse	20-7	Roy Danforth	23-9

NCAA Final Four (at San Diego Sports Arena): **Semifinals**—Kentucky 95, Syracuse 79; UCLA 75, Louisville 74 (OT). **Third Place**—Louisville 96, Syracuse 88 (OT). **Championship**—UCLA 92, Kentucky 85.
NIT Championship (at Madison Sq. Garden): Princeton 80, Providence 69. No Top 20 teams played in NIT.
CCA Championship (at Freedom Hall, Louisville): Drake 83, Arizona 76. No.14 Drake and No.18 USC were only Top 20 teams in CCA.

1976

		Before Tours	Head Coach	Final Record
1	**Indiana**	27-0	Bob Knight	32-0
2	Marquette	25-1	Al McGuire	27-2
3	UNLV	28-1	Jerry Tarkanian	29-2
4	Rutgers	28-0	Tom Young	31-2
5	UCLA	24-3	Gene Bartow	28-4
6	Alabama	22-4	C.M. Newton	23-5
7	Notre Dame	...22-5	Digger Phelps	23-6
8	North Carolina	..25-3	Dean Smith	25-4
9	Michigan	21-6	Johnny Orr	25-7
10	Western Mich.	..24-2	Eldon Miller	25-3
11	Maryland	22-6	Lefty Driesell	same
12	Cincinnati	25-5	Gale Catlett	25-6
13	Tennessee	...21-5	Ray Mears	21-6
14	Missouri	24-4	Norm Stewart	26-5
15	Arizona	22-8	Fred Snowden	24-9
16	Texas Tech	24-5	Gerald Myers	25-6
17	DePaul	19-8	Ray Meyer	20-9
18	Virginia	18-11	Terry Holland	18-12
19	Centenary	...22-5	Larry Little	same
20	Pepperdine	21-5	Gary Colson	22-6

NCAA Final Four (at the Spectrum, Phila.): **Semifinals**—Michigan 86, Rutgers 70; Indiana 65, UCLA 51. **Third Place**—UCLA 106, Rutgers 92. **Championship**—Indiana 86, Michigan 68.
NIT Championship (at Madison Square Garden): Kentucky 71, NC-Charlotte 67. No Top 20 teams played in NIT.

Associated Press Final Polls (Cont.)

1977

		Before Tourns	Head Coach	Final Record
1	Michigan	24-3	Johnny Orr	26-4
2	UCLA	24-3	Gene Bartow	25-4
3	Kentucky	24-3	Joe B. Hall	26-4
4	UNLV	25-2	Jerry Tarkanian	29-3
5	North Carolina	24-4	Dean Smith	28-5
6	Syracuse	25-3	Jim Boeheim	26-4
7	**Marquette**	20-7	Al McGuire	25-7
8	San Francisco	29-1	Bob Gaillard	29-2
9	Wake Forest	20-7	Carl Tacy	22-8
10	Notre Dame	21-6	Digger Phelps	22-7
11	Alabama	23-4	C.M. Newton	25-6
12	Detroit	24-3	Dick Vitale	25-4
13	Minnesota	24-3	Jim Dutcher	same*
14	Utah	22-6	Jerry Pimm	23-7
15	Tennessee	22-5	Ray Mears	22-6
16	Kansas St.	23-6	Jack Hartman	24-7
17	NC-Charlotte	25-3	Lee Rose	28-5
18	Arkansas	26-1	Eddie Sutton	26-2
19	Louisville	21-6	Denny Crum	21-7
20	VMI	25-3	Charlie Schmaus	26-4

*On probation

NCAA Final Four (at the Omni, Atlanta): **Semifinals**—Marquette 51, NC-Charlotte, 49; N. Carolina 84, UNLV 83. **Third Place**—UNLV 106, NC-Charlotte 94. **Championship**—Marquette 67, N. Carolina 59.
NIT Championship (at Madison Square Garden): St. Bonaventure 94, Houston 91. No.11 Alabama was only Top 20 team in NIT.

1979

		Before Tourns	Head Coach	Final Record
1	Indiana St.	29-0	Bill Hodges	33-1
2	UCLA	23-4	Gary Cunningham	25-5
3	**Michigan St.**	21-6	Jud Heathcote	26-6
4	Notre Dame	22-5	Digger Phelps	24-6
5	Arkansas	23-4	Eddie Sutton	25-5
6	DePaul	22-5	Ray Meyer	26-6
7	LSU	22-5	Dale Brown	23-6
8	Syracuse	25-3	Jim Boeheim	26-4
9	North Carolina	23-5	Dean Smith	23-6
10	Marquette	21-6	Hank Raymonds	22-7
11	Duke	22-7	Bill Foster	22-8
12	San Francisco	21-6	Dan Belluomini	22-7
13	Louisville	23-7	Denny Crum	24-8
14	Penn	21-5	Bob Weinhauer	25-7
15	Purdue	23-7	Lee Rose	27-8
16	Oklahoma	20-9	Dave Bliss	21-10
17	St. John's	18-10	Lou Carnesecca	21-11
18	Rutgers	21-8	Tom Young	22-9
19	Toledo	21-6	Bob Nichols	22-7
20	Iowa	20-7	Lute Olson	20-8

NCAA Final Four (at Special Events Center, Salt Lake City): **Semifinals**—Michigan St. 101, Penn 67; Indiana St. 76, DePaul 74; **Third Place**—DePaul 96, Penn 93; **Championship**—Michigan St. 75, Indiana St. 64.
NIT Championship (at Madison Square Garden): Indiana 53, Purdue 52. No. 15 Purdue was the only Top 20 team in NIT.

1978

		Before Tourns	Head Coach	Final Record
1	**Kentucky**	25-2	Joe B. Hall	30-2
2	UCLA	24-2	Gary Cunningham	25-3
3	DePaul	25-2	Ray Meyer	27-3
4	Michigan St.	23-4	Jud Heathcote	25-5
5	Arkansas	28-3	Eddie Sutton	32-3
6	Notre Dame	20-6	Digger Phelps	23-8
7	Duke	23-6	Bill Foster	27-7
8	Marquette	24-3	Hank Raymonds	24-4
9	Louisville	22-6	Denny Crum	23-7
10	Kansas	24-4	Ted Owens	24-5
11	San Francisco	22-5	Bob Gaillard	23-6
12	New Mexico	24-3	Norm Ellenberger	24-4
13	Indiana	20-7	Bob Knight	21-8
14	Utah	22-5	Jerry Pimm	23-6
15	Florida St.	23-5	Hugh Durham	23-6
16	North Carolina	23-7	Dean Smith	23-8
17	**Texas**	22-5	Abe Lemons	26-5
18	Detroit	24-3	Dave Gaines	25-4
19	Miami-OH	18-8	Darrell Hedric	19-9
20	Penn	19-7	Bob Weinhauer	20-8

NCAA Final Four (at the Checkerdome, St. Louis): **Semifinals**—Kentucky 64, Arkansas 59; Duke 90, Notre Dame 86. **Third Place**—Arkansas 71, Notre Dame 69. **Championship**—Kentucky 94, Duke 88.
NIT Championship (at Madison Square Garden): Texas 101, N.C. State 93. No. 17 Texas and No. 18 Detroit were only Top 20 teams in NIT.

1980

		Before Tourns	Head Coach	Final Record
1	DePaul	26-1	Ray Meyer	26-2
2	**Louisville**	28-3	Denny Crum	33-3
3	LSU	24-5	Dale Brown	26-6
4	Kentucky	28-5	Joe B. Hall	29-6
5	Oregon St.	26-3	Ralph Miller	26-4
6	Syracuse	25-3	Jim Boeheim	26-4
7	Indiana	20-7	Bob Knight	21-8
8	Maryland	23-6	Lefty Driesell	24-7
9	Notre Dame	20-7	Digger Phelps	20-8
10	Ohio St.	24-5	Eldon Miller	21-8
11	Georgetown	24-5	John Thompson	26-6
12	BYU	24-4	Frank Arnold	24-5
13	St. John's	24-4	Lou Carnesecca	24-5
14	Duke	22-8	Bill Foster	24-9
15	North Carolina	21-7	Dean Smith	21-8
16	Missouri	23-5	Norm Stewart	25-6
17	Weber St.	26-2	Neil McCarthy	26-3
18	Arizona St.	21-6	Ned Wulk	22-7
19	Iona	28-4	Jim Valvano	29-5
20	Purdue	19-9	Lee Rose	23-10

NCAA Final Four (at Market Square Arena, Indianapolis): **Semifinals**—Louisville 80, Iowa 72; UCLA 67, Purdue 62; **Championship**—Louisville 59, UCLA 54.
NIT Championship (at Madison Square Garden): Virginia 58, Minnesota 55. No Top 20 teams played in NIT.

1981

		Before Tourns	Head Coach	Final Record
1	DePaul	27-1	Ray Meyer	27-2
2	Oregon St.	26-1	Ralph Miller	26-2
3	Arizona St.	24-3	Ned Wulk	24-4
4	LSU	28-3	Dale Brown	31-5
5	Virginia	25-3	Terry Holland	29-4
6	North Carolina	25-7	Dean Smith	29-8
7	Notre Dame	22-5	Digger Phelps	23-6
8	Kentucky	22-5	Joe B. Hall	22-6
9	**Indiana**	21-9	Bob Knight	26-9
10	UCLA	20-6	Larry Brown	20-7
11	Wake Forest	22-6	Carl Tacy	22-7
12	Louisville	21-8	Denny Crum	21-9
13	Iowa	21-6	Lute Olson	21-7
14	Utah	24-4	Jerry Pimm	25-5
15	Tennessee	20-7	Don DeVoe	21-8
16	BYU	22-6	Frank Arnold	25-7
17	Wyoming	23-5	Jim Brandenburg	24-6
18	Maryland	20-9	Lefty Driesell	21-10
19	Illinois	20-7	Lou Henson	21-8
20	Arkansas	22-7	Eddie Sutton	24-8

NCAA Final Four (at the Spectrum, Phila.): **Semifinals**–N. Carolina 78; Virginia 65; Indiana 67, LSU 49. **Third Place**–Virginia 78, LSU 74. **Championship**–Indiana 63, N. Carolina 50.
NIT Championship (at Madison Square Garden): Tulsa 86, Syracuse 84. No Top 20 teams played in NIT.

1983

		Before Tourns	Head Coach	Final Record
1	Houston	27-2	Guy Lewis	31-3
2	Louisville	29-3	Denny Crum	32-4
3	St. John's	27-4	Lou Carnesecca	28-5
4	Virginia	27-4	Terry Holland	29-5
5	Indiana	23-5	Bob Knight	24-6
6	UNLV	28-2	Jerry Tarkanian	28-3
7	UCLA	23-5	Larry Farmer	23-6
8	North Carolina	26-7	Dean Smith	28-8
9	Arkansas	25-3	Eddie Sutton	26-4
10	Missouri	26-7	Norm Stewart	26-8
11	Boston College	24-6	Gary Williams	25-7
12	Kentucky	22-7	Joe B. Hall	23-8
13	Villanova	22-7	Rollie Massimino	24-8
14	Wichita St.	25-3	Gene Smithson	same*
15	Tenn.-Chatt.	26-3	Murray Arnold	26-4
16	**N.C. State**	20-10	Jim Valvano	26-10
17	Memphis St.	22-7	Dana Kirk	23-8
18	Georgia	21-9	Hugh Durham	24-10
19	Oklahoma St.	24-6	Paul Hansen	24-7
20	Georgetown	21-9	John Thompson	22-10

*On probation
NCAA Final Four (at The Pit, Albuquerque, NM): **Semifinals**–N.C. State 67, Georgia 60; Houston 94, Louisville 81. **Championship**–N.C. State 54, Houston 52.
NIT Championship (at Madison Square Garden): Fresno St. 69, DePaul 60. No Top 20 teams played in NIT.

1982

		Before Tourns	Head Coach	Final Record
1	**N. Carolina**	27-2	Dean Smith	32-2
2	DePaul	26-1	Ray Meyer	26-2
3	Virginia	29-3	Terry Holland	30-4
4	Oregon St.	23-4	Ralph Miller	25-5
5	Missouri	26-3	Norm Stewart	27-4
6	Georgetown	26-6	John Thompson	30-7
7	Minnesota	22-5	Jim Dutcher	23-6
8	Idaho	26-2	Don Monson	27-3
9	Memphis St.	23-4	Dana Kirk	24-5
10	Tulsa	24-5	Nolan Richardson	24-6
11	Fresno St.	26-2	Boyd Grant	27-3
12	Arkansas	23-5	Eddie Sutton	23-6
13	Alabama	23-6	Wimp Sanderson	24-7
14	West Virginia	26-3	Gale Catlett	27-4
15	Kentucky	22-7	Joe B. Hall	22-8
16	Iowa	20-7	Lute Olson	21-8
17	Ala-Birmingham	23-5	Gene Bartow	25-6
18	Wake Forest	20-8	Carl Tacy	21-9
19	UCLA	21-6	Larry Farmer	21-6
20	Louisville	20-9	Denny Crum	23-10

NCAA Final Four (at the Superdome, New Orleans): **Semifinals**–N. Carolina 68, Houston 63; Georgetown 50, Louisville 46. **Championship**–N. Carolina 63, Georgetown 62.
NIT Championship (at Madison Square Garden): Bradley 67, Purdue 58. No Top 20 teams played in NIT.

1984

		Before Tourns	Head Coach	Final Record
1	North Carolina	27-2	Dean Smith	28-3
2	**Georgetown**	29-3	John Thompson	34-3
3	Kentucky	26-4	Joe B. Hall	29-5
4	DePaul	26-2	Ray Meyer	27-3
5	Houston	28-4	Guy Lewis	32-5
6	Illinois	24-4	Lou Henson	26-5
7	Oklahoma	29-4	Billy Tubbs	29-5
8	Arkansas	25-6	Eddie Sutton	25-7
9	UTEP	27-3	Don Haskins	27-4
10	Purdue	22-6	Gene Keady	22-7
11	Maryland	23-7	Lefty Driesell	24-8
12	Tulsa	27-3	Nolan Richardson	27-4
13	UNLV	27-5	Jerry Tarkanian	29-6
14	Duke	24-9	Mike Krzyzewski	24-10
15	Washington	22-6	Marv Harshman	24-7
16	Memphis St.	24-6	Dana Kirk	26-7
17	Oregon St.	22-6	Ralph Miller	22-7
18	Syracuse	22-8	Jim Boeheim	23-9
19	Wake Forest	21-8	Carl Tacy	23-9
20	Temple	25-4	John Chaney	26-5

NCAA Final Four (at the Kingdome, Seattle): **Semifinals**–Houston 49, Virginia 47 (OT); Georgetown 53, Kentucky 40. **Championship**–Georgetown 84, Houston 75.
NIT Championship (at Madison Square Garden): Michigan 83, Notre Dame 63. No Top 20 teams played in NIT.

Highest-Rated College Games on TV

The dozen highest-rated college basketball games seen on U.S. television have been NCAA tournament championship games, led by the 1979 Michigan State-Indiana State final that featured Magic Johnson and Larry Bird.

Listed below are the finalists (winning team first), date of game, TV network, and TV rating and audience share (according to Nielson Media Research).

		Date	Net	Rtg/Sh			Date	Net	Rtg/Sh
1	Michigan St.-Indiana St.	3/26/79	NBC	24.1/38	7	N. Carolina-Georgetown	3/29/82	CBS	21.6/31
2	Villanova-Georgetown	4/1/85	CBS	23.3/33	8	UCLA-Kentucky	3/31/75	NBC	21.3/33
3	Duke-Michigan	4/6/92	CBS	22.7/35	9	Michigan-Seton Hall	4/3/89	CBS	21.3/33
4	N.C. State-Houston	4/4/83	CBS	22.3/32	10	Louisville-Duke	3/31/86	CBS	20.7/31
5	N. Carolina-Michigan	4/5/93	CBS	22.2/34	11	Indiana-N. Carolina	3/30/81	NBC	20.7/29
6	Arkansas-Duke	4/4/94	CBS	21.6/33	12	UCLA-Memphis St.	3/26/73	NBC	20.5/32

Associated Press Final Polls (Cont.)

1985

		Before Tourns	Head Coach	Final Record
1	Georgetown	.30-2	John Thompson	35-3
2	Michigan	.25-3	Bill Frieder	26-4
3	St. John's	.27-3	Lou Carnesecca	31-4
4	Oklahoma	.28-5	Billy Tubbs	31-6
5	Memphis St.	.27-3	Dana Kirk	31-4
6	Georgia Tech	.24-7	Bobby Cremins	27-8
7	North Carolina	.24-8	Dean Smith	27-9
8	Louisiana Tech	.27-2	Andy Russo	29-3
9	UNLV	.27-3	Jerry Tarkanian	28-4
10	Duke	.22-7	Mike Krzyzewski	23-8
11	VCU	.25-5	J.D. Barnett	26-6
12	Illinois	.24-8	Lou Henson	26-9
13	Kansas	.25-7	Larry Brown	26-8
14	Loyola-IL	.25-5	Gene Sullivan	27-6
15	Syracuse	.21-8	Jim Boeheim	22-9
16	N.C. State	.20-9	Jim Valvano	23-10
17	Texas Tech	.23-7	Gerald Myers	23-8
18	Tulsa	.23-7	Nolan Richardson	23-8
19	Georgia	.21-8	Hugh Durham	22-9
20	LSU	.19-9	Dale Brown	19-10

Note: Unranked **Villanova**, coached by Rollie Massimino, won the NCAAs. The Wildcats entered the tourney at 19-10 and had a final record of 25-10.

NCAA Final Four (at Rupp Arena, Lexington, KY): **Semifinals**– Georgetown 77, St. John's 59; Villanova 52, Memphis St. 45. **Championship**–Villanova 66, Georgetown 64.

NIT Championship (at Madison Square Garden): UCLA 65, Indiana 62. No Top 20 teams played in NIT.

1986

		Before Tourns	Head Coach	Final Record
1	Duke	.32-2	Mike Krzyzewski	37-3
2	Kansas	.31-3	Larry Brown	35-4
3	Kentucky	.29-3	Eddie Sutton	32-4
4	St. John's	.30-4	Lou Carnesecca	31-5
5	Michigan	.27-4	Bill Frieder	28-5
6	Georgia Tech	.25-6	Bobby Cremins	27-7
7	Louisville	.26-7	Denny Crum	32-7
8	North Carolina	.26-5	Dean Smith	28-6
9	Syracuse	.25-5	Jim Boeheim	26-6
10	Notre Dame	.23-5	Digger Phelps	23-6
11	UNLV	.31-4	Jerry Tarkanian	33-5
12	Memphis St.	.27-5	Dana Kirk	28-6
13	Georgetown	.23-7	John Thompson	24-8
14	Bradley	.31-2	Dick Versace	32-3
15	Oklahoma	.25-8	Billy Tubbs	26-9
16	Indiana	.21-7	Bob Knight	21-8
17	Navy	.27-4	Paul Evans	30-5
18	Michigan St.	.21-7	Jud Heathcote	23-8
19	Illinois	.21-9	Lou Henson	22-10
20	UTEP	.27-5	Don Haskins	27-6

NCAA Final Four (at Reunion Arena, Dallas): **Semifinals**–Duke 71, Kansas 67; Louisville 88, LSU 77. **Championship**–Louisville 72, Duke 69.

NIT Championship (at Madison Square Garden): Ohio St. 73, Wyoming 63. No Top 20 teams played in NIT.

1987

		Before Tourns	Head Coach	Final Record
1	UNLV	.33-1	Jerry Tarkanian	37-2
2	North Carolina	.29-3	Dean Smith	32-4
3	**Indiana**	.24-4	Bob Knight	30-4
4	Georgetown	.26-4	John Thompson	29-5
5	DePaul	.26-2	Joey Meyer	28-3
6	Iowa	.27-4	Tom Davis	30-5
7	Purdue	.24-4	Gene Keady	25-5
8	Temple	.31-3	John Chaney	32-4
9	Alabama	.26-4	Wimp Sanderson	28-5
10	Syracuse	.26-6	Jim Boeheim	31-7
11	Illinois	.23-7	Lou Henson	23-8
12	Pittsburgh	.24-7	Paul Evans	25-8
13	Clemson	.25-5	Cliff Ellis	25-6
14	Missouri	.24-9	Norm Stewart	24-10
15	UCLA	.24-6	Walt Hazzard	25-7
16	New Orleans	.25-3	Benny Dees	26-4
17	Duke	.22-8	Mike Krzyzewski	24-9
18	Notre Dame	.22-7	Digger Phelps	24-8
19	TCU	.23-6	Jim Killingsworth	24-7
20	Kansas	.23-10	Larry Brown	25-11

NCAA Final Four (at the Superdome, New Orleans): **Semifinals**–Syracuse 77, Providence 63; Indiana 97, UNLV 93. **Championship**–Indiana 74, Syracuse 73.

NIT Championship (at Madison Square Garden): Southern Miss. 84, La Salle 80. No Top 20 teams played in NIT.

1988

		Before Tourns	Head Coach	Final Record
1	Temple	.29-1	John Chaney	32-2
2	Arizona	.31-2	Lute Olson	35-3
3	Purdue	.27-3	Gene Keady	29-4
4	Oklahoma	.30-3	Billy Tubbs	35-4
5	Duke	.24-6	Mike Krzyzewski	28-7
6	Kentucky	.25-5	Eddie Sutton	27-6
7	North Carolina	.24-6	Dean Smith	27-7
8	Pittsburgh	.23-6	Paul Evans	24-7
9	Syracuse	.25-8	Jim Boeheim	26-9
10	Michigan	.24-7	Bill Frieder	26-8
11	Bradley	.26-4	Stan Albeck	26-5
12	UNLV	.27-5	Jerry Tarkanian	28-6
13	Wyoming	.26-5	Benny Dees	26-6
14	N.C. State	.24-7	Jim Valvano	24-8
15	Loyola-CA	.27-3	Paul Westhead	28-4
16	Illinois	.22-9	Lou Henson	23-10
17	Iowa	.22-9	Tom Davis	24-10
18	Xavier-OH	.26-3	Pete Gillen	26-4
19	BYU	.25-5	Ladell Andersen	26-6
20	Kansas St.	.22-8	Lon Kruger	25-9

Note: Unranked **Kansas**, coached by Larry Brown, won the NCAAs. The Jayhawks entered the tourney at 21-11 and had a final record of 27-11.

NCAA Final Four (at Kemper Arena, Kansas City): **Semifinals**–Kansas 66, Duke 59; Oklahoma 86, Arizona 78. **Championship**–Kansas 83, Oklahoma 79.

NIT Championship (at Madison Square Garden): Connecticut 72, Ohio St. 67. No Top 20 teams played in NIT.

1989

		Before Tourns	Head Coach	Final Record
1	Arizona	27-3	Lute Olson	29-4
2	Georgetown	26-4	John Thompson	29-5
3	Illinois	27-4	Lou Henson	31-5
4	Oklahoma	28-5	Billy Tubbs	30-6
5	North Carolina	27-7	Dean Smith	29-8
6	Missouri	27-7	Norm Stewart & Rich Daly*	29-8
7	Syracuse	27-7	Jim Boeheim	30-8
8	Indiana	25-7	Bob Knight	27-8
9	Duke	24-7	Mike Krzyzewski	28-8
10	**Michigan**	24-7	Bill Frieder (24-7) & Steve Fisher (6-0)	30-7
11	Seton Hall	26-6	P.J. Carlesimo	31-7
12	Louisville	22-8	Denny Crum	24-9
13	Stanford	26-6	Mike Montgomery	26-7
14	Iowa	22-9	Tom Davis	23-10
15	UNLV	26-7	Jerry Tarkanian	29-8
16	Florida St.	22-7	Pat Kennedy	22-8
17	West Virginia	25-4	Gale Catlett	26-5
18	Ball State	28-2	Rick Majerus	29-3
19	N.C. State	20-8	Jim Valvano	22-9
20	Alabama	23-7	Wimp Sanderson	23-8

NCAA Final Four (at The Kingdome, Seattle): **Semifinals**–Seton Hall 95, Duke 78; Michigan 83, Illinois 81. **Championship**–Michigan 80, Seton Hall 79 (OT).
NIT Championship (at Madison Square Garden): St. John's 73, St. Louis 65. No Top 20 teams played in NIT.

*Norm Stewart's assistant Rich Daly temporarily took over for his ailing boss (Daly coached the final 14 games of the season) but returned to his role as an assistant when Stewart recovered before the start of the following season.

1990

		Before Tourns	Head Coach	Final Record
1	Oklahoma	26-4	Billy Tubbs	27-5
2	UNLV	29-5	Jerry Tarkanian	35-5
3	Connecticut	28-5	Jim Calhoun	31-6
4	Michigan St.	26-5	Jud Heathcote	28-6
5	Kansas	29-4	Roy Williams	30-5
6	Syracuse	24-6	Jim Boeheim	26-7
7	Arkansas	26-4	Nolan Richardson	30-5
8	Georgetown	23-6	John Thompson	24-7
9	Georgia Tech	24-6	Bobby Cremins	28-7
10	Purdue	21-7	Gene Keady	22-8
11	Missouri	26-5	Norm Stewart	26-6
12	La Salle	29-1	Speedy Morris	30-2
13	Michigan	22-7	Steve Fisher	23-8
14	Arizona	24-6	Lute Olson	25-7
15	Duke	24-8	Mike Krzyzewski	29-9
16	Louisville	26-7	Denny Crum	27-8
17	Clemson	24-8	Cliff Ellis	26-9
18	Illinois	21-7	Lou Henson	21-8
19	LSU	22-8	Dale Brown	23-9
20	Minnesota	20-8	Clem Haskins	23-9
21	Loyola-CA	23-5	Paul Westhead	26-6
22	Oregon St.	22-6	Jim Anderson	22-7
23	Alabama	24-8	Wimp Sanderson	26-9
24	New Mexico St.	26-4	Neil McCarthy	26-5
25	Xavier-OH	26-4	Pete Gillen	28-5

NCAA Final Four (at McNichols Sports Arena, Denver): **Semifinals**–Duke 97, Arkansas 83; UNLV 90, Georgia Tech 81. **Championship**–UNLV 103, Duke 73.
NIT Championship (at Madison Square Garden): Vanderbilt 74, St.Louis 72. No Top 25 teams played in NIT.

1991

		Before Tourns	Head Coach	Final Record
1	UNLV	30-0	Jerry Tarkanian	34-1
2	Arkansas	31-3	Nolan Richardson	34-4
3	Indiana	27-4	Bob Knight	29-5
4	North Carolina	25-5	Dean Smith	29-6
5	Ohio St.	25-3	Randy Ayers	27-4
6	**Duke**	26-7	Mike Krzyzewski	32-7
7	Syracuse	26-5	Jim Boeheim	26-6
8	Arizona	26-6	Lute Olson	28-7
9	Kentucky	22-6	Rick Pitino	same*
10	Utah	28-3	Rick Majerus	30-4
11	Nebraska	26-7	Danny Nee	26-8
12	Kansas	22-7	Roy Williams	27-8
13	Seton Hall	22-8	P.J. Carlesimo	25-9
14	Oklahoma St.	22-7	Eddie Sutton	24-8
15	New Mexico St.	23-5	Neil McCarthy	23-6
16	UCLA	23-8	Jim Harrick	23-9
17	E.Tennessee St.	28-4	Alan LaForce	28-5
18	Princeton	24-2	Pete Carril	24-3
19	Alabama	21-9	Wimp Sanderson	23-10
20	St. John's	20-8	Lou Carnesecca	23-9
21	Mississippi St.	20-8	Richard Williams	20-9
22	LSU	20-9	Dale Brown	20-10
23	Texas	22-8	Tom Penders	23-9
24	DePaul	20-8	Joey Meyer	20-9
25	Southern Miss.	21-7	M.K. Turk	21-8

*On probation

NCAA Final Four (at the Hoosier Dome, Indianapolis): **Semifinals**–Kansas 79, North Carolina 73; Duke 79, UNLV 77. **Championship**–Duke 72, Kansas 65.
NIT Championship (at Madison Square Garden): Stanford 78, Oklahoma 72. No Top 25 teams played in NIT.

1992

		Before Tourns	Head Coach	Final Record
1	**Duke**	28-2	Mike Krzyzewski	34-2
2	Kansas	26-4	Roy Williams	27-5
3	Ohio St.	23-5	Randy Ayers	26-6
4	UCLA	25-4	Jim Harrick	28-5
5	Indiana	23-6	Bob Knight	27-7
6	Kentucky	26-6	Rick Pitino	29-7
7	UNLV	26-2	Jerry Tarkanian	same*
8	USC	23-5	George Raveling	24-6
9	Arkansas	25-7	Nolan Richardson	26-8
10	Arizona	24-6	Lute Olson	24-7
11	Oklahoma St.	26-7	Eddie Sutton	28-8
12	Cincinnati	25-4	Bob Huggins	29-5
13	Alabama	25-8	Wimp Sanderson	26-9
14	Michigan St.	21-7	Jud Heathcote	22-8
15	Michigan	20-8	Steve Fisher	25-9
16	Missouri	20-8	Norm Stewart	21-9
17	Massachusetts	28-4	John Calipari	30-5
18	North Carolina	21-9	Dean Smith	23-10
19	Seton Hall	21-8	P.J. Carlesimo	23-9
20	Florida St.	20-8	Pat Kennedy	22-10
21	Syracuse	21-9	Jim Boeheim	22-10
22	Georgetown	21-9	John Thompson	22-10
23	Oklahoma	20-8	Billy Tubbs	21-9
24	DePaul	20-8	Joey Meyer	20-9
25	LSU	20-9	Dale Brown	21-10

*On probation

NCAA Final Four (at the Metrodome, Minneapolis): **Semifinals**–Michigan 76, Cincinnati 72; Duke 81, Indiana 78. **Championship**–Duke 71, Michigan 51.
NIT Championship (at Madison Square Garden): Virginia 81, Notre Dame 76 (OT). No Top 25 teams played in NIT.

Associated Press Final Polls (Cont.)

1993

	Team	Before Tourns	Head Coach	Final Record
1	Indiana	28-3	Bob Knight	31-4
2	Kentucky	26-3	Rick Pitino	30-4
3	Michigan	26-4	Steve Fisher	31-5
4	**N. Carolina**	28-4	Dean Smith	34-4
5	Arizona	24-3	Lute Olson	24-4
6	Seton Hall	27-6	P.J. Carlesimo	28-7
7	Cincinnati	24-4	Bob Huggins	27-5
8	Vanderbilt	26-5	Eddie Fogler	28-6
9	Kansas	25-6	Roy Williams	29-7
10	Duke	23-7	Mike Krzyzewski	24-8
11	Florida St.	22-9	Pat Kennedy	25-10
12	Arkansas	20-8	Nolan Richardson	22-9
13	Iowa	22-8	Tom Davis	23-9
14	Massachusetts	23-6	John Calipari	24-7
15	Louisville	20-8	Denny Crum	22-9
16	Wake Forest	19-8	Dave Odom	21-9
17	New Orleans	26-3	Tim Floyd	26-4
18	Georgia Tech	19-10	Bobby Cremins	19-11
19	Utah	23-6	Rick Majerus	24-7
20	Western Ky.	24-5	Ralph Willard	26-6
21	New Mexico	24-6	Dave Bliss	24-7
22	Purdue	18-9	Gene Keady	18-10
23	Oklahoma St.	19-8	Eddie Sutton	20-9
24	New Mexico St.	25-7	Neil McCarthy	26-8
25	UNLV	21-7	Rollie Massimino	21-8

NCAA Final Four (at the Superdome, New Orleans): **Semifinals**–North Carolina 78, Kansas 68; Michigan 81, Kentucky 78 (OT). **Championship**–North Carolina 77, Michigan 71.

NIT Championship (at Madison Square Garden): Minnesota 62, Georgetown 61. No. 25 UNLV was the only Top 25 team that played in the NIT.

1995

	Team	Before Tourns	Head Coach	Final Record
1	**UCLA**	25-2	Jim Harrick	31-2
2	Kentucky	25-4	Rick Pitino	28-5
3	Wake Forest	24-5	Dave Odom	26-6
4	North Carolina	24-5	Dean Smith	28-6
5	Kansas	23-5	Roy Williams	25-6
6	Arkansas	27-6	Nolan Richardson	32-7
7	Massachusetts	26-4	John Calipari	26-5
8	Connecticut	25-4	Jim Calhoun	28-5
9	Villanova	25-7	Steve Lappas	25-8
10	Maryland	24-7	Gary Williams	26-8
11	Michigan St.	22-5	Jud Heathcote	22-6
12	Purdue	24-6	Gene Keady	25-7
13	Virginia	22-8	Jeff Jones	25-9
14	Oklahoma St.	23-9	Eddie Sutton	27-10
15	Arizona	23-7	Lute Olson	23-8
16	Arizona St.	22-8	Bill Frieder	24-9
17	Oklahoma	23-8	Kelvin Sampson	23-9
18	Mississippi St.	20-7	Richard Williams	22-8
19	Utah	27-5	Rick Majerus	28-6
20	Alabama	22-9	David Hobbs	23-10
21	Western Ky.	26-3	Matt Kilcullen	27-4
22	Georgetown	19-9	John Thompson	21-10
23	Missouri	19-8	Norm Stewart	20-9
24	Iowa St.	22-10	Tim Floyd	23-11
25	Syracuse	19-9	Jim Boeheim	20-10

NCAA Final Four (at the Kingdome, Seattle): **Semifinals**– UCLA 74, Oklahoma St. 61; Arkansas 75, North Carolina 68. **Championship**– UCLA 89, Arkansas 78.

NIT Championship (at Madison Square Garden): Virginia Tech 65, Marquette 64 (OT). No top 25 teams played in NIT.

1994

	Team	Before Tourns	Head Coach	Final Record
1	North Carolina	27-6	Dean Smith	28-7
2	**Arkansas**	25-3	Nolan Richardson	31-3
3	Purdue	26-4	Gene Keady	29-5
4	Connecticut	27-4	Jim Calhoun	29-5
5	Missouri	25-3	Norm Stewart	28-4
6	Duke	23-5	Mike Krzyzewski	28-6
7	Kentucky	26-6	Rick Pitino	27-7
8	Massachusetts	27-6	John Calipari	28-7
9	Arizona	25-5	Lute Olson	29-6
10	Louisville	26-5	Denny Crum	28-6
11	Michigan	21-7	Steve Fisher	24-8
12	Temple	22-7	John Chaney	23-8
13	Kansas	25-7	Roy Williams	27-8
14	Florida	25-7	Lon Kruger	29-8
15	Syracuse	21-6	Jim Boeheim	23-7
16	California	22-7	Todd Bozeman	22-8
17	UCLA	21-6	Jim Harrick	21-7
18	Indiana	19-8	Bob Knight	21-9
19	Oklahoma St.	23-9	Eddie Sutton	24-10
20	Texas	25-7	Tom Penders	26-8
21	Marquette	22-8	Kevin O'Neill	24-9
22	Nebraska	20-9	Danny Nee	20-10
23	Minnesota	20-11	Clem Haskins	21-12
24	Saint Louis	23-5	Charlie Spoonhour	23-6
25	Cincinnati	22-9	Bob Huggins	22-10

NCAA Final Four (at the Charlotte Coliseum): **Semifinals**– Arkansas 91, Arizona 82; Duke 70, Florida 65. **Championship**– Arkansas 76, Duke 72.

NIT Championship (at Madison Square Garden): Villanova 80, Vanderbilt 73. No top 25 teams played in NIT.

1996

	Team	Before Tourns	Head Coach	Final Record
1	Massachusetts	31-1	John Calipari	35-2
2	**Kentucky**	28-2	Rick Pitino	34-2
3	Connecticut	30-2	Jim Calhoun	32-3
4	Georgetown	26-7	John Thompson	29-8
5	Kansas	26-4	Roy Williams	29-5
6	Purdue	25-5	Gene Keady	26-6
7	Cincinnati	25-4	Bob Huggins	28-5
8	Texas Tech	28-1	James Dickey	30-2
9	Wake Forest	23-5	Dave Odom	26-6
10	Villanova	25-6	Steve Lappas	26-7
11	Arizona	24-6	Lute Olson	26-7
12	Utah	25-6	Rick Majerus	27-7
13	Georgia Tech	22-11	Bobby Cremins	24-12
14	UCLA	23-7	Jim Harrick	23-8
15	Syracuse	24-8	Jim Boeheim	29-9
16	Memphis	22-7	Larry Finch	22-8
17	Iowa St.	23-8	Tim Floyd	24-9
18	Penn St.	21-6	Jerry Dunn	21-7
19	Mississippi St.	22-7	Richard Williams	26-8
20	Marquette	22-7	Mike Deane	23-8
21	Iowa	22-8	Tom Davis	23-9
22	Virginia Tech	22-5	Bill Foster	23-6
23	New Mexico	27-4	Dave Bliss	28-5
24	Louisville	20-11	Denny Crum	22-12
25	North Carolina	20-10	Dean Smith	21-11

NCAA Final Four (at the Meadowlands, E. Rutherford, N.J.): **Semifinals**– Kentucky 81, Massachusetts 74; Syracuse 77, Mississippi St. 69. **Championship**– Kentucky 76, Syracuse 67.

NIT Championship (at Madison Square Garden): Nebraska 60, St. Joseph's 56. No top 25 teams played in NIT.

1997

	Before Tourns	Head Coach	Final Record
1	Kansas 32-1	Roy Williams	34-2
2	Utah 26-3	Rick Majerus	29-4
3	Minnesota 27-3	Clem Haskins	31-4
4	North Carolina .24-6	Dean Smith	28-7
5	Kentucky 30-4	Rick Pitino	35-5
6	South Carolina .24-7	Eddie Fogler	24-8
7	UCLA 21-7	Steve Lavin	24-8
8	Duke 23-8	Mike Krzyzewski	24-9
9	Wake Forest ...23-6	Dave Odom	24-7
10	Cincinnati 25-7	Bob Huggins	26-8
11	New Mexico ...24-7	Dave Bliss	25-8
12	St. Joseph's ...24-6	Phil Martelli	26-7
13	Xavier 22-5	Skip Prosser	23-6
14	Clemson 21-9	Rick Barnes	23-10
15	**Arizona** 19-9	Lute Olson	25-9
16	Charleston 28-2	John Kresse	29-3
17	Georgia 24-8	Tubby Smith	24-9
18	Iowa St. 20-8	Tim Floyd	22-9
19	Illinois 21-9	Lon Kruger	22-10
20	Villanova 23-9	Steve Lappas	24-10
21	Stanford 20-7	Mike Montgomery	22-8
22	Maryland 21-10	Gary Williams	21-11
23	Boston College .21-8	Jim O'Brien	22-9
24	Colorado 21-9	Ricardo Patton	22-10
25	Louisville 23-8	Denny Crum	26-9

NCAA Final Four (at the RCA Dome, Indianapolis): **Semifinals**– Kentucky 78, Minnesota 69; Arizona 66, North Carolina 58. **Championship**– Arizona 84, Kentucky 79 (OT).

NIT Championship (at Madison Square Garden): Michigan 82, Florida St. 72. No top 25 teams played in NIT.

1998

	Before Tourns	Head Coach	Final Record
1	North Carolina ..30-3	Bill Guthridge	34-4
2	Kansas 34-3	Roy Williams	35-4
3	Duke 29-3	Mike Krzyzewski	32-4
4	Arizona 27-4	Lute Olson	30-5
5	**Kentucky** 29-4	Tubby Smith	35-4
6	Connecticut ...29-4	Jim Calhoun	32-5
7	Utah 25-3	Rick Majerus	30-4
8	Princeton 26-1	Bill Carmody	27-2
9	Cincinnati 26-5	Bob Huggins	27-6
10	Stanford 26-4	Mike Montgomery	30-5
11	Purdue 26-7	Gene Keady	28-8
12	Michigan 24-8	Brian Ellerbe	25-9
13	Mississippi 22-6	Rob Evans	22-7
14	South Carolina .23-7	Eddie Fogler	23-8
15	TCU 27-5	Billy Tubbs	27-6
16	Michigan St. ...20-7	Tom Izzo	22-8
17	Arkansas 23-8	Nolan Richardson	24-9
18	New Mexico ...23-8	Dave Bliss	24-8
19	UCLA 22-8	Steve Lavin	24-9
20	Maryland 19-10	Gary Williams	21-11
21	Syracuse 24-8	Jim Boeheim	26-9
22	Illinois 22-9	Lon Kruger	23-10
23	Xavier 22-7	Skip Prosser	22-8
24	Temple 21-8	John Chaney	21-9
25	Murray St. 29-3	Mark Gottfried	29-4

NCAA Final Four (at the Alamodome, San Antonio): **Semifinals**– Kentucky 86, Stanford 85 (OT); Utah 65, North Carolina 59. **Championship**– Kentucky 78, Utah 69.

NIT Championship (at Madison Square Garden): Minnesota 79, Penn St. 72. No top 25 teams played in NIT.

1999

	Before Tourns	Head Coach	Final Record
1	Duke 32-1	Mike Krzyzewski	37-2
2	Michigan St. ...29-4	Tom Izzo	33-5
3	**Connecticut** ..28-2	Jim Calhoun	34-2
4	Auburn 27-3	Cliff Ellis	29-4
5	Maryland 26-5	Gary Williams	28-6
6	Utah 27-4	Rick Majerus	28-5
7	Stanford 25-6	Mike Montgomery	26-7
8	Kentucky 25-8	Tubby Smith	28-9
9	St. John's 25-8	Mike Jarvis	28-9
10	Miami-FL 22-6	Leonard Hamilton	23-7
11	Cincinnati 26-5	Bob Huggins	27-6
12	Arizona 22-6	Lute Olson	22-7
13	North Carolina .24-9	Bill Guthridge	24-10
14	Ohio St. 23-8	Jim O'Brien	27-9
15	UCLA 22-8	Steve Lavin	22-9
16	College of Charleston 28-2	John Kresse	28-3
17	Arkansas 22-10	Nolan Richardson	23-11
18	Wisconsin 22-9	Dick Bennett	22-10
19	Indiana 22-10	Bobby Knight	23-11
20	Tennessee 20-8	Jerry Green	21-9
21	Iowa 18-9	Tom Davis	20-10
22	Kansas 22-9	Roy Williams	23-10
23	Florida 20-8	Billy Donovan	22-9
24	NC-Charlotte ..22-10	Bob Lutz	23-11
25	New Mexico ...24-8	Dave Bliss	25-9

NCAA Final Four (at the Tropicana Field, St. Petersburg): **Semifinals**– Duke 68, Michigan St. 62; Connecticut 64, Ohio St. 58. **Championship**– Connecticut 77, Duke 74.

NIT Championship (at Madison Square Garden): California 61, Clemson 60. No top 25 teams played in NIT.

2000

	Before Tourns	Head Coach	Final Record
1	Duke 27-4	Mike Krzyzewski	29-5
2	**Michigan St.** ..26-7	Tom Izzo	32-7
3	Stanford 26-3	Mike Montgomery	27-4
4	Arizona 26-6	Lute Olson	27-7
5	Temple 26-5	John Chaney	27-6
6	Iowa St. 29-4	Larry Eustachy	32-5
7	Cincinnati 28-3	Bob Huggins	29-4
8	Ohio St. 22-6	Jim O'Brien	23-7
9	St. John's 24-7	Mike Jarvis	25-8
10	LSU 26-5	John Brady	28-6
11	Tennessee 24-6	Jerry Green	26-7
12	Oklahoma 26-6	Kelvin Sampson	27-7
13	Florida 24-7	Billy Donovan	29-8
14	Oklahoma St. ..24-6	Eddie Sutton	27-7
15	Texas 23-8	Rick Barnes	24-9
16	Syracuse 24-5	Jim Boeheim	26-6
17	Maryland 24-9	Gary Williams	25-10
18	Tulsa 29-4	Bill Self	32-5
19	Kentucky 22-9	Tubby Smith	23-10
20	Connecticut ...24-9	Jim Calhoun	25-10
21	Illinois 21-9	Lon Kruger	22-10
22	Indiana 20-8	Bobby Knight	20-9
23	Miami-FL 21-10	Leonard Hamilton	23-11
24	Auburn 23-9	Cliff Ellis	24-10
25	Purdue 21-9	Gene Keady	24-10

NCAA Final Four (at the RCA Dome, Indianapolis): **Semifinals**– Michigan St. 53, Wisconsin 41; Florida 71, North Carolina 59. **Championship**– Michigan St. 89, Florida 76.

NIT Championship (at Madison Square Garden): Wake Forest 71, Notre Dame 61. No top 25 teams played in NIT.

Associated Press Final Polls (Cont.)

2001

		Before Tourns	Head Coach	Final Record
1	**Duke**	.29-4	Mike Krzyzewski	35-4
2	Stanford	.28-2	Mike Montgomery	31-3
3	Michigan St.	.24-4	Tom Izzo	28-5
4	Illinois	.24-7	Bill Self	27-8
5	Arizona	.23-7	Lute Olson	28-8
6	North Carolina	.25-6	Matt Doherty	26-7
7	Boston College	.26-4	Al Skinner	27-5
8	Florida	.23-6	Billy Donovan	24-7
9	Kentucky	.22-9	Tubby Smith	24-10
10	Iowa St.	.25-5	Larry Eustachy	25-6
11	Maryland	.21-10	Gary Williams	25-11
12	Kansas	.24-6	Roy Williams	26-7
13	Oklahoma	.26-6	Kelvin Sampson	26-7
14	Mississippi	.25-7	Rod Barnes	27-8
15	UCLA	.21-8	Steve Lavin	23-9
16	Virginia	.20-8	Pete Gillen	20-9
17	Syracuse	.24-8	Jim Boeheim	25-9
18	Texas	.25-8	Rick Barnes	25-9
19	Notre Dame	.19-9	Mike Brey	20-10
20	Indiana	.21-12	Mike Davis	21-13
21	Georgetown	.23-7	Craig Esherick	25-8
22	St. Joseph's	.25-6	Phil Martelli	26-7
23	Wake Forest	.19-10	Dave Odom	19-11
24	Iowa	.22-11	Steve Alford	23-12
25	Wisconsin	18-10	Dick Bennett (2-1) & Brad Soderberg (16-10)	18-11

NCAA Final Four (at the HHH Metrodome, Minneapolis): **Semifinals**–Duke 95, Maryland 84; Arizona 80, Michigan St. 61. **Championship**–Duke 82, Arizona 72.
NIT Championship (at Madison Square Garden): Tulsa 79, Alabama 60. No top 25 teams played in NIT.

2002

		Before Tourns	Head Coach	Final Record
1	Duke	.29-3	Mike Krzyzewski	32-4
2	Kansas	.29-3	Roy Williams	33-4
3	Oklahoma	.27-4	Kelvin Sampson	31-5
4	**Maryland**	.26-4	Gary Williams	32-4
5	Cincinnati	.30-3	Bob Huggins	31-4
6	Gonzaga	.29-3	Mark Few	29-4
7	Arizona	.22-9	Lute Olson	24-10
8	Alabama	.26-7	Mark Gottfried	27-8
9	Pittsburgh	.27-5	Ben Howland	29-6
10	Connecticut	.24-6	Jim Calhoun	27-7
11	Oregon	.23-8	Ernie Kent	26-9
12	Marquette	.26-6	Tom Crean	26-7
13	Illinois	.24-8	Bill Self	26-9
14	Ohio St.	.23-7	Jim O'Brien	24-8
15	Florida	.22-8	Billy Donovan	22-9
16	Kentucky	.20-9	Tubby Smith	22-10
17	Mississippi St.	.26-7	Rick Stansbury	27-8
18	USC	.22-9	Henry Bibby	22-10
19	Western Ky.	.28-3	Dennis Felton	28-4
20	Oklahoma St.	.23-8	Eddie Sutton	23-9
21	Miami-FL	.24-7	Perry Clark	24-8
22	Xavier	.25-5	Thad Matta	26-6
23	Georgia	.21-9	Jim Harrick	22-10
24	Stanford	.19-9	Mike Montgomery	20-10
25	Hawaii	.27-5	Riley Wallace	27-6

NCAA Final Four (at the Georgia Dome, Atlanta): **Semifinals**–Maryland 97, Kansas 88; Indiana 73, Oklahoma 64. **Championship**–Maryland 64, Indiana 52.
NIT Championship (at Madison Square Garden): Memphis 72, South Carolina 62. No top 25 teams played in NIT.

2003

		Before Tourns	Head Coach	Final Record
1	Kentucky	.29-3	Tubby Smith	32-4
2	Arizona	.25-3	Lute Olson	28-4
3	Oklahoma	.24-6	Kelvin Sampson	27-7
4	Pittsburgh	.26-4	Ben Howland	28-5
5	Texas	.22-6	Rick Barnes	26-7
6	Kansas	.25-7	Roy Williams	30-8
7	Duke	.24-6	Mike Krzyzewski	26-7
8	Wake Forest	.24-5	Skip Prosser	25-6
9	Marquette	.23-5	Tom Crean	27-6
10	Florida	.24-7	Billy Donovan	25-8
11	Illinois	.24-6	Bill Self	25-7
12	Xavier	.25-5	Thad Matta	26-6
13	**Syracuse**	.24-5	Jim Boeheim	30-5
14	Louisville	.24-6	Rick Pitino	25-7
15	Creighton	.29-4	Dana Altman	29-5
16	Dayton	.25-5	Oliver Purnell	25-6
17	Maryland	.19-9	Gary Williams	21-10
18	Stanford	.23-8	Mike Montgomery	23-9
19	Memphis	.23-6	John Calipari	23-7
20	Mississippi St.	.21-9	Rick Stansbury	21-10
21	Wisconsin	.22-7	Bo Ryan	24-8
22	Notre Dame	.22-9	Mike Brey	24-10
23	Connecticut	.21-9	Jim Calhoun	23-10
24	Missouri	.21-10	Quin Snyder	22-11
25	Georgia	.19-8	Jim Harrick	same*

*Georgia chose not to participate in any postseason tournaments due to an investigation into academic fraud.

NCAA Final Four (at the Superdome, New Orleans): **Semifinals**–Syracuse 95, Texas 84; Kansas 94, Marquette 61. **Championship**–Syracuse 81, Kansas 78.
NIT Championship (at Madison Square Garden): St. John's 70, Georgetown 67. No top 25 teams played in NIT.

2004

		Before Tourns	Head Coach	Final Record
1	Stanford	.29-1	Mike Montgomery	30-2
2	Kentucky	.26-4	Tubby Smith	27-5
3	Gonzaga	.27-2	Mark Few	28-3
4	Oklahoma St.	.27-3	Eddie Sutton	31-4
5	St. Joseph's	.27-1	Phil Martelli	30-2
6	Duke	.27-5	Mike Krzyzewski	31-6
7	Connecticut	.27-6	Jim Calhoun	33-6
8	Mississippi St.	.25-3	Rick Stansbury	26-4
9	Pittsburgh	.29-4	Jamie Dixon	31-5
10	Wisconsin	.24-6	Bo Ryan	25-7
11	Cincinnati	.24-6	Bob Huggins	25-7
12	Texas	.23-7	Rick Barnes	25-8
13	Illinois	.24-6	Bruce Weber	26-7
14	Georgia Tech	.23-9	Paul Hewitt	28-10
15	N.C. State	.20-9	Herb Sendek	21-10
16	Kansas	.21-8	Bill Self	24-9
17	Wake Forest	.19-9	Skip Prosser	21-10
18	North Carolina	.18-10	Roy Williams	19-11
19	Maryland	.19-11	Gary Williams	20-12
20	Syracuse	.21-7	Jim Boeheim	23-8
21	Providence	.20-8	Tim Welsh	20-9
22	Arizona	.20-9	Lute Olson	20-10
23	So. Illinois	.25-4	Matt Painter	25-5
24	Memphis	.21-7	John Calipari	22-8
25	Boston College	.23-9	Al Skinner	24-10
	Utah St.	.25-3	Stew Morrill	25-4

NCAA Final Four (at the Alamodome, San Antonio): **Semifinals**–Georgia Tech 67, Oklahoma St. 65; Connecticut 79, Duke 78. **Championship**–Connecticut 82, Georgia Tech 73.
NIT Championship (at Madison Square Garden): Michigan 62, Rutgers 55. No. 25 Utah St. was the only Top 25 team that played in the NIT.

2005

	Before Tours	Head Coach	Final Record
1 Illinois	32-1	Bruce Weber	37-2
2 North Carolina	27-4	Roy Williams	33-4
3 Duke	25-5	Mike Krzyzewski	27-6
4 Louisville	29-4	Rick Pitino	33-5
5 Wake Forest	26-5	Skip Prosser	27-6
6 Oklahoma St.	24-6	Eddie Sutton	26-7
7 Kentucky	25-5	Tubby Smith	28-6
8 Washington	27-5	Lorenzo Romar	29-6
9 Arizona	27-6	Lute Olson	30-7
10 Gonzaga	25-4	Mark Few	26-5
11 Syracuse	27-6	Jim Boeheim	27-7
12 Kansas	23-6	Bill Self	23-7
13 Connecticut	22-7	Jim Calhoun	23-8
14 Boston College	24-4	Al Skinner	25-5
15 Michigan St.	24-6	Tom Izzo	26-7
16 Florida	23-7	Billy Donovan	24-8
17 Oklahoma	24-7	Kelvin Sampson	25-8
18 Utah	27-5	Ray Giacoletti	29-6
19 Villanova	22-7	Jay Wright	24-8
20 Wisconsin	22-8	Bo Ryan	25-9
21 Alabama	24-7	Mark Gottfried	24-8
22 Pacific	26-3	Bob Thomason	27-4
23 Cincinnati	24-7	Bob Huggins	25-8
24 Texas Tech	20-10	Bob Knight	22-11
25 Georgia Tech	19-11	Paul Hewitt	20-12

NCAA Final Four (at the Edward Jones Dome, St. Louis): **Semifinals**—Illinois 72, Louisville 57; North Carolina 87, Michigan St. 71. **Championship**—North Carolina 75, Illinois 70.

NIT Championship (at Madison Square Garden): South Carolina 60, St. Joseph's 57. No top 25 teams played in NIT.

2006

	Before Tours	Head Coach	Final Record
1 Duke	30-3	Mike Krzyzewski	32-4
2 Connecticut	27-3	Jim Calhoun	30-4
3 Villanova	25-4	Jay Wright	28-5
4 Memphis	30-3	John Calipari	33-4
5 Gonzaga	27-3	Mark Few	29-4
6 Ohio St.	25-5	Thad Matta	26-6
7 Boston College	26-7	Al Skinner	28-8
UCLA	27-6	Ben Howland	32-7
9 Texas	27-6	Rick Barnes	30-7
10 North Carolina	27-4	Roy Williams	33-4
11 Florida	23-7	Billy Donovan	24-8
12 Kansas	25-7	Bill Self	25-8
13 Illinois	25-6	Bruce Weber	26-7
14 Geo. Washington	26-2	Karl Hobbs	27-3
15 Iowa	25-8	Steve Alford	25-9
16 Pittsburgh	24-7	Jamie Dixon	25-8
17 Washington	24-6	Lorenzo Romar	26-7
18 Tennessee	21-7	Bruce Pearl	22-8
19 LSU	23-8	John Brady	27-9
20 Nevada	27-5	Mark Fox	27-6
21 Syracuse	23-11	Jim Boeheim	23-12
22 West Virginia	20-10	John Beilein	22-11
23 Georgetown	21-9	John Thompson III	23-10
24 Oklahoma	20-8	Kelvin Sampson	20-9
25 UAB	24-6	Mike Anderson	24-7

NCAA Final Four (at the RCA Dome, Indianapolis): **Semifinals**—Florida 73, George Mason 58; UCLA 59, LSU 45. **Championship**—Florida 73, UCLA 57.

NIT Championship (at Madison Square Garden): South Carolina 76, Michigan 64. No top 25 teams played in NIT.

2007

	Before Tours	Head Coach	Final Record
1 Ohio St.	27-3	Thad Matta	35-4
2 Kansas	30-4	Bill Self	33-5
3 Wisconsin	29-5	Bo Ryan	30-6
4 UCLA	26-5	Ben Howland	30-6
5 Memphis	30-3	John Calipari	33-4
6 Florida	29-5	Billy Donovan	35-5
7 Texas A&M	26-6	Billy Gillispie	26-7
8 North Carolina	28-6	Roy Williams	31-7
9 Georgetown	26-6	John Thompson III	30-7
10 Nevada	28-4	Mark Fox	29-5
11 Washington St.	25-7	Tony Bennett	26-8
12 Louisville	23-9	Rick Pitino	24-10
13 Pittsburgh	25-6	Jamie Dixon	27-7
14 Southern Illinois	27-6	Chris Lowery	29-7
15 Texas	24-9	Rick Barnes	25-10
16 Oregon	26-7	Ernie Kent	29-8
17 Maryland	24-8	Gary Williams	25-9
18 Marquette	24-9	Tom Crean	24-10
19 Butler	27-6	Todd Lickliter	29-7
20 Notre Dame	24-7	Mike Brey	24-8
21 Duke	22-10	Mike Krzyzewski	22-11
22 Tennessee	22-10	Bruce Pearl	24-11
23 Brigham Young	25-8	Dave Rose	25-9
24 Winthrop	28-4	Gregg Marshall	29-5
25 UNLV	28-6	Lon Kruger	30-7

NCAA Final Four (at the Georgia Dome, Atlanta): **Semifinals**—Ohio St. 67, Georgetown 60; Florida 76, UCLA 66. **Championship**—Florida 84, Ohio St. 75.

NIT Championship (at Madison Square Garden): West Virginia 78, Clemson 73. No top 25 teams played in NIT

2008

	Before Tours	Head Coach	Final Record
1 North Carolina	32-2	Roy Williams	36-3
2 Memphis	33-1	John Calipari	38-2
3 UCLA	31-3	Ben Howland	35-4
4 Kansas	31-3	Bill Self	37-3
5 Tennessee	29-4	Bruce Pearl	31-5
6 Wisconsin	29-5	Bo Ryan	31-5
7 Texas	28-6	Rick Barnes	31-7
8 Georgetown	27-5	John Thompson III	28-6
9 Duke	27-5	Mike Krzyzewski	28-6
10 Stanford	26-7	Trent Johnson	28-8
11 Butler	29-3	Todd Lickliter	30-4
12 Xavier	27-6	Sean Miller	30-7
13 Louisville	24-8	Rick Pitino	27-9
14 Drake	28-4	Keno Davis	28-5
15 Notre Dame	24-7	Mike Brey	25-8
16 Connecticut	24-8	Jim Calhoun	24-9
17 Pittsburgh	26-9	Jamie Dixon	27-10
18 Michigan St.	25-8	Tom Izzo	27-9
19 Vanderbilt	26-7	Kevin Stallings	26-8
20 Purdue	24-8	Matt Painter	25-9
21 Washington St.	24-8	Tony Bennett	26-9
22 Clemson	24-9	Oliver Purnell	24-10
23 Davidson	26-6	Bob McKillop	29-7
24 Gonzaga	25-7	Mark Few	25-8
25 Marquette	24-9	Tom Crean	25-10

NCAA Final Four (at the Alamodome, San Antonio): **Semifinals**—Memphis 78, UCLA 63; Kansas 84, North Carolina 66. **Championship**—Kansas 75, Memphis 68.

NIT Championship (at Madison Square Garden): Ohio St. 92, Massachusetts 85. No top 25 teams played in NIT

Annual NCAA Division I Leaders
Scoring

The NCAA did not begin keeping individual scoring records until the 1947-48 season. All averages include postseason games where applicable. **Multiple winners:** Pete Maravich and Oscar Robertson (3); Keydren Clark, Darrell Floyd, Charles Jones, Harry Kelly, Frank Selvy, Freeman Williams and Reggie Williams (2).

Year		Gm	Pts	Avg	Year		Gm	Pts	Avg
1948	Murray Wier, Iowa	19	399	21.0	1979	Lawrence Butler, Idaho St	27	812	30.1
1949	Tony Lavelli, Yale	30	671	22.4	1980	Tony Murphy, Southern-BR	29	932	32.J
1950	Paul Arizin, Villanova	29	735	25.3	1981	Zam Fredrick, S. Carolina	27	781	28.9
1951	Bill Mlkvy, Temple	25	731	29.2	1982	Harry Kelly, Texas Southern	29	862	29.7
1952	Clyde Lovellette, Kansas	28	795	28.4	1983	Harry Kelly, Texas Southern	29	835	28.8
1953	Frank Selvy, Furman	25	738	29.5	1984	Joe Jakubick, Akron	27	814	30.1
1954	Frank Selvy, Furman	29	1209	41.7	1985	Xavier McDaniel, Wichita St	31	844	27.2
1955	Darrell Floyd, Furman	25	897	35.9	1986	Terrance Bailey, Wagner	29	854	29.4
1956	Darrell Floyd, Furman	28	946	33.8	1987	Kevin Houston, Army	29	953	32.9
1957	Grady Wallace, S. Carolina	29	906	31.2	1988	Hersey Hawkins, Bradley	31	1125	36.3
1958	Oscar Robertson, Cincinnati	28	984	35.1	1989	Hank Gathers, Loyola-CA	31	1015	32.7
1959	Oscar Robertson, Cincinnati	30	978	32.6	1990	Bo Kimble, Loyola-CA	32	1131	35.3
1960	Oscar Robertson, Cincinnati	30	1011	33.7	1991	Kevin Bradshaw, US Int'l	28	1054	37.6
1961	Frank Burgess, Gonzaga	26	842	32.4	1992	Brett Roberts, Morehead St	29	815	28.1
1962	Billy McGill, Utah	26	1009	38.8	1993	Greg Guy, Texas-Pan Am	19	556	29.3
1963	Nick Werkman, Seton Hall	22	650	29.5	1994	Glenn Robinson, Purdue	34	1030	30.3
1964	Howie Komives, Bowling Green	23	844	36.7	1995	Kurt Thomas, TCU	27	781	28.9
1965	Rick Barry, Miami-FL	26	973	37.4	1996	Kevin Granger, Texas Southern	24	648	27.0
1966	Dave Schellhase, Purdue	24	781	32.5	1997	Charles Jones, LIU-Brooklyn	30	903	30.1
1967	Jimmy Walker, Providence	28	851	30.4	1998	Charles Jones, LIU-Brooklyn	30	869	29.0
1968	Pete Maravich, LSU	26	1138	43.8	1999	Alvin Young, Niagara	29	728	25.1
1969	Pete Maravich, LSU	26	1148	44.2	2000	Courtney Alexander, Fresno St.	27	669	24.8
1970	Pete Maravich, LSU	31	1381	44.5	2001	Ronnie McCollum, Centenary	27	787	29.1
1971	Johnny Neumann, Ole Miss	23	923	40.1	2002	Jason Conley, VMI	28	820	29.3
1972	Dwight Lamar, SW La	29	1054	36.3	2003	Ruben Douglas, New Mexico	28	783	28.0
1973	Bird Averitt, Pepperdine	25	848	33.9	2004	Keydren Clark, St. Peter's	29	775	26.7
1974	Larry Fogle, Canisius	25	835	33.4	2005	Keydren Clark, St. Peter's	28	721	25.8
1975	Bob McCurdy, Richmond	26	855	32.9	2006	Adam Morrison, Gonzaga	33	926	28.1
1976	Marshall Rodgers, Texas-Pan Am	25	919	36.8	2007	Reggie Williams, VMI	33	928	28.1
1977	Freeman Williams, Portland St.	26	1010	38.8	2008	Reggie Williams, VMI	25	695	27.8
1978	Freeman Williams, Portland St.	27	969	35.9					

Rebounds

The NCAA did not begin keeping individual rebounding records until the 1950-51 season. From 1956-62, the championship was decided on highest percentage of recoveries out of all rebounds made by both teams in all games. All averages include postseason games where applicable. **Multiple winners:** Paul Millsap (3); Artis Gilmore, Jerry Lucas, Xavier McDaniel, Kermit Washington and Leroy Wright (2).

Year		Gm	No	Avg	Year		Gm	No	Avg
1951	Ernie Beck, Penn	27	556	20.6	1980	Larry Smith, Alcorn State	26	392	15.1
1952	Bill Hannon, Army	17	355	20.9	1981	Darryl Watson, Miss. Valley St.	27	379	14.0
1953	Ed Conlin, Fordham	26	612	23.5	1982	LaSalle Thompson, Texas	27	365	13.5
1954	Art Quimby, Connecticut	26	588	22.6	1983	Xavier McDaniel, Wichita St.	28	403	14.4
1955	Charlie Slack, Marshall	21	538	25.6	1984	Akeem Olajuwon, Houston	37	500	13.5
1956	Joe Holup, G. Washington	26	604	25.6	1985	Xavier McDaniel, Wichita St.	31	460	14.8
1957	Elgin Baylor, Seattle	25	508	23.5	1986	David Robinson, Navy	35	455	13.0
1958	Alex Ellis, Niagara	25	536	26.2	1987	Jerome Lane, Pittsburgh	33	444	13.5
1959	Leroy Wright, Pacific	26	652	23.8	1988	Kenny Miller, Loyola-IL	29	395	13.6
1960	Leroy Wright, Pacific	17	380	23.4	1989	Hank Gathers, Loyola-CA	31	426	13.7
1961	Jerry Lucas, Ohio St.	27	470	19.8	1990	Anthony Bonner, St. Louis	33	456	13.8
1962	Jerry Lucas, Ohio St.	28	499	21.1	1991	Shaquille O'Neal, LSU	28	411	14.7
1963	Paul Silas, Creighton	27	557	20.6	1992	Popeye Jones, Murray St.	30	431	14.4
1964	Bob Pelkington, Xavier-OH	26	567	21.8	1993	Warren Kidd, Mid. Tenn. St.	26	386	14.8
1965	Toby Kimball, Connecticut	23	483	21.0	1994	Jerome Lambert, Baylor	24	355	14.8
1966	Jim Ware, Oklahoma City	29	607	20.9	1995	Kurt Thomas, TCU	27	393	14.6
1967	Dick Cunningham, Murray St.	22	479	21.8	1996	Marcus Mann, Miss. Valley St.	29	394	13.6
1968	Neal Walk, Florida	25	494	19.8	1997	Tim Duncan, Wake Forest	31	457	14.7
1969	Spencer Haywood, Detroit	22	472	21.5	1998	Ryan Perryman, Dayton	33	412	12.5
1970	Artis Gilmore, Jacksonville	28	621	22.2	1999	Ian McGinnis, Dartmouth	26	317	12.2
1971	Artis Gilmore, Jacksonville	26	603	23.2	2000	Darren Phillip, Fairfield	29	405	14.0
1972	Kermit Washington, American	23	455	19.8	2001	Chris Marcus, Western Ky.	31	374	12.1
1973	Kermit Washington, American	22	439	20.0	2002	Jeremy Bishop, Quinnipiac	29	347	12.0
1974	Marvin Barnes, Providence	32	597	18.7	2003	Brandon Hunter, Ohio	30	378	12.6
1975	John Irving, Hofstra	21	323	15.4	2004	Paul Millsap, Louisiana Tech	30	374	12.5
1976	Sam Pellom, Buffalo	26	420	16.2	2005	Paul Millsap, Louisiana Tech	29	360	12.4
1977	Glenn Mosley, Seton Hall	29	473	16.3	2006	Paul Millsap, Louisiana Tech	33	438	13.3
1978	Ken Williams, N. Texas	28	411	14.7	2007	Rashad Jones-Jennings, Ark-LR	30	392	13.1
1979	Monti Davis, Tennessee St.	26	421	16.2	2008	Michael Beasley, Kansas St.	33	408	12.4

Assists

The NCAA did not begin keeping individual assist records until the 1983-84 season. All averages include postseason games where applicable.

Multiple winner: Avery Johnson and Jared Jordan (2).

Year		Gm	No	Avg
1984	Craig Lathen, IL-Chicago	29	274	9.45
1985	Rob Weingard, Hofstra	24	228	9.50
1986	Mark Jackson, St. John's	36	328	9.11
1987	Avery Johnson, Southern-BR	31	333	10.74
1988	Avery Johnson, Southern-BR	30	399	13.30
1989	Glenn Williams, Holy Cross	28	278	9.93
1990	Todd Lehmann, Drexel	28	260	9.29
1991	Chris Corchiani, N.C. State	31	299	9.65
1992	Van Usher, Tennessee Tech	29	254	8.76
1993	Sam Crawford, N. Mexico St	34	310	9.12
1994	Jason Kidd, California	30	272	9.06
1995	Nelson Haggerty, Baylor	28	284	10.14
1996	Raimonds Miglinieks, UC-Irvine	27	230	8.52
1997	Kenny Mitchell, Dartmouth	26	203	7.81
1998	Ahlon Lewis, Arizona St.	32	294	9.19
1999	Doug Gottlieb, Oklahoma St.	34	299	8.79
2000	Mark Dickel, UNLV	31	280	9.03
2001	Markus Carr, CS-Northridge	32	286	8.94
2002	T.J. Ford, Texas	33	273	8.27
2003	Martell Bailey, Illinois-Chicago	30	244	8.13
2004	Greg Day, Troy St.	31	256	8.26
2005	Damitrius Coleman, Mercer	28	224	8.00
	& Will Funn, Portland State	28	224	8.00
2006	Jared Jordan, Marist	29	247	8.52
2007	Jared Jordan, Marist	33	286	8.67
2008	Jason Richards, Davidson	36	293	8.14

Blocked Shots

The NCAA did not begin keeping individual blocked shots records until the 1985-86 season. All averages include postseason games where applicable.

Multiple winners: Keith Closs, David Robinson and Tarvis Williams (2).

Year		Gm	No	Avg
1986	David Robinson, Navy	35	207	5.91
1987	David Robinson, Navy	32	144	4.50
1988	Rodney Blake, St. Joe's-PA	29	116	4.00
1989	Alonzo Mourning, G'town	34	169	4.97
1990	Kenny Green, Rhode Island	26	124	4.77
1991	Shawn Bradley, BYU	34	177	5.21
1992	Shaquille O'Neal, LSU	30	157	5.23
1993	Theo Ratliff, Wyoming	28	124	4.43
1994	Grady Livingston, Howard	26	115	4.42
1995	Keith Closs, Cen. Conn. St.	26	139	5.35
1996	Keith Closs, Cen. Conn. St.	28	178	6.36
1997	Adonal Foyle, Colgate	28	180	6.43
1998	Jerome James, Florida A&M	27	125	4.63
1999	Tarvis Williams, Hampton	27	135	5.00
2000	Ken Johnson, Ohio St.	30	161	5.37
2001	Tarvis Williams, Hampton	32	147	4.59
2002	Wojciech Myrda, La-Monroe	32	172	5.38
2003	Emeka Okafor, Connecticut	33	156	4.73
2004	Anwar Ferguson, Houston	27	111	4.11
2005	Deng Gai, Fairfield	30	165	5.50
2006	Shawn James, Northeastern	30	196	6.53
2007	Mickell Gladness, Alabama A&M	30	188	6.27
2008	Jarvis Varnado, Mississippi St.	34	157	4.62

All-Time NCAA Division I Individual Leaders

Through 2007-08; includes regular season and tournament games; **Last** column indicates final year played.

CAREER
Scoring

	Points	Yrs	Last	Gm	Pts
1	Pete Maravich, LSU	3	1970	83	3667
2	Freeman Williams, Port. St.	4	1978	106	3249
3	Lionel Simmons, La Salle	4	1990	131	3217
4	Alphonso Ford, Miss. Val. St.	4	1993	109	3165
5	Harry Kelly, Texas Southern	4	1983	110	3066
6	Hersey Hawkins, Bradley	4	1988	125	3008
7	Oscar Robertson, Cincinnati	3	1960	88	2973
8	Danny Manning, Kansas	4	1988	147	2951
9	Alfredrick Hughes, Loyola-IL	4	1985	120	2914
10	Elvin Hayes, Houston	3	1968	93	2884
11	Larry Bird, Indiana St.	3	1979	94	2850
12	Otis Birdsong, Houston	4	1977	116	2832
13	Kevin Bradshaw, Beth-Cook/US Int'l	4	1991	111	2804
14	Allan Houston, Tennessee	4	1993	128	2801
15	J.J. Redick, Duke	4	2006	139	2769
16	Hank Gathers, USC/Loyola-CA	4	1990	117	2723
17	Reggie Lewis, Northeastern	4	1987	122	2708
18	Daren Queenan, Lehigh	4	1988	118	2703
19	Byron Larkin, Xavier-OH	4	1988	121	2696
20	David Robinson, Navy	4	1987	127	2669

	Average	Yrs	Last	Pts	Avg
1	Pete Maravich, LSU	3	1970	3667	44.2
2	Austin Carr, Notre Dame	3	1971	2560	34.6
3	Oscar Robertson, Cinn	3	1960	2973	33.8
4	Calvin Murphy, Niagara	3	1970	2548	33.1
5	Dwight Lamar, SW La	2	1973	1862	32.7
6	Frank Selvy, Furman	3	1954	2538	32.5
7	Rick Mount, Purdue	3	1970	2323	32.3
8	Darrell Floyd, Furman	3	1956	2281	32.1
9	Nick Werkman, Seton Hall	3	1964	2273	32.0
10	Willie Humes, Idaho St.	2	1971	1510	31.5
11	William Averitt, Pepperdine	2	1973	1541	31.4
12	Elgin Baylor, Idaho/Seattle	3	1958	2500	31.3
13	Elvin Hayes, Houston	3	1968	2884	31.0
14	Freeman Williams, Port. St.	4	1978	3249	30.7
15	Larry Bird, Indiana St.	3	1979	2850	30.3
16	Bill Bradley, Princeton	3	1965	2503	30.2
17	Rich Fuqua, Oral Roberts	2	1973	1617	29.9
18	Wilt Chamberlain, Kansas	2	1958	1433	29.9
19	Rick Barry, Miami-FL	3	1965	2298	29.8
20	Doug Collins, Illinois St.	3	1973	2240	29.1

	Field Goal Pct.	Yrs	Last	FG	FGA	Pct
1	Steve Johnson, Ore. St.	4	1981	828	1222	.678
2	Michael Bradley, Kentucky/ Villanova	3	2001	441	651	.677
3	Murray Brown, Fla. St.	4	1980	566	847	.668
4	Lee Campbell, M.Tenn St./ SW Mo.St.	3	1990	411	618	.665
5	Warren Kidd, M.Tenn.St.	3	1993	496	747	.664
6	Todd MacCulloch, Wash.	4	1999	702	1058	.664
7	Joe Senser, West Chester	4	1979	476	719	.662
8	Kevin Magee, UC-Irvine	2	1982	552	841	.656
9	Orlando Phillips, Pepperdine	2	1983	404	618	.654
10	Bill Walton, UCLA	3	1974	747	1147	.651

Note: minimum 400 FGs made and an avg. of 4 per game.

	Free Throw Pct.	Yrs	Last	FT	FTA	Pct
1	Gary Buchanan, Villanova	4	2003	324	355	.913
2	J.J. Redick, Duke	4	2006	662	726	.912
3	Greg Starrick, Ky/So.Ill	4	1972	341	375	.909
4	Jack Moore, Nebraska	4	1982	446	495	.901
5	Steve Henson, Kansas St.	4	1990	361	401	.900
6	Steve Alford, Indiana	4	1987	535	596	.898
7	Bob Lloyd, Rutgers	3	1967	543	605	.898
8	Jim Barton, Dartmouth	4	1989	394	440	.895
9	Tommy Boyer, Arkansas	3	1963	315	353	.892
10	Kyle Korver, Creighton	4	2003	312	350	.891

Note: minimum 300 FTs made and an average of 2.5 per game.

All-Time NCAA Division I Individual Leaders (Cont.)
Rebounds

Total (before 1973)	Yrs	Last	Gm	No
1 Tom Gola, La Salle	4	1955	118	2201
2 Joe Holup, G. Washington	4	1956	104	2030
3 Charlie Slack, Marshall	4	1956	88	1916
4 Ed Conlin, Fordham	4	1955	102	1884
5 Dickie Hemric, Wake Forest	4	1955	104	1802
6 Paul Silas, Creighton	3	1964	81	1751
7 Art Quimby, Connecticut	4	1955	80	1716
8 Jerry Harper, Alabama	4	1956	93	1688
9 Jeff Cohen, Wm. & Mary	4	1961	103	1679
10 Steve Hamilton, Morehead St.	4	1958	102	1675

Average (before 1973)	Yrs	Last	No	Avg
1 Artis Gilmore, Jacksonville	2	1971	1224	22.7
2 Charlie Slack, Marshall	4	1956	1916	21.8
3 Paul Silas, Creighton	3	1964	1751	21.6
4 Leroy Wright, Pacific	3	1960	1442	21.5
5 Art Quimby, Connecticut	4	1955	1716	21.5

Note: minimum 800 rebounds.

Total (since 1973)	Yrs	Last	Gm	No
1 Tim Duncan, Wake Forest	4	1997	128	1570
2 Derrick Coleman, Syracuse	4	1990	143	1537
3 Malik Rose, Drexel	4	1996	120	1514
4 Ralph Sampson, Virginia	4	1983	132	1511
5 Pete Padgett, Nevada-Reno	4	1976	104	1464
6 Lionel Simmons, La Salle	4	1990	131	1429
7 Anthony Bonner, St. Louis	4	1990	133	1424
8 Tyrone Hill, Xavier-OH	4	1990	126	1380
9 Popeye Jones, Murray St.	4	1992	123	1374
10 Michael Brooks, La Salle	4	1980	114	1372

Average (since 1973)	Yrs	Last	No	Avg
1 Glenn Mosley, Seton Hall	4	1977	1263	15.2
2 Bill Campion, Manhattan	3	1975	1070	14.2
3 Pete Padgett, Nevada-Reno	4	1976	1464	14.1
4 Bob Warner, Maine	4	1976	1304	13.6
5 Shaquille O'Neal, LSU	3	1992	1217	13.5

Note: minimum 650 rebounds.

Assists

Total	Yrs	Last	Gm	No
1 Bobby Hurley, Duke	4	1993	140	1076
2 Chris Corchiani, N.C. State	4	1991	124	1038
3 Ed Cota, N. Carolina	4	2000	138	1030
4 Keith Jennings, E. Tenn. St.	4	1991	127	983
5 Steve Blake, Maryland	4	2003	138	972
6 Sherman Douglas, Syracuse	4	1989	138	960
7 Tony Miller, Marquette	4	1995	123	956
8 Aaron Miles, Kansas	4	2005	138	954
9 Greg Anthony, Portland/UNLV	4	1991	138	950
10 Doug Gottlieb, ND/Okla St.	4	2000	124	947

Average	Yrs	Last	No	Avg
1 Avery Johnson, Southern	2	1988	732	12.00
2 Sam Crawford, N. Mexico St.	2	1993	592	8.84
3 Mark Wade, Okla/UNLV	3	1987	693	8.77
4 Chris Corchiani, N.C. State	4	1991	1038	8.37
5 Taurence Chisholm, Delaware	4	1988	877	7.97
6 Van Usher, Tennessee Tech	3	1992	676	7.95
7 Anthony Manuel, Bradley	3	1989	855	7.92
8 Chico Fletcher, Ark. St.	4	2000	893	7.83
9 Gary Payton, Oregon St.	4	1990	938	7.82
10 Orlando Smart, San Francisco	4	1994	902	7.78

Note: minimum 550 assists.

Blocked Shots

Average	Yrs	Last	No	Avg
1 Keith Closs, Cen. Conn. St.	2	1996	317	5.87
2 Adonal Foyle, Colgate	3	1997	492	5.66
3 David Robinson, Navy	2	1987	351	5.24
4 Wojciech Mydra, LA-Monroe	4	2002	535	4.65
5 Shaquille O'Neal, LSU	3	1992	412	4.58

Note: minimum 225 blocked shots.

Steals

Average	Yrs	Last	No	Avg
1 Desmond Cambridge, Ala. A&M	3	2002	330	3.93
2 Mookie Blaylock, Oklahoma	2	1989	281	3.80
3 Ronn McMahon, Eastern Wash	3	1990	225	3.52
4 Eric Murdock, Providence	4	1991	376	3.21
5 Van Usher, Tennessee Tech	3	1992	270	3.18

Note: minimum 225 steals.

3-PT Field Goals

3-Pt Field Goals Made	Yrs	Last	Gm	3FG
1 J.J. Redick, Duke	4	2006	139	457
2 Curtis Staples, Virginia	4	1998	122	413
3 Keith Veney, Lamar/Marshall	4	1997	111	409
4 Doug Day, Radford	4	1993	117	401
5 Michael Watson, Missouri-KC	4	2004	117	391

3-Pt Field Goals/Game	Yrs	Last	3FG	Avg
1 Timothy Pollard, Miss. Vall	2	1989	256	4.57
2 Sydney Grider, LA-Lafayette	2	1990	253	4.36
3 Brian Merriweather, TX-Pan Am.	3	2001	332	3.95
4 Josh Heard, Tenn. Tech	2	2000	210	3.82
5 Kareem Townes, La Salle	3	1995	300	3.70

3-Pt Field Goal Pct.	Yrs	Last	3FG	Att	Pct
1 Tony Bennett, Wisc-GB	4	1992	290	584	.497
2 David Olson, Eastern Ill.	4	1992	262	562	.466
3 Ross Land, N. Arizona	4	2000	308	664	.464
4 Dan Dickau, Washington/ Gonzaga	4	2002	215	465	.462
5 Sean Jackson, Ohio/ Princeton	4	1992	243	528	.460

Note: minimum 200 3FGs made and an average of two per game.

SINGLE SEASON
Scoring

Points	Year	Gm	Pts
1 Pete Maravich, LSU	1970	31	1381
2 Elvin Hayes, Houston	1968	33	1214
3 Frank Selvy, Furman	1954	29	1209
4 Pete Maravich, LSU	1969	26	1148
5 Pete Maravich, LSU	1968	26	1138
6 Bo Kimble, Loyola-CA	1990	32	1131
7 Hersey Hawkins, Bradley	1988	31	1125
8 Austin Carr, Notre Dame	1970	29	1106
9 Austin Carr, Notre Dame	1971	29	1101
10 Otis Birdsong, Houston	1977	36	1090

Average	Year	Gm	Pts	Avg
1 Pete Maravich, LSU	1970	31	1381	44.5
2 Pete Maravich, LSU	1969	26	1148	44.2
3 Pete Maravich, LSU	1968	26	1138	43.8
4 Frank Selvy, Furman	1954	29	1209	41.7
5 Johnny Neumann, Ole Miss	1971	23	923	40.1
6 Freeman Williams, Port. St.	1977	26	1010	38.8
7 Billy McGill, Utah	1962	26	1009	38.8
8 Calvin Murphy, Niagara	1968	24	916	38.2
9 Austin Carr, Notre Dame	1970	29	1106	38.1
10 Austin Carr, Notre Dame	1971	29	1101	38.0

Field Goal Pct.

		Year	FG	FGA	Pct
1	Steve Johnson, Oregon St.	1981	235	315	.746
2	Dwayne Davis, Florida	1989	179	248	.722
3	Keith Walker, Utica	1985	154	216	.713
4	Steve Johnson, Oregon St.	1980	211	297	.710
5	Adam Mark, Belmont	2002	150	212	:708

Free Throw Pct.

		Year	FT	FTA	Pct
1	Blake Ahearn, SW Mo. St.	2004	117	120	.975
2	Derek Raivio, Gonzaga	2007	148	154	.961
3	Craig Collins, Penn St.	1985	94	98	.959
4	J.J. Redick, Duke	2004	143	150	.953
5	Rod Foster, UCLA	1982	95	100	.950

3-Pt Field Goal Pct.

		Year	3FG	Att	Pct
1	Glenn Tropf, Holy Cross	1988	52	82	.634
2	Sean Wightman, W. Mich	1992	48	76	.632
3	Keith Jennings, E. Tenn. St.	1991	84	142	.592
4	Dave Calloway, Monmouth	1989	48	82	.585
5	Steve Kerr, Arizona	1988	114	199	:573

Assists

	Average	Year	Gm	No	Avg
1	Avery Johnson, Southern-BR	1988	30	399	13.3
2	Anthony Manuel, Bradley	1988	31	373	12.0
3	Avery Johnson, Southern-BR	1987	31	333	10.7
4	Mark Wade, UNLV	1987	38	406	10.7
5	Nelson Haggerty, Baylor	1995	28	284	10.1
6	Glenn Williams, Holy Cross	1989	28	278	9.9
7	Chris Corchiani, N.C. State	1991	31	299	9.7
8	Tony Fairley, Charleston-So.	1987	28	270	9.6
9	Tyrone Bogues, Wake Forest	1987	29	276	9.5
10	Ron Weingard, Hofstra	1985	24	228	9.5

Rebounds

	Average (before 1973)	Year	Gm	No	Avg
1	Charlie Slack, Marshall	1955	21	538	25.6
2	Leroy Wright, Pacific	1959	26	652	25.1
3	Art Quimby, Connecticut	1955	25	611	24.4
4	Charlie Slack, Marshall	1956	22	520	23.6
5	Ed Conlin, Fordham	1953	26	612	23.5

	Average (since 1973)	Year	Gm	No	Avg
1	Kermit Washington, American	1973	25	511	20.4
2	Marvin Barnes, Providence	1973	30	571	19.0
3	Marvin Barnes, Providence	1974	32	597	18.7
4	Pete Padgett, Nevada	1973	26	462	17.8
5	Jim Bradley, Northern Ill	1973	24	426	17.8

Blocked Shots

	Average	Year	Gm	No	Avg
1	Shawn James, Northeastern	2006	30	196	6.53
2	Adonal Foyle, Colgate	1997	28	180	6.42
3	Keith Closs, Cen. Conn. St.	1996	28	178	6.36
4	Mickell Gladness, Ala. A&M	2007	30	188	6.27
5	David Robinson, Navy	1986	35	207	5.91

Steals

	Average	Year	Gm	No	Avg
1	Desmond Cambridge, Ala. A&M	2002	29	160	5.52
2	Darron Brittman, Chicago St.	1986	28	139	4.96
3	Aldwin Ware, Florida A&M	1988	29	142	4.90
4	John Linehan, Providence	2002	31	139	4.48
5	Ronn McMahon, East Wash.	1990	29	130	4.48

SINGLE GAME

Scoring

	Points vs Div. I Team	Year	Pts
1	Kevin Bradshaw, US Int'l vs Loyola-CA	1991	72
2	Pete Maravich, LSU vs Alabama	1970	69
3	Calvin Murphy, Niagara vs Syracuse	1969	68
4	Jay Handlan, Wash. & Lee vs Furman	1951	66
	Pete Maravich, LSU vs Tulane	1969	66
	Anthony Roberts, Oral Rbts vs N.C. A&T	1977	66
7	Anthony Roberts, Oral Rbts vs Ore	1977	65
	Scott Haffner, Evansville vs Dayton	1989	65
9	Pete Maravich, LSU vs Kentucky	1970	64
10	Johnny Neumann, Ole Miss vs LSU	1971	63
	Hersey Hawkins, Bradley vs Detroit	1988	63

	Points vs Non-Div. I Team	Year	Pts
1	Frank Selvy, Furman vs Newberry	1954	100
2	Paul Arizin, Villanova vs Phi. NAMC	1949	85
3	Freeman Williams, Port. St. vs Rocky Mt	1978	81
4	Bill Mlkvy, Temple vs Wilkes	1951	73
5	Freeman Williams, Port. St. vs So. Ore	1977	71
6	Darrell Floyd, Furman vs Morehead St.	1955	67

Note: Bevo Francis of Division II Rio Grande (Ohio) scored an overall collegiate record 113 points against Hillsdale in 1954. He also scored 84 against Alliance and 82 against Bluffton that same season.

3-Pt Field Goals

		Year	No
1	Keith Veney, Marshall vs Morehead St.	1996	15
2	Dave Jamerson, Ohio U. vs Charleston	1989	14
	Askia Jones, Kansas St. vs Fresno St.	1994	14
	Ronald Blackshear, Marshall vs. Akron	2002	14
5	Gary Bossert, Niagara vs Siena	1987	12
	Darrin Fitzgerald, Butler vs Detroit	1987	12
	Al Dillard, Arkansas vs Delaware St.	1993	12
	Mitch Taylor, South-BR vs La. Christian	1995	12
	David McMahan, Winthrop vs C. Carolina	1996	12
	Clarence Gilbert, Missouri vs Colorado	2002	12
	Terrence Woods, Fla. A&M vs Coppin St.	2003	12
	Michael Jenkins, Winthrop vs N.Greenville	2007	12

Assists

		Year	No
1	Tony Fairley, Baptist vs Armstrong St.	1987	22
	Avery Johnson, Southern-BR vs TX-South	1988	22
	Sherman Douglas, Syracuse vs Providence	1989	22
4	Mark Wade, UNLV vs Navy	1986	21
	Kelvin Scarborough, N. Mexico vs Hawaii	1987	21
	Anthony Manuel, Bradley vs UC-Irvine	1987	21
	Avery Johnson, Southern-BR vs Ala. St.	1988	21

Rebounds

	Total (before 1973)	Year	No
1	Bill Chambers, Wm. & Mary vs Virginia	1953	51
2	Charlie Slack, Marshall vs M. Harvey	1954	43
3	Tom Heinsohn, Holy Cross vs BC	1955	42
4	Art Quimby, UConn vs BU	1955	40
5	Three players tied with 39 each.		

	Total (since 1973)	Year	No
1	Larry Abney, Fresno St. vs SMU	2000	35
2	David Vaughn, Oral Roberts vs Brandeis	1973	34
3	Robert Parish, Centenary vs So. Miss	1973	33
4	Durand Macklin, LSU vs Tulane	1976	32
	Jervaughn Scales, South-BR vs Grambling	1994	32

Blocked Shots

		Year	No
1	Mickell Gladness, Ala. A&M vs. TX Southern	2007	16
2	David Robinson, Navy vs NC-Wilmington	1986	14
	Shawn Bradley, BYU vs Eastern Ky	1990	14
	Roy Rogers, Alabama vs Georgia	1996	14
	Loren Woods, Arizona vs Oregon	2000	14

Steals

		Year	No
1	Mookie Blaylock, Oklahoma vs Centenary	1987	13
	Mookie Blaylock, Oklahoma vs Loyola-CA	1988	13
3	Kenny Robertson, Cleve. St. vs Wagner	1988	12
	Terry Evans, Oklahoma vs Florida A&M	1993	12
	Richard Duncan, Mid. Tenn St. vs E. Ky.	1999	12
	Greedy Daniels, TCU vs Ark-Pine Bluff	2001	12
	Jehiel Lewis, Navy vs Bucknell	2002	12

Players of the Year and Top Draft Picks

Consensus College Players of the Year and first overall selections in NBA draft since the abolition of the NBA's territorial draft in 1966. Top draft picks who became Rookie of the Year are in **bold** type; (*) indicates top draft pick chosen as junior, (**) indicates top pick chosen as sophomore, (†) indicates top pick chosen as freshman, (‡) indicates top pick chosen as a high school senior. Only five players have been the unanimous college player of the year, the first overall pick in the NBA draft and then the NBA Rookie of the year.

Year	Player of the Year	Top Draft Pick	Year	Player of the Year	Top Draft Pick
1966	Cazzie Russell, Mich.	Cazzie Russell, NY	1989	Sean Elliott, Arizona	
1967	Lew Alcindor, UCLA	Jimmy Walker, Det.		& Danny Ferry, Duke	Pervis Ellison, Sac.
1968	Elvin Hayes, Houston	Elvin Hayes, SD	1990	Lionel Simmons, La Salle	**Derrick Coleman**, NJ
1969	Lew Alcindor, UCLA	**Lew Alcindor**, Mil.	1991	Larry Johnson, UNLV	
1970	Pete Maravich, LSU	Bob Lanier, Det.		& Shaquille O'Neal, LSU	**Larry Johnson**, Cha.
1971	Sidney Wicks, UCLA	Austin Carr, Cle.	1992	Christian Laettner, Duke	**Shaquille O'Neal**, Orl.*
1972	Bill Walton, UCLA	LaRue Martin, Por.	1993	Calbert Cheaney, Ind.	**Chris Webber**, Orl.**
1973	Bill Walton, UCLA	Doug Collins, Phi.	1994	Glenn Robinson, Purdue	Glenn Robinson, Mil.*
1974	Bill Walton, UCLA	Bill Walton, Por.	1995	Ed O'Bannon, UCLA	
1975	David Thompson, N.C. St.	David Thompson, Atl.		& Joe Smith, Maryland	Joe Smith, G. St.**
1976	Scott May, Indiana	John Lucas, Hou.	1996	Marcus Camby, UMass	**Allen Iverson**, Phi.**
1977	Marques Johnson, UCLA	Kent Benson, Ind.	1997	Tim Duncan, Wake Forest	**Tim Duncan**, SA
1978	Butch Lee, Marquette		1998	Antawn Jamison, N. Caro.	M. Olowokandi, LAC
	& Phil Ford, N. Caro.	Mychal Thompson, Por.	1999	Elton Brand, Duke	**Elton Brand**, Chi.**
1979	Larry Bird, Indiana St.	Magic Johnson, LAL**	2000	Kenyon Martin, Cincinnati	Kenyon Martin, NJ
1980	Mark Aguirre, DePaul	Joe Barry Carroll, G. St.	2001	Shane Battier, Duke	
1981	Ralph Sampson, Va.			& Jason Williams, Duke	Kwame Brown, Wash.‡
	& Danny Ainge, BYU	Mark Aguirre, Dal.	2002	Jason Williams, Duke	
1982	Ralph Sampson, Va.	James Worthy, LAL*		& Drew Gooden, Kansas	Yao Ming, Hou.
1983	Ralph Sampson, Va.	**Ralph Sampson**, Hou.	2003	T.J. Ford, Texas	
1984	Michael Jordan, N. Caro.	Akeem Olajuwon, Hou.		& David West, Xavier	**LeBron James**, Cle.‡
1985	Patrick Ewing, Georgetown		2004	Jameer Nelson, St. Joseph's	
	& Chris Mullin, St. John's	**Patrick Ewing**, NY		& Emeka Okafor, UConn	Dwight Howard, Orl.‡
1986	Walter Berry, St. John's	Brad Daugherty, Cle.	2005	Andrew Bogut, Utah	Andrew Bogut, Mil.**
1987	David Robinson, Navy	**David Robinson**, SA	2006	J.J. Redick, Duke	
1988	Hersey Hawkins, Bradley			& Adam Morrison, Gonz.	Andrea Bargnani, Tor.
	& Danny Manning, Kan.	Danny Manning, LAC	2007	Kevin Durant, Texas	Greg Oden, Ohio St.†
			2008	Tyler Hansbrough, UNC	Derrick Rose, Memphis†

Annual Awards

UPI picked the first national Division I Player of the Year in 1955. Since then, the U.S. Basketball Writers Assn. (1959), the Associated Press Player of the Year (1961), the Atlanta Tip-Off Club (1969), the National Assn. of Basketball Coaches (1975), and the LA Athletic Club's John Wooden Award (1977) have joined in. UPI discontinued its award in 1997. Since 1977, the first year all the following awards were given out, the same player has won all of them in the same season 16 times: Marques Johnson in 1977, Larry Bird in 1979, Ralph Sampson in both 1982 and '83, Michael Jordan in 1984, David Robinson in 1987, Lionel Simmons in 1990, Calbert Cheaney in 1993, Glenn Robinson in 1994, Tim Duncan in 1997, Antawn Jamison in 1998, Elton Brand in 1999, Kenyon Martin in 2000, Andrew Bogut in 2005, Kevin Durant in 2007 and Tyler Hansbrough in 2008.

Wooden Award

Voted on by a panel of coaches, sportswriters and broadcasters and first presented in 1977 by the Los Angeles Athletic Club in the name of former Purdue All-American and UCLA coach John Wooden. Unlike the other five player of the year awards, candidates for the Wooden must have a minimum grade point average of 2.00 (out of 4.00).

Multiple winner: Ralph Sampson (2).

Year		Year		Year	
1977	Marques Johnson, UCLA	1989	Sean Elliott, Arizona	2000	Kenyon Martin, Cincinnati
1978	Phil Ford, North Carolina	1990	Lionel Simmons, La Salle	2001	Shane Battier, Duke
1979	Larry Bird, Indiana St.	1991	Larry Johnson, UNLV	2002	Jason Williams, Duke
1980	Darrell Griffith, Louisville	1992	Christian Laettner, Duke	2003	T.J. Ford, Texas
1981	Danny Ainge, BYU	1993	Calbert Cheaney, Indiana	2004	Jameer Nelson, St. Joseph's
1982	Ralph Sampson, Virginia	1994	Glenn Robinson, Purdue	2005	Andrew Bogut, Utah
1983	Ralph Sampson, Virginia	1995	Ed O'Bannon, UCLA	2006	J.J. Redick, Duke
1984	Michael Jordan, N. Carolina	1996	Marcus Camby, UMass	2007	Kevin Durant, Texas
1985	Chris Mullin, St. John's	1997	Tim Duncan, Wake Forest	2008	Tyler Hansbrough, N. Carolina
1986	Walter Berry St. John's	1998	Antawn Jamison, N. Carolina		
1987	David Robinson, Navy	1999	Elton Brand, Duke		
1988	Danny Manning, Kansas				

United Press International

Voted on by a panel of UPI college basketball writers and first presented in 1955.
Multiple winners: Oscar Robertson, Ralph Sampson and Bill Walton (3); Lew Alcindor and Jerry Lucas (2).

Year		Year		Year	
1955	Tom Gola, La Salle	1961	Jerry Lucas, Ohio St.	1967	Lew Alcindor, UCLA
1956	Bill Russell, San Francisco	1962	Jerry Lucas, Ohio St.	1968	Elvin Hayes, Houston
1957	Chet Forte, Columbia	1963	Art Heyman, Duke	1969	Lew Alcindor, UCLA
1958	Oscar Robertson, Cincinnati	1964	Gary Bradds, Ohio St.	1970	Pete Maravich, LSU
1959	Oscar Robertson, Cincinnati	1965	Bill Bradley, Princeton	1971	Austin Carr, Notre Dame
1960	Oscar Robertson, Cincinnati	1966	Cazzie Russell, Michigan	1972	Bill Walton, UCLA

Year		Year		Year	
1973	Bill Walton, UCLA	1982	Ralph Sampson, Virginia	1991	Shaquille O'Neal, LSU
1974	Bill Walton, UCLA	1983	Ralph Sampson, Virginia	1992	Jim Jackson, Ohio St.
1975	David Thompson, N.C. State	1984	Michael Jordan, N. Carolina	1993	Calbert Cheaney, Indiana
1976	Scott May, Indiana	1985	Chris Mullin, St. John's	1994	Glenn Robinson, Purdue
1977	Marques Johnson, UCLA	1986	Walter Berry, St. John's	1995	Joe Smith, Maryland
1978	Butch Lee, Marquette	1987	David Robinson, Navy	1996	Ray Allen, UConn
1979	Larry Bird, Indiana St.	1988	Hersey Hawkins, Bradley	1997	award discontinued
1980	Mark Aguirre, DePaul	1989	Danny Ferry, Duke		
1981	Ralph Sampson, Virginia	1990	Lionel Simmons, La Salle		

U.S. Basketball Writers Association

Voted on by the USBWA and first presented in 1959.

Multiple winners: Ralph Sampson and Bill Walton (3); Lew Alcindor, Jerry Lucas and Oscar Robertson (2).

Year		Year		Year	
1959	Oscar Robertson, Cincinnati	1976	Adrian Dantley, Notre Dame	1993	Calbert Cheaney, Indiana
1960	Oscar Robertson, Cincinnati	1977	Marques Johnson, UCLA	1994	Glenn Robinson, Purdue
1961	Jerry Lucas, Ohio St.	1978	Phil Ford, North Carolina	1995	Ed O'Bannon, UCLA
1962	Jerry Lucas, Ohio St.	1979	Larry Bird, Indiana St.	1996	Marcus Camby, UMass
1963	Art Heyman, Duke	1980	Mark Aguirre, DePaul	1997	Tim Duncan, Wake Forest
1964	Walt Hazzard, UCLA	1981	Ralph Sampson, Virginia	1998	Antawn Jamison, N. Carolina
1965	Bill Bradley, Princeton	1982	Ralph Sampson, Virginia	1999	Elton Brand, Duke
1966	Cazzie Russell, Michigan	1983	Ralph Sampson, Virginia	2000	Kenyon Martin, Cincinnati
1967	Lew Alcindor, UCLA	1984	Michael Jordan, N. Carolina	2001	Shane Battier, Duke
1968	Elvin Hayes, Houston	1985	Chris Mullin, St. John's	2002	Jason Williams, Duke
1969	Lew Alcindor, UCLA	1986	Walter Berry, St. John's	2003	David West, Xavier
1970	Pete Maravich, LSU	1987	David Robinson, Navy	2004	Jameer Nelson, St. Joseph's
1971	Sidney Wicks, UCLA	1988	Hersey Hawkins, Bradley	2005	Andrew Bogut, Utah
1972	Bill Walton, UCLA	1989	Danny Ferry, Duke	2006	Adam Morrison, Gonzaga
1973	Bill Walton, UCLA	1990	Lionel Simmons, La Salle		& J.J. Redick, Duke
1974	Bill Walton, UCLA	1991	Larry Johnson, UNLV	2007	Kevin Durant, Texas
1975	David Thompson, N.C. State	1992	Christian Laettner, Duke	2008	Tyler Hansbrough, N. Carolina

Associated Press Player of the Year

Voted on by AP sportswriters and broadcasters.

Multiple winners: Ralph Sampson (3); Lew Alcindor, Jerry Lucas, David Thompson and Bill Walton (2).

Year		Year		Year	
1961	Jerry Lucas, Ohio St.	1977	Marques Johnson, UCLA	1993	Calbert Cheaney, Indiana
1962	Jerry Lucas, Ohio St.	1978	Butch Lee, Marquette	1994	Glenn Robinson, Purdue
1963	Art Heyman, Duke	1979	Larry Bird, Indiana St.	1995	Joe Smith, Maryland
1964	Gary Bradds, Ohio St.	1980	Mark Aguirre, DePaul	1996	Marcus Camby, UMass
1965	Bill Bradley, Princeton	1981	Ralph Sampson, Virginia	1997	Tim Duncan, Wake Forest
1966	Cazzie Russell, Michigan	1982	Ralph Sampson, Virginia	1998	Antawn Jamison, N. Carolina
1967	Lew Alcindor, UCLA	1983	Ralph Sampson, Virginia	1999	Elton Brand, Duke
1968	Elvin Hayes, Houston	1984	Michael Jordan, N. Carolina	2000	Kenyon Martin, Cincinnati
1969	Lew Alcindor, UCLA	1985	Patrick Ewing, Georgetown	2001	Shane Battier, Duke
1970	Pete Maravich, LSU	1986	Walter Berry, St. John's	2002	Jason Williams, Duke
1971	Austin Carr, Notre Dame	1987	David Robinson, Navy	2003	David West, Xavier
1972	Bill Walton, UCLA	1988	Hersey Hawkins, Bradley	2004	Jameer Nelson, St. Joseph's
1973	Bill Walton, UCLA	1989	Sean Elliott, Arizona	2005	Andrew Bogut, Utah
1974	David Thompson, N.C. State	1990	Lionel Simmons, La Salle	2006	J.J. Redick, Duke
1975	David Thompson, N.C. State	1991	Shaquille O'Neal, LSU	2007	Kevin Durant, Texas
1976	Scott May, Indiana	1992	Christian Laettner, Duke	2008	Tyler Hansbrough, N. Carolina

Naismith Award

Voted on by a panel of coaches, sportswriters and broadcasters and first presented in 1969 by the Atlanta Tip-Off Club in 1969 in the name of the inventor of basketball, Dr. James Naismith.

Multiple winners: Ralph Sampson and Bill Walton (3).

Year		Year		Year	
1969	Lew Alcindor, UCLA	1983	Ralph Sampson, Virginia	1997	Tim Duncan, Wake Forest
1970	Pete Maravich, LSU	1984	Michael Jordan, N. Carolina	1998	Antawn Jamison, N. Carolina
1971	Austin Carr, Notre Dame	1985	Patrick Ewing, Georgetown	1999	Elton Brand, Duke
1972	Bill Walton, UCLA	1986	Johnny Dawkins, Duke	2000	Kenyon Martin, Cincinnati
1973	Bill Walton, UCLA	1987	David Robinson, Navy	2001	Shane Battier, Duke
1974	Bill Walton, UCLA	1988	Danny Manning, Kansas	2002	Jason Williams, Duke
1975	David Thompson, N.C. State	1989	Danny Ferry, Duke	2003	T.J. Ford, Texas
1976	Scott May, Indiana	1990	Lionel Simmons, La Salle	2004	Jameer Nelson, St. Joseph's
1977	Marques Johnson, UCLA	1991	Larry Johnson, UNLV	2005	Andrew Bogut, Utah
1978	Butch Lee, Marquette	1992	Christian Laettner, Duke	2006	J.J. Redick, Duke
1979	Larry Bird, Indiana St.	1993	Calbert Cheaney, Indiana	2007	Kevin Durant, Texas
1980	Mark Aguirre, DePaul	1994	Glenn Robinson, Purdue	2008	Tyler Hansbrough, N. Carolina
1981	Ralph Sampson, Virginia	1995	Joe Smith, Maryland		
1982	Ralph Sampson, Virginia	1996	Marcus Camby, UMass		

National Association of Basketball Coaches

Voted on by the National Assn. of Basketball Coaches and presented by the Eastman Kodak Co. from 1975-94.
Multiple winners: Ralph Sampson and Jason Williams (2).

Year		Year		Year	
1975	David Thompson, N.C. State	1988	Danny Manning, Kansas	2001	Jason Williams, Duke
1976	Scott May, Indiana	1989	Sean Elliott, Arizona	2002	Jason Williams, Duke
1977	Marques Johnson, UCLA	1990	Lionel Simmons, La Salle		& Drew Gooden, Kansas
1978	Phil Ford, North Carolina	1991	Larry Johnson, UNLV	2003	Nick Collison, Kansas
1979	Larry Bird, Indiana St.	1992	Christian Laettner, Duke	2004	Jameer Nelson, St. Joseph's
1980	Michael Brooks, La Salle	1993	Calbert Cheaney, Indiana		& Emeka Okafor, Connecticut
1981	Danny Ainge, BYU	1994	Glenn Robinson, Purdue	2005	Andrew Bogut, Utah
1982	Ralph Sampson, Virginia	1995	Shawn Respert, Mich. St.	2006	J.J. Redick, Duke
1983	Ralph Sampson, Virginia	1996	Marcus Camby, UMass		& Adam Morrison, Gonzaga
1984	Michael Jordan, N. Carolina	1997	Tim Duncan, Wake Forest	2007	Kevin Durant, Texas
1985	Patrick Ewing, Georgetown	1998	Antawn Jamison, N. Carolina	2008	Tyler Hansbrough, N. Carolina
1986	Walter Berry, St. John's	1999	Elton Brand, Duke		
1987	David Robinson, Navy	2000	Kenyon Martin, Cincinnati		

All-Time Winningest Division I Coaches

Minimum of 10 seasons as Division I head coach; regular season and tournament games included; coaches active during 2007-08 in **bold** type.

Top 30 Winning Percentage

		Yrs	W	L	Pct
1	Clair Bee	.21	412	87	**.826**
2	Adolph Rupp	.41	876	190	**.822**
3	**Roy Williams**	.20	560	134	**.807**
4	John Wooden	.29	664	162	**.804**
5	John Kresse	.23	560	143	**.797**
6	Jerry Tarkanian	.31	729	201	**.784**
7	Francis Schmidt	.17	258	72	**.782**
8	Dean Smith	.36	879	254	**.776**
9	George Keogan	.27	414	127	**.765**
10	Jack Ramsay	.11	231	71	**.765**
11	Frank Keaney	.28	401	124	**.764**
12	Vic Bubas	.10	213	67	**.761**
13	Harry Fisher	.16	189	60	**.759**
14	**John Calipari**	.16	408	135	**.751**
15	**Mike Krzyzewski**	.33	803	267	**.750**
16	Fred Bennion	.11	95	32	**.748**
17	Chick Davies	.21	314	106	**.748**
18	Ray Mears	.21	399	135	**.747**
19	Edward McNichol	.10	186	63	**.747**
20	Rick Majerus	.20	422	147	**.742**
21	Al McGuire	.20	406	142	**.741**
22	Phog Allen	.48	746	264	**.739**
23	Everett Case	.19	377	134	**.738**
24	Arthur Schabinger	.19	245	88	**.736**
25	**Bob Huggins**	.26	616	222	**.735**
26	**Jim Boeheim**	.32	771	278	**.735**
27	G. Ott Romney	.13	283	102	**.735**
28	Walter Meanwell	.22	280	101	**.735**
29	**Rick Pitino**	.22	521	191	**.732**
30	Lute Olson	.35	799	295	**.730**

Top 30 Victories

		Yrs	W	L	Pct
1	**Bob Knight**	.42	902	371	.709
2	Dean Smith	.36	879	254	.776
3	Adolph Rupp	.41	876	190	.822
4	Jim Phelan	.49	830	524	.613
5	**Mike Krzyzewski**	.33	803	267	.750
6	**Lute Olson**	.35	799	295	.730
7	Eddie Sutton	.36	798	315	.717
8	Lefty Driesell	.41	786	394	.666
9	Lou Henson	.41	779	408	.656
10	**Jim Calhoun**	.36	774	337	.697
11	**Jim Boeheim**	.32	771	278	.735
12	Hank Iba	.41	767	338	.694
13	Ed Diddle	.42	759	302	.715
14	Phog Allen	.48	746	264	.739
15	John Chaney	.34	741	312	.704
16	Jerry Tarkanian	.31	729	201	.784
17	Norm Stewart	.38	728	374	.661
18	Ray Meyer	.42	724	354	.672
19	Don Haskins	.38	719	353	.671
20	Denny Crum	.30	675	295	.696
21	John Wooden	.29	664	162	.804
22	Ralph Miller	.38	657	382	.632
23	Gene Bartow	.34	647	353	.647
24	Billy Tubbs	.31	641	340	.653
25	Marv Harshman	.40	637	443	.590
26	Hugh Durham	.37	633	429	.596
27	Cam Henderson	.35	630	243	.722
28	Norm Sloan	.37	624	393	.614
29	**Bob Huggins**	.26	616	222	.735
30	**Tom Penders**	.34	608	410	.597

Note: Clarence (Bighouse) Gaines of Division II Winston-Salem St. (1947-93) retired after the 1992-93 season to finish his 47-year career ranked No. 3 on the all-time NCAA list of all coaches regardless of division. His record is 828-446 with a .650 winning percentage.

Where They Coached

Allen–Baker (1906-08), Kansas (1908-09), Haskell (1909), Central Mo. St. (1913-19), Kansas (1920-56); **Bartow**–Central Mo. St. (1962-64), Valparaiso (1965-70), Memphis St. (1971-74), Illinois (1975), UCLA (1976-77), UAB (1979-96); **Bennion**–BYU (1909-10), Utah (1911-14), Montana St. (1915-19); **Bee**–Rider (1929-31), LIU-Brooklyn (1932-45, 46-51); **Boeheim**–Syracuse (1977–); **Bubas**–Duke (1960-69); **Calhoun**–Northeastern (1973-86), Connecticut (1987–); **Calipari**–Massachusetts (1988-96), Memphis (2000–); **Case**–N.C. State (1947-64); **Chaney**–Cheyney St. (1973-82), Temple (1983-2006); **Crum**–Louisville (1972-01); **Davies**–Duquesne (1925-43, 47-48); **Diddle**–Western Ky. (1923-64); **Driesell**–Davidson (1961-69), Maryland (1970-86), J. Madison (1989-97), Georgia St. (1997-2003); **Durham**–Florida St. (1967-78), Georgia (1979-95), Jacksonville (1999-05); **Fisher**–Columbia (1907-16), Army (1922-23, 25). **Harshman**–Pacific Lutheran (1946-58), Wash. St. (1959-71), Washington (1972-85); **Haskins**–UTEP (1962-99); **Henderson**–Muskingum (1920-22), Davis & Elkins (1923-35), Marshall (1936-55); **Henson**–Hardin-Simmons (1963-66), N. Mexico St. (1967-75), Illinois (1976-96), N. Mexico St. (1997-05); **Huggins**–Walsh (1981-83), Akron (1985-89), Cincinnati (1990-05), Kansas St. (2006-07), West Virginia (2007–); **Iba**–NW Missouri St. (1930-33), Colorado (1934), Oklahoma St. (1935-70); **Keaney**–Rhode Island (1921-48); **Keogan**–St. Louis (1916), Allegheny (1919), Valparaiso (1920-21), Notre Dame (1924-43); **Knight**–Army (1966-71), Indiana (1972-00), Texas Tech (2001–); **Kresse**–Charleston (1979-2002); **Krzyzewski**–Army (1976-80), Duke (1981–); **Majerus**–Marquette (1984-86), Ball St. (1988-89), Utah (1991-2003), St.

ouis (2007–); **McGuire**–Belmont Abbey (1958-64), Marquette (1965-77); **Meanwell**– Wisconsin (1912-17, 21-34), Missouri (1918-20); **Mears**–Wittenberg (1957-62), Tennessee (1963-77); **Meyer**–DePaul (1943-84); **Miller**–Wichita St. (1952-64), Iowa (1965-70), Oregon St. (1971-89); **Olson**–Long Beach St. (1974), Iowa (1975-83), Arizona (1984–); **Penders**–Tufts (197-74), Columbia (1975-78), Fordham (1979-86), Rhode Island (1987-88), Texas (1989-98), George Washington (1999-2001), Houston (2005–); **Phelan**– Mount St. Mary's (1955-2003); **Pitino**–Boston Univ. (1979-83), Providence (1986-87), Kentucky (1989-97), Louisville (2001–).

Ramsay–St. Joseph's-PA (1956-66); **Romney**–Montana St. (1923-28), BYU (1929-35); **Rupp**–Kentucky (1931-72); **Sch-abinger**–Ottawa (1917-20), Emportia St. (1921-22), Creighton (1923-35); **Schmidt**–Tulsa (1916-17, 19-22), Arkansas (1924-29), TCU (1930-34); **Sloan**–Presbyterian (1952-55), Citadel (1957-60), Florida (1961-66), N.C. State (1967-80), Florida (1981-89); **Smith**– North Carolina (1962-97); **Stewart**–No. Iowa (1962-67), Missouri (1968-99); **Sutton**–Creighton (1970-74), Arkansas (1975-85), Kentucky (1986-89), Oklahoma St. (1991-2006); **Tarkanian**–Long Beach St. (1969-73), UNLV (1974-92), Fresno St. (1995-2002); **Tubbs**–Southwestern (1971-73), Lamar (1976-80, 2003-06), Oklahoma (1981-94), TCU (1995-2002); **Williams**–Kansas (1989-2003), North Carolina (2003–); **Wooden**–Indiana St. (1947-48), UCLA (1949-75).

Most NCAA Tournaments

Through 2008; listed are number of appearances, overall tournament record, times reaching Final Four, and number of NCAA championships. (*) denotes that actual records are different from official NCAA records.

App		W-L	F4	Championships
28	**Lute Olson***	46-28	5	1 (1997)
27	Dean Smith	65-27	11	2 (1982, 93)
27	**Bob Knight**	44-23	5	3 (1976, 81, 87)
26	Eddie Sutton*	39-26	4	None
25	**Jim Boeheim**	40-24	3	1 (2003)
24	**Mike Krzyzewski**	69-21	9	3 (1991-92, 2001)
23	Denny Crum	42-23	6	2 (1980, 86)
20	Adolph Rupp	30-18	6	4 (1948-49, 51, 58)
20	John Thompson	34-19	3	1 (1984)
20	**Jim Calhoun***	41-18	2	2 (1999, 2004)
19	Lou Henson	19-20	2	None
19	**Roy Williams**	51-17	6	2 (2005, 2008)
18	Lou Carnesecca	17-20	1	None
18	Jerry Tarkanian	38-18	4	1 (1990)
18	Gene Keady*	19-18	1	None
17	John Chaney	23-17	0	None
16	John Wooden	47-10	12	10 (1964-65, 67-73, 75)
16	Norm Stewart*	12-16	0	None
16	Nolan Richardson	26-15	3	1 (1994)
16	Jim Harrick	18-15	1	1 (1995)
16	**Bob Huggins**	21-15	1	None
16	**Rick Barnes**	18-16	1	None
15	Digger Phelps	17-17	1	None
15	**Gary Williams**	27-14	2	1 (2002)
14	Don Haskins	14-13	1	1 (1966)
14	Guy Lewis	26-18	5	None

Active Coaches' Victories

Minimum five seasons in Division I.

		Yrs	W	L	Pct
1	Mike Krzyzewski, Duke	33	803	267	.750
2	Lute Olson, Arizona	35	799	295	.730
3	Jim Calhoun, UConn	36	774	337	.697
4	Jim Boeheim, Syracuse	32	771	278	.735
5	Bob Huggins, Kansas St.	26	616	222	.735
6	Tom Penders, Houston	34	608	410	.597
7	Gary Williams, Maryland	30	604	343	.638
8	Homer Drew, Valparaiso	31	593	376	.612
9	Roy Williams, North Carolina	20	560	134	.807
10	Ben Braun, California	31	556	389	.588
	Bo Ryan, Wisconsin	24	556	163	.773
12	Cliff Ellis, Coastal Carolina	30	547	352	.608
	Pat Douglass, UC-Irvine	27	547	273	.667
14	Larry Hunter, Western Carolina	28	543	282	.658
15	Rick Byrd, Belmont	27	541	303	.641
16	Rick Pitino, Louisville	22	521	191	.732
17	Bobby Cremins, C. of Charleston	27	492	338	.593
18	John Beilein, Michigan	26	484	297	.620
19	Dave Bike, Sacred Heart	30	463	415	.527
20	Pat Kennedy, Towson	28	461	385	.545
21	Stew Morrill, Utah St.	22	455	224	.670
22	Don Maestri, Troy	26	454	313	.592
23	Rick Barnes, Texas	21	449	227	.664
24	Rick Majerus, St. Louis	21	438	162	.730
25	L. Vann Pettaway, Ala. A&M	22	421	229	.648
26	Mike Deane, Wagner	24	415	293	.586
27	Lon Kruger, UNLV	22	409	275	.598
28	John Calipari, Memphis	16	408	135	.751
29	Tubby Smith, Minnesota	17	407	159	.719
30	Tom Green, Fairleigh Dickinson	25	400	328	.549

Annual Awards

UPI picked the first national Division I Coach of the Year in 1955. Since then, the U.S. Basketball Writers Assn. (1959), AP (1967), the National Assn. of Basketball Coaches (1969), and the Atlanta Tip-Off Club (1987) have joined in. Since 1987, the first year all five awards were given out, no coach has won all of them in the same season.

United Press International

Voted on by a panel of UPI college basketball writers and first presented in 1955.

Multiple winners: John Wooden (6); Bob Knight, Ray Meyer, Adolph Rupp, Norm Stewart, Fred Taylor and Phil Woolpert (2).

Year	Year	Year
1955 Phil Woolpert, San Francisco	1970 John Wooden, UCLA	1985 Lou Carnesecca, St. John's
1956 Phil Woolpert, San Francisco	1971 Al McGuire, Marquette	1986 Mike Krzyzewski, Duke
1957 Frank McGuire, North Carolina	1972 John Wooden, UCLA	1987 John Thompson, Georgetown
1958 Tex Winter, Kansas St.	1973 John Wooden, UCLA	1988 John Chaney, Temple
1959 Adolph Rupp, Kentucky	1974 Digger Phelps, Notre Dame	1989 Bob Knight, Indiana
1960 Pete Newell, California	1975 Bob Knight, Indiana	1990 Jim Calhoun, Connecticut
1961 Fred Taylor, Ohio St.	1976 Tom Young, Rutgers	1991 Rick Majerus, Utah
1962 Fred Taylor, Ohio St.	1977 Bob Gaillard, San Francisco	1992 Perry Clark, Tulane
1963 Ed Jucker, Cincinnati	1978 Eddie Sutton, Arkansas	1993 Eddie Fogler, Vanderbilt
1964 John Wooden, UCLA	1979 Bill Hodges, Indiana St.	1994 Norm Stewart, Missouri
1965 Dave Strack, Michigan	1980 Ray Meyer, DePaul	1995 Leonard Hamilton, Miami-FL
1966 Adolph Rupp, Kentucky	1981 Ralph Miller, Oregon St.	1996 Gene Keady, Purdue
1967 John Wooden, UCLA	1982 Norm Stewart, Missouri	1997 award discontinued
1968 Guy Lewis, Houston	1983 Jerry Tarkanian, UNLV	
1969 John Wooden, UCLA	1984 Ray Meyer, DePaul	

Annual Awards (Cont.)

U.S. Basketball Writers Association

Voted on by the USBWA and first presented in 1959.

Multiple winners: John Wooden (5); Bob Knight (3); Lou Carnesecca, John Chaney, Ray Meyer, Fred Taylor and Roy Williams (2)

Year	Year	Year
1959 Eddie Hickey, Marquette	1976 Bob Knight, Indiana	1993 Eddie Fogler, Vanderbilt
1960 Pete Newell, California	1977 Eddie Sutton, Arkansas	1994 Charlie Spoonhour, St. Louis
1961 Fred Taylor, Ohio St.	1978 Ray Meyer, DePaul	1995 Kelvin Sampson, Oklahoma
1962 Fred Taylor, Ohio St.	1979 Dean Smith, North Carolina	1996 Gene Keady, Purdue
1963 Ed Jucker, Cincinnati	1980 Ray Meyer, DePaul	1997 Clem Haskins, Minnesota
1964 John Wooden, UCLA	1981 Ralph Miller, Oregon St.	1998 Tom Izzo, Michigan St.
1965 Butch van Breda Kolff, Princeton	1982 John Thompson, Georgetown	1999 Cliff Ellis, Auburn
1966 Adolph Rupp, Kentucky	1983 Lou Carnesecca, St. John's	2000 Larry Eustachy, Iowa St.
1967 John Wooden, UCLA	1984 Gene Keady, Purdue	2001 Al Skinner, Boston College
1968 Guy Lewis, Houston	1985 Lou Carnesecca, St. John's	2002 Ben Howland, Pittsburgh
1969 Maury John, Drake	1986 Dick Versace, Bradley	2003 Tubby Smith, Kentucky
1970 John Wooden, UCLA	1987 John Chaney, Temple	2004 Phil Martelli, St. Joseph's
1971 Al McGuire, Marquette	1988 John Chaney, Temple	2005 Bruce Weber, Illinois
1972 John Wooden, UCLA	1989 Bob Knight, Indiana	2006 Roy Williams, North Carolina
1973 John Wooden, UCLA	1990 Roy Williams, Kansas	2007 Tony Bennett, Washington St.
1974 Norm Sloan, N.C. State	1991 Randy Ayers, Ohio St.	2008 Keno Davis, Drake
1975 Bob Knight, Indiana	1992 Perry Clark, Tulane	

Associated Press

Voted on by AP sportswriters and broadcasters and first presented in 1967.

Multiple winners: John Wooden (5); Bob Knight (3); Guy Lewis, Ray Meyer, Ralph Miller, Eddie Sutton and Roy Williams (2)

Year	Year	Year
1967 John Wooden, UCLA	1981 Ralph Miller, Oregon St.	1995 Kelvin Sampson, Oklahoma
1968 Guy Lewis, Houston	1982 Ralph Miller, Oregon St.	1996 Gene Keady, Purdue
1969 John Wooden, UCLA	1983 Guy Lewis, Houston	1997 Clem Haskins, Minnesota
1970 John Wooden, UCLA	1984 Ray Meyer, DePaul	1998 Tom Izzo, Michigan St.
1971 Al McGuire, Marquette	1985 Bill Frieder, Michigan	1999 Cliff Ellis, Auburn
1972 John Wooden, UCLA	1986 Eddie Sutton, Kentucky	2000 Larry Eustachy, Iowa St.
1973 John Wooden, UCLA	1987 Tom Davis, Iowa	2001 Matt Doherty, North Carolina
1974 Norm Sloan, N.C. State	1988 John Chaney, Temple	2002 Ben Howland, Pittsburgh
1975 Bob Knight, Indiana	1989 Bob Knight, Indiana	2003 Tubby Smith, Kentucky
1976 Bob Knight, Indiana	1990 Jim Calhoun, Connecticut	2004 Phil Martelli, St. Joseph's
1977 Bob Gaillard, San Francisco	1991 Randy Ayers, Ohio St.	2005 Bruce Weber, Illinois
1978 Eddie Sutton, Arkansas	1992 Roy Williams, Kansas	2006 Roy Williams, North Carolina
1979 Bill Hodges, Indiana St.	1993 Eddie Fogler, Vanderbilt	2007 Tony Bennett, Washington St.
1980 Ray Meyer, DePaul	1994 Norm Stewart, Missouri	2008 Keno Davis, Drake

National Association of Basketball Coaches

Voted on by NABC membership and first presented in 1969.

Multiple winners: John Wooden (3); Gene Keady and Mike Krzyzewski (2).

Year	Year	Year
1969 John Wooden, UCLA	1982 Don Monson, Idaho	1996 John Calipari, UMass
1970 John Wooden, UCLA	1983 Lou Carnesecca, St. John's	1997 Clem Haskins, Minnesota
1971 Jack Kraft, Villanova	1984 Marv Harshman, Washington	1998 Bill Guthridge, N. Carolina
1972 John Wooden, UCLA	1985 John Thompson, Georgetown	1999 Mike Krzyzewski, Duke
1973 Gene Bartow, Memphis St.	1986 Eddie Sutton, Kentucky	& Jim O'Brien, Ohio St.
1974 Al McGuire, Marquette	1987 Rick Pitino, Providence	2000 Gene Keady, Purdue
1975 Bob Knight, Indiana	1988 John Chaney, Temple	2001 Tom Izzo, Michigan St.
1976 Johnny Orr, Michigan	1989 P.J. Carlesimo, Seton Hall	2002 Kelvin Sampson, Oklahoma
1977 Dean Smith, North Carolina	1990 Jud Heathcote, Michigan St.	2003 Tubby Smith, Kentucky
1978 Bill Foster, Duke	1991 Mike Krzyzewski, Duke	2004 Phil Martelli, St. Joseph's
& Abe Lemons, Texas	1992 George Raveling, USC	& Mike Montgomery, Stanford
1979 Ray Meyer, DePaul	1993 Eddie Fogler, Vanderbilt	2005 Bruce Weber, Illinois
1980 Lute Olson, Iowa	1994 Nolan Richardson, Arkansas	2006 Jay Wright, Villanova
1981 Ralph Miller, Oregon St.	& Gene Keady, Purdue	2007 Todd Lickliter, Butler
& Jack Hartman, Kansas St.	1995 Jim Harrick, UCLA	2008 Bob McKillop, Davidson

Naismith Award

Voted on by a panel of coaches, sportswriters and broadcasters and first presented by the Atlanta Tip-Off Club in 1987 in the name of the inventor of basketball, Dr. James Naismith. **Multiple winners:** Mike Krzyzewski (3); John Calipari (2).

Year	Year	Year
1987 Bob Knight, Indiana	1995 Jim Harrick, UCLA	2003 Tubby Smith, Kentucky
1988 Larry Brown, Kansas	1996 John Calipari, UMass	2004 Phil Martelli, St. Joseph's
1989 Mike Krzyzewski, Duke	1997 Roy Williams, Kansas	2005 Bruce Weber, Illinois
1990 Bobby Cremins, Georgia Tech	1998 Bill Guthridge, N. Carolina	2006 Jay Wright, Villanova
1991 Randy Ayers, Ohio St.	1999 Mike Krzyzewski, Duke	2007 Tony Bennett, Washington St.
1992 Mike Krzyzewski, Duke	2000 Mike Montgomery, Stanford	2008 John Calipari, Memphis
1993 Dean Smith, North Carolina	2001 Rod Barnes, Mississippi	
1994 Nolan Richardson, Arkansas	2002 Ben Howland, Pittsburgh	

Player of the Year and NBA MVP

College Players of the Year who have gone on to win the NBA's Most Valuable Player award:

Bill Russell COLLEGE–San Francisco (1956); PROS–Boston Celtics (1958, 1961, 1962, 1963 and 1965).
Oscar Robertson COLLEGE–Cincinnati (1958, 1959 and 1960); PROS–Cincinnati Royals (1964).
Kareem Abdul-Jabbar COLLEGE–UCLA (1967 and 1969); PROS–Milwaukee Bucks (1971, 1972 and 1974) and LA Lakers (1976, 1977 and 1980).
Bill Walton COLLEGE–UCLA (1972, 1973 and 1974); PROS–Portland Trail Blazers (1978).
Larry Bird COLLEGE–Indiana St. (1979); PROS–Boston Celtics (1984, 1985, and 1986).
Michael Jordan COLLEGE–North Carolina (1984); PROS–Chicago Bulls (1988, 1991, 1992, 1996 and 1998).
David Robinson COLLEGE–Navy (1987); PROS–San Antonio Spurs (1995).
Shaquille O'Neal COLLEGE–LSU (1991); PROS–LA Lakers (2000).
Tim Duncan COLLEGE–Wake Forest (1997); PROS–San Antonio Spurs (2002, 2003).

Other Men's Champions

The NCAA has sanctioned national championship tournaments for Division II since 1957 and Division III since 1975. The NAIA sanctioned a single tournament from 1937-91, then split into two divisions in 1992.

NCAA Div. II Finals

Multiple winners: Kentucky Wesleyan (8); Evansville (5); CS-Bakersfield and Virginia Union (3); Metropolitan State, North Alabama and Winona St. (2).

Year	Winner	Score	Loser	Year	Winner	Score	Loser
1957	Wheaton, IL	89-65	Ky. Wesleyan	1984	Central Mo. St.	81-77	St. Augustine's, NC
1958	South Dakota	75-53	St. Michael's, VT	1985	Jacksonville St.	74-73	South Dakota St.
1959	Evansville, IN	83-67	SW Missouri St.	1986	Sacred Heart, CT	93-87	SE Missouri St.
1960	Evansville	90-69	Chapman, CA	1987	Ky. Wesleyan	92-74	Gannon, PA
1961	Wittenberg, OH	42-38	SE Missouri St.	1988	Lowell, MA	75-72	AK-Anchorage
1962	Mt. St. Mary's, MD	58-57*	CS-Sacramento	1989	N.C. Central	73-46	SE Missouri St.
1963	South Dakota St.	42-40	Wittenberg, OH	1990	Ky. Wesleyan	93-79	CS-Bakersfield
1964	Evansville	72-59	Akron, OH	1991	North Alabama	79-72	Bridgeport, CT
1965	Evansville	85-82*	Southern Illinois	1992	Virginia Union	100-75	Bridgeport
1966	Ky. Wesleyan	54-51	Southern Illinois	1993	CS-Bakersfield	85-72	Troy St., AL
1967	Winston-Salem, NC	77-74	SW Missouri St.	1994	CS-Bakersfield	92-86	Southern Ind.
1968	Ky. Wesleyan	63-52	Indiana St.	1995	Southern Indiana	71-63	UC-Riverside
1969	Ky. Wesleyan	75-71	SW Missouri St.	1996	Fort Hays St.	70-63	N. Kentucky
1970	Phila. Textile	76-65	Tennessee St.	1997	CS-Bakersfield	57-56	N. Kentucky
1971	Evansville	97-82	Old Dominion, VA	1998	UC-Davis	83-77	Ky. Wesleyan
1972	Roanoke, VA	84-72	Akron, OH	1999	Ky. Wesleyan	75-60	Metropolitan St.
1973	Ky. Wesleyan	78-76*	Tennessee St.	2000	Metropolitan St.	97-79	Ky. Wesleyan
1974	Morgan St., MD	67-52	SW Missouri St.	2001	Ky. Wesleyan	72-63	Washburn, KS
1975	Old Dominion	76-74	New Orleans	2002	Metropolitan St.	80-72	Ky. Wesleyan
1976	Puget Sound, WA	83-74	Tennessee-Chatt.	2003	Northeastern St., OK	75-64	Ky. Wesleyan
1977	Tennessee-Chatt.	71-62	Randolph-Macon	2004	Kennesaw St., GA	84-59	Southern Indiana
1978	Cheyney, PA	47-40	WI-Green Bay	2005	Virginia Union	63-58	Bryant
1979	North Alabama	64-50	WI-Green Bay	2006	Winona St., MN	73-61	Virginia Union
1980	Virginia Union	80-74	New York Tech	2007	Barton	77-75	Winona St., MN
1981	Florida Southern	73-68	Mt. St. Mary's, MD	2008	Winona St., MN	87-76	Augusta St.
1982	Dist. of Columbia	73-63	Florida Southern		*Overtime		
1983	Wright St., OH	92-73	Dist. of Columbia				

NCAA Div. III Finals

Multiple winners: North Park (5); WI-Platteville (4); Calvin, Potsdam St., Scranton, WI-Stevens Point and WI-Whitewater (2).

Year	Winner	Score	Loser	Year	Winner	Score	Loser
1975	LeMoyne-Owen, TN	57-54	Glassboro St., NJ	1993	Ohio Northern	71-68	Augustana, IL
1976	Scranton, PA	60-57	Wittenberg, OH	1994	Lebanon Valley, PA	66-59*	NYU
1977	Wittenberg, OH	79-66	Oneonta St., NY	1995	WI-Platteville	69-55	Manchester, IN
1978	North Park, IL	69-57	Widener, PA	1996	Rowan, NJ	100-93	Hope, MI
1979	North Park, IL	66-62	Potsdam St., NY	1997	Illinois Wesleyan	89-86	Neb-Wesleyan
1980	North Park, IL	83-76	Upsala, NJ	1998	WI-Platteville	69-56	Hope, MI
1981	Potsdam St., NY	67-65*	Augustana, IL	1999	WI-Platteville	76-75**	Hampden-Sydney
1982	Wabash, IN	83-62	Potsdam St., NY	2000	Calvin, MI	79-74	WI-Eau Claire
1983	Scranton, PA	64-63	Wittenberg, OH	2001	Catholic, DC	76-62	Wm. Paterson
1984	WI-Whitewater	103-86	Clark, MA	2002	Otterbein	102-83	Elizabethtown
1985	North Park, IL	72-71	Potsdam St., NY	2003	Williams, MA	67-65	Gustavus Adolphus
1986	Potsdam St., NY	76-73	LeMoyne-Owen, TN	2004	WI-Stevens Point	84-82	Williams
1987	North Park, IL	106-100	Clark, MA	2005	WI-Stevens Point	73-49	Rochester
1988	Ohio Wesleyan	92-70	Scranton, PA	2006	Virginia Wesleyan	59-56	Wittenberg
1989	WI-Whitewater	94-86	Trenton St., NJ	2007	Amherst, MA	80-67	Virginia Wesleyan
1990	Rochester, NY	43-42	DePauw, IN	2008	Washington U.	90-68	Amherst
1991	WI-Platteville	81-74	Franklin Marshall		*Overtime		
1992	Calvin, MI	62-49	Rochester, NY		**Double overtime		

NAIA Finals, 1937-91

Multiple winners: Grand Canyon, Hamline, Kentucky St. and Tennessee St. (3); Central Missouri, Central St., Fort Hay St. and SW Missouri St. (2).

Year	Winner	Score	Loser
1937	Central Missouri	35-24	Morningside, IA
1938	Central Missouri	45-30	Roanoke, VA
1939	Southwestern, KS	32-31	San Diego St.
1940	Tarkio, MO	52-31	San Diego St.
1941	San Diego St.	36-32	Murray St., KY
1942	Hamline, MN	33-31	SE Oklahoma
1943	SE Missouri St.	34-32	NW Missouri St.
1944	Not held		
1945	Loyola-LA	49-36	Pepperdine, CA
1946	Southern Illinois	49-40	Indiana St.
1947	Marshall, WV	73-59	Mankato St., MN
1948	Louisville, KY	82-70	Indiana St.
1949	Hamline, MN	57-46	Regis, CO
1950	Indiana St.	61-47	East Central, OK
1951	Hamline, MN	69-61	Millikin, IL
1952	SW Missouri St.	73-64	Murray St., KY
1953	SW Missouri St.	79-71	Hamline, MN
1954	St. Benedict's, KS	62-56	Western Illinois
1955	East Texas St.	71-54	SE Oklahoma
1956	McNeese St., LA	60-55	Texas Southern
1957	Tennessee St.	92-73	SE Oklahoma
1958	Tennessee St.	85-73	Western Illinois
1959	Tennessee St.	97-87	Pacific-Luth., WA
1960	SW Texas St.	66-44	Westminster, PA
1961	Grambling, LA	95-75	Georgetown, KY
1962	Prairie View, TX	62-53	Westminster, PA
1963	Pan American, TX	73-62	Western Carolina
1964	Rockhurst, MO	66-56	Pan American, TX
1965	Central St., OH	85-51	Oklahoma Baptist
1966	Oklahoma Baptist	88-59	Georgia Southern
1967	St. Benedict's, KS	71-65	Oklahoma Baptist
1968	Central St., OH	51-48	Fairmont St., WV
1969	Eastern N. Mex	99-76	MD-Eastern Shore
1970	Kentucky St.	79-71	Central Wash.
1971	Kentucky St.	102-82	Eastern Michigan
1972	Kentucky St.	71-62	WI-Eau Claire
1973	Guilford, NC	99-96	MD-Eastern Shore
1974	West Georgia	97-79	Alcorn St., MS
1975	Grand Canyon, AZ	65-54	M'western St., TX

Year	Winner	Score	Loser
1976	Coppin St., MD	96-91	Henderson St., AR
1977	Texas Southern	71-44	Campbell, NC
1978	Grand Canyon	79-75	Kearney St., NE
1979	Drury, MO	60-54	Henderson St., AR
1980	Cameron, OK	84-77	Alabama St.
1981	Beth. Nazarene, OK	86-85*	AL-Huntsville
1982	SC-Spartanburg	51-38	Biola, CA
1983	Charleston, SC	57-53	WV-Wesleyan
1984	Fort Hays St., KS	48-46*	WI-Stevens Pt.
1985	Fort Hays St.	82-80*	Wayland Bapt., TX
1986	David Lipscomb, TN	67-54	AR-Monticello
1987	Washburn, KS	79-77	West Virginia St.
1988	Grand Canyon	88-86*	Auburn-Montg, AL
1989	St. Mary's, TX	61-58	East Central, OK
1990	Birm-Southern, AL	88-80	WI-Eau Claire
1991	Oklahoma City	77-74	Central Arkansas

NAIA Div. I Finals

NAIA split tournament into two divisions in 1992.

Multiple winners: Oklahoma City (4); Life, GA (3).

Year	Winner	Score	Loser
1992	Oklahoma City	82-73*	Central Arkansas
1993	Hawaii Pacific	88-83	Okla. Baptist
1994	Oklahoma City	99-81	Life, GA
1995	Birm-Southern	92-76	Pfeiffer, NC
1996	Oklahoma City	86-80	Georgetown, KY
1997	Life, GA	73-64	Okla. Baptist
1998	Georgetown, KY	83-69	So. Nazarene
1999	Life, GA	63-60	Mobile, AL
2000	Life, GA	61-59	Georgetown, KY
2001	Faulkner, AL	63-59	Science & Arts, OK
2002	Science & Arts, OK	96-79	Okla. Baptist
2003	Concordia, CA	88-84*	Mountain St., WV
2004	Mountain St., WV	74-70	Concordia, CA
2005	John Brown	65-55	Azusa Pacific
2006	Texas Wesleyan	67-65	Oklahoma City
2007	Oklahoma City	79-71	Concordia
2008	Oklahoma City	75-72	Mountain St., WV

*Overtime

NAIA Div. II Finals

NAIA split tournament into two divisions in 1992.

Multiple winners: Bethel, IN (3), Northwestern, IA and Oregon Tech (2).

Year	Winner	Score	Loser
1992	Grace, IN	85-79*	Northwestern, IA
1993	Williamette, OR	63-56	Northern St., SD
1994	Eureka, IL	98-95*	Northern St., SD
1995	Bethel, IN	103-95*	NW Nazarene, ID
1996	Albertson, ID	81-72*	Whitworth, WA
1997	Bethel, IN	95-94	Siena Heights, MI
1998	Bethel, IN	89-87	Oregon Tech
1999	Cornerstone, MI	113-109	Bethel
2000	Embry-Riddle, FL	75-63	Ozarks, MO

Year	Winner	Score	Loser
2001	Northwestern, IA	82-78	MidAm. Nazarene, KS
2002	Evangel, MO	84-61	Robert Morris, IL
2003	Northwestern, IA	77-57	Bethany, KS
2004	Oregon Tech	81-72	Bellevue, NE
2005	Walsh, OH	81-70	Concordia, NE
2006	Ozarks, MO	74-56	Huntington, IN
2007	MidAm. Nazarene	78-60	Mayville St.
2008	Oregon Tech	63-56	Bellevue, NE

WOMEN

NCAA Final Four

Replaced the Association of Intercollegiate Athletics for Women (AIAW) tournament in 1982 as the official playoff for the national championship.

Multiple winners: Tennessee (8); Connecticut (5); Louisiana Tech, Stanford and USC (2)

Year	Champion	Head Coach	Score	Runner-up	Third Place	
1982	Louisiana Tech	Sonya Hogg	76-62	Cheyney	Maryland	Tennessee
1983	USC	Linda Sharp	69-67	Louisiana Tech	Georgia	Old Dominion
1984	USC	Linda Sharp	72-61	Tennessee	Cheyney	Louisiana Tech
1985	Old Dominion	Marianne Stanley	70-65	Georgia	NE Louisiana	Western Ky.
1986	Texas	Jody Conradt	97-81	USC	Tennessee	Western Ky.
1987	Tennessee	Pat Summitt	67-44	Louisiana Tech	Long Beach St.	Texas
1988	Louisiana Tech	Leon Barmore	56-54	Auburn	Long Beach St.	Tennessee
1989	Tennessee	Pat Summitt	76-60	Auburn	Louisiana Tech	Maryland
1990	Stanford	Tara VanDerveer	88-81	Auburn	Louisiana Tech	Virginia

Year	Champion	Head Coach	Score	Runner-up		—Third Place—
1991	Tennessee	Pat Summitt	70-67 (OT)	Virginia	Connecticut	Stanford
1992	Stanford	Tara VanDerveer	78-62	Western Kentucky	SW Missouri St.	Virginia
1993	Texas Tech	Marsha Sharp	84-82	Ohio St.	Iowa	Vanderbilt
1994	N. Carolina	Sylvia Hatchell	60-59	Louisiana Tech	Alabama	Purdue
1995	Connecticut	Geno Auriemma	70-64	Tennessee	Georgia	Stanford
1996	Tennessee	Pat Summitt	83-65	Georgia	Connecticut	Stanford
1997	Tennessee	Pat Summitt	68-59	Old Dominion	Stanford	Notre Dame
1998	Tennessee	Pat Summitt	93-75	Louisiana Tech	Arkansas	N.C. State
1999	Purdue	Carolyn Peck	62-45	Duke	Louisiana Tech	Georgia
2000	Connecticut	Geno Auriemma	71-52	Tennessee	Penn St.	Rutgers
2001	Notre Dame	Muffet McGraw	68-66	Purdue	Connecticut	SW Missouri St.
2002	Connecticut	Geno Auriemma	82-70	Oklahoma	Tennessee	Duke
2003	Connecticut	Geno Auriemma	73-68	Tennessee	Texas	Duke
2004	Connecticut	Geno Auriemma	70-61	Tennessee	LSU	Minnesota
2005	Baylor	Kim Mulkey-Robertson	84-62	Michigan St.	LSU	Tennessee
2006	Maryland	Brenda Frese	78-75 (OT)	Duke	North Carolina	LSU
2007	Tennessee	Pat Summitt	59-46	Rutgers	LSU	North Carolina
2008	Tennessee	Pat Summitt	64-48	Stanford	Connecticut	LSU

Final Four sites: 1982 (Norfolk, Va.), **1983** (Norfolk, Va.), **1984** (Los Angeles), **1985** (Austin), **1986** (Lexington), **1987** (Austin), **1988** (Tacoma), **1989** (Tacoma), **1990** (Knoxville), **1991** (New Orleans), **1992** (Los Angeles), **1993** (Atlanta), **1994** (Richmond), **1995** (Minneapolis), **1996** (Charlotte), **1997** (Cincinnati), **1998** (Kansas City), **1999** (San Jose), **2000** (Philadelphia), **2001** (St. Louis), **2002** (San Antonio), **2003** (Atlanta), **2004** (New Orleans), **2005** (Indianapolis), **2006** (Boston), **2007** (Cleveland), **2008** (Tampa), **2009** (St. Louis), **2010** (San Antonio).

Most Outstanding Player

A Most Outstanding Player has been selected every year of the NCAA tournament. Winner who did not play for the tournament champion is listed in **bold** type.
Multiple winners: Chamique Holdsclaw, Cheryl Miller, Candace Parker and Diana Taurasi (2).

Year
1982 Janice Lawrence, La. Tech
1983 Cheryl Miller, USC
1984 Cheryl Miller, USC
1985 Tracy Claxton, Old Dominion
1986 Clarissa Davis, Texas
1987 Tonya Edwards, Tennessee
1988 Erica Westbrooks, La. Tech
1989 Bridgette Gordon, Tennessee
1990 Jennifer Azzi, Stanford

Year
1991 **Dawn Staley**, Virginia
1992 Molly Goodenbour, Stanford
1993 Sheryl Swoopes, Texas Tech
1994 Charlotte Smith, N. Carolina
1995 Rebecca Lobo, Connecticut
1996 Michelle Marciniak, Tennessee
1997 Chamique Holdsclaw, Tenn.
1998 Chamique Holdsclaw, Tenn.
1999 Ukari Figgs, Purdue

Year
2000 Shea Ralph, Connecticut
2001 Ruth Riley, Notre Dame
2002 Swin Cash, Connecticut
2003 Diana Taurasi, Connecticut
2004 Diana Taurasi, Connecticut
2005 Sophia Young, Baylor
2006 Laura Harper, Maryland
2007 Candace Parker, Tennessee
2008 Candace Parker, Tennessee

All-Time NCAA Division I Tournament Leaders

Through 2007-08; minimum of six games; **Last** column indicates final year played.

CAREER

Scoring

Total Points	Yrs	Last	Pts	Avg
1 Chamique Holdsclaw, Tennessee . .4		1999	**479**	21.8
2 Diana Taurasi, Connecticut 4		2004	**430**	18.7
3 Bridgette Gordon, Tenn 4		1989	**388**	21.6
4 Seimone Augustus, LSU 4		2006	**372**	19.6
5 Candice Wiggins, Stanford 4		2008	**367**	22.9
6 Alana Beard, Duke 4		2004	**352**	18.5
7 Cheryl Miller, USC 4		1986	**333**	20.8
8 Candace Parker, Tennessee 3		2008	**332**	21.0
9 Katie Douglas, Purdue 4		2001	**318**	14.4
10 Janice Lawrence, La. Tech 3		1984	**312**	22.3

Assists

Total Assists	Yrs	Last	No	Avg
1 Temeka Johnson, LSU 4		2005	**136**	8.5
2 Teresa Witherspoon, La. Tech 4		1988	**127**	7.9
3 Diana Taurasi, Connecticut 4		2004	**106**	4.3

Rebounds

Total Rebounds	Yrs	Last	No	Avg
1 Sylvia Fowles, LSU 4		2008	**221**	9.6
2 Chamique Holdsclaw, Tennessee . .4		1999	**198**	9.0
3 Cheryl Miller, USC 4		1986	**170**	10.6
4 Sheila Frost, Tennessee 4		1989	**162**	9.0
5 Val Whiting, Stanford 4		1993	**161**	10.1
6 Venus Lacy, La. Tech 3		1990	**148**	10.6
7 Bridgette Gordon, Tennessee 4		1989	**142**	7.9
	Tamika Catchings, Tennessee 3		2000	**142**	7.9
9 Kirsten Cummings, Long Beach St.	4	1985	**136**	10.5
10 Gwen Jackson, Tennessee 4		2003	**133**	6.7

Steals

Total Steals	Yrs	Last	No	Avg
1 Ticha Penicheiro, Old Dominion . .4		1998	**61**	4.7
2 Kelly Miller, Georgia 4		2001	**56**	4.7

SINGLE GAME

Scoring

	Year	Pts
1 Lorri Bauman, Drake vs Maryland	1982	50
2 Sheryl Swoopes, Texas Tech vs Ohio St	1993	47
3 Candice Wiggins, Stanford vs UTEP	2008	44
4 Barbara Kennedy, Clemson vs Penn St	1982	43
5 Jackie Stiles, SW Mo. St. vs. Duke	2001	41
Candice Wiggins, Stanford vs. Maryland .	2008	41

Rebounds

	Year	No
1 Cheryl Taylor, Tenn. Tech vs Georgia	1985	23
Charlotte Smith, N. Car. vs La. Tech	1994	23
3 Daedra Charles, Tenn. vs SW Missouri . . .	1991	22

Assists

	Year	No
1 Anne Troyan, Penn St. vs. N.C. State	1983	19
2 Tasha Pointer, Rutgers vs. S.F. Austin	2001	18
3 Three tied at 17 each.		

Associated Press Final Top 10 Polls

The Associated Press weekly women's college basketball poll was begun by Mel Greenberg of *The Philadelphia Inquirer* during the 1976-77 season. Although the poll was started as a Top 20 in 1977 and was expanded to a Top 25 in 1990, only the Top 10 from each poll are listed below due to space constraints. The Association of Intercollegiate Athletics for Women (AIAW) Tournament determined the Division I national champion from 1972-81. The NCAA began its women's Division I tournament in 1982. The final AP Polls were taken before the NCAA tournament. Eventual national champions are in **bold** type.

1977
1 **Delta St.**
2 Immaculata
3 St. Joseph's-PA
4 CS-Fullerton
5 Tennessee
6 Tennessee Tech
7 Wayland Baptist
8 Montclair St.
9 S.F. Austin St.
10 N.C. State

1978
1 Tennessee
2 Wayland Baptist
3 N.C. State
4 Montclair St.
5 **UCLA**
6 Maryland
7 Queens-NY
8 Valdosta St.
9 Delta St.
10 LSU

1979
1 **Old Dominion**
2 Louisiana Tech
3 Tennessee
4 Texas
5 S.F. Austin St.
6 UCLA
7 Rutgers
8 Maryland
9 Cheyney
10 Wayland Baptist

1980
1 **Old Dominion**
2 Tennessee
3 Louisiana Tech
4 South Carolina
5 S.F. Austin St.
6 Maryland
7 Texas
8 Rutgers
9 Long Beach St.
10 N.C. State

1981
1 **Louisiana Tech**
2 Tennessee
3 Old Dominion
4 USC
5 Cheyney
6 Long Beach St.
7 UCLA
8 Maryland
9 Rutgers
10 Kansas

1982
1 **Louisiana Tech**
2 Cheyney
3 Maryland
4 Tennessee
5 Texas
6 USC
7 Old Dominion
8 Rutgers
9 Long Beach St.
10 Penn St.

1983
1 USC
2 Louisiana Tech
3 Texas
4 Old Dominion
5 Cheyney
6 Long Beach St.
7 Maryland
8 Penn St.
9 Georgia
10 Tennessee

1984
1 Texas
2 Louisiana Tech
3 Georgia
4 Old Dominion
5 **USC**
6 Long Beach St.
7 Kansas St.
8 LSU
9 Cheyney
10 Mississippi

1985
1 Texas
2 NE Louisiana
3 Long Beach St.
4 Louisiana Tech
5 **Old Dominion**
6 Mississippi
7 Ohio St.
8 Georgia
9 Penn St.
10 Auburn

1986
1 **Texas**
2 Georgia
3 USC
4 Louisiana Tech
5 Western Ky.
6 Virginia
7 Auburn
8 Long Beach St.
9 LSU
10 Rutgers

1987
1 Texas
2 Auburn
3 Louisiana Tech
4 Long Beach St.
5 Rutgers
6 Georgia
7 **Tennessee**
8 Mississippi
9 Iowa
10 Ohio St.

1988
1 Tennessee
2 Iowa
3 Auburn
4 Texas
5 **Louisiana Tech**
6 Ohio St.
7 Long Beach St.
8 Rutgers
9 Maryland
10 Virginia

1989
1 **Tennessee**
2 Auburn
3 Louisiana Tech
4 Stanford
5 Maryland
6 Texas
7 Long Beach St.
8 Iowa
9 Colorado
10 Georgia

1990
1 Louisiana Tech
2 **Stanford**
3 Washington
4 Tennessee
5 UNLV
6 S.F. Austin St.
7 Georgia
8 Texas
9 Auburn
10 Iowa

1991
1 Penn St.
2 Virginia
3 Georgia
4 **Tennessee**
5 Purdue
6 Auburn
7 N.C. State
8 LSU
9 Arkansas
10 Western Ky.

1992
1 Virginia
2 Tennessee
3 **Stanford**
4 S.F. Austin St.
5 Mississippi
6 Miami-FL
7 Iowa
8 Maryland
9 Penn St.
10 SW Missouri St.

1993
1 Vanderbilt
2 Tennessee
3 Ohio St.
4 Iowa
5 **Texas Tech**
6 Stanford
7 Auburn
8 Penn St.
9 Virginia
10 Colorado

1994
1 Tennessee
2 Penn St.
3 Connecticut
4 **North Carolina**
5 Colorado
6 Louisiana Tech
7 USC
8 Purdue
9 Texas Tech
10 Virginia

1995
1 **Connecticut**
2 Colorado
3 Tennessee
4 Stanford
5 Texas Tech
6 Vanderbilt
7 Penn St.
8 Louisiana Tech
9 Western Ky.
10 Virginia

1996
1 Louisiana Tech
2 Connecticut
3 Stanford
4 **Tennessee**
5 Georgia
6 Old Dominion
7 Iowa
8 Penn St.
9 Texas Tech
10 Alabama

1997
1 Connecticut
2 Old Dominion
3 Stanford
4 North Carolina
5 Louisiana Tech
6 Georgia
7 Florida
8 Alabama
9 LSU
10 **Tennessee**

1998
1 **Tennessee**
2 Old Dominion
3 Connecticut
4 Louisiana Tech
5 Stanford
6 Texas Tech
7 North Carolina
8 Duke
9 Arizona
10 N.C. State

1999
1 **Purdue**
2 Tennessee
3 Louisiana Tech
4 Colorado St.
5 Old Dominion
6 Connecticut
7 Rutgers
8 Notre Dame
9 Texas Tech
10 Duke

2000
1 **Connecticut**
2 Tennessee
3 Louisiana Tech
4 Georgia
5 Notre Dame
6 Penn St.
7 Iowa St.
8 Rutgers
9 UC-Santa Barbara
10 Duke

2001
1 Connecticut
2 **Notre Dame**
3 Tennessee
4 Georgia
5 Duke
6 Louisiana Tech
7 Oklahoma
8 Iowa St.
9 Purdue
10 Vanderbilt

2002
1 **Connecticut**
2 Oklahoma
3 Duke
4 Vanderbilt
5 Stanford
6 Tennessee
7 Baylor
8 Louisiana Tech
9 Purdue
10 Iowa St.

2003
1 **Connecticut**
2 Duke
3 LSU
4 Tennessee
5 Texas
6 Louisiana Tech
7 Texas Tech
8 Kansas St.
9 Stanford
10 Purdue

2004
1 Duke
2 Tennessee
3 Purdue
4 Texas
5 Penn St.
6 **Connecticut**
7 Louisiana Tech
8 Kansas St.
9 Houston
10 Stanford

2005
1 Stanford
2 LSU
3 Tennessee
4 North Carolina
5 **Baylor**
6 Michigan St.
7 Duke
8 Ohio St.
9 Rutgers
10 Connecticut

2006
1 North Carolina
2 Ohio St.
3 **Maryland**
4 Duke
5 LSU
6 Tennessee
7 Oklahoma
8 Connecticut
9 Rutgers
10 Baylor

2007
1 Duke
2 Connecticut
3 North Carolina
4 **Tennessee**
5 Ohio St.
6 Stanford
7 Maryland
8 Arizona St.
9 Vanderbilt
10 LSU

2008
1 Connecticut
2 North Carolina
3 **Tennessee**
4 Stanford
5 Maryland
6 LSU
7 Rutgers
8 Texas A&M
9 Duke
10 California

All-Time AP Top 10

The composite AP Top 10 from the 1976-77 season through 2007-08, based on the final regular season rankings of each year. Team points are based on 10 points for all 1st place finishes, 9 for each 2nd, etc. Also listed are the number of times ranked No. 1 by AP going into the tournaments, and times ranked in the pre-tournament Top 10.

		Pts	No.1	Top 10			Pts	No.1	Top 10
1	Tennessee	226	5	30	6	Stanford	87	1	14
2	Louisiana Tech	173	4	24	7	Georgia	72	0	13
3	Connecticut	118	7	15	8	Duke	61	2	11
4	Texas	93	4	18	9	Penn St.	52	1	11
5	Old Dominion	81	2	11	10	Long Beach St.	45	0	10

All-Time Winningest Division I Teams

Division I schools with best winning percentages (with a minimum of 350 victories) and most victories through 2007-08 (including postseason tournaments). Although official NCAA women's basketball records didn't begin until the 1981-82 season, results from previous seasons are included below.

Top 15 Winning Percentage

		Yrs	W	L	Pct
1	Louisiana Tech	34	932	182	**.837**
2	Tennessee	63	1076	239	**.818**
3	Old Dominion	39	872	287	**.752**
4	Texas	34	843	285	**.747**
5	Montana	34	729	247	**.747**
6	Stanford	34	751	272	**.734**
7	Connecticut	34	749	284	**.725**
8	Utah	34	721	275	**.724**
9	Stephen F. Austin St.	39	806	313	**.720**
10	Rutgers	34	729	297	**.711**
11	Georgia	35	744	310	**.706**
12	Wisconsin-Green Bay	35	721	302	**.705**
13	Penn St.	44	752	331	**.694**
14	Auburn	37	730	325	**.692**
15	Texas Tech	33	736	331	**.690**

Top 15 Victories

		Yrs	W	L	Pct
1	Tennessee	63	**1076**	239	.818
2	Louisiana Tech	34	**932**	182	.837
3	Old Dominion	39	**872**	287	.752
4	Texas	34	**843**	285	.747
5	James Madison	86	**823**	488	.628
6	Stephen F. Austin St.	39	**806**	313	.720
7	Tennessee Tech	38	**791**	368	.682
8	Long Beach St.	46	**776**	392	.664
9	Ohio St.	43	**775**	391	.665
10	Western Kentucky	46	**769**	368	.676
11	Penn St.	44	**752**	331	.694
12	Richmond	88	**751**	527	.588
13	Georgia	35	**744**	310	.706
14	Kansas St.	40	**743**	441	.628
15	Texas Tech	33	**736**	331	.690

Annual NCAA Division I Leaders

All averages include postseason games

Scoring

Multiple winners: Cindy Blodgett, Andrea Congreaves and Jackie Stiles (2).

Year		Gm	Pts	Avg
1982	Barbara Kennedy, Clemson	31	908	29.3
1983	LaTaunya Pollard, L. Beach St	31	907	29.3
1984	Deborah Temple, Delta St	28	873	31.2
1985	Anucha Browne, Northwestern	28	855	30.5
1986	Wanda Ford, Drake	30	919	30.6
1987	Tresa Spaulding, BYU	28	810	28.9
1988	LeChandra LeDay, Grambling	28	850	30.4
1989	Patricia Hoskins, Miss. Valley	27	908	33.6
1990	Kim Perrot, SW Louisiana	28	839	30.0
1991	Jan Jensen, Drake	30	888	29.6
1992	Andrea Congreaves, Mercer	28	925	33.0
1993	Andrea Congreaves, Mercer	26	805	31.0
1994	Kristy Ryan, CS-Sacramento	26	727	28.0
1995	Koko Lahanas, CS-Fullerton	29	778	26.8
1996	Cindy Blodgett, Maine	32	889	27.8
1997	Cindy Blodgett, Maine	30	810	27.0
1998	Allison Feaster, Harvard	28	797	28.5
1999	Tamika Whitmore, Memphis	32	843	26.3
2000	Jackie Stiles, SW Missouri St.	32	890	27.8
2001	Jackie Stiles, SW Missouri St.	35	1062	30.3
2002	Kelly Mazzante, Penn St.	35	872	24.9
2003	Chandi Jones, Houston	28	770	27.5
2004	Emily Faurholt, Idaho	29	737	25.4
2005	Tan White, Mississippi St.	29	681	23.5
2006	Seimone Augustus, LSU	35	795	22.7
2007	Carrie Moore, Western Mich.	32	813	25.4
2008	Amber Holt, Middle Tennessee	34	930	27.4

Rebounds

Multiple winner: Patricia Hoskins and Courtney Paris (2).

Year		Gm	No	Avg
1982	Anne Donovan, Old Dominion	28	412	14.7
1983	Deborah Mitchell, Miss. Col	28	447	16.0
1984	Joy Kellog, Oklahoma City	23	373	16.2
1985	Rosina Pearson, Beth-Cookman	26	480	18.5
1986	Wanda Ford, Drake	30	506	16.9
1987	Patricia Hoskins, Miss. Valley St.	28	476	17.0
1988	Katie Beck, East Tenn. St.	25	441	17.6
1989	Patricia Hoskins, Miss. Valley St.	27	440	16.3
1990	Pam Hudson, Northwestern St	29	438	15.1
1991	Tarcha Hollis, Grambling	29	443	15.3
1992	Christy Greis, Evansville	28	383	13.7
1993	Ann Barry, Nevada	25	355	14.2
1994	DeShawne Blocker, E. Tenn. St.	26	450	17.3
1995	Tera Sheriff, Jackson St	29	401	13.8
1996	Dana Wynne, Seton Hall	29	372	12.8
1997	Etolia Mitchell, Georgia St.	25	330	13.2
1998	Alisha Hill, Howard	30	397	13.2
1999	Monica Logan, UMBC	27	364	13.5
2000	Malveata Johnson, N.C. A&T	27	363	13.4
2001	Andrea Gardner, Howard	31	439	14.2
2002	Mandi Carver, Idaho St.	27	336	12.4
2003	Jennifer Butler, Massachusetts	28	412	14.7
2004	Ashlee Kelly, Quinnipiac	29	392	13.5
2005	Sancho Lyttle, Houston	30	362	12.1
2006	Courtney Paris, Oklahoma	36	539	15.0
2007	Lachelle Lyles, SE Missouri St.	31	527	17.0
2008	Courtney Paris, Oklahoma	31	466	15.0

Note: Wanda Ford (1986) and Patricia Hoskins (1989) each led the country in scoring and rebounds in the same year.

All-Time NCAA Division I Individual Leaders

Through 2007-08; includes regular season and tournament games; Official NCAA women's basketball records began with 1981-82 season. Players who competed earlier than that are not included below; **Last** column indicates final year played.

CAREER

Scoring

	Average	Yrs	Last	Pts	Avg
1	Patricia Hoskins, Miss. Valley St.	.4	1989	3122	28.4
2	Sandra Hodge, New Orleans	...4	1984	2860	26.7
3	Jackie Stiles, SW Mo. St.	4	2001	3206	26.1
4	Lorri Bauman, Drake	4	1984	3115	26.0
5	Andrea Congreaves, Mercer	4	1993	2796	25.9
6	Cindy Blodgett, Maine	4	1998	3005	25.5
7	Valorie Whiteside, Aplach St.	...4	1988	2944	25.4
8	Joyce Walker, LSU	4	1984	2906	24.8
9	Tarcha Hollis, Grambling	4	1991	2058	24.2
10	Korie Hlede, Duquesne	4	1998	2631	24.1

Rebounds

	Average	Yrs	Last	Reb	Avg
1	Wanda Ford, Drake	4	1986	1887	16.1
2	Patricia Hoskins, Miss. Valley St.	..4	1989	1662	15.1
3	Tarcha Hollis, Grambling	4	1991	1185	13.9
4	Katie Beck, East Tenn. St.	4	1988	1404	13.4
5	Marilyn Stephens, Temple	4	1984	1519	13.0
6	Natalie Williams, UCLA	4	1994	1137	12.8
7	Cheryl Taylor, Tenn. Tech	4	1987	1532	12.8
8	DeShawne Blocker, E. Tenn. St.	..4	1995	1361	12.7
9	Olivia Bradley, West Virginia	..4	1985	1484	12.7
10	Judy Mosley, Hawaii	4	1990	1441	12.6

SINGLE SEASON

Scoring

	Average	Year	Gm	Pts	Avg
1	Patricia Hoskins, Miss.Valley St.	1989	27	908	33.6
2	Andrea Congreaves, Mercer	..1992	28	925	33.0
3	Deborah Temple, Delta St.	1984	28	873	31.2
4	Andrea Congreaves, Mercer	..1993	26	805	31.0
5	Wanda Ford, Drake	1986	30	919	30.6
6	Anucha Browne, Northwestern	.1985	28	855	30.5
7	LeChandra LeDay, Grambling	..1988	28	850	30.4
8	Jackie Stiles, SW Mo. St.	2001	35	1062	30.3
9	Kim Perrot, SW Louisiana	...1990	28	841	30.0
10	Tina Hutchinson, San Diego St.	1984	30	898	29.9

SINGLE GAME

Scoring

		Year	Pts
1	Cindy Brown, Long Beach St. vs San Jose St.	.1987	60
2	Lorri Bauman, Drake vs SW Missouri St.	...1984	58
	Kim Perrot, SW La. vs SE La	1990	58
4	Jackie Stiles, SW Mo. St. vs Evansville	...2000	56
5	Patricia Hoskins, Miss.Valley St. vs South-BR	.1989	55
	Patricia Hoskins, Miss.Valley St. vs Ala. St.	.1989	55

Rebounds (since 1982)

		Year	No
1	Deborah Temple, Delta St. vs. UAB	1983	40
2	Rosina Pearson, Bet-Cookman vs. Fla. Mem.	1984	37
3	Mauren Formico, Pepperdine vs. Loyola-CA	.1985	33

All-Time Winningest Division I Coaches

Minimum of 10 seasons as Division I head coach; regular season and tournament games included.

Top 10 Winning Percentage

		Yrs	W	L	Pct
1	Leon Barmore, La. Tech	20	576	87	**.869**
2	**Pat Summitt**, Tennessee	34	983	182	**.844**
3	**Geno Auriemma**, Connecticut	23	657	122	**.843**
4	**Tara VanDerveer**, Stanford	..29	724	188	**.794**
5	**Gail Goestenkors**, Texas	...16	418	112	**.789**
6	Bill Sheahan, Mt. St. Mary's	...17	372	104	**.782**
7	**Robin Selvig**, Montana	30	697	199	**.778**
8	Marsha Sharp, Texas Tech	...23	556	175	**.761**
9	**Andy Landers**, Georgia	29	707	225	**.759**
10	Jody Conradt, Texas	37	882	293	**.751**

Top 10 Victories

		Yrs	W	L	Pct
1	**Pat Summitt**, Tennessee	34	**983**	182	.844
2	Jody Conradt, Texas	37	**882**	293	.751
3	**C. Vivian Stringer**, Rutgers	.37	**804**	267	.751
4	**Sylvia Hatchell**, N. Carolina	.33	**784**	275	.740
5	**Kay Yow**, N.C. State	37	**729**	337	.686
6	**Tara VanDerveer**, Stanford	.29	**724**	188	.794
7	Sue Gunter, LSU	34	**708**	308	.697
8	**Andy Landers**, Georgia	29	**707**	225	.759
9	**Robin Selvig**, Montana	30	**697**	199	.778
10	Rene Portland, Penn St.	30	**681**	249	.732

Note: active coaches in **bold** type and listed with current teams. Retired coached listed with last team coached.

Annual Awards

The Broderick Award was first given out to the Women's Division I or Large School Player of the Year in 1977. Since then, the National Assn. for Girls and Women in Sports (1978), the Women's Basketball Coaches Assn. (1983), the Atlanta Tip-Off Club (1983) and the Associated Press (1995) have joined in.

Associated Press

Voted on by AP sportswriters and broadcasters and first presented in 1995.

Multiple winner: Seimone Augustus and Chamique Holdsclaw (2).

Year	Year	Year
1995 Rebecca Lobo, Connecticut	2000 Tamika Catchings, Tennessee	2004 Alana Beard, Duke
1996 Jennifer Rizzotti, Connecticut	2001 Ruth Riley, Notre Dame	2005 Seimone Augustus, LSU
1997 Kara Wolters, Connecticut	2002 Sue Bird, Connecticut	2006 Seimone Augustus, LSU
1998 Chamique Holdsclaw, Tennessee	2003 Diana Taurasi, Connecticut	2007 Courtney Paris, Oklahoma
1999 Chamique Holdsclaw, Tennessee		2008 Candace Parker, Tennessee

Broderick Award

Voted on by a national panel of women's collegiate athletic directors and first presented by the late Thomas Broderick, an athletic outfitter, in 1977. Honda has presented the award since 1987. Basketball Player of the Year is one of 10 nominated for Collegiate Woman Athlete of the Year; (*) indicates player also won Athlete of the Year.

Multiple winners: Seimone Augustus, Chamique Holdsclaw, Nancy Lieberman, Cheryl Miller, Candace Parker, Dawn Staley and Diana Taurasi (2).

Year	Year	Year
1977 Lucy Harris, Delta St.*	1988 Teresa Weatherspoon, La. Tech*	1999 Stephanie White-McCarty, Purdue
1978 Ann Meyers, UCLA*	1989 Bridgette Gordon, Tennessee	2000 Shea Ralph, Connecticut
1979 Nancy Lieberman, Old Dominion*	1990 Jennifer Azzi, Stanford	2001 Jackie Stiles, SW Missouri St.*
1980 Nancy Lieberman, Old Dominion*	1991 Dawn Staley, Virginia	2002 Sue Bird, Connecticut
1981 Lynette Woodard, Kansas	1992 Dawn Staley, Virginia	2003 Diana Taurasi, Connecticut
1982 Pam Kelly, La. Tech	1993 Sheryl Swoopes, Texas Tech	2004 Diana Taurasi, Connecticut
1983 Anne Donovan, Old Dominion	1994 Lisa Leslie, USC	2005 Seimone Augustus, LSU
1984 Cheryl Miller, USC*	1995 Rebecca Lobo, Connecticut	2006 Seimone Augustus, LSU
1985 Cheryl Miller, USC	1996 Jennifer Rizzotti, Connecticut	2007 Candace Parker, Tennessee
1986 Kamie Ethridge, Texas*	1997 Chamique Holdsclaw, Tennessee	2008 Candace Parker, Tennessee
1987 Katrina McClain, Georgia	1998 Chamique Holdsclaw, Tennessee*	

Women's Basketball Coaches Association

Voted on by the WBCA and first presented by Champion athletic outfitters in 1983. Merged with Wade Trophy in 2002.

Multiple winners: Chamique Holdsclaw, Cheryl Miller and Dawn Staley (2).

Year	Year	Year
1983 Anne Donovan, Old Dominion	1990 Venus Lacy, La. Tech	1996 Saudia Roundtree, Georgia
1984 Janice Lawrence, La. Tech	1991 Dawn Staley, Virgina	1997 Kate Starbird, Stanford
1985 Cheryl Miller, USC	1992 Dawn Staley, Virginia	1998 Chamique Holdsclaw, Tennessee
1986 Cheryl Miller, USC	1993 Sheryl Swoopes, Texas Tech	1999 Chamique Holdsclaw, Tennessee
1987 Katrina McClain, Georgia	1994 Lisa Leslie, USC	2000 Tamika Catchings, Tennessee
1988 Michelle Edwards, Iowa	1995 Rebecca Lobo, Connecticut	2001 Ruth Riley, Notre Dame
1989 Clarissa Davis, Texas		

Wade Trophy

Originally voted on by the National Assn. for Girls and Women in Sports (NAGWS) and awarded for academics and community service as well as player performance. First presented in 1978 in the name of former Delta St. coach Lily Margaret Wade. Since 2002, the trophy has been awarded to the Women's Basketball Coaches Association player of the year.

Multiple winner: Seimone Augustus and Nancy Lieberman (2).

Year	Year	Year
1978 Carol Blazejowski, Montclair St.	1989 Clarissa Davis, Texas	1999 Stephanie White-McCarty, Purdue
1979 Nancy Lieberman, Old Dominion	1990 Jennifer Azzi, Stanford	2000 Edwina Brown, Texas
1980 Nancy Lieberman, Old Dominion	1991 Daedra Charles, Tennessee	2001 Jackie Stiles, SW Missouri St.
1981 Lynette Woodard, Kansas	1992 Susan Robinson, Penn St.	2002 Sue Bird, Connecticut
1982 Pam Kelly, La. Tech	1993 Karen Jennings, Nebraska	2003 Diana Taurasi, Connecticut
1983 LaTaunya Pollard, L. Beach St.	1994 Carol Ann Shudlick, Minnesota	2004 Alana Beard, Duke
1984 Janice Lawrence, La. Tech	1995 Rebecca Lobo, Connecticut	2005 Seimone Augustus, LSU
1985 Cheryl Miller, USC	1996 Jennifer Rizzotti, Connecticut	2006 Seimone Augustus, LSU
1986 Kamie Ethridge, Texas	1997 DeLisha Milton, Florida	2007 Candace Parker, Tennessee
1987 Shelly Pennefather, Villanova	1998 Ticha Penicheiro, Old Dominion	2008 Candice Wiggins, Stanford
1988 Teresa Weatherspoon, La. Tech		

Naismith Trophy

Voted on by a panel of coaches, sportswriters and broadcasters and first presented in 1983 by the Atlanta Tip-Off Club in the name of the inventor of basketball, Dr. James Naismith.

Multiple winners: Cheryl Miller (3); Seimone Augustus, Clarissa Davis, Chamique Holdsclaw, Candace Parker, Dawn Staley and Diana Taurasi (2).

Year	Year	Year
1983 Anne Donovan, Old Dominion	1992 Dawn Staley, Virginia	2001 Ruth Riley, Notre Dame
1984 Cheryl Miller, USC	1993 Sheryl Swoopes, Texas Tech	2002 Sue Bird, Connecticut
1985 Cheryl Miller, USC	1994 Lisa Leslie, USC	2003 Diana Taurasi, Connecticut
1986 Cheryl Miller, USC	1995 Rebecca Lobo, Connecticut	2004 Diana Taurasi, Connecticut
1987 Clarissa Davis, Texas	1996 Saudia Roundtree, Georgia	2005 Seimone Augustus, LSU
1988 Sue Wicks, Rutgers	1997 Kate Starbird, Stanford	2006 Seimone Augustus, LSU
1989 Clarissa Davis, Texas	1998 Chamique Holdsclaw, Tennessee	2007 Candace Parker, Tennessee
1990 Jennifer Azzi, Stanford	1999 Chamique Holdsclaw, Tennessee	2008 Candace Parker, Tennessee
1991 Dawn Staley, Virgina	2000 Tamika Catchings, Tennessee	

Wooden Award

Voted on by a panel of coaches, sportswriters and broadcasters and first presented in 2004 by the Los Angeles Athletic Club in the name of former Purdue All-American and UCLA coach John Wooden. Unlike the other player of the year awards, candidates for the Wooden must have a minimum grade point average of 2.00 (out of 4.00).

Multiple winner: Seimone Augustus and Candace Parker (2).

Year	Year	Year
2004 Alana Beard, Duke	2006 Seimone Augustus, LSU	2007 Candace Parker, Tennessee
2005 Seimone Augustus, LSU		2008 Candace Parker, Tennessee

Coach of the Year Award

Voted on by the Women's Basketball Coaches Assn. and first presented by Converse athletic outfitters in 1983.

Multiple winners: Geno Auriemma (4); Pat Summitt (3), Jody Conradt, Gail Goestenkors, Rene Portland and Vivian Stringer (2).

Year	Year	Year
1983 Pat Summitt, Tennessee	1992 Ferne Labati, Miami-FL	2001 Muffet McGraw, Notre Dame
1984 Jody Conradt, Texas	1993 Vivian-Stringer, Iowa	2002 Geno Auriemma, Connecticut
1985 Jim Foster, St. Joseph's-PA	1994 Marsha Sharp, Texas Tech	2003 Gail Goestenkors, Duke
1986 Jody Conradt, Texas	1995 Pat Summitt, Tennessee	2004 Rene Portland, Penn St.
1987 Theresa Grentz, Rutgers	1996 Leon Barmore, La. Tech	2005 Pokey Chatman, LSU
1988 Vivian Stringer, Iowa	1997 Geno Auriemma, Connecticut	2006 Sylvia Hatchell, N. Carolina
1989 Tara VanDerveer, Stanford	1998 Pat Summitt, Tennessee	2007 Gail Goestenkors, Duke
1990 Kay Yow, N.C. State	1999 Carolyn Peck, Purdue	2008 Geno Auriemma, Connecticut
1991 Rene Portland, Penn St.	2000 Geno Auriemma, Connecticut	

Other Women's Champions

The NCAA has sanctioned national championship tournaments for Division II and Division III since 1982. The NAIA sanctioned a single tournament from 1981-91, then split in to two divisions in 1992. (*) denotes overtime

NCAA Div. II Finals

Multiple winners: North Dakota St. and Cal Poly Pomona (5); Delta St. and North Dakota (3).

Year	Winner	Score	Loser
1982	Cal Poly Pomona	93-74	Tuskegee, AL
1983	Virginia Union	73-60	Cal Poly Pomona
1984	Central Mo.St.	80-73	Virginia Union
1985	Cal Poly Pomona	80-69	Central Mo.St.
1986	Cal Poly Pomona	70-63	North Dakota St.
1987	New Haven, CT	77-75	Cal Poly Pomona
1988	Hampton, VA	65-48	West Texas St.
1989	Delta St., MS	88-58	Cal Poly Pomona
1990	Delta St., MS	77-43	Bentley, MA
1991	North Dakota St.	81-74	SE Missouri St.
1992	Delta St., MS	65-63	North Dakota St.
1993	North Dakota St.	95-63	Delta St.
1994	North Dakota St.	89-56	CS-San Bernadino
1995	North Dakota St.	98-85	Portland St.
1996	North Dakota St.	104-78	Shippensburg, PA
1997	North Dakota	94-78	S. Indiana
1998	North Dakota	92-76	Emporia St.
1999	North Dakota	80-63	Arkansas Tech
2000	Northern Kentucky	71-62	North Dakota St.
2001	Cal Poly Pomona	87-80*	North Dakota
2002	Cal Poly Pomona	74-62	SE Oklahoma St.
2003	South Dakota St.	65-60	Northern Kentucky
2004	California, PA	75-72	Drury
2005	Washburn	70-53	Seattle Pacific
2006	Grand Valley St.	58-52	AIC
2007	Southern Conn.	61-45	Florida Gulf Coast
2008	Northern Ky.	63-58	South Dakota

NCAA Div. III Finals

Multiple winners: Washington (4); Capital, Elizabethtown, Hope and WI-Stevens Point (2).

Year	Winner	Score	Loser
1982	Elizabethtown, PA	67-66*	NC-Greensboro
1983	North Central, IL	83-71	Elizabethtown, PA
1984	Rust College, MS	51-49	Elizabethtown, PA
1985	Scranton, PA	68-59	New Rochelle, NY
1986	Salem St., MA	89-85	Bishop, TX
1987	WI-Stevens Pt.	81-74	Concordia, MN
1988	Concordia, MN	65-57	St. John Fisher, NY
1989	Elizabethtown, PA	66-65	CS-Stanislaus
1990	Hope, MI	65-63	St. John Fisher
1991	St. Thomas, MN	73-55	Muskingum, OH
1992	Alma, MI	79-75	Moravian, PA
1993	Central Iowa	71-63	Capital, OH
1994	Capital, OH	82-63	Washington, MO
1995	Capital, OH	59-55	WI-Oshkosh
1996	WI-Oshkosh	66-50	Mt. Union, OH
1997	NYU	72-70	WI-Eau Claire
1998	Washington, MO	77-69	So. Maine
1999	Washington, MO	74-65	Col.of St. Benedict, MN
2000	Washington, MO	79-33	So. Maine
2001	Washington, MO	67-45	Messiah, PA
2002	WI-Stevens Pt.	67-65	St. Lawrence, NY
2003	Trinity, TX	60-58	E. Connecticut St.
2004	Wilmington	59-53	Bowdoin
2005	Millikin	70-50	Randolph-Macon
2006	Hope, MI	69-56	Southern Maine
2007	DePauw	55-52	Washington, MO
2008	Howard Payne, TX	68-54	Messiah, PA

AIAW Finals

The Association of Intercollegiate Athletics for Women Large College tournament determined the women's national champion for 10 years until supplanted by the NCAA. In 1982, most Division I teams entered the first NCAA tournament rather than the last one staged by the AIAW.

Year	Winner	Score	Loser	Year	Winner	Score	Loser
1972	Immaculata, PA	52-48	West Chester, PA	1978	UCLA	90-74	Maryland
1973	Immaculata, PA	59-52	Queens College, NY	1979	Old Dominion	75-65	Louisiana Tech
1974	Immaculata, PA	68-53	Mississippi College	1980	Old Dominion	68-53	Tennessee
1975	Delta St., MS	90-81	Immaculata, PA	1981	Louisiana Tech	79-59	Tennessee
1976	Delta St., MS	69-64	Immaculata, PA	1982	Rutgers	83-77	Texas
1977	Delta St., MS	68-55	LSU				

PRO
BASKETBALL

2007 / 2008 YEAR IN REVIEW

Doc Rivers got the rare indoor Gatorade shower from **Paul Pierce** following Game 6 of the NBA Finals.

NOTES

FROM A GOOD OL' FASHIONED GARDEN PARTY

The Celtics beat an old foe for their 17th banner and ended the leanest streak in the history of the NBA's proudest franchise.

by Bill Simmons

If legendary poet Tyrone Green rewrote "Images" about Game 6 of the 2008 NBA Finals, it could have gone something like this:

Dark and lonely on a summer night
Kill the Lakers
Kill the Lakers
Kobe barking, do he bite?
Kill the Lakers
Kill the Lakers
Raining 3s and and grabbing their neck
Then their hopes we start to wreck
Got every reason — what the heck?
Kill the Lakers
Kill the Lakers
C-I-L-L
The La-kers

This was an obliteration. There's no other word. Obliteration. The Celtics did more than just capture their 17th title Tuesday night, playing their finest game of the season and crushing the spirit of a long-time foe in the process. Boston 131, Los Angeles 92. And you know what? It wasn't even that close. For Celtics fans, the only way Game 6 could have been more satisfying was if Kobe flipped out in the fourth quarter and punched Sasha Vujacic during a timeout, then got dragged to the locker room by five teammates screaming, "This isn't over! This isn't over!" while Sasha sobbed into a towel. Maybe that didn't happen, but everything else did.

You know you attended a special game when you're trying to fall asleep that night and the following things are in place: Your palms are swollen and pink, almost like when someone allergic to shellfish accidentally touches a lobster. Your voice sounds more hoarse and scratchy than Lindsay Lohan after an all-night bender. Your body is caked in sweat, only you don't want to shower because it kinda feels like you played. You just lie there smiling and thinking about everything, and if you concentrate hard enough, you can still hear the crowd cheering and cheering. I climbed in my bed at 2:30 a.m. and didn't fall asleep until 4.

There are different ways to win a championship; all of them work, but ideally you'd like it to happen at home so the fans can share in the happiness, and you'd like

Bill Simmons is a columnist for ESPN.com and ESPN The Magazine.

AP Images

→ Celtic Pride returned to Boston with the franchise's 17th NBA banner, thanks in large part to the efforts of the new edition of **The Big Three** (from left): Kevin Garnett, Ray Allen and Paul Pierce.

a butt-whupping so everyone can spend a stress-free fourth quarter soaking it in, carrying on like maniacs, watching the boys celebrate on the bench and everything else. The Celtics clinched the 1986 title in Boston by effectively destroying the Sampson/ Olajuwon-era Rockets. The game happened 22 years ago almost to the day, and I just remember standing and cheering for three hours and thinking Larry Bird was superhuman. Everyone thought we were headed for another dynasty that day — we had the best player, one of the greatest teams ever, the No. 2 pick in the '86 draft ... I mean, life was good. Then Lenny Bias died from a cocaine overdose and sent the franchise into one of those Goose/ Maverick tailspins. Bird and McHale got injured, Reggie died and within seven years, the Celtics weren't the Celtics anymore.

On the surface, Tuesday night was about reclaiming old territory, a little like Avon Barksdale getting released from prison and reclaiming the streets of Baltimore. But it went much deeper than that. This was a generational thing. For older fans weaned on the Russell era (like my father), this was about stumbling into another banner well after the point when they had started wondering to themselves, "Good God, I don't know if I'm ever going to see another championship team." For fans weaned on the Hondo/Cowens teams or the Bird/McHale teams (like me), this felt like climbing into Doc Brown's DeLorean, back to those springs in New England when the weather started getting nice, pollen collected on the streets and everyone started getting geared up for a two-month run of Bruins and Celtics playoff games.

And for the under-30 fans, this was about breaking from the past and forming their own memories. Instead of hearing about the time Gerald Henderson stole the ball or Glenn McDonald saved the triple-

It was an MVP season for **Kobe Bryant** but that wasn't quite enough to carry the Lakers to victory in the Finals.

like we were attending some Celtics fan fantasy camp or something. I can't speak for everyone else, but I pounded my hands together for three solid hours. I jumped up in delight at least 50 times. I fought off a lump in my throat when Pierce and Doc Rivers were hugging near the end. I hugged people I didn't know and briefly turned into James Posey at one point.

Everything was a happy blur. Looking through my notebook Wednesday morning and trying to decipher the incoherent notes, fortunately, a few things from that happy blur stand out:

Note No. 1: "6/17"

If you're a numerology buff, then you'll enjoy this one: Game 6 was played on June 17 — in other words, "6" (the number for June, as well as the number of games in the Finals) and "17" (the number of Boston championships if you include one for 2008). Two of the four greatest Celtics of all-time — Bill Russell and John Havlicek — wore "6" and "17," respectively. And if you add 6+1+7, you'd get "14," the number worn by Bob Cousy, another one of the four greatest Celtics ever. (If you want to really stretch it, 3 + 3 = 6, and "33" was worn by Larry Bird, the fourth in the "greatest Celtics ever" group.) If that's not enough, the area code for Boston is "617." And on a somber note, the 1986 draft happened June 17 — really, the last day the Celtics felt like they were invincible. I don't know what all of this means, but it means something, right?

Note No. 2: "KG Head-Butt"

After a brutal Game 5, Kevin Garnett admitted afterward he "played like garbage." This made me happy. We need-

OT game, they finally had their own stories to tell, like the time Pierce dropped 41 on the Cavs in Game 7, or the time we came back from 24 down to beat the Lakers.

So everyone was three levels beyond euphoric Tuesday night. Say what you want about sports, but I can't think of anything else that brings random people together quite like winning. You should have seen Causeway Street before Game 6 — green everywhere you looked, everyone walking with a purpose, fans chanting different things, everyone just happy to be involved,

ed him to show up for Game 6, and as I wrote Tuesday, it sure seemed like he was either (A) shrinking from the moment or (B) totally worn down from keeping his engine in fifth gear for the duration of a grueling 107-game season. Before the opening tip, Garnett stood in front of the basket near Boston's bench, muttered a few things to psyche himself up and finally head-butted the basket support as hard as he could. Watching from about 50 feet away, my dad and I raced to make the "Uh-oh, I think we're getting the KG from the regular season tonight" comment.

Kobe and Co. looked like they wanted to catch a flight home at halftime.

And that's exactly what happened. Garnett finished with 26 points and 14 rebounds and played his usual terrific defense, but, more importantly, he found his swagger again, a level of passion and intensity that's unique to him and only him. Now I'm convinced Garnett just wore himself down as the playoffs went along. The whole thing meant too much to him; he wanted it too badly. By the end of Game 5, a cooked Garnett was standing flat-footed in the paint as key rebounds ricocheted by him in every direction. For someone who once averaged 15 boards a game, it seemed almost incomprehensible that he couldn't grab any of them. Was he choking? Was he injured? What the hell? Now we know the answer — if the season wore him down, then Tuesday night's crowd gave him one last energy boost, like 18,000 people were pouring a giant Red Bull down his throat. He ended up playing a monster game when Boston needed it most, and if there was a signature KG moment, it had to be the three-point play near the end of the first half when he hopped into the paint, got knocked to the floor and flung a line drive as he was falling that banked in, followed by Garnett lying on the floor with his arms raised, screaming at the ceiling.

Let the record show KG played one of his greatest games to help clinch a championship. It's something Elvin Hayes can't say, or Karl Malone, or Patrick Ewing, or Chris Webber, or anyone else from the not-so-clutch group that Garnett escaped. Much like John Elway after the '97 Super Bowl, any lingering questions about Garnett's ability to raise his game in big moments vanished into thin air for good Tuesday night. They will never be asked again. It's funny how a championship can do that.

Note No. 3: "Posey 3, 43-29, BED-LAM"

Here's where things started looking good — midway through the second quarter, after the Celtics survived a hot start from Kobe and some curious officiating — when the Celtics pulled away with some stifling defense and a few timely 3-pointers and finally rewarded a crowd that was ready to burst for a solid hour. You could actually see the Lakers wilting. I'm not kidding. They looked like they wanted to hop on the plane right then and there. More importantly, this was when the fans pushed themselves to another level — I know this sounds crazy, but, of all the sports, only in basketball can a crowd reach a point when everyone collectively decides, "There's no way we're losing tonight." You don't know when it's going to happen, you can't make it happen, but when it does happen ... you know.

43-29. Bedlam. That's when we knew.

Note No. 4: "84-53, 21 asts, 5 TO, 13 stls, 34-17 reb adv."

Here's when the night became a little surreal, with the Celtics leading by 31 in the third quarter and dominating the game statistically to the degree that I actually felt obligated to write those numbers down. The guy who keyed everything after halftime was Rajon Rondo, who played out of his mind and made the Lakers pay for the "let's cover everyone else and make Rondo beat us" strategy. If you applied my Table Test to Rondo's second season, you'd say he brought a ton of forks and plates to the table, and he definitely took off a bunch of knives and spoons. In other words, maybe he didn't give you everything you needed, but you could still eat dinner with him. If Rondo played well in the same game when Allen and/or Pierce were scoring and Garnett was controlling everything else, the 2008 Celtics were unbeatable at home. Repeat: Unbeatable. Just like Tuesday night.

No one in green and white deserved this title more than Paul Pierce.

Note No. 5: "PP — 'I'm tired'".

A direct quote from Paul Pierce after he airballed a 3-pointer with the Celtics winning by 30, got yanked for a much-needed sub and limped back to the bench. The guy was dead. You could see it.

Quick tangent: We're basically rooting for laundry in sports. Of the 10 best guys on this particular Boston team, seven of them weren't Celtics during last season's despicable tank job, and two of them weren't Celtics as recently as January. As much as I like the new guys and everything they brought to the team, I still feel like I'm getting to know them. Posey, House and Brown were hired guns. Garnett belongs to Minnesota. Allen belongs to Milwaukee and Seattle. Powe, Rondo and Big Baby just got here. This season was like having a great fantasy team — the guys were thrown together and made some magic happen, but, still, they were thrown together.

But Pierce …

I mean …

We watched that guy grow up. We watched him become a man. We believed in him, we gave up on him, and we believed in him again. I don't mean to sound like the old man in "Pretty Woman," but part of me wanted to walk onto the court Tuesday night and just tell Pierce, "It's hard for me to say this without sounding condescending, but I'm proud of you." The guy gave us everything he had, altered his NBA tombstone, earned a

place in the rafters and brought us a 17th title — just like he promised, by the way — and his sterling play in Games 4 and 5 ranks among the all-time greatest Celtic performances. We spend so much time complaining about sports and being disappointed that our favorite players never end up being who we wanted them to be, but in Pierce's case, he became everything we wanted him to be. When he held up the Finals MVP trophy after the game and screamed to the crowd in delight, I don't think I've ever been happier for a Boston athlete. How many guys stick with a crummy franchise for 10 solid years, then get a chance to lead that same team to a championship? Does that EVER happen in sports anymore?

Note: No. 6: "You feel safe?"

My dad asked me that one when we were leading, 89-60. My answer? No. The memory of the Game 2 meltdown still lingered. And, of course, the Lakers still had No. 24.

But as Bryant kept throwing up bricks and looking like Mike Tyson in Japan — remember when Buster Douglas kept clubbing Tyson in the head, and after the initial shock wore off, we came to the gradual realization that Tyson wasn't as dominant as we believed? — I started to feel safer and safer, and everything crested with those two Ray Allen 3s that practically caused the roof to cave in. Leading to …

Without the sudden resurrection of Ray Allen, Boston would not have won this series.

Note No. 7: "PJ smiling, PP nodding"

My favorite moment of the game, as well as the one I'll always remember. The Lakers called timeout after those Allen 3s with the Celtics leading, 101-70. (By the way, I can't remember another playoffs in any sport quite like the one Allen had; it was like watching a dead person climb out of a coffin at an open-casket funeral like nothing ever happened. Amazing. Twenty-two 3s in the Finals???? They would not have won the series without im, and that's an understatement.) Everyone ould smell the trophy at this point. It was oing to happen.

I glanced over to the Celtics' bench and oticed P.J. Brown just sitting there grinning; e looked like a proud parent watching a on or daughter giving an Oscars speech. le couldn't have been happier to be there. It vasn't possible. Standing next to him, Pierce uced the crowd behind the Celtics' bench, vatching everyone dance to the Jumbotron usic as he nodded happily. You could see im soaking in the moment. He wasn't even oing it for the cameras; it was one of those mes when you could study someone from a istance and read every single thing they vere thinking. He was thinking about the ast 10 years, and all the bad things that appened, and all the times he gave up ope, and now he was reminding himself to njoy the moment. You could see it. All of it.

Note No. 8: "Gino!!!!!!!!!"

They finally showed him with a little less han three minutes remaining. Once upon a me, we had Red Auerbach's cigar. Now, ve have a long-armed dancer with a creepy eard working his magic on an "American andstand" episode from 30 years ago. As oon as the music started, the crowd erupted nd Pierce quickly hopped onto a chair to lance along. This wouldn't have happened 2 years ago; back then, the players xchanged sweaty high-fives and hugs, the tadium played organ music, Red's cigar moke drifted toward the rafters and the fans repared to charge the court and eventually pend the rest of the night getting drunk at ne of the 50 bars surrounding the Garden. Now? We stay in our seats cheering and lapping, we can't celebrate after the game ecause nearly every bar was closed down or safety reasons, and we celebrate victories y dancing along with dead background ancers from long-defunct disco shows. hings are different now. S—- happens.

But you know what? I still loved every sec-

ond of it. I feel guilty about condoning anything about the Jumbotron era, but in this case, I gotta say ... it worked. Fifty years from now, everyone able to remember Game 6 of the 2008 Finals will remember Pierce and Gino dancing together. And that's just the way it is.

Note No. 9: "Deee-fense! Deee-fense!"

This chant happened after the game, when they were interviewing Doc Rivers on the podium after the celebration. (Important note: I was wrong about Terry Francona in 2004, and I was wrong about Doc in 2008. That's not earth-shattering news because I'm wrong many times. But this time, I was really, REALLY wrong. The guys gave him everything they had in the Finals. This had to be mentioned.) Doc mentioned that defense as the biggest reason for the victory, and out of nowhere, the fans started a "Deee-fense!" chant and drowned him out for the rest of the interview. It was the perfect way to end the season. Everything started with the defense this season, from Garnett's trade to Tom Thibodeau's hiring to Posey and Brown's signings to Pierce's emergence over these last few months as a truly great defensive player. Time and time again, the defense saved this season. If there's a lesson with the 2008 Celtics, it's one we already knew: Defense wins championships.

Note No. 10: "I gotta say, I never thought I'd see another championship in my lifetime."

My father said that during the celebration. He said it without a trace of seriousness, humor or emotion. Less than 13 months earlier, after our lottery hopes went down in flames and it looked like we were headed for the Yi Jianlian era, we both wondered if professional basketball effectively had been murdered in Boston. Dad bought a single season ticket for the Celtics for the 1973-74 season and carried me into the Garden for the next four years, sitting me on his lap and even letting me sleep on him during the famous triple-OT game against Phoenix in 1976. When I became too big to sit on his lap, he bought a second ticket even though we really didn't have any money at the time. And we've had those two tickets ever since. How do you repay someone for a lifelong experience like that? You don't. You can't.

For the past 15 years, he shelled out a substantial amount of money for one dreadful memory after another (with the exception of an improbable playoff run in 2002). What made him keep sending those checks with no daylight in sight? He hoped for another game like the famous Bird-Dominique duel in 1988, when Larry had come through enough times that you could actually feel it coming before it happened. After that masterpiece of a sporting event — really, it was a life experience — we were too wired to head right home, so we found an ice cream shop called Bailey's in Wellesley and ordered a couple hot fudge sundaes. I don't think we said anything for 20 solid minutes. We just kept eating ice cream and shaking our heads. What could you say? Can you put something like that into words? We were speechless. We were drained. We were lucky.

So maybe you can't walk away from the potential of more Bailey's moments, even if the NBA stacks heavy odds against such bliss happening for more than three or four franchises at the same time. After Reggie's death in the summer of '93, the Celtics stopped being lucky and they definitely stopped being smart. That didn't stop my father from steadfastly renewing those tickets every summer with his fingers crossed, hoping things would somehow revert to the way they were. Then the Allen trade happened, and McHale delivered KG on a silver platter, and Posey and House came aboard and, suddenly, we were alive again. Although the 17th title meant something different to everybody, for the lifers like my father and every other fan who kept their tickets as prices kept

rising and the team kept stumbling, Tuesd night resonated with them on a whole oth level. Had they given up, had they packed in, had they watched Game 6 happen on t evision and spent the whole time thinking, could have been there" ... now THAT wou have been cruel. Instead, they were insi the building and feeling part of everythi that was happening, mainly because th were.

Anyway, my father deserved the title much as anyone. I was somewhere betwe 100 and 500 times happier for him than was for anyone else. We parted ways aft the game, shared a hug and successful avoided getting choked up, although, in r rospect, that wouldn't have been a bo thing. I headed down to The Greatest Bar commemorate the victory with a packe house of deliriously happy Celtics fan threw down a few celebratory beers, turne down about 25 offers to do shots and had series of "Can you believe this?" convers tions with basically everyone in the ba Nobody really knew what to say. We a agreed that, as great as the night was, th it happened at the expense of the Lakers rea ly pushed everything over the top. Bosto fans hate the Yankees, we hate th Canadiens and we hate the Lakers. It's in ou DNA. It just is. Blowing the Lakers out of th building in Game 6 was the proverbial che ry on our hot fudge sundae. If it were th Jazz or the Spurs, it just wouldn't have bee the same.

At one point, someone asked me, "Ho are you gonna write about ... THAT? I mear how do you write about what just hap pened?"

I didn't know, and I didn't care. The Celtics were the champs. The Lakers had been vanquished. The city of Boston wa hopping. Everything was right with the worl again.

And that's when I decided to do a shot.

2007-2008
Season in Review

SPORTS ALMANAC

Final NBA Standings

Division champions (*) and playoff qualifiers (†) are noted. Number of seasons listed after each head coach refers to current tenure with club.

Western Conference

Northwest Div.	W	L	Pct	GB	Per Game For	Opp
*Utah	54	28	.659	–	106.2	99.3
†Denver	50	32	.610	4	110.7	107.0
Portland	41	41	.500	13	95.4	96.3
Minnesota	22	60	.268	32	95.6	102.4
Seattle	20	62	.244	34	97.5	106.3

Head Coaches: Utah—Jerry Sloan (20th season); **Den**—George Karl (4th); **Port**—Nate McMillan (3rd); **Min**—Randy Wittman (2nd); **Sea**—P.J. Carlesimo (1st).

Pacific Div.	W	L	Pct	GB	Per Game For	Opp
*LA Lakers	57	25	.695	–	108.6	101.3
†Phoenix	55	27	.671	2	110.1	105.0
Golden St.	48	34	.585	9	111.0	108.8
Sacramento	38	44	.463	19	102.5	104.8
LA Clippers	23	59	.280	34	93.8	101.1

Head Coaches: LAL—Phil Jackson (3rd season); **Pho**—Mike D'Antoni (5th); **G.St.**—Don Nelson (3rd); **Sac**—Reggie Theus (1st); **LAC**—Mike Dunleavy (5th).

Southwest Div.	W	L	Pct	GB	Per Game For	Opp
*New Orleans	56	26	.683	–	100.9	95.6
†San Antonio	56	26	.683	–	95.4	90.6
†Houston	55	27	.671	1	96.7	92.0
†Dallas	51	31	.622	5	100.4	95.9
Memphis	22	60	.268	34	100.7	106.9

Head Coaches: NO—Byron Scott (4th season); **SA**—Gregg Popovich (12th); **Hou**—Rick Adelman (1st); **Dal**—Avery Johnson (4th); **Mem**—Marc Iavaroni (1st).

Eastern Conference

Atlantic Div.	W	L	Pct	GB	Per Game For	Opp
*Boston	66	16	.805	–	100.5	90.3
†Toronto	41	41	.500	25	100.2	97.3
†Philadelphia	40	42	.488	26	96.6	96.2
New Jersey	34	48	.415	32	95.8	100.9
New York	23	59	.280	43	96.9	103.5

Head Coaches: Bos—Doc Rivers (4th season); **Tor**—Sam Mitchell (4th); **Phi**—Maurice Cheeks (3rd); **NJ**—Lawrence Frank (5th); ; **NY**—Isiah Thomas (2nd).

Central Div.	W	L	Pct	GB	Per Game For	Opp
*Detroit	59	53	.720	–	97.5	90.1
†Cleveland	45	37	.549	14	96.4	96.7
Indiana	36	46	.439	23	104.0	105.4
Chicago	33	49	.402	26	97.3	100.4
Milwaukee	26	56	.317	33	97.0	18-34

Head Coaches: Det—Flip Saunders (3rd season); **Cle**—Mike Brown (3rd); **Ind**—Jim O'Brien (1st); **Chi**—Scott Skiles (9-16) was fired on Dec. 22, 2007 and replaced by Pete Myers (0-1) then Jim Boylan (24-32) on an interim basis; **Mil**— Larry Krystkowiak (2nd).

Southeast Div.	W	L	Pct	GB	Per Game For	Opp
*Orlando	52	30	.634	–	104.5	99.0
†Washington	43	39	.524	9	98.8	99.2
†Atlanta	37	45	.451	15	98.2	100.0
Charlotte	32	50	.390	20	97.1	101.4
Miami	15	67	.183	37	91.4	100.0

Head Coaches: Orl—Stan Van Gundy (2nd season); **Wash**—Eddie Jordan (5th); **Atl**—Mike Woodson (4th); **Cha**—Sam Vincent (1st); **Mia**—Pat Riley (3rd).

Overall Conference Standings

Sixteen teams—eight from each conference—qualify for the NBA Playoffs; (*) indicates division champions.

Western Conference

		W	L	Home	Away	Conf	Div
1	LA Lakers*	57	25	30-11	27-14	37-15	12-4
2	New Orleans*	56	26	30-11	26-15	34-18	10-6
3	San Antonio	56	26	34-7	22-19	33-19	10-6
4	Utah*	54	28	37-4	17-24	33-19	10-6
5	Houston	55	27	31-10	24-17	33-19	8-8
6	Phoenix	55	27	30-11	25-16	31-21	10-6
7	Dallas	51	31	34-7	17-24	33-19	10-6
8	Denver	50	32	33-8	17-24	31-21	10-6
	Golden St.	48	34	27-14	21-20	28-24	10-6
	Portland	41	41	28-13	13-28	26-26	11-5
	Sacramento	38	44	26-15	12-29	21-31	3-13
	LA Clippers	23	59	13-28	10-31	13-39	5-11
	Minnesota	22	60	15-26	7-34	14-38	3-13
	Memphis	22	60	14-27	8-33	11-41	2-14
	Seattle	20	62	13-28	7-34	12-40	6-10

Eastern Conference

		W	L	Home	Away	Conf	Div
1	Boston*	66	16	35-6	31-10	41-11	14-2
2	Detroit*	59	23	34-7	25-16	37-15	11-5
3	Orlando*	52	30	25-16	27-14	38-14	12-4
4	Cleveland	45	37	27-14	18-23	28-24	7-9
5	Washington	43	39	25-16	18-23	29-23	10-6
6	Toronto	41	41	25-16	16-25	29-23	10-6
7	Philadelphia	40	42	22-19	18-23	25-27	7-9
8	Atlanta	37	45	25-16	12-29	24-28	9-7
	Indiana	36	46	21-20	15-26	24-28	5-11
	New Jersey	34	48	21-20	13-28	26-26	4-12
	Chicago	33	49	20-21	13-28	24-28	11-5
	Charlotte	32	50	21-10	11-30	19-33	7-9
	Milwaukee	26	56	19-22	7-34	18-34	6-10
	New York	23	59	15-26	8-33	20-32	5-11
	Miami	15	67	9-32	6-35	8-44	2-14

2008 NBA All-Star Game

East, 134-128

57th NBA All-Star Game. **Date:** Feb. 17, at New Orleans Arena in New Orleans; **Coaches:** Doc Rivers, Boston (East) and Byron Scott, New Orleans (West); **MVP:** LeBron James, East (27 points, 9 assists, 8 rebounds, 2 steals, 2 blocks); Starters chosen by fan vote, (Boston's Kevin Garnett was the leading vote-getter, receiving 2,399,148 votes); bench chosen by conference coaches' vote.

Western Conference

Pos	Starters	Min	FG M-A	Pts	Reb	A
G	Allen Iverson, Den	21	3-7	7	2	6
G	Kobe Bryant, LAL . . .	3	0-0	0	1	0
F	Tim Duncan, SA	22	2-7	4	9	1
F	Carmelo Anthony, Den	22	8-17	18	7	1
C	Yao Ming, Hou	13	2-5	6	5	1
	Bench					
F	Brandon Roy, Port	28	8-10	18	9	5
G	Chris Paul, NO	27	7-14	16	3	14
F	Dirk Nowitzki, Dal . . .	26	5-14	13	4	2
F	Amare Stoudamire, Pho	23	8-11	18	5	0
G	Steve Nash, Pho	20	4-8	8	0	6
F	Carlos Boozer, Utah . .	19	7-15	14	10	0
F	David West, NO	16	3-6	6	4	1
	TOTALS	240	57-114	128	59	37

Three-Point FG: 6-19 (Roy 2-3, Paul 2-6, Stoudemire 1-2, Nowitzki 1-2, Duncan 0-1, Nash 0-1); **Free Throws:** 8-14 (Ming 2-2, Nowitzki 2-2, Anthony 2-3, Iverson 1-2, Stoudemire 1-3, Boozer 0-2); **Percentages:** FG (.500), Three-Pt. FG (.316), Free Throws (.571); **Turnovers:** 21 (Iverson 6, Duncan 4, Anthony 2, Paul 2, Nowitzki 2, Ming, Stoudemire, Nash, Boozer, West); **Steals:** 11 (Iverson 4, Paul 4, Duncan, Roy, Stoudemire); **Blocked Shots:** 5 (Iverson, Duncan, Roy, Stoudemire, Nash); **Fouls:** 14 (Paul 5, Nash 3, Roy 2, Stoudemire 2, Duncan, West).

	1	2	3	4	F
East	34	40	32	28	**134**
West	28	37	28	35	**128**

Eastern Conference

Pos	Starters	Min	FG M-A	Pts	Reb	A
G	Jason Kidd, NJ	25	1-2	2	4	10
G	Dwyane Wade, Mia . .	22	7-12	14	4	3
F	LeBron James, Cle	30	12-22	27	8	9
F	Chris Bosh, Tor	22	7-15	14	7	1
C	Dwight Howard, Orl . .	31	7-7	16	9	3
	Bench					
G	Ray Allen, Bos	19	10-14	28	2	1
G	Chauncey Billups, Det .	18	3-10	6	1	4
G	Richard Hamilton, Det .	18	4-9	9	0	2
F	Rasheed Wallace, Det .	18	1-5	3	5	0
G	Joe Johnson, Atl	13	1-2	3	0	2
G	Paul Pierce, Bos	13	5-9	10	4	2
F	Antawn Jamison, Wash	12	1-3	2	1	0
	TOTALS	240	59-110	134	45	37

Three-Point FG: 10-36 (Allen 5-9, James 2-7, Wallace 1-5, Hamilton 1-1, Johnson 1-1, Kidd 0-1, Wade 0-1, Pierce 0-3, Jamison 0-2); **Free Throws:** 6-14 (Allen 3-5, Howard 2-3, James 1-1, Wade 0-2, Billups 0-1); **Percentages:** FG (.536), Three-Pt. FG (.278), Free Throws (.429); **Turnovers:** 16 (James 4, Wade 2, Kidd, Bosh, Howard, Billups, Wallace, Johnson); **Steals:** 13 (Kidd 4, Howard 3, James 2, Allen 2, Wallace, Johnson); **Blocked Shots:** 7 (James 2, Wallace 2, Wade, Howard, Jamison); **Fouls:** 13 (Howard 4, James 3, Wallace 2, Wade, Bosh, Billups, Johnson).

Halftime— East, 74-65; **Third Quarter—** East, 106-93; **Technical Fouls—** none; **Officials—** #36 David Jones, #32 Eddie Rush, #38 Michael Smith; **Attendance—** 16,271; **TV Rating—** 5.1 (TNT).

NBA 3-point Shootout

Six players are invited to compete in the annual three-point shooting contest held during All-Star Weekend, since 1986. Each shooter has 60 seconds to shoot the 25 balls in five racks outside the three-point line. Each ball is worth one point, except the last ball in each rack, which is worth two. Highest scores advance. First prize: $35,000.

First Round	Pts
Jason Kapono, Toronto	20
Daniel Gibson, Cleveland	17
Dirk Nowtizki, Dallas	17

Failed to advance	Pts
Peja Stojakovic, Sacramento	15
Richard Hamilton, Washington	14
Steve Nash, Phoenix	9

Finals	Pts
Jason Kapono	25
Daniel Gibson	17
Dirk Nowitzki	14

Slam Dunk Contest

The Dunk contest was held annually from 1984-97 before being replaced by the 2Ball competition. It made its return in 2000. The competitors are selected based on "the creativity and artistry they have displayed in dunking" over the course of the season. The dunks are judged by five judges on a scale from six to ten. The top two scorers from the first round advance to the final round and attempt two dunks. The winner was chosen via by a fan vote via text messaging. First prize: $35,000.

First Round	Pts
Dwight Howard, Orlando	100
Gerald Green, Minnesota	91

Failed to advance	Pts
Jamario Moon, Toronto	90
Rudy Gay, Memphis	85

Finals	Score
Dwight Howard def. Gerald Green	78%-22%

Cleveland
LeBron James
Scoring

Orlando
Dwight Howard
Rebounding

New Orleans
Chris Paul
Assists, Steals

Toronto
Jason Kapono
3-point FG pct.

NBA Regular Season Individual Leaders

Scoring
(*indicates rookie)

	Gm	Min	FG	FG%	3pt/Att	FT	FT%	Reb	Ast	Stl	Blk	Pts	Avg	Hi
LeBron James, Cle	75	3027	794	.484	113/359	549	.712	592	539	138	81	2250	30.0	51
Kobe Bryant, LAL	82	3192	775	.459	150/415	623	.840	517	441	151	40	2323	28.3	53
Allen Iverson, Den	82	3424	712	.458	95/275	645	.809	243	586	160	12	2164	26.4	51
Carmelo Anthony, Den	77	2806	728	.492	58/164	464	.786	571	259	98	39	1978	25.7	49
Amare Stoudemire, Pho	79	2677	714	.590	5/31	556	.805	719	118	64	163	1989	25.2	42
Kevin Martin, Sac	61	2216	417	.456	107/266	502	.869	273	129	62	5	1443	23.7	48
Dirk Nowitzki, Dal	77	2769	630	.479	79/220	478	.879	659	266	51	71	1817	23.6	37
Michael Redd, Mil	72	2702	550	.442	130/359	402	.820	309	247	65	13	1632	22.7	42
Richard Jefferson, NJ	82	3200	619	.466	77/213	542	.798	342	252	76	21	1857	22.6	36
Chris Bosh, Tor	67	2425	507	.494	10/25	472	.844	583	171	63	67	1496	22.3	42
Corey Maggette, LAC	70	2502	458	.458	78/203	553	.812	394	189	71	7	1547	22.1	35
Baron Davis, GSW	82	3196	650	.426	173/525	318	.750	385	623	191	43	1791	21.8	40
Jason Richardson, CHA	82	3149	648	.441	243/559	249	.752	441	258	116	57	1788	21.8	42
Joe Johnson, Atl	82	3343	647	.432	169/444	367	.834	367	474	84	18	1779	21.7	39
Tracy McGrady, Hou	66	2440	548	.419	86/295	245	.684	339	387	68	30	1427	21.6	47
Antawn Jamison, Wash	79	3061	618	.436	120/354	333	.760	806	120	106	34	1689	21.4	41
Vince Carter, NJ	76	2959	587	.456	98/273	350	.816	453	389	93	33	1622	21.3	39
Carlos Boozer, Utah	81	2827	709	.547	0/1	290	.738	844	233	100	41	1708	21.1	41
Chris Paul, NO	80	3006	630	.488	92/249	332	.851	321	925	217	4	1684	21.1	43
Al Jefferson, Min	82	2919	721	.500	0/5	284	.721	911	117	74	119	1726	21.0	40
Dwight Howard, Orl	82	3088	583	.599	0/4	529	.603	1161	110	74	176	1695	20.7	39
David West, NO	76	2870	629	.487	6/25	300	.850	675	177	62	99	1564	20.6	40
Jamal Crawford, NY	80	3190	570	.410	176/494	329	.864	207	398	81	17	1645	20.6	43
Kevin Durant*, Sea	80	2768	587	.430	59/205	391	.873	348	192	78	75	1624	20.3	42
Monta Ellis, G.St.	81	3071	652	.531	12/52	320	.767	404	315	124	27	1636	20.2	39
Rudy Gay, Mem	81	3000	625	.461	134/387	248	.785	499	158	111	79	1632	20.1	36
Stephen Jackson, G.St.	73	2855	488	.405	182/501	308	.832	318	300	92	29	1466	20.1	41
Josh Howard, Dal	76	2757	567	.455	67/210	312	.813	532	164	59	32	1513	19.9	47
Andre Iguodala, Phi	82	3542	582	.456	101/307	365	.721	446	391	171	49	1630	19.9	33
Paul Pierce, Bos	80	2874	509	.464	143/365	409	.843	411	363	101	36	1570	19.6	37

Rebounds

	Gm	Off	Def	Tot	Avg
Dwight Howard, Orl	82	279	882	1161	14.2
Marcus Camby, Den	79	230	807	1037	13.1
Tyson Chandler, NO	79	322	606	928	11.7
Tim Duncan, SA	78	237	644	881	11.3
Al Jefferson, Min	82	308	603	911	11.1
Emeka Okafor, Cha	82	255	621	876	10.7
Lamar Odom, LAL	77	197	622	819	10.6
Carlos Boozer, Utah	81	197	647	844	10.4
Samuel Dalembert, Phi	82	304	545	849	10.4
Antawn Jamison, Wash	79	215	591	806	10.2
Andris Biedrins, G.St.	76	256	488	744	9.8
Andrew Bogut, Milw	78	245	518	763	9.8
Al Horford*, Atl	81	248	537	785	9.7
Brad Miller, Sac	72	167	514	681	9.5
Nick Collison, Sea	78	254	476	730	9.4

Assists

	Gm	Ast	Avg
Chris Paul, NO	80	925	11.6
Steve Nash, Pho	81	898	11.1
Deron Williams, Utah	82	862	10.5
Jason Kidd, NJ-Dal	80	806	10.1
Jose Calderon, Tor	82	678	8.3
Baron Davis, G.St.	82	623	7.6
Raymond Felton, Cha	79	583	7.4
LeBron James, Cle	75	539	7.2
Allen Iverson, Den	82	586	7.1
Andre Miller, Phi	82	565	6.9
Earl Watson, Sea	78	531	6.8
Chauncey Billups, Det	78	529	6.8
Mo Williams, Milw	66	419	6.3
Kirk Hinrich, Chi	75	452	6.0
Tony Parker, SA	69	411	6.0

Field Goal Pct.

	Gm	FG	Att	Pct
Andris Biedrins, G.St.	.76	340	543	.626
Tyson Chandler, NO	.79	377	605	.623
Dwight Howard, Orl	.82	583	974	.599
Shaquille O'Neal, Mia-Pho	.61	331	558	.593
Amare Stoudemire, Pho	.79	714	1211	.590
Josh Childress, Atl	.76	327	573	.571
Ronnie Brewer, Utah	.76	354	634	.558
David Lee, NY	.81	341	618	.552
Carlos Boozer, Utah	.81	709	1297	.547
Kevin Garnett, Bos	.71	534	990	.539

Free Throw Pct.

	Gm	FT	Att	Pct
Peja Stojakovic, NO	.77	130	140	.929
Chauncey Billups, Det	.78	401	437	.918
Ben Gordon, Chi	.72	266	293	.908
Ray Allen, Bos	.73	215	237	.907
Steve Nash, Pho	.81	222	245	.906
Caron Butler, Wash	.58	236	262	.901
Jerry Stackhouse, Dal	.58	132	148	.892
Derek Fisher, LAL	.82	166	188	.883
Sam Cassell, LAC-Bos	.55	127	144	.882
Dirk Nowitzki, Dal	.77	478	544	.879

3-Point Field Goal Pct.

	Gm	3FG	Att	Pct
Jason Kapono, Tor	.81	57	118	.483
Steve Nash, Pho	.81	179	381	.470
James Jones, Port	.58	91	205	.444
Peja Stojakovic, NO	.77	231	524	.441
Daniel Gibson, Cle	.58	118	268	.440
Richard Hamilton, Det	.72	62	141	.440
Anthony Parker, Tor	.82	133	304	.438
Sasha Vujacic, LAL	.72	118	270	.437
Matt Carroll, Cha	.80	105	241	.436
Mike Miller, Mem	.70	155	359	.432

High-Point Games

	Opp	Date	FG-FT—Pts
Kobe Bryant, LAL	Mem	3/28/08	19-6—53
Kobe Bryant, LAL	Dal	3/2/08	15-20—52
LeBron James, Cle	Mem	1/15/08	18-9—51
Allen Iverson, Den	LAL	12/5/07	18-15—51

Blocked Shots

	Gm	Blk	Avg
Marcus Camby, Den	.79	285	3.61
Josh Smith, Atl	.81	227	2.80
Chris Kaman, LAC	.56	155	2.77
Samuel Dalembert, Phi	.82	192	2.34
Dwight Howard, Orl	.82	176	2.15
Amare Stoudemire, Pho	.79	163	2.06
Yao Ming, Hou	.55	111	2.02
Tim Duncan, SA	.78	152	1.95
Andrew Bogut, Milw	.78	135	1.73
Emeka Okafor, Cha	.82	138	1.68

Steals

	Gm	Stl	Avg
Chris Paul, NO	.80	217	2.71
Ron Artest, Sac	.57	133	2.33
Baron Davis, G. St.	.82	191	2.33
Caron Butler, Wash	.58	128	2.21
Gerald Wallace, Cha	.62	131	2.11
Andre Iguodala, Phi	.82	171	2.08
Shawn Marion, Pho	.63	125	1.98
Allen Iverson, Den	.82	160	1.95
Kobe Bryant, LAL	.82	151	1.84
LeBron James, Cle	.75	138	1.84

Rookie Leaders

Scoring	Gm	FG	FT	Pts	Avg
Kevin Durant, Sea	.80	587	391	1624	20.3
Al Thornton, LAC	.79	374	214	1005	12.7
J.C. Navarro, Mem	.82	308	156	896	10.9
Jeff Green, Sea	.80	320	177	838	10.5
Luis Scola, Hou	.82	345	157	847	10.3

Field Goal Pct.	Gm	FG	Att	Pct
Luis Scola, Hou	.82	345	670	.515
Al Horford, Atl	.81	333	668	.499
Kevin Durant, Sea	.80	587	1366	.430
Al Thornton, LAC	.79	374	871	.429
Jeff Green, Sea	.80	320	749	.427

Rebounds	Gm	Off	Def	Tot	Avg
Al Horford, Atl	.81	248	537	785	9.7
Luis Scola, Hou	.82	174	351	525	6.4
Jamario Moon, Tor	.78	92	392	484	6.2
Joakim Noah, Chi	.74	174	242	416	5.6
Jeff Green, Sea	.80	101	278	379	4.7

Assists	Gm	No	Avg
Kevin Durant, Sea	.80	192	2.4
JC Navarro, Mem	.82	177	2.2
Al Horford, Atl	.81	124	1.5
Jeff Green, Sea	.80	119	1.5
Corey Brewer, Min	.79	111	1.4

Personal Fouls

Mikki Moore, Sac	.310
Amare Stoudemire, Pho	.294
Carlos Boozer, Utah	.293
Danny Granger, Ind	.290
Dwight Howard, Orl	.274
Samuel Dalembert, Phi	.269
Paul Millsap, Utah	.269
Josh Smith, Atl	.269

Minutes

Allen Iverson, Den	.3423
Joe Johnson, Atl	.3342
Andre Iguodala, Phi	.3241
Richard Jefferson, NJ	.3200
Baron Davis, G.St.	.3196
Kobe Bryant, LAL	.3192
Jamal Crawford, NY	.3189
Jason Richardson, Cha	.3149

Turnovers

Steve Nash, Pho	.295
Deron Williams, Utah	.279
Jason Kidd, NJ-Dal	.266
Dwight Howard, Orl	.263
Kobe Bryant, LAL	.257
LeBron James, Cle	.255
Carmelo Anthony, Den	.253
Hedo Turkoglu, Orl	.246

Triple Doubles

Jason Kidd, NJ-Dal	.13
LeBron James, Cle	.7
Caron Butler, Wash	.3
Baron Davis, G.St.	.3
Marcus Camby, Den	.2
Hedo Turkoglu, Orl	.2
10 tied	.1

Double Doubles

Dwight Howard, Orl	.69
Chris Paul, NO	.56
Al Jefferson, Min	.55
Tim Duncan, SA	.53
Deron Williams, Utah	.52
Carlos Boozer, Utah	.51
Steve Nash, Pho	.48
Antawn Jamison, Wash	.44
Lamar Odom, LAL	.44

Technical Fouls

Kobe Bryant, LAL	.15
Baron Davis, G.St.	.12
Rasheed Wallace, Det	.12
Carmelo Anthony, Den	.11
Kenyon Martin, Den	.11
Brad Miller, Sac	.11
Cuttino Mobley, LAC	.11
Chris Paul, NO	.11
Amare Stoudamire, Pho	.11

Team by Team Statistics

Players who competed for more than one team during the regular season are listed with their final club; (*) indicates rookies.

Atlanta Hawks

(min. 10 gms)	Gm	FG%	Tpts	PPG	RPG	APG
Joe Johnson	.82	.432	1779	21.7	4.5	5.8
Josh Smith	.81	.457	1394	17.2	8.2	3.4
Marvin Williams	.80	.462	1185	14.8	5.7	1.7
Mike Bibby	.48	.411	667	13.9	3.3	6.0
Josh Childress	.76	.571	898	11.8	4.9	1.5
Al Horford	.81	.499	821	10.1	9.7	1.5
Salim Stoudamire	.35	.361	200	5.7	0.7	0.8
Zaza Pachulia	.62	.437	322	5.2	4.0	0.6
Acie Law	.56	.419	235	4.2	1.0	2.0
Jeremy Richardson	.19	.419	41	1.5	0.3	0.1
Solomon Jones	.35	.400	35	1.0	1.2	0.0
Mario West	.64	.429	59	0.9	0.8	0.8

Triple Doubles: Smith (1). **3-pt FG leader:** Johnson (169). **Steals leader:** Smith (123). **Blocks leader:** Smith (227).
Signed: Jeremy Richardson (Feb. 18).

Boston Celtics

(min. 10 gms)	Gm	FG%	Tpts	PPG	RPG	APG
Paul Pierce	.80	.464	1570	19.6	5.1	4.5
Kevin Garnett	.71	.539	1337	18.8	9.2	3.4
Ray Allen	.73	.445	1273	17.4	3.7	3.1
Sam Cassell	.55	.438	616	11.2	2.5	3.9
Rajon Rondo	.77	.492	814	10.6	4.2	5.1
Leon Powe	.56	.572	445	7.9	4.1	0.3
Eddie House	.78	.409	584	7.5	2.1	1.9
James Posey	.74	.418	545	7.4	4.4	1.5
Kendrick Perkins	.78	.615	542	6.9	6.1	1.1
Tony Allen	.75	.434	494	6.6	2.2	1.5
Glen Davis	.69	.484	313	4.5	3.0	0.4
P.J. Brown	.18	.341	39	2.2	3.8	0.6
Gabe Pruitt*	.15	.359	32	2.1	0.5	0.9
Scot Pollard	.22	.522	39	1.8	1.7	0.1
Brian Scalabrine	.48	.309	88	1.8	1.6	0.8

Triple Doubles: none. **3-pt FG leader:** Allen (180). **Steals leaders:** Rondo (129). **Blocks leader:** Perkins (114).

Charlotte Bobcats

	Gm	FG%	Tpts	PPG	RPG	APG
Jason Richardson	.82	.441	1788	21.8	5.4	3.1
Gerald Wallace	.62	.449	1200	19.4	6.0	3.5
Raymond Felton	.79	.413	1140	14.4	3.0	7.4
Emeka Okafor	.82	.535	1133	13.8	10.7	0.9
Matt Carroll	.80	.428	720	9.0	2.8	0.9
Nazr Mohammed	.82	.515	639	7.8	6.0	0.9
Jared Dudley	.73	.468	422	5.8	3.9	1.1
Earl Boykins	.36	.355	185	5.1	0.9	2.7
Derek Anderson	.28	.376	141	5.0	1.9	1.6
Jeff McInnis	.54	.434	242	4.5	1.8	4.1
Jermareo Davidson	.38	.408	120	3.2	1.6	0.3
Ryan Hollins	.60	.489	147	2.5	1.8	0.2
Othella Harrington	.22	.429	46	2.1	1.9	0.2

Triple Doubles: none. **3-pt FG leadLer:** Richardson (243). **Steals leaders:** Wallace (131). **Blocks leader:** Okafor (138).

Chicago Bulls

(min. 10 gms)	Gm	FG%	Tpts	PPG	RPG	APG
Ben Gordon	.72	.434	1336	18.6	3.1	3.0
Luol Deng	.63	.479	1070	17.0	6.3	2.5
Andres Nocioni	.82	.432	1080	13.2	4.2	1.2
Larry Hughes	.68	.381	827	12.2	3.4	2.7
Drew Gooden	.69	.449	826	12.0	8.6	1.2
Kirk Hinrich	.75	.414	862	11.5	3.3	6.0
Tyrus Thomas	.74	.423	502	6.8	4.6	1.2
Thabo Sefolosha	.69	.428	464	6.7	3.7	1.9
Joakim Noah	.74	.482	488	6.6	5.6	1.1
Chris Duhon	.66	.387	385	5.8	1.8	4.0
Aaron Gray	.61	.505	262	4.3	2.8	0.7
Shannon Brown	.21	.349	114	5.4	1.0	0.8
Demetris Nichols	.14	.261	15	1.1	0.4	0.1
Cedric Simmons	.14	.286	8	0.6	1.3	0.0

Triple Doubles: Hinrich (1). **3-pt FG leader:** Gordon (142). **Steals leader:** Hughes (99). **Blocks leader:** Thomas (72).

Cleveland Cavaliers

	Gm	FG%	Tpts	PPG	RPG	APG
LeBron James	.75	.484	2250	30.0	7.9	7.2
Zydrunas Ilgauskas	.73	.474	1029	14.1	9.3	1.4
Wally Szczerbiak	.75	.431	861	11.5	2.9	1.4
Daniel Gibson	.58	.432	605	10.4	2.3	2.5
Joe Smith	.77	.478	778	10.1	5.2	0.9
Delonte West	.61	.413	507	8.3	3.2	3.8
Devin Brown	.78	.409	586	7.5	3.4	2.2
Aleksandar Pavlovic	.51	.362	379	7.4	2.5	1.6
Anderson Varejao	.48	.461	321	6.7	8.3	1.1
Damon Jones	.67	.416	437	6.5	1.1	1.9
Ben Wallace	.72	.392	348	4.8	8.4	1.5
Dwayne Jones	.56	.532	78	1.4	2.5	0.2
Billy Thomas	.11	.235	14	1.3	0.2	0.0
Eric Snow	.22	.158	22	1.0	0.9	1.9

Triple Doubles: James (7). **3-pt FG leader:** Gibson (118). **Steals leader:** James (138). **Blocks leader:** Ilgauskas (120).

Dallas Mavericks

	Gm	FG%	Tpts	PPG	RPG	APG
Dirk Nowitzki	.77	.479	1817	23.6	8.6	3.5
Josh Howard	.76	.455	1513	19.9	7.0	2.2
Jason Terry	.82	.467	1269	15.5	2.5	3.2
Jason Kidd	.80	.385	864	10.8	7.5	10.1
Jerry Stackhouse	.58	.405	618	10.7	2.3	2.5
Brandon Bass	.79	.499	654	8.3	4.4	0.7
Antoine Wright	.56	.413	350	6.3	2.6	1.4
Erick Dampier	.72	.643	440	6.1	7.5	0.9
Tyronn Lue	.50	.447	290	5.8	1.1	1.5
Jose Barea	.44	.418	191	4.3	1.1	1.3
Eddie Jones	.47	.367	176	3.7	2.8	1.5
Devean George	.53	.357	194	3.7	2.6	0.7
Malik Allen	.73	.480	338	4.6	2.7	0.6
Jamaal Magloire	.31	.327	56	1.8	2.9	0.2
Juwan Howard	.50	.359	57	1.1	1.6	0.3

Triple Doubles: Kidd (13) and Nowitzki (1). **3-pt FG leader:** Terry (136). **Steals leader:** Kidd (136). **Blocks leader:** Dampier (106).

Denver Nuggets

	Gm	FG%	Tpts	PPG	RPG	APG
Allen Iverson	.82	.458	2164	26.4	3.0	7.1
Carmelo Anthony	.77	.492	1978	25.7	7.4	3.4
Kenyon Martin	.71	.538	877	12.4	6.5	1.3
J.R. Smith	.74	.461	907	12.3	2.1	1.7
Linas Kleiza	.79	.472	880	11.1	4.2	1.2
Marcus Camby	.79	.450	721	9.1	13.1	3.3
Eduardo Najera	.78	.473	464	5.9	4.3	1.2
Nene	.16	.408	85	5.3	5.4	0.9
Chucky Atkins	.24	.344	113	4.7	1.3	2.0
Bobby Jones	.47	.429	178	3.8	2.0	0.6
Yakhouba Diawara	.54	.410	153	2.8	1.1	0.7
Steve Hunter	.19	.536	39	2.1	1.5	0.0
Taurean Green	.7	.280	27	1.6	0.6	0.6
Jelani McCoy	.6	1.000	3	0.5	1.2	0.0

Triple Doubles: Camby (2). **3-pt FG leader:** Smith (157). **Steals leader:** Iverson (160). **Blocks leader:** Camby (285).

Detroit Pistons

	Gm	FG%	Tpts	PPG	RPG	APG
Richard Hamilton	.72	.484	1244	17.3	3.3	4.2
Chauncey Billups	.78	.448	1324	17.0	2.7	6.8
Tayshaun Prince	.82	.448	1080	13.2	4.9	3.3
Rasheed Wallace	.77	.432	979	12.7	6.6	1.8
Antonio McDyess	.78	.488	683	8.8	8.5	1.1
Jason Maxiell	.82	.538	651	7.9	5.3	0.6
Ronald Stuckey	.57	.401	436	7.6	2.3	2.8
Jarvis Hayes	.82	.431	552	6.7	2.2	0.8
Juan Dixon	.53	.668	263	5.0	1.4	1.8
Theo Ratliff	.26	.482	111	4.3	3.4	0.5
Arron Afflalo	.62	.411	276	3.7	1.8	0.7
Amir Johnson	.62	.558	221	3.6	3.8	0.5
Walter Hermann	.45	.389	153	3.4	1.6	0.4
Lindsey Hunter	.24	.344	58	2.4	0.5	1.4
Cheikh Samb	.4	.750	7	1.8	1.8	0.0

Triple Doubles: none. **3-pt FG leader:** Billups (137). **Steals leader:** Billups (101). **Blocks leader:** Wallace (129).

Golden St. Warriors

	Gm	FG%	Tpts	PPG	RPG	APG
Baron Davis	.82	.426	1791	21.8	4.7	7.6
Monta Ellis	.81	.531	1636	20.2	5.0	3.9
Stephen Jackson	.73	.405	1466	20.1	4.4	4.1
Al Harrington	.81	.434	1102	13.6	5.4	1.6
Andris Biedrins	.76	.626	796	10.5	9.8	1.0
Kelenaa Azubuike	.81	.445	692	8.5	4.0	0.9
Mickael Pietrus	.66	.439	472	7.2	3.7	0.7
Matt Barnes	.73	.423	486	6.7	4.4	1.9
Brandan Wright	.38	.554	151	4.0	2.6	0.2
Chris Webber	.9	.484	35	3.9	2.6	2.0
Austin Croshere	.44	.445	173	3.9	2.4	0.7
C.J. Watson	.32	.426	118	3.7	1.0	1.1
Troy Hudson	.9	.290	28	3.1	0.8	1.0
Marco Belinelli	.33	.387	95	2.9	0.4	0.5
Patrick O'Bryant	.24	.552	35	1.5	1.2	0.2
Kosta Perovic	.7	.300	10	1.4	0.9	0.0

Triple Doubles: none. **3-pt FG leader:** Jackson (182). **Steals leader:** Davis (191). **Blocks leader:** Biedrins (94).

Houston Rockets

	Gm	FG%	Tpts	PPG	RPG	APG
Yao Ming	.55	.507	1209	22.0	10.8	2.3
Tracy McGrady	.66	.419	1427	21.6	5.1	5.9
Rafer Alston	.74	.394	969	13.1	3.5	5.3
Luis Scola	.82	.515	847	10.3	6.4	1.3
Shane Battier	.80	.428	744	9.3	5.1	1.9
Bobby Jackson	.72	.403	553	7.7	2.5	1.9
Carl Landry	.42	.616	342	8.1	4.9	0.5
Luther Head	.73	.432	557	7.6	1.8	1.9
Steve Francis	.10	.333	55	5.5	2.3	3.0
Aaron Brooks	.51	.413	264	5.2	1.1	1.7
Gerald Green	.30	.344	153	5.1	2.1	1.0
Steve Novak	.35	.480	135	3.9	1.0	0.2
Mike Harris	.17	.500	62	3.6	3.2	0.2
Chuck Hayes	.79	.511	237	3.0	5.4	1.2
Dikembe Mutombo	.39	.538	118	3.0	5.1	0.1
Justin Williams	.23	.448	34	1.5	2.1	0.0
Loren Woods	.7	.600	6	0.9	0.1	0.3

Triple Doubles: McGrady (1). **3-pt FG leader:** Alston (143). **Steals leader:** Alston (98). **Blocks leader:** Ming (111).

Indiana Pacers

	Gm	FG%	Tpts	PPG	RPG	APG
Danny Granger	.80	.446	1567	19.6	6.1	2.1
Mike Dunleavy	.82	.476	1565	19.1	5.2	3.5
Jermaine O'Neal	.42	.439	571	13.6	6.7	2.2
Troy Murphy	.75	.455	916	12.2	7.2	2.2
Jamaal Tinsley	.39	.380	464	11.9	3.6	8.4
Ronald Murray	.42	.420	396	9.4	2.0	3.4
Kareem Rush	.71	.401	588	8.3	2.4	1.3
Marquis Daniels	.74	.430	606	8.2	2.9	1.9
Travis Diener	.66	.370	456	6.9	1.7	3.8
Shawne Williams	.65	.427	437	6.7	2.7	0.9
Jeff Foster	.77	.550	496	6.4	8.7	1.7
Ike Diogu	.30	.478	168	5.6	2.8	0.3
David Harrison	.55	.529	229	4.2	2.1	0.3
Andre Owens	.31	.374	123	4.0	1.5	1.5
Stephen Graham	.22	.586	87	4.0	1.0	0.4
Courtney Sims	.3	.000	0	0.0	0.7	0.3

Triple Doubles: none. **3-pt FG leader:** Granger (171). **Steals leader:** Granger (95). **Blocks leader:** O'Neal (87).

Los Angeles Clippers

(min. 5 gms)	Gm	FG%	Tpts	PPG	RPG	APG
Corey Maggette	.70	.458	1547	22.1	5.6	2.7
Elton Brand	.8	.456	141	17.6	8.0	2.0
Chris Kaman	.56	.483	878	15.7	12.7	1.9
Cuttino Mobley	.77	.433	984	12.8	3.6	2.6
Al Thornton	.79	.429	1005	12.7	4.5	1.2
Tim Thomas	.63	.413	780	12.4	5.1	2.7
Smush Parker	.28	.348	165	5.9	1.8	3.0
Josh Powell	.64	.460	353	5.5	5.2	0.7
Dan Dickau	.67	.419	352	5.3	1.4	2.6
Ruben Patterson	.20	.453	102	5.1	3.2	0.9
Richie Frahm	.10	.370	47	4.7	1.4	0.8
Brevin Knight	.74	.404	338	4.6	1.9	4.4
Quinton Ross	.76	.391	311	4.1	2.3	1.2
Nick Fazekas	.26	.561	107	4.1	3.4	0.4
Paul Davis	.22	.369	54	2.5	2.1	0.5
Aaron Williams	.30	.491	68	2.3	2.0	0.3
Marcus Williams	.11	.250	10	0.9	1.1	0.3
Guillermo Diaz	.6	.250	5	0.8	0.3	0.2

Triple Doubles: none. **3-pt FG leader:** Thomas (83). **Steals leader:** Knight (100). **Blocks leader:** Kamas (155).

Los Angeles Lakers

	Gm	FG%	Tpts	PPG	RPG	APG
Kobe Bryant	82	.459	2323	28.3	6.3	5.4
Pau Gasol	66	.534	1246	18.9	8.4	3.2
Lamar Odom	77	.525	1094	14.2	10.6	3.5
Andrew Bynum	35	.636	460	13.1	10.2	1.7
Derek Fisher	82	.436	956	11.7	2.1	2.9
Jordan Farmar	82	.461	749	9.1	2.2	2.7
Sasha Vujacic	72	.454	632	8.8	2.1	1.0
Vladimir Radmanovic	65	.453	543	8.4	3.3	1.9
Luke Walton	74	.450	535	7.2	3.9	2.9
Ronny Turiaf	78	.474	516	6.6	3.9	1.6
Trevor Ariza	35	.507	192	5.5	3.1	1.3
Chris Mihm	23	.337	82	3.6	3.3	0.6
Didier Ilunga-Mbenga	42	.464	83	2.0	1.7	0.2
Coby Karl	17	.346	30	1.8	0.8	0.5
Ira Newble	49	.437	188	3.8	2.6	0.4

Triple Doubles: Odom (1). **3-pt FG leader:** Bryant (150). **Steals leader:** Bryant (151). **Blocks leader:** Turiaf (108).

Memphis Grizzlies

	Gm	FG%	Tpts	PPG	RPG	APG
Rudy Gay	81	.462	1632	20.1	6.2	2.0
Mike Miller	70	.502	1147	16.4	6.7	3.4
Hakim Warrick	75	.502	852	11.4	4.7	0.7
Juan Carlos Navarro	82	.402	896	10.9	2.6	2.2
Kyle Lowry	82	.432	791	9.6	3.6	1.1
Mike Conley	53	.428	498	9.4	2.6	4.2
Darko Milicic	70	.438	505	7.2	6.1	0.8
Javaris Crittenton	50	.421	278	5.6	2.2	1.0
Tarence Kinsey	11	.421	40	3.6	1.1	0.2
Kwame Brown	15	.487	184	3.5	3.8	1.1
Brian Cardinal	37	.341	124	3.4	2.6	0.6
Andre Brown	33	.500	100	3.4	2.6	0.6
Jason Collins	74	.469	140	1.9	2.4	0.3
Casey Jacobsen	53	.339	107	2.0	1.2	0.4

Triple Doubles: none. **3-pt FG leader:** Navarro (156). **Steals leader:** Gay (111). **Blocks leader:** Milicic (114).

Miami Heat

	Gm	FG%	Tpts	PPG	RPG	APG
Dwyane Wade	51	.469	1254	24.6	4.2	6.9
Shawn Marion	63	.508	972	15.4	10.2	2.2
Ricky Davis	82	.433	1130	13.8	4.3	3.4
Udonis Haslem	49	.467	589	12.0	9.0	1.4
Daequan Cook	59	.381	518	8.8	3.0	1.3
Jason Williams	67	.384	588	8.8	1.9	4.6
Mark Blount	69	.462	581	8.4	3.8	0.6
Dorell Wright	44	.488	347	7.9	5.0	1.4
Chris Quinn	60	.424	465	7.8	2.0	3.0
Kasib Powell	11	.368	84	7.6	4.0	1.6
Earl Barron	46	.404	326	7.1	4.3	0.6
Marcus Banks	36	.450	239	6.6	1.3	1.7
Alonzo Mourning	25	.547	149	6.0	3.7	0.3
Luke Jackson	14	.325	79	5.6	2.4	1.2
Stephane Lasme	16	.451	83	5.2	3.3	0.2
Alexander Johnson	43	.488	179	4.2	2.2	0.3
Anfernee Hardaway	16	.367	60	3.8	2.2	2.2
Joel Anthony	24	.467	85	3.5	3.9	0.1

Triple Doubles: none. **3-pt FG leader:** Davis (135). **Steals leader:** Marion (125). **Blocks leader:** Marion (85).

Milwaukee Bucks

	Gm	FG%	Tpts	PPG	RPG	APG
Michael Redd	72	.442	1632	22.7	4.3	3.4
Mo Williams	66	.480	1137	17.2	3.5	6.3
Andrew Bogut	78	.511	1119	14.3	9.8	2.6
Charlie Villanueva	76	.435	886	11.7	6.1	1.0
Desmond Mason	59	.482	574	9.7	4.3	2.1
Yi Jianlian	66	.421	566	8.6	5.2	0.8
Ramon Sessions	17	.436	137	8.1	3.4	7.5
Charlie Bell	68	.381	514	7.6	2.5	3.1
Bobby Simmons	70	.421	531	7.6	3.2	1.1
Royal Ivey	75	.394	418	5.6	1.6	2.1
Awvee Storey	26	.438	92	3.5	2.1	0.6
Dan Gadzuric	51	.416	161	3.2	2.8	0.2
Jake Voskuhl	44	.463	98	2.2	2.2	0.3
Michael Ruffin	46	.532	91	2.0	4.0	0.5

Triple Doubles: none. **3-pt FG leader:** Bell (130). **Steals leader:** Redd (65). **Blocks leader:** Bogut (135).

Minnesota Timberwolves

	Gm	FG%	Tpts	PPG	RPG	APG
Al Jefferson	82	.500	1726	21.0	11.1	1.4
Rashad McCants	75	.453	1114	14.9	2.7	2.2
Randy Foye	39	.429	510	13.1	3.3	4.2
Ryan Gomes	82	.457	1033	12.6	5.8	1.8
Craig Smith	77	.563	727	9.4	4.6	0.8
Sebastian Telfair	60	.401	556	9.3	2.3	5.9
Marko Jaric	75	.430	621	8.3	3.0	4.1
Antoine Walker	46	.363	368	8.0	3.7	1.0
Kirk Snyder	36	.508	261	7.3	3.5	1.8
Corey Brewer	79	.374	459	5.8	3.7	1.4
Greg Buckner	31	.385	124	4.0	2.1	1.3
Michael Doleac	24	.444	57	2.4	2.0	0.3
Mark Madsen	20	.158	9	0.5	1.2	0.4

Triple Doubles: none. **3-pt FG leader:** McCants (142). **Steals leader:** Jaric (97). **Blocks leader:** Jefferson (119).

New Jersey Nets

	Gm	FG%	Tpts	PPG	RPG	APG
Richard Jefferson	82	.466	1857	22.6	4.2	3.1
Vince Carter	76	.456	1622	21.3	6.0	5.1
Devin Harris	64	.463	946	14.8	2.7	5.8
Bostjan Nachbar	75	.402	738	9.8	3.5	1.2
Josh Boone	70	.548	575	8.2	7.3	0.8
Nenad Krstic	45	.410	298	6.6	4.4	0.6
Stromile Swift	56	.509	343	6.1	3.6	0.5
Marcus Williams	53	.379	313	5.9	1.9	2.6
Sean Williams	73	.538	409	5.6	4.4	0.4
Maurice Ager	26	.323	51	2.0	0.5	0.3
DeSagana Diop	79	.522	226	2.9	5.0	0.5
Darrell Armstrong	50	.364	123	2.5	1.3	1.5
Trenton Hassell	63	.422	123	2.0	1.3	0.7

Triple Doubles: none. **3-pt FG leader:** Carter (98). **Steals leader:** Carter (93). **Blocks leaders:** Williams (106).

New Orleans Hornets

	Gm	FG%	Tpts	PPG	RPG	APG
Chris Paul	80	.488	1684	21.1	4.0	11.6
David West	76	.482	1564	20.6	8.9	2.3
Peja Stojakovic	77	.440	1263	16.4	4.3	1.2
Tyson Chandler	79	.623	929	11.8	11.7	1.0
Bonzi Wells	73	.443	662	9.1	4.5	1.3
Jannero Pargo	80	.390	644	8.1	1.6	2.4
Morris Peterson	76	.417	608	8.0	2.7	0.9
Mike James	54	.348	272	5.0	1.3	1.1
Rasual Butler	51	.350	252	4.9	2.0	0.7
Melvin Ely	52	.472	202	3.9	2.8	0.4
Julian Wright	57	.533	223	3.9	2.1	0.7
Hilton Armstrong	65	.453	178	2.7	2.5	0.4
Ryan Bowen	53	.490	114	2.2	1.9	0.5
Chris Andersen	5	.286	6	1.2	1.8	0.0

Triple Doubles: Paul (1). **3-pt FG leader:** Stojakovic (231). **Steals leader:** Paul (217). **Blocks leader:** West (99).

New York Knicks

	Gm	FG%	Tpts	PPG	RPG	APG
Jamal Crawford	80	.410	1645	20.6	2.6	5.0
Zach Randolph	69	.459	1217	17.6	10.3	2.0
Stephon Marbury	24	.419	333	13.9	2.5	4.7
Eddy Curry	59	.546	781	13.2	4.7	0.5
Nate Robinson	72	.423	913	12.7	3.1	2.9
David Lee	81	.552	876	10.8	8.9	1.2
Quentin Richardson	65	.359	527	8.1	4.8	1.8
Fred Jones	70	.421	532	7.6	2.4	2.4
Wilson Chandler	35	.438	255	7.3	3.6	0.9
Jared Jeffries	73	.400	269	3.7	3.3	0.9
Malik Rose	49	.367	171	3.5	2.1	0.6
Renaldo Balkman	65	.489	224	3.4	3.3	0.6
Mardy Collins	46	.326	145	3.2	1.6	1.9
Randolph Morris	18	.362	56	3.1	2.1	0.1
Jerome James	2	1.000	4	2.0	1.5	0.0

Triple Doubles: none. **3-pt FG leader:** Crawford (176). **Steals leader:** Crawford (81). **Blocks leader:** Balkman (30).

Orlando Magic

	Gm	FG%	Tpts	PPG	RPG	APG
Dwight Howard	82	.599	1695	20.7	14.2	1.3
Hedo Turkoglu	82	.456	1602	19.5	5.7	5.0
Rashard Lewis	81	.455	1476	18.2	5.4	2.4
Jameer Nelson	69	.469	755	10.9	3.5	5.6
Maurice Evans	75	.481	664	8.9	2.9	1.1
Keith Bogans	82	.410	711	8.7	3.2	1.3
Keyon Dooling	72	.468	581	8.1	1.4	1.8
Carlos Arroyo	62	.451	430	6.9	1.8	3.5
Brian Cook	51	.376	238	4.7	2.1	0.5
J.J. Redick	34	.444	140	4.1	0.7	0.5
Marcin Gortat	6	.471	18	3.0	2.7	0.3
Pat Garrity	31	.338	66	2.1	1.4	0.4
Bo Outlaw	2	.667	4	2.0	0.0	0.0
Adonal Foyle	82	.458	156	1.9	2.5	0.2
James Augustine	25	.529	40	1.6	1.2	0.1

Triple Doubles: Turkoglu (2). **3-pt FG leader:** Lewis (226). **Steals leader:** Lewis (99). **Blocks leader:** Howard (176).

Philadelphia 76ers

	Gm	FG%	Tpts	PPG	RPG	APG
Andre Iguodala	82	.456	1630	19.9	5.4	4.8
Andre Miller	82	.492	1398	17.0	4.0	6.9
Willie Green	74	.436	921	12.4	2.5	2.0
Louis Williams	80	.424	920	11.5	2.1	3.2
Samuel Dalembert	82	.513	864	10.5	10.4	0.5
Thaddeus Young	74	.539	610	8.2	4.2	0.8
Rodney Carney	70	.403	409	5.8	2.1	0.5
Reggie Evans	81	.439	425	5.2	7.5	0.8
Jason Smith	76	.455	340	4.5	3.0	0.3
Kevin Ollie	40	.420	70	1.8	0.5	1.0
Shavlik Randolph	9	.286	8	0.9	1.2	0.3
Calvin Booth	31	.333	24	0.8	1.2	0.3

Triple Doubles: none. **3-pt FG leader:** Iguodala (101). **Steals leader:** Iguodala (171). **Blocks leader:** Dalembert (192).

Phoenix Suns

	Gm	FG%	Tpts	PPG	RPG	APG
Amare Stoudemire	79	.590	1989	25.2	9.1	1.5
Steve Nash	81	.504	1371	16.9	3.5	11.1
Leandro Barbosa	82	.462	1283	15.6	2.8	2.6
Shaquille O'Neal	61	.593	832	13.6	9.1	1.5
Grant Hill	70	.503	919	13.1	5.0	2.9
Raja Bell	75	.421	889	11.9	3.7	2.2
Boris Diaw	82	.477	725	8.8	4.6	3.9
Gordan Giricek	56	.440	325	5.8	1.7	1.1
Alando Tucker	6	.364	22	3.7	1.3	0.0
Brian Skinner	66	.465	219	3.3	3.6	0.2
Sean Marks	19	.535	59	3.1	1.9	0.2
Linton Johnson III	8	.474	15	2.6	1.8	0.5
Eric Piatkowski	16	.364	39	2.4	0.8	0.6
D.J. Strawberry	33	.315	73	2.2	0.8	0.9

Triple Doubles: none. **3-pt FG leader:** Nash (179). **Steals leader:** Barbosa (75). **Blocks leader:** Stoudemire (163).

Portland Trail Blazers

	Gm	FG%	Tpts	PPG	RPG	APG
Brandon Roy	74	.454	1416	19.1	4.7	5.8
LaMarcus Aldridge	76	.484	1350	17.8	7.6	1.6
Travis Outlaw	82	.433	1092	13.3	4.6	1.3
Martell Webster	75	.422	799	10.7	3.9	1.2
Jarrett Jack	82	.431	814	9.9	2.9	3.8
Steve Blake	81	.408	692	8.5	2.4	5.1
James Jones	58	.437	463	8.0	2.8	0.6
Channing Frye	78	.488	530	6.8	4.5	0.7
Sergio Rodriguez	72	.352	180	2.5	0.8	1.7
Raef LaFrentz	39	.443	65	1.7	1.7	0.2
Von Wafer	29	.279	46	1.6	0.7	0.2
Josh McRoberts	8	.600	12	1.5	1.3	0.3

Triple Doubles: Roy (1). **3-pt FG leader:** Webster (123). **Steals leader:** Roy (79). **Blocks leader:** Aldridge (94).

NBA Points+Rebounds+Assists Leaders

	PPG	RPG	APG	Avg
LeBron James, Cle	30.0	7.9	7.2	45.1
Kobe Bryant, LAL	28.3	6.3	5.4	40.0
Chris Paul, NO	21.0	4.0	11.6	36.6
Allen Iverson, Den	26.4	3.0	7.1	36.5
Carmelo Anthony, Den	25.7	7.4	3.4	36.5
Dwight Howard, Orl	20.7	14.2	1.3	36.2
Amare Stoudemire, Pho	25.2	9.1	1.5	35.8

Sacramento Kings

	Gm	FG%	Tpts	PPG	RPG	APG
Kevin Martin	.61	.456	1443	23.7	4.5	2.1
Ron Artest	.57	.453	1168	20.5	5.8	3.5
Brad Miller	.72	.463	964	13.4	9.5	3.7
Beno Udrih	.65	.463	834	12.8	3.3	4.3
John Salmons	.81	.477	1015	12.5	4.3	2.6
Francisco Garcia	.79	.463	971	12.3	3.3	1.6
Mikki Moore	.82	.577	698	8.5	6.0	1.0
Anthony Johnson	.69	.437	387	5.6	2.0	3.8
Quincy Douby	.74	.394	354	4.8	1.1	0.7
Spencer Hawes	.71	.459	334	4.7	3.2	0.6
Shelden Williams	.64	.434	255	4.0	3.2	0.3
Dahntay Jones	.25	.434	81	3.2	1.4	0.5
Shareef Abdur-Rahim	.6	.214	10	1.7	1.7	0.7
Lorenzen Wright	.18	.286	15	1.7	2.1	0.2
Kenny Thomas	.23	.421	32	1.4	2.7	0.6
Darryl Watkins	.9	.333	12	1.3	1.3	0.0
Orien Greene	.7	.273	6	0.9	0.9	0.4

Triple Doubles: none. **3-pt FG leader:** Garcia (113).
Steals leader: Artest (133). **Blocks leaders:** Miller (74).

San Antonio Spurs

	Gm	FG%	Tpts	PPG	RPG	APG
Manu Ginobili	.74	.460	1442	19.5	4.8	4.5
Tim Duncan	.78	.497	1508	19.3	11.3	2.8
Tony Parker	.69	.494	1295	18.8	3.2	6.0
Michael Finley	.82	.414	826	10.1	3.1	1.4
Brent Barry	.31	.481	221	7.1	1.8	1.7
Kurt Thomas	.70	.492	443	6.3	7.2	1.0
Bruce Bowen	.81	.407	483	6.0	2.9	1.1
Ime Udoka	.73	.424	423	5.8	3.1	0.9
Damon Stoudamire	.60	.356	317	5.3	2.0	2.8
Matt Bonner	.68	.416	326	4.8	2.8	0.5
Fabricio Oberto	.82	.608	397	4.8	5.2	1.2
Jacque Vaughn	.74	.428	306	4.1	1.0	2.1
Ian Mahinmi	.6	.500	21	3.5	0.8	0.2
DerMarr Johnson	.5	.500	17	3.4	0.2	0.2
Darius Washington	.18	.438	53	2.9	1.1	0.8
Robery Horry	.45	.319	112	2.5	2.4	1.0
Keith Langford	.2	.250	2	1.0	1.0	0.0

Triple Doubles: none. **3-pt FG leaders:** Ginobili (156).
Steals leader: Ginobili (109). **Blocks leader:** Duncan (152).

Seattle Supersonics
(now Oklahoma City Thunder)

	Gm	FG%	Tpts	PPG	RPG	APG
Kevin Durant*	.80	.430	1624	20.3	4.4	2.4
Chris Wilcox	.62	.524	828	13.4	7.0	1.2
Earl Watson	.78	.454	836	10.7	2.9	6.8
Jeff Green	.80	.427	840	10.5	4.7	1.5
Nick Collison	.78	.502	767	9.8	9.4	1.4
Damien Wilkins	.76	.403	698	9.2	3.2	2.0
Luke Ridnour	.61	.399	393	6.4	1.5	4.0
Johan Petro	.72	.419	432	6.0	5.1	0.4
Mickael Gelabale	.39	.439	168	4.3	1.5	0.8
Donyell Marshall	.26	.327	98	3.8	2.9	0.4
Francisco Elson	.63	.390	210	3.3	3.2	0.4
Mike Wilks	.15	.472	41	2.7	1.3	0.9
Eddie Gill	.14	.387	38	2.7	1.6	1.6
Mouhamed Sene	.13	.458	30	2.3	1.2	0.1
Robert Swift	.8	.353	14	1.8	2.3	0.1
Ronald Dupree	.5	.333	4	0.8	1.6	0.2

Triple Doubles: Watson (1). **3-pt FG leader:** Durant (59). **Steals leader:** Durant (77). **Blocks leader:** Durant (75).

Toronto Raptors

	Gm	FG%	Tpts	PPG	RPG	APG
Chris Bosh	.67	.494	1496	22.3	8.7	2.6
Anthony Parker	.82	.476	1025	12.5	4.1	2.2
T.J. Ford	.51	.469	617	12.1	2.0	6.1
Jose Calderon	.82	.519	922	11.2	2.9	8.3
Andrea Bargnani	.78	.386	792	10.2	3.7	1.1
Carlos Delfino	.82	.397	738	9.0	4.4	1.8
Jamario Moon	.78	.485	661	8.5	6.8	1.2
Rasho Nesterovic	.71	.550	552	7.8	4.8	1.2
Jason Kapono	.81	.488	580	7.2	1.5	0.8
Kris Humphries	.70	.483	397	5.7	3.7	0.4
Joey Graham	.38	.434	138	3.6	1.8	0.4
Jorge Garbajosa	.7	.320	22	3.1	2.1	0.4
Maceo Baston	.15	.680	41	2.7	1.7	0.2
Primoz Brezec	.50	.468	112	2.2	1.6	0.2
Darrick Martin	.17	.233	27	1.6	0.4	1.2

Triple Doubles: none. **3-pt FG leader:** Parker (133).
Steals leader: Calderon (87). **Blocks leader:** Moon (108).

Utah Jazz

	Gm	FG%	Tpts	PPG	RPG	APG
Carlos Boozer	.81	.547	1708	21.1	10.4	2.9
Deron Williams	.82	.507	1545	18.8	3.0	10.5
Mehmet Okur	.72	.445	1047	14.5	7.7	2.0
Ronnie Brewer	.76	.558	914	12.0	2.9	1.8
Andrei Kirilenko	.72	.506	792	11.0	4.7	4.0
Kyle Korver	.75	.443	740	9.9	2.3	1.3
Matt Harpring	.76	.500	622	8.2	3.2	1.1
Paul Millsap	.82	.504	661	8.1	5.6	1.0
C.J. Miles	.60	.479	297	5.0	1.3	0.9
Ronnie Price	.61	.431	228	3.7	0.8	1.3
Jason Hart	.57	.322	165	2.9	1.0	1.5
Jarron Collins	.70	.439	118	1.7	1.7	0.5
Kyrylo Fesenko	.9	.375	14	1.6	2.8	0.2
Morris Almond	.9	.267	13	1.4	0.2	0.3

Triple Doubles: Boozer and Kirilenko (1). **3-pt FG leader:** Okur (114). **Steals leader:** Brewer (129). **Blocks leader:** Kirilenko (109).

Washington Wizards

	Gm	FG%	Tpts	PPG	RPG	APG
Antawn Jamison	.79	.436	1689	21.4	10.2	1.5
Caron Butler	.58	.466	1180	20.3	6.7	4.9
Gilbert Arenas	.13	.398	252	19.4	3.9	5.1
DeShawn Stevenson	.82	.386	917	11.2	2.9	3.1
Brendan Haywood	.80	.528	848	10.6	7.2	0.9
Roger Mason	.80	.443	724	9.1	1.6	1.7
Antonio Daniels	.71	.459	597	8.4	2.9	4.8
Nick Young	.75	.439	561	7.5	1.5	0.8
Andray Blatche	.82	.474	618	7.5	5.2	1.1
Darius Songaila	.80	.458	495	6.2	3.4	1.7
Oleksiy Pecherov	.35	.352	125	3.6	1.9	0.2
Dominic McGuire	.70	.379	93	1.3	2.0	0.6

Triple Doubles: Butler (3). **3-pt FG leader:** Stevenson (158). **Steals leader:** Butler (128). **Blocks leader:** Haywood (133).

NBA Regular Season Team Leaders

OFFENSE

WEST	Pts	Reb	Ast	FG%	3Pt%	FT%
Golden St.	111.0	43.2	22.4	.459	.348	.852
Denver	110.7	44.1	24.7	.470	.355	.751
Phoenix	110.1	41.5	26.7	.500	.393	.783
LA Lakers	108.6	44.1	24.4	.476	.378	.769
Utah	106.2	40.9	26.4	.497	.372	.759
Sacramento	102.5	40.1	19.1	.464	.373	.798
New Orleans	100.9	41.8	21.8	.466	.389	.769
Memphis	100.7	41.6	19.2	.454	.349	.723
Dallas	100.4	43.0	21.0	.464	.352	.814
Seattle	97.5	44.6	21.3	.444	.333	.770
Houston	96.7	44.6	21.4	.448	.342	.726
Minnesota	95.6	41.4	19.9	.451	.350	.736
Portland	95.4	40.7	21.1	.448	.377	.767
San Antonio	95.4	41.3	21.0	.457	.369	.761
LA Clippers	93.8	40.1	21.1	.438	.324	.781

EAST	Pts	Reb	Ast	FG%	3Pt%	FT%
Orlando	104.5	42.0	20.8	.474	.386	.721
Indiana	104.0	43.1	22.7	.444	.374	.768
Boston	100.5	42.0	22.4	.475	.381	.771
Toronto	100.2	40.1	23.8	.468	.392	.812
Washington	98.8	41.6	19.6	.446	.356	.782
Atlanta	98.2	42.2	22.0	.454	.356	.772
Detroit	97.5	41.4	22.3	.458	.366	.767
Chicago	97.3	43.0	22.1	.435	.363	.756
Charlotte	97.1	40.6	21.3	.452	.367	.714
Milwaukee	97.0	41.7	21.5	.449	.344	.733
New York	96.9	42.5	18.7	.439	.337	.727
Philadelphia	96.6	41.9	20.4	.460	.317	.706
Cleveland	96.4	44.6	20.0	.439	.358	.717
New Jersey	95.8	41.9	23.5	.443	.348	.736
Miami	91.4	37.6	20.0	.443	.358	.727

DEFENSE

WEST	Pts	Reb	Ast	FG%	3Pt%	FT%
San Antonio	90.6	40.3	18.2	.444	.342	.756
Houston	92.0	40.7	18.9	.433	.365	.737
New Orleans	95.6	40.8	21.7	.460	.351	.771
Dallas	95.9	40.3	18.9	.443	.349	.760
Portland	96.3	41.7	20.9	.451	.356	.766
Utah	99.3	37.8	19.9	.461	.357	.749
LA Clippers	101.1	43.6	22.4	.467	.349	.751
LA Lakers	101.3	42.8	21.9	.445	.362	.752
Minnesota	102.4	41.7	23.2	.472	.357	.769
Sacramento	104.8	41.9	22.9	.466	.373	.753
Phoenix	105.0	43.9	19.6	.456	.353	.749
Seattle	106.3	44.1	24.4	.461	.385	.749
Memphis	106.9	44.5	23.9	.480	.364	.774
Denver	107.0	45.4	25.7	.457	.363	.730
Golden State	108.8	47.0	23.6	.468	.368	.759

EAST	Pts	Reb	Ast	FG%	3Pt%	FT%
Detroit	90.1	39.1	19.1	.437	.332	.744
Boston	90.3	38.9	18.8	.419	.316	.743
Philadelphia	96.2	39.2	23.2	.461	.360	.772
Cleveland	96.7	40.4	21.0	.455	.357	.748
Toronto	97.3	41.6	21.9	.458	.368	.776
Orlando	99.0	41.7	21.5	.446	.358	.754
Washington	99.2	41.2	23.9	.461	.386	.754
Miami	100.0	43.1	22.2	.468	.369	.755
Atlanta	100.0	40.9	22.3	.463	.362	.752
Chicago	100.4	42.6	21.9	.453	.375	.766
New Jersey	100.9	41.6	22.1	.456	.369	.768
Charlotte	101.4	43.7	21.8	.466	.355	.747
New York	103.5	42.6	21.6	.474	.369	.739
Milwaukee	103.9	40.7	23.3	.480	.384	.766
Indiana	105.4	45.5	22.2	.454	.386	.757

Playoff Series Summaries

WESTERN CONFERENCE

FIRST ROUND (Best of 7)

(1) Los Angeles Lakers 4, (8) Denver Nuggets 0

Date	Winner	Home Court
Apr. 20	Lakers, 128-114	at Los Angeles
Apr. 23	Lakers, 122-107	at Los Angeles
Apr. 26	Lakers, 102-84	at Denver
Apr. 28	Lakers, 107-101	at Denver

(2) New Orleans Hornets 4, (7) Dallas Mavericks 1

Date	Winner	Home Court
Apr. 19	Hornets, 104-92	at N. Orleans
Apr. 22	Hornets, 127-103	at N. Orleans
Apr. 25	Mavericks, 99-87	at Dallas
Apr. 27	Hornets, 97-84	at Dallas
Apr. 29	Hornets, 99-94	at N. Orleans

(3) San Antonio Spurs 4, (6) Phoenix Suns 1

Date	Winner	Home Court
Apr. 19	Spurs, 117-115	at San Antonio
Apr. 22	Spurs, 102-96	at San Antonio
Apr. 25	Spurs, 115-99	at Phoenix
Apr. 27	Suns, 105-86	at Phoenix
Apr. 29	Spurs, 92-87	at San Antonio

(5) Utah Jazz 4, (4) Houston Rockets 2

Date	Winner	Home Court
Apr. 19	Jazz, 93-82	at Houston
Apr. 21	Jazz, 90-84	at Houston
Apr. 24	Rockets, 94-92	at Utah
Apr. 26	Jazz, 86-82	at Utah
Apr. 29	Rockets, 95-69	at Houston
May 2	Jazz, 113-91	at Utah

SEMIFINALS (Best of 7)

(1) Los Angeles Lakers 4, (5) Utah Jazz 2

Date	Winner	Home Court
May 4	Lakers, 109-98	at Los Angeles
May 7	Lakers 120-110	at Los Angeles
May 9	Jazz, 104-99	at Utah
May 11	Jazz, 123-115	at Utah
May 14	Lakers, 111-104	at Los Angeles
May 16	Lakers, 108-105	at Utah

(3) San Antonio Spurs 4, (2) New Orleans 3

Date	Winner	Home Court
May 3	Hornets, 101-82	at N. Orleans
May 5	Hornets, 102-84	at N. Orleans
May 8	Spurs, 110-99	at San Antonio
May 11	Spurs, 100-80	at San Antonio
May 13	Hornets, 101-79	at N. Orleans
May 15	Spurs, 99-80	at San Antonio
May 19	Spurs, 91-82	at N. Orleans

CHAMPIONSHIP (Best of 7)

(1) Los Angeles Lakers 4, (3) San Antonio 1

Date	Winner	Home Court
May 21	Lakers, 89-85	at Los Angeles
May 23	Lakers, 101-71	at Los Angeles
May 25	Spurs, 103-84	at San Antonio
May 27	Lakers, 93-91	at San Antonio
May 29	Lakers, 100-92	at Los Angeles

2008 NBA PLAYOFFS

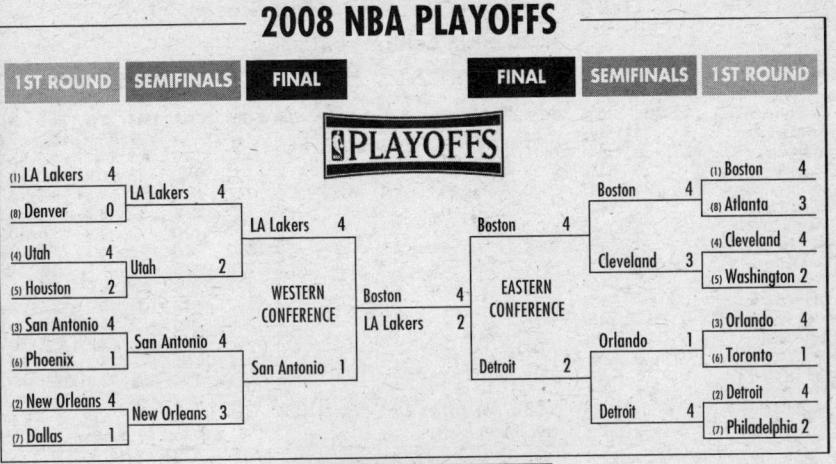

1ST ROUND	SEMIFINALS	FINAL		FINAL	SEMIFINALS	1ST ROUND

PLAYOFFS

(1) LA Lakers 4
(8) Denver 0
LA Lakers 4
(4) Utah 4
(5) Houston 2
Utah 2
LA Lakers 4

WESTERN CONFERENCE

(3) San Antonio 4
(6) Phoenix 1
San Antonio 4
(2) New Orleans 4
(7) Dallas 1
New Orleans 3
San Antonio 1

Boston 4
LA Lakers 2

Boston 4

EASTERN CONFERENCE

Detroit 2

Boston 4
Cleveland 3

Orlando 1

Detroit 4

(1) Boston 4
(8) Atlanta 3
(4) Cleveland 4
(5) Washington 2
(3) Orlando 4
(6) Toronto 1
(2) Detroit 4
(7) Philadelphia 2

EASTERN CONFERENCE

FIRST ROUND (Best of 7)

(1) Boston Celtics 4, (8) Atlanta Hawks 3

Date	Winner	Home Court
Apr. 20	Celtics, 104-81	at Boston
Apr. 23	Celtics, 96-77	at Boston
Apr. 26	Hawks, 102-93	at Atlanta
Apr. 28	Hawks, 97-92	at Atlanta
Apr. 30	Celtics, 110-85	at Boston
May 2	Hawks, 103-100	at Atlanta
May 4	Celtics, 99-65	at Boston

(3) Orlando Magic 4, (6) Toronto Raptors 1

Date	Winner	Home Court
Apr. 20	Magic, 114-100	at Orlando
Apr. 22	Magic 104-103	at Orlando
Apr. 24	Raptors, 108-94	at Toronto
Apr. 26	Magic, 106-94	at Toronto
Apr. 28	Magic, 102-92	at Orlando

(2) Detroit Pistons 4, (7) Philadelphia 76ers 2

Date	Winner	Home Court
Apr. 20	76ers, 90-86	at Detroit
Apr. 23	Pistons, 105-88	at Detroit
Apr. 25	76ers, 95-75	at Philadelphia
Apr. 27	Pistons, 93-84	at Philadelphia
Apr. 29	Pistons, 98-81	at Detroit
May 1	Pistons, 100-77	at Detroit

(4) Cleveland Cavaliers 4, (5) Wash. Wizards 2

Date	Winner	Home Court
Apr. 19	Cavaliers, 93-86	at Cleveland
Apr. 21	Cavaliers, 116-86	at Cleveland
Apr. 24	Wizards, 108-72	at Washington
Apr. 27	Cavaliers, 100-97	at Washington
Apr. 30	Wizards, 88-87	at Cleveland
May 2	Cavaliers, 105-88	at Washington

SEMIFINALS (Best of 7)

(1) Boston Celtics 4, (4) Cleveland Cavaliers 3

Date	Winner	Home Court
May 6	Celtics, 76-72	at Boston
May 8	Celtics, 89-73	at Boston
May 10	Cavaliers, 108-84	at Cleveland
May 12	Cavaliers, 88-77	at Cleveland
May 14	Celtics, 96-89	at Boston
May 16	Cavaliers, 74-69	at Cleveland
May 18	Celtics, 97-92	at Boston

(2) Detroit Pistons 4, (3) Orlando Magic 1

Date	Winner	Home Court
May 3	Pistons, 91-72	at Detroit
May 5	Pistons, 100-93	at Detroit
May 7	Magic, 111-86	at Orlando
May 10	Pistons, 90-89	at Orlando
May 13	Pistons, 91-86	at Detroit

CHAMPIONSHIP (Best of 7)

(1) Boston Celtics 4, (2) Detroit Pistons 2

Date	Winner	Home Court
May 20	Celtics, 88-79	at Boston
May 22	Pistons, 103-97	at Boston
May 24	Celtics, 94-80	at Detroit
May 26	Pistons, 94-75	at Detroit
May 28	Celtics, 106-102	at Boston
May 30	Celtics, 89-81	at Detroit

NBA FINALS (Best of 7)

	W-L	Avg.	Leading Scorer
Boston	4-2	102.2	P. Pierce (21.8)
LA Lakers	2-4	93.8	K. Bryant (25.7)

Date	Winner	Home Court
June 5	Celtics, 98-88	at Boston
June 8	Celtics, 108-102	at Boston
June 10	Lakers, 87-81	at Los Angeles
June 12	Celtics, 97-91	at Los Angeles
June 15	Lakers, 103-98	at Los Angeles
June 17	Celtics, 131-92	at Boston

Finals MVP

Paul Pierce, Boston, F
21.8 ppg, 4.5 rpg, 6.3 apg

NBA Finalists' Composite Box Scores

Boston Celtics (16-10)

(3 Game Min.)	Gm	FG%	3PT-A	TPts	Pts	Reb	Ast	Gm	FG%	3PT-A	TPts	Pts	Reb	As
		Overall Playoffs							Finals vs. Los Angeles					
Kevin Garnett	26	.495	2-8	530	20.4	10.5	3.3	6	.429	0-1	109	18.2	13.0	0.
Paul Pierce	26	.441	43-119	511	19.7	5.0	4.6	6	.432	11-28	131	21.8	4.5	6.
Ray Allen	26	.428	55-139	405	15.6	3.8	2.7	6	.507	22-42	122	20.3	5.0	2.
Rajon Rondo	26	.407	5-20	266	10.2	4.1	6.6	6	.377	0-3	56	9.3	3.8	6.7
James Posey	26	.437	35-88	174	6.7	3.6	1.1	6	.500	12-24	52	8.7	3.8	0.
Kendrick Perkins	25	.585	0-1	164	6.6	6.1	0.5	5	.571	0-0	20	4.0	3.6	0.4
Leon Powe	23	.493	0-0	116	5.0	2.7	0.2	6	.550	0-0	37	6.2	3.2	0.7
Sam Cassell	21	.333	6-28	94	4.5	0.7	1.2	5	.375	0-6	19	3.8	0.2	1.
P.J. Brown	25	.464	0-1	73	2.9	2.4	0.5	6	.391	0-0	24	4.0	3.2	0.7
Eddie House	21	.304	11-31	52	2.5	1.0	0.9	4	.357	7-17	32	8.0	2.5	2.
Glen Davis	17	.412	0-1	39	2.3	1.5	0.4	1	.500	0	3	3.0	4.0	0.0
Tony Allen	15	.563	0-1	20	1.3	0.2	0.2	3	.667	0-0	8	2.7	0.3	0.7
CELTICS	26	.447	157-437	2444	94.0	40.0	21.5	6	.444	52-121	613	102.2	42.2	23.0
OPPONENTS	26	.426	137-417	2308	88.8	36.3	18.5	6	.441	43-124	563	93.8	37.2	19.3

Los Angeles Lakers (14-7)

(3 Game Min.)	Gm	FG%	3PT-A	TPts	Pts	Reb	Ast	Gm	FG%	3PT-A	TPts	Pts	Reb	Ast
		Overall Playoffs							Finals vs. Boston					
Kobe Bryant	21	.479	32-106	633	30.1	5.7	5.6	6	.405	9-28	154	25.7	4.7	5.0
Pau Gasol	21	.530	0-0	354	16.9	9.3	4.0	6	.532	0-0	88	14.7	10.2	3.3
Lamar Odom	21	.491	3-11	301	14.3	10.0	3.0	6	.517	1-5	81	13.5	9.0	3.0
Derek Fisher	21	.452	22-50	215	10.2	2.2	2.5	6	.405	3-16	65	10.8	1.5	3.2
Sasha Vujacic	21	.399	31-79	171	8.1	2.2	0.8	6	.391	8-23	50	8.3	2.0	0.8
Vladimir Radmanovic	21	.444	29-78	168	8.0	3.8	1.5	6	.390	10-26	44	7.3	4.8	1.3
Luke Walton	21	.454	11-26	125	6.0	2.6	2.0	6	.313	2-6	15	2.5	1.0	1.2
Jordan Farmar	21	.383	17-44	119	5.7	1.6	1.3	6	.484	9-17	42	7.0	1.8	1.3
Trevor Ariza	8	.583	1-4	17	2.1	1.4	0.1	5	.556	1-3	13	2.6	1.8	0.2
Ronny Turiaf	19	.389	0-0	38	2.0	1.4	0.3	6	.500	0-0	11	1.8	0.7	0.0
Didier Ilunga-Mbenga	7	.625	0-0	10	1.4	1.3	0.0	0	.000	0-0	0	0.0	0.0	0.0
LAKERS	21	.468	146-398	2151	102.4	39.6	20.8	6	.441	43-124	563	93.8	37.2	19.3
OPPONENTS	21	.436	143-404	2105	100.2	43.4	21.9	6	.444	52-121	613	102.2	42.2	23.0

NBA Playoff Leaders

Scoring Average

	Gm	FG	FT	Pts	Avg
Kobe Bryant, LAL	21	222	157	633	30.1
LeBron James, Cle	13	113	122	366	28.2
Tracy McGrady, Hou	6	62	33	162	27.0
Dirk Nowitzki, Dal	5	43	42	134	26.8
Allen Iverson, Den	4	36	23	98	24.5
Chris Paul, NO	12	111	62	289	24.1
Chris Bosh, Tor	5	42	35	120	24.0
Amare Stoudemire, Pho	5	48	19	116	23.2
Carmelo Anthony, Den	4	32	24	90	22.5
Tony Parker, SA	17	152	70	381	22.4

Total Points

	Gm	FG	FT	Pts	Avg
Kobe Bryant, LAL	21	222	157	633	30.1
Kevin Garnett, Bos	26	217	94	530	20.4
Paul Pierce, Bos	26	163	142	511	19.7
Ray Allen, Bos	26	133	84	405	15.6
Tony Parker, SA	17	152	70	381	22.4

Rebounds

	Gm	Off	Def	Tot	Avg
Dwight Howard, Orl	10	60	98	158	15.8
Tim Duncan, SA	17	61	186	247	14.5
Marcus Camby, Den	4	11	42	53	13.2
Carlos Boozer, Utah	12	42	105	147	12.2
Antawn Jamison, Wash	6	19	53	72	12.0
Dirk Nowitzki, Dal	5	10	50	60	12.0

Assists

	Gm	No	Avg
Chris Paul, NO	12	135	11.2
Deron Williams, Utah	12	120	10.0
Steve Nash, Pho	5	39	7.8
LeBron James, Cle	13	99	7.6
Jose Calderon, Tor	5	35	7.0

Final Playoff Standings

ranked by victories

	Gm	W	L	Pct	Per Game For	Opp
Boston	26	16	10	.615	94.0	88.8
LA Lakers	21	14	7	.667	102.4	100.2
Detroit	17	10	7	.588	91.4	89.1
San Antonio	17	9	8	.529	94.1	94.9
New Orleans	12	7	5	.583	96.6	92.9
Cleveland	13	7	6	.538	89.9	87.8
Utah	12	6	6	.500	98.9	99.2
Orlando	10	5	5	.500	97.1	95.5
Atlanta	7	3	4	.429	87.1	99.1
Houston	6	2	4	.333	88.0	90.5
Washington	6	2	4	.333	92.2	95.5
Philadelphia	6	2	4	.333	85.8	92.8
Phoenix	5	1	4	.200	100.4	102.4
Dallas	5	1	4	.200	94.0	102.8
Denver	4	0	4	.000	101.5	114.8

Annual Awards

Most Valuable Player

The Maurice Podoloff Trophy; voting by 126-member panel of local and national pro basketball writers and broadcasters. Each ballot has five entries; points awarded on 10-7-5-3-1 basis.

	1st	2nd	3rd	4th	5th	Pts
Kobe Bryant, LA Lakers	82	32	10	2	-	1100
Chris Paul, New Orleans	28	64	32	2	-	894
Kevin Garnett, Boston	15	23	56	26	1	670
LeBron James, Cleveland	1	7	28	77	8	438
Dwight Howard, Orlando	-	-	7	39	60	
Amare Stoudemire, Phoenix	-	-	3	18	27	
Tim Duncan, San Antonio	-	-	2	19	25	
Tracy McGrady, Houston	-	-	2	13	19	
Steve Nash, Phoenix	-	-	4	6	18	
Manu Ginobili, San Antonio	-	-	-	9	9	
Dirk Nowitzki, Dallas	-	-	-	5	5	
Deron Williams, Utah	-	-	-	4	4	
Carmelo Anthony, Denver	-	-	1	-	3	
Paul Pierce, Boston	-	-	-	1	1	
Rasheed Wallace, Detroit	-	-	-	1	1	
Carlos Boozer, Utah	-	-	-	1	1	
Antawn Jamison, Washington	-	-	-	1	1	

All-NBA Teams

Voting by a 127-member panel of local and national pro basketball writers and broadcasters. Each ballot has entries for three teams; points awarded on 5-3-1 basis. First Team repeater from 2006-07 are in **bold** type.

Pos	First Team	1st	Pts
F	Kevin Garnett, Boston	118	612
F	LeBron James, Cleveland	117	610
C	Dwight Howard, Orlando	86	546
G	**Kobe Bryant**, LA Lakers	127	635
G	Chris Paul, New Orleans	124	629

Pos	Second Team	1st	Pts
F	Dirk Nowitzki, Dallas	1	189
F	Tim Duncan, San Antonio	25	397
C	Amare Stoudemire, Phoenix	30	412
G	Steve Nash, Phoenix	2	311
G	Deron Williams, Utah	0	228

Pos	Third Team	1st	Pts
F	Carlos Boozer, Utah	0	174
F	Paul Pierce, Boston	2	151
C	Yao Ming, Houston	2	71
G	Tracy McGrady, Houston	1	137
G	Manu Ginobili, San Antonio	0	123

Other players receiving votes (first team votes in parentheses): Allen Iverson, Denver, 116; Carmelo Anthony, Denver, 89; Marcus Camby, Denver, 59; Chauncey Billups, Detroit, 38; Baron Davis, Golden State, 32; David West, New Orleans, 24; Rasheed Wallace, Detroit, 22; Tyson Chandler, New Orleans, 18; Antawn Jamison, Washington, 15; Al Jefferson, Minnesota, 14; Chris Bosh, Toronto, 11; Joe Johnson, Atlanta 8; Andre Miller, Philadelphia, 7.

Rookie of the Year

The Eddie Gottlieb Trophy; voting by 125-member panel of local and national pro basketball writers and broadcasters. Each ballot has entries for three players; points awarded on 5-3-1 basis.

	1st	2nd	3rd	Pts
Kevin Durant, Seattle	90	30	5	545
Al Horford, Atlanta	30	74	18	390
Luis Scola, Houston	5	20	61	146
Al Thornton, LA Clippers	-	1	27	30
Jamario Moon, Toronto	-	-	7	7
Juan Carlos Navarro, Memphis	-	-	3	3
Thaddeus Young, Philadelphia	-	-	2	2
Carl Landry, Houston	-	-	1	1
Mike Conley, Memphis	-	-	1	1

All-Defensive Teams

Voting by NBA head coaches. Each ballot has entries for two teams; two points given for 1st team, one for 2nd. Coaches cannot vote for own players. First Team repeaters from 2006-07 are in **bold** type.

Pos	First Team	1st	Pts
F	Kevin Garnett, Boston	24	52
G	**Kobe Bryant**, LA Lakers	24	52
C	**Marcus Camby**, Denver	14	37
F	**Bruce Bowen**, San Antonio	13	36
F	**Tim Duncan**, San Antonio	12	33

Pos	Second Team	1st	Pts
F	Shane Battier, Houston	9	29
G	Chris Paul, New Orleans	10	26
C	Dwight Howard, Orlando	8	25
F	Tayshaun Prince, Detroit	3	20
G	Raja Bell, Phoenix	4	18

Other players receiving votes (first team votes in parentheses): Chauncey Billups, Detroit, 14 (5); Jason Kidd, Dallas, 13 (4); Rasheed Wallace, Detroit, 13 (3); Rajon Rondo, Boston, 11 (3); Deron Williams, Utah, 8, (3); Josh Smith, Atlanta, 8, (3); Ron Artest, Sacramento, 8 (2); Tyson Chandler, New Orleans, 8 (1).

Coach of the Year

The Red Auerbach Trophy; voting by a 125-member panel of local and national pro basketball writers and broadcasters.

Top Vote-getters	1st	2nd	3rd	Pts
Byron Scott, New Orleans	70	34	6	458
Doc Rivers, Boston	23	36	19	242
Rick Adelman, Houston	17	23	39	193
Maurice Cheeks, Philadelphia	5	12	20	81
Phil Jackson, LA Lakers	4	9	9	56
Jerry Sloan, Utah	6	4	7	49
Eddie Jordan, Washington	-	5	12	47
Stan Van Gundy, Orlando	2	8	14	
Nate McMillan, Portland	-	3	3	

All-Rookie Team

Voting by NBA's 30 head coaches, who cannot vote for players on their team. Each ballot has entries for two five-man teams, regardless of position; Coaches are not permitted to vote for players on their own team. two points given for 1st team, one for 2nd. First team votes in parentheses.

First Team	College	Pts
Al Horford, Atlanta (29)	Florida	58
Kevin Durant, Seattle (28)	Texas	57
Luis Scola, Houston (26)	none	53
Al Thornton, LA Clippers (20)	Florida St.	48
Jeff Green, Seattle (15)	Georgetown	43

Second Team	College	Pts
Jamario Moon, Toronto (12)	Meridian CC	38
Juan Carlos Navarro, Memphis (5)	none	24
Thaddeus Young, Philadelphia (4)	Georgia Tech	23
Rodney Stuckey, Detroit (5)	E. Washington	22
Carl Landry, Houston (1)	Purdue	18

Executive of the Year

The Sporting News Executive of the Year Award; voting done by a 47-member panel of NBA executives.

	Votes
Danny Ainge, Boston	18
Mitch Kupchak, LA Lakers	14
Jeff Bower, New Orleans	12

Sixth-Man Award

Voted on by a 124-member panel of local and national pro basketball writers and broadcasters. Each ballot has entries for three players; points awarded on 5-3-1 basis.

Top Vote-getters	1st	2nd	3rd	Pts
Manu Ginobili, San Antonio	123	-	-	615
Leandro Barbosa, Phoenix	1	84	26	283
Jason Terry, Dallas	-	9	17	44
Kyle Korver, Utah	-	7	13	34
Ben Gordon, Chicago	-	6	9	27
Josh Childress, Atlanta	-	5	8	23
J.R. Smith, Denver	-	4	10	22
James Posey, Boston	-	3	10	19
Jason Maxiell, Detroit	-	1	8	11
Travis Outlaw, Portland	-	-	11	11

Most Improved Player Award

Voted on by a 125-member panel of local and national pro basketball writers and broadcasters. Each ballot has entries for three players; points awarded on 5-3-1 basis.

Top Vote-getters	1st	2nd	3rd	Pts
Hedo Turkoglu, Orlando	61	22	9	380
Rudy Gay, Memphis	23	14	10	167
LaMarcus Aldridge, Portland	9	22	17	128
Al Jefferson, Minnesota	6	16	22	100
Rajon Rondo, Boston	6	10	17	77
Mike Dunleavy, Indiana	3	9	9	51
Jose Calderon, Toronto	2	10	5	45
Chris Paul, New Orleans	5	4	4	41
Beno Udrih, Sacramento	1	2	6	17
David West, New Orleans	1	2	4	15
Ronnie Brewer, Utah	1	2	1	12

Defensive Player of the Year Award

Voted on by a 124-member panel of local and national pro basketball writers and broadcasters.

Top Vote-getters	1st	2nd	3rd	Pts
Kevin Garnett, Boston	90	12	7	493
Marcus Camby, Denver	12	32	22	178
Shane Battier, Boston	11	33	21	175
Bruce Bowen, San Antonio	7	7	24	80
Kobe Bryant, LA Lakers	-	10	10	40
Josh Smith, Atlanta	1	6	11	34
Chris Paul, New Orleans	1	4	7	24
Dwight Howard, Orlando	1	4	7	24
Tim Duncan, San Antonio	-	6	4	22
Tayshaun Prince, Detroit	-	3	4	13

Sportsmanship Award

Each of the 30 NBA teams nominated a player from their roster "who best represents the ideals of sportsmanship on the court," then a panel of former players (Mike Bantom, Eddie Johnson, "Satch" Sanders, Kenny Smith and Steve Smith) selected the six divisional winners from the pool of nominees. The winner is chosen from the divisional winners in vote by current NBA players. The winner receives the Joe Dumars Trophy, named for the Pistons guard who won the inaugural sportsmanship award in 1996.

	1st	2nd	3rd	4th	5th	6th	Pts
Grant Hill, Phoenix	90	100	60	39	34	21	2628
Shane Battier, Hou	41	80	59	29	42	56	2318
Brandon Roy, Port	59	51	60	67	47	60	2064
Antonio McDyess, Det	44	47	55	65	69	64	1888
Antawn Jamison, Was	37	34	59	87	66	61	1820
Chris Bosh, Toronto	36	32	51	57	86	82	1666

2008 College Draft

First and second round picks at the 61st annual NBA Draft held June 26, 2008 in New York City at the Theatre at Madison Square Garden. The order of the first 14 positions were determined by a Draft Lottery held May 22, in Secaucus, N.J. Positions 15 through 30 reflect regular season records in reverse order.

First Round

	Team	Pos
1	Chicago ....Derrick Rose, Memphis	G
2	Miami ....Michael Beasley, Kansas St.	F
3	Minnesota ..............O.J. Mayo, USC	G
4	Seattle ....Russell Westbrook, UCLA	G
5	Memphis ....Kevin Love, UCLA	F
6	New York ....Danilo Gallinari, Italy	F
7	LA Clippers ....Eric Gordon, Indiana	G
8	Milwaukee ....Joe Alexander, West Va.	F
9	Charlotte ...........D.J. Augustin, Texas	G
10	New Jersey ....Brook Lopez, Stanford	C
11	Indiana ....Jerryd Bayless, Arizona	G
12	Sacramento ....Jason Thompson, Rider	F
13	Portland ....Brandon Rush, Kansas	G
14	Golden St. ....Anthony Randolph, LSU	F
15	Phoenix ....Robin Lopez, Stanford	F
16	Philadelphia ......Marreese Speights, Florida	F
17	Toronto ....Roy Hibbert, Georgetown	C
18	Washington ....JaVale McGee, Nevada	C
19	Cleveland ..........J.J. Hickson, N.C. State	F
20	Charlotte ....Alexis Ajinca, France	C
21	New Jersey ....Ryan Anderson, California	F
22	Orlando ....Courtney Lee, W. Kentucky	G
23	Utah ....Kosta Koufos, Ohio St.	C
24	Seattle ....Serge Ibaka, Spain	F
25	Houston ....Nicolas Batum, France	F
26	San Antonio ....George Hill, IUPUI	F
27	New Orleans ....Darrell Arthur, Kansas	F
28	Memphis ....Donte Greene, Syracuse	F
29	Detroit .............D.J. White, Indiana	F
30	Boston .........J.R. Giddens, New Mexico	G

Second Round

	Team	Pos
31	Minnesota ....Nikola Pekovic, Serbia	C
32	Seattle ....Walter Sharpe, UAB	F
33	Portland ....Joey Dorsey, Memphis	F
34	Minnesota ....Mario Chalmers, Kansas	G
35	LA Clippers ......DeAndre Jordan, Texas A&M	C
36	Portland ....Omer Asik, Turkey	C
37	Milwaukee ......Luc Mbah a Moute, UCLA	F
38	Charlotte ......Kyle Weaver, Washington St.	G
39	Chicago ....Sonny Weems, Arkansas	G
40	New Jersey ...Chris Douglas-Roberts, Memphis	G
41	Indiana ....Nathan Jawai, Australia	F
42	Sacramento ....Sean Singletary, Virginia	G
43	Sacramento ......Patrick Ewing Jr., Georgetown	F
44	Utah ....Ante Tomic, Croatia	C
45	San Antonio ....Goran Dragic, Slovenia	G
46	Seattle ....Trent Plaisted, BYU	F
47	Washington ....Bill Walkers, Kansas St.	F
48	Phoenix ....Malik Hairston, Oregon	G
49	Golden St. ....Richard Hendrix, Alabama	F
50	Seattle ....DeVon Hardin, California	C
51	Dallas ....Shan Foster, Vanderbilt	F
52	Miami ....Darnell Jackson, Kansas	F
53	Utah ....Tadija Dragicevic, Serbia	F
54	Houston ....Maarty Leunen, Oregon	F
55	Portland ....Mike Taylor, Iowa St.	G
56	Seattle ....Sasha Kaun, Kansas	C
57	San Antonio ....James Gist, Maryland	F
58	LA Lakers ....Joe Crawford, Kentucky	G
59	Detroit ....Deron Washington, Virginia Tech	F
60	Boston ....Semih Erden, Turkey	C

2008 Olympic Men's Basketball Tournament
Held Aug. 10-24, 2008 at Beijing, China.
Group Standings
Two points for a win and one for a loss; (*) indicated team advanced to semifinals.

Group A	W	L	For	Opp	Pts
*Lithuania	4	1	425	400	9
*Argentina	4	1	425	361	9
Croatia	3	2	399	380	8
Australia	3	2	457	405	8
Russia	1	4	387	406	6
Iran	0	5	323	464	5

PRELIMINARY RESULTS: **Aug. 10**–Russia 71, Iran 49; Lithuania 79, Argentina 75; Croatia 85, Australia 82; **Aug. 12**– Lithuania 99, Iran 67; Croatia 85, Russia 78; Argentina 85, Australia 68; **Aug. 14**–Australia 106, Iran 68; Lithuania 86, Russia 79; Argentina 77, Croatia 53; **Aug. 16**–Australia 95, Russia 80; Lithuania 86, Croatia 73; Argentina 97, Iran 82; **Aug. 18**–Croatia 91, Iran 57; Australia 106, Lithuania 75; Argentina 91, Russia 79.

Quarterfinals
Argentina 80	....	Greece 78
USA 116	....	Australia 85
Spain 72	....	Croatia 59
Lithuania 94	....	China 68

Semifinals
Argentina 101	....	USA 81
Spain 91	....	Lithuania 86

Group B	W	L	For	Opp	Pts
*United States	5	0	515	354	10
*Spain	4	1	418	369	9
Greece	3	2	415	375	8
China	2	3	366	400	7
Germany	1	4	330	390	6
Angola	0	5	321	477	5

PRELIMINARY RESULTS: **Aug. 10**–Germany 95, Angola 66; Greece 81, Greece 66; USA 101, China 70; **Aug. 12**–Greece 87, Germany 64; Spain 85, China 75; USA 97, Angola 76; **Aug. 14**–Spain 72, Germany 59; China 85, Angola 68; USA 92, Greece 69; **Aug. 16**–Greece 102, Angola 61; China 59, Germany 55; USA 119, Spain 82; **Aug. 18**–Greece 91, China 77; Spain 98, Angola 50; USA 106, Germany 57.

Bronze Medal Game
Argentina 87	....	Lithuania 75

Gold Medal Game
Aug. 24, 2008
USA 118	....	Spain 107

High Scorers–Dwyane Wade, USA 27 pts; Rudy Fernandez, Spain 22 pts.

Tournament Individual Leaders

Scoring	Gm	Pts	Avg
Pau Gasol, Spain	8	157	19.6
Yao Ming, China	6	114	19.0
Luis Scola, Argentina	8	151	18.9
Manu Ginobili, Argentina	7	124	17.7
J.R. Holden, Russia	5	88	17.6
Mohammadsamad Nijjhah, Iran	5	86	17.2
Dirk Nowitzki, Germany	5	85	17.0

Rebounding	Gm	Reb	Avg
Ehadadi Hamed, Iran	5	56	11.2
Dirk Nowitzki, Germany	5	42	8.4
Yao Ming, China	6	49	8.2
Yi Jiianlian, China	6	45	7.5
Pau Gasol, Spain	8	56	7.0

Assists	Gm	Ast	Avg
Sarunas Jasikevicius, Lithuania	8	42	5.3
J.R. Holden, Russia	5	24	4.8
Pablo Prigioni, Argentina	8	37	4.6
Chris Paul, USA	8	33	4.1
Manu Ginobili, Argentina	7	27	3.9
LeBron James, USA	8	30	3.8
Andrei Kirilenko, Russia	5	17	3.4

Field Goal Pct.	FG	FGA	Pct
Dwyane Wade, USA	47	70	.671
Pau Gasol, Spain	64	98	.653
LeBron James, USA	50	83	.602
Andrew Bogut, Australia	31	52	.596
Luis Scola, Argentina	63	107	.589

Women's National Basketball Association
2008 WNBA Final Standings
Conference champions (*) and playoff qualifiers (†) are noted. GB refers to Games Behind leader.

Eastern Conference
	W	L	Pct	GB	Home	Road
*Detroit	22	12	.647	–	14-3	8-9
†Connecticut	21	13	.618	1	13-4	8-9
†New York	19	15	.559	3	11-6	8-9
†Indiana	17	17	.500	5	11-6	6-11
Chicago	12	22	.353	10	8-9	4-13
Washington	10	24	.294	12	6-11	4-13
Atlanta	4	30	.118	18	1-16	3-14

2007 Standings: 1. Detroit (24-10); 2. Indiana (21-13); 3. Connecticut (18-16); 4. New York (16-18); 5. Washington (16-18); 6. Chicago (14-20).

Western Conference
	W	L	Pct	GB	Home	Road
*San Antonio	24	10	.706	–	15-2	9-8
†Seattle	22	12	.647	2	16-1	6-11
†Los Angeles	20	14	.588	4	12-5	8-9
†Sacramento	18	16	.529	6	13-4	5-12
Houston	17	17	.500	7	13-4	4-13
Phoenix	16	18	.471	8	10-7	6-11
Minnesota	16	18	.471	8	9-8	7-10

2007 Standings: 1. Phoenix (23-11); 2. San Antonio (20-14); 3. Sacramento (19-15); 4. Seattle (17-17); 5. Houston (13-21); 6. Minnesota (10-24); 7. Los Angeles (10-24).

WNBA Regular Season Individual Leaders

Scoring

	Gm	Pts	Avg
Diana Taurasi, Phoenix	34	820	24.1
Cappie Pondexter, Phoenix	32	679	21.2
Lauren Jackson, Seattle	21	425	20.2
Seimone Augustus, Minnesota	31	591	19.1
Candace Parker, Los Angeles	33	610	18.5
Tina Thompson, Hou	30	542	18.1

Field Goal Pct.

	FGM	FGA	Pct
Crystal Langhorne, Washington	68	109	.624
Erika DeSouza, Atlanta	48	82	.585
Sancho Lyttle, Houston	92	158	.582

Steals

	Gm	Stl	Avg
Alexis Hornbuckle, Detroit	34	79	2.32
Nicky Anosike, Minnesota	34	75	2.21
Ticha Penicheiro, Sacramento	32	65	2.03

Rebounds

	Gm	Reb	Avg
Candace Parker, Los Angeles	33	313	9.5
Lisa Leslie, Los Angeles	33	293	8.9
Cheryl Ford, Detroit	24	208	8.7
Candice Dupree, Chicago	34	267	7.9
Ebony Hoffman, Indiana	33	258	7.8
Sylvia Fowles, Chicago	17	127	7.5

Assists

	Gm	Ast	Avg
Lindsay Whalen, Connecticut	31	166	5.36
Ticha Penicheiro, Sacramento	32	166	5.19
Sue Bird, Seattle	33	169	5.12

Blocks

	Gm	Blk	Avg
Lisa Leslie, Los Angeles	33	97	2.94
Candace Parker, Los Angeles	33	75	2.27
Sylvia Fowles, Chicago	17	36	2.12

WNBA Playoffs

First Round (Best of 3)

Western Conference

(1) San Antonio vs. (4) Sacramento

Sept. 18 San Antonio 85 . . . . .at Sacramento 78
Sept. 21 Sacramento 84 . . . . .at San Antonio 67
Sept. 23 at San Antonio 86 . . . . .Sacramento 81
San Antonio wins series, 2-1

(2) Seattle vs. (3) Los Angeles

Sept. 20 at Los Angeles 77 . . . . .Seattle 69
Sept. 21 at Seattle 64 . . . . .Los Angeles 50
Sept. 23 Los Angeles 71 . . . . .at Seattle 64
Los Angeles wins series, 2-1

Eastern Conference

(1) Detroit vs. (4) Indiana

Sept. 19 Detroit 81 . . . . .at Indiana 72
Sept. 21 Indiana 89 . . . . .at Detroit 82
Sept. 23 at Detroit 80 . . . . .Indiana 61
Detroit wins series, 2-1

(2) Connecticut vs. (3) New York

Sept. 18 New York 72 . . . . .Connecticut 63
Sept. 20 at Connecticut 73 . . . . .New York 70
Sept. 22 New York 66 . . . . .at Connecticut 62
New York wins series, 2-1

Conference Finals (Best of 3)

Eastern

(1) Detroit vs. (3) New York

Sept. 26 at New York 60 . . . . .Detroit 56
Sept. 28 at Detroit 64 . . . . .New York 55
Sept. 29 at Detroit 75 . . . . .New York 73
Detroit wins series, 2-1

Western

(1) San Antonio vs. (3) Los Angeles

Sept. 25 at Los Angeles 85 . . . . .San Antonio 70
Sept. 27 at San Antonio 67 . . . . .Los Angeles 66
Sept. 28 at San Antonio 76 . . . . .Los Angeles 72
San Antonio wins series, 2-1

WNBA Finals (Best of 5)

Detroit vs. San Antonio

Detroit wins series, 3 games to 0

	W-L	Avg	Leading Scorer
S. Antonio Silver Stars	0-3	63.3	Wauters (16.0 ppg)
Detroit Shock	3-0	74.0	Smith (21.7 ppg)

Date		Winner	Home Court
Oct. 1	Shock, 77-69		at San Antonio
Oct. 3	Shock, 69-61		at San Antonio
Oct. 5	Shock, 76-60		at Detroit

Finals MVP: Katie Smith, Detroit, G (21.7 ppg, 6.7 rpg, 3.3 apg).

2008 WNBA Draft
First Round

Pick	Team	Player, College, Pos
1	Los Angeles	Candace Parker, Tennessee, F
2	Chicago	Sylvia Fowles, LSU, C
3	Minnesota	Candice Wiggins, Stanford, G
4	Detroit	Alexis Hornbuckle, Tennessee, G
5	Houston	Matee Ajavon, Rutgers, G
6	Washington	Crystal Langhorne, Maryland, F
7	New York	Essence Carson, Rutgers, G/F
8	Atlanta	Tamera Young, J. Madison, F
9	Connecticut	Amber Holt, Mid. Tenn St., F
10	Sacramento	Laura Harper, Maryland, F
11	Detroit	Tasha Humphrey, Georgia, F
12	Connecticut	Ketia Swanier, Connecticut, G
13	Phoenix	LaToya Pringle, N. Carolina, F
14	New York	Erlana Larkins, N. Carolina, F

Annual Awards

Most Valuable Player . . . . .Candace Parker, L.A., F
Rookie of the Year . . . . . . .Candace Parker, L.A., F
Most Improved . . . . .Ebony Hoffman, Ind., F
Def. Player of the Year . . . . . . .Lisa Leslie, L.A., C
Sixth Woman . . . . .Candice Wiggins, Minn., G
Coach of the Year . . . . .Mike Thibault, Conn.
Kim Perrot Sportsmanship Award . . . . .Vickie Johnson, S.A., G

All-WNBA First Team

Holdover from 2006-07 team is in **bold** type.

Pos		Pts
F	Candace Parker, Los Angeles	221
C	Lisa Leslie, Los Angeles	192
G	Lindsay Whalen, Connecticut	178
F	**Diana Taurasi, Phoenix**	178
F	Sophia Young, San Antonio	171

1938-2008
Through the Years

SPORTS ALMANAC

The NBA Finals

Although the National Basketball Association traces its first championship back to the 1946-47 season, the league was then called the Basketball Association of America (BAA). It did not become the NBA until after the 1948-49 season when the BAA and the National Basketball League (NBL) agreed to merge.

In the chart below, the Eastern finalists (representing the NBA Eastern Division from 1947-70, and the NBA Eastern Conference since 1971) are listed in CAPITAL letters. Also, each NBA champion's wins and losses are noted in parentheses after the series score.

Multiple winners: Boston (17); Minneapolis-LA Lakers (14); Chicago Bulls (6); San Antonio (4); Detroit, Phi-SF-Golden St. Warriors and Syracuse Nationals-Phi. 76ers (3); Houston and New York (2).

Year	Winner	Head Coach	Series	Loser	Head Coach
1947	PHILADELPHIA WARRIORS	Eddie Gottlieb	4-1 (WWWLW)	Chicago Stags	Harold Olsen
1948	Baltimore Bullets	Buddy Jeannette	4-2 (LWWWLW)	PHILA. WARRIORS	Eddie Gottlieb
1949	Minneapolis Lakers	John Kundla	4-2 (WWWLLW)	WASH. CAPITOLS	Red Auerbach
1950	Minneapolis Lakers	John Kundla	4-2 (WLWWLW)	SYRACUSE	Al Cervi
1951	Rochester	Les Harrison	4-3 (WWWLLLW)	NEW YORK	Joe Lapchick
1952	Minneapolis Lakers	John Kundla	4-3 (WLWLWLW)	NEW YORK	Joe Lapchick
1953	Minneapolis Lakers	John Kundla	4-1 (LWWWW)	NEW YORK	Joe Lapchick
1954	Minneapolis Lakers	John Kundla	4-3 (WLWWLLW)	SYRACUSE	Al Cervi
1955	SYRACUSE	Al Cervi	4-3 (WWLLLWW)	Ft. Wayne Pistons	Charley Eckman
1956	PHILADELPHIA WARRIORS	George Senesky	4-1 (WLWWW)	Ft. Wayne Pistons	Charley Eckman
1957	BOSTON	Red Auerbach	4-3 (WLWLWLW)	St. Louis Hawks	Alex Hannum
1958	St. Louis Hawks	Alex Hannum	4-2 (WLWLWW)	BOSTON	Red Auerbach
1959	BOSTON	Red Auerbach	4-0	Mpls. Lakers	John Kundla
1960	BOSTON	Red Auerbach	4-3 (WLWLWLW)	St. Louis Hawks	Ed Macauley
1961	BOSTON	Red Auerbach	4-1 (WWLWW)	St. Louis Hawks	Paul Seymour
1962	BOSTON	Red Auerbach	4-3 (WLLWLWW)	LA Lakers	Fred Schaus
1963	BOSTON	Red Auerbach	4-2 (WWLWLW)	LA Lakers	Fred Schaus
1964	BOSTON	Red Auerbach	4-1 (WWLWW)	SF Warriors	Alex Hannum
1965	BOSTON	Red Auerbach	4-1 (WWLWW)	LA Lakers	Fred Schaus
1966	BOSTON	Red Auerbach	4-3 (LWWWLLW)	LA Lakers	Fred Schaus
1967	PHILADELPHIA 76ERS	Alex Hannum	4-2 (WLWWLW)	SF Warriors	Bill Sharman
1968	BOSTON	Bill Russell	4-2 (LWLWLW)	LA Lakers	B.van Breda Kolff
1969	BOSTON	Bill Russell	4-3 (LLWWLWW)	LA Lakers	B.van Breda Kolff
1970	NEW YORK	Red Holzman	4-3 (WLWLWLW)	LA Lakers	Joe Mullaney
1971	Milwaukee	Larry Costello	4-0	BALT. BULLETS	Gene Shue
1972	LA Lakers	Bill Sharman	4-1 (LWWWW)	NEW YORK	Red Holzman
1973	NEW YORK	Red Holzman	4-1 (LWWWW)	LA Lakers	Bill Sharman
1974	BOSTON	Tommy Heinsohn	4-3 (WLWLWLW)	Milwaukee	Larry Costello
1975	Golden St. Warriors	Al Attles	4-0	WASH. BULLETS	K.C. Jones
1976	BOSTON	Tommy Heinsohn	4-2 (WWLLWW)	Phoenix	John MacLeod
1977	Portland	Jack Ramsay	4-2 (LLWWWW)	PHILA. 76ERS	Gene Shue
1978	WASHINGTON BULLETS	Dick Motta	4-3 (LWLWLWW)	Seattle	Lenny Wilkens
1979	Seattle	Lenny Wilkens	4-1 (LWWWW)	WASH. BULLETS	Dick Motta
1980	LA Lakers	Paul Westhead	4-2 (WLWLWW)	PHILA. 76ERS	Billy Cunningham
1981	BOSTON	Bill Fitch	4-2 (WLWLWW)	Houston	Del Harris
1982	LA Lakers	Pat Riley	4-2 (WLWLWW)	PHILA. 76ERS	Billy Cunningham
1983	PHILADELPHIA 76ERS	Billy Cunningham	4-0	LA Lakers	Pat Riley
1984	BOSTON	K.C. Jones	4-3 (LWLWLWW)	LA Lakers	Pat Riley
1985	LA Lakers	Pat Riley	4-2 (LWWWLW)	BOSTON	K.C. Jones
1986	BOSTON	K.C. Jones	4-2 (WWWLVW)	Houston	Bill Fitch
1987	LA Lakers	Pat Riley	4-2 (WWLWLW)	BOSTON	K.C. Jones
1988	LA Lakers	Pat Riley	4-3 (LWWLLWW)	DETROIT PISTONS	Chuck Daly
1989	DETROIT	Chuck Daly	4-0	LA Lakers	Pat Riley
1990	DETROIT	Chuck Daly	4-1 (WLWWW)	Portland	Rick Adelman
1991	CHICAGO	Phil Jackson	4-1 (LWWWW)	LA Lakers	Mike Dunleavy
1992	CHICAGO	Phil Jackson	4-2 (WLWW)	Portland	Rick Adelman
1993	CHICAGO	Phil Jackson	4-2 (WWWLWLW)	Phoenix	Paul Westphal
1994	Houston	Rudy Tomjanovich	4-3 (WLWLLWW)	NEW YORK	Pat Riley
1995	Houston	Rudy Tomjanovich	4-0	ORLANDO	Brian Hill
1996	CHICAGO	Phil Jackson	4-2 (WWWLLW)	Seattle	George Karl
1997	CHICAGO	Phil Jackson	4-2 (WWLWWW)	Utah	Jerry Sloan
1998	CHICAGO	Phil Jackson	4-2 (LWWWLW)	Utah	Jerry Sloan

The NBA Finals (Cont.)

Year	Winner	Head Coach	Series	Loser	Head Coach
1999	San Antonio	Gregg Popovich	4-1 (WWLWW)	NEW YORK	Jeff Van Gundy
2000	LA Lakers	Phil Jackson	4-2 (WWLWLW)	INDIANA	Larry Bird
2001	LA Lakers	Phil Jackson	4-1 (LWWW)	PHILA. 76ERS	Larry Brown
2002	LA Lakers	Phil Jackson	4-0	NEW JERSEY	Byron Scott
2003	San Antonio	Gregg Popovich	4-2 (WLWLWW)	NEW JERSEY	Byron Scott
2004	DETROIT	Larry Brown	4-1 (WLWWW)	LA Lakers	Phil Jackson
2005	San Antonio	Gregg Popovich	4-3 (WWLLWLW)	DETROIT	Larry Brown
2006	MIAMI	Pat Riley	4-2 (LLWWWW)	Dallas	Avery Johnson
2007	San Antonio	Gregg Popovich	4-0	Cleveland	Mike Brown
2008	BOSTON	Doc Rivers	4-2 (WWLWLW)	LA Lakers	Phil Jackson

Note: Four finalists were led by player-coaches: **1948**—Buddy Jeannette (guard) of Baltimore; **1950**—Al Cervi (guard) of Syracuse; **1968**—Bill Russell (center) of Boston; **1969**—Bill Russell (center) of Boston.

Finals Most Valuable Player

Winner who did not play for the NBA champion is in **bold** type.

Multiple winners: Michael Jordan (6); Tim Duncan, Magic Johnson and Shaquille O'Neal (3); Kareem Abdul-Jabbar, Larry Bird, Hakeem Olajuwon and Willis Reed (2).

Year		Year		Year	
1969	**Jerry West**, LA Lakers, G	1983	Moses Malone, Philadelphia, C	1997	Michael Jordan, Chicago, G
1970	Willis Reed, New York, C	1984	Larry Bird, Boston, F	1998	Michael Jordan, Chicago, G
1971	Lew Alcindor, Milwaukee, C	1985	K. Abdul-Jabbar, LA Lakers, C	1999	Tim Duncan, San Antonio, F/C
1972	Wilt Chamberlain, LA Lakers, C	1986	Larry Bird, Boston, F	2000	Shaquille O'Neal, LA Lakers, C
1973	Willis Reed, New York, C	1987	Magic Johnson, LA Lakers, G	2001	Shaquille O'Neal, LA Lakers, C
1974	John Havlicek, Boston, F	1988	James Worthy, LA Lakers, F	2002	Shaquille O'Neal, LA Lakers, C
1975	Rick Barry, Golden State, F	1989	Joe Dumars, Detroit, G	2003	Tim Duncan, San Antonio, F/C
1976	Jo Jo White, Boston, G	1990	Isiah Thomas, Detroit, G	2004	Chauncey Billups, Detroit, G
1977	Bill Walton, Portland, C	1991	Michael Jordan, Chicago, G	2005	Tim Duncan, San Antonio, F/C
1978	Wes Unseld, Washington, C	1992	Michael Jordan, Chicago, G	2006	Dwyane Wade, Miami, G
1979	Dennis Johnson, Seattle, G	1993	Michael Jordan, Chicago, G	2007	Tony Parker, San Antonio, G
1980	Magic Johnson, LA Lakers, G/C	1994	Hakeem Olajuwon, Houston, C	2008	Paul Pierce, Boston, F
1981	Cedric Maxwell, Boston, F	1995	Hakeem Olajuwon, Houston, C		
1982	Magic Johnson, LA Lakers, G	1996	Michael Jordan, Chicago, G		

Note: Lew Alcindor changed his name to Kareem Abdul-Jabbar after the 1970-71 season.

All-Time NBA Playoff Leaders

CAREER

Years listed indicate number of playoff appearances. Players active in 2008 in **bold** type. DNP indicates player that was active in 2008 but did not participate in playoffs.

Points

		Yrs	Gm	Pts	Avg
1	Michael Jordan	13	179	**5987**	33.4
2	Kareem Abdul-Jabbar	18	237	**5762**	24.3
3	**Shaquille O'Neal**	15	203	**5121**	25.2
4	Karl Malone	19	193	**4761**	24.7
5	Jerry West	13	153	**4457**	29.1
6	Larry Bird	12	164	**3897**	23.8
7	John Havlicek	13	172	**3776**	22.0
8	Hakeem Olajuwon	15	145	**3755**	25.9
9	Magic Johnson	13	190	**3701**	19.5
10	**Kobe Bryant**	11	152	**3686**	24.2
11	Scottie Pippen	16	208	**3642**	17.5
12	Elgin Baylor	12	134	**3623**	27.0
13	Wilt Chamberlain	13	160	**3607**	22.5
14	**Tim Duncan**	10	155	**3625**	23.4
15	Kevin McHale	13	169	**3182**	18.8
16	Dennis Johnson	13	180	**3116**	17.3
17	Julius Erving	11	141	**3088**	21.9
18	James Worthy	9	143	**3022**	21.1
19	Reggie Miller	15	144	**2972**	20.6
20	Clyde Drexler	15	145	**2963**	20.4

Scoring Average

Minimum of 25 games or 700 points.

		Yrs	Gm	Pts	Avg
1	Michael Jordan	13	179	5987	33.4
2	**Allen Iverson**	8	71	2111	29.7
3	Jerry West	13	153	4457	29.1
4	**Tracy McGrady**	7	38	1084	28.5
5	**LeBron James**	3	46	1267	27.5
6	Elgin Baylor	12	134	3623	27.0
7	George Gervin	9	59	1592	27.0
8	Hakeem Olajuwon	15	145	3755	25.9
9	**Vince Carter** (DNP)	6	42	1086	25.9
10	Bob Pettit	9	88	2240	25.5
11	Dominique Wilkins	10	56	1423	25.4
12	**Dirk Nowitzki**	10	87	2204	25.3
13	**Dwyane Wade** (DNP)	4	54	1366	25.3
14	**Shaquille O'Neal**	15	203	5121	25.2
15	**Amare Stoudemire**	4	36	903	25.1
16	Rick Barry	7	74	1833	24.8
17	Karl Malone	19	193	4761	24.7
18	Bernard King	5	28	687	24.5
19	Alex English	10	68	1661	24.4
20	Kareem Abdul-Jabbar	18	237	5762	24.3

Field Goals

		Yrs	FG	Att	Pct
1	Kareem Abdul-Jabbar	18	**2356**	4422	.533
2	Michael Jordan	13	**2188**	4497	.487
3	**Shaquille O'Neal**	15	**1992**	3532	.564
4	Karl Malone	19	**1743**	3768	.463
5	Jerry West	13	**1622**	3460	.469

Free Throws

		Yrs	FT	Att	Pct
1	Michael Jordan	13	**1463**	1766	.828
2	Karl Malone	19	**1269**	1725	.736
3	Jerry West	13	**1213**	1507	.805
4	**Shaquille O'Neal**	15	**1137**	2268	.501
5	Kareem Abdul-Jabbar	18	**1050**	1419	.740

Assists

		Yrs	Gm	No	Avg
1	Magic Johnson	13	190	**2346**	12.3
2	John Stockton	19	182	**1839**	10.1
3	Larry Bird	12	164	**1062**	6.5
4	Scottie Pippen	16	208	**1048**	5.0
5	Michael Jordan	13	179	**1022**	5.7

Rebounds

		Yrs	Gm	No	Avg
1	Bill Russell	13	165	**4104**	24.9
2	Wilt Chamberlain	13	160	**3913**	24.5
3	Kareem Abdul-Jabbar	18	237	**2481**	10.5
4	**Shaquille O'Neal**	15	203	**2447**	12.1
5	Karl Malone	19	193	**2062**	10.7

Steals

	No
Scottie Pippen	395
Michael Jordan	376
Magic Johnson	358
John Stockton	338
Larry Bird	296
Maurice Cheeks	295
Clyde Drexler	278

Blocks

	No
Hakeem Olajuwon	472
Shaquille O'Neal	446
Tim Duncan	415
K. Abdul-Jabbar	399
David Robinson	312
Patrick Ewing	303
Robert Parish	298

Games Played

	No		No
Robert Horry	244	Byron Scott	183
K. Abdul-Jabbar	237	John Stockton	182
Scottie Pippen	208	Dennis Johnson	180
Shaquille O'Neal	203	Michael Jordan	179
Danny Ainge	193	John Havlicek	172
Karl Malone	193	Horace Grant	170
Magic Johnson	190	Kevin McHale	169
Robert Parish	184	Dennis Rodman	169

SINGLE GAME

Points

	Date	FG-FT–Pts
Michael Jordan, Chi at Bos*	4/20/86	22-19-63
Elgin Baylor, LA at Bos	4/14/62	22-17–61
Wilt Chamberlain, Phi vs Syr	3/22/62	22-12–56
Michael Jordan, Chi at Mia	4/29/92	20-16-56
Charles Barkley, Pho vs G.St.	5/4/94	23- 7–56
Rick Barry, SF vs Phi	4/18/67	22-11–55
Michael Jordan, Chi vs Cle	5/1/88	24- 7–55
Michael Jordan, Chi vs Pho	4/16/93	21-13–55
Michael Jordan, Chi vs. Wash	4/27/97	22-10–55

*Double overtime.

Field Goals

	Date	FG	Att
Wilt Chamberlain, Phi vs Syr	3/14/60	24	42
John Havlicek, Bos vs Atl	4/1/73	24	36
Michael Jordan, Chi vs Cle	5/1/88	24	45

Eight tied with 22 each.

Miscellaneous

3-Pt Field Goals

	Date	No
Rex Chapman, Pho at Sea	4/25/97	9
Dan Majerle, Pho vs Sea	6/1/93	8
Allen Iverson, Phi vs Tor	5/16/01	8

Nine tied with 7 each.

Assists

	Date	No
Magic Johnson, LA vs Pho	5/15/84	24
John Stockton, Utah at LA Lakers	5/17/88	24
Magic Johnson, LA Lakers at Port	5/3/85	23
John Stockton, Utah vs Port	4/25/96	23
Doc Rivers, Atl vs Bos	5/16/88	22

Four tied with 21 each.

Rebounds

	Date	No
Wilt Chamberlain, Phi vs Bos	4/5/67	41
Bill Russell, Bos vs Phi	3/23/58	40
Bill Russell, Bos vs St.L	3/29/60	40
Bill Russell, Bos vs LA*	4/18/62	40

Three tied with 39 each.

*Overtime.

NBA FINALS

Points

Series		Year	Pts
4-Gm	Shaquille O'Neal, LAL vs NJ	2002	145
5-Gm	Allen Iverson, Phi vs LAL	2001	178
6-Gm	Michael Jordan, Chi vs Pho	1993	246
7-Gm	Elgin Baylor, LA vs Bos	1962	284

Field Goals

Series		Year	No
4-Gm	Hakeem Olajuwon, Hou vs Orl	1995	56
5-Gm	Allen Iverson, Phi vs LAL	2001	66
6-Gm	Michael Jordan, Chi vs Pho	1993	101
7-Gm	Elgin Baylor, LA vs Bos	1962	101

Assists

Series		Year	No
4-Gm	Bob Cousy, Bos vs Mpls	1959	51
5-Gm	Magic Johnson, LAL vs Chi	1991	62
6-Gm	Magic Johnson, LAL vs Bos	1985	84
7-Gm	Magic Johnson, LA vs Bos	1984	95

Rebounds

Series		Year	No
4-Gm	Bill Russell, Bos vs Mpls	1959	118
5-Gm	Bill Russell, Bos vs St.L	1961	144
6-Gm	Wilt Chamberlain, Phi vs SF	1967	171
7-Gm	Bill Russell, Bos vs LA	1962	189

Appearances in NBA Finals

Standings of all NBA teams that have reached the NBA Finals since 1947.

App		Titles	Last Won
29	Minneapolis-LA Lakers	14	2002
20	Boston Celtics	17	2008
9	Syracuse Nats-Phila. 76ers	3	1983
8	New York Knicks	2	1973
7	Ft. Wayne-Detroit Pistons	3	2004
6	Chicago Bulls	6	1998
6	Phila-SF-Golden St. Warriors	3	1975
6	Houston Rockets	2	1995
4	St. Louis Hawks	1	1958
4	Baltimore-Washington Bullets	1	1978
4	San Antonio Spurs	4	2007
3	Portland Trail Blazers	1	1977
3	Seattle SuperSonics	1	1979
2	Milwaukee Bucks	1	1971
2	New Jersey Nets	0	—
2	Phoenix Suns	0	—
2	Utah Jazz	0	—
1	Baltimore Bullets	1	1948
1	Rochester Royals	1	1951
1	Miami Heat	1	2006
1	Cleveland Cavaliers	0	—
1	Chicago Stags	0	—
1	Orlando Magic	0	—
1	Washington Capitols	0	—
1	Indiana Pacers	0	—

Change of address: The St. Louis Hawks now play in Atlanta, the Rochester Royals are now the Sacramento Kings and the Seattle SuperSonics are now the Oklahoma City Thunder.

Teams now defunct: Baltimore Bullets (1947-55), Chicago Stags (1946-50) and Washington Capitols (1946-51).

NBA All-Star Game

The NBA staged its first All-Star Game before 10,094 at Boston Garden on March 2, 1951. From that year on, the game has matched the best players in the East against the best in the West. Winning coaches are listed first. East leads series, 35-22.

Multiple MVP winners: Bob Pettit (4); Michael Jordan and Oscar Robertson (3); Kobe Bryant, Bob Cousy, Julius Erving, Allen Iverson, LeBron James, Magic Johnson, Karl Malone, Shaquille O'Neal and Isiah Thomas (2).

Year		Host	Coaches	Most Valuable Player
1951	East 111, West 94	Boston	Joe Lapchick, John Kundla	Ed Macauley, Boston
1952	East 108, West 91	Boston	Al Cervi, John Kundla	Paul Arizin, Philadelphia
1953	West 79, East 75	Ft. Wayne	John Kundla, Joe Lapchick	George Mikan, Minneapolis
1954	East 98, West 93 (OT)	New York	Joe Lapchick, John Kundla	Bob Cousy, Boston
1955	East 100, West 91	New York	Al Cervi, Charley Eckman	Bill Sharman, Boston
1956	West 108, East 94	Rochester	Charley Eckman, George Senesky	Bob Pettit, St. Louis
1957	East 109, West 97	Boston	Red Auerbach, Bobby Wanzer	Bob Cousy, Boston
1958	East 130, West 118	St. Louis	Red Auerbach, Alex Hannum	Bob Pettit, St. Louis
1959	West 124, East 108	Detroit	Ed Macauley, Red Auerbach	Bob Pettit, St. Louis & Elgin Baylor, Minneapolis
1960	East 125, West 115	Philadelphia	Red Auerbach, Ed Macauley	Wilt Chamberlain, Philadelphia
1961	West 153, East 131	Syracuse	Paul Seymour, Red Auerbach	Oscar Robertson, Cincinnati
1962	West 150, East 130	St. Louis	Fred Schaus, Red Auerbach	Bob Pettit, St. Louis
1963	East 115, West 108	Los Angeles	Red Auerbach, Fred Schaus	Bill Russell, Boston
1964	East 111, West 107	Boston	Red Auerbach, Fred Schaus	Oscar Robertson, Cincinnati
1965	East 124, West 123	St. Louis	Red Auerbach, Alex Hannum	Jerry Lucas, Cincinnati
1966	East 137, West 94	Cincinnati	Red Auerbach, Fred Schaus	Adrian Smith, Cincinnati
1967	West 135, East 120	San Francisco	Fred Schaus, Red Auerbach	Rick Barry, San Francisco
1968	East 144, West 124	New York	Alex Hannum, Bill Sharman	Hal Greer, Philadelphia
1969	East 123, West 112	Baltimore	Gene Shue, Richie Guerin	Oscar Robertson, Cincinnati
1970	East 142, West 135	Philadelphia	Red Holzman, Richie Guerin	Willis Reed, New York
1971	West 108, East 107	San Diego	Larry Costello, Red Holzman	Lenny Wilkens, Seattle
1972	West 112, East 110	Los Angeles	Bill Sharman, Tom Heinsohn	Jerry West, Los Angeles
1973	East 104, West 84	Chicago	Tom Heinsohn, Bill Sharman	Dave Cowens, Boston
1974	West 134, East 123	Seattle	Larry Costello, Tom Heinsohn	Bob Lanier, Detroit
1975	East 108, West 102	Phoenix	K.C. Jones, Al Attles	Walt Frazier, New York
1976	East 123, West 109	Philadelphia	Tom Heinsohn, Al Attles	Dave Bing, Washington
1977	West 125, East 124	Milwaukee	Larry Brown, Gene Shue	Julius Erving, Philadelphia
1978	East 133, West 125	Atlanta	Billy Cunningham, Jack Ramsay	Randy Smith, Buffalo
1979	West 134, East 129	Detroit	Lenny Wilkens, Dick Motta	David Thompson, Denver
1980	East 144, West 136 (OT)	Washington	Billy Cunningham, Lenny Wilkens	George Gervin, San Antonio
1981	East 123, West 120	Cleveland	Billy Cunningham, John MacLeod	Nate Archibald, Boston
1982	East 120, West 118	New Jersey	Bill Fitch, Pat Riley	Larry Bird, Boston
1983	East 132, West 123	Los Angeles	Billy Cunningham, Pat Riley	Julius Erving, Philadelphia
1984	East 154, West 145 (OT)	Denver	K.C. Jones, Frank Layden	Isiah Thomas, Detroit
1985	West 140, East 129	Indiana	Pat Riley, K.C. Jones	Ralph Sampson, Houston
1986	West 139, East 132	Dallas	K.C. Jones, Pat Riley	Isiah Thomas, Detroit
1987	West 154, East 149 (OT)	Seattle	Pat Riley, K.C. Jones	Tom Chambers, Seattle
1988	East 138, West 133	Chicago	Mike Fratello, Pat Riley	Michael Jordan, Chicago
1989	West 143, East 134	Houston	Pat Riley, Lenny Wilkens	Karl Malone, Utah
1990	East 130, West 113	Miami	Chuck Daly, Pat Riley	Magic Johnson, LA Lakers
1991	East 116, West 114	Charlotte	Chris Ford, Rick Adelman	Charles Barkley, Philadelphia
1992	West 153, East 113	Orlando	Don Nelson, Phil Jackson	Magic Johnson, LA Lakers
1993	West 135, East 132 (OT)	Salt Lake City	Paul Westphal, Pat Riley	Karl Malone, Utah & John Stockton, Utah
1994	East 127, West 118	Minneapolis	Lenny Wilkens, George Karl	Scottie Pippen, Chicago
1995	West 139, East 112	Phoenix	Paul Westphal, Brian Hill	Mitch Richmond, Sacramento
1996	East 129, West 118	San Antonio	Phil Jackson, George Karl	Michael Jordan, Chicago
1997	East 132, West 120	Cleveland	Doug Collins, Rudy Tomjanovich	Glen Rice, Charlotte
1998	East 135, West 114	New York	Larry Bird, George Karl	Michael Jordan, Chicago
1999	Not held–due to lockout			
2000	West 137, East 126	Oakland	Phil Jackson, Jeff Van Gundy	Tim Duncan, San Antonio & Shaquille O'Neal, LA Lakers
2001	East 111, West 110	Washington	Larry Brown, Rick Adelman	Allen Iverson, Philadelphia
2002	West 135, East 120	Philadelphia	Don Nelson, Byron Scott	Kobe Bryant, LA Lakers
2003	West 155, East 145 (2 OT)	Atlanta	Rick Adelman, Isiah Thomas	Kevin Garnett, Minnesota
2004	West 136, East 132	Los Angeles	Flip Saunders, Rick Carlisle	Shaquille O'Neal, LA Lakers
2005	East 125, West 115	Denver	Stan Van Gundy, Gregg Popovich	Allen Iverson, Philadelphia
2006	East 122, West 120	Houston	Flip Saunders, Avery Johnson	LeBron James, Cleveland
2007	West 153, East 132	Las Vegas	Mike D'Antoni, Eddie Jordan	Kobe Bryant, LA Lakers
2008	East 134, West 128	New Orleans	Doc Rivers, Byron Scott	LeBron James, Cleveland

NBA Franchise Origins

Here is what the current 30 teams in the National Basketball Association have to show for the years they have put in as members of the National Basketball League (NBL), Basketball Association of America (BAA), the NBA, and the American Basketball Association (ABA). League titles are noted by year won.

Western Conference

	First Season	League Titles	Franchise Stops
Dallas Mavericks	1980-81 (NBA)	None	•Dallas (1980–)
Denver Nuggets	1967-68 (ABA)	None	•Denver (1967–)
Golden St. Warriors	1946-47 (BAA)	1 BAA (1947)	•Philadelphia (1946-62)
		2 NBA (1956, 75)	San Francisco (1962-71)
			Oakland (1971–)
Houston Rockets	1967-68 (NBA)	2 NBA (1994-95)	•San Diego (1967-71)
			Houston (1971–)
Los Angeles Clippers	1970-71 (NBA)	None	•Buffalo (1970-78)
			San Diego (1978-84)
			Los Angeles (1984–)
Los Angeles Lakers	1947-48 (NBL)	1 NBL (1948)	•Minneapolis (1947-60)
		1 BAA (1949)	Los Angeles (1960-67)
		14 NBA (1950,52-54,72,	Inglewood, CA (1967-99)
		80,82,85,87-88,00-02)	Los Angeles (1999–)
Memphis Grizzlies	1995-96 (NBA)	None	•Vancouver (1995-01)
			Memphis, TN (2001–)
Minnesota Timberwolves	1989-90 (NBA)	None	•Minneapolis (1989–)
New Orleans Hornets	1988-89 (NBA)	None	•Charlotte (1988-2002)
			New Orleans (2002–)
			Oklahoma City (2005-07)
Oklahoma City Thunder	1967-68 (NBA)	1 NBA (1979)	•Seattle (1967-2008)
			Oklahoma City (2008–)
Phoenix Suns	1968-69 (NBA)	None	•Phoenix (1968–)
Portland Trail Blazers	1970-71 (NBA)	1 NBA (1977)	•Portland (1970–)
Sacramento Kings	1945-46 (NBL)	1 NBL (1946)	•Rochester, NY (1945-58)
		1 NBA (1951)	Cincinnati (1958-72)
			KC-Omaha (1972-75)
			Kansas City (1975-85)
			Sacramento (1985–)
San Antonio Spurs	1967-68 (ABA)	4 NBA (1999,2003,05,07)	•Dallas (1967-73)
			San Antonio (1973–)
Utah Jazz	1974-75 (NBA)	None	•New Orleans (1974-79)
			Salt Lake City (1979–)

Eastern Conference

	First Season	League Titles	Franchise Stops
Atlanta Hawks	1946-47 (NBL)	1 NBA (1958)	•Tri-Cities (1946-51)
			Milwaukee (1951-55)
			St. Louis (1955-68)
			Atlanta (1968–)
Boston Celtics	1946-47 (BAA)	17 NBA (1957,59-66,68-69	•Boston (1946–)
		74,76,81,84,86, 2008)	
Charlotte Bobcats	2004-05 (NBA)	None	•Charlotte (2004–)
Chicago Bulls	1966-67 (NBA)	6 NBA (1991-93,96-98)	•Chicago (1966–)
Cleveland Cavaliers	1970-71 (NBA)	None	•Cleveland (1970-74)
			Richfield, OH (1974-94)
			Cleveland (1994–)
Detroit Pistons	1941-42 (NBL)	2 NBL (1944-45)	•Ft. Wayne, IN (1941-57)
		3 NBA (1989-90, 2004)	Detroit (1957-78)
			Pontiac, MI (1978-88)
			Auburn Hills, MI (1988–)
Indiana Pacers	1967-68 (ABA)	3 ABA (1970,72-73)	•Indianapolis (1967–)
Miami Heat	1988-89 (NBA)	1 NBA (2006)	•Miami (1988–)
Milwaukee Bucks	1968-69 (NBA)	1 NBA (1971)	•Milwaukee (1968–)
New Jersey Nets	1967-68 (ABA)	2 ABA (1974,76)	•Teaneck, NJ (1967-68)
			Commack, NY (1968-69)
			W. Hempstead, NY (1969-71)
			Uniondale, NY (1971-77)
			Piscataway, NJ (1977-81)
			E. Rutherford, NJ (1981–)
New York Knicks	1946-47 (BAA)	2 NBA (1970,73)	•New York (1946–)
Orlando Magic	1989-90 (NBA)	None	•Orlando, FL (1989–)
Philadelphia 76ers	1949-50 (NBA)	3 NBA (1955,67,83)	•Syracuse, NY (1949-63)
			Philadelphia (1963–)
Toronto Raptors	1995-96 (NBA)	None	•Toronto (1995–)
Washington Wizards	1961-62 (NBA)	1 NBA (1978)	•Chicago (1961-63)
			Baltimore (1963-73)
			Landover, MD (1973–)

Note: The Tri-Cities Blackhawks represented Moline and Rock Island, Ill., and Davenport, Iowa.

The Growth of the NBA

Of the 11 franchises that comprised the Basketball Association of America (BAA) at the start of the 1946-47 season, only three remain—the Boston Celtics, New York Knickerbockers and Golden State Warriors (originally Philadelphia Warriors).

Just before the start of the 1948-49 season, four teams from the more established **National Basketball League** (NBL)—the Ft. Wayne Pistons (now Detroit), Indianapolis Jets, Minneapolis Lakers (now Los Angeles) and Rochester Royals (now Sacramento Kings)—joined the BAA.

A year later, the six remaining NBL franchises—Anderson (Ind.), Denver, Sheboygan (Wisc.), the Syracuse Nationals (now Philadelphia 76ers), Tri-Cities Blackhawks (now Atlanta Hawks) and Waterloo (Iowa)—joined along with the new Indianapolis Olympians and the BAA became the 17-team **National Basketball Association**.

The NBA was down to 10 teams by the 1950-51 season and slipped to eight by 1954-55 with Boston, New York, Philadelphia and Syracuse in the Eastern Division, and Ft. Wayne, Milwaukee (formerly Tri-Cities), Minneapolis and Rochester in the West.

By 1960, five of those surviving eight teams had moved to other cities but by the end of the decade the NBA was a 14-team league. It also had a rival, the **American Basketball Association**, which began play in 1967 with a red, white and blue ball, a three-point line and 11 teams. After a nine-year run, the ABA merged four clubs—the Denver Nuggets, Indiana Pacers, New York Nets and San Antonio Spurs—with the NBA following the 1975-76 season. The NBA adopted the three-point shot in 1979-80.

Expansion/Merger Timetable

For teams currently in NBA.

1948—Added NBL's Ft. Wayne Pistons (now Detroit), Minneapolis Lakers (now Los Angeles) and Rochester Royals (now Sacramento Kings); **1949**—Syracuse Nationals (now Philadelphia 76ers) and Tri-Cities Blackhawks (now Atlanta Hawks). **1961**—Chicago Packers (now Washington Wizards); **1966**—Chicago Bulls; **1967**—San Diego Rockets (now Houston) and Seattle SuperSonics; **1968**—Milwaukee Bucks and Phoenix Suns.

1970—Buffalo Braves (now Los Angeles Clippers), Cleveland Cavaliers and Portland Trail Blazers; **1974**—New Orleans Jazz (now Utah); **1976**—added ABA's Denver Nuggets, Indiana Pacers, New York Nets (now New Jersey) and San Antonio Spurs.

1980—Dallas Mavericks; **1988**—Charlotte Hornets and Miami Heat; **1989**—Minnesota Timberwolves and Orlando Magic.

1995—Toronto Raptors and Vancouver Grizzlies (Now Memphis).

2004—Charlotte Bobcats.

City and Nickname Changes

1951—Tri-Cities Blackhawks, who divided home games between Moline and Rock Island, Ill., and Davenport, Iowa, move to Milwaukee and become the Hawks; **1955**—Milwaukee Hawks move to St. Louis; **1957**—Ft. Wayne Pistons move to Detroit, while Rochester Royals move to Cincinnati.

1960—Minneapolis Lakers move to Los Angeles; **1962**—Chicago Packers renamed Zephyrs, while Philadelphia Warriors move to San Francisco; **1963**—Chicago Zephyrs move to Baltimore and become Bullets, while Syracuse Nationals move to Philadelphia and become 76ers; **1968**—St. Louis Hawks move to Atlanta.

1971—San Diego Rockets move to Houston, while San Francisco Warriors move to Oakland and become Golden State Warriors; **1972**—Cincinnati Royals move to Midwest, divide home games between Kansas City, Mo., and Omaha, Neb., and become Kings; **1973**—Baltimore Bullets move to Landover, Md., outside Washington and become Capital Bullets; **1974**—Capital Bullets renamed Washington Bullets; **1975**—KC-Omaha Kings settle in Kansas City; **1977**—New York Nets move from Uniondale, N.Y., to Piscataway, N.J. (later East Rutherford) and become New Jersey Nets; **1978**—Buffalo Braves move to San Diego and become Clippers; **1979**—New Orleans Jazz move to Salt Lake City and become Utah Jazz.

1984—San Diego Clippers move to Los Angeles; **1985**—Kansas City Kings move to Sacramento.

1997—Washington Bullets become Washington Wizards.

2001—Vancouver Grizzlies move to Memphis, Tenn.; **2002**—Charlotte Hornets move to New Orleans; **2005**—New Orleans Hornets become New Orleans/Oklahoma City Hornets and divide home games between New Orleans and Oklahoma City in aftermath of Hurricane Katrina; **2007**—Hornets move back to New Orleans full-time; **2008**—Sonics move to Oklahoma City and become the Oklahoma City Thunder.

Defunct NBA Teams

Teams that once played in the BAA and NBA, but no longer exist.

Anderson (Ind.)—Packers (1949-50); **Baltimore**—Bullets (1947-55); **Chicago**—Stags (1946-50); **Cleveland**—Rebels (1946-47); **Denver**—Nuggets (1949-50); **Detroit**—Falcons (1946-47); **Indianapolis**—Jets (1948-49) and Olympians (1949-53); **Pittsburgh**—Ironmen (1946-47); **Providence**—Steamrollers (1946-49); **St. Louis**—Bombers (1946-50); **Sheboygan (Wisc.)**—Redskins (1949-50); **Toronto**—Huskies (1946-47); **Washington**—Capitols (1946-51); **Waterloo (Iowa)**—Hawks (1949-50).

ABA Teams (1967-76)

Anaheim—Amigos (1967-68, moved to LA); **Baltimore**—Claws (1975, never played); **Carolina**—Cougars (1969-74, moved to St. Louis); **Dallas**—Chaparrals (1967-73, called Texas Chaparrals in 1970-71, moved to San Antonio); **Denver**—Rockets (1967-76, renamed Nuggets in 1974-76); **Miami**—Floridians (1968-72, called simply Floridians from 1970-72).

Houston—Mavericks (1967-69, moved to North Carolina); **Indiana**—Pacers (1967-76); **Kentucky**—Colonels (1967-76); **Los Angeles**—Stars (1968-70, moved to Utah); **Memphis**—Pros (1970-75, renamed Tams in 1972 and Sounds in 1974, moved to Baltimore); **Minnesota**—Muskies (1967-68, moved to Miami) and Pipers (1968-69, moved back to Pittsburgh); **New Jersey**—Americans (1967-68, moved to New York).

New Orleans—Buccaneers (1967-70, moved to Memphis); **New York**—Nets (1968-76); **Oakland**—Oaks (1967-69, moved to Washington); **Pittsburgh**—Pipers (1967-68, moved to Minnesota), Pipers (1969-72, renamed Condors in 1970); **St. Louis**—Spirits of St. Louis (1974-76); **San Antonio**—Spurs (1973-76); **San Diego**—Conquistadors (1972-75, renamed Sails in 1975); **Utah**—Stars (1970-75); **Virginia**—Squires (1970-76); **Washington**—Caps (1969-70, moved to Virginia).

Annual NBA Leaders
Scoring

Decided by total points from 1947-69, and per game average since 1970. A lockout in 1999 shortened the regular season to 50 games.

Multiple winners: Michael Jordan (10); Wilt Chamberlain (7); George Gervin and Allen Iverson (4); Neil Johnston, Bob McAdoo and George Mikan (3); Kareem Abdul-Jabbar, Paul Arizin, Kobe Bryant, Adrian Dantley, Tracy McGrady, Shaquille O'Neal and Bob Pettit (2).

Year		Gm	Pts	Avg	Year		Gm	Pts	Avg
1947	Joe Fulks, Phi	.60	1389	23.2	1979	George Gervin, SA	.80	2365	29.6
1948	Max Zaslofsky, Chi	.48	1007	21.0	1980	George Gervin, SA	.78	2585	33.1
1949	George Mikan, Mpls	.60	1698	28.3	1981	Adrian Dantley, Utah	.80	2452	30.7
1950	George Mikan, Mpls	.68	1865	27.4	1982	George Gervin, SA	.79	2551	32.3
1951	George Mikan, Mpls	.68	1932	28.4	1983	Alex English, Den	.82	2326	28.4
1952	Paul Arizin, Phi	.66	1674	25.4	1984	Adrian Dantley, Utah	.79	2418	30.6
1953	Neil Johnston, Phi	.70	1564	22.3	1985	Bernard King, NY	.55	1809	32.9
1954	Neil Johnston, Phi	.72	1759	24.4	1986	Dominique Wilkins, Atl	.78	2366	30.3
1955	Neil Johnston, Phi	.72	1631	22.7	1987	Michael Jordan, Chi	.82	3041	37.1
1956	Bob Pettit, St.L	.72	1849	25.7	1988	Michael Jordan, Chi	.82	2868	35.0
1957	Paul Arizin, Phi	.71	1817	25.6	1989	Michael Jordan, Chi	.81	2633	32.5
1958	George Yardley, Det	.72	2001	27.8	1990	Michael Jordan, Chi	.82	2753	33.6
1959	Bob Pettit, St.L	.72	2105	29.2	1991	Michael Jordan, Chi	.82	2580	31.5
1960	Wilt Chamberlain, Phi	.72	2707	37.6	1992	Michael Jordan, Chi	.80	2404	30.1
1961	Wilt Chamberlain, Phi	.79	3033	38.4	1993	Michael Jordan, Chi	.78	2541	32.6
1962	Wilt Chamberlain, Phi	.80	4029	50.4	1994	David Robinson, SA	.80	2383	29.8
1963	Wilt Chamberlain, SF	.80	3586	44.8	1995	Shaquille O'Neal, Orl	.79	2315	29.3
1964	Wilt Chamberlain, SF	.80	2948	36.9	1996	Michael Jordan, Chi	.82	2491	30.4
1965	Wilt Chamberlain, SF-Phi	.73	2534	34.7	1997	Michael Jordan, Chi	.82	2431	29.7
1966	Wilt Chamberlain, Phi	.79	2649	33.5	1998	Michael Jordan, Chi	.82	2357	28.7
1967	Rick Barry, SF	.78	2775	35.6	1999	Allen Iverson, Phi	.48	1284	26.8
1968	Dave Bing, Det	.79	2142	27.1	2000	Shaquille O'Neal, LAL	.79	2344	29.7
1969	Elvin Hayes, SD	.82	2327	28.4	2001	Allen Iverson, Phi	.71	2207	31.1
1970	Jerry West, LA	.74	2309	31.2	2002	Allen Iverson, Phi	.60	1883	31.4
1971	Lew Alcindor, Mil	.82	2596	31.7	2003	Tracy McGrady, Orl	.75	2407	32.1
1972	Kareem Abdul-Jabbar, Mil	.81	2822	34.8	2004	Tracy McGrady, Orl	.67	1878	28.0
1973	Nate Archibald, KC-Omaha	.80	2719	34.0	2005	Allen Iverson, Phi	.75	2302	30.7
1974	Bob McAdoo, Buf	.74	2261	30.6	2006	Kobe Bryant, LAL	.80	2832	35.4
1975	Bob McAdoo, Buf	.82	2831	34.5	2007	Kobe Bryant, LAL	.77	2430	31.6
1976	Bob McAdoo, Buf	.78	2427	31.1	2008	LeBron James, Cle	.75	2250	30.0
1977	Pete Maravich, NO	.73	2273	31.1					
1978	George Gervin, SA	.82	2232	27.2					

Note: Lew Alcindor changed his name to Kareem Abdul-Jabbar after the 1970-71 season.

Rebounds

Decided by total rebounds from 1951-69 and per game average since 1970.
Multiple winners: Wilt Chamberlain (11); Dennis Rodman (7); Moses Malone (6); Kevin Garnett and Bill Russell (4); Elvin Hayes, Dikembe Mutombo, Hakeem Olajuwon and Ben Wallace (2).

Year		Gm	No	Avg	Year		Gm	No	Avg
1951	Dolph Schayes, Syr	.66	1080	16.4	1970	Elvin Hayes, SD	.82	1386	16.9
1952	Larry Foust, Ft. Wayne	.66	880	13.3	1971	Wilt Chamberlain, LA	.82	1493	18.2
	& Mel Hutchins, Mil	.66	880	13.3	1972	Wilt Chamberlain, LA	.82	1572	19.2
1953	George Mikan, Mpls	.70	1007	14.4	1973	Wilt Chamberlain, LA	.82	1526	18.6
1954	Harry Gallatin, NY	.72	1098	15.3	1974	Elvin Hayes, Cap*	.81	1463	18.1
1955	Neil Johnston, Phi	.72	1085	15.1	1975	Wes Unseld, Wash	.73	1077	14.8
1956	Bob Pettit, St.L	.72	1164	16.2	1976	Kareem Abdul-Jabbar, LA	.82	1383	16.9
1957	Maurice Stokes, Roch	.72	1256	17.4	1977	Bill Walton, Port	.65	934	14.4
1958	Bill Russell, Bos	.69	1564	22.7	1978	Len Robinson, NO	.82	1288	15.7
1959	Bill Russell, Bos	.70	1612	23.0	1979	Moses Malone, Hou	.82	1444	17.6
1960	Wilt Chamberlain, Phi	.72	1941	27.0	1980	Swen Nater, SD	.81	1216	15.0
1961	Wilt Chamberlain, Phi	.79	2149	27.2	1981	Moses Malone, Hou	.80	1180	14.8
1962	Wilt Chamberlain, Phi	.80	2052	25.7	1982	Moses Malone, Hou	.81	1188	14.7
1963	Wilt Chamberlain, SF	.80	1946	24.3	1983	Moses Malone, Phi	.78	1194	15.3
1964	Bill Russell, Bos	.78	1930	24.7	1984	Moses Malone, Phi	.71	950	13.4
1965	Bill Russell, Bos	.78	1878	24.1	1985	Moses Malone, Phi	.79	1031	13.1
1966	Wilt Chamberlain, Phi	.79	1943	24.6	1986	Bill Laimbeer, Det	.82	1075	13.1
1967	Wilt Chamberlain, Phi	.81	1957	24.2	1987	Charles Barkley, Phi	.68	994	14.6
1968	Wilt Chamberlain, Phi	.82	1952	23.8	1988	Michael Cage, LAC	.72	938	13.0
1969	Wilt Chamberlain, LA	.81	1712	21.1	1989	Hakeem Olajuwon, Hou	.82	1105	13.5

*The Baltimore Bullets moved to Landover, Md. in 1973-74 and became first the Capital Bullets, then the Washington Bullets in 1974-75.

Rebounds (Cont.)

Year		Gm	No	Avg	Year		Gm	No	Avg
1990	Hakeem Olajuwon, Hou	82	1149	14.0	2000	Dikembe Mutombo, Atl	82	1157	14.1
1991	David Robinson, SA	82	1063	13.0	2001	Dikembe Mutombo, Atl-Phi	75	1015	13.5
1992	Dennis Rodman, Det	82	1530	18.7	2002	Ben Wallace, Det	80	1039	13.0
1993	Dennis Rodman, Det	62	1232	18.3	2003	Ben Wallace, Det	73	1126	15.4
1994	Dennis Rodman, SA	79	1132	17.3	2004	Kevin Garnett, Min	82	1139	13.9
1995	Dennis Rodman, SA	49	823	16.8	2005	Kevin Garnett, Min	82	1108	13.5
1996	Dennis Rodman, Chi	64	952	14.9	2006	Kevin Garnett, Min	76	966	12.7
1997	Dennis Rodman, Chi	55	883	16.1	2007	Kevin Garnett, Min	76	975	12.8
1998	Dennis Rodman, Chi	80	1201	15.0	2008	Dwight Howard, Orl	82	1161	14.2
1999	Chris Webber, Sac	42	545	13.0					

Assists

Decided by total assists from 1952-69 and per game average since 1970.

Multiple winners: John Stockton (9); Bob Cousy (8); Oscar Robertson (6); Jason Kidd (5); Magic Johnson and Kevin Porter (4); Steve Nash (3); Andy Phillip and Guy Rodgers (2).

Year		No	Year		No	Year		APG
1947	Ernie Calverley, Prov	202	1968	Wilt Chamberlain, Phi	702	1989	John Stockton, Utah	13.6
1948	Howie Dallmar, Phi	120	1969	Oscar Robertson, Cin	772	1990	John Stockton, Utah	14.5
1949	Bob Davies, Roch	321	1970	Lenny Wilkens, Sea	9.1	1991	John Stockton, Utah	14.2
1950	Dick McGuire, NY	386	1971	Norm Van Lier, Chi	10.1	1992	John Stockton, Utah	13.7
1951	Andy Phillip, Phi	414	1972	Jerry West, LA	9.7	1993	John Stockton, Utah	12.0
1952	Andy Phillip, Phi	539	1973	Nate Archibald, KC-O	11.4	1994	John Stockton, Utah	12.6
1953	Bob Cousy, Bos	547	1974	Ernie DiGregorio, Buf	8.2	1995	John Stockton, Utah	12.3
1954	Bob Cousy, Bos	518	1975	Kevin Porter, Wash	8.0	1996	John Stockton, Utah	11.2
1955	Bob Cousy, Bos	557	1976	Slick Watts, Sea	8.1	1997	Mark Jackson, Den-Ind	11.4
1956	Bob Cousy, Bos	642	1977	Don Buse, Ind	8.5	1998	Rod Strickland, Wash	10.5
1957	Bob Cousy, Bos	478	1978	Kevin Porter, Det-NJ	10.2	1999	Jason Kidd, Pho	10.8
1958	Bob Cousy, Bos	463	1979	Kevin Porter, Det	13.4	2000	Jason Kidd, Pho	10.1
1959	Bob Cousy, Bos	557	1980	M.R. Richardson, NY	10.1	2001	Jason Kidd, Pho	9.8
1960	Bob Cousy, Bos	715	1981	Kevin Porter, Wash	9.1	2002	Andre Miller, Cle	10.9
1961	Oscar Robertson, Cin	690	1982	Johnny Moore, SA	9.6	2003	Jason Kidd, NJ	8.9
1962	Oscar Robertson, Cin	899	1983	Magic Johnson, LA	10.5	2004	Jason Kidd, NJ	9.2
1963	Guy Rodgers, SF	825	1984	Magic Johnson, LA	13.1	2005	Steve Nash, Dal	11.5
1964	Neil Johnston, Cin	868	1985	Isiah Thomas, Det	13.9	2006	Steve Nash, Pho	10.5
1965	Oscar Robertson, Cin	861	1986	Magic Johnson, LAL	12.6	2007	Steve Nash, Pho	11.6
1966	Oscar Robertson, Cin	847	1987	Magic Johnson, LAL	12.2	2008	Chris Paul, NO	11.6
1967	Guy Rodgers, Chi	908	1988	John Stockton, Utah	13.8			

Field Goal Percentage

Multiple winners: Wilt Chamberlain and Shaquille O'Neal (9); Artis Gilmore (4); Neil Johnston (3); Bob Feerick, Johnny Green, Alex Groza, Cedric Maxwell, Kevin McHale, Gheorghe Muresan, Kenny Sears and Buck Williams (2).

Year		Pct	Year		Pct	Year		Pct
1947	Bob Feerick, Wash	.401	1968	Wilt Chamberlain, Phi	.595	1989	Dennis Rodman, Det	.595
1948	Bob Feerick, Wash	.340	1969	Wilt Chamberlain, LA	.583	1990	Mark West, Pho	.625
1949	Arnie Risen, Roch	.423	1970	Johnny Green, Cin	.559	1991	Buck Williams, Port	.602
1950	Alex Groza, Indpls	.478	1971	Johnny Green, Cin	.587	1992	Buck Williams, Port	.604
1951	Alex Groza, Indpls	.470	1972	Wilt Chamberlain, LA	.649	1993	Cedric Ceballos, Pho	.576
1952	Paul Arizin, Phi	.448	1973	Wilt Chamberlain, LA	.727	1994	Shaquille O'Neal, Orl	.599
1953	Neil Johnston, Phi	.452	1974	Bob McAdoo, Buf	.547	1995	Chris Gatling, G.St	.633
1954	Ed Macauley, Bos	.486	1975	Don Nelson, Bos	.539	1996	Gheorghe Muresan, Wash	.584
1955	Larry Foust, Ft.W	.487	1976	Wes Unseld, Wash	.561	1997	Gheorghe Muresan, Wash	.604
1956	Neil Johnston, Phi	.457	1977	K. Abdul-Jabbar, LA	.579	1998	Shaquille O'Neal, LAL	.584
1957	Neil Johnston, Phi	.447	1978	Bobby Jones, Den	.578	1999	Shaquille O'Neal, LAL	.576
1958	Jack Twyman, Cin	.452	1979	Cedric Maxwell, Bos	.584	2000	Shaquille O'Neal, LAL	.574
1959	Kenny Sears, NY	.490	1980	Cedric Maxwell, Bos	.609	2001	Shaquille O'Neal, LAL	.572
1960	Kenny Sears, NY	.477	1981	Artis Gilmore, Chi	.670	2002	Shaquille O'Neal, LAL	.579
1961	Wilt Chamberlain, Phi	.509	1982	Artis Gilmore, Chi	.652	2003	Eddy Curry, Chi	.585
1962	Walt Bellamy, Chi	.519	1983	Artis Gilmore, SA	.626	2004	Shaquille O'Neal, LAL	.584
1963	Wilt Chamberlain, SF	.528	1984	Artis Gilmore, SA	.631	2005	Shaquille O'Neal, Mia	.601
1964	Jerry Lucas, Cin	.527	1985	James Donaldson, LAC	.637	2006	Shaquille O'Neal, Mia	.600
1965	W. Chamberlain, SF-Phi	.510	1986	Steve Johnson, SA	.632	2007	Mikki Moore, NJ	.609
1966	Wilt Chamberlain, Phi	.540	1987	Kevin McHale, Bos	.604	2008	Andris Biedrins, G.St	.626
1967	Wilt Chamberlain, Phi	.683	1988	Kevin McHale, Bos	.604			

Free Throw Percentage

Multiple winners: Bill Sharman (7); Rick Barry (6); Reggie Miller (5); Larry Bird (4); Mark Price and Dolph Schayes (3); Mahmoud Abdul-Rauf, Larry Costello, Ernie DiGregorio, Bob Feerick, Kyle Macy, Calvin Murphy, Oscar Robertson, Larry Siegfried and Peja Stojakovic (2).

Year		Pct	Year		Pct	Year		Pct
1947	Fred Scolari, Wash	.811	1952	Bob Wanzer, Roch	.904	1957	Bill Sharman, Bos	.905
1948	Bob Feerick, Wash	.788	1953	Bill Sharman, Bos	.850	1958	Dolph Schayes, Syr	.904
1949	Bob Feerick, Wash	.859	1954	Bill Sharman, Bos	.844	1959	Bill Sharman, Bos	.932
1950	Max Zaslofsky, Chi	.843	1955	Bill Sharman, Bos	.897	1960	Dolph Schayes, Syr	.892
1951	Joe Fulks, Phi	.855	1956	Bill Sharman, Bos	.867	1961	Bill Sharman, Bos	.921

Free Throw Percentage (Cont.)

Year		Pct	Year		Pct	Year		Pct
1962	Dolph Schayes, Syr	.896	1978	Rick Barry, G.St.	.924	1994	M. Abdul-Rauf, Den	.956
1963	Larry Costello, Syr	.881	1979	Rick Barry, Hou	.947	1995	Spud Webb, Sac	.934
1964	Oscar Robertson, Cin	.853	1980	Rick Barry, Hou	.935	1996	M. Abdul-Rauf, Den	.930
1965	Larry Costello, Phi	.877	1981	Calvin Murphy, Hou	.958	1997	Mark Price, G.St.	.906
1966	Larry Siegfried, Bos	.881	1982	Kyle Macy, Pho	.899	1998	Chris Mullin, Ind.	.939
1967	Adrian Smith, Cin	.903	1983	Calvin Murphy, Hou	.920	1999	Reggie Miller, Ind	.915
1968	Oscar Robertson, Cin	.873	1984	Larry Bird, Bos	.888	2000	Jeff Hornacek, Utah	.950
1969	Larry Siegfried, NY	.864	1985	Kyle Macy, Pho	.907	2001	Reggie Miller, Ind	.928
1970	Flynn Robinson, Mil	.898	1986	Larry Bird, Bos	.896	2002	Reggie Miller, Ind	.911
1971	Chet Walker, Chi	.859	1987	Larry Bird, Bos	.910	2003	Allan Houston, NY	.919
1972	Jack Marin, Bal	.894	1988	Jack Sikma, Mil	.922	2004	Peja Stojakovic, Sac	.927
1973	Rick Barry, G.St.	.902	1989	Magic Johnson, LAL	.911	2005	Reggie Miller, Ind	.933
1974	Ernie DiGregorio, Buf	.902	1990	Larry Bird, Bos	.930	2006	Steve Nash, Pho	.921
1975	Rick Barry, G.St.	.904	1991	Reggie Miller, Ind	.918	2007	Kyle Korver, Phi	.914
1976	Rick Barry, G.St.	.923	1992	Mark Price, Cle	.947	2008	Peja Stojakovic, NO	.929
1977	Ernie DiGregorio, Buf	.945	1993	Mark Price, Cle	.948			

Three-Point Field Goal Percentage

Multiple winners: Craig Hodges, Jason Kapono, Steve Kerr (2)

Year		Pct	Year		Pct	Year		Pct
1980	Fred Brown, Sea	.443	1990	Steve Kerr, Cle	.507	2000	Hubert Davis, Dal	.491
1981	Brian Taylor, SD	.383	1991	Jim Les, Sac	.461	2001	Brent Barry, Sea	.476
1982	Campy Russell, NY	.439	1992	Dana Barros, Sea	.446	2002	Steve Smith, SA	.472
1983	Mike Dunleavy, SA	.345	1993	B.J. Armstrong, Chi	.453	2003	Bruce Bowen, SA	.441
1984	Darrell Griffith, Utah	.361	1994	Tracy Murray, Por	.459	2004	Anthony Peeler, Sac	.482
1985	Byron Scott, LAL	.433	1995	Steve Kerr, Chi	.524	2005	Fred Hoiberg, Min	.483
1986	Craig Hodges, Milw	.451	1996	Tim Legler, Wash	.522	2006	Richard Hamilton, Det	.458
1987	Kiki Vandeweghe, Por	.481	1997	Glen Rice, Cha	.470	2007	Jason Kapono, Mia	.514
1988	Craig Hodges, Milw-Pho	.491	1998	Dale Ellis, Sea	.464	2008	Jason Kapono, Tor	.483
1989	Jon Sundvold, Mia	.522	1999	Dell Curry, Milw	.476			

Blocked Shots

Multiple winners: Kareem Abdul-Jabbar, Mark Eaton and Marcus Camby (4); George Johnson, Dikembe Mutombo, Hakeem Olajuwon and Theo Ratliff (3); Manute Bol and Alonzo Mourning (2).

Year		Gm	No	Avg
1974	Elmore Smith, LA	.81	393	4.85
1975	Kareem Abdul-Jabbar, Mil	.65	212	3.26
1976	Kareem Abdul-Jabbar, LA	.82	338	4.12
1977	Bill Walton, Port	.65	211	3.25
1978	George Johnson, NJ	.81	274	3.38
1979	Kareem Abdul-Jabbar, LA	.80	316	3.95
1980	Kareem Abdul-Jabbar, LA	.82	280	3.41
1981	George Johnson, SA	.82	278	3.39
1982	George Johnson, SA	.75	234	3.12
1983	Tree Rollins, Atl	.80	343	4.29
1984	Mark Eaton, Utah	.82	351	4.28
1985	Mark Eaton, Utah	.82	456	5.56
1986	Manute Bol, Wash	.80	397	4.96
1987	Mark Eaton, Utah	.79	321	4.06
1988	Mark Eaton, Utah	.82	304	3.71
1989	Manute Bol, G.St.	.80	345	4.31
1990	Akeem Olajuwon, Hou	.82	376	4.59
1991	Hakeem Olajuwon, Hou	.56	221	3.95
1992	David Robinson, SA	.68	305	4.49
1993	Hakeem Olajuwon, Hou	.82	342	4.17
1994	Dikembe Mutombo, Den	.82	336	4.10
1995	Dikembe Mutombo, Den	.82	321	3.91
1996	Dikembe Mutombo, Den	.74	332	4.49
1997	Shawn Bradley, Dal-NJ	.73	248	3.40
1998	Marcus Camby, Tor	.63	230	3.65
1999	Alonzo Mourning, Mia	.46	180	3.91
2000	Alonzo Mourning, Mia	.79	294	3.72
2001	Theo Ratliff, Phi-Atl	.50	187	3.74
2002	Ben Wallace, Det	.80	278	3.48
2003	Theo Ratliff, Atl	.81	262	3.23
2004	Theo Ratliff, Atl-Port	.85	307	3.61
2005	Andrei Kirilenko, Utah	.41	136	3.32
2006	Marcus Camby, Den	.56	184	3.29
2007	Marcus Camby, Den	.70	231	3.30
2008	Marcus Camby, Den	.79	285	3.61

Steals

Multiple winners: Allen Iverson, Michael Jordan, Micheal Ray Richardson and Alvin Robertson (3); Mookie Blaylock, Baron Davis, Magic Johnson and John Stockton (2).

Year		Gm	No	Avg
1974	Larry Steele, Port	.81	217	2.68
1975	Rick Barry, G.St.	.80	228	2.85
1976	Slick Watts, Sea	.82	261	3.18
1977	Don Buse, Ind	.81	281	3.47
1978	Ron Lee, Pho	.82	225	2.74
1979	M.L. Carr, Det	.80	197	2.46
1980	Micheal Ray Richardson, NY	.82	265	3.23
1981	Magic Johnson, LA	.37	127	3.43
1982	Magic Johnson, LA	.78	208	2.67
1983	Micheal Ray Richardson, G. ST-NJ	.64	182	2.84
1984	Rickey Green, Utah	.81	215	2.65
1985	Micheal Ray Richardson, NJ	.82	243	2.96
1986	Alvin Robertson, SA	.82	301	3.67
1987	Alvin Robertson, SA	.81	260	3.21
1988	Michael Jordan, Chi	.82	259	3.16
1989	John Stockton, Utah	.82	263	3.21
1990	Michael Jordan, Chi	.82	227	2.77
1991	Alvin Robertson, SA	.81	246	3.04
1992	John Stockton, Utah	.82	244	2.98
1993	Michael Jordan, Chi	.78	221	2.83
1994	Nate McMillan, Sea	.73	216	2.96
1995	Scottie Pippen, Chi	.79	232	2.94
1996	Gary Payton, Sea	.81	231	2.85
1997	Mookie Blaylock, Atl	.78	212	2.72
1998	Mookie Blaylock, Atl.	.70	183	2.61
1999	Kendall Gill, NJ	.50	134	2.68
2000	Eddie Jones, Cha	.72	192	2.67
2001	Allen Iverson, Phi.	.71	178	2.51
2002	Allen Iverson, Phi.	.60	168	2.80
2003	Allen Iverson, Phi	.82	225	2.74
2004	Baron Davis, NO	.67	158	2.36
2005	Larry Hughes, Wash	.61	176	2.89
2006	Gerald Wallace, Cha	.55	138	2.51
2007	Baron Davis, G. St.	.63	135	2.14
2008	Chris Paul, NO	.80	217	2.71

All-Time NBA Regular Season Leaders

Through the 2007-08 regular season.

CAREER

Players active in 2007-08 in **bold** type.

Points

		Yrs	Gm	Pts	Avg
1	Kareem Abdul-Jabbar	20	1560	**38,387**	24.6
2	Karl Malone	19	1476	**36,928**	25.0
3	Michael Jordan	15	1072	**32,292**	30.1
4	Wilt Chamberlain	14	1045	**31,419**	30.1
5	Moses Malone	19	1329	**27,409**	20.6
6	Elvin Hayes	16	1303	**27,313**	21.0
7	Hakeem Olajuwon	18	1238	**26,946**	21.8
8	Oscar Robertson	14	1040	**26,710**	25.7
9	Dominique Wilkins	15	1074	**26,668**	24.8
10	John Havlicek	16	1270	**26,395**	20.8
11	**Shaquille O'Neal**	16	1042	**26,286**	25.2
12	Alex English	15	1193	**25,613**	21.5
13	Reggie Miller	18	1389	**25,279**	18.2
14	Jerry West	14	932	**25,192**	27.0
15	Patrick Ewing	17	1183	**24,815**	21.0
16	Charles Barkley	16	1073	**23,757**	22.1
17	Robert Parish	21	1611	**23,334**	14.5
18	Adrian Dantley	15	955	**23,177**	24.3
19	Elgin Baylor	14	846	**23,149**	27.4
20	**Allen Iverson**	12	829	**22,988**	27.7
21	Clyde Drexler	15	1086	**22,195**	20.4
22	Gary Payton	17	1335	**21,813**	16.3
23	Larry Bird	13	897	**21,791**	24.3
24	**Kobe Bryant**	12	866	**21,619**	25.0
25	Hal Greer	15	1122	**21,586**	19.2
26	Walt Bellamy	14	1043	**20,941**	20.1
27	Bob Pettit	11	792	**20,880**	26.4
28	David Robinson	14	987	**20,790**	21.1
29	George Gervin	10	791	**20,708**	26.2
30	Mitch Richmond	14	976	**20,497**	21.0

Scoring Average

Minimum of 400 games or 10,000 points.

		Yrs	Gm	Pts	Avg
1	Michael Jordan	15	1072	32,292	30.1
2	Wilt Chamberlain	14	1045	31,419	30.1
3	**Allen Iverson**	12	829	22,988	27.7
4	Elgin Baylor	14	846	23,149	27.4
5	**LeBron James**	5	391	10,689	27.3
6	Jerry West	14	932	25,192	27.0
7	Bob Pettit	11	792	20,880	26.4
8	George Gervin	10	791	20,708	26.2
9	Oscar Robertson	14	1040	26,710	25.7
10	**Shaquille O'Neal**	16	1042	26,286	25.2
11	Karl Malone	19	1476	36,928	25.0
12	**Kobe Bryant**	12	866	21,619	25.0
13	Dominique Wilkins	15	1074	26,668	24.8
14	Kareem Abdul-Jabbar	20	1560	38,387	24.6
15	Larry Bird	13	897	21,791	24.3
16	Adrian Dantley	15	955	23,177	24.3
17	Pete Maravich	10	658	15,948	24.2
18	**Vince Carter**	10	697	16,592	23.8
19	Rick Barry	10	794	18,395	23.2
20	**Paul Pierce**	10	732	16,945	23.1
21	Paul Arizin	10	713	16,266	22.8
22	**Gilbert Arenas**	7	431	9,827	22.8
23	George Mikan	9	520	11,764	22.6
24	Bernard King	14	874	19,655	22.5
25	**Dirk Nowitzki**	10	758	16990	22.4
26	**Tracy McGrady**	11	749	16,744	22.4
27	Charles Barkley	16	1073	23,757	22.1
28	David Thompson	8	509	11,264	22.1
29	Bob McAdoo	14	852	18,787	22.1
30	Julius Erving	11	836	18,364	22.0

Assists

		Yrs	Gm	No	Avg
1	John Stockton	19	1504	**15,806**	10.5
2	Mark Jackson	17	1296	**10,334**	8.0
3	Magic Johnson	13	906	**10,141**	11.2
4	Oscar Robertson	14	1040	**9,887**	9.5
5	**Jason Kidd**	14	1026	**9,497**	9.3
6	Isiah Thomas	13	979	**9,061**	9.3
7	Gary Payton	17	1335	**8,966**	6.7
8	Rod Strickland	17	1094	**7,987**	7.3
9	Maurice Cheeks	15	1101	**7,392**	6.7
10	Lenny Wilkens	15	1077	**7,211**	6.7
11	Terry Porter	17	1274	**7,160**	5.6
12	Tim Hardaway	13	867	**7,095**	8.2

Rebounds

		Yrs	Gm	No	Avg
1	Wilt Chamberlain	14	1045	**23,924**	22.9
2	Bill Russell	13	963	**21,620**	22.5
3	Kareem Abdul-Jabbar	20	1560	**17,440**	11.2
4	Elvin Hayes	16	1303	**16,279**	12.5
5	Moses Malone	19	1329	**16,212**	12.2
6	Karl Malone	19	1476	**14,968**	10.1
7	Robert Parish	21	1611	**14,715**	9.1
8	Nate Thurmond	14	964	**14,464**	15.0
9	Walt Bellamy	14	1043	**14,241**	13.7
10	Wes Unseld	13	984	**13,769**	14.0
11	Hakeem Olajuwon	18	1238	**13,748**	11.1
12	Buck Williams	17	1307	**13,017**	10.0

Note: If rebounds accumulated in the ABA are included, consider the following totals: Moses Malone (17,834) and Artis Gilmore (16,330).

Steals

		Yrs	Gm	No
1	John Stockton	19	1504	3265
2	Michael Jordan	15	1072	2514
3	Gary Payton	17	1335	2445
4	Maurice Cheeks	15	1101	2310
5	Scottie Pippen	17	1178	2307

Note: Steals have only been an official stat since the 1973-74 season.

Blocked Shots

		Yrs	Gm	No
1	Hakeem Olajuwon	18	1238	3830
2	**Dikembe Mutombo**	17	1187	3278
3	Kareem Abdul-Jabbar	20	1560	3189
4	Mark Eaton	11	875	3064
5	David Robinson	14	987	2954

Note: Blocked shots have only been an official stat since the 1973-74 season. Also, note that if ABA records are included, consider the following block totals: Artis Gilmore (3,178).

Games Played

		Yrs	Career	Gm
1	Robert Parish	21	1976-97	1611
2	Kareem Abdul-Jabbar	20	1970-89	1560
3	John Stockton	19	1984-03	1504
4	Karl Malone	19	1985-04	1476
5	Kevin Willis	20	1985-05,07	1424

Note: If ABA records are included, consider the following game totals: Moses Malone (1,455).

Field Goals

		Yrs	FG	Att	Pct
1	Kareem Abdul-Jabbar	20	**15,837**	28,307	.559
2	Karl Malone	19	**13,528**	26,210	.516
3	Wilt Chamberlain	14	**12,681**	23,497	.540
4	Michael Jordan	15	**12,192**	24,537	.497
5	Elvin Hayes	16	**10,976**	24,272	.452
6	Hakeem Olajuwon	18	**10,749**	20,991	.512
7	Alex English	15	**10,659**	21,036	.507
8	John Havlicek	16	**10,513**	23,930	.439
9	**Shaquille O'Neal**	16	**10,422**	17,952	.581
10	Dominique Wilkins	15	**9,963**	21,589	.461
11	Patrick Ewing	17	**9,702**	19,241	.504
12	Robert Parish	21	**9,614**	17,914	.537

Note: If field goals made in the ABA are included, consider these NBA-ABA totals: Julius Erving (11,818), Dan Issel (10,431), George Gervin (10,368), Moses Malone (10,277) and Rick Barry (9,695).

Free Throws

		Yrs	FT	Att	Pct
1	Karl Malone	19	**9787**	13,188	.742
2	Moses Malone	19	**8531**	11,090	.769
3	Oscar Robertson	14	**7694**	9,185	.838
4	Michael Jordan	15	**7327**	8,772	.835
5	Jerry West	14	**7160**	8,801	.814
6	Dolph Schayes	16	**6979**	8,273	.844
7	Adrian Dantley	15	**6832**	8,351	.818
8	Kareem Abdul-Jabbar	20	**6712**	9,304	.721
9	Charles Barkley	16	**6349**	8,643	.734
10	Reggie Miller	18	**6237**	7,026	.888
11	Bob Pettit	11	**6182**	8,119	.761
12	Wilt Chamberlain	14	**6057**	11,862	.511

Note: If free throws made in the ABA are included, consider these totals: Moses Malone (9,018), Dan Issel (6,591), and Julius Erving (6,256).

Free Throw Percentage

		Yrs	FT	Att	Pct
1	Mark Price	12	2135	2362	.904
2	Rick Barry	10	3818	4243	.900
3	**Steve Nash**	12	2170	2418	.897
4	**Peja Stojakovic**	10	2025	2264	.894
5	Calvin Murphy	13	3445	3864	.892

Note: If ABA records are included, consider the following free throw percentage: Rick Barry (5713-6397 for .893)

3-Pt Field Goal Pct.

(minimum 250 3-pt FGs made)

		Yrs	Gm	Pct	3FGM
1	**Jason Kapono**	5	321	**.464**	287
2	Steve Kerr	15	910	**.454**	726
3	Hubert Davis	12	685	**.441**	728
4	Drazen Petrovic	4	290	**.437**	255
5	**Steve Nash**	12	860	**.431**	1252

3-Pt Field Goals Made

		Yrs	Gm	Pct	3FGM
1	Reggie Miller	18	1389	.395	2560
2	**Ray Allen**	12	868	.397	2100
3	Dale Ellis	17	1209	.403	1719
4	Glen Rice	15	1000	.400	1559
5	**Eddie Jones**	14	954	.437	1546

Minutes Played

		Gm	MPG	Min
1	Kareem Abdul-Jabbar	1560	36.8	57,446
2	Karl Malone	1476	37.2	54,852
3	Elvin Hayes	1303	38.4	50,000
4	Wilt Chamberlain	1045	45.8	47,859
5	John Stockton	1504	31.8	47,764

Triple-Doubles

		Yrs	Gm	No
1	Oscar Robertson	14	1040	181
2	Magic Johnson	13	906	138
3	**Jason Kidd**	14	1026	100
4	Wilt Chamberlain	14	1045	78
5	Larry Bird	13	897	59

Note: The triple-double totals of Oscar Robertson and Wilt Chamberlain do not include games in which they may have recorded a triple-double with double-digit blocks and/or steals, since those stats have only been official since the 1973-74 season.

Personal Fouls

		Yrs	Gm	Fouls	DQ
1	Kareem Abdul-Jabbar	20	1560	**4657**	48
2	Karl Malone	19	1476	**4578**	28
3	Robert Parish	21	1611	**4443**	86
4	Charles Oakley	19	1282	**4421**	63
5	Hakeem Olajuwon	18	1238	**4383**	80

Note: If ABA records are included, consider the following personal foul totals: Artis Gilmore (4,529) and Caldwell Jones (4,436).

Disqualifications

		Yrs	Gm	No
1	Vern Mikkelsen	10	699	127
2	Walter Dukes	8	553	121
3	Shawn Kemp	14	1051	115
4	Charlie Share	8	555	105
5	Paul Arizin	10	713	101

NBA-ABA Top 20

Points

All-Time combined regular season scoring leaders, including ABA service (1968-76). NBA players with ABA experience are listed in CAPITAL letters. Players active during 2006-07 are in **bold** type.

		Yrs	Pts	Avg
1	Kareem Abdul-Jabbar	20	**38,387**	24.6
2	Karl Malone	19	**36,928**	25.0
3	Wilt Chamberlain	14	**31,419**	30.1
4	Michael Jordan	15	**32,292**	30.1
5	JULIUS ERVING	16	**30,026**	24.2
6	MOSES MALONE	21	**29,580**	20.3
7	DAN ISSEL	15	**27,482**	22.6
8	Elvin Hayes	16	**27,313**	21.0
9	Hakeem Olajuwon	18	**26,946**	21.8
10	Oscar Robertson	14	**26,710**	25.7
11	Dominique Wilkins	15	**26,668**	24.8
12	GEORGE GERVIN	14	**26,595**	25.1
13	John Havlicek	16	**26,395**	20.8
14	**Shaquille O'Neal**	16	**26,286**	25.2
15	Alex English	15	**25,613**	21.5
16	RICK BARRY	14	**25,279**	24.8
	Reggie Miller	18	**25,279**	18.2
18	Jerry West	14	**25,192**	27.0
19	ARTIS GILMORE	17	**24,941**	18.8
20	Patrick Ewing	17	**24,815**	21.0

ABA Totals: BARRY (4 yrs, 226 gm, 6884 pts, 30.5 avg); ERVING (5 yrs, 407 gm, 11,662 pts, 28.7 avg); GERVIN (4 yrs, 269 gm, 5887 pts, 21.9 avg); GILMORE (5 yrs, 420 gm, 9362 pts, 22.3 avg); ISSEL (6 yrs, 500 gm, 12,823 pts, 25.6 avg); MALONE (2 yrs, 126 gm, 2171 pts, 17.2 avg).

All-Time NBA Regular Season Leaders (Cont.)
SINGLE SEASON

Scoring Average

		Season	Avg
1	Wilt Chamberlain, Phi	1961-62	50.4
2	Wilt Chamberlain, SF	1962-63	44.8
3	Wilt Chamberlain, Phi	1960-61	38.4
4	Elgin Baylor, LA	1961-62	38.3
5	Wilt Chamberlain, Phi	1959-60	37.6
6	Michael Jordan, Chi	1986-87	37.1
7	Wilt Chamberlain, SF	1963-64	36.9
8	Rick Barry, SF	1966-67	35.6
9	Kobe Bryant, LAL	2005-06	35.4
10	Michael Jordan, Chi	1987-88	35.0

Field Goal Pct.

		Season	Pct
1	Wilt Chamberlain, LA	1972-73	.727
2	Wilt Chamberlain, SF	1966-67	.683
3	Artis Gilmore, Chi	1980-81	.670
4	Artis Gilmore, Chi	1981-82	.652
5	Wilt Chamberlain, LA	1971-72	.649

Free Throw Pct.

		Season	Pct
1	Calvin Murphy, Hou	1980-81	.958
2	Mahmoud Abdul-Rauf, Den.	1993-94	.956
3	Mark Price, Cle	1992-93	.948
4	Mark Price, Cle	1991-92	.947
	Rick Barry, Hou	1978-79	.947

3-Pt Field Goal Pct.

		Season	Pct
1	Steve Kerr, Chi	1994-95	.524
2	Jon Sundvold, Mia	1988-89	.522
3	Tim Legler, Wash	1995-96	.522
4	Steve Kerr, Chi	1995-96	.515
5	Jason Kapono, Mia	2006-07	.514

Personal Fouls

		Season	No
1	Darryl Dawkins, NJ	1983-84	386
2	Darryl Dawkins, NJ	1982-83	379

Assists

		Season	Avg
1	John Stockton, Utah	1989-90	14.5
2	John Stockton, Utah	1990-91	14.2
3	Isiah Thomas, Det	1984-85	13.9
4	John Stockton, Utah	1987-88	13.8
5	John Stockton, Utah	1991-92	13.7
6	John Stockton, Utah	1988-89	13.6
7	Kevin Porter, Det	1978-79	13.4
8	Magic Johnson, LAL	1983-84	13.1
9	Magic Johnson, LAL	1988-89	12.8
10	John Stockton, Utah	1993-94	12.6

Rebounds

		Season	Avg
1	Wilt Chamberlain, Phi	1960-61	27.2
2	Wilt Chamberlain, Phi	1959-60	27.0
3	Wilt Chamberlain, Phi	1961-62	25.7
4	Bill Russell, Bos	1963-64	24.7
5	Wilt Chamberlain, Phi	1965-66	24.6

Blocked Shots

		Season	Avg
1	Mark Eaton, Utah	1984-85	5.56
2	Manute Bol, Wash	1985-86	4.96
3	Elmore Smith, LA	1973-74	4.85
4	Mark Eaton, Utah	1985-86	4.61
5	Hakeem Olajuwon, Hou	1989-90	4.59

Steals

		Season	Avg
1	Alvin Robertson, SA	1985-86	3.67
2	Don Buse, Ind	1976-77	3.47
3	Magic Johnson, LAL	1980-81	3.43
4	Micheal Ray Richardson, NY	1979-80	3.23
5	Alvin Robertson, SA	1986-87	3.21

Turnovers

		Season	No
1	Artis Gilmore, Chi	1977-78	366
2	Kevin Porter, Det/NJ	1977-78	360

SINGLE GAME

Points

	Date	FG-FT	Pts
Wilt Chamberlain, Phi vs NY†	3/2/62	36-28-	100
Kobe Bryant, LAL vs. Tor	1/22/06	28-18-	81
Wilt Chamberlain, Phi vs LA***	12/8/61	31-16-	78
Wilt Chamberlain, Phi vs Chi	1/13/62	29-15-	73
Wilt Chamberlain, SF at NY	11/16/62	29-15-	73
David Thompson, Den at Det	4/9/78	28-17-	73
Wilt Chamberlain, SF at LA	11/3/62	29-14-	72
Elgin Baylor, LA at NY	11/15/60	28-15-	71
David Robinson, SA at LAC	4/24/94	26-18-	71
Wilt Chamberlain, SF at Syr	3/10/63	27-16-	70
Michael Jordan, Chi at Cle*	3/28/90	23-21-	69
Wilt Chamberlain, Phi at Chi	12/16/67	30-8-	68
Pete Maravich, NO vs NYK	2/25/77	26-16-	68
Wilt Chamberlain, Phi vs NY	3/9/61	27-13-	67
Wilt Chamberlain, Phi at St. L	2/17/62	26-15-	67
Wilt Chamberlain, Phi vs NY	2/25/62	25-17-	67
Wilt Chamberlain, SF vs LA	1/11/63	28-11-	67
Wilt Chamberlain, LA vs Pho	2/9/69	29-8-	66
Wilt Chamberlain, Phi at Cin	2/13/62	24-17-	65
Wilt Chamberlain, Phi at St. L	2/27/62	25-15-	65
Wilt Chamberlain, Phi vs LA	2/7/66	28-9-	65
Kobe Bryant, LAL vs Port	3/16/07	23-11-	65

*Overtime   ***Triple overtime.
†Game was played at Hershey, Penn.

Field Goals

	Date	FG	Att
Wilt Chamberlain, Phi vs NY	3/2/62	36	63
Wilt Chamberlain, Phi vs LA***	12/8/61	31	62
Wilt Chamberlain, Phi at Chi	12/16/67	30	40
Rick Barry, G.St. vs Port	2/26/74	30	45

Wilt Chamberlain made 29 four times.
***Triple overtime.

Free Throws

	Date	FT	Att
Wilt Chamberlain, Phi vs NY	3/2/62	28	32
Adrian Dantley, Utah vs Hou	1/4/84	28	29
Adrian Dantley, Utah vs Den	11/25/83	27	31
Adrian Dantley, Utah vs Dal	10/31/80	26	29
Michael Jordan, Chi vs NJ	2/26/87	26	27

3-Pt Field Goals

	Date	No
Kobe Bryant, LAL vs Sea	1/7/03	12
Donyell Marshall, Tor vs Phi	3/13/05	12
Dennis Scott, Orl vs Atl	4/18/96	11
Ray Allen, Milw vs Char	4/14/02	10
Brian Shaw, Mia at Mil	4/8/93	10
Joe Dumars, Det vs Min	11/8/94	10
George McCloud, Dal vs Pho	12/16/95	10*

Many tied with 9 each   * Overtime

Assists

	Date	No
Scott Skiles, Orl vs Den	12/30/90	30
Kevin Porter, NJ vs Hou	2/24/78	29
Bob Cousy, Bos vs Mpls	2/27/59	28
Guy Rodgers, SF vs St.L	3/14/63	28
John Stockton, Utah vs SA	1/15/91	28

Rebounds

	Date	No
Wilt Chamberlain, Phi vs Bos	11/24/60	55
Bill Russell, Bos vs Syr	2/5/60	51
Bill Russell, Bos vs Phi	11/16/57	49
Bill Russell, Bos vs Det	3/11/65	49
Wilt Chamberlain, Phi vs Syr	2/6/60	45
Wilt Chamberlain, Phi vs LA	1/21/61	45

Blocked Shots

	Date	No
Elmore Smith, LA vs Port	10/28/73	17
Manute Bol, Wash vs Atl	1/25/86	15
Manute Bol, Wash vs Ind	2/26/87	15
Shaquille O'Neal, Orl at NJ	11/20/93	15

Steals

	Date	No
Larry Kenon, San Antonio at KC	12/26/76	11
Kendall Gill, NJ vs Mia.	4/3/99	11

14 different players tied with 10 each, including Alvin Robertson, who had 10 steals in a game four times.

All-Time Winningest NBA Coaches

Top 25 NBA career victories through the 2007-08 season. Career, regular season and playoff records are noted along with NBA titles won. Coaches active during 2007-08 season in **bold** type.

		Career				Regular Season			Playoffs			
		Yrs	W	L	Pct	W	L	Pct	W	L	Pct	NBA Titles
1	Lenny Wilkens	32	1412	1253	.530	1332	1155	.536	80	98	.449	1 (1979)
2	Pat Riley	24	1381	805	.632	1210	694	.656	171	111	.606	5 (1982,85,87-88, 2006)
3	Don Nelson	29	1355	1045	.565	1280	954	.573	75	91	.452	None
4	Jerry Sloan	23	1182	811	.593	1089	711	.603	93	94	.497	None
5	Phil Jackson	17	1169	502	.700	976	418	.700	193	84	.697	9 (1991-93,96-98,00-02)
6	Larry Brown	23	1110	889	.555	1010	800	.558	100	89	.529	1 (2004)
7	Red Auerbach	20	1037	548	.654	938	479	.662	99	69	.589	9 (1957, 59-66)
8	Bill Fitch	25	999	1160	.463	944	1106	.460	55	54	.505	1 (1981)
9	Dick Motta	25	991	1087	.477	935	1017	.479	56	70	.444	1 (1978)
10	George Karl	20	941	697	.574	879	614	.589	62	83	.428	None
11	Jack Ramsay	21	908	841	.519	864	783	.525	44	58	.431	1 (1977)
12	Rick Adelman	16	879	580	.602	807	508	.614	72	72	.500	None
13	Cotton Fitzsimmons	21	867	824	.513	832	775	.518	35	49	.417	None
14	Gene Shue	22	814	908	.473	784	861	.477	30	47	.390	None
15	Red Holzman	18	754	652	.536	696	604	.535	58	48	.547	2 (1970, 73)
	John MacLeod	18	754	711	.515	707	657	.518	47	54	.465	None
17	Gregg Popovich	12	733	361	.670	632	302	.677	101	59	.631	4 (1999, 2003, 05, 07)
18	Chuck Daly	14	713	488	.594	638	437	.593	75	51	.595	2 (1989-90)
19	Mike Fratello	17	687	590	.538	667	548	.549	20	42	.323	None
20	Doug Moe	15	661	579	.533	628	529	.543	33	50	.398	None
21	Mike Dunleavy	15	611	658	.481	573	625	.783	38	33	.535	None
22	K.C. Jones	10	603	309	.661	522	252	.674	81	57	.587	2 (1984,86)
23	Del Harris	14	594	507	.540	556	457	.549	38	50	.432	None
24	Al Attles	14	588	548	.518	557	518	.518	31	30	.508	1 (1975)
25	Rudy Tomjanovich	13	578	455	.560	527	416	.559	51	39	.567	2 (1994-95)

Note: The NBA does not recognize records from the National Basketball League (1937-49), the American Basketball League (1961-62) or the American Basketball Assn. (1968-76), so the following NBL, ABL and ABA overall coaching records are not included above: NBL—**John Kundla** (51-19 and a title in 1 year). ABA—**Larry Brown** (249-129 in 4 yrs), **Alex Hannum** (194-164 and one title in 4 yrs), **K.C. Jones** (30-58 in 1 yr); **Kevin Loughery** (189-95 and one title in 3 yrs).

Where They Coached

Adelman—Portland (1988-94), Golden State (1995-97), Sacramento (1998-06), Houston (2007–); **Attles**—Golden St. (1970-80,80-83); **Auerbach**—Washington (1946-49), Tri-Cities (1949-50), Boston (1950-66); **Brown**—Denver (1976-79), New Jersey (1981-83), San Antonio (1988-92), LA Clippers (1992-93), Indiana (1993-97), Philadelphia (1997-2003), Detroit (2003-05), New York (2005-06), Charlotte (2008–); **Daly**—Cleveland (1981-82), Detroit (1983-92), New Jersey (1992-94), Orlando (1997-99); **Dunleavy**—L.A. Lakers (1990-91), Milwaukee (1992-1995), Portland (1997-2000), L.A. Clippers (2003–); **Fitch**—Cleveland (1970-79), Boston (1979-83), Houston (1983-88), New Jersey (1989-92), LA Clippers (1994-98); **Fitzsimmons**—Atlanta (1980-90), Cleveland (1993-99), Memphis (2004-06).

Harris—Houston (1979-83), Milwaukee (1987-92), LA Lakers (1994-99); **Holzman**—Milwaukee-St. Louis Hawks (1954-57), NY Knicks (1968-77,78-82); **Jackson**—Chicago (1989-98), LA Lakers (1999-2004, 05–); **Jones**—Washington (1973-76), Boston (1983-88), Seattle (1990-92); **Karl**—Cleveland (1984-86), Golden St. (1986-88), Seattle (1991-98), Milwaukee (1999-2003), Denver (2004—); **MacLeod**—Phoenix (1973-87), Dallas (1987-89), NY Knicks (1990-91); **Moe**—San Antonio (1976-80), Denver (1981-90), Philadelphia (1992-93).

Motta—Chicago (1968-76), Washington (1976-80), Dallas (1980-87), Sacramento (1990-91), Dallas (1994-96), Denver (1997); **Nelson**—Milwaukee (1976-87), Golden St. (1988-95, 2006—), New York (1995-96), Dallas (1997-2005); **Popovich**— San Antonio (1996—); **Ramsay**—Philadelphia (1968-72), Buffalo (1972-76), Portland (1976-86), Indiana (1986-89); **Riley**—LA Lakers (1981-90), New York (1991-95), Miami (1995-2003, 05-08); **Shue**—Baltimore (1967-73), Philadelphia (1973-77), San Diego Clippers (1978-80), Washington (1980-86), LA Clippers (1987-89); **Sloan**—Chicago (1979-82), Utah (1988—); **Tomjanovich**—Houston (1991-2003), LA Lakers (2004-05); **Wilkens**—Seattle (1969-72), Portland (1974-76), Seattle (1977-85), Cleveland (1986-93), Atlanta (1993-2000), Toronto (2000-03), New York (2004-05).

All-Time Winningest NBA Coaches (Cont.)

Top Winning Percentages

Minimum of 350 victories, including playoffs; coaches active during 2007-08 season in **bold** type.

		Yrs	W	L	Pct
1	Phil Jackson	17	1169	502	**.700**
2	Billy Cunningham	8	520	235	**.689**
3	**Gregg Popovich**	12	733	361	**.670**
4	K.C. Jones	10	603	309	**.661**
5	Red Auerbach	20	1037	548	**.654**
6	**Pat Riley**	24	1381	805	**.632**
7	Tommy Heinsohn	9	474	296	**.616**
8	**Rick Adelman**	16	879	580	**.602**
9	Chuck Daly	14	713	488	**.594**
10	**Jerry Sloan**	23	1182	811	**.593**
11	Larry Costello	10	467	323	**.591**
12	John Kundla	11	485	338	**.589**
13	**Phil "Flip" Saunders**	13	634	447	**.586**
14	Bill Sharman	7	368	267	**.580**
15	**George Karl**	20	941	697	**.574**
16	Al Cervi	9	359	267	**.573**
17	**Jeff Van Gundy**	11	474	362	**.567**
18	**Don Nelson**	29	1355	1045	**.565**
19	Joe Lapchick	9	356	277	**.562**
20	Rudy Tomjanovich	13	578	455	**.560**
21	Larry Brown	23	1110	889	**.555**
22	Bill Russell	8	375	317	**.542**
23	Del Harris	14	594	507	**.540**
24	Mike Fratello	17	687	590	**.538**
25	Alex Hannum	12	518	446	**.537**
26	Red Holzman	18	754	652	**.536**
27	Doug Moe	15	661	579	**.533**
28	Lenny Wilkens	32	1412	1253	**.530**
29	Richie Guerin	8	353	325	**.521**
30	Jack Ramsay	21	908	841	**.519**

Active Coaches' Victories

Through 2007-08 season, including playoffs.

		Yrs	W	L	Pct
1	Don Nelson, Golden St.	29	**1355**	1045	.565
2	Jerry Sloan, Utah	23	**1182**	811	.593
3	Phil Jackson, LA Lakers	17	**1169**	502	.700
4	Larry Brown, Charlotte	23	**1110**	889	.555
5	George Karl, Denver	20	**941**	697	.574
6	Rick Adelman, Houston	16	**879**	580	.602
7	Gregg Popovich, San Antonio	12	**733**	361	.670
8	Mike Dunleavy, LA Clippers	15	**611**	658	.481
9	Doc Rivers, Boston	9	**363**	352	.508
10	Byron Scott, New Orleans	8	**332**	336	.497
11	Nate McMillan, Portland	8	**314**	343	.478
12	Rick Carlisle, Dallas	6	**311**	243	.561
13	Scott Skiles, Milwaukee	8	**296**	271	.522
14	Mike D'Antoni, New York	6	**293**	198	.597
15	Maurice Cheeks, Philadelphia	7	**280**	283	.497
16	Eddie Jordan, Washington	7	**237**	296	.445
17	Jim O'Brien, Indiana	6	**232**	221	.512
18	Lawrence Frank, New Jersey	5	**209**	197	.515
19	P.J. Carlesimo, Oklahoma City	7	**206**	293	.413
20	Stan Van Gundy, Orlando	4	**186**	119	.610
21	Isiah Thomas, New York	3	**169**	174	.493
22	Mike Brown, Cleveland	3	**171**	121	.586
23	Sam Mitchell, Toronto	4	**151**	188	.445
24	Mike Woodson, Atlanta	4	**109**	226	.325
25	Randy Wittman, Minnesota	4	**96**	192	.333
26	Terry Porter, Phoenix	2	**72**	97	.426
27	Reggie Theus, Sacramento	1	**38**	44	.463
28	Marc Iavaroni, Memphis	1	**22**	60	.268
29	Michael Curry, Detroit	0	**0**	0	—
	Vinny Del Negro, Chicago	0	**0**	0	—
	Erik Spoelstra, Miami	0	**0**	0	—

Annual Awards
Most Valuable Player

The Maurice Podoloff Trophy for regular season MVP. Named after the first commissioner (then president) of the NBA. Winners first selected by the NBA players (1956-80) then a national panel of pro basketball writers and broadcasters (since 1981). Winners' scoring averages are provided; (*) indicates led league.

Multiple winners: Kareem Abdul-Jabbar (6); Michael Jordan and Bill Russell (5); Wilt Chamberlain (4); Larry Bird, Magic Johnson and Moses Malone (3); Tim Duncan, Karl Malone, Steve Nash and Bob Pettit (2).

Year		Avg	Year		Avg
1956	Bob Pettit, St. Louis, F	25.7*	1983	Moses Malone, Philadelphia, C	24.5
1957	Bob Cousy, Boston, G	20.6	1984	Larry Bird, Boston, F	24.2
1958	Bill Russell, Boston, C	16.6	1985	Larry Bird, Boston, F	28.7
1959	Bob Pettit, St. Louis, F	29.2*	1986	Larry Bird, Boston, F	25.8
1960	Wilt Chamberlain, Philadelphia, C	37.6*	1987	Magic Johnson, LAL, G	23.9
1961	Bill Russell, Boston, C	16.9	1988	Michael Jordan, Chicago, G	35.0*
1962	Bill Russell, Boston, C	18.9	1989	Magic Johnson, LAL, G	22.5
1963	Bill Russell, Boston, C	16.8	1990	Magic Johnson, LAL, G	22.3
1964	Oscar Robertson, Cincinnati, G	31.4	1991	Michael Jordan, Chicago, G	31.5*
1965	Bill Russell, Boston, C	14.1	1992	Michael Jordan, Chicago, G	30.1*
1966	Wilt Chamberlain, Philadelphia, C	33.5*	1993	Charles Barkley, Phoenix, F	25.6
1967	Wilt Chamberlain, Philadelphia, C	24.1	1994	Hakeem Olajuwon, Houston, C	27.3
1968	Wilt Chamberlain, Philadelphia, C	24.3	1995	David Robinson, San Antonio, C	27.6
1969	Wes Unseld, Baltimore, C	13.8	1996	Michael Jordan, Chicago, G	30.4*
1970	Willis Reed, New York, C	21.7	1997	Karl Malone, Utah, F	27.4
1971	Lew Alcindor, Milwaukee, C	31.7*	1998	Michael Jordan, Chicago, G	28.7*
1972	Kareem Abdul-Jabbar, Milwaukee, C	34.8*	1999	Karl Malone, Utah, F	23.8
1973	Dave Cowens, Boston, C	20.5	2000	Shaquille O'Neal, LAL, C	29.7*
1974	Kareem Abdul-Jabbar, Milwaukee, C	27.0	2001	Allen Iverson, Philadelphia, G	31.1*
1975	Bob McAdoo, Buffalo, F	34.5*	2002	Tim Duncan, San Antonio, F/C	25.5
1976	Kareem Abdul-Jabbar, LA, C	27.7	2003	Tim Duncan, San Antonio, F/C	23.3
1977	Kareem Abdul-Jabbar, LA, C	26.2	2004	Kevin Garnett, Minnesota, F	24.2
1978	Bill Walton, Portland, C	18.9	2005	Steve Nash, Phoenix, G	15.5
1979	Moses Malone, Houston, C	24.8	2006	Steve Nash, Phoenix, G	18.8
1980	Kareem Abdul-Jabbar, LA, C	24.8	2007	Dirk Nowitzki, Dallas, F	24.6
1981	Julius Erving, Philadelphia, F	24.6	2008	Kobe Bryant, LAL, G	28.3
1982	Moses Malone, Houston, C	31.1			

Note: Lew Alcindor changed his name to Kareem Abdul-Jabbar after the 1970-71 season.

Rookie of the Year

The Eddie Gottlieb Trophy for outstanding rookie of the regular season. Named after the pro basketball pioneer and owner-coach of the first NBA champion Philadelphia Warriors. Winners selected by a national panel of pro basketball writers and broadcasters. Winners' scoring averages provided; (*) indicates led league; winners who were also named MVP are in **bold** type.

Year		Avg	Year		Avg
1953	Don Meineke, Ft. Wayne, F	10.8	1982	Buck Williams, New Jersey, F	15.5
1954	Ray Felix, Baltimore, C	17.6	1983	Terry Cummings, San Diego, F	23.7
1955	Bob Pettit, Milwaukee Hawks, F	20.4	1984	Ralph Sampson, Houston, C	21.0
1956	Maurice Stokes, Rochester, F/C	16.8	1985	Michael Jordan, Chicago, G	28.2
1957	Tommy Heinsohn, Boston, F	16.2	1986	Patrick Ewing, New York, C	20.0
1958	Woody Sauldsberry, Philadelphia, F/C	12.8	1987	Chuck Person, Indiana, F	18.8
1959	Elgin Baylor, Minneapolis, F	24.9	1988	Mark Jackson, New York, G	13.6
1960	**Wilt Chamberlain**, Philadelphia, C	37.6*	1989	Mitch Richmond, Golden St., G	22.0
1961	Oscar Robertson, Cincinnati, G	30.5	1990	David Robinson, San Antonio, C	24.3
1962	Walt Bellamy, Chicago Packers, C	31.6	1991	Derrick Coleman, New Jersey, F	18.4
1963	Terry Dischinger, Chicago Zephyrs, F	25.5	1992	Larry Johnson, Charlotte, F	19.2
1964	Jerry Lucas, Cincinnati, F/C	17.7	1993	Shaquille O'Neal, Orlando,C	23.4
1965	Willis Reed, New York, C	19.5	1994	Chris Webber, Golden St., F	17.5
1966	Rick Barry, San Francisco, F	25.7	1995	Grant Hill, Detroit, F	19.9
1967	Dave Bing, Detroit, G	20.0		& Jason Kidd, Dallas, G	11.7
1968	Earl Monroe, Baltimore, G	24.3	1996	Damon Stoudamire, Toronto, G	19.0
1969	**Wes Unseld**, Baltimore, C	13.8	1997	Allen Iverson, Philadelphia, G	23.5
1970	Lew Alcindor, Milwaukee Bucks, C	28.8	1998	Tim Duncan, San Antonio, F/C	21.6
1971	Dave Cowens, Boston, C	17.0	1999	Vince Carter, Toronto, F	18.3
	& Geoff Petrie, Portland, G	24.8	2000	Elton Brand, Chicago, F	20.1
1972	Sidney Wicks, Portland, F	24.5		& Steve Francis, Houston, G	18.0
1973	Bob McAdoo, Buffalo, C/F	18.0	2001	Mike Miller, Orlando, G/F	11.9
1974	Ernie DiGregorio, Buffalo, G	15.2	2002	Pau Gasol, Memphis, F	17.6
1975	Keith Wilkes, Golden St., F	14.2	2003	Amare Stoudemire, Phoenix, F	13.5
1976	Alvan Adams, Phoenix, C	19.0	2004	LeBron James, Cleveland, F	20.9
1977	Adrian Dantley, Buffalo, F	20.3	2005	Emeka Okafor, Charlotte, F	15.1
1978	Walter Davis, Phoenix, G	24.2	2006	Chris Paul, NO/Okla. City, G	16.1
1979	Phil Ford, Kansas City, G	15.9	2007	Brandon Roy, Portland, G	16.8
1980	Larry Bird, Boston, F	21.3	2008	Kevin Durant, Seattle, F	20.3
1981	Darrell Griffith, Utah, G	20.6			

Note: The Chicago Packers changed their name to the Zephyrs after 1961-62 season. Also, Lew Alcindor changed his name to Kareem Abdul-Jabbar after the 1970-71 season.

Number One Draft Choices

Overall first choices in the NBA draft since the abolition of the territorial draft in 1966. Players who became Rookie of the Year are in **bold** type. The draft lottery began in 1985.

Year		Overall 1st Pick	Year		Overall 1st Pick
1966	New York	Cazzie Russell, Michigan	1988	LA Clippers	Danny Manning, Kansas
1967	Detroit	Jimmy Walker, Providence	1989	Sacramento	Pervis Ellison, Louisville
1968	San Diego	Elvin Hayes, Houston	1990	New Jersey	**Derrick Coleman**, Syracuse
1969	Milwaukee	**Lew Alcindor**, UCLA	1991	Charlotte	**Larry Johnson**, UNLV
1970	Detroit	Bob Lanier, St. Bonaventure	1992	Orlando	**Shaquille O'Neal**, LSU
1971	Cleveland	Austin Carr, Notre Dame	1993	Orlando	**Chris Webber**, Michigan
1972	Portland	LaRue Martin, Loyola-Chicago	1994	Milwaukee	Glenn Robinson, Purdue
1973	Philadelphia	Doug Collins, Illinois St.	1995	Golden St.	Joe Smith, Maryland
1974	Portland	Bill Walton, UCLA	1996	Philadelphia	**Allen Iverson**, Georgetown
1975	Atlanta	David Thompson, N.C. State	1997	San Antonio	**Tim Duncan**, Wake Forest
1976	Houston	John Lucas, Maryland	1998	LA Clippers	Michael Olowokandi, Pacific
1977	Milwaukee	Kent Benson, Indiana	1999	Chicago	**Elton Brand**, Duke
1978	Portland	Mychal Thompson, Minnesota	2000	New Jersey	Kenyon Martin, Cincinnati
1979	LA Lakers	Magic Johnson, Michigan St.	2001	Washington	Kwame Brown, Glynn Acad.
1980	Golden St	Joe Barry Carroll, Purdue	2002	Houston	Yao Ming, China
1981	Dallas	Mark Aguirre, DePaul	2003	Cleveland	**LeBron James**, St. Vincent/St. Mary
1982	LA Lakers	James Worthy, N. Carolina	2004	Orlando	Dwight Howard, SW Atlanta Christ.
1983	Houston	**Ralph Sampson**, Virginia	2005	Milwaukee	Andrew Bogut, Utah
1984	Houston	Akeem Olajuwon, Houston	2006	Toronto	Andrea Bargnani, Italy
1985	New York	**Patrick Ewing**, Georgetown	2007	Portland	Greg Oden, Ohio St.
1986	Cleveland	Brad Daugherty, N. Carolina	2008	Chicago	Derrick Rose, Memphis
1987	San Antonio	**David Robinson**, Navy			

Note: Lew Alcindor changed his name to Kareem Abdul-Jabbar after the 1970-71 season; Akeem Olajuwon changed his first name to Hakeem in 1991; in 1975 David Thompson signed with Denver of the ABA and did not play for Atlanta; David Robinson joined NBA for 1989-90 season after fulfilling military obligation.

Sixth Man Award

Awarded to the Best Player Off the Bench for the regular season. Winners selected by a national panel of pro basketba writers and broadcasters.

Multiple winners: Kevin McHale, Ricky Pierce and Detlef Schrempf (2).

Year	Year	Year
1983 Bobby Jones, Phi., F	1992 Detlef Schrempf, Ind., F	2001 Aaron McKie, Phi., G
1984 Kevin McHale, Bos., F	1993 Cliff Robinson, Port., F	2002 Corliss Williamson, Det., F
1985 Kevin McHale, Bos., F	1994 Dell Curry, Char., G	2003 Bobby Jackson, Sac., G
1986 Bill Walton, Bos., F/C	1995 Anthony Mason, NY, F	2004 Antawn Jamison, Dal., F
1987 Ricky Pierce, Mil., G/F	1996 Toni Kukoc, Chi., F	2005 Ben Gordon, Chi., G
1988 Roy Tarpley, Dal., F	1997 John Starks, NY, G	2006 Mike Miller, Mem., G
1989 Eddie Johnson, Pho., F	1998 Danny Manning, Pho., F	2007 Leandro Barbosa, Pho., G
1990 Ricky Pierce, Mil., G/F	1999 Darrell Armstrong, Orl., G	2008 Manu Ginobili, SA, G
1991 Detlef Schrempf, Ind., F	2000 Rodney Rogers, Pho., F	

Defensive Player of the Year

Awarded to the Best Defensive Player for the regular season. Winners selected by a national panel of pro basketball writers and broadcasters.

Multiple winners: Dikembe Mutombo and Ben Wallace (4); Mark Eaton, Sidney Moncrief, Alonzo Mourning, Hakeem Olajuwon and Dennis Rodman (2).

Year	Year	Year
1983 Sidney Moncrief, Mil., G	1992 David Robinson, SA, C	2000 Alonzo Mourning, Mia., C
1984 Sidney Moncrief, Mil., G	1993 Hakeem Olajuwon, Hou., C	2001 Dikembe Mutombo, Atl.-Phi., C
1985 Mark Eaton, Utah, C	1994 Hakeem Olajuwon, Hou., C	2002 Ben Wallace, Det., C/F
1986 Alvin Robertson, SA, G	1995 Dikembe Mutombo, Den., C	2003 Ben Wallace, Det., C/F
1987 Michael Cooper, LAL, F	1996 Gary Payton, Sea., G	2004 Ron Artest, Ind., F
1988 Michael Jordan, Chi., G	1997 Dikembe Mutombo, Atl., C	2005 Ben Wallace, Det., C/F
1989 Mark Eaton, Utah, C	1998 Dikembe Mutombo, Atl., C	2006 Ben Wallace, Det., C/F
1990 Dennis Rodman, Det., F	1999 Alonzo Mourning, Mia., C	2007 Marcus Camby, Den., C
1991 Dennis Rodman, Det., F		2008 Kevin Garnett, Bos, F

Most Improved Player

Awarded to the Most Improved Player for the regular season. Winners selected by a national panel of pro basketball writers and broadcasters.

Year	Year	Year
1986 Alvin Robertson, SA, G	1994 Don MacLean, Wash., F	2001 Tracy McGrady, Orl., F
1987 Dale Ellis, Sea., G	1995 Dana Barros, Phi., G	2002 Jermaine O'Neal, Ind., F
1988 Kevin Duckworth, Port., C	1996 Gheorghe Muresan, Wash., C	2003 Gilbert Arenas, G.St., G
1989 Kevin Johnson, Pho., G	1997 Isaac Austin, Miami, C	2004 Zach Randolph, Port., F
1990 Rony Seikaly, Mia., C	1998 Alan Henderson, Atl., F	2005 Bobby Simmons, LAC, F
1991 Scott Skiles, Orl., G	1999 Darrell Armstrong, Orl., G	2006 Boris Diaw, Pho., G
1992 Pervis Ellison, Wash., C	2000 Jalen Rose, Ind., G	2007 Monta Ellis, G. St., G
1993 Mahmoud Abdul-Rauf, Den., G		2008 Hedo Turkoglu, Orl., F

Coach of the Year

The Red Auerbach Trophy for outstanding coach of the year. Renamed in 1967 for the former Boston coach who led the Celtics to nine NBA titles. Winners selected by a national panel of pro basketball writers and broadcasters. Previous season and winning season records are provided; (*) indicates division title.

Multiple winners: Don Nelson and Pat Riley (3); Hubie Brown, Bill Fitch, Cotton Fitzsimmons and Gene Shue (2).

Year		Improvement		Year		Improvement	
1963 Harry Gallatin, St. L	.29-51	to	48-32	1986 Mike Fratello, Atl	.34-48	to	50-32
1964 Alex Hannum, SF	.31-49	to	48-32*	1987 Mike Schuler, Port	.40-42	to	49-33
1965 Red Auerbach, Bos	.59-21*	to	61-18*	1988 Doug Moe, Den	.37-45	to	54-28*
1966 Dolph Schayes, Phi	.40-40	to	55-25*	1989 Cotton Fitzsimmons, Pho	.28-54	to	55-27
1967 Johnny Kerr, Chi	.Expan.	to	33-48	1990 Pat Riley, LA Lakers	.57-25*	to	63-19*
1968 Richie Guerin, St. L	.39-42	to	56-26*	1991 Don Chaney, Hou	.41-41	to	52-30
1969 Gene Shue, Balt	.36-46	to	57-25*	1992 Don Nelson, GS	.44-38	to	55-27
1970 Red Holzman, NY	.54-28	to	60-22*	1993 Pat Riley, NY	.51-31	to	60-22
1971 Dick Motta, Chi	.39-43	to	51-31	1994 Lenny Wilkens, Atl	.43-39	to	57-25*
1972 Bill Sharman, LA	.48-34*	to	69-13*	1995 Del Harris, LA Lakers	.33-49	to	48-34
1973 Tommy Heinsohn, Bos	.56-26*	to	68-14*	1996 Phil Jackson, Chi	.47-35	to	72-10*
1974 Ray Scott, Det	.40-42	to	52-30	1997 Pat Riley, Mia	.42-40	to	61-21
1975 Phil Johnson, KC-Omaha	.33-49	to	44-38	1998 Larry Bird, Ind	.39-43	to	58-24
1976 Bill Fitch, Cle	.40-42	to	49-33*	1999 Mike Dunleavy, Port.	.46-36	to	35-15*
1977 Tom Nissalke, Hou	.40-42	to	49-33*	2000 Doc Rivers, Orlando	.33-17	to	41-41
1978 Hubie Brown, Atl	.31-51	to	41-41	2001 Larry Brown, Phila.	.49-33	to	56-26*
1979 Cotton Fitzsimmons, KC	.31-51	to	48-34*	2002 Rick Carlisle, Det	.32-50	to	50-32*
1980 Bill Fitch, Bos	.29-53	to	61-21*	2003 Gregg Popovich, SA	.58-24*	to	60-22*
1981 Jack McKinney, Ind	.37-45	to	44-38	2004 Hubie Brown, Mem.	.28-54	to	50-32
1982 Gene Shue, Wash	.39-43	to	43-39	2005 Mike D'Antoni, Pho	.29-53	to	62-30*
1983 Don Nelson, Mil	.55-27*	to	51-31*	2006 Avery Johnson, Dal	.58-24	to	60-22*
1984 Frank Layden, Utah	.30-52	to	45-37*	2007 Sam Mitchell, Tor	.27-55	to	47-35*
1985 Don Nelson, Mil	.50-32*	to	59-23*	2008 Byron Scott, NO	.39-43	to	56-26*

NBA's 50 Greatest Players

In October 1996, as part of its 50th anniversary celebration, the NBA named the 50 greatest players in league history. The voting was done by a league-approved panel of media, former players and coaches, current and former general managers and team executives. The players are listed alphabetically along with the dates of their professional careers and positions. Shaquille O'Neal, the only player active in 2007-08, is in **bold** type.

Player	Pos	Player	Pos	Player	Pos
Kareem Abdul-Jabbar, 1969-89	C	George Gervin, 1972-86	G	Robert Parish, 1976-97	C
Nate Archibald, 1970-84	G	Hal Greer, 1958-73	G	Bob Pettit, 1954-65	F/C
Paul Arizin, 1950-61	F/G	John Havlicek, 1962-78	F/G	Scottie Pippen, 1987-2005	F
Charles Barkley, 1984-00	F	Elvin Hayes, 1968-84	F/C	Willis Reed, 1964-74	C
Rick Barry, 1965-80	F	Magic Johnson, 1979-91, 96	G	Oscar Robertson, 1960-74	G
Elgin Baylor, 1958-72	F	Sam Jones, 1957-69	G	David Robinson, 1989-2003	C
Dave Bing, 1966-78	G	Michael Jordan, 1984-93,	G	Bill Russell, 1956-69	C
Larry Bird, 1979-92	F	95-98, 01-03		Dolph Schayes, 1948-64	F/C
Wilt Chamberlain, 1959-73	C	Jerry Lucas, 1963-74	F/C	Bill Sharman, 1950-61	G
Bob Cousy, 1950-63, 69-70	G	Karl Malone, 1985-2005	F	John Stockton, 1984-2003	G
Dave Cowens, 1970-80, 1982-83	C	Moses Malone, 1974-95	C	Isiah Thomas, 1981-94	G
Billy Cunningham, 1965-76	G	Pete Maravich, 1970-80	G	Nate Thurmond, 1963-77	C/F
Dave DeBusschere, 1962-74	F	Kevin McHale, 1980-93	F	Wes Unseld, 1968-81	C/F
Clyde Drexler, 1983-98	G	George Mikan, 1946-54, 55-56	C	Bill Walton, 1974-88	C
Julius Erving, 1971-87	F	Earl Monroe, 1967-80	G	Jerry West, 1960-74	G
Patrick Ewing, 1985-2002	C	Hakeem Olajuwon, 1984-2002	C	Lenny Wilkens, 1960-75	G
Walt Frazier, 1967-80	G	**Shaquille O'Neal**, 1992—	C	James Worthy, 1982-94	F

Note: Rick Barry, Billy Cunningham, Julius Erving, George Gervin and Moses Malone all played part of their pro careers in the ABA.

NBA's 10 Greatest Coaches

In December 1996, as part of its 50th anniversary celebration, the NBA named the 10 greatest coaches in league history. The voting was done by a league-approved panel of media. The coaches are listed alphabetically along with the dates of their professional coaching careers and overall records, including playoff games, and number of NBA titles won. Active coaches are in **bold** type.

Coach	W	L	Pct.	Titles	Coach	W	L	Pct.	Titles
Red Auerbach, 1946-66	1037	548	.654	9	John Kundla, 1947-59	485	338	.589	5
Chuck Daly, 1981-94, 97-99	713	488	.594	2	**Don Nelson**, 1976-96,				
Bill Fitch, 1970-98	999	1160	.463	1	97-05, 06—	1355	1045	.565	0
Red Holzman, 1953-82	754	652	.536	2	Jack Ramsay, 1968-89	908	841	.519	1
Phil Jackson, 1989-98,					Pat Riley, 1981-2003, 05-08	1381	805	.632	5
99-04, 05—	1169	502	.700	9	Lenny Wilkens, 1969-2005	1412	1253	.530	1
					TOTALS	10213	7632	.572	35

World Championships

The World Basketball Championships for men and women have been played regularly at four-year intervals (give or take a year) since 1970. The men's tournament began in 1950 and the women's in 1953. The Federation Internationale de Basketball Amateur (FIBA), which governs the World and Olympic tournaments, was founded in 1932. FIBA first allowed professional players from the NBA to participate in 1994. A team of collegians represented the USA in 1998.

Men

Multiple wins: Yugoslavia (5); Soviet Union and USA (3); Brazil (2).

Year	
1950	**Argentina**, United States, Chile
1954	**United States**, Brazil, Philippines
1959	**Brazil**, United States, Chile
1963	**Brazil**, Yugoslavia, Soviet Union
1967	**Soviet Union**, Yugoslavia, Brazil
1970	**Yugoslavia**, Brazil, Soviet Union
1974	**Soviet Union**, Yugoslavia, United States
1978	**Yugoslavia**, Soviet Union, Brazil
1982	**Soviet Union**, United States, Yugoslavia
1986	**United States**, Soviet Union, Yugoslavia
1990	**Yugoslavia**, Soviet Union, United States
1994	**United States**, Russia, Croatia
1998	**Yugoslavia**, Russia, United States
2002	**Yugoslavia**, Argentina, Germany
2006	**Spain**, Greece, United States
2010	at Turkey

Women

Multiple wins: USA (7); Soviet Union (6).

Year	
1953	**United States**, Chile, France
1957	**United States**, Soviet Union, Czechoslovakia
1959	**Soviet Union**, Bulgaria, Czechoslovakia
1964	**Soviet Union**, Czechoslovakia, Bulgaria
1967	**Soviet Union**, South Korea, Czechoslovakia
1971	**Soviet Union**, Czechoslovakia, Brazil
1975	**Soviet Union**, Japan, Czechoslovakia
1979	**United States**, South Korea, Canada
1983	**Soviet Union**, United States, China
1986	**United States**, Soviet Union, Canada
1990	**United States**, Yugoslavia, Cuba
1994	**Brazil**, China, United States
1998	**United States**, Russia, Australia
2002	**United States**, Russia, Australia
2006	**Australia**, Russia, United States
2010	at Czech Republic

American Basketball Association
ABA Finals

The original American Basketball Assn. began play in 1967-68 as a 10-team rival of the 21-year-old NBA. The ABA, which introduced the three-point basket, a multi-colored ball and the All-Star Game Slam Dunk Contest, lasted nine seasons before folding following the 1975-76 season. Four ABA teams—Denver, Indiana, New York and San Antonio—survived to enter the NBA in 1976-77. The NBA also adopted the three-point basket (in 1979-80) and the All-Star Game Slam Dunk Contest. The older league, however, refused to take in the ABA ball.

Multiple winners: Indiana (3); New York (2).

Year	Winner	Head Coach	Series	Loser	Head Coach
1968	Pittsburgh Pipers	Vince Cazzetta	4-3 (WLLWLWW)	New Orleans Bucs	Babe McCarthy
1969	Oakland Oaks	Alex Hannum	4-1 (WLWWW)	Indiana Pacers	Bob Leonard
1970	Indiana Pacers	Bob Leonard	4-2 (WWLLWW)	Los Angeles Stars	Bill Sharman
1971	Utah Stars	Bill Sharman	4-3 (WWLLWLW)	Kentucky Colonels	Frank Ramsey
1972	Indiana Pacers	Bob Leonard	4-2 (WLWLWW)	New York Nets	Lou Carnesecca
1973	Indiana Pacers	Bob Leonard	4-3 (WWLWLWW)	Kentucky Colonels	Joe Mullaney
1974	New York Nets	Kevin Loughery	4-1 (WWWLW)	Utah Stars	Joe Mullaney
1975	Kentucky Colonels	Hubie Brown	4-1 (WWWLW)	Indiana Pacers	Bob Leonard
1976	New York Nets	Kevin Loughery	4-2 (WLWLWLW)	Denver Nuggets	Larry Brown

Most Valuable Player

Winners' scoring averages provided; (*) indicates led league.

Multiple winners: Julius Erving (3); Mel Daniels (2).

Year		Avg
1968	Connie Hawkins, Pittsburgh, C	26.8*
1969	Mel Daniels, Indiana, C	24.0
1970	Spencer Haywood, Denver, C	30.0*
1971	Mel Daniels, Indiana, C	21.0
1972	Artis Gilmore, Kentucky, C	23.8
1973	Billy Cunningham, Carolina, F	24.1
1974	Julius Erving, New York, F	27.4*
1975	George McGinnis, Indiana, F	29.8*
	& Julius Erving, New York, F	27.9
1976	Julius Erving, New York, F	29.3*

Rookie of the Year

Winners' scoring averages provided; (*) indicates led league. Rookies who were also named Most Valuable Player are in **bold** type.

Year		Avg
1968	Mel Daniels, Minnesota, C	22.2
1969	Warren Armstrong, Oakland, G	21.5
1970	**Spencer Haywood**, Denver, C	30.0*
1971	Dan Issel, Kentucky, C	29.8*
	& Charlie Scott, Virginia, G	27.1
1972	**Artis Gilmore**, Kentucky, C	23.8
1973	Brian Taylor, New York, G	15.3
1974	Swen Nater, Virginia-SA, C	14.1
1975	Marvin Barnes, St. Louis, C	24.0
1976	David Thompson, Denver, F	26.0

Note: Warren Armstrong changed his name to Warren Jabali after the 1970-71 season.

Coach of the Year

Previous season and winning season records are provided; (*) indicates division title.

Multiple winner: Larry Brown (3).

Year		Improvement
1968	Vince Cazzetta, Pittsburgh	54-24*
1969	Alex Hannum, Oakland	22-56 to 60-18*
1970	Joe Belmont, Denver	44-34 to 51-33*
	& Bill Sharman, LA Stars	33-45 to 43-41
1971	Al Bianchi, Virginia	44-40 to 55-29*
1972	Tom Nissalke, Dallas	30-54 to 42-42
1973	Larry Brown, Carolina	35-49 to 57-27*
1974	Babe McCarthy, Kentucky	56-28 to 53-31
	& Joe Mullaney, Utah	55-29* to 51-33*
1975	Larry Brown, Denver	37-47 to 65-19*
1976	Larry Brown, Denver	65-19* to 60-24*

Scoring Leaders

Scoring championship decided by per game point average every season.

Multiple winner: Julius Erving (3).

Year		Gm	Avg	Pts
1968	Connie Hawkins, Pittsburgh	70	1875	26.8
1969	Rick Barry, Oakland	35	1190	34.0
1970	Spencer Haywood, Denver	84	2519	30.0
1971	Dan Issel, Kentucky	83	2480	29.8
1972	Charlie Scott, Virginia	73	2524	34.6
1973	Julius Erving, Virginia	71	2268	31.9
1974	Julius Erving, New York	84	2299	27.4
1975	George McGinnis, Indiana	79	2353	29.8
1976	Julius Erving, New York	84	2462	29.3

ABA All-Star Game

The ABA All-Star Game was an Eastern Division vs. Western Division contest from 1968-75. League membership had dropped to seven teams by 1976, the ABA's last season, so the team in first place at the break (Denver) played an All-Star team made up from the other six clubs.

Series: East won 5, West 3 and Denver 1.

Year	Result	Host	Coaches	Most Valuable Player
1968	East 126, West 120	Indiana	Jim Pollard, Babe McCarthy	Larry Brown, New Orleans
1969	West 133, East 127	Louisville	Alex Hannum, Gene Rhodes	John Beasley, Dallas
1970	West 128, East 98	Indiana	Babe McCarthy, Bob Leonard	Spencer Haywood, Denver
1971	East 126, West 122	Carolina	Al Bianchi, Bill Sharman	Mel Daniels, Indiana
1972	East 142, West 115	Louisville	Joe Mullaney, Ladell Andersen	Dan Issel, Kentucky
1973	West 123, East 111	Utah	Ladell Andersen, Larry Brown	Warren Jabali, Denver
1974	East 128, West 112	Virginia	Babe McCarthy, Joe Mullaney	Artis Gilmore, Kentucky
1975	East 151, West 124	San Antonio	Kevin Loughery, Larry Brown	Freddie Lewis, St. Louis
1976	Denver 144, ABA 138	Denver	Larry Brown, Kevin Loughery	David Thompson, Denver

Continental Basketball Association

Originally named the Eastern Pennsylvania Basketball League when it formed on April 23, 1946, the league changed names several times before becoming known as the Eastern Basketball Association. In 1978, the EBA was redubbed the CBA. The CBA suspended operations following the 2000 season but reorganized for the 2001-02 season.

Multiple champions: Allentown and Wilkes-Barre (8); Yakima/Yakama (5); Scranton, Tampa Bay, and Williamsport (3); Albany, Dakota, La Crosse, Pottsville, Rochester, Sioux Falls and Wilmington (2).

League Champions

Year		Year		Year		Year	
1947	Wilkes-Barre Barons	1964	Camden Bullets	1979	Rochester Zeniths	1995	Yakima Sun Kings
1948	Reading Keys	1965	Allentown Jets	1980	Anchorage Northern	1996	Sioux Falls Skyforce
1949	Pottsville Packers	1966	Wilmington Blue		Knights	1997	Oklahoma City
1950	Williamsport Billies		Bombers	1981	Rochester Zeniths		Calvary
1951	Sunbury Mercuries	1967	Wilmington Blue	1982	Lancaster Lightning	1998	Quad City Thunder
1952	Pottsville Packers		Bombers	1983	Detroit Spirits	1999	Connecticut Pride
1953	Williamsport Billies	1968	Allentown Jets	1984	Albany Patroons	2000	Yakima Sun Kings
1954	Williamsport Billies	1969	Wilkes-Barre Barons	1985	Tampa Bay Thrillers	2001	suspended play
1955	Wilkes-Barre Barons	1970	Allentown Jets	1986	Tampa Bay Thrillers	2002	Dakota Wizards
1956	Wilkes-Barre Barons	1971	Scranton Apollos	1987	Rapid City Thrillers*	2003	Yakima Sun Kings
1957	Scranton Miners	1972	Allentown Jets	1988	Albany Patroons	2004	Dakota Wizards
1958	Wilkes-Barre Barons	1973	Wilkes-Barre Barons	1989	Tulsa Fast Breakers	2005	Sioux Falls Skyforce
1959	Wilkes-Barre Barons	1974	Hartford Capitols	1990	La Crosse Catbirds	2006	Yakama Sun Kings
1960	Easton Madisons	1975	Allentown Jets	1991	Wichita Falls Texans	2007	Yakama Sun Kings
1961	Baltimore Bullets	1976	Allentown Jets	1992	La Crosse Catbirds	2008	Oklahoma Calvary
1962	Allentown Jets	1977	Scranton Apollos	1993	Omaha Racers		
1963	Allentown Jets	1978	Wilkes-Barre Barons	1994	Quad City Thunder		

*The Tampa Bay Thrillers moved to Rapid City, S.D. at the end of the 1987 regular season. The Yakima Sun Kings changed the spelling of their name to Yakama after they were purchased by the Yakama Indiana Nation in 2005.

National Basketball Association Development League

The D-League was founded in 2001 as an eight-team player and coach development league owned and operated by the NBA. Until recently, the individual teams did not have a direct relationship with NBA clubs but occasionally players and coaches were called up to the NBA. The NBDL champion was determined in a best-of-three championship series for the first two seasons of the league before changing the format to a single-game playoff in 2004. It reverted to a best-of-three in 2008.

The league has expanded and contracted in the years since its founding and some franchises have relocated. In 2005, the NBA announced that each D-League team would now be officially affiliated with one or more NBA teams, making it more of a true minor league system, where players can be sent down to gain experience and called-up when the big league team has a need. Four teams (The Colorado 14ers, Dakota Wizards, Idaho Stampede and Sioux Falls Skyforce) withdrew from the CBA and joined the D-League prior to the 2007 season. The league membership currently consists of 16 franchises.

League Champions

Multiple champions: Asheville (2).

Year	Champions	Head Coach	Score	Runners-up	Head Coach
2002	Greenville Groove	Milton Barnes	2-0	No. Charleston Lowgators	Alex English
2003	Mobile Revelers	Sam Vincent	2-1 (WLW)	Fayetteville Patriots	Jeff Capel
2004	Asheville Altitude	Joey Meyer	108-106 OT	Huntsville Flight	Ralph Lewis
2005	Asheville Altitude	Joey Meyer	90-67	Columbus Riverdragons	Jeff Malone
2006	Albuquerque Thunderbirds	Michael Cooper	119-108	Fort Worth Flyers	Sam Vincent
2007	Dakota Wizards	Dave Joerger	129-121	Colorado 14ers	Joe Wolf
2008	Idaho Stampeders	Bryan Gates	2-1 (LWW)	Austin Toros	Quin Snyder

Annual Awards

Most Valuable Player

Winner's scoring averages provided; (*) indicates led league.

Year		PPG
2002	Ansu Sesay, Greenville, F	16.5
2003	Devin Brown, Fayetteville, G	16.9
2004	Tierre Brown, Charleston, G	18.6
2005	Matt Carroll, Roanoke, G	20.1*
2006	Marcus Fizer, Austin, F	22.7
2007	Randy Livingston, Idaho, G	12.3
2008	Kasib Powell, Sioux Falls, F	22.3

Rookie of the Year

Year	
2002	Fred House, N. Charleston
2003	Devin Brown, Fayetteville
2004	Desmond Penigar, Asheville
2005	James Thomas, Roanoke
2006	Will Bynum, Roanoke
2007	Louis Amundson, Colorado
2008	Blake Ahearn, Dakota

Defensive Player of the Year

Year	
2002	Jeff Myers, Greenville
2003	Mikki Moore, Roanoke
2004	Karim Shabazz, Charleston
2005	Derrick Zimmerman, Columbus
2006	Derrick Zimmerman, Austin
2007	Renaldo Major, Dakota
2008	Stephane Lasme, Los Angeles & Mouhamed Sene, Idaho

Scoring Champion

Year		PPG
2002	Isaac Fontaine, Mobile	17.4
2003	Nate Johnson, Columbus	19.5
2004	Desmond Penigar, Asheville	19.6
2005	Isiah Victor, Roanoke	19.5
2006	Bracey Wright, Florida	22.0
2007	Roger Powell, Arkansas	22.3
2008	Morris Almond, Utah	25.6

WOMEN
Women's National Basketball Association

The WNBA, owned and operated by the NBA, began play in 1997 as an eight-team summer league. The league added two teams prior to its second season (1998), then added two more teams before its third season in 1999. Four additional teams were added before the 2000 season, bringing the total number of teams to 16. Prior to the 2003 season two franchises were relocated and two were contracted and one franchise folded before the 2004 season. One team (Chicago Sky) was added for the 2006 season bringing the total back to 14. The WNBA champion was determined by a single-game playoff in the league's 1997 inaugural season, before going to a best-of-three championship series in 1998 and a best-of-five championship series starting in 2005.

Multiple winners: Houston (4); Detroit (3); Los Angeles (2).

Year	Champions	Head Coach	Series	Runners-up	Head Coach
1997	Houston Comets	Van Chancellor	65-51	New York Liberty	Nancy Darsch
1998	Houston Comets	Van Chancellor	2-1 (LWW)	Phoenix Mercury	Cheryl Miller
1999	Houston Comets	Van Chancellor	2-1 (WLW)	New York Liberty	Richie Adubato
2000	Houston Comets	Van Chancellor	2-0	New York Liberty	Richie Adubato
2001	Los Angeles Sparks	Michael Cooper	2-0	Charlotte Sting	Anne Donovan
2002	Los Angeles Sparks	Michael Cooper	2-0	New York Liberty	Richie Adubato
2003	Detroit Shock	Bill Laimbeer	2-1 (LWW)	Los Angeles Sparks	Michael Cooper
2004	Seattle Storm	Anne Donovan	2-1 (LWW)	Connecticut Sun	Mike Thibault
2005	Sacramento Monarchs	John Whisenant	3-1 (WLWW)	Connecticut Sun	Mike Thibault
2006	Detroit Shock	Bill Laimbeer	3-2 (LWLWW)	Sacramento Monarchs	John Whisenant
2007	Phoenix Mercury	Paul Westhead	3-2 (LWLWW)	Dertoit Shock	Bill Laimbeer
2008	Detroit Shock	Bill Laimbeer	3-0	San Antonio Silver Stars	Dan Hughes

Championship MVPs: 1997-Cynthia Cooper, Houston; 1998-Cynthia Cooper, Houston; 1999-Cynthia Cooper, Houston; 2000-Cynthia Cooper, Houston; 2001-Lisa Leslie, Los Angeles; 2002-Lisa Leslie, Los Angeles; 2003-Ruth Riley, Detroit; 2004-Betty Lennox, Seattle; 2005-Yolanda Griffith, Sacramento; 2006-Deanna Nolan, Detroit; 2007-Cappie Pondexter, Phoenix; 2008-Katie Smith, Detroit.

Annual Awards
Most Valuable Player

Winner's scoring averages provided; (*) indicates led league.

Multiple winners: Sheryl Swoopes and Lisa Leslie (3); Cynthia Cooper (2).

Year		Avg
1997	Cynthia Cooper, Houston	22.2*
1998	Cynthia Cooper, Houston	22.7*
1999	Yolanda Griffith, Sacramento	18.8
2000	Sheryl Swoopes, Houston	20.7*
2001	Lisa Leslie, Los Angeles	19.5
2002	Sheryl Swoopes, Houston	18.5
2003	Lauren Jackson, Seattle	21.2*
2004	Lisa Leslie, Los Angeles	17.6
2005	Sheryl Swoopes, Houston	18.6*
2006	Lisa Leslie, Los Angeles	20.0
2007	Lauren Jackson, Seattle	23.8*
2008	Candace Parker, Los Angeles	18.5

Coach of the Year

Previous season and winning season's record are provided; (*) indicates division title.

Multiple winner: Van Chancellor (3); Mike Thibault (2).

Year		Improvement
1997	Van Chancellor, Houston	18-10*
1998	Van Chancellor, Houston	18-10 to 27-3*
1999	Van Chancellor, Houston	27-3 to 26-6*
2000	Michael Cooper, Los Angeles	20-12 to 28-4*
2001	Dan Hughes, Cleveland	17-15 to 22-10*
2002	Marianne Stanley, Washington	10-22 to 17-15
2003	Bill Laimbeer, Detroit	9-23 to 25-9*
2004	Suzie McConnell Serio, Minn.	18-16 to 18-16
2005	John Whisenant, Sacramento	18-16 to 25-9*
2006	Mike Thibault, Connecticut	26-8 to 26-8*
2007	Dan Hughes, San Antonio	13-21 to 20-14
2008	Mike Thibault, Connecticut	18-16 to 21-13

Rookie of the Year

Year		Year	
1998	Tracy Reid, Cha	2004	Diana Taurasi, Pho
1999	Chamique Holdsclaw, Wash	2005	Temeka Johnson, Was
2000	Betty Lennox, Minn	2006	Seimone Augustus, Minn
2001	Jackie Stiles, Port	2007	Armintie Price, Chi.
2002	Tamika Catchings, Ind	2008	Candace Parker, LA
2003	Cheryl Ford, Det		

Defensive Player of the Year

Multiple winners: Sheryl Swoopes (3); Tamika Catchings, Lisa Leslie and Teresa Weatherspoon (2).

Year		Year	
1997	T. Weatherspoon, NY	2003	Sheryl Swoopes, Hou
1998	T. Weatherspoon, NY	2004	Lisa Leslie, LA
1999	Yolanda Griffith, Sac	2005	Tamika Catchings, Ind
2000	Sheryl Swoopes, Hou	2006	Tamika Catchings, Ind
2001	Debbie Black, Mia	2007	Lauren Jackson, Sea.
2002	Sheryl Swoopes, Hou	2008	Lisa Leslie, LA

WNBA Number One Draft Picks

Year		Overall First Pick
1997	Utah Starzz	Dena Head
1998	Utah Starzz	Margo Dydek
1999	Washington Mystics	Chamique Holdsclaw
2000	Cleveland Rockers	Ann Wauters
2001	Seattle Storm	Lauren Jackson
2002	Seattle Storm	Sue Bird
2003	Cleveland Rockers	LaToya Thomas
2004	Phoenix Mercury	Diana Taurasi
2005	Charlotte Sting	Janel McCarville
2006	Minnesota Lynx	Seimone Augustus
2007	Phoenix Mercury	Lindsey Harding
2008	Los Angeles	Candace Parker

2007 / 2008 YEAR IN REVIEW

Pittsburgh's new dynamic duo, **Evgeni Malkin** (l) and Sidney Crosby, led the Pens to the Stanley Cup Finals in 2008.

WINGS
FLY HIGH

With a smart mix of fresh blood and familiar faces, the Red Wings skated with the Stanley Cup for the fourth time in 11 seasons.

by Scott Burnside

WHEN NICKLAS LIDSTROM TOOK THE STANLEY CUP from NHL commissioner Gary Bettman and presented it to his teammates, he became the first player born and trained in Europe to captain a Stanley Cup champion.

And, to be sure, this finely tuned Detroit team that finally beat back a stubborn Pittsburgh Penguins team by a 3-2 count in the decisive Game 6 has dispelled the old myth that you can't win a championship with a team frontloaded with European players.

But if you looked around the ice at Mellon Arena, at the players and their families and friends, many wiping back tears of joy or relief, you came to understand that this Detroit team wasn't built so much on drafting and developing European talent, but in fostering something much more powerful, something closely akin to family.

This was a team that didn't just talk about loyalty, they lived it.

How else to explain Chris Osgood, who now owns three Stanley Cup rings with the Red Wings, the previous two won 10 years apart.

Few other NHL clubs would be willing to bring back an aging goaltender for another kick at the can, yet GM Ken Holland embraced the 35-year-old's return after the lockout, understanding Osgood desperately wanted to come to his hockey home – Detroit.

And while Holland likely never imagined this scene, there was Osgood, winning his 14th game of these playoffs, fending off one final, valiant Pittsburgh thrust and raising his arms in the air to signal the Red Wings' fourth Stanley Cup win since 1997.

"It's been a long journey. Fifteen pounds later," Osgood said.

Osgood wasn't expected to be anywhere but on the end of the bench when the playoffs began, but with Dominik Hasek wobbling early in the first round, Red Wings coach Mike Babcock made the switch and Osgood rewarded him with stellar netminding night in and night out.

 Scott Burnside is an NHL writer for ESPN.com.

AP Images

Red Wings defenseman and captain **Nicklas Lidstrom** hoisted the Stanley Cup over his head for the fourth time in his Hall-of-Fame career.

"When you pull your goalie in the first round of the Stanley Cup playoffs, that usually means you're going fishing in about three days, and not 14 more wins or whatever we needed to get it done," Babcock said. "You've got to give him a lot of credit. He sat in my office at my house three years ago or two years ago, I guess, after the season, and talked about reinventing himself and finding a way, and he did."

Osgood is a decade older than the last time he held the Cup in his hands. He has a quiet confidence, in part because he is where he knew he belonged — in a Red Wings jersey.

"I'm much more mature," Osgood said. "I'm just going to take it all in. It's not about me, it's about guys like Dallas Drake."

A journeyman forward brought in to add some sand to the Red Wings' dressing room, Drake was the second player to handle the Stanley Cup, taking it from Lidstrom and holding it high above his head.

Drake played his first playoff game as an NHL player in 1993 as a member of the Red Wings. He'd played more than 1,000 regular-season games, but never made it even to a finals series. He came home to the Red Wings family to win his first Stanley Cup championship.

"My heart's still in my throat," the 39-year-old Drake said.

He recalled always managing to watch the final game of the playoffs every season just to watch the guys take their turns with the Cup. Suddenly, he was one of those guys.

No NHL player knows how to agitate quite like **Sean Avery**. In the 2008 playoffs, he got under Devils' goalie **Martin Brodeur's** skin — almost literally — causing the NHL to institute an immediate rule change.

"My legs are a little bit shaky. I was just trying to keep it [the cup] over my head," he said.

Asked about the frenetic final moments of the game after the Penguins had scored a power-play goal with 1:27 left to make the score 3-2 and then came within an inch or two of tying the game in the final seconds, Drake said, "Try sitting on the bench. I kept staring at my skates thinking time would go by faster but it didn't."

Among those Red Wings on the ice in that final, frenzied moment was Dan Cleary. He, too, is a player who might not have been anywhere in hockey if it weren't for the Detroit Red Wings and their willingness to give players a second or even third chance.

"I'll never forget this night as long as I live," said Cleary, who became the first Newfoundland native to win a Stanley Cup. "It feels like the entire weight of the world left me."

From a top prospect to chronic underachiever to a man without a contract three years ago, Cleary too has found a home in Detroit and, in return, has given them nothing but dedicated play.

"Here I am at the pinnacle of hockey," he said in disbelief.

As soon as he took the Cup from Drake, Cleary sought out his family in the stands and raised it to them.

"Oh my gosh, it's so surreal," said Cleary's wife Jelena, holding 22-month-old daughter Elle in her arms. "I'm just so happy for him."

Not far away on the ice was another player who came home to the Red Wings family this season. Darren McCarty played in only one game in the finals, but that did little to diminish the moment for him.

At the start of the season, McCarty was out of hockey, his life a virtual train wreck of financial woes and substance-abuse issues. Former teammate Kris Draper went to bat for him, and Holland — who drafted McCarty back in 1992 and has likened the rugged winger to a son — told McCarty he'd give him a chance if he was ready to get his life back together.

It paid off for both sides, but especially McCarty, who has reconnected with his ex-wife and four children. Two of them were at his side on the Mellon Arena ice as he talked about thinking of a montage of all the steps that led to this moment. McCarty was in Detroit for three championships in 1997, 1998 and 2002, but this one represents something greater, a victory in life.

"I've cried many tears already," McCarty's sister Melissa said as she watched her brother talk to reporters. "Just knowing how hard he's worked. Hockey's just the icing on the cake. We're so grateful to the Red Wing organization."

A few feet away from the McCarty family, former defenseman Jiri Fischer was embracing teammates and friends. He nearly died on the ice two years ago, but remains a part of the team.

Hasek came back to this team, too. He won a Cup here in 2002 and managed to put a lot of bad blood behind him to become the ultimate team player as Osgood took the Red Wings home.

Chris Chelios came here as a veteran expected to play out his career and yet has defied Father Time to win his second championship with the Red Wings. This might be it for him, since he was a healthy scratch for the finals. Despite his years in Chicago and Montreal, it's hard to think of Chelios as anything but a Red Wing.

In all, five Red Wings won their fourth Stanley Cup on this night. Those ties to the past tell almost as much of a story as the Wings' Euro-centrism. Six of the Red Wings' top nine scorers in the playoffs are from Sweden and another, Pavel Datsyuk, is from Russia.

And the presence of those talented Europeans proves there is not just one stylistic blueprint for success. Yet there is always one constant, regardless of whether your players are from Newfoundland or Stockholm — it's the willingness to commit to one another without question.

Lidstrom, of course, is the measured heart of this team, the tone-setter. And he proved he is a worthy successor to The Captain, Steve Yzerman, not just with his play, but with his complete understanding of his dressing room. Lidstrom said he started thinking about to whom he would hand the Cup back in the first round. Drake seemed a natural, he said.

"Looking at all the players on our team, Dallas is one of the first ones I played with," Lidstrom said. "He came in the year after I did. He's been in the league for 16 years. He had a long, good career. And he had never been to the finals before. So it felt natural to me to give it to him for all the effort and hours and everything he's put into the game, and not having a chance to hoist a Cup yet."

As for being the first European captain, Lidstrom has tried to downplay such talk, but he had to acknowledge it was something special, too.

"It's something I'm very proud of. I've been over here for a long time," he said. "I watched Steve Yzerman hoist it three times in the past, and I'm very proud of being the first European. I'm very proud of being a captain of the Red Wings. So much history with the team and great tradition, and we see some of the older players coming through. So I'm very proud to be the captain."

One of those experiencing this for the first time was coach Mike Babcock. He has a unique view of the team that has become his family and what it means to have won a championship with them.

"Well, you know, I probably haven't come to grips with that," he said. "But to be able to share this journey with the guys and to be able to share it with the city of Detroit and obviously my family, that's very emotional. And I'm sure I'm going to have some emotional moments in the next week just thinking about it."

10 Memorable Moments From The Postseason

by Scott Burnside

• Niklas Kronwall's crushing — and clean — open-ice hit on Pittsburgh's Ryan Malone near the Pittsburgh blue line early in Game 1 of the Stanley Cup finals. The hit broke Malone's nose for the third time in his career.

• Evgeni Malkin's short-handed slap-shot goal against Philadelphia in the opening game of the Eastern Conference finals. Malkin had been put down in the Flyers zone, but as he was coming back into the play, the Flyers turned the puck over and Sergei Gonchar hit a weary Malkin with a breakaway pass.

• Nicklas Lidstrom's long, wacky, bouncing goal on Dan Ellis of the Nashville Predators in the second period of Game 6 in the opening round of the playoffs.

• Sean Avery's strange puppet-boy dance in front of Devils goalie Martin Brodeur in the first round. The NHL stepped in to rewrite its rulebook in the middle of the playoffs, introducing what we like to call "The Nitwit Rule," which makes such behavior punishable by a minor penalty.

• Brenden Morrow's quadruple-overtime winner in Game 6 of the second round over San Jose.

• Alexander Ovechkin's steal of the puck and subsequent game-winning goal late in Game 1 of the Washington-Philadelphia first-round series.

• Ovechkin failing to shoot on a great chance from the slot late in the third period of Game 7 of the Caps' first-round loss to Philadelphia. He instead slid a pass to Sergei Fedorov, who was alone at the side of the net, but not looking for the pass.

• Evgeni Nabokov's sliding glove save early in the first overtime of Game 6 of the San Jose Sharks-Dallas Stars Western Conference semifinals series. Although the Sharks would later lose in quadruple overtime, the save was one for the ages.

• Jose Theodore's otherworldly performance against favored Minnesota in the first round, when he stopped 188 of 210 shots he faced in six games against the Wild.

• Speaking of goaltenders...all that fretting about whether rookie Carey Price could handle the load in Montreal seemed moot when he starred early in the first round against Boston. But the cracks that appeared in Price's game late in that seven-game series ruptured completely in the second round against Philadelphia.

2007-2008
Season in Review

Final NHL Standings

Division champions (*) and playoff qualifiers (†) are noted. Teams get two points for a win and one point for an overtime loss (OL) and a shootout loss (SL). Number of seasons listed after each head coach refers to current tenure with club through 2007-08 season.

Eastern Conference
Northeast Division

	W	L	OL	SL	Pts	GF	GA
*Montreal	47	25	4	6	104	262	222
†Ottawa	43	31	3	5	94	261	247
†Boston	41	29	5	7	94	212	222
Buffalo	39	31	3	9	90	255	242
Toronto	36	35	7	4	83	231	260

Head Coaches: Mon—Guy Carbonneau (2nd season); **Ott**—John Paddock (36-22-6) was fired on Feb. 28 and replaced by GM Bryan Murray (7-9-2); **Bos**—Claude Julien (1st); **Buf**—Lindy Ruff (10th); **Tor**—Paul Maurice (2nd).

Atlantic Division

	W	L	OL	SL	Pts	GF	GA
*Pittsburgh	47	27	4	4	102	247	216
†New Jersey	46	29	4	4	99	206	197
†NY Rangers	42	27	4	9	97	213	199
†Philadelphia	42	29	5	6	95	248	233
NY Islanders	35	38	6	3	79	194	243

Head Coaches: Pit—Michel Therrien (3rd season); **NJ**—Brent Sutter (1st); **NYR**—Tom Renney (4th); **Phi**—John Stevens (2nd); **NYI**—Ted Nolan (2nd).

Southeast Division

	W	L	OL	SL	Pts	GF	GA
*Washington	43	31	4	4	94	242	231
Carolina	43	33	3	3	92	252	249
Florida	38	35	6	3	85	216	226
Atlanta	34	40	2	6	76	216	272
Tampa Bay	31	42	8	1	71	223	267

Head Coaches: Wash—Glen Hanlon (4th; 6-14-1) was fired on Nov. 27 and replaced by Bruce Boudreau (37-17-7); **Car**—Peter Laviolette (4th); **Fla**—Jacques Martin (3rd); **Atl**—Bob Hartley (5th, 0-6-0) was fired on Oct. 17 and replaced by GM Don Waddell (34-34-8); **TB**—John Tortorella (7th).

Western Conference
Central Division

	W	L	OL	SL	Pts	GF	GA
*Detroit	54	21	2	5	115	257	184
†Nashville	41	32	4	5	91	230	229
Chicago	40	34	4	4	88	239	235
Columbus	34	36	4	8	80	193	218
St. Louis	33	36	8	5	79	205	237

Head Coaches: Det—Mike Babcock (3rd season); **Nash**—Barry Trotz (9th); **Chi**—Denis Savard (2nd); **Clb**—Ken Hitchcock (2nd); **St.L**—Andy Murray (2nd).

Northwest Division

	W	L	OL	SL	Pts	GF	GA
*Minnesota	44	28	2	8	98	223	218
†Colorado	44	31	4	3	95	231	219
†Calgary	42	30	7	3	94	229	227
Edmonton	41	35	2	4	88	235	251
Vancouver	39	33	1	9	88	213	215

Head Coaches: Min—Jacques Lemaire (7th season); **Col**—Joel Quenneville (3rd); **Calg**—Mike Keenan (1st); **Edm**—Craig MacTavish (7th); **Van**—Alain Vigneault (2nd).

Pacific Division

	W	L	OL	SL	Pts	GF	GA
*San Jose	49	23	4	6	108	222	193
†Anaheim	47	27	1	7	102	205	191
†Dallas	45	30	4	3	97	242	207
Phoenix	38	37	1	6	83	214	231
Los Angeles	32	43	4	3	71	231	266

Head Coaches: SJ—Ron Wilson (5th season); **Ana**—Randy Carlyle (3rd); **Dal**—Dave Tippett (5th); **Pho**—Wayne Gretzky (3rd); **LA**—Marc Crawford (2nd).

Home & Away, Division Records

Sixteen teams—eight from each conference—qualify for the Stanley Cup Playoffs; (*) indicates division champions.

Eastern Conference

		Pts	Home	Away	Div
1	Montreal*	104	22-13-6	25-12-4	20-11-1
2	Pittsburgh*	102	26-10-5	21-17-3	15-14-3
3	Washington*	94	23-15-3	20-16-5	18-11-3
4	New Jersey	99	25-14-2	21-15-5	13-15-4
5	NY Rangers	97	25-13-3	17-14-10	20-7-5
6	Philadelphia	95	21-14-6	21-15-5	17-12-3
7	Ottawa	94	22-15-4	21-16-4	18-13-1
8	Boston	94	21-16-4	20-13-8	13-13-6
	Carolina	92	24-13-4	19-20-2	19-11-2
	Buffalo	90	20-15-6	19-16-6	15-13-4
	Florida	85	18-15-8	20-20-1	16-14-2
	Toronto	83	18-17-6	18-18-5	14-13-5
	NY Islanders	79	18-18-5	17-20-4	15-15-2
	Atlanta	76	19-19-3	15-21-5	15-15-2
	Tampa Bay	71	20-18-3	11-24-6	12-17-3

Western Conference

		Pts	Home	Away	Div
1	Detroit*	115	29-9-3	25-12-4	17-12-3
2	San Jose*	108	22-13-6	27-10-4	16-10-6
3	Minnesota*	98	25-11-5	19-17-5	17-11-4
4	Anaheim	102	28-9-4	19-18-4	17-10-5
5	Dallas	97	23-16-2	22-14-5	16-11-5
6	Colorado	95	27-12-2	17-19-5	20-10-2
7	Calgary	94	21-11-9	21-19-1	16-12-4
8	Nashville	91	23-14-4	18-18-5	18-9-5
	Edmonton	88	23-17-1	18-18-5	13-16-3
	Chicago	88	23-16-2	17-18-6	19-11-2
	Vancouver	88	21-15-5	18-18-5	14-13-5
	Phoenix	83	17-20-4	21-17-3	19-11-2
	Columbus	80	20-14-7	14-22-5	11-18-3
	St. Louis	79	20-15-6	13-21-7	15-14-3
	Los Angeles	71	17-21-3	15-22-4	12-18-2

Washington Capitals
Alex Ovechkin
Scoring, Goals

San Jose Sharks
Joe Thornton
Assists

Chicago Blackhawks
Patrick Kane
Rookie Points

Detroit Red Wings
Chris Osgood
Goals Against Average

NHL Regular Season Individual Leaders

(*) indicates rookie eligible for Calder Trophy.

Scoring

	Pos	Gm	G	A	Pts	+/-	PM	PP	SH	GW	Shots	Pct
Alex Ovechkin, Washington	L	82	65	47	112	28	40	22	0	11	446	14.6
Evgeni Malkin, Pittsburgh	C	82	47	59	106	16	78	17	0	5	272	17.3
Jarome Iginla, Calgary	R	82	50	48	98	27	83	15	0	9	338	14.8
Pavel Datsyuk, Detroit	C	82	31	66	97	41	20	10	1	6	264	11.7
Joe Thornton, San Jose	C	82	29	67	96	18	59	11	0	5	178	16.3
Henrik Zetterberg, Detroit	L	75	43	49	92	30	34	16	1	7	358	12.0
Vincent Lecavalier, Tampa Bay	C	81	40	52	92	-17	89	10	1	7	318	12.6
Jason Spezza, Ottawa	C	76	34	58	92	26	66	11	0	6	210	16.2
Daniel Alfredsson, Ottawa	R	70	40	49	89	15	34	9	7	5	217	18.4
Ilya Kovalchuk, Atlanta	L	79	52	35	87	-12	52	16	2	4	283	18.4
Alex Kovalev, Montreal	R	82	35	49	84	18	70	17	0	5	230	15.2
Marian Gaborik, Minnesota	R	77	42	41	83	17	63	11	1	8	278	15.1
Mike Ribeiro, Dallas	C	76	27	56	83	21	46	7	0	5	107	25.2
Martin St. Louis, Tampa Bay	R	82	25	58	83	-23	26	10	2	5	241	10.4
Dany Heatley, Ottawa	L	71	41	41	82	33	76	13	0	8	224	18.3
Eric Staal, Carolina	C	82	38	44	82	-2	50	14	0	7	310	12.3
Ryan Getzlaf, Anaheim	C	77	24	58	82	32	94	4	1	2	185	13.0
Derek Roy, Buffalo	C	78	32	49	81	13	46	6	3	4	218	14.7
Jason Pominville, Buffalo	R	82	27	53	80	16	20	2	1	1	232	11.6

Three tied with 78 points.

Goals

Ovechkin, Wash ..... .65
Kovalchuk, Atl ..... .52
Iginla, Calg ..... .50
Malkin, Pit ..... .47
Zetterberg, Det ..... .43
Boyes, St.L ..... .43
Gaborik, Min ..... .42
Heatley, Ott ..... .41
Alfredsson, Ott ..... .40
Lecavalier, TB ..... .40
Nash, Clb ..... .38
Staal, Car ..... .38

Assists

Thornton, SJ ..... .67
Datsyuk, Det ..... .66
Savard, Bos ..... .63
H. Sedin, Van ..... .61
Lidstrom, Det ..... .60
Malkin, Pit ..... .59
Spezza, Ott ..... .58
Getzlaf, Ana ..... .58
St. Louis, TB ..... .58
Ribeiro, Dal ..... .56
Backstrom*, Wash ..... .55
Two tied with 54.

Defensemen Points

Lidstrom, Det ..... .70
Gonchar, Pit ..... .65
Streit, Mon ..... .62
Campbell, Buf-SJ ..... .62
Phaneuf, Calg ..... .60
Markov, Mon ..... .58
Green, Wash ..... .56
Rafalski, Det ..... .55
Kaberle, Tor ..... .53
Chara, Bos ..... .51
Jovanovski, Pho ..... .51

Rookie Points

Kane, Chi ..... .72
Backstrom, Wash ..... .69
Toews, Chi ..... .54
Mueller, Pho ..... .54
Gagner, Edm ..... .49
Cogliano, Edm ..... .45
Dubinsky, NYR ..... .40
Enstrom, Atl ..... .38
Hanzal, Pho ..... .35
Gilbert, Edm ..... .33
Johnson, St.L ..... .33
Dawes, NYR ..... .29

Plus/Minus

Datsyuk, Det ..... .41
Lidstrom, Det ..... .40
Heatley, Ott ..... .33
Getzlaf, Ana ..... .32
Zetterberg, Det ..... .30
Keith, Chi ..... .30
Ovechkin, Wash ..... .28
Kozlov, Wash ..... .28
Three tied at +27.

Game Winning Goals

Ovechkin, Wash ..... .11
Roenick, SJ ..... .10
Iginla, Calg 9
Boyes, St.L 9
Vanek, Buf 9
Nine tied with 8.

Power Play Goals

Ovechkin, Wash ..... .22
Vanek, Buf ..... .19
Jokinen, Fla ..... .18
Kovalev, Mon ..... .17
Malkin, Pit ..... .17
Zetterberg, Det ..... .16
Kovalchuk, Atl ..... .16
Three tied with 15.

Short-Handed Goals

Alfredsson, Ott 7
Sharp, Chi 7
Bourque, Chi 5
Richards, Phi 5
Nash, Clb 4
Park, NYI 4
Hagman, Dal 4
Fifteen tied with 3.

Shots

Ovechkin, Wash 446
Zetterberg, Det 358
Jokinen, Fla 341
Iginla, Calg 338
Blake, Tor 332
Nash, Clb 329
Lecavalier, TB 318
Staal, Car 310
Rolston, Min 289
Kovalchuk, Atl 283
Gaborik, Min 278

Shooting Pct.

(Min. 82 shots)

Ribeiro, Dal 25.2
Boyes, St.L 20.8
Svatos, Col 18.6
Kovalchuk, Atl 18.4
Alfredsson, Ott 18.4
Cogliano*, Edm 18.4
Heatley, Ott 18.3
Horcoff, Edm 18.3
Stastny, Col 17.4
Malkin, Pit 17.3

Penalty Minutes

Carcillo*, Pho 324
Boll*, Clb 226
Burish*, Chi 214
Cote*, Phi 202
Stortini, Edm 201
Neil, Ott 199
Clarkson*, NJ 183
Parros, Ana 183
Phaneuf, Calg 182
Burrows, Van 179
Godard, Calg 171

Minutes/Game

(Min. 50 Games)

Bouwmeester, Fla . . .27:28
Chara, Bos 26:50
Lidstrom, Det 26:43
Phaneuf, Calg 26:25
Pronger, Ana 26:00
McCabe, Tor 25:55
Gonchar, Pit 25:54
Keith, Chi 25:33
Beauchemin, Ana . .25:31
Ranger, TB 25:13

Goaltending

(Minimum 25 games)

	Gm	Min	GAA	Record	GA	Shots	Sv%	EN	Sho	G	A	Pts	PM
Chris Osgood, Detroit 43		2409	2.09	27-9-4	84	976	.914	1	4	0	3	3	0
Jean-Sebastien Giguere, Anaheim		3310	2.12	35-17-6	117	1508	.922	5	4	0	0	0	4
Evgeni Nabokov, San Jose 77		4561	2.14	46-21-8	163	1802	.910	6	6	0	2	2	12
Dominik Hasek, Detroit 41		2350	2.14	27-10-3	84	855	.902	3	5	0	1	1	12
Martin Brodeur, New Jersey 77		4635	2.17	44-27-6	168	2089	.920	8	4	0	4	4	6
Henrik Lundqvist, NY Rangers 72		4305	2.23	37-24-10	160	1823	.912	4	10	0	0	0	2
Pascal Leclaire, Columbus 54		2986	2.25	24-17-6	112	1379	.919	3	9	0	2	2	2
Niklas Backstrom, Minnesota 58		3409	2.31	33-13-8	131	1629	.920	2	4	0	0	0	0
Marty Turco, Dallas 62		3629	2.32	32-21-6	140	1543	.909	5	3	0	3	3	16
Cristobal Huet, Mon-Wash 52		3050	2.32	32-14-6	118	1479	.920	5	4	0	2	2	0
Marc-Andre Fleury, Pittsburgh . . .35		1857	2.33	19-10-2	72	909	.921	2	4	0	1	1	0
Dan Ellis, Nashville 44		2229	2.34	23-10-3	87	1147	.924	2	6	0	0	0	0
Roberto Luongo, Vancouver 73		4233	2.38	35-29-9	168	2029	.917	3	6	0	3	3	4
Manny Legace, St. Louis 66		3666	2.41	27-25-8	147	1648	.911	6	5	0	2	2	4
Jose Theodore, Col 53		3028	2.44	28-21-3	123	1367	.910	5	3	0	2	2	24

Wins

Nabokov, SJ 46
Brodeur, NJ 44
Kiprusoff, Calg 39
Lundqvist, NYR 37
Ward, Car 37
Miller, Buf 36
Luongo, Van 35
Giguere, Ana 35
Toskala, Tor 33
Backstrom, Min 33
Turco, Dal 32
Huet, Mon-Wash 32

Shutouts

Lundqvist, NYR 10
Leclaire, Clb 9
Nabokov, SJ 6
Luongo, Van 6
Ellis, Nash 6
Biron, Phi 5
Hasek, Det 5
Legace, St.L 5
Eleven tied with 4.

Save Pct.

Ellis, Nash 924
Conklin, Pit 923
Giguere, Ana 922
Thomas, Bos 921
Fleury, Pit 921
Brodeur, NJ 920
Bryzgalov, Pho-Ana . .920
Backstrom, Min 920
Huet, Mon-Wash 920
Price*, Mon 920
Vokoun, Fla 919
Leclaire, Clb 919

Minutes Played

Brodeur, NJ . . . . . +.4635
Nabokov, SJ 4561
Miller, Buf 4474
Kiprusoff, Calg 4398
Lundqvist, NYR 4305
Luongo, Van 4233
Vokoun, Fla 4031
Ward, Car 3930
Toskala, Tor 3837
DiPietro, NYI 3707
Legace, St.L 3666
Turco, Dal 3629

Power Play/Penalty Killing

Power play and penalty killing conversions. Power play: No—number of opportunities; GF—goals for; Pct—percentage. Penalty killing: No—number of times shorthanded; GA—goals against; Pct—percentage of penalties killed; SH—shorthanded goals for.

EASTERN	Power Play No	GF	Pct	Penalty Killing No	GA	Pct	SH	WESTERN	Power Play No	GF	Pct	Penalty Killing No	GA	Pct	SH
Montreal 372		90	24.2	342	60	82.5	8	Detroit 391		81	20.7	357	57	84.0	5
Philadelphia . . .385		84	21.8	388	65	83.2	13	Minnesota 338		64	18.9	330	49	85.2	3
Pittsburgh 378		77	20.4	357	68	81.0	6	San Jose 372		70	18.8	310	44	85.8	7
Tampa Bay 296		57	19.3	312	56	82.1	7	Phoenix 339		63	18.6	332	64	80.7	11
Florida 313		60	19.2	374	66	82.4	4	Dallas 354		64	18.1	352	51	85.5	13
Carolina 420		79	18.8	355	75	78.9	4	Los Angeles 366		64	17.5	309	68	78.0	11
Washington . . .346		65	18.8	349	68	80.5	5	Vancouver 369		63	17.1	368	64	82.6	8
Ottawa 328		60	18.3	380	72	81.1	18	Calgary 352		59	16.8	388	72	81.4	9
Buffalo 366		66	18.0	333	56	83.2	9	Anaheim 361		60	16.6	408	69	8.31	4
Toronto . . . . .·. .343		61	17.8	350	77	78.0	4	Edmonton 344		57	16.6	366	56	84.7	7
Boston 319		56	17.6	332	71	78.6	9	Chicago 365		58	15.9	385	69	82.1	17
NY Rangers . . .370		61	16.5	343	53	84.5	4	Columbus 356		53	14.9	378	63	83.3	8
Atlanta 316		52	16.5	354	75	78.8	13	Nashville 358		53	14.8	335	49	85.4	7
New Jersey 320		50	15.6	314	54	82.8	6	Colorado 335		49	14.6	301	56	81.4	2
NY Islanders . . .330		48	14.5	375	68	81.9	10	St. Louis 334		47	14.1	359	56	84.4	3

Shootout Records

A shootout decides the game's winner if the score is still tied after a five-minute, four-on-four sudden death overtime. In the shootout, each team takes three shots. The team with the most goals after those three shots is the winner. If the score remains tied, the shootout goes to a sudden death format.

Of the 1230 NHL games played in 2007-08, 156 were decided via the shootout (12.68 percent). Players attempted 1058 shots and scored 344 goals (32.51 percent). The tables below show each team's record in shootouts, along with their goals (G) and shots (Sh) for and against. Teams are ranked by wins.

Eastern Conference

	GP	Record	For G	For Sh	Against G	Against Sh
Atlanta	15	9-6	17	51	12	49
New Jersey	12	8-4	15	42	11	43
NY Rangers	17	8-9	15	53	16	53
Pittsburgh	11	7-4	17	44	13	44
Boston	13	6-7	8	35	11	36
NY Islanders	8	5-3	11	32	10	34
Florida	11	5-6	9	41	11	41
Montreal	11	5-6	9	37	10	38
Washington	8	4-4	10	39	11	39
Buffalo	13	4-9	12	43	17	43
Toronto	7	3-4	8	24	9	24
Ottawa	8	3-5	10	31	12	31
Philadelphia	9	3-6	10	25	13	23
Tampa Bay	3	2-1	4	10	3	9
Carolina	5	2-3	7	14	8	14

Western Conference

	GP	Record	For G	For Sh	Against G	Against Sh
Edmonton	19	15-4	24	65	12	69
Anaheim	15	8-7	16	48	16	45
Colorado	10	7-3	16	39	10	37
San Jose	12	6-6	18	41	18	40
Vancouver	15	6-9	13	56	17	58
Dallas	8	5-3	10	28	9	29
Los Angeles	8	5-3	12	29	10	28
Chicago	9	5-4	10	26	9	28
Detroit	10	5-5	12	30	11	28
Phoenix	11	5-6	12	39	12	42
Calgary	6	3-3	7	18	6	17
Nashville	8	3-5	6	21	9	22
St. Louis	8	3-5	5	27	6	26
Columbus	11	3-8	11	37	14	33
Minnesota	11	3-8	10	33	18	35

Individual Shootout Leaders

Leading shootout scorers (ranked by goals) and goaltenders (ranked by wins) during the 2007-08 season.

Shooters

	Goals	Shots	Pct	GDG
Patrick Kane*, Chi	7	9	77.8	3
Joe Pavelski, SJ	7	11	63.6	0
Erik Christensen, Atl	6	11	54.6	2
Ales Hemsky, Edm	6	16	37.5	4
Thirteen tied with 5 goals.				

Note: GDG denotes Game Deciding Goals

Goaltenders

	W-L	GA	Shots	SV%
Mathieu Garon, Edm	10-0	2	32	.938
Martin Brodeur, NJ	8-4	11	43	.744
Jose Theodore, Col	6-1	6	28	.786
J-S Giguere, Ana	6-5	10	30	.667
Evgeni Nabokov, SJ	6-6	18	40	.550
Henrik Lundqvist, NYR	6-7	13	42	.690
Roberto Luongo, Van	6-8	15	54	.722
Four tied with 5 wins.				

2008 NHL All-Star Game

56th NHL All-Star Game. **Date:** Jan. 27 at Philips Arena in Atlanta, Georgia. **Coaches:** Mike Babcock, Detroit (Western) and John Paddock, Ottawa (Eastern). Head coaches whose team had the best winning percentage in each conference on Jan. 4 (the half-way point of the season) were named all-star head coaches. **Attendance:** 18,644. **Time:** 2:16. **MVP:** Eric Staal, Carolina F (Eastern) — 2 goals, 1 assist.

Eastern 8, Western 7

	1	2	3	Final
Western Conference	1	2	4	7
Eastern Conference	5	0	3	8

1st Period: WEST—Rick Nash (unassisted), 0:12; EAST—Eric Staal (Brian Campbell, Evgeni Malkin), 1:20; EAST—Andrei Markov (Mike Richards, Marian Hossa), 9:43; EAST—Alex Ovechkin (Jason Spezza, Martin St. Louis), 13:35; EAST—Campbell (Malkin, Vincent Lecavalier), 15:10; EAST—Ovechkin 2 (St. Louis, Spezza), 17:49.

2nd Period: WEST—Nash 2 (Pavel Datsyuk), 9:34; WEST—Scott Niedermayer (Joe Thornton, Henrik Sedin), 15:08.

3rd Period: WEST—Ryan Getzlaf (Ed Jovanovski), 0:41; WEST—Nash 3 (Jarome Iginla), 1:56; EAST—Hossa (Scott Gomez, Zdeno Chara), 4:08; WEST—Dion Phaneuf (Getzlaf, Jason Arnott), 5:07; WEST—Marion Gaborik (Sedin), 10:57; EAST—Staal 2 (Ilya Kovalchuk, Marc Savard), 12:35; EAST—Savard (Campbell, Staal), 19:39.

Shots on Goal: Western—13-20-18—51; Eastern—16-8-9—33.

Power plays: none.

Goalies: Western—Chris Osgood (16 shots, 11 saves); Evgeni Nabokov (8 shots, 6 saves); Manny Legace (9 shots, 6 saves); Eastern—Rick DiPietro (13 shots, 12 saves), Tomas Vokoun (20 shots, 18 saves), Tim Thomas (18 shots, 14 saves).

Team by Team Statistics

High scorers and goaltenders with at least ten games played. Players who competed for more than one team during the regular season are listed with their final club; (*) indicates rookies eligible for Calder Trophy. Player positions are noted as follows: C—Center, L—Left wing, R—Right wing, D—Defenseman.

Anaheim Ducks

Top Scorers	Gm	G	A	Pts	+/-	PM	PP
Ryan Getzlaf, C	77	24	58	82	32	94	4
Corey Perry, R	70	29	25	54	12	108	11
Chris Kunitz, L	82	21	29	50	8	80	7
Chris Pronger, D	72	12	31	43	-1	128	8
Todd Bertuzzi, R	68	14	26	40	8	97	4
Mathieu Schneider, D	65	12	27	39	22	50	5
Doug Weight, C	67	10	15	25	4	32	2
ST.L	29	4	7	11	4	12	0
ANA	38	6	8	14	0	20	2
Scott Niedermayer, D	48	8	17	25	-2	16	7
Teemu Selanne, R	26	12	11	23	5	8	7
Francois Beauchemin, D	82	2	19	21	-9	59	0
Marc-Andre Bergeron, D	55	9	10	19	-16	20	8
NYI	46	9	9	18	-14	16	8
ANA	9	0	1	1	-2	4	0
Kent Huskins, D	76	4	15	19	23	59	1
Todd Marchant, C	75	9	7	16	-3	48	0
Rob Niedermayer, C	78	8	8	16	1	54	0
Samuel Pahlsson, C	56	6	9	15	-2	34	0
Bobby Ryan*, R	23	5	5	10	-1	6	3
Sean O'Donnell, D	82	2	7	9	9	84	0

Acquired: C Weight, L Michal Birner and an '08 7th-round pick from St.L for C Andy McDonald (Dec. 14); D Bergeron from NYI for an '08 3rd-round pick (Feb. 26).

Goalies (10 Gm)	Gm	Min	GAA	Record	SV%
Jonas Hiller*	23	1223	2.06	10-7-1	.927
Jean-Sebastien Giguere	58	3310	2.12	35-17-6	.922
ANAHEIM	82	5007	2.20	47-27-8	.920

Shutouts: Giguere (4). **Assists:** Hiller (1). **PM:** Giguere (4).

Atlanta Thrashers

Top Scorers	Gm	G	A	Pts	+/-	PM	PP
Ilya Kovalchuk, L	79	52	35	87	-12	52	16
Mark Recchi, R	72	14	34	48	-18	32	7
PIT	19	2	6	8	-2	12	2
ATL	53	12	28	40	-16	20	5
Eric Perrin, C	81	12	33	45	-5	26	2
Vyacheslav Kozlov, L	82	17	24	41	-10	26	5
Tobias Enstrom*, D	82	5	33	38	-5	42	4
Todd White, C	74	14	23	37	-12	36	6
Colby Armstrong, R	72	13	22	35	4	56	1
PIT	54	9	15	24	6	50	0
ATL	18	4	7	11	-2	6	1
Bobby Holik, C	82	15	19	34	-14	90	3
Erik Christensen, C	59	11	13	24	-10	30	2
PIT	49	9	11	20	-3	28	2
ATL	10	2	2	4	-7	2	0
Chris Thorburn, R	73	5	13	18	-4	92	0
Bryan Little*, C	48	6	10	16	-2	18	2
Niclas Havelid, D	81	1	13	14	2	42	0
Jim Slater, C	69	8	5	13	-10	41	0
Ken Klee, D	72	1	9	10	-5	60	0
Eric Boulton, L	74	4	5	9	-10	127	0

Acquired: R Armstrong, C Christensen, C Angelo Esposito and an '08 1st-round pick from Pit. for R Marian Hossa and R Pascal Dupuis (Feb. 26). **Claimed:** R Recchi off waivers from Pit. (Dec. 8).

Goalies (10 Gm)	Gm	Min	GAA	Record	SV%
Kari Lehtonen	48	2707	2.90	17-22-5	.916
Johan Hedberg	36	1927	3.46	14-15-3	.892
ATLANTA	82	5012	3.18	34-40-8	.904

Shutouts: Lehtonen (4), Hedberg (1). **Assists:** Lehtonen (2), Hedberg (1). **PM:** Hedberg (16), Lehtonen (4).

Boston Bruins

Top Scorers	Gm	G	A	Pts	+/-	PM	PP
Marc Savard, C	74	15	63	78	3	66	4
Marco Sturm, L	80	27	29	56	11	40	10
Zdeno Chara, D	77	17	34	51	14	114	9
Chuck Kobasew, R	73	22	17	39	6	29	6
Phil Kessel, C	82	19	18	37	-6	28	5
Dennis Wideman, D	81	13	23	36	11	70	9
Glen Metropolit, C	82	11	22	33	-3	36	1
Glen Murray, R	63	17	13	30	-4	50	7
P.J. Axelsson, L	75	13	16	29	11	15	0
Milan Lucic*, L	77	8	19	27	-2	89	1
David Krejci*, C	56	6	21	27	-3	20	1
Peter Schaefer, L	63	9	17	26	4	18	0
Andrew Ference, D	59	1	14	15	-14	50	0
Aaron Ward, D	65	5	8	13	9	54	0
Petteri Nokelainen*, C	57	7	3	10	0	19	0
Mark Stuart, D	82	4	4	8	2	81	0
Shane Hnidy, D	76	2	6	8	-2	71	0
ANA	33	1	2	3	2	30	0
BOS	43	1	4	5	-4	41	0

Three tied with 7 pts each.

Acquired: G Auld from Pho. for a minor leaguer and an '09 5th-round pick (Dec. 6); D Hnidy and an '08 6th-round pick from Ana. for R Brandon Bochenski (Jan. 2).

Goalies (10 Gm)	Gm	Min	GAA	Record	SV%
Alex Auld	32	1722	2.68	12-13-5	.907
PHO	9	509	3.54	3-6-0	.880
BOS	23	1213	2.32	9-7-5	.919
Tim Thomas	57	3442	2.44	28-19-6	.921
BOSTON	82	5003	2.58	41-29-12	.914

Shutouts: Thomas (3), Auld (3 incl. 1 with Pho.), Manny Fernandez (1). **Assists:** none. **PM:** Thomas (2).

Buffalo Sabres

Top Scorers	Gm	G	A	Pts	+/-	PM	PP
Derek Roy, C	78	32	49	81	13	46	6
Jason Pominville, R	82	27	53	80	16	20	2
Thomas Vanek, L	82	36	28	64	-5	64	19
Jochen Hecht, C	75	22	27	49	1	38	3
Ales Kotalik, R	79	23	20	43	-5	58	12
Tim Connolly, C	48	7	33	40	4	8	3
Drew Stafford, R	64	16	22	38	3	51	1
Paul Gaustad, C	82	10	26	36	-4	85	5
Daniel Paille, L	77	19	16	35	9	14	0
Steve Bernier, R	76	16	16	32	-1	64	4
SJ	59	13	10	23	-2	62	4
BUF	17	3	6	9	1	2	0
Jaroslav Spacek, D	60	9	23	32	7	42	7
Maxim Afinogenov, R	56	10	18	28	-16	42	1
Toni Lydman, D	82	4	22	26	1	74	3
Henrik Tallinder, D	71	1	17	18	5	48	0
Adam Mair, C	72	5	12	17	-2	66	0
Clarke MacArthur*, L	37	8	7	15	3	20	0
Nathan Paetsch, D	59	2	7	9	3	27	0
Michael Ryan*, C	46	4	4	8	-4	30	0
Andrej Sekera*, D	37	2	6	8	5	16	0
Dmitri Kalinin, D	46	1	7	8	-7	32	1

Acquired: R Bernier and an '08 1st-round pick for D Brian Campbell (Feb. 26).

Goalies (10 Gm)	Gm	Min	GAA	Record	Sv%
Ryan Miller	76	4474	2.64	36-27-10	.906
Jocelyn Thibault	12	507	3.31	3-4-2	.869
BUFFALO	82	5011	2.79	39-31-12	.900

Shutouts: Miller (3), Thibault (2). **Assists:** Miller (1). **PM:** Miller (6).

Calgary Flames

Top Scorers	Gm	G	A	Pts	+/-	PM	PP
Jarome Iginla, R	.82	50	48	98	27	83	15
Kristian Huselius, L	.81	25	41	66	10	40	6
Daymond Langkow, C	.80	30	35	65	16	19	14
Dion Phaneuf, D	.82	17	43	60	12	182	10
Alex Tanguay, L	.78	18	40	58	11	48	3
Matthew Lombardi, C	.82	14	22	36	-6	67	2
Adrian Aucoin, D	.76	10	25	35	13	37	5
Craig Conroy, C	.79	12	22	34	6	71	1
Owen Nolan, R	.77	16	16	32	6	71	1
Robyn Regehr, D	.82	5	15	20	11	79	1
Anders Eriksson, D	.61	1	17	18	-5	36	1
James Vandermeer, D	.75	3	14	17	6	110	2
CHI	.26	2	7	9	3	44	1
PHI	.28	1	5	6	-1	27	1
CALG	.21	0	2	2	4	39	0
Dustin Boyd*, C	.48	7	5	12	-11	6	0
Stephane Yelle, C	.74	3	9	12	-4	20	0
David Moss, L	.41	4	7	11	-4	10	0
Wayne Primeau, C	.43	3	7	10	-3	26	0
Eric Nystrom*, L	.44	3	7	10	-5	48	0
Cory Sarich, D	.80	2	5	7	2	135	0
Marcus Nilson, L	.47	3	2	5	2	4	0
Rhett Warrener, D	.31	1	3	4	-2	21	0
Mark Smith, C	.54	1	3	4	-6	59	0

Acquired: D Vandermeer from Phi. for an '09 3rd-round pick (Feb. 20).

Goalies (10 Gm)	Gm	Min	GAA	Record	SV%
Miikka Kiprusoff	.76	4398	2.69	39-26-10	.906
CALGARY	.82	4975	2.70	42-30-10	.904

Shutouts: Kiprusoff (2). **Assists:** Kiprusoff (2). **PM:** Kiprusoff (8), Curtis Joseph (2).

Carolina Hurricanes

Top Scorers	Gm	G	A	Pts	+/-	PM	PP
Eric Staal, C	.82	38	44	82	-2	50	14
Ray Whitney, L	.66	25	36	61	-6	30	6
Erik Cole, L	.73	22	29	51	5	76	10
Rod Brind'Amour, C	.59	19	32	51	0	38	6
Matt Cullen, C	.59	13	36	49	2	32	8
Joseph Corvo, D	.74	13	35	48	17	26	6
OTT	.51	6	21	27	13	18	1
CAR	.23	7	14	21	4	8	5
Sergei Samsonov, L	.61	14	22	36	-1	16	3
CHI	.23	0	4	4	-7	6	0
CAR	.38	14	18	32	6	10	3
Scott Walker, R	.58	14	18	32	-3	115	4
Tuomo Ruutu, C	.77	10	22	32	4	91	4
CHI	.60	6	15	21	3	75	1
CAR	.17	4	7	11	1	16	3
Justin Williams, R	.37	9	21	30	2	43	2
Jeff Hamilton, C	.58	9	15	24	-8	10	7
Chad LaRose, C	.58	11	12	23	6	46	0
Frantisek Kaberle, D	.80	0	22	22	-4	30	0
Tim Gleason, D	.80	3	16	19	5	84	0
Trevor Letowski, R	.75	9	9	18	-10	30	0
Bret Hedican, D	.66	2	15	17	17	70	0
Patrick Eaves, R	.37	5	10	15	-2	10	2
OTT	.26	4	6	10	0	6	1
CAR	.11	1	4	5	-2	4	1
Dennis Seidenberg, D	.47	0	15	15	6	18	0

Acquired: D Corvo and R Eaves from Ott. for L Cory Stillman and D Mike Commodore (Feb. 11); C Ruutu from Chi. for L Andrew Ladd (Feb. 26). **Claimed:** R Samsonov off waivers from Chi. (Jan. 9).

Goalies (10 Gm)	Gm	Min	GAA	Record	Sv%
Cam Ward	.69	3930	2.75	37-25-5	.904
John Grahame	.17	848	3.75	5-7-1	.875
CAROLINA	.82	4964	2.97	43-33-6	.896

Shutouts: Ward (4). **Assists:** Ward and Grahame (1); Ward (1). **PM:** Ward and Grahame (4).

Chicago Blackhawks

Top Scorers	Gm	G	A	Pts	+/-	PM	PP
Patrick Kane*, R	.82	21	51	72	-5	52	7
Patrick Sharp, R	.80	36	26	62	23	55	9
Jonathan Toews*, C	.64	24	30	54	11	44	7
Robert Lang, C	.76	21	33	54	9	50	7
Dustin Byfuglien, D	.67	19	17	36	-7	59	7
Jason Williams, C	.43	13	23	36	-2	22	6
Duncan Keith, D	.82	12	20	32	30	56	1
Brent Seabrook, D	.82	9	23	32	13	90	4
Andrew Ladd, L	.63	14	16	30	13	35	1
CAR	.43	9	9	18	9	31	0
CHI	.20	5	7	12	4	4	1
Martin Havlat, R	.35	10	17	27	4	22	3
James Wisniewski, D	.68	7	19	26	12	103	1
Rene Bourque, L	.62	10	14	24	6	42	0
Brent Sopel, D	.58	1	19	20	9	28	0
Cameron Barker, D	.45	6	12	18	-3	52	2
Dave Bolland*, C	.39	4	13	17	6	28	0
Yanic Perreault, C	.53	9	5	14	-1	24	0
Craig Adams, R	.75	4	7	11	-16	58	0
CAR	.40	2	3	5	-8	34	0
CHI	.35	2	4	6	-8	24	0
Adam Burish*, R	.81	4	4	8	-13	214	0
Jack Skille*, R	.16	3	2	5	1	0	0
Andrei Zyuzin, D	.32	2	3	5	-11	38	1
Petri Kontiola*, C	.12	0	5	5	0	0	0

Acquired: R Adams from Car. for an '09 conditional pick (Jan. 17); L Ladd from Car. for C Tuomo Ruutu (Feb. 26).

Goalies (10 Gm)	Gm	Min	GAA	Record	SV%
Nikolai Khabibulin	.50	2892	2.63	23-20-6	.909
Patrick Lalime	.32	1828	2.82	16-12-2	.897
CHICAGO	.82	4981	2.78	40-34-8	.902

Shutouts: Khabibulin (2), Lalime and Corey Crawford (1). **Assists:** Khabibulin (2). **PM:** Lalime (8), Khabibulin (4).

Colorado Avalanche

Top Scorers	Gm	G	A	Pts	+/-	PM	PP
Paul Stastny, C	.66	24	47	71	22	24	3
Andrew Brunette, L	.82	19	40	59	5	14	7
Milan Hejduk, R	.77	29	25	54	8	36	8
Wojtek Wolski, L	.77	18	30	48	10	14	4
Joe Sakic, C	.44	13	27	40	-4	20	5
Marek Svatos, R	.62	26	11	37	13	32	3
Ryan Smyth, L	.55	14	23	37	-4	50	2
John-Michael Liles, D	.81	6	26	32	2	26	5
Tyler Arnason, C	.70	10	21	31	-1	16	3
Ruslan Salei, D	.82	6	24	30	-4	98	1
FLA	.65	3	20	23	-5	75	1
COL	.17	3	4	7	1	23	0
Jaroslav Hlinka, C	.63	8	20	28	6	16	0
Ben Guite, C	.79	11	11	22	1	47	0
Brett Clark, D	.57	5	16	21	5	33	1
Scott Hannan, D	.82	2	19	21	-5	55	0
Jeff Finger, D	.72	8	11	19	12	40	1
Ian Laperriere, R	.70	4	15	19	-5	140	0
Adam Foote, D	.75	1	15	16	2	107	0
CLB	.63	1	14	15	3	95	0
COL	.12	0	1	1	-1	12	0
Peter Forsberg, C	.9	1	13	14	7	8	0
Jordan Leopold, D	.43	5	8	13	5	20	2
T.J. Hensick*, C	.31	6	5	11	-4	2	4
Cody McLeod*, L	.49	4	5	9	-6	120	0

Acquired: D Salei from Fla. for D Karlis Skrastins and an '08 3rd-round pick (Feb. 26); D Foote from Clb. for a conditional 1st-round pick in '08 or '09.

Goalies (10 Gm)	Gm	Min	GAA	Record	SV%
Jose Theodore	.53	3028	2.44	28-21-3	.910
Peter Budaj	.35	1912	2.57	16-10-4	.903
COLORADO	.82	4988	2.60	44-31-7	.903

Shutouts: Theodore (3). **Assists:** Theodore (2), Budaj (1). **PM:** Theodore and Budaj (2).

Columbus Blue Jackets

Top Scorers	Gm	G	A	Pts	+/-	PM	PP
Rick Nash, L	80	38	31	69	2	95	10
Nikolai Zherdev, R	82	26	35	61	-9	34	7
Michael Peca, C	65	8	26	34	-1	64	3
Ron Hainsey, D	78	8	24	32	-7	25	8
Jason Chimera, L	81	14	17	31	-5	98	1
Manny Malhotra, C	71	11	18	29	-3	34	2
David Vyborny, R	66	7	19	26	-8	34	2
Dan Fritsche, C	69	10	12	22	2	22	1
Jiri Novotny, C	65	8	14	22	-10	24	1
Rostislav Klesla, D	82	6	12	18	7	60	3
Dick Tarnstrom, D	48	3	11	14	-11	52	1
EDM	29	1	4	5	-6	40	0
CLB	19	2	7	9	-5	12	1
Jan Hejda, D	81	0	13	13	20	61	0
Fredrik Modin, L	23	6	6	12	1	20	2
Andrew Murray*, C	39	6	4	10	0	12	0
Jared Boll*, R	75	5	5	10	-4	226	0
Kris Russell*, D	67	2	8	10	-12	14	1
Gilbert Brule, C	61	1	8	9	-4	24	0
Joakim Lindstrom*, C	25	3	4	7	0	14	2
Ole-Kristian Tollefsen, D	51	2	2	4	-3	111	0
Duvie Westcott, D	23	1	3	4	-10	30	1

Five tied with 2 pts. each.

Acquired: D Tarnstrom from Edm. for L Curtis Glencross (Feb. 5).

Goalies (10 Gm)	Gm	Min	GAA	Record	SV%
Pascal Leclaire	54	2986	2.25	24-17-6	.919
Fredrik Norrena	37	1960	2.72	10-19-6	.896
COLUMBUS	82	4988	2.53	34-36-12	.907

Shutouts: Leclaire (9), Norrena (2). **Assists:** Leclaire (2), Norrena (1). **PM:** Leclaire (2).

Dallas Stars

Top Scorers	Gm	G	A	Pts	+/-	PM	PP
Mike Ribeiro, C	76	27	56	83	21	46	7
Brenden Morrow, L	82	32	42	74	23	105	12
Brad Richards, C	74	20	42	62	-27	15	9
TB	62	18	33	51	-25	15	9
DAL	12	2	9	11	-2	0	0
Mike Modano, C	82	21	36	57	-11	48	5
Niklas Hagman, L	82	27	14	41	4	51	4
Jere Lehtinen, R	48	15	22	37	9	14	9
Sergei Zubov, D	46	4	31	35	6	12	2
Antti Miettinen, R	69	15	19	34	4	34	5
Loui Eriksson, L	69	14	17	31	5	28	4
Stephane Robidas, D	82	9	17	26	0	85	7
Matt Niskanen*, D	78	7	19	26	22	36	2
Trevor Daley, D	82	5	19	24	-1	85	0
Stu Barnes, C	79	12	11	23	-3	26	0
Steve Ott, C	73	11	11	22	2	147	0
Joel Lundqvist, C	55	3	11	14	-3	22	0
Philippe Boucher, D	38	2	12	14	3	26	0
Mattias Norstrom, D	66	2	11	13	3	40	1
Nicklas Grossman*, D	62	0	7	7	10	22	0
Chris Conner*, R	22	3	2	5	0	6	0
Brad Winchester, L	41	1	2	3	-9	46	0
Krys Barch, R	48	1	2	3	-3	105	0
Toby Petersen, C	8	1	0	1	0	0	0

Acquired: C Richards and G Holmqvist from TB for G Mike Smith, C Jeff Halpern, L Jussi Jokinen and an '08 4th-round pick (Feb. 26).

Goalies (10 Gm)	Gm	Min	GAA	Record	SV%
Marty Turco	62	3629	2.31	32-21-6	.909
Johan Holmqvist	47	2549	3.04	21-16-6	.889
TB	45	2469	3.01	20-16-6	.890
DAL	2	80	3.75	1-0-0	.857
DALLAS	82	4975	2.46	45-30-7	.905

Shutouts: Turco (3), Holmqvist (2 with TB). **Assists:** Turco (3), Holmqvist (1 with TB). **PM:** Turco (16).

Detroit Red Wings

Top Scorers	Gm	G	A	Pts	+/-	PM	PP
Pavel Datsyuk, C	82	31	66	97	41	20	10
Henrik Zetterberg, L	75	43	49	92	30	34	16
Nicklas Lidstrom, D	76	10	60	70	40	40	5
Brian Rafalski, D	73	13	42	55	27	34	10
Daniel Cleary, R	63	20	22	42	21	33	5
Jiri Hudler, C	81	13	29	42	11	26	3
Tomas Holmstrom, L	59	20	20	40	9	58	11
Mikael Samuelsson, R	73	11	29	40	21	26	3
Johan Franzen, R	72	27	11	38	12	51	14
Valterri Filppula, C	78	19	17	36	16	28	3
Niklas Kronvall, D	65	7	28	35	25	44	0
Brad Stuart, D	72	6	17	23	-10	69	2
LA	63	5	16	21	-16	67	2
DET	9	1	1	2	6	2	0
Kris Draper, C	65	9	8	17	-2	68	0
Brett Ledba, D	78	3	11	14	-1	48	0
Tomas Kopecky, C	77	5	7	12	2	43	0
Chris Chelios, D	69	3	9	12	11	36	0
Andreas Lilja, D	79	2	10	12	-2	93	0
Kirk Maltby, L	61	6	4	10	-8	32	0
Dallas Drake, R	65	3	3	6	-12	41	0
Mark Hartigan, C	23	3	1	4	-2	16	0

Three tied with 3 pts. each.

Acquired: D Stuart from LA for an '08 2nd-round pick and an '09 4th-round pick (Feb. 26).

Goalies (10 Gm)	Gm	Min	GAA	Record	Sv%
Chris Osgood	43	2409	2.09	27-9-4	.914
Dominik Hasek	41	2350	2.14	27-10-3	.902
DETROIT	82	4979	2.16	54-21-7	.907

Shutouts: Hasek (5), Osgood (4). **Assists:** Osgood (3); Hasek (1). **PM:** Hasek (12).

Edmonton Oilers

Top Scorers	Gm	G	A	Pts	+/-	PM	PP
Ales Hemsky, R	74	20	51	71	-9	34	8
Shawn Horcoff, C	53	21	29	50	1	30	6
Sam Gagner*, C	79	13	36	49	-21	23	4
Dustin Penner, L	82	23	24	47	-12	45	13
Andrew Cogliano*, C	82	18	27	45	1	20	1
Robert Nilsson, L	71	10	31	41	8	20	3
Jarret Stoll, C	81	14	22	36	-23	74	8
Tom Gilbert*, D	82	13	20	33	-6	20	3
Kyle Brodziak, C	80	14	17	31	-6	33	0
Joni Pitkanen, D	63	8	18	26	-5	56	1
Curtis Glencross*, L	62	15	10	25	8	53	1
CLB	36	6	6	12	3	25	1
EDM	26	9	4	13	5	28	0
Marty Reasoner, C	82	11	14	25	-17	50	0
Fernando Pisani, R	56	13	9	22	-5	28	4
Denis Grebeshkov, D	71	3	15	18	2	22	1
Steve Staios, D	82	9	9	16	-14	121	1
Geoff Sanderson, L	41	3	10	13	-7	16	0
Zachery Stortini, R	66	3	9	12	3	201	0
Raffi Torres, L	32	5	6	11	-4	36	1
Sheldon Souray, D	26	3	7	10	-7	36	2
Ethan Moreau, L	25	5	4	9	-4	39	1
Marc-Antoine Pouliot, C	24	1	6	7	-1	12	0
Ladislav Smid, D	65	0	4	4	-15	58	0

Acquired: L Glencross from Clb. for D Dick Tarnstrom (Feb. 5).

Goalies (10 Gm)	Gm	Min	GAA	Record	Sv%
Mathieu Garon	47	2658	2.66	26-18-1	.913
Dwayne Roloson	43	2340	3.05	15-17-5	.901
EDMONTON	82	5035	2.94	41-35-6	.904

Shutouts: Garon (4). **Assists:** Roloson (1). **PM:** Garon (8), Roloson (2).

Florida Panthers

Top Scorers	Gm	G	A	Pts	+/-	PM	PP
Olli Jokinen, C	82	34	37	71	-19	67	18
Nathan Horton, R	82	27	35	62	15	85	9
Stephen Weiss, C	74	13	29	42	14	40	4
David Booth, L	73	22	18	40	13	26	1
Jay Bouwmeester, D	82	15	22	37	-5	72	4
Brett McLean, C	67	14	23	37	-5	34	3
Richard Zednik, R	54	15	11	26	-5	43	6
Rostislav Olesz, L	56	14	12	26	3	16	5
Kamil Kreps*, C	76	8	17	25	10	29	1
Steve Montador, D	73	8	15	23	1	73	2
Jozef Stumpel, L	52	7	13	20	-11	10	3
Ville Peltonen, L	56	5	15	20	-2	20	1
Gregory Campbell, C	81	5	13	18	-12	72	0
Radek Dvorak, R	67	8	9	17	-1	16	0
Cory Murphy, D	47	2	15	17	0	22	1
Bryan Allen, D	73	2	14	16	5	67	0
Magnus Johansson, D	45	0	14	14	-5	18	0
CHI	18	0	4	4	-5	4	0
FLA	27	0	10	10	0	14	0
Jassen Cullimore, D	65	3	10	13	21	38	0
Tomas Vokoun, G	69	0	6	6	0	4	0
Karlis Skrastins, D	60	2	3	5	-11	32	0
COL	43	1	3	4	-2	20	0
FLA	17	1	0	1	-9	12	0
Branislav Mezei, D	57	2	2	4	-13	64	0

Acquired: D Johansson from Chi. for an '09 seventh-round pick (Jan. 10); D Skrastins and an '08 3rd-round pick from Col. for D Ruslan Salei (Feb. 26);.

Goalies (10 Gm)	Gm	Min	GAA	Record	Sv%
Craig Anderson	17	935	2.25	8-6-1	.935
Tomas Vokoun	69	4031	2.68	30-29-8	.919
FLORIDA	82	4988	2.65	38-35-9	.920

Shutouts: Vokoun (4), Anderson (2). **Assists:** Vokoun (6), Anderson (1). **PM:** Vokoun (4), Anderson (2).

Los Angeles Kings

Top Scorers	Gm	G	A	Pts	+/-	PM	PP
Anze Kopitar, C	82	32	45	77	-15	22	12
Alexander Frolov, L	71	23	44	67	1	22	5
Dustin Brown, L	78	33	27	60	-13	55	12
Patrick O'Sullivan, C	82	22	31	53	-8	36	3
Mike Cammalleri, C	63	19	28	47	-16	30	10
Lubomir Visnovsky, D	82	8	33	41	-18	34	3
Derek Armstrong, C	77	8	27	35	4	63	1
Rob Blake, D	71	9	22	31	-19	98	5
Ladislav Nagy, L	38	9	17	26	-2	18	2
Tom Preissing, D	77	8	16	24	-6	16	6
Michal Handzus, C	82	7	14	21	-21	45	0
Kyle Calder, L	65	7	13	20	-11	18	3
Brian Willsie, R	53	4	8	12	-8	30	0
Jack Johnson*, D	74	3	8	11	-19	76	0
Matt Moulson*, L	22	5	4	9	2	4	0
Raitis Ivanans, L	73	6	2	8	-10	134	0
Scott Thornton, L	47	5	3	8	1	39	0
Matt Ellis, L	54	3	5	8	3	26	0
DET	35	2	4	6	1	12	0
LA	19	1	1	2	2	14	0
Kevin Dallman, D	34	3	4	7	4	4	0
Jeff Giuliano, L	53	0	6	6	-9	14	0
Brian Boyle*, C	8	4	1	5	4	4	0
Peter Harrold*, D	25	2	3	5	3	2	0

Claimed: L Ellis off waivers from Det. (Feb. 21).

Goalies (10 Gm)	Gm	Min	GAA	Record	Sv%
Erik Ersberg*	14	799	2.48	6-5-3	.927
Jason LaBarbera	45	2421	3.00	17-23-2	.910
Jean-Sebastien Aubin	19	828	3.19	5-6-1	.886
LOS ANGELES	82	4977	3.17	32-43-7	.900

Shutouts: Ersberg (2), LaBarbera (1). **Assists:** none. **PM:** LaBarbera and Dan Cloutier (2).

Minnesota Wild

Top Scorers	Gm	G	A	Pts	+/-	PM	PP
Marian Gaborik, R	77	42	41	83	17	63	11
Pierre-Marc Bouchard, C	81	13	50	63	-11	34	6
Brian Rolston, R	81	31	28	59	-1	53	11
Pavol Demitra, R	68	15	39	54	9	24	2
Brent Burns, D	82	15	28	43	12	80	8
Mikko Koivu, C	57	11	31	42	13	42	2
Eric Belanger, C	75	13	24	37	-6	30	7
Mark Parrish, R	66	16	14	30	2	16	7
Kim Johnsson, D	80	4	23	27	-4	42	2
Kurtis Foster, D	56	7	12	19	0	37	3
James Sheppard*, C	78	4	15	19	0	29	0
Stephane Veilleux, L	77	11	7	18	-13	61	0
Branko Radivojevic, R	73	7	10	17	-14	48	1
Nick Schultz, D	81	2	13	15	9	42	0
Aaron Voros, L	55	7	7	14	-7	141	0
Todd Fedoruk, L	69	6	7	13	2	139	2
DAL	11	0	2	2	2	33	0
MIN	58	6	5	11	0	106	2
Martin Skoula, D	80	3	8	11	-16	26	0
Keith Carney, D	61	1	10	11	8	42	0
Petteri Nummelin, D	27	2	7	9	-2	2	1
Sean Hill, D	35	2	7	9	-16	32	1
Matt Foy, R	28	4	4	8	-1	28	0
Wes Walz, C	11	1	3	4	-5	6	0
Benoit Pouliot*, L	11	2	1	3	-1	0	0
Chris Simon, L	38	1	2	3	-1	59	0
NYI	28	1	2	3	-1	43	0
MIN	10	0	0	0	-1	16	0

Acquired: L Simon from NYI for an '08 6th-round pick (Feb 26). **Claimed:** L Fedoruk off waivers from Dal. (Nov. 22).

Goalies (10 Gm)	Gm	Min	GAA	Record	Sv%
Niklas Backstrom	58	3409	2.31	33-13-8	.920
Josh Harding*	29	1571	2.94	11-15-2	.908
MINNESOTA	82	4994	2.52	44-28-10	.915

Shutouts: Backstrom (4), Harding (1). **Assists:** Harding (1). **PM:** Backstrom (2).

Montreal Canadiens

Top Scorers	Gm	G	A	Pts	+/-	PM	PP
Alex Kovalev, R	82	35	49	84	18	70	17
Tomas Plekanec, C	81	29	40	69	15	42	12
Mark Streit, D	81	13	49	62	-6	28	7
Andrei Markov, D	82	16	42	58	1	63	10
Saku Koivu, C	77	16	40	56	-4	93	8
Andrei Kostitsyn, L	78	26	27	53	15	29	12
Chris Higgins, L	82	27	25	52	0	22	12
Michael Ryder, R	70	14	17	31	-4	30	1
Guillaume Latendresse, R	73	16	11	27	-2	41	2
Sergei Kostitsyn*, L	52	9	18	27	9	51	3
Roman Hamrlik, D	77	5	21	26	7	38	3
Bryan Smolinski, C	64	8	17	25	-6	20	1
Maxim Lapierre, C	53	7	11	18	5	60	0
Michael Komisarek, D	75	4	13	17	9	101	0
Mathieu Dandenault, R	61	9	5	14	-11	34	0
Tom Kostopoulos, R	67	7	6	13	-3	113	0
Kyle Chipchura*, C	36	4	7	11	-1	10	0
Patrice Brisebois, D	43	3	8	11	-2	26	2
Mikhail Grabovski*, C	24	3	6	9	-4	8	0
Josh Gorges, D	62	0	9	9	0	32	0
Steve Begin, L	44	3	5	8	0	48	0
Francois Bouillon, D	74	2	6	8	9	61	0
Ryan O'Byrne, D	33	1	6	7	7	45	0

Goalies (10 Gm)	Gm	Min	GAA	Record	Sv%
Carey Price*	41	2413	2.56	24-12-3	.920
MONTREAL	82	4995	2.59	47-25-10	.917

Shutouts: Price (3), Jaroslav Halak (1). **Assists:** Price (2). **PM:** none.

Nashville Predators

Top Scorers	Gm	G	A	Pts	+/-	PM	PP
J.P. Dumont, R	.80	29	43	72	5	34	7
Jason Arnott, C	.79	28	44	72	19	54	13
Alexander Radulov, R	.81	26	32	58	7	44	4
Martin Erat, R	.76	23	34	57	-3	40	4
David Legwand, C	.65	15	29	44	-4	38	4
Marek Zidlicky, D	.79	5	38	43	-5	63	4
Jan Hlavac, L	.80	12	23	35	-1	40	0
TB	.62	9	13	22	-10	32	0
NASH	.18	3	10	13	9	8	0
Vernon Fiddler, C	.79	11	21	32	-4	47	2
Ryan Suter, D	.76	7	24	31	3	71	1
Radek Bonk, C	.79	14	15	29	-31	40	6
Dan Hamhuis, D	.80	4	23	27	-4	66	1
Martin Gelinas, L	.57	9	11	20	5	20	0
Shea Weber, D	.54	6	14	20	-6	49	5
Jordin Tootoo, R	.63	11	7	18	-8	100	0
Scott Nichol, C	.73	10	8	18	12	72	0
Ville Koistinen*, D	.48	4	13	17	13	18	2
Jerred Smithson, C	.81	7	9	16	-9	50	0
Greg De Vries, D	.77	4	11	15	7	71	0
Brandon Bochenski, R	.40	3	10	13	6	12	1
BOS	.20	0	6	6	2	6	0
ANA	.12	2	2	4	2	6	1
NASH	.8	1	2	3	2	0	0
Rich Peverley*, C	.33	5	5	10	4	8	0
Jed Ortmeyer, R	.51	4	4	8	-8	32	0
Greg Zanon, D	.78	0	5	5	-5	24	0
Darcy Hordichuk, L	.45	1	2	3	-1	60	0

Acquired: L Hlavac from TB for an '08 7th-round pick (Feb. 26); R Bochenski from Ana. for future considerations (Feb. 26).

Goalies (10 Gm)	Gm	Min	GAA	Record	Sv%
Dan Ellis	.44	2229	2.34	23-10-3	.924
Chris Mason	.51	2692	2.90	18-22-6	.898
NASHVILLE	.82	4983	2.70	41-32-9	.908

Shutouts: Ellis (6), Mason (4). **Assists:** Mason (1). **PM:** none.

New Jersey Devils

Top Scorers	Gm	G	A	Pts	+/-	PM	PP
Zach Parise, L	.81	32	33	65	13	25	10
Patrik Elias, L	.74	20	35	55	10	38	7
Brian Gionta, R	.82	22	31	53	1	46	8
John Madden, C	.80	20	23	43	1	26	3
Jamie Langenbrunner, R	.64	13	28	41	-1	30	5
Dainius Zubrus, R	.82	13	25	38	2	38	4
Travis Zajac, C	.82	14	20	34	-11	31	5
Paul Martin, D	.73	5	27	32	20	22	2
John Oduya, D	.75	6	20	26	27	46	2
Jay Pandolfo, L	.54	12	12	24	10	22	0
David Clarkson*, R	.81	9	13	22	1	183	0
Mike Mottau, D	.76	4	13	17	-11	48	1
Sergei Brylin, L	.82	6	10	16	-5	20	0
Karel Rachunek, D	.47	4	9	13	3	40	0
Bryce Salvador, D	.64	1	10	11	12	54	0
ST.L	.56	1	10	11	12	43	0
NJ	.8	0	0	0	0	11	0
Arron Asham, R	.77	6	4	10	-6	84	0
Colin White, D	.57	2	8	10	-5	26	0
Andy Greene*, D	.59	2	8	10	0	22	2
Michael Rupp, C	.64	3	6	9	-8	58	1
Sheldon Brookbank, D	.44	0	8	8	0	63	0
Vitaly Vishnevski, D	.69	2	5	7	-12	50	0
Rod Pelley*, L	.58	2	4	6	-3	19	0

Acquired: D Salvador from St.L for R Cam Janssen (Feb. 26).

Goalies (5 Gm)	Gm	Min	GAA	Record	Sv%
Martin Brodeur	.77	4635	2.17	44-27-6	.920
Kevin Weekes	.9	343	2.97	2-2-1	.894
NEW JERSEY	.82	5002	2.32	46-29-7	.914

Shutouts: Brodeur (4). **Assists:** Brodeur (4). **PM:** Brodeur (6), Weekes (2).

New York Islanders

Top Scorers	Gm	G	A	Pts	+/-	PM	PP
Mike Comrie, C	.76	21	28	49	-21	87	4
Bill Guerin, R	.81	23	21	44	-15	65	7
Miroslav Satan, R	.80	16	25	41	-11	39	5
Trent Hunter, R	.82	12	29	41	-17	43	2
Josef Vasicek, C	.81	16	19	35	1	53	0
Ruslan Fedotenko, L	.67	16	17	33	-9	40	8
Richard Park, R	.82	12	20	32	-4	20	1
Mike Sillinger, C	.52	14	12	26	-10	28	3
Sean Bergenheim, L	.78	10	12	22	-3	62	1
Bryan Berard, D	.54	5	17	22	-17	48	4
Chris Campoli, D	.46	4	14	18	-1	16	2
Andy Hilbert, L	.70	8	8	16	2	18	0
Blake Comeau*, R	.51	8	7	15	1	22	1
Radek Martinek, D	.69	0	15	15	-9	40	0
Bruno Gervais, D	.60	0	13	13	-5	34	0
Freddy Meyer, D	.57	3	9	12	2	22	0
PHO	.5	0	0	0	-4	0	0
NYI	.52	3	9	12	6	22	0
Andy Sutton, D	.58	1	7	8	-6	86	0
Brendan Witt, D	.59	2	5	7	-8	51	0
Kyle Okposo*, R	.9	2	3	5	3	2	1
Jeff Tambellini, L	.31	1	3	4	-9	8	0
Tim Jackman, R	.36	1	3	4	-3	57	0

Claimed: D Meyer off waivers from Pho. (Nov. 10).

Goalies (10 Gm)	Gm	Min	GAA	Record	Sv%
Wade Dubielewicz	.20	1132	2.70	9-9-1	.919
Rick DiPietro	.63	3707	2.82	26-28-7	.902
NY ISLANDERS	.82	4987	2.89	35-38-9	.904

Shutouts: DiPietro (3). **Assists:** DiPietro (6). **PM:** DiPietro (18).

New York Rangers

Top Scorers	Gm	G	A	Pts	+/-	PM	PP
Jaromir Jagr, R	.82	25	46	71	8	58	7
Scott Gomez, C	.81	16	54	70	3	36	7
Chris Drury, C	.82	25	33	58	-3	45	12
Brendan Shanahan, R	.73	23	23	46	-2	35	11
Martin Straka, L	.65	14	27	41	5	22	3
Brandon Dubinsky*, C	.82	14	26	40	8	79	1
Michal Rozsival, D	.80	13	25	38	0	80	6
Sean Avery, L	.57	15	18	33	6	154	2
Nigel Dawes*, L	.61	14	15	29	11	10	3
Daniel Girardi, D	.82	10	18	28	0	14	5
Fredrik Sjostrom, L	.69	12	9	21	-2	22	2
PHO	.51	10	9	19	-2	14	2
NYR	.18	2	0	2	0	8	0
Fedor Tyutin, D	.82	5	15	20	5	43	1
Christian Backman, D	.63	3	15	18	-2	50	1
ST.L	.45	1	9	10	-4	30	0
NYR	.18	2	6	8	2	20	1
Petr Prucha, L	.63	7	10	17	3	22	2
Paul Mara, D	.61	1	16	17	1	52	0
Ryan Callahan*, R	.52	8	5	13	7	31	0
Marek Malik, D	.42	2	8	10	7	48	0
Marc Staal*, D	.80	2	8	10	2	42	0
Blair Betts, C	.75	5	5	7	-4	20	0
Ryan Hollweg, L	.70	2	2	4	-12	96	0
Jason Strudwick, D	.52	1	1	2	0	40	0
Colton Orr, R	.74	1	1	2	-13	159	0

Acquired: L Sjostrom, G David LeNeveu, R Josh Gratton and an '09 conditional pick from Pho. for L Marcel Hossa and G Al Montoya (Feb. 26); D Backman from St.L for an '08 4th-round pick (Feb. 26).

Goalies (10 Gm)	Gm	Min	GAA	Record	SV%
Stephen Valiquette	.13	686	2.19	5-3-3	.916
Henrik Lundqvist	.72	4305	2.23	37-24-10	.912
NY RANGERS	.82	5018	2.27	42-27-13	.911

Shutouts: Lundqvist (10), Valiquette (2). **Assists:** none. **PM:** Lundqvist and Valiquette (2).

Ottawa Senators

Top Scorers	Gm	G	A	Pts	+/-	PM	PP
Jason Spezza, C	.76	34	58	92	26	66	11
Daniel Alfredsson, R	.70	40	49	89	15	34	9
Dany Heatley, L	.71	41	41	82	33	76	13
Cory Stillman, L	.79	24	41	65	-15	24	11
CAR	.55	21	25	46	-7	14	10
OTT	.24	3	16	19	-8	10	1
Antoine Vermette, L	.81	24	29	53	3	51	4
Mike Fisher, C	.79	23	24	47	-10	82	6
Wade Redden, D	.80	6	32	38	11	60	4
Andrej Meszaros, D	.82	9	27	36	5	50	6
Chris Kelly, C	.75	11	19	30	3	30	0
Randy Robitaille, C	.68	10	19	29	4	18	1
Christoph Schubert, D	.82	8	16	24	7	64	1
Dean McAmmond, C	.68	9	13	22	1	12	0
Chris Neil, R	.68	6	14	20	-3	199	0
Chris Phillips, D	.81	5	13	18	15	56	1
Anton Volchenkov, D	.67	1	14	15	14	55	0
Mike Commodore, D	.67	3	11	14	-7	100	0
CAR	.41	3	9	12	2	74	0
OTT	.26	0	2	2	-9	26	0
Martin Lapointe, R	.70	6	7	13	-5	70	1
CHI	.52	4	3	7	-3	47	0
OTT	.18	3	3	6	-2	23	1
Shean Donovan, R	.82	5	7	12	-3	73	0
Nick Foligno*, L	.45	6	3	9	0	20	0
Luke Richardson, D	.76	2	7	9	1	41	0

Acquired: L Stillman and D Commodore from Car. for D Joseph Corvo and R Patrick Eaves (Feb. 11); R Lapointe from Chi. for an '08 6th-round pick (Feb. 26).

Goalies (10 Gm)	Gm	Min	GAA	Record	Sv%
Martin Gerber	.57	3197	2.72	30-18-4	.910
Ray Emery	.31	1689	3.13	12-13-4	.890
OTTAWA	.82	4979	2.92	43-31-8	.901

Shutouts: Gerber (2), Emery and Gerber also shared a shutout. **Assists:** Gerber (2). **PM:** Gerber and Emery (6).

Philadelphia Flyers

Top Scorers	Gm	G	A	Pts	+/-	PM	PP
Mike Richards, C	.73	28	47	75	14	76	8
Daniel Briere, C	.79	31	41	72	-22	68	14
Vaclav Prospal, L	.80	33	38	71	0	45	10
TB	.62	29	28	57	-7	39	9
PHI	.18	4	10	14	7	6	1
Mike Knuble, R	.82	29	26	55	-3	72	15
Jeff Carter, C	.82	29	24	53	6	55	7
R.J. Umberger, C	.74	13	37	50	0	19	4
Joffrey Lupul, R	.56	20	26	46	2	35	7
Kimmo Timonen, D	.80	8	36	44	0	50	3
Scott Hartnell, L	.80	24	19	43	2	159	10
Braydon Coburn, D	.78	9	27	36	17	74	5
Randy Jones, D	.71	5	26	31	8	58	1
Scottie Upshall, R	.61	14	16	30	2	74	3
Simon Gagne, C	.25	7	11	18	-8	4	5
Steve Downie*, R	.32	6	6	12	2	73	0
Jim Dowd, C	.73	5	5	10	0	41	0
Jason Smith, D	.77	1	9	10	-4	86	0
Jaroslav Modry, D	.80	1	8	9	-9	50	0
LA	.61	1	5	6	2	42	0
PHI	.19	0	3	3	-11	8	0

Acquired: D Modry from LA for an '08 3rd-round pick (Feb. 19); L Prospal from TB for D Alexandre Picard and an '09 2nd-round pick (Feb. 25).

Goalies (10 Gm)	Gm	Min	GAA	Record	Sv%
Martin Biron	.62	3539	2.59	30-20-9	.918
Antero Niittymaki	.28	1424	2.91	12-9-2	.907
PHILADELPHIA	.82	4985	2.73	42-29-11	.913

Shutouts: Biron (5), Niittymaki (1). **Assists:** Biron (1). **PM:** Biron (8).

Phoenix Coyotes

Top Scorers	Gm	G	A	Pts	+/-	PM	PP
Shane Doan, R	.80	28	50	78	4	59	9
Radim Vrbata, R	.76	27	29	56	6	14	7
Peter Mueller*, C	.81	22	32	54	-13	32	7
Ed Jovanovski, D	.80	12	39	51	-13	73	6
Steve Reinprecht, C	.81	16	30	46	-3	26	5
Martin Hanzal*, C	.72	8	27	35	-7	28	1
Niko Kapanen, C	.79	10	18	28	-1	34	5
Daniel Winnik*, L	.79	11	15	26	-3	25	0
Derek Morris, D	.82	8	17	25	8	83	2
Daniel Carcillo*, L	.57	13	11	24	1	324	3
Keith Ballard, D	.82	6	15	21	7	85	2
Joel Perrault, C	.49	7	10	17	-11	48	3
Zbynek Michalek, D	.75	4	13	17	9	34	0
Michael York, L	.63	6	8	14	-8	4	4
Keith Yandle*, D	.43	5	7	12	-12	14	4
Nick Boynton, D	.79	3	9	12	-9	125	0
Mathias Tjarnqvist, L	.78	4	7	11	-1	34	0
Craig Weller, R	.59	3	8	11	-7	80	0
Marcel Hossa, R	.50	1	7	8	2	28	0
NYR	.36	1	7	8	8	24	0
PHO	.14	0	0	-6	4	0	

Acquired: L Hossa and G Al Montoya from NYR for L Fredrik Sjostrom, G David LeNeveu, R Josh Gratton and an '09 conditional pick (Feb. 26). **Claimed:** G Bryzgalov off waivers from Ana. (Nov. 17).

Goalies (10 Gm)	Gm	Min	GAA	Record	Sv%
Ilya Bryzgalov	.64	3613	2.44	28-25-6	.920
ANA		447	2.55	2-3-1	.909
PHO	.55	3167	2.43	26-22-5	.921
Mikael Tellqvist	.22	1224	2.75	9-8-2	.908
PHOENIX	.82	4995	2.70	38-37-7	.911

Shutouts: Bryzgalov (3); Tellqvist (2). **Assists:** Tellqvist (1). **PM:** Bryzgalov and Tellqvist (2).

Pittsburgh Penguins

Top Scorers	Gm	G	A	Pts	+/-	PM	PP
Evgeni Malkin, C	.82	47	59	106	16	78	17
Sidney Crosby, C	.53	24	48	72	18	39	6
Marian Hossa, R	.72	29	37	66	-14	36	8
ATL	.60	26	30	56	-14	30	8
PIT	.12	3	7	10	0	6	0
Sergei Gonchar, D	.78	12	53	65	13	66	8
Petr Sykora, R	.81	28	35	63	1	41	15
Ryan Malone, L	.77	27	24	51	14	103	11
Ryan Whitney, D	.76	12	28	40	-2	45	7
Jordan Staal, C	.82	12	16	28	-5	55	3
Pascal Dupuis, R	.78	12	15	27	0	32	0
ATL	.62	10	5	15	-4	24	0
PIT	.16	2	10	12	4	8	0
Maxime Talbot, C	.63	12	14	26	8	53	0
Hal Gill, D	.81	3	21	24	6	68	0
TOR	.63	2	18	20	0	52	0
PIT	.18	1	3	4	6	16	0
Tyler Kennedy*, C	.55	10	9	19	2	35	1
Kristopher Letang*, D	.63	6	11	17	-1	23	1
Jarkko Ruutu, L	.71	6	10	16	3	138	0
Gary Roberts, L	.38	5	12	15	-3	40	1
Georges Laraque, R	.71	4	9	13	0	141	0
Darryl Sydor, D	.74	1	12	13	1	26	1

Acquired: D Gill from Tor. for an '08 2nd-round pick and an '09 5th-round pick (Feb. 26); R Hossa and D Dupuis from Atl. for R Colby Armstrong, C Erik Christensen, C Angelo Esposito and an '08 1st-round pick (Feb. 26).

Goalies (10 Gm)	Gm	Min	GAA	Record	Sv%
Marc-Andre Fleury	.35	1857	2.33	19-10-2	.921
Ty Conklin	.33	1866	2.51	18-8-5	.923
Dany Sabourin	.24	1242	2.75	10-9-1	.904
PITTSBURGH	.82	4986	2.55	47-27-8	.916

Shutouts: Fleury (4); Conklin and Sabourin (2). **Assists:** Fleury and Conklin (1). **PM:** Conklin (4), Sabourin (2).

St. Louis Blues

Top Scorers	Gm	G	A	Pts	+/-	PM	PP
Brad Boyes, R	82	43	22	65	1	20	11
Paul Kariya, L	82	16	49	65	-10	50	5
Keith Tkachuk, C	79	27	31	58	-2	69	12
Andy McDonald, C	82	18	34	52	-21	62	3
ANA	33	4	12	16	-4	30	0
ST.L	49	14	22	36	-17	32	3
Lee Stempniak, R	80	13	25	38	0	40	3
Erik Johnson*, D	69	5	28	33	-9	28	4
David Backes, C	72	13	18	31	-11	99	3
David Perron*, L	62	13	14	27	16	38	3
Jamal Mayers, R	80	12	15	27	-19	91	0
Jay McClement, C	81	9	13	22	-17	26	0
Eric Brewer, D	77	1	21	22	-18	91	0
Ryan Johnson, C	79	5	13	18	-2	22	0
Martin Rucinsky, L	40	5	11	16	-9	40	1
Barret Jackman, D	78	2	14	16	-12	93	1
Dan Hinote, R	58	5	5	10	-3	42	0
Jay McKee, D	66	2	7	9	2	42	0
Steve Wagner*, D	24	2	6	8	-4	8	1
Jeff Woywitka*, D	27	2	6	8	2	12	0
Dwayne King, L	61	3	3	6	-4	100	0
Mike Johnson, R	21	2	3	5	-4	8	0

Three tied with 2 pts. each.

Acquired: C McDonald from Ana. for C Doug Weight, L Michal Birner and an '08 7th-round pick (Dec. 14).

Goalies (10 Gm)	Gm	Min	GAA	Record	SV%
Manny Legace	66	3666	2.41	27-25-8	.911
Hannu Toivonen	23	1202	3.44	6-10-5	.878
ST. LOUIS	82	4979	2.80	33-36-13	.897

Shutouts: Legace (5). **Assists:** Legace (2). **PM:** Legace (4), Toivonen (2).

San Jose Sharks

Top Scorers	Gm	G	A	Pts	+/-	PM	PP
Joe Thornton, C	82	29	67	96	18	59	11
Brian Campbell, D	83	8	54	62	8	20	5
BUF	63	5	38	43	-1	12	3
SJ	20	3	16	19	9	8	2
Milan Michalek, L	79	24	31	55	19	47	5
Patrick Marleau, C	78	19	29	48	-19	33	7
Joe Pavelski, C	82	19	21	40	1	28	8
Jonathan Cheechoo, R	69	23	14	37	11	46	10
Craig Rivet, D	74	5	30	35	3	104	2
Jeremy Roenick, C	69	14	19	33	-8	26	7
Mike Grier, R	78	9	13	22	-8	24	1
Christian Ehrhoff, D	77	1	21	22	-9	72	1
Torrey Mitchell*, C	82	10	10	20	-3	50	1
Devin Setoguchi*, R	44	11	6	17	6	8	3
Patrick Rissmiller, L	79	8	9	17	-8	30	0
Sandis Ozolinsh, D	39	3	13	16	-11	24	2
Matthew Carle, D	62	2	13	15	-8	26	2
Marc-Edouard Vlasic, D	82	2	12	14	-12	24	1
Kyle McLaren, D	61	3	8	11	3	84	0
Doug Murray, D	66	1	9	10	20	98	0
Curtis Brown, C	33	5	4	9	4	10	0
Marcel Goc, C	51	5	3	8	-15	12	0
Ryane Clowe, L	15	3	5	8	-14	22	2
Jody Shelley, L	62	1	6	7	-4	135	0
CLB	31	0	0	0	-2	44	0
SJ	31	1	6	7	-2	91	0
Alexei Semenov, D	22	1	3	4	-8	36	1

Acquired: L Shelley from Clb. for an '09 6-th round pick (Jan. 29); D Campbell from Buf. for R Steve Bernier and an '08 1st-round pick (Feb. 26).

Goalies (10 Gm)	Gm	Min	GAA	Record	Sv%
Evgeni Nabokov	77	4561	2.14	46-21-8	.910
SAN JOSE	82	5000	2.24	49-23-10	.906

Shutouts: Nabokov (6), Brian Boucher (1). **Assists:** Nabokov (2). **PM:** Nabokov (12).

Tampa Bay Lightning

Top Scorers	Gm	G	A	Pts	+/-	PM	PP
Vincent Lecavalier, C	81	40	52	92	-17	89	10
Martin St. Louis, R	82	25	58	83	-23	26	10
Jeff Halpern, C	83	20	22	42	0	54	4
DAL	64	10	14	24	-2	40	1
TB	19	10	8	18	2	14	3
Jussi Jokinen, L	72	16	26	42	-14	18	6
DAL	52	14	14	28	2	14	5
TB	20	2	12	14	-16	4	1
Michel Ouellet, R	64	17	19	36	11	12	5
Paul Ranger, D	72	10	21	31	-13	56	0
Filip Kuba, D	75	6	25	31	-8	40	2
Dan Boyle, D	37	4	21	25	-29	57	2
Mathieu Darche, L	73	7	15	22	-14	20	1
Chris Gratton, C	60	10	11	21	-7	77	1
Shane O'Brien, D	77	4	17	21	-2	154	0
Jason Ward, R	79	8	6	14	-18	42	1
Craig MacDonald, C	65	2	9	11	-10	16	0
Nick Tarnasky, C	80	6	4	10	-15	78	1
Andre Roy, R	63	4	3	7	-1	108	0
Brad Lukowich, D	59	1	6	7	-15	20	0
Alexandre Picard, D	24	3	3	6	-12	10	1
PHI	4	0	0	0	-3	2	0
TB	20	3	3	6	-9	8	1
Mike Lundin*, D	81	0	6	6	3	16	0

Acquired: D Picard and an '09 2nd-round pick from Phi. for L Vaclav Prospal (Feb. 25); G Smith, C Halpern, L Jokinen and an '08 4th-round pick from Dal. for C Brad Richards and G Johan Holmqvist (Feb. 26).

Goalies (10 Gm)	Gm	Min	GAA	Record	SV%
Mike Smith*	34	1946	2.59	15-19-0	.901
DAL	21	1172	2.46	12-9-0	.906
TB	13	774	2.79	3-10-0	.893
Karri Ramo*	22	1269	3.03	7-11-3	.890
Marc Denis	10	415	4.05	1-5-0	.859
TAMPA BAY	82	4963	3.22	31-42-9	.885

Shutouts: Smith (3, 2 with Dal.). **Assists:** Smith and Ramo (1). **PM:** Smith (12, 6 with Dal.), Ramo (4), Denis (2).

Toronto Maple Leafs

Top Scorers	Gm	G	A	Pts	+/-	PM	PP
Mats Sundin, C	74	32	46	78	17	76	10
Nik Antropov, R	72	26	30	56	10	92	12
Tomas Kaberle, D	82	8	45	53	-8	22	6
Jason Blake, L	82	15	37	52	-4	28	2
Alex Steen, L	76	15	27	42	0	32	2
Pavel Kubina, D	72	11	29	40	5	116	6
Alexei Ponikarovsky, L	66	18	17	35	3	36	1
Darcy Tucker, R	74	18	16	34	-8	100	7
Matt Stajan, C	82	16	17	33	-11	47	2
Bryan McCabe, D	54	5	18	23	-2	81	4
Kyle Wellwood, C	59	8	13	21	-12	0	5
Ian White, D	81	5	16	21	-9	44	0
Boyd Devereaux, C	62	7	11	18	-6	24	0
Chad Kilger, L	53	10	7	17	1	18	0
Dominic Moore, C	68	5	12	17	-4	24	1
MIN	30	1	2	3	-11	10	0
TOR	38	4	10	14	7	14	1
Jiri Tlusty*, C	58	10	6	16	-12	14	2
Mark Bell, L	35	4	6	10	-2	60	0
Anton Stralman*, D	50	3	6	9	-10	18	0
Andy Wozniewski, D	48	2	7	9	5	54	0
Carlo Colaiacovo, D	28	2	4	6	-4	10	0

Claimed: C Moore off waivers from Min. (Jan. 11).

Goalies (10 Gm)	Gm	Min	GAA	Record	Sv%
Vesa Toskala	66	3837	2.74	33-25-6	.904
Andrew Raycroft	19	965	3.92	2-9-5	.876
TORONTO	82	4991	3.08	36-35-11	.893

Shutouts: Toskala (3), Raycroft (1). **Assists:** Toskala (5). **PM:** Toskala (4).

Vancouver Canucks

Top Scorers	Gm	G	A	Pts	+/-	PM	PP
Henrik Sedin, C	82	15	61	76	6	56	4
Daniel Sedin, L	82	29	45	74	6	50	12
Markus Naslund, L . .	82	25	30	55	-7	46	9
Ryan Kesler, C	80	21	16	37	1	79	4
Taylor Pyatt, L	79	16	21	37	9	60	7
Alex Burrows, L	82	12	19	31	11	179	1
Brendan Morrison, C .	39	9	16	25	-3	18	3
Sami Salo, D	63	8	17	25	8	38	6
Mattias Ohlund, D . .	53	9	15	24	-1	79	4
Mason Raymond*, L . .	49	9	12	21	1	2	1
Alexander Edler*, D . .	75	8	12	20	6	42	4
Matt Pettinger, L . . .	76	6	7	13	-11	36	1
WASH	56	2	5	7	-11	25	1
VAN	20	4	2	6	0	11	0
Ryan Shannon, R . . .	27	5	8	13	-1	24	4
Trevor Linden, C	59	7	5	12	0	15	0
Kevin Bieksa, D	34	2	10	12	-11	90	1
Willie Mitchell, D . . .	72	2	10	12	6	81	0
Brad Isbister, L	55	6	5	11	-4	38	0
Byron Ritchie, L	71	3	8	11	-10	80	0
Lukas Krajicek, D . . .	39	2	9	11	-3	36	1
Aaron Miller, D	57	1	8	9	-4	32	0
Jason Jaffray, L	19	2	4	6	4	19	1

Acquired: L Pettinger from Wash. for L Matt Cooke (Feb. 26).

Goalies (10 Gm)	Gm	Min	GAA	Record	SV%
Roberto Luongo	73	4233	2.38	35-29-9	.917
Curtis Sanford	16	679	2.83	4-3-1	.898
VANCOUVER	82	5006	2.47	39-33-10	.913

Shutouts: Luongo (6). **Assists:** Luongo (3), Sanford (1).
PM: Luongo (4), Sanford (2).

Washington Capitals

Top Scorers	Gm	G	A	Pts	+/-	PM	PP
Alexander Ovechkin, L .	82	65	47	112	28	40	22
Nicklas Backstrom*, C .	82	14	55	69	13	24	3
Mike Green, D	82	18	38	56	6	62	8
Viktor Kozlov, C	81	16	38	54	28	18	2
Alexander Semin, L . .	63	26	16	42	-18	54	10
Sergei Fedorov, C . . .	68	11	30	41	-5	38	6
CLB	50	9	18	28	-3	30	5
WASH	18	2	11	13	-2	8	1
Brooks Laich, C	82	21	16	37	-3	35	8
Michael Nylander, C . .	40	11	26	37	-19	24	5
Tomas Fleischmann, L .	75	10	20	30	-7	18	1
Tom Poti, D	71	2	27	29	9	46	0
Matt Cooke, L	78	10	13	23	1	91	0
VAN	61	7	9	16	-4	64	0
WASH	17	3	4	7	5	27	0
Matt Bradley, R	77	7	11	18	1	74	1
Jeff Schultz, D	72	5	13	18	12	28	0
Boyd Gordon, C	67	7	9	16	5	12	0
Brian Pothier, D	38	5	9	14	5	20	1

Acquired: C Fedorov from Clb. for D Ted Ruth (Feb. 26); L Cooke from Van. for LW Matt Pettinger (Feb. 26); G Huet from Mon. for an '09 2nd-round pick (Feb. 26).

Goalies (10 Gm)	Gm	Min	GAA	Record	Sv%
Cristobal Huet	52	3049	2.32	32-14-6	.920
MON	39	2278	2.55	21-12-6	.916
WASH	13	771	1.63	11-2-0	.936
Brent Johnson	19	1032	2.67	7-8-2	.908
Olaf Kolzig	54	3154	2.91	25-21-6	.892
WASHINGTON	82	4987	2.73	43-31-8	.900

Shutouts: Huet (2), Kolzig (1). **Assists:** Kolzig (2); Huet (1). **PM:** Kolzig (8).

2008 NHL Entry Draft

Top 50 selections at the 46th annual NHL Entry Draft held June 20-21, 2008, at Scotiabank Place in Ottawa, Ontario. First 30 picks are first-round selections, 31-50 are second round. The order of the first 14 positions were determined by a draft lottery of non-playoff teams held April 7 in New York City. Only the worst five teams from the 2007-08 regular season had the chance to win the first overall pick. No team could move up more than four spots in the draft order or drop more than one position. Positions 15 through 30 reflect regular season records in reverse order.

Top 50 Selections

	Team	Player, Last Team	Pos
1	Tampa Bay	Steven Stamkos, Sarnia (OHL)	C
2	Los Angeles	Drew Doughty, Guelph (OHL)	D
3	Atlanta	Zach Bogosian, Peterborough (OHL)	D
4	St. Louis	Alex Pietrangelo, Niagara (OHL)	D
5	a-Toronto	Luke Schenn, Kelowna (WHL)	D
6	Columbus	Nikita Filatov, CSKA 2 (Rus)	L
7	b-Nashville	Colin Wilson, Boston U (HE)	C
8	Phoenix	Mikkel Boedker, Kitchener (OHL)	L
9	c-NY Islanders	Joshua Bailey, Windsor (OHL)	C
10	Vancouver	Cody Hodgson, Brampton (OHL)	C
11	Chicago	Kyle Beach, Everett (WHL)	C
12	d-Buffalo	Tyler Myers, Kelowna (WHL)	D
13	e-Los Angeles . . .	Colton Teubert, Regina (WHL)	D
14	Carolina	Zach Boychuk, Lethbridge (WHL)	C
15	f-Ottawa	Erik Karlsson, Frolunda Jr. (Swe)	D
16	Boston	Joe Colborne, Camrose (AJHL)	C
17	g-Anaheim	Jake Gardiner, Minnetonka, MN (HS)	D
18	h-Nashville	Chet Pickard, Tri-City (WHL)	G
19	i-Philadelphia	Luca Sbisa, Lethbridge (WHL)	D
20	NY Rangers . .	Michael Del Zotto, Oshawa (OHL)	D
21	j-Washington	Anton Gustafsson, Frolunda Jr. (Swe)	C
22	k-Edmonton	Jordan Eberle, Regina (WHL)	C
23	l-Minnesota	Tyler Cuma, Ottawa (OHL)	D
24	m-New Jersey . .	Mattias Tedenby, HV 71 (Swe)	L
25	n-Calgary	Greg Nemisz, Windsor (OHL)	C
26	o-Buffalo	Tyler Ennis, Medicine Hat (WHL)	C
27	p-Washington . . .	John Carlson, Indiana (USHL)	D
28	q-Phoenix	Viktor Tikhonov, Cherepovets (Rus)	W
29	r-Atlanta	Daultan Leveille, St. Catharines (GHL)	C
30	Detroit	Thomas McCollum, Guelph (OHL)	G
31	s-Florida	Jacob Markstrom, Brynas Jr. (Swe)	G
32	Los Angeles . . .	Vjateslav Voinov, Chelyabinsk (Rus)	D
33	t-St. Louis	Philip McRae, London (OHL)	C
34	St. Louis	Jake Allen, St. John's (QMJHL)	G
35	u-Anaheim . . N. Deschamps, Chicoutimi (QMJHL)		C
36	NY Islanders . . .	Corey Trivino, Stouffville (OPJHL)	C
37	Columbus	Cody Goloubef, Wisconsin (WCHA)	D
38	v-Nashville	Roman Josi, Bern (Swi)	D
39	w-Anaheim	Eric O'Dell, Sudbury (OHL)	C
40	x-NY Islanders . . .	Aaron Ness, Roseau, MN (HS)	D
41	Vancouver	Yann Sauve, Saint John (QMJHL)	D
42	y-Ottawa	Patrick Wiercioch, Omaha (USHL)	D
43	z-Anaheim	Justin Schultz, Westside (BCHL)	D
44	Buffalo	Luke Adam, St. John's (QMJHL)	C
45	Carolina	Zac Dalpe, Penticton (BCHL)	C
46	aa-Florida	Colby Robak, Brandon (WHL)	D
47	Boston	Maxime Sauve, Val D'Or (QMJHL)	C
48	Calgary	Mitch Wahl, Spokane (WHL)	C
49	bb-Phoenix	Jared Staal, Sudbury (OHL	R
50	Colorado	Cameron Guance, Miss. St.Michls (OHL)	C

Acquired picks: a—from NYI; **b**—from Tor; **c**—from Fla; **d**—from Edm; **e**—from Buf; **f**—from Nash; **g**—from Calg; **h**—from Ott; **i**—from Col; **j**—from NJ; **k**—from Ana; **l**—from Wash; **m**—from Min; **n**—from Mon; **o**—from SJ; **p**—from Phi.; **q**—from Dal; **r**—from Pit; **s**—from TB; **t**—from Atl; **u**—from Phi; **v**—from Tor; **w**—from Pho; **x**—from Fla; **y**—from Chi; **z**—from Edm; **aa**—from Nash; **bb**—from Tor.

Stanley Cup Playoffs

(1) Detroit 4						(1) Montreal 4
(8) Nashville 2	Detroit 4				Montreal 1	(8) Boston 3
(3) Colorado 4		Detroit 4		Philadelphia 1		(3) Washington 3
(6) Minnesota 2	Colorado 0				Philadelphia 4	(6) Philadelphia 4
		WESTERN CONFERENCE	Detroit 4	EASTERN CONFERENCE		
(2) San Jose 4			Pittsburgh 2			(2) Pittsburgh 4
(7) Calgary 3	San Jose 2				Pittsburgh 4	(7) Ottawa 0
(4) Anaheim 2		Dallas 2		Pittsburgh 4		(4) New Jersey 1
(5) Dallas 4	Dallas 4				NY Rangers 1	(5) NY Rangers 4

Stanley Cup Playoffs
Series Summaries
WESTERN CONFERENCE

QUARTERFINALS (Best of 7)

	W-L	GF	Leading Scorers
Detroit	4-2	17	Three tied with 5 pts.
Nashville	2-4	12	Three tied with 4 pts.

Date	Winner	Home Ice
April 10	Red Wings, 3-1	at Detroit
April 12	Red Wings, 4-2	at Detroit
April 14	Predators, 5-3	at Nashville
April 16	Predators, 3-2	at Nashville
April 18	Red Wings, 2-1 (OT)	at Detroit
April 20	Red Wings, 3-0	at Nashville

	W-L	GF	Leading Scorers
Colorado	4-2	17	Sakic (2-4-6)
Minnesota	2-4	12	Rolston (2-4-6)

Date	Winner	Home Ice
April 9	Avalanche, 3-2 (OT)	at Minnesota
April 11	Wild, 3-2 (OT)	at Minnesota
April 14	Wild, 3-2 (OT)	at Colorado
April 15	Avalanche, 5-1	at Colorado
April 17	Avalanche, 3-2	at Minnesota
April 19	Avalanche, 2-1	at Colorado

	W-L	GF	Leading Scorers
San Jose	4-3	19	Clowe (4-4-8)
Calgary	3-4	17	Iginla (4-5-9)

Date	Winner	Home Ice
April 9	Flames, 3-2	at San Jose
April 10	Sharks, 2-0	at San Jose
April 13	Flames, 4-3	at Calgary
April 15	Sharks, 3-2	at Calgary
April 17	Sharks, 4-3	at San Jose
April 20	Flames, 2-0	at Calgary
April 22	Sharks, 5-3	at San Jose

	W-L	GF	Leading Scorers
Dallas	4-2	20	Ribeiro (2-6-8)
Anaheim	2-4	13	Pronger (2-3-5)
			& Getzlaf (2-3-5)

Date	Winner	Home Ice
April 10	Stars, 4-0	at Anaheim
April 12	Stars, 5-2	at Anaheim
April 15	Ducks, 4-2	at Dallas
April 17	Stars, 3-1	at Dallas
April 18	Ducks, 5-2	at Anaheim
April 20	Stars, 4-1	at Dallas

SEMIFINALS (Best of 7)

	W-L	GF	Leading Scorers
Detroit	4-0	21	Franzen (9-1-10)
Colorado	0-4	9	Sakic (0-4-4)

Date	Winner	Home Ice
April 24	Red Wings, 4-3	at Detroit
April 26	Red Wings, 5-1	at Detroit
April 29	Red Wings, 4-3	at Colorado
May 1	Red Wings, 8-2	at Colorado

	W-L	GF	Leading Scorers
Dallas	4-2	15	Ribeiro (1-5-6)
			& Richards (1-5-6)
San Jose	2-4	11	Michalek (4-0-4)
			& Campbell (1-3-4)

Date	Winner	Home Ice
April 25	Stars, 3-2 (OT)	at San Jose
April 27	Stars, 5-2	at San Jose
April 29	Stars, 2-1 (OT)	at Dallas
April 30	Sharks, 2-1	at Dallas
May 2	Sharks, 3-2 (OT)	at San Jose
May 4	Stars, 2-1 (4OT)	at Dallas

CHAMPIONSHIP (Best of 7)

	W-L	GF	Leading Scorers
Detroit	4-2	17	Zetterberg (4-4—8)
Dallas	2-4	10	Morrow (2-2—4)
			& Richards (1-3—4)

Date	Winner	Home Ice
May 8	Red Wings, 4-1	at Detroit
May 10	Red Wings, 2-1	at Detroit
May 12	Red Wings, 5-2	at Dallas
May 14	Stars, 3-1	at Dallas
May 17	Stars, 2-1	at Detroit
May 19	Red Wings, 4-1	at Dallas

EASTERN CONFERENCE

QUARTERFINALS (Best of 7)

	W-L	GF	Leading Scorers
Montreal	4-3	19	S. Kostitsyn (3-3—6)
			& Kovalev (2-4—6)
Boston	3-4	15	Savard (1-5—6)

Date	Winner	Home Ice
April 10	Canadiens, 4-1	at Montreal
April 12	Canadiens, 3-2 (OT)	at Montreal
April 13	Bruins, 2-1 (OT)	at Boston
April 15	Canadiens, 1-0	at Boston
April 17	Bruins, 5-1	at Montreal
April 19	Bruins, 5-4	at Boston
April 21	Canadiens, 5-0	at Montreal

	W-L	GF	Leading Scorers
Philadelphia	4-3	23	Briere (6-5—11)
Washington	3-4	20	Ovechkin (4-5—9)

Date	Winner	Home Ice
April 11	Capitals, 5-4	at Washington
April 13	Flyers, 2-0	at Washington
April 15	Flyers, 6-3	at Philadelphia
April 17	Flyers, 4-3 (2OT)	at Philadelphia
April 19	Capitals, 3-2	at Washington
April 21	Capitals, 4-2	at Philadelphia
April 22	Flyers, 3-2 (OT)	at Washington

	W-L	GF	Leading Scorers
Pittsburgh	4-0	16	Crosby (2-6—8)
Ottawa	0-4	5	Stillman (2-0—2)
			& Commodore (0-2—2)

Date	Winner	Home Ice
April 9	Penguins, 4-0	at Pittsburgh
April 11	Penguins, 5-3	at Pittsburgh
April 14	Penguins, 4-1	at Ottawa
April 16	Penguins, 3-1	at Ottawa

	W-L	GF	Leading Scorers
NY Rangers	4-1	19	Jagr (2-6—8)
New Jersey	1-4	12	Elias (4-2—6)

Date	Winner	Home Ice
April 9	Rangers, 4-1	at New Jersey
April 11	Rangers, 2-1	at New Jersey
April 13	Devils, 4-3 (OT)	at New York
April 16	Rangers, 5-3	at New York
April 18	Rangers, 5-3	at New Jersey

SEMIFINALS (Best of 7)

	W-L	GF	Leading Scorers
Philadelphia	4-1	20	Umberger (8-1—9)
Montreal	1-4	14	Koivu (3-3—6)

Date	Winner	Home Ice
April 24	Canadiens, 4-3 (OT)	at Montreal
April 26	Flyers, 4-2	at Montreal
April 28	Flyers, 3-2	at Philadelphia
April 30	Flyers, 4-2	at Philadelphia
May 3	Flyers, 6-4	at Montreal

	W-L	GF	Leading Scorers
Pittsburgh	4-1	15	Malkin (4-3—7)
NY Rangers	1-4	12	Jagr (3-4—7)

Date	Winner	Home Ice
April 25	Penguins, 5-4	at Pittsburgh
April 27	Penguins, 2-0	at Pittsburgh
April 29	Penguins, 5-3	at New York
May 1	Rangers, 3-0	at New York
May 4	Penguins, 3-2 (OT)	at Pittsburgh

CHAMPIONSHIP (Best of 7)

	W-L	GF	Leading Scorers
Pittsburgh	4-1	20	Hossa (4-5—9)
Philadelphia	1-4	9	Lupul (2-2—4)
			& Umberger (1-3—4)

Date	Winner	Home Ice
May 9	Penguins, 4-2	at Pittsburgh
May 11	Penguins, 4-2	at Pittsburgh
May 13	Penguins, 4-1	at Philadelphia
May 15	Flyers, 4-2	at Philadelphia
May 18	Penguins, 6-0	at Pittsburgh

Conn Smythe Trophy
(Playoff MVP)

Henrik Zetterberg, Detroit, LW
22 games, 13 goals, 14 assists, 27 pts, +16

STANLEY CUP FINALS (Best of 7)

	W-L	GF	Leading Scorers
Detroit	4-2	17	Zetterberg (2-4—6)
Pittsburgh	2-4	10	Hossa (3-4—7)

Date	Winner	Home Ice
May 24	Red Wings, 4-0	at Detroit
May 26	Red Wings, 3-0	at Detroit
May 28	Penguins, 3-2	at Pittsburgh
May 31	Red Wings, 2-1	at Pittsburgh
June 2	Penguins, 4-3 (3OT)	at Detroit
June 4	Red Wings, 3-2	at Pittsburgh

Stanley Cup Finals Box Scores

Game 1

Saturday, May 24, at Detroit

Pittsburgh . . . . .0 0 0 — **0**
Detroit . . . . .0 1 3 — **4**

2nd Period: DET—Samuelsson 3 (unassisted), 13:01.

3rd Period: DET—Samuelsson 4 (unassisted), 13:01; DET—Cleary 2 (Stuart), 17:18 (sh); DET—Zetterberg 12 (Holmstrom, Lidstrom), 19:47 (pp).

Shots on Goal: Pittsburgh—12-4-3—19; Detroit—11-16-9—36. **Power plays:** Pittsburgh 0-5; Detroit 1-6. **Goalies:** Pittsburgh, Fleury (36 shots, 32 saves); Detroit, Osgood (19 shots, 19 saves). **Attendance:** 20,066.

Game 2

Monday, May 26, at Detroit

Pittsburgh . . . . .0 0 0 — **0**
Detroit . . . . .2 0 1 — **3**

1st Period: DET—Stuart 1 (Filppula), 6:55; DET—Holmstrom 4 (Zetterberg), 11:18.

3rd Period: DET—Fillpula 4 (Franzen), 8:48.

Shots on Goal: Pittsburgh—6-6-10—22; Detroit—12-11-11—34. **Power plays:** Pittsburgh 0-3; Detroit 0-8. **Goalies:** Pittsburgh, Fleury (34 shots, 31 saves); Detroit, Osgood (22 shots, 22 saves). **Attendance:** 20,066.

Game 3

Wednesday, May 28, at Pittsburgh

Detroit . . . . .0 1 1 — **2**
Pittsburgh . . . . .1 1 1 — **3**

1st Period: PIT—Crosby 5 (Hossa), 17:25.

2nd Period: PIT—Crosby 6 (Hossa), 2:34 (pp); DET—Franzen 13 (Lidstrom, Kronvall), 14:48 (pp).

3rd Period: PIT—Hall 3 (Talbot, Roberts), 7:18; DET—Samuelsson 5 (Stuart, Filppula), 13:37.

Shots on Goal: Detroit—9-9-16—34; Pittsburgh—6-13-5—24. **Power plays:** Detroit 1-5; Pittsburgh 1-3. **Goalies:** Detroit, Osgood (24 shots, 21 saves); Pittsburgh, Fleury (34 shots, 32 saves). **Attendance:** 17,132.

Stanley Cup Leaders

Scoring

(including all playoff games)

	Gm	G	A	Pts	+/-	PM	PP
Henrik Zetterberg, Det . . .	22	13	14	**27**	16	16	4
Sidney Crosby, Pit	20	6	21	**27**	7	12	2
Marian Hossa, Pit	20	12	14	**26**	8	12	5
Pavel Datsyuk, Det	22	10	13	**23**	13	6	4
Evgeni Malkin, Pit	20	10	12	**22**	3	24	5
Johan Franzen, Det	16	13	5	**18**	13	14	6
Mike Ribeiro, Dal	18	3	14	**17**	0	16	0
Daniel Briere, Phi	17	9	7	**16**	-3	20	6
Ryan Malone, Pit	20	6	10	**16**	4	25	3

Five tied with 15 pts.

Goaltending

(Minimum 7 games)

	Gm	W-L	ShO	GAA	Sv%
Chris Osgood, Det	19	14-4	3	**1.55**	.930
Marc-Andre Fleury, Pit . . .	20	14-6	3	**1.97**	.933
Marty Turco, Dal	18	10-8	1	**2.08**	.922
Evgeni Nabokov, SJ . . .	13	6-7	1	**2.18**	.907
Henrik Lundqvist, NYR . .	10	5-5	1	**2.57**	.909
Tim Thomas, Bos	7	3-4	0	**2.65**	.914

Game 4

Saturday, May 31, at Pittsburgh

Detroit . . . . .1 0 1 — **2**
Pittsburgh . . . . .1 0 0 — **1**

1st Period: PIT—Hossa 10 (Gonchar, Crosby), 2:51 (pp); DET—Lidstrom 3 (Rafalski, Datsyuk), 7:06.

3rd Period: DET—Hudler 5 (Helm, Stuart), 2:26.

Shots on Goal: Detroit—14-7-9—30; Pittsburgh—9-8-6—23. **Power plays:** Detroit 0-3; Pittsburgh 1-6. **Goalies:** Detroit, Osgood (23 shots, 22 saves); Pittsburgh, Fleury (30 shots, 28 saves). **Attendance:** 17,132.

Game 5

Monday, June 2, at Detroit

Pittsburgh . . . . .2 0 1 0 0 1 — **4**
Detroit . . . . .0 1 2 0 0 0 — **3**

1st Period: PIT—Hossa 11 (Crosby, Dupuis), 8:37; PIT—Hall 3 (unassisted), 14:41.

2nd Period: DET—Helm 2 (Maltby), 2:54.

3rd Period: DET—Datsyuk 10 (Zetterberg, Rafalski), 6:43 (pp); DET—Rafalski 3 (Franzen, Zetterberg), 9:23; PIT—Talbot 3 (Hossa, Crosby), 19:25.

3rd Overtime: PIT—Sykora 6 (Malkin, Gonchar), 9:57 (pp).

Shots on Goal: Pittsburgh—7-7-4-2-8-4—32; Detroit—8-12-14-13-7-4—58. **Power plays:** Pittsburgh 1-5; Detroit 1-5. **Goalies:** Pittsburgh, Fleury (58 shots, 55 saves); Detroit, Osgood (32 shots, 28 saves). **Attendance:** 20,066.

Game 6

Wednesday, June 4, at Pittsburgh

Detroit . . . . .1 1 1 — **3**
Pittsburgh . . . . .0 1 1 — **2**

1st Period: DET—Rafalski 4 (Zetterberg, Datsyuk), 5:03 (pp).

2nd Period: DET—Filppula 5 (Samuelsson, Kronwall), 8:07; PIT—Malkin 10 (Crosby, Hossa), 15:26 (pp).

3rd Period: DET—Zetterberg 13 (Datsyuk, Kronwall), 7:36; PIT—Hossa 12 (Gonchar, Malkin), 18:33 (pp).

Shots on Goal: Detroit—9-9-12—30; Pittsburgh—8-8-6—22. **Power plays:** Detroit 1-3; Pittsburgh 2-5. **Goalies:** Detroit, Osgood (22 shots, 20 saves); Pittsburgh, Fleury (30 shots, 27 saves). **Attendance:** 17,132.

Final Stanley Cup Standings

				—Goals—	
	Gm	W	L	For	Opp	Dif
Detroit	22	16	6	72	41	+31
Pittsburgh	20	14	6	61	43	+18
Dallas	18	10	8	45	41	+4
Philadelphia	17	9	8	52	54	-2
San Jose	13	6	7	30	32	-2
NY Rangers	10	5	5	31	27	+4
Montreal	12	5	7	33	35	-2
Colorado	10	4	6	26	33	-7
Calgary	7	3	4	17	19	-2
Washington	7	3	4	20	23	-3
Boston	7	3	4	15	19	-4
Nashville	6	2	4	12	17	-5
Minnesota	6	2	4	12	17	-5
Anaheim	6	2	4	13	20	-7
New Jersey	5	1	4	12	19	-7
Ottawa	4	0	4	5	16	-11

Finalists' Composite Box Scores
Detroit Red Wings (16-6)

Top Scorers	Pos	Overall Playoffs								Finals vs Pittsburgh							
		Gm	G	A	Pts	+/-	PM	PP	S	Gm	G	A	Pts	+/-	PM	PP	S
Henrik Zetterberg	C	22	13	14	27	16	16	4	116	6	2	4	6	1	2	1	32
Pavel Datsyuk	C	22	10	13	23	13	6	4	74	6	1	3	4	1	6	1	22
Johan Franzen	R	16	13	5	18	13	14	6	70	5	1	2	3	4	10	1	22
Niklas Kronwall	D	22	0	15	15	16	18	0	21	6	0	3	3	9	2	0	5
Jiri Hudler	C	22	5	9	14	-1	14	2	46	6	1	0	1	1	6	0	17
Brian Rafalski	D	22	4	10	14	6	12	2	58	6	2	2	4	0	6	1	15
Mikael Samuelsson	R	22	5	8	13	8	8	0	79	6	3	1	4	3	0	0	21
Nicklas Lidstrom	D	22	3	10	13	8	14	1	41	6	1	2	3	-1	4	0	10
Tomas Holmstrom	L	21	4	8	12	4	26	1	41	5	1	1	2	-1	6	0	8
Valterri Filppula	C	22	5	6	11	7	2	0	39	6	2	2	4	3	0	0	15
Brad Stuart	D	21	1	6	7	15	14	0	25	6	1	4	5	9	2	0	7
Kris Draper	C	22	3	1	4	0	10	0	37	6	0	0	0	3	4	0	7
Darren Helm	C	18	2	2	4	2	2	0	21	6	1	1	2	1	2	0	7
Dallas Drake	R	22	1	3	4	2	12	0	27	6	0	0	0	2	6	0	7
Daniel Cleary	R	22	2	1	3	1	4	0	54	6	1	0	1	2	4	0	16
Darren McCarty	R	17	1	1	2	1	19	0	14	2	0	0	0	1	0	0	0
Brett Lebda	D	19	0	2	2	0	6	0	12	6	0	0	0	0	2	0	3
Mark Hartigan	C	10	1	0	1	0	0	0	5	0	0	0	0	0	0	0	0
Kirk Maltby	L	12	0	1	1	0	10	0	6	6	0	1	1	1	6	0	6
Andreas Lilja	D	12	0	1	1	3	6	0	7	6	0	0	0	-1	6	0	2
Chris Chelios	D	14	0	0	0	2	10	0	11	6	0	0	0	0	0	0	0

Overtime goals—OVERALL (Franzen); FINALS (none). **Shorthanded goals**—OVERALL (Zetterberg and Franzen 2, Lidstrom and Cleary 1); FINALS (Cleary). **Power Play conversions**—OVERALL (20 for 106, 18.9%); FINALS (4 for 30, 13.3%).

Goaltending	Gm	Min	GAA	GA	SA	Sv%	W-L	Gm	Min	GAA	GA	SA	Sv%	W-L
Chris Osgood	19	1160	1.55	30	430	.930	14-4	6	409	1.47	10	142	.930	4-2
Dominik Hasek	4	206	2.91	10	89	.888	2-2	0	0	0	—	0	0	0-0
TOTAL	22	1372	1.79	41	520	.921	16-6	6	409	1.47	10	142	.930	4-2

Empty Net Goals—OVERALL (1), FINALS (none). **Shutouts**—OVERALL (Osgood 3), FINALS (Osgood 2). **Assists**—OVERALL (none), FINALS (none). **Penalty Minutes**—OVERALL (Hasek 2), FINALS (none).

Pittsburgh Penguins (14-6)

Top Scorers	Pos	Overall Playoffs								Finals vs Detroit							
		Gm	G	A	Pts	+/-	PM	PP	S	Gm	G	A	Pts	+/-	PM	PP	S
Sidney Crosby	C	20	6	21	27	7	12	2	59	6	2	4	6	1	4	1	18
Marian Hossa	R	20	12	14	26	8	12	5	76	6	3	4	7	1	2	2	18
Evgeni Malkin	C	20	10	12	22	3	24	5	75	6	1	2	3	-2	6	1	16
Ryan Malone	L	20	6	10	16	4	25	3	43	6	0	1	1	-2	8	0	6
Sergei Gonchar	D	20	1	13	14	0	8	1	40	6	0	3	3	-4	2	0	10
Petr Sykora	R	20	6	3	9	2	42	1	42	6	1	0	1	-4	4	1	6
Maxime Talbot	C	17	3	6	9	4	36	0	16	6	1	1	2	-1	18	0	3
Jordan Staal	C	20	6	1	7	-4	14	1	34	6	0	0	0	-6	4	0	6
Pascal Dupuis	R	20	2	5	7	5	18	0	38	6	0	1	1	-2	2	0	10
Ryan Whitney	D	20	1	5	6	8	25	1	37	6	0	0	0	-4	0	0	16
Adam Hall	R	17	3	1	4	-1	8	0	14	6	2	0	2	0	2	0	7
Gary Roberts	L	11	2	2	4	-4	32	1	9	5	0	1	1	-2	16	0	4
Tyler Kennedy	C	20	0	4	4	0	13	0	34	6	0	0	0	-3	2	0	4
Jarkko Ruutu	L	20	2	1	3	-1	26	0	23	6	0	0	0	-1	2	0	5
Georges Laraque	R	15	1	2	3	-1	4	0	4	1	0	0	0	0	2	0	1
Rob Scuderi	D	20	0	3	3	5	2	0	6	6	0	0	0	-3	0	0	1
Kristopher Letang	D	16	0	2	2	5	12	0	14	2	0	0	0	-2	0	0	3
Brooks Orpik	D	20	0	2	2	-3	18	0	14	6	0	0	0	-5	8	0	5
Hal Gill	D	20	0	1	1	0	12	0	16	6	0	0	0	-3	6	0	2
Darryl Sydor	D	4	0	0	0	1	2	0	2	4	0	0	0	1	2	0	2

Overtime goals—OVERALL (Hossa, Sykora); FINALS (Sykora). **Shorthanded goals**—OVERALL (Malkin); FINALS (none). **Power Play conversions**—OVERALL (21 for 92, 22.8%); FINALS (5 for 27, 18.5%).

Goaltending	Gm	Min	GAA	GA	SA	Sv%	W-L	Gm	Min	GAA	GA	SA	Sv%	W-L
Marc-Andre Fleury	20	1251	1.97	41	610	.933	14-6	6	406	2.51	17	222	.923	2-4
TOTAL	20	1257	2.05	43	612	.930	14-6	6	409	2.49	17	222	.923	2-4

Empty Net Goals—OVERALL (2), FINALS (none). **Shutouts**—OVERALL (Fleury 3), FINALS (none). **Assists**—OVERALL (none), FINALS (none). **Penalty Minutes**—OVERALL (Fleury 2), FINALS (Fleury 2).

Annual Awards

Voting for the Hart, Calder, Norris, Lady Byng, Selke, and Masterton Trophies is conducted after the regular season by the Professional Hockey Writers' Association. The Vezina Trophy is selected by the NHL general managers, while the Jack Adams Award is selected by NHL broadcasters. Points are awarded on 10–7–5–3–1 basis except for the Vezina Trophy and the Adams Award which are awarded 5–3–1.

Hart Trophy
For Most Valuable Player

	Pos	1st	2nd	3rd	4th	5th	Pts
Alex Ovechkin, Wash	.L	128	4	1	0	0—	1313
Evgeni Malkin, Pit	.C	1	66	27	13	13—	659
Jarome Iginla, Calg	.R	2	41	33	26	15—	565
Nicklas Lidstrom, Det	.D	2	7	17	24	20—	246
Martin Brodeur, NJ	.G	1	8	19	21	15—	239

Calder Trophy
For Rookie of the Year

	Pos	1st	2nd	3rd	4th	5th	Pts
Patrick Kane, Chi	.R	71	34	26	0	0—	1078
N. Backstrom, Wash	.C	30	51	35	12	4—	872
Jonathan Toews, Chi	.C	19	-26	30	38	11—	647
Carey Price, Mon	.G	11	16	26	30	19—	461
Peter Mueller, Pho	.C	0	2	12	31	28—	195

Norris Trophy
For Best Defenseman

	1st	2nd	3rd	4th	5th	Pts
Nicklas Lidstrom, Det	127	5	1	1	0—	1313
Dion Phaneuf, Calg	2	38	37	26	12—	561
Zdeno Chara, Bos	3	38	23	21	12—	486
Sergei Gonchar, Pit	1	24	21	21	24—	370
Brian Campbell, Buf-SJ	1	18	16	31	24—	333

Vezina Trophy
For Outstanding Goaltender

	1st	2nd	3rd	Pts
Martin Brodeur, NJ	.15	12	2—	113
Evgeni Nabokov, SJ	.13	13	2—	106
Henrik Lundqvist, NYR	.1	0	8—	13
Jean-Sebastien Giguere, Ana	.0	1	8—	11
Miikka Kiprusoff, Calg	.1	0	2—	7

Lady Byng Trophy
For Sportsmanship and Gentlemanly Play

	Pos	1st	2nd	3rd	4th	5th	Pts
Pavel Dastyuk, Det	.C	75	21	13	7	1—	984
Martin St. Louis, TB	.R	2	17	15	11	14—	261
Jason Pominville, Buf	.R	3	12	15	18	10—	253
Nicklas Lidstrom, Det	.D	9	9	7	6	5—	211
Henrik Zetterberg, Det	.L	6	9	6	9	5—	185

Selke Trophy
For Best Defensive Forward

	Pos	1st	2nd	3rd	4th	5th	Pts
Pavel Datsyuk, Det	.C	43	9	7	3	0—	537
John Madden, NJ	.C	18	18	16	17	10—	447
Henrik Zetterberg, Det	.L	22	20	6	10	5—	425
Patrick Sharp, Chi	.R	10	14	13	8	3—	290
Mike Richards, Phi	.C	10	6	6	13	9—	220

Adams Award
For Coach of the Year

	1st	2nd	3rd	Pts
Bruce Boudreau, Wash	.31	15	8—	208
Guy Carbonneau, Mon	.24	23	7—	196
Mike Babcock, Det	.6	8	11—	65
Barry Trotz, Nash	.4	8	16—	60
Ron Wilson, SJ	.2	5	7—	32

AP Images

Alex Ovechkin took home the Richard, Lester B. Pearson, Hart and Art Ross Trophies at the 2008 NHL Awards Ceremony.

Other Awards

Lester B. Pearson Award (NHL Players Assn. MVP)— Alex Ovechkin, Wash.
Jennings Trophy (goaltenders with a minimum of 25 games played for team with fewest goals against)— Dominik Hasek and Chris Osgood, Det.
Maurice "Rocket" Richard Trophy (regular season goal-scoring leader)—Alex Ovechkin, Wash.
Art Ross Trophy (regular season points leader)— Alex Ovechkin, Wash.
Masterton Trophy (perseverance, sportsmanship, and dedication to hockey)—Jason Blake, Tor.
King Clancy Trophy (leadership and humanitarian contributions to community)—Vincent Lecavalier, TB
Lester Patrick Trophy (outstanding service to hockey in the U.S.)—Brian Leetch, Cammi Granato, Stan Fischler and John Halligan. (Awarded in 2007)

All-NHL Team

Voting by PHWA. Holdovers from 2006-07 first team in **bold**.

	First Team		Second Team
G	Evgeni Nabokov, SJ	G	**Martin Brodeur**, NJ
D	**Nicklas Lidstrom**, Det	D	Brian Campbell, Buf-SJ
D	Dion Phaneuf, Calg	D	Zdeno Chara, Bos
C	Evgeni Malkin, Pit	C	Joe Thornton, SJ
R	Jarome Iginla, Calg	R	Alex Kovalev, Mon
L	**Alex Ovechkin**, Wash	L	Henrik Zetterberg, Det

All-Rookie Team

Voting by PHWA.

Pos		Pos	
G	Carey Price, Mon	F	Nicklas Backstrom, Wash
D	Tobias Enstrom, Atl	F	Patrick Kane, Chi
D	Tom Gilbert, Edm	F	Jonathan Toews, Chi

COLLEGE HOCKEY

NCAA Men's Division I

Final regular season standings; overall records, including all postseason tournament games, in parentheses.

Atlantic Hockey

	W	L	T	Pts	GF	GA
Army (19-14-4) 17	8	3	37	84	51
R.I.T. (19-12-6) 15	8	5	35	87	72
*Air Force (21-12-6) 14	9	5	33	89	65
Sacred Heart (16-19-3) . .14	11	3	31	91	79
Mercyhurst (15-19-7) 11	10	7	29	83	89
Connecticut (13-21-3) 11	14	3	25	62	84
Canisius (11-20-6) 10	13	5	25	80	79
Bentley (9-21-6) 9	13	6	24	81	88
Holy Cross (10-19-7) 9	15	4	22	66	85
American Int'l (8-23-5) . . .8	17	3	19	87	98

Conf. Tourney Final: Air Force 5, Mercyhurst 4 (2OT).
*NCAA Tourney (0-1): Air Force (0-1).

Central Collegiate Hockey Assn.

	W	L	T	Pts	GF	GA
*Michigan (33-6-4) 20	4	4	44	107	62
*Miami-OH (33-8-1) 21	6	1	43	114	56
*Michigan St. (25-12-5) . . .19	6	3	41	92	58
*Notre Dame (27-16-4) . . .15	9	4	34	74	57
Ferris St. (18-16-5) 12	12	4	28	77	72
N. Michigan (20-20-4) 12	13	3	27	76	78
Bowling Green (18-21-0) . .13	15	0	26	73	84
Nebraska-Omaha (17-19-4) .11	13	4	26	87	99
Alaska-Fairbanks (9-21-5) 8	16	4	20	61	80
Lake Superior (10-20-7) . . .7	15	6	20	65	101
Ohio State (12-25-4) 7	18	3	17	61	93
W. Michigan (8-27-3) 4	22	2	10	53	100

Conf. Tourney Final: Michigan 2, Miami-OH 1.
*NCAA Tourney (7-4): Michigan (2-1); Miami-OH (1-1); Michigan St. (1-1); Notre Dame (3-1).

College Hockey America

	W	L	T	Pts	GF	GA
Bemidji State (17-16-3) . . .13	4	3	29	71	39
*Niagara (22-11-4) 12	6	2	26	71	51
Robert Morris (15-15-4) . .10	7	3	23	67	67
Wayne State (11-25-2) 6	14	0	12	54	71
Alab.-Huntsville (6-21-4) 3	13	4	10	40	75

Conf. Tourney Final: Niagara 3, Bemidji State 2.
*NCAA Tourney (0-1): Niagara (0-1).

ECAC Hockey League

	W	L	T	Pts	GF	GA
*Clarkson (22-13-4) 15	4	3	33	72	47
*Princeton (21-14-0) 14	8	0	28	75	57
Harvard (17-13-4) 12	7	3	27	59	41
Cornell (19-14-3) 12	9	1	25	60	43
Union (15-14-6) 10	7	5	25	50	57
Quinnipiac (20-15-4) 9	9	4	22	62	67
Yale (16-14-4) 9	9	4	22	58	61
Colgate (18-18-6) 8	9	5	21	58	55
St. Lawrence (13-20-4) 7	13	2	16	58	68
Brown (6-21-4) 6	13	3	15	50	68
Dartmouth (12-16-4) 6	13	3	15	64	78
Rensselaer (11-23-4) 6	13	3	15	45	69

Conf. Tourney Final: Princeton 4, Harvard 1.
*NCAA Tourney (1-2): Clarkson (1-1); Princeton (0-1).

Hockey East Association

	W	L	T	Pts	GF	GA
*New Hampshire (25-10-3) 19	5	3	41	84	54
Boston University (19-17-4) 15	9	3	33	97	72
Vermont (17-15-7) 13	9	5	31	67	78
*Boston College (25-11-8) .11	9	7	29	82	67
Providence (14-17-5) 11	11	5	27	66	66
Northeastern (16-18-3) . . .12	13	2	26	73	80
UMass-Lowell (16-17-4) . .10	13	4	24	70	76
UMass-Amherst (14-16-6) . .9	13	5	23	73	71
Maine (13-18-3) 9	15	3	21	59	73
Merrimack (12-18-4) 6	18	3	15	48	82

Conf. Tourney Final: Boston College 4, Vermont 0.
*NCAA Tourney (4-1): New Hampshire (0-1); Boston College (4-0).

Western Collegiate Hockey Assn.

	W	L	T	Pts	GF	GA
*Colorado College (28-12-1) 21	6	1	43	95	52
*North Dakota (28-11-4) . . .18	7	3	39	85	53
*Denver (26-14-1) 16	11	1	33	75	67
Minnesota St. (19-16-4) . . .12	12	4	28	71	75
*St. Cloud St. (19-16-5) 12	12	4	28	79	74
*Wisconsin (16-17-7) 11	12	5	27	68	68
*Minnesota (19-17-9) 9	12	7	25	64	70
Minnesota Duluth (13-17-6) . .9	14	5	23	55	76
Michigan Tech (14-20-5) 9	15	4	22	55	77
Alaska-Anchorage (7-21-8) . . .3	19	6	12	54	89

Conf. Tourney Final: Denver 2, Minnesota 1.
*NCAA Tourney (3-6): Colorado College (0-1): North Dakota (2-1); Denver (0-1); St. Cloud St. (0-1); Wisconsin (1-1); Minnesota (0-1).

USCHO.com/CSTV
Division I Men's Poll

Compiled March 24, 2008, **before** the NCAA tournament. Voting panel consists of 28 Division I coaches and 12 writers from across the country. First place votes are in parentheses. Teams in **bold** type went on to reach the NCAA Frozen Four. Top-10 shown.

	League	W	L	T	Pts
1 Michigan (50) . . . . .CCHA	31	5	4	1000
2 Miami-OH . . . . .CCHA	32	7	1	926
3 North Dakota . . . . . . .WCHA	26	10	4	861
4 Denver . . . . .WCHA	26	13	1	818
5 New Hampshire . . . . . . .HEA	25	9	3	813
6 Colorado College . . . .WCHA	28	11	1	795
7 Boston College . . . . . . .HEA	21	11	8	722
8 St. Cloud St. . . . . .WCHA	19	15	5	601
9 Michigan St. . . . . .CCHA	24	11	5	575
10 Minnesota . . . . .WCHA	19	16	9	512

Hobey Baker Award

For men's College Hockey Player of the Year. Voting is done by a 25-member panel of college hockey personnel, national media, and pro scouts, plus a one percent fan vote.

		Cl	Pos
Winner: Kevin Porter, Michigan . . . . .Sr.	F

NCAA Division I Tournament

Regional seeds in parentheses

East Regional

Held in Albany, N.Y., March 28-29.

First Round

(1) Michigan 5 . . . .(4) Niagara 1
(3) Clarkson 2 . . . .(2) St. Cloud St. 1

Second Round

Michigan 2 . . . . .Clarkson 0

Northeast Regional

Held in Worcester, Mass., March 29-30.

First Round

(1) Miami-OH 3 . . . . .OT . . . .(4) Air Force 2
(2) Boston College 5 . . . .(3) Minnesota 2

Second Round

Boston College 4 . . . . . . .OT . . . . .Miami-OH 3

West Regional

Held in Colorado Springs, Colo., March 28-29.

First Round

(4) Notre Dame 4 . . . .(1) New Hampshire 1
(3) Michigan St. 3 . . . .(2) Colorado College 1

Second Round

Notre Dame 3 . . . . .Michigan St. 1

Midwest Regional

Held in Madison Wis., March 29-30.

First Round

(1) North Dakota 5 . . . .(4) Princeton 1
(3) Wisconsin 6 . . . .(2) Denver 2

Second Round

North Dakota 3 . . . . . . .OT . . . . .Wisconsin 2

The Frozen Four

Held at the Pepsi Center in Denver, Colo., April 10 and April 12. Single elimination; no consolation game.

Semifinals

Notre Dame 5 . . . . .OT . . . . .Michigan 4
Boston College 6 . . . . .North Dakota 1

Championship Game

Boston College, 4-1

Notre Dame (CCHA) 0   1   0   —1
Boston College (HEA) 0   3   1   —4

2nd Period: BC—Gerbe 34 (Gibbons, Smith), 2:23; BC—Gerbe 35 (Smith, Bertram), 5:37 (pp); BC—Whitney 11 (Gerbe, Ferriero), 8:11 (pp); ND—Deeth 11 (Lawson, Cole), 9:07.
3rd Period: BC—Smith 25 (Gerbe, Gibbons), 5:31.

Shots on Goal: Notre Dame—5-8-8—21; Boston College—7-11-5—23. **Power plays:** Notre Dame 0-8; Boston College 2-4.

Goalies: Notre Dame—Pearce (23 shots, 19 saves); Boston College—Muse (21 shots, 20 saves).

Attendance: 18,632. **Time:** 2:45.

Most Outstanding Player: Nathan Gerbe, Boston College junior forward.

All-Tournament Team: Gerbe, F Ben Smith, D Mike Brennan and G John Muse of Boston College; F Kevin Deeth and D Kyle Lawson of Notre Dame.

Division I Leaders

Scoring

(Minimum 20 games)	Cl	Gm	G	A	Pts	Avg
Nathan Gerbe, BC	Jr	43	35	33	68	1.58
Kevin Porter, Michigan	Sr	43	33	30	63	1.47
Ryan Cruthers, Robert Morr.	So	34	22	27	49	1.44
Chad Kolarik, Michigan	Sr	39	30	26	56	1.44
Bryan Marshall, Neb.-Omaha	Sr	30	13	30	43	1.43

Goaltending

(Minimum 15 games)	Cl	Record	Sv%	GAA
Jeff Zatkoff, Miami-OH	Jr	27-8-1	.933	1.72
Philippe Lamoureux, N. Dak.	Sr	27-11-4	.932	1.75
Richard Bachman, Colo. Col.	Fr	25-9-1	.931	1.85
Josh Kassel, Army	Jr	18-10-2	.925	1.92
Billy Sauer, Michigan	Jr	30-4-3	.924	1.95

Division III Championship

March 22-23 at Herb Brooks Arena in Lake Placid, N.Y.

Semifinals

St. Norbert (Wis.) 3 . . . . .Norwich (Vt.) 0
Plattsburgh St. (N.Y.) 6 . . . . .Elmira (N.Y.) 3

Championship

St. Norbert 2 .Plattsburgh St. 0

Final records: St. Norbert (27-1-4); Plattsburgh St. (25-5-0); Norwich (23-7-0); Elmira (20-4-5).

Women's College Hockey

NCAA Division I Frozen Four

March 20 and 22 at the Duluth Entertainment and Convention Center in Duluth, Minn.

Semifinals

Wisconsin 4 . . . . .Harvard 1
Minnesota Duluth 3 . . . . .New Hampshire 2

Championship

Minnesota Duluth 4 . . . . .Wisconsin 0

Final records: Minnesota Duluth (34-4-1); Wisconsin (29-9-3); New Hampshire (33-4-1); Harvard (32-2-0).

All-Tournament Team: G Kim Martin (Most Outstanding Player), F Laura Fridfinnson, F Sara O'Toole, D Myriam Trepanier and D Heidi Pelttari of UMD; F Erika Lawler of Wisconsin.

NCAA Division III Championship

March 21-22 at Stafford Ice Arena in Plattsburgh, N.Y.

Semifinals

Manhattanville (N.Y.) 4 . . . . .OT . . . . . . .Wis.-Superior 3
Plattsburgh St. (N.Y.) 2 . . . . .Elmira (N.Y.) 0

Third Place

Elmira 3 . . . . .Wis.-Superior 0

Championship

Plattsburgh St. 3 . . . . .Manhattanville 2

Final records: Plattsburgh St. (25-3-1); Manhattanville (24-7-0); Elmira (23-6-1); Wis.-Superior (23-6-1).

Patty Kazmaier Award

For women's college hockey Player of the Year. Voting is done by a 13-member panel of national media, varsity coaches, and one USA Hockey member.

	Cl	Pos
Winner: Sarah Vaillancourt, Harvard	Jr.	F

MINOR LEAGUE HOCKEY

American Hockey League

Division champions (*) and playoff qualifiers (†) are noted. **OTL** denotes any game that was tied at the end of regulation and lost during a five-minute overtime period. If the game is tied after the overtime period, a shootout ensues with each team getting five attempts to score on a breakaway from the red line. Shootout Losses are listed as **SOL**. Teams are awarded two points for a win (regulation, overtime or shootout), one point for an OTL or SOL, and zero points for a regulation loss.

Eastern Conference

Atlantic Division

Team (Affiliate)	W	L	OTL	SOL	Pts
*Providence (Bos)	55	18	3	4	117
†Hartford (NYR)	50	20	2	8	110
†Portland (Ana)	45	26	5	4	99
†Manchester (LA)	39	31	5	5	88
Springfield (Edm)	35	35	5	5	80
Worcester (SJ)	32	37	5	6	75
Lowell (NJ)	25	43	7	5	62

East Division

Team (Affiliate)	W	L	OTL	SOL	Pts
*Wilkes-Barre/Scran. (Pit)	47	26	3	4	101
†Philadelphia (Phi)	46	27	4	3	99
†Albany (Car)	43	30	3	4	93
†Hershey (Wash)	42	30	2	6	92
Bridgeport Sound (NYI)	40	36	1	3	84
Binghamton (Ott)	34	32	9	5	82
Norfolk (TB)	29	44	2	5	65

Scoring Leaders

	Gm	G	A	Pts	PM
Jason Krog, Chi	80	39	73	**112**	30
Martin St. Pierre, Rock	69	21	67	**88**	80
Teddy Purcell, Manc	67	25	58	**83**	34
Pierre-Alexandre Parentrau, Har.	75	34	47	**81**	81
Cal O'Reilly, Mil	80	16	63	**79**	22

Goaltending Leaders

(At least 1560 minutes)	GP	GAA	Sv%	Record
Nolan Schaefer, Hou	34	**2.06**	.924	19-13-0
Jaroslav Halak, Ham	28	**2.10**	.929	15-10-2
Michael Leighton, Alb	58	**2.10**	.931	28-25-4

Western Conference

North Division

Team (Affiliate)	W	L	OTL	SOL	Pts
*Toronto (Tor)	50	21	3	6	109
†Syracuse (Clb)	46	26	2	6	100
†Manitoba (Van)	46	27	3	4	99
Hamilton (Mon)	36	34	3	7	82
Grand Rapids (Det)	31	41	2	6	70
Lake Erie (Col)	26	41	6	7	65
Rochester (Buf/Fla)	24	46	6	4	58

West Division

Team (Affiliate)	W	L	OTL	SOL	Pts
*Chicago (Atl)	53	22	2	3	111
†Rockford (Chi)	44	26	4	6	98
†Houston (Min)	45	29	2	4	96
†Milwaukee (Nash)	44	29	4	3	95
†San Antonio (Pho)	42	28	3	7	94
Quad City (Calg)	38	32	3	7	86
Peoria (St.L)	38	33	4	5	85
Iowa (Dal)	35	37	5	3	78

Calder Cup Finals

	W-L	GF	Leading Scorers
Chicago	4-2	23	Krog (3-7—10)
Wilkes-Barre/Scranton	2-4	17	Goligoski (1-7—8)

Date	Winner	Home Ice
May 29	Chicago, 5-4	at Chicago
June 1	Chicago, 4-2	at Chicago
June 4	Chicago, 6-1	at W-B/Scranton
June 6	W-B/Scranton, 3-2	at W-B/Scranton
June 7	W-B/Scranton, 5-1	at W-B/Scranton
June 10	Chicago, 5-2	at Chicago

Playoff MVP: Jason Krog, Chicago, C

IIHF World Hockey Championships

Playoff Round results from the 2008 IIHF Men's and Women's World Hockey Championships.

MEN

Held May 2-18 in Quebec City and Halifax, Canada.

Quarterfinals

Sweden 3 . . . . OT . . . . . Czech Republic 2
Canada 8 . . . . Norway 2
Russia 6 . . . . Switzerland 0
Finland 3 . . . . OT . . . . United States 2

Semifinals

Russia 4 . . . . Finland 0
Canada 5 . . . . Sweden 4

Bronze Medal Game

Finland 4 . . . . Sweden 0

Gold Medal Game

Russia 5 . . . . OT . . . . Canada 4

All-Star Team (selected by media): **G**— Evgeni Nabokov, Russia; **D**— Mike Green, Canada and Tomas Kaberle, Czech Republic; **F**— Rick Nash, Canada, Dany Heatley, Canada (MVP) and Alex Ovechkin, Russia.

Scoring Leaders

	Gm	G	A	Pts
Dany Heatley, Canada	9	12	8	20
Ryan Getzlaf, Canada	9	3	11	14
Rick Nash, Canada	9	6	7	13
Alexander Semin, Russia	9	6	7	13
Mattias Weinhandl, Sweden	9	5	8	13

Three tied with 12 points each.

WOMEN

Held April 4-12 in Harbin, China.

Bronze Medal Game

Finland 4 . . . . Switzerland 1

Gold Medal Game

United States 4 . . . . Canada 3

All-Star Team (selected by media): **G**— Noora Raty, Finland (MVP); **D**— Emma Laaksonen, Finland and Julie Chu, USA; **F**— Hayley Wickenheiser, Canada, Natalie Darwitz, USA and Jayna Hefford, Canada.

1893-2008
Through the Years

SPORTS ALMANAC

The Stanley Cup

The Stanley Cup was originally donated to the Canadian Amateur Hockey Association by Sir Frederick Arthur Stanley, Lord Stanley of Preston and 16th Earl of Derby, who had become interested in the sport while Governor General of Canada from 1888 to 1893. Stanley wanted the trophy to be a challenge cup, contested for each year by the best amateur hockey teams in Canada.

In 1893, the Cup was presented without a challenge to the AHA champion Montreal Amateur Athletic Association team. Every year since, however, there has been a playoff. In 1914, Cup trustees limited the field challenging for the trophy to the champion of the eastern professional National Hockey Association (NHA, organized in 1910) and the western professional Pacific Coast Hockey Association (PCHA, organized in 1912).

The NHA disbanded in 1917 and the National Hockey League (NHL) was formed. From 1918 to 1926, the NHL and PCHA champions played for the Cup with the Western Canada Hockey League (WCHL) champion joining in a three-way challenge in 1923 and '24. The PCHA disbanded in 1924, while the WCHL became the Western Hockey League (WHL) for the 1925-26 season and folded the following year. The NHL playoffs have decided the winner of the Stanley Cup ever since.

Champions, 1893-1917

Multiple winners: Montreal Victorias and Montreal Wanderers (4); Montreal Amateur Athletic Association and Ottawa Silver Seven (3); Montreal Shamrocks, Ottawa Senators, Quebec Bulldogs and Winnipeg Victorias (2).

Year		Year		Year	
1893	Montreal AAA	1901	Winnipeg Victorias	1909	Ottawa Senators
1894	Montreal AAA	1902	Montreal AAA	1910	Montreal Wanderers
1895	Montreal Victorias	1903	Ottawa Silver Seven	1911	Ottawa Senators
1896	(Feb.) Winnipeg Victorias	1904	Ottawa Silver Seven	1912	Quebec Bulldogs
	(Dec.) Montreal Victorias	1905	Ottawa Silver Seven	1913	Quebec Bulldogs
1897	Montreal Victorias	1906	Montreal Wanderers	1914	Toronto Blueshirts (NHA)
1898	Montreal Victorias	1907	(Jan.) Kenora Thistles	1915	Vancouver Millionaires (PCHA)
1899	Montreal Shamrocks		(Mar.) Montreal Wanderers	1916	Montreal Canadiens (NHA)
1900	Montreal Shamrocks	1908	Montreal Wanderers	1917	Seattle Metropolitans (PCHA)

Champions Since 1918

Multiple winners: Montreal Canadiens (23); Toronto Arenas-St. Pats-Maple Leafs (13); Detroit Red Wings (11); Boston Bruins and Edmonton Oilers (5); NY Islanders, NY Rangers and Ottawa Senators (4); Chicago Blackhawks and New Jersey Devils (3); Colorado Avalanche, Montreal Maroons, Philadelphia Flyers and Pittsburgh Penguins (2).

Year	Winner	Head Coach	Series		Loser	Head Coach
1918	Toronto Arenas	Dick Carroll	3-2 (WLWLW)		Vancouver (PCHA)	Frank Patrick
1919	No Decision*					
1920	Ottawa	Pete Green	3-2 (WWLLW)		Seattle (PCHA)	Pete Muldoon
1921	Ottawa	Pete Green	3-2 (LWWLW)		Vancouver (PCHA)	Frank Patrick
1922	Toronto St. Pats	Eddie Powers	3-2 (LWLWW)		Vancouver (PCHA)	Frank Patrick
1923	Ottawa	Pete Green	3-1 (WLWW)		Vancouver (PCHA)	Frank Patrick
			2-0		Edmonton (WCHL)	K.C. McKenzie
1924	Montreal	Leo Dandurand	2-0		Vancouver (PCHA)	Frank Patrick
			2-0		Calgary (WCHL)	Eddie Oatman
1925	Victoria (WCHL)	Lester Patrick	3-1 (WWLW)		Montreal	Leo Dandurand
1926	Montreal Maroons	Eddie Gerard	3-1 (WWLW)		Victoria (WHL)	Lester Patrick
1927	Ottawa	Dave Gill	2-0-2 (TWTW)		Boston	Art Ross
1928	NY Rangers	Lester Patrick	3-2 (LWLWW)		Montreal Maroons	Eddie Gerard
1929	Boston	Cy Denneny	2-0		NY Rangers	Lester Patrick
1930	Montreal	Cecil Hart	2-0		Boston	Art Ross
1931	Montreal	Cecil Hart	3-2 (WLLWW)		Chicago	Art Duncan
1932	Toronto	Dick Irvin	3-0		NY Rangers	Lester Patrick
1933	NY Rangers	Lester Patrick	3-1 (WWLW)		Toronto	Dick Irvin
1934	Chicago	Tommy Gorman	3-1 (WWLW)		Detroit	Jack Adams
1935	Montreal Maroons	Tommy Gorman	3-0		Toronto	Dick Irvin
1936	Detroit	Jack Adams	3-1 (WWLW)		Toronto	Dick Irvin
1937	Detroit	Jack Adams	3-2 (LWLWW)		NY Rangers	Lester Patrick
1938	Chicago	Bill Stewart	3-1 (WWLW)		Toronto	Dick Irvin
1939	Boston	Art Ross	4-1 (WLWWW)		Toronto	Dick Irvin
1940	NY Rangers	Frank Boucher	4-2 (WWLLWW)		Toronto	Dick Irvin

* The 1919 finals were cancelled after five games due to an influenza epidemic with Montreal and Seattle (PCHA) tied at 2-2-1.

The Stanley Cup (Cont.)

Year	Winner	Head Coach	Series	Loser	Head Coach
1941	Boston	Cooney Weiland	4-0	Detroit	Jack Adams
1942	Toronto	Hap Day	4-3 (LLLWWWW)	Detroit	Jack Adams
1943	Detroit	Ebbie Goodfellow	4-0	Boston	Art Ross
1944	Montreal	Dick Irvin	4-0	Chicago	Paul Thompson
1945	Toronto	Hap Day	4-3 (WWWWLLLW)	Detroit	Jack Adams
1946	Montreal	Dick Irvin	4-1 (WWWLW)	Boston	Dit Clapper
1947	Toronto	Hap Day	4-2 (LWWWLW)	Montreal	Dick Irvin
1948	Toronto	Hap Day	4-0	Detroit	Tommy Ivan
1949	Toronto	Hap Day	4-0	Detroit	Tommy Ivan
1950	Detroit	Tommy Ivan	4-3 (WLWLLWW)	NY Rangers	Lynn Patrick
1951	Toronto	Joe Primeau	4-1 (WLWWW)	Montreal	Dick Irvin
1952	Detroit	Tommy Ivan	4-0	Montreal	Dick Irvin
1953	Montreal	Dick Irvin	4-1 (WLWWW)	Boston	Lynn Patrick
1954	Detroit	Tommy Ivan	4-3 (WLWWLLW)	Montreal	Dick Irvin
1955	Detroit	Jimmy Skinner	4-3 (WWLLWLW)	Montreal	Dick Irvin
1956	Montreal	Toe Blake	4-1 (WWLWW)	Detroit	Jimmy Skinner
1957	Montreal	Toe Blake	4-1 (WWWLW)	Boston	Milt Schmidt
1958	Montreal	Toe Blake	4-2 (WLWLWW)	Boston	Milt Schmidt
1959	Montreal	Toe Blake	4-1 (WWLWW)	Toronto	Punch Imlach
1960	Montreal	Toe Blake	4-0	Toronto	Punch Imlach
1961	Chicago	Rudy Pilous	4-2 (WLWLWW)	Detroit	Sid Abel
1962	Toronto	Punch Imlach	4-2 (WWLLWW)	Chicago	Rudy Pilous
1963	Toronto	Punch Imlach	4-1 (WWWLW)	Detroit	Sid Abel
1964	Toronto	Punch Imlach	4-3 (WLLWLWW)	Detroit	Sid Abel
1965	Montreal	Toe Blake	4-3 (WWWLLWLW)	Chicago	Billy Reay
1966	Montreal	Toe Blake	4-2 (LLWWWW)	Detroit	Sid Abel
1967	Toronto	Punch Imlach	4-2 (LWWLWW)	Montreal	Toe Blake
1968	Montreal	Toe Blake	4-0	St. Louis	Scotty Bowman
1969	Montreal	Claude Ruel	4-0	St. Louis	Scotty Bowman
1970	Boston	Harry Sinden	4-0	St. Louis	Scotty Bowman
1971	Montreal	Al MacNeil	4-3 (LLWWWLWW)	Chicago	Billy Reay
1972	Boston	Tom Johnson	4-2 (WWWLWLW)	NY Rangers	Emile Francis
1973	Montreal	Scotty Bowman	4-2 (WWLWLW)	Chicago	Billy Reay
1974	Philadelphia	Fred Shero	4-2 (LWWLWW)	Boston	Bep Guidolin
1975	Philadelphia	Fred Shero	4-2 (WWLLWW)	Buffalo	Floyd Smith
1976	Montreal	Scotty Bowman	4-0	Philadelphia	Fred Shero
1977	Montreal	Scotty Bowman	4-0	Boston	Don Cherry
1978	Montreal	Scotty Bowman	4-2 (WWLWLW)	Boston	Don Cherry
1979	Montreal	Scotty Bowman	4-1 (LWWLW)	NY Rangers	Fred Shero
1980	NY Islanders	Al Arbour	4-2 (WLWWLW)	Philadelphia	Pat Quinn
1981	NY Islanders	Al Arbour	4-1 (WWWLW)	Minnesota	Glen Sonmor
1982	NY Islanders	Al Arbour	4-0	Vancouver	Roger Neilson
1983	NY Islanders	Al Arbour	4-0	Edmonton	Glen Sather
1984	Edmonton	Glen Sather	4-1 (WLWWW)	NY Islanders	Al Arbour
1985	Edmonton	Glen Sather	4-1 (LWWWW)	Philadelphia	Mike Keenan
1986	Montreal	Jean Perron	4-1 (LWWWW)	Calgary	Bob Johnson
1987	Edmonton	Glen Sather	4-3 (WWLWLLW)	Philadelphia	Mike Keenan
1988	Edmonton	Glen Sather	4-0	Boston	Terry O'Reilly
1989	Calgary	Terry Crisp	4-2 (WLLWWW)	Montreal	Pat Burns
1990	Edmonton	John Muckler	4-1 (WWLWW)	Boston	Mike Milbury
1991	Pittsburgh	Bob Johnson	4-2 (LWLWWW)	Minnesota	Bob Gainey
1992	Pittsburgh	Scotty Bowman	4-0	Chicago	Mike Keenan
1993	Montreal	Jacques Demers	4-1 (LWWWW)	Los Angeles	Barry Melrose
1994	NY Rangers	Mike Keenan	4-3 (LWWWLLW)	Vancouver	Pat Quinn
1995	New Jersey	Jacques Lemaire	4-0	Detroit	Scotty Bowman
1996	Colorado	Marc Crawford	4-0	Florida	Doug MacLean
1997	Detroit	Scotty Bowman	4-0	Philadelphia	Terry Murray
1998	Detroit	Scotty Bowman	4-0	Washington	Ron Wilson
1999	Dallas	Ken Hitchcock	4-2 (LWWLWW)	Buffalo	Lindy Ruff
2000	New Jersey	Larry Robinson	4-2 (WLWWLW)	Dallas	Ken Hitchcock
2001	Colorado	Bob Hartley	4-3 (WLWLLWW)	New Jersey	Larry Robinson
2002	Detroit	Scotty Bowman	4-1 (LWWWW)	Carolina	Paul Maurice
2003	New Jersey	Pat Burns	4-3 (WLWLWLW)	Anaheim	Mike Babcock
2004	Tampa Bay	John Tortorella	4-3 (LWLWLWW)	Calgary	Darryl Sutter
2005	Not held*				
2006	Carolina	Peter Laviolette	4-3 (WWLWLLW)	Edmonton	Craig MacTavish
2007	Anaheim	Randy Carlyle	4-1 (WWLWW)	Ottawa	Bryan Murray
2008	Detroit	Mike Babcock	4-2 (WWLWLW)	Pittsburgh	Michel Therrien

* The lack of a labor agreement between the owners and NHLPA and the ensuing owners' lockout canceled the 2004-05 season.

M.J. O'Brien Trophy

Donated by Canadian mining magnate M.J. O'Brien, whose son Ambrose founded the National Hockey Association in 1910. Originally presented to the NHA champion until the league's demise in 1917, the trophy then passed to the NHL champion through 1927. It was awarded to the NHL's Canadian Division winner from 1927-38 and the Stanley Cup runner-up from 1939-50 before being retired in 1950.

NHA winners included the Montreal Wanderers (1910), original Ottawa Senators (1911 and '15), Quebec Bulldogs (1912 and '13), Toronto Blueshirts (1914) and Montreal Canadiens (1916 and '17).

Conn Smythe Trophy

The Most Valuable Player of the Stanley Cup Playoffs, as selected by the Pro Hockey Writers Association. Presented since 1965 by Maple Leaf Gardens Limited in the name of the former Toronto coach, GM and owner, Conn Smythe. Winners who did not play for the Cup champion are in **bold** type.

Multiple winners: Patrick Roy (3); Wayne Gretzky, Mario Lemieux, Bobby Orr and Bernie Parent (2).

Year		Year		Year	
1965	Jean Beliveau, Mon., C	1980	Bryan Trottier, NYI, C	1995	Claude Lemieux, NJ, RW
1966	**Roger Crozier**, Det., G	1981	Butch Goring, NYI, C	1996	Joe Sakic, Col., C
1967	Dave Keon, Tor., C	1982	Mike Bossy, NYI, RW	1997	Mike Vernon, Det., G
1968	**Glenn Hall**, St.L., G	1983	Billy Smith, NYI, G	1998	Steve Yzerman, Det., C
1969	Serge Savard, Mon., D	1984	Mark Messier, Edm., LW	1999	Joe Nieuwendyk, Dal., C
1970	Bobby Orr, Bos., D	1985	Wayne Gretzky, Edm., C	2000	Scott Stevens, NJ, D
1971	Ken Dryden, Mon., G	1986	Patrick Roy, Mon., G	2001	Patrick Roy, Col., G
1972	Bobby Orr, Bos., D	1987	**Ron Hextall**, Phi., G	2002	Nicklas Lidstrom, Det., D
1973	Yvan Cournoyer, Mon., RW	1988	Wayne Gretzky, Edm., C	2003	**J-S Giguere**, Ana., G
1974	Bernie Parent, Phi., G	1989	Al MacInnis, Calg., D	2004	Brad Richards, TB, C
1975	Bernie Parent, Phi., G	1990	Bill Ranford, Edm., G	2005	Not awarded
1976	**Reggie Leach**, Phi., RW	1991	Mario Lemieux, Pit., C	2006	Cam Ward, Car., G
1977	Guy Lafleur, Mon., RW	1992	Mario Lemieux, Pit., C	2007	Scott Niedermayer, Ana., D
1978	Larry Robinson, Mon., D	1993	Patrick Roy, Mon., G	2008	Henrik Zetterberg, Det., LW
1979	Bob Gainey, Mon., LW	1994	Brian Leetch, NYR, D		

Note: Ken Dryden (1971), Patrick Roy (1986), Ron Hextall (1987) and Cam Ward (2006) are the only players to win as rookies.

All-Time Stanley Cup Playoff Leaders

CAREER

Stanley Cup Playoff leaders through 2008. Years listed indicate number of playoff appearances. Players active in 2007-08 are in **bold** type; (DNP) indicates player that was active in 2007-08 but did not participate in playoffs.

Scoring

Points

		Yrs	Gm	G	A	Pts
1	Wayne Gretzky	16	208	122	260	382
2	Mark Messier	17	236	109	186	295
3	Jari Kurri	14	200	106	127	233
4	Glenn Anderson	15	225	93	121	214
5	Paul Coffey	16	194	59	137	196
6	Brett Hull	19	202	103	87	190
7	**Joe Sakic**	13	172	84	104	188
8	Doug Gilmour	17	182	60	128	188
9	Steve Yzerman	20	196	70	115	185
10	Bryan Trottier	17	221	71	113	184
11	**Jaromir Jagr**	15	169	77	104	181
12	Ray Bourque	21	214	41	139	180
13	Jean Beliveau	17	162	79	97	176
14	Denis Savard	16	169	66	109	175
15	Mario Lemieux	8	107	76	96	172
16	**Peter Forsberg**	13	151	64	107	171
17	**Sergei Fedorov**	14	169	51	117	168
18	Denis Potvin	14	185	56	108	164
19	Mike Bossy	10	129	85	75	160
	Gordie Howe	20	157	68	92	160
	Bobby Smith	13	184	64	96	160
	Al MacInnis	19	177	39	121	160
23	Claude Lemieux	17	233	80	77	157
24	Adam Oates	15	163	42	114	156
25	Larry Murphy	20	215	37	115	152

Goals

		Yrs	Gm	G
1	Wayne Gretzky	16	208	122
2	Mark Messier	17	236	109
3	Jari Kurri	15	200	106
4	Brett Hull	19	202	103
5	Glenn Anderson	15	225	93
6	Mike Bossy	10	129	85
7	**Joe Sakic**	13	172	84
8	Maurice Richard	15	133	82
9	Claude Lemieux	17	233	80
10	Jean Beliveau	17	162	79

Assists

		Yrs	Gm	A
1	Wayne Gretzky	16	208	260
2	Mark Messier	17	236	186
3	Ray Bourque	21	214	139
4	Paul Coffey	16	194	137
5	Doug Gilmour	17	182	128
6	Jari Kurri	15	200	127
7	Glenn Anderson	15	225	121
	Al MacInnis	19	177	121
9	**Sergei Fedorov**	14	169	117
10	Larry Robinson	20	227	116

The Stanley Cup (Cont.)

Goaltending
Wins

		Gm	W-L	Pct	GAA
1	Patrick Roy	247	151-94	.616	2.30
2	**Martin Brodeur**	169	95-74	.562	1.96
3	Grant Fuhr	150	92-50	.648	2.92
4	Billy Smith	132	88-36	.710	2.73
	Ed Belfour	161	88-68	.564	2.17
6	Ken Dryden	112	80-32	.714	2.40
7	Mike Vernon	138	77-56	.579	2.68
8	Jacques Plante	112	71-37	.657	2.17
9	Andy Moog	132	68-57	.544	3.04
10	**Dominik Hasek**	119	65-49	.570	2.02

Shutouts

		Gm	GAA	No
1	Patrick Roy	247	2.30	23
2	**Martin Brodeur**	169	1.96	22
3	**Curtis Joseph**	133	2.42	16
4	Clint Benedict	48	1.80	15
	Jacques Plante	112	2.17	15

Appearances in Cup Finals

Standings of all teams that have reached the Stanley Cup championship round, since 1918.

App		Cups	Last Won
32	Montreal Canadiens	23 *	1993
23	Detroit Red Wings	11	2008
21	Toronto Maple Leafs	13 †	1967
17	Boston Bruins	5	1972
10	New York Rangers	4	1994
10	Chicago Blackhawks	3	1961
7	Edmonton Oilers	5	1990
7	Philadelphia Flyers	2	1975
5	New York Islanders	4	1983
5	Vancouver Millionaires (PCHA)	0	—
4	(original) Ottawa Senators	4	1927
4	Minnesota/Dallas (North) Stars	1	1999
4	New Jersey Devils	3	2003
3	Pittsburgh Penguins	2	1992
3	Montreal Maroons	2	1935
3	Calgary Flames	1	1989
3	St. Louis Blues	0	—
2	Colorado Avalanche	2	2001
2	Anaheim Ducks	1	2007
2	Carolina Hurricanes	1	2006
2	Victoria Cougars (WCHL-WHL)	1	1925
2	Buffalo Sabres	0	—
2	Seattle Metropolitans (PCHA)	0	—
2	Vancouver Canucks	0	—
1	Tampa Bay Lightning	1	2004
1	Calgary Tigers (WCHL)	0	—
1	Edmonton Eskimos (WCHL)	0	—
1	Florida Panthers	0	—
1	Los Angeles Kings	0	—
1	Ottawa Senators	0	—
1	Washington Capitals	0	—

*Les Canadiens also won the Cup in 1916 for a total of 24. Also, their final with Seattle in 1919 was cancelled due to an influenza epidemic that claimed the life of the Habs' Joe Hall.

†Toronto has won the Cup under three nicknames—Arenas (1918), St. Pats (1922) and Maple Leafs (1932,42,45,47-49,51,62-64,67).

Teams now defunct (7): Calgary Tigers, Edmonton Eskimos, Montreal Maroons, (original) Ottawa Senators, Seattle, Vancouver Millionaires and Victoria. Edmonton (1923) and Calgary (1924) represented the WCHL and later the WHL, while Vancouver (1918,1921-24) and Seattle (1919-20) played out of the PCHA.

Goals Against Average
Minimum of 50 games played

		Gm	Min	GA	GAA
1	George Hainsworth	52	3486	112	1.93
2	**Martin Brodeur**	169	10,520	344	1.96
3	Turk Broda	101	6389	211	1.98
4	**Dominik Hasek**	119	7317	246	2.02
5	J-S Giguere	51	3150	110	2.10
6	**Chris Osgood**	106	6245	220	2.11
7	Jacques Plante	112	6652	240	2.16
8	**Ed Belfour**	161	9945	359	2.17
9	**Evgeni Nabokov**	59	3567	129	2.17
10	**Miikka Kiprusoff**	50	2960	108	2.19

Note: Clint Benedict had an average of 1.80 but played in only 48 games.

Games Played
(Goalies only)

		Yrs	Gm
1	Patrick Roy, Mon-Col	17	247
2	**Martin Brodeur**, New Jersey	14	169
3	Ed Belfour, Chi-Dal-Tor	13	161
4	Grant Fuhr, Edm-Buf-St.L	14	150
5	Mike Vernon, Calg-Det-SJ-Fla	14	138

Miscellaneous
Championships

		Yrs	Cups
1	Henri Richard, Montreal	18	11
2	Yvan Cournoyer, Montreal	15	10
	Jean Beliveau, Montreal	17	10
4	Claude Provost, Montreal	14	9
5	Jacques Lemaire, Montreal	11	8
	Maurice Richard, Montreal	15	8
	Red Kelly, Detroit-Toronto	19	8

Years in Playoffs

		Yrs	Gm
1	**Chris Chelios**, Mon-Chi-Det	23	260
	Ray Bourque, Boston-Colorado	21	214
3	Gordie Howe, Detroit-Hartford	20	157
	Larry Robinson, Montreal-Los Angeles	20	227
	Larry Murphy, LA-Wash-Min-Pit-Tor-Det	20	215
	Scott Stevens, Wash-St.L-NJ	20	233
	Steve Yzerman, Detroit	20	196

Games Played

		Yrs	Gm
1	**Chris Chelios**, Mon-Chi-Det	23	260
2	Patrick Roy, Montreal-Colorado	17	247
3	Mark Messier, Edm-NYR-Van	17	236
4	Claude Lemieux, Mon-NJ-Col-Pho-Dal	17	233
	Scott Stevens, Wash-St.L-NJ	20	233

Penalty Minutes

		Yrs	Gm	Min
1	Dale Hunter, Que-Wash-Col	18	186	729
2	Chris Nilan, Mon-NYR-Bos-Mon	12	111	541
3	Claude Lemieux, Mon-NJ-Col-Pho-Dal	17	233	529
4	Rick Tocchet, Phi-Pit-Bos-Pho	13	145	471
5	Willi Plett, Atl-Calg-Min-Bos	10	83	466

SINGLE SEASON

Points

		Year	Gm	G	A	Pts
1	Wayne Gretzky, Edm	1985	18	17	30	47
2	Mario Lemieux, Pit	1991	23	16	28	44
3	Wayne Gretzky, Edm	1988	19	12	31	43
4	Wayne Gretzky, LA	1993	24	15	25	40
5	Wayne Gretzky, Edm	1983	16	12	26	38
6	Paul Coffey, Edm	1985	18	12	25	37
7	Mike Bossy, NYI	1981	18	17	18	35
	Wayne Gretzky, Edm	1984	19	13	22	35
	Doug Gilmour, Tor	1993	21	10	25	35
10	Six tied with 34 each.					

Goals

		Year	Gm	No
1	Reggie Leach, Philadelphia	1976	16	19
	Jari Kurri, Edmonton	1985	18	19
3	Joe Sakic, Colorado	1996	22	18
4	Seven tied with 17 each, incl. 3 times by Mike Bossy.			

Assists

		Year	Gm	No
1	Wayne Gretzky, Edmonton	1988	19	31
2	Wayne Gretzky, Edmonton	1985	18	30
3	Wayne Gretzky, Edmonton	1987	21	29
4	Mario Lemieux, Pittsburgh	1991	23	28
5	Wayne Gretzky, Edmonton	1983	16	26

Goaltending

Wins

1 Sixteen tied with 16 each.

Shutouts

		Year	Gm	No
1	Martin Brodeur, New Jersey	2003	24	7
2	Dominik Hasek, Detroit	2002	23	6
3	J-S Giguere, Anaheim	2003	21	5
	Nikolai Khabibulin, Tampa Bay	2004	23	5
	Miikka Kiprusoff, Calgary	2004	26	5

Goals Against Average

	(Min. 8 games played)	Year	Gm	Min	GA	GAA
1	Terry Sawchuk, Det	1952	8	480	5	0.63
2	Clint Benedict, Mon-M	1928	9	555	8	0.89
3	Turk Broda, Tor	1951	9	509	9	1.06
4	Dave Kerr, NYR	1937	9	553	10	1.11
5	Jacques Plante, Mon	1960	8	489	11	1.35

Note: Average determined by games played through 1942-43 season and by minutes played since then.

SINGLE SERIES

Points

	Year	Rd	G-A—Pts
Rick Middleton, Bos vs Buf	1983	DF	5-14—19
Wayne Gretzky, Edm vs Chi	1985	CF	4-14—18
Mario Lemieux, Pit vs Wash	1992	DSF	7-10—17
Barry Pedersen, Bos vs Buf	1983	DF	7-9—16
Doug Gilmour, Tor vs SJ	1994	CSF	3-13—16

Goals

	Year	Rd	No
Jari Kurri, Edm vs Chi	1985	CF	12
Newsy Lalonde, Mon vs Ott	1919	SF*	11
Tim Kerr, Phi vs Pit	1989	DF	10
Five tied with 9 each.			

*NHL final prior to Stanley Cup series with Seattle (PCHA).

Assists

	Year	Rd	No
Rick Middleton, Bos vs Buf	1983	DF	14
Wayne Gretzky, Edm vs Chi	1985	CF	14
Wayne Gretzky, Edm vs LA	1987	DSF	13
Doug Gilmour, Tor vs SJ	1994	CSF	13
Four tied with 11 each.			

SINGLE GAME

Points

	Date	G	A	Pts
Patrik Sundstrom, NJ vs Wash	4/22/88	3	5	8
Mario Lemieux, Pit vs Phi	4/25/89	5	3	8
Wayne Gretzky, Edm at Calg	4/17/83	4	3	7
Wayne Gretzky, Edm at Win	4/25/85	3	4	7
Wayne Gretzky, Edm vs LA	4/9/87	1	6	7

Goals

	Date	No
Newsy Lalonde, Mon vs Ott	3/1/19	5
Maurice Richard, Mon vs Tor	3/23/44	5
Darryl Sittler, Tor vs Phi	4/22/76	5
Reggie Leach, Phi vs Bos	5/6/76	5
Mario Lemieux, Pit vs Phi	4/25/89	5

Assists

	Date	No
Mikko Leinonen, NYR vs Phi	4/8/82	6
Wayne Gretzky, Edm vs LA	4/9/87	6
11 tied with 5 each.		

NHL All-Star Game

Three benefit NHL All-Star Games were staged in the 1930s for forward Ace Bailey and the families of Howie Morenz and Babe Siebert. Bailey, of Toronto, suffered a fractured skull on a career-ending check by Boston's Eddie Shore. Morenz, the Montreal Canadiens' legend, died of a heart attack at 35 after a severely broken leg ended his career. Siebert, who played with both Montreal teams, drowned at age 35.

The All-Star Game was revived at the start of the 1947-48 season as an annual exhibition match between the defending Stanley Cup champion and all-stars from the league's other five teams. The format has changed several times since then. The game was moved to midseason in 1966-67 and became an East vs. West contest in 1968-69. The Eastern (East, 1968-1974; Wales, 1975-93) Conference leads the series 20-9-1. From 1998-2002, the East-West format was abandoned for one pitting North America vs. the rest of the world (N. America leads that series 3-2). In 2003 the game returned to East vs. West. Since 2006, the game is no longer played during Olympic years.

Benefit Games

Date	Occasion		Host	Coaches
2/14/34	Ace Bailey Benefit	Toronto 7, All-Stars 3	Toronto	Dick Irvin, Lester Patrick
11/3/37	Howie Morenz Memorial	All-Stars 6, Montreals* 5	Montreal	Jack Adams, Cecil Hart
10/29/39	Babe Siebert Memorial	All-Stars 5, Canadiens 3	Montreal	Art Ross, Pit Lepine

*Combined squad of Montreal Canadiens and Montreal Maroons.

NHL All-Star Game (Cont.)

All-Star Games

Multiple MVP winners: Wayne Gretzky and Mario Lemieux (3); Bobby Hull and Frank Mahovlich (2).

Year		Host	Coaches	Most Valuable Player
1947	All-Stars 4, Toronto 3	Toronto	Dick Irvin, Hap Day	No award
1948	All-Stars 3, Toronto 1	Chicago	Tommy Ivan, Hap Day	No award
1949	All-Stars 3, Toronto 1	Toronto	Tommy Ivan, Hap Day	No award
1950	Detroit 7, All-Stars 1	Detroit	Tommy Ivan, Lynn Patrick	No award
1951	1st Team 2, 2nd Team 2	Toronto	Joe Primeau, Hap Day	No award
1952	1st Team 1, 2nd Team 1	Detroit	Tommy Ivan, Dick Irvin	No award
1953	All-Stars 3, Montreal 1	Montreal	Lynn Patrick, Dick Irvin	No award
1954	All-Stars 2, Detroit 2	Detroit	King Clancy, Jim Skinner	No award
1955	Detroit 3, All-Stars 1	Detroit	Jim Skinner, Dick Irvin	No award
1956	All-Stars 1, Montreal 1	Montreal	Jim Skinner, Toe Blake	No award
1957	All-Stars 5, Montreal 3	Montreal	Milt Schmidt, Toe Blake	No award
1958	Montreal 6, All-Stars 3	Montreal	Toe Blake, Milt Schmidt	No award
1959	Montreal 6, All-Stars 1	Montreal	Toe Blake, Punch Imlach	No award
1960	All-Stars 2, Montreal 1	Montreal	Punch Imlach, Toe Blake	No award
1961	All-Stars 3, Chicago 1	Chicago	Sid Abel, Rudy Pilous	No award
1962	Toronto 4, All-Stars 1	Toronto	Punch Imlach, Rudy Pilous	Eddie Shack, Tor., RW
1963	All-Stars 3, Toronto 3	Toronto	Sid Abel, Punch Imlach	Frank Mahovlich, Tor., LW
1964	All-Stars 3, Toronto 2	Toronto	Sid Abel, Punch Imlach	Jean Beliveau, Mon., C
1965	All-Stars 5, Montreal 2	Montreal	Billy Reay, Toe Blake	Gordie Howe, Det., RW
1966	No game (see below)			
1967	Montreal 3, All-Stars 0	Montreal	Toe Blake, Sid Abel	Henri Richard, Mon., C
1968	Toronto 4, All-Stars 3	Toronto	Punch Imlach, Toe Blake	Bruce Gamble, Tor., G
1969	West 3, East 3	Montreal	Scotty Bowman, Toe Blake	Frank Mahovlich, Det., LW
1970	East 4, West 1	St. Louis	Claude Ruel, Scotty Bowman	Bobby Hull, Chi., LW
1971	West 2, East 1	Boston	Scotty Bowman, Harry Sinden	Bobby Hull, Chi., LW
1972	East 3, West 2	Minnesota	Al MacNeil, Billy Reay	Bobby Orr, Bos., D
1973	East 5, West 4	NY Rangers	Tom Johnson, Billy Reay	Greg Polis, Pit., LW
1974	West 6, East 4	Chicago	Billy Reay, Scotty Bowman	Garry Unger, St.L., C
1975	Wales 7, Campbell 1	Montreal	Bep Guidolin, Fred Shero	Syl Apps Jr., Pit., C
1976	Wales 7, Campbell 5	Philadelphia	Floyd Smith, Fred Shero	Peter Mahovlich, Mon., C
1977	Wales 4, Campbell 3	Vancouver	Scotty Bowman, Fred Shero	Rick Martin, Buf., LW
1978	Wales 3, Campbell 2 (OT)	Buffalo	Scotty Bowman, Fred Shero	Billy Smith, NYI, G
1979	No game (see below)			
1980	Wales 6, Campbell 3	Detroit	Scotty Bowman, Al Arbour	Reggie Leach, Phi., RW
1981	Campbell 4, Wales 1	Los Angeles	Pat Quinn, Scotty Bowman	Mike Liut, Hart., G
1982	Wales 4, Campbell 2	Washington	Al Arbour, Glen Sonmor	Mike Bossy, NYI, RW
1983	Campbell 9, Wales 3	NY Islanders	Roger Neilson, Al Arbour	Wayne Gretzky, Edm., C
1984	Wales 7, Campbell 6	New Jersey	Al Arbour, Glen Sather	Don Maloney, NYR, LW
1985	Wales 6, Campbell 4	Calgary	Al Arbour, Glen Sather	Mario Lemieux, Pit., C
1986	Wales 4, Campbell 3 (OT)	Hartford	Mike Keenan, Glen Sather	Grant Fuhr, Edm., G
1987	No game (see below)			
1988	Wales 6, Campbell 5 (OT)	St. Louis	Mike Keenan, Glen Sather	Mario Lemieux, Pit., C
1989	Campbell 9, Wales 5	Edmonton	Glen Sather, Terry O'Reilly	Wayne Gretzky, LA, C
1990	Wales 12, Campbell 7	Pittsburgh	Pat Burns, Terry Crisp	Mario Lemieux, Pit., C
1991	Campbell 11, Wales 5	Chicago	John Muckler, Mike Milbury	Vincent Damphousse, Tor., LW
1992	Campbell 10, Wales 6	Philadelphia	Bob Gainey, Scotty Bowman	Brett Hull, St.L., RW
1993	Wales 16, Campbell 6	Montreal	Scotty Bowman, Mike Keenan	Mike Gartner, NYR, RW
1994	East 9, West 8	NY Rangers	Jacques Demers, Barry Melrose	Mike Richter, NYR, G
1995	No game (see below)			
1996	East 5, West 4	Boston	Doug MacLean, Scotty Bowman	Ray Bourque, Bos., D
1997	East 11, West 7	San Jose	Doug MacLean, Ken Hitchcock	Mark Recchi, Mon., RW
1998	North America 8, World 7	Vancouver	Jacques Lemaire, Ken Hitchcock	Teemu Selanne, Ana., RW
1999	North America 8, World 6	Tampa	Ken Hitchcock, Lindy Ruff	Wayne Gretzky, NYR, C
2000	World 9, North America 4	Toronto	Scotty Bowman, Pat Quinn	Pavel Bure, Fla., RW
2001	North America 14, World 12	Denver	Joel Quenneville, Jacques Martin	Bill Guerin, Bos., RW
2002	World 8, North America 5	Los Angeles	Scotty Bowman, Pat Quinn	Eric Daze, Chi., LW
2003	West 6, East 5 (OT)†	Florida	Marc Crawford, Jacques Martin	Dany Heatley, Atl., RW
2004	East 6, West 4	Minnesota	Pat Quinn, Dave Lewis	Joe Sakic, Col., C
2005	No game (see below)			
2006	No game (see below)			
2007	West 12, East 9	Dallas	Randy Carlyle, Lindy Ruff	Daniel Briere, Buf., C
2008	East 8, West 7	Atlanta	John Paddock, Mike Babcock	Eric Staal, Car., C

†After a five-minute scoreless overtime, the game was settled by a shootout. The West outscored the East, 3-1.

No All-Star Game: in 1966 (moved from start of season to mid-season); in 1979 (replaced by Challenge Cup series with USSR); in 1987 (replaced by Rendez-Vous '87 series with USSR); in 1995 (canceled when NHL lockout shortened season to 48 games); in 2005 (NHL lockout canceled the entire season); in 2006 (game no longer played in Olympic years).

NHL Franchise Origins

Here is what the current 30 teams in the National Hockey League have to show for the years they have put in as members of the NHL, the early National Hockey Association (NHA) and the more recent World Hockey Association (WHA). League titles and Stanley Cup championships are noted by year won. The Stanley Cup has automatically gone to the NHL champion since the 1926-27 season. Following the 1992-93 season, the NHL renamed the Clarence Campbell Conference the Western Conference, while the Prince of Wales Conference became the Eastern Conference.

Western Conference

	First Season	League Titles	Franchise Stops
Anaheim Ducks	1993-94 (NHL)	1 Cup (2007)	•Anaheim, CA (1993—)
Calgary Flames	1972-73 (NHL)	1 Cup (1989)	•Atlanta (1972-80)
			Calgary (1980—)
Chicago Blackhawks	1926-27 (NHL)	3 Cups (1934,38,61)	•Chicago (1926—)
Colorado Avalanche	1972-73 (WHA)	1 WHA (1977)	•Quebec City (1972-95)
		2 Cups (1996, 2001)	Denver (1995—)
Columbus Blue Jackets	2000-01 (NHL)	None	•Columbus, OH (2000—)
Dallas Stars	1967-68 (NHL)	1 Cup (1999)	•Bloomington, MN (1967-93)
			Dallas (1993—)
Detroit Red Wings	1926-27 (NHL)	11 Cups (1936-37,43,50,52,54-55,97,98, 2002,08)	•Detroit (1926—)
Edmonton Oilers	1972-73 (WHA)	5 Cups (1984-85,87-88,90)	•Edmonton (1972—)
Los Angeles Kings	1967-68 (NHL)	None	•Inglewood, CA (1967-99)
			Los Angeles (1999—)
Minnesota Wild	2000-01 (NHL)	None	•St. Paul, MN (2000—)
Nashville Predators	1998-99 (NHL)	None	•Nashville, TN (1998—)
Phoenix Coyotes	1972-73 (WHA)	3 WHA (1976, 78-79)	•Winnipeg (1972-96)
			Phoenix (1996—)
St. Louis Blues	1967-68 (NHL)	None	•St. Louis (1967—)
San Jose Sharks	1991-92 (NHL)	None	•San Francisco (1991-93)
			San Jose (1993—)
Vancouver Canucks	1970-71 (NHL)	None	•Vancouver (1970—)

Eastern Conference

	First Season	League Titles	Franchise Stops
Atlanta Thrashers	1999-00 (NHL)	None	•Atlanta (1999—)
Boston Bruins	1924-25 (NHL)	5 Cups (1929,39,41,70,72)	•Boston (1924—)
Buffalo Sabres	1970-71 (NHL)	None	•Buffalo (1970—)
Carolina Hurricanes	1972-73 (WHA)	1 WHA (1973)	•Boston (1972-74)
		1 Cup (2006)	W. Springfield, MA (1974-75)
			Hartford, CT (1975-78)
			Springfield, MA (1978-80)
			Hartford (1980-97)
			Greensboro, NC (1997-99)
			Raleigh, NC (1999—)
Florida Panthers	1993-94 (NHL)	None	•Miami (1993-98)
			Sunrise, FL (1998—)
Montreal Canadiens	1909-10 (NHA)	2 NHA (1916-17) 2 NHL (1924-25) 24 Cups (1916,24,30-31,44,46,53,56-60,65-66,68-69,71,73,76-79,86,93)	•Montreal (1909—)
New Jersey Devils	1974-75 (NHL)	3 Cups (1995, 2000,03)	•Kansas City (1974-76)
			Denver (1976-82)
			E. Rutherford, NJ (1982—)
New York Islanders	1972-73 (NHL)	4 Cups (1980-83)	•Uniondale, NY (1972—)
New York Rangers	1926-27 (NHL)	4 Cups (1928,33,40,94)	•New York (1926—)
Ottawa Senators	1992-93 (NHL)	None	•Ottawa (1992-1996)
			Kanata, Ont. (1996—)
Philadelphia Flyers	1967-68 (NHL)	2 Cups (1974-75)	•Philadelphia (1967—)
Pittsburgh Penguins	1967-68 (NHL)	2 Cups (1991-92)	•Pittsburgh (1967—)
Tampa Bay Lightning	1992-93 (NHL)	1 Cup (2004)	•Tampa, FL (1992-93)
			St. Petersburg, FL (1993-96)
			Tampa, FL (1996—)
Toronto Maple Leafs	1916-17 (NHA)	2 NHL (1918,22) 13 Cups (1918,22,32,42,45, 47-49,51,62-64,67)	•Toronto (1916—)
Washington Capitals	1974-75 (NHL)	None	•Landover, MD (1974-97)
			Washington, D.C. (1997—)

Note: The Hartford Civic Center roof collapsed after a snowstorm in January 1978, forcing the Whalers to move their home games to Springfield, Mass., for two years.

The Growth of the NHL

Of the four franchises that comprised the National Hockey League (NHL) at the start of the 1917-18 season, only two remain—the Montreal Canadiens and the Toronto Maple Leafs (originally the Toronto Arenas). From 1919-26, eight new teams joined the league, but only four—the Boston Bruins, Chicago Blackhawks (originally Black Hawks), Detroit Red Wings (originally Cougars) and New York Rangers—survived.

It was 41 years before the NHL expanded again, doubling in size for the 1967-68 season with new teams in Bloomington (Minn.), Los Angeles, Oakland, Philadelphia, Pittsburgh and St. Louis. The league had 16 clubs by the start of the 1972-73 season, but it also had a rival in the **World Hockey Association,** which debuted that year with 12 teams.

The NHL added two more teams in 1974 and merged the struggling Cleveland Barons (originally the Oakland Seals) and Minnesota North Stars in 1978, before absorbing four WHA clubs—the Edmonton Oilers, Hartford Whalers, Quebec Nordiques and Winnipeg Jets—in time for the 1979-80 season. Seven expansion teams joined the league in the 1990s, with two more being added in 2000 to make it an even 30.

Expansion/Merger Timetable

For teams currently in NHL.

1919—Quebec Bulldogs finally take the ice after sitting out NHL's first two seasons; **1924**—Boston Bruins and Montreal Maroons; **1925**—New York Americans and Pittsburgh Pirates; **1926**—Chicago Black Hawks (now Blackhawks), Detroit Cougars (now Red Wings) and New York Rangers; **1932**—Ottawa Senators return after sitting out 1931-32 season.

1967—California-Oakland Seals (later Cleveland Barons), Los Angeles Kings, Minnesota North Stars, Philadelphia Flyers, Pittsburgh Penguins and St. Louis Blues.

1970—Buffalo Sabres and Vancouver Canucks; **1972**—Atlanta Flames (now Calgary) and New York Islanders; **1974**—Kansas City Scouts (now New Jersey Devils) and Washington Capitals; **1978**—Cleveland Barons merge with Minnesota North Stars (now Dallas Stars) and team remains in Minnesota; **1979**—added WHA's Edmonton Oilers, Hartford Whalers (now Carolina Hurricanes), Quebec Nordiques (now Colorado Avalanche) and Winnipeg Jets (now Phoenix Coyotes).

1991—San Jose Sharks; **1992**—Ottawa Senators and Tampa Bay Lightning; **1993**—Mighty Ducks of Anaheim and Florida Panthers; **1998**—Nashville Predators; **1999**—Atlanta Thrashers.

2000—Columbus Blue Jackets and Minnesota Wild.

City and Nickname Changes

1919—Toronto Arenas renamed St. Pats; **1920**—Quebec Bulldogs move to Hamilton and become Tigers (will fold in 1925); **1926**—Toronto St. Pats renamed Maple Leafs; **1929**—Detroit Cougars renamed Falcons.

1930—Pittsburgh Pirates move to Philadelphia and become Quakers (will fold in 1931); **1932**—Detroit Falcons renamed Red Wings; **1934**—Ottawa Senators move to St. Louis and become Eagles (will fold in 1935); **1941**—New York Americans renamed Brooklyn Americans (will fold in 1942).

1967—California Seals renamed Oakland Seals three months into first season; **1970**—Oakland Seals renamed California Golden Seals; **1975**—California Golden Seals renamed Seals; **1976**—California Seals move to Cleveland and become Barons, while Kansas City Scouts move to Denver and become Colorado Rockies; **1978**—Cleveland Barons merge with Minnesota North Stars and become Minnesota North Stars.

1980—Atlanta Flames move to Calgary; **1982**—Colorado Rockies move to East Rutherford, N.J., and become New Jersey Devils; **1986**—Chicago Black Hawks renamed Blackhawks; **1993**—Minnesota North Stars move to Dallas and become Stars. **1995**—Quebec Nordiques move to Denver and become Colorado Avalanche; **1996**—Winnipeg Jets move to Phoenix and become Coyotes; **1997**—Hartford Whalers move to Greensboro, N.C. and become Carolina Hurricanes; **1999**—Carolina Hurricanes move to Raleigh, N.C.; **2006**—Mighty Ducks of Anaheim renamed Anaheim Ducks.

Defunct NHL Teams

Teams that once played in the NHL, but no longer exist.

Brooklyn—Americans (1941-42, formerly NY Americans from 1925-41); **Cleveland**—Barons (1976-78, originally California-Oakland Seals from 1967-76); **Hamilton (Ont.)**—Tigers (1920-25, originally Quebec Bulldogs from 1919-20); **Montreal**—Maroons (1924-38) and Wanderers (1917-18); **New York**—Americans (1925-41, later Brooklyn Americans for 1941-42); **Oakland**—Seals (1967-76, also known as California Seals and Golden Seals and later Cleveland Barons from 1976-78); **Ottawa**—Senators (1917-31 and 1932-34, later St. Louis Eagles for 1934-35); **Philadelphia**—Quakers (1930-31, originally Pittsburgh Pirates from 1925-30); **Pittsburgh**—Pirates (1925-30, later Philadelphia Quakers for 1930-31); **Quebec**—Bulldogs (1919-20, later Hamilton Tigers from 1920-25); **St. Louis**—Eagles (1934-35), originally Ottawa Senators (1917-31 and 1932-34).

WHA Teams (1972-79)

Baltimore—Blades (1975); **Birmingham**—Bulls (1976-78); **Calgary**—Cowboys (1975-77); **Chicago**—Cougars (1972-75); **Cincinnati**—Stingers (1975-79); **Cleveland**—Crusaders (1972-76, moved to Minnesota); **Denver**—Spurs (1975-76, moved to Ottawa); **Edmonton**—Oilers (1972-79, originally called Alberta Oilers in 1972-73); **Houston**—Aeros (1972-78); **Indianapolis**—Racers (1974-78).

Los Angeles—Sharks (1972-74, moved to Michigan); **Michigan**—Stags (1974-75, moved to Baltimore); **Minnesota**—Fighting Saints (1972-76) and New Fighting Saints (1976-77); **New England**—Whalers (1972-79, played in Boston from 1972-74, West Springfield, MA from 1974-75, Hartford from 1975-78 and Springfield, MA in 1979); **New Jersey**—Knights (1973-74, moved to San Diego); **New York**—Raiders (1972-74, renamed Golden Blades in 1973, moved to New Jersey).

Ottawa—Nationals (1972-73, moved to Toronto) and Civics (1976); **Philadelphia**—Blazers (1972-73, moved to Vancouver); **Phoenix**—Roadrunners (1974-77); **Quebec**—Nordiques (1972-79); **San Diego**—Mariners (1974-77); **Toronto**—Toros (1973-76, moved to Birmingham, AL); **Vancouver**—Blazers (1973-75, moved to Calgary); **Winnipeg**—Jets (1972-79).

Annual NHL Leaders

Art Ross Trophy (Scoring)

Given to the player who leads the league in points scored and named after the former Boston Bruins general manager-coach. First presented in 1948, names of prior leading scorers have been added retroactively. A tie for the scoring championship is broken three ways: 1. total goals; 2. fewest games played; 3. first goal scored.

Multiple winners: Wayne Gretzky (10); Gordie Howe and Mario Lemieux (6); Phil Esposito and Jaromir Jagr (5); Stan Mikita (4); Bobby Hull and Guy Lafleur (3); Max Bentley, Charlie Conacher, Bill Cook, Babe Dye, Bernie Geoffrion, Elmer Lach, Newsy Lalonde, Joe Malone, Dickie Moore, Howie Morenz, Bobby Orr and Sweeney Schriner (2).

Year		Gm	G	A	Pts	Year		Gm	G	A	Pts
1918	Joe Malone, Mon	20	44	0	44	1963	Gordie Howe, Det	70	38	48	86
1919	Newsy Lalonde, Mon	17	23	9	32	1964	Stan Mikita, Chi	70	39	50	89
1920	Joe Malone, Que	24	39	6	45	1965	Stan Mikita, Chi	70	28	59	87
1921	Newsy Lalonde, Mon	24	33	8	41	1966	Bobby Hull, Chi	65	54	43	97
1922	Punch Broadbent, Ott	24	32	14	46	1967	Stan Mikita, Chi	70	35	62	97
1923	Babe Dye, Tor	22	26	11	37	1968	Stan Mikita, Chi	72	40	47	87
1924	Cy Denneny, Ott	21	22	1	23	1969	Phil Esposito, Bos	74	49	77	126
1925	Babe Dye, Tor	29	38	6	44	1970	Bobby Orr, Bos	76	33	87	120
1926	Nels Stewart, Maroons	36	34	8	42	1971	Phil Esposito, Bos	78	76	76	152
1927	Bill Cook, NYR	44	33	4	37	1972	Phil Esposito, Bos	76	66	67	133
1928	Howie Morenz, Mon	43	33	18	51	1973	Phil Esposito, Bos	78	55	75	130
1929	Ace Bailey, Tor	44	22	10	32	1974	Phil Esposito, Bos	78	68	77	145
1930	Cooney Weiland, Bos	44	43	30	73	1975	Bobby Orr, Bos	80	46	89	135
1931	Howie Morenz, Mon	39	28	23	51	1976	Guy Lafleur, Mon	80	56	69	125
1932	Busher Jackson, Tor	48	28	25	53	1977	Guy Lafleur, Mon	80	56	80	136
1933	Bill Cook, NYR	48	28	22	50	1978	Guy Lafleur, Mon	79	60	72	132
1934	Charlie Conacher, Tor	42	32	20	52	1979	Bryan Trottier, NYI	76	47	87	134
1935	Charlie Conacher, Tor	47	36	21	57	1980	Marcel Dionne, LA	80	53	84	137
1936	Sweeney Schriner, NYA	48	19	26	45	1981	Wayne Gretzky, Edm	80	55	109	164
1937	Sweeney Schriner, NYA	48	21	25	46	1982	Wayne Gretzky, Edm	80	92	120	212
1938	Gordie Drillon, Tor	48	26	26	52	1983	Wayne Gretzky, Edm	80	71	125	196
1939	Toe Blake, Mon	48	24	23	47	1984	Wayne Gretzky, Edm	74	87	118	205
1940	Milt Schmidt, Bos	48	22	30	52	1985	Wayne Gretzky, Edm	80	73	135	208
1941	Bill Cowley, Bos	46	17	45	62	1986	Wayne Gretzky, Edm	80	52	163	215
1942	Bryan Hextall, NYR	48	24	32	56	1987	Wayne Gretzky, Edm	79	62	121	183
1943	Doug Bentley, Chi	50	33	40	73	1988	Mario Lemieux, Pit	77	70	98	168
1944	Herbie Cain, Bos	48	36	46	82	1989	Mario Lemieux, Pit	76	85	114	199
1945	Elmer Lach, Mon	50	26	54	80	1990	Wayne Gretzky, LA	73	40	102	142
1946	Max Bentley, Chi	47	31	30	61	1991	Wayne Gretzky, LA	78	41	122	163
1947	Max Bentley, Chi	60	29	43	72	1992	Mario Lemieux, Pit	64	44	87	131
1948	Elmer Lach, Mon	60	30	31	61	1993	Mario Lemieux, Pit	60	69	91	160
1949	Roy Conacher, Chi	60	26	42	68	1994	Wayne Gretzky, LA	81	38	92	130
1950	Ted Lindsay, Det	69	23	55	78	1995	Jaromir Jagr, Pit	48	32	38	70
1951	Gordie Howe, Det	70	43	43	86	1996	Mario Lemieux, Pit	70	69	92	161
1952	Gordie Howe, Det	70	47	39	86	1997	Mario Lemieux, Pit	76	50	72	122
1953	Gordie Howe, Det	70	49	46	95	1998	Jaromir Jagr, Pit	77	35	67	102
1954	Gordie Howe, Det	70	33	48	81	1999	Jaromir Jagr, Pit	81	44	83	127
1955	Bernie Geoffrion, Mon	70	38	37	75	2000	Jaromir Jagr, Pit	63	42	54	96
1956	Jean Beliveau, Mon	70	47	41	88	2001	Jaromir Jagr, Pit	81	52	69	121
1957	Gordie Howe, Det	70	44	45	89	2002	Jarome Iginla, Calg	82	52	44	96
1958	Dickie Moore, Mon	70	36	48	84	2003	Peter Forsberg, Col	75	29	77	106
1959	Dickie Moore, Mon	70	41	55	96	2004	Martin St. Louis, TB	82	38	56	94
1960	Bobby Hull, Chi	70	39	42	81	2006	Joe Thornton, Bos-SJ	81	29	96	125
1961	Bernie Geoffrion, Mon	64	50	45	95	2007	Sidney Crosby, Pit	79	36	84	120
1962	Bobby Hull, Chi	70	50	34	84	2008	Alex Ovechkin, Wash	82	65	47	112

Note: The three times players have tied for total points in one season the player with more goals has won the trophy. In 1961-62, Hull outscored Andy Bathgate of NY Rangers, 50 goals to 28. In 1979-80, Dionne outscored Wayne Gretzky of Edmonton, 53-51. In 1995, Jagr outscored Eric Lindros of Philadelphia, 32-29.

Goals

Multiple winners: Bobby Hull (7); Phil Esposito (6); Charlie Conacher, Wayne Gretzky, Gordie Howe and Maurice Richard (5); Bill Cooke, Babe Dye, Brett Hull, Mario Lemieux, Pavel Bure and Teemu Selanne (3); Jean Beliveau, Doug Bentley, Peter Bondra, Mike Bossy, Bernie Geoffrion, Bryan Hextall, Jarome Iginla, Joe Malone and Nels Stewart (2).

Year		No	Year		No	Year		No
1918	Joe Malone, Mon	44	1927	Bill Cook, NYR	33	1936	Charlie Conacher, Tor	23
1919	Odie Cleghorn, Mon	23	1928	Howie Morenz, Mon	33		& Bill Thoms, Tor	23
	& Newsy Lalonde, Mon	23	1929	Ace Bailey, Tor	22	1937	Larry Aurie, Det	23
1920	Joe Malone, Que	39	1930	Cooney Weiland, Bos	43		& Nels Stewart, Bos-NYA	23
1921	Babe Dye, Ham-Tor	35	1931	Charlie Conacher, Tor	31	1938	Gordie Drillon, Tor	26
1922	Punch Broadbent, Ott	32	1932	Charlie Conacher, Tor	34	1939	Roy Conacher, Bos	26
1923	Babe Dye, Tor	26		& Bill Cook, NYR	34	1940	Bryan Hextall, NYR	24
1924	Cy Denneny, Ott	22	1933	Bill Cook, NYR	28	1941	Bryan Hextall, NYR	26
1925	Babe Dye, Tor	38	1934	Charlie Conacher, Tor	32	1942	Lynn Patrick, NYR	32
1926	Nels Stewart, Maroons	34	1935	Charlie Conacher, Tor	36	1943	Doug Bentley, Chi	33

Annual NHL Leaders (Cont.)

Year		No	Year		No	Year		No
1944	Doug Bentley, Chi	38	1966	Bobby Hull, Chi	54	1988	Mario Lemieux, Pit	70
1945	Maurice Richard, Mon	50	1967	Bobby Hull, Chi	52	1989	Mario Lemieux, Pit	85
1946	Gaye Stewart, Tor	37	1968	Bobby Hull, Chi	44			
1947	Maurice Richard, Mon	45	1969	Bobby Hull, Chi	58	1990	Brett Hull, St.L	72
1948	Ted Lindsay, Det	33				1991	Brett Hull, St.L	86
1949	Sid Abel, Det	28	1970	Phil Esposito, Bos	43	1992	Brett Hull, St.L	70
			1971	Phil Esposito, Bos	76	1993	Alexander Mogilny, Buf	76
1950	Maurice Richard, Mon	43	1972	Phil Esposito, Bos	66		& Teemu Selanne, Win	76
1951	Gordie Howe, Det	43	1973	Phil Esposito, Bos	55	1994	Pavel Bure, Van	60
1952	Gordie Howe, Det	47	1974	Phil Esposito, Bos	68	1995	Peter Bondra, Wash	34
1953	Gordie Howe, Det	49	1975	Phil Esposito, Bos	61	1996	Mario Lemieux, Pit	69
1954	Maurice Richard, Mon	37	1976	Reggie Leach, Phi	61	1997	Keith Tkachuk, Pho	52
1955	Bernie Geoffrion, Mon	38	1977	Steve Shutt, Mon	60	1998	Teemu Selanne, Ana	52
	& Maurice Richard, Mon	38	1978	Guy Lafleur, Mon	60		& Peter Bondra, Wash	52
1956	Jean Beliveau, Mon	47	1979	Mike Bossy, NYI	69	1999	Teemu Selanne, Ana	47
1957	Gordie Howe, Det	44						
1958	Dickie Moore, Mon	36	1980	Danny Gare, Buf	56	2000	Pavel Bure, Fla	58
1959	Jean Beliveau, Mon	45		Charlie Simmer, LA	56	2001	Pavel Bure, Fla	59
				& Blaine Stoughton, Hart	56	2002	Jarome Iginla, Calg	52
1960	Bronco Horvath, Bos	39	1981	Mike Bossy, NYI	68	2003	Milan Hejduk, Col	50
	& Bobby Hull, Chi	39	1982	Wayne Gretzky, Edm	92	2004	Jarome Iginla, Calg	52
1961	Bernie Geoffrion, Mon	50	1983	Wayne Gretzky, Edm	71		Ilya Kovalchuk, Atl	41
1962	Bobby Hull, Chi	50	1984	Wayne Gretzky, Edm	87		& Rick Nash, Clb	41
1963	Gordie Howe, Det	38	1985	Wayne Gretzky, Edm	73	2006	Jonathan Cheechoo, SJ	56
1964	Bobby Hull, Chi	43	1986	Jari Kurri, Edm	68	2007	Vincent Lecavalier, TB	52
1965	Norm Ullman, Tor	42	1987	Wayne Gretzky, Edm	62	2008	Alex Ovechkin, Wash	65

Assists

Multiple winners: Wayne Gretzky (16); Bobby Orr (5); Adam Oates, Frank Boucher, Bill Cowley, Phil Esposito, Gordie Howe, Jaromir Jagr, Elmer Lach, Mario Lemieux, Stan Mikita, Joe Primeau and Joe Thornton (3); Syl Apps, Andy Bathgate, Jean Beliveau, Doug Bentley, Art Chapman, Bobby Clarke, Ron Francis, Ted Lindsay, Bert Olmstead, Henri Richard and Bryan Trottier (2).

Year		No	Year		No	Year		No
1918	No official records kept.		1950	Ted Lindsay, Det	55	1980	Wayne Gretzky, Edm	86
1919	Newsy Lalonde, Mon	9	1951	Gordie Howe, Det	43	1981	Wayne Gretzky, Edm	109
1920	Corbett Denneny, Tor	12		& Teeder Kennedy, Tor	43	1982	Wayne Gretzky, Edm	120
1921	Louis Berlinquette, Mon	9	1952	Elmer Lach, Mon	50	1983	Wayne Gretzky, Edm	125
	Harry Cameron, Tor	9	1953	Gordie Howe, Det	46	1984	Wayne Gretzky, Edm	118
	& Joe Matte, Ham	9	1954	Gordie Howe, Det	48	1985	Wayne Gretzky, Edm	135
1922	Punch Broadbent, Ott	14	1955	Bert Olmstead, Mon	48	1986	Wayne Gretzky, Edm	163
	& Leo Reise, Ham	14	1956	Bert Olmstead, Mon	56	1987	Wayne Gretzky, Edm	121
1923	Ed Bouchard, Ham	12	1957	Ted Lindsay, Det	55	1988	Wayne Gretzky, Edm	109
1924	King Clancy, Ott	8	1958	Henri Richard, Mon	52	1989	Wayne Gretzky, LA	114
1925	Cy Denneny, Ott	15	1959	Dickie Moore, Mon	55		& Mario Lemieux, Pit	114
1926	Frank Nighbor, Ott	13	1960	Don McKenney, Bos	49	1990	Wayne Gretzky, LA	102
1927	Dick Irvin, Chi	18	1961	Jean Beliveau, Mon	58	1991	Wayne Gretzky, LA	122
1928	Howie Morenz, Mon	18	1962	Andy Bathgate, NYR	56	1992	Wayne Gretzky, LA	90
1929	Frank Boucher, NYR	16	1963	Henri Richard, Mon	50	1993	Adam Oates, Bos	97
1930	Frank Boucher, NYR	36	1964	Andy Bathgate, NYR-Tor	58	1994	Wayne Gretzky, LA	92
1931	Joe Primeau, Tor	32	1965	Stan Mikita, Chi	59	1995	Ron Francis, Pit	48
1932	Joe Primeau, Tor	37	1966	Jean Beliveau, Mon	48	1996	Ron Francis, Pit	92
1933	Frank Boucher, NYR	28		Stan Mikita, Chi	48		& Mario Lemieux, Pit	92
1934	Joe Primeau, Tor	32		& Bobby Rousseau, Mon	48	1997	Mario Lemieux, Pit	72
1935	Art Chapman, NYA	34	1967	Stan Mikita, Chi	62		& Wayne Gretzky, NYR	72
1936	Art Chapman, NYA	28	1968	Phil Esposito, Bos	49	1998	Jaromir Jagr, Pit	67
1937	Syl Apps, Tor	29	1969	Phil Esposito, Bos	77		& Wayne Gretzky, NYR	67
1938	Syl Apps, Tor	29	1970	Bobby Orr, Bos	87	1999	Jaromir Jagr, Pit	83
1939	Bill Cowley, Bos	34	1971	Bobby Orr, Bos	102	2000	Mark Recchi, Phi	63
1940	Milt Schmidt, Bos	30	1972	Bobby Orr, Bos	80	2001	Jaromir Jagr, Pit	69
1941	Bill Cowley, Bos	45	1973	Phil Esposito, Bos	75		& Adam Oates, Wash	69
1942	Phil Watson, NYR	37	1974	Bobby Orr, Bos	90	2002	Adam Oates, Wash-Phi	64
1943	Bill Cowley, Bos	45	1975	Bobby Clarke, Phi	89	2003	Peter Forsberg, Col	56
1944	Clint Smith, Chi	49		& Bobby Orr, Bos	89	2004	Scott Gomez, NJ	56
1945	Elmer Lach, Mon	54	1976	Bobby Clarke, Phi	89		& Martin St. Louis, TB	56
1946	Elmer Lach, Mon	34	1977	Guy Lafleur, Mon	80	2006	Joe Thornton, Bos-SJ	96
1947	Billy Taylor, Det	46	1978	Bryan Trottier, NYI	77	2007	Joe Thornton, SJ	92
1948	Doug Bentley, Chi	37	1979	Bryan Trottier, NYI	87	2008	Joe Thornton, SJ	67
1949	Doug Bentley, Chi	43						

Goals Against Average

Average determined by games played through 1942-43 season and by minutes played since then. Minimum of 15 games from 1917-18 season through 1925-26; minimum of 25 games since 1926-27 season. Not to be confused with the Vezina Trophy. Goaltenders who posted the season's lowest goals against average, but did not win the Vezina are in **bold** type.

Multiple winners: Jacques Plante (9); Clint Benedict and Bill Durnan (6); Johnny Bower, Ken Dryden and Tiny Thompson (4); Patrick Roy and Georges Vezina (3); Ed Belfour, Frankie Brimsek, Turk Broda, George Hainsworth, Dominik Hasek, Miikka Kiprusoff, Harry Lumley, Bernie Parent, Pete Peeters, Terry Sawchuk and Marty Turco (2).

Year		GAA	Year		GAA	Year		GAA
1918	Georges Vezina, Mon	3.82	1948	Turk Broda, Tor	2.38	1978	Ken Dryden, Mon	2.05
1919	Clint Benedict, Ott	2.94	1949	Bill Durnan, Mon	2.10	1979	Ken Dryden, Mon	2.30
1920	Clint Benedict, Ott	2.67	1950	Bill Durnan, Mon	2.20	1980	Bob Sauve, Buf	2.36
1921	Clint Benedict, Ott	3.13	1951	Al Rollins, Tor	1.77	1981	Richard Sevigny, Mon	2.40
1922	Clint Benedict, Ott	3.50	1952	Terry Sawchuk, Det	1.90	1982	**Denis Herron**, Mon	2.64
1923	Clint Benedict, Ott	2.25	1953	Terry Sawchuk, Det	1.90	1983	Pete Peeters, Bos	2.36
1924	Georges Vezina, Mon	2.00	1954	Harry Lumley, Tor	1.86	1984	**Pat Riggin**, Wash	2.66
1925	Georges Vezina, Mon	1.87	1955	**Harry Lumley**, Tor	1.94	1985	**Tom Barrasso**, Buf	2.66
1926	Alex Connell, Ott	1.17	1956	Jacques Plante, Mon	1.86	1986	**Bob Froese**, Phi	2.55
1927	**Clint Benedict**, Mon-M	1.51	1957	Jacques Plante, Mon	2.02	1987	**Brian Hayward**, Mon	2.81
1928	Geo. Hainsworth, Mon	1.09	1958	Jacques Plante, Mon	2.11	1988	**Pete Peeters**, Wash	2.78
1929	Geo. Hainsworth, Mon	0.98	1959	Jacques Plante, Mon	2.16	1989	Patrick Roy, Mon	2.47
1930	Tiny Thompson, Bos	2.23	1960	Jacques Plante, Mon	2.54	1990	**Mike Liut**, Hart-Wash	2.53
1931	Roy Worters, NYA	1.68	1961	Johnny Bower, Tor	2.50	1991	Ed Belfour, Chi	2.47
1932	Chuck Gardiner, Chi	1.92	1962	Jacques Plante, Mon	2.37	1992	Patrick Roy, Mon	2.36
1933	Tiny Thompson, Bos	1.83	1963	**Jacques Plante**, Mon	2.49	1993	**Felix Potvin**, Tor	2.50
1934	**Wilf Cude**, Det-Mon	1.57	1964	**Johnny Bower**, Tor	2.11	1994	Dominik Hasek, Buf	1.95
1935	Lorne Chabot, Chi	1.83	1965	Johnny Bower, Tor	2.38	1995	Dominik Hasek, Buf	2.11
1936	Tiny Thompson, Bos	1.71	1966	**Johnny Bower**, Tor	2.25	1996	**Ron Hextall**, Phi	2.17
1937	Norm Smith, Det	2.13	1967	Glenn Hall, Chi	2.38	1997	**Martin Brodeur**, NJ	1.88
1938	Tiny Thompson, Bos	1.85	1968	Gump Worsley, Mon	1.98	1998	**Ed Belfour**, Dal	1.88
1939	Frankie Brimsek, Bos	1.58	1969	**Jacques Plante**, St.L.	1.96	1999	**Ron Tugnutt**, Ott	1.79
1940	Dave Kerr, NYR	1.60	1970	**Ernie Wakely**, St.L	2.11	2000	Brian Boucher, Phi	1.91
1941	Turk Broda, Tor	2.06	1971	**Jacques Plante**, Tor	1.88	2001	**Marty Turco**, Dal	1.90
1942	Frankie Brimsek, Bos	2.45	1972	Tony Esposito, Chi	1.77	2002	**Patrick Roy**, Col	1.94
1943	John Mowers, Det	2.47	1973	Ken Dryden, Mon	2.26	2003	**Marty Turco**, Dal	1.72
1944	Bill Durnan, Mon	2.18	1974	Bernie Parent, Phi	1.89	2004	**Miikka Kiprusoff**, Calg	1.69
1945	Bill Durnan, Mon	2.42	1975	Bernie Parent, Phi	2.03	2006	Miikka Kiprusoff, Calg	2.07
1946	Bill Durnan, Mon	2.60	1976	Ken Dryden, Mon	2.03	2007	**Niklas Backstrom**, Min	1.97
1947	Bill Durnan, Mon	2.30	1977	Bunny Larocque, Mon	2.09	2008	**Chris Osgood**, Det	2.09

Penalty Minutes

Multiple winners: Red Horner (8); Gus Mortson and Dave Schultz (4); Bert Corbeau, Lou Fontinato and Tiger Williams (3); Sean Avery, Matthew Barnaby, Billy Boucher, Carl Brewer, Red Dutton, Pat Egan, Bill Ezinicki, Joe Hall, Tim Hunter, Keith Magnuson, Chris Nilan, Jimmy Orlando and Rob Ray (2).

Year		Min	Year		Min	Year		Min
1918	Joe Hall, Mon	60	1948	Bill Barilko, Tor	147	1978	Dave Schultz, LA-Pit	405
1919	Joe Hall, Mon	85	1949	Bill Ezinicki, Tor	145	1979	Tiger Williams, Tor	298
1920	Cully Wilson, Tor	79	1950	Bill Ezinicki, Tor	144	1980	Jimmy Mann, Win	287
1921	Bert Corbeau, Mon	86	1951	Gus Mortson, Tor	142	1981	Tiger Williams, Van	343
1922	Sprague Cleghorn, Mon	63	1952	Gus Kyle, Bos	127	1982	Paul Baxter, Pit	409
1923	Billy Boucher, Mon	52	1953	Maurice Richard, Mon	112	1983	Randy Holt, Wash	275
1924	Bert Corbeau, Tor	55	1954	Gus Mortson, Chi	132	1984	Chris Nilan, Mon	338
1925	Billy Boucher, Mon	92	1955	Fern Flaman, Bos	150	1985	Chris Nilan, Mon	358
1926	Bert Corbeau, Tor	121	1956	Lou Fontinato, NYR	202	1986	Joey Kocur, Det	377
1927	Nels Stewart, Mon-M	133	1957	Gus Mortson, Chi	147	1987	Tim Hunter, Calg	361
1928	Eddie Shore, Bos	165	1958	Lou Fontinato, NYR	152	1988	Bob Probert, Det	398
1929	Red Dutton, Mon-M	139	1959	Ted Lindsay, Chi	184	1989	Tim Hunter, Calg	375
1930	Joe Lamb, Ott	119	1960	Carl Brewer, Tor	150	1990	Basil McRae, Min	351
1931	Harvey Rockburn, Det	118	1961	Pierre Pilote, Chi	165	1991	Rob Ray, Buf	350
1932	Red Dutton, NYA	107	1962	Lou Fontinato, Mon	167	1992	Mike Peluso, Chi	408
1933	Red Horner, Tor	144	1963	Howie Young, Det	273	1993	Marty McSorley, LA	399
1934	Red Horner, Tor	146	1964	Vic Hadfield, NYR	151	1994	Tie Domi, Win	347
1935	Red Horner, Tor	125	1965	Carl Brewer, Tor	177	1995	Enrico Ciccone, TB	225
1936	Red Horner, Tor	167	1966	Reg Fleming, Bos-NYR	166	1996	Matthew Barnaby, Buf.	335
1937	Red Horner, Tor	124	1967	John Ferguson, Mon	177	1997	Gino Odjick, Van	371
1938	Red Horner, Tor	82	1968	Barclay Plager, St.L.	153	1998	Donald Brashear, Van	372
1939	Red Horner, Tor	85	1969	Forbes Kennedy, Phi-Tor	219	1999	Rob Ray, Buf	261
1940	Red Horner, Tor	87	1970	Keith Magnuson, Chi	213	2000	Denny Lambert, Atl	219
1941	Jimmy Orlando, Det	99	1971	Keith Magnuson, Chi	291	2001	Matthew Barnaby, Pit-TB	265
1942	Pat Egan, NYA	124	1972	Bryan Watson, Pit	212	2002	Peter Worrell, Fla	354
1943	Jimmy Orlando, Det	99	1973	Dave Schultz, Phi	259	2003	Jody Shelley, Clb	249
1944	Mike McMahon, Mon	98	1974	Dave Schultz, Phi	348	2004	Sean Avery, LA	261
1945	Pat Egan, Bos	86	1975	Dave Schultz, Phi	472	2006	Sean Avery, LA	257
1946	Jack Stewart, Det	73	1976	Steve Durbano, Pit-KC	370	2007	Ben Eager, Phi	233
1947	Gus Mortson, Tor	133	1977	Tiger Williams, Tor	338	2008	Daniel Carcillo, Pho	324

All-Time NHL Regular Season Leaders

Through 2008 regular season.

CAREER

Players active during 2008 season in **bold** type.

Points

		Yrs	Gm	G	A	Pts
1	Wayne Gretzky	20	1487	894	1963	2857
2	Mark Messier	25	1756	694	1193	1887
3	Gordie Howe	26	1767	801	1049	1850
4	Ron Francis	23	1731	549	1249	1798
5	Marcel Dionne	18	1348	731	1040	1771
6	Steve Yzerman	22	1514	692	1063	1755
7	Mario Lemieux	17	915	690	1033	1723
8	**Joe Sakic**	19	1363	623	1006	1629
9	**Jaromir Jagr**	17	1273	646	953	1599
10	Phil Esposito	18	1282	717	873	1590
11	Ray Bourque	22	1612	410	1169	1579
12	Paul Coffey	21	1409	396	1135	1531
13	Stan Mikita	22	1394	541	926	1467
14	Bryan Trottier	18	1279	524	901	1425
15	Adam Oates	19	1337	341	1079	1420
16	Doug Gilmour	20	1474	450	964	1414
17	Dale Hawerchuk	16	1188	518	891	1409
18	Jari Kurri	17	1251	601	797	1398
19	Luc Robitaille	19	1431	668	726	1394
20	Brett Hull	20	1269	741	650	1391
21	**Mark Recchi**	19	1410	522	859	1381
22	John Bucyk	23	1540	556	813	1369
23	Guy Lafleur	17	1126	560	793	1353
24	**Brendan Shanahan**	20	1490	650	690	1340
25	Dave Andreychuk	23	1639	640	698	1338
	Denis Savard	17	1196	473	865	1338
27	Mike Gartner	19	1432	708	627	1335
28	Pierre Turgeon	19	1294	515	812	1327
29	Gilbert Perreault	17	1191	512	814	1326
30	**Mats Sundin**	17	1305	555	766	1321

Goals

		Yrs	Gm	No
1	Wayne Gretzky	20	1487	894
2	Gordie Howe	26	1767	801
3	Brett Hull	20	1269	741
4	Marcel Dionne	18	1348	731
5	Phil Esposito	18	1282	717
6	Mike Gartner	19	1432	708
7	Mark Messier	25	1756	694
8	Steve Yzerman	22	1514	692
9	Mario Lemieux	17	915	690
10	Luc Robitaille	19	1431	668
11	**Brendan Shanahan**	20	1490	650
12	**Jaromir Jagr**	17	1273	646
13	Dave Andreychuk	23	1639	640
14	**Joe Sakic**	19	1363	623
15	Bobby Hull	16	1063	610
16	Dino Ciccarelli	19	1232	608
17	Jari Kurri	17	1251	601
18	Mike Bossy	10	752	573
19	Joe Nieuwendyk	20	1257	564
20	Guy Lafleur	17	1126	560
21	John Bucyk	23	1540	556
22	**Mats Sundin**	17	1305	555
23	**Teemu Selanne**	15	1067	552
24	Ron Francis	23	1731	549
25	Michel Goulet	15	1089	548
26	Maurice Richard	18	978	544
27	Stan Mikita	22	1394	541
28	Frank Mahovlich	18	1181	533
29	**Mike Modano**	18	1320	528
30	Bryan Trottier	18	1279	524

Assists

		Yrs	Gm	No
1	Wayne Gretzky	20	1487	1963
2	Ron Francis	23	1731	1249
3	Mark Messier	25	1756	1193
4	Ray Bourque	22	1612	1169
5	Paul Coffey	21	1409	1135
6	Adam Oates	19	1337	1079
7	Steve Yzerman	22	1514	1063
8	Gordie Howe	26	1767	1049
9	Marcel Dionne	18	1348	1040
10	Mario Lemieux	17	915	1033
11	**Joe Sakic**	19	1363	1006
12	Doug Gilmour	20	1474	964
13	**Jaromir Jagr**	17	1273	953
14	Al MacInnis	23	1416	934
15	Larry Murphy	21	1615	929
16	Stan Mikita	22	1394	926
17	Bryan Trottier	18	1279	901
18	Phil Housley	21	1495	894
19	Dale Hawerchuk	16	1188	891
20	Phil Esposito	18	1281	873

Penalty Minutes

		Yrs	Gm	Min
1	Tiger Williams	14	962	3966
2	Dale Hunter	19	1407	3565
3	Tie Domi	16	1020	3515
4	Marty McSorley	17	961	3381
5	Bob Probert	16	935	3300
6	Rob Ray	15	900	3207
7	Craig Berube	17	1054	3149
8	Tim Hunter	16	815	3146
9	Chris Nilan	13	688	3043
10	Rick Tocchet	18	1144	2972
11	Pat Verbeek	20	1424	2905
12	**Chris Chelios**	24	1616	2873
13	Dave Manson	16	1103	2792
14	Scott Stevens	22	1635	2785
15	Willi Plett	12	834	2572

NHL-WHA Top 10

All-time regular season scoring leaders, including games played in World Hockey Association (1972-79). NHL players with WHA experience are listed in CAPITAL letters. Players active during 2008 are in **bold** type.

Points

		Yrs	G	A	Pts
1	WAYNE GRETZKY	21	940	2027	2967
2	GORDIE HOWE	32	975	1383	2358
3	MARK MESSIER	26	695	1203	1898
4	BOBBY HULL	23	913	895	1808
5	Ron Francis	23	549	1249	1798
6	Marcel Dionne	18	731	1040	1771
7	Steve Yzerman	22	692	1063	1755
8	Mario Lemieux	17	690	1033	1723
9	**Joe Sakic**	19	623	1006	1629
10	**Jaromir Jagr**	17	646	953	1599

WHA Totals: GRETZKY (1 yr, 80 gm, 46-64—110); HOWE (6 yrs; 419 gm, 174-334—508); MESSIER (1 yr, 52 gm, 1-10—11); HULL (7 yrs, 411 gm, 303-335—638).

Years Played

		Yrs	Career	Gm
1	Gordie Howe	26	1946-71, 79-80	1767
2	Mark Messier	25	1979-2004	1756
3	**Chris Chelios**	24	1984–	1616
	Alex Delvecchio	24	1950-74	1549
	Tim Horton	24	1949-50, 51-74	1446
6	Ron Francis	23	1981-2004	1731
	Dave Andreychuk	23	1982-2006	1639
	John Bucyk	23	1955-78	1540
	Al MacInnis	23	1982-2004	1416
10	Scott Stevens	22	1982-2004	1635
	Ray Bourque	22	1979-2001	1612
	Steve Yzerman	22	1983-2006	1514
	Stan Mikita	22	1958-80	1394
	Doug Mohns	22	1953-75	1390
	Dean Prentice	22	1952-74	1378

Note: Combined NHL-WHA years played: Howe (32); Messier (26); Harry Howell (24); Bobby Hull (23); Norm Ullman, Eric Nesterenko, Frank Mahovlich and Dave Keon (22).

Games Played

		Yrs	Career	Gm
1	Gordie Howe	26	1946-71, 79-80	1767
2	Mark Messier	25	1979-2004	1756
3	Ron Francis	23	1981-2004	1731
4	Dave Andreychuk	23	1982-2006	1639
5	Scott Stevens	22	1982-2004	1635
6	**Chris Chelios**	24	1984–	1616
7	Larry Murphy	21	1980-2001	1615
8	Ray Bourque	22	1979-2001	1612
9	Alex Delvecchio	24	1950-74	1549
10	John Bucyk	23	1955-78	1540
11	Steve Yzerman	22	1983-2006	1514
12	Phil Housley	21	1982-2003	1495
13	**Brendan Shanahan**	20	1987–	1490
14	Wayne Gretzky	20	1979-99	1487
15	Doug Gilmour	20	1983-2003	1474

Note: Combined NHL-WHA games played: Howe (2,186), Messier (1,808), Dave Keon (1,597), Harry Howell (1,581), Gretzky (1,567), Norm Ullman (1,554), Mike Gartner (1,510) and Bobby Hull (1,474).

Goaltending

Wins

		Yrs	Gm	W	L	T	Pct
1	Patrick Roy	19	1029	**551**	315	131	.618
2	**Martin Brodeur**	15	968	**538**	290	105	.633
3	Ed Belfour	18	963	**484**	320	111	.602
4	**Curtis Joseph**	18	922	**449**	343	90	.560
5	Terry Sawchuk	21	971	**447**	330	172	.562
6	Jacques Plante	18	837	**434**	247	146	.614
7	Tony Esposito	16	886	**423**	306	152	.566
8	Glenn Hall	18	906	**407**	326	163	.545
9	Grant Fuhr	19	868	**403**	295	114	.567
10	**Dominik Hasek**	16	735	**389**	223	82	.620
11	Mike Vernon	19	781	**385**	273	92	.575
12	John Vanbiesbrouck	20	882	**374**	346	119	.517
13	Andy Moog	18	713	**372**	209	88	.622
14	Tom Barrasso	19	777	**369**	277	86	.563
15	**Chris Osgood**	14	664	**363**	195	66	.635
16	Rogie Vachon	16	795	**355**	291	127	.541
17	Gump Worsley	21	861	**335**	352	150	.490
18	Harry Lumley	16	804	**330**	329	143	.501
19	Sean Burke	18	820	**324**	341	101	.487
20	Billy Smith	18	680	**305**	233	105	.556

Note: Beginning with the 2005-06 season, NHL ties were eliminated as shootouts decided games that were still tied after a five-minute overtime. Note that overtime losses and shootout losses are not included in the tables above or below.

Losses

		Yrs	Gm	W	L	T	Pct
1	Gump Worsley	21	861	335	**352**	150	.490
2	Gilles Meloche	18	788	270	**351**	131	.446
3	John Vanbiesbrouck	20	882	374	**346**	119	.517
4	**Curtis Joseph**	18	922	449	**343**	90	.560
5	Sean Burke	18	820	324	**341**	101	.487

Shutouts

		Yrs	Games	No
1	Terry Sawchuk	21	971	103
2	**Martin Brodeur**	15	968	96
3	George Hainsworth	11	465	94
4	Glenn Hall	18	906	84
5	Jacques Plante	18	837	82
6	Alex Connell	12	417	81
	Tiny Thompson	12	553	81
	Dominik Hasek	16	735	81
9	Tony Esposito	16	886	76
	Ed Belfour	18	963	76

Goals Against Average

Minimum of 300 games played.

Before 1950

		Gm	Min	GA	GAA
1	George Hainsworth	465	29,415	937	1.91
2	Alex Connell	417	26,050	830	1.91
3	Chuck Gardiner	316	19,687	664	2.02
4	Lorne Chabot	411	25,307	860	2.04
5	Tiny Thompson	553	34,175	1183	2.08

Since 1950

		Gm	Min	GA	GAA
1	**Marty Turco**	382	21,648	775	2.15
2	**Martin Brodeur**	968	57,207	2099	2.20
3	**Dominik Hasek**	735	42,836	1572	2.20
4	Ken Dryden	397	23,352	870	2.24
5	Roman Turek	328	19,095	734	2.31
6	**Manny Legace**	308	17,215	663	2.31
7	**Miikka Kiprusoff**	309	17,888	707	2.37
8	**Evgeni Nabokov**	430	24,610	974	2.37
9	Jacques Plante	837	49,533	1965	2.38
10	**Jean-Sebastien Giguere**	411	23,664	957	2.43

NHL-WHA Top 10

All-time regular season wins leaders, including games played in World Hockey Association (1972-79). NHL goaltenders with WHA experience are listed in CAPITAL letters. Players active during 2008 are in bold type.

Wins

		Yrs	W	L	T	Pct
1	Patrick Roy	19	**551**	315	131	.618
2	**Martin Brodeur**	15	**538**	290	105	.633
3	Ed Belfour	18	**484**	320	111	.602
4	JACQUES PLANTE	19	**449**	261	147	.610
	Curtis Joseph	18	**449**	343	90	.560
6	Terry Sawchuk	21	**447**	330	172	.562
7	Tony Esposito	16	**423**	306	152	.566
8	Glenn Hall	18	**407**	326	163	.545
9	Grant Fuhr	19	**403**	295	114	.567
10	**Dominik Hasek**	16	**389**	223	82	.620

WHA Totals: PLANTE (1 yr, 31 gm, 15-14-1).

All-Time NHL Regular Season Leaders (Cont.)
SINGLE SEASON

Scoring
Points

		Season	G	A	Pts
1	Wayne Gretzky, Edm	1985-86	52	163	215
2	Wayne Gretzky, Edm	1981-82	92	120	212
3	Wayne Gretzky, Edm	1984-85	73	135	208
4	Wayne Gretzky, Edm	1983-84	87	118	205
5	Mario Lemieux, Pit	1988-89	85	114	199
6	Wayne Gretzky, Edm	1982-83	71	125	196
7	Wayne Gretzky, Edm	1986-87	62	121	183
8	Mario Lemieux, Pit	1987-88	70	98	168
	Wayne Gretzky, LA	1988-89	54	114	168
10	Wayne Gretzky, Edm	1980-81	55	109	164
11	Wayne Gretzky, LA	1990-91	41	122	163
12	Mario Lemieux, Pit	1995-96	69	92	161
13	Mario Lemieux, Pit	1992-93	69	91	160
14	Steve Yzerman, Det	1988-89	65	90	155
15	Phil Esposito, Bos	1970-71	76	76	152
16	Bernie Nicholls, LA	1988-89	70	80	150
17	Jaromir Jagr, Pit	1995-96	62	87	149
	Wayne Gretzky, Edm	1987-88	40	109	149
19	Pat LaFontaine, Buf	1992-93	53	95	148
20	Mike Bossy, NYI	1981-82	64	83	147

WHA 150 points or more: 154—Marc Tardif, Que. (1977-78).

Goals

		Season	Gm	No
1	Wayne Gretzky, Edm	1981-82	80	92
2	Wayne Gretzky, Edm	1983-84	74	87
3	Brett Hull, St.L	1990-91	78	86
4	Mario Lemieux, Pit	1988-89	76	85
5	Alexander Mogilny, Buf.	1992-93	77	76
	Phil Esposito, Bos	1970-71	78	76
	Teemu Selanne, Win	1992-93	84	76
8	Wayne Gretzky, Edm	1984-85	80	73
9	Brett Hull, St.L	1989-90	80	72
10	Jari Kurri, Edm	1984-85	73	71
	Wayne Gretzky, Edm	1982-83	80	71
12	Brett Hull, St.L	1991-92	73	70
	Mario Lemieux, Pit	1987-88	77	70
	Bernie Nicholls, LA	1988-89	79	70
15	Mario Lemieux, Pit	1992-93	60	69
	Mario Lemieux, Pit	1995-96	70	69
	Mike Bossy, NYI	1978-79	80	69
18	Phil Esposito, Bos	1973-74	78	68
	Jari Kurri, Edm	1985-86	78	68
	Mike Bossy, NYI	1980-81	79	68

WHA 70 goals or more: 77—Bobby Hull, Win. (1974-75); 75—Real Cloutier, Que. (1978-79); 71—Marc Tardif, Que. (1975-76); 70—Anders Hedberg, Win. (1976-77).

Assists

		Season	Gm	No
1	Wayne Gretzky, Edm	1985-86	80	163
2	Wayne Gretzky, Edm	1984-85	80	135
3	Wayne Gretzky, Edm	1982-83	80	125
4	Wayne Gretzky, LA	1990-91	78	122
5	Wayne Gretzky, Edm	1986-87	79	121
6	Wayne Gretzky, Edm	1981-82	80	120
7	Wayne Gretzky, Edm	1983-84	74	118
8	Mario Lemieux, Pit	1988-89	76	114
	Wayne Gretzky, LA	1988-89	78	114
10	Wayne Gretzky, Edm	1987-88	64	109
	Wayne Gretzky, Edm	1980-81	80	109
12	Wayne Gretzky, LA	1989-90	73	102
	Bobby Orr, Bos	1970-71	78	102
14	Mario Lemieux, Pit	1987-88	77	98
15	Adam Oates, Bos	1992-93	84	97

WHA 95 assists or more: 106—Andre Lacroix, San Diego (1974-75).

Goaltending
Wins

		Season	Record
1	Martin Brodeur, NJ	2006-07	48-23-0
2	Bernie Parent, Phi	1973-74	47-13-12
	Roberto Luongo, Van	2006-07	47-22-0
4	**Evgeni Nabokov, SJ**	2007-08	46-21-8
5	Bernie Parent, Phi	1974-75	44-14-9
	Terry Sawchuk, Det	1950-51	44-13-13
	Terry Sawchuk, Det	1951-52	44-14-12
	Martin Brodeur, NJ	2007-08	44-27-6
9	Martin Brodeur, NJ	1999-00	43-20-8
	Martin Brodeur, NJ	1997-98	43-17-8
	Martin Brodeur, NJ	2005-06	43-23-0
	Tom Barrasso, Pit	1992-93	43-14-5
	Ed Belfour, Chi	1990-91	43-19-7

Most WHA wins in one season: 44—Richard Brodeur, Que. (1975-76).

Losses

		Season	Record
1	Gary Smith, Cal	1970-71	19-48-4
2	Al Rollins, Chi	1953-54	12-47-7
3	Peter Sidorkiewicz, Ott	1992-93	8-46-3
4	Harry Lumley, Chi	1951-52	17-44-9
5	Three tied with 41 losses each.		

Most WHA losses in one season: 36—Don McLeod, Van. (1974-75) and Andy Brown, Ind. (1974-75).

Shutouts

		Season	Gm	No
1	George Hainsworth, Mon	1928-29	44	22
2	Alex Connell, Ott	1925-26	36	15
	Alex Connell, Ott	1927-28	44	15
	Hal Winkler, Bos	1927-28	44	15
	Tony Esposito, Chi	1969-70	63	15

Most WHA shutouts in one season: 5—Gerry Cheevers, Cle. (1972-73) and Joe Daly, Win. (1975-76).

Goals Against Average
Before 1950

		Season	Gm	GAA
1	George Hainsworth, Mon	1928-29	44	0.98
2	George Hainsworth, Mon	1927-28	44	1.09
3	Alex Connell, Ott	1925-26	36	1.17
4	Tiny Thompson, Bos	1928-29	44	1.18
5	Roy Worters, NY Americans	1928-29	38	1.21

Since 1950

		Season	Gm	GAA
1	Miikka Kiprusoff, Calg	2003-04	38	1.69
2	Marty Turco, Dal	2002-03	55	1.72
3	Tony Esposito, Chi	1971-72	48	1.77
4	Al Rollins, Tor	1950-51	40	1.77
5	Ron Tugnutt, Ott	1998-99	43	1.79

Penalty Minutes

		Season	PM
1	Dave Schultz, Phi	1974-75	472
2	Paul Baxter, Pit	1981-82	409
3	Mike Peluso, Chi	1991-92	408
4	Dave Schultz, LA-Pit	1977-78	405
5	Marty McSorley, LA	1992-93	399
6	Bob Probert, Det	1987-88	398
7	Basil McRae, Min	1987-88	382
8	Joey Kocur, Det	1985-86	377
9	Tim Hunter, Calg	1988-89	375
10	Donald Brashear, Van	1997-98	372

WHA 355 minutes or more: 365—Curt Brackenbury, Min-Que. (1975-76).

SINGLE GAME

Points

	Date	G-A—Pts
Darryl Sittler, Tor vs Bos	2/7/76	6-4—10
Maurice Richard, Mon vs Det	12/28/44	5-3— 8
Bert Olmstead, Mon vs Chi	1/9/54	4-4— 8
Tom Bladon, Phi vs Cle	12/11/77	4-4— 8
Bryan Trottier, NYI vs NYR	12/23/78	5-3— 8
Peter Stastny, Que at Wash	2/22/81	4-4— 8
Anton Stastny, Que at Wash	2/22/81	3-5— 8
Wayne Gretzky, Edm vs NJ	11/19/83	3-5— 8
Wayne Gretzky, Edm vs Min	1/4/84	4-4— 8
Paul Coffey, Edm vs Det	3/14/86	2-6— 8
Mario Lemieux, Pit vs St.L	10/15/88	2-6— 8
Bernie Nicholls, LA vs Tor	12/1/88	2-6— 8
Mario Lemieux, Pit vs NJ	12/31/88	5-3— 8

Goals

	Date	No
Joe Malone, Que vs Tor	1/31/20	7
Newsy Lalonde, Mon vs Tor	1/10/20	6
Joe Malone, Que vs Ott	3/10/20	6
Corb Denneny, Tor vs Ham	1/26/21	6
Cy Denneny, Ott vs Ham	3/7/21	6
Syd Howe, Det vs NYR	2/3/44	6
Red Berenson, St.L at Phi	11/7/68	6
Darryl Sittler, Tor vs Bos	2/7/76	6

Assists

	Date	No
Billy Taylor, Det at Chi	3/16/47	7
Wayne Gretzky, Edm vs Wash	2/15/80	7
Wayne Gretzky, Edm at Chi	12/11/85	7
Wayne Gretzky, Edm vs Que	2/14/86	7
24 players tied with 6 each.		

Penalty Minutes

	Date	Min
Randy Holt, LA at Phi	3/11/79	67
Brad Smith, Tor vs Det	11/15/86	57
Reed Low, St.L at Calg	2/28/02	57
Frank Bathe, Phi vs LA	3/11/79	55
Reed Low, St.L at Det	12/31/02	53
Russ Anderson, Pit vs Edm	1/19/80	51

Penalties

	Date	No
Chris Nilan, Bos vs Har	3/31/91	10*
Nine tied with 9 each.		

* Nilan accumulated six minors, two majors, one 10-minute misconduct and one game misconduct.

All-Time Winningest NHL Coaches

Top 20 NHL career victories through the 2007-08 season. Career, regular season and playoff records are noted along with NHL titles won. Coaches active during 2007-08 season in **bold** type. In the following tables, overtime and shootout losses are considered losses.

		Career				Regular Season				Playoffs				
		Yrs	W	L	T	Pct	W	L	T	Pct	W	L	T	Pct	Stanley Cups
1	Scotty Bowman	30	**1467**	714	313	.651	1244	584	313	.654	223	130	0	.632	9 (1973, 76-79, 92, 97-98, 2002)
2	**Al Arbour**	23	**905**	663	248	.567	782	577	248	.564	123	86	0	.589	4 (1980-83)
3	Dick Irvin	26	**790**	609	228	.556	690	521	226	.559	100	88	2	.532	4 (1932,44,46,53)
4	Pat Quinn	19	**751**	596	154	.552	657	507	154	.557	94	89	0	.514	None
5	**Mike Keenan**	19	**720**	604	147	.539	626	531	147	.536	94	73	0	.563	1 (1994)
6	**Bryan Murray**	17	**672**	548	131	.546	620	488	131	.553	52	60	0	.464	None
7	Billy Reay	16	**599**	445	175	.563	542	385	175	.571	57	60	0	.487	None
8	Glen Sather	13	**586**	351	122	.611	497	314	121	.598	89	37	1	.705	4 (1984-85,87-88)
9	Toe Blake	13	**582**	292	159	.640	500	255	159	.634	82	37	0	.689	8 (1956-60,65-66,68)
10	Pat Burns	14	**579**	438	151	.560	501	367	151	.566	78	71	0	.523	1 (2003)
11	**Ron Wilson**	14	**565**	520	101	.519	518	472	101	.521	47	48	0	.495	None
12	**Jacques Lemaire**	14	**560**	477	124	.536	500	425	124	.536	60	52	0	.536	1 (1995)
13	**Jacques Martin**	14	**555**	509	119	.519	517	462	119	.525	38	47	0	.447	None
14	**Ken Hitchcock**	12	**536**	394	88	.570	470	343	88	.570	66	51	0	.564	1 (1999)
15	**Marc Crawford**	13	**513**	454	103	.528	470	414	103	.528	43	40	0	.518	1 (1996)
16	Roger Neilson	17	**511**	436	159	.534	460	381	159	.540	51	55	0	.481	None
17	**Joel Quenneville**	11	**480**	370	77	.559	438	325	77	.567	42	45	0	.483	None
18	Brian Sutter	13	**479**	477	140	.501	451	437	140	.507	28	40	0	.412	None
19	Jack Adams	21	**465**	442	162	.511	413	390	161	.512	52	52	1	.500	3 (1936-37, 43)
20	Jacques Demers	14	**464**	510	130	.479	409	467	130	.471	55	43	0	.561	1 (1993)

Where They Coached

Adams—Toronto (1922-23), Detroit (1927-47); **Arbour**—St. Louis (1970-73), NY Islanders (1973-86,88-94,2007*); **Blake**—Montreal (1955-68); **Bowman**—St. Louis (1967-71), Montreal (1971-79), Buffalo (1979-87), Pittsburgh (1991-93), Detroit (1993-2002); **Burns**—Montreal (1988-92), Toronto (1992-96), Boston (1997-2000), New Jersey (2002-05); **Crawford**—Quebec/Colorado (1994-98), Vancouver (98-2006), Los Angeles (2006-08); **Demers**—Quebec (1979-80), St. Louis (1983-86), Detroit (1986-90), Montreal (1992-95), Tampa Bay (1997-99).

    Hitchcock—Dallas (1996-2002), Philadelphia (2002-06), Columbus (2006-); **Irvin**—Chicago (1930-31,55-56), Toronto (1931-40), Montreal (1940-55); **Keenan**—Philadelphia (1984-88), Chicago (1988-92), NY Rangers (1993-94), St. Louis (1994-96), Vancouver (1997-99), Boston (2000-01), Florida (2001-03), Calgary (2007-); **Lemaire**— Montreal (1984-85), New Jersey (1993-98), Minnesota (2000-); **Martin**—St. Louis (1986-88), Ottawa (1995-2004), Florida (2004-08); **Murray**—Washington (1982-90), Detroit (1990-93), Florida (1997-98), Anaheim (2001-02), Ottawa (2004-07,08).

    Neilson—Toronto (1977-79), Buffalo (1979-81), Vancouver (1982-83), Los Angeles (1984), NY Rangers (1989-93), Florida (1993-95), Philadelphia (1998-00), Ottawa (2002); **Quenneville**—St. Louis (1996-2004), Colorado (2005-2008); **Quinn**—Philadelphia (1978-82), Los Angeles (1984-87), Vancouver (1990-94, 96), Toronto (1998-2006); **Reay**—Toronto (1957-59), Chicago (1963-77); **Sather**—Edmonton (1979-89, 93-94), NY Rangers (2003-04); **B. Sutter**—St. Louis (1988-92), Boston (1992-95), Calgary (1997-2000), Chicago (2001-05); **Wilson**—Anaheim (1993-97), Washington (1997-2002), San Jose (2002-08), Toronto (2008-).

    Note: Arbour returned to the bench for one game on Nov. 3, 2007 to coach his 1,500th game for the Islanders.

Top Winning Percentages

Minimum of 275 victories, including playoffs.

		Yrs	W	L	T	Pct.
1	Scotty Bowman	30	1467	714	313	.651
2	Toe Blake	13	582	292	159	.640
3	Glen Sather	13	586	351	122	.611
4	Fred Shero	10	451	272	119	.606
5	Don Cherry	6	281	177	77	.597
6	Tommy Ivan	9	324	205	111	.593
7	Ken Hitchcock	12	536	394	88	.570
8	Al Arbour	23	905	663	248	.567
9	Billy Reay	16	599	445	175	.563
10	Emile Francis	13	433	326	112	.561
11	Joel Quenneville	11	480	370	77	.559
12	Bob Hartley	9	378	295	61	.557
13	Pat Burns	14	579	438	151	.560
14	Hap Day	10	308	237	81	.557
15	Dick Irvin	26	790	609	228	.556
16	Lester Patrick	13	312	242	115	.552
17	Art Ross	18	393	310	95	.552
18	Pat Quinn	19	751	596	154	.552
19	Bob Johnson	6	275	223	58	.547
20	Bryan Murray	17	672	548	131	.546
21	Terry Murray	11	406	331	89	.545
22	Mike Keenan	19	720	604	147	.539
23	Lindy Ruff	10	449	381	78	.537
24	Jacques Lemaire	14	560	477	124	.536
25	Roger Neilson	16	511	436	159	.534
26	Punch Imlach	15	439	384	148	.528
27	Marc Crawford	13	513	454	103	.528
28	Darryl Sutter	11	456	404	101	.527
29	Jacques Martin	14	555	509	119	.519
30	Ron Wilson	14	565	520	101	.519

Active Coaches' Victories

Records through 2007-08 season, including playoffs.

		Yrs	W	L	T	Pct.
1	Mike Keenan, Calg.	19	720	604	147	.539
2	Ron Wilson, Tor	14	565	520	101	.519
3	Jacques Lemaire, Min.	14	560	477	124	.536
4	Ken Hitchcock, Clb.	12	536	394	88	.570
5	Lindy Ruff, Buf.	10	449	381	78	.537
6	Terry Murray, LA	11	406	331	89	.545
7	Barry Trotz, Nash.	9	330	370	60	.474
8	Andy Murray, St.L	7	285	297	58	.491
9	Craig MacTavish, Edm.	7	282	281	47	.501
10	Mike Babcock, Det.	7	274	184	19	.594
11	Dave Tippett, Dal.	5	256	173	28	.591
12	Peter Laviolette, Car.	6	252	222	25	.530
13	Alain Vigneault, Van.	6	206	211	35	.494
	Michel Therrien, Pit.	6	206	213	23	.492
15	Craig Hartsburg, Ott.	6	192	202	69	.489
16	Tom Renney, NYR	6	183	199	9	.480
17	Claude Julien, Bos	5	167	161	11	.509
18	Randy Carlyle, Ana.	3	165	124	0	.571
19	Wayne Gretzky, Pho.	3	107	139	0	.435
20	Guy Carbonneau, Mon.	2	94	82	0	.534
21	Barry Melrose, TB	3	92	112	29	.457
22	Tony Granato, Col	2	81	53	17	.593
23	John Stevens, Phi	2	72	101	0	.416
24	Denis Savard, Chi.	2	64	79	0	.448
25	Brent Sutter, NJ	1	47	40	0	.540
26	Bruce Boudreau, Wash.	1	40	28	0	.588
27	John Anderson, Atl	0	0	0	0	.000
	Peter DeBoer, Fla.	0	0	0	0	.000
	Scott Gordon, NYI	0	0	0*	0	.000
	Todd McLellan, SJ	0	0	0	0	.000

Annual Awards

Hart Memorial Trophy

Awarded to the player "adjudged to be the most valuable to his team" and named after Cecil Hart, the former manager-coach of the Montreal Canadiens. Winners selected by Pro Hockey Writers Assn. (PHWA). Winners' scoring statistics or goaltender W-L records and goals against average are provided; (*) indicates led or tied for league lead.

Multiple winners: Wayne Gretzky (9); Gordie Howe (6); Eddie Shore (4); Bobby Clarke, Mario Lemieux, Howie Morenz and Bobby Orr (3); Jean Beliveau, Bill Cowley, Phil Esposito, Dominik Hasek, Bobby Hull, Guy Lafleur, Mark Messier, Stan Mikita and Nels Stewart (2).

Year		G	A	Pts	Year		G	A	Pts
1924	Frank Nighbor, Ottawa, C	10	3	13	1952	Gordie Howe, Det., RW	47	39	86*
1925	Billy Burch, Hamilton, C	20	4	24	1953	Gordie Howe, Det., RW	49	46	95*
1926	Nels Stewart, Maroons, C	34	8	42*	1954	Al Rollins, Chi., G	12-47-7;		3.23
1927	Herb Gardiner, Mon., D	6	6	12	1955	Ted Kennedy, Tor., C	10	42	52
1928	Howie Morenz, Mon., C	33	18	51	1956	Jean Beliveau, Mon., C	47	41	88
1929	Roy Worters, NYA, G	16-13-9;		1.21	1957	Gordie Howe, Det.,RW	44	45	89*
1930	Nels Stewart, Maroons, C	39	16	55	1958	Gordie Howe, Det., RW	33	44	77
1931	Howie Morenz, Mon., C	28	23	51*	1959	Andy Bathgate, NYR, RW	40	48	88
1932	Howie Morenz, Mon., C	24	25	49	1960	Gordie Howe., Det., RW	28	45	73
1933	Eddie Shore, Bos., D	8	27	35	1961	Bernie Geoffrion, Mon., RW	50	45	95*
1934	Aurel Joliat, Mon., LW	22	15	37	1962	Jacques Plante, Mon., G	42-14-14;		2.37*
1935	Eddie Shore, Bos., D	7	26	33	1963	Gordie Howe, Det., RW	38	48	86*
1936	Eddie Shore, Bos., D	3	16	19	1964	Jean Beliveau, Mon., C	28	50	78
1937	Babe Siebert, Mon., D	8	20	28	1965	Bobby Hull, Chi., LW	39	32	71
1938	Eddie Shore, Bos., D	3	14	17	1966	Bobby Hull, Chi., LW	54	43	97*
1939	Toe Blake, Mon., LW	24	23	47*	1967	Stan Mikita, Chi., C	35	62	97*
1940	Ebbie Goodfellow, Det., C	11	17	28	1968	Stan Mikita, Chi., C	40	47	87*
1941	Bill Cowley, Bos., C	17	45	62*	1969	Phil Esposito, Bos., C	49	77	126*
1942	Tommy Anderson, NYA, D	12	29	41	1970	Bobby Orr, Bos., D	33	87	120*
1943	Bill Cowley, Bos., C	27	45	72	1971	Bobby Orr, Bos., D	37	102	139
1944	Babe Pratt, Tor., D	17	40	57	1972	Bobby Orr, Bos., D	37	80	117
1945	Elmer Lach, Mon., C	26	54	80*	1973	Bobby Clarke, Phi., C	37	67	104
1946	Max Bentley, Chi., C	31	30	61*	1974	Phil Esposito, Bos., C	68	77	145*
1947	Maurice Richard, Mon., RW	45	26	71	1975	Bobby Clarke, Phi., C	27	89	116
1948	Buddy O'Connor, NYR, C	24	36	60	1976	Bobby Clarke, Phi., C	30	89	119
1949	Sid Abel, Det., C	28	26	54	1977	Guy Lafleur, Mon., RW	56	80	136*
1950	Chuck Rayner, NYR, G	28-30-11;		2.62	1978	Guy Lafleur, Mon., RW	60	72	132*
1951	Milt Schmidt, Bos., C	22	39	61	1979	Bryan Trottier, NYI., C	47	87	134*

Year		G	A	Pts	Year		G	A	Pts
1980	Wayne Gretzky, Edm., C	51	86	137*	1994	Sergei Fedorov, Det., C	56	64	120
1981	Wayne Gretzky, Edm., C	55	109	164*	1995	Eric Lindros, Phi., C	29	41	70*
1982	Wayne Gretzky, Edm., C	92	120	212*	1996	Mario Lemieux, Pit., C	69	92	161*
1983	Wayne Gretzky, Edm., C	71	125	196*	1997	Dominik Hasek, Buf., G	37-20-10;		2.27
1984	Wayne Gretzky, Edm., C	87	118	205*	1998	Dominik Hasek, Buf., G	33-23-13;		2.09
1985	Wayne Gretzky, Edm., C	73	135	208*	1999	Jaromir Jagr, Pit., RW	44	83	127*
1986	Wayne Gretzky, Edm., C	52	163	215*	2000	Chris Pronger, St.L, D	14	48	62
1987	Wayne Gretzky, Edm., C	62	121	183*	2001	Joe Sakic, Col., C	54	64	118
1988	Mario Lemieux, Pit., C	70	98	168*	2002	Jose Theodore, Mon., G	30-24-10;		2.11
1989	Wayne Gretzky, LA, C	54	114	168	2003	Peter Forsberg, Col., C	29	77	106*
1990	Mark Messier, Edm., C	45	84	129	2004	Martin St. Louis, TB, RW	38	56	94*
1991	Brett Hull, St. L., RW	86	45	131	2006	Joe Thornton, Bos-SJ, C	29	96	125*
1992	Mark Messier, NYR, C	35	72	107	2007	Sidney Crosby, Pit., C	36	84	120*
1993	Mario Lemieux, Pit., C	69	91	160*	2008	Alex Ovechkin, Wash., L	65	47	112*

Calder Memorial Trophy

Awarded to the most outstanding rookie of the year and named after Frank Calder, the late NHL president (1917-43). Since the 1990-91 season, all eligible candidates must not have attained their 26th birthday by Sept. 15 of their rookie year. Winners selected by PHWA. Winners' scoring statistics or goaltender W-L record & goals against average are provided.

Year		G	A	Pts	Year		G	A	Pts
1933	Carl Voss, NYR-Det., C	8	15	23	1971	Gilbert Perreault, Buf., C	38	34	72
1934	Russ Blinco, Maroons, C	14	9	23	1972	Ken Dryden, Mon., G	39-8-15;		2.24
1935	Sweeney Schriner, NYA, LW	18	22	40	1973	Steve Vickers, NYR, LW	30	23	53
1936	Mike Karakas, Chi., G	21-19-8;		1.92	1974	Denis Potvin, NYI, D	17	37	54
1937	Syl Apps, Tor., C	16	29	45	1975	Eric Vail, Atl., LW	39	21	60
1938	Cully Dahlstrom, Chi., C	10	9	19	1976	Bryan Trottier, NYI, C	32	63	95
1939	Frankie Brimsek, Bos., G	33-9-1;		1.58	1977	Willi Plett, Atl., RW	33	23	56
1940	Kilby MacDonald, NYR, LW	15	13	28	1978	Mike Bossy, NYI, RW	53	38	91
1941	John Quilty, Mon., C	18	16	34	1979	Bobby Smith, Min., C	30	44	74
1942	Knobby Warwick, NYR, RW	16	17	33	1980	Ray Bourque, Bos., D	17	48	65
1943	Gaye Stewart, Tor., LW	24	23	47	1981	Peter Stastny, Que., C	39	70	109
1944	Gus Bodnar, Tor., C	22	40	62	1982	Dale Hawerchuk, Win., C	45	58	103
1945	Frank McCool, Tor., G	24-22-4;		3.22	1983	Steve Larmer, Chi., RW	43	47	90
1946	Edgar Laprade, NYR, C	15	19	34	1984	Tom Barrasso, Buf., G	26-12-3;		2.84
1947	Howie Meeker, Tor., RW	27	18	45	1985	Mario Lemieux, Pit., C	43	57	100
1948	Jim McFadden, Det., C	24	24	48	1986	Gary Suter, Calg., D	18	50	68
1949	Penny Lund, NYR, RW	14	16	30	1987	Luc Robitaille, LA, LW	45	39	84
1950	Jack Gelineau, Bos., G	22-30-15;		3.28	1988	Joe Nieuwendyk, Calg., C	51	41	92
1951	Terry Sawchuk, Det., G	44-13-13;		1.99	1989	Brian Leetch, NYR, D	23	48	71
1952	Bernie Geoffrion, Mon., RW	30	24	54	1990	Sergei Makarov, Calg., RW	24	62	86
1953	Gump Worsley, NYR, G	13-29-8;		3.06	1991	Ed Belfour, Chi., G	43-19-7;		2.47
1954	Camille Henry, NYR, LW	24	15	39	1992	Pavel Bure, Van., RW	34	26	60
1955	Ed Litzenberger, Mon-Chi., RW	23	28	51	1993	Teemu Selanne, Win., RW	76	56	132
1956	Glenn Hall, Det., G	30-24-16;		2.11	1994	Martin Brodeur, NJ, G	27-11-8;		2.40
1957	Larry Regan, Bos., RW	14	19	33	1995	Peter Forsberg, Que., C	15	35	50
1958	Frank Mahovlich, Tor., LW	20	16	36	1996	Daniel Alfredsson, Ott., RW	26	35	61
1959	Ralph Backstrom, Mon., C	18	22	40	1997	Bryan Berard, NYI, D	8	40	48
1960	Billy Hay, Chi., C	18	37	55	1998	Sergei Samsonov, Bos., LW	22	25	47
1961	Dave Keon, Tor., C	20	25	45	1999	Chris Drury, Col., C	20	24	44
1962	Bobby Rousseau, Mon., RW	21	24	45	2000	Scott Gomez, NJ, C	19	51	70
1963	Kent Douglas, Tor., D	7	15	22	2001	Evgeni Nabokov, SJ, G	32-21-7;		2.19
1964	Jacques Laperriere, Mon., D	2	28	30	2002	Dany Heatley, Atl., RW	26	41	67
1965	Roger Crozier, Det., G	40-23-7;		2.42	2003	Barret Jackman, St.L, D	3	16	19
1966	Brit Selby, Tor., LW	14	13	27	2004	Andrew Raycroft, Bos., G	29-18-9;		2.05
1967	Bobby Orr, Bos., D	13	28	41	2006	Alex Ovechkin, Wash., L	52	54	106
1968	Derek Sanderson, Bos., C	24	25	49	2007	Evgeni Malkin, Pit., C	33	52	85
1969	Danny Grant, Min., LW	34	31	65	2008	Patrick Kane, Chi., R	21	51	72
1970	Tony Esposito, Chi., G	38-17-8;		2.17					

Vezina Trophy

From 1927-80, given to the principal goaltender(s) on the team allowing the fewest goals during the regular season. Trophy named after 1920's great Georges Vezina of the Montreal Canadiens, who died of tuberculosis in 1926. Since the 1980-81 season, the trophy has been awarded to the most outstanding goaltender of the year as selected by the league's general managers.

Multiple Winners: Jacques Plante (7, one of them shared); Bill Durnan and Dominik Hasek (6); Ken Dryden (5, three shared); Bunny Larocque (4, all shared); Terry Sawchuk (4, one shared); Martin Brodeur and Tiny Thompson (4); Tony Esposito (3, one shared); George Hainsworth (3); Glenn Hall (3, two shared); Patrick Roy (3); Ed Belfour (2); Johnny Bower (2, one shared); Frankie Brimsek (2); Turk Broda (2); Chuck Gardiner (2); Charlie Hodge (2, one shared); Bernie Parent (2, one shared); Gump Worsley (2, both shared).

Year		Record	GAA	Year		Record	GAA
1927	George Hainsworth, Mon	28-14-2	1.52	1930	Tiny Thompson, Bos	38-5-1	2.23
1928	George Hainsworth, Mon	26-11-7	1.09	1931	Roy Worters, NYA	18-16-10	1.68
1929	George Hainsworth, Mon	22-7-15	0.98	1932	Chuck Gardiner, Chi	18-19-11	1.92

Year		Record	GAA	Year		Record	GAA
1933	Tiny Thompson, Bos	25-15-8	1.83	1972	Tony Esposito, Chi	31-10-6	1.77
1934	Chuck Gardiner, Chi	20-17-11	1.73		& Gary Smith, Chi	14-5-6	2.42
1935	Lorne Chabot, Chi	26-17-5	1.83	1973	Ken Dryden, Mon	33-7-13	2.26
1936	Tiny Thompson, Bos	22-20-6	1.71	1974	(Tie) Bernie Parent, Phi	47-13-12	1.89
1937	Norm Smith, Det	25-14-9	2.13		Tony Esposito, Chi	34-14-21	2.04
1938	Tiny Thompson, Bos	30-11-7	1.85	1975	Bernie Parent, Phi	44-14-10	2.03
1939	Frankie Brimsek, Bos	33-9-1	1.58	1976	Ken Dryden, Mon	42-10-8	2.03
1940	Dave Kerr, NYR	27-11-10	1.60	1977	Ken Dryden, Mon	41-6-8	2.14
1941	Turk Broda, Tor	28-14-6	2.06		& Bunny Larocque, Mon	19-2-4	2.09
1942	Frankie Brimsek, Bos	24-17-6	2.45	1978	Ken Dryden, Mon	37-7-7	2.05
1943	John Mowers, Det	25-14-11	2.47		& Bunny Larocque, Mon	22-3-4	2.67
1944	Bill Durnan, Mon	38-5-7	2.18	1979	Ken Dryden, Mon	30-10-7	2.30
1945	Bill Durnan, Mon	38-8-4	2.42		& Bunny Larocque, Mon	22-7-4	2.84
1946	Bill Durnan, Mon	24-11-5	2.60	1980	Bob Sauve, Buf	20-8-4	2.36
1947	Bill Durnan, Mon	34-16-10	2.30		& Don Edwards, Buf.	27-9-12	2.57
1948	Turk Broda, Tor	32-15-13	2.38	1981	Richard Sevigny, Mon	20-4-3	2.40
1949	Bill Durnan, Mon	28-23-9	2.10		Denis Herron, Mon.	6-9-6	3.50
1950	Bill Durnan, Mon	26-21-17	2.20		& Bunny Larocque, Mon.	16-9-3	3.03
1951	Al Rollins, Tor.	27-5-8	1.77	1982	Billy Smith, NYI	32-9-4	2.97
1952	Terry Sawchuk, Det.	44-14-12	1.90	1983	Pete Peeters, Bos	40-11-9	2.36
1953	Terry Sawchuk, Det.	32-15-16	1.90	1984	Tom Barrasso, Buf.	26-12-3	2.84
1954	Harry Lumley, Tor	32-24-13	1.86	1985	Pelle Lindbergh, Phi	40-17-7	3.02
1955	Terry Sawchuk, Det.	40-17-11	1.96	1986	John Vanbiesbrouck, NYR	31-21-5	3.32
1956	Jacques Plante, Mon.	42-12-10	1.86	1987	Ron Hextall, Phi	37-21-6	3.00
1957	Jacques Plante, Mon.	31-18-12	2.02	1988	Grant Fuhr, Edm.	40-24-9	3.43
1958	Jacques Plante, Mon.	34-14-8	2.11	1989	Patrick Roy, Mon	33-5-6	2.47
1959	Jacques Plante, Mon.	38-16-13	2.16	1990	Patrick Roy, Mon	31-16-5	2.53
1960	Jacques Plante, Mon.	40-17-12	2.54	1991	Ed Belfour, Chi.	43-19-7	2.47
1961	Johnny Bower, Tor	33-15-10	2.50	1992	Patrick Roy, Mon	36-22-8	2.36
1962	Jacques Plante, Mon.	42-14-14	2.37	1993	Ed Belfour, Chi.	41-18-11	2.59
1963	Glenn Hall, Chi	30-20-16	2.55	1994	Dominik Hasek, Buf	30-20-6	1.95
1964	Charlie Hodge, Mon	33-18-11	2.26	1995	Dominik Hasek, Buf	19-14-7	2.11
1965	Johnny Bower, Tor	13-13-8	2.38	1996	Jim Carey, Wash	35-24-9	2.26
	& Terry Sawchuk, Tor	17-13-6	2.56	1997	Dominik Hasek, Buf	37-20-10	2.27
1966	Gump Worsley, Mon	29-14-6	2.36	1998	Dominik Hasek, Buf	33-23-13	2.09
	& Charlie Hodge, Mon	12-7-2	2.58	1999	Dominik Hasek, Buf	30-18-14	1.87
1967	Glenn Hall, Chi	19-5-5	2.38	2000	Olaf Kolzig, Wash	41-20-11	2.24
	& Denis Dejordy, Chi	22-12-7	2.46	2001	Dominik Hasek, Buf	37-24-4	2.11
1968	Gump Worsley, Mon	19-9-8	1.98	2002	Jose Theodore, Mon.	30-24-10	2.11
	& Rogie Vachon, Mon	23-13-2	2.48	2003	Martin Brodeur, N.J.	41-23-9	2.02
1969	Jacques Plante, St.L	18-12-6	1.96	2004	Martin Brodeur, N.J.	38-26-11	2.03
	& Glenn Hall, St.L	19-12-8	2.17	2006	Miikka Kiprusoff, Calg	42-20-11	2.07
1970	Tony Esposito, Chi	38-17-8	2.17	2007	Martin Brodeur, N.J.	48-23-7	2.18
1971	Ed Giacomin, NYR	27-10-7	2.16	2008	Martin Brodeur, N.J.	44-27-6	2.17
	& Gilles Villemure, NYR	22-8-4	2.30				

Lady Byng Memorial Trophy

Awarded to the player "adjudged to have exhibited the best type of sportsmanship and gentlemanly conduct combined with a high standard of playing ability" and named after Lady Evelyn Byng, the wife of former Canadian Governor General (1921-26) Baron Byng of Vimy. Winners selected by PHWA.

Multiple winners: Frank Boucher (7); Wayne Gretzky (5); Red Kelly (4); Bobby Bauer, Mike Bossy, Pavel Datsyuk, Alex Delvecchio and Ron Francis (3); Johnny Bucyk, Marcel Dionne, Paul Kariya, Dave Keon, Joey Mullen, Frank Nighbor, Jean Ratelle, Clint Smith and Sid Smith (2). **Note:** Bill Quackenbush and Red Kelly are the only defensemen to win.

Year		Year		Year	
1925	Frank Nighbor, Ott., C	1944	Clint Smith, Chi., C	1963	Dave Keon, Tor., C
1926	Frank Nighbor, Ott., C	1945	Bill Mosienko, Chi., RW	1964	Ken Wharram, Chi., RW
1927	Billy Burch, NYA, C	1946	Toe Blake, Mon., LW	1965	Bobby Hull, Chi., LW
1928	Frank Boucher, NYR, C	1947	Bobby Bauer, Bos., RW	1966	Alex Delvecchio, Det., LW
1929	Frank Boucher, NYR, C	1948	Buddy O'Connor, NYR, C	1967	Stan Mikita, Chi., C
1930	Frank Boucher, NYR, C	1949	Bill Quackenbush, Det., D	1968	Stan Mikita, Chi., C
1931	Frank Boucher, NYR, C	1950	Edgar Laprade, NYR, C	1969	Alex Delvecchio, Det., LW
1932	Joe Primeau, Tor., C	1951	Red Kelly, Det., D	1970	Phil Goyette, St.L., C
1933	Frank Boucher, NYR, C	1952	Sid Smith, Tor., LW	1971	Johnny Bucyk, Bos., LW
1934	Frank Boucher, NYR, C	1953	Red Kelly, Det., D	1972	Jean Ratelle, NYR, C
1935	Frank Boucher, NYR, C	1954	Red Kelly, Det., D	1973	Gilbert Perreault, Buf., C
1936	Doc Romnes, Chi., F	1955	Sid Smith, Tor., LW	1974	Johnny Bucyk, Bos., LW
1937	Marty Barry, Det., C	1956	Earl Reibel, Det., C	1975	Marcel Dionne, Det., C
1938	Gordie Drillon, Tor., RW	1957	Andy Hebenton, NYR, RW	1976	Jean Ratelle, NY-Bos., C
1939	Clint Smith, NYR, C	1958	Camille Henry, NYR, LW	1977	Marcel Dionne, LA, C
1940	Bobby Bauer, Bos., RW	1959	Alex Delvecchio, Det., LW	1978	Butch Goring, LA, C
1941	Bobby Bauer, Bos., RW	1960	Don McKenney, Bos., C	1979	Bob MacMillan, Atl., RW
1942	Syl Apps, Tor., C	1961	Red Kelly, Tor., D	1980	Wayne Gretzky, Edm., C
1943	Max Bentley, Chi., C	1962	Dave Keon, Tor., C	1981	Rick Kehoe, Pit., RW

Year		Year		Year	
1982	Rick Middleton, Bos., RW	1991	Wayne Gretzky, LA, C	2000	Pavol Demitra, St.L., RW
1983	Mike Bossy, NYI, RW	1992	Wayne Gretzky, LA, C	2001	Joe Sakic, Col., C
1984	Mike Bossy, NYI, RW	1993	Pierre Turgeon, NYI, C	2002	Ron Francis, Car., C
1985	Jari Kurri, Edm., RW	1994	Wayne Gretzky, LA, C	2003	Alexander Mogilny, Tor., RW
1986	Mike Bossy, NYI, RW	1995	Ron Francis, Pit., C	2004	Brad Richards, TB, C
1987	Joey Mullen, Calg., RW	1996	Paul Kariya, Ana., LW	2006	Pavel Datsyuk, Det., C
1988	Mats Naslund, Mon., LW	1997	Paul Kariya, Ana., LW	2007	Pavel Datsyuk, Det., C
1989	Joey Mullen, Calg., RW	1998	Ron Francis, Pit., C	2008	Pavel Datsyuk, Det., C
1990	Brett Hull, St.L., RW	1999	Wayne Gretzky, NYR, C		

James Norris Memorial Trophy

Awarded to the most outstanding defenseman of the year and named after James Norris, the late Detroit Red Wings owner-president. Winners selected by PHWA.

Multiple winners: Bobby Orr (8); Doug Harvey (7); Nicklas Lidstrom (6); Ray Bourque (5); Chris Chelios, Paul Coffey, Pierre Pilote and Denis Potvin (3); Rod Langway, Brian Leetch and Larry Robinson (2).

Year		Year		Year	
1954	Red Kelly, Detroit	1972	Bobby Orr, Boston	1990	Ray Bourque, Boston
1955	Doug Harvey, Montreal	1973	Bobby Orr, Boston	1991	Ray Bourque, Boston
1956	Doug Harvey, Montreal	1974	Bobby Orr, Boston	1992	Brian Leetch, NY Rangers
1957	Doug Harvey, Montreal	1975	Bobby Orr, Boston	1993	Chris Chelios, Chicago
1958	Doug Harvey, Montreal	1976	Denis Potvin, NY Islanders	1994	Ray Bourque, Boston
1959	Tom Johnson, Montreal	1977	Larry Robinson, Montreal	1995	Paul Coffey, Detroit
1960	Doug Harvey, Montreal	1978	Denis Potvin, NY Islanders	1996	Chris Chelios, Chicago
1961	Doug Harvey, Montreal	1979	Denis Potvin, NY Islanders	1997	Brian Leetch, NY Rangers
1962	Doug Harvey, NY Rangers	1980	Larry Robinson, Montreal	1998	Rob Blake, Los Angeles
1963	Pierre Pilote, Chicago	1981	Randy Carlyle, Pittsburgh	1999	Al MacInnis, St. Louis
1964	Pierre Pilote, Chicago	1982	Doug Wilson, Chicago	2000	Chris Pronger, St. Louis
1965	Pierre Pilote, Chicago	1983	Rod Langway, Washington	2001	Nicklas Lidstrom, Detroit
1966	Jacques Laperriere, Montreal	1984	Rod Langway, Washington	2002	Nicklas Lidstrom, Detroit
1967	Harry Howell, NY Rangers	1985	Paul Coffey, Edmonton	2003	Nicklas Lidstrom, Detroit
1968	Bobby Orr, Boston	1986	Paul Coffey, Edmonton	2004	Scott Niedermayer, NJ
1969	Bobby Orr, Boston	1987	Ray Bourque, Boston	2006	Nicklas Lidstrom, Detroit
1970	Bobby Orr, Boston	1988	Ray Bourque, Boston	2007	Nicklas Lidstrom, Detroit
1971	Bobby Orr, Boston	1989	Chris Chelios, Montreal	2008	Nicklas Lidstrom, Detroit

Frank Selke Trophy

Awarded to the outstanding defensive forward of the year and named after the late Montreal Canadiens general manager. Winners selected by the PHWA. **Multiple winners:** Bob Gainey (4); Guy Carbonneau and Jere Lehtinen (3); Rod Brind'Amour, Sergei Fedorov and Michael Peca (2).

Year		Year		Year	
1978	Bob Gainey, Mon., LW	1988	Guy Carbonneau, Mon., C	1998	Jere Lehtinen, Dal., RW
1979	Bob Gainey, Mon., LW	1989	Guy Carbonneau, Mon., C	1999	Jere Lehtinen, Dal., RW
1980	Bob Gainey, Mon., LW	1990	Rick Meagher, St.L., C	2000	Steve Yzerman, Det., C
1981	Bob Gainey, Mon., LW	1991	Dirk Graham, Chi., RW	2001	John Madden, NJ, LW
1982	Steve Kasper, Bos., C	1992	Guy Carbonneau, Mon., C	2002	Michael Peca, NYI, C
1983	Bobby Clarke, Phi., C	1993	Doug Gilmour, Tor., C	2003	Jere Lehtinen, Dal., RW
1984	Doug Jarvis, Wash., C	1994	Sergei Fedorov, Det., C	2004	Kris Draper, Det., C
1985	Craig Ramsay, Buf., LW	1995	Ron Francis, Pit., C	2006	Rod Brind'Amour, Car., C
1986	Troy Murray, Chi., C	1996	Sergei Fedorov, Det., C	2007	Rod Brind'Amour, Car., C
1987	Dave Poulin, Phi., C	1997	Michael Peca, Buf., C	2008	Pavel Datsyuk, Det., C

Jack Adams Award

Awarded to the coach "adjudged to have contributed the most to his team's success" and named after the late Detroit Red Wings coach and general manager. Winners selected by NHL Broadcasters' Assn.; (*) indicates division champion.

Multiple winners: Pat Burns (3); Scotty Bowman, Jacques Demers and Pat Quinn (2).

Year		Improvement		Year		Improvement	
1974	Fred Shero, Phi.	37-30-11	to 50-16-12*	1991	Brian Sutter, St.L	37-34-9	to 47-22-11
1975	Bob Pulford, LA.	41-14-23	to 37-35-8	1992	Pat Quinn, Van.	28-43-9	to 42-26-12*
1976	Don Cherry, Bos.	40-26-14	to 48-15-17*	1993	Pat Burns, Tor.	30-43-7	to 44-29-11
1977	Scotty Bowman, Mon	58-11-11*	to 60-8-12*	1994	Jacques Lemaire, NJ	40-37-7	to 47-25-12
1978	Bobby Kromm, Det	6-55-9	to 32-34-14	1995	Marc Crawford, Que	34-42-8	to 30-13-5*
1979	Al Arbour, NYI	48-17-15*	to 51-15-14*	1996	Scotty Bowman, Det	33-11-4*	to 62-13-7*
1980	Pat Quinn, Phi	40-25-15	to 48-12-20*	1997	Ted Nolan, Buf	33-42-7	to 40-30-12*
1981	Red Berenson, St.L.	34-34-12	to 45-18-17*	1998	Pat Burns, Bos.	26-47-9	to 39-30-13
1982	Tom Watt, Win	9-57-14	to 33-33-14	1999	Jacques Martin, Ott.	34-33-15	to 44-23-15*
1983	Orval Tessier, Chi	30-38-12	to 47-23-10	2000	Joel Quenneville, St.L.	37-32-13	to 51-20-11*
1984	Bryan Murray, Wash.	39-25-16	to 48-27-5	2001	Bill Barber, Phi	45-25-12	to 43-25-11-3
1985	Mike Keenan, Phi	44-26-10	to 53-20-7*	2002	Bob Francis, Pho	35-27-17-3	to 40-27-9-6
1986	Glen Sather, Edm	49-20-11*	to 56-17-7*	2003	Jacques Lemaire, Minn.	26-35-12-9	to 42-29-10-1
1987	Jacques Demers, Det	17-57-6	to 34-36-10	2004	John Tortorella, TB.	36-25-16-5	to 46-22-8-6*
1988	Jacques Demers, Det	34-36-10	to 41-28-11*	2006	Lindy Ruff, Buf	37-34-7-4	to 52-24-1-5
1989	Pat Burns, Mon	45-22-13	to 53-18- 9*	2007	Alain Vigneault, Van.	42-32-4-4	to 49-26-3-4
1990	Bob Murdoch, Win	26-42-12	to 37-32-11	2008	Bruce Boudreau, Wash.	28-40-3-11	to 43-31-4-4*

Lester B. Pearson Award

Awarded to the season's most outstanding player and named after the former diplomat, Nobel Peace Prize winner and Canadian prime minister. Winners selected by the NHL Players Association.

Multiple winners: Wayne Gretzky (5); Mario Lemieux (4); Jaromir Jagr and Guy Lafleur (3); Marcel Dionne, Phil Esposito, Dominik Hasek and Mark Messier (2).

Year		Year		Year	
1971	Phil Esposito, Bos., C	1984	Wayne Gretzky, Edm., C	1997	Dominik Hasek, Buf., G
1972	Jean Ratelle, NYR, C	1985	Wayne Gretzky, Edm., C	1998	Dominik Hasek, Buf., G
1973	Bobby Clarke, Phi., C	1986	Mario Lemieux, Pit., C	1999	Jaromir Jagr, Pit., RW
1974	Phil Esposito, Bos., C	1987	Wayne Gretzky, Edm., C	2000	Jaromir Jagr, Pit., RW
1975	Bobby Orr, Bos., D	1988	Mario Lemieux, Pit., C	2001	Joe Sakic, Col., C
1976	Guy Lafleur, Mon., RW	1989	Steve Yzerman, Det., C	2002	Jarome Iginla, Calg., RW
1977	Guy Lafleur, Mon., RW	1990	Mark Messier, Edm., C	2003	Markus Naslund, Van., LW
1978	Guy Lafleur, Mon., RW	1991	Brett Hull, St.L., RW	2004	Martin St. Louis, TB, RW
1979	Marcel Dionne, LA, C	1992	Mark Messier, NYR, C	2006	Jaromir Jagr, NYR, RW
1980	Marcel Dionne, LA, C	1993	Mario Lemieux, Pit., C	2007	Sidney Crosby, Pit., C
1981	Mike Liut, St.L., G	1994	Sergei Fedorov, Det., C	2008	Alex Ovechkin, Wash., L
1982	Wayne Gretzky, Edm., C	1995	Eric Lindros, Phi., C		
1983	Wayne Gretzky, Edm., C	1996	Mario Lemieux, Pit., C		

King Clancy Memorial Trophy

Awarded to the player who "best exemplifies leadership on and off the ice and who has made a noteworthy humanitarian contribution to his community" and named after former player, coach, official and executive Frank "King" Clancy. Presented by the NHL's Board of Governors.

Year		Year		Year	
1988	Lanny McDonald, Calg., RW	1995	Joe Nieuwendyk, Calg., C	2002	Ron Francis, Car., C
1989	Bryan Trottier, NYI, C	1996	Kris King, Win., LW	2003	Brendan Shanahan, Det., LW
1990	Kevin Lowe, Edm., D	1997	Trevor Linden, Van., C	2004	Jarome Iginla, Calg., RW
1991	Dave Taylor, LA, RW	1998	Kelly Chase, St.L, RW	2006	Olaf Kolzig, Wash., G
1992	Ray Bourque, Bos., D	1999	Rob Ray, Buf., RW	2007	Saku Koivu, Mon., C
1993	Dave Poulin, Bos., C	2000	Curtis Joseph, Tor., G	2008	Vincent Lecavalier, TB, C
1994	Adam Graves, NYR, LW	2001	Shjon Podein, Col., LW		

Bill Masterton Trophy

Awarded to the player who "best exemplifies the qualities of perseverance, sportsmanship and dedication to hockey" and named after the 29-year-old rookie center of the Minnesota North Stars who died of a head injury sustained in a 1968 NHL game. Presented by the PHWA.

Year		Year		Year	
1968	Claude Provost, Mon., RW	1982	Chico Resch, Colo., G	1996	Gary Roberts, Calg., LW
1969	Ted Hampson, Oak., C	1983	Lanny McDonald, Calg., RW	1997	Tony Granato, SJ, LW
1970	Pit Martin, Chi., C	1984	Brad Park, Det., D	1998	Jamie McLennan, St.L, G
1971	Jean Ratelle, NYR, C	1985	Anders Hedberg, NYR, RW	1999	John Cullen, TB, C
1972	Bobby Clarke, Phi., C	1986	Charlie Simmer, Bos., LW	2000	Ken Daneyko, NJ, D
1973	Lowell MacDonald, Pit., RW	1987	Doug Jarvis, Hart., C	2001	Adam Graves, NYR, LW
1974	Henri Richard, Mon., C	1988	Bob Bourne, LA, C	2002	Saku Koivu, Mon., C
1975	Don Luce, Buf., C	1989	Tim Kerr, Phi., C	2003	Steve Yzerman, Det., C
1976	Rod Gilbert, NYR, RW	1990	Gord Kluzak, Bos., D	2004	Bryan Berard, Chi., D
1977	Ed Westfall, NYI, RW	1991	Dave Taylor, LA, RW	2006	Teemu Selanne, Ana., RW
1978	Butch Goring, LA, C	1992	Mark Fitzpatrick, NYI, G	2007	Phil Kessel, Bos., C
1979	Serge Savard, Mon., D	1993	Mario Lemieux, Pit., C	2008	Jason Blake, Tor., L
1980	Al MacAdam, Min., RW	1994	Cam Neely, Bos., RW		
1981	Blake Dunlop, St.L., C	1995	Pat LaFontaine, Buf., C		

Number One Draft Choices

Overall first choices in the NHL draft since the league staged its first universal amateur draft in 1969. Players are listed with team that selected them; those who became Rookie of the Year are in **bold** type.

Year		Year		Year	
1969	Rejean Houle, Mon., LW	1983	Brian Lawton, Min., C	1997	Joe Thornton, Bos., C
1970	**Gilbert Perreault,** Buf., C	1984	**Mario Lemieux,** Pit., C	1998	Vincent Lecavalier, TB, C
1971	Guy Lafleur, Mon., RW	1985	Wendel Clark, Tor., LW/D	1999	Patrik Stefan, Atl., C
1972	Billy Harris, NYI, RW	1986	Joe Murphy, Det., C	2000	Rick DiPietro, NYI, G
1973	**Denis Pótvin,** NYI, D	1987	Pierre Turgeon, Buf., C	2001	Ilya Kovalchuk, Atl., RW
1974	Greg Joly, Wash., D	1988	Mike Modano, Min., C	2002	Rick Nash, Clb., LW
1975	Mel Bridgman, Phi., C	1989	Mats Sundin, Que., RW	2003	Marc-Andre Fleury, Pit., G
1976	Rick Green, Wash., D	1990	Owen Nolan, Que., RW	2004	**Alex Ovechkin**, Wash., LW
1977	Dale McCourt, Det., C	1991	Eric Lindros, Que., C	2005	Sidney Crosby, Pit., C
1978	**Bobby Smith,** Min., C	1992	Roman Hamrlik, TB, D	2006	Erik Johnson, St.L, D
1979	Rob Ramage, Colo., D	1993	Alexandre Daigle, Ott., C	2007	**Patrick Kane**, Chi., RW
1980	Doug Wickenheiser, Mon., C	1994	Ed Jovanovski, Fla., D	2008	Steven Stamkos, TB, C
1981	**Dale Hawerchuk,** Win., C	1995	**Bryan Berard,** Ott., D		
1982	Gord Kluzak, Bos., D	1996	Chris Phillips, Ott., D		

World Hockey Association

WHA Finals

The World Hockey Association began play in 1972-73 as a 12-team rival of the 56-year-old NHL. The WHA played for the AVCO World Trophy in its seven playoff finals (Avco Financial Services underwrote the playoffs).

Multiple winners: Winnipeg (3); Houston (2).

Year	Winner	Head Coach	Series	Loser	Head Coach
1973	New England Whalers	Jack Kelley	4-1 (WWLWW)	Winnipeg Jets	Bobby Hull
1974	Houston Aeros	Bill Dineen	4-0	Chicago Cougars	Pat Stapleton
1975	Houston Aeros	Bill Dineen	4-0	Quebec Nordiques	Jean-Guy Gendron
1976	Winnipeg Jets	Bobby Kromm	4-0	Houston Aeros	Bill Dineen
1977	Quebec Nordiques	Marc Boileau	4-3 (LWLWWLW)	Winnipeg Jets	Bobby Kromm
1978	Winnipeg Jets	Larry Hillman	4-0	NE Whalers	Harry Neale
1979	Winnipeg Jets	Larry Hillman	4-2 (WWLWLW)	Edmonton Oilers	Glen Sather

Playoff MVPs—1973—No award; **1974**—No award; **1975**—Ron Grahame, Houston, G; **1976**—Ulf Nilsson, Winnipeg, C; **1977**—Serg Bernier, Quebec, C; **1978**—Bobby Guindon, Winnipeg, C; **1979**—Rich Preston, Winnipeg, RW.

Most Valuable Player

(Gordie Howe Trophy, 1976-79)

Year		G	A	Pts
1973	Bobby Hull, Win., LW	51	52	103
1974	Gordie Howe, Hou., RW	31	69	100
1975	Bobby Hull, Win., LW	77	65	142
1976	Marc Tardif, Que., LW	71	77	148
1977	Robbie Ftorek, Pho., C	46	71	117
1978	Marc Tardif, Que., LW	65	89	154
1979	Dave Dryden, Edm., G	41-17-2; 2.89		

Scoring Leaders

Year		Gm	G	A	Pts
1973	Andre Lacroix, Phi	78	50	74	124
1974	Mike Walton, Min	78	57	60	117
1975	Andre Lacroix, S. Diego	78	41	106	147
1976	Marc Tardif, Que	81	71	77	148
1977	Real Cloutier, Que	76	66	75	141
1978	Marc Tardif, Que	78	65	89	154
1979	Real Cloutier, Que	77	75	54	129

Note: In 1979, 18 year-old Rookie of the Year Wayne Gretzky finished third in scoring (46-64—110).

Rookie of the Year

Year		G	A	Pts
1973	Terry Caffery, N. Eng., C	39	61	100
1974	Mark Howe, Hou., LW	38	41	79
1975	Anders Hedberg, Win., RW	53	47	100
1976	Mark Napier, Tor., RW	43	50	93
1977	George Lyle, N. Eng., LW	39	33	72
1978	Kent Nilsson, Win., C	42	65	107
1979	Wayne Gretzky, Ind.-Edm., C	46	64	110

Best Goaltender

Year		Record	GAA
1973	Gerry Cheevers, Cleveland	32-20-0	2.84
1974	Don McLeod, Houston	33-13-3	2.56
1975	Ron Grahame, Houston	33-10-0	3.03
1976	Michel Dion, Indianapolis	14-15-1	2.74
1977	Ron Grahame, Houston	27-10-2	2.74
1978	Al Smith, New England	30-20-3	3.22
1979	Dave Dryden, Edmonton	41-17-2	2.89

Best Defenseman

Year	
1973	J.C. Tremblay, Quebec
1974	Pat Stapleton, Chicago
1975	J.C. Tremblay, Quebec
1976	Paul Shmyr, Cleveland
1977	Ron Plumb, Cincinnati
1978	Lars-Erik Sjoberg, Winnipeg
1979	Rick Ley, New England

Coach of the Year

Year		Improvement		
1973	Jack Kelley, N. Eng			46-30-2*
1974	Billy Harris, Tor	35-39-4	to	41-33-4
1975	Sandy Hucul, Pho	Expan.	to	39-31-8
1976	Bobby Kromm, Win	38-35-5	to	52-27-2*
1977	Bill Dineen, Hou	53-27-0 *	to	50-24-6*
1978	Bill Dineen, Hou	50-24-6 *	to	42-34-4
1979	John Brophy, Birm	36-41-3	to	32-42-6

*Won Division.

WHA All-Star Game

The WHA All-Star Game was an Eastern Division vs Western Division contest from 1973-75. In 1976, the league's five Canadian-based teams played the nine teams in the US. Over the final three seasons–East played West in 1977; AVCO Cup champion Quebec played a WHA All-Star team in 1978; and in 1979, a full WHA All-Star team played a three-game series with Moscow Dynamo of the Soviet Union.

Year	Result	Host	Coaches	Most Valuable Player
1973	East 6, West 2	Quebec	Jack Kelley, Bobby Hull	Wayne Carleton, Ottawa
1974	East 8, West 4	St. Paul, MN	Jack Kelley, Bobby Hull	Mike Walton, Minnesota
1975	West 6, East 4	Edmonton	Bill Dineen, Ron Ryan	Rejean Houle, Quebec
1976	Canada 6, USA 1	Cleveland	Jean-Guy Gendron, Bill Dineen	Can—Real Cloutier, Que. USA—Paul Shmyr, Cleve.
1977	East 4, West 2	Hartford	Jacques Demers, Bobby Kromm	East—L. Levasseur, Min. West—W. Lindstrom, Win.
1978	Quebec 5, WHA 4	Quebec	Marc Boileau, Bill Dineen	Quebec—Marc Tardif WHA—Mark Howe, NE
1979	WHA def. Moscow Dynamo 3 games to none (4-2, 4-2, 4-3)	Edmonton	Larry Hillman, P. Iburtovich	No awards

World Championship

Men

The World Hockey Championship tournament has been played regularly since 1930. The International Ice Hockey Federation (IIHF), which governs both the World and Winter Olympic tournaments, considers the Olympic champions from 1920-68 to also be the World champions. However the IIHF has not recognized an Olympic champion as World champion since 1968. The IIHF has sanctioned separate World Championships in Olympic years four times—in 1972, 1976, 1992 and 2002. The world championship is officially vacant for the three Olympic years from 1980-88.

Multiple winners: Canada and Soviet Union/Russia (24); Sweden (8); Czechoslovakia (6) Czech Republic (5), USA (2).

Year		Year		Year		Year	
1920	Canada	1952	Canada	1971	Soviet Union	1990	Soviet Union
1924	Canada	1953	Sweden	1972	Czechoslovakia	1991	Sweden
1928	Canada	1954	Soviet Union	1973	Soviet Union	1992	Sweden
1930	Canada	1955	Canada	1974	Soviet Union	1993	Russia
1931	Canada	1956	Soviet Union	1975	Soviet Union	1994	Canada
1932	Canada	1957	Sweden	1976	Czechoslovakia	1995	Finland
1933	United States	1958	Canada	1977	Czechoslovakia	1996	Czech Republic
1934	Canada	1959	Canada	1978	Czechoslovakia	1997	Canada
1935	Canada	1960	United States	1979	Soviet Union	1998	Sweden
1936	Great Britain	1961	Canada	1980	Not held	1999	Czech Republic
1937	Canada	1962	Sweden	1981	Soviet Union	2000	Czech Republic
1938	Canada	1963	Soviet Union	1982	Soviet Union	2001	Czech Republic
1939	Canada	1964	Soviet Union	1983	Soviet Union	2002	Slovakia
1940-46	Not held	1965	Soviet Union	1984	Not held	2003	Canada
1947	Czechoslovakia	1966	Soviet Union	1985	Czechoslovakia	2004	Canada
1948	Czechoslovakia	1967	Soviet Union	1986	Soviet Union	2005	Czech Republic
1949	Czechoslovakia	1968	Soviet Union	1987	Sweden	2006	Sweden
1950	Canada	1969	Soviet Union	1988	Not held	2007	Canada
1951	Canada	1970	Soviet Union	1989	Soviet Union	2008	Russia

Women

The women's World Hockey Championship tournament is governed by the International Ice Hockey Federation (IIHF).

Multiple winners: Canada (9); United States (2).

Year		Year		Year		Year		Year	
1990	Canada	1997	Canada	2001	Canada	2005	United States	2008	United States
1992	Canada	1999	Canada	2004	Canada	2007	Canada		
1994	Canada	2000	Canada						

Canada vs. USSR Summits

The first competition between the Soviet National Team and the NHL took place Sept. 2-28, 1972. A team of NHL All-Stars emerged as the winner of the heralded 8-game series, but just barely—winning with a record of 4-3-1 after trailing 1-3-1.

Two years later a WHA All-Star team played the Soviet Nationals and could win only one game and tie three others in eight contests. Two other Canada vs USSR series took place during NHL All-Star breaks: the three-game Challenge Cup at New York in 1979, and the two-game Rendez-Vous '87 in Quebec City in 1987.

The NHL All-Stars played the USSR in a three-game Challenge Cup series in 1979.

1972 Team Canada vs. USSR

NHL All-Stars vs Soviet National Team.

Date	City	Result	Goaltenders
9/2	Montreal	USSR, 7-3	Tretiak/Dryden
9/4	Toronto	Canada, 4-1	Esposito/Tretiak
9/6	Winnipeg	Tie, 4-4	Tretiak/Esposito
9/8	Vancouver	USSR, 5-3	Tretiak/Dryden
9/22	Moscow	USSR, 5-4	Tretiak/Esposito
9/24	Moscow	Canada, 3-2	Dryden/Tretiak
9/26	Moscow	Canada, 4-3	Esposito/Tretiak
9/28	Moscow	Canada, 6-5	Dryden/Tretiak

Standings

	W	L	T	Pts	GF	GA
Team Canada (NHL)	4	3	1	9	32	32
Soviet Union	3	4	1	7	32	32

Leading Scorers

1. Phil Esposito, Canada, (7-6—13); **2.** Aleksandr Yakushev, USSR (7-4—11); **3.** Paul Henderson, Canada (7-2—9); **4.** Boris Shadrin, USSR (3-5—8); **5.** Valeri Kharlamov, USSR (3-4—7) and Vladimir Petrov, USSR (3-4—7).

1974 Team Canada vs. USSR

WHA All-Stars vs Soviet National Team.

Date	City	Result	Goaltenders
9/17	Quebec City	Tie, 3-3	Tretiak/Cheevers
9/19	Toronto	Canada, 4-1	Cheevers/Tretiak
9/21	Winnipeg	USSR, 8-5	Tretiak/McLeod
9/23	Vancouver	Tie, 5-5	Tretiak/Cheevers
10/1	Moscow	USSR, 3-2	Tretiak/Cheevers
10/3	Moscow	USSR, 5-2	Tretiak/Cheevers
10/5	Moscow	Tie, 4-4	Cheevers/Tretiak
10/6	Moscow	USSR, 3-2	Sidelinkov/Cheevers

Standings

	W	L	T	Pts	GF	GA
Soviet Union	4	1	3	11	32	27
Team Canada (WHA)	1	4	3	5	27	32

Leading Scorers

1. Bobby Hull, Canada (7-2—9); **2.** Aleksandr Yakushev, USSR (6-2—8), Ralph Backstrom, Canada (4-4—8) and Valeri Kharlamov, USSR (2-6—8); **5.** Gordie Howe, Canada (3-4—7), Andre Lacroix, Canada (1-6—7) and Vladimi Petrov, USSR (1-6—7).

1979 Challenge Cup Series

NHL All-Stars vs Soviet National Team

Date	City	Result	Goaltenders
2/8	New York	NHL, 4-2	K. Dryden/Tretiak
2/10	New York	USSR, 5-4	Tretiak/K. Dryden
2/11	New York	USSR, 6-0	Myshkin/Cheevers

Rendez-Vous '87

NHL All-Stars vs Soviet National Team

Date	City	Result	Goaltenders
2/11	Quebec	NHL, 4-3	Fuhr/Belosheykhin
2/13	Quebec	USSR, 5-3	Belosheykhin/Fuhr

The Canada Cup

After organizing the historic 8-game Team Canada-Soviet Union series of 1972, NHL Players Association executive director Alan Eagleson and the NHL created the Canada Cup in 1976. For the first time, the best players from the world's six major hockey powers—Canada, Czechoslovakia, Finland, Russia, Sweden and the USA—competed together in one tournament.

1976
Round Robin Standings

	W	L	T	Pts	GF	GA
Canada	4	1	0	8	22	6
Czechoslovakia	3	1	1	7	19	9
Soviet Union	2	2	1	5	23	14
Sweden	2	2	1	5	16	18
United States	1	3	1	3	14	21
Finland	1	4	0	2	16	42

Finals (Best of 3)

Date	City	Score
9/13	Toronto	Canada 6, Czechoslovakia 0
9/15	Montreal	Canada 5, Czechoslovakia 4 (OT)

Note: Darryl Sittler scored the winning goal for Canada at 11:33 in overtime to clinch the Cup, 2 games to none.

Leading Scorers

1. Victor Hluktov, USSR (5-4—9), Bobby Orr, Canada (2-7—9) and Denis Potvin, Canada (1-8—9); **4.** Bobby Hull, Canada (5-3—8) and Milan Novy, Czechoslovakia (5-3—8).

Team MVPs

Canada—Rogie Vachon   Sweden—Borje Salming
Czech.—Milan Novy   USA—Robbie Ftorek
USSR—Alexandr Maltsev   Finland—Matti Hagman
Tournament MVP—Bobby Orr, Canada

1981
Round Robin Standings

	W	L	T	Pts	GF	GA
Canada	4	0	1	9	32	13
Soviet Union	3	1	1	7	20	13
Czechoslovakia	2	1	2	6	21	13
United States	2	2	1	5	17	19
Sweden	1	4	0	2	13	20
Finland	0	4	1	1	6	31

Semifinals

Date	City	Score
9/11	Ottawa	USSR 4, Czechoslovakia 1
9/11	Montreal	Canada 4, United States 1

Finals

Date	City	Score
9/13	Montreal	USSR 8, Canada 1

Leading Scorers

1. Wayne Gretzky, Canada (5-7—12); **2.** Mike Bossy, Canada (8-3—11), Bryan Trottier, Canada (3-8—11), Guy Lafleur, Canada (2-9—11), Alexei Kasatonov, USSR (1-10—11).

All-Star Team

Goal—Vladislav Tretiak, USSR; **Defense**—Arnold Kadlec, Czech. and Alexei Kasatonov, USSR; **Forwards**—Mike Bossy, Canada, Gil Perreault, Canada, and Sergei Shepelev, USSR. **Tournament MVP**—Tretiak.

1984
Round Robin Standings

	W	L	T	Pts	GF	GA
Soviet Union	5	0	0	10	22	7
United States	3	1	1	7	21	13
Sweden	3	2	0	6	15	16
Canada	2	2	1	5	23	18
West Germany	0	4	1	1	13	29
Czechoslovakia	0	4	1	1	10	21

Semifinals

Date	City	Score
9/12	Edmonton	Sweden 9, United States 2
9/15	Montreal	Canada 3, USSR 2 (OT)

Note: Mike Bossy scored the winning goal for Canada at 12:29 in overtime.

Finals (Best of 3)

Date	City	Score
9/16	Calgary	Canada 5, Sweden 2
9/18	Edmonton	Canada 6, Sweden 5

Leading Scorers

1. Wayne Gretzky, Canada (5-7—12); **2.** Michel Goulet, Canada (5-6—11), Kent Nilsson, Sweden (3-8—11), Paul Coffey, Canada (3-8—11); **5.** Hakan Loob, Sweden (6-4—10).

All-Star Team

Goal—Vladimir Myshkin, USSR; **Defense**—Paul Coffey, Canada and Rod Langway, USA; **Forwards**—Wayne Gretzky, Canada, John Tonelli, Canada, and Sergei Makarov, USSR. **Tournament MVP**—Tonelli.

1987
Round Robin Standings

	W	L	T	Pts	GF	GA
Canada	3	0	2	8	19	13
Soviet Union	3	1	1	7	22	13
Sweden	3	2	0	6	17	14
Czechoslovakia	2	2	1	5	12	15
United States	2	3	0	4	13	14
Finland	0	5	0	0	9	23

Semifinals

Date	City	Score
9/8	Hamilton	USSR 4, Sweden 2
9/9	Montreal	Canada 5, Czechoslovakia 3

Finals (Best of 3)

Date	City	Score
9/11	Montreal	USSR 6, Canada 5 (OT)
9/13	Hamilton	Canada 6, USSR 5 (2 OT)
9/15	Hamilton	Canada 6, USSR 5

Note: In Game 1, Alexander Semak of USSR scored at 5:33 in overtime. In Game 2, Mario Lemieux of Canada scored at 10:01 in the second overtime period. Lemieux also won Game 3 on a goal with 1:26 left in regulation time.

Leading Scorers

1. Wayne Gretzky, Canada (3-18—21); **2.** Mario Lemieux, Canada (11-7—18); **3.** Sergei Makarov, USSR (7-8—15); **4.** Vladimir Krutov, USSR (7-7—14); **5.** Viacheslav Bykov, USSR (2-7—9); **6.** Ray Bourque, Canada (2-6—8).

All-Star Team

Goal—Grant Fuhr, Canada; **Defense**—Ray Bourque, Canada and Viacheslav Fetisov, USSR; **Forwards**—Wayne Gretzky, Canada, Mario Lemieux, Canada, and Vladimir Krutov, USSR. **Tournament MVP**—Gretzky.

1991

Round Robin Standings

	W	L	T	Pts	GF	GA
Canada	3	0	2	8	21	11
United States	4	1	0	8	19	15
Finland	2	2	1	5	10	13
Sweden	2	3	0	4	13	17
Soviet Union	1	3	1	3	14	14
Czechoslovakia	1	4	0	2	11	18

Semifinals

Date	City	Score
9/11	Hamilton	United States 7, Finland 3
9/12	Toronto	Canada 4, Sweden 0

Finals (Best of 3)

Date	City	Score
9/14	Montreal	Canada 4, United States 1
9/16	Hamilton	Canada 4, United States 2

Leading Scorers

1. Wayne Gretzky, Canada (4-8—12); **2.** Steve Larmer, Canada (6-5—11); **3.** Brett Hull, USA (2-7—9); **4.** Mike Modano, USA (2-7—9); **5.** Mark Messier, Canada (2-6—8).

All-Star Team

Goal—Bill Ranford, Canada; **Defense**—Al MacInnis, Canada and Chris Chelios, USA; **Forwards**—Wayne Gretzky, Canada, Jeremy Roenick, USA and Mats Sundin, Sweden. **Tournament MVP**—Bill Ranford.

The World Cup

Formed jointly by the NHL and the NHL Players Association in cooperation with the International Ice Hockey Federation. The inaugural World Cup held games in nine different cities throughout North America and Europe, the most ever by a single international hockey tournament.

1996

Round Robin Standings

European Pool	W	L	T	Pts	GF	GA
Sweden	3	0	0	6	14	3
Finland	2	1	0	4	17	11
Germany	1	2	0	2	11	15
Czech Republic	0	3	0	0	4	17

North American Pool	W	L	T	Pts	GF	GA
United States	3	0	0	6	19	8
Canada	2	1	0	4	11	10
Russia	1	2	0	2	12	14
Slovakia	0	3	0	0	10	18

Semifinals

Date	City	Score
9/7	Philadelphia	Canada 3, Sweden 2 (OT)
9/8	Ottawa	United States 5, Russia 2

Finals (Best of 3)

Date	City	Score
9/10	Philadelphia	Canada 4, United States 3 (OT)
9/12	Montreal	United States 5, Canada 2
9/14	Montreal	United States 5, Canada 2

Leading Scorers

1. Brett Hull, USA (7-4—11); **2.** John LeClair, USA (6-4—10); **3.** Mats Sundin, Sweden (4-3—7); Wayne Gretzky, Canada (3-4—7); Doug Weight, USA (3-4—7); Paul Coffey, Canada (0-7—7); Brian Leetch, USA (0-7—7).

All-Tournament Team

Goal—Mike Richter, USA; **Defense**—Calle Johansson, Sweden and Chris Chelios, USA; **Forwards**—Brett Hull, USA; John LeClair, USA and Mats Sundin, Sweden. **Tournament MVP**—Mike Richter, USA.

2004

Round Robin Standings

European Pool	W	L	T	Pts	GF	GA
Finland	2	0	1	5	11	4
Sweden	2	0	1	5	13	9
Czech Republic	1	2	0	2	10	10
Germany	0	3	0	0	4	15

North American Pool	W	L	T	Pts	GF	GA
Canada	3	0	0	6	10	3
Russia	2	1	0	4	9	6
United States	1	2	0	2	5	6
Slovakia	0	3	0	0	4	13

Semifinals

Date	City	Score
9/10	St. Paul, Minn.	Finland 2, United States 1
9/11	Toronto	Canada 4, Czech Rep. 3 (OT)

Championship Game

Date	City	Score
9/14	Toronto	Canada 3, Finland 2

Leading Scorers

1. Fredrik Modin, Sweden (4-4—8); **2.** Vincent Lecavalier, Canada (2-5—7); **3.** Keith Tkachuk, USA (5-1—6); Joe Sakic, Canada (4-2—6); Martin Havlat, Czech Republic (3-3—6); Kimmo Timonen, Finland (1-5—6); Joe Thornton, Canada (1-5—6); Mike Modano, USA (0-6—6); Daniel Alfredsson, Sweden (0-6—6).

All-Tournament Team

Goal—Martin Brodeur, Canada; **Defense**—Kimmo Timonen, Finland and Adam Foote, Canada; **Forwards**—Vincent Lecavalier, Canada; Saku Koivu, Finland and Fredrik Modin, Sweden. **Tournament MVP**—Vincent Lecavalier, Canada.

Note: See Olympics chapter for all men's and women's Olympic hockey results.

U.S. DIVISION I COLLEGE HOCKEY

NCAA Men's Frozen Four

The NCAA Division I hockey tournament began in 1948 and was played at the Broadmoor Ice Palace in Colorado Springs from 1948-57. Since 1958, the tournament has moved around the country, stopping for consecutive years only at Boston Garden from 1972-74. Consolation games to determine third place were played from 1949-89 and discontinued in 1990.

Multiple winners: Michigan (9); North Dakota and Denver (7); Wisconsin (6); Minnesota (5); Boston University (4); Boston College, Lake Superior St., Michigan St. and Michigan Tech (3); Colorado College, Cornell, Maine and RPI (2).

Year	Champion	Head Coach	Score	Runner-up	Third Place		
1948	Michigan	Vic Heyliger	8-4	Dartmouth	Colorado College and Boston College		

Year	Champion	Head Coach	Score	Runner-up	Third Place	Score	Fourth Place
1949	Boston College	Snooks Kelley	4-3	Dartmouth	Michigan	10-4	Colorado Col.
1950	Colorado College	Cheddy Thompson	13-4	Boston Univ.	Michigan	10-6	Boston College
1951	Michigan	Vic Heyliger	7-1	Brown	Boston Univ.	7-4	Colorado College
1952	Michigan	Vic Heyliger	4-1	Colorado Col.	Yale	4-1	St. Lawrence
1953	Michigan	Vic Heyliger	7-3	Minnesota	RPI	6-3	Boston Univ.
1954	RPI	Ned Harkness	5-4 *	Minnesota	Michigan	7-2	Boston College
1955	Michigan	Vic Heyliger	5-3	Colorado Col.	Harvard	6-3	St. Lawrence
1956	Michigan	Vic Heyliger	7-5	Michigan Tech	St. Lawrence	6-2	Boston College
1957	Colorado College	Tom Bedecki	13-6	Michigan	Clarkson	2-1	Harvard
1958	Denver	Murray Armstrong	6-2	North Dakota	Clarkson	5-1	Harvard
1959	North Dakota	Bob May	4-3 *	Michigan St.	Boston College	7-6	St. Lawrence
1960	Denver	Murray Armstrong	5-3	Michigan Tech	Boston Univ.	7-6	St. Lawrence
1961	Denver	Murray Armstrong	12-2	St. Lawrence	Minnesota	4-3	RPI
1962	Michigan Tech	John MacInnes	7-1	Clarkson	Michigan	5-1	St. Lawrence
1963	North Dakota	Barry Thorndycraft	6-5	Denver	Clarkson	5-3	Boston College
1964	Michigan	Allen Renfrew	6-3	Denver	RPI	2-1	Providence
1965	Michigan Tech	John MacInnes	8-2	Boston College	North Dakota	9-5	Brown
1966	Michigan St.	Amo Bessone	6-1	Clarkson	Denver	4-3	Boston Univ.
1967	Cornell	Ned Harkness	4-1	Boston Univ.	Michigan St.	6-1	North Dakota
1968	Denver	Murray Armstrong	4-0	North Dakota	Cornell	6-1	Boston College
1969	Denver	Murray Armstrong	4-3	Cornell	Harvard	6-5	Michigan Tech
1970	Cornell	Ned Harkness	6-4	Clarkson	Wisconsin	6-5	Michigan Tech
1971	Boston Univ.	Jack Kelley	4-2	Minnesota	Denver	1-0	Harvard
1972	Boston Univ.	Jack Kelley	4-0	Cornell	Wisconsin	5-2	Denver
1973	Wisconsin	Bob Johnson	4-2	Denver	Boston College	3-1	Cornell
1974	Minnesota	Herb Brooks	4-2	Michigan Tech	Boston Univ.	7-5	Harvard
1975	Michigan Tech	John MacInnes	6-1	Minnesota	Boston Univ.	10-5	Harvard
1976	Minnesota	Herb Brooks	6-4	Michigan Tech	Brown	8-7	Boston Univ.
1977	Wisconsin	Bob Johnson	6-5 *	Michigan	Boston Univ.	6-5	N. Hampshire
1978	Boston Univ.	Jack Parker	5-3	Boston College	Bowl. Green	4-3	Wisconsin
1979	Minnesota	Herb Brooks	4-3	North Dakota	Dartmouth	7-3	N. Hampshire
1980	North Dakota	Gino Gasparini	5-2	N. Michigan	Dartmouth	8-4	Cornell
1981	Wisconsin	Bob Johnson	6-3	Minnesota	Mich. Tech	5-2	N. Michigan
1982	North Dakota	Gino Gasparini	5-2	Wisconsin	Northeastern	10-4	N. Hampshire
1983	Wisconsin	Jeff Sauer	6-2	Harvard	Providence	4-3	Minnesota
1984	Bowling Green	Jerry York	5-4 #	Minn-Duluth	North Dakota	6-5	Michigan St.
1985	RPI	Mike Addesa	2-1	Providence	Minn. Duluth	7-6	Boston College
1986	Michigan St.	Ron Mason	6-5	Harvard	Minnesota	6-4	Denver
1987	North Dakota	Gino Gasparini	5-3	Michigan St.	Minnesota	6-3	Harvard
1988	Lake Superior St.	Frank Anzalone	4-3 *	St. Lawrence	Maine	5-2	Minnesota
1989	Harvard	Billy Cleary	4-3 *	Minnesota	Michigan St.	7-4	Maine

Year	Champion	Head Coach	Score	Runner-up	Third Place
1990	Wisconsin	Jeff Sauer	7-3	Colgate	Boston College and Boston Univ.
1991	Northern Michigan	Rick Comley	8-7 †	Boston Univ.	Maine and Clarkson
1992	Lake Superior St.	Jeff Jackson	5-3	Wisconsin	Michigan and Michigan St.
1993	Maine	Shawn Walsh	5-4	Lake Superior St.	Boston Univ. and Michigan
1994	Lake Superior St.	Jeff Jackson	9-1	Boston Univ.	Harvard and Minnesota
1995	Boston Univ.	Jack Parker	6-2	Maine	Michigan and Minnesota
1996	Michigan	Red Berenson	3-2 *	Colorado Col.	Vermont and Boston Univ.
1997	North Dakota	Dean Blais	6-4	Boston Univ.	Colorado College and Michigan
1998	Michigan	Red Berenson	3-2 *	Boston College	New Hampshire and Ohio St.
1999	Maine	Shawn Walsh	3-2 *	New Hampshire	Boston College and Michigan St.
2000	North Dakota	Dean Blais	4-2	Boston College	St. Lawrence and Maine
2001	Boston College	Jerry York	3-2 *	North Dakota	Michigan and Michigan St.
2002	Minnesota	Don Lucia	4-3 *	Maine	Michigan and New Hampshire
2003	Minnesota	Don Lucia	5-1	New Hampshire	Michigan and Cornell
2004	Denver	George Gwozdecky	1-0	Maine	Minnesota Duluth and Boston College
2005	Denver	George Gwozdecky	4-1	North Dakota	Colorado College and Minnesota
2006	Wisconsin	Mike Eaves	2-1	Boston College	North Dakota and Maine
2007	Michigan St.	Rick Comley	3-1	Boston College	North Dakota and Maine
2008	Boston College	Jerry York	4-1	Notre Dame	North Dakota and Michigan

* Overtime   † 3rd Overtime   # 4th Overtime

Note: Runners-up Denver (1973) and Wisconsin (1992) had participation voided by the NCAA for using ineligible players.

U.S. Division I College Hockey (Cont.)

Tournament Most Outstanding Player

The Most Outstanding Players of each NCAA Div. I tournament since 1948. Winners of the award who did not play for the tournament champion in **bold** type. In 1960, three players, none on the winning team, shared the award.
   Multiple winners: Lou Angotti and Marc Behrend (2).

Year	Year	Year
1948 **Joe Riley,** Dartmouth, F	1967 Walt Stanowski, Cornell, D	1988 Bruce Hoffort, Lk. Superior, G
1949 **Dick Desmond,** Dart., G	1968 Gerry Powers, Denver, G	1989 Ted Donato, Harvard, F
1950 **Ralph Bevins,** Boston U., G	1969 Keith Magnuson, Denver, D	1990 Chris Tancill, Wisconsin, F
1951 **Ed Whiston,** Brown, G	1970 Dan Lodboa, Cornell, D	1991 Scott Beattie, No. Mich., F
1952 **Ken Kinsley,** Colo. Col., G	1971 Dan Brady, Boston U., G	1992 Paul Constantin, Lk. Superior, F
1953 John Matchefts, Mich., F	1972 Tim Regan, Boston, U., G	1993 Jim Montgomery, Maine, F
1954 Abbie Moore, RPI, F	1973 Dean Talafous, Wisc., F	1994 Sean Tallaire, Lk. Superior, F
1955 **Phil Hilton,** Colo. Col., D	1974 Brad Shelstad, Minn., G	1995 Chris O'Sullivan, Boston U., F
1956 Lorne Howes, Mich., G	1975 Jim Warden, Mich. Tech, G	1996 Brendan Morrison, Michigan, F
1957 Bob McCusker, Colo. Col., F	1976 Tom Vannelli, Minn., F	1997 Matt Henderson, N. Dakota, F
1958 Murray Massier, Denver, F	1977 Julian Baretta, Wisc., G	1998 Marty Turco, Michigan, G
1959 Reg Morelli, N. Dakota, F	1978 Jack O'Callahan, Boston U., D	1999 Alfie Michaud, Maine, G
1960 **Lou Angotti,** Mich. Tech., F;	1979 Steve Janaszak, Minn., G	2000 Lee Goren, N. Dakota, F
Bob Marquis, Boston U., F;	1980 Doug Smail, N. Dakota, F	2001 Chuck Kobasew, Boston College, F
& **Barry Urbanski,** BU, G	1981 Marc Behrend, Wisc., G	2002 Grant Potulny, Minnesota, F
1961 Bill Masterton, Denver, F	1982 Phil Sykes, N. Dakota, F	2003 Thomas Vanek, Minnesota, F
1962 Lou Angotti, Mich. Tech, F	1983 Marc Behrend, Wisc., G	2004 Adam Berkhoel, Denver, G
1963 Al McLean, N. Dakota, F	1984 Gary Kruzich, Bowl. Green, G	2005 Peter Mannino, Denver, G
1964 Bob Gray, Michigan, G	1985 **Chris Terreri,** Prov., G	2006 Robbie Earl, Wisconsin, F
1965 Gary Milroy, Mich. Tech, F	1986 Mike Donnelly, Mich. St., F	2007 Justin Abdelkader, Michigan St., F
1966 Gaye Cooley, Mich. St., G	1987 Tony Hrkac, N. Dakota, F	2008 Nathan Gerbe, Boston College, F

Hobey Baker Award

College hockey's Player of the Year award; voted on by a national panel of sportswriters, broadcasters, college coaches and pro scouts (plus a fan vote beginning in 2003). First presented in 1981 by the Decathlon Athletic Club of Bloomington, Minn., in the name of the Princeton collegiate hockey and football star who was killed in a plane crash.

Year	Year	Year
1981 Neal Broten, Minnesota, F	1991 Dave Emma, Boston College, F	2001 Ryan Miller, Michigan St., G
1982 George McPhee, Bowl. Green, F	1992 Scott Pellerin, Maine, F	2002 Jordan Leopold, Minnesota, D
1983 Mark Fusco, Harvard, D	1993 Paul Kariya, Maine, F	2003 Peter Sejna, Colorado Coll.,·F
1984 Tom Kurvers, Minn. Duluth, D	1994 Chris Marinucci, Minn. Duluth, F	2004 Junior Lessard, Minn. Duluth, F
1985 Bill Watson, Minn. Duluth, F	1995 Brian Holzinger, Bowl. Green, F	2005 Marty Sertich, Colorado Coll., F
1986 Scott Fusco, Harvard, F	1996 Brian Bonin, Minnesota, F	2006 Matt Carle, Denver, D
1987 Tony Hrkac, North Dakota, F	1997 Brendan Morrison, Michigan, F	2007 Ryan Duncan, North Dakota, F
1988 Robb Stauber, Minnesota, G	1998 Chris Drury, Boston U., F	2008 Kevin Porter, Michigan, F
1989 Lane MacDonald, Harvard, F	1999 Jason Krog, UNH, F	
1990 Kip Miller, Michigan St., F	2000 Mike Mottau, Boston College, D	

NCAA Women's Frozen Four

Women's college hockey was officially introduced as an NCAA Division I sport in 2000-01.
   Multiple winner: Minnesota-Duluth (4); Minnesota and Wisconsin (2).

Year	Champion	Head Coach	Score	Runner-up	Third Place	Score	Fourth Place
2001	Minnesota Duluth	Shannon Miller	4-2	St. Lawrence	Harvard	3-2	Dartmouth
2002	Minnesota Duluth	Shannon Miller	3-2	Brown	(tie) Niagara and Minnesota, .2-2		
2003	Minnesota Duluth	Shannon Miller	4-3*	Harvard	Dartmouth	4-2	Minnesota
2004	Minnesota	Laura Halldorson	6-2	Harvard	St. Lawrence	2-1	Dartmouth
2005	Minnesota	Laura Halldorson	4-3	Harvard	St. Lawrence	5-1	Dartmouth
2006	Wisconsin	Mark Johnson	3-0	Minnesota	New Hampshire and St. Lawrence (no game)		
2007	Wisconsin	Mark Johnson	4-1	Minnesota Duluth	Boston College and St. Lawrence (no·game)		
2008	Minnesota Duluth	Shannon Miller	4-0	Wisconsin	New Hampshire and Harvard (no game)		

* 2nd OT

Patty Kazmaier Award

Awarded annually to the women's Division I player who displays the highest standards of personal and team excellence during the season; voted on by a 13-member panel of national media, college coaches and one USA Hockey member. First presented in 1998, in the name of the Princeton collegiate hockey and lacrosse star who died in 1990 of a rare blood disease.
   Multiple winner: Jennifer Botterill (2).

Year	Year	Year
1998 Brandy Fisher, New Hampshire, F	2002 Brooke Whitney, Northeastern, F	2006 Sara Bauer, Wisconsin, F
1999 A.J. Mleczko, Harvard, F	2003 Jennifer Botterill, Harvard, F	2007 Julie Chu, Harvard, F.
2000 Ali Brewer, Brown, G	2004 Angela Ruggiero, Harvard, D	2008 Sarah Vaillancourt, Harvard, F
2001 Jennifer Botterill, Harvard, F	2005 Krissy Wendell, Minnesota, F	

Late-round pick/waiver-wire pickup **Cliff Lee** rewarded owners with 22 wins and a 2.54 ERA.

FANTASY SPORTS HAVE HIT A WALL

Now the real fun starts.

by Peter Keating

THERE ARE TWO KINDS OF FANTASY PLAYERS: CONTROLLED ADDICTS AND BINGE TWEAKERS. Controlled Addicts are the guys who check rosters and make trades as part of their daily routine; friends and family are aware of waiver deadlines and know better than to interrupt a draft. CAs may participate in multiple leagues, but probably the same ones they've been in for years. Their fiercest rivals are among their closest pals. When Pedro Martinez went down, the Addict who owned him thought, "Maybe this gives me a chance to start Edinson Volquez."

Binge Tweakers, on the other hand, are always looking for new action. They crave the high of serial competition more than the satisfaction of winning. BTs join as many leagues as they can, compete online against people they don't know and are

game for any sport. When Martinez went down, the Binger who owned him thought, "I've got healthy hurlers on my seven other teams. And I'm still alive in three NCAA pools!"

Well, after years of trying to hook more CAs, the fantasy industry has shifted its focus to the BTs. Until recently, you see, so many new players signed up for leagues each year that the industry found it easy to boost revenues, which hit $2 billion in 2007, according to the Fantasy Sports Trade Association. But now standard-issue fantasy football and baseball have become what economists call mature markets. They've gathered about as many players as they're ever going to get.

In 2007, the number of Americans who started playing fantasy football was matched by the number who dropped the habit, and the number of teams managed by fantasy football players stayed level. Companies realize they have to devise new ways to get their most excitable existing customers—the BTs—to spend more cash.

Peter Keating writes "The Biz" column for *ESPN The Magazine* and is the author of "Dingers! A Short History of the Long Ball."

Cheat sheets? Check. Cheese puffs? Check. $20 trophy. Check. Thirteen guys in a basement? Check. If this scene looks familiar to you, you're probably one of North America's 19.4 million fantasy players.

If you're a CA, this is no biggie. You might find that a new outfit is running your league, because businesses that run fantasy apps will start to gobble each other up to bring in more money. But consolidation won't affect your chances of drafting Edwin Encarnacion.

If you're a BT, though, get ready. Here's what's coming down the pike:

1. "Fantasy sports" will soon cover every kind of competition imaginable. There's already fantasy Madden, fantasy fashion and fantasy Survivor. Leagues are popping up around everything from movie box-office receipts to congressional voting to assembling the cast for Saturday Night Live. But beyond all the bizarre ideas out there, two sports stand a fairly good chance of breaking out: golf and bass fishing. Seriously. Both have tours of periodic events and are quite addictive once you start following them. Fantasy bass fishing has major money behind it too: FLW Fantasy Fishing (which is free to play) has Wal-Mart as a title sponsor and is offering $1.7 million in prize money in 2008, the biggest fantasy payout ever.

2. Stakes will be raised to feed the rush. The World Championship of Fantasy Football already holds drafts on casino floors, and

an outfit calling itself "THE Fantasy Football League" plans to charge players 20 grand for a chance at a $150,000 purse. Yes, it's pricey, but in the early days of new industries, startups sell creative products at crazy prices, and jonesing BTs might just pay for it.

3. You'll get ever more real-time access to fantasy data. That equals more sugar for BTs and means it will be even easier to play at work. Increasingly, players are making friends at the office through fantasy leagues or talking about them around the watercooler, according to FSTA surveys. It's why CBS Sports made all NCAA Tourney games available for free over the web this year and why the fantasy sections at ESPN.com are dedicated to providing users with nonstop news in those few hours between SportsCenters.

It's all about feeding the obsession. Of course, while the number of supervisors who play fantasy is rising, so is the number of firms trying to ban access to fantasy sites from cubicleland. So you'll have to befriend your IT department to keep access to your fantasy info—or invite your boss to play.

One last thing about the two kinds of fantasy players: Over time, they can change. Binge Tweakers settle down; Controlled Addicts get restless, especially if they find new opportunities. You might be in just one baseball league today, but a year from now, you might be researching the best holes for anglers at Lake Tohopekaliga.

Fantasy Fast Facts

- 19.4 million people age 12 and up are now playing fantasy sports in the U.S. and Canada.

- Over 2 million of those 19.4 million are teenagers.

- 34 million people are either playing or have at one time played fantasy sports.

- Players spend an average of $467.60 per year on fantasy sports.

- 92 percent are male, 77 percent are married

- Total market size is estimated at more than $1.5 billion, including sponsorships, endorsements, contest management and advertising.

- 80% of people that play fantasy sports play fantasy football, followed by baseball at 30% and auto racing at 26%.

- Average player age is 36.

- 71 percent have a bachelor's degree.

- Avg. fantasy player owns two teams.

Source:
Fantasy Sports Trade Association

Fantasy Football Top Performers (1996-2007)

Time to relive all of your draft-day steals for the past 12 years. Listed are the top 20 fantasy football performers from 1996-2007. The scoring system used to devise the rankings is based on a combination of yardage accumulated and touchdowns scored/thrown. Note that TD shown below refer to passing touchdowns for quarterbacks, and total touchdowns for all others. (*) denotes rookie.

1996

Favre dominates in his only Super Bowl-winning season. Terry Allen explodes for 21 rushing touchdowns with the 'Skins.

	Player	Pos	Key Statistics
1	Brett Favre, GB	QB	3899 passing yards, 39 TD
2	Vinny Testaverde, Bal.	QB	4177 passing yards, 33 TD
3	Terry Allen, Wash.	RB	1353 rushing yards, 21 TD
4	Terrell Davis, Den.	RB	1538 rushing yards, 15 TD
5	Mark Brunell, Jax	QB	4367 passing yards, 19 TD
6	Ricky Watters, Phi.	RB	1411 rushing yards, 13 TD
7	John Elway, Den.	QB	3328 passing yards, 26 TD
8	Jeff Blake, Cin.	QB	3624 passing yards, 24 TD
9	Curtis Martin, NE	RB	1152 rushing yards, 17 TD
10	Drew Bledsoe, NE	QB	4086 passing yards, 27 TD
11	Emmitt Smith, Dal.	RB	1204 rushing yards, 15 TD
12	Barry Sanders, Det.	RB	1553 rushing yards, 10 TD
13	Jerome Bettis, Pit.	RB	1431 rushing yards, 11 TD
14	Michael Jackson, Bal.	WR	1201 receiving yards, 14 TD
15	Tony Martin, SD	WR	1171 receiving yards, 14 TD
16	Eddie George*, Hou.	RB	1368 rushing yards, 8 TD
17	Steve Young, SF	QB	2410 passing yards, 14 TD
18	Carl Pickens, Cin.	WR	1180 receiving yards, 12 TD
19	Jeff Hostetler, Oak.	QB	2548 passing yards, 23 TD
20	Jerry Rice, SF	WR	1254 receiving yards, 9 TD

1997

Electrifying Lion Barry Sanders joins the 2000-yard club.

	Player	Pos	Key Statistics
1	Barry Sanders, Det.	RB	2053 rushing yards, 14 TD
2	Terrell Davis, Den.	RB	1750 rushing yards, 15 TD
3	Brett Favre, GB	QB	3867 passing yards, 35 TD
4	Kordell Stewart, Pit.	QB	21 passing TD, 11 rushing
5	Jeff George, Oak.	QB	3917 passing yards, 29 TD
6	Dorsey Levens, GB	RB	1435 rushing yards, 12 TD
7	John Elway, Den.	QB	3635 passing yards, 27 TD
8	Steve McNair, Ten.	QB	14 passing TD, 8 rushing
9	Drew Bledsoe, NE	QB	3706 passing yards, 28 TD
10	Steve Young, SF	QB	3029 passing yards, 19 TD
11	Mark Brunell, Jax	QB	3281 passing yards, 18 TD
12	Jerome Bettis, Pit.	RB	1665 rushing yards, 9 TD
13	Warren Moon, Sea.	QB	3678 passing yards, 25 TD
14	K. Abdul-Jabbar, Mia.	RB	892 rushing yards, 16 TD
15	N. Kaufman, Oak.	RB	1294 rushing yards, 8 TD
16	Rob Moore, Ari.	WR	1584 receiving yards, 8 TD
17	Corey Dillon*, Cin.	RB	1129 rushing yards, 10 TD
18	Antonio Freeman, GB	WR	1243 receiving yards, 12 TD
19	Marshall Faulk, Ind.	RB	1054 rushing yards, 8 TD
20	Brad Johnson, Min.	QB	3036 passing yards, 20 TD

1998

TD cracks 2000; welcome to the top-20 Moss and Owens.

	Player	Pos	Key Statistics
1	Terrell Davis, Den.	RB	2008 rushing yards, 21 TD
2	Steve Young, SF	QB	36 passing TD, 6 rushing TD
3	Jamal Anderson, Atl	RB	1846 rushing yards, 14 TD
4	R. Cunningham, Min	QB	3704 passing yards, 34 TD
5	Marshall Faulk, Ind.	RB	2227 all-purpose yards, 10 TD
6	Fred Taylor*, Jax	RB	1223 rushing yards, 17 TD
7	Brett Favre, GB	QB	4212 passing yards, 31 TD
8	Garrison Hearst, SF	RB	1570 rushing yards, 9 TD
9	Steve McNair, Ten	QB	3228 passing yards, 15 TD
10	Vinny Testaverde, NYJ	QB	3256 passing yards, 29 TD

	Player	Pos	Key Statistics
11	Emmitt Smith, Dal.	RB	1332 rushing yards, 15 TD
12	Randy Moss*, Min.	WR	1313 receiving yards, 17 TD
13	Antonio Freeman, GB	WR	1424 receiving yards, 14 TD
14	Chris Chandler, Atl.	QB	3154 passing yards, 25 TD
15	Curtis Martin, NYJ	RB	1287 rushing yards, 9 TD
16	Trent Green, Wash.	QB	3441 passing yards, 23 TD
17	Ricky Watters, Sea.	RB	1239 rushing yards, 9 TD
18	Robert Edwards*, NE	RB	1115 rushing yards, 12 TD
19	Jake Plummer, Ari.	QB	3737 passing yards, 17 TD
20	Terrell Owens, SF	WR	1097 receiving yards, 15 TD

1999

Warner breaks out with the most surprising year in fantasy football history. Manning and Harrison join the party.

	Player	Pos	Key Statistics
1	Kurt Warner, St.L	QB	4353 passing yards, 41 TD
2	Marshall Faulk, St.L	RB	2429 all-purpose yards, 12 TD
3	Edgerrin James*, Ind.	RB	1553 rushing yards, 17 TD
4	Steve Beuerlein, Car.	QB	4436 passing yards, 36 TD
5	Rich Gannon, Oak.	QB	3840 passing yards, 24 TD
6	Peyton Manning, Ind.	QB	4135 passing yards, 26 TD
7	Stephen Davis, Wash.	RB	1405 rushing yards, 17 TD
8	Eddie George, Ten.	RB	1304 rushing yards, 13 TD
9	Marvin Harrison, Ind.	WR	1663 receiving yards, 12 TD
10	Brad Johnson, Wash.	QB	4005 passing yards, 24 TD
11	Emmitt Smith, Dal.	RB	1397 rushing yards, 13 TD
12	Randy Moss, Min.	WR	1413 receiving yards, 12 TD
13	Doug Flutie, Buf.	QB	3171 passing yards, 19 TD
14	Brett Favre, GB	QB	4091 passing yards, 22 TD
15	Dorsey Levens, GB	RB	1034 rushing yards, 10 TD
16	Charlie Garner, SF	RB	1229 rushing yards, 6 TD
17	Cris Carter, Min.	WR	1241 receiving yards, 13 TD
18	Curtis Martin, NYJ	RB	1464 rushing yards, 5 TD
19	Steve McNair, Ten.	QB	12 passing TD, 8 rushing TD
20	Jimmy Smith, Jax	WR	1636 receiving yards, 6 TD

2000

Faulk scores 26 total touchdowns (18 rushing, 8 receiving) to break Emmitt Smith's former single-season record of 25.

	Player	Pos	Key Statistics
1	Marshall Faulk, St.L	RB	2207 all-purpose yards, 26 TD
2	D. Culpepper, Min.	QB	33 passing TD, 7 rushing TD
3	Jeff Garcia, SF	QB	4278 passing yards, 31 TD
4	Edgerrin James, Ind.	RB	1709 rushing yards, 18 TD
5	Peyton Manning, Ind.	QB	4413 passing yards, 33 TD
6	Rich Gannon, Oak.	QB	3430 passing yards, 28 TD
7	Eddie George, Ten.	RB	1509 rushing yards, 16 TD
8	D. McNabb, Phi.	QB	21 passing TD, 6 rushing TD
9	Elvis Grbac, KC	QB	4169 passing yards, 28 TD
10	Mike Anderson*, Den.	RB	1500 rushing yards, 15 TD
11	Robert Smith, Min.	RB	1521 rushing yards, 10 TD
12	Fred Taylor, Jax	RB	1399 rushing yards, 14 TD
13	Ahman Green, GB	RB	1175 rushing yards, 13 TD
14	Curtis Martin, NYJ	RB	1204 rushing yards, 11 TD
15	Ricky Watters, Sea.	RB	1242 rushing yards, 9 TD
16	Randy Moss, Min.	WR	1437 receiving yards, 15 TD
17	Charlie Garner, SF	RB	1142 rushing yards, 10 TD
18	Mark Brunell, Jax	QB	3640 passing yards, 20 TD
19	Lamar Smith, Mia.	RB	1139 rushing yards, 16 TD
20	Marvin Harrison, Ind.	WR	1413 receiving yards, 14 TD

Fantasy Football Top Performers (Cont.)

2001

The Rams are at it again, at least until their meeting with the Pats in the Super Bowl; Priest Holmes has his bust-out season; how did Jay Fiedler get in there?

Player	Pos	Key Statistics
1 Marshall Faulk, St.L	RB	2147 all-purpose yards, 21 TD
2 Kurt Warner, St.L	QB	4830 passing yards, 36 TD
3 Jeff Garcia, SF	QB	3538 passing yards, 32 TD
4 Priest Holmes, KC	RB	2169 all-purpose yards, 10 TD
5 Rich Gannon, Oak.	QB	3828 passing yards, 27 TD
6 Steve McNair, Ten.	QB	21 passing TD, 5 rushing TD
7 D. McNabb, Phi.	QB	3233 passing yards, 25 TD
8 Peyton Manning, Ind.	QB	4131 passing yards, 26 TD
9 Ahman Green, Gb	RB	1387 rushing yards, 11 TD
10 Brett Favre, GB	QB	3921 passing yards, 32 TD
11 Aaron Brooks, NO	QB	3832 passing yards, 26 TD
12 Shaun Alexander, Sea.	RB	1318 rushing yards, 16 TD
13 Curtis Martin, NYJ	RB	1513 rushing yards, 10 TD
14 Marvin Harrison, Ind.	WR	1524 receiving yards, 15 TD
15 Terrell Owens, SF	WR	1412 receiving yards, 16 TD
16 Kordell Stewart, Pit.	QB	14 passing TD, 5 rushing TD
17 Jay Fiedler, Mia.	QB	20 passing TD, 4 rushing TD
18 Corey Dillon, Cin.	RB	1315 rushing yards, 13 TD
19 L. Tomlinson*, SD	RB	1236 rushing yards, 10 TD
20 David Boston, Ari.	WR	1598 receiving yards, 8 TD

2002

Priest Holmes solidifies himself as a top pick; Ricky Williams enjoys South Beach; Clinton Portis has a fine rookie season.

Player	Pos	Key Statistics
1 Priest Holmes, KC	RB	2287 all-purpose yards, 24 TD
2 Ricky Williams, Mia.	RB	1853 rushing yards, 17 TD
3 L. Tomlinson, SD	RB	1683 rushing yards, 15 TD
4 Rich Gannon, Oak.	QB	4689 passing yards, 26 TD
5 Michael Vick, Atl.	QB	16 passing TD, 8 rushing TD
6 D. Culpepper, Min.	QB	18 passing TD, 10 rushing TD
7 Clinton Portis*, Den.	RB	1508 rushing yards, 17 TD
8 Shaun Alexander, Sea.	RB	1175 rushing yards, 18 TD
9 Deuce McAllister, NO	RB	1388 rushing yards, 16 TD
10 Peyton Manning, Ind.	QB	4200 passing yards, 27 TD
11 Charlie Garner, Oak.	RB	1903 all-purpose yards, 11 TD
12 Steve McNair, Ten.	QB	3387 passing yards, 22 TD
13 Trent Green, KC	QB	3690 passing yards, 26 TD
14 Drew Bledsoe, Buf.	QB	4359 passing yards, 24 TD
15 Tiki Barber, NYG	RB	1989 all-purpose yards, 11 TD
16 Aaron Brooks, NO	QB	3572 passing yards, 26 TD
17 Jeff Garcia, SF	QB	3344 passing yards, 21 TD
18 Tom Brady, NE	QB	3764 passing yards, 28 TD
19 Travis Henry, Buf.	RB	1438 rushing yards, 14 TD
20 Marvin Harrison, Ind.	WR	1722 receiving yards, 11 TD

2003

Holmes sets a new single-season touchdown record; Jamal Lewis misses the single-season rushing mark by 39 yards.

Player	Pos	Key Statistics
1 Priest Holmes, KC	RB	2110 all-purpose yards, 27 TD
2 L. Tomlinson, SD	RB	2370 all-purpose yards, 17 TD
3 Ahman Green, GB	RB	1883 rushing yards, 20 TD
4 Jamal Lewis, Bal.	RB	2066 rushing yards, 14 TD
5 D. Culpepper, Min.	QB	3479 passing yards, 25 TD
6 Clinton Portis, Den.	RB	1591 rushing yards, 14 TD
7 Peyton Manning, Ind.	QB	4267 passing yards, 29 TD
8 Randy Moss, Min.	WR	1632 receiving yards, 17 TD
9 Shaun Alexander, Sea.	RB	1435 rushing yards, 16 TD
10 Deuce McAllister, NO	RB	1641 rushing yards, 8 TD

Player	Pos	Key Statistics
11 Trent Green, KC	QB	4039 passing yards, 24 TD
12 Matt Hasselbeck, Sea.	QB	3841 passing yards, 26 TD
13 Torry Holt, St.L	WR	1696 receiving yards, 12 TD
14 Steve McNair, Ten.	QB	24 passing TD, 4 rushing TD
15 Aaron Brooks, NO	QB	3546 passing yards, 24 TD
16 Fred Taylor, Jax	RB	1572 rushing yards, 7 TD
17 Jon Kitna, Cin.	QB	3591 passing yards, 26 TD
18 Jeff Garcia, SF	QB	18 passing TD, 7 rushing TD
19 Ricky Williams, Mia.	RB	1372 rushing yards, 10 TD
20 Brett Favre, GB	QB	3361 passing yards, 32 TD

2004

Manning breaks Marino's record for TD passes, still beaten out by Culpepper as the top fantasy scorer; Ricky Williams sticks it to keeper-league owners everywhere by retiring just before training camp.

Player	Pos	Key Statistics
1 D. Culpepper, Min.	QB	4717 passing yards, 39 TD
2 Peyton Manning, Ind.	QB	4557 passing yards, 49 TD
3 Shaun Alexander, Sea.	RB	1696 rushing yards, 20 TD
4 Tiki Barber, NYG	RB	2096 all-purpose yards, 15 TD
5 D. McNabb, Phi.	QB	3875 passing yards, 31 TD
6 L. Tomlinson, SD	RB	1335 rushing yards, 18 TD
7 Curtis Martin, NYJ	RB	1697 rushing yards, 14 TD
8 Trent Green, KC	QB	4591 passing yards, 27 TD
9 Jake Plummer, Den.	QB	4089 passing yards, 27 TD
10 Domanick Davis, Hou.	RB	1188 rushing yards, 14 TD
11 Edgerrin James, Ind.	RB	1548 rushing yards, 9 TD
12 Brett Favre, GB	QB	4088 passing yards, 30 TD
13 Jake Delhomme, Car.	QB	3886 passing yards, 29 TD
14 Corey Dillon, NE	RB	1635 rushing yards, 13 TD
15 Aaron Brooks, NO	QB	21 passing TD, 4 rushing TD
16 Drew Brees, SD	QB	3159 passing yards, 27 TD
17 M. Muhammad, Car.	WR	1405 receiving yards, 16 TD
18 Marc Bulger, St.L	QB	3964 passing yards, 21 TD
19 Tom Brady, NE	QB	3692 passing yards, 28 TD
20 Michael Vick, Atl.	QB	2313 passing yards, 14 TD

2005

It's Shaun Alexander's turn to set a new single-season touchdown record (28); Larry Johnson takes advantage of the KC offensive line; Carson Palmer is the top-scoring fantasy quarterback of the year.

Player	Pos	Key Statistics
1 Shaun Alexander, Sea.	RB	1880 rushing yards, 28 TD
2 Larry Johnson, KC	RB	1750 rushing yards, 21 TD
3 L. Tomlinson, SD	RB	1462 rushing yards, 20 TD
4 Tiki Barber, NYG	RB	2390 all-purpose yards, 11 TD
5 Edgerrin James, Ind.	RB	1506 rushing yards, 14 TD
6 Carson Palmer, Cin.	QB	3836 passing yards, 32 TD
7 Tom Brady, NE	QB	4110 passing yards, 26 TD
8 Peyton Manning, Ind.	QB	3747 passing yards, 28 TD
9 Clinton Portis, Wash.	RB	1516 rushing yards, 11 TD
10 Steve Smith, Car.	WR	1563 receiving yards, 13 TD
11 Matt Hasselbeck, Sea.	QB	3459 passing yards, 24 TD
12 Rudi Johnson, Cin.	RB	1458 rushing yards, 12 TD
13 Eli Manning, NYG	QB	3762 passing yards, 24 TD
14 LaMont Jordan, Oak.	RB	1025 rushing yards, 11 TD
15 Jake Plummer, Den.	QB	3366 passing yards, 18 TD
16 Michael Vick, Atl.	QB	15 passing TD, 6 rushing TD
17 Drew Brees, SD	QB	3576 passing yards, 24 TD
18 Trent Green, KC	QB	4014 passing yards, 17 TD
19 Kerry Collins, Oak.	QB	3759 passing yards, 20 TD
20 Drew Bledsoe, Dal.	QB	3639 passing yards, 23 TD

Colts QB **Peyton Manning** became a top-ten fantasy performer and first-round fantasy draft pick in 1999...and he's been there ever since.

2006

Tomlinson has a season for the ages, smashing the single season record for TD with 31; Manning continues to be his usual stellar self, leading the Colts to Super Bowl; Brees does his part to help the city of New Orleans recover.

	Player	Pos	Key Statistics
1	L. Tomlinson, SD	RB	2323 all-purpose yards, 31 TD
2	Peyton Manning, Ind.	QB	4397 passing yards, 31 TD
3	Larry Johnson, KC	RB	2199 all-purpose yards, 19 TD
4	Drew Brees, NO	QB	4418 passing yards, 26 TD
5	Steven Jackson, St.L	RB	2334 all-purpose yards, 16 TD
6	Jon Kitna, Det	QB	4208 passing yards, 21 TD
7	Michael Vick, Atl	QB	2272 pass/1039 rush yards
8	Carson Palmer, Cin	QB	4035 passing yards, 28 TD
9	Marc Bulger, St.L	QB	4301 passing yards, 24 TD
10	Tom Brady, NE	QB	3529 passing yards, 24 TD
11	Brett Favre, GB	QB	3885 passing yards, 18 TD
12	Frank Gore, SF	RB	2180 all-purpose yards, 9 TD
13	B. Roethlisberger, Pit.	QB	2513 passing yards, 18 TD
14	Willie Parker, Pit	RB	1494 rushing yards, 16 TD
15	M. Jones-Drew, Jax	RB	2250 all-purpose yards, 16 TD
16	Philip Rivers, SD	QB	3388 passing yards, 22 TD
17	Eli Manning, NYG	QB	3244 passing yards, 24 TD
18	Brian Westbrook, Phi	RB	1955 all-purpose yards, 11 TD
19	Tiki Barber, NYG	RB	2127 all-purpose yards, 5 TD
20	Marvin Harrison, Ind.	WR	1366 receiving yards, 12 TD

2007

Brady and Moss enjoy their first season together, setting new NFL marks for TD thrown and caught; Tomlinson is still on his game; Favre has a resurgence; and rookie Peterson enters the top 20, where he's likely to stay for the foreseeable future.

	Player	Pos	Key Statistics
1	Tom Brady, NE	QB	4806 passing yards, 50 TD
2	L. Tomlinson, SD	RB	1474 rushing yards, 18 TD
3	Tony Romo, Dal.	QB	4211 passing yards, 36 TD
4	Randy Moss, NE	WR	1493 receiving yards, 23 TD
5	Brian Westbrook, Phi.	RB	2104 all-purpose yards, 12 TD
6	Peyton Manning, Ind.	QB	4040 passing yards, 31 TD
7	Ben Roethlisberger, Pit.	QB	3154 passing yards, 32 TD
8	Drew Brees, NO	QB	4428 passing yards, 28 TD
9	Derek Anderson, Cle.	QB	3787 passing yards, 29 TD
10	Brett Favre, GB	QB	4155 passing yards, 28 TD
11	Matt Hasselbeck, Sea.	QB	2966 passing yards, 28 TD
12	Joseph Addai, Ind.	RB	1072 rushing yards, 15 TD
13	Adrian Peterson, Min.	RB	1341 rushing yards, 13 TD
14	Carson Palmer, Cin.	QB	4131 passing yards, 26 TD
15	Terrell Owens, Dal.	WR	1355 receiving yards, 15 TD
16	Braylon Edwards, Cle.	WR	1289 receiving yards, 16 TD
17	Clinton Portis, Wash.	RB	1262 rushing yards, 11 TD
18	Jamal Lewis, Bal.	RB	1304 rushing yards, 11 TD
19	Kurt Warner, Ari.	QB	3417 passing yards, 27 TD
20	Reggie Wayne, Ind.	WR	1510 receiving yards, 10 TD

Fantasy Baseball Top Performers (1996-2008)

Listed are the top 10 fantasy baseball positional players and top five fantasy pitchers from 1996-2008. The rankings are based on a typical 5 x 5 scoring system, where the following stats are used: batting average, home runs, runs batted in, runs, stolen bases for hitters; and wins, saves, strikeouts, earned run average and WHIP (walks + hits per inning pitched) for pitchers. (*) denotes rookie.

1996

Coors Field provides three memorable performances, and who can forget the Brady Anderson 50-homer year?

Hitter	Pos	Avg	HR	RBI	SB	R
1 Ellis Burks, Col.	OF	.344	40	128	32	142
2 Barry Bonds, SF	OF	.308	42	129	40	122
3 Alex Rodriguez, Sea.	SS	.358	36	123	15	141
4 A. Galarraga, Col.	1B	.304	47	150	18	119
5 Ken Griffey Jr., Sea.	OF	.303	49	140	16	125
6 Albert Belle, Cle.	OF	.311	48	148	11	124
7 Brady Anderson, Bal.	OF	.297	50	110	21	117
8 Kenny Lofton, Cle.	OF	.317	14	67	75	132
9 Dante Bichette, Col.	OF	.313	31	141	31	114
10 Mo Vaughn, Bos.	1B	.326	44	143	2	118

Pitcher	Pos	W	Sv	ERA	WHIP	K
1 John Smoltz, Atl.	SP	24	0	2.94	1.00	276
2 Kevin Brown, Fla.	SP	17	0	1.89	0.94	159
3 Greg Maddux, Atl.	SP	15	0	2.72	1.03	172
4 Hideo Nomo, LA	SP	16	0	3.19	1.16	234
5 Trevor Hoffman, SD	RP	9	42	2.25	0.92	111

1997

Griffey's best season still not enough to win, while Rocket's first year in Canada takes pitching honors.

Hitter	Pos	Avg	HR	RBI	SB	R
1 Larry Walker, Col.	OF	.366	49	130	33	143
2 Ken Griffey Jr., Sea.	OF	.304	56	147	15	125
3 Jeff Bagwell, Hou.	1B	.286	43	135	31	109
4 A. Galarraga, Col.	1B	.318	41	140	15	120
5 Barry Bonds, SF	OF	.291	40	101	37	123
6 Mike Piazza, LA	C	.362	40	124	5	104
7 Craig Biggio, Hou.	2B	.309	22	81	47	146
8 M. McGwire, Oak.-St.L	1B	.274	58	123	3	86
9 Frank Thomas, ChW	DH	.347	35	125	1	110
10 Raul Mondesi, LA	OF	.310	30	87	32	95

Pitcher	Pos	W	Sv	ERA	WHIP	K
1 Roger Clemens, Tor.	SP	21	0	2.05	1.03	292
2 Pedro Martinez, Mon.	SP	17	0	1.90	0.93	305
3 Randy Johnson, Sea.	SP	20	0	2.28	1.05	291
4 Curt Schilling, Phi.	SP	17	0	2.97	1.05	319
5 Greg Maddux, Atl.	SP	19	0	2.20	0.95	177

1998

The single-season homer mark gets broken by two hitters, but Sosa gets the nod with his stolen bases.

Hitter	Pos	Avg	HR	RBI	SB	R
1 Sammy Sosa, ChC	OF	.308	66	158	18	134
2 Alex Rodriguez, Sea.	SS	.310	42	124	46	123
3 Mark McGwire, St.L	1B	.299	70	147	1	130
4 Ken Griffey Jr., Sea.	OF	.284	56	146	20	120
5 Albert Belle, ChW	OF	.328	49	152	6	113
6 Vinny Castilla, Col.	3B	.319	46	144	5	108
7 Juan Gonzalez, Tex.	OF	.318	45	157	2	110
8 Barry Bonds, SF	OF	.303	37	122	28	120
9 Craig Biggio, Hou.	2B	.325	20	88	50	123
10 V. Guerrero, Mon.	OF	.324	38	109	11	108

Pitcher	Pos	W	Sv	ERA	WHIP	K
1 Greg Maddux, Atl.	SP	18	0	2.22	0.98	204
2 Roger Clemens, Tor.	SP	20	0	2.65	1.10	271
3 Kevin Brown, SD	SP	18	0	2.38	1.07	257
4 Pedro Martinez, Bos.	SP	19	0	2.89	1.09	251
5 Curt Schilling, Phi.	SP	15	0	3.25	1.11	300

1999

The power of power is evident as Bagwell's second 30-30 season gets trumped by Slammin' Sammy.

Hitter	Pos	Avg	HR	RBI	SB	R
1 Sammy Sosa, ChC	OF	.288	63	141	7	114
2 Jeff Bagwell, Hou.	1B	.304	42	126	30	143
3 Chipper Jones, Atl.	3B	.319	45	110	25	116
4 Mark McGwire, St.L	1B	.278	65	147	0	118
5 Ken Griffey Jr., Sea.	OF	.285	48	134	24	123
6 Manny Ramirez, Cle.	OF	.333	44	165	2	131
7 Shawn Green, Tor.	OF	.309	42	123	20	134
8 Ivan Rodriguez, Tex.	C	.332	35	113	25	116
9 Larry Walker, Col.	OF	.379	37	115	11	108
10 Roberto Alomar, Cle.	2B	.323	24	120	37	138

Pitcher	Pos	W	Sv	ERA	WHIP	K
1 Pedro Martinez, Bos.	SP	23	0	2.07	0.92	313
2 Randy Johnson, Ari.	SP	17	0	2.48	1.02	364
3 Kevin Millwood, Atl.	SP	18	0	2.68	1.00	205
4 Kevin Brown, LA	SP	18	0	3.00	1.07	221
5 Billy Wagner, Hou.	RP	4	39	1.57	0.78	124

2000

Todd Helton enjoys his best season to keep Jeff Bagwell at No. 2, while Pedro edges the Big Unit for the second straight season.

Hitter	Pos	Avg	HR	RBI	SB	R
1 Todd Helton, Col.	1B	.372	42	147	5	138
2 Jeff Bagwell, Hou.	1B	.310	47	132	9	152
3 Sammy Sosa, Chc	OF	.320	50	138	7	106
4 V. Guerrero, Mon.	OF	.345	44	123	9	101
5 Alex Rodriguez, Sea.	SS	.316	41	132	15	134
6 Darin Erstad, Ana.	OF	.355	25	100	28	121
7 Richard Hidalgo, Hou.	OF	.314	44	122	13	118
8 Barry Bonds, SF	OF	.306	49	106	11	129
9 Carlos Delgado, Tor.	1B	.344	41	137	0	115
10 Frank Thomas, ChW	DH	.328	43	143	1	115

Pitcher	Pos	W	Sv	ERA	WHIP	K
1 Pedro Martinez, Bos.	SP	18	0	1.74	0.74	284
2 Randy Johnson, Ari.	SP	19	0	2.64	1.12	347
3 Kevin Brown, LA	SP	13	0	2.58	0.99	216
4 Greg Maddux, Atl.	SP	19	0	3.00	1.07	190
5 Robb Nen, SF	RP	4	41	1.50	0.85	92

2001

Bonds breaks HR record for his only time as fantasy's top hitter

Hitter	Pos	Avg	HR	RBI	SB	R
1 Barry Bonds, SF	OF	.328	73	137	13	129
2 Sammy Sosa, ChC	OF	.328	64	160	0	146
3 Alex Rodriguez, Tex.	SS	.318	52	135	18	133
4 Luis Gonzalez, Ari.	OF	.325	57	142	1	128
5 Todd Helton, Col.	1B	.336	49	146	7	132
6 Shawn Green, LA	OF	.297	49	125	20	121
7 V. Guerrero, Mon.	OF	.307	34	108	37	107
8 Larry Walker, Col.	OF	.350	38	123	14	107
9 Ichiro Suzuki, Sea.	OF	.350	8	69	56	127
10 Bret Boone, Sea.	2B	.331	37	141	5	118

Pitcher	Pos	W	Sv	ERA	WHIP	K
1 Randy Johnson, Ari.	SP	21	0	2.49	1.01	372
2 Curt Schilling, Ari.	SP	22	0	2.98	1.08	293
3 Mike Mussina, NYY	SP	17	0	3.15	1.07	214
4 Greg Maddux, Atl.	SP	17	0	3.05	1.06	173
5 Javier Vazquez, Mon.	SP	16	0	3.42	1.08	208

Grabbing **Alex Rodriguez** with your first-round pick is about as close as you can get to a sure thing. The slugging third baseman has been one of the top ten fantasy hitters ten times in the last 13 years.

2002

One homer from 40-40, Vlad keeps A-Rod a runner up, while a pair of Arizona hurlers dominate the mound again.

	Hitter	Pos	Avg	HR	RBI	SB	R
1	V. Guerrero, Mon.	OF	.336	39	111	40	106
2	Alex Rodriguez, Tex.	SS	.300	57	142	9	125
3	Alfonso Soriano, NYY	2B	.300	39	102	41	128
4	Barry Bonds, SF	OF	.370	46	110	9	117
5	Jim Thome, Cle,	1B	.304	52	118	1	101
6	M. Ordonez, ChW	OF	.320	38	135	7	116
7	Jason Giambi, NYY	1B	.314	41	122	2	120
8	Sammy Sosa, ChC	OF	.288	49	108	2	122
9	Lance Berkman, Hou.	OF	.292	42	128	8	106
10	Miguel Tejada, Oak.	SS	.308	34	131	7	108

	Pitcher	Pos	W	Sv	ERA	WHIP	K
1	Randy Johnson, Ari.	SP	24	0	2.32	1.03	334
2	Curt Schilling, Ari.	SP	23	0	3.23	0.97	316
3	Pedro Martinez, Bos.	SP	20	0	2.26	0.92	239
4	Eric Gagne, LA	RP	4	52	1.97	0.86	114
5	Barry Zito, Oak.	SP	23	0	2.75	1.13	182

2003

Welcome to the list, Albert. Two top-10 newcomers (Pujols and Schmidt) are tops for the year.

	Hitter	Pos	Avg	HR	RBI	SB	R
1	Albert Pujols. St.L	1B	.359	43	124	5	137
2	Gary Sheffield, Atl.	OF	.330	39	132.	18	126
3	Alex Rodriguez, Tex.	SS	.298	47	118	17	124
4	Alfonso Soriano, NYY	2B	.290	38	91	35	114
5	Todd Helton, Col.	1B	.358	33	117	0	135
6	Barry Bonds, SF	OF	.341	45	90	7	111
7	Carlos Beltran, KC	OF	.307	26	100	41	102
8	Carlos Delgado, Tor.	1B	.302	42	145	0	117
9	Manny Ramirez, Bos.	OF	.325	37	104	3	117
10	Bret Boone, Sea.	2B	.294	35	117	16	111

	Pitcher	Pos	W	Sv	ERA	WHIP	K
1	Jason Schmidt, SF	SP	17	0	2.34	0.95	208
2	Eric Gagne, LA	RP	2	55	1.20	0.69	137
3	Mark Prior, ChC	SP	18	0	2.43	1.10	245
4	Roy Halladay, Tor.	SP	22	0	3.25	1.07	204
5	Esteban Loaiza, ChW	SP	21	0	2.90	1.11	207

2004

The Twins' Johan Santana finishes No. 1 among all players, a feat that will be duplicated the following two seasons.

	Hitter	Pos	Avg	HR	RBI	SB	R
1	V. Guerrero, Mon.	OF	.336	39	111	40	106
2	Alex Rodriguez, Tex.	SS	.300	57	142	9	125
3	Alfonso Soriano, NYY	2B	.300	39	102	41	128
4	Barry Bonds, SF	OF	.370	46	110	9	117
5	Jim Thome, Cle,	1B	.304	52	118	1	101
6	M. Ordonez, ChW	OF	.320	38	135	7	116
7	Jason Giambi, NYY	1B	.314	41	122	2	120
8	Sammy Sosa, ChC	OF	.288	49	108	2	122
9	Lance Berkman, Hou.	OF	.292	42	128	8	106
10	Miguel Tejada, Oak.	SS	.308	34	131	7	108

	Pitcher	Pos	W	Sv	ERA	WHIP	K
1	Randy Johnson, Ari.	SP	24	0	2.32	1.03	334
2	Curt Schilling, Ari.	SP	23	0	3.23	0.97	316
3	Pedro Martinez, Bos.	SP	20	0	2.26	0.92	239
4	Eric Gagne, LA	RP	4	52	1.97	0.86	114
5	Barry Zito, Oak.	SP	23	0	2.75	1.13	182

Fantasy Baseball Top Performers (Cont.)

2005

A-Rod's third best season finally results in top fantasy hitter honors. Santana plays sweet music again.

Hitter	Pos	Avg	HR	RBI	SB	R
1 A. Rodriguez, NYY	3B	.321	48	130	21	124
2 Derrek Lee, ChC	1B	.335	46	107	15	120
3 Albert Pujols, St.L	1B	.330	41	117	16	129
4 David Ortiz, Bos.	DH	.300	47	148	1	119
5 Mark Texeira, Tex.	1B	.301	43	144	4	112
6 Manny Ramirez, Bos.	OF	.292	45	144	1	112
7 Jason Bay, Pit.	OF	.306	32	101	21	110
8 Andruw Jones, Atl.	OF	.263	51	128	5	95
9 Alfonso Soriano, Tex.	2B	.268	36	104	30	102
10 V. Guerrero, LAA	OF	.317	32	108	13	95

Pitcher	Pos	W	Sv	ERA	WHIP	K
1 Johan Santana, Min.	SP	16	0	2.87	0.97	238
2 Chris Carpenter, St.L	SP	21	0	2.83	1.06	213
3 Roger Clemens, Hou.	SP	13	0	1.87	1.01	185
4 Pedro Martinez, NYM	SP	15	0	2.82	0.95	208
5 Dontrelle Willis, Fla.	SP	22	0	2.63	1.13	170

2006

Pujols holds off the HR champ, SB leader and 40-40 entrant for his second fantasy hitting title.

Hitter	Pos	Avg	HR	RBI	SB	R
1 Albert Pujols, St.L	1B	.331	49	137	7	119
2 Ryan Howard, Phi.	1B	.313	58	149	0	104
3 Jose Reyes, NYM	SS	.300	19	81	64	122
4 A. Soriano, Wash.	OF	.277	46	95	41	119
5 David Ortiz, Bos.	DH	.287	54	137	1	115
6 Derek Jeter, NYY	SS	.343	14	97	34	118
7 Matt Holliday, Col.	OF	.326	34	114	10	119
8 Carlos Beltran, NYM	OF	.275	41	116	18	127
9 Chase Utley, Phi.	2B	.309	32	102	15	131
10 Lance Berkman, Hou.	OF	.315	45	136	3	95

Pitcher	Pos	W	Sv	ERA	WHIP	K
1 Johan Santana, Min.	SP	19	0	2.77	0.98	245
2 Chris Carpenter, St.L	SP	15	0	3.09	1.07	184
3 Brandon Webb, Ari.	SP	16	0	3.10	1.13	178
4 John Smoltz, Atl.	SP	16	0	3.49	1.19	211
5 Roy Oswalt, Hou.	SP	15	0	2.98	1.17	166

2007

After a relatively tough 2006, A-Rod puts up a monster season in his contract year.

Hitter	Pos	Avg	HR	RBI	SB	R
1 A. Rodriguez, NYY	3B	.314	54	156	24	143
2 Hanley Ramirez, Fla.	SS	.332	29	81	51	125
3 Matt Holiday, Col.	OF	.340	36	137	11	120
4 M. Ordonez, Det.	OF	.363	28	139	4	117
5 David Wright, NYM	3B	.325	30	107	34	113
6 Jimmy Rollins, Phi	SS	.296	30	94	41	139
7 David Ortiz, Bos.	DH	.332	35	117	3	116
8 Prince Fielder, Mil.	1B	.288	50	119	2	109
9 Jose Reyes, NYM	SS	.280	12	57	78	119
10 Brandon Phillips, Cin.	2B	.288	30	94	32	107

Pitcher	Pos	W	Sv	ERA	WHIP	K
1 Jake Peavy, SD	SP	19	0	2.54	1.06	240
2 C.C. Sabathia, Cle.	SP	19	0	3.21	1.14	209
3 Johan Santana, Min.	SP	15	0	3.33	1.07	235
4 Josh Beckett, Bos.	SP	20	0	3.27	1.14	194
5 Brandon Webb, Ari.	SP	18	0	3.01	1.19	194

2008

Pujols grabs top billing for the third time with his blend of average and power, while Halladay puts it all together for the Jays.

Hitter	Pos	Avg	HR	RBI	SB	R
1 Albert Pujols, St.L	1B	.357	37	116	7	100
2 Jose Reyes, NYM	SS	.297	16	68	56	113
3 Hanley Ramirez, Fla	SS	.301	33	67	35	125
4 Matt Holliday, Col	OF	.321	25	88	28	107
5 David Wright, NYM	3B	.302	33	124	15	115
6 M. Ramirez, Bos-LAD	OF	.332	37	121	3	102
7 Lance Berkman, Hou	1B	.312	29	106	18	114
8 Dustin Pedroia, Bos	2B	.326	17	83	20	118
9 Alex Rodriguez, NYY	3B	.302	35	103	18	104
10 Grady Sizemore, Cle	OF	.268	33	90	38	101

Pitcher	Pos	W	Sv	ERA	WHIP	K
1 Roy Halladay, Tor	SP	20	0	2.78	1.05	206
2 CC Sabathia, Cle-Mil	SP	17	0	2.70	1.11	251
3 Tim Lincecum, SF	SP	18	0	2.62	1.17	265
4 Cliff Lee, Cle	SP	22	0	2.54	1.11	170
5 Mariano Rivera, NYY	RP	6	39	1.40	0.67	77

So Why Is It Called "Rotisserie" Baseball?

As legend has it, publishing executive and Rotisserie Baseball founding father Dan Okrent typed out the preliminary rules in the late 70s and presented them to a group of friends and colleagues at Manhattan's **La Rotisserie Francaise** on East 52nd Street (since shut down).

"An extremely undistinguished French restaurant," Okrent says.

Okrent, himself, can't confirm the exact dates (Dickson's Baseball Dictionary claims Rotisserie was born Nov. 17, 1979), but says the idea came to him during a flight between Hartford and Austin in the fall of 1979.

The original league consisted of 10 teams that included Okrent, Robert Sklar, Lee Eisenberg, Rob Fleder, Thomas Guinzberg, Cork Smith, Valerie Salembier, Peter Gethers, Bruce McCall, Michael Pollett and Glen Waggoner.

Sources: *New York Times, USA Today, ESPN The Magazine*

COLLEGE SPORTS

2007 / 2008 YEAR IN REVIEW

Utah's **Ashley Postell** won the women's all-around title at the NCAA gymnastics championships in April.

ACT OF SPORTSMANSHIP

Sara Tucholsky's first career home run will be remembered less for the actual hit and more for the way she circled the bases.

by Graham Hays

WESTERN OREGON SENIOR SARA TUCHOLSKY HAD NEVER HIT A HOME RUN IN HER CAREER.

Central Washington senior Mallory Holtman was already her school's career leader in them. But when a twist of fate and a torn knee ligament brought them face to face with each other and face to face with the end of their playing days, they combined on a home run trot that celebrated the collective human spirit far more than individual athletic achievement.

Both schools compete as Division II softball programs in the Great Northwest Athletic Conference. Neither had ever reached the NCAA tournament at the Division II level. But when they arrived for their conference doubleheader at Central Washington's 300-seat stadium in Ellensburg, a small town 100 miles and a mountain range removed from Seattle, the hosts resided one game behind the visitors at the top of the conference standings. As was the case at dozens of other diamonds across the map, two largely anonymous groups prepared to play the most meaningful games of their seasons.

It was a typical Saturday of softball in April, right down to a few overzealous fans heckling an easy target, the diminutive Tucholsky, when she came to the plate in the top of the second inning of the second game with two runners on base and the game still scoreless after Western Oregon's 8-1 win in the first game of the afternoon.

"I just remember trying to block them out," Tucholsky said of the hecklers. "The first pitch I took, it was a strike. And then I really don't remember where the home run pitch was at all; [I] just remember hitting it, and I knew it was out."

A part-time starter in the outfield throughout her four years, Tucholsky had been caught in a numbers game this season on a deep roster that

Graham Hays is a writer and contributor for ESPN.com's women's basketball, softball and soccer coverage.

215

Western Oregon's **Sara Tucholsky** is carried around the bases by Central Washington's **Liz Wallace**, left, and **Mallory Holtman** after injuring her knee following her home run on April 26.

entered the weekend hitting better than .280 and having won nine games in a row. Prior to the pitch she sent over the centerfield fence, she had just three hits in 34 at-bats this season. And in that respect, her hitting heroics would have made for a pleasing, if familiar, story line on their own: an unsung player steps up in one of her final games and lifts her team's postseason chances.

But it was what happened after an overly excited Tucholsky missed first base on her home run trot and reversed direction to tag the bag that proved unforgettable.

"Sara is small — she's like 5-2, really tiny," Western Oregon coach Pam Knox said. "So you would never think that she would hit a home run. The score was 0-0, and Sara hit a shot over centerfield. And I'm coaching third and I'm high-fiving the other two runners that came by — then all of a sudden, I look up, and I'm like, 'Where's Sara?' And I look over, and she's in a heap beyond first base."

While she was doubling back to tag first base, Tucholsky's right knee gave out. The two runners who had been on base already had crossed home plate, leaving her the only offensive player on the field of play, even as she lay crumpled

AP Images

Central Washington softball players **Liz Wallace**, left, and **Mallory Holtman**, right, join Western Oregon softball player **Sara Tucholsky** to accept the award for best moment at the ESPYs Awards on July 16, 2008 in Los Angeles.

in the dirt a few feet from first base and a long way from home plate. First base coach Shannon Prochaska — Tucholsky's teammate for three seasons and the only voice she later remembered hearing in the ensuing conversation — checked to see whether she could crawl back to the base under her own power.

As Knox explained, "It went through my mind, I thought, 'If I touch her, she's going to kill me.' It's her only home run in four years. I didn't want to take that from her, but at the same time, I was worried about her."

Umpires confirmed that the only option available under the rules was to replace Tucholsky at first base with a pinch runner and have the hit recorded as a two-run single instead of a three-run homer. Any assistance from coaches or trainers while she was an active runner would result in an out. So with no choice, Knox prepared to make the substitution, taking both the run and the memory from Tucholsky.

"And right then," Knox said, "I heard, 'Excuse me, would it be OK if we carried her around and she touched each bag?'"

The voice belonged to Holtman, a four-year starter who owns just about every major offensive record there is to claim in Central Washington's record book. She also is staring down a pair of knee surgeries as soon as the season ends. Her knees ache after every game, but having already used a redshirt season earlier in her career, and ready to move on to graduate school and coaching at Central, she put the operations on hold so as to avoid missing any of her final season. Now, with her own opportunity for a first postseason appearance very much hinging on the outcome of the game — her final game at home — she stepped up to help a player she knew only as an opponent for four years.

"Honestly, it's one of those things that I hope anyone would do it for me," Holtman said. "She hit the ball over her fence. She's a senior; it's her last year...I don't know, it's just one of those things I guess that maybe because compared to everyone on the field at the time, I had been playing longer and knew we could touch her, it was my idea first. But I think anyone who knew that we could touch her would have offered to do it, just because it's the right thing to do. She was obviously in agony."

Holtman and shortstop Liz Wallace lifted Tucholsky off the ground and supported her weight between them as they began a slow trip around the bases, stopping at each one so Tucholsky's left foot could secure her passage onward. Even with Tucholsky feeling the pain of what trainers subsequently came to believe was a torn ACL, the surreal quality of perhaps the longest and most crowded home run trot in the game's history hit all three players.

"We all started to laugh at one point, I think when we touched the first base," Holtman said. "I don't know what it looked like to observers, but it was kind of funny because Liz and I were carrying her on both sides and we'd get to a base and gently, barely tap her left foot, and we'd all of a sudden start to get the giggles a little bit."

Accompanied by a standing ovation from the fans, they finally reached home plate and passed the home run hitter into the arms of her own teammates.

Then Holtman and Wallace returned to their positions and tried to win the game.

Hollywood would have a difficult time deciding how such a script should end, whether to leave Tucholsky's home run as the decisive blow or reward the selfless actions of her opponents. Reality has less room for such philosophical quandaries. Central Washington did rally for two runs in the bottom of the second — runs that might have tied the game had Knox been forced to replace Tucholsky — but Western Oregon held on for a 4-2 win.

But unlike a movie, the credits didn't roll after the final out, and the story that continues has little to do with those final scores.

"It kept everything in perspective and the fact that we're never bigger than the game," Knox said of the experience. "It was such a lesson that we learned — that it's not all about winning. And we forget that, because as coaches, we're always trying to get to the top. We forget that. But I will never, ever forget this moment. It's changed me, and I'm sure it's changed my players."

For her part, Holtman seems not altogether sure what all the fuss is about. She seems to genuinely believe that any player in her position on any field on any day would have done the same thing. Which helps explains why it did happen on that day and on that field.

.And she appreciates the knowledge that while the results of that game and her senior season soon will fade into the dust and depth of old media guides and Internet archives, the story of what happened. in her final game at home will live on far longer.

"I think that happening on Senior Day, it showed the character of our team," Holtman said. "Because granted I thought of it, but everyone else would have done it. It's something people will talk about for Senior Day. They won't talk about who got hits and what happened and who won; they'll talk about that. And it's kind of a nice way to go out, because it shows what our program is about and the kind of people we have here."

Underdogs to Wonderdogs
Notes from Fresno State's improbable NCAA Baseball title

• The Bulldogs survived six elimination games on their way to the title, including two against finals opponent Georgia.

• The Bulldogs lost 12 of their first 20 games.

• Fresno State entered the WAC tournament with a 33-27 record. The Bulldogs weren't even on the bubble for an at-large spot in the NCAA tournament, and only advanced because of their win in the conference tourney.

• The Bulldogs were a No. 4 regional seed in the NCAA tourney (there are only four teams in each region), which is the equivalent of being seeded in the 13-16 range for the NCAA basketball tournament.

• Fresno State is the lowest seed in any sport to win an NCAA championship.

• Fresno State's 31 losses are the most by an NCAA baseball champion.

Source: ESPN Research

See more details of the 2008 College World Series in the Baseball chapter (page 91).

Rank 'Em: Cinderella Teams

Rank		Year	Points
1	USA hockey	1980	361,329
2	Fresno St. baseball	2008	315,897
3	N.C. State basketball	1983	273,735
4	Villanova basketball	1985	271,416
5	N.Y. Giants	2007	227,089
6	Denmark soccer	1992	162,522
7	UCSB men's soccer	2006	145,336
8	Houston Rockets	1995	139,544
9	St. Louis Cardinals	2006	137,878
10	N.J. Devils	1995	136,341

Total Votes: 40,953

NCAA Schools & Champions

SPORTS ALMANAC

NCAA Football Bowl Subdivision Schools
(Formerly Division I-A)

2008 Season

Conferences and coaches as of Sept. 30, 2008.

Joining Sun Belt in 2009: WESTERN KENTUCKY from FCS (affiliate member in 2007 & 2008).
Joining Sun Belt in 2013: SOUTH ALABAMA (new program beginning in 2009).

	Nickname	Conference	Head Coach	Location	Colors
Air Force	Falcons	Mountain West	Troy Calhoun	Colo. Springs, CO	Blue/Silver
Akron	Zips	Mid-American	J.D. Brookhart	Akron, OH	Blue/Gold
Alabama	Crimson Tide	SEC-West	Nick Saban	Tuscaloosa, AL	Crimson/White
Arizona	Wildcats	Pac-10	Mike Stoops	Tucson, AZ	Cardinal/Navy
Arizona St.	Sun Devils	Pac-10	Dennis Erickson	Tempe, AZ	Maroon/Gold
Arkansas	Razorbacks	SEC-West	Bobby Petrino	Fayetteville, AR	Cardinal/White
Arkansas St.	Indians	Sun Belt	Steve Roberts	State Univ., AR	Scarlet/Black
Army	Cadets, Black Knights	Independent	Stan Brock	West Point, NY	Black/Gold/Gray
Auburn	Tigers	SEC-West	Tommy Tuberville	Auburn, AL	Orange/Blue
Ball St.	Cardinals	Mid-American	Brady Hoke	Muncie, IN	Cardinal/White
Baylor	Bears	Big 12	Art Briles	Waco, TX	Green/Gold
Boise St.	Broncos	WAC	Chris Petersen	Boise, ID	Orange/Blue
Boston College	Eagles	ACC	Jeff Jagodzinski	Chestnut Hill, MA	Maroon/Gold
Bowling Green	Falcons	Mid-American	Gregg Brandon	Bowling Green, OH	Orange/Brown
Brigham Young	Cougars	Mountain West	Bronco Mendenhall	Provo, UT	Blue/White/Tan
Buffalo	Bulls	Mid-American	Turner Gill	Buffalo, NY	Royal Blue/White
California	Golden Bears	Pac-10	Jeff Tedford	Berkeley, CA	Blue/Gold
Central Florida	Golden Knights	USA	George O'Leary	Orlando, FL	Black/Gold
Central Michigan	Chippewas	Mid-American	Butch Jones	Mt. Pleasant, MI	Maroon/Gold
Cincinnati	Bearcats	Big East	Brian Kelly	Cincinnati, OH	Red/Black
Clemson	Tigers	ACC	Tommy Bowden	Clemson, SC	Purple/Orange
Colorado	Buffaloes	Big 12	Dan Hawkins	Boulder, CO	Silver/Gold/Black
Colorado St.	Rams	Mountain West	Steve Fairchild	Ft. Collins, CO	Green/Gold
Connecticut	Huskies	Big East	Randy Edsall	Storrs, CT	Blue/White
Duke	Blue Devils	ACC	David Cutcliffe	Durham, NC	Royal Blue/White
East Carolina	Pirates	USA	Skip Holtz	Greenville, NC	Purple/Gold
Eastern Michigan	Eagles	Mid-American	Jeff Genyk	Ypsilanti, MI	Green/White
Florida	Gators	SEC-East	Urban Meyer	Gainesville, FL	Orange/Blue
Florida Atlantic	Owls	Sun Belt	H. Schnellenberger	Boca Raton, FL	Blue/Red
Florida Int'l	Golden Panthers	Sun Belt	Mario Cristobal	Miami, FL	Blue/Gold
Florida St.	Seminoles	ACC	Bobby Bowden	Tallahassee, FL	Garnet/Gold
Fresno St.	Bulldogs	WAC	Pat Hill	Fresno, CA	Red/Blue
Georgia	Bulldogs	SEC-East	Mark Richt	Athens, GA	Red/Black
Georgia Tech	Yellow Jackets	ACC	Paul Johnson	Atlanta, GA	Old Gold/White
Hawaii	Warriors	WAC	Greg McMackin	Honolulu, HI	Green/White
Houston	Cougars	USA	Kevin Sumlin	Houston, TX	Scarlet/White
Idaho	Vandals	WAC	Robb Akey	Moscow, ID	Silver/Gold
Illinois	Fighting Illini	Big Ten	Ron Zook	Champaign, IL	Orange/Blue
Indiana	Hoosiers	Big Ten	Bill Lynch	Bloomington, IN	Cream/Crimson
Iowa	Hawkeyes	Big Ten	Kirk Ferentz	Iowa City, IA	Old Gold/Black
Iowa St.	Cyclones	Big 12	Gene Chizik	Ames, IA	Cardinal/Gold
Kansas	Jayhawks	Big 12	Mark Mangino	Lawrence, KS	Crimson/Blue
Kansas St.	Wildcats	Big 12	Ron Prince	Manhattan, KS	Purple/White
Kent St.	Golden Flashes	Mid-American	Doug Martin	Kent, OH	Navy Blue/Gold
Kentucky	Wildcats	SEC-East	Rich Brooks	Lexington, KY	Blue/White
LSU	Fighting Tigers	SEC-West	Les Miles	Baton Rouge, LA	Purple/Gold
LA-Lafayette	Ragin' Cajuns	Sun Belt	Rickey Bustle	Lafayette, LA	Vermilion/White
LA-Monroe	Warhawks	Sun Belt	Charlie Weatherbie	Monroe, LA	Maroon/Gold
Louisiana Tech	Bulldogs	WAC	Derek Dooley	Ruston, LA	Red/Blue
Louisville	Cardinals	Big East	Steve Kragthorpe	Louisville, KY	Red/Black/White

	Nickname	Conference	Head Coach	Location	Colors
Marshall	Thundering Herd	USA	Mark Snyder	Huntington, WV	Green/White
Maryland	Terrapins, Terps	ACC	Ralph Friedgen	College Park, MD	Red/White/Black/Gold
Memphis	Tigers	USA	Tommy West	Memphis, TN	Blue/Gray
Miami-FL	Hurricanes	ACC	Randy Shannon	Coral Gables, FL	Orange/Grn./Wt.
Miami-OH	RedHawks	Mid-American	Shane Montgomery	Oxford, OH	Red/White
Michigan	Wolverines	Big Ten	Rich Rodriguez	Ann Arbor, MI	Maize/Blue
Michigan St.	Spartans	Big Ten	Mark Dantonio	E. Lansing, MI	Green/White
Middle Tennessee	Blue Raiders	Sun Belt	Rick Stockstill	Murfreesboro, TN	Royal Blue/White
Minnesota	Golden Gophers	Big Ten	Tim Brewster	Minneapolis, MN	Maroon/Gold
Mississippi	Ole Miss, Rebels	SEC-West	Houston Nutt	Oxford, MS	Cardinal/Navy Bl.
Mississippi St.	Bulldogs	SEC-West	Sylvester Croom	Starkville, MS	Maroon/White
Missouri	Tigers	Big 12	Gary Pinkel	Columbia, MO	Old Gold/Black
Navy	Midshipmen	Independent	Ken Niumatalolo	Annapolis, MD	Navy Blue/Gold
Nebraska	Cornhuskers	Big 12	Bo Pelini	Lincoln, NE	Scarlet/Cream
Nevada	Wolf Pack	WAC	Chris Ault	Reno, NV	Silver/Blue
New Mexico	Lobos	Mountain West	Rocky Long	Albuquerque, NM	Cherry/Silver
New Mexico St.	Aggies	WAC	Hal Mumme	Las Cruces, NM	Crimson/White
North Carolina	Tar Heels	ACC	Butch Davis	Chapel Hill, NC	Carolina Blue/Wt.
North Carolina St.	Wolfpack	ACC	Tom O'Brien	Raleigh, NC	Red/White
North Texas	Mean Green	Sun Belt	Todd Dodge	Denton, TX	Green/White
Northern Illinois	Huskies	Mid-American	Jerry Kill	DeKalb, IL	Cardinal/Black
Northwestern	Wildcats	Big Ten	Pat Fitzgerald	Evanston, IL	Purple/White
Notre Dame	Fighting Irish	Independent	Charlie Weis	Notre Dame, IN	Gold/Blue
Ohio University	Bobcats	Mid-American	Frank Solich	Athens, OH	Hunter Green/Wt.
Ohio St.	Buckeyes	Big Ten	Jim Tressel	Columbus, OH	Scarlet/Gray
Oklahoma	Sooners	Big 12	Bob Stoops	Norman, OK	Crimson/Cream
Oklahoma St.	Cowboys	Big 12	Mike Gundy	Stillwater, OK	Orange/Black
Oregon	Ducks	Pac-10	Mike Bellotti	Eugene, OR	Green/Yellow
Oregon St.	Beavers	Pac-10	Mike Riley	Corvallis, OR	Orange/Black
Penn St.	Nittany Lions	Big Ten	Joe Paterno	University Park, PA	Blue/White
Pittsburgh	Panthers	Big East	Dave Wannstedt	Pittsburgh, PA	Blue/Gold
Purdue	Boilermakers	Big Ten	Joe Tiller	W. Lafayette, IN	Old Gold/Black
Rice	Owls	USA	David Bailiff	Houston, TX	Blue/Gray
Rutgers	Scarlet Knights	Big East	Greg Schiano	New Brunswick, NJ	Scarlet
San Diego St.	Aztecs	Mountain West	Chuck Long	San Diego, CA	Scarlet/Black
San Jose St.	Spartans	WAC	Dick Tomey	San Jose, CA	Gold/White/Blue
South Carolina	Gamecocks	SEC-East	Steve Spurrier	Columbia, SC	Garnet/Black
South Florida	Bulls	Big East	Jim Leavitt	Tampa, FL	Green/Gold
SMU	Mustangs	USA	June Jones	Dallas, TX	Red/Blue
Southern Miss.	Golden Eagles	USA	Larry Fedora	Hattiesburg, MS	Black/Gold
Stanford	Cardinal	Pac-10	Jim Harbaugh	Stanford, CA	Cardinal/White
Syracuse	Orange	Big East	Greg Robinson	Syracuse, NY	Orange
Temple	Owls	Mid-American	Al Golden	Philadelphia, PA	Cherry/White
Tennessee	Volunteers	SEC-East	Phillip Fulmer	Knoxville, TN	Orange/White
Texas	Longhorns	Big 12	Mack Brown	Austin, TX	Burnt Orange/Wt.
Texas A&M	Aggies	Big 12	Mike Sherman	College Station, TX	Maroon/White
TCU	Horned Frogs	Mountain West	Gary Patterson	Ft. Worth, TX	Purple/White
Texas Tech	Red Raiders	Big 12	Mike Leach	Lubbock, TX	Scarlet/Black
Toledo	Rockets	Mid-American	Tom Amstutz	Toledo, OH	Blue/Gold
Troy	Trojans	Sun Belt	Larry Blakeney	Troy, AL	Cardinal/Slvr./Blk.
Tulane	Green Wave	USA	Bob Toledo	New Orleans, LA	Olive Grn./Sky Bl.
Tulsa	Golden Hurricane	USA	Todd Graham	Tulsa, OK	Blue/Gold/Crimson
UAB	Blazers	USA	Neil Callaway	Birmingham, AL	Green/Gold
UCLA	Bruins	Pac-10	Rick Neuheisel	Los Angeles, CA	Blue/Gold
UNLV	Rebels	Mountain West	Mike Sanford	Las Vegas, NV	Scarlet/Gray
USC	Trojans	Pac-10	Pete Carroll	Los Angeles, CA	Cardinal/Gold
Utah	Utes	Mountain West	Kyle Whittingham	Salt Lake City, UT	Crimson/White
Utah St.	Aggies	WAC	Brent Guy	Logan, UT	Navy Blue/White
UTEP	Miners	USA	Mike Price	El Paso, TX	Orange/Blue/Silver
Vanderbilt	Commodores	SEC-East	Bobby Johnson	Nashville, TN	Black/Gold
Virginia	Cavaliers	ACC	Al Groh	Charlottesville, VA	Orange/Blue
Virginia Tech	Hokies, Gobblers	ACC	Frank Beamer	Blacksburg, VA	Orange/Maroon
Wake Forest	Demon Deacons	ACC	Jim Grobe	Winston-Salem, NC	Old Gold/Black
Washington	Huskies	Pac-10	Tyrone Willingham	Seattle, WA	Purple/Gold
Washington St.	Cougars	Pac-10	Paul Wulff	Pullman, WA	Crimson/Gray
West Virginia	Mountaineers	Big East	Bill Stewart	Morgantown, WV	Old Gold/Blue
Western Kentucky	Hilltoppers	Independent	David Elson	Bowling Green, KY	Red/White
Western Michigan	Broncos	Mid-American	Bill Cubit	Kalamazoo, MI	Brown/Gold
Wisconsin	Badgers	Big Ten	Bret Bielema	Madison, WI	Cardinal/White
Wyoming	Cowboys	Mountain West	Joe Glenn	Laramie, WY	Brown/Gold

NCAA Football Championship Subdivision Schools

(Formerly Division I-AA)

2008 Season

Conferences and coaches as of Sept. 30, 2008.

Name Change in 2008: Gateway Conference changes name to Missouri Valley Football Conference.
Metro Atlantic Conference disbanded: IONA to FCS Independent; DUQUESNE joining Northeast; LA SALLE disbanded its program; MARIST joining Pioneer in 2009 (FCS Independent in 2008); SAINT PETER'S disbanded its program.
Joining Big South in 2008: STONY BROOK from Northeast (FCS Independent in 2007).
Joining Missouri Valley in 2008: NORTH DAKOTA ST. and SOUTH DAKOTA ST. from Great West.
Joining Great West in 2008: NORTH DAKOTA and SOUTH DAKOTA from Division II.
Joining Pioneer in 2008: CAMPBELL (resurrecting its program).
Joining Southern in 2008: SAMFORD from Ohio Valley.
Joining FCS in 2008: BRYANT from Division II (joining the Northeast Conference in 2012).
Joining FCS in 2009: OLD DOMINION (new program, joining the Colonial Athletic Association in 2011).
Joining FCS in 2010: GEORGIA STATE (new program, joining the Colonial Athletic Association in 2012); LAMAR (resurrecting its program, joining the Southland Conference in 2010).

	Nickname	Conference	Head Coach	Location	Colors
Alabama A&M	Bulldogs	SWAC	Anthony Jones	Huntsville, AL	Maroon/White
Alabama St.	Hornets	SWAC	Reggie Barlow	Montgomery, AL	Black/Gold
Albany	Great Danes	Northeast	Bob Ford	Albany, NY	Purple/Gold
Alcorn St.	Braves	SWAC	Ernest Jones	Lorman, MS	Purple/Gold
Appalachian St.	Mountaineers	Southern	Jerry Moore	Boone, NC	Black/Gold
Ark.-Pine Bluff	Golden Lions	SWAC	Monte Coleman	Pine Bluff, AR	Black/Gold
Austin Peay St.	Governors	Ohio Valley	Rick Christophel	Clarksville, TN	Red/White
Bethune-Cookman	Wildcats	Mid-Eastern	Alvin Wyatt	Daytona Beach, FL	Maroon/Gold
Brown	Bears	Ivy	Phil Estes	Providence, RI	Brown/Red/White
Bryant	Bulldogs	Independent	Marty Fine	Smithfield, RI	Black/Gold/White
Bucknell	Bison	Patriot	Tim Landis	Lewisburg, PA	Orange/Blue
Butler	Bulldogs	Pioneer	Jeff Voris	Indianapolis, IN	Blue/White
Cal Poly	Mustangs	Great West	Rich Ellerson	San Luis Obispo, CA	Green/Gold
Campbell	Camels	Pioneer	Dale Steele	Buies Creek, NC	Orange/Black
Central Arkansas	Bears	Southland	Clint Conque	Conway, AR	Purple/Gray
Central Conn. St.	Blue Devils	Northeast	Jeff McInerney	New Britain, CT	Blue/White
Charleston So.	Buccaneers	Big South	Jay Mills	Charleston, SC	Blue/Gold
Chattanooga	Mocs	Southern	Rodney Allison	Chattanooga, TN	Navy Blue/Old Gold
The Citadel	Bulldogs	Southern	Kevin Higgins	Charleston, SC	Blue/White
Coastal Carolina	Chanticleers	Big South	David Bennett	Conway, SC	Green/Bronze/Black
Colgate	Raiders	Patriot	Dick Biddle	Hamilton, NY	Maroon/White/Gray
Columbia	Lions	Ivy	Norries Wilson	New York, NY	Lt. Blue/White
Cornell	Big Red	Ivy	Jim Knowles	Ithaca, NY	Carnelian/White
Dartmouth	Big Green	Ivy	Buddy Teevens	Hanover, NH	Green/White
Davidson	Wildcats	Pioneer	Tripp Merritt	Davidson, NC	Red/Black
Dayton	Flyers	Pioneer	Rick Chamberlin	Dayton, OH	Red/Blue
Delaware	Blue Hens	Colonial	K.C. Keeler	Newark, DE	Blue/Gold
Delaware St.	Hornets	Mid-Eastern	Al Lavan	Dover, DE	Red/Blue
Drake	Bulldogs	Pioneer	Chris Creighton	Des Moines, IA	Blue/White
Duquesne	Dukes	Northeast	Jerry Schmitt	Pittsburgh, PA	Red/Blue
Eastern Illinois	Panthers	Ohio Valley	Bob Spoo	Charleston, IL	Blue/Gray
Eastern Kentucky	Colonels	Ohio Valley	Dean Hood	Richmond, KY	Maroon/White
Eastern Washington	Eagles	Big Sky	Beau Baldwin	Cheney, WA	Red/White
Elon	Phoenix	Southern	Pete Lembo	Elon, NC	Maroon/Gold
Florida A&M	Rattlers	Mid-Eastern	Joe Taylor	Tallahassee, FL	Orange/Green
Fordham	Rams	Patriot	Tom Masella	Bronx, NY	Maroon/White
Furman	Paladins	Southern	Bobby Lamb	Greenville, SC	Purple/White
Gardner-Webb	Bulldogs	Big South	Steve Patton	Boiling Springs, NC	Scarlet/Black
Georgetown	Hoyas	Patriot	Kevin Kelly	Washington, DC	Blue/Gray
Georgia Southern	Eagles	Southern	Chris Hatcher	Statesboro, GA	Blue/White
Grambling St.	Tigers	SWAC	Rod Broadway	Grambling, LA	Black/Gold
Hampton	Pirates	Mid-Eastern	Jerry Holmes	Hampton, VA	Royal Blue/White
Harvard	Crimson	Ivy	Tim Murphy	Cambridge, MA	Crimson/Black/White
Hofstra	Pride	Colonial	Dave Cohen	Hempstead, NY	Gold/White/Blue
Holy Cross	Crusaders	Patriot	Tom Gilmore	Worcester, MA	Royal Purple
Howard	Bison	Mid-Eastern	Carey Bailey	Washington, DC	Blue/Wt./Red
Idaho St.	Bengals	Big Sky	John Zamberlin	Pocatello, ID	Orange/Black
Illinois St.	Redbirds	Missouri Valley	Denver Johnson	Normal, IL	Red/White
Indiana St.	Sycamores	Missouri Valley	Trent Miles	Terre Haute, IN	Royal Blue/White
Iona	Gaels	Independent	Fred Mariani	New Rochelle, NY	Maroon/Gold
Jackson St.	Tigers	SWAC	Rick Comegy	Jackson, MS	Blue/White
Jacksonville	Dolphins	Pioneer	Kerwin Bell	Jacksonville, FL	Green/White
Jacksonville St.	Gamecocks	Ohio Valley	Jack Crowe	Jacksonville, AL	Red/White
James Madison	Dukes	Colonial	Mickey Matthews	Harrisonburg, VA	Purple/Gold

	Nickname	Conference	Head Coach	Location	Colors
Lafayette	Leopards	Patriot	Frank Tavani	Easton, PA	Maroon/White
Lehigh	Mountain Hawks	Patriot	Andy Coen	Bethlehem, PA	Brown/White
Liberty	Flames	Big South	Danny Rocco	Lynchburg, VA	Red/White/Blue
Maine	Black Bears	Colonial	Jack Cosgrove	Orono, ME	Blue/White
Marist	Red Foxes	Independent	Jim Parady	Poughkeepsie, NY	Red/White
Massachusetts	Minutemen	Colonial	Don Brown	Amherst, MA	Maroon/White
McNeese St.	Cowboys	Southland	Matt Viator	Lake Charles, LA	Blue/Gold
Miss. Valley St.	Delta Devils	SWAC	Willie Totten	Itta Bena, MS	Green/White
Missouri St.	Bears	Missouri Valley	Terry Allen	Springfield, MO	Maroon/White
Monmouth	Hawks	Northeast	Kevin Callahan	W. Long Branch, NJ	Royal Blue/White
Montana	Grizzlies	Big Sky	Bobby Hauck	Missoula, MT	Maroon/Silver
Montana St.	Bobcats	Big Sky	Rob Ash	Bozeman, MT	Blue/Gold
Morehead St.	Eagles	Pioneer	Matt Ballard	Morehead, KY	Blue/Gold
Morgan St.	Bears	Mid-Eastern	Donald Hill-Eley	Baltimore, MD	Blue/Orange
Murray St.	Racers	Ohio Valley	Matt Griffin	Murray, KY	Blue/Gold
New Hampshire	Wildcats	Colonial	Sean McDonnell	Durham, NH	Blue/White
Nicholls St.	Colonels	Southland	Jay Thomas	Thibodaux, LA	Red/Gray
Norfolk State	Spartans	Mid-Eastern	Pete Adrian	Norfolk, VA	Green/Gold
North Carolina A&T	Aggies	Mid-Eastern	Lee Fobbs	Greensboro, NC	Blue/Gold
NC Central	Eagles	Independent	Mose Rison	Durham, NC	Maroon/Gray
North Dakota	Fighting Sioux	Great West	Chris Mussman	Grand Forks, ND	Kelly Green/White
North Dakota St.	Bison	Missouri Valley	Craig Bohl	Fargo, ND	Green/Yellow
Northeastern	Huskies	Colonial	Rocky Hager	Boston, MA	Red/Black
Northern Arizona	Lumberjacks	Big Sky	Jerome Souers	Flagstaff, AZ	Blue/Gold
Northern Colorado	Bears	Big Sky	Scott Downing	Greeley, CO	Blue/Gold
Northern Iowa	Panthers	Missouri Valley	Mark Farley	Cedar Falls, IA	Purple/Old Gold
Northwestern St.	Demons	Southland	Scott Stoker	Natchitoches, LA	Purple/White
Pennsylvania	Quakers	Ivy	Al Bagnoli	Philadelphia, PA	Red/Blue
Portland St.	Vikings	Big Sky	Jerry Glanville	Portland, OR	Green/White
Prairie View A&M	Panthers	SWAC	Henry Frazier	Prairie View, TX	Purple/Gold
Presbyterian	Blue Hose	Big South	Bobby Bentley	Clinton, SC	Garnet/Blue
Princeton	Tigers	Ivy	Roger Hughes	Princeton, NJ	Orange/Black
Rhode Island	Rams	Colonial	Darren Rizzi	Kingston, RI	Light Blue/Navy/Wt.
Richmond	Spiders	Colonial	Mike London	Richmond, VA	Red/Blue
Robert Morris	Colonials	Northeast	Joe Walton	Moon Township, PA	Blue/White
Sacramento St.	Hornets	Big Sky	Marshall Sperbeck	Sacramento, CA	Green/Gold
Sacred Heart	Pioneers	Northeast	Paul Gorham	Fairfield, CT	Scarlet/White
St. Francis-PA	Red Flash	Northeast	Dave Opfar	Loretto, PA	Red/White
Sam Houston St.	Bearkats	Southland	Todd Whitten	Huntsville, TX	Orange/White
Samford	Bulldogs	Southern	Pat Sullivan	Birmingham, AL	Crimson/Blue
San Diego	Toreros	Pioneer	Ron Caragher	San Diego, CA	Lt. Blue/Navy
Savannah St.	Tigers	Independent	Robert Wells	Savannah, GA	Orange/Blue
South Carolina St.	Bulldogs	Mid-Eastern	Oliver Pough	Orangeburg, SC	Garnet/Blue
South Dakota	Coyotes	Great West	Ed Meierkort	Vermillion, SD	Red/White
South Dakota St.	Jackrabbits	Missouri Valley	John Stiegelmeier	Brookings, SD	Yellow/Blue
SE Missouri St.	Redhawks	Ohio Valley	Tony Samuel	Cape Girardeau, MO	Red/Black
Southeastern Louisiana	Lions	Southland	Mike Lucas	Hammond, LA	Green/Gold
Southern-BR	Jaguars	SWAC	Pete Richardson	Baton Rouge, LA	Blue/Gold
Southern Illinois	Salukis	Missouri Valley	Dale Lennon	Cardondale, IL	Maroon/White
Southern Utah	Thunderbirds	Great West	Ed Lamb	Cedar City, UT	Scarlet/White
Stephen F. Austin	Lumberjacks	Southland	J.C. Harper	Nacogdoches, TX	Purple/White
Stony Brook	Seawolves	Big South	Chuck Priore	Stony Brook, NY	Scarlet/Gray
Tennessee-Martin	Skyhawks	Ohio Valley	Jason Simpson	Martin, TN	Orange/White/Blue
Tennessee St.	Tigers	Ohio Valley	James Webster	Nashville, TN	Blue/White
Tennessee Tech	Golden Eagles	Ohio Valley	Watson Brown	Cookeville, TN	Purple/Gold
Texas Southern	Tigers	SWAC	Johnnie Cole	Houston, TX	Maroon/Gray
Texas St.	Bobcats	Southland	Brad Wright	San Marcos, TX	Maroon/Gold
Towson	Tigers	Colonial	Gordy Combs	Towson, MD	Gold/White
UC-Davis	Aggies	Great West	Bob Biggs	Davis, CA	Yale Blue/Gold
Valparaiso	Crusaders	Pioneer	Stacy Adams	Valparaiso, IN	Brown/Gold
Villanova	Wildcats	Colonial	Andy Talley	Villanova, PA	Blue/White
VMI	Keydets	Big South	Sparky Woods	Lexington, VA	Red/White/Yellow
Wagner	Seahawks	Northeast	Walt Hameline	Staten Island, NY	Green/White
Weber St.	Wildcats	Big Sky	Ron McBride	Ogden, UT	Royal Purple/White
Western Carolina	Catamounts	Southern	Dennis Wagner	Cullowhee, NC	Purple/Gold
Western Illinois	Leathernecks	Missouri Valley	Don Patterson	Macomb, IL	Purple/Gold
William & Mary	Tribe	Colonial	Jimmye Laycock	Williamsburg, VA	Green/Gold/Silver
Winston-Salem St.	Rams	Mid-Eastern	Kermit Blount	Winston-Salem, NC	Red/White
Wofford	Terriers	Southern	Mike Ayers	Spartanburg, SC	Old Gold/Black
Yale	Bulldogs, Elis	Ivy	Jack Siedlecki	New Haven, CT	Yale Blue/White
Youngstown St.	Penguins	Missouri Valley	Jon Heacock	Youngstown, OH	Red/White

NCAA Division I Basketball Schools
2008-2009 Season
Conferences and coaches as of Sept. 30, 2008.

Joining Big South in 2008-09: GARDNER-WEBB from Atlantic Sun.
Joining Division II in 2008-09: BRYANT from Division II (joining the Northeast Conference in 2012).
Joining Ohio Valley in 2008-09: SOUTHERN ILLINOIS EDWARDSVILLE from Division II.
Joining Southern in 2008-09: SAMFORD from Ohio Valley.
New Conference beginning in 2008-09: Great West Conference — HOUSTON BAPTIST from Division II, NEW JERSEY INSTITUTE OF TECHNOLOGY from Independent; NORTH DAKOTA from Division II; SOUTH DAKOTA from Division II; TEXAS PAN AMERICAN from Independent; UTAH VALLEY from Independent.

	Nickname	Conference	Head Coach	Location	Colors
Air Force	Falcons	Mountain West	Jeff Reynolds	Colo. Springs, CO	Blue/Silver
Akron	Zips	Mid-American	Keith Dambrot	Akron, OH	Blue/Gold
Alabama	Crimson Tide	SEC-West	Mark Gottfried	Tuscaloosa, AL	Crimson/White
Alabama A&M	Bulldogs	SWAC	Vann Pettaway	Huntsville, AL	Maroon/White
Alabama St.	Hornets	SWAC	Lewis Jackson	Montgomery, AL	Black/Gold
Albany	Great Danes	America East	Will Brown	Albany, NY	Purple/Gold
Alcorn St.	Braves	SWAC	Larry Smith	Lorman, MS	Purple/Gold
American	Eagles	Patriot	Jeff Jones	Washington, DC	Red/Blue
Appalachian St.	Mountaineers	Southern	Houston Fancher	Boone, NC	Black/Gold
Arizona	Wildcats	Pac-10	Lute Olson	Tucson, AZ	Cardinal/Navy
Arizona St.	Sun Devils	Pac-10	Herb Sendek	Tempe, AZ	Maroon/Gold
Arkansas	Razorbacks	SEC-West	John Pelphrey	Fayetteville, AR	Cardinal/White
Ark.-Little Rock	Trojans	Sun Belt	Steve Shields	Little Rock, AR	Silver/Black/Maroon
Ark.-Pine Bluff	Golden Lions	SWAC	George Ivory	Pine Bluff, AR	Black/Gold
Arkansas St.	Indians	Sun Belt	John Brady	State Univ., AR	Scarlet/Black
Army	Black Knights	Patriot	Jim Crews	West Point, NY	Black/Gold/Gray
Auburn	Tigers	SEC-West	Jeff Lebo	Auburn, AL	Orange/Blue
Austin Peay St.	Governors	Ohio Valley	Dave Loos	Clarksville, TN	Red/White
Ball St.	Cardinals	Mid-American	Billy Taylor	Muncie, IN	Cardinal/White
Baylor	Bears	Big 12	Scott Drew	Waco, TX	Green/Gold
Belmont	Bruins	Atlantic Sun	Rick Byrd	Nashville, TN	Navy Blue/Red
Bethune-Cookman	Wildcats	Mid-Eastern	Clifford Reed	Daytona Beach, FL	Maroon/Gold
Binghamton	Bearcats	America East	Kevin Broadus	Binghamton, NY	Green/Black/White
Boise St.	Broncos	WAC	Greg Graham	Boise, ID	Orange/Blue
Boston College	Eagles	ACC	Al Skinner	Chestnut Hill, MA	Maroon/Gold
Boston University	Terriers	America East	Dennis Wolff	Boston, MA	Scarlet/White
Bowling Green	Falcons	Mid-American	Louis Orr	Bowling Green, OH	Orange/Brown
Bradley	Braves	Mo. Valley	Jim Les	Peoria, IL	Red/White
Brigham Young	Cougars	Mountain West	Dave Rose	Provo, UT	Blue/White/Tan
Brown	Bears	Ivy	Jesse Agel	Providence, RI	Brown/Cardinal/White
Bryant	Bulldogs	Independent	Tim O'Shea	Smithfield, RI	Black/Gold/White
Bucknell	Bison	Patriot	Dave Paulsen	Lewisburg, PA	Orange/Blue
Buffalo	Bulls	Mid-American	R. Witherspoon	Buffalo, NY	Royal Blue/White
Butler	Bulldogs	Horizon	Brad Stevens	Indianapolis, IN	Blue/White
California	Golden Bears	Pac-10	Mike Montgomery	Berkeley, CA	Blue/Gold
Cal Poly	Mustangs	Big West	Kevin Bromley	San Luis Obispo, CA	Green/Gold
CS-Bakersfield	Roadrunners	Independent	Keith Brown	Bakersfield, CA	Blue/Gold
CS-Fullerton	Titans	Big West	Bob Burton	Fullerton, CA	Blue/Orange/White
CS-Northridge	Matadors	Big West	Bobby Braswell	Northridge, CA	Red/White/Black
Campbell	Camels	Atlantic Sun	Robbie Laing	Buies Creek, NC	Orange/Black
Canisius	Golden Griffins	Metro Atlantic	Tom Parrotta	Buffalo, NY	Blue/Gold
Centenary	Gents, Gentlemen	Summit	Greg Gary	Shreveport, LA	Maroon/White
Central Arkansas	Bears	Southland	Rand Chappell	Conway, AR	Purple/Gray
Central Conn. St.	Blue Devils	Northeast	Howie Dickenman	New Britain, CT	Blue/White
Central Florida	Golden Knights	USA	Kirk Speraw	Orlando, FL	Black/Gold
Central Michigan	Chippewas	Mid-American	Ernie Zeigler	Mt. Pleasant, MI	Maroon/Gold
Charleston So.	Buccaneers	Big South	Barclay Radebaugh	Charleston, SC	Blue/Gold
Charlotte	49ers	Atlantic 10	Bobby Lutz	Charlotte, NC	Green/White
Chattanooga	Mocs	Southern	John Shulman	Chattanooga, TN	Navy Blue/Old Gold
Chicago St.	Cougars	Independent	Benjy Taylor	Chicago, IL	Green/White
Cincinnati	Bearcats	Big East	Mick Cronin	Cincinnati, OH	Red/Black
The Citadel	Bulldogs	Southern	Ed Conroy	Charleston, SC	Blue/White
Clemson	Tigers	ACC	Oliver Purnell	Clemson, SC	Purple/Orange
Cleveland St.	Vikings	Horizon	Gary Waters	Cleveland, OH	Forest Green/White
Coastal Carolina	Chanticleers	Big South	Cliff Ellis	Conway, SC	Green/Bronze/Black
Colgate	Raiders	Patriot	Emmett Davis	Hamilton, NY	Maroon/Gray/White
College of Charleston	Cougars	Southern	Bobby Cremins	Charleston, SC	Maroon/White
Colorado	Buffaloes	Big 12	Jeff Bzdelik	Boulder, CO	Silver/Gold/Black
Colorado St.	Rams	Mountain West	Tim Miles	Ft. Collins, CO	Green/Gold

	Nickname	Conference	Head Coach	Location	Colors
Columbia	Lions	Ivy	Joseph Jones	New York, NY	Lt. Blue/White
Connecticut	Huskies	Big East	Jim Calhoun	Storrs, CT	Blue/White
Coppin St.	Eagles	Mid-Eastern	Ron Mitchell	Baltimore, MD	Royal Blue/Gold
Cornell	Big Red	Ivy	Steve Donahue	Ithaca, NY	Carnelian/White
Creighton	Bluejays	Mo. Valley	Dana Altman	Omaha, NE	Blue/White
Dartmouth	Big Green	Ivy	Terry Dunn	Hanover, NH	Green/White
Davidson	Wildcats	Southern	Bob McKillop	Davidson, NC	Red/Black
Dayton	Flyers	Atlantic 10	Brian Gregory	Dayton, OH	Red/Blue
Delaware	Fightin' Blue Hens	Colonial	Monte Ross	Newark, DE	Blue/Gold
Delaware St.	Hornets	Mid-Eastern	Greg Jackson	Dover, DE	Red/Columbia Blue
Denver	Pioneers	Sun Belt	Joe Scott	Denver, CO	Crimson/Gold
DePaul	Blue Demons	Big East	Jerry Wainwright	Chicago, IL	Scarlet/Blue
Detroit Mercy	Titans	Horizon	Ray McCallum	Detroit, MI	Red/White/Blue
Drake	Bulldogs	Mo. Valley	Mark Phelps	Des Moines, IA	Blue/White
Drexel	Dragons	Colonial	Bruiser Flint	Philadelphia, PA	Navy Blue/Gold
Duke	Blue Devils	ACC	Mike Krzyzewski	Durham, NC	Royal Blue/White
Duquesne	Dukes	Atlantic 10	Ron Everhart	Pittsburgh, PA	Red/Blue
East Carolina	Pirates	USA	Mack McCarthy	Greenville, NC	Purple/Gold
East Tenn. St.	Buccaneers	Atlantic Sun	Murry Bartow	Johnson City, TN	Blue/Gold
Eastern Illinois	Panthers	Ohio Valley	Mike Miller	Charleston, IL	Blue/Gray
Eastern Kentucky	Colonels	Ohio Valley	Jeff Neubauer	Richmond, KY	Maroon/White
Eastern Michigan	Eagles	Mid-American	Charles Ramsey	Ypsilanti, MI	Green/White
Eastern Washington	Eagles	Big Sky	Kirk Earlywine	Cheney, WA	Red/White
Elon	Phoenix	Southern	Ernie Nestor	Elon, NC	Maroon/Gold
Evansville	Aces	Mo. Valley	Marty Simmons	Evansville, IN	Purple/White
Fairfield	Stags	Metro Atlantic	Ed Cooley	Fairfield, CT	Cardinal Red
Fairleigh Dickinson	Knights	Northeast	Tom Green	Teaneck, NJ	Maroon/Blue
Florida	Gators	SEC-East	Billy Donovan	Gainesville, FL	Orange/Blue
Florida A&M	Rattlers	Mid-Eastern	Eugene Harris	Tallahassee, FL	Orange/Green
Florida Atlantic	Owls	Sun Belt	Mike Jarvis	Boca Raton, FL	Blue/Red
Florida Gulf Coast	Eagles	Atlantic Sun	Dave Balza	Fort Myers, FL	Kelly Green/Royal Blue
Florida Int'l	Golden Panthers	Sun Belt	Sergio Rouco	Miami, FL	Blue/Gold
Florida St.	Seminoles	ACC	Leonard Hamilton	Tallahassee, FL	Garnet/Gold
Fordham	Rams	Atlantic 10	Dereck Whittenburg	Bronx, NY	Maroon/White
Fresno St.	Bulldogs	WAC	Steve Cleveland	Fresno, CA	Red/Blue
Furman	Paladins	Southern	Jeff Jackson	Greenville, SC	Purple/White
Gardner-Webb	Bulldogs	Big South	Rick Scruggs	Boiling Springs, NC	Scarlet/Black
George Mason	Patriots	Colonial	Jim Larranaga	Fairfax, VA	Green/Gold
George Washington	Colonials	Atlantic 10	Karl Hobbs	Washington, DC	Buff/Blue
Georgetown	Hoyas	Big East	John Thompson III	Washington, DC	Blue/Gray
Georgia	Bulldogs, 'Dawgs	SEC-East	Dennis Felton	Athens, GA	Red/Black
Georgia Southern	Eagles	Southern	Jeff Price	Statesboro, GA	Blue/White
Georgia St.	Panthers	Colonial	Rod Barnes	Atlanta, GA	Roy. Blue/White
Georgia Tech	Yellow Jackets	ACC	Paul Hewitt	Atlanta, GA	Old Gold/White
Gonzaga	Bulldogs, Zags	West Coast	Mark Few	Spokane, WA	Blue/White/Red
Grambling St.	Tigers	SWAC	Rick Duckett	Grambling, LA	Black/Gold
Hampton	Pirates	Mid-Eastern	Kevin Nickelberry	Hampton, VA	Royal Blue/White
Hartford	Hawks	America East	Dan Leibovitz	W. Hartford, CT	Scarlet/White
Harvard	Crimson	Ivy	Tommy Amaker	Cambridge, MA	Crimson/Black/White
Hawaii	Rainbow Warriors	WAC	Bob Nash	Honolulu, HI	Green/White
High Point	Panthers	Big South	Bart Lundy	High Point, NC	Purple/White
Hofstra	Pride	Colonial	Tom Pecora	Hempstead, NY	Blue/Gold/White
Holy Cross	Crusaders	Patriot	Ralph Willard	Worcester, MA	Royal Purple
Houston	Cougars	USA	Tom Penders	Houston, TX	Scarlet/White
Houston Baptist	Huskies	Great West	Ron Cottrell	Houston, TX	Royal Blue/Orange
Howard	Bison	Mid-Eastern	Gil Jackson	Washington, DC	Blue/White/Red
Idaho	Vandals	WAC	Don Verlin	Moscow, ID	Silver/Gold
Idaho St.	Bengals	Big Sky	Joe O'Brien	Pocatello, ID	Orange/Black
Illinois	Fighting Illini	Big Ten	Bruce Weber	Champaign, IL	Orange/Blue
Illinois-Chicago	Flames	Horizon	Jim Collins	Chicago, IL	Navy Blue/Red
Illinois St.	Redbirds	Mo. Valley	Tom Jankovich	Normal, IL	Red/White
Indiana	Hoosiers	Big Ten	Tom Crean	Bloomington, IN	Cream/Crimson
IPFW	Mastodons	Summit	Dane Fife	Fort Wayne, IN	Royal Blue/White
IUPUI	Jaguars	Summit	Ron Hunter	Indianapolis, IN	Red/Gold
Indiana St.	Sycamores	Mo. Valley	Kevin McKenna	Terre Haute, IN	Blue/White
Iona	Gaels	Metro Atlantic	Kevin Willard	New Rochelle, NY	Maroon/Gold
Iowa	Hawkeyes	Big Ten	Todd Lickliter	Iowa City, IA	Old Gold/Black
Iowa St.	Cyclones	Big 12	Greg McDermott	Ames, IA	Cardinal/Gold
Jackson St.	Tigers	SWAC	Tevester Anderson	Jackson, MS	Blue/White
Jacksonville	Dolphins	Atlantic Sun	Cliff Warren	Jacksonville, FL	Green/White
Jacksonville St.	Gamecocks	Ohio Valley	James Green	Jacksonville, AL	Red/White

	Nickname	Conference	Head Coach	Location	Colors
James Madison	Dukes	Colonial	Matt Brady	Harrisonburg, VA	Purple/Gold
Kansas	Jayhawks	Big 12	Bill Self	Lawrence, KS	Crimson/Blue
Kansas St.	Wildcats	Big 12	Frank Martin	Manhattan, KS	Purple/White
Kennesaw St.	Owls	Atlantic Sun	Tony Ingle	Kennesaw, GA	Black/Gold
Kent St.	Golden Flashes	Mid-American	Geno Ford	Kent, OH	Navy Blue/Gold
Kentucky	Wildcats	SEC-East	Billy Gillispie	Lexington, KY	Blue/White
La Salle	Explorers	Atlantic 10	John Giannini	Philadelphia, PA	Blue/Gold
Lafayette	Leopards	Patriot	Fran O'Hanlon	Easton, PA	Maroon/White
Lamar	Cardinals	Southland	Steve Roccaforte	Beaumont, TX	Red/White
Lehigh	Mountain Hawks	Patriot	Brett Reed	Bethlehem, PA	Brown/White
Liberty	Flames	Big South	Ritchie McKay	Lynchburg, VA	Red/White/Blue
Lipscomb	Bisons	Atlantic Sun	Scott Sanderson	Nashville, TN	Purple/Gold
Long Beach St.	49ers	Big West	Dan Monson	Long Beach, CA	Black/Gold
Long Island	Blackbirds	Northeast	Jim Ferry	Brooklyn, NY	Black/Silver/Blue
Longwood	Lancers	Independent	Mike Gillian	Farmville, VA	Blue/White
LSU	Fighting Tigers	SEC-West	Trent Johnson	Baton Rouge, LA	Purple/Gold
LA-Lafayette	Ragin' Cajuns	Sun Belt	Robert Lee	Lafayette, LA	Vermilion/White
LA-Monroe	Warhawks	Sun Belt	Orlando Early	Monroe, LA	Maroon/Gold
Louisiana Tech	Bulldogs	WAC	Kerry Rupp	Ruston, LA	Red/Blue
Louisville	Cardinals	Big East	Rick Pitino	Louisville, KY	Red/Black/White
Loyola Chicago	Ramblers	Horizon	Jim Whitesell	Chicago, IL	Maroon/Gold
Loyola Maryland	Greyhounds	Metro Atlantic	Jimmy Patsos	Baltimore, MD	Green/Gray
Loyola Marymount	Lions	West Coast	Bill Bayno	Los Angeles, CA	Crimson/Blue
Maine	Black Bears	America East	Ted Woodward	Orono, ME	Blue/White
Manhattan	Jaspers	Metro Atlantic	Barry Rohrssen	Riverdale, NY	Kelly Green/White
Marist	Red Foxes	Metro Atlantic	Chuck Martin	Poughkeepsie, NY	Red/White
Marquette	Golden Eagles	Big East	Buzz Williams	Milwaukee, WI	Blue/Gold
Marshall	Thundering Herd	USA	Donnie Jones	Huntington, WV	Green/White
Maryland	Terrapins, Terps	ACC	Gary Williams	College Park, MD	Red/Wt./Black/Gold
MD-Balt. County	Retrievers	America East	Randy Monroe	Baltimore, MD	Black/Gold/Red
MD-Eastern Shore	Hawks	Mid-Eastern	Frankie Allen	Princess Anne, MD	Maroon/Gray
Massachusetts	Minutemen	Atlantic 10	Derek Kellogg	Amherst, MA	Maroon/White
McNeese St.	Cowboys	Southland	Dave Simmons	Lake Charles, LA	Blue/Gold
Memphis	Tigers	USA	John Calipari	Memphis, TN	Blue/Gray
Mercer	Bears	Atlantic Sun	Bob Hoffman	Macon, GA	Orange/Black
Miami-FL	Hurricanes	ACC	Frank Haith	Coral Gables, FL	Orange/Grn./White
Miami-OH	RedHawks	Mid-American	Charlie Coles	Oxford, OH	Red/White
Michigan	Wolverines	Big Ten	John Beilein	Ann Arbor, MI	Maize/Blue
Michigan St.	Spartans	Big Ten	Tom Izzo	East Lansing, MI	Green/White
Middle Tennessee	Blue Raiders	Sun Belt	Kermit Davis Jr.	Murfreesboro, TN	Royal Blue/White
Minnesota	Golden Gophers	Big Ten	Tubby Smith	Minneapolis, MN	Maroon/Gold
Mississippi	Ole Miss, Rebels	SEC-West	Andy Kennedy	Oxford, MS	Cardinal/Navy Blue
Mississippi St.	Bulldogs	SEC-West	Rick Stansbury	Starkville, MS	Maroon/White
Miss. Valley St.	Delta Devils	SWAC	Sean Woods	Itta Bena, MS	Green/White
Missouri	Tigers	Big 12	Mike Anderson	Columbia, MO	Old Gold/Black
Missouri St.	Bears	Mo. Valley	Cuonzo Martin	Springfield, MO	Maroon/White
Missouri-KC	Kangaroos	Summit	Matt Brown	Kansas City, MO	Blue/Gold
Monmouth	Hawks	Northeast	Dave Calloway	W. Long Branch, NJ	Midnight Blue/White
Montana	Grizzlies	Big Sky	Wayne Tinkle	Missoula, MT	Copper/Silver/Gold
Montana St.	Bobcats	Big Sky	Brad Huse	Bozeman, MT	Blue/Gold
Morehead St.	Eagles	Ohio Valley	Donnie Tyndall	Morehead, KY	Blue/Gold
Morgan St.	Bears	Mid-Eastern	Todd Bozeman	Baltimore, MD	Blue/Orange
Mt. St. Mary's	Mountaineers	Northeast	Milan Brown	Emmitsburg, MD	Blue/White
Murray St.	Racers	Ohio Valley	Billy Kennedy	Murray, KY	Blue/Gold
Navy	Midshipmen	Patriot	Billy Lange	Annapolis, MD	Navy Blue/Gold
Nebraska	Cornhuskers	Big 12	Doc Sadler	Lincoln, NE	Scarlet/Cream
Nevada	Wolf Pack	WAC	Mark Fox	Reno, NV	Silver/Blue
New Hampshire	Wildcats	America East	Bill Herrion	Durham, NH	Blue/White
NJ Inst. of Tech.	Highlanders	Independent	Jim Engles	Newark, NJ	Red/White
New Mexico	Lobos	Mountain West	Steve Alford	Albuquerque, NM	Cherry/Silver
New Mexico St.	Aggies	WAC	Marvin Menzies	Las Cruces, NM	Crimson/White
New Orleans	Privateers	Sun Belt	Joe Pasternack	New Orleans, LA	Royal Blue/Silver
Niagara	Purple Eagles	Metro Atlantic	Joe Mihalich	Lewiston, NY	Purple/White/Gold
Nicholls St.	Colonels	Southland	J.P. Piper	Thibodaux, LA	Red/Gray
Norfolk St.	Spartans	Mid-Eastern	Anthony Evans	Norfolk, VA	Green/Gold
North Carolina	Tar Heels	ACC	Roy Williams	Chapel Hill, NC	Carolina Blue/Wht.
North Carolina A&T	Aggies	Mid-Eastern	Jerry Eaves	Greensboro, NC	Blue/Gold
North Carolina St.	Wolfpack	ACC	Sidney Lowe	Raleigh, NC	Red/White
NC-Asheville	Bulldogs	Big South	Eddie Biedenbach	Asheville, NC	Royal Blue/White
NC-Central	Eagles	Independent	Henry Dickerson	Durham, NC	Maroon/Gray
NC-Greensboro	Spartans	Southern	Mike Dement	Greensboro, NC	Gold/White/Navy

	Nickname	Conference	Head Coach	Location	Colors
NC-Wilmington	Seahawks	Colonial	Benny Moss	Wilmington, NC	Green/Gold/Navy
North Dakota	Fighting Sioux	Great West	Brian Jones	Grand Forks, ND	Kelly Green/White
North Dakota St.	Bison	Summit	Saul Phillips	Fargo, ND	Yellow/Green
North Florida	Ospreys	Atlantic Sun	Matt Kilcullen	Jacksonville, FL	Navy Blue/Gray
North Texas	Mean Green	Sun Belt	Johnny Jones	Denton, TX	Green/White
Northeastern	Huskies	Colonial	Bill Coen	Boston, MA	Red/Black
Northern Arizona	Lumberjacks	Big Sky	Mike Adras	Flagstaff, AZ	Blue/Gold
Northern Colorado	Bears	Big Sky	Tad Boyle	Greeley, CO	Blue/Gold
Northern Illinois	Huskies	Mid-American	Ricardo Patton	DeKalb, IL	Cardinal/Black
Northern Iowa	Panthers	Mo. Valley	Ben Jacobson	Cedar Falls, IA	Purple/Old Gold
Northwestern	Wildcats	Big Ten	Bill Carmody	Evanston, IL	Purple/White
Northwestern St.	Demons	Southland	Mike McConathy	Natchitoches, LA	Purple/Orange/Wt.
Notre Dame	Fighting Irish	Big East	Mike Brey	Notre Dame, IN	Gold/Blue
Oakland-MI	Golden Grizzlies	Summit	Greg Kampe	Rochester, MI	Black/Gold
Ohio University	Bobcats	Mid-American	John Groce	Athens, OH	Hunter Green/White
Ohio St.	Buckeyes	Big Ten	Thad Matta	Columbus, OH	Scarlet/Gray
Oklahoma	Sooners	Big 12	Jeff Capel	Norman, OK	Crimson/Cream
Oklahoma St.	Cowboys	Big 12	Travis Ford	Stillwater, OK	Orange/Black
Old Dominion	Monarchs	Colonial	Blaine Taylor	Norfolk, VA	Slate Blue/Silver
Oral Roberts	Golden Eagles	Summit	Scott Sutton	Tulsa, OK	Navy Blue/White
Oregon	Ducks	Pac-10	Ernie Kent	Eugene, OR	Green/Yellow
Oregon St.	Beavers	Pac-10	Craig Robinson	Corvallis, OR	Orange/Black
Pacific	Tigers	Big West	Bob Thomason	Stockton, CA	Orange/Black
Pennsylvania	Quakers	Ivy	Glen Miller	Philadelphia, PA	Red/Blue
Penn St.	Nittany Lions	Big Ten	Ed DeChellis	University Park, PA	Blue/White
Pepperdine	Waves	West Coast	Tom Asbury	Malibu, CA	Blue/Orange
Pittsburgh	Panthers	Big East	Jamie Dixon	Pittsburgh, PA	Gold/Blue
Portland	Pilots	West Coast	Eric Reveno	Portland, OR	Purple/White
Portland St.	Vikings	Big Sky	Ken Bone	Portland, OR	Green/White
Prairie View A&M	Panthers	SWAC	Byron Rimm II	Prairie View, TX	Purple/Gold
Presbyterian	Blue Hose	Big South	Gregg Nibert	Clinton, SC	Garnet/Blue
Princeton	Tigers	Ivy	Sydney Johnson	Princeton, NJ	Orange/Black
Providence	Friars	Big East	Keno Davis	Providence, RI	Black/White
Purdue	Boilermakers	Big Ten	Matt Painter	W. Lafayette, IN	Old Gold/Black
Quinnipiac	Bobcats	Northeast	Tom Moore	Hamden, CT	Navy/Gold
Radford	Highlanders	Big South	Brad Greenberg	Radford, VA	Blue/Red/Green/Wt.
Rhode Island	Rams	Atlantic 10	Jim Baron	Kingston, RI	Lt. Blue/White/Navy
Rice	Owls	USA	Ben Braun	Houston, TX	Blue/Gray
Richmond	Spiders	Atlantic 10	Chris Mooney	Richmond, VA	Red/Blue
Rider	Broncs	Metro Atlantic	Tommy Dempsey	Lawrenceville, NJ	Cranberry/White
Robert Morris	Colonials	Northeast	Mike Rice	Moon Township, PA	Blue/Red/White
Rutgers	Scarlet Knights	Big East	Fred Hill Jr.	New Brunswick, NJ	Scarlet
Sacramento St.	Hornets	Big Sky	Brian Katz	Sacramento, CA	Green/Gold
Sacred Heart	Pioneers	Northeast	Dave Bike	Fairfield, CT	Scarlet/White
St. Bonaventure	Bonnies	Atlantic 10	Mark Schmidt	St. Bonaventure, NY	Brown/White
St. Francis-NY	Terriers	Northeast	Brian Nash	Brooklyn, NY	Red/Blue
St. Francis-PA	Red Flash	Northeast	Don Friday	Loretto, PA	Red/White
St. John's	Red Storm	Big East	Norm Roberts	Jamaica, NY	Red/White
Saint Joseph's	Hawks	Atlantic 10	Phil Martelli	Philadelphia, PA	Crimson/Gray
Saint Louis	Billikens	Atlantic 10	Rick Majerus	St. Louis, MO	Blue/White
Saint Mary's-CA	Gaels	West Coast	Randy Bennett	Moraga, CA	Red/Blue
Saint Peter's	Peacocks	Metro Atlantic	John Dunne	Jersey City, NJ	Blue/White
Sam Houston St.	Bearkats	Southland	Bob Marlin	Huntsville, TX	Orange/White
Samford	Bulldogs	Southern	Jimmy Tillette	Birmingham, AL	Red/Blue
San Diego	Toreros	West Coast	Bill Grier	San Diego, CA	Lt. Blue/Navy
San Diego St.	Aztecs	Mountain West	Steve Fisher	San Diego, CA	Scarlet/Black
San Francisco	Dons	West Coast	Rex Walters	San Francisco, CA	Green/Gold
San Jose St.	Spartans	WAC	George Nessman	San Jose, CA	Gold/White/Blue
Santa Clara	Broncos	West Coast	Kerry Keating	Santa Clara, CA	Bronco Red/White
Savannah St.	Tigers	Independent	Horace Broadnax	Savannah, GA	Orange/Blue
Seton Hall	Pirates	Big East	Bobby Gonzalez	South Orange, NJ	Blue/White
Siena	Saints	Metro Atlantic	Fran McCaffery	Loudonville, NY	Green/Gold
South Alabama	Jaguars	Sun Belt	Ronnie Arrow	Mobile, AL	Red/White/Blue
South Carolina	Gamecocks	SEC-East	Darrin Horn	Columbia, SC	Garnet/Black
South Carolina St.	Bulldogs	Mid-Eastern	Tim Carter	Orangeburg, SC	Garnet/Blue
South Carolina Upstate	Spartans	Atlantic Sun	Eddie Payne	Spartanburg, SC	Green/White/Black
South Dakota St.	Jackrabbits	Summit	Scott Nagy	Brookings, SD	Yellow/Blue
South Dakota	Coyotes	Great West	Dave Boots	Vermillion, SD	Red/White
South Florida	Bulls	Big East	Stan Heath	Tampa, FL	Green/Gold
SE Missouri St.	Redhawks	Ohio Valley	Scott Edgar	Cape Girardeau, MO	Red/Black
Southeastern Louisiana	Lions	Southland	Jim Yarbrough Jr.	Hammond, LA	Green/Gold
Southern-BR	Jaguars	SWAC	Rob Spivery	Baton Rouge, LA	Blue/Gold

	Nickname	Conference	Head Coach	Location	Colors
Southern Illinois	Salukis	Mo. Valley	Chris Lowery	Carbondale, IL	Maroon/White
SIU-Edwardsville	Cougars	Ohio Valley	Lennox Forrester	Edwardsville, IL	Red/White
SMU	Mustangs	USA	Matt Doherty	Dallas, TX	Red/Blue
Southern Miss	Golden Eagles	USA	Larry Eustachy	Hattiesburg, MS	Black/Gold
Southern Utah	Thunderbirds	Summit	Roger Reid	Cedar City, UT	Scarlet/White
Stanford	Cardinal	Pac-10	Johnny Dawkins	Stanford, CA	Cardinal/White
S.F. Austin St.	Lumberjacks	Southland	Danny Kaspar	Nacogdoches, TX	Purple/White
Stetson	Hatters	Atlantic Sun	Derek Waugh	DeLand, FL	Green/White
Stony Brook	Seawolves	America East	Steve Pikiell	Stony Brook, NY	Scarlet/Gray
Syracuse	Orange	Big East	Jim Boeheim	Syracuse, NY	Orange
Temple	Owls	Atlantic 10	Fran Dunphy	Philadelphia, PA	Cherry/White
Tennessee	Volunteers	SEC-East	Bruce Pearl	Knoxville, TN	Orange/White
Tenn-Martin	Skyhawks	Ohio Valley	Bret Campbell	Martin, TN	Orange/Wt./Blue
Tennessee St.	Tigers	Ohio Valley	Cy Alexander	Nashville, TN	Blue/White
Tennessee Tech	Golden Eagles	Ohio Valley	Mike Sutton	Cookeville, TN	Purple/Gold
Texas	Longhorns	Big 12	Rick Barnes	Austin, TX	Burnt Orange/White
Texas A&M	Aggies	Big 12	Mark Turgeon	College Station, TX	Maroon/White
TX A&M Corpus-Christi	Islanders	Southland	Perry Clark	Corpus Christi, TX	Blue/Green/Silver
TCU	Horned Frogs	Mountain West	Jim Christian	Ft. Worth, TX	Purple/White
Texas Southern	Tigers	SWAC	Tony Harvey	Houston, TX	Maroon/Gray
Texas St.	Bobcats	Southland	Doug Davalos	San Marcos, TX	Maroon/Gold
Texas Tech	Red Raiders	Big 12	Pat Knight	Lubbock, TX	Scarlet/Black
TX-Arlington	Mavericks	Southland	Scott Cross	Arlington, TX	Royal Blue/White
TX-Pan American	Broncs	Great West	Tom Schuberth	Edinburg, TX	Green/White
TX-San Antonio	Roadrunners	Southland	Brooks Thompson	San Antonio, TX	Orange/Navy/White
Toledo	Rockets	Mid-American	Gene Cross	Toledo, OH	Blue/Gold
Towson	Tigers	Colonial	Pat Kennedy	Towson, MD	Gold/White/Black
Troy	Trojans	Sun Belt	Don Maestri	Troy, AL	Cardinal/Silver/Black
Tulane	Green Wave	USA	Dave Dickerson	New Orleans, LA	Olive Grn./Sky Blue
Tulsa	Golden Hurricane	USA	Doug Wojcik	Tulsa, OK	Blue/Gold/Crimson
UAB	Blazers	USA	Mike Davis	Birmingham, AL	Green/Gold
UC-Irvine	Anteaters	Big West	Pat Douglass	Irvine, CA	Blue/Gold
UCLA	Bruins	Pac-10	Ben Howland	Los Angeles, CA	Blue/Gold
UC-Davis	Aggies	Big West	Gary Stewart	Davis, CA	Yale Blue/Gold
UC-Riverside	Highlanders	Big West	Jim Wooldridge	Riverside, CA	Blue/Gold
UC-Santa Barbara	Gauchos	Big West	Bob Williams	Santa Barbara, CA	Blue/Gold
UNLV	Runnin' Rebels	Mountain West	Lon Kruger	Las Vegas, NV	Scarlet/Gray
USC	Trojans	Pac-10	Tim Floyd	Los Angeles, CA	Cardinal/Gold
Utah	Utes, Runnin' Utes	Mountain West	Jim Boylen	Salt Lake City, UT	Crimson/White
Utah St.	Aggies	WAC	Stew Morrill	Logan, UT	Navy Blue/White
Utah Valley	Wolverines	Great West	Dick Hunsaker	Orem, UT	Green/Gold/White
UTEP	Miners	USA	Tony Barbee	El Paso, TX	Orange/Blue/Silver
Valparaiso	Crusaders	Horizon	Homer Drew	Valparaiso, IN	Brown/Gold
Vanderbilt	Commodores	SEC-East	Kevin Stallings	Nashville, TN	Black/Gold
Vermont	Catamounts	America East	Mike Lonergan	Burlington, VT	Green/Gold
Villanova	Wildcats	Big East	Jay Wright	Villanova, PA	Blue/White
Virginia	Cavaliers	ACC	Dave Leitao	Charlottesville, VA	Orange/Blue
VCU	Rams	Colonial	Anthony Grant	Richmond, VA	Black/Gold
VMI	Keydets	Big South	Duggar Baucom	Lexington, VA	Red/White/Yellow
Virginia Tech	Hokies, Gobblers	ACC	Seth Greenberg	Blacksburg, VA	Orange/Maroon
Wagner	Seahawks	Northeast	Mike Deane	Staten Island, NY	Green/White
Wake Forest	Demon Deacons	ACC	Dino Gaudio	Winston-Salem, NC	Old Gold/Black
Washington	Huskies	Pac-10	Lorenzo Romar	Seattle, WA	Purple/Gold
Washington St.	Cougars	Pac-10	Tony Bennett	Pullman, WA	Crimson/Gray
Weber St.	Wildcats	Big Sky	Randy Rahe	Ogden, UT	Purple/White
West Virginia	Mountaineers	Big East	Bob Huggins	Morgantown, WV	Old Gold/Blue
Western Carolina	Catamounts	Southern	Larry Hunter	Cullowhee, NC	Purple/Gold
Western Illinois	Leathernecks	Summit	Jim Molinari	Macomb, IL	Purple/Gold
Western Kentucky	Hilltoppers	Sun Belt	Ken McDonald	Bowling Green, KY	Red/White
Western Michigan	Broncos	Mid-American	Steve Hawkins	Kalamazoo, MI	Brown/Gold
Wichita St.	Shockers	Mo. Valley	Gregg Marshall	Wichita, KS	Yellow/Black
William & Mary	Tribe	Colonial	Tony Shaver	Williamsburg, VA	Green/Gold/Silver
Winston-Salem St.	Rams	Mid-Eastern	Bobby Collins	Winston-Salem, NC	Red/White
Winthrop	Eagles	Big South	Randy Peele	Rock Hill, SC	Garnet/Gold
Wisconsin	Badgers	Big Ten	Bo Ryan	Madison, WI	Cardinal/White
WI-Green Bay	Phoenix	Horizon	Tod Kowalczyk	Green Bay, WI	Green/White/Red
WI-Milwaukee	Panthers	Horizon	Rob Jeter	Milwaukee, WI	Black/Gold
Wofford	Terriers	Southern	Mike Young	Spartanburg, SC	Old Gold/Black
Wright St.	Raiders	Horizon	Brad Brownell	Dayton, OH	Green/Gold
Wyoming	Cowboys	Mountain West	Heath Schroyer	Laramie, WY	Brown/Gold
Xavier	Musketeers	Atlantic 10	Sean Miller	Cincinnati, OH	Blue/Gray/White
Yale	Bulldogs, Elis	Ivy	James Jones	New Haven, CT	Yale Blue/White
Youngstown St.	Penguins	Horizon	Jerry Slocum	Youngstown, OH	Red/White

Scouts Inc. Evaluations

Listed are the top recruiting prospects for the 2009 high school graduating class for boys basketball, and the 2008 and 2009 graduating classes for football, as graded by the members of ESPN's Scouts Inc.

The analysts and talent evaluators at Scouts Inc. watch games, break down film and use their extensive experience and contacts in their respective sports to provide the deepest and most detailed scouting reports available.

For basketball grades, 98-100 is a high-major plus prospect while 94-97 is a high-major prospect.

For football grades, 90-100 is a rare prospect while 80-89 is an outstanding prospect.

For expanded lists and in-depth information on each recruit, go to the "High School" tab on ESPN.com.

Basketball Top 30 — High School Class of 2009

List is as of Oct. 10, 2008 and subject to change. *NCAA schools listed have been given only a verbal commitment at press time.

	Name	Hometown	Position	HT	WT	Rank	Grade	NCAA School*
1	Xavier Henry	Oklahoma City, OK	SG	6-6	225	SG#1	99	undeclared
2	Derrick Favors	Atlanta, GA	PF	6-9	220	PF#1	98	undeclared
3	John Henson	Tampa, FL	PF	6-10	195	PF#2	98	North Carolina
4	DeMarcus Cousins	Mobile, AL	C	6-9	260	C#1	98	UAB
5	Renardo Sidney	Los Angeles, CA	PF	6-9	260	PF#3	98	undeclared
6	John Wall	Raleigh, NC	PG	6-3	180	PG#1	98	undeclared
7	Lance Stephenson	Brooklyn, NY	SG	6-5	220	SG#2	98	undeclared
8	Jordan Hamilton	Compton, CA	SF	6-6	195	SF#1	98	Texas
9	Mason Plumlee	Arden, NC	PF	6-10	215	PF#4	97	Duke
10	Daniel Orton	Oklahoma City, OK	C	6-10	260	C#2	97	undeclared
11	Dominic Cheek	Jersey City, NJ	SG	6-6	185	SG#3	97	undeclared
12	Ryan Kelly	Raleigh, NC	PF	6-9	210	PF#5	97	Duke
13	Kenny Boynton Jr.	Pompano Beach, FL	SG	6-3	190	SG#4	97	undeclared
14	Abdul Gaddy	Tacoma, WA	PG	6-3	180	PG#2	97	Arizona
15	Avery Bradley	Tacoma, WA	SG	6-3	180	SG#5	97	Texas
16	Milton Jennings	Summerville, SC	SF	6-9	200	SF#2	97	Clemson
17	Wallace Judge	Washington, DC	PF	6-8	195	PF#6	97	Kansas St.
18	Dante Taylor	Greenburgh, NY	PF	6-9	220	PF#7	97	Pittsburgh
19	Dexter Strickland	Elizabeth, NJ	SG	6-3	185	SG#6	97	North Carolina
20	Alex Oriakhi	Lowell, MA	PF	6-8	230	PF#8	96	Connecticut
21	Keith Gallon	Houston, TX	C	6-9	290	C#3	96	undeclared
22	Maalik Wayns	Philadelphia, PA	PG	6-0	185	PG#3	96	Villanova
23	Royce White	Minnetonka, MN	SF	6-7	220	SF#3	96	Minnesota
24	Erik Murphy	South Kingstown, RI	PF	6-10	225	PF#9	96	Florida
25	Leslie McDonald	Memphis, TN	SG	6-5	200	SG#7	96	North Carolina
26	Christian Watford	Birmingham, AL	SF	6-8	215	SF#4	95	Indiana
27	Mouphtaou Yarou	Rockville, MD	PF	6-9	230	PF#10	95	Villanova
28	Peyton Siva	Seattle WA	PG	5-11	180	PG#4	95	Louisville
29	Rodney Williams	New Hope, MN	SF	6-7	185	SF#5	95	Minnesota
30	Michael Snaer	Moreno Valley, CA	SG	6-5	200	SG#8	94	undeclared

Top 25 NCAA Football Recruiting Classes of 2008

Listed are the NCAA programs with the best recruiting classes from the pool of 2008 high school seniors. These grades and rankings are purely subjective and were assigned by Scouts Inc.'s Tom Luginbill, Craig Haubert, Billy Tucker and Bill Conley.

	School		School		School		School
1	Miami-FL	8	Oklahoma	15	Virginia Tech	22	Nebraska
2	Clemson	9	Notre Dame	16	Illinois	23	Minnesota
3	Alabama	10	Texas	17	Arizona St.	24	Colorado
4	Florida	11	LSU	18	Arkansas	25	Texas A&M
5	Georgia	12	Florida St.	19	Auburn		
6	Ohio St.	13	Michigan	20	N.C. State		
7	USC	14	UCLA	21	Pittsburgh		

Football Top 30 — High School Class of 2008

	Name	Hometown	Position	HT	WT	Rank	Grade	NCAA School
1	DaQuan Bowers	Bamberg, SC	DE	6-4	265	DE#1	95	Clemson
2	Julio Jones	Foley, AL	WR	6-4	215	WR#1	95	Alabama
3	Will Hill	West Orange, NJ	S	6-3	203	S#1	94	Florida
4	Terrelle Pryor	Jeannette, PA	QB	6-6	227	QB#1	93	Ohio St.
5	A.J. Green	Ridgeville, SC	WR	6-4	184	WR#2	91	Georgia
6	Arthur Brown	Wichita, KS	OLB	6-1	210	OLB#1	90	Miami-FL
7	Jermie Calhoun	Van, TX	RB	6-0	210	RB#1	90	Oklahoma
8	Patrick Johnson	Pembroke Pines, FL	CB	6-1	193	CB#1	90	LSU
9	Darrell Scott	Moorpark, CA	RB	6-0	204	RB#2	89	Colorado
10	Dee Finley	Auburn, AL	S	6-3	210	S#2	88	Florida
11	R.J. Washington	Keller, TX	DE	6-3	245	DE#2	87	Oklahoma
12	Jamie Harper	Jacksonville, FL	RB	6-0	220	RB#3	86	Clemson
13	Josh Jarboe	Decatur, GA	WR	6-2	200	WR#3	86	Oklahoma
14	Chancey Aghayere	Garland, TX	DE	6-4	244	DE#3	86	LSU
15	Brice Butler	Norcross, GA	WR	6-2	178	WR#4	86	USC
16	D.J. Grant	Austin, TX	WR	6-3	200	WR#5	85	Texas
17	Dan Buckner	Allen, TX	WR	6-4	209	WR#6	85	Texas
18	Etienne Sabino	Miami, FL	ILB	6-3	228	ILB#1	85	Ohio St.
19	Burton Scott	Prichard, AL	ATH	5-11	194	ATH#1	84	Alabama
20	Blake Ayles	Orange, CA	TE	6-4	240	TE#1	84	USC
21	Sean Spence	Miami, FL	OLB	6-0	190	OLB#2	84	Miami-FL
22	Dayne Crist	Canoga Park, CA	QB	6-5	228	QB#2	84	Notre Dame
23	DeAndre Brown	Ocean Springs, MS	WR	6-6	208	WR#7	84	Southern Miss
24	T.J. Bryant	Tallahassee, FL	CB	6-0	180	CB#2	83	USC
25	Jonathan Baldwin	Aliquippa, PA	WR	6-6	220	TE#2	83	Pittsburgh
26	Ryan Williams	Manassas, VA	RB	5-10	192	RB#4	83	Virginia Tech
27	Marcus Forston	Miami, FL	DT	6-2	286	DT#1	83	Miami-FL
28	Brandon Harris	Miami, FL	CB	5-10	174	CB#3	83	Miami-FL
29	Mike Floyd	St. Paul, MN	WR	6-4	195	WR#8	83	Notre Dame
30	Courtney Upshaw	Eufaula, AL	DE	6-2	225	DE#4	83	Alabama

Football Top 30 — High School Class of 2009

List is as of Oct. 8, 2008 and subject to change. *Note that 2009 National Signing Day is in February, so the NCAA schools listed have been given only a verbal commitment at press time.

	Name	Hometown	Position	HT	WT	Rank	Grade	NCAA School*
1	Matt Barkley	Santa Ana, CA	QB	6-3	222	QB#1	93	USC
2	Russell Shepard	Houston, TX	ATH	6-1	183	ATH#1	93	LSU
3	Aaron Murray	Tampa, FL	QB	6-1	198	QB#2	93	Georgia
4	Devon Kennard	Phoenix, AZ	DE	6-3	257	DE#1	91	undeclared
5	Dre Kirkpatrick	Gadsden, AL	CB	6-2	180	CB#1	90	undeclared
6	Manti Te'o	Honolulu, HI	OLB	6-2	230	OLB#1	88	undeclared
7	Jacobbi McDaniel	Greenville, FL	DT	6-0	267	DT#1	87	Florida St.
8	Craig Loston	Aldine, TX	S	6-2	193	S#1	87	Clemson
9	Jelani Jenkins	Wheaton, MD	OLB	6-1	210	OLB#2	86	undeclared
10	Reuben Randle	Bastrop, LA	WR	6-3	195	WR#1	86	undeclared
11	Jaamal Berry	Miami, FL	RB	5-11	185	RB#1	86	Ohio St.
12	Trent Richardson	Pensacola, FL	RB	5-11	219	RB#2	85	Alabama
13	Mason Walters	Wolfforth, TX	OT	6-7	285	OT#1	85	Texas
14	Bryce Brown	Wichita, KS	RB	6-0	215	RB#3	85	Miami-FL
15	Damario Jeffrey	Columbia, SC	S	6-3	210	S#2	85	South Carolina
16	Dorian Bell	Monroeville, PA	OLB	6-0	220	OLB#3	85	Ohio St.
17	Marlon Brown	Memphis, TN	WR	6-5	205	WR#2	85	undeclared
18	Ray Ray Armstrong	Sanford, FL	ATH	6-4	215	ATH#2	84	undeclared
19	Garrett Gilbert	Austin, TX	QB	6-4	195	QB#3	84	Texas
20	Devonte Holloman	Rock Hill, SC	S	6-2	213	S#3	84	Clemson
21	Vontaze Burfict	Corona, CA	ILB	6-2	244	ILB#1	84	USC
22	Shaquelle Evans	Inglewood, CA	WR	6-1	203	WR#3	84	undeclared
23	Sam Montgomery	Greenwood, SC	DE	6-4	220	DE#2	84	undeclared
24	Cierre Woods	Oxnard, CA	ATH	6-0	192	ATH#3	84	Notre Dame
25	Nico Johnson	Andalusia, AL	ILB	6-2	220	ILB#2	84	Alabama
26	Darius Winston	Helena, AR	CB	6-0	180	CB#2	84	Arkansas
27	Paden Kelley	Austin, TX	OT	6-6	280	OT#2	84	Texas
28	Eric Fields	Warner Robbins, GA	OLB	6-1	210	OLB #4	83	Clemson
29	Stavion Lowe	Brownwood, TX	OT	6-6	294	OT#3	83	LSU
30	Andre Debose	Sanford, FL	WR	6-0	180	WR#4	83	undeclared

2007-08 Directors' Cup

Sponsored by the United States Sports Academy (USSA). Developed as a joint effort between the National Association of Collegiate Directors of Athletics (NACDA) and USA Today. Introduced in 1993-94 to honor the nation's best overall NCAA Division I athletic department (combining men's and women's sports). Winners in NCAA Division II and III and NAIA were named for the first time following the 1995-96 season.

Standings are computed by NACDA with points awarded for each Div. I school's finish in 20 sports (top 10 scoring sports for both men and women). Div. II schools are awarded points in 14 sports (top 7 scoring sports for both men and women). Div III schools are awarded points in 18 sports (top 9 scoring sports for both men and women). NAIA schools are awarded points in 12 sports (top 6 scoring sports for both men and women). National champions in each sport earn 100 points, while 2nd through 64th-place finishers earn decreasing points depending on the size of the tournament field. Division I-A football points are based on the final USA Today Coaches' Top 25 poll, as well as non-Top 25 bowl participants. Listed below are team conferences (for Div. I only), combined Final Four finishes (1st through 4th place) for men's and women's programs, overall points in **bold** type, and the previous year's ranking (for Div. I only).

Multiple winners: Stanford (14); Williams, MA (12); Simon Fraser, BC and UC-Davis (6); Grand Valley St., MI (5); Azusa Pacific, CA (4); Lindenwood, MO (2).

Division I

		Conf	1-2-3-4	Pts	06-07 Rank			Conf	1-2-3-4	Pts	06-07 Rank
1	Stanford	Pac-10	1-4-4-0	**1461.00**	1	14	North Carolina	ACC	1-0-2-0	**977.50**	3
2	UCLA	Pac-10	3-1-3-0	**1182.00**	2	15	Florida St.	ACC	1-2-1-0	**970.50**	15
3	Michigan	Big Ten	0-0-2-0	**1161.00**	4	16	Tennessee	SEC	1-0-0-0	**952.75**	7
4	Arizona St.	Pac-10	3-1-0-1	**1146.00**	10	17	Virginia	ACC	0-0-2-0	**869.00**	13
5	Texas	Big 12	0-2-1-2	**1129.50**	8	18	Wisconsin	Big Ten	0-1-0-0	**829.50**	16
6	Florida	SEC	0-0-2-1	**1126.75**	6	19	Duke	ACC	0-0-3-0	**820.00**	11
7	California	Pac-10	1-1-2-1	**1119.00**	9	20	Auburn	SEC	0-2-0-0	**761.50**	19
8	LSU	SEC	2-2-1-1	**1081.66**	17	21	Notre Dame	Big East	2-2-1-0	**760.50**	22
9	Penn St.	Big Ten	2-1-0-3	**1041.00**	21	22	Washington	Pac-10	0-1-0-0	**745.25**	29
10	Georgia	SEC	2-1-1-0	**1040.00**	12	23	Oklahoma	Big 12	1-0-0-0	**713.00**	25
11	Ohio St.	Big Ten	1-1-1-1	**1033.75**	14	24	Arkansas	SEC	0-0-0-0	**696.00**	31
12	Texas A&M	Big 12	0-1-1-1	**1031.00**	18	25	Alabama	SEC	0-0-1-0	**683.00**	43
13	USC	Pac-10	2-3-2-0	**1011.25**	5						

Division II

		1-2-3-4	Pts			1-2-3-4	Pts
1	Grand Valley St., MI	0-0-4-2	**1028.75**	14	Southern Ill. Edwardsville	0-0-0-1	**521.50**
2	Abilene Christian, TX	3-1-0-0	**858.00**	15	Indianapolis	0-0-0-0	**495.25**
3	Minnesota St.-Mankato	0-1-0-0	**813.75**	16	Nebraska-Kearney	1-0-0-0	**494.50**
4	UC San Diego	0-1-0-2	**752.00**	17	Bryant, RI	0-0-1-0	**482.00**
5	Tampa, FL	1-0-0-0	**654.50**	18	Central Missouri	0-0-1-0	**477.00**
6	Adams St., CO	2-2-1-1	**617.50**	19	Drury, MO	1-1-1-0	**476.00**
7	Nebraska-Omaha	0-0-1-0	**612.00**	20	Western Washington	1-1-0-0	**466.75**
8	California, PA	0-0-1-0	**607.50**	21	Northern Kentucky	1-0-0-0	**459.50**
9	Ashland, OH	0-0-1-0	**603.00**	22	Western St., CO	0-1-0-0	**457.50**
10	North Dakota	0-0-1-0	**582.50**	23	Wayne St., MI	0-0-0-0	**449.50**
11	Emporia St, KS	0-1-0-0	**568.50**	24	Truman St., MO	1-0-0-0	**437.50**
12	West Chester, PA	1-0-1-0	**555.50**	25	Cal State-Chico	0-0-0-1	**437.00**
13	South Dakota	0-1-0-0	**529.75**				

Division III

		1-2-3-4	Pts			1-2-3-4	Pts
1	Williams, MA	2-0-0-0	**1120.25**	14	Ithaca, NY	0-0-2-1	**588.00**
2	Washington, MO	3-0-2-0	**899.00**	15	Wisconsin Stevens Point	0-0-0-0	**587.25**
3	New Jersey	0-0-2-0	**825.25**	16	Tufts, MA	0-0-0-0	**580.00**
4	Amherst, MA	1-2-0-0	**815.00**	17	Johns Hopkins, MD	0-3-0-0	**577.50**
5	Middlebury, VT	1-1-1-0	**813.50**	18	DePauw, IN	0-1-0-0	**570.00**
6	Wisconsin Whitewater	1-2-0-0	**808.00**	19	Wisconsin La Crosse	1-1-0-1	**566.50**
7	Emory, GA	0-1-0-2	**752.50**	20	Illinois Wesleyan	2-0-0-1	**565.50**
8	Wartburg, IA	1-1-1-0	**722.00**	21	Wisconsin Oshkosh	0-0-1-0	**538.75**
9	Cortland St., NY	0-2-1-0	**712.50**	22	Gustavus Adolphus, MN	0-0-0-0	**524.25**
10	Wisconsin Eau Claire	1-0-0-0	**628.00**	23	Salisbury, MD	1-0-2-0	**487.00**
11	Messiah, PA	0-2-1-0	**615.25**	24	Calvin, MI	0-0-0-2	**483.25**
12	St. Thomas, MN	0-0-0-0	**594.25**	25	Bowdoin, ME	1-0-0-0	**469.00**
13	Trinity, TX	0-1-0-0	**589.50**				

NAIA

		1-2-3-4	Pts			1-2-3-4	Pts
1	Azusa Pacific, CA	3-2-1-1	947.00	14	Dickinson St., ND	0-1-2-0	555.75
2	Simon Fraser, B.C.	1-3-2-1	818.00	15	Wayland Baptist, TX	2-0-0-0	537.50
3	Embry Riddle, FL	0-1-1-0	736.25	16	Oklahoma Baptist	0-1-1-1	537.25
4	Fresno Pacific, CA	1-2-0-0	684.00	17	Black Hills St., SD	0-1-0-0	533.00
5	Concordia, CA	0-1-1-0	679.50		Morningside, IA	0-0-1-0	533.00
6	California Baptist	2-1-1-0	679.00	19	Olivet Nazarene, IL	0-0-0-0	531.50
7	Lindenwood, MO	1-0-1-1	666.00	20	Cedarville, OH	0-1-0-0	509.50
8	Savannah Art & Design, GA	0-0-2-0	652.00	21	Shorter, GA	0-0-0-0	509.25
9	Malone, OH	1-0-0-1	625.75	22	Cumberlands, KY	0-0-0-1	491.75
10	Point Loma Nazarene, CA	0-0-1-0	618.25	23	Lewis Clark St., ID	1-0-0-0	490.00
11	Oklahoma City	2-0-2-0	617.00	24	Indiana Wesleyan	0-0-0-0	478.00
12	McKendree, IL	0-1-0-0	611.50	25	Lindsey Wilson, KY	0-0-2-0	476.75
13	Northwestern, IA	1-0-1-0	577.00				

NCAA Division I Schools on Probation

As of Sept. 30, 2008, there were 26 Division I member institutions serving NCAA probations.

School	Sport	Yrs	Penalty To End	School	Sport	Yrs	Penalty To End
McNeese St.	M Basketball	2	2/7/09	Ball St.	Football	2	10/15/09
	M & W X Country	2	2/7/09		M Tennis	2	10/15/09
	M & W Indoor	2	2/7/09		Softball	2	10/15/09
	M & W Outdoor	2	2/7/09	Florida A&M	Numerous	4	1/31/10
Ohio St.	M & W Basketball	3	3/9/09	Texas Christian	M Tennis	2	2/26/10
	Football	3	3/9/09	Fresno St.	M Basketball	4	4/25/10
Louisiana-Lafayette	Football	2	4/18/09	Middle Tennessee	W Volleyball	5	5/21/10
	Basketball	2	4/18/09	Oklahoma	Football	2	5/23/10
West Virginia	M Soccer	2	4/29/09	Southeast Missouri St.	W Basketball	2	6/17/10
Nicholls St.	M Basketball	4	5/9/09	Baylor	M Basketball	5	6/22/10
	Football	4	5/9/09		Football	5	6/22/10
Temple	M Tennis	5	5/9/09	Arkansas	M Indoor	3	10/24/10
Savannah St.	Football	3	5/18/09		M Outdoor	3	10/24/10
Colorado	Football	2	6/20/09	Long Beach St.	M Basketball	3	3/5/11
Alcorn St.	W Basketball	3	6/28/09	Brigham Young	M Volleyball	3	3/10/11
Purdue	W Basketball	2	8/21/09	New Mexico	Football	3	8/19/11
Kansas	Football	3	10/11/09	Prairie View A&M	W Basketball	4	1/7/12
	M Basketball	3	10/11/09	Florida International	Numerous	4	5/5/12
				Texas Southern	M & W Tennis	4	7/15/12
					Softball	4	7/15/12

Remaining postseason and TV sanctions

2008-2009 postseason bans: Texas Southern softball.
2008-2009 television bans: None.

NCAA Graduation Rates

The following table compares graduation rates of NCAA Division I student athletes with the entire student body in those schools. **Years** given denote the year in which students entered college. **Rates** are based on students who enrolled as freshmen, received an athletics scholarship and graduated in six years or less. All figures are percentages.

Source: NCAA Graduation Rates Report, 2007.

	1995	1996	1997	1998	1999	2000
All Student Athletes	60	62	62	62	63	63
Entire Student Body	58	59	60	60	61	62
Male Student Athletes	54	55	55	55	56	55
Male Student Body	56	56	57	57	58	59
Female Student Athletes	69	70	70	71	71	71
Female Student Body	61	62	63	63	64	64
FBS (1-A) Football Players	53	54	57	54	54	55
Male Basketball Players	43	44	44	43	46	46
Female Basketball Players	65	66	64	63	64	64

2007-08 NCAA Team Champions

The NCAA administers 88 championships in 23 sports (not including Division I-A football). In 2007-08, 70 different schools won titles and 14 won multiple titles (including I-A football champ LSU).

Multiple winners: Three—ABILENE CHRISTIAN (Div. II men's cross country, men's and women's outdoor track); ARIZONA ST. (Div. I softball and men's and women's indoor track); UCLA (Div. I men's golf, women's tennis and National Div. women's water polo); WASHINGTON, MO (Div. III women's volleyball, men's basketball and tennis). **Two**—ADAMS ST., CO (Div. II women's cross country and women's indoor track); ARIZONA (Div. I men's and women's swimming & diving); ARMSTRONG ATLANTIC ST. (Div. II men's and women's tennis); GEORGIA (Div. I men's tennis and National Div. women's gymnastics); ILL.-WESLEYAN (Div. III women's indoor and outdoor track); KENYON, OH (Div. III men's and women's swimming & diving); LSU (FBS football and Div. I women's outdoor track); PENN ST. (Div. 1 women's volleyball and National Div. men's volleyball); USC (Div. I women's soccer and women's golf); WILLIAMS, MA (Div. III rowing and women's tennis).

Overall titles in parentheses; (*) indicates defending champions.

FALL

Cross Country

Men

Div.	Winner		Runner-Up	Score
I	Oregon	(5)	Iona	85-113
II	Abilene Christian	(2)	Tie	59-66
III	NYU	(1)	Haverford, PA	128-150

Women

Div.	Winner		Runner-Up	Score
I	Stanford*	(5)	Oregon	145-177
II	Adams St., CO*	(13)	Seattle Pacific	63-178
III	Amherst, MA	(1)	Plattsburgh St., NY	120-159

Field Hockey

Div.	Winner		Runner-Up	Score
I	North Carolina	(5)	Penn St.	3-0
II	Bloomsburg, PA	(14)	UMass-Lowell	5-2
III	Bowdoin, ME	(1)	Middlebury, VT	4-3

Football

Div.	Winner		Runner-Up	Score
FBS	LSU	(3)	Ohio St.	38-24
FCS	Appalachian St.*	(3)	Delaware	49-21
II	Valdosta St., GA		Northwest Mo. St.	25-20
III	Wis.-Whitewater	(1)	Mount Union, OH*	31-21

Note: There is no official FBS playoff. Florida defeated Ohio St. in the BCS Championship Game.

Soccer

Men

Div.	Winner		Runner-Up	Score
I	Wake Forest	(1)	Ohio St.	2-1
II	Franklin Pierce, NH	(1)	Lincoln Memorial, TN	1-0
III	Middlebury, VT	(1)	Trinity, TX	0-0 (4-3)

Women

Div.	Winner		Runner-Up	Score
I	USC	(1)	Florida St.	2-0
II	Tampa	(1)	Franklin Pierce	0-0 (3-1)
III	Wheaton, IL*	(3)	Messiah, PA	1-0

Volleyball

Women

Div.	Winner		Runner-Up	Score
I	Penn St.	(2)	Stanford	3-2
II	Concordia-St.Paul	(1)	Western Washington	3-1
III	Washington, MO	(10)	Wis-Whitewater	3-2

Water Polo

Men

Div.	Winner		Runner-Up	Score
National	California*	(13)	USC	8-6

WINTER

Basketball

Men

Div.	Winner		Runner-Up	Score
I	Kansas	(3)	Memphis	75-68 (OT)
II	Winona St., MN	(2)	Augusta St., GA	87-76
III	Washington, MO	(1)	Amherst, MA*	90-68

Women

Div.	Winner		Runner-Up	Score
I	Tennessee*	(8)	Stanford	64-48
II	Northern Kentucky	(2)	South Dakota	63-58
III	Howard Payne, TX	(1)	Messiah, PA	68-54

Bowling

Women

Div.	Winner		Runner-Up	Score
Nat'l	MD-Eastern Shore	(1)	Arkansas St.	4-2

Fencing

Div.	Winner		Runner-Up	Score
Combined	Ohio St.	(2)	Notre Dame	185-176

Gymnastics

Div.	Winner		Runner-Up	Margin
Men	Oklahoma	(8)	Stanford	by .450
Women	Georgia*	(9)	Utah	by .325

Ice Hockey

Men

Div.	Winner		Runner-Up	Score
I	Boston College	(3)	Notre Dame	4-1
III	St. Norbert, WI	(1)	Plattsburgh St., NY	2-0

Women

Div.	Winner		Runner-Up	Score
I	Minnesota Duluth	(4)	Wisconsin*	4-0
III	Plattsburgh St., NY*	(2)	Manhattanville, NY	3-2

Rifle

Div.	Winner		Runner-Up	Score
Combined	AK-Fairbanks*	(10)	Army	4662-4652

Skiing

Div.	Winner		Runner-Up	Score
Combined	Denver	(19)	Colorado	649.5-619

Swimming & Diving

Men

Div.	Winner		Runner-Up	Score
I	Arizona	(1)	Texas	500.5-406
II	Drury, MO	(6)	Missouri S&T	523.5-336
III	Kenyon, OH*	(29)	Johns Hopkins	635-330

Women

Div.	Winner		Runner-Up	Score
.........Arizona	(1)	Auburn*	484-348
I ....Truman St., MO	(7)	Drury, MO*	461.5-449
II .....Kenyon, OH*	(22)	Amherst, MA	566.5-341

Indoor Track
Men

Div.	Winner		Runner-Up	Score
......Arizona St.	(1)	Florida St.	44-41
II ..St. Augustine's, NC*	(11)	Abilene Christian, TX	68-49
III .....Wis-La Crosse	(14)	Monmouth, NJ	43-33

Women

Div.	Winner		Runner-Up	Score
......Arizona St.*	(2)	LSU	51-43
II ....Adams St., CO	(1)	St. Augustine's, NC*	55-48
III ...Illinois Wesleyan	(1)	Wartburg, IA	30-27

Wrestling
Men

Div.	Winner		Runner-Up	Score
...........Iowa	(21)	Ohio St.	117.5-79
II ..Nebraska-Kearney	(1)	Minn. St.-Mank.	108.5-108
III .....Wartburg, IA	(6)	Wis.-La Crosse	147-100

SPRING

Baseball

Div.	Winner		Runner-Up	Score
.......Fresno St.	(1)	Georgia	6-7, 19-10, 6-1
II ....Mount Olive, NC	(1)	Ouachita Baptist, AR	6-2
III ......Trinity, CT	(1)	Johns Hopkins	5-4

Note: The Division I Championship Series is best-of-three.

Golf
Men

Div.	Winner		Runner-Up	Score
.........UCLA	(2)	Stanford	1194-1195
II ......West Florida	(2)	N. Fla & St. Edward's	playoff
III ....St. John's, MN*	(2)	Redlands, CA	1192-1195

Women

Div.	Winner		Runner-Up	Score
.........USC	(2)	UCLA	1168-1174
II ....Rollins, FL	(5)	Nova SE	1181-1188
III ....Methodist, NC*	(12)	DePauw, IN	1219-1258

Lacrosse
Men

Div.	Winner		Runner-Up	Score
......Syracuse	(9)	Johns Hopkins*	13-10
II ....NY Inst. of Tech.	(4)	Le Moyne, NY*	16-11
III .....Salisbury, MD*	(8)	Cortland, NY	19-13

Women

Div.	Winner		Runner-Up	Score
......Northwestern*	(4)	Pennsylvania	10-6
II ...West Chester, PA	(2)	C.W. Post, NY*	13-12
III ...Hamilton, NY	(1)	Franklin & Marshall*	13-6

Rowing
Women

Div.	Winner		Runner-Up	Score
............Brown*	(6)	Washington	67-59
II .Western Washington*	(4)	UC-San Diego	20-15
III ......Williams, MA*	(4)	Trinity, CT	25-21

Softball

Div.	Winner		Runner-Up	Score
.........Arizona St.	(1)	Texas A&M	3-0, 11-0
II ....Humboldt St., CA	(2)	Emporia St., KS	1-0
III ...Wis.-Eau Claire	(1)	Wis.-Whitewater	4-3 (9 inn)

Note: The Division I Championship Series is best-of-three.

Tennis
Men

Div.	Winner		Runner-Up	Score
...........Georgia*	(6)	Texas	4-2
II .Armstrong Atlantic St.	(1)	Barry, FL	5-0
III ....Washington, MO	(1)	Emory, GA	5-3

Women

Div.	Winner		Runner-Up	Score
.............UCLA	(1)	California	4-0
II .Armstrong Atlantic St.	(4)	Lynn, FL	5-1
III ....Williams, MA	(3)	Washington & Lee, VA*	5-4

Outdoor Track
Men

Div.	Winner		Runner-Up	Score
...........Florida St.*	(3)	LSU	52-44
II ....Abilene Christian*	(18)	St Augustine's	108.5-102
III ......McMurry, TX	(1)	Cortland, NY	35-33

Women

Div.	Winner		Runner-Up	Score
..............LSU	(14)	Arizona St.*	67-63
II ....Abilene Christian	(10)	Adams St, CO	76.5-55
III Illinois Wesleyan and Wis.-River Falls tie with 35 pts.			

Volleyball
Men

Div.	Winner		Runner-Up	Score
National ..... Penn St.	(2)	Pepperdine	3-1

Water Polo
Women

Div.	Winner		Runner-Up	Score
National ....UCLA*	(6)	USC	6-3

All-Time Team Champions
Division I - Top Ten

Combined NCAA Division I men's, women's and coed team champions through spring 2008.

School	Men's	Women's	Coed	Total
1 UCLA 71	32	0	103
2 Stanford 58	37	0	95
3 USC 73	13	0	86
4 Oklahoma St. ..48	0	0	48
5 Arkansas 43	0	0	43
6 LSU 16	25	0	41
7 Texas 17	22	0	39
8 Penn State 19	5	10	34
9 North Carolina ..9	24	0	33
10 Michigan 30	2	0	32

Note: Totals above do not reflect Division I-A football championships, which are not conducted by the NCAA. Coed championships include rifle, skiing and fencing (since 1990).

Source: NCAA

Texas Tech
Sally Kipyego
Cross Country, Track

Utah
Ashley Postell
Gymnastics

Iowa
Brent Metcalf
Wrestling

Auburn
Cesar Cielo
Swimming

2007-08 Division I Individual Champions
Repeat champions in **bold** type.

FALL

Cross Country

Men (10,000 meters)	Time
1 Josh McDougal, Liberty	29:22.4
2 Galen Rupp, Oregon	29:23.4
3 Lopez Lomong, Northern Arizona	29:45.5

Women (6,000 meters)	Time
1 **Sally Kipyego**, Texas Tech	19:30.9
2 Jenny Barringer, Colorado	19:47.8
3 Susan Kuijken, Florida St.	19:57.3

WINTER

Fencing
Men

Event		Score
Foil	**Andras Horanyi**, Ohio St.	14-7
Epee	**Slava Zingerman**, Wayne St.	15-7
Sabre	Jeff Spear, Columbia	15-10

Women

Event		Score
Foil	Monika Golebiewski, St. John's	15-7
Epee	Kelley Hurley, Notre Dame	11-10
Sabre	Sarah Borrmann, Notre Dame	15-11

Gymnastics
Men

Event		Points
All-Around	Casey Sandy, Penn St.	91.350
Floor Exercise	Steven Legendre, Oklahoma	16.100
Pommel Horse	**Tim McNeill**, California	15.625
Rings	Jonathan Horton, Oklahoma	16.125
Vault	Steven Legendre, Oklahoma	16.400
Parallel Bars	**Tim McNeill**, California	15.650
High Bar	Paul Ruggeri, Illinois	15.000

Women

Event		Points
All-Around	Ashley Postell, Utah	39.750
Vault	Susan Jackson, LSU	9.8563
Uneven Bars	Tasha Schwikert, UCLA	9.9375
Balance Beam	Grace Taylor, Georgia	9.9500
Floor Exercise	Courtney McCool, Georgia	9.9625

Rifle
Combined
Smallbore

		Points
1	Chris Abalo, Army	687.6
2	Brian Kern, Army	681.6
3	Steven Scherer, Army	680.6

Air Rifle

		Points
1	Patrik Sartz, Alaska-Fairbanks	696.4
2	Josh Albright, Navy	693.9
3	Christofer Olofsson, Alaska-Fairbanks	693.8

Skiing
Men

Event		Time
Slalom	John Buchar, Denver	1:42.10
Giant Slalom	John Buchar, Denver	1:39.85
10-k Freestyle	Glenn Randall, Dartmouth	30:37.3
20-k Classic	Marius Korthauer, AK-Fairbanks	1:03:07.6

Women

Event		Time
Slalom	Lucie Zikova, Colorado	1:27.09
Giant Slalom	Lucie Zikova, Colorado	1:44.88
5-k Freestyle	Maria Grevsgaard, Colorado	17:09.8
15-k Classic	Maria Grevsgaard, Colorado	55:04.6

Wrestling

Wgt	Champion	Runner-Up
125	Angel Escobedo, Indiana	J. Ness, Minnesota
133	Coleman Scott, Okla. St.	J. Slaton, Iowa
141	J Jaggers, Ohio St.	C. Mendes, Cal Poly
149	Brent Metcalf, Iowa	B. Jenkins, Penn St.
157	Jordan Leen, Cornell	M. Poeta, Illinois
165	**Mark Perry**, Iowa	E. Tannenbaum, Michigan
174	Keith Gavin, Pittsburgh	S. Luke, Michigan
184	Mike Pucillo, Ohio St.	J. Varner, Iowa St.
197	Phil Davis, Penn St.	W. Michalak, Central Mich.
285	Dustin Fox, Northwestern	J. Bergman, Ohio St.

USC
Rebecca Soni
Swimming

Arizona St.
Jacquelyn Johnson
Track & Field

Arizona St.
Azahara Munoz
Golf

Virginia
Somdev Devvarman
Tennis

Swimming & Diving
(*) indicates meet record.

Men

Event (yards)		Time
50 free	**Cesar Cielo**, Auburn	18.52*
100 free	**Cesar Cielo**, Auburn	40.92*
200 free	Dave Walters, Texas	1:32.56
500 free	Sebastien Rouault, Georgia	4:09.48
1650 free	Sebastien Rouault, Georgia	14:26.86
100 back	Ben Hesen, Indiana	44.72
200 back	Patrick Schirk, Penn St.	1:40.22
100 breast	Paul Kornfeld, Stanford	52.03
200 breast	Paul Kornfeld, Stanford	1:53.11
100 butterfly	**Albert Subirats**, Arizona	45.07
200 butterfly	Gil Stovall, Georgia	1:41.33*
200 IM	Darian Townsend, Arizona	1:42.72
400 IM	**Alex Vanderkaay**, Michigan	3:41.58
200 free relay	**Auburn**	1:15.66
400 free relay	Arizona	2:49.01
800 free relay	**Arizona**	6:12.85*
200 medley relay	**Auburn**	1:23.24*
400 medley relay	Arizona	3:04.43

Diving		Points
1-meter	Chris Colwill, Georgia	407.25
3-meter	Reuben Ross, Miami-FL	466.80*
Platform	Sean Moore, Ohio St.	478.20*

Women

Event (yards)		Time
50 free	Lara Jackson, Arizona	21.69
100 free	Lacey Nymeyer, Arizona	47.50
200 free	Caroline Burckle, Florida	1:43.10
500 free	Caroline Burckle, Florida	4:33.60*
1650 free	Emily Brunemann, Michigan	15:53.69
100 back	Gemma Spofforth, Florida	51.78
200 back	**Gemma Spofforth**, Florida	1:50.70
100 breast	Rebecca Soni, USC	59.19
200 breast	**Rebecca Soni**, USC	2:06.32*
100 butterfly	Christine Magnuson, Tennessee	50.70
200 butterfly	Saori Haruguchi, Oregon St.	1:52.39*
200 IM	Ava Ohlgren, Auburn	1:53.94
400 IM	Julia Smit, Stanford	4:02.41
200 free relay	**Arizona**	1:26.90*
400 free relay	Arizona	3:11.34*
800 free relay	Arizona	6:59.69*
200 medley relay	**Arizona**	1:35.29*
400 medley relay	Arizona	3:29.06*

Diving		Points
1-meter	Emma Friesen, Hawaii	336.20
3-meter	Chelsea Davis, Ohio St.	365.85
Platform	Brittany Viola, Miami-FL	362.60

Indoor Track
(*) indicates meet record.

Men

Event		Time
60 meters	Richard Thompson, LSU	6.51*
200 meters	Rubin Williams, Tennessee	20.36
400 meters	Andretti Bain, Oral Roberts	46.19
800 meters	Tyler Mulder, Northern Iowa	1:49.20
Mile	**Leonel Manzano**, Texas	4:04.45
3000 meters	Kyle Alcorn, Arizona St.	8:00.82
5000 meters	Shadrack Songok, Tex. A&M-CC	13:51.26
60-m hurdles	Drew Brunson, Florida St.	7.53
4x400-m relay	**Baylor**	3:05.66
Distance medley relay	Texas	9:32.04

Event		Hgt/Dist
High Jump	Dusty Jonas, Nebraska	7-7
Pole Vault	Rory Quiller, Binghamton	18-0½
Long Jump	Reindell Cole, CS-Northridge	26-7¾
Triple Jump	Nkosinza Balumbu, Arkansas	54-3¼
Shot Put	Ryan Whiting, Arizona St.	71-3½
35-lb Throw	**Egor Agafonov**, Kansas	74-6¼
Heptathlon	Gonzalo Barroilhet, Florida St.	5951 pts.

Women

Event		Time
60 meters	Kelly-Ann Baptiste, LSU	7.17
200 meters	Bianca Knight, Texas	22.40*
400 meters	Krista Simkins, Miami-FL	52.16
800 meters	Latavia Thomas, LSU	2:05.07
Mile	Hannah England, Florida St.	4:35.30
3000 meters	Susan Kuijken, Florida St.	8:58.14
5000 meters	**Sally Kipyego**, Texas Tech	15:31.91
60-m hurdles	Tiffany Ofili, Michigan	7.94
4x400-m relay	**LSU**	3:31.14
Distance medley relay	Tennessee	11:01.97

Event		Hgt/Dist
High Jump	Ebba Jungmark, Washington St.	6-2¼
Pole Vault	**Ellie Rudy**, Montana St.	14-1¼
Long Jump	Brittney Reese, Mississippi	22-2¼
Triple Jump	**Erica McLain**, Stanford	46-7¼
Shot Put	Mariam Kevkhishvili, Florida	58-6
20-lb Throw	**Brittany Riley**, Southern Illinois	83-1¾
Pentathlon	**Jacquelyn Johnson**, Ariz. St.	4496 pts.*

SPRING
Golf
Men

			Total
1	Kevin Chappell, UCLA	69-73-68-76—	286
2	Nick Taylor, Washington	75-66-73-75—	289
	Jorge Campillo, Indiana	75-70-72-72—	289

Golf (cont.)

Women

		Total
1	Azahara Munoz, Arizona St. 69-72-73-73	287*
2	Tiffany Joh, UCLA 74-69-72-72	287
3	Garrett Phillips, Georgia 71-74-71-73	289

* Munoz defeated Joh in the 1st hole of a sudden death playoff.

Tennis

Men

Singles— **Somdev Devvarman** (Virginia) def. J.P. Smith (Tennessee), 6-3, 6-2.

Doubles— Robert Farah & Kaes Van't Hof (USC) def. Jonas Berg & Erling Tveit (Mississippi), 7-6(10), 7-6(6).

Women

Singles— Amanda McDowell (Georgia Tech) def. Zuzana Zemenova (Baylor), 6-2, 6-3.

Doubles— Tracey Lin & Riza Zalameda (UCLA) def. Melanie Gloria & Tinesta Rowe (Fresno St.), 6-2, 4-6, 6-3.

Outdoor Track

(*) indicates meet record

Men

Event		Time
100 meters	Richard Thompson, LSU	10.12
200 meters	**Walter Dix**, Florida St.	20.40
400 meters	Andretti Bain, Oral Roberts	44.62
800 meters	Jacob Hernandez, Texas	1:45.31
1500 meters	Leonel Manzano, Texas	3:41.25
5000 meters	Robert Curtis, Villanova	13:33.93
10,000 meters	**S. Songok**, Texas A&M-CC	28:46.69
110-m hurdles	Jason Richardson, S. Carolina	13.40
400-m hurdles	Jeshua Anderson, Wash. St.	48.51
3000-m steeple	Kyle Alcorn, Arizona St.	8:28.26
4x100-m relay	LSU	38.42
4x400-m relay	**Baylor**	3:00.22

Event		Hgt/Dist
High Jump	Mickael Hanany, UTEP	7-7¼
Pole Vault	Maston Wallace, Texas	17-6½
Long Jump	Ngonidzashe Makusha, Fla. St.	27-2¾
Triple Jump	Muhammad Halim, Cornell	54-8
Shot Put	Cory Martin, Auburn	66-9¼
Discus	Rashaud Scott, Kentucky	199-8
Javelin	Chris Hill, Georgia	257-3
Hammer	Cory Martin, Auburn	243-2
Decathlon	Ashton Eaton, Oregon	8055 pts.

Women

Event		Time
100 meters	Kelly-Ann Baptiste, LSU	11.20
200 meters	Simone Facey, Texas A&M	22.63
400 meters	Shana Cox, Penn St.	50.97
800 meters	Geena Gall, Michigan	2:03.91
1500 meters	Hannah England, Florida St.	4:06.19*
5000 meters	Sally Kipyego, Texas Tech	15:15.08*
10,000 meters	Lisa Koll, Iowa St.	32:44.95
100-m hurdles	**Tiffany Ofili**, Michigan	12.84
400-m hurdles	Nickiesha Wilson, LSU	54.45
3000-m steeple	Jenny Barringer, Colorado	9:29.20*
4x100-m relay	**Texas A&M**	42.59
4x400-m relay	Penn St.	3:27.69

Event		Hgt/Dist
High Jump	Elizabeth Patterson, Arizona	6-11¼
Pole Vault	Katie Morgan, California	13-9¼
Long Jump	Brittney Reese, Mississippi	22-9
Triple Jump	Erica McLain, Stanford	47-11*
Shot Put	**Jessica Pressley**, Arizona St.	59-5¾
Discus	Sarah Stevens, Arizona St.	184-2
Javelin	Rachel Yurkovich, Oregon	185-7
Hammer	Eva Orban, USC	225-5
Heptathlon	**Jacquelyn Johnson**, Ariz. St.	6053 pts.

Championships
Most Outstanding Players

Men

Baseball	Tommy Mendonca, Fresno St.
Basketball	Mario Chalmers, Kansas
Cross Country	Josh McDougal, Liberty*
Golf	Kevin Chappell, UCLA*
Gymnastics	Casey Sandy, Penn St.*
Ice Hockey	Nathan Gerbe, Boston College
Lacrosse	Mike Leveille, Syracuse
Soccer: Offense	Marcus Tracy, Wake Forest
Soccer: Defense	Brian Edwards, Wake Forest
Swimming	Cesar Cielo, Auburn†
& Diving	Chris Colwill, Georgia†
Tennis	Somdev Devvarman, Virginia*
Track: Indoor	Leonel Manzano, Texas†
Track: Outdoor	Richard Thompson, LSU†
Volleyball	Matt Anderson, Penn St.
Water Polo	Michael Sharf, California
Wrestling	Brent Metcalf, Iowa

Women

Basketball	Candace Parker, Tennessee
Bowling	Jessica Worsley, Md.-Eastern Shore
Cross Country	Sally Kipyego, Texas Tech*
Golf	Azahara Munoz, Arizona St.*
Gymnastics	Ashley Postell, Utah*
Ice Hockey	Kim Martin, Minnesota Duluth
Lacrosse	Hilary Bowen, Northwestern
Soccer: Offense	Amy Rodriguez, USC
Soccer: Defense	Kristin Olsen, USC
Softball	Katie Burkhart, Arizona St.
Swimming	Caroline Burckle, Florida†
& Diving	Emma Friesen, Hawaii†
Tennis	Amanda McDowell, Georgia Tech*
Track: Indoor	Lativia Thomas, LSU†
Track: Outdoor	Simone Facey, Texas A&M†
Volleyball	Megan Hodge, Penn St.
Water Polo	Tanya Gandy, UCLA

(*) indicates won individual or all-around NCAA championship; There were no official Outstanding Players in fencing, field hockey, I-AA football, rifle, rowing and skiing. (†) Outstanding players in Swimming & Diving and Indoor and Outdoor Track are the individuals earning the most points in the Championships.

2007-08 NAIA Team Champions

Total NAIA titles in that sport in parentheses.

FALL

Cross Country: MEN'S–Malone, OH (2); WOMEN'S–Simon Fraser, BC (10). **Football:** MEN'S– Carroll, MT (5). **Soccer:** MEN'S–Azusa Pacific, CA (1); WOMEN'S–Martin Methodist, TN (2). **Volleyball:** WOMENS–Fresno Pacific, CA (3).

WINTER

Basketball: MEN'S–Division I: Oklahoma City (6) and Division II: Oregon Tech (2); WOMEN'S–Division I: Vanguard, CA (1) and Division II: Northwestern, IA (2). **Swimming & Diving:** MEN'S–California Baptist (3); WOMEN'S– California Baptist (4). **Indoor Track:** MEN'S–Azusa Pacific, CA (6); WOMEN'S–Wayland Baptist, TX (4). **Wrestling:** MEN'S–Lindenwood, MO (4).

SPRING

Baseball: MEN'S–Lewis-Clark St., ID (16). **Golf:** MEN'S–British Columbia (1); WOMEN'S–Oklahoma City (4). **Softball:** WOMEN'S–Lubbock Christian, TX (1). **Tennis:** MEN'S–Auburn-Montgomery (8); WOMEN'S–Auburn-Montgomery (9). **Outdoor Track:** MEN'S–Azusa Pacific, CA (14); WOMEN'S–Wayland Baptist, TX (1).

Annual NCAA Division I Team Champions

Men's and women's NCAA Division I team champions from bowling to wrestling. Also see team champions for baseball, basketball, football, golf, ice hockey, soccer and tennis in the appropriate chapters throughout the almanac. See pages 474-476 for the list of 2007-08 individual champions.

BOWLING

Women

Down 2 games to 1, Maryland-Eastern Shore roared back to win three straight to defeat Arkansas State for their first NCAA bowling title. It's the first NCAA title of any kind for the Hawks, as well as the first for the Mid-eastern Athletic Conference. Senior Jessica Worsley took home the Most Valuable Bowler award, while coach Sharon Brummell became the first female head coach to guide her team to an NCAA bowling title. (*Omaha, NE; April 10-12, 2008.*)

Multiple winner: Nebraska (2).

Year	Year	Year	Year	Year
2004 Nebraska	2005 Nebraska	2006 F. Dickinson	2007 Vanderbilt	2008 MD-East. Shore

CROSS COUNTRY

Men

Oregon placed all five of its scorers in the top 30 and rolled to its fifth Division I men's cross country championship. Junior Galen Rupp led the Ducks with a second-place overall finish, just one second behind race winner Josh MacDougal of Liberty. Oregon finished with 85 points to defeat runner-up Iona (113) and Oklahoma State (180). Northern Arizona's Lopez Lomong placed finished in third. (*Terre Haute, IN; Nov. 17, 2007.*)

Multiple winners: Arkansas (11); Michigan St. (8); UTEP (7); Oregon (5); Stanford, Villanova and Wisconsin (4); Colorado, Drake, Indiana and Penn St. (3); Iowa St., San Jose St. and Western Michigan (2).

Year	Year	Year	Year	Year
1938 Indiana	1952 Michigan St.	1967 Villanova	1982 Wisconsin	1997 Stanford
1939 Michigan St.	1953 Kansas	1968 Villanova	1983 Vacated	1998 Arkansas
1940 Indiana	1954 Oklahoma St.	1969 UTEP	1984 Arkansas	1999 Arkansas
1941 Rhode Island	1955 Michigan St.	1970 Villanova	1985 Wisconsin	2000 Arkansas
1942 Indiana	1956 Michigan St.	1971 Oregon	1986 Arkansas	2001 Colorado
& Penn St.	1957 Notre Dame	1972 Tennessee	1987 Arkansas	2002 Stanford
1943 Not held	1958 Michigan St.	1973 Oregon	1988 Wisconsin	2003 Stanford
1944 Drake	1959 Michigan St.	1974 Oregon	1989 Iowa St.	2004 Colorado
1945 Drake	1960 Houston	1975 UTEP	1990 Arkansas	2005 Wisconsin
1946 Drake	1961 Oregon St.	1976 UTEP	1991 Arkansas	2006 Colorado
1947 Penn St.	1962 San Jose St.	1977 Oregon	1992 Arkansas	2007 Oregon
1948 Michigan St.	1963 San Jose St.	1978 UTEP	1993 Arkansas	
1949 Michigan St.	1964 Western Mich.	1979 UTEP	1994 Iowa St.	
1950 Penn St.	1965 Western Mich.	1980 UTEP	1995 Arkansas	
1951 Syracuse	1966 Villanova	1981 UTEP	1996 Stanford	

Women

Senior Arianna Lambie's third straight top-10 finish carried Stanford to its third straight NCAA Division I women's cross country title and fourth overall. Lambie finished in ninth as the Cardinal finished with 145 points to better runner-up Oregon (177) and third place Florida State (236). Texas Tech's Sally Kipyego set a new course record as she took the individual title for the second consecutive year. (*Terre Haute, IN; Nov. 19, 2007.*)

Multiple winners: Villanova (7); Stanford (5); BYU (4); Colorado, Oregon, Virginia and Wisconsin (2).

Year	Year	Year	Year	Year
1981 Virginia	1987 Oregon	1993 Villanova	1999 BYU	2005 Stanford
1982 Virginia	1988 Kentucky	1994 Villanova	2000 Colorado	2006 Stanford
1983 Oregon	1989 Villanova	1995 Providence	2001 BYU	2007 Stanford
1984 Wisconsin	1990 Villanova	1996 Stanford	2002 BYU	
1985 Wisconsin	1991 Villanova	1997 BYU	2003 Stanford	
1986 Texas	1992 Villanova	1998 Villanova	2004 Colorado	

FENCING

Men & Women

Junior Jason Pryor defeated Harvard's Terry Sherrill in mens' epee to clinch Ohio State's third NCAA fencing championship. The Buckeyes amassed 185 points to edge runner-up Notre Dame with 176 (*Madison, NJ; Mar. 12-16, 2008.*)

Multiple winners: Penn St. (10); Notre Dame (3); Columbia/Barnard and Ohio St. (2). **Note:** Prior to 1990, men and women held separate championships. Men's multiple winners included: NYU (12); Columbia (11); Wayne St. (7); Navy, Notre Dame and Penn (3); Illinois (2). Women's multiple winners included: Wayne St. (3); Yale (2).

Year	Year	Year	Year
1990 Penn St.	1995 Penn St.	2000 Penn St.	2005 Notre Dame
1991 Penn St.	1996 Penn St.	2001 St. John's	2006 Harvard
1992 Columbia/Barnard	1997 Penn St.	2002 Penn St.	2007 Penn St.
1993 Columbia/Barnard	1998 Penn St.	2003 Notre Dame	2008 Ohio St.
1994 Notre Dame	1999 Penn St.	2004 Ohio St.	

Annual NCAA Division I Team Champions (Cont.)

FIELD HOCKEY

Women

Katelyn Falgowski gave top-ranked North Carolina an early lead and the Tar Heels clamped down on defense to defeat Penn State, 3-0, en route to their fifth NCAA field hockey championship and first since 1997. The win capped a perfect 24-0 season for North Carolina as they became the fifth team to win the title without a loss or a tie. (*College Park, MD; Nov. 18, 2007.*)

Multiple winners: Old Dominion (9); Maryland and North Carolina (5); Wake Forest (3); Connecticut (2).

Year	Year	Year	Year	Year
1981 Connecticut	1987 Maryland	1993 Maryland	1999 Maryland	2005 Maryland
1982 Old Dominion	1988 Old Dominion	1994 J. Madison	2000 Old Dominion	2006 Maryland
1983 Old Dominion	1989 North Carolina	1995 North Carolina	2001 Michigan	2007 North Carolina
1984 Old Dominion	1990 Old Dominion	1996 North Carolina	2002 Wake Forest	
1985 Connecticut	1991 Old Dominion	1997 North Carolina	2003 Wake Forest	
1986 Iowa	1992 Old Dominion	1998 Old Dominion	2004 Wake Forest	

GYMNASTICS

Men

Olympian Jonathan Horton stuck his dismount in the rings to lead Oklahoma to its eighth NCAA gymnastics title and fifth in the last seven years. The title came down to the meet's final event as the Sooners edged Stanford by just .450 points. Taqiy Abdullah-Simmons also came through with a clutch performance in the rings. (*Stanford, CA; Apr. 17-19, 2008.*)

Multiple winners: Penn St. (12); Illinois (9); Nebraska and Oklahoma (8); California and So. Illinois (4); Iowa St., Michigan, Ohio St. and Stanford (3); Florida St and UCLA (2).

Year	Year	Year	Year	Year
1938 Chicago	1957 Penn St.	1970 Michigan	1983 Nebraska	1998 California
1939 Illinois	1958 Michigan St.	& Michigan (T)	1984 UCLA	1999 Michigan
1940 Illinois	& Illinois	1971 Iowa St.	1985 Ohio St.	2000 Penn St.
1941 Illinois	1959 Penn St.	1972 So. Illinois	1986 Arizona St.	2001 Ohio St.
1942 Illinois	1960 Penn St.	1973 Iowa St.	1987 UCLA	2002 Oklahoma
1943-47 Not held	1961 Penn St.	1974 Iowa St.	1988 Nebraska	2003 Oklahoma
1948 Penn St.	1962 USC	1975 California	1989 Illinois	2004 Penn St.
1949 Temple	1963 Michigan	1976 Penn St.	1990 Nebraska	2005 Oklahoma
1950 Illinois	1964 So. Illinois	1977 Indiana St.	1991 Oklahoma	2006 Oklahoma
1951 Florida St.	1965 Penn St.	& Oklahoma	1992 Stanford	2007 Penn St.
1952 Florida St.	1966 So. Illinois	1978 Oklahoma	1993 Stanford	2008 Oklahoma
1953 Penn St.	1967 So. Illinois	1979 Nebraska	1994 Stanford	
1954 Penn St.	1968 California	1980 Nebraska	1995 Stanford	(T) indicates won tram-
1955 Illinois	1969 Iowa	1981 Nebraska	1996 Ohio St.	poline competition
1956 Illinois	& Michigan (T)	1982 Nebraska	1997 California	(1969-70).

Women

Georgia scored 197.450 points to win its fourth straight NCAA women's gymnastics title under head coach Suzanne Yoculan and record-tying ninth overall. Utah finished second with a 197.125 followed by Stanford (196.750). Since 1982, only four schools have won the title. (*Athens, GA; Apr. 25-27, 2008.*)

Multiple winners: Georgia and Utah (9); UCLA (5); Alabama (4).

Year	Year	Year	Year	Year
1982 Utah	1988 Alabama	1994 Utah	2000 UCLA	2006 Georgia
1983 Utah	1989 Georgia	1995 Utah	2001 UCLA	2007 Georgia
1984 Utah	1990 Utah	1996 Alabama	2002 Alabama	2008 Georgia
1985 Utah	1991 Alabama	1997 UCLA	2003 UCLA	
1986 Utah	1992 Utah	1998 Georgia	2004 UCLA	
1987 Georgia	1993 Georgia	1999 Georgia	2005 Georgia	

LACROSSE

Men

Syracuse defeated defending champ Johns Hopkins, 13-10, in front of a record crowd of 48,970 for its ninth NCAA Division I lacrosse title. Junior Dan Hardy scored three goals to lead the Orange, while tournament MVP Mike Leveille added a goal and two assists. Syracuse ended the year at 16-2, while Johns Hopkins dropped to 11-6. (*Foxboro, MA; May 24, 2008.*)

Multiple winners: Johns Hopkins and Syracuse (9); Princeton (6); North Carolina and Virginia (4); Cornell (3); Maryland (2).

Year	Year	Year	Year	Year
1971 Cornell	1979 Johns Hopkins	1987 Johns Hopkins	1995 Syracuse	2003 Virginia
1972 Virginia	1980 Johns Hopkins	1988 Syracuse	1996 Princeton	2004 Syracuse
1973 Maryland	1981 North Carolina	1989 Syracuse	1997 Princeton	2005 Johns Hopkins
1974 Johns Hopkins	1982 North Carolina	1990 Syracuse*	1998 Princeton	2006 Virginia
1975 Maryland	1983 Syracuse	1991 North Carolina	1999 Virginia	2007 Johns Hopkins
1976 Cornell	1984 Johns Hopkins	1992 Princeton	2000 Syracuse	2008 Syracuse
1977 Cornell	1985 Johns Hopkins	1993 Syracuse	2001 Princeton	
1978 Johns Hopkins	1986 North Carolina	1994 Princeton	2002 Syracuse	

*Title was later vacated due to action by the NCAA Committee on Infractions.

Women

Northwestern won its fourth consecutive Division I women's lacrosse title with a 10-6 victory over Penn. The Wildcats finished the season at 21-1 as they avenged their season's only blemish, an 11-7 to the Quakers less than a month earlier. Junior Hannah Neilsen and tournament Most Outstanding Player Hilary Bowen each netted three goals for the Wildcats. Morgan Lathrop made 11 saves to backbone the Northwestern defensive effort. (Towson, MD; May 25, 2008.)

Multiple winners: Maryland (9); Northwestern (4); Princeton and Virginia (3); Penn St. and Temple (2).

Year	Year	Year	Year	Year
1982 Massachusetts	1988 Temple	1994 Princeton	2000 Maryland	2006 Northwestern
1983 Delaware	1989 Penn St.	1995 Maryland	2001 Maryland	2007 Northwestern
1984 Temple	1990 Harvard	1996 Maryland	2002 Princeton	2008 Northwestern
1985 New Hampshire	1991 Virginia	1997 Maryland	2003 Princeton	
1986 Maryland	1992 Maryland	1998 Maryland	2004 Virginia	
1987 Penn St.	1993 Virginia	1999 Maryland	2005 Northwestern	

RIFLE

Men & Women

Patrik Sartz and Christofer Olofsson placed first and third in the air rifle competition to lead Alaska-Fairbanks to its fourth consecutive NCAA rifle championship and tenth overall. The Nanooks trailed host Army by six points heading into the final day but their performance in the air rifle was enough to complete the comeback. (West Point, NY; Mar. 14-15, 2008.)

Multiple winners: West Virginia (13); Alaska-Fairbanks (10); Tennessee Tech (3); Murray St. (2).

Year	Year	Year	Year	Year
1980 Tenn. Tech	1986 West Virginia	1992 West Virginia	1998 West Virginia	2004 AK-Fairbanks
1981 Tenn. Tech	1987 Murray St.	1993 West Virginia	1999 AK-Fairbanks	2005 Army
1982 Tenn. Tech	1988 West Virginia	1994 AK-Fairbanks	2000 AK-Fairbanks	2006 AK-Fairbanks
1983 West Virginia	1989 West Virginia	1995 West Virginia	2001 AK-Fairbanks	2007 AK-Fairbanks
1984 West Virginia	1990 West Virginia	1996 West Virginia	2002 AK-Fairbanks	2008 AK-Fairbanks
1985 Murray St.	1991 West Virginia	1997 West Virginia	2003 AK-Fairbanks	

ROWING

Intercollegiate Rowing Association Regatta
VARSITY EIGHTS
Men

The Wisconsin crew sprinted past Washington in the final 500 meters to finish eight seats ahead of the Huskies for its first IRA Varsity Eights title in 18 years. Washington won the Ten Eyck points trophy (Cooper River, Camden, NJ; June 5-7, 2008.)

The IRA was formed in 1895 by several Northeastern colleges after Harvard and Yale quit the Rowing Association (established in 1871) to stage an annual race of their own. Since then the IRA Regatta has been contested over courses of varying lengths in Poughkeepsie, N.Y., Marietta, Ohio, Syracuse, N.Y. and Camden, N.J.

Distances: 4 miles (1895-97,1899-1916,1925-41); 3 miles (1898,1921-24,1947-49,1952-63,1965-67); 2 miles (1920,1950-51); 2000 meters (1964, since 1968).

Multiple winners: Cornell (24); California (15); Navy (13); Washington (12); Penn (9); Wisconsin (8); Brown (7); Syracuse (6); Columbia (4); Harvard and Princeton (3); Northeastern (2).

Year	Year	Year	Year	Year
1895 Columbia	1917-19 Not held	1941 Washington	1967 Penn	1989 Penn
1896 Cornell	1920 Syracuse	1942-46 Not held	1968 Penn	1990 Wisconsin
1897 Cornell	1921 Navy	1947 Navy	1969 Penn	1991 Northeastern
1898 Penn	1922 Navy	1948 Washington	1970 Washington	1992 Dartmouth, Navy & Penn†
1899 Penn	1923 Washington	1949 California	1971 Cornell	
1900 Penn	1924 Washington	1950 Washington	1972 Penn	1993 Brown
1901 Cornell	1925 Navy	1951 Wisconsin	1973 Wisconsin	1994 Brown
1902 Cornell	1926 Washington	1952 Navy	1974 Wisconsin	1995 Brown
1903 Cornell	1927 Columbia	1953 Navy	1975 Wisconsin	1996 Princeton
1904 Syracuse	1928 California	1954 Navy*	1976 California	1997 Washington
1905 Syracuse	1929 Columbia	1955 Cornell	1977 Cornell	1998 Princeton
1906 Cornell	1930 Cornell	1956 Cornell	1978 Syracuse	1999 California
1907 Cornell	1931 Navy	1957 Cornell	1979 Brown	2000 California
1908 Syracuse	1932 California	1958 Cornell	1980 Navy	2001 California
1909 Cornell	1933 Not held	1959 Wisconsin	1981 Cornell	2002 California
1910 Cornell	1934 California	1960 California	1982 Cornell	2003 Harvard
1911 Cornell	1935 California	1961 California	1983 Brown	2004 Harvard
1912 Cornell	1936 Washington	1962 Cornell	1984 Navy	2005 Harvard
1913 Syracuse	1937 Washington	1963 California	1985 Princeton	2006 California
1914 Columbia	1938 Navy	1964 California	1986 Brown	2007 Washington
1915 Cornell	1939 California	1965 Navy	1987 Brown	2008 Wisconsin
1916 Syracuse	1940 Washington	1966 Wisconsin	1988 Northeastern	

*In 1954, Navy was disqualified because of an ineligible coxswain; no trophies were given.
†First dead heat in history of IRA Regatta.

Annual NCAA Division I Team Champions (Cont.)
NCAA Rowing Championships
Women

As it normally does, the 2008 NCAA Rowing Championships came down to the Varsity Eights race, and as usual, Brown did what it needed to do for the title. The Bears placed third in the race behind Yale and Stanford, but it gave them all the points they needed to win their sixth overall championship. Brown finished with 67 points overall, ahead of Washington (59), Cal (53) and Yale (51). (*Gold River, CA; May 29-June 1, 2008.*)

Multiple winners: Brown (6); Washington (3); California (2).

Year	Overall winner	Varsity Eights	Year	Overall winner	Varsity Eights
1997	Washington	Washington	2003	Harvard	Harvard
1998	Washington	Washington	2004	Brown	Brown
1999	Brown	Brown	2005	California	California
2000	Brown	Brown	2006	California	Princeton
2001	Washington	Washington	2007	Brown	Yale
2002	Brown	Washington	2008	Brown	Yale

National Rowing Championship
VARSITY EIGHTS
Men

National championship raced annually from 1982-96 in Bantam, Ohio over a 2,000-meter course on Lake Harsha. Winner received the Herschede Cup. Regatta discontinued in 1997.

Multiple winners: Harvard (6); Brown (3); Wisconsin (2).

Year	Champion	Time	Runner-up	Time	Year	Champion	Time	Runner-up	Time
1982	Yale	5:50.8	Cornell	5:54.15	1990	Wisconsin	5:52.5	Harvard	5:56.84
1983	Harvard	5:59.6	Washington	6:00.0	1991	Penn	5:58.21	Northeastern	5:58.48
1984	Washington	5:51.1	Yale	5:55.6	1992	Harvard	5:33.97	Dartmouth	5:34.28
1985	Harvard	5:44.4	Princeton	5:44.87	1993	Brown	5:54.15	Penn	5:56.98
1986	Wisconsin	5:57.8	Brown	5:59.9	1994	Brown	5:24.52	Harvard	5:25.83
1987	Harvard	5:35.17	Brown	5:35.63	1995	Brown	5:23.40	Princeton	5:25.83
1988	Harvard	5:35.98	Northeastern	5:37.07	1996	Princeton	5:57.47	Penn	6:03.28
1989	Harvard	5:36.6	Washington	5:38.93	1997	discontinued			

Women

National championship held over various distances at 10 different venues from 1979-96. Distances– 1000 meters (1979-81); 1500 meters (1982-83); 1000 meters (1984); 1750 meters (1985); 2000 meters (1986-88, 1991-96); 1852 meters (1989-90). Winner received the Ferguson Bowl. Regatta discontinued in 1997.

Multiple winners: Washington (7); Princeton (4); Boston University (2).

Year	Champion	Time	Runner-up	Time	Year	Champion	Time	Runner-up	Time
1979	Yale	3:06	California	3:08.6	1988	Washington	6:41.0	Yale	6:42.37
1980	California	3:05.4	Oregon St.	3:05.8	1989	Cornell	5:34.9	Wisconsin	5:37.5
1981	Washington	3:20.6	Yale	3:22.9	1990	Boston Univ.	7:03.2	Cornell	7:06.21
1982	Washington	4:56.4	Wisconsin	4:59.83	1991	Boston Univ.	6:28.79	Cornell	6:32.79
1983	Washington	4:57.5	Dartmouth	5:03.02	1992	Princeton	6:40.75	Washington	6:43.86
1984	Washington	3:29.48	Radcliffe	3:31.08	1993	Princeton	6:11.38	Yale	6:14.46
1985	Washington	5:28.4	Wisconsin	5:32.0	1994	Princeton	6:11.93	Washington	6:12.69
1986	Wisconsin	6:53.28	Radcliffe	6:53.34	1995	Brown	6:45.7	Princeton	6:49.3
1987	Washington	6:33.8	Yale	6:37.4	1996				
					1997	discontinued			

SKIING
Men & Women

Denver's John Buchar won the men's slalom and giant slalom to lift the Pioneers to their 19th NCAA skiing title and fifth of the decade. Denver trailed rival Colorado by 17.5 points heading into the final day but turned that deficit into a 30.5 win thanks to its stellar alpine performance. (*Bozeman, MN; March 5-8, 2008.*)

Multiple winners: Denver (19); Colorado (16); Utah (10); Vermont (5); Dartmouth (3); Wyoming (2).

Year		Year		Year		Year		Year	
1954	Denver	1966	Denver	1977	Colorado	1989	Vermont	2001	Denver
1955	Denver	1967	Denver	1978	Colorado	1990	Vermont	2002	Denver
1956	Denver	1968	Wyoming	1979	Colorado	1991	Colorado	2003	Utah
1957	Denver	1969	Denver	1980	Vermont	1992	Vermont	2004	New Mexico
1958	Dartmouth	1970	Denver	1981	Utah	1993	Utah	2005	Denver
1959	Colorado	1971	Denver	1982	Colorado	1994	Vermont	2006	Colorado
1960	Colorado	1972	Colorado	1983	Utah	1995	Colorado	2007	Dartmouth
1961	Denver	1973	Colorado	1984	Utah	1996	Utah	2008	Denver
1962	Denver	1974	Colorado	1985	Wyoming	1997	Utah		
1963	Denver	1975	Colorado	1986	Utah	1998	Colorado		
1964	Denver	1976	Colorado	1987	Utah	1999	Colorado		
1965	Denver		& Dartmouth	1988	Utah	2000	Denver		

SOFTBALL

Women

Arizona State routed Texas A&M, 11-0, a day after blanking them, 3-0, to sweep the best-of-3 series and win its first Division I softball title. Sun Devil ace and tournament Most Outstanding Player Katie Burkhart whiffed 13 batters and allowed just four hits in the series-clinching shutout. Slugger Katie Cochran, who was intentionally walked six straight times earlier in the tournament, belted a three-run homer to pace the offense. Arizona State finished the year at 66-5, while fifth-seeded Texas A&M fell to 57-10. (Oklahoma City, OK; May 29-June 3, 2008.)

Multiple winners: UCLA (10); Arizona (8); Texas A&M (2).

Year	Year	Year	Year	Year
1982 UCLA	1988 UCLA	1994 Arizona	2000 Oklahoma	2006 Arizona
1983 Texas A&M	1989 UCLA	1995 UCLA*	2001 Arizona	2007 Arizona
1984 UCLA	1990 UCLA	1996 Arizona	2002 California	2008 Arizona St.
1985 UCLA	1991 Arizona	1997 Arizona	2003 UCLA	
1986 CS-Fullerton	1992 UCLA	1998 Fresno St.	2004 UCLA	
1987 Texas A&M	1993 Arizona	1999 UCLA	2005 Michigan	

*Title was later vacated due to action by the NCAA Committee on Infractions.

SWIMMING & DIVING

Men

Albert Subirats successfully defended his title in the 100-yd butterfly and Darian Townsend won the 200-yd IM to lead Arizona to its first NCAA Division I men's swimming championship. The Wildcats amassed a total of 500.5 points to cruise to the victory over runner-up Texas (406) and third place Stanford (344). Arizona also won three of the meet's five relays. Auburn star Cesar Cielo grabbed four titles — two individual and two relays, while Georgia's Sebastien Rouault and Stanford's Paul Kornfeld were the meet's other two individual double winners. (Federal Way, WA; Mar. 27-29, 2008.)

Multiple winners: Michigan and Ohio St. (11); Texas and USC (9); Stanford (8); Auburn (7); Indiana (6); Yale (4); California and Florida (2).

Year	Year	Year	Year	Year
1937 Michigan	1952 Ohio St.	1967 Stanford	1982 UCLA	1997 Auburn
1938 Michigan	1953 Yale	1968 Indiana	1983 Florida	1998 Stanford
1939 Michigan	1954 Ohio St.	1969 Indiana	1984 Florida	1999 Auburn
1940 Michigan	1955 Ohio St.	1970 Indiana	1985 Stanford	2000 Texas
1941 Michigan	1956 Ohio St.	1971 Indiana	1986 Stanford	2001 Texas
1942 Yale	1957 Michigan	1972 Indiana	1987 Stanford	2002 Texas
1943 Ohio St.	1958 Michigan	1973 Indiana	1988 Texas	2003 Auburn
1944 Yale	1959 Michigan	1974 USC	1989 Texas	2004 Auburn
1945 Ohio St.	1960 USC	1975 USC	1990 Texas	2005 Auburn
1946 Ohio St.	1961 Michigan	1976 USC	1991 Texas	2006 Auburn
1947 Ohio St.	1962 Ohio St.	1977 USC	1992 Stanford	2007 Auburn
1948 Michigan	1963 USC	1978 Tennessee	1993 Stanford	2008 Arizona
1949 Ohio St.	1964 USC	1979 California	1994 Stanford	
1950 Ohio St.	1965 USC	1980 California	1995 Michigan	
1951 Yale	1966 USC	1981 Texas	1996 Texas	

Women

Arizona, who lost the 2007 championship on the final day, finally captured its first NCAA Division I women's swimming title in dominating fashion. Lara Jackson (50-yd free) and Lacey Nymeyer (100-yd free) were individual winners for the Wildcats, but it was the relays where Arizona truly excelled, sweeping all five events and setting a new meet record in each. Arizona finished with 484 points to defeat runner-up and defending champ Auburn (348) and third place Stanford (343). USC's Rebecca Soni and Florida's Caroline Burckle and Gemma Spofforth all won two events each. (Columbus, OH; Mar. 20-22, 2008.)

Multiple winners: Stanford (8); Texas (7); Auburn (5); Georgia (4).

Year	Year	Year	Year	Year
1982 Florida	1988 Texas	1994 Stanford	2000 Georgia	2006 Auburn
1983 Stanford	1989 Stanford	1995 Stanford	2001 Georgia	2007 Auburn
1984 Texas	1990 Texas	1996 Stanford	2002 Auburn	2008 Arizona
1985 Texas	1991 Texas	1997 USC	2003 Auburn	
1986 Texas	1992 Stanford	1998 Stanford	2004 Auburn	
1987 Texas	1993 Stanford	1999 Georgia	2005 Georgia	

The Harvard-Yale Regatta

Harvard's Varsity Eights crew took the lead at the two-mile mark and held on to beat Yale by 7.5 seconds at the 143rd running of the Harvard/Yale Regatta, held June 13-14, 2008 on the Thames River in New London, Conn. The Crimson finished the four-mile race in 18:54.1, while the Bulldogs came in at 19:01.6. The win completed a four-race sweep for the Crimson, who also took the two-mile Combination Race, the two-mile Freshman Race and the three-mile Junior Varsity Race. The Harvard/Yale Regatta is the nation's oldest intercollegiate sporting event. Harvard holds an 89-54 series edge.

Annual NCAA Division I Team Champions (Cont.)

INDOOR TRACK

Men

Arizona State placed third in the meet's final event, the 4 x 400-meter relay, which was good enough to clinch their first Division I indoor track championship. The Sun Devils just needed to finish ahead of Florida State in the relay, and they did just that with the Seminoles coming in sixth. Arizona State accumulated 44 points to edge runner-up Florida State (41) and third place Texas (34). LSU (33) and Tennessee (26) rounded out the Top 5. Kyle Alcorn paced the Sun Devils with a win in the 3000-meter run (8:00.82), while Ryan Whiting won the shot put with a throw of 71-3½. *(Fayetteville, AR; Mar. 10-15, 2008.)*

Multiple winners: Arkansas (19); UTEP (7); Kansas and Villanova (3); LSU and USC (2).

Year	Year	Year	Year	Year
1965 Missouri	1974 UTEP	1983 SMU	1992 Arkansas	2001 LSU
1966 Kansas	1975 UTEP	1984 Arkansas	1993 Arkansas	2002 Tennessee
1967 USC	1976 UTEP	1985 Arkansas	1994 Arkansas	2003 Arkansas
1968 Villanova	1977 Washington St.	1986 Arkansas	1995 Arkansas	2004 LSU
1969 Kansas	1978 UTEP	1987 Arkansas	1996 George Mason	2005 Arkansas
1970 Kansas	1979 Villanova	1988 Arkansas	1997 Arkansas	2006 Arkansas
1971 Villanova	1980 UTEP	1989 Arkansas	1998 Arkansas	2007 Wisconsin
1972 USC	1981 UTEP	1990 Arkansas	1999 Arkansas	2008 Arizona St.
1973 Manhattan	1982 UTEP	1991 Arkansas	2000 Arkansas	

Women

Jacquelyn Johnson became the first three-time winner of the indoor pentathlon in leading Arizona State to its second straight Division I women's indoor track championship. The Sun Devils scored 51 points to outpace runner-up LSU (43) for the second consecutive year. Michigan (39), Texas (35) and Stanford (32) rounded out the Top 5. Johnson amassed 4,496 points to set an all-time NCAA meet and collegiate record. Arizona State already had the title clinched before the last event, the 4 x 400-meter relay, in which they placed third. Texas Tech distance runner extraordinaire Sally Kipyego successfully defended her title in the 5000-meter run with a time of 15:31.91. *(Fayetteville, AR; Mar. 10-15, 2008.)*

Multiple winners: LSU (11); Texas (6); Arizona St., Nebraska and UCLA (2).

Year	Year	Year	Year	Year
1983 Nebraska	1989 LSU	1995 LSU	2001 UCLA	2007 Arizona St.
1984 Nebraska	1990 Texas	1996 LSU	2002 LSU	2008 Arizona St.
1985 Florida St.	1991 LSU	1997 LSU	2003 LSU	
1986 Texas	1992 Florida	1998 Texas	2004 LSU	
1987 LSU	1993 LSU	1999 Texas	2005 Tennessee	
1988 Texas	1994 LSU	2000 UCLA	2006 Texas	

OUTDOOR TRACK

Men

Olympian sprinter Walter Dix successfully defended his title in the 200-meter event (20.40) to carry Florida State to its third straight NCAA Division I outdoor track title. Dix also finished fourth in the 100-meter dash, which was won by LSU's Richard Thompson in 10.12. The Seminoles scored 52 points to get past runners-up LSU and Auburn (tied at 44). Texas (35) and Texas A&M (32) rounded out the top 5. Long jumper Ngonidzashe Makusha was the other individual winner for Florida State, grabbing first with a leap of 27-2¾. Shadrack Songok of Texas A&M-Corpus Christi repeated as champion in the 10,000-meter run with a time of 28:46.69. *(Des Moines, IA; June 11-14, 2008.)*

Multiple winners: USC (26); Arkansas (12); UCLA (8); UTEP (6); Illinois and Oregon (5); LSU and Stanford (4); Florida St., Kansas and Tennessee (3); SMU (2).

Year	Year	Year	Year	Year
1921 Illinois	1939 USC	1957 Villanova	1974 Tennessee	1992 Arkansas
1922 California	1940 USC	1958 USC	1975 UTEP	1993 Arkansas
1923 Michigan	1941 USC	1959 Kansas	1976 USC	1994 Arkansas
1924 Not held	1942 USC	1960 Kansas	1977 Arizona St.	1995 Arkansas
1925 Stanford*	1943 USC	1961 USC	1978 UCLA & UTEP	1996 Arkansas
1926 USC*	1944 Illinois	1962 Oregon	1979 UTEP	1997 Arkansas
1927 Illinois*	1945 Navy	1963 USC	1980 UTEP	1998 Arkansas
1928 Stanford	1946 Illinois	1964 Oregon	1981 UTEP	1999 Arkansas
1929 Ohio St.	1947 Illinois	1965 Oregon & USC	1982 UTEP	
1930 USC	1948 Minnesota	1966 UCLA	1983 SMU	2000 Stanford
1931 USC	1949 USC	1967 USC	1984 Oregon	2001 Tennessee
1932 Indiana	1950 USC	1968 USC	1985 Arkansas	2002 LSU
1933 LSU	1951 USC	1969 San Jose St.	1986 SMU	2003 Arkansas
1934 Stanford	1952 USC	1970 BYU, Kansas	1987 UCLA	2004 Arkansas
1935 USC	1953 USC	& Oregon	1988 UCLA	2005 Arkansas
1936 USC	1954 USC	1971 UCLA	1989 LSU	2006 Florida St.
1937 USC	1955 USC	1972 UCLA	1990 LSU	2007 Florida St.
1938 USC	1956 UCLA	1973 UCLA	1991 Tennessee	2008 Florida St.

(*) indicates unofficial championship.

Women

LSU edged Arizona St., 67-63, to win its 14th overall NCAA Division I outdoor track title and first since 2003. Texas A&M (48), Penn St. (39) and Texas Tech (32) rounded out the top 5. The Lady Tigers and Sun Devils were tied heading into the meet's final event, the 4 x 400m relay. Penn St. won the event, but perhaps more importantly, LSU placed second and Arizona St. placed fifth to clinch the title for LSU. Kelly-Ann Baptiste (11.20) won the 100-m dash, and Nickiesha Wilson won the 400-m hurdles in 54.45 to lead LSU to victory. (Des Moines, IA; June 11-14, 2008.)

Multiple winners: LSU (14); Texas (4); UCLA (3).

Year	Year	Year	Year	Year
1982 UCLA	1988 LSU	1994 LSU	2000 LSU	2006 Auburn
1983 UCLA	1989 LSU	1995 LSU	2001 USC	2007 Arizona St.
1984 Florida St.	1990 LSU	1996 LSU	2002 South Carolina	2008 LSU
1985 Oregon	1991 LSU	1997 LSU	2003 LSU	
1986 Texas	1992 LSU	1998 Texas	2004 UCLA	
1987 LSU	1993 LSU	1999 Texas	2005 Texas	

VOLLEYBALL

Men

Penn State dropped the first game of its championship match with Pepperdine, then rallied to win three straight for their its second overall men's volleyball title. It's the first win since 1994 for the Nittany Lions, who took the title, 27-30, 33-31, 30-25, 30-23. Senior setter Luke Murray recorded 63 assists, 12 digs and 11 blocks to lead Penn State, while teammate Matt Anderson pounded 29 kills with a .451 hitting percentage to earn the tournament's Most Outstanding Player award. Paul Carroll led Pepperdine with 35 kills. (Irvine, CA; May 3, 2008.)

Multiple winners: UCLA (19); Pepperdine (5); USC (4); BYU (3); Penn St. (2).

Year	Year	Year	Year	Year
1970 UCLA	1978 Pepperdine	1986 Pepperdine	1994 Penn St.	2002 Hawaii†
1971 UCLA	1979 UCLA	1987 UCLA	1995 UCLA	2003 Lewis, IL*
1972 UCLA	1980 USC	1988 USC	1996 UCLA	2004 BYU
1973 San Diego St.	1981 UCLA	1989 UCLA	1997 Stanford	2005 Pepperdine
1974 UCLA	1982 UCLA	1990 USC	1998 UCLA	2006 UCLA
1975 UCLA	1983 UCLA	1991 Long Beach St.	1999 BYU	2007 UC Irvine
1976 UCLA	1984 UCLA	1992 Pepperdine	2000 UCLA	2008 Penn St.
1977 USC	1985 Pepperdine	1993 UCLA	2001 BYU	

†Title was later vacated due to action by the NCAA Committee on Infractions.
*Division II

The Most Common College Nicknames

	Name	Examples	No.		Name	Examples	No.		Name	Examples	No.
1	Eagles	B.C., Biola	64	9	Crusaders	Susquehanna	30	16	Hawks	Monmouth	18
2	Tigers	LSU, Occidental	46	10	Pioneers	Denver	27		Rams	Colorado St.	18
3	Bulldogs	Yale, The Citadel	40	11	Knights	Fair. Dickinson	24	18	Vikings	Cleveland St.	17
4	Lions	Columbia	37	12	Bears	Brown, Shaw	21	19	Golden		
5	Wildcats	Arizona	33		Falcons	Air Force	21		Eagles	Marquette	16
6	Warriors	Winona St.	32	14	Saints	Marymount	20		Spartans	Michigan St.	16
7	Cougars	Houston	31	15	Cardinals	Ball St.	19				
	Panthers	Pitt, York	31								

...And Some of the More Uncommon

(all nicknames below belong to just one school)

Auggies — Augsburg College
Banana Slugs — Cal-Santa Cruz
Battlin' Beavers — Blackburn Coll.
Bloodhounds — John Jay College
　of Criminal Justice
Blueboys — Illinois College
Chanticleers — Coastal Carolina
Eutectics — St. Louis College
　of Pharmacy

Fords — Haverford
Gorloks — Webster
Judges — Brandeis
Jumbos — Tufts
Nanooks — Alaska-Fairbanks
Otters — CS-Monterey Bay
Paladins — Furman
Pelicans — Spalding

Phantoms — East-West
Pilgrims — New England College
Profs — Rowan
Silverswords — Chaminade
Stormy Petrels — Oglethorpe
Violets — NYU.
White Mules — Colby College

Sources:
Pete Fournier, The Handbook of Mascots and Nicknames
(via) 23 Ways To Get To First Base: The ESPN Uncyclopedia

Annual NCAA Division I Team Champions (Cont.)

Women

Top-ranked Penn State won a thrilling 5-game final match with Stanford to capture its second NCAA women's volleyball title and first since 1999. The Nittany Lions won, 30-25, 30-26, 23-20, 19-30, 15-8, and avenged their five-game loss to the Cardinal three months before. Megan Hodge led Penn State with 26 kills, while Alisha Glass added 65 assists. Alex Klineman and Foluke Akinradewo led the Cardinal with 18 kills apiece. (*Sacramento, CA; Dec. 15, 2007.*)

Multiple winners: Stanford (6); Hawaii, Long Beach St., Nebraska, UCLA and USC (3); Pacific and Penn St. (2).

Year	Year	Year	Year	Year
1981 USC	1987 Hawaii	1993 Long Beach St.	1999 Penn St.	2005 Washington
1982 Hawaii	1988 Texas	1994 Stanford	2000 Nebraska	2006 Nebraska
1983 Hawaii	1989 Long Beach St.	1995 Nebraska	2001 Stanford	2007 Penn St.
1984 UCLA	1990 UCLA	1996 Stanford	2002 USC	
1985 Pacific	1991 UCLA	1997 Stanford	2003 USC	
1986 Pacific	1992 Stanford	1998 Long Beach St.	2004 Stanford	

WATER POLO

Men

California successfully defended its title with an 8-6 win over USC at the NCAA Men's Water Polo Championship. Seniors Adam Haley and Zac Monsees led the Bear attack with two goals each, and goalie Mark Sheredy turned away 11 USC shots to backbone the defense. J.W. Krumpholz added 2 goals for the Trojans. (*Stanford, CA; Dec. 2, 2007.*)

Multiple winners: California (13); Stanford (10); UCLA (8); UC-Irvine and USC (3).

Year	Year	Year	Year	Year
1969 UCLA	1977 California	1985 Stanford	1993 Stanford	2001 Stanford
1970 UC-Irvine	1978 Stanford	1986 Stanford	1994 Stanford	2002 Stanford
1971 UCLA	1979 UC-S. Barbara	1987 California	1995 UCLA	2003 USC
1972 UCLA	1980 Stanford	1988 California	1996 UCLA	2004 UCLA
1973 California	1981 Stanford	1989 UC-Irvine	1997 Pepperdine	2005 USC
1974 California	1982 UC-Irvine	1990 California	1998 USC	2006 California
1975 California	1983 California	1991 California	1999 UCLA	2007 California
1976 Stanford	1984 California	1992 California	2000 UCLA	

Women

UCLA capped off its undefeated season with a decisive 6-3 victory over USC to win its fourth straight women's water polo title and sixth overall. The Bruins (33-0) jumped out to a 3-0 first quarter lead on goals by Tanya Gandy, Courtney Mathewson and Gabrielle Domanic, then increased the lead to 5-1 at the half. Gandy, who added a second goal, was named tournament MVP. Brittany Fullen made 6 saves to lead the Bruins to victory. (*Stanford, CA; May 11, 2008.*)

Multiple winner: UCLA (6).

Year	Year	Year	Year	Year
2001 UCLA	2003 UCLA	2005 UCLA	2007 UCLA	2008 UCLA
2002 Stanford	2004 USC	2006 UCLA		

WRESTLING

Men

Senior Mark Perry and sophomore Brent Metcalf won individual title in their weight classed and the Iowa Hawkeyes won NCAA wrestling title no. 21 by over 38 points. The Hawkeyes amassed 117½ points to defeat runner-up Ohio State (79) and Penn State (75). Metcalf beat Penn State's Bubba Jenkins, 14-8, in the 149-pound finals, while Perry took down Michigan's Eric Tannenbaum, 5-2, in the 165-pound finals. (*St. Louis, MO; Mar. 20-22, 2008.*)

Multiple winners: Oklahoma St. (34); Iowa (21); Iowa St. (8); Oklahoma (7); Minnesota (3).

Year	Year	Year	Year	Year
1928 Okla. A&M*	1943-45 Not held	1961 Okla. St.	1977 Iowa St.	1993 Iowa
1929 Okla. A&M	1946 Okla. A&M	1962 Okla. St.	1978 Iowa	1994 Okla. St.
1930 Okla. A&M	1947 Cornell Col.	1963 Oklahoma	1979 Iowa	1995 Iowa
1931 Okla. A&M*	1948 Okla. A&M	1964 Okla. St.	1980 Iowa	1996 Iowa
1932 Indiana*	1949 Okla. A&M	1965 Iowa St.	1981 Iowa	1997 Iowa
1933 Okla. A&M*	1950 Northern Iowa	1966 Okla. St.	1982 Iowa	1998 Iowa
& Iowa St.*	1951 Oklahoma	1967 Michigan St.	1983 Iowa	1999 Iowa
1934 Okla. A&M	1952 Oklahoma	1968 Okla. St.	1984 Iowa	2000 Iowa
1935 Okla. A&M	1953 Penn St.	1969 Iowa St.	1985 Iowa	2001 Minnesota
1936 Oklahoma	1954 Okla. A&M	1970 Iowa St.	1986 Iowa	2002 Minnesota
1937 Okla. A&M	1955 Okla. A&M	1971 Okla. St.	1987 Iowa St.	2003 Okla. St.
1938 Okla. A&M	1956 Okla. A&M	1972 Iowa St.	1988 Arizona St.	2004 Okla. St.
1939 Okla. A&M	1957 Oklahoma	1973 Iowa St.	1989 Okla. St.	2005 Okla. St.
1940 Okla. A&M	1958 Okla. St.	1974 Oklahoma	1990 Okla. St.	2006 Okla. St.
1941 Okla. A&M	1959 Okla. St.	1975 Iowa	1991 Iowa	2007 Minnesota
1942 Okla. A&M	1960 Oklahoma	1976 Iowa	1992 Iowa	2008 Iowa

(*) indicates unofficial champions. **Note:** Oklahoma A&M became Oklahoma St. in 1958.

HALLS of FAME
& AWARDS

It was finally good for the Goose in Cooperstown, N.Y. After missing out eight times, he made the cut in 2008.

BASEBALL

National Baseball Hall of Fame & Museum

Established in 1935 by Major League Baseball to celebrate the game's 100th anniversary. **Address:** 25 Main Street, Cooperstown, NY 13326. **Telephone:** (607) 547-7200. **Web:** www.baseballhalloffame.org

Eligibility: In August 2001, the Hall of Fame announced changes in the way players are elected via the Veterans Committee. The voting done by Baseball Writers' Association of America remains unchanged. Nominated players must have played at least parts of 10 seasons in the major leagues and be retired for at least five. Certain nominated players not elected by the writers can become eligible via the Veterans Committee. The new Veterans Committee will be comprised of all living Hall of Famers as well as all living winners of the Ford Frick and J.G. Taylor Spink. Awards and three members of the old 15-member Veterans Committee with unexpired terms. There was no Veterans Committee vote in 2002. Beginning in 2003 the new Veterans Committee votes every two years on former players and every four years on managers, umpires and executives. Previously, the committee voted annually.

Also, the eligibility of all players that had been dropped from the ballots for not receiving five percent of the vote was restored and those players can now be immediately considered by the new Veterans Committee. The players on baseball's ineligible list are still excluded from consideration. Pete Rose is the only living ex-player on that list.

Class of 2008 (1): BBWAA vote— **Rich "Goose" Gossage**, Chicago White Sox (1972-76), Pittsburgh Pirates (1977), N.Y. Yankees (1978-83, 1989), San Diego Padres (1984-87), Chicago Cubs (1988), San Francisco Giants (1989), Texas Rangers (1991), Oakland Athletics (1992-93), Seattle Mariners (1994).

2008 Top vote-getters (543 BBWAA ballots cast, 408 needed to elect, 27 to remain on ballot): 1. **Rich Gossage** (466), 2. **Jim Rice** (392); 3. **Andre Dawson** (358), 4. **Bert Blyleven** (336), 5. **Lee Smith** (235), 6. **Jack Morris** (233), 7. **Tommy John** (158), 8. **Tim Raines** (132), 9. **Mark McGwire** (128), 10. **Alan Trammell** (99), 11. **Dave Concepcion** (88), 12. **Don Mattingly** (86), 13. **Dave Parker** (82), 14. **Dale Murphy** (75), 15. **Harold Baines** (28).

Elected first year on ballot (43): Hank Aaron, Ernie Banks, Johnny Bench, Wade Boggs, George Brett, Lou Brock, Rod Carew, Steve Carlton, Ty Cobb, Dennis Eckersley, Bob Feller, Bob Gibson, Tony Gwynn, Reggie Jackson, Walter Johnson, Al Kaline, Sandy Koufax, Mickey Mantle, Christy Mathewson, Willie Mays, Willie McCovey, Paul Molitor, Joe Morgan, Eddie Murray, Stan Musial, Jim Palmer, Kirby Puckett, Cal Ripken Jr., Brooks Robinson, Frank Robinson, Jackie Robinson, Babe Ruth, Nolan Ryan, Mike Schmidt, Tom Seaver, Ozzie Smith, Warren Spahn, Willie Stargell, Honus Wagner, Ted Williams, Dave Winfield, Carl Yastrzemski and Robin Yount.

Members are listed with years of induction; (+) indicates deceased members.

Catchers

Bench, Johnny 1989	+ Cochrane, Mickey 1947	+ Hartnett, Gabby 1955
Berra, Yogi 1972	+ Dickey, Bill 1954	+ Lombardi, Ernie 1986
+ Bresnahan, Roger 1945	Ewing, Buck 1939	+ Schalk, Ray 1955
+ Campanella, Roy 1969	+ Ferrell, Rick 1984	
Carter, Gary 2003	Fisk, Carlton 2000	

1st Basemen

+ Anson, Cap 1939	+ Connor, Roger 1976	McCovey, Willie 1986
+ Beckley, Jake 1971	+ Foxx, Jimmie 1951	+ Mize, Johnny 1981
+ Bottomley, Jim 1974	+ Gehrig, Lou 1939	Murray, Eddie 2003
+ Brouthers, Dan 1945	+ Greenberg, Hank 1956	Perez, Tony 2000
Cepeda, Orlando 1999	+ Kelly, George 1973	+ Sisler, George 1939
+ Chance, Frank 1946	Killebrew, Harmon 1984	+ Terry, Bill 1954

2nd Basemen

Carew, Rod 1991	+ Herman, Billy 1975	+ Robinson, Jackie 1962
+ Collins, Eddie 1939	+ Hornsby, Rogers 1942	Sandberg, Ryne 2005
Doerr, Bobby 1986	+ Lajoie, Nap 1937	Schoendienst, Red 1989
+ Evers, Johnny 1946	+ Lazzeri, Tony 1991	
+ Fox, Nellie 1997	Mazeroski, Bill 2001	### Designated Hitters
+ Frisch, Frankie 1947	+ McPhee, Bid 2000	Molitor, Paul 2004
+ Gehringer, Charlie 1949	Morgan, Joe 1990	

Shortstops

Aparicio, Luis 1984	+ Jackson, Travis 1982	Smith, Ozzie 2002
+ Appling, Luke 1964	+ Jennings, Hugh 1945	+ Tinker, Joe 1946
+ Bancroft, Dave 1971	+ Maranville, Rabbit 1954	+ Vaughan, Arky 1985
Banks, Ernie 1977	+ Reese, Pee Wee 1984	+ Wagner, Honus 1936
+ Boudreau, Lou 1970	Ripken Jr., Cal 2007	+ Wallace, Bobby 1953
+ Cronin, Joe 1956	+ Rizzuto, Phil 1994	+ Ward, Monte 1964
+ Davis, George 1998	+ Sewell, Joe 1977	Yount, Robin 1999

3rd Basemen

+ Baker, Frank 1955	Kell, George 1983	Schmidt, Mike 1995
Boggs, Wade 2005	+ Lindstrom, Fred 1976	+ Traynor, Pie 1948
Brett, George 1999	+ Mathews, Eddie 1978	
+ Collins, Jimmy 1945	Robinson, Brooks 1983	

Center Fielders

+ Ashburn, Richie 1995	+ Doby, Larry 1998	+ Roush, Edd 1962
+ Averill, Earl 1975	+ Duffy, Hugh 1945	Snider, Duke 1980
+ Carey, Max 1961	+ Hamilton, Billy 1961	+ Speaker, Tris 1937
+ Cobb, Ty 1936	+ Mantle, Mickey 1974	+ Waner, Lloyd 1967
+ Combs, Earle 1970	Mays, Willie 1979	+ Wilson, Hack 1979
+ DiMaggio, Joe 1955	+ Puckett, Kirby 2001	

Left Fielders

Brock, Lou 1985	+ Kelley, Joe 1971	+ Simmons, Al 1953
+ Burkett, Jesse 1946	Kiner, Ralph 1975	+ Stargell, Willie 1988
+ Clarke, Fred 1945	+ Manush, Heinie 1964	+ Wheat, Zack 1959
+ Delahanty, Ed 1945	+ Medwick, Joe 1968	Williams, Billy 1987
+ Goslin, Goose 1968	Musial, Stan 1969	+ Williams, Ted 1966
+ Hafey, Chick 1971	+ O'Rourke, Jim 1945	Yastrzemski, Carl 1989

Right Fielders

Aaron, Hank 1982	Jackson, Reggie 1993	Robinson, Frank 1982
+ Clemente, Roberto 1973	Kaline, Al 1980	+ Ruth, Babe 1936
+ Crawford, Sam 1957	+ Keeler, Willie 1939	+ Slaughter, Enos 1985
+ Cuyler, Kiki 1968	+ Kelly, King 1945	+ Thompson, Sam 1974
+ Flick, Elmer 1963	+ Klein, Chuck 1980	+ Waner, Paul 1952
Gwynn, Tony 2007	+ McCarthy, Tommy 1946	Winfield, Dave 2001
+ Heilmann, Harry 1952	+ Ott, Mel 1951	+ Youngs, Ross 1972
+ Hooper, Harry 1971	+ Rice, Sam 1963	

Major League Baseball's All-Time Team — 1969 and 1997

The Baseball Writers' Association of America originally selected an all-time team as part of major league baseball's 100th anniversary, announcing the outcome of its vote on July 21, 1969. Vote totals were not released. Another vote was released when a panel of 36 BWAA members picked an all-time team for the *Classic Sports Network* just before the 1997 All-Star Game. This time vote totals were given, the single outfield category was divided into three (left, center and right) and two recently popularized positions—the designated hitter and relief pitcher—were added. In the most recent vote two points were awarded for first-place votes and one point for second place. Point totals follow the names with the number of first-place votes in parentheses. All-time team members are listed in **bold** type

1969 Vote

C **Mickey Cochrane**, Bill Dickey, Roy Campanella
1B **Lou Gehrig**, George Sisler, Stan Musial
2B **Rogers Hornsby**, Charlie Gehringer, Eddie Collins
SS **Honus Wagner**, Joe Cronin, Ernie Banks
3B **Pie Traynor**, Brooks Robinson, Jackie Robinson
OF **Babe Ruth**, **Ty Cobb**, **Joe DiMaggio**, Ted Williams, Tris Speaker, Willie Mays

RHP **Walter Johnson**, Christy Mathewson, Cy Young
LHP **Lefty Grove**, Sandy Koufax, Carl Hubbell
Mgr. **John McGraw**, Casey Stengel, Joe McCarthy

1969 Vote All-Time Outstanding Player: **Ruth**, Cobb, Wagner, DiMaggio

1997 Vote

C **Johnny Bench** (24) 52; Yogi Berra (4) 22; Roy Campanella (4) 17; Mickey Cochrane (1) 5; Bill Dickey (1) 4; Gabby Hartnett (1) 3; Carlton Fisk 2.

1B **Lou Gehrig** (31) 661/2; Jimmie Foxx (3) 19; George Sisler (2) 8; Willie McCovey 6; Hank Greenberg 21/2; Stan Musial, Eddie Murray, Mark McGwire and Frank Thomas 1.

2B **Rogers Hornsby** (17) 44; Joe Morgan (6) 23; Jackie Robinson (6) 15; Charley Gehringer (4) and Napoleon Lajoie (3) 11; Eddie Collins (1) 3; Rod Carew 2; Ryne Sandberg 1.

SS **Honus Wagner** (23) 55; Cal Ripken Jr. (6) 24; Ozzie Smith (5) 16; Ernie Banks (1) 8; Lou Boudreau and Luke Appling 1.

3B **Mike Schmidt** (21) 50; Brooks Robinson (13) 37; Eddie Mathews 5; George Brett (1) 8; Pie Traynor 3; Pete Rose (1) 2; Frank Baker, Al Rosen and Wade Boggs 1.

LF **Ted Williams** (32) 68; Stan Musial (4) 36; Pete Rose, Ralph Kiner, Rickey Henderson and Barry Bonds 1.

CF **Willie Mays** (25) 57; Ty Cobb (7) 22; Joe DiMaggio (3) 17; Mickey Mantle (1) 10; Tris Speaker 2.

RF **Babe Ruth** (31) 67; Hank Aaron (5) 36; Frank Robinson 2; Al Kaline, Roberto Clemente and Tony Gwynn 1.

DH **Paul Molitor** (22) 48; Harold Baines (3) 12; Don Baylor (1) 10; Edgar Martinez (2) 9; Ty Cobb (2) 6; Hal McRae (1) 5; Mickey Mantle (1) and Dave Parker (1) 3; Joe DiMaggio (1) 2; Lee May, Frank Robinson and Tony Oliva 1.

RHP **Walter Johnson** (9) 30, Cy Young (12) 25; Christy Mathewson (5) 18; Bob Feller (4) 10; Bob Gibson 2; Nolan Ryan (2) 7; Tom Seaver (1) 3; Greg Maddux (1), Grover Cleveland Alexander and Juan Marichal 1.

LHP **Sandy Koufax** (11) 32; Warren Spahn (11) 28; Lefty Grove (8) 25; Steve Carlton (4) 12; Carl Hubbell 6; Whitey Ford (1) 3; Eddie Plank (1) 2.

RP **Dennis Eckersley** (16) 40; Rollie Fingers (9) 29; Lee Smith (4) 13; Hoyt Wilhelm (3) 10; Rich Gossage (3) 9; Bruce Sutter (1) 6, Dan Quisenberry 1.

Mgr. **Casey Stengel** (6) 22, Joe McCarthy (6) 18; Connie Mack (7) 17; John McGraw (6) 14; Sparky Anderson (3) 11; Leo Durocher (2) 6; Dick Williams (1) 4; Billy Martin (1) 3; Al Lopez (1), Ned Hanlon (1), Whitey Herzog (1), Earl Weaver and Bobby Cox 2; Tony La Russa 1.

Baseball (Cont.)
Pitchers

+ Alexander, Grover 1938
+ Bender, Chief 1953
+ Brown, Mordecai 1949
  Bunning, Jim 1996
  Carlton, Steve 1994
+ Chesbro, Jack 1946
+ Clarkson, John 1963
+ Coveleski, Stan 1969
+ Dean, Dizzy 1953
+ Drysdale, Don 1984
  Eckersley, Dennis 2004
+ Faber, Red 1964
  Feller, Bob 1962
  Fingers, Rollie 1992
  Ford, Whitey 1974
+ Galvin, Pud 1965
  Gibson, Bob 1981
+ Gomez, Lefty 1972
  Gossage, Rich 2008
+ Grimes, Burleigh 1964
+ Grove, Lefty 1947

+ Haines, Jess 1970
+ Hoyt, Waite 1969
+ Hubbell, Carl 1947
+ Hunter, Catfish 1987
  Jenkins, Ferguson 1991
+ Johnson, Walter 1936
+ Joss, Addie 1978
+ Keefe, Tim 1964
  Koufax, Sandy 1972
+ Lemon, Bob 1976
+ Lyons, Ted 1955
  Marichal, Juan 1983
+ Marquard, Rube 1971
+ Mathewson, Christy 1936
+ McGinnity, Joe 1946
  Niekro, Phil 1997
+ Newhouser, Hal 1992
+ Nichols, Kid 1949
  Palmer, Jim 1990
+ Pennock, Herb 1948
  Perry, Gaylord 1991

+ Plank, Eddie 1946
+ Radbourne, Old Hoss 1939
+ Rixey, Eppa 1963
  Roberts, Robin 1976
+ Ruffing, Red 1967
+ Rusie, Amos 1977
  Ryan, Nolan 1999
  Seaver, Tom 1992
+ Spahn, Warren 1973
  Sutter, Bruce 2006
  Sutton, Don 1998
+ Vance, Dazzy 1955
+ Waddell, Rube 1946
+ Walsh, Ed 1946
+ Welch, Mickey 1973
+ Wilhelm, Hoyt 1985
+ Willis, Vic 1995
+ Wynn, Early 1972
+ Young, Cy 1937

Managers

+ Alston, Walter 1983
  Anderson, Sparky 2000
+ Durocher, Leo 1994
+ Hanlon, Ned 1996
+ Harris, Bucky 1975
+ Huggins, Miller 1964

  Lasorda, Tommy 1997
  Lopez, Al 1977
+ Mack, Connie 1937
+ McCarthy, Joe 1957
+ McGraw, John 1937
+ McKechnie, Bill 1962

+ Robinson, Wilbert 1945
+ Selee, Frank 1999
+ Stengel, Casey 1966
  Weaver, Earl 1996

Umpires

+ Barlick, Al 1989
+ Chylak, Nestor 1999
+ Conlan, Jocko 1974

+ Connolly, Tom 1953
+ Evans, Billy 1973
+ Hubbard, Cal 1976

+ Klem, Bill 1953
+ McGowan, Bill 1992

From Negro Leagues

+ Bell, Cool Papa (OF) 1974
+ Brown, Ray (P) 2006
+ Brown, Willard (OF) 2006
+ Cooper, Andy (P) 2006
+ Charleston, Oscar (1B-OF) .. 1976
+ Dandridge, Ray (3B) 1987
+ Day, Leon (P-OF-2B) 1995
+ Dihigo, Martin (P-OF) ... 1977
+ Foster, Rube (P-Mgr) 1981
+ Foster, Willie (P) 1996

+ Gibson, Josh (C) 1972
+ Grant, Frank (2B) 2006
+ Hill, Pete (OF) 2006
  Irvin, Monte (OF) 1973
+ Johnson, Judy (3B) 1975
+ Leonard, Buck (1B) 1972
+ Lloyd, Pop (SS) 1977
+ Mackey, Biz (C) 2006
+ Mendez, Jose (P) 2006
+ Paige, Satchel (P) 1971

+ Rogan, Wilber (P) 1998
+ Santop, Luis (C) 2006
+ Smith, Hilton 2001
+ Stearnes, Turkey (OF) 2000
+ Suttles, Mule (1B) 2006
+ Taylor, Ben (1B) 2006
+ Torriente, Cristobal (OF) .. 2006
+ Wells, Willie (SS) 1997
+ Williams, Joe (P) 1999
+ Wilson, Jud (3B) 2006

Pioneers and Executives

+ Barrow, Ed 1953
+ Bulkeley, Morgan 1937
+ Cartwright, Alexander 1938
+ Chadwick, Henry 1938
+ Chandler, Happy 1982
+ Comiskey, Charles 1939
+ Cummings, Candy 1939
+ Frick, Ford 1970
+ Giles, Warren 1979
+ Griffith, Clark 1946

+ Harridge, Will 1972
+ Hulbert, William 1995
+ Johnson, Ban 1937
+ Landis, Kenesaw 1944
+ MacPhail, Larry 1978
  MacPhail, Lee 1998
+ Manley, Effa 2006
+ Pompez, Alex 2006
+ Posey, Cumberland 2006
+ Rickey, Branch 1967

+ Spalding, Al 1939
+ White, Sol 2006
+ Veeck, Bill 1991
+ Weiss, George 1971
+ Wilkinson, J.L. 2006
+ Wright, George 1937
+ Wright, Harry 1953
+ Yawkey, Tom 1980

BASKETBALL

Naismith Memorial Basketball Hall of Fame

Established in 1949 by the National Association of Basketball Coaches in memory of the sport's inventor, Dr. James Naismith. Original Hall opened in 1968 and a renovated version of the Hall opened in 1985. A completely new building opened Sept. 28, 2002. **Address:** 1000 West Columbus Avenue, Springfield, MA 01105. **Telephone:** (413) 781-6500. **Web:** www.hoophall.com.

Eligibility: Nominated players and referees must be retired for five years, coaches must have coached 25 years or be retired for five, and contributors must have already completed their noteworthy service to the game. Voting done by 24-member honors committee made up of media representatives, Hall of Fame members and trustees. Any nominee not elected after five years becomes eligible for consideration by the Veterans' Committee after a five-year wait.

Class of 2008 (7): PLAYERS—**Adrian Dantley, Patrick Ewing, Hakeem Olajuwon**; COACHES—**Pat Riley** and **Cathy Rush**; CONTRIBUTOR—**William Davidson** and **Dick Vitale**

2008 finalists (nominated but not elected): PLAYERS—Dennis Johnson, Richie Guerin, Chris Mullin and Maciel Ubiratan Pereira. COACHES—Don Nelson and Togo Soares. CONTRIBUTOR—Victor Bubas and Johnny 'Red' Kerr.

Note: **John Wooden, Lenny Wilkens** and **Bill Sharman** are the only members to be inducted as both a player and a coach.

Members are listed with years of induction; (+) indicates deceased members.

Men

Abdul-Jabbar, Kareem ..1995	Gola, Tom 1975	Monroe, Earl 1990
Archibald, Nate 1991	Goodrich, Gail 1996	Murphy, Calvin 1993
+ Arizin, Paul 1977	Greer, Hal 1981	+ Murphy, Charles (Stretch) 1960
Barkley, Charles 2006	+ Gruenig, Robert 1963	Olajuwon, Hakeem 2008
+ Barlow, Thomas (Babe) 1980	Hagan, Cliff 1977	+ Page, Harlan (Pat) ...1962
Barry, Rick 1987	+ Hanson, Victor 1960	Parish, Robert 2003
Baylor, Elgin 1976	Havlicek, John 1983	+ Petrovic, Drazen 2002
Beckman, John 1972	Hawkins, Connie 1992	Pettit, Bob 1970
Bellamy, Walt 1993	Hayes, Elvin 1990	+ Phillip, Andy 1961
Belov, Sergei 1992	Haynes, Marques 1998	+ Pollard, Jim 1977
Bing, Dave 1990	Heinsohn, Tom 1986	Ramsey, Frank 1981
Bird, Larry 1998	+ Holman, Nat 1964	Reed, Willis 1981
+ Borgmann, Bennie 1961	Houbregs, Bob 1987	Risen, Arnie 1998
Bradley, Bill 1982	Howell, Bailey 1997	Robertson, Oscar 1979
Cervi, Al 1984	+ Hyatt, Chuck 1959	+ Roosma, John 1961
+ Brennan, Joe 1974	Issel, Dan 1993	Russell, Bill 1974
+ Chamberlain, Wilt 1978	+ Jeannette, Buddy 1994	+ Russell, John (Honey) .1964
+ Cooper, Charles (Tarzan) 1976	+ Johnson, Bill (Skinny) ...1976	Schayes, Dolph 1972
+ Cosic, Kresimir 1996	Johnson, Earvin (Magic) .2002	+ Schmidt, Ernest J 1973
Cousy, Bob 1970	+ Johnston, Neil 1990	+ Schommer, John 1959
Cowens, Dave 1991	Jones, K. C 1989	+ Sedran, Barney 1962
Cunningham, Billy 1986	Jones, Sam 1983	Sharman, Bill 1975
Dantley, Adrian 2008	+ Krause, Edward (Moose) .1975	+ Steinmetz, Christian ...1961
+ Davies, Bob 1969	Kurland, Bob 1961	Thomas, Isiah 2000
+ DeBernardi, Forrest ..1961	Lanier, Bob 1992	Thompson, David 1996
+ DeBusschere, Dave ...1982	+ Lapchick, Joe 1966	+ Thompson, John (Cat) ..1962
+ Dehnert, Dutch 1968	Lovellette, Clyde 1988	Thurmond, Nate 1984
Drexler, Clyde 2004	Lucas, Jerry 1979	Twyman, Jack 1982
Dumars, Joe 2006	Luisetti, Hank 1959	Unseld, Wes 1988
+ Endacott, Paul 1971	Macauley, Ed 1960	+ Vandivier, Robert (Fuzzy) 1974
English, Alex 1997	Malone, Moses 2001	+ Wachter, Ed 1961
Erving, Julius (Dr. J) .1993	+ Maravich, Pete 1987	Walton, Bill 1993
Ewing, Patrick 2008	Martin, Slater 1981	Wanzer, Bobby 1987
+ Foster, Bud 1964	McAdoo, Bob 2000	West, Jerry 1979
Frazier, Walt 1987	+ McCracken, Branch ...1960	Wilkens, Lenny 1989
+ Friedman, Marty 1971	+ McCracken, Jack 1962	Wilkins, Dominique ...2006
+ Fulks, Joe 1977	+ McDermott, Bobby 1988	Wooden, John 1960
Gale, Laddie 1976	McGuire, Dick 1993	Worthy, James 2003
Gallatin, Harry 1991	McHale, Kevin 1999	+ Yardley, George 1996
+ Gates, William (Pop) .1989	+ Mikan, George 1959	
Gervin, George 1996	Mikkelsen, Vern 1995	

Women

Blazejowski, Carol 1994	Marcari, Hortencia 2005
Crawford, Joan 1997	Meyers, Ann 1993
Curry, Denise 1997	Miller, Cheryl 1995
Donovan, Anne 1995	Semenova, Uljana 1993
Harris-Stewart, Lucia ...1992	White, Nera 1992
Lieberman, Nancy 1996	Woodard, Lynette 2004

Teams

Buffalo Germans 1961
First Team 1959
Harlem Globetrotters 2002
New York Renaissance ...1963
Original Celtics 1959
Texas Western (1966) ...2007

Referees

+ Enright, Jim 1978
+ Hepbron, George 1960
+ Hoyt, George 1961
. Kennedy, Pat 1959
+ Leith, Lloyd 1982

+ Mihalik, Red 1986
+ Nucatola, John 1977
+ Quigley, Ernest (Quig) 1961
+ Rudolph, Marvin (Mendy) . .2007
+ Shirley, J. Dallas 1979

+ Strom, Earl 1995
+ Tobey, Dave 1961
+ Walsh, David 1961

Coaches

+ Allen, Forrest (Phog) 1959
+ Anderson, Harold (Andy) . .1984
+ Auerbach, Red . . . . .1968 *
    Auriemma, Geno 2006
    Barmore, Leon 2003
+ Barry, Sam 1978
+ Blood, Ernest (Prof) 1960
    Boeheim, Jim 2005
    Brown, Larry 2002
    Calhoun, Jim 2005
+ Cann, Howard 1967
+ Carlson, Henry (Doc) 1959
    Carnesecca, Lou 1992
    Carnevale, Ben 1969
    Carril, Pete 1997
+ Case, Everett 1981
    Chancellor, Van 2007
    Chaney, John 2001
    Conradt, Jody 1998
    Crum, Denny 1994
    Daly, Chuck 1994
+ Dean, Everett 1966
+ Diaz-Miguel, Antonio 1997
+ Diddle, Ed 1971
+ Drake, Bruce 1972
    Ferrandiz, Pedro 2007
    Gaines, Clarence (Bighouse) .1981

+ Gardner, Jack 1983
+ Gill, Amory (Slats) 1967
+ Gomelsky, Aleksandr 1995
+ Gunter, Sue 2005
+ Hannum, Alex 1998
    Harshman, Marv 1984
+ Haskins, Don 1997
+ Hickey, Eddie 1978
+ Hobson, Howard (Hobby) . .1965
+ Holzman, Red 1986
+ Iba, Hank 1968
    Jackson, Phil 2007
+ Julian, Alvin (Doggie) 1967
+ Keaney, Frank 1960
+ Keogan, George 1961
    Knight, Bob 1991
    Krzyzewski, Mike 2001
    Kundla, John 1995
+ Lambert, Ward (Piggy) 1960
+ Litwack, Harry 1975
+ Loeffler, Ken 1964
+ Lonborg, Dutch 1972
. McCutchan, Arad 1980
+ McGuire, Al 1992
+ McGuire, Frank 1976
. McLendon, John 1978
+ Meanwell, Walter (Doc) 1959

    Meyer, Ray 1978
+ Miller, Ralph 1988
    Moore, Billie 1999
    Newell, Pete 1978
+ Nikolic, Aleksandar 1998
    Novosel, Mirko 2007
    Olson, Lute 2002
    Ramsay, Jack 1992
    Riley, Pat 2008
    Rubini, Cesare 1994
+ Rupp, Adolph 1968
    Rush, Cathy 2008
+ Sachs, Leonard 1961
    Sharman, Bill 2004
+ Shelton, Everett 1979
    Smith, Dean 1982
    Summitt, Pat 2000
+ Taylor, Fred 1986
    Thompson, John 1999
+ Wade, Margaret 1984
    Watts, Stan 1985
    Wilkens, Lenny 1998
    Williams, Roy 2007
    Wooden, John 1972
+ Woolpert, Phil 1992
    Wootten, Morgan 2000
    Yow, Kay 2002

Contributors

+ Abbott, Senda Berenson . . .1984
+ Bee, Clair 1967
+ Biasone, Danny 2000
    Brown, Hubie 2005
+ Brown, Walter A 1965
+ Bunn, John 1964
    Colangelo, Jerry 2004
    Davidson, Bill 2008
+ Douglas, Bob 1971
+ Duer, Al 1981
    Embry, Wayne 1999
+ Fagan, Clifford B 1983
+ Fisher, Harry 1973
+ Fleisher, Larry 1991
    Gavitt, Dave 2006
+ Gottlieb, Eddie 1971
+ Gulick, Luther 1959
+ Harrison, Les 1979

+ Hearn, Francis (Chick) 2003
+ Hepp, Ferenc 1980
+ Hickox, Ed 1959
+ Hinkle, Tony 1965
+ Irish, Ned 1964
+ Jones, R. William 1964
+ Kennedy, Walter 1980
    Lemon, Meadowlark 2003
+ Liston, Emil (Liz) 1974
+ Mokray, Bill 1965
+ Morgan, Ralph 1959
+ Morgenweck, Frank (Pop) . . .1962
+ Naismith, James 1959
    Newton, Charles M. 2000
+ O'Brien, John J. (Jack) 1961
+ O'Brien, Larry 1991
+ Olsen, Harold G 1959
+ Podoloff, Maurice 1973

+ Porter, Henry (H.V.) 1960
+ Reid, William A 1963
+ Ripley, Elmer 1972
+ St. John, Lynn W 1962
+ Saperstein, Abe 1970
+ Schabinger, Arthur 1961
+ Stagg, Amos Alonzo 1959
    Stankovic, Boris 1991
+ Steitz, Ed 1983
+ Taylor, Chuck 1968
. Teague, Bertha 1984
+ Tower, Oswald 1959
+ Trester, Arthur (A.L.) 1961
    Vitale, Dick 2008
+ Wells, Cliff 1971
. Wilke, Lou 1982
+ Zollner, Fred 1999

Curt Gowdy Award

First presented in 1990 by the Hall of Fame Board of Trustees for meritorious contributions by the media. Named in honor of the former NBC sportscaster, the Gowdy Award does not constitute induction into the Hall of Fame.

Year		Year		Year	
1990	Curt Gowdy & Dick Herbert	1998	Dick Vitale, Larry Donald & Dick Weiss	2004	Phil Jasner & Max Falkenstein
1991	Dave Dorr & Marty Glickman			2005	Jack McCallum & Bill Campbell
1992	Sam Goldaper & Chick Hearn	1999	Smith Barrier & Bob Costas		
1993	Leonard Lewin & Johnny Most	2000	Dave Kindred & Hubie Brown	2006	Bill Raftery & Mark Heisler
1994	Leonard Koppett & Cawood Ledford	2001	Dick Stockton & Curry Kirkpatrick	2007	Al McCoy & Malcolm Moran
1995	Dick Enberg & Bob Hammel	2002	Jim Nantz & Jim O'Connell		
1996	Billy Packer & Bob Hentzen	2003	Sid Hartman & Hot Rod Hundley	2008	Bob Wolff & David Dupree
1997	Marv Albert & Bob Ryan				

BOWLING

International Bowling Hall of Fame & Museum

The International Bowling Hall is one museum with separate wings for honorees of the American Bowling Congress (ABC), Professional Bowlers' Association (PBA), Women's International Bowling Congress (WIBC) and Professional Women Bowlers Association (PWBA). In 2005 the ABC and WIBC merged, becoming the United States Bowling Congress. In November 2008, the museum moved from its longtime location in St. Louis, Mo. to a new building in Arlington, Texas alongside the USBC and BPAA.

Professional Bowlers Association

Established in 1975. **Eligibility:** The criteria was revamped in 2002. Nominees must now be retired from full-time competition on the PBA Tour for a minimum of at least five years, or reached the age of 50, and must have won a minimum of 10 PBA Tour titles or two major titles. Those inducted under the meritorius service category have been omitted due to space constraints.

Members are listed with years of induction; (+) indicates deceased members.

Performance

+. Allen, Bill	+ Fazio, Buzz 1976	Roth, Mark 1987
+ Anthony, Earl ... 1986	Ferraro, Dave 1997	Salvino, Carmen ... 1975
Aulby, Mike ... 1996	+ Godman, Jim 1987	Semiz, Teata ... 1998
Berardi, Joe ... 1990	Hardwick, Billy ... 1977	Smith, Harry ... 1975
Bluth, Ray ... 1975	Holman, Marshall ... 1990	Soutar, Dave ... 1979
Bohn, Parker III ... 2000	Hudson, Tommy ... 1989	Stefanich, Jim ... 1980
Buckley, Roy ... 1992	Husted, Dave ... 1996	Voss, Brian ... 1994
Burton, Nelson Jr ... 1979	Johnson, Don ... 1977	Webb, Wayne ... 1993
Carter, Don ... 1975	Laub, Larry ... 1985	+ Weber, Dick ... 1975
Colwell, Paul ... 1991	Monacelli, Amleto ... 1997	Weber, Pete ... 1998
Cook, Steve ... 1993	Ozio, David ... 1995	+ Welu, Billy ... 1975
Davis, Dave ... 1978	Pappas, George ... 1986	Williams, Mark ... 1999
Dickinson, Gary ... 1988	Petraglia, John ... 1982	Williams, Walter Ray Jr. ... 1995
Durbin, Mike ... 1984	Ritger, Dick ... 1978	Zahn, Wayne ... 1981

Veterans

Allison, Glenn ... 1984	+ Joseph, Joe ... 1985	Schlegel, Ernie ... 1997
Asher, Barry ... 1988	Limongello, Mike ... 1994	+ St. John, Jim ... 1989
Baker, Tom ... 1999	Marzich, Andy ... 1990	Strampe, Bob ... 1987
Foremsky, Skee ... 1992	McCune, Don ... 1991	
Guenther, Johnny ... 1986	McGrath, Mike ... 1988	

United States Bowling Congress

Established in 2005 with the merger of the American Bowling Congress and Women's International Bowling Congress.
Class of 2008: PERFORMANCE— Parker Bohn III, Brian Voss, Leanne Barrette Hulsenberg, Carolyn Dorin-Ballard.

Performance

Bohn III, Parker ... 2008	Vadakin, Gordon ... 2007
Dorin-Ballard, Carolyn ... 2008	Voss, Brian ... 2008
Fehr, Nancy ... 2006	### Meritorious Service
Hulsenber, Leanne Barrette ... 2008	Deken, Fran ... 2006
Pollard, Rick ... 2006	Marchione, Connie ... 2007
Pollard, Ron ... 2006	Sommer Jr., John ... 2006

American Bowling Congress

Established in 1941 and open to professional and amateur bowlers, now part of the USBC Hall of Fame. **Eligibility:** Nominated bowlers must have competed in at least 20 years of ABC tournaments.

Members are listed with years of induction; (+) indicates deceased members.

Performance

Allison, Glenn ... 1979	+ Brosius, Eddie ... 1976	+ Crimmins, Johnny ... 1962
+ Anthony, Earl ... 1986	+ Bujack, Fred ... 1967	Davis, Dave ... 1990
Asher, Barry ... 1998	Bunetta, Bill ... 1968	+ Daw, Charlie ... 1941
+ Asplund, Harold ... 1978	Burton, Nelson Jr ... 1981	+ Day, Ned ... 1952
Aulby, Mike ... 2001	+ Burton, Nelson Sr ... 1964	Dickinson, Gary ... 1992
Baer, Gordy ... 1987	+ Campi, Lou ... 1968	Duke, Norm ... 2002
Beach, Bill ... 1991	+ Carlson, Adolph ... 1941	+ Easter, Sarge ... 1963
+ Benkovic, Frank ... 1958	Carter, Don ... 1970	Ellis, Don ... 1981
Berlin, Mike ... 1994	+ Caruana, Frank ... 1977	+ Falcaro, Joe ... 1968
+ Billick, George ... 1982	+ Cassio, Marty ... 1972	+ Faragalli, Lindy ... 1968
+ Blouin, Jimmy ... 1953	+ Castellano, Graz ... 1976	+ Fazio, Buzz ... 1963
Bluth, Ray ... 1973	Chamberlain, Bob ... 2005	Fehr, Steve ... 1993
+ Bodis, Joe ... 1941	+ Clause, Frank ... 1980	+ Gersonde, Russ ... 1968
+ Bomar, Buddy ... 1966	Cohn, Alfred ... 1985	+ Gibson, Therm ... 1965
Bower, Gary ... 2001	Colwell, Paul ... 1999	+ Godman, Jim ... 1987
+ Brandt, Allie ... 1960	Couture, Pete ... 2004	Goike, Robert ... 1996

Bowling (Cont.)

+ Golembiewski, Billy 1979
  Griffo, Greg 1995
  Guenther, Johnny 1988
  Hanson, Bob 2004
  Hardwick, Billy 1985
  Hart, Bob 1994
+ Hennessey, Tom 1976
  Hoover, Dick 1974
  Horn, Bud 1992
  Howard, George 1986
  Jackson, Eddie 1988
+ Jackson, Lowell 2003
+ Johnson, Don 1982
  Johnson, Earl 1987
+ Joseph, Joe 1969
+ Jouglard, Lee 1979
+ Kartheiser, Frank 1967
+ Kawolics, Ed 1968
+ Kissoff, Joe 1976
+ Klares, John 1982
+ Knox, Billy 1954
+ Koster, John 1941
+ Krems, Eddie 1973
  Kristof, Joe 1968
+ Krumske, Paul 1968
+ Lange, Herb 1941
+ Lauman, Hank 1976
  Lewis, Mark 2004
  Lillard, Bill 1972
  Lindemann, Tony 1979
+ Lindsey, Mort 1941

+ Lippe, Harry 1989
  Lubanski, Ed 1971
+ Lucci, Vince Sr 1978
+ Marino, Hank 1941
+ Martino, John 1969
  Marzich, Andy 1993
  McGrath, Mike 1993
+ McMahon, Junie 1967
+ Meisel, Darold 1998
+ Mercurio, Skang 1967
+ Meyers, Norm 1984
+ Nagy, Steve 1963
+ Norris, Joe 1954
+ O'Donnell, Chuck 1968
  Pappas, George 1989
+ Patterson, Pat 1974
+ Powell, John (Junior) 2000
  Ritger, Dick 1984
+ Rogoznica, Andy 1993
  Salvino, Carmen 1979
  Savoy, Todd 2005
  Schissler, Les 1991
  Schlegel, Ernie 1997
  Schroeder, Jim 1990
+ Schwoegler, Connie 1968
  Scudder, Don 1999
  Semiz, Teata 1991
+ Sielaff, Lou 1968
+ Sinke, Joe 1977
+ Sixty, Billy 1961
  Smith, Harry 1978

+ Smith, Jimmy 1941
  Soutar, Dave 1985
+ Sparando, Tony 1968
  Spigner, Bill 2001
+ Spinella, Barney 1968
+ Steers, Harry 1941
  Stefanich, Jim 1983
+ Stein, Otto Jr 1971
  Stoudt, Bud 1991
  Strampe, Bob 1977
+ Thoma, Sykes 1971
  Toft, Rod 1991
+ Totsky, Mike 1996
  Tountas, Pete 1989
  Tucker, Bill 1988
  Tuttle, Tommy 1995
+ Varipapa, Andy 1957
+ Ward, Walter 1959
+ Weber, Dick 1970
  Weber, Pete 2002
+ Welu, Billy 1975
  Wilcox, John 1999
  Williams, Walter Ray Jr. 2005
+ Wilman, Joe 1951
+ Wolf, Phil 1961
  Wonders, Rich 1990
+ Young, George 1959
  Zahn, Wayne 1980
  Zikes, Les 1983
+ Zunker, Gil 1941

Pioneers

+ Hall, William Sr. 1994
  Hirashima, Hiroto 1995
+ Karpf, Samuel 1993
+ Moore, Henry 1996
+ Pasdeloup, Frank 1993
+ Rhodman, Bill 1997

+ Satow, Masao 1994
+ Schutte, Louis 1993
  Shimada, Fuzzy 1997
+ Stein, Louis 1997
+ Thompson, William V. 1993
+ Timm, Dr. Henry 1993

Meritorious Service

+ Franklin, Bill 1992
+ Hagerty, Jack 1963
+ Hattstrom, H.A. (Doc) 1980
+ Hermann, Cornelius 1968
+ Howley, Pete 1941
  James, Steve 2005
  Jensen, Mark 2002
  Jowdy, John 2001
+ Kennedy, Bob 1981
+ Langtry, Abe 1963
+ Levine, Sam 1971
+ Luby, David 1969
  Luby, Mort Jr. 1988
+ Luby, Mort Sr. 1974
  Matzelle, Al 1995
+ McCullough, Howard 1971
  Mormando, Nick 2003

+ Patterson, Morehead 1985
+ Petersen, Louie 1963
  Pezzano, Chuck 1982
  Picchietti, Remo 1993
  Pluckhahn, Bruce 1989
+ Raymer, Milt 1972
+ Reed, Elmer 1978
  Reichert, Jack 1998
  Rudo, Milt 1984
  Schenkel, Chris 1988
  Skelton, Max 2002
+ Sweeney, Dennis 1974
  Tessman, Roger 1994
+ Thum, Joe 1980
  Weinstein, Sam 1970
+ Whitney, Eli 1975
+ Wolf, Fred 1976

+ Allen, Lafayette Jr. 1994
+ Briell, Frank 1996
+ Carow, Rev. Charles 1995
+ Celestine, Sydney 1993
+ Curtis, Thomas 1993
+ de Freitas, Eric 1994

+ Allen, Harold 1966
  Archibald, John 1996
+ Baker, Frank 1975
+ Baumgarten, Elmer 1963
+ Bellisimo, Lou 1986
+ Bensinger, Bob 1969
  Borden, Fred 2002
+ Chase, LeRoy 1972
+ Coker, John 1980
+ Collier, Chuck 1963
+ Cruchon, Steve 1983
+ Ditzen, Walt 1973
+ Dobs, Darold 1999
+ Doehrman, Bill 1968
+ Elias, Eddie 1985
  Esposito, Frank 1997
  Evans, Dick 1992

Women's International Bowling Congress

Established in 1953. **Eligibility:** Performance nominees must have won at least one WIBC Championship Tournament title, a WIBC Queens tournament title or an international competition title and have bowled in at least 15 national WIBC Championship Tournaments (unless injury or illness cut career short).

Members are listed with years of induction; (+) indicates deceased members.

Performance

  Abel, Joy 1984
  Adamek, Donna 1996
  Ann, Patty 1995
  Bolt, Mae 1978
  Bouvia, Gloria 1987
  Boxberger, Loa 1984

  Buckner, Pam 1990
+ Burling, Catherine 1958
+ Burns, Nina 1977
  Cantaline, Anita 1979
  Carter, LaVerne 1977
  Carter, Paula 1994

  Coburn, Doris 1976
  Coburn-Carroll, Cindy 1998
  Costello, Pat 1986
  Costello, Patty 1989
  Daniels, Cheryl 2002
  Dryer, Pat 1978

Duggan, Anne Marie 2005
Duval, Helen 1970
Fellmeth, Catherine 1970
Fiebig, Cora 2004
Fothergill, Dotty 1980
Fulton, Louise 2001
Fritz, Deane 1966
Garms, Shirley 1971
Gianulias, Nikki 1997
Gloor, Olga 1976
Gonzalez, Ashie 1998
Graham, Linda 1992
Graham, Mary Lou 1989
Greenwald, Goldie 1953
Grinfelds, Vesma 1991
Harman, Janet 1985
Hartrick, Stella 1972
Hatch, Grayce 1953
Havlish, Jean 1987
Hoffman, Martha 1979
Holm, Joan 1974
Humphreys, Birdie 1979
Ignizio, Millie Martorella . .1975
Jacobson, D.D 1981
Jaeger, Emma 1953

Johnson, Tish 2002
Kelly, Annese 1985
Kelly, Linda 2003
+ Knechtges, Doris 1983
Kuczynski, Betty 1981
Ladewig, Marion 1964
+ Matthews, Merle 1974
McCutcheon, Floretta 1956
Merrick, Marge 1980
+ Mikiel, Val 1979
Miller-Mackey, Dana 2000
Miller, Carol 1997
+ Miller, Dorothy 1954
Mivelaz, Betty 1991
Mohacsi, Mary 1994
Morris, Betty 1983
Naccarato, Jeanne 1999
Nichols, Lorrie Koch 1989
Norman, Carol 2001
Norman, Edie Jo 1993
Norton, Virginia 1988
Notaro, Phyllis 1979
Ortner, Bev 1972
+ Powers, Connie 1973
Reichley, Susie 2000

Rickard, Robbie 1994
+ Robinson, Leona 1969
Romeo, Robin 1995
+ Rump, Anita 1962
+ Ruschmeyer, Addie 1961
+ Ryan, Esther 1963
+ Sablatnik, Ethel 1979
Sandelin, Lucy 1999
+ Schulte, Myrtle 1965
+ Shablis, Helen 1977
Sill, Aleta 1996
+ Simon, Violet (Billy) 1960
+ Small, Tess 1971
+ Smith, Grace 1968
Soutar, Judy 1976
+ Stockdale, Louise 1953
Toepfer, Elvira 1976
+ Twyford, Sally 1964
Wagner, Lisa 2000
+ Warmbier, Marie 1953
Wene-Martin, Sylvia 1966
Wilkinson, Dorothy 1990
+ Winandy, Cecelia 1975
Zimmerman, Donna 1982

Meritorious Service

Baetz, Helen 1977
Baker, Helen 1989
Banker, Gladys 1994
Bayley, Clover 1992
Bennie, Bernice 2003
Berger, Winifred 1976
Bohlen, Philena 1955
Borschuk, Lo 1988
Botkin, Freda 1986
Broyles, Sylvia 2005
Chapman, Emily 1957
Chapman, Nancy 2002
Crowe, Alberta 1982
Deitch, Joyce 2003
+ Dornblaser, Gertrude 1979
Duffy, Agnes 1987
Finke, Gertrude 1990
+ Fisk, Rae 1983

+ Haas, Dorothy 1977
Hagin, Elaine 2000
+ Herold, Mitzi 1998
+ Higley, Margaret 1969
+ Hochstadter, Bee 1967
+ Kay, Nora 1964
Keller, Pearl 1999
+ Kelly, Ellen 1979
Kelone, Theresa 1978
+ Knepprath, Jeannette 1963
+ Lasher, Iolia 1967
+ Marrs, Mabel 1979
+ McBride, Bertha 1968
McLeary, Hazel 2000
+ Menne, Catherine 1979
Mitchell, Flora 1996
Morton, Clara 2001
+ Mraz, Jo 1959

O'Connor, Billie 1992
+ Phaler, Emma 1965
+ Porter, Cora 1986
+ Quin, Zoe 1979
+ Rishling, Gertrude 1972
Robinson, Jeanette 2000
Rowe, Dorothy 2004
Simone, Anne 1991
Sloan, Catherine 1985
+ Speck, Berdie 1966
Spitalnick, Mildred 1994
+ Spring, Alma 1979
+ Switzer, Pearl 1973
+ Todd, Trudy 1993
+ Veatch, Georgia 1974
+ White, Mildred 1975
+ Wood, Ann 1970

Professional Women Bowlers Hall of Fame

Established in 1995 by the Ladies Pro Bowlers Tour. The LPBT has since been renamed the Professional Women Bowlers Association and the PWBA Hall of Fame has since been folded into the International Bowling Hall of Fame. The PWBA has not inducted any new members since 2003.

Eligibility: Nominees in performance category must have at least five titles from organizations including All-Star, World Invitational, LPBT, WPBA, PWBA, TPA and LPBA.

Members are listed with year of induction; (+) indicates deceased member.

Performance

Adamek, Donna 1995
Coburn-Carroll, Cindy 1997
Costello, Pat 1997
Costello, Patty 1995
Duggan, Anne Marie 2003
Fothergill, Dotty 1995
Gianulias, Nikki 1996

Grinfelds, Vesma 1997
Johnson, Tish 1998
Ladewig, Marion 1995
Martorella, Millie 1995
Miller-Mackey, Dana 2002
Morris, Betty 1995
Naccarato, Jeanne 2002

Nichols, Lorrie 1996
Norton, Virginia 2003
Romeo, Robin 1996
Sill, Aleta 1998
Wagner, Lisa 1996

Pioneers

Able, Joy 1998
Boxberger, Loa 1997
Carter, LaVerne 1995

Coburn, Doris 1996
Duval, Helen 1995
Garms, Shirley 1995

Ortner, Bev 1998
Soutar, Judy 1997
Zimmerman, Donna 1996

Builders

+ Buehler, Janet 1996
Keller, Pearl 1997

Robinson, Jeanette 1996
Sommer Jr., John 1997

+ Veatch, Georgia 1995

BOXING

International Boxing Hall of Fame

Established in 1984 and opened in 1989. **Address:** 1 Hall of Fame Drive, Canastota, NY. 13032. **Telephone:** (315) 69
7095. **Web:** www.ibhof.com.

Eligibility: All nominees must be retired for five years. Voting done by 142-member panel made up of Boxing Writers' Ass
ciation members and world-wide boxing historians.

Class of 2008 (13): MODERN ERA—**Larry Holmes, Eddie Perkins** and **Holman Williams.** OLD TIMERS—**Le
Harvey, Frank Klaus** and **Harry Lewis.** PIONEER—**Dan Donnelly**; NON-PARTICIPANTS—**Bill Gore** and **Moge
Palle.** OBSERVERS—**Dave Anderson** and **Joe Koizumi.**

Members are listed with year of induction; (+) indicates deceased member.

Modern Era

Ali, Muhammad	1990
+ Angott, Sammy	1998
+ Apostoli, Fred	2003
Arguello, Alexis	1992
+ Armstrong, Henry	1990
Basilio, Carmen	1990
Benitez, Wilfredo	1996
Benvenuti, Nino	1992
+ Berg, Jackie (Kid)	1994
Bivins, Jimmy	1999
+ Brown, Joe	1996
Buchanan, Ken	2000
+ Burley, Charley	1992
Canto, Miguel	1998
Carbajal, Michael	2006
+ Carter, Jimmy	2000
+ Cerdan, Marcel	1991
Cervantes, Antonio	1998
Chacon, Bobby	2005
Chandler, Jeff	2000
+ Charles, Ezzard	1990
Cokes, Curtis	2003
+ Conn, Billy	1990
Cuevas, Pipino	2002
Duran, Roberto	2007
+ Elorde, Gabriel (Flash)	1993
Fenech, Jeff	2002
Foreman, George	2003
Foster, Bob	1990
Frazier, Joe	1990
Fullmer, Gene	1991
Galaxy, Khaosai	1999
+ Galindez, Victor	2002
Gavilan, Kid	1990
Giardello, Joey	1993
Gomez, Wilfredo	1995

Gonzalez, Humberto	2006
+ Graham, Billy	1992
+ Graziano, Rocky	1991
Griffith, Emile	1990
Hagler, Marvelous Marvin	1993
Harada, Masahiko (Fighting)	1995
Holmes, Larry	2008
Jack, Beau	1991
+ Jenkins, Lew	1999
Jofre, Eder	1992
Johansson, Ingemar	2002
Johnson, Harold	1993
Laguna, Ismael	2001
LaMotta, Jake	1990
Leonard, Sugar Ray	1997
+ Liston, Sonny	1991
+ Locche, Nicolino	2003
Loi, Duilio	2005
Lopez, Ricardo	2007
+ Louis, Joe	1990
+ Marciano, Rocky	1990
+ Maxim, Joey	1994
McCallum, Mike	2003
McGuigan, Barry	2005
+ Montgomery, Bob	1995
+ Monzon, Carlos	1990
+ Moore, Archie	1990
Muhammad, Matthew Saad	1998
Napoles, Jose	1990
Nelson, Azumah	2004
Norris, Terry	2005
Norton, Ken	1992
Olivares, Ruben	1991
+ Olson, Carl (Bobo)	2000
Ortiz, Carlos	1991
+ Ortiz, Manuel	1996

Palomino, Carlos	200
Papp, Laszlo	200
+ Pastrano, Willie	200
Patterson, Floyd	199
Pedroza, Eusebio	199
+ Pep, Willie	199
+ Perez, Pascual	199
Perkins, Eddie	200
Pryor, Aaron	199
Qawi, Dwight Muhammad	200
Ramos, Ultiminio	200
+ Robinson, Sugar Ray	199
+ Rodriguez, Luis	199
+ Rosario, Edwin	200
+ Saddler, Sandy	199
+ Saldivar, Vicente	199
+ Sanchez, Salvador	199
+ Schmeling, Max	199
Spinks, Michael	199
+ Tiger, Dick	199
Torres, Jose	199
+ Turpin, Randy	200
+ Walcott, Jersey Joe	1990
Whitaker, Pernell	200
Williams, Holman	200
+ Williams, Ike	1990
+ Wright, Chalky	199
+ Zale, Tony	199
Zaragoza, Daniel	200
Zarate, Carlos	199
+ Zivic, Fritzie	199

Old-Timers

+ Ambers, Lou	1992
+ Arizmendi, Baby	2004
+ Attell, Abe	1990
+ Baer, Max	1995
+ Barry, Jimmy	2000
+ Bass, Benny	2002
+ Battalino, Battling	2003
+ Berlenbach, Paul	2001
+ Braddock, Jim	2001
+ Britton, Jack	1990
+ Brouillard, Lou	2006
+ Brown, Aaron (Dixie Kid)	2002
+ Brown, Panama Al	1992
+ Burns, Tommy	1996
+ Canzoneri, Tony	1990
+ Carpentier, Georges	1991
+ Chocolate, Kid	1991
+ Choynski, Joe	1998
+ Corbett, James J.	1990
+ Corbett III, Young	2004
+ Coulon, Johnny	1999

+ Criqui, Eugene	2005
+ Darcy, Les	1993
+ Delaney, Jack	1996
+ Dempsey, Jack	1990
+ Dempsey, Jack (Nonpareil)	1992
+ Dillon, Jack	1995
+ Dixon, George	1990
+ Driscoll, Jim	1990
+ Dundee, Johnny	1991
+ Escobar, Sixto	2002
+ Fields, Jackie	2004
+ Fitzsimmons, Bob	1990
+ Flowers, Theodore (Tiger)	1993
+ Gans, Joe	1990
+ Genaro, Frankie	1998
+ Gibbons, Mike	1992
+ Gibbons, Tommy	1993
+ Godfrey, George	2007
+ Greb, Harry	1990
+ Griffo, Young	1991
+ Harris, Harry	2002

+ Harvey, Len	2008
+ Herman, Pete	1997
+ Jackson, Peter	1990
+ Jeanette, Joe	1997
+ Jeffries, James J	1990
+ Johnson, Jack	1990
+ Kaplan, Louis (Kid)	2003
+ Ketchel, Stanley	1990
+ Klaus, Frank	2008
+ Kilbane, Johnny	1995
+ LaBarba, Fidel	1996
+ Langford, Sam	1990
+ Lavigne, George (Kid)	1998
+ Leonard, Benny	1990
+ Levinsky, Battling	2000
+ Lewis, Harry	2008
+ Lewis, John Henry	1994
+ Lewis, Ted (Kid)	1992
+ Loughran, Tommy	1991
+ Lynch, Benny	1998
+ Lynch, Joe	2005

+ Mandell, Sammy	1998	+ Papke, Billy	2001	+ Thil, Marcel	2005
+ McAuliffe, Jack	1995	+ Petrolle, Billy	2000	+ Tunney, Gene	1990
+ McCoy, Charles (Kid)	1991	+ Ritchie, Willie	2004	+ Villa, Pancho	1994
+ McFarland, Packey	1992	+ Rosenbloom, Maxie	1993	+ Walcott, Joe (Barbados)	1991
+ McGovern, Terry	1990	+ Ross, Barney	1990	+ Walker, Mickey	1990
+ McLarnin, Jimmy	1991	+ Ryan, Tommy	1991	+ Welsh, Freddie	1997
+ McVey, Sam	1999	+ Sharkey, Jack	1994	+ Wilde, Jimmy	1990
+ Miller, Freddie	1997	+ Sharkey, Tom	2003	+ Willard, Jess	2003
+ Mitchell, Charley	2002	+ Slattery, Jimmy	2006	+ Williams, Kid	1996
+ Montanez, Pedro	2007	+ Steele, Freddie	1999	+ Wills, Harry	1992
+ Moran, Owen	2002	+ Stribling, Young	1996	+ Wolgast, Ad	2000
+ Nelson, Battling	1992	+ Taylor, Charles (Bud)	2005	+ Wolgast, Midget	2001
+ Norfolk, Kid	2007	+ Tendler, Lew	1999	+ Yarosz, Teddy	2006
+ O'Brien, Philadelphia Jack	1994		

Pioneers

+ Aaron, Barney	2001	+ Donovan, Prof. Mike	1998	+ Molineaux, Tom	1997
+ Aaron, Young Barney	2007	+ Duffy, Paddy	1994	+ Morrissey, John	1996
+ Baldwin, Caleb	2003	+ Goss, Joe	2003	+ Pearce, Henry	1993
+ Belcher, Jem	1992	+ Edwards, Billy	2004	+ Randall, Jack	2005
+ Brain, Ben	1994	+ Figg, James	1992	+ Richmond, Bill	1999
+ Broughton, Jack	1990	+ Heenan, John C.	2002	+ Sam, Dutch	1997
+ Burke, James (Deaf)	1992	+ Jackson, Gentleman John	1992	+ Sam, Young Dutch	2002
+ Carney, Jem	2006	+ Johnson, Tom	1995	+ Sayers, Tom	1990
+ Chambers, Arthur	2000	+ King, Tom	1992	+ Spring, Tom	1992
+ Cribb, Tom	1991	+ Langham, Nat	1992	+ Sullivan, John L	1990
+ Curtis, Dick	2007	+ Mace, Jem	1990	+ Thompson, William	1991
+ Donnelly, Dan	2008	+ Mendoza, Daniel	1990	+ Ward, Jem	1995

Non-Participants

+ Andrews, Thomas S	1992	+ Dundee, Chris	1994	+ Markson, Harry	1992
+ Arcel, Ray	1991	+ Dunphy, Don	1993	Mercante, Arthur	1995
Arum, Bob	1999	+ Duva, Dan	2003	+ Morgan, Dan	2000
Astaire, Jarvis	2006	Duva, Lou	1998	+ Muldoon, William	1996
+ Ballarati, Giuseppe	1999	+ Eaton, Aileen	2002	Neiman, LeRoy	2007
Benton, George	2001	+ Egan, Pierce	1991	Odd, Gilbert	1995
+ Bimstein, Whitey	2006	+ Fleischer, Nat	1990	+ O'Rourke, Tom	1999
+ Blackburn, Jack	1992	+ Fox, Richard K.	1997	+ Parker, Dan	1996
+ Brady, William A.	1998	+ Fragetta, Dewey	2003	+ Parnassus, George	1991
+ Branchini, Umberto	2004	Fraser, Don	2005	Peltz, J. Russell	2004
Brenner, Teddy	1993	+ Futch, Eddie	1994	+ Queensberry, Marquis of	1990
Brusa, Amilcar	2007	+ Goldman, Charley	1992	+ Rickard, Tex	1990
+ Cayton, Bill	2005	+ Goldstein, Ruby	1994	+ Rudd, Irving	1999
+ Chambers, John Graham	1990	Goodman, Murray	1999	+ Sabbatini, Rodolfo	2006
Chargin, Don	2001	+ Gore, Bill	2008	+ Sarreal Lope	2005
Christodolou, Stanley	2004	+ Humphreys, Joe	1997	+ Siler, George	1995
Clancy, Gil	1993	+ Ichinose, Sam	2001	+ Silverman, Sam	2002
+ Coffroth, James W.	1991	+ Jacobs, Jimmy	1993	+ Solomons, Jack	1995
+ Cohen, Irving	2002	+ Jacobs, Mike	1990	Steward, Emanuel	1996
+ Conde, Cuco	2007	+ Johnston, Jimmy	1999	Sulaiman, Jose	2007
+ D'Amato, Cus.	1995	+ Kearns, Jack (Doc)	1990	+ Taub, Sam	1994
Dickson, Jeff	2000	King, Don	1997	+ Taylor, Herman	1998
+ Donovan, Arthur	1993	Lectoure, Tito	2000	+ Viscusi, Lou	2004
Duff, Mickey	1999	+ Liebling, A.J	1992	+ Walker, James J. (Jimmy)	1992
Dundee, Angelo	1992	+ Lonsdale, Lord	1990	+ Weill, Al	2003

Observers

Anderson, Dave	2008	Gutteridge, Reg	2002	+ Runyon, Damon	2002
+ Bromberg, Lester	2001	Heinz, W.C.	2004	Schulberg, Budd	2003
+ Cannon, Jimmy	2002	+ Jones, Jersey	2005	Sugar, Bert	2005
+ Citro, Ralph	2001	Kaplan, Hank	2006	+ Weston, Stanley	2006
+ Dorgan, Tad	2007	Koizumi, Joe	2008	
Fiske, Jack	2003	+ Mullan, Harry	2005	
Gallo, Bill	2001	+ Nagler, Barney	2004	

FOOTBALL

College Football Hall of Fame

Established in 1955 by the National Football Foundation. **Address:** 111 South St. Joseph St., South Bend, IN 46601. **Telephone:** (574) 235-9999. **Web:** www.collegefootball.org

Eligibility: Nominated players must be out of college 10 years and a first team All-America pick by a major selector during their careers; coaches must be retired three years or active and over 75 years old. Voting done by 12-member panel of athletic directors, conference and bowl officials and media representatives. The first year representatives from NCAA Div. I-AA, II, and III, and the NAIA were eligible for induction was 1996.

Class of 2008 (15): LARGE COLLEGE—QB **Troy Aikman**, UCLA (1987-88); RB **Bill Cannon**, LSU (1957-59); OT **Jim Dombrowski**, Virginia (1982-85); LB **Pat Fitzgerald**, Northwestern (1994-96); LB **Wilber Marshall**, Florida (1980-83); RB **Rueben Mayes**, Washington St. (1982-85); OG **Randall McDaniel**, Arizona St. (1984-87); QB **Don McPherson**, Syracuse (1984-87); TE **Jay Novacek**, Wyoming (1982-84); SE **Dave Parks**, Texas Tech (1961-63); NG **Ron Simmons**, Florida St. (1977-80); RB **Thurman Thomas**, Oklahoma St. (1984-87); QB **Arnold Tucker**, Army (1944-46); COACHES—**John Cooper**, Tulsa (1977-84), Arizona St. (1985-87), Ohio St. (1988-2000); **Lou Holtz**, William & Mary (1969-71), N.C. State (1972-75), Arkansas (1977-83), Minnesota (1984-85), Notre Dame (1986-96), South Carolina (1999-2004).

Note: Bobby Dodd and **Amos Alonzo Stagg** are the only members to be honored as both players and coaches. Players are listed with *final year they played* in college and coaches are listed with year of induction; (+) indicates deceased members.

Players

+ Abell, Earl-Colgate 1915	+ Benbrook, Al-Michigan 1910	Cannon, Bill-LSU 1959
Agase, Alex-Purdue/Ill 1946	Bennett, Cornelius-Alabama 1986	+ Cannon, Jack-N.Dame 1929
Agganis, Harry-Boston U . . .1952	+ Berry, Charlie-Lafayette 1924	Cappelletti, John-Penn St . . .1973
Aikman, Troy-UCLA 1988	+ Bertelli, Angelo-N.Dame 1943	+ Carideo, Frank-N.Dame 1930
Albert, Frank-Stanford 1941	+ Berwanger, Jay-Chicago 1935	Carney, Charles-Illinois . . . .1921.
+ Aldrich, Ki-TCU 1938	+ Bettencourt, L.-St.Mary's . . .1927	Caroline, J.C.-Illinois 1954
+ Aldrich, Malcolm-Yale 1921	Biletnikoff, Fred-Fla.St. 1964	Carpenter, Bill-Army 1959
+ Alexander, Joe-Syracuse 1920	Blades, Benny-Miami,FL 1987	+ Carpenter, Hunter-NC/
Allen, Marcus-USC 1981	Blanchard, Doc-Army 1946	Va. Tech 1905
Alworth, Lance-Arkansas 1961	+ Blozis, Al-Georgetown 1941	Carroll, Chas.-Washington . . .1928
+ Ameche, Alan-Wisconsin . . .1954	Bock, Ed-Iowa St 1938	Carter, Anthony-Michigan . . .1982
+ Ames, Knowlton-Princeton . .1889	Bomar, Lynn-Vanderbilt 1924	Casanova, Tommy-LSU 1971
+ Amling, Warren-Ohio St 1946	+ Bomeisler, Bo-Yale 1912	+ Casey, Edward-Harvard 1919
Anderson, Bob P.-Army 1959	+ Booth, Albie-Yale 1931	Casillas, Tony-Oklahoma 1985
Anderson, Bobby-Colorado .1969	+ Borries, Fred-Navy 1934	Cassady, Howard-Ohio St . . .1955
Anderson, Dick-Colorado . . .1967	+ Bosley, Bruce-West Va 1955	+ Chamberlin, Guy-Neb.Wes./
Anderson, Donny-Tex.Tech . .1965	Bosseler, Don-Miami,FL 1956	Nebraska 1915
+ Anderson, Hunk-N.Dame . . .1921	Bottari, Vic-California 1938	Chapman, Sam-California . .1937
Arnett, Jon-USC 1956	Bowden, Murry-Dartmouth . .1970	Chappuis, Bob-Michigan . . .1947
Atkins, Doug-Tennessee 1952	+ Boynton, Ben-Williams 1920	+ Christman, Paul-Missouri . . .1940
Babich, Bob-Miami-OH 1968	Brahaney, Tom-Oklahoma . . .1972	+ Clark, Dutch-Colo. Col. 1929
+ Bacon, Everett-Wesleyan . . .1912	+ Brewer, Charles-Harvard . . .1895	Cleary, Paul-USC 1947
+ Bagnell, Reds-Penn 1950	+ Bright, Johnny-Drake 1951	+ Clevenger, Zora-Indiana . . .1903
+ Baker, Hobey-Princeton . . · .1913	Brodie, John-Stanford 1956	Cloud, Jack-Wm. & Mary . .1949
+ Baker, John-USC 1931	+ Brooke, George-Penn 1895	+ Cochran, Gary-Princeton . . .1897
+ Baker, Moon-N'western 1926	Brosky, Al-Illinois 1952	+ Cody, Josh-Vanderbilt 1919
Baker, Terry-Oregon St 1962	Brown, Bob-Nebraska 1963	Coleman, Don-Mich.St 1951
+ Ballin, Harold-Princeton 1914	+ Brown, Dave-Michigan 1974	+ Conerly, Charlie-Miss 1947
+ Banker, Bill-Tulane 1929	Brown, Geo-Navy/S.Diego St .1947	Connor, George-HC/ND 1947
Banonis, Vince-Detroit 1941	+ Brown, Gordon-Yale 1900	+ Corbin, William-Yale 1888
+ Barnes, Stan-California 1921	Brown, Jim-Syracuse 1956	Corbus, William-Stanford . . .1933
+ Barrett, Charles-Cornell 1915	+ Brown, John, Jr.-Navy 1913	Covert, Jimbo-Pittsburgh . . .1983
+ Baston, Bert-Minnesota 1916	+ Brown, Johnny Mack-Ala . . .1925	+ Cowan, Hector-Princeton . . .1889
+ Battles, Cliff-WV Wesleyan .1931	+ Brown, Tay-USC 1932	+ Coy, Edward (Ted)-Yale 1909
Baugh, Sammy-TCU 1936	Brown, Tom-Minnesota 1960	+ Crawford, Fred-Duke 1933
Baughan, Maxie-Ga.Tech . . .1959	Browner, Ross-Notre Dame .1977	Crow, John David-Tex.A&M . .1957
+ Bausch, James-Wichita/	Budde, Brad-USC 1979	+ Crowley, Jim-Notre Dame . . .1924
Kansas 1930	+ Bunker, Paul-Army 1902	Csonka, Larry-Syracuse 1967
Beagle, Ron-Navy 1955	Burford, Chris-Stanford 1959	Curtis, Tom-Michigan 1969
Beasley, Terry-Auburn 1971	+ Burris, Kurt-Oklahoma 1954	+ Cutter, Slade-Navy 1934
Beban, Gary-UCLA 1967	Burton, Ron-N'western 1959	Czarobski, Ziggie-N.Dame . .1947
Bechtol, Hub-Tex.Tech/Texas 1946	Butkus, Dick-Illinois 1964	Dale, Carroll-Va.Tech 1959
+ Beck, Ray-Ga. Tech 1951	Butler, Kevin-Georgia 1984	Dalrymple, Gerald-Tulane . .1931
+ Beckett, John-Oregon 1916	+ Butler, Robert-Wisconsin . . .1913	+ Dalton, John-Navy 1911
Bednarik, Chuck-Penn 1948	+ Cafego, George-Tenn 1939	+ Daly, Chas.-Harvard/Army .1902
Behm, Forrest-Nebraska 1940	Cagle, Red-SWLa/Army 1929	Daniell, Averell-Pitt 1936
Bell, Bobby-Minnesota 1962	+ Cain, John-Alabama 1932	Daniell, James-Ohio St 1941
Bell, Ricky-USC 1976	Cameron, Ed-Wash.& Lee . .1924	+ Davies, Tom-Pittsburgh 1921
Bellino, Joe-Navy 1960	+ Campbell, David-Harvard . . .1901	Davis, Anthony-USC 1974
Below, Marty-Wisconsin 1923	Campbell, Earl-Texas 1977	+ Davis, Ernie-Syracuse 1961

College Football Hall of Fame (Cont.)

College Football Hall of Fame (Cont.)

Coaches

+ Aillet, Joe 1989	+ Gustafson, Andy 1985	+ Norton, Homer 1971
+ Alexander, Bill 1951	+ Hall, Edward 1951	+ O'Neill, Frank (Buck) 1951
+ Anderson, Ed 1971	+ Harding, Jack 1980	+ Osborne, Tom 1998
+ Armstrong, Ike 1957	+ Harlow, Richard 1954	+ Owen, Bennie 1951
+ Bachman, Charlie 1978	+ Harman, Harvey 1981	Parseghian, Ara 1980
+ Banks, Earl 1992	+ Harper, Jesse 1971	Paterno, Joe 2007
+ Baujan, Harry 1990	+ Haughton, Percy 1951	+ Perry, Doyt 1988
+ Bell, Matty 1955	+ Hayes, Woody 1983	+ Phelan, Jimmy 1973
+ Bezdek, Hugo 1954	+ Heisman, John W 1954	+ Prothro, Tommy 1991
+ Bible, Dana X 1951	+ Higgins, Robert 1954	Ralston, John 1992
+ Bierman, Bernie 1955	+ Hollingberry, Babe 1979	+ Robinson, E.N. 1955
Blackman, Bob 1987	Holtz, Lou 2008	+ Rockne, Knute 1951
+ Blaik, Earl (Red) 1965	+ Howard, Frank 1989	+ Romney, Dick 1954
Bowden, Bobby 2006	+ Ingram, Bill 1973	+ Roper, Bill 1951
Broyles, Frank 1983	James, Don 1997	Royal, Darrell 1983
Bruce, Earle 2002	+ Jennings, Morley 1973	+ Sanders, Henry (Red) 1996
+ Bryant, Paul (Bear) 1986	+ Jones, Biff 1954	+ Sanford, George 1971
+ Butts, Wally 1997	+ Jones, Howard 1951	Schembechler, Bo 1993
+ Caldwell, Charlie 1961	+ Jones, Tad 1958	+ Schmidt, Francis 1971
+ Camp, Walter 1951	+ Jordan, Lloyd 1978	+ Schwartzwalder, Ben 1982
Casanova, Len 1977	+ Jordan, Ralph (Shug) 1982	+ Shaughnessy, Clark 1968
+ Cavanaugh, Frank 1954	+ Kerr, Andy 1951	+ Shaw, Buck 1972
+ Claiborne, Jerry 1999	Kush, Frank 1995	+ Smith, Andy 1951
+ Colman, Dick 1990	+ Leahy, Frank 1970	+ Snavely, Carl 1965
Cooper, John 2008	+ Little, George 1955	+ Stagg, Amos Alonzo 1951
Coryell, Don 1999	+ Little, Lou 1960	+ Sutherland, Jock 1951
Cozza, Carmen 2002	+ Madigan, Slip 1974	Switzer, Barry 2001
+ Crisler, Fritz 1954	Maurer, Dave 1991	+ Tatum, Jim 1984
+ Daugherty, Duffy 1984	+ McClendon, Charley 1986	Teaff, Grant 2001
+ Devaney, Bob 1981	+ McCracken, Herb 1973	+ Thomas, Frank 1951
+ Devine, Dan 1985	+ McGugin, Dan 1951	+ Vann, Thad 1987
Deromedi, Herb 2007	+ McKay, John 1988	Vaught, Johnny 1979
Dickey, Doug 2003	+ McKeen, Allyn 1991	+ Wade, Wallace 1955
+ Dobie, Gil 1951	+ McLaughry, Tuss 1962	+ Waldorf, Lynn (Pappy) 1966
+ Dodd, Bobby 1993	+ Merritt, John 1994	+ Warner, Glenn (Pop) 1951
Donahue, Tom 2000	+ Meyer, Dutch 1956	Welsh, George 2004
+ Donohue, Michael 1951	+ Mollenkopf, Jack 1988	+ Wieman, E.E. (Tad) 1956
Dooley, Vince 1994	+ Moore, Bernie 1954	+ Wilce, John 1954
+ Dorais, Gus 1954	+ Moore, Scrappy 1980	+ Wilkinson, Bud 1969
Dye, Pat 2005	+ Morrison, Ray 1954	+ Williams, Henry 1951
+ Edwards, Bill 1986	+ Munger, George 1976	+ Woodruff, George 1963
Edwards, LaVell 2004	+ Munn, Clarence (Biggie) . . .1959	+ Woodson, Warren 1989
+ Engle, Rip 1973	+ Murray, Bill 1974	+ Wyatt, Bowden 1997
Evashevski, Forest 2000	+ Murray, Frank 1983	Yeoman, Bill 2001
Faurot, Don 1961	+ Mylin, Ed (Hooks) 1974	+ Yost, Fielding (Hurry Up) . . .1951
Fry, Hayden 2003	+ Neale, Earle (Greasy) 1967	Young, Jim 1999
+ Gaither, Jake 1973	+ Neely, Jess 1971	+ Zuppke, Bob 1951
Gillman, Sid 1989	Nehlen, Don 2005	
+ Godfrey, Ernest 1972	+ Nelson, David 1987	
Graves, Ray 1990	+ Neyland, Robert 1956	

Pro Football Hall of Fame

Established in 1963 by National Football League to commemorate the sport's professional origins. **Address:** 2121 George Halas Drive NW, Canton, OH 44708. **Telephone:** (330) 456-8207. **Web:** www.profootballhof.com

Eligibility: Nominated players must be retired five years, coaches must be retired, and contributors can still be active. Voting done by 39-member panel made up of media representatives from all 31 NFL cities (two from New York), one PFWA representative and six selectors-at-large.

Class of 2008 (6): PLAYERS—DE **Fred Dean**, San Diego Chargers (1975-81), San Francisco 49ers (1981-85); CB **Darrell Green**, Washington Redskins (1983-2002); WR **Art Monk**, Washington Redskins (1980-93), New York Jets (1994), Philadelphia Eagles (1995); CB **Emmitt Thomas**, Kansas City Chiefs (1966-78); LB **Andre Tippett**, New England Patriots (1982-93); OT **Gary Zimmerman**, Minnesota Vikings (1986-92), Denver Broncos (1993-97).

Quarterbacks

Aikman, Troy 2006	+ Graham, Otto 1965	Namath, Joe 1985
Baugh, Sammy 1963	+ Griese, Bob 1990	Parker, Clarence (Ace) . . .1972
Blanda, George (also PK) . .1981	+ Herber, Arnie 1966	Starr, Bart 1977
Bradshaw, Terry 1989	Jurgensen, Sonny 1983	Staubach, Roger 1985
+ Clark, Dutch 1963	Kelly, Jim 2002	Tarkenton, Fran 1986
+ Conzelman, Jimmy 1964	+ Layne, Bobby 1967	Tittle, Y.A 1971
Dawson, Len 1987	+ Luckman, Sid 1965	+ Unitas, Johnny 1979
+ Driscoll, Paddy 1965	Marino, Dan 2005	+ Van Brocklin, Norm 1971
Elway, John 2004	Montana, Joe 2000	+ Waterfield, Bob 1965
Fouts, Dan 1993	Moon, Warren 2006	Young, Steve 2005
+ Friedman, Benny 2005		

Running Backs

Allen, Marcus 2003	Hornung, Paul 1986	Perry, Joe 1969
+ Battles, Cliff 1968	Johnson, John Henry 1987	+ Pollard, Fritz 2005
Brown, Jim 1971	Kelly, Leroy 1994	Riggins, John 1992
Campbell, Earl 1991	+ Leemans, Tuffy 1978	Sanders, Barry 2004
Canadeo, Tony 1974	Matson, Ollie 1972	Sayers, Gale 1977
Csonka, Larry 1987	McAfee, George 1966	Simpson, O.J 1985
Dickerson, Eric 1999	McElhenny, Hugh 1970	+ Strong, Ken 1967
Dorsett, Tony 1994	+ McNally, Johnny (Blood) . .1963	Taylor, Jim 1976
Dudley, Bill 1966	Moore, Lenny 1975	Thomas, Thurman 2007
Gifford, Frank 1977	+ Motley, Marion 1968	+ Thorpe, Jim 1963
+ Grange, Red 1963	+ Nagurski, Bronko 1963	Trippi, Charley 1968
+ Guyon, Joe 1966	+ Nevers, Ernie 1963	Van Buren, Steve 1965
Harris, Franco 1990	+ Payton, Walter 1993	+ Walker, Doak 1986
+ Hinkle, Clarke 1964		

Ends & Wide Receivers

Alworth, Lance 1978	Irvin, Michael 2007	Newsome, Ozzie 1999
+ Badgro, Red 1981	Joiner, Charlie 1996	Pihos, Pete 1970
Berry, Raymond 1973	Largent, Steve 1995	Sanders, Charlie 2007
Biletnikoff, Fred 1988	Lavelli, Dante 1975	Smith, Jackie 1994
Casper, Dave 2002	Lofton, James 2003	Stallworth, John 2002
+ Chamberlin, Guy 1965	Mackey, John 1992	Swann, Lynn 2001
Ditka, Mike 1988	Maynard, Don 1987	Taylor, Charley 1984
+ Fears, Tom 1970	McDonald, Tommy 1998	Warfield, Paul 1983
+ Hewitt, Bill 1971	+ Millner, Wayne 1968	Winslow, Kellen 1995
Hirsch, Elroy (Crazylegs) . .1968	Mitchell, Bobby 1983	
+ Hutson, Don 1963	Monk, Art 2008	

Offensive Linemen

Bednarik, Chuck (C-LB) 1967	Langer, Jim (C) 1987	Ringo, Jim (C) 1981
Brown, Bob (T) 2004	Little, Larry (G) 1993	+ St. Clair, Bob (T) 1990
Brown, Roosevelt (T) 1975	Mack, Tom (G) 1999	Shaw, Billy (G) 1999
DeLamielleure, Joe (G) 2003	Matthews, Bruce (G-T-C) . . .2007	Shell, Art (T) 1989
Dierdorf, Dan (T) 1996	McCormack, Mike (T) 1984	Slater, Jackie (T) 2001
Gatski, Frank (C) 1985	Mix, Ron (T-G) 1979	Stephenson, Dwight (C) . . .1998
Gregg, Forrest (T-G) 1977	Munchak, Mike (G) 2001	+ Upshaw, Gene (G) 1987
+ Groza, Lou (T-PK) 1974	Munoz, Anthony (T) 1998	Yary, Ron (T) 2001
Hannah, John (G) 1991	+ Musso, George (T-G) 1982	+ Webster, Mike (C) 1997
Hickerson, Gene (G) 2007	Otto, Jim (C) 1980	Wright, Rayfield (T) 2006
Jones, Stan (T-G-DT) 1991	Parker, Jim (G) 1973	Zimmerman, Gary (T) 2008

Linemen (pre-World War II)

+ Edwards, Turk (T) 1969
+ Fortmann, Dan (G) 1985
+ Healey, Ed (T) 1964
+ Hein, Mel (C) 1963
+ Henry, Pete (T) 1963

+ Hubbard, Cal (T) 1963
+ Kiesling, Walt (G) 1966
+ Kinard, Bruiser (T) 1971
+ Lyman, Link (T) 1964
+ Michalske, Mike (G) 1964

+ Musso, George (T-G) 1982
+ Stydahar, Joe (T) 1967
+ Trafton, George (C) 1964
+ Turner, Bulldog (C) 1966
+ Wojciechowicz, Alex (C) . .1968

Defensive Linemen

Atkins, Doug 1982
Bethea, Elvin 2003
+ Buchanan, Buck 1990
Creekmur, Lou 1996
Davis, Willie 1981
Dean, Fred 2008
Donovan, Art 1968
Eller, Carl 2004
+ Ford, Len 1976

Greene, Joe 1987
Hampton, Dan 2002
Jones, Deacon 1980
+ Jordan, Henry 1995
Lilly, Bob 1980
Long, Howie 2000
Marchetti, Gino 1972
+ Nomellini, Leo 1969
Olsen, Merlin 1982

Page, Alan 1988
Robustelli, Andy 1971
Selmon, Lee Roy 1995
Stautner, Ernie 1969
+ Weinmeister, Arnie 1984
White, Randy 1994
+ White, Reggie 2006
Willis, Bill 1977
Youngblood, Jack 2001

Linebackers

Bell, Bobby 1983
Buoniconti, Nick 2001
Butkus, Dick 1979
Carson, Harry 2006
Connor, George (DT-OT) . . .1975
+ George, Bill 1974

Ham, Jack 1988
Hendricks, Ted 1990
Huff, Sam 1982
Lambert, Jack 1990
Lanier, Willie 1986
+ Nitschke, Ray 1978

Schmidt, Joe 1973
Singletary, Mike 1998
Taylor, Lawrence 1999
Tippett, Andre 2008
Wilcox, Dave 2000

Defensive Backs

Adderley, Herb 1980
Barney, Lem 1992
Blount, Mel 1989
Brown, Willie 1984
+ Christiansen, Jack 1970
Green, Darrell 2008
Haynes, Michael 1997
Houston, Ken 1986

Johnson, Jimmy 1994
Krause, Paul 1998
+ Lane, Dick (Night Train) . . .1974
Lary, Yale 1979
Lott, Ronnie 2000
Renfro, Mel 1996
Thomas, Emmitt 2008
+ Tunnell, Emlen 1967

Wehrli, Roger 2007
Wilson, Larry 1978
Wood, Willie 1989

Placekicker

Stenerud, Jan 1991

Coaches

+ Allen, George 2002
+ Brown, Paul 1967
+ Ewbank, Weeb 1978
+ Flaherty, Ray 1976
Gibbs, Joe 1996
Gillman, Sid 1983
Grant, Bud 1994

+ Halas, George 1963
+ Lambeau, Curly 1963
+ Landry, Tom 1990
Levy, Marv 2001
+ Lombardi, Vince 1971
Madden, John 2006
+ Neale, Earle (Greasy) 1969

Noll, Chuck 1993
+ Owen, Steve 1966
Shula, Don 1997
Stram, Hank 2003
+ Walsh, Bill 1993

Contributors

+ Bell, Bert 1963
+ Bidwill, Charles 1967
+ Carr, Joe 1963
Davis, Al 1992
+ Finks, Jim 1995
+ Halas, George 1963

+ Hunt, Lamar 1972
+ Mara, Tim 1963
+ Mara, Wellington 1997
+ Marshall, George 1963
+ Ray, Hugh (Shorty) 1966
+ Reeves, Dan 1967

+ Rooney, Art 1964
Rooney, Dan 2000
+ Rozelle, Pete 1985
Schramm, Tex 1991

NFL's All-Time Team

Selected by the Pro Football Hall of Fame voters and released Aug. 1, 2000 as part of the NFL Century celebration.

Offense

Wide Receivers: Don Hutson and Jerry Rice
Tight End: John Mackey
Tackles: Roosevelt Brown and Anthony Munoz
Guards: John Hannah and Jim Parker
Center: Mike Webster
Quarterback: Johnny Unitas
Running Backs: Jim Brown and Walter Payton

Defense

Ends: Deacon Jones and Reggie White
Tackles: Joe Greene and Bob Lilly
Linebackers: Dick Butkus, Jack Ham and Lawrence Taylor
Cornerbacks: Mel Blount and Dick (Night Train) Lane
Safeties: Ronnie Lott and Larry Wilson

Specialists

Placekicker: Jan Stenerud
Punter: Ray Guy
Kick Returner: Gale Sayers

Punt Returner: Deion Sanders
Special Teams: Steve Tasker

GOLF

World Golf Hall of Fame

The World Golf Hall of Fame opened its doors in 1998 at the World Golf Village outside of Jacksonville, Fla. **Address:** One World Golf Place, St. Augustine, FL 32092. **Telephone:** (904) 940-4000. **Web:** www.wghof.com/hof/hof.php **Eligibility:** Professionals have three avenues into the WGHF. A PGA Tour player qualifies for the ballot if he has at least 10 victories in approved tournaments, or at least two victories among The Players Championship, Masters, U.S. Open, British Open and PGA Championship, is at least 40 years old and has been a member of the Tour for 10 years. A senior PGA Tour player qualifies if he has been a Senior Tour member for five years and has 20 wins between the PGA Tour and Senior Tour or five wins among the PGA majors, the Players Championship and the senior majors (U.S. Senior Open, Tradition, PGA Seniors' Championship and Senior Players Championship). Final selections for both Veteran's (for players who played bulk of their career before 1974) and Lifetime Achievement Categories are made by the Executive Committee of the World Golf Hall of Fame, which includes leaders from the major golf organizations.

Any player qualifying for the LPGA Hall automatically qualifies for the WGHF. Until 1999, nominees must have had played 10 years on the LPGA tour and won 30 official events, including two major championships; 35 official events and one major; or 40 official events and no majors. The eligibility requirements were loosened somewhat in 1999. The new guidelines are based on a system which awards two points for winning a major and one point for winning other tournaments, the Vare trophy (for lowest scoring average) and the player of the year award. Players must win at least one major, Vare trophy, or player of the year award and accumulate a total of 27 points to be inducted. For players not eligible for either the PGA Tour or the LPGA Hall of Fame, a body of over 300 international golf writers and historians will vote each year.

Members are listed with year of induction; (+) indicates deceased members.

Class of 2008 (6): MEN—**Craig Wood**; VETERAN'S—**Bob Charles** and **Denny Shute.** LIFETIME ACHIEVE-MENT—**Pete Dye, Carol Semple Thompson** and **Herbert Warren Wind**.

Men

+ Anderson, Willie	1975	Green, Hubert	2007	+ Ouimet, Francis	1974
Aoki, Isao	2004	+ Guldahl, Ralph	1981	Palmer, Arnold	1974
+ Armour, Tommy	1976	+ Hagen, Walter	1974	+ Park, Willie Sr.	2005
+ Ball, John, Jr	1977	+ Hilton, Harold	1978	+ Picard, Henry	2006
Ballesteros, Seve	1999	+ Hogan, Ben	1974	Player, Gary	1974
Barnes, Jim	1989	Irwin, Hale	1992	Price, Nick	2003
Beman, Deane	2000	Jacklin, Tony	2002	+ Robertson, Allan	2001
Bolt, Tommy	2002	Jacobs, John	2000	+ Runyan, Paul	1990
Bonallack, Sir Michael	2000	+ Jones, Bobby	1974	+ Sarazen, Gene	1974
+ Boros, Julius	1982	Kite, Tom	2004	+ Shute, Denny	2008
+ Braid, James	1976	Langer, Bernhard	2002	Sifford, Charlie	2004
Burke, Jack Jr.	2000	+ Little, Lawson	1980	Singh, Vijay	2006
Casper, Billy	1978	Littler, Gene	1990	+ Smith, Horton	1990
Charles, Bob	2008	+ Locke, Bobby	1977	+ Snead, Sam	1974
Coles, Neil	2000	+ Mangrum, Lloyd	1998	+ Stewart, Payne	2001
+ Cooper, Lighthorse Harry	1992	+ Middlecoff, Cary	1986	Strange, Curtis	2007
+ Cotton, Sir Henry	1980	Miller, Johnny	1996	+ Taylor, John H	1975
Crenshaw, Ben	2002	+ Morris, Tom Jr	1975	Thomson, Peter	1988
+ Demaret, Jimmy	1983	+ Morris, Tom Sr	1976	+ Travers, Jerry	1976
De Vicenzo, Roberto	1989	Nagle, Kel	2007	Travis, Walter	1979
+ Diegel, Leo	2003	+ Nelson, Byron	1974	Trevino, Lee	1981
+ Evans, Chick	1975	Nelson, Larry	2006	+ Vardon, Harry	1974
Faldo, Nick	1997	Nicklaus, Jack	1974	Watson, Tom	1988
Floyd, Ray	1989	Norman, Greg	2001	+ Wood, Craig	2008

Women

Alcott, Amy	1999	Inkster, Julie	2000	Smith, Marilynn	2006
+ Berg, Patty	1974	Jameson, Betty	1951	Sorenstam, Annika	2003
Bradley, Pat	1986	King, Betsy	1995	Streit, Marlene Stewart	2004
Carner, JoAnne	1985	Lopez, Nancy	1989	Suggs, Louise	1979
Caponi, Donna	2001	Mann, Carol	1977	+ Vare, Glenna Collett	1975
Daniel, Beth	1999	Okamoto, Ayako	2005	Webb, Karrie	2005
Hagge, Marlene	2002	Pak, Se Ri	2007	+ Wethered, Joyce	1975
Haynie, Sandra	1977	Rankin, Judy	2000	Whitworth, Kathy	1982
Higuchi, Chako	2003	Rawls, Betsy	1987	Wright, Mickey	1976
+ Howe, Dorothy C.H	1978	Sheehan, Patty	1993	+ Zaharias, Babe Didrikson	1974

Lifetime Achievement

Bell, Judy	2001	+ Graffis, Herb	1977	+ Roberts, Clifford	1978
Campbell, William	1990	+ Harlow, Robert	1988	Rodriguez, Chi Chi	1992
+ Carr, Joe	2007	+ Hope, Bob	1983	+ Ross, Donald	1977
+ Corcoran, Fred	1975	+ Jones, Robert Trent	1987	+ Solheim, Karsten	2001
+ Crosby, Bing	1978	+ Macdonald, Charles Blair	2007	+ Shore, Dinah	1994
+ Darwin, Bernard	2005	+ MacKenzie, Alister	2005	Thompson, Carol Semple	2008
+ Dey, Joe	1975	+ McCormack, Mark	2006	+ Tufts, Richard	1992
Dye, Peter	2008	+ Penick, Harvey	2002	+ Wind, Herbert Warren	2008

HOCKEY

Hockey Hall of Fame

Established in 1945 by the National Hockey League and opened in 1961. **Address:** BCE Place, 30 Yonge Street, Toronto, Ontario, M5E 1X8. **Telephone:** (416) 360-7735. **Web:** www.hhof.com

Eligibility: Nominated players and referees must be retired three years. However that waiting period has now been waived 10 times. Players that have had the waiting period waived are indicated with an asterisk. Voting done by 18-member panel made up of pro and amateur hockey personalities and media representatives. A 15-member Veterans Committee that selected older players was eliminated in 2000.

Class of 2008 (4): PLAYERS—F **Glenn Anderson**, Edmonton Oilers (1981-1991,96), Toronto Maple Leafs (1992-94), New York Rangers (1994); St. Louis (1995, 96); F **Igor Larionov**, CSKA Moscow (1981-89), Vancouver Canucks (1990-92), San Jose Sharks (1994-96), Detroit Red Wings (1996-2000, 2001-03), Florida Panthers (2001), New Jersey Devils (2004). BUILDER—**Ed Chynoweth**, executive; REFEREE/LINESMAN—**Ray Scapinello**.

Members are listed with year of induction; (+) indicates deceased members.

Forwards

+ Abel, Sid 1969	+ Gardner, Jimmy 1962	Mullen, Joe 2000
+ Adams, Jack 1959	Gartner, Mike 2001	Neely, Cam 2005
Anderson, Glenn 2008	+ Geoffrion, Bernie 1972	+ Nighbor, Frank 1947
+ Apps, Syl 1961	+ Gerard, Eddie 1945	+ Noble, Reg 1962
Armstrong, George 1975	Gilbert, Rod 1982	+ O'Connor, Buddy 1988
+ Bailey, Ace 1975	Gillies, Clark 2002	+ Oliver, Harry 1967
+ Bain, Dan 1945	+ Gilmour, Billy 1962	Olmstead, Bert 1985
+ Baker, Hobey 1945	Goulet, Michel 1998	+ Patrick, Lynn 1980
Barber, Bill 1990	Gretzky, Wayne* 1999	Perreault, Gilbert 1990
+ Barry, Marty 1965	+ Griffis, Si 1950	+ Phillips, Tom 1945
Bathgate, Andy 1978	Hawerchuk, Dale 2001	+ Primeau, Joe 1963
+ Bauer, Bobby 1996	+ Hay, George 1958	Pulford, Bob 1991
Beliveau, Jean* 1972	+ Hextall, Bryan 1969	+ Rankin, Frank 1961
+ Bentley, Doug 1964	+ Hooper, Tom 1962	Ratelle, Jean 1985
+ Bentley, Max 1966	+ Howe, Gordie* 1972	Richard, Henri 1979
+ Blake, Toe 1966	+ Howe, Syd 1965	+ Richard, Maurice (Rocket)* . .1961
Bossy, Mike 1991	Hull, Bobby 1983	+ Richardson, George 1950
+ Boucher, Frank 1958	+ Hyland, Harry 1962	+ Roberts, Gordie 1971
+ Bowie, Dubbie 1945	+ Irvin, Dick 1958	+ Russel, Blair 1965
+ Broadbent, Punch 1962	+ Jackson, Busher 1971	+ Russell, Ernie 1965
Bucyk, John (Chief) 1981	+ Joliat, Aurel 1947	+ Ruttan, Jack 1962
+ Burch, Billy 1974	+ Keats, Duke 1958	Savard, Denis 2000
Clarke, Bobby 1987	Kennedy, Ted (Teeder) 1966	+ Scanlan, Fred 1965
+ Colville, Neil 1967	Keon, Dave 1986	Schmidt, Milt 1961
+ Conacher, Charlie 1961	+ Kharlamov, Valeri 2005	+ Schriner, Sweeney 1962
Conacher, Roy 1998	Kurri, Jari 2001	+ Seibert, Oliver 1961
+ Cook, Bill 1952	Lach, Elmer 1966	Shutt, Steve 1993
+ Cook, Bun 1995	Lafleur, Guy 1988	+ Siebert, Babe 1964
Cournoyer, Yvan 1982	LaFontaine, Pat 2003	Sittler, Darryl 1989
+ Cowley, Bill 1968	+ Lalonde, Newsy 1950	+ Smith, Alf 1962
+ Crawford, Rusty 1962	Laprade, Edgar 1993	Smith, Clint 1991
+ Darragh, Jack 1962	Larionov, Igor 2008	+ Smith, Hooley 1972
+ Davidson, Scotty 1950	Lemaire, Jacques 1984	+ Smith, Tommy 1973
+ Day, Hap 1961	Lemieux, Mario* 1997	+ Stanley, Barney 1962
Delvecchio, Alex 1977	+ Lewis, Herbie 1989	Stastny, Peter 1998
+ Denneny, Cy 1959	Lindsay, Ted* 1966	+ Stewart, Nels 1962
Dionne, Marcel 1992	+ MacKay, Mickey 1952	+ Stuart, Bruce 1961
+ Drillon, Gordie 1975	Mahovlich, Frank 1981	+ Taylor, Fred (Cyclone) 1947
+ Drinkwater, Graham 1950	+ Malone, Joe 1950	+ Trihey, Harry 1950
Duff, Dick 2006	+ Marshall, Jack 1965	Trottier, Bryan 1997
Dumart, Woody 1992	+ Maxwell, Fred 1962	Ullman, Norm 1982
+ Dunderdale, Tommy 1974	McDonald, Lanny 1992	+ Walker, Jack 1960
+ Dye, Babe 1970	+ McGee, Frank 1945	+ Walsh, Marty 1962
Esposito, Phil 1984	+ McGimsie, Billy 1962	+ Watson, Harry (Whipper) . . .1994
+ Farrell, Arthur 1965	Messier, Mark 2007	+ Watson, Harry (Moose) 1962
Federko, Bernie 2002	Mikita, Stan 1983	+ Weiland, Cooney 1971
+ Foyston, Frank 1958	Moore, Dickie 1974	+ Westwick, Harry (Rat) 1962
Francis, Ron 2007	+ Morenz, Howie 1945	+ Whitcroft, Fred 1962
+ Frederickson, Frank 1958	+ Mosienko, Bill 1965	
Gainey, Bob 1992		

Referees & Linesmen

Armstrong, Neil 1991	+ Hayes, George 1988	Scapinello, Ray 2008
Ashley, John 1981	+ Hewitson, Bobby 1963	+ Smeaton, J. Cooper 1961
Chadwick, Bill 1964	+ Ion, Mickey 1961	Storey, Red 1967
D'Amico, John 1993	Pavelich, Matt 1987	Udvari, Frank 1973
+ Elliott, Chaucer 1961	+ Rodden, Mike 1962	van Hellemond, Andy 1999

Goaltenders

+ Benedict, Clint 1965	Giacomin, Eddie 1987	+ Plante, Jacques 1978
Bower, Johnny 1976	+ Hainsworth, George 1961	+ Rayner, Chuck 1973
+ Brimsek, Frankie 1966	Hall, Glenn 1975	Roy, Patrick 2006
+ Broda, Turk 1967	+ Hern, Riley 1962	+ Sawchuk, Terry* 1971
Cheevers, Gerry 1985	+ Holmes, Hap 1972	Smith, Billy 1993
+ Connell, Alex 1958	+ Hutton, J.B. (Bouse) 1962	+ Thompson, Tiny 1959
Dryden, Ken 1983	+ Lehman, Hughie 1958	Tretiak, Vladislav 1989
+ Durnan, Bill 1964	+ LeSueur, Percy 1961	+ Vezina, Georges 1945
Esposito, Tony 1988	+ Lumley, Harry 1980	+ Worsley, Gump 1980
Fuhr, Grant 2003	+ Moran, Paddy 1958	+ Worters, Roy 1969
+ Gardiner, Chuck 1945	Parent, Bernie 1984	

Defensemen

Boivin, Leo 1986	+ Hall, Joe 1961	+ Pitre, Didier 1962
+ Boon, Dickie 1952	+ Harvey, Doug 1973	Potvin, Denis 1991
Bouchard, Butch 1966	Horner, Red 1965	+ Pratt, Babe 1966
+ Boucher, George 1960	+ Horton, Tim 1977	Pronovost, Marcel 1978
Bourque, Ray 2004	Howell, Harry 1979	+ Pulford, Harvey 1945
+ Cameron, Harry 1962	+ Johnson, Ching 1958	+ Quackenbush, Bill 1976
+ Clancy, King 1958	+ Johnson, Ernie 1952	Reardon, Kenny 1966
+ Clapper, Dit* 1947	+ Johnson, Tom 1970	Robinson, Larry 1995
+ Cleghorn, Sprague 1958	Kelly, Red* 1969	+ Ross, Art 1945
Coffey, Paul 2004	Langway, Rod 2002	Salming, Borje 1996
+ Conacher, Lionel 1994	+ Laperriere, Jacques 1987	Savard, Serge 1986
+ Coulter, Art 1974	Lapointe, Guy 1993	+ Seibert, Earl 1963
+ Dutton, Red 1958	+ Laviolette, Jack 1962	+ Shore, Eddie 1947
Fetisov, Viacheslav 2001	+ MacInnis, Al 2007	+ Simpson, Joe 1962
Flaman, Fernie 1990	+ Mantha, Sylvio 1960	Stanley, Allan 1981
Gadsby, Bill 1970	+ McNamara, George 1958	Stevens, Scott 2007
+ Gardiner, Herb 1958	Murphy, Larry 2004	+ Stewart, Jack 1964
+ Goheen, F.X. (Moose) 1952	Orr, Bobby* 1979	+ Stuart, Hod 1945
+ Goodfellow, Ebbie 1963	Park, Brad 1988	+ Wilson, Gordon (Phat) 1962
+ Grant, Mike 1950	+ Patrick, Lester 1947	
+ Green, Wilf (Shorty) 1962	Pilote, Pierre 1975	

Builders

+ Adams, Charles 1960	+ Hanley, Bill 1986	+ O'Brien, J.A 1962
+ Adams, Weston W. Sr 1972	+ Hay, Charles 1984	O'Neill, Brian 1994
+ Ahearn, Frank 1962	+ Hendy, Jim 1968	Page, Fred 1993
+ Aherne, J.F. (Bunny) 1977	+ Hewitt, Foster 1965	Patrick, Craig 2001
+ Allan, Sir Montagu 1945	+ Hewitt, W.A 1945	+ Patrick, Frank 1958
Allen, Keith 1992	Hotchkiss, Harley 2006	+ Pickard, Allan 1958
Arbour, Al 1996	+ Hume, Fred 1962	Pilous, Rudy 1985
+ Ballard, Harold 1977	Ilitch, Mike 2003	Poile, Bud 1990
+ Bauer, Fr. David 1989	+ Imlach, Punch 1984	- Pollock, Sam 1978
+ Bickell, J.P. 1978	+ Ivan, Tommy 1964	+ Raymond, Donat 1958
Bowman, Scotty 1991	+ Jennings, Bill 1975	+ Robertson, John Ross 1945
+ Brooks, Herb 2006	+ Johnson, Bob 1992	+ Robinson, Claude 1945
+ Brown, George 1961	+ Juckes, Gordon 1979	Ross, Philip 1976
+ Brown, Walter 1962	+ Kilpatrick, John 1960	+ Sabetzki, Gunther 1995
+ Buckland, Frank 1975	+ Kilrea, Brian 2003	Sather, Glen 1997
Bush, Walter 2000	+ Knox, Seymour III 1993	+ Selke, Frank 1960
Butterfield, Jack 1980	+ Leader, Al 1969	Sinden, Harry 1983
+ Calder, Frank 1945	+ LeBel, Bob 1970	+ Smith, Frank 1962
+ Campbell, Angus 1964	+ Lockhart, Tom 1965	+ Smythe, Conn 1958
+ Campbell, Clarence 1966	+ Loicq, Paul 1961	Snider, Ed 1988
+ Cattarinich, Joseph 1977	+ Mariucci, John 1985	+ Stanley, Lord of Preston . . .1945
+ Chynoweth, Ed 2008	Mathers, Frank 1992	+ Sutherland, James 1945
Costello, Murray 2005	+ McLaughlin, Frederic 1963	+ Tarasov, Anatoli 1974
+ Dandurand, Leo 1963	+ Milford, Jake 1984	Torrey, Bill 1995
+ Dilio, Frank 1964	+ Molson, Hartland 1973	+ Turner, Lloyd 1958
+ Dudley, George 1958	Morrison, Ian (Scotty) 1999	+ Tutt, William Thayer 1978
+ Dunn, James 1968	+ Murray, Athol (Pere) 1998	+ Voss, Carl 1974
Fletcher, Cliff 2004	+ Nelson, Francis 1945	+ Waghorne, Fred 1961
Francis, Emile 1982	+ Neilson, Roger 2002	+ Wirtz, Arthur 1971
+ Gibson, Jack 1976	+ Norris, Bruce 1969	+ Wirtz, Bill 1976
+ Gorman, Tommy 1963	+ Norris, James D 1962	Ziegler, John 1987
Gregory, Jim 2007	+ Norris, James Sr 1958	
+ Griffiths, Frank A. 1993	+ Northey, William 1945	

Note: Alan Eagleson was inducted into the Hockey Hall of Fame in 1989 but resigned in 1998 after being found guilty of fraud.

U.S. Hockey Hall of Fame

Established in 1968 by the Eveleth (Minn.) Civic Association Project H Committee and opened in 1973. **Address:** 801 Hat Trick Ave., P.O. Box 657, Eveleth, MN 55734. **Telephone:** (218) 744-5167. **Web:** www.ushockeyhall.com

Eligibility: Nominated players and referees must be American-born and retired five years; coaches must be American-born and must have coached predominantly American teams. Voting done by 12-member panel made up of Hall of Fame members and U.S. hockey officials.

Class of 2008 (4): PLAYERS—**Cammi Granato, Brett Hull, Brian Leetch** and **Mike Richter.**

Members are listed with year of induction; (+) indicates deceased members.

Players

+ Abel, Clarence (Taffy) 1973	Fusco, Scott 2002	+ Mather, Bruce 1998
+ Baker, Hobey 1973	Gambucci, Gary 2007	Mayasich, John 1976
Bartholome, Earl 1977	+ Garrison, John 1974	McCartan, Jack 1983
+ Bessone, Peter 1978	Garrity, Jack 1986	Milbury, Mike 2007
Blake, Bob 1985	+ Goheen, Frank (Moose) ...1973	Moe, Bill 1974
Boucha, Henry 1995	Granato, Cammi 2008	Morrow, Ken 1995
+ Brimsek, Frankie 1973	Grant, Wally 1994	+ Moseley, Fred 1975
+ Brink, Milton (Curly) 2007	+ Harding, Austie 1975	Mullen, Joe 1998
Broten, Neal 2000	Housley, Phil 2004	+ Murray, Hugh (Muzz) Sr ..1987
Cavanagh, Joe 1994	Howe, Mark 2003	+ Nelson, Hub 1978
+ Chaisson, Ray 1974	Hull, Brett 2008	+ Nyrop, William D. 1997
Chase, John 1973	Iglehart, Stewart 1975	Olson, Eddie 1977
Christian, Bill 1984	Ikola, Willard 1990	+ Owen, George 1973
Christian, Dave 2001	Johnson, Mark 2004	+ Palmer, Winthrop 1973
Christian, Roger 1989	Johnson, Paul 2001	Paradise, Bob 1989
Christiansen, Keith 2005	Johnson, Virgil 1974	+ Purpur, Clifford (Fido) ...1974
Cleary, Bill 1976	+ Karakas, Mike 1973	Ramsey, Mike 2001
Cleary, Bob 1981	Kirrane, Jack 1987	Richter, Mike 2008
+ Conroy, Tony 1975	LaFontaine, Pat 2003	Riley, Bill 1977
Coppo, Paul 2004	+ Lane, Myles 1973	Riley, Joe 2002
Curran, Mike 1998	Langevin, Dave 1993	+ Roberts, Maurice 2005
+ Dahlstrom, Carl (Cully) ...1973	Langway, Rod 1999	+ Romnes, Elwin (Doc) 1973
+ Desjardins, Vic 1974	Larson, Reed 1996	+ Rondeau, Dick 1985
+ Desmond, Richard 1988	Leetch, Brian 2008	Sheehy, Timothy 1997
+ Dill, Bob 1979	+ Linder, Joe 1975	Watson, Gordie 1999
Dougherty, Richard 2003	+ LoPresti, Sam 1973	+ Williams, Tom 1981
+ Everett, Doug 1974	MacDonald, Lane 2005	Williamson, Murray 2005
Ftorek, Robbie 1991	+ Mariucci, John 1973	+ Winters, Frank (Coddy) ...1973
Fusco, Mark 2002	Matchefts, John 1991	+ Yackel, Ken 1986

Coaches

+ Almquist, Oscar 1983	Heyliger, Vic 1974	Pleban, Connie 1990
Bessone, Amo 1992	+ Holt Jr., Charles E. 1997	Ramsay, Mike 2001
+ Brooks, Herb 1990	Ikola, Willard 1990	Riley, Jack 1979
Ceglarski, Len 1992	+ Jeremiah, Eddie 1973	+ Ross, Larry 1988
+ Cunniff, John 2003	+ Johnson, Bob 1991	+ Thompson, Cliff 1973
+ Fullerton, James 1992	Johnson, Paul 2001	+ Stewart, Bill 1982
Gambucci, Sergio 1996	Kelley, Jack 1993	Watson, Sid 1999
+ Gordon, Malcolm 1973	+ Kelly, John (Snooks) 1974	+ Winsor, Ralph 1973
Harkness, Ned 1994	Nanne, Lou 1998	Woog, Doug 2002

Referee

Chadwick, Bill 1974

Contributor

+ Schulz, Charles M. 1993

Administrators

+ Brown, George 1973	+ Jennings, Bill 1981	Ridder, Bob 1976
+ Brown, Walter 1973	+ Kahler, Nick 1980	Trumble, Hal 1970
Bush, Walter 1980	+ Lockhart, Tom 1973	+ Tutt, Thayer 1973
+ Clark, Don 1978	Marvin, Cal 1982	+ Wirtz, Bill 1967
Claypool, Jim 1995	Palazzari, Doug 2000	+ Wright, Lyle 1973
+ Gibson, J.L. (Doc) 1973	Patrick, Craig 1996	
Ilitch, Mike 2004	Pleau, Larry 2000	

HORSE RACING

National Museum of Racing and Hall of Fame

Established in 1950 by the Saratoga Springs Racing Association and opened in 1955. **Address:** National Museum of Racing and Hall of Fame, 191 Union Ave., Saratoga Springs, NY 12866. **Telephone:** (518) 584-0400.
Web: www.racingmuseum.org

Eligibility: Nominated horses must be retired five years; jockeys must be active at least 15 years; trainers must be active at least 25 years. Voting done by 125-member panel of horse racing media.

Class of 2008 (6): JOCKEYS—**Edgar Prado** and **Milo Valenzuela**; TRAINERS—**Carl Nafzger**. HORSES—**Ancient Hill, Inside Information** and **Manila**.

Members are listed with year of induction; (+) indicates deceased members.

Jockeys

+ Adams, Frank (Dooley)* 1970	+ Garner, Andrew (Mack) 1969	Prado, Edgar 2008
+ Adams, John 1965	+ Garrison, Snapper 1955	+ Purdy, Sam 1970
+ Aitcheson, Joe Jr.* 1978	+ Gomez, Avelino 1982	+ Reiff, John 1956
+ Arcaro, Eddie 1958	+ Griffin, Henry 1956	+ Robertson, Alfred 1971
Atkinson, Ted 1957	+ Guerin, Eric 1972	Rotz, John L. 1983
Baeza, Braulio 1976	+ Hartack, Bill 1959	+ Sande, Earl 1955
Bailey, Jerry 1995	Hawley, Sandy 1992	Santos, Jose 2007
+ Barbee, George 1996	+ Johnson, Albert 1971	Sellers, John 2007
+ Bassett, Carroll* 1972	+ Knapp, Willie 1969	+ Shilling, Carroll 1970
Baze, Russell 1999	Krone, Julie 2000	+ Shoemaker, Bill 1958
+ Blum, Walter 1987	+ Kummer, Clarence 1972	+ Simms, Willie 1977
Boland, Bill 2006	+ Kurtsinger, Charley 1967	+ Sloan, Todhunter 1955
+ Bostwick, George H.* ...1968	+ Loftus, Johnny 1959	Smith, Mike 2003
+ Boulmetis, Sam 1973	Longden, Johnny 1958	+ Smithwick, A. Patrick* ..1973
+ Brooks, Steve 1963	Maher, Danny 1955	Stevens, Gary 1997
Brumfield, Don 1996	+ McAtee, Linus 1956	+ Stout, James 1968
+ Burns, Tommy 1983	McCarron, Chris 1989	+ Taral, Fred 1955
+ Butwell, Jimmy 1984	+ McCreary, Conn 1975	+ Tuckerman, Bayard Jr.* ..1973
+ Byers, J.D. (Dolly) 1967	+ McKinney, Rigan 1968	Turcotte, Ron 1979
Cauthen, Steve 1994	+ McLaughlin, James 1955	+ Turner, Nash 1955
+ Coltiletti, Frank 1970	+ Miller, Walter 1955	Ussery, Robert 1980
Cordero, Angel Jr. 1988	+ Murphy, Isaac 1955	+ Valenzuela, Milo 2008
+ Crawford, Robert (Specs)* ..1973	+ Neves, Ralph 1960	Vasquez, Jacinto 1998
Day, Pat 1991	+ Notter, Joe 1963	Velasquez, Jorge 1990
Delahoussaye, Eddie ...1993	+ O'Connor, Winnie 1956	Walsh, Thomas* 2005
Desormeaux, Kent 2004	+ Odom, George 1955	+ Westrope, Jack 2002
+ Ensor, Lavelle (Buddy) ..1962	+ O'Neill, Frank 1956	+ Woolf, George 1955
+ Fator, Laverne 1955	+ Parke, Ivan 1978	+ Workman, Raymond 1956
Fires, Earlie 2001	+ Patrick, Gil 1970	Ycaza, Manuel 1977
Fishback, Jerry* 1992	Pincay, Laffit Jr. 1975	
		*Steeplechase jockey

Trainers

+ Barrera, Laz 1979	+ Hirsch, W.J. (Buddy) ...1982	+ Miller, MacKenzie 1987
+ Bedwell, H. Guy 1971	+ Hitchcock, Thomas Sr. ..1973	+ Molter, William, Jr. 1960
+ Brown, Edward D. 1984	+ Hughes, Hollie 1973	Mott, Bill 1998
Burch, Elliot 1980	+ Hyland, John 1956	+ Mulholland, Winbert 1967
+ Burch, Preston M. 1963	+ Jacobs, Hirsch 1958	Nafzger, Carl 2008
+ Burch, W.P. 1955	Jerkens, H. Allen 1975	+ Neloy, Eddie 1983
+ Burlew, Fred 1973	Johnson, Philip 1997	Nerud, John 1972
+ Childs, Frank E. 1968	+ Johnson, William R. ...1986	+ Parke, Burley 1986
+ Clark, Henry 1982	+ Jolley, LeRoy 1987	+ Penna, Angel Sr. 1988
+ Cocks, W. Burling 1985	+ Jones, Ben A. 1958	+ Pincus, Jacob 1988
Conway, James P. 1996	+ Jones, H.A. (Jimmy) ...1959	+ Rogers, John 1955
Croll, Jimmy 1994	+ Joyner, Andrew 1955	+ Rowe, James Sr. 1955
Delp, Bud 2002	Kelly, Tom 1993	Schulhofer, Scotty 1992
Drysdale, Neil 2000	+ Laurin, Lucien 1977	Sheppard, Jonathan 1990
+ Duke, William 1956	+ Lewis, J. Howard 1969	+ Smith, Robert A. 1976
+ Feustel, Louis 1964	Lukas, D. Wayne 1999	Smith, Tom 2001
+ Fitzsimmons, J. (Sunny Jim) .1958	+ Luro, Horatio 1980	+ Smithwick, Mike 1976
+ Forrest, Henry 2007	Mandella, Richard 2001	+ Stephens, Woody 1976
Frankel, Bobby 1995	+ Madden, John 1983	Tenny, Mesh 1991
+ Gaver, John M. 1966	+ Maloney, Jim 1989	+ Thompson, H.J. 1969
Hanford, Carl 2006	Martin, Frank (Pancho) ..1981	+ Trotsek, Harry 1984
+ Healey, Thomas 1955	McAnally, Ron 1990	Van Berg, Jack 1985
+ Hildreth, Samuel 1955	+ McCabe, Frank 2007	+ Van Berg, Marion 1970
+ Hine, Hubert (Sonny) ..2003	+ McDaniel, Henry 1956	Veitch, John 2007
+ Hirsch, Max 1959	McGaughey, Shug 2004	+ Veitch, Sylvester 1977

Horse Racing (Cont.)
Trainers (Cont.)

+ Walden, Robert 1970	Watters, Sidney Jr. 2005	+ Williamson, Ansel 1998
Walsh, Michael 1997	Whiteley, Frank Jr. 1978	Winfrey, W.C. (Bill) 1971
+ Ward, Sherrill 1978	+ Whittingham, Charlie 1974	Zito, Nick 2005

Horses
Year foaled in parentheses.

A.P. Indy (1989) 2000	+ Elkridge (1938) 1966	+ Neji (1950) 1966
+ Ack Ack (1966) 1986	+ Emperor of Norfolk (1885) .1988	+ Noor (1945) 2002
Affectionately (1960) 1989	+ Equipoise (1928) 1957	+ Northern Dancer (1961) ...1976
+ Affirmed (1975) 1980	+ Exceller (1973) 1999	+ Oedipus (1941) 1978
All-Along (1979) 1990	+ Exterminator (1915) 1957	+ Old Rosebud (1911) 1968
+ Alsab (1939) 1976	+ Fairmount (1921) 1985	+ Omaha (1932) 1965
+ Alydar (1975) 1989	+ Fair Play (1905) 1956	+ Pan Zareta (1910) 1972
Alysheba (1984) 1993	+ Firenze (1885) 1981	+ Parole (1873) 1984
+ American Eclipse (1814) ..1970	Flatterer (1979) 1994	Personal Ensign (1984) ..1993
+ Ancient Title (1971) 2008	Flawlessly (1989) 2004	Paseana (1987) 2001
+ Armed (1941) 1963	+ Foolish Pleasure (1972) ..1995	+ Peter Pan (1904) 1956
+ Artful (1902) 1956	+ Forego (1971) 1979	Precisionist (1983) 2003
+ Arts and Letters (1966) ..1994	+ Fort Marcy (1964) 1998	Princess Rooney (1980) ..1991
+ Assault (1943) 1964	+ Gallant Bloom (1966) 1977	+ Real Delight (1949) 1987
+ Battleship (1927) 1969	+ Gallant Fox (1927) 1957	+ Regret (1912) 1957
+ Bayakoa (1984) 1998	+ Gallant Man (1954) 1987	+ Reigh Count (1925) 1978
+ Bed O'Roses (1947) 1976	+ Gallorette (1942) 1962	Riva Ridge (1969) 1998
+ Beldame (1901) 1956	+ Gamely (1964) 1980	+ Roamer (1911) 1981
+ Ben Brush (1893) 1955	Genuine Risk (1977) 1986	+ Roseben (1901) 1956
+ Bewitch (1945) 1977	+ Good and Plenty (1900) ..1956	+ Round Table (1954) 1972
+ Bimelech (1937) 1990	+ Go For Wand (1987) 1996	+ Ruffian (1972) 1976
+ Black Gold (1919) 1989	+ Granville (1933) 1997	+ Ruthless (1864) 1975
+ Black Helen (1932) 1991	+ Grey Lag (1918) 1957	+ Salvator (1886) 1955
+ Blue Larkspur (1926) 1957	+ Gun Bow (1960) 1999	+ Sarazen (1921) 1957
+ Bold 'n Determined (1977) .1997	+ Hamburg (1895) 1986	+ Seabiscuit (1933) 1958
+ Bold Ruler (1954) 1973	+ Hanover (1884) 1955	+ Searching (1952) 1978
+ Bon Nouvel (1960) 1976	+ Henry of Navarre (1891) ..1985	+ Seattle Slew (1974) 1981
+ Boston (1833) 1955	+ Hill Prince (1947) 1991	+ Secretariat (1970) 1974
+ Broomstick (1901) 1956	+ Hindoo (1878) 1955	Serena's Song (1992) 2002
+ Buckpasser (1963) 1970	Holy Bull (1991) 2001	+ Shuvee (1966) 1975
+ Busher (1942) 1964	+ Imp (1894) 1965	Silver Charm (1995) 2007
+ Bushranger (1930) 1967	Inside Information (1991) ..2008	+ Silver Spoon (1956) 1978
+ Cafe Prince (1970) 1985	+ Jay Trump (1957) 1971	+ Sir Archy (1805) 1955
+ Carry Back (1958) 1975	John Henry (1975) 1990	+ Sir Barton (1916) 1957
+ Cavalcade (1931) 1993	+ Johnstown (1936) 1992	Skip Away (1993) 2004
+ Challendon (1936) 1977	+ Jolly Roger (1922) 1965	Slew o' Gold (1980) 1992
+ Chris Evert (1971) 1988	+ Kingston (1884) 1955	+ Stymie (1941) 1975
+ Cicada (1959) 1967	+ Kelso (1957) 1967	+ Sun Beau (1925) 1996
Cigar (1990) 2002	+ Kentucky (1861) 1983	+ Sunday Silence (1986) 1996
+ Citation (1945) 1959	Lady's Secret (1982) 1992	+ Susan's Girl (1969) 1976
+ Coaltown (1945) 1983	+ La Prevoyante (1970) 1995	+ Swaps (1952) 1966
+ Colin (1905) 1956	+ L'Escargot (1963) 1977	+ Swoon's Son (1952) 2007
+ Commando (1898) 1956	+ Lexington (1850) 1955	+ Sword Dancer (1956) 1977
Cougar II (1969) 2006	Lonesome Glory (1989) ..2005	+ Sysonby (1902) 1956
+ Count Fleet (1940) 1961	+ Longfellow (1867) 1971	+ Ta Wee (1966) 1994
+ Crusader (1923) 1995	+ Luke Blackburn (1877) ...1956	+ Tim Tam (1955) 1985
+ Dahlia (1971) 1981	+ Majestic Prince (1966) ...1988	+ Tom Fool (1949) 1960
+ Damascus (1964) 1974	+ Man o' War (1917) 1957	+ Top Flight (1929) 1966
Dance Smartly (1989) ...2003	Manila (1984) 2008	+ Tosmah (1961) 1984
+ Dark Mirage (1965) 1974	+ Maskette (1906) 2001	+ Twenty Grand (1928) 1957
+ Davona Dale (1976) 1985	Miesque (1984) 1999	+ Twilight Tear (1941) 1963
+ Desert Vixen (1970) 1979	+ Miss Woodford (1880) 1967	+ War Admiral (1934) 1958
+ Devil Diver (1939) 1980	Mom's Command (1983) ..2007	+ Whirlaway (1938) 1959
+ Discovery (1931) 1969	+ Myrtlewood (1933) 1979	+ Whisk Broom II (1907) 1979
+ Domino (1891) 1955	+ Nashua (1952) 1965	Winning Colors (1985) ...2000
+ Dr. Fager (1964) 1971	+ Native Dancer (1950) 1963	Zaccio (1976) 1990
Easy Goer (1986) 1997	+ Native Diver (1959) 1978	+ Zev (1920) 1983
+ Eight 30 (1936) 1994	+ Needles (1953) 2000	

Exemplars of Racing

+ Hanes, John W 1982	+ Mellon, Paul 1989	Widener, George D 1971
+ Jeffords, Walter M 1973		

MEDIA

National Sportscasters and Sportswriters Hall of Fame

Established in 1959 by the National Sportscasters and Sportswriters Association. **Address:** 322 East Innes St., Salisbury, NC 28144. **Telephone:** (704) 633-4275. **Web:** www.nssahalloffame.com. **Eligibility:** Nominees must be active for at least 25 years. Voting done by NSSA membership and other media representatives. Members are listed with year of induction; (+) indicates deceased members.

Sportscasters

+ Allen, Mel 1972	+ Gowdy, Curt 1981	+ Murphy, Bob 2002
+ Barber, Walter (Red) 1973	Harwell, Ernie 1989	+ Nelson, Lindsey 1979
Brennaman, Marty 2005	+ Hearn, Chick 1997	+ Prince, Bob 1986
+ Brickhouse, Jack 1983	+ Hodges, Russ 1975	+ Rizzuto, Phil 2006
+ Buck, Jack 1990	+ Hoyt, Waite 1987	+ Schenkel, Chris 1981
+ Caray, Harry 1989	+ Husing, Ted 1963	+ Scott, Ray 1982
+ Cosell, Howard 1993	Jackson, Keith 1995	Scully, Vin 1991
+ Dean, Dizzy 1976	Lundquist, Vern 2007	Simpson, Jim 2000
+ Dunphy, Don 1986	+ McCarthy, Clem 1970	+ Stern, Bill 1974
+ Elson, Bob 1995	+ McKay, Jim 1987	Summerall, Pat 1994
Enberg, Dick 1996	+ McNamee, Graham 1964	Whitaker, Jack 2001
Garagiola, Joe 2004	Michaels, Al 1998	Wolff, Bob 2003
+ Glickman, Marty 1992	Miller, Jon 1999	

Sportswriters

Anderson, Dave 1990	+ Grimsley, Will 1987	+ Parker, Dan 1975
Bisher, Furman 1989	+ Heinz, W.C. 2001	Pope, Edwin 1994
Broeg, Bob 1997	+ Holtzman, Jerome 2004	+ Povich, Shirley 1984
+ Burick, Si 1985	Izenberg, Jerry 2000	+ Rice, Grantland 1962
+ Cannon, Jimmy 1986	Jenkins, Dan 1996	+ Runyon, Damon 1964
+ Carmichael, John P. 1994	Jenkins, Sally 2005	Russell, Fred 1988
Collins, Bud 2002	+ Kieran, John 1971	Sherrod, Blackie 1991
+ Connor, Dick 1992	Kindred, Dave 2007	+ Smith, Walter (Red) 1977
+ Considine, Bob 1980	+ Lardner, Ring 1967	+ Spink, J.G. Taylor 1969
+ Daley, Arthur 1976	+ McDonough, Will 2003	+ Steadman, John 1999
Deford, Frank 1998	McGeehan, W.O. 2006	Vecsey, George 2001
Durslag, Mel 1995	+ Murphy, Jack 1988	+ Ward, Arch 1973
+ Gould, Alan 1990	+ Murray, Jim 1978	+ Woodward, Stanley 1974
+ Graham, Frank Sr. 1995	Olderman, Murray 1993	

MOTORSPORTS

Motorsports Hall of Fame of America

Established in 1989. **Mailing Address:** P.O. Box 194, Novi, MI 48376. **Telephone:** (248) 349-7223. **Web:** www.mshf.com. **Eligibility:** Nominees must be retired at least three years or engaged in their area of motorsports for at least 20 years. Areas include: open wheel, stock car, dragster, sports car, motorcycle, off road, power boat, air racing, land speed records, historic and at-large.

Class of 2008 (7): DRIVERS—**Michael Andretti, Buddy Baker, John Force, Richie Ginther, Wayne Rainey, Paul Goldsmith, Betty Skelton.** Members are listed with year of induction; (+) indicates deceased members.

Drivers

Allison, Bobby 1992	+ DePalma, Ralph 1992	Hill, Eddie 2002
Amato, Joe 2004	+ DePaolo, Peter 1995	Hill, Phil 1989
Andretti, Mario 1990	+ Donahue, Mark 1990	+ Hinnershitz, Tommy 2003
Andretti, Michael 2008	+ Earnhardt, Dale 2002	+ Holbert, Al 1993
+ Arfons, Art 1991	Elliott, Bill 2007	+ Horn, Ted 1993
+ Baker, Buck 1998	Fittipaldi, Emerson 2001	+ Hulme, Denis 1998
Baker, Buddy 2008	Flock, Tim 1999	Ivo, Tommy 2005
+ Baker, Cannonball 1989	Follmer, George 1999	Jarrett, Ned 1997
+ Bettenhausen, Tony 1997	Forbes-Robinson, Elliott 2006	Jenkins, Bill (Grumpy) 1996
Brabham, Geoff 2004	Force, John 2008	Johncock, Gordon 2002
Breedlove, Craig 1993	Foster, Danny 2005	Johnson, Junior 1991
Bryan, Jimmy 1999	Foyt, A.J. 1989	Jones, Parnelli 1992
+ Campbell, Sir Malcolm 1994	Garlits, Don 1989	Kalitta, Connie 1992
+ Cantrell, Bill 1992	Glidden, Bob 1994	Karamesines, Chris 2006
+ Chenoweth, Dean 1991	Ginther, Richie 2008	Kenyon, Mel 2003
+ Chevrolet, Gaston 2002	Goldsmith, Paul 2008	+ Kurtis, Frank 1999
Chrisman, Art 1997	+ Gregg, Peter 2000	Lawson, Eddie 2002
+ Clark, Jim 1990	Gurney, Dan 1991	Leonard, Joe 1991
+ Cook, Betty 1996	Hanauer, Chip 1995	+ Lockhart, Frank 1999
+ Cooper, Earl 2001	Hannah, Bob 2000	Lorenzen, Fred 2001
Cunningham, Briggs 1997	Hanks, Sam 2000	+ McLaren, Bruce 1995
+ Davis, Jim 1997	+ Harroun, Ray 2000	Mann, Dick 1993
D'Eath, Tom 2000	Hart, C.J. 1999	Mansell, Nigel 2006
DeCoster, Roger 1994	Haywood, Hurley 2005	Markle, Bart 1999

Motorsports (Cont.)

Martin, Buddy	.2007	
+ Mays, Rex	.1995	
McEwen, Tom	.2001	
McGriff, Hershel	.2006	
Mears, Rick	.1998	
+ Meyer, Louis	.1993	
+ Miles, Ken	.2001	
+ Milton, Tommy	.1998	
Muldowney, Shirley	.1990	
+ Muncy, Bill	.1989	
+ Murphy, Jimmy	.1998	
+ Musson, Ron	.1993	
Nickelson, Don	.1998	
Nixon, Gary	.2003	
+ Nordskog, Bob	.1997	
+ Oldfield, Barney	.1989	
Ongais, Danny	.2000	
+ Parks, Wally	.1993	
Parsons, Benny	.2005	

+ Parsons, Johnnie	.2004
Pearson, David	.1993
+ Petrali, Joe	.1992
+ Petty, Lee	.1996
Petty, Richard	.1989
Prudhomme, Don	.1991
Rahal, Bobby	.2004
Rainey, Wayne	.2008
Rathman, Jim	.2007
Resweber, Carroll	.1998
Redman, Brian	.2002
Revson, Peter	.1996
+ Roberts, Fireball	.1995
Roberts, Kenny	.1990
Rutherford, Johnny	.1996
+ Ruttman, Troy	.2005
Seebold, Bill	.1999
+ Shaw, Wilbur	.1991

Shobert, Bubba	.2007
Skelton, Betty	.2008
Slovak, Mira	.2001
Smith, Malcolm	.1996
Sneva, Tom	.2005
Sox, Ronnie	.2007
Spencer, Freddie	.2001
Springsteen, Jay	.2005
+ Thompson, Mickey	.1990
+ Turner, Curtis	.2006
Unser, Al	.1991
Unser, Bobby	.1994
Vesco, Don	.2004
+ Vukovich, Bill Sr	.1992
Waltrip, Darrell	.2003
Ward, Jeff	.2006
Ward, Rodger	.1995
+ Wood, Gar	.1990
Yarborough, Cale	.1994

Contributors

+ Agajanian, J.C	.1992
Bignotti, George	.1993
+ Black, Keith	.1995
Bondurant, Bob	.2003
+ Brawner, Clint	.1998
Carnegie, Tom	.2006
Chapman, Colin	.1997
+ Chevrolet, Louis	.1995
+ Donovan, Ed	.2003
Duesenberg, Fred	.1997
Economaki, Chris	.1994
+ Ford, Henry	.1996

+ France, Bill Jr.	.2004
+ France, Bill Sr.	.1990
Glick, Shav	.2004
Granatelli, Andy	.2001
Hall, Jim	.1994
+ Holman, John	.2005
+ Hulman, Tony	.1991
+ Jones, Ted	.2003
+ Kiekhaefer, Carl	.1998
Little, Bernie	.1994
McGee, Jim	.2007
Mehl, Leo	.2007

+ Miller, Harry	.1999
+ Moody, Ralph	.2005
+ Offenhauser, Fred	.2002
Penske, Roger	.1995
+ Rickenbacker, Eddie	.1994
+ Rose, Mauri	.1996
Shelby, Carroll	.1992
Simpson, Bill	.2003
Watson, A.J.	.1996
Wood, Glen	.2000
Wood, Leonard	.2000
+ Yunick, Smokey	.2000

International Motorsports Hall of Fame

Established in 1990 by the International Motorsports Hall of Fame Commission. **Mailing Address:** P.O. Box 1018, Talladega, AL 35161. **Telephone:** (256) 362-5002. **Web:** www.motorsportshalloffame.com.

Eligibility: Nominees must be retired from their specialty in motorsports for five years. Voting done by 150-member panel made up of the world-wide auto racing media. Members are listed with year of induction; (+) indicates deceased members.

Class of 2008 (6): DRIVERS—**Art Arfons, Robert "Red" Byron** and **Everett "Cotton" Owens**; CONTRIBUTORS—**Bill "Grumpy" Jenkins, Frank Kurtis** and **Ralph Seagraves**.

Drivers

Allison, Bobby	.1993
Amato, Joe	.2005
Andretti, Mario	.2000
+ Arfons, Art	.2008
+ Ascari, Alberto	.1992
+ Baker, Buck	.1990
Bonnett, Neil	.2001
+ Bettenhausen, Tony	.1991
Brabham, Jack	.1990
Bryan, Jimmy	.2001
+ Byron, Robert	.2008
+ Campbell, Sir Malcolm	.1990
+ Caracciola, Rudolph	.1998
+ Clark, Jim	.1990
+ DePalma, Ralph	.1991
+ Donahue, Mark	.1990
Donlavey, Junie	.2007
+ Earnhardt, Dale	.2006
Evans, Richie	.1996
+ Fangio, Juan Manuel	.1990
Farmer, Charles	.2004
Fittipaldi, Emerson	.2003
+ Flock, Tim	.1991
Foyt, A.J.	.2000
Gant, Harry	.2006
Glidden, Bob	.2005
+ Gregg, Peter	.1992
Gurney, Dan	.1990
Guthrie, Janet	.2006
Hailwood, Mike	.2001

+ Haley, Donald	.1996
Hanauer, Chip	.2005
+ Hendrick, Ray	.2007
+ Hill, Graham	.1990
Hill, Phil	.1991
+ Holbert, Al	.1993
+ Hulme, Denis	.2002
Ickx, Jacky	.2002
Ingram, Jack	.2007
+ Isaac, Bobby	.1996
Jarrett, Ned	.1991
Johncock, Gordon	.1999
Johnson, Junior	.1990
Johnson, Warren	.2007
Jones, Parnelli	.1990
Kenyon, Mel	.2003
+ Kulwicki, Alan	.2002
Lauda, Niki	.1993
Lorenzen, Fred	.1991
+ Lund, Tiny	.1994
Mansell, Chip	.2005
+ Mays, Rex	.1993
+ McLaren, Bruce	.1991
+ Meyer, Louis	.1992
Moss, Stirling	.1990
Muldowney, Shirley	.2004
+ Muncey, Bill	.2004
+ Nuvolari, Tazio	.1998
+ Oldfield, Barney	.1990
Owens, Everett	.2008

Parsons, Benny	.1994
Pearson, David	.1993
+ Petty, Lee	.1990
Piquet, Nelson	.2000
Prodhomme, Don	.2000
Prost, Alain	.1999
Rahal, Bobby	.2004
Rainey, Wayne	.2007
+ Richmond, Tim	.2002
+ Roberts, Fireball	.1990
Roberts, Kenny	.1992
Rose, Mauri	.1994
Rutherford, Johnny	.1996
Scott, Wendell	.1999
+ Senna, Ayrton	.2000
+ Shaw, Wilbur	.1991
Smith, Louise	.1999
Stewart, Jackie	.1990
Surtees, John	.1996
+ Thomas, Herb	.1995
+ Turner, Curtis	.1992
Unser, Al Sr.	.1998
Unser, Bobby	.1990
+ Vukovich, Bill	.1991
Waltrip, Darrell	.2005
Ward, Rodger	.1992
+ Weatherly, Joe	.1994
Wood, Glen	.2002
Yarborough, Cale	.1993

OLYMPICS

U.S. Olympic Hall of Fame

Established in 1983 by the United States Olympic Committee. **Mailing Address:** U.S. Olympic Committee, 1750 East Boulder Street, Colorado Springs, CO 80909. Plans for a permanent museum site have been suspended due to lack of funding. **Telephone:** (719) 866-4529. **Web:** www.usoc.org

Eligibility: Nominated athletes must be four years removed from their last Olympic competition. Voting for membership in the Hall was suspended in 1993 but resumed in 2004. Voting from 1983-92 was done by National Sportscasters and Sportswriters Association, Hall of Fame members and the USOC board members of directors. Beginning in 2004 the voting weight was divided among U.S. Olympians, select U.S. Olympic family/media and fans.

Class of 2008: ATHLETES—**Bruce Baumgartner** (wrestling); **Joan Benoit** (track & field); **Brian Boitano** (figure skating); **Oscar de La Hoya** (boxing); **Karch Kiraly** (volleyball), **J. Michael Plumb** (Equestrian), **David Robinson** (basketball), **Amy Van Dyken** (swimming), **Lones W. Wigger Jr.** (shooting); COACH—**Carlo Fassi**. VETERAN—**Carol Heiss Jenkins**. SPECIAL CONTRIBUTOR— **Frank Marshall**. TEAM—**1996 Women's Gymnastics**

Members are listed with year of induction; (+) indicates deceased members.

Teams

1956 Basketball Dick Boushka, Carl Cain, Chuck Darling, Bill Evans, Gib Ford, Burdy Haldorson, Bill Hougland, Bob Jeangerard, K.C. Jones, Bill Russell, Ron Tomsic, +Jim Walsh and coach +Gerald Tucker.

1960 Basketball Jay Arnette, Walt Bellamy, Bob Boozer, Terry Dischinger, Burdy Haldorson, Darrall Imhoff, Allen Kelley, +Lester Lane, Jerry Lucas, Oscar Robertson, Adrian Smith, Jerry West and coach Pete Newell.

1964 Basketball Jim Barnes, Bill Bradley, Larry Brown, Joe Caldwell, Mel Counts, Richard Davies, Walt Hazzard, Luke Jackson, John McCaffrey, Jeff Mullins, Jerry Shipp, George Wilson and coach +Hank Iba.

1960 Ice Hockey Billy Christian, Roger Christian, Billy Cleary, Bob Cleary, Gene Grazia, Paul Johnson, Jack Kirrane, John Mayasich, Jack McCartan, Bob McKay, Dick Meredith, Weldon Olson, Ed Owen, Rod Paavola, Larry Palmer, Dick Rodenheiser, +Tom Williams and coach Jack Riley.

1980 Ice Hockey Bill Baker, Neal Broten, Dave Christian, Steve Christoff, Jim Craig, Mike Eruzione, John Harrington, Steve Janaszak, Mark Johnson, Ken Morrow, Rob McClanahan, Jack O'Callahan, Mark Pavelich, Mike Ramsey, Buzz Schneider, Dave Silk, Eric Strobel, Bob Suter, Phil Verchota, Mark Wells and coach +Herb Brooks.

1996 Women's Soccer Michelle Akers, Brandi Chastain, Amanda Cromwell, Joy Fawcett, Julie Foudy, Carin Gabarra, Mia Hamm, Mary Harvey, Kristine Lilly, Shannon MacMillan, Tiffeny Milbrett, Carla Overbeck, Cindy Parlow, Tiffany Roberts, Briana Scurry, Thori Staples Bryan, Tisha Venturini, Saskia Webber, Staci Wilson and coach Tony DiCicco

1996 Women's Gymnastics Amanda Borden, Amy Chow, Dominique Dawes, Shannon Miller, Dominique Moceanu, Jaycie Phelps and Kerri Strug

Alpine Skiing
Mahre, Phil 1992

Basketball
Robinson, David 2008

Bobsled
+ Eagan, Eddie (see Boxing) .1983

Boxing
De La Hoya, Oscar 2008
Clay, Cassius 1983
+ Eagan, Eddie (see Bobsled) .1983
Foreman, George 1990
Frazier, Joe 1989
Leonard, Sugar Ray 1985
· Patterson, Floyd 1987

Coaches
+ Brooks, Herb 2006
Fassi, Carlo 2008

Cycling
Carpenter-Phinney, Connie .1992

Diving
King, Miki 1992
Lee, Sammy 1990
Louganis, Greg 1985
McCormick, Pat 1985

Equestrian
Plumb, J. Michael 2008

Figure Skating
Albright, Tenley 1988
Boitano, Brian 2008
Button, Dick 1983
Fleming, Peggy 1983
Hamill, Dorothy 1991
Hamilton, Scott 1990
Yamaguchi, Kristi 2006

Gymnastics
Conner, Bart 1991
Retton, Mary Lou 1985
Miller, Shannon 2006
Vidmar, Peter 1991

Paralympian
Golden-Brosnihan, Diana . .2006

Rowing
+ Kelly, Jack Sr. 1990

Shooting
Wigger Jr., Lones 2008

Speed Skating
Blair, Bonnie 2004
Heiden, Eric 1983
Jansen, Dan 2004

Volleyball
Kiraly, Karch 2008

Veterans
Heiss Jenkins, Carol 2008
+ Shea, Jack 2006

Wrestling
Baumgartner, Bruce 2008
Gable, Dan 1985

Swimming
Babashoff, Shirley 1987
Biondi, Matt 2004
Caulkins, Tracy 1990
+ Daniels, Charles 1988
de Varona, Donna 1987
Evans, Janet 2004
Gaines, Rowdy 2006
+ Kahanamoku, Duke 1984
+ Madison, Helene 1992
Meyer, Debbie 1986
Naber, John 1984

Schollander, Don 1983
Spitz, Mark 1983
Van Dyken, Amy 2008
+ Weissmuller, Johnny 1983

Weightlifting
+ Davis, John 1989
Kono, Tommy 1990

Track & Field
Ashford, Evelyn 2006
Beamon, Bob 1983
Benoit, Joan 2008
Boston, Ralph 1985
+ Calhoun, Lee 1991
Campbell, Milt 1992
Coachman, Alice 2004
+ Davenport, Willie 1991
Davis, Glenn 1986
+ Didrikson, Babe 1983
Dillard, Harrison 1983
Evans, Lee 1989
+ Ewry, Ray 1983
Fosbury, Dick 1992
+ Hayes, Bob 2006
Jenner, Bruce 1986
Johnson, Rafer 1983
+ Joyner, Florence Griffith . .2004
Joyner-Kersee, Jackie 2004
+ Kraenzlein, Alvin 1985
Lewis, Carl 1985
Mathias, Bob 1983
Mills, Billy 1984
Morrow, Bobby 1989
Moses, Edwin 1985
O'Brien, Parry 1984
+ Oerter, Al 1983
+ Owens, Jesse 1983
+ Paddock, Charley 1991

U.S. Olympic Hall of Fame (Cont.)
Track & Field (Cont.)

Richards, Bob	1983	Shorter, Frank	1984	Tyus, Wyomia	1985
+ Rudolph, Wilma	1983	+ Thorpe, Jim	1983	Whitfield, Mal	1988
+ Sheppard, Mel	1989	Toomey, Bill	1984	+ Wykoff, Frank	1984

Contributors

+ Arledge, Roone	1989	Hull, Col. Don	1992	+ McKay, Jim	1988
+ Brundage, Avery	1983	+ Iba, Hank	1985	Miller, Don	1984
+ Bushnell, Asa	1990	+ Kane, Robert	1986	+ Simon, William	1991
Ebersol, Dick	2006	+ Kelly, Jack Jr.	1992	Walker, LeRoy	1987
Greenspan, Bud	2004	Marshall, Frank	2008		

SOCCER

National Soccer Hall of Fame

Established in 1950 by the Philadelphia Oldtimers Association. First exhibit unveiled in Oneonta, NY in 1982. Moved into new Hall of Fame building in the summer of 1999. **Address:** 18 Stadium Circle, Oneonta, NY 13820. **Telephone:** (607) 432-3351. **Web:** www.soccerhall.org

Eligibility: Players must have been retired as a player for at least three years, but for no more than 10 years He or she must have played at least 20 full international games for the United States. He or she must have played at least five seasons in an American first-division professional league (NASL or MLS), and won the league championship, won the U.S. Open Cup or been a league all-star at least once. Other categories include Veterans (included under Players) and Builders. Voting done by a committee made up of Hall of Famers, U.S. Soccer officials and members of the national media.

Class of 2008 (2): **Hugo Perez** and **Anson Dorrance.**

Members are listed with home state and year of induction; (+) indicates deceased members.

Players

Akers, Michelle	2004	+ Fricker, Werner	1992	Nanoski, Jukey	1993
Alberto, Carlos	2003	+ Fryer, William J.	1951	Nelson, Johnny	2005
Annis, Robert	1976	Gabarra, Carin	2000	Nilsen, werner	2005
+ Auld, Andrew	1986	+ Gaetjens, Joe	1976	+ Ntsoelengoe, Ace (S.Afr.)	2003
Bachmeier, Adolph	2002	Gallagher, James	1986	O'Brien, Shamus	1990
Bahr, Walter	1976	Gard, Gino	1976	Olaff, Gene	1971
Balboa, Marcelo	2005	+ Gentle, James	1986	+ Oliver, Arnie	1968
+ Barr, George	1983	Getzinger, Rudy	1991	Oliver, Len	1996
+ Beardsworth, Fred	1965	+ Glover, Teddy	1965	Overbeck, Carla	2006
Beckenbauer, Franz (Ger)	1998	+ Gonsalves, Billy	1950	Pariani, Gino	1976
Bernabei, Ray	1978	Gormley, Bob	1989	+ Patenaude, Bert	1971
Bogicevic, Vladislav (Yug)	2002	+ Govier, Sheldon	1950	Pel|fe (Brazil)	1993
+ Bookie, Michael	1986	Granitza, Karl-Heinz (Ger)	2003	Perez, Hugo	2008
Borghi, Frank	1976	Gryzik, Joe	1973	Ramos, Tab	2005
+ Boulos, Frenchy	1980	Hamm, Mia	2007	+ Ratican, Harry	1950
+ Brittan, Harold	1951	+ Harker, Al	1979	+ Renzulli, Pete	1951
+ Brown, David	1951	Harkes, John	2005	Roe, Jimmy	1997
Brown, George	1995	Heinrichs, April	1998	Roth, Werner	1989
+ Brown, James	1986	Higgins, Shannon	2002	Roy, Willy	1989
Caligiuri, Paul	2004	Howard, Ted	2003	+ Ryan, Hun	1958
+\. Carenza, Joe	1982	Hynes, John	1977	Salcedo Frabie	2005
+ Caraffi, Ralph	1959	+ Japp, John	1953	Schaller, Willy	1995
Chacurian, Chico	1992	Keough, Harry	1976	Slone, Philip	1986
+ Chesney, Stan	1966	Kropfelder, Nicholas	1996	Smith, Bobby	2007
Child, Paul (Eng)	2003	+ Kunter, Rudy	1963	+ Souza, Ed	1976
Chinaglia, Giorgio (Italy)	2000	Lalas, Alexi	2006	Souza, Clarkie	1976
Clavijo, Fernando	2005	Lang, Millard	1950	+ Spalding, Dick	1951
+ Colombo, Charlie	1976	Lenarduzzi, Bob (Can)	2003	+ Stark, Archie	1950
Coombes, Geoff	1976	+ Looby, Bill	2001	+ Swords, Thomas	1951
+ Craddock Jr., Robert	1976	+ Maca, Joe	1976	+ Tintle, Joseph	1952
Danilo, Paul	1997	Mausser, Arnie	2003	+ Tracey, Ralph	1986
Davis, Rick	2001	McBride, Pat	1994	Trost, Al	2006
+ Dick, Walter	1989	+ McGhee, Bart	1986	+ Vaughn, David	1986
Diorio, Nick	1974	+ McGuire, John	1951	+ Wallace, Frank	1976
+ Donelli, Buff	1954	+ McIlveney, Eddie	1976	+ Weir, Alex	1975
Douglas, Jimmy	1953	McLaughlin, Bennie	1977	Willey, Alan (Eng)	2003
+ Duggan, Thomas	1951	+ Mieth, Werner	1974	Wilson, Bruce (Can)	2003
+ Dunn, James	1974	+ Millar, Robert	1950	+ Wilson, Peter	1950
Ely, Alexander	1997	Monsen, Lloyd	1994	Wolanin, Adam	1976
+ Ferguson, John	1950	Moore, Johnny	1997	+ Wood, Alex	1986
Fleming, Tom (Whitey)	2005	+ Moorehouse, George	1986	Wynalda, Eric	2004
+ Florie, Thomas	1986	+ Morrison, Robert	1951	Zerhusen, Al	1978
Foudy, Julie	2007	Murphy, Edward	1998		

Builders

Abronzino, Umberto 1971	+ Fowler, Dan 1970	+ Netto, Fred 1958
Aimi, Milton 1991	+ Fowler, Peg 1979	Newman, Ron 1992
+ Alonso, Julie 1972	+ Garcia, Pete 1964	+ Niotis, D.J. 1963
+ Andersen, William 1956	+ Giesler, Walter 1962	+ Palmer, William 1952
Anschutz, Philip 2006	+ Gould, David L. 1953	+ Pearson, Eddie 1990
+ Ardizzone, John 1971	+ Greer, Don 1985	+ Peel, Peter 1951
+ Armstrong, James 1952	+ Guelker, Bob 1980	+ Peters, Wally 1967
+ Barriskill, Joe 1953	Guennel, Joe 1980	Phillipson, Don 1987
Berling, Clay 1995	+ Healey, George 1951	+ Piscopo, Giorgio 1978
+ Best, John O. 1982	Heilpern, Herb 1988	+ Pomeroy, Edgar 1955
+ Booth, Joseph 1952	+ Hemmings, William 1961	+ Ramsden, Arnold 1957
+ Boxer, Matt 1961	Hermann, Robert 2001	+ Reese, Doc 1957
Bradley, Gordon (Eng) ...1996	+ Hudson, Maurice 1966	Ringsdorf, Gene 1979
+ Briggs, Lawrence E. 1978	+ Hunt, Lamar 1982	Robbie, Elizabeth 2003
+ Brock, John 1950	+ Iglehart, Alfredda 1951	+ Robbie, Joe 2003
+ Brown, Andrew M. 1950	+ Jeffrey, William 1951	Ross, Steve 2003
+ Cahill, Thomas W 1950	+ Johnston, Jack 1952	Rothenberg, Alan 2007
+ Chyzowych, Walter 1997	+ Kabanica, Mike 1987	+ Rottenberg, Jack 1971
+ Coll, John 1986	Kehoe, Bob 1990	+ Sager, Tom 1968
Collins, George M. 1951	+ Kelly, Frank 1994	Saunders, Harry 1981
Collins, Peter 1998	+ Kempton, George 1950	Schellscheidt, Mannie ...1990
+ Commander, Colin 1967	+ Klein, Paul 1953	+ Schillinger, Emil 1960
+ Cordery, Ted 1975	Kleinaitis, Al 1995	+ Schroeder, Elmer 1951
+ Craddock, Robert 1959	+ Kozma, Oscar 1964	+ Schwarz, Erno 1951
+ Craggs, Edmund 1969	+ Kracher, Frank 1983	+ Shields, Fred 1968
Craggs, George 1981	Kraft, Granny 1984	+ Single, Erwin 1981
+ Cummings, Wilfred R. ..1953	+ Kraus, Harry 1963	+ Smith, Alfred 1951
+ Delach, Joseph 1973	+ Lamm, Kurt 1979	Smith, Patrick 1998
DeLuca, Anthony 1979	Larson, Bert 1988	Spath, Reinhold 1997
+ Donaghy, Edward J. ...1951	+ Lewis, H. Edgar 1950	+ Steelink, Nicolaas 1971
+ Donnelly, George 1989	Lombardo, Joe 1984	Steinbrecher, Hank 2005
Dorrance, Anson 2008	Long, Denny 1993	Stern, Lee 2003
+ Dresmich, John W. 1968	+ MacEwan, John J. 1953	+ Steur, August 1969
+ Duff, Duncan 1972	+ Magnozzi, Enzo 1977	+ Stewart, Douglas 1950
+ Edwards, Gene 1985	+ Maher, Jack 1970	+ Stone, Robert T 1971
Epperleim, Rudy 1951	+ Manning, Dr. Randolf ..1950	Toye, Clive 2003
+ Ertegun, Ahmet 2003	+ Marre, John 1953	+ Triner, Joseph 1951
Ertegun, Nesuhi 2003	+ McClay, Allan 1971	+ Walder, Jimmy 1971
+ Fairfield, Harry 1951	+ McGrath, Frank 1978	+ Washauer, Adolph 1977
Feibusch, Ernst 1984	+ McGuire, Jimmy 1951	+ Webb, Tom 1987
+ Fernley, John A. 1951	+ McSkimming, Dent 1951	+ Weston, Victor 1956
+ Ferro, Charles 1958	Merovich, Pete 1971	+ Woods, John W. 1952
+ Fishwick, George E. ...1974	Miller, Al 1995	Woosnam, Phil 1997
+ Flamhaft, Jack 1964	+ Miller, Milton 1971	Yeagley, Jerry 1989
+ Fleming, Harry G. 1967	+ Mills, Jimmy 1954	+ Young, John 1958
+ Foulds, Pal 1953	+ Moore, James F. 1971	+ Zampini, Dan 1963
+ Foulds, Sam 1969	+ Morrissette, Bill 1967	

SWIMMING

International Swimming Hall of Fame

Established in 1965 by the U.S. College Coaches' Swim Forum. **Address:** One Hall of Fame Drive, Ft. Lauderdale, FL 33316. **Telephone:** (954) 462-6536. **Web:** www.ishof.org.

Categories for induction are: swimming, diving, water polo, synchronized swimming, coaching, pioneers and contributors. Coaches and contributors are not included in the following list. Only U.S. men and women listed below.

Class of 2008 (2): U.S. WOMEN—**Anita Nall** and **Jill Savery.**

Members are listed with year of induction; (+) indicates deceased members.

U.S. Men

+ Anderson, Miller 1967	Clark, Earl 1972	Edgar, David 1996
Barrowman, Mike 1997	Clark, Steve 1966	+ Faricy, John 1990
Berkoff, David 2005	+ Cleveland, Dick 1991	+ Farrell, Jeff 1968
Biondi, Matt 1997	Clotworthy, Robert 1980	+ Fick, Peter 1978
Boggs, Phil 1985	+ Crabbe, Buster 1965	+ Flanagan, Ralph 1978
Bottom, Joe 2006	+ Daniels, Charlie 1965	Ford, Alan 1966
Breen, George 1975	Degener, Dick 1971	Furniss, Bruce 1987
+ Browning, Skippy 1975	DeMont, Rick 1990	Gaines, Rowdy 1995
Bruner, Mike 1988	Dempsey, Frank 1996	Garton, Tim 1997
Burton, Mike 1977	+ Desjardins, Pete 1966	+ Glancy, Harrison 1990
+ Cann, Tedford 1967	Dolan, Tom 2006	Goodell, Brian 1986
Carey, Rick 1993	Dysdale, Taylor 1994	+ Goodwin, Budd 1971

Graef, Jed 1988
Haines, George 1977
Hall Sr., Gary 1981
+ Harlan, Bruce 1973
Harper, Don 1998
+ Hebner, Harry 1968
+ Heidenreich, Jerry 1992
Hencken, John 1988
Hickcox, Charles 1976
Higgins, John 1971
+ Holiday, Harry 1991
Hough, Richard 1970
Irwin, Juno Stover 1980
Graham, Johnston 1998
Jager, Tom 2001
Jastremski, Chet 1977
+ Kahanamoku, Duke 1965
+ Kealoha, Warren 1968
Kiefer, Adolph 1965
Kinsella, John 1986
+ Kojac, George 1968
Konno, Ford 1972
+ Kruger, Stubby 1986
+ Kuehn, Louis 1988
+ Langer, Ludy 1988
+ Langner, G. Harold 1995
Larson, Lance 1980
Laufer, Walter 1973
Lee, Dr. Sammy 1968
Lemmon, Kelley 1999
+ LeMoyne, Harry 1988
Lenzi, Mark 2003

Louganis, Greg 1993
Lundquist, Steve 1990
Mann, Thompson 1984
+ Martin, G. Harold 1999
McCormick, Pat 1965
+ McDermott, Turk 1969
+ McGillivray, Perry 1981
McKee, Tim 1998
McKenzie, Don 1989
McKinney, Frank 1975
McLane, Jimmy 1970
+ Medica, Jack 1966
Montgomery, Jim 1986
Morales, Pablo 1998
Mulliken, Bill 1984
Naber, John 1982
Nakama, Keo 1975
+ O'Connor, Wally 1966
Oyakawa, Yoshi 1973
+ Patnik, Al 1969
Prew, William 1998
+ Riley, Mickey 1977
+ Ris, Wally 1966
Robie, Carl 1976
Ross, Clarence 1988
+ Ross, Norman 1967
Roth, Dick 1987
Rouse, Jeff 2001
+ Ruddy Sr., Joe 1986
Russell, Doug 1985
Saari, Roy 1976
+ Schaeffer, E. Carroll 1968

Scholes, Clarke 1980
Schollander, Don 1965
Schroeder, Terry 2002
Shaw, Tim 1989
+ Sheldon, George 1989
Sitzberger, Ken 1994
+ Skelton, Robert 1988
Smith, Bill 1966
+ Smith, Dutch 1979
+ Smith, Jimmy 1992
Spitz, Mark 1977
+ Stack, Allen 1979
Stewart, Melvin 2002
Stickles, Ted 1995
Stock, Tom 1989
+ Swendsen, Clyde 1991
Taft, Ray 1996
Tobian, Gary 1978
Troy, Mike 1971
Vande Weghe, Albert 1990
Vassallo, Jesse 1997
+ Verdeur, Joe 1966
Vogel, Matt 1996
+ Vollmer, Hal 1990
+ Wayne, Marshall 1981
Webster, Bob 1970
+ Weissmuller, Johnny 1965
+ White, Al 1965
Wilson, Craig 2005
Wiggins, Al 1994
Wrightson, Bernie 1984
Yorzyk, Bill 1971

U.S. Women

Andersen, Teresa 1986
Atwood, Sue 1992
Babashoff, Shirley 1982
Babb-Sprague, Kristen 1999
Ball, Catie 1976
+ Bauer, Sybil 1967
Bean, Dawn Pawson 1996
Belote, Melissa 1983
Bleibtrey, Ethelda 1967
+ Boyle, Charlotte 1988
Bruner, Jayne Owen 1998
Burke, Lynn 1978
Bush, Lesley 1986
Callen, Gloria 1984
Caretto, Patty 1987
Carr, Cathy 1988
Caulkins, Tracy 1990
+ Chadwick, Florence 1970
Chandler, Jennifer 1987
Cohen, Tiffany 1996
+ Coleman, Georgia 1966
Cone, Carin 1984
Costie, Candy 1995
Cox, Lynne 2000
Crlenkovich, Helen 1981
Curtis, Ann 1966
Daniel, Ellie 1997
de Varona, Donna 1969
Dean, Penny 1996
+ Dorfner, Olga 1970
Draves, Vickie 1969
Duenkel, Ginny 1985
Dunbar, Barbara 2000
Dyroen-Lancer, Becky 2004
Ederle, Gertrude 1965
Ellis, Kathy 1991
Elsener, Patty 2002
Evans, Janet 2001
Fauntz, Jane 1991
Ferguson, Cathy 1978
Finneran, Sharon 1985

+ Fulton, Patty Robinson 2001
+ Galligan, Claire 1970
+ Garatti-Seville, Eleanor 1992
Gestring, Marjorie 1976
Gossick, Sue 1988
+ Guest, Irene 1990
Gundling, Buelah 1965
Hall, Kaye 1979
Henne, Jan 1979
Hogan, Peg 2002
Hogshead, Nancy 1994
Holm, Eleanor 1966
Hunt-Newman, Virginia 1993
Johnson, Gail 1983
Josephson, Karen 1997
Josephson, Sarah 1997
+ Kaufman, Beth 1967
+ Kight, Lenore 1981
King, Micki 1978
Kolb, Claudia 1975
+ Lackie, Ethel 1969
+ Landon, Alice Lord 1993
Linehan, Kim 1997
+ Madison, Helene 1966
Mann, Shelly 1966
McCormick, Kelly 1999
McGrath, Margo 1989
McKim, Josephine 1991
Meagher, Mary T. 1993
+ Meany, Helen 1971
Merlino, Maxine 1999
Meyer, Debbie 1977
Mitchell, Betsy 1998
Mitchell, Michele 1995
Moe, Karen 1992
Morris, Pam 1965
Mueller, Ardeth 1996
Nall, Anita 2008
Neilson, Sandra 1986
Neyer, Megan 1997
+ Norelius, Martha 1967

Olsen, Zoe Ann 1989
O'Rourke, Heidi 1980
+ Osipowich, Albina 1986
Pedersen, Susan 1995
Pinkston, Betty Becker 1967
Pope, Paula Jean Meyers . . .1979
Potter, Cynthia 1987
+ Poynton, Dorothy 1968
+ Rawls, Katherine 1965
Redmond, Carol 1989
Riggin, Aileen 1967
Roper, Gail 1997
Ross, Anne 1984
Rothhammer, Keena 1991
Ruiz-Conforto, Tracie 1993
Ruuska, Sylvia 1976
Sanders, Summer 2002
Savery, Jill 2008
Schuler, Carolyn 1989
Seller, Peg 1988
+ Smith, Caroline 1988
Steinseifer, Carrie 1999
Sterkel, Jill 2002
Stouder, Sharon 1972
+ Toner, Vee 1995
Val, Laura 2003
Van Dyken, Amy 2007
+ Vilen, Kay 1978
Von Saltza, Chris 1966
+ Wainwright, Helen 1972
Walker, Clara Lamore 1995
+ Watson, Lillian (Pokey) 1984
Wayte, Mary 2000
Wehselau, Mariechen 1989
Welshons, Kim 1988
Wichman, Sharon 1991
Williams, Esther 1966
+ Woodbridge, Margaret 1989
Woodhead, Cynthia 1994
Wyland, Wendy 2001

TENNIS

International Tennis Hall of Fame

Originally the National Tennis Hall of Fame. Established in 1953 by James Van Alen and sanctioned by the U.S. Tennis Association in 1954. Renamed the International Tennis Hall of Fame in 1976. **Address:** 194 Bellevue Ave., Newport, RI 02840. **Telephone:** (401) 849-3990. **Web:** www.tennisfame.com

Eligibility: Nominated players must be five years removed from being a "significant factor" in competitive tennis. Voting done by members of the international tennis media. Due to space constraints only players are listed below.

Class of 2008 (3): Michael Chang, Mark McCormack and **Eugene Scott.**

Members are listed with year of induction; (+) indicates deceased members.

Men

+ Adee, George 1964	+ Gonzales, Pancho 1968	+ Perry, Fred 1975
+ Alexander, Fred 1961	+ Grant, Bryan (Bitsy) 1972	+ Pettitt, Tom 1982
+ Allison, Wilmer 1963	+ Griffin, Clarence 1970	Pietrangeli, Nicola 1986
+ Alonso, Manuel 1977	+ Hackett, Harold 1961	+ Quist, Adrian 1984
Anderson, Malcolm 2000	Hewitt, Bob 1992	Rafter, Patrick 2006
+ Ashe, Arthur 1985	+ Hoad, Lew 1980	Ralston, Dennis 1987
+ Austin, Bunny 1997	+ Hovey, Fred 1974	+ Renshaw, Ernest 1983
Becker, Boris 2003	+ Hunt, Joe 1966	+ Renshaw, William 1983
+ Behr, Karl 1969	+ Hunter, Frank 1961	+ Richards, Vincent 1961
Borg, Bjorn 1987	+ Johnston, Bill 1958	+ Riggs, Bobby 1967
+ Borotra, Jean 1976	+ Jones, Perry 1970	Roche, Tony 1986
+ Bromwich, John 1984	Kelleher, Robert 2000	Rose, Mervyn 2001
+ Brookes, Norman 1977	Kodes, Jan 1990	Rosewall, Ken 1980
+ Brugnon, Jacques 1976	+ Kramer, Jack 1968	Sampras, Pete 2007
+ Budge, Don 1964	+ Lacoste, Rene 1976	Santana, Manuel 1984
+ Campbell, Oliver 1955	+ Larned, William 1956	Savitt, Dick 1976
+ Chace, Malcolm 1961	Larsen, Art 1969	Schroeder, Ted 1966
Chang, Michael 2008	Laver, Rod 1981	+ Sears, Richard 1955
+ Clark, Clarence 1983	Lendl, Ivan 2001	Sedgman, Frank 1979
+ Clark, Joseph 1955	+ Lott, George 1964	Segura, Pancho 1984
+ Clothier, William 1956	Mako, Gene 1973	Seixas, Vic 1971
+ Cochet, Henri 1976	McEnroe, John 1999	+ Shields, Frank 1964
Connors, Jimmy 1998	McGregor, Ken 1999	+ Slocum, Henry 1955
Cooper, Ashley 1991	+ McKinley, Chuck 1986	Smith, Stan 1987
Courier, Jim 2005	+ McLoughlin, Maurice 1957	Stolle, Fred 1985
+ Crawford, Jack 1979	McMillan, Frew 1992	+ Talbert, Bill 1967
+ David, Herman 1998	+ McNeill, Don 1965	+ Tilden, Bill 1959
Davidson, Sven 2007	Mulloy, Gardnar 1972	Trabert, Tony 1970
+ Doeg, John 1962	+ Murray, Lindley 1958	+ Van Ryn, John 1963
+ Doherty, Lawrence 1980	Myrick, Julian 1963	Vilas, Guillermo 1991
+ Doherty, Reginald 1980	Nastase, Ilie 1991	+ Vines, Ellsworth 1962
+ Drobny, Jaroslav 1983	Newcombe, John 1986	+ von Cramm, Gottfried 1977
+ Dwight, James 1955	+ Nielsen, Arthur 1971	+ Ward, Holcombe 1956
Edberg, Stefan 2004	Noah, Yannick 2005	+ Washburn, Watson 1965
Emerson, Roy 1982	Olmedo, Alex 1987	+ Whitman, Malcolm 1955
+ Etchebaster, Pierre 1978	+ Osuna, Rafael 1979	Wilander, Mats 2002
Falkenburg, Bob 1974	+ Parker, Frank 1966	+ Wilding, Anthony 1978
Fraser, Neale 1984	+ Patterson, Gerald 1989	+ Williams, Richard 2nd 1957
+ Garland, Chuck 1969	Patty, Budge 1977	Wood, Sidney 1964

Women

+ Atkinson, Juliette 1974	Goolagong Cawley, Evonne 1988	Osborne duPont, Margaret .1967
Austin, Tracy 1992	Graf, Steffi 2004	+ Palfrey Danzig, Sarah 1963
+ Barger-Wallach, Maud . . .1958	+ Hansell, Ellen 1965	Richey, Nancy 2003
Betz Addie, Pauline 1965	Hard, Darlene 1973	+ Roosevelt, Ellen 1975
+ Bjurstedt Mallory, Molla . . .1958	Hart, Doris 1969	+ Round Little, Dorothy 1986
Bowrey, Lesley Turner 1997	Haydon Jones, Ann 1985	+ Ryan, Elizabeth 1972
Brough Clapp, Louise 1967	Heldman, Gladys 1979	Sabatini, Gabriela 2006
+ Browne, Mary 1957	+ Hotchkiss Wightman, Hazel 1957	Sanchez-Vicario, Arantxa . .2007
Bueno, Maria 1978	+ Jacobs, Helen Hull 1962	+ Sears, Eleanora 1968
+ Cahill, Mabel 1976	King, Billie Jean 1987	Shriver, Pam 2002
Casals, Rosie 1996	+ Lenglen, Suzanne 1978	Smith Court, Margaret 1979
Cheney, Dorothy (Dodo) . . .2004	Mandlikova, Hana 1994	+ Sutton Bundy, May 1956
+ Connolly Brinker, Maureen .1968	+ Marble, Alice 1964	+ Townsend Toulmin, Bertha .1974
+ Dod, Charlotte (Lottie) 1983	+ McKane Godfree, Kitty 1978	Wade, Virginia 1989
+ Douglass Chambers, Dorothy1981	+ Moore, Elisabeth 1971	+ Wagner, Marie 1969
Dürr, Françoise 2003	Mortimer Barrett, Angela . .1993	+ Wills Moody Roark, Helen .1959
Evert, Chris 1995	Novotna, Jana 2005	
Fry Irvin, Shirley 1970	Navratilova, Martina 2000	
Gibson, Althea 1971	+ Nuthall Shoemaker, Betty . .1977	

TRACK & FIELD

National Track & Field Hall of Fame

Established in 1974 by the The Athletics Congress (now USA Track & Field). **Address:** 216 Fort Washington Ave., New York, NY 10032. **Telephone:** (212) 923-1803, ext. 10. **Web:** www.usatf.org.
Eligibility: Nominated athletes must be retired three years and coaches must have coached at least 20 years if retired or 35 years if still coaching. Voting done by 800-member panel made up of Hall of Fame and USA Track & Field officials, Hall of Fame members, current U.S. champions and members of the Track & Field Writers of America. Due to space contraints, the coaches and contributors are not listed below. Members are listed with year of induction; (+) indicates deceased members.

Class of 2007 (5): MEN—**Elvin C. "Ducky" Drake** (coach), **Glenn Morris** (decathlon), **Calvin Smith** (sprints), **George Woods** (shot put). WOMEN—**Jane Frederick** (combined events).

Men

+ Albritton, Dave 1980
  Ashenfelter, Horace 1975
  Banks, Willie 1999
+ Bausch, James 1979
  Beamon, Bob 1977
  Beatty, Jim 1990
  Bell, Earl 2002
  Bell, Greg 1988
+ Boeckmann, Dee 1976
  Boston, Ralph 1974
+ Borican, Jonn 2000
  Bragg, Don 1996
+ Calhoun, Lee 1974
  Campbell, Milt 1989
  Carlos, John 2003
  Carr, Henry 1997
  Cawley, Rex 2006
+ Clark, Ellery 1991
  Conley, Mike 2004
  Connolly, Harold 1984
  Courtney, Tom 1978
+ Cunningham, Glenn 1974
+ Curtis, William 1979
+ Davenport, Willie 1982
  Davis, Glenn 1974
  Davis, Harold 1974
  Davis, Jack 2004
  Davis, Otis 2004
  Dillard, Harrison 1974
  Dumas, Charles 1990
+ Eastman, Ben 2006
  Evans, Lee 1983
+ Ewell, Barney 1986
+ Ewry, Ray 1974
+ Flanagan, John 1975
  Fosbury, Dick 1981
  Foster, Greg 1998
  Fuchs, Jim 2005
+ Gordien, Fortune 1979
  Greene, Charles 1992
+ Hahn, Archie 1983
+ Hardin, Glenn 1978
+ Hayes, Bob 1976
  Held, Bud 1987
  Hines, Jim 1979
+ Houser, Bud 1979
+ Hubbard, DeHart 1979
  James, Larry 2003

  Jenkins, Charlie 1992
  Jenner, Bruce 1980
+ Johnson, Cornelius 1994
  Johnson, Michael 2004
  Johnson, Rafer 1974
  Jones, Hayes 1976
+ Kelley, John A. 1980
  Kingdom, Roger 2005
+ Kiviat, Abel 1985
+ Kraenzlein, Alvin 1974
  Laird, Ron 1986
  Larrabee, Mike 2003
+ Lash, Don 1995
+ Laskau, Henry 1997
  Lewis, Carl 2001
  Lindgren, Gerry 2004
  Liquori, Marty 1995
  Long, Dr. Dallas 1996
  Marsh, Henry 2001
+ Mathias, Bob 1974
  Matson, Randy 1984
  McCluskey, Joe 1996
  McGrath, Matt 2006
+ Meadows, Earle 1996
+ Meredith, Ted 1982
+ Metcalfe, Ralph 1975
+ Milborn, Rod 1993
  Mills, Billy 1976
  Moore, Charles 1999
  Morris, Glenn 2008
  Moore, Tom 1988
  Morrow, Bobby 1975
+ Mortensen, Jess 1992
  Moses, Edwin 1994
+ Myers, Lawrence 1974
  Myricks, Larry 2001
  Nehemiah, Renaldo 1997
  Nieder, Bill 2006
  O'Brien, Dan 2006
  O'Brien, Parry 1974
+ Oerter, Al 1974
+ Osborn, Harold 1974
+ Owens, Jesse 1974
+ Paddock, Charlie 1976
  Patton, Mel 1985
+ Peacock, Eulace 1987
  Penel, John 2004

  Powell, Mike 2005
+ Prefontaine, Steve 1976
  Prinstein, Meyer 2000
+ Ray, Joie 1976
+ Rice, Greg 1977
  Richards, Rev. Bob 1975
  Robinson, Arnie 2000
  Rodgers, Bill 1999
+ Rose, Ralph 1976
  Ryun, Jim 1980
  Salazar, Alberto 2001
  Santee, Wes 2005
+ Scholz, Jackson 1977
  Schul, Bob 1991
  Scott, Steve 2002
  Seagren, Bob 1986
+ Sheppard, Mel 1976
+ Sheridan, Martin 1988
  Shorter, Frank 1989
  Silvester, Jay 1998
  Sime, Dave 1981
+ Simpson, Robert 1974
  Smith, Calvin 2008
  Smith, Tommie 1978
+ Stanfield, Andy 1977
  Steers, Les 1974
  Stones, Dwight 1998
+ Taylor, Frederick Morgan . .2000
+ Tewksbury, Dr. Walter 1996
  Thomas, John 1985
+ Thomson, Earl 1977
+ Thorpe, Jim 1975
+ Tolan, Eddie 1982
  Toomey, Bill 1975
+ Towns, Forrest (Spec) 1976
  Warmerdam, Cornelius 1974
  Whitfield, Mal 1974
  Wilkins, Mac 1993
+ Williams, Archie 1992
  Wohlhuter, Rick 1990
  Wolcott, Fred 2005
  Woodruff, John 1978
  Woods, George 2008
  Wottle, Dave 1982
+ Wykoff, Frank 1977
  Young, George 1981
  Young, Kevin 2006
  Young, Larry 2002

Women

  Ashford, Evelyn 1997
  Brisco, Valerie 1995
  Brown, Earlene 2005
  Cheeseborough, Chandra . . .2000
  Coachman, Alice 1975
+ Copeland, Lillian 1994
+ Didrikson, Babe 1974
+ Faggs, Mae 1976
  Ferrell, Barbara 1988
  Frederick, Jane 2008
+ Griffith Joyner, Florence 1995
+ Hall Adams, Evelyne 1988

  Heritage, Doris Brown 1990
+ Jackson, Nell 1989
  Jennings, Lynn 2006
  Joyner-Kersee, Jackie 2004
  Larrieu Smith, Francie 1998
  Manning-Mims, Madeline . . .1984
  McDaniel, Mildred 1983
  McGuire, Edith 1979
  Ritter, Louise 1995
+ Robinson, Betty 1977
+ Rudolph, Wilma 1974
  Samuelson, Joan 2004

  Schmidt, Kate 1994
  Seidler, Maren 2000
+ Shiley Newhouse, Jean 1993
  Slaney, Mary 2003
+ Stephens, Helen 1975
  Torrence, Gwen 2002
  Tyus, Wyomia 1980
+ Walsh, Stella 1975
  Watson, Martha 1987
  White, Willye 1981

WOMEN

International Women's Sports Hall of Fame

Established in 1980 by the Women's Sports Foundation. **Address:** Women's Sports Foundation, Eisenhower Park, East Meadow, NY 11554. **Telephone:** (516) 542-4700.

Eligibility: Nominees' achievements and commitment to the development of women's sports must be internationally recognized. Athletes are elected in two categories—Pioneer (before 1960) and Contemporary (since 1960). Members are divided below by sport for the sake of easy reference; (*) indicates member inducted in Pioneer category. Coaching nominees must have coached at least 10 years. Members are listed with year of induction; (+) indicates deceased members.

Class of 2008 (4): CONTEMPORARY—**Hisako "Chako" Higuchi** (golf); **Hassiba Boulmerka** (track & field); **Shannon Miller** (gymnastics); COACH—**Sue Enquist** (softball).

Alpine Skiing
Cranz, Christl* 1991
+ Golden Brosnihan, Diana . .1997
Lawrence, Andrea Mead* .1983
Moser-Proell, Annemarie . . .1982

Auto Racing
Guthrie, Janet 1980

Aviation
+ Coleman, Bessie* 1992
+ Earhart, Amelia* 1980
+ Marvingt, Marie* 1987

Badminton
Hashman, Judy Devlin* . . .1995

Baseball
Stone, Toni* 1993

Basketball
Meyers, Ann 1985
Miller, Cheryl 1991
Stewart, Lusia Harris 2005

Bowling
Ladewig, Marion* 1984

Coaches
+ Applebee, Constance 1991
Backus, Sharron 1993
Carver, Chris 2001
Conradt, Judy 1995
Emery, Gail 1997
Franke, Nikki 2002
Green, Tina Sloan 1999
Grossfeld, Muriel 1991
Holum, Diana 1996
Jacket, Barbara 1995
+ Jackson, Nell 1990
Kanakogi, Rusty 1994
Kearney, Beverly 2004
Stringer, C. Vivian 2006
Summitt, Pat Head 1990
VanDerveer, Tara 1998
Vollstedt, Linda 2003
+ Wade, Margaret 1992
Wright, Marjorie 2005

Cycling
Carpenter Phinney, Connie .1990

Diving
Gao, Min 2003
King, Micki 1983
McCormick, Pat* 1984
Riggin, Aileen* 1988

Equestrian
Hartel, Lis 1994

Fencing
Schacherer-Elek, Ilona* . . .1989

Figure Skating
Albright, Tenley* 1983
+ Blanchard, Theresa Weld* .1989
Fleming, Peggy 1981
+ Heiss Jenkins, Carol* 1992
+ Henie, Sonja* 1982
Protopopov, Ludmila 1992
Rodnina, Irena 1988
Scott-King, Barbara Ann* . .1997
Torvill, Jayne 2002
Witt, Katarina* 2005

Golf
Berg, Patty* 1980
Carner, JoAnne 1987
Haynie, Sandra 1999
Hicks, Betty* 1995
Higuchi, Hisako 2008
Jameson, Betty* 1999
Mann, Carol 1982
Rawls, Betsy* 1986
+ Sears, Eleanora 1984
Suggs, Louise* 1987
+ Vare, Glenna Collett* 1981
Whitworth, Kathy 1984
Wright, Mickey 1981
+ Zaharias, Babe Didrikson* .1980

Gymnastics
Caslavska, Vera 1991
Comaneci, Nadia 1990
Korbut, Olga 1982
Latynina, Larysa* 1985
Miller, Shanon 2008
Retton, Mary Lou 1993
Tourischeva, Lyudmila 1987

Orienteering
Kringstad, Annichen 1995

Shooting
Murdock, Margaret 1988

Softball
Joyce, Joan 1989

Speed Skating
+ Klein Outland, Kit* 1993
Young, Sheila 1981

Squash
McKay, Heather* 2003

Swimming
Caulkins, Tracy 1986
+ Chadwick, Florence* 1996
Curtis Cuneo, Ann* 1985
de Varona, Donna 1983
Ederle, Gertrude* 1980
Fraser, Dawn 1985
Gould, Shane 2006
Hogshead-Makar, Nancy . .2004
Holm, Eleanor* 1980
Meagher, Mary T. 1993
Meyer-Reyes, Debbie 1987
Nyad, Diana 2006
Ruiz-Confronto, Tracie 2001

Tennis
Bueno, Maria Esther 2004
+ Connolly, Maureen* 1987
+ Dod, Charlotte (Lottie)* 1986
Evert, Chris 1981
+ Gibson, Althea* 1980
Goolagong Cawley, Evonne 1989
+ Hotchkiss Wightman, Hazel*1986
King, Billie Jean 1980
+ Lenglen, Suzanne* 1984
Navratilova, Martina 1984
Osbourne du Pont,Margaret*1998
+ Sears, Eleanora* 1984
Smith Court, Margaret 1986

Track & Field
Ashford, Evelyn 1997
Blankers-Koen, Fanny* 1982
Boulmerka, Hassiba 2008
Brisco, Valerie 2002
Cheng, Chi 1994
Coachman Davis, Alice* . . .1991
Cuthbert, Betty* 2002
+ Faggs Star, Aeriwentha Mae* 1996
+ Griffith Joyner, Florence . . .1998
Joyner-Kersee, Jackie 2003
Manning Mims, Madeline . .1987
Moutawakel, Nawal El 2006
Nelson, Marjorie Jackson* . .2001
+ Rudolph, Wilma 1980
Samuelson, Joan Benoit . . .1999
+ Stephens, Helen* 1983
Strickland de la Hunty, Shirley*1998
Szewinska, Irena 1992
Tyus, Wyomia 1981
Waitz, Grete 1995
White, Willye 1988
+ Zaharias, Babe Didrikson* .1980

Volleyball
+ Hyman, Flo 1986

Water Skiing
McGuire, Willa Worthington* 1990

RETIRED NUMBERS

Major League Baseball

The New York Yankees have retired the most uniform numbers (14) in the major leagues; followed by the Brooklyn/Los Angeles Dodgers (10), the St. Louis Cardinals (9), the Chicago White Sox, the Pittsburgh Pirates and New York/San Francisco Giants (8). **Jackie Robinson** had his #42 retired by Major League Baseball in 1997. Players who were already wearing the number were allowed to continue to do so. Los Angeles had already retired Robinson's number so he's only listed with the Dodgers below. **Nolan Ryan** has had his number retired by three teams—#34 by Texas and Houston and #30 by California (now Los Angeles Angels of Anaheim). Six players and a manager have had their numbers retired by two teams: **Hank Aaron**—#44 by the Boston/Milwaukee/Atlanta Braves and the Milwaukee Brewers; **Rod Carew**—#29 by Minnesota and California (now Anaheim); **Rollie Fingers**—#34 by Milwaukee and Oakland; **Carlton Fisk**—#27 by Boston and #72 by the Chicago White Sox; **Reggie Jackson**— #9 by the Oakland Athletics and #44 by the New York Yankees; **Frank Robinson**—#20 by Cincinnati and Baltimore; **Casey Stengel**—#37 by the New York Yankees and New York Mets.

Numbers retired in 2008 (2): BOSTON RED SOX—#6 worn by **Johnny Pesky** (1942, 1946-52 with Red Sox); HOUSTON ASTROS—#7 worn by **Craig Biggio** (1988-2007 with Astros).

American League

Two AL teams—the Seattle Mariners and the Toronto Blue Jays—have not retired any numbers. The Blue Jays have a "level of excellence" which includes Joe Carter (#29), Tony Fernandez (#1), Dave Stieb (#11), George Bell (#37), and Cito Gaston (#43). All numbers have been used in recent years, however.

Baltimore Orioles
- 4   Earl Weaver
- 5   Brooks Robinson
- 8   Cal Ripken Jr.
- 20   Frank Robinson
- 22   Jim Palmer
- 33   Eddie Murray

Boston Red Sox
- 1   Bobby Doerr
- 4   Joe Cronin
- 6   Johnny Pesky
- 8   Carl Yastrzemski
- 9   Ted Williams
- 27   Carlton Fisk

Chicago White Sox
- 2   Nellie Fox
- 3   Harold Baines
- 4   Luke Appling
- 9   Minnie Minoso
- 11   Luis Aparicio
- 16   Ted Lyons
- 19   Billy Pierce
- 72   Carlton Fisk

Cleveland Indians
- 3   Earl Averill
- 5   Lou Boudreau
- 14   Larry Doby
- 18   Mel Harder
- 19   Bob Feller
- 21   Bob Lemon
- 455   Fans (# of consecutive sellouts)

Detroit Tigers
- 2   Charlie Gehringer
- 5   Hank Greenberg
- 6   Al Kaline
- 16   Hal Newhouser
- 23   Willie Horton

Kansas City Royals
- 5   George Brett
- 10   Dick Howser
- 20   Frank White

LA Angels of Anaheim
- 11   Jim Fregosi
- 26   Gene Autry
- 29   Rod Carew
- 30   Nolan Ryan
- 50   Jimmie Reese

Minnesota Twins
- 3   Harmon Killebrew
- 6   Tony Oliva
- 14   Kent Hrbek
- 29   Rod Carew
- 34   Kirby Puckett

Oakland Athletics
- 9   Reggie Jackson
- 27   Catfish Hunter
- 34   Rollie Fingers
- 43   Dennis Eckersley

New York Yankees
- 1   Billy Martin
- 3   Babe Ruth
- 4   Lou Gehrig
- 5   Joe DiMaggio
- 7   Mickey Mantle
- 8   Yogi Berra & Bill Dickey
- 9   Roger Maris
- 10   Phil Rizzuto
- 15   Thurman Munson
- 16   Whitey Ford
- 23   Don Mattingly
- 32   Elston Howard
- 37   Casey Stengel
- 44   Reggie Jackson
- 49   Ron Guidry

Tampa Bay Rays
- 12   Wade Boggs

Texas Rangers
- 26   Johnny Oates
- 34   Nolan Ryan

National League

Three NL teams—the Arizona Diamondbacks, Colorado Rockies and Washington Nationals—have not retired any numbers. San Francisco has honored former NY Giants Christy Mathewson and John McGraw even though they played before numbers were worn. As did the Philadelphia Phillies for Grover Cleveland Alexander and Chuck Klein. The Montreal Expos had retired #8 for Gary Carter, #10 for Rusty Staub and Andre Dawson and #30 for Tim Raines but Washington has used those numbers.

Atlanta Braves
- 3   Dale Murphy
- 21   Warren Spahn
- 35   Phil Niekro
- 41   Eddie Mathews
- 44   Hank Aaron

Chicago Cubs
- 10   Ron Santo
- 14   Ernie Banks
- 23   Ryne Sandberg
- 26   Billy Williams

Cincinnati Reds
- 1   Fred Hutchinson
- 5   Johnny Bench
- 8   Joe Morgan
- 10   Sparky Anderson
- 13   Dave Concepcion
- 18   Ted Kluszewski
- 20   Frank Robinson
- 24   Tony Perez

Florida Marlins
- 5   Carl Barger

Houston Astros
- 5   Jeff Bagwell
- 7   Craig Biggio
- 24   Jimmy Wynn
- 25   Jose Cruz
- 32   Jim Umbricht
- 33   Mike Scott
- 34   Nolan Ryan
- 40   Don Wilson
- 49   Larry Dierker

Los Angeles Dodgers
- 1   Pee Wee Reese
- 2   Tommy Lasorda
- 4   Duke Snider
- 19   Jim Gilliam
- 20   Don Sutton
- 24   Walter Alston
- 32   Sandy Koufax
- 39   Roy Campanella
- 42   Jackie Robinson
- 53   Don Drysdale

Milwaukee Brewers
- 4   Paul Molitor
- 19   Robin Yount
- 34   Rollie Fingers
- 44   Hank Aaron

New York Mets
- 14   Gil Hodges
- 37   Casey Stengel
- 41   Tom Seaver

Philadelphia Phillies
- 1   Richie Ashburn
- 14   Jim Bunning
- 20   Mike Schmidt
- 32   Steve Carlton
- 36   Robin Roberts

Pittsburgh Pirates
- 1   Billy Meyer
- 4   Ralph Kiner
- 8   Willie Stargell
- 9   Bill Mazeroski
- 11   Paul Waner
- 20   Pie Traynor
- 21   Roberto Clemente
- 33   Honus Wagner
- 40   Danny Murtaugh

San Diego Padres
- 6   Steve Garvey
- 19   Tony Gwynn
- 31   Dave Winfield
- 35   Randy Jones

San Francisco Giants
- 3   Bill Terry
- 4   Mel Ott
- 11   Carl Hubbell
- 24   Willie Mays
- 27   Juan Marichal
- 30   Orlando Cepeda
- 36   Gaylord Perry
- 44   Willie McCovey

St. Louis Cardinals
- 1   Ozzie Smith
- 2   Red Schoendienst
- 6   Stan Musial
- 9   Enos Slaughter
- 14   Ken Boyer
- 17   Dizzy Dean
- 20   Lou Brock
- 42   Bruce Sutter
- 45   Bob Gibson
- 85   August (Gussie) Busch (age)

National Basketball Association

Boston has retired the most numbers (21) in the NBA, followed by Portland (9); the Rochester/Cincinnati Royals/K.C./Sacramento Kings, Syracuse Nats/Philadelphia 76ers and New York Knicks (8); Detroit, Los Angeles Lakers, Milwaukee and Phoenix Suns have (7); Cleveland and New Jersey have (6). **Wilt Chamberlain** is the only player to have his number retired by three teams: #13 by the LA Lakers, Golden State and Philadelphia; Nine players have had their numbers retired by two teams: **Kareem Abdul-Jabbar**—#33 by LA Lakers and Milwaukee; **Charles Barkley**—#34 by Philadelphia and Phoenix; **Clyde Drexler**—#22 by Houston and Portland; **Julius Erving**—#6 by Philadelphia and #32 by New Jersey; **Michael Jordan**—#23 by Chicago and Miami (in his honor); **Bob Lanier**—#16 by Detroit and Milwaukee; **Pete Maravich**—#7 by Utah and New Orleans; **Oscar Robertson**—#1 by Milwaukee and #14 by Sacramento; **Nate Thurmond**—#42 by Cleveland and Golden State. Miami retired #23 for **Michael Jordan** eventhough he never played for the team.

Numbers retired in 2007-08 (3): SAN ANTONIO—#6 worn by **Avery Johnson** (1990-92, 1992-93, 1994-2001 with Spurs); WASHINGTON—#10 worn by **Earl Monroe** (1967-73 with Baltimore Bullets).

Eastern Conference

Two Eastern teams—the Charlotte Bobcats and Toronto Raptors—have not retired any numbers.

Atlanta Hawks
- 9 Bob Pettit
- 17 Ted Turner
- 21 Dominique Wilkins
- 23 Lou Hudson
- 40 Jason Collier

Chicago Bulls
- 4 Jerry Sloan
- 10 Bob Love
- 23 Michael Jordan
- 33 Scottie Pippen

Cleveland Cavaliers
- 7 Bingo Smith
- 22 Larry Nance
- 25 Mark Price
- 34 Austin Carr
- 42 Nate Thurmond
- 43 Brad Daugherty

Detroit Pistons
- 2 Chuck Daly
- 4 Joe Dumars
- 11 Isiah Thomas
- 15 Vinnie Johnson
- 16 Bob Lanier
- 21 Dave Bing
- 40 Bill Laimbeer

Boston Celtics
- 1 Walter A. Brown
- 2 Red Auerbach
- 3 Dennis Johnson
- 6 Bill Russell
- 10 Jo Jo White
- 14 Bob Cousy
- 15 Tom Heinsohn
- 16 Tom (Satch) Sanders
- 17 John Havlicek
- 18 Dave Cowens
- 19 Don Nelson
- 21 Bill Sharman
- 22 Ed Macauley
- 23 Frank Ramsey
- 24 Sam Jones
- 25 K.C. Jones
- 31 Cedric Maxwell
- 32 Kevin McHale
- 33 Larry Bird
- 35 Reggie Lewis
- 00 Robert Parish
- **Loscy** Jim Loscutoff (#18)
- **Radio mic** Johnny Most

Indiana Pacers
- 30 George McGinnis
- 31 Reggie Miller
- 34 Mel Daniels
- 35 Roger Brown
- 529 Bob "Slick" Leonard

Miami Heat
- 23 Michael Jordan

Milwaukee Bucks
- 1 Oscar Robertson
- 2 Junior Bridgeman
- 4 Sidney Moncrief
- 14 Jon McGlocklin
- 16 Bob Lanier
- 32 Brian Winters
- 33 Kareem Abdul-Jabbar

New York Knicks
- 10 Walt Frazier
- 12 Dick Barnett
- 15 Dick McGuire & Earl Monroe
- 19 Willis Reed
- 22 Dave DeBusschere
- 24 Bill Bradley
- 33 Patrick Ewing
- 613 Red Holzman

New Jersey Nets
- 3 Drazen Petrovic
- 4 Wendell Ladner
- 23 John Williamson
- 25 Bill Melchionni
- 32 Julius Erving
- 52 Buck Williams

Orlando Magic
- 6 Fans ("Sixth Man")

Philadelphia 76ers
- 2 Moses Malone
- 6 Julius Erving
- 10 Maurice Cheeks
- 13 Wilt Chamberlain
- 15 Hal Greer
- 24 Bobby Jones
- 32 Billy Cunningham
- 34 Charles Barkley
- **P.A. mic** Dave Zinkoff

Washington Wizards
- 10 Earl Monroe
- 11 Elvin Hayes
- 25 Gus Johnson
- 41 Wes Unseld

Western Conference

Two Western teams—the Los Angeles Clippers and Memphis Grizzlies—have not retired any numbers.

Dallas Mavericks
- 15 Brad Davis
- 22 Rolando Blackman

Denver Nuggets
- 2 Alex English
- 33 David Thompson
- 40 Byron Beck
- 44 Dan Issel
- 432 Doug Moe

Golden St. Warriors
- 13 Wilt Chamberlain
- 14 Tom Meschery
- 16 Al Attles
- 24 Rick Barry
- 42 Nate Thurmond

Houston Rockets
- 22 Clyde Drexler
- 23 Calvin Murphy
- 24 Moses Malone
- 34 Hakeem Olajuwon
- 45 Rudy Tomjanovich

Los Angeles Lakers
- 13 Wilt Chamberlain
- 22 Elgin Baylor
- 25 Gail Goodrich
- 32 Magic Johnson
- 33 Kareem Abdul-Jabbar
- 42 James Worthy
- 44 Jerry West
- **Radio mic** Chick Hearn

Minn. Timberwolves
- 2 Malik Sealy

New Orleans Hornets
- 7 Pete Maravich
- 13 Bobby Phills

Phoenix Suns
- 5 Dick Van Arsdale
- 6 Walter Davis
- 7 Kevin Johnson
- 9 Dan Majerle
- 24 Tom Chambers
- 33 Alvan Adams
- 34 Charles Barkley
- 42 Connie Hawkins
- 44 Paul Westphal
- 832 Cotton Fitzsimmons

Portland Trail Blazers
- 1 Larry Weinberg
- 13 Dave Twardzik
- 14 Lionel Hollins
- 15 Larry Steele
- 20 Maurice Lucas
- 22 Clyde Drexler
- 32 Bill Walton
- 36 Lloyd Neal
- 45 Geoff Petrie
- 77 Jack Ramsay

Sacramento Kings
- 1 Nate Archibald
- 2 Mitch Richmond
- 6 Fans ("Sixth Man")
- 11 Bob Davies
- 12 Maurice Stokes
- 14 Oscar Robertson
- 27 Jack Twyman
- 44 Sam Lacey

San Antonio Spurs
- 6 Avery Johnson
- 13 James Silas
- 32 Sean Elliott
- 44 George Gervin
- 50 David Robinson
- 00 Johnny Moore

Oklahoma City Thunder
- 1 Gus Williams
- 10 Nate McMillan
- 19 Lenny Wilkens
- 24 Spencer Haywood
- 32 Fred Brown
- 43 Jack Sikma
- **Radio mic** Bob Blackburn

Utah Jazz
- 1 Frank Layden
- 4 Adrian Dantley
- 7 Pete Maravich
- 12 John Stockton
- 14 Jeff Hornacek
- 32 Karl Malone
- 35 Darrell Griffith
- 53 Mark Eaton

Retired Numbers (Cont.)
National Football League

The Chicago Bears have retired the most uniform numbers (13) in the NFL; followed by the New York Giants (11); San Francisco (9); the Dallas Texans/Kansas City Chiefs, Boston-New England Patriots (8); the Baltimore-Indianapolis Colts (7); Detroit and Philadelphia (6); Cleveland (5). No player has ever had his number retired by more than one NFL team.

Numbers retired in 2007-08 (2): ST. LOUIS—#28 worn by **Marshall Faulk** (1999-2005 with Rams); SAN FRANCISCO—#8 worn by Steve Young (1987-99 with 49ers).

AFC

Four AFC teams—the Baltimore Ravens, Houston Texans, Jacksonville Jaguars and Oakland Raiders—have not retired any numbers.

Buffalo Bills		**Indianapolis Colts**		**Miami Dolphins**		**New York Jets**	
12	Jim Kelly	19	Johnny Unitas	12	Bob Griese	12	Joe Namath
		22	Buddy Young	13	Dan Marino	13	Don Maynard
Cincinnati Bengals		24	Lenny Moore	39	Larry Csonka	73	Joe Klecko
54	Bob Johnson	70	Art Donovan				
		77	Jim Parker	**New England Patriots**		**Pittsburgh Steelers**	
Cleveland Browns		82	Raymond Berry	20	Gino Cappelletti	70	Ernie Stautner
14	Otto Graham	89	Gino Marchetti	40	Mike Haynes		
32	Jim Brown			56	Andre Tippett	**San Diego Chargers**	
45	Ernie Davis	**Kansas City Chiefs**		57	Steve Nelson	14	Dan Fouts
46	Don Fleming	3	Jan Stenerud	73	John Hannah	19	Lance Alworth
76	Lou Groza	16	Len Dawson	78	Bruce Armstrong		
		28	Abner Haynes	79	Jim Lee Hunt	**Tennessee Titans**	
Denver Broncos		33	Stone Johnson	89	Bob Dee	1	Warren Moon
7	John Elway	36	Mack Lee Hill			34	Earl Campbell
18	Frank Tripucka	63	Willie Lanier			43	Jim Norton
44	Floyd Little	78	Bobby Bell			63	Mike Munchak
		86	Buck Buchanan			65	Elvin Bethea
						74	Bruce Matthews

NFC

Dallas is the only NFC team that hasn't officially retired any numbers. The Falcons haven't issued uniform #10 (Steve Bartkowski) and #78 (Mike Kenn) since those players retired. The Cowboys have a "Ring of Honor" at Texas Stadium that includes 15 players, one coach and one president/GM—Troy Aikman, Tony Dorsett, Cliff Harris, Bob Hayes, Chuck Howley, Michael Irvin, Lee Roy Jordan, Tom Landry, Bob Lilly, Don Meredith, Don Perkins, Mel Renfro, Tex Schramm, Emmitt Smith, Roger Staubach, Randy White and Rayfield Wright.

Arizona Cardinals		**Detroit Lions**		**New York Giants**		**St. Louis Rams**	
8	Larry Wilson	7	Dutch Clark	1	Ray Flaherty	7	Bob Waterfield
40	Pat Tillman	20	Barry Sanders	4	Tuffy Leemans	28	Marshall Faulk
77	Stan Mauldin	22	Bobby Layne	7	Mel Hein	29	Eric Dickerson
88	J.V. Cain	37	Doak Walker	11	Phil Simms	74	Merlin Olsen
99	Marshall Goldberg	56	Joe Schmidt	14	Y.A. Tittle	78	Jackie Slater
		85	Chuck Hughes	16	Frank Gifford	85	Jack Youngblood
Atlanta Falcons		88	Charlie Sanders	32	Al Blozis		
31	William Andrews			40	Joe Morrison	**San Francisco 49ers**	
57	Jeff Van Note	**Green Bay Packers**		42	Charlie Conerly	8	Steve Young
60	Tommy Nobis	3	Tony Canadeo	50	Ken Strong	12	John Brodie
		14	Don Hutson	56	Lawrence Taylor	16	Joe Montana
Carolina Panthers		15	Bart Starr			34	Joe Perry
51	Sam Mills	66	Ray Nitschke	**Philadelphia Eagles**		37	Jimmy Johnson
		92	Reggie White	15	Steve Van Buren	39	Hugh McElhenny
Chicago Bears				40	Tom Brookshier	42	Ronnie Lott
3	Bronko Nagurski	**Minnesota Vikings**		44	Pete Retzlaff	70	Charlie Krueger
5	George McAfee	10	Fran Tarkenton	60	Chuck Bednarik	73	Leo Nomellini
7	George Halas	53	Mick Tingelhoff	70	Al Wistert	79	Bob St. Clair
28	Willie Galimore	70	Jim Marshall	92	Reggie White	87	Dwight Clark
34	Walter Payton	77	Korey Stringer	99	Jerome Brown		
40	Gale Sayers	80	Cris Carter			**Seattle Seahawks**	
41	Brian Piccolo	88	Alan Page			12	Fans ("12th Man")
42	Sid Luckman					80	Steve Largent
51	Dick Butkus	**New Orleans Saints**					
56	Bill Hewitt	31	Jim Taylor			**Tampa Bay Buccaneers**	
61	Bill George	81	Doug Atkins			63	Lee Roy Selmon
66	Bulldog Turner						
77	Red Grange					**Washington Redskins**	
						33	Sammy Baugh

National Hockey League

The Montreal Canadiens have retired the most uniform numbers (14) in the NHL; followed by Boston (10); NY Rangers (7); Buffalo, Detroit and N.Y. Islanders (6). Following his retirement in 1999, the NHL announced that the league would retire **Wayne Gretzky**'s #99. Five other players have had their numbers retired by two teams: **Gordie Howe**—#9 by Detroit and Hartford; **Bobby Hull**—#9 by Chicago and Winnipeg (now Phoenix); **Ray Bourque**—#77 by Boston and Colorado; **Mark Messier**—#11 by Edmonton and NY Rangers; **Patrick Roy**—#33 by Montreal and Colorado.

Numbers retired in 2008-09 (2): NY RANGERS—#9 worn by **Adam Graves** (1991-2001 with Rangers) and **Andy Bathgate** (1952-63 with Rangers); #3 worn by **Harry Howell** (1952-69 with Rangers); VANCOUVER—#16 worn by **Trevor Linden** (1988-97, 2001-08 with Canucks).

Eastern Conference

Three Eastern teams—the Atlanta Thrashers, Florida Panthers, and Tampa Bay Lightning—have not retired any numbers. The Hartford Whalers had retired three numbers: #2 Rick Ley, #9 Gordie Howe and #19 John McKenzie.

Boston Bruins
- 2 Eddie Shore
- 3 Lionel Hitchman
- 4 Bobby Orr
- 5 Dit Clapper
- 7 Phil Esposito
- 8 Cam Neely
- 9 John Bucyk
- 15 Milt Schmidt
- 24 Terry O'Reilly
- 77 Ray Bourque

Buffalo Sabres
- 2 Tim Horton
- 7 Rick Martin
- 11 Gilbert Perreault
- 14 Rene Robert
- 16 Pat LaFontaine
- 18 Danny Gare

Carolina Hurricanes
- 10 Ron Francis

Montreal Canadiens
- 1 Jacques Plante
- 2 Doug Harvey
- 4 Jean Beliveau
- 5 Bernard Geoffrion
- 9 Howie Morenz
- 9 Maurice Richard
- 10 Guy Lafleur
- 12 Dickie Moore
-    Yvan Cournoyer
- 16 Henri Richard
- 18 Serge Savard
- 19 Larry Robinson
- 23 Bob Gainey
- 29 Ken Dryden

New Jersey Devils
- 3 Ken Daneyko
- 4 Scott Stevens

New York Islanders
- 5 Denis Potvin
- 9 Clark Gillies
- 19 Bryan Trottier
- 22 Mike Bossy
- 23 Bob Nystrom
- 31 Billy Smith

New York Rangers
- 1 Eddie Giacomin
- 2 Brian Leetch
- 3 Harry Howell
- 7 Rod Gilbert
- 9 Adam Graves
-    Andy Bathgate
- 11 Mark Messier
- 35 Mike Richter

Ottawa Senators
- 8 Frank Finnigan

Philadelphia Flyers
- 1 Bernie Parent
- 4 Barry Ashbee
- 7 Bill Barber
- 16 Bobby Clarke

Pittsburgh Penguins
- 21 Michel Briere
- 66 Mario Lemieux

Toronto Maple Leafs
- 5 Bill Barilko
- 6 Ace Bailey

Washington Capitals
- 5 Rod Langway
- 7 Yvon Labre
- 11 Mike Gartner
- 32 Dale Hunter

Western Conference

Four Western teams—the Columbus Blue Jackets, Anaheim Ducks, Nashville Predators and San Jose Sharks—have not retired any numbers. Note, the Quebec Nordiques retired the numbers of J.C. Tremblay (3), Marc Tardif (8) and Michel Goulet (16) but these numbers have been worn since the team moved to Colorado. Detroit has not officially retired the numbers of Larry Aurie (6) and Vladimir Konstantinov (16) but has kept them "out of circulation." Similarly, St. Louis has not officially retired the number of Doug Wickenheiser (14) but has kept it out of circulation since his death in 1999.

Calgary Flames
- 9 Lanny McDonald
- 30 Mike Vernon

Chicago Blackhawks
- 1 Glenn Hall
- 9 Bobby Hull
- 18 Denis Savard
- 21 Stan Mikita
- 35 Tony Esposito

Colorado Avalanche
- 33 Patrick Roy
- 77 Ray Bourque

Dallas Stars
- 7 Neal Broten
- 8 Bill Goldsworthy
- 19 Bill Masterton

Detroit Red Wings
- 1 Terry Sawchuk
- 7 Ted Lindsay
- 9 Gordie Howe
- 10 Alex Delvecchio
- 12 Sid Abel
- 19 Steve Yzerman

Edmonton Oilers
- 3 Al Hamilton
- 7 Paul Coffey
- 11 Mark Messier
- 17 Jari Kurri
- 31 Grant Fuhr
- 99 Wayne Gretzky

Los Angeles Kings
- 16 Marcel Dionne
- 18 Dave Taylor
- 20 Luc Robitaille
- 30 Rogie Vachon
- 99 Wayne Gretzky

Minnesota Wild
- 1 Fans

Phoenix Coyotes
- 9 Bobby Hull
- 25 Thomas Steen

St. Louis Blues
- 2 Al MacInnis
- 3 Bob Gassoff
- 8 Barclay Plager
- 11 Brian Sutter
- 16 Brett Hull
- 24 Bernie Federko

Vancouver Canucks
- 12 Stan Smyl
- 16 Trevor Linden

AWARDS

Associated Press Athletes of the Year

Selected annually by AP newspaper sports editors since 1931.

Male

The top 5 vote-getters: 1. **Tom Brady**, football, 51 points; 2. **Roger Federer**, tennis, 33; 3. **Tiger Woods**, golf, 29; 4. **Barry Bonds**, baseball, 8; 5. **Peyton Manning**, football and **Josh Beckett**, baseball, 7.

Multiple winners: Lance Armstrong and Tiger Woods (4); Michael Jordan (3); Don Budge, Sandy Koufax, Carl Lewis, Joe Montana and Byron Nelson (2).

Year		Year		Year	
1931	**Pepper Martin**, baseball	1941	**Joe DiMaggio**, baseball	1951	**Dick Kazmaier**, col. football
1932	**Gene Sarazen**, golf	1942	**Frank Sinkwich**, col. football	1952	**Bob Mathias**, track
1933	**Carl Hubbell**, baseball	1943	**Gunder Haegg**, track	1953	**Ben Hogan**, golf
1934	**Dizzy Dean**, baseball	1944	**Byron Nelson**, golf	1954	**Willie Mays**, baseball
1935	**Joe Louis**, boxing	1945	**Byron Nelson**, golf	1955	**Hopalong Cassady**, col. football
1936	**Jesse Owens**, track	1946	**Glenn Davis**, college football	1956	**Mickey Mantle**, baseball
1937	**Don Budge**, tennis	1947	**Johnny Lujack**, col. football	1957	**Ted Williams**, baseball
1938	**Don Budge**, tennis	1948	**Lou Boudreau**, baseball	1958	**Herb Elliott**, track
1939	**Nile Kinnick**, college football	1949	**Leon Hart**, college football	1959	**Ingemar Johansson**, boxing
1940	**Tom Harmon**, college football	1950	**Jim Konstanty**, baseball		

Awards (Cont.)

Year		Year		Year	
1960	**Rafer Johnson**, track	1976	**Bruce Jenner**, track	1992	**Michael Jordan**, pro basketball
1961	**Roger Maris**, baseball	1977	**Steve Cauthen**, horse racing	1993	**Michael Jordan**, pro basketball
1962	**Maury Wills**, baseball	1978	**Ron Guidry**, baseball	1994	**George Foreman**, boxing
1963	**Sandy Koufax**, baseball	1979	**Willie Stargell**, baseball	1995	**Cal Ripken Jr.**, baseball
1964	**Don Schollander**, swimming	1980	**U.S. Olympic hockey team**	1996	**Michael Johnson**, track
1965	**Sandy Koufax**, baseball	1981	**John McEnroe**, tennis	1997	**Tiger Woods**, golf
1966	**Frank Robinson**, baseball	1982	**Wayne Gretzky**, hockey	1998	**Mark McGwire**, baseball
1967	**Carl Yastrzemski**, baseball	1983	**Carl Lewis**, track	1999	**Tiger Woods**, golf
1968	**Denny McLain**, baseball	1984	**Carl Lewis**, track	2000	**Tiger Woods**, golf
1969	**Tom Seaver**, baseball	1985	**Dwight Gooden**, baseball	2001	**Barry Bonds**, baseball
1970	**George Blanda**, pro football	1986	**Larry Bird**, pro basketball	2002	**Lance Armstrong**, cycling
1971	**Lee Trevino**, golf	1987	**Ben Johnson**, track	2003	**Lance Armstrong**, cycling
1972	**Mark Spitz**, swimming	1988	**Orel Hershiser**, baseball	2004	**Lance Armstrong**, cycling
1973	**O.J. Simpson**, pro football	1989	**Joe Montana**, pro football	2005	**Lance Armstrong**, cycling
1974	**Muhammad Ali**, boxing	1990	**Joe Montana**, pro football	2006	**Tiger Woods**, golf
1975	**Fred Lynn**, baseball	1991	**Michael Jordan**, pro basketball	2007	**Tom Brady**, football

Female

The top 5 vote-getters: 1. **Lorena Ochoa**, golf, 71 points; 2. **Justine Henin**, tennis, 18; 3. **Paula Radcliffe**, track, 16; 4. **Candace Parker**, basketball, 14; 5. **Allyson Felix**, track, 8.

Multiple winners: Babe Didrikson Zaharias (6); Chris Evert (4); Patty Berg, Maureen Connolly and Annika Sorenstam (3); Tracy Austin, Althea Gibson, Billie Jean King, Nancy Lopez, Alice Marble, Martina Navratilova, Lorena Ochoa, Wilma Rudolph, Monica Seles, Kathy Whitworth and Mickey Wright (2).

Year		Year		Year	
1931	**Helene Madison**, swimming	1957	**Althea Gibson**, tennis	1983	**Martina Navratilova**, tennis
1932	**Babe Didrikson**, track	1958	**Althea Gibson**, tennis	1984	**Mary Lou Retton**, gymnastics
1933	**Helen Jacobs**, tennis	1959	**Maria Bueno**, tennis	1985	**Nancy Lopez**, golf
1934	**Virginia Van Wie**, golf	1960	**Wilma Rudolph**, track	1986	**Martina Navratilova**, tennis
1935	**Helen Wills Moody**, tennis	1961	**Wilma Rudolph**, track	1987	**Jackie Joyner-Kersee**, track
1936	**Helen Stephens**, track	1962	**Dawn Fraser**, swimming	1988	**Florence Griffith Joyner**, track
1937	**Katherine Rawls**, swimming	1963	**Mickey Wright**, golf	1989	**Steffi Graf**, tennis
1938	**Patty Berg**, golf	1964	**Mickey Wright**, golf	1990	**Beth Daniel**, golf
1939	**Alice Marble**, tennis	1965	**Kathy Whitworth**, golf	1991	**Monica Seles**, tennis
1940	**Alice Marble**, tennis	1966	**Kathy Whitworth**, golf	1992	**Monica Seles**, tennis
1941	**Betty Hicks Newell**, golf	1967	**Billie Jean King**, tennis	1993	**Sheryl Swoopes**, basketball
1942	**Gloria Callen**, swimming	1968	**Peggy Fleming**, skating	1994	**Bonnie Blair**, speed skating
1943	**Patty Berg**, golf	1969	**Debbie Meyer**, swimming	1995	**Rebecca Lobo**, col. basketball
1944	**Ann Curtis**, swimming	1970	**Chi Cheng**, track	1996	**Amy Van Dyken**, swimming
1945	**Babe Didrikson Zaharias**, golf	1971	**Evonne Goolagong**, tennis	1997	**Martina Hingis**, tennis
1946	**Babe Didrikson Zaharias**, golf	1972	**Olga Korbut**, gymnastics	1998	**Se Ri Pak**, golf
1947	**Babe Didrikson Zaharias**, golf	1973	**Billie Jean King**, tennis	1999	**U.S. Soccer Team**
1948	**Fanny Blankers-Koen**, track	1974	**Chris Evert**, tennis	2000	**Marion Jones**, track
1949	**Marlene Bauer**, golf	1975	**Chris Evert**, tennis	2001	**Jennifer Capriati**, tennis
1950	**Babe Didrikson Zaharias**, golf	1976	**Nadia Comaneci**, gymnastics	2002	**Serena Williams**, tennis
1951	**Maureen Connolly**, tennis	1977	**Chris Evert**, tennis	2003	**Annika Sorenstam**, golf
1952	**Maureen Connolly**, tennis	1978	**Nancy Lopez**, golf	2004	**Annika Sorenstam**, golf
1953	**Maureen Connolly**, tennis	1979	**Tracy Austin**, tennis	2005	**Annika Sorenstam**, golf
1954	**Babe Didrikson Zaharias**, golf	1980	**Chris Evert Lloyd**, tennis	2006	**Lorena Ochoa**, golf
1955	**Patty Berg**, golf	1981	**Tracy Austin**, tennis	2007	**Lorena Ochoa**, golf
1956	**Pat McCormick**, diving	1982	**Mary Decker Tabb**, track		

USOC Sportsman & Sportswoman of the Year

To the outstanding overall male and female athletes from within the U.S. Olympic Committee member organizations. Winners are chosen from nominees of the national governing bodies for Olympic and Pan American Games and affiliated organizations. Voting is done by members of the national media, USOC board of directors and Athletes' Advisory Council.

Sportsman

Multiple winners: Lance Armstrong (4); Eric Heiden and Michael Johnson (3); Matt Biondi and Greg Louganis (2).

Year		Year		Year	
1974	**Jim Bolding**, track	1986	**Matt Biondi**, swimming	1998	**Jonny Moseley**, skiing
1975	**Clint Jackson**, boxing	1987	**Greg Louganis**, diving	1999	**Lance Armstrong**, cycling
1976	**John Naber**, swimming	1988	**Matt Biondi**, swimming	2000	**Rulon Gardner**, wrestling
1977	**Eric Heiden**, speed skating	1989	**Roger Kingdom**, track	2001	**Lance Armstrong**, cycling
1978	**Bruce Davidson**, equestrian	1990	**John Smith**, wrestling	2002	**Lance Armstrong**, cycling
1979	**Eric Heiden**, speed skating	1991	**Carl Lewis**, track	2003	**Lance Armstrong**, cycling
1980	**Eric Heiden**, speed skating	1992	**Pablo Morales**, swimming	2004	**Michael Phelps**, swimming
1981	**Scott Hamilton**, fig. skating	1993	**Michael Johnson**, track	2005	**Hunter Kemper**, triathlon
1982	**Greg Louganis**, diving	1994	**Dan Jansen**, speed skating	2006	**Joey Cheek**, speedskating
1983	**Rick McKinney**, archery	1995	**Michael Johnson**, track	2007	**Tyson Gay**, track
1984	**Edwin Moses**, track	1996	**Michael Johnson**, track		
1985	**Willie Banks**, track	1997	**Pete Sampras**, tennis		

Sportswoman

Multiple winners: Bonnie Blair, Tracy Caulkins, Katie Hoff, Jackie Joyner-Kersee, Picabo Street and Sheila Young Ochowicz (2).

Year		Year		Year	
1974	**Shirley Babashoff**, swimming	1985	**Mary Decker Slaney**, track	1997	**Tara Lipinski**, figure skating
1975	**Kathy Heddy**, swimming	1986	**Jackie Joyner-Kersee**, track	1998	**Picabo Street**, skiing
1976	**Sheila Young**, speedskating	1987	**Jackie Joyner-Kersee**, track	1999	**Jenny Thompson**, swimming
1977	**Linda Fratianne**, fig. skating	1988	**Florence Griffith Joyner**, track	2000	**Marion Jones**, track
1978	**Tracy Caulkins**, swimming	1989	**Janet Evans**, swimming	2001	**Jennifer Capriati**, tennis
1979	**Sippy Woodhead**, swimming	1990	**Lynn Jennings**, track	2002	**Sarah Hughes**, figure skating
1980	**Beth Heiden**, speed skating	1991	**Kim Zmeskal**, gymnastics	2003	**Michelle Kwan**, figure skating
1981	**Sheila Ochowicz**, speed skating & cycling	1992	**Bonnie Blair**, speed skating	2004	**Carly Patterson**, gymnastics
1982	**Melanie Smith**, equestrian	1993	**Gail Devers**, track	2005	**Katie Hoff**, swimming
1983	**Tamara McKinney**, skiing	1994	**Bonnie Blair**, speed skating	2006	**Hannah Teter**, snowboarding
1984	**Tracy Caulkins**, swimming	1995	**Picabo Street**, skiing	2007	**Katie Hoff**, swimming
		1996	**Amy Van Dyken**, swimming		

UPI International Athletes of the Year

Selected annually by United Press International's European newspaper sports editors from 1974-95.

Male

Multiple winners: Sebastian Coe, Alberto Juantorena and Carl Lewis (2).

Year		Year		Year	
1974	**Muhammad Ali**, boxing	1982	**Daley Thompson**, track	1990	**Stefan Edberg**, tennis
1975	**Joao Oliveira**, track	1983	**Carl Lewis**, track	1991	**Sergei Bubka**, track
1976	**Alberto Juantorena**, track	1984	**Carl Lewis**, track	1992	**Kevin Young**, track
1977	**Alberto Juantorena**, track	1985	**Steve Cram**, track	1993	**Miguel Indurain**, cycling
1978	**Henry Rono**, track	1986	**Diego Maradona**, soccer	1994	**Johann Olav Koss**, speed skating
1979	**Sebastian Coe**, track	1987	**Ben Johnson**, track	1995	**Jonathan Edwards**, track
1980	**Eric Heiden**, speed skating	1988	**Matt Biondi**, swimming	1996	discontinued
1981	**Sebastian Coe**, track	1989	**Boris Becker**, tennis		

Female

Multiple winners: Nadia Comaneci, Steffi Graf, Marita Koch and Monica Seles (2).

Year		Year		Year	
1974	**Irena Szewinska**, track	1982	**Marita Koch**, track	1990	**Merlene Ottey**, track
1975	**Nadia Comaneci**, gymnastics	1983	**Jarmila Kratochvilova**, track	1991	**Monica Seles**, tennis
1976	**Nadia Comaneci**, gymnastics	1984	**Martina Navratilova**, tennis	1992	**Monica Seles**, tennis
1977	**Rosie Ackermann**, track	1985	**Mary Decker Slaney**, track	1993	**Wang Junxia**, track
1978	**Tracy Caulkins**, swimming	1986	**Heike Drechsler**, track	1994	**Le Jingyi**, swimming
1979	**Marita Koch**, track	1987	**Steffi Graf**, tennis	1995	**Gwen Torrence**, track
1980	**Hanni Wenzel**, alpine skiing	1988	**Florence Griffith Joyner**, track	1996	discontinued
1981	**Chris Evert Lloyd**, tennis	1989	**Steffi Graf**, tennis		

Honda-Broderick Cup

To the outstanding collegiate woman athlete of the year in NCAA competition. Winner is chosen from nominees in each of the NCAA's 10 competitive sports. Final voting is done by member athletic directors. Award is named after founder and sportswear manufacturer Thomas Broderick.

Multiple winner: Tracy Caulkins (2).

Year			Year		
1977	**Lucy Harris**, Delta St	basketball	1993	**Lisa Fernandez**, UCLA	softball
1978	**Ann Meyers**, UCLA	basketball	1994	**Mia Hamm**, North Carolina	soccer
1979	**Nancy Lieberman**, Old Dominion	basketball	1995	**Rebecca Lobo**, UConn	basketball
1980	**Julie Shea**, N.C. State	track & field	1996	**Jennifer Rizzotti**, UConn	basketball
1981	**Jill Sterkel**, Texas	swimming	1997	**Cindy Daws**, Notre Dame	soccer
1982	**Tracy Caulkins**, Florida	swimming	1998	**Chamique Holdsclaw**, Tennessee	basketball
1983	**Deitre Collins**, Hawaii	volleyball	1999	**Misty May**, Long Beach St.	volleyball
1984	**Tracy Caulkins**, Florida & **Cheryl Miller**, USC	swimming basketball	2000	**Cristina Teuscher**, Columbia	swimming
1985	**Jackie Joyner**, UCLA	track & field	2001	**Jackie Stiles**, SW Missouri St.	basketball
1986	**Kamie Ethridge**, Texas	basketball	2002	**Angela Williams**, USC	track
1987	**Mary T. Meagher**, California	swimming	2003	**Natasha Watley**, UCLA	softball
1988	**Teresa Weatherspoon**, La. Tech	basketball	2004	**Tara Kirk**, Stanford	swimming
1989	**Vicki Huber**, Villanova	track	2005	**Ogonna Nnamani**, Stanford	volleyball
1990	**Suzy Favor**, Wisconsin	track	2006	**Christine Sinclair**, Portland	soccer
1991	**Dawn Staley**, Virginia	basketball	2007	**Sarah Pavan**, Nebraska	volleyball
1992	**Missy Marlowe**, Utah	gymnastics	2008	**Candace Parker**, Tennessee	basketball

Awards (Cont.)

Flo Hyman Award

Presented annually since 1987 by the Women's Sports Foundation for "exemplifying dignity, spirit and commitment to excellence" and named in honor of the late captain of the 1984 U.S. Women's Volleyball team. Voting by WSF members.

Year		Year		Year	
1987	**Martina Navratilova**, tennis	1993	**Lynette Woodard**, basketball	1999	**Bonnie Blair**, speed skating
1988	**Jackie Joyner-Kersee**, track	1994	**Patty Sheehan**, golf	2000	**Monica Seles**, tennis
1989	**Evelyn Ashford**, track	1995	**Mary Lou Retton**, gymnastics	2001	**Lisa Leslie**, basketball
1990	**Chris Evert**, tennis	1996	**Donna de Varona**, swimming	2002	**Dot Richardson**, softball
1991	**Diana Golden**, skiing	1997	**Billie Jean King**, tennis	2003	**Nawal El Moutawakel**, track
1992	**Nancy Lopez**, golf	1998	**Nadia Comaneci**, gymnastics	2004	**Kristi Yamaguchi**, fig. skating

James E. Sullivan Memorial Award

Presented annually by the Amateur Athletic Union since 1930. The Sullivan Award is named after the former AAU president and given to the athlete who, "by his or her performance, example and influence as an amateur, has done the most during the year to advance the cause of sportsmanship."

Year		Year		Year	
1930	**Bobby Jones**, golf	1957	**Bobby Morrow**, track	1984	**Greg Louganis**, diving
1931	**Barney Berlinger**, track	1958	**Glenn Davis**, track	1985	**Joan B. Samuelson**, track
1932	**Jim Bausch**, track	1959	**Parry O'Brien**, track	1986	**Jackie Joyner-Kersee**, track
1933	**Glenn Cunningham**, track	1960	**Rafer Johnson**, track	1987	**Jim Abbott**, baseball
1934	**Bill Bonthron**, track	1961	**Wilma Rudolph**, track	1988	**Florence Griffith Joyner**, track
1935	**Lawson Little**, golf	1962	**Jim Beatty**, track	1989	**Janet Evans**, swimming
1936	**Glenn Morris**, track	1963	**John Pennel**, track	1990	**John Smith**, wrestling
1937	**Don Budge**, tennis	1964	**Don Schollander**, swimming	1991	**Mike Powell**, track
1938	**Don Lash**, track	1965	**Bill Bradley**, basketball	1992	**Bonnie Blair**, speed skating
1939	**Joe Burk**, rowing	1966	**Jim Ryun**, track	1993	**Charlie Ward**, football
1940	**Greg Rice**, track	1967	**Randy Matson**, track	1994	**Dan Jansen**, speed skating
1941	**Leslie MacMitchell**, track	1968	**Debbie Meyer**, swimming	1995	**Bruce Baumgartner**, wrestling
1942	**Cornelius Warmerdam**, track	1969	**Bill Toomey**, track	1996	**Michael Johnson**, track
1943	**Gilbert Dodds**, track	1970	**John Kinsella**, swimming	1997	**Peyton Manning**, football
1944	**Ann Curtis**, swimming	1971	**Mark Spitz**, swimming	1998	**Chamique Holdsclaw**, basketball
1945	**Doc Blanchard**, football	1972	**Frank Shorter**, track		
1946	**Arnold Tucker**, football	1973	**Bill Walton**, basketball	1999	**Coco and Kelly Miller**, basketball
1947	**John B. Kelly, Jr.**, rowing	1974	**Rich Wohlhuter**, track		
1948	**Bob Mathias**, track	1975	**Tim Shaw**, swimming	2000	**Rulon Gardner**, wrestling
1949	**Dick Button**, skating	1976	**Bruce Jenner**, track	2001	**Michelle Kwan**, figure skating
1950	**Fred Wilt**, track	1977	**John Naber**, swimming	2002	**Sarah Hughes**, figure skating
1951	**Bob Richards**, track	1978	**Tracy Caulkins**, swimming	2003	**Michael Phelps**, swimming
1952	**Horace Ashenfelter**, track	1979	**Kurt Thomas**, gymnastics	2004	**Paul Hamm**, gymnastics
1953	**Sammy Lee**, diving	1980	**Eric Heiden**, speed skating	2005	**J.J. Redick**, basketball
1954	**Mal Whitfield**, track	1981	**Carl Lewis**, track	2006	**Jessica Long**, paralympic swimmer
1955	**Harrison Dillard**, track	1982	**Mary Decker**, track		
1956	**Pat McCormick**, diving	1983	**Edwin Moses**, track	2007	**Tim Tebow**, football

ESPY Awards

The ESPY Awards, which represent the convergence of the sports and entertainment communities, were created by ESPN in 1993 and are given for Excellence in Sports Performance Yearly in more than 30 categories. Until 2004, ESPYs were awarded by a panel of sports executives, journalists and retired athletes whose decisions are based on the performances of the nominees during the year preceding the awards ceremony. Currently, online balloting is used. Note that not all categories are listed below.

Breakthrough Athlete

Year		Year	
1993	Gary Sheffield, San Diego Padres	2001	Daunte Culpepper, Minnesota Vikings
1994	Mike Piazza, Los Angeles Dodgers	2002	Tom Brady, New England Patriots
1995	Jeff Bagwell, Houston Astros	2003	Alfonso Soriano, New York Yankees
1996	Hideo Nomo, Los Angeles Dodgers	2004	LeBron James, Cleveland Cavaliers
1997	Tiger Woods, golf	2005	Dwyane Wade, Miami Heat
1998	Nomar Garciaparra, Boston Red Sox	2006	Chris Paul, New Orleans Hornets
1999	Randy Moss, Minnesota Vikings	2007	Devin Hester, Chicago Bears
2000	Kurt Warner, St. Louis Rams	2008	Adrian Peterson, Minnesota Vikings

Outstanding Performance Under Pressure

Year		Year	
1993	Christian Laettner, Duke	1997	Kerri Strug, Olympic gymnast
1994	Joe Carter, Toronto Blue Jays	1998	Terrell Davis, Denver Broncos
1995	Mark Messier, New York Rangers	1999	Mark O'Meara, golf
1996	Martin Brodeur, New Jersey Devils		

Best Coach/Manager

Year	
1993	Jimmy Johnson, Dallas Cowboys
1994	Jimmy Johnson, Dallas Cowboys
1995	George Siefert, San Francisco 49ers
1996	Gary Barnett, Northwestern
1997	Joe Torre, New York Yankees
1998	Jim Leyland, Florida Marlins
1999	Joe Torre, New York Yankees
2000	Joe Torre, New York Yankees
2001	Joe Torre, New York Yankees
2002	Phil Jackson, Los Angeles Lakers
2003	Jon Gruden, Tampa Bay Buccaneers
2004	Larry Brown, Detroit Pistons
2005	Bill Belichick, New England Patriots
2006	Bill Cowher, Pittsburgh Steelers
2007	Tony Dungy, Indianapolis Colts
2008	Pat Summitt, Tennessee

Best Comeback Athlete

Year	
1993	Dave Winfield, Toronto Blue Jays
1994	Mario Lemieux, Pittsburgh Penguins
1995	Dan Marino, Miami Dolphins
1996	Michael Jordan, Chicago Bulls
1997	Evander Holyfield, boxer
1998	Roger Clemens, Toronto Blue Jays
1999	Eric Davis, Baltimore Orioles
2000	Lance Armstrong, cycling
2001	Andres Galarraga, baseball
2002	Jennifer Capriati, tennis
2003	Tommy Maddox, Pittsburgh Steelers
2004	Bethany Hamilton, surfing
2005	Mark Fields, Carolina Panthers
2006	Tedy Bruschi, New England Patriots
2008	Josh Hamilton, Texas Rangers

Best Female Athlete

Year		Year	
1993	Monica Seles, tennis	2001	Marion Jones, track
1994	Julie Krone, jockey	2002	V. Williams, tennis
1995	Bonnie Blair, speed skater	2003	S. Williams, tennis
1996	Rebecca Lobo, basketball	2004	Diana Taurasi, basketball
1997	Amy Van Dyken, swimming	2005	Annika Sorenstam, golf
1998	Mia Hamm, soccer	2006	Annika Sorenstam, golf
1999	C. Holdsclaw, college basketball	2007	Taryne Mowatt, softball
2000	Mia Hamm, soccer	2008	Candace Parker, basketballl

Best Male Athlete

Year	
1993	Michael Jordan, Chicago Bulls
1994	Barry Bonds, San Francisco Giants
1995	Steve Young, San Francisco 49ers
1996	Cal Ripken, Baltimore Orioles
1997	Michael Johnson, Olympic sprinter
1998	Tiger Woods, golf
1999	Mark McGwire, St. Louis Cardinals
2000	Tiger Woods, golf
2001	Tiger Woods, golf
2002	Tiger Woods, golf
2003	Lance Armstrong, cycling
2004	Lance Armstrong, cycling
2005	Lance Armstrong, cycling
2006	Lance Armstrong, cycling
2007	LaDainian Tomlinson, San Diego Chargers
2008	Tiger Woods, golf

Best Team

Year		Year	
1993	Dallas Cowboys	2001	NY Yankees & Oklahoma football
1994	Toronto Blue Jays	2002	Los Angeles Lakers
1995	New York Rangers	2003	Anaheim Angels
1996	UConn women's basketball	2004	Detroit Pistons
1997	New York Yankees	2005	Boston Red Sox
1998	Denver Broncos	2006	Pittsburgh Steelers
1999	New York Yankees	2007	Indianapolis Colts
2000	U.S. Women's World Cup Team	2008	Boston Celtics

Best Baseball Player

Year		Year	
1993	Dennis Eckersley, Oak	2001	Pedro Martinez, Bos.
1994	Barry Bonds, S.F.	2002	Barry Bonds, S.F.
1995	Jeff Bagwell, Hou.	2003	Barry Bonds, S.F.
1996	Greg Maddux, Atl.	2004	Barry Bonds, S.F.
1997	Ken Caminiti, S.D.	2005	Albert Pujols, St. L.
1998	Larry Walker, Colo.	2006	Albert Pujols, St. L.
1999	Mark McGwire, St.L	2007	Derek Jeter, NYY
2000	Pedro Martinez, Bos.	2008	Alex Rodriguez, NYY

Best NFL Player

Year		Year	
1993	Emmitt Smith, Dal.	2002	Marshall Faulk, St. L
1994	Emmitt Smith, Dal.	2003	Michael Vick, Atl.
1995	Barry Sanders, Det.	2004	Peyton Manning, Ind
1996	Brett Favre, G.B.	2005	Peyton Manning, Ind
1997	Brett Favre, G.B.	2006	Shaun Alexander, Sea
1998	Barry Sanders, Det.	2007	LaDainian Tomlinson, S.D.
1999	Terrell Davis, Den.		
2000	Kurt Warner, St. L.		
2001	Marshall Faulk, St. L	2008	Tom Brady, NE

Best NBA Player

Year		Year	
1993	Michael Jordan, Chi.	2001	Shaquille O'Neal, LAL
1994	Charles Barkley, Pho.	2002	Shaquille O'Neal, LAL
1995	Hakeem Olajuwon, Hou.	2003	Tim Duncan, S.A.
1996	Hakeem Olajuwon, Hou.	2004	Kevin Garnett, Min.
1997	Michael Jordan, Chi.	2005	Steve Nash, Pho.
1998	Michael Jordan, Chi.	2006	Dwyane Wade, Mia.
1999	Michael Jordan, Chi.	2007	LeBron James, Cle.
2000	Tim Duncan, S.A.	2008	Kobe Bryant, LAL

Best WNBA Player

Year		Year	
1998	Cynthia Cooper, Hou.	2002	Lisa Leslie, L.A.
		2003	Lisa Leslie, L.A.
1999	Cynthia Cooper, Hou.	2004	Lauren Jackson, Sea.
		2005	Lauren Jackson, Sea.
2000	Cynthia Cooper, Hou.	2006	Sheryl Swoopes, Hou.
2001	Sheryl Swoopes, Hou.	2007	Lisa Leslie, L.A.
		2008	Lauren Jackson, Sea

Best NHL Player

Year		Year	
1993	Mario Lemieux, Pit.	2001	Chris Pronger, St. L
1994	Mario Lemieux, Pit.	2002	Jarome Iginla, Cal.
1995	Mark Messier, NYR	2003	Jean-Sebastien Giguere, Ana.
1996	Eric Lindros, Phi.		
1997	Joe Sakic, Col.	2004	Jarome Iginla, Cal.
1998	Mario Lemieux, Pit.	2005	not awarded
1999	Dominik Hasek, Buf.	2006	Jaromir Jagr, NYR
2000	Dominik Hasek, Buf.	2007	Sidney Crosby, Pit.
		2008	Sidney Crosby, Pit.

Outstanding College Football Performer of the Year

Year	
1993	Garrison Hearst, Georgia
1994	Charlie Ward, Florida State
1995	Rashaan Salaam, Colorado
1996	Eddie George, Ohio State
1997	Danny Wuerffel, Florida
1998	Peyton Manning, Tennessee
1999	Ricky Williams, Texas
2000	Michael Vick, Virginia Tech
2001	Chris Weinke, Florida State

Outstanding Men's College Basketball Performer of the Year

Year		Year	
1993	Christian Laettner, Duke	1998	Keith Van Horn, Utah
1994	Bobby Hurley, Duke	1999	Antawn Jamison, N. Carolina
1995	Grant Hill, Duke	2000	Elton Brand, Duke
1996	Ed O'Bannon, UCLA	2001	Kenyon Martin, Cincinnati
1997	Tim Duncan, Wake Forest		

Outstanding Women's College Basketball Performer of the Year

Year	
1993	Dawn Staley, Virginia
1994	Sheryl Swoopes, Texas Tech
1995	Charlotte Smith, North Carolina
1996	Rebecca Lobo, Connecticut
1997	Saudia Roundtree, Georgia
1998	Chamique Holdsclaw, Tennessee
1999	Chamique Holdsclaw, Tennessee
2000	Chamique Holdsclaw, Tennessee
2001	Tamika Catchings, Tennessee

Best Men's Tennis Player

Year		Year	
1993	Jim Courier	2001	Pete Sampras
1994	Pete Sampras	2002	Lleyton Hewitt
1995	Pete Sampras	2003	Andre Agassi
1996	Pete Sampras	2004	Andy Roddick
1997	Pete Sampras	2005	Roger Federer
1998	Pete Sampras	2006	Roger Federer
1999	Pete Sampras	2007	Roger Federer
2000	Andre Agassi	2008	Roger Federer

Best Women's Tennis Player

Year		Year	
1993	Monica Seles	2001	Venus Williams
1994	Steffi Graf	2002	Venus Williams
1995	A. Sanchez Vicario	2003	Serena Williams
1996	Steffi Graf	2004	Serena Williams
1997	Steffi Graf	2005	Maria Sharapova
1998	Martina Hingis	2006	Venus Williams
1999	Lindsay Davenport	2007	Maria Sharapova
2000	Lindsay Davenport	2008	Maria Sharapova

Best Men's Golfer

Year		Year	
1993	Fred Couples	1999	Mark O'Meara
1994	Nick Price	2000	Tiger Woods
1995	Nick Price	2001	Tiger Woods
1996	Corey Pavin	2002	Tiger Woods
1997	Tom Lehman	2003	Tiger Woods
1998	Tiger Woods	2004	Phil Mickelson

Best Golfer

Year		Year	
2004	Tiger Woods	2007	Tiger Woods
2005	Tiger Woods	2008	Tiger Woods
2006	Tiger Woods		

Best Women's Golfer

Year		Year	
1993	Dottie Mochrie	1999	Annika Sorenstam
1994	Betsy King	2000	Julie Inkster
1995	Laura Davies	2001	Karrie Webb
1996	Annika Sorenstam	2002	Annika Sorenstam
1997	Karrie Webb	2003	Annika Sorenstam
1998	Annika Sorenstam	2004	Annika Sorenstam

Best Jockey

Year		Year	
1994	Mike Smith	2002	Victor Espinoza
1995	Chris McCarron	2003	Jose Santos
1996	Jerry Bailey	2004	Stewart Elliot
1997	Jerry Bailey	2005	Jeremy Rose
1998	Gary Stevens	2006	Edgar Prado
1999	Kent Desormeaux	2007	Calvin Borel
2000	Chris Antley	2008	Kent Desormeaux
2001	Kent Desormeaux		

Best Bowler

Year		Year	
1995	Norm Duke	2002	Pete Weber
1996	Mike Aulby	2003	Walter Ray Williams
1997	Bob Learn Jr.	2004	Pete Weber
1998	Walter Ray Williams	2005	Walter Ray Williams
1999	Walter Ray Williams	2006	Walter Ray Williams
2000	Parker Bohn III	2007	Norm Duke
2001	Walter Ray Williams	2008	Norm Duke

Best Men's Track Athlete

Year		Year	
1993	Kevin Young	2000	Michael Johnson
1994	Michael Johnson	2001	Maurice Greene
1995	Dennis Mitchell	2002	Maurice Greene
1996	Michael Johnson	2003	Tim Montgomery
1997	Michael Johnson	2004	Tom Pappas
1998	Wilson Kipketer	2005	not awarded
1999	Maurice Greene	2006	Justin Gatlin

Best Women's Track Athlete

Year		Year	
1993	Evelyn Ashford	2000	Marion Jones
1994	Gail Devers	2001	Marion Jones
1995	Gwen Torrence	2002	Marion Jones
1996	Kim Batten	2003	Gail Devers
1997	Marie-Jose Perec	2004	Gail Devers
1998	Marion Jones	2005	not awarded
1999	Marion Jones	2006	Allyson Felix

Best Track and Field Athlete

Year		Year	
2007	Jeremy Wariner	2008	Tyson Gay

Best U.S. Olympian

Year	
2006	Shaun White, snowboarding

Best Driver

Year		Year	
1993	Nigel Mansell	2001	Bobby Labonte
1994	Nigel Mansell	2002	Michael Schumacher
1995	Al Unser Jr.	2003	Tony Stewart
1996	Jeff Gordon	2004	Dale Earnhardt Jr.
1997	Jimmy Vasser	2005	Michael Schumacher
1998	Jeff Gordon	2006	Tony Stewart
1999	Jeff Gordon	2007	Jeff Gordon
2000	Dale Jarrett	2008	Jimmie Johnson

Game of the Year

Year	
1996	AFC championship between Colts and Steelers
1997	Rose Bowl, Ohio State edges Arizona St.
1998	Super Bowl XXXII, Broncos over Packers
1999-2001	not awarded
2002	World Series Game 7, Diamondbacks-Yankees
2003	Fiesta Bowl, Ohio State beat Miami-FL in OT
2004	Super Bowl XXXVIII, Patriots over Panthers
2005	ALCS Game 5, Red Sox beat Yankees
2006	Rose Bowl, Texas beat USC
2007	Fiesta Bowl, Boise State beat Oklahoma
2008	Super Bowl XLII, Giants upset Patriots

Best Play

Year	
2002	Derek Jeter's throw in World Series Game 3.
2003	LSU's Hail Mary TD.
2004	New Orleans Saints' lateral
2005	Blake Hoffarber's last second 3-pointer from back.
2006	Tyrone Prothro's behind-the-back catch
2007	Boise State's Fiesta Bowl Statue of Liberty play
2008	Eli Manning's pass to David Tyree in SB XLII

Best Boxer

Year		Year	
1993	Riddick Bowe	2001	Felix Trinidad
1994	Evander Holyfield	2002	Lennox Lewis
1995	George Foreman	2003	Roy Jones Jr.
1996	Roy Jones Jr.	2004	Antonio Tarver
1997	Evander Holyfield	2005	Bernard Hopkins
1998	Evander Holyfield	2006	Oscar De La Hoya
1999	Oscar De La Hoya	2007	Floyd Mayweather
2000	Roy Jones Jr.	2008	Floyd Mayweather

Best Male College Athlete

Year	
2002	Cael Sanderson, Iowa St. wrestling
2003	Carmelo Anthony, Syracuse basketball
2004	Emeka Okafor, UConn basketball
2005	Matt Leinart, USC football
2006	Reggie Bush, USC football
2007	Kevin Durant, Texas basketball
2008	Tim Tebow, Florida football

Best Female College Athlete

Year	
2002	Sue Bird, UConn basketball
2003	Diana Taurasi, UConn basketball
2004	Diana Taurasi, UConn basketball
2005	Cat Osterman, Texas softball
2006	Cat Osterman, Texas softball
2007	Taryne Mowatt, Arizona softball
2008	Candace Parker, Tennessee

Best Male Soccer Player

Year		Year	
2002	Landon Donovan	2004	David Beckham
2003	Ronaldo		

Best Female Soccer Player

Year		Year	
2002	Tiffeny Milbrett	2004	Mia Hamm
2003	Katia		

Best Soccer Player

Year		Year	
2005	Mia Hamm, USA	2006	Ronaldinho, Brazil

Best MLS Player

Year		Year	
2006	Landon Donovan, LA	2007	Landon Donovan, LA
		2008	David Beckham, LA

Best Outdoors Athlete

Year		Year	
2002	Kevin VanDam, fishing	2005	J.R. Salzman, lumberjack
2003	Jay Yelas, fishing	2008	Scott Smiley, mountaineer
2004	Tina Bosworth, log rolling		

Best Action Sports Athlete

Year		Year	
2002	Kelly Clark, snowboarding	2003	Shaun White, snowboarding

Best Male Action Sports Athlete

Year		Year	
2004	Ryan Nyquist, bike	2007	Travis Pastrana, motocross
2005	Dave Mirra, bike		
2006	Shaun White, snowboarding	2008	Shaun White, snowboarding

Best Female Action Sports Athlete

Year		Year	
2004	Dallas Friday, wakeboarding	2006	Hannah Teter, snowboarding
2005	Sofia Mulanovich, surfing	2007	Sarah Burke, skiing
		2008	Gretchen Bleiler, snowbaording

Best Male Athlete with a Disability

Year		Year	
2005	Marlon Shirley, track	2007	Casey Tubbs, track
2006	Bobby Martin, football	2008	Ryan Kocer, wrestling

Best Female Athlete with a Disability

Year	
2005	Erin Popovich, swimming
2006	Sarah Reinertsen, triathon
2007	Jessica Long, swimming
2008	Shay Oberg, softball

Best Sports Movie

Year		Year	
2002	The Rookie	2006	Glory Road
2003	Bend it like Beckham	2007	Talladega Nights
2004	Miracle	2008	Semi-Pro
2005	Friday Night Lights		

Best Record-Breaking Performance

Year	
2001	Pete Sampras, Grand Slam singles titles
2002	Tiger Woods, four straight Majors
2003	Emmitt Smith, NFL rushing record
2004	Eric Gagne, baseball consecutive saves
2005	Peyton Manning, NFL single-season TD passes
2006	Shaun Alexander, NFL single-season TDs scored
2007	LaDainian Tomlinson, NFL single-season TDs scored
2008	Brett Favre, NFL career TD passes

Best Upset

Year	
2004	Pistons over Lakers in NBA Finals
2005	#14 Bucknell over #3 Kansas in NCAA tournament
2006	not awarded
2007	Warriors over Mavericks in NBA Playoffs
2008	Giants over Patriots in Super Bowl XLII

Best Moment

Year	
2006	Jason McElwaine, Greece-Athena HS basketball
2007	Saints return home, beat Falcons on MNF
2008	Mallory Holtman and Liz Wallace carry Sara Tucholsky around the bases

Arthur Ashe Award for Courage

Presented since 1993 on the annual ESPN "ESPYs" telecast. Given to a member of the sports community who has exemplified the same courage, spirit and determination to help others despite personal hardship that characterized Arthur Ashe, the late tennis champion and humanitarian. Voting done by select 26-member committee of media and sports personalities.

Year		Year		Year	
1993	**Jim Valvano**, basketball	2001	**Cathy Freeman**, track	2006	**Afghanistan female soccer**
1994	**Steve Palermo**, baseball	2002	**Todd Beamer, Mark**	2007	**Trevor Ringland** & **David**
1995	**Howard Cosell**, TV & radio		**Bingham, Tom Burnett** &		**Cullen**, Peace Players International
1996	**Loretta Clairborne**, special		**Jeremy Glick**, Flight 93		
	olympics	2003	**Pat Tillman**, football	2008	**John Carlos** and **Tommie**
1997	**Muhammad Ali**, boxing		& **Kevin Tillman**, baseball		**Smith,** 1968 Olympians
1998	**Dean Smith**, college basketball	2004	**George Weah**, soccer		
1999	**Billie Jean King**, tennis	2005	**Emmanuel Ofosu Yeboah** &		
2000	**Dave Sanders**, Columbine H.S. coach		**Jim MacLaren**, disabled athletes		

The Hickok Belt

Officially known as the S. Rae Hickok Professional Athlete of the Year Award and presented by the Kickik Manufacturing Co. of Arlington, Texas, from 1950-76. The trophy was a large belt of gold, diamonds and other jewels, reportedly worth $30,000 in 1976, the last year it was handed out. Voting was done by 270 newspaper sports editors from around the country.

Multiple winner: Sandy Koufax (2).

Year		Year		Year	
1950	**Phil Rizzuto**, baseball	1960	**Arnold Palmer**, golf	1970	**Brooks Robinson**, baseball
1951	**Allie Reynolds**, baseball	1961	**Roger Maris**, baseball	1971	**Lee Trevino**, golf
1952	**Rocky Marciano**, boxing	1962	**Maury Wills**, baseball	1972	**Steve Carlton**, baseball
1953	**Ben Hogan**, golf	1963	**Sandy Koufax**, baseball	1973	**O.J. Simpson**, football
1954	**Willie Mays**, baseball	1964	**Jim Brown**, football	1974	**Muhammad Ali**, boxing
1955	**Otto Graham**, football	1965	**Sandy Koufax**, baseball	1975	**Pete Rose**, baseball
1956	**Mickey Mantle**, baseball	1966	**Frank Robinson**, baseball	1976	**Ken Stabler**, football
1957	**Carmen Basilio**, boxing	1967	**Carl Yastrzemski**, baseball	1977	Discontinued
1958	**Bob Turley**, baseball	1968	**Joe Namath**, football		
1959	**Ingemar Johansson**, boxing	1969	**Tom Seaver**, baseball		

Presidential Medal of Freedom

Since President John F. Kennedy established the Medal of Freedom as America's highest civilian honor in 1963, only 17 sports figures have won the award. Note that (*) indicates the presentation was made posthumously.

Year		President	Year		President
1963	**Bob Kiphuth**, swimming	Kennedy	2002	**Hank Aaron**, baseball	G.W. Bush
1976	**Jesse Owens**, track & field	Ford	2003	**John Wooden**, basketball	G.W. Bush
1977	**Joe DiMaggio**, baseball	Ford	2003	**Roberto Clemente***, baseball	G.W. Bush
1983	**Paul (Bear) Bryant***, football	Reagan	2004	**Arnold Palmer**, golf	G.W. Bush
1984	**Jackie Robinson***, baseball	Reagan	2005	**Muhammad Ali**, boxing	G.W. Bush
1986	**Earl (Red) Blaik**, football	Reagan	2005	**Jack Nicklaus**, golf	G.W. Bush
1991	**Ted Williams**, baseball	G. Bush	2005	**Frank Robinson**, baseball	G.W. Bush
1992	**Richard Petty**, auto racing	G. Bush	2006	**John "Buck" O'Neill***, baseball	G.W. Bush
1993	**Arthur Ashe***, tennis	Clinton			

Congressional Gold Medal

Since the American Revolution, the U.S. Congress has commissioned gold medals as its highest expression of national appreciation for distinguished achievements and contributions. The medals are produced by the U.S. Mint. Each medal honors a particular individual, institution or event. Only five sports figure have won the award but note that track legend **Wilma Rudolph** and golfer **Arnold Palmer** have been nominated for, but not yet awarded, the Congressional gold medal.

Year		Year	
1973	**Roberto Clemente**, baseball	2005	**Jackie Robinson**, baseball
1982	**Joe Louis**, boxing	2007	**Byron Nelson**, golf
1988	**Jesse Owens**, track & field		

Time Person of the Year

Since Charles Lindbergh was named *Time* magazine's first Man of the Year for 1927, two individuals with significant sports credentials have won the honor.

Year	
1984	**Peter Ueberroth**, president of the Los Angeles Olympic Organizing Committee.
1991	**Ted Turner**, owner-president of Turner Broadcasting System, founder of CNN cable news network, owner of the Atlanta Braves (NL) and Atlanta Hawks (NBA), and former winning America's Cup skipper.

Soccer legend **Pele** and quarterback **Joe Namath** try their hands (and heads) at each other's sports on Aug. 5, 1975.

Sports Personalities

Nine hundred seventy-three entries dating back to the 19th century. Entries updated through Oct. 1, 2008.

Hank Aaron (b. Feb. 5, 1934): Baseball OF; led NL in HRs and RBI 4 times each and batting twice with Milwaukee and Atlanta Braves; MVP in 1957; played in 24 All-Star Games; was all-time leader in HRs (755) until being passed by Barry Bonds in 2007; all-time leader in RBI (2,297), total bases (6,856), 3rd in hits (3,771); won 3 Gold Gloves.

Kareem Abdul-Jabbar (b. Lew Alcindor, Apr. 16, 1947): Basketball C; led UCLA to 3 NCAA titles (1967-69); Final 4 MOP 3 times; Player of Year twice; led Milwaukee (1) and LA Lakers (5) to 6 NBA titles; playoff MVP twice (1971,85), regular season MVP 6 times (1971-72,74,76-77,80); retired in 1989 after 20 seasons as all-time leader in over 20 categories.

Andre Agassi (b. Apr. 29, 1970): Tennis; 60 career tournament wins including the career grand slam; Wimbledon (1992), U.S. Open (1994,99), Australian Open (1995,2000,01,03), French Open (1999); helped U.S. win 2 Davis Cup finals (1990,92); regained the world No. 1 ranking in 1999 for the first time since 1996; retired after the 2006 U.S. Open; married to former tennis star Steffi Graf.

Troy Aikman (b. Nov. 21, 1966): Football QB; consensus All-America at UCLA (1988); 1st overall pick in 1989 NFL Draft (by Dallas); led Cowboys to 3 Super Bowl titles (1992,93,95 seasons); MVP of Super Bowl XXVII; inducted into Pro Football HOF in 2006.

Marv Albert (b. June 12, 1941): Radio-TV; NBC announcer and radio broadcaster for the New York Knicks, Rangers and Giants who pleaded guilty to a misdemeanor assault charge amid embarrassing allegations of his sex life. Rehired to MSG and Turner networks in 1998 and NBC in '99.

Tenley Albright (b. July 18, 1935): Figure skater; 2-time world champion (1953,55); won Olympic silver (1952) and gold (1956) medals; became a surgeon.

Amy Alcott (b. Feb. 22, 1956): Golfer; 29 career wins, including five majors; inducted into World Golf Hall of Fame in 1999.

Grover Cleveland (Pete) Alexander (b. Feb. 26, 1887, d. Nov. 4, 1950): Baseball RHP; won 20 or more games 9 times; 373 career wins and 90 shutouts.

Muhammad Ali (b. Cassius Clay, Jan. 17, 1942): Boxer; 1960 Olympic light heavyweight champion; 3-time world heavyweight champ (1964-67, 1974-78,1978-79); defeated Sonny Liston (1964), George Foreman (1974) and Leon Spinks (1978) for title; fought Joe Frazier in 3 memorable bouts (1971-75), winning twice; adopted Black Muslim faith in 1964 and changed name; stripped of title in 1967 after conviction for refusing induction into U.S. Army; verdict reversed by Supreme Court in 1971; career record of 56-5 with 37 KOs and 19 successful title defenses; lit the flaming cauldron to signal the beginning of the 1996 Summer Olympics in Atlanta.

Forrest (Phog) Allen (b. Nov. 18, 1885, d. Sept. 16, 1974): Basketball; college coach 48 years; directed Kansas to NCAA title (1952); 746 wins.

Bobby Allison (b. Dec. 3, 1937): Auto racer; 3-time winner of Daytona 500 (1978,82,88); NASCAR national champ in 1983; father of Davey.

Davey Allison (b. Feb. 25, 1961, d. July 13, 1993): Auto racer; stock car Rookie of Year (1987); winner of 19 NASCAR races, including 1992 Daytona 500; killed at age 32 in helicopter accident at Talladega Superspeedway; son of Bobby.

Roberto Alomar (b. Feb. 5, 1968): Baseball; 10-time Gold Glove second baseman; MVP of 1992 ALCS; became known well beyond baseball for spitting in the face of umpire John Hirschbeck.

Walter Alston (b. Dec. 1, 1911, d. Oct. 1, 1984): Baseball; managed Brooklyn-LA Dodgers 23 years, won 7 pennants and 4 World Series (1955,59,63,65); retired after 1976 season with 2,063 wins (2,040 regular season and 23 postseason).

Morten Andersen (b. Aug 19, 1960): Football K; all-time leading scorer in NFL history; played in more games than anyone in NFL history (382 entering 2008 season); signed by Falcons in Sept, 2007 – at age 47.

Gary Anderson (b. July 16, 1959): Football K; 2nd leading scorer in NFL history; had perfect regular season in 1998 (59/59 PAT, 35/35 FG); led AFC in scoring 3 times and NFC once.

Sparky Anderson (b. Feb. 22, 1934): Baseball; one of two managers (La Russa) to win World Series in each league—Cincinnati in NL (1975-76) and Detroit in AL (1984); 6th-ranked skipper on career list with 2,228 wins (2,194 regular season and 34 postseason; inducted into the Baseball Hall of Fame in 2000.

Mario Andretti (b. Feb. 28, 1940): Auto racer; 4-time USAC-CART national champion (1965-66,69,84); only driver to win Daytona 500 (1967), Indy 500 (1969) and Formula One world title (1978); Indy 500 Rookie of Year (1965); retired after 1994 racing season ranked 1st in poles (67) and starts (407) and 2nd in wins (52) on all-time CART list; father of Michael and Jeff, uncle of John, grandfather of Marco.

Michael Andretti (b. Oct. 5, 1962): Auto racer; 1991 CART national champion with single-season record 8 wins; Indy 500 Rookie of Year (1984); left IndyCar for ill-fated Formula One try in 1993; returned to IndyCar in 1994; son of Mario, father of Marco.

Earl Anthony (b. Apr. 27, 1938, d. Aug. 14, 2001): Bowler; 6-time PBA Bowler of Year; 41 career titles; first to earn $100,000 in 1 season (1975); first to earn $1 million in career; won 10 Majors (2 Tournament of Champions, 6 PBA National Championships and 2 ABC Masters).

Said Aouita (b. Nov. 2, 1959): Moroccan runner; won gold (5000m) and bronze (800m) in 1984 Olympics; won 5000m at 1987 World Championships; formerly held 2 world records recognized by IAAF—2000m and 5000m.

Luis Aparicio (b. Apr. 29, 1934): Baseball SS; retired as all-time leader in most games, assists and double plays by shortstop; led AL in stolen bases 9 times (1956-64); 506 career steals.

Al Arbour (b. Nov. 1, 1932): Hockey; coached NY Islanders to 4 straight Stanley Cup titles (1980-83); retired after 1993-94 season; 2nd on all-time career list with 905 wins (782 regular season and 123 postseason); elected to Hockey Hall of Fame in 1996; returned in 2007 to coach his 1500th game with NYI.

Eddie Arcaro (b. Feb. 19, 1916, d. Nov. 14, 1997): Jockey; 2-time Triple Crown winner (Whirlaway in 1941, Citation in '48); he won Kentucky Derby 5 times, Preakness and Belmont 6 times each.

Roone Arledge (b. July 8, 1931, d. Dec. 5, 2002): Sports TV pioneer; innovator of live events, anthology shows, Olympic coverage, "Monday Night Football" and "Wide World of Sports"; ran ABC Sports from 1968-86; ran ABC News from 1977-98.

Henry Armstrong (b. Dec. 12, 1912, d. Oct. 22, 1988): Boxer; held feather-, light- and welterweight titles in 1938; pro record 152-21-8 with 100 KOs.

Lance Armstrong (b. Sept. 18, 1971): Cyclist; Texan who made cycling history becoming the first 6-time, then 7-time winner of the Tour de France (1999-2005); returned from treatment for testicular cancer to become the world's top cyclist; 4-time AP Male Athlete of the Year.

Arthur Ashe (b. July 10, 1943, d. Feb. 6, 1993): Tennis; first black man to win U.S. Championship (1968) and Wimbledon (1975); 1st U.S. player to earn $100,000 in 1 year (1970); won Davis Cup as player (1968-70) and captain (1981-82); wrote black sports history, Hard Road to Glory; announced in 1992 that he was infected with AIDS virus from a blood transfusion during 1983 heart surgery; in 1997, the new home for the U.S. Open was named Arthur Ashe Stadium.

Evelyn Ashford (b. Apr. 15, 1957): Track & Field; winner of 4 Olympic gold medals—100m in 1984, and 4x100m in 1984, '88 and '92; also won silver medal in 100m in '88; member of 5 U.S. Olympic teams (1976-92); Inducted into Track and Field and Women's Sports Halls of Fame in 1997.

Red Auerbach (b. Sept. 20, 1917, d. Oct. 28, 2006): Basketball; retired as winningest all-time coach (regular season and playoffs) in NBA history (now 7th); won 1,037 times in 20 years; as coach-GM, led Boston to a record 9 NBA titles, including 8 in a row (1959-66); also coached defunct Washington Capitols (1946-49); NBA Coach of the Year award named after him; retired as Celtics coach in 1966 and as GM in '84; club president from 1970 to 1997 and then again from 2001 until his death in 2006.

Tracy Austin (b. Dec. 12, 1962): Tennis; youngest player to win U.S. Open (age 16 in 1979); won 2nd U.S. Open in '81; named AP Female Athlete of Year twice before she was 20; recurring neck and back injuries shortened career after 1983; youngest player ever inducted into Tennis Hall of Fame (age 29 in 1992).

Paul Azinger (b. Jan. 6, 1960): Golf; PGA Player of Year (1987); 12 career wins, including '93 PGA Championship; missed most of '94 season overcoming lymphoma in right shoulder blade; member of 4 U.S. Ryder Cup teams (1989,91,93,2002); captained U.S. team to Ryder Cup win in 2008.

Bob Baffert (b. Jan. 13, 1953): Horse racing; 3-time Eclipse Award winner as outstanding trainer (1997-99); trained 3 Kentucky Derby winners (1997,98,02), 4 Preakness winners (1997,98,01,02) and 1 Belmont Stakes winner (2001); 4-time leading annual money leader for trainers (1998-01).

Donovan Bailey (b. Dec. 16, 1967): Track; Jamaican-born Canadian sprinter who set world record in the 100m (9.84) in gold medal-winning performance at 1996 Olympics which stood until '99; set indoor record in 50m (5.56) in 1996; member of Canadian 4x100 relay that won gold in 1996 Olympics.

Oksana Baiul (b. Feb. 26, 1977): Ukrainian figure skater; 1993 world champion at age 15; edged Nancy Kerrigan by a 5-4 judges' vote for 1994 Olympic gold medal.

Hobey Baker (b. Jan. 15, 1892, d. Dec. 21, 1918): Football and hockey star at Princeton (1911-14); member of college football and pro hockey Halls of Fame; college hockey Player of Year award named after him; killed in plane crash.

Seve Ballesteros (b. Apr. 9, 1957): Spanish golfer; has won British Open 3 times (1979,84,88) and Masters twice (1980,83); 3-time European Golfer of Year (1986,88,91); led Europe to 5 Ryder Cup titles (1985,87,89,95,97).

Ernie Banks (b. Jan. 31, 1931): Baseball SS-1B; led NL in home runs and RBI twice each; 2-time MVP (1958-59) with Chicago Cubs; 512 career HRs.

Roger Bannister (b. Mar. 23, 1929): British runner; first to run mile in less than 4 minutes (3:59.4 on May 6, 1954).

Walter (Red) Barber (b. Feb. 17, 1908, d. Oct. 22, 1992): Radio-TV; renowned baseball play-by-play broadcaster for Cincinnati, Brooklyn and N.Y. Yankees from 1934-66; won Peabody Award for radio commentary in 1991.

Charles Barkley (b. Feb. 20, 1963): Basketball F; 5-time All-NBA 1st team with Philadelphia and Phoenix; U.S. Olympic Dream Team member in '92; NBA regular season MVP in 1993; currently a basketball announcer for TNT; inducted into Basketball Hall of Fame in 2006.

Rick Barry (b. Mar. 28, 1944): Basketball F; only player to lead both NBA and ABA in scoring; 5-time All-NBA 1st team; Finals MVP with Golden St. in 1975. Perfected the underhand foul shot.

Sammy Baugh (b. Mar. 17, 1914): Football QB-DB-P; led Washington to NFL titles in 1937 (his rookie year) and '42; led league in passing 6 times, punting 4 times and interceptions once.

Elgin Baylor (b. Sept. 16, 1934): Basketball F; Most Outstanding Player of Final Four in 1958; led Minneapolis-LA Lakers to 8 NBA Finals; 10-time All-NBA 1st team (1959-65,67-69); LA Clippers' Vice President of Basketball Ops until Oct. 2008.

Bob Beamon (b. Aug. 29, 1946): Track & Field; won 1968 Olympic gold medal in long jump with world record (29-ft, 2½ in.) that shattered old mark by nearly 2 feet; record finally broken by 2 inches in 1991 by Mike Powell.

Franz Beckenbauer (b. Sept. 11, 1945): Soccer; captain of West German World Cup champions in 1974 then coached West Germany to World Cup title in 1990; invented sweeper position; played in U.S. for NY Cosmos (1977-80,83).

David Beckham (b. May 2, 1975): Soccer; English star perhaps known more for his good looks, his 1999 marriage to former Spice Girl, Victoria Adams (Posh Spice), and his trademark free kick; captain of the English national team from 2000-2006; scored goals in 3 different World Cups (1998,2002,2006); played for Manchester United (1993-95, 1995-2003) then Real Madrid (2003-07) before coming to America in 2007 to join the MLS' Los Angeles Galaxy.

Boris Becker (b. Nov. 22, 1967): German tennis player; 3-time Wimbledon champ (1985-86,89); youngest male (17) to win Wimbledon; led country to 1st Davis Cup win in 1988; has also won U.S. (1989) and Australian (1991,96) Opens.

Chuck Bednarik (b. May 1, 1925): Football C-LB; 2-time All-America at Penn and 7-time All-Pro with NFL Eagles as both center (1950) and linebacker (1951-56); missed only 3 games in 14 seasons; led Eagles to 1960 NFL title as a 35-year-old two-way player.

Clair Bee (b. Mar. 2, 1896, d. May 20, 1983): Basketball coach who led LIU to 2 undefeated seasons (1936,39) and 2 NIT titles (1939,41); his teams won 95 percent of their games between 1931-51, including 43 in a row from 1935-37; coached NBA Baltimore Bullets from 1952-54, but was only 34-116; contributions to game include 1-3-1 zone defense, 3-second rule and NBA 24-second clock.

Bill Belichick (b. Apr. 16, 1952): Football; longtime assistant to Bill Parcells who became head coach of N.E. Patriots in 2000 and went on to win 3 Super Bowls; gained unwanted attention in Sept. 2007 after a Patriots cameraman was found to have videotaped the NY Jets sidelines in an attempt to obtain signals; 142 wins entering 2008 (15-4 postseason).

Jean Beliveau (b. Aug. 31, 1931): Hockey C; led Montreal to 10 Stanley Cups in 17 playoffs; playoff MVP (1965); 2-time regular season MVP (1956,64).

Bert Bell (b. Feb. 25, 1895, d. Oct. 11, 1959): Football; team owner and 2nd NFL commissioner (1946-59); proposed college draft in 1935 and instituted TV blackout rule.

James (Cool Papa) Bell (b. May 17, 1903, d. Mar. 8, 1991): Baseball; member of the Negro Leagues; widely considered the fastest player ever to play baseball; also coached for the Kansas City Monarchs, teaching such players as Jackie Robinson; member of the National Baseball Hall of Fame.

Deane Beman (b. Apr. 22, 1938): Golf; 1st commissioner of PGA Tour (1974-94); introduced "stadium golf" and created The Players Championship; as player, won U.S. Amateur twice and British Amateur once; inducted into the World Golf Hall of Fame in 2000.

Johnny Bench (b. Dec. 7, 1947): Baseball C; led NL in HRs twice and RBI 3 times; 2-time regular season MVP (1970,72) with Cincinnati, World Series MVP in 1976; 389 career HRs.

Patty Berg (b. Feb. 13, 1918, d. Sept. 10, 2006): Golfer; 60 career pro wins, including 15 majors; 3-time AP Female Athlete of Year (1938,43,55).

Chris Berman (b. May 10, 1955): Radio-TV; 6-time National Sportscaster of Year famous for his nicknames and jovial studio anchoring on ESPN; play-by-play man first year Brown University football team won the Ivy League (1976).

* **Yogi Berra** (b. May 12, 1925): Baseball C; played on 10 World Series winners with NY Yankees; holds WS records for games played (75), at bats (259) and hits (71); 3-time AL MVP (1951,54-55); managed both Yankees (1964) and NY Mets (1973) to pennants.

Jay Berwanger (b. Mar. 19, 1914, d. June 26, 2002): Football HB; Univ. of Chicago star; won 1st Heisman Trophy in 1935; top selection in the 1st-ever NFL Draft (1936).

Gary Bettman (b. June 2, 1952): Hockey; former NBA executive, who was named first commissioner of NHL on Dec. 11, 1992; took office on Feb. 1, 1993; commissioner during NHL lockout of 2004-05.

Abebe Bikila (b. Aug. 7, 1932, d. Oct. 25, 1973): Ethiopian runner; 1st to win consecutive Olympic marathons (1960,64).

Matt Biondi (b. Oct. 8, 1965): Swimmer; won 7 medals in 1988 Olympics, including 5 gold (2 individual, 3 relay); won a total of 11 medals (8 gold, 2 silver and a bronze) in 3 Olympics (1984,88,92).

Larry Bird (b. Dec. 7, 1956): Basketball F; college Player of Year (1979) at Indiana St.; 1980 NBA Rookie of Year; 9-time All-NBA 1st team; 3-time regular season MVP (1984-86); led Boston to 3 NBA titles (1981,84, 86); 2-time Finals MVP (1984,86); U.S. Olympic Dream Team member in '92; inducted into Hall of Fame in 1998; in 1997, named coach of Indiana Pacers and won Coach of the Year honors in first season; led the Pacers to the NBA Finals in 2000 but lost in 6 games to the Lakers and retired; named president of basketball operations of Pacers in 2003.

The Black Sox: Eight Chicago White Sox players who were banned from baseball for life in 1921 for allegedly throwing the 1919 World Series— RHP Eddie Cicotte (1884-1969), OF Happy Felsch (1891-1964), 1B Chick Gandil (1887-1970), OF Shoeless Joe Jackson (1889-1951), INF Fred McMullin (1891-1952), SS Swede Risberg (1894-1975), 3B-SS Buck Weaver (1890-1956), and LHP Lefty Williams (1893-1959).

Earl (Red) Blaik (b. Feb. 15, 1897, d. May 6, 1989): Football; coached Army to consecutive national titles in 1944-45; 166 career wins and 3 Heisman winners (Blanchard, Davis, Dawkins).

Bonnie Blair (b. Mar. 18, 1964): Speed skater; only American woman to win 5 Olympic gold medals in Winter Games; won 500-meters in 1988, then 500m and 1,000m in both 1992 and '94; added 1,000m bronze in 1988; Sullivan Award winner (1992); retired on 31st birthday as reigning world sprint champ.

Hector (Toe) Blake (b. Aug. 21, 1912, d. May 17, 1995): Hockey LW; led Montreal to 2 Stanley Cups as a player and 8 more as coach; 1939 NHL MVP.

Felix (Doc) Blanchard (b. Dec. 11, 1924): Football FB; 3-time All-America; led Army to national titles in 1944-45; Glenn Davis' running mate; won Heisman Trophy and Sullivan Award in 1945.

George Blanda (b. Sept. 17, 1927): Football QB-PK; was pro football's all-time leading scorer (2,002 points) until 2000 when he was finally passed by kicker Gary Anderson; led Houston to 2 AFL titles (1960-61); played 26 pro seasons; retired at age 48.

Fanny Blankers-Koen (b. Apr. 26, 1918, d. Jan. 25, 2004): Dutch sprinter; 30-year-old mother of two, who won 4 gold medals (100m, 200m, 800m hurdles and 4x100m relay) at 1948 Olympics.

Drew Bledsoe (b. Feb. 14, 1972): Football QB; 1st overall pick in 1993 NFL draft (N.E. Patriots); one of only 11 QBs in NFL history with 40,000 career passing yards; played with Buffalo (2002-04) then Dallas (2005-06); retired in April, 2007.

Jim Boeheim (b. Nov. 17, 1944): Basketball; long-time coach at Syracuse; won 1st NCAA title in 2003; one of 19 Div. I coaches with 700 career victories.

Wade Boggs (b. June 15, 1958): Baseball 3B; 5 AL batting titles (1983,85-88) with Boston Red Sox; 11-time All-Star; two Gold Gloves; later played with NY Yankees and Tampa Bay; retired in 1999 with 3,010 hits (3,000th hit was a HR); inducted into Hall of Fame in 2005.

Usain Bolt (b. Aug. 21, 1986): Track & Field; Jamaican sprinter who took the Beijing Olympics by storm in 2008, winning 3 gold medals (100, 200m and 4 x100m) and breaking world records in the 100m (9.69) and 200m (19.30).

Barry Bonds (b. July 24, 1964): Baseball OF; MLB all-time and single-season home run leader; broke Hank Aaron's career record with his 756th HR on Aug. 7, 2007 — a shot to right-center off Washington lefty Mike Bacsik; set MLB single-season HR record in 2001 with 73; 7-time NL MVP, 2 with Pittsburgh (1990,92) and 5 with San Francisco (1993,2001-04); one of only 4 men with 40 HRs and 40 SBs in same season (1996); holds major league record for single season (2004) and career walks; hit .370 in 2002 at age 38; finished 2007 season with 762 HR; polarizing and controversial, he is viewed by many as a poster child for baseball's steroid problems; son of Bobby.

Bjorn Borg (b. June 6, 1956): Swedish tennis player; 2-time Player of Year (1979-80); won 6 French Opens and 5 straight Wimbledons (1976-80); led Sweden to 1st Davis Cup win in 1975; retired in 1983 at age 26; attempted unsuccessful comeback in 1991.

Mike Bossy (b. Jan. 22, 1957): Hockey RW; led NY Isles to 4 Stanley Cups; playoff MVP in 1982; 50 goals or more 9 straight years; 573 career goals.

Ralph Boston (b. May 9, 1939): Track & Field; medaled in 3 consecutive Olympic long jumps— gold (1960), silver (1964), bronze (1968).

Ray Bourque (b. Dec. 28, 1960): Hockey D; 12-time All-NHL 1st team; won 5 Norris Trophies (1987-88,1990-91,94) with Boston; '96 All-Star Game MVP; all-time leader for points and assists by a defenseman; won 2001 Stanley Cup with Colorado then retired; elected to Hall of Fame in 2004.

Bobby Bowden (b. Nov. 8, 1929): Football; coached Florida St. to 2 national titles (1993,99); entered 2008 season as all-time wins leader in college football history with 373 victories including a 20-10-1 bowl record in 42 years as coach at Samford, West Va. and FSU; father of Clemson head coach Tommy and former Auburn coach Terry.

Riddick Bowe (b. Aug. 10, 1967): Boxer; former undisputed heavyweight champ who fought career-defining trilogy with Evander Holyfield (1992-1995); won 1st meeting by decision, lost rematch in "Fan Man Fight," won last Holyfield fight by 8th-round KO.

Scotty Bowman (b. Sept. 18, 1933): Hockey coach; all-time winningest NHL coach in both regular season (1,244) and playoffs (223) over 30 seasons; coached a record nine Stanley Cup winners with Montreal (1973,76-79), Pittsburgh (1992) and Detroit (1997,98,2002); retired after 2001-02 season.

Jack Brabham (b. Apr. 2, 1926): Australian auto racer; 3-time Formula One champion (1959-60,66); 14 career wins; member of the Hall of Fame.

James J. Braddock (b. June 7, 1905, d. Nov. 29, 1974): Boxer; journeyman who won heavyweight belt in 10-1 upset of hard-hitting Max Baer in 1935.

Bill Bradley (b. July 28, 1943): Basketball F; 2-time All-America at Princeton; Player of the Year and Final 4 MOP in 1965; captain of gold medal-winning 1964 Olympic team; Sullivan Award winner (1965); led NY Knicks to 2 NBA titles (1970,73); U.S. Senator (D NJ) 1979-95; ran for President in 2000.

Pat Bradley (b. Mar. 24, 1951): Golfer; 2-time LPGA Player of Year (1986,91); won career LPGA grand slam, including 3 du Maurier Classics; inducted into the LPGA Hall of Fame on Jan. 18, 1992; 31 LPGA tournament wins.

Terry Bradshaw (b. Sept. 2, 1948): Football QB; led Pittsburgh to 4 Super Bowl titles (1975-76,79-80); 2-time Super Bowl MVP (1979-80) and regular season MVP in 1978; Fox TV studio analyst.

Tom Brady (b. Aug. 3, 1977): Football QB; 6th-round draft pick (Michigan) who became 3-time Super Bowl winner with N.E. Patriots, 2-time Super Bowl MVP; won NFL MVP award in 2007 after setting the single-season record for TD passes (50).

George Brett (b. May 15, 1953): Baseball 3B-1B; AL batting champion in 3 different decades (1976,80,90); MVP in 1980; led KC to World Series title in 1985; retired after 1993 season with 3,154 hits and .305 average; inducted into Hall of Fame in 1999.

Valerie Brisco-Hooks (b. July 6, 1960): Track & Field; won three gold medals at the 1984 Olympics (200 meters, 400 meters and 4x100 relay); first athlete to ever win the 200 and 400 in the same Olympics.

Lou Brock (b. June 18, 1939): Baseball OF; former all-time SB leader (938); led NL in SBs 8 times; led St. Louis to 2 WS titles (1964,67); 3,023 career hits.

Martin Brodeur (b. May 6, 1972): Hockey G; led New Jersey Devils to 3 Stanley Cup titles (1995,2000,2003); won Vezina Trophy 4 times (2003-04, 2007-08) and led NHL in goals against average in 1997 (1.88); entered 2008-09 with 538 wins (2nd behind Roy) and 96 shutouts (2nd behind Sawchuk).

Herb Brooks (b. Aug. 5, 1937, d. Aug. 11, 2003): Hockey; former U.S. Olympic player (1964,68) who coached 1980 "Miracle on Ice" team to gold medal and 2002 U.S. team to silver medal; coached Minnesota to 3 NCAA titles (1974,76,78); also coached 4 NHL teams.

Jim Brown (b. Feb. 17, 1936): Football FB; All-America at Syracuse (1956) and NFL Rookie of Year (1957); led NFL in rushing 8 times; 8-time All-Pro (1957-61,63-65); 3-time MVP (1958,63,65) with Cleveland; ran for 12,312 yards and scored 126 touchdowns in just 9 seasons; first player to reach the 100-touchdown milestone; member of pro and college football halls of fame.

Larry Brown (b. Sept. 14, 1940): Basketball; played in ACC, AAU, 1964 Olympics and ABA; 3-time assist leader (1968-70) and 3-time Coach of Year (1973,75-76) in ABA; coached ABA's Carolina and Denver and NBA's Denver, N.J., San Antonio, LA Clippers, Indiana, Philadelphia, Detroit, N.Y. Knicks and now Charlotte Bobcats; won the 2004 NBA title with Pistons; also coached UCLA to NCAA Final (1980), Kansas to NCAA title (1988) and the USA men's basketball team to a disappointing bronze medal in Athens in 2004.

Mordecai (Three-Finger) Brown (b. Oct. 18, 1876, d. Feb. 14, 1948): Baseball; nickname derived from injury in a childhood accident that left him with three digits on right hand; injury gave him a particularly nasty curve ball; in 1908, first pitcher to record 4 consecutive shutouts and finished at 29-9; career record of 239-130 with lifetime ERA of 2.06; member of Hall of Fame.

Paul Brown (b. Sept. 7, 1908, d. Aug. 5, 1991): Football innovator; coached Ohio St. to national title in 1942; in pros, directed Cleveland Browns to 4 straight AAFC titles (1946-49) and 3 NFL titles (1950,54-55); formed Cincinnati Bengals as head coach and part owner in 1968 (reached playoffs in '70).

Valery Brumel (b. Apr. 14, 1942, d. Jan. 26, 2003): Soviet high jumper; dominated event from 1961-64; broke world record 5 times; won silver in 1960 Olympics and gold in 1964; highest jump was 7-5¾.

Avery Brundage (b. Sept. 28, 1887, d. May 5, 1975): Amateur sports czar for over 40 years as president of AAU (1928-35), U.S. Olympic Committee (1929-53) and Int'l Olympic Committee (1952-72).

Kobe Bryant (b. Aug. 23, 1978): Basketball; G/F for the LA Lakers; graduated from Lower Merion (Penn.) HS and made the jump directly to the NBA; youngest player (18 yrs., 2 mos., 11 days) ever to appear in an NBA game; youngest all-star in NBA history; won 3 consecutive titles with the Lakers (2000,01,02); accused of rape in 2003 but charges were dropped in 2004; won NBA MVP award in 2007-08.

Paul (Bear) Bryant (b. Sept. 11, 1913, d. Jan. 26, 1983): Football; coached at 4 colleges over 38 years; directed Alabama to 6 national titles (1961,64-65,73,78-79); retired as the winningest coach of all-time (323-85-17 record) finally passed by Joe Paterno in 2001; 15 bowl wins, including 8 Sugar Bowls.

Sergey Bubka (b. Dec. 4, 1963): Ukrainian pole vaulter; 1st man to clear 20 feet both indoors and out (1991); holder of indoor (20-2) and outdoor (20-1¾) world records; 6-time world champion (1983, 87, 91, 93, 95, 97); won Olympic gold medal in 1988.

Buck Buchanan (b. Sept. 10, 1940, d. July 16, 1992): Football DT; played both ways in college at Grambling; first pick in the first AFL draft by the Dallas Texans; missed one game in 13 seasons; star of KC Chiefs team that won Super Bowl IV; later coached Saints and Browns; member of Pro Football HOF.

Jack Buck (b. Aug. 21, 1924, d. June 18, 2002): Radio-TV; broadcast baseball games for St. Louis Cardinals from 1954-2001; CBS Radio voice for Monday Night Football (1978-96) and announcer for 1st televised AFL game in 1960; recipient of Baseball Hall of Fame's Ford Frick Award (1987) and Football Hall of Fame's Pete Rozelle Award (1996); received the Purple Heart in WWII; father of sportscaster Joe.

Don Budge (b. June 13, 1915, d. Jan. 26, 2000): Tennis; in 1938 became 1st player to win the Grand Slam— the French, Wimbledon, U.S. and Australian titles in 1 year; led U.S. to 2 Davis Cups (1937-38); turned pro in late '38.

Maria Bueno (b. Oct. 11, 1939): Brazilian tennis player; won 4 U.S. Championships (1959,63-64,66) and 3 Wimbledons (1959-60,64).

Leroy Burrell (b. Feb. 21, 1967: Track & Field; set former world record of 9.85 in 100 meters, July 6, 1994; previously held record (9.90) in 1991; member of 4 world record-breaking 4x100m relay teams.

Susan Butcher (b. Dec. 26, 1954, d. Aug. 5, 2006): Sled Dog racer; 4-time winner of Iditarod Trail race (1986-88,90).

Dick Butkus (b. Dec. 9, 1942): Football LB; 2-time All-America at Illinois (1963-64); All-Pro 7 of 9 NFL seasons with Chicago Bears; worked with XFL in 2001.

Dick Button (b. July 18, 1929): Figure skater; 5-time world champion (1948-52); 2-time Olympic champ (1948,52); Sullivan Award winner (1949); won Emmy Award as Best Analyst for 1980-81 TV season.

Walter Byers (b. Mar. 13, 1922): College athletics; 1st executive director of NCAA, serving from 1951-88.

Frank Calder (b. Nov. 17, 1877, d. Feb. 4, 1943): Hockey; 1st NHL president (1917-43); guided league through its formative years; NHL's Rookie of the Year award named after him.

Jim Calhoun (b. May 10, 1942): Basketball; has coached UConn to 2 NCAA titles (1999, 2004); inducted into Basketball Hall of Fame in 2005.

Lee Calhoun (b. Feb. 23, 1933, d. June 22, 1989): Track & Field; won consecutive Olympic gold medals in the 110m hurdles (1956,60).

Walter Camp (b. Apr. 7, 1859, d. Mar. 14, 1925): Football coach and innovator; established scrimmage line, center snap, downs, 11 players per side; selected 1st All-America team (1889).

Roy Campanella (b. Nov. 19, 1921, d. June 26, 1993): Baseball C; 3-time NL MVP (1951,53,55); led Brooklyn to 5 pennants and 1st World Series title (1955); career tragically cut short when he was paralyzed in a 1958 car crash.

Clarence Campbell (b. July 9, 1905, d. June 24, 1984): Hockey; 3rd NHL president (1946-77), league tripled in size from 6 to 18 teams during his tenure.

Earl Campbell (b. Mar. 29, 1955): Football RB; won Heisman Trophy in 1977; led NFL in rushing 3 times (1978-80); 3-time All-Pro; 2-time MVP (1978-79) at Houston; rushed for 9,407 yards and 74 touchdowns over his 8-year career.

John Campbell (b. Apr. 8, 1955): Harness racing; 6-time winner of Hambletonian (1987,88,90,95,98, 2006); 3-time Driver of Year; first driver to go over $100 million in career winnings.

Milt Campbell (b. Dec. 9, 1933): Track & Field; won silver medal in 1952 Olympic decathlon and gold medal in '56.

Jimmy Cannon (b. 1910, d. Dec. 5, 1973): Tough, opinionated New York sportswriter and essayist who viewed sports as an extension of show business; protégé of Damon Runyon; covered World War II for *Stars & Stripes.*

Jose Canseco (b. July 2, 1964): Baseball OF/DH; 1986 AL ROY and 1988 MVP with the Oakland A's; became the 1st player in MLB history with 40 HRs and 40 steals in a season (1988); retired in 2003 with 462 career HRs; admitted steroid use and implicated various other major league players in his 2005 book, "Juiced."

Tony Canzoneri (b. Nov. 6, 1908, d. Dec. 9, 1959): Boxer; 2-time world lightweight champion (1930-33,35-36); pro record 141-24-10 with 44 KOs.

Jennifer Capriati (b. Mar. 29, 1976): Tennis; youngest Grand Slam semifinalist ever (age 14 in 1990 French Open); surprise gold medalist at 1992 Olympics; left Tour from 1994-96 due to personal problems; waged successful comeback, winning French Open (2001) and 2 Australian Opens (2001,02).

Harry Caray (b. Mar. 1, 1917, d. Feb. 18, 1998): Radio-TV; baseball play-by-play broadcaster for St. Louis Cardinals, Oakland, Chicago White Sox and Cubs 1945-98; father of late sportscaster Skip and grandfather of sportscaster Chip.

Rod Carew (b. Oct. 1, 1945): Baseball 2B-1B; led AL in batting 7 times (1969,72-75,77-78) with Minnesota; MVP in 1977; had 3,053 career hits; elected to Hall of Fame in 1991.

Steve Carlton (b. Dec. 22, 1944): Baseball LHP; "Lefty"; won 20 or more games 6 times; 4-time Cy Young winner (1972,77,80,82) with Philadelphia; 329-244 career record; 4,136 career Ks; elected to Hall of Fame in 1994.

JoAnne Carner (b. Apr. 4, 1939): Golfer; 5-time U.S. Amateur champion; 2-time U.S. Open champ; 3-time LPGA Player of Year (1974,81-82); 43 career wins.

Cris Carter (b. Nov. 25, 1965): Football; WR with Philadelphia (1987-89), Minnesota (1990-2001) and Miami (2002); twice caught 122 passes in a season (1994, '95), the first time establishing an NFL record for catches in a season that was beaten a year later; 2nd player to reach 1,000 career catches.

Don Carter (b. July 29, 1926): Bowler; 6-time Bowler of Year (1953-54,57-58,60,62); voted Greatest of All-Time in 1970.

Joe Carter (b. Mar. 7, 1960): Baseball OF; 3-time All-America at Wichita St. (1979-81); won 1993 World Series for Toronto with 3-run HR in bottom of the 9th of Game 6.

Alexander Cartwright (b. Apr. 17, 1820, d. July 12, 1892): Baseball; engineer and draftsman who spread gospel of baseball from New York City to California gold fields; widely regarded as the father of modern game; his guidelines included setting 3 strikes for an out and 3 outs for each half inning.

Billy Casper (b. June 24, 1931): Golfer; 2-time PGA Player of Year (1966,70); has won U.S. Open (1959,66), Masters (1970), U.S. Senior Open (1983); compiled 51 PGA Tour wins and 9 on Senior Tour.

Tracy Caulkins (b. Jan. 11, 1963): Swimmer; won 3 gold medals (2 individual) at 1984 Olympics; set 5 world records and won 48 U.S. national titles from 1978-84; Sullivan Award winner (1978); 2-time Honda Broderick Cup winner (1982,84).

Steve Cauthen (b. May 1, 1960): Jockey; became youngest jockey (18) to win the Triple Crown with Affirmed in 1978; won a record $6.1 million in 1977, winning the Eclipse Award as the nation's top rider and the award for AP male athlete of the year.

Evonne Goolagong Cawley (b. July 31, 1951): Australian tennis player; won Australian Open 4 times, Wimbledon twice (1971,80), French once (1971).

Florence Chadwick (b. Nov. 9, 1917, d. Mar. 15, 1995): Dominant distance swimmer of 1950s; set English Channel records from France to England (1950) and England to France (1951 and '55).

Wilt Chamberlain (b. Aug. 21, 1936, d. Oct. 12, 1999): Basketball C; consensus All-America in 1957 and '58 at Kansas; Final Four MOP in 1957; led NBA in scoring 7 times and rebounding 11 times; 7-time All-NBA first team; 4-time MVP (1960,66-68) in Philadelphia; scored 100 points vs. NY Knicks in Hershey, Pa.; Mar. 2, 1962; led 76ers (1967) and LA Lakers (1972) to NBA titles; Finals MVP in 1972.

A.B. (Happy) Chandler (b. July 14, 1898, d. June 15, 1991): Baseball; former Kentucky governor and U.S. Senator who succeeded Judge Landis as commissioner in 1945; backed Branch Rickey's move in 1947 to make Jackie Robinson 1st black player in major leagues; deemed too pro-player and ousted by owners in 1951.

Michael Chang (b. Feb. 22, 1972): Tennis; won the 1989 French Open, becoming the youngest men's champion of a grand slam event (17 years, 3 months.); went 11 consecutive years (1988-98) with at least one title; finished in top 10 in the ATP year-end rankings from 1992-97 (career high no. 2 in 1996).

Julio Cesar Chavez (b. July 12, 1962): Mexican boxer; world jr. welterweight champ (1989-94); also held titles as jr. lightweight (1984-87) and lightweight (1987-89); won over 100 bouts; 90-bout unbeaten streak ended 1/29/94 when Frankie Randall won title on split decision; Chavez won title back 4 months later.

Linford Christie (b. Apr. 2, 1960): British sprinter; won 100-meter gold medals at both 1992 Olympics (9.96) and '93 World Championships (9.87).

Jim Clark (b. Mar. 14, 1936, d. Apr. 7, 1968): Scottish auto racer; 2-time Formula One world champ (1963,65); won Indy 500 in 1965; killed in car crash.

Bobby Clarke (b. Aug. 13, 1949): Hockey C; led Philadelphia Flyers to consecutive Stanley Cups in 1974-75; 3-time regular season MVP (1973,75-76); currently Flyers Senior Vice President.

Ron Clarke (b. Feb. 21, 1937): Australian runner; from 1963-70 set 17 world records in races from 2 miles to 20,000m; never won Olympic gold medal.

Roger Clemens (b. Aug. 4, 1962): Baseball RHP; twice fanned MLB record 20 batters in 9-inning game (April 29, 1986 & Sept. 18, 1996); won a record 7 Cy Young Awards with Boston (1986-87,91), Toronto (1997,98), N.Y. Yankees (2001) and Houston (2004); AL MVP in 1986; won 2 World Series with N.Y. (1999-2000); led majors in ERA in 2005 at age 43; won 354 games; struck out 4672 batters; became embroiled in steroid controversy in 2008 after being accused in the Mitchell Report by former-trainer Brian McNamee.

Roberto Clemente (b. Aug. 18, 1934, d. Dec. 31, 1972): Baseball OF; hit over .300 13 times with Pittsburgh; led NL in batting 4 times; World Series MVP in 1971; regular season MVP in 1966; had 3,000 career hits; killed in plane crash; MLB Man of the Year award is named for him.

Alice Coachman (b. Nov. 9, 1923): Track & Field; became the first black woman to win Olympic gold with her 1948 high jump win (London); broke the HS and college high jump records despite not wearing any shoes; member of National Track & Field Hall of Fame.

Ty Cobb (b. Dec. 18, 1886, d. July 17, 1961): Baseball OF; all-time highest career batting average (.366); hit over .400 3 times; led AL in batting 12 times and stolen bases 6 times with Detroit; MVP in 1911; had 4,189 career hits, 2,246 career runs and 892 steals; played 24 years (22 with Detroit, 2 with Philadelphia); nicknamed "The Georgia Peach"; part of Baseball Hall of Fame's inaugural class.

Mickey Cochrane (b. Apr. 6, 1903, d. June 28, 1962): Baseball C; led Philadelphia A's (1929-30) and Detroit (1935) to 3 World Series titles; 2-time AL MVP (1928,34).

Sebastian Coe (b. Sept. 29, 1956): British runner; won gold medal in 1500m and silver medal in 800m at both 1980 and '84 Olympics; long-time world record holder in 800m and 1000m; elected to Parliament as Conservative in 1992.

Paul Coffey (b. June 1, 1961): Hockey D; 3-time Norris Trophy winner; member of 4 Stanley Cup champions at Edmonton (1984-85,87) and Pittsburgh (1991); scored 1,531 points in 21 NHL seasons; elected to Hall of Fame in 2004.

Rocky Colavito (b. August 10, 1933): Baseball OF; six-time all-star who hit 374 HRs over his 14-year career; hugely popular in Cleveland where he played from 1955-59 and then 1965-67; led the league in HRs in 1959 with 42 and RBI in 1965 with 108; hit four consecutive HRs in one game.

Eddie Collins (b. May 2, 1887, d. Mar. 25, 1951): Baseball 2B; led Philadelphia A's (1910-11) and Chicago White Sox (1917) to 3 World Series titles; AL MVP in 1914; had 3,311 career hits and 743 stolen bases.

Nadia Comaneci (b. Nov. 12, 1961): Romanian gymnast; first to record perfect 10 in Olympics; won 3 individual golds at 1976 Olympics and 2 more in '80.

Lionel Conacher (b. May 24, 1901, d. May 26, 1954): Canada's greatest all-around athlete; NHL hockey (2 Stanley Cups), CFL football (1 Grey Cup), minor league baseball, soccer, lacrosse, track, amateur boxing champion; member of Parliament (1949-54).

Tony Conigliaro (b. Jan. 7, 1945, d. Feb. 24, 1990): Baseball OF; youngest (20 years old) to lead the AL in HRs (32 in 1965); hit in the face with a fastball in 1967; came back to hit 36 HRs in 1970 with Red Sox, but was never the same.

Gene Conley (b. Nov. 10, 1930): Baseball and Basketball; played for World Series and NBA champions with Milwaukee Braves (1957) and Boston Celtics (1959-61); losing pitcher in 1954 All-Star Game and winning pitcher in 1955 Game; 91-96 record in 11 seasons.

Billy Conn (b. Oct. 8, 1917, d. May 29, 1993): Boxer; Pittsburgh native and world light heavyweight champion from 1939-41; nearly upset heavyweight champ Joe Louis in 1941 title bout, but was knocked out in 13th round; pro record 63-11-1 with 14 KOs.

Dennis Conner (b. Sept. 16, 1942): Sailing; 3-time America's Cup-winning skipper aboard *Freedom* (1980), *Stars & Stripes* (1987) and the *Stars & Stripes* catamaran (1988); only American skipper to lose Cup, first in 1983 when *Australia II* beat *Liberty* and again in '95 when New Zealand's *Black Magic* swept Conner and his *Stars & Stripes* crew aboard the borrowed *Young America.*

Maureen Connolly (b. Sept. 17, 1934, d. June 21, 1969): Tennis; 1st woman to win Grand Slam (in 1953 at age 18); horse riding accident ended her career in '54 at age 19; won 3 Wimbledons (1952-54), 3 U.S. Opens (1951-53), 2 French Opens (1953-54) and 1 Australian Open (1953); 3-time AP Female Athlete of Year (1951-53).

Jimmy Connors (b. Sept. 2, 1952): Tennis; No.1 player in world 5 times (1974-78); won 5 U.S. Opens, 2 Wimbledons and 1 Australian; rose from No. 936 at the close of 1990 to U.S. Open semifinals in 1991 at age 39; NCAA singles champ (1971); all-time leader in pro singles titles (109) and matches won at U.S. Open (98) and Wimbledon (84).

Jack Kent Cooke (b. Oct. 25, 1912, d. April 6, 1997): Football; sole owner of NFL Washington Redskins from 1985-97; teams won 2 Super Bowls (1988,92); also owned NBA Lakers and NHL Kings in LA; built LA Forum for $12 million in 1967.

Cynthia Cooper (b. April 14, 1963): Women's basketball G; won two NCAA basketball titles at USC (1983-84); won gold medal with U.S. team in 1988; 2-time WNBA MVP and 4-time league champion with Houston Comets; coach of WNBA's Phoenix Mercury 2001-02; coach of Prairie View A&M since 2005.

Angel Cordero Jr. (b. Nov. 8, 1942): Jockey; retired third on all-time list with 7,057 wins in 38,646 starts; won Kentucky Derby 3 times (1974,76,85), Preakness twice and Belmont once; 2-time Eclipse Award winner (1982-83).

Howard Cosell (b. Mar. 25, 1920, d. Apr. 23, 1995): Radio-TV; former ABC commentator on *Monday Night Football* and *Wide World of Sports,* who energized TV sports journalism with abrasive "tell it like it is" style.

Bob Costas (b. Mar. 22, 1952): Radio-TV; NBC broadcaster who has been anchor for NBA, NFL and Olympics as well as baseball play-by-play man; 15-time Emmy winner as studio host/play-by-play and 8-time National Sportscaster of Year.

James (Doc) Counsilman (b. Dec. 28, 1920, d. Jan. 4, 2004): Swimming; coached Indiana men's swim team to 6 NCAA championships (1968-73); coached the 1964 and '76 U.S. men's Olympic teams that won a combined 21 of 24 gold medals; in 1979 became oldest person (59) to swim English Channel; retired in 1990 with dual meet record of 287-36-1.

Fred Couples (b. Oct. 3, 1959): Golfer; 2-time PGA Tour Player of the Year (1991,92); 15 Tour victories, including 1992 Masters.

Jim Courier (b. Aug. 17, 1970): Tennis; No. 1 player in world in 1992, won 2 Australian Opens (1992-93) and 2 French Opens (1991-92); played on 1992 Davis Cup winner; Nick Bollettieri Academy classmate of Andre Agassi; entered Hall of Fame in 2005.

Margaret Smith Court (b. July 16, 1942): Australian tennis player; won Grand Slam in both singles (1970) and mixed doubles (1963 with Ken Fletcher); record 24 Grand Slam singles titles—11 Australian, 5 U.S., 5 French and 3 Wimbledon.

Bob Cousy (b. Aug. 9, 1928): Basketball G; led NBA in assists 8 times; 10-time All-NBA 1st team; 1957 MVP; led Boston to 6 NBA titles (1957,59-63); elected to Hall of Fame in 1970, one of NBA's 50 Greatest Players.

Buster Crabbe (b. Feb. 7, 1908, d. Apr. 23, 1983): Swimmer; 2-time Olympic freestyle medalist with bronze in 1928 (1500m) and gold in '32 (400m); became movie star and King of Serials as Flash Gordon and Buck Rogers.

Ben Crenshaw (b. Jan. 11, 1952): Golfer; co-NCAA champion with Tom Kite in 1972; battled Graves' disease in mid-1980s; 19 career Tour victories; won Masters for second time in 1995 and dedicated it to 90-year-old mentor Harvey Penick, who had died a week earlier; captain of 1999 Ryder Cup team.

Joe Cronin (b. Oct. 12, 1906, d. Sept. 7, 1984): Baseball SS; hit over .300 and drove in over 100 runs 8 times each; player-manager in Washington and Boston (1933-47); AL president (1959-73); No. 4 retired by Red Sox in 1984.

Larry Csonka (b. Dec. 25, 1946): Football RB; powerful runner and blocker who gained 8,081 yards in 11 seasons in the AFL and NFL; won two consecutive Super Bowls with the Miami Dolphins (1973-74) and was named MVP in the latter, rushing for 145 yards and two TDs; member of the College and Pro Football Halls of Fame; rescued from storm-tossed vessel by Coast Guard in Bering Sea in 2005.

Mark Cuban (b. July 31, 1958): Basketball; enthusiastic, outspoken owner of the Dallas Mavericks; co-creator of Broadcast.com, which he sold to Yahoo! in 1999 for roughly $5 billion in Yahoo! stock; purchased the Mavericks in 2000 for $280 million; has spent slightly less than that in fines to the NBA for, among other things, criticizing officials and getting involved in on-court fracases.

Ann Curtis (b. Mar. 6, 1926): Swimming; won two gold medals and one silver in 1948 Olympics; set four world and 18 U.S. records during career; first woman and swimmer to win Sullivan Award (1944).

Betty Cuthbert (b. Apr. 20, 1938): Australian runner; won gold medals in 100 and 200 meters and 4x100m relay at 1956 Olympics; also won 400m gold at 1964 Olympics.

Bjorn Dählie (b. June 19, 1967): Norwegian cross-country skier; winner of a record eight gold and 12 overall Winter Olympic medals from 1992-98.

Chuck Daly (b. July 20, 1930): Basketball; coached Detroit to two NBA titles (1989-90); also coached NBA "Dream Team" to gold medal in 1992 Olympics; retired in 1994 but returned in 1997 to coach Orlando Magic for two seasons.

John Daly (b. Apr. 28, 1966): Golfer; big hitter who was surprise winner of 1991 PGA Championship as unknown 25-year old; battled through personal troubles in 1994 to return in '95 and won 2nd major at British Open, beating Italy's Costantino Rocca in 4-hole playoff; won first PGA Tour event in nine years at 2004 Buick Invitational; has admitted to accumulating somewhere in the range of $50-60 million in gambling losses. ·

Johnny Damon (b. Nov. 5, 1973): Baseball CF; long-haired lead-off man for the 2004 World Series champion Boston Red Sox who became a short-haired lead-off man when he was signed by the New York Yankees in 2006.

Stanley Dancer (b. July 25, 1927, d. Sept. 8, 2005): Harness racing; winner of 4 Hambletonians; trainer-driver of Triple Crown winners in trotting (Nevele Pride in 1968 and Super Bowl in '72) and pacing (Most Happy Fella in 1970).

Beth Daniel (b. Oct. 14, 1956): Golfer; 33 career wins, including 1 major; inducted into World Golf Hall of Fame in 1999.

Alvin Dark (b. Jan. 7, 1922): Baseball IF and MGR; hit .322 to win the NL Rookie of the Year award in 1948 with the Boston Braves; won 994 games as a manager and led the Oakland A's to a World Series win in 1974.

Tamas Darnyi (b. June 3, 1967): Hungarian swimmer; 2-time double gold medal winner in 200m and 400m individual medley at 1988 and '92 Olympics; also won both events in 1986 and '91 world championships; set world records in both at '91 worlds; 1st swimmer to break 2 minutes in 200m IM (1:59:36).

Lindsay Davenport (b. June 8, 1976): Tennis player; became first American female ranked No. 1 in the world (1998) since Chris Evert in 1985; won U.S. Open (1998), Wimbledon (1999) and Australian Open (2000); won Olympic gold medal in 1996; passed Steffi Graf in 2008 to become the WTA Tour's all-time leading money winner.

Al Davis (b. July 4, 1929): Football; GM-coach of Oakland 1963-66; helped force AFL-NFL merger as AFL commissioner in 1966; returned to Oakland as managing general partner and directed club to 3 Super Bowl wins (1977,81,84); defied fellow NFL owners and moved Raiders to LA in 1982; turned down owners' 1995 offer to build him a new stadium in LA and moved back to Oakland instead.

Dwight Davis (b. July 5, 1879, d. Nov. 28, 1945): Tennis; donor of Davis Cup; played for winning U.S. team in 1st two Cup finals (1900,02); won U.S. and Wimbledon doubles titles in 1901; Secretary of War (1925-29) under President Coolidge.

Ernie Davis (b. Dec. 14, 1939, d. May 18, 1963): Football; star running back at Syracuse University; first black player to win the Heisman Trophy in 1961; drafted by the Washington Redskins and traded to Cleveland but died the following year of leukemia before playing a pro game.

Glenn Davis (b. Dec. 26, 1924, d. Mar. 9, 2005): Football HB; 3-time All-America; led Army to national titles in 1944-45; Doc Blanchard's running mate; won Heisman Trophy in 1946.

John Davis (b. Jan. 12, 1921, d. July 13, 1984): Weightlifting; 6-time world champion; 2-time Olympic super-heavyweight champ (1948,52); undefeated from 1938-53.

Terrell Davis (b. Oct. 28, 1972): Football RB; 1998 NFL MVP, rushing for a league-leading 2,008 yards (4th all-time); played for two Super Bowl winners in Denver (XXXII and XXXIII), earning MVP honors in the former with Super Bowl-record 3 rushing touchdowns.

Pat Day (b. Oct. 13, 1953): Jockey; four-time Eclipse award winner (1984,86,87,91); became all-time leader in earnings in 2002; has 8,803 career victories; won Kentucky Derby (1992), five Preaknesses (1985,90,94-96) and three Belmonts (1989,94,2000); inducted into Hall of Fame in 1991; retired in 2005.

Ron Dayne (b. Mar. 14, 1978): Football RB; NCAA Div. I-A all-time leading rusher, gaining 6,397 yards at Wisconsin (1996-99); 1999 Heisman Trophy winner; selected in 1st round (11th overall) of 2000 NFL draft by NY Giants.

Dizzy Dean (b. Jan. 16 1911, d. July 17, 1974): Baseball RHP; led NL in strikeouts and complete games four times; last NL pitcher to win 30 games (30-7 in 1934); MVP in 1934 with St. Louis; 150-83 all-time record.

Dave DeBusschere (b. Oct. 16, 1940, d. May, 14, 2003): Basketball F; youngest coach in NBA history (24 in 1964); player-coach of Detroit Pistons (1964-67); played in 8 All-Star games; won 2 NBA titles as player with NY Knicks (1970, 73); ABA commissioner (1975-76); also pitched 2 seasons for Chicago White Sox (1962-63) with 3-4 record.

Pierre de Coubertin (b. Jan. 1, 1863, d. Sept. 2, 1937): French educator; father of the Modern Olympic Games; IOC president from 1896-1925.

Brian Deegan (b. May 9, 1975): Freestyle Motocross Rider; early pioneer of FMX; winner of 10 combined X Games medals; first rider to land a 360 in competition; WFA Series champ (1999); L.A. Coliseum Supercross winner (1999–125cc); experienced numerous life-threatening crashes; featured in over 20 motocross videos.

Anita DeFrantz (b. Oct. 4, 1952): Olympics; attorney who became the International Olympic Committee's first female vice president in 1997; first woman to represent U.S. on IOC (elected in 1986); member of USOC Executive Committee; member of bronze medal U.S. women's eight-oared shell at Montreal in 1976.

Oscar De La Hoya (b. Feb. 4, 1973): Boxer; 1992 Olympic gold medallist (lightweight); has held world titles in 4 weight classes; was unbeaten until losing WBC Welterweight belt to Felix Trinidad in a majority decision in 1999; later moved to jr. middleweight and won WBA and WBC belts; TKO'd in by Bernard Hopkins in their undisputed middleweight title fight in 2004; defeated Ricardo Mayorga in 2005 for WBC Super Welterweight title, then lost title to Floyd Mayweather Jr. in a split decision in May 2007.

Cedric Dempsey (b. Apr. 14, 1932): College sports; succeeded Dick Schultz as NCAA executive director (title later changed to president) in 1993 and served until the end of 2002; former athletic director at Pacific (1967-79), San Diego St. (1979), Houston (1979-82) and Arizona (1983-93).

Jack Dempsey (b. June 24, 1895, d. May 31, 1983): Boxer; world heavyweight champion from 1919-26; lost title to Gene Tunney, then lost "Long Count" rematch in 1927 when he floored Tunney in 7th round but failed to retreat to neutral corner; pro record 64-6-9 with 49 KOs.

Bob Devaney (b. April 13, 1915, d. May 9, 1997): Football; head coach at Wyoming from 1957-1961; from 1962 to 1972 built Nebraska into a college football power; won 2 consecutive national titles in 1970-71; later served as Nebraska's A.D.

Donna de Varona (b. Apr. 26, 1947): Swimming; won gold medals in 400 IM and 400 freestyle relay at 1964 Olympics; set 18 world records during career; co-founder of Women's Sports Foundation in 1974.

Gail Devers (b. Nov. 19, 1966): Track & Field; won Olympic gold medal in 100 meters in 1992 and '96; world champion in 100 meters (1993) and 100-meter hurdles (1993,95,99); overcame thyroid disorder (Graves' disease) that sidelined her in 1989-90 and nearly resulted in having both feet amputated.

Eric Dickerson (b. Sept. 2, 1960): Football RB; led NFL in rushing 4 times (1983-84,86,88); ran for single-season record 2,105 yards in 1984; NFC Rookie of Year in 1983; All-Pro 5 times; traded from LA Rams to Indianapolis (Oct. 31, 1987) in 3-team, 10-player deal (including draft picks); 6th on all-time career rushing list with 13,259 yards in 11 seasons.

Harrison Dillard (b. July 8, 1923): Track & Field; only man to win Olympic gold medals in both sprints (100m in 1948) and hurdles (110m in 1952).

Joe DiMaggio (b. Nov. 25, 1914, d. Mar. 8, 1999): Baseball OF; hit safely in 56 straight games (1941); led AL in batting, HRs and RBI twice each; 3-time MVP (1939,41,47); hit .325 with 361 HRs over 13 seasons; led NY Yankees to 10 World Series titles.

Marcel Dionne (b. Aug. 3, 1951): Hockey C; fifth on NHL's all-time points list (1,771) and fourth on goals list (731) through 2008; tied Wayne Gretzky for the league lead in points (137) in 1980; scored 50 goals in a season 6 times; member of the Hockey HOF.

Mike Ditka (b. Oct. 18, 1939): Football; All-America at Pitt (1960); NFL Rookie of Year (1961); 5-time Pro Bowl tight end for Chicago Bears; returned to Chicago as head coach in 1982 and to Super Bowl XX in 1986; left Bears in 1992 and worked as a broadcaster at NBC for four years; coached the New Orleans Saints from 1997-99; compiled 127-101-0 record in 14 seasons; currently an ESPN analyst.

Larry Doby (b. Dec. 13, 1924, d. June 18, 2003): Baseball OF; first black player in the AL; joined the Cleveland Indians in July 1947, three months after Jackie Robinson entered the Majors with the NL's Brooklyn Dodgers; an all-star centerfielder from 1949-55; managed the Chicago White Sox in 1978, becoming the second black major league manager; inducted into the Hall of Fame in 1998.

Charlotte (Lottie) Dod (b. Sept. 24, 1871, d. June 27, 1960): British athlete; 5-time Wimbledon singles champion (1887-88,91-93); youngest player ever to win Wimbledon (15 in 1887); archery silver medalist at 1908 Olympics; member of national field hockey team in 1899; 1904 British Amateur golf champ.

Tim Donaghy (b. Jan. 7, 1967): Basketball; NBA referee from 1994-2007; rocked the NBA in 2007 when he plead guilty to betting on games, including some he officiated, and providing inside information to other bettors.

Tony Dorsett (b. Apr. 7, 1954): Football RB; won Heisman Trophy leading Pitt to national title in 1976; 3rd all-time in NCAA Div. I-A rushing with 6,082 yards; led Dallas to Super Bowl title as NFC Rookie of Year (1977); NFC Player of Year (1981); rushed for 12,739 yards in 12 years.

James (Buster) Douglas (b. Apr. 7, 1960): Boxer; 42-1 shot who knocked out undefeated Mike Tyson in 10th round on Feb. 10, 1990 to win heavyweight title in Tokyo; 8½ months later, lost only title defense to Evander Holyfield by KO in 3rd round.

Vicki Manalo Draves (b. Dec. 31, 1924): Diver; First woman in olympic history to win gold medals in both platform diving and springboard diving; inducted into Int'l Swimming Hall of Fame in 1969.

The Dream Team Head coach Chuck Daly's "Best Ever" 12-man NBA All-Star squad that headlined the 1992 Summer Olympics in Barcelona and easily won the basketball gold medal; co-captained by Larry Bird and Magic Johnson, with veterans Charles Barkley, Clyde Drexler, Patrick Ewing, Michael Jordan, Karl Malone, Chris Mullin, Scottie Pippen, David Robinson, John Stockton and Duke's Christian Laettner.

Heike Drechsler (b. Dec. 16, 1964): German long jumper and sprinter; East German before reunification in 1991; set world long jump record (24-2¼) in 1988; won long jump gold medals at 1992 Olympics and 1983 and '93 World Championships.

Ken Dryden (b. Aug. 8, 1947): Hockey G; led Montreal to 6 Stanley Cup titles; playoff MVP as rookie in 1971; won or shared 5 Vezina trophies; 2.24 career GAA; Canadian politician, lawyer and businessman.

Don Drysdale (b. July 23, 1936, d. July 3, 1993): Baseball RHP; led NL in strikeouts 3 times and games started 4 straight years; pitched record 6 shutouts in a row in 1968; won Cy Young (1962); had 209-166 record and hit 29 HRs in 14 years.

Charley Dumas (b. Feb. 12, 1937): U.S. high jumper; first man to clear 7 feet (7-0½) on June 29, 1956; won gold medal at 1956 Olympics.

Tim Duncan (b. Apr. 25, 1976): Basketball C/F; drafted first overall by San Antonio in 1997 NBA Draft; 7-footer who dominates on offense and defense; has won 4 NBA titles (1999, 2003, 2005, 2007) earning Finals MVP honors each time; 2-time NBA MVP (2002-03); 1997 College Player of the Year at Wake Forest; 1998 NBA Rookie of the Year.

Margaret Osborne du Pont (b. Mar. 4, 1918): Tennis; won 5 French, 7 Wimbledon and an unprecedented 25 U.S. national titles in singles, doubles and mixed doubles from 1941-62.

Roberto Duran (b. June 16, 1951): Panamanian boxer; one of only 6 fighters to hold 4 different world titles— lightweight (1972-79), welterweight (1980), junior middleweight (1983) and middleweight (1989-90); lost famous "No Mas" welterweight title bout when he quit in 8th round against Sugar Ray Leonard (1980); retired in 2002 at age 50 (104-16, 69 KOs).

Tony Dungy (b. Oct. 6, 1955): Football; Coach of Tampa Bay Buccaneers from 1996-2001 and current coach of Indianapolis Colts since 2002; became first black head coach in NFL history to win a Super Bowl with the Colts' victory over the Bears in 2007; also won Super Bowl as a player with Steelers (1978).

Leo Durocher (b. July 27, 1905, d. Oct. 7, 1991): Baseball; managed in NL 24 years; won 2,015 games, including postseason; 3 pennants with Brooklyn (1941) and NY Giants (1951,54); won World Series in 1954.

Eddie Eagan (b. Apr. 26, 1898, d. June 14, 1967): Only athlete to win gold medals in both Summer and Winter Olympics (Boxing—1920, Bobsled—1932).

Alan Eagleson (b. Apr. 24, 1933): Hockey; Toronto lawyer, agent and 1st executive director of NHL Players Assn. (1967-90); midwifed Team Canada vs. Soviet series (1972) and Canada Cup; charged with racketeering and defrauding NHLPA in 1994; sentenced to 18 months in jail after pleading guilty but only served 6 months; resigned from Hall of Fame.

Dale Earnhardt (b. Apr. 29, 1951, d. Feb. 18, 2001): Auto racer; 7-time NASCAR national champion (1980,86-87,90-91,93-94); Rookie of Year in 1979; was all-time NASCAR money leader with over $34 million won and 76 career wins when he died; finally won Daytona 500 in 1998 on 20th attempt; died in last lap crash at the 2001 Daytona 500.

James Easton (b. July 26, 1935): Olympics; archer and sporting goods manufacturer (Easton softball bats); one of 4 American delegates to the International Olympic Committee; member of LA Olympic Organizing Committee in 1984.

Dennis Eckersley (b. Oct. 3, 1954): Baseball P; began his career as a starter in 1975 with Cleveland; no-hit Angels in 1977; won 20 games in 1978 with Boston; moved to the bullpen after 12 seasons as a starter and became one of the best closers of all-time with Oakland; won 1992 AL Cy Young and MVP.

Stefan Edberg (b. Jan. 19, 1966): Swedish tennis player; 2-time No.1 player (1990-91); 2-time winner of Australian Open (1985,87), Wimbledon (1988,90) and U.S. Open (1991-92).

Gertrude Ederle (b. Oct. 23, 1906, d. Nov. 30, 2003): Swimmer; 1st woman to swim English Channel, breaking men's record by 2 hours in 1926; won 3 medals in 1924 Olympics.

Krisztina Egerszegi (b. Aug. 16, 1974): Hungarian swimmer; 3-time gold medal winner (100m and 200m backstroke and 400m IM) at 1992 Olympics; also won a gold (200m back) and silver (100m back) at 1988 Games; youngest (14) ever to win swimming gold. Won fifth gold medal (200m back) at '96 Games.

Lee Elder (b. July 14, 1934): Golf; in 1975, became the first black golfer to play in the Masters Tournament; also played in the 1977 Masters; member of the 1979 U.S. Ryder Cup team; played in South Africa's first integrated tournament in 1972.

Todd Eldredge (b. Aug. 28, 1971): Figure Skater; 6-time U.S. champion (1990,91,95,97,98,2002); 1996 World Champion; won U.S. titles at all three levels (novice, junior and senior); most decorated American figure skater without an Olympic medal.

Bill Elliott (b. Oct. 8, 1955): Auto racer; 2-time winner of Daytona 500 (1985,87); NASCAR national champ in 1988; 44 career NASCAR wins.

Herb Elliott (b. Feb. 25, 1938): Australian runner; undefeated from 1958-60; ran 17 sub-4:00 miles; 3 world records; won gold medal in 1500 meters at 1960 Olympics; retired at age 22.

Ernie Els (b. Oct. 17, 1969): Golfer; sweet swinging South African; 1994 PGA Tour Rookie of the Year and European Golfer of the Year; 2-time U.S. Open winner (1994,97); won 3rd major in 2002 British Open playoff; 16 PGA Tour wins.

John Elway (b. June 28, 1960): Football QB; All-American at Stanford; #1 overall pick in the famous quarterback draft of 1983; known for his last-minute, game-winning scoring drives; led Broncos to 3 Super Bowl losses before back-to-back wins in Super Bowl XXXII and XXXIII; 1987 NFL MVP; 4-time Pro Bowler; one of only three quarterbacks (Favre & Marino) to throw for over 50,000 yards.

Roy Emerson (b. Nov. 3, 1936): Australian tennis player; won 12 majors in singles— 6 Australian, 2 French, 2 Wimbledon and 2 U.S. from 1961-67.

Kornelia Ender (b. Oct. 25, 1958): East German swimmer; 1st woman to win 4 gold medals at one Olympics (1976), all in world-record time.

Julius Erving (b. Feb. 22, 1950): Basketball F; "Dr. J"; changed game in the ABA, then NBA with his "above-the-rim" style of play; in ABA (1971-76): 3-time MVP, 2-time playoff MVP, led NY Nets to 2 titles (1974,76); in NBA (1976-87): 5-time All-NBA 1st team, MVP in 1981, led Philadelphia 76ers to 1983 NBA title.

Phil Esposito (b. Feb. 20, 1942): Hockey C; 1st NHL player to score 100 points in a season (126 in 1969); 6-time All-NHL 1st team with Boston (1969-74); 2-time MVP (1969,74); 5-time scoring champ; star of 1972 Canada-Soviet series; former president-GM of Tampa Bay Lightning.

Janet Evans (b. Aug. 28, 1971): Swimmer; won 3 individual gold medals (400m & 800m freestyle, 400m IM) at 1988 Olympics; 1989 Sullivan Award winner; won 1 gold (800m) and 1 silver (400m) at 1992 Olympics.

Lee Evans (b. Feb. 25, 1947): Track & Field; dominant quarter-miler in world from 1966-72; world record in 400m set at 1968 Olympics stood 20 years.

Chris Evert (b. Dec. 21, 1954): Tennis; No. 1 player in world 5 times (1975-77,80-81); won at least 1 Grand Slam singles-title every year from 1974-86; 18 majors in all— 7 French, 6 U.S., 3 Wimbledon and 2 Australian; retired after 1989 season with 154 singles titles and $8,896,195 in career earnings.

Weeb Ewbank (b. May 6, 1907, d. Nov. 18, 1998): Football; only coach to win NFL and AFL titles; led Baltimore to 2 NFL titles (1958-59) and NY Jets to Super Bowl III win.

Patrick Ewing (b. Aug. 5, 1962): Basketball C; 3-time All-America; led Georgetown to 3 NCAA Finals and 1984 title; Final 4 MOP in '84; 1986 NBA Rookie of Year with New York; All-NBA (1990); on U.S. Olympic gold medal-winning teams in 1984 and '92; named one of the NBA's 50 Greatest Players; inducted into Hall of Fame in 2008.

Ray Ewry (b. Oct. 14, 1873, d. Sept. 29, 1937): Track & Field; won 10 gold medals (although 2 are not recognized by IOC) over 4 consecutive Olympics (1900,04,06,08); all events he won (Standing HJ, LJ and TJ) were discontinued in 1912.

Nick Faldo (b. July 18, 1957): British golfer; 3-time winner of British Open (1987,90,92) and Masters (1989, 90, 96); 3-time European Golfer of Year (1989-90,92); PGA Player of Year in 1990.

Juan Manuel Fangio (b. June 24, 1911, d. July 17, 1995): Argentine auto racer; 5-time F1 world champ (1951,54-57); 24 career wins, retired in 1958.

Marshall Faulk (b. Feb. 26, 1973): Football RB; 3-time consensus All-America at San Diego St.; 2-time NCAA Div. I-A rushing leader (1991-92); 2nd overall pick (Indianapolis) of the 1994 NFL draft; traded to St.L Rams in 1999; NFL MVP in 2000 (AP/PFWA) and 2001 (Bell/PFWA); scored 26 TDs in 2000.

Brett Favre (b. Oct. 10, 1969): Football; Strong-armed Southern Miss. QB drafted in 1991 in the 2nd round (33rd overall) by Atlanta; traded to Green Bay in 1992; 3-time league MVP (1995-97); 8-time Pro Bowl QB; led Packers to Super Bowl victory over New England in 1997; became NFL all-time leader in passing yards and TD passes in 2007; also holds marks for most completions, attempts, interceptions and wins as a starting QB; holds NFL quarterback record for consecutive games started, with over 250...and counting; traded to NY Jets in 2008.

Sergei Fedorov (b. Dec. 13, 1969): Hockey C; first Russian to win NHL Hart Trophy as 1993-94 regular season MVP; 5-time All-Star and 3-time Stanley Cup winner (1997,98,2002) with Detroit.

Roger Federer (b. Aug. 8, 1981): Tennis; top-ranked men's tennis player for a record 237 straight weeks from February 2004 to August 2008; winner of 13 Grand Slam events (behind only Pete Sampras' 14): Australian Open (2004,06,07), Wimbledon (2003-07); U.S. Open (2004-08); recorded a 55-match win streak in North America; 4-time ATP Player of the Year (2004-07); Olympic gold medalist (doubles) in Beijing in 2008.

Donald Fehr (b. July 18, 1948): Baseball labor leader; protégé of Marvin Miller; executive director and general counsel of Major League Players Assn. since 1983; led players in 1994 "salary cap" strike that lasted eight months and resulted in first cancellation of World Series since 1904.

Bob Feller (b. Nov. 3, 1918): Baseball RHP; Hall of Fame fire-baller who led AL in strikeouts 7 times and wins 6 times with Cleveland Indians; threw 3 no-hitters and major league record 12 one-hitters; 266-162 record; amassed 2,581 Ks despite missing four seasons to military service during WWII.

Tom Ferguson (b. Dec. 20, 1950): Rodeo; 6-time All-Around champion (1974-79); 1st cowboy to win $100,000 in one season (1978); 1st to win $1 million in career (1986).

Herve Filion (b. Feb. 1, 1940): Harness racing; 10-time Driver of Year; first driver to win over 15,000 races.

Rollie Fingers (b. Aug. 25, 1946): Baseball RHP; mustachioed relief ace with 341 career saves; won AL MVP and Cy Young awards in 1981 with Milwaukee; World Series MVP in 1974 with Oakland; elected to Hall of Fame in 1992.

Charles O. Finley (b. Feb. 22, 1918, d. Feb. 19, 1997): Baseball owner; moved KC A's to Oakland in 1968; won 3 straight World Series from 1972-74; also owned teams in NHL and ABA.

Bobby Fischer (b. Mar. 9, 1943, d. Jan. 17, 2008): Chess; at 15, became youngest international grandmaster in chess history; only American to hold world championship (1972-75); was stripped of title in 1975 after refusing to defend against Anatoly Karpov and became recluse; re-emerged to defeat old foe and former world champion Boris Spassky in 1992.

Carlton Fisk (b. Dec. 26, 1947): Baseball C; holds all-time major league record for games caught (2,226); also held HR record for catchers (351) until 2004 (Mike Piazza); AL Rookie of Year (1972) and 10-time All-Star; hit epic, 12th-inning Game 6 homer for Boston Red Sox in 1975 World Series; elected to the Hall of Fame in 2000.

Emerson Fittipaldi (b. Dec. 12, 1946): Brazilian auto racer; 2-time Formula One world champion (1972,74); 2-time winner of Indy 500 (1989,93); won overall IndyCar title in 1989.

Bob Fitzsimmons (b. May 26, 1863, d. Oct. 22, 1917): British boxer; held 3 world titles— middleweight (1881-97), heavyweight (1897-99) and light heavyweight (1903-05); pro record 40-11 with 32 KOs.

James (Sunny Jim) Fitzsimmons (b. July 23, 1874, d. Mar. 11, 1966): Horse racing; trained horses that won over 2,275 races, including 2 Triple Crown winners—Gallant Fox in 1930 and Omaha in '35.

Jim Fixx (b. Apr. 23, 1932, d. July 20, 1984): Running; author who popularized the sport of running; his 1977 bestseller *The Complete Book of Running*, is credited with helping start America's fitness revolution; ironically died of a heart attack while running.

Larry Fleisher (b. Sept. 26, 1930, d. May 4, 1989): Basketball; led NBA players union from 1961-89; increased average yearly salary from $9,400 in 1967 to $600,000 without a strike.

Peggy Fleming (b. July 27, 1948): Figure skating; 3-time world champion (1966-68); won Olympic gold medal in 1968.

Curt Flood (b. Jan. 18, 1938, d. Jan. 20, 1997): Baseball OF; played 15 years (1956-69,71) mainly with St. Louis; hit over .300 6 times with 7 Gold Gloves; refused trade to Phillies in 1969; lost challenge to baseball's reserve clause in Supreme Court in 1972 but his case helped bring free agency to MLB.

Ray Floyd (b. Sept. 14, 1942): Golfer; has 22 PGA victories in 4 decades; joined Senior PGA Tour in 1992 and has 14 Senior wins; has won Masters (1976), U.S. Open (1986), PGA twice (1969,82) and PGA Seniors Championship (1995); first player to win on PGA and Senior tours in same year (1992); member of 8 Ryder Cup teams and captain in 1989.

Doug Flutie (b. Oct. 23, 1962): Football QB; Boston College QB who threw famous 48-yard "Hail Mary" to defeat Miami on Nov. 23, 1984; 1984 Heisman Trophy winner; played in USFL, NFL and CFL; 6-time CFL MVP; led Calgary (1992) and Toronto (1996-97) to Grey Cup titles; on Jan. 1, 2007, recorded the NFL's first drop kick since 1941.

Whitey Ford (b. Oct. 21, 1928): Baseball LHP; all-time leader in World Series wins (10); led AL in wins 3 times; won Cy Young and World Series MVP in 1961 with NY Yankees; 236-106 record.

George Foreman (b. Jan. 10, 1949): Boxer; Olympic heavyweight champ (1968); world heavyweight champ (1973-74, 94-95); lost title to Muhammad Ali (KO-8th) in '74; recaptured it on Nov. 5, 1994 at age 45 with a 10-round KO of WBA/IBF champ Michael Moorer, becoming the oldest man to win heavyweight crown; named AP Male Athlete of Year 20 years after losing title to Ali; stripped of WBA title in 1995 after declining to fight No. 1 contender; successfully defended title at age 46 against 26-year-old Axel Schulz in controversial maj. decision; gave up IBF title after refusing rematch with Schulz.

Dick Fosbury (b. Mar. 6, 1947): Track & Field; revolutionized high jump with back-first "Fosbury Flop"; won gold medal at 1968 Olympics.

Greg Foster (b. Aug. 4, 1958): Track & Field; 3-time winner of World Championship in 110-m hurdles (1983,87,91); won silver in 1984 Olympics; world indoor champion in 1991.

The Four Horsemen Senior backfield that led Notre Dame to national collegiate football championship in 1924; put together as sophomores by Irish coach Knute Rockne; immortalized by sportswriter Grantland Rice, whose report of the Oct. 19, 1924, Notre Dame-Army game began: "Outlined against a blue, gray October sky the Four Horsemen rode again..."; HB Jim Crowley (b. Sept. 10, 1902, d. Jan. 15, 1986), FB Elmer Layden (b. May 4, 1903, d. June 30, 1973), HB Don Miller (b. May 30, 1902, d. July 28, 1979) and QB Harry Stuhldreher (b. Oct. 14, 1901, d. Jan. 26, 1965).

The Four Musketeers French quartet that dominated men's tennis in 1920s and '30s, winning 8 straight French singles titles (1925-32), 6 Wimbledons in a row (1924-29) and 6 consecutive Davis Cups (1927-32)— Jean Borotra (b. Aug. 13, 1898, d. July 17, 1994), Jacques Brugnon (b. May 11, 1895, d. Mar. 20, 1978), Henri Cochet (b. Dec. 14, 1901, d. Apr. 1, 1987), Rene Lacoste (b. July 2, 1905, d. Oct. 13, 1996).

Nellie Fox (b. Dec. 25, 1927, d. Dec. 1, 1975): Baseball 2B; batted .306 in 1959 to win the AL MVP award with the pennant-winning Chicago White Sox; led the league in fielding percentage six times, hits four times and triples once; ended his 19-year career with 2,663 hits, 1,279 runs and .288 average.

Jimmie Foxx (b. Oct. 22, 1907, d. July 21, 1967): Baseball 1B; led AL in home runs 4 times and batting average twice; won Triple Crown in 1933; 3-time MVP (1932-33,38) with Philadelphia and Boston; hit 30 HRs or more 12 years in a row; 534 career HRs.

A.J. Foyt (b. Jan. 16, 1935): Auto racer; 7-time USAC-CART national champion (1960-61,63-64, 67,75,79); 4-time Indy 500 winner (1961,64, 67,77); only driver in history to win Indy 500, Daytona 500 (1972) and 24 Hours of LeMans (1967 with Dan Gurney); retired in 1993 as all-time CART wins leader with 67.

Bill France Sr. (b. Sept. 26, 1909, d. June 7, 1992): Stock car pioneer and promoter; founded NASCAR in 1948; guided race circuit through formative years; built both Daytona (Fla.) Int'l Speedway and Talladega (Ala.) Superspeedway.

Dawn Fraser (b. Sept. 4, 1937): Australian swimmer; won gold medals in 100m freestyle at 3 consecutive Olympics (1956,60,64).

Joe Frazier (b. Jan. 12, 1944): Boxer; 1964 Olympic heavyweight champion; world heavyweight champ (1970-73); decisioned former champ Muhammad Ali in March 1971 in one of the most anticipated prizefights in history, fought Ali twice more, losing both times including the "Thrilla in Manila" in 1975; pro record 32-4-1 with 27 KOs.

Walt Frazier (b. March 29, 1945): Basketball G; won the NBA championship twice (1970 and 73) with the New York Knicks; stole spotlight from teammate Willis Reed in Game 7 of 1970 Finals vs. the Lakers with 36 points, 19 assists and 5 steals; averaged 18.9 PPG and 6.1 APG over his career; four-time all-NBA and a member of the Hall of Fame; nicknamed "Clyde" after well-dressed gangster Clyde Barrow.

Cathy Freeman (b. Feb. 16, 1973): Track & Field; Australian Aborigine who lit the cauldron at the start of the 2000 Olympic Games in Sydney and later won gold in the 400-meters on her home soil; 2-time world champion in the 400-meters (1997,99).

Ford Frick (b. Dec. 19, 1894, d. Apr. 8, 1978): Baseball; sportswriter and radio announcer who served as NL president (1934-51) and commissioner (1951-65); convinced record-keepers to list Roger Maris' and Babe Ruth's season records separately; major leagues moved to West Coast and expanded from 16 to 20 teams during his tenure.

Frankie Frisch (b. Sept. 9, 1898, d. Mar. 12, 1973): Baseball 2B; played on 8 NL pennant winners in 19 years with NY and St. Louis; hit .300 or better 11 years in a row (1921-31); MVP in 1931; player-manager from 1933-37.

Dan Gable (b. Oct. 25, 1948): Wrestling; career wrestling record of 118-1 (Larry Owings beat him in his final collegiate match) at Iowa St., where he was a 2-time NCAA champ (1968,69) and tourney MVP in 1969 (137 lbs); won gold medal (149 lbs) at 1972 Olympics; coached Iowa to 9 straight NCAA titles (1978-86) and 15 overall in 21 years.

Eddie Gaedel (b. June 8, 1925, d. June 18, 1961): Baseball PH; St. Louis Browns' 3-foot-7 player whose career lasted one at bat (he walked) on Aug 19, 1951; hired as a publicity stunt by owner Bill Veeck.

Clarence (Big House) Gaines (b. May 21, 1924, d. April 18, 2005): Basketball; 828-447 record in 47 years as coach of Div. II Winston-Salem.

Alonzo (Jake) Gaither (b. Apr. 11, 1903, d. Feb. 18, 1994): Football; head coach at Florida A&M for 25 years; led Rattlers to 6 national black college titles; retired after 1969 season with record of 203-36-4 and a winning percentage of .844; coined phrase, "I like my boys agile, mobile and hostile."

Rulon Gardner (b. Aug. 16, 1971): Olympic wrestler; surprise winner of the super heavyweight Greco-Roman gold medal at the 2000 Sydney Games; beat unbeatable Russian legend Alexandre Kareline, 1-0; won 2000 Sullivan Award and USOC Sportsman of the Year Award; lost a toe to frostbite in 2002 but still took bronze medal in Athens (2004).

Cito Gaston (b. Mar. 17, 1944): Baseball; managed Toronto to consecutive World Series titles (1992-93); first black manager to win Series.

Justin Gatlin (b. Feb. 10, 1982): American sprinter; won 100m gold medal and 200m bronze at 2004 Summer Olympics in Athens; tied 100-m record (9.77) in May 2006 but that mark was later anulled; serving an 4-year ban for a 2nd positive drug test.

Lou Gehrig (b. June 19, 1903, d. June 2, 1941): Baseball 1B; played in 2,130 consecutive games from 1925-39 a major league record until Cal Ripken Jr. surpassed it in 1995; led AL in RBI 5 times and HRs 3 times; drove in 100 runs or more 13 years in a row; 2-time MVP (1927,36); hit .340 with 493 HRs over 17 seasons; led NY Yankees to 6 World Series titles; died at age 37 of Amyotrophic Lateral Sclerosis (ALS), a rare and incurable disease of the nervous system now better known as Lou Gehrig's disease.

Bernie Geoffrion (b. Feb. 14, 1931, d. Mar. 11, 2006): Hockey RW; credited with popularizing the slap shot, earning his nickname "Boom Boom"; scored 30 goals in 1952 to win the NHL's Calder Trophy (Rookie of the Year Award); won the MVP award (Hart) in 1955; became the second player in history to score 50 goals in one season; led the league in points in 1955 and 61; won 6 Stanley Cups with Montreal; member of the Hockey Hall of Fame.

George Gervin (b. April 27, 1952): Basketball G/F; joined the ABA in 1972 and came to the NBA with San Antonio in 1976; a five-time NBA all-star; led the league in scoring four times; scored 26,595 points with an average of 25.1 per game; known as the "Iceman" because of his cool style; elected to the Hall of Fame in 1996.

A. Bartlett Giamatti (b. Apr. 14, 1938, d. Sept. 1, 1989): Scholar and seventh commissioner of baseball; banned Pete Rose for life for betting on Major League games and associating with known gamblers; also served as the president of Yale (1978-86) and the NL (1986-89); father of character actor Paul.

Joe Gibbs (b. Nov. 25, 1940): Football; coached Washington to 3 Super Bowl titles in 12 seasons before retiring in 1993; owner of NASCAR racing team that won 1993 Daytona 500 and 2000 Winston Cup title; lured out of retirement to coach Redskins from 2004-07; retired after 2007 season with 171 wins, 10th on the all-time list.

Althea Gibson (b. Aug. 25, 1927, d. Sept. 28, 2003): Tennis; won both Wimbledon and U.S. championships in 1957 and '58; 1st African-American to play in either tourney and 1st to win each title.

Bob Gibson (b. Nov. 9, 1935): Baseball RHP; won 20 or more games 5 times; won 2 NL Cy Youngs (1968,70); MVP in 1968; led St. Louis to 2 World Series titles (1964,67); his ERA of 1.12 in 1968 is the lowest for a starter since 1914; 251-174 record.

Josh Gibson (b. Dec. 21, 1911, d. Jan. 20, 1947): Baseball C; the "Babe Ruth of the Negro Leagues"; Satchel Paige's battery mate with Pittsburgh Crawfords. The Negro Leagues did not keep accurate records but Gibson hit 84 home runs in one season and his Baseball Hall of Fame plaque says he hit "almost 800" home runs in his 17-year career.

Kirk Gibson (b. May 28, 1957): Baseball OF; All-America flanker at Mich. St. in 1978; chose baseball career and was AL playoff MVP with Detroit in 1984 and NL regular season MVP with Los Angeles in 1988; hit famous pinch-hit home run against Oakland's Dennis Eckersley in Game 1 of the 1988 World Series to vault the Dodgers to the title.

Frank Gifford (b. Aug. 16, 1930): Football HB; 4-time All-Pro (1955-57,59); NFL MVP in 1956; led NY Giants to 3 NFL title games; longtime TV sportscaster, beginning career in 1958 while still a player; scandal struck the married Gifford after he was videotaped in a compromising position with a former stewardess in 1997.

Sid Gillman (b. Oct. 26, 1911, d. Jan. 3, 2003): Football innovator; coach elected to both College and Pro Football Halls of Fame; led college teams at Miami-OH and Cincinnati to combined 81-19-2 record from 1944-54; coached LA Rams (1955-59) in NFL, then led LA-San Diego Chargers to 5 Western titles and 1 league championship in first six years of AFL.

George Gipp (b. Feb. 18, 1895, d. Dec. 14, 1920): Football HB; died of throat infection 2 weeks before he made All-America at Notre Dame; rushed for 2,341 yards, scored 156 points and averaged 38 yards a punt in 4 years (1917-20); inspiration for Knute Rockne's "Win one for the Gipper" speech.

Marc Girardelli (b. July 18, 1963): Luxembourg Alpine skier; Austrian native who refused to join Austrian Ski Federation because he wanted to be coached by his father; won unprecedented 5th overall World Cup title in 1993; winless at Olympics, although he won 2 silver medals in 1992.

Tom Glavine (b. Mar. 26, 1966): Baseball LHP; led the majors in wins from 1991-95 with 91; NL Cy Young winner in 1991 and '98; eighth-time All-Star; World Series MVP with Atlanta in 1995; one of only 23 pitchers in MLB history to record 300 wins.

Tom Gola (b. Jan. 13, 1933): Basketball F; 4-time All-America and 1955 Player of Year at La Salle; MOP in 1952 NIT and '54 NCAA Final 4, leading Explorers to both titles; won NBA title as rookie with Philadelphia Warriors in 1956; 4-time NBA All-Star.

Marshall Goldberg (b. Oct. 24, 1917, d. Apr. 3, 2006): Football HB; 2-time consensus All-America at Pittsburgh (1937-38); led Pitt to national championship in 1937; played on NFL champion Chicago Cardinals 10 years later.

Lefty Gomez (b. Nov. 26, 1908, d. Feb. 17, 1989): Baseball LHP; 4-time 20-game winner with NY Yankees; holds World Series record for most wins (6) without a defeat; pitched on 5 world championship clubs in 1930s.

Pancho Gonzales (b. May 9, 1928, d. July 3, 1995): Tennis; won consecutive U.S. Championships in 1948-49 before turning pro at 21; dominated pro tour from 1950-61; in 1969 at age 41, played longest Wimbledon match ever (5:12), beating Charlie Pasarell 22-24,1-6,16-14,6-3,11-9.

Bob Goodenow (b. Oct. 29, 1952): Hockey; succeeded Alan Eagleson as executive director of NHL Players Association in 1990; led players on 10-day strike in 1992, during 103-day owners' lockout in 1994-95 and lockout in 2004; resigned in 2005.

Roger Goodell (b. Feb. 19, 1959): Football; former NFL intern who rose quickly through the ranks and was elected to succeed Paul Tagliabue as the Commissioner of the league on Aug. 8, 2006; joined the NFL as an intern in 1981 after graduating from Washington & Jefferson College; also worked in P.R. for the N.Y. Jets, as assistant to AFC president Lamar Hunt, and in many positions for Tagliabue including Executive V.P. and COO from 2001-06.

Gail Goodrich (b. April 23, 1943): Basketball G; starred at UCLA and won two national championships in 1964 and 1965 under legendary coach John Wooden's tutelage; won the NBA championship with the L.A. Lakers in 1972 and led the team in scoring (25.9 ppg); averaged 18.6 ppg over his 14-year career.

Jeff Gordon (b. Aug. 4, 1971): Auto racer; 1993 NASCAR Rookie of Year; 4-time Winston Cup champion (1995,97,98,2001); won inaugural Brickyard 400 in 1994; became youngest winner (25) of the Daytona 500 in 1997, won Daytona 500 again in 1999 and 2005; in 1998 he tied Richard Petty for the modern-era record for wins in a single season with 13; NASCAR's all-time leading money winner; has 81 Winston/Nextel Cup career wins as of Sept. 2008.

Rich (Goose) Gossage (b. July 5, 1951): Baseball RHP; Nine-time All-Star (1975-78, 80-82, 84-85); intimidating relief pitcher; Fireman of the Year in 1975 with White Sox and 1978 with Yankees; led AL in saves with 26 (1975), 27 (1978); 1,002 career appearances; 310 saves; elected to Baseball Hall of Fame in 2008.

Shane Gould (b. Nov. 23, 1956): Australian swimmer; set world records in 5 different women's freestyle events between July 1971 and Jan. 1972; won 3 gold medals, a silver and bronze in 1972 Olympics then retired at age 16.

Alf Goullet (b. Apr. 5, 1891, d. Mar. 11, 1995): Cycling; Australian who gained fame and fortune early in century as premier performer on U.S. 6-day bike race circuit; won 8 annual races at Madison Square Garden with 6 different partners from 1913-23.

Curt Gowdy (b. July 31, 1919, d. Feb. 20, 2006): Radio-TV; former radio voice of NY Yankees and then Boston Red Sox from 1949-66; TV play-by-play man for AFL, NFL and major league baseball; has broadcast World Series, All-Star Games, Rose Bowls, Super Bowls, Olympics and NCAA Final Fours for 3 networks; hosted "The American Sportsman."

Steffi Graf (b. June 14, 1969): German tennis player; won Grand Slam and Olympic gold medal in 1988 at age 19; won three of four majors in 1993, '95 and '96; won 22 Grand Slam singles titles— 7 at Wimbledon, 6 French, 5 U.S. and 4 Australian Opens, retired in 1999 as 3rd all-time with 107 career singles titles and as all-time tour leader in career earnings with over $21 million in prize money (passed in 2008); married to fellow tennis great Andre Agassi.

Otto Graham (b. Dec. 6, 1921, d. Dec. 17, 2003): Football QB and basketball All-America at Northwestern; in pro ball, led Cleveland Browns to 7 league titles in 10 years, winning 4 AAFC championships (1946-49) and 3 NFL (1950,54-55); 5-time All-Pro; 2-time NFL MVP (1953,55).

Cammi Granato (b. Mar. 25, 1971): Hockey; American women's hockey pioneer; captain of U.S. team that won gold in the inaugural Olympic women's hockey competition in 1998 in Nagano; sister of NHL veteran Tony.

Red Grange (b. June 13, 1903, d. Jan. 28, 1991): Football HB; 3-time All-America at Illinois who brought 1st huge crowds to pro football when he signed with Chicago Bears in 1925; formed 1st AFL with manager-promoter C.C. Pyle in 1926, but league folded and he returned to Bears.

Bud Grant (b. May 20, 1927): Football and Basketball; only coach to win 100 games in both CFL and NFL and only member of both CFL and U.S. Pro Football Halls of Fame; led Winnipeg to 4 Grey Cup titles (1958-59,61-62) in 6 appearances, but his Minnesota Vikings lost all 4 Super Bowl attempts in 1970s; accumulated 122 CFL wins and 168 NFL wins; also All-Big Ten at Minnesota in both football and basketball in late 1940s; a 3-time CFL All-Star offensive end; also member of 1950 NBA champion Minneapolis Lakers.

Rocky Graziano (b. June 7, 1922, d. May 22, 1990): Boxer; world middleweight champion (1946-47); fought Tony Zale for title 3 times in 21 months, losing twice; pro record 67-10-6 with 52 KOs; movie "Somebody Up There Likes Me" based on his life.

Hank Greenberg (b. Jan. 1, 1911, d. Sept. 4, 1986): Baseball 1B/LF; slugging right-hander who led AL in HRs and RBI 4 times each; 2-time MVP (1935, 40) with Detroit; 331 career HRs, including 58 in 1938; elected to Hall of Fame in 1956.

Joe Greene (b. Sept. 24, 1946): Football DT; 5-time All-Pro (1972-74,77,79); led Pittsburgh to 4 Super Bowl titles in 1970s; nicknamed "Mean Joe."

Maurice Greene (b. July 23, 1974): Track & Field; former world record holder (9.79) in the 100m; won the gold medal in the 100m and 4x100m at the 2000 Sydney Olympics; took 100m bronze in 2004 (Athens).

Bud Greenspan (b. Sept. 18, 1926): Filmmaker specializing in the Olympic Games; has won Emmy awards for 22-part "The Olympiad" (1976-77) and historical vignettes for ABC/TV's coverage of 1980 Winter Games; won 1994 Emmy award for edited special on Lillehammer Winter Olympics; won The Peabody Award in 1996 for his outstanding service in chronicling the Olympic Games.

Wayne Gretzky (b. Jan. 26, 1961): Hockey C; 10-time NHL scoring champion; 9-time regular season MVP (1979-87,89) and 9-time All-NHL first team; scored 200 points or more in a season 4 times; led Edmonton to 4 Stanley Cups (1984-85,87-88); 2-time playoff MVP (1985,88); traded to LA Kings (Aug. 9, 1988); broke Gordie Howe's all-time NHL goal scoring record of 801 on Mar. 23, 1994; all-time NHL leader in points (2857), goals (894) and assists (1963); also all-time Stanley Cup leader in points, goals and assists; spent the end of the 1996 season with the St. Louis Blues then signed a free agent contract with the New York Rangers; retired in 1999 with 61 NHL scoring records; became part-owner of NHL's Coyotes in 2000 and became head coach in 2005.

Bob Griese (b. Feb. 3, 1945): Football QB; 2-time All-Pro (1971,77); led Miami to undefeated season (17-0) in 1972 and consecutive Super Bowl titles (1973-74); father of Brian.

Ken Griffey Jr. (b. Nov. 21, 1969): Baseball OF; overall 1st pick of 1987 draft by Seattle; 10-time Gold Glove winner; 13-time All-Star; 1997 AL MVP; MVP of 1992 All-Star game at age 23; hit home runs in 8 consecutive games in 1993; son of Ken Sr. and in 1990 they became the first father-son combination to appear in the same major league lineup; traded to the Cincinnati Reds before the 2000 season, then to the Chicago White Sox in 2008; hit the 600th home run of his career on June 9, 2008.

Archie Griffin (b. Aug. 21, 1954): Football RB; only college player to win two Heisman Trophies (1974-75); rushed for 5,177 yards in career at Ohio St. and played in four straight Rose Bowls; drafted by Cincinnati Bengals and played 8 years in NFL.

Emile Griffith (b. Feb. 3, 1938): Boxer; world welterweight champion (1961,62-63,63-65); world middleweight champ (1966-67,67-68); pro record 85-24-2 with 23 KOs.

Dick Groat (b. Nov. 4, 1930): Basketball G and Baseball SS; 2-time basketball All-America at Duke and college Player of Year in 1951; won NL MVP award as shortstop with Pittsburgh in 1960; won World Series with Pirates (1960) and St. Louis (1964).

Lefty Grove (b. Mar. 6, 1900, d. May 23, 1975): Baseball LHP; won 20 or more games 8 times; led AL in ERA 9 times and strikeouts 7 times; 31-4 record and MVP in 1931 with Philadelphia; 300-141 record; real name: Robert Moses Grove.

Lou Groza (b. Jan. 25, 1924, d. Nov. 29, 2000): Football T-PK; 6-time All-Pro; played in 13 championship games for Cleveland from 1946-67; kicked winning field goal in 1950 NFL title game; 1,608 career points (1,349 in NFL).

Janet Guthrie (b. Mar. 7, 1938): Auto racer; in 1977, became 1st woman to race in Indianapolis 500; placed 9th at Indy in 1978.

Tony Gwynn (b. May 9, 1960): Baseball OF; 8-time NL batting champion (1984,87-89,94-97) with San Diego; 15-time All-Star; got 3,000th career hit Aug. 6, 1999 at Montreal; played basketball at San Diego St. leaving as school's all-time assist leader; drafted in 10th round of 1981 NBA draft by then San Diego Clippers; retired with 3,141 career hits; inducted into the Baseball Hall of Fame in 2007.

Harvey Haddix (b. Sept. 18, 1925, d. Jan. 9, 1994): Baseball LHP; pitched 12 perfect innings for Pittsburgh, but lost to Milwaukee in the 13th, 1-0 (May 26, 1959); won Game 7 of 1960 World Series.

Walter Hagen (b. Dec. 21, 1892, d. Oct. 5, 1969): Pro golf pioneer; won 2 U.S. Opens (1914,19), 4 British Opens (1922,24,28-29), 5 PGA Championships (1921,24-27) and 5 Western Opens; 44 career PGA wins; 6-time U.S. Ryder Cup captain.

Marvin Hagler (b. May 23, 1954): Boxer; hard-punching world middleweight champion from 1980-87; enjoyed his nickname "Marvelous Marvin" so much he had his name legally changed; pro record of 62-3-2 with 52 KOs; retired after suffering 1987 upset loss to Sugar Ray Leonard.

Mika Hakkinen (b. Sept. 28, 1968): Finnish auto racer; won two consecutive Formula One world drivers championships in 1998 and '99; recorded eight wins in '98 and five in '99; 20 F1 wins.

George Halas (b. Feb. 2, 1895, d. Oct. 31, 1983): Football pioneer; MVP in 1919 Rose Bowl; player-coach-owner of Chicago Bears from 1920-83; signed Red Grange in 1925; coached Bears for 40 seasons and won 8 NFL titles (1921,32-33,40-41,43,46,63); 2nd on all-time career list with 324 wins; elected to NFL Hall of Fame in 1963.

Dorothy Hamill (b. July 26, 1956): Figure skater; won Olympic gold medal and world championship in 1976; Ice Capades headliner from 1977-84; bought the financially-strapped Ice Capades in 1993 and sold it several years later.

Scott Hamilton (b. Aug. 28, 1958): Figure skater; 4-time world champion (1981-84); won gold medal at 1984 Olympics.

Mia Hamm (b. Mar. 17, 1972): Soccer F; all-time leading international scorer with 158 goals; member of three U.S. Olympic teams (1996,2000,04), and four U.S. World Cup teams (1991,95,99,2003); made the U.S. National Team at 15; a three-time collegiate All-American; led North Carolina to four national titles (1989,90, 92,93); Two-time FIFA Women's World Player of the Year (2001-02); inducted into National Hall of Fame in 2007; married to baseball's Nomar Garciaparra.

Tonya Harding (b. Nov. 12, 1970): Figure skater; 1991 and 1994 U.S. women's champion; involved in plot hatched by ex-husband Jeff Gillooly to injure rival Nancy Kerrigan and keep her off Olympic team; won '94 U.S. title in Kerrigan's absence; denied any role in assault and sued USOC to keep her spot in Olympics; finished 8th at Lillehammer (Kerrigan recovered and won silver medal); pleaded guilty on Mar. 16 to conspiracy to hinder investigation; stripped of 1994 title by U.S. Figure Skating Association.

Tom Harmon (b. Sept. 28, 1919, d. Mar. 17, 1990): Football HB; 2-time All-America at Michigan; won Heisman Trophy in 1940; played with AFL NY Americans in 1941 and NFL LA Rams (1946-47);World War II fighter pilot who won Silver Star and Purple Heart; became radio-TV commentator.

Franco Harris (b. Mar. 7, 1950): Football RB; ran for over 1,000 yards in a season 8 times; rushed for 12,120 yards in 13 years; led Pittsburgh to 4 Super Bowl titles.

Leon Hart (b. Nov. 2, 1928, d. Sept. 24, 2002): Football E; only player to win 3 national championships in college and 3 more in the NFL; won his titles at Notre Dame (1946-47,49) and with Detroit Lions (1952-53,57); 3-time All-America and last lineman to win Heisman Trophy (1949); All-Pro on both offense and defense in 1951.

Bill Hartack (b. Dec. 9, 1932, d. Nov. 26, 2007): Jockey; won Kentucky Derby 5 times (1957 ,60,62,64,69), Preakness 3 times (1956,64,69), and the Belmont once (1960).

Doug Harvey (b. Dec. 19, 1924, d. Dec. 26, 1989): Hockey D; 10-time All-NHL 1st team; won Norris Trophy 7 times (1955-58,60-62); led Montreal to 6 Stanley Cups.

Dominik Hasek (b. Jan. 29, 1965): Czech hockey goaltender; 2-time NHL MVP (1997,98) with Buffalo; 6-time Vezina Trophy winner (1994,95,97,98,99, 2001); led Czech Republic to Olympic gold medal in 1998; won Stanley Cup with Detroit in 2002.

Billy Haughton (b. Nov. 2, 1923, d. July 15, 1986): Harness racing; 4-time winner of Hambletonian; trainer-driver of one Pacing Triple Crown winner (1968); 4,910 career wins.

João Havelange (b. May 8, 1916): Soccer; Brazilian-born president of Federation Internationale de Football Assoc. (FIFA) 1974-98; also member of International Olympic Committee.

John Havlicek (b. Apr. 8, 1940): Basketball F; played in three NCAA final fours (1960-62); led Boston to eight NBA titles (1963-66,68-69,74,76); Finals MVP in 1974; four-time All-NBA 1st team; #17 retired by the Celtics.

Tony Hawk (b. May 12, 1968): Skateboarder; winner of 16 X Games medals; top-ranked ranked vert skater for 12 consecutive years; in 1999, became the first person to land the 900; credited with inventing nearly 100 tricks; creator, Tony Hawk's Pro Skater best-selling video game franchise ($1billion+ in sales), autobiography appeared on *The New York Times* bestseller list (2000).

Bob Hayes (b. Dec. 20, 1942, d. Sept. 18, 2002): Track & Field and Football; won gold medal in 100m at 1964 Olympics; all-pro SE for Dallas in 1966; won Super Bowl with Cowboys in 1972; convicted of drug trafficking in 1979 and served 18 months of a 5-year sentence.

Elvin Hayes (b. Nov. 17, 1945): Basketball C; Known as "the Big E"; Overall number one pick of the 1968 NBA draft; three-time All-NBA first team (1975,77,79); 1978 Finals MVP; 12-time NBA all-star (1969-80); named to NBA's 50 Greatest Players; amassed 27,313 points and 16,279 rebounds; member of basketball Hall of Fame.

Woody Hayes (b. Feb. 14, 1913, d. Mar. 12, 1987): Football; coached Ohio St. to 6 national titles (1954,57,61,68,70) and 4 Rose Bowl victories; 238 career wins in 28 seasons at Denison, Miami-OH and OSU; his coaching career ended abruptly in 1978 after he attacked an opposing player on the sidelines after an interception.

Thomas Hearns (b. Oct. 18, 1958): Boxer; held world titles as welterweight, junior middleweight, middleweight and light heavyweight; four career losses came against Ray Leonard, Marvin Hagler and twice to Iran Barkley; pro record of 60-4-1, 46 KOs.

Eric Heiden (b. June 14, 1958): Speed skater; 3-time overall world champion (1977-79); won all 5 men's speed skating gold medals at 1980 Olympics, setting records in each; Sullivan Award winner (1980).

Mel Hein (b. Aug. 22, 1909, d. Jan. 31, 1992): Football C; NFL All-Pro 8 straight years (1933-40); MVP in 1938 with Giants; didn't miss a game in 15 years.

John W. Heisman (b. Oct. 23, 1869, d. Oct. 3, 1936): Football; coached at 9 colleges from 1892-1927; won 185 games; Director of Athletics at Downtown Athletic Club in NYC (1928-36); DAC named Heisman Trophy after him.

Carol Heiss (b. Jan. 20, 1940): Figure skater; 5-time world champion (1956-60); won Olympic silver medal in 1956 and gold in '60; married 1956 men's gold medalist Hayes Jenkins.

Rickey Henderson (b. Dec. 25, 1958): Baseball OF; AL playoff MVP (1989) and AL regular season MVP (1990); set single-season base stealing record of 130 in 1982; led AL in steals a record 12 times; broke Lou Brock's all-time record of 938 on May 1, 1991; holds all-time MLB records in runs (2295), stolen bases (1406), and HRs as leadoff batter (81).

Sonja Henie (b. Apr. 8, 1912, d. Oct. 12, 1969): Norwegian figure skater; 10-time world champion (1927-36); won 3 consecutive Olympic gold medals (1928,32,36); became movie star.

Foster Hewitt (b. Nov. 21, 1902, d. Apr. 21, 1985): Radio-TV; Canada's premier hockey play-by-play broadcaster from 1923-81; coined phrase, "He shoots, he scores!"

Damon Hill (b. Sept. 17, 1960): British auto racer; 1996 Formula 1 champion; 22 F1 wins places him 10th all-time; son of Graham.

Graham Hill (b. Feb. 15, 1929, d. Nov. 29, 1975): British auto racer; 2-time Formula One world champion (1962,68); won Indy 500 in 1966; killed in plane crash; father of Damon.

Phil Hill (b. Apr. 20, 1927, d. Aug. 28, 2008): Auto racer; first U.S. driver to win Formula One championship (1961); 3 career wins (1958-64).

Sir Edmund Hillary (b. July 20, 1919, d. Jan. 11, 2008): New Zealand mountaineer; On May 29, 1953, along with Sherpa Tenzing Norgay, Hillary became the first to reach summit of Mt. Everest, the world's highest peak.

Martina Hingis (b. Sept. 30, 1980): Swiss tennis player; in March 1997 at 16 years, 6 months, she became the youngest No. 1 ranked player since the ranking system began in 1975; won Wimbledon (1997), U.S. Open (1997) and 3 Australian Opens (1997,98,99); first woman to surpass the $3 million mark in earnings for one season (1997).

Max Hirsch (b. July 30, 1880, d. Apr. 3, 1969): Horse racing; trained 1,933 winners from 1908-68; won Triple Crown with Assault in 1946.

Tommy Hitchcock (b. Feb. 11, 1900, d. Apr. 19, 1944): Polo; world class player at 20; achieved 10-goal rating 18 times from 1922-40.

Lew Hoad (b. Nov. 23, 1934, d. July 3, 1994): Australian tennis player; 2-time Wimbledon winner (1956-57); won Australian, French and Wimbledon titles in 1956, but missed capturing Grand Slam at Forest Hills when beaten by Ken Rosewall in 4-set final.

Gil Hodges (b. Apr. 4, 1924, d. Apr. 2, 1972): Baseball 1B-Manager; tied Major League record with four home runs in one game on Aug 31, 1950; won three Gold Gloves (1957-59); drove in 100 runs in seven consecutive seasons (1949-55); hit 370 home runs and 1,274 RBIs lifetime; won 660 games as a manager (Senators and Mets).

Mat Hoffman (b. Jan. 9, 1972): BMX; youngest pro in BMX history at age 16, world record holder for High Air on a BMX Bike (26.5 feet out of a 24-foot quarterpipe in 2001); invented over 100 staple BMX tricks; started the Bike Stunt Series (1992-televised by ESPN starting in 1995); founded the Hoffman Sports Association.

Trevor Hoffman (b. Oct. 13, 1967): Baseball RHP; 2-time NL saves leader (1998, 2006); earned his 479th save on Sept, 24, 2006 to pass Lee Smith as the all-time major league leader; recorded eight 40-save seasons and one 50-save season (53 in 1998).

Ben Hogan (b. Aug. 13, 1912, d. July 25, 1997): Golfer; 4-time PGA Player of Year; one of only five players to win all four Grand Slam titles (others are Nicklaus, Player, Sarazen and Woods); won 4 U.S. Opens, 2 Masters, 2 PGAs and 1 British Open between 1946-53; nearly killed in Feb. 2, 1949 car accident, but came back to win 1950 U.S. Open just 16 months later; one of only two players (Woods) to win three of the four current majors in one year when he won Masters, U.S. Open and British Open in 1953 at age 41; third on all-time list with 64 career wins.

Chamique Holdsclaw (b. Aug. 9, 1977): Basketball F; 2-time national player of the year, leading Tennessee to 3 straight national championships (1996-98); 1998 Sullivan Award winner; top selection by the Washington Mystics in the 1999 WNBA draft; 1999 WNBA Rookie of the Year; unexpectedly retired a few weeks into the 2007 season.

Eleanor Holm (b. Dec. 6, 1913, d. Jan. 31, 2004): Swimmer; won gold medal in 100m backstroke at 1932 Olympics; thrown off '36 U.S. team for drinking champagne in public and shooting craps on boat to Germany.

Nat Holman (b. Oct. 18, 1896, d. Feb. 12, 1995): Basketball pioneer; played with Original Celtics (1920-28); coached CCNY to both NCAA and NIT titles in 1950 (a year later, several of his players were caught up in a point-shaving scandal); 423 career wins.

Larry Holmes (b. Nov. 3, 1949): Boxer; heavyweight champion (WBC or IBF) from 1978-85; beat Gerry Cooney on a 13th-round TKO in their 1982 mega-fight; successfully defended title 20 times before losing to Michael Spinks; returned from first retirement in 1988 and was KO'd in 4th by champ Mike Tyson; launched second comeback in 1991; fought and lost title bids against Evander Holyfield in '92 and Oliver McCall in '95; pro record of 69-6 and 44 KOs.

Lou Holtz (b. Jan. 6, 1937): Football; coached Notre Dame to national title in 1988; 2-time Coach of Year (1977,88); also coached NFL's NY Jets for 13 games (3-10) in 1976.

Evander Holyfield (b. Oct. 19, 1962): Boxer; only man to win (and lose) world heavyweight title 4 times; Wore belt off and on from 1990-2001; defeated former champ Mike Tyson in 1996 to win WBA belt; in 1997 rematch, Tyson was DQ'd for twice biting his ear; former undisputed cruiserweight world (1987-88) champ before moving to heavyweight; returned to ring in Aug. 2006 with a 2nd-round TKO of Jeremy Bates.

Red Holzman (b. Aug. 10, 1920, d. Nov. 13, 1998): Basketball; played for NBL and NBA champions at Rochester (1946,51); coached NY Knicks to 2 NBA titles (1970,73); Coach of Year (1970); 754 career NBA wins.

Bernard Hopkins (b. Jan. 15, 1965): Boxer; became first undisputed world middleweight champion since Marvin Hagler when he upset undefeated Felix Trinidad in 2001; defended title a division-record 20 times before losing belts on a split decision to Jermain Taylor in 2005; won decision over Antonio Tarver in June, 2006, then retired; promptly unretired in 2007 with a unanimous decision over Winky Wright; lost decision to Joe Calzaghe in April, 2008; 48-5-1 (32 KOs).

Rogers Hornsby (b. Apr. 27, 1896, d. Jan. 5, 1963): Baseball 2B; hit .400 3 times, including .424 in 1924; led NL in batting 7 times; 2-time MVP (1925,29); career BA of .358 over 23 years is highest in NL.

Paul Hornung (b. Dec. 23, 1935): Football HB-PK; only Heisman Trophy winner to play for losing team (2-8 Notre Dame in 1956); 3-time NFL scoring leader (1959-61) at Green Bay; 176 points in 1960, an all-time record; MVP in 1961; suspended by NFL for 1963 season for betting on his own team.

Gordie Howe (b. Mar. 31, 1928): Hockey RW; played 32 seasons in NHL and WHA from 1946-80; led NHL in scoring 6 times; all-NHL 1st team 12 times; MVP 6 times in NHL (1952-53,57-58,60,63) with Detroit and once in WHA (1974) with Houston; ranks 2nd on all-time NHL list in goals (801) and 3rd in points (1,850); played with sons Mark and Marty at Houston (1973-77) and New England-Hartford (1977-80).

Cal Hubbard (b. Oct. 31, 1900, d. Oct. 17, 1977): Member of college football, pro football and baseball halls of fame; 9 years in NFL; 4-time All-Pro at end and tackle; AL umpire (1936-51).

William DeHart Hubbard (b. Nov. 25, 1903, d. June 23, 1976): Track & Field; won the long jump at the 1924 Olympics, becoming the first black athlete to win an Olympic gold medal in an individual event; set the long jump world record in 1925 (25-10¾) and tied the 100-yd dash record (9.6) in 1926.

Carl Hubbell (b. June 22, 1903, d. Nov. 21, 1988): Baseball LHP; led NL in wins and ERA 3 times each; 2-time MVP (1933,36) with NY Giants; fanned Ruth, Gehrig, Foxx, Simmons and Cronin in succession in 1934 All-Star Game; 253-154 career record.

Sam Huff (b. Oct. 4, 1934): Football LB; glamorized NFL's middle linebacker position with NY Giants from 1956-63; subject of "The Violent World of Sam Huff" TV special in 1961; helped club win 6 division titles and a world championship (1956).

Miller Huggins (b. Mar. 27, 1878, d. Sept. 25, 1929): Baseball; managed NY Yankees from 1918 until his death late in '29 season; led Yanks to 6 pennants and 3 World Series titles from 1921-28.

Bobby Hull (b. Jan. 3, 1939): Hockey LW; led NHL in scoring 3 times; 2-time MVP (1965-66) with Chicago; All-NHL first team 10 times; jumped to WHA in 1972, 2-time MVP there (1973,75) with Winnipeg; scored 913 goals in both leagues; father of Brett.

Brett Hull (b. Aug. 9, 1964): Hockey RW; NHL MVP in 1991 with St. Louis; holds single season RW scoring record with 86 goals; he and father Bobby have both won Hart (MVP), Lady Byng (sportsmanship) and All-Star Game MVP trophies; won 2 Stanley Cups.

Lamar Hunt (b. Aug. 2, 1932, d. Dec. 13, 2006): Football/Soccer; Founder of the Kansas City Chiefs (formerly Dallas Texans); instrumental in forming the AFL in 1959 and merging the league with NFL in 1966; elected to the Pro Football HOF in 1972; AFC Championship trophy bear his name; investor/operator in MLS; also member of National Soccer HOF.

Jim (Catfish) Hunter (b. Apr. 8, 1946, d. Sept. 9, 1999): Baseball RHP; won 20 games or more 5 times (1971-75); played on 5 World Series winners with Oakland and NY Yankees; threw perfect game in 1968; won AL Cy Young Award in 1974; 224-166 career record.

Ibrahim Hussein (b. June 3, 1958): Kenyan distance runner; 3-time winner of Boston Marathon (1988,91-92) and 1st African runner to win in Boston; won New York Marathon in 1987.

Don Hutson (b. Jan. 31, 1913, d. June 24, 1997): Football E-PK; led NFL in receptions 8 times and interceptions once; 9-time All-Pro (1936,38-45) for Green Bay; 99 career TD catches.

Flo Hyman (b. July 31, 1954 d. Jan. 24, 1986): Volleyball; 3-time All-America spiker at Houston and captain of 1984 U.S. Women's Olympic team; died of heart attack caused by Marfan Syndrome during a match in Japan in 1986; namesake of award given out annually by the Women's Sports Foundation.

Hank Iba (b. Aug. 6, 1904, d. Jan. 15, 1993): Basketball; coached Oklahoma A&M to 2 straight NCAA titles (1945-46); 767 career wins in 41 years; coached U.S. Olympic team to 2 gold medals (1964,68), but lost to Soviets in controversial '72 final.

Punch Imlach (b. Mar. 15, 1918, d. Dec. 1, 1987): Hockey; directed Toronto to 4 Stanley Cups (1962-64,67) in 11 seasons as GM-coach.

Miguel Induráin (b. July 16, 1964): Spanish cyclist; won 5 straight Tour de Frances (1991-95), won gold in time trial at '96 Olympics; retired in 1997.

Juli Inkster (b. June 24, 1960): Golfer; 31 career LPGA victories; winner of 7 major LPGA tournaments and 3 consecutive U.S. Women's Amateur tournaments (1980-82); inducted into the World Golf Hall of Fame in 2000; LPGA Rookie of the Year in 1984.

Hale Irwin (b. June 3, 1945): Golfer; oldest player ever to win U.S. Open (45 in 1990); NCAA champion in 1967; 20 PGA victories, including 3 U.S. Opens (1974,79,90); 5-time Ryder Cup team member; joined Senior PGA Tour in 1995 and has already won 45 titles.

Allen Iverson (b. June 7, 1975): Basketball G; former Georgetown Hoya chosen first overall by the Philadelphia 76ers in the 1996 NBA Draft; NBA Rookie of the Year (1997); 3-time NBA scoring leader (2001-02,05) and steals leader (2001-02); voted regular season MVP in 2001 and led 76ers to NBA Finals; traded to Denver Nuggets in December 2006.

Bo Jackson (b. Nov. 30, 1962): Baseball OF and Football RB; won Heisman Trophy in 1985 and MVP of baseball All-Star Game in 1989; starter for both baseball's KC Royals and NFL's LA Raiders in 1988 and '89; severely injured left hip Jan. 13, 1991, in NFL playoffs; waived by Royals but signed by Chicago White Sox in 1991; missed entire 1992 season recovering from hip surgery; played for White Sox in 1993 and California in '94 before retiring.

Joe Jackson (b. July 16, 1889, d. Dec. 5, 1951): Baseball OF; hit .300 or better 11 times; nicknamed "Shoeless Joe"; career average of .356, third highest all-time; was placed on MLB's ineligible list in 1921 following the Black Sox scandal in which he and 7 teammates were accused of fixing 1919 World Series.

Phil Jackson (b. Sept. 17, 1945): Basketball; NBA champion as reserve forward with New York in 1973 (injured when Knicks won in '70); coached Chicago to six NBA titles in eight years (1991-93, 96-98); coach of the year in 1996 and 97; returned to coach the LA Lakers in 1999 and won 3 more titles (2000,01,02); all-time leader in winning pct. for NBA coaches with 350 or more wins; left Lakers after 2004 Finals loss to Detroit but returned after one season; all-time NBA leader in playoff wins (193).

Reggie Jackson (b. May 18, 1946): Baseball OF; "Mr. October"; led AL in HRs 4 times; MVP in 1973; played on 5 World Series winners with Oakland and NY Yankees; 1977 Series MVP with 5 HRs; 563 career HRs; all-time strikeout leader (2,597); member of the Hall of Fame.

Dr. Robert Jackson (b. Aug. 6, 1932): Surgeon; revolutionized sports medicine by popularizing the use of arthroscopic surgery to treat injuries; learned technique from Japanese physician that allowed athletes to return quickly from potentially career-ending injuries.

Helen Jacobs (b. Aug. 6, 1908, d. June 2, 1997): Tennis; 4-time winner of U.S. Championship (1932-35); Wimbledon winner in 1936; lost 4 Wimbledon finals to arch-rival Helen Wills Moody.

Jaromir Jagr (b. Feb. 15, 1972): Czech Hockey RW; fifth overall pick by Pittsburgh (1990); NHL All-Rookie team (1991); NHL MVP (1999); Won Art Ross Trophy (1995,98,99,00,01); 7-time All-NHL First Team; NHL single season record for most points by a right wing (149); NHL single season record for most assists by a RW (87); 646 goals, 1,599 points; left NHL in 2008 to play with Russian team Avangard Omsk.

LeBron James (b. Dec. 30, 1984): Basketball; mega-hyped top overall pick in 2003 NBA Draft (Cleveland) straight out of high school; youngest-ever NBA Rookie of the Year (2004); led Cavs to Finals in 2007 (loss to Spurs); scored 48 points (including team's final 25) in a win over Pistons in 2007 conference finals; won gold medal with U.S. team in 2008.

Dan Jansen (b. June 17, 1965): Speed skater; fell in 500m and 1,000m in 1988 Olympics just after sister Jane's death; placed 4th in 500m and didn't attempt 1,000m in 1992; fell in 500m at '94 Games, but finally won an Olympic medal with world record (1:12.43) effort in 1,000m.

Dale Jarrett (b. Nov. 26, 1956): Auto racer; 1999 Winston Cup champion; 3-time Daytona 500 champion (1993,96,2000); son of driver Ned Jarrett.

James J. Jeffries (b. Apr. 15, 1875, d. Mar. 3, 1953): Boxer; world heavyweight champion (1899-1905); retired undefeated but came back to fight Jack Johnson in 1910 and lost (KO, 15th).

David Jenkins (b. June 29, 1936): Figure skater; brother of Hayes; 3-time world champion (1957-59); won gold medal at 1960 Olympics.

Hayes Jenkins (b. Mar. 23, 1933): Figure skater; 4-time world champion (1953-56); won gold medal at 1956 Olympics; married skater Carol Heiss.

Bruce Jenner (b. Oct. 28, 1949): Track & Field; won gold medal in 1976 Olympic decathlon.

Jackie Jensen (b. Mar. 9, 1927, d. July 14, 1982): Football RB and Baseball OF; All-America at Cal in 1948; AL MVP with Boston Red Sox in 1958.

Derek Jeter (b. June 26, 1974): Baseball SS; 1st-round draft choice (6th overall) of the N.Y. Yankees in 1992; became Yankees' everyday starting shortstop in 1996 and the team hasn't missed the postseason since; won 4 World Series championships in his first 5 seasons (1996, 98-2000); MVP of the 2000 All-Star Game and World Series; named captain of the Yankees in 2003; all-time postseason hits leader; recorded more hits in Yankee Stadium than anyone else.

Ben Johnson (b. Dec. 30, 1961): Canadian sprinter; set 100m world record (9.83) at 1987 World Championships; won 100m at 1988 Olympics, but flunked drug test and forfeited gold medal; banned for life by IAAF in 1993 for testing positive again.

Bob Johnson (b. Mar. 4, 1931, d. Nov. 26, 1991): Hockey; coached Pittsburgh Penguins to 1st Stanley Cup title in 1991; led Wisconsin to 3 NCAA titles (1973,77,81); also coached 1976 U.S. Olympic team and NHL Calgary Flames (1982-87).

Earvin (Magic) Johnson (b. Aug. 14, 1959): Basketball G; led Michigan St. to NCAA title in 1979 and was Final 4 MOP; All-NBA 1st team 9 times; 3-time MVP (1987,89-90); led LA Lakers to 5 NBA titles; 3-time Finals MVP (1980, 82, 87); 3rd all-time in NBA assists with 10,141; retired on Nov. 7, 1991 after announcing he was HIV-positive; returned to score 25 points in 1992 NBA All-Star Game; U.S. Olympic Dream Team co-captain; announced NBA comeback then retired again before start of 1992-93 season; named head coach of Lakers on Mar. 23, 1994, but finished season at 5-11 and quit; later became minority owner of team; came back a final time and played 32 games during 1995-96 season.

Jack Johnson (b. Mar. 31, 1878, d. June 10, 1946): Boxer; heavyweight champion (1908-15) and 1st black to hold title; defeated Tommy Burns for crown at age 30; fled to Europe in 1913 after Mann Act conviction; lost title to Jess Willard in Havana, but claimed to have taken a dive; 78-8-12 with 45 KOs.

Jimmy Johnson (b. July 16, 1943): Football; All-SWC defensive lineman on Arkansas' 1964 national championship team; coached U. of Miami-FL to national title in 1987; college record of 81-34-3 in 10 years; hired by old pal Jerry Jones to succeed Tom Landry in 1989; went 1-15 in '89, then led Cowboys to consecutive Super Bowl victories (1993-94); quit in 1994 after feuding with Jones; replaced Don Shula as Miami Dolphins head coach from 1996-99.

Judy Johnson (b. Oct. 26, 1899, d. June 13, 1989): Baseball IF; one of the great stars of the Negro Leagues; a terrific fielding third baseman who regularly batted over .300; when baseball integrated Johnson's playing days were over but he coached and scouted for the Philadelphia Athletics, Boston Braves and Philadelphia Phillies; member of Hall of Fame.

Junior Johnson (b. June 28, 1931): Auto Racing; won Daytona 500 in 1960; also won 13 NASCAR races in 1965, including the Rebel 300 at Darlington; retired from racing to become a highly successful car owner; his first driver was Bobby Allison.

Michael Johnson (b. Sep 13, 1967): Track & Field; Shattered world record in 200m (19.32) and set Olympic record in 400m (43.49) to become first man to win the gold in both races in the same Olympic Games at Atlanta in 1996; two-time world champion in 200 (1991,95) and four-time world champ in 400 (1993,95,97,99); set world record in 400m (43.18) at '99 world championships in Seville; won the 400 in Sydney in 2000 to become the only man to win the event in two consecutive Olympics; retired in 2001.

Randy Johnson (b. Sept. 10, 1963): Baseball LHP; 6'10" flamethrower; struck out over 300 batters 6 times (1993,98,99,00,01,02); led AL in Ks 4 times (1992-95) and NL 5 times (1999-2002,04); struck out 20 batters in a game (5/8/01); 5-time Cy Young Award winner with Seattle and Arizona (AL-1995, NL-1999-2002); won 3 games and co-MVP honors (Curt Schilling) in 2001 World Series; became oldest in baseball history to pitch a perfect game at age 40; pitched for N.Y. Yankees 2005-06, Arizona 2007—.

Walter Johnson (b. Nov. 6, 1887, d. Dec. 10, 1946): Baseball RHP; nicknamed "Big Train" Johnson had an overpowering fastball; won 20 games or more 10 straight years; led AL in ERA 5 times, wins 6 times and strikeouts 12 times; twice MVP (1913, 24) with Washington Senators; all-time leader in shutouts (110) and 2nd in wins (417); part of the Hall of Fame's inaugural class of 1936.

Ben A. Jones (b. Dec. 31, 1882, d. June 13, 1961): Horse racing; Calumet Farm trainer (1939-47); saddled 6 Kentucky Derby champions, including 2 Triple Crown winners—Whirlaway in 1941 and Citation in '48.

Bobby Jones (b. Mar. 17, 1902, d. Dec. 18, 1971): Won U.S. and British Opens plus U.S. and British Amateurs in 1930 to become golf's only Grand Slam winner ever; between 1922-30, he won 4 U.S. Opens, 5 U.S. Amateurs, 3 British Opens, and 1 British Amateur for 13 Major titles in all, a record that stood until Jack Nicklaus broke it; played in 6 Walker Cups; designed Augusta National (with Alister Mackenzie) and founded Masters tournament in 1934.

Deacon Jones (b. Dec. 9, 1938): Football DE; 5-time All-Pro (1965-69) with LA Rams; unofficially 3rd all-time in NFL sacks with 173½ in 14 years; inducted into Pro Football Hall of Fame in 1980.

Jerry Jones (b. Oct. 13, 1942): Football; owner-GM of Dallas Cowboys; maverick who bought declining team (3-13) and Texas Stadium for $140 million in 1989; hired pal Jimmy Johnson to replace legendary coach Tom Landry; their partnership led to 2 Super Bowl titles (1993-94); when feud developed, he fired Johnson and hired Barry Switzer and won Super Bowl in 1996; hired Bill Parcells as head coach in 2003, then Wade Phillips in 2007.

Marion Jones (b. Oct. 12, 1975): Track & Field; American sprinter who won 3 golds (100m, 200m, 4x100m) at 2000 Sydney Olympics; 5-time world champion: 100m (1997,99), 200m (2001), 4x100m (1997, 2001); voted Women's Athlete of the Year by *Track & Field News* in 1997,98 and 2000; 1999 Jesse Owens Award winner; 2000 AP and USOC Female Athlete of the Year; after years of lying to the media, federal agents and two grand juries, finally admitted to steroid use in October 2007; subsequently had all Olympic medals stripped and all results nullified since 2000; served 6 months in jail in 2008.

Roy Jones Jr. (b. Jan. 16, 1969): Boxing; robbed of gold medal at 1988 Olympics on a scoring error; still voted Outstanding Boxer of the Games; won IBF middleweight crown, beating Bernard Hopkins in 1993; moved up to super middleweight and won IBF title from James Toney in 1994; moved up to light heavyweight, winning WBC (1997), WBA (1998) and IBF titles (1999); made temporary move to heavyweight in 2003 and decisioned John Ruiz for WBA belt; lost WBC light heavyweight belt to Antonio Tarver in a 2nd round KO in 2004; knocked out in comeback fight with Glen Johnson in 2004; fought Tarver for a 3rd time in 2005.

Michael Jordan (b. Feb. 17, 1963): Basketball G; College Player of Year with North Carolina in 1984; NBA Rookie of the Year (1985); led NBA in scoring 7 years in a row (1987-93) and also 1996-98; 10-time All-NBA 1st team; 5-time regular season MVP (1988,91-92,96,98) and 6-time MVP of NBA Finals (1991-93,96-98); 3-time AP Male Athlete of Year; led U.S. Olympic team to gold in 1984 and '92; stunned sports world when he retired at age 30 on Oct. 6, 1993; signed as OF with Chi. White Sox and spent summer of '94 in AA with Birmingham; struggled with .204 average; made one of the most anticipated comebacks in sports history when he returned to the Bulls lineup on Mar. 19, 1995 but Bulls were eliminated by Orlando in 2nd round of playoffs later that season; led Bulls to NBA titles for the next 3 years for 6 titles in all (1991-93,96-98); retired in 1999; became pres. of Wash. Wizards before unretiring again in 2001 and returning to play with Wizards for 2 seasons; became part-owner of the Charlotte Bobcats in June, 2006.

Florence Griffith Joyner (b. Dec. 21, 1959, d. Sept. 21, 1998): Track & Field; set world records in 100 and 200m in 1988; won 3 gold medals at '88 Olympics (100m, 200m, 4x100m relay); Sullivan Award winner (1988); retired in 1989; named as co-chairperson of President's Council on Physical Fitness and Sports in 1993; sister-in-law of Jackie Joyner-Kersee; died of suffocation during an epileptic seizure in 1998.

Jackie Joyner-Kersee (b. Mar. 3, 1962): Track & Field; 2-time world champion in both long jump (1987,91) and heptathlon (1987,93); won heptathlon gold medals at 1988 and '92 Olympics and LJ gold at '88 Games; also won Olympic silver (1984) in heptathlon and bronze (1992,96) in LJ; Sullivan Award winner (1986); only woman to receive *The Sporting News* Man of Year award.

Alberto Juantorena (b. Nov. 21, 1950): Cuban runner; won 400m and 800m golds at 1976 Olympics.

Sonny Jurgensen (b. Aug. 23, 1934): Football QB; played 18 seasons with Philadelphia and Washington; led NFL in passing totals (1967,69); All-Pro in 1961; 255 career TD passes.

Duke Kahanamoku (b. Aug. 24, 1890, d. Jan. 22, 1968): Swimmer; won 3 gold medals and 2 silver over 3 Olympics (1912,20,24); also surfing pioneer.

Al Kaline (b. Dec. 19, 1934): Baseball; youngest player (at age 20) to win batting title (led AL with .340 in 1955); had 3,007 hits, 399 HRs in 22 years with Detroit.

Anatoly Karpov (b. May 23, 1951): Chess; Soviet world champion from 1975-85; regained International Chess Federation (FIDE) championship in 1993 when Garry Kasparov was stripped of title after forming new Professional Chess Association; held FIDE title until 1999.

Garry Kasparov (b. Apr. 13, 1963): Chess; Azerbaijani who became youngest player (22 years, 210 days) ever to win world championship as Soviet in 1985; defeated countryman Anatoly Karpov for title; split with International Chess Federation (FIDE) to form Professional Chess Association (PCA) in 1993; stripped of FIDE title in '93 but successfully defended PCA title against Briton Nigel Short; beat IBM supercomputer "Deep Blue" 4 games to 2 in 1996 much-publicized match in New York; lost rematch to computer in 1997; finally lost world title to Vladimir Kramnik in 2000.

Mike Keenan (b. Oct. 21, 1949): Hockey; coach who led NY Rangers to Stanley Cup title in 1994 after 53 unsuccessful seasons; 5th all-time on NHL coaching wins list; hired as coach of Calgary Flames in 2007.

Kipchoge (Kip) Keino (b. Jan. 17, 1940): Kenyan runner; policeman who beat USA's Jim Ryun to win 1,500m gold medal at 1968 Olympics; won again in steeplechase at 1972 Summer Games; his success spawned long line of distance champions from Kenya.

Johnny A. Kelley (b. Sept. 6, 1907, d. Oct. 7, 2004): Distance runner; ran in his 61st and final Boston Marathon at age 84 in 1992, finishing in 5:58:36; won Boston twice (1935,45) and was 2nd seven times.

Jim Kelly (b. Feb. 14, 1960): Football QB; led Buffalo to four straight Super Bowls, and is only QB to lose four times; named to AFC Pro Bowl team 5 times; inducted into Pro Football Hall of Fame in 2002.

Leroy Kelly (b. May 20, 1942): Football; replaced Jim Brown in the Cleveland Browns backfield in 1967, he led the NFL in rushing yards (1,205), rushing average (5.5 per carry) and rushing touchdowns (11).

Walter Kennedy (b. June 8, 1912, d. June 26, 1977): Basketball; 2nd NBA commissioner (1963-75), league doubled in size to 18 teams during his tenure.

Nancy Kerrigan (b. Oct. 13, 1969): Figure skating; 1993 U.S. women's champion and Olympic medalist in 1992 (bronze) and '94 (silver); victim of Jan. 6, 1994 assault at U.S. nationals in Detroit when Shane Stant clubbed her right knee with a baton after a practice session; conspiracy hatched by Jeff Gillooly, ex-husband of rival Tonya Harding; though unable to compete in nationals, she recovered and was granted berth on Olympic team; finished 2nd in Lillehammer to Oksana Baiul of Ukraine by a 5-4 judges' vote.

Billy Kidd (b. Apr. 13, 1943): Skiing; the first great Amercian male Alpine skier; first American male to win an Olympic medal when he won a silver in the slalom and a bronze in the Alpine combined in 1964; competed respectably with the great Jean-Claude Killy; won the world Alpine combined event in 1970, which was the first world championship for an American male.

Harmon Killebrew (b. June 29, 1936): Baseball 3B-1B; led AL in HRs 6 times and RBI 3 times; MVP in 1969 with Minnesota; 573 career HRs.

Jean-Claude Killy (b. Aug. 30, 1943): French alpine skier; 2-time World Cup champion (1967-68); won 3 gold medals at 1968 Olympics in Grenoble; co-president of 1992 Winter Games in Albertville; president of coordination commission for 2006 Turin Games.

Ralph Kiner (b. Oct. 27, 1922): Baseball OF; led NL in home runs 7 straight years (1946-52) with Pittsburgh; 369 career HRs and 1,015 RBI in 10 seasons; long-time NY Mets announcer.

Betsy King (b. Aug. 13, 1955): Golfer; 2-time LPGA Player of Year (1984,89); 3-time winner of Dinah Shore (1987,90,97) and 2-time winner of U.S. Open (1989,90); 34 overall Tour wins; 1st player in LPGA history to break $5 million mark in career earnings; member of LPGA Hall of Fame.

Billie Jean King (b. Nov. 22, 1943): Tennis; women's rights pioneer; Wimbledon singles champ 6 times; U.S. champ 4 times; first woman athlete to earn $100,000 in a year (1971); beat 55-year-old Bobby Riggs 6-4,6-3,6-3, in "Battle of the Sexes" to win $100,000 at Astrodome in 1973; founded the Women's Sports Foundation in 1974; captained the U.S. Olympic team in 1996 and 2000.

Don King (b. Aug. 20, 1931): Boxing promoter; first major black promoter who has controlled heavyweight title off and on since 1978; first big promotion was Muhammad Ali's fight against George Foreman in 1974; former numbers operator who served 4 years for manslaughter (1967-70); acquitted of tax evasion and fraud in 1985; also promoted Larry Holmes, Mike Tyson, Evander Holyfield, Roberto Duran and Julio Cesar Chavez among others; has been accused of bilking his fighters out of money; famous for his gravity-defying hairstyle and his catchphrase "Only in America!"

Karch Kiraly (b. Nov. 3, 1960): Volleyball; USA's preeminent volleyball player; led UCLA to three NCAA championships (1979,81,82); played on US national teams that won Olympic gold medals in 1984 and '88, world championships in '82 and '86; won the inaugural gold medal for Olympic beach volleyball with Kent Steffes in 1996.

Tom Kite (b. Dec. 9, 1949): Golfer; co-NCAA champion with Ben Crenshaw (1972); PGA Rookie of Year (1973); PGA Player of Year (1989); finally won 1st major with victory in 1992 U.S. Open at Pebble Beach; captain of 1997 US Ryder Cup team; 19 career PGA wins, played on the Champions tour since 2000 (currently has 10 wins).

Gene Klein (b. Jan. 29, 1921, d. Mar. 12, 1990): Horseman; won 3 Eclipse awards as top owner (1985-87); his filly Winning Colors won 1988 Kentucky Derby; also owned San Diego Chargers football team (1966-84).

Bob Knight (b. Oct. 25, 1940): Basketball; all-time NCAA Div. I coaching leader with 902 wins in 42 years; coached Indiana to 3 NCAA titles (1976,81,87); 3-time Coach of Year (1975-76,89); coached 1984 U.S. Olympic team to gold medal; his volatile temper finally cost him when he was fired from Indiana in Sept. 2000 after a string of unacceptable incidents that included choking one of his players; returned to coaching with Texas Tech in 2001; retired from coaching on Feb. 4, 2008.

Phil Knight (b. Feb. 24, 1938): Founder and chairman of Nike, Inc., the multi-billion dollar shoe and fitness company founded in 1972 and based in Beaverton, Ore.; named "The Most Powerful Man in Sports" by *The Sporting News* in 1992.

Bill Koch (b. June 7, 1955): Cross country skiing; first highly accomplished American male in his sport; first American male to win a cross country Olympic medal when he took home a silver in the 30-kilometer race in 1976; in 1982, he was the first American male to win the Nordic World Cup.

Tommy Kono (b. June 27, 1930): weight lifter; won 2 olympic gold medals for U.S. (1952,56) and 1 silver (1960); all 3 medals were in different weight classes; set world records in four different classes; inducted into U.S. Olympic Hall of Fame in 1990.

Olga Korbut (b. May 16, 1955): Soviet gymnast; became the media darling of the 1972 Olympics in Munich by winning 3 gold medals (balance beam, floor exercise and team all-around); came back in the 1976 Olympics in Montreal and was a part of the USSR's gold medal winning all-around team; first to perform back somersault on balance beam; was inducted into the International Women's Sports Hall of Fame in 1982, the first gymnast to be inducted.

Johann Olav Koss (b. Oct. 29, 1968): Norwegian speed skater; won three gold medals at 1994 Olympics in Lillehammer with world records in the 1,500m, 5,000m and 10,000m; also won 1,500m gold and 10,000m silver in 1992 Games; retired shortly after '94 Olympics.

Sandy Koufax (b. Dec. 30, 1935): Baseball LHP; led NL in strikeouts 4 times and ERA 5 straight years; won 3 Cy Young Awards (1963,65,66) with LA Dodgers; MVP in 1963; 2-time World Series MVP (1963, 65); threw perfect game against Chicago Cubs (1-0, Sept. 9, 1965) and had 3 other no-hitters, 40 shutouts and 137 complete games in a career that ended prematurely due to an arm injury.

Alvin Kraenzlein (b. Dec. 12, 1876, d. Jan. 6, 1928): Track & Field; won 4 individual gold medals in 1900 Olympics (60m, long jump and the 110m and 200m hurdles).

Jack Kramer (b. Aug. 1, 1921): Tennis; Wimbledon singles champ 1947; U.S. champ 1946-47; promoter and Open pioneer.

Lenny Krayzelburg (b. Sept. 28, 1975): Swimmer; won gold for U.S. in the 100m and 200m backstrokes and the 4x100m medley relay at the 2000 Sydney Games.

Ingrid Kristiansen (b. Mar. 21, 1956): Norwegian runner; 2-time Boston Marathon winner (1986,89); won New York City Marathon in 1989; former world record holder in the marathon.

Julie Krone (b. July 24, 1963): Jockey; only woman to ride winner in a Triple Crown race when she took 1993 Belmont Stakes aboard Colonial Affair; retired in 1999 as all-time winningest female jockey with over 3,000 wins; became the first female jockey named to hall of fame in 2000; came out of retirement in 2002, winning 2003 Breeders Cup race aboard Halfbridled.

Mike Krzyzewski (b. Feb. 13, 1947): Basketball; has coached Duke to 10 Final Four appearances and 3 NCAA titles (1991-92,2001); has coached at Army (1976-80) and Duke (1981-); inducted into Hall of Fame in 2001; coached U.S. team to Olympic gold medal in Beijing in 2008.

Bowie Kuhn (b. Oct. 28, 1926, d. March 15, 2007): Baseball Commissioner; Elected commissioner on Feb. 4, 1969 and served until Sept. 30, 1984; kept Willie Mays and Mickey Mantle out of baseball for their employment with casinos; handed down one-year suspensions of several players for drug involvement; nixed Charlie Finley's sale of three players for $3.5 million; baseball enjoyed unprecedented attendance and television contracts during his reign.

Alan Kulwicki (b. Dec. 14, 1954, d. Apr. 1, 1993): Auto racer; 1992 NASCAR national champion; 1st college grad and Northerner to win title; NASCAR Rookie of Year in 1986; famous for driving car backwards on victory lap; killed at age 38 in plane crash near Bristol, Tenn.

Michelle Kwan (b. July 7, 1980): Figure Skater; 1998 Olympic silver medalist at Nagano and 2002 bronze medalist at Salt Lake City; 9-time U.S. Champion (1996,98-05) and 5-time World Champ (1996,98,00,01,03); holds U.S. record with 8 career overall medals at the World Championships (5 gold, 3 silver); was U.S. alternate to the Olympics in 1994 as a 13-year-old.

Tony La Russa (b. Oct. 4, 1944): Baseball; former manager of the White Sox and A's and now current manager of the St. Louis Cardinals (since 1996); led A's (1989) and Cardinals (2006) to World Series titles; 2nd manager to win WS title with both AL and NL teams; ranks No. 3 all-time on coaching wins list.

Marion Ladewig (b. Oct. 30, 1914): Bowler; named Woman Bowler of the Year 9 times (1950-54,57-59,63).

Guy Lafleur (b. Sept. 20, 1951): Hockey RW; led NHL in scoring 3 times (1976-78); 2-time MVP (1977-78), played for 5 Stanley Cup winners in Montreal; playoff MVP in 1977; returned to NHL as player in 1988 after election to Hall of Fame; retired again in 1991 with 560 goals and 1,353 points.

Napoleon (Nap) Lajoie (b. Sept. 5, 1874, d. Feb. 7, 1959): Baseball 2B; led AL in batting 3 times (1901,03-04); batted .422 in 1901; hit .339 for career with 3,251 hits.

Jack Lambert (b. July 8, 1952): Football LB; 6-time All-Pro (1975-76,79-82); led Pittsburgh to 4 Super Bowl titles.

Floyd Landis (b. Oct. 14, 1975): Cycling; had his surprising 2006 Tour de France win stripped after it was revealed that two of his urine samples taken during the race tested positive for high testosterone levels.

Kenesaw Mountain Landis (b. Nov. 20, 1866, d. Nov. 25, 1944): U.S. District Court judge who became first baseball commissioner (1920-44); banned eight Chicago "Black Sox" from baseball for life for throwing 1919 World Series.

Tom Landry (b. Sept. 11, 1924, d. Feb. 12, 2000): Football; All-Pro DB for NY Giants (1954); coached Dallas for 29 years (1960-88); won 2 Super Bowls (1972,78); 3rd on NFL all-time list with 270 wins.

Steve Largent (b. Sept. 28, 1954): Football WR; retired in 1989 after 14 years in Seattle with then NFL records in passes caught (819) and TD passes caught (100); elected to U.S. House of Representatives (R, Okla.) in 1994 and Pro Football Hall of Fame in '95; ran for governor of Oklahoma in 2002 but suffered a narrow defeat.

Don Larsen (b. Aug. 7, 1929): Baseball RHP; NY Yankees hurler who pitched the only perfect game in World Series history—a 2-0 victory over Brooklyn in Game 5 of the 1956 Series; Series MVP that year.

Tommy Lasorda (b. Sept. 22, 1927): Baseball; managed LA Dodgers to 2 World Series titles (1981,88) in 4 appearances; retired as manager during 1996 season with 1,599 regular-season wins in 21 years; named interim GM of Dodgers in 1998; member of Baseball Hall of Fame; managed gold-medal winning U.S. Olympic team in 2000 at Sydney.

Larissa Latynina (b. Dec. 27, 1934): Soviet gymnast; won total of 18 medals, (9 gold) in 3 Olympics (1956,60,64).

Nikki Lauda (b. Feb. 22, 1949): Austrian auto racer; 3-time world Formula One champion (1975, 77,84); 25 career wins from 1971-85.

Rod Laver (b. Aug. 9, 1938): Australian tennis player; undersized but big-hitting left-hander is only player to win Grand Slam twice (1962,69); Wimbledon champion 4 times; first to earn $1 million in career prize money, won 11 Grand Slam and 47 professional singles titles.

Bobby Layne (b. Dec. 19, 1926, d. Dec. 1, 1986): Football QB; college star at Texas; master of 2-minute offense; led Detroit to 4 divisional titles and 3 NFL championships in 1950s.

Frank Leahy (b. Aug. 27, 1908, d. June 21, 1973): Football; coached Notre Dame to four national titles (1943,46-47,49); career record of 107-13-9 for a winning pct. of .864.

Sammy Lee (b. Aug. 1, 1920): Diving; won Olympic gold medals for U.S. in the platform diving event in 1948 and 1952, the first male diver in history to win 2 golds in that event; Sullivan Award winner (1953); former Dr. in U.S. Army; trained Greg Louganis.

Brian Leetch (b. Mar. 3, 1968): Hockey D; NHL Rookie of Year in 1989; won Norris Trophy as top defenseman in 1992; Conn Smythe Trophy winner as playoffs' MVP in 1994 when he helped lead NY Rangers to 1st Stanley Cup title in 54 years.

Jacques Lemaire (b. Sept. 7, 1945): Hockey C; member of 8 Stanley Cup champions in Montreal; scored 366 goals in 12 seasons; coached Canadiens (1983-85) and NJ Devils (1993-98), won 1995 Stanley Cup with New Jersey; returned to coaching with the expansion Minnesota Wild in 2000.

Mario Lemieux (b. Oct. 5, 1965): Hockey C; 6-time NHL scoring leader (1988-89,92-93,96-97); Rookie of Year (1985), 4-time All-NHL 1st team (1988-89,93,96), 3-time regular season MVP (1988,93,96); 3-time All-Star Game MVP; led Pittsburgh to consecutive Stanley Cup titles (1991 and '92) and was playoff MVP both years; won 1993 scoring title despite missing 24 games to undergo radiation treatments for Hodgkin's disease; missed 62 games during 1993-94 season and entire 1994-95 season due to back injuries and fatigue; returned in 1995-96 to lead NHL in scoring and win the MVP trophy; retired after 1996-97 season and inducted into the Hall of Fame; headed group of investors that bought bankrupt Penguins in 1999; made surprising return to the ice in 2001 as owner-player with Penguins; retired again in 2006.

Greg LeMond (b. June 26, 1961): American cyclist; 3-time Tour de France winner (1986,89-90); only non-European to win the event until Lance Armstrong in 1999; retired in Dec. 1994 after being diagnosed with a rare muscular disease known as mitochondrial myopathy.

Ivan Lendl (b. Mar. 7, 1960): Czech tennis player; No. 1 player in world 4 times (1985-87,89); won both French and U.S. Opens 3 times and Australian twice; owns 94 career tournament wins.

Suzanne Lenglen (b. May 24, 1899, d. July 4, 1938): French tennis player; dominated women's tennis from 1919-26; won both Wimbledon and French singles titles 6 times.

Sugar Ray Leonard (b. May 17, 1956): Boxer; light welterweight Olympic champ (1976); won world welterweight title in 1979 and 4 more titles; in 1987 he upset Marvin Hagler for the middleweight crown; retired and unretired several times, before ending his career for good in 1997 with record of 36-3-1 and 25 KOs following a TKO loss to Hector Camacho.

Walter (Buck) Leonard (b. Sept. 8, 1907, d. Nov. 27, 1997): Baseball 1B; won Negro League championship nine years in a row with the Homestead Grays; hit .391 in 1948 to lead the league; usually batted cleanup behind Josh Gibson; retired at the age of 48; member of the National Baseball Hall of Fame.

Lisa Leslie (b. July 7, 1972): Basketball C; 2-time WNBA Finals MVP (2001-02) with the champion Los Angeles Sparks; 3-time regular season MVP (2001,2004,2006); 3-time WNBA All-Star Game MVP (1999,2001-02); 3-time Olympic gold medalist (1996,2000,2004); consensus National Player of the Year at USC (1994).

Marv Levy (b. Aug. 3, 1928): Football; coached Buffalo to four consecutive Super Bowls, but is one of two coaches who are 0-4 (Bud Grant is other); won 50 games and two CFL Grey Cups with Montreal (1974,77); returned to Bills as GM from 2006-08.

Bill Lewis (b. Nov. 30, 1868, d. Jan. 1, 1949): Football; college star at Amherst College and then Harvard; first black player to be selected as an All-American (1892-93); also the first black admitted to the American Bar Association (1911); was U.S. Assistant Attorney General.

Carl Lewis (b. July 1, 1961): Track & Field; won 9 Olympic gold medals; 4 in 1984 (100m, 200m, 4x100m, LJ), 2 in '88 (100m, LJ), 2 in '92 (4x100m, LJ) and 1 in '96 (LJ); has record 8 World Championship titles and 10 medals; all Sullivan Award winner (1981); two-time AP Athlete of the Year (1983-84); in 1991, set world record in 100m with a 9.86.

Lennox Lewis (b. Sept. 2, 1965): British boxer; won 1988 Olympic super heavyweight gold medal for Canada; was awarded WBC heavyweight belt when Riddick Bowe tossed it in a London trash can in 1993; lost title in a 2nd round TKO loss to Oliver McCall; won rematch 3 years later when McCall suffered emotional breakdown in the ring; unified titles in his rematch with Evander Holyfield in Nov. 1999; lost belts in upset loss to Hasim Rahman in April 2001 but took them back 7 months later; recorded 8th-round KO of Mike Tyson in June 2002.

Nancy Lieberman (b. July 1, 1958): Basketball; 3-time All-America and 2-time Player of Year (1979-80); led Old Dominion to consecutive AIAW titles in 1979 and '80; played in defunct WPBL and WABA and became 1st woman to play in men's pro league (USBL) in 1986; played in the inaugural season of the WNBA for the Phoenix Mercury and served as coach/GM of Detroit Shock (1998-2000).

Eric Lindros (b. Feb. 28, 1973): Hockey C; No. 1 pick in 1991 NHL draft by Quebec but sat out 1991-92 season rather than play for Nordiques; traded to Philadelphia in 1992 for 6 players, 2 No. 1 picks and $15 million; elected Flyers captain at age 22; NHL MVP in 1995; 6-time NHL all-star; suffered series of concussions; retired in 2007.

Tara Lipinski (b. June 10, 1982): Figure Skater; won the 1998 women's figure skating gold medal at the Olympics in Nagano, becoming the youngest in history (15 yrs., 7 mos.) to do so; she and Michelle Kwan gave the U.S. its first 1-2 finish in that event since 1956; 1997 U.S. and World champion.

Sonny Liston (b. May 8, 1932, d. Dec. 30, 1970): Boxer; heavyweight champion (1962-64), who knocked out Floyd Patterson twice in the first round, then lost title to Muhammad Ali (then Cassius Clay) in 1964; pro record of 50-4 with 39 KOs.

Vince Lombardi (b. June 11, 1913, d. Sept. 3, 1970): Football; coached Green Bay to five NFL titles; won first two Super Bowls (1967-68); died as NFL's alltime winningest coach with percentage of .740 (105-35-6); Super Bowl trophy named in his honor.

Johnny Longden (b. Feb. 14, 1907, d. Feb. 14, 2003): Jockey; first to win 6,000 races; rode Count Fleet to Triple Crown in 1943.

Jeannie Longo (b. Oct. 31, 1958): French cyclist; 12-time world cycling champion and 1996 olympic road race gold medallist.

Nancy Lopez (b. Jan. 6, 1957): Golfer; 4-time LPGA Player of the Year (1978-79,85,88); Rookie of Year (1977); 3-time winner of LPGA Championship; reached Hall of Fame by age 30 with 35 victories; 48 career wins.

Donna Lopiano (b. Sept. 11, 1946): Former basketball and softball star who was women's athletic director at Texas for 18 years before leaving to become executive director of Women's Sports Foundation in 1992; resigned from that position in 2007.

Greg Louganis (b. Jan. 29, 1960): U.S. diver; widely considered the greatest diver in history; won platform and springboard gold medals at both 1984 and '88 Olympics; also won a silver medal at the 1976 Olympics at the age of 16; won five world championships and 47 U.S. National Diving titles; revealed on Feb. 22, 1995 that he has AIDS.

Joe Louis (b. May 13, 1914, d. Apr. 12, 1981): Boxer; world heavyweight champion from June 22, 1937 to Mar. 1, 1949; his reign of 11 years, 8 months longest in division history; successfully defended title 25 times; retired in 1949, but returned to lose title shot against successor Ezzard Charles in 1950 and then to Rocky Marciano in '51; pro record of 63-3 with 49 KOs.

Sid Luckman (b. Nov. 21, 1916, d. July 5, 1998): Football QB; 6-time All-Pro; led Chicago Bears to 4 NFL titles (1940-41,43,46); MVP in 1943.

Hank Luisetti (b. June 16, 1916, d. Dec. 17, 2002): Basketball F; 3-time All-America at Stanford (1936-38); revolutionized game with one-handed shot.

Johnny Lujack (b. Jan. 4, 1925): Football QB; led Notre Dame to three national titles (1943,46-47); won Heisman Trophy in 1947.

Darrell Wayne Lukas (b. Sept. 2, 1935): Horse racing; four-time Eclipse-winning trainer who saddled Horses of Year Lady's Secret in 1988 and Criminal Type in 1990; first trainer to earn over $100 million in purses; led nation in earnings 14 times since 1983; Grindstone's Kentucky Derby win in 1996 gave him six Triple Crown wins in a row; has won Preakness five times, Kentucky Derby four times and Belmont four times; his most recent Triple Crown victory came in the 2000 Belmont with Commendable; 16 Breeders' Cup victories.

Gen. Douglas MacArthur (b. Jan. 26, 1880, d. Apr. 5, 1964): Controversial U.S. general of World War II and Korea; president of U.S. Olympic Committee (1927-28); college football devotee, National Football Foundation MacArthur Bowl named after him.

Connie Mack (b. Dec. 22, 1862, d. Feb. 8, 1956): Baseball owner; managed Philadelphia A's until he was 87 (1901-50); all-time major league wins leader with 3,755, including World Series; won 9 AL pennants and 5 World Series (1910-11,13,29-30); also finished last 17 times.

Andy MacPhail (b. Apr. 5, 1953): Baseball; Baltimore Orioles president of baseball operations; former Chicago Cubs president/CEO; was GM of 2 World Series champions in Minnesota (1987,91); won first title at age 34; son of Lee, grandson of Larry.

Larry MacPhail (b. Feb. 3, 1890, d. Oct. 1, 1975): Baseball executive and innovator; introduced major leagues to night games at Cincinnati (May 24, 1935); won pennant in Brooklyn (1941) and World Series with NY Yankees (1947); father of Lee, grandfather of Andy.

Lee MacPhail (b. Oct. 25, 1917): Baseball; AL president (1974-83); president of owners' Player Relations Committee (1984-85); also GM of Baltimore (1959-65) and NY Yankees (1967-74); son of Larry and father of Andy.

Wendy Macpherson (b. Jan. 28, 1968): Bowling; voted Bowler of the Decade for the 1990s; Major titles include the 1986 BPAA U.S. Open, 1988, 2000 and 2003 WIBC Queens and 1999 Sam's Town Invitational; annual PWBA money winner 4 times.

John Madden (b. Apr. 10, 1936): Football and Radio-TV; won 112 games and a Super Bowl (1976 season) as coach of Oakland Raiders; has won 16 Emmy Awards since 1982 as NFL analyst; signed 4-year, $32 million deal with Fox in 1994— a richer contract than any NFL player at the time; joined Al Michaels in ABC's Monday Night Football booth in 2002 after 21 seasons alongside Pat Summerall; joined NBC for Sunday Night Football beginning in 2006.

Greg Maddux (b. Apr. 14, 1966): Baseball RHP; won unprecedented 4 straight NL Cy Young Awards with Cubs (1992) and Atlanta (1993-95); has led NL in ERA four times (1993-95,98); owner of a record 17 gold gloves; only pitcher to win at least 15 games in 17 straight seasons (1988-2004); got his 300th win in 2004; one of nine pitchers with over 350 wins.

Larry Mahan (b. Nov. 21, 1943): Rodeo; 6-time All-Around world champion cowboy (1966-70,73).

Phil Mahre (b. May 10, 1957): Alpine skier; 3-time World Cup overall champ (1981-83); finished 1-2 with twin brother Steve in 1984 Olympic slalom.

Karl Malone (b. July 24, 1963): Basketball F; 11-time All-NBA 1st team (1989-99) with Utah; 2-time NBA MVP (1997,99); all-time NBA leader in free throws made (9,787), 2nd in career points (36,928) and field goals made (13,528); member of the 1992 and '96 Olympic gold medal teams; named one of the NBA's 50 greatest players.

Moses Malone (b. Mar. 23, 1955): Basketball C; signed with Utah of ABA out of high school at age 19; led NBA in rebounding 6 times; 4-time All-NBA 1st team; 3-time NBA MVP (1979,82-83); Finals MVP with Philadelphia in 1983; played 21 pro seasons.

Peyton Manning (b. Mar. 24, 1976): Football QB; top overall pick (out of Tennessee) by the Indianapolis Colts in the 1998 draft; 2-time Associated Press NFL MVP (2003-04); led AFC in passing efficiency 4 times (1998,2004-06); entered 2008 with 306 touchdown passes, 4th on the all-time list; threw an NFL record 49 TD passes in 2004 (broken in 2007); led Colts to long-awaited Super Bowl title in Feb. 2007 (XLI); son of Archie, brother of Eli.

Nigel Mansell (b. Aug. 8, 1953): British auto racer; won 1992 Formula One driving championship with record 9 victories and 14 poles; quit Grand Prix circuit to race Indy cars in 1993; 1st rookie to win IndyCar title; 3rd driver to win IndyCar and F1 titles; returned to F1 after 1994 IndyCar season and won '94 Australian Grand Prix; left F1 again on May 23, 1995 with 31 wins and 32 poles in 15 years.

Mickey Mantle (b. Oct. 20, 1931, d. Aug. 13, 1995): Baseball CF; led AL in home runs 4 times; won Triple Crown in 1956; hit 52 HRs in 1956 and 54 in '61; 3-time MVP (1956-57,62); hit 536 career HRs; played in 12 World Series with NY Yankees and won 7 times; all-time World Series leader in HRs (18), RBI (40), runs (42) and strikeouts (54); inducted into Baseball Hall of Fame in 1974.

Diego Maradona (b. Oct. 30, 1960): Soccer F; captain and MVP of 1986 World Cup champion Argentina; also led national team to 1990 World Cup final; consensus Player of Decade in 1980s; led Napoli to 2 Italian League titles (1987,90) and UEFA Cup (1989); tested positive for cocaine and suspended 15 months by FIFA in 1991; returned to World Cup as Argentine captain in 1994, but was kicked out after 2 games for using banned substances.

Pete Maravich (b. June 27, 1947, d. Jan. 5, 1988): Basketball; NCAA scoring leader 3 times at LSU (1968-70); averaged NCAA-record 44.2 points a game over career; Player of Year in 1970; NBA scoring champ in '77 with New Orleans.

Alice Marble (b. Sept. 28, 1913, d. Dec. 13, 1990): Tennis; 4-time U.S. champion (1936,38-40); won Wimbledon in 1939; swept U.S. singles, doubles and mixed doubles from 1938-40.

Gino Marchetti (b. Jan. 2, 1927): Football DE; 8-time NFL All-Pro (1957-64) with Baltimore Colts.

Rocky Marciano (b. Sept. 1, 1923, d. Aug. 31, 1969): Boxer; heavyweight champion (1952-56); only heavyweight champ in history to retire undefeated; pro record of 49-0 with 43 KOs; killed in plane crash.

Juan Marichal (b. Oct. 20, 1938): Baseball RHP; won 21 or more games 6 times for S.F. Giants from 1963-69; ended 16-year career at 243-142.

Dan Marino (b. Sept. 15, 1961): Football QB; 2nd all-time (to Favre) in career NFL TD passes (420), attempts (8,358), completions (4,967) and passing yards (61,361); 4-time leading passer in AFC (1983-84,86,89); set NFL single-season records for TD passes (48, since broken) and passing yards (5,084) in 1984.

Roger Maris (b. Sept. 10, 1934, d. Dec. 14, 1985): Baseball OF; broke Babe Ruth's season HR record with 61 in 1961 and held record until 1998 (Mark McGwire); 2-time AL MVP (1960-61) with NY Yankees; 275 HRs in 12 years.

Jim Marshall (b. Dec. 30, 1937): Football; long-time Vikings DE and NFL ironman; played in 282 consecutive games (1960-1979); also famous for picking up a fumble and running 66 yards the wrong way into the opponent's (49ers) endzone.

Billy Martin (b. May 16, 1928, d. Dec. 25, 1989): Baseball; 5-time manager of NY Yankees; won 2 pennants and 1 World Series (1977); also managed Minnesota, Detroit, Texas and Oakland; played on 5 Yankee world champions in 1950s.

Pedro Martinez (b. Oct. 25, 1971): Baseball RHP; won 1997 NL Cy Young award with Montreal; traded to Boston Red Sox in Nov. 1997; 2-time AL Cy Young Award winner with Boston (1999,2000); signed with NY Mets in 2005.

Eddie Mathews (b. Oct. 13, 1931, d. Feb. 18, 2001): Baseball 3B; led NL in HRs twice (1953,59); hit 30 or more HRs 9 straight years; 512 career HRs.

Christy Mathewson (b. Aug. 12, 1880, d. Oct. 7, 1925): Baseball RHP; won 22 or more games 12 straight years (1903-14); 373 career wins; pitched 3 shutouts in 1905 World Series.

Bob Mathias (b. Nov. 17, 1930, d. Sept. 2, 2006): Track & Field; youngest winner of decathlon with gold medal in 1948 Olympics at age 17; first to repeat as decathlon champ in 1952; Sullivan Award winner (1948); 4-term member of U.S. Congress (R, Calif.) from 1967-74.

Ollie Matson (b. May 1, 1930): Football HB; All-America at San Francisco (1951); bronze medal winner in 400m at 1952 Olympics; 4-time All-Pro for NFL Chicago Cardinals (1954-57); traded to LA Rams for 9 players in 1959; accounted for 12,884 all-purpose yards and scored 73 TDs in 14 seasons.

Don Mattingly (b. Apr. 20, 1961): Baseball 1B; AL MVP (1985); won AL batting title in 1984 (.343); led majors with 145 RBI in 1985; led AL with 238 hits (Yankee record) and 53 doubles in 1986; won 9 Gold Glove Awards at 1B (1985-89, 91-94).

Willie Mays (b. May 6, 1931): Baseball OF; nicknamed the "Say Hey Kid"; led NL in HRs and stolen bases 4 times each; 2-time MVP (1954,65) with NY-SF Giants; Hall of Famer who played in 24 All-Star Games, earning MVP honors twice (1963,68); 12-time Gold Glove winner; 660 HRs, 1,903 RBI and 3,283 hits in career.

Floyd Mayweather Jr. (b. Feb. 24, 1977): Boxer; *Ring Magazine* Fighter of the Year in 1998 and 2007; held junior lightweight, lightweight, junior welterweight, welterweight and junior middleweight titles during his 12-year pro career; retired in 2008 with career mark of 39-0 and 25 KO; Olympic bronze medalist in 1996.

Bill Mazeroski (b. Sept. 5, 1936): Baseball 2B; career .260 hitter who won the 1960 World Series for Pittsburgh with a lead-off HR in the bottom of the 9th inning of Game 7; the pitcher was Ralph Terry of the NY Yankees, the count was 1-0 and the score was tied 9-9; also a sure-fielder, Maz won 8 Gold Gloves in 17 seasons.

Bob McAdoo (b. Sept. 25, 1951): Basketball F/C; 1972 *Sporting News* First Team All-American; NBA Rookie of the Year (1973); NBA MVP (1975); All-NBA First Team (1975); Led NBA in scoring three consecutive years (1974-76); 5-time All-Star (1974-78); two championships with LA Lakers (1982,85).

Joe McCarthy (b. Apr. 21, 1887, d. Jan. 13, 1978): Baseball; first manager to win pennants in both leagues (Chicago Cubs in 1929 and NY Yankees in 1932); greatest success came with Yankees when he won seven pennants and six World Series championships from 1936 to 1943; first manager to win four World Series in a row (1936-39); finished his career with the Boston Red Sox (1948-50); lifetime record of 2125-1333; member of Baseball Hall of Fame.

Pat McCormick (b. May 12, 1930): U.S. diver; won women's platform and springboard gold medals in both 1952 and '56 Olympics.

Willie McCovey (b. Jan. 10, 1938): Baseball 1B; led NL in HRs 3 times and RBI twice; MVP in 1969 with SF; 521 career HRs; "McCovey Cove," the bay outside the rightfield fence at San Francisco's AT&T Park is named for him.

John McEnroe (b. Feb. 16, 1959): Tennis; No.1 player in the world 4 times (1981-84); 4-time U.S. Open champ (1979-81,84); 3-time Wimbledon champ (1981,83-84); played on 5 Davis Cup winners (1978,79,81,82,92); won NCAA singles title (1978); finished career with 77 singles championships and 77 more in men's doubles (including 9 Grand Slam titles).

John McGraw (b. Apr. 7, 1873, d. Feb. 25, 1934): Baseball; managed NY Giants to 9 NL pennants between 1905-24; won 3 World Series (1905,21-22); 2nd on all-time career list with 2,866 wins in 33 seasons (2,840 regular season and 26 World Series).

Frank McGuire (b. Nov. 8, 1916, d. Oct. 11, 1994): Basketball; winner of 731 games as high school, college and pro coach; won at least 100 games at 3 colleges— St. John's (103), North Carolina (164) and South Carolina (283); won 550 games in 30 college seasons; 1957 UNC team went 32-0 and beat Kansas 54-53 in triple OT to win NCAA title; coached NBA Philadelphia Warriors to 49-31 record in 1961-62, but refused to move with team to San Francisco.

Mark McGwire (b. Oct. 1, 1963): Baseball 1B; Member of 1984 U.S. Olympic baseball team; won AL Rookie of the Year and hit rookie-record 49 HRs in 1987; shattered Roger Maris' season home run record (61) in 1998 with St. Louis (70); followed that with 65 HRs in 1999; retired in 2001 with 583 HR; took a tremendous media hit and became a target for steroid accusations after he stood up in Congress in 2005 and refused to "talk about the past."

Jim McKay (b. Sept. 24, 1921, d. June 7, 2008): Radio-TV; host and commentator of ABC's Olympic coverage and "Wide World of Sports" show beginning in 1961; covered 12 Olympics, including the 1972 Munich games in which 11 Israeli athletes were killed; 12-time Emmy winner; also given Peabody Award in 1988 and Life Achievement Emmy in 1990; became part owner of Baltimore Orioles in 1993.

Tamara McKinney (b. Oct. 16, 1962): Skiing; first American woman to win overall Alpine World Cup championship (1983); won World Cup slalom (1984) and giant slalom titles twice (1981,83).

Denny McLain (b. Mar. 29, 1944): Baseball RHP; last pitcher to win 30 games (1968); 2-time Cy Young winner (1968-69) with Detroit; convicted of racketeering, extortion and drug possession in 1985, served 29 months of 25-year jail term, sentence overturned when court ruled he had not received a fair trial; he has faced subsequent legal troubles.

Rick Mears (b. Dec. 3, 1951): Auto racer; 3-time CART national champ (1979,81-82); 4-time winner of Indy 500 (1979,84,88,91) and only driver to win 6 Indy 500 poles; Indy 500 Rookie of Year (1978); retired in 1992 with 29 CART wins and 40 poles.

Mark Messier (b. Jan. 18, 1961): Hockey C; 2-time NHL MVP with Edmonton (1990) and NY Rangers (1992); captain of 1994 Rangers team that won 1st Stanley Cup since 1940; ranks 2nd in all-time play-off points, goals and assists; 2nd on all-time regular season points list (1,887); retired in 2005.

Mike Metzger (b. Nov. 19, 1975): Freestyle Motocross Rider; AMA National mini-bike champion (1990), credited as "The Godfather" of FMX for his early creative influences and trick inventions; first to land back-to-back backflips in competition (2002 X Games), winner of five X Games medals.

Debbie Meyer (b. Aug. 14, 1952): Swimmer; 1st swimmer to win 3 individual golds at 1 Olympics (1968).

Ann Meyers (b. Mar. 26, 1955): Basketball G; In 1974, became first high schooler to play for U.S. national team; 4-time All-American at UCLA (1976-79); member of 1976 U.S. Olympic team; Broderick Award and Cup winner (1978); Signed $50,000 no cut contract with NBA's Indiana Pacers (1980); married Dodger great Don Drysdale.

Phil Mickelson (b. June 16, 1970): Golfer; "Lefty;" won 3 individual NCAA championships at Arizona St. (1989,90,92); 3rd all-time on PGA Tour career money list with over $50 million and counting; finally broke through with his first major title with his Masters win in 2004; added a PGA Championship title in 2005 and a second Masters win in 2006.

George Mikan (b. June 18, 1924, d. June 2, 2005): Basketball C; 3-time All-America (1944-46); led DePaul to NIT title (1945); led Minneapolis Lakers to 5 NBA titles in 6 years (1949-54); first commissioner of ABA (1967-69).

Stan Mikita (b. May 20, 1940): Hockey C; led NHL in scoring 4 times; won both MVP and Lady Byng awards in 1967 and '68 with Chicago.

Bode Miller (b. Oct. 12, 1977): Alpine Skier; Overall World Cup champion in 2005 and 2008; won 2 silver medals at 2002 Winter Olympics; 2 golds, 1 silver at 2003 World Championships; 2004 Giant Slalom World Cup champion; came up empty at Turin Olympic Games in 2006; 2007 Super G World Cup champ.

Cheryl Miller (b. Jan. 3, 1964): Basketball; 3-time College Player of Year (1984-86); led USC to NCAA title and U.S. to Olympic gold medal in 1984; coached USC to 44-14 record in 2 years; coached WNBA's Phoenix Mercury for 4 years; sister of NBA's Reggie.

Del Miller (b. July 5, 1913, d. Aug. 19, 1996): Harness racing; driver, trainer, owner, breeder, seller and track owner; drove to 2,441 wins from 1929-90.

Marvin Miller (b. Apr. 14, 1917): Baseball labor leader; executive director of Players' Assn. from 1966-82; increased average salary from $19,000 to over $240,000; led 13-day strike in 1972 and 50-day walkout in '81.

Shannon Miller (b. Mar. 10, 1977): Gymnast; won 5 medals in 1992 Olympics and 2 golds in '96 Games; All-Around champion in 1993 and '94.

Billy Mills (b. June 30, 1938): Track & Field; Native American who was upset winner of 10,000m gold medal at 1964 Olympics.

Bora Milutinovic (b. Sept. 7, 1944): Soccer; Serbian who coached U.S. national team from 1991-95; led Mexico (1986), Costa Rica ('90), USA ('94) and Nigeria ('98) into the 2nd round of the World Cup; coached China in 2002 but was ousted in 1st round.

Dave Mirra (b. Apr. 4, 1974): BMX; medaled in every summer X Games since 1995; has 20 X Games medals (14 gold); first to do a double backflip on a BMX bike; nicknamed "Miracle Boy" after his brush with death when he was hit by a drunk driver (1994).

Tommy Moe (b. Feb. 17, 1970): Alpine skier; won Downhill gold and Super-G silver at 1994 Winter Olympics; 1st U.S. man to win 2 Olympic alpine medals in one year.

Paul Molitor (b. Aug. 22, 1956): Baseball DH-1B; All-America SS at Minnesota in 1976; spent 15 years with Milwaukee, then 3 each with Toronto and Minnesota; led Blue Jays to 2nd straight World Series title as MVP (1993); hit .418 in 2 Series appearances (1982,93); holds World Series game record with 5 hits.

Joe Montana (b. June 11, 1956): Football QB; led Notre Dame to national title in 1977; led San Francisco to 4 Super Bowl titles in 1980s; only 3-time Super Bowl MVP; 2-time NFL MVP (1989-90); led NFL in passing 5 times; traded to K.C. in 1993; ranks 5th all-time in passing efficiency (92.3); 273 career TD passes and 40,551 passing yards; inducted into Pro Football Hall of Fame in 2000.

Helen Wills Moody (b. Oct. 6, 1905, d. Jan. 1, 1998): Tennis; won 8 Wimbledon singles titles, 7 U.S. and 4 French from 1923-38.

Warren Moon (b. Nov. 18, 1956): Football QB; MVP of 1978 Rose Bowl with Washington; MVP of CFL with Edmonton in 1983; led Eskimos to 5 consecutive Grey Cup titles (1978-82) and was playoff MVP twice (1980,82); entered NFL in 1984 and played for 4 different teams; 9-time Pro Bowler; 49,325 NFL passing yards; inducted into Hall of Fame in 2006.

Archie Moore (b. Dec. 13, 1913, d. Dec. 9, 1998): Boxer; world light heavyweight champion (1952-60); pro record 199-26-8 with a record 145 KOs.

Noureddine Morceli (b. Feb. 28, 1970): Algerian runner; 3-time world champion at 1,500 meters (1991,93,95) and 1996 Olympic gold medal winner; held world records in several middle distance events.

Howie Morenz (b. June 21, 1902, d. Mar. 8, 1937): Hockey C; 3-time NHL MVP (1928,31,32); led Montreal Canadiens to 3 Stanley Cups; voted Outstanding Player of the Half-Century in 1950.

Joe Morgan (b. Sept. 19, 1943): Baseball 2B; regular-season MVP both years he led Cincinnati to World Series titles (1975-76); 1,865 career walks; led NL in walks 4 times; ESPN baseball announcer.

Bobby Morrow (b. Oct. 15, 1935): Track & Field; won 3 gold medals at 1956 Olympics (100m, 200m and 4x400m relay).

Willie Mosconi (b. June 27, 1913, d. Sept. 12, 1993): Pocket Billiards; 14-time world champ (1941-57).

Annemarie Moser-Pröll (b. Mar. 27, 1953): Austrian alpine skier; won World Cup overall title 6 times (1971-75,79); all-time women's World Cup leader in career wins with 61; won Downhill in 1980 Olympics.

Edwin Moses (b. Aug. 31, 1955): Track & Field; won 400m hurdles at 1976 and '84 Olympics, bronze medal in '88; also winner of 122 consecutive races from 1977-87.

Stirling Moss (b. Sept. 17, 1929): Auto racer; won 194 of 466 career races and 16 Formula One events, but was never world champion.

Marion Motley (b. June 5, 1920, d. June 27, 1999): Football FB/LB; hard-charging runner who was all-time leading AAFC rusher; ran for over 4,700 yards and 31 TDs for Cleveland Browns (1946-53), leading the NFL in 1950; first black member of the Pro Football Hall of Fame.

Shirley Muldowney (b. June 19, 1940): Drag Racer; "Cha Cha"; women's racing pioneer; 3-time Winston drag racing Top Fuel champion (1977,80,82); recorded 18 career NHRA National Event Victories.

Anthony Munoz (b. Aug. 19, 1958): Football OT; drafted 3rd overall in 1980 out of USC; 11-time All-Pro with Cincinnati; member of NFL 75th Anniv. All-Time Team; elected to Hall of Fame in 1998.

Calvin Murphy (b. May 9, 1948): Basketball G; NBA All-Rookie team (1971); holds NBA single season free throw percentage (.958); has all-time career free throw pct. of .892; elected to Basketball Hall of Fame in 1992; only 5'9" and 165 pounds.

Dale Murphy (b. Mar. 12, 1956): Baseball OF; led NL in HRs and RBI twice; 2-time MVP (1982-83) with Atlanta; also played with Philadelphia and Colorado; retired in 1993 with 398 HRs.

Jack Murphy (b. Feb. 5, 1923, d. Sept. 24, 1980): Sports editor and columnist of *The San Diego Union* from 1951-80; instrumental in bringing AFL Chargers south from LA in 1961, landing Padres as NL expansion team in '69; and lobbying for San Diego stadium that would later bear his name.

Eddie Murray (b. Feb. 24, 1956): Baseball 1B-DH; AL Rookie of Year in 1977; became 20th player in history, but only 2nd switch hitter (after Pete Rose) to get 3,000 hits; one of only 4 men (Aaron, Mays and Palmeiro) with 500 HRs and 3,000 hits.

Jim Murray (b. Dec. 29, 1919, d. Aug. 16, 1998): Sports columnist for *LA Times* 1961-98; 14-time Sportswriter of the Year; won Pulitzer Prize for commentary in 1990.

Ty Murray (b. Oct. 11, 1969): Rodeo cowboy; 7-time All-Around world champion (1989-94,98); Rookie of Year in 1988; youngest (age 20) to win All-Around title; career hampered by injury; married pop singer Jewel in 2008.

Stan Musial (b. Nov. 21, 1920): Baseball OF-1B; led NL in batting 7 times and RBI 2 times; 3-time MVP (1943,46,48) with St. Louis; played in 24 All-Star Games; had 3,630 career hits (4th all-time) and .331 average.

John Naber (b. Jan. 20, 1956): Swimmer; won 4 gold medals and a silver in 1976 Olympics.

Rafael Nadal (b. June 3, 1986): Spanish tennis player; winner of 5 Grand Slam singles titles: French Open (2005-08) and Wimbledon (2008); overtook rival Roger Federer as the top-ranked men's tennis player on Aug. 18, 2008; Olympic gold medalist (2008).

Bronko Nagurski (b. Nov. 3, 1908, d. Jan. 7, 1990): Football FB-T; All-America at Minnesota (1929); All-Pro with Chicago Bears (1932-34); charter member of college and pro Halls of Fame.

James Naismith (b. Nov. 6, 1861, d. Nov. 28, 1939): Canadian physical education instructor who invented basketball in 1891 at the YMCA Training School (now Springfield College) in Springfield, Mass.

Joe Namath (b. May 31, 1943): Football QB; "Broadway Joe;" signed for unheard-of $400,000 as rookie with AFL's NY Jets in 1965; 2-time All-AFL (1968-69) and All-NFL (1972); led Jets to a 16-7 upset over the heavily-favored Baltimore Colts in Super Bowl III (1969) after making brash prediction of victory; selected Super Bowl MVP.

Ilie Nastase (b. July 19, 1946): Romanian tennis player; No.1 in the world twice (1972-73); won U.S. (1972) and French (1973) Opens; has since entered Romanian politics.

Martina Navratilova (b. Oct. 18, 1956): Tennis player; No.1 player in the world 7 times (1978-79,82-86); won her record 9th Wimbledon singles title in 1990; also won 4 U.S. Opens, 3 Australian and 2 French; in all, won 18 Grand Slam singles titles, 41 Grand Slam doubles titles; all-time leader among men and women in singles titles (167); won over $21 million in career earnings; inducted into Int'l Tennis Hall of Fame in 2000; retired in 2006 after winning U.S. Open mixed doubles title.

Cosmas Ndeti (b. Nov. 24, 1971): Kenyan distance runner; winner of three consecutive Boston Marathons (1993-95); set course record in 1994 — 2:07:15 (since broken in 2006).

Earle (Greasy) Neale (b. Nov. 5, 1891, d. Nov. 2, 1973): Baseball and Football; hit .357 for Cincinnati in 1919 World Series; also played with pre-NFL Canton Bulldogs; later coached Philadelphia Eagles to 2 NFL titles (1948-49).

Primo Nebiolo (b. July 14, 1923, d. Nov. 7, 1999): Italian president of International Amateur Athletic Federation (IAAF) since 1981; also an at-large member of International Olympic Committee; regarded as dictatorial, but credited with elevating track & field to world class financial status.

Byron Nelson (b. Feb. 4, 1912, d. Sept. 26, 2006): Golfer; 2-time winner of both Masters (1937,42) and PGA (1940,45); also U.S. Open champion in 1939; won 19 tournaments in 1945, including 11 in a row; also set all-time PGA stroke average with 68.33 strokes per round over 120 rounds in '45.

Lindsey Nelson (b. May 25, 1919, d. June 10, 1995): Radio-TV; all-purpose play-by-play broadcaster for CBS, NBC and others; 4-time Sportscaster of the Year (1959-62); voice of Cotton Bowl for 25 years and NY Mets from 1962-78; given Life Achievement Emmy Award in 1991.

Ernie Nevers (b. June 11, 1903, d. May 3, 1976): Football FB; earned 11 letters in four sports at Stanford; played pro football, baseball and basketball; scored 40 points for Chicago Cardinals in one NFL game (1929).

Paula Newby-Fraser (b. June 2, 1962): Zimbabwean triathlete; 8-time winner of Ironman Triathlon in Hawaii; established women's record of 8:55:28 in 1992.

John Newcombe (b. May 23, 1944): Australian tennis player; No.1 player in world 3 times (1967,70-71); won Wimbledon 3 times and U.S. and Australian championships twice each.

Pete Newell (b. Aug. 31, 1915): Basketball; coached at Univ. of San Francisco, Michigan St. and the Univ. of California; first coach to win NIT (San Francisco-1949), NCAA (California-1959) and Olympic gold medal (1960); later served as the general manager of the San Diego Rockets and LA Lakers in the NBA; member of Basketball Hall of Fame.

Jack Nicklaus (b. Jan. 21, 1940): Golfer; all-time leader in major tournament wins with 18— 6 Masters, 5 PGAs, 4 U.S. Opens and 3 British Opens; oldest player to win Masters (46 in 1986); PGA Player of Year 5 times (1967,72-73,75-76); named Golfer of the Century by PGA in 1988; 6-time Ryder Cup player and 2-time captain (1983,87); won NCAA title (1961) and 2 U.S. Amateurs (1959,61); 73 PGA Tour wins (2nd to Sam Snead's 82); fourth win in Tradition in 1996 gave him 8 majors on Senior PGA Tour; nicknamed "the Golden Bear."

Chuck Noll (b. Jan. 5, 1932): Football; coached Pittsburgh to 4 Super Bowl titles (1975-76,79-80); retired after 1991 season with 209 career wins (including playoffs) in 23 years.

Greg Norman (b. Feb. 10, 1955): Australian golfer; 73 tournament wins worldwide including 20 PGA Tour victories; 2-time British Open winner (1986,93); lost Masters by a stroke in both 1986 (to Jack Nicklaus) and '87 (to Larry Mize in sudden death); 1995 PGA Tour Player of the Year; surprising 3rd-place British Open finisher in 2008; married to former tennis champ Chris Evert.

James D. Norris (b. Nov. 6, 1906, d. Feb. 25, 1966): Boxing promoter and NHL owner; president of International Boxing Club from 1949 until U.S. Supreme Court ordered its break-up (for anti-trust violations) in 1958; only NHL owner to win Stanley Cups in two cities: Detroit (1936-37,43) and Chicago (1961).

Paavo Nurmi (b. June 13, 1897, d. Oct. 2, 1973): Finnish runner; won 9 gold medals (6 individual) in 1920, '24 and '28 Olympics; from 1921-31 broke 23 world outdoor records in events ranging from 1,500 to 20,000 meters.

Dan O'Brien (b. July 18, 1966): Track & Field; Olympic decathlon gold medalist (1996); set former world record in decathlon (8,891 pts) in 1992, after shockingly failing to qualify for event at U.S. Olympic Trials; three-time world champion (1991,93,95).

Larry O'Brien (b. July 7, 1917, d. Sept. 27, 1990): Basketball; former U.S. Postmaster General and 3rd NBA commissioner (1975-84); league absorbed 4 ABA teams and created salary cap during his term in office.

Parry O'Brien (b. Jan. 28, 1932): Track & Field; in 4 consecutive Olympics, won two gold medals, a silver and placed 4th in the shot put (1952-64).

Al Oerter (b. Sept. 19, 1936, d. Oct. 1, 2007): Track & Field; won 4 discus gold medals in consecutive Olympics from 1956-68.

Sadaharu Oh (b. May 20, 1940): Baseball 1B; led Japan League in HRs 15 times; 9-time MVP for Tokyo Giants; all-time Japan League HR leader with 868 in 22 years.

Hakeem Olajuwon (b. Jan. 21, 1963): Basketball C; Nigerian native who was All-America in 1984 and Final Four MOP in 1983 for Houston; overall 1st pick by Houston Rockets in 1984 NBA draft; led Rockets to back-to-back NBA titles (1994-95); regular season MVP (1994) and 2-time Finals MVP ('94-95); 6-time All-NBA 1st team (1987-89,93-95); all-time NBA blocks leader.

Jose Maria Olazabal (b. Feb. 5, 1966): Spanish golfer; has 29 worldwide victories including 2 Masters (1994,99); played on 6 European Ryder Cup teams.

Barney Oldfield (b. Jan. 29, 1878, d. Oct. 4, 1946): Auto racing pioneer; drove cars built by Henry Ford; first man to drive car a mile per minute (1903).

Walter O'Malley (b. Oct. 9, 1903, d. Aug. 9, 1979): Baseball owner; moved Brooklyn Dodgers to Los Angeles after 1957 season; won 4 World Series (1955,59,63,65).

Shaquille O'Neal (b. Mar. 6, 1972): Basketball C; 2-time All-America at LSU (1991-92); overall 1st pick (as a junior) by Orlando in 1992 NBA draft; Rookie of Year in 1993; 2-time NBA scoring leader (1995,2000); regular season MVP (2000) and 3-time NBA Finals MVP (2000,01,02) with Lakers; named one of the NBA's 50 Greatest Players; traded to Miami in 2004 and won a title with the Heat in 2006; traded to Phoenix Suns in 2008.

Bobby Orr (b. Mar. 20, 1948): Hockey D; league's only 8-time Norris Trophy winner as best defenseman (1968-75); credited with revolutionizing the position; 3-time Hart Trophy winner as NHL regular season MVP (1970-72); led NHL in scoring twice and assists 5 times; All-NHL 1st team 8 times; playoff MVP twice (1970,72) with Boston; career cut short due to a series of knee injuries.

Tom Osborne (b. Feb. 23, 1937): Football; Nebraska head coach from 1973-97; retired with career record of 255-49-3 and winning percentage of .836; won national championships in 1994 and '95 and shared national title with Michigan in '97; member of U.S. Congress (R., Neb.) from 2000-06; Nebraska athletic director since 2007.

Mel Ott (b. Mar. 2, 1909, d. Nov. 21, 1958): Baseball OF; joined NY Giants at age 16; led NL in HRs 6 times; had 511 HRs and 1,860 RBI in 22 years.

Kristin Otto (b. Feb. 7, 1966): East German swimmer; 1st woman to win 6 gold medals (4 individual) at one Olympics (1988).

Francis Ouimet (b. May 8, 1893, d. Sept. 3, 1967): Golfer; won 1913 U.S. Open as 20-year-old amateur playing in Brookline, Mass. course where he used to caddie; won U.S. Amateur twice; 8-time Walker Cup player.

Jesse Owens (b. Sept. 12, 1913, d. Mar. 31, 1980): Track & Field; set 4 world records in one afternoon competing for Ohio State at the Big Ten Championships (May 25, 1935); a year later, he soundly debunked Adolf Hitler's "master race" claims, winning 4 gold medals (100m, 200m, 4x100m relay and long jump) at 1936 Summer Olympics in Berlin.

Terrell Owens (b. Dec. 7, 1973): Football WR; "T.O.;" never-boring wide receiver sometimes known more for his elaborate touchdown celebrations and his outspokenness; entered 2008 season with 882 receptions (9th all-time) and 131 TD (tied for 5th all-time); played for 49ers, Eagles and now Dallas Cowboys.

Alan Page (b. Aug. 7, 1945): Football DE; All-America at Notre Dame in 1966 and member of two national championship teams; 6-time NFL All-Pro and 1971 Player of Year with Minnesota Vikings; later a lawyer who was elected to Minnesota Supreme Court in 1992.

Satchel Paige (b. July 7, 1906, d. June 6, 1982): Baseball RHP; pitched 55 career no-hitters over 20 seasons in Negro Leagues, entered major leagues with Cleveland in 1948 at age 42; had 28-31 record in 5 years; returned to AL at age 59 to start 1 game for Kansas City in 1965 (went 3 innings, gave up a hit and got a strikeout); elected to Baseball Hall of Fame in 1971.

Se Ri Pak (b. Sept. 28, 1977): Golfer; won two Majors as an LPGA rookie in 1998 (LPGA Championship and U.S. Open); youngest player to win the U.S. Open (20); has won 5 majors overall; inducted into the World Golf Hall of Fame in 2007.

Arnold Palmer (b. Sept. 10, 1929): Golfer; winner of 4 Masters, 2 British Opens and a U.S. Open; 2-time PGA Player of Year (1960,62); 1st player to earn over $1 million in career (1968); annual PGA Tour money leader award named after him; 62 wins on PGA Tour and 10 more on Champions Tour; made 48 consecutive Masters starts.

Jim Palmer (b. Oct. 15, 1945): Baseball RHP; 3-time Cy Young Award winner (1973,75-76); won 20 or more games 8 times with Baltimore; elected to the Baseball Hall of Fame in 1990.

Bill Parcells (b. Aug. 22, 1941): Football; coached NY Giants to 2 Super Bowl titles (1987,91); retired after 1990 season then returned in 1993 as coach of New England; took hapless Pats from 2-14 in 1992 to Super Bowl (loss to Green Bay); coached the Jets for 3 seasons (1997-99), turning them from 1-15 doormat to AFC East champ in 2 years; retired again in 2000; returned to coach the Dallas Cowboys from 2003-07; Executive VP of Miami Dolphins since 2008.

Jack Pardee (b. Apr. 19, 1936): Football; All-America LB at Texas A&M; All-Pro with LA Rams (1963) and Washington (1971); 2-time NFL Coach of Year (1976,79); won 87 games in 11 seasons; only man hired as head coach in NFL, WFL, USFL and CFL.

Bernie Parent (b. Apr. 3, 1945): Hockey G; led Philadelphia Flyers to 2 Stanley Cups as playoff MVP (1974,75); 2-time Vezina Trophy winner; posted 55 career shutouts and 2.55 GAA in 13 seasons.

Joe Paterno (b. Dec. 21, 1926): Football; passed Bear Bryant in 2001 as all-time wins leader in college football (since passed by Bobby Bowden); has coached Penn St. to 372-125-3 record, 23-10-1 bowl record and 2 national titles (1982,86) in 42 years; also had three unbeaten teams that didn't finish No. 1; 4-time Coach of Year (1982,78,82,86).

Craig Patrick (b. May 20, 1946): Hockey; 3rd generation Patrick to have name inscribed on Stanley Cup; GM of 2-time Cup champion Pittsburgh Penguins (1991-92); also captain of 1969 NCAA champion at Denver; assistant coach-GM of 1980 gold medal-winning U.S. Olympic team; grandson of Lester.

Danica Patrick (b. March 25, 1982): Auto racer; IndyCar Rookie of the Year in 2005; became the 4th woman to race in the Indianapolis 500 and finished in 4th (2005); won the Indy Japan 300 on April 20, 2008, making her the first woman to win an IndyCar race.

Lester Patrick (b. Dec. 30, 1883, d. June 1, 1960): Hockey; pro hockey pioneer as player, coach and general manager for 43 years; led NY Rangers to Stanley Cups as coach (1928,33) and GM (1940); grandfather of Craig.

Carly Patterson (b. Feb. 4, 1988): American gymnast; Olympic women's all-around champion at Athens in 2004.

Floyd Patterson (b. Jan. 4, 1935, d. May 11, 2006): Boxer; Olympic middleweight champ in 1952; world heavyweight champ (1956-59,60-62); 1st to regain heavyweight crown; fought Ingemar Johansson 3 times in 22 months from 1959-61, won last 2; pro record 55-8-1 (40 KOs).

Walter Payton (b. July 25, 1954, d. Nov. 1, 1999): Football RB; formerly NFL's all-time leading rusher with 16,726 yards (1984-2002, passed by Emmitt Smith); scored 125 career TDs; All-Pro 7 times with Chicago; led NFC in rushing 5 times (1976-80); league MVP in 1977 (AP & PFWA) and 1985 (Bell); won ring with Bears in Super Bowl XX; known as superb runner, receiver and blocker; nicknamed "Sweetness".

Calvin Peete (b. July 18, 1943): Golf; began playing golf at age 23; over $2 million in career earnings; selected to 2 U.S. Ryder Cup teams (1983,85).

Pelé (b. Oct. 23, 1940): Brazilian soccer F; given name— Edson Arantes do Nascimento; led Brazil to 3 World Cup titles (1958,62,70); came to U.S. in 1975 to play for NY Cosmos in NASL; scored 1,281 goals in 22 years including 12 goals in the World Cup; served as Brazil's minister of sport (1990-98); named IOC Athlete of the Century and FIFA's co-Player of the Century (along with Diego Maradona).

Roger Penske (b. Feb. 20, 1937): Auto racing; national sports car driving champion (1964); established racing team in 1961; co-founder of CART; Penske Racing has won 14 Indianapolis 500s and 11 CART points titles; announced move to IRL for 2002 season; won IRL points title with Sam Hornish Jr. in 2006.

Willie Pep (b. Sept. 19, 1922, d. Nov. 23, 2006): Boxer; 2-time world featherweight champion (1942-48,49-50); pro record 230-11-1 with 65 KOs.

Marie-Jose Perec (b. May 9, 1968): Track & Field; French sprinter who became 2nd woman to win the 200m and 400m events in the same Olympics (1996); also won the 400 in 1992 Games.

Fred Perry (b. May 18, 1909, d. Feb. 2, 1995): British tennis player; 3-time Wimbledon champ (1934-36); 1st player to win all four Grand Slam singles titles, though not in same year; last native to win All-England men's title.

Gaylord Perry (b. Sept. 15, 1938): Baseball RHP; one of only four pitchers to win the Cy Young Award in both leagues; retired in 1983 with 314-265 record and 3,534 K over 22 years with 8 teams; brother Jim won 215 games for family total of 529.

Bob Pettit (b. Dec. 12, 1932): Basketball F; All-NBA 1st team 10 times (1955-64); 2-time MVP (1956,59) with St. Louis Hawks; first player to score 20,000 points.

Richard Petty (b. July 2, 1937): Auto racer; 7-time winner of Daytona 500; 7-time NASCAR national champ (1964,67,71-72,74-75,79); first stock car driver to win $1 million in career; all-time NASCAR leader in races won (200), poles (126) and wins in a single season (27 in 1967); son of Lee (55 career wins), father of Kyle (8 career wins), grandfather of Adam; nicknamed "The King".

Michael Phelps (b. June 30, 1985): American swimmer who won 8 gold medals at the 2008 Olympics in Beijing, breaking Mark Spitz's 26-year-old Olympic record of 7; attempted to break Spitz's record in 2004 in Athens but "settled" for 6 golds and two bronzes; his 14 golds make him the all-time leading gold medalist in Summer Olympic history; also won 7 golds at the 2007 World Championships in Melbourne.

Mike Piazza (b. Sept. 4, 1968): Baseball C; slugger who broke Carlton Fisk's MLB record for HRs by a catcher in 2004 with his 352nd; was the 62nd-round selection by the LA Dodgers in the 1988 draft; 1993 NL Rookie of the Year; 11-time All-Star; recorded an RBI in 15 straight games in 2000; retired in May, 2008 with 427 HR and .308 avg.

Laffit Pincay Jr. (b. Dec. 29, 1946): Jockey; 5-time Eclipse Award winner (1971,73-74,79,85); winner of 3 Belmonts and 1 Kentucky Derby (aboard Swale in 1984); retired as all-time winningest jockey with 9,530 career wins (passed in 2006, Baze).

Scottie Pippen (b. Sept. 25, 1965): Basketball F; started on 6 NBA champions with Chicago (1991-93, 96-98); 3-time All-NBA first team (1994-96). Voted one of NBA's 50 Greatest Players.

Rick Pitino (b. Sept. 18, 1952): Basketball coach; won 1996 NCAA title at Kentucky; coach and president of NBA's Celtics (1997-2001); returned to college with Louisville and in 2005 became the first coach to take 3 schools to the Final Four (Providence, Kentucky, Louisville).

Jacques Plante (b. Jan. 17, 1929, d. Feb. 27, 1986): Hockey G; led Montreal to 6 Stanley Cups (1953,56-60); won 7 Vezina Trophies; MVP in 1962; first goalie to regularly wear a mask; posted 82 shutouts with 2.38 GAA.

Gary Player (b. Nov. 1, 1936): South African golfer; 3-time winner of Masters (1961,74,78) and British Open (1959,68,74); one of only 5 players to win career Grand Slam (Hogan, Nicklaus, Sarazen and Woods); also won 2 PGAs, a U.S. Open and 2 U.S. Senior Opens.

Jim Plunkett (b. Dec. 5, 1947): Football QB; Heisman Trophy winner (Stanford) in 1970; AFL Rookie of the Year in 1971; led Oakland-LA Raiders to Super Bowl wins in 1981 and '84; MVP in '81.

Maurice Podoloff (b. Aug. 18, 1890, d. Nov. 24, 1985): Basketball; engineered merger of Basketball Assn. of America and National Basketball League into NBA in 1949; NBA commissioner (1949-63); league MVP trophy named after him.

Fritz Pollard (b. Jan. 27, 1894, d. May 11, 1986): Football; 1st black All-America RB (1916 at Brown); 1st black player in Rose Bowl; 7-year NFL pro (1920-26); 1st black NFL coach.

Sam Pollock (b. Dec. 15, 1925): Hockey GM; managed NHL Montreal Canadiens to 9 Stanley Cups in 14 years (1965-78).

Denis Potvin (b. Oct. 29, 1953): Hockey D; won Norris Trophy 3 times (1976,78-79); 5-time All-NHL 1st-team; led NY Islanders to 4 Stanley Cups.

Asafa Powell (b. Nov. 11, 1982): Track & Field; Jamaican sprinter who broke world record in 100m with a 9.77 on June 14, 2005; ran 9.77 two more times, then shattered his own mark by running a 9.74 in in Sept. 2007 (mark since broken, Bolt, 2008).

Mike Powell (b. Nov. 10, 1963): Track & Field; broke Bob Beamon's 23-year-old long jump world record by 2 inches with leap of 29-ft., 4½ in. at the 1991 World Championships; Sullivan Award winner (1991); won long jump silver medals in 1988 and '92 Olympics; repeated as world champ in 1993.

Steve Prefontaine (b. Jan. 25, 1951, d. May 30, 1975): Track & Field; All-America distance runner at Oregon; first athlete to win same event at NCAA championships 4 straight years (5,000 meters from 1970-73); finished 4th in 5,000 at 1972 Munich Olympics; first athlete to endorse Nike running shoes; killed in a one-car accident.

Nick Price (b. Jan. 28, 1957): Zimbabwean golfer; PGA Tour Player of Year in 1993 and '94; won PGA Championship in 1992 and '94, British Open in 1994.

Alain Prost (b. Feb. 24, 1955): French auto racer; 4-time Formula One world champion (1985-86,89,93); retired after '93 season as all-time F1 wins leader with 51 (passed by Michael Schumacher in 2001).

Kirby Puckett (b. Mar. 14, 1961, d. Mar. 6, 2006): Baseball OF; led Minnesota Twins to World Series titles in 1987 and '91; retired in 1996 due to an eye ailment with a batting title (1989), 2,304 hits and a .318 career average in 12 seasons; elected to Hall of Fame in 2001.

Albert Pujols (b. Jan. 16, 1980): Baseball 1B; 5th fastest to 300 HR in MLB history; NL Rookie of the Year in 2001; NL batting champion in 2003 (.359); NL MVP in 2005; won WS with Cardinals in 2006.

C.C. Pyle (b. 1882, d. Feb. 3, 1939): Promoter; known as "Cash and Carry"; hyped Red Grange's pro football debut by arranging 1925 barnstorming tour with Bears; had Grange bolt NFL for new AFL in 1926 (AFL folded in '27); also staged 2 transcontinental footraces (1928-29), known as "Bunion Derbies."

Bobby Rahal (b. Jan. 10, 1953): Auto racer; 3-time PPG Cup champ (1986,87,92); 24 career Indy-Car wins, including 1986 Indy 500; current IRL team owner with TV's David Letterman; acted as interim president-CEO of CART in 2000.

Manny Ramirez (b. May 30, 1972): Baseball OF; enigmatic slugger who helped lead the Red Sox to their first World Series title in 86 years (2004); named World Series MVP; also won title with Boston in 2007; played first 8 seasons in Cleveland; all-time postseason HR leader; hit his 500th HR on May 31, 2008; traded to LA Dodgers on July 31, 2008.

Jack Ramsay (b. Feb. 21, 1925): Basketball; coach who won 239 college games with St. Joe's-PA in 11 seasons and 906 NBA games (including playoffs) with 4 teams over 21 years; led Portland to 1977 NBA title; placed 3rd in 1961 Final Four (later vacated).

Bill Rassmussen (b. Oct. 15, 1932): Radio-TV; unemployed radio broadcaster who founded ESPN, the nation's first 24-hour all-sports cable-TV network, in 1978; bought out by Getty Oil in 1981.

Willis Reed (b. June 25, 1942): Basketball C; led NY Knicks to NBA titles in 1970 and '73; Finals MVP both years; 1970 regular season MVP. Voted one of NBA's 50 Greatest Players; fought off serious injury and limped onto court just prior to Game 7 of the 1970 Finals, his dramatic entrance helped inspire his team to victory over Wilt Chamberlain's Lakers.

Pee Wee Reese (b. July 23, 1918, d. Aug. 14, 1999): Baseball SS; member of Brooklyn/Los Angeles Dodgers from 1940-58; led NL in runs scored (132) in 1949 and stolen bases (30) in 1952; hit over .300 in a season once (.309 in 1954); led the NL in putouts four times; real name was Harold H. Reese.

Mary Lou Retton (b. Jan. 24, 1968): Gymnast; won gold medal in women's All-Around at the 1984 Olympics; also won 2 silvers and 2 bronzes.

Grantland Rice (b. Nov. 1, 1880, d. July 13, 1954): First celebrated American sportswriter; chronicled the Golden Age of Sport in 1920s; immortalized Notre Dame's "Four Horsemen."

Jerry Rice (b. Oct. 13, 1962): Football WR; 2-time Div. I-AA All-America at Mississippi Valley St. (1983-84); won 3 Super Bowls with San Francisco (1989,90,95); 10-time All-Pro; regular season MVP in 1987 and Super Bowl MVP in 1989; all-time NFL leader in touchdowns (208), receptions (1549) and receiving yards (22,895); retired in 2005 after a 20-year NFL career.

Henri Richard (b. Feb. 29, 1936): Hockey C; leap year baby who played on more Stanley Cup championship teams (11) than anybody else; at 5-foot-7, known as the "Pocket Rocket"; brother of Maurice.

Maurice Richard (b. Aug. 4, 1921, d. May 27, 2000): Hockey RW; the "Rocket"; 8-time NHL 1st team All-Star; MVP in 1947; 1st to score 50 goals in one season (1944-45); 544 career goals; played on 8 Stanley Cup winners in Montreal.

Bob Richards (b. Feb. 2, 1926): Track & Field; pole vaulter, ordained minister and original *Wheaties* pitchman, remains only 2-time men's Olympic pole vault champ (1952,56).

Tex Rickard (b. Jan. 2, 1870, d. Jan. 6, 1929): Promoter who handled boxing's first $1 million gate (Dempsey vs. Carpentier in 1921); built Madison Square Garden in 1925; founded NY Rangers as Garden tenant in 1926 and named NHL team after himself (Tex's Rangers); also built Boston Garden in 1928.

Eddie Rickenbacker (b. Oct. 8, 1890, d. July 23, 1973): Mechanic and auto racer; became America's top flying ace (22 kills) in World War I; owned Indianapolis Speedway (1927-45) and ran Eastern Air Lines (1938-59).

Branch Rickey (b. Dec. 20, 1881, d. Dec. 9, 1965): Baseball innovator; revolutionized game with creation of modern farm system while GM of St. Louis Cardinals (1917-42); integrated major leagues in 1947 as president-GM of Brooklyn Dodgers when he brought up Jackie Robinson (whom he had signed on Oct. 23, 1945); later GM of Pittsburgh Pirates.

Leni Riefenstahl (b. Aug. 22, 1902, d. Sept. 8, 2003): German filmmaker of 1930s; directed classic sports documentary "Olympia" on 1936 Berlin Summer Olympics; infamous, however, for also making 1934 Hitler propaganda film "Triumph of the Will."

Roy Riegels (b. Apr. 4, 1908, d. Mar. 26, 1993): Football; California center who picked up fumble in 2nd quarter of 1929 Rose Bowl and raced 70 yards in the wrong direction to set up a 2-point safety in 8-7 loss to Georgia Tech.

Bobby Riggs (b. Feb. 25, 1918, d. Oct. 25, 1995): Tennis; won Wimbledon (1939) and U.S. title twice (1939,41); legendary hustler who made his biggest score in 1973 as 55-year-old male chauvinist challenging the best women players; beat No. 1 Margaret Smith Court 6-2,6-1, but was thrashed by No. 2 Billie Jean King, 6-4,6-3,6-3 in nationally televised "Battle of the Sexes" on Sept. 20, before 30,492 at the Astrodome.

Pat Riley (b. Mar. 20, 1945): Basketball; coached LA Lakers to 4 of their 5 NBA titles in 1980s (1982,85,87-88); coached New York Knicks from 1991-95, then signed with Miami Heat as coach, team president and part-owner; coached Heat to NBA title in 2006; 3-time Coach of Year (1990,93,97); 2nd on list of all-time coaching victories behind Lenny Wilkens.

Cal Ripken Jr. (b. Aug. 24, 1960): Baseball SS; broke Lou Gehrig's major league Iron Man record of 2,130 consecutive games played on Sept. 6, 1995; record streak began on May 30, 1982 and ended Sept. 19, 1998 after 2,632 games; 2-time AL MVP (1983,91) for Baltimore; AL Rookie of Year (1982); AL starter in All-Star Game from 1984-2001; 2-time All-Star Game MVP (1991,2001); holds record for career HR by a shortstop; inducted into Hall of Fame in 2007.

Mariano Rivera (b. Nov. 29, 1969): Baseball RP; dominant closer who rode his cut fastball to 4 World Series titles with the Yankees (1996,1998-2000); MVP of the 1999 World Series and 2003 ALCS; all-time postseason and World Series saves leader; 2nd on all-time regular season saves list (behind Trevor Hoffman); threw last pitch in Yankee Stadium.

Phil Rizzuto (b. Sept. 25, 1918, d. Aug. 13, 2007): Baseball SS; nicknamed "the Scooter"; AL MVP with the Yankees in 1950; 5-time All-Star; retired in 1956 and became Yankees radio and television announcer; elected to the Hall of Fame in 1994.

Oscar Robertson (b. Nov. 24, 1938): Basketball G; 3-time College Player of Year (1958-60) at Cincinnati; led 1960 U.S. Olympic team to gold medal; NBA Rookie of Year (1961); 9-time All-NBA 1st team; MVP in 1964 with Cincinnati Royals; NBA champion in 1971 with Milwaukee Bucks; 6-time annual NBA assist leader; 4th in career assists with 9,887; 8th in career points with 26,710.

Paul Robeson (b. Apr. 8, 1898, d. Jan. 23, 1976): Black 4-sport star and 2-time football All-America (1917-18) at Rutgers; 3-year NFL pro; also scholar, lawyer, singer, actor and political activist; long-tainted by Communist sympathies, he was finally inducted into College Football Hall of Fame in 1995.

Brooks Robinson (b. May 18, 1937): Baseball 3B; led AL in fielding 12 times from 1960-72 with Baltimore; AL MVP in 1964; World Series MVP in 1970; 16 Gold Gloves; entered Hall of Fame in 1983.

David Robinson (b. Aug. 6, 1965): Basketball C; 1987 College Player of Year at Navy; overall 1st pick by San Antonio in 1987 NBA draft; served in military (1987-89); NBA Rookie of Year (1990) and MVP (1995); 2-time All-NBA 1st team (1991,92); led NBA in scoring in 1994; member of 1988, '92 and '96 U.S. Olympic teams; won 2 NBA titles (1999, 2003).

Eddie Robinson (b. Feb. 13, 1919, d. Apr. 3, 2007): Football; head coach at Div. I-AA Grambling from 1941-97; retired as winningest coach in college history (408-165-15, win total since broken); led Tigers to 8 national black college titles.

Frank Robinson (b. Aug. 31, 1935): Baseball OF; won MVP in NL (1961) and AL (1966); Triple Crown winner and World Series MVP in 1966 with Baltimore; 7th on all-time home run list with 586; 1st black manager in major leagues with Cleveland in 1975; has also managed in San Francisco, Baltimore and Montreal/Washington; served as the league's VP of on-field operations (2000-01).

Jackie Robinson (b. Jan. 31, 1919, d. Oct. 24, 1972): Baseball 1B-2B-3B; 4-sport athlete at UCLA (baseball, basketball, football and track); hit .387 with Kansas City Monarchs of Negro Leagues in 1945; signed by Brooklyn Dodgers' Branch Rickey on Oct. 23, 1945. Played in minors (Montreal) in 1946 and broke Major League Baseball's color line in 1947; Rookie of Year in 1947 and NL's MVP in 1949; hit .311 over 10 seasons. His #42 was retired by Major League Baseball in 1997.

Sugar Ray Robinson (b. May 3, 1921, d. Apr. 12, 1989): Boxer; arguably the greatest pound-for-pound prizefighter of all-time; world welterweight champion (1946-51); 5-time middleweight champ; retired at age 45 with pro record of 174-19-6 (109 KOs).

Knute Rockne (b. Mar. 4, 1888, d. Mar. 31, 1931): Football; coached Notre Dame to 3 consensus national titles (1924,29,30), highest winning percentage in college history (.881) with record of 105-12-5 over 13 seasons; killed in plane crash.

Bill Rodgers (b. Dec. 23, 1947): Distance runner; won Boston and New York City marathons 4 times each from 1975-80.

Dennis Rodman (b. May 13, 1961): Basketball F; superb rebounder and defender; known for dyeing his hair and getting suspended; in 1997, he was suspended for 11 games for kicking a cameraman; led NBA in rebounding 7 straight years (1992-98); won 5 NBA titles with Detroit (1989,90) and Chicago (1996-98); 2-time defensive player of the year (1990-91).

Irina Rodnina (b. Sept. 12, 1949): Soviet figure skater; won 10 world championships and 3 Olympic gold medals in pairs competition from 1969-80.

Alex Rodriguez (b. July 27, 1975): Baseball 3B; led AL in hitting (.358) his first full season in the majors (1996); in 1998 became third player ever with 40 HRs and 40 steals in one season; signed a 10-year, $252 mil deal (the biggest in U.S. sports history) with Texas in 2000; won AL MVP in 2003; was traded to NY Yankees in 2004 and won AL MVP in 2005 and his third in 2007; youngest player to 500 HR (32).

Juan (Chi Chi) Rodriguez (b. Oct. 23, 1935): Golfer; popular player with 8 PGA Tour victories and 22 Senior Tour wins; 1973 U.S. Ryder Cup Team.

Ronaldo (b. Sept. 22, 1976): Brazilian soccer F; named to the Brazilian National Team when he was 17; 3-time FIFA World Player of the Year (1996,97,2002); European Player of the Year in 1997 and 2002; named 1998 World Cup MVP; led Brazil to World Cup title in 2002, scoring 8 times including both of Brazil's goals in its win over Germany in the final; all-time leading scorer in World Cup history with 15 in 4 World Cups.

Art Rooney (b. Jan. 27, 1901, d. Aug. 25, 1988): Race track legend and pro football pioneer; bought Pittsburgh Steelers franchise in 1933 for $2,500; finally won NFL title with 1st of 4 Super Bowls in 1974 season.

Theodore Roosevelt (b. Oct. 27, 1858, d. Jan. 6, 1919): 26th President of the U.S.; physical fitness buff who boxed as undergraduate at Harvard; credited with presidential assist in forming of Intercollegiate Athletic Assn. (now NCAA) in 1905-06.

Mauri Rose (b. May 26, 1906, d. Jan. 1, 1981): Auto racer; 3-time winner of Indy 500 (1941,47-48).

Murray Rose (b. Jan. 6, 1939): Australian swimmer; won 3 gold medals at 1956 Olympics; added a gold, silver and bronze in 1960.

Pete Rose (b. Apr. 14, 1941): Baseball OF-IF; all-time hits leader with 4,256 and games leader with 3,562; led NL in batting 3 times; regular-season MVP in 1973; World Series MVP in 1975; had 44-game hitting streak in '78; managed Cincinnati (1984-89); banned for life in 1989 for conduct detrimental to baseball (betting on baseball); convicted of tax evasion in 1990 and sentenced to 5 months in prison.

Ken Rosewall (b. Nov. 2, 1934): Tennis; won French and Australian singles titles at age 18; U.S. champ twice, but never won Wimbledon.

Mark Roth (b. Apr. 10, 1951): Bowler; 4-time PBA Player of Year (1977-79,84); has 34 tournament wins and over $1.6 million in career earnings.

Alan Rothenberg (b. Apr. 10, 1939): Soccer; president of U.S. Soccer 1990-98; surprised European skeptics by directing hugely successful 1994 World Cup tournament; successfully got oft-delayed outdoor Major League Soccer off ground in 1996.

Chad Rowan (Akebono) (b. May 8, 1969): Sumo Wrestling; 6-foot-9, 510-pound naturalized Japanese citizen born in Hawaii; first foreign grand champion in sumo wrestling's 2,000-year history.

Patrick Roy (b. Oct. 5, 1965): Hockey G; led Montreal to 2 Stanley Cup titles (1986,93) and won 3rd and 4th Cups with Colorado (1996,2001); 3-time playoff MVP (as rookie in 1986,93,2001); won Vezina Trophy 3 times (1989-90,92); led NHL in goals against average 3 times (1989,92,2002); all-time leader in career regular season wins (551) and playoff wins (151).

Pete Rozelle (b. Mar. 1, 1926, d. December 6, 1996): Football; NFL Commissioner from 1960-89; presided over growth of league from 12 to 28 teams, merger with AFL, creation of Super Bowl and advent of huge TV rights fees.

Wilma Rudolph (b. June 23, 1940, d. Nov. 12, 1994): Track & Field; won 3 gold medals (100m, 200m and 4x100m relay) at 1960 Olympics; also won relay silver in '56 Games at age 16; 2-time AP Athlete of Year (1960-61) and Sullivan Award winner in 1961; suffered from polio and wore leg braces until she was 9.

John Ruiz (b. Jan. 4, 1972): Boxer; defeated Evander Holyfield by decision in 2001 for the WBA heavyweight title; the first-ever Hispanic heavyweight champ; lost belt to Roy Jones Jr. on unanimous dec. in 2003.

Damon Runyon (b. Oct. 4, 1884, d. Dec. 10, 1946): Kansas native who gained fame as New York journalist, sports columnist and short-story writer; best known for 1932 story collection, "Guys and Dolls."

Adolph Rupp (b. Sept. 2, 1901, d. Dec. 10, 1977): Basketball; 3rd in all-time college coaching wins with 876; led Kentucky to 4 NCAA championships (1948-49,51,58) and 1 NIT title (1946).

Bill Russell (b. Feb. 12, 1934): Basketball C; won titles in college (with San Francisco in 1955,56), Olympics (1956) and pros; 5-time NBA MVP (1958,61,62,63,65); led Boston Celtics to an amazing 11 titles from 1957-69; 4-time NBA rebound leader (1958-59,64-65); 2nd on all-time rebound list with 21,620; became first black NBA (and major professional sports) head coach in 1966.

Babe Ruth (b. Feb. 6, 1895, d. Aug. 16, 1948): Baseball LHP-OF; two-time 20-game winner with Boston Red Sox (1916-17); had a 94-46 record with a 2.28 ERA, while he was 3-0 in the World Series with an ERA of 0.87; sold to New York Yankees for $100,000 in 1920; AL MVP in 1923; led AL in slugging average 13 times, HRs 12 times, RBI 6 times and batting once (.378 in 1924); hit 60 HRs in 1927 and at least 54 3 other times; ended career with Boston Braves in 1935 with 714 HRs, 2,211 RBI, 2,062 walks and a batting average of .342; remains all-time leader in slugging percentage (.690); member of the Hall of Fame's inaugural class of 1936.

Johnny Rutherford (b. Mar. 12, 1938): Auto racer; 3-time winner of Indy 500 (1974,76,80); CART national champion in 1980.

Nolan Ryan (b. Jan. 31, 1947): Baseball RHP; recorded 7 no-hitters against Kansas City and Detroit (1973), Minnesota (1974), Baltimore (1975), LA Dodgers (1981), Oakland A's (1990) and Toronto (1991 at age 44); 2-time 20-game winner (1973-74); 2-time NL leader in ERA (1981,87); led AL in strikeouts 9 times and NL twice in 27 years; retired after 1993 season with 324 wins, 292 losses and all-time records for strikeouts (5,714) and walks (2,795); number retired by three teams (California, Houston, Texas).

Samuel Ryder (b. Mar. 24, 1858, d. Jan. 2, 1936): Golf; English seed merchant who donated the Ryder Cup in 1927 for competition between pro golfers from Great Britain and the U.S.; made his fortune by coming up with idea of selling seeds in small packages.

Toni Sailer (b. Nov. 17, 1935): Austrian skier; 1st to win 3 alpine gold medals in Winter Olympics— taking downhill, slalom and giant slalom events in 1956.

Alberto Salazar (b. Aug. 7, 1958): Track and Field; broke 12-year-old record at New York Marathon in 1981 and broke Boston Marathon record in 1982; won three straight NY Marathons (1980-82).

Juan Antonio Samaranch (b. July 17, 1920): president of International Olympic Committee (1980-2001); the native of Barcelona was re-elected in 1996 after IOC's move in '95 to bump membership age limit to 80; replaced by Belgian Jacques Rogge.

Pete Sampras (b. Aug. 12, 1971): Tennis; No.1 in world (1993-98); youngest ever U.S. Open men's champ (19 years, 28 days) in 1990; his win at 2002 U.S. Open was record 14th grand slam singles title; won 2 Australian Opens (1994,97), 7 Wimbledons (1993-95, 1997-2000) and 5 U.S. Opens (1990,93, 95-96,2002); earned $43.3 million on the ATP Tour.

Joan Benoit Samuelson (b. May 16, 1957): Distance runner; won Boston Marathon twice (1979,83); won first women's Olympic marathon in 1984 Games; Sullivan Award recipient in 1985.

Arantxa Sanchez-Vicario (b. Dec. 18, 1971): Spanish tennis player; won 29 singles titles including 3 French Opens (1989,94,98) and 1 U.S. Open (1994); 6 doubles and 4 mixed doubles grand slam titles.

Earl Sande (b. Nov. 13, 1898, d. Aug. 19, 1968): Jockey; rode Gallant Fox to Triple Crown in 1930; won 5 Belmonts and 3 Kentucky Derbies.

Barry Sanders (b. July 16, 1968): Football RB; won 1988 Heisman Trophy as junior at Oklahoma St.; all-time NCAA single season leader in rushing (2,628 yards), scoring (234 points) and TDs (39); 4-time NFL rushing leader with Detroit Lions (1990,94,96,97); NFC Rookie of Year (1988); 2-time NFL Player of Year (1991,97); NFC MVP (1997); rushed for 2,053 yards in 1997; No. 3 all-time rusher (15,269 yds); retired prior to 1999 season; inducted into Pro Football Hall of Fame in 2004.

Deion Sanders (b. Aug. 9, 1967): Baseball OF and Football DB-KR-WR; 7-time NFL All-Pro CB with Atlanta, San Fran. and Dallas (1991-94,96-98); led majors in triples (14) with Braves in 1992 and hit .533 in World Series that year; played on 2 Super Bowl winners (SF in XXIX, and Dallas in XXX); first 2-way starter in NFL since 1962 (Chuck Bednarik); only athlete to play in both World Series and Super Bowl.

Cael Sanderson (b. June 20, 1979): Wrestling; first 4-time undefeated NCAA college wrestling champion (1999-2002); went 159-0 during 4-year career at Iowa State; 4-time NCAA Most Outstanding Wrestler; won gold medal at Athens Games in 2004.

Abe Saperstein (b. July 4, 1901, d. Mar. 15, 1966): Basketball; founded all-black, Harlem Globetrotters barnstorming team in 1927; coached sharpshooting comedians to 1940 world pro title in Chicago and established troupe as game's foremost goodwill ambassadors; also served as 1st commissioner of American Basketball League (1961-62).

Gene Sarazen (b. Feb. 27, 1902, d. May 13, 1999): Golfer; one of only five players to win all four Grand Slam titles (others are Hogan, Nicklaus, Player and Woods); won Masters, British Open, 2 U.S. Opens and 3 PGA titles between 1922-35; invented sand wedge in 1930.

Glen Sather (b. Sept. 2, 1943): Hockey; GM-coach of 4 Stanley Cup winners in Edmonton (1984-85,87-88) and GM-only for another in 1990; ranks 8th on all-time NHL coaching list with 586 wins (including playoffs); entered Hockey Hall of Fame in 1997; named President-GM of NY Rangers in 2000.

Terry Sawchuk (b. Dec. 28, 1929, d. May 31, 1970): Hockey G; recorded 103 shutouts in 21 NHL seasons; 4-time Vezina Trophy winner; played on 4 Stanley Cup winners at Detroit and Toronto; posted career 2.52 GAA.

Gale Sayers (b. May 30, 1943): Football HB; 2-time All-America at Kansas; NFL Rookie of Year (1965) and 5-time All-Pro with Chicago; scored then-record 22 TDs in rookie year; led league in rushing twice (1966,69).

Chris Schenkel (b. Aug. 21, 1923, d. Sept. 11, 2005): Radio-TV; 4-time Sportscaster of Year; easygoing baritone who covered basketball, bowling, football, golf and the Olympics for ABC and CBS; host of ABC's Pro Bowlers Tour for 33 years; received lifetime achievement Emmy Award in 1992.

Vitaly Scherbo (b. Jan. 13, 1972): Russian gymnast; winner of unprecedented 6 gold medals in gymnastics, including men's All-Around, for Unified Team in 1992 Olympics; also won 3 bronze in '96 Games.

Curt Schilling (b. Nov. 14, 1966): Baseball RHP; led majors in strikeouts twice (1997-98) with Philadelphia; shared 2001 World Series MVP award with Arizona teammate Randy Johnson; traded to Boston in 2003; helped Red Sox end 86-year championship drought in 2004; widely known for gutsy "bloody sock" performance in 2004 ALCS vs Yankees; won World Series with Boston again in 2007.

Mike Schmidt (b. Sept. 27, 1949): Baseball 3B; led NL in HRs 8 times; 3-time MVP (1980,81,86) with Philadelphia; 548 career HRs and 10 Gold Gloves; inducted into Hall of Fame in 1995.

Don Schollander (b. Apr. 30, 1946): Swimming; won 4 gold medals at 1964 Olympics, plus one gold and one silver in 1968; won Sullivan Award in 1964.

Dick Schultz (b. Sept. 5, 1929): Executive director of NCAA from 1988-93; resigned on May 11, 1993 in wake of special investigator's report citing Univ. of Virginia with improper student-athlete loan program during Schultz's tenure as athletic director (1981-87); executive director of USOC 1995-2000.

Michael Schumacher (b. Jan. 3, 1969): German auto racer; Formula One's all-time win leader with 84 grand prix victories; 7-time world champion (1994-95,2000-04); broke his own Formula One single-season record with 13 wins in 2004; retired at the end of the 2006 F1 season.

Bob Seagren (b. Oct. 17, 1946): Track & Field; won gold medal in pole vault at 1968 Olympics; broke world outdoor record 5 times.

Tom Seaver (b. Nov. 17, 1944): Baseball RHP; won 3 Cy Young Awards (1969,73,75); led NL in K 5 times (1970,71,73,75,76); pitched no-hitter in 1978 for Cin.; had 311 wins, 3,640 strikeouts and 2.86 ERA over 20 years.

Peter Seitz (b. May 17, 1905, d. Oct. 17, 1983): Baseball arbitrator; ruled on Dec. 23, 1975 that players who perform for one season without a signed contract can become free agents; decision ushered in big money era for players.

Monica Seles (b. Dec. 2, 1973): Tennis; No. 1 in the world in 1991 and '92 after winning Australian, French and U.S. Opens both years; won 4 Australian, 3 French and 2 US Opens; winner of 30 singles titles in just 5 years before she was stabbed in the back by Steffi Graf fan Gunter Parche on Apr. 30, 1993 during match in Hamburg, Germany; spent remainder of 1993, all of '94 and most of '95 recovering; returned to tennis with win at the 1995 Canadian Open; won 1996 Australian Open; winner of 53 WTA tournaments.

Bud Selig (b. July 30, 1934): Baseball; Milwaukee car dealer who bought AL Seattle Pilots for $10.8 million in 1970 and moved team to Midwest; as de facto commissioner, he presided over 232-day players' strike that resulted in cancellation of World Series for first time since 1904; officially elected baseball's ninth commissioner on July 9, 1998; has overseen many changes in MLB including interleague play, wild card playoffs, and new steroid testing policy.

Frank Selke (b. May 7, 1893, d. July 3, 1985): Hockey; GM of 6 Stanley Cup champions in Montreal (1953,56-60); the annual NHL trophy for best defensive forward bears his name.

Ayrton Senna (b. Mar. 21, 1960, d. May 1, 1994): Brazilian auto racer; 3-time Formula One champion (1988,90-91); died as all-time F1 leader in poles (65) and 2nd in wins (41, currently in 3rd); killed in crash at Imola, Italy during '94 San Marino GP.

Wilbur Shaw (b. Oct. 13, 1902, d. Oct. 30, 1954): Auto racer; 3-time winner and 3-time runner-up of Indy 500 from 1933-1940.

Patty Sheehan (b. Oct. 27, 1956): Golfer; LPGA Player of Year in 1983; clinched entry into LPGA Hall of Fame with her 30th career win in 1993; her 6 major titles include 3 LPGA Champ. (1983-84,93), 2 U.S. Opens (1992,94) 1 Dinah Shore (1996).

Bill Shoemaker (b. Aug. 19, 1931, d. Oct. 12, 2003): Jockey; ranks 3rd all-time in career wins with 8,833; 3-time Eclipse Award winner as jockey (1981) and special award recipient (1976,81); won 5 Belmonts, 4 Kentucky Derbys and 2 Preaknesses; oldest jockey to win Kentucky Derby (age 54, aboard Ferdinand in 1986); retired in 1990 to become trainer; paralyzed in 1991 auto accident but continued to train horses.

Eddie Shore (b. Nov. 25, 1902, d. Mar. 16, 1985): Hockey D; only NHL defenseman to win Hart Trophy as MVP 4 times (1933,35-36,38); led Boston Bruins to Stanley Cup titles in 1929 and '39; had 105 goals and 1,047 penalty minutes in 14 seasons.

Frank Shorter (b. Oct. 31, 1947): Track & Field; won gold medal in marathon at 1972 Olympics, 1st American to win in 64 years.

Don Shula (b. Jan. 4, 1930): Football; retired after 1995 season with an NFL-record 347 career wins (including playoffs) and a winning percentage of .665; took six teams to Super Bowl and won twice with Miami (VII, VIII); 4-time Coach of Year, twice with Baltimore (1964,68) and twice with Miami (1970-71); coached 1972 Dolphins to 17-0 record, the only undefeated team in NFL history.

Charlie Sifford (b. June 2, 1922): Golf; won the Hartford Open in 1967 with a final-round 64, becoming the first black player to win a PGA event; amassed over $1 million in career earnings; published his autobiography "Just Let Me Play" in 1992.

Al Simmons (b. May 22, 1902, d. May 26, 1956): Baseball OF; led AL in batting twice (1930-31) with Philadelphia A's and knocked in 100 runs or more 11 straight years (1924-34).

O.J. Simpson (b. July 9, 1947): Football RB; won Heisman Trophy in 1968 at USC; ran for 2,003 yards in NFL in 1973; All-Pro 5 times; MVP in 1973; rushed for 11,236 career yards; TV analyst and actor after career ended; arrested June 17, 1994 as suspect in double murder of ex-wife Nicole Brown Simpson and her friend Ronald Goldman; acquitted on Oct. 3, 1995 by a Los Angeles jury in criminal trial but forced to make financial reparations after losing wrongful death suit; arrested in Sept. 2007 for robbery and assault for reportedly storming into a Las Vegas hotel room and demanding sports memorabilia that he claimed belonged to him; found guilty on all charges on Oct. 3, 2008; sentencing is scheduled for Dec. 5, 2008.

Vijay Singh (b. Feb. 22, 1963): Fijian golfer; temporarily dethroned Tiger Woods as world's top-ranked player in 2004; has 34 career PGA Tour wins including 1998 and 2004 PGA championships and 2000 Masters; 2003-04 PGA Tour money leader.

George Sisler (b. Mar. 24, 1893, d. Mar. 26, 1973): Baseball 1B; hit over .400 twice (1920,22) and batted over .300 in 13 of his 15 seasons; his MLB record of 257 hits (1920) was finally broken by Seattle's Ichiro Suzuki (262) in 2004; played most of his career with the St. Louis Browns; inducted into Baseball Hall of Fame in 1939.

Mary Decker Slaney (b. Aug. 4, 1958): U.S. middle distance runner; has held 7 separate American track & field records from the 800 to 10,000 meters; won both 1,500 and 3,000 meters at 1983 World Championships in Helsinki, but no Olympic medals.

Kelly Slater (b. Feb. 11, 1972): Surfer; 8-time world champion; member of the Surfers' Hall of Fame; holds records for being the youngest (1992) and oldest (2005) world champion; earned the only perfect two-wave score at a WCT event; tied for most WCT event wins in a tour season; most career WCT event wins, highest money-earner in the history of the ASP (Association of Surfing Professionals).

Raisa Smetanina (b. Feb. 29, 1952): Russian Nordic skier; all-time leading female Winter Olympics medalist with 10 cross country medals (4 gold, 5 silver and a bronze) in 5 appearances (1976,80,84,88,92) for USSR and Unified Team.

Billy Smith (b. Dec. 12, 1950): Hockey G; led NY Islanders to 4 consecutive Stanley Cups (1980-83); won Vezina Trophy in 1982; Stanley Cup MVP in 1983.

Dean Smith (b. Feb. 28, 1931): Basketball; No. 2 on all-time NCAA coaches victory list (879 wins, previous leader until he was passed in 2007 by Bobby Knight); led North Carolina to 25 NCAA tournaments in 34 years, reaching Final Four 10 times and winning championship twice (1982,93); coached U.S. Olympic team to gold medal in 1976.

Emmitt Smith (b. May 15, 1969): Football RB; NFL's all-time leading rusher (18,355 yards); also holds all-time record for rushing TDs (164); 4-time NFL rushing leader (1991-93,95); recorded 11 straight 1,000-yard seasons (1991-2001) with Dallas Cowboys; regular season and Super Bowl MVP in 1993; played on three Super Bowl champions (1993,94,96); retired in 2005 after 15 seasons.

John Smith (b. Aug. 9, 1965): Wrestler; 2-time NCAA champion for Oklahoma St. at 134 lbs (1987-88) and Most Outstanding Wrestler of '88 championships; 3-time world champion; gold medal winner at 1988 and '92 Olympics at 137 lbs; won Sullivan Award (1990); coached Oklahoma St. to 1994 NCAA title and brother Pat was Most Outstanding Wrestler.

Lee Smith (b. Dec. 4, 1957): Baseball RHP; 3-time NL saves leader (1983,91-92); retired as all-time saves leader with 478 (now 3rd all-time); 10 seasons with 30+ saves, 3 times saved over 40.

Ozzie Smith (b. Dec. 26, 1954): Baseball SS; won 13 straight Gold Gloves (1980-92); played in 12 straight All-Star Games (1981-92); MVP of 1985 NL playoffs; all-time MLB assist leader (8,375); inducted into Baseball Hall of Fame in 2002.

Walter (Red) Smith (b. Sept. 25, 1905, d. Jan. 15, 1982): Sportswriter for newspapers in Philadelphia and New York from 1936-82; won Pulitzer Prize for commentary in 1976.

Conn Smythe (b. Feb. 1, 1895, d. Nov. 18, 1980): Hockey pioneer; built Maple Leaf Gardens in 1931; managed Toronto to 7 Stanley Cups.

Sam Snead (b. May 27, 1912, d. May 23, 2002): Golfer; won both Masters and PGA 3 times and British Open once; runner-up in U.S. Open 4 times; PGA Player of Year in 1949; oldest player (52 years, 10 months) to win PGA event with Greater Greensboro Open title in 1965; all-time PGA Tour career victory leader with 82.

Peter Snell (b. Dec. 17, 1938): Track & Field; New Zealander who won gold medal in 800m at 1960 Olympics, then won both the 800m and 1,500m at 1964 Games.

Duke Snider (b. Sept. 19, 1926): Baseball OF; hit 40 or more home runs five straight seasons (1953-57); led the league in runs scored 1953-55; played in six World Series with the Dodgers and batted .286 with 11 home runs; nicknamed "Duke of Flatbush"; in 18 seasons hit 407 home runs, scored 1,259 runs and had 1,333 RBI.

Annika Sorenstam (b. Oct. 9, 1970): Swedish golfer; has won 10 women's majors; 8-time Rolex Player of the Year (1995,97-98, 2001-05); shot an LPGA-record 59 in round 2 of the 2001 Standard Register Ping; LPGA all-time leading money winner; in 2003 she became first woman in 58 years to play on men's PGA Tour (via a sponsor's exemption); shot 71-74 but missed the cut at the Colonial by 4 strokes.

Sammy Sosa (b. Nov. 12, 1968): Baseball OF; slugging Chicago Cub who surpassed Roger Maris' season home run record (61), just after Mark McGwire did in 1998 and finished the year with 66; followed that up with seasons of 63, 50 and 64 HRs; 1998 NL MVP; 7-time All-Star; 609 career homers.

Javier Sotomayor (b. Oct. 13, 1967): Cuban high jumper; first man to clear 8 feet (8-0) on July 29, 1989; won gold medal at 1992 Olympics with jump of only 7-ft, 8-in.; broke world record with leap of 8-0½ in 1993; had a controversial drug suspension reduced, which allowed him to participate in 2000 Olympics; won the silver medal in Sydney with a leap of 7-7¼.

Warren Spahn (b. Apr. 23, 1921, d. Nov. 23, 2003): Baseball LHP; led NL in wins 8 times; won 20 or more games 13 times; Cy Young winner in 1957; most career wins (363) by a lefthander.

Tris Speaker (b. Apr. 4, 1888, d. Dec. 8, 1958): Baseball OF; all-time leader in outfield assists (449) and doubles (792); had .344 career BA and 3,515 hits.

J.G. Taylor Spink (b. Nov. 6, 1888, d. Dec. 7, 1962): Publisher of *The Sporting News* from 1914-62; BBWAA annual meritorious service award named after him.

Leon Spinks (b. July 11, 1953): Boxing; won heavyweight crown in split decision over Muhammad Ali in Feb. 1978; Ali regained title seven months later; won gold medal in light heavyweight division at 1976 Olympics; brother Michael won the heavyweight title in 1983; were the only brothers to hold world titles; known more for frequent traffic violations and lavish lifestyle than bouts late in career; filed for bankruptcy in 1986.

Mark Spitz (b. Feb. 10, 1950): American swimmer; set 23 world and 35 U.S. records; won what was all-time record of 7 gold medals (4 individual, 3 relay) in 1972 Olympics (broken by Michael Phelps' 8 in 2008); also won 4 medals (2 gold, a silver and a bronze) in 1968 Games for a total of 11.

Latrell Sprewell (b. Sept. 8, 1970): Basketball G; former NBA All-Star who made headlines in 1997 for attacking Golden State Warriors head coach P.J. Carlesimo during a practice.

Lyn St. James (b. Mar. 13, 1947): Auto racer; one of just 5 women to qualify for the Indianapolis 500; best finish in the race came in 1992 when she came in 11th and won Indianapolis 500 Rookie of the Year.

Amos Alonzo Stagg (b. Aug. 16, 1862, d. Mar. 17, 1965): Football innovator; coached at U. of Chicago for 41 seasons and College of the Pacific for 14 more; 314-199-35 record; elected to both college football and basketball Halls of Fame.

Willie Stargell (b. Mar. 6, 1940, d. Apr. 9, 2001): Baseball OF-1B; "Pops"; led NL in home runs twice (1971,73); 475 career HRs; NL co-MVP and World Series MVP in 1979.

Bart Starr (b. Jan. 9, 1934): Football QB; led Green Bay to 5 NFL titles and 2 Super Bowl wins from 1961-67; regular season MVP in 1966; MVP of Super Bowls I and II.

Roger Staubach (b. Feb. 5, 1942): Football QB; Heisman Trophy winner as Navy junior in 1963; led Dallas to 2 Super Bowl titles (1972,78) and was Super Bowl MVP in 1972; 5-time leading passer in NFC (1971,73,77-79).

George Steinbrenner (b. July 4, 1930): Baseball; principal owner of NY Yankees since 1973; teams have won 10 pennants and 6 World Series (1977-78,96,98,99,00); ordered by commissioner Fay Vincent in 1990 to surrender control of club for dealings with small-time gambler; reinstated in 1993; demanding and highly successful, he once claimed, "Winning is the most important thing in my life, after breathing."

Casey Stengel (b. July 30, 1890, d. Sept. 29, 1975): Baseball; player for 14 years and manager for 25; outfielder and lifetime .284 hitter with 5 clubs (1912-25); guided NY Yankees to 10 AL pennants and 7 World Series titles from 1949-60; 1st NY Mets skipper from 1962-65.

Ingemar Stenmark (b. Mar. 18, 1956): Swedish alpine skier; 3-time World Cup overall champ (1976-78); posted 86 World Cup wins in 16 years; won 2 gold medals at 1980 Olympics.

Helen Stephens (b. Feb. 3, 1918, d. Jan. 17, 1994): Track & Field; set 3 world records in 100-yard dash and 4 more in 100 meters in 1935-36; won gold medals in 100 meters and 4x100-meter relay in 1936 Olympics; retired in 1937.

Woody Stephens (b. Sept. 1, 1913, d. Aug. 22, 1998): Horse racing; trainer who saddled an unprecedented 5 straight winners in Belmont Stakes (1982-86); also had two Kentucky Derby winners (1974,84) and one Preakness winner (1952); trained 1982 Horse of Year Conquistador Cielo; won Eclipse award as nation's top trainer in 1983.

David Stern (b. Sept. 22, 1942): Basketball; marketing expert and NBA commissioner since 1984; took office the year Michael Jordan turned pro; league has grown from 23 teams to 30 during his watch and opened offices worldwide; oversaw launch of WNBA in 1997.

Teófilo Stevenson (b. Mar. 29, 1952): Cuban boxer; won 3 consecutive gold medals as Olympic heavyweight (1972,76,80); was denied a chance to win a fourth when Cuba boycotted 1984 Los Angeles Games; did not turn pro.

Jackie Stewart (b. June 11, 1939): Auto racer; won 27 Formula One races and 3 world driving titles from 1965-73.

John Stockton (b. Mar 26, 1962): Basketball G; all-time NBA leader in every major assist category, including most in a season (1,164) and most in a career (15,806); also the NBA's all-time leader in steals (3,265); All-NBA team in '94 and '95; member of 1992 and '96 US Olympic basketball teams; 10-time All-Star; played 19 seasons with Utah Jazz—18 of them with Karl Malone—perfecting the pick and roll.

Curtis Strange (b. Jan. 30, 1955): Golfer; won consecutive U.S. Open titles (1988-89); 3-time leading money winner on PGA Tour (1985,87-88); first PGA player to win $1 million in one year (1988); captain of the 2002 U.S. Ryder Cup team.

Picabo Street (b. Apr. 3, 1971): Skiing; 2-time Olympic medalist, gold (Super G in 1998) and silver (downhill in 1994); her 1995 World Cup downhill series title first-ever by U.S. woman, she repeated the feat in 1996.

Kerri Strug (b. Nov. 19, 1977): Gymnastics; delivered the most dramatic moment of the 1996 Summer Olympics when she completed a vault (9.712) after spraining her ankle; the second vault helped assure the first all-around gold medal for a US Women's gymnastics team.

Louise Suggs (b. Sept. 7, 1923): Golfer; won 11 majors and 58 LPGA events overall from 1949-62; founder and charter member of the LPGA; first woman elected to LPGA Hall of Fame (1951).

James E. Sullivan (b. Nov. 18, 1862, d. Sept. 16, 1914): Track & Field; pioneer who founded Amateur Athletic Union (AAU) in 1888; director of St. Louis Olympic Games in 1904; AAU's annual Sullivan Award for performance and sportsmanship named after him.

John L. Sullivan (b. Oct. 15, 1858, d. Feb. 2, 1918): Boxer; nicknamed "The Boston Strong Boy"; world heavyweight champion (1882-92); last of bare-knuckle champions, beating Jake Kilrain after 75 rounds in 1889; was knocked out by "Gentleman" Jim Corbett in the 21st round in 1892, never fought again.

Pat Summitt (b. June 14, 1952): Basketball; women's basketball coach at Tennessee (1974—); entered 2008-09 season as all-time leader in career victories with 983; coached 1984 US women's basketball team to its first Olympic gold medal; has coached Lady Vols to 8 national championships (1987, 89,91,96,97,98,2007,08); her Lady Vols have made 11 of the last 14 Final Fours.

Don Sutton (b. April 2, 1945): Baseball RHP; won 324 games and tossed 58 shutouts in his 23-year career; recorded NL record five career 1-hitters; played with Dodgers, Astros, Brewers, Athletics, Angels and was a 4-time All-Star; elected to Hall of Fame in 1998.

Ichiro Suzuki (b. Oct. 22, 1973): Baseball OF; became the 2nd player (Fred Lynn) to win AL Rookie of the Year and MVP in same year (2001); 1st Japanese-born position player to play in MLB; won 7 consecutive Japanese batting titles (1994-2000) and has won two more in AL with Seattle (2001,04); broke George Sisler's 84-year-old hits record with 262 in 2004; MVP of 2007 All-Star Game (hit inside-the-park HR); has 200+ hits in each of his 8 MLB seasons.

Lynn Swann (b. Mar. 7, 1952): Football WR; played nine seasons with Pittsburgh (1974-82); appeared in four Super Bowls and had 16 catches for 364 yards and three TDs; named MVP of Super Bowl X for 4 catch, 161 yard, 1 TD performance.

Barry Switzer (b. Oct. 5, 1937): Football; coached Oklahoma to 3 national titles (1974-75,85); all-time winning percentage of .837 (157-29-4); resigned in 1989 after OU was slapped with 3-year NCAA probation; hired as Dallas Cowboys head coach in 1994 and led team to victory in Super Bowl XXX in 1996.

Sheryl Swoopes (b. Mar. 25, 1971): Basketball; forward for WNBA's Houston Comets; 4-time WNBA regular season MVP (2000,02,03,05); 3-time Olympic gold medalist (1996,2000,2004); led Texas Tech to Div. I NCAA championship in 1993; consensus National Player of the Year in 1993.

Paul Tagliabue (b. Nov. 24, 1940): Football; NFL attorney who was elected league's 4th commissioner in 1989 and served until his retirement in 2006; ushered in salary cap in 1994; the league expanded from 28 teams to 32 in his tenure.

Anatoli Tarasov (b. 1918, d. June 23, 1995): Hockey; coached Soviet Union to 9 straight world championships and 3 Olympic gold medals (1964, 68,72).

Jerry Tarkanian (b. Aug. 30, 1930): Basketball; amassed 778 wins in 31 years at Long Beach St., UNLV and Fresno St.; led UNLV to 4 Final Fours and 1 national title (1990); fought battle with NCAA over purity of UNLV program; quit as coach after going 26-2 in 1991-92; fired after 20 games (9-11) as coach of NBA San Antonio Spurs in 1992.

Fran Tarkenton (b. Feb. 3, 1940): Football QB; scrambling two-time NFL All-Pro (1973,75); 1975 Player of the Year; threw for 47,003 yards and 342 TDs (both former NFL records) in 18 seasons with Vikings and N.Y. Giants; selected to 9 Pro Bowls; inducted into Pro Football Hall of Fame in 1986.

Chuck Taylor (b. June 24, 1901, d. June 23, 1969): Converse traveling salesman whose name came to grace the classic, high-top canvas basketball sneakers known as "Chucks"; over 750 million pairs have been sold since 1917; he also ran clinics worldwide and edited Converse Basketball Yearbook (1922-68).

Lawrence Taylor (b. Feb. 4, 1959): Football LB; All-America at North Carolina (1980); only defensive player in NFL history to be consensus Player of Year (1986); led N.Y. Giants to Super Bowl titles in 1986 and '90 seasons; played in 10 Pro Bowls (1981-90); retired after 1993 season with 132½ sacks; had several drug-related arrests in retirement; inducted into Hall of Fame in 1999.

Marshall (Major) Taylor (b. Nov. 26, 1878, d. June 21, 1932): Cyclist; Considered one of the first African-American sports heroes; held 7 world cycling records at the turn of the century, racing mostly in Europe, Australia and New Zealand after being barred from many events in the U.S. due to racial prejudices; won the world one-mile championship in 1899.

Gustavo Thoeni (b. Feb. 28, 1951): Italian alpine skier; 4-time World Cup overall champion (1971-73,75); won giant slalom at 1972 Olympics.

Isiah Thomas (b. Apr. 30, 1961): Basketball; led Indiana to NCAA title as sophomore and Final 4 MOP in 1981; consensus All-America guard in '81; led Detroit to 2 NBA titles (1989,1990); NBA Finals MVP in 1990; 3-time All-NBA 1st team (1984-86); elected to Hall of Fame in 2000; CBA owner from 1998-2000; former coach of the Indiana Pacers and former president and head coach of the N.Y. Knicks.

Thurman Thomas (b. May 16, 1966): Football RB; 3-time AFC rushing leader (1990-91,93); 2-time All-Pro (1990-91); 1991 NFL Player of Year; led Buffalo to 4 straight Super Bowls (1991-94).

Daley Thompson (b. July 30, 1958): British Track & Field; won consecutive gold medals in decathlon at 1980 and '84 Olympics.

Jenny Thompson (b. Feb. 26, 1973): American swimmer; 8-time Olympic gold medalist (all in relays); winner of 12 Olympic medals overall, tied for the most by an American woman (w/Dara Torres); competed in 5 Olympic Games (1988,92,96,2000,04).

John Thompson (b. Sept. 2, 1941): Basketball; coached centers Patrick Ewing, Alonzo Mourning and Dikembe Mutombo at Georgetown; reached NCAA tourney final 3 out of 4 years with Ewing, winning title in 1984; also led Hoyas to 6 Big East tourney titles; coached 1988 U.S. Olympic team to bronze medal; retired abruptly during 1999 season with 27-year mark of 596-239.

Bobby Thomson (b. Oct. 25, 1923): Baseball OF; career .270 hitter who won the 1951 NL pennant for the NY Giants with a 1-out, 3-run HR in the bottom of the 9th inning of Game 3 of a best-of-3 playoff with Brooklyn; the pitcher was Ralph Branca, the count was 0-1 and the Dodgers were ahead 4-2; the Giants had trailed Brooklyn by 13½ games on Aug. 11.

Ian Thorpe (b. Oct. 13, 1982): Australian swimmer; 5-time gold medalist; won 400m free at Sydney Olympics (breaking his own world record) and silver in 200m free; won gold and broke the world record in the 4x100m and 4x200 free relays; won 200m free and 400m free Olympic gold at Athens in 2004; 2002 Jesse Owens Award winner.

Jim Thorpe (b. May 28, 1887, d. Mar. 28, 1953): Native American multi-sport superstar; 2-time All-America halfback at Carlisle; won both pentathlon and decathlon gold medals at 1912 Olympics; stripped of medals a month later for playing semi-pro baseball prior to Games (medals restored in 1982); played major league baseball (1913-19) and pro football (1920-26,28); became first president of NFL (then known as the APFA) in 1920; chosen "Athlete of the Half Century" by AP in 1950.

Bill Tilden (b. Feb. 10, 1893, d. June 5, 1953): Tennis; won 7 U.S. and 3 Wimbledon titles in 1920s; led U.S. to 7 straight Davis Cup victories (1920-26).

Tinker to Evers to Chance Chicago Cubs double play combination from 1903-10; immortalized in poem by New York sportswriter Franklin P. Adams—SS Joe Tinker (1880-1948), 2B Johnny Evers (1883-1947) and 1B Frank Chance (1877-1924); all 3 managed the Cubs and made the Hall of Fame.

Y.A. Tittle (b. Oct. 24, 1926): Football QB; Yelberton Abraham; played 17 years in AAFC and NFL; All-Pro 4 times; league MVP with San Francisco (1957) and NY Giants (1962, 63); 28,339 career passing yards.

Alberto Tomba (b. Dec. 19, 1966): Italian alpine skier; winner of 5 Olympic medals (3 gold, 2 silver); 1st alpine skier to win gold medals in 2 consecutive Winter Games (1988 and '92).

Dara Torres (b. April 15, 1967): Swimmer; her 12 career Olympic medals (4G, 4S, 4B) are tied for the most by an American woman (w/Jenny Thompson); made stunning comeback at the Beijing Olympics in 2008, winning 3 silver medals and setting an America record in the 50-freestyle at the age of 41.

Vladislav Tretiak (b. Apr. 25, 1952): Hockey G; led USSR to Olympic gold medals in 1972 and '76; starred for Soviets against Team Canada in 1972, and again in 2 Canada Cups (1976,81).

Lee Trevino (b. Dec. 1, 1939): Golfer; 2-time winner of 3 majors—U.S. Open (1968, 71), British Open (1971-72) and PGA (1974,84); PGA Tour Player of the Year (1971) and 3 times with Seniors (1990,92,94); 29 PGA Tour and 29 Champions Tour wins.

Felix Trinidad (b. Jan. 10, 1973): Puerto Rican boxer; former WBC/IBF welterweight champion; won WBC belt with a maj. dec. over Oscar De La Hoya in 1999; stepped up to jr. middleweight and won the WBA title from David Reid in 2000; moved to middleweight and captured WBA title from William Joppy; 42-3 record with 35 KO through Sept., 2008.

Bryan Trottier (b. July 17, 1956): Hockey C; led NY Islanders to 4 straight Stanley Cups (1980-83); Rookie of Year (1976); scoring champion (134 points) and regular season MVP in 1979; playoff MVP (1980); added 5th and 6th Cups with Pittsburgh in 1991 and '92; entered Hockey Hall of Fame in 1997.

Gene Tunney (b. May 25, 1897, d. Nov. 7, 1978): Boxer; world heavyweight champion from 1926-28; beat 31-year-old champ Jack Dempsey in unanimous 10 round decision in 1926; beat him again in famous "long count" rematch in '27; quit while still champion in 1928 with 65-1-1 record and 47 KOs.

Ted Turner (b. Nov. 19, 1938): Sportsman and TV mogul; skippered Courageous to America's Cup win in 1977; one-time owner of MLB Braves, NBA Hawks and NHL Thrashers; founder of CNN, TNT and TBS; founder of Goodwill Games; 1991 Time Man of Year.

Mike Tyson (b. June 30, 1966): Boxer; youngest (19) heavyweight champion ever (WBC in 1986); undisputed champ from 1987 until upset loss to 42-1 shot Buster Douglas on Feb. 10, 1990, in Tokyo; found guilty on Feb. 10, 1992, of raping 18-year-old Miss Black America contestant Desiree Washington in Indianapolis on July 19, 1991; sentenced to 6-year prison term; released May 9, 1995 after serving 3 years; reclaimed WBC and WBA belts with wins over Frank Bruno and Bruce Seldon in 1996; lost WBA title to Evander Holyfield in 1996; bit Holyfield's ear twice during their 1997 WBA title rematch; KO'd in 8th round by Lennox Lewis in 2002; 50-6 with 44 KO.

Wyomia Tyus (b. Aug. 29, 1945): Track & Field; 1st woman to win consecutive Olympic gold medals in 100m (1964-68).

Peter Ueberroth (b. Sept. 2, 1937): Organizer of 1984 Summer Olympics in LA; 1984 *Time* Man of Year; baseball commissioner from 1984-89; headed Rebuild Los Angeles for one year after 1992 riots; currently chairman of USOC.

Johnny Unitas (b. May 7, 1933, d. Sept. 11, 2002): Football QB; Big-game field general who led Baltimore Colts to 2 NFL titles (1958-59) and a Super Bowl win (1971); All-Pro 5 times; 3-time MVP (1959,64,67); selected to 10 Pro Bowls; passed for 40,239 career yards and 290 TDs.

Al Unser Jr. (b. Apr. 19, 1962): Auto racer; 2-time CART-IndyCar national champion (1990,94); 2-time Indy 500 winer (1992,94), giving Unser family 9 overall titles at the Brickyard; retired in 2004 with 31 CART wins in 19 years; left CART for Indy Racing League in 2000; son of Al and nephew of Bobby.

Al Unser Sr. (b. May 29, 1939): Auto racer; 3-time USAC-CART national champion (1970,83,85); 4-time winner of Indy 500 (1970-71,78,87); retired in 1994 with 39 wins; younger brother of Bobby and father of Al Jr.

Bobby Unser (b. Feb. 20, 1934): Auto racer; 2-time USAC-CART national champion (1968,74); 3-time winner of Indy 500 (1968,75,81); retired after 1981 season; recorded 35 career wins.

Gene Upshaw (b. Aug. 15, 1945, d. Aug. 20, 2008): Football G; 2-time All-AFL and 3-time All-NFL selection with Oakland; helped lead Raiders to 2 Super Bowl titles in 1976 and '80 seasons; executive director of NFL Players Assn. from 1987 until his death in 2008; agreed to application of salary cap in 1994.

Jim Valvano (b. Mar. 10, 1946, d. Apr. 28, 1993): Basketball; coach at N.C. State whose team upset Houston to win national title in 1983; in 19 seasons as a coach appeared in 8 NCAA tournaments; twice voted ACC Coach of the Year; career record 346-212; AD at N.C. State (1986-89) when a recruiting and admissions scandal forced him out of the job; worked as a broadcaster for ESPN and ABC; died after a year-long battle with cancer; The V Foundation for cancer research is named for him.

Norm Van Brocklin (b. Mar. 15, 1926, d. May 2, 1983): Football QB-P; led NFL in passing 3 times and punting twice; led LA Rams (1951) and Philadelphia (1960) to NFL titles; MVP in 1960.

Amy Van Dyken (b. Feb. 17, 1973): Swimming; first American woman to win four gold medals in one Olympics (1996); also won gold at Sydney in 2000.

Johnny Vander Meer (b. Nov. 2, 1914, d. Oct. 6, 1997): Baseball LHP; only major leaguer to pitch consecutive no-hitters (June 11 & 15, 1938).

Harold S. Vanderbilt (b. July 6, 1884, d. July 4, 1970): Sportsman; successfully defended America's Cup 3 times (1930, 34,37); also invented contract bridge in 1926.

Glenna Collett Vare (b. June 20, 1903, d. Feb. 10, 1989): Golfer; won record 6 U.S. Women's Amateur titles from 1922-35; "the female Bobby Jones."

Andy Varipapa (b. Mar. 31, 1891, d. Aug. 25, 1984): Bowler; trick-shot artist; won consecutive All-Star match game titles (1947-48) at age 55 and 56.

Bill Veeck (b. Feb. 9, 1914, d. Jan. 2, 1986): Maverick baseball executive; owned AL teams in Cleveland, St. Louis and Chicago from 1946-80; introduced ballpark giveaways, exploding scoreboards, Wrigley Field's ivy-covered walls and midget Eddie Gaedel; won World Series with Indians (1948) and pennant with White Sox (1959).

Michael Vick (b. June 26, 1980): Football QB; 1st overall pick in 2001 NFL draft out of Virginia Tech; led Atlanta Falcons to NFC Championship Game in 2004; in 2006 became the first QB to rush for over 1,000 yards in single season; became well-known outside of sports world in 2007 after pleading guilty to financing and operating an interstate dogfighting ring.

Jacques Villeneuve (b. Apr. 9, 1971): Canadian auto racer; won Indy 500 and IndyCar driving championship in 1995; jumped to Formula One racing in 1996 and won the F1 title in 1997.

Fay Vincent (b. May 29, 1938): Baseball; became 8th commissioner after death of A. Bartlett Giamatti in 1989; presided over World Series earthquake, owners' lockout and banishment of NY Yankees owner George Steinbrenner in his first year on the job; contentious relationship with owners resulted in his resignation on Sept. 7, 1992, four days after 18-9 "no confidence" vote.

Lasse Viren (b. July 22, 1949): Finnish runner; won gold medals at 5,000 and 10,000 meters in 1972 Munich Olympics; repeated 5,000/10,000 double in 1976 Games and added a fifth place finish in the marathon.

Dick Vitale (b. June 9, 1939): Broadcaster; Radio and television commentator for ESPN and ABC Sports known for his enthusiastic, almost spastic style; had successful college and pro basketball coaching career with the University of Detroit (1973-77) and the Detroit Pistons (1978-79).

Lanny Wadkins (b. Dec. 5, 1949): Golfer; member of 8 U.S. Ryder Cup teams (captain in 1995); won 1977 PGA Championship; 21 PGA Tour wins.

Honus Wagner (b. Feb. 24, 1874, d. Dec. 6, 1955): Baseball SS; hit .300 for 17 consecutive seasons (1897-1913) with Louisville and Pittsburgh; led NL in batting 8 times; ended career with 3,430 career hits, a .329 average and 722 stolen bases.

Grete Waitz (b. Oct. 1, 1953): Norwegian runner; 9-time winner of New York City Marathon from 1978-88; won silver medal at 1984 Olympics.

Jersey Joe Walcott (b. Jan. 31, 1914, d. Feb. 27, 1994): Boxer; oldest heavyweight (37) to win the championship until George Foreman surpassed him in 1994; lost four championship bouts before knocking out Ezzard Charles in the seventh round in 1951; lost the title the following year to Rocky Marciano; pro career record of 50-17-1 with 30 KOs; later became sheriff of Camden County, NJ.

Doak Walker (b. Jan. 1, 1927, d. Sept. 27, 1998): Football HB; won Heisman Trophy as SMU junior in 1948; led Detroit to 2 NFL titles (1952-53); All-Pro 4 times in 6 years.

Herschel Walker (b. Mar. 3, 1962): Football RB; led Georgia to national title as freshman in 1980; won Heisman in 1982 then jumped to upstart USFL in '83; signed by Dallas Cowboys after USFL folded; led NFL in rushing in 1988; traded to Minnesota in 1989 for 5 players and 6 draft picks.

Rusty Wallace (b. Aug. 14, 1956): Auto racing; NASCAR Winston Cup champ in 1989 and runner-up in 1980, 1988 and 1993; recorded 55 victories and won over $40 million in earnings in more than 25 years of racing; currently a racing analyst for ESPN.

Bill Walsh (b. Nov. 30, 1931, d. July 30, 2007): Football; Hall of Fame coach and GM of 3 Super Bowl winners with San Francisco (1982,85,89); retired after 1989 Super Bowl; returned to college coaching in 1992 for his second stint at Stanford; retired again after 1994 season; returned as 49er GM from 1999-2001; known as "The Genius"; devised what would later become known as the West Coast offense; created the Minority Coaching Fellowship in 1987.

Bill Walton (b. Nov. 5, 1952): Basketball C; 3-time College Player of Year (1972-74); led UCLA to 2 national titles (1972-73); led Portland to NBA title as MVP in 1977; regular season MVP in 1978; won 1986 NBA title with Boston.

Darrell Waltrip (b. Feb. 5, 1947): Auto racing; 3-time NASCAR Winston Cup champion (1981,82,85); 84 career Winston Cup wins and 59 poles.

Arch Ward (b. Dec. 27, 1896, d. July 9, 1955): Promoter and sports editor of *Chicago Tribune* from 1930-55; founder of baseball All-Star Game (1933), Chicago College All-Star Football Game (1934) and the All-America Football Conference (1946-49).

Charlie Ward (b. Oct. 12, 1970): Football QB and Basketball G; 1993 Heisman winner with national champion Florida St.; won Sullivan Award (1993); 3-year starter for FSU basketball team; 1st round pick of NY Knicks in 1994 NBA draft.

Glenn (Pop) Warner (b. Apr. 5, 1871, d. Sept. 7, 1954): Football innovator; coached at 7 colleges over 49 years; 319 career wins, 4th all-time; produced 47 All-Americas, including Jim Thorpe and Ernie Nevers.

Kurt Warner (b. June 22, 1971): Football QB; former Arena leaguer who led the St. Louis Rams to 2000 Super Bowl win; threw for a record 414 yards and was Super Bowl MVP; 2-time NFL MVP (1999,2001).

Tom Watson (b. Sept. 4, 1949): Golfer; 6-time PGA Player of the Year (1977-80,82,84); has won 5 British Opens, 2 Masters and a U.S. Open; 4-time Ryder Cup member and captain of 1993 team; 39 PGA tour wins; 12 Champions tour wins.

Danny Way (b. Apr. 15, 1974): Skateboarder; conceived the Megaramp (2002) and brought the Big Air event to the X Games (2004); set world records for longest distance jumped (79 feet–2004), height out of a ramp (23.5 feet– 2003), and highest bomb drop (28 feet–2006, from the guitar outside the Hard Rock Hotel in Las Vegas); first person to jump over the Great Wall of China without motorized aid (2005), two-time Thrasher Magazine Skater of the Year (1991, 2004).

Earl Weaver (b. Aug. 14, 1930): Baseball; managed the Baltimore Orioles to 6 Eastern Division titles, four AL pennants and a World Series victory in 1970; was ejected 91 times and suspended four times for outbursts against umpires; record of 1,480-1,060 from 1968-82 and 1985-86.

Alan Webb (b. Jan. 13, 1983): Track; in 2001, he ran a mile in 3:53.43 to break Jim Ryun's 36-year-old national high school record; ran 3:46.91 in July, 2007 to set a new American record.

Karrie Webb (b. Dec. 21, 1974): Australian golfer; youngest woman (26) to win career Grand Slam; her win in the 2002 British Open made her the first player to win the "Super Grand Slam" (5 different majors) and gave her 6 major titles; won the 2006 Kraft Nabisco Championship to make it 7 majors; 2-time Rolex Player of the Year (1999-2000); entered Hall of Fame in 2005.

Dick Weber (b. Dec. 23, 1929, d. Feb. 13, 2005): Bowler; 3-time PBA Bowler of the Year (1961,63,65); won 30 PBA titles in 4 decades; father of Pete.

Pete Weber (b. Aug. 21, 1962): Bowler; 2nd on all-time PBA money list; 1990 PBA Rookie of the Year; inducted into PBA Hall of Fame (1998); winner of 34 PBA titles; son of Dick.

Johnny Weissmuller (b. June 2, 1904, d. Jan. 20 1984): American swimmer; won 3 gold medals (100m free, 400m free, 4x200m free) at 1924 Olympics and 2 more at 1928 Games (100m free and 4x200m free); set 51 world records; became Hollywood's most famous Tarzan.

Jerry West (b. May 28, 1938): Basketball G; 2-time All-America and NCAA Final 4 MOP (1959) at West Virginia; led 1960 U.S. Olympic team to gold medal; 10-time All-NBA 1st-team; NBA finals MVP (1969); led LA Lakers to NBA title once as player (1972) and then 6 more times (1980,82,85,87,88,00) as an executive in various positions with the club; President of Basketball Ops. for Memphis Grizzlies from 2002-07; his silhouette serves as the NBA's logo.

Pernell Whitaker (b. Jan. 2, 1964): Boxer; won Olympic gold medal as lightweight in 1984; won 4 world championships as lightweight, jr. welterweight, welterweight and jr. middleweight; outfought but failed to beat Julio Cesar Chavez when 1993 welterweight title defense ended in controversial draw; pro record of 41-3-1 (17 KOs); nicknamed "Sweet Pea."

Bill White (b. Jan. 28, 1934): Baseball; former NL president and highest ranking black executive in sports from 1989-94; as 1st baseman, won 7 Gold Gloves and hit .286 with 202 HRs in 13 seasons.

Byron (Whizzer) White (b. June 8, 1917, d. Apr. 15, 2002): Football; All-America HB at Colorado (1937); signed with Pittsburgh in 1938 for the then largest contract in pro history ($15,800); took Rhodes Scholarship in 1939; returned to NFL in 1940 to lead league in rushing and retired in 1941; named to U.S. Supreme Court by President Kennedy in 1962 and stepped down in 1993.

Reggie White (b. Dec. 19, 1961, d. Dec. 26, 2004): Football DE; nicknamed the "Minister of Defense"; consensus All-America in 1983 at Tennessee; 7-time All-NFL (1986-92) with Philadelphia; won Super Bowl with Green Bay in 1997; 2nd all-time in career NFL sacks (198).

Shaun White (b. Sept. 3, 1986): Snowboarder/Skateboarder; first athlete to compete in both Winter and Summer X Games; winner of 14 combined X Games medals (11 snowboarding, 3 skateboarding); won an Olympic gold medal in 2006 for Halfpipe; nicknamed "The Flying Tomato."

Kathy Whitworth (b. Sept. 27, 1939): Golf; 7-time LPGA Player of the Year (1966-69,71-73); won 6 majors; 88 tour wins, most on LPGA or PGA tour.

Hoyt Wilhelm (b. July 26, 1923, d. Aug. 23, 2002): Baseball RHP; Knuckleballer who is 1st in games won in relief (123); career ERA of 2.52, 227 saves and 651 games finished; 1st reliever inducted into Hall of Fame (1985); threw no-hitter vs. NY Yankees (1958); hit lone HR of career in first major league at bat (1952); won Purple Heart at Battle of the Bulge.

Lenny Wilkens (b. Oct. 28, 1937): Basketball; NBA's all-time winningest coach; MVP of 1960 NIT as Providence guard; played 15 years in NBA, including 4 as player-coach; 9-time All-Star and MVP of 1971 game; coached Seattle to 1979 NBA title; Coach of Year in 1994 with Atlanta; career record of 1412-1253 including playoffs with 7 NBA teams; coached USA basketball team to gold medal in 1996; member of the basketball hall of fame as player and coach.

Dominique Wilkins (b. Jan. 12, 1960): Basketball F; prolific scorer and ferocious dunker who led NBA in scoring (30.3 ppg) in 1986 with Atlanta; All-NBA 1st team in 1986; 2-time NBA slam dunk champion; nicknamed "The Human Highlight Film"; inducted into Basketball Hall of Fame in 2006.

Bud Wilkinson (b. Apr. 23, 1916, d. Feb. 9, 1994): Football; played on 1936 national championship team at Minnesota; coached Oklahoma to 3 national titles (1950, 55, 56); won 4 Orange and 2 Sugar Bowls; teams had winning streaks of 47 (1953-57) and 31 (1948-50); retired after 1963 season with 145-29-4 record in 17 years; also coached St. Louis of NFL to 9-20 record from 1978-79.

Ricky Williams (b. May 21, 1977): Football RB; became all-time NCAA Div. I-A leader in rushing yards (6,279) and TDs (75) at Texas but has been passed in both categories; 1998 Heisman Trophy winner; 5th overall in 1999 NFL draft by Saints; traded to Miami in 2002; stunned teammates when he retired suddenly just prior to 2004 season; returned in 2005; suspended from the NFL for 2006 and part of 2007.

Serena Williams (b. Sept. 26, 1981): Tennis; first African-American woman to win a Grand Slam title since Althea Gibson in 1958 by winning the 1999 U.S. Open; has 9 career Grand Slam titles: 2 Wimbledons (2002-03), French Open (2002), 3 U.S. Opens (1999,02,08) and 3 Australian Opens (2003,05,07); won doubles Olympic gold with Venus in 2000.

Ted Williams (b. Aug. 30, 1918, d. July 5, 2002): Baseball OF; led AL in batting 6 times, and HRs and RBI 4 times each; won Triple Crown twice (1942,47); 2-time MVP (1946,49); last player to bat .400 when he hit .406 in 1941; Marine Corps combat pilot who missed 3 full seasons during WWII (1943-45) and most of two others (1952-53) during Korean War; hit .344 lifetime with 521 HRs in 19 years with Boston Red Sox; also known as avid fisherman; furor erupted following his death when plans to keep his body frozen at a cryogenic lab were made public.

Venus Williams (b. June 17, 1980): Tennis; won Wimbledon (2000,01,05,07,08) and 2 U.S. Open 2000-01) singles titles; 2000 Olympic singles and doubles gold medalist; 2008 Olympic doubles gold medalist; recorded fastest serve in main-draw match history with 129 mph blast in 2008 Wimbledon; won career doubles grand slam with Serena.

Walter Ray Williams Jr. (b. Oct. 6, 1959): Bowling and Horseshoes; 6-time PBA Bowler of Year (986,93,96,97,98,2003); all-time leading money winner on the PBA Tour; has 44 all-time record PBA titles; also won 6 World Horseshoe Pitching titles.

Hack Wilson (b. Apr. 26, 1900, d. Nov. 23, 948): Baseball; as a Chicago Cub, he produced one f baseball's most outstanding seasons in 1930 with 6 home runs, .356 batting average, 105 walks and, most amazingly, a major league record 191 RBIs that till stands; finished career with 244 HRs, 1,062 RBIs.

Dave Winfield (b. Oct. 3, 1951): Baseball OF—NFL, NBA, ABA, and MLB; chose baseball and played n 12 All-Star Games over 22-year career; won World eries with Toronto in 1992; career 3,110 hits and 465 HRs; inducted into Baseball Hall of Fame in 2001.

Katarina Witt (b. Dec. 3, 1965): East German gure skater; 4-time world champion (1984-85,87-88); von consecutive Olympic gold medals (1984,88).

John Wooden (b. Oct. 14, 1910): Basketball; College Player of Year at Purdue in 1932; coached UCLA o 88 straight wins (1971-74), 10 national titles (1964-65,67-73,75); inducted into the Hall of Fame as both player and coach; career college coaching record of 664-162 over 29 years.

Tiger Woods (b. Dec. 30, 1975): Golfer; 3-time winner of U.S. Amateur (1994-96); won 6 events and broke the single season money record in his 1st full season on PGA Tour; won 1997 Masters by a record 18-under par and 13 strokes; won 2nd major at 1999 PGA Championship; in 2000 won the U.S. Open at Pebble Beach by a record 15 strokes, the British Open by 8 strokes and the PGA Championship in a playoff; held all 4 Major titles simultaneously with his win at 2001 Masters; has since won 8 more majors for a total of 14: 2 Masters (2002,05), 2 British Opens (2005-06), 2 PGA Championships (2006-07) and 2 U.S. Opens (2002,08); all-time PGA Tour money leader with over $82 million; 1 of only 5 players to win all 4 Grand Slam titles (others are Hogan, Nicklaus, Player and Sarazen); winner of PGA Tour's first FedEx Cup n 2007; 9-time PGA Tour Player of the Year; 65 wins.

Mickey Wright (b. Feb. 14, 1935): Golfer; won 3 of 4 majors (LPGA, U.S. Open, Titleholders) in 1961; 4-time winner of both U.S. Open and LPGA titles; 82 career wins including 13 majors.

Early Wynn (b. Jan. 6, 1920, d. Mar. 4, 1999): Baseball RHP; won 20 games 5 times; Cy Young winner in 1959; 300-244 record in 23 years.

Kristi Yamaguchi (b. July 12, 1971): Figure Skating; 1991 world champion; then the national, world and Olympic titles in 1992, then turned professional.

Cale Yarborough (b. Mar. 27, 1940): Auto racer; 3-time NASCAR national champion (1976-78); 4-time winner of Daytona 500 (1968,77,83-84); 83 career NASCAR wins.

Carl Yastrzemski (b. Aug. 22, 1939): Baseball OF; led AL in batting 3 times; won Triple Crown and MVP in 1967; had 3,419 hits and 452 HRs in 23 years with Boston Red Sox; member of Hall of Fame.

Cy Young (b. Mar. 29, 1867, d. Nov. 4, 1955): Baseball RHP; all-time leader in wins (511), losses (313), complete games (751) and innings pitched (7,356); had career 2.63 ERA in 22 years (1890-1911); 30-game winner 5 times and 20-game winner 11 other times; threw three no-hitters and a perfect game (1904); annual AL/NL pitching awards are named after him.

Dick Young (b. Oct. 17, 1917, d. Aug. 31, 1987): Confrontational sportswriter for 44 years with NY tabloids; as baseball beat writer and columnist, he led change from flowery prose to hard-nosed reporting.

Sheila Young (b. Oct. 14, 1950): Speed skater and cyclist; 1st U.S. athlete to win 3 medals at Winter Olympics (1976); won speed skating overall and sprint cycling world titles in 1976.

Steve Young (b. Oct. 11, 1961): Football QB; All-America at BYU (1983); NFL Player of Year (1992) with SF 49ers; only QB to lead NFL in passer rating 4 straight years (1991-94); rating of 112.8 in 1994 is highest ever; threw record 6 TD passes in MVP performance in Super Bowl XXIX; retired with NFL records for highest passer rating (96.8) and completion pct. (64.4); 232 career TD passes and 33,124 yards.

Robin Yount (b. Sept. 16, 1955): Baseball SS-OF; AL MVP at 2 positions—as SS in 1982 and OF in '89; retired after 1993 season with 3,142 hits, 251 HRs and a major-league-record 123 sacrifice flies after 20 seasons with Brewers; inducted into Hall of Fame in 1999.

Steve Yzerman (b. May 9, 1965): Hockey C; Captained the Detroit Red Wings to 3 Stanley Cup wins (1997-98,2002); won the Conn Smythe Trophy as the playoff MVP in 1998; one of 17 NHL players to score more than 600 goals; retired after 2005-06 with 692 goals and 1,755 career points.

Mario Zagallo (b. Aug. 9, 1931): Soccer; Brazilian forward who is one of only two men (Franz Beckenbauer is the other) to serve as both captain (1962) and coach (1970,94) of World Cup champion.

Babe Didrikson Zaharias (b. June 26, 1911, d. Sept. 27, 1956): All-around athlete who was chosen AP Female Athlete of Year 6 times from 1932-54; won 2 gold medals (javelin and 80-meter hurdles) and a silver (high jump) at 1932 Olympics; played baseball and acquired the nickname "Babe" for her tape measure home runs; real first name was Mildred; took up golf in 1935 and went on to win 55 pro and amateur events; won 10 majors, including 3 U.S. Opens (1948,50,54); helped found LPGA in 1949; chosen female "Athlete of the Half Century" by AP in 1950; when asked if there was anything she didn't play, she replied, "Yeah, dolls."

Tony Zale (b. May 29, 1913, d. March 20, 1997): Boxer; 2-time world middleweight champion (1941-47,48); fought Rocky Graziano for title 3 times in 21 months in 1947-48, winning twice; pro record 67-18-2 with 44 KOs.

Frank Zamboni (b. Jan. 16, 1901, d. July 27, 1988): Mechanic, ice salesman and skating rink owner in Paramount, Calif.; invented ice-resurfacing machine in 1949; now there are few skating rinks without one as thousands have been sold in over 35 countries.

Emil Zatopek (b. Sept. 19, 1922, d. Nov. 22, 2000): Czech distance runner; winner of 1948 Olympic gold medal at 10,000 meters; 4 years later, won unprecedented Olympic triple crown (5,000 meters, 10,000 meters and marathon) at 1952 Games in Helsinki.

Zinedine Zidane (b. June 23, 1972): French soccer player; 3-time FIFA World Player of the Year (1998, 2000, 2003); led host nation France to 1998 World Cup title, scoring twice in final against Brazil; a record $64m transfer fee sent the midfielder from Juventus to Real Madrid in 2001; led France to the World Cup final in 2006 (loss to Italy in penalty kicks); won Golden Ball as the tournament's most outstanding player, despite being given a red card in the 110th minute of the final for his notorious headbutt into the chest of Italy's Marco Materazzi.

John Ziegler (b. Feb. 9, 1934): Hockey; NHL president from 1977-92; negotiated settlement with rival WHA in 1979 that led to inviting four WHA teams (Edmonton, Hartford, Quebec and Winnipeg) to join NHL; stepped down June 12, 1992, 2 months after settling 10-day players' strike.

Pirmin Zurbriggen (b. Feb. 4, 1963): Swiss alpine skier; 4-time World Cup overall champ (1984,87-88,90) and 3-time runner-up; 40 World Cup wins in 10 years; won gold and bronze medals at 1988 Olympics.

Minority Firsts

Jackie Robinson's breaking of the baseball color barrier took on mythic status, but many other athletes of color entered their chosen sport or won major championships with decidedly less fanfare. This list attempts to chronicle their successes. Official sources were used where available; some entries are based on published reports at the time or anecdotal information.

African-American

Auto Racing

NASCAR driver: Charlie Scott, Daytona Beach, Fla., 1956
NASCAR winner: Wendell Scott, Jacksonville, Fla., 1963

Baseball

MLB player: Jackie Robinson, Brooklyn Dodgers, 1947
MLB coach: Buck O'Neil, Chicago Cubs, 1962
MLB manager: Frank Robinson, Cleveland Indians, 1975
Hall of Fame: Jackie Robinson, 1962

Boxing

Heavyweight champion: Jack Johnson, 1908

College Football

Player, major college: George Jewett, Michigan, 1890
Head coach, Div. I-A: Willie Jeffries, Wichita State, 1979
Heisman Trophy: Ernie Davis, Syracuse, 1961
Hall of Fame: Fritz Pollard, 1954

Golf

PGA Tour: Charlie Sifford, 1961
PGA winner: Peter Brown, Waco Open, 1964
Major winner: Tiger Woods, Masters, 1997
World Hall of Fame: Charlie Sifford, 2004
LPGA Tour: Althea Gibson, 1963

NBA

Player: Earl Lloyd, Washington Capitols, 1950
Coach: Bill Russell, Boston Celtics, 1968
Hall of Fame: Bill Russell, Boston Celtics, 1975

NFL

Player, pre-merger: Charles Follis, Shelby Athletic Club, 1902
QB: Willie Thrower, Chicago Bears, 1953
Head coach, pre-merger: Fritz Pollard, Akron Pros, 1921
Hall of Fame: Emlen Tunnell, New York Giants, 1967

NHL

Player: Willie O'Ree, Boston Bruins, 1958 (Canadian); Val James, Buffalo Sabres, 1982 (American)
Coach: Dirk Graham, Chicago Blackhawks, 1998 (Canadian)
Hall of Fame: Grant Fuhr (Canadian), Edmonton Oilers, 2003

Olympics

Summer Games
Gold medalist (men): DeHart Hubbard, long jump, 1924
Gold medalist (women): Alice Coachman, high jump, 1948
Winter Games
Gold medalist (men): Shani Davis, speedskating, 2006
Gold medalist (women): Vonetta Flowers, bobsled, 2002

Tennis

Grand Slam event: Althea Gibson, French Open, 1956; Arthur Ashe, U.S. Open, 1968
Hall of Fame: Althea Gibson, 1971; Arthur Ashe, 1985

Hispanic

Auto Racing

NASCAR driver: Frank Mundy, Strictly Stock Race #1 at Charlotte (N.C.) Speedway, 1949

Baseball

Player: Esteban Bellán, Troy, N.Y. Haymakers, 1871
Manager: Mike Gonzalez, St. Louis Cardinals, 1940
Hall of Fame: Roberto Clemente, 1973

Boxing

Heavyweight champion: John Ruiz, WBA, 2001

College Football

QB, starting, major college: Tom Flores, Pacific; Joe Kapp, California, 1956
Heisman Trophy: Jim Plunkett, Stanford, 1970
Head coach, major coll.: Marcelino Huerta, Wichita St., 1962

Golf

PGA Tour winner: Chi Chi Rodriguez, Denver Open, 1963
LPGA Tour winner: Fay Crocker, Serbin Open (Miami), 1955

NBA

Player: Butch Lee, Atlanta Hawks, 1979
Coach: Dick Versace, Indiana Pacers, 1989

NFL

Player: Lou Molinet, Frankford Yellowjackets, 1927
Quarterback: Tom Flores, Oakland Raiders (AFL), 1960
Head coach: Tom Fears, New Orleans Saints, 1967

NHL

Player: Bill Guerin, New Jersey Devils, 1991

Olympics

Summer Games
Medalist (men): Miguel Capriles, fencing, bronze, 1932
Winter Games
Gold medalist (men): Derek Parra, speedskating, 2006
Medalist (women): Jennifer Rodriguez, speedskating, bronze, 2002

Tennis

Grand Slam event: Pancho Gonzalez, U.S. Champ's, 1948

Asian

Auto Racing

NASCAR driver: George Tet, Grand National race #21, Charlotte (N.C.) Motor Speedway, 1960

Baseball

Player: Masanori Murakami, San Francisco Giants, 1964 (Japanese); Ryan Kurosaki, St. Louis Cardinals, 1975 (Japanese-American)

College Football

QB, starting: Roman Gabriel, NC State, 1959

Golf

PGA Tour winner: Isao Aoki, Hawaiian Open, 1983
LPGA Major winner: Chako Higuchi, LPGA Champ., 1977

NBA

Player: Wataru Misaka, New York Knicks, 1947

NFL

Player: Walter Achiu, Dayton Triangles, 1927
QB: Roman Gabriel, Los Angeles Rams, 1962

NHL

Player: Larry Kwong, New York Rangers, 1948 (Canadian)

Olympics

Summer Games
Gold medalist (men): Sammy Lee, diving, 1948
Gold medalist (women): Victoria Manalo Draves, diving, 1948
Winter Games
Gold medalist (men): Apolo Anton Ohno, short-track speed skating, 2002
Gold medalist (women): Kristi Yamaguchi, figure skating, 1992

Tennis

Grand Slam event: Michael Chang, French Open, 1988

BALLPARKS & ARENAS

The Indianapolis Colts said goodbye to the RCA Dome and opened up shop at **Lucas Oil Stadium** in 2008.

Coming Attractions

SPORTS ALMANAC

2008

BASEBALL

Washington (NL): Nationals Park opened Mar. 30, 2008 with a 3-2 Nats win over the Braves on Ryan Zimmerman's walk-off homer. The stadium cost $611 million (paid for with largely public funds) and boasts an environmentally friendly design. Located in Southeast Washington near the Navy Yard, it is owned by the D.C. Sports & Entertainment Commission. The exterior design includes a lot of glass, similar to the new Washington Convention Center. Included in the ballpark's 41,888-seat capacity are approximately 22,000 seats in the lower bowl, 12,100 in the upper seating bowl, from where fans can see the U.S. Capitol building, 2,500 club seats and 1,112 suite seats. The stadium includes a 4,500 square foot high-definition scoreboard. The joint venture team of HOK/Devrouax-Purnell Architects designed the stadium and borrowed an odd right-angled jog into the right-center field fence from the old Griffith Stadium, the former home of the Washington Senators.

NFL FOOTBALL

Indianapolis (AFC): Lucas Oil Stadium opened for business on Aug. 22, 2008 with an Indiana high school football double-header. Lucas Oil bought the stadium naming rights for 20 years for $122 million. The new glass and brick stadium, designed by HKS, Inc., features a retro look that is shared by several other sports venues in Indianpolis including Conseco Fieldhouse, home to the Pacers. LOS seats 63,000 (expandable to 70,000 for the Super Bowl and Final Four) and cost an estimated $720 million. It features a retractable roof and FieldTurf surface. It is located in the parking lot across South Street from the former site of the RCA Dome.

2009

BASEBALL

New York (AL): The new retro-styled park is scheduled to open April 16, 2009 with a Yankees game against Cleveland. The new stadium will have 53,000 seats, fewer than "The House that Ruth Built" but it will have a lot more luxury suites. HOK Sport is the architect and the stadium is to be located on the sites of Macombs Dam and Mullaly Parks across from the original Yankee Stadium. The Yankees agreed to privately finance the new $1.6 billion facility with the city chipping in $135 million to replace parkland (and make the necessary infrastructure improvements) and the State on the hook for $70 million for the construction of new parking facilities.

New York (NL): Citi Field (Citigroup Inc. will pay $400 million over 20 years for the naming rights) is scheduled to open on April 13, 2009 with a Mets game against the San Diego Padres. The replacement for Shea Stadium will seat approximately 45,000 (with 54 luxury suites) and feature natural grass. Although the park will be located in Willets Point, Queens between Shea Stadium and 126th Street it will be designed to evoke memories of Brooklyn's beloved but long lost Ebbets Field. The asymmetrical outfield walls and generous dimensions (LF-335'; LC-379'; CF-408'; RC-383'; RF-330') should make for a traditional pitcher's park. The estimated cost of the ballpark and infrastructure improvements is $800 million. The Mets are expected to cover about $600 million of the total. The deal includes a 40-year lease that will keep the Mets in New York until at least 2049.

NFL FOOTBALL

Dallas (NFC): Construction on a new publicly funded stadium for the Cowboys in Arlington, Texas is well under way. The 80,000-seat stadium will be located south of the Tom Landry Freeway, next door to the Texas Rangers Ballpark. Designed by HKS, Inc., the distinctive hole in the roof from Texas Stadium will be replicated with a retractable roof. The stadium will be expandable to hold close to 100,000 fans and cost an estimated $1.1 billion. The stadium will also feature an enormous 60-yard long videoboard. Adjacent to the new stadium will be a 1.2 million-square-foot shopping area called Glorypark. Construction will be partially funded by the sale of personal seat licenses. The home opener is set for the fall of 2009 and the NFL has awarded the stadium Super Bowl XLV (Feb. 6, 2011).

2010

BASEBALL

Minnesota (AL): The Twins broke ground on a new ball park Aug. 30, 2007; The stadium will be known as Target Field (Target Stores is the title sponsor). The open-air, natural grass park will cover 40,000 including 72 suites and 4,000 club seats. It will be located behind the Target Center (home to the NBA's Minnesota Timberwolves). The preliminary field dimensions are as follows: LF-339'; LC-377'; CF-404'; RC-367'; RF-328'. Estimated cost of the project is $518 million; The home opener is scheduled for 2010.

NFL FOOTBALL

New York (AFC/NFC): Ground was officially broken on a new stadium that will be shared by the New York Jets and New York Giants on Sept. 5, 2007. The new 82,500-seat stadium will be located in the Meadowlands adjacent to the existing Giants Stadium. The stadium will include 9,200 club seats and 200 luxury suites. Design plans include ways to customize the theme of the stadium including a distinctive lighting system that will illuminate the stadium and will switch colors (green for the Jets, blue for the Giants) depending on who is playing. The price tag for the privately financed stadium is $1.3 billion. Construction is scheduled for completion in 2010. Talks with the German company Allianz for stadium naming rights broke down when the company's former ties to the Nazis during World War II became more widely known.

NBA BASKETBALL

Orlando (East): Construction on the new Orlando Events Center (title sponsor pending), the future home of the Magic, is underway. The 18,500-seat arena (expandable up to 20,000) will be located at the corner of Church Street and Hughey Avenue. The total cost of the project is $481 million and opening is scheduled for October 2010.

AP Images

Yankee Stadium wasn't the only baseball cathedral to close it's doors in 2008. The New York Mets said goodbye to Shea Stadium (left) and will move next door and begin play at the brand new **Citi Field** (foreground) in 2009.

NHL HOCKEY

Pittsburgh (East): Groundbreaking on the new Penguins arena in downtown Pittsburgh at the site adjacent to the existing Mellon Arena bordering Centre Avenue, Washington Place and Fifth Avenue took place Aug. 14, 2008. The $290 million building will serve as the Pens' new home until at least 2040. The arena was designed by famed stadium architects HOK Sport and will seat 18,087 (in honor of Sidney Crosby's number) for hockey; home opener is scheduled for 2010.

2011

BASEBALL

Oakland (AL): The Oakland A's announced plans for the new Cisco Field (Cisco Systems is the title sponsor) to be located at Pacific Commons, west of Interstate 880 in Fremont, Calif. about 20 miles south of McAfee Coliseum where they will continue to play through at least 2010. The park will seat between 32,000-35,000, feature a natural grass field and cost an estimated $450 million. The stadium is expected to offer some of the closest vantage points in the majors; The projected opening is for the 2011 season.

NBA BASKETBALL

New Jersey (East): The Barclays Center (Barclays Bank PLC agreed to pay a reported $400 million over 20 years for the naming rights) would be located in Brooklyn's Prospect Heights as part of Atlantic Yards, a $4.2 billion office, residential and shopping complex. The complex has met considerable resistance from community activists and could be scaled down somewhat if it's built at all. The 19,000-seat, Frank Gehry-designed arena is aiming to be open for business for the 2010-11 season. The Nets have the option to extend their lease through the 2012-13 season should the project hit further delays. The team is likely to be redubbed the Brooklyn Nets and the relocation could be the best chance for the Nets to land highly coveted potential free agent LeBron James.

Other Ballpark & Stadia in the Works

The **Florida Marlins** think they have the funding and political will to realize their decade-old dream of a new ballpark in South Florida but things have been held up in court. A lawsuit was brought against the county to block use of public monies to help fund the $525 million new stadium. The current lease that the Marlins hold at Dolphin Stadium will expire in 2010. The former site of the Orange Bowl in **Little Havana** will be the location for the proposed 37,000-seat retractable-roof ballpark and the team could be redubbed the Miami Marlins following the move. Earliest opening day will likely be April 2011.

The **Kansas City Royals** have undertaken a **major renovation to Kauffman Stadium**. The project, which will occur in several stages over the next few years is expected to be completed by 2009. The improvements, designed by HOK Sport, will include altering the layout of the bullpens, new, wider fan concourses, a high-def scoreboard, an outdoor plaza and new premium seating areas and luxury suites. The total pricetag is expected to be $250 million.

The **San Francisco 49ers** are moving forward with plans to build a new stadium 45 miles south of the city in Santa Clara, Calif., where the team's headquarters and training facility currently reside. Many issues still need to be resolved and the earliest opening for a new stadium would be 2012. The team is advocating that a special election be held in 2009 to decide on public financing for the project.

The **Minnesota Vikings** have hired HKS Architects, designers of Lucas Oil Stadium in Indianapolis and the new Cowboys stadium in Dallas to design a new retractable-roof stadium for the team. The team's lease at the Metrodome expires after the 2011 season and the new stadium could be located on the same site. Funding and legislative approval for the project still need to be secured.

The **San Diego Chargers** have stepped up efforts to leave Qualcomm Stadium and recently announced interest in moving south of the city to **Chula Vista** where a vote on whether to approve a stadium for the Marine Terminal area was set for Nov. 4, 2008.

Home, Sweet Home

The home fields, home courts and home ice of the AL, NL, NBA, NFL, NHL, NCAA Division I-A college football and Division I basketball.

Attendance figures for the 2007 NFL regular season and the 2007-08 NBA and NHL regular seasons are provided. See Baseball chapter for 2008 AL and NL attendance figures.

MAJOR LEAGUE BASEBALL

American League

		Built	Capacity	LF	LCF	CF	RCF	RF	Field
						—Outfield Fences—			
Baltimore Orioles	Oriole Park at Camden Yards	1992	48,876	337	376	406	391	320	Grass
Boston Red Sox	Fenway Park	1912	39,928	310	379	390*	380	302	Grass
Chicago White Sox	U.S. Cellular Field	1991	40,615	330	377	400	372	335	Grass
Cleveland Indians	Progressive Field	1994	43,345	325	370	405	375	325	Grass
Detroit Tigers	Comerica Park	2000	40,950	345	370	420	365	330	Grass
Kansas City Royals	Kauffman Stadium	1973	39,000	330	375	400	375	330	Grass
Los Angeles Angels of Anaheim	Angel Stadium of Anaheim	1966	45,050	365	387	400	370	365	Grass
Minnesota Twins	Hubert H. Humphrey Metrodome	1982	48,678	343	385	408	367	327	Turf
New York Yankees	Yankee Stadium	2009	52,325	318	399	408	385	314	Grass
Oakland Athletics	Oakland-Alameda County Coliseum	1966	35,067†	330	367	400	367	330	Grass
Seattle Mariners	SAFECO Field	1999	47,116	331	390	405	387	327	Grass
Tampa Bay Rays	Tropicana Field	1990	36,048†	315	370	404	370	322	Turf
Texas Rangers	Rangers Ballpark in Arlington	1994	49,115	332	390	400	381	325	Grass
Toronto Blue Jays	Rogers Centre	1989	50,516	328	375	400	375	328	Turf

*The straightaway center-field fence at Fenway Park is 390 feet from home plate but the deepest part of center-field, a.k.a. "the Triangle," is 420 feet away. The left-field fence, known as "the Green Monster," is 37 feet tall. Two hundred and seventy seats were added to the top of the wall in 2003 replacing the 23-foot screen that previously topped the Monster.

†The Oakland A's and Tampa Bay Rays have closed off portions of their upper decks and covered the seats with a tarp. The stadiums could accomodate more fans (Oakland:43,662; Tampa Bay: 45,365) if those sections were reopened.

National League

		Built	Capacity	LF	LCF	CF	RCF	RF	Field
					—Outfield Fences—				
Arizona Diamondbacks	Chase Field	1998	49,033	330	376	407	376	334	Grass
Atlanta Braves	Turner Field	1996	50,091	335	380	401	390	330	Grass
Chicago Cubs	Wrigley Field	1914	41,160	355	368	400	368	353	Grass
Cincinnati Reds	Great American Ball Park	2003	42,059	328	379	404	370	325	Grass
Colorado Rockies	Coors Field	1995	50,445	347	390	415	375	350	Grass
Florida Marlins	Dolphin Stadium	1987	36,331	330	385	434	385	345	Grass
Houston Astros	Minute Maid Park	2000	40,950	315	362	436	373	326	Grass
Los Angeles Dodgers	Dodger Stadium	1962	56,000	330	385	395	385	330	Grass
Milwaukee Brewers	Miller Park	2001	42,400	340	374	400	378	345	Grass
New York Mets	Citi Field	2009	45,000	335	379	408	383	330	Grass
Philadelphia Phillies	Citizens Bank Park	2004	43,647	329	369	401*	369	330	Grass
Pittsburgh Pirates	PNC Park	2001	38,496	326	368	399*	375	324	Grass
St. Louis Cardinals	Busch Stadium	2006	46,861	336	390	400	390	335	Grass
San Diego Padres	PETCO Park	2004	42,445	336	367	396*	387	322	Grass
San Francisco Giants	AT&T Park	2000	41,503	339	364	399	421	309	Grass
Washington Nationals	Nationals Park	2008	41,888	336	377	402	370	335	Grass

*The deepest part of PNC Park is 410 feet between straightaway center and left-center. The deepest part of Citizens Bank Park is 409 feet in part of left-center. The deepest part of PETCO Park is 411 feet in part of right-center.

Rank by Capacity

AL		NL	
New York	52,325	Los Angeles	56,000
Toronto	50,516	Colorado	50,445
Texas	49,115	Atlanta	50,091
Baltimore	48,876	Arizona	49,033
Minnesota	48,678	St. Louis	46,861
Seattle	47,116	New York	45,000
Los Angeles	45,050	Philadelphia	43,647
Cleveland	43,345	San Diego	42,445
Detroit	40,950	Milwaukee	42,400
Chicago	40,615	Cincinnati	42,059
Boston	39,928	Washington	41,888
Kansas City	39,000	San Francisco	41,503
Tampa Bay	36,048	Chicago	41,160
Oakland	35,067	Houston	40,950
		Pittsburgh	38,496
		Florida	36,331

Rank by Age

AL		NL	
Boston	1912	Chicago	1914
Los Angeles	1966	Los Angeles	1962
Oakland	1966	Florida	1987
Kansas City	1973	Atlanta	1993
Minnesota	1982	Colorado	1995
Toronto	1989	Arizona	1998
Tampa Bay	1990	Houston	2000
Chicago	1991	San Francisco	2000
Baltimore	1992	Milwaukee	2001
Cleveland	1994	Pittsburgh	2001
Texas	1994	Cincinnati	2003
Seattle	1999	Philadelphia	2004
Detroit	2000	San Diego	2004
New York	2009	St. Louis	2006
		Washington	2008
		New York	2009

Home Fields

Listed below are the principal home fields used through the years by current American and National League teams. The NL became a major league in 1876, the AL in 1901. The capacity figures in the right-hand column indicate the largest seating capacity of the ballpark while the club played there. Capacity figures before 1915 (and the introduction of concrete grandstands) are sketchy at best and have been left blank.

American League

Baltimore Orioles

1901	Lloyd Street Grounds (Milwaukee) . . .	—
1902–53	Sportsman's Park II (St. Louis)	.30,500
1954–91	Memorial Stadium (Baltimore)	.53,371
1992–	Oriole Park at Camden Yards	.48,876

Boston Red Sox

1901–11	Huntington Ave. Grounds	—
1912–	Fenway Park	.39,928
	(1934 capacity—27,000)	

Chicago White Sox

1901–10	Southside Park	—
1910–90	Comiskey Park I	.43,931
1991–	U.S. Cellular Field	.40,615
	(2003 capacity—46,943)	

Cleveland Indians

1901–09	League Park I	—
1910–46	League Park II	.21,414
1932–93	Cleveland Stadium	.74,483
1994–	Progressive Field	.43,345

Detroit Tigers

1901–11	Bennett Park	—
1912–99	Tiger Stadium	.46,945
2000–	Comerica Park	.40,950
	(1912 capacity—23,000)	

Kansas City Royals

1969–72	Municipal Stadium	.35,020
1973–	Kauffman Stadium	.39,000
	(1973 capacity—40,762)	

Los Angeles Angels of Anaheim

1961	Wrigley Field (Los Angeles)	.20,457
1962-65	Dodger Stadium	.56,000
1966–	Angel Stadium of Anaheim	.45,050
	(1966 capacity—43,250)	

Minnesota Twins

1901-02	American League Park (Washington, DC)	—
1903-60	Griffith Stadium	.27,410
1960-81	Metropolitan Stadium (Bloomington, MN)	.45,919
1982–	HHH Metrodome (Minneapolis)	.48,678
	(1982 capacity—54,000)	

New York Yankees

1901–02	Oriole Park (Baltimore)	—
1903–12	Hilltop Park (New York)	—
1913–22	Polo Grounds II	.38,000
1923–73	Yankee Stadium I	.67,224
1974–75	Shea Stadium	.55,101
1976–2008	Yankee Stadium II	.57,478
2009–	Yankee Stadium III	.52,325

Oakland Athletics

1901–08	Columbia Park (Philadelphia)	—
1909–54	Shibe Park	.33,608
1955–67	Municipal Stadium (Kansas City)	.35,020
1968–	Oakland-Alameda County Coliseum	.35,067
	(1968 capacity—48,621)	

Seattle Mariners

1977–99	The Kingdome	.59,166
1999–	SAFECO Field	.47,116

Tampa Bay Rays

1990–	Tropicana Field	.36,048
	(1999 capacity—43,761)	

Texas Rangers

1961	Griffith Stadium (Washington, DC)	.27,410
1962–71	RFK Stadium	.45,016
1972–93	Arlington Stadium (Texas)	.43,521
1994–	Rangers Ballpark in Arlington	.49,115

Toronto Blue Jays

1977–89	Exhibition Stadium	.43,737
1989–	Rogers Centre	.50,516
	(1989 capacity—49,500)	

Ballpark Name Changes: ANAHEIM—**Angel Stadium of Anaheim**, originally Anaheim Stadium (1966-98), then Edison International Field of Anaheim (1998-2003); CHICAGO—**Comiskey Park I** originally White Sox Park (1910-12), then Comiskey Park in 1913, then White Sox Park again in 1962, then Comiskey Park again in 1976; **U.S. Cellular Field** originally Comiskey Park (1991-2002); CLEVELAND—**League Park** renamed Dunn Field in 1920, then League Park again in 1928; **Cleveland Stadium** originally Municipal Stadium (1932-74); **Progressive Field** originally Jacobs Field (1994-2007); DETROIT—**Tiger Stadium** originally Navin Field (1912-37), then Briggs Stadium (1938-60); KANSAS CITY—**Kauffman Stadium** originally Royals Stadium (1973-93); LOS ANGELES—**Dodger Stadium** referred to as Chavez Revine by AL while Angels played there (1962-65); OAKLAND—**Oakland-Alameda County Coliseum** originally Oakland Alameda Coliseum (1968-98), then Network Associates Coliseum (1998-2004), then McAfee Coliseum (2004-2008); PHILADELPHIA—**Shibe Park** renamed Connie Mack Stadium in 1953; ST. LOUIS—**Sportsman's Park** renamed Busch Stadium in 1953; WASHINGTON—**Griffith Stadium** originally National Park (1892-1920), **RFK Stadium** originally D.C. Stadium (1961-68); TEXAS—**Rangers Ballpark in Arlington** originally The Ballpark in Arlington (1994-2004), then Ameriquest Field in Arlington (2004-07); TORONTO—**Rogers Centre** originally Skydome (1989-2005).

National League

Arizona Diamondbacks

1998–	Chase Field	.49,033

Atlanta Braves

1876–94	South End Grounds I (Boston)	—
1894–1914	South End Grounds II	—
1915–52	Braves Field	.40,000
1953–65	County Stadium (Milwaukee)	.43,394
1966–96	Atlanta-Fulton County Stadium	.52,769
	(1966 capacity—50,000)	
1997–	Turner Field	.50,091

Chicago Cubs

1876–77	State Street Grounds	—
1878–84	Lakefront Park	—
1885–91	West Side Park	—
1891–93	Brotherhood Park	—
1893–1915	West Side Grounds	—
1916–	Wrigley Field	.41,160
	(1916 capacity—16,000)	

Cincinnati Reds

1876–79	Avenue Grounds	—
1880	Bank Street Grounds	—
1890–1901	Redland Field I	—
1902–11	Palace of the Fans	—
1912–70	Crosley Field	.29,603
1970–2002	Cinergy Field	.40,007
	(1970 capacity—52,000)	
2003–	Great American Ball Park	.42,059

Major League Baseball (Cont.)

Colorado Rockies

1993–94	Mile High Stadium (Denver)	76,100
1995–	Coors Field	50,445

Florida Marlins

1993–	Dolphin Stadium (Miami)	36,331
	(1993 capacity—47,662)	

Houston Astros

1962–64	Colt Stadium	32,601
1965–99	The Astrodome	54,370
	(1965 capacity—45,011)	
2000–	Minute Maid Park	40,950

Los Angeles Dodgers

1890	Washington Park I (Brooklyn)	—
1891–97	Eastern Park	—
1898–1912	Washington Park II	—
1913–55	Ebbets Field	31,497
1956–57	Ebbets Field	31,497
	& Roosevelt Stadium (Jersey City)	24,167
1958–61	Memorial Coliseum (Los Angeles)	93,600
1962–	Dodger Stadium	56,000

Milwaukee Brewers

1969	Sick's Stadium (Seattle)	59,166
1970–	County Stadium (Milwaukee)	53,192
2000	(1970 capacity—46,620)	
2001–	Miller Park	42,400

New York Mets

1962–63	Polo Grounds	55,987
1964–2008	Shea Stadium	56,749
2009–	Citi Field	45,000

Philadelphia Phillies

1883–86	Recreation Park	—
1887–94	Huntingdon Ave. Grounds	—
1895–1938	Baker Bowl	18,800
1938–70	Shibe Park	33,608

Philadelphia Phillies (Cont.)

1971–2003	Veterans Stadium	62,418
2004–	Citizens Bank Park	43,647

Pittsburgh Pirates

1887–90	Recreation Park	—
1891–1909	Exposition Park	—
1909–70	Forbes Field	35,000
1970–2000	Three Rivers Stadium	47,687
	(1970 capacity—50,235)	
2001–	PNC Park	38,496

St. Louis Cardinals

1876–77	Sportsman's Park I	—
1885–86	Vandeventer Lot	—
1892–1920	Robison Field	18,000
1920–66	Sportsman's Park II	30,500
1966–2005	Busch Stadium	49,814
2006–	Busch Stadium II	46,861

San Diego Padres

1969–2003	Qualcomm Stadium	66,083
2004–	PETCO Park	42,445

San Francisco Giants

1876	Union Grounds (Brooklyn)	—
1883–88	Polo Grounds I (New York)	—
1889–90	Manhattan Field	—
1891–1957	Polo Grounds II	55,987
1958–59	Seals Stadium (San Francisco)	22,900
1960–99	3Com Park	63,000
	(1960 capacity—42,553)	
2000–	AT&T Park	41,503

Washington Nationals

1969–76	Jarry Park (Montreal)	28,000
1977–2002	Olympic Stadium	46,500
2003–04	Olympic Stadium	46,500
	& Hiram Bithon Stadium (San Juan)	18,000
2005–07	RFK Stadium (Washington D.C.)	45,250
2008–	Nationals Ballpark	41,888

Ballpark Name Changes: ARIZONA—**Chase Field** originally named Bank One Ballpark (1998-2005); ATLANTA—**Atlanta-Fulton County Stadium** originally Atlanta Stadium (1966-74), **Turner Field** originally Centennial Olympic Stadium (1996); CHICAGO—**Wrigley Field** originally Weeghman Park (1914-17), then Cubs Park (1918-25); CINCINNATI—**Redland Field** originally League Park (1890-93), **Crosley Field** originally Redland Field II (1912-33) and **Cinergy Field** originally Riverfront Stadium (1970-96); FLORIDA—**Dolphin Stadium** originally Joe Robbie Stadium (1987-96), then Pro Player Stadium (1997-2004), then Dolphins Stadium (2004-06); HOUSTON—**Astrodome** originally Harris County Domed Stadium before it opened in 1965; **Enron Field** renamed Astros briefly and then Minute Maid Park in 2002; PHILADELPHIA—**Baker Field** originally Philadelphia Park (1895-1912), **Shibe Park** renamed Connie Mack Stadium in 1953; ST. LOUIS—**Robison Field** originally Vandeventer Lot, then League Park, then Cardinal Park all before becoming Robison Field in 1901, **Sportsman's Park** renamed Busch Stadium in 1953, and **Busch Stadium** originally Busch Memorial Stadium (1966-82); SAN DIEGO—**Qualcomm Stadium** originally San Diego Stadium (1967-81) and San Diego/Jack Murphy Stadium (1982-96); SAN FRANCISCO—**3Com Park** originally Candlestick Park (1960-95), **AT&T Park** originally Pacific Bell Park (2000-03), then SBC Park (2003-06).

NATIONAL BASKETBALL ASSOCIATION

Western Conference

		Location	Built	Capacity
Dallas Mavericks	**American Airlines Center**	Dallas, Texas	2001	**19,200**
Denver Nuggets	**Pepsi Center**	Denver, Colo.	1999	**19,099**
Golden State Warriors	**Oracle Arena**	Oakland, Calif.	1997	**19,596**
Houston Rockets	**Toyota Center**	Houston, Texas	2003	**18,300**
Los Angeles Clippers	**Staples Center**	Los Angeles, Calif.	1999	**18,694**
Los Angeles Lakers	**Staples Center**	Los Angeles, Calif.	1999	**18,997**
Memphis Grizzlies	**FedEx Forum**	Memphis, Tenn.	2004	**18,400**
Minnesota Timberwolves	**Target Center**	Minneapolis, Minn.	1990	**19,006**
New Orleans Hornets	**New Orleans Arena**	New Orleans, La.	1999	**18,500**
Oklahoma City Thunder	**Ford Center**	Oklahoma City, Okla.	2002	**19,599**
Phoenix Suns	**U.S. Airways Center**	Phoenix, Ariz.	1992	**19,023**
Portland Trail Blazers	**Rose Garden**	Portland, Ore.	1995	**19,980**
Sacramento Kings	**ARCO Arena**	Sacramento, Calif.	1988	**17,317**
San Antonio Spurs	**AT&T Center**	San Antonio, Texas	2002	**18,500**
Utah Jazz	**EnergySolutions Arena**	Salt Lake City, Utah	1991	**19,911**

Notes: Seattle's KeyArena was originally the Seattle Center Coliseum before being rebuilt in 1995; The Staples Center has different listed capacities for Clippers games and Lakers games because of different floor seating arrangements.

Eastern Conference

		Location	Built	Capacity
Atlanta Hawks	**Philips Arena**	Atlanta, Ga.	1999	**19,445**
Boston Celtics	**TD Banknorth Garden**	Boston, Mass.	1995	**18,624**
Charlotte Bobcats	**Time Warner Cable Arena**	Charlotte, N.C.	2005	**18,500**
Chicago Bulls	**United Center**	Chicago, Ill.	1994	**21,711**
Cleveland Cavaliers	**The Quicken Loans Arena**	Cleveland, Ohio	1994	**20,562**
Detroit Pistons	**The Palace of Auburn Hills**	Auburn Hills, Mich.	1988	**22,076**
Indiana Pacers	**Conseco Fieldhouse**	Indianapolis, Ind.	1999	**18,345**
Miami Heat	**AmericanAirlines Arena**	Miami, Fla.	1999	**16,500**
Milwaukee Bucks	**Bradley Center**	Milwaukee, Wisc.	1988	**18,717**
New Jersey Nets	**Izod Center**	E. Rutherford, N.J.	1981	**20,049**
New York Knicks	**Madison Square Garden**	New York, N.Y.	1968	**19,763**
Orlando Magic	**Amway Arena**	Orlando, Fla.	1989	**17,248**
Philadelphia 76ers	**Wachovia Center**	Philadelphia, Penn.	1996	**20,444**
Toronto Raptors	**Air Canada Centre**	Toronto, Ont.	1999	**19,800**
Washington Wizards	**Verizon Center**	Washington, D.C.	1997	**20,674**

Rank by Capacity

Western		Eastern	
Portland	19,980	Detroit	22,076
Utah	19,911	Chicago	21,711
New Orleans	19,675	Washington	20,674
Oklahoma City	19,599	Cleveland	20,562
Golden State	19,596	Philadelphia	20,444
Dallas	19,200	New Jersey	20,049
Denver	19,099	Toronto	19,800
Phoenix	19,023	New York	19,763
Minnesota	19,006	Atlanta	19,445
LA Lakers	18,997	Milwaukee	18,717
LA Clippers	18,694	Boston	18,624
San Antonio	18,500	Charlotte	18,500
Memphis	18,400	Indiana	18,345
Houston	18,300	Orlando	17,248
Sacramento	17,317	Miami	16,500

Rank by Age

Western		Eastern	
Sacramento	1988	New York	1968
Minnesota	1990	New Jersey	1981
Utah	1991	Detroit	1988
Phoenix	1992	Milwaukee	1988
Portland	1995	Orlando	1989
Golden St.	1997	Chicago	1994
Denver	1999	Cleveland	1994
LA Clippers	1999	Boston	1995
LA Lakers	1999	Philadelphia	1996
Dallas	2001	Washington	1997
San Antonio	2002	Toronto	1999
New Orleans	2002	Atlanta	1999
Oklahoma City	2002	Indiana	1999
Houston	2003	Miami	1999
Memphis	2004	Charlotte	2005

2007-08 NBA Attendance

Official overall attendance in the NBA for the 2007-08 season was 21,394,770 for an average per game crowd of 17,394 over 1,230 games. Teams in each conference are ranked by attendance over 41 home games based on total tickets distributed. Rank column refers to rank in entire league. Numbers in parentheses indicate conference rank in 2006-07.

Western Conference

		Attendance	Rank	Average
1	Dallas (1)	831,738	4	20,286
2	Utah (2)	816,211	5	19,907
3	Golden St. (7)	804,864	6	19,630
4	Portland (12)	801,566	7	19,550
5	LA Lakers (3)	778,877	11	18,997
6	San Antonio (4)	761,149	13	18,564
7	Phoenix (5)	755,302	14	18,422
8	Houston (11)	718,524	16	17,524
9	Denver (10)	411,962	17	17,364
10	LA Clippers (6)	692,408	19	16,888
11	Minnesota (14)	593,537	25	14,476
12	New Orleans (8)	581,432	26	14,181
13	Sacramento (9)	580,178	27	14,150
14	Seattle (13)	547,556	28	13,355
15	Memphis (15)	523,578	29	12,770
	TOTAL	679,925	—	16,584

Eastern Conference

		Attendance	Rank	Average
1	Detroit (2)	905,116	1	22,076
2	Chicago (1)	901,502	2	21,987
3	Cleveland (3)	839,074	3	20,465
4	Miami (4)	798,004	8	19,463
5	Toronto (7)	796,835	9	19,435
6	New York (5)	782,993	10	19,097
7	Boston (10)	763,584	12	18,624
8	Washington (6)	736,391	15	17,960
9	Orlando (8)	709,346	18	17,301
10	Atlanta (12)	763,584	20	16,280
11	New Jersey (9)	641,921	21	15,666
12	Milwaukee (11)	639,421	22	15,595
13	Philadelphia (15)	609,675	23	14,870
14	Charlotte (13)	603,403	24	14,717
15	Indiana (14)	501,092	30	12,221
	TOTAL	746,393	—	18,204

Home Courts

Listed below are the principal home courts used through the years by current NBA teams. The largest capacity of each arena is noted in the right-hand column. ABA arenas (1967-76) are included for Denver, Indiana, New Jersey and San Antonio.

Western Conference

Dallas Mavericks

1980–2000	Reunion Arena	18,187
2001–	American Airlines Center	19,200

Denver Nuggets

1967–75	Auditorium Arena	6,841
1975–99	McNichols Sports Arena	17,171
	(1975 capacity—16,700)	
1999–	Pepsi Center	19,099

Golden State Warriors

1946–52	Philadelphia Arena	7,777
1952–62	Convention Hall (Philadelphia)	9,200
	& Philadelphia Arena	7,777
1962–64	Cow Palace (San Francisco)	13,862
1964–66	Civic Auditorium	7,500
	& (USF Memorial Gym)	6,000
1966–67	Cow Palace, Civic Auditorium	
	& Oakland Coliseum Arena	15,000
1967–71	Cow Palace	14,500
1971–96	Oakland Coliseum Arena	15,025
	(1971 capacity—12,905)	
1996–97	San Jose Arena	18,500
1997–	Oracle Arena	19,596

Houston Rockets

1967–71	San Diego Sports Arena	14,000
1971–72	Hofheinz Pavilion (Houston)	10,218
1972–73	Hofheinz Pavilion	10,218
	& HemisFair Arena (San Antonio)	10,446
1973–75	Hofheinz Pavilion	10,218
1975–2002	Compaq Center	16,285
2003–	Toyota Center	18,300

Los Angeles Clippers

1970–78	Memorial Auditorium (Buffalo)	17,300
1978–84	San Diego Sports Arena	12,167
1985–94	Los Angeles Sports Arena	16,005
1994–99	Los Angeles Sports Arena	16,021
	& Arrowhead Pond	18,211
1999–	Staples Center	18,694

Los Angeles Lakers

1948–60	Minneapolis Auditorium	10,000
1960–67	Los Angeles Sports Arena	14,781
1967–99	Great Western Forum (Inglewood, CA)	17,505
	(1967 capacity—17,086)	
1999–	Staples Center	18,997

Memphis Grizzlies

1995–2001	General Motors Place (Vancouver)	19,193
2001–03	The Pyramid (Memphis, TN)	19,342
2004–	FedEx Forum	18,400

Minnesota Timberwolves

1989–90	Hubert H. Humphrey Metrodome	23,000
1990–	Target Center	19,006

New Orleans Hornets

1988–2002	Charlotte Coliseum	19,925
	(1988 capacity—23,500)	
2002-05	New Orleans Arena	18,500

New Orleans (Cont.)

2005-06	Ford Center (Oklahoma City)	19,675
	& Maravich Center (Baton Rouge)	14,164
2007–	New Orleans Arena	18,500

Oklahoma City Thunder

1967–78	Seattle Center Coliseum	14,098
1978–85	Kingdome	40,192
1985–94	Seattle Center Coliseum	14,252
1994–95	Tacoma Dome	19,000
1995–2007	KeyArena at Seattle Center	17,072
2008–	Ford Center (Okla. City, Okla)	19,599

Phoenix Suns

1968–92	Arizona Veterans' Memorial Coliseum	14,487
1992–	U.S. Airways Center	19,023

Portland Trail Blazers

1970–95	Memorial Coliseum	12,888
1995–	Rose Garden	19,980
	(1995 capacity—21,538)	

Sacramento Kings

1948–55	Edgarton Park Arena (Rochester, NY)	5,000
1955–58	Rochester War Memorial	10,000
1958–72	Cincinnati Gardens	11,438
1972–74	Municipal Auditorium (Kansas City)	9,929
	& Omaha (NE) Civic Auditorium	9,136
1974–78	Kemper Arena (Kansas City)	16,785
	& Omaha Civic Auditorium	9,136
1978–85	Kemper Arena	16,886
1985–88	ARCO Arena I	10,333
1988–	ARCO Arena II	17,317
	(1988 capacity—16,517)	

San Antonio Spurs

1967–70	Memorial Auditorium (Dallas)	8,088
	& Moody Coliseum (Dallas)	8,500
1970–71	Moody Coliseum	8,500
	Tarrant County	
	Convention Center (Ft. Worth)	13,500
	& Municipal Coliseum (Lubbock)	10,400
1971–73	Moody Coliseum	9,500
	& Memorial Auditorium	8,088
1973–93	HemisFair Arena (San Antonio)	16,057
1993–2002	The Alamodome	20,557
2002–	AT&T Center	18,500

Utah Jazz

1974–75	Municipal Auditorium (New Orleans)	7,853
	& Louisiana Superdome	47,284
1975–79	Superdome	47,284
1979–83	Salt Palace (Salt Lake City)	12,519
1983–84	Salt Palace	12,519
	& Thomas & Mack Center (Las Vegas)	18,500
1984–91	Salt Palace	12,616
1991–	EnergySolutions Arena	19,911

Note: The Sacramento (then Kansas City) Kings played 30 home games at Kansas City Municipal Auditorium during the 1979-80 season after the Kemper Auditorium roof collapsed during a severe rain and wind storm on June 4, 1979.

Eastern Conference

Atlanta Hawks

1949–51	Wharton Field House (Moline, IL)	6,000
1951–55	Milwaukee Arena	11,000
1955–68	Kiel Auditorium (St. Louis)	10,000
1968–72	Alexander Mem. Coliseum (Atlanta)	7,166
1972–96	The Omni	16,378
1997–99	Georgia Dome	21,570
	& Alexander Mem. Coliseum	9,300
1999–	Philips Arena	19,445

Boston Celtics

1946–95	Boston Garden	14,890
1995–	TD Banknorth Garden	18,624

Note: From 1975-95 the Celtics played some regular season games at the Hartford Civic Center (15,418).

Charlotte Bobcats

2004-05	Charlotte Coliseum	19,925
2005–	Time Warner Cable Arena	18,500

Chicago Bulls

1966–67	Chicago Amphitheater	11,002
1967–94	Chicago Stadium	18,676
1994–	United Center	21,711

Cleveland Cavaliers

1970–74	Cleveland Arena	11,000
1974–94	The Coliseum (Richfield, OH)	20,273
1994–	The Quicken Loans Arena	20,562

Detroit Pistons

1948–52	North Side H.S. Gym (Ft. Wayne, IN)	3,800
1952–57	Memorial Coliseum (Ft. Wayne)	9,306
1957–61	Olympia Stadium (Detroit)	14,000
1961–78	Cobo Arena	11,147
1978–88	Silverdome (Pontiac, MI)	22,366
1988–	The Palace of Auburn Hills	22,076

Indiana Pacers

1967–74	State Fairgrounds (Indianapolis)	9,479
1974–99	Market Square Arena	16,530
	(1974 capacity—17,287)	
1999–	Conseco Fieldhouse	18,345

Miami Heat

1988–99	Miami Arena	15,200
2000–	AmericanAirlines Arena	16,500

Milwaukee Bucks

1968–88	Milwaukee Arena (The Mecca)	11,052
1988–	Bradley Center	18,717

New Jersey Nets

1967–68	Teaneck (NJ) Armory	3,500
1968–69	Long Island Arena (Commack, NY)	6,500
1969–71	Island Garden (W. Hempstead, NY)	5,200
1971–77	Nassau Coliseum (Uniondale, NY)	15,500
1977–81	Rutgers Ath. Center (Piscataway, NJ)	9,050
1981–	Izod Center (E. Ruth., NJ)	20,049

New York Knicks

1946–68	Madison Sq. Garden III (50th St.)	18,496
1968–	Madison Sq. Garden IV (33rd St.)	19,763
	(1968 capacity—19,694)	

Orlando Magic

1989–	Amway Arena	17,248

Philadelphia 76ers

1949–51	State Fair Coliseum (Syracuse, NY)	7,500
1951–63	Onondaga County (NY) War Memorial	8,000
1963–67	Convention Hall (Philadelphia)	12,000
	& Philadelphia Arena	7,777
1967–96	CoreStates Spectrum	18,136
1996–	Wachovia Center	20,444

Toronto Raptors

1995–99	SkyDome	20,125
1999–	Air Canada Centre	19,800

Washington Wizards

1961–62	Chicago Amphitheater	11,000
1962–63	Chicago Coliseum	7,100
1963–73	Baltimore Civic Center	12,289
1973–97	USAir Arena (Landover, MD)	18,756
1997–	Verizon Center	20,674

Note: From 1988-96 the Wizards (then Bullets) played four regular season games at Baltimore Arena (12,756).

Building Name Changes: BOSTON—**TD Banknorth Garden** originally FleetCenter (1995-2005); CLEVELAND—**The Quicken Loans Arena** originally Gund Arena (1994-2005); GOLDEN ST—**Oracle Arena** originally The Arena in Oakland (1997-2007); HOUSTON—**Compaq Center** originally The Summit (1975-97); NEW JERSEY—**Izod Center** originally Byrne Meadowlands Arena (1981-96) then Continental Airlines Arena (1997-2007); ORLANDO—**Amway Arena** originally Orlando Arena (1989-99) then TD Waterhouse Centre (1999-2007); PHILADELPHIA—**Wachovia Center** originally the CoreStates Center (1996-98), then the First Union Center (1998-2003) and **CoreStates Spectrum** originally The Spectrum (1967-94); SAN ANTONIO—**AT&T Center** originally SBC Center (2002-07); UTAH—**EnergySolutions Arena** originally Delta Center (199-12007); WASHINGTON—**USAir Arena** originally Capital Centre (1973-93); **Verizon Center** originally MCI Center (1997-2006).

NATIONAL FOOTBALL LEAGUE

American Football Conference

		Location	Built	Capacity	Field
Baltimore Ravens	**M&T Bank Stadium**	Baltimore, Md.	1998	**69,084**	Grass
Buffalo Bills	**Ralph Wilson Stadium**	Orchard Park, N.Y.	1973	**73,967**	Turf
Cincinnati Bengals	**Paul Brown Stadium**	Cincinnati, Ohio	2000	**65,352**	Grass
Cleveland Browns	**Cleveland Browns Stadium**	Cleveland, Ohio	1999	**73,200**	Grass
Denver Broncos	**INVESCO Field at Mile High**	Denver, Colo.	2001	**76,125**	Grass
Houston Texans	**Reliant Stadium**	Houston, Tex.	2002	**69,500**	Grass
Indianapolis Colts	**Lucas Oil Stadium**	Indianapolis, Ind.	2008	**63,000**	Turf
Jacksonville Jaguars	**Jacksonville Municipal Stadium**	Jacksonville, Fla.	1995	**67,164**	Grass
Kansas City Chiefs	**Arrowhead Stadium**	Kansas City, Mo.	1972	**79,451**	Grass
Miami Dolphins	**Dolphin Stadium**	Miami, Fla.	1987	**75,540**	Grass
New England Patriots	**Gillette Stadium**	Foxboro, Mass.	2002	**68,000**	Turf
New York Jets	**Giants Stadium**	E. Rutherford, N.J.	1976	**80,062**	Grass
Oakland Raiders	**McAfee Coliseum**	Oakland, Calif.	1966	**63,132**	Grass
Pittsburgh Steelers	**Heinz Field**	Pittsburgh, Pa.	2001	**64,450**	Grass
San Diego Chargers	**Qualcomm Stadium**	San Diego, Calif.	1967	**71,294**	Grass
Tennessee Titans	**LP Field**	Nashville, Tenn.	1999	**68,798**	Grass

National Football Conference

		Location	Built	Capacity	Field
Arizona Cardinals	**University of Phoenix Stadium**	Glendale, Ariz.	2006	**63,500***	Grass
Atlanta Falcons	**Georgia Dome**	Atlanta, Ga.	1992	**71,228**	Turf
Carolina Panthers	**Bank of America Stadium**	Charlotte, N.C.	1996	**73,500**	Grass
Chicago Bears	**Soldier Field**	Chicago, Ill.	1924	**63,000**	Grass
Dallas Cowboys	**Texas Stadium**	Irving, Texas	1971	**65,639**	Turf
Detroit Lions	**Ford Field**	Detroit, Mich.	2002	**65,000**	Turf
Green Bay Packers	**Lambeau Field**	Green Bay, Wis.	1957	**72,515**	Grass
Minnesota Vikings	**Hubert H. Humphrey Metrodome**	Minneapolis, Minn.	1982	**64,121**	Turf
New Orleans Saints	**Louisiana Superdome**	New Orleans, La.	1975	**69,703**	Turf
New York Giants	**Giants Stadium**	E. Rutherford, N.J.	1976	**80,062**	Grass
Philadelphia Eagles	**Lincoln Financial Field**	Philadelphia, Pa.	2003	**68,532**	Grass
St. Louis Rams	**Edward Jones Dome**	St. Louis, Mo.	1995	**66,000**	Turf
San Francisco 49ers	**Monster Park**	San Francisco, Calif.	1960	**69,400**	Grass
Seattle Seahawks	**Qwest Field**	Seattle, Wash.	2002	**67,000**	Grass
Tampa Bay Buccaneers	**Raymond James Stadium**	Tampa, Fla.	1998	**65,657**	Grass
Washington Redskins	**FedEx Field**	Raljon, Md.	1997	**86,484**	Grass

*Cardinals Stadium is expandable to 73,000.

National Football League (Cont.)

Rank by Capacity

AFC		NFC	
NY Jets	.80,062	Washington	.86,484
Kansas City	.79,451	NY Giants	.80,062
Denver	.76,125	Carolina	.73,500
Miami	.75,540	Green Bay	.72,515
Buffalo	.73,967	Atlanta	.71,228
Cleveland	.73,200	New Orleans	.69,703
San Diego	.71,294	San Francisco	.69,400
Houston	.69,500	Philadelphia	.68,532
Baltimore	.69,084	Seattle	.67,000
Tennessee	.68,798	St. Louis	.66,000
New England	.68,000	Tampa Bay	.65,657
Jacksonville	.67,164	Dallas	.65,639
Cincinnati	.65,352	Detroit	.65,000
Pittsburgh	.64,450	Minnesota	.64,121
Oakland	.63,132	Arizona	.63,500
Indianapolis	.63,000	Chicago	.63,000

Rank by Age

AFC		NFC	
Oakland	.1966	Chicago	.1924
San Diego	.1967	Green Bay	.1957
Kansas City	.1972	San Francisco	.1960
Buffalo	.1973	Dallas	.1971
NY Jets	.1976	New Orleans	.1975
Miami	.1987	NY Giants	.1976
Jacksonville	.1995	Minnesota	.1982
Baltimore	.1998	Atlanta	.1992
Cleveland	.1999	St. Louis	.1995
Tennessee	.1999	Carolina	.1996
Cincinnati	.2000	Washington	.1997
Denver	.2001	Tampa Bay	.1998
Pittsburgh	.2001	Seattle	.2002
New England	.2002	Detroit	.2002
Houston	.2002	Philadelphia	.2003
Indianapolis	.2008	Arizona	.2006

Notes: Chicago's Soldier Field was rebuilt and Green Bay's Lambeau Field was renovated in 2003.

2007 NFL Attendance

Overall paid attendance in the NFL for the 2007 season was 17,345,205 for an average per game crowd of 67,775 over 256 games. Teams in each conference are ranked by attendance over eight home games. Rank column indicates rank in entire league. Numbers in parentheses indicate conference rank in 2006.

AFC

		Attendance	Rank	Average
1	N.Y. Jets (2)	.616,856	3	77,107
2	Kansas City (1)	.614,216	4	76,777
3	Denver (3)	.612,896	5	76,612
4	Cleveland (5)	.584,008	7	73,001
5	Miami (4)	.577,832	8	72,229
6	Baltimore (6)	.572,104	9	71,513
7	Buffalo (10)	.568,440	10	71,055
8	Houston (7)	.564,160	12	70,520
9	Tennessee (8)	.553,144	14	69,143
10	New England (9)	.550,048	15	68,756
11	Cincinnati (13)	.526,320	20	65,790
12	San Diego (12)	.524,016	21	65,502
13	Jacksonville (11)	.522,408	23	65,301
14	Pittsburgh (14)	.496,672	29	62,084
15	Oakland (15)	.472,880	31	59,110
16	Indianapolis (16)	.458,440	32	57,305
	TOTAL	.8,790,440	—	68,675

NFC

		Attendance	Rank	Average
1	Washington (1)	.704,720	1	88,090
2	N.Y. Giants (2)	.629,848	2	73,731
3	Carolina (3)	.587,224	6	73,403
4	Green Bay (5)	.566,440	11	70,805
5	New Orleans (7)	.560,040	13	70,005
6	Atlanta (4)	.547,168	16	68,396
7	Seattle (9)	.545,552	17	68,194
8	Philadelphia (6)	.545,360	18	68,170
9	San Francisco (8)	.544,224	19	68,028
10	Tampa Bay (10)	.522,528	22	65,316
11	Arizona (13)	.516,648	24	64,581
12	Dallas (14)	.508,280	25	63,535
13	St. Louis (11)	.504,352	27	63,044
14	Minnesota (12)	.506,048	26	63,256
15	Chicago (15)	.497,264	28	62,158
16	Detroit (16)	.490,440	30	61,305
	TOTAL	.8,554,765	—	66,834

Home Fields

Listed below are the principal home fields used through the years by current NFL teams. The largest capacity of each stadium is noted in the right-hand column. All-America Football Conference stadiums (1946-49) are included for Cleveland and San Francisco.

AFC

Baltimore Ravens

1996–97	Memorial Stadium	.65,000
1998–	M&T Bank Stadium	.69,084

Buffalo Bills

1960–72	War Memorial Stadium	.45,748
1973–	Ralph Wilson Stadium (Orchard Park, NY)	.73,967
	(1973 capacity—80,020)	

Cincinnati Bengals

1968–69	Nippert Stadium (Univ. of Cincinnati)	.26,500
1970–99	Cinergy Field	.60,389
	(1970 capacity—56,200)	
2000–	Paul Brown Stadium	.65,352

Cleveland Browns

1946–95	Cleveland Stadium	.78,512
	(1946 capacity—85,703)	
1999–	Cleveland Browns Stadium	.73,200

Denver Broncos

1960–2000	Mile High Stadium	.76,123
	(1960 capacity—34,000)	
2001–	INVESCO Field at Mile High	.76,125

Houston Texans

2002–	Reliant Stadium	.69,500

Indianapolis Colts

1953–83	Memorial Stadium (Baltimore)	.60,020
1984–2007	RCA Dome (Indianapolis)	.56,127
2008–	Lucas Oil Stadium	.63,000

Jacksonville Jaguars

1995–	Jacksonville Municipal Stadium	.67,164
	(1995 capacity—73,000)	

Kansas City Chiefs

1960–62	Cotton Bowl (Dallas)	.72,000
1963–71	Municipal Stadium (Kansas City)	.47,000
1972–	Arrowhead Stadium	.79,451
	(1972 capacity—78,097)	

Miami Dolphins

1966–86	Orange Bowl	75,206
1987–	Dolphin Stadium	75,540

New England Patriots

1960–62	Nickerson Field (Boston Univ.)	17,369
1963–68	Fenway Park	33,379
1969	Alumni Stadium (Boston College)	26,000
1970	Harvard Stadium	37,300
1971-2001	Foxboro Stadium	60,292
	(1971 capacity—61,114)	
2002–	Gillette Stadium (Foxboro, Mass.)	68,000

New York Jets

1960–63	Polo Grounds	55,987
1964–83	Shea Stadium	60,372
1984–	Giants Stadium (E. Rutherford, NJ)	80,062

Oakland Raiders

1960	Kesar Stadium (San Francisco)	59,636
1961	Candlestick Park	42,500
1962–65	Frank Youell Field (Oakland)	20,000
1966–81	Oakland-Alameda County Coliseum	54,587
1982–94	Memorial Coliseum (Los Angeles)	67,800
1995–	McAfee Coliseum	63,132

Pittsburgh Steelers

1933–57	Forbes Field	35,000
1958–63	Forbes Field	35,000
	& Pitt Stadium	54,500
1964–69	Pitt Stadium	54,500
1970–	Three Rivers Stadium	59,600
2000	(1970 capacity—49,000)	
2001–	Heinz Field	64,450

San Diego Chargers

1960	Memorial Coliseum (Los Angeles)	92,604
1961–66	Balboa Stadium (San Diego)	34,000
1967–	Qualcomm Stadium	71,294
	(1967 capacity—54,000)	

Tennessee Titans

1960–64	Jeppesen Stadium (Houston)	23,500
1965–67	Rice Stadium (Rice Univ.)	70,000
1968–96	Astrodome	59,969
1997	Liberty Bowl (Memphis)	62,380
1998	Vanderbilt Stadium (Nashville)	41,600
1999–	LP Field (Nashville)	68,798

Stadium Name Changes: BALTIMORE—**M&T Bank Stadium** was originally named Ravens Stadium (1998-99) then was renamed PSInet Stadium (1999-2002) and renamed Ravens Stadium (2002-03); BUFFALO—**Ralph Wilson Stadium** originally Rich Stadium (1973-99); CINCINNATI—Cinergy Field originally Riverfront Stadium (1970-96); CLEVELAND—Cleveland Stadium originally Municipal Stadium (1932-74); DENVER—**Mile High Stadium** originally Bears Stadium (1948-66); INDIANAPOLIS—**RCA Dome** originally Hoosier Dome (1984-94); JACKSONVILLE—**Jacksonville Municipal Stadium** (1995-97, 2007—) was formerly named ALLTEL Stadium (1997-2007); MIAMI—**Dolphins Stadium** originally Joe Robbie Stadium (1987-96), then Pro Player Stadium (1996-2005); NEW ENGLAND—Foxboro Stadium originally Schaefer Stadium (1971-82), then Sullivan Stadium (1983-89); **Gillette Stadium** originally CMGI Field; OAKLAND—**McAfee Coliseum** originally Oakland Alameda Coliseum (1995-99), Network Associates Coliseum (1999-2004); SAN DIEGO—**Qualcomm Stadium** originally San Diego Stadium (1967-81) then San Diego/Jack Murphy Stadium (1981-96); TENNESSEE—**LP Field** originally Adelphia Coliseum (1999-2001), then The Coliseum (2001-06).

NFC

Arizona Cardinals

1920–21	Normal Field (Chicago)	7,500
1922–25	Comiskey Park	28,000
1926–28	Normal Field	7,500
1929–59	Comiskey Park	52,000
1960–65	Busch Stadium (St. Louis)	34,000
1966–87	Busch Memorial Stadium	54,392
1988–2005	Sun Devil Stadium (Tempe, AZ)	73,273
2006—	Univ. of Phoenix Stadium (Glendale)	63,500

Atlanta Falcons

1966-91	Atlanta-Fulton County Stadium	59,643
1992–	Georgia Dome	71,228

Carolina Panthers

1995	Memorial Stadium (Clemson, SC)	81,473
1996–	Bank of America Stadium	73,500

Chicago Bears

1920	Staley Field (Decatur, IL)	—
1921–70	Wrigley Field (Chicago)	37,741
1971–2001	Soldier Field	66,944
	(1971 capacity—55,049)	
2002	Memorial Stadium (Champaign, IL)	69,249
2003–	Soldier Field	63,000

Dallas Cowboys

1960–70	Cotton Bowl	72,132
1971–	Texas Stadium (Irving, TX)	65,639
	(1971 capacity—65,101)	

Detroit Lions

1930–33	Spartan Stadium (Portsmouth, OH)	8,200
1934–37	Univ. of Detroit Stadium	25,000
1938–74	Tiger Stadium	54,468
1975-2001	Pontiac Silverdome	80,311
	(1975 capacity—80,638)	
2002–	Ford Field	65,000

Green Bay Packers

1921–22	Hagemeister Brewery Park	—
1923–24	Bellevue Park	—
1925–56	City Stadium I	24,800
1957–	Lambeau Field	72,515
	(1957 capacity—32,150)	
	(2002 capacity—62,500)	

Note: The Packers played games in Milwaukee from 1933-94: at Borchert Field, State Fair Park and Marquette Stadium (1933-52), and County Stadium (1953-94).

Minnesota Vikings

1961–81	Metropolitan Stadium (Bloomington)	48,446
1982–	HHH Metrodome (Minneapolis)	64,121
	(1982 capacity—62,220)	

New Orleans Saints

1967–74	Tulane Stadium	80,997
1975–2004	Louisiana Superdome	69,703
	(1975 capacity—74,472)	
2005	Tiger Stadium (Baton Rouge)	91,644
	& Alamodome (San Antonio)	65,000
2006—	Louisiana Superdome	69,703

Note: The Saints were unable to play at the Louisiana Superdome in the wake of Hurricane Katrina and played four home games at LSU's Tiger Stadium and three at the Alamodome in San Antonio in 2005.

New York Giants

1925–55	Polo Grounds II	55,200
1956–73	Yankee Stadium I	63,800
1973–74	Yale Bowl (New Haven, CT)	70,896
1975	Shea Stadium	60,372
1976–	Giants Stadium (E. Rutherford, NJ)	80,062
	(1976 capacity—76,800)	

National Football League (Cont.)

Philadelphia Eagles

1933–35	Baker Bowl	18,800
1936–39	Municipal Stadium	73,702
1940	Shibe Park	33,608
1941	Municipal Stadium	73,702
1942	Shibe Park	33,608
1943	Forbes Field (Pittsburgh)	34,528
1944–57	Shibe Park	33,608
1958–70	Franklin Field (Univ. of Penn.)	60,546
1971–2002	Veterans Stadium	65,352
2003–	Lincoln Financial Field	68,532

St. Louis Rams

1937–42	Municipal Stadium (Cleveland)	85,703
1937	League Park (Cleveland)	—
1938*	Shaw Stadium (Cleveland)	—
1937	League Park	—
1943	Suspended operations for one year.	
1944–45	Municipal Stadium	85,703
1946–79	Memorial Coliseum (Los Angeles)	92,604
1980–94	Anaheim Stadium	69,008
1995	Busch Stadium	60,000
1995–	Edward Jones Dome	66,000

San Francisco 49ers

1946–70	Kezar Stadium	59,636
1971–	Monster Park	69,400
	(1971 capacity—61,246)	

Seattle Seahawks

1976–94	Kingdome	66,000
1994	Kingdome	66,400
	& Husky Stadium	72,500
1995–99	Kingdome	66,400
2000-01	Husky Stadium	72,500
2002–	Qwest Field	67,000

Tampa Bay Buccaneers

1976–97	Houlihan's Stadium	74,300
1998–	Raymond James Stadium	65,657

Washington Redskins

1932	Braves Field (Boston)	40,000
1933–36	Fenway Park	27,000
1937–60	Griffith Stadium (Washington, DC)	35,000
1961–97	RFK Stadium	56,454
1997–	FedEx Field (Raljon, MD)	86,484

Stadium Name Changes: ATLANTA—**Atlanta-Fulton County Stadium** originally Atlanta Stadium (1966-74); CAROLINA—**Bank of America Stadium** originally Ericsson Stadium (1996-2004); CHICAGO—**Wrigley Field** originally Cubs Park (1916-25); DETROIT—**Tiger Stadium** originally Navin Field (1912-37), then Briggs Stadium (1938-60), also, **Pontiac Silverdome** originally Pontiac Metropolitan Stadium (1975); GREEN BAY—**Lambeau Field** originally City Stadium II (1957-64); PHILADELPHIA—**Shibe Park** renamed Connie Mack Stadium in 1953; ST. LOUIS—**Busch Memorial Stadium** renamed Busch Stadium in 1983; **Edward Jones Dome** originally Trans World Dome (1995-99), then The Dome at America's Center (2000-01); SAN FRANCISCO—**Monster Park** originally Candlestick Park (1960-94), then 3Com Park (1995-2001) and again Candlestick Park (2001-04); SEATTLE—**Qwest Field** originally Seahawks Stadium (2002-04); TAMPA BAY—**Raymond James Stadium** originally Tampa Stadium (1976-96), then **Houlihan's Stadium** (1996-98); WASHINGTON—**RFK Stadium** originally D.C. Stadium (1961-68), also, **FedEx Field** originally Jack Kent Cooke Stadium (1997-99).

NATIONAL HOCKEY LEAGUE

Western Conference

		Location	Built	Capacity
Anaheim Ducks	**Honda Center**	Anaheim, Calif.	1993	**17,174**
Calgary Flames	**Pengrowth Saddledome**	Calgary, Alb.	1983	**17,135**
Chicago Blackhawks	**United Center**	Chicago, Ill.	1994	**20,500**
Colorado Avalanche	**Pepsi Center**	Denver, Colo.	1999	**18,007**
Columbus Blue Jackets	**Nationwide Arena**	Columbus, Ohio	2000	**18,136**
Dallas Stars	**American Airlines Center**	Dallas, Texas	2001	**18,532**
Detroit Red Wings	**Joe Louis Arena**	Detroit, Mich.	1979	**20,058**
Edmonton Oilers	**Rexall Place**	Edmonton, Alb.	1974	**16,839**
Los Angeles Kings	**Staples Center**	Los Angeles, Calif.	1999	**18,118**
Minnesota Wild	**Xcel Energy Center**	St. Paul, Minn.	2000	**18,064**
Nashville Predators	**Sommet Center**	Nashville, Tenn.	1996	**17,113**
Phoenix Coyotes	**Jobing.com Arena**	Glendale, Ariz.	2003	**17,799**
St. Louis Blues	**Scottrade Center**	St. Louis, Mo.	1994	**19,022**
San Jose Sharks	**HP Pavilion at San Jose**	San Jose, Calif.	1993	**17,496**
Vancouver Canucks	**General Motors Place**	Vancouver, B.C.	1995	**18,422**

Eastern Conference

		Location	Built	Capacity
Atlanta Thrashers	**Philips Arena**	Atlanta, Ga.	1999	**18,545**
Boston Bruins	**TD Banknorth Garden**	Boston, Mass.	1995	**17,565**
Buffalo Sabres	**HSBC Arena**	Buffalo, N.Y.	1996	**18,690**
Carolina Hurricanes	**RBC Center**	Raleigh, N.C.	1999	**18,730**
Florida Panthers	**BankAtlantic Center**	Sunrise, Fla.	1998	**19,250**
Montreal Canadiens	**Bell Centre**	Montreal, Que.	1996	**21,273**
New Jersey Devils	**Prudential Center**	Newark, N.J.	2007	**17,625**
New York Islanders	**Nassau Veterans' Mem. Coliseum**	Uniondale, N.Y.	1972	**16,234**
New York Rangers	**Madison Square Garden**	New York, N.Y.	1968	**18,200**
Ottawa Senators	**Scotiabank Place**	Kanata, Ont.	1996	**19,311**
Philadelphia Flyers	**Wachovia Center**	Philadelphia, Penn.	1996	**18,523**
Pittsburgh Penguins	**Mellon Arena**	Pittsburgh, Penn.	1961	**16,958**
Tampa Bay Lightning	**St. Pete Times Forum**	Tampa Bay, Fla.	1996	**19,758**
Toronto Maple Leafs	**Air Canada Centre**	Toronto, Ont.	1999	**18,819**
Washington Capitals	**Verizon Center**	Washington, D.C.	1997	**18,672**

Rank by Capacity

Western		Eastern	
Chicago	20,500	Montreal	21,273
Detroit	20,058	Tampa Bay	19,758
St. Louis	19,022	Florida	19,250
Dallas	18,532	Toronto	18,819
Vancouver	18,422	Carolina	18,730
Columbus	18,136	Buffalo	18,690
Los Angeles	18,118	Washington	18,672
Minnesota	18,064	Atlanta	18,545
Colorado	18,007	Philadelphia	18,523
Phoenix	17,799	Ottawa	18,500
San Jose	17,496	NY Rangers	18,200
Anaheim	17,174	New Jersey	17,625
Calgary	17,135	Boston	17,565
Nashville	17,113	Pittsburgh	16,958
Edmonton	16,839	NY Islanders	16,234

Rank by Age

Western		Eastern	
Edmonton	1974	Pittsburgh	1961
Detroit	1979	NY Rangers	1968
Calgary	1983	NY Islanders	1972
Anaheim	1993	Boston	1995
San Jose	1993	Montreal	1996
Chicago	1994	Ottawa	1996
St. Louis	1994	Buffalo	1996
Nashville	1994	Philadelphia	1996
Vancouver	1995	Tampa Bay	1996
Colorado	1999	Washington	1997
Los Angeles	1999	Florida	1998
Columbus	2000	Toronto	1999
Minnesota	2000	Carolina	1999
Dallas	2001	Atlanta	1999
Phoenix	2003	New Jersey	2007

2007-08 NHL Attendance

Official overall paid attendance for the 2007-08 season according to the NHL accounting office was 21,288,601 (paid tickets) for an average per game crowd of 17,308 over 1,230 games. Teams in each conference are ranked by attendance over 41 home games. Rank column refers to rank in entire league. Numbers in parentheses indicate conference rank in 2006-07.

Western Conference

		Attendance	Rank	Average
1	Detroit (1)	773,696	7	18,870
2	Calgary (2)	790,849	6	19,289
3	Vancouver (3)	763,830	9	18,630
4	Minnesota (4)	761,288	10	18,568
5	Dallas (5)	739,585	12	18,038
6	St. Louis (15)	722,021	13	17,610
7	San Jose (7)	713,863	14	17,411
8	Anaheim (11)	704,932	15	17,193
9	Colorado (6)	690,552	17	16,842
10	Edmonton (9)	690,399	18	16,839
11	Chicago (14)	689,377	19	16,814
12	Los Angeles (8)	680,877	21	16,606
13	Nashville (12)	611,328	27	14,910
14	Columbus (10)	607,757	28	14,823
15	Phoenix (13)	607,638	29	14,820
	TOTAL	10,547,992	—	17,151

Eastern Conference

		Attendance	Rank	Average
1	Montreal (1)	872,193	1	21,273
2	Buffalo (6)	817,956	2	19,950
3	Ottawa (4)	812,665	3	19,821
4	Philadelphia (5)	801,797	4	19,556
5	Toronto (3)	796,803	5	19,434
6	Tampa Bay (2)	766,412	8	18,692
7	N.Y. Rangers (7)	746,200	11	18,200
8	Pittsburgh (9)	700,137	16	17,076
9	Carolina (8)	681,962	17	16,633
10	Atlanta (10)	649,081	22	15,831
11	New Jersey (13)	638,144	23	15,564
12	Washington (14)	634,381	24	15,472
13	Florida (11)	632,881	25	15,436
14	Boston (12)	630,750	26	15,384
15	N.Y. Islanders (15)	559,247	30	13,640
	TOTAL	10,740,609	—	17,464

Home Ice

Listed below are the principal home buildings used through the years by current NHL teams. The largest capacity of each arena is noted in the right hand column. World Hockey Association arenas (1972-79) are included for Edmonton, Hartford (now Carolina), Quebec (now Colorado) and Winnipeg (now Phoenix).

Western Conference

Anaheim Ducks

1993–	Honda Center	17,174

Calgary Flames

1972–80	The Omni (Atlanta)	15,278
1980–83	Calgary Corral	7,424
1983–	Pengrowth Saddledome (1983 capacity—16,674)	17,135

Chicago Blackhawks

1926–29	Chicago Coliseum	5,000
1929–94	Chicago Stadium	17,317
1994–	United Center	20,500

Colorado Avalanche

1972–95	Le Colisee de Quebec	15,399
1995–99	McNichols Arena (Denver)	16,061
1999–	Pepsi Center	18,007

Columbus Blue Jackets

2000–	Nationwide Arena	18,136

Dallas Stars

1967–93	Met Center (Bloomington, MN)	15,174
1993–2000	Reunion Arena (Dallas)	17,001
2001–	American Airlines Center	18,532

Detroit Red Wings

1926–27	Border Cities Arena (Windsor, Ont.)	3,200
1927–79	Olympia Stadium (Detroit)	16,700
1979–	Joe Louis Arena	20,058

Edmonton Oilers

1972–74	Edmonton Gardens	7,200
1974–	Rexall Place (1974 capacity—15,513)	16,839

Los Angeles Kings

1967–99	Great Western Forum (Inglewood) (1967 capacity—15,651)	16,005
1999–	Staples Center	18,118

Note: The Kings played 17 games at Long Beach Sports Arena and LA Sports Arena at the start of the 1967-68 season.

Minnesota Wild

2000–	Xcel Energy Center (St. Paul)	18,064

Nashville Predators

1998–	Sommet Center	17,113

National Hockey League (Cont.)

Phoenix Coyotes

1972–96	Winnipeg Arena	15,393
	(1972 capacity—10,177)	
1996–2002	America West (Phoenix)	16,210
2003–	Jobing.com Arena (Glendale, Ariz.) ..	17,799

St. Louis Blues

1967–94	St. Louis Arena	17,188
1994–	Scottrade Center	19,022

San Jose Sharks

1991–93	Cow Palace (Daly City, CA)	11,100
1993–	HP Pavilion at San Jose	17,496

Vancouver Canucks

1970–95	Pacific Coliseum	16,150
1995–	General Motors Place	18,422

Building Name Changes: ANAHEIM—**Honda Center** originally Arrowhead Pond (1993-2006); CALGARY—**Pengrowth Saddledome** formerly named Canadian Airlines Saddledome (1996-2000) which was originally Olympic Saddledome (1983-95); DALLAS—**Met Center** in Minneapolis originally Metropolitan Sports Center (1967-82); EDMONTON—**Rexall Place** was formerly named Skyreach Centre (1999-2004) which was formerly named Edmonton Coliseum (1995-99) which was originally Northlands Coliseum (1974-94); LOS ANGELES—**Great Western Forum** originally The Forum (1967-88); NASHVILLE—**Sommet Center** originally Nashville Arena (1994-99), then Gaylord Entertainment Center (1999-2007); PHOENIX—**Jobing.com Arena** originally Glendale Arena (2003-07); ST. LOUIS—**Scottrade Center** originally Kiel Center (1994-2000) then Savvis Center (2000-06), **St. Louis Arena** renamed The Checkerdome in 1977, then St. Louis Arena again in 1982; SAN JOSE—**HP Pavilion at San Jose** originally San Jose Arena (1993-2000), then Compaq Center at San Jose (2000-03).

Eastern Conference

Atlanta Thrashers

1999–	Philips Arena	18,545

Boston Bruins

1924–28	Boston Arena	6,200
1928–95	Boston Garden	14,448
1995–	TD Banknorth Garden	17,565

Buffalo Sabres

1970–96	Memorial Auditorium (The Aud)	16,284
	(1970 capacity—10,429)	
1996–	HSBC Arena	18,690

Carolina Hurricanes

1972–73	Boston Garden	14,442
1973–74	Boston Garden (regular season) ...	14,442
	West Springfield (MA) Big E (playoffs)	5,513
1974–75	West Springfield Big E	5,513
	& Hartford (CT) Civic Center ...	10,507
1975–77	Hartford Civic Center	10,507
1977–78	Hartford Civic Center	10,507
	& Springfield (MA) Civic Center ...	7,725
1978–79	Springfield Civic Center	7,725
1979–80	Springfield Civic Center	7,725
	& Hartford Civic Center II ...	14,250
1980–97	Hartford Civic Center II	15,635
1997–99	Greensboro Coliseum	21,500
1999–	RBC Center	18,730

Note: The Hartford Civic Center roof caved in January 1978, forcing the Whalers to move their home games to Springfield, MA for two years.

Florida Panthers

1993–98	Miami Arena	14,703
1998–	BankAtlantic Center	19,250

Montreal Canadiens

1910–21	Jubilee Arena	3,200
1913–18	Montreal Arena (Westmount)	6,000
1918–26	Mount Royal Arena	6,750
1926–68	Montreal Forum I	15,500
1968–96	Montreal Forum II	17,959
1996–	Bell Centre	21,273

New Jersey Devils

1974–76	Kemper Arena (Kansas City)	16,300
1976–82	McNichols Arena (Denver)	15,900
1982-2006	Continental Airlines Arena	19,040
	(1982 capacity—19,023)	
2007–	Prudential Center	17,625

New York Islanders

1972–	Nassau Veterans' Mem. Coliseum ..	16,234
	(1972 capacity—14,500)	

New York Rangers

1925–68	Madison Square Garden III	15,925
1968–	Madison Square Garden IV	18,200
	(1968 capacity—17,250)	

Ottawa Senators

1992–96	Ottawa Civic Center	10,755
1996–	Scotiabank Place (Kanata)	19,311
	(1996 capacity—18,500)	

Philadelphia Flyers

1967–96	CoreStates Spectrum	17,380
	(1967 capacity—14,558)	
1996–	Wachovia Center	18,523

Pittsburgh Penguins

1967–	Mellon Arena	16,958
	(1967 capacity—12,508)	

Tampa Bay Lightning

1992–93	Expo Hall (Tampa)	10,500
1993–96	ThunderDome (St. Petersburg)	26,000
1996–	St. Pete Times Forum	19,758

Toronto Maple Leafs

1917–31	Mutual Street Arena	8,000
1931–99	Maple Leaf Gardens	15,746
	(1931 capacity—13,542)	
1999–	Air Canada Centre	18,819

Washington Capitals

1974–97	USAir Arena (Landover, MD)	18,130
1997–	Verizon Center	18,672

Building Name Changes: BOSTON—**TD Banknorth Garden** originally FleetCenter (1995-2005); BUFFALO—**HSBC Arena** originally Marine Midland Arena (1996-99); CALGARY—**Pengrowth Saddledome** originally Canadian Airlines Arena (1983-2000); CAROLINA—**RBC Center** originally Raleigh Entertainment and Sports Arena (1999-2002); DALLAS—**American Airlines Center** originally Reunion Arena (1993-2000); FLORIDA—**BankAtlantic Center** formerly named Office Depot Center (2002-05) and originally National Car Rental Center (1998-2002); MONTREAL—**Bell Centre** originally Molson Centre (1996-2002); NEW JERSEY—**Continental Airlines Arena** originally Meadowlands Arena (1982-96); OTTAWA—**Scotiabank Place** originally Corel Centre (1996-2006); PHILADELPHIA—**Wachovia Center** originally the CoreStates Center (1996-98), then First Union Center (1998-2003) and **CoreStates Spectrum** originally The Spectrum (1967-94); PITTSBURGH—**Mellon Arena** originally Civic Arena (1967-2000); TAMPA BAY—**St. Pete Times Forum** originally Ice Palace (1996-2002); WASHINGTON—**USAir Arena** originally Capital Centre (1974-93); **Verizon Center** originally MCI Center (1997-2006).

Horse Racing
Triple Crown race tracks

Race	Racetrack	Seats	Infield
Kentucky Derby	Churchill Downs	48,500	65,000
Preakness Stakes	Pimlico Race Course	13,047	60,000
Belmont Stakes	Belmont Park	32,941	N/A

Record crowds: Kentucky Derby—163,628 (1974); Preakness—112,668 (2004); Belmont—120,139 (2004).
Note: Belmont Park does not open infield for Belmont Stakes.

Tennis
Grand Slam center courts

Event	Main Stadium	Seats
Australian Open	Melbourne Park	15,021
French Open	Stade Roland Garros	16,300
Wimbledon	Centre Court	13,813
U.S. Open	Arthur Ashe Stadium	22,547

COLLEGE BASKETBALL

The 50 Largest Arenas

The 50 largest arenas in Division I for the 2008-09 NCAA regular season. Note that (*) indicates part-time home court.

		Seats	Home Team
1	Carrier Dome	33,000	Syracuse
2	Thompson-Boling Arena	24,535	Tennessee
3	Rupp Arena	23,500	Kentucky
4	Marriott Center	22,700	BYU
5	Dean Smith Center	21,750	N. Carolina
6	Verizon Center	20,674	Georgetown*
7	RBC Center	19,722	N.C. State
8	Value City Arena	19,500	Ohio St.
9	Bud Walton Arena	19,200	Arkansas
10	Wachovia Center	19,010	Villanova*
11	Freedom Hall	18,865	Louisville
12	Bradley Center	18,717	Marquette
13	Thomas & Mack Center	18,500	UNLV
14	Madison Square Garden	18,470	St. John's*
15	FedEx Forum	18,400	Memphis
16	University Arena (The Pit)	18,018	New Mexico
17	Prudential Center	18,000	Seton Hall
18	Comcast Center	17,950	Maryland
19	Colonial Center	17,600	South Carolina
20	Qwest Center Omaha	17,560	Creighton
21	Allstate Arena	17,500	DePaul
22	Assembly Hall	17,456	Indiana
23	Herb Kohl Center	17,142	Wisconsin
24	Frank Erwin Center	16,755	Texas
25	Assembly Hall	16,450	Illinois
26	Allen Fieldhouse	16,300	Kansas
27	XL Center	16,294	UConn*
28	Save Mart Center	16,116	Fresno St.
29	JVM Arena	16,000	Jacksonville
30	Carver-Hawkeye Arena	15,500	Iowa
	Times Union Center	15,500	Siena
32	Bryce Jordan Center	15,261	Penn St.
33	John Paul Jones Arena	15,219	Virginia
34	United Spirit Arena	15,098	Texas Tech
35	Breslin Events Center	15,085	Michigan St.
36	Mizzou Arena	15,061	Missouri
37	Coleman Coliseum	15,043	Alabama
38	Arena-Auditorium	15,028	Wyoming
39	Huntsman Center	15,000	Utah
40	LJVM Coliseum	14,665	Wake Forest & Winston-Salem*
41	Williams Arena	14,625	Minnesota
42	McKale Center	14,545	Arizona
43	Maravich Assembly Ctr	14,236	LSU
44	Wells Fargo Arena	14,198	Arizona St.
45	Memorial Gym	14,168	Vanderbilt
46	Mackey Arena	14,123	Purdue
47	James H. Hilton Coliseum	14,092	Iowa St.
48	WVU Coliseum	14,000	West Virginia
49	Crisler Arena	13,751	Michigan
50	Wolstein Center	13,610	Cleveland St.

Division I Conference Home Courts

NCAA Division I conferences for the 2008-09 season. Teams with home games in more than one arena are noted.

America East

	Home Floor	Seats
Albany	SEFCU Arena	4,538
Binghamton	BU Events Center	5,142
Boston University	Case Gym	1,800
	& Agganis Arena	5,687
Hartford	Reich Family Pavilion	3,977
Maine	Alfond Arena	5,712
MD-Balt. County	RAC Arena	4,024
New Hampshire	Lundholm Gym	3,500
Stony Brook	Pritchard Gym	2,000
	& SB Sports Complex	4,103
Vermont	Patrick Gym	3,266

Atlantic Coast

	Home Floor	Seats
Boston College	Silvio O. Conte Forum	8,606
Clemson	Littlejohn Coliseum	9,749
Duke	Cameron Indoor Stadium	9,314
Florida St.	Donald L. Tucker Center	12,200
Georgia Tech	Alexander Memorial Coliseum	9,191
Maryland	Comcast Center	17,950
Miami-FL	BankUnited Center	7,000
North Carolina	Dean Smith Center	21,750
N.C. State	RBC Center	19,722
Virginia	John Paul Jones Arena	15,219
Virginia Tech	Cassell Coliseum	10,052
Wake Forest	LJVM Coliseum	14,665

Atlantic Sun

	Home Floor	Seats
Belmont	Curb Event Center	5,000
Campbell	Carter Gym	1,050
East Tennessee St.	Memorial Center	12,000
Florida Gulf Coast	Alico Arena	4,000
Jacksonville	JVM Arena	16,000
Kennesaw St.	KSU Convocation Center	4,500
Lipscomb	Allen Arena	5,028
Mercer	University Center	3,200
North Florida	UNF Arena	5,800
Stetson	Edmunds Center	5,000
So. Carolina-Upstate	G.B. Hodge Center	1,535

Men's Basketball Attendance Leaders

Schools ranked by average attendance for 2007-08 season.

	Team (2006-07 rank)	Gms	Average
1	Kentucky (1)	18	22,554
2	North Carolina (3)	16	20,497
3	Syracuse (2)	22	20,345
4	Tennessee (4)	16	20,267
5	Louisville (5)	17	19,481
6	Maryland (8)	19	17,950
7	Wisconsin (7)	18	17,190

College Basketball (Cont.)

Atlantic 10

	Home Floor	Seats
Charlotte	Halton Arena	9,105
Dayton	U. of Dayton Arena	13,266
Duquesne	Palumbo Center	6,200
Fordham	Rose Hill Gym	3,470
George Washington	Smith Center	5,000
La Salle	Tom Gola Arena	4,000
Massachusetts	Mullins Center	9,493
Rhode Island	Ryan Center	7,657
Richmond	Robins Center	9,071
St. Bonaventure	Reilly Center	6,000
Saint Louis	Chaifetz Arena	10,600
St. Joseph's	The Palestra*	8,700
Temple	Liacouras Center	10,206
Xavier-OH	Cintas Center	10,250

*St. Joe's will play the 2008-09 season here while renovations of its on-campus facility (Hagan Arena) takes place.

Big East

	Home Floor	Seats
Cincinnati	Fifth Third Arena	13,176
Connecticut	Gampel Pavilion	10,167
	& XL Center	16,294
DePaul	Allstate Arena	17,500
Georgetown	Verizon Center	20,674
Louisville	Freedom Hall	18,865
Marquette	Bradley Center	18,717
Notre Dame	Joyce Center	11,418
Pittsburgh	Petersen Event Center	12,500
Providence	Dunkin Donuts Center	12,993
Rutgers	Louis Brown Athletic Center (The RAC)	9,000
St. John's	Carnesecca Arena	6,008
	& Madison Square Garden	18,470
Seton Hall	Prudential Center	18,000
South Florida	Sun Dome	10,411
Syracuse	Carrier Dome	33,000
Villanova	The Pavilion	6,500
	& Wachovia Center	19,010
West Virginia	WVU Coliseum	14,000

Big Sky

	Home Floor	Seats
Eastern Wash.	Reese Court	6,000
Idaho St.	Holt Arena	8,000
Montana	Dahlberg Arena	7,321
Montana St.	Worthington Arena	7,250
Northern Arizona	Walkup Skydome	7,000
Northern Colorado	Butler-Hancock Sports Pavilion	4,500
Portland St.	Stott Center	1,500
Sacramento St.	Colberg Court	1,200
Weber St.	Dee Events Center	12,000

Big South

	Home Floor	Seats
Charleston Southern	CSU Fieldhouse	789
Coastal Carolina	Kimbel Arena	1,037
Gardner-Webb	Paul Porter Arena	5,000
High Point	Millis Center	2,565
Liberty	Vines Center	9,000
NC-Asheville	Justice Center	1,200
Presbyterian	Pinson Arena	2,000
Radford	Dedmon Center	5,000
VMI	Cameron Hall	5,800
Winthrop	Winthrop Coliseum	6,100

Big Ten

	Home Floor	Seats
Illinois	Assembly Hall	16,450
Indiana	Assembly Hall	17,456
Iowa	Carver-Hawkeye Arena	15,500
Michigan	Crisler Arena	13,751
Michigan St.	Breslin Events Center	15,085
Minnesota	Williams Arena	14,625
Northwestern	Welsh-Ryan Arena	8,117
Ohio St.	Value City Arena	19,500
Penn St.	Bryce Jordan Center	15,261
Purdue	Mackey Arena	14,123
Wisconsin	Kohl Center	17,142

Big 12

	Home Floor	Seats
Baylor	Ferrell Center	10,284
Colorado	Coors Events Conference Ctr.	11,064
Iowa St.	Hilton Coliseum	14,092
Kansas	Allen Fieldhouse	16,300
Kansas St.	Bramlage Coliseum	13,595
Missouri	Mizzou Arena	15,061
Nebraska	Devaney Sports Center	13,500
Oklahoma	Lloyd Noble Center	12,000
Oklahoma St.	Gallagher-Iba Arena	13,611
Texas	Erwin Center	16,755
Texas A&M	Reed Arena	12,500
Texas Tech	United Spirit Arena	15,098

Big West

	Home Floor	Seats
Cal Poly	Mott Gym	3,032
CS-Fullerton	Titan Gym	4,000
CS-Northridge	The Matadome	1,600
Long Beach St.	The Walter Pyramid	5,000
Pacific	Alex G. Spanos Center	6,150
UC-Davis	The Pavilion	7,200
UC-Irvine	Bren Events Center	4,984
UC-Riverside	Student Rec. Center	3,168
UC-Santa Barbara	The Thunderdome	6,000

Colonial Athletic Association

	Home Floor	Seats
Delaware	Bob Carpenter Center	5,000
Drexel	Daskalakis Athletic Center	2,300
George Mason	Patriot Center	10,000
Georgia St.	GSU Sports Arena	4,500
Hofstra	Hofstra Arena	5,124
James Madison	JMU Convocation Center	7,156
Northeastern	Solomon Court	1,500
	& Matthews Arena	6,000
NC-Wilmington	Trask Coliseum	6,100
Old Dominion	Ted Constant Convocation Ctr.	8,650
Towson	Towson Center	5,000
VCU	Siegel Center	7,500
William & Mary	Kaplan Arena	8,600

Conference USA

	Home Floor	Seats
UAB	Bartow Arena	8,508
Central Fla.	UCF Arena	9,465
East Carolina	Minges Coliseum	8,000
Houston	Hofheinz Pavilion	8,479
Marshall	Cam Henderson Center	9,043
Memphis	FedEx Forum	18,400
Rice	Autry Court	5,000
SMU	Moody Coliseum	8,998
Southern Miss	Reed Green Coliseum	8,095
Tulane	Fogelman Arena	3,600
Tulsa	Reynolds Center	8,355
UTEP	Haskins Center	12,000

Longest Home Court Win Streaks

Wins	Team	Seasons	Ended By
129	Kentucky	1943-55	Ga. Tech, 59-58
99	St. Bonaventure	1948-61	Niagara, 87-77
98	UCLA	1970-76	Oregon, 65-45
86	Cincinnati	1957-64	Bradley, 87-77

Horizon League

	Home Floor	Seats
Butler	Hinkle Fieldhouse	11,043
Cleveland St.	Wolstein Center	13,610
Detroit Mercy	Calihan Hall	8,837
IL-Chicago	UIC Pavilion	8,000
Loyola-IL	Gentile Center	5,200
Valparaiso	Athletics-Recreation Center	5,000
WI-Green Bay	Resch Center	10,400
WI-Milwaukee	U.S. Cellular Arena	10,783
Wright St.	Nutter Center	10,632
Youngstown St.	Beeghly Center	6,500

Ivy League

	Home Floor	Seats
Brown	Pizzitola Sports Center	2,800
Columbia	Levien Gymnasium	3,408
Cornell	Newman Arena	4,473
Dartmouth	Leede Arena	2,100
Harvard	Lavietes Pavilion	2,195
Penn	The Palestra	8,700
Princeton	Jadwin Gymnasium	6,854
Yale	Payne Whitney Gym	3,100

Metro Atlantic Athletic

	Home Floor	Seats
Canisius	Koessler Athletic Center	2,176
Fairfield	Arena at Harbor Yard	9,000
Iona	Hynes Athletic Center	2,611
Loyola-MD	Reitz Arena	3,000
Manhattan	Draddy Gymnasium	3,000
Marist	McCann Field House	3,944
Niagara	Gallagher Center	2,400
Rider	Alumni Gymnasium	1,650
St. Peter's	Yanitelli Center	3,200
Siena	Times Union Center	15,500

Mid-American

	Home Floor	Seats
Akron	JAR Arena	5,942
Ball St.	John E. Worthen Arena	11,500
Bowling Green	Anderson Arena	5,000
Buffalo	Alumni Arena	6,100
Central Mich.	Rose Arena	5,200
Eastern Mich.	Convocation Center	8,824
Kent St.	MAC Center	6,327
Miami-OH	Millett Hall	9,200
Northern Illinois	Convocation Center	9,100
Ohio Univ.	Convocation Center	13,000
Toledo	Savage Hall	9,000
Western Mich.	University Arena	5,421

Mid-Eastern Athletic

	Home Floor	Seats
Bethune-Cookman	Moore Gym	3,000
Coppin St.	Coppin Center	1,720
Delaware St.	Memorial Hall	3,000
Florida A&M	Gaither Gym	3,365
Hampton	Hampton Convocation Center	7,500
Howard	Burr Gym	2,200
MD-East.Shore	W.P. Hytche Center	5,500
Morgan St.	Hill Fieldhouse	4,500
Norfolk St.	Echols Hall	7,600
N. Carolina A&T	Corbett Sports Center	6,700
South Carolina St.	SHM Center	3,200
Winston-Salem St.	LJVM Coliseum Annex	4,200

Missouri Valley

	Home Floor	Seats
Bradley	Carver Arena	11,300
Creighton	Qwest Center Omaha	17,560
Drake	Knapp Center	7,002
Evansville	Roberts Stadium	11,600
Illinois St.	Redbird Arena	10,200
Indiana St.	Hulman Center	10,200
Missouri St.	JQH Arena	11,000
Northern Iowa	McLeod Center	7,018
Southern Ill.	SIU Arena	10,000
Wichita St.	Charles Koch Arena	10,400

Mountain West

	Home Floor	Seats
Air Force	Clune Arena	6,002
BYU	Marriott Center	22,700
Colorado St.	Moby Arena	8,745
UNLV	Thomas & Mack Center	18,500
New Mexico	The Pit	18,018
San Diego St.	Cox Arena at the Aztec Bowl	12,414
TCU	Daniel-Meyer Coliseum	7,201
Utah	Jon M. Huntsman Center	15,000
Wyoming	Arena-Auditorium	15,028

Northeast

	Home Floor	Seats
Central Conn. St.	Detrick Gym	3,200
Farleigh Dickinson	Rothman Center	5,000
LIU-Brooklyn	ARW Center	3,000
Monmouth	Boylan Gym	2,500
Mt. St. Mary's	Knott Arena	3,121
Quinnipiac	TD Banknorth Sports Center	3,570
Robert Morris	Sewall Center	3,056
Sacred Heart	Pitt Center	2,100
St. Francis-NY	Pope Center	1,200
St. Francis-PA	DeGol Arena	3,500
Wagner	Spiro Sports Center	2,100

Ohio Valley

	Home Floor	Seats
Austin Peay	Dunn Center	9,000
Eastern Illinois	Lantz Arena	5,300
Eastern Ky.	McBrayer Arena	6,500
Jacksonville St.	Mathews Coliseum	5,500
Morehead St.	Johnson Arena	6,500
Murray St.	Regional Special Events Ctr.	8,602
SE Missouri St.	Show Me Center	7,000
SIU-Edwardsville	Vadalabene Center	4,000
Tennessee-Martin	Skyhawk Arena	6,700
Tennessee St.	Gentry Complex	10,500
Tennessee Tech	Eblen Center	10,152

Pacific-10

	Home Floor	Seats
Arizona	McKale Center	14,545
Arizona St.	Wells Fargo Arena	14,198
California	Haas Pavillion	11,877
Oregon	McArthur Court	9,087
Oregon St.	Gill Coliseum	10,400
Stanford	Maples Pavilion	7,391
UCLA	Pauley Pavilion	12,819
USC	Galen Center	10,258
Washington	Bank of America Arena	10,000
Washington St.	Friel Court	11,566

Future NCAA Final Four Sites

	Men				Women		
Year	Arena	Seats	Location	Year	Arena	Seats	Location
2009	Ford Field	65,000	Detroit	2009	Edward Jones Dome	66,000	St. Louis
2010	Lucas Oil Stadium	63,000	Indianapolis	2010	Alamodome	36,500	San Antonio
2011	Reliant Stadium	69,500	Houston	2011	Lucas Oil Stadium	63,000	Indianapolis

College Basketball (Cont.)

Patriot League

	Home Floor	Seats
American	Bender Arena	4,500
Army	Christl Arena	5,043
Bucknell	Gary A. Sojka Pavilion	4,000
Colgate	Cotterell Court	3,000
Holy Cross	Hart Recreation Center	3,600
Lafayette	Kirby Sports Center	3,500
Lehigh	Stabler Arena	5,600
Navy	Alumni Hall	5,710

Southeastern

Eastern	Home Floor	Seats
Florida	O'Connell Center	12,000
Georgia	Stegeman Coliseum	10,523
Kentucky	Rupp Arena	23,500
South Carolina	Colonial Center	17,600
Tennessee	Thompson-Boling Arena	24,535
Vanderbilt	Memorial Gymnasium	14,168

Western	Home Floor	Seats
Alabama	Coleman Coliseum	15,043
Arkansas	Bud Walton Arena	19,200
Auburn	Beard-Eaves-Memorial Coliseum	10,500
LSU	Maravich Assembly Center	14,164
Mississippi	Tad Smith Coliseum	8,700
Mississippi St.	Humphrey Coliseum	10,500

Southern

	Home Floor	Seats
Appalachian St.	Seby Jones Arena	8,325
Chattanooga	McKenzie Arena	11,218
The Citadel	McAlister Field House	6,200
Coll. of Charleston	John Kresse Arena	5,000
Davidson	Belk Arena	5,700
Elon	Alumni Gym	1,558
Furman	Timmons Arena	5,000
Ga. Southern	Hanner Fieldhouse	5,500
NC-Greensboro	Fleming Gymnasium	2,320
Samford	Corts Arena	5,000
W. Carolina	Ramsey Center	7,286
Wofford	Johnson Arena	3,500

Southland

	Home Floor	Seats
Central Arkansas	Farris Center	5,500
Lamar	Montagne Center	10,080
McNeese St.	Burton Coliseum	8,000
Nicholls St.	Stopher Gym	3,800
Northwestern St.	Prather Coliseum	4,300
Sam Houston St.	Johnson Coliseum	6,172
SE Louisiana	University Center	7,500
S.F. Austin St.	W.R. Johnson Coliseum	7,200
Texas A&M-Corpus Christi	American Bank Center	8,156
TX-Arlington	Texas Hall	4,200
TX-San Antonio	Convocation Center	5,100
Texas St.	Strahan Coliseum	7,200

Southwestern Athletic

	Home Floor	Seats
Alabama A&M	Elmore Gymnasium	6,000
Alabama St.	Joe Reed Acadome	8,000
Alcorn St.	Whitney Complex	7,000
Arkansas-Pine Bluff	K.L. Johnson Complex	4,500
Grambling St.	Health & P.E. Building	7,500
	& Memorial Gym	2,200
Jackson St.	Williams Center	8,000
Miss.Valley St.	Harrison HPER Athletic Complex	6,000
Prairie View A&M	William Nicks Building	5,520
Southern-BR	Clark Activity Center	7,500
TX Southern	Health & P.E. Building	8,100

The Summit League

	Home Floor	Seats
Centenary	Gold Dome	3,000
IUPUI	IUPUI Gym	2,000
IPFW	Memorial Coliseum	11,500
Missouri-KC	Municipal Auditorium	9,827
North Dakota St.	Bison Sports Arena	6,000
Oakland	Athletics Center O'Rena	4,005
Oral Roberts	Mabee Center	10,575
South Dakota St.	Frost Arena	8,500
Southern Utah	Centrum	5,300
Western Ill.	Western Hall	5,139

Sun Belt

	Home Floor	Seats
Arkansas-Little Rock	Stephens Center	5,600
Arkansas St.	Convocation Center	10,563
Denver	Magness Arena	7,200
Fla. Atlantic	FAU Gym	5,000
Florida International	FIU Arena	5,000
LA-Lafayette	The Cajundome	11,550
LA-Monroe	Fant-Ewing Coliseum	7,085
Middle Tennessee	Murphy Center	11,520
New Orleans	Lakefront Arena	8,933
North Texas	The Super Pit	10,032
South Alabama	Mitchell Center	10,000
Troy	Trojan Arena	4,000
Western Ky.	E.A. Diddle Arena	7,326

West Coast

	Home Floor	Seats
Gonzaga	McCarthey Athletic Center	6,000
Loyola Marymount	Gersten Pavilion	4,156
Pepperdine	Firestone Fieldhouse	3,104
Portland	Chiles Center	5,000
St. Mary's-CA	McKeon Pavilion	3,500
San Diego	Jenny Craig Pavilion	5,100
San Francisco	War Memorial Gym	5,300
Santa Clara	Leavey Center	5,000

Western Athletic

	Home Floor	Seats
Boise St.	Taco Bell Arena	12,380
Fresno St.	Save Mart Center	16,116
Hawaii	Stan Sheriff Center	10,300
Idaho	Cowan Spectrum	7,000
Louisiana Tech	Thomas Assembly Center	8,000
Nevada	Lawlor Events Center	11,200
New Mexico St.	Pan American Center	13,071
San Jose St.	The Event Center	5,000
Utah St.	Dee Glen Smith Spectrum	10,270

Independents

	Home Floor	Seats
Cal State Bakersfield	Rabobank Arena	8,848
Chicago St.	Jones Convocation Center	7,000
Houston Baptist	Sharp Gym	1,500
Longwood	Henry I. Willet Jr. Hall	2,522
N.C. Central	McLendon-McDougald Gym	3,056
Savannah St.	Tiger Arena	6,000
Texas-Pan Am	UTPA Fieldhouse	4,000
Utah Valley	McKay Center	8,500
UC Davis	The Pavilion	7,580
N.J.I.T	Fleisher Athletic Center	1,500

COLLEGE FOOTBALL

The 40 Largest I-A Stadiums

The 40 largest stadiums in NCAA Division I-A college football (officially Football Bowl Subdivision) heading into the 2008 season. Note that (*) indicates stadium not on campus.

		Location	Seats	Home Team	Conference	Built	Field
1	Beaver Stadium	University Park, Penn.	107,282	Penn St.	Big Ten	1960	Grass
2	Michigan Stadium	Ann Arbor, Mich.	106,201†	Michigan	Big Ten	1927	Turf
3	Neyland Stadium	Knoxville, Tenn.	104,079	Tennessee	SEC-East	1921	Grass
4	Ohio Stadium	Columbus, Ohio	102,329	Ohio St.	Big Ten	1922	Grass
5	LA Memorial Coliseum*	Los Angeles, Calif.	93,607	USC	Pac-10	1923	Grass
6	Sanford Stadium	Athens, Ga.	92,746	Georgia	SEC-East	1929	Grass
7	Tiger Stadium	Baton Rouge, La.	92,400	LSU	SEC-West	1924	Grass
8	Bryant-Denny Stadium	Tuscaloosa, Ala.	92,158	Alabama	SEC-West	1929	Grass
9	Rose Bowl*	Pasadena, Calif.	91,136	UCLA	Pac-10	1922	Grass
10	Griffin Stadium at Florida Field	Gainesville, Fla.	88,548	Florida	SEC-East	1929	Grass
11	Jordan-Hare Stadium	Auburn, Ala.	87,451	Auburn	SEC-West	1939	Grass
12	Memorial Stadium	Lincoln, Neb.	85,157	Nebraska	Big 12-North	1923	Turf
13	Royal-Texas Memorial Stadium	Austin, Texas	85,123	Texas	Big 12-South	1924	Grass
14	Kyle Field	College Station, Texas	82,600	Texas A&M	Big 12-South	1925	Grass
15	Doak Campbell Stadium	Tallahasse, Fla.	82,300	Florida St.	ACC	1950	Grass
16	Gaylord Family-Oklahoma Memorial Stadium	Norman, Okla.	82,112	Oklahoma	Big 12-South	1924	Grass
17	Notre Dame Stadium	Notre Dame, Ind.	80,795	Notre Dame	Independent	1930	Grass
18	Camp Randall Stadium	Madison, Wis.	80,321	Wisconsin	Big Ten	1917	Turf
19	Memorial Stadium	Clemson, S.C.	80,301	Clemson	ACC	1942	Grass
20	Williams-Brice Stadium	Columbia, S.C.	80,250	South Carolina	SEC-East	1934	Grass
21	Dolphin Stadium	Miami, Fla.	76,500	Miami-FL	ACC-Coastal	1987	Grass
22	Razorback Stadium	Fayetteville, Ark.	76,000	Arkansas	SEC-West	1938	Grass
23	Spartan Stadium	East Lansing, Mich.	75,005	Michigan St.	Big Ten	1957	Turf
24	Memorial Stadium	Berkeley, Calif.	73,347	California	Pac-10	1923	Turf
25	Husky Stadium	Seattle, Wash.	72,500	Washington	Pac-10	1920	Turf
26	Sun Devil Stadium	Tempe, Ariz.	71,706	Arizona St.	Pac-10	1959	Grass
27	Legion Field*	Birmingham, Ala.	71,594	UAB	USA	1927	Grass
28	Qualcomm Stadium	San Diego, Calif.	71,295	San Diego St.	Mountain West	1967	Grass
29	Kinnick Stadium	Iowa City, Iowa	70,585	Iowa	Big Ten	1929	Grass
30	Citrus Bowl*	Orlando, Fla.	70,188	Central Florida	USA	1936	Grass
31	Rice Stadium	Houston, Texas	70,000	Rice	USA	1950	Turf
32	Louisiana Superdome*	New Orleans, La.	69,767	Tulane	USA	1975	Turf
33	Memorial Stadium	Champaign, Ill.	69,249	Illinois	Big Ten	1923	Turf
34	Lincoln Financial Field*	Philadelphia, Penn.	68,532	Temple	Mid-American	2003	Grass
35	Memorial Stadium	Columbia, Mo.	68,349	Missouri	Big 12-North	1926	Turf
36	Commonwealth	Lexington, Ky.	67,606	Kentucky	SEC-East	1973	Grass
37	Lane Stadium	Blacksburg, Va.	66,233	Va. Tech	ACC	1965	Grass
38	Raymond James Stadium*	Tampa, Fla.	65,657	South Florida	Big East	1998	Grass
39	LaVell Edwards Stadium	Provo, Utah	65,524	BYU	Mountain West	1964	Grass
40	Heinz Field*	Pittsburgh, Penn.	64,450	Pittsburgh	Big East	2001	Grass

†The capacity of Michigan Stadium has been temporarily downsized during renovations.

2008 Conference Home Fields

NCAA Division I-A (FBS) conference by conference listing includes member teams heading into the 2008 season. Note that (*) indicates stadium is not on campus. For the purposes of this list anything other than natural grass is called turf.

Atlantic Coast

Atlantic	Stadium	Built	Seats	Field
Boston College	Alumni	1957	44,500	Turf
Clemson	Memorial	1942	80,301	Grass
Florida St.	Doak Campbell	1950	82,300	Grass
Maryland	Byrd	1950	51,500	Grass
N.C. State	Carter-Finley	1966	55,571	Grass
Wake Forest	BB&T Field	1968	31,500	Turf
Coastal	**Stadium**	**Built**	**Seats**	**Field**
Duke	Wallace Wade	1929	33,941	Grass
Georgia Tech	Bobby Dodd	1913	55,000	Grass
Miami-FL	Dolphin Stadium	1987	76,500	Grass
No. Carolina	Kenan Memorial	1927	60,000	Grass
Virginia	Scott	1931	61,500	Grass
Virginia Tech	Lane	1965	66,233	Grass

Big East

	Stadium	Built	Seats	Field
Cincinnati	Nippert	1924	35,000	Turf
Connecticut	Rentschler Field*	2003	40,000	Grass
Louisville	Papa John's Cardinal	1998	42,000	Turf
Pittsburgh	Heinz Field*	2001	64,450	Grass
Rutgers	Rutgers	1994	41,500	Grass
South Florida	Raymond James*	1988	65,657	Grass
Syracuse	Carrier Dome	1980	51,000	Turf
West Virginia	Mountaineer Field	1980	60,000	Turf

Independents

	Stadium	Built	Seats	Field
Army	Michie	1924	39,929	Turf
Navy	Navy-Marine Corps Memorial	1959	30,000	Turf
Notre Dame	Notre Dame	1930	80,795	Grass
Western Ky.	Houchens Industries –L.T. Smith	1968	22,000	Turf

College Football (Cont.)

Big Ten

	Stadium	Built	Seats	Field
Illinois	Memorial	1923	69,249	Turf
Indiana	Memorial	1960	52,354	Turf
Iowa	Kinnick	1929	70,585	Grass
Michigan	Michigan	1927	106,201	Turf
Michigan St.	Spartan	1957	75,005	Grass
Minnesota	HHH Metrodome*	1982	64,172	Turf
Northwestern	Ryan Field	1926	49,256	Grass
Ohio St.	Ohio	1922	102,329	Grass
Penn St.	Beaver	1960	107,282	Grass
Purdue	Ross-Ade	1924	62,500	Grass
Wisconsin	Camp Randall	1917	80,320	Turf

Big 12

North	Stadium	Built	Seats	Field
Colorado	Folsom Field	1924	53,750	Turf
Iowa St.	Jack Trice Field	1975	55,000	Grass
Kansas	Memorial	1921	50,071	Turf
Kansas St.	Snyder Family	1968	52,000	Turf
Missouri	Memorial	1926	68,349	Turf
Nebraska	Memorial	1923	85,157	Turf
South	Stadium	Built	Seats	Field
Baylor	Floyd Casey	1950	50,000	Grass
Oklahoma	Gaylord Family-Oklahoma Memorial	1924	82,112	Grass
Oklahoma St.	Boone Pickens	1920	60,000	Turf
Texas	Royal-Memorial	1924	85,123	Grass
Texas A&M	Kyle Field	1925	82,600	Grass
Texas Tech	Jones AT&T	1947	53,702	Turf

Note: The annual Oklahoma-Texas game has been played at the Cotton Bowl (capacity 68,252) in Dallas since 1937.

Conference USA

East	Stadium	Built	Seats	Field
UAB	Legion Field	1927	71,594	Grass
C. Florida	Bright House Networks	2007	45,031	Grass
E. Carolina	Dowdy-Ficklen	1963	43,000	Grass
Marshall	Joan C. Edwards	1991	38,019	Turf
Memphis	Liberty Bowl*	1965	62,380	Grass
Southern Miss	M.M. Roberts	1976	33,000	Grass
West	Stadium	Built	Seats	Field
Houston	Robertson	1942	32,000	Grass
Rice	Rice	1950	70,000	Turf
SMU	Gerald J. Ford Stadium	2000	32,000	Grass
Tulane	Superdome*	1975	69,767	Turf
Tulsa	H.A. Chapman	1930	35,542	Grass
UTEP	Sun Bowl*	1963	51,500	Turf

Mid-American

	Stadium	Built	Seats	Field
Akron	Rubber Bowl*	1940	35,202	Turf
Ball St.	Scheumann	1967	25,400	Grass
Bowling Green	Doyt Perry	1966	24,000	Turf
Buffalo	U. at Buffalo	1993	29,013	Turf
Central Mich.	Kelly/Shorts	1972	30,199	Turf
Eastern Mich.	Rynearson	1969	30,200	Turf
Kent	Dix	1969	29,287	Turf
Miami-OH	Fred Yager	1983	24,286	Turf
Northern Ill.	Huskie	1965	31,000	Turf
Ohio Univ.	Peden	1929	24,000	Turf
Temple	Lincoln Financial Field*	2003	68,532	Grass
Toledo	Glass Bowl	1937	26,248	Turf
Western Mich.	Waldo	1939	30,200	Turf

Mountain West

	Stadium	Built	Seats	Field
Air Force	Falcon	1962	52,480	Turf
BYU	LaVell Edwards	1964	65,524	Grass
Colorado St.	Hughes	1968	34,000	Turf
New Mexico	University	1960	40,094	Grass
San Diego St.	Qualcomm*	1967	71,295	Grass
TCU	Amon G. Carter	1929	46,083	Grass
UNLV	Sam Boyd*	1971	36,800	Grass
Utah	Rice-Eccles	1927	45,017	Turf
Wyoming	War Memorial	1950	32,580	Turf

Pacific-10

	Stadium	Built	Seats	Field
Arizona	Arizona	1928	57,803	Grass
Arizona St.	Sun Devil	1958	71,706	Grass
California	Memorial	1923	73,347	Turf
Oregon	Autzen	1967	53,800	Turf
Oregon St.	Reser	1953	45,674	Grass
Stanford	Stanford	1921	50,000	Grass
UCLA	Rose Bowl*	1922	91,136	Grass
USC	LA Memorial Coliseum*	1923	93,607	Grass
Washington	Husky	1920	72,500	Turf
Washington St.	Martin	1972	37,600	Turf

Southeastern

East	Stadium	Built	Seats	Field
Florida	Florida Field	1929	88,548	Grass
Georgia	Sanford	1929	92,746	Grass
Kentucky	Commonwealth	1973	67,530	Grass
South Carolina	Williams-Brice	1934	80,250	Grass
Tennessee	Neyland	1921	104,079	Grass
Vanderbilt	Vanderbilt	1981	39,790	Grass
West	Stadium	Built	Seats	Field
Alabama	Bryant-Denny	1929	92,158	Grass
Arkansas	Razorback & War Memorial*	1938 1948	76,000 53,727	Grass Grass
Auburn	Jordan-Hare	1939	87,451	Grass
LSU	Tiger	1924	92,400	Grass
Mississippi	Vaught-Hemingway	1915	60,580	Grass
Miss. St.	Davis Wade	1915	55,082	Grass

Note: EAST–Vanderbilt Stadium was rebuilt in 1981.

Sun Belt

	Stadium	Built	Seats	Field
Arkansas St.	Indian	1974	33,410	Turf
Florida Atlantic	Lockhart	1959	20,450	Grass
Florida International	FIU	1995	23,500	Turf
LA-Lafayette	Cajun Field	1971	31,000	Grass
LA-Monroe	Malone	1978	30,427	Grass
Mid. Tenn. St.	Johnny 'Red' Floyd	1933	30,788	Turf
North Texas	Fouts Field	1952	30,500	Turf
Troy	Movie Gallery Veterans	1950	30,000	Turf

Western Athletic

	Stadium	Built	Seats	Field
Boise St.	Bronco	1970	32,000	Turf
Fresno St.	Bulldog	1980	41,031	Grass
Hawaii	Aloha*	1975	50,000	Turf
Idaho	Kibbie Dome	1975	16,000	Turf
Louisiana Tech	Joe Aillet	1968	30,600	Grass
Nevada	Mackay	1967	31,900	Grass
New Mexico St.	Aggie Memorial	1978	30,343	Grass
San Jose St.	Spartan	1933	30,456	Grass
Utah St.	Romney	1968	30,257	Grass

BUSINESS

Seattle SuperSonics owner **Clay Bennett** is all smiles as he announces his team's move to Oklahoma City in 2008.

SONICS
BOLT

The Sonics franchise was moved from Seattle to Oklahoma City beginning in 2008-09, which begs the question, "Who's Next?"

WHO'S HAVE THUNK IT?

Other than Clay Bennett, that is. The Sonics have left Seattle after 41 years and one NBA title, and hordes of hoops fans in the Pacific Northwest are in mourning.

Can you feel their pain? You should make the effort, because someday you could lose your favorite home team, too. And if you do, you'll want Sonics fans' support just as much they want yours now.

Franchise relocation doesn't happen every day in major professional sports. In most cases, you can always count on your home team to be there for you when you need it. Maybe your favorite club is locked into a long-term lease, has a thriving fan base, just signed a sweet stadium deal in the heart of downtown and has a civic-minded owner. Good for you. It's hard to find greener pastures than that. But if the Seattle situation teaches us anything, it's that nothing lasts forever.

So we took a look around the sports landscape and compiled a list of 10 less-than-stable franchises whose owners just might be watching the developments in Seattle and Oklahoma City with some special interest.

There's nothing scientific about this list. We don't have any more inside info than you do. But to us, these look like the likeliest candidates to be next, even if you'll never hear Bud Selig, Roger Goodell, David Stern or Gary Bettman admit to the possibility on the record. (That just wouldn't be the politically correct thing to do.)

One note: We didn't include the New Jersey Nets on our list because their proposed move to Brooklyn would keep them within the same metropolitan area.

1. Nashville Predators, NHL

It drives the local ownership group crazy whenever anyone suggests the Predators are a prime target to relocate, but they are. Poor fan support, poor corporate support and a major investor (William "Boots" Del Biaggio III) who may go to jail for financial shenanigans all add up to a tenuous future in Nashville, no matter how angry it makes the locals when they hear it.

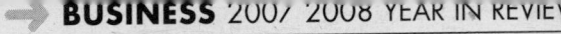

Sonics fans show their displeasure towards owner Clay Bennett's decision to move the team from Seattle to Oklahoma City.

2. New Orleans Hornets, NBA

NBA basketball in New Orleans was a tough sell even before Hurricane Katrina. Now three-plus years removed from the disaster, the long-term viability of the NBA in the Big Easy remains murky. In January 2008, the Hornets negotiated the right to opt out of their New Orleans Arena lease if the average attendance were to fall short of 14,735 from Dec. 1, 2007 to the end of the 2008-09 season. Some saw this new arrangement as the precursor to a move to another city. Indeed, the Hornets averaged only 14,181 in ticket sales during the 2007-08 season, fifth-worst in the league. But New Orleans did see a surge in attendance thanks to its hosting of the 2008 All-Star Game and the team's strong playoff push. And the Hornets recently announced they've sold more than 5,000 new season tickets for the 2008-09 season. The current prevailing view is that the Hornets and the NBA hope to keep the team in New Orleans.

3. Buffalo Bills, NFL

According to The Associated Press, the Bills will receive $78 million —

more than double their calculated 2006 operating income — to play eight games in Toronto the next five years. The Bills say they need to exploit the nearby Canadian market for the team in the NFL's third-smallest market to compete with teams in metropolises. Still, fans worry this market expansion is the first step toward leaving Buffalo, a charter city in the old American Football League. NFL commissioner Roger Goodell dismissed fears that the Bills will relocate to Toronto, adding that he believes the franchise's future is more secure with the additional revenue it generates from playing an annual game north of the border. He also said he expects the team to play in western New York for a long time.

4. Florida Panthers, NHL

Principal owner Alan Cohen has a long and attractive lease at BankAtlantic Center. But at some point, won't he get tired of owning the worst-run team in the NHL in the league's worst market? The Panthers regularly have fewer than 10,000 real human bodies in attendance for games, haven't made the playoffs since 2000 and have won more than one playoff round only once in their history. The real question is whether anyone would notice if the Panthers were gone.

5. Sacramento Kings, NBA

Despite ongoing efforts by the NBA and local authorities to get funding for a new arena in Sacramento, the writing could be on the wall. Arco Arena is the third-smallest in capacity. An attempt to get a $600 million arena deal in Sacramento was shot down by voters in 2006. Other indicators: The Kings finished with the fourth-worst home attendance in the league in 2008, and their owners, the Maloofs, spend much of their time in Las Vegas overseeing their casinos. So it's clear why there is so much speculation about an eventual move to Sin City. The NBA already has tested the Vegas waters by placing the 2007 All-Star Game and other events there, while Sacramento still has yet to host an All-Star Game.

6. Atlanta Thrashers, NHL

Fan support, never strong to begin with, has dwindled as the team has mismanaged viable prospects. Season-ticket support has fallen dramatically. The Thrashers have made the playoffs just once in their history and have failed to win a single postseason game. Ownership squabbles also continue to dog this franchise, which should have been able to take better advantage of the oodles of corporate money that resides in Atlanta.

7. Minnesota Vikings, NFL

The Vikings have proposed a $954 million complex to be built in downtown Minneapolis, and a retractable-roof stadium was at the heart of the proposal. But in December 2007, the Vikings and stadium proponents got the cold shoulder from the Minnesota legislature about the idea of the state funding the new building. Afterward, Vikings owner Zygi Wilf said the issue "needs to be resolved in the near future." Meanwhile, the Vikings' lease at the Metrodome expires in 2011.

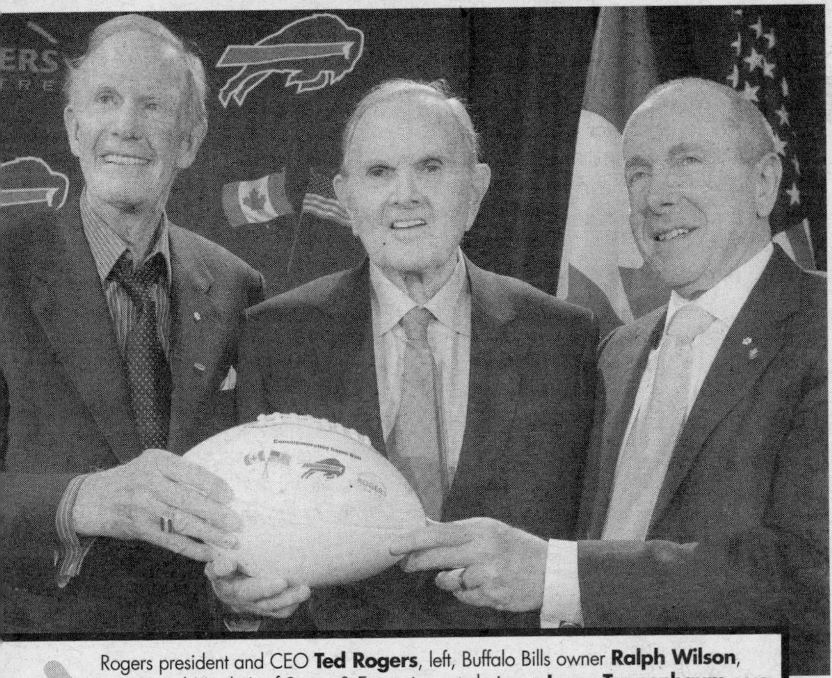

Rogers president and CEO **Ted Rogers**, left, Buffalo Bills owner **Ralph Wilson**, center, and Maple Leaf Sports & Entertainment chairman **Larry Tannenbaum** pose after announcing that the Bills will play eight games in the next five years in Toronto. Some are uneasy that this is a step towards a permanent move across the border.

8. Oakland Athletics, MLB

There have been very few updates on A's owner Lewis Wolff's ambitious proposal to construct a $1.8 billion ballpark village in nearby Fremont, Calif. The proposal has yet to be finalized and is contingent on an environmental report that could take several months to complete, pushing back the potential opening of a new ballpark as far into the future as 2012. Given that the A's have long played second fiddle to the Giants in the Bay Area and have struggled for years to secure any ballpark deal, one would surmise that the A's chances of relocation, while still very, very small, are stronger than most in baseball.

9. Memphis Grizzlies, NBA

Since its inception in Vancouver, the Grizzlies franchise has been troubled. In speculation about which teams might move to Las Vegas, Seattle, Anaheim, San Jose or Kansas City, the Grizzlies often are named. Team owner Michael Heisley has tried in vain to sell the team and remains on the lookout for potential buyers. Since he moved the team to Memphis in 2001, Heisley has been disappointed with fan and sponsor support there. Likewise, local fans have become disenchanted with the management of the team under Heisley. But under any owner, moving the Grizzlies would not be an easy task. Several significant hurdles are in place, including a "shall not relocate" clause that local authorities can try to enforce. The Seattle situation proves that leases and other contractual bonds can be negotiated away, but a move from Memphis does not appear imminent.

10. Tampa Bay Rays, MLB

The Rays recently abandoned their plans to build a $450 million waterfront stadium. That doesn't mean they're automatically a relocation candidate. But despite their 2008 on-field success, they still have less security now than they had while they were pushing through their ballpark proposal.

Also Receiving Consideration

Milwaukee Bucks, NBA

The Bucks have several factors that have led to speculation about an eventual move. Owner Herb Kohl has actively shopped the franchise at times and almost sold it to a group led by Michael Jordan in 2003. Also, Milwaukee is one of the smallest NBA markets. And the Bucks play in the fourth-oldest NBA arena, with a proposed $300 million downtown facility not receiving much local support. With its reasonable payroll and short-term arena lease, the Bucks could be an attractive franchise for a prospective buyer.

New York Islanders, NHL

This storied franchise plays in one of the worst buildings in the NHL — Pittsburgh is close, but a new facility is in the works there — and there seems to be no real timetable for either retrofitting crumbling Nassau Veterans Memorial Coliseum or building a new facility in the Uniondale, N.Y., area.

Owner Charles Wang remains committed to the market. But at some point, the situation simply becomes unworkable, and both the league and the team might be better off packing up those Stanley Cup banners and heading elsewhere.

San Diego Chargers, NFL

The team's already-constant complaints about Qualcomm Stadium have grown louder (is that possible?) ever since the Padres moved out of Qualcomm and into their beautiful new baseball digs at Petco Park. The team is exploring plans to build a $1.2 billion complex in nearby Chula Vista, Calif., but that plan faces obstacles. Chargers ownership maintains that it wants to keep the team in San Diego, despite the $800 million Los Angeles-area stadium plan unveiled by Ed Roski — a close friend of the Spanos family, which owns the Chargers.

Jacksonville Jaguars, NFL

Funny thing about the Jaguars in Jacksonville: They win but still can't consistently sell out in college-football-obsessed Florida. According to the Florida Times-Union, the Jaguars were ranked 28th out of 32 teams in NFL revenue last season. The team's home, Jacksonville Municipal Stadium, doesn't have a naming-rights deal. But the Sports Business Daily reports that Jaguars season-ticket renewals are at a record 84 percent, an increase from 75 percent in 2007.

Florida Marlins, MLB

Long a strong candidate for relocation, the Marlins appear to have a reasonably secure ballpark deal in place. The new stadium, to be built on the site of the Orange Bowl, is scheduled to open in 2011.

Source: ESPN.com

2007-08 Top 50 Network TV Sports Events

al 2007-08 network television ratings for the top nationally telecast sports events, according to Nielsen Media Research.
vers period from Sept. 1, 2007 through Aug. 31, 2008. Events are listed with ratings points and audience share; each
ings point represents 1,128,000 households and shares indicate percentage of TV sets in use.
Multiple entries: SPORTS—NFL Football (34); Summer Olympics (13); Major League Baseball (2). NETWORKS—FOX
d NBC (18); CBS (15).

	Date	Net	Rtg/Sh
Super Bowl XLII			
(Giants vs Patriots) 2/3/08	FOX	43.1/65
NFC Championship Game			
(Giants at Packers) 1/20/08	FOX	29.0/43
AFC Championship Game			
(Chargers at Patriots) . . .1/20/08	CBS	25.7/46
NFC Div. Playoff Game			
(Giants at Cowboys) 1/13/08	FOX	23.6/40
AFC Div. Playoff Game			
(Chargers at Colts) 1/13/08	CBS	20.2/41
NFL Regular Season Late Game			
(Patriots at Colts/various) .11/4/07	CBS	20.1/36
Summer Olympics			
(Women's gymnastics team final & men's swimming 200 fly, 4x200 relay) . . .8/12/08	NBC	20.0/34
NFL Regular Season Late Game			
(Various teams) 12/9/07	CBS	18.4/32
Summer Olympics			
(Women's gymnastics, men's & women's swimming) . . .8/10/08	NBC	18.1/31
NFL Regular Season Late Game			
(Various teams) 10/14/07	CBS	18.0/34
AFC Div. Playoff Game			
(Jaguars at Patriots) 1/12/08	CBS	17.9/30
Summer Olympics			
(Women's gymnastics, men's & women's swimming, w beach volleyball) 8/14/08	NBC	17.9/30
Summer Olympics			
(Men's & women's swimming, men's track & field 100m final) 8/16/08	NBC	17.8/32
Summer Olympics			
(Men's gymnastics, Men's & women's swimming, beach volleyball) 8/11/08	NBC	17.6/29
NFC Div. Playoff Game			
(Seahawks at Packers) . . .1/12/08	FOX	17.0/34
AFC Wild Card Game			
(Titans at Chargers) 1/6/08	CBS	16.7/30
Summer Olympics			
(Men's gymnastics, Men's & women's swimming, w beach volleyball) 8/13/08	NBC	16.7/28
Summer Olympics			
(Men's & women's gymnastics, Men's & women's track & field 8/19/08	NBC	16.3/27
Summer Olympics			
(Men's & women's gymnastics, women's track & field, women's diving) 8/17/08	NBC	16.0/27
Summer Olympics			
(Men's & women's gymnastics, w beach volleyball semis) 8/18/08	NBC	15.8/26
NFL Regular Season Late Game			
(Various teams) 11/11/07	FOX	15.6/30
Summer Olympics			
(Men's & women's swimming, men's track & field) 8/15/08	NBC	15.4/28
Summer Olympics			
(Men's & women's track & field, w beach volleyball gold medal match) 8/20/08	NBC	15.2/26
NFC Wild Card Game			
(Giants at Buccaneers) 1/6/08	FOX	15.1/33
NFL Regular Season Late Game			
(Various teams) 11/18/07	FOX	15.0/28
AFC Wild Card Game			
(Jaguars at Steelers) 1/5/08	NBC	15.0/25
NFL Regular Season Late Game			
(Various teams) 12/16/07	FOX	14.6/26

	Date	Net	Rtg/Sh
28 **NFL Regular Season Late Game**			
(Various teams) 10/21/07	FOX	14.5/29
29 **Allstate BCS Championship Game**			
(LSU vs Ohio St.) 1/7/08	FOX	14.4/22
30 **NFC Wild Card Game**			
(Redskins at Seahawks) . . .1/5/08	NBC	14.0/27
31 **Summer Olympics**			
(Men's & women's swimming, men's gymnastics, w beach volleyball) 8/9/08	NBC	13.9/27
32 **NFL Regular Season Late Game**			
(Various teams) 12/2/07	FOX	13.8/25
Summer Olympics			
(Men's & women's track & field, women's diving, men's beach volleyball) . .8/21/08	NBC	13.8/23
34 **NFL Regular Season Late Game**			
(Various teams) 11/25/07	CBS	13.7/25
35 **NFL Regular Season Late Game**			
(Various teams) 9/9/07	FOX	13.6/26
36 **NFL Sunday Night Football**			
(Eagles at Patriots) 11/25/07	NBC	13.4/21
37 **NFL Regular Season Early Game**			
(Various teams) 12/016/07	CBS	13.3/27
38 **NFL Regular Season Late Game**			
(Various teams) 12/30/07	FOX	13.2/25
NFL Thanksgiving Day Early Game			
(Packers at Lions) 11/22/07	FOX	13.2/33
40 **NFL Regular Season Late Game**			
(Various teams) 10/28/07	FOX	13.1/26
41 **NFL Regular Season Early Game**			
(Various teams) 12/9/07	FOX	12.9/27
42 **MLB World Series—Game 4**			
(Red Sox at Rockies) . . .10/28/07	FOX	12.6/21
43 **NFL Regular Season Late Game**			
(Various teams) 12/23/07	CBS	12.5/26
44 **NFL Regular Season Late Game**			
(Various teams) 9/30/07	CBS	12.2/24
45 **NCAA Men's Basketball Championship Game**			
(Kansas vs Memphis) 4/7/08	CBS	12.1/20
46 **NFL Thanksgiving Day Late Game**			
(Jets at Cowboys) 11/22/07	CBS	12.0/31
47 **NFL Sunday Night Football**			
(Cowboys at Bears) 9/23/07	NBC	11.8/19
48 **MLB ALCS—Game 7**			
(Indians at Red Sox) . . .10/21/07	FOX	11.7/19
49 **NFL Regular Season Early Game**			
(Various teams) 9/23/07	CBS	11.6/26
NFL Regular Season Early Game			
(Various teams) 12/2/07	CBS	11.6/24
NFL Sunday Night Football			
(Giants at Cowboys) 9/9/07	NBC	11.6/19

Other top non-NFL TV sports events

	Date	Net	Rtg/Sh
56 **Rose Bowl**			
(Illinois vs USC) 1/1/08	ABC	11.1/19
MLB World Series—Game 2			
(Rockies at Red Sox) . . .10/25/07	FOX	11.1/18
61 **NBA Finals—Game 6**			
(Lakers at Celtics) 6/17/08	ABC	10.7/19
Summer Olympics			
(Men's & women's track & field, men's diving) 8/22/08	NBC	10.7/19
64 **MLB World Series—Game 1**			
(Rockies at Red Sox) . . .10/24/07	FOX	10.5/18

All-Time Top-Rated TV Programs

NFL Football dominates television's All-Time Top-Rated 50 Programs with 23 Super Bowls and the 1981 NFC Champions Game making the list. Rankings based on surveys taken from January 1961 through August 31, 2008; include only sponsor programs seen on individual networks; and programs under 30 minutes scheduled duration are excluded. Programs are lis with ratings points, audience share and number of households watching, according to Nielsen Media Research.

Multiple entries: The Super Bowl (23); "Roots" (7); "The Beverly Hillbillies" and "The Thorn Birds" (3); "The Bob Ho Christmas Show," "The Ed Sullivan Show," "Gone With The Wind" and 1994 Winter Olympics (2).

	Program	Episode/Game	Net	Date	Rating	Share	Househol
1	M*A*S*H (series)	Final episode	CBS	2/28/83	**60.2**	77	50,150,0
2	Dallas (series)	"Who Shot J.R.?"	CBS	11/21/80	**53.3**	76	41,470,0
3	Roots (mini-series)	Part 8	ABC	1/30/77	**51.1**	71	36,380,0
4	Super Bowl XVI	49ers 26, Bengals 21	CBS	1/24/82	**49.1**	73	40,020,0
5	Super Bowl XVII	Redskins 27, Dolphins 17	NBC	1/30/83	**48.6**	69	40,480,0
6	XVII Winter Olympics	Women's Figure Skating	CBS	2/23/94	**48.5**	64	45,690,0
7	Super Bowl XX	Bears 46, Patriots 10	NBC	1/26/86	**48.3**	70	41,490,0
8	Gone With the Wind (movie)	Part 1	NBC	11/7/76	**47.7**	65	33,960,0
9	Gone With the Wind (movie)	Part 2	NBC	11/8/76	**47.4**	64	33,750,0
10	Super Bowl XII	Cowboys 27, Broncos 10	CBS	1/15/78	**47.2**	67	34,410,0
11	Super Bowl XIII	Steelers 35, Cowboys 31	NBC	1/21/79	**47.1**	74	35,090,0
12	Bob Hope Special	Christmas Show	NBC	1/15/70	**46.6**	64	27,260,0
13	Super Bowl XVIII	Raiders 38, Redskins 9	CBS	1/22/84	**46.4**	71	38,800,0
	Super Bowl XIX	49ers 38, Dolphins 16	ABC	1/20/85	**46.4**	63	39,390,0
15	Super Bowl XIV	Steelers 31, Rams 19	CBS	1/20/80	**46.3**	67	35,330,0
16	Super Bowl XXX	Cowboys 27, Steelers 17	NBC	1/28/96	**46.0**	68	44,114,4
	ABC Theater (special)	"The Day After"	ABC	11/20/83	**46.0**	62	38,550,0
18	Roots (mini-series)	Part 6	ABC	1/28/77	**45.9**	66	32,680,0
	The Fugitive (series)	Final episode	ABC	8/29/67	**45.9**	72	25,700,0
20	Super Bowl XXI	Giants 39, Broncos 20	CBS	1/25/87	**45.8**	66	40,030,0
21	Roots (mini-series)	Part 5	ABC	1/27/77	**45.7**	71	32,540,0
22	Super Bowl XXVIII	Cowboys 30, Bills 13	NBC	1/30/94	**45.5**	66	42,860,0
	Cheers (series)	Final episode	NBC	5/20/93	**45.5**	64	42,360,5
24	The Ed Sullivan Show	Beatles' 1st appearance	CBS	2/9/64	**45.3**	60	23,240,0
25	Super Bowl XXVII	Cowboys 52, Bills 17	NBC	1/31/93	**45.1**	66	41,988,1
26	Bob Hope Special	Christmas Show	NBC	1/14/71	**45.0**	61	27,050,0
27	Roots (mini-series)	Part 3	ABC	1/25/77	**44.8**	68	31,900,0
28	Super Bowl XXXII	Broncos 31, Packers 24	NBC	1/25/98	**44.5**	67	43,630,0
29	Super Bowl XI	Raiders 32, Vikings 14	NBC	1/9/77	**44.4**	73	31,610,0
	Super Bowl XV	Raiders 27, Eagles 10	NBC	1/25/81	**44.4**	63	34,540,0
31	Super Bowl VI	Cowboys 24, Dolphins 3	CBS	1/16/72	**44.2**	74	27,450,0
32	XVII Winter Olympics	Women's Figure Skating	CBS	2/25/94	**44.1**	64	41,540,0
	Roots (mini-series)	Part 2	ABC	1/24/77	**44.1**	62	31,400,0
34	The Beverly Hillbillies (series)	Regular episode	CBS	1/8/64	**44.0**	65	22,570,0
35	Roots (mini-series)	Part 4	ABC	1/26/77	**43.8**	66	31,190,0
	The Ed Sullivan Show	Beatles' 2nd appearance	CBS	2/16/64	**43.8**	60	22,445,0
37	Super Bowl XXIII	49ers 20, Bengals 16	NBC	1/22/89	**43.5**	68	39,320,0
38	The Academy Awards	John Wayne wins Oscar	ABC	4/7/70	**43.4**	78	25,390,0
39	Super Bowl XXXI	Packers 35, Patriots 21	FOX	1/26/97	**43.3**	65	42,000,0
	Super Bowl XXXIV	Rams 23, Titans 16	ABC	1/30/00	**43.3**	63	43,618,0
41	The Thorn Birds (mini-series)	Part 3	ABC	3/29/83	**43.2**	62	35,990,0
42	Super Bowl XLII	Giants 17, Patriots 14	FOX	2/3/08	**43.1**	65	48,655,0
	The Thorn Birds (mini-series)	Part 4	ABC	3/30/83	**43.1**	62	35,900,0
44	NFC Championship Game	49ers 28, Cowboys 27	CBS	1/10/82	**42.9**	62	34,940,0
45	The Beverly Hillbillies (series)	Regular episode	CBS	1/15/64	**42.8**	62	21,960,0
46	Super Bowl VII	Dolphins 14, Redskins 7	NBC	1/14/73	**42.7**	72	27,670,0
47	The Thorn Birds (mini-series)	Part 2	ABC	3/28/83	**42.5**	59	35,400,0
48	Super Bowl IX	Steelers 16, Vikings 6	NBC	1/12/75	**42.4**	72	29,040,0
	The Beverly Hillbillies (series)	Regular episode	CBS	2/26/64	**42.4**	60	21,750,0
50	Five shows tied with a 42.3 rating.						

All-Time Top-Rated Cable TV Sports Events

All-time cable television for sports events, according to ESPN, Turner Sports research and *The Sports Business Daily*. Covers period from Sept. 1, 1980 through Aug. 31, 2008.

NFL Telecasts

		Date	Net	Rtg
1	Chicago at Minnesota	12/6/87	ESPN	17.6
2	Detroit at Miami	12/25/94	ESPN	15.1
3	Chicago at Minnesota	12/3/89	ESPN	14.7
4	Cleveland at San Fran	11/29/87	ESPN	14.2
5	Pittsburgh at Houston	12/30/90	ESPN	13.8

Non-NFL Telecasts

		Date	Net	Rtg
1	MLB: Chicago (NL)-St. Louis	9/7/98	ESPN	9.5
2	NBA: Detroit-Boston	6/1/88	TBS	8.8
3	NBA: Chicago-Detroit	5/31/89	TBS	8.2
4	NBA: Detroit-Boston	5/26/88	TBS	8.1
	MLB: Giants-Chicago (NL)	9/28/98	ESPN	8.0

Note: The September 15, 2008 *Monday Night Football* game on ESPN between the Cowboys and Eagles earned a 13.3 rating and was watched in 12,953,000 households, the largest audience in the history of cable television. The total broke the record of 12,529,000 households, held by the Patriots-Ravens *Monday Night Football* game on December 3, 2007.

Screen Gems

The Top-Grossing Sports Movies of All Time (as of Sept. 20, 2008)

Movie (Year)	Domestic Revenue	Movie (Year)	Domestic Revenue
1 The Waterboy (1998)	$161,491,646	11 The Karate Kid, Part II (1986)	$115,103,979
2 The Longest Yard (2005)	158,119,460	12 Dodgeball: A True Underdog	
3 Jerry Maguire (1996)	153,952,592	Story (2004)	114,326,736
4 Talladega Nights: The Ballad		13 A League of Their Own (1992)	107,533,928
of Ricky Bobby (2006)	148,213,377	14 Million Dollar Baby (2004)	100,492,203
5 Rocky IV (1985)	127,873,716	15 The Karate Kid (1984)	90,815,558
6 Rocky III (1982)	125,049,125	16 The Game Plan (2007)	90,636,983
7 Seabiscuit (2003)	120,277,854	17 Space Jam (1996)	90,418,342
8 Blades of Glory (2007)	118,594,548	18 Rocky II (1979)	85,182,160
9 Rocky (1976)	117,235,147	19 Days of Thunder (1990)	82,670,733
10 Remember the Titans (2000)	115,654,751	20 Nacho Libre (2006)	80,197,993

Source: boxofficemojo.com and 23 Ways To Get To First Base: The ESPN Uncyclopedia

Oscar Might

Sports Movies Nominated For Best Picture

Movie	Sport	Year	Movie	Sport	Year
The Champ	Boxing	1931	Raging Bull	Boxing	1980
Here Comes Mr. Jordan	Boxing	1941	Chariots of Fire	Track	1981*
The Pride of the Yankees	Baseball	1942	Field of Dreams	Baseball	1989
The Hustler	Billiards	1961	Jerry Maguire	Football	1996
Rocky	Boxing	1976*	Seabiscuit	Horse Racing	2003
Heaven Can Wait	Football	1978	Million Dollar Baby	Boxing	2004
Breaking Away	Cycling	1979	* won Academy Award		

Saturday Night Live Hosts

Sports personalities who have hosted NBC's *Saturday Night Live* since the show's first telecast in 1975.

Athlete	Sport	Year	Athlete	Sport	Year
Michael Phelps	Swimming	2008	Michael Jordan	Basketball	1991
LeBron James	Basketball	2007	George Steinbrenner	Baseball	1990
Peyton Manning	Football	2007	Chris Evert	Tennis	1989
Lance Armstrong	Cycling	2005	Wayne Gretzky	Hockey	1989
Tom Brady	Football	2005	Joe Montana	Football	1987
Andy Roddick	Tennis	2003	Bob Uecker	Baseball	1984
Jeff Gordon	Auto Racing	2003	Alex Karras	Football	1985
Jonny Mosely	Freestyle Skiing	2002	Howard Cosell	Announcing	1985
Derek Jeter	Baseball	2001	John Madden	Football	1982
Deion Sanders	Football	1995	Bill Russell	Basketball	1979
George Foreman	Boxing	1994	O.J. Simpson	Football	1978
Charles Barkley	Basketball	1993	Fran Tarkenton	Football	1977

Source: NBC.com

Visionary Moments

Sports Television Firsts

The first sporting event ever televised in the United States was a baseball game between Columbia University and Princeton University on May 17, 1939. Here are some other firsts in televised sports:

BOXING
Max Baer vs Lou Nova, Yankee Stadium; June 1, 1939

TENNIS
Eastern Grass Court championship matches; Westchester (New York) Country Club, August 9, 1939

FOOTBALL
Fordham University vs Waynesburg College; New York City, September 30, 1939

HOCKEY
New York Rangers vs Montreal Canadiens; Madison Square Garden, February 28, 1940

BASKETBALL
Fordham University vs University of Pittsburgh; Madison Square Garden, February 28, 1940

TRACK & FIELD
AAAA Track & Field Championships; Madison Square Garden, March 2, 1940

OLYMPICS
Winter Games, Squaw Valley (California), February 18, 1960

Source: 23 Ways To Get To First Base: The ESPN Uncyclopedia

ESPN The Magazine's Ultimate Standings
Fan Satisfaction Rankings

ESPN The Magazine, in conjunction with SportsNation, surveyed over 80,000 fans in order to rank the current 122 major men's professional sports franchises (MLB, NFL, NBA, NHL). The following eight criteria were used:

Bang for the Buck: Revenues directly from fans divided by wins in the past three years; **Fan Relations**: Ease of access to players, coaches and management; **Ownership**: Honesty; loyalty to players and city; **Affordability**: Price of tickets, parking and concessions; **Stadium Experience**: Friendliness of environment, quality of game-day promotions; **Players**: Effort on the field, likability off it; **Coach/Manager**: Strong on-field leadership; **Title Track**: Titles already won or expected soon.

Results from last four years are provided. Note that no NHL teams were ranked in 2005 and 2006 due to the 2004-05 lockout.

Team	2005	2006	2007	2008
Indianapolis Colts	3	4	4	1
San Antonio Spurs	2	1	2	2
New Orleans Hornets	83	55	44	3
Green Bay Packers	8	30	23	4
Anaheim Ducks	—	—	6	5
Los Angeles Angels	5	5	7	6
Detroit Tigers	53	76	12	7
Detroit Pistons	1	2	5	8
Jacksonville Jaguars	28	16	25	9
Arizona Diamondbacks	32	51	43	10
New England Patriots	4	10	31	11
Detroit Red Wings	—	—	18	12
Milwaukee Brewers	45	17	16	13
St. Louis Blues	—	—	63	14
Utah Jazz	20	35	26	15
Cleveland Indians	42	25	33	16
Carolina Hurricanes	—	—	10	17
Seattle Seahawks	59	24	13	18
Dallas Mavericks	13	15	3	19
Golden State Warriors	80	58	89	20
Atlanta Braves	16	9	15	21
Dallas Stars	—	—	20	22
Buffalo Sabres	—	—	1	23
Pittsburgh Penguins	—	—	35	24
Pittsburgh Steelers	9	3	9	25
Colorado Rockies	85	75	85	26
San Jose Sharks	—	—	22	27
Phoenix Suns	21	20	11	28
Ottawa Senators	—	—	34	29
Portland Trail Blazers	79	89	92	30
Minnesota Wild	—	—	29	31
Colorado Avalanche	—	—	40	32
Houston Rockets	56	21	27	33
San Diego Chargers	37	45	59	34
Washington Wizards	62	59	47	35
Tampa Bay Lightning	—	—	17	36
Nashville Predators	—	—	8	37
Phoenix Coyotes	—	—	71	38
Minnesota Twins	29	38	14	39
New Jersey Devils	—	—	54	40
Denver Nuggets	48	29	51	41
Orlando Magic	44	77	58	42
Boston Celtics	63	70	112	43
Toronto Raptors	75	84	45	44
Washington Capitals	—	—	65	45
Dallas Cowboys	39	27	82	46
Charlotte Bobcats	—	—	80	47
New York Giants	71	33	101	48
Cleveland Cavaliers	34	46	36	49
Tennessee Titans	19	34	62	50
Kansas City Royals	58	74	68	51
Columbus Blue Jackets	—	—	76	52
New Orleans Saints	87	91	42	53
Calgary Flames	—	—	38	54
San Diego Padres	47	49	64	55
Houston Texans	—	79	93	56
Buffalo Bills	15	31	56	57
Chicago White Sox	70	13	28	58
Cincinnati Reds	54	60	57	59
St. Louis Cardinals	11	7	19	60
Los Angeles Lakers	49	61	67	61
Philadelphia Phillies	78	83	69	62
Washington Nationals	68	64	78	63
Cleveland Browns	90	66	116	64
New York Yankees	17	28	48	65
Philadelphia Eagles	6	18	49	66
Toronto Blue Jays	67	47	41	67
Tampa Bay Buccaneers	36	22	72	68
Houston Astros	27	11	30	69
Atlanta Thrashers	—	—	55	70
Philadelphia Flyers	—	—	96	71
Denver Broncos	26	14	24	72
Montreal Canadiens	—	—	70	73
New York Islanders	—	—	87	74
Tampa Bay Rays	73	85	86	75
Baltimore Ravens	22	54	32	76
Los Angeles Dodgers	52	82	60	77
Carolina Panthers	12	8	37	78
New York Rangers	—	—	83	79
Edmonton Oilers	—	—	46	80
Chicago Bears	69	43	50	81
Los Angeles Clippers	65	78	77	82
Seattle Mariners	61	72	90	83
Arizona Cardinals	82	86	97	84
Oakland Athletics	38	42	52	85
Atlanta Hawks	88	87	113	86
Miami Heat	18	23	21	87
Chicago Blackhawks	—	—	118	88
Boston Red Sox	46	62	88	89
Texas Rangers	31	41	53	90
Vancouver Canucks	—	—	74	91
Washington Redskins	60	37	108	92
New York Mets	86	67	61	93
Philadelphia 76ers	40	48	115	94
Chicago Cubs	57	73	98	95
Sacramento Kings	23	40	110	96
Chicago Bulls	74	44	39	97
Florida Panthers	—	—	107	98
Florida Marlins	25	53	84	99
New Jersey Nets	76	65	104	100
Kansas City Chiefs	24	26	66	101
San Francisco 49ers	89	81	100	102
Pittsburgh Pirates	64	68	75	103
San Francisco Giants	35	56	91	104
New York Jets	41	63	79	105
Boston Bruins	—	—	117	106
Los Angeles Kings	—	—	103	107
Miami Dolphins	55	36	73	108
Milwaukee Bucks	51	52	94	109
Minnesota Vikings	81	90	119	110
St. Louis Rams	66	50	81	111
Indiana Pacers	10	12	114	112
Memphis Grizzlies	30	32	95	113
Baltimore Orioles	50	80	105	114
Cincinnati Bengals	43	19	102	115
Seattle SuperSonics	33	57	111	116
Oakland Raiders	84	71	121	117
Minnesota Timberwolves	14	39	109	118
Atlanta Falcons	7	6	106	119
Detroit Lions	72	69	122	120
Toronto Maple Leafs	—	—	99	121
New York Knicks	77	88	120	122

Costliest Collectibles

Listed are the most expensive pieces of sports memorabilia ever sold, according to the following auction houses and other sources: Lelands, Guernsey's, Sotheby's, Christie's, Gotta Have It! Collectibles, Grey Flannel Auctions, Mastro Auctions and Hunt Auctions. Figures are as of Sept. 30, 2008. (*) indicates estimated amount paid.

	Item	Sold For
1	Mark McGwire 70th HR ball, 1998 HR chase (purchased by Todd McFarlane)	$3,005,000
2	Honus Wagner 1909 American Tobacco Co. T206 PSA-8 baseball card (sale 2007)	2,800,000
3	Honus Wagner 1909 American Tobacco Co. T206 PSA-8 baseball card (sale 2007)	2,350,000
4	Honus Wagner 1909 American Tobacco Co. T206 PSA-8 baseball card (sale 2008)	1,620,000
5	Honus Wagner 1909 American Tobacco Co. T206 PSA-8 baseball card (sale 2000)	1,265,000
	Babe Ruth bat, first HR in Yankee Stadium	1,265,000
7	Babe Ruth sale contract (Red Sox to Yankees)	996,000
8	Babe Ruth 1933 inaugural All-Star Game HR ball	805,000
9	Barry Bonds 700th HR ball	804,129
10	SGC co. 1914 Cracker Jack complete baseball card set	800,000
11	Babe Ruth 1934 Tour of Japan Game Worn Uniform	787,859
12	Barry Bonds record-breaking 756th home run ball	752,467
13	Hank Aaron 755th home run ball	650,000
14	Honus Wagner 1909 American Tobacco Co. T206 PSA-8 baseball card (sale 1996)	640,500
15	Shoeless Joe Jackson "Black Betsy" game-used bat (sale 2001)	577,610
16	Barry Bonds 73rd HR (purchased by Todd McFarlane)	517,500
17	Honus Wagner 1909 American Tobacco Co. T206 PSA-8 baseball card (sale 1995)	500,000*
18	1921 Bath Ruth bat used in hitting record setting 59th HR	483,000
19	1869 Cincinnati Red Stockings Trophy Ball Collection (17)	473,383
20	Honus Wagner American Tobacco Co. "Frank Nagy" T206 GAI 3.5 baseball card	456,057

Top-Selling NFL Jerseys

Listed are the 25 top-selling jerseys at NFLShop.com between April 1 and August 11, 2008. Sourse: NFLShop.com

1 Brett Favre, NY Jets
2 Brett Favre, Green Bay
3 Tony Romo, Dallas
4 Tom Brady, New England
5 Eli Manning, NY Giants
6 Peyton Manning, Indianapolis
7 Adrian Peterson, Minnesota
8 LaDainian Tomlinson, San Diego
9 Marion Barber, Dallas
10 Darren McFadden, Oakland
11 Ben Roethlisberger, Pittsburgh
12 Brian Urlacher, Chicago
13 Devin Hester, Chicago
14 Randy Moss, New England
15 Troy Polamalu, Pittsburgh
16 Michael Strahan, NY Giants
17 Brian Westbrook, Philadelphia
18 Terrell Owens, Dallas
19 Osi Umenyiora, NY Giants
20 Jason Witten, Dallas
21 DeMarcus Ware, Dallas
22 Reggie Bush, New Orleans
23 Patrick Willis, San Francisco
24 Jay Cutler, Denver
25 JaMarcus Russell, Oakland

Top-Selling NBA Jerseys (1998-2008)

Listed are the top 10 jersey sales since the NBA store in New York City opened its doors on Sept. 18, 1998

1 Michael Jordan
2 Kobe Bryant
3 Allen Iverson
4 LeBron James
5 Shaquille O'Neal
6 Tracy McGrady
7 Dwyane Wade
8 Jason Kidd
9 Vince Carter
10 Tim Duncan

Teams Bought in 2008

Major league clubs acquiring new majority owners from Oct. 1, 2007 through Sept. 30, 2008.

NHL Hockey

Edmonton Oilers: On June 19 the NHL's Board of Governors unanimously approved the sale of the Oilers from the 34-member Edmonton Investors Group to Rexall pharmacy billionaire Daryl Katz. The deal is said to be worth approximately $200 million. Katz had made five previous offers to purchase the team over a ten-month span and finally came through with an offer EIG couldn't pass up.

Nashville Predators: On November 29, 2007 the NHL's Board of Governors approved the sale of the Predators from Craig Leipold to a nine-member group of investors led by David Freeman. The deal is worth approximately $193 million and includes the team's arena, the Sommet Center. Freeman is chairman and governor of the investors group known as Predators Holdings LLC, while William "Boots" Del Biaggio and local businessman Herb Fritch are alternate governors.

Tampa Bay Lightning: On June 19 the NHL's Board of Governors unanimously approved the sale of the Lightning from Palace Sports & Entertainment (PS&E) to Absolute Hockey Enterprises. In addition to the Lightning, the deal also included the team's lease agreement with Hillsborough County — owners of the St. Pete Times Forum, and two pieces of adjacent land. Absolute Hockey includes former NHL coach Doug MacLean, real estate developer Jeff Sherrin, TV producer Oren Koules and Tampa attorney Steve Burton. Absolute reportedly paid $206 million.

Also of Note:

Chicago Blackhawks (NHL): Longtime team owner and chairman Bill Wirtz died of cancer on September 26, 2007. His son Rocky Wirtz, 55, has taken over as the team chairman.

Miami Dolphins (NFL): On February 22 owner Wayne Huizenga sold 50 percent of the team, Dolphin Stadium and surrounding land to lawyer and real estate developer Stephen Ross for a total of $550 million.

St. Louis Rams (NFL): Team owner Georgia Frontiere died of breast cancer on January 18, 2008. Her two children, Chip Rosenbloom and Lucia Rodriguez inherited 60 percent of the team. Vice Chairman Stan Kroenke owns the remaining 40 percent.

Team Payrolls

Team payrolls for active players during the 2007-08 season for the NBA and NHL, the 2007 season for the NFL and the 2008 season (as of opening day) for Major League Baseball. Figures are in millions of dollars. **Note:** The NFL, NHL and NBA use a salary cap to limit payrolls. The NFL's cap was $109 million in 2007, the NHL's cap was $50.3 million in 2007-08; and the NBA's cap was $58.68 million, though teams can circumvent the cap via bonuses and other exceptions. Note, however, that the totals listed below reflect actual player salaries, not salary cap numbers. **Sources**: USA Today and Sports Business Daily.

	NBA		MLB		NHL		NFL
1	New York $95.3	1	NY Yankees ..$209.1	1	Colorado $61.3	1	Washington ...$123.4
2	Dallas 94.3	2	NY Mets 137.8	2	Philadelphia 57.0	2	New England ...118.0
3	Denver 83.8	3	Detroit 137.7	3	NY Rangers 56.7	3	New Orleans ...110.4
4	Miami 74.9	4	Boston 133.4	4	Calgary 50.9	4	Buffalo 108.9
5	Boston 74.4	5	Chi. White Sox ..121.2	5	Anaheim 50.8	5	Kansas City 108.5
6	Philadelphia 73.8	6	LA Angels 119.2	6	Ottawa 50.0	6	Dallas 107.4
7	Cleveland 71.6	7	LA Dodgers 118.6	7	Carolina 49.9	7	San Francisco ..106.9
8	Portland 71.1	8	Chi. Cubs 118.3	8	Boston 49.5	8	Detroit 106.7
9	LA Lakers 71.0	9	Seattle 117.7	9	Dallas 49.4	9	Pittsburgh 106.3
10	Phoenix 70.8	10	Atlanta 102.4	10	New Jersey 47.6	10	Baltimore 105.0
11	Houston 69.4	11	St. Louis 99.6	11	Edmonton 46.9	11	Chicago 104.2
12	New Jersey 69.0	12	Philadelphia 98.3	12	Toronto 46.4	12	Indianapolis 102.8
13	Washington 67.8	13	Toronto 97.8	13	Minnesota 46.2	13	San Diego 102.5
14	San Antonio 67.5	14	Houston 88.9	14	Buffalo 46.0	14	Cleveland 102.4
15	Indiana 67.2	15	Milwaukee 80.9	15	Vancouver 45.7	15	Denver 102.2
16	Detroit 67.2	16	Cleveland 79.0	16	Detroit 44.6	16	Philadelphia 100.8
17	Toronto 67.1	17	San Francisco ...76.6	17	Washington 44.3	17	St. Louis 100.3
18	LA Clippers 64.5	18	Cincinnati 74.1	18	Montreal 42.3	18	NY Jets 100.0
19	Minnesota 64.4	19	San Diego 73.7	19	San Jose 41.5	19	Seattle 100.0
20	Sacramento 64.4	20	Colorado 68.7	20	Pittsburgh 41.4	20	Arizona 98.7
21	Chicago 64.2	21	Texas 67.7	21	Los Angeles 40.5	21	Cincinnati 98.5
22	Seattle 63.5	22	Baltimore 67.2	22	Florida 39.7	22	Houston 98.2
23	Milwaukee 62.7	23	Arizona 66.2	23	St. Louis 39.0	23	Tampa Bay 98.1
24	New Orleans 60.8	24	Kansas City 58.2	24	NY Islanders 39.0	24	Green Bay 97.7
25	Utah 59.2	25	Minnesota 56.9	25	Tampa Bay 39.0	25	Tennessee 97.1
26	Golden St. 58.6	26	Washington 55.0	26	Atlanta 36.6	26	Jacksonville 94.0
27	Orlando 56.5	27	Pittsburgh 48.7	27	Phoenix 35.7	27	Carolina 93.9
28	Memphis 55.6	28	Oakland 48.0	28	Chicago 34.8	28	Miami 92.6
29	Atlanta 54.5	29	Tampa Bay 43.8	29	Nashville 30.3	29	Minnesota 92.2
30	Charlotte 52.9	30	Florida 21.8	30	Columbus 28.0	30	Oakland 90.9
						31	Atlanta 83.8
						32	NY Giants 75.8

Top 10 Salaries In Each Sport

The top 10 highest paid athletes in the NBA and NHL (2007-08 season), Major League Baseball (2008 - opening day) and the NFL (2007). Figures are in millions of dollars. Note that NFL figures include signing bonuses.
Sources: USA Today, Street & Smith's SportsBusiness Journal, NHLPA and AP.

NFL

		Position	Team	Salary
1	Dwight Freeney	Def. Lineman	Indianapolis	$30.750
2	Marc Bulger	Quarterback	St. Louis	17.502
3	Leonard Davis	Off. Lineman	Dallas	17.006
4	Gaines Adams	Def. Lineman	Tampa Bay	15.434
5	Robert Geathers	Def. Lineman	Cincinnati	14.000
6	Cory Redding	Def. Lineman	Detroit	13.625
7	Derrick Dockery	Off. Lineman	Buffalo	13.505
8	Reggie Bush	Running Back	New Orleans	13.376
9	Kris Dielman	Off. Lineman	San Diego	13.305
10	Larry Johnson	Running Back	Kansas City	13.300
	League Avg			1.400

MLB

		Position	Team	Salary
1	Alex Rodriguez	Third Base	NY Yankees	$28.000
2	Jason Giambi	First Base	NY Yankees	23.429
3	Derek Jeter	Shortstop	NY Yankees	21.600
4	Manny Ramirez	Left Field	Boston	18.930
5	Carlos Beltran	Center Field	NY Mets	18.623
6	Ichiro Suzuki	Right Field	Seattle	17.102
7	Johan Santana	Pitcher	NY Mets	16.984
8	Todd Helton	First Base	Colorado	16.600
9	Torii Hunter	Center Field	LA Angels	16.500
10	Four tied			16.000
	League Avg			3.150

NBA

		Position	Team	Salary
1	Kevin Garnett	Forward	Boston	$23.750
2	Michael Finley	Forward	San Antonio	20.460
3	Shaquille O'Neal	Center	Miami	20.000
4	Jermaine O'Neal	Forward	Indiana	19.720
5	Jason Kidd	Guard	New Jersey	19.720
6	Kobe Bryant	Guard	LA Lakers	19.490
7	Tim Duncan	Center	San Antonio	19.010
	Allen Iverson	Guard	Denver	19.010
	Stephon Marbury	Guard	New York	19.010
10	Tracy McGrady	Guard	Houston	18.250
	League Avg			4.650

NHL

		Position	Team	Salary
1	Daniel Briere	Center	Philadelphia	$10.000
	Scott Gomez	Center	NY Rangers	10.000
	Thomas Vanek	Left Wing	Buffalo	10.000
4	Jaromir Jagr	Right Wing	NY Rangers	8.360
5	Kimmo Timonen	Defense	Philadelphia	8.000
6	Brad Richards	Center	Dallas	7.800
7	Nicklas Lidstrom	Defense	Detroit	7.600
8	Zdeno Chara	Defense	Boston	7.500
	Patrik Elias	Left Wing	New Jersey	7.500
	Ryan Smyth	Left Wing	Colorado	7.500
	League Avg			1.907

Collective Bargaining Agreements

Listed are highlights from the collective bargaining agreements (CBAs) of the four major sports leagues.

Sources: League CBAs, league players' associations, *USA Today*

Expiration: Current agreement expires December 11, 2011.

Salary cap: None, though it does tax teams whose payrolls exceed agreed-upon limits, which vary from year to year.

Maximum player salary: None.

Minimum player salary: $390,000 (2008).

Free Agency: A player can become eligible for free agency after six years of MLB service.

Revenue Sharing: Each team contributes 31% of its Net Local Revenue into a pool, which is then divided equally among all teams.

Luxury Tax: Referred to by MLB as the "Competitive Balance Tax." In 2008 the tax threshold was $155 million. The amount of tax is charged on the difference between the threshold and the team's payroll and depends upon how many consecutive years the team has exceeded the tax threshold.

Steroid Policy: 50-game suspension for first offense, 100 games for second, lifetime ban for third. One spring training and at least one regular season test.

Expiration: Current agreement is valid through the 2010-11 season, with a league option for an additional season.

Salary cap: In 2008-09, the cap is set at $58.68 million, while the minimum (75% of max.) is $44.01 million. The NBA operates under a soft salary cap and contains exceptions that allow teams to exceed the cap. For example, the Larry Bird exception allows a team to exceed the salary cap to re-sign its own free agents up to the players' maximum salary.

Maximum player salary: Depends on the number of years played, but rookie maximum in 2007-08 is $13.041 million and the maximum for a veteran with more than ten years played is $18.258 million (without bonuses).

Minimum player salary: Depends on the number of years played, but rookie minimum in 2007-08 is $427,163 and the minimum for a veteran with more than ten years played is $1.22 million.

Steroid Policy: 10-game suspension for first offense, 25 games for second, one year for third and a lifetime ban for a fourth. Up to four random tests per season.

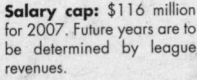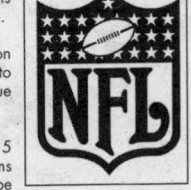

Expiration: Agreement signed in March, 2006 is valid through 2011 season.

Salary cap: $116 million for 2007. Future years are to be determined by league revenues.

Revenue Sharing: Top 15 revenue-generating teams contribute to a pool that is be dispersed to the lower-revenue teams, with the top five teams giving the most. Expected to add $850-900 million over the life of the contract.

Rookies: Players drafted in the first round of the draft can sign contracts longer than five years. Those drafted in rounds 2-7 can sign only four-year deals, preventing teams from locking up players who prove to be worth more than their initial contract allows.

Franchise Players: Teams can no longer protect a player with the "franchise" tag for more than two years. "Franchise" player becomes a "transition" player in the third year of his contract, so it's easier for him to leave.

Steroid Policy: Four-game suspension for first offense, eight games for second offense, one-year ban for third offense. Players subject to at least one test per season.

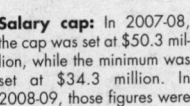

Expiration: Agreement is valid until Sept. 15, 2011. However, the NHLPA has the option to terminate it on Sept. 15, 2009 or extend it to 2012.

Salary cap: In 2007-08, the cap was set at $50.3 million, while the minimum was set at $34.3 million. In 2008-09, those figures were upped to $56.7 million (maximum) and $40.7 million (minimum).

Maximum player salary: Players can earn no more than 20 percent of the salary cap (or $11.34 million in 2008-09).

Minimum player salary: $450,000 for 2005-06 and 2006-07, $475,000 in 2007-09 and $500,000 for 2009-11.

Revenue Sharing: All clubs are eligible for revenue sharing that are ranked in the bottom half (bottom 15) in league revenue and those that operate in cities with a demographic of 2.5 million or fewer TV households.

Steroid Policy: 20-game suspension for first offense, 60 games for second offense, lifetime ban for third offense. Players subject to up to two tests per season.

Highest and Lowest Ticket Prices

The most expensive and least expensive average ticket prices for NFL, MLB, NBA and NHL franchises. Average ticket prices for each league are as follows: **NFL** $72.20, **MLB** $25.43, **NBA** $48.83 and **NHL** $48.72.

Source: Team Marketing Report

NFL

	Highest	Venue	Avg. Price
1	New England	Gillette Stadium	$117.84
2	Tampa Bay	Raymond James Stadium	90.13
3	Chicago	Soldier Field	88.33
4	NY Giants	Giants Stadium	88.06
5	NY Jets	Giants Stadium	86.99

	Lowest	Venue	Avg. Price
1	Buffalo	Ralph Wilson Stadium	$51.24
2	Cleveland	Cleveland Browns Stadium	54.41
3	Jacksonville	Jacksonville Mun. Stadium	55.30
4	Tennessee	LP Field	58.55
5	Seattle	Qwest Field	61.25

MLB

	Highest	Venue	Avg. Price
1	Boston	Fenway Park	$48.80
2	Chicago Cubs	Wrigley Field	42.49
3	NY Yankees	Yankee Stadium	41.40
4	NY Mets	Shea Stadium	34.05
5	Chi. White Sox	U.S. Cellular Field	30.28

	Lowest	Venue	Avg. Price
1	Arizona	Chase Field	$15.96
2	Atlanta	Turner Field	17.05
3	Pittsburgh	PNC Park	17.07
4	Tampa Bay	Tropicana Field	17.23
5	Kansas City	Kauffman Stadium	17.54

NBA

	Highest	Venue	Avg. Price
1	LA Lakers	Staples Center	$89.24
2	New York	Madison Sq. Garden	70.51
3	Boston	TD Banknorth Garden	65.43
4	Chicago	United Center	63.00
5	New Jersey	Continental Airlines Arena	60.98

	Lowest	Venue	Avg. Price
1	New Orleans	New Orleans Arena	$24.58
2	Charlotte	Charlotte Bobcats Arena	29.10
3	Washington	Verizon Center	30.89
4	Golden St.	Oracle Arena	31.13
5	Seattle	KeyArena	35.00

NHL

	Highest	Venue	Avg. Price
1	Toronto	Air Canada Centre	$88.32
2	Vancouver	General Motors Place	71.39
3	Montreal	Bell Centre	67.65
4	New Jersey	Continental Airlines Arena	64.17
5	Edmonton	Rexall Place	61.69

	Lowest	Venue	Avg. Price
1	St. Louis	Scottrade Center	$25.48
2	Buffalo	HSBC Arena	32.56
3	Chicago	United Center	34.88
4	Carolina	RBC Center	34.89
5	Dallas	American Airlines Center	36.85

Commissioners and Presidents

Chief Executives of Established Major Sports Organizations since 1876. (*) indicates died in office.

Major League Baseball

Commissioner	Tenure
Kenesaw Mountain Landis*	1920–44
Albert (Happy) Chandler	1945–51
Ford Frick	1951–65
William Eckert	1965–68
Bowie Kuhn	1969–84
Peter Ueberroth	1984–89
A. Bartlett Giamatti*	1989
Fay Vincent	1989–92
Bud Selig†	1998–

†Served as interim commissioner from 1992-98.

National League

President	Tenure
Morgan G. Bulkeley	1876
William A. Hulbert*	1877–82
A.G. Mills	1883–84
Nicholas Young	1885–1902
Henry Pulliam*	1903–09
Thomas J. Lynch	1910–13
John K. Tener	1914–18
John A. Heydler	1918–34
Ford Frick	1935–51
Warren Giles	1951–69
Charles (Chub) Feeney	1970–86
A. Bartlett Giamatti	1987–89
Bill White	1989–94
Leonard Coleman	1994–99

Note: League president jobs were eliminated after the 1999 season.

American League

President	Tenure
Bancroft (Ban) Johnson	1901–27
Ernest Barnard*	1927–31
William Harridge	1931–59
Joe Cronin	1959–73
Lee McPhail	1974–83
Bobby Brown	1984–94
Gene Budig	1994–99

Note: League president jobs were eliminated after the 1999 season.

NBA

Commissioner	Tenure
Maurice Podoloff	1949–63
Walter Kennedy	1963–75
Larry O'Brien	1975–84
David Stern	1984–

NFL

President	Tenure
Jim Thorpe	1920
Joe Carr	1921–39
Carl Storck	1939–41

Commissioner	
Elmer Layden	1941–46
Bert Bell*	1946–59
Austin Gunsel	1959–60
Pete Rozelle	1960–89
Paul Tagliabue	1989-2006
Roger Goodell	2006–

NHL

President	Tenure
Frank Calder*	1917–43
Red Dutton	1943–46
Clarence Campbell	1946–77
John Ziegler	1977–92
Gil Stein	1992–93

Commissioner	
Gary Bettman	1993–

NCAA

President	Tenure
Walter Byers	1951–88
Dick Schultz	1988–93
Cedric Dempsey	1993–2002
Myles Brand	2003–

Note: Office was known as Executive Director until 1998.

IOC

President	Tenure
Demetrius Vikelas, Greece	1894–96
Baron Pierre de Coubertin, France	1896–1925
Count Henri de Baillet-Latour, Belgium	1925–42
Vacant	1942–46
J. Sigfried Edstrom, Sweden	1946–52
Avery Brundage, USA	1952–72
Lord Michael Killanin, Ireland	1972–80
Juan Antonio Samaranch, Spain	1980–2001
Jacques Rogge, Belgium	2001–

Pro Stadium Naming Rights

isted are the most lucrative stadium sponsorship deals to date, ranked by the total amount over the life of the contract. Totals are in millions. As of Sept. 30, 2008. **Source:** *Street & Smith's SportsBusiness Journal* research.

	Facility	Sponsor	Home Teams	Price	Years	Avg/Yr	Expires
1	Citi Field#, Queens	Citigroup	Mets	$400.0†	20	$20.00	2028
	Barclays Center#, Brooklyn	Barclays	Nets	400.0†	20	20.00	2028
3	Reliant Stadium, Houston	Reliant Energy	Texans	300.0	30	10.00	2032
4	FedEx Field, Raljon, MD	Federal Express	Redskins	205.0	27	7.60	2025
5	American Airlines Center, Dallas	American Airlines	Mavericks, Stars	195.0	30	6.50	2030
6	Philips Arena, Atlanta	Royal Philips Electron.	Hawks, Thrashers	185.0	20	9.25	2019
7	Minute Maid Park, Houston	Minute Maid	Astros	170.0	28	6.07	2029
8	U. of Phoenix Stadium, Glendale	University of Phoenix	Cardinals	154.5	20	7.73	2025
9	Bank of America Stadium, Charlotte	Bank of America	Car. Panthers	140.0	20	7.00	2023
10	Lincoln Financial Field, Phila.	Lincoln Financial Group	Eagles	139.6	20	6.98	2022
11	Nationwide Arena, Columbus	Nationwide Insurance	Blue Jackets	135.0	indefinitely		
12	Lucas Oil Stadium, Indianapolis	Lucas Oil Products	Colts	121.5	20	6.08	2028
13	Invesco Field at Mile High, Denver	Invesco Funds	Broncos	120.0	20	6.00	2021
	TD Banknorth Garden, Boston	TD Banknorth	Bruins, Celtics	120.0	20	6.00	2025
	Cisco Field@, Fremont	Cisco Systems	A's	120.0	30	4.00	2040
16	Staples Center, Los Angeles	Staples	Lakers, Clippers, LA Kings	116.0	20	5.80	2019
17	Prudential Center, Newark	Prudential	Devils	105.3	20	5.27	2026
18	Citizens Bank Park, Philadelphia	Citizens Bank	Phillies	95.0	25	3.80	2029
	Toyota Center, Houston	Toyota	Rockets	95.0	20	4.75	2022
20	FedEx Forum, Memphis	Federal Express	Grizzlies	90.0	23	3.91	2026
	Gillette Stadium, Foxborough, MA	Gillette	Patriots	90.0	15	6.00	2016
22	Gaylord Ent. Center, Memphis	Gaylord Entertainment	Predators	80.0	20	4.00	2018
	RBC Center, Raleigh	RBC Centura Banks	Hurricanes	80.0	20	4.00	2022
24	Qwest Field, Seattle	Qwest Communications	Seahawks	75.0	15	5.00	2018
	Great American Ball Park, Cincinnati	Great American Ins.	Reds	75.0	30	2.50	2032
	M&T Bank Stadium, Baltimore	M&T Bank	Ravens	75.0	15	5.00	2017
	Xcel Energy Center, St. Paul	Xcel Energy	Wild	75.0	25	3.00	2024

† estimated.   #scheduled to open in 2009.   @scheduled to open in 2011.

Note: In September, 2008, Target won the naming rights for the Minnesota Twins new park, scheduled to open in 2010. Terms were not disclosed but are estimated to be $100-125 million over 25 years. Also, upcoming stadiums in Dallas (Cowboys) and New York (Giants/Jets) are expected garner yearly naming rights fees in the $20 million range, but as of press time, no deals had been announced.

Television Rights

Major sports and their television deals as of Sept. 30, 2008.

League	Network	Yrs (Ends)	Amount	League	Network	Yrs (Ends)	Amount
NFL	ESPN (MNF)	8 (2013)	$8.8 billion	NHL	NBC	3 (2009)	— †
	NBC (Sun. nights)	6 (2011)	3.6 billion		Versus	3 (2011)	undisclosed
	FOX (Sundays)	6 (2011)	4.4 billion	NCAA Men's Hoops			
	CBS (Sundays)	6 (2011)	3.7 billion	Tournament	CBS	11 (2013)	$6 billion
	DirecTV (Sundays)	5 (2010)	3.5 billion	NCAA Women's Hoops			
NBA	ABC/ESPN	8 (2016)	undisclosed	Tournament	ESPN	11 (2013)	$200 million@
	TNT	8 (2016)	undisclosed	NCAA Football BCS	ABC	8 (2014)	$300 million%
MLB	ESPN	8 (2013)	$2.368 billion		FOX	6 (2010)	320 million%
	FOX	7 (2013)	undisclosed				
	TBS	7 (2013)	undisclosed	NASCAR	FOX, TNT ABC, ESPN, SPEED	8 (2014)	$4.48 billion
				Olympics	NBC	13 (2008)	$3.5 billion #
					NBC	9 (2012)	2.2 billion #
				PGA Tour	CBS, NBC,	6 (2012)	undisclosed
					The Golf Channel	15 (2021)	undisclosed

Super Bowl TV Rights

2007	CBS	2009	NBC	2011	FOX
2008	FOX	2010	CBS	2012	NBC

† NBC and the NHL agreed to a deal whereby the two entities share advertising revenues. NBC paid no rights fees.

@ Also included are all rights to the College World Series and various other NCAA championships.

% ABC and the Rose Bowl agreed to an eight-year deal (2007-2014) to include eight Rose Bowls and two other BCS title games. FOX and the BCS inked a deal worth an estimated $320 million which gives them rights to the Fiesta, Orange and Sugar bowls from 2007-10 and the BCS National Championship Game from 2007-09.

NBC paid approximately $3.5 billion for exclusive rights to the 1996 Summer Games (Atlanta), the 2000 Summer Games (Sydney), the 2002 Winter Games (Salt Lake City), the 2004 Summer Games (Athens), the 2006 Winter Games (Turin) and the 2008 Summer Games (Beijing). In July 2003, NBC announced a deal worth $2.2 billion which also gave them rights to the 2010 Winter Games (Vancouver) and the 2012 Summer Games (London).

Note: The NFL and NBA also have league-owned channels. The NFL Network shows preseason games, as well as an eight-game regular season package. NBA TV will offer 96 NBA regular season games during the 2008-09 season.

AWARDS

The Peabody Award

Presented annually since 1940 for outstanding achievement in radio and television broadcasting. Named after Georgia banke and philanthropist George Foster Peabody, the awards are administered by the Henry W. Grady College of Journalism and Mass Communication at the University of Georgia.

Television

Year

1960 **CBS** for coverage of 1960 Winter and Summer Olympic Games

1966 ABC's **"Wide World of Sports"** (for Outstanding Achievement in Promotion of International Understanding).

1968 **ABC Sports** coverage of both the 1968 Winter and Summer Olympic Games.

1972 **ABC Sports** coverage of the 1972 Summer Olympics in Munich.

1973 **Joe Garagiola** of NBC Sports (for "The Baseball World of Joe Garagiola").

1976 **ABC Sports** coverage of both the 1976 Winter and Summer Olympic Games.

1984 **Roone Arledge**, president of ABC News & Sports (for significant contributions to news and sports programming)

1986 **WFAA-TV**, Dallas for its investigation of the Southern Methodist University football program.

1988 **Jim McKay** of ABC Sports (for pioneering efforts and career accomplishments in the world of TV sports).

1991 **CBS Sports** coverage of the 1991 Masters golf tournament
     & **HBO Sports** and **Black Canyon Productions** for the baseball special "When It Was A Game."

1995 **Kartemquin Educational Films** and **KTCA-TV** in St. Paul, MN, presented on PBS for "Hoop Dreams"
     & **Turner Original Productions** for the baseball special "Hank Aaron: Chasing the Dream."

1996 **HBO Sports** for its documentary "The Journey of the African-American Athlete"
     & **Bud Greenspan**, a personal award for excellence in chronicling the Olympic Games.

1997 **HBO Pictures** and **The Thomas Carter Company** for the original movie "Don King: Only in America."

1998 **KTVX-TV**, Salt Lake City for its investigation into the policies and practices of the IOC during the Olympic bribery scandal & **HBO Sports** for its ongoing series of sports documentaries.

1999 **WCPO-TV**, Cincinnati for its investigation of fraud and misrepresentation in the construction of new sports stadiums, **HBO Sports** for its documentary "Dare to Compete: The Struggle of Women in Sports," and its documentary "Fists of Freedom: The Story of the '68 Summer Games" & **ESPN** for its "SportsCentury" series.

2000 **HBO Sports** for its documentary "Ali-Frazier 1: One Nation...Divisible."

2001 **The Ciesla Foundation** and **Cinemax** for the documentary "The Life and Times of Hank Greenberg."

2002 **ESPN** for "The Complete Angler," its documentary celebrating nature, art and fly-fishing.

2005 **Showtime** and **Red Rock Entertainment** for the original movie "Edge of America," about an African-American teacher who agrees to coach the girls basketball team at an American Indian-reservation school in Utah.

2006 **CBS News** for its "60 Minutes" segment on the allegations of rape against Duke University lacrosse players and its role in stopping a prosecutorial rush to judgment, **HBO Sports** for its sports biography, "Billie Jean King: Portrait of a Pioneer," & **NBC Universal Television Studio** in association with **Imagine Entertainment** and **Film 44** for its dramatic series, "Friday Night Lights," based around high-school football in a Texas town.

Radio

Year

1974 **WSB** radio in Atlanta for "Henry Aaron: A Man with a Mission."

1991 **Red Barber** of National Public Radio (for his six decades as a broadcaster and his 10 years as a commentator on NPR's "Morning Edition").

National Emmy Awards
Sports Programming

Presented by the Academy of Television Arts and Sciences since 1948. Eligibility period covered the calendar year from 1948-57 and since 1988. Note that due to space constraints, not every award is listed below.

Multiple major award winners: ABC "Wide World of Sports" (20), ESPN "SportsCenter" and NFL Films Football coverage (17); HBO "Real Sports with Bryant Gumbel" (16); NBC Olympics coverage (11); CBS NFL Football coverage and FOX MLB coverage (10); ABC Olympics coverage and ABC "Monday Night Football" (9); ESPN "Outside the Lines" (8); ESPN "GameDay/Sunday NFL Countdown (7); CBS NCAA Basketball coverage (6); CBS "NFL Today" (5); ESPN "SportsCentury" series, NBC Ironman Triathlon coverage and The NBA on TNT (4); ABC "The American Sportsman," ABC Indianapolis 500 coverage, CBS Golf coverage, CBS Tour de France coverage, FOX "NFL Sunday," and HBO "Inside the NFL" (3); ABC Kentucky Derby coverage, ABC "Sportsbeat," Bud Greenspan Olympic specials, CBS Olympics coverage, ESPN "Speedworld," ESPN Sunday Night Football, ESPN Wimbledon coverage, MTV Sports series, NASCAR on FOX, The NBA on NBC and NBC World Series coverage (2).

1949	**1966-67**
Coverage—"Wrestling" (KTLA, Los Angeles)	Program—"Wide World of Sports" (ABC)
1950	**1967-68**
Program—"Rams Football" (KNBH-TV, Los Angeles)	Program—"Wide World of Sports" (ABC)
1954	**1968-69**
Program—"Gillette Cavalcade of Sports" (NBC)	Program—"1968 Summer Olympics" (ABC)
1965-66	**1969-70**
Programs—"Wide World of Sports" (ABC), "Shell's Wonderful World of Golf" (NBC) and "CBS Golf Classic" (CBS)	Programs—"NFL Football" (CBS) and "Wide World" of Sports" (ABC)

1970-71

Program—"Wide World of Sports" (ABC)

1971-72

Program—"Wide World of Sports" (ABC)

1972-73

News Special—"Coverage of Munich Olympic Tragedy" (ABC)

Sports Programs—"1972 Summer Olympics" (ABC) and "Wide World of Sports" (ABC)

1973-74

Program—"Wide World of Sports" (ABC)

1974-75

Non-Edited Program—"Jimmy Connors vs. Rod Laver Tennis Challenge" (CBS)

Edited Program—"Wide World of Sports" (ABC)

1975-76

Live Special—"1975 World Series: Cincinnati vs. Boston" (NBC)

Live Series—"NFL Monday Night Football" (ABC)

Edited Specials—"1976 Winter Olympics" (ABC) and "Triumph and Tragedy: The Olympic Experience" (ABC)

Edited Series—"Wide World of Sports" (ABC)

1976-77

Live Special—"1976 Summer Olympics" (ABC)

Live Series—"The NFL Today/NFL Football" (CBS)

Edited Special—"1976 Summer Olympics Preview" (ABC)

Edited Series—"The Olympiad" (PBS)

1977-78

Live Special—"Muhammad Ali vs. Leon Spinks Heavyweight Championship Fight" (CBS)

Live Series—"The NFL Today/NFL Football" (CBS)

Edited Special—"The Impossible Dream: Ballooning Across the Atlantic" (CBS)

Edited Series—"The Way It Was" (PBS)

1978-79

Live Special—"Super Bowl XIII: Pittsburgh vs Dallas" (NBC)

Live Series—"NFL Monday Night Football" (ABC)

Edited Special—"Spirit of '78: The Flight of Double Eagle II" (ABC)

Edited Series—"The American Sportsman" (ABC)

1979-80

Live Special—"1980 Winter Olympics" (ABC)

Live Series—"NCAA College Football" (ABC)

Edited Special—"Gossamer Albatross: Flight of Imagination" (CBS)

Edited Series—"NFL Game of the Week" (NFL Films)

1980-81

Live Special—"1981 Kentucky Derby" (ABC)

Live Series—"PGA Golf Tour" (CBS)

Edited Special—"Wide World of Sports 20th Anniversary Show" (ABC)

Edited Series—"The American Sportsman" (ABC)

1981-82

Live Special—"1982 NCAA Basketball Final: North Carolina vs Georgetown" (CBS)

Live Series—"NFL Football" (CBS)

Edited Special—"1982 Indianapolis 500" (ABC)

Edited Series—"Wide World of Sports" (ABC)

1982-83

Live Special—"1982 World Series: St. Louis vs Milwaukee" (NBC)

Live Series—"NFL Football" (CBS)

Edited Special—"Wimbledon '83" (NBC)

Edited Series—"Wide World of Sports" (ABC)

Journalism—"ABC Sportsbeat" (ABC)

1983-84

No awards given

1984-85

Live Special—"1984 Summer Olympics" (ABC)

Live Series—No award given

Edited Special—"Road to the Super Bowl '85" (NFL Films)

Edited Series—"The American Sportsman" (ABC)

Journalism—"ABC Sportsbeat" (ABC), "CBS Sports Sunday" (CBS), Dick Schaap features (ABC) and 1984 Summer Olympic features (ABC)

1985-86

No awards given

1986-87

Live Special—"1987 Daytona 500" (CBS)

Live Series—"NFL Football" (CBS)

Edited Special—"Wide World of Sports 25th Anniversary Special" (ABC)

Edited Series—"Wide World of Sports" (ABC)

1987-88

Live Special—"1987 Kentucky Derby" (ABC)

Live Series—"NFL Monday Night Football" (ABC)

Edited Special—"Paris-Roubaix Bike Race" (CBS)

Edited Series—"Wide World of Sports" (ABC)

1988

Live Special—"1988 Summer Olympics" (NBC)

Live Series—"1988 NCAA Basketball" (CBS)

Edited Special—"Road to the Super Bowl '88" (NFL Films)

Edited Series—"Wide World of Sports" (ABC)

Studio Show—"NFL GameDay" (ESPN)

Journalism—1988 Summer Olympic reporting (NBC)

1989

Live Special—"1989 Indianapolis 500" (ABC)

Live Series—"NFL Monday Night Football" (ABC)

Edited Special—"Trans-Antarctical The International Expedition" (ABC)

Edited Series—"This is the NFL" (NFL Films)

Studio Show—"NFL Today" (CBS)

Journalism—1989 World Series Game 3 earthquake coverage (ABC)

1990

Live Special—"1990 Indianapolis 500" (ABC)

Live Series—"1990 NCAA Basketball Tournament" (CBS)

Edited Special—"Road to Super Bowl XXIV" (NFL Films)

Edited Series—"Wide World of Sports" (ABC)

Studio Show—"SportsCenter" (ESPN)

Journalism—"Outside the Lines: The Autograph Game" (ESPN)

National Emmy Awards (Cont.)

1991

Live Special—"1991 NBA Finals: Chicago vs LA Lakers" (NBC)
Live Series—"1991 NCAA Basketball Tournament" (CBS)
Edited Special—"Wide World of Sports 30th Anniversary Special" (ABC)
Edited Series—"This is the NFL" (NFL Films)
Studio Show—"NFL GameDay" (ESPN) and "NFL Live" (NBC)
Journalism—"Outside the Lines: Steroids—Whatever It Takes" (ESPN)

1992

Live Special—"1992 Breeders' Cup" (NBC)
Live Series—"1992 NCAA Basketball Tournament" (CBS)
Edited Special—"1992 Summer Olympics" (NBC)
Edited Series—"MTV Sports" (MTV)
Studio Show—"The NFL Today" (CBS)
Journalism—"Outside the Lines: Portraits in Black and White" (ESPN)

1993

Live Special—"1993 World Series" (CBS)
Live Series—"Monday Night Football" (ABC)
Edited Special—"Road to the Super Bowl" (NFL Films)
Edited Series—"This is the NFL" (NFL Films)
Studio Show—"The NFL Today" (CBS)
Journalism (TIE)—"Outside the Lines: Mitch Ivey Feature" (ESPN) and "SportsCenter: University of Houston Football" (ESPN).
Feature—"Arthur Ashe: His Life, His Legacy" (NBC).

1994

Live Special—"NHL Stanley Cup Finals" (ESPN)
Live Series—"Monday Night Football" (ABC)
Edited Special—"Lillehammer '94: 16 Days of Glory" (Disney/Cappy Productions)
Edited Series—"MTV Sports" (MTV)
Studio Show—"NFL GameDay" (ESPN)
Journalism—"1994 Winter Olympic Games: Mossad feature" (CBS)
Feature (TIE)—"Heroes of Telemark" on Winter Olympic Games (CBS); and "SportsCenter: Vanderbilt running back Brad Gaines" (ESPN).

1995

Live Special—"Cal Ripken 2131" (ESPN)
Live Series—"ESPN Speedworld" (ESPN)
Edited Special (quick turn-around)—"Outside the Lines: Play-ball—Opening Day in America" (ESPN)
Edited Special (long turn-around)—"Lillehammer, an Olympic Diary" (CBS)
Edited Series—"NFL Films Presents" (NFL Films)
Studio Show (TIE)—"NFL GameDay" (ESPN) and "FOX NFL Sunday" (FOX)
Journalism—"Real Sports with Bryant Gumbel: Broken Promises" (HBO)
Feature (TIE)—"SportsCenter: Jerry Quarry" (ESPN) and "Real Sports with Bryant Gumbel: Coach" (HBO).

1996

Live Special—"1996 World Series" (FOX)
Live Series—"ESPN Speedworld" (ESPN)
Edited Special—"Football America" (TNT/NFL Films)
Edited Series—"NFL Films Presents" (NFL Films)
Live Event Turnaround—"The Centennial Olympic Games" (NBC)
Studio Show—"SportsCenter" (ESPN)
Journalism—"Outside the Lines: AIDS in Sports" (ESPN)
Feature—"Real Sports with Bryant Gumbel: 1966 Texas Western NCAA Champs" (HBO).

1997

Live Special—"The NBA Finals" (NBC)
Live Series—"NFL Monday Night Football" (ABC)
Edited Special—"Ironman Triathlon World Championship" (NBC/World Triathlon Corporation)
Edited Series—"NFL Films Presents" (NFL Films)
Live Event Turnaround—"Outside The Lines: Inside The Kentucky Derby" (ESPN)
Studio Show—"FOX NFL Sunday" (FOX)
Journalism—"Real Sports with Bryant Gumbel: Pros and Cons" (HBO)
Feature—"NFL Films Presents: Eddie George" (NFL Films).

1998

Live Special—"McGwire's 62nd Home Run Game" (FOX)
Live Series—"NBC Golf Tour" (NBC)
Edited Special—"A Cinderella Season: The Lady Vols Fight Back" (HBO)
Edited Series—"Real Sports with Bryant Gumbel" (HBO)
Live Event Turnaround—"Wimbledon '98" (NBC)
Studio Show—"FOX NFL Sunday" (FOX)
Journalism (TIE)—"Real Sports with Bryant Gumbel: Winning At All Costs" (HBO) and "Real Sports with Bryant Gumbel: Diamond Bucks" (HBO)
Feature—"NFL Films Presents: Steve Mariucci" (ESPN2 and NFL Films).

1999

Live Special—"2000 MLB All-Star Game" (FOX)
Live Series—"MLB Regular Season" (FOX)
Edited Special—"Ironman Triathlon World Championship" (NBC)
Edited Series—"SportsCentury: 50 Greatest Athletes" (ESPN)
Live Event Turnaround—"The World Track & Field Championships" (NBC)
Studio Show—"MLB Pre-Game Show" (FOX)
Journalism—"Real Sports with Bryant Gumbel: Fake Golf Clubs" (HBO)
Feature—"NFL Films Presents: Lt. Kalsu" (ESPN2)

2000

Live Special—"2000 World Series" (FOX)
Live Series—"NFL Sunday Night Football" (ESPN)
Edited Special—"Hoops and Hoosiers: The Story of the Final Four 2000" (CBS)
Edited Series—"SportsCentury: The Top 50 & Beyond" (ESPN)
Live Event Turnaround—"The Games of the XXVII Olympiad" (NBC)
Studio Show—"FOX NFL Sunday" (FOX)
Journalism—"Real Sports with Bryant Gumbel: Dominican Free-For-All" (HBO)
Feature—"The Games of the XXVII Olympiad" (NBC)

"Baseball" Wins Prime Time Emmy

Ken Burns's miniseries "Baseball" won the 1994 Emmy Award for Outstanding Informational Series. The nine-part documentary aired from Sept. 18-28, 1994 and ran more than 18 hours, drawing the largest audience in PBS history.

2001

Live Special—"2001 World Series" (FOX)
Live Series—"NASCAR on FOX" (FOX)
Edited Special—"ABC's Wide World of Sports 40th Anniversary Special" (ABC)
Edited Series—"SportsCentury" (ESPN Classic)
Live Event Turnaround—"Tour de France" (CBS)
Studio Show—Weekly—"Sunday NFL Countdown" (ESPN)
Studio Show—Daily—"Inside the NBA" (TNT/TBS)
Journalism—"Real Sports with Bryant Gumbel: Amare Stoudemire" (HBO)
Feature—"NFL Films Presents: Gerry Faust—The Golden Dream" (ESPN2)
Documentary—"Do You Believe in Miracles? The Story of the 1980 U.S. Hockey Team" (HBO)

2002

Live Special—"XIX Olympic Winter Games" (NBC)
Live Series—"The NBA on NBC" (NBC)
Edited Special—"America's Heroes: The Bravest vs. The Finest" (NBC)
Edited Series—"Real Sports with Bryant Gumbel" (HBO)
Live Event Turnaround—"Tour de France" (CBS)
Studio Show—Weekly—"Inside the NFL" (HBO & NFL Films)
Studio Show—Daily—"Baseball Tonight" (ESPN)
Journalism—"Outside the Lines, Weekly: Eligibility for Sale" (ESPN) and "Outside the Lines, Weekly: Iraqi Atletes, Tales of Torture" (ESPN)
Long Feature—"SportsCenter: Flight 93" (ESPN)
Short Feature—"SportsCenter: Chris Paul" (ESPN), "XIX Olympic Winter Games: Bill Johnson" (NBC) and "XIX Olympic Winter Games: The Sheas" (NBC)
Documentary—"Our Greatest Hopes, Our Worst Fears: The Tragedy of the Munich Games" (ABC)

2003

Live Special— "MLB on FOX: Post Season" (FOX)
Live Series— "ESPN NFL Sunday Night Football" (ESPN)
Edited Special— "Ironman Triathlon World Championship" (NBC/World Triathlon Corporation)
Edited Series/Anthology—Legendary Nights" (HBO)
Live Event Turnaround—"Tour de France" (CBS)
Studio Show—Weekly—"Sunday NFL Countdown" (ESPN)
Studio Show—Daily—"SportsCenter" (ESPN)
Journalism—"Real Sports with Bryant Gumbel: Marcus Dixon" (HBO)
Editing—"Jim McKay — My World in My Words " (HBO)
The Dick Schaap Outstanding Writing Award—"Wimbledon — Where is Wimbledon" (ESPN)
Long Feature—"NFL Films Presents on The NFL Network: Big Charlie's" (NFL Network/NFL Films) and "Real Sports with Bryant Gumbel: Alex Zanardi" (HBO)
Short Feature—"SportsCenter: Picking Up Butch" (ESPN)
Documentary—"The Curse of the Bambino" (HBO/Black Canyon Productions/Clear Channel Entertainment Television)

2004

Live Special—"The Masters" (CBS)
Live Series—"ABC's NFL Monday Night Football" (ABC)
Edited Special—"Ironman Triathlon World Championship" (NBC/Ironman Productions)
Edited Series/Anthology—"Real Sports with Bryant Gumbel" (HBO)
Live Event Turnaround—"The Games of the XXVIII Olympiad" (NBC)
Studio Show—Weekly—"Inside the NFL" (HBO)
Studio Show—Daily—"SportsCenter" (ESPN)
Journalism—"Real Sports with Bryant Gumbel: Sport of Sheikhs" (HBO)
Editing (TIE)—"NFL Films Presents on NFL Network: Michael Zagaris" (NFL Network/NFL Films) and "Wimbledon on NBC: Patrick Stewart Tease and Closing Thoughts" (NBC)

The Dick Schaap Outstanding Writing Award—"Wimbledon on ESPN2—Wimbledon Reflections" (ESPN2)
Long Feature—"SportsCenter: Ben Comen" (ESPN)
Short Feature—"The Super Bowl Today: NFL Quarterbacks" (CBS)
Documentary—"The Games of the XXVIII Olympiad: Stylianos Kryiakides, The Journey of a Warrior" (NBC)

2005

Live Special—"134th British Open Championship" (TNT)
Live Series—"NASCAR on FOX" (FOX)
Edited Special—"CostasNOW: David Robinson—A Man In Full" (HBO)
Edited Series/Anthology—"SportsCentury" (ESPN Classic)
Live Event Turnaround—"Best of Winter X Games Nine" (ABC & ESPN Productions)
Studio Show—Weekly—"Inside the NFL" (HBO)
Studio Show—Daily—"Inside the NBA, Playoffs" (TNT)
Journalism—"Real Sports with Bryant Gumbel: Soccer Racism" (HBO)
Editing—"PGA Tour Sunday: Kevin Hall" (USA & PGA Tour Productions)
The Dick Schaap Outstanding Writing Award—"SportsCenter: Finding Bobby Fischer" (Jeremy Schaap, ESPN)
Long Feature—"Real Sports with Bryant Gumbel: The Hoyts" (HBO)
Short Feature—"Timeless: Lama Kunga" (ESPN2 & Red Line Films)
Documentary—"Rhythym in the Rope" (ESPN2)

2006

Live Special— "MLB on FOX: Post Season" (FOX)
Live Series— "NASCAR on TNT & NBC" (TNT/NBC)
Edited Special— "2006 Ford Ironman World Championships" (NBC/Ironman Productions)
Edited Series/Anthology— "Real Sports with Bryant Gumbel" (HBO)
Live Event Turnaround— "Beyond the Wheel" (NASCAR Images/Speed)
Studio Show—Weekly— "Sunday NFL Countdown" (ESPN)
Studio Show—Daily— "Inside the NBA - Playoffs" (TNT)
Journalism— "Real Sports with Bryant Gumbel: Uninsured" (HBO)
Editing—"NBA on TNT" (TNT)
The Dick Schaap Outstanding Writing Award— "One of a Kind: The Rise and Fall of Stu Ungar" (ESPN/Red Line Films)
Long Feature— "SportsCenter: Travis Roy" (ESPN)
Short Feature— "NCAA Men's Basketball Tournament" (CBS)
Documentary— "One of a Kind: The Rise and Fall of Stu Ungar" (ESPN/Red Line Films)

2007

Live Special— "MLB on FOX: Tostitos Fiesta Bowl" (FOX)
Live Series— "NASCAR on FOX" (FOX)
Edited Special— "De La Hoya/Mayweather 24/7" (HBO)
Edited Series/Anthology— "America's Game: The Super Bowl Champions" (NFL Network/NFL Films)
Live Event Turnaround— "Quest for the Cup" (NASCAR Images/VOOM)
Studio Show—Weekly— "College Gameday" (ESPN)
Studio Show—Daily— "Inside the NBA" (TNT)
Journalism— "Real Sports with Bryant Gumbel: Headgames: The NFL Concussion Crisis" (HBO)
Editing— "Ali's 65" (ESPN/Televersemedia)
The Dick Schaap Outstanding Writing Award— "Mayweather/Hatton 24/7" (HBO)
Long Feature— "NFL Films Presents: Finding Your Butkus" (NFL Network/NFL Films)
Short Feature— "Sunday NFL Countdown: Fear" (ESPN/Bluefoot Entertainment)
Documentary— "Ghosts of Flatbush" (HBO)

Sportscasters of the Year
National Emmy Awards

An Emmy Award for Sportscasters was first introduced in 1968 and given for Outstanding Host/Commentator for the 1967-68 TV season. Two awards, one for Outstanding Host or Play-by-Play and the other for Outstanding Analyst, were first presented in 1981 for the 1980-81 season. Three awards, for Outstanding Studio Host, Play-by-Play and Studio Analyst, have been given since the 1993 season, and one more, Sports Event Analyst, was added in 1997.

Multiple winners: John Madden (16); Bob Costas (15); Cris Collinsworth and Jim McKay (9); Joe Buck and Al Michaels (6); Dick Enberg (4); James Brown, Keith Jackson and Tim McCarver (3); Terry Bradshaw, Ernie Johnson and Joe Morgan (2). Note that Jim McKay has won a total of 12 Emmy awards: eight for Host/Commentator, one for Host/Play-by-Play, two for Sports Writing and one for News Commentary.

Season	Host/Commentator	Season	Host/Play-by-Play	Season	Analyst
1967-68	Jim McKay, ABC	1980-81	Dick Enberg, NBC	1980-81	Dick Button, ABC
1968-69	No award	1981-82	Jim McKay, ABC	1981-82	John Madden, CBS
1969-70	No award	1982-83	Dick Enberg, NBC	1982-83	John Madden, CBS
1970-71	Jim McKay, ABC	1983-84	No award	1983-84	No award
	& Don Meredith, ABC	1984-85	George Michael, NBC	1984-85	No award
1971-72	No award	1985-86	No award	1985-86	No award
1972-73	Jim McKay, ABC	1986-87	Al Michaels, ABC	1986-87	John Madden, CBS
1973-74	Jim McKay, ABC	1987-88	Bob Costas, NBC	1987-88	John Madden, CBS
1974-75	Jim McKay, ABC	1988	Bob Costas, NBC	1988	John Madden, CBS
1975-76	Jim McKay, ABC	1989	Al Michaels, ABC	1989	John Madden, CBS
1976-77	Frank Gifford, ABC	1990	Dick Enberg, NBC	1990	John Madden, CBS
1977-78	Jack Whitaker, CBS	1991	Bob Costas, NBC	1991	John Madden, CBS
1978-79	Jim McKay, ABC	1992	Bob Costas, NBC	1992	John Madden, CBS
1979-80	Jim McKay, ABC				

Studio Host

Year		Year		Year	
1993	Bob Costas, NBC	1999	James Brown, FOX	2004	Bob Costas, HBO/NBC
1994	Bob Costas, NBC	2000	Bob Costas, NBC	2005	Bob Costas, HBO/NBC
1995	Bob Costas, NBC	2001	Bob Costas, HBO &	2006	Ernie Johnson, TNT
1996	Bob Costas, NBC		Ernie Johnson, TNT/TBS	2007	James Brown, CBS
1997	Dan Patrick, ESPN	2002	Bob Costas, HBO/NBC		
1998	James Brown, FOX	2003	Bob Costas, HBO/NBC		

Play-by-Play

Year		Year		Year	
1993	Dick Enberg, NBC	1998	Keith Jackson, ABC	2003	Joe Buck, FOX
1994	Keith Jackson, ABC	1999	Joe Buck, FOX	2004	Joe Buck, FOX
1995	Al Michaels, ABC	2000	Al Michaels, ABC	2005	Joe Buck, FOX
1996	Keith Jackson, ABC	2001	Joe Buck, FOX	2006	Al Michaels, ABC/NBC
1997	Bob Costas, NBC	2002	Joe Buck, FOX	2007	Al Michaels, NBC

Studio Analyst

Year		Year		Year	
1993	Billy Packer, CBS	1998	Cris Collinsworth, HBO/FOX	2003	Cris Collinsworth, HBO
1994	John Madden, FOX	1999	Terry Bradshaw, FOX	2004	Cris Collinsworth, HBO
1995	John Madden, FOX	2000	Steve Lyons, FOX	2005	Cris Collinsworth, HBO
1996	Howie Long, FOX	2001	Terry Bradshaw, FOX	2006	Cris Collinsworth, HBO/NBC
1997	Cris Collinsworth, HBO/NBC	2002	Cris Collinsworth, HBO	2007	Cris Collinsworth, HBO/NBC

Sports Events Analyst

Year		Year		Year	
1997	Joe Morgan, ESPN	2001	Tim McCarver, FOX	2005	John Madden, ABC
1998	John Madden, FOX	2002	Tim McCarver, FOX	2006	Cris Collinsworth, NFL Network
1999	John Madden, FOX	2003	John Madden, ABC	2007	John Madden, NBC
2000	Tim McCarver, FOX	2004	Joe Morgan, ESPN		

Lifetime Achievement Emmy Award

Year		Year		Year		Year	
1989	Jim McKay	1994	Howard Cosell	1999	Jack Buck	2004	Chet Simmons
1990	Lindsey Nelson	1995	Vin Scully	2000	Dick Enberg	2005	Bud Greenspan
1991	Curt Gowdy	1996	Frank Gifford	2001	Herb Granath	2006	Don Ohlmeyer
1992	Chris Schenkel	1997	Jim Simpson	2002	Roone Arledge*	2007	Frank Chirkinian
1993	Pat Summerall	1998	Keith Jackson	2003	Ed and Steve Sabol		

*Arledge is the only recipient of two Lifetime Achievement Emmy Awards. In addition to sports, he won the lifetime award for "News and Documentary" in 2002.

Sportscaster of the Year

Presented annually since 1959 by the National Sportscasters and Sportswriters Association, based in Salisbury, N.C. Voting is done by NSSA members and selected national media.

Multiple winners: Bob Costas (8); Chris Berman (6) Keith Jackson (5); Joe Buck, Lindsey Nelson and Chris Schenkel (4); Dick Enberg, Al Michaels, Jim Nantz and Vin Scully (3); Curt Gowdy and Ray Scott (2).

Year		Year		Year		Year	
1959	Lindsey Nelson	1972	Keith Jackson	1984	John Madden	1997	Bob Costas
1960	Lindsey Nelson	1973	Keith Jackson	1985	Bob Costas	1998	Jim Nantz
1961	Lindsey Nelson	1974	Keith Jackson	1986	Al Michaels	1999	Dan Patrick
1962	Lindsey Nelson	1975	Keith Jackson	1987	Bob Costas	2000	Bob Costas
1963	Chris Schenkel	1976	Keith Jackson	1988	Bob Costas	2001	Chris Berman
1964	Chris Schenkel	1977	Pat Summerall	1989	Chris Berman	2002	Joe Buck
1965	Vin Scully	1978	Vin Scully	1990	Chris Berman	2003	Joe Buck
1966	Curt Gowdy	1979	Dick Enberg	1991	Bob Costas	2004	Joe Buck
1967	Chris Schenkel	1980	Dick Enberg	1992	Bob Costas	2005	Jim Nantz
1968	Ray Scott		& Al Michaels	1993	Chris Berman	2006	Joe Buck
1969	Curt Gowdy	1981	Dick Enberg	1994	Chris Berman	2007	Jim Nantz
1970	Chris Schenkel	1982	Vin Scully	1995	Bob Costas		
1971	Ray Scott	1983	Al Michaels	1996	Chris Berman		

The Pulitzer Prize

The Pulitzer Prizes for journalism, letters, drama and music have been presented annually since 1917 in the name of Joseph Pulitzer (1847-1911), the publisher of the *New York World*. Sixteen Pulitzers have been awarded for newspaper sports reporting, sports commentary and sports photography.

News Coverage

1935 **Bill Taylor,** *NY Herald Tribune,* for his reporting on the 1934 America's Cup yacht races.

Special Citation

1952 **Max Kase,** *NY Journal-American,* for his reporting on the 1951 college basketball point-shaving scandal.

Meritorious Public Service

1954 *Newsday* (Garden City, N.Y.) for its expose of New York State's race track scandals and labor racketeering.

General Reporting

1956 **Arthur Daley,** *NY Times,* for his 1955 columns.

Investigative Reporting

1981 **Clark Hallas** & **Robert Lowe,** *(Tucson) Arizona Daily Star,* for their 1980 investigation of the University of Arizona athletic department.

1986 **Jeffrey Marx** & **Michael York,** Lexington (Ky.) *Herald-Leader,* for its 1985 investigation of the basketball program at the University of Kentucky and other major colleges.

Photography

1949 **Nat Fein,** *NY Herald Tribune,* for his photo, "Babe Ruth Bows Out."

1952 **John Robinson** & **Don Ultang,** Des Moines (Iowa) *Register and Tribune,* for their sequence of six pictures of the 1951 Drake-Oklahoma A&M football game, in which Drake's Johnny Bright broke his jaw.

Specialized Reporting

1985 **Randall Savage** & **Jackie Crosby,** Macon (Ga.) *Telegraph and News,* for their 1984 investigation of athletics and academics at the University of Georgia and Georgia Tech.

Beat Reporting

2000 **George Dohrmann,** St. Paul (Min.) *Pioneer Press,* for his investigation that revealed academic fraud in the men's basketball program at the University of Minnesota.

Feature Writing

1997 **Lisa Pollak,** *Baltimore Sun,* for her story about baseball umpire John Hirschbeck dealing with the death of one son and the illness of another from the same disease.

Commentary

1976 **Red Smith,** *NY Times,* for his 1975 columns.
1981 **Dave Anderson,** *NY Times,* for his 1980 columns.
1990 **Jim Murray,** *LA Times,* for his 1989 columns.

1985 **The Photography Staff** of the *Orange County* (Calif.) *Register,* for their coverage of the 1984 Summer Olympics in Los Angeles.

1993 **William Snyder** & **Ken Geiger,** *The Dallas Morning News,* for their coverage of the 1992 Summer Olympics in Barcelona, Spain.

Red Smith Award

Presented annually by the Associated Press Sports Editors (APSE) to a person who has made "major contributions to sports journalism" and named in honor of the late newspaper columnist for the *New York Herald-Tribune* and *New York Times.*

Year		Year		Year	
1981	Red Smith, *NY Times*	1991	Dave Kindred, *Nat'l Sports Daily*	2002	Dick Schaap, *ESPN* "The Sports Reporters"
1982	Jim Murray, *LA Times*	1992	Ed Storin, *Miami Herald*	2003	George Solomon, *Washington Post*
1983	Shirley Povich, *Washington Post*	1993	Tom McEwen, *Tampa Tribune*	2004	Jimmy Cannon, NYC columnist
1984	Fred Russell, *Nashville Banner*	1994	Dave Anderson, *NY Times*	2005	Mary Garber, *Winston-Salem Journal*
1985	Blackie Sherrod, *Dallas Morning News*	1995	Richard Sandler, *Newsday*	2006	Joe McGuff, *Kansas City Star*
		1996	Bill Dwyre, *LA Times*	2007	Van McKenzie, *Orlando Sentinel*
1986	Si Burick, *Dayton Daily News*	1997	Jerome Holtzman, *Chicago Tribune*	2008	W.C. Heinz, *New York Sun*
1987	Will Grimsley, *AP*	1998	Sam Lacy, *Baltimore Afro-American*		
1988	Furman Bisher, *Atlanta Journal*	1999	Bud Collins, *Boston Globe*		
1989	Edwin Pope, *Miami Herald*	2000	Jerry Izenberg, *Newark Star Ledger*		
1990	Dave Smith, *Dallas Morning News*	2001	John Steadman, *Baltimore Sun*		

Sportswriter of the Year
NSSA Award

Presented annually since 1959 by the National Sportscasters and Sportswriters Association, based in Salisbury, N.C. Voting is done by NSSA members and selected national media.

Multiple winners: Jim Murray (14); Rick Reilly (11); Frank Deford (6); Red Smith (5); Will Grimsley (4); Peter Gammons (3); Bob Ryan (2).

Year		Year		Year	
1959	Red Smith, *NY Herald-Tribune*	1976	Jim Murray, *LA Times*	1993	Peter Gammons, *Boston Globe*
1960	Red Smith, *NY Herald-Tribune*	1977	Jim Murray, *LA Times*	1994	Rick Reilly, *Sports Ill.*
1961	Red Smith, *NY Herald-Tribune*	1978	Will Grimsley, AP	1995	Rick Reilly, *Sports Ill.*
1962	Red Smith, *NY Herald-Tribune*	1979	Jim Murray, *LA Times*	1996	Rick Reilly, *Sports Ill.*
1963	Arthur Daley, *NY Times*	1980	Will Grimsley, AP	1997	Dave Kindred, *The Sporting News*
1964	Jim Murray, *LA Times*	1981	Will Grimsley, AP		
1965	Red Smith, *NY Herald-Tribune*	1982	Frank Deford, *Sports Ill.*	1998	Mitch Albom, *Detroit Free Press*
1966	Jim Murray, *LA Times*	1983	Will Grimsley, AP	1999	Rick Reilly, *Sports Ill.*
1967	Jim Murray, *LA Times*	1984	Frank Deford, *Sports Ill.*	2000	Bob Ryan, *Boston Globe*
1968	Jim Murray, *LA Times*	1985	Frank Deford, *Sports Ill.*	2001	Rick Reilly, *Sports Ill.*
1969	Jim Murray, *LA Times*	1986	Frank Deford, *Sports Ill.*	2002	Rick Reilly, *Sports Ill.*
1970	Jim Murray, *LA Times*	1987	Frank Deford, *Sports Ill.*	2003	Rick Reilly, *Sports Ill.*
1971	Jim Murray, *LA Times*	1988	Frank Deford, *Sports Ill.*	2004	Rick Reilly, *Sports Ill.*
1972	Jim Murray, *LA Times*	1989	Peter Gammons, *Sports Ill.*	2005	Steve Rushin, *Sports Ill.*
1973	Jim Murray, *LA Times*	1990	Peter Gammons, *Boston Globe*	2006	Bob Reilly, *Boston Globe*
1974	Jim Murray, *LA Times*	1991	Rick Reilly, *Sports Ill.*	2007	Bob Ryan, *Boston Globe*
1975	Jim Murray, *LA Times*	1992	Rick Reilly, *Sports Ill.*		

Best Newspaper Sports Sections of 2007

Winners of the annual Associated Press Sports Editors contest for best daily and Sunday sports sections. Awards are divided into different categories, based on circulation figures. Selections are made by a committee of APSE members.

Circulation Over 250,000

Top 10 Daily		Top 10 Sunday	
Boston Globe	Los Angeles Times	Atlanta Journal-Constitution	Kansas City Star
Chicago Tribune	Orlando Sentinel	Baltimore Sun	Miami Herald
Dallas Morning News	San Jose Mercury News	Boston Globe	New York Daily News
Fort Worth Star-Telegram	USA Today	Chicago Sun-Times	Newark Star Ledger
Kansas City Star	Washington Post	Dallas Morning News	Washington Post

Circulation 100,000-250,000

Top 10 Daily		Top 10 Sunday	
Buffalo News	Times Picayune	Charlotte Observer	San Antonio Express-News
Contra Costa Times	(New Orleans)	Des Moines Register	St. Paul Pioneer Press
Des Moines Register	Palm Beach Post	(Columbia, SC)	Tampa Tribune
Detroit News	Salt Lake Tribune	Omaha World Herald	The State (Columbia, SC)
Record (Hackensack, NJ)	Seattle Times	Palm Beach Post	Times Picayune
	Tampa Tribune	Salt Lake Tribune	(New Orleans)

Best Sportswriting of 2007

Winners of the annual Associated Press Sports Editors Contest for best sportswriting in 2007. Eventual winners were chosen from five finalists in each writing division. Selections are made by a committee of APSE members. Note the investigative writing division included all circulation categories.

Circulation over 250,000

Column:	Bill Plaschke, *Los Angeles Times*	**Game story:**	Bill Reiter, *Kansas City Star*
Feature:	Dave Scheiber, *St. Petersburg Times*	**Explanatory:**	Mark Zeigler, *San Diego Union-Tribune*
Breaking News:	Amy Shipley, *Washington Post*	**Project:**	Alan Schwarz, *New York Times*

Circulation 100,000-250,000

Column:	Ted Miller, *Seattle Post-Intelligencer*	**Explanatory:**	Ron Higgins, *Memphis Commercial Appeal*
Feature:	Kelsie Smith, *St. Paul Pioneer Press*	**Project:**	Doug Harris, Joanne Huist Smith, Lucas Sullivan and Michael Cooper, *Dayton Daily News* and *Springfield News Sun*
Breaking News:	Andy Boogaard, *Fresno Bee*		
Game story:	Kevin Robbins, *Austin American-Statesman*		

All Categories

Investigative: Eduardo Encina, Abbie Vansickle, Mark Topkin, Carrie Weimar, Rebecca Catalanello, Kevin Graham, S.I. Rosenbaum and Graham Brink, *St. Petersburg Times*

INTERNATIONAL SPORTS

2007 / 2008 YEAR IN REVIEW

Lindsey Vonn and **Bode Miller** became the first Americans to sweep the men's and women's World Cup overall titles in 25 years.

SCENIC FINISH
UGLY JOURNEY

Carlos Sastre coasted down the beautiful Champs-Elysees to win the 2008 Tour de France. The rest of the race wasn't quite so beautiful.

by Bonnie D. Ford

ONE OF THE MOST TIMELESS MOMENTS IN THE TOUR DE FRANCE comes after the three-week endurance test is over and the teams slowly parade up and around the long, cobblestoned sweep of the Champs-Elysees, where the top sprinters in the peloton just finished trying to beat each others' brains out.

No matter what the weather is throughout the final Sunday, this ritual always seems to unfold in a dreamy silver haze with dusk falling on the broad avenue that was a battleground when Paris was liberated during World War II.

Riders roll at a deliberate pace with their arms around one another, waving and grinning in obvious relief. This year, there was ecstatic Team CSC-Saxo Bank, clearly the deepest and most astute squad in the race, flanking its soft-spoken matador Carlos Sastre, who won the Tour with one well-timed attack on Alpe d'Huez.

At the other end of the spectrum was beleaguered Barloworld, which had just four of nine riders left at the end, decimated by crashes and a positive doping test.

Somewhere in between were U.S.-based Garmin-Chipotle and Team Columbia. Garmin leader Christian Vande Velde, who entered this race still loitering on the edge of self-confidence and emerged from it forever changed, wore an American flag like a cape. His elite stature is now confirmed by a fifth-place overall finish, and Garmin proved it belonged in the race. Columbia heads home with five stage wins courtesy of its young sprinters and has at least initially succeeded in distancing itself from a troubled previous incarnation as T-Mobile.

It was all very picturesque here after the final official ceremony. That was in direct contrast to the ugly free-for-all the night before, when the race was really won.

In a quirk of athletic etiquette well known to cycling devotees, the Tour's

Bonnie D. Ford covers tennis and Olympic sports for ESPN.com.

AP Images

Carlos Sastre of Spain, wearing the overall leader's yellow jersey, and **Cadel Evans** of Australia, right, ride past the Arc de Triomphe during the 21st stage of the Tour de France.

overall results are decided on its penultimate day. The time gaps after the final individual time trial are allowed to stand, and Sunday's Stage 21, while not entirely uncompetitive, always comes down to a sprinters' duel with the peloton finishing just behind them in a massed, multicolored peacock's tail and all riders in it awarded the same time.

When Sastre — against most conventional wisdom — performed well enough in the time trial to stave off Australia's Cadel Evans, among others, he was able to slip on the yellow jersey knowing it would be his the next day as well unless he were to suffer a freak accident. He beamed from the podium. Then Sastre entered the

fenced-off area where he, Evans, third-place finisher Bernard Kohl of Austria, Denis Menchov, Vande Velde and several other top contenders underwent drug testing.

A cluster of reporters and photographers 10 deep engulfed the enclosure, waiting for the men to finish surrendering their bodily fluids. This is cycling's equivalent of the red-carpet rite. Imagine World Series or Super Bowl victors trooping into the white van before they spoke to the media. The players' unions wouldn't stand for it, and neither would the networks.

Evans finally emerged, surrounded by a human chain of police officers and accompanied by the same stocky bodyguard who once protected Lance

Armstrong and Alexander Vinokourov. Sastre went to his winner's news conference, part of which concerned his relationship with Manolo Saiz, the discredited former manager of ONCE, the powerful Spanish outfit where Sastre came of age, and with Liberty Seguros.

Sastre refused to repudiate his ex-boss, who was tainted by the still less-than-fully resolved Operacion Puerto doping investigation in Spain. Saiz, a master of training riders for the time-trial event, taught Sastre the fundamentals. Sastre added that they haven't been in touch in a few years because they've "taken different paths." Sastre is a veteran of CSC and the aggressive anti-doping program insisted upon by owner Bjarne Riis, who last year confessed to having used performance-enhancing substances on the way to his 1996 Tour win and thus knows firsthand how destructive the burden of lying and cheating can be.

It was all a reminder of the sticky wickets cycling is passing through as it ricochets from the sublime images of the Champs-Elysees to the more prosaic daily spectacle of finish-line testing. It's challenging to be a competitor in this sport under these circumstances, it's a challenging sport to cover, and at times it's an achingly difficult sport for fans to commit to.

For the second straight year, the Tour's route on its last day went through Chatenay-Malabry, the suburban Paris location of the national laboratory that conducts anti-doping tests on samples taken at the Tour.

Four positive tests were announced during the race. The number is no different from last year's Tour, although erstwhile 2007 race leader Michael Rasmussen's sensational in-race dismissal for allegedly trying to avoid drug testing ratcheted up the drama.

So why did things feel different? Should they have? The anti-doping programs undertaken by Garmin, Columbia and CSC provided some assurance that teams were trying to turn things around. But then again, earlier that week, customs officials theatrically stopped and searched a car on the race course that was driven by the father of CSC's fraternal one-two punch of Andy and Frank Schleck. The authorities found nothing, but the action couldn't help but foster unease.

Perhaps that was the point. The French cycling federation wrestled control of the race from the international governing body and put national anti-doping officials in charge of testing. Under the new regime, speculation about who is suspect has become open debate as some of the same riders had their numbers pulled for testing day after day. Denial about the sport's dirty secrets has gradually evolved into a kick-butt-and-post-names approach that could unfairly smear some riders. That might be the price the sport has to pay at this point.

The question anyone mulling these matters should pose is when other sports will pony up the same cash. Sastre's iconic yellow jersey reminds us of something else. Cycling is the canary in a grimy coal mine right now, still capable of hitting sweet notes, yet in tenuous health from the dangerous fumes still lingering underground. If only athletes, managers and owners in other sports would become brave enough to take the same risks.

Lance Is On The Comeback Trail

by Bonnie D. Ford

Lance Armstrong's longtime coach Chris Carmichael said Tuesday that Armstrong is as driven as he was when he first returned to the peloton as a cancer survivor 10 years ago.

"It's like 1999 again," Carmichael told ESPN.com. "I don't know if I've ever seen him this motivated. He knows it's a big challenge. He knows he has to use his time well and he can't screw around with it."

Carmichael will help the soon-to-be 37-year-old try to regain his former supremacy at the Tour de France after three years away from professional cycling. Armstrong won his first Tour de France in '99 after returning to cycling in '98.

Armstrong's preparation for and second-place finish to a world champion at the Leadville Trail 100 mountain bike race in August sealed his desire to come back, Carmichael said, although he had already begun to lay the groundwork by registering for out-of-competition drug testing with the U.S. Anti-Doping Agency.

Carmichael and Armstrong spent three weeks together in Colorado training for the 100-mile race, which takes place at altitudes above 10,000 feet. "At first it was, 'Let's see how I do,' and then with about a week to go, it was just like, 'Man, I gotta figure out how to win this thing,'" Carmichael said of Armstrong's evolving attitude.

That period coincided with the end of the Tour de France, which they watched with keen interest.

"I know how to push his hot buttons," Carmichael said. "Basically, I said, 'Look who's there at the end. These are all guys you raced with.' I felt like there was no reason he couldn't come back to where he was. Not to take away from [2008 Tour winner Carlos] Sastre or any of the top guys, but all that was within his grasp."

Veteran rider Bobby Julich, a teammate of Armstrong's at Motorola in the 1990s, told ESPN.com he saw Armstrong in Nice, France, this summer and noticed that he looked extremely fit. The second-place finish in Leadville also impressed Julich from afar, but he said he never would have guessed Armstrong would launch a full comeback.

"He left at the pinnacle of the sport, a total ride-into-the-sunset finish, but obviously he didn't get it all out," said Julich, 36, who recently announced his own retirement. "I don't doubt for a second that he'll be right there. I don't think he'll have a problem with the physical part of it. He's the toughest son of a gun I'll ever meet."

On balance, Julich said, the increased attention Armstrong could bring to the sport is probably good, but he wondered whether younger riders like 2007 Tour champion Alberto Contador of Spain might feel it is their turn to be in the spotlight.

"Maybe he's doing it to prove that the Tour de France needs him, and he needs the Tour," Julich said.

It's currently unclear how Armstrong intends to back up a pledge to "create" an independent testing program — in addition to tests conducted by official agencies — that will show he is racing clean.

Armstrong told *Vanity Fair* that "revenge" against those who think he used performance-enhancing drugs is part of his motivation.

Tour de France race director Christian Prudhomme told The Associated Press that Armstrong and his team will have to "follow all the rules today, that are much more strict than they were."

Prudhomme noted the suspicions of drug use that followed Armstrong and suggested that it wasn't guaranteed that the former champion would make it to the start line next July.

"Suspicion has followed Lance Armstrong since 1999, everyone knows that. But in this proposed comeback...you have to remember we are in mid-September and that much water will run under the bridge until the Tour de France departure in Monaco," Prudhomme said.

In the *Vanity Fair* story, he admitted he has been "combative," "unavailable" and "arrogant" with the media in the past, and vowed he would mend his ways.

Armstrong has competed in three marathons (all completed under three hours) since his retirement and continued to enter local races as well as the recent grind at Leadville. He is concentrating on core training at the moment to build muscle, which naturally erodes with age, but come January will focus almost exclusively on training on the bike.

Carmichael said altitude training would be a priority. Armstrong recently purchased a home in Aspen, Colo., to facilitate that, and when he's at sea level will continue his past practice of sleeping in a hypoxic tent, where lower oxygen levels mimic conditions at altitude.

The coach shot down the notion that Armstrong has been bored in retirement, but said this was the ideal time for a comeback. Armstrong's foundation is well-established, his three children are school-age and he is single — a status continually noted by the tabloid press, which has delighted in detailing his high-profile dating escapades.

The *Vanity Fair* interview indicated that Armstrong is confident his age will not be an impediment. He cited recent examples like 41-year-old swimmer Dara Torres. "Athletes at 30, 35 mentally get tired," he said. "They've done their sport for 20, 25 years and they're like, 'I've had enough.' But there's no evidence to support that when you're 38, you're any slower than when you were 32."

"I think it's great," said longtime teammate George Hincapie. "He's done more than anyone for the sport, especially in America and around the world."

2007-2008 Season in Review

SPORTS ALMANAC

TRACK & FIELD

2008 IAAF World Athletics Final

The 6th annual IAAF World Athletics Final held in Stuttgart, Germany, Sept. 13-14, 2008. Total prize fund for the event is $3,020,000 with anyone setting a world record receiving an additional $100,000. Participants are decided according to the IAAF rankings in each event. Note that (WR) indicates world record and (CR) indicates championship meet record.

MEN

Event		Time	
100 meters	Asafa Powell, JAM	9.87	
200 meters	Stephane Buckland, MAU	20.57	
400 meters	LaShawn Merritt, USA	44.50	
800 meters	Alfred Kirwa Yego, KEN	1:49.05	
1500 meters	Haron Keitany, KEN	3:37.92	
3000 meters	Bernard Lagat, USA	8:02.97	
5000 meters	Edwin Cheruiyot Soi, KEN	13:22.81	
110m hurdles	David Oliver, USA	13.22	
400m hurdles	Kerron Clement, USA	48.96	
3000m steeple	Paul Kipsiele Koech, KEN	8:05.35	

Event		Hgt/Dist	
High Jump	Andrey Silnov, RUS	7-8½	**CR**
Pole Vault	Derek Miles, USA	19-0½	
Long Jump	Fabrice Lapierre, AUS	26-8½	
Triple Jump	Nelson Evora, POR	56-6¾	
Shot Put	Tomasz Majewski, POL	68-6	
Discus	Gerd Kanter, EST	224-4	
Hammer	Primoz Kozmus, SLO	262-5	
Javelin	Vadims Vasilevskis, LAT	284-3	

WOMEN

Event		Time	
100 meters	Shelly-Ann Fraser, JAM	10.94	
200 meters	Sanya Richards, USA	22.50	
400 meters	Sanya Richards, USA	50.41	
800 meters	Pamela Jelimo, KEN	1:56.23	**CR**
1500 meters	Maryam Yusuf Jamal, BRN	4:06.59	
3000 meters	Meseret Defar, ETH	8:43.60	
5000 meters	Meseret Defar, ETH	14:53.82	
100m hurdles	Josephine Onyia, ESP	12.54	
400m hurdles	Melaine Walker, JAM	54.06	
3000m steeple	Gulnara Galkina, RUS	9:21.73	**CR**

Event		Hgt/Dist	
High Jump	Blanka Vlasic, CRO	6-7	**CR**
Pole Vault	Silke Spiegelburg, GER	15-5	
Long Jump	Naide Gomes, POR	22-0¼	
Triple Jump	Anna Pyatykh, RUS	48-6	
Shot Put	Valerie Vili, NZ	64-7¼	
Discus	Yarelis Barrios, CUB	212-10	
Hammer	Yipsi Moreno, CUB	243-1	
Javelin	Barbora Spotakova, CZE	237-2	**WR**

2008 IAAF World Cross Country Championships

The 36th IAAF World Cross Country Championships held in Edinburgh, Scotland (March 30).

MEN

12 km	1. Kenenisa Bekele, Ethiopia	34:38
(7.45 mi)	2. Leonard Patrick Komon, Kenya	34:41
	3. Zersenay Tadese, Eritrea	34:43
	Best USA—Jorge Torres, 19th	36:03

WOMEN

8 km	1. Tirunesh Dibaba, Ethiopia	25:10
(4.97 mi)	2. Mestawet Tufa, Ethiopia	25:15
	3. Linet Chepkwemoi Masai, Kenya	25:18
	Best USA—Emily Brown, 18th	26:36

World Outdoor Records Set in 2008

World outdoor records set or equaled between Oct. 1, 2007 and Sept. 30, 2008; (p) indicates record is pending ratification by the IAAF.

MEN

Event	Name	Record	Old Mark	Date
100 meters	**Usain Bolt**, JAM	9.72	9.74	May 31, 2008
	Usain Bolt, JAM	9.69p	9.72	August 16, 2008
200 meters	**Usain Bolt**, JAM	19.30p	19.32	August 20, 2008
4 x 100m	**JAM** (Carter, Frater, Bolt, Powell)	37.10p	37.40	August 22, 2008
110m hurdles	**Dayron Robles**, CUB	12.87	12.88	June 12, 2008
20km race walk	**Sergey Morozov**, RUS	1:16:43p	1:17:16	June 8, 2008
50km race walk	**Denis Nizhegorodov**, RUS	3:34:14p	3:35:47	May 11, 2008
Marathon	**Haile Gebrselassie**, ETH	2:03:59p	2:04:26	Sept. 28, 2008

WOMEN

Event	Name	Record	Old Mark	Date
5,000 meters	**Tirunesh Dibaba**, ETH	14:11.15p	14:16.63	June 6, 2008
Steeplechase	**G. Samitova-Galkina**, RUS	8:58.81p	9:01.59	August 17, 2008
Pole Vault	**Yelena Isinbayeva**, RUS	16-6	16-5¼	July 11, 2008
	Yelena Isinbayeva, RUS	16-6½	16-6	July 29, 2008
	Yelena Isinbayeva, RUS	16-6¾p	16-6½	August 18, 2008
Javelin	**Barbora Spotakova**, CZE	237-2p	235-3	September 13, 2008

World, Olympic and American Outdoor Records
As of Sept. 30, 2008

World outdoor records officially recognized by the International Amateur Athletics Federation (IAAF); (p) indicates record is pending ratification. Note that marathon records are not officially recognized by the IAAF.

MEN
Running

Event		Time		Date Set	Location
100 meters:	**World**	9.69p	**Usain Bolt**, Jamaica	Aug. 16, 2008	Beijing
	Olympic	9.69	Bolt (same as World)	—	—
	American	9.77	Tyson Gay	June 28, 2008	Eugene, Ore.
200 meters:	**World**	19.30p	**Usain Bolt**, Jamaica	Aug. 20, 2008	Beijing
	Olympic	19.30	Bolt (same as World)	—	—
	American	19.32	Michael Johnson, USA	Aug. 1, 1996	Atlanta
400 meters:	**World**	43.18	**Michael Johnson**, USA	Aug. 26, 1999	Seville
	Olympic	43.49	Michael Johnson, USA	July 29, 1996	Atlanta
	American	43.18	Johnson (same as World)	—	—
800 meters:	**World**	1:41.11	**Wilson Kipketer**, Denmark	Aug. 24, 1997	Cologne
	Olympic	1:42.58	Vebjoern Rodal, Norway	July 31, 1996	Atlanta
	American	1:42.60	Johnny Gray	Aug. 28, 1985	Koblenz, W. Ger.
1000 meters:	**World**	2:11.96	**Noah Ngeny**, Kenya	Sept. 5, 1999	Rieti, ITA
	Olympic		Not an event	—	—
	American	2:13.9	Rick Wohlhuter	July 30, 1974	Oslo
1500 meters:	**World**	3:26.00	**Hicham El Guerrouj**, Morocco	July 14, 1998	Rome
	Olympic	3:32.07	Noah Ngeny, Kenya	Sept. 29, 2000	Sydney
	American	3:29.30	Bernard Lagat	Aug. 28, 2005	Rieti, ITA
Mile:	**World**	3:43.13	**Hicham El Guerrouj**, Morocco	July 7, 1999	Rome
	Olympic		Not an event	—	—
	American	3:46.91	Alan Webb	July 21, 2007	Brasschaa, BEL
2000 meters:	**World**	4:44.79	**Hicham El Guerrouj**, Morocco	Sept. 7, 1999	Berlin
	Olympic		Not an event	—	—
	American	4:52.44	Jim Spivey	Sept. 15, 1987	Lausanne, SWI
3000 meters:	**World**	7:20.67	**Daniel Komen**, Kenya	Sept. 1, 1996	Rieti, ITA
	Olympic		Not an event	—	—
	American	7:30.84	Bob Kennedy	Aug. 8, 1998	Monte Carlo
5000 meters:	**World**	12:37.35	**Kenenisa Bekele**, Ethiopia	May 31, 2004	Hengelo, NED
	Olympic	12:57.82	Kenenisa Bekele, Ethiopia	Aug. 23, 2008	Beijing
	American	12:58.21	Bob Kennedy	Aug. 14, 1996	Zurich
10,000 meters:	**World**	26:17.53	**Kenenisa Bekele**, Ethiopia	Aug. 26, 2005	Brussels
	Olympic	27:01.17	Kenenisa Bekele, Ethiopia	Aug. 17, 2008	Beijing
	American	27:13.98	Meb Keflezighi	May 4, 2001	Stanford, Calif.
20,000 meters:	**World**	56:26.0	**Haile Gebrselassie**, Ethiopia	June 27, 2007	Ostrava, CZR
	Olympic		Not an event	—	—
	American	58:15.0	Bill Rodgers	Aug. 9, 1977	Boston
Marathon:	**World**	2:03:59p	**Haile Gebrselassie**, Ethiopia	Sept. 28, 2008	Berlin
	Olympic	2:06:32	Samuel Kamau Wanjiru, Kenya	Aug. 24, 2008	Beijing
	American	2:05:38	Khalid Khannouchi	Apr. 14, 2002	London

Relays

Event		Time		Date Set	Location
4 x 100m:	**World**	37.10p	**Jamaica** (Carter, Frater, Bolt, Powell)	Aug. 22, 2008	Beijing
	Olympic	37.10	Jamaica (same as World)	—	—
	American	37.40	USA (Marsh, Burrell, Mitchell, C. Lewis)	Aug. 8, 1992	Barcelona
		37.40	USA (Drummond, Cason, Mitchell, Burrell)	Aug. 21, 1993	Stuttgart
4 x 200m:	**World**	1:18.68	**USA** (Marsh, Burrell, Heard, C. Lewis)	Apr. 17, 1994	Walnut, Calif.
	Olympic		Not an event	—	—
	American	1:18.68	USA (same as World)	—	—
4 x 400m:	**World**	2:54.29	**USA** (Valmon, Watts, Reynolds, Johnson)	July 22, 1993	Stuttgart
	Olympic	2:55.39	USA (Merritt, Taylor, Neville, Wariner)	Aug. 23, 2008	Beijing
	American	2:54.29	USA (same as World)	—	—
4 x 800m:	**World**	7:02.43	**Kenya** (Mutua, Yiampoy, Kombich, Bungei)	Aug. 25, 2006	Brussels
	Olympic		Not an event	—	—
	American	7:02.82	USA (Harris, Robinson, Burley, Krummenacker)	Aug. 25, 2006	Brussels
4 x 1500m:	**World**	14:38.8	**West Germany** (Wessinghage, Hudak, Lederer, Fleschen)	Aug. 17, 1977	Cologne
	Olympic		Not an event	—	—
	American	14:46.3	USA (Aldredge, Clifford, Harbour, Duits)	June 24, 1979	Bourges, FRA

Note: On August 12, 2008 the IAAF stripped the United States' 1998 world record in the 4 x 400m (2:54.20) due to Antonio Pettigrew's doping admission. Also on that team were Jerome Young, Tyree Washington and Michael Johnson.

Steeplechase

Event		Time		Date Set	Location
3000 meters:	**World**	7:53.63	**Saif Saaeed Shaheen**, Qatar	Sept. 3, 2004	Brussels
	Olympic	8:05.51	Julius Kariuki, Kenya	Sept. 30, 1988	Seoul
	American	8:08.82	Daniel Lincoln	July 14, 2006	Rome

Note: A men's steeplechase course consists of 28 hurdles (3 feet high) and seven water jumps (12 feet long).

Hurdles

Event		Time		Date Set	Location
110 meters:	**World**	12.87	**Dayron Robles**, Cuba	June 11, 2008	Ostrava, CZR
	Olympic	12.91	Xiang Liu, China	Aug. 27, 2004	Athens
	American	12.90	Dominique Arnold	July 11, 2006	Lausanne
400 meters:	**World**	46.78	**Kevin Young**, USA	Aug. 6, 1992	Barcelona
	Olympic	46.78	Young (same as World)	—	—
	American	46.78	Young (same as World)	—	—

Note: The 10 hurdles at 110 meters are 3 feet, 6 inches high and those at 400 meters are 3 feet.

Walking

Event		Time		Date Set	Location
20 km:	**World**	1:16:43	**Sergey Morozov**, Russia	June 8, 2008	Saransk, RUS
	Olympic	1:18:59	Robert Korzeniowski, Poland	Sept. 22, 2000	Sydney
	American	1:23:40	Tim Seaman	Aug. 19, 2000	San Diego
50 km:	**World**	3:34:14	**Denis Nizhegorodov**, Russia	May 11, 2008	Cheboksary, RUS
	Olympic	3:37:09	Alex Schwazer, Italy	Aug. 22, 2008	Beijing
	American	3:48:04	Curt Clausen	May 2, 1999	Deauville, FRA

Field Events

Event		Mark		Date Set	Location
High Jump:	**World**	8-0½	**Javier Sotomayor**, Cuba	July 27, 1993	Salamanca, SPA
	Olympic	7-10	Charles Austin, USA	July 28, 1996	Atlanta
	American	7-10½	Charles Austin	Aug. 7, 1991	Zurich
Pole Vault:	**World**	20-1¾	**Sergey Bubka**, Ukraine	July 31, 1994	Sestriere, ITA
	Olympic	19-6½	Steven Hooker, Australia	Aug. 22, 2008	Beijing
	American	19-9¾	Brad Walker	June 8, 2008	Eugene, Ore.
Long Jump:	**World**	29-4½	**Mike Powell**, USA	Aug. 30, 1991	Tokyo
	Olympic	29-2½	Bob Beamon, USA	Oct. 18, 1968	Mexico City
	American	29-4½	Powell (same as World)	—	—
Triple Jump:	**World**	60-0¼	**Jonathan Edwards**, GBR	Aug. 7, 1995	Göteborg, SWE
	Olympic	59-4¼	Kenny Harrison, USA	July 27, 1996	Atlanta
	American	59-4¼	Kenny Harrison (same as Olympic)	—	—
Shot Put:	**World**	75-10¼	**Randy Barnes**, USA	May 20, 1990	Los Angeles
	Olympic	73-8¾	Ulf Timmermann, East Germany	Sept. 23, 1988	Seoul
	American	75-10¼	Barnes (same as World)	—	—
Discus:	**World**	243-0	**Jurgen Schult**, East Germany	June 6, 1986	Neubrandenburg
	Olympic	229-3½	Virgilijus Alekna, Lithuania	Aug. 23, 2004	Athens
	American	237-4	Ben Plucknett	July 7, 1981	Stockholm
Javelin:	**World**	323-1	**Jan Zelezny**, Czech Republic	May 25, 1996	Jena, GER
	Olympic	297-1	Andreas Thorkildsen, Norway	Aug. 23, 2008	Beijing
	American	299-6	Breaux Greer	June 21, 2007	Indianapolis
Hammer:	**World**	284-7	**Yuriy Sedykh**, USSR	Aug. 30, 1986	Stuttgart
	Olympic	278-2	Sergey Litvinov, USSR	Sept. 26, 1988	Seoul
	American	270-9	Lance Deal	Sept. 7, 1996	Milan

Note: The international weights for men—**Shot** (16 lbs); **Discus** (4 lbs/6.55 oz); **Javelin** (minimum 1 lb/12¼ oz.); **Hammer** (16 lbs).

Decathlon

Event		Points		Date Set	Location
Ten Events:	**World**	9026	**Roman Sebrle**, Czech Republic	May 26-27, 2001	Gotzis, AUT
	Olympic	8893	Roman Sebrle, Czech Republic	Aug. 23-24, 2004	Athens
	American	8891	Dan O'Brien	Sept. 4-5, 1992	Talence, FRA

Note: Sebrle's WR times and distances, in order over two days—**100m** (10.64); **LJ** (26-7¼); **Shot** (50-3½); **HJ** (6-11½); **400m** (47.79); **110m H** (13.92); **Discus** (157-3); **PV** (15-9); **Jav** (230-2); **1500m** (4:21.98).

World, Olympic and American Outdoor Records (Cont.)

WOMEN
Running

Event		Time		Date Set	Location
100 meters:	World	10.49	**Florence Griffith Joyner**, USA	July 16, 1988	Indianapolis
	Olympic	10.62	Florence Griffith Joyner, USA	Sept. 24, 1988	Seoul
	American	10.49	Griffith Joyner (same as World)	—	—
200 meters:	World	21.34	**Florence Griffith Joyner**, USA	Sept. 29, 1988	Seoul
	Olympic	21.34	Griffith Joyner (same as World)	—	—
	American	21.34	Griffith Joyner (same as World)	—	—
400 meters:	World	47.60	**Marita Koch**, East Germany	Oct. 6, 1985	Canberra, AUS
	Olympic	48.25	Marie-Jose Perec, France	July 29, 1996	Atlanta
	American	48.70	Sanya Richards	Sept. 16, 2006	Athens
800 meters:	World	1:53.28	**Jarmila Kratochvilova**, Czech.	July 26, 1983	Munich
	Olympic	1:53.42	Nadezhda Olizarenko, USSR	July 27, 1980	Moscow
	American	1:56.40	Jearl Miles-Clark	Aug. 11, 1999	Zurich
1000 meters:	World	2:28.98	**Svetlana Masterkova**, Russia	Aug. 23, 1996	Brussels
	Olympic		Not an event		
	American	2:31.80	Regina Jacobs	July 3, 1999	Brunswick, Me.
1500 meters:	World	3:50.46	**Qu Yunxia**, China	Sept. 11, 1993	Beijing
	Olympic	3:53.96	Paula Ivan, Romania	Oct. 1, 1988	Seoul
	American	3:57.12	Mary Slaney	July 26, 1983	Stockholm
Mile:	World	4:12.56	**Svetlana Masterkova**, Russia	Aug. 14, 1996	Zurich
	Olympic		Not an event		
	American	4:16.71	Mary Slaney	Aug. 21, 1985	Zurich
2000 meters:	World	5:25.36	**Sonia O'Sullivan**, Ireland	July 8, 1994	Edinburgh
	Olympic		Not an event	—	—
	American	5:32.7	Mary Slaney	Aug. 3, 1984	Eugene, Ore.
3000 meters:	World	8:06.11	**Wang Junxia**, China	Sept. 13, 1993	Beijing
	Olympic	8:26.53	Tatyana Samolenko, USSR	Sept. 25, 1988	Seoul
	American	8:25.83	Mary Slaney	Sept. 7, 1985	Rome
5000 meters:	World	14:11.15p	**Tirunesh Dibaba**, Ethiopia	June 6, 2008	Oslo
	Olympic	14:40.79	Gabriela Szabo, Romania	Sept. 25, 2000	Sydney
	American	14:44.80	Shalane Flanagan	April 13, 2007	Sacramento
10,000 meters:	World	29:31.78	**Wang Junxia**, China	Sept. 8, 1993.	Beijing
	Olympic	29:54.66	Tirunesh Dibaba, Ethiopia	Aug. 15, 2008	Beijing
	American	30:22.22	Shalane Flanagan	Aug. 15, 2008	Beijing
Marathon:	World	2:15:25	**Paula Radcliffe**, Great Britain	Apr. 13, 2003	London
	Olympic	2:23:14	Naoko Takahashi, Japan	Sept. 24, 2000	Sydney
	American	2:19:36	Deena Kastor	Apr. 23, 2006	London

Relays

Event		Time		Date Set	Location
4 x 100m:	World	41.37	**East Germany** (Gladisch, Rieger, Auerswald, Gohr)	Oct. 6, 1985	Canberra, AUS
	Olympic	41.60	East Germany (Muller, Wockel, Auerswald, Gohr)	Aug. 1, 1980	Moscow
	American	41.47	USA (Gaines, Jones, Miller, Devers)	Aug. 9, 1997	Athens
4 x 200m:	World	1:27.46	**USA** (Jenkins, Colander-Richardson, Perry, Jones)	Apr. 29, 2000	Philadelphia
	Olympic		Not an event	—	—
	American	1:27.46	USA (same as World)	—	—
4 x 400m:	World	3:15.17	**USSR** (Ledovskaya, Nazarova, Pinigina, Bryzgina)	Oct. 1, 1988	Seoul
	Olympic	3:15.17	USSR (same as World)	—	—
	American	3:15.51	USA (Howard, Dixon, Brisco, Griffith Joyner)	Oct. 1, 1988	Seoul
4 x 800m:	World	7:50.17	**USSR** (Olizarenko, Gurina, Borisova, Podyalovskaya)	Aug. 5, 1984	Moscow
	Olympic		Not an event	—	—
	American	8:17.09	Athletics West (Addison, Arbogast, Decker Slaney, Mullen)	Apr. 24, 1983	Walnut, Calif.

Hurdles

Event		Time		Date Set	Location
100 meters:	World	12.21	**Yordanka Donkova**, Bulgaria	Aug. 20, 1988	Stara Zagora, BUL
	Olympic	12.37	Joanna Hayes, USA	Aug. 24, 2004	Athens
	American	12.33	Gail Devers	July 23, 2000	Sacramento

400 meters:	World	52.34	**Yuliya Pechenkina**, Russia	Aug. 8, 2003	Tula, RUS
	Olympic	52.64	Melanie Walker, Jamaica	Aug. 20, 2008	Beijing
	American	52.61	Kim Batten	Aug. 11, 1995	Göteborg, SWE

Note: The 10 hurdles at 110 meters are 3 feet, 6 inches high and those at 400 meters are 3 feet.

Walking

Event		Time		Date Set	Location
20 km:	World	1:25:41	**Olimpiada Ivanova**, Russia	Aug. 7, 2005	Helsinki
	Olympic	1:29:05	Wang Liping, China	Sept. 28, 2000	Sydney
	American	1:31:51	Michelle Rohl	May 13, 2000	Kenosha, Wis.

Note: On Feb. 23, 2008 Russian Olga Kaniskina recorded the fastest 20k walk in history, 1:25:11, but it cannot be registered as the world record because only Russian and no international judges were present.

Steeplechase

Event		Time		Date Set	Location
3000 meters:	World	8:58.81p	**G. Samitova-Galkina**, Russia	Aug. 17, 2008	Beijing
	Olympic	8:58.81	Samitova-Galkina (same as World)	—	—
	American	9:22.26	Jennifer Barringer	Aug. 17, 2008	Beijing

Note: A women's steeplechase course consists of 28 hurdles (30 inches high) and seven water jumps (10 feet long).

Field Events

Event		Mark		Date Set	Location
High Jump:	World	6-10¼	**Stefka Kostadinova**, Bulgaria	Aug. 30, 1987	Rome
	Olympic	6-9	Yelena Slesarenko, Russia	Aug. 28, 2004	Athens
	American	6-8	Louise Ritter	July 8, 1988	Austin, Texas
		6-8	Louise Ritter	Sept. 30, 1988	Seoul
Pole Vault:	World	16-6¾	**Yelena Isinbayeva**, Russia	Aug. 18, 2008	Beijing
	Olympic	16-6¾	Isinbayeva, Russia (same as World)	—	—
	American	16-1¾	Jenn Stuczynski	July 6, 2008	Eugene, Ore.
Long Jump:	World	24-8¼	**Galina Chistyakova**, USSR	June 11, 1988	Leningrad
	Olympic	24-3¼	Jackie Joyner-Kersee, USA	Sept. 29, 1988	Seoul
	American	24-7	Jackie Joyner-Kersee	May 22, 1994	New York
Triple Jump:	World	50-10¼	**Inessa Kravets**, Ukraine	Aug. 10, 1995	Göteborg, SWE
	Olympic	50-6	Francoise Mbango-Etone, Cameroon	Aug. 17, 2008	Beijing
	American	47-5	Tiombe Hurd	July 11, 2004	Sacramento, Calif.
Shot Put:	World	74-3	**Natalya Lisovskaya**, USSR	June 7, 1987	Moscow
	Olympic	73-6¼	Ilona Slupianek, E. Germany	July 24, 1980	Moscow
	American	66-2½	Ramona Pagel	June 25, 1988	San Diego
Discus:	World	252-0	**Gabriele Reinsch**, E. Germany	July 9, 1988	Neubrandenburg
	Olympic	237-2½	Martina Hellmann, E. Germany	Sept. 29, 1988	Seoul-Roos
	American	222-0	Suzy Powell-Roos	Apr. 14, 2007	Wailuku, Hawaii
Javelin:	World	237-2p	**Barbora Spotakova**, Czech Rep.	Sept. 13, 2008	Stuttgart
	Olympic	234-8	Osleidys Menendez, Cuba	Aug. 27, 2004	Athens
	American	210-7	Kim Kreiner	May 17, 2007	Fortaleza, BRA
Hammer:	World	257-11	**Tatyana Lysenko**, Russia	May 26, 2007	Sochi, RUS
	Olympic	250-5	Aksana Miankova, Belarus	Aug. 20, 2008	Beijing
	American	242-4	Erin Gilreath	June 25, 2005	Carson, Calif.

Note: The international weights for women—**Shot** (8 lbs/13 oz); **Discus** (2 lbs/3.27 oz); **Javelin** (minimum 1 lb/5.16 oz); **Hammer** (8 lbs/13 oz).

Heptathlon

Event		Points		Date Set	Location
Seven Events:	World	7291	**Jackie Joyner-Kersee**, USA	Sept. 23-24, 1988	Seoul
	Olympic	7291	Joyner-Kersee (same as World)	—	—
	American	7291	Joyner-Kersee (same as World)	—	—

Note: Joyner-Kersee's WR times and distances, in order over two days—**100m H** (12.69); **HJ** (61¼); **Shot** (51-10); **200m** (22.56); **LJ** (23-10¼); **Jav** (149-10); **800m** (2:08.51).

World Indoor Records Set in 2008

World indoor records set or equaled between Oct. 1, 2007 and Sept. 30, 2008. (p) indicates pending ratification.

MEN

No world records set.

WOMEN

Event	Name	Record	Old Mark	Date
1500 meters	**Yelena Soboleva**, RUS	3:58.05	3:58.28	February 10, 2008
	Yelena Soboleva, RUS	3:57.71	3:58.05	March 9, 2008
60-meter hurdles	**Susanna Kallur**, SWE	7.68	7.69	February 10, 2008
4 x 800-meter relay	**Russia**	8:14.53p	8:18.54	February 10, 2008
Pole Vault	**Yelena Isinbayeva**, RUS	16-2¾	16-2	February 10, 2008

World and American Indoor Records

As of Sept. 30, 2008

World indoor records officially recognized by the International Amateur Athletics Federation (IAAF); (p) indicates record is pending ratification by the IAAF; (a) indicates record was set at an altitude over 1000 meters.

MEN
Running

Event		Time		Date Set	Location
50 meters:	World	5.56a	**Donovan Bailey**, Canada	Feb. 9, 1996	Reno, Nev.
		5.56	**Maurice Greene**, USA	Feb. 13, 1999	Los Angeles
	American	5.56	Greene (same as World)	Feb. 13, 1999	Los Angeles
60 meters:	World	6.39	**Maurice Greene**, USA	Feb. 3, 1998	Madrid
		6.39	**Maurice Greene**, USA	Mar. 3, 2001	Atlanta
	American	6.39	Greene (same as World)	—	—
200 meters:	World	19.92	**Frankie Fredericks**, Namibia	Feb. 18, 1996	Lievin, FRA
	American	20.10	Wallace Spearmon	Mar. 11, 2005	Fayetteville, Ark.
400 meters:	World	44.57	**Kerron Clement**, USA	Mar. 12, 2005	Fayetteville, Ark.
	American	44.57	Clement (same as World)	—	—
800 meters:	World	1:42.67	**Wilson Kipketer**, Denmark	Mar. 9, 1997	Paris
	American	1:45.00	Johnny Gray	Mar. 8, 1992	Sindelfingen, GER
1000 meters:	World	2:14.96	**Wilson Kipketer**, Denmark	Feb. 20, 2000	Birmingham, ENG
	American	2:17.86	David Krummenacker	Jan. 27, 2002	Boston
1500 meters:	World	3:31.18	**Hicham El Guerrouj**, Morocco	Feb. 2, 1997	Stuttgart
	American	3:33.34	Bernard Lagat	Feb. 11, 2005	Fayetteville, Ark.
Mile:	World	3:48.45	**Hicham El Guerrouj**, Morocco	Feb. 12, 1997	Ghent, BEL
	American	3:49.89	Bernard Lagat	Feb. 11, 2005	Fayetteville, Ark.
3000 meters:	World	7:24.90	**Daniel Komen**, Kenya	Feb. 6, 1998	Budapest
	American	7:32.43	Bernard Lagat	Feb. 17, 2007	Birmingham, ENG
5000 meters:	World	12:49.60	**Kenenisa Bekele**, Ethiopia	Feb. 20, 2004	Birmingham, ENG
	American	13:20.55	Doug Padilla	Feb. 12, 1982	New York

Note: The Mile run is 1,609.344 meters.

Hurdles

Event		Time		Date Set	Location
50 meters:	World	6.25	**Mark McKoy**, Canada	Mar. 5, 1986	Kobe, JPN
	American	6.35	Greg Foster	Jan. 27, 1985	Rosemont, Ill.
		6.35	Greg Foster	Jan. 31, 1987	Ottawa
60 meters:	World	7.30	**Colin Jackson**, Great Britain	Mar. 6, 1994	Sindelfingen, GER
	American	7.36	Greg Foster	Jan. 16, 1987	Los Angeles
		7.36	Allen Johnson	March 6, 2004	Budapest

Note: The hurdles for both distances are 3 feet, 6 inches high. There are four hurdles in the 50 meters and five in the 60.

Walking

Event		Time		Date Set	Location
5000 meters:	World	18:07.08	**Mikhail Shchennikov**, Russia	Feb. 14, 1995	Moscow
	American	19:15.88	Tim Seaman	Feb. 25, 2006	Boston

Relays

Event		Time		Date Set	Location
4 x 200 meters:	World	1:22.11	**Great Britain**	Mar. 3, 1991	Glasgow
	American	1:22.71	National Team	Mar. 3, 1991	Glasgow
4 x 400 meters:	World	3:02.83	**United States**	Mar. 7, 1999	Maebashi, JPN
	American	3:01.96	National Team	Feb. 11, 2006	Fayetteville, Ark.
4 x 800 meters:	World	7:13.94	**United States**	Feb. 6, 2000	Boston
	American	7:13.94	Global Athletics (same as World)	Feb. 6, 2000	Boston

Note: The 4 x 400-meter American record of 3:01.96 was not ratified as a World record because no EPO testing was done.

Field Events

Event		Mark		Date Set	Location
High Jump:	World	7-11½	**Javier Sotomayor**, Cuba	Mar. 4, 1989	Budapest
	American	7-10½	Hollis Conway	Mar. 10, 1991	Seville
Pole Vault:	World	20-2	**Sergey Bubka**, Ukraine	Feb. 21, 1993	Donyetsk, UKR
	American	19-9p	Jeff Hartwig	Mar. 10, 2002	Sindelfingen, GER
Long Jump:	World	28-10¼	**Carl Lewis**, USA	Jan. 27, 1984	New York
	American	28-10¼	Lewis (same as World)	—	—
Triple Jump:	World	58-6	**Aliecer Urrutia**, Cuba	Mar. 1, 1997	Sindelfingen, GER
		58-6	**Christian Olsson**, Sweden	Mar. 7, 2004	Budapest
	American	58-3¼	Mike Conley	Feb. 27, 1987	New York
Shot Put:	World	74-4¼	**Randy Barnes**, USA	Jan. 20, 1989	Los Angeles
	American	74-4¼	Barnes (same as World)	—	—

Note: The international shot put weight for men is 16 lbs.

Heptathlon

	Points		Date Set	Location
Seven Events:	**World** 6476	**Dan O'Brien**, USA	Mar. 13-14, 1993	Toronto
	American 6476	O'Brien (same as World)		

Note: O'Brien's WR times and distances, in order over two days—**60m** (6.67); **LJ** (25-8¾); **SP** (52-6¾); **HJ** (6-11¾); **60m H** (7.85); **PV** (17-0¾); **1000m** (2:57.96).

WOMEN
Running

Event	Time		Date Set	Location
50 meters:	**World** 5.96	**Irina Privalova**, Russia	Feb. 9, 1995	Madrid
	American 6.02	Gail Devers	Feb. 21, 1999	Lievin, FRA
60 meters:	**World** 6.92	**Irina Privalova**, Russia	Feb. 11, 1993	Madrid
	6.92	**Irina Privalova**, Russia	Feb. 9, 1995	Madrid
	American 6.95	Gail Devers	Mar. 12, 1993	Toronto
	6.95	Marion Jones	Mar. 7, 1998	Maebashi, JPN
200 meters:	**World** 21.87	**Merlene Ottey**, Jamaica	Feb. 13, 1993	Lievin, FRA
	American 22.18	Michelle Collins	Mar. 15, 2003	Birmingham, ENG
400 meters:	**World** 49.59	**Jarmila Kratochvilova**, Czech.	Mar. 7, 1982	Milan
	American 50.64	Diane Dixon	Mar. 10, 1991	Seville
800 meters:	**World** 1:55.82	**Jolanda Ceplak**, Slovenia	Mar. 3, 2002	Vienna
	American . . .1:58.71	Nicole Teter	Mar. 2, 2002	New York
1000 meters:	**World** 2:30.94	**Maria Mutola**, Mozambique	Feb. 25, 1999	Stockholm
	American . . .2:34.19	Jennifer Toomey	Feb. 20, 2004	Birmingham, ENG
1500 meters:	**World** . . .3:57.71	**Yelena Soboleva**, Russia	March 9, 2008	Moscow
	American . . .3:59.98	Regina Jacobs	Feb. 1, 2003	Boston
Mile:	**World** 4:17.14	**Doina Melinte**, Romania	Feb. 9, 1990	E. Rutherford, N.J.
	American 4:20.5	Mary Slaney	Feb. 19, 1982	San Diego
3000 meters:	**World** 8:23.72	**Meseret Defar**, Ethiopia	Feb. 3, 2007	Stuttgart
	American . . .8:33.25	Shalane Flanagan	Jan. 27, 2007	Boston
5000 meters:	**World** . . .14:27.42	**Tirunesh Dibaba**, Ethiopia	Jan. 27, 2007	Boston
	American . .15:07.44	Marla Runyan	Feb. 18, 2001	New York City

Note: The Mile run is 1,609.344 meters.

Hurdles

Event	Time		Date Set	Location
50 meters:	**World** 6.58	**Cornelia Oschkenat**, E. Ger.	Feb. 20, 1988	East Berlin
	American 6.67a	Jackie Joyner-Kersee	Feb. 10, 1995	Reno, Nev.
60 meters:	**World** 7.68	**Susanna Kallur**, Sweden	Feb. 10, 2008	Karlsruhe, GER
	American 7.74	Gail Devers	Mar. 1, 2003	Boston

Note: The hurdles for both distances are 2 feet, 9 inches high. There are four hurdles in the 50 meters and five in the 60.

Walking

Event	Time		Date Set	Location
3000 meters:	**World** . . .11:40.33	**Claudia Stef**, Romania	Jan. 30, 1999	Bucharest
	American . .12:20.79	Debbi Lawrence	Mar. 12, 1993	Toronto

Relays

Event	Time		Date Set	Location
4 x 200 meters:	**World** 1:32.41	**Russia**	Jan. 29, 2005	Glasgow
	American 1:33.24	National Team	Feb. 12, 1994	Glasgow
4 x 400 meters:	**World** 3:23.37	**Russia**	Jan. 28, 2006	Glasgow
	American 3:27.59	National Team	Mar. 7, 1999	Maebashi, JPN
4 x 800 meters:	**World** . . . .8:14.53 p	**Russia**	Feb. 10, 2008	Moscow, RUS
	American . . . 8:25.5	Villanova	Feb. 7, 1987	Gainesville, Fla.

Field Events

Event	Mark		Date Set	Location
High Jump:	**World** 6-9¾	**Kajsa Bergqvist**, Sweden	Feb. 4, 2006	Arnstadt, GER
	American 6-7	Tisha Waller	Feb. 28, 1998	Atlanta
Pole Vault:	**World** 16-2¾	**Yelena Isinbayeva**, Russia	Feb. 16, 2008	Donetsk, UKR
	American 15-9¼	Stacy Dragila, USA	Mar. 6, 2004	Budapest
Long Jump:	**World** 24-2¼	**Heike Drechsler**, E. Germany	Feb. 13, 1988	Vienna
	American 23-4¾	Jackie Joyner-Kersee	Mar. 5, 1994	Atlanta
Triple Jump:	**World** 50-4¾	**Tatyana Lebedeva**, Russia	Mar. 6, 2004	Budapest
	American 46-8¼	Sheila Hudson	Mar. 4, 1995	Atlanta
Shot Put:	**World** 73-10	**Helena Fibingerova**, Czech.	Feb. 19, 1977	Jablonec, CZE
	American 65-0¾	Ramona Pagel	Feb. 20, 1987	Inglewood, Calif.

Note: The international shotput weight for women is 8 lbs. and 13 oz.

Pentathlon

	Points		Date Set	Location
Five Events:	**World** 4991	**Irina Byelova**, Russia	Feb. 14-15, 1992	Berlin
	American 4753	DeDee Nathan	Mar. 4-5, 1999	Maebashi, JPN

Note: Byelova's WR times and distances, in order over two days—**60m H** (8.22); **HJ** (6-4); **SP** (43-5¾); **LJ** (21-1¾); **800m** (2:10.26).

SWIMMING

World Swimming Records Set in 2008

World long course records set or equaled between Oct. 1, 2007 and Sept. 30, 2008; (p) indicates record is awaiting ratification. (r) indicates relay leadoff split.

MEN

Event	Name	Record	Old Mark	Date
50m freestyle (1)	**Eamon Sullivan**, AUS	21.56	21.64	Feb. 17, 2008
50m freestyle (2)	**Alain Bernard**, FRA	21.50	21.56	March 13, 2008
50m freestyle (3)	**Eamon Sullivan**, AUS	21.28p	21.50	March 22, 2008
100m freestyle (1)	**Jason Lezak**, USA	47.58	47.84	July 2, 2008
100m freestyle (2)	**Eamon Sullivan**, AUS	47.05p	47.58	Aug. 13, 2008
200m freestyle	**Michael Phelps**, USA	1:42.96p	1:43.86	Aug. 10, 2008
50m backstroke	**Liam Tancock**, GBR	24.47	24.80	March 31, 2008
100m backstroke (1)	**Nicholas Thoman**, USA	52.91	52.98	Aug. 1, 2008
100m backstroke (2)	**Aaron Peirsol**, USA	52.54p	52.91	Aug. 12, 2008
200m backstroke	**Ryan Lochte**, USA	1:53.94p	1:54.32	Aug. 13, 2008
100m breaststroke	**Kosuke Kitajima**, JPN	58.91p	59.13	Aug. 11, 2008
200m butterfly	**Michael Phelps**, USA	1:52.03p	1:52.09	Aug. 13, 2008
200m IM	**Michael Phelps**, USA	1:54.23p	1:54.98	Aug. 15, 2008
400m IM (1)	**Michael Phelps**, USA	4:05.25	4:06.22	June 29, 2008
400m IM (2)	**Michael Phelps**, USA	4:03.84p	4:05.25	Aug. 10, 2008
4x100m freestyle relay	**USA** (Phelps, Weber-Gale, Jones, Lezak)	3:08.24p	3:12.46	Aug. 11, 2008
4x200m freestyle relay	**USA** (Phelps, Lochte, Berens, Vanderkaay)	6:58.56p	7:03.24	Aug. 13, 2008
4x100m medley relay	**USA** (Peirsol, Hansen, Phelps, Lezak)	3:29.34p	3:30.68	Aug. 17, 2008

WOMEN

Event	Name	Record	Old Mark	Date
50m freestyle	**Libby Trickett**, AUS	23.97p	24.13	March 29, 2008
100m freestyle	**Libby Trickett**, AUS	52.88p	53.30	March 27, 2008
200m freestyle	**Federica Pellegrini**, ITA	1:54.82p	1:55.52	August 13, 2008
400m freestyle	**Federica Pellegrini**, ITA	4:01.53p	4:02.13	March 24, 2008
800m freestyle	**Rebecca Adlington**, GBR	8:14.10p	8:16.22	August 16, 2008
50m backstroke	**Sophie Edington**, AUS	27.67p	28.16	March 23, 2008
100m backstroke	**Kirsty Coventry**, ZIM	58.77p	59.44	August 11, 2008
200m backstroke (1)	**Kirsty Coventry**, ZIM	2:06.39	2:06.62	February 16, 2008
200m backstroke (2)	**Margaret Hoelzer**, USA	2:06.09	2:06.39	July 5, 2008
200m backstroke (3)	**Kirsty Coventry**, ZIM	2:05.24p	2:06.09	August 16, 2008
200m breaststroke	**Rebecca Soni**, USA	2:20.22p	2:20.54	August 15, 2008
200m butterfly	**Liu Zige**, CHN	2:04.18p	2:05.40	August 14, 2008
200m IM (1)	**Stephanie Rice**, AUS	2:08.92	2:09.72	March 25, 2008
200m IM (2)	**Stephanie Rice**, AUS	2:08.45p	2:08.92	August 13, 2008
400m IM (1)	**Stephanie Rice**, AUS	4:31.46	4:32.89	March 22, 2008
400m IM (2)	**Katie Hoff**, USA	4:31.12	4:31.46	June 30, 2008
400m IM (3)	**Stephanie Rice**, AUS	4:29.45p	4:31.12	August 10, 2008
4x100m freestyle relay	**NED** (Dekker, Kromowidjojo, Heemskerk, Veldhuis)	3:33.62p	3:35.22	August 10, 2008
4x200m freestyle relay	**AUS** (Rice, Barratt, Palmer, Mackenzie)	7:44.31p	7:50.09	August 14, 2008
4x100m medley relay	**AUS** (Seebohm, Jones, Schipper, Trickett)	3:52.69p	3:55.74	August 17, 2008

DID YOU KNOW?

*American **Michael Phelps** consumes roughly 12,000 calories per day during his training. To put that into perspective, the men's recommended daily amount is generally between 2,500 and 3,000. A usual day for Phelps consisted of* **(breakfast)** *three fried egg sandwiches with cheese, lettuce, tomatoes, fried onions, and mayo, one five-egg omelet, a bowl of grits, three slices of French toast with powdered sugar, three chocolate chip pancakes, two cups of coffee;* **(lunch)** *1,000 calories worth of energy drinks, one pound of pasta with tomato sauce and two large ham and cheese sandwiches with mayo on white bread;* **(dinner)** *an entire pizza, another pound of pasta with tomato sauce, and 1,000 calories of energy drinks.*

World, Olympic and American Records
As of September 30, 2008

World long course records officially recognized by the Federation Internationale de Natation Amateur (FINA). Note that (p) denotes that a record is awaiting ratification and (r) is a relay lead-off split.

MEN

Freestyle

Distance		Time		Date Set	Location
50 meters:	World	21.28p	**Eamon Sullivan**, Australia	Mar. 22, 2008	Sydney
	Olympic	21.30	Cesar Cielo Filho, Brazil	Aug. 16, 2008	Beijing
	American	21.47	Garrett Weber-Gale	July 4, 2008	Omaha
100 meters:	World	47.05p	**Eamon Sullivan**, Australia	Aug. 12, 2008	Beijing
	Olympic	47.05	Sullivan (same as World)	—	—
	American	47.51r	Michael Phelps	Aug. 11, 2008	Beijing
200 meters:	World	1:42.96p	**Michael Phelps**, USA	Aug. 10, 2008	Beijing
	Olympic	1:42.96	Phelps (same as World)	—	—
	American	1:42.96	Phelps (same as World)	—	—
400 meters:	World	3:40.08	**Ian Thorpe**, Australia	July 30, 2002	Manchester, GBR
	Olympic	3:40.59	Ian Thorpe, Australia	Sept. 16, 2000	Sydney
	American	3:42.78	Larsen Jensen	Aug. 9, 2008	Beijing
800 meters:	World	7:38.65	**Grant Hackett**, Australia	July 27, 2005	Montreal
	Olympic		Not an event	—	—
	American	7:45.63	Larsen Jensen	July 27, 2005	Montreal
1500 meters:	World	14:34.56	**Grant Hackett**, Australia	July 29, 2001	Fukuoka, JPN
	Olympic	14:38.92	Grant Hackett, Australia	Aug. 15, 2008	Beijing
	American	14:45.29	Larsen Jensen	Aug. 21, 2004	Athens

Backstroke

Distance		Time		Date Set	Location
50 meters:	World	24.47	**Liam Tancock**, Great Britian	April 2, 2008	Sheffield, GBR
	Olympic		Not an event	—	—
	American	24.71	Ben Hesen	July 4, 2008	Omaha
100 meters:	World	52.54p	**Aaron Peirsol**, USA	Aug. 12, 2008	Beijing
	Olympic	52.54	Peirsol (same as World)	—	—
	American	52.54	Peirsol (same as World)	—	—
200 meters:	World	1:53.94p	**Ryan Lochte**, USA	Aug. 13, 2008	Beijing
	Olympic	1:53.94	Lochte (same as World)	—	—
	American	1:53.94	Lochte (same as World)	—	—

Breaststroke

Distance		Time		Date Set	Location
50 meters:	World	27.18	**Oleg Lisogor**, Ukraine	Aug. 1, 2002	Berlin
	Olympic		Not an event	—	—
	American	27.39	Ed Moses	Mar. 31, 2001	Austin, Texas
100 meters:	World	58.91p	**Kosuke Kitajima**, JPN	Aug. 11, 2008	Beijing
	Olympic	58.91	Kitajima (same as World)	—	—
	American	59.13	Brendan Hansen, USA	Aug. 1, 2006	Irvine, Calif.
200 meters:	World	2:07.51	**Kosuke Kitajima**, JPN	June 8, 2008	Tokyo
	Olympic	2:07.64	Kosuke Kitajima, Japan	Aug. 14, 2008	Beijing
	American	2:08.50	Brendan Hansen, USA	Aug. 20, 2006	Victoria, B.C.

Butterfly

Distance		Time		Date Set	Location
50 meters:	World	22.96	**Roland Schoeman**, South Africa	July 25, 2005	Montreal
	Olympic		Not an event	—	—
	American	23.12	Ian Crocker	July 25, 2005	Montreal
100 meters:	World	50.40	**Ian Crocker**, USA	July 30, 2005	Montreal
	Olympic	50.58	Michael Phelps	Aug. 16, 2008	Beijing
	American	50.40	Crocker (same as World)	—	—
200 meters:	World	1:52.03p	**Michael Phelps**, USA	Aug. 13, 2008	Beijing
	Olympic	1:52.03	Phelps (same as World)	—	—
	American	1:52.03	Phelps (same as World)	—	—

Individual Medley

Distance		Time		Date Set	Location
200 meters:	World	1:54.23	**Michael Phelps**, USA	Aug. 15. 2008	Beijing
	Olympic	1:54.23	Phelps (same as World)	—	—
	American	1:54.23	Phelps (same as World)	—	—
400 meters:	World	4:03.84	**Michael Phelps**, USA	Aug. 10, 2008	Beijing
	Olympic	4:03.84	Phelps (same as World)	—	—
	American	4:03.84	Phelps (same as World)	—	—

Swimming (Cont.)
Relays

Distance		Time		Date Set	Location
4x100m free:	**World**	3:08.24p	**USA** (Phelps, Weber-Gale, Jones, Lezak)	Aug. 11, 2008	Beijing
	Olympic	3:08.24	USA (same as World)	—	—
	American	3:08.24	USA (same as World)	—	—
4x200m free:	**World**	6:58.56p	**USA** (Phelps, Lochte, Berens, Vanderkaay)	Aug. 13, 2008	Beijing
	Olympic	6:58.56	USA (same as World)	—	—
	American	6:58.56	USA (same as World)	—	—
4x100m medley:	**World**	3:29.34p	**USA** (Peirsol, Hansen, Phelps, Lezak)	Aug. 17, 2008	Beijing
	Olympic	3:29.34	USA (same as World)	—	—
	American	3:29.34	USA (same as World)	—	—

WOMEN

Freestyle

Distance		Time		Date Set	Location
50 meters:	**World**	23.97p	**Libby Trickett**, Australia	Mar. 29, 2008	Sydney
	Olympic	24.06	Britta Steffen, Germany	Aug. 17, 2008	Beijing
	American	24.07	Dara Torres	Aug. 17, 2008	Beijing
100 meters:	**World**	52.88p	**Libby Trickett**, Australia	Mar. 27, 2008	Sydney
	Olympic	53.12	Britta Steffen, Germany	Aug. 15, 2008	Beijing
	American	53.39	Natalie Coughlin	Aug. 15, 2008	Beijing
200 meters:	**World**	1:54.82p	**Federica Pellegrini**, Italy	Aug. 13, 2008	Beijing
	Olympic	1:57.65	Pellegrini (same as World)	—	—
	American	1:55.78	Katie Hoff	Aug. 13, 2008	Eindhoven, NED
400 meters:	**World**	4:01.53	**Federica Pellegrini**, Italy	Mar. 24, 2008	Budapest
	Olympic	4:02.24	Rebecca Adlington, Great Britain	Aug. 10, 2008	Beijing
	American	4:02.20	Katie Hoff	Feb. 15, 2008	Columbia, Mo.
800 meters:	**World**	8:14.10	**Rebecca Adlington**, GBR	Aug. 16, 2008	Beijing
	Olympic	8:14.10	Adlington (same as World)	—	—
	American	8:16.22	Janet Evans, USA	Aug. 20, 1989	Tokyo
1500 meters:	**World**	15:42.54	**Kate Ziegler**, USA	June 17, 2007	Mission Viejo, CA
	Olympic		Not an event		
	American	15:42.54	Ziegler (same as World)	—	—

Backstroke

Distance		Time		Date Set	Location
50 meters:	**World**	27.67p	**Sophie Edington**, Australia	Mar. 23, 2008	Sydney
	Olympic		Not an event	—	—
	American	27.80p	Haley McGregory	June 7, 2008	Austin, Texas
100 meters:	**World**	58.77	**Kirsty Coventry**, Zimbabwe	Aug. 11, 2008	Beijing
	Olympic	58.77	Coventry (same as World)	—	—
	American	58.94r	Natalie Coughlin	Aug. 17, 2008	Beijing
200 meters:	**World**	2:05.24p	**Kirsty Coventry**, Zimbabwe	Aug. 16, 2008	Beijing
	Olympic	2:05.24	Coventry (same as World)	—	—
	American	2:06.09	Margaret Hoelzer	July 5, 2008	Omaha

Breaststroke

Distance		Time		Date Set	Location
50 meters:	**World**	30.31	**Jade Edmistone**, Australia	Jan. 30, 2006	Melbourne, AUS
	Olympic		Not an event	—	—
	American	30.53	Jessica Hardy	July 1, 2008	Omaha
100 meters:	**World**	1:05.09	**Leisel Jones**, Australia	Mar. 20, 2006	Melbourne, AUS
	Olympic	1:05.17	Leisel Jones, Australia	Aug. 12, 2008	Beijing
	American	1:06.20	Jessica Hardy	July 26, 2005	Montreal
200 meters:	**World**	2:20.22	**Rebecca Soni**, USA	Aug. 15, 2008	Beijing
	Olympic	2:20.22	Soni (same as World)	—	—
	American	2:20.22	Soni (same as World)	—	—

Butterfly

Distance		Time		Date Set	Location
50 meters:	World	25.46	**Therese Alshammar**, Sweden	June 13, 2007	Barcelona
	Olympic		Not an event	—	—
	American	26.00	Jenny Thompson	July 26, 2003	Barcelona
100 meters:	World	56.61	**Inge de Bruijn**, Netherlands	Sept. 17, 2000	Sydney
	Olympic	56.61	de Bruijn (same as World)	—	—
	American	57.08	Christine Magnuson	Aug. 10, 2008	Beijing
200 meters:	World	2:04.18p	**Liu Zige**, China	Aug. 14, 2008	Beijing
	Olympic	2:04.18	Liu (same as World)	—	—
	American	2:05.88	Misty Hyman, USA	Sept. 20, 2000	Sydney

Individual Medley

Distance		Time		Date Set	Location
200 meters:	World	2:08.45p	**Stephanie Rice**, Australia	Aug. 13, 2008	Beijing
	Olympic	2:08.45	Rice (same as World)	—	—
	American	2:09.71	Katie Hoff	July 2, 2008	Omaha
400 meters:	World	4:29.45p	**Stephanie Rice**, Australia	Aug. 13, 2008	Beijing
	Olympic	4:29.45	Rice (same as World)	—	—
	American	4:31.12	Katie Hoff	June 29, 2008	Omaha

Relays

Distance		Time		Date Set	Location
4x100m free:	World	3:33.62	**Netherlands** (Dekker, Kromowidjojo, Heemskerk, Veldhuis)	Mar. 18, 2008	Eindhoven, NED
	Olympic	3:33.76	Netherlands (Dekker, Kromowidjojo, Heemskerk, Veldhuis)	Aug. 10, 2008	Beijing
	American	3:34.33	USA (Coughlin, Nymeyer, Joyce, Torres)	Aug. 10, 2008	Beijing
4x200m free:	World	7:44.31p	**Australia** (Rice, Barratt, Palmer, Mackenzie)	Aug. 14. 2008	Beijing
	Olympic	7:44.31	Australia (same as World)	—	—
	American	7:46.33	USA (Schmitt, Coughlin, Burckle, Hoff)	Aug. 14, 2008	Beijing
4x100m medley:	World	3:52.69	**Australia** (Seebohm, Jones, Schipper, Trickett)	Aug. 17, 2008	Beijing
	Olympic	3:52.69	Australia (same as World)	—	—
	American	3:53.30	USA (Coughlin, Soni, Magnuson, Torres)	Aug. 17. 2008	Beijing

2008 FINA Short Course World Championships

The 9th FINA Short Course (25m) World Championships held in Manchester, Great Britain, April 9-13, 2008. Note that (WR) indicates world record, (CR) indicates championships meet record and (=CR) indicates tied championships meet record.

MEN

Event		Time	
50m free	Duje Draganja, CRO	20.81	**WR**
100m free	Nathan Adrian, USA	46.67	**CR**
200m free	Kenrick Monk, AUS	1:43.46	
400m free	Yuriy Prilukov, RUS	3:37.35	
1500m free	Yuriy Prilukov, RUS	14:22.98	**CR**
50m back	Peter Marshall, USA	23.49	
100m back	Liam Tancock, GBR	50.14	
200m back	Markus Rogan, AUT	1:47.84	**WR**
50m breast	Oleg Lisogor, UKR	26.46	
100m breast	Igor Borysik, UKR	57.74	**CR**
200m breast	Kristopher Gilchrist, GBR	2:06.18	
50m fly	Adam Pine, AUS	22.78	
100m fly	Peter Mankoc, SLO	50.04	**CR**
200m fly	Moss Burmester, NZL	1:51.05	**CR**
100m I.M.	Ryan Lochte, USA	51.15	**WR**
200m I.M.	Ryan Lochte, USA	1:51.56	**WR**
400m I.M	Ryan Lochte, USA	4:03.21	
4x100m free	United States	3:08.44	**WR**
4x200m free	Australia	6:55.65	**CR**
4x100m medley	Russia	3:24.29	**WR**

WOMEN

Event		Time	
50m free	Marleen Veldhuis, NED	23.25	**WR**
100m free	Marleen Veldhuis, NED	52.17	**=CR**
200m free	Kylie Palmer, AUS	1:54.41	
400m free	Kylie Palmer, AUS	3:59.23	**CR**
1500m free	Rebecca Adlington, GBR	8:08.25	**CR**
50m back	Sanja Jovanovic, CRO	26.37	**WR**
100m back	Kirsty Coventry, ZIM	57.10	**CR**
200m back	Kirsty Coventry, ZIM	2:00.91	**WR**
50m breast	Jessica Hardy, USA	29.58	**WR**
100m breast	Jessica Hardy, USA	1:04.22	**CR**
200m breast	Suzaan Van Biljon, RSA	2:18.73	**CR**
50m fly	Felicity Galvez, AUS	25.32	**WR**
100m fly	Felicity Galvez, AUS	55.89	**WR**
200m fly	Mary DeScenza, USA	2:04.27	**CR**
100m I.M.	Shayne Reese, AUS	59.58	
200m I.M.	Kirsty Coventry, ZIM	2:06.13	**WR**
400m I.M	Kirsty Coventry, ZIM	4:26.52	**WR**
4x100m free	Netherlands	3:29.42	**WR**
4x200m free	Netherlands	7:38.90	**WR**
4x100m medley	United States	3:51.36	**WR**

WINTER SPORTS

Alpine Skiing
World Cup Champions
Top Five Standings
MEN

Overall 1. Bode Miller, USA (1409 pts); 2. Benjamin Raich, AUT (1298); 3. Didier Cuche, SUI (1263); 4. Manfred Moelgg, ITA (924); 5. Ted Ligety, USA (898).

Downhill 1. Didier Cuche, SUI (584 pts); 2. Bode Miller, USA (579); 3. Michael Walchhofer, AUT (407); 4. Marco Sullivan, USA (278); 5. Werner Heel, ITA (273).

Slalom 1. Manfred Moelgg, ITA (531 pts); 2. Jean-Baptiste Grange, FRA (512); 3. Reinfried Herbst, AUT (450); 4. Mario Matt, AUT (427); 5. Ivica Kostelic, CRO (425). *Best USA*—Ted Ligety (9th, 274 pts).

Giant Slalom 1. Ted Ligety, USA (485 pts); 2. Benjamin Raich, AUT (438); 3. Manfred Moelgg, ITA (376); 4. Didier Cuche, SUI (293); 5. Daniel Albrecht, SUI (284).

Super G 1. Hannes Reichelt, AUT (341 pts); 2. Didier Cuche, SUI (340); 3. Benjamin Raich, AUT (286); 4. Didier Defago, SUI (262); 5. Christoph Gruber, AUT (251). *Best USA*—Bode Miller (8th, 211 pts).

Combined 1. Bode Miller, USA (410 pts); 2. Ivica Kostelic, CRO (256); 3. Daniel Albrecht, SUI (245); 4. Jean-Baptiste Grange, FRA (220); 5. Rainer Schoenfelder, AUT (206).

Nation's Cup Champion: Austria

WOMEN

Overall 1. Lindsey Vonn, USA (1403 pts); 2. Nicole Hosp, AUT (1183); 3. Maria Riesch, GER (1146); 4. Elisabeth Goergl, AUT (1137); 5. Marlies Schild, AUT (1120).

Downhill 1. Lindsey Vonn, USA (755 pts); 2. Renate Goetschl, AUT (448); 3. Britt Janyk, CAN (390); 4. Anja Paerson, SWE (331); 5. Kelly Vanderbeek, CAN (323).

Slalom 1. Marlies Schild, AUT (640 pts); 2. Nicole Hosp, AUT (515); 3. Veronika Zuzulova, SVK (501); 4. Tanja Poutiainen, FIN (484); 5. Sarka Zahrobska, CZE (392). *Best USA*—Resi Stiegler (18th, 111 pts).

Giant Slalom 1. Denise Karbon, ITA (592 pts); 2. Elisabeth Goergl, AUT (479); 3. Manuela Moelgg, ITA (359); 4. Tanja Poutiainen, FIN (297); 5. Julia Mancuso, USA (253).

Super G 1. Maria Riesch, GER (374 pts); 2. Elisabeth Goergl, AUT (326); 3. Fabienne Suter, SUI (305); 4. Renate Goetschl, AUT (283); 5. Emily Brydon, CAN (270). *Best USA*—Lindsey Vonn (6th, 262 pts).

Combined 1. Maria Riesch, GER (260 pts); 2. Lindsey Vonn, USA (200); 3. Anja Paerson, SWE (160); 4. Sandrine Aubert, FRA (110); 5. Marlies Schild, AUT (106).

Nation's Cup Champion: Austria

2008 U.S. Alpine Championships
at Sugarloaf, Maine (March 19-26)
MEN

Downhill	T.J. Lanning, Park City, UT
Slalom	Jimmy Cochran, Keene, NH
Giant Slalom	Tim Jitloff, Reno, NV
Super G	Kevin Francis, Bend, OR
Combined	Jimmy Cochran, Keene, NH

WOMEN

Downhill	Stacey Cook, Mammoth, CA
Slalom	Lindsey Vonn, Vail, CO
Giant Slalom	Lauren Ross, Stowe, VT
Super G	Stacey Cook, Mammoth, CA
Combined	Lindsey Vonn, Vail, CO

Freestyle Skiing
World Cup Champions
MEN

Overall	Steve Omischl, Canada
Aerials	Steve Omischl, Canada
Moguls	Dale Begg-Smith, Australia
Ski Cross	Tomas Kraus, Czech Republic
Halfpipe	Matthew Hayward, Canada

WOMEN

Overall	Ophelie David, France
Aerials	Jacqui Cooper, Australia
Moguls	Aiko Uemura, Japan
Ski Cross	Ophelie David, France
Halfpipe	Sarah Burke, Canada

2008 U.S. Freestyle Championships
at Park City, Utah (March 27-30)
MEN

Aerials	Ryan St. Onge, Winter Park, CO
Moguls	Michael Morse, Duxbury, MA
Dual Moguls	Michael Morse, Duxbury, MA
Halfpipe	David Wise, Caldwell, ID

WOMEN

Aerials	Emily Cook, Belmont, MA
Moguls	Emiko Torito, Steamboat, CO
Dual Moguls	Michelle Roark, Denver, CO
Halfpipe	Jennifer Hudak, Park City, UT

Snowboarding
World Cup Champions
MEN

Overall	Benjamin Karl, Austria
Halfpipe	Iouri Podladtchikov, Switzerland
Parallel Slalom	Benjamin Karl, Austria
Snowboardcross	Pierre Vaultier, France
Big Air	Stefan Gimpl, Austria

WOMEN

Overall	Nicolien Sauerbreij, Netherlands
Halfpipe	Manuela Laura Pesko, Switzerland
Parallel Slalom	Nicolien Sauerbreij, Netherlands
Snowboardcross	Maelle Ricker, Canada

2008 U.S. Open Snowboarding Championships
at Stratton, Vermont (March 17-23)
MEN

Halfpipe	Shaun White, Carlsbad, CA
Slopestyle	Shaun White, Carlsbad, CA
Big Air	Tim Humphreys, Basking Ridge, NJ

WOMEN

Halfpipe	Torah Bright, Australia
Slopestyle	Kjersti Oestgaard Buaas, Norway
Big Air	Cheryl Maas, Netherlands

Nordic Skiing

World Cup Champions
MEN

Cross Country - Overall .... Lukas Bauer, Czech Republic
Cross Country - Distance ... Lukas Bauer, Czech Republic
Cross Country - Sprint .... Ola Vigen Hattestad, Norway

Nordic Combined - Overall .. Ronny Ackermann, Germany
Nordic Combined - Sprint .. Ronny Ackermann, Germany

Ski Jumping - Overall ...... Thomas Morgenstern, Austria
Ski Jumping - Four Hills .... Janne Ahonen, Finland
Ski Jumping - Nordic Tourn. .Gregor Schlierenzauer, Austria

WOMEN

Cross Country - Overall .... Virpi Kuitunen, Finland
Cross Country - Distance ...... Virpi Kuitunen, Finland
Cross Country - Sprint .... Petra Majdic, Slovenia

2008 U.S. Cross Country Championship
at Houghton, Michigan (Jan. 1-6)
MEN

Sprint .... Andy Newell, Shaftsbury, VT
15-k Classic .... Lars Flora, Anchorage, AK
10-k Freestyle .... Leif Zimmerman, Bozeman, MT
Team Sprint .... Torin Koos, Leavenworth, WA
    & Andrew Newell, Shaftsbury, VT

WOMEN

Sprint .... Kikkan Randall, Anchorage, AK
10-k Classic .... Kikkan Randall, Anchorage, AK
5-k Freestyle .... Caitlin Compton, Minneapolis, MN
Team Sprint .... Lindsey Dehlin, Mahtomedi, MN
    & Lindsay Williams, Hastings, MN

2008 U.S. Ski Jumping/ Nordic Combined Championships
at Park City, Utah (March 15-16)
MEN

Nordic Combined .... Bill Demong, Vermontville, NY
Normal Hill (100m) Johnny Spillane, Steamboat Springs, CO
Large Hill (134m) .... Anders Johnson, Park City, UT

WOMEN

Nordic Combined (Exhibition) . Jessica Jerome, Park City, UT
Normal Hill (100m) ...... Jessica Jerome, Park City, UT
Large Hill (134m) .... Jessica Jerome, Park City, UT

Speed Skating

World Cup Champions
MEN

100 meters .... Kang-Seok Lee, Korea
500 meters .... Jeremy Wotherspoon, Canada
1000 meters .... Shani Davis, United States
1500 meters .... Shani Davis, United States
5000/10,000 meters .... Havard Bokko, Norway
Team Pursuit .... Netherlands

WOMEN

100 meters .... Jenny Wolf, Germany
500 meters .... Jenny Wolf, Germany
1000 meters .... Anni Friesinger, Germany
1500 meters .... Kristina Groves, Canada
3000/5000 meters .. Martina Sablikova, Czech Republic
Team Pursuit .... Canada

2008 World Allround Championships
at Berlin, Germany (Feb. 9-10)
MEN

500 meters .... Denny Morrison, Canada
1500 meters .... Shani Davis, United States
5000 meters .... Sven Kramer, Netherlands
10,000 meters .... Sven Kramer, Netherlands

WOMEN

500 meters .... Christine Nesbitt, Canada
1500 meters .... Ireen Wust, Netherlands
3000 meters ...... Paulien van Deutekom, Netherlands
5000 meters .... Martina Sablikova, Czech Republic

2008 World Short Track Championships
at Gangneung City, South Korea (Mar. 7-9)
MEN

500 meters .... Apolo Anton Ohno, United States
1000 meters .... Lee Ho-Suk, Korea
1500 meters .... Song Kyung-Taek, Korea
3000 meters .... Lee Seung-Hoon, Korea
5000 meter relay .... Korea
All-Around .... Apolo Anton Ohno, United States

WOMEN

500 meters .... Wang Meng, China
1000 meters .... Wang Meng, China
1500 meters .... Wang Meng, China
3000 meters .... Zhou Yang, China
3000 meter relay .... Korea
All-Around .... Wang Meng, China

Figure Skating

World Championships
at Goteborg, Sweden (March 18-23)

Men's —1. Jeffrey Buttle, Canada; 2. Brian Joubert, France; 3. Johnny Weir, USA; 4. Daisuke Takahashi, Japan; 5. Stephane Lambiel, Switzerland.

Women's —1. Mao Asada, Japan; 2. Carolina Kostner, Italy; 3. Kim Yu-Na, Korea; 4. Yukari Nakano, Japan; 5. Joannie Rochette, Canada.

Pairs —1. Aliona Savchenko & Robin Szolkowy, Germany; 2. Zhang Dan & Zhang Hao, China; 3. Jessica Dube & Bryce Davison, Canada; 4. Yuko Kawaguchi & Alexander Smirnov, Russia; 5. Pang Qing & Tong Jian, China.

Ice Dance —1. Isabelle Delobel & Olivier Schoenfelder, France; 2. Tessa Virtue & Scott Moir, Canada; 3. Jana Khokhlova & Sergei Novitski, Russia; 4. Tanith Belbin & Benjamin Agosto, USA; 5. Federica Faiella & Massimo Scali, Italy.

U.S. Championships
at St. Paul, Minnesota (Jan. 20-27)

Men's .... Evan Lysacek
Women's .... Mirai Nagasu
Pairs .... Keauna McLaughlin
    & Rockne Brubaker
Ice Dance .... Tanith Belbin
    & Benjamin Agosto

European Championships
at Zagreb, Croatia (Jan. 21-27)

Men's .... Tomas Verner, Czech Republic
Women's .... Carolina Kostner, Italy
Pairs .... Aliona Savchenko
    & Robin Szolkowy, Germany
Ice Dance .... Oksana Domnina
    & Maxim Shabalin, Russia

Cycling
2008 Tour de France

The 95th Tour de France (July 5-27) ran 21 stages, covering 3,558 kilometers (2,212 miles) starting in the northwest city of Brest in the Brittany region, winding through the French countryside, making a brief visit to Italy, and finishing in Paris on the Avenue des Champs-Elysees.

Team CSC's Carlos Sastre became the third consecutive Spaniard and seventh overall to win the Tour, with a 58-second win over runner-up Cadel Evans of Australia. The race was sadly marred once again by failed drug tests, random searches and ensuing disqualifications. Last year's champion Alberto Contador was notably absent after his entire team Astana was barred from the race. Spaniards Manuel Beltran and Moises Duenas, Italian Riccardo Ricco and Kazakh rider Dmitriy Fofonov also tested positive at various stages. Sastre took the lead during the 17th stage, with an aggressive move at the base of the gruelling climb to Alpe d'Huez, then held on to win the title in 87 hours, 52 minutes and 52 seconds.

		Team	Behind				Team	Behind
1	Carlos Sastre, ESP	CSC	—		6	Frank Schleck, LUX	CSC	4:28
2	Cadel Evans, AUS	Silence-Lotto	0:58		7	Samuel Sanchez Gonxalez, ESP	Euskaltel	6:25
3	Bernhard Kohl, AUT	Gerolsteiner	1:13		8	Kim Kirchen, LUX	Columbia	6:55
4	Denis Menchov, RUS	Rabobank	2:10		9	Alejandro Valverde, ESP	Caisse d'Epargne	7:12
5	Christian Vande Velde, USA	Garmin-Chipotle	3:05		10	Tadej Valjavec, SLO	AG2R La Mondiale	9:05

Other Worldwide Champions

2008 Major UCI (Union Cycliste Internationale) Road results through Sept. 21. Note that in some instances, the date shown below is the final day of that particular race.

MEN

Race	Winner	Race	Winner
Jan. 27: Tour Down Under (AUS)	Andre Greipel, GER	Apr. 20: Amstel Gold Race (NED)	Damiano Cunego, ITA
Feb. 17: Tour de Langwaki (MAS)	Ruslan Ivanov, MLDV	Apr. 27 Fleche Wallonne (BEL)	Kim Kirchen, LUX
Feb. 17: Mediterranean Tour (FRA)	A. Botcharov, RUS	Apr. 29: Liege-Bastogne-Liege (BEL)	Alejandro Valverde, ESP
Feb. 21: Ruta del Sol (ESP)	Pablo Lastras Garcia, ESP	May 4: Tour de Romandie (SWI)	Andreas Klöden, GER
Mar. 1: Tour of Valencia (ESP)	Rubén Plaza, ESP	May 11: Four Days of Dunkirk (FRA)	Stéphane Augé, FRA
Mar. 1: Omloop Het Volk (BEL)	Philippe Gilbert, BEL	May 25: Tour of Catalunya (ESP)	José Luis Carrasco, ESP
Mar. 16: Paris-Nice (FRA)	Davide Rebellin, ITA	June 1: Giro d'Italia (ITA)	Alberto Contador, ESP
Mar. 18: Tirreno-Adriatico (ITA)	Fabian Cancellara, SWI	June 15: Dauphine Libere (FRA)	Alejandro Valverde, ESP
Mar. 22: Milan-San Remo (ITA)	Fabian Cancellara, SWI	June 22: Tour of Switzerland (SWI)	Roman Kreuziger, CZE
Mar. 30: Criterium Int'l (FRA)	Jens Voigt, GER	Aug. 2: San Sebastian Classic (ESP)	Alejandro Valverde, ESP
Apr. 6: Tour of Flanders (BEL)	Stijn Devolder, BEL	Sept. 6: Tour of Germany (GER)	Linus Gerdemann, GER
Apr. 9: Gent-Wevelgem (BEL)	Oscar Freire, ESP	Sept. 7: Vattenfall Cyclassics (GER)	Robbie McEwen, AUS
Apr. 13: Paris-Roubaix (FRA)	Tom Boonen, BEL	Sept. 21: Tour of Spain (ESP)	Alberto Contador, ESP

WOMEN

Race	Winner	Race	Winner
Feb. 22: Geelong Women's Tour (AUS)	Christiane Soeder, AUT	May 25: Tour de L'Aude (FRA)	Judith Arndt, GER
Mar. 2: Tour of New Zealand (NZ)	Kristin Armstrong, USA	May 31: Montreal World Cup (CAN)	Judith Arndt, GER
Apr. 6: Tour de Flanders (BEL)	Judith Arndt, GER	July 13: Giro d'Italia Femminile (ITA)	Fabiana Luperini, ITA
Apr. 12: Ronde van Drenthe (NED)	Chantal Beltman, NED	July 30: Vagarda Open (SWE)	Kori Kelley-Seehafer, USA
Apr. 23: Fleche Wallonne (BEL)	Marianne Vos, NED	Aug. 24: GP of Plouay (FRA)	Fabiana Luperini, ITA
May 4: Tour de Berne (SWI)	Susanne Ljungskog, SWE	Sept. 14: Tour of Nuremberg (GER)	Judith Arndt, GER

Gymnastics
2008 Visa Championships

MEN

Held May 22-24, 2008 at Reliant Park in Houston, Texas

All-Around	David Sender, Arlington Heights, IL
High Bar	Joseph Hagerty, Rio Rancho, NM
Parallel Bars	Justin Spring, Burke, VA
Vault	David Sender, Arlington Heights, IL
Pommel Horse	Yewki Tomita, Tucson, AZ
Rings	Kevin Tan, Fremont, CA
Floor Exercise	Morgan Hamm, Waukesha, WI

WOMEN

Held June 5-7, 2008 at Agganis Arena in Boston, Mass.

All-Around	Shawn Johnson, West Des Moines, IA
Vault	Alicia Sacramone, Winchester, MA
Uneven Bars	Nastia Liukin, Parker, TX
Balance Beam	Nastia Liukin, Parker, TX
Floor Exercise	Shawn Johnson, West Des Moines, IA

Marathons
2008 Boston Marathon

The 112th edition of the Boston Marathon was held Monday, April 21, 2008 and run, as always, from Hopkinton through Ashland, Framingham, Natick, Wellesley, Newton and Brookline to Boston, Mass. Kenya's Robert Kipkoech Cheruiyot led the race virtually wire-to-wire, extending his lead to 30 seconds in the Newton Hills, then increasing it to well over a minute by the time he reached the Boylston St. finish. It was his third straight victory in Boston and his fourth overall. Unlike last year's rainy, blustery weather, the conditions were exceptional as Cheruiyot cruised to the sixth-fastest Boston time ever (2:07:46).

In the women's division, Ethiopian Dire Tune and Russian Alevtina Biktimirova sprinted down Boylston side-by-side toward the finish line in one of the most thrilling finishes in race history. Tune opened up a slight lead towards the finish line and broke the tape in 2:25:25, just two seconds faster than Biktimirova. It was the closest women's finish in the history of the race. Tune and Cheruiyot each earned $150,000 for their victories. **Distance:** 26.2 miles.

	MEN	Time		WOMEN	Time
1	Robert Cheruiyot, Kenya	2:07:46	1	Dire Tune, Ethiopia	2:25:25
2	Abderrahime Bouramdane, Morocco	2:09:04	2	Alevtina Biktimirova, Russia	2:25:27
3	Khalid El Boumlili, Morocco	2:10:35	3	Rita Jeptoo, Kenya	2:26:34
4	Gashaw Asfaw, Ethiopia	2:10:47	4	Jelena Prokopcuka, Latvia	2:28:12
5	Kasime Adillo, Ethiopia	2:12:24	5	Askale Tafa Magarsa, Ethiopia	2:29:48

Best USA: 10th—Nicholas Arciniaga, Mich. 2:16:13

Best USA: 10th—Stephanie Hood, Ill. 2:44:44

World Marathon Majors

On January 23, 2006, the Boston, London, Berlin, Chicago and New York City marathons collectively launched the World Marathon Majors – with a $1 million prize purse to be split equally between the top male and female marathoners in the world. The inaugural 2006-2007 series was won by Kenyan Robert Cheruiyot and Ethiopian Gete Wami. The 2007-08 series will conclude at the New York City Marathon on November 2, 2008.

Other 2008 Winners

Osaka
Jan. 27	Women	Mara Yamauchi, GBR		2:25:10

(No men's division)

Tokyo
Feb. 17	Men	Viktor Rothlin, SWI		2:07:23

(No women's division)

Los Angeles
Mar. 2	Men	Moiben Laban, KEN		2:13:50
	Women	Tatiana Aryasova, RUS		2:29:09

Rome
Mar. 16	Men	Jonathan Yego Kiptoo, KEN		2:09:58
	Women	Galina Bogomolova, RUS		2:22:53

Paris
Apr. 6	Men	Tsegaye Kebede, ETH		2:06:40
	Women	Martha Komu, KEN		2:25:33

Rotterdam
Apr. 13	Men	William Kipsang, KEN		2:05:49
	Women	Lyubov Morgunova, RUS		2:25:12

London
Apr. 13	Men	Martin Lel, KEN		2:05:15
	Women	Irina Mikitenko, GER		2:24:14

Berlin
Sept. 28	Men	Haile Gebrselassie, ETH		2:03:59*
	Women	Irina Mikitenko, GER		2:19:19

* World Record

Late 2007

Chicago
Oct. 7	Men	Patrick Ivuti, KEN		2:11:11
	Women	Berhane Adere, ETH		2:33:49

New York City
Nov. 4	Men	Martin Lel, KEN		2:09:04
	Women	Paula Radcliffe, GBR		2:23:09

Tokyo Women's
Nov. 18	Women	Mizuki Noguchi		2:21:37

Fukuoka
Dec. 3	Men	Samuel Wanjiru, JPN		2:06:39

(No women's division)

Rowing
2008 World Championships
at Linz and Ottensheim, Austria (July 22-27)

MEN		WOMEN	
Coxed Pairs	Canada, 7:06.69	Coxless Fours	Belarus, 6:39.89
Light Eights	United States, 5:50.29	Light Single Sculls	Pamela Weisshaupt,
Light Coxless Pairs	Greece, 6:40.92		Switzerland, 7:43.26
Light Single Sculls	Duncan Grant,	Light Quad Sculls	Australia, 6:36.41
	New Zealand, 6:52.38		
Light Quad Sculls	Italy, 5:57.30		

1882-2008
Through the Years

SPORTS ALMANAC

TRACK & FIELD

IAAF World Championships

While the Summer Olympics have served as the unofficial world outdoor championships for track and field throughout the centuries, a separate World Championship meet was started in 1983 by the International Amateur Athletic Federation (IAAF). The meet was held every four years from 1983-91, but began an every-other-year cycle in 1993. Sites include Helsinki (1983, 2005), Rome (1987), Tokyo (1991), Stuttgart (1993), Göteborg, Sweden (1995), Athens (1997), Seville, Spain (1999), Edmonton (2001), Paris (2003) and Osaka, Japan (2007). Looking forward, the Championships will be held in Berlin (2009), Daegu, South Korea (2011) and Moscow (2013). Note that (WR) indicates world record and (CR) indicates championship meet record. (W) indicates wind-aided.

MEN

Most gold medals (at least three, including relays): Michael Johnson (9); Carl Lewis (8); Sergey Bubka (6); Maurice Greene and Lars Riedel (5); Hicham El Guerrouj, Haile Gebrselassie, Allen Johnson, Ivan Pedroso, Antonio Pettigrew, Calvin Smith and Jeremy Wariner (4); Donovan Bailey, Kenenisa Bekele, Tomas Dvorak, Greg Foster, Tyson Gay, John Godina, Werner Gunthor, Wilson Kipketer, Moses Kiptanui, Robert Korzeniowski, Dennis Mitchell, Noureddine Morceli, Dan O'Brien, Jefferson Perez, Butch Reynolds, Ivan Tikhon and Jan Zelezny (3).

100 Meters

Year		Time	
1983	Carl Lewis, USA	10.07	
1987	Carl Lewis, USA	9.93*	
1991	Carl Lewis, USA	9.86	WR
1993	Linford Christie, GBR	9.87	
1995	Donovan Bailey, CAN	9.97	
1997	Maurice Greene, USA	9.86	
1999	Maurice Greene, USA	9.80	CR
2001	Maurice Greene, USA	9.82	
2003	Kim Collins, SKN	10.07	
2005	Justin Gatlin, USA	9.88	
2007	Tyson Gay, USA	9.85	

*Original winner Ben Johnson, CAN, was stripped of his medal.

200 Meters

Year		Time	
1983	Calvin Smith, USA	20.14	
1987	Calvin Smith, USA	20.16	
1991	Michael Johnson, USA	20.01	
1993	Frank Fredericks, NAM	19.85	
1995	Michael Johnson, USA	19.79	
1997	Ato Boldon, USA	20.04	
1999	Maurice Greene, USA	19.90	
2001	Konstantinos Kenteris, GRE	20.04	
2003	John Capel, USA	20.30	
2005	Justin Gatlin, USA	20.04	
2007	Tyson Gay, USA	19.76	CR

400 Meters

Year		Time	
1983	Bert Cameron, JAM	45.05	
1987	Thomas Schonlebe, E. Ger	44.33	
1991	Antonio Pettigrew, USA	44.57	
1993	Michael Johnson, USA	43.65	
1995	Michael Johnson, USA	43.39	
1997	Michael Johnson, USA	44.12	
1999	Michael Johnson, USA	43.18	WR
2001	Avard Moncur, BAH	44.64	
2003	Jerome Young, USA	44.50	
2005	Jeremy Wariner, USA	43.93	
2007	Jeremy Wariner, USA	43.45	

800 Meters

Year		Time	
1983	Willi Wülbeck, W. Ger	1:43.65	
1987	Billy Konchellah, KEN	1:43.06	CR
1991	Billy Konchellah, KEN	1:43.99	
1993	Paul Ruto, KEN	1:44.71	
1995	Wilson Kipketer, DEN	1:45.08	
1997	Wilson Kipketer, DEN	1:43.38	
1999	Wilson Kipketer, DEN	1:43.30	
2001	Andre Bucher, SWI	1:43.70	
2003	Djabir Said-Guerni, ALG	1:44.81	
2005	Rashid Ramzi, BRN	1:44.24	
2007	Alfred Kirwa Yego, KEN	1:47.09	

1500 Meters

Year		Time	
1983	Steve Cram, GBR	3:41.59	
1987	Abdi Bile, SOM	3:36.80	
1991	Noureddine Morceli, ALG	3:32.84	
1993	Noureddine Morceli, ALG	3:34.24	
1995	Noureddine Morceli, ALG	3:33.73	
1997	Hicham El Guerrouj, MOR	3:35.83	
1999	Hicham El Guerrouj, MOR	3:27.65	CR
2001	Hicham El Guerrouj, MOR	3:30.68	
2003	Hicham El Guerrouj, MOR	3:31.77	
2005	Rashid Ramzi, BRN	3:37.88	
2007	Bernard Lagat, USA	3:34.77	

5000 Meters

Year		Time	
1983	Eammon Coghlan, IRL	13:28.53	
1987	Said Aouita, MOR	13:26.44	
1991	Yobes Ondieki, KEN	13:14.45	
1993	Ismael Kirui, KEN	13:02.75	
1995	Ismael Kirui, KEN	13:16.77	
1997	Daniel Komen, KEN	13:07.38	
1999	Salah Hissou, MOR	12:58.13	
2001	Richard Limo, KEN	13:00.77	
2003	Eliud Kipchoge, KEN	12:52.79	CR
2005	Benjamin Limo, KEN	13:32.55	
2007	Bernard Lagat, USA	13:45.87	

10,000 Meters

Year		Time	
1983	Alberto Cova, ITA	28:01.04	
1987	Paul Kipkoech, KEN	27:38.63	
1991	Moses Tanui, KEN	27:38.74	
1993	Haile Gebrselassie, ETH	27:46.02	
1995	Haile Gebrselassie, ETH	27:12.95	
1997	Haile Gebrselassie, ETH	27:24.58	
1999	Abel Anton, SPA	27:57.27	
2001	Charles Kamathi, KEN	27:53.25	
2003	Kenenisa Bekele, ETH	26:49.57	CR
2005	Kenenisa Bekele, ETH	27:08.33	
2007	Kenenisa Bekele, ETH	27:05.90	

Marathon

Year		Time	
1983	Rob de Castella, AUS	2:10:03	
1987	Douglas Wakiihuri, KEN	2:11:48	
1991	Hiromi Taniguchi, JPN	2:14:57	
1993	Mark Plaatjes, USA	2:13:57	
1995	Martin Fíz, SPA	2:11:41	
1997	Abel Anton, SPA	2:13:16	
1999	Abel Anton, SPA	2:13:36	
2001	Gezahegne Abera, ETH	2:12:42	
2003	Jaouad Gharib, MOR	2:08:31	CR
2005	Jaouad Gharib, MOR	2:10:10	
2007	Luke Kibet, KEN	2:15:59	

110-Meter Hurdles

Year		Time	
1983	Greg Foster, USA	13.42	
1987	Greg Foster, USA	13.21	
1991	Greg Foster, USA	13.06	
1993	Colin Jackson, GBR	12.91	WR
1995	Allen Johnson, USA	13.00	
1997	Allen Johnson, USA	12.93	
1999	Colin Jackson, GBR	13.04	
2001	Allen Johnson, USA	13.04	
2003	Allen Johnson, USA	13.12	
2005	Ladji Doucoure, FRA	13.07	
2007	Xiang Liu, CHN	12.95	

400-Meter Hurdles

Year		Time	
1983	Edwin Moses, USA	47.50	
1987	Edwin Moses, USA	47.46	
1991	Samuel Matete, ZAM	47.64	
1993	Kevin Young, USA	47.18	CR
1995	Derrick Adkins, USA	47.98	
1997	Stephane Diagana, FRA	47.70	
1999	Fabrizio Mori, ITA	47.72	
2001	Felix Sanchez, DOM	47.49	
2003	Felix Sanchez, DOM	47.25	
2005	Bershawn Jackson, USA	47.30	
2007	Kerron Clement, USA	47.61	

3000-Meter Steeplechase

Year		Time	
1983	Patriz Ilg, W. Ger	8:15.06	
1987	Francesco Panetta, ITA	8:08.57	
1991	Moses Kiptanui, KEN	8:12.59	
1993	Moses Kiptanui, KEN	8:06.36	
1995	Moses Kiptanui, KEN	8:04.16	CR
1997	Wilson B. Kipketer, KEN	8:05.84	
1999	Christopher Koskei, KEN	8:11.76	
2001	Reuben Kosgei, KEN	8:15.16	
2003	Saif Saaeed Shaheen, QAT	8:04.39	
2005	Saif Saaeed Shaheen, QAT	8:13.31	
2007	Brimin Kiprop Kipruto, KEN	8:13.82	

4 x 100-Meter Relay

Year		Time	
1983	United States	37.86	WR
1987	United States	37.90	
1991	United States	37.50	WR
1993	United States	37.48	CR
1995	Canada	38.31	
1997	Canada	37.86	
1999	United States	37.59	
2001	United States	37.96	
2003	United States	38.06	
2005	France	38.08	
2007	United States	37.78	

4 x 400-Meter Relay

Year		Time	
1983	Soviet Union	3:00.79	
1987	United States	2:57.29	
1991	Great Britain	2:57.53	
1993	United States	2:54.29	WR
1995	United States	2:57.32	
1997	United States	2:56.47*	
1999	United States	2:56.45*	
2001	United States	2:57.54	
2003	France	2:58.88*	
2005	United States	2:56.91	
2007	United States	2:55.56	

*The United States was stripped of its 2003 gold after lead runner Calvin Harrison's second doping violation. The 1997 and 99 golds are currently in question after Antonio Pettigrew's doping admission, but at press time, no decision had been made.

20-Kilometer Walk

Year		Time	
1983	Ernesto Canto, MEX	1:20:49	
1987	Maurizio Damilano, ITA	1:20:45	
1991	Maurizio Damilano, ITA	1:19:37	
1993	Valentin Massana, SPA	1:22:31	
1995	Michele Didoni, ITA	1:19:59	
1997	Daniel Garcia, MEX	1:21:43	
1999	Ilya Markov, RUS	1:23:34	
2001	Roman Rasskazov, RUS	1:20:31	
2003	Jefferson Perez, ECU	1:17:21	WR
2005	Jefferson Perez, ECU	1:18:35	
2007	Jefferson Perez, ECU	1:22:20	

50-Kilometer Walk

Year		Time	
1983	Ronald Weigel, E. Ger	3:43:08	
1987	Hartwig Gauder, E. Ger	3:40:53	
1991	Aleksandr Potashov, USSR	3:53:09	
1993	Jesus Angel Garcia, SPA	3:41:41	
1995	Valentin Kononen, FIN	3:43:42	
1997	Robert Korzeniowski, POL	3:44:46	
1999	Ivano Brugnetti, ITA	3:47:54*	
2001	Robert Korzeniowski, POL	3:42:08	
2003	Robert Korzeniowski, POL	3:36:03	WR
2005	Sergey Kirdyapkin, RUS	3:38:08	
2007	Nathan Deakes, AUS	3:43:53	

* Original winner German Skurygin, RUS, was stripped of his 1999 title after testing positive for a banned substance.

High Jump

Year		Height	
1983	Gennedy Avdeyenko, USSR	7- 7¼	
1987	Patrik Sjoberg, SWE	7- 9¾	
1991	Charles Austin, USA	7- 9¾	
1993	Javier Sotomayor, CUB	7-10½	CR
1995	Troy Kemp, BAH	7- 9¼	
1997	Javier Sotomayor, CUB	7- 9¼	
1999	Vyacheslav Voronin, RUS	7- 9¼	
2001	Martin Buss, GER	7- 8¾	
2003	Jacques Freitag, RSA	7- 8½	
2005	Yuriy Krymarenko, UKR	7- 7¼	
2007	Donald Thomas, BAH	7- 8½	

Pole Vault

Year		Height	
1983	Sergey Bubka, USSR	18- 8¼	
1987	Sergey Bubka, USSR	19- 2¼	
1991	Sergey Bubka, USSR	19- 6¼	
1993	Sergey Bubka, UKR	19- 8¼	
1995	Sergey Bubka, UKR	19- 5	
1997	Sergey Bubka, UKR	19- 8½	
1999	Maksim Tarasov, RUS	19- 9	
2001	Dmitri Markov, AUS	19-10¼	CR
2003	Giuseppe Gibilisco, ITA	19- 4¼	
2005	Rens Blom, NED	19- 0½	
2007	Brad Walker, USA	19- 2¾	

Long Jump

Year		Distance	
1983	Carl Lewis, USA	28- 0¾	
1987	Carl Lewis, USA	28- 0¼	
1991	Mike Powell, USA	29- 4½	WR
1993	Mike Powell, USA	28- 2¼	
1995	Ivan Pedroso, CUB	28- 6½	
1997	Ivan Pedroso, CUB	27- 7½	
1999	Ivan Pedroso, CUB	28- 1	
2001	Ivan Pedroso, CUB	27- 6¾	
2003	Dwight Phillips, USA	27- 3¾	
2005	Dwight Phillips, USA	28- 2¾	
2007	Irving Saladino, PAN	28- 1¾	

Triple Jump

Year		Distance	
1983	Zdzislaw Hoffmann, POL	57- 2	
1987	Khristo Markov, BUL	58- 9	
1991	Kenny Harrison, USA	58- 4	
1993	Mike Conley, USA	58- 7¼	
1995	Jonathan Edwards, GBR	60- 0¼	WR
1997	Yoelvis Quesada, CUB	58- 6¾	
1999	Charles Michael Friedek, GER	57- 8½	
2001	Jonathan Edwards, GBR	58- 9½	
2003	Christian Olsson, SWE	58- 1¾	
2005	Walter Davis, USA	57- 7¾	
2007	Nelson Evora, POR	58- 2½	

Shot Put

Year		Distance	
1983	Edward Sarul, POL	70- 2¼	
1987	Werner Günthör SWI	72-11¼	CR
1991	Werner Günthör, SWI	71- 1¼	
1993	Werner Günthör, SWI	72- 1	
1995	John Godina, USA	70- 5¼	
1997	John Godina, USA	70- 4¼	
1999	C.J. Hunter, USA	71- 6	
2001	John Godina, USA	71- 9	
2003	Andrei Mikhnevich, BLR	71- 2	
2005	Adam Nelson, USA	71- 3½	
2007	Reese Hoffa, USA	72- 3¾	

Discus

Year		Distance	
1983	Imrich Bugar, CZE	222- 2	
1987	Jurgen Schult, E. Ger	225- 6	
1991	Lars Riedel, GER	217- 2	
1993	Lars Riedel, GER	222- 2	
1995	Lars Riedel, GER	225- 7	
1997	Lars Riedel, GER	224-10	
1999	Anthony Washington, USA	226- 7	
2001	Lars Riedel, GER	228- 9	
2003	Virgilijus Alekena, LIT	228- 7	
2005	Virgilijus Alekena, LIT	230- 2	CR
2007	Gerd Kanter, EST	226- 2	

Hammer Throw

Year		Distance	
1983	Sergey Litvinov, USSR	271- 3	
1987	Sergey Litvinov, USSR	272- 6	
1991	Yuri Sedykh, USSR	268- 0	
1993	Andrey Abduvaliyev, TAJ	267-10	
1995	Andrey Abduvaliyev, TAJ	267- 7	
1997	Heinz Weis, GER	268- 4	
1999	Karsten Kobs, GER	263- 3	
2001	Szymon Ziolkowski, POL	273- 7	
2003	Ivan Tikhon, BLR	272- 5	
2005	Ivan Tikhon, BLR	275- 2	CR
2007	Ivan Tikhon, BLR	274- 4	

Javelin

Year		Distance	
1983	Detlef Michel, E. Ger	293-7	
1987	Seppo Raty, FIN	274-1	
1991	Kimmo Kinnunen, FIN	297-11	
1993	Jan Zelezny, CZR	282-1	
1995	Jan Zelezny, CZR	293-11	
1997	Marius Corbett, S. Afr.	290-0	
1999	Aki Parviainen, FIN	293-8	
2001	Jan Zelezny, CZR	304- 5	CR
2003	Sergey Makarov, RUS	280- 3	
2005	Andrus Varnik, EST	286- 0	
2007	Tero Pitkamaki, FIN	296- 4	

Decathlon

Year		Points	
1983	Daley Thompson, GBR	8714	
1987	Torsten Voss, E. Ger	8680	
1991	Dan O'Brien, USA	8812	
1993	Dan O'Brien, USA	8817	
1995	Dan O'Brien, USA	8695	
1997	Tomas Dvorak, CZR	8837	
1999	Tomas Dvorak, CZR	8744	
2001	Tomas Dvorak, CZR	8902	CR
2003	Tom Pappas, USA	8750	
2005	Bryan Clay, USA	8732	
2007	Roman Sebrle, CZR	8676	

WOMEN

Multiple gold medals (at least 3, including relays): Gail Devers (5), Jearl Miles Clark, Tirunesh Dibaba, Allyson Felix, Jackie Joyner-Kersee and Marion Jones (4); Franka Dietzsch, Tatyana Samolenko Dorovskikh, Silke Gladisch, Marita Koch, Carolina Kluft, Astrid Kumbernuss, Tatyana Lebedeva, Maria Mutola, Merlene Ottey, Gabriela Szabo, Gwen Torrence and Lauryn Williams (3).

100 Meters

Year		Time	
1983	Marlies Gohr, E. Ger	10.97	
1987	Silke Gladisch, E. Ger	10.90	
1991	Katrin Krabbe, GER	10.99	
1993	Gail Devers, USA	10.81	
1995	Gwen Torrence, USA	10.85	
1997	Marion Jones, USA	10.83	
1999	Marion Jones, USA	10.70	CR
2001	Zhanna Pintusevich-Block, UKR	10.82	
2003	Torri Edwards, USA	10.93*	
2005	Lauryn Williams, USA	10.93	
2007	Veronica Campbell, JAM	11.01	

*Original winner Kelli White, USA, was stripped of her medal.

200 Meters

Year		Time	
1983	Marita Koch, E. Ger	22.13	
1987	Silke Gladisch, E. Ger	21.74	CR
1991	Katrin Krabbe, GER	22.09	
1993	Merlene Ottey, JAM	21.98	
1995	Merlene Ottey, JAM	22.12	
1997	Zhanna Pintusevich, UKR	22.32	
1999	Inger Miller, USA	21.77	
2001	Marion Jones, USA	22.39	
2003	Anastasiya Kapachinskaya, RUS	22.38*	
2005	Allyson Felix, USA	22.16	
2007	Allyson Felix, USA	21.81	

*Original winner Kelli White, USA, was stripped of her medal.

400 Meters

Year		Time	
1983	Jarmila Kratochvilova, CZE	47.99	WR
1987	Olga Bryzgina, USSR	49.38	
1991	Marie-José Pérec, FRA	49.13	
1993	Jearl Miles, USA	49.82	
1995	Marie-José Pérec, FRA	49.28	
1997	Cathy Freeman, AUS	49.77	
1999	Cathy Freeman, AUS	49.67	
2001	Amy Mbacke Thiam, SEN	49.86	
2003	Ana Guevara, MEX	48.89	
2005	Tonique Williams-Darling, BAH	49.55	
2007	Christine Ohuruogu, GBR	49.61	

800 Meters

Year		Time	
1983	Jarmila Kratochvilova, CZE	1:54.68	CR
1987	Sigrun Wodars, E. Ger	1:55.26	
1991	Lilia Nurutdinova, USSR	1:57.50	
1993	Maria Mutola, MOZ	1:55.43	
1995	Ana Quirot, CUB	1:56.11	
1997	Ana Quirot, CUB	1:57.14	
1999	Ludmila Formanova, CZR	1:56.68	
2001	Maria Mutola, MOZ	1:57.17	
2003	Maria Mutola, MOZ	1:59.89	
2005	Zulia Calatayud, CUB	1:58.82	
2007	Janeth Jepkosgei, KEN	1:56.04	

1500 Meters

Year		Time	
1983	Mary Decker, USA	4:00.90	
1987	Tatiana Samolenko, USSR	3:58.56	
1991	Hassiba Boulmerka, ALG	4:02.21	
1993	Liu Dong, CHN	4:00.50	
1995	Hassiba Boulmerka, ALG	4:02.42	
1997	Carla Sacramento, POR	4:04.24	
1999	Svetlana Masterkova, RUS	3:59.53	
2001	Gabriela Szabo, ROM	4:00.57	
2003	Tatyana Tomashova, RUS	3:58.52	CR
2005	Tatyana Tomashova, RUS	4:00.35	
2007	Maryam Yusuf Jamal, BRN	3:58.75	

5000 Meters

Held as 3000-meter race from 1983-93

Year		Time	
1983	Mary Decker, USA	8:34.62	
1987	Tatyana Samolenko, USSR	8:38.73	
1991	T. Samolenko Dorovskikh, USSR	8:35.82	
1993	Qu Yunxia, CHN	8:28.71	
1995	Sonia O'Sullivan, IRL	14:46.47	
1997	Gabriela Szabo, ROM	14:57.68	
1999	Gabriela Szabo, ROM	14:41.82	
2001	Olga Yegorova, RUS	15:03.39	
2003	Tirunesh Dibaba, ETH	14:51.72	
2005	Tirunesh Dibaba, ETH	14:38.59	CR
2007	Meseret Defar, ETH	14:57.91	

10,000 Meters

Year		Time	
1983	Not held		
1987	Ingrid Kristiansen, NOR	31:05.85	
1991	Liz McColgan, GBR	31:14.31	
1993	Wang Junxia, CHN	30:49.30	
1995	Fernanda Ribeiro, POR	31:04.99	
1997	Sally Barsosio, KEN	31:32.92	
1999	Gete Wami, ETH	30:24.56	
2001	Derartu Tulu, ETH	31:48.81	
2003	Berhane Adere, ETH	30:04.18	CR
2005	Tirunesh Dibaba, ETH	30:24.02	
2007	Tirunesh Dibaba, ETH	31:55.41	

3000-Meter Steeplechase

Year		Time	
2005	Docus Inzikuru, UGA	9:18.24	
2007	Yekaterina Volkova, RUS	9:06.57	CR

Marathon

Year		Time	
1983	Grete Waitz, NOR	2:28:09	
1987	Rose Mota, POR	2:25:17	
1991	Wanda Panfil, POL	2:29:53	
1993	Junko Asari, JPN	2:30:03	
1995	Manuela Machado, POR	2:25:39	
1997	Hiromi Suzuki, JPN	2:29:48	
1999	Jong Song-Ok, N. Kor	2:26:59	
2001	Lidia Simon, ROM	2:26:01	
2003	Catherine Ndereba, KEN	2:23:55	
2005	Paula Radcliffe, GBR	2:20:57	CR
2007	Catherine Ndereba, KEN	2:30:37	

100-Meter Hurdles

Year		Time	
1983	Bettine Jahn, E. Ger	12.35w	
1987	Ginka Zagorcheva, BUL	12.34	CR
1991	Lyudmila Narozhilenko, USSR	12.59	
1993	Gail Devers, USA	12.46	
1995	Gail Devers, USA	12.68	
1997	Ludmila Enquist, SWE	12.50	
1999	Gail Devers, USA	12.37	
2001	Anjanette Kirkland, USA	12.42	
2003	Perdita Felicien, CAN	12.53	
2005	Michelle Perry, USA	12.66	
2007	Michelle Perry, USA	12.46	

400-Meter Hurdles

Year		Time	
1983	Yekaterina Fesenko, USSR	54.14	
1987	Sabine Busch, E. Ger	53.62	
1991	Tatiana Ledovskaya, USSR	53.11	
1993	Sally Gunnell, GBR	52.74	WR
1995	Kim Batten, USA	52.61	WR
1997	Nezha Bidouane, MOR	52.97	
1999	Daima Pernia, CUB	52.89	
2001	Nezha Bidouane, MOR	53.34	
2003	Jana Pittman, AUS	53.22	
2005	Yuliya Pechonkina, RUS	52.90	
2007	Jana Rawlinson, AUS	53.31	

4 x 100-Meter Relay

Year		Time	
1983	East Germany	41.76	
1987	United States	41.58	
1991	Jamaica	41.94	
1993	Russia	41.49	
1995	United States	42.12	
1997	United States	41.47	CR
1999	Bahamas	41.92	
2001	Germany	42.32*	
2003	France	41.78	
2005	United States	41.78	
2007	United States	41.98	

*The United States was stripped of its 2001 gold after lead runner Kelli White tested positive for a stimulant.

4 x 400-Meter Relay

Year		Time	
1983	East Germany	3:19.73	
1987	East Germany	3:18.63	
1991	Soviet Union	3:18.43	
1993	United States	3:16.71	CR
1995	United States	3:22.39	
1997	Germany	3:20.92	
1999	Russia	3:21.98	
2001	Jamaica	3:20.65	
2003	United States	3:22.63	
2005	Russia	3:20.95	
2007	United States	3:18.55	

20-Kilometer Walk

Held as 10-Kilometer race from 1987-97

Year		Time	
1983	Not held		
1987	Irina Strakhova, USSR	44:12	
1991	Alina Ivanova, USSR	42:57	
1993	Sari Essayah, FIN	42:59	
1995	Irina Stankina, RUS	42:13	
1997	Anna Sidoti, ITA	42:55	
1999	Hongyu Liu, CHN	1:30:50	
2001	Olimpiada Ivanova, RUS	1:27:48	
2003	Yelena Nikolayeva, RUS	1:26:52	
2005	Olimpiada Ivanova, RUS	1:25:41	WR
2007	Olga Kaniskina, RUS	1:30:09	

High Jump

Year		Height	
1983	Tamara Bykova, USSR	6- 7	
1987	Stefka Kostadinova, BUL	6-10¼	WR
1991	Heike Henkel, GER	6- 8¾	
1993	Ioamnet Quintero, CUB	6- 6¼	
1995	Stefka Kostadinova, BUL	6- 7	
1997	Hanne Haugland, NOR	6- 6¼	
1999	Inga Babakova, UKR	6- 6¼	
2001	Hestrie Cloete, RSA	6- 6¾	
2003	Hestrie Cloete, RSA	6- 9	
2005	Kajsa Bergqvist, SWE	6- 7½	
2007	Blanka Vlasic, CRO	6- 8½	

Pole Vault

Year		Height	
1999	Stacy Dragila, USA	15- 1	
2001	Stacy Dragila, USA	15- 7	
2003	Svetlana Feofanova, RUS	15- 7	
2005	Yelena Isinbayeva, RUS	16- 5¼	WR
2007	Yelena Isinbayeva, RUS	15- 9	

Long Jump

Year		Distance	
1983	Heike Daute, E. Ger	23-10¼[W]	
1987	Jackie Joyner-Kersee, USA	24- 1¾	CR
1991	Jackie Joyner-Kersee, USA	24- 0¼	
1993	Heike Drechsler, GER	23- 4	
1995	Fiona May, ITA	22-10¾[W]	
1997	Lyudmila Galkina, RUS	23- 1¾	
1999	Niurka Montalvo, SPA	23- 2	
2001	Fiona May, ITA	23- 0½	
2003	Eunice Barber, FRA	22-11¼	
2005	Tianna Madison, USA	22- 7¼	
2007	Tatyana Lebedeva, RUS	23- 0¾	

Triple Jump

Year		Distance	
1993	Ana Biryukova, RUS	46- 6¼	
1995	Inessa Kravets, UKR	50- 10¾	WR
1997	Sarka Kasparkova, CZR	49- 10½	
1999	Paraskevi Tsiamita, GRE	48- 10	
2001	Tatyana Lebedeva, RUS	50- 0½	
2003	Tatyana Lebedeva, RUS	49- 9¾	
2005	Trecia Smith, JAM	49- 7	
2007	Yargelis Savigne, CUB	50- 1½	

Shot Put

Year		Distance	
1983	Helena Fibingerova, CZE	69- 0	
1987	Natalia Lisovskaya, USSR	69- 8	CR
1991	Huang Zhihong, CHN	68- 4	
1993	Huang Zhihong, CHN	67- 6	
1995	Astrid Kumbernuss, GER	69- 7½	
1997	Astrid Kumbernuss, GER	67- 11½	
1999	Astrid Kumbernuss, GER	65- 1½	
2001	Yanina Korolchik, BLR	67- 7½	
2003	Svetlana Krivelyova, RUS	67- 8¼	
2005	Nadezhda Ostapchuk, BLR	67- 3½	
2007	Valerie Vili, NZ	67- 4¾	

Discus

Year		Distance	
1983	Martina Opitz, E. Ger	226- 2	
1987	Martina Opitz Hellmann, E. Ger	235- 0	CR
1991	Tsvetanka Khristova, BUL	233- 0	
1993	Olga Burova, RUS	221- 1	
1995	Ellina Zvereva, BLR	225- 2	
1997	Beatrice Faumuina, NZE	219- 3	
1999	Franka Dietzsch, GER	223- 6	
2001	Natalya Sadova, RUS	224-11	
2003	Irina Yatchenko, BLR	220-10	
2005	Franka Dietzsch, GER	218- 4	
2007	Franka Dietzsch, GER	218- 6	

Hammer Throw

Year		Distance	
1999	Mihaela Melinte, ROM	246-8¾	CR
2001	Yipsi Moreno, CUB	231- 9	
2003	Yipsi Moreno, CUB	240- 7	
2005	Olga Kuzenkova, RUS	246- 5	
2007	Betty Heidler, GER	245- 3	

Javelin

Year		Distance	
1983	Tiina Lillak, FIN	232- 4	
1987	Fatima Whitbread, GBR	251- 5	CR
1991	Xu Demei, CHN	225- 8	
1993	Trine Hattestad, NOR	227- 0	
1995	Natalya Shikolenko, BLR	221- 8	
1997	Trine Hattestad, NOR	225- 8	
1999	Mirela Manjani-Tzelili, GRE	220- 1	
2001	Osleidys Menendez, CUB	228- 1	
2003	Mirela Manjani, GRE	218- 3	
2005	Osleidys Menendez, CUB	235- 3	WR
2007	Barbora Spotakova, CZR	220- 0	

Heptathlon

Year		Points	
1983	Ramona Neubert, E. Ger	6770	
1987	Jackie Joyner-Kersee, USA	7128	CR
1991	Sabine Braun, GER	6672	
1993	Jackie Joyner-Kersee, USA	6837	
1995	Ghada Shouaa, SYR	6651	
1997	Sabine Braun, GER	6739	
1999	Eunice Barber, FRA	6861	
2001	Yelena Prokhorova, RUS	6694	
2003	Carolina Kluft, SWE	7001	
2005	Carolina Kluft, SWE	6887	
2007	Carolina Kluft, SWE	7032	

World Cross Country Championships

MEN

Multiple winners: Kenenisa Bekele (6); John Ngugi and Paul Tergat (5); Carlos Lopes (3); Mohammed Mourhit, Khalid Skah, William Sigei, John Treacy and Craig Virgin (2).

Year	
1973	Pekka Paivarinta, Finland
1974	Eric DeBeck, Belgium
1975	Ian Stewart, Scotland
1976	Carlos Lopes, Portugal
1977	Leon Schots, Belgium
1978	John Treacy, Ireland
1979	John Treacy, Ireland
1980	Craig Virgin, USA
1981	Craig Virgin, USA
1982	Mohammed Kedir, Ethiopia
1983	Bekele Debele, Ethiopia
1984	Carlos Lopes, Portugal
1985	Carlos Lopes, Portugal
1986	John Ngugi, Kenya
1987	John Ngugi, Kenya

Year		Year		Year	
1988	John Ngugi, Kenya	1995	Paul Tergat, Kenya	2002	Kenenisa Bekele, Ethiopia
1989	John Ngugi, Kenya	1996	Paul Tergat, Kenya	2003	Kenenisa Bekele, Ethiopia
1990	Khalid Skah, Morocco	1997	Paul Tergat, Kenya	2004	Kenenisa Bekele, Ethiopia
1991	Khalid Skah, Morocco	1998	Paul Tergat, Kenya	2005	Kenenisa Bekele, Ethiopia
1992	John Ngugi, Kenya	1999	Paul Tergat, Kenya	2006	Kenenisa Bekele, Ethiopia
1993	William Sigei, Kenya	2000	Mohammed Mourhit, Belgium	2007	Zersenay Tadesse, Eritrea
1994	William Sigei, Kenya	2001	Mohammed Mourhit, Belgium	2008	Kenenisa Bekele, Ethiopia

WOMEN

Multiple winners: Grete Waitz (5); Tirunesh Dibaba, Lynn Jennings and Derartu Tulu (3); Zola Budd, Paola Cacchi, Maricica Puica, Paula Radcliffe, Annette Sergent, Carmen Valero and Gete Wami (2).

Year		Year		Year	
1973	Paola Cacchi, Italy	1985	Zola Budd, England	1997	Derartu Tulu, Ethiopia
1974	Paola Cacchi, Italy	1986	Zola Budd, England	1998	Sonia O'Sullivan, Ireland
1975	Julie Brown, USA	1987	Annette Sergent, France	1999	Gete Wami, Ethiopia
1976	Carmen Valero, Spain	1988	Ingrid Kristiansen, Norway	2000	Derartu Tulu, Ethiopia
1977	Carmen Valero, Spain	1989	Annette Sergent, France	2001	Paula Radcliffe, Gr. Britain
1978	Grete Waitz, Norway	1990	Lynn Jennings, USA	2002	Paula Radcliffe, Gr. Britain
1979	Grete Waitz, Norway	1991	Lynn Jennings, USA	2003	Werknesh Kidane, Ethiopia
1980	Grete Waitz, Norway	1992	Lynn Jennings, USA	2004	Benita Johnson, Australia
1981	Grete Waitz, Norway	1993	Albertina Dias, Portugal	2005	Tirunesh Dibaba, Ethiopia
1982	Maricica Puica, Romania	1994	Helen Chepngeno, Kenya	2006	Tirunesh Dibaba, Ethiopia
1983	Grete Waitz, Norway	1995	Derartu Tulu, Ethiopia	2007	Lornah Kiplagat, Netherlands
1984	Maricica Puica, Romania	1996	Gete Wami, Ethiopia	2008	Tirunesh Dibaba, Ethiopia

Marathons

Boston

America's oldest regularly contested foot race, the Boston Marathon is held on Patriots' Day every April. It has been run at four different distances: 24 miles, 1232 yards (1897-1923); 26 miles, 209 yards (1924-26); 26 miles, 385 yards (1927-52, since 1957); 25 miles, 958 yards (1953-56).

MEN

Multiple winners: Clarence DeMar (7); Robert Kipkoech Cheruiyot, Gerard Cote and Bill Rodgers (4); Ibrahim Hussein, Cosmas Ndeti, Eino Oksanen and Leslie Pawson (3); Tarzan Brown, Jim Caffrey, John A. Kelley, John Miles, Toshihiko Seko, Geoff Smith, Moses Tanui and Aurele Vandendriessche (2).

Year		Time	Year		Time
1897	John McDermott, New York	2:55:10	1932	Paul deBruyn, Germany	2:33:36
1898	Ronald McDonald, Massachusetts	2:42:00	1933	Leslie Pawson, Rhode Island	2:31:01
1899	Lawrence Brignolia, Massachusetts	2:54:38	1934	Dave Komonen, Canada	2:32:53
1900	Jim Caffrey, Canada	2:39:44	1935	John A. Kelley, Massachusetts	2:32:07
1901	Jim Caffrey, Canada	2:29:23	1936	Ellison (Tarzan) Brown, Rhode Island	2:33:40
1902	Sam Mellor, New York	2:43:12	1937	Walter Young, Canada	2:33:20
1903	J.C. Lorden, Massachusetts	2:41:29	1938	Leslie Pawson, Rhode Island	2:35:34
1904	Mike Spring, New York	2:38:04	1939	Ellison (Tarzan) Brown, Rhode Island	2:28:51
1905	Fred Lorz, New York	2:38:25			
1906	Tim Ford, Massachusetts	2:45:45	1940	Gerard Cote, Canada	2:28:28
1907	Tom Longboat, Canada	2:24:24	1941	Leslie Pawson, Rhode Island	2:30:38
1908	Tom Morrissey, New York	2:25:43	1942	Joe Smith, Massachusetts	2:26:51
1909	Henri Renaud, New Hampshire	2:53:36	1943	Gerard Cote, Canada	2:28:25
			1944	Gerard Cote, Canada	2:31:50
1910	Fred Cameron, Nova Scotia	2:28:52	1945	John A. Kelley, Massachusetts	2:30:40
1911	Clarence DeMar, Massachusetts	2:21:39	1946	Stylianos Kyriakides, Greece	2:29:27
1912	Mike Ryan, Illinois	2:21:18	1947	Yun Bok Suh, Korea	2:25:39
1913	Fritz Carlson, Minnesota	2:25:14	1948	Gerard Cote, Canada	2:31:02
1914	James Duffy, Canada	2:25:01	1949	Karle Leandersson, Sweden	2:31:50
1915	Edouard Fabre, Canada	2:31:41			
1916	Arthur Roth, Massachusetts	2:27:16	1950	Kee Yonh Ham, Korea	2:32:39
1917	Bill Kennedy, New York	2:28:37	1951	Shigeki Tanaka, Japan	2:27:45
1918	World War relay race		1952	Doroteo Flores, Guatemala	2:31:53
1919	Carl Linder, Massachusetts	2:29:13	1953	Keizo Yamada, Japan	2:18:51
1920	Peter Trivoulidas, New York	2:29:31	1954	Veiko Karvonen, Finland	2:20:39
1921	Frank Zuna, New Jersey	2:18:57	1955	Hideo Hamamura, Japan	2:18:22
1922	Clarence DeMar, Massachusetts	2:18:10	1956	Antti Viskari, Finland	2:14:14
1923	Clarence DeMar, Massachusetts	2:23:37	1957	John J. Kelley, Connecticut	2:20:05
1924	Clarence DeMar, Massachusetts	2:29:40	1958	Franjo Mihalic, Yugoslavia	2:25:54
1925	Charles Mellor, Illinois	2:33:00	1959	Eino Oksanen, Finland	2:22:42
1926	John Miles, Nova Scotia	2:25:40			
1927	Clarence DeMar, Massachusetts	2:40:22	1960	Paavo Kotila, Finland	2:20:54
1928	Clarence DeMar, Massachusetts	2:37:07	1961	Eino Oksanen, Finland	2:23:39
1929	John Miles, Nova Scotia	2:33:08	1962	Eino Oksanen, Finland	2:23:48
			1963	Aurele Vandendriessche, Belgium	2:18:58
1930	Clarence DeMar, Massachusetts	2:34:48	1964	Aurele Vandendriessche, Belgium	2:19:59
1931	James Henigan, Massachusetts	2:46:45	1965	Morio Shigematsu, Japan	2:16:33
			1966	Kenji Kimihara, Japan	2:17:11

Boston Marathon (Cont.)

Year		Time	Year		Time
1967	David McKenzie, New Zealand	2:15:45	1989	Abebe Mekonnen, Ethiopia	2:09:06
1968	Amby Burfoot, Connecticut	2:22:17	1990	Gelindo Bordin, Italy	2:08:19
1969	Yoshiaki Unetani, Japan	2:13:49	1991	Ibrahim Hussein, Kenya	2:11:06
1970	Ron Hill, England	2:10:30	1992	Ibrahim Hussein, Kenya	2:08:14
1971	Alvaro Mejia, Colombia	2:18:45	1993	Cosmas Ndeti, Kenya	2:09:33
1972	Olavi Suomalainen, Finland	2:15:39	1994	Cosmas Ndeti, Kenya	2:07:15
1973	Jon Anderson, Oregon	2:16:03	1995	Cosmas Ndeti, Kenya	2:09:22
1974	Neil Cusack, Ireland	2:13:39	1996	Moses Tanui, Kenya	2:09:16
1975	Bill Rodgers, Massachusetts	2:09:55	1997	Lameck Aguta, Kenya	2:10:34
1976	Jack Fultz, Pennsylvania	2:20:19	1998	Moses Tanui, Kenya	2:07:34
1977	Jerome Drayton, Canada	2:14:46	1999	Joseph Chebet, Kenya	2:09:52
1978	Bill Rodgers, Massachusetts	2:10:13	2000	Elijah Lagat, Kenya	2:09:47
1979	Bill Rodgers, Massachusetts	2:09:27 ·	2001	Lee Bong-Ju, South Korea	2:09:43
1980	Bill Rodgers, Massachusetts	2:12:11	2002	Rodgers Rop, Kenya	2:09:02
1981	Toshihiko Seko, Japan	2:09:26	2003	Robert Kipkoech Cheruiyot, Kenya	2:10:11
1982	Alberto Salazar, Oregon	2:08:52	2004	Timothy Cherigat, Kenya	2:10:37
1983	Greg Meyer, New Jersey	2:09:00	2005	Hailu Negussie, Ethiopia	2:11:45
1984	Geoff Smith, England	2:10:34	2006	Robert Kipkoech Cheruiyot, Kenya	2:07:14*
1985	Geoff Smith, England	2:14:05	2007	Robert Kipkoech Cheruiyot, Kenya	2:14:13
1986	Rob de Castella, Australia	2:07:51	2008	Robert Kipkoech Cheruiyot, Kenya	2:07:46
1987	Toshihiko Seko, Japan	2:11:50		*Course record.	
1988	Ibrahim Hussein, Kenya	2:08:43			

WOMEN

Multiple winners: Catherine Ndereba (4); Rosa Mota, Uta Pippig and Fatuma Roba (3); Joan Benoit, Miki Gorman, Ingrid Kristiansen and Olga Markova (2).

Year		Time	Year		Time
1972	Nina Kuscsik, New York	3:08:58	1991	Wanda Panfil, Poland	2:24:18
1973	Jacqueline Hansen, California	3:05:59	1992	Olga Markova, CIS	2:23:43
1974	Miki Gorman, California	2:47:11	1993	Olga Markova, Russia	2:25:27
1975	Liane Winter, West Germany	2:42:24	1994	Uta Pippig, Germany	2:21:45
1976	Kim Merritt, Wisconsin	2:47:10	1995	Uta Pippig, Germany	2:25:11
1977	Miki Gorman, California	2:48:33	1996	Uta Pippig, Germany	2:27:12
1978	Gayle Barron, Georgia	2:44:52	1997	Fatuma Roba, Ethiopia	2:26:23
1979	Joan Benoit, Maine	2:35:15	1998	Fatuma Roba, Ethiopia	2:23:21
1980	Jacqueline Gareau, Canada	2:34:28	1999	Fatuma Roba, Ethiopia	2:23:25
1981	Allison Roe, New Zealand	2:26:46	2000	Catherine Ndereba, Kenya	2:26:11
1982	Charlotte Teske, West Germany	2:29:33	2001	Catherine Ndereba, Kenya	2:23:53
1983	Joan Benoit, Maine	2:22:43	2002	Margaret Okayo, Kenya	2:20:43*
1984	Lorraine Moller, New Zealand	2:29:28	2003	Svetlana Zakharova, Russia	2:25:20
1985	Lisa Larsen Weidenbach, Mass	2:34:06	2004	Catherine Ndereba, Kenya	2:24:27
1986	Ingrid Kristiansen, Norway	2:24:55	2005	Catherine Ndereba, Kenya	2:25:13
1987	Rosa Mota, Portugal	2:25:21	2006	Rita Jeptoo, Kenya	2:23:38
1988	Rosa Mota, Portugal	2:24:30	2007	Lidiya Grigoryeva, Russia	2:29:18
1989	Ingrid Kristiansen, Norway	2:24:33	2008	Dire Tune, Ethiopia	2:25:25
1990	Rosa Mota, Portugal	2:25:23		*Course record.	

New York City

Started in 1970, the New York City Marathon is run in the fall, usually on the first Sunday in November. The route winds through all of the city's five boroughs and finishes in Central Park.

MEN

Multiple winners: Bill Rodgers (4); Alberto Salazar (3); Tom Fleming, John Kagwe, Martin Lel, Orlando Pizzolato and German Silva (2).

Year		Time	Year		Time	Year		Time
1970	Gary Muhrcke, USA	2:31:38	1984	Orlando Pizzolato, ITA	2:14:53	1998	John Kagwe, KEN	2:08:45
1971	Norman Higgins, USA	2:22:54	1985	Orlando Pizzolato, ITA	2:11:34	1999	Joseph Chebet, KEN	2:09:14
1972	Sheldon Karlin, USA	2:27:52	1986	Gianni Poli, ITA	2:11:06	2000	Abdelkhader El Mouaziz, MOR	2:10:08
1973	Tom Fleming, USA	2:21:54	1987	Ibrahim Hussein, KEN	2:11:01			
1974	Norbert Sander, USA	2:26:30	1988	Steve Jones, WAL	2:08:20	2001	Tesfaye Jifar, ETH	2:07:43*
1975	Tom Fleming, USA	2:19:27	1989	Juma Ikangaa, TAN	2:08:01	2002	Rodgers Rop, KEN	2:08:07
1976	Bill Rodgers, USA	2:10:09	1990	Douglas Wakiihuri, KEN	2:12:39	2003	Martin Lel, KEN	2:10:30
1977	Bill Rodgers, USA	2:11:28	1991	Salvador Garcia, MEX	2:09:28	2004	Hendrik Ramaala, RSA	2:09:28
1978	Bill Rodgers, USA	2:12:12	1992	Willie Mtolo, S. Afr.	2:09:29	2005	Paul Tergat, KEN	2:09:30
1979	Bill Rodgers, USA	2:11:42	1993	Andres Espinosa, MEX	2:10:04	2006	M. Gomes dos Santos, BRA	2:09:58
1980	Alberto Salazar, USA	2:09:41	1994	German Silva, MEX	2:11:21			
1981	Alberto Salazar, USA	2:08:13	1995	German Silva, MEX	2:11:00	2007	Martin Lel, KEN	2:09:04
1982	Alberto Salazar, USA	2:09:29	1996	Giacomo Leone, ITA	2:09:54		*Course record.	
1983	Rod Dixon, NZE	2:08:59	1997	John Kagwe, KEN	2:08:12			

WOMEN

Multiple winners: Grete Waitz (9); Miki Gorman, Nina Kuscsik, Tegla Loroupe, Margaret Okayo, Jelena Prokopcuka and Paula Radcliffe (2).

Year		Time	Year		Time	Year		Time
1970	No Finisher		1983	Grete Waitz, NOR	2:27:00	1996	Anuta Catuna, ROM	2:28:18
1971	Beth Bonner, USA	2:55:22	1984	Grete Waitz, NOR	2:29:30	1997	F. Rochat-Moser, SWI	2:28:43
1972	Nina Kuscsik, USA	3:08:41	1985	Grete Waitz, NOR	2:28:34	1998	Franca Fiacconi, ITA	2:25:17
1973	Nina Kuscsik, USA	2:57:07	1986	Grete Waitz, NOR	2:28:34	1999	Adriana Fernandez, MEX	2:25:06
1974	Katherine Switzer, USA	3:07:29	1987	Priscilla Welch, GBR	2:30:17	2000	Ludmila Petrova, RUS	2:25:45
1975	Kim Merritt, USA	2:46:14	1988	Grete Waitz, NOR	2:28:07	2001	Margaret Okayo, KEN	2:24:21
1976	Miki Gorman, USA	2:39:11	1989	Ingrid Kristiansen, NOR	2:25:30	2002	Joyce Chepchumba, KEN	2:25:56
1977	Miki Gorman, USA	2:43:10	1990	Wanda Panfil, POL	2:30:45	2003	Margaret Okayo, KEN	2:22:31*
1978	Grete Waitz, NOR	2:32:30	1991	Liz McColgan, GBR	2:27:23	2004	Paula Radcliffe, GBR	2:23:10
1979	Grete Waitz, NOR	2:27:33	1992	Lisa Ondieki, AUS	2:24:40	2005	Jelena Prokopcuka, LAT	2:24:41
1980	Grete Waitz, NOR	2:25:41	1993	Uta Pippig, GER	2:26:24	2006	Jelena Prokopcuka, LAT	2:25:05
1981	Allison Roe, NZE	2:25:29	1994	Tegla Loroupe, KEN	2:27:37	2007	Paula Radcliffe, GBR	2:23:09
1982	Grete Waitz, NOR	2:27:14	1995	Tegla Loroupe, KEN	2:28:06	*Course record.		

Annual Awards

Track & Field News Athletes of the Year

Voted on by an international panel of track and field experts and presented since 1959 for men and 1974 for women.

MEN

Multiple winners: Hicham El Guerrouj and Carl Lewis (3); Kenenisa Bekele, Sergey Bubka, Sebastian Coe, Haile Gebrselassie, Michael Johnson, Alberto Juantorena, Noureddine Morceli, Jim Ryun and Peter Snell (2).

Year		Event	Year		Event
1959	Martin Lauer, W. Germany	110H/Decathlon	1984	Carl Lewis, USA	100/200/Long Jump
1960	Rafer Johnson, USA	Decathlon	1985	Said Aouita, Morocco	1500/5000
1961	Ralph Boston, USA	Long Jump/110 Hurdles	1986	Yuri Sedykh, USSR	Hammer Throw
1962	Peter Snell, New Zealand	800/1500	1987	Ben Johnson, Canada	100
1963	C.K. Yang, Taiwan	Decathlon/Pole Vault	1988	Sergey Bubka, USSR	Pole Vault
1964	Peter Snell, New Zealand	800/1500	1989	Roger Kingdom, USA	110 Hurdles
1965	Ron Clarke, Australia	5000/10,000	1990	Michael Johnson, USA	200/400
1966	Jim Ryun, USA	800/1500	1991	Sergey Bubka, USSR	Pole Vault
1967	Jim Ryun, USA	1500	1992	Kevin Young, USA	400 Hurdles
1968	Bob Beamon, USA	Long Jump	1993	Noureddine Morceli, Algeria	Mile/1500/3000
1969	Bill Toomey, USA	Decathlon	1994	Noureddine Morceli, Algeria	Mile/1500/3000
1970	Randy Matson, USA	Shot Put	1995	Haile Gebrselassie, Ethiopia	5000/10,000
1971	Rod Milburn, USA	110 Hurdles	1996	Michael Johnson, USA	200/400
1972	Lasse Viren, Finland	5000/10,000	1997	Wilson Kipketer, Denmark	800
1973	Ben Jipcho, Kenya	1500/5000/Steeplechase	1998	Haile Gebrselassie, Ethiopia	3000/5000/10,000
1974	Rick Wohlhuter, USA	800/1500	1999	Hicham El Guerrouj, Morocco	Mile/1500
1975	John Walker, New Zealand	800/1500	2000	Virgilijus Alekna, Lithuania	Discus
1976	Alberto Juantorena, Cuba	400/800	2001	Hicham El Guerrouj, Morocco	Mile/1500
1977	Alberto Juantorena, Cuba	400/800	2002	Hicham El Guerrouj, Morocco	Mile/1500
1978	Henry Rono, Kenya	5000/10,000/Steeplechase	2003	Felix Sanchez, Dominican Republic	400 Hurdles
1979	Sebastian Coe, Great Britain	800/1500	2004	Kenenisa Bekele, Ethiopia	5000/10,000
1980	Edwin Moses, USA	400 Hurdles	2005	Kenenisa Bekele, Ethiopia	5000/10,000
1981	Sebastian Coe, Great Britain	800/1500	2006	Asafa Powell, Jamaica	100
1982	Carl Lewis, USA	100/200/Long Jump	2007	Tyson Gay, USA	100/200
1983	Carl Lewis, USA	100/200/Long Jump			

WOMEN

Multiple winners: Marita Koch (4); Marion Jones and Jackie Joyner-Kersee (3); Evelyn Ashford and Yelena Isinbayeva (2).

Year		Event	Year		Event
1974	Irena Szewinska, Poland	100/200/400	1991	Heike Henkel, Germany	High Jump
1975	Faina Melnik, USSR	Shot Put/Discus	1992	Heike Drechsler, Germany	Long Jump
1976	Tatiana Kazankina, USSR	800/1500	1993	Wang Junxia, China	1500/3000/10,000
1977	Rosemarie Ackermann, E. Germany	High Jump	1994	Jackie Joyner-Kersee, USA	100H/Heptathlon/LJ
1978	Marita Koch, E. Germany	100/200/400	1995	Sonia O'Sullivan, Ireland	1500/3000/5000
1979	Marita Koch, E. Germany	100/200/400	1996	Svetlana Masterkova, Russia	800/1500
1980	Ilona Briesenick, E. Germany	Shot Put	1997	Marion Jones, USA	100/200
1981	Evelyn Ashford, USA	100/200	1998	Marion Jones, USA	100/200/LJ
1982	Marita Koch, E. Germany	100/200/400	1999	Gabriela Szabo, Romania	3000/5000
1983	Jarmila Kratochvilova, Czech	200/400/800	2000	Marion Jones, USA	100/200/LJ
1984	Evelyn Ashford, USA	100	2001	Stacy Dragila, USA	Pole Vault
1985	Marita Koch, E. Germany	100/200/400	2002	Paula Radcliffe, Gr. Britain	3000/5000/10k/Mar
1986	Jackie Joyner-Kersee, USA	Heptathlon/Long Jump	2003	Maria Mutola, Mozambique	800
1987	Jackie Joyner-Kersee, USA	100H/Heptathlon/LJ	2004	Yelena Isinbayeva, Russia	Pole Vault
1988	Florence Griffith Joyner, USA	100/200	2005	Yelena Isinbayeva, Russia	Pole Vault
1989	Ana Quirot, Cuba	400/800	2006	Sanya Richards, USA	200/400
1990	Merlene Ottey, Jamaica	100/200	2007	Meseret Defar, Ethiopia	3000/5000

SWIMMING & DIVING

FINA World Championships

While the Summer Olympics have served as the unofficial world championships for swimming and diving throughout the centuries, a separate World Championship meet was started in 1973 by the Federation Internationale de Natation Amateur (FINA). The meet has varied between being held every two years, every three years or every four years. Currently it is held every two years. Sites have been Belgrade (1973); Cali, COL (1975); West Berlin (1978); Guayaquil, ECU (1982); Madrid (1986); Perth (1991 & 98), Rome (1994), Fukuoka, JPN (2001), Barcelona (2003), Montreal (2005) and Melbourne (2007). Looking forward, the Championships will be held in Rome (2009) and Shanghai (2011).

MEN

Most gold medals (including relays): Michael Phelps (15); Ian Thorpe (11); Grant Hackett (10); Aaron Peirsol (8); Jim Montgomery (7); Matt Biondi, Michael Klim and Aleksandr Popov (6); Rowdy Gaines, Brendan Hansen and Matt Welsh (5); Joe Bottom, Ian Crocker, Tamas Darnyi, Michael Gross, Tom Jager, Jason Lezak, David McCagg, Vladimir Salnikov and Tim Shaw (4); Billy Forrester, Andras Hargitay, Kosuke Kitajima, Ryan Lochte, Roland Matthes, John Murphy, Jeff Rouse, Norbert Rozsa and David Wilkie (3).

50-Meter Freestyle

Year		Time	
1973-82	Not held		
1986	Tom Jager, USA	.22.49	
1991	Tom Jager, USA	.22.16	
1994	Aleksandr Popov, RUS	.22.17	
1998	Bill Pilczuk, USA	.22.29	
2001	Anthony Ervin, USA	.22.09	
2003	Aleksandr Popov, RUS	.21.92	
2005	Roland Schoeman, RSA	.21.69	CR
2007	Benjamin Wildman-Tobriner, USA	.21.88	

100-Meter Freestyle

Year		Time	
1973	Jim Montgomery, USA	.51.70	
1975	Tim Shaw, USA	.51.25	
1978	David McCagg, USA	.50.24	
1982	Jorg Woithe, E. Ger	.50.18	
1986	Matt Biondi, USA	.48.94	
1991	Matt Biondi, USA	.49.18	
1994	Aleksandr Popov, RUS	.49.12	
1998	Aleksandr Popov, RUS	.48.93	
2001	Anthony Ervin, USA	.48.33	
2003	Aleksandr Popov, RUS	.48.42	
2005	Filippo Magnini, ITA	.48.12	CR
2007	Filippo Magnini, ITA	.48.43	

200-Meter Freestyle

Year		Time	
1973	Jim Montgomery, USA	1:53.02	
1975	Tim Shaw, USA	1:52.04	
1978	Billy Forrester, USA	1:51.02	
1982	Michael Gross, W. Ger	1:49.84	
1986	Michael Gross, W. Ger	1:47.92	
1991	Giorgio Lamberti, ITA	1:47.27	
1994	Antti Kasvio, FIN	1:47.32	
1998	Michael Klim, AUS	1:47.41	
2001	Ian Thorpe, AUS	1:44.06	WR
2003	Ian Thorpe, AUS	1:45.14	
2005	Michael Phelps, USA	1:45.20	
2007	Michael Phelps, USA	1:43.86	WR

400-Meter Freestyle

Year		Time	
1973	Rick DeMont, USA	3:58.18	
1975	Tim Shaw, USA	3:54.88	
1978	Vladimir Salnikov, USSR	3:51.94	
1982	Vladimir Salnikov, USSR	3:51.30	
1986	Rainer Henkel, W. Ger	3:50.05	
1991	Jorg Hoffman, GER	3:48.04	
1994	Kieren Perkins, AUS	3:43.80	
1998	Ian Thorpe, AUS	3:46.29	
2001	Ian Thorpe, AUS	3:40.17	WR
2003	Ian Thorpe, AUS	3:42.58	
2005	Grant Hackett, AUS	3:42.91	
2007	Tae Hwan Park, KOR	3:44.30	

800-Meter Freestyle

Year		Time	
1973-98	Not held		
2001	Ian Thorpe, AUS	7:39.16	
2003	Grant Hackett, AUS	7:43.82	
2005	Grant Hackett, AUS	7:38.65	WR
2007	Oussama Mellouli, TUN	7:46.95	

1500-Meter Freestyle

Year		Time	
1973	Stephen Holland, AUS	15:31.85	
1975	Tim Shaw, USA	15:28.92	
1978	Vladimir Salnikov, USSR	15:03.99	
1982	Vladimir Salnikov, USSR	15:01.77	
1986	Rainer Henkel, W. Ger	15:05.31	
1991	Jorg Hoffman, GER	14:50.36	
1994	Kieren Perkins, AUS	14:50.52	
1998	Grant Hackett, AUS	14:51.70	
2001	Grant Hackett, AUS	14:34.56	WR
2003	Grant Hackett, AUS	14:43.14	
2005	Grant Hackett, AUS	14:42.58	
2007	Mateusz Sawrymowicz, POL	14:45.94	

50-Meter Backstroke

Year		Time	
1973-98	Not held		
2001	Randall Bal, USA	.25.34	
2003	Thomas Rupprath, GER	.24.80	WR
2005	Aristeidis Grigoriadis, GRE	.24.95	
2007	Gerhard Zandberg, RSA	.24.98	

100-Meter Backstroke

Year		Time	
1973	Roland Matthes, E. Ger	.57.47	
1975	Roland Matthes, E. Ger	.58.15	
1978	Bob Jackson, USA	.56.36	
1982	Dirk Richter, E. Ger	.55.95	
1986	Igor Polianski, USSR	.55.58	
1991	Jeff Rouse, USA	.55.23	
1994	Martin Lopez-Zubero, SPA	.55.17	
1998	Lenny Krayzelburg, USA	.55.00	
2001	Matt Welsh, AUS	.54.31	
2003	Aaron Peirsol, USA	.53.61	
2005	Aaron Peirsol, USA	.53.62	
2007	Aaron Peirsol, USA	.52.98	WR

200-Meter Backstroke

Year		Time	
1973	Roland Matthes, E. Ger	2:01.87	
1975	Zoltan Varraszto, HUN	2:05.05	
1978	Jesse Vassallo, USA	2:02.16	
1982	Rick Carey, USA	2:00.82	
1986	Igor Polianski, USSR	1:58.78	
1991	Martin Zubero, SPA	1:59.52	
1994	Vladimir Selkov, RUS	1:57.42	
1998	Lenny Krayzelburg, USA	1:58.84	
2001	Aaron Peirsol, USA	1:57.13	
2003	Aaron Peirsol, USA	1:55.92	
2005	Aaron Peirsol, USA	1:54.66	
2007	Ryan Lochte, USA	1:54.32	WR

50-Meter Breaststroke

Year		Time
1973-98 Not held		
2001	Oleg Lisogor, UKR	27.52
2003	James Gibson, GBR	27.56
2005	Mark Warnecke, GER	27.63
2007	Oleg Lisogor, UKR	27.66

100-Meter Breaststroke

Year		Time	
1973	John Hencken, USA	1:04.02	
1975	David Wilkie, GBR	1:04.26	
1978	Walter Kusch, W. Ger	1:03.56	
1982	Steve Lundquist, USA	1:02.75	
1986	Victor Davis, CAN	1:02.71	
1991	Norbert Rozsa, HUN	1:01.45	
1994	Norbert Rozsa, HUN	1:01.24	
1998	Frederik deBurghgraeve, BEL	1:01.34	
2001	Roman Sloudnov, RUS	1:00.16	
2003	Kosuke Kitajima, JPN	59.78	
2005	Brendan Hansen, USA	59.37	CR
2007	Brendan Hansen, USA	59.80	

200-Meter Breaststroke

Year		Time	
1973	David Wilkie, GBR	2:19.28	
1975	David Wilkie, GBR	2:18.23	
1978	Nick Nevid, USA	2:18.37	
1982	Victor Davis, CAN	2:14.77	
1986	Jozsef Szabo, HUN	2:14.27	
1991	Mike Barrowman, USA	2:11.23	
1994	Norbert Rozsa, HUN	2:12.81	
1998	Kurt Grote, USA	2:13.40	
2001	Brendan Hansen, USA	2:10.69	
2003	Kosuke Kitajima, JPN	2:09.42	WR
2005	Brendan Hansen, USA	2:09.85	
2007	Kosuke Kitajima, JPN	2:09.80	

50-Meter Butterfly

Year		Time	
1973-98 Not held			
2001	Geoff Huegill, AUS	23.50	
2003	Matt Welsh, AUS	23.43	
2005	Roland Schoeman, RSA	22.96	WR
2007	Roland Schoeman, RSA	23.18	

100-Meter Butterfly

Year		Time	
1973	Bruce Robertson, CAN	55.69	
1975	Greg Jagenburg, USA	55.63	
1978	Joe Bottom, USA	54.30	
1982	Matt Gribble, USA	53.88	
1986	Pablo Morales, USA	53.54	
1991	Anthony Nesty, SUR	53.29	
1994	Rafal Szukala, POL	53.51	
1998	Michael Klim, AUS	52.25	
2001	Lars Frolander, SWE	52.10	
2003	Ian Crocker, USA	50.98	
2005	Ian Crocker, USA	50.40	WR
2007	Michael Phelps, USA	50.77	

200-Meter Butterfly

Year		Time	
1973	Robin Backhaus, USA	2:03.32	
1975	Billy Forrester, USA	2:01.95	
1978	Mike Bruner, USA	1:59.38	
1982	Michael Gross, W. Ger	1:58.85	
1986	Michael Gross, W. Ger	1:56.53	
1991	Melvin Stewart, USA	1:55.69	WR
1994	Denis Pankratov, RUS	1:56.54	
1998	Denys Sylantyev, UKR	1:56.61	
2001	Michael Phelps, USA	1:54.58	WR
2003	Michael Phelps, USA	1:54.35	
2005	Pawel Korzeniowski, POL	1:55.02	
2007	Michael Phelps, USA	1:52.09	

200-Meter Individual Medley

Year		Time	
1973	Gunnar Larsson, SWE	2:08.36	
1975	Andras Hargitay, HUN	2:07.72	
1978	Graham Smith, CAN	2:03.65	
1982	Alexander Sidorenko, USSR	2:03.30	
1986	Tamás Darnyi, HUN	2:01.57	
1991	Tamás Darnyi, HUN	1:59.36	
1994	Janis Sievinen, FIN	1:58.16	
1998	Marcel Wouda, NET	2:01.18	
2001	Massimiliano Rosolino, ITA	1:59.71	
2003	Michael Phelps, USA	1:56.04	WR
2005	Michael Phelps, USA	1:56.68	
2007	Michael Phelps, USA	1:54.98	WR

400-Meter Individual Medley

Year		Time	
1973	Andras Hargitay, HUN	4:31.11	
1975	Andras Hargitay, HUN	4:32.57	
1978	Jesse Vassallo, USA	4:20.05	
1982	Ricardo Prado, BRA	4:19.78	
1986	Tamás Darnyi, HUN	4:18.98	
1991	Tamás Darnyi, HUN	4:12.36	
1994	Tom Dolan, USA	4:12.30	
1998	Tom Dolan, USA	4:14.95	
2001	Alessio Boggiatto, ITA	4:13.15	
2003	Michael Phelps, USA	4:09.09	WR
2005	Laszlo Cseh, HUN	4:09.63	
2007	Michael Phelps, USA	4:06.22	WR

4 x 100-Meter Freestyle Relay

Year		Time	
1973	United States	3:27.18	
1975	United States	3:24.85	
1978	United States	3:19.74	
1982	United States	3:19.26	
1986	United States	3:19.98	
1991	United States	3:17.15	
1994	United States	3:16.90	
1998	United States	3:16.69	
2001	Australia	3:14.10	
2003	Russia	3:14.06	
2005	United States	3:13.77	
2007	United States	3:12.72	CR

4 x 200-Meter Freestyle Relay

Year		Time	
1973	United States	7:33.22	
1975	West Germany	7:39.44	
1978	United States	7:20.82	
1982	United States	7:21.09	
1986	East Germany	7:15.91	
1991	Germany	7:13.50	
1994	Sweden	7:17.34	
1998	Australia	7:12.48	
2001	Australia	7:04.66	WR
2003	Australia	7:08.58	
2005	United States	7:06.58	
2007	United States	7:03.24	WR

4 x 100-Meter Medley Relay

Year		Time	
1973	United States	3:49.49	
1975	United States	3:49.00	
1978	United States	3:44.63	
1982	United States	3:40.84	
1986	United States	3:41.25	
1991	United States	3:39.66	
1994	United States	3:37.74	
1998	Australia	3:37.98	
2001	Australia	3:35.35	
2003	United States	3:31.54	WR
2005	United States	3:31.85	
2007	Australia	3:34.93	

WOMEN

Most gold medals (including relays): Kornelia Ender and Lisbeth Lenton (8); Leisel Jones and Kristin Otto (7); Katie Hoff and Jenny Thompson (6); Natalie Coughlin, Inge De Bruijn, Hannah Stockbauer and Luo Xuejuan (5); Tracy Caulkins, Heike Friedrich, Le Jingyi, Jana Klochkova, Rosemarie Kother, Ulrike Richter and Kate Ziegler (4).

50-Meter Freestyle

Year		Time	
1973-82	Not held		
1986	Tamara Costache, ROM	.25.28	
1991	Zhuang Yong, CHN	.25.47	
1994	Le Jingyi, CHN	.24.51	WR
1998	Amy Van Dyken, USA	.25.15	
2001	Inge de Bruijn, NED	.24.47	
2003	Inge de Bruijn, NED	.24.47	
2005	Lisbeth Lenton, AUS	.24.59	
2007	Lisbeth Lenton, AUS	.24.53	

100-Meter Freestyle

Year		Time	
1973	Kornelia Ender, E. Ger	.57.54	
1975	Kornelia Ender, E. Ger	.56.50	
1978	Barbara Krause, E. Ger	.55.68	
1982	Birgit Meineke, E. Ger	.55.79	
1986	Kristin Otto, E. Ger	.55.05	
1991	Nicole Haislett, USA	.55.17	
1994	Le Jingyi, CHN	.54.01	WR
1998	Jenny Thompson, USA	.54.95	
2001	Inge de Bruijn, NED	.54.18	
2003	Hanna-Maria Seppala, FIN	.54.37	
2005	Jodie Henry, AUS	.54.18	
2007	Lisbeth Lenton, AUS	.53.40	CR

200-Meter Freestyle

Year		Time	
1973	Keena Rothhammer, USA	2:04.99	
1975	Shirley Babashoff, USA	2:02.50	
1978	Cynthia Woodhead, USA	1:58.53	
1982	Annemarie Verstappen, NED	1:59.53	
1986	Heike Friedrich, E. Ger	1:58.26	
1991	Hayley Lewis, AUS	2:00.48	
1994	Franziska Van Almsick, GER	1:56.78	WR
1998	Claudia Poll, CRC	1:58.90	
2001	Giaan Rooney, AUS	1:58.57	
2003	Alena Popchenko, BLR	1:58.32	
2005	Solenne Figues, FRA	1:58.60	
2007	Laure Manaudou, FRA	1:55.52	WR

400-Meter Freestyle

Year		Time	
1973	Heather Greenwood, USA	4:20.28	
1975	Shirley Babashoff, USA	4:22.70	
1978	Tracey Wickham, AUS	4:06.28	WR
1982	Carmela Schmidt. E. Ger	4:08.98	
1986	Heike Friedrich, E. Ger	4:07.45	
1991	Janet Evans, USA	4:08.63	
1994	Yang Aihua, CHN	4:09.64	
1998	Yan Chen, CHN	4:06.72	
2001	Yana Klochkova, UKR	4:07.30	
2003	Hannah Stockbauer, GER	4:06.75	
2005	Laure Manaudou. FRA	4:06.44	
2007	Laure Manaudou, FRA	4:02.61	CR

800-Meter Freestyle

Year		Time	
1973	Novella Calligaris, ITA	8:52.97	
1975	Jenny Turrall, AUS	8:44.75	
1978	Tracey Wickham, AUS	8:25.94	
1982	Kim Linehan, USA	8:27.48	
1986	Astrid Strauss, E. Ger	8:28.24	
1991	Janet Evans, USA	8:24.05	
1994	Janet Evans, USA	8:29.85	
1998	Brooke Bennett, USA	8:28.71	
2001	Hannah Stockbauer, GER	8:24.66	
2003	Hannah Stockbauer, GER	8:23.66	CR
2005	Kate Ziegler, USA	8:25.31	
2007	Kate Ziegler, USA	8:18.52	CR

1500-Meter Freestyle

Year		Time	
1973-98	Not held		
2001	Hannah Stockbauer, GER	16:01.02	
2003	Hannah Stockbauer, GER	16:00.18	CR
2005	Kate Ziegler, USA	16:00.41	CR
2007	Kate Ziegler, USA	15:53.05	CR

50-Meter Backstroke

Year		Time	
1973-98	Not held		
2001	Haley Cope, USA	.28.51	
2003	Nina Zhivanevskaya, ESP	.28.48	CR
2005	Giaan Rooney, AUS	.28.63	
2007	Leila Vaziri, USA	.28.16	WR

100-Meter Backstroke

Year		Time	
1973	Ulrike Richter, E. Ger	1:05.42	
1975	Ulrike Richter, E. Ger	1:03.30	
1978	Linda Jezek, USA	1:02.55	
1982	Kristin Otto, E. Ger	1:01.30	
1986	Betsy Mitchell, USA	1:01.74	
1991	Krisztina Egerszegi, HUN	1:01.78	
1994	He Cihong, CHN	1:00.57	
1998	Lea Maurer, USA	1:01.16	
2001	Natalie Coughlin, USA	1:00.37	
2003	Antje Buschschulte, GER	1:00.50	
2005	Kirsty Coventry, ZIM	1:00.24	
2007	Natalie Coughlin, USA	.59.44	WR

200-Meter Backstroke

Year		Time	
1973	Melissa Belote, USA	2:20.52	
1975	Birgit Treiber, E. Ger	2:15.46	
1978	Linda Jezek, USA	2:11.93	
1982	Cornelia Sirch, E. Ger	2:09.91	
1986	Cornelia Sirch, E. Ger	2:11.37	
1991	Krisztina Egerszegi, HUN	2:09.15	
1994	He Cihong, CHN	2:07.40	CR
1998	Roxanna Maracineanu, FRA	2:11.26	
2001	Diana Iuliana Mocanu, ROM	2:09.94	
2003	Katy Sexton, GBR	2:08.74	
2005	Kirsty Coventry, ZIM	2:08.52	
2007	Margaret Hoelzer, USA	2:07.16	CR

50-Meter Breaststroke

Year		Time	
1973-82	Not held		
2001	Luo Xuejuan, CHN	.30.84	
2003	Luo Xuejuan, CHN	.30.67	
2005	Jade Edmistone, AUS	.30.45	WR
2007	Jessica Hardy, USA	.30.63	

100-Meter Breaststroke

Year		Time	
1973	Renate Vogel, E. Ger	1:13.74	
1975	Hannalore Anke, E. Ger	1:12.72	
1978	Julia Bogdanova, USSR	1:10.31	
1982	Ute Geweniger, E. Ger	1:09.14	
1986	Sylvia Gerasch, E. Ger	1:08.11	
1991	Linley Frame, AUS	1:08.81	
1994	Samantha Riley, AUS	1:07.69	
1998	Kristy Kowal, USA	1:08.42	
2001	Luo Xuejuan, CHN	1:07.18	
2003	Luo Xuejuan, CHN	1:06.80	
2005	Leisel Jones, AUS	1:06.25	
2007	Leisel Jones, AUS	1:05.72	CR

200-Meter Breaststroke

Year		Time
1973	Renate Vogel, E. Ger	2:40.01
1975	Hannalore Anke, E. Ger	2:37.25
1978	Lina Kachushite, USSR	2:31.42
1982	Svetlana Varganova, USSR	2:28.82
1986	Silke Hoerner, E. Ger	2:27.40
1991	Elena Volkova, USSR	2:29.53
1994	Samantha Riley, AUS	2:26.87
1998	Agnes Kovacs, HUN	2:25.45
2001	Agnes Kovacs, HUN	2:24.90
2003	Amanda Beard, USA	2:22.99
2005	Leisel Jones, AUS	2:21.72 WR
2007	Leisel Jones, AUS	2:21.84

50-Meter Butterfly

Year		Time
1973-98 Not held		
2001	Inge de Bruijn, NED	25.90
2003	Inge de Bruijn, NED	25.84 CR
2005	Danni Miatke, AUS	26.11
2007	Therese Alshammar, SWE	25.91

100-Meter Butterfly

Year		Time
1973	Kornelia Ender, E. Ger	1:02.53
1975	Kornelia Ender, E. Ger	1:01.24
1978	Joan Pennington, USA	1:00.20
1982	Mary T. Meagher, USA	59.41
1986	Kornelia Gressler, E. Ger	59.51
1991	Qian Hong, CHN	59.68
1994	Liu Limin, CHN	58.98
1998	Jenny Thompson, USA	58.46
2001	Petria Thomas, AUS	58.27
2003	Jenny Thompson, USA	57.96
2005	Jessicah Schipper, AUS	57.23 CR
2007	Lisbeth Lenton, AUS	57.15 WR

200-Meter Butterfly

Year		Time
1973	Rosemarie Kother, E. Ger	2:13.76
1975	Rosemarie Kother, E. Ger	2:15.92
1978	Tracy Caulkins, USA	2:09.78
1982	Ines Geissler, E. Ger	2:08.66
1986	Mary T. Meagher, USA	2:08.41
1991	Summer Sanders, USA	2:09.24
1994	Liu Limin, CHN	2:07.25
1998	Susie O'Neill, AUS	2:07.93
2001	Petria Thomas, AUS	2:06.73
2003	Otylia Jedrzejczak, POL	2:07.56
2005	Otylia Jedrzejczak, POL	2:05.61 WR
2007	Jessicah Schipper, AUS	2:06.39

200-Meter Individual Medley

Year		Time
1973	Andre Huebner, E. Ger	2:20.51
1975	Kathy Heddy, USA	2:19.80
1978	Tracy Caulkins, USA	2:19.80
1982	Petra Schneider, E. Ger	2:11.79
1986	Kristin Otto, E. Ger	2:15.56
1991	Lin Li, CHN	2:13.40
1994	Lu Bin, CHN	2:12.34
1998	Yanyan Wu, CHN	2:10.88
2001	Maggie Bowen, USA	2:11.93
2003	Yana Klochkova, UKR	2:10.75
2005	Katie Hoff, USA	2:10.41 WR
2007	Katie Hoff, USA	2:10.13 CR

400-Meter Individual Medley

Year		Time
1973	Gudrun Wegner, E. Ger	4:57.71
1975	Ulrike Tauber, E. Ger	4:52.76
1978	Tracy Caulkins, USA	4:40.83
1982	Petra Schneider, E. Ger	4:36.10
1986	Kathleen Nord, E. Ger	4:43.75
1991	Lin Li, CHN	4:41.45
1994	Dai Guohong, CHN	4:39.14
1998	Yan Chen, CHN	4:36.66
2001	Yana Klochkova, UKR	4:36.98
2003	Yana Klochkova, UKR	4:36.74
2005	Katie Hoff, USA	4:36.07 CR
2007	Katie Hoff, USA	4:32.89 CR

4 x 100-Meter Freestyle Relay

Year		Time
1973	East Germany	3:52.45
1975	East Germany	3:49.37
1978	United States	3:43.43
1982	United States	3:43.97
1986	East Germany	3:40.57
1991	United States	3:43.26
1994	China	3:37.91
1998	United States	3:42.11
2001	Germany	3:39.58
2003	United States	3:38.09
2005	Australia	3:37.32 CR
2007	Australia	3:35.48 CR

4 x 200-Meter Freestyle Relay

Year		Time
1973-82 Not held		
1986	East Germany	7:59.33
1991	Germany	8:02.56
1994	China	7:57.96
1998	Germany	8:01.46
2001	Great Britain	7:58.69
2003	United States	7:55.70
2005	United States	7:53.70 CR
2007	United States	7:50.09 WR

4 x 100-Meter Medley Relay

Year		Time
1973	East Germany	4:16.84
1975	East Germany	4:14.74
1978	United States	4:08.21
1982	East Germany	4:05.80
1986	East Germany	4:04.82
1991	United States	4:06.51
1994	China	4:01.67
1998	United States	4:01.93
2001	Australia	4:01.50
2003	China	3:59.89
2005	Australia	3:57.47 CR
2007	Australia	3:55.74 WR

Diving

Most Gold Medals: MEN–Greg Louganis and Dmitri Sautin (5); Phil Boggs, Alexandre Despatie and Wang Feng (3). WOMEN–Guo Jingjing (8); Irina Kalinina, Gao Min and Wu Minxia (3).

MEN

1-Meter Springboard

Year		Pts
1973-86 Not Held		
1991	Edwin Jongejans, NED	588.51
1994	Evan Stewart, ZIM	382.14
1998	Yu Zhuocheng, CHN	417.54
2001	Wang Feng, CHN	444.03
2003	Xu Xiang, CHN	431.94
2005	Alexandre Despatie, CAN	489.69
2007	Luo Yutong, CHN	477.40

3-Meter Springboard

Year		Pts
1973	Phil Boggs, USA	618.57
1975	Phil Boggs, USA	597.12
1978	Phil Boggs, USA	913.95
1982	Greg Louganis, USA	752.67
1986	Greg Louganis, USA	750.06
1991	Kent Ferguson, USA	650.25

3-Meter Springboard (Cont.)

Year		Pts
1994	Yu Zhuocheng, CHN	.655.44
1998	Dmitri Sautin, RUS	.746.79
2001	Dmitri Sautin, RUS	.725.82
2003	Alexander Dobroskok, RUS	.788.37
2005	Alexandre Despatie, CAN	.813.60
2007	Qin Kai, CHN	.545.35

Platform

Year		Pts
1973	Klaus Dibiasi, ITA	.559.53
1975	Klaus Dibiasi, ITA	.547.98
1978	Greg Louganis, USA	.844.11
1982	Greg Louganis, USA	.634.26
1986	Greg Louganis, USA	.668.58
1991	Sun Shuwei, CHN	.626.79
1994	Dmitri Sautin, RUS	.634.71
1998	Dmitri Sautin, RUS	.750.99
2001	Tian Liang, CHN	.688.77
2003	Alexandre Despatie, CAN	.716.91
2005	Hu Jia, CHN	.698.01
2007	Gleb Galperin, RUS	.544.70

3-Meter Synchronized

Year		Pts
1973-98	Not held	
2001	Peng Bo & Wang Kenan, CHN	.342.63
2003	A. Dobroskok & D. Sautin, RUS	.369.18
2005	He Chong & Wang Feng, CHN	.384.42
2007	Qin Kai & Wang Feng, CHN	.458.76

10-Meter Synchronized

Year		Pts
1973-98	Not held	
2001	Tian Liang & Hu Jia, CHN	.361.41
2003	M. Helm & R. Newbery, AUS	.384.60
2005	D. Dobrosok & G. Galperin, RUS	.392.88
2007	Huo Liang & Lin Yue, CHN	.489.48

WOMEN

1-Meter Springboard

Year		Pts
1973-86	Not held	
1991	Gao Min, CHN	.478.26
1994	Chen Lixia, CHN	.279.30
1998	Irina Lashko, RUS	.296.07
2001	Blythe Hartley, CAN	.300.81
2003	Irina Lashko, AUS	.299.97
2005	Blythe Hartley, CAN	.325.65
2007	He Zi, CHN	.316.65

3-Meter Springboard

Year		Pts
1973	Christa Koehler, E. Ger	.442.17
1975	Irina Kalinina, USSR	.489.81
1978	Irina Kalinina, USSR	.691.43
1982	Megan Neyer, USA	.501.03
1986	Gao Min, CHN	.582.90
1991	Gao Min, CHN	.539.01
1994	Tan Shuping, CHN	.548.49
1998	Yulia Pakhalina, RUS	.544.52
2001	Guo Jingjing, CHN	.596.67
2003	Guo Jingjing, CHN	.617.94
2005	Guo Jingjing, CHN	.645.54
2007	Guo Jingjing, CHN	.381.75

Platform

Year		Pts
1973	Ulrike Knape, SWE	.406.77
1975	Janet Ely, USA	.403.89
1978	Irina Kalinina, USSR	.412.71
1982	Wendy Wyland, USA	.438.79
1986	Chen Lin, CHN	.449.67
1991	Fu Mingxia, CHN	.426.51
1994	Fu Mingxia, CHN	.434.04
1998	Olena Zhupyna	.550.41
2001	Xu Mian, CHN	.532.65
2003	Emilie Heymans, CAN	.597.45
2005	Laura Wilkinson, USA	.564.87
2007	Wang Xin, CHN	.432.85

3-Meter Synchronized

Year		Pts
1973-98	Not held	
2001	Wu Minxia & Guo Jingjing, CHN	.347.31
2003	Wu Minxia & Guo Jingjing, CHN	.357.30
2005	Li Ting & Guo Jingjing, CHN	.351.60
2007	Wu Minxia & Guo Jingjing, CHN	.355.80

10-Meter Synchronized

Year		Pts
1973-98	Not held	
2001	Duan Qing & Sang Xue, CHN	.329.94
2003	Lao Lishi & Li Ting, CHN	.344.58
2005	Jia Tong & Yuan Pei Lin, CHN	.344.58
2007	Jia Tong & Chen Ruolin, CHN	.361.32

ALPINE SKIING

World Cup Overall Champions

World Cup Overall Champions (downhill and slalom events combined) since the tour was organized in 1967.

MEN

Multiple winners: Marc Girardelli (5); Hermann Maier, Gustavo Thoeni and Pirmin Zurbriggen (4); Phil Mahre and Ingemar Stenmark (3); Stephan Eberharter, Jean-Claude Killy, Lasse Kjus, Bode Miller and Karl Schranz (2).

Year		Year		Year	
1967	Jean-Claude Killy, France	1981	Phil Mahre, USA	1995	Alberto Tomba, Italy
1968	Jean-Claude Killy, France	1982	Phil Mahre, USA	1996	Lasse Kjus, Norway
1969	Karl Schranz, Austria	1983	Phil Mahre, USA	1997	Luc Alphand, France
1970	Karl Schranz, Austria	1984	Pirmin Zurbriggen, Switzerland	1998	Hermann Maier, Austria
1971	Gustavo Thoeni, Italy	1985	Marc Girardelli, Luxembourg	1999	Lasse Kjus, Norway
1972	Gustavo Thoeni, Italy	1986	Marc Girardelli, Luxembourg	2000	Hermann Maier, Austria
1973	Gustavo Thoeni, Italy	1987	Pirmin Zurbriggen, Switzerland	2001	Hermann Maier, Austria
1974	Piero Gros, Italy	1988	Pirmin Zurbriggen, Switzerland	2002	Stephan Eberharter, Austria
1975	Gustavo Thoeni, Italy	1989	Marc Girardelli, Luxembourg	2003	Stephan Eberharter, Austria
1976	Ingemar Stenmark, Sweden	1990	Pirmin Zurbriggen, Switzerland	2004	Hermann Maier, Austria
1977	Ingemar Stenmark, Sweden	1991	Marc Girardelli, Luxembourg	2005	Bode Miller, USA
1978	Ingemar Stenmark, Sweden	1992	Paul Accola, Switzerland	2006	Benjamin Raich, Austria
1979	Peter Luescher, Switzerland	1993	Marc Girardelli, Luxembourg	2007	Aksel Lund Svindal, Norway
1980	Andreas Wenzel, Liechtenstein	1994	Kjetil Andre Aamodt, Norway	2008	Bode Miller, USA

WOMEN

Multiple winners: Annemarie Moser-Pröll (6); Janica Kostelic, Petra Kronberger and Vreni Schneider (3); Michela Figini, Nancy Greene, Erika Hess, Anja Paerson, Katja Seizinger, Maria Walliser and Hanni Wenzel (2).

Year		Year		Year	
1967	Nancy Greene, Canada	1981	Marie-Therese Nadig, SWI	1995	Vreni Schneider, Switzerland
1968	Nancy Greene, Canada	1982	Erika Hess, Switzerland	1996	Katja Seizinger, Germany
1969	Gertrud Gabi, Austria	1983	Tamara McKinney, USA	1997	Pernilla Wiberg, Sweden
1970	Michele Jacot, France	1984	Erika Hess, Switzerland	1998	Katja Seizinger, Germany
1971	Annemarie Pröll, Austria	1985	Michela Figini, Switzerland	1999	Alexandra Meissnitzer, Austria
1972	Annemarie Pröll, Austria	1986	Maria Walliser, Switzerland	2000	Renate Goetschl, Austria
1973	Annemarie Pröll, Austria	1987	Maria Walliser, Switzerland	2001	Janica Kostelic, Croatia
1974	Annemarie Pröll, Austria	1988	Michela Figini, Switzerland	2002	Michaela Dorfmeister, Austria
1975	Annemarie Moser-Pröll, Austria	1989	Vreni Schneider, Switzerland	2003	Janica Kostelic, Croatia
1976	Rosi Mittermaier, W. Germany	1990	Petra Kronberger, Austria	2004	Anja Paerson, Sweden
1977	Lise-Marie Morerod, Switzerland	1991	Petra Kronberger, Austria	2005	Anja Paerson, Sweden
1978	Hanni Wenzel, Liechtenstein	1992	Petra Kronberger, Austria	2006	Janica Kostelic, Croatia
1979	Annemarie Moser-Pröll, Austria	1993	Anita Wachter, Austria	2007	Nicole Hosp, Austria
1980	Hanni Wenzel, Liechtenstein	1994	Vreni Schneider, Switzerland	2008	Lindsey Vonn, USA

World Cup Event Champions

MEN

Downhill

Multiple winners: Franz Klammer (5); Luc Alphand, Stephan Eberharter, Franz Heinzer and Peter Muller (3); Roland Collumbin, Didier Cuche, Marc Girardelli, Helmut Hoflehner, Hermann Maier, Bernard Russi, Karl Schranz, Michael Walchhofer and Pirmin Zurbriggen (2).

Year		Year		Year	
1967	Jean-Claude Killy, France	1981	Harti Weirather, Austria	1995	Luc Alphand, France
1968	Gerhard Nenning, Austria	1982	Steve Podborski, Canada	1996	Luc Alphand, France
1969	Karl Schranz, Austria		Peter Muller, Switzerland	1997	Luc Alphand, France
1970	Karl Schranz, Austria	1983	Franz Klammer, Austria	1998	Andreas Schifferer, Austria
	Karl Cordin, Austria	1984	Urs Raber, Switzerland	1999	Lasse Kjus, Norway
1971	Bernard Russi, Switzerland	1985	Helmut Hoflehner, Austria	2000	Hermann Maier, Austria
1972	Bernard Russi, Switzerland	1986	Peter Wirnsberger, Austria	2001	Hermann Maier, Austria
1973	Roland Collumbin, Switzerland	1987	Pirmin Zurbriggen, Switzerland	2002	Stephan Eberharter, Austria
1974	Roland Collumbin, Switzerland	1988	Pirmin Zurbriggen, Switzerland	2003	Stephan Eberharter, Austria
1975	Franz Klammer, Austria	1989	Marc Girardelli, Luxembourg	2004	Stephan Eberharter, Austria
1976	Franz Klammer, Austria	1990	Helmut Hoflehner, Austria	2005	Michael Walchhofer, Austria
1977	Franz Klammer, Austria	1991	Franz Heinzer, Switzerland	2006	Michael Walchhofer, Austria
1978	Franz Klammer, Austria	1992	Franz Heinzer, Switzerland	2007	Didier Cuche, Switzerland
1979	Peter Muller, Switzerland	1993	Franz Heinzer, Switzerland	2008	Didier Cuche, Switzerland
1980	Peter Muller, Switzerland	1994	Marc Girardelli, Luxembourg		

Slalom

Multiple winners: Ingemar Stenmark (8); Alberto Tomba (4); Jean-Noel Augert, Marc Girardelli and Benjamin Raich (3); Armin Bittner, Thomas Sykora and Gustavo Thoeni (2).

Year		Year		Year	
1967	Jean-Claude Killy, France	1981	Ingemar Stenmark, Sweden	1996	Sebastien Amiez, France
1968	Domeng Giovanoli, Switzerland	1982	Phil Mahre, USA	1997	Thomas Sykora, Austria
1969	Jean-Noel Augert, France	1983	Ingemar Stenmark, Sweden	1998	Thomas Sykora, Austria
1970	Patrick Russel, France	1984	Marc Girardelli, Luxembourg	1999	Thomas Stangassinger, Austria
	Alain Penz, France	1985	Marc Girardelli, Luxembourg	2000	Kjetil Andre Aamodt, Norway
1971	Jean-Noel Augert, France	1986	Rok Petrovic, Yugoslavia	2001	Benjamin Raich, Austria
1972	Jean-Noel Augert, France	1987	Bojan Krizaj, Yugoslavia	2002	Ivica Kostelic, Croatia
1973	Gustavo Thoeni, Italy	1988	Alberto Tomba, Italy	2003	Kalle Palander, Finland
1974	Gustavo Thoeni, Italy	1989	Armin Bittner, West Germany	2004	Rainer Schoenfelder, Austria
1975	Ingemar Stenmark, Sweden	1990	Armin Bittner, West Germany	2005	Benjamin Raich, Austria
1976	Ingemar Stenmark, Sweden	1991	Marc Girardelli, Luxembourg	2006	Giorgio Rocca, Italy
1977	Ingemar Stenmark, Sweden	1992	Alberto Tomba, Italy	2007	Benjamin Raich, Austria
1978	Ingemar Stenmark, Sweden	1993	Tomas Fogdof, Sweden	2008	Manfred Moelgg, Italy
1979	Ingemar Stenmark, Sweden	1994	Alberto Tomba, Italy		
1980	Ingemar Stenmark, Sweden	1995	Alberto Tomba, Italy		

Giant Slalom

Multiple winners: Ingemar Stenmark (8); Michael von Gruenigen and Alberto Tomba (4); Hermann Maier and Pirmin Zurbriggen (3); Joel Gaspoz, Jean-Claude Killy, Phil Mahre, Benjamin Raich and Gustavo Thoeni (2).

Year		Year		Year	
1967	Jean-Claude Killy, France	1976	Ingemar Stenmark, Sweden	1984	Ingemar Stenmark, Sweden
1968	Jean-Claude Killy, France	1977	Heini Hemmi, Switzerland		Pirmin Zurbriggen, Switzerland
1969	Karl Schranz, Austria		Ingemar Stenmark, Sweden	1985	Marc Girardelli, Luxembourg
1970	Gustavo Thoeni, Italy	1978	Ingemar Stenmark, Sweden	1986	Joel Gaspoz, Switzerland
1971	Patrick Russel, France	1979	Ingemar Stenmark, Sweden	1987	Joel Gaspoz, Switzerland
1972	Gustavo Thoeni, Italy	1980	Ingemar Stenmark, Sweden		Pirmin Zurbriggen, Switzerland
1973	Hans Hinterseer, Austria	1981	Ingemar Stenmark, Sweden	1988	Alberto Tomba, Italy
1974	Piero Gros, Italy	1982	Phil Mahre, USA	1989	Pirmin Zurbriggen, Switzerland
1975	Ingemar Stenmark, Sweden	1983	Phil Mahre, USA		

Giant Slalom (Cont.)

Year		Year		Year	
1990	Ole-Cristian Furuseth, Norway	1996	Michael von Gruenigen, SWI	2003	Michael von Gruenigen, SWI
	Gunther Mader, Austria	1997	Michael von Gruenigen, SWI	2004	Bode Miller, USA
1991	Alberto Tomba, Italy	1998	Hermann Maier, Austria	2005	Benjamin Raich, Austria
1992	Alberto Tomba, Italy	1999	Michael von Gruenigen, SWI	2006	Benjamin Raich, Austria
1993	Kjetil Andre Aamodt, Norway	2000	Hermann Maier, Austria	2007	Aksel Lund Svindal, Norway
1994	Christian Mayer, Austria	2001	Hermann Maier, Austria	2008	Ted Ligety, USA
1995	Alberto Tomba, Italy	2002	Frederic Covili, France		

Super G

Multiple winners: Hermann Maier (5); Pirmin Zurbriggen (4); Stephan Eberharter and Bode Miller (2).

Year		Year		Year	
1986	Markus Wasmeier, W. Ger.	1994	Jan Einar Thorsen, Norway	2002	Stephan Eberharter, Austria
1987	Pirmin Zurbriggen, Switzerland	1995	Peter Runggaldier, Italy	2003	Stephan Eberharter, Austria
1988	Pirmin Zurbriggen, Switzerland	1996	Atle Skaardal, Norway	2004	Hermann Maier, Austria
1989	Pirmin Zurbriggen, Switzerland	1997	Luc Alphand, France	2005	Bode Miller, USA
1990	Pirmin Zurbriggen, Switzerland	1998	Hermann Maier, Austria	2006	Aksel Lund Svindal, Norway
1991	Franz Heinzer, Switzerland	1999	Hermann Maier, Austria	2007	Bode Miller, USA
1992	Paul Accola, Switzerland	2000	Hermann Maier, Austria	2008	Hannes Reichelt, Austria
1993	Kjetil Andre Aamodt, Norway	2001	Hermann Maier, Austria		

Combined

Multiple winners: Marc Girardelli and Andreas Wenzel (4); Kjetil Andre Aamodt, Phil Mahre and Bode Miller (3); Benjamin Raich and Pirmin Zurbriggen (2). Note that the Combined title was not awarded from 1997-99.

Year		Year		Year	
1979	Andreas Wenzel, Liechtenstein	1988	Hubert Strolz, Austria	2000	Kjetil Andre Aamodt, Norway
1980	Andreas Wenzel, Liechtenstein	1989	Marc Girardelli, Luxembourg	2001	Lasse Kjus, Norway
1981	Phil Mahre, USA	1990	Pirmin Zurbriggen, Switzerland	2002	Kjetil Andre Aamodt, Norway
1982	Phil Mahre, USA	1991	Marc Girardelli, Luxembourg	2003	Bode Miller, USA
1983	Phil Mahre, USA	1992	Paul Accola, Switzerland	2004	Bode Miller, USA
1984	Andreas Wenzel, Liechtenstein	1993	Marc Girardelli, Luxembourg	2005	Benjamin Raich, Austria
1985	Andreas Wenzel, Liechtenstein	1994	Kjetil Andre Aamodt, Norway	2006	Benjamin Raich, Austria
1986	Markus Wasmeier, W. Ger	1995	Marc Girardelli, Luxembourg	2007	Aksel Lund Svindal, Norway
1987	Pirmin Zurbriggen, Switzerland	1996	Gunther Mader, Austria	2008	Bode Miller, USA

WOMEN

Downhill

Multiple winners: Annemarie Moser-Pröll (7); Renate Goetschl (5); Michela Figini and Katja Seizinger (4); Michaela Dorfmeister, Isolde Kostner, Isabelle Mir, Marie-Therese Nadig, Picabo Street, Bridgitte Totschnig-Habersatter and Maria Walliser (2).

Year		Year		Year	
1967	Marielle Goitschel, France	1981	Marie-Therese Nadig, SWI	1995	Picabo Street, USA
1968	Isabelle Mir, France	1982	Marie-Cecile Gros-Gaudenier, FRA	1996	Picabo Street, USA
	Olga Pall, Austria	1983	Doris De Agostini, Switzerland	1997	Renate Goetschl, Austria
1969	Wiltrud Drexel, Austria	1984	Maria Walliser, Switzerland	1998	Katja Seizinger, Germany
1970	Isabelle Mir, France	1985	Michela Figini, Switzerland	1999	Renate Goetschl, Austria
1971	Annemarie Pröll, Austria	1986	Maria Walliser, Switzerland	2000	Regina Haeusl, Germany
1972	Annemarie Pröll, Austria	1987	Michela Figini, Switzerland	2001	Isolde Kostner, Italy
1973	Annemarie Pröll, Austria	1988	Michela Figini, Switzerland	2002	Isolde Kostner, Italy
1974	Annemarie Pröll, Austria	1989	Michela Figini, Switzerland	2003	Michaela Dorfmeister, Austria
1975	Annemarie Moser-Pröll, Austria	1990	Katrin Gutensohn-Knopf, GER	2004	Renate Goetschl, Austria
1976	Bridgitte Totschnig-Habersatter, AUT	1991	Chantal Bournissen, SWI	2005	Renate Goetschl, Austria
1977	Bridgitte Totschnig-Habersatter, AUT	1992	Katja Seizinger, Germany	2006	Michaela Dorfmeister, Austria
1978	Annemarie Moser-Pröll, Austria	1993	Katja Seizinger, Germany	2007	Renate Goetschl, Austria
1979	Annemarie Moser-Pröll, Austria	1994	Katja Seizinger, Germany	2008	Lindsey Vonn, USA
1980	Marie-Therese Nadig, SWI				

Slalom

Multiple winners: Vreni Schneider (6); Erika Hess (5); Janica Kostelic (3); Marielle Goitschel, Britt Lafforgue, Lisa-Marie Morerod, Marlies Schild and Roswitha Steiner (2).

Year		Year		Year	
1967	Marielle Goitschel, France	1982	Erika Hess, Switzerland	1995	Vreni Schneider, Switzerland
1968	Marielle Goitschel, France	1983	Erika Hess, Switzerland	1996	Elfi Eder, Austria
1969	Gertrud Gabl, Austria	1984	Tamara McKinney, USA	1997	Pernilla Wiberg, Sweden
1970	Ingrid Lafforgue, France	1985	Erika Hess, Switzerland	1998	Ylva Nowen, Sweden
1971	Britt Lafforgue, France	1986	Roswitha Steiner, Austria	1999	Sabine Egger, Austria
1972	Britt Lafforgue, France		Erika Hess, Switzerland	2000	Spela Pretnar, Slovenia
1973	Patricia Emonet, France	1987	Corrine Schmidhauser,	2001	Janica Kostelic, Croatia
1974	Christa Zechmeister, W. Germany		Switzerland	2002	Laure Pequegnot, France
1975	Lisa-Marie Morerod, Switzerland	1988	Roswitha Steiner, Austria	2003	Janica Kostelic, Croatia
1976	Rosi Mittermaier, W. Germany	1989	Vreni Schneider, Switzerland	2004	Anja Paerson, Sweden
1977	Lisa-Marie Morerod, Switzerland	1990	Vreni Schneider, Switzerland	2005	Tanja Poutiainen, Finland
1978	Hanni Wenzel, Liechtenstein	1991	Petra Kronberger, Austria	2006	Janica Kostelic, Croatia
1979	Regina Sackl, Austria	1992	Vreni Schneider, Switzerland	2007	Marlies Schild, Austria
1980	Perrine Pelene, France	1993	Vreni Schneider, Switzerland	2008	Marlies Schild, Austria
1981	Erika Hess, Switzerland	1994	Vreni Schneider, Switzerland		

Giant Slalom

Multiple winners: Vreni Schneider (5); Lisa-Marie Morerod, Annemarie Moser-Pröll and Anja Paerson (3); Martina Ertl, Nancy Greene, Carole Merle, Sonja Nef, Anita Wachter and Hanni Wenzel (2).

Year		Year		Year	
1967	Nancy Greene, Canada	1981	Marie-Therese Nadig, SWI	1994	Anita Wachter, Austria
1968	Nancy Greene, Canada	1982	Irene Epple, West Germany	1995	Vreni Schneider, Switzerland
1969	Marilyn Cochran, USA	1983	Tamara McKinney, USA	1996	Martina Ertl, Germany
1970	Michele Jacot, France	1984	Erika Hess, Switzerland	1997	Deborah Compagnoni, Italy
	Francoise Macchi, France	1985	Maria Keihl, West Germany	1998	Martina Ertl, Germany
1971	Annemarie Pröll, Austria		Michela Figini, Switzerland	1999	Alexandra Meissnitzer, Austria
1972	Annemarie Pröll, Austria	1986	Vreni Schneider, Switzerland	2000	Michaela Dorfmeister, Austria
1973	Monika Kaserer, Austria	1987	Vreni Schneider, Switzerland	2001	Sonja Nef, Switzerland
1974	Hanni Wenzel, Liechtenstein		Maria Walliser, Switzerland	2002	Sonja Nef, Switzerland
1975	Annemarie Moser-Pröll, Austria	1988	Mateja Svet, Yugoslavia	2003	Anja Paerson, Sweden
1976	Lisa-Marie Morerod, SWI	1989	Vreni Schneider, Switzerland	2004	Anja Paerson, Sweden
1977	Lisa-Marie Morerod, SWI	1990	Anita Wachter, Austria	2005	Tanja Poutiainen, Finland
1978	Lisa-Marie Morerod, SWI	1991	Vreni Schneider, Switzerland	2006	Anja Paerson, Sweden
1979	Christa Kinshofer, W. Ger.	1992	Carole Merle, France	2007	Nicole Hosp, Austria
1980	Hanni Wenzel, Liechtenstein	1993	Carole Merle, France	2008	Denise Karbon, Italy

Super G

Multiple winners: Katja Seizinger (5); Carole Merle (4); Renate Goetschl (3); Michaela Dorfmeister and Hilde Gerg (2).

Year		Year		Year	
1986	Maria Kiehl, West Germany	1994	Katja Seizinger, Germany	2002	Hilde Gerg, Germany
1987	Maria Walliser, Switzerland	1995	Katja Seizinger, Germany	2003	Carole Montillet, France
1988	Michela Figini, Switzerland	1996	Katja Seizinger, Germany	2004	Renate Goetschl, Austria
1989	Carole Merle, France	1997	Hilde Gerg, Germany	2005	Michaela Dorfmeister, Austria
1990	Carole Merle, France	1998	Katja Seizinger, Germany	2006	Michaela Dorfmeister, Austria
1991	Carole Merle, France	1999	Alexandra Meissnitzer, Austria	2007	Renate Goetschl, Austria
1992	Carole Merle, France	2000	Renate Goetschl, Austria	2008	Maria Riesch, Germany
1993	Katja Seizinger, Germany	2001	Regine Cavagnoud, France		

Combined

Multiple winners: Brigitte Oertli (5); Janica Kostelic (4); Anita Wachter and Hanni Wenzel (3); Sabine Ginther, Renate Goetschl and Pernilla Wiberg (2). Note that the Combined title was not awarded from 1997-99 or in 2004.

Year		Year		Year	
1979	Annemarie Moser-Pröll, Austria	1987	Brigitte Oertli, Switzerland	1996	Anita Wachter, Austria
	Hanni Wenzel, Liechtenstein	1988	Brigitte Oertli, Switzerland	2000	Renate Goetschl, Austria
1980	Hanni Wenzel, Liechtenstein	1989	Brigitte Oertli, Switzerland	2001	Janica Kostelic, Croatia
1981	Maria-Therese Nadig,	1989	Brigitte Oertli, Switzerland	2002	Renate Goetschl, Austria
	Switzerland	1990	Anita Wachter, Austria	2003	Janica Kostelic, Croatia
1982	Irene Epple, West Germany	1991	Sabine Ginther, Austria	2005	Janica Kostelic, Croatia
1983	Hanni Wenzel, Liechtenstein	1992	Sabine Ginther, Austria	2006	Janica Kostelic, Croatia
1984	Erika Hess, Switzerland	1993	Anita Wachter, Austria	2007	Marlies Schild, Austria
1985	Brigitte Oertli, Switzerland	1994	Pernilla Wiberg, Sweden	2008	Maria Riesch, Germany
1986	Maria Walliser, Switzerland	1995	Pernilla Wiberg, Sweden		

FIGURE SKATING

World Champions

Skaters who won World and Olympic championships in the same year are listed in **bold** type.

MEN

Multiple winners: Ulrich Salchow (10); Karl Schafer (7); Dick Button (5); Willy Bockl, Kurt Browning, Scott Hamilton and Hayes Jenkins and Alexei Yagudin (4); Emmerich Danzer, Gillis Grafstrom, Gustav Hugel, David Jenkins, Fritz Kachler, Ondrej Nepela, Evgeni Plushenko and Elvis Stojko (3); Brian Boitano, Gilbert Fuchs, Jan Hoffmann, Felix Kaspar, Vladimir Kovalev, Stephane Lambiel and Tim Wood (2).

Year		Year		Year	
1896	Gilbert Fuchs, Germany	1907	Ulrich Salchow, Sweden	1924	**Gillis Grafstrom,** Sweden
1897	Gustav Hugel, Austria	1908	**Ulrich Salchow,** Sweden	1925	Willy Bockl, Austria
1898	Henning Grenander, Sweden	1909	Ulrich Salchow, Sweden	1926	Willy Bockl, Austria
1899	Gustav Hugel, Austria	1910	Ulrich Salchow, Sweden	1927	Willy Bockl, Austria
1900	Gustav Hugel, Austria	1911	Ulrich Salchow, Sweden	1928	Willy Bockl, Austria
1901	Ulrich Salchow, Sweden	1912	Fritz Kachler, Austria	1929	Gillis Grafstrom, Sweden
1902	Ulrich Salchow, Sweden	1913	Fritz Kachler, Austria	1930	Karl Schafer, Austria
1903	Ulrich Salchow, Sweden	1914	Gosta Sandhal, Sweden	1931	Karl Schafer, Austria
1904	Ulrich Salchow, Sweden	1915-21	Not held	1932	**Karl Schafer,** Austria
1905	Ulrich Salchow, Sweden	1922	Gillis Grafstrom, Sweden	1933	Karl Schafer, Austria
1906	Gilbert Fuchs, Germany	1923	Fritz Kachler, Austria	1934	Karl Schafer, Austria

Figure Skating (Cont.)

Year		Year		Year	
1935	Karl Schafer, Austria	1965	Alain Calmat, France	1990	Kurt Browning, Canada
1936	**Karl Schafer**, Austria	1966	Emmerich Danzer, Austria	1991	Kurt Browning, Canada
1937	Felix Kaspar, Austria	1967	Emmerich Danzer, Austria	1992	**Viktor Petrenko**, CIS
1938	Felix Kaspar, Austria	1968	Emmerich Danzer, Austria	1993	Kurt Browning, Canada
1939	Graham Sharp, Britain	1969	Tim Wood, USA	1994	Elvis Stojko, Canada
1940-46	Not held	1970	Tim Wood, USA	1995	Elvis Stojko, Canada
1947	Hans Gerschwiler, Switzerland	1971	Ondrej Nepela, Czechoslovakia	1996	Todd Eldredge, USA
1948	**Dick Button**, USA	1972	**Ondrej Nepela**, Czechoslovakia	1997	Elvis Stojko, Canada
1949	Dick Button, USA	1973	Ondrej Nepela, Czechoslovakia	1998	Alexei Yagudin, Russia
1950	Dick Button, USA	1974	Jan Hoffmann, E. Germany	1999	Alexei Yagudin, Russia
1951	Dick Button, USA	1975	Sergie Volkov, USSR	2000	Alexei Yagudin, Russia
1952	**Dick Button**, USA	1976	**John Curry**, Britain	2001	Evgeni Plushenko, Russia
1953	Hayes Jenkins, USA	1977	Vladimir Kovalev, USSR	2002	**Alexei Yagudin**, Russia
1954	Hayes Jenkins, USA	1978	Charles Tickner, USA	2003	Evgeni Plushenko, Russia
1955	Hayes Jenkins, USA	1979	Vladimir Kovalev, USSR	2004	Evgeni Plushenko, Russia
1956	**Hayes Jenkins**, USA	1980	Jan Hoffmann, E. Germany	2005	Stephane Lambiel, Switzerland
1957	David Jenkins, USA	1981	Scott Hamilton, USA	2006	Stephane Lambiel, Switzerland
1958	David Jenkins, USA	1982	Scott Hamilton, USA	2007	Brian Joubert, France
1959	David Jenkins, USA	1983	Scott Hamilton, USA	2008	Jeffrey Buttle, Canada
1960	Alan Giletti, France	1984	**Scott Hamilton**, USA		
1961	Not held	1985	Alexander Fadeev, USSR		
1962	Donald Jackson, Canada	1986	Brian Boitano, USA		
1963	Donald McPherson, Canada	1987	Brian Orser, Canada		
1964	**Manfred Schnelldorfer**, W. Germany	1988	**Brian Boitano**, USA		
		1989	Kurt Browning, Canada		

WOMEN

Multiple winners: Sonja Henie (10); Carol Heiss, Michelle Kwan and Herma Planck Szabo (5); Lily Kronberger and Katarina Witt (4); Sjoukje Dijkstra, Peggy Fleming and Meray Horvath (3); Tenley Albright, Linda Fratianne, Anett Poetzsch, Beatrix Schuba, Barbara Ann Scott, Gabriele Seyfert, Irina Slutskaya, Megan Taylor, Alena Vrzanova and Kristi Yamaguchi (2).

Year		Year		Year	
1906	Madge Syers, Britain	1949	Alena Vrzanova, Czechoslovakia	1980	**Anett Poetzsch**, E. Germany
1907	Madge Syers, Britain	1950	Alena Vrzanova, Czechoslovakia	1981	Denise Biellmann, Switzerland
1908	Lily Kronberger, Hungary	1951	Jeannette Altwegg, Britain	1982	Elaine Zayak, USA
1909	Lily Kronberger, Hungary	1952	Jacqueline Du Bief, France	1983	Rosalyn Sumners, USA
1910	Lily Kronberger, Hungary	1953	Tenley Albright, USA	1984	**Katarina Witt**, E. Germany
1911	Lily Kronberger, Hungary	1954	Gundi Busch, W. Germany	1985	Katarina Witt, E. Germany
1912	Meray Horvath, Hungary	1955	Tenley Albright, USA	1986	Debi Thomas, USA
1913	Meray Horvath, Hungary	1956	Carol Heiss, USA	1987	Katarina Witt, E. Germany
1914	Meray Horvath, Hungary	1957	Carol Heiss, USA	1988	**Katarina Witt**, E. Germany
1915-21	Not held	1958	Carol Heiss, USA	1989	Midori Ito, Japan
1922	Herma Planck-Szabo, Austria	1959	Carol Heiss, USA	1990	Jill Trenary, USA
1923	Herma Planck-Szabo, Austria	1960	**Carol Heiss**, USA	1991	Kristi Yamaguchi, USA
1924	**Herma Planck-Szabo**, AUT	1961	Not held	1992	**Kristi Yamaguchi**, USA
1925	Herma Planck-Szabo, Austria	1962	Sjoukje Dijkstra, Netherlands	1993	Oksana Baiul, Ukraine
1926	Herma Planck-Szabo, Austria	1963	Sjoukje Dijkstra, Netherlands	1994	Yuka Sato, Japan
1927	Sonja Henie, Norway	1964	**Sjoukje Dijkstra**, Netherlands	1995	Lu Chen, China
1928	**Sonja Henie**, Norway	1965	Petra Burka, Canada	1996	Michelle Kwan, USA
1929	Sonja Henie, Norway	1966	Peggy Fleming, USA	1997	Tara Lipinski, USA
1930	Sonja Henie, Norway	1967	Peggy Fleming, USA	1998	Michelle Kwan, USA
1931	Sonja Henie, Norway	1968	**Peggy Fleming**, USA	1999	Maria Butyrskaya, Russia
1932	**Sonja Henie**, Norway	1969	Gabriele Seyfert, E. Germany	2000	Michelle Kwan, USA
1933	Sonja Henie, Norway	1970	Gabriele Seyfert, E. Germany	2001	Michelle Kwan, USA
1934	Sonja Henie, Norway	1971	Beatrix Schuba, Austria	2002	Irina Slutskaya, Russia
1935	Sonja Henie, Norway	1972	**Beatrix Schuba**, Austria	2003	Michelle Kwan, USA
1936	**Sonja Henie**, Norway	1973	Karen Magnussen, Canada	2004	Shizuka Arakawa, Japan
1937	Cecilia Colledge, Britain	1974	Christine Errath, E. Germany	2005	Irina Slutskaya, Russia
1938	Megan Taylor, Britain	1975	Dianne DeLeeuw, Netherlands	2006	Kimmie Meissner, USA
1939	Megan Taylor, Britain	1976	**Dorothy Hamill**, USA	2007	Miki Ando, Japan
1940-46	Not held	1977	Linda Fratianne, USA	2008	Mao Asada, Japan
1947	Barbara Ann Scott, Canada	1978	Anett Poetzsch, E. Germany		
1948	**Barbara Ann Scott**, Canada	1979	Linda Fratianne, USA		

U.S. Champions

Skaters who won U.S., World and Olympic championships in same year are in **bold** type.

MEN

Multiple winners: Dick Button and Roger Turner (7); Todd Eldredge (6); Sherwin Badger and Robin Lee (5); Brian Boitano, Scott Hamilton, David Jenkins, Hayes Jenkins and Charles Tickner (4); Gordon McKellen, Nathaniel Niles, Johnny Weir, Michael Weiss and Tim Wood (3); Scott Allen, Christopher Bowman, Scott Davis, Evan Lysacek, Eugene Turner and Gary Visconti (2).

Year		Year		Year		Year	
1914	Norman Scott	1940	Eugene Turner	1965	Gary Visconti	1989	Christopher Bowman
1915-17	Not held	1941	Eugene Turner	1966	Scott Allen	1990	Todd Eldredge
1918	Nathaniel Niles	1942	Robert Specht	1967	Gary Visconti	1991	Todd Eldredge
1919	Not held	1943	Arthur Vaughn	1968	Tim Wood	1992	Christopher Bowman
1920	Sherwin Badger	1944-45	Not held	1969	Tim Wood	1993	Scott Davis
1921	Sherwin Badger	1946	Dick Button	1970	Tim Wood	1994	Scott Davis
1922	Sherwin Badger	1947	Dick Button	1971	John (Misha) Petkevich	1995	Todd Eldredge
1923	Sherwin Badger	1948	**Dick Button**	1972	Ken Shelley	1996	Rudy Galindo
1924	Sherwin Badger	1949	Dick Button	1973	Gordon McKellen	1997	Todd Eldredge
1925	Nathaniel Niles	1950	Dick Button	1974	Gordon McKellen	1998	Todd Eldredge
1926	Chris Christenson	1951	Dick Button	1975	Gordon McKellen	1999	Michael Weiss
1927	Nathaniel Niles	1952	**Dick Button**	1976	Terry Kubicka	2000	Michael Weiss
1928	Roger Turner	1953	Hayes Jenkins	1977	Charles Tickner	2001	Tim Goebel
1929	Roger Turner	1954	Hayes Jenkins	1978	Charles Tickner	2002	Todd Eldredge
1930	Roger Turner	1955	Hayes Jenkins	1979	Charles Tickner	2003	Michael Weiss
1931	Roger Turner	1956	**Hayes Jenkins**	1980	Charles Tickner	2004	Johnny Weir
1932	Roger Turner	1957	David Jenkins	1981	Scott Hamilton	2005	Johnny Weir
1933	Roger Turner	1958	David Jenkins	1982	Scott Hamilton	2006	Johnny Weir
1934	Roger Turner	1959	David Jenkins	1983	Scott Hamilton	2007	Evan Lysacek
1935	Robin Lee	1960	David Jenkins	1984	**Scott Hamilton**	2008	Evan Lysacek
1936	Robin Lee	1961	Bradley Lord	1985	Brian Boitano		
1937	Robin Lee	1962	Monty Hoyt	1986	Brian Boitano		
1938	Robin Lee	1963	Thomas Litz	1987	Brian Boitano		
1939	Robin Lee	1964	Scott Allen	1988	**Brian Boitano**		

WOMEN

Multiple winners: Michelle Kwan and Maribel Vinson (9); Theresa Weld Blanchard and Gretchen Merrill (6); Tenley Albright, Peggy Fleming and Janet Lynn (5); Linda Fratianne and Carol Heiss (4); Dorothy Hamill, Beatrix Loughran, Rosalyn Summers, Joan Tozzer and Jill Trenary (3); Yvonne Sherman and Debi Thomas (2).

Year		Year		Year		Year	
1914	Theresa Weld	1940	Joan Tozzer	1964	Peggy Fleming	1988	Debi Thomas
1915-17	Not held	1941	Jane Vaughn	1965	Peggy Fleming	1989	Jill Trenary
1918	Rosemary Beresford	1942	Jane Sullivan	1966	Peggy Fleming	1990	Jill Trenary
1919	Not held	1943	Gretchen Merrill	1967	Peggy Fleming	1991	Tonya Harding
1920	Theresa Weld	1944	Gretchen Merrill	1968	**Peggy Fleming**	1992	**Kristi Yamaguchi**
1921	Theresa Blanchard	1945	Gretchen Merrill	1969	Janet Lynn	1993	Nancy Kerrigan
1922	Theresa Blanchard	1946	Gretchen Merrill	1970	Janet Lynn	1994	vacated*
1923	Theresa Blanchard	1947	Gretchen Merrill	1971	Janet Lynn	1995	Nicole Bobek
1924	Theresa Blanchard	1948	Gretchen Merrill	1972	Janet Lynn	1996	Michelle Kwan
1925	Beatrix Loughran	1949	Yvonne Sherman	1973	Janet Lynn	1997	Tara Lipinski
1926	Beatrix Loughran	1950	Yvonne Sherman	1974	Dorothy Hamill	1998	Michelle Kwan
1927	Beatrix Loughran	1951	Sonya Klopfer	1975	Dorothy Hamill	1999	Michelle Kwan
1928	Maribel Vinson	1952	Tenley Albright	1976	**Dorothy Hamill**	2000	Michelle Kwan
1929	Maribel Vinson	1953	Tenley Albright	1977	Linda Fratianne	2001	Michelle Kwan
1930	Maribel Vinson	1954	Tenley Albright	1978	Linda Fratianne	2002	Michelle Kwan
1931	Maribel Vinson	1955	Tenley Albright	1979	Linda Fratianne	2003	Michelle Kwan
1932	Maribel Vinson	1956	Tenley Albright	1980	Linda Fratianne	2004	Michelle Kwan
1933	Maribel Vinson	1957	Carol Heiss	1981	Elaine Zayak	2005	Michelle Kwan
1934	Suzanne Davis	1958	Carol Heiss	1982	Rosalyn Sumners	2006	Sasha Cohen
1935	Maribel Vinson	1959	Carol Heiss	1983	Rosalyn Sumners	2007	Kimmie Meissner
1936	Maribel Vinson	1960	**Carol Heiss**	1984	Rosalyn Sumners	2008	Mirai Nagasu
1937	Maribel Vinson	1961	Laurence Owen	1985	Tiffany Chin		
1938	Joan Tozzer	1962	Barbara Pursley	1986	Debi Thomas		
1939	Joan Tozzer	1963	Lorraine Hanlon	1987	Jill Trenary		

* Tonya Harding was stripped of the 1994 women's title and banned from membership in the U.S. Figure Skating Assn. for life on June 30, 1994 for violating the USFSA Code of Ethics after she pleaded guilty to a charge of conspiracy to hinder the prosecution related to the Jan. 6, 1994 attack on Nancy Kerrigan.

TOUR DE FRANCE

The world's premier cycling event, the Tour de France is staged throughout the country (sometimes passing through neighboring countries) over four weeks. The 1946 Tour, however, the first after World War II, was only a five-day race.

Multiple winners: Lance Armstrong (7); Jacques Anquetil, Bernard Hinault, Miguel Induráin and Eddy Merckx (5); Louison Bobet, Greg LeMond and Philippe Thys (3); Gino Bartali Ottavio Bottecchia, Fausto Coppi, Laurent Fignon, Nicholas Frantz, Firmin Lambot, André Leducq, Sylvere Maes, Antonin Magne, Lucien Petit-Breton and Bernard Thevenet (2).

Year		Time (hrs:min:sec)	Year		Time (hrs:min:sec)
1903	Maurice Garin, France	94:33:14	1972	Eddy Merckx, Belgium	108:17:18
1904	Henri Cornet, France	96:05:55	1973	Luis Ocana, Spain	122:25:34
1905	Louis Trousselier, France	112:18:09	1974	Eddy Merckx, Belgium	116:16:58
1906	René Pottier, France	185:47:26	1975	Bernard Thevenet, France	114:35:31
1907	Lucien Petit-Breton, France	156:22:30	1976	Lucien van Impe, Belgium	116:22:23
1908	Lucien Petit-Breton, France	156:09:31	1977	Bernard Thevenet, France	115:38:30
1909	Francois Faber, Luxembourg	156:55:10	1978	Bernard Hinault, France	108:18:00
1910	Octave Lapize, France	163:52:38	1979	Bernard Hinault, France	103:06:50
1911	Gustave Garrigou, France	195:35:25	1980	Joop Zoetemelk, Netherlands	109:19:14
1912	Odile Defraye, Belgium	184:50:00	1981	Bernard Hinault, France	96:19:38
1913	Philippe Thys, Belgium	197:54:00	1982	Bernard Hinault, France	92:08:46
1914	Philippe Thys, Belgium	200:28:49	1983	Laurent Fignon, France	105:07:52
1915-18	Not held		1984	Laurent Fignon, France	112:03:40
1919	Firmin Lambot, Belgium	231:07:15	1985	Bernard Hinault, France	113:24:23
1920	Philippe Thys, Belgium	228:36:13	1986	Greg LeMond, USA	110:35:19
1921	Léon Scieur, Belgium	221:50:00	1987	Stephen Roche, Ireland	115:27:42
1922	Firmin Lambot, Belgium	222:08:06	1988	Pedro Delgado, Spain	84:27:53
1923	Henri Pelissier, France	222:15:30	1989	Greg LeMond, USA	87:38:35
1924	Ottavio Bottecchia, Italy	226:18:21	1990	Greg LeMond, USA	90:43:20
1925	Ottavio Bottecchia, Italy	219:10:13	1991	Miguel Induráin, Spain	101:01:20
1926	Lucien Buysse, Belgium	238:44:25	1992	Miguel Induráin, Spain	100:49:30
1927	Nicholas Frantz, Luxembourg	198:16:42	1993	Miguel Induráin, Spain	95:57:09
1928	Nicholas Frantz, Luxembourg	192:48:58	1994	Miguel Induráin, Spain	103:38:38
1929	Maurice Dewaele, Belgium	186:39:16	1995	Miguel Induráin, Spain	92:44:59
1930	André Leducq, France	172:12:10	1996	Bjarne Riis, Denmark	95:57:16
1931	Antonin Magne, France	177:10:03	1997	Jan Ullrich, Germany	100:30:35
1932	André Leducq, France	154:11:49	1998	Marco Pantani, Italy	92:49:46
1933	Georges Speicher, France	147:51:37	1999	Lance Armstrong, USA	91:32:16
1934	Antonin Magne, France	147:03:58	2000	Lance Armstrong, USA	92:33:08
1935	Romain Maes, Belgium	141:32:00	2001	Lance Armstrong, USA	86:17:28
1936	Sylvere Maes, Belgium	142:47:32	2002	Lance Armstrong, USA	82:05:12
1937	Roger Lapebie, France	138:58:31	2003	Lance Armstrong, USA	83:41:12
1938	Gino Bartali, Italy	148:29:12	2004	Lance Armstrong, USA	83:36:02
1939	Sylvere Maes, Belgium	132:03:17	2005	Lance Armstrong, USA	86:15:02
1940-45	Not held		2006	Oscar Pereiro, Spain	89:40:27
1946	Jean Lazarides, France	44:31:42	2007	Alberto Contador, Spain	91:00:26
1947	Jean Robic, France	148:11:25	2008	Carlos Sastre, Spain	87:52:52
1948	Gino Bartali, Italy	147:10:36			
1949	Fausto Coppi, Italy	149:40:49			
1950	Ferdinand Kubler, Switzerland	145:36:56			
1951	Hugo Koblet, Switzerland	142:20:14			
1952	Fausto Coppi, Italy	151:57:20			
1953	Louison Bobet, France	129:23:25			
1954	Louison Bobet, France	140:06:50			
1955	Louison Bobet, France	130:29:26			
1956	Roger Walkowiak, France	124:01:16			
1957	Jacques Anquetil, France	135:44:42			
1958	Charly Gaul, Luxembourg	116:59:05			
1959	Federico Bahamontes, Spain	113:50:54			
1960	Gastone Nencini, Italy	112:08:42			
1961	Jacques Anquetil, France	122:01:33			
1962	Jacques Anquetil, France	114:31:54			
1963	Jacques Anquetil, France	113:30:05			
1964	Jacques Anquetil, France	127:09:44			
1965	Felice Gimondi, Italy	116:42:06			
1966	Lucien Aimar, France	117:34:21			
1967	Roger Pingeon, France	136:53:50			
1968	Jan Janssen, Netherlands	133:49:42			
1969	Eddy Merckx, Belgium	116:16:02			
1970	Eddy Merckx, Belgium	119:31:48			
1971	Eddy Merckx, Belgium	96:45:14			

Tour de France Dress Code

Yellow Jersey
Leader in the overall standings

Green Jersey
Leader in the points standings

Red Polka-Dot Jersey
King of the Mountains (best climber)

White Jersey
Highest-ranking rider under the age of 25

Yellow Helmet
Entire team that is leading in the standings

Red Number
Most aggressive rider in each stage

Note: Riders leading in more than one category wear only the highest-ranking jersey, in this order: yellow, green, red polka-dot, white.

Source:
23 Ways To Get To First Base: The ESPN Uncyclopedia

OLYMPIC GAMES

2008 BEIJING IN REVIEW

The Bird's Nest was the site for a stunning **Opening Ceremonies** at the 2008 Summer Games in Beijing.

CHINA GOLD

The 2008 Summer Games in Beijing had plenty of memorable moments...and ESPN.com's Pat Forde ran his Forde-Yard Dash through all of them. Well, nearly all of them.

by Pat Forde

Forty names, games, countries and minutiae that made news at the Beijing Olympics (forged birth certificates sold separately):

Douse the flame. The Metric Dash has ridden in the last lost taxi, slept on the last concrete mattress and imbibed the last watery beer for these Games. No more noodles for a while. No more rushing to catch the 3 a.m. bus from the Main Press Center that never, ever departed at 3:01 – that would be late.

You know it's time to go when even the supernaturally enthusiastic volunteers are losing their hospitality. Time to trade in Georgia (No. 32 in the medals standings) for Georgia (No. 1 in the AP and USA Today polls).

But the 958 medals doled out by the International Olympic Committee weren't quite enough. Time now for a few more gold, silver and bronze to be distributed by Baron Pierre de Metric Dash.

Overachievers

Forget figuring out which countries had the most medals – that's easy. Which countries won the most medals per competitor brought to Beijing? (Medal counts as of 8 p.m. Saturday, Beijing time.)

Gold: Zimbabwe (1). Thirteen athletes, four medals; one medal for every 3.3 athletes.

Silver: Kenya (2). Forty-six athletes, 13 medals; one medal for every 3.5 athletes.

Bronze: Armenia (3). Twenty-five athletes, six medals; one medal for every 4.2 athletes.

Underachievers

Which countries won the least medals per competitor?

Gold: South Africa (4). One medal, 142 athletes.

Silver: Egypt (5). One medal, 104 athletes.

Bronze: Belgium (6). It brought 103 athletes to Beijing but won only two

 Pat Forde is a senior writer at ESPN.com

American swimmer **Michael Phelps'** record haul of eight gold medals was more than 195 countries and his spot in the record books, like the one you are holding now is secure.

medals. Time to drink even more of that excellent Belgian beer.

Biggest studs in Beijing: Male Division

Gold: Michael Phelps (7), United States. His was simply the best athletic performance The Metric Dash has ever seen. If Phelps were a country, he'd have finished 25th in the medals standings.

Silver: Usain Bolt (8), Jamaica. Ran three finals, set three world records. You'll hear a lot of talk in the upcoming football season about speed, but you won't see anyone nearly as fleet as Bolt was in the Bird's Nest. No human has ever moved faster.

Bronze: Maarten van der Weijden (9), Netherlands. The open-water swimmer was diagnosed with leukemia in 2001 and at one point was given a slim chance to live. He spent two years out of his sport combating the disease, at times simply hoping to survive it. Last week, he won the .10k open-water swim gold medal.

Biggest studs in Beijing: Female Division

Gold: Yukiko Ueno (10), Japan. The bionic softball pitcher threw the final 28 innings of the tournament for the Japanese over two days – 21 of them in a single day. The final seven came in what might have been the biggest upset of the entire Olympics, a 3-1 win over the United States in the gold-medal game.

Silver: Misty May-Treanor and Kerri Walsh (11), United States. John Wooden once won 88 straight basketball games. Sounds impressive until you compare it to this beach volleyball tandem, which leaves Beijing with a 108-match winning streak.

Bronze: Olga Kharlan (12), Ukraine. In the most exciting Olympic event nobody saw – except The Metric Dash,

Jamaican sprinter **Usain Bolt** demolished the competition and, for moments at least, made folks forget about Phelps.

ated for a long time and declared no point just moments earlier.

Biggest duds in Beijing: Male Division

Gold: Tyson Gay (13), United States. When the summer began, a lot of people thought Gay could win both the 100- and 200-meter dashes. But since injuring himself while running in a 200 prelim at the U.S. trials, it's been all downhill. He failed to make the 100 final in Beijing, then was a co-conspirator in a dropped baton that disqualified the American 4x100 relay. Brutal.

Silver: U.S. boxing (14). Muhammad Ali, George Foreman, Sugar Ray Leonard and other former gold medalists from the United States must be aghast. The Americans won one medal – a bronze by heavyweight Deontay Wilder – in their worst performance in Olympic boxing history.

Bronze: Grant Hackett (15), Australia. The swimming legend was picked by *USA Today* and *Sports Illustrated* to sweep the 400 and 1,500 freestyle events. He finished sixth in the 400 and second in the 1,500, beaten by a Tunisian in the latter. Competing in his third Olympics, the 28-year-old Hackett suddenly looked old.

Biggest duds in Beijing: Female Division

Gold: France (16). The French men won 30 medals in these Games. The women? Seven. Biggest fall from grace goes to swimmer Laure Manaudou, who failed to medal in three individual events after winning five individual medals

who was pulled in watching on TV one afternoon in the Main Press Center – Kharlan led a ridiculous comeback to give Ukraine the team saber gold medal over China. The Chinese led 25-15 until Kharlan started swashbuckling like Zorro on amphetamines. Kharlan single-handedly outscored the entire Chinese team the rest of the way, 21-20, and scored 21 of Ukraine's final 30 points. She entered the final match against Tan Xue down four points and ended up winning to give her team a 45-44 victory. The final touch came after the judges deliber-

three gold) at the 2007 world championships.

Silver: Lyudmila Blonska (17), Ukraine. The heptathlete won the silver medal – then had it stripped after testing positive for drugs. She'd previously tested positive at an international competition in 2003. Welcome to Banned for Lifeville, sister.

Bronze: Katie Hoff and Kate Ziegler (18), United States. The American swimmers were expected to win up to eight medals, with three or four of them gold. They won three medals – all by Hoff, none of them gold. Ziegler didn't even make a final in either the 400 or 800 freestyle.

Best supporting actors

Gold: Jason Lezak (19), United States. What Lezak did to pull out the 400 freestyle relay will go down as one of the greatest clutch performances in Olympic history. Overhauling the former world-record holder, smack-talking Frenchman Alain Bernard, was a feat of such adrenal force that it was reminiscent of those stories you hear about women lifting cars to free their trapped children. Lezak couldn't swim back to that level in the individual 100 freestyle (he took home bronze), but nobody will forget the relay swim that kept Phelps' great eight quest alive.

Silver: Milorad Cavic (20), Serbia. The Californian swimming for his parents' home country was on nobody's radar coming into these Games. But he earned his niche in history, first for suggesting that Phelps needed to lose for the good of the sport, then for very nearly making it happen. Cavic lost gold in the 100 butterfly by one-hundredth of a second in a race that

Coach **Hugh McCutcheon** lost his father-in-law in a bizarre knife attack. Two weeks later his USA volleyball squad defeated Brazil in the gold-medal match.

somehow eclipsed the aforementioned relay as the most memorable of the Olympics.

Bronze: Carli Lloyd (21), United States. The face of the women's soccer team was goalkeeper Hope Solo. She had the back-story – her public blasting of former U.S. coach Greg Ryan and goalie Briana Scurry at last year's Women's World Cup. She had the front story – her shutout of the powerful Brazilians cinched the gold medal. But it was Olympic rookie Lloyd who scored the only goal in a key Olympic match against Japan, and it was Lloyd who scored the goal that won it against Brazil.

American Olympians

Three Yanks who ennobled the Games by their actions:

Gold: David Neville (22). His headfirst dive to the finish line for bronze in the 400-meter track final was the living symbol of how badly someone can want a medal. Couldn't happen to a nicer guy, and it completed an American sweep of the event – a rare triumphant moment for the U.S. at the track venue.

Silver: Brendan Hansen (23). America's best breaststroker had a brutal summer – he failed to make the Olympic team in the 200 breast and failed to win a medal in the 100, an event in which he held the world record. After finishing fourth and watching bitter rival Kosuke Kitajima of Japan win the gold and take his world record, Hansen could have quickly exited the pool and left the painful scene. Instead, he crossed two lanes to congratulate Kitajima. That's class.

Bronze: Jessica Mendoza (24). The softball left fielder was crushed when the U.S. was stunned by Japan in the gold-medal game, but she overcame it for the greater cause of Olympic softball. She quickly organized the Japanese and bronze medalist Australia to place softballs in the shape of the numbers "2016" in the infield, then had the teams pose behind them. The point: to bring back softball, which is being booted from the Olympics in part because of – oops – American dominance.

Biggest buffoon of the Games

Gold: Jacques Rogge (25), IOC president. The fool who runs these Games has generally feigned powerlessness in response to Chinese clampdowns on free speech and human rights – but the peacock crowed in dismay when Usain Bolt dared enjoy himself after winning the 100-meter gold. Rogge clucked his tongue at Bolt's lavish celebration – which, it should be noted, was not done in a demeaning way toward any of his competitors. It was, anything, a re-enactment of Muhammad Ali's shortest poem: "Me, Whee!" For Rogge to finally find a conscience about something so harmless and trivial speaks volumes about the lack of perspective in the IOC ivory tower.

Silver: Spanish basketball team (26). For some reason, the Spaniards thought it would be a great idea to pose for an advertising picture pulling their eyelids to the sides, approximating the "slant-eyed" look of Asians. They also saw nothing to apologize for, after the ad launched a small firestorm in the United States. The Chinese didn't take offense, which should perhaps be the final word on the matter – but it still seems like a wildly insensitive stunt to The Metric Dash.

Bronze: Ara Abrahamian (27), Swedish wrestler. Abrahamian was so displeased with his bronze medal after a controversial loss in the 84-kilogram Greco-Roman event that he took it off, dropped it to the mat and walked off during the ceremony. The IOC correctly kept it. No bronze for that baby.

Biggest breakthroughs

Gold: Iceland (28). As the name suggests, this is not a Summer Olympics power. But there it was Sunday, playing in the men's team handball final, gunning for the first Summer gold medal in the nation's history. France won, but Iceland took home the silver. That should melt a few hearts up around the Arctic Circle.

Silver: American volleyball (29). Gold medals in men's and women's beach volleyball. Berths in the indoors gold-medal games, with the men winning gold and the women taking silver. The bumping, setting and spiking have never been better in the U.S. than right now.

Bronze: Asian swimming (30). China's six medals tied for third-most at the Water Cube. Japan's five tied for sixth-most. South Korea chipped in with two. The three combined for four golds. The sport is more than just the U.S., Australia and an assortment of Europeans these days.

Most overrated Chinese story lines

Gold: Smog (31). Yeah, it was sci-fi horrible the first few days. And everyone obsessed on it, because there were no competitions yet and there was nothing else to do. But then it cleared, and pretty much never came back. We had a ton of blue sky the past two weeks, and the heat was overrated, too.

Silver: Liu Xiang (32). The country's hero never cleared a single hurdle in competition here, pulling out with an injury in the prelims. Talk about a letdown.

Bronze: Project 119 (33). Shortly after China was awarded the Games in 2001, officials came up with Project 119 – 119 represents the number of gold medals awarded at the 2000 Sydney Olympics in swimming, track and field and other water-based events like canoe and kayak. In Beijing, the number of golds increased to 122. In Sydney, China won just one gold within those sports. In Athens, that number increased to four. So, how did the Chinese fare on home soil? Overall, it had a smashing Games, racking up a world-best 51 golds. But it didn't come close in the "119" sports, taking home only one gold each in the women's 200-meter fly, men's canoe/kayak, women's rowing and women's sailing.

Coach K and the **"Redeem Team"** brought home the gold in men's basketball after falling short in Athens four years ago.

Most notable Chinese traits

Gold: Seriousness (34). The folks here don't exactly cut up like, say, the Aussies in Sydney in 2000. The Olympic pastime among them was taking their picture in front of the venues, and 80 percent of them weren't smiling for the camera. There was one moment of humor Saturday, when Jeff Duncan of the *New Orleans Times-Picayune* went to the Main Press Center help desk to get his going-away media gift: a genuine bronze medal. Jeff's playing question, "Why not a gold?" was met with a surprisingly playful response from a volunteer: "Work harder next time." That prompted The Metric Dash to chuckle and

National icon **Yao Ming** carried the flag for China at the Opening Ceremonies, accompanied by a young earthquake survivor.

of a cab, and figured it was lost forever. Yet, 24 hours later, a note was in the hotel room inquiring about ownership of said BlackBerry. How the cabbie and the hotel managed to track down The Metric Dash remains a mystery. Regardless, it's not the kind of thing you see happening in Manhattan every lunar eclipse. (The flip side of that anecdote was the dozen cab drivers who meandered around Beijing hopelessly lost. The Metric Dash has never seen so many cabbies with no idea where anything is.)

Best Chinese things to experience

Gold: The Great Wall (37). Nothing else like it, anywhere.

Silver: The Silk Market (38). This is full-contact shopping like nothing in the Western world. It's five stories of booths manned by astonishingly aggressive shop girls, who literally will grab you and drag you into their micro-store in an attempt to sell you everything from shirts to jeans to shoes to luggage to, yes, silk dresses. Once you're in, expect a hard-core bartering battle conducted on a calculator – you pressing buttons, them countering – with prices starting at roughly 10 times what you might end up paying if you play hardball. The saleswomen alternate between flirtation and anger, depending on how the negotiations are going.

Bronze: Opening Ceremony (39). They sure seemed great, back before we heard how much was fake and how badly some of the participants were treated. But the flame-lighting remains an all-time show stopper.

Point after ...

When hungry in Beijing, The Metric Dash has one place not to recommend, on name alone: Country Ass (40). In general, there is a lot of food not to recommend there. The Metric Dash is ready for some barbecued ribs, please.

hold up a hand for a high five from the volunteer. She looked at the hand as if it were radioactive. End of high jinks.

Silver: Helpfulness (35). The Chinese service industry generally bent over backward to please. Of course, when you have volunteers on every street corner, in every hotel lobby and crawling around every venue, things tend to work well. One thing China never runs out of is manpower. One night at the patio bar of The Metric Dash's hotel, there were 17 patrons and 15 workers. Not too difficult to get a waiter's attention with a ratio like that.

Bronze: Diligence (36). One night, The Metric Dash left his BlackBerry in the back

2008 BEIJING
Games in Review

ESPN
SPORTS ALMANAC

Final Medal Standings

National Medal Standings are not recognized by the IOC. The unofficial point totals are based on three points for every gold medal, two for each silver and one for each bronze.

		G	S	B	Total	Points			G	S	B	Total	Points
1	China	51	21	28	100	223		Mexico	2	0	1	3	7
2	**United States**	36	38	36	110	220		Croatia	0	2	3	5	7
3	Russia	23	21	28	72	139		Lithuania	0	2	3	5	7
4	Great Britain	19	13	15	47	98	48	Latvia	1	1	1	3	6
5	Australia	14	15	17	46	89		Greece	0	2	2	4	6
6	Germany	16	10	15	41	83		Armenia	0	0	6	6	6
7	South Korea	13	10	8	31	67	51	Belgium	1	1	0	2	5
8	France	7	16	17	40	60		Dominican Republic	1	1	0	2	5
9	Italy	8	10	10	28	54		Estonia	1	1	0	2	5
10	Japan	9	6	10	25	49		Portugal	1	1	0	2	5
11	Ukraine	7	5	15	27	46		India	1	0	2	3	5
12	Cuba	2	11	11	24	39		Nigeria	0	1	3	4	5
13	Spain	5	10	3	18	38	57	Iran	1	0	1	2	4
14	Netherlands	7	5	4	16	35		Trinidad & Tobago	0	2	0	2	4
15	Canada	3	9	6	18	33		Austria	0	1	2	3	4
16	Belarus	4	5	10	19	32		Ireland	0	1	2	3	4
17	Kenya	5	5	4	14	29		Serbia	0	1	2	3	4
18	Jamaica	6	3	2	11	26		Chinese Taipei	0	0	4	4	4
19	Brazil	3	4	8	15	25		Israel	1	0	1	2	4
20	Poland	3	6	1	10	22	64	Bahrain	1	0	0	1	3
21	Hungary	3	5	2	10	21		Cameroon	1	0	0	1	3
	Norway	3	5	2	10	21		Panama	1	0	0	1	3
	Kazakhstan	2	4	7	13	21		Tunisia	1	0	0	1	3
24	Romania	4	1	3	8	17		Algeria	0	1	1	2	3
25	Ethiopia	4	1	2	7	16		Bahamas	0	1	1	2	3
	New Zealand	3	1	5	9	16		Colombia	0	1	1	2	3
27	Czech Republic	3	3	0	6	15		Krygyzstan	0	1	1	2	3
28	Slovakia	3	2	1	6	14		Morocco	0	1	1	2	3
	Turkey	1	4	3	8	14		Tajikistan	0	1	1	2	3
30	Denmark	2	2	3	7	13	74	Chile	0	1	0	1	2
31	Georgia	3	0	3	6	12		Ecuador	0	1	0	1	2
32	North Korea	2	1	3	6	11		Iceland	0	1	0	1	2
	Azerbaijan	1	2	4	7	11		Malaysia	0	1	0	1	2
34	Mongolia	2	2	0	4	10		South Africa	0	1	0	1	2
	Thailand	2	2	0	4	10		Singapore	0	1	0	1	2
	Argentina	2	0	4	6	10		Sudan	0	1	0	1	2
	Switzerland	2	0	4	6	10		Vietnam	0	1	0	1	2
	Uzbekistan	1	2	3	6	10	82	Afghanistan	0	0	1	1	1
39	Zimbabwe	1	3	0	4	9		Egypt	0	0	1	1	1
	Slovenia	1	2	2	5	9		Moldova	0	0	1	1	1
	Sweden	0	4	1	5	9		Mauritius	0	0	1	1	1
42	Bulgaria	1	1	3	5	8		Togo	0	0	1	1	1
	Indonesia	1	1	3	5	8		Venezuela	0	0	1	1	1
44	Finland	1	1	2	4	7							

Leading Medal Winners

USA medalists in bold type.

Men

No		Sport	G-S-B	No.		Sport	G-S-B
8	**Michael Phelps**, USA	Swimming	8-0-0	3	Kosuke Kitajima, JPN	Swimming	2-0-1
4	**Ryan Lochte**, USA	Swimming	2-0-2	3	Laszlo Cseh, HUN	Swimming	0-3-0
3	Chris Hoy, GBR	Cycling	3-0-0	3	**Matt Grevers**, USA	Swimming	2-1-0
3	Kai Zou, CHN	Gymnastics	3-0-0	3	Wei Yang, CHN	Gymnastics	2-1-0
3	Usain Bolt, JAM	Track and Field	3-0-0	3	Alain Bernard, FRA	Swimming	1-1-1
3	**Jason Lezak**, USA	Swimming	2-0-1	3	Eamon Sullivan, AUS	Swimming	0-2-1
3	**Aaron Peirsol**, USA	Swimming	2-1-0	3	Andrew Lauterstein, AUS	Swimming	0-1-2

Leading Medal Winners (Cont.)

Men

No		Sport	G-S-B	No		Sport	G-S-B
2	**LaShawn Merritt**, USA	Track and Field	2-0-0	2	Peter Vanderkaay, USA	Swimming	1-0-1
2	**Angelo Taylor**, USA	Track and Field	2-0-0	2	Tim Brabants, GBR	Kayak	1-0-1
2	**Garrett Weber-Gale**, USA	Track and Field	2-0-0	2	Ken Wallace, AUS	Kayak	1-0-1
2	Kenenisa Bekele, ETH	Track and Field	2-0-0	2	Kai Qin, CHN	Diving	1-0-1
2	Bradley Wiggins, GBR	Cycling	2-0-0	2	Ligin Wang, CHN	Table Tennis	1-0-1
2	Yibing Chen, CHN	Gymnastics	2-0-0	2	Breton Rickard, AUS	Swimming	0-2-0
2	Xiaopeng Li, CHN	Gymnastics	2-0-0	2	David Cal, SPA	Canoe	0-2-0
2	Qin Xiao, CHN	Gymnastics	2-0-0	2	Kohei Uchimura, JPN	Gymnastics	0-2-0
2	Lin Ma, CHN	Table Tennis	2-0-0	2	Amaury Leveaux, FRA	Swimming	0-2-0
2	Fabrice Jeannet, FRA	Fencing	1-1-0	2	Richard Thompson, T&T	Track and Field	0-2-0
2	Nicolas Lopez, FRA	Fencing	1-1-0	2	Thomasz Wylenzek, GER	Canoe	0-1-1
2	Eric Lamaze, CAN	Equestrian	1-1-0	2	Christian Gille, GER	Canoe	0-1-1
2	Joan Llaneras, SPA	Cycling	1-1-0	2	Jared Tallent, AUS	Track and Field	0-1-1
2	**Jeremy Wariner**, USA	Track and Field	1-1-0	2	Matt Targett, AUS	Swimming	0-1-1
2	Jason Kenny, GBR	Cycling	1-1-0	2	Hayden Roulston, NZE	Cycling	0-1-1
2	Kyung-Mo Park, KOR	Archery	1-1-0	2	**Jonathan Horton**, USA	Gymnastics	0-1-1
2	Jong Oh Jin, KOR	Shooting	1-1-0	2	Hayden Stoeckel, AUS	Swimming	0-1-1
2	Taehwan Park, KOR	Swimming	1-1-0	2	Grant Hackett, AUS	Swimming	0-1-1
2	Hao Wang, CHN	Table Tennis	1-1-0	2	Gleb Galperin, RUS	Diving	0-0-2
2	Cesar Cielo Filho, BRA	Swimming	1-0-1	2	Anton Golotsutskov, RUS	Gymnastics	0-0-2
2	Matteo Tagliariol, ITA	Fencing	1-0-1	2	Arkady Vyatchanin, RUS	Swimming	0-0-2
2	Fabian Cancellara, SUI	Cycling	1-0-1	2	Leith Brodie, AUS	Swimming	0-0-2
2	Vadzim Makhneu, BLR	Kayak	1-0-1	2	Patrick Murphy, AUS	Swimming	0-0-2
2	Raman Piatrushenka, BLR	Kayak	1-0-1	2	Hugues Duboscq, FRA	Swimming	0-0-2
2	**David Neville**, USA	Track and Field	1-0-1	2	**Walter Dix**, USA	Track and Field	0-0-2

Women

No		Sport	G-S-B	No		Sport	G-S-B
6	**Natalie Coughlin**, USA	Swimming	1-2-3	2	Katalin Kovacs, HUN	Kayak	1-1-0
5	**Nastia Liukin**, USA	Gymnastics	1-3-1	2	Juan Juan Zhang, CHN	Archery	1-1-0
4	Lisbeth Trickett, AUS	Swimming	2-1-1	2	Nan Weng, CHN	Table Tennis	1-1-0
4	**Shawn Johnson**, USA	Gymnastics	1-3-0	2	Katrin Wagner-Augustin, GER	Kayak	1-0-1
4	Kirsty Coventry, ZIM	Swimming	1-3-0	2	Heike Kemmer, GER	Equestrian	1-0-1
3	Stephanie Rice, AUS	Swimming	3-0-0	2	Sandra Izbasa, ROM	Gymnastics	1-0-1
3	Leisel Jones, AUS	Swimming	2-1-0	2	Georgeta Andrunache, ROM	Rowing	1-0-1
3	**Rebecca Soni**, USA	Swimming	1-2-0	2	Viorica Susanu, ROM	Rowing	1-0-1
3	Jessicah Schipper, AUS	Swimming	1-0-2	2	Maria Valentina Vezzali, ITA	Fencing	1-0-1
3	Fei Cheng, CHN	Gymnastics	1-0-2	2	Shayne Reese, AUS	Swimming	1-0-1
3	Yilin Yang, CHN	Gymnastics	1-0-2	2	Melanie Schlanger, AUS	Swimming	1-0-1
3	**Dara Torres**, USA	Swimming	0-3-0	2	**Beezie Madden**, USA	Equestrian	1-0-1
3	**Margaret Hoelzer**, USA	Swimming	0-2-1	2	**Sanya Richards**, USA	Track and Field	1-0-1
3	**Katie Hoff**, USA	Swimming	0-1-2	2	**Mariel Zagunis**, USA	Fencing	1-0-1
3	Jiaying Pang, CHN	Swimming	0-1-2	2	Ok-Hee Yun, KOR	Archery	1-0-1
2	Anastasia Davydova, RUS	Synch. Swimming	2-0-0	2	Minxia Wu, CHN	Diving	1-0-1
2	Anastasia Ermakova, RUS	Synch. Swimming	2-0-0	2	Xin Wang, CHN	Diving	1-0-1
2	Britta Steffen, GER	Swimming	2-0-0	2	Yue Guo, CHN	Table Tennis	1-0-1
2	Hinrich Romeike, GER	Equestrian	2-0-0	2	Yang Yu, CHN	Badminton	1-0-1
2	Tirunesh Dibaba, ETH	Track and Field	2-0-0	2	Julia Pakhalina, RUS	Diving	0-2-0
2	Rebecca Adlington, GBR	Swimming	2-0-0	2	Tatyana Lebedeva, RUS	Track and Field	0-2-0
2	Felicity Galvez, AUS	Swimming	2-0-0	2	Gemma Mengual, SPA	Synch. Swimming	0-2-0
2	Kexin He, CHN	Gymnastics	2-0-0	2	Christine Magnuson, USA	Swimming	0-2-0
2	Jingjing Guo, CHN	Diving	2-0-0	2	Andrea Fuentes, SPA	Synch. Swimming	0-2-0
2	Ruolin Chen, CHN	Diving	2-0-0	2	**Kara Lynn Joyce**, USA	Swimming	0-2-0
2	Yining Zhang, CHN	Table Tennis	2-0-0	2	Elvan Abeylegesse, TUR	Track and Field	0-2-0
2	Yulia Gushchina, RUS	Track and Field	1-1-0	2	**Sada Jacobson**, USA	Fencing	0-1-1
2	Isabell Werth, GER	Equestrian	1-1-0	2	**Julia Smit**, USA	Swimming	0-1-1
2	Katerina Emmons, CZE	Shooting	1-1-0	2	Shericka Williams, JAM	Track and Field	0-1-1
2	Anky van Grunsven, NED	Equestrian	1-1-0	2	Kerron Stewart, JAM	Track and Field	0-1-1
2	**Allyson Felix**, USA	Track and Field	1-1-0	2	Margherita Granbassi, ITA	Fencing	0-0-2
2	Sung-Hyun Park, KOR	Table Tennis	1-1-0	2	Cate Campbell, AUS	Swimming	0-0-2
2	Hyojung Lee, KOR	Badminton	1-1-0	2	Kristina Cook, GBR	Equestrian	0-0-2
2	Natasa Janic, HUN	Kayak	1-1-0	2	**Becca Ward**, USA	Fencing	0-0-2

MEDAL SPORTS

Medal winners in individual sports contested at Beijing, China from Aug. 8-24, 2008. Team Sports summaries from Baseball to Water Polo begin on page 667.

ARCHERY

(70 meters)

MEN

Individual: 1. Viktor Ruban, UKR def. **2.** Park Kyung-Mo, KOR (113-112); **3.** Bair Badenov, RUS def. Juan Rene Serrano, MEX (115-110).
Team: 1. South Korea def. **2.** Italy (227-225); **3.** China def. Ukraine (222-219).

WOMEN

Individual: 1. Juan Juan Zhang, CHN def. **2.** Sung-Hyun Park, KOR (110-109); **3.** Ok-Hee Yun, KOR def. Un Sil Kwon, PRK (109-106).
Team: 1. South Korea def. **2.** China (224-215); **3.** France def. Great Britain (203-201).

BADMINTON

MEN

Singles: 1. Lin Dan, CHN def. **2.** Chong Wei Lee, MAL; **3.** Chen Jin, CHN def. Lee Hyunil, KOR.
Doubles: 1. Indonesia (Markis Kido & Hendra Setiawan), def. **2.** China (Fu Haifeng & Cai Yun); **3.** South Korea (Lee Jaejin & Hwang Jiman) def. Denmark (Jonas Rasmussen & Lars Paaske).

WOMEN

Singles: 1. Zhang Ning, CHN def. **2.** Xie Xingfang, CHN; **3.** Maria Kristin Yulianti, INA def. Lu Lan, CHN.
Doubles: 1. China (Du Jing & Yu Yang) def. **2.** South Korea (Lee Hyojung & Lee Kyungwon); **3.** China (Wei Yili & Zhang Yawen) def. Japan (Satoko Suetsuna & Miyuki Maeda)

MIXED

Doubles: 1. South Korea (Lee Yongdae & Lee Hyojung) def. **2.** Indonesia (Nova Widianto); **3.** China (He Hanbin & Yu Yang) def. Indonesia (Flandy Limpele & Vita Marissa).

BEACH VOLLEYBALL

Men: 1. Phil Dalhausser & Todd Rogers, USA def. **2.** Marcio Araujo & Fabio Magalhaes, BRA; **3.** Emanuel Rego & Richardo Santos def. Jorge Terceiro & Renato Gomes, GEO.
Women: 1. Kerri Walsh & Misty May, USA def. **2.** Tian Jia & Wang Jie, CHN; **3.** Zhang Xi & Xue Chen, CHN def. Renata Ribeiro & Talita Rocha, BRA.

BOXING

Light Flyweight (106 lbs): **1.** Shiming Zou, CHN def. **2.** Serdama Purevdorj, MGL; **3.** Paddy Barnes, IRL and Yampier Hernandez, CUB.
Flyweight (112 lbs): **1.** Somjit Jongjohor, THA def. **2.** Andris Laffita Hernandez, CUB; **3.** Georgy Balakshin, RUS and Vincenzo Picardi, ITA.
Batamweight (119 lbs): **1.** Badar-Uugan Enkhbat, MGL def. **2.** Yankiel Leon Alarcon, CUB **3.** Bruno Julie, MRI and Veaceslav Gojan, MDA.
Featherweight (125 lbs): **1.** Vasyl Lomachenko, UKR def. **2.** Khedafi Djelkhir, FRA; **3.** Yakup Kilic, TUR and Shahin Imranov, AZE.
Lightweight (132 lbs): **1.** Alexey Tishchenko, RUS def. **2.** Daouda Sow, FRA; **3.** Yordenis Ugas, CUB and Hrachik Javakhyan, ARM.
Light Welterweight (141 lbs): **1.** Felix Diaz, DOM def. **2.** Manus Boonjumnong, THA; **3.** Roniel Iglesias Sotolongo, CUB and Alexis Fastine, FRA.
Welterweight (152 lbs): **1.** Bakhyt Sarsekbayev, KAZ def. **2.** Carlos Banteaux Suarez, CUB; **3.** Silamu Hanati, CHN and Jungjoo Kim, KOR.
Middleweight (165 lbs): **1.** James Degale, GBR def. **2.** Emilio Correa Bayeaux, CUB; **3.** Darren John Sutherland, IRL and Vijender Kumar, IND.
Light Heavyweight (178 lbs): **1.** Xiaoping Zhang def. **2.** Kenny Egan, IRL; **3.** Yerkebulan Shynaliyev, KAZ and Tony Jeffries, GBR.
Heavyweight (201 lbs): **1.** Rakhim Chakhkiev, RUS def. **2.** Clemente Russo, ITA; **3.** Deontay Wilder, USA and Osmai Acosta Duarte, CUB.
Super Heavyweight (over 201 lbs): **1.** Roberto Cammarelle, ITA def. **2.** Zhilei Zhang, CHN; **3.** Vyacheslav Glazkov, UKR def. David Price, GBR.

CANOE/KAYAK

MEN'S FLATWATER

Canoe 500m Singles: 1. Maxim Opaley, RUS (1:47.140); **2.** David Cal, SPA (1:48.397); **3.** Iurii Cheban, UKR (1:48.776).
Canoe 1000m Singles: 1. Attila Sandor Vajda, HUN (3:50.467); **2.** David Cal, SPA (3:52.751); **3.** Thomas Hall, CAN (3:53.653).
Canoe 500m Doubles: 1. Meng Guanliang & Yang Wenjun, CHN (1:41.282); **2.** Alexander Kostoglod & Sergey Ulegin, RUS (1:41.282); **3.** Christian Gille & Thomasz Wylenzek, GER (1:41.964).
Canoe 1000m Doubles: 1. Aliaksandr Bahdanovich & Andrei Bahdanovich, BLR (3:36.365); **2.** Christian Gille & Thomasz Wylenzek, GER (3:36.588); **3.** Gyorgy Kozmann & Tamas Kiss, HUN (3:40.258).
Kayak 500m Singles: 1. Ken Wallace, AUS (1:37.252); **2.** Adam van Koeverden, CAN (1:37.630); **3.** Tim Brabants, GBR (1:37.671).
Kayak 500m Doubles: 1. Saul Craviotto & Carlos Perez, SPA (1:28.736); **2.** Ronald Rauhe & Tim Wieskotter, GER (1:28.827); **3.** Raman Piatrushenka & Vadzim Makhneu, BLR (1:30.005).

Kayak 1000m Singles: 1. Tim Brabants, GBR (3:26.323); **2.** Eirik Veraas Larsen, NOR (3:27.342); **3.** Ken Wallace, AUS (3:27.485).

Kayak 1000m Doubles: 1. Andreas Ihle & Martin Hollstein, GER (3:11.809); **2.** Kim Wraae Knudsen & Rene Holten Poulsen, DEN (3:13.580); **3.** Andrea Facchin & Antonio Massimiliano Scaduto, ITA (3:14.750).

Kayak 1000m Fours: 1. Belarus (2:55.714); **2.** Slovakia (2:56.593); **3.** Germany (2:56.676).

WOMEN'S FLAT WATER

Kayak 500m Singles: 1. Inna Osypenki-Radomska, UKR (1:50.673); **2.** Josefa Idem, ITA (1:50.677); **3.** Katrin Wagner-Augustin, GER (1:51.022).

Kayak 500m Doubles: 1. Katalin Kovacs & Natasa Janic, HUN (1:41.308); **2.** Aneta Pastuszka & Beata Mikolajczyk, POL (1:42.092); **3.** Marie Delattre & Anne-Laure Viard, FRA (1:42.128).

Kayak Sprint 500m Fours: 1. Germany (1:32.231); **2.** Hungary (1:32.971); **3.** Australia (1:34.704).

MEN'S SLALOM

Canoe Singles: 1. Michal Martikan, SVK (87.76); **2.** David Florence, GBR (88.15); **3.** Robin Bell, AUS (89.43).

Canoe Doubles: 1. Pavol Hochschorner & Peter Hochschorner, SVK; **2.** Jaroslav Volf & Ondrej Stepanek, CZE; **3.** Mikhail Kuznetsov & Dmitry Larionov, RUS.

Kayak Singles: 1. Alexander Grimm, GER (84.39); **2.** Fabien Lefevre, FRA (86.09); **3.** Benjamin Boukepti, Togo (87.37).

WOMEN'S SLALOM

Kayak Singles: 1. Elena Kaliska, SVK (95.51); **2.** Jacqueline Lawrence, AUS (103.54); **3.** Violetta Oblinger Peters, AUS (104.12).

CYCLING

MEN
BMX

Individual: 1. Maris Strombergs, LAT (36.190); **2.** Mike Day, USA (36.606); **3.** Donny Robinson, USA (36.972).

Mountain Bike

Cross Country (35.6 km): **1.** Julien Absalon, FRA (1:55:59); **2.** Jean-Christophe Peraud, FRA (1:57:06); **3.** Nino Schurter, SUI (1:57:52).

Road

Individual Road Race: 1. Samuel Sanchez, SPA (6:23:49); **2.** Davide Rebellin, ITA (6:23:49); **3.** Fabian Cancellara, SUI (6:23:49).

Individual Time Trial: 1. Fabian Cancellara, SUI (1:02:11.43); **2.** Gustav Larsson, SWE (1:02:44.79); **3.** Levi Leipheimer, USA (1:03:21.11).

Track

Time Trial (1 km): **1.** Chris Hoy, GBR; **2.** Jason Kenny, GBR; **3.** Mickael Bourgain, FRA.

Individual Match Sprint (3 laps): **1.** Ryan Bayley, AUS; **2.** Theo Bos, NED; **3.** Rene Wolff, GER.

Keirin (8 laps): **1.** Chris Hoy, GBR; **2.** Ross Edgar, GBR; **3.** Kiyofumi Nagai, JPN.

Individual Points Race (40 km): **1.** Juan Llaneras, SPA; **2.** Roger Kluge, GER; **3.** Chris Newton, GBR.

Individual Pursuit (4000 m): **1.** Bradley Wiggins, GBR **2.** Hayden Roulston, NZE **3.** Steve Burke, GBR.

Team Sprint (3 laps): **1.** Great Britain **2.** France; **3.** Germany.

Team Pursuit (4 km): **1.** Great Britain (3:53.314) def. **2.** Denmark; **3.** New Zealand.

Madison (50 km): **1.** Juan Esteban Curuchet & Walter Fernando Perez, ARG; **2.** Juan Llanderas & Antonio Tauler, SPA; **3.** Alexey Markov & Mikhail Ignatyev, RUS.

WOMEN
BMX

Individual: 1. Anne-Caroline Chausson, FRA (35:976); **2.** Laetitia le Corguille, FRA (38.042); **3.** Jill Kitner, USA (38.674).

Mountain Bike

Cross Country (26.7 km): **1.** Sabine Spitz, GER (1:45:11); **2.** Maja Wloszczowska, POL (1:45:52); **3.** Irina Kalentyeva, RUS (1:46:28).

Road

Individual Road Race: 1. Nicole Cook, GBR (3:32:24); **2.** Emma Johansson, SWE (3:32:24); **3.** Tatiana Guderzo, ITA (3:32:24).

Individual Time Trial: 1. Kristin Armstrong, USA (34:51.72); 2. Emma Pooley, GBR (35:16.01); 3. Karin Thurig, SUI (35:50.99).

Track

Individual Match Sprint (3 laps): **1.** Victoria Pendleton; **2.** Anna Meares, AUS; **3.** Guo Shuang, CHN.

Individual Pursuit (3 km): **1.** Rebecca Romero, GBR; **2.** Wendy Houvenaghel, GBR; **3.** Lesya Kalitovska, UKR

Individual Points Race: 1. Marianne Vos, NED; **2.** Yoanka Gonzalez, CUB **3.** Leire Olaverria, SPA.

DIVING

MEN

3m Springboard: 1. Chong He, CHN (572.90 pts); **2.** Alexandre Despatie, CAN (536.65); **3.** Kai Qin, CHN (530.10).

10m Platform: 1. Matthew Mitcham, AUS (537.95 pts); **2.** Mathew Helm, AUS (730.56); **3.** Tian Liang, CHN (729.66).

Synchronized 3m Springboard: 1. Feng Wang & Kai Qin, CHN (469.08 pts); **2.** Dmitry Sautin & Yuriy Kunakov, RUS (421.98); **3.** Ilya Kvasha & Oleksiy Prygorov, UKR (415.05).

Synchronized 10m Platform: 1. Yue Lin & Liang Huo, CHN (468.18 pts); **2.** Patrick Hausding & Sascha Klein, GER (450.42); **3.** Gleb Galperin & Dmitriy Dobroskok, RUS (445.26).

WOMEN

3m Springboard: 1. Guo Jingjing, CHN (415.35 pts); **2.** Julia Pakhalina, RUS (398.60); **3.** Minxia Wu, CHN (389.85).

10m Platform: 1. Ruolin Chen, CHN (447.70 pts); **2.** Emilie Heymans, CAN (437.05); **3.** Xin Wang, CHN (429.90).

Synchronized 3m Springboard: 1. Wu Minxia & Guo Jingjing, CHN (343.50 pts); **2.** Julia Pakhalina & Anastasia Pozdnyakova, RUS (323.61); **3.** Ditte Kotzian & Heike Fischer, GER (318.90).

Synchronized 10m Platform: 1. Xin Wang & Ruolin Chen, CHN (363.54 pts); **2.** Briony Cole & Melissa Wu, AUS (335.16); **3.** Paola Espinosa & Tatiana Ortiz, MEX (330.06).

EQUESTRIAN

Horses in parentheses.

Individual Dressage: 1. Anky van Grunsven, (Salinero) NED; **2.** Isabell Werth, (Satchmo) GER; **3.** Heike Kemmer (Bonaparte) GER.

Team Dressage: 1. Germany (72.917); **2.** Netherlands (71.75); **3.** Denmark (68.875).

Individual Show Jumping: 1. Eric Lamaze, (Hickstead) CAN (38.39); **2.** Rolf-Goran Bengtsson, (Ninja) SWE (38.39); **3.** Beezie Madden, (Authentic) USA (35.25).

Team Show Jumping: 1. United States; **2.** Canada; **3.** Norway.

Individual 3-Day Eventing: 1. Hinrich Romeike, (Marius) GER (54.2); **2.** Gina Miles, (McKinlaigh) USA (56.1); **3.** Kristina Cook, (Miners Frolic) GBR (57.4).

Team 3-Day Eventing: 1. Germany (166.10); **2.** Australia (171.2); **3.** Great Britain (185.70).

USA Entry: Laura Kraut, Mclain Ward, Beezie Madden, Will Simpson.

FENCING

MEN

Individual Epée: 1. Matteo Taliariol, ITA def. **2.** Fabrice Jeannet, FRA (15-9); **3.** Jose Luis Abajo, SPA def. Gabor Boczko, HUN (8-7).

Team Epée: 1. France def. **2.** Poland (45-29); **3.** Italy def. China (45-35).

Individual Foil: 1. Benjamin Kleibrink, GER, def. **2.** Yuki Ota, JPN (15-9); **3.** Salvatore Sanzo, ITA def. Jun Zhu, CHN (15-14).

Team Foil: 1. Italy def. China (45-42); **3.** Russia def. United States (45-38).

Individual Sabre: 1. Man Zhong, CHN, def. **2.** Nicolas Lopez, FRA (15-9); **3.** Mihai Covaliu, ROU def. Julien Pillet, FRA (15-11).

Team Sabre: 1. France def. **2.** USA (45-37); **3.** Italy def. Russia (45-44).

WOMEN

Individual Epée: 1. Britta Heidemann, GER, def. **2.** Ana Maria Branza, ROU (15-11); **3.** Ildiko Mincza-Nebald, HUN def. Na Li, CHN (15-11).

Team Epée: 1. Russia def. **2.** Germany (34-28); **3.** France def. Canada (45-37).

Individual Foil: 1. Maria Valentina Vezzali, ITA def. **2.** Hyunhee Nam, KOR (6-5); **3.** Margherita Granbassi, ITA, def. Giovanna Trillini, ITA (15-12).

Team Foil: 1. Russia def. USA (28-11); **3.** Italy def. Hungary (32-23).

Individual Sabre: 1. Mariel Zagunis, USA def. **2.** Sada Jacobson, USA (15-8); **3.** Becca Ward, USA def. Sofiya Velikaya, RUS (15-14).

Team Sabre: 1. Ukraine def. **2.** China (45-44); **3.** United States def. France (45-38).

GYMNASTICS

MEN
All-Around

		Points
1	Wei Yang, CHN	94.575
2	Kohei Uchimura, JPN	91.975
3	Benoît Caranobe, FRA	91.925

Top 10 USA: 9th—Jonathan Horton (91.575).

Floor Exercise

		Points
1	Kai Zou, CHN	16.050
2	Gervasio Deferr, SPA	15.775
3	Anton Golotsutskov, RUS	15.725

Horizontal Bar

		Points
1	Kai Zou, CHN	16.200
2	Jonathan Horton, USA	16.175
3	Fabian Hambuechen, GER	15.875

Parallel Bars

		Points
1	Xiaopeng Li, CHN	16.450
2	Wonchul Yoo, KOR	16.250
3	Anton Fokin, UZB	16.200

Pommel Horse

		Points
1	Qin Xiao, CHN	15.875
2	Filip Ude, CRO	15.725
3	Louis Smith, GBR	15.725

Top 8 USA: 7th—Alexander Artemev (14.975).

Rings

		Points
1	Yibing Chen, CHN	16.600
2	Wei Yang, CHN	16.425
3	Oleksander Vorobiov, UKR	16.325

Vault

		Points
1	Leszek Blanik, POL	16.537
2	Thomas Bouhail, FRA	16.537
3	Anton Golotsutskov, RUS	16.475

Team

		Points
1	China	286.125
2	Japan	278.875
3	United States	275.850

USA entry: Alexander Artemev, Raj Bhavsar, Joey Hagerty, Jonathan Horton, Justin Spring, Kai Wen Tan.

WOMEN
All-Around

		Points
1	Nastia Liukin, USA	63.325
2	Shawn Johnson, USA	62.725
3	Yilin Yang, CHN	62.650

Floor Exercise

		Points
1	Sandra Izbasa, ROM	15.650
2	Shawn Johnson, USA	15.500
3	Nastia Liukin, USA	15.425

Balance Beam

		Points
1	Shawn Johnson, USA	16.225
2	Nastia Liukin, USA	16.025
3	Fei Cheng, CHN	15.950

Uneven Bars

		Points
1	Kexin He, CHN	16.725
2	Nastia Liukin, USA	16.725
3	Yilin Yang, CHN	16.650

Vault

		Points
1	Un Jong Hong, PRK	15.650
2	Oksana Chusovitina, GER	15.575
3	Fei Cheng, CHN	15.562

Team

		Points
1	China	188.900
2	United States	186.525
3	Romania	181.525

USA entry: Shawn Johnson, Nastia Liukin, Chellsie Memmel, Samanthia Peszek, Alicia Sacramone, Bridget Sloan.

RHYTHMIC GYMNASTICS

Individual All-Around

		Points
1	Evgeniya Kanaeva, RUS	75.500
2	Inna Zhukova, BLR	71.925
3	Anna Bessonova, UKR	71.875

Team

		Points
1	Russia	35.550
2	China	35.225
3	Belarus	34.900

TRAMPOLINE

Men

		Points
1	Chunlong Lu, CHN	41.00
2	Jason Burnett, CAN	40.70
3	Dong Dong, CHN	40.60

Women

		Points
1	Wenna He, CHN	37.80
2	Karen Cockburn, CAN	37.00
3	Ekaterina Khilko, UZB	36.90

JUDO

MEN

Extra Lightweight (132 lbs)**: 1.** Minho Choi, KOR **2.** Ludwig Paischer, AUS; **3.** Rishod Sobirov, UZB and Ruben Houkes, NED.

Half-Lightweight (143 lbs)**: 1**. Masato Uchishiba, JPN; **2.** Benjamin Darbelet, FRA; **3.** Yordanis Arencibia, CUB and Chol Min.Pak, PRK.

Lightweight (157 lbs)**: 1.** Elnur Mammadli, AZB; **2.** Kichun Wang, KOR; **3.** Rasul Boqiev, TAJ and Leandro Guilheiro, BRA.

Half-Middleweight (172 lbs)**: 1.** Ole Bischof, GER; **2.** Jaebum Kim, KOR; **3.** Tiago Camilo, BRA and Roman Gontiuk, UKR.

Middleweight (190 lbs)**: 1.** Irakli Tsirekidze, GEO; **2.** Amar Benikhlef, ALG; **3.** Hesham Mesbah, EGY and Sergei Aschwanden, SUI.

Half-Heavyweight (209 lbs)**: 1.** Tuvshinbayar Naidan, MGL; **2.** Askhat Zhitkeyev, KAZ; **3.** Movlud Miraliyev, AZB and Henk Grol, NED.

Heavyweight (over 209 lbs)**: 1.** Satoshi Ishii, JPN; **2.** Abdullo Tangriev; **3.** Oscar Brayson, CUB and Teddy Riner, FRA.

WOMEN

Extra Lightweight (106 lbs)**: 1.** Alina Alexandra Dumitru, ROM; **2.** Yanet Bermoy, CUB; **3.** Paula Belen PAreto, ARG and Ryoko Tani, JPN.

Half-Lightweight (115 lbs)**: 1**. Xian Dongmei, CHN; **2.** Kum Ae An, PRK; **3.** Soraya Haddad, ALG and Misato Nakamura, JPN.

Lightweight (123 lbs)**: 1.** Giulia Quintavalle, ITA; **2.** Deborah Gravenstijn, NED; **3.** Ketleyn Quadros, BRA and Yan Xu, CHN.

Half-Middleweight (134 lbs)**: 1.** Ayumi Tanimoto, JPN; **2.** Lucie Decosse, FRA; **3.** Elisabeth Willeboordse, NED and Ok Im Won, PRK.

Middleweight (146 lbs)**: 1.** Masae Ueno, JPN; **2.** Anaysi Hernandez, CUB; **3.** Ronda Rousey, USA and Edith Bosch, NED.

Half-Heavyweight (159 lbs)**: 1.** Xiuli Yang, CHN; **2.** Yalennis Castillo, CUB; **3.** Gyeongmi Jeong, KOR and Stephanie Possamai, FRA.

Heavyweight (over 159 lbs)**: 1.** Wen Tong, CHN; **2.** Maki Tsukada JPN; **3.** Lucija Polavder, SLO and Idalys Ortiz, CUB.

MODERN PENTATHLON

Five events in one day—shooting (4.5mm air pistol), fencing (one-touch epée), swimming (200m freestyle), riding (450m stadium course with 15 jumps), and running (3,000m cross-country).

MEN

1. Andrey Moiseev, RUS (5,632 pts); **2.** Edvinas Krungolcas, LTU (5,548); **3.** Andrejus Zadneprovskis, LTU (5,524).

Top USA entrant—18th, Sam Sacksen (5,272).

WOMEN

1. Lena Schoneborn, GER (5,792 pts); **2.** Heather Fell, GBR (5,752); **3.** Victoria Tereshuk, UKR (5,672).

Top USA entrant—19th, Sheila Taormina (5,304).

ROWING

(2000-meter course)

MEN

Single Sculls: 1. Olaf Tufte, NOR; **2.** Ondrej Synek, CZE; **3.** Mahe Drysdale, NZE.

Lightweight Double Sculls: 1. Zac Purchase & Mark Hunter, GBR; **2.** Dimitrios Mouglos & Vasileios Polymeros; **3.** Mads Reinholdt Rasmussen & Rasmus Nicholai Quist Hansen, DEN.

Double Sculls: 1. David Crawshay & Scott Brennan, AUS; **2.** Tonu Endrekson & Juri Jaanson, EST; **3.** Matthew Wells & Stephen Rowbotham, GBR.

Quadruple Sculls: 1. Poland; **2.** Italy; **3.** France.

Coxless Pairs: 1. Drew Ginn & Duncan Free, AUS; **2.** David Calderm & Scott Grandsen, CAN; **3.** Nathan Twaddle & George Bridgewater, NZE.

Coxless Fours: 1. Great Britain; **2.** Australia; **3.** France.

Coxed Eight: 1. Canada; **2.** Great Britain; **3.** United States. **USA entry:** Beau Hoopman, Matt Schnobrich, Micah Boyd, Wyatt Allen, Daniel Walsh, Steven Coppola, Josh Inman, Bryan Volpenhein, Marcus Mc Elhenney.

WOMEN

Single Sculls: 1. Rumyana Neykova, BLG; **2.** Michelle Guerrette, USA; **3.** Ekaterina Karsten, BLR.

Lightweight Double Sculls: 1. Kirsten van der Kolk & Marit van Eupen, NED; **2.** Sanna Sten & Minna Nieminen, FIN; **3.** Melanie Kok & Tracy Cameron, CAN.

Double Sculls: 1. Georgina Evers-Swindell & Caroline Evers-Swindell, NZE; **2.** Annekatrin Thiele & Christiane Huth, GER; **3.** Elise Laverick & Anna Bebington, GBR.

Quadruple Sculls: 1. China; **2.** Great Britain; **3.** Germany.

Coxless Pairs: 1. Georgeta Andrunache & Viorica Susanu, ROM; **2.** You Wu & Yulan Gao, CHN; **3.** Yuliya Bichyk & Natallia Helakh, BLR.

Coxed Eights: 1. United Statee; **2.** Netherlands; **3.** Romania. **USA entry:** Erin Cafaro, Lindsay Shoop, Anna Goodale, Elle Logan, Anne Cummins, Susan Francia, Caroline Lind, Caryn Davies, Mary Whipple.

SAILING

OPEN

Finn: 1. Ben Ainslie, GBR; **2.** Zach Railey, USA; **3.** Guillaume Florent, FRA.

Tornado: 1. Fernando Echavarri & Anton Paz, SPA; **2.** Darren Bundock & Glenn Ashby, AUS; **3.** Santiago Lange & Carlos Espinola, ARG.

49er: 1. Jonas Warrer & Martin Kirketerp Ibsen, DEN; **2.** Iker Martinez de Lizarduy & Xabier Fernand, SPA; **3.** Jan Peter Peckolt & Hans Peckolt, GER.

MEN

Windsurfer: 1. Tom Ashley, NZE; **2.** Julien Bontemps, FRA; **3.** Shahar Zubari, ISR.

470: 1. Nathan Wilmot & Malcolm Page, AUS; **2.** Nick Rogers & Joe Glanfield, GBR; **3.** Nicolas Charbonnier & Olivier Bausset, FRA.

Laser: 1. Paul Goodison, GBR; **2.** Vasilij Zbogar, SLO; **3.** Diego Romero, ITA.

Star: 1. Iain Percy & Andrew Simpson, GBR; **2.** Robert Scheidt & Bruno Prada, BRA; **3.** Fredrik Loof & Anders Ekstrom, SWE.

WOMEN

Windsurfer: 1. Jian Yin, CHN; **2.** Alessandra Sensini, ITA; **3.** Bryony Shaw, GBR.

470: 1. Elise Rechichi & Tessa Parkinson, AUS; **2.** Marcelien de Koning, NED; **3.** Fernanda Oliveira & Isabel Swan, BRA.

Europe: 1. Anna Tunnicliffe, USA; **2.** Gintare Volungeviciute, LTU; **3.** Lijia Xu, CHN.

Mistral: 1. Faustine Merret, FRA; **2.** Jian Yin, CHN; **3.** Alessandra Sensini, ITA.

Yngling: 1. Great Britain; **2.** Netherlands; **3.** Greece.

SHOOTING

MEN

50m Free Pistol: 1. Jong Oh Jin, KOR (660.4 pts); **2.** Zongliang Tan, CHN (659.5); **3.** Vladimir Isakov, RUS (658.9).

50m Free Rifle/3 Positions: 1. Jian Qiu, CHN (1272.5 pts); **2.** Jury Sukhorukov, UKR (1272.4); **3.** Rajmond Debevec, SLO (1271.7).

50m Free Rifle/Prone: 1. Arthur Ayvazian, UKR (702.7 pts); **2.** Matthew Emmons, USA (701.7); **3.** Warren Potent, AUS (700.5).

25m Rapid Fire Pistol: 1. Oleksandr Petriv, UKR (780.2 pts); **2.** Ralf Schumann, GER (779.5); **3.** Christian Reitz, GER (779.3).

10m Running Game Target: 1. Manfred Kurzer, GER (682.4 pts); **2.** Alexander Blinov, RUS (678.0); **3.** Dimitri Lykin, RUS (677.1).

10m Air Pistol: 1. Wenjun Guo, CHN (492.3 pts); **2.** Natalia Paderina, RUS (489.1); **3.** Nino Salukvadze, GEO (487.4).

10m Air Rifle: 1. Abhinav Bindra, IND (700.5 pts); **2.** Qinan Zhu, CHN (699.7); **3.** Henri Hakkinen, FIN (699.4).

Trap: 1. David Kostelecky, CZE (146 pts); **2.** Giovanni Pellielo, ITA (143); **3.** Alexey Alipov, RUS (142).

Double Trap: 1. Walton Eller, USA (190 pts); **2.** Francesco D Aniello, ITA (187); **3.** Binyuan Hu, CHN (184).

Skeet: 1. Vincent Hancock, USA (145 pts, won shoot-off); **2.** Tore Brovold, NOR (145); **3.** Anthony Terras, FRA (144).

WOMEN

25m Sport Pistol: 1. Ying Chen, CHN (793.4 pts); **2.** Gundegmass Otryad, MGL (792.2); **3.** Munkhbayar Dorjsuren, GER (789.2).

10m Air Pistol: 1. Olga Klochneva, RUS (483.3 pts, won shoot-off); **2.** Jasna Sekaric, SBM (483.3); **3.** Maria Grozdeva, BUL (482.3).

50m smallbore/3 Positions: 1. Li Du, CHN (690.3 pts); **2.** Katerina Emmons, CZE (687.7); **3.** Eglis Yaima Cruz, CUB (687.6).

10m Air Rifle: 1. Katerina Emmons, CZE (503.5 pts); **2.** Lioubov Galkina, RUS (501.5); **3.** Snjezana Pejcic, CRO (500.9).

Trap: 1. Satu Makela-Nummela, FIN (91 pts); **2.** Zuzana Stefecekova, SVK (89); **3.** Corey Cogdell, USA (862).

Skeet: 1. Chiara Cainero, ITA (93 pts, won shootout); **2.** Kimberly Rhode, USA (93); **3.** Christine Brinker, GER (93).

SWIMMING

MEN
50-meter Freestyle

		Time
1	Cesar Cielo Filho, BRA	21.30
2	Amaury Leveaux, FRA	21.45
3	Alain Bernard, FRA	21.49

100-meter Freestyle

		Time
1	Alain Bernard, FRA	47.21
2	Eamon Sullivan, AUS	47.32
3	Jason Lezak, USA	47.67
	Cesar Cielo Filho, BRA	47.67

200-meter Freestyle

		Time	
1	Michael Phelps, USA	1:42.96	WR
2	Taehwan Park, KOR	1:44.85	
3	Peter Vanderkaay, USA	1:45.14	

400-meter Freestyle

		Time
1	Taehwan Park, KOR	3:41.86
2	Lin Zhang, CHN	3:42.44
3	Larsen Jensen, USA	3:42.78

1500-meter Freestyle

		Time
1	Oussama Mellouli, TUN	14:40.84
2	Grant Hackett, AUS	14:41.53
3	Ryan Cochrane, CAN	14:42.69

100-meter Backstroke

		Time	
1	Aaron Peirsol, USA	52.54	WR
2	Matt Grevers, USA	53.11	
3	Arkady Vyatchanin, RUS	53.18	
	Hayden Stoeckel, AUS	53.18	

200-meter Backstroke

		Time	
1	Ryan Lochte, USA	1:53.94	WR
2	Aaron Peirsol, USA	1:54.33	
3	Arkady Vyatchanin, RUS	1:54.93	

100-meter Breaststroke

		Time	
1	Kosuke Kitajima, JPN	58.91	WR
2	Alexander Dale Oen, NOR	59.20	
3	Hugues Duboscq, FRA	59.37	

200-meter Breaststroke

		Time	
1	Kosuke Kitajima, JPN	2:07.64	OR
2	Brenton Rickard, AUS	2:08.88	
3	Hugues Duboscq, FRA	2:08.94	

100-meter Butterfly

		Time	
1	Michael Phelps, USA	50.58	OR
2	Milorad Cavic, SER	50.59	
3	Andrew Lauterstein, AUS	51.12	

200-meter Butterfly

		Time	
1	Michael Phelps, USA	1:52.03	WR
2	Laszlo Cseh, HUN	1:52.70	
3	Takeshi Matsuda, JPN	1:52.97	

200-meter Individual Medley

		Time	
1	Michael Phelps, USA	1:54.23	WR
2	Laszlo Cseh, HUN	1:56.52	
3	Ryan Lochte, USA	1:56.53	

400-meter Individual Medley

		Time	
1	Michael Phelps USA	4:03.84	WR
2	Laszlo Cseh, HUN	4:06.16	
3	Ryan Lochte, USA	4:08.09	

4x100-meter Freestyle Relay

		Time	
1	United States	3:08.24	WR
2	France	3:08.32	
3	Australia	3:09.91	

USA—Michael Phelps, Garrett Weber-Gale, Cullen Jones, Jason Lezak; **FRA**—Amaury Leveaux, Fabien Gilot, Frederick Bousquet, Alain Bernard; **AUS**—Eamon Sullivan, Andrew Lauterstein, Ashley Callus, Matt Targett.

4x200-meter Freestyle Relay

		Time	
1	United States	6:58.56	WR
2	Russia	7:03.70	
3	Australia	7:04.98	

USA—Michael Phelps, Ryan Lochte, Ricky Berens, Peter Vanderkaay; **RUS**—Nikita Lobintsev, Evgeniy Lagunov, Danila Izotov, Alexander Sukhorukov; **AUS**—Patrick Murphy, Grant Hackett, Grant Brits, Nick Ffrost.

4x100-meter Medley Relay

		Time	
1	United States	3:29.34	WR
2	Australia	3:30.04	
3	Japan	3:31.18	

USA—Aaron Perisol, Brendan Hansen, Michael Phelps, Jason Lezak; **AUS**—Hayden Stoeckel, Brenton Rickard, Andrew Lauterstein, Eamon Sullivan; **JPN**—Junichi Miyashita, Kosuke Kitajima, Takuro Fujii, Hisayoshi Sato.

10-km Marathon Swim

		Time
1	Maarten van der Weijden, NED	1:51:51.6
2	David Davies, GBR	1:51:53.1
3	Thomas Lurz, GER	1:51:53.6

WOMEN
50-meter Freestyle

		Time	
1	Britta Steffen, GER	24.06	OR
2	Dara Torres, USA	24.07	
3	Cate Campbell, AUS	24.17	

100-meter Freestyle

		Time	
1	Britta Steffen, GER	53.12	OR
2	Lisbeth Trickett, AUS	53.16	
3	Natalie Coughlin, USA	53.39	

200-meter Freestyle

		Time
1	Federica Pellegrini, ITA	1:54.82
2	Sara Isakovic, SLO	1:54.97
3	Jiaying Pang, CHN	1:55.05

400-meter Freestyle

		Time
1	Rebecca Adlington, GBR	4:03.22
2	Katie Hoff, USA	4:03.29
3	Joanne Jackson, GBR	4:03.52

800-meter Freestyle

		Time	
1	Rebecca Adlington, GBR	8:14.10	WR
2	Alessia Filippi, ITA	8:20.23	
3	Lotte Friis, DEN	8:23.03	

100-meter Backstroke

		Time
1	Natalie Coughlin, USA	58.96
2	Kirsty Coventry, ZIM	59.19
3	Margaret Hoelzer, USA	59.34

200-meter Backstroke

		Time	
1	Kirsty Coventry, ZIM	2:05.24	WR
2	Margaret Hoelzer, USA	2:06.23	
3	Reiko Nakamura, JPN	2:07.13	

100-meter Breaststroke

		Time	
1	Leisel Jones, AUS	1:05.17	OR
2	Rebecca Soni, USA	1:06.73	
3	Mirna Jukic, AUS	1:07.34	

200-meter Breaststroke

		Time	
1	Rebecca Soni, USA	2:20.22	OR
2	Leisel Jones, AUS	2:22.05	
3	Sara Nordenstam, NOR	2:23.02	

100-meter Butterfly

		Time
1	Lisbeth Trickett, AUS	56.73
2	Christine Magnuson, USA	57.10
3	Jessicah Schipper, AUS	57.25

200-meter Butterfly

		Time	
1	Zige Liu, CHN	2:04.18	WR
2	Liuyang Jiao, CHN	2:04.72	
3	Jessicah Schipper, AUS	2:06.26	

200-meter Individual Medley

		Time	
1	Stephanie Rice, AUS	2:08.45	WR
2	Kirsty Coventry, ZIM	2:08.59	
3	Natalie Coughlin, USA	2:10.34	

400-meter Individual Medley

		Time	
1	Stephanie Rice, AUS	4:29.45	WR
2	Kirsty Coventry, ZIM	4:29.89	
3	Katie Hoff, USA	4:37.71	

4x 100-meter Freestyle Relay

		Time	
1	Netherlands	3:33.76	OR
2	United States	3:34.33	
3	Australia	3:35.05	

NED—Inge Dekker, Ranomi Kromowidjojo, Femke Heemskerk, Marleen Veldhuis; **USA**—Natalie Coughlin, Lacey Nymeyer, Kara Lynn Joyce, Dara Torres; **AUS**—Cate Campbell, Alice Mills, Melanie Schlanger, Lisbeth Trickett.

4x 200-meter Freestyle Relay

		Time	
1	Australia	7:44.31	WR
2	China	7:45.93	
3	United States	7:46.33	

AUS—Stephanie Rice, Bronte Barratt, Kylie Palmer, Linda Mackenzie; **CHN**—Yu Yang, Qianwei Zhu, Miao Tan, Jiaying Pang; **USA**—Alison Schmitt, Natalie Coughlin, Caroline Burckle, Katie Hoff.

4x 100-meter Medley Relay

		Time	
1	Australia	3:52.69	WR
2	United States	3:53.30	
3	China	3:56.11	

AUS—Emily Seebohm, Leisel Jones, Jessicah Schipper, Lisbeth Trickett; **USA**—Natalie Coughlin, Rebecca Soni, Christine Magnuson, Dara Torres; **CHN**—Jing Zhao, Ye Sun, Yafaei Zhou, Jiaying Pang.

10-km Marathon Swim

		Time
1	Larisa Ilchenko, RUS	1:59:27.7
2	Keri-Anne Payne, GBR	1:59:29.2
3	Cassandra Patten, GBR	1:59:31.0

Synchronized Swimming

Duet: 1. Anastasia Davydova & Anastasia Ermakova, RUS (99.251 pts); **2.** Andrea Fuentes & Gemma Mengual, SPA (98.334); **3.** Saho Harada & Emiko Suzuki, JPN (97.167)

Team: 1. Russia (99.500 pts); **2.** Spain (98.251); **3.** China (97.334).

TABLE TENNIS

MEN

Singles: 1. Lin Ma, CHN def. **2.** Wang Hao, CHN (4-1); **3.** Wang Liqin, CHN def. Jorgen Persson, SWE (4-0).

Teams: 1. China def. **2.** Germany (3-0); **3.** South Korea def. Austria (3-1).

WOMEN

Singles: 1. Yining Zhang, CHN def. **2.** Nan Wang, CHN (4-1); **3.** Yue Guo, CHN def. Jia Wei Li, SIN (4-2).

Teams: 1. China def. **2.** Singapore (3-0); **3.** South Korea def. Japan, (3-0).

TAE KWON DO

MEN

128 pounds: 1. Guillermo Perez, MEX; **2.** Yulis Gabriel Mercedes, DOM; **3.** Mu-Yen Chu, TPE and Rohullash Nikpai, AFG

150 pounds: 1. Taejin Son, KOR; **2.** Mark Lopez, USA; **3.** Yu-Chi Sung, TPE and Servet Tazegul, TUR

176 pounds: 1. Hadi Saei, IRA; **2.** Mauro Sarmiento, ITA; **3.** Steven Lopez, USA and Guo Zhu, CHN.

Over 176 pounds: 1. Dongmin Cha, KOR **2.** Alexandros Nikolaidis, GRE; **3.** Arman Chilmanov, KAZ and Chika Yagazie Chukwumerije, NGR.

WOMEN

108 pounds: 1. Jingyu Wu, CHN; **2.** Buttree Puedpong, THA; **3.** Dalia Contreras Rivero, VEN def. Daynelis Montejo, CUB.

125 pounds: 1. Sujeong Lim, KOR **2.** Azize Tanrikulu, TUR; **3.** Diana Lopez, USA and Martina Zubcic, CRO.

147 pounds: 1. Kyungseon Hwang, KOR; **2.** Karine Sergerie, CAN; **3.** Gwladys Patience Epangue, FRA and Sandra Saric, CRO

Over 147 pounds: 1. Maria del Rosario Espinoza, MEX; **2.** Nina Solheim, NOR; **3.** Natalia Falavigna, BRA and Sarah Stevenson, GBR.

TENNIS

MEN

Singles: 1. Rafael Nadal, SPA def. **2.** Fernando Gonzalez, CHI 6-3, 7-6 (7-2), 6-3; **3.** Novak Djokovic, SRB def. James Blake, USA 6-3, 7-6 (7-4).

Doubles: 1. Roger Federer & Stanislas Wawrinka, SUI, def. **2.** Simon Aspelin & Thomas Johansson, SWE 6-3, 6-4, 6-7 (4-7), 6-3; **3.** Bob Bryan & Mike Bryan, USA def. Arnaud Clement & Michael Llodra, FRA 3-6, 6-3, 6-4.

WOMEN

Singles: 1. Elena Dementieva, RUS, def. **2.** Dinara Safina, RUS, 3-6, 7-5 6-3; **3.** Vera Zvonareva, RUS def. Na Li, CHN 6-0, 7-5.

Doubles: 1. Venus Williams & Serena Williams, USA, def. **2.** Anabel Medina Garrigues & Virginia Ruano Pascual, SPA, 6-2, 6-0; **3.** Zi Yan & Jie Zheng, CHN def. Alona Bondarenko & Kateryna Bondarenko, UKR 6-2, 6-2.

TRACK & FIELD

MEN
100 meters

		Time
1	Usain Bolt, JAM	9.69 **WR**
2	Richard Thompson, Trinidad & Tobago	9.89
3	Walter Dix, USA	9.91

Other Top 8 USA—8th Davis Patton (10.03).

200 meters

		Time
1	Usain Bolt, JAM	19.30 **WR**
2	Shawn Crawford, USA	19.96
3	Walter Dix, USA	19.98

400 meters

		Time
1	LaShawn Merritt, USA	43.75
2	Jeremy Wariner, USA	44.74
3	David Neville, USA	44.80

800 meters

		Time
1	Wilfred Bungei, KEN	1:44.65
2	Ismail Ahmed Ismail, SUD	1:44.70
3	Alfred Kirwa Yego, KEN	1:44.82

1500 meters

		Time
1	Rashid Ramzi, BAH	3:32.94
2	Asbel Kipruto Kiprop, KEN	3:33.11
3	Nicholas Willis, NZE	3:34.16

5000 meters

		Time
1	Kenenisa Bekele, ETH	12:57.82 **OR**
2	Eliud Kipchoge, KEN	13:02.80
3	Edwin Cheruiyot Soi, KEN	13:06.22

10,000 meters

		Time
1	Kenenisa Bekele, ETH	27:01.17 **OR**
2	Sileshi Sihine, ETH	27:02.77
3	Micah Kogo, KEN	27:04.11

Marathon

		Time
1	Samuel Kamau Wansiru, KEN	2:06:32 **OR**
2	Jaouad Gharib, MOR	2:07:16
3	Tsegay Kebede, ETH	2:10:00

Top USA—9th Dathan Ritzenhein (2:11:59); 10th Ryan Hall (2:12:33).

4x100-meter Relay

		Time
1	Jamaica	37.10 **WR**
2	Trinidad & Tobago	38.06
3	Japan	38.15

JAM—Nesta Carter, Michael Frater, Usain Bolt, Asafa Powell; **T&T**—Keston Bledman, Marc Burns, Emmanuel Callender; **JPN**—Naoki Tsukahara, Shingo Suetsugu, Shinji Takahira, Nobuharu Asahara

4x400-meter Relay

		Time
1	United States	2:55.39 **OR**
2	Bahamas	2:58.04
3	Russia	2:58.06

USA—LaShawn Merritt, Angelo Taylor, David Neville, Jeremy Wariner; **BAH**—Andretti Bain, Michael Mathieu, Andrae Williams, Christoper Brown; **RUS**—Maksim Dyldin, Vladislav Frolov, Anton Kokorin, Denis Alexeev.

110-meter Hurdles

		Time
1	Dayron Robles, CUB	12.93
2	David Payne, USA	13.17
3	David Oliver, USA	13.18

400-meter Hurdles

		Time
1	Angelo Taylor, USA	47.25
2	Kerron Clement, USA	47.98
3	Bershawn Jackson, USA	48.06

3000-meter Steeplechase

		Time
1	Brimin Kiprop Kipruto, KEN	8:10.34
2	M. Mekhissi-Benabbad, FRA	8:10.49
3	Richard Kipkemboi Mateelong, KEN	8:11.01

USA Top 15—13th Anthony Famiglietti (8:31.21)

20-kilometer Walk

		Time
1	Valeriy Borchin, RUS	1:19:01
2	Jefferson Perez, ECU	1:19:15
3	Jared Tallent, AUS :	1:19:42

USA Entrants—43th Kevin Eastler (1:28:44).

50-kilometer Walk

		Time
1	Alex Schwazer, ITA	3:37:09 **OR**
2	Jared Tallent, AUS	3:39:27
3	Denis Nizhegorodov, RUS	3:40:14

USA Entrants—39th Phillip Dunn (4:08:32).

High Jump

		Height
1	Andrey Silnov, RUS	2.36m
2	Germaine Mason, GBR	2.34m
3	Yaroslav Rybakov, RUS	2.34m

Note: Second and third place cleared the same height, order of finish was decided by number of misses.

Pole Vault

		Height
1	Steve Hooker, AUS	5.76m **OR**
2	Evgeny Lukyanenko, RUS	5.85m
3	Denys Yurchenko, UKR	5.70m

Long Jump

		Distance
1	Irving Jahir Saladino Aranda, PAN	8.34m
2	Khotso Mokoena, RSA	8.24m
3	Ibrahim Camejo, CUB	8.20m

Triple Jump

		Distance
1	Nelson Evora, POR	17.67m
2	Phillips Idowu, GBR	17.62m
3	Leevan Sands, BAH	17.59m

Shot Put

		Distance
1	Tomasz Majewski, POL	21.51m
2	Christian Cantwell, USA	21.09m
3	Andrei Mikhnevich, BLR	21.05m

Other Top 10 USA—7th Reese Hoffa (20.53).

Discus

		Distance
1	Gerd Kanter, EST	68.82m
2	Piotr Malachowski, POL	67.82m
3	Virgilijus Alekna, LTU	67.79m

Hammer Throw

		Distance
1	Primoz Kozmus, SLO	82.02m
2	Vadim Devyatovskiy, BLR	81.61m
3	Ivan Tsikhan, BLR	81.51m

Javelin

		Distance
1	Andreas Thorkildsen, NOR	90.57m **OR**
2	Ainars Kovals, LAT	86.64m
3	Tero Pitkamaki, FIN	86.16m

Decathlon

		Points
1	Bryan Clay, USA	8791
2	Andrei Krauchanka, BLR	8551
3	Leonel Suarez, CUB	8527

WOMEN

100 meters

		Time
1	Shelly-ann Fraser, JAM	10.78
2	Sherone Simpson, JAM	10.98
	Kerron Stewart, JAM	10.98

Top 10 USA—4th Lauryn Williams (11.03); 5th Muna Lee (11.07); 8th Torri Edwards (11.20).

200 meters

		Time
1	Veronica Campbell-Brown, JAM	21.74
2	Allyson Felix, USA	21.93
3	Kerron Stewart, JAM	22.00

Top 10 USA—4th Muna Lee (22.01); 5th Marshevet Hooker (22.34).

400 meters

		Time
1	Christine Ohuruogu, GBR	49.62
2	Shericka Williams, JAM	49.69
3	Sanya Richards, USA	49.93

800 meters

		Time
1	Pamela Jelimo, KEN	1:54.87
2	Janeth Jepkosgei Busienei, KEN	1:56.07
3	Hasna Benhassi, MOR	1:56.73

1500 meters

		Time
1	Nancy Jebet Langat, KEN	4:00.23
2	Iryna Lishchynska, UKR	4:01.63
3	Nataliya Tobias, UKR	4:01.78

Top 10 USA—7th Shannon Rowbury (4:03.58).

5000 meters

		Time
1	Tirunesh Dibaba, ETH	15:41.40
2	Elvan Abeylegesse, TUR	15:42.74
3	Meseret Defar, ETH	15:44.12

Top 10 USA—9th Kara Goucher (15:49.39); 10th Shalane Flanagan (15:50.80).

10,000 meters

		Time
1	Tirunesh Dibaba, ETH	29:54.66
2	Elvan Abeylegesse, TUR	29:56.34
3	Shalane Flanagan, USA	30:22.22

Marathon

		Time
1	Constantina Tomescu, ROM	2:26:44
2	Catherine Ndereba, KEN	2:27:06
3	Chunxiu Zhou, CHN	2:27:07

Top USA—27th Blake Russell (2:33:13).

4x100-meter Relay

		Time
1	Russia	42.31
2	Belgium	42.54
3	Nigeria	43.04

RUS—Evgeniya Polyakova, Aleksandra Fedoriva, Yulia Gushchina, Yuliya Chermoshanskaya; **BEL**—Olivia Borlee, Hanna Marien, Elodie Ouerdraogo, Kim Gevaert; **NGR**—Franca Idoko, Glorida Kemasuode, Halimat Ismaila, Oludamola Osayomi.

4x400-meter Relay

		Time
1	United States	3:18.54
2	Russia	3:18.82
3	Jamaica	3:20.40

USA—Mary Wineberg, Allyson Felix, Monique Henderson, Sanya Richards; **RUS**—Yulia Gushchina, Liudmila Litvinova, Tatiana Firova, Anastasia Kapachinskaya; **JAM**—Shericka Williams, Shereefa Lloyd, Rosemarie Whyte, Novelene Williams.

100-meter Hurdles

		Time
1	Dawn Harper, USA	12.54
2	Sally Mclellan, AUS	12.64
3	Priscilla Lopes-Schliep, CAN	12.64

Other Top 10 USA—4th Damu Cherry (12.65); 7th Lolo Jones (12.72).

400-meter Hurdles

		Time
1	Melanie Walker, JAM	52.64
2	Sheena Tosta, USA	53.70
3	Tasha Danvers, GBR	53.84

20-kilometer Walk

		Time
1	Olga Kaniskina, RUS	1:26:31 **OR**
2	Kjersti Platzer, NOR	1:27:07
3	Elisa Rigaudo, ITA	1:27:12

Top USA—31st Joanne Dow (1:34:15).

High Jump

		Distance
1	Tia Hellebaut, BEL	2.05m
2	Blanka Vlasic, CRO	2.05m
3	Anna Chicherova, RUS	2.03m

Top USA—6th Chaunte Howard (1.99m).

Long Jump

		Distance
1	Maurren Higa Maggi, BRA	7.04m
2	Tatyanna Lebedeva, RUS	7.03m
3	Blessing Okagbare, NGR	6.91m

Top USA—5th Brittney Reese (6.76m), 8th Grace Upshaw (6.58m).

Triple Jump

		Distance
1	Francoise Mbango Etone, CMR	15.39m
2	Tatyana Lebedeva, RUS	15.32m
3	Hrysopiyi Devetzi, GRE	15.23m

Shot Put

		Distance
1	Valerie Vili, NZE	20.56m
2	Natalia Mikhnevich, BLR	20.28m
3	Nadzeya Ostapchuk, BLR	19.86m

Discus

		Distance
1	Stephanie Brown Trafton, USA	64.74m
2	Yarelys Barrios, CUB	63.64m
3	Olena Antonova, UKR	62.59m

Other Top 10 USA—10th Aretha Thurmond (59.80)

Javelin

		Distance
1	Barbora Spotakova, CZE	71.42m
2	Maria Abakumova, RUS	70.78m
3	Christina Obergfoll, GER	66.13m

Pole Vault

		Distance
1	Yelena Isinbaeva, RUS	5.05m **WR**
2	Jennifer Stuczynski, USA	4.80m
3	Svetlana Feofanova, RUS	4.75m

Hammer Throw

		Distance
1	Aksana Miankova, BLR	76.34m **OR**
2	Yipsi Moreno, CUB	75.20m
3	Wenxiu Zhang, CHN	74.32m

Heptathlon

		Points
1	Nataliia Dobrynska, UKR	6733
2	Hyleas Fountain, USA	6619
3	Tatiana Chernova, RUS	6591

TRIATHLON

1.5 km swim, 40 km bicycle ride, 10 km run

MEN

		Time
1	Jan Frodeno, GER	1:48:53.28
2	Simon Whitfield, CAN	1:48:58.47
3	Bevan Docherty, NZE	1:49:05.59

Top USA—7th Hunter Kemper (1:49:48.75), 18th Jarrod Shoemaker (1:50:46.39).

WOMEN

		Time
1	Emma Snowsill, AUS	1:58:27.66
2	Vanessa Fernandes, POR	1:59:34.63
3	Emma Moffatt, AUS	1:59:55.84

Top USA—4th Laura Bennett (2:00:21.54); 11th Sarah Haskins (2:01:22.57)

WEIGHTLIFTING

56 kg: 1. Qingquan Long, CHN (292 kg); **2.** Anh. Tuan Hoang, VIE (290); **3.** Eko Yuli Irawan, IND (288).

62 kg: 1. Xiangxiang Zhang, CHN (319 kg); **2.** Diego Salazar, COL (305); **3.** Tritatno, INA (298).

69 kg: 1. Hui Liao, CHN (348 kg); **2.** Vencelas Dabaya-Tientcheu, FRA (338); **3.** Tigran Gevorg Matrirosyan, ARM (338).

77 kg: 1. Jaehyouk Sa, KOR (366 kg); **2.** Jongli Li, CHN (366); **3.** Gevorg Davtyan, ARM (360).

85 kg: 1. Yong Lu, CHN (394 kg); **2.** Andrei Rybakou, BLR (394); **3.** Tigran Varban Martirosyan, ARM (380).

94 kg: 1. Ilya Ilin, KAZ (406 kg); **2.** Szymon Kolecki, POL (403); **3.** Khadzhimurat Akkaev, RUS (399).

105 kg: 1. Andrei Aramnau, BLR (436 kg); **2.** Dmitriy Klokov, RUS (423); **3.** Dmitriy Lapikov, RUS (420).

106+ kg: 1. Matthias Steiner, GER (461 kg); **2.** Evgeny Chigishev, RUS (460); **3.** Viktors Scerbatihs, LAT (448).

WOMEN

48 kg: 1. Xiexia Chen, CHN (212 kg); **2.** Sibel Ozkan, TUR (199); **3.** Wei-Ling Chen, TPE (196).

53 kg: 1. Prapawadee Jaroenrattanatarakoon, THA (221 kg); **2.** Jinhee Yoon, KOR (213); **3.** Nastassia Novikava, BLR (213).

58 kg: 1. Yanqing Chen, CHN (244 kg); **2.** Marina Shainova, RUS (227); **3.** Jong Ae O, PRK (226).

63 kg: 1. Hyon Suk Pak, PRK (241 kg); **2.** Irina Nekrassova, KAZ (240); **3.** Ying-Chi Lu, TPE (231).

69 kg: 1. Chunhong Liu, CHN (286 kg); **2.** Oxana Slivenko, RUS (255); **3.** Natalya Davydova, UKR (250).

75 kg: 1. Lei Cao, CHN (282 kg); **2.** Alla Vazhenina, KAZ (266); **3.** Nadezda Evstyukhina, RUS (264).

76+ kg: 1. Miran Jang, KOR (326 kg); **2.** Olha Korobka, UKR (277); **3.** Mariya Grabovetskaya, KAZ (270).

WRESTLING

Freestyle
MEN

55 kg: 1. Henry Cejudo, USA; **2.** Tomohiro Matsunaga, JPN; **3.** Besik Kudukhov, RUS and Radoslav Velikov, BUL.

60 kg: 1. Mavlet Batirov, RUS; **2.** Vasyl Fedoryshyn, UKR; **3.** Kenichi Yumoto, JPN and Seyedmorad Mohammadi, IRA.

66 kg: 1. Ramazan Sahin, TUR; **2.** Andriy Stadnik, UKR; **3.** Otar Tushishvili, GEO and Sushil Kumar, IND.

74 kg: 1. Buvaysa Saytiev, RUS; **2.** Soslan Tigiev, UZB **3.** Kiril Terziev, BUL and Murad Gaidarov, BLR.

84 kg: 1. Revazi Mindorashvili, GEO; **2.** Yusup Abdusalomov, TJK; **3.** Georgy Ketoev, RUS and Taras Danko, UKR.

96 kg: 1. Shirvani Muradov, RUS; **2.** Taimuraz Tigiyev, KAZ; **3.** George Gogshelidze, GEO and Khetag Gazyumova, AZB

120 kg: 1. Artur Taymazov, UZB; **2.** Bakhtiyar Akmedov, RUS; **3.** David Musulbes, SLO and Marid Mutalimove, KAZ.

WOMEN

48 kg: 1. Carol Huynh, CAN; **2.** Chiharu Icho, JPN; **3.** Mariya Stadnik, AZB and Irini Merleni, UKR.

55 kg: 1. Saori Yoshida, JPN; **2.** Li Xu, CHN; **3.** Jackeline Renteria, COL and Tonya Verbeek, CAN.

63 kg: 1. Kaori Icho, JPN; **2.** Alena Kartashova, RUS; **3.** Randi Miller, USA and Yelena Shalygina, KAZ.

72 kg: 1. Jiao Wang, CHN; **2.** Stanka Zlateva, BUL; **3.** Agnieszka Wieszczek, POL and Kyoko Hamaguchi, JPN.

Greco-Roman
MEN

55 kg: 1. Nazyr Mankiev, RUS; **2.** Rovshan Bayramov, AZB; **3.** Eun-Chul Park, KOR and Roman Amoyan, ARM.

60 kg: 1. Islam-Beka Albiev, RUS; **2.** Vitaliy Rahimov, AZB; **3.** Nurbakyt Tengizbayev, KAZ and Ruslan Tiumenbaev, KYR.

66 kg: 1. Steeve Guenot, FRA; **2.** Kanatbek Begaliev, KYR; **3.** Mikhail Siamionau, BLR and Armen Vardanyan, UKR.

74 kg: 1. Manuchar Kvirkelia, GEO; **2.** Yongxhiang Chang, CHN **3.** Yavor Yanakiev, BUL and Christophe Guenot, FRA.

84 kg: 1. Andrea Minguzzi, ITA; **2.** Zotan Fodor, HUN; **3.** Nazmi Avluca, TUR.

96 kg: 1. Aslanbek Khushtov, RUS; **2.** Mirko Englich, GER; **3.** Asset Mambetov, KAZ and Adam Wheeler, USA.

120 kg: 1. Mijan Lopez, CUB; **2.** Khasan Baroev, RUS; **3.** Yuri Patrikeev, ARM and Mindaugas Mizgaitis, LTU.

TEAM SPORTS

BASEBALL

Round Robin Standings

Top four teams advance to medal round. Note that RS stands for Runs Scored and RA stands for Runs Against. (*) indicates team advanced to the medal round.

	Gm	W	L	Pct	RS	RA	Medal Round
*South Korea	7	7	0	1.000	41	22	2-0
*Cuba	7	6	1	.857	52	23	1-1
*United States	7	5	2	.714	40	22	1-1
*Japan	7	4	3	.571	30	14	0-2
Canada	7	2	5	.286	29	20	–
Chinese Taipei	7	2	5	.286	29	33	–
China	7	1	6	.143	14	60	–
Netherlands	7	1	6	.143	9	50	–

Semifinals

South Korea 6 .... Japan 2
Cuba 10 .... United States 2

Bronze Medal

United States 8 .... Japan 4

Gold Medal

South Korea 3 .... Cuba 2

Team USA Batting

	Pos	Avg	AB	R	H	HR	RBI
Jason Donald	IF	.381	21	4	8	1	5
Terry Tiffee	IF	.324	37	4	12	0	5
Louis Marson	C	.308	13	3	4	0	0
Matthew Brown	IF	.281	32	4	9	2	10
Brian Barden	IF	.265	34	8	9	1	5
Dexter Fowler	OF	.250	28	5	7	0	2
John Gall	OF	.242	33	5	8	1	5
Nate Schierholtz	OF	.216	37	7	8	1	6
Jayson Nix	2B	.214	14	3	3	1	1
Taylor Teagarden	C	.188	16	2	3	0	4
Matt LaPorta	OF	.158	19	3	3	2	4
Mike Hessman	IF	.091	22	2	2	1	1
TOTALS		.248	306	50	76	10	48
OPPONENTS		.214	299	36	64	10	33

Team USA Pitching

	ERA	Gm	W-L	SV	IP	BB	SO
Jake Arrieta	0.00	1	1-0	0	6.0	2	7
Kevin Jepsen	0.00	4	0-0	1	5.2	2	5
Mike Koplove	0.00	4	0-0	0	5.1	1	6
Casey Weathers	0.00	3	0-0	0	3.0	1	5
Brian Duensing	1.17	4	1-0	0	7.2	2	5
Jeremy Cummings	1.80	2	0-0	0	5.0	0	2
Trevor Cahill	2.25	2	0-0	0	8.0	5	5
Stephen Strasburg	2.45	2	1-1	0	11.0	1	16
Brett Anderson	4.97	2	1-0	0	12.2	3	10
Brandon Knight	5.91	2	1-0	0	10.2	4	7
Blaine Neal	7.36	3	0-0	0	3.2	0	2
Jeff Stevens	9.00	4	1-2	0	4.0	1	2
TOTALS	3.05	9	6-3	1	82.2	22	72
OPPONENTS	4.97	9	3-6	1	79.2	34	80

BASKETBALL

MEN

Round Robin Standings

Top four teams advance to medal round.

Group A	Gm	W	L	Pts	Points For	Opp	Medal Round
*Lithuania	5	4	1	9	425	400	1-2
*Argentina	5	4	1	9	425	361	2-1
*Croatia	5	3	2	8	399	380	0-1
*Australia	5	3	2	8	457	405	0-1
Russia	5	1	4	6	387	406	–
Iran	5	0	5	5	323	464	–

Group B	Gm	W	L	Pts	Points For	Opp	Medal Round
*United States	5	5	0	10	515	354	3-0
*Spain	5	4	1	9	418	369	2-1
*Greece	5	3	2	8	415	375	0-1
*China	5	2	3	7	366	400	0-1
Germany	5	1	4	6	330	390	–
Angola	5	0	5	5	321	477	–

Quarterfinals

Argentina 80 ....Greece 78
USA 116 ....Australia 85
Spain 72 ....Croatia 59
Lithuania 94 ....China 68

Semifinals

USA 101 ....Argentina 81
Spain 91 ....Lithuania 86

Bronze Medal

Argentina 87 ....Lithuania 75

Gold Medal

United States 118 ....Spain 107

Team USA Scoring

	Gm	FG%	FT%	—Per Game— Min	Pts	Reb	Ast
Dwyane Wade	8	.671	.634	18.8	16.0	4.0	1.9
LeBron James	8	.602	.458	24.8	15.5	5.3	3.8
Kobe Bryant	8	.462	.583	23.5	15.0	2.8	2.1
Carmelo Anthony	8	.422	.828	19.1	11.5	4.3	0.4
Dwight Howard	8	.745	.459	16.1	10.9	5.8	0.5
Chris Bosh	8	.774	.862	17.3	9.1	6.1	0.3
Deron Williams	8	.442	.900	19.0	8.0	2.3	2.8
Chris Paul	8	.500	.917	21.9	8.0	3.6	4.1
Tayshaun Prince	8	.591	.500	11.0	4.3	1.9	0.3
Carlos Boozer	8	.556	.750	6.0	3.3	1.9	0.3
Michael Redd	8	.323	.000	9.1	3.1	1.1	0.5
Jason Kidd	8	.857	.000	13.5	1.6	1.6	2.0
TOTALS	8	.550	.377	200.0	106.2	41.5	18.8
OPPONENTS	8	.403	.299	200.0	78.4	35.9	10.6

WOMEN

Round Robin Standings

Top four teams advance to medal round.

Group A	Gm	W	L	Pts	Points For	Opp	Medal Round
*Australia	5	5	0	10	424	319	2-1
*Russia	5	4	1	9	339	333	2-1
*Belarus	5	2	3	7	324	332	0-1
*South Korea	5	2	3	7	327	360	0-1
Latvia	5	1	4	6	334	387	–
Brazil	5	1	4	6	337	354	–

Group B	Gm	W	L	Pts	Points For	Opp	Medal Round
*United States	5	5	0	10	491	276	3-0
*China	5	4	1	9	358	346	1-2
*Spain	5	3	2	8	357	324	0-1
*Czech Republic	5	2	3	7	346	356	0-1
New Zealand	5	1	4	6	320	423	–
Mali	5	0	5	5	255	402	–

Quarterfinals

China 77 ....Belarus 62
Australia 79 ....Czech Republic 46
USA 104 ....South Korea 50
Russia 84 ....Spain 65

Semifinals

United States 67 ....Russia 52
Australia 90 ....China 56

Bronze Medal

Russia 94 ....China 81

Gold Medal

United States 92 ....Australia 65

Team USA Scoring

	Gm	FG%	FT%	Min	Pts	Reb	Ast
					—Per Game—		
Sylvia Fowles	8	.643	.680	17.9	13.4	8.4	0.9
Tina Thompson	8	.494	.739	21.9	12.8	3.9	1.5
Diana Taurasi	8	.492	1.000	19.5	10.9	3.9	2.4
Lisa Leslie	8	.576	.417	17.9	9.4	4.5	0.5
Candace Parker	8	.614	.677	16.5	9.4	4.5	0.8
Seimone Augustus	8	.466	.818	17.8	7.9	2.3	1.4
Kara Lawson	8	.656	1.000	16.3	7.0	2.0	3.0
Tamika Catchings	8	.724	.583	16.0	6.8	4.4	1.8
Cappie Pondexter	8	.579	.750	11.6	6.4	0.9	2.1
Katie Smith	8	.421	1.000	18.0	4.9	2.5	1.9
Sue Bird	8	.323	.500	18.5	3.0	2.3	1.8
DeLisha Milton-Jones	7	.556	.714	9.4	2.1	1.3	0.4
TOTALS	8	.542	.719	200.0	94.2	43.0	18.3
OPPONENTS	8	.339	.650	200.0	56.6	30.4	10.1

FIELD HOCKEY

MEN

Round Robin Standings

Top two teams advance to medal round.

Group A	Gm	W	L	T	Pts	GF	GA	Medal Round
*Spain	5	4	1	0	12	9	5	1-1
*Germany	5	3	0	2	11	12	6	2-0
New Zealand	5	2	2	1	7	10	9	—
South Korea	5	2	2	1	7	13	11	—
Belgium	5	1	3	1	4	9	13	—
China	5	0	4	1	1	7	16	—

Group B	Gm	W	L	T	Pts	GF	GA	Medal Round
*Netherlands	5	4	0	1	13	16	6	0-2
*Australia	5	3	0	2	11	24	7	1-1
Great Britain	5	2	1	2	8	10	7	—
Pakistan	5	2	3	0	6	11	13	—
Canada	5	1	3	1	4	10	17	—
South Africa	5	0	5	0	0	4	25	—

Semifinals

Germany 4 .... Netherlands 3
Spain 3 .... Australia 2

Bronze Medal

Australia 6 .... Netherlands 2

Gold Medal

Germany 1 .... Spain 0

WOMEN

Round Robin Standings

Top two teams advance to medal round.

Group A	Gm	W	L	T	Pts	GF	GA	Medal Round
*Netherlands	5	5	0	0	15	14	3	2-0
*China	5	3	1	1	10	14	4	1-1
Australia	5	3	1	1	10	17	9	—
Spain	5	2	3	0	6	4	12	—
South Korea	5	1	4	0	3	13	18	—
South Africa	5	0	5	0	0	2	18	—

BASKETBALL (Group B)

Group B	Gm	W	L	T	Pts	GF	GA	Medal Round
*Germany	5	4	1	0	12	12	8	0-2
*Argentina	5	3	0	2	11	13	7	1-1
Great Britain	5	2	1	2	8	7	9	—
United States	5	1	1	3	6	9	8	—
Japan	5	1	3	1	4	5	7	—
New Zealand	5	0	5	0	0	6	13	—

Semifinals

Netherlands 5 ....,.... Argentina 2
China 3 .... Germany 2

Bronze Medal

Argentina 3 .... Germany 1

Gold Medal

Netherlands 2 .... China 0

SOCCER

MEN

Group A	Gm	W	L	T	Pts	GF	GA	Medal Round
*Argentina	3	3	0	0	9	5	1	3-0
*Ivory Coast	3	2	1	0	6	6	4	0-1
Australia	3	0	2	1	1	3	—
Serbia	3	0	2	1	1	3	7	—

Group B	Gm	W	L	T	Pts	GF	GA	Medal Round
*Nigeria	3	2	0	1	7	4	2	2-1
*Netherlands	3	1	0	2	5	3	2	0-1
United States	3	1	1	1	4	4	4	—
Japan	3	0	3	0	0	1	4	—

Group C	Gm	W	L	T	Pts	GF	GA	Medal Round
*Brazil	3	3	0	0	9	9	0	2-1
*Belgium	3	2	1	3	6	3	1	1-2
China	3	0	2	1	1	6	1	—
New Zealand	3	0	2	1	1	7	1	—

Group D	Gm	W	L	T	Pts	GF	GA	Medal Round
*Italy	3	2	0	1	7	6	0	0-1
*Cameroon	3	1	0	2	5	2	1	0-1
South Korea	3	1	1	1	4	2	4	—
Honduras	3	0	3	0	0	0	5	—

Quarterfinals

Brazil 2 .... Cameroon 0
Belgium 3 .... Italy 2
Argentina 2 .... OT .... Netherlands 1
Nigeria 2 .... Ivory Coast 0

Semifinals

Argentina 3 .... Brazil 0
Nigeria 4 .... Belgium 1

Bronze Medal

Brazil 3 .... Belgium 0

Gold Medal

Argentina 1 .... Nigeria 0

WOMEN

Group E	Gm	W	L	T	Pts	GF	GA	Medal Round
*China	3	2	0	1	7	5	2	0-1
*Sweden	3	2	1	0	4	3	3	0-1
*Canada	3	1	1	1	4	4	4	0-1
Argentina	3	0	3	0	0	1	5	–

Group F	Gm	W	L	T	Pts	GF	GA	Medal Round
*Brazil	3	2	0	1	7	5	2	2-1
*Germany	3	2	0	1	7	2	0	2-1
North Korea	3	1	2	0	3	2	3	–
Nigeria	3	0	3	0	0	1	2	–

Group G	Gm	W	L	T	Pts	GF	GA	Medal Round
*Norway	3	2	1	0	6	4	5	0-1
*United States	3	2	1	0	6	5	3	3-0
*Japan	3	1	1	1	4	7	4	1-2
New Zealand	3	0	2	1	1	2	7	–

Quarterfinals

Japan 2	China 0
Germany 2 ....OT	Sweden 0
United States 2 .....OT	Canada 1
Brazil 2	Norway 1

Semifinals

Brazil 4	Germany 1
United States 4	Japan 2

Bronze Medal

Germany 2	Japan 0

Gold Medal

United States 1 .....OT	Brazil 0

SOFTBALL

Top four teams advance to semifinals.

	Gm	W	L	RF	RA	Medal Round
*United States	7	7	0	53	15	1-1
*Japan	7	6	1	23	13	2-1
*Australia	7	5	2	30	11	1-1
*Canada	7	3	4	17	23	0-1
Venezuela	7	2	5	15	35	–
China	7	2	5	19	21	–
Taiwan	7	2	5	10	23	–
Netherlands	7	1	6	8	48	–

Semifinals

United States 4	Japan 1
Australia 5	Canada 3

Bronze Medal
(loser gets medal)

Japan 4	Australia 3 (12 inn.)

Gold Medal

Japan 3	United States 1

Olympic Baseball and Softball No More

In July 2005, the International Olympic Committee voted baseball and softball out of the Olympic Games effective in 2012 in London. A large reason for the decision was the total American dominance in softball. Ironically, the USA would lose the gold medal match to Japan in 2008.

TEAM HANDBALL

Top four teams in each group advance to medal round.

MEN

Group A	Gm	W	L	T	Pts	GF	GA	Medal Round
*France	5	4	0	1	9	148	115	3-0
*Poland	5	3	1	1	7	147	128	0-1
*Croatia	5	3	2	0	6	140	115	1-2
*Spain	5	3	2	0	6	152	145	2-1
Brazil	5	1	4	0	2	129	153	–
China	0	0	5	0	0	104	164	–

Group B	Gm	W	L	T	Pts	GF	GA	Medal Round
*South Korea	5	3	2	0	6	122	129	0-1
*Iceland	5	2	1	2	6	151	146	2-1
*Denmark	5	2	1	2	6	137	131	0-1
*Russia	5	2	2	1	5	136	131	0-1
Germany	5	2	2	1	5	126	130	–
Egypt	5	0	3	2	2	127	132	–

Quarterfinals

France 27	Russia 24
Iceland 32	Poland 30
Croatia 26	Denmark 24
Spain 29	South Korea 24

Semifinals

France 25	Croatia 23
Iceland 36	Spain 30

Bronze Medal

Spain 35	Croatia 29

Gold Medal

France 28	Iceland 23

WOMEN

Group A	Gm	W	L	T	Pts	GF	GA	Medal Round
*Norway	5	5	0	0	10	154	106	3-0
*Romania	5	4	1	0	8	150	112	0-1
*China	5	2	3	0	4	122	135	0-1
*France	5	2	3	0	4	121	128	0-1
Kazakhstan	5	1	3	1	3	109	137	–
Angola	5	0	4	1	1	109	147	–

Group B	Gm	W	L	T	Pts	GF	GA	Medal Round
*Russia	5	4	0	1	9	148	125	2-1
*South Korea	5	3	1	1	7	155	127	2-1
*Hungary	5	2	2	1	5	129	142	1-2
*Sweden	5	2	3	0	4	123	137	0-1
Brazil	5	1	3	1	3	124	137	–
Germany	5	1	4	0	2	123	134	–

Quarterfinals

Norway 31	Sweden 24
Hungary 34	Romania 30
South Korea 31	China 23
Russia 32	France 31

Semifinals

Norway 29	South Korea 28
Russia 22	Hungary 20

Bronze Medal

South Korea 33	Hungary 28

Gold Medal

Norway 34	Russia 27

VOLLEYBALL

Top four teams advance to quarterfinals. Note that SF stands for Sets For and SA stands for Sets Against.

MEN

Group A	Gm	W	L	Pts	SF	SA	Medal Round
*United States	5	5	0	10	15	4	3-0
*Italy	5	4	1	9	13	6	1-2
*Bulgaria	5	3	2	8	10	9	0-1
*China	5	2	3	7	9	13	0-1
Venezuela	5	1	4	6	8	12	–
Japan	5	0	5	0	4	15	–

Group B	Gm	W	L	Pts	SF	SA	Medal Round
*Brazil	5	4	1	9	13	4	2-1
*Russia	5	4	1	9	14	7	2-1
*Poland	5	4	1	9	12	6	0-1
*Serbia	5	2	3	9	10	7	0-1
Germany	5	1	4	6	6	12	–
Egypt	5	0	5	5	0	15	–

Quarterfinals

United States 3 ....Serbia 2
(20-25, 25-23, 21-25, 25-18, 15-12)
Italy 3 ....Poland 2
(25-19, 25-22, 18-25, 26-28, 17-15)
Brazil 3 ....China 0
(25-17, 25-15, 25-16)
Russia 3 ....Bulgaria 1
(20-25, 25-16, 25-22, 25-21)

Semifinals

United States 3 ....Russia 2
(25-22, 25-21, 25-27, 22-25, 15-13)
Brazil 3 ....Italy 1
(19-25, 25-18, 25-21, 25-22)

Bronze Medal

Russia 3 ....Italy 0
(25-22, 25-19, 25-23)

Gold Medal

United States 3 ....Brazil 1
(20-25, 25-22, 25-21, 25-23)

WOMEN

Group A	Gm	W	L	Pts	SF	SA	Medal Round
*Cuba	5	5	0	10	15	3	1-2
*United States	5	4	1	9	12	9	2-1
*China	5	3	2	8	13	7	2-1
*Japan	5	2	3	7	7	11	0-1
Poland	5	1	4	6	9	12	–
Venezuela	5	0	5	5	1	15	–

Group B	Gm	W	L	Pts	SF	SA	Medal Round
*Brazil	5	5	0	10	15	0	3-0
*Italy	5	4	1	9	12	4	0-1
*Russia	5	3	2	8	10	6	0-1
*Serbia	5	2	3	7	6	10	0-1
Kazakhstan	5	1	4	6	4	13	–
Algeria	5	0	5	5	1	15	–

Quarterfinals

Cuba 3 ....Serbia 0
(26-24, 25-19, 26-24)
Brazil 3 ....Japan 0
(25-12, 25-20, 25-16)
China 3 ....Russia 0
(25-22, 27-25, 25-19)
United States 3 ....Italy 2
(20-25, 25-21, 19-25, 25-18, 15-6)

Semifinals

Brazil 3 ....China 0
(27-25, 25-2, 25-14)
United States 3 ....Cuba 0
(25-20, 25-16, 25-17)

Bronze Medal

China 3 ....Cuba 1
(25-16, 21-25, 25-13, 25-20)

Gold Medal

Brazil 3 ....United States 1
(25-15, 18-25, 25-13, 25-21)

WATER POLO

MEN

Round Robin Standings

Top three teams in each group advance.

Group A	Gm	W	L	T	Pts	GF	GA	Medal Round
*Hungary	5	4	0	1	9	60	36	2-0
*Spain	5	4	1	0	8	52	34	0-1
*Montenegro	5	2	1	2	6	43	33	1-2
Australia	5	2	2	1	5	45	40	–
Greece	5	1	4	0	2	39	56	–
Canada	5	0	5	0	0	21	61	–

Group B	Gm	W	L	T	Pts	GF	GA	Medal Round
*United States	5	4	1	0	8	37	31	1-1
*Croatia	5	4	1	0	8	56	31	0-1
*Serbia	5	3	2	0	6	50	38	2-1
Germany	5	2	3	0	4	33	44	–
Italy	5	2	3	0	4	57	50	–
China	5	0	5	0	0	25	64	–

Quarterfinals

Montenegro 7 ....Croatia 6
Serbia 9 ....Spain 5

Semifinals

United States 10 ....Serbia 5
Hungary 11 ....Montenegro 9

Bronze Medal

Serbia 6 ....Montenegro 4

Gold Medal

Hungary 14 ....United States 10

WOMEN

Round Robin Standings

Top three teams in each group advance.

Group A	Gm	W	L	T	Pts	GF	GA	Medal Round
*United States	3	2	0	1	5	33	27	1-1
*Italy	3	2	0	1	5	28	26	0-1
*China	3	1	2	0	2	33	33	0-1
Russia	3	0	3	0	0	26	34	–

Group B	Gm	W	L	T	Pts	GF	GA	Medal Round
*Hungary	3	2	0	1	5	28	20	0-2
*Australia	3	2	0	1	5	25	22	2-1
*Netherlands	3	1	2	0	2	27	27	3-0
Greece	3	0	3	0	0	16	27	–

Quarterfinals

Netherlands 13 ....Italy 11
Australia 12 ....China 11

Semifinals

Netherlands 8 ....Hungary 7
United States 9 ....Australia 8

Bronze Medal

Australia 12 ....Hungary 11

Gold Medal

Netherlands 9 ....United States 8

1896-2008
Through the Years

SPORTS ALMANAC

Modern Olympic Games

The original Olympic Games were celebrated as a religious festival from 776 B.C. until 393 A.D., when Roman emperor Theo-dosius I banned all pagan festivals (the Olympics celebrated the Greek god Zeus). On June 23, 1894, French educator Baron Pierre de Coubertin, speaking at the Sorbonne in Paris to a gathering of international sports leaders, proposed that the ancient games be revived on an international scale. The idea was enthusiastically received and the Modern Olympics were born. The first Olympics were held two years later in Athens, where 245 athletes from 14 nations competed in the ancient Panathenaic stadium to large and ardent crowds. Americans captured nine out of 12 track and field events, but Greece won the most medals with 47.

The Summer Olympics

Year	No	Location	Dates	Nations	Most medals	USA medals	
1896	I	Athens, GRE	Apr. 6-15	14	Greece (10-19-18—47)	11- 6- 2— 19	(2nd)
1900	II	Paris, FRA	May 20-Oct. 28	26	France (26-37-32—95)	18-14-15— 47	(2nd)
1904	III	St. Louis, USA. . . .	July 1-Nov. 23	13	USA (78-84-82—244)	78-84-82—244	(1st)
1906-a	—	Athens, GRE	Apr. 22-May 2	20	France (15-9-16—40)	12-6- 6— 24	(3rd)
1908	IV	London, GBR	Apr. 27-Oct. 31	22	Britain (54-46-38—138)	23-12-12— 47	(2nd)
1912	V	Stockholm, SWE . .	May 5-July 22	28	Sweden (23-24-17—64)	25-18-20— 63	(2nd)
1916	VI	Berlin, GER	Cancelled (WWI)				
1920	VII	Antwerp, BEL	Apr. 20-Sept. 12	29	USA (41-27-27—95)	41-27-27— 95	(1st)
1924	VIII	Paris, FRA	May 4-July 27	44	USA (45-27-27—99)	45-27-27— 99	(1st)
1928	IX	Amsterdam, NED . .	May 17-Aug. 12	46	USA (22-18-16—56)	22-18-16— 56	(1st)
1932	X	Los Angeles, USA. .	July 30-Aug. 14	37	USA (41-32-30—103)	41-32-30—103	(1st)
1936	XI	Berlin, GER	Aug. 1-16	49	Germany (33-26-30—89)	24-20-12— 56	(2nd)
1940-b	XII	Tokyo, JPN	Cancelled (WWII)				
1944	XIII	London, GBR	Cancelled (WWII)				
1948	XIV	London, GBR	July 29-Aug. 14 .	59	USA (38-27-19—84)	38-27-19— 84	(1st)
1952-cd	XV	Helsinki, FIN	July 19-Aug. 3	69	USA (40-19-17—76)	40-19-17— 76	(1st)
1956-e	XVI	Melbourne, AUS . .	Nov. 22-Dec. 8	72	USSR (37-29-32—98)	32-25-17— 74	(2nd)
1960	XVII	Rome, ITA	Aug. 25-Sept. 11	83	USSR (43-29-31—103)	34-21-16— 71	(2nd)
1964	XVIII	Tokyo, JPN	Oct. 10-24	93	USSR (30-31-35—96)	36-26-28— 90	(2nd)
1968-f	XIX	Mexico City, MEX	Oct. 12-27	112	USA (45-28-34—107)	45-28-34—107	(1st)
1972	XX	Munich, W. GER . .	Aug. 26-Sept. 10	121	USSR (50-27-22—99)	33-31-30— 94	(2nd)
1976-g	XXI	Montreal, CAN . . .	July 17-Aug. 1	92	USSR (49-41-35—125)	34-35-25— 94	(3rd)
1980-h	XXII	Moscow, USSR . . .	July 19-Aug. 3	80	USSR (80-69-46—195)	Boycotted games	
1984-i	XXIII	Los Angeles, USA .	July 28-Aug. 12	140	USA (83-61-30—174)	83-61-30—174	(1st)
1988.	XXIV	Seoul, S. KOR . . .	Sept. 17-Oct. 2	159	USSR (55-31-46—132)	36-31-27— 94	(3rd)
1992-j	XXV	Barcelona, SPA . . .	July 25-Aug. 9	169	UT (45-38-29—112)	37-34-37—108	(2nd)
1996	XXVI	Atlanta, USA	July 20-Aug. 4	197	USA (44-32-25—101)	44-32-25—101	(1st)
2000	XXVII	Sydney, AUS	Sept. 15-Oct. 1	199	USA (40-24-33—97)	40-24-33— 97	(1st)
2004	XXVIII	Athens, GRE	Aug. 13-29	202	USA (35-39-29—103)	35-39-29—103	(1st)
2008	XXIX	Beijing, CHN	Aug. 8-24	204	USA (36-38-36—110)	36-38-36—110	(1st)
2012	XXX	London, ENG	July 27-Aug. 12				

a—The 1906 Intercalated Games in Athens are considered unofficial by the IOC because they did not take place in the four-year cycle established in 1896. However, most record books include these interim games with the others.

b—The 1940 Summer Games are originally scheduled for Tokyo, but Japan resigns as host after the outbreak of the Sino-Japanese War in 1937. Helsinki is the next choice, but the IOC cancels the Games after Soviet troops invade Finland in 1939.

c—Germany and Japan are allowed to rejoin the Olympic community for the first Summer Games since 1936. Though a divided country, the Germans send a joint East-West team until 1964.

d—The Soviet Union (USSR) participates in its first Olympics, Winter or Summer, since the Russian revolution in 1917 and takes home the second most medals (22-30-19—71).

e—Due to Australian quarantine laws, the equestrian events for the 1956 Games are held in Stockholm, June 10-17.

f—East Germany and West Germany send separate teams for the first time and will continue to do so through 1988.

g—The 1976 Games are boycotted by 32 nations, most of them from black Africa, because the IOC will not ban New Zealand. Earlier that year, a rugby team from New Zealand had toured racially segregated South Africa.

h—The 1980 Games are boycotted by 64 nations, led by the USA, to protest the Soviet invasion of Afghanistan on Dec. 27, 1979.

i—The 1984 Games are boycotted by 14 Eastern Bloc nations, led by the USSR, to protest America's overcommercialization of the Games, inadequate security and an anti-Soviet attitude by the U.S. government. Most believe, however, the communist walkout is simply revenge for 1980.

j—Germany sends a single team after East and West German reunification in 1990 and the USSR competes as the Unified Team after the breakup of the Soviet Union in 1991.

Event-by-Event

Gold medal winners from 1896-2008 in the following events: Baseball, Basketball, Boxing, Diving, Field Hockey, Gymnastics, Soccer, Softball, Swimming, Tennis and Track & Field.

BASEBALL

Multiple gold medals: Cuba (3).

Year		Year	
1992	**Cuba**, Taiwan, Japan	2004	**Cuba**, Australia, Japan
1996	**Cuba**, Japan, United States	2008	**South Korea**, Cuba, United States
2000	**United States**, Cuba, South Korea		

U.S. Medal-Winning Baseball Teams

1996 (bronze medal): P–Kris Benson, R.A. Dickey, Seth Greisinger, Billy Koch, Braden Looper, Jim Parque and Jeff Weaver; C–A.J. Hinch, Matt LeCroy and Brian Lloyd; INF–Troy Glaus, Kip Harkrider, Travis Lee, Warren Morris, Augie Ojeda and Jason Williams; OF–Chad Allen, Chad Green, Jacque Jones and Mark Kotsay; Manager–Skip Bertman. Final: Cuba over Japan, 13-9

2000 (gold medal): P–Kurt Ainsworth, Ryan Franklin, Chris George, Shane Heams, Rick Krivda, Roy Oswalt, Jon Rauch, Bobby Seay, Ben Sheets, Todd Williams and Tim Young; C–Pat Borders, Marcus Jensen and Mike Kinkade; INF–Brent Abernathy, Sean Burroughs, Jim Cotton, Gookie Dawkins, Adam Everett and Doug Mientkiewicz; OF–Mike Neill, Anthony Sanders, Brad Wilkerson and Ernie Young; Manager–Tommy Lasorda. Final: USA over Cuba, 4-0.

2008 (bronze medal): P–Brett Anderson, Jake Arrieta, Trevor Cahill, Jeremy Cummings, Brian Duensing, Kevin Jepsen, Brandon Knight, Mike Koplove, Blaine Neal, Jeff Stevens, Stephen Strasburg, Casey Weathers; C–Lou Marson, Taylor Teagarden; INF–Brian Barden, Matthew Brown, Jason Donald, Mike Hessman, Jayson Nix, Terry Tiffee; OF–Dexter Fowler, John Gall, Matt LaPorta, Nate Schierholtz; Manager–Davey Johnson. Final: South Korea over Cuba, 3-2.

BASKETBALL

MEN

Multiple gold medals: USA (13), USSR (2).

Year		Year	
1936	**United States**, Canada, Mexico	1980	**Yugoslavia**, Italy, Soviet Union
1948	**United States**, France, Brazil	1984	**United States**, Spain, Yugoslavia
1952	**United States**, Soviet Union, Uruguay	1988	**Soviet Union**, Yugoslavia, United States
1956	**United States**, Soviet Union, Uruguay	1992	**United States**, Croatia, Lithuania
1960	**United States**, Soviet Union, Brazil	1996	**United States**, Yugoslavia, Lithuania
1964	**United States**, Soviet Union, Brazil	2000	**United States**, France, Lithuania
1968	**United States**, Yugoslavia, Soviet Union	2004	**Argentina**, Italy, United States
1972	**Soviet Union**, United States, Cuba	2008	**United States**, Spain, Argentina
1976	**United States**, Yugoslavia, Soviet Union		

U.S. Medal-Winning Men's Basketball Teams

1936 (gold medal): Sam Balter, Ralph Bishop, Joe Fortenberry, Tex Gibbons, Francis Johnson, Carl Knowles, Frank Lubin, Art Mollner, Don Piper, Jack Ragland, Carl Shy, Willard Schmidt, Duane Swanson and William Wheatley. Coach–Jim Needles; Assistant–Gene Johnson. Final: USA over Canada, 19-8.

1948 (gold medal): Cliff Barker, Don Barksdale, Ralph Beard, Louis Beck, Vince Boryla, Gordon Carpenter, Alex Groza, Wallace Jones, Bob Kurland, Ray Lumpp, R.C. Pitts, Jesse Renick, Robert (Jackie) Robinson and Ken Rollins. Coach–Omar Browning; Assistant–Adolph Rupp. Final: USA over France, 65-21.

1952 (gold medal): Ron Bontemps, Mark Freiberger, Wayne Glasgow, Charlie Hoag, Bill Hougland, John Keller, Dean Kelley, Bob Kenney, Bob Kurland, Bill Lienhard, Clyde Lovellette, Frank McCabe, Dan Pippin and Howie Williams. Coach–Warren Womble; Assistant–Forrest (Phog) Allen. Final: USA over USSR, 36-25.

1956 (gold medal): Dick Boushka, Carl Cain, Chuck Darling, Bill Evans, Gib Ford, Burdy Haldorson, Bill Hougland, Bob Jeangerard, K.C. Jones, Bill Russell, Ron Tomsic and Jim Walsh. Coach–Gerald Tucker; Assistant–Bruce Drake. Final: USA over USSR, 89-55.

1960 (gold medal): Jay Arnette, Walt Bellamy, Bob Boozer, Terry Dischinger, Jerry Lucas, Oscar Robertson, Adrian Smith, Burdy Haldorson, Darrall Imhoff, Allen Kelley, Lester Lane and Jerry West. Coach–Pete Newell; Assistant–Warren Womble. Final round: USA defeated USSR (81-57), Italy (112-81) and Brazil (90-63) in round robin.

1964 (gold medal): Jim (Bad News) Barnes, Bill Bradley, Larry Brown, Joe Caldwell, Mel Counts, Dick Davies, Walt Hazzard, Lucious Jackson, Pete McCaffrey, Jeff Mullins, Jerry Shipp and George Wilson. Coach–Hank Iba; Assistant–Henry Vaughn. Final: USA over USSR, 73-59.

1968 (gold medal): Mike Barrett, John Clawson, Don Dee, Cal Fowler, Spencer Haywood, Bill Hosket, Jim King, Glynn Saulters, Charlie Scott, Mike Silliman, Ken Spain, and Jo Jo White. Coach–Hank Iba; Assistant–Henry Vaughn. Final: USA over Yugoslavia, 65-50.

1972 (silver medal refused): Mike Bantom, Jim Brewer, Tom Burleson, Doug Collins, Kenny Davis, Jim Forbes, Tom Henderson, Bobby Jones, Dwight Jones, Kevin Joyce, Tom McMillen and Ed Ratleff. Coach–Hank Iba; Assistants– John Bach and Don Haskins. Final: USSR over USA, 51-50.

1976 (gold medal): Tate Armstrong, Quinn Buckner, Kenny Carr, Adrian Dantley, Walter Davis, Phil Ford, Ernie Grunfeld, Phil Hubbard, Mitch Kupchak, Tommy LaGarde, Scott May and Steve Sheppard. Coach–Dean Smith; Assistants–Bill Guthridge and John Thompson. Final: USA over Yugoslavia, 95-74.

1980 (no medal): USA boycotted Moscow Games. Final: Yugoslavia over Italy, 86-77.

1984 (gold medal): Steve Alford, Patrick Ewing, Vern Fleming, Michael Jordan, Joe Kleine, Jon Koncak, Chris Mullin, Sam Perkins, Alvin Robertson, Wayman Tisdale, Jeff Turner and Leon Wood. Coach–Bobby Knight; Assistants– Don Donoher and George Raveling. Final: USA over Spain, 96-65.

1988 (bronze medal): Stacey Augmon, Willie Anderson, Bimbo Coles, Jeff Grayer, Hersey Hawkins, Dan Majerle, Danny Manning, Mitch Richmond, J.R. Reid, David Robinson, Charles D. Smith and Charles E. Smith. Coach–John Thompson; Assistants–George Raveling and Mary Fenlon. Final: USSR over Yugoslavia, 76-63.

Basketball (Cont.)

1992 (gold medal): Charles Barkley, Larry Bird, Clyde Drexler, Patrick Ewing, Magic Johnson, Michael Jordan, Christian Laettner, Karl Malone, Chris Mullin, Scottie Pippen, David Robinson and John Stockton. Coach—Chuck Daly; Assistants—Lenny Wilkens, Mike Krzyzewski and P.J. Carlesimo. Final: USA over Croatia, 117-85.

1996 (gold medal): Charles Barkley, Anfernee Hardaway, Grant Hill, Karl Malone, Reggie Miller, Hakeem Olajuwon, Shaquille O'Neal, Gary Payton, Scottie Pippen, David Robinson and John Stockton. Coach—Lenny Wilkens; Assistants—Bobby Cremins, Clem Haskins and Jerry Sloan. Final: USA over Yugoslavia, 95-69.

2000 (gold medal): Shareef Abdur-Rahim, Ray Allen, Vin Baker, Vince Carter, Kevin Garnett, Tim Hardaway, Allan Houston, Jason Kidd, Antonio McDyess, Alonzo Mourning, Gary Payton and Steve Smith. Coach—Rudy Tomjanovich; Assistants—Larry Brown, Gene Keady and Tubby Smith. Final: USA over France, 85-75.

2004 (bronze medal): Carmelo Anthony, Carlos Boozer, Tim Duncan, Allen Iverson, LeBron James, Richard Jefferson, Stephon Marbury, Shawn Marion, Lamar Odom, Emeka Okafor, Amare Stoudemire, Dwyane Wade. Coach—Larry Brown; Assistants—Gregg Popovich, Roy Williams, Oliver Purnell, Dr. Sheldon Burns. Final—Argentina over Italy, 84-69.

2008 (gold medal): Carmelo Anthony, Carlos Boozer, Chris Bosh, Kobe Bryant, Dwight Howard, LeBron James, Jason Kidd, Chris Paul, Tayshaun Prince, Michael Redd, Dwyane Wade, Deron Williams. Coach—Mike Krzyzewski; Assistants—Jim Boeheim, Mike D'Antoni, Nate McMillan. Final: USA over Spain, 118-107.

WOMEN

Multiple gold medals: USA (6), USSR/UT (3).

Year		Year	
1976	**Soviet Union**, United States, Bulgaria	1996	**United States**, Brazil, Australia
1980	**Soviet Union**, Bulgaria, Yugoslavia	2000	**United States**, Australia, Brazil
1984	**United States**, South Korea, China	2004	**United States**, Australia, Russia
1988	**United States**, Yugoslavia, Soviet Union	2008	**United States**, Australia, Russia
1992	**Unified Team**, China, Unified Team		

BOXING

Multiple gold medals: László Papp, Felix Savon and Teófilo Stevenson (3); Ariel Hernandez, Angel Herrera, Mario Kindelan, Oliver Kirk, Jerzy Kulej, Boris Lagutin, Harry Mallin, Guillermo Rigondeaux, Oleg Saitov and Hector Vinent (2). All fighters won titles in consecutive Olympics, except Kirk, who won both the bantamweight and featherweight titles in 1904 (he only had to fight once in each division).

Light Flyweight (106 lbs)

Year		Final Match	Year		Final Match
1968	Francisco Rodriguez, VEN	Decision, 3-2	1992	Rogelio Marcelo, CUB	Decision, 24-10
1972	György Gedó, HUN	Decision, 5-0	1996	Daniel Petrov Bojilov, BUL	Decision, 19-6
1976	Jorge Hernandez, CUB	Decision, 4-1	2000	Brahim Asloum, FRA	Decision, 23-10
1980	Shamil Sabyrov, USSR	Decision, 3-2	2004	Yan Bhartelemy, CUB	Decision, 21-16
1984	Paul Gonzales, USA	Default	2008	Shiming Zou, CHN	Retired, 2nd
1988	Ivailo Hristov, BUL	Decision, 5-0			

Flyweight (112 lbs)

Year		Final Match	Year		Final Match
1904	George Finnegan, USA	Stopped, 1st	1968	Ricardo Delgado, MEX	Decision, 5-0
1920	Frank Di Gennara, USA	Decision	1972	Georgi Kostadinov, BUL	Decision, 5-0
1924	Fidel LaBarba, USA	Decision	1976	Leo Randolph, USA	Decision, 3-2
1928	Antal Kocsis, HUN	Decision	1980	Peter Lessov, BUL	Stopped, 2nd
1932	István Énekes, HUN	Decision	1984	Steve McCrory, USA	Decision, 4-1
1936	Willi Kaiser, GER	Decision	1988	Kim Kwang-Sun, S. Kor	Decision, 4-1
1948	Pascual Perez, ARG	Decision	1992	Su Choi-Chol, N. Kor	Decision, 12-2
1952	Nate Brooks, USA	Decision, 3-0	1996	Maikro Romero, CUB	Decision, 12-11
1956	Terence Spinks, GBR	Decision	2000	Wijan Ponlid, THA	Decision, 19-12
1960	Gyula Török, HUN	Decision, 3-2	2004	Yuriorkis Gamboa, CUB	Decision, 38-23
1964	Fernando Atzori, ITA	Decision, 4-1	2008	Somjit JongJohor, THA	Decision, 8-2

Bantamweight (119 lbs)

Year		Final Match	Year		Final Match
1904	Oliver Kirk, USA	Stopped, 3rd	1968	Valery Sokolov, USSR	Stopped, 2nd
1908	Henry Thomas, GBR	Decision	1972	Orlando Martinez, CUB	Decision, 5-0
1920	Clarence Walker, RSA	Decision	1976	Gu Yong-Ju, N. Kor	Decision, 5-0
1924	William Smith, RSA	Decision	1980	Juan Hernandez, CUB	Decision, 5-0
1928	Vittorio Tamagnini, ITA	Decision	1984	Maurizio Stecca, ITA	Decision, 4-1
1932	Horace Gwynne, CAN	Decision	1988	Kennedy McKinney, USA	Decision, 5-0
1936	Ulderico Sergo, ITA	Decision	1992	Joel Casamayor, CUB	Decision, 14-8
1948	Tibor Csik, HUN	Decision	1996	Istvan Kovacs, HUN	Decision, 14-7
1952	Pentti Hämäläinen, FIN	Decision, 2-1	2000	Guillermo Rigondeaux, CUB	Decision, 18-12
1956	Wolfgang Behrendt, GER	Decision	2004	Guillermo Rigondeaux, CUB	Decision, 22-13
1960	Oleg Grigoryev, USSR	Decision	2008	Badar-Uugan Enkhbat, MON	Decision, 16-5
1964	Takao Sakurai, JPN	Stopped, 2nd			

Featherweight (125 lbs)

Year		Final Match	Year		Final Match
1904	Oliver Kirk, USA	Decision	1968	Antonio Roldan, MEX	Won on Disq.
1908	Richard Gunn, GBR	Decision	1972	Boris Kousnetsov, USSR	Decision, 3-2
1920	Paul Fritsch, FRA	Decision	1976	Angel Herrera, CUB	KO, 2nd
1924	John Fields, USA	Decision	1980	Rudi Fink, E. Ger	Decision, 4-1
1928	Lambertus van Klaveren, NED	Decision	1984	Meldrick Taylor, USA	Decision, 5-0
1932	Carmelo Robledo, ARG	Decision	1988	Giovanni Parisi, ITA	Stopped, 1st
1936	Oscar Casanovas, ARG	Decision	1992	Andreas Tews, GER	Decision, 16-7
1948	Ernesto Formenti, ITA	Decision	1996	Somluck Kamsing, THA	Decision, 8-5
1952	Jan Zachara, CZE	Decision, 2-1	2000	Bekzat Sattarkhanov, KAZ	Decision, 22-14
1956	Vladimir Safronov, USSR	Decision	2004	Alexei Tichtchenko, RUS	Decision, 39-17
1960	Francesco Musso, ITA	Decision, 4-1	2008	Vasyl Lomachenko, UKR	TKO, 1st
1964	Stanislav Stepashkin, USSR	Decision, 3-2			

Lightweight (132 lbs)

Year		Final Match	Year		Final Match
1904	Harry Spanger, USA	Decision	1968	Ronnie Harris, USA	Decision, 5-0
1908	Frederick Grace, GBR	Decision	1972	Jan Szczepanski, POL	Decision, 5-0
1920	Samuel Mosberg, USA	Decision	1976	Howard Davis, USA	Decision, 5-0
1924	Hans Nielsen, DEN	Decision	1980	Angel Herrera, CUB	Stopped, 3rd
1928	Carlo Orlandi, ITA	Decision	1984	Pernell Whitaker, USA	Foe quit, 2nd
1932	Lawrence Stevens, S. Afr	Decision	1988	Andreas Zuelow, E. Ger	Decision, 5-0
1936	Imre Harangi, HUN	Decision	1992	Oscar De La Hoya, USA	Decision, 7-2
1948	Gerald Dreyer, S. Afr	Decision	1996	Hocine Soltani, ALG	Tiebreak, 3-3
1952	Aureliano Bolognesi, ITA	Decision, 2-1	2000	Mario Kindelan, CUB	Decision, 14-4
1956	Richard McTaggart, GBR	Decision	2004	Mario Kindelan, CUB	Decision, 30-22
1960	Kazimierz Pazdzior, POL	Decision, 4-1	2008	Alexey Tishchenko, RUS	Decision, 11-9
1964	József Grudzien, POL	Decision, 5-0			

Light Welterweight (141 lbs)

Year		Final Match	Year		Final Match
1952	Charles Adkins, USA	Decision, 2-1	1984	Jerry Page, USA	Decision, 5-0
1956	Vladimir Yengibaryan, USSR	Decision	1988	Vyacheslav Yanovsky, USSR	Decision, 5-0
1960	Bohumil Nemecek, CZE	Decision, 5-0	1992	Hector Vinent, CUB	Decision, 11-1
1964	Jerzy Kulej, POL	Decision, 5-0	1996	Hector Vinent, CUB	Decision, 20-13
1968	Jerzy Kulej, POL	Decision, 3-2	2000	Mahamadkadyz Abdullaev, UZB	Decision, 27-20
1972	Ray Seales, USA	Decision, 3-2	2004	Manus Boonjumnong, THA	Decision, 17-11
1976	Ray Leonard, USA	Decision, 5-0	2008	Felix Diaz, DRP	Decision, 12-4
1980	Patrizio Oliva, ITA	Decision, 4-1			

Welterweight (152 lbs)

Year		Final Match	Year		Final Match
1904	Albert Young, USA	Decision	1968	Manfred Wolke, E. Ger	Decision, 4-1
1920	Bert Schneider, CAN	Decision	1972	Emilio Correa, CUB	Decision, 5-0
1924	Jean Delarge, BEL	Decision	1976	Jochen Bachfeld, E. Ger	Decision, 3-2
1928	Edward Morgan, NZE	Decision	1980	Andrés Aldama, CUB	Decision, 4-1
1932	Edward Flynn, USA	Decision	1984	Mark Breland, USA	Decision, 5-0
1936	Sten Suvio, FIN	Decision	1988	Robert Wangila, KEN	KO, 2nd
1948	Julius Torma, CZE	Decision	1992	Michael Carruth, IRE	Decision, 13-10
1952	Zygmunt Chychla, POL	Decision, 3-0	1996	Oleg Saitov, RUS	Decision, 14-9
1956	Nicolae Linca, ROM	Decision	2000	Oleg Saitov, RUS	Decision, 24-16
1960	Nino Benvenuti, ITA	Decision, 4-1	2004	Bakhtiyar Artayev, KAZ	Decision, 36-26
1964	Marian Kasprzyk, POL	Decision, 4-1	2008	Bakhyt Sarsekbayev, KAZ	Decision, 10-6

Light Middleweight (156 lbs)

Year		Final Match	Year		Final Match
1952	László Papp, HUN	Decision, 3-0	1980	Armando Martinez, CUB	Decision, 4-1
1956	László Papp, HUN	Decision	1984	Frank Tate, USA	Decision, 5-0
1960	Skeeter McClure, USA	Decision, 4-1	1988	Park Si-Hun, S. Kor	Decision, 3-2
1964	Boris Lagutin, USSR	Decision, 4-1	1992	Juan Lemus, CUB	Decision, 6-1
1968	Boris Lagutin, USSR	Decision, 5-0	1996	David Reid, USA	KO, 3rd
1972	Dieter Kottysch, W. Ger	Decision, 3-2	2000	Yermakhan Ibraimov, KAZ	Decision, 25-23
1976	Jerzy Rybicki, POL	Decision, 5-0	2004	weight class eliminated.	

Middleweight (165 lbs)

Year		Final Match	Year		Final Match
1904	Charles Mayer, USA	Stopped, 3rd	1952	Floyd Patterson, USA	KO, 1st
1908	John Douglas, GBR	Decision	1956	Gennady Schatkov, USSR	KO, 1st
1920	Harry Mallin, GBR	Decision	1960	Eddie Crook, USA	Decision, 3-2
1924	Harry Mallin, GBR	Decision	1964	Valery Popenchenko, USSR	Stopped, 1st
1928	Piero Toscani, ITA	Decision	1968	Christopher Finnegan, GBR	Decision, 3-2
1932	Carmen Barth, USA	Decision	1972	Vyacheslav Lemechev, USSR	KO, 1st
1936	Jean Despeaux, FRA	Decision	1976	Michael Spinks, USA	Stopped, 3rd
1948	László Papp, HUN	Decision	1980	José Gomez, CUB	Decision, 4-1

Boxing (Cont.)
Middleweight (Cont.)

Year		Final Match	Year		Final Match
1992	Ariel Hernandez, CUB	Decision, 12-7	1996	Ariel Hernandez, CUB	Decision, 11-3
1984	Shin Joon-Sup, S. Kor	Decision, 3-2	2000	Jorge Gutierrez, CUB	Decision, 17-15
1988	Henry Maske, E. Ger	Decision, 5-0	2004	Gaydarbek Gaydarbekov, RUS	Decision, 28-18
1992	Ariel Hernandez, CUB	Decision, 12-7	2008	James Degale, GBR	Decision, 16-14

Light Heavyweight (178 lbs)

Year		Final Match	Year		Final Match
1920	Eddie Eagan, USA	Decision	1972	Mate Parlov, YUG	Stopped, 2nd
1924	Harry Mitchell, GBR	Decision	1976	Leon Spinks, USA	Stopped, 3rd
1928	Victor Avendaño, ARG	Decision	1980	Slobodan Kacar, YUG	Decision, 4-1
1932	David Carstens, S. Afr	Decision	1984	Anton Josipovic, YUG	Default
1936	Roger Michelot, FRA	Decision	1988	Andrew Maynard, USA	Decision, 5-0
1948	George Hunter, S. Afr	Decision	1992	Torsten May, GER	Decision, 8-3
1952	Norvel Lee, USA	Decision, 3-0	1996	Vasilii Jirov, KAZ	Decision, 17-4
1956	Jim Boyd, USA	Decision	2000	Alexander Lebziak, RUS	Decision, 20-6
1960	Cassius Clay, USA	Decision, 5-0	2004	Andre Ward, USA	Decision, 20-13
1964	Cosimo Pinto, ITA	Decision, 3-2	2008	Xiaoping Zhang, CHN	Decision, 11-7
1968	Dan Poznjak, USSR	Default			

Note: Cassius Clay changed his name to Muhammad Ali after winning the world heavyweight championship in 1964.

Heavyweight (201 lbs)

Year		Final Match	Year		Final Match
1984	Henry Tillman, USA	Decision, 5-0	1996	Felix Savon, CUB	Decision, 20-2
1988	Ray Mercer, USA	KO, 1st	2000	Felix Savon, CUB	Decision, 21-13
1992	Felix Savon, CUB	Decision, 14-1	2004	Odlanier Solis, CUB	Decision, 22-13

Super Heavyweight (Unlimited)

Year		Final Match	Year		Final Match
1904	Samuel Berger, USA	Decision	1968	George Foreman, USA	Stopped, 2nd
1908	Albert Oldham, GBR	KO, 1st	1972	Teófilo Stevenson, CUB	Default
1920	Ronald Rawson, GBR	Decision	1976	Teófilo Stevenson, CUB	KO, 3rd
1924	Otto von Porat, NOR	Decision	1980	Teófilo Stevenson, CUB	Decision, 4-1
1928	Arturo Rodriguez Jurado, ARG	Stopped, 1st	1984	Tyrell Biggs, USA	Decision, 4-1
1932	Santiago Lovell, ARG	Decision	1988	Lennox Lewis, CAN	Stopped, 2nd
1936	Herbert Runge, GER	Decision	1992	Roberto Balado, CUB	Decision, 13-2
1948	Rafael Iglesias, ARG	KO, 2nd	1996	Vladimir Klichko, UKR	Decision, 7-3
1952	Ed Sanders, USA	Won on Disq.*	2000	Audley Harrison, GBR	Decision, 30-16
1956	Pete Rademacher, USA	Stopped, 1st	2004	Alexander Povetkin, RUS	walkover†
1960	Franco De Piccoli, ITA	KO, 1st	2008	Roberto Cammarele, ITA	Stopped, 4th
1964	Joe Frazier, USA	Decision, 3-2			

*Sanders' opponent, Ingemar Johansson, was disqualified in 2nd round for not trying.
†Povetkin was awarded the gold when his opponet Mohamed Aly failed a pre-fight physical due to a shoulder injury.
Note: Super Heavyweight was called heavyweight through 1980.

DIVING

MEN

Multiple gold medals: Greg Louganis (4); Klaus Dibiasi and Xiong Ni (3); Pete Desjardins, Sammy Lee, Tian Liang, Bob Webster and Albert White (2).

Springboard

Year		Points	Year		Points
1908	Albert Zürner, GER	85.5	1968	Bernie Wrightson, USA	170.15
1912	Paul Günther, GER	79.23	1972	Vladimir Vasin, USSR	594.09
1920	Louis Kuehn, USA	675.4	1976	Phil Boggs, USA	619.05
1924	Albert White, USA	696.4	1980	Aleksandr Portnov, USSR	905.03
1928	Pete Desjardins, USA	185.04	1984	Greg Louganis, USA	754.41
1932	Michael Galitzen, USA	161.38	1988	Greg Louganis, USA	730.80
1936	Richard Degener, USA	163.57	1992	Mark Lenzi, USA	676.53
1948	Bruce Harlan, USA	163.64	1996	Xiong Ni, CHN	701.46
1952	David Browning, USA	205.29	2000	Xiong Ni, CHN	708.72
1956	Bob Clotworthy, USA	159.56	2004	Peng Bo, CHN	787.38
1960	Gary Tobian, USA	170.00	2008	Chong He, CHN	572.90
1964	Ken Sitzberger, USA	159.90			

Platform

Year		Points	Year		Points
1904	George Sheldon, USA	12.66	1920	Clarence Pinkston, USA	100.67
1906	Gottlob Walz, GER	156.0	1924	Albert White, USA	97.46
1908	Hjalmar Johansson, SWE	83.75	1928	Pete Desjardins, USA	98.74
1912	Erik Adlerz, SWE	73.94	1932	Harold Smith, USA	124.80

Year		Points
1936	Marshall Wayne, USA	113.58
1948	Sammy Lee, USA	130.05
1952	Sammy Lee, USA	156.28
1956	Joaquin Capilla, MEX	152.44
1960	Bob Webster, USA	165.56
1964	Bob Webster, USA	148.58
1968	Klaus Dibiasi, ITA	164.18
1972	Klaus Dibiasi, ITA	504.12
1976	Klaus Dibiasi, ITA	600.51

Year		Points
1980	Falk Hoffmann, E. Ger	835.65
1984	Greg Louganis, USA	710.91
1988	Greg Louganis, USA	638.61
1992	Sun Shuwei, CHN	677.31
1996	Dmitri Sautin, RUS	692.34
2000	Tian Liang, CHN	724.53
2004	Hu Jia, CHN	748.08
2008	Matthew Mitcham, AUS	537.95

WOMEN

Multiple gold medals: Pat McCormick and Fu Mingxia (4); Ingrid Engel-Krämer and Guo Jingjing (3); Vicki Draves, Dorothy Poynton Hill and Gao Min (2).

Springboard

Year		Points
1920	Aileen Riggin, USA	539.9
1924	Elizabeth Becker, USA	474.5
1928	Helen Meany, USA	78.62
1932	Georgia Coleman, USA	87.52
1936	Marjorie Gestring, USA	89.27
1948	Vicki Draves, USA	108.74
1952	Pat McCormick, USA	147.30
1956	Pat McCormick, USA	142.36
1960	Ingrid Krämer, GER	155.81
1964	Ingrid Engel-Krämer, GER	145.00
1968	Sue Gossick, USA	150.77

Year		Points
1972	Micki King, USA	450.03
1976	Jennifer Chandler, USA	506.19
1980	Irina Kalinina, USSR	725.91
1984	Sylvie Bernier, CAN	530.70
1988	Gao Min, CHN	580.23
1992	Gao Min, CHN	572.40
1996	Fu Mingxia, CHN	547.68
2000	Fu Mingxia, CHN	609.42
2004	Guo Jingjing, CHN	633.15
2008	Guo Jingjing, CHN	415.35

Platform

Year		Points
1912	Greta Johansson, SWE	39.9
1920	Stefani Fryland-Clausen, DEN	34.6
1924	Caroline Smith, USA	33.2
1928	Elizabeth Becker Pinkston, USA	31.6
1932	Dorothy Poynton, USA	40.26
1936	Dorothy Poynton Hill, USA	33.93
1948	Vicki Draves, USA	68.87
1952	Pat McCormick, USA	79.37
1956	Pat McCormick, USA	84.85
1960	Ingrid Krämer, GER	91.28
1964	Lesley Bush, USA	99.80

Year		Points
1968	Milena Duchková, CZE	109.59
1972	Ulrika Knape, SWE	390.00
1976	Elena Vaytsekhovskaya, USSR	406.59
1980	Martina Jäschke, E. Ger	596.25
1984	Zhou Jihong, CHN	435.51
1988	Xu Yanmei, CHN	445.20
1992	Fu Mingxia, CHN	461.43
1996	Fu Mingxia, CHN	521.58
2000	Laura Wilkinson, USA	543.75
2004	Chantelle Newberry, AUS	590.31
2008	Ruolin Chen, CHN	447.70

FIELD HOCKEY

MEN

Multiple gold medals: India (8); Great Britain, Pakistan and West Germany/Germany (3); Netherlands (2).

Year	
1908	**Great Britain**, Ireland, Scotland
1920	**Great Britain**, Denmark, Belgium
1928	**India**, Netherlands, Germany
1932	**India**, Japan, United States
1936	**India**, Germany, Netherlands
1948	**India**, Great Britain, Netherlands
1952	**India**, Netherlands, Great Britain
1956	**India**, Pakistan, Germany
1960	**Pakistan**, India, Spain
1964	**India**, Pakistan, Australia
1968	**Pakistan**, Australia, India

Year	
1972	**West Germany**, Pakistan, India
1976	**New Zealand**, Australia, Pakistan
1980	**India**, Spain, Soviet Union
1984	**Pakistan**, West Germany, Great Britain
1988	**Great Britain**, West Germany, Netherlands
1992	**Germany**, Australia, Pakistan
1996	**Netherlands**, Spain, Australia
2000	**Netherlands**, South Korea, Australia
2004	**Australia**, Netherlands, Germany
2008	**Germany**, Spain, Australia

WOMEN

Multiple gold medals: Australia (3); Netherlands (2).

Year	
1980	**Zimbabwe**, Czechoslovakia, Soviet Union
1984	**Netherlands**, West Germany, United States
1988	**Australia**, South Korea, Netherlands
1992	**Spain**, Germany, Great Britain

Year	
1996	**Australia**, South Korea, Netherlands
2000	**Australia**, Argentina, Netherlands
2004	**Germany**, Netherlands, Argentina
2008	**Netherlands**, China, Argentina

GYMNASTICS

MEN

At least 4 gold medals (including team events): Sawao Kato (8); Nikolai Andrianov, Viktor Chukarin and Boris Shakhlin (7); Akinori Nakayama and Vitaly Scherbo (6); Yukio Endo, Anton Heida, Mitsuo Tsukahara and Takashi Ono (5); Vladimir Artemov, Georges Miez, Valentin Muratov and Alexei Nemov (4).

All-Around

Year		Points	Year		Points
1900	Gustave Sandras, FRA	.302	1960	Boris Shakhlin, USSR	.115.95
1904	Julius Lenhart, AUT	.69.80	1964	Yukio Endo, JPN	.115.95
1906	Pierre Payssé, FRA	.97.0	1968	Sawao Kato, JPN	.115.9
1908	Alberto Braglia, ITA	.317.0	1972	Sawao Kato, JPN	.114.650
1912	Alberto Braglia, ITA	.135.0	1976	Nikolai Andrianov, USSR	.116.65
1920	Giorgio Zampori, ITA	.88.35	1980	Aleksandr Dityatin, USSR	.118.65
1924	Leon Stukelj, YUG	.110.340	1984	Koji Gushiken, JPN	.118.7
1928	Georges Miez, SWI	.247.500	1988	Vladimir Artemov, USSR	.119.125
1932	Romeo Neri, ITA	.140.625	1992	Vitaly Scherbo, UT	.59.025
1936	Alfred Schwarzmann, GER	.113.100	1996	Li Xiaosahuang, CHN	.58.423
1948	Veikko Huhtanen, FIN	.229.7	2000	Alexei Nemov, RUS	.58.474
1952	Viktor Chukarin, USSR	.115.7	2004	Paul Hamm, USA*	.57.823
1956	Viktor Chukarin, USSR	.114.25	2008	Wei Yang, CHN	.94.575

*Paul Hamm won the all-around gold but following the event it was discovered that a scoring error made by the judges in Athens and bronze medallist Yang Tae Young of South Korea was shorted a tenth of a point in the start value of his parallel bar routine. That difference could have given the South Korean the gold medal. The matter eventually ended when the Court of the Arbitration for Sport decided the result would stand and Hamm would keep his gold.

High Bar

Year		Points	Year		Points
1896	Hermann Weingärtner, GER	.—	1968	(TIE) Akinori Nakayama, JPN	.19.55
1904	(TIE) Anton Heida, USA	.40		& Mikhail Voronin, USSR	.19.55
	& Edward Hennig, USA	.40	1972	Mitsuo Tsukahara, JPN	.19.725
1924	Leon Stukelj, YUG	.19.73	1976	Mitsuo Tsukahara, JPN	.19.675
1928	Georges Miez, SWI	.19.17	1980	Stoyan Deltchev, BUL	.19.825
1932	Dallas Bixler, USA	.18.33	1984	Shinji Morisue, JPN	.20.00
1936	Aleksanteri Saarvala, FIN	.19.367	1988	(TIE) Vladimir Artemov, USSR	.19.900
1948	Josef Stalder, SWI	.19.85		& Valeri Lyukin, USSR	.19.900
1952	Jack Günthard, SWI	.19.55	1992	Trent Dimas, USA	.9.875
1956	Takashi Ono, JPN	.19.60	1996	Andreas Wecker, GER	.9.850
1960	Takashi Ono, JPN	.19.60	2000	Alexei Nemov, RUS	.9.787
1964	Boris Shakhlin, USSR	.19.625	2004	Igor Cassina, ITA	.9.812
			2008	Kai Zou, CHN	.16.200

Parallel Bars

Year		Points	Year		Points
1896	Alfred Flatow, GER	.—	1968	Akinori Nakayama, JPN	.19.475
1904	George Eyser, USA	.44	1972	Sawao Kato, JPN	.19.475
1924	August Güttinger, SWI	.21.63	1976	Sawao Kato, JPN	.19.675
1928	Ladislav Vácha, CZE	.18.83	1980	Aleksandr Tkachyov, USSR	.19.775
1932	Romeo Neri, ITA	.18.97	1984	Bart Conner, USA	.19.95
1936	Konrad Frey, GER	.19.067	1988	Vladimir Artemov, USSR	.19.925
1948	Michael Reusch, SWI	.19.75	1992	Vitaly Scherbo, UT	.9.900
1952	Hans Eugster, SWI	.19.65	1996	Rustam Sharipov, UKR	.9.837
1956	Viktor Chukarin, USSR	.19.20	2000	Li Xiaopeng, CHN	.9.825
1960	Boris Shakhlin, USSR	.19.40	2004	Valeri Goncharov, UKR	.9.787
1964	Yukio Endo, JPN	.19.675	2008	Li Xiaopeng, CHN	.16.450

Vault

Year		Points	Year		Points
1896	Karl Schumann, GER	.—	1964	Haruhiro Yamashita, JPN	.19.60
1904	(TIE) George Eyser, USA	.36	1968	Mikhail Voronin, USSR	.19.00
	& Anton Heida, USA	.36	1972	Klaus Köste, E. Ger	.18.85
1924	Frank Kriz, USA	.9.98	1976	Nikolai Andrianov, USSR	.19.45
1928	Eugen Mack, SWI	.9.58	1980	Nikolai Andrianov, USSR	.19.825
1932	Savino Guglielmetti, ITA	.18.03	1984	Lou Yun, CHN	.19.95
1936	Alfred Schwarzmann, GER	.19.20	1988	Lou Yun, CHN	.19.875
1948	Paavo Aaltonen, FIN	.19.55	1992	Vitaly Scherbo, UT	.9.856
1952	Viktor Chukarin, USSR	.19.20	1996	Alexei Nemov, RUS	.9.787
1956	(TIE) Helmut Bantz, GER	.18.85	2000	Gervasio Deferr, SPA	.9.712
	& Valentin Muratov, USSR	.18.85	2004	Gervasio Deferr, SPA	.9.737
1960	(TIE) Takashi Ono, JPN	.19.35	2008	Leszek Blanik, POL	.16.537
	& Boris Shakhlin, USSR	.19.35			

Pommel Horse

Year		Points
1896	Louis Zutter, SWI	–
1904	Anton Heida, USA	.42
1924	Josef Wilhelm, SWI	.21.23
1928	Hermann Hänggi, SWI	.19.75
1932	István Pelle, HUN	.19.07
1936	Konrad Frey, GER	.19.333
1948	(TIE) Paavo Aaltonen, FIN	.19.35
	Veikko Huhtanen, FIN	.19.35
	& Heikki Savolainen, FIN	.19.35
1952	Viktor Chukarin, USSR	.19.50
1956	Boris Shakhlin, USSR	.19.25
1960	(TIE) Eugen Ekman, FIN	.19.375
	& Boris Shakhlin, USSR	.19.375
1964	Miroslav Cerar, YUG	.19.525
1968	Miroslav Cerar, YUG	.19.325

Year		Points
1972	Viktor Klimenko, SOV	.19.125
1976	Zoltán Magyar, HUN	.19.70
1980	Zoltán Magyar, HUN	.19.925
1984	(TIE) Li Ning, CHN	.19.95
	& Peter Vidmar, USA	.19.95
1988	(TIE) Dmitri Bilozerchev, USSR,	.19.95
	Zsolt Borkai, HUN	.19.95
	& Lyubomir Geraskov, BUL	.19.95
1992	(TIE) Pae Gil-Su, N. Kor	.9.925
	& Vitaly Scherbo, UT	.9.925
1996	Li Donghua, SWI	.9.875
2000	Marius Urzica, ROM	.9.862
2004	Teng Haibin, CHN	.9.837
2008	Qin Xiao, CHN	.15.875

Rings

Year		Points
1896	Ioannis Mitropoulos, GRE	–
1904	Hermann Glass, USA	.45
1924	Francesco Martino, ITA	.21.553
1928	Leon Stukelj, YUG	.19.25
1932	George Gulack, USA	.18.97
1936	Alois Hudec, CZE	.19.433
1948	Karl Frei, SWI	.19.80
1952	Grant Shaginyan, USSR	.19.75
1956	Albert Azaryan, USSR	.19.35
1960	Albert Azaryan, USSR	.19.725
1964	Takuji Haytta, JPN	.19.475
1968	Akinori Nakayama, JPN	.19.45

Year		Points
1972	Akinori Nakayama, JPN	.19.35
1976	Nikolai Andrianov, USSR	.19.65
1980	Aleksandr Dityatin, USSR	.19.875
1984	(TIE) Koji Gushiken, JPN	.19.85
	& Li Ning, CHN	.19.85
1988	(TIE) Holger Behrendt, E. Ger	.19.925
	& Dmitri Bilozerchev, USSR	.19.925
1992	Vitaly Scherbo, UT	.9.937
1996	Yuri Chechi, ITA	.9.887
2000	Szilveszter Csollany, HUN	.9.850
2004	Dimonsthenis Tampakos, GRE	.9.862
2008	Yibing Chen, CHN	.16.600

Floor Exercise

Year		Points
1932	Istvan Pelle, HUN	.9.60
1936	Georges Miez, SWI	.18.666
1948	Ferenc Pataki, HUN	.19.35
1952	William Thoresson, SWE	.19.25
1956	Valentin Muratov, USSR	.19.20
1960	Nobuyuki Aihara, JPN	.19.45
1964	Franco Menichelli, ITA	.19.45
1968	Sawao Kato, JPN	.19.475
1972	Nikolai Andrianov, USSR	.19.175

Year		Points
1976	Nikolai Andrianov, USSR	.19.45
1980	Roland Brückner, E. Ger	.19.75
1984	Li Ning, CHN	.19.925
1988	Sergei Kharkov, USSR	.19.925
1992	Li Xiaosahuang, CHN	.9.925
1996	Ioannis Melissanidis, GRE	.9.850
2000	Igors Vihrovs, LAT	.9.812
2004	Kyle Shewfelt, CAN	.9.787
2008	Kai Zou, CHN	.16.050

Team Combined Exercises

Year		Points
1904	United States	.374.43
1906	Norway	.19.00
1908	Sweden	.438
1912	Italy	.265.75
1920	Italy	.359.855
1924	Italy	.839.058
1928	Switzerland	.1718.625
1932	Italy	.541.850
1936	Germany	.657.430
1948	Finland	.1358.30
1952	Soviet Union	.574.40
1956	Soviet Union	.568.25
1960	Japan	.575.20

Year		Points
1964	Japan	.577.95
1968	Japan	.575.90
1972	Japan	.571.25
1976	Japan	.576.85
1980	Soviet Union	.598.60
1984	United States	.591.40
1988	Soviet Union	.593.35
1992	Unified Team	.585.45
1996	Russia	.576.778
2000	China	.231.919
2004	Japan	.173.821
2008	China	.286.125

WOMEN

At least 4 gold medals (including team events): Larissa Latynina (9); Vera Cáslavská (7); Polina Astakhova, Nadia Comaneci, Agnes Keleti and Nelli Kim (5); Olga Korbut, Ecaterina Szabó and Lyudmila Tourischeva (4).

All-Around

Year		Points	Year		Points
1952	Maria Gorokhovskaya, USSR	76.78	1984	Mary Lou Retton, USA	79.175
1956	Larissa Latynina, USSR	74.933	1988	Yelena Shushunova, USSR	79.662
1960	Larissa Latynina, USSR	77.031	1992	Tatiana Gutsu, UT	39.737
1964	Vera Cáslavská, CZE	77.564	1996	Lilia Podkopayeva, UKR	39.255
1968	Vera Cáslavská, CZE	78.25	2000	Simona Amanar, ROM*	38.642
1972	Lyudmila Tourischeva, USSR	77.025	2004	Carly Patterson, USA	38.387
1976	Nadia Comaneci, ROM	79.275	2008	Nastia Liukin, USA	63.325
1980	Yelena Davydova, USSR	79.15			

*Amanar finished second to **Andreea Raducan**, Romania, who was disqualified for testing positive for pseudo-ephedrine, a drug banned by the IOC and found in Nurofen—an over-the-counter medicine she purportedly took to treat a cold.

Vault

Year		Points	Year		Points
1952	Yekaterina Kalinchuk, USSR	19.20	1984	Ecaterina Szabó, ROM	19.875
1956	Larissa Latynina, USSR	18.833	1988	Svetlana Boginskaya, USSR	19.905
1960	Margarita Nikolayeva, USSR	19.316	1992	(TIE) Henrietta Onodi, HUN	9.925
1964	Vera Cáslavská, CZE	19.483		& Lavinia Milosovici, ROM	9.925
1968	Vera Cáslavská, CZE	19.775	1996	Simona Amanar, ROM	9.775
1972	Karin Janz, E. Ger	19.525	2000	Elena Zamolodtchikova, RUS	9.731
1976	Nelli Kim, USSR	19.80	2004	Monica Rosu, ROM	9.656
1980	Natalia Shaposhnikova, USSR	19.725	2008	Un John Hong, N. Kor	15.650

Uneven Bars

Year		Points	Year		Points
1952	Margit Korondi, HUN	19.40	1984	(TIE) Julianne McNamora, USA	19.95
1956	Agnes Keleti, HUN	18.966		& Ma Yanhong, CHN	19.95
1960	Polina Astakhova, USSR	19.616	1988	Daniela Silivas, ROM	20.00
1964	Polina Astakhova, USSR	19.332	1992	Lu Li, CHN	10.00
1968	Vera Cáslavská, CZE	19.65	1996	Svetlana Khorkina, RUS	9.850
1972	Karin Janz, E. Ger	19.675	2000	Svetlana Khorkina, RUS	9.862
1976	Nadia Comaneci, ROM	20.00	2004	Emilie Lepennec, FRA	9.687
1980	Maxi Gnauck, E. Ger	19.875	2008	Kexin He, CHN	16.725

Balance Beam

Year		Points	Year		Points
1952	Nina Bocharova, USSR	19.22	1984	(TIE) Simona Pauca, ROM	19.80
1956	Agnes Keleti, HUN	18.80		& Ecaterina Szabó, ROM	19.80
1960	Eva Bosakova, CZE	19.283	1988	Daniela Silivas, ROM	19.924
1964	Vera Cáslavská, CZE	19.449	1992	Tatiana Lyssenko, UT	9.975
1968	Natalya Kuchinskaya, USSR	19.65	1996	Shannon Miller, USA	9.862
1972	Olga Korbut, USSR	19.40	2000	Liu Xuan, CHN	9.825
1976	Nadia Comaneci, ROM	19.95	2004	Catalina Ponor, ROM	9.787
1980	Nadia Comaneci, ROM	19.80	2008	Shawn Johnson, USA	16.225

Floor Exercise

Year		Points	Year		Points
1952	Agnes Keleti, HUN	19.36	1980	(TIE) Nadia Comaneci, ROM	19.875
1956	(TIE) Agnes Keleti, HUN	18.733		& Nelli Kim, USSR	19.875
	& Larissa Latynina, USSR	18.733	1984	Ecaterina Szabó, ROM	19.975
1960	Larissa Latynina, USSR	19.583	1988	Daniela Silivas, ROM	19.937
1964	Larissa Latynina, USSR	19.599	1992	Lavinia Milosovici, ROM	10.000
1968	(TIE) Vera Cáslavská, CZE	19.675	1996	Lilia Podkopayeva, UKR	9.887
	& Larissa Petrik, USSR	19.675	2000	Elena Zamolodtchikova, RUS	9.850
1972	Olga Korbut, USSR	19.575	2004	Catalina Ponor, ROM	9.750
1976	Nelli Kim, USSR	19.85	2008	Sandra Izbasa, ROM	15.650

Team Combined Exercises

Year		Points	Year		Points
1928	Netherlands	316.75	1976	Soviet Union	466.00
1936	Germany	506.50	1980	Soviet Union	394.90
1948	Czechoslovakia	445.45	1984	Romania	392.02
1952	Soviet Union	527.03	1988	Soviet Union	395.475
1956	Soviet Union	444.800	1992	Unified Team	395.666
1960	Soviet Union	382.320	1996	United States	389.225
1964	Soviet Union	280.890	2000	Romania	154.608
1968	Soviet Union	382.85	2004	Romania	114.283
1972	Soviet Union	380.50	2008	China	188.900

SOCCER
MEN

Multiple gold medals: Great Britain and Hungary (3); Uruguay and USSR (2).

Year		Year	
1900	**Great Britain**, France, Belgium	1964	**Hungary**, Czechoslovakia, Germany
1904	**Canada**, USA I, USA II	1968	**Hungary**, Bulgaria, Japan
1906	**Denmark**, Smyrna (Int'l entry), Greece	1972	**Poland**, Hungary, East Germany & Soviet Union
1908	**Great Britain**, Denmark, Netherlands	1976	**East Germany**, Poland, Soviet Union
1912	**Great Britain**, Denmark, Netherlands	1980	**Czechoslovakia**, East Germany, Soviet Union
1920	**Belgium**, Spain, Netherlands	1984	**France**, Brazil, Yugoslavia
1924	**Uruguay**, Switzerland, Sweden	1988	**Soviet Union**, Brazil, West Germany
1928	**Uruguay**, Argentina, Italy	1992	**Spain**, Poland, Ghana
1936	**Italy**, Austria, Norway	1996	**Nigeria**, Argentina, Brazil
1948	**Sweden**, Yugoslavia, Denmark	2000	**Cameroon**, Spain, Chile
1952	**Hungary**, Yugoslavia, Sweden	2004	**Argentina**, Paraguay, Italy
1956	**Soviet Union**, Yugoslavia, Bulgaria	2008	**Argentina**, Nigeria, Brazil
1960	**Yugoslavia**, Denmark, Hungary		

WOMEN

Multiple gold medals: United States (2).

Year		Year	
1996	**United States**, China, Norway	2004	**United States**, Brazil, Germany
2000	**Norway**, United States, Germany	2008	**United States**, Brazil, Germany

SOFTBALL

Multiple gold medals: United States (3).

Year		Year	
1996	**United States**, China, Australia	2004	**United States**, Australia, Japan
2000	**United States**, Japan, Australia	2008	**Japan**, United States, Australia

SWIMMING

World and Olympic records below that appear to be broken or equaled by winning times in subsequent years, but are not so indicated, were all broken in preliminary heats leading up to the finals. Some events were not held at every Olympics.

MEN

At least 4 gold medals (including relays): Michael Phelps (14); Mark Spitz (9); Matt Biondi (8); Gary Hall Jr. (6); Charles Daniels, Tom Jager, Don Schollander, Ian Thorpe and Johnny Weissmuller (5); Tamás Darnyi, Roland Matthes, John Naber, Aleksandr Popov, Murray Rose, Vladimir Salnikov and Henry Taylor (4).

50-meter Freestyle

Year	Time		Year	Time	
1904 Zoltán Halmay, HUN (50 yds)	28.0		2000 (TIE) Anthony Ervin, USA	21.98	
1906-84 Not held			& Gary Hall Jr., USA	21.98	
1988 Matt Biondi, USA	22.14	**WR**	2004 Gary Hall Jr., USA	21.93	
1992 Aleksandr Popov, UT	21.91	**OR**	2008 Cesar Cielo Filho, BRA	21.30	**OR**
1996 Aleksandr Popov, RUS	22.13				

100-meter Freestyle

Year	Time		Year	Time	
1896 Alfréd Hajós, HUN	1:22.2	**OR**	1960 John Devitt, AUS	55.2	**OR**
1904 Zoltán Halmay, HUN (100 yds)	1:02.8		1964 Don Schollander, USA	53.4	**OR**
1906 Charles Daniels, USA	1:13.4		1968 Michael Wenden, AUS	52.2	**WR**
1908 Charles Daniels, USA	1:05.6	**WR**	1972 Mark Spitz, USA	51.22	**WR**
1912 Duke Kahanamoku, USA	1:03.4		1976 Jim Montgomery, USA	49.99	
1920 Duke Kahanamoku, USA	1:00.4	**WR**	1980 Jorg Woithe, E. Ger	50.40	
1924 Johnny Weissmuller, USA	59.0	**OR**	1984 Rowdy Gaines, USA	49.80	**OR**
1928 Johnny Weissmuller, USA	58.6	**OR**	1988 Matt Biondi, USA	48.63	**OR**
1932 Yasuji Miyazaki, JPN	58.2		1992 Aleksandr Popov, UT	49.02	
1936 Ferenc Csik, HUN	57.6		1996 Aleksandr Popov, RUS	48.74	
1948 Wally Ris, USA	57.3	**OR**	2000 Pieter van den Hoogenband, NED	48.30	
1952 Clarke Scholes, USA	57.4		2004 Pieter van den Hoogenband, NED	48.17	
1956 Jon Henricks, AUS	55.4	**OR**	2008 Alain Bernard, FRA	47.21	

200-meter Freestyle

Year	Time		Year	Time	
1900 Frederick Lane, AUS (220 yds)	2:25.2	**OR**	1976 Bruce Furniss, USA	1:50.29	**WR**
1904 Charles Daniels, USA (220 yds)	2:44.2		1980 Sergei Kopliakov, USSR	1:49.81	**OR**
1968 Michael Wenden, AUS	1:55.2	**OR**	1984 Michael Gross, W. Ger	1:47.44	**WR**
1972 Mark Spitz, USA	1:52.78	**WR**	1988 Duncan Armstrong, AUS	1:47.25	**WR**

Swimming (Cont.)
200-meter Freestyle (Cont.)

Year	Time		Year	Time	
1992 Yevgeny Sadovyi, UT	1:46.70	OR	2004 Ian Thorpe, AUS	1:44.71	OR
1996 Danyon Loader, NZE	1:47.63		2004 Ian Thorpe, AUS	1:44.71	
2000 Pieter van den Hoogenband, NED	1:45.35	WR	2008 Michael Phelps, USA	1:42.96	WR

400-meter Freestyle

Year	Time		Year	Time	
1896 Paul Neumann, AUT (550m)	8:12.6		1960 Murray Rose, AUS	4:18.3	OR
1904 Charles Daniels, USA (440 yds)	6:16.2		1964 Don Schollander, USA	4:12.2	WR
1906 Otto Scheff, AUT	6:23.8		1968 Mike Burton, USA	4:09.0	OR
1908 Henry Taylor, GBR	5:36.8		1972 Bradford Cooper, AUS*	4:00.27	OR
1912 George Hodgson, CAN	5:24.4		1976 Brian Goodell, USA	3:51.93	WR
1920 Norman Ross, USA	5:26.8		1980 Vladimir Salnikov, USSR	3:51.31	OR
1924 Johnny Weissmuller, USA	5:04.2	OR	1984 George DiCarlo, USA	3:51.23	OR
1928 Alberto Zorilla, ARG	5:01.6	OR	1988 Uwe Dassler, E. Ger	3:46.95	WR
1932 Buster Crabbe, USA	4:48.4	OR	1992 Yevgeny Sadovyi, UT	3:45.00	WR
1936 Jack Medica, USA	4:44.5	OR	1996 Danyon Loader, NZE	3:47.97	
1948 Bill Smith, USA	4:41.0	OR	2000 Ian Thorpe, AUS	3:40.59	WR
1952 Jean Boiteux, FRA	4:30.7	OR	2004 Ian Thorpe, AUS	3:43.10	
1956 Murray Rose, AUS	4:27.3	OR	2008 Taehwan Park, S. Kor	3:41.86	

*Cooper finished second to Rick DeMont of the U.S., who was disqualified when he flunked the post-race drug test (his asthma medication was on the IOC's banned list).

1500-meter Freestyle

Year	Time		Year	Time	
1896 Alfréd Hajós, HUN (1200m)	18:22.2	OR	1960 Jon Konrads, AUS	17:19.6	OR
1900 John Arthur Jarvis, GBR (1000m)	13:40.2		1964 Robert Windle, AUS	17:01.7	OR
1904 Emil Rausch, GER (1 mile)	27:18.2		1968 Mike Burton, USA	16:38.9	OR
1906 Henry Taylor, GBR (1 mile)	28:28.0		1972 Mike Burton, USA	15:52.58	WR
1908 Henry Taylor, GBR	22:48.4	WR	1976 Brian Goodell, USA	15:02.40	WR
1912 George Hodgson, CAN	22:00.0	WR	1980 Vladimir Salnikov, USSR	14:58.27	WR
1920 Norman Ross, USA	22:23.2		1984 Mike O'Brien, USA	15:05.20	
1924 Andrew (Boy) Charlton, AUS	20:06.6	WR	1988 Vladimir Salnikov, USSR	15:00.40	
1928 Arne Borge, SWE	19:51.8	OR	1992 Kieren Perkins, AUS	14:43.48	WR
1932 Kusuo Kitamura, JPN	19:12.4	OR	1996 Kieren Perkins, AUS	14:56.40	
1936 Noboru Terada, JPN	19:13.7		2000 Grant Hackett, AUS	14:48.33	
1948 James McLane, USA	19:18.5		2004 Grant Hackett, AUS	14:43.40	
1952 Ford Konno, USA	18:30.3	OR	2008 Oussama Mellouli, TUN	14:40.84	
1956 Murray Rose, AUS	17:58.9				

100-meter Backstroke

Year	Time		Year	Time	
1904 Walter Brack, GER (100 yds)	1:16.8		1968 Roland Matthes, E. Ger	.58.7	OR
1908 Arno Bieberstein, GER	1:24.6	WR	1972 Roland Matthes, E. Ger	.56.58	OR
1912 Harry Hebner, USA	1:21.2		1976 John Naber, USA	.55.49	WR
1920 Warren Kealoha, USA	1:15.2		1980 Bengt Baron, SWE	.56.33	
1924 Warren Kealoha, USA	1:13.2	OR	1984 Rick Carey, USA	.55.79	
1928 George Kojac, USA	1:08.2	WR	1988 Daichi Suzuki, JPN	.55.05	
1932 Masaji Kiyokawa, JPN	1:08.6		1992 Mark Tewksbury, CAN	.53.98	OR
1936 Adolf Kiefer, USA	1:05.9	OR	1996 Jeff Rouse, USA	.54.10	
1948 Allen Stack, USA	1:06.4		2000 Lenny Krayzelburg, USA	.53.72	OR
1952 Yoshinobu Oyakawa, USA	1:05.4	OR	2004 Aaron Peirsol, USA	.54.06	
1956 David Theile, AUS	1:02.2	OR	2008 Aaron Peirsol, USA	.52.54	WR
1960 David Theile, AUS	1:01.9	OR			

200-meter Backstroke

Year	Time		Year	Time	
1900 Ernst Hoppenberg, GER	2:47.0		1988 Igor Poliansky, USSR	1:59.37	
1964 Jed Graef, USA	2:10.3	WR	1992 Martin Lopez-Zubero, SPA	1:58.47	OR
1968 Roland Matthes, E. Ger	2:09.6	OR	1996 Brad Bridgewater, USA	1:58.54	
1972 Roland Matthes, E. Ger	2:02.82	=WR	2000 Lenny Krayzelburg, USA	1:56.76	OR
1976 John Naber, USA	1:59.19	WR	2004 Aaron Peirsol, USA	1:54.95	OR
1980 Sándor Wládar, HUN	2:01.93		2008 Ryan Lochte, USA	1:53.94	WR
1984 Rick Carey, USA	2:00.23				

100-meter Breaststroke

Year	Time		Year	Time	
1968 Don McKenzie, USA	1:07.7	OR	1992 Nelson Diebel, USA	1:01.50	OR
1972 Nobutaka Taguchi, JPN	1:04.94	WR	1996 Fred deBurghgraeve, BEL	1:00.60	
1976 John Hencken, USA	1:03.11	WR	2000 Domenico Fioravanti, ITA	1:00.46	OR
1980 Duncan Goodhew, GBR	1:03.44		2004 Kosuke Kitajima, JPN	1:00.08	
1984 Steve Lundquist, USA	1:01.65	WR	2008 Kosuke Kitajima, JPN	.58.91	WR
1988 Adrian Moorhouse, GBR	1:02.04				

200-meter Breaststroke

Year		Time		Year		Time	
1908	Frederick Holman, GBR	3:09.2	WR	1968	Felipe Muñoz, MEX	2:28.7	
1912	Walter Bathe, GER	3:01.8	OR	1972	John Hencken, USA	2:21.55	WR
1920	Hakan Malmroth, SWE	3:04.4		1976	David Wilkie, GBR	2:15.11	WR
1924	Robert Skelton, USA	2:56.6		1980	Robertas Zhulpa, USSR	2:15.85	
1928	Yoshiyuki Tsuruta, JPN	2:48.8	OR	1984	Victor Davis, CAN	2:13.34	WR
1932	Yoshiyuki Tsuruta, JPN	2:45.4		1988	József Szabó, HUN	2:13.52	
1936	Tetsuo Hamuro, JPN	2:41.5	OR	1992	Mike Barrowman, USA	2:10.16	WR
1948	Joseph Verdeur, USA	2:39.3	OR	1996	Norbert Rozsa, HUN	2:12.57	
1952	John Davies, AUS	2:34.4	OR	2000	Domenico Fioravanti, ITA	2:10.87	
1956	Masaru Furukawa, JPN	2:34.7*	OR	2004	Kosuke Kitajima, JPN	2:09.44	OR
1960	Bill Mulliken, USA	2:37.4		2008	Kosuke Kitajima, JPN	2:07.64	OR
1964	Ian O'Brien, AUS	2:27.8	WR				

*In 1956, the butterfly stroke and breaststroke were separated into two different events.

100-meter Butterfly

Year		Time		Year		Time	
1968	Doug Russell, USA	55.9	OR	1992	Pablo Morales, USA	53.32	
1972	Mark Spitz, USA	54.27	WR	1996	Dennis Pankratov, RUS	52.27	
1976	Matt Vogel, USA	54.35		2000	Lars Frolander, SWE	52.00	
1980	Pär Arvidsson, SWE	54.92		2004	Michael Phelps, USA	51.25	OR
1984	Michael Gross, W. Ger	53.08	WR	2008	Michael Phelps, USA	50.58	OR
1988	Anthony Nesty, SUR	53.0	OR				

200-meter Butterfly

Year		Time		Year		Time	
1956	Bill Yorzyk, USA	2:19.3	OR	1984	Jon Sieben, AUS	1:57.04	WR
1960	Mike Troy, USA	2:12.8	WR	1988	Michael Gross, W. Ger	1:56.94	OR
1964	Kevin Berry, AUS	2:06.6	WR	1992	Melvin Stewart, USA	1:56.26	OR
1968	Carl Robie, USA	2:08.7		1996	Dennis Pankratov, RUS	1:56.51	
1972	Mark Spitz, USA	2:00.70	WR	2000	Tom Malchow, USA	1:55.35	OR
1976	Mike Bruner, USA	1:59.23	WR	2004	Michael Phelps, USA	1:54.04	OR
1980	Sergei Fesenko, USSR	1:59.76		2008	Michael Phelps, USA	1:52.03	WR

200-meter Individual Medley

Year		Time		Year		Time	
1968	Charles Hickcox, USA	2:12.0	OR	1996	Attila Czene, HUN	1:59.91	
1972	Gunnar Larsson, SWE	2:07.17	WR	2000	Massimiliano Rosolino, ITA	1:58.98	OR
1984	Alex Baumann, CAN	2:01.42	WR	2004	Michael Phelps, USA	1:57.14	OR
1988	Tamás Darnyi, HUN	2:00.17	WR	2008	Michael Phelps, USA	1:54.23	WR
1992	Tamás Darnyi, HUN	2:00.76					

400-meter Individual Medley

Year		Time		Year		Time	
1964	Richard Roth, USA	4:45.4	WR	1988	Tamás Darnyi, HUN	4:14.75	WR
1968	Charles Hickcox, USA	4:48.4		1992	Tamás Darnyi, HUN	4:14.23	OR
1972	Gunnar Larsson, SWE	4:31.98	OR	1996	Tom Dolan, USA	4:14.90	
1976	Rod Strachan, USA	4:23.68	WR	2000	Tom Dolan, USA	4:11.76	WR
1980	Aleksandr Sidorenko, USSR	4:22.89	OR	2004	Michael Phelps, USA	4:08.26	WR
1984	Alex Baumann, CAN	4:17.41	WR	2008	Michael Phelps, USA	4:03.84	WR

4x100-meter Freestyle Relay

Year		Time		Year		Time	
1964	United States	3:32.2	WR	1992	United States	3:16.74	
1968	United States	3:31.7	WR	1996	United States	3:15.41	
1972	United States	3:26.42	WR	2000	Australia	3:13.67	WR
1976-80	Not held			2004	South Africa	3:13.17	WR
1984	United States	3:19.03	WR	2008	United States	3:08.24	WR
1988	United States	3:16.53	WR				

4x200-meter Freestyle Relay

Year		Time		Year		Time	
1906	Hungary (x250m)	16:52.4		1964	United States	7:52.1	WR
1908	Great Britain	10:55.6	WR	1968	United States	7:52.33	
1912	Australia/New Zealand	10:11.6	WR	1972	United States	7:35.78	WR
1920	United States	10:04.4	WR	1976	United States	7:23.22	
1924	United States	9:53.4	WR	1980	Soviet Union	7:23.50	
1928	United States	9:36.2	WR	1984	United States	7:15.69	WR
1932	Japan	8:58.4	WR	1988	United States	7:12.51	WR
1936	Japan	8:51.5	WR	1992	Unified Team	7:11.95	WR
1948	United States	8:46.0	WR	1996	United States	7:14.84	
1952	United States	8:31.1	OR	2000	Australia	7:07.05	WR
1956	Australia	8:23.6	WR	2004	United States	7:07.33	
1960	United States	8:10.2	WR	2008	United States	6:58.56	WR

Swimming (Cont.)
4x100-meter Medley Relay

Year		Time		Year		Time	
1960	United States	4:05.4	**WR**	1988	United States	3:36.93	**WR**
1964	United States	3:58.4	**WR**	1992	United States	3:36.93	**=WR**
1968	United States	3:54.9	**WR**	1996	United States	3:34.84	
1972	United States	3:48.16	**WR**	2000	United States	3:33.73	**WR**
1976	United States	3:42.22	**WR**	2004	United States	3:30.68	**WR**
1980	Australia	3:45.70		2008	United States	3:29.34	**WR**
1984	United States	3:39.30	**WR**				

WOMEN

At least 4 gold medals (including relays): Jenny Thompson (8); Kristin Otto and Amy Van Dyken (6); Krisztina Egerszegi (5), Kornelia Ender, Janet Evans, Dawn Fraser and Dara Torres (4).

50-meter Freestyle

Year		Time		Year		Time	
1988	Kristin Otto, E. Ger	25.49	**OR**	2000	Inge de Bruijn, NED	24.32	
1992	Yang Wenyi, CHN	24.79	**WR**	2004	Inge de Bruijn, NED	24.58	
1996	Amy Van Dyken, USA	24.87		2008	Britta Steffen, GER	24.06	**OR**

100-meter Freestyle

Year		Time		Year		Time	
1912	Fanny Durack, AUS	1:22.2		1972	Sandra Neilson, USA	58.59	**OR**
1920	Ethelda Bleibtrey, USA	1:13.6	**WR**	1976	Kornelia Ender, E. Ger	55.65	**WR**
1924	Ethel Lackie, USA	1:12.4		1980	Barbara Krause, E. Ger	54.79	**WR**
1928	Albina Osipowich, USA	1:11.0	**OR**	1984	(TIE) Nancy Hogshead, USA	55.92	
1932	Helene Madison, USA	1:06.8	**OR**		& Carrie Steinseifer, USA	55.92	
1936	Rie Mastenbroek, NED	1:05.9	**OR**	1988	Kristin Otto, E. Ger	54.93	
1948	Greta Andersen, DEN	1:06.3		1992	Zhuang Yong, CHN	54.65	**OR**
1952	Katalin Szöke, HUN	1:06.8		1996	Le Jingyi, CHN	54.50	
1956	Dawn Fraser, AUS	1:02.0	**OR**	2000	Inge de Bruijn, NED	53.83	
1960	Dawn Fraser, AUS	1:01.2	**OR**	2004	Jodie Henry, AUS	53.84	
1964	Dawn Fraser, AUS	59.5	**OR**	2008	Britta Steffen, GER	53.12	**OR**
1968	Jan Henne, USA	1:00.0					

200-meter Freestyle

Year		Time		Year		Time	
1968	Debbie Meyer, USA	2:10.5	**OR**	1992	Nicole Haislett, USA	1:57.90	
1972	Shane Gould, AUS	2:03.56	**WR**	1996	Claudia Poll, CRC	1:58.16	
1976	Kornelia Ender, E. Ger	1:59.26	**WR**	2000	Susie O'Neill, AUS	1:58.24	
1980	Barbara Krause, E. Ger	1:58.33	**OR**	2004	Camelia Potec, ROM	1:58.03	
1984	Mary Wayte, USA	1:59.23		2008	Federica Pellegrini, ITA	1:54.82	**WR**
1988	Heike Friedrich, E. Ger	1:57.65	**OR**				

400-meter Freestyle

Year		Time		Year		Time	
1920	Ethelda Bleibtrey, USA (300m)	4:34.0	**WR**	1972	Shane Gould, AUS	4:19.44	**WR**
1924	Martha Norelius, USA	6:02.2	**OR**	1976	Petra Thümer, E. Ger	4:09.89	**WR**
1928	Martha Norelius, USA	5:42.8	**WR**	1980	Ines Diers, E. Ger	4:08.76	**OR**
1932	Helene Madison, USA	5:28.5	**WR**	1984	Tiffany Cohen, USA	4:07.10	**OR**
1936	Rie Mastenbroek, NED	5:26.4	**OR**	1988	Janet Evans, USA	4:03.85	**WR**
1948	Ann Curtis, USA	5:17.8	**OR**	1992	Dagmar Hase, GER	4:07.18	
1952	Valéria Gyenge, HUN	5:12.1	**OR**	1996	Michelle Smith, IRE	4:07.25	
1956	Lorraine Crapp, AUS	4:54.6	**OR**	2000	Brooke Bennett, USA	4:05.80	
1960	Chris von Saltza, USA	4:50.6	**OR**	2004	Laure Manaudou, FRA	4:05.34	
1964	Ginny Duenkel, USA	4:43.3	**OR**	2008	Rebecca Adlington, GBR	4:03.22	
1968	Debbie Meyer, USA	4:31.8	**OR**				

800-meter Freestyle

Year		Time		Year		Time	
1968	Debbie Meyer, USA	9:24.0	**OR**	1992	Janet Evans, USA	8:25.52	
1972	Keena Rothhammer, USA	8:53.68	**WR**	1996	Brooke Bennett, USA	8:27.89	
1976	Petra Thümer, E. Ger	8:37.14	**WR**	2000	Brooke Bennett, USA	8:19.67	**OR**
1980	Michelle Ford, AUS	8:28.90	**OR**	2004	Ai Shibata, JPN	8:24.54	
1984	Tiffany Cohen, USA	8:24.95	**OR**	2008	Rebecca Adlington, GBR	8:14.10	**WR**
1988	Janet Evans, USA	8:20.20	**OR**				

100-meter Backstroke

Year		Time		Year		Time	
1924	Sybil Bauer, USA	1:23.2	**OR**	1972	Melissa Belote, USA	1:05.78	**OR**
1928	Maria Braun, NED	1:22.0		1976	Ulrike Richter, E. Ger	1:01.83	**OR**
1932	Eleanor Holm, USA	1:19.4		1980	Rica Reinisch, E. Ger	1:00.86	**WR**
1936	Dina Senff, NED	1:18.9		1984	Theresa Andrews, USA	1:02.55	
1948	Karen-Margrete Harup, DEN	1:14.4	**OR**	1988	Kristin Otto, E. Ger	1:00.89	
1952	Joan Harrison, S. Afr.	1:14.3		1992	Krisztina Egerszegi, HUN	1:00.68	**OR**
1956	Judy Grinham, GBR	1:12.9	**OR**	1996	Beth Botsford, USA	1:01.19	
1960	Lynn Burke, USA	1:09.3	**OR**	2000	Diana Mocanu, ROM	1:00.21	**OR**
1964	Cathy Ferguson, USA	1:07.7	**WR**	2004	Natalie Coughlin, USA	1:03.37	
1968	Kaye Hall, USA	1:06.2	**WR**	2008	Natalie Coughlin, USA	58.96	

200-meter Backstroke

Year	Time		Year	Time	
1968 Pokey Watson, USA	2:24.8	OR	1992 Krisztina Egerszegi, HUN	2:07.06	OR
1972 Melissa Belote, USA	2:19.19	WR	1996 Krisztina Egerszegi, HUN	2:07.83	
1976 Ulrike Richter, E. Ger	2:13.43	OR	2000 Diana Mocanu, ROM	2:08.16	
1980 Rica Reinisch, E. Ger	2:11.77	WR	2004 Kirsty Coventry, ZIM	2:09.19	
1984 Jolanda de Rover, NED	2:12.38		2008 Kirsty Coventry, ZIM	2:05.24	WR
1988 Krisztina Egerszegi, HUN	2:09.29	OR			

100-meter Breaststroke

Year	Time		Year	Time	
1968 Djurdjica Bjedov, YUG	1:15.8	OR	1992 Yelena Rudkovskaya, UT	1:08.00	
1972 Cathy Carr, USA	1:13.58	WR	1996 Penny Heyns, RSA.	1:07.73	
1976 Hannelore Anke, E. Ger	1:11.16		2000 Megan Quann, USA	1:07.05	
1980 Ute Geweniger, E. Ger	1:10.22		2004 Luo Xuejuan, CHN	1:06.64	OR
1984 Petra van Staveren, NED	1:09.88	OR	2008 Leisel Jones, AUS	1:05.17	OR
1988 Tania Dangalakova, BUL	1:07.95	OR			

200-meter Breaststroke

Year	Time		Year	Time	
1924 Lucy Morton, GBR	3:33.2	OR	1972 Beverley Whitfield, AUS	2:41.71	OR
1928 Hilde Schrader, GER	3:12.6		1976 Marina Koshevaya, USSR	2:33.35	WR
1932 Clare Dennis, AUS	3:06.3	OR	1980 Lina Kaciusyte, USSR	2:29.54	OR
1936 Hideko Maehata, JPN	3:03.6		1984 Anne Ottenbrite, CAN	2:30.38	
1948 Petronella van Vliet, NED	2:57.2		1988 Silke Hörner, E. Ger	2:26.71	WR
1952 éva Székely, HUN	2:51.7	OR	1992 Kyoko Iwasaki, JPN	2:26.65	OR
1956 Ursula Happe, GER	2:53.1	OR	1996 Penny Heyns, RSA	2:25.41	
1960 Anita Lonsbrough, GBR	2:49.5	WR	2000 Agnes Kovacs, HUN	2:24.35	
1964 Galina Prozumenshikova, USSR	2:46.4	OR	2004 Amanda Beard, USA	2:23.37	OR
1968 Sharon Wichman, USA	2:44.4	OR	2008 Rebecca Soni, USA	2:20.22	WR

100-meter Butterfly

Year	Time		Year	Time	
1956 Shelley Mann, USA	1:11.0	OR	1984 Mary T. Meagher, USA	.59.26	
1960 Carolyn Schuler, USA	1:09.5	OR	1988 Kristin Otto, E. Ger	.59.00	OR
1964 Sharon Stouder, USA	1:04.7	WR	1992 Qian Hong, CHN	.58.62	OR
1968 Lynn McClements, AUS	1:05.5		1996 Amy Van Dyken, USA	.59.13	
1972 Mayumi Aoki, JPN	1:03.34	WR	2000 Inge de Bruijn, NED	.56.61	WR
1976 Kornelia Ender, E. Ger	1:00.13	=WR	2004 Petria Thomas, AUS	.57.72	
1980 Caren Metschuck, E. Ger	1:00.42		2008 Lisbeth Trickett, AUS	.56.73	

200-meter Butterfly

Year	Time		Year	Time	
1968 Ada Kok, NED	2:24.7	OR	1992 Summer Sanders, USA	2:08.67	
1972 Karen Moe, USA	2:15.57	WR	1996 Susie O'Neill, AUS	2:07.76	
1976 Andrea Pollack, E. Ger	2:11.41	OR	2000 Misty Hyman, USA	2:05.88	OR
1980 Ines Geissler, E. Ger	2:10.44	OR	2004 Otylia Jedrzejczak, POL	2:06.05	
1984 Mary T. Meagher, USA	2:06.90	OR	2008 Zige Liu, CHN	2:04.18	WR
1988 Kathleen Nord, E. Ger	2:09.51				

200-meter Individual Medley

Year	Time		Year	Time	
1968 Claudia Kolb, USA	2:24.7	OR	1996 Michelle Smith, IRE	2:13.93	
1972 Shane Gould, AUS	2:23.07	WR	2000 Yana Klochkova, UKR	2:10.68	OR
1984 Tracy Caulkins, USA	2:12.64	OR	2004 Yana Klochkova, UKR	2:11.14	
1988 Daniela Hunger, E. Ger	2:12.59	OR	2008 Stephanie Rice, AUS	2:08.45	WR
1992 Lin Li, CHN	2:11.65	WR			

400-meter Individual Medley

Year	Time		Year	Time	
1964 Donna de Varona, USA	5:18.7	OR	1988 Janet Evans, USA	4:37.76	
1968 Claudia Kolb, USA	5:08.5	OR	1992 Krisztina Egerszegi, HUN	4:36.54	
1972 Gail Neall, AUS	5:02.97	WR	1996 Michelle Smith, IRE	4:39.18	
1976 Ulrike Tauber, E. Ger	4:42.77	WR	2000 Yana Klochkova, UKR	4:33.59	WR
1980 Petra Schneider, E. Ger	4:36'29	WR	2004 Yana Klochkova, UKR	4:34.83	
1984 Tracy Caulkins, USA	4:39.24		2008 Stephanie Rice, AUS	4:29.45	WR

4x100-meter Freestyle Relay

Year	Time		Year	Time	
1912 Great Britain	5:52.8	WR	1952 Hungary	4:24.4	WR
1920 United States	5:11.6	WR	1956 Australia	4:17.1	WR
1924 United States	4:58.8	WR	1960 United States	4:08.9	WR
1928 United States	4:47.6	WR	1964 United States	4:03.8	WR
1932 United States	4:38.0	WR	1968 United States	4:02.5	OR
1936 Netherlands	4:36.0	OR	1972 United States	3:55.19	WR
1948 United States	4:29.2	OR	1976 United States	3:44.82	WR

Swimming (Cont.)

4x100-meter Freestyle Relay (Cont.)

Year		Time		Year		Time	
1980	East Germany	3:42.71	WR	1996	United States	3:39.29	
1984	United States	3:43.43		2000	United States	3:36.61	WR
1988	East Germany	3:40.63	OR	2004	Australia	3:35.94	WR
1992	United States	3:39.46	WR	2008	Netherlands	3:33.76	OR

4x200-meter Freestyle Relay

Year		Time		Year		Time	
1996	United States	7:59.87		2004	United States	7:53.42	WR
2000	United States	7:57.80	OR	2008	Australia	7:44.31	WR

4x100-meter Medley Relay

Year		Time		Year		Time	
1960	United States	4:41.1	WR	1988	East Germany	4:03.74	OR
1964	United States	4:33.9	WR	1992	United States	4:02.54	WR
1968	United States	4:28.3	OR	1996	United States	4:02.88	
1972	United States	4:20.75	WR	2000	United States	3:58.30	WR
1976	East Germany	4:07.95	WR	2004	Australia	3:57.32	WR
1980	East Germany	4:06.67	WR	2008	Australia	3:52.69	WR
1984	United States	4:08.34					

TENNIS

MEN

Multiple gold medals (including men's doubles): John Boland, Max Decugis, Laurie Doherty, Reggie Doherty, Arthur Gore, Andre Grobert, Nicolas Massu, Vincent Richards, Charles Winslow and Beals Wright (2).

Singles

Year			Year		
1896	John Boland	Great Britain/Ireland	1924	Vincent Richards	United States
1900	Laurie Doherty,	Great Britain	1928-84	Not held	
1904	Beals Wright	United States	1988	Miloslav Mecir	Czechoslovakia
1906	Max Decugis	France	1992	Marc Rosset	Switzerland
1908	Josiah Ritchie	Great Britain	1996	Andre Agassi	United States
	(Indoor) Arthur Gore	Great Britain	2000	Yevgeny Kafelnikov	Russia
1912	Charles Winslow	South Africa	2004	Nicolas Massu	Chile
	(Indoor) André Gobert	France	2008	Rafael Nadal	Spain
1920	Louis Raymond	South Africa			

Doubles

Year		Year	
1896	John Boland, IRE & Fritz Traun, GER	1924	Vincent Richards & Frank Hunter, USA
1900	Laurie and Reggie Doherty, GBR	1928-84	Not held
1904	Edgar Leonard & Beals Wright, USA	1988	Ken Flach & Robert Seguso, USA
1906	Max Decugis & Maurice Germot, FRA	1992	Boris Becker & Michael Stich, GER
1908	George Hillyard & Reggie Doherty, GBR	1996	Todd Woodbridge & Mark Woodforde, AUS
	(Indoor) Arthur Gore & Herbert Barrett, GBR	2000	Sebastien Lareau & Daniel Nestor, CAN
1912	Charles Winslow & Harold Kitson, S. Afr.	2004	Fernando Gonzalez & Nicolas Massu, CHI
	(Indoor) Andre Gobert & Maurice Germot, FRA	2008	Roger Federer & Stanislas Wawrinka, SUI
1920	Noel Turnbull & Max Woosnam, GBR		

WOMEN

Multiple gold medals (including women's doubles): Venus Williams (3); Serena Williams, Helen Wills, Gigi Fernandez, Mary Joe Fernandez (2).

Singles

Year			Year		
1900	Charlotte Cooper	Great Britain	1928-84	Not held	
1906	Esmee Simiriotou	Greece	1988	Steffi Graf	West Germany
1908	Dorothea Chambers	Great Britain	1992	Jennifer Capriati	United States
	(Indoor) Gwen Eastlake-Smith	Great Britain	1996	Lindsay Davenport	United States
1912	Marguerite Broquedis	France	2000	Venus Williams	United States
	(Indoor) Edith Hannam	Great Britain	2004	Justine Henin-Hardenne	Belgium
1920	Suzanne Lenglen	France	2008	Elena Dementieva	Russia
1924	Helen Wills	United States			

Doubles

Year		Year	
1920	Winifred McNair & Kitty McKane, GBR	1996	Gigi Fernandez & Mary Joe Fernandez, USA
1924	Hazel Wightman & Helen Wills, USA	2000	Serena Williams & Venus Williams, USA
1928-84	Not held	2004	Li Ting & Sun Tian Tian, CHN
1988	Pam Shriver & Zina Garrison, USA	2008	Serena Williams & Venus Williams, USA
1992	Gigi Fernandez & Mary Joe Fernandez, USA		

TRACK & FIELD

MEN

At least 4 gold medals (including relays and discontinued events): Ray Ewry (10); Carl Lewis and Paavo Nurmi (9); Ville Ritola and Martin Sheridan (5); Harrison Dillard, Archie Hahn, Michael Johnson, Hannes Kolehmainen, Alvin Kraenzlein, Eric Lemming, Jim Lightbody, Al Oerter, Jesse Owens, Meyer Prinstein, Mel Sheppard, Lasse Viren and Emil Zátopek (4). Note that all of Ewry's gold medals came before 1912, in the Standing High Jump, Standing Long Jump and Standing Triple Jump.

100 meters

Year		Time		Year		Time	
1896	Tom Burke, USA	12.0		1960	Armin Hary, GER	10.2	**OR**
1900	Frank Jarvis, USA	11.0		1964	Bob Hayes, USA	10.0	**=WR**
1904	Archie Hahn, USA	11.0		1968	Jim Hines, USA	9.95	**WR**
1906	Archie Hahn, USA	11.2		1972	Valery Borzov, USSR	10.14	
1908	Reggie Walker, S. Afr.	10.8	**=OR**	1976	Hasely Crawford, TRI	10.06	
1912	Ralph Craig, USA	10.8		1980	Allan Wells, GBR	10.25	
1920	Charley Paddock, USA	10.8		1984	Carl Lewis, USA	9.99	
1924	Harold Abrahams, GBR	10.6	**=OR**	1988	Carl Lewis, USA*	9.92	**WR**
1928	Percy Williams, CAN	10.8		1992	Linford Christie, GBR	9.96	
1932	Eddie Tolan, USA	10.3	**OR**	1996	Donovan Bailey, CAN	9.84	**WR**
1936	Jesse Owens, USA	10.3w		2000	Maurice Greene, USA	9.87	
1948	Harrison Dillard, USA	10.3	**=OR**	2004	Justin Gatlin, USA	9.85	
1952	Lindy Remigino, USA	10.4		2008	Usain Bolt, JAM	9.69	**WR**
1956	Bobby Morrow, USA	10.5					

w indicates wind-aided.

*Lewis finished second to Ben Johnson of Canada, who set a world record of 9.79 seconds. Two days later, Johnson was stripped of his gold medal and his record when he tested positive for steroid use in a post-race drug test.

200 meters

Year		Time		Year		Time	
1900	Walter Tewksbury, USA	22.2		1964	Henry Carr, USA	20.3	**OR**
1904	Archie Hahn, USA	21.6	**OR**	1968	Tommie Smith, USA	19.83	**WR**
1908	Bobby Kerr, CAN	22.6		1972	Valery Borzov, USSR	20.00	
1912	Ralph Craig, USA	21.7		1976	Donald Quarrie, JAM	20.23	
1920	Allen Woodring, USA	22.0		1980	Pietro Mennea, ITA	20.19	
1924	Jackson Scholz, USA	21.6		1984	Carl Lewis, USA	19.80	**OR**
1928	Percy Williams, CAN	21.8		1988	Joe DeLoach, USA	19.75	**OR**
1932	Eddie Tolan, USA	21.2	**OR**	1992	Mike Marsh, USA	20.01	
1936	Jesse Owens, USA	20.7	**OR**	1996	Michael Johnson, USA	19.32	**WR**
1948	Mel Patton, USA	21.1		2000	Konstantinos Kenteris, GRE	20.09	
1952	Andy Stanfield, USA	20.7		2004	Shawn Crawford, USA	19.79	
1956	Bobby Morrow, USA	20.6	**OR**	2008	Usain Bolt, JAM	19.30	**WR**
1960	Livio Berruti, ITA	20.5	**=WR**				

400 meters

Year		Time		Year		Time	
1896	Tom Burke, USA	54.2		1960	Otis Davis, USA	44.9	**WR**
1900	Maxey Long, USA	49.4	**OR**	1964	Mike Larrabee, USA	45.1	
1904	Harry Hillman, USA	49.2	**OR**	1968	Lee Evans, USA	43.86	**WR**
1906	Paul Pilgrim, USA	53.2		1972	Vince Matthews, USA	44.66	
1908	Wyndham Halswelle, GBR	50.0		1976	Alberto Juantorena, CUB	44.26	
1912	Charlie Reidpath, USA	48.2	**OR**	1980	Viktor Markin, USSR	44.60	
1920	Bevil Rudd, S. Afr.	49.6		1984	Alonzo Babers, USA	44.27	
1924	Eric Liddell, GBR	47.6	**OR**	1988	Steve Lewis, USA	43.87	
1928	Ray Barbuti, USA	47.8		1992	Quincy Watts, USA	43.50	**OR**
1932	Bill Carr, USA	46.2	**WR**	1996	Michael Johnson, USA	43.49	**OR**
1936	Archie Williams, USA	46.5		2000	Michael Johnson, USA	43.84	
1948	Arthur Wint, JAM	46.2		2004	Jeremy Wariner, USA	44.00	
1952	George Rhoden, JAM	45.9	**OR**	2008	LaShawn Merritt, USA	43.75	
1956	Charley Jenkins, USA	46.7					

800 meters

Year		Time		Year		Time	
1896	Teddy Flack, AUS	2:11.0		1960	Peter Snell, NZE	1:46.3	**OR**
1900	Alfred Tysoe, GBR	2:01.2		1964	Peter Snell, NZE	1:45.1	**OR**
1904	Jim Lightbody, USA	1:56.0	**OR**	1968	Ralph Doubell, AUS	1:44.3	**=WR**
1906	Paul Pilgrim, USA	2:01.5		1972	Dave Wottle, USA	1:45.9	
1908	Mel Sheppard, USA	1:52.8	**WR**	1976	Alberto Juantorena, CUB	1:43.50	**WR**
1912	Ted Meredith, USA	1:51.9	**WR**	1980	Steve Ovett, GBR	1:45.4	
1920	Albert Hill, GBR	1:53.4		1984	Joaquim Cruz, BRA	1:43.00	**OR**
1924	Douglas Lowe, GBR	1:52.4		1988	Paul Ereng, KEN	1:43.45	
1928	Douglas Lowe, GBR	1:51.8	**OR**	1992	William Tanui, KEN	1:43.66	
1932	Tommy Hampson, GBR	1:49.7	**WR**	1996	Vebjoern Rodal, NOR	1:42.58	**OR**
1936	John Woodruff, USA	1:52.9		2000	Nils Schumann, GER	1:45.08	
1948	Mal Whitfield, USA	1:49.2	**OR**	2004	Yuriy Borzakovskiy, RUS	1:44.45	
1952	Mal Whitfield, USA	1:49.2	**=OR**	2008	Wilfred Bungei, KEN	1:44.65	
1956	Tom Courtney, USA	1:47.7	**OR**				

1500 meters

Year		Time		Year		Time	
1896	Teddy Flack, AUS	4:33.2		1960	Herb Elliott, AUS	3:35.6	WR
1900	Charles Bennett, GBR	4:06.2	WR	1964	Peter Snell, NZE	3:38.1	
1904	Jim Lightbody, USA	4:05.4	WR	1968	Kip Keino, KEN	3:34.9	OR
1906	Jim Lightbody, USA	4:12.0		1972	Pekka Vasala, FIN	3:36.3	
1908	Mel Sheppard, USA	4:03.4	OR	1976	John Walker, NZE	3:39.17	
1912	Arnold Jackson, GBR	3:56.8	OR	1980	Sebastian Coe, GBR	3:38.4	
1920	Albert Hill, GBR	4:01.8		1984	Sebastian Coe, GBR	3:32.53	OR
1924	Paavo Nurmi, FIN	3:53.6	OR	1988	Peter Rono, KEN	3:35.96	
1928	Harry Larva, FIN	3:53.2	OR	1992	Fermin Cacho, SPA	3:40.12	
1932	Luigi Beccali, ITA	3:51.2	OR	1996	Noureddine Morceli, ALG	3:35.78	
1936	John Lovelock, NZE	3:47.8	WR	2000	Noah Ngeny, KEN	3:32.07	OR
1948	Henry Eriksson, SWE	3:49.8		2004	Hicham El Guerrouj, MOR	3:34.18	
1952	Josy Barthel, LUX	3:45.1	OR	2008	Rashid Ramzi, BAH	3:32.94	
1956	Ron Delany, IRE	3:41.2	OR				

5000 meters

Year		Time		Year		Time	
1912	Hannes Kolehmainen, FIN	14:36.6	WR	1968	Mohamed Gammoudi, TUN	14:05.0	
1920	Joseph Guillemot, FRA	14:55.6		1972	Lasse Viren, FIN	13:26.4	OR
1924	Paavo Nurmi, FIN	14:31.2	OR	1976	Lasse Viren, FIN	13:24.76	
1928	Ville Ritola, FIN	14:38.0		1980	Miruts Yifter, ETH	13:21.0	
1932	Lauri Lehtinen, FIN	14:30.0	OR	1984	Said Aouita, MOR	13:05.59	OR
1936	Gunnar Höckert, FIN	14:22.2	OR	1988	John Ngugi, KEN	13:11.70	
1948	Gaston Reiff, BEL	14:17.6	OR	1992	Dieter Baumann, GER	13:12.52	
1952	Emil Zátopek, CZE	14:06.6	OR	1996	Venuste Niyongabo, BUR	13:07.96	
1956	Vladimir Kuts, USSR	13:39.6	OR	2000	Millon Wolde, ETH	13:35.49	
1960	Murray Halberg, NZE	13:43.4		2004	Hicham El Guerrouj, MOR	13:14.39	
1964	Bob Schul, USA	13:48.8		2008	Kenenisa Bekele, ETH	12:57.82	OR

10,000 meters

Year		Time		Year		Time	
1912	Hannes Kolehmainen, FIN	31:20.8		1968	Naftali Temu, KEN	29:27.4	
1920	Paavo Nurmi, FIN	31:45.8		1972	Lasse Viren, FIN	27:38.4	WR
1924	Ville Ritola, FIN	30:23.2	WR	1976	Lasse Viren, FIN	27:40.38	
1928	Paavo Nurmi, FIN	30:18.8	OR	1980	Miruts Yifter, ETH	27:42.7	
1932	Janusz Kusocinski, POL	30:11.4	OR	1984	Alberto Cova, ITA	27:47.54	
1936	Ilmari Salminen, FIN	30:15.4		1988	Brahim Boutaib, MOR	27:21.46	OR
1948	Emil Zátopek, CZE	29:59.6	OR	1992	Khalid Skah, MOR	27:46.70	
1952	Emil Zátopek, CZE	29:17.0	OR	1996	Haile Gebrselassie, ETH	27:07.34	OR
1956	Vladimir Kuts, USSR	28:45.6	OR	2000	Haile Gebrselassie, ETH	27:18.20	
1960	Pyotr Bolotnikov, USSR	28:32.2	OR	2004	Kenenisa Bekele, ETH	27:05.10	OR
1964	Billy Mills, USA	28:24.4	OR	2008	Kenenisa Bekele, ETH	27:01.17	OR

Marathon

Year		Time		Year		Time	
1896	Spiridon Louis, GRE	2:58:50		1960	Abebe Bikila, ETH	2:15:16.2	WB
1900	Michel Théato, FRA	2:59:45		1964	Abebe Bikila, ETH	2:12:11.2	WB
1904	Thomas Hicks, USA	3:28:53		1968	Mamo Wolde, ETH	2:20:26.4	
1906	Billy Sherring, CAN	2:51:23.6		1972	Frank Shorter, USA	2:12:19.8	
1908	Johnny Hayes, USA*	2:55:18.4	OR	1976	Waldemar Cierpinski, E. Ger	2:09:55.0	OR
1912	Kenneth McArthur, S. Afr.	2:36:54.8		1980	Waldemar Cierpinski, E. Ger	2:11:03.0	
1920	Hannes Kolehmainen, FIN	2:32:35.8	WB	1984	Carlos Lopes, POR	2:09:21.0	OR
1924	Albin Stenroos, FIN	2:41:22.6		1988	Gelindo Bordin, ITA	2:10:32	
1928	Boughéra El Ouafi, FRA	2:32:57.0		1992	Hwang Young-Cho, S. Kor	2:13:23	
1932	Juan Carlos Zabala, ARG	2:31:36.0	OR	1996	Josia Thugwane, RSA.	2:12:36	
1936	Sohn Kee-Chung, JPN†	2:29:19.2	OR	2000	Gezahegne Abera, ETH	2:10:11	
1948	Delfo Cabrera, ARG	2:34:51.6		2004	Stefano Baldini, ITA	2:10:55	
1952	Emil Zátopek, CZE	2:23:03.2	OR	2008	Samuel Kamau Wansiru, KEN	2:06:32	OR
1956	Alain Mimoun, FRA	2:25:00.0					

*Dorando Pietri of Italy placed first, but was disqualified for being helped across the finish line.

†Sohn was a Korean, but he was forced to compete under the name Kitei Son by Japan, which occupied Korea at the time.

Note: Marathon distances–40,000 meters (1896,1904); 40,260 meters (1900); 41,860 meters (1906); 42,195 meters (1908 and since 1924); 40,200 meters (1912); 42,750 meters (1920). Current distance of 42,195 meters measures 26 miles, 385 yards.

110-meter Hurdles

Year		Time		Year		Time	
1896	Tom Curtis, USA	17.6		1936	Forrest (Spec) Towns, USA	14.2	
1900	Alvin Kraenzlein, USA	15.4	OR	1948	William Porter, USA	13.9	OR
1904	Frederick Schule, USA	16.0		1952	Harrison Dillard, USA	13.7	OR
1906	Robert Leavitt, USA	16.2		1956	Lee Calhoun, USA	13.5	OR
1908	Forrest Smithson, USA	15.0	WR	1960	Lee Calhoun, USA	13.8	
1912	Frederick Kelly, USA	15.1		1964	Hayes Jones, USA	13.6	
1920	Earl Thomson, CAN	14.8	WR	1968	Willie Davenport, USA	13.3	OR
1924	Daniel Kinsey, USA	15.0		1972	Rod Milburn, USA	13.24	=WR
1928	Syd Atkinson, S. Afr.	14.8		1976	Guy Drut, FRA	13.30	
1932	George Saling, USA	14.6		1980	Thomas Munkelt, E. Ger	13.39	

1984 Roger Kingdom, USA ....13.20 **OR**	2000 Anier Garcia, CUB 13.00
1988 Roger Kingdom, USA ....12.98 **OR**	2004 Liu Xiang, CHN ....12.91 **OR**
1992 Mark McKoy, CAN 13.12	2008 Dayron Robles, CUB 12.93
1996 Allen Johnson, USA ....12.95 **OR**	

400-meter Hurdles

Year	Time		Year	Time	
1900 Walter Tewksbury, USA	.57.6		1964 Rex Cawley, USA	.49.6	
1904 Harry Hillman, USA	.53.0		1968 David Hemery, GBR	.48.12	**WR**
1908 Charley Bacon, USA	.55.0	**WR**	1972 John Akii-Bua, UGA	.47.82	**WR**
1920 Frank Loomis, USA	.54.0	**WR**	1976 Edwin Moses, USA	.47.64	**WR**
1924 Morgan Taylor, USA	.52.6		1980 Volker Beck, E. Ger	.48.70	
1928 David Burghley, GBR	.53.4	**OR**	1984 Edwin Moses, USA	.47.75	
1932 Bob Tisdall, IRE	.51.7		1988 Andre Phillips, USA	.47.19	**OR**
1936 Glenn Hardin, USA	.52.4		1992 Kevin Young, USA	.46.78	**WR**
1948 Roy Cochran, USA	.51.1	**OR**	1996 Derrick Adkins, USA	.47.54	
1952 Charley Moore, USA	.50.8	**OR**	2000 Angelo Taylor, USA	.47.50	
1956 Glenn Davis, USA	.50.1	**=OR**	2004 Felix Sanchez, DOM	.47.63	
1960 Glenn Davis, USA	.49.3	**OR**	2008 Angelo Taylor, USA	.47.25	

3000-meter Steeplechase

Year	Time		Year	Time	
1900 George Orton, CAN	.7:34.4		1964 Gaston Roelants, BEL	.8:30.8	**OR**
1904 Jim Lightbody, USA	.7:39.6		1968 Amos Biwott, KEN	.8:51.0	
1908 Arthur Russell, GBR	.10:47.8		1972 Kip Keino, KEN	.8:23.6	**OR**
1920 Percy Hodge, GBR	.10:00.4	**OR**	1976 Anders Gärderud, SWE	.8:08.2	**WR**
1924 Ville Ritola, FIN	.9:33.6		1980 Bronislaw Malinowski, POL	.8:09.7	
1928 Toivo Loukola, FIN	.9:21.8	**WR**	1984 Julius Korir, KEN	.8:11.80	
1932 Volmari Iso-Hollo, FIN	.10:33.4*		1988 Julius Kariuki, KEN	.8:05.51	**OR**
1936 Volmari Iso-Hollo, FIN	.9:03.8	**WR**	1992 Matthew Birir, KEN	.8:08.84	
1948 Thore Sjöstrand, SWE	.9:04.6		1996 Joseph Keter, KEN	.8:07.12	
1952 Horace Ashenfelter, USA	.8:45.4	**WR**	2000 Reuben Kosgei, KEN	.8:21.43	
1956 Chris Brasher, GBR	.8:41.2	**OR**	2004 Ezekiel Kemboi, KEN	.8:05.81	
1960 Zdzislaw Krzyszkowiak, POL	.8:34.2	**OR**	2008 Birmin Kiprop Kipruto, KEN	.8:10.34	

*Iso-Hollo ran one extra lap due to lap counter's mistake.
Other steeplechase distances: 2500 meters (1900); 2590 meters (1904); 3200 meters (1908) and 3460 meters (1932).

4x100-meter Relay

Year	Time		Year	Time	
1912 Great Britain	.42.4		1968 United States	.38.23	**WR**
1920 United States	.42.2	**WR**	1972 United States	.38.19	**WR**
1924 United States	.41.0	**=WR**	1976 United States	.38.33	
1928 United States	.41.0	**=WR**	1980 Soviet Union	.38.26	
1932 United States	.40.0	**WR**	1984 United States	.37.83	**WR**
1936 United States	.39.8	**WR**	1988 Soviet Union	.38.19	
1948 United States	.40.6		1992 United States	.37.40	**WR**
1952 United States	.40.1		1996 Canada	.37.69	
1956 United States	.39.5	**WR**	2000 United States	.37.61	
1960 Germany	.39.5	**=WR**	2004 Great Britain	.38.07	
1964 United States	.39.0	**WR**	2008 Jamaica	.37.10	**WR**

4x400-meter Relay

Year	Time		Year	Time	
1908 United States	.3:29.4		1968 United States	.2:56.16	**WR**
1912 United States	.3:16.6	**WR**	1972 Kenya	.2:59.8	
1920 Great Britain	.3:22.2		1976 United States	.2:58.65	
1924 United States	.3:16.0	**WR**	1980 Soviet Union	.3:01.1	
1928 United States	.3:14.2	**WR**	1984 United States	.2:57.91	
1932 United States	.3:08.2	**WR**	1988 United States	.2:56.16	**=WR**
1936 Great Britain	.3:09.0		1992 United States	.2:55.74	**WR**
1948 United States	.3:10.4		1996 United States	.2:55.99	
1952 Jamaica	.3:03.9	**WR**	2000 United States	.2:56.35	
1956 United States	.3:04.8		2004 United States	.2:55.91	
1960 United States	.3:02.2	**WR**	2008 United States	.2:55.39	**OR**
1964 United States	.3:00.7	**WR**			

20-kilometer Walk

Year	Time		Year	Time	
1956 Leonid Spirin, USSR	.1:31:27.4		1984 Ernesto Canto, MEX	.1:23:13	**OR**
1960 Vladimir Golubnichiy, USSR	.1:34:07.2		1988 Jozef Pribilinec, CZE	.1:19:57	**OR**
1964 Ken Matthews, GBR	.1:29:34.0	**OR**	1992 Daniel Plaza Montero, SPA	.1:21:45	
1968 Vladimir Golubnichiy, USSR	.1:33:58.4		1996 Jefferson Perez, ECU	.1:20:07	
1972 Peter Frenkel, E. Ger	.1:26:42.4	**OR**	2000 Robert Korzeniowski, POL	.1:18:59	**OR**
1976 Daniel Bautista, MEX	.1:24:40.6	**OR**	2004 Ivano Brugnetti, ITA	.1:19:40	
1980 Maurizio Damilano, ITA	.1:23:35.5	**OR**	2008 Valeriy Borchin, RUS	.1:19:01	

Track & Field (Cont.)

50-kilometer Walk

Year		Time	
1932	Thomas Green, GBR	4:50:10	
1936	Harold Whitlock, GBR	4:30:41.4	OR
1948	John Ljunggren, SWE	4:41:52	
1952	Giuseppe Dordoni, ITA	4:28:07.8	OR
1956	Norman Read, NZE	4:30:42.8	
1960	Don Thompson, GBR	4:25:30.0	OR
1964	Abdon Pamich, ITA	4:11:12.4	OR
1968	Christoph Höhne, E. Ger	4:20:13.6	
1972	Bernd Kannenberg, W. Ger	3:56:11.6	OR

Year		Time	
1976	Not held		
1980	Hartwig Gauder, E. Ger	3:49:24.0	OR
1984	Raul Gonzalez, MEX	3:47:26	OR
1988	Vyacheslav Ivanenko, USSR	3:38:29	OR
1992	Andrei Perlov, UT	3:50:13	
1996	Robert Korzeniowski, POL	3:43:30	
2000	Robert Korzeniowski, POL	3:42:22	
2004	Robert Korzeniowski, POL	3:38:46	
2008	Alex Schwazer, ITA	3:37:09	OR

High Jump

Year		Height	
1896	Ellery Clark, USA	5-11¼	
1900	Irving Baxter, USA	6- 2¾	OR
1904	Sam Jones, USA	5-11	
1906	Cornelius Leahy, GBR/IRE	5-10	
1908	Harry Porter, USA	6- 3	OR
1912	Alma Richards, USA	6- 4	OR
1920	Richmond Landon, USA	6- 4	=OR
1924	Harold Osborn, USA	6- 6	OR
1928	Bob King, USA	6- 4½	
1932	Duncan McNaughton, CAN	6- 5½	
1936	Cornelius Johnson, USA	6- 8	OR
1948	John Winter, AUS	6- 6	
1952	Walt Davis, USA	6- 8½	OR
1956	Charley Dumas, USA	6-11½	OR

Year		Height	
1960	Robert Shavlakadze, USSR	7- 1	OR
1964	Valery Brumel, USSR	7- 1¾	OR
1968	Dick Fosbury, USA	7- 4¼	OR
1972	Yuri Tarmak, USSR	7- 3¾	
1976	Jacek Wszola, POL	7- 4½	OR
1980	Gerd Wessig, E. Ger	7- 8¾	WR
1984	Dietmar Mögenburg, W. Ger	7- 8½	
1988	Gennady Avdeyenko, USSR	7- 9¾	OR
1992	Javier Sotomayor, CUB	7- 8	
1996	Charles Austin, USA	7-10	OR
2000	Sergey Klugin, RUS	7- 8½	
2004	Stefan Holm, SWE	7- 8¾	
2008	Andrey Silnov, RUS	2.36m	

Pole Vault

Year		Height	
1896	William Hoyt, USA	10-10	
1900	Irving Baxter, USA	10-10	
1904	Charles Dvorak, USA	11- 5¾	
1906	Fernand Gonder, FRA	11- 5¾	
1908	(TIE) Edward Cooke, USA	12- 2	
	& Alfred Gilbert, USA	12- 2	OR
1912	Harry Babcock, USA	12-11½	OR
1920	Frank Foss, USA	13- 5	WR
1924	Lee Barnes, USA	12-11½	
1928	Sabin Carr, USA	13- 9¼	OR
1932	Bill Miller, USA	14-1¾	OR
1936	Earle Meadows, USA	14- 3¼	OR
1948	Guinn Smith, USA	14-1¼	
1952	Bob Richards, USA	14-11	OR

Year		Height	
1956	Bob Richards, USA	14-11½	OR
1960	Don Bragg, USA	15- 5	OR
1964	Fred Hansen, USA	16- 8¾	OR
1968	Bob Seagren, USA	17-8½	OR
1972	Wolfgang Nordwig, E. Ger	18- 0½	OR
1976	Tadeusz Slusarski, POL	18- 0½	=OR
1980	Wladyslaw Kozakiewicz, POL	18-11½	WR
1984	Pierre Quinon, FRA	18-10¼	
1988	Sergey Bubka, USSR	19- 4¼	OR
1992	Maksim Tarasov, UT	19-0¼	
1996	Jean Galfione, FRA	19- 5¼	OR
2000	Nick Hysong, USA	19-4¼	
2004	Timothy Mack, USA	19-6¼	OR
2008	Steve Hooker, AUS	5.76m	OR

Long Jump

Year		Distance	
1896	Ellery Clark, USA	20-10	
1900	Alvin Kraenzlein, USA	23- 6¾	OR
1904	Meyer Prinstein, USA	24- 1	OR
1906	Meyer Prinstein, USA	23- 7½	
1908	Frank Irons, USA	24- 6½	OR
1912	Albert Gutterson, USA	24-11¼	OR
1920	William Petersson, SWE	23-5½	
1924	De Hart Hubbard, USA	24- 5	
1928	Ed Hamm, USA	25- 4½	OR
1932	Ed Gordon, USA	25- 0¾	
1936	Jesse Owens, USA	26-5½	OR
1948	Willie Steele, USA	25- 8	
1952	Jerome Biffle, USA	24-10	
1956	Greg Bell, USA	25- 8¼	

Year		Distance	
1960	Ralph Boston, USA	26-7¾	OR
1964	Lynn Davies, GBR	26- 5¾	
1968	Bob Beamon, USA	29- 2½	WR
1972	Randy Williams, USA	27-0½	
1976	Arnie Robinson, USA	27- 4¾	
1980	Lutz Dombrowski, E. Ger	28- 0¼	
1984	Carl Lewis, USA	28-0¼	
1988	Carl Lewis, USA	28- 7¼	
1992	Carl Lewis, USA	28- 5½	
1996	Carl Lewis, USA	27-10¾	
2000	Ivan Pedroso, CUB	28- 0¾	
2004	Dwight Phillips, USA	28- 2¼	
2008	Irving Jahir Saladino Aranda, PAN	8.34m	

Triple Jump

Year	Distance		Year	Distance	
1896 James Connolly, USA	44-11¾		1960 Józef Schmidt, POL	55- 2	
1900 Meyer Prinstein, USA	47- 5¾	**OR**	1964 Józef Schmidt, POL	55-3½	**OR**
1904 Meyer Prinstein, USA	47- 1		1968 Viktor Saneyev, USSR	57- 0¾	**WR**
1906 Peter O'Connor, GBR/IRE	46-2¼		1972 Viktor Saneyev, USSR	56-11¼	
1908 Timothy Ahearne, GBR/IRE	48-11¼	**OR**	1976 Viktor Saneyev, USSR	56- 8¾	
1912 Gustaf Lindblom, SWE	48-5¼		1980 Jack Uudmäe, USSR	56-11¼	
1920 Vilho Tuulos, FIN	47- 7		1984 Al Joyner, USA	56-7½	
1924 Nick Winter, AUS	50-11¼	**WR**	1988 Khristo Markov, BUL	57- 9¼	**OR**
1928 Mikio Oda, JPN	49-11		1992 Mike Conley, USA	59-7½W	**OR**
1932 Chuhei Nambu, JPN	51- 7	**WR**	1996 Kenny Harrison, USA	59-4¼	**OR**
1936 Naoto Tajima, JPN	52- 6	**WR**	2000 Jonathan Edwards, GBR	58-1¼	
1948 Arne Ahman, SWE	50- 6¼		2004 Christian Olsson, SWE	58-4½	
1952 Adhemar da Silva, BRA	53-2¾	**WR**	2008 Nelson Evora, POR	17.67m	
1956 Adhemar da Silva, BRA	53- 7¾	**OR**	Windicates wind-aided.		

Shot Put

Year	Distance		Year	Distance	
1896 Bob Garrett, USA	36- 9¾		1960 Bill Nieder, USA	64-6¾	**OR**
1900 Richard Sheldon, USA	46- 3¼	**OR**	1964 Dallas Long, USA	66- 8½	**OR**
1904 Ralph Rose, USA	48- 7	**WR**	1968 Randy Matson, USA	67-4¾	
1906 Martin Sheridan, USA	40- 5¼		1972 Wladyslaw Komar, POL	69- 6	**OR**
1908 Ralph Rose, USA	46-7½		1976 Udo Beyer, E. Ger	69- 0¾	
1912 Patrick McDonald, USA	50- 4	**OR**	1980 Vladimir Kiselyov, USSR	70- 0½	**OR**
1920 Ville Pörhölä, FIN	48-7¼		1984 Alessandro Andrei, ITA	69- 9	
1924 Bud Houser, USA	49- 2¼		1988 Ulf Timmermann, E. Ger	73- 8¾	**OR**
1928 John Kuck, USA	52- 0¾	**WR**	1992 Mike Stulce, USA	71-2½	
1932 Leo Sexton, USA	52- 6	**OR**	1996 Randy Barnes, USA	70-11¼	
1936 Hans Woellke, GER	53- 1¾	**OR**	2000 Arsi Harju, FIN	69-10¼	
1948 Wilbur Thompson, USA	56- 2	**OR**	2004 Yuriy Bilonog, UKR	69-5¼	
1952 Parry O'Brien, USA	57- 1½	**OR**	2008 Tomasz Majewski, POL	21.51m	
1956 Parry O'Brien, USA	60-11¼	**OR**			

Discus Throw

Year	Distance		Year	Distance	
1896 Bob Garrett, USA	95- 7½		1960 Al Oerter, USA	194- 2	**OR**
1900 Rudolf Bauer, HUN	118- 3	**OR**	1964 Al Oerter, USA	200- 1	**OR**
1904 Martin Sheridan, USA	128-10½	**OR**	1968 Al Oerter, USA	212- 6	**OR**
1906 Martin Sheridan, USA	136- 0		1972 Ludvik Danek, CZE	211- 3	
1908 Martin Sheridan, USA	134- 2	**OR**	1976 Mac Wilkins, USA	221- 5	
1912 Armas Taipale, FIN	148- 3	**OR**	1980 Viktor Rashchupkin, USSR	218- 8	
1920 Elmer Niklander, FIN	146-7		1984 Rolf Danneberg, W. Ger	218- 6	
1924 Bud Houser, USA	151- 4	**OR**	1988 Jürgen Schult, E. Ger	225- 9	**OR**
1928 Bud Houser, USA	155- 3	**OR**	1992 Romas Ubartas, LIT	213- 8	
1932 John Anderson, USA	162- 4	**OR**	1996 Lars Riedel, GER	227-8	
1936 Ken Carpenter, USA	165- 7	**OR**	2000 Virgilijus Alekna, LIT	227-4	
1948 Adolfo Consolini, ITA	173- 2	**OR**	2004 Virgilijus Alekna, LIT*	229-3	**OR**
1952 Sim Iness, USA	180- 6	**OR**	2008 Gerd Kanter, EST	68.82m	
1956 Al Oerter, USA	184-11	**OR**			

*Hungary's **Robert Fazekas** had a throw of 232 feet, 8 inches, and was initially declared the winner, but he was disqualified for failing to submit to a drug test following the competition.

Hammer Throw

Year	Distance		Year	Distance	
1900 John Flanagan, USA	163- 1		1964 Romuald Klim, USSR	228-10	**OR**
1904 John Flanagan, USA	168- 1	**OR**	1968 Gyula Zsivótzky, HUN	240- 8	**OR**
1908 John Flanagan, USA	170- 4	**OR**	1972 Anatoly Bondarchuk, USSR	247- 8	**OR**
1912 Matt McGrath, USA	179- 7	**OR**	1976 Yuri Sedykh, USSR	254- 4	**OR**
1920 Pat Ryan, USA	173- 5		1980 Yuri Sedykh, USSR	268- 4	**WR**
1924 Fred Tootell, USA	174-10		1984 Juha Tiainen, FIN	256- 2	
1928 Pat O'Callaghan, IRE	168- 7		1988 Sergey Litvinov, USSR	278- 2	**OR**
1932 Pat O'Callaghan, IRE	176-11		1992 Andrei Abduvaliyev, UT	270- 9	
1936 Karl Hein, GER	185- 4	**OR**	1996 Balazs Kiss, HUN	266-6	
1948 Imre Németh, HUN	183-11		2000 Szymon Ziolkowski, POL	262-6	
1952 József Csérmák, HUN	197-11	**WR**	2004 Koji Murofushi, JPN*	272-0	
1956 Harold Connolly, USA	207- 3	**OR**	2008 Primoz Kozmus, SLO	82.02m	
1960 Vasily Rudenkov, USSR	220- 2	**OR**			

Hungary's **Adrian Annus** was initially awarded the gold medal for his throw of 272-11, but after questions were raised about the legitimacy of his post-competition drug test, and he failed to submit to a follow-up test, he was disqualified and stripped of the gold.

Track & Field (Cont.)

Javelin Throw

Year		Distance		Year		Distance	
1908	Eric Lemming, SWE	179-10	WR	1968	Jänis Lüsis, USSR	295-7	OR
1912	Eric Lemming, SWE	198-11	WR	1972	Klaus Wolfermann, W. Ger	296-10	OR
1920	Jonni Myyrä, FIN	215-10	OR	1976	Miklos Németh, HUN	310-4	WR
1924	Jonni Myyrä, FIN	206-7		1980	Dainis Kula, USSR	299-2	
1928	Erik Lundkvist, SWE	218-6	OR	1984	Arto Härkönen, FIN	284-8	
1932	Matti Järvinen, FIN	238-6	OR	1988	Tapio Korjus, FIN	276-6	
1936	Gerhard Stöck, GER	235-8		1992	Jan Zelezny, CZE	294-2*	OR
1948	Kai Tapio Rautavaara, FIN	228-10		1996	Jan Zelezny, CZR	289-3	
1952	Cy Young, USA	242-1	OR	2000	Jan Zelezny, CZR	295-10	OR
1956	Egil Danielson, NOR	281-2	WR	2004	Andreas Thorkildsen, NOR	283-9	
1960	Viktor Tsibulenko, USSR	277-8		2008	Andreas Thorkildsen, NOR	90.57m	
1964	Pauli Nevala, FIN	271-2					

*In 1986 the balance point of the javelin was modified and new records have been kept since.

Decathlon

Year		Points		Year		Points	
1904	Thomas Kiely, IRE	6036		1964	Willi Holdorf, GER	7887	
1906-08	Not held			1968	Bill Toomey, USA	8193	OR
1912	Jim Thorpe, USA	8412	WR	1972	Nikolai Avilov, USSR	8454	WR
1920	Helge Lövland, NOR	6803		1976	Bruce Jenner, USA	8617	WR
1924	Harold Osborn, USA	7711	WR	1980	Daley Thompson, GBR	8495	
1928	Paavo Yrjölä, FIN	8053	WR	1984	Daley Thompson, GBR	8798	=WR
1932	Jim Bausch, USA	8462	WR	1988	Christian Schenk, E. Ger	8488	
1936	Glenn Morris, USA	7900	WR	1992	Robert Zmelik, CZE	8611	
1948	Bob Mathias, USA	7139		1996	Dan O'Brien, USA	8824	
1952	Bob Mathias, USA	7887	WR	2000	Erki Nool, EST	8641	
1956	Milt Campbell, USA	7937	OR	2004	Roman Sebrle, CZE	8893	OR
1960	Rafer Johnson, USA	8392	OR	2008	Bryan Clay, USA	8791	

WOMEN

At least 4 gold medals (including relays): Evelyn Ashford, Fanny Blankers-Koen, Betty Cuthbert and Bärbel Eckert Wöckel (4).

100 meters

Year		Time		Year		Time	
1928	Betty Robinson, USA	12.2	=WR	1976	Annegret Richter, W. Ger	11.08	
1932	Stella Walsh, POL*	11.9	=WR	1980	Lyudmila Kondratyeva, USSR	11.06	
1936	Helen Stephens, USA	11.5w		1984	Evelyn Ashford, USA	10.97	OR
1948	Fanny Blankers-Koen, NED	11.9		1988	Florence Griffith Joyner, USA	10.54w	
1952	Marjorie Jackson, AUS	11.5	=WR	1992	Gail Devers, USA	10.82	OR
1956	Betty Cuthbert, AUS	11.5		1996	Gail Devers, USA	10.94	
1960	Wilma Rudolph, USA	11.0w		2000	Ekaterina Thanou, GRE†	11.12	
1964	Wyomia Tyus, USA	11.4		2004	Yuliya Nesterenko, BLR	10.93	
1968	Wyomia Tyus, USA	11.08	WR	2008	Shelly-ann Fraser, JAM	10.78	
1972	Renate Stecher, E. Ger	11.07					

*An autopsy performed after Walsh's death in 1980 revealed that she was a man.
windicates wind-aided.

†Marion Jones won the gold (10.75) but later admitted to using performance-enhancing drugs and was stripped of the gold.

200 meters

Year		Time		Year		Time	
1948	Fanny Blankers-Koen, NED	24.4		1980	Bärbel Eckert Wockel, E. Ger	22.03	OR
1952	Marjorie Jackson, AUS	23.7	OR	1984	Valerie Brisco-Hooks, USA	21.81	OR
1956	Betty Cuthbert, AUS	23.4	=OR	1988	Florence Griffith Joyner, USA	21.34	WR
1960	Wilma Rudolph, USA	24.0		1992	Gwen Torrence, USA	21.81	
1964	Edith McGuire, USA	23.0	OR	1996	Marie-Jose Perec, FRA	22.12	
1968	Irena Szewinska, POL	22.5	WR	2000	Pauline Davis-Thompson, BAH†	22.27	
1972	Renate Stecher, E. Ger	22.40	=WR	2004	Veronica Campbell, JAM	22.05	
1976	Bärbel Eckert, E. Ger	22.37	OR	2008	Veronica Campbell-Brown, JAM	21.74	

†Marion Jones won the gold (21.84) but later admitted to using performance-enhancing drugs and was stripped of the gold.

400 meters

Year		Time		Year		Time	
1964	Betty Cuthbert, AUS	52.0		1988	Olga Bryzgina, USSR	48.65	OR
1968	Colette Besson, FRA	52.03	=OR	1992	Marie-Jose Perec, FRA	48.83	
1972	Monika Zehrt, E. Ger	51.08	OR	1996	Marie-Jose Perec, FRA	48.25	OR
1976	Irena Szewinska, POL	49.29	WR	2000	Cathy Freeman, AUS	49.11	
1980	Marita Koch, E. Ger	48.88	OR	2004	Tonique Williams-Darling, BAH	49.41	
1984	Valerie Brisco-Hooks, USA	48.83	OR	2008	Christine Ohuruogu, GBR	49.62	

800 meters

Year	Time		Year	Time	
1928 Lina Radke, GER	2:16.8	WR	1984 Doina Melinte, ROM	1:57.60	
1932-56 Not held			1988 Sigrun Wodars, E. Ger	1:56.10	
1960 Lyudmila Shevtsova, USSR	2:04.3	=WR	1992 Ellen van Langen, NED	1:55.54	
1964 Ann Packer, GBR	2:01.1	OR	1996 Svetlana Masterkova, RUS	1:57.73	
1968 Madeline Manning, USA	2:00.9	OR	2000 Maria Mutola, MOZ	1:56.15	
1972 Hildegard Falck, W. Ger	1:58.55	OR	2004 Kelly Holmes, GBR	1:56.38	
1976 Tatyana Kazankina, USSR	1:54.94	WR	2008 Pamela Jelirro, KEN	1:54.87	
1980 Nadezhda Olizarenko, USSR	1:53.42	WR			

1500 meters

Year	Time		Year	Time	
1972 Lyudmila Bragina, USSR	4:01.4	WR	1992 Hassiba Boulmerka, ALG	3:55.30	
1976 Tatyana Kazankina, USSR	4:05.48		1996 Svetlana Masterkova, RUS	4:00.83	
1980 Tatyana Kazankina, USSR	3:56.6	OR	2000 Nouria Merah-Benida, ALG	4:05.10	
1984 Gabriella Dorio, ITA	4:03.25		2004 Kelly Holmes, GBR	3:57.90	
1988 Paula Ivan, ROM	3:53.96	OR	2008 Nancy Jebet Langat, KEN	4:00.23	

5000 meters

Year	Time		Year	Time	
1984 Maricica Puica, ROM	8:35.96		1996 Wang Junxia, CHN	14:59.88	
1988 Tatyana Samolenko, USSR	8:26.53	OR	2000 Gabriela Szabo, ROM	14:40.79	OR
1992 Elena Romanova, UT	8:46.04		2004 Meseret Defar, ETH	14:45.65	
Note: Event held over 3000 meters from 1984-92.			2008 Tirunesh Dibaba, ETH	15:41.40	

10,000 meters

Year	Time		Year	Time	
1988 Olga Bondarenko, USSR	31:05.21	OR	2000 Derartu Tulu, ETH	30:17.49	OR
1992 Derartu Tulu, ETH	31:06.02		2004 Xing Huina, CHN	30:24.36	
1996 Fernanda Ribeiro, POR	31:01.63	OR	2008 Tirunesh Dibaba, ETH	29:54.66	

Marathon

Year	Time	Year	Time
1984 Joan Benoit, USA	2:24:52	2000 Naoko Takahashi, JPN	2:23:14
1988 Rosa Mota, POR	2:25:40	2004 Mizuki Noguchi, JPN	2:26:20
1992 Valentina Yegorova, UT	2:32:41	2008 Constantina Tomescu, ROM	2:26:44
1996 Fatuma Roba, ETH	2:26:05		

100-meter Hurdles

Year	Time		Year	Time	
1932 Babe Didrikson, USA	11.7	WR	1980 Vera Komisova, USSR	12.56	OR
1936 Trebisonda Valla, ITA	11.7		1984 Benita Fitzgerald-Brown, USA	12.84	
1948 Fanny Blankers-Koen, NED	11.2	OR	1988 Yordanka Donkova, BUL	12.38	OR
1952 Shirley Strickland, AUS	10.9	WR	1992 Paraskevi Patoulidou, GRE	12.64	
1956 Shirley Strickland, AUS	10.7	OR	1996 Ludmila Enquist, SWE	12.58	
1960 Irina Press, USSR	10.8		2000 Olga Shishigina, KAZ	12.65	
1964 Karin Balzer, GER	10.5ᵂ		2004 Joanna Hayes, USA	12.37	OR
1968 Maureen Caird, AUS	10.3	OR	2008 Dawn Harper, USA	12.54	
1972 Annelie Ehrhardt, E. Ger	12.59	WR	ᵂindicates wind-aided.		
1976 Johanna Schaller, E. Ger	12.77		**Note:** Event held over 80 meters from 1932-68.		

400-meter Hurdles

Year	Time		Year	Time	
1984 Nawal El Moutawakel, MOR	54.61	OR	2000 Irina Privalova, RUS	53.02	
1988 Debra Flintoff-King, AUS	53.17	OR	2004 Fani Halkia, GRE	52.82	
1992 Sally Gunnell, GBR	53.23		2008 Melanie Walker, JAM	52.64	
1996 Deon Hemmings, JAM	52.82	OR			

4x100-meter Relay

Year	Time		Year	Time	
1928 Canada	48.4	WR	1976 East Germany	42.55	OR
1932 United States	46.9	WR	1980 East Germany	41.60	WR
1936 United States	46.9		1984 United States	41.65	
1948 Holland	47.5		1988 United States	41.98	
1952 United States	45.9	WR	1992 United States	42.11	
1956 Australia	44.5	WR	1996 United States	41.95	
1960 United States	44.5		2000 Bahamas	42.20	
1964 Poland	43.6		2004 Jamaica	41.73	
1968 United States	42.87	WR	2008 Russia	42.31	
1972 West Germany	42.81	WR			

Track & Field (Cont.)

4x400-meter Relay

Year		Time		Year		Time	
1972	East Germany	3:23.0	WR	1992	Unified Team	3:20.20	
1976	East Germany	3:19.23	WR	1996	United States	3:20.91	
1980	Soviet Union	3:20.2		2000	Jamaica†	3:23.25	
1984	United States	3:18.29	OR	2004	United States	3:19.01	
1988	Soviet Union	3:15.18	WR	2008	United States	3:18.54	

†The United States won the gold in Sydney but American Marion Jones would later admit to using performance-enhancing drugs and the United States relay squad (3:22.62) was stripped of the gold.

20-kilometer Walk

Year		Time	Year		Time
1992	Chen Yueling, CHN	44:32	2000	Wang Liping, CHN	1:29:05
1996	Yelena Ninikolayeva, RUS	41:49	2004	Athanasia Tsoumeleka, GRE	1:29:12
			2008	Olga Kaniskina, RUS	1:26:31

Note: Event was held over 10 kilometers from 1992-96.

Pole Vault

Year		Height		Year		Height	
2000	Stacy Dragila, USA	15-1	OR	2008	Yelena Isinbayeva, RUS	5.05m	WR
2004	Yelena Isinbayeva, RUS	16-1¼	WR				

High Jump

Year		Height		Year		Height	
1928	Ethel Catherwood, CAN	5-2½		1976	Rosemarie Ackermann, E. Ger	6-4	OR
1932	Jean Shiley, USA	5-5¼	WR	1980	Sara Simeoni, ITA	6-5½	OR
1936	Ibolya Csák, HUN	5-3		1984	Ulrike Meyfarth, W. Ger	6-7½	OR
1948	Alice Coachman, USA	5-6	OR	1988	Louise Ritter, USA	6-8	OR
1952	Esther Brand, RSA	5-5¾		1992	Heike Henkel, GER	6-7½	
1956	Mildred McDaniel, USA	5-9¼	WR	1996	Stefka Kostadinova, BUL	6-8¾	
1960	Iolanda Balas, ROM	6-0¾	OR	2000	Yelena Yelesina, RUS	6-7	
1964	Iolanda Balas, ROM	6-2¾	OR	2004	Yelena Slesarenko, RUS	6-9	OR
1968	Miloslava Rezkova, CZE	5-11½		2008	Tia Hellebaut, BEL	2.05m	
1972	Ulrike Meyfarth, W. Ger	6-3½	=WR				

Long Jump

Year		Distance		Year		Distance	
1948	Olga Gyarmati, HUN	18-8¼		1980	Tatyana Kolpakova, USSR	23-2	OR
1952	Yvette Williams, NZE	20-5¾	OR	1984	Anisoara Cusmir-Stanciu, ROM	22-10	
1956	Elzbieta Krzesinska, POL	20-10	=WR	1988	Jackie Joyner-Kersee, USA	24-3¼	OR
1960	Vyera Krepkina, USSR	20-10¾	OR	1992	Heike Drechsler, GER	23-5¼	
1964	Mary Rand, GBR	22-2¼	WR	1996	Chioma Ajunwa, NGR	23-4½	
1968	Viorica Viscopoleanu, ROM	22-4½	WR	2000	Heike Drechsler, GER	22-11¼	
1972	Heidemarie Rosendahl, W. Ger	22-3		2004	Tatyana Lebedeva, RUS	23-2½	
1976	Angela Voigt, E. Ger	22-0¾		2008	Maureen Higa Maggi, BRA	7.04m	

Triple Jump

Year		Distance	Year		Distance
1996	Inessa Kravets, UKR	50-3½	2004	Francoise Mbango Etone, CMR	50-2½
2000	Tereza Marinova, BUL	49-10½	2008	Francoise Mbango Etone, CMR	15.39m

Shot Put

Year		Distance		Year		Distance	
1948	Micheline Ostermeyer, FRA	45-1½		1980	Ilona Slupianek, E. Ger	73-6¼	OR
1952	Galina Zybina, USSR	50-1¾	WR	1984	Claudia Losch, W. Ger	67-2¼	
1956	Tamara Tyshkevich, USSR	54-5	OR	1988	Natalia Lisovskaya, USSR	72-11¾	
1960	Tamara Press, USSR	56-10	OR	1992	Svetlana Krivaleva, UT	69-1¼	
1964	Tamara Press, USSR	59-6¼	OR	1996	Astrid Kumbernuss, GER	67-5½	
1968	Margitta Gummel, E. Ger	64-4	WR	2000	Yanina Korolchik, BLR	67-5½	
1972	Nadezhda Chizhova, USSR	69-0	WR	2004	Yumileidi Cumba, CUB*	64-3¼	
1976	Ivanka Hristova, BUL	69-5¼	OR	2008	Valerie Vili, NZE	20.56m	

*Russia's Irina Korzhanenko (69-1¼) was stripped of the gold for failing a post-competition drug test.

Discus Throw

Year		Distance		Year		Distance	
1928	Halina Konopacka, POL	129-11¾	WR	1964	Tamara Press, USSR	187-10	OR
1932	Lillian Copeland, USA	133-2	OR	1968	Lia Manoliu, ROM	191-2	OR
1936	Gisela Mauermayer, GER	156-3	OR	1972	Faina Melnik, USSR	218-7	OR
1948	Micheline Ostermeyer, FRA	137-6		1976	Evelin Schlaak, E. Ger	226-4	OR
1952	Nina Romaschkova, USSR	168-8	OR	1980	Evelin Schlaak Jahl, E. Ger	229-6	OR
1956	Olga Fikotová, CZE	176-1	OR	1984	Ria Stalman, NED	214-5	
1960	Nina Ponomaryeva, USSR	180-9	OR	1988	Martina Hellmann, E. Ger	237-2½	OR

Year		Distance	Year		Distance
1992	Maritza Marten, CUB	229-10	2004	Natalya Sadova, RUS	219-10
1996	Ilke Wyludda, GER	228-6	2008	Stefanie Brown Trafton, USA	64.74m
2000	Ellina Zvereva, BLR	224-5			

Hammer Throw

Year		Distance		Year		Distance	
2000	Kamila Skolimowska, POL	233- 5¾	OR	2008	Aksana Miankova, BLR	76.34m	OR
2004	Olga Kuzenkova, RUS	246-1	OR				

Javelin Throw

Year		Distance		Year		Distance	
1932	Babe Didrikson, USA	143- 4		1976	Ruth Fuchs, E. Ger	216- 4	OR
1936	Tilly Fleischer, GER	148- 3	OR	1980	Maria Colon Rueñes, CUB	224- 5	OR
1948	Herma Bauma, AUT	149- 6	OR	1984	Tessa Sanderson, GBR	228- 2	OR
1952	Dana Zátopková, CZE	165- 7	OR	1988	Petra Felke, E. Ger	245- 0	OR
1956	Ineze Jaunzeme, USSR	176- 8	OR	1992	Silke Renk, GER	224-2	
1960	Elvira Ozolina, USSR	183- 8	OR	1996	Heli Rantanen, FIN	222-11	
1964	Mihaela Penes, ROM	198- 7	OR	2000	Trine Hattestad, NOR	226-1	OR
1968	Angéla Németh, HUN	198- 0		2004	Osleidys Menendez, CUB	234-8	OR
1972	Ruth Fuchs, E. Ger	209- 7	OR	2008	Barbora Spotakova, CZE	71.42m	

Heptathlon

Year		Points		Year		Points	
1964	Irina Press, USSR	5246	WR	1988	Jackie Joyner-Kersee, USA	7291	WR
1968	Ingrid Becker, W. Ger	5098		1992	Jackie Joyner-Kersee, USA	7044	
1972	Mary Peters, GBR	4801	WR	1996	Ghada Shouaa, SYR	6780	
1976	Siegrun Siegl, E. Ger	4745		2000	Denise Lewis, GBR	6584	
1980	Nadezhda Tkachenko, USSR	5083	WR	2004	Carolina Kluft, SWE	6952	
1984	Glynis Nunn, AUS	6390	OR	2008	Nataliia Dobrynska, UKR	6733	

Note: Seven-event Heptathlon replaced five-event Pentathlon in 1984.

All-Time Leading Medal Winners – Single Games

Athletes who have won the most medals in a single Summer Olympics. Totals include individual, relay and team medals. U.S. athletes are in **bold** type.

MEN

No		Sport	G-S-B	No		Sport	G-S-B
8	**Michael Phelps**, USA (2008)	Swim	8-0-0	6	Takashi Ono, JPN (1960)	Gym	3-1-2
8†	**Michael Phelps**, USA (2004)	Swim	6-0-2	6	Viktor Chukarin, USSR (1956)	Gym	4-2-0
8	Aleksandr Dityatin, USSR (1980)	Gym	3-4-1	6	Konrad Frey, GER (1936)	Gym	3-1-2
7	**Mark Spitz**, USA (1972)	Swim	7-0-0	6	Ville Ritola, FIN (1924)	Track	4-2-0
7	**Willis Lee**, USA (1920)	Shoot	5-1-1	6	Hubert Van Innis, BEL (1920)	Arch	4-2-0
7	**Matt Biondi**, USA (1988)	Swim	5-1-1	6	**Carl Osburn**, USA (1920)	Shoot	4-1-1
7	Boris Shakhlin, USSR (1960)	Gym	4-2-1	6	Louis Richardet, SWI (1906)	Shoot	3-3-0
7	**Lloyd Spooner**, USA (1920)	Shoot	4-1-2	6	**Anton Heida**, USA (1904)	Gym	5-1-0
7	Mikhail Voronin, USSR (1968)	Gym	2-4-1	6	**George Eyser**, USA (1904)	Gym	3-2-1
7	Nikolai Andrianov, USSR (1976)	Gym	2-4-1	6	**Burton Downing**, USA (1904)	Cycle	2-3-1
6	Vitaly Scherbo, UT (1992)	Gym	6-0-0	6	Alexei Nemov, RUS (1996)	Gym	2-1-3
6	Li Ning, CHN (1984)	Gym	3-2-1	6	Alexei Nemov, RUS (2000)	Gym	2-1-3
6	Akinori Nakayama, JPN (1968)	Gym	4-1-1				

†Includes gold medal as preliminary member of 1st-place relay team.

WOMEN

No		Sport	G-S-B	No		Sport	G-S-B
7	Maria Gorokhovskaya, USSR (1952)	Gym	2-5-0	5	Shane Gould, AUS (1972)	Swim	3-1-1
6	Kristin Otto, E. Ger (1988)	Swim	6-0-0	5	Nadia Comaneci, ROM (1976)	Gym	3-1-1
6	Agnes Keleti, HUN (1956)	Gym	4-2-0	5	Karin Janz, E. Ger (1972)	Gym	2-2-1
6	Vera Cáslavská, CZE (1968)	Gym	4-2-0	5	Ines Diers, E. Ger (1980)	Swim	2-2-1
6	Larisa Latynina, USSR (1956)	Gym	4-1-1	5	**Shirley Babashoff**, USA (1976)	Swim	1-4-0
6	Larisa Latynina, USSR (1960)	Gym	3-2-1	5	**Mary Lou Retton**, USA (1984)	Gym	1-2-2
6	Daniela Silivas, ROM (1988)	Gym	3-2-1	5	**Shannon Miller**, USA (1992)	Gym	0-2-3
6	Larisa Latynina, USSR (1964)	Gym	2-2-2	5	**Marion Jones**†, USA (2000)	Track	3-0-2
6	**Natalie Coughlin**, USA (2008)	Swim	1-2-3	5	**Dara Torres**, USA (2000)	Swim	2-0-3
6	Margit Korondi, HUN (1956)	Gym	1-1-4	5	**Natalie Coughlin**, USA (2004)	Swim	2-2-1
6	Kornelia Ender, E. Ger (1976)	Swim	4-1-0	5	**Nastia Liukin**, USA (2008)	Gym	1-3-1
6	Ecaterina Szabó, ROM (1984)	Gym	4-1-0				

†Jones admitted to using performance-enhancing drugs and has been stripped of her medals.

All-Time Leading Medal Winners – Career

MEN

No		Sport	G-S-B	No		Sport	G-S-
16†	**Michael Phelps**, USA	Swimming	14-0-2	10	**Carl Lewis**, USA	Track/Field	9-1-
15	Nikolai Andrianov, USSR	Gymnastics	7-5-3	10	Aladár Gerevich, HUN	Fencing	7-1-
13	Boris Shakhlin, USSR	Gymnastics	7-4-2	10	Akinori Nakayama, JPN	Gymnastics	6-2-
13	Edoardo Mangiarotti, ITA	Fencing	6-5-2	10	Aleksandr Dityatin, USSR	Gymnastics	3-6-
13	Takashi Ono, JPN	Gymnastics	5-4-4	9	Vitaly Scherbo, BLR	Gymnastics	6-0-
12	Paavo Nurmi, FIN	Track/Field	9-3-0	9	**Gary Hall Jr.**, USA	Swimming	5-3-
12	Sawao Kato, JPN	Gymnastics	8-3-1	9*	**Martin Sheridan**, USA	Track/Field	5-3-
12	Alexei Nemov, RUS	Gymnastics	4-2-6	9*	Zoltán Halmay, HUN	Swimming	5-3-
11	**Mark Spitz**, USA	Swimming	9-1-1	9	Giulio Gaudini, ITA	Fencing	3-4-
11†	**Matt Biondi**, USA	Swimming	8-2-1	9	Mikhail Voronin, USSR	Gymnastics	2-6-
11	Viktor Chukarin, USSR	Gymnastics	7-3-1	9	Heikki Savolainen, FIN	Gymnastics	2-1-
11	**Carl Osburn**, USA	Shooting	5-4-2	9	Yuri Titov, USSR	Gymnastics	1-5-
10*	**Ray Ewry**, USA	Track/Field	10-0-0	9	Alexander Popov, UT/RUS	Swimming	4-5-

†Includes gold medal as preliminary member of 1st-place relay team.
*Medals won by Ewry (2-0-0), Sheridan (2-3-0) and Halmay (1-1-0) at the 1906 Intercalated games are not officially recognized by the IOC.

Games Participated In

Andrianov (1972,76,80); **Biondi** (1984,88,92); **Chukarin** (1952,56); **Dityatin** (1976,80); **Ewry** (1900,04,06,08); **Gerevich** (1932,36,48,52,56,60); **Gaudini** (1928,32,36); **Hall Jr.** (1996,2000,04); **Halmay** (1900,04,06,08); **Kato** (1968,72,76); **Lewis** (1984,88,92,96); **Mangiarotti** (1936,48,52,56,60); **Nakayama** (1968,72); **Nemov** (1996,2000); **Nurmi** (1920,24,28); **Ono** (1952,56,60,64); **Osburn** (1912,20, 24); **Phelps** (2004,08); **Popov** (1992,96,2000); **Savolainen** (1928,32,36,48,52); **Scherbo** (1992,96); **Shakhlin** (1956,60,64); **Sheridan** (1904,06,08); **Spitz** (1968,72); **Titov** (1956,60,64); **Voronin** (1968,72).

WOMEN

No		Sport	G-S-B	No		Sport	G-S-B
18	Larissa Latynina, USSR	Gymnastics	9-5-4	8	Dawn Fraser, AUS	Swimming	4-4-0
12	Birgit Fischer, GER	Canoe/Kayak	8-4-0	8	**Shirley Babashoff**, USA	Swimming	2-6-0
12	**Jenny Thompson**, USA	Swimming	8-3-1	8	Sofia Muratova, USSR	Gymnastics	2-2-4
12	**Dara Torres**, USA	Swimming	4-4-4	7	Inge de Bruijn, NED	Swimming	4-2-2
11	Vera Cáslavská, CZE	Gymnastics	7-4-0	7	Krisztina Egerszegi, HUN	Swimming	5-1-1
11	**Natalie Coughlin**, USA	Swimming	3-4-4	7	Irena Kirszenstein Szewinska, POL	Track/Field	3-2-2
10	Agnes Keleti, HUN	Gymnastics	5-3-2	7	Shirley Strickland, AUS	Track/Field	3-1-3
10	Polina Astakhova, USSR	Gymnastics	5-2-3	7	Maria Gorokhovskaya, USSR	Gymnastics	2-5-0
10	Franziska van Almsick, GER	Swimming	0-4-6	7	Ildiko Sagine-Ujlaki-Rejto, HUN	Fencing	2-3-2
9	Nadia Comaneci, ROM	Gymnastics	5-3-1	7	**Shannon Miller**, USA	Gymnastics	2-2-3
9	Lyudmila Tourischeva, USSR	Gymnastics	4-3-2	7	Susie O'Neill, AUS	Swimming	2-4-1
8	Isabell Werth, GER	Equestrian	5-3-0	7	Merlene Ottey, JAM	Track/Field	0-2-5
8	Kornelia Ender, E. Ger	Swimming	4-4-0				

Games Participated In

Astakhova (1956,60,64); **Babashoff** (1972,76); **Cáslavská** (1960,64,68); **Comaneci** (1976,80); **Coughlin** (2004,08); **de Bruijn** (2000,04); **Egerszegi** (1988,92,96); **Ender** (1972,76); **Fischer** (1980,92,96,2000,04); **Fraser** (1956,60,64); **Gorokhovskaya** (1952); **Keleti** (1952,56); **Latynina** (1956,60,64); **Miller** (1992,96); **Muratova** (1956,60); **O'Neill** (1996,2000); **Ottey** (1980,84,88,92,96); **Sagine-Ujlaki-Rejto** (1960,64,68,72,76); **Strickland** (1948,52,56); **Szewinska** (1964,68,72,76,80); **Thompson** (1992,96,2000,04); **Torres** (1984,88,92,2000,08); **Tourischeva** (1968, 72,76); **van Almsick** (1992,96,2000,04).

Most Gold Medals

MEN

No		Sport	G-S-B	No		Sport	G-S-B
14†	**Michael Phelps**, USA	Swimming	14-0-2	7	Nikolai Andrianov, USSR	Gymnastics	7-5-3
10*	**Ray Ewry**, USA	Track/Field	10-0-0	7	Boris Shakhlin, USSR	Gymnastics	7-4-2
9	Paavo Nurmi, FIN	Track/Field	9-3-0	7	Viktor Chukarin, USSR	Gymnastics	7-3-1
9	**Mark Spitz**, USA	Swimming	9-1-1	7	Aladar Gerevich, HUN	Fencing	7-1-2
9	**Carl Lewis**, USA	Track/Field	9-1-0				
8	Sawao Kato, JPN	Gymnastics	8-3-1				
8†	**Matt Biondi**, USA	Swimming	8-2-1				

*Medals won by Ewry (2-0-0) at the 1906 Intercalated games are not officially recognized by the IOC.
†Includes gold medal as preliminary member of 1st-place relay team.

WOMEN

No		Sport	G-S-B	No		Sport	G-S-B
9	Larissa Latynina, USSR	Gymnastics	9-5-4	5	Agnes Keleti, HUN	Gymnastics	5-3-2
8	**Jenny Thompson**, USA	Swimming	8-3-1	5	Nadia Comaneci, ROM	Gymnastics	5-3-1
8	Vera Cáslavská, CZE	Gymnastics	7-4-0	5	Polina Astakhova, USSR	Gymnastics	5-2-3
8	Birgit Fischer, GER	Canoe/Kayak	8-4-0	5	Krisztina Egerszegi, HUN	Swimming	5-1-1
6†	Kristin Otto, E. Ger	Swimming	6-0-0				
6†	**Amy Van Dyken**, USA	Swimming	6-0-0				

†Includes gold medal as preliminary member of 1st-place relay team.

Most Silver Medals

MEN				WOMEN		
No		Sport	G-S-B	No		Sport	G-S-B
6	Alexandr Dityatin, USSR	Gymnastics	3-6-1	6	**Shirley Babashoff**, USA	Swimming	2-6-0
6	Mikhail Voronin, USSR	Gymnastics	2-6-1	5	Larissa Latynina, USSR	Gymnastics	9-5-4
5	Nikolai Andrianov, USSR	Gymnastics	7-5-3	5	Maria Gorokhovskaya, USSR	Gymnastics	2-5-0
5	Edoardo Mangiarotti, ITA	Fencing	6-5-2	5	Dagmar Hase, GER	Swimming	1-5-1
5	Zoltán Halmay, HUN	Swimming	3-5-1	4	Vera Cáslavská, CZE	Gymnastics	7-4-0
5	Gustavo Marzi, ITA	Fencing	2-5-0	4	Kornelia Ender, E. Ger	Swimming	4-4-0
5	Yuri Titov, USSR	Gymnastics	1-5-3	4	Dawn Fraser, AUS	Swimming	4-4-0
5	Viktor Lisitsky, USSR	Gymnastics	0-5-0	4	Erica Zuchold, E. Ger	Gymnastics	0-4-1
5	Alexander Popov, UT/RUS	Swimming	4-5-0				

Most Bronze Medals

MEN				WOMEN		
No		Sport	G-S-B	No		Sport	G-S-B
6	Alexei Nemov, RUS	Gymnastics	4-2-6	6	Franziska van Almsick, GER	Swimming	0-4-6
6	Heikki Savolainen, FIN	Gymnastics	2-1-6	5	Merlene Ottey, JAM	Track/Field	0-2-5
5	Daniel Revenu, FRA	Fencing	1-0-5	5	Larissa Latynina, USSR	Gymnastics	9-5-4
5	Philip Edwards, CAN	Track/Field	0-0-5	4	**Dara Torres**, USA	Swimming	4-4-4
5	Adrianus De Jong, NED	Fencing	0-0-5	4	Sofia Muratova, USSR	Gymnastics	2-2-4

All-Time Leading USA Medal Winners

Most Overall Medals

MEN

No		Sport	G-S-B	No		Sport	G-S-B
16†	Michael Phelps	Swimming	14-0-2	6	Anton Heida	Gymnastics	5-1-0
11	Mark Spitz	Swimming	9-1-1	6	Don Schollander	Swimming	5-1-0
11†	Matt Biondi	Swimming	8-2-1	6	Johnny Weissmuller	Swim/Water Polo	5-0-1
11	Carl Osburn	Shooting	5-4-2	6	Alfred Lane	Shooting	5-0-1
10*	Ray Ewry	Track/Field	10-0-0	6	Jim Lightbody	Track/Field	4-2-0
10	Carl Lewis	Track/Field	9-1-0	6	George Eyser	Gymnastics	3-2-1
9	Gary Hall Jr.	Swimming	5-3-1	6	Ralph Rose	Track/Field	3-2-1
9*	Martin Sheridan	Track/Field	5-3-1	6	Michael Plumb	Equestrian	2-4-0
8	Charles Daniels	Swimming	5-1-2	6	Burton Downing	Cycling	2-3-1
7‡	Tom Jager	Swimming	5-1-1	6	Bob Garrett	Track/Field	2-2-2
7	Willis Lee	Shooting	5-1-1				
7	Lloyd Spooner	Shooting	4-1-2				

†Includes gold medal as prelim. member of 1st-place relay team.
*Medals won by Ewry (2-0-0) and Sheridan (2-3-0) at the 1906 Intercalated games are not officially recognized by the IOC.
‡Includes 3 gold medals as prelim. member of 1st-place relay teams.

Games Participated In

Biondi (1984,88,92); **Daniels** (1904,06,08); **Downing** (1904); **Ewry** (1900,04,06,08); **Eyser** (1904); **Garrett** (1896,1900); **Hall Jr.** (1996,2000,04) **Heida** (1904); **Jager** (1984,88,92); **Lane** (1912,20); **Lewis** (1984,88,92,96); **Lightbody** (1904,06); **Osburn** (1912,20,24); **Phelps** (2004,08); **Plumb** (1960, 64,68,72,76,84); **Rose** (1904,08,12); **Schollander** (1964, 68); **Sheridan** (1904,06,08); **Spitz** (1968,72); **Spooner** (1920); **Weissmuller** (1924,28).

WOMEN

No		Sport	G-S-B	No		Sport	G-S-B
12	Jenny Thompson	Swimming	8-3-1	6	Angel Martino	Swimming	3-0-3
12	Dara Torres	Swimming	4-4-4	5	Evelyn Ashford	Track/Field	4-1-0
11	Natalie Coughlin	Swimming	3-4-4	5	Janet Evans	Swimming	4-1-0
8	Shirley Babashoff	Swimming	2-6-0	5	Florence Griffith Joyner	Track/Field	3-2-0
7	Shannon Miller	Gymnastics	2-2-3	5†	Mary T. Meagher	Swimming	3-1-1
7	Amanda Beard	Swimming	2-4-1	5	Gwen Torrence	Track/Field	3-2-0
6†	Amy Van Dyken	Swimming	6-0-0	5	Marion Jones‡	Track/Field	3-0-2
6	Jackie Joyner-Kersee	Track/Field	3-1-2	5	Mary Lou Retton	Gymnastics	1-2-2

†Includes gold medal as prelim. member of 1st-place relay team.
‡Jones admitted to using performance-enhancing drugs and has been stripped of her medals.

Games Participated In

Ashford (1976,84,88,92); **Babashoff** (1972,76); **Beard** (1996,2000,04); **Coughlin** (2004), **Evans** (1988,92,96); **Griffith Joyner** (1984,88); **Jones** (2000); **Joyner-Kersee** (1984,88,92,96); **Martino** (1992,96); **McCormick** (1952,56); **Meagher** (1984,88); **Miller** (1992,96); **Retton** (1984); **Thompson** (1988,92,96,2000,04); **Torrence** (1988,92,96); **Torres** (1984,88,92,2000,08); **Van Dyken** (1996,2000).

Most Gold Medals

MEN

No		Sport	G-S-B
14†	Michael Phelps	Swimming	14-0-2
10*	Raymond Ewry	Track/Field	10-0-0
9	Mark Spitz	Swimming	9-1-1
9	Carl Lewis	Track/Field	9-1-0
8†	Matt Biondi	Swimming	8-2-1
5	Carl Osburn	Shooting	5-4-2
5*	Martin Sheridan	Track/Field	5-3-1
5	Charles Daniels	Swimming	5-1-2
5‡	Tom Jager	Swimming	5-1-1
5	Willis Lee	Shooting	5-1-1
5	Anton Heida	Gymnastics	5-1-0
5	Don Schollander	Swimming	5-1-0
5	Johnny Weissmuller	Swim/Water Polo	5-0-1
5	Alfred Lane	Shooting	5-0-1
5	Morris Fisher	Shooting	5-0-0
5	Gary Hall Jr.	Swimming	5-3-1
4	Jim Lightbody	Track/Field	4-2-0
4	Lloyd Spooner	Shooting	4-1-2
4	Greg Louganis	Diving	4-1-0
4	John Naber	Swimming	4-1-0
4	Meyer Prinstein	Track/Field	4-1-0
4	Mel Sheppard	Track/Field	4-1-0
4	Marcus Hurley	Cycling	4-0-1
4†	Jon Olsen	Swimming	4-0-1
4	Archie Hahn	Track/Field	4-0-0
4	Alvin Kraenzlein	Track/Field	4-0-0
4	Al Oerter	Track/Field	4-0-0
4	Jesse Owens	Track/Field	4-0-0

*Medals won by Ewry (2-0-0) and Sheridan (2-3-0) at the 1906 Intercalated games are not officially recognized by the IOC.
†Includes gold medal as preliminary member of 1st-place relay team.
‡Includes 3 gold medals as preliminary member of 1st-place relay teams.

WOMEN

No		Sport	G-S-B
8	Jenny Thompson	Swimming	8-3-
6†	Amy Van Dyken	Swimming	6-0-
4	Dara Torres	Swimming	4-4-
4	Evelyn Ashford	Track/Field	4-1-
4	Janet Evans	Swimming	4-1-
4	Pat McCormick	Diving	4-0-
3	Natalie Coughlin	Swimming	3-4-
3	Florence Griffith Joyner	Track/Field	3-2-
3	Jackie Joyner-Kersee	Track/Field	3-1-
3†	Mary T. Meagher	Swimming	3-1-
3	Gwen Torrence	Track/Field	3-1-
3	Marion Jones*	Track/Field	3-0-
3	Valerie Brisco-Hooks	Track/Field	3-1-
3	Nancy Hogshead	Swimming	3-1-
3	Sharon Stouder	Swimming	3-1-
3	Wyomia Tyus	Track/Field	3-1-
3	Chris von Saltza	Swimming	3-1-
3	Wilma Rudolph	Track/Field	3-0-
3	Melissa Belote	Swimming	3-0-
3	Ethelda Bleibtrey	Swimming	3-0-
3	Tracy Caulkins	Swimming	3-0-
3†	Nicole Haislett	Swimming	3-0-
3	Helen Madison	Swimming	3-0-
3	Debbie Meyer	Swimming	3-0-
3	Sandra Neilson	Swimming	3-0-
3	Martha Norelius	Swimming	3-0-
3†	Carrie Steinseifer	Swimming	3-0-
3‡	Ashley Tappin	Swimming	3-0-

†Includes gold medal as preliminary member of 1st-place relay team.
‡Includes 3 gold medals as preliminary member of 1st-place relay teams.
*Jones was stripped of the five medals she won in 2000 after admitting to using performance-enhancing drugs.

Most Silver Medals

MEN

No		Sport	G-S-B
4	Carl Osburn	Shooting	5-4-2
4	Michael Plumb	Equestrian	2-4-0
3	Martin Sheridan	Track/Field	5-3-1
3	Burton Downing	Cycling	2-3-1
3	Irving Baxter	Track/Field	2-3-0

No		Sport	G-S-B
3	Earl Thomson	Equestrian	2-3-0
3	Alexander McKee	Swimming	0-3-0

WOMEN

No		Sport	G-S-B
6	Shirley Babashoff	Swimming	2-6-0

All-Time Medal Standings, 1896-2008

All-time Summer Games medal standings, based on *The Golden Book of the Olympic Games*. Medal counts include the 1906 Intercalated Games, which are not recognized by the IOC.

		G	S	B	Total
1	**United States**	943	735	651	2329
2	USSR (1952-88)	395	319	296	1010
3	Great Britain	201	255	252	715
4	France	206	218	247	671
5	Italy	197	164	178	539
6	Germany (1896-64,92–)	167	164	193	524
7	Sweden	140	161	180	481
8	Hungary	161	146	163	470
9	East Germany (1968-88)	159	150	136	445
	Australia	133	141	171	445
11	China	163	117	106	386
12	Japan	122	112	124	358
13	Russia (1896-1912, 96–)	108	100	112	320
14	Finland	102	84	116	302
15	West Germany (1968-88)	77	104	120	301
16	Romania	86	89	117	292
17	Poland	62	80	119	261
18	Canada	57	96	107	260
19	Netherlands	72	81	98	250
20	South Korea	68	74	73	215
21	Bulgaria	51	84	77	212
22	Switzerland	50	76	68	194
23	Cuba	66	62	60	188
24	Denmark	44	65	67	176
25	Norway	57	49	44	150
26	Greece	38	56	52	146
27	Belgium	39	52	54	145
28	Czechoslovakia (1924-92)	49	49	44	142
29	Unified Team (1992)	45	38	29	112
	Spain	33	49	30	112
31	Austria	22	37	37	96
32	Yugoslavia (1924-88,96-2000)	28	32	33	93
33	Brazil	19	26	46	91
34	New Zealand	36	15	37	88
35	Turkey	37	23	22	82
36	South Africa (1904-60, 92–)	20	24	26	70

		G	S	B	Total
37	Kenya	22	29	24	75
38	Ukraine	19	20	34	73
39	Argentina	17	23	26	66
40	Mexico	12	18	24	54
41	Jamaica	13	24	16	53
42	Belarus	9	14	28	51
43	Iran	11	15	22	48
44	North Korea	10	12	19	41
45	Ethiopia	18	6	14	38
46	Czech Republic	10	12	11	33
47	Estonia	9	8	14	31
48	Kazakhstan	6	12	10	28
49	Indonesia	6	9	10	25
50	Ireland	9	7	8	24
51	Nigeria	2	9	12	23
52	Egypt	7	6	9	22
53	Portugal	4	7	11	22
54	Thailand	7	4	10	21
55	Morocco	6	5	10	21
56	Great Britain/Ireland	6	11	3	20
	India	9	4	7	20
	Slovakia	7	8	5	20
59	Chinese Taipei	2	6	11	19
	Mongolia	2	7	10	19
61	Georgia	5	2	11	18
62	Latvia	2	11	4	17
	Lithuania	4	4	9	17
	Croatia	3	6	8	17
	Uzbekistan	4	5	8	17
66	Azerbaijan	4	3	9	16
67	Slovenia	3	5	7	15
68	Algeria	4	2	8	14
	Trinidad & Tobago	1	5	8	14
70	Chile	2	7	4	13
71	Venezuela	1	2	8	11
72	Pakistan	3	3	4	10
	Uruguay	2	2	6	10
	Bahamas	3	3	4	10
	Colombia	1	3	6	10
76	Philippines	0	2	7	9
77	Israel	2	1	5	8
	Zimbabwe	3	4	1	8
79	Tunisia	2	2	3	7
80	Uganda	1	3	2	6
	Bohemia	0	1	5	6
	Puerto Rico	0	1	5	6
	Cameroon	4	1	1	6
84	Moldova	0	2	3	5
85	Peru	1	3	0	4
	Costa Rica	1	1	2	4
	Dominican Republic	2	1	1	4
	Namibia	0	4	0	4
	Lebanon	0	2	2	4
	Ghana	0	1	3	4
91	Serbia	0	1	2	3
	Luxembourg	2	1	0	3
	Armenia	1	1	1	3
	Panama	1	0	2	3
	Iceland	0	1	2	3
	Malaysia	0	1	2	3
	Syria	1	1	1	3
98	Hong Kong	1	1	0	2

		G	S	B	Total
	Japan/Korea	1	0	1	2
	Mozambique	1	0	1	2
	Surinam	1	0	1	2
	Serbia & Montenegro	0	2	0	2
	Tanzania	0	2	0	2
	Krygyzstan	0	1	1	2
	Great Britain/USA	0	1	1	2
	Haiti	0	1	1	2
	Russia/Estonia	0	1	1	2
	Saudi Arabia	0	1	1	2
	United Arab Republic	0	1	1	2
	Zambia	0	1	1	2
	The Antilles	0	0	2	2
	Qatar	0	0	2	2
	Singapore	0	2	0	2
114	Australia/New Zealand	1	0	0	1
	Burkina Faso	1	0	0	1
	Cuba/USA	1	0	0	1
	Denmark/Sweden	1	0	0	1
	Ecuador	1	0	0	1
	Gr. Britain/Ireland/Germany	1	0	0	1
	Gr. Britain/Ireland/USA	1	0	0	1
	Ireland/USA	1	0	0	1
	United Arab Emirates	1	0	0	1
	Belgium/Greece	0	1	0	1
	Ceylon	0	1	0	1
	France/USA	0	1	0	1
	France/Gr. Britain/Ireland	0	1	0	1
	Ivory Coast	0	1	0	1
	Netherlands Antilles	0	1	0	1
	Paraguay	0	1	0	1
	Senegal	0	1	0	1
	Smyrna	0	1	0	1
	Sudan	0	1	0	1
	Tonga	0	1	0	1
	Vietnam	0	1	0	1
	Virgin Islands	0	1	0	1
	Afghanistan	0	0	1	1
	Australia/Great Britain	0	0	1	1
	Barbados	0	0	1	1
	Bermuda	0	0	1	1
	Bohemia/Great Britain	0	0	1	1
	Djibouti	0	0	1	1
	Eritrea	0	0	1	1
	France/Great Britain	0	0	1	1
	Guyana	0	0	1	1
	Iraq	0	0	1	1
	Kuwait	0	0	1	1
	Kyrgyzstan	0	0	1	1
	Macedonia	0	0	1	1
	Mauritius	0	0	1	1
	Mexico/Spain	0	0	1	1
	Niger	0	0	1	1
	Scotland	0	0	1	1
	Sri Lanka	0	0	1	1
	Thessalonika	0	0	1	1
	Togo	0	0	1	1
	Wales	0	0	1	1

Combined totals:	G	S	B	Total
USSR/UT/Russia	548	457	437	1440
Germany/E. Ger/W. Ger	404	418	449	1271

Notes: Athletes from the USSR participated in the Summer Games from 1952-88, returned as the Unified Team in 1992 after the breakup of the Soviet Union (in 1991) and have competed as independent republics since the 1994 Winter Games. Germany was barred from the Olympics in 1924 and 1948 following World Wars I and II. Divided into East and West Germany after WWII, both countries competed together from 1952-64, then separately from 1968-88. Germany was reunified in 1990. Czechoslovakia split into Slovakia and the Czech Republic in 1993. Croatia and Bosnia-Herzegovina gained independence from Yugoslavia in 1991. Yugoslavia was not invited to the 1992 games (though Serbian and Montenegrin athletes were allowed to compete as independent athletes) but returned in 1996 and competed under the name Serbia & Montenegro starting in 2004. South Africa was banned from 1964-88 for using the apartheid policy in the selection of its teams. It returned in 1992 as the Republic of South Africa (RSA).

1924-2006
Through the Years

SPORTS ALMANAC

The Winter Olympics

The move toward a winter version of the Olympics began in 1908 when figure skating made an appearance at the Summer Games in London. Ten-time world champion Ulrich Salchow of Sweden, who originated the backwards, one revolution jump that bears his name, and Madge Syers of Britain were the first singles champions. Germans Anna Hubler and Heinrich Berger won the pairs competition.

Organizers of the 1916 Summer Games in Berlin planned to introduce a "Skiing Olympia," featuring nordic events in the Black Forest, but the Games were cancelled after the outbreak of World War I in 1914.

The Games resumed in 1920 at Antwerp, Belgium, where figure skating returned and ice hockey was added as a medal event. Sweden's Gillis Grafstrom and Magda Julin took individual honors, while Ludovika and Walter Jakobsson were the top pair. In hockey, Canada won the gold medal with the United States second and Czechoslovakia third.

Despite the objections of Modern Olympics' founder Baron Pierre de Coubertin and the resistance of the Scandinavian countries, which had staged their own Nordic championships every four or five years from 1901-26 in Sweden, the International Olympic Committee sanctioned an "International Winter Sports Week" at Chamonix, France, in 1924. The 11-day event, which included nordic skiing, speed skating, figure skating, ice hockey and bobsledding, was a huge success and was retroactively called the first Olympic Winter Games.

Seventy years after those first cold weather Games, the 17th edition of the Winter Olympics took place in Lillehammer, Norway, in 1994. The event ended the four-year Olympic cycle of staging both Winter and Summer Games in the same year and began a new schedule that calls for the two Games to alternate every two years.

Year	No	Location	Dates	Nations	Most medals	USA medals
1924	I	Chamonix, FRA	Jan. 25-Feb. 4	16	Norway (4-7-6–17)	1-2-1–4 (3rd)
1928	II	St. Moritz, SWI	Feb. 11-19	25	Norway (6-4-5–15)	2-2-2– 6 (2nd)
1932	III	Lake Placid, USA	Feb. 4-15	17	USA (6-4-2–12)	6-4-2–12 (1st)
1936	IV	Garmisch-Partenkirchen, GER .	Feb. 6-16	28	Norway (7-5-3–15)	1-0-3– 4 (T-5th)
1940-a	–	Sapporo, JPN	Cancelled (WWII)			
1944	–	Cortina d'Ampezzo, ITA	Cancelled (WWII)			
1948	V	St. Moritz, SWI	Jan. 30-Feb. 8	28	Norway (4-3-3–10), Sweden (4-3-3–10) & Switzerland (3-4-3–10)	3-4-2– 9 (4th)
1952-b	VI	Oslo, NOR	Feb. 14-25	30	Norway (7-3-6–16)	4-6-1–11 (2nd)
1956-c	VII	Cortina d'Ampezzo, ITA	Jan. 26-Feb. 5	32	USSR (7-3-6–16)	2-3-2– 7 (T-4th)
1960	VIII	Squaw Valley, USA	Feb. 18-28	30	USSR (7-5-9–21)	3-4-3–10 (2nd)
1964	IX	Innsbruck, AUT	Jan. 29-Feb. 9	36	USSR (11-8-6–25)	1-2-3– 6 (7th)
1968-d	X	Grenoble, FRA	Feb. 6-18	37	Norway (6-6-2–14)	1-5-1– 7 (T-7th)
1972	XI	Sapporo, JPN	Feb. 3-13	35	USSR (8-5-3–16)	3-2-3– 8 (6th)
1976-e	XII	Innsbruck, AUT	Feb. 4-15	37	USSR (13-6-8–27)	3-3-4–10 (T-3rd)
1980	XIII	Lake Placid, USA	Feb. 14-23	37	E. Germany (9-7-7–23)	6-4-2–12 (3rd)
1984	XIV	Sarajevo, YUG	Feb. 7-19	49	USSR (6-10-9–25)	4-4-0– 8 (T-5th)
1988	XV	Calgary, CAN	Feb. 13-28	57	USSR (11-9-9–29)	2-1-3– 6 (T-8th)
1992-f	XVI	Albertville, FRA	Feb. 8-23	63	Germany (10-10-6–26)	5-4-2–11 (6th)
1994-g	XVII	Lillehammer, NOR	Feb. 12-27	67	Norway (10-11-5–26)	6-5-2–13 (T-5th)
1998	XVIII	Nagano, JPN	Feb. 7-22	72	Germany (12-9-8–29)	6-3-4–13 (5th)
2002	XIX	Salt Lake City, USA	Feb. 8-24	78	Germany (12-16-7–35)	10-13-11–34 (2nd)
2006	XX	Turin, ITA	Feb. 10-26	87	Germany (11-12-6–29)	9-9-7–25 (2nd)
2010	XXI	Vancouver, CAN	Feb. 12-28			
2014	XXII	Sochi, RUS	Feb. 7-23			

a–The 1940 Winter Games are originally scheduled for Sapporo, but Japan resigns as host in 1937 when the Sino-Japanese war breaks out. St. Moritz is the next choice, but the Swiss feel that ski instructors should not be considered professionals and the IOC withdraws its offer. Finally, Garmisch-Partenkirchen is asked to serve again as host, but the Germans invade Poland in 1939 and the Games are eventually cancelled.

b–Germany and Japan are allowed to rejoin the Olympic community for the first time since World War II. Though a divided country, the Germans send a joint East-West team through 1964.

c–The Soviet Union (USSR) participates in its first Winter Olympics and takes home the most medals, including the gold medal in ice hockey.

d–East Germany and West Germany officially send separate teams for the first time and will continue to do so through 1988.

e–The IOC grants the 1976 Winter Games to Denver in May 1970, but in 1972 Colorado voters reject a $5 million bond issue to finance the undertaking. Denver immediately withdraws as host and the IOC selects Innsbruck, the site of the 1964 Games, to take over.

f–Germany sends a single team after East and West German reunification in 1990 and the USSR competes as the Unified Team after the breakup of the Soviet Union in 1991.

g–The IOC moves the Winter Games' four-year cycle ahead two years in order to separate them from the Summer Games and alternate Olympics every two years.

Event-by-Event

Gold medal winners from 1924-2006 in the following events: Alpine Skiing, Biathlon, Bobsled, Cross Country Skiing, Curling, Figure Skating, Freestyle Skiing, Ice Hockey, Luge, Nordic Combined, Skeleton, Ski Jumping, Snowboarding and Speed Skating.

ALPINE SKIING

MEN

Multiple gold medals: Kjetil Andre Aamodt (4); Jean-Claude Killy, Toni Sailer and Alberto Tomba (3); Hermann Maier, Henri Oreiller, Benjamin Raich, Ingemar Stenmark and Markus Wasmeier (2).

Downhill

Year		Time	Year		Time
1948	Henri Oreiller, FRA	2:55.0	1980	Leonhard Stock, AUS	1:45.50
1952	Zeno Colò, ITA	2:30.8	1984	Bill Johnson, USA	1:45.59
1956	Toni Sailer, AUT	2:52.2	1988	Pirmin Zurbriggen, SWI	1:59.63
1960	Jean Vuarnet, FRA	2:06.0	1992	Patrick Ortlieb, AUT	1:50.37
1964	Egon Zimmermann, AUT	2:18.16	1994	Tommy Moe, USA	1:45.75
1968	Jean-Claude Killy, FRA	1:59.85	1998	Jean-Luc Cretier, FRA	1:50.11
1972	Bernhard Russi, SWI	1:51.43	2002	Fritz Strobl, AUT	1:39.13
1976	Franz Klammer AUT	1:45.73	2006	Antoine Deneriaz, FRA	1:48.80

Slalom

Year		Time	Year		Time
1948	Edi Reinalter, SWI	2:10.3	1980	Ingemar Stenmark, SWE	1:44.26
1952	Othmar Schneider, AUT	2:00.0	1984	Phil Mahre, USA	1:39.41
1956	Toni Sailer, AUT	3:14.7	1988	Alberto Tomba, ITA	1:39.47
1960	Ernst Hinterseer, AUT	2:08.9	1992	Finn Christian Jagge, NOR	1:44.39
1964	Pepi Stiegler, AUT	2:11.13	1994	Thomas Stangassinger, AUT	2:02.02
1968	Jean-Claude Killy, FRA	1:39.73	1998	Hans-Petter Buraas, NOR	1:49.31
1972	Francisco Ochoa, SPA	1:49.27	2002	Jean-Pierre Vidal, FRA	1:41.06
1976	Piero Gros, ITA	2:03.29	2006	Benjamin Raich, AUT	1:43.14

Giant Slalom

Year		Time	Year		Time
1952	Stein Eriksen, NOR	2:25.0	1984	Max Julen, SWI	2:41.18
1956	Toni Sailer, AUS	3:00.1	1988	Alberto Tomba, ITA	2:06.37
1960	Roger Staub, SWI	1:48.3	1992	Alberto Tomba, ITA	2:06.98
1964	Francois Bonlieu, FRA	1:46.71	1994	Markus Wasmeier, GER	2:52.46
1968	Jean-Claude Killy, FRA	3:29.28	1998	Hermann Maier, AUT	2:38.51
1972	Gustav Thöni, ITA	3:09.62	2002	Stephan Eberharter, AUT	2:23.28
1976	Heini Hemmi, SWI	3:26.97	2006	Benjamin Raich, AUT	2:35.00
1980	Ingemar Stenmark, SWE	2:40.74			

Super G

Year		Time	Year		Time
1988	Frank Piccard, FRA	1:39.66	1998	Hermann Maier, AUT	1:34.82
1992	Kjetil Andre Aamodt, NOR	1:13.04	2002	Kjetil Andre Aamodt, NOR	1:21.58
1994	Markus Wasmeier, GER	1:32.53	2006	Kjetil Andre Aamodt, NOR	1:30.65

Alpine Combined

Year		Points	Year		Time
1936	Franz Pfnür, GER	99.25	1994	Lasse Kjus, NOR	3:17.53
1948	Henri Oreiller, FRA	3.27	1998	Mario Reiter, AUT	3:08.06
1952-84	Not held		2002	Kjetil Andre Aamodt, NOR	3:17.56
1988	Hubert Strolz, AUT	36.55	2006	Ted Ligety, USA	3:09.35
1992	Josef Polig, ITA	14.58			

Athletes with Winter and Summer Medals

Only four athletes have won medals in **both** the Winter and Summer Olympics:

Eddie Eagan, USA–Light Heavyweight Boxing gold (1920) and Four-man Bobsled gold (1932).

Jacob Tullin Thams, Norway–Ski Jumping gold (1924) and 8-meter Yachting silver (1936).

Christa Luding-Rothenburger, East Germany–Speed Skating gold at 500 meters (1984) and 1,000m (1988), silver at 500m (1988) and bronze at 500m (1992) and Match Sprint Cycling silver (1988). Luding-Rothenburger is the only athlete to ever win medals in both Winter and Summer Games in the same year.

Clara Hughes, Canada–Cycling bronzes in Road Race and Time Trial (1996) and Speed Skating bronze at 5,000m (2002) and Speed Skating gold at 5,000m and silver in Team Pursuit (2006).

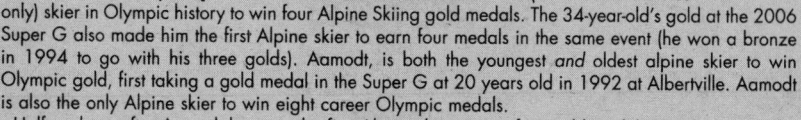

Gold Strike in the Mountains

With his age-defying gold medal performance at Sestriere, Italy in 2006, Norway's **Kjetil Andre Aamodt** became the first (and for 30 minutes only) skier in Olympic history to win four Alpine Skiing gold medals. The 34-year-old's gold at the 2006 Super G also made him the first Alpine skier to earn four medals in the same event (he won a bronze in 1994 to go with his three golds). Aamodt, is both the youngest *and* oldest alpine skier to win Olympic gold, first taking a gold medal in the Super G at 20 years old in 1992 at Albertville. Aamodt is also the only Alpine skier to win eight career Olympic medals.

Half an hour after Aamodt became the first Alpine skier to win four gold medals, **Janica Kostelic** of Croatia won the Alpine Combined to become the first woman to achieve the same feat. She also took the silver medal in the Super G and placed fourth in the slalom.

WOMEN

Multiple gold medals: Janica Kostelic (4), Deborah Compagnoni, Vreni Schneider and Katja Seizinger (3); Michaela Dorfmeister, Marielle Goitschel, Trude Jochum-Beiser, Petra Kronberger, Andrea Mead Lawrence, Rosi Mittermaier, Marie-Theres Nadig, Hanni Wenzel and Pernilla Wiberg (2).

Downhill

Year		Time	Year		Time
1948	Hedy Schlunegger, SWI	2:28.3	1980	Annemarie Moser-Pröll, AUT	1:37.52
1952	Trude Jochum-Beiser, AUT	1:47.1	1984	Michela Figini, SWI	1:13.36
1956	Madeleine Berthod, SWI	1:40.7	1988	Marina Kiehl, W. Ger	1:25.86
1960	Heidi Biebl, GER	1:37.6	1992	Kerrin Lee-Gartner, CAN	1:52.55
1964	Christl Haas, AUT	1:55.39	1994	Katja Seizinger, GER	1:35.93
1968	Olga Pall, AUT	1:40.87	1998	Katja Seizinger, GER	1:28.89
1972	Marie-Theres Nadig, SWI	1:36.68	2002	Carole Montillet, FRA	1:39.56
1976	Rosi Mittermaier, W. Ger	1:46.16	2006	Michaela Dorfmeister, AUT	1:56.49

Slalom

Year		Time	Year		Time
1948	Gretchen Fraser, USA	1:57.2	1980	Hanni Wenzel, LIE	1:25.09
1952	Andrea Mead Lawrence, USA	2:10.6	1984	Paoletta Magoni, ITA	1:36.47
1956	Renée Colliard, SWI	1:52.3	1988	Vreni Schneider, SWI	1:36.69
1960	Anne Heggtveit, CAN	1:49.6	1992	Petra Kronberger, AUT	1:32.68
1964	Christine Goitschel, FRA	1:29.86	1994	Vreni Schneider, SWI	1:56.01
1968	Marielle Goitschel, FRA	1:25.86	1998	Hilde Gerg, GER	1:32.40
1972	Barbara Cochran, USA	1:31.24	2002	Janica Kostelic, CRO	1:46.10
1976	Rosi Mittermaier, W. Ger	1:30.54	2006	Anja Paerson, SWE	1:29.04

Giant Slalom

Year		Time	Year		Time
1952	Andrea Mead Lawrence, USA	2:06.8	1984	Debbie Armstrong, USA	2:20.98
1956	Ossi Reichert, GER	1:56.5	1988	Vreni Schneider, SWI	2:06.49
1960	Yvonne Rügg, SWI	1:39.9	1992	Pernilla Wiberg, SWE	2:12.74
1964	Marielle Goitschel, FRA	1:52.24	1994	Deborah Compagnoni, ITA	2:30.97
1968	Nancy Greene, CAN	1:51.97	1998	Deborah Compagnoni, ITA	2:50.59
1972	Marie-Theres Nadig, SWI	1:29.90	2002	Janica Kostelic, CRO	2:30.01
1976	Kathy Kreiner, CAN	1:29.13	2006	Julia Mancuso, USA	2:09.19
1980	Hanni Wenzel, LIE	2:41.66			

Super G

Year		Time	Year		Time
1988	Sigrid Wolf, AUT	1:19.03	1998	Picabo Street, USA	1:18.02
1992	Deborah Compagnoni, ITA	1:21.22	2002	Daniela Ceccarelli, ITA	1:13.59
1994	Diann Roffe-Steinrotter, USA	1:22.15	2006	Michaela Dorfmeister, AUT	1:32.47

Alpine Combined

Year		Points	Year		Time
1936	Christl Cranz, GER	97.06	1994	Pernilla Wiberg, SWE	3:05.16
1948	Trude Beiser, AUT	6.58	1998	Katja Seizinger, GER	2:40.74
1952-84	Not held		2002	Janica Kostelic, CRO	2:43.28
1988	Anita Wachter, AUT	29.25	2006	Janica Kostelic, CRO	2:51.08
1992	Petra Kronberger, AUT	2.55			

BIATHLON
MEN

Multiple gold medals (including relays): Ole Einar Bjoerndalen (5); Aleksandr Tikhonov (4); Mark Kirchner, Michael Greis and Ricco Gross (3); Anatoly Alyabyev, Ivan Biakov, Sergei Chepikov, Sven Fischer, Halvard Hanevold, Frank Luck, Viktor Mamatov, Frank-Peter Roetsch, Magnar Solberg and Dmitri Vasilyev (2).

10 kilometers

Year		Time	Year		Time
1980	Frank Ulrich, E. Ger	32:10.69	1994	Sergei Chepikov, RUS	28:07.0
1984	Erik Kvalfoss, NOR	30:53.8	1998	Ole Einar Bjoerndalen, NOR	27:16.2
1988	Frank-Peter Roetsch, E. Ger	25:08.1	2002	Ole Einar Bjoerndalen, NOR	24:51.3
1992	Mark Kirchner, GER	26:02.3	2006	Sven Fischer, GER	26:11.6

12.5 kilometers

Year		Time	Year		Time
2002	Ole Einar Bjoerndalen, NOR	32:34.6	2006	Vincent Defrasne, FRA	35:20.2

15 kilometers

Year		Time
2006	Michael Greis, GER	47:20.0

20 kilometers

Year		Time	Year		Time
1960	Klas Lestander, SWE	1:33:21.6	1988	Frank-Peter Roetsch, E. Ger	56:33.3
1964	Vladimir Melanin, USSR	1:20:26.8	1992	Yevgeny Redkine, UT	57:34.4
1968	Magnar Solberg, NOR	1:13:45.9	1994	Sergei Tarasov, RUS	57:25.3
1972	Magnar Solberg, NOR	1:15:55.50	1998	Halvard Hanevold, NOR	56:16.4
1976	Nikolai Kruglov, USSR	1:14:12.26	2002	Ole Einar Bjoerndalen, NOR	51:03.3
1980	Anatoly Alyabyev, USSR	1:08:16.31	2006	Michael Greis, GER	54:23.0
1984	Peter Angerer, W. Ger	1:11:52.7			

4x7.5-kilometer Relay

Year		Time	Year		Time	Year		Time
1968	Soviet Union	2:13:02.4	1984	Soviet Union	1:38:51.7	1998	Germany	1:21:36.2
1972	Soviet Union	1:51:44.92	1988	Soviet Union	1:22:30.0	2002	Norway	1:23:42.3
1976	Soviet Union	1:57:55.64	1992	Germany	1:24:43.5	2006	Germany	1:21:51.5
1980	Soviet Union	1:34:03.27	1994	Germany	1:30:22.1			

WOMEN

Multiple gold medals (including relays): Myriam Bedard, Andrea Henkel, Svetlana Ishmouratova, Anfisa Reztsova and Kati Wilhelm (2). Note that Reztsova won a third gold medal in 1988 in the cross country 4x5-kilometer relay.

7.5 kilometers

Year		Time	Year		Time
1992	Anfisa Reztsova, UT	24:29.2	2002	Kati Wilhelm, GER	20:41.4
1994	Myriam Bedard, CAN	26:08.8	2006	Florence Baverel-Robert, FRA	22:31.4
1998	Galina Koukleva, RUS	23:08.0			

10 kilometers

Year		Time	Year		Time
2002	Olga Pyleva, RUS	31:07.7	2006	Kati Wilhelm, GER	36:43.6

12.5 kilometers

Year		Time
2006	Anna Carin Olofsson, SWE	40:36.5

15 kilometers

Year		Time	Year		Time
1992	Antje Misersky, GER	51:47.2	2002	Andrea Henkel, GER	47:29.1
1994	Myriam Bedard, CAN	52:06.6	2006	Svetlana Ishmouratova, RUS	49:24.1
1998	Ekaterina Dafovska, BUL	54:52.0			

4x7.5-kilometer Relay

Year		Time	Year		Time
1992	France	1:15:55.6	2002	Germany	1:27:55.0
1994	Russia	1:47:19.5	2006	Russia	1:16:12.5
1998	Germany	1:40:13.6	**Note:** Event featured three skiers per team in 1992.		

BOBSLED

A two-woman bobsled event was added in 2002. Only drivers are listed in parentheses.

Multiple gold medals: DRIVERS–Andre Lange and Meinhard Nehmer (3); Billy Fiske, Wolfgang Hoppe, Christoph Langen, Eugenio Monti, Andreas Ostler and Gustav Weder (2). CREW–Bernard Germeshausen (3); Donat Acklin, Luciano De Paolis, Cliff Gray, Lorenz Nieberl and Dietmar Schauerhammer (2).

Two-Man

Year		Time	Year		Time
1932	United States (Hubert Stevens)	8:14.74	1980	Switzerland (Erich Schärer)	4:09.36
1936	United States (Ivan Brown)	5:29.29	1984	East Germany (Wolfgang Hoppe)	3:25.56
1948	Switzerland (Felix Endrich)	5:29.2	1988	Soviet Union (Janis Kipurs)	3:54.19
1952	Germany (Andreas Ostler)	5:24.54	1992	Switzerland I (Gustav Weder)	4:03.26
1956	Italy (Lamberto Dalla Costa)	5:30.14	1994	Switzerland I (Gustav Weder)	3:30.81
1960	Not held		1998	(TIE) Italy I (Guenther Huber)	3:37.24
1964	Great Britain (Anthony Nash)	4:21.90		& Canada I (Pierre Lueders)	3:37.24
1968	Italy (Eugenio Monti)	4:41.54	2002	Germany I (Christoph Langen)	3:10.11
1972	West Germany (Wolfgang Zimmerer)	4:57.07	2006	Germany I (Andre Lange)	3:43.38
1976	East Germany (Meinhard Nehmer)	3:44.42			

Two-Woman

Year		Time	Year		Time
2002	United States II (Jill Bakken)	1:37.76	2006	Germany I (Sandra Kiriasis)	3:49.98

Four-Man

Year		Time	Year		Time
1924	Switzerland (Eduard Scherrer)	5:45.54	1972	Switzerland (Jean Wicki)	4:43.07
1928	United States (Billy Fiske)	3:20.5	1976	East Germany (Meinhard Nehmer)	3:40.43
1932	United States (Billy Fiske)	7:53.68	1980	East Germany (Meinhard Nehmer)	3:59.92
1936	Switzerland (Pierre Musy)	5:19.85	1984	East Germany (Wolfgang Hoppe)	3:20.22
1948	United States (Francis Tyler)	5:20.1	1988	Switzerland (Ekkehard Fasser)	3:47.51
1952	Germany (Andreas Ostler)	5:07.84	1992	Austria I (Ingo Appelt)	3:53.90
1956	Switzerland (Franz Kapus)	5:10.44	1994	Germany II (Harald Czudaj)	3:27.78
1960	Not held		1998	Germany II (Christoph Langen)	2:39.41
1964	Canada (Vic Emery)	4:14.46	2002	Germany II (Andre Lange)	3:07.51
1968	Italy (Eugenio Monti)	2:17.39	2006	Germany I (Andre Lange)	3:40.42

Note: Five-man sleds were used in 1928.

CROSS COUNTRY SKIING

Starting with the 1988 Winter Games in Calgary, the classical and freestyle (i.e., skating) techniques were designated for specific events. The Pursuit race was introduced in 1992 and revamped after the 1998 Nagano Games. The Sprint was added in 2002 and the distances have differed slightly (1.5k in 2002 and 1.4k in 2006). The Team Sprint was added in 2006

MEN

Multiple gold medals (including relays): Bjorn Dählie (8); Thomas Alsgaard, Sixten Jernberg, Gunde Svan, Thomas Wassberg and Nikolai Zimyatov (4); Veikko Hakulinen, Eero Mäntyranta and Vegard Ulvang (3); Hallgeir Brenden, Harald Grönningen, Thorleif Haug, Bjoern Lind, Johann Muehlegg, Jan Ottoson, Kristen Skjeldal, Pål Tyldum, Andrus Veerpalu and Vyacheslav Vedenine (2).

Multiple gold medals (including Nordic Combined): Johan Gröttumsbråten and Thorleif Haug (3).

Sprint

Held as a freestyle event.

Year		Time	Year		Time
2002	Tor Arne Hetland, NOR	2:56.9	2006	Bjoern Lind, SWE	2:26.5

Team Sprint (3x1.4 km)

Held as a classical event.

Year		Time
2006	Sweden	17:02.9

10 kilometers

Held as a classical event.

Year		Time	Year		Time
1992	Vegard Ulvang, NOR	27:36.0	1998	Bjorn Dählie, NOR	27:24.5
1994	Bjorn Dählie, NOR	24:20.1	2002	discontinued	

Combined Pursuit

From 1992-98 the pursuit included a 10-km classical race and a 15-km freestyle race contested on separate days. In 2002, the pursuit was shortened to two 10-km races held on the same day. In 2006, the Combined Pursuit was comprised of back-to-back 15-km classical and freestyle races.

Year		Time	Year		Time
1992	Bjorn Dählie, NOR	1:05:37.9	2002	Johann Muehlegg, SPA	.49:20.4
1994	Bjorn Dählie, NOR	1:00:08.8	2006	Eugeni Dementiev, RUS	1:17:00.8
1998	Thomas Alsgaard, NOR	1:07:01.7			

15 kilometers

Held over 18 kilometers from 1924-52. Held as a classical event from 1956-88, and since 2002. Replaced by the 15-km combined pursuit (1992-98).

Year		Time	Year		Time
1924	Thorleif Haug, NOR	1:14:31.0	1968	Harald Grönningen, NOR	.47:54.2
1928	Johan Gröttumsbräten, NOR	1:37:01.0	1972	Sven-Ake Lundback, SWE	.45:28.24
1932	Sven Utterström, SWE	1:23:07.0	1976	Nikolai Bazhukov, USSR	.43:58.47
1936	Erik-August Larsson, SWE	1:14:38.0	1980	Thomas Wassberg, SWE	.41:57.63
1948	Martin Lundström, SWE	1:13:50.0	1984	Gunde Svan, SWE	.41:25.6
1952	Hallgeir Brenden, NOR	1:01:34.0	1988	Mikhail Devyatyarov, USSR	.41:18.9
1956	Hallgeir Brenden, NOR	.49:39.0	1992-98	Not held	
1960	Hakon Brusveen, NOR	.51:55.5	2002	Andrus Veerpalu, EST	.37:07.4
1964	Eero Mäntyranta, FIN	.50:54.1	2006	Andrus Veerpalu, EST	.38:01.3

30 kilometers

Held as a freestyle event from 1956-94, and in 2002. Held as a classical event in 1998.

Year		Time	Year		Time
1956	Veikko Hakulinen, FIN	1:44:06.0	1984	Nikolai Zimyatov, USSR	1:28:56.3
1960	Sixten Jernberg, SWE	1:51:03.9	1988	Alexei Prokurorov, USSR	1:24:26.3
1964	Eero Mäntyranta, FIN	1:30:50.7	1992	Vegard Ulvang, NOR	1:22:27.8
1968	Franco Nones, ITA	1:35:39.2	1994	Thomas Alsgaard, NOR	1:12:26.4
1972	Vyacheslav Vedenine, USSR	1:36:31.15	1998	Mika Myllylae, FIN	1:33:55.8
1976	Sergei Saveliev, USSR	1:30:29.38	2002	Johann Muehlegg, SPA	1:09:28.9
1980	Nikolai Zimyatov, USSR	1:27:02.80	2006	discontinued	

50 kilometers

Held as a classical event from 1924-94, and since 2002. Held as a freestyle event in 1998.

Year		Time	Year		Time
1924	Thorleif Haug, NOR	3:44:32.0	1972	Päl Tyldum, NOR	2:43:14.75
1928	Per Erik Hedlund, SWE	4:52:03.0	1976	Ivar Formo, NOR	2:37:30.05
1932	Veli Saarinen, FIN	4:28:00.0	1980	Nikolai Zimyatov, USSR	2:27:24.60
1936	Elis Wiklund, SWE	3:30:11.0	1984	Thomas Wassberg, SWE	2:15:55.8
1948	Nils Karlsson, SWE	3:47:48.0	1988	Gunde Svan, SWE	2:04:30.9
1952	Veikko Hakulinen, FIN	3:33:33.0	1992	Bjorn Dählie, NOR	2:03:41.5
1956	Sixten Jernberg, SWE	2:50:27.0	1994	Vladimir Smirnov, KAZ	2:07:20.3
1960	Kalevi Hämäläinen, FIN	2:59:06.3	1998	Bjorn Dählie, NOR	2:05:08.2
1964	Sixten Jernberg, SWE	2:43:52.6	2002	Mikhail Ivanov, RUS*	2:06:20.8
1968	Ole Ellefsaeter, NOR	2:28:45.8	2006	Giorgio Di Centa, ITA	2:06:11.8

*Ivanov finished second to Johann Muehlegg of Spain, who was disqualified for failing a drug test.

4x10-kilometer Mixed Relay

Two classical and two freestyle legs.

Year		Time	Year		Time	Year		Time
1936	Finland	2:41:33.0	1968	Norway	2:08:33.5	1992	Norway	1:39:26.0
1948	Sweden	2:32:08.0	1972	Soviet Union	2:04:47.94	1994	Italy	1:41:15.0
1952	Finland	2:20:16.0	1976	Finland	2:07:59.72	1998	Norway	1:40:55.7
1956	Soviet Union	2:15:30.0	1980	Soviet Union	1:57:03.46	2002	Norway	1:32:45.5
1960	Finland	2:18:45.6	1984	Sweden	1:55:06.3	2006	Italy	1:43:45.7
1964	Sweden	2:18:34.6	1988	Sweden	1:43:58.6			

WOMEN

Multiple gold medals (including relays): Lyubov Egorova (6); Larissa Lazutina (5); Galina Kulakova and Raisa Smetanina (4); Claudia Boyarskikh, Olga Danilova and Marja-Liisa Hämäläinen and Elena Valbe (3); Stefania Belmondo, Manuela Di Centa, Nina Gavriluk, Toini Gustafsson, Barbara Petzold, Kristina Smigun and Julija Tchepalova (2).

Multiple gold medals (including relays and Biathlon): Anfisa Reztsova (2).

Cross Country (Cont.)

Sprint

The Sprint was added in 2002 and the distances have differed slightly (1.5km in 2002 and 1.2km in 2006). The Team Sprint was added in 2006

Year		Time	Year		Time
2002	Julija Tchepalova, RUS	.3:10.6	2006	Chandra Crawford, CAN	.2:12.3

Team Sprint (3x1.2km)

Year		Time
2006	Sweden	.16:36.9

5 kilometers

Held as a classical event from 1964-98. From 1992-98 it was half of the combined pursuit event. Discontinued after 1998.

Year		Time	Year		Time
1964	Claudia Boyarskikh, USSR	.17:50.5	1984	Marja-Liisa Hämäläinen, FIN	.17:04.0
1968	Toini Gustafsson, SWE	.16:45.2	1988	Marjo Matikainen, FIN	.15:04.0
1972	Galina Kulakova, USSR	.17:00.50	1992	Marjut Lukkarinen, FIN	.14:13.8
1976	Helena Takalo, FIN	.15:48.69	1994	Lyubov Egorova, RUS	.14:08.8
1980	Raisa Smetanina, USSR	.15:06.92	1998	Larissa Lazutina, RUS	.17:37.9

Combined Pursuit

From 1992-98 the pursuit consisted of a 10-km freestyle race in which the starting order was determined by order of finish in the 5-km classical race contested on separate days. In 2002, the pursuit was shortened to a 5-km classical race followed by a 5-km freestyle race contested on the same day. The 5-km classical is no longer a separate medal event. In 2006, the Combined Pursuit was comprised of back-to-back 7½-km classical and freestyle races.

Year		Time	Year		Time
1992	Lyubov Egorova, UT	.40:07.7	2002	Olga Danilova, RUS	.24:52.1
1994	Lyubov Egorova, RUS	.41:38.1	2006	Kristina Smigun, EST	.42:48.7
1998	Larissa Lazutina, RUS	.46:06.9			

10 kilometers

Held as a classical event from 1952-88, and since 2002. Replaced by 10-km combined pursuit from 1992-98.

Year		Time	Year		Time
1952	Lydia Wideman, FIN	.41:40.0	1980	Barbara Petzold, E. Ger	.30:31.54
1956	Lyubov Kosyreva, USSR	.38:11.0	1984	Marja-Liisa Hämäläinen, FIN	.31:44.2
1960	Maria Gusakova, USSR	.39:46.6	1988	Vida Venciene, USSR	.30:08.3
1964	Claudia Boyarskikh, USSR	.40:24.3	1992-98	Not held	
1968	Toini Gustafsson, SWE	.36:46.5	2002	Bente Skari, NOR	.28:05.6
1972	Galina Kulakova, USSR	.34:17.82	2006	Kristina Smigun, EST	.27:51.4
1976	Raisa Smetanina, USSR	.30:13.41			

15 kilometers

Held as a freestyle event from 1992-94, and 2002. Held as a classical event in 1998.

Year		Time	Year		Time
1992	Lyubov Egorova, UT	.42:20.8	1998	Olga Danilova, RUS	.46:55.4
1994	Manuela Di Centa, ITA	.39:44.5	2002	Stefania Belmondo, ITA	.39:54.4

20 kilometers

Held as a classical event from 1984-88. Discontinued in 1992 and replaced by the 30-kilometer freestyle.

Year		Time	Year		Time
1984	Marja-Liisa Hämäläinen, FIN	1:01:45.0	1988	Tamara Tikhonova, USSR	.55:53.6

30 kilometers

Replaced 20-km classical event in 1992. Held as a freestyle event 1992-98 and 2006. Held as a classical event in 2002.

Year		Time	Year		Time
1992	Stefania Belmondo, ITA	1:22:30.1	2002	Gabriella Paruzzi, ITA*	1:30:57.1
1994	Manuela Di Centa, ITA	1:25:41.6	2006	Katerina Neumannova, CZE	1:22:25.4
1998	Julija Tchepalova, RUS	1:22:01.5			

*Paruzzi finished second to Larissa Lazutina of Russia, who was disqualified after failing a drug test.

4x5-kilometer Relay

Two classical and two freestyle legs since 1992. Event featured three skiers per team from 1956-72.

Year		Time	Year		Time	Year		Time
1956	Finland	1:09:01.0	1976	Soviet Union	1:07:49.75	1994	Russia	.57:12.5
1960	Sweden	1:04:21.4	1980	East Germany	1:02:11.10	1998	Russia	.55:13.5
1964	Soviet Union	.59:20.2	1984	Norway	1:06:49.7	2002	Germany	.49:30.6
1968	Norway	.57:30.0	1988	Soviet Union	.59:51.1	2006	Russia	.54:47.7
1972	Soviet Union	.48:46.15	1992	Unified Team	.59:34.8			

CURLING

MEN

Year		
1998	**Switzerland**, Canada, Norway	
2002	**Norway**, Canada, Switzerland	
2006	**Canada**, Finland, United States	

WOMEN

Year		
1998	**Canada**, Denmark, Sweden	
2002	**Great Britain**, Switzerland, Canada	
2006	**Sweden**, Switzerland, Canada	

FIGURE SKATING

MEN

Multiple gold medals: Gillis Grafström (3); Dick Button and Karl Schäfer (2).

Year		Year		Year	
1908	Ulrich Salchow ....SWE	1952	Dick Button ....USA	1984	Scott Hamilton ....USA
1912	Not held	1956	Hayes Alan Jenkins .....USA	1988	Brian Boitano ....USA
1920	Gillis Grafström ....SWE	1960	David Jenkins ....USA	1992	Victor Petrenko ....UT-
1924	Gillis Grafström ....SWE	1964	Manfred Schnelldorfer ...GER	1994	Alexei Urmanov ....RUS
1928	Gillis Grafström ....SWE	1968	Wolfgang Schwarz .....AUT	1998	Ilia Kulik ....RUS
1932	Karl Schäfer ....AUT	1972	Ondrej Nepela ....CZE	2002	Alexei Yagudin ....RUS
1936	Karl Schäfer ....AUT	1976	John Curry ....GBR	2006	Yevgeny Plushenko .....RUS
1948	Dick Button ....USA	1980	Robin Cousins ....GBR		

WOMEN

Multiple gold medals: Sonja Henie (3); Katarina Witt (2).

Year		Year		Year	
1908	Madge Syers ....GBR	1952	Jeanette Altwegg ....GBR	1984	Katarina Witt ....E. Ger
1912	Not held	1956	Tenley Albright ....USA	1988	Katarina Witt ....E. Ger
1920	Magda Julin-Mauroy ....SWE	1960	Carol Heiss ....USA	1992	Kristi Yamaguchi ....USA
1924	Herma Planck-Szabö ....AUT	1964	Sjoukje Dijkstra ....NED	1994	Oksana Baiul ....UKR
1928	Sonja Henie ....NOR	1968	Peggy Fleming ....USA	1998	Tara Lipinski ....USA
1932	Sonja Henie ....NOR	1972	Beatrix Schuba ....AUT	2002	Sarah Hughes ....USA
1936	Sonja Henie ....NOR	1976	Dorothy Hamill ....USA	2006	Shizuka Arakawa ....JPN
1948	Barbara Ann Scott ......CAN	1980	Anett Poetzsch ....E. Ger		

Pairs

Multiple gold medals: MEN–Pierre Brunet, Artur Dmitriev, Sergei Grinkov, Oleg Protopopov and Aleksandr Zaitsev (2). WOMEN–Irina Rodnina (3); Ludmila Belousova, Ekaterina Gordeeva and Andree Joly Brunet (2).

Year		Year	
1908	Anna Hübler & Heinrich Burger ....Germany	1968	Ludmila Belousova & Oleg Protopopov ......USSR
1912	Not held	1972	Irina Rodnina & Aleksei Ulanov ....USSR
1920	Ludovika & Walter Jakobsson ....Finland	1976	Irina Rodnina & Aleksandr Zaitsev ....USSR
1924	Helene Engelmann & Alfred Berger ....Austria	1980	Irina Rodnina & Aleksandr Zaitsev ....USSR
1928	Andrée Joly & Pierre Brunet ....France	1984	Elena Valova & Oleg Vasiliev ....USSR
1932	Andrée & Pierre Brunet ....France	1988	Ekaterina Gordeeva & Sergei Grinkov ......USSR
1936	Maxi Herber & Ernst Baier ....Germany	1992	Natalia Mishkutienok & Arthur Dmitriev ......UT
1948	Micheline Lannoy & Pierre Baugniet ......Belgium	1994	Ekaterina Gordeeva & Sergei Grinkov ......RUS
1952	Ria & Paul Falk ....Germany	1998	Oksana Kazakova & Artur Dmitriev ....RUS
1956	Elisabeth Schwartz & Kurt Oppelt ....Austria	2002	Elena Berezhnaya & Anton Sikharulidze ......RUS
1960	Barbara Wagner & Robert Paul ....Canada		Jamie Sale & David Pelletier* ....CAN
1964	Ludmila Belousova & Oleg Protopopov .....USSR	2006	Tatyana Totmiyanina & Maxim Marinin ......RUS

*Originally awarded silver medals, Sale & Pelletier later had them upgraded to gold after an investigation by the International Olympic Committee and the International Skating Union concluded that a judge was guilty of misconduct.

Ice Dancing

Multiple gold medals: Oksana Grishuk & Yevgeny Platov (2).

Year		Year	
1976	Lyudmila Pakhomova & Aleksandr Gorshkov ..USSR	1994	Oksana Grishuk & Yevgeny Platov ....RUS
1980	Natalia Linichuk & Gennady Karponosov ....USSR	1998	Oksana Grishuk & Yevgeny Platov ....RUS
1984	Jayne Torvill & Christopher Dean .....Great Britain	2002	Marina Anissina & Gwendal Peizerat ....FRA
1988	Natalia Bestemianova & Andrei Bukin ......USSR	2006	Tatyana Navka & Roman Kostomarov ....RUS
1992	Marina Klimova & Sergei Ponomarenko ....UT		

FREESTYLE SKIING

MEN

Aerials

Year		Points
1994	Andreas Schoebaechler, SWI	234.67
1998	Eric Bergoust, USA	255.64
2002	Ales Valenta, CZR	257.02
2006	Xiaopeng Han, CHN	250.77

Moguls

Year		Points
1994	Jean-Luc Brassard, CAN	27.24
1998	Jonny Moseley, USA	26.93
2002	Janne Lahtela, FIN	27.97
2006	Dale Begg-Smith, AUS	26.77

WOMEN

Aerials

Year		Points
1994	Lina Cherjazova, UZB	166.84
1998	Nikki Stone, USA	193.00
2002	Alisa Camplin, AUS	193.47
2006	Evelyne Leu, SWI	202.55

Moguls

Year		Points
1994	Stine Lise Hattestad, NOR	25.97
1998	Tae Satoya, JPN	25.06
2002	Kari Traa, NOR	25.94
2006	Jennifer Heil, CAN	26.50

ICE HOCKEY

MEN

Multiple gold medals: Soviet Union/Unified Team (8); Canada (7); Sweden and United States (2).

Year	
1920	**Canada**, United States Czechoslovakia
1924	**Canada**, United States, Great Britain
1928	**Canada**, Sweden, Switzerland
1932	**Canada**, United States, Germany
1936	**Great Britain**, Canada, United States
1948	**Canada**, Czechoslovakia, Switzerland
1952	**Canada**, United States, Sweden
1956	**Soviet Union**, United States, Canada
1960	**United States**, Canada, Soviet Union
1964	**Soviet Union**, Sweden, Czechoslovakia
1968	**Soviet Union**, Czechoslovakia, Canada
1972	**Soviet Union**, United States, Czechoslovakia
1976	**Soviet Union**, Czechoslovakia, West Germany

Year	
1980	**United States**, Soviet Union, Sweden
1984	**Soviet Union**, Czechoslovakia, Sweden
1988	**Soviet Union**, Finland, Sweden
1992	**Unified Team**, Canada, Czechoslovakia
1994	**Sweden**, Canada, Finland
1998	**Czech Republic**, Russia, Finland
2002	**Canada**, United States, Russia
2006	**Sweden**, Finland, Czech Republic

WOMEN

Year	
1998	**United States**, Canada, Finland
2002	**Canada**, United States, Sweden
2006	**Canada**, Sweden, United States

U.S. Gold Medal Hockey Teams

MEN

1960

Forwards: Billy Christian, Roger Christian, Billy Cleary, Gene Grazia, Paul Johnson, Bob McVey, Dick Meredith, Weldy Olson, Dick Rodenheiser and Tom Williams. **Defensemen:** Bob Cleary, Jack Kirrane (captain), John Mayasich, Bob Owen and Rod Paavola. **Goaltenders:** Jack McCartan and Larry Palmer. **Coach:** Jack Riley.

1980

Forwards: Neal Broten, Steve Christoff, Mike Eruzione (captain), John Harrington, Mark Johnson, Rob McClanahan, Mark Pavelich, Buzz Schneider, Dave Silk, Eric Strobel, Phil Verchota and Mark Wells. **Defensemen:** Bill Baker, Dave Christian, Ken Morrow, Jack O'Callahan, Mike Ramsey and Bob Suter. **Goaltenders:** Jim Craig and Steve Janaszak. **Coach:** Herb Brooks.

WOMEN

1998

Forwards: Laurie Baker, Alana Blahoski, Lisa Brown-Miller, Karen Bye, Tricia Dunn, Cammi Granato, Katie King, Shelley Looney, A.J. Mleczko, Jenny Schmidgall, Gretchen Ulion, Sandra Whyte. **Defensemen:** Chris Bailey, Colleen Coyne, Sue Mertz, Tara Mounsey, Vicki Movessian, Angela Ruggiero. **Goaltenders:** Sarah DeCosta and Sarah Tueting. **Coach:** Ben Smith.

LUGE
MEN

Multiple gold medals: (including doubles): Georg Hackl (3); Jan Behrendt, Norbert Hahn, Paul Hildgartner, Thomas Köhler, Stefan Krausse, Hans Rinn and Armin Zoeggeler (2).

Singles

Year		Time	Year		Time
1964	Thomas Köhler, GER	3:26.77	1988	Jens Müller, E. Ger	3:05.548
1968	Manfred Schmid, AUT	2:52.48	1992	Georg Hackl, GER	3:02.363
1972	Wolfgang Scheidel, E. Ger	3:27.58	1994	Georg Hackl, GER	3:21.571
1976	Dettlef Günther, E. Ger	3:27.688	1998	Georg Hackl, GER	3:18.436
1980	Bernhard Glass, E. Ger	2:54.796	2002	Armin Zoeggeler, ITA	2:57.941
1984	Paul Hildgartner, ITA	3:04.258	2006	Armin Zoeggeler, ITA	3:26.088

Doubles

Year		Time	Year		Time
1964	Josef Feistmantl & Manfred Stengl, AUT	1:41.62	1988	Joerg Hoffmann & Jochen Pietzsch, E. Ger.	1:31.940
1968	Klaus Bonsack & Thomas Köhler, E. Ger.	1:35.85	1992	Jan Behrendt & Stefan Krausse, GER	1:32.053
1972	(TIE) Paul Hildgartner/Walter Plaikner, ITA	1:28.35	1994	Kurt Brugger & Wilfred Huber, ITA	1:36.720
	& Richard Bredow/Horst Hornlein, E. Ger.	1:28.35	1998	Jan Behrendt & Stefan Krausse, GER	1:41.105
1976	Norbert Hahn & Hans Rinn, E. Ger.	1:25.604	2002	Patric-Fritz Leitner & Alexander Resch, GER	1:26.082
1980	Norbert Hahn & Hans Rinn, E. Ger.	1:19.331	2006	Andreas Linger & Wolfgang Linger, AUT	1:34.497
1984	Hans Stangassinger & Franz Wembacher, W. Ger.	1:23.620			

WOMEN

Multiple gold medals: Sylke Otto and Steffi Martin Walter (2).

Singles

Year		Time	Year		Time
1964	Ortrun Enderlein, GER	3:24.67	1988	Steffi Martin Walter, E. Ger	3:03.973
1968	Erica Lechner, ITA	2:28.66	1992	Doris Neuner, AUT	3:06.696
1972	Anna-Maria Müller, E. Ger	2:59.18	1994	Gerda Weissensteiner, ITA	3:15.517
1976	Margit Schumann, E. Ger	2:50.621	1998	Silke Kraushaar, GER	3:23.779
1980	Vera Zozulya, USSR	2:36.537	2002	Sylke Otto, GER	2:52.464
1984	Steffi Martin, E. Ger	2:46.570	2006	Sylke Otto, GER	3:07.979

NORDIC COMBINED

Ski jumping followed by a cross country race. Judges stopped converting cross country times into points after the 1994 Games. The times listed are final cross country times adjusted to include the competitors' staggered start time. The staggered start is determined by the Gundersen Method, which is a table that converts final ski jumping point differentials into time intervals.

Multiple gold medals: Samppa Lajunen and Ulrich Wehling (3); Bjarte Engen Vik, Felix Gottwald, Johan Gröttumsbråten, Fred Boerre Lundberg, Takanori Kono and Kenji Ogiwara (2).

Individual

Year		Points	Year		Points
1924	Thorleif Haug, NOR	18.906	1976	Ulrich Wehling, E. Ger	423.39
1928	Johan Gröttumsbråten, NOR	17.833	1980	Ulrich Wehling, E. Ger	432.200
1932	Johan Gröttumsbråten, NOR	446.00	1984	Tom Sandberg, NOR	422.595
1936	Oddbjörn Hagen, NOR	430.3	1988	Hippolyt Kempf, SWI	432.230
1948	Heikki Hasu, FIN	448.80	1992	Fabrice Guy, FRA	426.470
1952	Simon Slattvik, NOR	451.621	1994	Fred Boerre Lundberg, NOR	457.970
1956	Sverre Stenersen, NOR	455.000			**Time**
1960	Georg Thoma, GER	457.952	1998	Bjarte Engen Vik, NOR	41:21.1
1964	Tormod Knutsen, NOR	469.28	2002	Samppa Lajunen, FIN	39:11.7
1968	Franz Keller, W. Ger	449.04	2006	Georg Hettich, GER	39:44.6
1972	Ulrich Wehling, E. Ger	413.340			

Sprint

New event in 2002.

Year		Time	Year		Time
2002	Samppa Lajunen, FIN	16:40.1	2006	Felix Gottwald, AUT	18:29.0

Team

Year		Points	Year		Time
1988	West Germany	792.08	1998	Norway	54:11.5
1992	Japan	1247.180	2002	Finland	48:42.2
1994	Japan	1368.860	2006	Austria	49:52.6

SKELETON

MEN
Singles

Year		Time
1928	Jennison Heaton, USA	3:01.8
1932-36	Not held	
1948	Nino Bibbia, ITA	5:23.2
1952-98	Not held	
2002	Jim Shea, USA	1:41.96
2006	Duff Gibson, CAN	1:55.88

WOMEN
Singles

Year		Time
2002	Tristan Gale, USA	1:45.11
2006	Maya Pedersen, SWI	1:59.83

Note: This event was called Cresta when it was held in 1928 and 1948.

SKI JUMPING

Multiple gold medals (including team jumping): Matti Nykänen (4); Jens Weissflog (3); Simon Ammann, Birger Ruud, Thomas Morgenstern and Toni Nieminen (2).

Normal Hill (90 Meters)

Year		Points	Year		Points
1924-60	Not held		1988	Matti Nykänen, FIN	229.1
1964	Veikko Kankkonen, FIN	229.9	1992	Ernst Vettori, AUT	222.8
1968	Jiri Raska, CZE	216.5	1994	Espen Bredesen, NOR	282.0
1972	Yukio Kasaya, JPN	244.2	1998	Jani Soininen, FIN	234.5
1976	Hans-Georg Aschenbach, E. Ger	252.0	2002	Simon Ammann, SWI	269.0
1980	Anton Innauer, AUT	266.3	2006	Lars Bystoel, NOR	266.5
1984	Jens Weissflog, E. Ger	215.2			

Note: Jump held at 70 meters from 1964-92.

Large Hill (120 Meters)

Year		Points	Year		Points
1924	Jacob Tullin Thams, NOR	18.960	1972	Wojciech Fortuna, POL	219.9
1928	Alf Andersen, NOR	19.208	1976	Karl Schäabl, AUT	234.8
1932	Birger Ruud, NOR	228.1	1980	Jouko Törmänen, FIN	271.0
1936	Birger Ruud, NOR	232.0	1984	Matti Nykänen, FIN	231.2
1948	Petter Hugsted, NOR	228.1	1988	Matti Nykänen, FIN	224.0
1952	Arnfinn Bergmann, NOR	226.0	1992	Toni Nieminen, FIN	239.5
1956	Antti Hyvärinen, FIN	227.0	1994	Jens Weissflog, GER	274.5
1960	Helmut Recknagel, GER	227.2	1998	Kazuyoshi Funaki, JPN	272.3
1964	Toralf Engan, NOR	230.7	2002	Simon Ammann, SWI	281.4
1968	Vladimir Beloussov, USSR	231.3	2006	Thomas Morgenstern, AUT	276.9

Note: Jump held at various lengths from 1924-56; at 80 meters from 1960-64; and at 90 meters from 1968-88.

Team (Large Hill)

Year		Points	Year		Points
1988	Finland	634.4	1998	Japan	933.0
1992	Finland	644.4	2002	Germany	974.1
1994	Germany	970.1	2006	Austria	984.0

Skicross In for 2010 Games

Men's and Women's **Skicross** will be the only new event to make its debut at the 2010 Winter Games in Vancouver, Canada. Women's ski jumping, which was thought to have a decent chance at inclusion, was passed over.

The Vancouver skicross events will feature 32 men and 16 women competing in the same format as the snowboard version, where multiple skiers race down a winding, banked course side-by-side. The two gold medals will bring the total of medal events in Vancouver to 86.

Ski jumping, and by extension nordic combined, remain the only Winter Olympic sports that do not have events for women. The IOC also denied a proposed team event in Alpine skiing, mixed relay in biathlon, team competitions in bobsled and skeleton, a team luge competition and mixed doubles in curling.

In other Winter Olympic news, **Sochi, Russia** was named the host city for the 2014 Games. Sochi beat out competing bids from Salzburg, Austria and PyeongChang, South Korea.

SNOWBOARDING

Multiple gold medals: Philipp Schoch (2).

MEN

Halfpipe

Year		Points
1998	Gian Simmen, SWI	85.2
2002	Ross Powers, USA	46.1
2006	Shaun White, USA	46.8

Giant Slalom

Discontinued after 1998, replaced by Parallel Giant Slalom.

Year		Time
1998	Ross Rebagliati, CAN	2:03.96

Parallel Giant Slalom

Year		
2002	Philipp Schoch	SWI
2006	Philipp Schoch	SWI

Snowboard Cross

Added in 2006.

Year		
2006	Seth Wescott	USA

WOMEN

Halfpipe

Year		Points
1998	Nicola Thost, GER	74.6
2002	Kelly Clark, USA	47.9
2006	Hannah Teter, USA	46.4

Giant Slalom

Discontinued after 1998, replaced by Parallel Giant Slalom.

Year		Time
1998	Karine Ruby, FRA	2:17.34

Parallel Giant Slalom

Year		
2002	Isabelle Blanc	FRA
2006	Daniela Meuli	SWI

Snowboard Cross

Added in 2006.

Year		
2006	Tanja Frieden	SWI

SPEED SKATING

MEN

Multiple gold medals: Eric Heiden and Clas Thunberg (5); Ivar Ballangrud, Yevgeny Grishin and Johann Olav Koss (4); Hjalmar Andersen, Tomas Gustafson, Irving Jaffee and Ard Schenk (3); Gaétan Boucher, Enrico Fabris, Knut Johannesen, Erhard Keller, Uwe-Jens Mey, Gianni Romme, Jack Shea and Jochem Uytdehaage (2). Note that Thunberg's total includes the All-Around, which was contested for the only time in 1924.

500 meters

Year		Time		Year		Time	
1924	Charles Jewtraw, USA	44.0		1972	Erhard Keller, W. Ger	39.44	**OR**
1928	(TIE) Bernt Evensen, NOR	43.4	**OR**	1976	Yevgeny Kulikov, USSR	39.17	**OR**
	& Clas Thunberg, FIN	43.4	**OR**	1980	Eric Heiden, USA	38.03	**OR**
1932	Jack Shea, USA	43.4	**=OR**	1984	Sergei Fokichev, USSR	38.19	
1936	Ivar Ballangrud, NOR	43.4	**=OR**	1988	Uwe-Jens Mey, E. Ger	36.45	**WR**
1948	Finn Helgesen, NOR	43.1	**OR**	1992	Uwe-Jens Mey, GER	37.14	
1952	Ken Henry, USA	43.2		1994	Aleksandr Golubev, RUS	36.33	**OR**
1956	Yevgeny Grishin, USSR	40.2	**=WR**	1998	Hiroyashu Shimizu, JPN	71.35*	**OR**
1960	Yevgeny Grishin, USSR	40.2	**=WR**	2002	Casey FitzRandolph, USA	69.23	**OR**
1964	Terry McDermott, USA	40.1	**OR**	2006	Joey Cheek, USA	69.76	
1968	Erhard Keller, W. Ger	40.3					

*The two-race final was introduced; skater with the lowest combined time wins gold.

1000 meters

Year		Time		Year		Time	
1924-72	Not held			1992	Olaf Zinke, GER	1:14.85	
1976	Peter Mueller, USA	1:19.32		1994	Dan Jansen, USA	1:12.43	**WR**
1980	Eric Heiden, USA	1:15.18	**OR**	1998	Ids Postma, NED	1:10.64	**OR**
1984	Gaétan Boucher, CAN	1:15.80		2002	Gerard van Velde, NED	1:07.18	**WR**
1988	Nikolai Gulyaev, USSR	1:13.03	**OR**	2006	Shani Davis, USA	1:08.89	

1500 meters

Year		Time		Year		Time	
1924	Clas Thunberg, FIN	2:20.8		1968	Kees Verkerk, NED	2:03.4	**OR**
1928	Clas Thunberg, FIN	2:21.1		1972	Ard Schenk, NED	2:02.96	**OR**
1932	Jack Shea, USA	2:57.5		1976	Jan Egil Storholt, NOR	1:59.38	**OR**
1936	Charles Mathisen, NOR	2:19.2	**OR**	1980	Eric Heiden, USA	1:55.44	**OR**
1948	Sverre Farstad, NOR	2:17.6	**OR**	1984	Gaétan Boucher, CAN	1:58.36	
1952	Hjalmar Andersen, NOR	2:20.4		1988	Andre Hoffman, E. Ger	1:52.06	**WR**
1956	(TIE) Yevgeny Grishin, USSR	2:08.6	**WR**	1992	Johann Olav Koss, NOR	1:54.81	
	& Yuri Mikhailov, USSR	2:08.6	**WR**	1994	Johann Olav Koss, NOR	1:51.29	**WR**
1960	(TIE) Roald Aas, NOR	2:10.4		1998	Aadne Sondral, NOR	1:47.87	**WR**
	& Yevgeny Grishin, USSR	2:10.4		2002	Derek Parra, USA	1:43.95	**WR**
1964	Ants Antson, USSR	2:10.3		2006	Enrico Fabris, ITA	1:45.97	

5000 meters

Year		Time		Year		Time	
1924	Clas Thunberg, FIN	8:39.0		1972	Ard Schenk, NED	7:23.61	
1928	Ivar Ballangrud, NOR	8:50.5		1976	Sten Stensen, NOR	7:24.48	
1932	Irving Jaffee, USA	9:40.8		1980	Eric Heiden, USA	7:02.29	OR
1936	Ivar Ballangrud, NOR	8:19.6	OR	1984	Tomas Gustafson, SWE	7:12.28	
1948	Reidar Liaklev, NOR	8:29.4		1988	Tomas Gustafson, SWE	6:44.63	WR
1952	Hjalmar Andersen, NOR	8:10.6	OR	1992	Geir Karlstad, NOR	6:59.97	
1956	Boris Shilkov, USSR	7:48.7	OR	1994	Johann Olav Koss, NOR	6:34.96	WR
1960	Viktor Kosichkin, USSR	7:51.3		1998	Gianni Romme, NED	6:22.20	WR
1964	Knut Johannesen, NOR	7:38.4	OR	2002	Jochem Uytdehaage, NED	6:14.66	WR
1968	Fred Anton Maier, NOR	7:22.4	WR	2006	Chad Hedrick, USA	6:14.68	

10,000 meters

Year		Time		Year		Time	
1924	Julius Skutnabb, FIN	18:04.8		1972	Ard Schenk, NED	15:01.35	OR
1928	Irving Jaffee, USA*	18:36.5		1976	Piet Kleine, NED	14:50.59	OR
1932	Irving Jaffee, USA	19:13.6		1980	Eric Heiden, USA	14:28.13	WR
1936	Ivar Ballangrud, NOR	17:24.3	OR	1984	Igor Malkov, USSR	14:39.90	
1948	Ake Seyffarth, SWE	17:26.3		1988	Tomas Gustafson, SWE	13:48.20	WR
1952	Hjalmar Andersen, NOR	16:45.8	OR	1992	Bart Veldkamp, NED	14:12.12	
1956	Sigvard Ericsson, SWE	16:35.9	OR	1994	Johann Olav Koss, NOR	13:30.55	WR
1960	Knut Johannesen, NOR	15:46.6	WR	1998	Gianni Romme, NED	13:15.33	WR
1964	Jonny Nilsson, SWE	15:50.1		2002	Jochem Uytdehaage, NED	12:58.92	WR
1968	Johnny Höglin, SWE	15:23.6	OR	2006	Bob De Jong, NED	13:01.57	

*Unofficial, according to the IOC. Jaffee recorded the fastest time, but the event was called off in progress due to thawing ice.

Team Pursuit

Added in 2006.

Year
2006 **Italy**, Canada, Netherlands

WOMEN

Multiple gold medals: Lydia Skoblikova (6); Bonnie Blair (5); Claudia Pechstein (4); Karin Enke, Gunda Niemann-Stirnemann and Yvonne van Gennip (3); Tatiana Averina, Catriona Lemay-Doan, Christa Rothenburger and Marianne Timmer (2).

500 meters

Year		Time		Year		Time	
1960	Helga Haase, GER	45.9		1988	Bonnie Blair, USA	39.10	WR
1964	Lydia Skoblikova, USSR	45.0	OR	1992	Bonnie Blair, USA	40.33	
1968	Lyudmila Titova, USSR	46.1		1994	Bonnie Blair, USA	39.25	
1972	Anne Henning, USA	43.33	OR	1998	Catriona Lemay-Doan, CAN	76.60*	OR
1976	Sheila Young, USA	42.76	OR	2002	Catriona Lemay-Doan, CAN	74.75	OR
1980	Karin Enke, E. Ger	41.78	OR	2006	Svetlana Zhurova, RUS	76.57	
1984	Christa Rothenburger, E. Ger	41.02	OR				

*The two-race final was introduced; skater with the lowest combined time wins gold.

1000 meters

Year		Time		Year		Time	
1960	Klara Guseva, USSR	1:34.1		1988	Christa Rothenburger, E. Ger	1:17.65	WR
1964	Lydia Skoblikova, USSR	1:33.2	OR	1992	Bonnie Blair, USA	1:21.90	
1968	Carolina Geijssen, NED	1:32.6	OR	1994	Bonnie Blair, USA	1:18.74	
1972	Monika Pflug, W. Ger	1:31.40	OR	1998	Marianne Timmer, NED	1:16.51	OR
1976	Tatiana Averina, USSR	1:28.43	OR	2002	Chris Witty, USA	1:13.83	WR
1980	Natalia Petruseva, USSR	1:24.10	OR	2006	Marianne Timmer, NED	1:16.05	
1984	Karin Enke, E. Ger	1:21.61	OR				

1500 meters

Year		Time		Year		Time	
1960	Lydia Skoblikova, USSR	2:25.2	WR	1988	Yvonne van Gennip, NED	2:00.68	OR
1964	Lydia Skoblikova, USSR	2:22.6	OR	1992	Jacqueline Börner, GER	2:05.87	
1968	Kaija Mustonen, FIN	2:22.4	OR	1994	Emese Hunyady, AUT	2:02.19	
1972	Dianne Holum, USA	2:20.85	OR	1998	Marianne Timmer, NED	1:57.58	WR
1976	Galina Stepanskaya, USSR	2:16.58	OR	2002	Anni Friesinger, GER	1:54.02	WR
1980	Annie Borckink, NED	2:10.95	OR	2006	Cindy Klassen, CAN	1:55.27	
1984	Karin Enke, E. Ger	2:03.42	WR				

Speed Skating (Cont.)
3000 meters

Year		Time	
1960	Lydia Skoblikova, USSR	5:14.3	
1964	Lydia Skoblikova, USSR	5:14.9	
1968	Johanna Schut, NED	4:56.2	OR
1972	Christina Baas-Kaiser, NED	4:52.14	OR
1976	Tatiana Averina, USSR	4:45.19	OR
1980	Bjorg Eva Jensen, NOR	4:32.13	OR
1984	Andrea Schöne, E. Ger	4:24.79	OR

Year		Time	
1988	Yvonne van Gennip, NED	4:11.94	WR
1992	Gunda Niemann, GER	4:19.90	
1994	Svetlana Bazhanova, RUS	4:17.43	
1998	Gunda Niemann-Stirnemann, GER	4:07.29	OR
2002	Claudia Pechstein, GER	3:57.70	WR
2006	Ireen Wust, NED	4:02.43	

5000 meters

Year		Time	
1960-84 Not held			
1988	Yvonne van Gennip, NED	7:14.13	WR
1992	Gunda Niemann, GER	7:31.57	
1994	Claudia Pechstein, GER	7:14.37	

Year		Time	
1998	Claudia Pechstein, GER	6:59.61	WR
2002	Claudia Pechstein, GER	6:46.91	WR
2006	Clara Hughes, CAN	6:59.07	

Team Pursuit
Added in 2006.

Year	
2006	**Germany**, Canada, Russia

SHORT TRACK SPEED SKATING

MEN

Multiple gold medals (including relays): Hyun-Soo Ahn, Marc Gagnon and Kim Ki-Hoon (3); Apolo Anton Ohno (2).

500 meters
added in 1994.

Year		Time	
1994	Chae Ji-Hoon, S. Kor.	43.45	
1998	Takafumi Nishitani, JPN	42.862	
2002	Marc Gagnon, CAN	41.802	OR
2006	Apolo Anton Ohno, USA	41.935	

1000 meters

Year		Time	
1992	Kim Ki-Hoon, S. Kor.	1:30.76	WR
1994	Kim Ki-Hoon, S. Kor.	1:34.57	
1998	Kim Dong-Sung, S. Kor.	1:32.375	
2002	Steven Bradbury, AUS	1:29.109	
2006	Hyun-Soo Ahn, S. Kor.	1:26.739	

1500 meters
added in 2002.

Year		Time
2002	Apolo Anton Ohno, USA*	2:18.541
2006	Hyun-Soo Ahn, S. Kor.	2:25.341

*Ohno finished second to South Korea's Kim Dong-Sung, who was disqualifed for cross-tracking.

5000-m Relay

Year		Time	
1992	South Korea	7:14.02	WR
1994	Italy	7:11.74	OR
1998	Canada	7:06.075	
2002	Canada	6:51.579	
2006	South Korea	6:43.376	

WOMEN

Multiple gold medals (including relays): Chun Lee-Kyung (4); Sun-Yu Jin (3); Kim Yun-Mi, Annie Perrault, Cathy Turner, Won Hye-Kyung and Yang Yang (A) (2)

500 meters

Year		Time	
1992	Cathy Turner, USA	47.04	
1994	Cathy Turner, USA	45.98	OR
1998	Annie Perrault, CAN	46.568	
2002	Yang Yang (A), CHN	44.187	
2006	Meng Wang, CHN	44.345	

1000 meters
added in 1994.

Year		Time
1994	Chun Lee-Kyung, S. Kor.	1:36.87
1998	Chun Lee-Kyung, S. Kor.	1:42.776
2002	Yang Yang (A), CHN	1:36.391
2006	Sun-Yu Jin, S. Kor.	1:32.859

1500 meters
added in 2002.

Year		Time
2002	Ko Gi-Hyun, S. Kor.	2:31.581
2006	Sun-Yu Jin, S. Kor.	2:23.494

3000-m Relay

Year		Time	
1992	Canada	4:36.62	
1994	South Korea	4:26.64	WR
1998	South Korea	4:16.260	WR
2002	South Korea	4:12.793	WR
2006	South Korea	4:17.040	

All-Time Leading Medal Winners

MEN

No		Sport	G-S-B
12	Bjorn Dählie, NOR	Cross Country	8-4-0
9	Sixten Jernberg, SWE	Cross Country	4-3-2
8	Kjetil Andre Aamodt, NOR	Alpine	4-2-2
7	Clas Thunberg, FIN	Speed Skating	5-1-1
7	Ivar Ballangrud, NOR	Speed Skating	4-2-1
7	Ricco Gross, GER	Biathlon	3-3-1
7	Veikko Hakulinen, FIN	Cross Country	3-3-1
7	Eero Mäntyranta, FIN	Cross Country	3-2-2
7	Bogdan Musiol, E. Ger/GER	Bobsled	1-5-1
6	Ole Einar Bjoerndalen, NOR	Biathlon	5-1-0
6	Thomas Alsgaard, NOR	Cross Country	4-2-0
6	Gunde Svan, SWE	Cross Country	4-1-1
6	Vegard Ulvang, NOR	Cross Country	3-2-1
6	Johan Gröttumsbråten, NOR	Nordic	3-1-2
6	Wolfgang Hoppe, E. Ger/GER	Bobsled	2-3-1
6	Eugenio Monti, ITA	Bobsled	2-2-2
6	Felix Gottwald, AUT	Nordic	2-1-3
6	Vladimir Smirnov, USSR/UT/KAZ	X-country	1-4-1
6	Mika Myllylae, FIN	Cross Country	1-1-4
6	Roald Larsen, NOR	Speed Skating	0-2-4
6	Harri Kirvesniemi, FIN	Cross Country	0-0-6

No		Sport	G-S-B
5	Eric Heiden, USA	Speed Skating	5-0-0
5	Yevgeny Grishin, USSR	Speed Skating	4-1-0
5	Johann Olav Koss, NOR	Speed Skating	4-1-0
5	Matti Nykänen, FIN	Ski Jumping	4-1-0
5	Aleksandr Tikhonov, USSR	Biathlon	4-1-0
5	Nikolai Zimyatov, USSR	Cross Country	4-1-0
5	Georg Hackl, GER	Luge	3-2-0
5	Samppa Lajunen, FIN	Cross Country	3-2-0
5	Alberto Tomba, ITA	Alpine	3-2-0
5	Marc Gagnon, CAN	ST Sp. Skating	3-0-2
5	Harald Grönningen, NOR	Cross Country	2-3-0
5	Frank Luck, GER	Biathlon	2-3-0
5	Päl Tyldum, NOR	Cross Country	2-3-0
5	Sven Fischer, GER	Biathlon	2-2-1
5	Knut Johannesen, NOR	Speed Skating	2-2-1
5	Lasse Kjus, NOR	Alpine	1-3-1
5	Peter Angerer, W. Ger/GER	Biathlon	1-2-2
5	Juha Mieto, FIN	Cross Country	1-2-2
5	Fritz Feierabend, SWI	Bobsled	0-3-2
5	Rintje Ritsma, NED	Speed Skating	0-2-3

WOMEN

No		Sport	G-S-B
10	Raisa Smetanina, USSR/UT	Cross Country	4-5-1
9	Lyubov Egorova, UT/RUS	Cross Country	6-3-0
9	Larissa Lazutina, UT/RUS	Cross Country	5-3-1
9	Stefania Belmondo, ITA	Cross Country	2-3-4
8	Galina Kulakova, USSR	Cross Country	4-2-2
8	Karin (Enke) Kania, E. Ger	Speed Skating	3-4-1
8	Gunda Neimann-Stirnemann, GER	Speed Skating	3-4-1
8	Ursula Disl, GER	Biathlon	2-4-2
8	Claudia Pechstein, GER	Speed Skating	4-1-2
7	Marja-Liisa (Hämäläinen) Kirvesniemi, FIN	Cross Country	3-0-4
7	Elena Valbe, UT/RUS	Cross Country	3-0-4
7	Andrea (Mitscherlich, Schöne) Ehrig, E. Ger	Speed Skating	1-5-1
6	Lydia Skoblikova, USSR	Speed Skating	6-0-0

No		Sport	G-S-B
6	Bonnie Blair, USA	Speed Skating	5-0-1
6	Janica Kostelic, CRO	Alpine	4-2-0
6	Manuela Di Centa, ITA	Cross Country	2-2-2
6	Cindy Klassen, CAN	Speed Skating	1-2-3
5	Lee-Kyung Chun, S. Kor	ST Sp. Skating	4-0-1
5	Olga Danilova, RUS	Cross Country	3-2-0
5	Anfisa Reztsova, USSR/UT	CC/Biathlon	3-1-1
5	Vreni Schneider, SWI	Alpine	3-1-1
5	Katja Seizinger, GER	Alpine	3-0-2
5	Kati Wilhelm, GER	Biathlon	2-3-0
5	Helena Takalo, FIN	Cross Country	1-3-1
5	Bente (Martinsen) Skari, NOR	Cross Country	1-2-2
5	Alevtina Kolchina, USSR	Cross Country	1-1-3
5	Anja Paerson, SWE	Alpine	1-1-3
5	Yang Yang (S), CHN	ST Sp. Skating	0-4-1
5	Anita Moen, NOR	Cross Country	0-3-2

Games Medaled In

MEN–**Aamodt** (1992,94,2002,2006); **Alsgaard** (1994,98,2002); **Angerer** (1980,84,88); **Ballangrud** (1928,32,36); **Bjoerndalen** (1998,2002); **Dählie** (1992,94,98); **Feierabend** (1936,48,52); **Fischer** (1994,98,2002); **Gagnon** (1994,98,2002); **Gottwald** (2002,06); **Grishin** (1956,60,64); **Gross** (1992,94,98,2002); **Gröttumsbråten** (1924,28,32); **Grönningen** (1960,64,68); **Hackl** (1988,92,94,98,2002); **Hakulinen** (1952,56,60); **Heiden** (1980); **Hoppe** (1984,88,92,94); **Jernberg** (1956,60,64); **Johannesen** (1956,60,64); **Kirvesniemi** (1980,84,92,94,98); **Kjus** (1994,98,2002); **Koss** (1992,94); **Lajunen** (1998,2002); **Larsen** (1924,28); **Luck** (1994,98,2002); **Mäntyranta** (1960,64,68); **Mieto** (1976,80,84); **Monti** (1956,60,64,68); **Musiol** (1980,84,88,92); **Myllylae** (1994,98); **Nykänen** (1984,88); **Ritsma** (1994,98); **Smirnov** (1988,92,94,98); **Svan** (1984,88); **Thunberg** (1924,28); **Tikhonov** (1968,72,76,80); **Tomba** (1988,92,94); **Tyldum** (1968,72,76); **Ulvang** (1988,92,94); **Zimyatov** (1980,84).

WOMEN–**Belmondo** (1992,94,98,2002); **Blair** (1988,92,94); **Chun** (1994,98); **Danilova** (1998,2002); **Di Centa** (1992,94); **Disl** (1992,94,98,2002); **Egorova** (1992,94); **Ehrig** (1976,80,84,88); **Kania** (1980,84,88); **Kirvesniemi** (1984,88,94); **Klassen** (2002,06); **Kolchina** (1964,68); **Kulakova** (1968,72,76,80); **Lazutina** (1992,94,98,2002); **Moen** (1994,98,2002); **Niemann-Stirnemann** (1992,94,98); **Paerson** (2002,06); **Pechstein** (1992,94,98,2002); **Reztsova** (1988,92,94); **Schneider** (1988,92,94); **Seizinger** (1992,94,98); **Skari** (1998,2002); **Skoblikova** (1960,64); **Smetanina** (1976,80,84,88,92); **Takalo** (1972,76,80); **Valbe** (1992,94,98); **Wilhelm** (2002,06); **Yang** (1998,2002).

All-Time Leading USA Medalists

MEN

No		Sport	G-S-B	No		Sport	G-S-B
5	Eric Heiden	Speed Skating	5-0-0	2	Terry McDermott	Speed Skating	1-1-0
5	Apolo Anton Ohno	ST Sp. Skating	2-1-2	2	Dick Meredith	Ice Hockey	1-1-0
3*	Irving Jaffee	Speed Skating	3-0-0	2	Tommy Moe	Alpine	1-1-0
3	Pat Martin	Bobsled	1-2-0	2	Weldy Olson	Ice Hockey	1-1-0
3	Joey Cheek	Speed Skating	1-1-1	2	Derek Parra	Speed Skating	1-1-0
3	Chad Hendrick	Speed Skatng	1-1-1	2	Dick Rodenheiser	Ice Hockey	1-1-0
3	John Heaton	Bobsled/Skeleton	0-2-1	2	Shani Davis	Speed Skating	1-1-0
2	Dick Button	Figure Skating	2-0-0	2	Ross Powers	Snowboarding	1-0-1
2†	Eddie Eagan	Boxing/Bobsled	2-0-0	2	Stan Benham	Bobsled	0-2-0
2	Billy Fiske	Bobsled	2-0-0	2	Herb Drury	Ice Hockey	0-2-0
2	Cliff Gray	Bobsled	2-0-0	2	Eric Flaim	Sp. Skate/ST Sp. Skate	0-2-0
2	Jack Shea	Speed Skating	2-0-0	2	Bode Miller	Alpine	0-2-0
2	Billy Cleary	Ice Hockey	1-1-0	2	Frank Synott	Ice Hockey	0-2-0
2	Jennison Heaton	Bobsled/Skeleton	1-1-0	2	Danny Kass	Snowboarding	0-2-0
2	David Jenkins	Figure Skating	1-1-0	2	John Garrison	Ice Hockey	0-1-1
2	John Mayasich	Ice Hockey	1-1-0	2	Rusty Smith	ST Sp. Skating	0-0-2

*Jaffee is generally given credit for a third gold medal in the 10,000-meter Speed Skating race of 1928. He had the fastest time before the race was cancelled due to thawing ice. The IOC considers the race unofficial.

†Eagan won the light heavyweight boxing title at the 1920 Summer Games in Antwerp and the four-man Bobsled at the 1932 Winter Games in Lake Placid. He is the only athlete ever to win gold medals in both the Winter and Summer Olympics.

WOMEN

No		Sport	G-S-B	No		Sport	G-S-B
6	Bonnie Blair	Speed Skating	5-0-1	2	Cammi Granato	Ice Hockey	1-1-0
4	Cathy Turner	ST Sp. Skating	2-1-1	2	Carol Heiss	Figure Skating	1-1-0
4	Dianne Holum	Speed Skating	1-2-1	2	Shelley Looney	Ice Hockey	1-1-0
3	Chris Witty	Speed Skating	1-1-1	2	Sue Merz	Ice Hockey	1-1-0
3	Sheila Young	Speed Skating	1-1-1	2	A.J. Mleczko	Ice Hockey	1-1-0
3	Angela Ruggiero	Ice Hockey	1-1-1	2	Tara Mounsey	Ice Hockey	1-1-0
3	Katie King	Ice Hockey	1-1-1	2	Diann Roffe-Steinrotter	Alpine	1-1-0
3	Tricia Dunn	Ice Hockey	1-1-1	2	Picabo Street	Alpine	1-1-0
3	Jenny Potter	Ice Hockey	1-1-1	2	Sarah Teuting	Ice Hockey	1-1-0
3	Leah Poulos Mueller	Speed Skating	0-3-0	2	Anne Henning	Speed Skating	1-0-1
3	Beatrix Loughran	Figure Skating	0-2-1	2	Penny Pitou	Alpine	0-2-0
3	Amy Peterson	ST Sp. Skating	0-2-1	2	Nancy Kerrigan	Figure Skating	0-1-1
2	Andrea Mead Lawrence	Alpine	2-0-0	2	Michelle Kwan	Figure Skating	0-1-1
2	Tenley Albright	Figure Skating	1-1-0	2	Jean Saubert	Alpine	0-1-1
2	Chris Bailey	Ice Hockey	1-1-0	2	Nikki Ziegelmeyer	ST Sp. Skating	0-1-1
2	Laurie Baker	Ice Hockey	1-1-0	2	Jennifer Rodriguez	Speed Skating	0-0-2
2	Karyn Bye	Ice Hockey	1-1-0				
2	Sara DeCosta	Ice Hockey	1-1-0				
2	Gretchen Fraser	Alpine	1-1-0				

Note: The term ST Sp. Skating refers to Short Track (or pack) Speed Skating.

Most Gold Medals

MEN

No		Sport	G-S-B
8	Bjorn Dählie, NOR	Cross Country	8-4-0
5	Clas Thunberg, FIN	Speed Skating	5-1-1
5	Ole Einar Bjoerndalen, NOR	Biathlon	5-1-0
5	**Eric Heiden, USA**	Speed Skating	5-0-0
4	Sixten Jernberg, SWE	Cross Country	4-3-2
4	Kjetil Andre Aamodt, NOR	Alpine	4-2-2
4	Ivar Ballangrud, NOR	Speed Skating	4-2-1
4	Thomas Alsgaard, NOR	Cross Country	4-2-0
4	Gunde Svan, SWE	Cross Country	4-1-1
4	Yevgeny Grishin, USSR	Speed Skating	4-1-0
4	Johann Olav Koss, NOR	Speed Skating	4-1-0
4	Matti Nykänen, FIN	Ski Jumping	4-1-0
4	Aleksandr Tikhonov, USSR	Biathlon	4-1-0
4	Nikolai Zimyatov, USSR	Cross Country	4-1-0
4	Thomas Wassberg, SWE	Cross Country	4-0-0

WOMEN

No		Sport	G-S-B
6	Lyubov Egorova, UT/RUS	Cross Country	6-3-0
6	Lydia Skoblikova, USSR	Speed Skating	6-0-0
5	Larissa Lanina, USSR/UT	Cross Country	4-5-1
4	Galina Kulakova, USSR	Cross Country	4-2-2
4	Janica Kostelic, CRO	Alpine	4-2-0
4	Claudia Pechstein, GER	ST Sp. Skating	4-1-2
4	Lee-Kyung Chun, S. Kor.	ST Sp. Skating	4-0-1

All-Time Medal Standings, 1924-2006

All-time Winter Games medal standings, according to *The Golden Book of the Olympic Games*. Medal counts include figure skating medals (1908 and '20) and hockey medals (1920) awarded at the Summer Games. National medal standings for the Winter and Summer Games are not recognized by the IOC.

		G	S	B	Total
1	Norway	96	102	84	282
2	**United States**	78	81	59	218
3	Soviet Union (1956-88)	78	57	59	194
4	Austria	50	64	71	185
5	Germany (1928-36, 52-64, 1992–)	58	58	38	154
6	Finland	42	57	52	151
7	Sweden	46	32	44	122
8	Canada	38	38	44	120
9	East Germany (1968-88)	43	39	36	118
10	Switzerland	37	37	43	117
11	Italy	36	31	33	100
12	France	25	24	32	81
13	Russia (1994–)	33	26	19	80
14	Netherlands	25	30	23	78
15	West Germany (1968-88)	18	20	19	57
16	China	4	16	13	33
17	Japan	9	10	13	32
18	South Korea	17	8	6	31
19	Great Britain	8	5	14	27
20	Czechoslovakia (1924-92)	2	8	16	26
21	Unified Team (1992)	9	6	8	23
22	Czech Republic (1998–)	3	3	3	9
23	Liechtenstein	2	2	5	9
24	Poland	1	3	4	8
25	Estonia	4	1	1	6
	Hungary	0	2	4	6
	Bulgaria	1	2	3	6
	Belarus (1994–)	0	3	3	6
	Australia	3	0	3	6
30	Kazakhstan (1994–)	1	2	2	5
	Belgium	1	1	3	5
	Ukraine (1994–)	1	1	3	5
33	Croatia	3	1	0	4
	Spain	3	0	1	4
	Yugoslavia (1924-88)	0	3	1	4
	Slovenia	0	0	4	4
	Slovenia (1992–)	0	0	3	3
38	Luxembourg	0	2	0	2
	North Korea	0	1	1	2
40	Uzbekistan (1994–)	1	0	0	1
	Slovakia	0	1	0	1
	Denmark	0	1	0	1
	New Zealand	0	1	0	1
	Romania	0	0	1	1
	Latvia	0	0	1	1

Combined totals	G	S	B	Total
Germany/East Germany/West Germany	119	117	93	329
USSR/Unified Team/Russia	122	89	86	297

Notes: Athletes from the USSR participated in the Winter Games from 1956-88, returned as the Unified Team in 1992 after the breakup of the Soviet Union (in 1991) and then competed for the independent republics of Belarus, Kazakhstan, Russia, Ukraine, Uzbekistan and three others in 1994. Yugoslavia divided into Croatia and Bosnia-Herzegovina in 1992, while Czechoslovakia split into Slovakia and the Czech Republic in 1993.

Germany was barred from the Olympics in 1924 and 1948 as an aggressor nation in both World Wars I and II. Divided into East and West Germany after WWII, both countries competed under one flag from 1952-64, then as separate teams from 1968-88. Germany was reunified in 1990.

SOCCER

Manchester United keeper **Edwin Van der Sar** saved the final penalty kick and the day against Chelsea in the Champions League.

SPANISH FLY

Spain's upset of Germany at EURO 2008 could be the start of something big for the perennial underachievers.

By Gerry Brown

SPAIN FINALLY CAME THROUGH ON EUROPE'S BIGGEST STAGE AND DELIVERED ON SO MUCH UNFULFILLED PROMISE with its first major championship win since 1964 when they beat Germany, 1-0, in the final of Euro 2008 in Vienna.

The Spanish survived a shaky start then controlled the ball for much of the match against a solid German squad that was weakened (we'll never know how much) by the injury to its formidable captain Michael Ballack — the midfielder with the iron will and the gimpy calf.

It was Spain's brilliant young striker Fernando Torres, the scoring sensation who scored 33 goals for Liverpool in the English Premier League, that struck the decisive blow past German keeper Jens Lehmann in, coincidentally, the 33rd minute.

Torres had been outshined by countryman David Villa for most of the tournament but Villa missed the final when he was sidelined with an injury. Torres picked up the load and lived up to the reputation he earned as a rookie in the EPL.

Now the only question left about Spain is how wary the soccer world should be when they reconvene in South Africa in 2010. After 44 years of disappointment, the Spanish may just be getting started. They will have to do so without outgoing 69-year-old head coach Luis Aragones, who announced his plans to leave his post.

Spain's King Juan Carlos put words to his country's long painful wait.

"We suffered, but in the end, it was worth the pain," he told Cuatro TV.

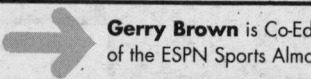

Gerry Brown is Co-Editor of the ESPN Sports Almanac.

AP Images

→ Spanish striker **Fernando Torres** flew past the German defense and scored the tournament-winner at EURO 2008 in Vienna.

SUMMER OLYMPICS

Africa won its first soccer gold medal when Nigeria stunned Argentina at Atlanta in 1996. But the Beijing rematch between the two nations 12 years later was a different story.

Argentina's Lionel Messi saw to that. After almost missing the tournament due to a dispute between the national team and Barcelona, his European club team, "The Flea" drew blood at the Bird's Nest and got the key touch of the ball to set-up the gold winning goal for Argentina. The match was played in intense midday heat (107 degrees) and was actually halted briefly by the referee in the 30th minute to allow the players to rest and take in fluids. Unfortunately for the Nigerians it was only a temporary delay before Argentina got a measure of revenge for Atlanta.

The story on these shores was not as satisfying, as Team USA failed to advance out of group play, finishing third in Group B behind Nigeria and the Netherlands with a 1-1-1 record.

A win or tie against Nigeria in their final match would have sent them onto the quarterfinals, but defender Michael Orozco was hit with a red card on a high elbow just three minutes in and the team played with 10 the rest of the way.

USA keeper **Hope Solo** saved the match single-handedly (right-handedly, actually) with her save on Marta in the 72nd minute.

WOMEN'S

The American women made it two straight gold medals with an exciting 1-0 slippery-pitch win over Marta and arch rivals Brazil in overtime.

The two sides have had a number of memorable meetings previously, most recently in China at the 2007 Women's World Cup where the Hope Solo Saga couldn't quite upstage the brilliant Brazilians.

This time Solo was back in goal and the result was reversed, if not the score.

Solo was superb and the American defense was stifling. And after a scoreless 90 minutes, Carli Lloyd netted the game winner outside the box early in the first overtime period. The defense finished the job and the USA took the gold.

CHAMPIONS LEAGUE

In the first All-English final of the Champions League, Manchester United and Chelsea battled fiercely but were still tied after 120 minutes, and went on to a shootout.

With a chance to win the match for the Blues in the shootout, Chelsea captain John Terry slipped on the wet turf and his PK banged off the post.

Then after the teams traded successful kicks, Man. U keeper Edwin Van der Sar stopped Nicolas Anelka's bid, giving United its third European title, 6-5.

Team USA made things interesting at the finish with a flurry of scoring chances but, ultimately, couldn't deliver.

The U.S. still could have advanced despite the loss to Nigeria if Japan got past Holland, but the Dutch won, 1-0, on a penalty kick.

One bright spot for the U.S. was the play of goalkeeper Brad Guzan who made more than his share of special saves and could be a key part of the future for the U.S. team.

AP Images

SOLO NO MORE

Goalkeeper regains starting spot and teammates' trust

By all appearances, the hug is sincere. Two ponytails, two smiles, one quick lock. They don't have to be best friends, coach Pia Sundhage tells them. They can run and kick and expose their souls for 90 minutes, then adjourn for the day like business partners.

The well-traveled road from Qinhuangdao to Beijing is 4.5 hours by bus, a slow crawl through green marshes, ginkgos and the occasional sheep, and this is the quick route to see the U.S. women's soccer team. Nineteen women have been isolated, far away from the glare of the Olympics, and they like it that way. Here, there are no questions about friendships, team dynamics or, most importantly, Hope Solo. Here, Solo has faded into anonymity, unique only by virtue of her green jersey.

It is the Saturday after the Opening Ceremony, the Americans have just averted what surely would have been dissected as an Olympic collapse, and Solo leans against a fence, nose ring shining, and eyeballs the team bus as it fills. She has nothing salacious to say. Eleven months ago, on Chinese soil, Solo vented and a freshly scrubbed American institution shook.

The headstrong goalkeeper bristled about her benching during the World Cup, questioned her coach and took what was perceived to be a deep dig at a beloved teammate. She was banished from the team, isolated from her peers.

Her teammates roll their eyes now when the Solo scandal is broached. "That's history," they'll say. They need her. Ask Solo whether it's true, whether she has won their trust back, and she pauses, choosing her words carefully.

"Time helps with everything," she says. "I've gotten a lot closer with my teammates over the last couple of months.

"A lot can happen in a year. A lot can change mentally and in your heart."

When Lesle Gallimore recruited Solo, she thought the kid hated her. The University of Washington coach had called her out at a camp once, as she did most 14-year-olds, and made Solo cry.

It didn't take Gallimore long to realize Solo wasn't the typical teenager. She was a forward in high school and could dazzle at any position on the field. Goalkeeper is a grueling position, Gallimore says, one that requires unwavering focus during long blocks of solitude.

Solo never seemed to get distracted. Not when her dad, a homeless Vietnam veteran, stood in the corner of the field before every Huskies home game, watching her warm up. Not when the average teen might've been embarrassed to claim the rumpled man who occasionally was accompanied by a foul whiff. Her teammates, for the most part, didn't know that Jeffrey Solo was his daughter's best friend and that she'd go to the woods and visit him, feeding him macaroni and cheese.

"She has so much unconditional love for her family," Gallimore says. "It didn't matter to her.

"She's an extremely resilient person who has been through a lot in her life. She has sort of ... I wouldn't say it's a thick skin. But she's had a lot of things in her life that are way worse than what happened in China."

In 2007, a few months before the World Cup, Jeffrey Solo died of unknown causes. Hope dedicated the Cup to her father, and spread his ashes near the goal before every game.

"I played out of my mind," she says. "It was something immediate that I could give back to him. He was more excited about the World Cup than I was; he was so proud of me. He carried me through it."

Solo went more than 300 minutes without giving up a goal, and led the U.S. to the semifinals. During a team dinner just before the Americans were to play Brazil, coach Greg Ryan tapped Solo on the shoulder and told her they needed to talk.

Ryan had decided to sit Solo in favor of Briana Scurry, the goalkeeper who had led the Americans to gold medals in Atlanta and Athens. Scurry had past success against Brazil. The U.S. lost the game, 4-0.

Had Solo held her tongue, contained the emotions boiling inside of her, Gallimore is convinced the national focus would've been on Ryan's questionable coaching decision. It wouldn't have escalated into a YouTube favorite.

But Solo, still hurting from her father's death, couldn't hold it in.

"It was the wrong decision, and I think anybody that knows anything about the game knows that," Solo said then. "There's no doubt in my mind I would have made those saves. And the fact of the matter is, it's not 2004 anymore."

And with that, Solo became an outcast. She was banned from team meals and the third-place game against Norway. She wasn't allowed to fly back with the Americans.

Solo issued a handful of apologies, and it didn't seem to be enough. With one short outburst, she violated an unwritten code in high-level women's athletics.

"Women have to get along," says sports psychologist Jack Stark. "There can be a lot more individualism on male teams; it's almost promoted sometimes.

"[Women] are supposed to be very aggressive and physical, then go in the locker room and put on makeup and be feminine. In elite women's athletics, you have to be diplomatic or you get the team coming down on top of you."

The MySpace page hasn't had a log-in since December 2007. At the top is a picture of Solo smiling and holding a soccer ball. Beside it is a quote:

"If you truly expect to realize your dreams, abandon the need for blanket approval. If conforming to everyone else's expectations is the number one goal, you have sacrificed your uniqueness and, therefor[e] your excellence."

In the days after the World Cup, Solo thought about quitting, running away from the clique that shunned her. She'd barely had time to mourn her father. She was isolated and depressed. Back home, Gallimore was shocked by the juice the controversy had created. She wasn't angry at Solo for speaking her mind. She was mad at Ryan for denying her star a chance at a World Cup title.

A month after China, U.S. Soccer President Sunil Gulati announced that Ryan's contract wouldn't be extended. Sundhage, a former Swedish footballer, eventually was hired to lead the Americans.

One of Sundhage's first tasks was to call in Solo, Scurry and backup goalkeeper Nicole Barnhart for separate meetings.

"To ignore it, I think that would be arrogant," Sundhage says.

"I listened to their stories, and I asked them two questions: Do you want to win? Yes. Do we need good goalkeepers? Yes."

Solo regained her starting job, surrendering just six goals in 1,170 minutes. The Americans will face Japan in the Olympic semifinals Monday, and their quiet rise in faraway venues in Shanghai and Qinhuangdao has turned into sort of a feelgood story. Just before the Olympics, the U.S. lost scoring whiz Abby Wambach to a broken leg.

In the opening game, the Americans did not look like the powerhouse that has never failed to medal in the Olympics. Solo gave up two goals in the first four minutes of a 2-0 loss to Norway.

As Solo looked up at the scoreboard in the final minutes, she said she felt sick to her stomach.

"The energy in the locker room was different," Solo says. "You could feel the nerves.

"There was a lot of pressure, I think, after everything that was said last year. I got that game under my belt and came up fine."

It is Sunday, 24 hours before the Americans play Japan for a shot at the championship game, and they are finally in Beijing. They assemble for a news conference with Sundhage and four selected players. Solo is not among them.

The conversation bounces from Wambach's injury to the Norway game to how the team has been building chemistry with every Olympic match. And that, maybe, is a sign that the Solo scandal has finally subsided. Or are they just better at keeping their emotions in check?

"We couldn't move forward and be where we are today without that trust being there," co-captain Kate Markgraf says. "She's one of the 19 we have. You know what? We all have to be strong together. And that trust is totally regained."

Somewhere away from the prying cameras, Solo wants to believe that. She doesn't need 18 deep friendships; she just wants respect.

-Elizabeth Merrill, ESPN.com

2007-2008
Season in Review

SPORTS ALMANAC

2008 UEFA European Championships

The UEFA European Football Championships are held every four years to determine the best national team on the European continent. In 2008 it was contested for the 13th time since its inception in 1960. Held June 7-29, 2008 in Austria/Switzerland.

First Round

Round robin; each team played the other three teams in its group once. Note that three points were awarded for a win and one point for a tie. (*) indicates team advanced to second round.

Group A	W	L	T	Pts	GF	GA
*Portugal	2	1	0	6	5	3
*Turkey	2	1	0	6	5	5
Czech Republic	1	2	0	3	4	6
Switzerland	1	2	0	3	3	3

Results

Date	Site	Result
June 7	Basel	Czech Republic 1, Switzerland 0
June 7	Geneva	Portugal 2, Turkey 0
June 11	Geneva	Portugal 3, Czech Republic 1
June 11	Basel	Turkey 2, Switzerland 1
June 15	Basel	Switzerland 2, Portugal 0
June 15	Geneva	Turkey 3, Czech Republic 2

Group B	W	L	T	Pts	GF	GA
*Croatia	3	0	0	9	4	1
*Germany	2	1	0	6	4	2
Austria	0	2	1	1	1	3
Poland	0	2	1	1	1	4

Results

Date	Site	Result
June 8	Vienna	Croatia 1, Austria 0
June 8	Klagenfurt	Germany 2, Poland 0
June 12	Klagenfurt	Croatia 2, Germany 1
June 12	Vienna	Austria 1, Poland 1
June 16	Vienna	Germany 1, Austria 0
June 16	Klagenfurt	Croatia 1, Poland 0

Group C	W	L	T	Pts	GF	GA
*Netherlands	3	0	0	9	9	1
*Italy	1	1	1	4	3	4
Romania	0	1	2	2	1	3
France	0	2	1	1	1	6

Results

Date	Site	Result
June 9	Zurich	Romania 0, France 0
June 9	Bern	Netherlands 3, Italy 0
June 13	Zurich	Italy 1, Romania 1
June 13	Bern	Netherlands 4, France 1
June 17	Bern	Netherlands 2, Romania 0
June 17	Zurich	Italy 2, France 0

Group D	W	L	T	Pts	GF	GA
*Spain	3	0	0	9	8	3
*Russia	2	1	0	6	4	4
Sweden	1	2	0	3	3	4
Greece	0	3	0	0	1	5

Results

Date	Site	Result
June 10	Innsbruck	Spain 4, Russia 1
June 10	Salzburg	Sweden 2, Greece 0
June 14	Innsbruck	Spain 2, Sweden 1
June 14	Salzburg	Russia 1, Greece 0
June 18	Salzburg	Spain 2, Greece 1
June 18	Innsbruck	Russia 2, Sweden 0

Quarterfinals

Date	Site	Result
June 19	Basel	Germany 3, Portugal 2
June 20	Vienna	Turkey 1, Croatia 1 (3-1)
June 21	Basel	Russia 3, Netherlands 1 OT
June 22	Vienna	Spain 0, Italy 0 (4-2)

Semifinals

Date	Site	Result
June 25	Basel	Germany 3, Turkey 2
June 26	Vienna	Spain 3, Russia 0

Final

Date	Site	Result
June 29	Vienna	Spain 1, Germany 0

Goals: ESP—Fernando Torres (33').
Referee: Roberto Rosetti, Italy
Attendance: 51,428

Tournament Leaders

Leading Goal Scorers	Gms	Goals
David Villa, Spain	6	4
Hakan Yakin, Switzerland	3	3
Semih Senturk, Turkey	5	3
Roman Pavlyuchenko, Russia	5	3
Lukas Podolski, Germany	6	3

Most Valuable Player
Xavi, Spain

Team of the Tournament

GK: Gianluigi Buffon, Italy; Iker Casillas, Spain; Edwin van der Sar, Netherlands; **DEF:** Bosingwa, Portugal; Philipp Lahm, Germany; Carlos Marchena, Spain; Pepe, Portugal; Carles Puyol, Spain; Yuri Zhirkov, Russia; **MF:** Hamit Altintop, Turkey; Luka Modric, Croatia; Marcos Senna, Spain; Xavi Hernández, Spain; Konstantin Zyryanov, Russia; Michael Ballack, Germany; Cesc Fàbregas, Spain; Andrés Iniesta, Spain; Lukas Podolski, Germany; Wesley Sneijder, Netherlands; **FWD:** Andrei Arshavin, Russia; Roman Pavlyuchenko, Russia; Fernando Torres, Spain; David Villa, Spain.

FIFA Top 50 World Rankings

FIFA announced a new monthly world ranking system on Aug. 13, 1993 designed to "provide a constant international comparison of national team performances." The rankings are based on a mathematical formula that weighs strength of schedule, importance of matches and goals scored for and against. Games considered include World Cup qualifying and final rounds, Continental championship qualifying and final rounds, and friendly matches.

The formula has been altered somewhat over the years. Following a change in July 2006, the rankings now take into account all International "A" matches from the last four years. At the end of the year, FIFA designates a Team of the Year. Teams of the Year so far have been Germany (1993), Brazil (1994-2000, 2002-06), France (2001) and Argentina (2007). The USA reached their highest-ever ranking (6th) in July 2005.

2007

		Points	2006 Rank			Points	2006 Rank			Points	2006 Rank
1	Argentina	1523	3	18	Bulgaria	881	43	35	Ireland	731	49
2	Brazil	1502	1	19	USA	876	31	36	Finland	697	52
3	Italy	1498	2	20	Nigeria	875	9	37	Ivory Coast	688	18
4	Spain	1349	12	21	Paraguay	873	35	38	Senegal	687	41
5	Germany	1298	6	22	Poland	862	24	39	Egypt	686	27
6	Czech Republic	1290	10	23	Russia	861	22		Morocco	686	39
7	France	1243	4	24	Sweden	853	14	41	Iran	677	38
8	Portugal	1241	8	25	Cameroon	853	11	42	South Korea	663	51
9	Netherlands	1170	7	26	Israel	852	44	43	Ghana	659	28
10	Croatia	1129	15	27	Serbia	844	33	44	Switzerland	657	17
11	Greece	1114	16	28	Uruguay	831	29	45	Chile	655	41
12	England	1113	5	29	Norway	827	50	46	Mali	652	36
13	Romania	1088	19	30	Ukraine	824	13	47	Tunisia	639	32
14	Scotland	990	25	31	Denmark	797	21	48	Australia	607	39
15	Mexico	982	13	32	Northern Ireland	780	48	49	Belgium	600	53
16	Turkey	924	26	33	Guinea	758	23	50	Hungary	588	62
17	Colombia	907	34	34	Japan	748	47				

2008 (as of Oct. 8)

		Points	2007 Rank			Points	2007 Rank			Points	2007 Rank
1	Spain	1643	4	18	Romania	927	13	35	Northern Ireland	721	32
2	Italy	1365	3	19	Ukraine	893	30	36	Chile	714	45
3	Germany	1336	5	20	Uruguay	887	28	37	Lithuania	706	59
4	Brazil	1280	2	21	USA	861	19	38	Ireland	701	35
5	Netherlands	1258	9	22	Egypt	860	39	39	Norway	680	29
6	Croatia	1223	10	23	Paraguay	860	21	40	Serbia	673	27
7	Argentina	1200	1	24	Mexico	841	15	41	Guinea	670	33
8	Czech Republic	1111	6	25	Ghana	839	43	42	Ecuador	661	56
9	Russia	1076	23	26	Scotland	820	14	43	Morocco	642	39
10	Portugal	1075	8	27	Nigeria	818	20		Finland	642	36
11	France	1035	7	28	Sweden	794	24	45	Switzerland	641	44
12	Cameroon	1027	25	29	Ivory Coast	779	37	46	Macedonia	637	58
13	Turkey	1021	16	30	Poland	763	22	47	Tunisia	624	47
14	England	982	12	31	Denmark	760	31	48	Iran	619	41
15	Bulgaria	969	18	32	Japan	747	34	49	Senegal	615	38
16	Israel	961	26	33	Colombia	739	17	50	Honduras	601	53
17	Greece	945	11	34	Australia	737	48				

FIFA Women's World Rankings

As part of its growing recognition of women's soccer FIFA began ranking the women's national teams in 2002 following the inaugural FIFA Women's U19 World Championship in Canada. The rankings are currently released four times a year and are calculated in a similar manner to the men's rankings. The first women's international was held on April 17, 1971 (France vs. the Netherlands). The Top 30 teams are listed below.

2008 (as of Sept. 5)

		Points	2007 Rank			Points	2007 Rank			Points	2007 Rank
1	USA	2211	2	11	England	1939	10	21	Czech Republic	1807	19
2	Germany	2152	1	12	China	1915	13	22	Mexico	1774	22
3	Brazil	2131	4	13	Italy	1905	14	23	South Korea	1765	25
4	Sweden	2063	3	14	Australia	1898	12	24	New Zealand	1745	23
5	North Korea	2026	6	15	Russia	1890	15	25	Nigeria	1728	24
6	Norway	2021	5	16	Ukraine	1869	17	26	Scotland	1714	26
7	France	1999	7	17	Finland	1852	16	27	Switzerland	1667	28
8	Denmark	1988	8	18	Iceland	1830	21	28	Ireland	1654	31
9	Japan	1985	11	19	Spain	1819	20		Argentina	1654	29
10	Canada	1944	9	20	Netherlands	1808	18	30	Poland	1629	27

2008 FIFA Indoor World Cup

Officially the FIFA Futsal World Cup, contested for the 6th time since its inception in 1989. Held Sept. 30-Oct. 19, 2008 in Brazil.

First Round

Round robin; each team played the other three teams in its group once. Note that three points were awarded for a win and one point for a tie. (*) indicates team advanced to second round.

Group A	W	L	T	Pts	GF	GA
*Brazil	4	0	0	12	49	1
*Russia	3	1	0	9	50	15
Japan	2	2	0	6	13	24
Cuba	1	3	0	3	16	25
Solomon Islands	0	4	0	0	6	69

Group C	W	L	T	Pts	GF	GA
*Ukraine	3	0	1	10	17	7
*Argentina	3	0	1	10	13	5
Guatemala	2	2	0	6	14	9
Egypt	1	3	0	3	9	12
China	0	4	0	0	5	25

Group B	W	L	T	Pts	GF	GA
*Paraguay	3	1	0	9	19	5
*Italy	3	1	0	9	12	6
Portugal	3	1	0	9	15	8
Thailand	1	3	0	3	7	15
USA	0	4	0	0	5	24

Group D	W	L	T	Pts	GF	GA
*Spain	3	0	1	10	13	3
*Iran	3	0	1	10	14	9
Czech Republic	2	2	0	6	10	10
Libya	0	3	1	1	7	14
Uruguay	0	3	1	1	6	14

Second Round

Round robin; each team played the other three teams in its group once. Note that three points were awarded for a win and one point for a tie. (*) indicates team advanced to semifinals.

Group E	W	L	T	Pts	GF	GA
*Brazil	3	0	0	9	9	3
*Italy	1	1	1	4	9	8
Iran	1	1	1	4	10	10
Ukraine	0	3	0	0	7	14

Group F	W	L	T	Pts	GF	GA
*Spain	3	0	0	9	11	4
*Russia	1	1	1	4	9	11
Argentina	0	1	2	2	6	7
Paraguay	0	2	1	1	8	12

Semifinals

Date	Site	Result
Oct. 16	Rio De Janeiro	Brazil 4, Russia 2
Oct. 16	Rio De Janeiro	Spain 3, Italy 2 OT

Third Place

Date	Site	Result
Oct. 18	Rio De Janeiro	Italy 2, Russia 1

Final

Date	Site	Result
Oct. 19	Rio De Janeiro	Brazil 2, Spain 2

Brazil won championship, 4-3, in a penalty shootout

Goal Scoring Leaders

	Goals
Pula, Russia	16
Falcao, Brazil	15
Lenisio, Brazil	11
Damir Khamadiev, Russia	10
Schumacher, Brazil	10
Vladislav Shayakhmetov, Russia	9

2008 FIFA Beach Soccer World Cup

Held July 17-27, 2008 in Marseille, France.

Quarterfinals (July 24)

Portugal 6	Uruguay 3
Brazil 6	Russia 4
Italy 5	France 2
Spain 2	Argentina 0

Semifinals (July 26)

Brazil 5	Portugal 4
Italy 4	Spain 4

Italy advanced, 1-0, in a penalty shootout

Third Place (July 27)

Portugal 5	Spain 4

Final (July 27)

Brazil 5	Italy 3

2010 World Cup South Africa

32 teams will compete for the next World Cup to be held in 2010 in South Africa. Qualification will not be fully complete until Nov. 2009 but the teams will be allocated among the six FIFA confederations as follows:

Europe: 13 teams   **Africa:** 5 teams + host
South America: 4-5 teams   **Oceania:** 0-1 team
Asia: 4-5 teams   **No./Cent. America:** 3-4 teams

Important Dates

Preliminary Draw: Nov. 25, 2007
Opening Match: June 11, 2010
Final Match: July 11, 2010 in Johannesburg

U.S. Men's National Team
2008 Schedule and Results

Through Sept. 10, 2008. Games in **bold** type are World Cup qualifiers.

Date		Result	USA Goals	Site	Attendance
Jan. 19	Sweden	W, 2-0	Robinson, Donovan	Carson, Calif.	14,878
Feb. 6	Mexico	T, 2-2	Onyewu, Altidore	Houston, Texas	70,103
Mar. 26	Poland	W, 3-0	Bocanegra, Onyewu, Lewis	Krakow, Poland	20,000
May 28	England	L, 0-2	—	London, England	71,233
June 4	Spain	L, 0-1	—	Santander, Spain	14,232
June 8	Argentina	T, 0-0	—	East Rutherford, N.J.	78,682
June 15	**Barbados**	W, 8-0	Dempsey (2) Bradley, Ching (2), Donovan, own goal, Johnson	Carson, Calif.	11,476
June 22	**Barbados**	W, 1-0	Lewis	Bridgetown, Barbados	—
Aug. 20	**Guatemala**	W, 1-0	Bocanegra	Guatemala City	25,000
Sept. 6	**Cuba**	W, 1-0	Dempsey	Havana, Cuba	—
Sept. 10	**Trinidad & Tobago**	W, 3-0	Bradley, Dempsey, Ching	Bridgeview, Ill.	11,452
Nov. 19	**Guatemala**			Commerce City, Colo.	

Overall record: 7-2-2. **Team scoring:** Goals for–21; Goals against–5.

U.S. Women's National Team
2008 Schedule and Results

Games in **bold** type are from the 2008 Summer Olympics in China.

Date		Result	USA Goals	Site	Attendance
Jan. 16	Canada	W, 4-0	Rodriguez (2), Tarpley (2)	Guangzhou, China	1,000
Jan. 18	Finland	W, 4-1	Tarpley (2), Cheney, Wozniak	Guangzhou, China	500
Jan. 20	China	W, 1-0	Boxx	Guangzhou, China	3,000
Mar. 5	China	W, 4-0	Tarpley, Heath, Wambach, Lloyd	Abufeira, Portugal	—
Mar. 7	Italy	W, 2-0	Tarpley, O'Reilly	Alvor, Portugal	—
Mar. 10	Norway	W, 4-0	Kai, Wambach, O'Reilly, Rodriguez	Alvor, Portugal	—
Mar. 12	Denmark	W, 2-1	Kai, Wambach	VR de SA, Portugal	—
Apr. 4	Jamaica	W, 6-0	Lloyd, Cheney, Wambach (2), O'Reilly, Heath	Juarez, Mexico	5,083
Apr. 6	Mexico	W, 3-1	Kai, Wambach	Juarez, Mexico	22,280
Apr. 9	Costa Rica	W, 3-0	Kai (2), O'Reilly	Juarez, Mexico	22,280
Apr. 12	Canada	T, 1-1 (6-5)	Lloyd	Juarez, Mexico	4,151
Apr. 27	Australia	W, 3-2	Kai, Wambach, Lloyd	Cary, N.C.	3,698
May 3	Australia	W, 5-4	Tarpley (2), Wambach (2), Hucles	Birmingham, Ala.	5,000
May 10	Canada	W, 6-0	Tarpley, Kai (3), Lloyd, Osborne	Washington, D.C.	9,332
June 15	Australia	W, 2-1	Kai, Wambach	Suwon, So. Korea	1,357
June 17	Brazil	W, 1-0	Rodriguez	Suwon, So. Korea	1,158
June 19	Italy	W, 2-0	Wambach (2)	Suwon, So. Korea	1,075
June 21	Canada	W, 1-0	Hucles	Suwon, So. Korea	25,280
July 2	Norway	W, 4-0	Tarpley, Lloyd, Hucles, Wambach	Fredrikstad, Norway	1,900
July 5	Sweden	W, 1-0	Lloyd	Skelleftea, Sweden	4,313
July 13	Brazil	W, 1-0	Rodriguez	Commerce City, Colo.	15,071
July 16	Brazil	W, 1-0	Kai	San Diego, Calif.	7,502
Aug. 6	Norway	L, 0-2	—	Qinhuangdao, China	17,673
Aug. 9	**Japan**	W, 1-0	Lloyd	Qinhuangdao, China	16,912
Aug. 12	**New Zealand**	W, 4-0	O'Reilly, Rodriguez, Tarpley, Hucles	Qinhuangdao, China	12,453
Aug. 15	**Canada**	W, 2-1 (OT)	Huccles, Kai	Shanghai, China	26,129
Aug. 18	**Japan**	W, 4-2	Hucles (2), Chalupny, O'Reilly	Beijing, China	50,937
Aug. 21	**Brazil**	W, 1-0 (OT)	Lloyd	Beijing, China	51,612
Sept. 13	Ireland	W, 2-0	Kai, O'Reilly	Philadelphia, Penn.	13,176
Sept. 17	Ireland	W, 1-0	Kai	E. Rutherford, N.J.	4,227
Sept. 20	Ireland	W, 2-0	Chalupny, Markgraf	Bridgeview, Ill.	5,390
Nov. 1	South Korea			Richmond, Va.	
Nov. 5	South Korea			Cincinnati, Ohio	
Nov. 8	South Korea			Tampa, Fla.	

Overall record: 29-1-1. **Team Scoring:** Goals for–78; Goals against–16.

Club Team Competition
2007 FIFA Club World Championship

The FIFA Club World Championship (now officially the FIFA Club World Championship TOYOTA Cup Japan) merged with the Toyota Cup (a.k.a. European/South American Cup) in 2005 and is open to the champions from the African, Asian, Oceanic and North/Central American soccer federations as well as Europe and South America. The European and South American clubs get byes into the semifinals. In 2007, FIFA introduced a play-in round for entry into the quarterfinals between the club from Oceania and the host nation's J-League in Japan. However to avoid having two teams from one country compete when a Japanese team won the berth from Asia, they took the highest-ranked non-Japanese team from Asia (Iran's **Sepahan**).

The 2007 FIFA Club World Championship TOYOTA Cup took place December 6-16. The teams representing their continents were as follows: EUROPE—**AC Milan** (Italy), NORTH/CENTRAL AMERICA—**Pachuca** (Mexico), SOUTH AMERICA—**Boca Juniors** (Argentina), OCEANIA—**Waitakere United** (New Zealand), ASIA—**Urawa Red Diamonds** (Japan), AFRICA—**Etoile Sportive Du Sahel** (Tunisia). As the European and South American teams, respectively, AC Milan and Boca Juniors received byes into the semifinals.

Play-in
Sepahan 3 . . . . .Waitakere United 1

Quarterfinals
Etoile Sportive du Sahel 1 . . . . .Pachuca 0
Urawa Red Diamons 3 . . . . .Sepahan 1

Semifinals
Boca Juniors 1 . . . . .Etoile Sportive du Sahel 0
AC Milan 1 . . . . .Urawa Red Diamonds 0

3rd Place Match
Urawa Red Diamonds 2 . . . . . .Etoile Sportive du Sahel 2
Urawa Red Diamonds won 4-2 in a penalty shootout

Final
Dec. 16 at Yokohama, Japan.
Attendance: 68,263

AC Milan 4 . . . . Boca Juniors 2

Scoring
AC Milan—Filippo Inzaghi (21', 71'); Alessandro Nesta (50'); Kaka (61').
Boca Juniors—Rodrigo Palacio (22'); Pablo Ledesma (85').

SOUTH AMERICA

2007 Libertadores Cup

Contested by the league champions of South America's football union. Two-leg Semifinals and two-leg Final; home teams listed first. LDU Quito of Ecuador qualified for the 2008 FIFA Club World Championship in Japan in December.

Final Four: Fluminese (Brazil), América (Mexico), Boca Juniors (Argentina) and LDU Quito (Ecuador).

Semifinals

Fluminese vs. Boca Juniors
Boca Juniors 1 . . . . .Fluminese 3
Fluminese 2 . . . . .Boca Juniors 2
Fluminese advanced 5-3 on aggregate

LDU Quito vs. América
América 1 . . . . .LDU Quito 1
LDU Quito 0 . . . . .América 0
Aggregate tied 1-1, LDU Quito advanced on away goals

Final

Matches played June 25 in Quito, Ecuador and July 2 in Rio de Janeiro.
LDU Quito 4 . . . . .Fluminese 2
Fluminese 3 . . . . .LDU Quito 1
Aggregate tied 5-5, LDU Quito won 3-1 in a penalty shootout

2008 Lamar Hunt U.S. Open Cup

Dating back to 1914, the U.S. Open Cup is the oldest soccer competition in the United States and is among the oldest in the world. The U.S. Open Cup is a single-elimination tournament open to all amateur and professional teams in the United States. Forty teams (24 professional and 16 amateur) competed in the 2008 Lamar Hunt U.S. Open Cup. The tournament was renamed for the U.S. Soccer pioneer and MLS Team owner in 1999. All teams listed below are from the MLS unless otherwise noted.

Quarterfinals
D.C. United def. Chicago Fire, 2-1
N.E. Revolution def. Crystal Palace Balt. (USL-2) on PKs
Charleston Battery (USL-1) def. FC Dallas, 3-1
Seattle Sounders (USL-1) def. KC Wizards on PKs

Semifinals
D.C. United def. New England Revolution, 3-1
Charleston Battery def. Seattle Sounders on PKs

Final (Aug. 26, 2008)
D.C. United def. Charleston Battery, 2-1

There are two major European club competitions sanctioned by the Union of European Football Associations (UEFA). The constantly evolving **Champions League** is currently a 76-team tournament made up from UEFA member countries. The teams are ranked 1-74 depending on how they finish in their own domestic leagues. UEFA ranks the quality of the 53 European national football associations (from No. 1 Italy to No. 53 Montenegro) and assigns each association a number of teams they may enter weighted by their respective ranking (UEFA calls this number a coefficient). Associations 1-3 (Spain, Italy, England) get 4 teams in, Nos. 4-6 (France, Germany, Portugal) get three teams; Nos. 7-15 get two teams and 16-53 get one team apiece.

The 28 teams from associations 25-53 play two-leg, total goal elimination series. The 14 survivors advance to the Second Qualifying Phase and join the 8 teams from associations 17-24 and the 6 runners up from associations 10-16; The 14 clubs that survive this phase join the seven champions from associations 10-16, three runners up from 7-9, six third-place teams from associations 1-6 and two fourth-place teams from 1-3 to play in the Third Qualifying Phase. The winning clubs from the 16 two-leg, total goal elimination series join the defending champion, nine champions from associations 1-9 and 6 runners up from associations 1-6 advance to the 32-team Group Stage.

The 32 teams are separated into eight groups of four and play a round-robin series of home-and-home matches. The eight group winners and eight group runners-up advance to the next round where they are paired and play two home-and-home matches. The home-and-home series are played through the semifinals until ultimately a single championship match for the European club championship is held.

The updated **UEFA Cup**, which is basically a combination of the what was once known as the Cup Winners' Cup (played between national cup champions) and the old UEFA Cup (sort of a "best of the rest" tournament), is single-elimination throughout and features 121 additional teams plus teams that have been already eliminated from the Champions League.

2007-08 Champions League

Round of 16
Two legs, total goals; home team listed first.

Schalke vs. Porto
Feb. 19   Schalke 1 . . . . Porto 0
Mar. 5   Porto 1 . . . . Schalke 0
Aggregate tied 1-1, Schalke wins 4-1 on PKs

Roma vs. Real Madrid
Feb. 19   Roma 2 . . . . Real Madrid 1
Mar. 5   Real Madrid 1 . . . . Roma 2
Roma wins 4-2 on aggregate

Olympiacos vs. Chelsea
Feb. 19   Olympiacos 0 . . . . Chelsea 0
Mar. 5   Chelsea 3 . . . . Olympiacos 0
Aggregate tied 2-2, Valencia wins on away goals

Liverpool vs. Internazionale
Feb. 19   Liverpool 3 . . . . Internazionale 0
Mar. 5   Internazionale 0 . . . . Liverpool 1
Liverpool wins 3-0 on aggregate

Celtic vs. Barcelona
Feb. 20   Celtic 2 . . . . Barcelona 3
Mar. 4   Barcelona 1 . . . . Celtic 0
Barcelona wins 4-2 on aggregate

Manchester United vs. Lyon
Feb. 20   Lyon 1 . . . . Manchester United 1
Mar. 4   Manchester United 1 . . . . Lyon 0
Manchester wins 2-1 on aggregate

Fenerbache vs. Sevilla
Feb. 20   Fenerbache 3 . . . . Sevilla 2
Mar. 4   Sevilla 3 . . . . Fenerbache 2
Aggregate tied 5-5, Fenerbache wins 3-2 on PKs

Arsenal vs. Milan
Feb. 20   Arsenal 0 . . . . Milan 0
Mar. 4   Milan 0 . . . . Arsenal 2
Aresenal wins 2-0 on aggregate

Quarterfinals
Two legs, total goals; home team listed first.

Roma vs. Manchester United
Apr. 1   Roma 0 . . . . Manchester United 2
Apr. 9   Manchester United 1 . . . . Roma 0
Manchester United 3-0 on aggregate

Schalke vs. Barcelona
Apr. 1   Schalke 0 . . . . Barcelona 1
Apr. 9   Barcelona 1 . . . . Schalke 0
Barcelona wins 2-0 on aggregate

Chelsea vs. Fenerbache
Apr. 2   Fenerbache 2 . . . . Chelsea 1
Apr. 8   Chelsea 2 . . . . Fenerbache 0
Chelsea wins 3-2 on aggregate

Arsenal vs. Liverpool
Apr. 2   Arsenal 1 . . . . Liverpool 1
Apr. 8   Liverpool 4 . . . . Arsenal 2
Liverpool wins 5-3 on aggregate

Semifinals
Two legs, total goals; home team listed first.

Liverpool vs. Chelsea
Apr. 22   Liverpool 1 . . . . Chelsea 1
Apr. 30   Chelsea 3 . . . . Liverpool 2
Chelsea wins 4-3 on aggregate

Barcelona vs. Manchester United
Apr. 23   Barcelona 0 . . . . Manchester United 0
Apr. 29   Manchester United 1 . . . . Barcelona 0
Manchester United wins 1-0 on aggregate

2008 Champions League Final
Manchester United vs. Chelsea
May 21, 2008 at Luzhniki Stadium in Moscow. **Attendance:** 67,310

Manchester United 1 . . . . Chelsea 1

Scoring:
MAN U—Cristiano Ronaldo (26'); CHELSEA— Frank Lampard (45')

Manchester United wins 6-5 on PKs

2008 UEFA Cup
Two-leg Quarterfinals and Semifinals, one-game Final; home team listed first.

Final Eight: Zenit St. Petersburg (Russia), Bayern (Germany), Bayer Leverkusen (Germany), Rangers (Scotland), Sporting (Portugal), Getafe (Spain), Fiorentina (Italy); PSV Eindhoven (The Netherlands).

Quarterfinals

Bayer Leverkusen vs. Zenit
Apr. 3 Leverkusen 1 . . . . Zenit 4
Apr. 10 Zenit 0 . . . . Leverkusen 1
Zenit wins 4-2 on aggregate

Bayern vs. Getafe
Apr. 3 Bayern 1 . . . . Getafe 1
Apr. 10 Getafe 3 . . . . Bayern 3
Aggregate tied 4-4, Bayern wins on away goals

Rangers vs. Sporting
Apr. 3 Rangers 0 . . . . Sporting 0
Apr. 10 Sporting 0 . . . . Rangers 2
Rangers wins 2-0 on aggregate

Fiorentina vs. PSV
Apr. 3 Fiorentina 1 . . . . PSV 1
Apr. 10 PSV 0 . . . . Fiorentina 2
Fiorentina wins 3-1 on aggregate

Semifinals

Bayern vs. Zenit
Apr. 24 Bayern 1 . . . . Zenit 1
May 1 Zenit 4 . . . . Bayern 0
Zenit wins 5-1 on aggregate

Fiorentina vs. Rangers
Apr. 24 Rangers 0 . . . . Fiorentina 0
May 1 Fiorentina 0 . . . . Rangers 0
Rangers wins 4-2 on PKs

Final
Zenit vs. Rangers
May 14, 2008 in City of Manchester, Manchester. **Attendance:** 43,878

Zenit 2 . . . . Rangers 0

Scoring:
ZENIT—Denisov (72') and Zyryanov (94')

2008 FA Cup
May 17, 2008 at Wembley Stadium, London, England. **Attendance:** 89,874

Portsmouth 1 . . . . Cardiff City 0

Scoring:
PORTSMOUTH—Kanu (37')

International Soccer events scheduled for Late 2008 and 2009

Dates	Tournament
Oct. 28-Nov. 16, 2008	FIFA U-17 Women's World Cup (New Zealand)
Nov. 19-Dec. 7, 2008	FIFA U-20 Women's World Cup (Chile)
Dec. 11-21, 2008	FIFA Club World Cup (Japan)
June 14-29, 2009	FIFA Confederations Cup (South Africa)
Sept. 25-Oct. 16, 2009	FIFA U-20 World Cup (Egypt)
Oct. 24-Nov. 15, 2009	FIFA U-17 World Cup (Nigeria)

Major League Soccer
2008 Final Regular Season Standings

Conference champions (*) and playoff qualifiers (†) are noted. Teams receive three points for a win and one for a tie. The GF and GA columns refer to Goals For and Goals Against in regulation play. Number of seasons listed after each head coach refers to current tenure with club through the 2008 season.

Eastern Conference

Team	W	L	T	Pts	GF	GA
*Columbus Crew	17	7	6	57	50	36
†Chicago Fire	13	10	7	46	44	33
†N.E. Revolution	12	11	7	43	40	43
†Kansas City Wizards	11	10	9	42	37	39
†New York Red Bulls	10	11	9	39	42	48
D.C. United	11	15	4	37	43	51
Toronto FC	9	13	8	35	34	43

Head Coaches: Clb—Sigi Schmid (3rd season); **Chi**—Denis Hamlett (1st); **NE**—Steve Nicol (8th); **KC**—Curt Onalfo (2nd); **NY**—Juan Carlos Osaoria (1st); **DC**—Tom Soehn (2nd); **Tor**—John Carver (1st).

Western Conference

Team	W	L	T	Pts	GF	GA
*Houston Dynamo	13	5	12	51	45	32
†Chivas USA	12	11	7	43	40	41
†Real Salt Lake	10	10	10	40	40	39
Colorado Rapids	11	14	5	38	44	45
FC Dallas	8	10	12	36	45	41
Los Angeles Galaxy	8	13	9	33	55	62
San Jose Earthquakes	8	13	9	33	32	38

Head Coaches: Hou—Dominic Kinnear (5th season); **Chv**—Preki Radosavljevic (2nd); **RSL**—Jason Kreis (2nd); **Colo**—Fernando Clavijo (4th, 7-10-3 resigned on Aug. 20, 2008 and was replaced by Gary Smith (4-4-2); **Dal**—Steve Morrow (2nd); **LA**—Ruud Gullit (1st, 6-4-2) resigned and was replaced by Bruce Arena (1st); **SJ**—Frank Yallop (1st).

Leading Scorers

Goals

	Gm	No
Landon Donovan, LA	25	20
Kenny Cooper, Dal	30	18
Edson Buddle, LA	27	15
Juan Pablo Angel, NY	23	14
Brian Ching, Hou	25	13
Conor Casey, Col	21	11
Luciano Emilio, DC	27	11
Jaime Moreno, DC	25	10
Chad Barrett, Tor	29	9
Alejandro Moreno, Clb	27	9
Chris Rolfe, Chi	26	9

Assists

	Gm	No
Guillermo Barros Schelotto, Clb	27	19
Javier Morales, RSL	29	15
Terry Cooke, Col	24	12
Cuauhtemoc Blanco, Chi	27	11
David Beckham, LA	25	10
Jaime Moreno, DC	25	10
Landon Donovan, LA	25	9
Brad Davis, Hou	26	8
Andre Rocha, Dal	27	8
Justin Mapp, Chi	30	8

Shots

	Gm	No
Kenny Cooper, Dal	30	119
Dwayne De Rosario, Hou	24	78
Juan Pablo Angel, NY	23	76
Luciano Emilio, DC	27	76
Edson Buddle, LA	27	74
Robbie Rogers, Clb	27	70
Yura Movsisyan, RSL	22	69
Claudio Lopez, KC	28	67
Chad Barrett, Tor	29	66
Landon Donovan, LA	25	65

Shots on Goal

	Gm	No
Kenny Cooper, Dal	30	60
Juan Pablo Angel, NY	23	41
Landon Donovan, LA	25	40
Luciano Emilio, DC	27	39
Edson Buddle, LA	27	38
Dwayne De Rosario, Hou	24	34
Yura Movsisyan, RSL	22	33
Robbie Rogers, Clb	27	33
Chad Barrett, Tor	29	32
Brian Ching, Hou	25	29

Multi-Goal Games

	Gm	MGG
Landon Donovan, LA	25	6
Kenny Cooper, Dal	30	4
Juan Pablo Angel, NY	23	2
Chad Barrett, Tor	29	2
Edson Buddle, LA	27	2
Conor Casey, Col	21	2
Brian Ching, Hou	25	2
Luciano Emilio, DC	27	2
Rohan Ricketts, Tor	27	2
Robbie Rogers, Clb	27	2
Chris Rolfe, Chi	26	2

Hat Tricks

	Gm	Hats
Edson Buddle, LA	27	2
Landon Donovan, LA	25	2
Conor Casey, Col	21	1
Luciano Emilio, DC	27	1
Chris Rolfe, Chi	26	1

2008 MLS Attendance

Number in parentheses indicates last year's rank.

	Gm	Total	Avg
Los Angeles (1)	15	390,132	26,009
Toronto (3)	15	301,541	20,103
D.C. United (2)	15	297,531	19,835
New England (4)	15	263,706	17,580
Chicago (6)	15	255,511	17,034
Houston (8)	15	254,083	16,939
Real Salt Lake (7)	15	242,690	16,179
New York (5)	15	238,925	15,928
Chivas USA (12)	15	226,717	15,114
Columbus (9)	15	219,332	14,622
San Jose (*)	15	205,695	13,713
Colorado (11)	15	204,884	13,659
Dallas (10)	15	195,356	13,024
Kansas City (13)	15	160,286	10,686
TOTALS	210	3,456,389	16,459

*San Jose was an expansion team in 2008.

Fouls Committed

	Gm	No
Atiba Harris, Chv	.28	73
Andre Rocha, Dal	.27	52
Fred, DC	.23	50
Javier Morales, RSL	.29	49
Carl Robinson, Tor	.27	49
Shalrie Joseph, NE	.27	47
Paulo Nagamura, Chv	.24	47
Kevin Goldthwaite, NY	.28	42
Jeff Larentowicz, NE	.28	42
Marcelo Saragosa, Dal	.25	41

Fouls Suffered

	Gm	No
Cuauhtemoc Blanco, Chi	.27	76
Robbie Rogers, Clb	.27	73
Alejandro Moreno, Clb	.27	69
Guillermo Barros Schelotto, Clb	.27	63
Javier Morales, RSL	.29	59
Davy Arnaud, KC	.24	58
Atiba Harris, Chv	.28	50
Brian Ching, Hou	.25	49
Kenny Cooper, Dal	.30	48
Kei Kamara, Hou	.22	47

Offsides

	Gm	Offs
Kenny Cooper, Dal	.30	39
Jeff Cunningham, Dal	.27	39
Dwayne De Rosario, Hou	.24	35
Scott Sealy, SJ	.27	35
Edson Buddle, LA	.27	30
Juan Pablo Angel, NY	.23	27
Danny Dichio, Tor	.23	26
Alejandro Moreno, Clb	.27	25
Claudio Lopez, KC	.28	24
Chad Barett, Tor	.29	23
Brian Ching, Hou	.25	23

Cautions (Yellow Cards)

	Gm	No
Bakary Soumare, Chi	.28	10
Frankie Hejduk, Clb	.24	9
Jamison Olave, RSL	.23	9
Marcelo Saragosa, Dal	.25	9
Five players tied with 8 each.		

Ejections (Red Cards)

	Gm	No
Roger Espinoza, KC	.22	2
Bryan Namoff, DC	.27	2
Pablo Ricchetti, Dal	.27	2
James Riley, SJ	.24	2
Eddie Robinson, Hou	.20	2
Marco Velez, Tor	.23	2

Corner Kicks

	Gm	CKs
Guillermo Barros Schelotto, Clb	.27	126
Javier Morales, RSL	.29	112
Terry Cooke, Col	.24	88
Steve Ralston, NE	.21	75
David Beckham, LA	.25	69
Claudio Lopez, KC	.28	65
Dave van den Bergh, NY	.26	65
Brad Davis, Hou	.26	61
Andre Rocha, Dal	.27	60
Ronnie O'Brien, SJ	.28	60

Game-Winning Goals

	Gm	GWG
Juan Pablo Angel, NY	.23	4
Chad Barrett, Tor	.29	4
Kenny Cooper, Dal	.30	4
Luciano Emilio, DC	.27	4
Steve Ralston, NE	.21	4

Game-Winning Assists

	Gm	GWA
Guillermo Barros Schelotto, Clb	.27	5
Steve Ralston, NE	.21	5
Brad Davis, Hou	.26	4
Andre Rocha, Dal	.27	4
Eight players tied with 3 each.		

Minutes Played

	Mins
Jon Busch, Chi	.2700
Joe Cannon, SJ	.2700
Jimmy Conrad, KC	.2700
Kevin Hartman, KC	.2700
Jay Heaps, NE	.2700
Nick Rimando, RSL	.2700
Clyde Simms, DC	.2697
Brian Carroll, Clb	.2692

Leading Goaltenders

Goals Against Average

	Gm	Min	Shts	Svs	GAA	W-L-T
Pat Onstad, Hou	.24	2098	100	76	1.03	10-4-9
Jon Busch, Chi	.30	2700	155	122	1.10	13-10-7
William Hesmer, Clb	.29	2610	130	97	1.14	17-6-6
Bouna Coundoul, Col	.17	1530	75	54	1.24	6-8-3
Joe Cannon, SJ	.30	2700	162	124	1.27	8-13-9
Kevin Hartman, KC	.30	2700	156	117	1.30	11-10-9
Nick Rimando, RSL	.30	2700	135	96	1.30	10-10-10
Dario Sala, Dal	.28	2520	129	92	1.32	8-8-12
Brad Guzan, Chv	.15	1350	68	48	1.33	6-5-4
Matt Reis, NE	.28	2485	145	107	1.38	11-11-6
Greg Sutton, Tor	.24	2160	151	116	1.46	7-10-7
Jon Conway, NY	.28	2520	140	98	1.50	9-10-9

Save Percentage

	Svs	SOG	SV Pct
Jon Busch, Chi	.122	156	78.2
Joe Cannon, SJ	.124	166	74.7
William Hesmer, Clb	.97	132	73.5
Greg Sutton, Tor	.116	160	72.5
Pat Onstad, Hou	.76	105	72.4
Kevin Hartman, KC	.117	162	72.2
Matt Reis, NE	.92	131	70.2

Saves

	Gm	No
Joe Cannon, SJ	.30	124
Jon Busch, Chi	.30	122
Kevin Hartman, KC	.30	117
Greg Sutton, Tor	.24	116
Matt Reis, NE	.28	107

Shutouts

	Gm	No
Jon Busch, Chi	.30	10
Kevin Hartman, KC	.30	10
Williams Hesmer, Clb	.29	10
Joe Cannon, SJ	.30	9
Nick Rimando, RSL	.30	8

Wins

	Gm	No
William Hesmer, Clb	.29	17
Jon Busch, Chi	.30	13
Kevin Hartman, KC	.30	11
Matt Reis, NE	.28	11
Pat Onstad, Hou	.24	10
Nick Rimando, RSL	.30	10

Major League Soccer (Cont.)

Team-by-Team Statistics

Chicago Fire

(min. 10 Gms)	Pos	Gm	Min	G	A	Sht
Chris Rolfe	.F	26	1960	9	7	42
Cuauhtemoc Blanco	.M	27	2398	7	11	46
Chad Barrett	.F	16	1174	5	4	35
Brian McBride	.F	11	932	5	2	30
John Thorrington	.M	23	1881	5	2	24
Tomasz Frankowski	.F	17	628	2	2	14
Stephen King	.M	20	854	2	1	13
Justin Mapp	.M	30	2229	2	8	42
Gonzalo Segares	.D	23	2013	2	2	16
Wilman Conde	.D	22	1750	1	1	7
Mike Banner	.M	11	288	0	0	5
Diego Gutierrez	.M	20	1660	0	1	2
Andy Herron	.F	17	529	0	0	15
Logan Pause	.M	27	2430	0	0	5
Brandon Prideaux	.D	27	2254	0	1	10
Bakary Soumare	.D	28	2514	0	1	5

Top Goalkeepers	Gm	Min	W-L-T	Shts	Svs	GAA
Jon Busch	30	2700	13-10-7	156	122	1.10

Chivas USA

(min. 10 Gms)	Pos	Gm	Min	G	A	Sht
Alecko Eskandarian	.F	11	656	5	2	23
Sacha Kljestan	.M	22	1941	5	7	36
Ante Razov	.F	22	1415	5	6	51
Justin Braun	.F	24	1219	4	2	32
Jesse March	.M	25	2138	4	0	15
Jorge Flores	.M	11	590	3	0	4
Atiba Harris	.F	28	2014	3	5	42
Jonathan Bornstein	.D	21	1679	2	2	10
Paulo Nagamura	.M	24	2062	2	3	17
Jim Curtin	.D	18	1382	1	0	7
Maykel Galindo	.F	10	549	1	2	12
Carey Talley	.M	16	1298	1	2	11
Bobby Burling	.D	20	1659	0	0	7
Francisco Mendoza	.M	28	2434	0	4	15
Claudio Suarez	.D	14	1080	0	0	5
Shavar Thomas	.D	19	1553	0	0	7

Goalkeepers	Gm	Min	W-L-T	Shts	Svs	GAA
Brad Guzan	15	1350	6-5-4	71	48	1.33
Dan Kennedy	9	699	4-3-0	32	22	1.03
Zach Thornton	8	651	2-3-3	146	86	1.37

Colorado Rapids

(min. 10 Gms)	Pos	Gm	Min	G	A	Sht
Conor Casey	.F	21	1313	11	2	51
Omar Cummings	.F	26	1629	6	4	56
Colin Clark	.M	29	2325	5	3	46
Tom McManus	.F	22	1307	5	2	44
Christian Gomez	.M	20	1423	3	6	36
Herculez Gomez	.M	17	644	2	1	23
Nick LaBrocca	.M	30	2396	2	0	24
Mike Petke	.D	11	831	2	0	4
Mehdi Ballouchy	.M	19	1200	1	4	20
Jose Burciaga Jr.	.D	12	818	1	1	10
Terry Cooke	.M	24	1698	1	12	22
John DiRaimondo	.M	11	714	1	0	5
Facundo Erpen	.D	23	1854	1	1	18
Jacob Peterson	.M	17	762	1	0	15
Jordan Harvey	.D	15	1180	0	1	2
Ugo Ihemelu	.D	18	1493	0	0	2
Kosuke Kimura	.D	18	1438	0	0	2
Pablo Mastroeni	.M/D	25	2004	0	0	6

Goalkeepers	Gm	Min	W-L-T	Shts	Svs	GAA
Bouna Coundoul	17	1530	6-8-3	77	54	1.24
Preston Burpo	13	1170	5-6-2	63	37	1.85

Columbus Crew

(min. 10 Gms)	Pos	Gm	Min	G	A	Sht
Alejandro Moreno	.F	27	2428	9	4	46
Guillermo Barros Schelotto	.F	27	2216	7	19	54
Robbie Rogers	.M	27	2334	6	3	70
Brad Evans	.F	26	1756	5	1	37
Steve Lenhart	.F	10	278	4	0	8
Chad Marshall	.D	29	2485	4	2	23
Jason Garey	.F	10	128	3	0	11
Eddie Gaven	.M/F	24	1848	3	2	30
Emmanuel Ekpo	.M	17	742	2	1	14
Brian Carroll	.M	30	2692	1	2	17
Frankie Hejduk	.D	24	2135	1	4	22
Andy Iro	.D	18	1079	1	0	9
Pat Noonan	.M/F	11	531	1	2	9
Ezra Hendrickson	.D	13	688	0	0	5
Stefani Miglioranzi	.D/M	14	471	0	1	2
Danny O'Rourke	.D	28	2452	0	4	2
Gino Padula	.D	14	1227	0	0	8

Top Goalkeepers	Gm	Min	W-L-T	Shts	Svs	GAA
Will Hesmer	29	2610	17-6-6	132	97	1.14

D.C. United

(min. 10 Gms)	Pos	Gm	Min	G	A	Sht
Luciano Emilio	.F	27	2141	11	5	76
Jaime Moreno	.F	25	1861	10	10	36
Santino Quaranta	.M	27	1963	5	4	45
Marcelo Gallardo	.M	15	1161	4	3	31
Fred	.M	23	1690	2	4	29
Francis Doe	.F	12	435	2	0	9
Clyde Simms	.M/D	30	2697	2	2	24
Quavas Kirk	.F	10	135	1	0	3
Gonzalo Martinez	.D	26	2102	1	2	9
Devon McTavish	.D/M	26	2223	1	4	11
Bryan Namoff	.D	27	2398	1	0	13
Gonzalo Peralta	.D	18	1514	1	0	6
Marc Burch	.D	28	1817	0	3	13
Rod Dyachenko	.F	19	776	0	3	7
Ivan Guerrero	.M/D	13	1149	0	4	8

Top Goalkeepers	Gm	Min	W-L-T	Shts	Svs	GAA
Zach Wells	17	1530	8-8-1	85	56	1.65
Louis Crayton	12	1080	3-6-3	64	43	1.58

FC Dallas

(min. 10 Gms)	Pos	Gm	Min	G	A	Sht
Kenny Cooper	.F	30	2622	18	3	119
Jeff Cunningham	.F	11	951	5	2	24
Dominic Oduro	.F	25	992	5	2	28
Arturo Alvarez	.M	16	931	3	3	22
Andre Rocha	.M	27	2151	3	8	47
Abe Thompson	.F	13	427	1	1	12
Drew Moor	.D	27	2430	2	1	18
Juan Toja	.M	16	1283	2	2	21
Bruno Guarda	.M	12	822	1	1	10
Aaron Pitchkolan	.D	21	1345	1	0	6
Marcelo Saragosa	.M	25	1809	1	2	14
Eric Avila	.M	14	508	0	2	4
Duilio Davino	.D	23	1958	0	1	5
Dax McCarty	.M	17	821	0	2	2
Pablo Ricchetti	.M	27	2252	0	3	10
Adrian Serioux	.D	24	1926	0	4	8
Blake Wagner	.D	24	2068	0	0	6

Goalkeepers	Gm	Min	W-L-T	Shts	Svs	GAA
Dario Sala	28	2520	8-8-12	131	92	1.32

Houston Dynamo

(min. 10 Gms)	Pos	Gm	Min	G	A	Sht
Brian Ching	F	25	2096	13	5	57
Dwayne De Rosario	M	24	1948	7	2	78
Nate Jaqua	F	14	901	4	4	10
Brad Davis	M	26	1800	3	8	42
Stuart Holden	M	27	1652	3	4	35
Brian Mullan	M	30	2343	3	5	18
Franco Caraccio	F	10	602	2	1	13
Ricardo Clark	M	23	2205	2	1	25
Kei Kamara	F	10	555	2	2	18
Corey Ashe	M	22	847	1	1	13
Bobby Boswell	D	29	2610	1	1	15
Geoff Cameron	M	23	921	1	2	13
Wade Barrett	D	26	2328	0	0	2
Patrick Ianni	D	17	1010	0	1	1
Richard Mulrooney	D	23	2025	0	4	5
Eddie Robinson	D	20	1570	0	0	8
Craig Waibel	D	14	1245	0	3	9

Goalkeeper	Gm	Min	W-L-T	Shts	Svs	GAA
Pat Onstad	24	2098	10-4-9	105	76	1.03
Tony Caig	7	602	3-1-3	36	24	1.20

Kansas City Wizards

(min. 10 Gms)	Pos	Gm	Min	G	A	Sht
Davy Arnaud	M/F	24	2019	7	3	44
Jimmy Conrad	D	30	2700	6	0	16
Claudio Lopez	F	28	2265	6	7	67
Jack Jewsbury	M	29	2548	3	7	17
Michael Harrington	D	30	2597	2	2	5
Scott Sealy	F	13	853	2	0	19
Michael Harrington	D	30	2597	2	2	5
Scott Sealy	F	13	853	2	0	19
Roger Espinoza	M	22	1169	1	3	16
Ivan Trujillo	F	17	700	1	0	10
Sasha Victorine	M	16	1126	1	0	22
Aaron Hohlbein	D/M	14	1158	0	1	1
Jonathan Leathers	D	15	1093	0	0	4
Carlos Marinelli	M	15	778	0	3	14
Kurt Morsink	M	21	1215	0	3	16
Chance Myers	D	10	681	0	0	5
Ryan Pore	M	14	485	0	1	6
Tyson Wahl	D	16	1327	0	0	3
Kerry Zavagnin	M	17	1116	0	1	5

Top Goalkeeper	Gm	Min	W-L-T	Shts	Svs	GAA
Kevin Hartman	30	2700	11-10-9	162	117	1.30

Los Angeles Galaxy

(min. 10 Gms)	Pos	Gm	Min	G	A	Sht
Landon Donovan	F	25	2136	20	9	65
Edson Buddle	F	27	2218	15	3	74
David Beckham	M	25	2248	5	10	35
Alan Gordon	F	26	1314	5	7	46
Ely Allen	M	12	848	1	1	15
Alvaro Pires	M	19	1253	1	1	9
Chris Klein	D	30	2685	1	7	19
Brandon McDonald	M	16	1036	1	1	12
Carlos Ruiz	F	10	386	1	0	9
Peter Vagenas	M	14	933	1	3	7
Joe Franchino	M	15	886	0	0	6
Sean Franklin	D	27	2385	0	1	12
Ante Jazic	D	15	1172	0	3	3
Mike Randolph	D	20	1468	0	3	13
Troy Roberts	M	17	1316	0	0	3
Greg Vanney	D	25	2050	0	1	7
Abel Xavier	D	10	854	0	1	1

Top Goalkeeper	Gm	Min	W-L-T	Shts	Svs	GAA
Steve Cronin	22	1935	6-9-6	141	92	2.05
Josh Wicks	6	495	1-2-3	33	20	2.18

New England Revolution

(min. 10 Gms)	Pos	Gm	Min	G	A	Sht
Steve Ralston	M	21	1715	8	7	21
Taylor Twellman	F	16	1211	8	2	42
Adam Cristman	F	18	1300	6	1	39
Kheli Dube	F	21	1252	4	4	29
Jeff Larentowicz	M	28	2437	4	2	24
Kenny Mansally	F	17	979	3	1	14
Sainey Nyassi	M	25	1661	2	1	28
Khano Smith	M	23	1515	2	3	26
Shalrie Joseph	M	27	2384	1	1	27
Chris Albright	D	26	2340	0	0	10
Mauricio Castro	M	24	1584	0	3	29
Jay Heaps	D	30	2700	0	1	15
Amaechi Igwe	D	11	568	0	0	2
Michael Parkhurst	D	28	2520	0	1	4
Pat Phelan	M/D	11	467	0	0	1
Wells Thompson	M	19	786	0	1	9

Goalkeeper	Gm	Min	W-L-T	Shts	Svs	GAA
Matt Reis	28	2485	11-11-6	150	107	1.38

New York Red Bulls

(min. 10 Gms)	Pos	Gm	Min	G	A	Sht
Juan Pablo Angel	F	23	1955	14	3	76
Dave van den Bergh	M	26	2228	7	5	36
Mike Magee	F/M	26	1665	5	1	35
Dane Richards	M	23	1553	3	6	28
Danleigh Borman	M	15	721	2	0	16
Kevin Goldthwaite	D	28	2438	2	2	17
Seth Stammler	M/D	26	2195	1	4	25
Sinisa Ubiparipovic	M	16	821	1	2	12
Andrew Boyens	D	19	1506	0	0	5
Hunter Freeman	D	14	953	0	1	1
Chris Leitch	D	17	1259	0	2	1
Carlos Mendes	M/D	17	964	0	0	2
Jeff Parke	D	24	2025	0	0	12
Juan Pietravallo	M	13	889	0	1	6
Jorge Rojas	M	11	825	0	5	13
Luke Sassano	M/D	18	954	0	0	8
John Wolyniec	F	19	726	0	1	18

Goalkeepers	Gm	Min	W-L-T	Shts	Svs	GAA
Jon Conway	28	2520	9-10-9	146	98	1.50

Real Salt Lake

(min. 10 Gms)	Pos	Gm	Min	G	A	Sht
Yura Movsisyan	F	22	1229	7	1	69
Robbie Findley	F	29	1493	6	5	44
Javier Morales	M	29	2511	6	15	48
Fabian Espindola	F	12	642	5	0	25
Kyle Beckerman	M	30	2683	3	2	45
Kenny Deuchar	F	29	1557	3	2	41
Jamison Olave	D	23	2006	2	0	10
Dema Kovalenko	M	22	1668	1	2	25
Andy Williams	M	26	1602	1	3	41
Tony Beltran	D	15	936	0	1	4
Nat Borchers	D	29	2610	0	1	13
Kenny Cutler	M	11	454	0	0	3
Ian Joy	D	19	1377	0	0	3
Clint Mathis	M/F	11	590	0	0	12
Robbie Russell	M/D	11	683	0	0	6
Chris Wingert	D	29	2589	0	3	10

Top Goalkeeper	Gm	Min	W-L-T	Shts	Svs	GAA
Nick Rimando	30	2700	10-10-10	140	96	1.30

Major League Soccer (Cont.)

San Jose Earthquakes

(min. 10 Gms)	.Pos	Gm	Min	G	A	Sht
Darren Huckerby	.M	14	1211	6	4	31
Ryan Johnson	.F/M	28	1535	5	1	29
Ronnie O'Brien	.M	28	2286	4	6	62
Arturo Alvarez	.F	12	864	3	3	18
Scott Sealy	.F	14	1168	3	3	26
Ryan Cochrane	.D	19	1535	2	1	3
Ramiro Corrales	.M/D	22	1895	2	2	29
John Cunliffe	.F	12	389	2	0	10
Kei Kamara	.F	12	997	2	0	28
Shea Salinas	.M	23	544	2	0	12
Ivan Guerrero	.M/D	14	1014	1	0	8
Eric Denton	.D	26	2209	0	2	3
Nick Garcia	.D	24	2151	0	2	0
Ned Grabavoy	.M	24	1709	0	4	14
Kelly Gray	.D	13	742	0	0	13
Jason Hernandez	.D	28	2451	0	1	5
Francisco Lima	.M	14	1183	0	2	8
James Riley	.D/F	24	2055	0	2	7

Top Goalkeeper	**Gm**	**Min**	**W-L-T**	**Shts**	**Svs**	**GAA**
Joe Cannon	.30	2700	8-13-9	166	124	1.27

Toronto FC

(min. 10 Gms)	Pos	Gm	Min	G	A	Sht
Danny Dichio	.F	23	1445	5	3	20
Chad Barrett	.F	13	998	4	3	31
Amado Guevara	.M	21	1819	4	4	41
Rohan Ricketts	.M	27	2139	4	4	29
Jeff Cunningham	.F	16	747	3	0	19
Abdus Ibrahim	.F	12	486	2	0	13
Marco Velez	.D	23	1973	2	0	6
Marvell Wynne	.D	24	2115	2	2	9
Jim Brennan	.D	28	2462	1	3	18
Maurice Edu	.M	13	1104	1	1	17
Julius James	.D	13	899	1	0	6
Laurent Robert	.M	17	1364	1	3	31
Carl Robinson	.M	27	2426	1	1	8
Jarrod Smith	.F	20	728	1	0	14
Kevin Harmse	.M	16	1077	0	0	7
Tyrone Marshall	.D	24	2019	0	0	2
Johann Smith	.F	10	371	0	1	5

Top Goalkeeper	**Gm**	**Min**	**W-L-T**	**Shts**	**Svs**	**GAA**
Greg Sutton	.24	2160	7-7-10	160	116	1.46
Brian Edwards	.6	540	2-3-1	31	23	1.33

SuperLiga

Created in 2007, the SuperLiga is a competition between teams from Major League Soccer and Mexico's Primera Division. Eight clubs—four each from MLS and the Primera Division—took part in the second competition held July 12-Aug. 5. Though the first edition of SuperLiga in 2007 was set up by invitation to specific teams, going forward the leagues determine future SuperLiga berths. The games were played at American stadiums. The winning club, CF Pachuca of Mexico, received $1 million. (*) denotes that club advanced to the knockout stage.

Group Stage

Group A	W	L	T	Pts
*Houston Dynamo (MLS)	2	1	0	6
*Atlante (Primera)	2	1	0	6
Guadalajara (Primera)	2	1	0	6
D.C. United (MLS)	0	3	0	0

RESULTS: July 12–DC United 1, Guadalaja 2; Houston 4, Atlante 0; July 15–DC United 2, Atlante 3; Houston 0, Guadalajara 1; July 19–DC United 1, Houston 3; Atlante 2, Guadalajara 0.

Group B	W	L	T	Pts
*N.E. Revolution (MLS)	2	0	1	7
*Pachuca (Primera)	1	1	1	4
Chivas USA (MLS)	1	1	1	4
Santos Laguna (Primera)	0	1	2	2

RESULTS: July 13– NE Revolution 1, Santos Laguna 0; Chivas 1, Pachuca 2; July 16–NE Revolution 1, Pachuca 0; Chivas USA 1, Santos Laguna 0; July 20–Chivas USA 1, NE Revolution 1; Santos Laguna 1, Pachuca 1.

Semifinals

July 29

at Houston Dynamo 2 . . . . .Pachuca 0

July 30

at N.E. Revolution 1 . . . . .Atlante 0

Final

Aug. 5 at Gillette Stadium, Foxboro, Mass.

N.E. Revolution 2 . . . . .Houston Dynamo 2

Revolution wins, 6-5, on penalty kicks

Scoring

NE REVS: Steve Ralston (41'), Shalrie Joseph (102')
HOU: Nate Jacqua (18'), Kei Kamara (98')

SHOOTOUT

New England	Houston
Steve Ralston (Goal)	Craig Weibel (Goal)
Matt Reis (Miss)	C. Wondolowski (Goal)
Shalrie Joseph (Goal)	D. De Rosario (Saved)
Taylor Twellman (Goal)	Brian Ching (Goal)
Khano Smith (Saved)	Ricardo Clark (Goal)
Jeff Larentowicz (Goal)	Wade Barrett (Goal)
Chris Tierney (Goal)	Kei Kamara (Goal)
Chris Albright (Goal)	Corey Ashe (Missed)

Colleges

MEN

2007 NCAA Division I Tournament

First Round (Nov. 23-24)

Ill-Chicago 0 . . . . .St. Louis 0
Ill-Chicago advanced on PKs
California 2 . . . . .2OT . . . . .Cal-Davis 1
South Florida 2 . . . . .Colgate 1
Louisville 1 . . . . .Duke 0
Virginia 3 . . . . .St. Peter's 1
Massachusetts 2 . . . . .Boston University 1
Washington 1 . . . . .Portland 0
SMU 1 . . . . .Gonzaga 0
Central Conn. St. 3 . . . . .Harvard 2
UCLA 1 . . . . .New Mexico 0
Bradley 2 . . . . .DePaul 0
Vermont 1 . . . . .Dartmouth 1
Vermont advanced on PKs
Furman 2 . . . . .Campbell 0
Loyola 2 . . . . .Liberty 0
Oakland 2 .Michigan St. 1
Old Dominion 1 . . . . .Providence 0

Second Round (Nov. 28)

Connecticut 2 . . . . .Vermont 0
Santa Clara 3 . . . . .UCLA 1
Wake Forest 1 . . . . .Furman 0
Massachusetts 2 . . . . .Boston College 1
Old Dominion 2 . . . . .2 OT . . . . .Brown 1
Bradley 1 . . . . .Indiana 0
Bradley advanced on PKs
Central Conn. St. 3 .Tulsa 2
Creighton 3 . . . . .SMU 0
Notre Dame 2 .Oakland 1
Ohio St. 1 . . . . .Louisville 0
Cal-Santa Barbara 1 . . . . .Washington 0
Va. Tech 3 . . . . .California 2
Ill-Chicago 2 .Northwestern 0
South Florida 1 . . . . .2 OT . . . . .Akron 0
West Virginia 1 . . . . .Virginia 0
Maryland 0 . . . . .Loyola 0
Maryland advanced on PKs

Third Round (Dec. 1-2)

Connecticut 5 .South Florida 0
Wake Forest 3 . . . . .West Virginia 1
Ohio St. 4 . . . . .2 OT . . .Cal-Santa Barbara 3
Va. Tech 1 . . . . : . .Old Dominion 0
Bradley 3 . . . . .2 OT . . . . .Maryland 2
Massachusetts 3 . . . . .Central Conn. St. 1
Notre Dame 2 . . . . .Santa Clara 0
Illinois-Chicago 2 . . . . .Creighton 0

Quarterfinals (Dec. 7-8-9)

Massachusetts 2 . . . . .Ill-Chicago 1
Ohio St. 4 . . . . .Bradley 0
Va. Tech 1 . . . . .Connecticut 0
Wake Forest 1 . . . . .OT . . . . .Notre Dame 0

2007 College Cup
at Cary, N.C. (Dec. 14 & 16)

Semifinals

Ohio St. 1 . . . . .Massachusetts 0
Wake Forest 2 . . . . .Va. Tech 0

Championship

Wake Forest 2 . . . . .Ohio St. 1

Scoring

1st Half: OSU—Roger Espinoza (Doug Verhoff), 12:02
2nd Half: WF—Tracy Marcus (Cody Arnoux), 65:59;
Zack Schilawaski, (Marcus), 77:13.

Attendance: 8,172
Final records: WF (21-2-2), Ohio St. (17-4-5).
Most Outstanding Off. Player: Marcus Tracy, WF
Most Outstanding Def. Player: Brian Edwards, WF

2007 Annual Awards

Men's Players of the Year

M.A.C. Hermann Trophy . . . . . .O'Brian White, UConn, F
Soccer America . . . . .O'Brian White, UConn, F

NSCAA Coach of the Year

Men's Div. I . . . . .Jay Vidovich, Wake Forest

Division I All-America Teams

MEN

The 2007 first team All-America selections of the National Soccer Coaches Association of America (NSCAA).

GOALKEEPER—Stefan Frei, USC.

DEFENDERS—Eric Brunner, Ohio St.; Julius James, Connecticut; Pat Phelan, Wake Forest.

MIDFIELDERS—Reuben Ayarna, Boston College; Alejandro Bedoya, Boston College; Andrew Jacobson, California; Peter Lowry, Santa Clara.

FORWARDS—Xavier Balc, Ohio St.; Joseph Lapira, Notre Dame; Patrick Nyarko, Va. Tech; O'Brian White, Connecticut.

WOMEN
2007 NCAA Division I Tournament

First Round (Nov. 15-16)
Texas A&M 4 .Stephen F. Austin 1
Texas 2 . . . . .BYU 0
UCLA 3 . . . . .CS-Fullerton 1
North Carolina 6 .High Point 1
Portland 5 . . . . .Denver 0
Stanford 7 .Sacramento St. 0
Purdue 4 . . . . .Oakland (Mich.) 0
Penn St. 4 . . . . .Monmouth 0
USC 3 . . . . .Creighton 1
Virginia 4 . . . . .Loyola-MD 1
Florida 3 . . . . .Miami-FL 0
Oklahoma St. 2 .San Diego 1
Notre Dame 3 . . . . .Loyola-Chicago 0
Florida St. 3 .Kennesaw St. 0
West Va. 4 . . . . .Navy 0
Georgia 6 . . . . .Alabama A&M 1
California 2 . . . . .Santa Clara 0
Tennessee 2 . . . . .Furman 0
Connecticut 0 . . . . .Boston College 0
Connecticut advanced on PKs
Wake Forest 2 . . . . .Boston University 1
Missouri 1 .SE Missouri St. 1
Missouri advanced on PKs
Central Florida 3 . . . . .Auburn 1
Clemson 4 . . . . .Charlotte 2
Colorado 2 . . . . .Hawaii 0
Duke 1 . . . . .South Carolina 1
Duke advanced on PKs
Hofstra 1 . . . . .Ohio St. 0
Illinois 1 . . . . .OT . . . . .Louisville 0
Indiana 3 . . . . .2 OT . . . . .Toledo 2
James Madison 2 . . . . .Pennsylvania 0
LSU 1 . . . . .2 OT . . . . .Samford 0
NC-Greensboro 1 . . . . .Memphis 0
Williams & Mary 2 . . . . .Georgetown 1

Second Round (Nov. 17-18)
UCLA 4 . . . . .Oklahoma St. 0
North Carolina 3 . . . . .NC-Greensboro 1
Portland 1 . . . . .Colorado 0
Stanford 1 . . . . .California 1
Stanford advanced on PKs
Indiana 0 . . . . .Purdue 0
Indiana advanced on PKs
USC 1 . . . . .2 OT . . . . .Missouri 0
Virginia 1 .William & Mary 0

Florida 0 . . . . .Central Florida 0
Florida advanced on PKs
Notre Dame 2 . . . . .Illinois 0
Florida St. 4 . . . . .LSU 0
West Va. 2 .James Madison 0
Duke 1 . . . . .Georgia 0
Tennessee 1 . . . . .2 OT . . . . .Clemson 0
Connecticut 2 . . . . .Wake Forest 0
Penn St. 2 . . . . .OT . . . . .Hofstra 1

Third Round (Nov. 24-25)
UCLA 2 . . . . .OT . . . . .Virginia 1
Connecticut 2 . . . . .Stanford 0
Florida St. 4 . . . . .Texas 0
Notre Dame 3 . . . . .North Carolina 2
Portland 3 . . . . .Tennessee 0
West Va. 1 . . . . .Penn St. 0
USC 1 . . . . .Florida 0
Duke 2 . . . . .Indiana 0

Quarterfinals (Nov. 30)
UCLA 3 . . . . .2 OT . . . . .Portland 2
USC 1 . . . . .West Va. 0
Notre Dame 3 . . . . .Duke 2
Florida St. 3 . . . . .2 OT . . . . .Connecticut 2

2007 College Cup
at College Station, Texas (Dec. 7 & 9)
Semifinals
Florida St. 3 .Notre Dame 2
USC 2 . . . . .UCLA 1

Championship
USC 2 . . . . .Florida St. 0
Scoring
1st Half: USC—Marihelen Tomer (unassisted), 24:45.
2nd Half: USC—Janessa Currier (unassisted), 75:02.
Final records: Florida St. (18-6-3), USC (20-3-2).

2007 Annual Awards
Women's Players of the Year
M.A.C. Hermann Trophy . . . Mami Yamaguchi, Fla. St., MF
Soccer America . . . . .Lauren Cheney, UCLA, F
NSCAA Coach of the Year
Women's Div. I . . . . .Ali Khosroshahin, USC

Division I All-America Teams
The 2007 first team All-America selections of the National Soccer Coaches Association of America (NSCAA).

GOALKEEPER—Alyssa Naeher, Penn St.
DEFENDERS—Nikki Krzysik, Virginia; Stephanie Lopez, Portland; Becky Sauerbrunn, Virginia; Brittany Taylor, Connecticut.
MIDFIELDERS—Yael Averbuch, North Carolina; Tobin Heath, North Carolina; Meghan Schnur, Connecticut; Brittany Block, Notre Dame.
FORWARDS—Lauren Cheyney, UCLA; Parrissa Eyorokon, Purdue; Kerri Hanks, Notre Dame; Mami Yamaguchi, Florida St.

1900-2008
Through the Years

ESPN SPORTS ALMANAC

The World Cup

The Federation Internationale de Football Association (FIFA) began the World Cup championship tournament in 1930 with a 13-team field in Uruguay. Sixty-four years later, 138 countries competed in qualifying rounds to fill 24 berths in the 1994 World Cup finals. FIFA increased the World Cup '98 tournament field from 24 to 32 teams, and it remained at 32 in 2006 including automatic berths for defending champion Brazil and host Germany. The other 30 slots were allotted by region: Europe (12), Africa (5), South America (4), CONCACAF (3), Asia (4), the two remaining positions were determined via two home-and-away playoff series. One was between the #4 CONCACAF team (Trinidad & Tobago) and the #5 Asian team (Bahrain) and the other was between the #5 South American team (Uruguay) and the champion of Oceania (Australia).

Tournaments have been played once in Asia (Japan/South Korea), three times in North America (Mexico 2 and U.S.), four times in South America (Argentina, Chile, Brazil and Uruguay) and nine times in Europe (France 2, Italy 2, England, Spain, Sweden, Switzerland and West Germany). Following an outcry when Germany was awarded the 2006 World Cup over South Africa, FIFA announced that, starting in 2010, the World Cup will be rotated among six continents.

Brazil retired the first World Cup (called the Jules Rimet Trophy after FIFA's first president) in 1970 after winning it for the third time. The new trophy, first presented in 1974, is known as simply the World Cup.

Multiple winners: Brazil (5); Italy (4); West Germany (3); Argentina and Uruguay (2).

Year	Champion	Manager	Score	Runner-up	Host Country	Third Place
1930	Uruguay	Alberto Suppici	4-2	Argentina	Uruguay	No game
1934	Italy	Vittório Pozzo	2-1*	Czechoslovakia	Italy	Germany 3, Austria 2
1938	Italy	Vittório Pozzo	4-2	Hungary	France	Brazil 4, Sweden 2
1942-46 Not held						
1950	Uruguay	Juan Lopez	2-1	Brazil	Brazil	No game
1954	West Germany	Sepp Herberger	3-2	Hungary	Switzerland	Austria 3, Uruguay 1
1958	Brazil	Vicente Feola	5-2	Sweden	Sweden	France 6, W. Ger. 3
1962	Brazil	Aimoré Moreira	3-1	Czechoslovakia	Chile	Chile 1, Yugoslavia 0
1966	England	Alf Ramsey	4-2*	W. Germany	England	Portugal 2, USSR 1
1970	Brazil	Mario Zagalo	4-1	Italy	Mexico	W. Ger. 1, Uruguay 0
1974	West Germany	Helmut Schoen	2-1	Netherlands	W. Germany	Poland 1, Brazil 0
1978	Argentina	Cesar Menotti	3-1*	Netherlands	Argentina	Brazil 2, Italy 1
1982	Italy	Enzo Bearzot	3-1	W. Germany	Spain	Poland 3, France 2
1986	Argentina	Carlos Bilardo	3-2	W. Germany	Mexico	France 4, Belgium 2*
1990	West Germany	Franz Beckenbauer	1-0	Argentina	Italy	Italy 2, England 1
1994	Brazil	Carlos Parreira	0-0†	Italy	USA	Sweden 4, Bulgaria 0
1998	France	Aimé Jacquet	3-0	Brazil	France	Croatia 2, Netherlands 1
2002	Brazil	Luiz Felipe Scolari	2-0	Germany	Japan/S. Korea	Turkey 3, S. Korea 2
2006	Brazil	Marcelo Lippi	1-1‡	France	Germany	Germany 3, Portugal 1
2010	at South Africa (June 11-July 11)					
2014	at Brazil (TBD)					

*Winning goals scored in overtime (no sudden death); †Brazil def. Italy in shootout (3-2); ‡Italy def. France in shootout (5-3).

All-Time World Cup Leaders

Career Goals

World Cup scoring leaders through 2006. Years listed are years played in World Cup.

	No
Ronaldo, Brazil (1994, 98, 2002, 06)	15
Gerd Müller, West Germany (1970, 74)	14
Just Fontaine, France (1958)	13
Pelé, Brazil (1958, 62, 66, 70)	12
Sandor Kocsis, Hungary (1954)	11
Juergen Klinsmann, Germany (1990, 94, 98)	11
Six Players tied with 10 each.	

Most Valuable Player

Officially, the Golden Ball Award, the Most Valuable Player of the World Cup tournament has been selected since 1982 by a panel of international soccer journalists.

Year		Year	
1982	Paolo Rossi, Italy	1998	Ronaldo, Brazil
1986	Diego Maradona, Arg.	2002	Oliver Kahn, Germany
1990	Toto Schillaci, Italy	2006	Zinedine Zidane, France
1994	Romario, Brazil		

Single Tournament Goals

Year		Gm	No
1930	Guillermo Stabile, Argentina	4	8
1934	Angelo Schiavio, Italy	3	4
	Oldrich Nejedly, Czechoslovakia	4	4
	Edmund Conen, Germany	4	4
1938	Leônidas, Brazil	3	8
1950	Ademir, Brazil	6	7
1954	Sandor Kocsis, Hungary	5	11
1958	Just Fontaine, France	6	13
1962	Drazen Jerkovic, Yugoslavia	6	6
1966	Eusébio, Portugal	6	9
1970	Gerd Müller, West Germany	6	10
1974	Grzegorz Lato, Poland	7	7
1978	Mario Kempes, Argentina	7	6
1982	Paolo Rossi, Italy	7	6
1986	Gary Lineker, England	5	6
1990	Toto Schillaci, Italy	7	6
1994	Oleg Salenko, Russia	3	6
	Hristo Stoitchkov, Bulgaria	7	6
1998	Davor Suker, Croatia	7	6
2002	Ronaldo, Brazil	7	8
2006	Miroslav Klose, Germany	7	5

All-Time World Cup Ranking Table

Since the first World Cup in 1930, Brazil is the only country to play in all 17 final tournaments. The FIFA all-time table below ranks all nations that have ever qualified for a World Cup final tournament by points earned through 2006. Victories, which earned two points from 1930-90, were awarded three points starting in 1994. Note that Germany's appearances include 10 made by West Germany from 1954-90. Participants in the 2006 World Cup final are in **bold** type.

#	Team	App	Gm	W	L	T	Pts	GF	GA
1	**Brazil**	18	92	64	14	14	153	201	84
2	**Germany**	16	92	56	18	19	142	190	110
3	**Italy**	16	76	56	17	19	115	122	68
4	**Argentina**	14	64	33	20	12	83	113	74
5	**England**	12	55	27	14	16	71	74	47
6	**Spain**	12	49	23	16	10	63	80	57
	France	12	51	25	17	9	63	95	64
8	Sweden	11	46	16	17	12	47	74	69
9	**Netherlands**	8	34	16	10	10	44	59	38
10	Russia	9	37	17	14	6	41	64	44
11	Yugoslavia	9	37	16	13	8	40	60	46
	Uruguay	10	40	15	15	10	40	65	57
13	**Poland**	7	31	15	11	5	37	44	40
	Mexico	13	44	11	22	12	37	48	85
15	Hungary	9	32	15	14	3	33	87	57
16	Belgium	11	36	10	17	9	30	46	63
	Czech Republic	9	33	12	16	5	30	47	49
18	Austria	7	29	12	13	4	28	43	47
19	**Portugal**	4	19	12	7	0	27	31	19
20	**Switzerland**	8	26	8	14	4	22	37	51
21	Romania	7	21	8	8	5	21	30	32
	Paraguay	7	22	6	10	6	21	27	36
	South Korea	7	24	5	13	6	21	22	53
24	Chile	7	25	7	12	6	20	31	40
25	Denmark	3	13	7	4	2	18	24	18
26	**USA**	8	25	6	16	3	17	27	51
27	Cameroon	5	17	4	6	7	16	15	29
28	Scotland	8	23	4	12	7	15	25	41
	Turkey	2	10	4	4	1	15	20	17
	Croatia	3	13	6	5	2	15	15	11
31	Bulgaria	7	26	3	15	8	14	22	53
32	Ireland	3	13	2	4	7	12	10	10
33	Peru	4	15	4	8	3	11	19	31
	No. Ireland	3	13	3	5	5	11	13	23
35	Nigeria	3	11	4	6	1	9	14	16
	Ukraine	1	5	3	2	0	9	5	7
37	Morocco	4	13	2	7	4	8	12	18
	Colombia	4	13	3	8	2	8	14	23
	Costa Rica	3	10	3	6	1	8	12	21
	Senegal	1	5	2	1	2	8	7	6
	Japan	3	10	2	6	2	8	8	14
	Ecuador	2	7	3	4	0	8	7	8
43	Norway	2	8	3	2	3	7	7	8
44	East Germany	1	6	2	2	2	6	5	5
	South Africa	2	6	1	2	3	6	8	11
	Saudi Arabia	4	13	2	9	2	6	9	32
	Tunisia	4	12	1	7	4	6	8	17
	Ghana	1	3	2	0	1	6	4	3
49	Algeria	2	6	2	3	1	5	6	10
	Wales	1	5	1	1	3	5	4	4
	Australia	2	6	1	4	2	5	5	11
52	**Iran**	3	9	1	6	2	4	6	18
53	North Korea	1	4	1	2	1	3	5	9
	Cuba	1	3	1	1	1	3	5	12
	Jamaica	1	3	1	2	0	3	3	9
	Ivory Coast	1	3	1	2	0	3	5	6
57	Egypt	2	4	0	2	2	2	3	6
	Honduras	1	3	0	1	2	2	2	3
	Israel	1	3	0	1	2	2	1	3
	Angola	1	3	0	1	2	2	1	2
61	Bolivia	3	6	0	5	1	1	1	20
	Kuwait	1	3	0	2	1	1	2	6
	Trinidad & Tobago	1	3	0	2	1	1	0	4
64	El Salvador	2	6	0	6	0	0	1	22
	Canada	1	3	0	3	0	0	0	5
	East Indies	1	1	0	1	0	0	0	6
	Greece	1	3	0	3	0	0	0	10
	Haiti	1	3	0	3	0	0	2	14
	Iraq	1	3	0	3	0	0	1	4
	Slovenia	1	3	0	2	1	0	2	7
	New Zealand	1	3	0	2	1	0	2	12
	UAE	1	3	0	3	0	0	2	11
	China	1	3	0	3	0	0	0	9
	Zaire	1	3	0	3	0	0	0	14
	Serbia & Montenegro	1	3	0	3	0	0	2	10
	Togo	1	3	0	3	0	0	1	6

The United States in the World Cup

While the United States has fielded a national team every year of the World Cup, only seven of those teams have been able to make it past the preliminary competition and qualify for the final World Cup tournament. The 1994 national team automatically qualified because the U.S. served as host of the event for the first time. The U.S. played in three of the first four World Cups (1930, '34 and '50) and each of the last five (1990, '94, '98, 2002 and 2006). The Americans have a record of 6-16-3 in 25 World Cup matches.

1930
1st Round Matches
United States 3 . . . . Belgium 0
United States 3 . . . . Paraguay 0
Semifinals
Argentina 6 . . . . United States 1
U.S. Scoring—Bert Patenaude (3), Bart McGhee (2), James Brown and Thomas Florie.

1934
1st Round Match
Italy 7 . . . . United States 1
U.S. Scoring—Buff Donelli (who later became a noted college and NFL football coach).

1950
1st Round Matches
Spain 3 . . . . United States 1
United States 1 . . . . England 0
Chile 5 . . . . United States 2
U.S. Scoring—Joe Gaetjens, Joe Maca, John Souza and Frank Wallace.

1990
1st Round Matches
Czechoslovakia 5 . . . . United States 1
Italy 1 . . . . United States 0
Austria 2 . . . . United States 1
U.S. Scoring—Paul Caligiuri and Bruce Murray.

1994
1st Round Matches

United States 1 . . . . .Switzerland 1
United States 2 . . . . .Colombia 1
Romania 1 .United States 0

Round of 16

Brazil 1 . . . . .United States 0
U.S. Scoring–Eric Wynalda, Earnie Stewart and own goal
(Colombia defender Andres Escobar).

1998
1st Round Matches

Germany 2 .United States 0
Iran 2 . . . . .United States 1
Yugoslavia 1 . . . . .United States 0
U.S. Scoring–Brian McBride.

2002
1st Round Matches

United States 3 .Portugal 2
United States 1 .So. Korea 1
Poland 3 . . . . .United States 1

Round of 16

United States 2 . . . . Mexico 0

Round of 8

Germany 1 .United States 0
U.S. Scoring– Landon Donovan (2), Brian McBride (2),
John O'Brien, own goal (Portugal defender Jorge Costa) and
Clint Mathis.

2006
1st Round Matches

Czech Republic 3 . . . . .United States 0
Italy 1 . . . . .United States 1
Ghana 2 . . . . .United States 1
U.S. Scoring–own goal (Italian defender Christian Zaccardo), Clint Dempsey.

World Cup Finals

Brazil and Germany (formerly West Germany) have played in the most Cup finals with seven but faced each other for the first time in a final in 2002. Note that a four-team round robin determined the 1950 championship–the deciding game turned out to be the last one of the tournament between Uruguay and Brazil.

1930
Uruguay 4, Argentina 2
(at Montevideo, Uruguay)

		1	2–T
July 30	Uruguay (4-0) 1		3–4
	Argentina (4-1) 2		0–2

Goals: Uruguay–Pablo Dorado (12th minute), Pedro Cea (54th), Santos Iriarte (68th), Castro (89th); Argentina–Carlos Peucelle (20th), Guillermo Stabile (37th).

Uruguay–Ballesteros, Nasazzi, Mascheroni, Andrade, Fernandez, Gestido, Dorado, Scarone, Castro, Cea, Iriarte.

Argentina–Botasso, Della Torre, Paternoster, J. Evaristo, Monti, Suarez, Peucelle, Varallo, Stabile, Ferreira, M. Evaristo.

Attendance: 90,000. **Referee:** Langenus (Belgium).

1934
Italy 2, Czechoslovakia 1 (OT)
(at Rome)

		1	2	OT–T
June 10	Italy (4-0-1) 0		1	1–2
	Czechoslovakia (3-1) 0		0	0–1

Goals: Italy–Raimondo Orsi (80th minute), Angelo Schiavio (95th); Czechoslovakia–Puc (70th).

Italy–Combi, Monzeglio, Allemandi, Ferraris IV, Monti, Bertolini, Guaita, Meazza, Schiavio, Ferrari, Orsi.

Czechoslovakia–Planicka, Zenisek, Ctyroky, Kostalek, Cambal, Krcil, Junek, Svoboda, Sobotka, Nejedly, Puc.

Attendance: 55,000. **Referee:** Eklind (Sweden).

1938
Italy 4, Hungary 2
(at Paris)

		1	2–T
June 19	Italy (4-0) 3		1–4
	Hungary (3-1) 1		1–2

Goals: Italy–Gino Colaussi (5th minute), Silvio Piola (16th), Colaussi (35th), Piola (82nd); Hungary–Titkos (7th), Georges Sarosi (70th).

Italy–Olivieri, Foni, Rava, Serantoni, Andreolo, Locatelli, Biavati, Meazza, Piola, Ferrari, Colaussi.

Hungary–Szabo, Polgar, Biro, Szalay, Szucs, Lazar, Sas, Vincze, G. Sarosi, Szengeller, Titkos.

Attendance: 65,000. **Referee:** Capdeville (France).

1950
Uruguay 2, Brazil 1
(at Rio de Janeiro)

		1	2–T
July 16	Uruguay (3-0-1) 0		2–2
	Brazil (4-1-1) 0		1–1

Goals: Uruguay–Juan Schiaffino (66th minute), Chico Ghiggia (79th); Brazil–Friaca (47th).

Uruguay–Maspoli, M. Gonzales, Tejera, Gambetta, Varela, Andrade, Ghiggia, Perez, Miguez, Schiaffino, Moran.

Brazil–Barbosa, Augusto, Juvenal, Bauer, Danilo, Bigode, Friaça, Zizinho, Ademir, Jair, Chico.

Attendance: 199,854. **Referee:** Reader (England).

DID YOU KNOW?

*Italy won the last **World Cup** (in 1938) before World War II and held the trophy until the return of the tournament in 1950. **Did you know** that during the war Dr. Ottorino Barassi, the Italian Vice President of FIFA, actually hid the World Cup trophy in a shoe box under his bed to save it from falling into the hands of occupying troops?*

World Cup Finals (Cont.)

1954
West Germany 3, Hungary 2
(at Berne, Switzerland)

		1	2–T
July 4	West Germany (4-1)	2	1–3
	Hungary (4-1)	2	0–2

Goals: West Germany–Max Morlock (10th minute), Helmut Rahn (18th), Rahn (84th); Hungary–Ferenc Puskas (4th), Zoltan Czibor (9th).

West Germany–Turek, Posipal, Liebrich, Kohlmeyer, Eckel, Mai, Rahn, Morlock, O. Walter, F. Walter, Schaefer.

Hungary–Grosics, Buzansky, Lorant, Lantos, Bozsik, Zakarias, Czibor, Kocsis, Hidegkuti, Puskas, J. Toth.

Attendance: 60,000. **Referee:** Ling (England).

1958
Brazil 5, Sweden 2
(at Stockholm)

		1	2–T
June 29	Brazil (5-0-1)	2	3–5
	Sweden (4-1-1)	1	1–2

Goals: Brazil–Vava (9th minute), Vava (32nd), Pelé (55th), Mario Zagalo (68th), Pelé (90th); Sweden–Nils Liedholm (3rd), Agne Simonsson (80th).

Brazil–Gilmar, D. Santos, N. Santos, Zito, Bellini, Orlando, Garrincha, Didi, Vava, Pelé, Zagalo.

Sweden–Svensson, Bergmark, Axbom, Boerjesson, Gustavsson, Parling, Hamrin, Gren, Simonsson, Liedholm, Skoglund.

Attendance: 49,737. **Referee:** Guigue (France).

1962
Brazil 3, Czechoslovakia 1
(at Santiago, Chile)

		1	2–T
June 17	Brazil (5-0-1)	1	2–3
	Czechoslovakia (3-2-1)	1	0–1

Goals: Brazil–Amarildo (17th minute), Zito (68th), Vava (77th); Czechoslovakia–Josef Masopust (15th).

Brazil–Gilmar, D. Santos, N. Santos, Zito, Mauro, Zozimo, Garrincha, Didi, Vava, Amarildo, Zagalo.

Czechoslovakia–Schroiff, Tichy, Novak, Pluskal, Popluhar, Masopust, Pospichal, Scherer, Kvasniak, Kadraba, Jelinek.

Attendance: 68,679. **Referee:** Latishev (USSR).

1966
England 4, West Germany 2 (OT)
(at London)

		1	2	OT–T
July 30	England (5-0-1)	1	1	2–4
	West Germany (4-1-1)	1	1	0–2

Goals: England–Geoff Hurst (18th minute), Martin Peters (78th), Hurst (101st), Hurst (120th); West Germany–Helmut Haller (12th), Wolfgang Weber (90th).

England–Banks, Cohen, Wilson, Stiles, J. Charlton, Moore, Ball, Hurst, B. Charlton, Hunt, Peters.

West Germany–Tilkowski, Hottges, Schnellinger, Beckenbauer, Schulz, Weber, Haller, Seeler, Held, Overath, Emmerich.

Attendance: 93,802. **Referee:** Dienst (Switzerland).

1970
Brazil 4, Italy 1
(at Mexico City)

		1	2–T
June 21	Brazil (6-0)	1	3–4
	Italy (3-1-2)	1	0–1

Goals: Brazil–Pelé (18th minute), Gerson (65th), Jairzinho (70th), Carlos Alberto (86th); Italy–Roberto Boninsegna (37th).

Brazil–Felix, C. Alberto, Everaldo, Clodoaldo, Brito, Piazza, Jairzinho, Gerson, Tostão, Pelé, Rivelino.

Italy–Albertosi, Burgnich, Facchetti, Bertini (Juliano, 73rd), Rosato, Cera, Domenghini, Mazzola, Boninsegna (Rivera, 84th), De Sisti, Riva.

Attendance: 107,412. **Referee:** Glockner (E. Germany).

1974
West Germany 2, Netherlands 1
(at Munich)

		1	2–T
July 7	West Germany (6-1)	2	0–2
	Netherlands (5-1-1)	1	0–1

Goals: West Germany–Paul Breitner (25th minute, penalty kick), Gerd Müller (43rd); Netherlands–Johan Neeskens (1st, penalty kick).

West Germany–Maier, Beckenbauer, Vogts, Breitner, Schwarzenbeck, Overath, Bonhof, Hoeness, Grabowski, Muller, Holzenbein.

Netherlands–Jongbloed, Suurbier, Rijsbergen (De Jong, 58th), Krol, Haan, Jansen, Van Hanegem, Neeskens, Rep, Cruyff, Rensenbrink (R. Van de Kerkhof, 46th).

Attendance: 77,833. **Referee:** Taylor (England).

1978
Argentina 3, Netherlands 1 (OT)
(at Buenos Aires)

		1	2	OT–T
June 25	Argentina (5-1-1)	1	0	2–3
	Netherlands (3-2-2)	0	1	0–1

Goals: Argentina–Mario Kempes (37th minute), Kempes (104th), Daniel Bertoni (114th); Netherlands–Dirk Nanninga (81st).

Argentina–Fillol, Olguin, L. Galvan, Passarella, Tarantini, Ardiles (Larrosa, 65th), Gallego, Kempes, Luque, Bertoni, Ortiz (Houseman, 77th).

Netherlands–Jongbloed, Jansen (Suurbier, 72nd), Brandts, Krol, Poortvliet, Haan, Neeskens, W. Van de Kerkhof, R. Van de Kerkhof, Rep (Nanninga, 58th), Rensenbrink.

Attendance: 77,260. **Referee:** Gonella (Italy).

1982
Italy 3, West Germany 1
(at Madrid)

		1	2–T
July 11	Italy (4-0-3)	0	3–3
	West Germany (4-2-1)	0	1–1

Goals: Italy–Paolo Rossi (57th minute), Marco Tardelli (68th), Alessandro Altobelli (81st); West Germany–Paul Breitner (83rd).

Italy–Zoff, Scirea, Gentile, Cabrini, Collovati, Bergomi, Tardelli, Oriali, Conti, Rossi, Graziani (Altobelli, 8th, and Causio, 89th).

West Germany–Schumacher, Stielike, Kaltz, Briegel, K.H. Forster, B. Forster, Breitner, Dremmler (Hrubesch, 61st), Littbarski, Fischer, Rummenigge (Muller, 69th).

Attendance: 90,080. **Referee:** Coelho (Brazil).

1986
Argentina 3, West Germany 2
(at Mexico City)

		1	2–T
June 29	Argentina (6-0-1) 1	2–3
	West Germany (4-2-1) 0	2–2

Goals: Argentina–Jose Brown (22nd minute), Jorge Valdano (55th), Jorge Burruchaga (83rd); West Germany–Karl-Heinz Rummenigge (73rd), Rudi Voller (81st).

Argentina–Pumpido, Cuciuffo, Olarticoechea, Ruggeri, Brown, Batista, Burruchaga (Trobbiani, 89th), Giusti, Enrique, Maradona, Valdano.

West Germany–Schumacher, Jakobs, B. Forster, Berthold, Briegel, Eder, Brehme, Matthaus, Rummenigge, Magath (Hoeness, 61st), Allofs (Voller, 46th).

Attendance: 114,590. **Referee:** Filho (Brazil).

1990
West Germany 1, Argentina 0
(at Rome)

		1	2–T
July 8	West Germany (6-0-1) 0	1–1
	Argentina (4-2-1) 0	0–0

Goals: West Germany–Andreas Brehme (85th minute, penalty kick).

West Germany–Illgner, Berthold (Reuter, 73rd), Kohler, Augenthaler, Buchwald, Brehme, Haessler, Matthaus, Littbarski, Klinsmann, Voller.

Argentina–Goycoechea, Ruggeri (Monzon, 46th), Simon, Serrizuela, Lorenzo, Basualdo, Troglio, Burruchaga (Calderon, 53rd), Sensini, Dezotti, Maradona.

Attendance: 73,603. **Referee:** Codesal (Mexico).

1994
Brazil 0, Italy 0 (Shoot-out)
(at Pasadena, Calif.)

		1	2	OT–T
July 17	Brazil (6-0-1) 0	0	0–0*
	Italy (4-2-1) 0	0	0–0

*Brazil wins shootout, 3-2.

Shootout (five shots each, alternating): ITA–Baresi (miss, 0-0); BRA–Santos (blocked, 0-0); ITA–Albertini (goal, 0-0); BRA–Romario (goal, 1-1); ITA–Evani (goal, 2-1); BRA–Branco (goal, 2-2); ITA–Massaro (blocked, 2-2); BRA–Dunga (goal, 2-3); ITA–R. Baggio (miss, 2-3).

Brazil–Taffarel, Jorginho (Cafu, 21st minute), Branco, Aldair, Santos, Mazinho, Silva, Dunga, Zinho (Viola, 106th), Bebeto, Romario.

Italy–Pagliuca, Mussi (Apolloni, 35th minute), Baresi, Benarrivo, Maldini, Albertini, D. Baggio (Evani, 95th), Berti, Donadoni, R. Baggio, Massaro.

Attendance: 94,194. **Referee:** Puhl (Hungary).

1998
France 3, Brazil 0
(at Paris)

		1	2–	T
July 12	Brazil (6-1) 0	0–	0
	France (7-0) 2	1–	3

Goals: France–Zinedine Zidane (27th and 46th minutes), Petit (92).

Brazil–Taffarel, Cafu, Aldair, Baiano, Carlos, Sampaio (Edmundo, 74th minute), Dunga, Rivaldo, Leonardo (Denilson, 46th minute), Bebeto, Ronaldo.

France–Barthez, Lizarazu, Desailly, Thuram, Leboeuf, Djorkaeff (Viera, 75th minute), Deschamps, Petit, Karembeu (Boghossian, 57th minute), Guivarc'h, Dugarry.

Attendance: 75,000. **Referee:** Belqola (Morocco).

2002
Brazil 2, Germany 0
(at Yokohama, Japan)

		1	2–	T
June 30	Germany (5-2) 0	0–	0
	Brazil (7-0) 0	2–	2

Goals: Brazil–Ronaldo (67th and 79th minutes).

Germany–Kahn, Linke, Ramelow, Neuville, Hamann, Klose (Bierhoff, 74th minute), Jeremies (Asamoah, 77th minute), Bode (Ziege, 84th minute), Schneider, Metzelder, Frings.

Brazil–Marcos, Cafu, Lucio, Junior, Edmilson, Carlos, Silva, Ronaldo (Denilson, 90th minute), Rivaldo, Ronaldinho (Paulista, 85th minute), Kleberson.

Attendance: 69,029. **Referee:** Collina (Italy).

2006
Italy 1, France 1 (Shoot-out)
(at Berlin)

		1	2	OT–	T
July 9	Italy (5-2) 1	0	0–1*
	France (7-0) 1	0	0–1

*Italy wins shootout, 5-4.

Goals: France–Zinedine Zidane (7th minute); Italy—Marco Materazzi (19th).

Shootout (five shots each, alternating): ITA–Pirlo (goal, 1-0); FRA–Wiltord (goal, 1-1); ITA– Materazzi (goal, 2-1); FRA–Trezeguet miss, 1-2); ITA– De Rossi (goal, 3-1); FRA–Abidal (goal, 2-3); ITA– Del Piero (goal, 4-2); FRA–Sagnol (goal, 3-4); ITA–Grosso (goal, 5-3).

Italy–Buffon, Gross, Cannavaro, Gattuso, Toni, Totti (De Rossi, 61st minute), Camoranesi (Del Piero, 86th), Zambrotta, Perrotta (Iaquinta), Pirlo, Materazzi.

France–Barthez, Abidal, Vieira (Diarra, 56th minute), Gallas, Makelele, Malouda, Zidane, Henry (Wiltord 107th), Thuram, Sagnol, Ribery (Trezeguet 100th).

Attendance: 69,000. **Referee:** Elizondo (Argentina).

World Cup Shoot-outs
Introduced in 1982; winning sides in **bold** type.

Year	Round		Final	SO	Year	Round		Final	SO
1982	Semi	**W. Germany** vs. France	3-3	(5-4)	1998	Second	**Argentina** vs. England	2-2	(4-3)
1986	Quarter	**Belgium** vs. Spain	1-1	(5-4)		Quarter	**France** vs. Italy	0-0	(4-3)
	Quarter	**France** vs. Brazil	1-1	(4-3)	2002	Second	**Spain** vs. Ireland	1-1	(3-2)
	Quarter	**W. Germany** vs. Mexico	0-0	(4-1)		Quarter	**So. Korea** vs. Spain	0-0	(5-3)
1990	Second	**Ireland** vs. Romania	0-0	(5-4)	2006	Second	**Ukraine** vs. Switzerland	0-0	(3-0)
	Quarter	**Argentina** vs. Yugoslavia	0-0	(3-2)		Quarter	**Germany** vs. Argentina	1-1	(4-2)
	Semi	**Argentina** vs. Italy	1-1	(4-3)		Quarter	**Portugal** vs. England	0-0	(3-1)
	Semi	**W. Germany** vs. England	1-1	(4-3)		Final	**Italy** vs. France	1-1	(5-3)
1994	Second	**Bulgaria** vs. Mexico	1-1	(3-1)					
	Quarter	**Sweden** vs. Romania	2-2	(5-4)					
	Final	**Brazil** vs. Italy	0-0	(3-2)					

World Cup (Cont.)
Year-by-Year Comparisons

How the 18 World Cup tournaments have compared in nations qualifying, matches played, players participating, goals scored, average goals per game, overall attendance and attendance per game.

Year	Host	Continent	Nations	Matches	Players	Goals Scored	Goals Per Game	Attendance Overall	Attendance Per Game
1930	Uruguay	So. America	13	18	189	70	3.8	589,300	32,739
1934	Italy	Europe	16	17	208	70	4.1	361,000	21,235
1938	France	Europe	15	18	210	84	4.7	376,000	20,889
1942-46	Not held								
1950	Brazil	So. America	13	22	192	88	4.0	1,044,763	47,489
1954	Switzerland	Europe	16	26	233	140	5.3	872,000	33,538
1958	Sweden	Europe	16	35	241	126	3.6	819,402	23,411
1962	Chile	So. America	16	32	252	89	2.8	892,812	27,900
1966	England	Europe	16	32	254	89	2.8	1,464,944	45,780
1970	Mexico	No. America	16	32	270	95	3.0	1,690,890	52,840
1974	West Germany	Europe	16	38	264	97	2.6	1,809,953	47,630
1978	Argentina	So. America	16	38	277	102	2.7	1,685,602	44,358
1982	Spain	Europe	24	52	396	146	2.8	2,108,723	40,552
1986	Mexico	No. America	24	52	414	132	2.5	2,393,031	46,020
1990	Italy	Europe	24	52	413	115	2.2	2,516,354	48,391
1994	United States	No. America	24	52	437	140	2.7	3,587,088	68,982
1998	France	Europe	32	64	704	171	2.7	2,775,400	43,366
2002	Japan/So. Korea	Asia	32	64	736	161	2.5	2,705,197	42,269
2006	Germany	Europe	32	64	736	147	2.3	3,353,655	52,401

OTHER WORLDWIDE COMPETITION

The Olympic Games

Held every four years since 1896, except during World War I (1916) and World War II (1940-44). Soccer was not a medal sport in 1896 at Athens or in 1932 at Los Angeles. By agreement between FIFA and the IOC, Olympic soccer competition is currently limited to players 23 years old and under with a few exceptions.

Multiple winners: England and Hungary (3); Argentina, Soviet Union and Uruguay (2).

MEN

Year	
1900	**England**, France, Belgium
1904	**Canada**, USA I, USA II
1906	**Denmark**, Smyrna (Int'l entry), Greece
1908	**England**, Denmark, Netherlands
1912	**England**, Denmark, Netherlands
1920	**Belgium**, Spain, Netherlands
1924	**Uruguay**, Switzerland, Sweden
1928	**Uruguay**, Argentina, Italy
1936	**Italy**, Austria, Norway
1948	**Sweden**, Yugoslavia, Denmark
1952	**Hungary**, Yugoslavia, Sweden
1956	**Soviet Union**, Yugoslavia, Bulgaria
1960	**Yugoslavia**, Denmark, Hungary

Year	
1964	**Hungary**, Czechoslovakia, Germany
1968	**Hungary**, Bulgaria, Japan
1972	**Poland**, Hungary, East Germany & Soviet Union
1976	**East Germany**, Poland, Soviet Union
1980	**Czechoslovakia**, East Germany, Soviet Union
1984	**France**, Brazil, Yugoslavia
1988	**Soviet Union**, Brazil, West Germany
1992	**Spain**, Poland, Ghana
1996	**Nigeria**, Argentina, Brazil
2000	**Cameroon**, Spain, Chile
2004	**Argentina**, Paraguay, Italy
2008	**Argentina**, Nigeria, Brazil

WOMEN

Multiple winners: United States (3).

Year	
1996	**USA**, China, Norway
2000	**Norway**, USA, Germany

Year	
2004	**USA**, Brazil, Germany
2008	**USA**, Brazil, Germany

The Under-20 World Cup

Held every two years since 1977. Officially, the FIFA World Youth Championship.

Multiple winners: Argentina (6); Brazil (3); Portugal (2).

Year		Year		Year		Year	
1977	Soviet Union	1985	Brazil	1993	Brazil	2001	Argentina
1979	Argentina	1987	Yugoslavia	1995	Argentina	2003	Brazil
1981	West Germany	1989	Portugal	1997	Argentina	2005	Argentina
1983	Brazil	1991	Portugal	1999	Spain	2007	Argentina

The Under-17 World Cup

Held every two years since 1985. Officially, the FIFA U-17 World Championship.
Multiple winners: Brazil and Nigeria (3); Ghana (2).

Year		Year	
1985	Nigeria	1997	Brazil
1987	Soviet Union	1999	Brazil
1989	Saudi Arabia	2001	France
1991	Ghana	2003	Brazil
1993	Nigeria	2005	Mexico
1995	Ghana	2007	Nigeria

Indoor World Championship

First held in 1989. Officially. the FIFA Futsal World Championship.
Multiple winners: Brazil (4), Spain (2).

Year		Year	
1989	Brazil	2000	Spain
1992	Brazil	2004	Spain
1996	Brazil	2008	Brazil

Women's World Cup

First held in 1991. Officially, the FIFA Women's World Championship.
Multiple winner: Germany and United States (2).

Year		Year	
1991	United States	2003	Germany
1995	Norway	2007	Germany
1999	United States		

Confederations Cup

First held in 1992. Contested by the Continental champions of Africa, Asia, Europe, North America and South America and originally called the Intercontinental Championship for the King Fahd Cup until it was redubbed the FIFA/Confederations Cup for the King Fahd Trophy in 1997.
Multiple winners: Brazil and France (2).

Year		Year	
1992	Argentina	2001	France
1995	Denmark	2003	France
1997	Brazil	2005	Brazil
1999	Mexico		

CONTINENTAL COMPETITION

European Championship

Held every four years since 1960. Officially, the European Football Championship. Winners receive the Henri Delaunay trophy, named for the Frenchman who first proposed the idea of a European Soccer Championship in 1927. The first one would not be played until five years after his death in 1955.
Multiple winners: Germany/West Germany (3); France and Spain (2).

Year		Year		Year		Year	
1960	Soviet Union	1976	Czechoslovakia	1988	Netherlands	2000	France
1964	Spain	1980	West Germany	1992	Denmark	2004	Greece
1968	Italy	1984	France	1996	Germany	2008	Spain
1972	West Germany						

Copa America

Held irregularly since 1916. Unofficially, the Championship of South America.
Multiple winners: Argentina and Uruguay (14); Brazil (8); Paraguay and Peru (2).

Year		Year		Year		Year		Year	
1916	Uruguay	1926	Uruguay	1946	Argentina	1963	Bolivia	1995	Uruguay
1917	Uruguay	1927	Argentina	1947	Argentina	1967	Uruguay	1997	Brazil
1919	Brazil	1929	Argentina	1949	Brazil	1975	Peru	1999	Brazil
1920	Uruguay	1935	Uruguay	1953	Paraguay	1979	Paraguay	2001	Colombia
1921	Argentina	1937	Argentina	1955	Argentina	1983	Uruguay	2004	Brazil
1922	Brazil	1939	Peru	1956	Uruguay	1987	Uruguay	2007	Brazil
1923	Uruguay	1941	Argentina	1957	Argentina	1989	Brazil		
1924	Uruguay	1942	Uruguay	1958	Argentina	1991	Argentina		
1925	Argentina	1945	Argentina	1959	Uruguay	1993	Argentina		

African Nations Cup

Contested since 1957 and held every two years since 1968.
Multiple winners: Egypt (6); Cameroon and Ghana (4); Congo/Zaire (3); Nigeria (2).

Year		Year		Year		Year		Year	
1957	Egypt	1970	Sudan	1982	Ghana	1994	Nigeria	2004	Tunisia
1959	Egypt	1972	Congo	1984	Cameroon	1996	South Africa	2006	Egypt
1962	Ethiopia	1974	Zaire	1986	Egypt	1998	Egypt	2008	Egypt
1963	Ghana	1976	Morocco	1988	Cameroon	2000	Cameroon		
1965	Ghana	1978	Ghana	1990	Algeria	2002	Cameroon		
1968	Zaire	1980	Nigeria	1992	Ivory Coast				

CONCACAF Gold Cup

The Confederation of North, Central American and Caribbean Football Championship. Contested irregularly from 1963-81 and revived as CONCACAF Gold Cup in 1991.
Multiple winners: Mexico (7); United States (4); Costa Rica (2).

Year		Year		Year		Year		Year	
1963	Costa Rica	1971	Mexico	1991	United States	2000	Canada	2007	United States
1965	Mexico	1973	Haiti	1993	Mexico	2002	United States		
1967	Guatemala	1977	Mexico	1996	Mexico	2003	Mexico		
1969	Costa Rica	1981	Honduras	1998	Mexico	2005	United States		

CLUB COMPETITION
FIFA Club World Cup

The FIFA Club World Championship merged with the Toyota Cup in 2005. The Toyota Cup held each December in Japan had previously served as the unofficial world club championship and was played between the champions of Europe and South America. But FIFA took over the tournament starting in 2005 and is now open to the champions from the African, Asian, Oceanic and North/Central American soccer federations as well as Europe and South America. From now on the new six-team tournament will be played each December in Japan. Note that FIFA held an eight-team world club championship tournament in 2000 but the tournament was not held again until late 2005 when it officially merged with the Toyota Cup.

Year	**Year**	**Year**	**Year**
2000 Corinthians (Brazil)	2005 São Paulo (Brazil)	2006 Internacional (Brazil)	2007 AC Milan

Toyota Cup

Also known as the **European/South American Cup** and Intercontinental Cup. Until 2005, it was contested annually in December between the winners of the European Champions League (formerly European Cup) and South America's Copa Libertadores for the unofficial World Club Championship. Four European Cup winners refused to participate in the championship match in the 1970s and were replaced each time by the European Cup runner-up: Panathinaikos (Greece) for Ajax Amsterdam (Netherlands) in 1971; Juventus (Italy) for Ajax in 1973; Atlético Madrid (Spain) for Bayern Munich (West Germany) in 1974; and Malmo (Sweden) for Nottingham Forest (England) in 1979. Another European Cup winner, Marseille of France, was prohibited by the Union of European Football Associations (UEFA) from playing for the 1993 Toyota Cup because of its involvement in a match-rigging scandal. Best-of-three game format from 1960-68, then a two-game/total goals format from 1969-79. Toyota became Cup sponsor in 1980, changed the format to a one-game championship and moved it to Toyko.

Multiple winners: AC Milan, Boca Juniors, Nacional, Penarol and Real Madrid (3); Ajax Amsterdam, Bayern Munich, FC Porto, Independiente, Inter Milan, Juventus, Santos and Sao Paulo (2).

Year	**Year**	**Year**
1960 Real Madrid (Spain)	1975 Not held	1990 AC Milan (Italy)
1961 Penarol (Uruguay)	1976 Bayern Munich (W. Germany)	1991 Red Star (Yugoslavia)
1962 Santos (Brazil)	1977 Boca Juniors (Argentina)	1992 Sao Paulo (Brazil)
1963 Santos (Brazil)	1978 Not held	1993 Sao Paulo (Brazil)
1964 Inter Milan (Italy)	1979 Olimpia (Paraguay)	1994 Velez Sarsfield (Argentina)
1965 Inter Milan (Italy)	1980 Nacional (Uruguay)	1995 Ajax Amsterdam (Netherlands)
1966 Penarol (Uruguay)	1981 Flamengo (Brazil)	1996 Juventus (Italy)
1967 Racing Club (Argentina)	1982 Penarol (Uruguay)	1997 Borussia Dortmund (Germany)
1968 Estudiantes (Argentina)	1983 Gremio (Brazil)	1998 Real Madrid (Spain)
1969 AC Milan (Italy)	1984 Independiente (Argentina)	1999 Manchester United (England)
1970 Feyenoord (Netherlands)	1985 Juventus (Italy)	2000 Boca Juniors (Argentina)
1971 Nacional (Uruguay)	1986 River Plate (Argentina)	2001 Bayern Munich (Germany)
1972 Ajax Amsterdam (Netherlands)	1987 FC Porto (Portugal)	2002 Real Madrid (Spain)
1973 Independiente (Argentina)	1988 Nacional (Uruguay)	2003 Boca Juniors (Argentina)
1974 Atlético Madrid (Spain)	1989 AC Milan (Italy)	2004 FC Porto (Portugal)

European Cup/UEFA Champions League

Contested annually since the 1955-56 season by the league champions of the member countries of the Union of European Football Associations (UEFA). In 1999, UEFA announced the formation of a new competition called the UEFA Champions League to take the place of the Cup competition.

Multiple winners: Real Madrid (9); AC Milan (7); Ajax Amsterdam, Bayern Munich and Liverpool (4); Manchester United (3); Barcelona, Benfica, FC Porto, Inter Milan, Juventus and Nottingham Forest (2).

Year	**Year**	**Year**
1956 Real Madrid (Spain)	1974 Bayern Munich (W. Germany)	1992 Barcelona (Spain)
1957 Real Madrid (Spain)	1975 Bayern Munich (W. Germany)	1993 Marseille (France)*
1958 Real Madrid (Spain)	1976 Bayern Munich (W. Germany)	1994 AC Milan (Italy)
1959 Real Madrid (Spain)	1977 Liverpool (England)	1995 Ajax Amsterdam (Netherlands)
1960 Real Madrid (Spain)	1978 Liverpool (England)	1996 Juventus (Italy)
1961 Benfica (Portugal)	1979 Nottingham Forest (England)	1997 Borussia Dortmund (Germany)
1962 Benfica (Portugal)	1980 Nottingham Forest (England)	1998 Real Madrid (Spain)
1963 AC Milan (Italy)	1981 Liverpool (England)	1999 Manchester United (England)
1964 Inter Milan (Italy)	1982 Aston Villa (England)	2000 Real Madrid (Spain)
1965 Inter Milan (Italy)	1983 SV Hamburg (W. Germany)	2001 Bayern Munich (Germany)
1966 Real Madrid (Spain)	1984 Liverpool (England)	2002 Real Madrid (Spain)
1967 Glasgow Celtic (Scotland)	1985 Juventus (Italy)	2003 AC Milan (Italy)
1968 Manchester United (England)	1986 Steaua Bucharest (Romania)	2004 FC Porto (Portugal)
1969 AC Milan (Italy)	1987 FC Porto (Portugal)	2005 Liverpool (England)
1970 Feyenoord (Netherlands)	1988 PSV Eindhoven (Netherlands)	2006 Barcelona (Spain)
1971 Ajax Amsterdam (Netherlands)	1989 AC Milan (Italy)	2007 AC Milan (Italy)
1972 Ajax Amsterdam (Netherlands)	1990 AC Milan (Italy)	2008 Manchester United (England)
1973 Ajax Amsterdam (Netherlands)	1991 Red Star Belgrade (Yugo.)	*title vacated

European Cup Winner's Cup

Contested annually from the 1960-61 season through the 1999-2000 season by the cup winners of the member countries of the Union of European Football Associations (UEFA). The Cup Winner's Cup was absorbed by the UEFA Cup in 2000.

Multiple winners: Barcelona (4); AC Milan, RSC Anderlecht, Chelsea and Dinamo Kiev (2).

Year		Year		Year	
1961	Fiorentina (Italy)	1974	FC Magdeburg (E. Germany)	1987	Ajax Amsterdam (Netherlands)
1962	Atletico Madrid (Spain)	1975	Dinamo Kiev (USSR)	1988	Mechelen (Belgium)
1963	Tottenham Hotspur (England)	1976	RSC Anderlecht (Belgium)	1989	Barcelona (Spain)
1964	Sporting Lisbon (Portugal)	1977	SV Hamburg (W. Germany)	1990	Sampdoria (Italy)
1965	West Ham United (England)	1978	RSC Anderlecht (Belgium)	1991	Manchester United (England)
1966	Borussia Dortmund (W.Germany)	1979	Barcelona (Spain)	1992	Werder Bremen (Germany)
1967	Bayern Munich (W. Germany)	1980	Valencia (Spain)	1993	Parma (Italy)
1968	AC Milan (Italy)	1981	Dinamo Tbilisi (USSR)	1994	Arsenal (England)
1969	Slovan Bratislava (Czech.)	1982	Barcelona (Spain)	1995	Real Zaragoza (Spain)
1970	Manchester City (England)	1983	Aberdeen (Scotland)	1996	Paris St. Germain (France)
1971	Chelsea (England)	1984	Juventus (Italy)	1997	Barcelona (Spain)
1972	Glasgow Rangers (Scotland)	1985	Everton (England)	1998	Chelsea (England)
1973	AC Milan (Italy)	1986	Dinamo Kiev (USSR)	1999	Lazio (Italy)

UEFA Cup

Contested annually since the 1957-58 season by teams other than league champions and cup winners of the Union of European Football Associations (UEFA). Teams selected by UEFA based on each country's previous performance in the tournament. Teams from England were banned from UEFA Cup play from 1985-90 for the criminal behavior of their supporters. In 1999, with the formation of the new Champions League, UEFA announced that the UEFA Cup would be expanded and include any teams that would have normally played in the Cup Winner's Cup.

Multiple winners: Barcelona, Inter Milan, Juventus, Liverpool and Valencia (3); Borussia Mönchengladbach, Feyenoord, IFK Göteborg, Leeds United, Parma, Real Madrid and Tottenham Hotspur (2).

Year		Year		Year	
1958	Barcelona (Spain)	1976	Liverpool (England)	1994	Inter Milan (Italy)
1959	Not held	1977	Juventus (Italy)	1995	Parma (Italy)
1960	Barcelona (Spain)	1978	PSV Eindhoven (Netherlands)	1996	Bayern Munich (Germany)
1961	AS Roma (Italy)	1979	Borussia Mönchengladbach (W.	1997	Schalke 04 (Germany)
1962	Valencia (Spain)		Germany)	1998	Inter Milan (Italy)
1963	Valencia (Spain)	1980	Eintracht Frankfurt (W. Germany)	1999	Parma (Italy)
1964	Real Zaragoza (Spain)	1981	Ipswich Town (England)	2000	Galatasaray (Turkey)
1965	Ferencvaros (Hungary)	1982	IFK Göteborg (Sweden)	2001	Liverpool (England)
1966	Barcelona (Spain)	1983	RSC Anderlecht (Belgium)	2002	Feyenoord (Netherlands)
1967	Dinamo Zagreb (Yugoslavia)	1984	Tottenham Hotspur (England)	2003	FC Porto (Portugal)
1968	Leeds United (England)	1985	Real Madrid (Spain)	2004	Valencia (Spain)
1969	Newcastle United (England)	1986	Real Madrid (Spain)	2005	CSKA Moscow (Russia)
1970	Arsenal (England)	1987	IFK Göteborg (Sweden)	2006	Sevilla (Spain)
1971	Leeds United (England)	1988	Bayer Leverkusen (W. Germany)	2007	Espanyol (Spain)
1972	Tottenham Hotspur (England)	1989	Napoli (Italy)	2008	Zenit St. Petersburg (Russia)
1973	Liverpool (England)	1990	Juventus (Italy)		
1974	Feyenoord (Netherlands)	1991	Inter Milan (Italy)		
1975	Borussia Mönchengladbach (W. Germany)	1992	Ajax Amsterdam (Netherlands)		
		1993	Juventus (Italy)		

Copa Libertadores

Contested annually since the 1955-56 season by the league champions of South America's football union.

Multiple winners: Independiente (7); Boca Juniors and Peñarol (5); Estudiantes, Nacional-Uruguay, Olimpia and São Paulo (3); Cruzeiro, Gremio, River Plate and Santos (2).

Year		Year		Year	
1960	Peñarol (Uruguay)	1977	Boca Juniors (Argentina)	1994	Velez Sarsfield (Argentina)
1961	Peñarol (Uruguay)	1978	Boca Juniors (Argentina)	1995	Gremio (Brazil)
1962	Santos (Brazil)	1979	Olimpia (Paraguay)	1996	River Plate (Argentina)
1963	Santos (Brazil)	1980	Nacional (Uruguay)	1997	Cruzeiro (Brazil)
1964	Independiente (Argentina)	1981	Flamengo (Brazil)	1998	Vasco da Gama (Brazil)
1965	Independiente (Argentina)	1982	Peñarol (Uruguay)	1999	Palmeiras (Brazil)
1966	Peñarol (Uruguay)	1983	Gremio (Brazil)	2000	Boca Juniors (Argentina)
1967	Racing Club (Argentina)	1984	Independiente (Argentina)	2001	Boca Juniors (Argentina)
1968	Estudiantes de la Plata (Argentina)	1985	Argentinos Jrs. (Argentina)	2002	Olimpia (Paraguay)
1969	Estudiantes de la Plata (Argentina)	1986	River Plate (Argentina)	2003	Boca Juniors (Argentina)
1970	Estudiantes de la Plata (Argentina)	1987	Peñarol (Uruguay)	2004	Once Caldas (Colombia)
1971	Nacional (Uruguay)	1988	Nacional (Uruguay)	2005	São Paulo (Brazil)
1972	Independiente (Argentina)	1989	Nacional Medellin (Colombia)	2006	Internacional (Brazil)
1973	Independiente (Argentina)	1990	Olimpia (Paraguay)	2007	Boca Juniors (Argentina)
1974	Independiente (Argentina)	1991	Colo Colo (Chile)	2008	LDU Quito (Ecuador)
1975	Independiente (Argentina)	1992	São Paulo (Brazil)		
1976	Cruzeiro (Brazil)	1993	São Paulo (Brazil)		

Annual Awards
World Player of the Year

Presented by FIFA, the European Sports Magazine Association (ESM) and Adidas, the sports equipment manufacturer, since 1991. Winners are selected by national team coaches and captains from around the world.

Multiple winners: Ronaldo and Zinedine Zidane (3); Ronaldinho (2).

Year		Nat'l Team	Year		Nat'l Team
1991	Lothar Matthäus, Inter Milan	Germany	2000	Zinedine Zidane, Juventus	France
1992	Marco Van Basten, AC Milan	Netherlands	2001	Luis Figo, Real Madrid	Portugal
1993	Roberto Baggio, Juventus	Italy	2002	Ronaldo, Real Madrid	Brazil
1994	Romario, Barcelona	Brazil	2003	Zinedine Zidane, Real Madrid	France
1995	George Weah, AC Milan	Liberia	2004	Ronaldinho, Barcelona	Brazil
1996	Ronaldo, Barcelona	Brazil	2005	Ronaldinho, Barcelona	Brazil
1997	Ronaldo, Inter Milan	Brazil	2006	Fabio Cannavaro, Juventus/Real Madrid	Italy
1998	Zinedine Zidane, Juventus	France	2007	Kaká, AC Milan	Brazil
1999	Rivaldo, Barcelona	Brazil			

Women's World Player of the Year

Presented by FIFA since 2001. Winners are selected by national team coaches from around the world.

Multiple winners: Birgit Prinz (3), Marta and Mia Hamm (2).

Year		Nat'l Team	Year		Nat'l Team
2001	Mia Hamm, Washington Freedom	USA	2005	Birgit Prinz, FFC Frankfurt	Germany
2002	Mia Hamm, Washington Freedom	USA	2006	Marta, Umea IK	Brazil
2003	Birgit Prinz, FFC Frankfurt	Germany	2007	Marta, Umea IK	Brazil
2004	Birgit Prinz, FFC Frankfurt	Germany			

European Player of the Year

Officially, the "Ballon d'Or," or "Golden Ball," and presented by *France Football* magazine since 1956. Candidates were limited to European players in European league suntil 1995 and winners are selected by a poll of European soccer journalists.

Multiple winners: Johan Cruyff, Michel Platini and Marco Van Basten (3); Franz Beckenbauer, Alfredo di Stéfano, Kevin Keegan, Ronaldo and Karl-Heinz Rummenigge (2).

Year		Nat'l Team	Year		Nat'l Team
1956	Stanley Matthews, Blackpool	England	1982	Paolo Rossi, Juventus	Italy
1957	Alfredo di Stéfano, Real Madrid	Arg./Spain	1983	Michel Platini, Juventus	France
1958	Raymond Kopa, Real Madrid	France	1984	Michel Platini, Juventus	France
1959	Alfredo di Stéfano, Real Madrid	Arg./Spain	1985	Michel Platini, Juventus	France
1960	Luis Suarez, Barcelona	Spain	1986	Igor Belanov, Dinamo Kiev	Soviet Union
1961	Enrique Sivori, Juventus	Arg./Italy	1987	Ruud Gullit, AC Milan	Netherlands
1962	Josef Masopust, Dukla Prague	Czech.	1988	Marco Van Basten, AC Milan	Netherlands
1963	Lev Yashin, Dinamo Moscow	Soviet Union	1989	Marco Van Basten, AC Milan	Netherlands
1964	Denis Law, Manchester United	Scotland	1990	Lothar Matthäus, Inter Milan	W. Ger.
1965	Eusébio, Benfica	Portugal	1991	Jean-Pierre Papin, Marseille	France
1966	Bobby Charlton, Manchester United	England	1992	Marco Van Basten, AC Milan	Netherlands
1967	Florian Albert, Ferencvaros	Hungary	1993	Roberto Baggio, Juventus	Italy
1968	George Best, Manchester United	No. Ireland	1994	Hristo Stoitchkov, Barcelona	Bulgaria
1969	Gianni Rivera, AC Milan	Italy	1995	George Weah, AC Milan	Liberia
1970	Gerd Müller, Bayern Munich	W. Ger.	1996	Matthias Sammer, Bor. Dortmund	Germany
1971	Johan Cruyff, Ajax Amsterdam	Netherlands	1997	Ronaldo, Inter Milan	Brazil
1972	Franz Beckenbauer, Bayern Munich	W. Ger.	1998	Zinedine Zidane, Juventus	France
1973	Johan Cruyff, Barcelona	Netherlands	1999	Rivaldo, Barcelona	Brazil
1974	Johan Cruyff, Barcelona	Netherlands	2000	Luis Figo, Real Madrid	Portugal
1975	Oleg Blokhin, Dinamo Kiev	Soviet Union	2001	Michael Owen, Liverpool	England
1976	Franz Beckenbauer, Bayern Munich	W. Ger.	2002	Ronaldo, Real Madrid	Brazil
1977	Allan Simonsen, B. Mönchengladbach	Denmark	2003	Pavel Nedved, Juventus	Czech Republic
1978	Kevin Keegan, SV Hamburg	England	2004	Andriy Schevchenko, AC Milan	Ukraine
1979	Kevin Keegan, SV Hamburg	England	2005	Ronaldinho, Barcelona	Brazil
1980	K.H. Rummenigge, Bayern Munich	W. Ger.	2006	Fabio Cannavaro, Juventus/Real Madrid	Italy
1981	K.H. Rummenigge, Bayern Munich	W. Ger.	2007	Kaká, AC Milan	Brazil

U.S. Player of the Year

Presented by Honda and the Spanish-speaking radio show "Futbol de Primera" since 1991. Candidates are limited to American players who have played with the U.S. National Team and winners are selected by a panel of U.S. soccer journalists.

Multiple winners: Landon Donovan (4); Clint Dempsey and Eric Wynalda (2).

Year		Year		Year		Year	
1991	Hugo Perez	1996	Eric Wynalda	2001	Earnie Stewart	2006	Clint Dempsey
1992	Eric Wynalda	1997	Eddie Pope	2002	Landon Donovan	2007	Landon Donovan
1993	Thomas Dooley	1998	Cobi Jones	2003	Landon Donovan		
1994	Marcelo Balboa	1999	Kasey Keller	2004	Landon Donovan		
1995	Alexi Lalas	2000	Claudio Reyna	2005	Clint Dempsey		

South American Player of the Year

Presented by *El Mundo* of Venezuela from 1971-1985 and *El Pais* of Uruguay since 1986. Candidates are limited to South American players in South American or Mexican leagues and winners are selected by a poll of South American sports editors.

Multiple winners: Elias Figueroa, Carlos Tevez and Zico (3); Enzo Francescoli, Diego Maradona and Carlos Valderrama (2).

Year		Nat'l Team	Year		Nat'l Team
1971	Tostao, Cruzeiro	Brazil	1990	Raul Amarilla, Olimpia	Paraguay
1972	Teofilo Cubillas, Alianza Lima	Peru	1991	Oscar Ruggeri, Velez Sarsfield	Argentina
1973	Pelé, Santos	Brazil	1992	Rai, Sao Paulo	Brazil
1974	Elias Figueroa, Internacional	Chile	1993	Carlos Valderrama, Atl. Junior	Colombia
1975	Elias Figueroa, Internacional	Chile	1994	Cafu, Sao Paulo	Brazil
1976	Elias Figueroa, Internacional	Chile	1995	Enzo Francescoli, River Plate	Uruguay
1977	Zico, Flamengo	Brazil	1996	Jose Luis Chilavert, Velez Sarsfield	Paraguay
1978	Mario Kempes, Valencia	Argentina	1997	Marcelo Salas, River Plate	Chile
1979	Diego Maradona, Argentinos Juniors	Argentina	1998	Martin Palermo, Boca Juniors	Argentina
1980	Diego Maradona, Boca Juniors	Argentina	1999	Javier Saviola, River Plate	Argentina
1981	Zico, Flamengo	Brazil	2000	Romario, Vasco da Gama	Brazil
1982	Zico, Flamengo	Brazil	2001	Juan Roman Riquelme, Boca Juniors	Argentina
1983	Socrates, Corinthians	Brazil	2002	Jose Cardozo, Toluca	Paraguay
1984	Enzo Francescoli, River Plate	Uruguay	2003	Carlos Tevez, Boca Juniors	Argentina
1985	Julio Cesar Romero, Fluminense	Paraguay	2004	Carlos Tevez, Boca Juniors	Argentina
1986	Antonio Alzamendi, River Plate	Uruguay	2005	Carlos Tevez, Corinthians	Argentina
1987	Carlos Valderrama, Deportivo Cali	Colombia	2006	Matias Fernandez, Colo Coco	Chile
1988	Ruben Paz, Racing Buenos Aires	Uruguay	2007	Salvador Cabañas, America	Mexico
1989	Bebeto, Vasco da Gama	Brazil			

Asian Player of the Year

Presented by the Asian Football Confederation since 1994. Prior to 1994 it was awarded unoffically.

Multiple winners: Kim Joo-Sung (3); Hidetoshi Nakata (2).

Year		Year		Year	
1988	Ahmed Radhi, Iraq	1995	Masami Ihara, Japan	2002	Shinji Ono, Japan
1989	Kim Joo-Sung, South Korea	1996	Khodadad Azizi, Iran	2003	Mehdi Mahdavikia, Iran
1990	Kim Joo-Sung, South Korea	1997	Hidetoshi Nakata, Japan	2004	Ali Karimi, Iran
1991	Kim Joo-Sung, South Korea	1998	Hidetoshi Nakata, Japan	2005	Hamad Al-Montashari, S. Arabia
1992	no award	1999	Ali Daei, Iran	2006	Khalfan Ibrahim, Qatar
1993	Kazuyoshi Miura, Japan	2000	Nawaf Al-Temyat, S. Arabia	2007	Yasser Al-Qahtani, S. Arabia
1994	Saeed Al-Owairan, S. Arabia	2001	Fan Zhiyi, China		

African Player of the Year

Officially, the African "Ballon d'Or" and presented by *France Football* magazine from 1970-96. The African Player of the Year award has been presented by the CAF (African Football Confederation) since 1997. All African players are eligible for the award.

Multiple winners: George Weah and Abedi Pelé (3); El Hadji Diouf, Samuel Eto'o, Nwankwo Kanu, Roger Milla and Thomas N'Kono (2).

Year		Year		Year	
1970	Salif Keita, Mali	1983	Mahmoud Al-Khatib, Egypt	1996	Nwankwo Kanu, Nigeria
1971	Ibrahim Sunday, Ghana	1984	Theophile Abega, Cameroon	1997	Victor Ikpeba, Nigeria
1972	Cherif Souleymane, Guinea	1985	Mohamed Timoumi, Morocco	1998	Mustapha Hadji, Morocco
1973	Tshimimu Bwanga, Zaire	1986	Badou Zaki, Morocco	1999	Nwankwo Kanu, Nigeria
1974	Paul Moukila, Congo	1987	Rabah Madjer, Algeria	2000	Patrick Mboma, Cameroon
1975	Ahmed Faras, Morocco	1988	Kalusha Bwalya, Zambia	2001	El Hadji Diouf, Senegal
1976	Roger Milla, Cameroon	1989	George Weah, Liberia	2002	El Hadji Diouf, Senegal
1977	Dhiab Tarak, Tunisia	1990	Roger Milla, Cameroon	2003	Samuel Eto'o, Cameroon
1978	Abdul Razak, Ghana	1991	Abedi Pelé, Ghana	2004	Samuel Eto'o, Cameroon
1979	Thomas N'Kono, Cameroon	1992	Abedi Pelé, Ghana	2005	Samuel Eto'o, Cameroon
1980	Jean Manga Onguene, Cameroon	1993	Abedi Pelé, Ghana	2006	Didier Drogba, Ivory Coast
1981	Lakhdar Belloumi, Algeria	1994	George Weah, Liberia	2007	Frédéric Kanouté, Mali
1982	Thomas N'Kono, Cameroon	1995	George Weah, Liberia		

U.S. PRO LEAGUES

OUTDOOR
Major League Soccer

Sanctioned by U.S. Soccer and FIFA, the international soccer federation. MLS was founded on the heels of the successful 1994 World Cup tournament hosted by the United States and it remains the only FIFA-sanctioned division I outdoor league in the United States. The annual MLS title game is known as the MLS Cup.

Multiple winners: D.C. United (4); Houston, Los Angeles and San Jose (2).

MLS Cup

Year	Winner	Head Coach	Score	Loser	Head Coach	Site
1996	D.C. United	Bruce Arena	3-2 OT	Los Angeles Galaxy	Lothar Osiander	Foxboro, Mass.
1997	D.C. United	Bruce Arena	2-1	Colorado Rapids	Glen Myernick	Washington, D.C.
1998	Chicago Fire	Bob Bradley	2-0	D.C. United	Bruce Arena	Pasadena, Calif.
1999	D.C. United	Thomas Rongen	2-0	Los Angeles Galaxy	Sigi Schmid	Foxboro, Mass.
2000	Kansas City Wizards	Bob Gansler	1-0	Chicago Fire	Bob Bradley	Washington, D.C.
2001	San Jose Earthquakes	Frank Yallop	2-1 OT	Los Angeles Galaxy	Sigi Schmid	Columbus, Ohio
2002	Los Angeles Galaxy	Sigi Schmid	1-0 2OT	N.E. Revolution	Steve Nicol	Foxboro, Mass.
2003	San Jose Earthquakes	Frank Yallop	4-2	Chicago Fire	Dave Sarachan	Carson, Calif.
2004	D.C. United	Peter Nowak	3-2	Kansas City Wizards	Bob Gansler	Carson, Calif.
2005	Los Angeles Galaxy	Steve Sampson	1-0 OT	N.E. Revolution	Steve Nicol	Frisco, Texas
2006	Houston Dynamo	Dominic Kinnear	1-1 2OT*	N.E. Revolution	Steve Nicol	Frisco, Texas
2007	Houston Dynamo	Dominic Kinnear	2-1	N.E. Revolution	Steve Nicol	Washington, D.C.

*Dynamo won on penalty kicks, 4-3.

MLS Cup '96
D.C. United, 3-2 (OT)
Oct. 20 at Foxboro Stadium, Foxboro, Mass.
Attendance: 34,643

	1	2	OT	
Los Angeles Galaxy	1	1	0	—2
D.C. United	0	2	1	—3

First Half: LA–Eduardo Hurtado (Mauricio Cienfuegos), 5th minute.
Second Half: LA–Chris Armas (unassisted), 56th; DC–Tony Sanneh (Marco Etcheverry), 73rd; DC–Shawn Medved (unassisted), 82nd.
Overtime: DC–Eddie Pope (Etcheverry), 94th.
MVP: Marco Etcheverry, D.C. United, Midfielder

MLS Cup '97
D.C. United, 2-1
Oct. 26 at RFK Stadium, Washington, D.C.
Attendance: 57,431

	1	2	
Colorado Rapids	0	1	—1
D.C. United	1	1	—2

First Half: DC–Jaime Moreno (Tony Sanneh, David Vaudreuil), 37th minute.
Second Half: DC–Sanneh (John Harkes, Richie Williams), 68th; COL–Adrian Paz (David Patino, Matt Kmosko), 75th.
MVP: Jaime Moreno, D.C. United, Forward

MLS Cup '98
Chicago Fire, 2-0
Oct. 25 at the Rose Bowl, Pasadena, Calif.
Attendance: 51,350

	1	2	
D.C. United	0	0	—0
Chicago	2	0	—2

First Half: CHI–Jerzy Podbrozny (Peter Nowak, Ante Razov), 29th minute; CHI–Diego Gutierrez (Nowak), 45th.
MVP: Nowak, Chicago, Midfielder

MLS Cup '99
D.C. United, 2-0
Nov. 21 at Foxboro Stadium, Foxboro, Mass.
Attendance: 44,910

	1	2	
D.C. United	2	0	—2
Los Angeles	0	0	—0

First Half: DC–Jaime Moreno (Roy Lassiter), 19th minute; DC–Ben Olsen (unassisted), 48th
MVP: Olsen, D.C. United, Midfielder

MLS Cup 2000
Kansas City Wizards, 1-0
Oct. 15 at RFK Stadium, Washington, D.C.
Attendance: 39,159

	1	2	
Chicago	0	0	—0
Kansas City	1	0	—1

First Half: DC– Miklos Molnar (Chris Klein), 11th minute.
MVP: Tony Meola, Kansas City, Goalkeeper

MLS Cup 2001
San Jose Earthquakes, 2-1 (OT)
Oct. 21 at Crew Stadium, Columbus, Ohio
Attendance: 21,626

	1	2	OT	
San Jose	1	0	1	—2
Los Angeles	1	0	0	—1

First Half: LA–Luis Hernandez (Greg Vanney, Kevin Hartman), 21st minute; SJ–Landon Donovan (Ian Russell, Richard Mulrooney), 43rd. **Overtime:** SJ–Dwayne DeRosario (Ronnie Ekelund, Zak Ibsen), 96th.
MVP: Dwayne DeRosario, San Jose, Forward

MLS Cup 2002
Los Angeles Galaxy, 1-0 (2 OT)
Oct. 20 at Gillette Stadium, Foxboro, Mass.
Attendance: 61,316

	1	2	1OT	2OT	
Los Angeles	0	0	0	1	—1
New England	0	0	0	0	—0

2nd OT: LA–Carlos Ruiz, (Tyrone Marshall, Chris Albright), 113th minute.
MVP: Carlos Ruiz, Los Angeles, F

MLS Cup 2003
San Jose Earthquakes, 4-2
Nov. 23 at Home Depot Center, Carson, Calif.
Attendance: 27,000

	1	2	
San Jose	.2	2	—4
Chicago	.0	2	—2

First Half: SJ– Ronnie Ekelund (unassisted), 5th minute; SJ–Landon Donovan (Jamil Walker), 38th.

Second Half: CHI–DaMarcus Beasley (Andy Williams), 49th; SJ–Richard Mulrooney (Craig Waibel), 50th; CHI–own goal (Chris Roner), 54th; SJ–Donovan (Dwayne De Rosario, Brian Mullan), 71st.

MVP: Landon Donovan, San Jose, F

MLS Cup 2004
D.C. United, 3-2
Nov. 14 at Home Depot Center, Carson, Calif.
Attendance: 25,797

	1	2	
D.C. United	.3	0	—3
Kansas City	.1	1	—2

First Half: KC– Jose Burciaga Jr. (unassisted), 6th minute; DC–Alecko Eskandarian (Brian Carroll), 19th. DC–Alecko Eskandarian (unassisted), 23rd. DC–own goal (Alex Zotinca), 26th.

Second Half: KC–Josh Wolff (penalty kick), 58th.

MVP: Alecko Eskandarian, D.C. United, F

MLS Cup 2005
Los Angeles Galaxy, 1-0 (OT)
Nov. 13 at Pizza Hut Park, Frisco, Texas
Attendance: 21,193

	1	2	OT	
Los Angeles	.1	0	1	—1
New England	.0	0	0	—0

Overtime: LA–Guillermo Ramirez (unassisted), 107th.
MVP: Guillermo "Pando" Ramirez, Los Angeles, F

MLS Cup 2006
Houston Dynamo, 1-1, won on PKs, 4-3
Nov. 12 at Pizza Hut Park, Frisco, Texas
Attendance: 22,427

	1	2	OT	2OT	
New England	.0	.0	0	1	—1
Houston	.0	.0	0	1	—1

2nd Overtime: NE–Taylor Twellman, 113th. HOU–Brian Ching, 114th. **MVP:** Brian Ching, Houston, F

MLS Cup 2007
Houston Dynamo, 2-1
Nov. 18 at RFK Stadium, Washington, D.C.
Attendance: 39,859

	1	2	
Houston	.0	2	—2
New England	.1	0	—1

First Half: NE–Taylor Twellman, 20th.
Second Half: HOU–Ngwenya 61st; De Rosario, 74th.
MVP: Dwayne De Rosario, Houston, MF

Regular Season

Most Valuable Player
1996 Carlos Valderrama, Tampa Bay
1997 Preki, Kansas City
1998 Marco Etcheverry, D.C.
1999 Jason Kreis, Dallas
2000 Tony Meola, Kansas City
2001 Alex Pineda Chacón, Miami
2002 Carlos Ruiz, LA
2003 Preki, Kansas City
2004 Amado Guevara, MetroStars
2005 Taylor Twellman, New England
2006 Christian Gomez, D.C. United
2007 Luciano Emilio, D.C. United

Coach of the Year
1996 Thomas Rongen, Tampa Bay
1997 Bruce Arena, D.C.
1998 Bob Bradley, Chicago
1999 Sigi Schmid, Los Angeles
2000 Bob Gansler, Kansas City
2001 Frank Yallop, San Jose
2002 Steve Nicol, New England
2003 Dave Sarachan, Chicago
2004 Greg Andrulis, Columbus
2005 Dominic Kinnear, San Jose
2006 Bob Bradley, Chivas USA
2007 Preki, Chivas USA

Defender of the Year
1996 John Doyle, San Jose
1997 Eddie Pope, D.C.
1998 Lubos Kubik, Chicago
1999 Robin Fraser, Los Angeles
2000 Peter Vermes, Kansas City
2001 Jeff Agoos, San Jose
2002 Carlos Bocanegra, Chicago
2003 Carlos Bocanegra, Chicago
2004 Robin Fraser, Columbus
2005 Jimmy Conrad, Kansas City
2006 Bobby Bosewell, D.C. United
2007 Michael Parkhurst, New-England

Leading Scorer

	G	A	Pts
1996 Roy Lassiter, Tampa Bay	.27	4	58
1997 Preki, Kansas City	.12	17	41
1998 Stern John, Columbus	.26	5	57
1999 Jason Kreis, Dallas	.18	15	51
2000 Mamadou Diallo, Tampa Bay	.26	4	56
2001 Alex Pineda Chacón, Miami	.19	9	47
2002 Taylor Twellman, New England	.23	6	52
2003 Preki, Kansas City	.12	17	41
2004 Pat Noonan, New England	.11	8	30
& Amado Guevara, MetroStars	.10	10	30
2005 Taylor Twellman, New England	.17	7	41
2006 Jeff Cunningham, Real Salt Lake	.16	11	43
2007 Luciano Emilio, D.C. United	.20	1	41

Goalkeeper of the Year
1996 Mark Dodd, Dallas
1997 Brad Friedel, Columbus
1998 Zach Thornton, Chicago
1999 Kevin Hartman, Los Angeles
2000 Tony Meola, Kansas City
2001 Tim Howard, MetroStars
2002 Joe Cannon, San Jose
2003 Pat Onstad, San Jose
2004 Joe Cannon, Colorado
2005 Pat Onstad, San Jose
2006 Troy Perkins, D.C. United
2007 Brad Guzan, Chivas USA

Rookie of the Year
1996 Steve Ralston, Tampa Bay
1997 Mike Duhaney, Tampa Bay
1998 Ben Olsen, D.C.
1999 Jay Heaps, Miami
2000 Carlos Bocanegra, Chicago
2001 Rodrigo Faria, MetroStars
2002 Kyle Martino, Columbus
2003 Damani Ralph, Chicago
2004 Clint Dempsey, New England
2005 Michael Parkhurst, New England
2006 Jonathan Bornstein, Chivas USA
2007 Maurice Edu, Toronto FC

Other U.S. Pro Leagues (Cont.)
National Professional Soccer League (1967)

Not sanctioned by FIFA, the international soccer federation. The NPSL recruited individual players to fill the rosters of its 10 teams. The league lasted only one season.

	Playoff Final			**Regular Season**			
Year	Winner	Scores	Loser	Leading Scorer	G	A	Pts
1967	Oakland Clippers	0-1, 4-1	Baltimore Bays	Yanko Daucik, Toronto 20		8	48

United Soccer Association (1967)

Sanctioned by FIFA. Originally called the North American Soccer League, it became the USA to avoid being confused with the National Professional Soccer League (see above). Instead of recruiting individual players, the USA imported 12 entire teams from Europe to represent its 12 franchises. It, too, only lasted a season. The league champion Los Angeles Wolves were actually Wolverhampton of England and the runner-up Washington Whips were Aberdeen of Scotland.

	Playoff Final			**Regular Season**			
Year	Winner	Score	Loser	Leading Scorer	G	A	Pts
1967	Los Angeles Wolves	6-5 (OT)	Washington Whips	Roberto Boninsegna, Chicago 10		1	21

North American Soccer League (1968-84)

The NPSL and USA merged to form the NASL in 1968 and the new league lasted through 1984. The NASL championship was known as the Soccer Bowl from 1975-84. One game decided the NASL title every year but five. There were no playoffs in 1969; a two-game/aggregate goals format was used in 1968 and '70; and a best-of-three games format was used in 1971 and '84; (*) indicates overtime and (†) indicates game decided by shootout.

Multiple winners: NY Cosmos (5); Chicago (2).

	Playoff Final			**Regular Season**			
Year	Winner	Score(s)	Loser	Leading Scorer	G	A	Pts
1968	Atlanta Chiefs	0-0, 3-0	San Diego Toros	John Kowalik, Chicago 30		9	69
1969	Kansas City Spurs	No game	Atlanta Chiefs	Kaiser Motaung, Atlanta 16		4	36
1970	Rochester Lancers	3-0,1-3	Washington Darts	Kirk Apostolidis, Dallas 16		3	35
1971	Dallas Tornado	1-2*, 4-1,2-0	Atlanta Chiefs	Carlos Metidieri, Rochester 19		8	46
1972	New York Cosmos	2-1	St. Louis Stars	Randy Horton, New York 9		4	22
1973	Philadelphia Atoms	2-0	Dallas Tornado	Kyle Rote Jr., Dallas 10		10	30
1974	Los Angeles Aztecs	3-3†	Miami Toros	Paul Child, San Jose 15		6	36
1975	Tampa Bay Rowdies	2-0	Portland Timbers	Steve David, Miami 23		6	52
1976	Toronto Metros	3-0	Minnesota Kicks	Giorgio Chinaglia, New York 19		11	49
1977	New York Cosmos	2-1	Seattle Sounders	Steve David, Los Angeles 26		6	58
1978	New York Cosmos	3-1	Tampa Bay Rowdies	Giorgio Chinaglia, New York 34		11	79
1979	Vancouver Whitecaps	2-1	Tampa Bay Rowdies	Oscar Fabbiani, Tampa Bay 25		8	58
1980	New York Cosmos	3-0	Ft. Laud. Strikers	Giorgio Chinaglia, New York 32		13	77
1981	Chicago Sting	0-0†	New York Cosmos	Giorgio Chinaglia, New York 29		16	74
1982	New York Cosmos	1-0	Seattle Sounders	Giorgio Chinaglia, New York 20		15	55
1983	Tulsa Roughnecks	2-0	Toronto Blizzard	Roberto Cabanas, New York 25		16	66
1984	Chicago Sting	2-1,3-2	Toronto Blizzard	Steve Zungul, Golden Bay 20		10	50

Note: In 1969, Kansas City won the NASL regular season championship with 110 points to 109 for Atlanta. There were no playoffs.

Regular Season MVP
Regular season Most Valuable Player as designated by the NASL.

Multiple winner: Carlos Metidieri (2).

Year	Year	Year
1967 Rueben Navarro, Phila (NPSL)	1973 Warren Archibald, Miami	1979 Johan Cruyff, Los Angeles
1968 John Kowalik, Chicago	1974 Peter Silvester, Baltimore	1980 Roger Davies, Seattle
1969 Cirilio Fernandez, KC	1975 Steve David, Miami	1981 Giorgio Chinaglia, New York
1970 Carlos Metidieri, Rochester	1976 Pelé, New York	1982 Peter Ward, Seattle
1971 Carlos Metidieri, Rochester	1977 Franz Beckenbauer, New York	1983 Roberto Cabanas, New York
1972 Randy Horton, New York	1978 Mike Flanagan, New England	1984 Steve Zungul, Golden Bay

USL First Division/A-League

The American Professional Soccer League was formed in 1990 with the merger of the Western Soccer League and the New American Soccer League. The APSL was officially sanctioned as an outdoor pro league in 1992 and changed its name to the A-League in 1995. The league was reorganized under the umbrella of the United Soccer Leagues and renamed the USL First Division in 2005.

Multiple winners: Seattle (4); Rochester (3); Colorado, Milwaukee and Montreal (2).

Year	Year	Year
1990 Maryland Bays	1996 Seattle Sounders	2002 Milwaukee Rampage
1991 SF Bay Blackhawks	1997 Milwaukee Rampage	2003 Charleston Battery
1992 Colorado Foxes	1998 Rochester Rhinos	2004 Montreal Impact
1993 Colorado Foxes	1999 Minnesota Thunder	2005 Seattle Sounders
1994 Montreal Impact	2000 Rochester Rhinos	2006 Vancouver Whitecaps
1995 Seattle Sounders	2001 Rochester Rhinos	2007 Seattle Sounders

Women's United Soccer Association (2001-03)

The eight-team WUSA was formed in 2000 as the top women's outdoor professional league and play began in 2001. The league championship game is known as the Founders Cup. The league folded following the 2003 season.

Founders Cup

Year	Winner	Score	Loser	Site
2001	Bay Area CyberRays	3-3*	Atlanta Beat	Foxboro, Mass.
2002	Carolina Courage	3-2	Washington Freedom	Atlanta, Ga.
2003	Washington Freedom	2-1 OT	Atlanta Beat	San Diego, Calif.

*Bay Area won shoot-out, 4-2.

Regular Season

WUSA Most Valuable Player

2001 Tiffeny Milbrett, New York
2002 Marinette Pichon, Philadelphia
2003 Maren Meinert, Boston

WUSA Leading Scorer

		G	A	Pts
2001	Tiffeny Milbrett, New York	16	3	35
2002	Katia, San Jose	15	5	35
2003	Mia Hamm, Washington	11	11	33
	& Abby Wambach, Washington	13	7	33

INDOOR
Major Soccer League (1978-92)

Originally the Major Indoor Soccer League from 1978-79 season through 1989-90. The MISL championship was decided by one game in 1980 and 1981; a best-of-three games series in 1979, best-of-five games in 1982 and 1983; and best-of-seven games since 1984. The MSL folded after the 1991-92 season.

Multiple winners: San Diego (8); New York (4).

Playoff Final

Year	Winner	Series	Loser
1979	New York Arrows	2-0	Philadelphia
1980	New York Arrows	7-4 (1 game)	Houston
1981	New York Arrows	6-5 (1 game)	St. Louis
1982	New York Arrows	3-2 (LWWLW)	St. Louis
1983	San Diego Sockers	3-2 (WWLLW)	Baltimore
1984	Baltimore Blast	4-1 (LWWWW)	St. Louis
1985	San Diego Sockers	4-1 (WWWLW)	Baltimore
1986	San Diego Sockers	4-3 (WLLLWWW)	Minnesota
1987	Dallas Sidekicks	4-3 (LLWWLWW)	Tacoma
1988	San Diego Sockers	4-0	Cleveland
1989	San Diego Sockers	4-3 (LWWWLLW)	Baltimore
1990	San Diego Sockers	4-2 (LWWWLW)	Baltimore
1991	San Diego Sockers	4-2 (WLWLWW)	Cleveland
1992	San Diego Sockers	4-2 (WWWLLW)	Dallas

Regular Season

Leading Scorer	G	A	Pts
Fred Grgurev, Philadelphia	46	28	74
Steve Zungul, New York	90	46	136
Steve Zungul, New York	108	44	152
Steve Zungul, New York	103	60	163
Steve Zungul, NY/Golden Bay	75	47	122
Stan Stamenkovic, Baltimore	34	63	97
Steve Zungul, San Diego	68	68	136
Steve Zungul, Tacoma	55	60	115
Tatu, Dallas	73	38	111
Eric Rasmussen, Wichita	55	57	112
Preki, Tacoma	51	53	104
Tatu, Dallas	64	49	113
Tatu, Dallas	78	66	144
Zoran Karic, Cleveland	39	63	102

Playoff MVPs

MSL playoff Most Valuable Players, selected by a panel of soccer media covering the playoffs.

Multiple winners: Steve Zungul (4); Brian Quinn (2).

Year		Year	
1979	Shep Messing, NY	1986	Brian Quinn, SD
1980	Steve Zungul, NY	1987	Tatu, Dallas
1981	Steve Zungul, NY	1988	Hugo Perez, SD
1982	Steve Zungul, NY	1989	Victor Nogueira, SD
1983	Juli Veee, SD	1990	Brian Quinn, SD
1984	Scott Manning, Bal.	1991	Ben Collins, SD
1985	Steve Zungul, SD	1992	Thompson Usiyan, SD

Regular Season MVPs

MSL regular-season Most Valuable Players, selected by a panel of soccer media from every city in the league.

Multiple winners: Steve Zungul (6); Victor Nogueira and Tatu (2).

Year		Year	
1979	Steve Zungul, NY	1986	Steve Zungul, SD/Tac.
1980	Steve Zungul, NY	1987	Tatu, Dallas
1981	Steve Zungul, NY	1988	Erik Rasmussen, Wich.
1982	Steve Zungul, NY	1989	Preki, Tacoma
	& Stan Terlecki, Pit.	1990	Tatu, Dallas
1983	Alan Mayer, SD	1991	Victor Nogueira, SD
1984	Stan Stamenkovic, Bal.	1992	Victor Nogueira, SD
1985	Steve Zungul, SD		

NASL Indoor Champions (1980-84)

The North American Soccer League started an indoor league in the fall of 1979. The indoor NASL, which featured many of the same teams and players who played in the outdoor NASL, crowned champions from 1980-82 before suspending play. It was revived for the 1983-84 indoor season but folded for good in 1984. The NASL held indoor tournaments in 1975 (San Jose Earthquakes won) and 1976 (Tampa Bay Rowdies won) before the indoor league was started.

Multiple winner: San Diego (2).

Year		Year		Year		Year	
1980	Tampa Bay Rowdies	1982	San Diego Sockers	1983	Play suspended	1984	San Diego Sockers
1981	Edmonton Drillers						

Major Indoor Soccer League (1984-2008)

The winter indoor MISL began as the American Indoor Soccer Association in 1984-85, then changed its name to the National Professional Soccer League in 1989-90 and was known as the NPSL until 2001 when the name was changed again and the league was relaunched as the MISL. The league ceased operation in May of 2008.

Multiple winners: Canton (5); Baltimore and Milwaukee (4); Cleveland (3); Kansas City and Philadelphia (2).

Year		Year		Year		Year	
1985	Canton (OH) Invaders	1991	Chicago Power	1997	Kansas City Attack	2003	Baltimore Blast
1986	Canton Invaders	1992	Detroit Rockers	1998	Milwaukee Wave	2004	Baltimore Blast
1987	Louisville Thunder	1993	Kansas City Attack	1999	Cleveland Crunch	2005	Milwaukee Wave
1988	Canton Invaders	1994	Cleveland Crunch	2000	Milwaukee Wave	2006	Baltimore Blast
1989	Canton Invaders	1995	St. Louis Ambush	2001	Milwaukee Wave	2007	Philadelphia Kixx
1990	Canton Invaders	1996	Cleveland Crunch	2002	Philadelphia Kixx	2008	Baltimore Blast

Continental Indoor Soccer League (1993-97)

The summer indoor CISL played its first season in 1993 and folded following the 1997 season.

Multiple winner: Monterrey (2).

Year		Year		Year	
1993	Dallas Sidekicks	1995	Monterrey La Raza	1997	Seattle Seadogs
1994	Las Vegas Dustdevils	1996	Monterrey La Raza		

U.S. COLLEGES

NCAA Men's Division I Champions

NCAA Division I champions since the first title was contested in 1959. The championship has been shared three times—in 1967, 1968 and 1989. There was a playoff for third place from 1974-81.

Multiple winners: Saint Louis (10); Indiana (7); San Francisco and Virginia (5); UCLA (4); Clemson, Connecticut, Howard and Michigan St. (2).

Year	Winner	Head Coach	Score	Runner-up	Host/Site	Semifinalists
1959	Saint Louis	Bob Guelker	5-2	Bridgeport	Connecticut	West Chester, CCNY
1960	Saint Louis	Bob Guelker	3-2	Maryland	Brooklyn	West Chester, Connecticut
1961	West Chester	Mel Lorback	2-0	Saint Louis	Saint Louis	Bridgeport, Rutgers
1962	Saint Louis	Bob Guelker	4-3	Maryland	Saint Louis	Mich. St., Springfield
1963	Saint Louis	Bob Guelker	3-0	Navy	Rutgers	Army, Maryland
1964	Navy	F.H. Warner	1-0	Michigan St.	Brown	Army, Saint Louis
1965	Saint Louis	Bob Guelker	1-0	Michigan St.	Saint Louis	Army, Navy
1966	San Francisco	Steve Negoesco	5-2	LIU-Brooklyn	California	Army, Mich. St.
1967-a	Michigan St. & Saint Louis	Gene Kenney Harry Keough	0-0	—	Saint Louis	LIU-Bklyn, Navy
1968-b	Michigan St. & Maryland	Gene Kenney Doyle Royal	2-2 (2 OT)	—	Ga. Tech	Brown, San Jose St.
1969	Saint Louis	Harry Keough	4-0	San Francisco	San Jose St.	Harvard, Maryland
1970	Saint Louis	Harry Keough	1-0	UCLA	SIU-Ed'sville	Hartwick, Howard
1971-c	Howard	Lincoln Phillips	3-2	Saint Louis	Miami	Harvard, San Fran.
1972	Saint Louis	Harry Keough	4-2	UCLA	Miami	Cornell, Howard
1973	Saint Louis	Harry Keough	2-1 (OT)	UCLA	Miami	Brown, Clemson

Year	Winner	Head Coach	Score	Runner-up	Host/Site	Third Place
1974	Howard	Lincoln Phillips	2-1 (4OT)	Saint Louis	Saint Louis	Hartwick 3, UCLA 1
1975	San Francisco	Steve Negoesco	4-0	SIU-Ed'sville	SIU-Ed'sville	Brown 2, Howard 0
1976	San Francisco	Steve Negoesco	1-0	Indiana	Penn	Hartwick 4, Clemson 3
1977	Hartwick	Jim Lennox	2-1	San Francisco	California	SIU-Ed'sville 3, Brown 2
1978-d	San Francisco	Steve Negoesco	4-3 (OT)	Indiana	Tampa	Clemson 6, Phi. Textile 2
1979	SIU-Ed'sville	Bob Guelker	3-2	Clemson	Tampa	Penn St. 2, Columbia 1
1980	San Francisco	Steve Negoesco	4-3 (OT)	Indiana	Tampa	Ala. A&M 2, Hartwick 0
1981	Connecticut	Joe Morrone	2-1 (OT)	Alabama A&M	Stanford	East. Ill. 4, Phi. Textile 2

Year	Winner	Head Coach	Score	Runner-up	Host/Site	Semifinalists
1982	Indiana	Jerry Yeagley	2-1 (8 OT)	Duke	Ft. Lauderdale	Connecticut, SIU-Ed'sville
1983	Indiana	Jerry Yeagley	1-0 (2 OT)	Columbia	Ft. Lauderdale	Connecticut, Virginia
1984	Clemson	I.M. Ibrahim	2-1	Indiana	Seattle	Hartwick, UCLA
1985	UCLA	Sigi Schmid	1-0 (8 OT)	American	Seattle	Evansville, Hartwick
1986	Duke	John Rennie	1-0	Akron	Tacoma	Fresno St., Harvard
1987	Clemson	I.M. Ibrahim	2-0	San Diego St.	Clemson	Harvard, N. Carolina
1988	Indiana	Jerry Yeagley	1-0	Howard	Indiana	Portland, S. Carolina
1989-e	Santa Clara & Virginia	Steve Sampson Bruce Arena	1-1 (2 OT)	—	Rutgers	Indiana, Rutgers
1990-f	UCLA	Sigi Schmid	0-0 (PKs)	Rutgers	South Fla.	Evansville, N.C. State
1991-g	Virginia	Bruce Arena	0-0 (PKs)	Santa Clara	Tampa	Indiana, Saint Louis
1992	Virginia	Bruce Arena	2-0	San Diego	Davidson	Davidson, Duke
1993	Virginia	Bruce Arena	2-0	South Carolina	Davidson	CS-Fullerton, Princeton
1994	Virginia	Bruce Arena	1-0	Indiana	Davidson	Rutgers, UCLA

Year	Winner	Head Coach	Score	Runner-up	Host/Site	Semifinalists
1995	Wisconsin	Jim Launder	2-0	Duke	Richmond	Portland, Virginia
1996	St. John's	Dave Masur	4-1	Fla. International	Richmond	Creighton, NC-Charlotte
1997	UCLA	Sigi Schmid	2-0	Virginia	Richmond	Indiana, Saint Louis
1998	Indiana	Jerry Yeagley	3-1	Stanford	Richmond	Maryland, Santa Clara
1999	Indiana	Jerry Yeagley	1-0	Santa Clara	Charlotte	Connecticut, UCLA
2000	Connecticut	Ray Reid	2-0	Creighton	Charlotte	Indiana, Southern Methodist
2001	North Carolina	Elmar Bolowich	2-0	Indiana	Columbus	St. John's, Stanford
2002	UCLA	Tom Fitzgerald	1-0	Stanford	Dallas	Creighton, Maryland
2003	Indiana	Jerry Yeagley	2-1	St. John's	Columbus	Maryland, Santa Clara
2004-h	Indiana	Mike Freitag	1-1 (PKs)	UCSB	Carson, Calif.	Duke, Maryland
2005	Maryland	Sasho Cirovski	1-0	New Mexico	Cary, N.C.	Clemson, SMU
2006	UCSB	Tim Vom Steeg	2-1	UCLA	St. Louis, Mo.	Virginia, Wake Forest
2007	Wake Forest	Jay Vidovich	2-1	Ohio St.	Cary, N.C.	Massachusetts, Va. Tech

a–game declared a draw due to inclement weather after regulation time; **b**–game declared a draw after two overtimes; **c**–Howard vacated title for using ineligible player; **d**–San Francisco vacated title for using ineligible player; **e**–game declared a draw due to inclement weather after two overtimes. **f**–UCLA wins on penalty kicks (4-3) after four overtimes; **g**–Virginia wins on penalty kicks (3-1) after four overtimes; **h**–Indiana wins on penalty kicks (3-2) after two overtimes.

Women's NCAA Division I Champions

NCAA Division I women's champions since the first tournament was contested in 1982.

Multiple winner: North Carolina (18).

Year	Winner	Coach	Score	Runner-up	Host/Site
1982	North Carolina	Anson Dorrance	2-0	Central Florida	Central Florida
1983	North Carolina	Anson Dorrance	4-0	George Mason	Central Florida
1984	North Carolina	Anson Dorrance	2-0	Connecticut	North Carolina
1985	George Mason	Hank Leung	2-0	North Carolina	George Mason
1986	North Carolina	Anson Dorrance	2-0	Colorado College	George Mason
1987	North Carolina	Anson Dorrance	1-0	Massachusetts	Massachusetts
1988	North Carolina	Anson Dorrance	4-1	N.C. State	North Carolina
1989	North Carolina	Anson Dorrance	2-0	Colorado College	N.C. State
1990	North Carolina	Anson Dorrance	6-0	Connecticut	North Carolina
1991	North Carolina	Anson Dorrance	3-1	Wisconsin	North Carolina
1992	North Carolina	Anson Dorrance	9-1	Duke	North Carolina
1993	North Carolina	Anson Dorrance	6-0	George Mason	North Carolina
1994	North Carolina	Anson Dorrance	5-0	Notre Dame	Portland
1995	Notre Dame	Chris Petrucelli	1-0 (3OT)	Portland	North Carolina
1996	North Carolina	Anson Dorrance	1-0 (2OT)	Notre Dame	Santa Clara
1997	North Carolina	Anson Dorrance	2-0	Connecticut	NC-Greensboro
1998	Florida	Becky Burleigh	1-0	North Carolina	NC-Greensboro
1999	North Carolina	Anson Dorrance	2-0	Notre Dame	San Jose, Calif.
2000	North Carolina	Anson Dorrance	2-1	UCLA	San Jose, Calif.
2001	Santa Clara	Jerry Smith	1-0	North Carolina	Dallas
2002	Portland	Clive Charles	2-1 (2OT)	Santa Clara	Austin
2003	North Carolina	Anson Dorrance	6-0	Connecticut	Cary, N.C.
2004-a	Notre Dame	Randy Waldrum	1-1 (PKs)	UCLA	Cary, N.C.
2005	Portland	Bill Irwin	4-0	UCLA	College Station, Tex.
2006	North Carolina	Anson Dorrance	2-1	Notre Dame	Cary, N.C.
2007	USC	Ali Khosroshahin	2-0	Florida St.	College Station, Tex.

a–Notre Dame wins on penalty kicks (4-3) after two overtimes.

Annual Awards
MEN
Hermann Trophy

College Player of the Year. Voted on by Division I college coaches and selected sportswriters and first presented in 1967 in the name of Robert Hermann, one of the founders of the North American Soccer League.

Multiple winners: Mike Fisher, Mike Seerey, Ken Snow and Al Trost (2).

Year		Year		Year	
1967	Dov Markus, LIU	1981	Armando Betancourt, Indiana	1995	Mike Fisher, Virginia
1968	Manuel Hernandez, San Jose St.	1982	Joe Ulrich, Duke	1996	Mike Fisher, Virginia
1969	Al Trost, Saint Louis	1983	Mike Jeffries, Duke	1997	Johnny Torres, Creighton
1970	Al Trost, Saint Louis	1984	Amr Aly, Columbia	1998	Wojtek Krakowiak, Clemson
1971	Mike Seerey, Saint Louis	1985	Tom Kain, Duke	1999	Ali Curtis, Duke
1972	Mike Seerey, Saint Louis	1986	John Kerr, Duke	2000	Chris Gbandi, Connecticut
1973	Dan Counce, Saint Louis	1987	Bruce Murray, Clemson	2001	Luchi Gonzalez, SMU
1974	Farrukh Quraishi, Oneonta St.	1988	Ken Snow, Indiana	2002	Alecko Eskandarian, Virginia
1975	Steve Ralbovsky, Brown	1989	Tony Meola, Virginia	2003	Chris Wingert, St. John's
1976	Glenn Myernick, Hartwick	1990	Ken Snow, Indiana	2004	Danny O'Rourke, Indiana
1977	Billy Gazonas, Hartwick	1991	Alexi Lalas, Rutgers	2005	Jason Garey, Maryland
1978	Angelo DiBernardo, Indiana	1992	Brad Friedel, UCLA	2006	Joseph Lapira, Notre Dame
1979	Jim Stamatis, Penn St.	1993	Claudio Reyna, Virginia	2007	O'Brian White, Connecticut
1980	Joe Morrone, Jr. Connecticut	1994	Brian Maisonneuve, Indiana		

Missouri Athletic Club Award

College Player of the Year. Voted on by men's team coaches around the country from Division I to junior college level and first presented in 1986 by the Missouri Athletic Club of St. Louis.

Multiple winners: Claudio Reyna and Ken Snow (2).

Year		Year		Year	
1986	John Kerr, Duke	1992	Claudio Reyna, Virginia	1998	Jay Heaps, Duke
1987	John Harkes, Virginia	1993	Claudio Reyna, Virginia	1999	Sasha Victorine, UCLA
1988	Ken Snow, Indiana	1994	Todd Yeagley, Indiana	2000	Ali Curtis, Duke
1989	Tony Meola, Virginia	1995	Matt McKeon, St. Louis	2001	Luchi Gonzalez, SMU
1990	Ken Snow, Indiana	1996	Mike Fisher, Virginia	2002	merged with Hermann Trophy.
1991	Alexi Lalas, Rutgers	1997	Johnny Torres, Creighton		

Coach of the Year

Men's Coach of the Year. Voted on by the National Soccer Coaches Association of America. From 1973-81 all Senior College coaches were eligible. In 1982, the award split into several divisions. The Division I Coach of the Year is listed since 1982.

Multiple winner: Jerry Yeagley (6), Tim Vom Steeg (2).

Year		Year		Year	
1973	Robert Guelker, SIU-Edwardsville	1985	Peter Mehleft, American	1997	Sigi Schmid, UCLA
1974	Jack MacKenzie, Quincy College	1986	Steve Parker, Akron	1998	Jerry Yeagley, Indiana
1975	Paul Reinhardt, Vermont	1987	Anson Dorrance, N. Carolina	1999	Jerry Yeagley, Indiana
1976	Jerry Yeagley, Indiana	1988	Keith Tucker, Howard	2000	Ray Reid, Connecticut
1977	Klass Deboer, Cleveland St.	1989	Steve Sampson, Santa Clara	2001	Elmar Bolowich, North Carolina
1978	Cliff McCrath, Seattle Pacific	1990	Bob Reasso, Rutgers	2002	Tom Fitzgerald, UCLA
1979	Walter Bahr, Penn St.	1991	Mitch Murray, Santa Clara	2003	Jerry Yeagley, Indiana
1980	Jerry Yeagley, Indiana	1992	Charles Slagle, Davidson	2004	Tim Vom Steeg, UCSB
1981	Schellas Hyndman, E. Illinois	1993	Bob Bradley, Princeton	2005	Sasho Cirovski, Maryland
1982	John Rennie, Duke	1994	Jerry Yeagley, Indiana	2006	Tim Vom Steeg, UCSB
1983	Dieter Ficken, Columbia	1995	Jim Launder, Wisconsin	2007	Jay Vidovich, Wake Forest
1984	James Lennox, Hartwick	1996	Dave Masur, St. John's		

WOMEN
Hermann Trophy

Women's College Player of the year. Voted on by Division I college coaches and selected sportswriters and first presented in 1988 in the name of Robert Hermann, one of the founders of the North American Soccer League.

Multiple winners: Mia Hamm, Cindy Parlow and Christine Sinclair (2).

Year		Year		Year	
1988	Michelle Akers, Central Fla.	1995	Shannon McMillan, Portland	2002	Aly Wagner, Santa Clara
1989	Shannon Higgins, N. Carolina	1996	Cindy Daws, Notre Dame	2003	Catherine Reddick, N. Carolina
1990	April Kater, Massachusetts	1997	Cindy Parlow, N. Carolina	2004	Christine Sinclair, Portland
1991	Kristine Lilly, N. Carolina	1998	Cindy Parlow, N. Carolina	2005	Christine Sinclair, Portland
1992	Mia Hamm, N. Carolina	1999	Mandy Clemens, Santa Clara	2006	Kerri Hanks, Notre Dame
1993	Mia Hamm, N. Carolina	2000	Anne Makinen, Notre Dame	2007	Mami Yamaguchi, Florida St.
1994	Tisha Venturini, N. Carolina	2001	Christie Welsh, Penn St.		

Missouri Athletic Club Award

Women's College Player of the Year. Voted on by women's team coaches around the country from Division I to junior college level and first presented in 1991 by the Missouri Athletic Club of St. Louis.

Multiple winners: Mia Hamm and Cindy Parlow (2).

Year		Year		Year	
1991	Kristine Lilly, N. Carolina	1995	Shannon McMillan, Portland	1999	Mandy Clemens, Santa Clara
1992	Mia Hamm, N. Carolina	1996	Cindy Daws, Notre Dame	2000	Anne Makinen, Notre Dame
1993	Mia Hamm, N. Carolina	1997	Cindy Parlow, N. Carolina	2001	Christie Welsh, Penn St.
1994	Tisha Venturini, N. Carolina	1998	Cindy Parlow, N. Carolina	2002	merged with Hermann Trophy.

Coach of the Year

Women's Coach of the Year. Voted on by the National Soccer Coaches Association of America. From 1982-87 all Senior College coaches were eligible. In 1988, the award was split into several divisions. The Division I Coach of the Year is listed since 1988.

Multiple winners: Anson Dorrance (4); Kalenkeni M. Banda and Chris Petrucelli (2).

Year		Year		Year	
1982	Anson Dorrance, N. Carolina	1991	Greg Ryan, Wisc-Madison	2000	Jillian Ellis, UCLA
1983	David Lombardo, Keene St.	1992	Bell Hempen, Duke	2001	Jerry Smith, Santa Clara
1984	Phillip Picince, Brown	1993	Jac Cicala, George Mason	2002	Clive Charles, Portland
1985	Kalenkeni M. Banda, UMass	1994	Chris Petrucelli, Norte Dame	2003	Anson Dorrance, N. Carolina
1986	Anson Dorrance, N. Carolina	1995	Chris Petrucelli, Norte Dame	2004	Julie Shackford, Princeton
1987	Kalenkeni M. Banda, UMass	1996	John Walker, Nebraska	2005	Paula Wilkins, Penn St.
1988	Larry Gross, N.C. State	1997	Len Tsantiris, Connecticut	2006	Anson Dorrance, N. Carolina
1989	Austin Daniels, Hartford	1998	Becky Burleigh, Florida	2007	Ali Khosroshahin, USC
1990	Lauren Gregg, Virginia	1999	Patrick Farmer, Penn St.		

ACTION SPORTS

2007 / 2008 YEAR IN REVIEW

Snowboarder **Gretchen Bleiler** had plenty to celebrate after her gold medal run in the SuperPipe at Winter X 12.

THE SKINNY FROM X GAMES 14

By Mary Buckheit

Hey sports fans, it's time for your yearly dose of cool in the summer heat. And with more than a decade's worth of X Games in the history books, we suggest you pay attention this time. So before you stick-and-ball purists throw up your paws and return to the usually scheduled programming, may I remind you that a little bad-assery never hurt anybody. And if you're still running for the hills, might I suggest that if it's too loud — you're too old!

Don't be scared, even old dogs need some new tricks.

Mary Buckheit
is a Page 2 Columnist

SKATEBOARD

STREET: Ryan Sheckler 2. Paul Rodriguez 3. Greg Lutzka

A little more bling came into the life of Ryan when he skated to his first Street gold. Back in 2003, toddler Sheckler (now 18), became the youngest skateboard gold medalist the X Games had ever seen when he took the Park title back to his crib.

BIG AIR: Bob Burnquist 2. Danny Way 3. Jake Brown

All eyes were on Jake Brown's triumphant return to The STAPLES Center sky a year after his infamous tumble from it, but it was Bob Burnquist who nabbed the mega

It wasn't quite as bad as Jake Brown's fall in 2007 but **Danny Way** hit hard enough. And then got back on his deck for a Big Air silver medal at XG14.

AP Images

ramp spoils. The Brazilian banged out a dramatic and e-bro-tional victory by clinching the title (his second-ever in Big Air) on his last run, which was also the last run of the entire competition. The walk-off win was so sweet, it reduced Bob B. to a pile of kneepads and man tears, but we don't judge here. What we will say is that if anyone should have been crying, it was Danny Way, who had two gnarly crashes in the comp, and no business dropping in after either one of them—but he did, and he proceeded to stomp a silver (some argue gold-worthy) run.

VERT: Pierre Luc Gagnon 2. Bucky Lasek 3. Shaun White

PLG delivered one clean run after another in the new jam-format finals, besting four-time Vert gold medalist, Bucky Lasek ('99, '00, '03, '04) and the defending golden boy, Shaun White. Oh Canada, he stands on guard for thee.

SUPERPARK: Rune Gilfberg 2. Andy Macdonald 3. Tony Trjillo

Coming in to XG14, the Great Dane, was the most medaled athlete NOT to have a gold. He came to Los Angeles with eight medals. He'll be leaving with nine. And most importantly, the new addition is finally made of gold.

Josh Hansen styled on his way to X Games gold in Moto X Racing in 2008.

WOMEN'S STREET: Elissa Steamer 2. Marisa Dal Santo 3. Amy Caron

Elissa Steamer reclaimed her reign over the Street, picking up her fourth gold in five years ('04, '05, '06, '08). Last year, skating on her 21st birthday, Marisa Dal Santo snuck in and stole the top-billing, but this time around she settled for silver.

WOMEN'S VERT: Karen Jones 2. Lyn-z Adams Hawkins 3. Mimi Knoop

Podium regulars like Lyn-z and Mimi were in the hunt, but newbie Karen Jones took the top step in 2008.

MOTO X

BEST TRICK: Kyle Loza 2. Jeremey Lusk 3. Todd Potter

22-year-old Kyle Loza became the first back-to-back champ of the Moto summit. Jim DeChamp boldly attempted to land the first front flip ever to see the light of X, and Scott Murray tried to join a select few ever to land a double-backflip but in the end, it was Loza's new varial (The Electric Doom) executed to perfection that took home the hardware. These photos will make you nauseous:

STEP UP: Ricky Carmichael 2. Ronnie Renner 3. Tommy Clowers

It feels unfair to call Moto legend Ricky Carmichael a rookie, but it was his first-ever Step Up X competition. The dirt bike deity destroyed the field, topping defending champ Ronnie Renner by a foot, although it felt more like a mile.

FREESTYLE: Jeremy Lusk
2. Mat Rebeaud 3. Mike Mason

Jeremy Lusk cruised to victory over Swiss sensation, Mat Rebeaud, adding another gold to the Metal Mulisha family mantle. Lusk's Metal Mulisha bro, Jeremy Stenberg had a mid-run motorcycle malfunction and proceeded to twitch into a tantrum of cone-kicking proportions.

SPEED & STYLE: Kevin Johnson 2. Ronnie Renner 3. Jeremy Stenberg

Kevin Johnson, the pride of Albuquerque, N.M., defeated freestyle vet Ronnie Renner at the Home Depot Center to take home the first-ever Speed & Style title on the history books.

SUPERMOTO: Jeff Ward 2. Robbie Horton 3. Brandon Currie

The event that rewards super speed on dirt and asphalt went to the wise Jeff Ward. At the ripe age of 47, Ward becomes one of the oldest competitors in the X Games ever to win a gold medal (second only to unknown Angelika Casteneda, who competed and won the Xventure Race (XG2) at 53-years-old!).

RACING (Men): Josh Hansen 2. Jeremy McGrath 3. Josh Grant

SoCal boy Josh Hansen may have been fired by Joe Gibbs Racing, but the Metal Mulisha has never been afraid of the stone that the builders refused. That's why they picked him up a few weeks ago, just in time for him to bring them Moto X Racing gold. It should be noted that defending champ Ricky Carmichael did not enter the event this year.

RACING (Women): Tarah Geiger
2. Sherri Cruse 3. Tatum Sik

X Games 14 played host to the Moto X debut of the fairer sex. The event—a five lap race to the finish line, as opposed to the gentlemen's 10-lap circuit—opened up when Sherri Cruse went down and Tarah Geiger capitalized.

BMX

BIG AIR: Chad Kagy 2. Dave Mirra 3. Kevin Robinson

Neither defending champ Kevin Robinson, nor Mr. Dave Mirra, the most decorated athlete in X Games history (22 total medals), could top Chad Kagy and his new collarbone on the mega ramp. After crashing in last year's competition, Kagy came back in '08 with a repaired wing and a mission to add a few more medals to his stash. Mission accomplished.

VERT: Jamie Bestwick 2. Chad Kagy 3. Steve McCann

It was more glory for Australia and Jamie Bestwick. The 36-year-old veteran of Vert picked up another gold, his fifth XG Vert title and sixth gold medal overall (he won Best Trick gold in '05). While he's no stranger to 24-karats, this Vert victory is special as it marks

ESPN Media

Levi LaVallee showed speed and style on his snowmachine and won gold for his efforts at Winter X 12.

the first time Jamie has ever won back-to-back top-billing. He now has eight total XG medals.

SUPERPARK: Daniel Dhers 2. Diogo Canina 3. Rob Darden

The Venezuelan vet Daniel Dhers continued down the BMX golden brick road winning his second XG gold, and third medal overall. After winning BMX Park last year, he nabbed the first BMX SuperPark gold medal ever given away at an X Games. Smells like a dynasty is brewin'.

STREET: Garrett Reynolds 2. Van Homan 3. Sean Sexton

In his sophomore year at Summer X, 17-year-old Garrett Reynolds earned his first medal on the eve of his 18th year. Saturday's Birthday Boy earned gold on Friday, while maintaining the distinction of the youngest rider in the final.

Congratulations, kiddo. You have arrived.

RALLY CAR

RACING: Travis Pastrana 2. Tanner Foust 3. Dave Mirra

Travis Pastrana and last-minute stand-in co-driver, Carolyn Bosley took gold with authority, while Tanner Faust and Ms. Chrissie Beavis nabbed silver, but the fun part of this one was all the peripheral carnage on the course. Andrew Comrie-Picard rolled his Subaru tail-over-tea kettle and Dave Mirra competed on a front axel so bent out of shape he needed five-point-turns to negotiate the course's curvature.

2007-2008 Season in Review

SPORTS ALMANAC

Summer X Games 14

The annual action sports showcase originally founded by ESPN in 1995. The 14th edition of the Summer X Games was held July 31-Aug. 3, 2008 at the Staples Center and Home Depot Center in Los Angeles, Calif. Medal winners from each event listed below.

Skateboarding

Men's Street

		Score
1	Ryan Scheckler	92.00
2	Paul Rodriguez	90.91
3	Greg Lutzka	87.50

Women's Street

		Score
1	Elissa Steamer	87.83
2	Marisa Dal Santo	81.50
3	Amy Caron	80.00

Men's Vert

		Total
1	Pierre Luc Gagnon	120
2	Bucky Lasek	104
3	Shaun White	101

Women's Vert

1	Karen Jones
2	Lyn-z Adams Hawkins
3	Mimi Knoop

SuperPark

1	Rune Glifberg
2	Andy Macdonald
3	Tony Trujillo

Big Air

		Score
1	Bob Burnquist	96.00
2	Danny Way	94.00
3	Jake Brown	91.33

Rally Car Racing

1	Travis Pastrana
2	Tanner Foust
3	Dave Mirra and Ken Block

BMX

Vert

		Score
1	Jamie Bestwick	111
2	Chad Kagy	105
3	Steve McCann	103

Freestyle Street

1	Garrett Reynolds
2	Van Homan
3	Sean Sexton

Freestyle SuperPark

		Total
1	Daniel Dhers	101
2	Diogo Canina	90
3	Rob Darden	85

Big Air

		Score
1	Chad Kagy	96.00
2	Dave Mirra	94.66
3	Kevin Robinson	91.00

Moto X

Freestyle

1	Jeremy Lusk
2	Mat Rebeau
3	Mike Mason & Jeremy Stenberg

Step Up

		Height
1	Ricky Carmichael	33'
2	Ronnie Renner	32'
3	Tommy Clowers	30'
4	Brian Deegan	30'
5	Mike Mason	30'

Best Trick

		Score
1	Kyle Loza	94.40
2	Jeremy Lusk	92.80
3	Todd Potter	90.00

SuperMoto

1	Jeff Ward
2	Robbie Horton
3	Brandon Currie

Speed & Style

		Total
1	Kevin Johnson	90.70
2	Ronnie Renner	87.75
3	Jeremy Stenberg	92.40

Men's Racing

		Total
1	Josh Hansen	628.56
2	Jeremy McGrath	636.57
3	Josh Grant	638.23

Women's Racing

		Total
1	Tarah Gieger	400.86
2	Sherri Cruse	416.71
3	Tatum Silk	424.67

Winter X Games 12

Held January 23-27, 2008 at Aspen, Colorado. Medal winners from each event listed below.

Snowboarding

Men's Snowboarder X

		Winning Time
1	Nate Holland	.93.48
2	Markus Schairer	.93.81
3	David Speiser	.95.80

Women's Snowboarder X

		Winning Time
1	Lindsey Jacobellis	102.00
2	Tanja Fredien	102.67
3	Sandra Frei	104.33

Men's Slopestyle

		Score
1	Andreas Wiig	.92.00
2	Kevin Pearce	.88.33
3	Shaun White	.83.33

Women's Slopestyle

		Score
1	Jamie Anderson	.90.66
2	Claudia Fliri	.86.33
3	Spencer O'Brien	.80.00

Men's SuperPipe

		Score
1	Shaun White	.96.66
2	Ryoh Aono	.88.00
3	Kevin Pearce	.85.66

Women's SuperPipe

		Score
1	Gretchen Bleiler	.93.33
2	Torah Bright	.92.66
3	Kelly Clark	.90.00

Big Air

Semifinals: Kevin Pearce def. Andreas Wiig, 3-0; Torstein Horgmo def. Travis Rice, 2-1.
Gold Medal Match: Torstein Horgmo def. Kevin Pearce, 3-0

Skiing

Men's Skier X

		Time
1	Daron Rahlves	.86.05
2	Stanley Hayer	.86.27
3	Casey Puckett	.86.61

Women's Skier X

		Time
1	Ophelie David	.92.19
2	Hedda Bernsten	.92.70
3	Magdalena Jonsson	.93.56

Men's SuperPipe

		Score
1	Tanner Hall	.92.33
2	Simon Dumont	.91.00
3	Colby West	.85.00

Women's SuperPipe

		Score
1	Sarah Burke	.92.00
2	Mirjam Jaeger	.81.33
3	Jen Hudak	.78.33

Men's Slopestyle

		Score
1	Andrea Hatveit	.94.00
2	Jossi Wells	.90.00
3	Jon Olsson	.87.00

Mono Skier X

		Score
1	Kees-Jan van der Klooster	117.77
2	Tyler Walker	121.52
3	Chris Devlin-Young	161.61

Snowmobiling

SnoCross

1	Tucker Hibbert
2	Brett Turcotte
3	D.J. Eckstrom

Freestyle

Gold Medal Match (loser wins Silver)—Levi LaVallee def. Joe Parsons, 87.66 def. 87.33; **Bronze Medal**—Heath Frisby def. Daniel Bodin 84.00-65.00.

Speed & Style

Gold Medal Match (loser wins Silver)—Levi LaVallee def. Sam Rogers, 91.00 to 82.07; **Bronze Medal**—Joe Parson def. Heath Frisby, 92.33 to 80.19.

Mountain Dew Action Sports Tour

2008 Dew Tour Locations: Panasonic Open, Baltimore, Md. (June 19-22); Right Guard Open, Cleveland, Ohio (July 17-20); Wendy's Invitational, Portland, Ore. (Aug. 21-24); Toyota Challenge, Salt Lake City, Utah (Sept. 11-14); Playstation Pro, Orlando, Fla. (Oct. 16-19).

Panasonic Open
June 19-22 at Baltimore, Md.

Skate Vert

		Score
1	Bucky Lasek	93.75
2	Pierre-Luc Gagnon	93.50
3	Bob Burnquist	84.75

Skate Park

		Score
1	Ryan Sheckler	94.65
2	Paul Rodriguez	89.80
3	Chaz Ortiz	89.55

BMX Vert

		Score
1	Jamie Bestwick	96.00
2	Chad Kagy	93.17
3	Simon Tabron	92.00

BMX Park

		Score
1	Daniel Dhers	93.33
2	Ryan Guettler	92.50
3	Mike Spinner	92.33

BMX Dirt

		Score
1	Ryan Nyquist	95.42
2	James Foster	95.09
3	Cameron White	94.00

FMX

		Score
1	Blake Williams	90.33
2	Nate Adams	89.33
3	Matieu Rebeaud	89.00

Right Guard Open
July 17-20 at Cleveland, Ohio

Skate Vert

		Score
1	Shaun White	92.00
2	Bucky Lasek	88.25
3	Andy Macdonald	87.25

Skate Park

		Score
1	Paul Rodriguez	90.75
2	Chaz Ortiz	90.70
3	Radolfo Ramos	88.50

BMX Vert

		Score
1	Jamei Bestwick	94.50
2	Chad Kagy	94.50
3	Steven McCann	93.33

BMX Park

		Score
1	Daniel Dhers	92.67
2	Mike Spinner	91.17
3	Rob Darden	91.17

BMX Dirt

		Score
1	Cameron White	93.92
2	Ryan Guettler	92.50
3	Ryan Nyquist	91.59

Wendy's Invitational
Aug. 21-24 at Portland, Ore.

Skate Vert

		Score
1	Bob Burnquist	91.25
2	Pierre-Luc Gagnon	89.75
3	Bucky Lasek	86.50

BMX Dirt

		Score
1	Luke Parslow	92.25
2	Cory Nastazio	91.09
3	Corey Bohan	90.75

Skate Park

		Score
1	Ryan Sheckler	90.10
2	Paul Rodriguez	87.25
3	Greg Lutzka	86.45

BMX Park

		Score
1	Daniel Dhers	93.83
2	Mike Spinner	92.67
3	Rob Darden	91.33

BMX Vert

		Score
1	Chad Kagy	95.00
2	Jamie Bestwick	94.17
3	Steve McCann	91.50

Mountain Dew Action Sports Tour (Cont.)

Toyota Challenge
Sept. 11-14 at Salt Lake City, Utah

Skate Vert
		Score
1	Andy Macdonald	90.50
2	Pierre-Luc Gagnon	90.25
3	Bob Burnquist	88.25

BMX Dirt
		Score
1	Mike Aitken	92.08
2	Corey Bohan	91.92
3	Cameron White	91.92

Skate Park
		Score
1	Chaz Ortiz	93.05
2	Ryan Sheckler	90.00
3	Rodolfo Ramos	85.90

BMX Park
		Score
1	Daniel Dhers	93.33
2	Mike Spinner	93.00
3	Garrett Reynolds	92.00

BMX Vert
		Score
1	Jamie Bestwick	93.00
2	Chad Kagy	93.00
3	Simon Tabron	92.17

FMX
		Score
1	Adam Jones	94.17
2	Robbie Maddison	92.13
3	Jeremy Lusk	91.50

PlayStation Pro
Oct. 16-19 at Orlando, Fla.

Skate Vert
		Score
1	Pierre-Luc Gagnon	96.00
2	Andy Macdonald	86.00
3	Danny Mayer	86.00

Skate Park
		Score
1	Chaz Ortiz	92.75
2	Paul Rodriguez	95.25
3	Greg Lutzka	87.75

BMX Vert
		Score
1	Jamie Bestwick	94.00
2	Chad Kagy	92.67
3	Simon Tabron	91.50

BMX Park
		Score
1	Ryan Nyquist	95.00
2	Daniel Dhers	93.33
3	Austin Coleman	92.67

BMX Dirt
		Score
1	Dennis Enarson	81.50
2	Corey Bohan	93.50
3	Cameron White	92.67

FMX
		Score
1	Adam Jones	93.67
2	Robbie Maddison	93.10
3	Jeremy Lusk	92.57

2008 Mountain Dew Tour Final Points Standings

In each discipline (SKATE, BMX and FMX), athletes who qualify into each event (Vert, Park, Dirt or FMX) receive points based on the Final results from that event. Riders are awarded points corresponding to their final placing.

Skate Vert
		Pts
1	Pierre-Luc Gagnon	408
2	Andy Macdonald	395
3	Bob Burnquist	381
4	Bucky Lasek	370
5	Adam Taylor	322

BMX Park
		Pts
1	Daniel Dhers	485
2	Mike Spinner	379
3	Ryan Nyquist	322
4	Rob Darden	322
5	Garrett Reynolds	282

Skate Park
		Pts
1	Chaz Ortiz	430
2	Paul Rodriguez	408
3	Ryan Sheckler	387
4	Greg Lutzka	360
5	Austen Seaholm	310

BMX Dirt
		Pts
1	Cameron White	378
2	Corey Bohan	363
3	Dennis Enarson	362
4	Luke Parslow	340
5	Ryan Nyquist	321

BMX Vert
		Pts
1	Jamie Bestwick	485
2	Chad Kagy	440
3	Simon Tabron	365
4	Steven McCann	321
5	Dennis McCoy	310

FMX
		Pts
1	Adam Jones	265
2	Robbie Maddison	235
3	Jeremy Lusk	220
4	Beau Bamburg	190
5	two tied	180

Surfing
2008 ASP World Championship Tour
MEN

Quiksilver Pro at Gold Coast

	Finals	Pts
1	Kelly Slater	17.94
2	Mick Fanning	15.23

Rip Curl Pro at Bells Beach

	Finals	Pts
1	Kelly Slater	15.63
2	Bede Durbridge	15.16

Billabong Pro Teahupoo

	Finals	Pts
1	Bruno Santos	9.16
2	Manoa Drollet	6.83

Globe Pro, Fiji

	Finals	Pts
1	Kelly Slater	16.67
2	C.J. Hobgood	13.27

Billabong Pro at Jeffreys Bay

	Finals	Pts
1	Kelly Slater	16.73
2	Mick Fanning	9.40

Rip Curl Pro Search, Bali

	Finals	Pts
1	Bruce Irons	17.66
2	Fredrick Patacchia	11.16

Boost Mobil Pro, Trestles, Calif

	Finals	Pts
1	Kelly Slater	18.97
2	Taj Burrow	18.63

Quiksilver Pro France

	Finals	Pts
1	Adrian Buchan	15.74
2	Kelly Slater	18.97

Billabong Pro Spain

	Finals	Pts
1	C.J. Hobgood	18.51
2	Joel Parkinson	15.83

Ratings
through Billabong Pro Spain (Oct. 12)

		Pts
1	Kelly Slater, USA	8042
2	Taj Burrow, AUS	6324
3	Joel Parkinson, AUS	6180
4	Bede Durbridge, AUS	5990
5	Adriano de Souza, BRA	5748
6	C.J. Hobgood, USA	5670
7	Adrian Buchan, AUS	5370
8	Mick Fanning, AUS	5310
9	Bobby Martinez, USA	5282

Remaining Men's Events: Hang Loose Santa Catarina Pro, Oct. 28-Nov. 5; Billabong Pipeline Masters at Oahu, Dec. 8-20.

WOMEN

Roxy Pro at Gold Coast

	Finals	Pts
1	Sofia Mulanovich	17.34
2	Samantha Cornish	7.83

Rip Curl Pro at Bells Beach

	Finals	Pts
1	Stephanie Gilmore	16.50
2	Sofia Mulanovich	16.17

Billabong Pro Mademoiselle

	Finals	Pts
1	Stephanie Gilmore	16.66
2	Layne Beachley	11.00

Beachley Classic at Manly Beach

	Finals	Pts
1	Tyler Wright	13.64
2	Silvana Lima	12.84

Ratings
through Beachley Classic (Oct. 14)

		Pts
1	Sofia Mulanovich, PER	4411
2	Stephanie Gilmore, AUS	3948
3	Layne Beachley, AUS	3698
4	Amee Donohoe, AUS	3331
5	Silvana Lima, BRA	3194
6	Samantha Cornish, AUS	3060
7	Melanie Bartels, USA	2544
8	Jacqueline Silva, BRA	2486
9	Rebecca Woods, AUS	2294
10	Jessi Miley-Dyer, AUS	2268

Remaining Women's Events: Mancora Peru Classic, Nov.3-8; Roxy Pro at Sunset Beach, Nov. 24-Dec. 6; Billabong Pro at Honolua Bay, Dec. 8-20.

Snowboarding
Chevrolet Grand Prix Series

Breckenridge, Colo. (Dec. 15, 2007); Tamarack Resort, Idaho (Feb. 9-10, 2008); Killington, Vt. (Mar. 16, 2008)

Breckenridge

Men's Pipe Finals

		Pts
1	Shaun White	48.4
2	Steve Fisher	47.8
3	Elijah Teter	44.5

Women's Pipe Finals

		Pts
1	Gretchen Bleiler	45.3
2	Kelly Clark	42.6
3	Hannah Teter	41.9

Tamarack

Men's Pipe Finals

		Pts
1	Louie Vito	45.8
2	Greg Brentz	44.5
3	Elijah Teter	43.5

Women's Pipe Finals

		Pts
1	Kelly Clark	45.2
2	Clair Bidez	39.4
3	Ellery Hollingsworth	35.5

Men's Boarder Cross Finals

1	Seth Westcott
2	Shaun Palmer
3	Graham Watanabe

Women's Boarder Cross Finals

1	Lindsey Jacobellis
2	Michelle Brodeur
3	Kim Krahulec

Killington

Men's Pipe Finals

		Pts
1	Louie Vito	45.8
2	Greg Brentz	44.5
3	Peetu Piroinen	43.9

Women's Pipe Finals

		Pts
1	Kelly Clark	46.4
2	Ellery Hollingsworth	43.6
3	Clair Bidez	39.9

See the **International Sports** chapter for results from the 2008 Snowboarding World Cup.

1995-2008
Through the Years

SPORTS ALMANAC

X GAMES

The ESPN Extreme Games, originally envisioned as a biannual showcase for "alternative" sports, were first held June 24-July 1, 1995 in Newport and Providence, R.I. and Mt. Snow, Vt. The success of the inaugural event prompted organizers to make it an annual competition. Newport would again serve as host for the redubbed X Games in 1996. The X Games has evolved rapidly since its inception and have been held in several cities since. New sports and events have been added while others have been dropped.

SUMMER X GAMES

Summer X Games sites: 1995–Newport/Providence, R.I. (and Mt. Snow, Vt.); 1996–Newport/Providence, R.I.; 1997–San Diego; 1998–San Diego; 1999–San Francisco; 2000–San Francisco; 2001–Philadelphia; 2002–Philadelphia; 2003–Los Angeles; 2004–Los Angeles; 2005–Los Angeles; 2006–Los Angeles; 2007–Los Angeles; 2008–Los Angeles

BMX

Multiple winners: Dave Mirra (13); Jamie Bestwick (5); Ryan Nyquist (4); Corey Bohan, Martti Kuoppa and Trevor Meyer (3); Daniel Dhers, Matt Hoffman, T.J. Lavin, Brandon Meadows and Kevin Robinson (2)

Year	Vert
1995	Matt Hoffman
1996	Matt Hoffman
1997	Dave Mirra
1998	Dave Mirra
1999	Dave Mirra
2000	Jamie Bestwick
2001	Dave Mirra
2002	Dave Mirra
2003	Jamie·Bestwick
2004	Dave Mirra
2005	Jamie Bestwick
2006	Chad Kagy
2007	Jamie Bestwick
2008	Jamie Bestwick

Year	Vert Best Trick
2005	Jamie Bestwick
2006	Kevin Robinson
2007	not held

Year	Big Air
2006	Kevin Robinson
2007	Kevin Robinson
2008	Chad Kagy

Year	Street/Stunt Park
1996	Dave Mirra
1997	Dave Mirra
1998	Dave Mirra
1999	Dave Mirra
2000	Dave Mirra
2001	Bruce Crisman
2002	Ryan Nyquist
2003	Ryan Nyquist
2004	Dave Mirra
2005	Dave Mirra
2006	Scotty Cranmer
2007	Daniel Dhers
2008	Garrett Reynolds

Year	SuperPark
2008	Daniel Dhers

Year	Downhill
2001	Brandon Meadows
2002	Robbie Miranda
2003	Brandon Meadows
2004	event discontinued

Year	Dirt
1995	Jay Miron
1996	Joey Garcia
1997	T.J. Lavin
1998	Brian Foster
1999	T.J. Lavin
2000	Ryan Nyquist
2001	Stephen Murray
2002	Allan Cooke
2003	Ryan Nyquist
2004	Corey Bohan
2005	Corey Bohan
2006	Corey Bohan
2007	not held

Year	Flatland
1997	Trevor Meyer
1998	Trevor Meyer
1999	Trevor Meyer
2000	Martti Kuoppa
2001	Martti Kuoppa
2002	Martti Kuoppa
2003	Simon O'Brien
2004	event discontinued

Moto X

Year	Freestyle
1999	Travis Pastrana
2000	Travis Pastrana
2001	Travis Pastrana
2002	Mike Metzger
2003	Travis Pastrana
2004	Nate Adams
2005	Travis Pastrana
2006	Jeremy Stenberg
2007	Adam Jones
2008	Jeremy Lusk

Rally Car Racing

Year	
2006	Travis Pastrana/ Christian Edstrom
2007	Tanner Foust/ Christine Beavis
2008	Travis Pastrana

Year	Step Up
2001	Tommy Clowers
2002	Tommy Clowers
2003	Matt Buyten
2004	Jeremy McGrath
2005	Tommy Clowers
2006	Matt Buyten
2007	Ronnie Renner
2008	Ricky Carmichael

Year	Men's Racing
2007	Ricky Carmichael
2008	Josh Hansen

Year	Women's Racing
2008	Tarah Gieger

Year	Speed & Style
2008	Kevin Johnson

Year	Big Air
2001	Kenny Bartman
2002	Mike Metzger
2003	Brian Deegan

Year	Super Moto
2004	Ben Bostrom
2005	Doug Henry
2006	Jeff Ward
2007	Mark Burkhart
2008	Jeff Ward

Year	Best Trick
2004	Chuck Carothers
2005	not held
2006	Travis Pastrana
2007	Adam Jones
2008	Kyle Loza

Skateboarding

Multiple winners: Tony Hawk (9); Andy Macdonald (8); Bucky Lasek (6); Bob Burnquist, Elissa Steamer and Pierre-Luc Gagnon (4); Rodil de Araujo Jr., and Danny Way (3); Cara-Beth Burnside, Sandro Dias, Paul Rodriguez and Chris Senn (2).

Year	Vert Singles	Year	Vert Doubles	Year	Men's Street
1995	Tony Hawk	1997	Hawk/Macdonald	2003	Eric Koston
1996	Andy Macdonald	1998	Hawk/Macdonald	2004	Paul Rodriguez
1997	Tony Hawk	1999	Hawk/Macdonald	2005	Paul Rodriguez
1998	Andy Macdonald	2000	Hawk/Macdonald	2006	Chris Cole
1999	Bucky Lasek	2001	Hawk/Macdonald	2007	Chris Cole
2000	Bucky Lasek	2002	Hawk/Macdonald	2008	Ryan Scheckler
2001	Bob Burnquist	2003	Lasek/Burnquist	**Year**	**Women's Street**
2002	Pierre-Luc Gagnon	2004	event discontinued	2004	Elissa Steamer
2003	Bucky Lasek			2005	Elissa Steamer
2004	Bucky Lasek	**Year**	**Vert Best Trick**	2006	Elissa Steamer
2005	Pierre-Luc Gagnon	2000	Bob Burnquist	2007	Marisa Dal Santo
2006	Sandro Dias	2001	Matt Dove	2008	Elissa Steamer
2007	Shaun White	2002	Pierre-Luc Gagnon	**Year**	**Big Air**
2008	Pierre-Luc Gagnon	2003	Tony Hawk	2004	Danny Way
Year	**Women's Vert**	2004	Sandro Dias	2005	Danny Way
2004	L. Adams Hawkins	2005	Bob Burnquist	2006	Danny Way
2005	Cara-Beth Burnside	2006	Bucky Lasek	2007	Bob Burnquist
2006	Cara-Beth Burnside	2007	not held	2008	Bob Burnquist
2007	Lyn-z Adams Hawkins	**Year**	**Park**	**Year**	**Street/Park**
2008	Karen Jonas	2003	Ryan Scheckler	1995	Chris Senn
Year	**Street Best Trick**	**Year**	**SuperPark**	1996	Rodil de Araujo Jr.
2001	Kerry Getz	2008	Rune Gilfberg	1997	Chris Senn
2002	Rodil de Araujo Jr.	**Year**	**Women's Park**	1998	Rodil de Araujo Jr.
2003	Chad Muska	2003	Vanessa Torres	1999	Chris Senn
2004	event discontinued	2004	event discontinued	2000	Eric Koston
				2001	Kerry Getz
				2002	Rodil de Araujo Jr.

Street Luge

Multiple winners: Biker Sherlock (5); Dennis Derammelaere and Rat Sult (2)

Year	Dual	Year	Mass	Year	Super Mass
1995	Bob Pereyra	1995	Shawn Gilbert	1997	Biker Sherlock
1996	Shawn Goular	1996	Biker Sherlock	1998	Rat Sult
1997	Biker Sherlock	1997	Biker Sherlock	1999	David Rogers
1998	Biker Sherlock	1998	Rat Sult	2000	Bob Pereyra
1999	Dennis Derammelaere	1999	event discontinued	2001	Brent DeKeyser
2000	Bob Ozman	**Year**	**King of the Hill**	2002	event discontinued
2001	event discontinued	2001	Dennis Derammelaere		
		2002	event discontinued		

Sportclimbing

Multiple winners: Katie Brown, Hans Florine and Elena Ovtchinnikova (3); Maxim Stenkovoy (2).

Year	Men's Difficulty	Year	Men's Speed	Year	Women's Speed
1995	Ian Vickers	1995	Hans Florine	1995	Elena Ovtchinnikova
1996	Arnaud Petit	1996	Hans Florine	1996	Cecile Le Flem
1997	Francois Legrand	1997	Hans Florine	1997	Elena Ovtchinnikova
1998	Christian Core	1998	Vladimir Netsvetaev	1998	Elena Ovtchinnikova
1999	Chris Sharma	1999	Aaron Shamy	1999	Renata Piszczek
2000	event discontinued	2000	Vladimir Zakharov	2000	Etti Hendrawati
Year	**Women's Difficulty**	2001	Maxim Stenkovoy	2001	Elena Repko
1995	Robyn Erbersfield	2002	Maxim Stenkovoy	2002	Tori Allen
1996	Katie Brown	2003	event discontinued	2003	event discontinued
1997	Katie Brown				
1998	Katie Brown				
1999	Stephanie Bodet				
2000	event discontinued				

X-Venture Race		Bungee Jumping		Big-Air Snowboarding	
Year		**Year**		**Year**	**Men**
1995	Team Threadbo	1995	Doug Anderson	1997	Peter Line
1996	Team Kobeer	1996	Peter Bihun	1998	Kevin Jones
1997	Team Presidio	1997	event discontinued	1999	Peter Line
1998	event discontinued			**Year**	**Women**
				1997	Tina Dixon
				1998	Janet Matthews
				1999	Barrett Christy

Note: Snowboarding was held at the Summer X Games from 1997-99.

Summer X Games (Cont.)

In-Line Skating

Multiple winners: Fabiola da Silva (7); Eito Yasutoko (3), Derek Downing, Jaren Grob, Martina Svobodova, Gypsy Tidwell (2).

Year	Men's Vert
1995	Tom Fry
1996	Rene Hulgreen
1997	Tim Ward
1998	Cesar Mora
1999	Eito Yasutoko
2000	Eito Yasutoko
2001	Taig Khris

Year	Women's Vert
1995	Tash Hodgeson
1996	Fabiola da Silva
1997	Fabiola da Silva
1998	Fabiola da Silva
1999	Ayumi Kawasaki
2000	Fabiola da Silva
2001	Fabiola da Silva

Year	Combined Vert
2002	Takeshi Yasutoko
2003	Eito Yasutoko
2004	Takeshi Yasutoko
2005	event discontinued

Note: In 2002 the men's and women's vert events were combined.

Year	Men's Park
1995	Matt Salerno
1996	Arlo Eisenberg
1997	Arron Feinberg
1998	Jonathan Bergeron
1999	Nicky Adams
2000	Sven Boekhorst
2001	Jaren Grob
2002	Jaren Grob
2003	Bruno Lowe
2004	event discontinued

Year	Women's Park
1997	Sayaka Yabe
1998	Jenny Curry
1999	Sayaka Yabe
2000	Fabiola da Silva
2001	Martina Svobodova
2002	Martina Svobodova
2003	Fabiola da Silva
2004	event discontinued

Year	Vert Triples
1998	Malina/Fogarty/Popa
1999	Khris/Bujanda/Boekhorst
2000	event discontinued

Year	Men's Downhill
1995	Derek Downing
1996	Dante Muse
1997	Derek Downing
1998	Patrick Naylor
1999	event discontinued

Year	Women's Downhill
1995	Julie Brandt
1996	Gypsy Tidwell
1997	Gypsy Tidwell
1998	Julie Brandt
1999	event discontinued

Watersports

Multiple winners: Dallas Friday and Danny Harf (4); Parks Bonifay, Peter Fleck, Tara Hamilton and Darin Shapiro (2).

Year	Barefoot Waterski Jumping
1995	Justin Seers
1996	Ron Scarpa
1997	Peter Fleck
1998	Peter Fleck
1999	event discontinued

Year	Men's Wakeboarding
1996	Parks Bonifay
1997	Jeremy Kovak
1998	Darin Shapiro
1999	Parks Bonifay
2000	Darin Shapiro
2001	Danny Harf
2002	Danny Harf
2003	Danny Harf
2004	Phillip Soven
2005	Danny Harf
2006	event discontinued

Year	Women's Wakeboarding
1997	Tara Hamilton
1998	Andrea Gaytan
1999	Meaghan Major
2000	Tara Hamilton
2001	Dallas Friday
2002	Emily Copeland
2003	Dallas Friday
2004	Dallas Friday
2005	Dallas Friday
2006	event discontinued

Skysurfing

Year	
1995	Fradet/Zipser
1996	Furrer/Scmid
1997	Hartman/Pappadato
1998	Rozov/Burch
1999	Fradet/Iodice
2000	Klaus/Rogers
2001	event discontinued

Surfing

Year	Men	Year	Women
2003	East Coast	2007	Team USA
2003	East Coast		
2004	East Coast		
2005	East Coast		
2006	West Coast		
2007	Team USA		

Note: The X Games surfing competition was held between teams from the East and West Coasts (2003-2006) and between Team USA and Team World (2007).

WINTER X GAMES

Winter X Games sites: 1997–Snow Summit Mountain Resort, Big Bear Lake, Calif.; 1998–Crested Butte, Colo.; 1999–Crested Butte, Colo.; 2000– Mt. Snow, Vt.; 2001–Mt. Snow, Vt.; 2002–Aspen, Colo.; 2003–Aspen, Colo.; 2004–Aspen, Colo.; 2005–Aspen, Colo; 2006–Aspen, Colo; 2007–Aspen, Colo.

Snowboarding

Multiple winners: Tara Dakides and Shaun White (5); Janna Meyen (4); Lindsey Jacobellis and Shaun Palmer (3); Gretchen Bleiler, Barrett Christy, Kelly Clark, Steve Fisher, Kevin Jones, Ueli Kestenholz, Todd Richards and Maelle Ricker (2).

Year	Men's Big Air
1997	Jimmy Halopoff
1998	Jason Borgstede
1999	Kevin Sansalone
2000	Peter Line
2001	Jussi Oksanen

Year	Women's Big Air
1997	Barrett Christy
1998	Tina Basich
1999	Barrett Christy
2000	Tara Dakides
2001	Tara Dakides

Year	Best Trick
2007	Andreas Wiig

Year	Men's Boarder X	Year	Women's Boarder X	Year	Men's Slopestyle	Year	Women's Slopestyle
1997	Shaun Palmer	1997	Jennie Waara	1997	Daniel Franck	1997	Barrett Christy
1998	Shaun Palmer	1998	Tina Dixon	1998	Ross Powers	1998	Jennie Waara
1999	Shaun Palmer	1999	Maelle Ricker	1999	Peter Line	1999	Tara Dakides
2000	Drew Neilson	2000	Leslee Olson	2000	Kevin Jones	2000	Tara Dakides
2001	Scott Gaffney	2001	Line Oestvold	2001	Kevin Jones	2001	Jaime MacLeod
2002	Philippe Conte	2002	Ine Poetzl	2002	Travis Rice	2002	Tara Dakides
2003	Ueli Kestenholz	2003	Lindsey Jacobellis	2003	Shaun White	2003	Janna Meyen
2004	Ueli Kestenholz	2004	Lindsey Jacobellis	2004	Shaun White	2004	Janna Meyen
2005	Xavier de le Rue	2005	Lindsey Jacobellis	2005	Shaun White	2005	Janna Meyen
2006	Nate Holland	2006	Maelle Ricker	2006	Shaun White	2006	Janna Meyen
2007	Nate Holland	2007	Joanie Anderson	2007	Andreas Wiig	2007	Jamie Anderson
2008	Nate Holland	2008	Lindsey Jacobellis	2008	Andreas Wiig	2008	Jamie Anderson

Year	Men's Halfpipe	Year	Women's Halfpipe	Year	Men's Superpipe	Year	Women's Superpipe
1997	Todd Richards	1997	Shannon Dunn	2001	Dan Kass	2001	Shannon Dunn
1998	Ross Powers	1998	Cara-Beth Burnside	2002	J.J. Thomas	2002	Kelly Clark
1999	Jimi Scott	1999	Michele Taggart	2003	Shaun White	2003	Gretchen Bleiler
2000	Todd Richards	2000	S. Brun Kjeldaas	2004	Steve Fisher	2004	Hannah Teter
				2005	Antti Autti	2005	Gretchen Bleiler
				2006	Shaun White	2006	Kelly Clark
				2007	Steve Fisher	2007	Torah Bright
				2008	Shaun White	2008	Jamie Anderson

Skiing

Multiple winners: Aleisha Cline (4); Simon Dumont and Tanner Hall (3); Reggie Crist, Grete Eliassen, , Lars Lewen (2).

Year	Men's Big Air	Year	Women's Skier X	Year	Women's SuperPipe
1999	J.F. Cusson	1999	Aleisha Cline	2005	Grete Eliassen
2000	Candide Thovex	2000	Anik Demers	2006	Grete Eliassen
2001	Tanner Hall	2001	Aleisha Cline	2007	Sarah Burke
2002	event discontinued	2002	Aleisha Cline	2008	Sarah Burke

Year	Men's Skier X	Year		Year	Men's Speed
1998	Dennis Rey	2003	Aleisha Cline	1997	Phil Tintsman
1999	Enak Gavaggio	2004	Karin Huttary	1998	Jurgen Beneke
2000	Shaun Palmer	2005	Sanna Tidstrand	1999	event discontinued
2001	Zach Crist	2006	Karin Huttary		
2002	Reggie Crist	2007	Ophelie David	Year	Men's Slopestyle
2003	Lars Lewen	2008	Ophelie David	2002	Tanner Hall
2004	Casey Puckett	Year	SuperPipe	2003	Not held
2005	Reggie Crist	2002	Jon Olsson	2004	Simon Dumont
2006	Lars Lewen	2003	Candide Thovex	2005	Charles Gagnier
2007	Casey Puckett	2004	Simon Dumont	2006	not held
2008	Daron Rahlves	Year	Men's SuperPipe	2007	Candide Thovex
Year	Mono Skier X (Coed)	2005	Simon Dumont	2008	Andrea HAtveit
2007	Tyler Walker	2006	Tanner Hall		
2008	Kees-Jan van der Klooster	2007	Tanner Hall	Year	Women's Speed
		2008	Tanner Hall	1997	Cheri Elliott
				1998	Elke Brutsaert
				1999	event discontinued

Snomobiling

Year	Snocross	Year	Hillcross
1998	Toni Haikonen	2001	Carl Kuster
1999	Chris Vincent	2002	Carl Kuster
2000	Tucker Hibbert	2003	T.J. Kullas
2001	Blair Morgan	2003	Mike Metzger
2002	Blair Morgan	2004	Levi LaVallee
2003	Not held	2005	event discontinued
2004	Michael Island	Year	Freestyle
2005	Blair Morgan	2007	Chris Burandt
2006	Blair Morgan	2008	Levi LaVallee
2007	Tucker Hibbert	Year	Speed & Style
2008	Tucker Hibbert	20008	Levi LaVallee

Ice Climbing

Year	Men's Difficulty
1997	Jaren Ogden
1998	Will Gadd
1999	Will Gadd
2000	event discontinued

Year	Women's Difficulty
1997	Bird Lew
1998	Kim Csizmazia
1999	Kim Csizmazia
2000	event discontinued

Year	Men's Speed
1997	Jared Ogden
1998	Will Gadd
1999	event discontinued

Year	Women's Speed
1997	Bird Lew
1998	Kim Csizmazia
1999	event discontinued

Snow Mountain Bike Racing

Year	Men's Downhill	Year	Men's Biker X
1997	Shaun Palmer	1999	Steve Peat
1998	Andrew Shandro	2000	Myles Rockwell
1999	event discontinued	2001	event discontinued

Year	Women's Downhill	Year	Women's Biker X
1997	Missy Giove	1999	Tara Llanes
1998	Marla Streb	2000	Katrina Miller
1999	event discontinued	2001	event discontinued

Winter X Games (Cont.)

Super-modified Shovel Racing

Year	
1997	Don Adkins
1999	event discontinued

CrossOver

Year	
1997	Brian Patch
1998	event discontinued

Skiboarding

Year	
1998	Mike Nick
1999	Chris Hawks
2000	Neal Lyons
2001	event discontinued

Moto X

Year	Big Air
2001	Mike Jones
2002	Brian Deegan
Year	**Best Trick**
2004	Caleb Wyatt
2005	Jeremy Stenberg
2006	Jeremy Stenberg

UltraCross

Year	
2000	McLain/Lind
2001	Palmer/Takizawa
2002	Wescott/Lind
2003	Delerue/Zackrisson
2004	Holland/Crist
2005	Huser/Andersson
2006	event discontinued

Mountain Dew Action Sports Tour
All-Time Winners

Panasonic Open

Skate Vert
2005	Bucky Lasek	2007	Shaun White
2006	Bob Burnquist	2008	Bucky Lasek

Skate Park
2005	Ryan Sheckler	2007	Ryan Sheckler
2006	Ryan Sheckler	2008	Ryan Sheckler

BMX Vert
2005	Jamie Bestwick	2007	Jamie Bestwick
2006	Simon Tabron	2008	Jamie Beswick

BMX Park
2005	Ryan Guettler	2007	Daniel Dhers
2006	Scotty Cranmer	2008	Daniel Dhers

BMX Dirt
2005	Ryan Guettler	2007	Ryan Nyquist
2006	Anthony Napolitan	2008	Ryan Nyquist

FMX
2005	Kenny Batram	2007	Nate Adams
2006	Nate Adams	2008	Blake Williams

Wendy's Invitational

Skate Vert
2005	Bucky Lasek	2007	Shaun White
2006	Sandro Dias	2008	Bob Burnquist

Skate Park
2005	Greg Lutzka	2007	Greg Lutzka
2006	Ryan Sheckler	2008	Ryan Sheckler

BMX Vert
2005	Jamie Bestwick	2007	Jamie Bestwick
2006	Jamie Bestwick	2008	Chad Kagy

BMX Park
2005	Ryan Nyquist	2007	Mike Spinner
2006	Ryan Nyquist	2008	Daniel Dhers

BMX Dirt
2005	Ryan Guettler	2007	Dennis Earson
2006	Cameron White	2008	Luke Parslow

FMX
2005	Kenny Batram	2007	Adam Jones
2006	Travis Pastrana	2008	not held

Righ Guard Open

Skate Vert
2005	Bucky Lasek	2007	Shaun White
2006	Shaun White	2008	Shaun White

Skate Park
2005	Ryan Sheckler	2007	Ryan Sheckler
2006	Jereme Rogers	2008	Paul Rodriguez

BMX Vert
2005	Jamie Bestwick	2007	Simon Tabron
2006	Jamie Bestwick	2008	Jamie Bestwick

BMX Park
2005	Ryan Guettler	2007	Daniel Dhers
2006	Daniel Dhers	2008	Daniel Dhers

BMX Dirt
2005	Ryan Guettler	2007	Ryan Nyquist
2006	Ryan Nyquist	2008	Luke Parslow

FMX
2005	Kenny Batram	2007	Nate Adams
2006	Travis Pastrana	2008	not held

Toyota Challenge

Skate Vert
2005	Pierre-Luc Gagnon	2007	Pierre-Luc Gagnon
2006	Bucky Lasek	2008	ndy Macdonald

Skate Park
2005	Ryan Sheckler	2007	Ryan Sheckler
2006	Ryan Sheckler	2008	Chaz Ortiz

BMX Vert
2005	Jamie Bestwick	2007	Jamie Bestwick
2006	Jamie Bestwick	2008	Jamie Bestwick

BMX Park
2005	Dave Mirra	2007	Scotty Cranmer
2006	Scotty Cranmer	2008	Daniel Dhers

BMX Dirt
2005	Ryan Guettler	2007	James Foster
2006	Ryan Guettler	2008	Mike Aitken

FMX
2005	Jeremy Stenberg	2007	Nate Adams
2006	Nate Adams	2008	Adam Jones

Playstation Pro

Skate Vert
2005	Pierre-Luc Gagnon	2007	Bucky Lasek
2006	Bucky Lasek	2008	Pierre-Luc Gagnon

Skate Park
2005	Jereme Rogers	2007	Greg Lutzka
2006	Jereme Rogers	2008	Chaz Ortiz

BMX Vert
2005	Jamie Bestwick	2007	Chad Kagy
2006	Jamie Bestwick	2008	Jamie Bestwick

BMX Park
2005	Scotty Cranmer	2007	Daniel Dhers
2006	Daniel Dhers	2008	Ryan Nyquist

BMX Dirt
2005	Ryan Nyquist	2007	Luke Parslow
2006	Anthony Napolitan	2008	Dennis Enarson

FMX
2005	Kenny Bartram	2007	Nate Adams
2006	Mike Mason	2008	Adam Jones

HORSE RACING

2007 / 2008 YEAR IN REVIEW

Kent Desormeaux rode **Big Brown** to victory in the 134th Kentucky Derby at Churchill Downs.

BROWN OUT

Big Brown tempted racing fans with a serious run at the Triple Crown. As usual, however, hopes were dashed at the Belmont.

By Pat Forde

HOW NOW, BROWN CROWN?

How now, Rick Dutrow, do you explain the biggest bust since Morganna the Kissing Bandit?

How now does it feel to be the freshly humbled fool of thoroughbred racing, after your waltz to the Triple Crown turned into a disaster, a last-place finish, a Brownout? How now do you justify all the obnoxious bragging about your horse, Big Brown? How now do you possibly answer for having flagrantly disrespected the difficulty of the task before you?

You remember, babe: Winning the Belmont and the first Triple Crown in 30 years was a "foregone conclusion." You dismissed the field by saying, "These horses just cannot run with Big Brown." You envisioned winning this race "by daylight, easily. I just don't see no dogfight in this race."

It might not have been a dogfight. But there was one dog in the race: the Brown Bomber. This was the worst performance by a Brown since W. told Mike he was doing a heck of a job handling Katrina.

When it was over and Big Brown had been eased by jockey Kent Desormeaux while long shot Da' Tara won wire-to-wire, the disbelief at the mammoth old track was palpable. Dutrow walked with the colt back to the stable area with his blue shirt plastered to his skin. It was the definition of flop sweat.

The cocky trainer, who had all the answers for five weeks, had none. If bettors had a dollar for every time Dutrow said, "I don't know" when he finally talked to the media Saturday evening, they might have won back everything they lost on Big Brown.

The only thing he did know is that he doesn't regret all the pre-race smugness.

"I just went by what I was feeling,"

 Pat Forde is a senior writer for ESPN.com

AP Images

Big Brown trainer **Rick Dutrow**, center, had some serious 'splaining to do after his horse didn't finish the Belmont Stakes on June 7 after winning the first two legs of the Triple Crown.

Dutrow said. "I'm sure that didn't get him beat or have him pull up."

No, talking trash didn't get Big Brown beat. But it came back to smack Dutrow in his fresh mouth when the foregone conclusion fell apart.

Make no mistake, a lot of people in the racing game enjoyed seeing Dutrow and the slickster owners from IEAH Stables go down in ignominious fashion. Dutrow has a long list of medication infractions, and it came out in recent weeks that IEAH front man Michael Iavarone was fined and suspended himself for making unauthorized penny stock trades on Wall Street. They weren't the most lovable group to dally with the Triple Crown.

But beyond that was the simple lack of tact that characterized this campaign.

Someone asked trainer David Carroll, whose Denis of Cork finished second, whether he felt bad about helping spoil a Triple Crown.

"No, I don't," Carroll said. "Not one little bit. There's a right way and a wrong way. You win with class and you lose with class.

"Basically what [Dutrow] has been saying is, [Denis of Cork] is a P.O.S. And he isn't. He rubbed me the wrong way."

The biggest Belmont favorite since Spectacular Bid in 1979 (he went off at 3-10) flamed out in stunning fashion, with Desormeaux easing him up

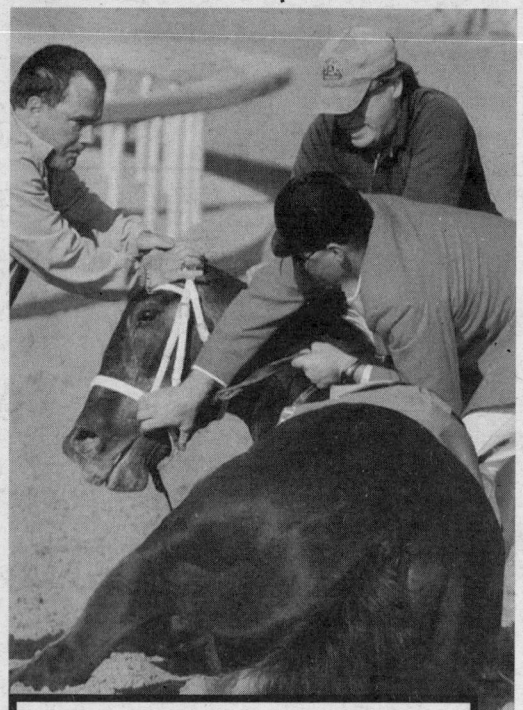

Eight Belles was euthanized after breaking both front ankles following a second-place finish in the Kentucky Derby.

on the dejected walk through the tunnel from the paddock to the stable area, and then spent about 40 minutes leaning on a sawhorse and watching Big Brown walk the shedrow at the security barn.

After checking out his colt, Dutrow could find nothing wrong. He'd heard second-hand about the TV reports saying Big Brown possibly was kicked when Desormeaux swung him wide off the rail going into the first turn, trying to escape the box opposing riders had put him in. He planned to have Big Brown's lungs scoped Sunday, but said there was no sign of a cough or other pulmonary problems.

"I don't see a problem," Dutrow said, "and I looked for one."

coming out of the second turn and into the stretch. That's normally the sign of a horse in distress, and anxiety exploded through the Belmont grandstand at the sight of Big Brown being pulled out of contention.

After the Eight Belles trauma at the Kentucky Derby five weeks earlier, the sight of a blooming hero being eased was more than many racing fans could bear – among them Jill Baffert, wife of standout trainer Bob Baffert, who burst into tears while watching near the finish line. This could have been the knockout blow for racing.

Fortunately, Big Brown appears to be OK. Dutrow watched him intently

Problem is, Dutrow never entertained the possibility of a problem during this Triple Crown run. Even after watching all the Triple Crown near-misses of recent years – Silver Charm in 1997, Real Quiet in '98, Charismatic in '99, War Emblem in 2002, Funny Cide in '03 and Smarty Jones in '04 – he failed to absorb the singular truth of this three-race series:

It's incredibly hard to win. That's why it's been done just 11 times in the history of the sport. That's why great horses like Spectacular Bid and Point Given didn't get it done.

"I can't fathom what kind of freaks those 11 Triple Crown winners were," Desormeaux said.

But Dutrow thumbed his nose at history and talked like a guy who thought he knew better than everyone else.

The training time missed after suffering a quarter crack in his left front hoof? Not a problem.

The third race in five weeks, against fresher rivals? Not a problem.

The possible tactics employed to make this race the roughest of Big Brown's inexperienced life? Not a problem.

Dutrow, we had a problem. We don't know the answer right now and might never know, but it was obvious that this race had gone badly wrong for the previously unbeaten horse as they entered the far turn.

By then, Desormeaux was laying in third place behind pace-setter Da' Tara and Tale of Ekati through a moderate first three-quarters of a mile. That's when Desormeaux began working on Big Brown's neck, urging him forward, while Eibar Coa was sitting still atop Tale of Ekati.

And they weren't changing positions.

The push-button acceleration that made Big Brown's Kentucky Derby and Preakness victories memorable was missing. Desormeaux was working hard, and his colt was going nowhere. For whatever reason, Big Brown was done and the Triple Crown drought was extended yet again.

If anyone won – beyond the remarkable Nick Zito, who now has foiled two straight Triple tries after upsetting Smarty Jones in 2004 – it was racing itself.

True, it was a letdown for all the fans who turned out to see a coronation. And it was a maddening day for the fans who found many of the toilets at Belmont rendered inoperable – lending new meaning to the racing slogan, "Go, Baby, Go!" But this was perhaps the ultimate proof that the Triple Crown must be approached with the utmost respect.

Dutrow and IEAH – newcomers to this level of success – ignorantly swaggered into their home turf of New York thinking they had it won. And they made a naked money grab along the way.

IEAH savvily coaxed a reported $50 million out of Three Chimneys Farm in Kentucky for the breeding rights to Big Brown after his race career is over. (If anyone felt anywhere near as badly as Dutrow and Desormeaux Saturday night, it was Three Chimneys owner Robert Clay. You overpaid, Bob.)

The Big Brown camp plastered the UPS logo on Desormeaux's silks and the colt's saddle cloth. Dutrow showed up in the paddock for the Belmont wearing a hat flacking for the Trump Taj Mahal casino. And there was a deal with Hooters as well, but Belmont nixed the idea of having hotties in orange pants prancing through the paddock.

They turned the Belmont Stakes into a crass NASCAR race. Then blew an engine after guaranteeing victory.

The response from the New York crowd was part sympathy for the horse, part disdain for the people. Some fans booed and threw cups. Some cussed at Dutrow as he escorted the horse away from the track.

And somewhere – wherever the racing gods live – there was unabated laughter at this comeuppance. Karma's a bitch, babe, and so is the Triple Crown.

Tragedy on the Track
by Pat Forde

A bad step.

That's the most common explanation given in thoroughbred racing when a horse breaks down: It was just a bad step.

A sad thing, but a fluke thing. An unpredictable thing, they say. An unpreventable thing, they insist.

There is some truth to that. Sometimes, even the greatest of care cannot prevent a tragedy. The physics of race horses leaves their very existences fraught with peril: large, muscular animals running very fast on very thin legs. Bad steps do happen, and when they do, they can be lethal.

But racing is taking its own bad steps if it thinks it can continue dismissing the fatal breakdowns of star animals with shoulder shrugs and some sympathetic words. If racing wants to act as though it is powerless to prevent – or at least significantly limit – these gruesome occurrences, it will run itself right out of business as a legitimate American sport.

Amid the fallout from Eight Belles' fatal breakdown after the Kentucky Derby, the NTRA pumped out some protective spin. Part of the information it passed on was a statistic attributed to the American Association of Equine Practitioners, stating American racing suffers approximately 1.6 fatalities for every 1,000 horses that start a race. That's an illuminative stat. But here's the only stat that matters to most casual racing fans: Too many horses are dying on the sport's biggest days.

Millions of people tune into horse racing no more than four days a year: the three Triple Crown races, plus the Breeders' Cup. If you watched the past 13 of those Saturdays, dating to the 2005 Breeders' Cup, you had a 38.5 percent chance of witnessing a fatal breakdown.

In '05 at Belmont, Funfair broke a hind leg in the Breeders' Cup Mile and was euthanized that day. (That race was on turf, not dirt.)

In '06, we had the Barbaro disaster at the Preakness, followed by the long and ultimately unsuccessful attempt to save the Derby champion's life. While that was still ongoing, we saw Pine Island's fatal breakdown in the Breeders' Cup Distaff that fall.

In '07, two-time European champion George Washington broke down in the Breeders' Cup Classic and was euthanized on the scene.

And now we have the Eight Belles breakdown, the first fatality at the Kentucky Derby anyone can remember.

Yeah, athletes can die in other sports, too. Auto racing and boxing come to mind. But fans of those sports haven't seen five deaths in the past 13 runnings of the Daytona 500 or the Indy 500, or the past 13 title fights.

A balkanized industry needs to coalesce and put every conceivable solution on the table. It took some steps after the Barbaro breakdown two years ago, but more are needed.

Among the items that should be up for serious discussion:

• Racing surface. Within the past couple of years, several tracks have switched from dirt to a synthetic surface that theoretically is more consistent and less punitive on horses' joints.

• The demands of the Triple Crown on the modern race horse. As recently as 10 years ago, Derby champion Real Quiet ran nine times as a 2-year-old and six more times at age 3. This year's Derby champion, Big Brown, ran once at age 2 and ran just his fourth career race in winning the roses.

• The current state of American breeding. This is the big one. American race horses are bred (and inbred) for speed racing on dirt tracks, not for durability. The collective gene pool has been reduced, and physical infirmities are being passed along like hair color in humans. Take a look at Eight Belles' pedigree. Her grandsire is Unbridled, winner of the 1990 Kentucky Derby. But his offspring have been both precocious and often brittle.

He sired Grindstone, who won the '96 Derby but never raced again after being injured shortly after the Derby. He also sired '96 Derby favorite Unbridled's Song, whose chances in that race were compromised by foot problems. Unbridled's Song then sired Eight Belles.

Does that mean Eight Belles was doomed by pedigree to meet her tragic demise at Churchill Downs? Not necessarily. It really might have been just a bad step.

But racing has been plagued by so many high-profile "bad steps" lately that it must examine the trend and do whatever it can to reverse it.

2007-2008 Season in Review

ESPN SPORTS ALMANAC

Thoroughbred Racing
Major Stakes Races

Winners of major stakes races from Nov. 1, 2007 through Sept. 28, 2008; (T) indicates turf race course; F indicates furlongs.

Late 2007

Date	Race	Track	Miles	Winner	Jockey	Purse
Nov. 23	Clark Handicap	Churchill Downs	1⅛	A.P. Arrow	Ramon Dominguez	$500,000

2008 (through Sept. 28)

Date	Race	Track	Miles	Winner	Jockey	Purse
Jan. 26	Sunshine Millions Sprint	Gulfstream	6F	Benny the Bull	Edgar Prado	$300,000
Jan. 26	Sunshine Millions Oaks	Gulfstream	6F	American County	Edgar Prado	250,000
Jan. 26	Sunshine Mill. Filly/Mare T	Santa Anita	1⅛ (T)	Quite a Bride	Garrett Gomez	500,000
Jan. 26	Sunshine Mill. Filly/Mare Sp	Santa Anita	6F	Dearest Trickski	Mike Smith	300,000
Jan. 26	Sunshine Millions Dash	Santa Anita	6F	Bob Black Jack	David Flores	250,000
Jan. 26	Sunshine Millions Oaks	Gulfstream	1⅛	Ginger Punch	Rafael Bejarano	500,000
Jan. 26	Sunshine Millions Turf	Gulfstream	1⅛ (T)	War Monger	Kent Desormeaux	500,000
Jan. 26	Sunshine Millions Classic	Gulfstream	1⅛	Go Between	Garrett Gomez	1,000,000
Feb. 2	Charles H. Strub Stakes	Santa Anita	1⅛	Monterey Jazz	David Flores	300,000
Feb. 2	Donn Handicap	Gulfstream	1⅛	Spring At Last	Eibar Coa	500,000
Feb. 9	Santa Maria Handicap	Santa Anita	1 1/16	Double Trouble	Rafael Bejarano	250,000
Feb. 24	Fountain of Youth Stakes	Gulfstream	1⅛	Cool Coal Man	Kent Desormeaux	350,000
Mar. 1	Santa Anita Handicap	Santa Anita	1¼	Heatseeker	Rafael Bejarano	1,000,000
Mar. 8	Louisiana Derby	Fair Grounds	1 1/16	Pyro	Shaun Bridgmohan	600,000
Mar. 8	Santa Anita Oaks	Santa Anita	1 1/16	Ariege	Corey Nakatani	300,000
Mar. 9	Santa Margarita Handicap	Santa Anita	1⅛	Nashoba's Key	Garrett Gomez	300,000
Mar. 15	Rebel Stakes	Oaklawn	1 1/16	Sierra Sunset	Christopher Emigh	300,000
Mar. 15	Tampa Bay Derby	Tampa Bay	1 1/16	Big Truck	Eibar Coa	300,000
Mar. 16	WinStar Derby	Sunland	1⅛	Liberty Bull	Eddie Razo Jr.	600,000
Mar. 22	Lane's End Stakes	Turfway	1⅛	Adriano	Edgar Prado	500,000
Mar. 29	Dubai World Cup	Nad al-Sheba	1¼	Curlin	Robby Albarado	6,000,000
Mar. 29	Dubai Golden Shaheen	Nad al-Sheba	¾	Benny the Bull	Edgar Prado	2,000,000
Mar. 29	Dubai Duty Free	Nad al-Sheba	1⅛	Jay Peg	Anton Marcus	5,000,000
Mar. 29	Dubai Sheema Classic	Nad al-Sheba	1½	Sun Classique	Kevin Shea	5,000,000
Mar. 29	UAE Derby	Nad al-Sheba	1⅛	Honour Devil	John Murtagh	2,000,000
Mar. 29	Florida Derby	Gulfstream	1⅛	Big Brown	Kent Desormeaux	1,000,000
Apr. 5	Santa Anita Derby	Santa Anita	1⅛	Colonel John	Corey Nakatani	750,000
Apr. 5	Ashland Stakes	Keeneland	1 1/16	Little Belle	Rajiv Maragh	500,000
Apr. 5	Oaklawn Handicap	Oaklawn	1⅛	Tiago	Mike Smith	500,000
Apr. 5	Apple Blossom Handicap	Oaklawn	1 1/16	Zenyatta	Mike Smith	500,000
Apr. 5	Illinois Derby	Hawthorne	1⅛	Recapturetheglory	E.T. Baird	500,000
Apr. 5	Wood Memorial	Aqueduct	1⅛	Tale of Ekati	Edgar Prado	750,000
Apr. 12	Blue Grass Stakes	Keeneland	1⅛	Monba	Edgar Prado	750,000
Apr. 12	Arkansas Derby	Oaklawn	1⅛	Gayego	Mike Smith	1,000,000
Apr. 19	Coolmore Lexington Stakes	Keeneland	1 1/16	Behindatthebar	David Flores	325,000
Apr. 27	Queen Elizabeth II Cup	Sha Tin	1¼ (T)	Archipenko	Kevin Shea	1,797,600
May 2	Kentucky Oaks	Churchill Downs	1⅛	Proud Spell	Gabriel Saez	500,000
May 3	**Kentucky Derby**	Churchill Downs	1¼	Big Brown	Kent Desormeaux	2,000,000
May 3	Woodford Reserve Classic	Churchill Downs	1⅛ (T)	Einstein	Robby Albarado	500,000
May 16	Black-Eyed Susan Stakes	Pimlico	1⅛	Sweet Vendetta	Channing Hill	200,000
May 17	**Preakness Stakes**	Pimlico	1 3/16	Big Brown	Kent Desormeaux	1,000,000
May 26	Gamely BC Handicap	Hollywood Park	1⅛ (T)	Precious Kitten	Rafael Bejarano	250,000
May 26	Shoemaker BC Mile	Hollywood Park	1 (T)	Daytona	Alex Solis	250,000
May 26	Metropolitan Handicap	Belmont	1	Divine Park	Alan Garcia	600,000
June 7	Epsom Derby	Epsom Downs	1½ (T)	New Approach	Kevin Manning	2,573,000
June 7	**Belmont Stakes**	Belmont	1½	Da' Tara	Alan Garcia	1,000,000
June 7	Manhattan Handicap	Belmont	1¼ (T)	Dancing Forever	Rene Douglas	400,000
June 7	Just a Game Stakes	Belmont	1 (T)	Ventura	Garrett Gomez	400,000
June 7	Acorn Stakes	Belmont	1	Zaftig	John Velazquez	250,000
June 7	Charles Whittingham H	Hollywood Park	1¼ (T)	Artiste Royal	David Flores	300,000

Major Stakes Races (Cont.)

Date	Race	Track	Miles	Winner	Jockey	Purse
June 14	Stephen Foster Handicap	Churchill Downs	1⅛	Curlin	Robby Albarado	$1,000,000
June 14	Ogden Phipps Handicap	Belmont	1¹⁄₁₆	Ginger Punch	Rafael Bejarano	300,000
June 21	Colonial Turf Cup Stakes	Colonial Downs	1³⁄₁₆ (T)	Sailor's Cap	Alan Garcia	600,000
June 22	Queen's Plate	Woodbine	1¼	Not Bourbon	Jono Jones	1,000,000
June 28	Suburban Handicap	Belmont	1¼	Frost Giant	Rudy Rodriguez	400,000
June 28	Mother Goose Stakes	Belmont	1⅛	Music Note	Javier Castellano	250,000
June 28	Hollywood Gold Cup	Hollywood Park	1¼	Mast Track	Tyler Baze	750,000
July 5	CashCall Mile	Hollywood Park	1 (T)	Diamond Diva	David Flores	750,000
July 5	American Oaks	Hollywood Park	1¼ (T)	Pure Clan	Julien Leparoux	750,000
July 5	United Nations Stakes	Monmouth Park	1⅜ (T)	Presious Passion	Eddie Castro	750,000
July 12	Princess Rooney Handicap	Calder	6 F	Mistical Plan	Corey Nakatani	400,000
July 12	Smile Sprint Handicap	Calder	6 F	Benny the Bull	Edgar Prado	400,000
June 29	Irish Derby	Curragh	1½ (T)	Frozen Fire	Seamus Heffernan	2,350,000
July 12	Swaps BC Stakes	Hollywood Park	1⅛	Tres Borrachos	Tyler Baze	350,000
July 12	Delaware Oaks	Delaware	1¹⁄₁₆	Proud Spell	Gabriel Saez	500,000
July 12	Man o' War Stakes	Belmont	1⅜ (T)	Red Rocks	Javier Castellano	500,000
July 13	Delaware Handicap	Delaware	1¼	Hysticalady	Garrett Gomez	1,000,000
July 19	Virginia Derby	Colonial Downs	1¼ (T)	Gio Ponti	Garrett Gomez	750,000
July 19	Coaching Club Am. Oaks	Belmont	1¼	Music Note	Javier Castellano	300,000
July 20	Eddie Read Handicap	Del Mar	1⅛ (T)	Monzante	Rafael Bejarano	400,000
July 26	K. George VI and Q. Elizabeth Diamond Stakes	Ascot	1½ (T)	Duke of Marmalade	Johnny Murtagh	1,700,000
July 26	Diana Stakes	Saratoga	1⅛ (T)	Forever Together	Julien Leparoux	500,000
July 26	Go for Wand Handicap	Saratoga	1⅛	Ginger Punch	Rafael Bejarano	250,000
July 26	Whitney Handicap	Saratoga	1⅛	Commentator	John Velazquez	750,000
July 27	Jim Dandy Stakes	Saratoga	1⅛	Macho Again	Julien Leparoux	500,000
Aug. 2	West Virginia Derby	Mountaineer Park	1⅛	Ready Set	Julien Leparoux	750,000
Aug. 3	Haskell Invitational	Monmouth	1⅛	Big Brown	Kent Desormeaux	1,000,000
Aug. 3	John C. Mabee Handicap	Del Mar	1⅛ (T)	Black Mamba	Garrett Gomez	400,000
Aug. 9	Arlington Million	Arlington	1¼ (T)	Spirit One	Ioritz Mendizabal	1,000,000
Aug. 9	Beverly D. Stakes	Arlington	1³⁄₁₆ (T)	Mauralakana	Kent Desormeaux	750,000
Aug. 9	Secretariat Stakes	Arlington	1¼ (T)	Winchester	Rene Douglas	400,000
Aug. 16	Alabama Stakes	Saratoga	1¼	Proud Spell	Gabriel Saez	600,000
Aug. 16	Sword Dancer Invitational	Saratoga	1½ (T)	Grand Couturier	Alan Garcia	500,000
Aug. 22	Personal Ensign Handicap	Saratoga	1¼	Ginger Punch	Rafael Bejarano	400,000
Aug. 23	Travers Stakes	Saratoga	1¼	Colonel John	Garrett Gomez	1,000,000
Aug. 24	Pacific Classic	Del Mar	1¼	Go Between	Garrett Gomez	1,000,000
Aug. 30	The Woodward Stakes	Saratoga	1⅛	Curlin	Robby Albarado	500,000
Sept. 1	Pennsylvania Derby	Philadelphia	1⅛	Anak Nakal	Joe Bravo	1,000,000
Sept. 6	Irish Champion Stakes	Leopardstown	1¼ (T)	New Approach	Kevin Manning	1,360,000
Sept. 6	Ruffian Handicap	Belmont	1¹⁄₁₆	Tough Tiz's Sis	Edgar Prado	300,000
Sept. 7	Woodbine Mile	Woodbine	1 (T)	Rahy's Attorney	Slade Callaghan	1,000,000
Sept. 13	Monmouth Stakes	Monmouth	1⅛ (T)	Big Brown	Kent Desormeaux	500,000
Sept. 20	Massachusetts Handicap	Suffolk Downs	1⅛	Commentator	John Velazquez	500,000
Sept. 20	Super Derby	Louisiana Downs	1⅛	My Pal Charlie	Curt Bourque	500,000
Sept. 27	Hawthorne Gold Cup	Hawthorne	1¼	Fairbanks	Richard Migliore	500,000
Sept. 27	Goodwood Handicap	Santa Anita	1⅛	Well Armed	Aaron Gryder	500,000
Sept. 27	Jockey Club Gold Cup	Belmont	1¼	Curlin	Robby Albarado	750,000

NTRA National Thoroughbred Poll

The NTRA Thoroughbred Poll conducted by National Thoroughbred Racing Association, covering races through Sept. 28, 2008. Rankings are based on the votes of horse racing media representatives on a 10-9-8-7-6-5-4-3-2-1 basis. First place votes are in parentheses.

		Pts	Age	Sex	'08 Record Sts—1-2-3	Owner	Trainer
1	Curlin (17)	188	4	Colt	6—5-1-0	Stonestreet Stables LLC	Steven Asmussen
2	Zenyatta (2)	159	4	Filly	6—6-0-0	Mr. & Mrs. Jerome S. Moss	John Shirreffs
3	Big Brown	145	3	Colt	7—6-0-0	IEAH Stables and Paul P. Pompa Jr.	Richard Dutrow Jr.
4	Commentator	117	7	Gelding	5—4-1-0	Tracy Farmer	Nick Zito
5	Ginger Punch	60	5	Mare	7—5-1-1	Stronach Stables	Bobby Frankel
6	Colonel John	55	3	Colt	5—3-0-1	WinStar Farm LLC	Eoin G. Harty
7	Indian Blessing	47	3	Filly	7—5-2-0	Patti & Hal J. Earnhardt III	Bob Baffert
8	Go Between	39	5	Horse	5—2-3-0	Peter Vegso	Bill Mott
9	Well Armed	38	5	Gelding	6—3-2-1	WinStar Farm LLC	Eoin G. Harty
10	Proud Spell	29	3	Filly	8—4-2-2	Brereton C. Jones	J. Larry Jones

Others receiving votes: Music Note (27); Grand Couturier (23); Wait A While (16); Cocoa Beach (12); Benny The Bull, Hysticalady and Kip Deville (11); Red Rocks (10); Einstein (9); Tiago (7); First Defence, Red Giant and Stardom Bound (6); Mauralakana (5); Intangaroo and Macho Again (3); Dorimefasollatido and Tom Lin (1).

The 2008 Triple Crown

134TH KENTUCKY DERBY

Grade I for three-year-olds; 10th race at Churchill Downs in Louisville. **Date**—May 3, 2008; **Distance**—1¼ miles; **Stakes Purse**—$2,211,800 ($1,451,800 to winner; $400,000 for 2nd; $200,000 for 3rd; $100,000 for 4th; $60,000 for 5th); **Track**—Fast; **Off**—6:15 p.m. EDT; **Favorite**—Big Brown (7-2 odds); **Field**—20 horses; **Time**—2:01.82; **Start**—Good for all but Visionaire and Smooth Air; **Won**—Driving; **Sire**—Boundary (Danzig); **Dam**—Mien (Nureyev); **Record** (going into race)—3 starts, 3 wins, 0 second, 0 third; **Last start**—1st in Florida Derby (March 29); **Breeder**—Monticule (Ky.).

Order of Finish	Jockey	PP	1/4	1/2	3/4	Mile	Stretch	Finish	To $1
Big Brown	Kent Desormeaux	20	4-½	6-1½	6-½	1-hd	1-2½	1-4¾	2.40
Eight Belles	Gabriel Saez	5	5-hd	5-½	5-2	4-½	2-2	2-3½	13.10
Denis of Cork	Calvin Borel	16	20	20	20	13-hd	6-1	3-2¾	27.20
Tale of Ekati	Eibar Coa	2	9-½	7-hd	7-1	5-1	4-½	4-¾	37.40
Recapturetheglory	E.T. Baird	18	3-½	3-hd	3-hd	2-hd	3-2	5-2-½	49.00
Colonel John	Corey Nakatani	10	17-½	16-hd	10-½	6-½	7-½	6-¾	4.70
Anak Nakal	Rafael Bejarano	3	16-½	15-1½	17-1	12-hd	11-2	7-no	53.90
Pyro	Shaun Bridgmohan	9	18-1½	17-hd	18-1½	15-2	9-½	8-¾	5.70
Cowboy Cal	John Velazquez	17	2-½	2-½	2-1	3-½	5-½	9-3¾	39.20
Z Fortune	Robby Albarado	6	7-hd	8-½	8-1	8-2	8-2½	10-1½	19.20
Smooth Air	Manoel Cruz	12	15-½	18-4	11-hd	10-½	10-hd	11-1¾	42.00
Visionaire	Jose Lezcano	8	19-4	19-3	19-hd	18-2½	16-3	12-1½	25.30
Court Vision	Garrett Gomez	4	13-½	12-½	15-1½	14-1½	12-hd	13-nk	17.70
Z Humor	Rene Douglas	11	14-1	13-1½	16-½	16-2	15-½	14-7¼	63.60
Cool Coal Man	Julien Leparoux	1	6-½	4-½	4-hd	9-4	14-1	15-nk	44.10
Bob Black Jack	Richard Migliore	13	1-½	1-1	1-½	7-hd	13-2	16-4¾	29.40
Gayego	Mike Smith	19	8-1	9-2	9-1½	11-½	17-4	17-12	18.90
Big Truck	Javier Castellano	7	10-hd	10-½	12-½	17-½	18-3	18-2	28.60
Adriano	Edgar Prado	15	11-hd	14-½	14-½	19-4	19-4	19-8¾	28.90
Monba	Ramon Dominguez	14	12-1½	11-1	13-½	20	20	20	31.60

Times—23.30; 47.04; 1:11.14; 1:36.56; 2:01.82.

$2 Mutuel Prices—#20 Big Brown ($6.80, $5.00, $4.80); #5 Eight Belles ($10.60, $6.40); #16 Denis of Cork ($11.60). **Exacta**—(20-5) for $141.60; **Trifecta**—(20-5-16) for $3,445.60; **$2 Superfecta**—(20-5-16-2) for $58,737.80; **Scratched**—none; **Overweights**—none. **Attendance**—157,770; **TV Rating**—8.8 (NBC).

Trainers & Owners (by finish): **1**—Richard Dutrow Jr. & IEAH Stables and Paul P. Pompa Jr.; **2**—J. Larry Jones & Fox Hill Farms Inc.; **3**—David Carroll & Mr. and Mrs. William K. Warren Jr.; **4**—Barclay Tagg and Charles E. Fipke; **5**—Louie J. Roussel III & Ronnie Lamarque; **6**—Eoin Harty & WinStar Farm LLC; **7**—Nick Zito & Four Roses Thoroughbreds; **8**—Steven M. Asmussen & Winchell Thoroughbreds LLC; **9**—Todd Pletcher & Stonerside Stable; **10**—Steven M. Asmussen & Zayat Stables LLC; **11**—Bennie F. Stutts Jr. & Mount Joy Stables Inc.; **12**—Michael Matz & Team Valor International and Vision Racing LLC; **13**—William I. Mott & IEAH Stables, Michael Iavarone and WinStar Farm LLC, Bill Casner et al.; **14**—William I. Mott & Zayat Stables LLC; **15**—Nick Zito & Robert V. LaPenta; **16**—James M. Kasparoff & Jeff Harmon and Tim Kasparoff; **17**—Paulo H. Lobo & Cubanacan Stables, Carlos Juelle and Jose N. Prieto; **18**—Barclay Tagg & Eric Fein and Barry Elberg; **19**—Graham H. Motion & Courtlandt Farms; **20**—Todd Pletcher & Starlight, Lucarelli and Saylor.

133RD PREAKNESS STAKES

Grade I for three-year-olds; 12th race at Pimlico in Baltimore. **Date**—May 17, 2008; **Distance**—1 3/16 miles; **Stakes Purse**—$1,000,000 ($600,000 to winner; $200,000 for 2nd; $110,000 for 3rd; $60,000 for 4th; $30,000 for 5th); **Track**—Fast; **Off**—6:17 p.m. EDT; **Favorite**—Big Brown (1-5 odds); **Field**—12 horses; **Time**—1:54.80; **Start**—Good for all but Tres Borrachos and Kentucky Bear; **Won**—Ridden out; **Sire**—Boundary (Danzig); **Dam**—Mien (Nureyev); **Record** (going into race)—4 starts, 4 wins, 0 second, 0 third; **Last start**—1st in Kentucky Derby (May 3); **Breeder**—Monticule (Ky.).

Order of Finish	Jockey	PP	1/4	1/2	3/4	Stretch	Finish	To $1
Big Brown	Kent Desormeaux	6	3-½	3-1½	3-2	1-5½	1-5¼	0.20
Macho Again	Julien Leparoux	1	6-hd	6-hd	8-2	4-hd	2-½	39.90
Icabad Crane	Jeremy Rose	3	10-hd	12	9-hd	5-3	3-¾	22.20
Racecar Rhapsody	Robby Albarado	5	9-2	9-2½	10-2	2-½	4-4¼	25.10
Stevil	John Velazquez	8	5-1	5-1	4-½	3-1	5-3¾	40.60
Kentucky Bear	Jamie Theriot	7	8-hd	8-½	6-½	7-1½	6-½	13.90
Hey Byrn	C.C. Lopez	12	4-1½	4-1	5-hd	6-1	7-1¾	34.30
Giant Moon	Ramon Dominguez	10	7-3	7-1	7-½	11-1½	8-¾	36.60
Tres Borrachos	Tyler Baze	2	12	11-hd	12	10-hd	9-1¼	43.20
Yankee Bravo	Alex Solis	4	11-hd	10-hd	11-hd	9-1	10-7¼	23.70
Gayego	Mike Smith	11	1-1½	1-1½	1-hd	12	11-nk	9.20
Riley Tucker	Edgar Prado	9	2-1½	2-2½	2-1	8-1	12	36.40

Times—23.59; 46.81; 1:10.48; 1:35.72; 1:54.80.

$2 Mutuel Prices—#7 Big Brown ($2.40, $2.60, $2.40); #1 Macho Again ($17.20, $10.40); #3 Icabad Crane ($5.60). **Exacta**—(7-1) for $36.60; **Trifecta**—(7-1-3) for $336.80; **$1 Superfecta**—(7-1-3-6) for $1,192.30; **Scratched**—Behindatthebar; **Overweights**—none. **Attendance**—112,222; **TV Rating**—5.5 (NBC).

Trainers & Owners (by finish): **1**—Richard Dutrow Jr. & IEAH Stables and Paul P. Pompa Jr.; **2**—Dallas Stewart & West Point Thoroughbreds; **3**—Graham H. Motion & Earle I. Mack; **4**—Kenneth G. McPeek & Jerry Carroll, Stan Kaplan, Ronald Plattner and Mark Guilfoyle; **5**—Nick Zito & Robert V. LaPenta; **6**—Reade Baker & Bear Stables Ltd.; **7**—Edward Plesa Jr. & Beatrice Oxenberg; **8**—Richard Schosberg & Albert Fried Jr.; **9**—Beau Greely & Beau Greely, John J. Greely IV and Phil Houchens; **10**—Patrick Gallagher & Bienstock and Winner Stables and Richard Duggan; **11**—Paulo Lobo & Cubanacan Stables; **12**—Bill Mott & Zayat Stables LLC.

The 2008 Triple Crown (Cont.)

140TH BELMONT STAKES

Grade I for three-year-olds; 11th race at Belmont Park in Elmont, N.Y. **Date**—June 7, 2008; **Distance**—1½ miles; **Stakes Purse**—$1,000,000 ($600,000 to winner; $200,000 for 2nd; $85,000 for 3rd; $85,000 for 4th; $30,000 for 5th); **Track**—Fast; **Off**—6:31 p.m. EDT; **Favorite**—Big Brown (1-4 odds); **Field**—9 horses; **Time**—2:29.65; **Start**—Good; **Won**—Driving; **Sire**—Tiznow (Cee's Tizzy); **Dam**—Torchera (Pirate's Bounty); **Record** (going into race)—7 starts, 1 win, 2 seconds, 1 third; **Last Start**—2nd in Barbaro Stakes (May 17); **Breeder**—WinStar Farm LLC.

Order of Finish	Jockey	PP	1/4	1/2	Mile	1-1/4	Stretch	Finish	To $1
Da'Tara	Alan Garcia	5	1-3	1-1	1-2	1-5	1-4	1-5¼	38.50
Denis of Cork	Robby Albarado	4	6-hd	6-1	5-½	2-½	2-2	2-2¾	7.20
Anak Nakal (dead heat)	Julien Leparoux	7	4-2	4-6	4-2	3-½	3-½	3	34.25
Ready's Echo (dead heat)	John Velazquez	8	8-½	8-2	8-1½	6-1½	5-4	3-3	28.75
Macho Again	Garrett Gomez	3	5-2	5-1½	6-hd	5-1½	4-1	5-7¼	17.40
Tale of Ekati	Eibar Coa	6	2-1	2-1	2-½	4-½	6-8	6-6½	14.50
Guadalcanal	Javier Castellano	2	7-1	7-hd	9	9	8	7-½	25.00
Icabad Crane	Jeremy Rose	9	9	9	7-3	7-4	7-½	8	17.00
Big Brown	Kent Desormeaux	1	3-1½	3-2	3-2½	8-½	—	—	0.30

Times—23.82; 48.30; 1:12.90; 1:37.96; 2:03.21; 2:29.65.

$2 Mutuel Prices: #6 Da'Tara ($79.00, $28.00, $14.80); #4 Denis of Cork ($5.40, $4.10); #8 Anak Nakal ($7.60) and Ready's Echo ($6.20). **Exacta**—(6-4) for $659.00; **Trifecta**—(6-4-8) for $3,703.00 and (6-4-9) for 3,954.00; **Superfecta**—(6-4-8-9) for $48,637.00; **Scratched**—Casino Drive; **Overweights**—none; **Attendance**—94,476; **TV Rating**—8.2 (ABC).

Trainers & Owners (by finish): **1**—Nick Zito & Robert LaPenta; **2**—David Carroll & Mr. and Mrs. William K. Warren Jr.; **3**—Nick Zito & Four Roses Thoroughbreds; **4**—Todd Pletcher & Let's Go Stable; **5**—Dallas Stewart & West Point Thoroughbreds; **6**—Barclay Tagg & Charles E. Fipke; **7**—Fred Seitz & Fred Seitz; **8**—Graham H. Motion & Earle Mack; **9**—Richard Dutrow Jr. & IEAH Stables and Paul P. Pompa Jr.

2007-08 Money Leaders

Official Top 10 standings for 2007 and unofficial Top 10 standings for 2008, through Sept. 28. Results are based on North American races plus select international races. Source: *Equibase Company.*

FINAL 2007

HORSES	Age	Sts	1-2-3	Earnings
Curlin	3	9	6-1-2	$5,102,800
Invasor (ARG)	5	2	2-0-0	3,900,000
Street Sense	3	8	4-3-0	3,205,000
Vengeance of Rain (NZ)	7	1	1-0-0	3,000,000
Admire Moon (JPN)	4	1	1-0-0	3,000,000
English Channel	5	7	4-2-0	2,640,000
Hard Spun	3	10	4-3-1	2,572,500
Kip Deville	4	7	3-1-1	1,965,780
Ginger Punch	4	8	5-2-1	1,827,060
Cloudy's Knight	7	9	3-3-1	1,762,868

JOCKEYS	Mts	1st	Earnings
Garrett Gomez	1262	266	$23,800,074
Robby Albarado	1260	253	19,399,249
John Velazquez	1131	199	18,119,713
Cornelio Velasquez	1619	262	15,997,913
Rafael Bejarano	1469	241	15,892,188
Ramon Dominguez	1333	319	15,343,920
Eibar Coa	1628	285	14,237,059
Edgar Prado	1117	207	13,662,743
Kent Desormeaux	1093	206	13,322,428
Javier Castellano	1107	168	12,551,303

TRAINERS	Sts	1st	Earnings
Todd Pletcher	1233	289	$28,571,697
Steven Asmussen	2273	488	23,898,844
Kiaran McLaughlin	525	119	12,905,403
Bobby Frankel	566	123	12,168,647
Doug O'Neill	1049	153	10,856,219
Bill Mott	774	156	9,949,267
Scott Lake	2345	485	9,724,556
Richard Dutrow Jr.	659	166	9,604,524
Gary Contessa	1230	176	7,597,499
Jerry Hollendorfer	1012	244	7,309,698

2008 (Through Sept. 28)

HORSES	Age	Sts	1-2-3	Earnings
Curlin	4	6	5-1-0	$5,039,000
Big Brown	3	7	6-0-0	3,576,700
Benny the Bull	5	4	4-0-0	1,753,000
Go Between	5	5	2-3-0	1,530,000
Proud Spell	3	8	4-2-2	1,514,840
Well Armed	6	6	3-2-1	1,460,000
Colonel John	3	5	3-0-1	1,213,530
Hystericalady	5	7	4-1-1	1,182,053
Ginger Punch	5	7	5-1-1	1,163,924
Mauralakana (FRA)	5	7	5-2-0	1,066,920

JOCKEYS	Mts	1st	Earnings
Garrett Gomez	821	161	$16,885,919
Kent Desormeaux	801	138	13,110,611
Alan Garcia	1030	187	12,314,944
Edgar Prado	1018	177	12,257,052
Rafael Bejarano	916	182	12,077,858
John Velazquez	1023	191	11,417,146
Ramon Dominguez	1084	262	11,059,777
Robby Albarado	851	172	10,389,465
Eibar Coa	1139	205	9,889,049
Javier Castellano	853	138	9,520,490

TRAINERS	Sts	1st	Earnings
Steven Asmussen	2263	485	$19,313,344
Todd Pletcher	852	170	11,061,609
Richard Dutrow Jr.	568	138	10,138,804
Bobby Frankel	395	77	9,322,067
Bill Mott	642	94	8,434,008
Scott Lake	1554	336	7,291,513
Jerry Hollendorfer	833	200	6,973,909
Kiaran McLaughlin	438	102	6,633,333
Gary Contessa	985	130	6,079,171
Anthony Dutrow	564	137	5,993,881

The $25.5 million Breeders' Cup World Championships were held October 24-25 at Santa Anita Park in California. See Updates chapter (973-975) for results.

Harness Racing
2007-08 Major Stakes Races

Winners of major stakes races from Oct. 14, 2007 through Sept. 28, 2008; all paces and trots cover one mile; (BC) indicates year-end Breeders' Crown series.

Late 2007

Date	Race	Raceway	Winner	Time	Driver	Purse
Oct. 27	**Messenger Stakes**	Yonkers	Always A Virgin	1:52	Brian Sears	725,480
Nov. 24	BC 3-Yr-Old Colt Pace	Meadowlands	Artist's View	1:50⁴/₅	George Brennan	$555,000
Nov. 24	BC 3-Yr-Old Filly Pace	Meadowlands	Artcotic	1:51²/₅	Brian Sears	500,000
Nov. 24	BC 3-Yr-Old Colt Trot	Meadowlands	Arch Madness	1:52⁴/₅	Brian Sears	610,000
Nov. 24	BC 3-Yr-Old Filly Trot	Meadowlands	Southwind Serena	1:55²/₅	Yannick Gingras	500,000
Nov. 24	BC 2-Yr-Old Colt Pace	Meadowlands	Santanna Blue Chip	1:51³/₅	Jody Jamieson	650,000
Nov. 24	BC 2-Yr-Old Filly Pace	Meadowlands	Stylish Artist	1:53	George Brennan	650,000
Nov. 24	BC 2-Yr-Old Colt Trot	Meadowlands	Deweycheatumnhowe	1:57²/₅	Ray Schnittker	650,000
Nov. 24	BC 2-Yr-Old Filly Trot	Meadowlands	Snow White	1:55¹/₅	John Campbell	650,000

2008 (through Sept. 28)

Date	Race	Raceway	Winner	Time	Driver	Purse
May 31	New Jersey Classic	Meadowlands	McCedes	1:49⁴/₅	Cat Manzi	$500,000
June 14	North America Cup	Mohawk	Somebeachsomewhere	1:49	Paul MacDonell	1,500,000
June 28	**Yonkers Trot**	Yonkers	Napoleon	1:57¹/₅	Stephane Bouchard	605,854
June 28	Hoosier Cup	Hoosier Park	Art Official	1:51¹/₅	Ryan Anderson	500,000
July 5	Art Rooney Pace	Yonkers	Badlands Nitro	1:52⁴/₅	Brian Sears	538,270
July 12	William Haughton Open Pace	Meadowlands	Mister Big	1:49	Brian Sears	600,000
July 19	Meadowlands Pace	Meadowlands	Art Official	1:47	Ron Pierce	1,100,000
July 31	Peter Haughton Memorial	Meadowlands	Muscle Hill	1:55	Brian Sears	500,000
July 31	Merrie Annabelle Final	Meadowlands	Honorable Daughter	1:55⁴/₅	John Campbell	523,600
Aug. 1	Sweetheart Pace	Meadowlands	Pedigree Snob	1:51⁴/₅	Tim Tetrick	431,000
Aug. 1	Woodrow Wilson Pace	Meadowlands	Major In Art	1:50⁴/₅	Brian Sears	350,000
Aug. 2	**Hambletonian**	Meadowlands	Deweycheatumnhowe	1:52	Ray Schnittker	1,500,000
Aug. 2	Hambletonian Oaks	Meadowlands	Creamy Mimi	1:53⁴/₅	Andy Miller	750,000
Aug. 2	Mistletoe Shalee	Meadowlands	Stylish Artist	1:51	Eric Goodell	407,000
Aug. 2	Nat Ray	Meadowlands	Misterizi	1:51	Tim Tetrick	300,000
Aug. 2	U.S. Pacing Championship	Meadowlands	Mister Big	1:48²/₅	Brian Sears	332,000
Aug. 16	Canadian Pacing Derby	Mohawk	Mister Big	1:50	Brian Sears	679,245
Aug. 17	Confederation Cup	Flamboro	Somebeachsomewhere	1:49²/₅	Paul MacDonell	628,931
Aug. 30	BC Open Pace	Mohawk	Mister Big	1:50	Brian Sears	532,150
Aug. 30	BC Mare Trot	Mohawk	Brigham Dream	1:53⁴/₅	Luc Ouellette	352,815
Aug. 30	BC Open Trot	Mohawk	Corleone Kosmos	1:51¹/₅	John Campbell	638,580
Aug. 30	BC Mare Pace	Mohawk	My Little Dragon	1:50¹/₅	Brian Sears	352,815
Aug. 30	World Trotting Derby	DuQuoin	Deweycheatumnhowe	1:50⁴/₅	Ray Schnittker	565,000
Aug. 30	Metro Pace	Mohawk	Major In Art	1:51²/₅	Brian Sears	1,000,000
Sept. 1	**Cane Pace**	Freehold	Art Official	1:51¹/₅	Ron Pierce	392,850
Sept. 13	Canadian Trotting Classic	Mohawk	Deweycheatumnhowe	1:53²/₅	Ray Schnittker	1,000,000
Sept. 18	**Little Brown Jug**	Delaware	Shadow Play	1:50¹/₅	David Miller	551,225
Sept. 20	Maple Leaf Trot	Mohawk	Arch Madness	1:52	Brian Sears	704,983

2007-08 Money Leaders

Official Top 10 standings for 2007 and unofficial Top 10 standings for 2008 through Sept. 28.

FINAL 2007

HORSES	Age	Sts	1-2-3	Earnings
Donato Hanover	3th	13	11-1-1	$2,336,190
Tell All	3ph	22	12-2-4	1,509,227
Southwind Lynx	3ph	17	5-5-1	1,356,150
Mister Big	4ph	28	12-9-3	1,310,914
Snow White	2tm	13	11-0-1	1,252,646
Maltese Artist	6pg	27	13-4-5	1,053,830
Always A Virgin	3ph	20	13-2-2	1,022,703
Pampered Princess	3tm	15	6-7-1	1,022,118
Lis Mara	5ph	17	9-2-1	974,355
Adrian Chip	3th	14	9-4-1	962,550

DRIVERS	Mts	1st	Earnings
Tim Tetrick	4728	1189	$18,350,047
Ron Pierce	2529	399	13,369,514
Brian Sears	2033	389	12,909,976
David Miller	2755	368	10,763,443
Anthony Morgan	4109	879	10,455,993
John Campbell	1122	166	10,127,507
Jody Jamieson	2258	386	10,053,205
Yannick Gingras	2627	449	9,671,846
George Brennan	2242	356	9,065,239
Cat Manzi	3624	602	8,265,926

2008 (through Sept. 28)

HORSES	Age	Sts	1-2-3	Earnings
Deweycheatumnhowe	3	11	10-1-0	$1,979,355
Somebeachsomewhere	3	11	10-1-0	1,603,503
Art Official	3	19	12-4-1	1,355,895
Badlands Nitro	3	14	9-3-1	1,287,184
Mister Big	5	10	8-2-0	1,276,932
Artistic Fella	5	14	5-7-1	937,580
Lantern Kronos	3	15	12-2-0	897,664
My Little Dragon	5	22	10-4-5	817,567
Crazed	3	10	6-1-2	813,150
Arch Madness	4	11	3-6-0	810,846

DRIVERS	Mts	1st	Earnings
Tim Tetrick	3291	742	$16,311,945
Brian Sears	1904	394	14,131,742
Ron Pierce	1848	264	9,372,252
David Miller	2157	302	8,786,283
Anthony Morgan	3454	763	8,345,970
Andy Miller	2530	354	8,193,466
Yannick Gingras	2040	257	7,820,200
David Palone	2190	692	7,544,843
John Campbell	1142	152	7,472,858
Eric Goodell	2419	329	6,994,223

1867-2008
Through the Years

SPORTS ALMANAC

Thoroughbred Racing

The Triple Crown

The term "Triple Crown" was coined by sportswriter Charles Hatton while covering the 1930 victories of Gallant Fox in the Kentucky Derby, Preakness Stakes and Belmont Stakes. Before then, only Sir Barton (1919) had won all three races in the same year. Since then, nine horses have won the Triple Crown. Two trainers, James (Sunny Jim) Fitzsimmons and Ben A. Jones, have saddled two Triple Crown champions, while Eddie Arcaro is the only jockey to ride two champions.

Year		Jockey	Trainer	Owner	Sire/Dam
1919	**Sir Barton**	Johnny Loftus	H. Guy Bedwell	J.K.L. Ross	Star Shoot/Lady Sterling
1930	**Gallant Fox**	Earl Sande	J.E. Fitzsimmons	Belair Stud	Sir Gallahad III/Marguerite
1935	**Omaha**	Willie Saunders	J.E. Fitzsimmons	Belair Stud	Gallant Fox/Flambino
1937	**War Admiral**	Charley Kurtsinger	George Conway	Samuel Riddle	Man o' War/Brushup
1941	**Whirlaway**	Eddie Arcaro	Ben A. Jones	Calumet Farm	Blenheim II/Dustwhirl
1943	**Count Fleet**	Johnny Longden	Don Cameron	Mrs. J.D. Hertz	Reigh Count/Quickly
1946	**Assault**	Warren Mehrtens	Max Hirsch	King Ranch	Bold Venture/Igual
1948	**Citation**	Eddie Arcaro	Ben A. Jones	Calumet Farm	Bull Lea/Hydroplane II
1973	**Secretariat**	Ron Turcotte	Lucien Laurin	Meadow Stable	Bold Ruler/Somethingroyal
1977	**Seattle Slew**	Jean Cruguet	Billy Turner	Karen Taylor	Bold Reasoning/My Charmer
1978	**Affirmed**	Steve Cauthen	Laz Barrera	Harbor View Farm	Exclusive Native/Won't Tell You

Note: Gallant Fox (1930) is the only Triple Crown winner to sire another Triple Crown winner, Omaha (1935). Wm. Woodward Sr., owner of Belair Stud, was breeder-owner of both horses and both were trained by Sunny Jim Fitzsimmons.

Triple Crown Near Misses

Fifty horses have won two legs of the Triple Crown. Of those, nineteen won the Kentucky Derby (KD) and Preakness Stakes (PS) only to be beaten in the Belmont Stakes (BS). Two others, Burgoo King (1932) and Bold Venture (1936), won the Derby and Preakness, but were forced out of the Belmont with the same injury—a bowed tendon—that effectively ended their racing careers. In 1978, Alydar finished second to Affirmed in all three races, the only time that has happened. Note that the Preakness preceded the Kentucky Derby in 1922, '23 and '31; (*) indicates won on disqualification.

Year		KD	PS	BS	Year		KD	PS	BS
1877	**Cloverbrook**	DNS	won	won	1967	**Damascus**	3rd	won	won
1878	**Duke of Magenta**	DNS	won	won	1968	**Forward Pass**	won*	won	2nd
1880	**Grenada**	DNS	won	won	1969	**Majestic Prince**	won	won	2nd
1881	**Saunterer**	DNS	won	won	1971	**Canonero II**	won	won	4th
1895	**Belmar**	DNS	won	won	1972	**Riva Ridge**	won	4th	won
1920	**Man o' War**	DNS	won	won	1974	**Little Current**	5th	won	won
1922	**Pillory**	DNS	won	won	1976	**Bold Forbes**	won	3rd	won
1923	**Zev**	won	12th	won	1979	**Spectacular Bid**	won	won	3rd
1931	**Twenty Grand**	won	2nd	won	1981	**Pleasant Colony**	won	won	3rd
1932	**Burgoo King**	won	won	DNS	1984	**Swale**	won	7th	won
1936	**Bold Venture**	won	won	DNS	1987	**Alysheba**	won	won	4th
1939	**Johnstown**	won	5th	won	1988	**Risen Star**	3rd	won	won
1940	**Bimelech**	2nd	won	won	1989	**Sunday Silence**	won	won	2nd
1942	**Shut Out**	won	5th	won	1991	**Hansel**	10th	won	won
1944	**Pensive**	won	won	2nd	1994	**Tabasco Cat**	6th	won	won
1949	**Capot**	2nd	won	won	1995	**Thunder Gulch**	won	3rd	won
1950	**Middleground**	won	2nd	won	1997	**Silver Charm**	won	won	2nd
1953	**Native Dancer**	2nd	won	won	1998	**Real Quiet**	won	won	2nd
1955	**Nashua**	2nd	won	won	1999	**Charismatic**	won	won	3rd
1956	**Needles**	won	2nd	won	2001	**Point Given**	5th	won	won
1958	**Tim Tam**	won	won	2nd	2002	**War Emblem**	won	won	8th
1961	**Carry Back**	won	won	7th	2003	**Funny Cide**	won	won	3rd
1963	**Chateaugay**	won	2nd	won	2004	**Smarty Jones**	won	won	2nd
1964	**Northern Dancer**	won	won	3rd	2005	**Afleet Alex**	3rd	won	won
1966	**Kauai King**	won	won	4th	2008	**Big Brown**	won	won	DNF

The Triple Crown Challenge (1987-93)

Seeking to make the Triple Crown more than just a media event and to insure that owners would not be attracted to more lucrative races, officials at Churchill Downs, the Maryland Jockey Club and the New York Racing Association created Triple Crown Productions in 1985 and announced that a $1 million bonus would be given to the horse that performs best in the Kentucky Derby, Preakness Stakes and Belmont Stakes. Furthermore, a bonus of $5 million would be presented to any horse winning all three races.

Revised in 1991, the rules stated that the winning horse must: 1. finish all three races; 2. earn points by finishing first, second, third or fourth in at least one of the three races; and 3. earn the highest number of points based on the following system—10 points to win, five to place, three to show and one to finish fourth. In the event of a tie, the $1 million is distributed equally among the top point-getters. From 1987-90, the system was five points to win, three to place and one to show. The Triple Crown Challenge was discontinued in 1994.

Year		KD	PS	BS	Pts	Year		KD	PS	BS	Pts
1987	1 Bet Twice	2nd	2nd	1st—	11	1991	1 Hansel	10th	1st	1st—	20
	2 Alysheba	1st	1st	4th—	10		2 Strike the Gold	1st	6th	2nd—	15
	3 Cryptoclearance	4th	3rd	2nd—	4		3 Mane Minister	3rd	3rd	3rd—	9
1988	1 Risen Star	3rd	1st	1st—	11	1992	1 Pine Bluff	5th	1st	3rd—	13
	2 Winning Colors	1st	3rd	6th—	6		2 Casual Lies	2nd	3rd	5th—	8
	3 Brian's Time	6th	2nd	3rd—	4		(No other horses ran all three races.)					
1989	1 Sunday Silence	1st	1st	2nd—	13	1993	1 Sea Hero	1st	5th	7th—	10
	2 Easy Goer	2nd	2nd	1st—	11		2 Wild Gale	3rd	8th	3rd—	6
	3 Hawkster	5th	5th	5th—	0		(No other horses ran all three races.)					
1990	1 Unbridled	1st	2nd	4th—	8						
	2 Summer Squall	2nd	1st	DNR—	8						
	3 Go and Go	DNR	DNR	1st—	5						
	(Unbridled was only horse to run all three races.)										

Kentucky Derby

For three-year-olds. Held the first Saturday in May at Churchill Downs in Louisville, Ky. Inaugurated in 1875.

Originally run at 1½ miles (1875-95), shortened to present 1¼ miles in 1896.

Trainers with most wins: Ben Jones (6); D. Wayne Lukas and Dick Thompson (4); Bob Baffert, Sunny Jim Fitzsimmons and Max Hirsch (3).

Jockeys with most wins: Eddie Arcaro and Bill Hartack (5); Bill Shoemaker (4); Angel Cordero Jr., Kent Desormeaux, Issac Murphy, Earl Sande and Gary Stevens (3).

Winning fillies: Regret (1915), Genuine Risk (1980) and Winning Colors (1988).

Year	Winner (Margin)	Time	Jockey	Trainer	2nd place	3rd place
1875	Aristides (1)	2:37¾	Oliver Lewis	Ansel Anderson	Volcano	Verdigris
1876	Vagrant (2)	2:38¼	Bobby Swim	James Williams	Creedmore	Harry Hill
1877	Baden-Baden (2)	2:38	Billy Walker	Ed Brown	Leonard	King William
1878	Day Star (2)	2:37¼	Jimmy Carter	Lee Paul	Himyar	Leveler
1879	Lord Murphy (1)	2:37	Charlie Shauer	George Rice	Falsetto	Strathmore
1880	Fonso (1)	2:37½	George Lewis	Tice Hutsell	Kimball	Bancroft
1881	Hindoo (4)	2:40	Jim McLaughlin	James Rowe Sr.	Lelex	Alfambra
1882	Apollo (½)	2:40¼	Babe Hurd	Green Morris	Runnymede	Bengal
1883	Leonatus (3)	2:43	Billy Donohue	John McGinty	Drake Carter	Lord Raglan
1884	Buchanan (2)	2:40¼	Isaac Murphy	William Bird	Loftin	Audrain
1885	Joe Cotton (nk)	2:37¼	Babe Henderson	Alex Perry	Bersan	Ten Booker
1886	Ben Ali (½)	2:36½	Paul Duffy	Jim Murphy	Blue Wing	Free Knight
1887	Montrose (2)	2:39¼	Isaac Lewis	John McGinty	Jim Gore	Jacobin
1888	MacBeth II (1)	2:38¼	George Covington	John Campbell	Gallifet	White
1889	Spokane (ns)	2:34½	Thomas Kiley	John Rodegap	Proctor Knott	Once Again
1890	Riley (2)	2:45	Isaac Murphy	Edward Corrigan	Bill Letcher	Robespierre
1891	Kingman (1)	2:52¼	Isaac Murphy	Dud Allen	Balgowan	High Tariff
1892	Azra (ns)	2:41½	Lonnie Clayton	John Morris	Huron	Phil Dwyer
1893	Lookout (5)	2:39¼	Eddie Kunze	Wm. McDaniel	Plutus	Boundless
1894	Chant (2)	2:41	Frank Goodale	Eugene Leigh	Pearl Song	Sigurd
1895	Halma (3)	2:37½	Soup Perkins	Byron McClelland	Basso	Laureate
1896	Ben Brush (ns)	2:07¾	Willie Simms	Hardy Campbell	Ben Eder	Semper Ego
1897	Typhoon II (hd)	2:12½	Buttons Garner	J.C. Cahn	Ornament	Dr. Catlett
1898	Plaudit (nk)	2:09	Willie Simms	John E. Madden	Lieber Karl	Isabey
1899	Manuel (2)	2:12	Fred Taral	Robert Walden	Corsini	Mazo
1900	Lieut. Gibson (4)	2:06¼	Jimmy Boland	Charles Hughes	Florizar	Thrive
1901	His Eminence (2)	2:07¾	Jimmy Winkfield	F.B. Van Meter	Sannazarro	Driscoll
1902	Alan-a-Dale (ns)	2:08¾	Jimmy Winkfield	T.C. McDowell	Inventor	The Rival
1903	Judge Himes (¾)	2:09	Hal Booker	J.P. Mayberry	Early	Bourbon
1904	Elwood (½)	2:08½	Shorty Prior	C.E. Durnell	Ed Tierney	Brancas
1905	Agile (3)	2:10¾	Jack Martin	Robert Tucker	Ram's Horn	Layson
1906	Sir Huon (2)	2:08⅘	Roscoe Troxler	Pete Coyne	Lady Navarre	James Reddick
1907	Pink Star (2)	2:12⅗	Andy Minder	W.H. Fizer	Zal	Ovelando
1908	Stone Street (1)	2:15⅕	Arthur Pickens	J.W. Hall	Sir Cleges	Dunvegan
1909	Wintergreen (4)	2:08⅕	Vincent Powers	Charles Mack	Miami	Dr. Barkley

Kentucky Derby (Cont.)

Year	Winner (Margin)	Time	Jockey	Trainer	2nd place	3rd place
1910	**Donau** (½)	2:06⅖	Fred Herbert	George Ham	Joe Morris	Fighting Bob
1911	**Meridian** (¾)	2:05	George Archibald	Albert Ewing	Governor Gray	Colston
1912	**Worth** (nk)	2:09⅖	C.H. Shilling	Frank Taylor	Duval	Flamma
1913	**Donerail** (½)	2:04⅘	Roscoe Goose	Thomas Hayes	Ten Point	Gowell
1914	**Old Rosebud** (8)	2:03⅖	John McCabe	F.D. Weir	Hodge	Bronzewing
1915	**Regret** (2)	2:05⅖	Joe Notter	James Rowe Sr.	Pebbles	Sharpshooter
1916	**George Smith** (nk)	2:04	Johnny Loftus	Hollie Hughes	Star Hawk	Franklin
1917	**Omar Khayyam** (2)	2:04⅗	Charles Borel	C.T. Patterson	Ticket	Midway
1918	**Exterminator** (1)	2:10⅘	William Knapp	Henry McDaniel	Escoba	Viva America
1919	**SIR BARTON** (5)	2:09⅘	Johnny Loftus	H. Guy Bedwell	Billy Kelly	Under Fire
1920	**Paul Jones** (hd)	2:09	Ted Rice	Billy Garth	Upset	On Watch
1921	**Behave Yourself** (hd)	2:04⅕	Charles Thompson	Dick Thompson	Black Servant	Prudery
1922	**Morvich** (1½)	2:04⅗	Albert Johnson	Fred Burlew	Bet Mosie	John Finn
1923	**Zev** (1½)	2:05⅖	Earl Sande	David Leary	Martingale	Vigil
1924	**Black Gold** (½)	2:05⅕	John Mooney	Hanly Webb	Chilhowee	Beau Butler
1925	**Flying Ebony** (1½)	2:07⅗	Earl Sande	William Duke	Captain Hal	Son of John
1926	**Bubbling Over** (5)	2:03⅘	Albert Johnson	Dick Thompson	Bagenbaggage	Rock Man
1927	**Whiskery** (hd)	2:06	Linus McAtee	Fred Hopkins	Osmand	Jock
1928	**Reigh Count** (3)	2:10⅖	Chick Lang	Bert Michell	Misstep	Toro
1929	**Clyde Van Dusen** (2)	2:10⅘	Linus McAtee	Clyde Van Dusen	Naishapur	Panchio
1930	**GALLANT FOX** (2)	2:07⅗	Earl Sande	Jim Fitzsimmons	Gallant Knight	Ned O.
1931	**Twenty Grand** (4)	2:01⅘	Charley Kurtsinger	James Rowe Jr.	Sweep All	Mate
1932	**Burgoo King** (5)	2:05⅕	Eugene James	Dick Thompson	Economic	Stepenfetchit
1933	**Brokers Tip** (ns)	2:06⅘	Don Meade	Dick Thompson	Head Play	Charley O.
1934	**Cavalcade** (2½)	2:04	Mack Garner	Bob Smith	Discovery	Agrarian
1935	**OMAHA** (1½)	2:05	Willie Saunders	Jim Fitzsimmons	Roman Soldier	Whiskolo
1936	**Bold Venture** (hd)	2:03⅗	Ira Hanford	Max Hirsch	Brevity	Indian Broom
1937	**WAR ADMIRAL** (1¾)	2:03⅕	Charley Kurtsinger	George Conway	Pompoon	Reaping Reward
1938	**Lawrin** (1)	2:04⅘	Eddie Arcaro	Ben Jones	Dauber	Can't Wait
1939	**Johnstown** (8)	2:03⅖	James Stout	Jim Fitzsimmons	Challedon	Heather Broom
1940	**Gallahadion** (1½)	2:05	Carroll Bierman	Roy Waldron	Bimelech	Dit
1941	**WHIRLAWAY** (8)	2:01⅖	Eddie Arcaro	Ben Jones	Staretor	Market Wise
1942	**Shut Out** (2½)	2:04⅖	Wayne Wright	John Gaver	Alsab	Valdina Orphan
1943	**COUNT FLEET** (3)	2:04	Johnny Longden	Don Cameron	Blue Swords	Slide Rule
1944	**Pensive** (4½)	2:04⅕	Conn McCreary	Ben Jones	Broadcloth	Stir Up
1945	**Hoop Jr** (6)	2:07	Eddie Arcaro	Ivan Parke	Pot O'Luck	Darby Dieppe
1946	**ASSAULT** (8)	2:06⅗	Warren Mehrtens	Max Hirsch	Spy Song	Hampden
1947	**Jet Pilot** (hd)	2:06⅘	Eric Guerin	Tom Smith	Phalanx	Faultless
1948	**CITATION** (3½)	2:05⅖	Eddie Arcaro	Ben Jones	Coaltown	My Request
1949	**Ponder** (3)	2:04⅕	Steve Brooks	Ben Jones	Capot	Palestinian
1950	**Middleground** (1¼)	2:01⅗	William Boland	Max Hirsch	Hill Prince	Mr. Trouble
1951	**Count Turf** (4)	2:02⅗	Conn McCreary	Sol Rutchick	Royal Mustang	Ruhe
1952	**Hill Gail** (2)	2:01⅗	Eddie Arcaro	Ben Jones	Sub Fleet	Blue Man
1953	**Dark Star** (hd)	2:02	Hank Moreno	Eddie Hayward	Native Dancer	Invigorator
1954	**Determine** (1½)	2:03	Raymond York	Willie Molter	Hasty Road	Hasseyampa
1955	**Swaps** (1½)	2:01⅘	Bill Shoemaker	Mesh Tenney	Nashua	Summer Tan
1956	**Needles** (¾)	2:03⅖	David Erb	Hugh Fontaine	Fabius	Come On Red
1957	**Iron Liege** (ns)	2:02⅕	Bill Hartack	Jimmy Jones	Gallant Man	Round Table
1958	**Tim Tam** (½)	2:05	Ismael Valenzuela	Jimmy Jones	Lincoln Road	Noureddin
1959	**Tomy Lee** (ns)	2:02⅕	Bill Shoemaker	Frank Childs	Sword Dancer	First Landing
1960	**Venetian Way** (3½)	2:02⅖	Bill Hartack	Victor Sovinski	Bally Ache	Victoria Park
1961	**Carry Back** (¾)	2:04	John Sellers	Jack Price	Crozier	Bass Clef
1962	**Decidedly** (2¼)	2:00⅖	Bill Hartack	Horatio Luro	Roman Line	Ridan
1963	**Chateaugay** (1¼)	2:01⅘	Braulio Baeza	James Conway	Never Bend	Candy Spots
1964	**Northern Dancer** (nk)	2:00	Bill Hartack	Horatio Luro	Hill Rise	The Scoundrel
1965	**Lucky Debonair** (nk)	2:01⅕	Bill Shoemaker	Frank Catrone	Dapper Dan	Tom Rolfe
1966	**Kauai King** (½)	2:02	Don Brumfield	Henry Forrest	Advocator	Blue Skyer
1967	**Proud Clarion** (1)	2:00⅗	Bobby Ussery	Loyd Gentry	Barbs Delight	Damascus
1968	**Forward Pass*** (nk)	—	Ismael Valenzuela	Henry Forrest	Francie's Hat	T.V. Commercial
1969	**Majestic Prince** (nk)	2:01⅘	Bill Hartack	Johnny Longden	Arts and Letters	Dike
1970	**Dust Commander** (5)	2:03⅖	Mike Manganello	Don Combs	My Dad George	High Echelon
1971	**Canonero II** (3¼)	2:03⅕	Gustavo Avila	Juan Arias	Jim French	Bold Reason
1972	**Riva Ridge** (3¼)	2:01⅘	Ron Turcotte	Lucien Laurin	No Le Hace	Hold Your Peace
1973	**SECRETARIAT** (2½)	1:59⅖	Ron Turcotte	Lucien Laurin	Sham	Our Native
1974	**Cannonade** (2¼)	2:04	Angel Cordero Jr.	Woody Stephens	Hudson County	Agitate
1975	**Foolish Pleasure** (1¾)	2:02	Jacinto Vasquez	LeRoy Jolley	Avatar	Diabolo
1976	**Bold Forbes** (1)	2:01⅗	Angel Cordero Jr.	Laz Barrera	Honest Pleasure	Elocutionist
1977	**SEATTLE SLEW** (1¾)	2:02⅕	Jean Cruguet	Billy Turner	Run Dusty Run	Sanhedrin
1978	**AFFIRMED** (1½)	2:01⅕	Steve Cauthen	Laz Barrera	Alydar	Believe It
1979	**Spectacular Bid** (2¾)	2:02⅖	Ron Franklin	Bud Delp	General Assembly	Golden Act

Year	Winner (Margin)	Time	Jockey	Trainer	2nd place	3rd place
1980	**Genuine Risk** (1)	2:02	Jacinto Vasquez	LeRoy Jolley	Rumbo	Jaklin Klugman
1981	**Pleasant Colony** (3/4)	2:02	Jorge Velasquez	John Campo	Woodchopper	Partez
1982	**Gato Del Sol** (2½)	2:02⅖	E. Delahoussaye	Eddie Gregson	Laser Light	Reinvested
1983	**Sunny's Halo** (2)	2:02⅕	E. Delahoussaye	David Cross Jr.	Desert Wine	Caveat
1984	**Swale** (3¼)	2:02⅖	Laffit Pincay Jr.	Woody Stephens	Coax Me Chad	At The Threshold
1985	**Spend A Buck** (5¼)	2:00⅕	Angel Cordero Jr.	Cam Gambolati	Stephan's Odyssey	Chief's Crown
1986	**Ferdinand** (2¼)	2:02⅘	Bill Shoemaker	Chas. Whittingham	Bold Arrangement	Broad Brush
1987	**Alysheba** (3/4)	2:03⅖	Chris McCarron	Jack Van Berg	Bet Twice	Avies Copy
1988	**Winning Colors** (nk)	2:02⅕	Gary Stevens	D. Wayne Lukas	Forty Niner	Risen Star
1989	**Sunday Silence** (2½)	2:05	Pat Valenzuela	Chas. Whittingham	Easy Goer	Awe Inspiring
1990	**Unbridled** (3½)	2:02	Craig Perret	Carl Nafzger	Summer Squall	Pleasant Tap
1991	**Strike the Gold** (1¾)	2:03	Chris Antley	Nick Zito	Best Pal	Mane Minister
1992	**Lil E. Tee** (1)	2:03	Pat Day	Lynn Whiting	Casual Lies	Dance Floor
1993	**Sea Hero** (2½)	2:02⅖	Jerry Bailey	Mack Miller	Prairie Bayou	Wild Gale
1994	**Go For Gin** (2)	2:03⅗	Chris McCarron	Nick Zito	Strodes Creek	Blumin Affair
1995	**Thunder Gulch** (2¼)	2:01⅕	Gary Stevens	D. Wayne Lukas	Tejano Run	Timber Country
1996	**Grindstone** (ns)	2:01	Jerry Bailey	D. Wayne Lukas	Cavonnier	Prince of Thieves
1997	**Silver Charm** (hd)	2:02⅖	Gary Stevens	Bob Baffert	Captain Bodgit	Free House
1998	**Real Quiet** (½)	2:02⅕	Kent Desormeaux	Bob Baffert	Victory Gallop	Indian Charlie
1999	**Charismatic** (nk)	2:03⅕	Chris Antley	D. Wayne Lukas	Menifee	Cat Thief
2000	**Fusaichi Pegasus** (1½)	2:01⅕	Kent Desormeaux	Neil Drysdale	Aptitude	Impeachment
2001	**Monarchos** (4¾)	1:59⅘	Jorge Chavez	John Ward Jr.	Invisible Ink	Congaree
2002	**War Emblem** (4)	2:01	Victor Espinoza	Bob Baffert	Proud Citizen	Perfect Drift
2003	**Funny Cide** (1¾)	2:01	Jose Santos	Barclay Tagg	Empire Maker	Peace Rules
2004	**Smarty Jones** (2¾)	2:04	Stewart Elliott	John Servis	Lion Heart	Imperialism
2005	**Giacomo** (½)	2:02¾	Mike Smith	John Shirreffs	Closing Argument	Afleet Alex
2006	**Barbaro** (6½)	2:01⅖	Edgar Prado	Michael Matz	Blue Grass Cat	Steppenwolfer
2007	**Street Sense** (2¼)	2:02⅕	Calvin Borel	Carl Nafzger	Hard Spun	Curlin
2008	**Big Brown** (4¾)	2:01⅘	Kent Desormeaux	Richard Dutrow Jr.	Eight Belles	Denis of Cork

*Dancer's Image finished first (in 2:02⅕), but was disqualified after traces of prohibited medication were found in his system.

Preakness Stakes

For three-year-olds. Held two weeks after the Kentucky Derby at Pimlico Race Course in Baltimore. Inaugurated 1873. Note that the 1918 race was held over two divisions. Originally run at 1½ miles (1873-88), then at 1¼ miles (1889), 1½ miles (1890), 1 1/16 miles (1894-1900), 1 mile & 70 yards (1901-07), 1 1/16 miles (1908), 1 mile (1909-1910), 1⅛ miles (1911-24), and the present 1 3/16 miles since 1925.

Trainers with most wins: Robert W. Walden (7); T.J. Healey and D. Wayne Lukas (5); Bob Baffert, Sunny Jim Fitzsimmons and Jimmy Jones (4); J. Whalen (3).

Jockeys with most wins: Eddie Arcaro (6); Pat Day (5); G. Barbee, Bill Hartack and Lloyd Hughes (3).

Winning fillies: Flocarline (1903), Whimsical (1906), Rhine Maiden (1915) and Nellie Morse (1924).

Year	Winner (Margin)	Time	Jockey	Trainer	2nd place	3rd place
1873	**Survivor** (10)	2:43	G. Barbee	A.D. Pryor	John Boulger	Artist
1874	**Culpepper** (3/4)	2:56½	W. Donohue	H. Gaffney	King Amadeus	Scratch
1875	**Tom Ochiltree** (2)	2:43½	L. Hughes	R.W. Walden	Viator	Bay Final
1876	**Shirley** (4)	2:44¾	G. Barbee	W. Brown	Rappahannock	Compliment
1877	**Cloverbrook** (2)	2:45½	C. Holloway	J. Walden	Bombast	Lucifer
1878	**Duke of Magenta** (2)	2:41¾	C. Holloway	R.W. Walden	Bayard	Albert
1879	**Harold** (1)	2:40½	L. Hughes	R.W. Walden	Jericho	Rochester
1880	**Grenada** (3/4)	2:40½	L. Hughes	R.W. Walden	Oden	Emily F.
1881	**Saunterer** (½)	2:40½	T. Costello	R.W. Walden	Compensation	Baltic
1882	**Vanguard** (nk)	2:44½	T. Costello	R.W. Walden	Heck	Col. Watson
1883	**Jacobus** (4)	2:42½	G. Barbee	R. Dwyer	Parnell	(2-horse race)
1884	**Knight of Ellerslie** (2)	2:39½	S. Fisher	T.B. Doswell	Welcher	(2-horse race)
1885	**Tecumseh** (2)	2:49	Jim McLaughlin	C. Littlefield	Wickham	John C.
1886	**The Bard** (3)	2:45	S. Fisher	J. Huggins	Eurus	Elkwood
1887	**Dunboyne** (1)	2:39½	W. Donohue	W. Jennings	Mahoney	Raymond
1888	**Refund** (3)	2:49	F. Littlefield	R.W. Walden	Bertha B.*	Glendale
1889	**Buddhist** (8)	2:17½	W. Anderson	J. Rogers	Japhet	(2-horse race)
1890	**Montague** (3)	2:36¾	W. Martin	E. Feakes	Philosophy	Barrister
1891-93	Not held					
1894	**Assignee** (3)	1:49¼	F. Taral	W. Lakeland	Potentate	Ed Kearney
1895	**Belmar** (1)	1:50½	F. Taral	E. Feakes	April Fool	Sue Kittie
1896	**Margrave** (1)	1:51	H. Griffin	Byron McClelland	Hamilton II	Intermission
1897	**Paul Kauvar** (1½)	1:51¼	T. Thorpe	T.P. Hayes	Elkins	On Deck
1898	**Sly Fox** (2)	1:49¾	W. Simms	H. Campbell	The Huguenot	Nuto
1899	**Half Time** (1)	1:47	R. Clawson	F. McCabe	Filigrane	Lackland
1900	**Hindus** (hd)	1:48⅖	H. Spencer	J.H. Morris	Sarmatian	Ten Candles
1901	**The Parader** (2)	1:47⅕	F. Landry	T.J. Healey	Sadie S.	Dr. Barlow
1902	**Old England** (ns)	1:45⅘	L. Jackson	G.B. Morris	Maj. Daingerfield	Namtor
1903	**Flocarline** (½)	1:44⅘	W. Gannon	H.C. Riddle	Mackey Dwyer	Rightful

Preakness Stakes (Cont.)

Year	Winner (Margin)	Time	Jockey	Trainer	2nd place	3rd place
1904	**Bryn Mawr** (1)	1:44⅕	E. Hildebrand	W.F. Presgrave	Wotan	Dolly Spanker
1905	**Cairngorm** (hd)	1:45⅘	W. Davis	A.J. Joyner	Kiamesha	Coy Maid
1906	**Whimsical** (4)	1:45	Walter Miller	T.J. Gaynor	Content	Larabie
1907	**Don Enrique** (1)	1:45⅖	G. Mountain	J. Whalen	Ethon	Zambesi
1908	**Royal Tourist** (4)	1:46⅖	Eddie Dugan	A.J. Joyner	Live Wire	Robert Cooper
1909	**Effendi** (1)	1:39⅘	Willie Doyle	F.C. Frisbie	Fashion Plate	Hill Top
1910	**Layminster** (½)	1:40⅗	R. Estep	J.S. Healy	Dalhousie	Sager
1911	**Watervale** (1)	1:51	Eddie Dugan	J. Whalen	Zeus	The Nigger
1912	**Colonel Holloway** (5)	1:56⅗	C. Turner	D. Woodford	Bwana Tumbo	Tipsand
1913	**Buskin** (nk)	1:53⅖	James Butwell	J. Whalen	Kleburne	Barnegat
1914	**Holiday** (¾)	1:53⅘	A. Schuttinger	J.S. Healy	Brave Cunarder	Defendum
1915	**Rhine Maiden** (1½)	1:58	Douglas Hoffman	F. Devers	Half Rock	Runes
1916	**Damrosch** (1½)	1:54⅘	Linus McAtee	A.G. Weston	Greenwood	Achievement
1917	**Kalitan** (2)	1:54⅖	E. Haynes	Bill Hurley	Al M. Dick	Kentucky Boy
1918	**War Cloud** (¾)	1:53⅗	Johnny Loftus	W.B. Jennings	Sunny Slope	Lanius
1918	**Jack Hare Jr** (2)	1:53⅖	Charles Peak	F.D. Weir	The Porter	Kate Bright
1919	**SIR BARTON** (4)	1:53	Johnny Loftus	H. Guy Bedwell	Eternal	Sweep On
1920	**Man o' War** (1½)	1:51⅗	Clarence Kummer	L. Feustel	Upset	Wildair
1921	**Broomspun** (¾)	1:54⅕	F. Coltiletti	James Rowe Sr.	Polly Ann	Jeg
1922	**Pillory** (hd)	1:51⅗	L. Morris	Thomas Healey	Hea	June Grass
1923	**Vigil** (1¼)	1:53⅗	B. Marinelli	Thomas Healey	General Thatcher	Rialto
1924	**Nellie Morse** (1½)	1:57⅕	John Merimee	A.B. Gordon	Transmute	Mad Play
1925	**Coventry** (4)	1:59	Clarence Kummer	William Duke	Backbone	Almadel
1926	**Display** (hd)	1:59⅘	John Maiben	Thomas Healey	Blondin	Mars
1927	**Bostonian** (½)	2:01⅗	Whitey Abel	Fred Hopkins	Sir Harry	Whiskery
1928	**Victorian** (ns)	2:00⅕	Sonny Workman	James Rowe Jr.	Toro	Solace
1929	**Dr. Freeland** (1)	2:01⅗	Louis Schaefer	Thomas Healey	Minotaur	African
1930	**GALLANT FOX** (¾)	2:00⅗	Earl Sande	Jim Fitzsimmons	Crack Brigade	Snowflake
1931	**Mate** (1½)	1:59	George Ellis	J.W. Healy	Twenty Grand	Ladder
1932	**Burgoo King** (hd)	1:59⅘	Eugene James	Dick Thompson	Tick On	Boatswain
1933	**Head Play** (4)	2:02	Charley Kurtsinger	Thomas Hayes	Ladysman	Utopian
1934	**High Quest** (ns)	1:58⅕	Robert Jones	Bob Smith	Cavalcade	Discovery
1935	**OMAHA** (6)	1:58⅖	Willie Saunders	Jim Fitzsimmons	Firethorn	Psychic Bid
1936	**Bold Venture** (ns)	1:59	George Woolf	Max Hirsch	Granville	Jean Bart
1937	**WAR ADMIRAL** (hd)	1:58⅖	Charley Kurtsinger	George Conway	Pompoon	Flying Scot
1938	**Dauber** (7)	1:59⅘	Maurice Peters	Dick Handlen	Cravat	Menow
1939	**Challedon** (1¼)	1:59⅘	George Seabo	Louis Schaefer	Gilded Knight	Volitant
1940	**Bimelech** (3)	1:58⅗	F.A. Smith	Bill Hurley	Mioland	Gallahadion
1941	**WHIRLAWAY** (5½)	1:58⅘	Eddie Arcaro	Ben Jones	King Cole	Our Boots
1942	**Alsab** (1)	1:57	Basil James	Sarge Swenke	Requested & Sun Again (dead heat)	
1943	**COUNT FLEET** (8)	1:57⅖	Johnny Longden	Don Cameron	Blue Swords	Vincentive
1944	**Pensive** (¾)	1:59⅕	Conn McCreary	Ben Jones	Platter	Stir Up
1945	**Polynesian** (2½)	1:58⅘	W.D. Wright	Morris Dixon	Hoop Jr.	Darby Dieppe
1946	**ASSAULT** (nk)	2:01⅖	Warren Mehrtens	Max Hirsch	Lord Boswell	Hampden
1947	**Faultless** (1¼)	1:59	Doug Dodson	Jimmy Jones	On Trust	Phalanx
1948	**CITATION** (5½)	2:02⅖	Eddie Arcaro	Jimmy Jones	Vulcan's Forge	Bovard
1949	**Capot** (hd)	1:56	Ted Atkinson	J.M. Gaver	Palestinian	Noble Impulse
1950	**Hill Prince** (5)	1:59⅕	Eddie Arcaro	Casey Hayes	Middleground	Dooly
1951	**Bold** (7)	1:56⅖	Eddie Arcaro	Preston Burch	Counterpoint	Alerted
1952	**Blue Man** (3½)	1:57⅖	Conn McCreary	Woody Stephens	Jampol	One Count
1953	**Native Dancer** (nk)	1:57⅘	Eric Guerin	Bill Winfrey	Jamie K.	Royal Bay Gem
1954	**Hasty Road** (nk)	1:57⅖	Johnny Adams	Harry Trotsek	Correlation	Hasseyampa
1955	**Nashua** (1)	1:54⅗	Eddie Arcaro	Jim Fitzsimmons	Saratoga	Traffic Judge
1956	**Fabius** (¾)	1:58⅖	Bill Hartack	Jimmy Jones	Needles	No Regrets
1957	**Bold Ruler** (2)	1:56⅕	Eddie Arcaro	Jim Fitzsimmons	Iron Liege	Inside Tract
1958	**Tim Tam** (1½)	1:57⅕	Ismael Valenzuela	Jimmy Jones	Lincoln Road	Gone Fishin'
1959	**Royal Orbit** (4)	1:57	William Harmatz	R. Cornell	Sword Dancer	Dunce
1960	**Bally Ache** (4)	1:57⅗	Bobby Ussery	Jimmy Pitt	Victoria Park	Celtic Ash
1961	**Carry Back** (¾)	1:57⅗	Johnny Sellers	Jack Price	Globemaster	Crozier
1962	**Greek Money** (ns)	1:56⅕	John Rotz	V.W. Raines	Ridan	Roman Line
1963	**Candy Spots** (3½)	1:56⅕	Bill Shoemaker	Mesh Tenney	Chateaugay	Never Bend
1964	**Northern Dancer** (2¼)	1:56⅘	Bill Hartack	Horatio Luro	The Scoundrel	Hill Rise
1965	**Tom Rolfe** (nk)	1:56⅕	Ron Turcotte	Frank Whiteley	Dapper Dan	Hail To All
1966	**Kauai King** (1¾)	1:55⅖	Don Brumfield	Henry Forrest	Stupendous	Amberoid
1967	**Damascus** (2¼)	1:55⅕	Bill Shoemaker	Frank Whiteley	In Reality	Proud Clarion
1968	**Forward Pass** (6)	1:56⅘	Ismael Valenzuela	Henry Forrest	Out Of the Way	Nodouble
1969	**Majestic Prince** (hd)	1:55⅗	Bill Hartack	Johnny Longden	Arts and Letters	Jay Ray
1970	**Personality** (nk)	1:56⅕	Eddie Belmonte	John Jacobs	My Dad George	Silent Screen
1971	**Canonero II** (1½)	1:54	Gustavo Avila	Juan Arias	Eastern Fleet	Jim French

AP Images

***Affirmed** (with jockey Steve Cauthen) wins the 103rd running of the Preakness on May 20, 1978 by a neck over Alydar. Affirmed is the last horse to win the Triple Crown.*

Year	**Winner** (Margin)	Time	Jockey	Trainer	2nd place	3rd place
1972	**Bee Bee Bee** (1 1/4)	1:55 3/5	Eldon Nelson	Red Carroll	No Le Hace	Key To The Mint
1973	**SECRETARIAT** (2 1/2)	1:54 2/5	Ron Turcotte	Lucien Laurin	Sham	Our Native
1974	**Little Current** (7)	1:54 3/5	Miguel Rivera	Lou Rondinello	Neapolitan Way	Cannonade
1975	**Master Derby** (1)	1:56 2/5	Darrel McHargue	Smiley Adams	Foolish Pleasure	Diabolo
1976	**Elocutionist** (3 1/2)	1:55	John Lively	Paul Adwell	Play The Red	Bold Forbes
1977	**SEATTLE SLEW** (1 1/2)	1:54 2/5	Jean Cruguet	Billy Turner	Iron Constitution	Run Dusty Run
1978	**AFFIRMED** (nk)	1:54 2/5	Steve Cauthen	Laz Barrera	Alydar	Believe It
1979	**Spectacular Bid** (3 1/2)	1:54 1/5	Ron Franklin	Bud Delp	Golden Act	Screen King
1980	**Codex** (4 3/4)	1:54 1/5	Angel Cordero Jr.	D. Wayne Lukas	Genuine Risk	Colonel Moran
1981	**Pleasant Colony** (1)	1:54 3/5	Jorge Velasquez	John Campo	Bold Ego	Paristo
1982	**Aloma's Ruler** (1/2)	1:55 2/5	Jack Kaenel	John Lenzini Jr.	Linkage	Cut Away
1983	**Deputed Testamony** (2 3/4)	1:55 2/5*	Donald Miller Jr.	Bill Boniface	Desert Wine	High Honors
1984	**Gate Dancer** (1 1/2)	1:53 3/5	Angel Cordero Jr.	Jack Van Berg	Play On	Fight Over
1985	**Tank's Prospect** (hd)	1:53 2/5	Pat Day	D. Wayne Lukas	Chief's Crown	Eternal Prince
1986	**Snow Chief** (4)	1:54 4/5	Alex Solis	Melvin Stute	Ferdinand	Broad Brush
1987	**Alysheba** (1/2)	1:55 4/5	Chris McCarron	Jack Van Berg	Bet Twice	Cryptoclearance
1988	**Risen Star** (1 1/4)	1:56 1/5	E. Delahoussaye	Louie Roussel III	Brian's Time	Winning Colors
1989	**Sunday Silence** (ns)	1:53 4/5	Pat Valenzuela	Chas. Whittingham	Easy Goer	Rock Point
1990	**Summer Squall** (2 1/4)	1:53 3/5	Pat Day	Neil Howard	Unbridled	Mister Frisky
1991	**Hansel** (7)	1:54	Jerry Bailey	Frank Brothers	Corporate Report	Mane Minister
1992	**Pine Bluff** (3/4)	1:55 3/5	Chris McCarron	Tom Bohannan	Alydeed	Casual Lies
1993	**Prairie Bayou** (1/2)	1:56 3/5	Mike Smith	Tom Bohannan	Cherokee Run	El Bakan
1994	**Tabasco Cat** (3/4)	1:56 2/5	Pat Day	D. Wayne Lukas	Go For Gin	Concern
1995	**Timber Country** (1/2)	1:54 2/5	Pat Day	D. Wayne Lukas	Oliver's Twist	Thunder Gulch
1996	**Louis Quatorze** (3 1/4)	1:53 2/5	Pat Day	Nick Zito	Skip Away	Editor's Note
1997	**Silver Charm** (hd)	1:54 2/5	Gary Stevens	Bob Baffert	Free House	Captain Bodgit
1998	**Real Quiet** (2 1/4)	1:54 4/5	Kent Desormeaux	Bob Baffert	Victory Gallop	Classic Cat
1999	**Charismatic** (1 1/2)	1:55 1/5	Chris Antley	D. Wayne Lukas	Menifee	Badge
2000	**Red Bullet** (3 3/4)	1:56	Jerry Bailey	Joe Orseno	Fusaichi Pegasus	Impeachment
2001	**Point Given** (2 1/4)	1:55 2/5	Gary Stevens	Bob Baffert	A P Valentine	Congaree
2002	**War Emblem** (3/4)	1:56 1/5	Victor Espinoza	Bob Baffert	Magic Weisner	Proud Citizen
2003	**Funny Cide** (9 3/4)	1:55 3/5	Jose Santos	Barclay Tagg	Midway Road	Scrimshaw
2004	**Smarty Jones** (11 1/2)	1:55 2/5	Stewart Elliott	John Servis	Rock Hard Ten	Eddington
2005	**Afleet Alex** (4 3/4)	1:55	Jeremy Rose	Tim Ritchey	Scrappy T	Giacomo
2006	**Bernardini** (5 1/4)	1:54 3/5	Javier Castellano	Thomas Albertrani	Sweetnorthernsaint	Hemingway's Key
2007	**Curlin** (hd)	1:53 2/5	Robby Albarado	Steven Asmussen	Street Sense	Hard Spun
2008	**Big Brown** (5 1/4)	1:54 4/5	Kent Desormeaux	Richard Dutrow Jr.	Macho Again	Icabad Crane

* Later named Judge Murray.

Belmont Stakes

For three-year-olds. Held three weeks after Preakness Stakes at Belmont Park in Elmont, N.Y. Inaugurated in 1867 at Jerome Park, moved to Morris Park in 1890 and then to Belmont Park in 1905.

Originally run at 1 mile and 5 furlongs (1867-89), then 1¼ miles (1890-1905), 1⅜ miles (1906-25), and the present 1½ miles since 1926.

Trainers with most wins: James Rowe Sr. (8); Sam Hildreth (7); Sunny Jim Fitzsimmons (6); Woody Stephens (5); Max Hirsch, D. Wayne Lukas and Robert W. Walden (4); Elliott Burch, Lucien Laurin, F. McCabe and D. McDaniel (3).

Jockeys with most wins: Eddie Arcaro and Jim McLaughlin (6); Earl Sande and Bill Shoemaker (5); Braulio Baeza; Pat Day, Laffit Pincay Jr., Gary Stevens and James Stout (3).

Winning fillies: Ruthless (1867), Tanya (1905) and Rags to Riches (2007).

Year	Winner (Margin)	Time	Jockey	Trainer	2nd place	3rd place
1867	**Ruthless** (½)	3:05	J. Gilpatrick	A.J. Minor	DeCourcey	Rivoli
1868	**General Duke** (2)	3:02	Bobby Swim	A. Thompson	Northumberland	Fanny Ludlow
1869	**Fenian** (6)	3:04¼	C. Miller	J. Pincus	Glenelg	Invercauld
1870	**Kingfisher** (nk)	2:59½	W. Dick	R. Colston	Foster	Midday
1871	**Harry Bassett** (3)	2:56	W. Miller	D. McDaniel	Stockwood	By the Sea
1872	**Joe Daniels** (¾)	2:58¼	James Roe	D. McDaniel	Meteor	Shylock
1873	**Springbok** (¾)	3:01¾	James Roe	D. McDaniel	Count d'Orsay	Strachino
1874	**Saxon** (nk)	2:39½	G. Barbee	W. Prior	Grinstead	Aaron Pennington
1875	**Calvin** (2)	2:42¼	Bobby Swim	A. Williams	Aristides	Milner
1876	**Algerine** (½)	2:40½	Billy Donohue	Major Doswell	Fiddlesticks	Barricade
1877	**Cloverbrook** (1)	2:46	C. Holloway	J. Walden	Loiterer	Baden-Baden
1878	**Duke of Magenta** (2)	2:43½	L. Hughes	R.W. Walden	Bramble	Sparta
1879	**Spendthrift** (6)	2:42¾	George Evans	T. Puryear	Monitor	Jericho
1880	**Grenada** (nk)	2:47	L. Hughes	R.W. Walden	Ferncliffe	Turenne
1881	**Saunterer** (nk)	2:47	T. Costello	R.W. Walden	Eole	Baltic
1882	**Forester** (5)	2:43	Jim McLaughlin	L. Stuart	Babcock	Wyoming
1883	**George Kinney** (3)	2:42½	Jim McLaughlin	James Rowe Sr.	Trombone	Renegade
1884	**Panique** (nk)	2:42	Jim McLaughlin	James Rowe Sr.	Knight of Ellerslie	Himalaya
1885	**Tyrant** (3)	2:43	Paul Duffy	W. Claypool	St. Augustine	Tecumseh
1886	**Inspector B** (1)	2:41	Jim McLaughlin	F. McCabe	The Bard	Linden
1887	**Hanover** (15)	2:43½	Jim McLaughlin	F. McCabe	Oneko	(2-horse race)
1888	**Sir Dixon** (15)	2:40¼	Jim McLaughlin	F. McCabe	Prince Royal	(2-horse race)
1889	**Eric** (½)	2:47¼	W. Hayward	J. Huggins	Diablo	Zephyrus
1890	**Burlington** (2)	2:07¾	Pike Barnes	A. Cooper	Devotee	Padishah
1891	**Foxford** (nk)	2:08¾	Ed Garrison	M. Donavan	Montana	Laurestan
1892	**Patron** (6)	2:12	W. Hayward	L. Stuart	Shellbark	(2-horse race)
1893	**Commanche** (hd)	1:53¼	Willie Simms	G. Hannon	Dr. Rice	Rainbow
1894	**Henry of Navarre** (1½)	1:56½	Willie Simms	B. McClelland	Prig	Assignee
1895	**Belmar** (hd)	2:11½	Fred Taral	E. Feakes	Counter Tenor	Nanki Poo
1896	**Hastings** (hd)	2:24½	H. Griffin	J.J. Hyland	Handspring	Hamilton II
1897	**Scottish Chieftain** (1)	2:23¼	J. Scherrer	M. Byrnes	On Deck	Octagon
1898	**Bowling Brook** (6)	2:32	F. Littlefield	R.W. Walden	Previous	Hamburg
1899	**Jean Beraud** (hd)	2:23	R. Clawson	Sam Hildreth	Half Time	Glengar
1900	**Ildrim** (ns)	2:21¼	Nash Turner	H.E. Leigh	Petruchio	Missionary
1901	**Commando** (2)	2:21	H. Spencer	James Rowe Sr.	The Parader	All Green
1902	**Masterman** (2)	2:22⅗	John Bullman	J.J. Hyland	Renald	King Hanover
1903	**Africander** (2)	2:21¾	John Bullman	R. Miller	Whorler	Red Knight
1904	**Delhi** (4)	2:06⅗	George Odom	James Rowe Sr.	Graziallo	Rapid Water
1905	**Tanya** (½)	2:08	E. Hildebrand	J.W. Rogers	Blandy	Hot Shot
1906	**Burgomaster** (4)	2:20	Lucien Lyne	J.W. Rogers	The Quail	Accountant
1907	**Peter Pan** (1)	N/A	G. Mountain	James Rowe Sr.	Superman	Frank Gill
1908	**Colin** (hd)	N/A	Joe Notter	James Rowe Sr.	Fair Play	King James
1909	**Joe Madden** (8)	2:21⅗	E. Dugan	Sam Hildreth	Wise Mason	Donald MacDonald
1910	**Sweep** (6)	2:22	James Butwell	James Rowe Sr.	Duke of Ormonde	(2-horse race)
1911-12	Not held					
1913	**Prince Eugene** (½)	2:18	Roscoe Troxler	James Rowe Sr.	Rock View	Flying Fairy
1914	**Luke McLuke** (8)	2:20	Merritt Buxton	J.F. Schorr	Gainer	Charlestonian
1915	**The Finn** (4)	2:18⅖	George Byrne	E.W. Heffner	Half Rock	Pebbles
1916	**Friar Rock** (3)	2:22	E. Haynes	Sam Hildreth	Spur	Churchill
1917	**Hourless** (10)	2:17⅘	James Butwell	Sam Hildreth	Skeptic	Wonderful
1918	**Johren** (2)	2:20⅖	Frank Robinson	A. Simons	War Cloud	Cum Sah
1919	**SIR BARTON** (5)	2:17⅖	John Loftus	H. Guy Bedwell	Sweep On	Natural Bridge
1920	**Man o' War** (20)	2:14⅕	Clarence Kummer	L. Feustel	Donnacona	(2-horse race)
1921	**Grey Lag** (3)	2:16⅘	Earl Sande	Sam Hildreth	Sporting Blood	Leonardo II
1922	**Pillory** (2)	2:18⅘	C.H. Miller	T.J. Healey	Snob II	Hea
1923	**Zev** (1½)	2:19	Earl Sande	Sam Hildreth	Chickvale	Rialto
1924	**Mad Play** (2)	2:18⅘	Earl Sande	Sam Hildreth	Mr. Mutt	Modest
1925	**American Flag** (8)	2:16⅘	Albert Johnson	G.R. Tompkins	Dangerous	Swope
1926	**Crusader** (1)	2:32⅕	Albert Johnson	George Conway	Espino	Haste

Year	Winner (Margin)	Time	Jockey	Trainer	2nd place	3rd place
1927	**Chance Shot** (1½)	2:32⅖	Earl Sande	Pete Coyne	Bois de Rose	Flambino
1928	**Vito** (3)	2:33⅕	Clarence Kummer	Max Hirsch	Genie	Diavolo
1929	**Blue Larkspur** (¾)	2:32⅘	Mack Garner	C. Hastings	African	Jack High
1930	**GALLANT FOX** (3)	2:31⅗	Earl Sande	Jim Fitzsimmons	Whichone	Questionnaire
1931	**Twenty Grand** (10)	2:29⅗	Charley Kurtsinger	James Rowe Jr.	Sun Meadow	Jamestown
1932	**Faireno** (1½)	2:32⅘	Tom Malley	Jim Fitzsimmons	Osculator	Flag Pole
1933	**Hurryoff** (1½)	2:32⅗	Mack Garner	H. McDaniel	Nimbus	Union
1934	**Peace Chance** (6)	2:29⅕	W.D. Wright	Pete Coyne	High Quest	Good Goods
1935	**OMAHA** (1½)	2:30⅗	Willie Saunders	Jim Fitzsimmons	Firethorn	Rosemont
1936	**Granville** (ns)	2:30	James Stout	Jim Fitzsimmons	Mr. Bones	Hollyrood
1937	**WAR ADMIRAL** (3)	2:28⅗	Charley Kurtsinger	George Conway	Sceneshifter	Vamoose
1938	**Pasteurized** (nk)	2:29⅖	James Stout	George Odom	Dauber	Cravat
1939	**Johnstown** (5)	2:29⅗	James Stout	Jim Fitzsimmons	Belay	Gilded Knight
1940	**Bimelech** (¾)	2:29⅗	Fred Smith	Bill Hurley	Your Chance	Andy K.
1941	**WHIRLAWAY** (2½)	2:31	Eddie Arcaro	Ben Jones	Robert Morris	Yankee Chance
1942	**Shut Out** (2)	2:29⅕	Eddie Arcaro	John Gaver	Alsab	Lochinvar
1943	**COUNT FLEET** (25)	2:28⅕	Johnny Longden	Don Cameron	Fairy Manhurst	Deseronto
1944	**Bounding Home** (½)	2:32⅕	G.L. Smith	Matt Brady	Pensive	Bull Dandy
1945	**Pavot** (5)	2:30⅕	Eddie Arcaro	Oscar White	Wildlife	Jeep
1946	**ASSAULT** (3)	2:30⅘	Warren Mehrtens	Max Hirsch	Natchez	Cable
1947	**Phalanx** (5)	2:29⅖	R. Donoso	Syl Veitch	Tide Rips	Tailspin
1948	**CITATION** (8)	2:28⅕	Eddie Arcaro	Jimmy Jones	Better Self	Escadru
1949	**Capot** (½)	2:30⅕	Ted Atkinson	John Gaver	Ponder	Palestinian
1950	**Middleground** (1)	2:28⅗	William Boland	Max Hirsch	Lights Up	Mr. Trouble
1951	**Counterpoint** (4)	2:29	David Gorman	Syl Veitch	Battlefield	Battle Morn
1952	**One Count** (2½)	2:30⅕	Eddie Arcaro	Oscar White	Blue Man	Armageddon
1953	**Native Dancer** (nk)	2:28⅗	Eric Guerin	Bill Winfrey	Jamie K.	Royal Bay Gem
1954	**High Gun** (nk)	2:30⅘	Eric Guerin	Max Hirsch	Fisherman	Limelight
1955	**Nashua** (9)	2:29	Eddie Arcaro	Jim Fitzsimmons	Blazing Count	Portersville
1956	**Needles** (nk)	2:29⅘	David Erb	Hugh Fontaine	Career Boy	Fabius
1957	**Gallant Man** (8)	2:26⅗	Bill Shoemaker	John Nerud	Inside Tract	Bold Ruler
1958	**Cavan** (6)	2:30⅕	Pete Anderson	Tom Barry	Tim Tam	Flamingo
1959	**Sword Dancer** (¾)	2:28⅖	Bill Shoemaker	Elliott Burch	Bagdad	Royal Orbit
1960	**Celtic Ash** (5½)	2:29⅕	Bill Hartack	Tom Barry	Venetian Way	Disperse
1961	**Sherluck** (2¼)	2:29⅕	Braulio Baeza	Harold Young	Globemaster	Guadalcanal
1962	**Jaipur** (ns)	2:28⅘	Bill Shoemaker	B. Mulholland	Admiral's Voyage	Crimson Satan
1963	**Chateaugay** (2½)	2:30⅕	Braulio Baeza	James Conway	Candy Spots	Choker
1964	**Quadrangle** (2)	2:28⅖	Manuel Ycaza	Elliott Burch	Roman Brother	Northern Dancer
1965	**Hail to All** (nk)	2:28⅖	John Sellers	Eddie Yowell	Tom Rolfe	First Family
1966	**Amberoid** (2½)	2:29⅗	William Boland	Lucien Laurin	Buffle	Advocator
1967	**Damascus** (2½)	2:28⅘	Bill Shoemaker	F.Y. Whiteley Jr.	Cool Reception	Gentleman James
1968	**Stage Door Johnny** (1¼)	2:27⅕	Gus Gustines	John Gaver	Forward Pass	Call Me Prince
1969	**Arts and Letters** (5½)	2:28⅘	Braulio Baeza	Elliott Burch	Majestic Prince	Dike
1970	**High Echelon** (¾)	2:34	John Rotz	John Jacobs	Needles N Pens	Naskra
1971	**Pass Catcher** (¾)	2:30⅖	Walter Blum	Eddie Yowell	Jim French	Bold Reason
1972	**Riva Ridge** (7)	2:28	Ron Turcotte	Lucien Laurin	Ruritania	Cloudy Dawn
1973	**SECRETARIAT** (31)	2:24	Ron Turcotte	Lucien Laurin	Twice A Prince	My Gallant
1974	**Little Current** (7)	2:29⅕	Miguel Rivera	Lou Rondinello	Jolly Johu	Cannonade
1975	**Avatar** (nk)	2:28⅕	Bill Shoemaker	Tommy Doyle	Foolish Pleasure	Master Derby
1976	**Bold Forbes** (nk)	2:29	Angel Cordero Jr.	Laz Barrera	McKenzie Bridge	Great Contractor
1977	**SEATTLE SLEW** (4)	2:29⅗	Jean Cruguet	Billy Turner	Run Dusty Run	Sanhedrin
1978	**AFFIRMED** (hd)	2:26⅘	Steve Cauthen	Laz Barrera	Alydar	Darby Creek Road
1979	**Coastal** (3¼)	2:28⅗	Ruben Hernandez	David Whiteley	Golden Act	Spectacular Bid
1980	**Temperence Hill** (2)	2:29⅘	Eddie Maple	Joseph Cantey	Genuine Risk	Rockhill Native
1981	**Summing** (nk)	2:29	George Martens	Luis Barerra	Highland Blade	Pleasant Colony
1982	**Conquistador Cielo** (14)	2:28⅕	Laffit Pincay Jr.	Woody Stephens	Gato Del Sol	Illuminate
1983	**Caveat** (3½)	2:27⅘	Laffit Pincay Jr.	Woody Stephens	Slew o' Gold	Barberstown
1984	**Swale** (4)	2:27⅕	Laffit Pincay Jr.	Woody Stephens	Pine Circle	Morning Bob
1985	**Creme Fraiche** (½)	2:27	Eddie Maple	Woody Stephens	Stephan's Odyssey	Chief's Crown
1986	**Danzig Connection** (1¼)	2:29⅘	Chris McCarron	Woody Stephens	Johns Treasure	Ferdinand
1987	**Bet Twice** (14)	2:28⅕	Craig Perret	Jimmy Croll	Cryptoclearance	Gulch
1988	**Risen Star** (14¾)	2:26⅖	E. Delahoussaye	Louie Roussel III	Kingpost	Brian's Time
1989	**Easy Goer** (8)	2:26	Pat Day	Shug McGaughey	Sunday Silence	Le Voyageur
1990	**Go And Go** (8¼)	2:27⅕	Michael Kinane	Dermot Weld	Thirty Six Red	Baron de Vaux
1991	**Hansel** (hd)	2:28	Jerry Bailey	Frank Brothers	Strike the Gold	Mane Minister
1992	**A.P. Indy** (¾)	2:26	E. Delahoussaye	Neil Drysdale	My Memoirs	Pine Bluff
1993	**Colonial Affair** (2)	2:29⅘	Julie Krone	Scotty Schulhofer	Kissin Kris	Wild Gale
1994	**Tabasco Cat** (2)	2:26⅘	Pat Day	D. Wayne Lukas	Go For Gin	Strodes Creek
1995	**Thunder Gulch** (2)	2:32	Gary Stevens	D. Wayne Lukas	Star Standard	Citadeed
1996	**Editor's Note** (1)	2:28⅘	Rene Douglas	D. Wayne Lukas	Skip Away	My Flag
1997	**Touch Gold** (¾)	2:28⅘	Chris McCarron	David Hofmans	Silver Charm	Free House

Belmont Stakes (Cont.)

Year	Winner (Margin)	Time	Jockey	Trainer	2nd place	3rd place
1998	**Victory Gallop** (ns)	2:29	Gary Stevens	Elliott Walden	Real Quiet	Thomas Jo
1999	**Lemon Drop Kid** (hd)	2:27$\frac{4}{5}$	Jose Santos	Scotty Schulhofer	Vision and Verse	Charismatic
2000	**Commendable** (1$\frac{1}{2}$)	2:31$\frac{1}{5}$	Pat Day	D. Wayne Lukas	Aptitude	Unshaded
2001	**Point Given** (12$\frac{1}{4}$)	2:26$\frac{2}{5}$	Gary Stevens	Bob Baffert	A P Valentine	Monarchos
2002	**Sarava** ($\frac{1}{2}$)	2:29$\frac{3}{5}$	Edgar Prado	Ken McPeek	Medaglia d'Oro	Sunday Break
2003	**Empire Maker** ($\frac{3}{4}$)	2:28$\frac{1}{5}$	Jerry Bailey	Bobby Frankel	Ten Most Wanted	Funny Cide
2004	**Birdstone** (1)	2:27$\frac{2}{5}$	Edgar Prado	Nick Zito	Smarty Jones	Royal Assault
2005	**Afleet Alex** (7)	2:28$\frac{3}{5}$	Jeremy Rose	Tim Ritchey	Andromeda's Hero	Nolan's Cat
2006	**Jazil** (1$\frac{1}{4}$)	2:27$\frac{4}{5}$	Fernando Jara	Kiaran McLaughlin	Bluegrass Cat	Sunriver
2007	**Rags to Riches** (hd)	2:28$\frac{4}{5}$	John Velazquez	Todd Pletcher	Curlin	Tiago
2008	**Da'Tara** (5$\frac{1}{4}$)	2:29$\frac{3}{5}$	Alan Garcia	Nick Zito	Denis of Cork	Anak Nakal & Ready's Echo

Breeders' Cup World Championships

Inaugurated on Nov. 10, 1984, the Breeders' Cup World Championships consists of 11 races (14 beginning in 2008) on one track on one day late in the year to determine thoroughbred racing's principle champions.

The Breeders' Cup has been (will be) held at the following tracks: Aqueduct Racetrack (N.Y.) in 1985; Arlington Park (Ill.) in 2002; Belmont Park (N.Y.) in 1990, '95, 2001 and '05; Churchill Downs (Ky.) in 1988, '91, '94, '98, 2000 and '06; Gulfstream Park (Fla.) in 1989, '92 and '99; Hollywood Park (Calif.) in 1984, '87 and '97; Lone Star Park (Texas) in 2004; Monmouth Park (N.J.) in 2007; Santa Anita Park (Calif.) in 1986, '93, 2003 and '08; and Woodbine (Toronto) in 1996.

Horses with most wins: Bayakoa, Da Hoss, High Chaparral, Lure, Miesque and Tiznow (2).

Trainers with most wins: D. Wayne Lukas (18); Shug McGaughey (9); Neil Drysdale and Richard Mandella (6); Bob Baffert, Bobby Frankel and Bill Mott (5); Andre Fabre and Ron McAnally (4); Pascal Bary, Francois Boutin, Patrick Byrne, Julio Canani, Richard Dutrow Jr., Aidan O'Brien, Doug O'Neill, Todd Pletcher and Sir Michael Stoute (3).

Jockeys with most wins: Jerry Bailey (15); Pat Day (12); Mike Smith (10); Chris McCarron (9); Gary Stevens (8); Eddie Delahoussaye, Corey Nakatani, Laffit Pincay Jr., Jose Santos and Pat Valenzuela (7); Frankie Dettori and John Velazquez (6); Angel Cordero Jr., Garrett Gomez and Craig Perret (4); Kent Desormeaux, David Flores, Michael Kinane, Edgar Prado, Randy Romero, Alex Solis and Cornelio Velasquez (3).

Juvenile

Distances: one mile (1984-85, 87); 1$\frac{1}{16}$ miles (1986, 1988-2001, 2003–), 1$\frac{1}{8}$ miles (2002).

Year	Winner (Margin)	Time	Jockey	Trainer	2nd place	3rd place
1984	**Chief's Crown** ($\frac{3}{4}$)	1:36$\frac{1}{5}$	Don MacBeth	Roger Laurin	Tank's Prospect	Spend A Buck
1985	**Tasso** (ns)	1:36$\frac{1}{5}$	Laffit Pincay Jr.	Neil Drysdale	Storm Cat	Scat Dancer
1986	**Capote** (1$\frac{1}{4}$)	1:43$\frac{4}{5}$	Laffit Pincay Jr.	D. Wayne Lukas	Qualify	Alysheba
1987	**Success Express** (1$\frac{3}{4}$)	1:35$\frac{1}{5}$	Jose Santos	D. Wayne Lukas	Regal Classic	Tejano
1988	**Is It True** (1$\frac{1}{4}$)	1:46$\frac{3}{5}$	Laffit Pincay Jr.	D. Wayne Lukas	Easy Goer	Tagel
1989	**Rhythm** (2)	1:43$\frac{3}{5}$	Craig Perret	Shug McGaughey	Grand Canyon	Slavic
1990	**Fly So Free** (3)	1:43$\frac{2}{5}$	Jose Santos	Scotty Schulhofer	Take Me Out	Lost Mountain
1991	**Arazi** (4$\frac{3}{4}$)	1:44$\frac{3}{5}$	Pat Valenzuela	Francois Boutin	Bertrando	Snappy Landing
1992	**Gilded Time** ($\frac{3}{4}$)	1:43$\frac{2}{5}$	Chris McCarron	Darrell Vienna	It'sali'lknownfact	River Special
1993	**Brocco** (5)	1:42$\frac{4}{5}$	Gary Stevens	Randy Winick	Blumin Affair	Tabasco Cat
1994	**Timber Country** ($\frac{1}{2}$)	1:44$\frac{2}{5}$	Pat Day	D. Wayne Lukas	Eltish	Tejano Run
1995	**Unbridled's Song** (nk)	1:41$\frac{3}{5}$	Mike Smith	James Ryerson	Hennessy	Editor's Note
1996	**Boston Harbor** (nk)	1:43$\frac{2}{5}$	Jerry Bailey	D. Wayne Lukas	Acceptable	Ordway
1997	**Favorite Trick** (5$\frac{1}{2}$)	1:41$\frac{2}{5}$	Pat Day	Patrick Byrne	Dawson's Legacy	Nationalore
1998	**Answer Lively** (hd)	1:44	Jerry Bailey	Bobby Barnett	Aly's Alley	Cat Thief
1999	**Anees** (2$\frac{1}{2}$)	1:42$\frac{1}{5}$	Gary Stevens	Alex Hassinger Jr.	Chief Seattle	High Yield
2000	**Macho Uno** (ns)	1:42	Jerry Bailey	Joe Orseno	Point Given	Street Cry
2001	**Johannesburg** (2$\frac{1}{4}$)	1:42$\frac{1}{5}$	Michael Kinane	Aidan O'Brien	Repent	Siphonic
2002	**Vindication** (2$\frac{3}{4}$)	1:49$\frac{3}{5}$	Mike Smith	Bob Baffert	Kafwain	Hold That Tiger
2003	**Action This Day** (2$\frac{1}{4}$)	1:43$\frac{3}{5}$	David Flores	Richard Mandella	Minister Eric	Chapel Royal
2004	**Wilko** ($\frac{3}{4}$)	1:42	Frankie Dettori	Jeremy Noseda	Afleet Alex	Sun King
2005	**Stevie Wonderboy** (1$\frac{1}{4}$)	1:41$\frac{3}{5}$	Garrett Gomez	Doug O'Neill	Henny Hughes	First Samurai
2006	**Street Sense** (10)	1:43$\frac{4}{5}$	Calvin Borel	Carl Nafzger	Circular Quay	Great Hunter
2007	**War Pass** (4$\frac{3}{4}$)	1:42$\frac{3}{5}$	Cornelio Velasquez	Nick Zito	Pyro	Kodiak Kowboy

Juvenile Fillies

Distances: one mile (1984-85, 87); 1$\frac{1}{16}$ miles (1986, 1988-2001, 2003–); 1$\frac{1}{8}$ miles (2002).

Year	Winner (Margin)	Time	Jockey	Trainer	2nd place	3rd place
1984	**Outstandingly***	1:37$\frac{4}{5}$	Walter Guerra	Pancho Martin	Dusty Heart	Fine Spirit
1985	**Twilight Ridge** (1)	1:35$\frac{4}{5}$	Jorge Velasquez	D. Wayne Lukas	Family Style	Steal A Kiss
1986	**Brave Raj** (5$\frac{1}{2}$)	1:43$\frac{1}{5}$	Pat Valenzuela	Melvin Stute	Tappiano	Saros Brig
1987	**Epitome** (ns)	1:36$\frac{2}{5}$	Pat Day	Phil Hauswald	Jeanne Jones	Dream Team
1988	**Open Mind** (1$\frac{3}{4}$)	1:46$\frac{3}{5}$	Angel Cordero Jr.	D. Wayne Lukas	Darby Shuffle	Lea Lucinda
1989	**Go for Wand** (2$\frac{3}{4}$)	1:44$\frac{1}{5}$	Randy Romero	Wm. Badgett Jr.	Sweet Roberta	Stella Madrid
1990	**Meadow Star** (5)	1:44	Jose Santos	LeRoy Jolley	Private Treasure	Dance Smartly
1991	**Pleasant Stage** (nk)	1:46$\frac{2}{5}$	E. Delahoussaye	Chris Speckert	La Spia	Cadillac Women
1992	**Eliza** (nk)	1:42$\frac{4}{5}$	Pat Valenzuela	Alex Hassinger	Educated Risk	Boots 'n Jackie
1993	**Phone Chatter** (hd)	1:43	Laffit Pincay Jr.	Richard Mandella	Sardula	Heavenly Prize

Year	Winner (Margin)	Time	Jockey	Trainer	2nd place	3rd place
1994	**Flanders** (hd)	1:45⅕	Pat Day	D. Wayne Lukas	Serena's Song	Stormy Blues
1995	**My Flag** (½)	1:42⅖	Jerry Bailey	Shug McGaughey	Cara Rafaela	Golden Attraction
1996	**Storm Song** (4½)	1:43⅗	Craig Perret	Nick Zito	Love That Jazz	Critical Factor
1997	**Countess Diana** (8½)	1:42⅕	Shane Sellers	Patrick Byrne	Career Collection	Primaly
1998	**Silverbulletday** (½)	1:43⅗	Gary Stevens	Bob Baffert	Excellent Meeting	Three Ring
1999	**Cash Run** (1¼)	1:43⅕	Jerry Bailey	D. Wayne Lukas	Chilukki	Surfside
2000	**Caressing** (½)	1:42⅗	John Velazquez	David Vance	Platinum Tiara	She's a Devil Due
2001	**Tempera** (1½)	1:41⅖	David Flores	Eoin Harty	Imperial Gesture	Bella Bellucci
2002	**Storm Flag Flying** (½)	1:49⅗	John Velazquez	Shug McGaughey	Composure	Santa Catarina
2003	**Halfbridled** (2½)	1:42⅗	Julie Krone	Richard Mandella	Ashado	Victory U.S.A.
2004	**Sweet Catomine** (3¾)	1:41⅗	Corey Nakatani	Julio Canani	Balletto	Runway Model
2005	**Folklore** (1¼)	1:43⅘	Edgar Prado	D. Wayne Lukas	Wild Fit	Original Spin
2006	**Dreaming of Anna** (1½)	1:43⅘	Rene Douglas	Wayne Catalano	Octave	Cotton Blossom
2007	**Indian Blessing** (3½)	1:44⅗	Garrett Gomez	Bob Baffert	Proud Spell	Backseat Rhythm

*In 1984, winner Fran's Valentine was disqualified for interference in the stretch and placed 10th.

Sprint

Distance: six furlongs (since 1984).

Year	Winner (Margin)	Time	Jockey	Trainer	2nd place	3rd place
1984	**Eillo** (ns)	1:10⅕	Craig Perret	Budd Lepman	Commemorate	Fighting Fit
1985	**Precisionist** (¾)	1:08⅖	Chris McCarron	L.R. Fenstermaker	Smile	Mt. Livermore
1986	**Smile** (1¼)	1:08⅖	Jacinto Vasquez	Scotty Schulhofer	Pine Tree Lane	Bedside Promise
1987	**Very Subtle** (4)	1:08⅘	Pat Valenzuela	Melvin Stute	Groovy	Exclusive Enough
1988	**Gulch** (¾)	1:10⅖	Angel Cordero Jr.	D. Wayne Lukas	Play The King	Afleet
1989	**Dancing Spree** (nk)	1:09	Angel Cordero Jr.	Shug McGaughey	Safely Kept	Dispersal
1990	**Safely Kept** (nk)	1:09⅗	Craig Perret	Alan Goldberg	Dayjur	Black Tie Affair
1991	**Sheikh Albadou** (nk)	1:09⅕	Pat Eddery	Alexander Scott	Pleasant Tap	Robyn Dancer
1992	**Thirty Slews** (nk)	1:08⅕	Eddie Delahoussaye	Bob Baffert	Meafara	Rubiano
1993	**Cardmania** (nk)	1:08⅗	Eddie Delahoussaye	Derek Meredith	Meafara	Gilded Time
1994	**Cherokee Run** (nk)	1:09⅖	Mike Smith	Frank Alexander	Soviet Problem	Cardmania
1995	**Desert Stormer** (nk)	1:09	Kent Desormeaux	Frank Lyons	Mr. Greeley	Lit de Justice
1996	**Lit de Justice** (1¼)	1:08⅗	Corey Nakatani	Jenine Sahadi	Paying Dues	Honour and Glory
1997	**Elmhurst** ½)	1:08⅕	Corey Nakatani	Jenine Sahadi	Hesabull	Bet On Sunshine
1998	**Reraise** (2)	1:09	Corey Nakatani	Craig Dollase	Grand Slam	Kona Gold
1999	**Artax** (½)	1:07⅘	Jorge Chavez	Louis Albertrani	Kona Gold	Big Jag
2000	**Kona Gold** (½)	1:07⅗	Alex Solis	Bruce Headley	Honest Lady	Bet On Sunshine
2001	**Squirtle Squirt** (½)	1:08⅖	Jerry Bailey	Bobby Frankel	Xtra Heat	Caller One
2002	**Orientate** (½)	1:08⅘	Jerry Bailey	D. Wayne Lukas	Thunderello	Crafty C.T.
2003	**Cajun Beat** (2¼)	1:07⅗	Cornelio Velasquez	Stephen Margolis	Bluesthestandard	Shake You Down
2004	**Speightstown** (1¼)	1:08	John Velazquez	Todd Pletcher	Kela	My Cousin Matt
2005	**Silver Train** (hd)	1:08⅘	Edgar Prado	Richard Dutrow Jr.	Taste of Paradise	Lion Tamer
2006	**Thor's Echo** (4)	1:08⅘	Corey Nakatani	Doug O'Neill	Friendly Island	Nightmare Affair
2007	**Midnight Lute** (4¾)	1:09	Garrett Gomez	Bob Baffert	Idiot Proof	Talent Search

Mile

Year	Winner (Margin)	Time	Jockey	Trainer	2nd place	3rd place
1984	**Royal Heroine** (1½)	1:32⅗	Fernando Toro	John Gosden	Star Choice	Cozzene
1985	**Cozzene** (2¼)	1:35	Walter Guerra	Jan Nerud	Al Mamoon*	Shadeed
1986	**Last Tycoon** (hd)	1:35⅕	Yves St.-Martin	Robert Collet	Palace Music	Fred Astaire
1987	**Miesque** (3½)	1:32⅘	Freddie Head	Francois Boutin	Show Dancer	Sonic Lady
1988	**Miesque** (4)	1:38⅗	Freddie Head	Francois Boutin	Steinlen	Simply Majestic
1989	**Steinlen** (¾)	1:37⅕	Jose Santos	D. Wayne Lukas	Sabona	Most Welcome
1990	**Royal Academy** (nk)	1:35⅕	Lester Piggott	M.V. O'Brien	Itsallgreektome	Priolo
1991	**Opening Verse** (2¼)	1:37⅖	Pat Valenzuela	Dick Lundy	Val des Bois	Star of Cozzene
1992	**Lure** (3)	1:32⅘	Mike Smith	Shug McGaughey	Paradise Creek	Brief Truce
1993	**Lure** (2¼)	1:33⅖	Mike Smith	Shug McGaughey	Ski Paradise	Fourstars Allstar
1994	**Barathea** (hd)	1:34⅖	Frankie Dettori	Luca Cumani	Johann Quatz	Unfinished Symph
1995	**Ridgewood Pearl** (2)	1:43⅗	John Murtagh	John Oxx	Fastness	Sayyedati
1996	**Da Hoss** (1½)	1:35⅘	Gary Stevens	Michael Dickinson	Spinning World	Same Old Wish
1997	**Spinning World** (2)	1:32⅗	Cash Asmussen	Jonathan Pease	Geri	Decorated Hero
1998	**Da Hoss** (hd)	1:35⅕	John Velazquez	Michael Dickinson	Hawksley Hill	Labeeb
1999	**Silic** (nk)	1:34⅕	Corey Nakatani	Julio Canani	Tuzla	Docksider
2000	**War Chant** (nk)	1:34⅗	Gary Stevens	Neil Drysdale	North East Bound	Dansili
2001	**Val Royal** (1¾)	1:32	Jose Valdivia	Julio Canani	Forbidden Apple	Bach
2002	**Domedriver** (¾)	1:36⅘	Thierry Thulliez	Pascal Bary	Rock of Gibraltar	Good Journey
2003	**Six Perfections** (¾)	1:33⅘	Jerry Bailey	Pascal Bary	Touch of the Blues	Century City
2004	**Singletary** (½)	1:36⅘	David Flores	Donald Chatlos Jr.	Antonius Pius	Six Perfections
2005	**Artie Schiller** (¾)	1:36⅕	Garrett Gomez	James Jerkens	Leroidesanimaux	Gorella
2006	**Miesque's Approval** (4)	1:34⅗	Eddie Castro	Martin Wolfson	Aragorn	Badge of Silver
2007	**Kip Deville** (1)	1:39⅗	Cornelio Velasquez	Richard Dutrow Jr.	Excellent Art	Cosmonaut

*In 1985, 2nd place finisher Palace Music was disqualified for interference and placed 9th.

Breeders' Cup Championship (Cont.)

Ladies' Classic

Formerly known as the Distaff (1984-2007). Distances: 1¼ miles (1984-87); 1⅛ miles (since 1988).

Year	Winner (Margin)	Time	Jockey	Trainer	2nd place	3rd place
1984	**Princess Rooney** (7)	2:02⅖	Eddie Delahoussaye	Neil Drysdale	Life's Magic	Adored
1985	**Life's Magic** (6¼)	2:02	Angel Cordero Jr.	D. Wayne Lukas	Lady's Secret	DontstopThemusic
1986	**Lady's Secret** (2½)	2:01⅕	Pat Day	D. Wayne Lukas	Fran's Valentine	Outstandingly
1987	**Sacahuista** (2¼)	2:02⅘	Randy Romero	D. Wayne Lukas	Clabber Girl	Oueee Bebe
1988	**Personal Ensign** (ns)	1:52	Randy Romero	Shug McGaughey	Winning Colors	Goodbye Halo
1989	**Bayakoa** (1½)	1:47⅖	Laffit Pincay Jr.	Ron McAnally	Gorgeous	Open Mind
1990	**Bayakoa** (6¾)	1:49⅕	Laffit Pincay Jr.	Ron McAnally	Colonial Waters	Valay Maid
1991	**Dance Smartly** (½)	1:50⅘	Pat Day	Jim Day	Versailles Treaty	Brought to Mind
1992	**Paseana** (4)	1:48	Chris McCarron	Ron McAnally	Versailles Treaty	Magical Maiden
1993	**Hollywood Wildcat** (ns)	1:48⅕	Eddie Delahoussaye	Neil Drysdale	Paseana	Re Toss
1994	**One Dreamer** (nk)	1:50⅗	Gary Stevens	Thomas Proctor	Heavenly Prize	Miss Dominique
1995	**Inside Information** (13½)	1:46	Mike Smith	Shug McGaughey	Heavenly Prize	Lakeway
1996	**Jewel Princess** (1½)	1:48⅕	Corey Nakatani	Wallace Dollase	Serena's Song	Different
1997	**Ajina** (2)	1:47⅕	Mike Smith	Bill Mott	Sharp Cat	Escena
1998	**Escena** (ns)	1:49⅘	Gary Stevens	Bill Mott	Banshee Breeze	Keeper Hill
1999	**Beautiful Pleasure** (¾)	1:47⅖	Jorge Chavez	John Ward Jr.	Banshee Breeze	Heritage of Gold
2000	**Spain** (1½)	1:47⅗	Victor Espinoza	D. Wayne Lukas	Surfside	Heritage of Gold
2001	**Unbridled Elaine** (hd)	1:49⅕	Pat Day	Dallas Stewart	Spain	Two Item Limit
2002	**Azeri** (5)	1:48⅗	Mike Smith	Laura de Seroux	Farda Amiga	Imperial Gesture
2003	**Adoration** (4½)	1:49⅕	Pat Valenzuela	David Hofmans	Elloluv	Got Koko
2004	**Ashado** (1¼)	1:48⅕	John Velazquez	Todd Pletcher	Storm Flag Flying	Stellar Jayne
2005	**Pleasant Home** (9¼)	1:48⅖	Cornelio Velasquez	Shug McGaughey	Society Selection	Ashado
2006	**Round Pond** (5½)	1:50⅖	Edgar Prado	Michael Matz	Asi Siempre	Happy Ticket
2007	**Ginger Punch** (nk)	1:50	Rafael Bejarano	Bobby Frankel	Hystericalady	Octave

Turf

Distance: 1½ miles (since 1984).

Year	Winner (Margin)	Time	Jockey	Trainer	2nd place	3rd place
1984	**Lashkari** (nk)	2:25⅕	Yves St.-Martin	de Royer-Dupre	All Along	Raami
1985	**Pebbles** (nk)	2:27	Pat Eddery	Clive Brittain	StrawberryRoad II	Mourjane
1986	**Manila** (nk)	2:25⅖	Jose Santos	Leroy Jolley	Theatrical	Estrapade
1987	**Theatrical** (½)	2:24⅖	Pat Day	Bill Mott	Trempolino	Village Star II
1988	**Gt. Communicator** (½)	2:35⅕	Ray Sibille	Thad Ackel	Sunshine Forever	Indian Skimmer
1989	**Prized** (hd)	2:28	Eddie Delahoussaye	Neil Drysdale	Sierra Roberta	Star Lift
1990	**In The Wings** (½)	2:29⅗	Gary Stevens	Andre Fabre	With Approval	El Senor
1991	**Miss Alleged** (2)	2:30⅘	Eric Legrix	Pascal Bary	Itsallgreektome	Quest for Fame
1992	**Fraise** (ns)	2:24	Pat Valenzuela	Bill Mott	Sky Classic	Quest for Fame
1993	**Kotashaan** (½)	2:25	Kent Desormeaux	Richard Mandella	Bien Bien	Luazur
1994	**Tikkanen** (1½)	2:26⅖	Mike Smith	Jonathan Pease	Hatoof	Paradise Creek
1995	**Northern Spur** (nk)	2:42	Chris McCarron	Ron McAnally	Freedom Cry	Carnegie
1996	**Pilsudski** (1¼)	2:30⅕	Walter Swinburn	Sir Michael Stoute	Singspiel	Swain
1997	**Chief Bearhart** (¾)	2:24	Jose Santos	Mark Frostad	Borgia	Flag Down
1998	**Buck's Boy** (1¼)	2:28⅗	Shane Sellers	Noel Hickey	Yagli	Dushyantor
1999	**Daylami** (2½)	2:24⅗	Frankie Dettori	Saeed bin Suroor	Royal Anthem	Buck's Boy
2000	**Kalanisi** (½)	2:26⅘	John Murtagh	Sir Michael Stoute	Quiet Resolve	John's Call
2001	**Fantastic Light** (¾)	2:24⅕	Frankie Dettori	Saeed bin Suroor	Milan	Timboroa
2002	**High Chaparral** (1¼)	2:30⅕	Michael Kinane	Aidan O'Brien	With Anticipation	Falcon Flight
2003	**High Chaparral***	2:24⅕	Michael Kinane	Aidan O'Brien	—	Falbrav
	& **Johar***	2:24⅕	Alex Solis	Richard Mandella		
2004	**Better Talk Now** (1¾)	2:29⅗	Ramon Dominguez	H. Graham Motion	Kitten's Joy	Powerscourt
2005	**Shirocco** (1¾)	2:29⅖	Christophe Soumillon	Andre Fabre	Ace	Azamour
2006	**Red Rocks** (½)	2:27⅕	Frankie Dettori	Brian Meehan	Better Talk Now	English Channel
2007	**English Channel** (7)	2:36⅘	John Velazquez	Todd Pletcher	Shamdinan	Red Rocks

*in 2003, High Chaparral and Johar finished in a dead heat, the first in Breeders' Cup history.

Filly & Mare Turf

Distance: 1⅜ miles (1999-2000,04,06-07); 1¼ miles (2001-03,05).

Year	Winner (Margin)	Time	Jockey	Trainer	2nd place	3rd place
1999	**Soaring Softly** (¾)	2:13⅘	Jerry Bailey	James J. Toner	Coretta	Zomarradah
2000	**Perfect Sting** (¾)	2:13	Jerry Bailey	Joe Orseno	Tout Charmant	Catella
2001	**Banks Hill** (5½)	2:00⅕	Olivier Peslier	Andre Fabre	Spook Express	Spring Oak
2002	**Starine** (1½)	2:03⅗	John Velazquez	Bobby Frankel	Banks Hill	Islington
2003	**Islington** (nk)	1:59	Kieren Fallon	Sir Michael Stoute	L'Ancresse	Yesterday
2004	**Ouija Board** (1½)	2:18⅕	Kieren Fallon	Edward Dunlop	Film Maker	Wonder Again
2005	**Intercontinental** (1¼)	2:02⅖	Rafael Bejarano	Bobby Frankel	Ouija Board	Film Maker
2006	**Ouija Board** (2¼)	2:14⅖	Frankie Dettori	Edward Dunlop	Film Maker	Honey Ryder
2007	**Lahudood** (¾)	2:22⅗	Alan Garcia	Kiaran McLaughlin	Honey Ryder	Passage of Time

Classic

Distance: 1¼ miles (since 1984).

Year	Winner (Margin)	Time	Jockey	Trainer	2nd place	3rd place
1984	**Wild Again** (hd)	2:03⅖	Pat Day	Vincent Timphony	Slew o' Gold	Gate Dancer*
1985	**Proud Truth** (hd)	2:00⅘	Jorge Velasquez	John Veitch	Gate Dancer	Turkoman
1986	**Skywalker** (1¼)	2:00⅖	Laffit Pincay Jr.	M. Whittingham	Turkoman	Precisionist
1987	**Ferdinand** (ns)	2:01⅖	Bill Shoemaker	C. Whittingham	Alysheba	Judge Angelucci
1988	**Alysheba** (ns)	2:04⅘	Chris McCarron	Jack Van Berg	Seeking the Gold	Waquoit
1989	**Sunday Silence** (½)	2:00⅕	Chris McCarron	C. Whittingham	Easy Goer	Blushing John
1990	**Unbridled** (1)	2:02⅕	Pat Day	Carl Nafzger	Ibn Bey	Thirty Six Red
1991	**Black Tie Affair** (1¼)	2:02⅘	Jerry Bailey	Ernie Poulos	Twilight Agenda	Unbridled
1992	**A.P. Indy** (2)	2:00⅕	Eddie Delahoussaye	Neil Drysdale	Pleasant Tap	Jolypha
1993	**Arcangues** (2)	2:00⅘	Jerry Bailey	Andre Fabre	Bertrando	Kissin Kris
1994	**Concern** (nk)	2:02⅖	Jerry Bailey	Richard Small	Tabasco Cat	Dramatic Gold
1995	**Cigar** (2½)	1:59⅖	Jerry Bailey	Bill Mott	L'Carriere	Unaccounted For
1996	**Alphabet Soup** (ns)	2:01	Chris McCarron	David Hofmans	Louis Quatorze	Cigar
1997	**Skip Away** (6)	1:59⅕	Mike Smith	Hubert Hine	Deputy Commander	Dowty
1998	**Awesome Again** (¾)	2:02	Pat Day	Patrick Byrne	Silver Charm	Swain
1999	**Cat Thief** (1¼)	1:59⅖	Pat Day	D. Wayne Lukas	Budroyale	Golden Missile
2000	**Tiznow** (nk)	2:00⅗	Chris McCarron	Jay Robbins	Giant's Causeway	Captain Steve
2001	**Tiznow** (ns)	2:00⅗	Chris McCarron	Jay Robbins	Sakhee	Albert the Great
2002	**Volponi** (6½)	2:01⅖	Jose Santos	Philip Johnson	Medaglia d'Oro	Milwaukee Brew
2003	**Pleasantly Perfect** (1½)	1:59⅘	Alex Solis	Richard Mandella	Medaglia d'Oro	Dynever
2004	**Ghostzapper** (3)	1:59	Javier Castellano	Bobby Frankel	Roses in May	Pleasantly Perfect
2005	**Saint Liam** (1)	2:01⅖	Jerry Bailey	Richard Dutrow Jr.	Flower Alley	Perfect Drift
2006	**Invasor** (1)	2:02	Fernando Jara	Kiaran McLaughlin	Bernardini	Premium Tap
2007	**Curlin** (4½)	2:00⅖	Robby Albarado	Steven Asmussen	Hard Spun	Awesome Gem

*In 1984, 2nd place finisher Gate Dancer was disqualified for interference and placed 3rd.

Filly & Mare Sprint

Distance: 6 furlongs (since 2007).

Year	Winner (Margin)	Time	Jockey	Trainer	2nd place	3rd place
2007	**Maryfield** (½)	1:09⅘	Elvis Trujillo	Doug O'Neill	Miraculous Miss	Miss Macy Sue

Juvenile Turf

Distance: 1 mile (since 2007).

Year	Winner (Margin)	Time	Jockey	Trainer	2nd place	3rd place
2007	**Nownownow** (½)	1:40⅖	Julien Leparoux	Francois Parisel	Archill Island	Cannonball

Dirt Mile

Year	Winner (Margin)	Time	Jockey	Trainer	2nd place	3rd place
2007	**Corinthian** (hd)	2:03⅖	Kent Desormeaux	James Jerkens	Gottcha Gold	Discreet Cat

Annual Money Leaders

Horses

Annual money-leading horses since 1910, according to *The American Racing Manual.*

Multiple leaders: Round Table, Buckpasser, Alysheba and Cigar (2).

Year		Age	Sts	1-2-3	Earnings
1910	Novelty	2	16	11—	$72,630
1911	Worth	2	13	10—	16,645
1912	Star Charter	4	17	6—	14,655
1913	Old Rosebud	2	14	12—	19,057
1914	Roamer	3	16	12—	29,105
1915	Borrow	7	9	4—	20,195
1916	Campfire	2	9	6—	49,735
1917	Sun Briar	2	9	5—	59,505
1918	Eternal	2	8	6—	56,173
1919	Sir Barton	3	13	8-3-2	88,250
1920	Man o' War	3	11	11-0-0	166,140
1921	Morvich	2	11	11-0-0	115,234
1922	Pillory	3	7	4-1-1	95,654
1923	Zev	3	14	12-1-0	272,008
1924	Sarzen	3	12	8-1-1	95,640
1925	Pompey	2	10	7-2-0	121,630
1926	Crusader	3	15	9-4-0	166,033
1927	Anita Peabody	2	7	6-0-1	111,905
1928	High Strung	2	6	5-0-0	153,590
1929	Blue Larkspur	3	6	4-1-0	153,450
1930	Gallant Fox	3	10	9-1-0	308,275
1931	Gallant Flight	2	7	7-0-0	219,000
1932	Gusto	3	16	4-3-2	145,940
1933	Singing Wood	2	9	3-2-2	88,050
1934	Cavalcade	3	7	6-1-0	$111,235
1935	Omaha	3	9	6-1-2	142,255
1936	Granville	3	11	7-3-0	110,295
1937	Seabiscuit	4	15	11-2-2	168,580
1938	Stagehand	3	15	8-2-3	189,710
1939	Challedon	3	15	9-2-3	184,535
1940	Bimelech	3	7	4-2-1	110,005
1941	Whirlaway	3	20	13-5-2	272,386
1942	Shut Out	3	12	8-2-0	238,872
1943	Count Fleet	3	6	6-0-0	174,055
1944	Pavot	2	8	8-0-0	179,040
1945	Busher	3	13	10-2-1	273,735
1946	Assault	3	15	8-2-3	424,195
1947	Armed	6	17	11-4-1	376,325
1948	Citation	3	20	19-1-0	709,470
1949	Ponder	3	21	9-5-2	321,825
1950	Noor	5	12	7-4-1	346,940
1951	Counterpoint	3	15	7-2-1	250,525
1952	Crafty Admiral	4	16	9-4-1	277,225
1953	Native Dancer	3	10	9-1-0	513,425
1954	Determine	3	15	10-3-2	328,700
1955	Nashua	3	12	10-1-1	752,550
1956	Needles	3	8	4-2-0	440,850
1957	Round Table	3	22	15-1-3	600,383

Annual Money Leaders — Horses (Cont.)

Year		Age	Sts	1-2-3	Earnings	Year		Age	Sts	1-2-3	Earnings
1958	Round Table	4	20	14-4-0	$662,780	1983	All Along (FRA)	4	7	4-1-1	$2,138,963
1959	Sword Dancer	3	13	8-4-0	537,004	1984	Slew o' Gold	4	6	5-1-0	2,627,944
1960	Bally Ache	3	15	10-3-1	445,045	1985	Spend A Buck	3	7	5-1-1	3,552,704
1961	Carry Back	3	16	9-1-3	565,349	1986	Snow Chief	3	9	6-1-1	1,875,200
1962	Never Bend	2	10	7-1-2	402,969	1987	Alysheba	3	10	3-2-1	2,511,156
1963	Candy Spots	3	12	7-2-1	604,481	1988	Alysheba	4	9	7-1-0	3,808,600
1964	Gun Bow	4	16	8-4-2	580,100	1989	Sunday Silence	3	9	7-2-0	4,578,454
1965	Buckpasser	2	11	9-1-0	568,096	1990	Unbridled	3	11	4-3-2	3,718,149
1966	Buckpasser	3	14	13-1-0	669,078	1991	Dance Smartly	3	8	8-0-0	2,876,821
1967	Damascus	3	16	12-3-1	817,941	1992	A.P. Indy	3	7	5-0-1	2,622,560
1968	Forward Pass	3	13	7-2-0	546,674	1993	Kotashaan (FRA)	5	10	6-3-0	2,619,014
1969	Arts and Letters	3	14	8-5-1	555,604	1994	Paradise Creek	5	11	8-2-1	2,610,451
1970	Personality	3	18	8-2-1	444,049	1995	Cigar	5	10	10-0-0	4,819,800
1971	Riva Ridge	2	9	7-0-0	503,263	1996	Cigar	6	8	5-2-1	4,910,000
1972	Droll Role	4	19	7-3-4	471,633	1997	Skip Away	4	11	4-5-2	4,089,000
1973	Secretariat	3	12	9-2-1	860,404	1998	Silver Charm	4	9	6-2-0	4,696,506
1974	Chris Evert	3	8	5-1-2	551,063	1999	Almutawakel	4	4	1-1-1	3,290,000
1975	Foolish Pleasure	3	11	5-4-1	716,278	2000	Dubai Millennium (GBR)	4	1	1-0-0	3,600,000
1976	Forego	6	8	6-1-1	401,701	2001	Captain Steve	4	6	2-1-1	4,201,200
1977	Seattle Slew	3	7	6-1-1	641,370	2002	Street Cry (IRE)	4	3	2-1-0	4,266,615
1978	Affirmed	3	11	8-2-0	901,541	2003	Moon Ballad (IRE)	4	3	1-0-0	3,651,101
1979	Spectacular Bid	3	12	10-1-1	1,279,334	2004	Smarty Jones	3	7	6-1-0	7,563,535
1980	Temperence Hill	3	17	8-3-1	1,130,452	2005	Saint Liam	5	6	4-1-0	3,696,960
1981	John Henry	6	10	8-0-0	1,798,030	2006	Invasor (ARG)	4	4	4-0-0	3,690,000
1982	Perrault (GBR)	5	8	4-1-2	1,197,400	2007	Curlin	3	9	6-1-2	5,102,800

Jockeys

Annual money-leading jockeys since 1910, according to *The American Racing Manual*.

Multiple leaders: Bill Shoemaker (10); Laffit Pincay Jr. (7); Eddie Arcaro and Jerry Bailey (6); Braulio Baeza (5); Chris McCarron and Jose Santos (4); Angel Cordero Jr. and Earl Sande (3); Ted Atkinson, Pat Day, Laverne Fator, Mack Garner, Garrett Gomez, Bill Hartack, Charley Kurtsinger, Johnny Longden, Mike Smith, Gary Stevens, John Velazquez, Sonny Workman and Wayne Wright (2).

Year		Mts	Wins	Earnings	Year		Mts	Wins	Earnings
1910	Carroll Shilling	506	172	$176,030	1946	Ted Atkinson	1377	233	$1,036,825
1911	Ted Koerner	813	162	88,308	1947	Douglas Dodson	646	141	1,429,949
1912	Jimmy Butwell	684	144	79,843	1948	Eddie Arcaro	726	188	1,686,230
1913	Merritt Buxton	887	146	82,552	1949	Steve Brooks	906	209	1,316,817
1914	J. McCahey	824	155	121,845	1950	Eddie Arcaro	888	195	1,410,160
1915	Mack Garner	775	151	96,628	1951	Bill Shoemaker	1161	257	1,329,890
1916	John McTaggart	832	150	155,055	1952	Eddie Arcaro	807	188	1,859,591
1917	Frank Robinson	731	147	148,057	1953	Bill Shoemaker	1683	485	1,784,187
1918	Lucien Luke	756	178	201,864	1954	Bill Shoemaker	1251	380	1,876,760
1919	John Loftus	177	65	252,707	1955	Eddie Arcaro	820	158	1,864,796
1920	Clarence Kummer	353	87	292,376	1956	Bill Hartack	1387	347	2,343,955
1921	Earl Sande	340	112	263,043	1957	Bill Hartack	1238	341	3,060,501
1922	Albert Johnson	297	43	345,054	1958	Bill Shoemaker	1133	300	2,961,693
1923	Earl Sande	430	122	569,394	1959	Bill Shoemaker	1285	347	2,843,133
1924	Ivan Parke	844	205	290,395	1960	Bill Shoemaker	1227	274	2,123,961
1925	Laverne Fator	315	81	305,775	1961	Bill Shoemaker	1256	304	2,690,819
1926	Laverne Fator	511	143	361,435	1962	Bill Shoemaker	1126	311	2,916,844
1927	Earl Sande	179	49	277,877	1963	Bill Shoemaker	1203	271	2,526,925
1928	Linus McAtee	235	55	301,295	1964	Bill Shoemaker	1056	246	2,649,553
1929	Mack Garner	274	57	314,975	1965	Braulio Baeza	1245	270	2,582,702
1930	Sonny Workman	571	152	420,438	1966	Braulio Baeza	1341	298	2,951,022
1931	Charley Kurtsinger	519	93	392,095	1967	Braulio Baeza	1064	256	3,088,888
1932	Sonny Workman	378	87	385,070	1968	Braulio Baeza	1089	201	2,835,108
1933	Robert Jones	471	63	226,285	1969	Jorge Velasquez	1442	258	2,542,315
1934	Wayne Wright	919	174	287,185	1970	Laffit Pincay Jr.	1328	269	2,626,526
1935	Silvio Coucci	749	141	319,760	1971	Laffit Pincay Jr.	1627	380	3,784,377
1936	Wayne Wright	670	100	264,000	1972	Laffit Pincay Jr.	1388	289	3,225,827
1937	Charley Kurtsinger	765	120	384,202	1973	Laffit Pincay Jr.	1444	350	4,093,492
1938	Nick Wall	658	97	385,161	1974	Laffit Pincay Jr.	1278	341	4,251,060
1939	Basil James	904	191	353,333	1975	Braulio Baeza	1190	196	3,674,398
1940	Eddie Arcaro	783	132	343,661	1976	Angel Cordero Jr.	1534	274	4,709,500
1941	Don Meade	1164	210	398,627	1977	Steve Cauthen	2075	487	6,151,750
1942	Eddie Arcaro	687	123	481,949	1978	Darrel McHargue	1762	375	6,188,353
1943	Johnny Longden	871	173	573,276	1979	Laffit Pincay Jr.	1708	420	8,183,535
1944	Ted Atkinson	1539	287	899,101	1980	Chris McCarron	1964	405	7,666,100
1945	Johnny Longden	778	180	981,977	1981	Chris McCarron	1494	326	8,397,604

Year		Mts	Wins	Earnings
1982	Angel Cordero Jr.	1838	397	$9,702,520
1983	Angel Cordero Jr.	1792	362	10,116,807
1984	Chris McCarron	1565	356	12,038,213
1985	Laffit Pincay Jr.	1409	289	13,415,049
1986	Jose Santos	1636	329	11,329,297
1987	Jose Santos	1639	305	12,407,355
1988	Jose Santos	1867	370	14,877,298
1989	Jose Santos	1459	285	13,847,003
1990	Gary Stevens	1504	283	13,881,198
1991	Chris McCarron	1440	265	14,456,073
1992	Kent Desormeaux	1568	361	14,193,006
1993	Mike Smith	1510	343	14,024,815
1994	Mike Smith	1484	317	15,979,820
1995	Jerry Bailey	1367	287	$16,311,876
1996	Jerry Bailey	1187	298	19,465,376
1997	Jerry Bailey	1136	269	18,206,013
1998	Gary Stevens	869	178	19,358,840
1999	Pat Day	1265	254	18,092,845
2000	Pat Day	1219	267	17,479,838
2001	Jerry Bailey	912	227	22,597,720
2002	Jerry Bailey	833	214	22,871,814
2003	Jerry Bailey	776	206	23,354,960
2004	John Velazquez	1327	335	22,248,661
2005	John Velazquez	1148	251	24,459,923
2006	Garrett Gomez	1270	261	20,122,592
2007	Garrett Gomez	1262	266	23,800,074

Trainers

Annual money-leading trainers since 1908, according to *The American Racing Manual.*

Multiple Leaders: D. Wayne Lukas (14); Sam Hildreth (9); Charlie Whittingham (7); Sunny Jim Fitzsimmons and Jimmy Jones (5); Bob Baffert, Laz Barrera, Ben Jones, Todd Pletcher and Willie Molter (4); Hirsch Jacobs, Eddie Neloy and James Rowe Sr. (3); H. Guy Bedwell, Bobby Frankel, Jack Gaver, John Schorr, Humming Bob Smith, Silent Tom Smith and Mesh Tenney (2).

Year		Wins	Earnings
1908	James Rowe Sr.	50	$284,335
1909	Sam Hildreth	73	123,942
1910	Sam Hildreth	84	148,010
1911	Sam Hildreth	67	49,418
1912	John Schorr	63	58,110
1913	James Rowe Sr.	18	45,936
1914	R.C. Benson	45	59,315
1915	James Rowe Sr.	19	75,596
1916	Sam Hildreth	39	70,950
1917	Sam Hildreth	23	61,698
1918	H. Guy Bedwell	53	80,296
1919	H. Guy Bedwell	63	208,728
1920	Louis Feustel	22	186,087
1921	Sam Hildreth	85	262,768
1922	Sam Hildreth	74	247,014
1923	Sam Hildreth	75	392,124
1924	Sam Hildreth	77	255,608
1925	G.R. Tompkins	30	199,245
1926	Scott Harlan	21	205,681
1927	W.H. Bringloe	63	216,563
1928	John Schorr	65	258,425
1929	James Rowe Jr.	25	314,881
1930	Sunny Jim Fitzsimmons	47	397,355
1931	Big Jim Healy	33	297,300
1932	Sunny Jim Fitzsimmons	68	266,650
1933	Humming Bob Smith	53	135,720
1934	Humming Bob Smith	43	249,938
1935	Bud Stotler	87	303,005
1936	Sunny Jim Fitzsimmons	42	193,415
1937	Robert McGarvey	46	209,925
1938	Earl Sande	15	226,495
1939	Sunny Jim Fitzsimmons	45	266,205
1940	Silent Tom Smith	14	269,200
1941	Ben Jones	70	475,318
1942	Jack Gaver	48	406,547
1943	Ben Jones	73	267,915
1944	Ben Jones	60	601,660
1945	Silent Tom Smith	52	510,655
1946	Hirsch Jacobs	99	560,077
1947	Jimmy Jones	85	1,334,805
1948	Jimmy Jones	81	1,118,670
1949	Jimmy Jones	76	978,587
1950	Preston Burch	96	637,754
1951	Jack Gaver	42	616,392
1952	Ben Jones	29	662,137
1953	Harry Trotsek	54	1,028,873
1954	Willie Molter	136	1,107,860
1955	Sunny Jim Fitzsimmons	66	1,270,055
1956	Willie Molter	142	1,227,402
1957	Jimmy Jones	70	1,150,910
1958	Willie Molter	69	1,116,544

Year		Wins	Earnings
1959	Willie Molter	71	$847,290
1960	Hirsch Jacobs	97	748,349
1961	Jimmy Jones	62	759,856
1962	Mesh Tenney	58	1,099,474

Year		Sts	Wins	Earnings
1963	Mesh Tenney	192	40	$860,703
1964	Bill Winfrey	287	61	1,350,534
1965	Hirsch Jacobs	610	91	1,331,628
1966	Eddie Neloy	282	93	2,456,250
1967	Eddie Neloy	262	72	1,776,089
1968	Eddie Neloy	212	52	1,233,101
1969	Elliott Burch	156	26	1,067,936
1970	Charlie Whittingham	551	82	1,302,354
1971	Charlie Whittingham	393	77	1,737,115
1972	Charlie Whittingham	429	79	1,734,020
1973	Charlie Whittingham	423	85	1,865,385
1974	Pancho Martin	846	166	2,408,419
1975	Charlie Whittingham	487	3	2,437,244
1976	Jack Van Berg	2362	496	2,976,196
1977	Laz Barrera	781	127	2,715,848
1978	Laz Barrera	592	100	3,307,164
1979	Laz Barrera	492	98	3,608,517
1980	Laz Barrera	559	99	2,969,151
1981	Charlie Whittingham	376	74	3,993,302
1982	Charlie Whittingham	410	63	4,587,457
1983	D. Wayne Lukas	595	78	4,267,261
1984	D. Wayne Lukas	805	131	5,835,921
1985	D. Wayne Lukas	1140	218	11,155,188
1986	D. Wayne Lukas	1510	259	12,345,180
1987	D. Wayne Lukas	1735	343	17,502,110
1988	D. Wayne Lukas	1500	318	17,842,358
1989	D. Wayne Lukas	1398	305	16,103,998
1990	D. Wayne Lukas	1396	267	14,508,871
1991	D. Wayne Lukas	1497	289	15,942,223
1992	D. Wayne Lukas	1349	230	9,806,436
1993	Bobby Frankel	345	79	8,933,252
1994	D. Wayne Lukas	693	147	9,247,457
1995	D. Wayne Lukas	837	194	12,834,483
1996	D. Wayne Lukas	1006	192	15,966,344
1997	D. Wayne Lukas	824	169	9,993,569
1998	Bob Baffert	538	139	15,000,870
1999	Bob Baffert	735	169	16,934,607
2000	Bob Baffert	678	146	11,831,605
2001	Bob Baffert	660	138	16,354,996
2002	Bobby Frankel	480	117	17,748,340
2003	Bobby Frankel	413	114	19,143,289
2004	Todd Pletcher	948	240	17,511,923
2005	Todd Pletcher	1039	257	20,867,842
2006	Todd Pletcher	1168	294	26,820,243
2007	Todd Pletcher	1233	289	28,571,697

All-Time Leaders

The all-time leading horses, trainers and jockeys of North America. Records are courtesy of the *Equibase Company* and include all available earnings from races in foreign countries. Horses must have had at least one start in the United States or Canada. Note that horses, jockeys and trainers who were active in 2008 are in **bold** type.

Records are through Sept. 29, 2008.

Top 20 Horses—Earnings

		Sts	1st	2nd	3rd	Earnings
1	**Curlin**	.15	11	2	2	$10,246,800
2	Cigar	.33	19	4	5	9,999,815
3	Skip Away	.38	18	10	6	9,616,360
4	Fantastic Light	.25	12	5	3	8,486,957
5	Invasor (ARG)	.12	11	0	0	7,804,070
6	Pleasantly Perfect	.18	9	3	2	7,789,880
7	Smarty Jones	.9	8	1	0	7,613,155
8	Silver Charm	.24	12	7	6	6,944,369
9	Captain Steve	.25	9	3	7	6,828,356
10	Alysheba	.26	11	8	2	6,679,242

Top 10 Jockeys — Races Won

		Yrs	Wins	Earnings
1	**Russell Baze**	.35	10,269	$157,828,600
2	Laffit Pincay Jr.	.37	9530	237,120,625
3	Bill Shoemaker	.42	8833	123,375,524
4	Pat Day	.33	8803	297,912,019
5	David Gall	.43	7396	24,972,821
6	Chris McCarron	.29	7141	263,985,505
7	Angel Cordero Jr.	.35	7057	164,570,227
8	Jorge Velasquez	.33	6795	125,544,379
9	**Earlie Fires**	.34	6470	86,392,977
10	Sandy Hawley	.31	6449	88,681,292

Top 10 Jockeys — Earnings

		Yrs	Wins	Earnings
1	Pat Day	.33	8803	$297,912,019
2	Jerry Bailey	.31	5893	296,104,129
3	Chris McCarron	.29	7141	263,985,505
4	Laffit Pincay Jr.	.37	9530	237,120,625
5	Gary Stevens	.27	4888	221,207,064
6	**Edgar Prado**	.22	6155	213,174,276
7	**Kent Desormeaux**	.23	5031	212,948,230
8	**Alex Solis**	.28	4618	210,349,049
9	**John Velazquez**	.19	4006	207,784,703
10	Eddie Delahoussaye	.36	6384	195,884,940

Top 10 Trainers — Races Won

		Wins	Earnings
1	Dale Baird	.9445	$35,326,403
2	Jack Van Berg	.6387	82,071,504
3	King Leatherbury	.6256	56,862,284
4	**Jerry Hollendorfer**	.5205	100,388,030
5	Richard Hazelton	.4715	40,068,141
6	D. Wayne Lukas	.4506	251,367,476
7	Scott Lake	.4419	79,637,294
8	**Steven Asmussen**	.4402	127,358,142
9	Frank Merrill Jr.	.3974	16,980,632
10	**Bill Mott**	.3791	170,294,540

Top 10 Trainers — Earnings

		Wins	Earnings
1	D. Wayne Lukas	.4506	$251,367,476
2	**Bobby Frankel**	.3596	218,981,621
3	**Bill Mott**	.3791	170,294,540
4	**Todd Pletcher**	.2158	153,787,744
5	**Bob Baffert**	.1748	131,044,475
6	**Steven Asmussen**	.4402	127,358,142
7	**Ron McAnally**	.2531	120,431,956
8	**Richard Mandella**	.1776	109,224,130
9	Charles Whittingham	.2534	109,215,527
10	**Jerry Hollendorfer**	.5205	100,388,030

Horse of the Year (1936-70)

In 1971, the *Daily Racing Form*, the Thoroughbred Racing Associations, and the National Turf Writers Assn. joined forces to create the Eclipse Awards. Before then, however, the *Racing Form* (1936-70) and the TRA (1950-70) issued separate selections for Horse of the Year. Their picks differed only four times from 1950-70 and are so noted. Horses listed in CAPITAL letters are Triple Crown winners; (f) indicates female.

Multiple winners: Kelso (5); Challedon, Native Dancer and Whirlaway (2).

Year		Year		Year		Year	
1936	Granville	1946	ASSAULT	1955	Nashua	1964	Kelso
1937	WAR ADMIRAL	1947	Armed	1956	Swaps	1965	Roman Brother (DRF)
1938	Seabiscuit	1948	CITATION	1957	Bold Ruler (DRF)		Moccasin (TRA)
1939	Challedon	1949	Capot		Dedicate (TRA)	1966	Buckpasser
1940	Challedon	1950	Hill Prince	1958	Round Table	1967	Damascus
1941	WHIRLAWAY	1951	Counterpoint	1959	Sword Dancer	1968	Dr. Fager
1942	Whirlaway	1952	One Count (DRF)	1960	Kelso	1969	Arts and Letters
1943	COUNT FLEET		Native Dancer (TRA)	1961	Kelso	1970	Fort Marcy (DRF)
1944	Twilight Tear (f)	1953	Tom Fool	1962	Kelso		Personality (TRA)
1945	Busher (f)	1954	Native Dancer	1963	Kelso		

Eclipse Awards

The Eclipse Awards, honoring the Horse of the Year and other champions of the sport, are sponsored by the National Thoroughbred Racing Association (NTRA), *Daily Racing Form* and the National Turf Writers Assn. In 1998, the NTRA replaced the Thoroughbred Racing Associations of North America as co-sponsor.

The awards are named after the 18th century racehorse and sire, Eclipse, who began racing at age five and was unbeaten in 18 starts (eight wins were walkovers). As a stallion, Eclipse sired winners of 344 races, including three Epsom Derby champions.

Horses listed in CAPITAL letters won the Triple Crown that year. Age of horse in parentheses where necessary.

Multiple winners: (horses): Forego (8); John Henry (7); Affirmed, Lonesome Glory and Secretariat (5); Azeri, Cigar, Flatterer, Seattle Slew, Skip Away and Spectacular Bid (4); Ack Ack, McDynamo, Susan's Girl, Tiznow and Zaccio (3); All Along, Alysheba, Ashado, Bayakoa, Black Tie Affair, Cafe Prince, Charismatic, Conquistador Cielo, Curlin, Desert Vixen, Favorite Trick, Ferdinand, Flawlessly, Flat Top, Ghostzapper, Go for Wand, High Chaparral, Holy Bull, Housebuster, Invasor, Kotashaan, Lady's Secret, Life's Magic, Miesque, Mineshaft, Morley Street, Open Mind, Ouija Board, Paseana, Point Given, Riva Ridge, Saint Liam, Silverbulletday, Slew o' Gold and Spend A Buck (2).

Multiple winners: (people): Jerry Bailey (7); Juddmonte Farms and Laffit Pincay Jr. (6); Bobby Frankel (5); Adena Springs, Laz Barrera, Pat Day, John Franks, D. Wayne Lukas, Allen Paulson, Ogden Phipps, Todd Pletcher and Frank Stronach (4); Bob Baffert, Steve Cauthen, Harbor View Farm, Fred W. Hooper, Nelson Bunker Hunt, Mr. & Mrs. Gene Klein, Dan Lasater, John & Betty Mabee, Paul Mellon, Bill Shoemaker, Edward Taylor and Charlie Whittingham (3); Braulio Baeza, C.T. Chenery, Claiborne Farm, Angel Cordero Jr., Kent Desormeaux, Richard Englander, William S. Farish, John W. Galbreath, Chris McCarron, Bill Mott, Mike Smith and John Velazquez (2).

Horse of the Year

Year		Year		Year		Year	
1971	Ack Ack (5)	1981	John Henry (6)	1991	Black Tie Affair (5)	2001	Point Given (3)
1972	Secretariat (2)	1982	Conquistador Cielo (3)	1992	A.P. Indy (3)	2002	Azeri (4)
1973	SECRETARIAT (3)	1983	All Along (4)	1993	Kotashaan (5)	2003	Mineshaft (4)
1974	Forego (4)	1984	John Henry (9)	1994	Holy Bull (3)	2004	Ghostzapper (4)
1975	Forego (5)	1985	Spend A Buck (3)	1995	Cigar (5)	2005	Saint Liam (5)
1976	Forego (6)	1986	Lady's Secret (4)	1996	Cigar (6)	2006	Invasor (4)
1977	SEATTLE SLEW (3)	1987	Ferdinand (4)	1997	Favorite Trick (2)	2007	Curlin (3)
1978	AFFIRMED (3)	1988	Alysheba (4)	1998	Skip Away (5)		
1979	Affirmed (4)	1989	Sunday Silence (3)	1999	Charismatic (3)		
1980	Spectacular Bid (4)	1990	Criminal Type (5)	2000	Tiznow (3)		

Older Male

Year		Year		Year		Year	
1971	Ack Ack (5)	1981	John Henry (6)	1991	Black Tie Affair (5)	2001	Tiznow (4)
1972	Autobiography (4)	1982	Lemhi Gold (4)	1992	Pleasant Tap (5)	2002	Left Bank (5)
1973	Riva Ridge (4)	1983	Bates Motel (4)	1993	Bertrando (4)	2003	Mineshaft (4)
1974	Forego (4)	1984	Slew o' Gold (4)	1994	The Wicked North (4)	2004	Ghostzapper (4)
1975	Forego (5)	1985	Vanlandingham (4)	1995	Cigar (5)	2005	Saint Liam (5)
1976	Forego (6)	1986	Turkoman (4)	1996	Cigar (6)	2006	Invasor (4)
1977	Forego (7)	1987	Ferdinand (4)	1997	Skip Away (4)	2007	Lawyer Ron (4)
1978	Seattle Slew (4)	1988	Alysheba (4)	1998	Skip Away (5)		
1979	Affirmed (4)	1989	Blushing John (4)	1999	Victory Gallop (4)		
1980	Spectacular Bid (4)	1990	Criminal Type (5)	2000	Lemon Drop Kid (4)		

Older Female

Year		Year		Year		Year	
1971	Shuvee (5)	1981	Relaxing (5)	1991	Queena (5)	2001	Gourmet Girl (6)
1972	Typecast (6)	1982	Track Robbery (6)	1992	Paseana (5)	2002	Azeri (4)
1973	Susan's Girl (4)	1983	Amb. of Luck (4)	1993	Paseana (6)	2003	Azeri (5)
1974	Desert Vixen (4)	1984	Princess Rooney (4)	1994	Sky Beauty (4)	2004	Azeri (6)
1975	Susan's Girl (6)	1985	Life's Magic (4)	1995	Inside Information (4)	2005	Ashado (4)
1976	Proud Delta (4)	1986	Lady's Secret (4)	1996	Jewel Princess (4)	2006	Fleet Indian (5)
1977	Cascapedia (4)	1987	North Sider (5)	1997	Hidden Lake (4)	2007	Ginger Punch (4)
1978	Late Bloomer (4)	1988	Personal Ensign (4)	1998	Escena (5)		
1979	Waya (5)	1989	Bayakoa (5)	1999	Beautiful Pleasure (4)		
1980	Glorious Song (4)	1990	Bayakoa (6)	2000	Riboletta (5)		

3-Year-Old Male

Year		Year		Year		Year	
1971	Canonero II	1981	Pleasant Colony	1991	Hansel	2001	Point Given
1972	Key to the Mint	1982	Conquistador Cielo	1992	A.P. Indy	2002	War Emblem
1973	SECRETARIAT	1983	Slew o' Gold	1993	Prairie Bayou	2003	Funny Cide
1974	Little Current	1984	Swale	1994	Holy Bull	2004	Smarty Jones
1975	Wajima	1985	Spend A Buck	1995	Thunder Gulch	2005	Afleet Alex
1976	Bold Forbes	1986	Snow Chief	1996	Skip Away	2006	Bernardini
1977	SEATTLE SLEW	1987	Alysheba	1997	Silver Charm	2007	Curlin
1978	AFFIRMED	1988	Risen Star	1998	Real Quiet		
1979	Spectacular Bid	1989	Sunday Silence	1999	Charismatic		
1980	Temperence Hill	1990	Unbridled	2000	Tiznow		

Eclipse Awards (Cont.)

3-Year-Old Female

Year		Year		Year		Year	
1971	Turkish Trousers	1981	Wayward Lass	1991	Dance Smartly	2001	Xtra Heat
1972	Susan's Girl	1982	Christmas Past	1992	Saratoga Dew	2002	Farda Amiga
1973	Desert Vixen	1983	Heartlight No. One	1993	Hollywood Wildcat	2003	Bird Town
1974	Chris Evert	1984	Life's Magic	1994	Heavenly Prize	2004	Ashado
1975	Ruffian	1985	Mom's Command	1995	Serena's Song	2005	Smuggler
1976	Revidere	1986	Tiffany Lass	1996	Yanks Music	2006	Wait a While
1977	Our Mims	1987	Sacahuista	1997	Ajina	2007	Rags to Riches
1978	Tempest Queen	1988	Winning Colors	1998	Banshee Breeze		
1979	Davona Dale	1989	Open Mind	1999	Silverbulletday		
1980	Genuine Risk	1990	Go for Wand	2000	Surfside		

2-Year-Old Male

Year		Year		Year		Year	
1971	Riva Ridge	1981	Deputy Minister	1991	Arazi	2001	Johannesburg
1972	Secretariat	1982	Roving Boy	1992	Gilded Time	2002	Vindication
1973	Protagonist	1983	Devil's Bag	1993	Dehere	2003	Action This Day
1974	Foolish Pleasure	1984	Chief's Crown	1994	Timber Country	2004	Declan's Moon
1975	Honest Pleasure	1985	Tasso	1995	Maria's Mon	2005	Stevie Wonderboy
1976	Seattle Slew	1986	Capote	1996	Boston Harbor	2006	Street Sense
1977	Affirmed	1987	Forty Niner	1997	Favorite Trick	2007	War Pass
1978	Spectacular Bid	1988	Easy Goer	1998	Answer Lively		
1979	Rockhill Native	1989	Rhythm	1999	Anees		
1980	Lord Avie	1990	Fly So Free	2000	Macho Uno		

2-Year-Old Female

Year		Year		Year		Year	
1971	Numbered Account	1980	Heavenly Cause	1990	Meadow Star	2000	Caressing
1972	La Prevoyante	1981	Before Dawn	1991	Pleasant Stage	2001	Tempera
1973	Talking Picture	1982	Landaluce	1992	Eliza	2002	Storm Flag Flying
1974	Ruffian	1983	Althea	1993	Phone Chatter	2003	Halfbridled
1975	Dearly Precious	1984	Outstandingly	1994	Flanders	2004	Sweet Catomine
1976	Sensational	1985	Family Style	1995	Golden Attraction	2005	Folklore
1977	Lakeville Miss	1986	Brave Raj	1996	Storm Song	2006	Dreaming of Anna
1978	(TIE) Candy Eclair	1987	Epitome	1997	Countess Diana	2007	Indian Blessing
	& It's in the Air	1988	Open Mind	1998	Silverbulletday		
1979	Smart Angle	1989	Go for Wand	1999	Chilukki		

Sprinter

Year		Year		Year		Year	
1971	Ack Ack (5)	1980	Plugged Nickle (3)	1990	Housebuster (3)	2000	Kona Gold (6)
1972	Chou Croute (4)	1981	Guilty Conscience (5)	1991	Housebuster (4)	2001	Squirtle Squirt (3)
1973	Shecky Greene (3)	1982	Gold Beauty (3)	1992	Rubiano (5)	2002	Orientate (4)
1974	Forego (4)	1983	Chinook Pass (4)	1993	Cardmania (7)	2003	Aldebaran (5)
1975	Gallant Bob (3)	1984	Eillo (4)	1994	Cherokee Run (4)	2004	Speightstown (6)
1976	My Juliet (4)	1985	Precisionist (4)	1995	Not Surprising (4)	2005	Lost in the Fog (3)
1977	What a Summer (4)	1986	Smile (6)	1996	Lit de Justice (6)	2006	Thor's Echo (4)
1978	(TIE) Dr. Patches (4)	1987	Groovy (4)	1997	Smoke Glacken (3)	2007	(M) Midnight Lute (4)
	& J.O. Tobin (4)	1988	Gulch (4)	1998	Reraise (3)		(F) Maryfield (6)
1979	Star de Naskra (4)	1989	Safely Kept (3)	1999	Artax (4)		

Note: In 2007, awards for Male and Female Sprinter were given.

Champion Turf Horse

Year		Year		Year		Year	
1971	Run the Gantlet (3)	1973	SECRETARIAT (3)	1975	Snow Knight (4)	1977	Johnny D (3)
1972	Cougar II (6)	1974	Dahlia (4)	1976	Youth (3)	1978	Mac Diarmida (3)

Champion Male Turf Horse

Year		Year		Year		Year	
1979	Bowl Game (5)	1987	Theatrical (5)	1995	Northern Spur (4)	2003	High Chaparral (4)
1980	John Henry (5)	1988	Sunshine Forever (3)	1996	Singspiel (4)	2004	Kitten's Joy (3)
1981	John Henry (6)	1989	Steinlen (6)	1997	Chief Bearhart (4)	2005	Leroidesanimaux (5)
1982	Perrault (4)	1990	Itsallgreektome (3)	1998	Buck's Boy (5)	2006	Miesque's Approval (7)
1983	John Henry (8)	1991	Tight Spot (4)	1999	Daylami (5)	2007	English Channel (5)
1984	John Henry (9)	1992	Sky Classic (5)	2000	Kalanisi (5)		
1985	Cozzene (4)	1993	Kotashaan (5)	2001	Fantastic Light (5)		
1986	Manila (3)	1994	Paradise Creek (5)	2002	High Chaparral (3)		

Champion Female Turf Horse

Year		Year		Year		Year	
1979	Trillion (5)	1987	Miesque (3)	1995	Possibly Perfect (5)	2003	Islington (5)
1980	Just A Game II (4)	1988	Miesque (4)	1996	Wandesta (5)	2004	Ouija Board (3)
1981	De La Rose (3)	1989	Brown Bess (7)	1997	Ryafan (3)	2005	Intercontinental (5)
1982	April Run (4)	1990	Laugh and Be Merry (5)	1998	Fiji (4)	2006	Ouija Board (5)
1983	All Along (4)	1991	Miss Alleged (4)	1999	Soaring Softly (4)	2007	Lahudood (4)
1984	Royal Heroine (4)	1992	Flawlessly (4)	2000	Perfect Sting (4)		
1985	Pebbles (4)	1993	Flawlessly (5)	2001	Banks Hill (3)		
1986	Estrapade (6)	1994	Hatoof (5)	2002	Golden Apples (4)		

Steeplechase or Hurdle Horse

Year		Year		Year		Year	
1971	Shadow Brook (7)	1981	Zaccio (5)	1991	Morley Street (7)	2001	Pompeyo (8)
1972	Soothsayer (5)	1982	Zaccio (6)	1992	Lonesome Glory (4)	2002	Flat Top (9)
1973	Athenian Idol (5)	1983	Flatterer (4)	1993	Lonesome Glory (5)	2003	McDynamo (6)
1974	Gran Kan (8)	1984	Flatterer (5)	1994	Warm Spell (6)	2004	Hirapour (6)
1975	Life's Illusion (4)	1985	Flatterer (6)	1995	Lonesome Glory (7)	2005	McDynamo (8)
1976	Straight and True (6)	1986	Flatterer (7)	1996	Correggio (5)	2006	McDynamo (9)
1977	Cafe Prince (7)	1987	Inlander (6)	1997	Lonesome Glory (9)	2007	Good Night Shirt (6)
1978	Cafe Prince (8)	1988	Jimmy Lorenzo (6)	1998	Flat Top (5)		
1979	Martie's Anger (4)	1989	Highland Bud (4)	1999	Lonesome Glory (11)		
1980	Zaccio (4)	1990	Morley Street (6)	2000	All Gong (6)		

Outstanding Jockey

Year		Year		Year		Year	
1971	Laffit Pincay Jr.	1981	Bill Shoemaker	1991	Pat Day	2001	Jerry Bailey
1972	Braulio Baeza	1982	Angel Cordero Jr.	1992	Kent Desormeaux	2002	Jerry Bailey
1973	Laffit Pincay Jr.	1983	Angel Cordero Jr.	1993	Mike Smith	2003	Jerry Bailey
1974	Laffit Pincay Jr.	1984	Pat Day	1994	Mike Smith	2004	John Velazquez
1975	Braulio Baeza	1985	Laffit Pincay Jr.	1995	Jerry Bailey	2005	John Velazquez
1976	Sandy Hawley	1986	Pat Day	1996	Jerry Bailey	2006	Edgar Prado
1977	Steve Cauthen	1987	Pat Day	1997	Jerry Bailey	2007	Garrett Gomez
1978	Darrel McHargue	1988	Jose Santos	1998	Gary Stevens		
1979	Laffit Pincay Jr.	1989	Kent Desormeaux	1999	Jorge Chavez		
1980	Chris McCarron	1990	Craig Perret	2000	Jerry Bailey		

Outstanding Apprentice Jockey

Year		Year		Year		Year	
1971	Gene St. Leon	1981	Richard Migliore	1991	Mickey Walls	2000	Tyler Baze
1972	Thomas Wallis	1982	Alberto Delgado	1992	Rosemary Homeister	2001	Jeremy Rose
1973	Steve Valdez	1983	Declan Murphy	1993	Juan Umana	2002	Ryan Fogelsonger
1974	Chris McCarron	1984	Wesley Ward	1994	Dale Beckner	2003	Eddie Castro
1975	Jimmy Edwards	1985	Art Madrid Jr.	1995	Ramon B. Perez	2004	Brian Hernandez Jr.
1976	George Martens	1986	Allen Stacy	1996	Neil Poznansky	2005	Emma-Jayne Wilson
1977	Steve Cauthen	1987	Kent Desormeaux	1997	Roberto Rosado	2006	Julien Leparoux
1978	Ron Franklin	1988	Steve Capanas		& Philip Teator	2007	Joe Talamo
1979	Cash Asmussen	1989	Michael Luzzi	1998	Shaun Bridgmohan		
1980	Frank Lovato Jr.	1990	Mark Johnston	1999	Ariel Smith		

Outstanding Trainer

Year		Year		Year		Year	
1971	Charlie Whittingham	1981	Ron McAnally	1991	Ron McAnally	2001	Bobby Frankel
1972	Lucien Laurin	1982	Charlie Whittingham	1992	Ron McAnally	2002	Bobby Frankel
1973	H. Allen Jerkens	1983	Woody Stephens	1993	Bobby Frankel	2003	Bobby Frankel
1974	Sherill Ward	1984	Jack Van Berg	1994	D. Wayne Lukas	2004	Todd Pletcher
1975	Steve DiMauro	1985	D. Wayne Lukas	1995	Bill Mott	2005	Todd Pletcher
1976	Laz Barrera	1986	D. Wayne Lukas	1996	Bill Mott	2006	Todd Pletcher
1977	Laz Barrera	1987	D. Wayne Lukas	1997	Bob Baffert	2007	Todd Pletcher
1978	Laz Barrera	1988	Shug McGaughey	1998	Bob Baffert		
1979	Laz Barrera	1989	Charlie Whittingham	1999	Bob Baffert		
1980	Bud Delp	1990	Carl Nafzger	2000	Bobby Frankel		

Outstanding Owner

Year		Year		Year		Year	
1971	Mr. & Mrs. E.E. Fogleson	1981	Dotsam Stable	1991	Sam-Son Farms	2001	Richard Englander
1972-73	No award	1982	Viola Sommer	1992	Juddmonte Farms	2002	Richard Englander
1974	Dan Lasater	1983	John Franks	1993	John Franks	2003	Juddmonte Farms
1975	Dan Lasater	1984	John Franks	1994	John Franks	2004	Ken & Sarah Ramsey
1976	Dan Lasater	1985	Mr. & Mrs. Gene Klein	1995	Allen Paulson	2005	Michael Gill
1977	Maxwell Gluck	1986	Mr. & Mrs. Gene Klein	1996	Allen Paulson	2006	Darley & Lael Stables
1978	Harbor View Farm	1987	Mr. & Mrs. Gene Klein	1997	Carolyn Hine	2007	Shadwell Stable
1979	Harbor View Farm	1988	Ogden Phipps	1998	Frank Stronach		
1980	Mr. & Mrs. B. Firestone	1989	Ogden Phipps	1999	Frank Stronach		
		1990	Frances Genter	2000	Frank Stronach		

Eclipse Awards (Cont.)
Outstanding Breeder

Year		Year		Year		Year	
1971	Paul Mellon	1981	Golden Chance Farm	1991	John & Betty Mabee	2001	Juddmonte Farms
1972	C.T. Chenery	1982	Fred W. Hooper	1992	William S. Farish	2002	Juddmonte Farms
1973	C.T. Chenery	1983	Edward P. Taylor	1993	Allan Paulson	2003	Juddmonte Farms
1974	John W. Galbreath	1984	Claiborne Farm	1994	William T. Young	2004	Adena Springs
1975	Fred W. Hooper	1985	Nelson Bunker Hunt	1995	Juddmonte Farms	2005	Adena Springs
1976	Nelson Bunker Hunt	1986	Paul Mellon	1996	Farnsworth Farms	2006	Adena Springs
1977	Edward P. Taylor	1987	Nelson Bunker Hunt	1997	John & Betty Mabee	2007	Adena Springs
1978	Harbor View Farm	1988	Ogden Phipps	1998	John & Betty Mabee		
1979	Claiborne Farm	1989	North Ridge Farm	1999	William S. Farish		
1980	Mrs. Henry Paxson	1990	Calumet Farm	2000	Frank Stronach		

Award of Merit

Year		Year		Year		Year	
1976	Jack J. Dreyfus	1987	J.B. Faulconer	1995	Ted Bassett III	2003	Richard Duchossois
1977	Steve Cauthen	1988	John Forsythe	1996	Allen Paulson	2004	Oaklawn Park &
1978	Dinny Phipps	1989	Michael Sandler	1997	Bob & Beverly Lewis		the Cella family
1979	Jimmy Kilroe	1990	Warner L. Jones	1998	D.G. Van Clief Jr.	2005	Penny Chenery
1980	John D. Shapiro	1991	Fred W. Hooper	2000	Jim McKay	2006	John Nerud
1981	Bill Shoemaker	1992	Joe Hirsch	2001	Pete Pederson		
1984	John Gaines		& Robert P. Strub		& Harry T. Mangurian		
1985	Keene Daingerfield	1993	Paul Mellon	2002	Ogden Phipps		
1986	Herman Cohen	1994	Alfred G. Vanderbilt		& Howard Battle		

Special Award

Year		Year		Year		Year	
1971	Robert J. Kleberg	1987	Anheuser-Busch	1998	Oak Tree Racing	2004	Dale Baird
1974	Charles Hatton	1988	Edward J. DeBartolo Sr.		Association	2005	Cash is King Stable
1976	Bill Shoemaker	1989	Richard Duchossois	1999	Laffit Pincay Jr.	2006	Roy & Gretchen
1980	John T. Landry	1994	Eddie Arcaro	2000	John Hettinger		Jackson
	& Pierre E. Bellocq		& John Longden	2001	Sheikh Mohammed	2007	Kentucky Horse Park
1984	C.V. Whitney	1995	Russell Baze		al-Maktoum		
1985	Arlington Park			2002	Keeneland Library		

HARNESS RACING

Triple Crown Winners
PACERS

Ten three-year-olds have won the Cane Pace, Little Brown Jug and Messenger Stakes in the same year since the Pacing Triple Crown was established in 1956. No trainer or driver has won it more than once.

Year		Driver	Trainer	Owner
1959	**Adios Butler**	Clint Hodgins	Paige West	Paige West & Angelo Pellillo
1965	**Bret Hanover**	Frank Ervin	Frank Ervin	Richard Downing
1966	**Romeo Hanover**	Bill Myer & George Sholty*	Jerry Silverman	Lucky Star Stables & Morton Finder
1968	**Rum Customer**	Billy Haughton	Billy Haughton	Kennilworth Farms & L.C. Mancuso
1970	**Most Happy Fella**	Stanley Dancer	Stanley Dancer	Egyptian Acres Stable
1980	**Niatross**	Clint Galbraith	Clint Galbraith	Niagara Acres, Niatross Stables
				& Clint Galbraith
1983	**Ralph Hanover**	Ron Waples	Stew Firlotte	Waples Stable, Pointsetta Stable,
				Grant's Direct Stable & P.J. Baugh
1997	**Western Dreamer**	Mike Lachance	Bill Robinson Stable	Matthew, Daniel and Patrick Daly
1999	**Blissful Hall**	Ron Pierce	Benn Wallace	Daniel Plouffe
2003	**No Pan Intended**	David Miller	Ivan Sugg	Bob Glazer

*Myer drove Romeo Hanover in the Cane, Sholty in the other two races.

TROTTERS

Eight three-year-olds have won the Yonkers Trot, Hambletonian and Kentucky Futurity in the same year since the Trotting Triple Crown was established in 1955. Stanley Dancer is the only driver/trainer to win it twice.

Year		Driver/Trainer	Owner
1955	**Scott Frost**	Joe O'Brien	S.A. Camp Farms
1963	**Speedy Scot**	Ralph Baldwin	Castleton Farms
1964	**Ayres**	John Simpson Sr.	Charlotte Sheppard
1968	**Nevele Pride**	Stanley Dancer	Nevele Acres & Lou Resnick
1969	**Lindy's Pride**	Howard Beissinger	Lindy Farms
1972	**Super Bowl**	Stanley Dancer	Rachel Dancer & Rose Hild Breeding Farm
2004	**Windsong's Legacy**	Trond Smedshammer	Fredrick Lindegaard
2006	**Glidemaster**	John Campbell & George Brennan*	Bob Burgess, Karin Olsson-Burgess,
			Marsha Cohen & Brittany Farms

*Brennan drove Glidemaster in the Yonkers Trot, Campbell in the other two races.

Triple Crown Near Misses

PACERS

Nine horses have won the first two legs of the Triple Crown, but not the third. The Cane Pace (CP), Little Brown Jug (LBJ), and Messenger Stakes (MS) have not always been run in the same order so numbers after races won indicate sequence for that year.

Year		CP	LBJ	MS	Year		CP	LBJ	MS
1957	**Torpid**	won, 1	won, 2	DNF*	1990	**Jake and Elwood** . . .	won, 1	NE	won, 2
1960	**Countess Adios**	won, 2	NE	won, 1	1992	**Western Hanover** . . .	won, 1	2nd*	won, 2
1971	**Albatross**	won, 2	2nd*	won, 1	1993	**Rijadh**	won, 1	2nd*	won, 2
1976	**Keystone Ore**	won, 1	won, 2	2nd*	1998	**Shady Character**	won, 1	won, 2	6th*
1986	**Barberry Spur**	won, 1	won, 2	2nd*					

*Winning horses: Meadow Lands (1957), Nansemond (1971), Windshield Wiper (1976), Amity Chef (1986), Fake Left (1992), Life Sign (1993), Fit for Life (1998).

Note: Torpid (1957) scratched before the final heat; Countess Adios (1960) and Jake and Elwood (1990) not eligible for Little Brown Jug.

TROTTERS

Eight horses have won the first two legs of the Triple Crown– the Yonkers Trot (YT) and the Hambletonian (Ham)–but not the third. The winner of the Kentucky Futurity (KF) is listed.

Year		YT	Ham	KF	Year		YT	Ham	KF
1962	**A.C.'s Viking**	won	won	Safe Mission	1987	**Mack Lobell**	won	won	Napoletano
1976	**Steve Lobell**	won	won	Quick Pay	1993	**American Winner**	won	won	Pine Chip
1977	**Green Speed**	won	won	Texas	1996	**Continentalvictory**	won	won	Running Sea
1978	**Speedy Somolli**	won	won	Doublemint	1998	**Muscles Yankee**	won	won	Trade Balance

Note: Green Speed (1977) was not eligible for the Kentucky Futurity; Continentalvictory (1996) was withdrawn from the Kentucky Futurity due to a leg injury.

The Hambletonian

For three-year-old trotters. Inaugurated in 1926 in Syracuse, N.Y.; Lexington, Ky.; Goshen, N.Y.; Yonkers, N.Y.; Du Quoin, Ill.; and since 1981 at The Meadowlands in East Rutherford, N.J.

Run at one mile since 1947. Winning horse must win two heats.

Drivers with most wins: John Campbell (6); Stanley Dancer, Billy Haughton, Mike Lachance and Ben White (4); Howard Beissinger, Del Cameron and Henry Thomas (3).

Year	Horse	Driver	Fastest Heat	Year	Horse	Driver	Fastest Heat
1926	**Guy McKinney**	Nat Ray	2:04¾	1961	**Harlan Dean**	James Arthur	1:58⅖
1927	**Iosola's Worthy** . . .	Marvin Childs	2:03¾	1962	**A.C.'s Viking**	Sanders Russell	1:59⅗
1928	**Spencer**	W.H. Lessee	2:02½	1963	**Speedy Scot**	Ralph Baldwin	1:57⅗
1929	**Walter Dear**	Walter Cox	2:02¾	1964	**Ayres**	John Simpson Sr.	1:56⅘
1930	**Hanover's Bertha** . .	Tom Berry	2:03	1965	**Egyptian Candor** . .	Del Cameron	2:03⅘
1931	**Calumet Butler** . . .	R.D. McMahon	2:03¼	1966	**Kerry Way**	Frank Ervin	1:58⅘
1932	**The Marchioness** . .	Will Caton	2:01¼	1967	**Speedy Streak** . . .	Del Cameron	2:00
1933	**Mary Reynolds** . . .	Ben White	2:03¾	1968	**Nevele Pride**	Stanley Dancer	1:59⅖
1934	**Lord Jim**	Doc Parshall	2:02¾	1969	**Lindy's Pride**	Howard Beissinger	1:57⅗
1935	**Greyhound**	Sep Palin	2:02¼	1970	**Timothy T**	John Simpson Jr.	1:58⅖
1936	**Rosalind**	Ben White	2:01¾	1971	**Speedy Crown** . . .	Howard Beissinger	1:57⅖
1937	**Shirley Hanover** . .	Henry Thomas	2:01½	1972	**Super Bowl**	Stanley Dancer	1:56⅖
1938	**McLin Hanover** . . .	Henry Tomas	2:02¼	1973	**Flirth**	Ralph Baldwin	1:57⅕
1939	**Peter Astra**	Doc Parshall	2:04¼	1974	**Christopher T**	Billy Haughton	1:58⅗
1940	**Spencer Scott** . . .	Fred Egan	2:02	1975	**Bonefish**	Stanley Dancer	1:59
1941	**Bill Gallon**	Lee Smith	2:05	1976	**Steve Lobell**	Billy Haughton	1:56⅖
1942	**The Ambassador** . .	Ben White	2:04	1977	**Green Speed**	Billy Haughton	1:55⅗
1943	**Volo Song**	Ben White	2:02½	1978	**Speedy Somolli** . . .	Howard Beissinger	1:55
1944	**Yankee Maid**	Henry Thomas	2:04	1979	**Legend Hanover** . .	George Sholty	1:56⅕
1945	**Titan Hanover**	Harry Pownall Sr.	2:04	1980	**Burgomeister**	Billy Haughton	1:56⅗
1946	**Chestertown**	Thomas Berry	2:02½	1981	**Shiaway St. Pat** . .	Ray Remmen	2:01⅕
1947	**Hoot Mon**	Sep Palin	2:00	1982	**Speed Bowl**	Tommy Haughton	1:56⅘
1948	**Demon Hanover** . .	Harrison Hoyt	2:02	1983	**Duenna**	Stanley Dancer	1:57⅖.
1949	**Miss Tilly**	Fred Egan	2:01⅖	1984	**Historic Freight** . .	Ben Webster	1:56⅖
1950	**Lusty Song**	Del Miller	2:02	1985	**Prakas**	Bill O'Donnell	1:54⅗
1951	**Mainliner**	Guy Crippen	2:02⅗	1986	**Nuclear Kosmos** . .	Ulf Thoresen	1:55⅖
1952	**Sharp Note**	Bion Shively	2:02⅗	1987	**Mack Lobell**	John Campbell	1:53⅖
1953	**Helicopter**	Harry Harvey	2:01⅗	1988	**Armbro Goal**	John Campbell	1:54⅗
1954	**Newport Dream** . .	Del Cameron	2:02⅘	1989	**Park Avenue Joe** . .	Ron Waples	1:54⅗
1955	**Scott Frost**	Joe O'Brien	2:00⅗		& **Probe** *	Bill Fahy	
1956	**The Intruder**	Ned Bower	2:01⅘	1990	**Harmonious**	John Campbell	1:54⅕
1957	**Hickory Smoke** . . .	John Simpson Sr.	2:00⅕	1991	**Giant Victory**	Jack Moiseyev	1:54⅘
1958	**Emily's Pride**	Flave Nipe	1:59⅘	1992	**Alf Palema**	Mickey McNichol	1:56⅖
1959	**Diller Hanover** . . .	Frank Ervin	2:01⅕	1993	**American Winner** . .	Ron Pierce	1:53⅕
1960	**Blaze Hanover** . . .	Joe O'Brien	1:59⅗	1994	**Victory Dream** . . .	Mike Lachance	1:54⅕

*In 1989, Park Avenue Joe and Probe finished in a dead heat in the race-off. They were later declared co-winners, but Park Avenue Joe was awarded 1st place money because his three-race summary (2-1-1) was better than Probe's (1-9-1).

The Hambletonian (Cont.)

Year		Driver	Fastest Heat	Year		Driver	Fastest Heat
1995	**Tagliabue**	John Campbell	1:54⅘	2002	**Chip Chip Hooray**	Eric Ledford	1:53⅗
1996	**Continentalvictory**	Mike Lachance	1:52⅘	2003	**Amigo Hall**	Mike Lachance	1:54
1997	**Malabar Man**	Mal Burroughs	1:55	2004	**Windsong's Legacy**	T. Smedshammer	1:54⅕
1998	**Muscles Yankee**	John Campbell	1:52⅖	2005	**Vivid Photo**	Roger Hammer	1:52⅗
1999	**Self Possessed**	Mike Lachance	1:51⅗	2006	**Glidemaster**	John Campbell	1:51⅕
2000	**Yankee Paco**	Trevor Ritchie	1:53⅖	2007	**Donato Hanover**	Ron Pierce	1:53⅖
2001	**Scarlet Knight**	Stefan Melander	1:53⅘	2008	**Deweycheatumnhowe**	Ray Schnittker	1:52

The Little Brown Jug

Harness racing's most prestigious race for three-year-old pacers. Inaugurated in 1946 and held annually at the Delaware, Ohio County Fairgrounds. Winning horse must win two heats.

Year		Year		Year		Year	
1946	Ensign Hanover	1962	Lehigh Hanover	1978	Happy Escort	1994	Magical Mike
1947	Forbes Chief	1963	Overtrick	1979	Hot Hitter	1995	Nick's Fantasy
1948	Knight Dream	1964	Vicar Hanover	1980	Niatross	1996	Armbro Operative
1949	Good Time	1965	Bret Hanover	1981	Fan Hanover	1997	Western Dreamer
1950	Dudley Hanover	1966	Romeo Hanover	1982	Merger	1998	Shady Character
1951	Tar Heel	1967	Best Of All	1983	Ralph Hanover	1999	Blissful Hall
1952	Meadow Rice	1968	Rum Customer	1984	Colt Fortysix	2000	Astreos
1953	Keystoner	1969	Laverne Hanover	1985	Nihilator	2001	Bettor's Delight
1954	Adios Harry	1970	Most Happy Fella	1986	Barberry Spur	2002	Million Dollar Cam
1955	Quick Chief	1971	Nansemond	1987	Jaguar Spur	2003	No Pan Intended
1956	Noble Adios	1972	Strike Out	1988	B.J. Scoot	2004	Timesarechanging
1957	Torpid	1973	Melvin's Woe	1989	Goalie Jeff	2005	P-Forty-Seven
1958	Shadow Wave	1974	Armbro Omaha	1990	Beach Towel	2006	Mr. Feelgood
1959	Adios Butler	1975	Seatrain	1991	Precious Bunny	2007	Tell All
1960	Bullet Hanover	1976	Keystone Ore	1992	Fake Left	2008	Shadow Play
1961	Henry T. Adios	1977	Governor Skipper	1993	Life Sign		

Annual Awards
Harness Horse of the Year

Selected since 1947 by U.S. Trotting Association and the U.S. Harness Writers Association; age of winning horse is noted; (t) indicates trotter and (p) indicates pacer. **Multiple winners:** Bret Hanover and Nevele Pride (3); Adios Butler, Albatross, Cam Fella, Good Time, Mack Lobell, Moni Maker, Niatross and Scott Frost (2).

Year		Year		Year		Year	
1947	Victory Song (4t)	1963	Speedy Scot (3t)	1979	Niatross (2p)	1995	CR Kay Suzie (3t)
1948	Rodney (4t)	1964	Bret Hanover (2p)	1980	Niatross (3p)	1996	Continentalvictory (3t)
1949	Good Time (3p)	1965	Bret Hanover (3p)	1981	Fan Hanover (3p)	1997	Malabar Man (3t)
1950	Proximity (8t)	1966	Bret Hanover (4p)	1982	Cam Fella (3p)	1998	Moni Maker (5t)
1951	Pronto Don (6t)	1967	Nevele Pride (2t)	1983	Cam Fella (4p)	1999	Moni Maker (6t)
1952	Good Time (6p)	1968	Nevele Pride (3t)	1984	Fancy Crown (3t)	2000	Gallo Blue Chip (3p)
1953	Hi Lo's Forbes (5p)	1969	Nevele Pride (4t)	1985	Nihilator (3p)	2001	Bunny Lake (3p)
1954	Stenographer (3t)	1970	Fresh Yankee (7t)	1986	Forrest Skipper (4p)	2002	Real Desire (4p)
1955	Scott Frost (3t)	1971	Albatross (3p)	1987	Mack Lobell (3t)	2003	No Pan Intended (3p)
1956	Scott Frost (4t)	1972	Albatross (4p)	1988	Mack Lobell (4t)	2004	Rainbow Blue (3p)
1957	Torpid (3p)	1973	Sir Dalrae (4p)	1989	Matt's Scooter (4p)	2005	Rocknroll Hanover (3p)
1958	Emily's Pride (3t)	1974	Delmonica Hanover (5t)	1990	Beach Towel (3p)	2006	Glidemaster (3t)
1959	Bye Bye Byrd (4p)	1975	Savoir (7t)	1991	Precious Bunny (3p)	2007	Donato Hanover (3t)
1960	Adios Butler (3p)	1976	Keystone Ore (3p)	1992	Artsplace (4p)		
1961	Adios Butler (5p)	1977	Green Speed (3t)	1993	Staying Together (4p)		
1962	Su Mac Lad (8t)	1978	Abercrombie (3p)	1994	Cam's Card Shark (3p)		

Driver of the Year

Determined by Universal Driving Rating System (UDR) and presented by the Harness Tracks of America since 1968. Eligible drivers must have at least 1,000 starts for the season. **Multiple winners:** Hervé Filion (10); Dave Palone (4); John Campbell, Walter Case Jr. and Mike Lachance (3); Tony Morgan, Bill O'Donnell, Luc Ouellette and Ron Waples (2).

Year		Year		Year		Year	
1968	Stanley Dancer	1979	Ron Waples	1991	Walter Case Jr.	2002	Tony Morgan
1969	Herve Filion	1980	Ron Waples	1992	Walter Case Jr.	2003	Dave Palone
1970	Herve Filion	1981	Herve Filion	1993	Jack Moiseyev	2004	Dave Palone
1971	Herve Filion	1982	Bill O'Donnell	1994	Dave Magee	2005	Cat Manzi
1972	Herve Filion	1983	John Campbell	1995	Luc Ouellette	2006	Jim Morrill Jr.
1973	Herve Filion	1984	Bill O'Donnell	1996	Tony Morgan & Luc Ouellette	2007	Tim Tetrick
1974	Herve Filion	1985	Mike Lachance	1997	Tony Morgan		
1975	Joe O'Brien	1986	Mike Lachance	1998	Walter Case Jr.		
1976	Herve Filion	1987	Mike Lachance	1999	Dave Palone		
1977	Donald Dancer	1988	John Campbell	2000	Dave Palone		
1978	Carmine Abbatiello & Herve Filion	1989	Herve Filion	2001	Stephane Bouchard		
		1990	John Campbell				

TENNIS

2007 / 2008 YEAR IN REVIEW

Serena Williams won the 2008 U.S. Open for her ninth career Grand Slam singles title.

SPANISH
CLASS

With two Grand Slam titles in 2008, Rafael Nadal ascends to the World's No. 1 men's ranking. And that's just the beginning.

by Greg Garber

HE WAS A 15-YEAR-OLD KID playing in his first ATP-level tournament, but already you could see the power — that left arm was freakishly muscular, reminiscent of another lefty, Rod Laver — the quickness, the ball-striking ability. Oh, and the hunger. It burned in his brown eyes with a startling intensity.

Rafael Nadal's first-round opponent on April 29, 2002, was Ramon Delgado of Paraguay, a legitimate pro ranked No. 81 in the world. Four years earlier, Delgado had stunned No. 1 Pete Sampras in the second round of the French Open (in straight sets). Playing in Mallorca, the sun-splashed Spanish island on which he was born, Nadal schooled Delgado, 6-4, 6-4.

Benito Perez-Barbadillo, working for the ATP communications department that week, had heard about Nadal. Earlier that year, in Kitzbuhel, Austria, Miguel Angel Nadal, a member of the Spanish national soccer team, had bragged to him about his nephew, say-ing he wanted to play professional tennis. Carlos Moya, Nadal's mentor, a French Open champion and fellow Mallorcan, also had talked him up. Still, Perez-Barbadillo wasn't fully prepared for the complete player he saw defeat Delgado.

"Here's this little kid, beating this 20-something guy, one very solid pro," Perez-Barbadillo said recently from his office in Monte Carlo, Monaco. "The thing I remember is that his serve was not working that great. But the movement, the shots. He was really good.

"And you could see he really wanted to win."

Nadal lost his second-round match, to Olivier Rochus of Belgium, but he soon proved to be a Mozartian prodigy. Rafa won his first Grand Slam event, the 2005 French Open, a week after he turned 19. Six weeks later, he

Greg Garber has been with ESPN since 1991 and is a Senior Writer for ESPN.com.

Spain's **Rafael Nadal** won his fourth straight French Open, then proved he was more than a clay court specialist with his first Wimbledon title.

became the world's No. 2-ranked player, behind Roger Federer.

Now, at the age of 22, Nadal completes his long journey to the top of men's professional tennis with a freshly minted Olympic gold medal hanging around his neck. After sitting behind Federer for a record 160 consecutive weeks — Nadal has been No. 2 longer than it took him to reach that spot from No. 466 — he is finally No. 1 in the ATP rankings.

Nadal has taken every opportunity to downplay his displacement of Federer.

"I feel happy because, for sure, to be No. 1 is hard work from a long, long time ago," Nadal said in Cincinnati after his elevation was guaranteed. "But no time to be excited and be happy and enjoy. I am in a good [position.] The goal is only continuing playing like this and continuing to improve my tennis, to have chances to continue winning important tournaments on this surface."

Perez-Barbadillo, now Rafa's confidant and press agent, confirms that the No. 1 ranking is not Nadal's driving motivation.

"Every tennis player wants to be No. 1 player, yes," Perez-Barbadillo said. "But the way he thinks is, 'If I win big titles, the ranking comes with that.' He knows that titles are what really will mark his career.

AP Images

Roger Federer may have lost his No. 1 ranking in 2008, but his sixth straight U.S. Open title showed he wasn't going anywhere.

"If you have a No. 1 like Roger Federer in front of you, you have to understand there is nothing more you can do. I remember him saying once that he was the No. 1 player in the world. I said, 'What do you mean?'

"He said, 'Roger Federer is from another world.'"

Todd Martin, a two-time Grand Slam finalist, admitted he was slightly surprised by Nadal's ultimate ascension.

"A year ago the discussion was what happens first — will Nadal reach No. 1, or will [Novak] Djokovic become No. 2?" said Martin, who played some senior singles matches at the U.S. Open. "I thought Djokovic would make the run before Nadal. I bought into some of the weaknesses that Rafael showed in the second half of 2007. I also thought losing to [Jo-Wilfried] Tsonga at the Australian Open would hurt him more than it did.

"At the core of it, he has the greatest weapon in the game — that's his heart. His heart, I think, dictates how good his focus is on a day-to-day, point-to-point basis. His heart is so in it, his mind is never out of it."

Nadal, at 22 years, 2 months and 2 weeks, was more than three months younger than Federer was when he became No. 1. Nadal has already won five Grand Slam singles titles — four French Opens and one at Wimbledon. At his exact age, Federer had only one.

Powerful prodigy

Sixteen months after his first ATP-level victory, Nadal came to New York for the 2003 U.S. Open. Spectators, eating ice cream and sipping drinks, watched Carlos Moya hitting balls on Practice Court 5. Golfer Sergio Garcia, a good friend of the Spaniard's, worked the baseline as a ball boy. Onlookers paid little attention to Moya's practice partner, the strapping kid with long brown hair on the other side of the net. But who was the guy consistently outhitting the 1998 French Open champion?

Seventeen-year-old Rafael Nadal.

Yes, the very player who earlier that year qualified his way into the main draw at Hamburg, then beat his idol, Moya, in the first round.

Nadal won his first-round match at the U.S. Open in straight sets over Fernando Vicente, but lost to the eccentric Moroccan Younes El Aynaoui, also in straights — but Rafa pushed him to two tiebreakers. On one point, Nadal whiffed on an overhead with his back to the net, then sprinted past the baseline, whirled, and hit a spectacular forehand winner. El Aynaoui could only shake his head and throw him a thumbs-up.

"I knew Rafa would become No. 1 sooner or later," Moya said two weeks ago in Los Angeles. "I can't say that I really helped Rafa so much, maybe a bit when I was 24 and practicing with him. That motivated me — you don't want to lose to a kid. He's helped me to be a better player by his intensity in training and his desire."

"After he won Wimbledon, it doesn't matter what the rankings say," said Paul Annacone, the men's head coach for Great Britain's Lawn Tennis Association, "that guy with two Slams [this year] is probably the No. 1 player in the world. He's relentless about his improvement. He's checked all the clichéd boxes to get better. It's amazing how diligent he is."

Nadal was always a natural on clay, but he quickly adapted his game of attrition to the slippery slope of grass, a surface on which the ball skids and footing can be treacherous. He forced himself out of his clay comfort zone, and learned to be more offensive and take greater risks.

He reached the finals at the All England Club in 2006 and 2007, losing to Federer both times, but then broke through with an epic victory back in July. Nadal prevailed in a breathtaking five-set final that was the longest (4 hours, 48 minutes) and, what many believe, the best in Wimbledon history.

While Nadal has mastered clay, and now grass, he had struggled — in light of his success, it's a highly relative term — on hard courts. At least until he won nine straight matches in the hard-court heat of ATP Masters Series events in Toronto and Cincinnati, running his consecutive match victory total to 32. He took the title in Canada, but looked exhausted in losing to Djokovic in the Cincinnati semifinals.

Even in defeat, Martin was impressed with Nadal.

"He's so invested in every single second he's on the tennis court," Martin observed. "He missed one particular volley against Djokovic. He doesn't miss volleys he should make, and this one to me was a focus error, a count-your-chickens-before-they-hatch error.

"Rafael is the only guy who I'd notice, watching from my sofa, that specific error. His eyes are absolutely wide for every ball that comes his way. He's 100 percent ready to play every day, which is astonishing."

Nadal, however, vindicated that loss to Djokovic, defeating the Serb in the Olympic semifinals. Nadal, fittingly, then took Fernando Gonzalez down in the final, becoming the first Spanish player to capture Olympic gold.

Men's tennis has been remarkably stable at the very top. In the three years that Federer and Nadal have been 1-2, the No. 1 spot in the women's game has changed no fewer than 13 times — and featured seven different players. But now, the men's world order changes.

Federer will not likely equal Sampras' record of finishing six straight years at No. 1 (1993 to 1998). With Federer chaffing at his second-class status, and inevitable pressure from the hard-charging Djokovic, how long will Nadal reign?

More than likely, not as long as Federer's record 237 weeks. Nadal played 85 matches last year, second only to Djokovic's 87. Through the Olympics, a victim of his own success, he had logged a staggering 78 matches — 17 more than anyone else.

When Nadal unleashes a forehand — Andy Murray calls it the "heaviest ball in tennis" — you wonder if his muscles and tendons will survive the effort.

"I'm not so concerned about the way he hits the ball, it's the way he moves and the body type he has," said Annacone, who coached Sampras for eight years. "He's a big, huge, strong athlete, but there's a lot of muscle mass to carry around. Like Boris Becker, he's big and he's doing all that stopping and starting, pounding side to side.

"The guys that reach that level the most efficiently and easily tend to have the longevity. That's Roger and Pete [Sampras] and Andre [Agassi], to an extent. Rafa can play at really high levels. But it takes more out of him to do so. I'd say he is incrementally more vulnerable than someone like a Federer."

Said Martin, "I just don't think Roger's going away. I've never bought into the idea that this is the beginning of the swan song. He needs to ask some pretty tough questions of himself. Is he willing to do what's necessary to again improve more than Nadal and the others?

"Rafael staying at No. 1, it's not so much a tennis question as a math answer. He'll have to sustain a level of play on the hard courts that he hasn't shown yet. The first six months of the year he dominated on two surfaces. He has to prove he's at least the second-best on hard courts in the world.

2007-2008
Season in Review

SPORTS ALMANAC

Tournament Results

Winners of men's and women's pro singles championships from Nov. 5, 2007 through Sept. 29, 2008.

Men's ATP Tour

Late 2007

Finals	Tournament	Winner	Earnings	Runner-Up	Score
Nov. 5	TMS—Paris	David Nalbandian	$496,720	R. Nadal	64 60
Nov. 26	Tennis Masters Cup (Shanghai)	Roger Federer	1,200,000	D. Ferrer	62 63 62
Dec. 2	Davis Cup Final (Portland, Ore.)	United States	—	Russia	4-1

2008 (through Sept. 29)

Finals	Tournament	Winner	Earnings	Runner-Up	Score
Jan. 5	Qatar ExxonMobil Open (Doha)	Andy Murray	$171,000	S. Wawrinka	64 46 62
Jan. 6	Next Generation Hardcourts (Adelaide)	Michael Llodra	73,900	J. Nieminen	63 64
Jan. 6	Chennai Open	Mikhail Youzhny	68,800	R. Nadal	60 61
Jan. 13	Medibank International (Sydney)	Dmitry Tursunov	73,900	C. Guccione	76 76
Jan. 13	Heineken Open (Auckland)	Phillip Kohlschreiber	73,700	J.C. Ferrero	76 75
Jan. 27	**Australian Open** (Melbourne)	Novak Djokovic	1,281,000	J-W Tsonga	46 64 63 76
Feb. 3	Movistar Open (Vina Del Mar)	Fernando Gonzalez	73,500	J. Monaco	walkover
Feb. 17	Delray Beach Int'l Champs	Kei Nishikori	68,800	J. Blake	36 61 64
Feb. 17	Brasil Open (Costa Do Sauipe)	Nicolas Almagro	77,300	C. Moya	76 36 75
Feb. 17	Open 13 (Marseille)	Andy Murray	125,050	M. Ancic	63 64
Feb. 24	Copa Telmex (Buenos Aires)	David Nalbandian	74,000	J. Acasuso	36 76 64
Feb. 24	ABN/AMRO World Tennis Tournament (Rotterdam)	Michael Llodra	249,667	R. Soderling	67 63 76
Feb. 24	SAP Open (San Jose)	Andy Roddick	68,800	R. Stepanek	64 75
Mar. 2	Mexican Open (Acapulco)	Nicolas Almagro	163,750	D. Nalbandian	61 76
Mar. 2	Regions Morgan Keegan Champs (Memphis)	Steve Darcis	163,750	R. Soderling	63 76
Mar. 2	PBZ Zagreb Indoors	Sergiy Stakhovsky	86,300	I. Ljubicic	75 64
Mar. 8	Barclays Dubai Tennis Championships	Andy Roddick	300,000	F. Lopez	67 64 62
Mar. 9	Tennis Channel Open (Las Vegas)	Samuel Querrey	68,800	K. Anderson	46 63 64
Mar. 24	TMS—Indian Wells	Novak Djokovic	555,000	M. Fish	62 57 63
Apr. 6	TMS—Sony Ericsson Open (Miami)	Nikolay Davydenko	590,000	R. Nadal	64 62
Apr. 20	Valencia Open	David Ferrer	86,300	N. Almagro	46 62 76
Apr. 20	U.S. Clay Court Championships (Houston)	Marcel Granollers-Pujol	68,800	J. Blake	64 16 75
Apr. 20	Estoril Open	Roger Federer	86,300	N. Davydenko	76 12 (ret.)
Apr. 27	TMS—Monte Carlo	Rafael Nadal	525,600	R. Federer	75 75
May 4	Open Sabadell Atlantico (Barcelona)	Rafael Nadal	199,000	D. Ferrer	61 46 61
May 4	BMW Open (Munich)	Fernando Gonzalez	86,300	S. Bolelli	76 67 63
May 11	TMS—Internazionali BNL d'Italia (Rome)	Novak Djokovic	525,000	S. Wawrinka	46 63 63
May 18	TMS—Hamburg	Rafael Nadal	525,500	R. Federer	75 67 63
May 24	Grand Prix Hassan II (Casablanca)	Gilles Simon	86,300	J. Benneteau	75 62
May 24	Hypo Group Tennis Int'l (Portschach)	Nikolay Davydenko	86,300	J. Monaco	62 26 62
May 24	World Team Championship (Dusseldorf)	Sweden	—	Russia	2-1
June 8	**French Open** (Roland Garros)	Rafael Nadal	1,460,050	R. Federer	61 63 60
June 15	Gerry Weber Open (Halle)	Roger Federer	168,600	P. Kohlschreiber	63 64
June 15	Stella Artois Championships (London)	Rafael Nadal	123,400	N. Djokovic	76 75
June 16	Orange Warsaw Open	Nikolay Davydenko	99,000	T. Robredo	63 63
June 21	Slazenger Open (Nottingham)	Ivo Karlovic	86,300	F. Verdasco	75 67 76
June 21	Ordina Open ('s-Hertogenbosch)	David Ferrer	86,300	M. Gicquel	64 62
July 6	**Wimbledon** (London)	Rafael Nadal	1,288,000	R. Federer	64 64 67 67 97
July 13	Allianz Swiss Open (Gstaad)	Victor Hanescu	94,900	I. Andreev	63 64
July 13	Hall of Fame Championships (Newport)	Fabrice Santoro	64,000	P. Amritraj	63 75
July 13	Catella Swedish Open (Bastad)	Tommy Robredo	79,200	T. Berdych	64 61
July 13	Mercedes Cup (Stuttgart)	Juan Martin del Potro	172,285	R. Gasquet	64 75
July 20	Croatia Open (Umag)	Fernando Verdasco	79,200	I. Andreev	36 64 76
July 20	Austrian Open (Kitzbuhel)	Juan Martin del Potro	170,825	J. Melzer	62 61

Tournament Results (Cont.)

Finals	Tournament	Winner	Earnings	Runner-Up	Score
July 20	Indianapolis Tennis Championships	Gilles Simon	$83,500	D. Tursunov	64 64
July 20	Dutch Open (Amersfoort)	Albert Montanes	79,200	S. Darcis	16 75 63
July 27	TMS—Rogers Masters (Toronto)	Rafael Nadal	420,000	N. Kiefer	63 62
Aug. 3	TMS—Western & Southern Financial Group Masters (Cincinnati)	Andy Murray	420,000	N. Djokovic	76 76
Aug. 10	Countrywide Classic (Los Angeles)	Juan Martin del Potro	79,000	A. Roddick	61 76
Aug. 17	Legg Mason Classic (Washington D.C.)	Juan Martin del Potro	80,650	V. Troicki	63 63
Aug. 17	Olympic Gold Medal Match (Beijing)	Rafael Nadal	—	F. Gonzalez	63 76 63
Aug. 23	Pilot Pen (New Haven)	Marin Cilic	94,000	M. Fish	64 46 62
Sept. 8	**U.S. Open** (Flushing)	Roger Federer	1,200,000	A. Murray	62 75 62
Sept. 14	BCR Romanian Open (Bucharest)	Gilles Simon	86,300	C. Moya	63 64
Sept. 28	China Open (Beijing)	Andy Roddick	85,000	D. Sela	64 67 63
Sept. 28	Thailand Open (Bangkok)	Jo-Wilfried Tsonga	94,000	N. Djokovic	76 64

Note: TMS indicates tournament is part of the ATP Tennis Masters Series.

Women's WTA Tour

Late 2007

Finals	Tournament	Winner	Earnings	Runner-Up	Score
Nov. 5	Bell Challenge (Quebec)	Lindsay Davenport	$25,840	J. Vakulenko	64 61
Nov. 11	Sony Ericsson Championships (Madrid)	Justine Henin	1,000,000	M. Sharapova	57 75 63

2008 (through Sept. 29)

Finals	Tournament	Winner	Earnings	Runner-Up	Score
Jan. 5	Mondial Australian Hardcourts (Gold Coast)	Li Na	$28,000	V. Azarenka	46 63 64
Jan. 5	ASB Bank Classic (Auckland)	Lindsay Davenport	22,900	A. Rezai	62 62
Jan. 11	Moorilla International (Hobart)	Elena Daniilidou	25,650	V. Zvonareva	walkover
Jan. 11	Medibank International (Sydney)	Justine Henin	95,500	S. Kuznetsova	46 62 64
Jan. 27	**Australian Open** (Melbourne)	Maria Sharapova	1,200,000	A. Ivanovic	75 63
Feb. 10	Pattaya Open (Pattaya City)	Agnieszka Radwanska	25,650	J. Craybas	62 16 76
Feb. 10	Open Gaz de France (Paris)	Anna Chakvetadze	95,500	A. Szavay	63 26 62
Feb. 17	Proximus Diamond Games (Antwerp)	Justine Henin	95,500	K. Knapp	63 63
Feb. 17	Cachantun Cup (Vina Del Mar)	Flavia Pennetta	30,500	K. Zakopalova	64 54 (ret.)
Feb. 24	Copa Colsanitas (Bogota)	Nuria Llagostera Vives	29,000	M.E. Salerni	60 64
Feb. 24	Qatar Total Open (Doha)	Maria Sharapova	414,000	V. Zvonareva	61 26 60
Mar. 1	Barclay's Dubai Championships	Elena Dementieva	250,000	S. Kuznetsova	46 63 62
Mar. 2	Regions Morgan Keegan Championships and Cellular South Cup (Memphis)	Lindsay Davenport	28,000	O. Govortsova	62 61
Mar. 2	Abierto Mexicano de Tenis (Acapulco)	Flavia Pennetta	28,700	A. Cornet	60 46 61
Mar. 9	Bangalore Open	Serena Williams	95,500	P. Schnyder	75 63
Mar. 23	Pacific Life Open (Indian Wells)	Ana Ivanovic	332,000	S. Kuznetsova	64 63
Apr. 6	Sony Ericsson Open (Miami)	Serena Williams	590,000	J. Jankovic	61 57 63
Apr. 13	Bausch & Lomb Championships (Amelia Island)	Maria Sharapova	95,500	D. Cibulkova	76 63
Apr. 20	Family Circle Cup (Charleston)	Serena Williams	196,900	V. Zvonareva	64 36 63
Apr. 20	Estoril Open	Maria Kirilenko	22,900	I. Benesova	64 62
May 4	ECM Prague Open	Vera Zvonareva	22,900	V. Azarenka	76 62
May 4	Grand Prix De S.A.R. (Fes)	Gisela Dulko	22,900	A. Medina Garrigues	76 65 76
May 11	Qatar Telecom German Open (Berlin)	Dinara Safina	196,900	E. Dementieva	36 62 63
May 18	Internazionali BNL d'Italia (Rome)	Jelena Jankovic	196,900	A. Cornet	62 62
May 24	Strasbourg International	A. Medina Garrigues	28,000	K. Srebotnik	46 76 60
May 24	Istanbul Cup	Agnieszka Radwanska	30,500	E. Dementieva	63 62
June 8	**French Open** (Roland Garros)	Ana Ivanovic	1,570,000	D. Safina	64 63
June 15	Barcelona KIA	Maria Kirilenko	22,900	M. J. Martinez Sanchez	60 62
June 15	DFS Classic (Birmingham)	Kateryna Bondarenko	31,000	Y. Wickmayer	76 36 76
June 21	Ordina Open ('s-Hertogenbosch)	Tamarine Tanasugarn	28,000	D. Safina	75 63
June 21	International Women's Open (Eastbourne)	Agnieszka Radwanska	95,500	N. Petrova	64 67 64
July 6	**Wimbledon** (London)	Venus Williams	1,490,000	S. Williams	75 64
July 13	Palermo International	Sara Errani	22,000	M. Koryttseva	62 63
July 13	Gaz de France GP (Budapest)	Alize Cornet	28,000	A. Klepac	76 63
July 20	Bank of the West Classic (Stanford)	Aleksandra Wozniak	95,500	M. Bartoli	75 63
July 20	Gastein Ladies (Bad Gastein)	Pauline Parmentier	28,000	L. Hradecka	64 64
July 27	East West Bank Classic (Los Angeles)	Dinara Safina	95,500	F. Pennetta	64 62
July 27	Banka Koper Slovenia Open (Portoroz)	Sara Errani	22,900	A. Medina Garrigues	63 63
Aug. 3	Nordea Nordic Light Open (Stockholm)	Caroline Wozniacki	22,925	V. Dushevina	60 62

Finals	Tournament	Winner	Earnings	Runner-Up	Score
Aug. 3	Rogers Cup (Montreal)	Dinara Safina	$196,900	D. Cibulkova	62 61
Aug. 17	Olympics Gold Medal Match (Beijing)	Elena Dementieva	—	D. Safina	36 75 63
Aug. 17	Western & Southern Open (Cincinnati)	Nadia Petrova	28,000	N. Dechy	62 61
Aug. 23	Pilot Pen Tennis (New Haven)	Caroline Wozniacki	95,500	A. Chakvetadze	36 64 61
Aug. 23	Forest Hills Women's Tennis Classic	Lucie Safarova	22,000	Peng Shuai	64 62
Sept. 8	**U.S. Open** (Flushing)	Serena Williams	1,500,000	J. Jankovic	64 75
Sept. 14	2008 Fed Cup Final (Madrid)	Russia	—	Spain	4-0
Sept. 14	Commonwealth Bank Classic (Bali)	Patty Schnyder	35,000	T. Paszek	63 60
Sept. 21	Toray Pan Pacific Open (Tokyo)	Dinara Safina	196,900	S. Kuznetsova	61 63
Sept. 21	Guangzhou International	Vera Zvonareva	28,000	Peng Shuai	67 60 62
Sept. 28	China Open (Beijing)	Jelena Jankovic	95,500	S. Kuznetsova	63 62
Sept. 28	Hansol Korea Open (Seoul)	Maria Kirilenko	22,900	S. Stosur	26 61 64

2008 Grand Slam Tournaments

Australian Open

MEN'S SINGLES

FINAL EIGHT—#1 Roger Federer; #2 Rafael Nadal; #3 Novak Djokovic; #5 David Ferrer; #12 James Blake; #14 Mikhail Youzhny; #24 Jarkko Nieminen; plus unseeded Jo-Wilifried Tsonga.

Quarterfinals

Nadal def. Nieminen	.75 63 61
Djokovic def. Ferrer	.60 63 75
Federer def. Blake	.75 76(5) 64
Tsonga def. Youzhny	.75 60 76(6)

Semifinals

Tsonga def. Nadal	.62 63 62
Djokovic def. Federer	.75 63 76(5)

Final

Djokovic def. Tsonga	.46 64 63 76(2)

MEN'S DOUBLES FINALS

#8 Jonathan Erlich & Andy Ram def. #7 Arnaud Clement & Michael Llodra, 7-5, 7-6(4).

WOMEN'S SINGLES

FINAL EIGHT—#1 Justine Henin; #3 Jelena Jankovic; #4 Ana Ivanovic; #5 Maria Sharapova; #7 Serena Williams; #8 Venus Williams; #9 Daniela Hantuchova; #29 Agnieszka Radwanska.

Quarterfinals

Hantuchova def. Radwanska	.62 62
Jankovic def. S. Williams	.63 64
Ivanovic def. V. Williams	.76(3) 64
Sharapova def. Henin	.64 60

Semifinals

Sharapova def. Jankovic	.63 61
Ivanovic def. Hantuchova	.06 63 64

Final

Sharapova def. Ivanovic	.75 63

WOMEN'S DOUBLES FINALS

Alona Bondarenko & Kateryna Bondarenko def. #12 Victoria Azarenka & Shahar Peer, 2-6, 6-1, 6-4.

MIXED DOUBLES FINALS

#5 Tian Tian Sun & Nenad Zimonjic def. Sania Mirza & Mahesh Bhupathi, 7-6(4), 6-4.

French Open

MEN'S SINGLES

FINAL EIGHT—#1 Roger Federer; #2 Rafael Nadal; #3 Novak Djokovic; #5 David Ferrer; #19 Nicolas Almagro; #24 Fernando Gonzalez; plus unseeded Ernests Gulbis and Gael Monfils.

Quarterfinals

Nadal def. Almagro	.61 61 61
Monfils def. Ferrer	.63 36 63 61
Djokovic def. Gulbis	.75 76(3) 75
Federer def. Gonzalez	.26 62 63 64

Semifinals

Nadal def. Djokovic	.64 62 76(3)
Federer def. Monfils	.62 57 63 75

Final

Nadal def. Federer	.61 63 60

MEN'S DOUBLES FINALS

Pablo Cuevas & Luis Horna def. #2 Daniel Nestor & Nenad Zimonjic, 6-2, 6-3.

WOMEN'S SINGLES

FINAL EIGHT—#2 Ana Ivanovic; #3 Jelena Jankovic; #4 Svetlana Kuznetsova; #7 Elena Dementieva; #10 Patty Schnyder; #13 Dinara Safina; plus unseeded Carla Suarez-Navarro and Kaia Kanepi.

Quarterfinals

Ivanovic def. Schnyder	.63 62
Safina def. Dementieva	.46 76(5) 60
Jankovic def. Suarez-Navarro	.63 62
Kuznetsova def. Kanepi	.75 62

Semifinals

Safina def. Kuznetsova	.63 62
Ivanovic def. Jankovic	.64 36 64

Final

Ivanovic def. Safina	.64 63

WOMEN'S DOUBLES FINALS

#10 Anabel Medina Garrigues & Virginia Ruano Pascual def. Casey Dellacqua & Francesca Schiavone, 2-6, 7-5, 6-4.

MIXED DOUBLES FINALS

#3 Victoria Azarenka & Bob Bryan def. #1 Katarina Srebotnik & Nenad Zimonjic, 6-2, 7-6(4).

Wimbledon

MEN'S SINGLES

FINAL EIGHT—# 1 Roger Federer; #2 Rafael Nadal; #9 Rainer Schuettler; #12 Andy Murray; #31 Feliciano Lopez; plus unseeded Mario Ancic, Arnaud Clement and Marat Safin.

Quarterfinals

Nadal def. Murray .63 62 64
Safin def. Lopez . . . . .36 75 76(1) 63
Federer def. Ancic 61 75 64
Schuettler def. Clement . . . .63 57 76(6) 67(7) 86

Semifinals

Federer def. Safin . . . . .63 76(3) 64
Nadal def. Schuettler . . . .· . . . . .61 76(3) 64

Final

Nadal def. Federer . . . . .64 64 67(5) 67(8) 97

MEN'S DOUBLES FINALS

#2 Daniel Nestor & Nenad Zimonjic def. #8 Jonas Bjorkman & Kevin Ullyett, 7-6(12) 6-7(3) 6-3 6-3.

WOMEN'S SINGLES

FINAL EIGHT—#5 Elena Dementieva; #6 Serena Williams; #7 Venus Williams; #14 Agnieszka Radwanska; #18 Nicole Vaidisova; #21 Nadia Petrova; plus unseeded Zheng Jie and Tamarine Tanasugarn.

Quarterfinals

S. Williams def. Radwanska 64 60
Dementieva def. Petrova . . . . .61 67(6) 63
Zheng def. Vaidisova 62 57 61
V. Williams def. Tanasugarn 64 63

Semifinals

S. Williams def. Zheng . . . . .62 76(5)
V. Williams def. Dementieva . . . . .61 76(3)

Final

V. Williams def. S. Williams 75 64

WOMEN'S DOUBLES FINALS

#11 Serena Williams & Venus Williams def. #16 Lisa Raymond & Samantha Stosur, 6-2, 6-2.

MIXED DOUBLES FINALS

Bob Bryan & Samantha Stosur def. #1 Mike Bryan & Katarina Srebotnik, 7-5, 6-4.

U.S. Open

MEN'S SINGLES

FINAL EIGHT—#1 Rafael Nadal; #2 Roger Federer; #3 Novak Djokovic; #6 Andy Murray; #8 Andy Roddick; #17 Juan Martin del Potro; plus unseeded Mardy Fish and Gilles Muller.

Quarterfinals

Murray def. del Potro . . . . .76(2) 76(1) 46 75
Federer def. Muller . . . . .76(5) 64 76(5)
Nadal def. Fish .36 61 64 62
Djokovic def. Roddick . . . . .62 63 36 76(5)

Semifinals

Federer def. Djokovic 63 57 75 62
Murray def. Nadal . . . . .62 76(5) 46 64

Final

Federer def. Murray .62 75 62

MEN'S DOUBLES FINALS

#2 Bob Bryan & Mike Bryan def. #7 Lukas Dlouhy & Leander Paes, 7-6(5), 7-6(10).

WOMEN'S SINGLES

FINAL EIGHT—#2 Jelena Jankovic; #4 Serena Williams; #5 Elena Dementieva; #6 Dinara Safina; #7 Venus Williams; #15 Patty Schnyder; #16 Flavia Pennetta; #29 Sybille Bammer.

Quarterfinals

Dementieva def. Schnyder 62 63
Safina def. Pennetta 62 63
Jankovic def. Bammer 61 64
S. Williams def. V. Williams . . . . .76(6) 76(7)

Semifinals

Jankovic def. Dementieva 64 64
S. Williams def. Safina 63 62

Final

S. Williams def. Jankovic 64 75

WOMEN'S DOUBLES FINALS

#1 Cara Black & Liezel Huber def. Lisa Raymond & Samantha Stosur, 6-3, 7-6(6).

MIXED DOUBLES FINALS

#5 Cara Black & Leander Paes def. Liezel Huber & Jamie Murray, 7-6(6), 6-4.

2008 Fed Cup

Originally the Federation Cup and started in 1963 by the International Tennis Federation as the Davis Cup of women's tennis.

Quarterfinals (Feb. 2-3)

Winner	Loser
Russia 4 . . . . .at Israel 1	
at United States 4 . . . . .Germany 1	
at China 3 . . . . .France 2	
Spain 3 . . . . .at Italy 2	

Semifinals (Aptil 26-27)

Winner	Loser
at Russia 3 . . . . .United States 2	
Spain 4 . . . . .at China 1	

Finals

(in Madrid, Spain, Sept. 13-14)

Russia 4, Spain 0

Singles—Vera Zvonareva (RUS) def. Anabel Medina Garrigues (ESP) 6-3, 6-4; Svetlana Kuznetsova (RUS) def. Carla Suarez-Navarro (ESP) 6-3, 6-1; Kuznetsova (RUS) def. Medina Garrigues (ESP) 5-7, 6-3, 6-4.

Doubles—Ekaterina Makarova & Elena Vesnina (RUS) def. Nuria Llagostera Vives & Suarez Navarro (ESP) 6-2, 6-1.

Singles Leaders

Official Top 20 rankings and money leaders of men's and women's tours for 2007 and unofficial rankings for 2008 (through Sept. 29), as compiled by the ATP Tour (Association of Tennis Professionals) and WTA (Women's Tennis Association). Note that money lists include doubles earnings.

Final 2007 Rankings and Money Won

Listed are events won and times a finalist and semifinalist (Finish; 1-2-SF), match record (W-L), and earnings for the year.

MEN

		Finish 1-2-S	W-L	Earnings
1	Roger Federer	8-4-0	68-9	$7,430,620
2	Rafael Nadal	6-3-3	70-15	5,646,935
3	Novak Djokovic	5-2-4	68-19	3,927,700
4	Nikolay Davydenko	1-0-6	53-31	2,051,775
5	David Ferrer	3-2-2	61-23	1,955,252
6	Andy Roddick	2-1-5	54-16	1,532,070
7	Fernando Gonzalez	1-2-0	37-24	1,437,130
8	Richard Gasquet	1-2-3	49-24	1,284,790
9	David Nalbandian	2-0-0	31-18	1,230,465
10	Tommy Robredo	2-2-1	49-26	1,027,147
11	Andy Murray	2-2-3	43-14	880,905
12	Tommy Haas	1-0-3	39-17	974,350
13	James Blake	2-3-2	54-24	966,585
14	Tomas Berdych	1-0-4	46-24	1,126,070
15	Marcos Baghdatis	1-2-3	48-22	890,330
16	Carlos Moya	1-2-3	42-23	867,315
17	Ivan Ljubicic	2-2-2	44-23	963,445
18	Guillermo Canas	1-2-2	39-21	919,940
19	Mikhail Youzhny	1-2-3	50-24	1,028,900
20	Juan Ignacio Chela	1-0-2	40-25	987,765

WOMEN

		Finish 1-2-SF	W-L	Earnings
1	Justine Henin	10-1-2	63-4	$5,429,586
2	Svetlana Kuznetsova	1-5-4	55-20	2,287,487
3	Jelena Jankovic	4-4-7	72-25	1,831,012
4	Ana Ivanovic	3-2-3	51-18	1,960,354
5	Maria Sharapova	1-3-4	40-11	1,758,550
6	Anna Chakvetadze	4-0-5	59-20	1,406,266
7	Serena Williams	2-1-0	35-10	2,102,642
8	Venus Williams	3-1-3	50-10	1,878,187
9	Daniela Hantuchova	2-2-5	52-28	1,205,487
10	Marion Bartoli	0-2-5	47-31	1,246,906
11	Elena Dementieva	2-0-3	41-18	863,241
12	Nicole Vaidisova	0-0-4	37-14	875,623
13	Tatiana Golovin	2-2-2	46-18	583,975
14	Nadia Petrova	1-2-1	38-19	810,962
15	Dinara Safina	1-1-2	43-22	1,017,267
16	Patty Schnyder	0-2-1	45-25	1,000,625
17	Shahar Peer	0-1-2	46-22	817,765
18	Amelie Mauresmo	1-3-1	28-15	736,354
19	Martina Hingis	1-1-0	24-13	625,295
20	Agnes Szavay	3-1-1	56-14	527,866

2008 Tour Rankings (through Sept. 29)

Listed are tournaments won and times a finalist and semifinalist (Finish; 1-2-SF), match record (W-L), and points earned (Pts). The **Indesit ATP Race** replaced the men's pro tennis tour's 27-year-old computer ranking system in 2000. Under the new system players start from zero on Jan. 1 and accumulate points during the calendar year with the player accumulating the most points becoming the World No. 1. Points are awarded in 18 tournaments: nine Tennis Masters Series events, four Grand Slams and five other International Series events. The Tennis Master Cup will count as a 19th tournament for those that qualify.

MEN

Final ATP Tour singles rankings will be based on points earned from 18 tournaments played in 2008. Tournaments, titles and match won-lost records are for 2008 only.

Rank 08	(07)		Finish 1-2-SF	W-L	Pts
1	2	Rafael Nadal	8-2-4	77-9	1265
2	1	Roger Federer	3-4-2	55-12	921
3	3	Novak Djokovic	3-3-6	58-14	899
4	19	Andy Murray	3-1-1	43-14	520
5	4	Nikolay Davydenko	3-1-3	47-16	417
6	5	Andy Roddick	3-1-3	41-13	352
7	6	David Ferrer	2-1-1	42-19	337
8	9	James Blake	0-2-3	43-21	309
9	35	Stanislas Wawrinka	0-2-2	37-17	286
10	42	Juan Martin del Potro	4-0-1	34-9	272
11	7	Fernando Gonzalez	2-1-0	35-12	271
12	29	Gilles Simon	3-0-2	40-20	261
13	28	Nicolas Almagro	2-1-0	35-15	253
	26	Fernando Verdasco	1-1-2	40-23	253
15		Jo-Wilfried Tsonga	1-1-2	23-9	250
16	32	Igor Andreev	0-2-0	39-28	239
17	37	Mardy Fish	0-2-1	30-21	226
18	8	Tommy Robredo	1-1-1	33-19	225
19		Marin Cilic	1-0-2	33-22	205
20	45	Gael Monfils	1-0-3	22-14	204

WOMEN

WTA Tour singles ranking system based on total Round and Quality Points for each tournament played during the last 12 months (capped at 17 tournaments). Tournaments, titles and match won-lost records, however, are for 2008 only.

Rank 08	(07)		Finish 1-2-SF	W-L	Pts
1	7	Serena Williams	4-1-1	43-6	4091
2	3	Jelena Jankovic	2-2-5	55-16	4070
3	17	Dinara Safina	4-3-1	52-15	3747
4	14	Elena Dementieva	2-2-5	46-13	3470
5	5	Ana Ivanovic	2-1-2	32-11	3328
6	4	Maria Sharapova	3-0-2	32-4	3041
7	2	Svetlana Kuznetsova	0-5-2	42-19	3000
8	8	Venus Williams	1-0-1	28-9	2271
9	22	Vera Zvonareva	2-3-3	52-17	2167
10	26	Agnieszka Radwanska	3-0-2	49-17	2146
11	15	Patty Schnyder	1-1-1	33-19	1797
12	6	Anna Chakvetadze	1-1-1	27-20	1747
13	9	Daniela Hantuchova	0-0-2	19-16	1650
14	12	Marion Bartoli	0-1-3	24-22	1570
15	39	Flavia Pennetta	2-1-2	42-20	1540
16	60	Caroline Wozniacki	2-0-1	43-17	1483
17	30	Victoria Azarenka	0-2-2	35-17	1474
18	10	Nadia Petrova	1-1-2	34-19	1449
19		Alize Cornet	1-2-3	35-20	1423
20	51	Dominika Cibulkova	0-2-0	37-24	1262

2008 Money Winners

Amounts include singles and doubles earnings through Sept. 29, 2008.

MEN

		Earnings			Earnings			Earnings
1	Rafael Nadal	$6,583,074	11	James Blake	$850,081	21	Bob Bryan	$742,112
2	Roger Federer	4,561,341	12	Fernando Verdasco	837,885		Mike Bryan	742,112
3	Novak Djokovic	3,883,382	13	Nicolas Almagro	836,458	23	Dmitry Tursunov	725,063
4	Andy Murray	2,334,965	14	Tommy Robredo	818,265	24	Daniel Nestor	713,058
5	Nikolay Davydenko	1,521,606	15	Igor Andreev	806,554	25	Nenad Zimonjic	711,175
6	Andy Roddick	1,132,237	16	Mardy Fish	806,227	26	Gael Monfils	695,254
7	David Ferrer	1,104,268	17	Michael Llodra	790,557	27	Fernando Gonzalez	691,876
8	Jo-Wilfried Tsonga	942,506	18	Gilles Simon	785,001	28	Richard Gasquet	665,952
9	Stanislas Wawrinka	918,781	19	Robin Soderling	776,451	29	Feliciano Lopez	657,128
10	Juan Martin del Potro	889,333	20	Mikhail Youzhny	759,197	30	Marat Safin	654,182

WOMEN

		Earnings			Earnings			Earnings
1	Serena Williams	$3,641,548	11	Zheng Jie	$760,744	21	Flavia Pennetta	$606,154
2	Ana Ivanovic	2,594,645	12	Katarina Srebotnik	760,670	22	Anna Chakvetadze	564,144
3	Jelena Jankovic	2,459,745	13	A. Medina Garrigues	719,047	23	Daniela Hantuchova	556,641
4	Dinara Safina	2,342,820	14	Cara Black	693,505	24	Alona Bondarenko	536,318
5	Venus Williams	2,272,130	15	Victoria Azarenka	693,269	25	Shahar Peer	522,822
6	Maria Sharapova	1,937,879	16	Nadia Petrova	679,300	26	Dominika Cibulkova	516,189
7	Elena Dementieva	1,513,479	17	Patty Schnyder	676,514	27	Samantha Stosur	513,946
8	Svetlana Kuznetsova	1,317,484	18	Liezel Huber	666,302	28	V. Ruano Pascual	512,576
9	Agnieszka Radwanska	966,247	19	Ai Sugiyama	649,611	29	Marion Bartoli	503,071
10	Vera Zvonareva	878,155	20	Carolina Wozniacki	618,882	30	Kateryna Bondarenko	489,763

Davis Cup

2007 FINAL

United States 4, Russia 1

at Portland, Oregon (Nov. 30 - Dec. 2)

Day One—Andy Roddick (USA) def. Dmitry Tursunov (RUS) 6-4, 6-4, 6-2; James Blake (USA) def. Mikhail Youzhny (RUS) 6-3, 7-6(4), 6-7(3), 7-6(3).

Day Two—Bob Bryan & Mike Bryan (USA) def. Igor Andreev & Nikolay Davydenko (RUS) 7-6(4), 6-4, 6-2.

Day Three—Andreev (RUS) def. B. Bryan (USA) 6-3, 7-6(4); Blake (USA) def. Tursunov (RUS) 1-6, 6-3, 7-5.

2008

FIRST ROUND
(February 8-10)

Winner	Loser
at Russia 3	Serbia 2
at Czech Republic 3	Belgium 2
at Argentina 4	Great Britain 1
Sweden 3	at Israel 2
at Germany 3	Korea 2
Spain 5	at Peru 0
France 5	at Romania 0
United States 4	at Austria 1

QUARTERFINALS
(April 11-13)

Winner	Loser
at Russia 3	Czech Republic 2
at Argentina 4	Sweden 1
Spain 4	at Germany 1
at United States 4	France 1

SEMIFINALS

Argentina 3, Russia 2

at Buenos Aures, Argentina (Sept. 19-21)

Day One—David Nalbandian (ARG) def. Igor Andreev (RUS) 7-6(5) 6-2, 6-4; Juan Martin del Potro (ARG) def. Nikolay Davydenko (RUS) 6-1, 6-4, 6-2.

Day Two—Igor Kunitsyn & Dmitry Tursunov (RUS) def. Guillermo Canas & Nalbandian (ARG) 6-2, 6-1, 6-7(9), 3-6, 8-6.

Day Three—Davydenko (RUS) def. Nalbandian (ARG) 3-6, 6-3, 7-6(2), 6-0; del Potro (ARG) def. Andreev (RUS) 6-4, 6-2, 6-1.

Spain 4, United States 1

at Madrid, Spain (Sept. 19-21)

Day One—Rafael Nadal (ESP) def. Sam Querrey (USA) 6-7(5), 6-4, 6-3, 6-4; David Ferrer (ESP) def. Andy Roddick (USA) 7-6(5), 2-6, 1-6, 6-4, 8-6.

Day Two—Mike Bryan & Mardy Fish (USA) def. Feliciano Lopez & Fernando Verdasco (ESP) 4-6, 6-4, 6-3, 4-6, 6-4.

Day Three—Nadal (ESP) def. Roddick (USA) 6-4, 6-0, 6-4; Lopez (ESP) def. Querrey (USA) 7-6(3), 7-6(4).

2008 FINAL

Argentina vs. Spain: scheduled for Nov. 21-23 in Buenos Aires, Argentina.

1877-2008 Through the Years

Grand Slam Championships
Australian Open
MEN

Became an Open Championship in 1969. Two tournaments were held in 1977; the first in January, the second in December. Tournament moved back to January in 1987, so no championship was decided in 1986. **Surface:** Synpave Rebound Ace (hardcourt surface composed of polyurethane and synthetic rubber).

Multiple winners: Roy Emerson (6); Andre Agassi, Jack Crawford and Ken Rosewall (4); James Anderson, Roger Federer, Rod Laver, Adrian Quist, Mats Wilander and Pat Wood (3); Boris Becker, Jack Bromwich, Ashley Cooper, Jim Courier, Stefan Edberg, Rodney Heath, Johan Kriek, Ivan Lendl, John Newcombe, Pete Sampras, Frank Sedgman, Guillermo Vilas and Tony Wilding (2).

Year	Winner	Loser	Score	Year	Winner	Loser	Score
1905	Rodney Heath	A. Curtis	46 63 64 64	1961	Roy Emerson	R. Laver	16 63 75 64
1906	Tony Wilding	H. Parker	60 64 64	1962	Rod Laver	R. Emerson	86 06 64 64
1907	Horace Rice	H. Parker	63 64 64	1963	Roy Emerson	K. Fletcher	63 63 61
1908	Fred Alexander	A. Dunlop	36 36 60 62 63	1964	Roy Emerson	F. Stolle	63 64 62
1909	Tony Wilding	E. Parker	61 75 62	1965	Roy Emerson	F. Stolle	79 26 64 75 61
1910	Rodney Heath	H. Rice	64 63 62	1966	Roy Emerson	A. Ashe	64 68 62 63
1911	Norman Brookes	H. Rice	61 62 63	1967	Roy Emerson	A. Ashe	64 61 61
1912	J. Cecil Parke	A. Beamish	36 63 16 61 75	1968	Bill Bowrey	J. Gisbert	75 26 97 64
1913	Ernie Parker	H. Parker	26 61 62 63	1969	Rod Laver	A. Gimeno	63 63 75
1914	Pat Wood	G. Patterson	64 63 57 61	1970	Arthur Ashe	D. Crealy	64 97 62
1915	Gordon Lowe	H. Rice	46 61 61 64	1971	Ken Rosewall	A. Ashe	61 75 63
1916-18	Not held World War I			1972	Ken Rosewall	M. Anderson	78 63 75
1919	A.R.F. Kingscote	E. Pockley	64 60 63	1973	John Newcombe	O. Parun	63 67 75 61
1920	Pat Wood	R. Thomas	63 46 68 61 63	1974	Jimmy Connors	P. Dent	76 64 46 63
1921	Rhys Gemmell	A. Hedeman	75 61 64	1975	John Newcombe	J. Connors	75 36 64 75
1922	James Anderson	G. Patterson	60 36 36 63 62	1976	Mark Edmondson	J. Newcombe	67 63 76 61
1923	Pat Wood	C.B. St. John	61 61 63	1977	Roscoe Tanner	G. Vilas	63 63 63
1924	James Anderson	R. Schlesinger	63 64 36 57 63		Vitas Gerulaitis	J. Lloyd	63 76 57 36 62
1925	James Anderson	G. Patterson	11-9 26 62 63	1978	Guillermo Vilas	J. Marks	64 64 36 63
1926	John Hawkes	J. Willard	61 63 61	1979	Guillermo Vilas	J. Sadri	76 63 62
1927	Gerald Patterson	J. Hawkes	36 64 36 18-16 63	1980	Brian Teacher	K. Warwick	75 76 63
1928	Jean Borotra	R.O. Cummings	64 61 46 57 63	1981	Johan Kriek	S. Denton	62 76 67 64
1929	John Gregory	R. Schlesinger	62 62 57 75	1982	Johan Kriek	S. Denton	63 63 62
1930	Gar Moon	H. Hopman	63 61 63	1983	Mats Wilander	I. Lendl	61 64 64
1931	Jack Crawford	H. Hopman	64 62 26 61	1984	Mats Wilander	K. Curren	67 64 76 62
1932	Jack Crawford	H. Hopman	46 63 36 63 61	1985	Stefan Edberg	M. Wilander	64 63 63
1933	Jack Crawford	K. Gledhill	26 75 63 62	1986	Not held		
1934	Fred Perry	J. Crawford	63 75 61	1987	Stefan Edberg	P. Cash	63 64 36 57 63
1935	Jack Crawford	F. Perry	26 64 64 64	1988	Mats Wilander	P. Cash	63 67 36 61 86
1936	Adrian Quist	J. Crawford	62 63 46 36 97	1989	Ivan Lendl	M. Mecir	62 62 62
1937	Viv McGrath	J. Bromwich	63 16 60 26 61	1990	Ivan Lendl	S. Edberg	46 76 52 (ret.)
1938	Don Budge	J. Bromwich	64 62 61	1991	Boris Becker	I. Lendl	16 64 64 64
1939	Jack Bromwich	A. Quist	64 61 63	1992	Jim Courier	S. Edberg	63 36 64 62
1940	Adrian Quist	J. Crawford	63 61 62	1993	Jim Courier	S. Edberg	62 61 26 75
1941-45	Not held World War II			1994	Pete Sampras	T. Martin	76 64 64
1946	Jack Bromwich	D. Pails	57 63 75 36 62	1995	Andre Agassi	P. Sampras	46 61 76 64
1947	Dinny Pails	J. Bromwich	46 64 36 75 86	1996	Boris Becker	M. Chang	62 64 26 62
1948	Adrian Quist	J. Bromwich	64 36 63 26 63	1997	Pete Sampras	C. Moya	62 63 63
1949	Frank Sedgman	J. Bromwich	63 63 63	1998	Petr Korda	M. Rios	62 62 62
1950	Frank Sedgman	K. McGregor	63 64 46 61	1999	Yevgeny Kafelnikov	T. Enqvist	46 60 63 76
1951	Dick Savitt	K. McGregor	63 26 63 61	2000	Andre Agassi	Y. Kafelnikov	36 63 62 64
1952	Ken McGregor	F. Sedgman	75 12-10 26 62	2001	Andre Agassi	A. Clement	64 62 62
1953	Ken Rosewall	M. Rose	60 63 64	2002	Thomas Johansson	M. Safin	36 64 64 76
1954	Mervyn Rose	R. Hartwig	62 06 64 62	2003	Andre Agassi	R. Schuettler	62 62 61
1955	Ken Rosewall	L. Hoad	97 64 64	2004	Roger Federer	M. Safin	76 64 62
1956	Lew Hoad	K. Rosewall	64 36 64 75	2005	Marat Safin	L. Hewitt	16 63 64 64
1957	Ashley Cooper	N. Fraser	63 9-11 64 62	2006	Roger Federer	M. Baghdatis	57 75 60 62
1958	Ashley Cooper	M. Anderson	75 63 64	2007	Roger Federer	F. Gonzalez	76 64 64
1959	Alex Olmedo	N. Fraser	61 62 36 63	2008	Novak Djokovic	J-W Tsonga	46 64 63 76
1960	Rod Laver	N. Fraser	57 36 63 86 86				

WOMEN

Became an Open Championship in 1969. Two tournaments were held in 1977, the first in January, the second in December. Tournament moved back to January in 1987, so no championship was decided in 1986.

Multiple winners: Margaret Smith Court (11); Nancye Wynne Bolton (6); Daphne Akhurst (5); Evonne Goolagong Cawley, Steffi Graf and Monica Seles (4); Joan Hartigan, Martina Hingis, Martina Navratilova and Serena Williams (3); Coral Buttsworth, Jennifer Capriati, Chris Evert Lloyd, Thelma Long, Hana Mandlikova, Mall Molesworth and Mary Carter Reitano (2).

Year	Winner	Loser	Score	Year	Winner	Loser	Score
1922	Mall Molesworth	E. Boyd	63 10-8	1968	Billie Jean King	M. Smith	61 62
1923	Mall Molesworth	E. Boyd	61 75	1969	Margaret Court	B.J. King	64 61
1924	Sylvia Lance	E. Boyd	63 36 64	1970	Margaret Court	K. Melville	61 63
1925	Daphne Akhurst	E. Boyd	16 86 64	1971	Margaret Court	E. Goolagong	26 76 75
1926	Daphne Akhurst	E. Boyd	61 63	1972	Virginia Wade	E. Goolagong	64 64
1927	Esna Boyd	S. Harper	57 61 62	1973	Margaret Court	E. Goolagong	64 75
1928	Daphne Akhurst	E. Boyd	75 62	1974	Evonne Goolagong	C. Evert	76 46 60
1929	Daphne Akhurst	L. Bickerton	61 57 62	1975	Evonne Goolagong	M. Navratilova	63 62
1930	Daphne Akhurst	S. Harper	10-8 26 75	1976	Evonne Cawley	R. Tomanova	62 62
1931	Coral Buttsworth	M. Crawford	16 63 64	1977	Kerry Reid	D. Balestrat	75 62
1932	Coral Buttsworth	K. Le Messurier	97 64		Evonne Cawley	H. Gourlay	63 60
1933	Joan Hartigan	C. Buttsworth	64 63	1978	Chris O'Neil	B. Nagelsen	63 76
1934	Joan Hartigan	M. Molesworth	61 64	1979	Barbara Jordan	S. Walsh	63 63
1935	Dorothy Round	N. Lyle	16 61 63	1980	Hana Mandlikova	W. Turnbull	60 75
1936	Joan Hartigan	N. Wynne	64 64	1981	Martina Navratilova	C. Evert Lloyd	67 64 75
1937	Nancye Wynne	E. Westacott	63 57 64	1982	Chris Evert Lloyd	M. Navratilova	63 26 63
1938	Dorothy Bundy	D. Stevenson	63 62	1983	Martina Navratilova	K. Jordan	62 76
1939	Emily Westacott	N. Hopman	61 62	1984	Chris Evert Lloyd	H. Sukova	67 61 63
1940	Nancye Wynne	T. Coyne	57 64 60	1985	Martina Navratilova	C. Evert Lloyd	62 46 62
1941-45 Not held World War II				1986	Not held		
1946	Nancye Bolton	J. Fitch	64 64	1987	Hana Mandlikova	M. Navratilova	75 76
1947	Nancye Bolton	N. Hopman	63 62	1988	Steffi Graf	C. Evert	61 76
1948	Nancye Bolton	M. Toomey	63 61	1989	Steffi Graf	H. Sukova	64 64
1949	Doris Hart	N. Bolton	63 64	1990	Steffi Graf	M.J. Fernandez	64 64
1950	Louise Brough	D. Hart	64 36 64	1991	Monica Seles	J. Novotna	57 63 61
1951	Nancye Bolton	T. Long	61 75	1992	Monica Seles	M.J. Fernandez	62 63
1952	Thelma Long	H. Angwin	62 63	1993	Monica Seles	S. Graf	46 63 62
1953	Maureen Connolly	J. Sampson	63 62	1994	Steffi Graf	A.S. Vicario	60 62
1954	Thelma Long	J. Staley	63 64	1995	Mary Pierce	A.S. Vicario	63 62
1955	Beryl Penrose	T. Long	64 63	1996	Monica Seles	A. Huber	64 61
1956	Mary Carter	T. Long	36 62 97	1997	Martina Hingis	M. Pierce	62 62
1957	Shirley Fry	A. Gibson	63 64	1998	Martina Hingis	C. Martinez	63 63
1958	Angela Mortimer	L. Coghlan	63 64	1999	Martina Hingis	A. Mauresmo	62 63
1959	Mary Reitano	R. Schuurman	62 63	2000	Lindsay Davenport	M. Hingis	61 75
1960	Margaret Smith	J. Lehane	75 62	2001	Jennifer Capriati	M. Hingis	64 63
1961	Margaret Smith	J. Lehane	61 64	2002	Jennifer Capriati	M. Hingis	46 76 62
1962	Margaret Smith	J. Lehane	60 62	2003	Serena Williams	V. Williams	76 36 64
1963	Margaret Smith	J. Lehane	62 62	2004	J. Henin-Hardenne	K. Clijsters	63 46 63
1964	Margaret Smith	L. Turner	63 62	2005	Serena Williams	L. Davenport	26 63 60
1965	Margaret Smith	M. Bueno	57 64 52 (ret)	2006	Amelie Mauresmo	J. Henin-Hardenne	61 20 (ret)
1966	Margaret Smith	N. Richey	walkover	2007	Serena Williams	M. Sharapova	61 62
1967	Nancy Richey	L. Turner	61 64	2008	Maria Sharapova	A. Ivanovic	75 63

French Open
MEN

From 1891 to 1925, entry was restricted to members of French clubs. Became an Open Championship in 1968, but closed to contract pros in 1972. Note that Max Decugis won eight tournaments before 1925 (1903-04, 1907-09, 1912-14) to lead all men. **Surface:** Red clay.

Multiple winners (since 1925): Bjorn Borg (6); Henri Cochet and Rafael Nadal (4); Gustavo Kuerten, Rene Lacoste, Ivan Lendl and Mats Wilander (3); Sergi Bruguera, Jim Courier, Jaroslav Drobny, Roy Emerson, Jan Kodes, Rod Laver, Frank Parker, Nicola Pietrangeli, Ken Rosewall, Manuel Santana, Tony Trabert and Gottfried von Cramm (2).

Year	Winner	Loser	Score	Year	Winner	Loser	Score
1925	Rene Lacoste	J. Borotra	75 61 64	1939	Don McNeill	B. Riggs	75 60 63
1926	Henri Cochet	R. Lacoste	62 64 63	1940-45 Not held World War II			
1927	Rene Lacoste	B. Tilden	64 46 57 63 11-9	1946	Marcel Bernard	J. Drobny	36 26 61 64 63
1928	Henri Cochet	R. Lacoste	57 63 61 63	1947	Joseph Asboth	E. Sturgess	86 75 64
1929	Rene Lacoste	J. Borotra	63 26 60 26 86	1948	Frank Parker	J. Drobny	64 75 57 86
1930	Henri Cochet	B. Tilden	36 86 63 61	1949	Frank Parker	B. Patty	63 16 61 64
1931	Jean Borotra	C. Boussus	26 64 75 64	1950	Budge Patty	J. Drobny	61 62 36 57 75
1932	Henri Cochet	G. de Stefani	60 64 46 63	1951	Jaroslav Drobny	E. Sturgess	63 63
1933	Jack Crawford	H. Cochet	86 61 63	1952	Jaroslav Drobny	F. Sedgman	62 60 36 64
1934	Gottfried von Cramm	J. Crawford	64 79 36 75 63	1953	Ken Rosewall	V. Seixas	63 6416 62
1935	Fred Perry	G. von Cramm	63 36 61 63	1954	Tony Trabert	A. Larsen	64 75 61
1936	Gottfried von Cramm	F. Perry	60 26 62 60	1955	Tony Trabert	S. Davidson	26 61 64 62
1937	Henner Henkel	H. Austin	61 64 63	1956	Lew Hoad	S. Davidson	64 86 63
1938	Don Budge	R. Menzel	63 62 64	1957	Sven Davidson	H. Flam	63 64 64

Year	Winner	Loser	Score
1958	Mervyn Rose	L. Ayala	63 64 64
1959	Nicola Pietrangeli	I. Vermaak	36 63 64 61
1960	Nicola Pietrangeli	L. Ayala	36 63 64 46 63
1961	Manuel Santana	N. Pietrangeli	46 61 36 60 62
1962	Rod Laver	R. Emerson	36 26 63 97 62
1963	Roy Emerson	P. Darmon	36 61 64 64
1964	Manuel Santana	N. Pietrangeli	63 61 46 75
1965	Fred Stolle	T. Roche	36 60 62 63
1966	Tony Roche	I. Gulyas	61 64 75
1967	Roy Emerson	T. Roche	61 64 26 62
1968	Ken Rosewall	R. Laver	63 61 26 62
1969	Rod Laver	K. Rosewall	64 63 64
1970	Jan Kodes	Z. Franulovic	62 64 60
1971	Jan Kodes	I. Nastase	86 62 26 75
1972	Andres Gimeno	P. Proisy	46 63 61 61
1973	Ilie Nastase	N. Pilic	63 63 60
1974	Bjorn Borg	M. Orantes	26 67 60 61 61
1975	Bjorn Borg	G. Vilas	62 63 64
1976	Adriano Panatta	H. Solomon	61 64 46 76
1977	Guillermo Vilas	B. Gottfried	60 63 60
1978	Bjorn Borg	G. Vilas	61 61 63
1979	Bjorn Borg	V. Pecci	63 61 67 64
1980	Bjorn Borg	V. Gerulaitis	64 61 62
1981	Bjorn Borg	I. Lendl	61 46 62 36 61
1982	Mats Wilander	G. Vilas	16 76 60 64
1983	Yannick Noah	M. Wilander	62 75 76
1984	Ivan Lendl	J. McEnroe	36 26 64 75 75
1985	Mats Wilander	I. Lendl	36 64 62 62
1986	Ivan Lendl	M. Pernfors	63 62 64
1987	Ivan Lendl	M. Wilander	75 62 36 76
1988	Mats Wilander	H. Leconte	75 62 61
1989	Michael Chang	S. Edberg	61 36 46 64 62
1990	Andres Gomez	A. Agassi	63 26 64 64
1991	Jim Courier	A. Agassi	36 64 26 61 64
1992	Jim Courier	P. Korda	75 62 61
1993	Sergi Bruguera	J. Courier	64 26 62 36 63
1994	Sergi Bruguera	A. Berasategui	63 75 26 61
1995	Thomas Muster	M. Chang	75 62 64
1996	Yevgeny Kafelnikov	M. Stich	76 75 76
1997	Gustavo Kuerten	S. Bruguera	63 64 62
1998	Carlos Moya	A. Corretja	63 75 63
1999	Andre Agassi	A. Medvedev	16 26 64 63 64
2000	Gustavo Kuerten	M. Norman	62 63 26 76
2001	Gustavo Kuerten	A. Corretja	67 75 62 60
2002	Albert Costa	J. C. Ferrero	61 60 46 63
2003	Juan Carlos Ferrero	M. Verkerk	61 63 62
2004	Gaston Gaudio	G. Coria	06 36 64 61 86
2005	Rafael Nadal	M. Puerta	67 63 61 75
2006	Rafael Nadal	R. Federer	16 61 64 76
2007	Rafael Nadal	R. Federer	63 46 63 64
2008	Rafael Nadal	R. Federer	61 63 60

WOMEN

From 1897 to 1925, entry was restricted to members of French clubs. Became an Open Championship in 1968, but closed to contract pros in 1972. Note that Suzanne Lenglen won two titles prior to 1925, giving her six total.

Multiple winners (since 1925): Chris Evert Lloyd (7); Steffi Graf (6); Margaret Smith Court (5); Justine Henin and Helen Wills Moody (4); Arantxa Sanchez Vicario, Monica Seles and Hilde Sperling (3); Maureen Connolly, Margaret Osborne du Pont, Doris Hart, Ann Haydon Jones, Suzanne Lenglen, Simone Mathieu, Margaret Scriven, Martina Navratilova and Lesley Turner (2).

Year	Winner	Loser	Score
1925	Suzanne Lenglen	K. McKane	61 62
1926	Suzanne Lenglen	M. Browne	61 60
1927	Kea Bouman	I. Peacock	62 64
1928	Helen Wills	E. Bennett	61 62
1929	Helen Wills	S. Mathieu	63 64
1930	Helen Moody	H. Jacobs	62 61
1931	Cilly Aussem	B. Nuthall	86 61
1932	Helen Moody	S. Mathieu	75 61
1933	Margaret Scriven	S. Mathieu	62 46 64
1934	Margaret Scriven	H. Jacobs	75 46 61
1935	Hilde Sperling	S. Mathieu	62 61
1936	Hilde Sperling	S. Mathieu	63 64
1937	Hilde Sperling	S. Mathieu	62 64
1938	Simone Mathieu	N. Landry	60 63
1939	Simone Mathieu	J. Jedrzejowska	63 86
1940-45	Not held World War II		
1946	Margaret Osborne	P. Betz	16 86 75
1947	Patricia Todd	D. Hart	63 36 64
1948	Nelly Landry	S. Fry	62 06 60
1949	Margaret du Pont	N. Adamson	75 62
1950	Doris Hart	P. Todd	64 46 62
1951	Shirley Fry	D.,Hart	63 36 63
1952	Doris Hart	S. Fry	64 64
1953	Maureen Connolly	D. Hart	62 64
1954	Maureen Connolly	G. Bucaille	64 61
1955	Angela Mortimer	D. Knode	26 75 10-8
1956	Althea Gibson	A. Mortimer	60 12-10
1957	Shirley Bloomer	D. Knode	61 63
1958	Suzi Kormoczi	S. Bloomer	64 16 62
1959	Christine Truman	S. Kormoczi	64 75
1960	Darlene Hard	Y. Ramirez	63 64
1961	Ann Haydon	Y. Ramirez	62 61
1962	Margaret Smith	L. Turner	63 36 75
1963	Lesley Turner	A. Jones	26 63 75
1964	Margaret Smith	M. Bueno	57 61 62
1965	Lesley Turner	M. Smith	63 64
1966	Ann Jones	N. Richey	63 61
1967	Francoise Durr	L. Turner	46 63 64
1968	Nancy Richey	A. Jones	57 64 61
1969	Margaret Court	A. Jones	61 46 63
1970	Margaret Court	H. Niessen	62 64
1971	Evonne Goolagong	H. Gourlay	63 75
1972	Billie Jean King	E. Goolagong	63 63
1973	Margaret Court	C. Evert	67 76 64
1974	Chris Evert	O. Morozova	61 62
1975	Chris Evert	M. Navratilova	26 62 61
1976	Sue Barker	R. Tomanova	62 06 62
1977	Mima Jausovec	F. Mihai	62 67 61
1978	Virginia Ruzici	M. Jausovec	62 62
1979	Chris Evert Lloyd	W. Turnbull	62 60
1980	Chris Evert Lloyd	V. Ruzici	60 63
1981	Hana Mandlikova	S. Hanika	62 64
1982	Martina Navratilova	A. Jaeger	76 61
1983	Chris Evert Lloyd	M. Jausovec	61 62
1984	Martina Navratilova	C. Evert Lloyd	61 62
1985	Chris Evert Lloyd	M. Navratilova	63 67 75
1986	Chris Evert Lloyd	M. Navratilova	26 63 63
1987	Steffi Graf	M. Navratilova	64 46 86
1988	Steffi Graf	N. Zvereva	60 60
1989	A. Sanchez Vicario	S. Graf	76 36 75
1990	Monica Seles	S. Graf	76 64
1991	Monica Seles	A.S. Vicario	63 64
1992	Monica Seles	S. Graf	62 36 10-8
1993	Steffi Graf	M.J. Fernandez	46 62 64
1994	A. Sanchez Vicario	M. Pierce	64 64
1995	Steffi Graf	A.S. Vicario	76 46 60
1996	Steffi Graf	A.S. Vicario	63 67 10-8
1997	Iva Majoli	M. Hingis	64 62
1998	A. Sanchez Vicario	M. Seles	76 06 62
1999	Steffi Graf	M. Hingis	46 75 62
2000	Mary Pierce	C. Martinez	62 75
2001	Jennifer Capriati	K. Clijsters	16 64 1210
2002	Serena Williams	V. Williams	75 63
2003	J. Henin-Hardenne	K. Clijsters	60 64
2004	Anastasia Myskina	E. Dementieva	61 62
2005	J. Henin-Hardenne	M. Pierce	61 61
2006	J. Henin-Hardenne	S. Kuznetsova	64 64
2007	Justine Henin	A. Ivanovic	61 62
2008	Ana Ivanovic	D. Safina	64 63

Wimbledon
MEN

Officially called "The Lawn Tennis Championships" at the All England Club, Wimbledon. Challenge round system (defending champion qualified for following year's final) used from 1877-1921. Became an Open Championship in 1968, but closed to contract pros in 1972. **Surface:** Grass.

Multiple winners: Willie Renshaw and Pete Sampras (7); Bjorn Borg, Laurie Doherty and Roger Federer (5); Reggie Doherty, Rod Laver and Tony Wilding (4); Wilfred Baddeley, Boris Becker, Arthur Gore, John McEnroe, John Newcombe, Fred Perry and Bill Tilden (3); Jean Borotra, Norman Brookes, Don Budge, Henri Cochet, Jimmy Connors, Stefan Edberg, Roy Emerson, John Hartley, Lew Hoad, Rene Lacoste, Gerald Patterson and Joshua Pim (2).

Year	Winner	Loser	Score	Year	Winner	Loser	Score
1877	Spencer Gore	W. Marshall	61 62 64	1947	Jack Kramer	T. Brown	61 63 62
1878	Frank Hadow	S. Gore	75 61 97	1948	Bob Falkenburg	J. Bromwich	75 06 62 36 75
1879	John Hartley	V. St. L. Goold	62 64 62	1949	Ted Schroeder	J. Drobny	36 60 63 46 64
1880	John Hartley	H. Lawford	60 62 26 63	1950	Budge Patty	F. Sedgman	61 8-10 62 63
1881	Willie Renshaw	J. Hartley	60 61 61	1951	Dick Savitt	K. McGregor	64 64 64
1882	Willie Renshaw	E. Renshaw	61 26 46 62 62	1952	Frank Sedgman	J. Drobny	46 62 63 62
1883	Willie Renshaw	E. Renshaw	26 63 63 46 63	1953	Vic Seixas	K. Nielsen	97 63 64
1884	Willie Renshaw	H. Lawford	60 64 97	1954	Jaroslav Drobny	K. Rosewall	13-11 46 62 97
1885	Willie Renshaw	H. Lawford	75 62 46 75	1955	Tony Trabert	K. Nielsen	63 75 61
1886	Willie Renshaw	H. Lawford	60 57 63 64	1956	Lew Hoad	K. Rosewall	62 46 75 64
1887	Herbert Lawford	E. Renshaw	16 63 36 64 64	1957	Lew Hoad	A. Cooper	62 61 62
1888	Ernest Renshaw	H. Lawford	63 75 60	1958	Ashley Cooper	N. Fraser	36 63 64 13-11
1889	Willie Renshaw	E. Renshaw	64 61 36 60	1959	Alex Olmedo	R. Laver	64 63 64
1890	Willoughby Hamilton	W. Renshaw	68 62 36 61	1960	Neale Fraser	R. Laver	64 36 97 75
1891	Wilfred Baddeley	J. Pim	64 16 75 60	1961	Rod Laver	C. McKinley	63 61 64
1892	Wilfred Baddeley	J. Pim	46 63 63 62	1962	Rod Laver	M. Mulligan	62 62 61
1893	Joshua Pim	W. Baddeley	36 61 63 62	1963	Chuck McKinley	F. Stolle	97 61 64
1894	Joshua Pim	W. Baddeley	10-8 62 86	1964	Roy Emerson	F. Stolle	64 12-10 46 63
1895	Wilfred Baddeley	W. Eaves	46 26 86 62 63	1965	Roy Emerson	F. Stolle	62 64 64
1896	Harold Mahony	W. Baddeley	62 68 57 86 63	1966	Manuel Santana	D. Ralston	64 11-9 64
1897	Reggie Doherty	H. Mahony	64 64 63	1967	John Newcombe	W. Bungert	63 61 61
1898	Reggie Doherty	L. Doherty	63 63 26 57 61	1968	Rod Laver	T. Roche	63 64 62
1899	Reggie Doherty	A. Gore	16 46 62 63 63	1969	Rod Laver	J. Newcombe	64 57 64 64
1900	Reggie Doherty	S. Smith	68 63 61 62	1970	John Newcombe	K. Rosewall	57 63 62 36 61
1901	Arthur Gore	R. Doherty	46 75 64 64	1971	John Newcombe	S. Smith	63 57 26 64 64
1902	Laurie Doherty	A. Gore	64 63 36 60	1972	Stan Smith	I. Nastase	46 63 63 46 75
1903	Laurie Doherty	F. Riseley	75 63 60	1973	Jan Kodes	A. Metreveli	61 98 63
1904	Laurie Doherty	F. Riseley	61 75 86	1974	Jimmy Connors	K. Rosewall	61 61 64
1905	Laurie Doherty	N. Brookes	86 62 64	1975	Arthur Ashe	J. Connors	61 61 57 64
1906	Laurie Doherty	F. Riseley	64 46 62 63	1976	Bjorn Borg	I. Nastase	64 62 97
1907	Norman Brookes	A. Gore	64 62 62	1977	Bjorn Borg	J. Connors	36 62 61 57 64
1908	Arthur Gore	R. Barrett	63 62 46 36 64	1978	Bjorn Borg	J. Connors	62 62 63
1909	Arthur Gore	M. Ritchie	68 16 62 62 62	1979	Bjorn Borg	R. Tanner	67 61 36 63 64
1910	Tony Wilding	A. Gore	64 75 46 62	1980	Bjorn Borg	J. McEnroe	16 75 63 67 86
1911	Tony Wilding	R. Barrett	64 46 26 62 (ret)	1981	John McEnroe	B. Borg	46 76 76 64
1912	Tony Wilding	A. Gore	64 44 75 62	1982	Jimmy Connors	J. McEnroe	36 63 67 76 64
1913	Tony Wilding	M. McLoughlin	86 63 10-8	1983	John McEnroe	C. Lewis	62 62 62
1914	Norman Brookes	T. Wilding	64 64 75	1984	John McEnroe	J. Connors	61 61 62
1915-18	Not held World War I			1985	Boris Becker	K. Curren	63 67 76 64
1919	Gerald Patterson	N. Brookes	63 75 62	1986	Boris Becker	I. Lendl	64 63 75
1920	Bill Tilden	G. Patterson	26 63 62 64	1987	Pat Cash	I. Lendl	76 62 75
1921	Bill Tilden	B. Norton	46 26 61 60 75	1988	Stefan Edberg	B. Becker	46 76 64 62
1922	Gerald Patterson	R. Lycett	63 64 62	1989	Boris Becker	S. Edberg	60 76 64
1923	Bill Johnston	F. Hunter	60 63 61	1990	Stefan Edberg	B. Becker	62 62 36 36 64
1924	Jean Borotra	R. Lacoste	61 36 61 36 64	1991	Michael Stich	B. Becker	64 76 64
1925	Rene Lacoste	J. Borotra	63 63 46 86	1992	Andre Agassi	G. Ivanisevic	67 64 64 16 64
1926	Jean Borotra	H. Kinsey	86 61 63	1993	Pete Sampras	J. Courier	76 76 36 63
1927	Henri Cochet	J. Borotra	46 46 63 64 75	1994	Pete Sampras	G. Ivanisevic	76 76 60
1928	Rene Lacoste	H. Cochet	61 46 64 62	1995	Pete Sampras	B. Becker	67 62 64 62
1929	Henri Cochet	J. Borotra	64 63 64	1996	Richard Krajicek	M. Washington	63 64 63
1930	Bill Tilden	W. Allison	63 97 64	1997	Pete Sampras	C. Pioline	64 62 64
1931	Sidney Wood	F. Shields	walkover	1998	Pete Sampras	G. Ivanisevic	67 76 64 36 62
1932	Ellsworth Vines	H. Austin	64 62 60	1999	Pete Sampras	A. Agassi	63 64 75
1933	Jack Crawford	E. Vines	46 11-9 62 26 64	2000	Pete Sampras	P. Rafter	67 76 64 62
1934	Fred Perry	J. Crawford	63 60 75	2001	Goran Ivanisevic	P. Rafter	63 36 63 26 97
1935	Fred Perry	G. von Cramm	62 64 64	2002	Lleyton Hewitt	D. Nalbandian	61 63 62
1936	Fred Perry	G. von Cramm	61 61 60	2003	Roger Federer	M. Philippoussis	76 62'76
1937	Don Budge	G. von Cramm	63 64 62	2004	Roger Federer	A. Roddick	46 75 76 64
1938	Don Budge	H. Austin	61 60 63	2005	Roger Federer	A. Roddick	62 76 64
1939	Bobby Riggs	E. Cooke	26 86 36 63 62	2006	Roger Federer	R. Nadal	60 76 67 63
1940-45	Not held World War II			2007	Roger Federer	R. Nadal	76 46 76 26 62
1946	Yvon Petra	G. Brown	62 64 79 57 64	2008	Rafael Nadal	R. Federer	64 64 67 67 97

WOMEN

Officially called "The Lawn Tennis Championships" at the All England Club, Wimbledon. Challenge round system (defending champion qualified for following year's final) used from 1877-1921. Became an Open Championship in 1968, but closed to contract pros in 1972.

Multiple winners: Martina Navratilova (9); Helen Wills Moody (8); Dorothea Douglass Chambers and Steffi Graf (7); Blanche Bingley Hillyard, Billie Jean King and Suzanne Lenglen (6); Lottie Dod, Charlotte Cooper Sterry and Venus Williams (5); Louise Brough (4); Maria Bueno, Maureen Connolly, Margaret Smith Court and Chris Evert Lloyd (3); Evonne Goolagong Cawley, Althea Gibson, Kitty McKane Godfree, Dorothy Round, May Sutton, Maud Watson and Serena Williams (2).

Year	Winner	Loser	Score
1884	Maud Watson	L. Watson	68 63 63
1885	Maud Watson	B. Bingley	61 75
1886	Blanche Bingley	M. Watson	63 63
1887	Lottie Dod	B. Bingley	62 60
1888	Lottie Dod	B. Hillyard	63 63
1889	Blanche Hillyard	L. Rice	46 86 64
1890	Lena Rice	M. Jacks	64 61
1891	Lottie Dod	B. Hillyard	62 61
1892	Lottie Dod	B. Hillyard	61 61
1893	Lottie Dod	B. Hillyard	68 61 64
1894	Blanche Hillyard	E. Austin	61 61
1895	Charlotte Cooper	H. Jackson	75 86
1896	Charlotte Cooper	A. Pickering	62 63
1897	Blanche Hillyard	C. Cooper	57 75 62
1898	Charlotte Cooper	L. Martin	64 64
1899	Blanche Hillyard	C. Cooper	62 63
1900	Blanche Hillyard	C. Cooper	46 64 64
1901	Charlotte Sterry	B. Hillyard	62 62
1902	Muriel Robb	C. Sterry	75 61
1903	Dorothea Douglass	E. Thomson	46 64 62
1904	Dorothea Douglass	C. Sterry	60 63
1905	May Sutton	D. Douglass	63 64
1906	Dorothea Douglass	M. Sutton	63 97
1907	May Sutton	D. Chambers	61 64
1908	Charlotte Sterry	A. Morton	64 64
1909	Dora Boothby	A. Morton	64 46 86
1910	Dorothea Chambers	D. Boothby	62 62
1911	Dorothea Chambers	D. Boothby	60 60
1912	Ethel Larcombe	C. Sterry	63 61
1913	Dorothea Chambers	R. McNair	60 64
1914	Dorothea Chambers	E. Larcombe	75 64
1915-18	Not held World War I		
1919	Suzanne Lenglen	D. Chambers	10-8 46 97
1920	Suzanne Lenglen	D. Chambers	63 60
1921	Suzanne Lenglen	E. Ryan	62 60
1922	Suzanne Lenglen	M. Mallory	62 60
1923	Suzanne Lenglen	K. McKane	62 62
1924	Kitty McKane	H. Wills	46 64 64
1925	Suzanne Lenglen	J. Fry	62 60
1926	Kitty Godfree	L. de Alvarez	62 46 63
1927	Helen Wills	L. de Alvarez	62 64
1928	Helen Wills	L. de Alvarez	62 63
1929	Helen Wills	H. Jacobs	61 62
1930	Helen Moody	E. Ryan	62 62
1931	Cilly Aussem	H. Krahwinkel	62 75
1932	Helen Moody	H. Jacobs	63 61
1933	Helen Moody	D. Round	64 68 63
1934	Dorothy Round	H. Jacobs	62 57 63
1935	Helen Moody	H. Jacobs	63 36 75
1936	Helen Jacobs	H.K. Sperling	62 46 75
1937	Dorothy Round	J. Jedrzejowska	62 26 75
1938	Helen Moody	H. Jacobs	64 60
1939	Alice Marble	K. Stammers	62 60
1940-45	Not held World War II		
1946	Pauline Betz	L. Brough	62 64
1947	Margaret Osborne	D. Hart	62 64
1948	Louise Brough	D. Hart	63 86
1949	Louise Brough	M. du Pont	10-8 16 10-8

Year	Winner	Loser	Score
1950	Louise Brough	M. du Pont	61 36 61
1951	Doris Hart	S. Fry	61 60
1952	Maureen Connolly	L. Brough	75 63
1953	Maureen Connolly	D. Hart	86 75
1954	Maureen Connolly	L. Brough	62 75
1955	Louise Brough	B. Fleitz	75 86
1956	Shirley Fry	A. Buxton	63 61
1957	Althea Gibson	D. Hard	63 62
1958	Althea Gibson	A. Mortimer	86 62
1959	Maria Bueno	D. Hard	64 63
1960	Maria Bueno	S. Reynolds	86 60
1961	Angela Mortimer	C. Truman	46 64 75
1962	Karen Susman	V. Sukova	64 64
1963	Margaret Smith	B.J. Moffitt	63 64
1964	Maria Bueno	M. Smith	64 79 63
1965	Margaret Smith	M. Bueno	64 75
1966	Billie Jean King	M. Bueno	63 36 61
1967	Billie Jean King	A. Jones	63 64
1968	Billie Jean King	J. Tegart	97 75
1969	Ann Jones	B.J. King	36 63 62
1970	Margaret Court	B.J. King	14-12 11-9
1971	Evonne Goolagong	M. Court	64 61
1972	Billie Jean King	E. Goolagong	63 63
1973	Billie Jean King	C. Evert	60 75
1974	Chris Evert	O. Morozova	60 64
1975	Billie Jean King	E. Cawley	60 61
1976	Chris Evert	E. Cawley	63 46 86
1977	Virginia Wade	B. Stove	46 63 61
1978	Martina Navratilova	C. Evert	26 64 75
1979	Martina Navratilova	C. Evert Lloyd	64 64
1980	Evonne Cawley	C. Evert Lloyd	61 76
1981	Chris Evert Lloyd	H. Mandlikova	62 62
1982	Martina Navratilova	C. Evert Lloyd	61 36 62
1983	Martina Navratilova	A. Jaeger	60 63
1984	Martina Navratilova	C. Evert Lloyd	76 62
1985	Martina Navratilova	C. Evert Lloyd	46 63 62
1986	Martina Navratilova	H. Mandlikova	76 63
1987	Martina Navratilova	S. Graf	75 63
1988	Steffi Graf	M. Navratilova	57 62 61
1989	Steffi Graf	M. Navratilova	62 67 61
1990	Martina Navratilova	Z. Garrison	64 61
1991	Steffi Graf	G. Sabatini	64 36 86
1992	Steffi Graf	M. Seles	62 61
1993	Steffi Graf	J. Novotna	76 16 64
1994	Conchita Martinez	M. Navratilova	64 36 63
1995	Steffi Graf	A.S. Vicario	46 61 75
1996	Steffi Graf	A.S. Vicario	63 75
1997	Martina Hingis	J. Novotna	26 63 63
1998	Jana Novotna	N. Tauziat	64 76
1999	Lindsay Davenport	S. Graf	64 75
2000	Venus Williams	L. Davenport	63 76
2001	Venus Williams	J. Henin	61 36 60
2002	Serena Williams	V. Williams	76 63
2003	Serena Williams	V. Williams	46 64 62
2004	Maria Sharapova	S. Williams	61 64
2005	Venus Williams	L. Davenport	46 76 97
2006	Amelie Mauresmo	J. Henin-Hardenne	26 63 64
2007	Venus Williams	M. Bartoli	64 61
2008	Venus Williams	S. Williams	75 64

U.S. Open
MEN

Challenge round system (defending champion qualified for following year's final) used from 1884 to 1911. Known as the Patriotic Tournament in 1917 during World War I. Amateur and Open Championships held in 1968 and '69. Became an exclusively Open Championship in 1970. **Surface:** Decoturf II (acrylic cement).

Multiple winners: Bill Larned, Richard Sears and Bill Tilden (7); Jimmy Connors, Roger Federer and Pete Sampras (5); John McEnroe and Robert Wrenn (4); Oliver Campbell, Ivan Lendl, Fred Perry and Malcolm Whitman (3); Andre Agassi, Don Budge, Stefan Edberg, Roy Emerson, Neale Fraser, Pancho Gonzales, Bill Johnston, Jack Kramer, Rene Lacoste, Rod Laver, Maurice McLoughlin, Lindley Murray, John Newcombe, Frank Parker, Patrick Rafter, Bobby Riggs, Ken Rosewall, Frank Sedgman, Henry Slocum Jr., Tony Trabert, Ellsworth Vines and Dick Williams (2).

Year	Winner	Loser	Score	Year	Winner	Loser	Score
1881	Richard Sears	W. Glyn	60 63 62	1946	Jack Kramer	T. Brown, Jr.	97 63 60
1882	Richard Sears	C. Clark	61 64 60	1947	Jack Kramer	F. Parker	46 26 61 60 63
1883	Richard Sears	J. Dwight	62 60 97	1948	Pancho Gonzales	E. Sturgess	62 63 14-12
1884	Richard Sears	H. Taylor	60 16 60 62	1949	Pancho Gonzales	F. Schroeder	16-18 26 61 62 64
1885	Richard Sears	G. Brinley	63 46 60 63	1950	Arthur Larsen	H. Flam	63 46 57 64 63
1886	Richard Sears	R. Beeckman	46 61 63 64	1951	Frank Sedgman	V. Seixas	64 61 61
1887	Richard Sears	H. Slocum Jr.	61 63 62	1952	Frank Sedgman	G. Mulloy	61 62 63
1888	Henry Slocum Jr.	H. Taylor	64 61 60	1953	Tony Trabert	V. Seixas	63 62 63
1889	Henry Slocum Jr.	Q. Shaw	63 61 46 62	1954	Vic Seixas	R. Hartwig	36 62 64 64
1890	Oliver Campbell	H. Slocum Jr.	62 46 63 61	1955	Tony Trabert	K. Rosewall	97 63 63
1891	Oliver Campbell	C. Hobart	26 75 79 61 62	1956	Ken Rosewall	L. Hoad	46 62 63 63
1892	Oliver Campbell	F. Hovey	75 36 63 75	1957	Mal Anderson	A. Cooper	10-8 75 64
1893	Robert Wrenn	F. Hovey	64 36 64 64	1958	Ashley Cooper	M. Anderson	62 36 46 10-8 86
1894	Robert Wrenn	M. Goodbody	68 61 64 64	1959	Neale Fraser	A. Olmedo	63 57 62 64
1895	Fred Hovey	R. Wrenn	63 62 64	1960	Neale Fraser	R. Laver	64 64 97
1896	Robert Wrenn	F. Hovey	75 36 60 16 61	1961	Roy Emerson	R. Laver	75 63 62
1897	Robert Wrenn	W. Eaves	46 86 63 26 62	1962	Rod Laver	R. Emerson	62 64 57 64
1898	Malcolm Whitman	D. Davis	36 62 62 61	1963	Rafael Osuna	F. Froehling	75 64 62
1899	Malcolm Whitman	P. Paret	61 62 36 75	1964	Roy Emerson	F. Stolle	64 62 64
1900	Malcolm Whitman	B. Larned	64 16 62 62	1965	Manuel Santana	C. Drysdale	62 79 75 61
1901	Bill Larned	B. Wright	62 68 64 64	1966	Fred Stolle	J. Newcombe	46 12-10 63 64
1902	Bill Larned	R. Doherty	46 62 64 86	1967	John Newcombe	C. Graebner	64 64 86
1903	Laurie Doherty	B. Larned	60 63 10-8	1968	Am-Arthur Ashe	B. Lutz	46 63 8-10 60 64
1904	Holcombe Ward	B. Clothier	10-8 64 97		Op-Arthur Ashe	T. Okker	14-12 57 63 36 63
1905	Beals Wright	H. Ward	62 61 11-9	1969	Am-Stan Smith	B. Lutz	97 63 61
1906	Bill Clothier	B. Wright	63 60 64		Op-Rod Laver	T. Roche	79 61 63 62
1907	Bill Larned	R. LeRoy	62 62 64	1970	Ken Rosewall	T. Roche	26 64 76 63
1908	Bill Larned	B. Wright	61 62 86	1971	Stan Smith	J. Kodes	36 63 62 76
1909	Bill Larned	B. Clothier	61 62 57 16 61	1972	Ilie Nastase	A. Ashe	36 63 67 64 63
1910	Bill Larned	T. Bundy	61 57 60 68 61	1973	John Newcombe	J. Kodes	64 16 46 62 63
1911	Bill Larned	M. McLoughlin	64 64 62	1974	Jimmy Connors	K. Rosewall	61 60 61
1912	Maurice McLoughlin	W.F. Johnson	36 26 62 64 62	1975	Manuel Orantes	J. Connors	64 63 63
1913	Maurice McLoughlin	R. Williams	64 57 63 61	1976	Jimmy Connors	B. Borg	64 36 76 64
1914	Dick Williams	M. McLoughlin	63 86 10-8	1977	Guillermo Vilas	J. Connors	26 63 76 60
1915	Bill Johnston	M. McLoughlin	16 60 75 10-8	1978	Jimmy Connors	B. Borg	64 62 62
1916	Dick Williams	B. Johnston	46 64 06 62 64	1979	John McEnroe	V. Gerulaitis	75 63 63
1917	Lindley Murray	N. Niles	57 86 63 63	1980	John McEnroe	B. Borg	76 61 67 57 64
1918	Lindley Murray	B. Tilden	63 61 75	1981	John McEnroe	B. Borg	46 62 64 63
1919	Bill Johnston	B. Tilden	64 64 64	1982	Jimmy Connors	I. Lendl	63 62 46 64
1920	Bill Tilden	B. Johnston	61 16 75 57 63	1983	Jimmy Connors	I. Lendl	63 67 75 60
1921	Bill Tilden	W. Johnson	61 63 61	1984	John McEnroe	I. Lendl	63 64 61
1922	Bill Tilden	B. Johnston	46 36 62 63 64	1985	Ivan Lendl	J. McEnroe	76 63 64
1923	Bill Tilden	B. Johnston	64 61 64	1986	Ivan Lendl	M. Mecir	64 62 60
1924	Bill Tilden	B. Johnston	61 97 62	1987	Ivan Lendl	M. Wilander	67 60 76 64
1925	Bill Tilden	B. Johnston	46 11-9 63 46 63	1988	Mats Wilander	I. Lendl	64 46 63 57 64
1926	Rene Lacoste	J. Borotra	64 60 64	1989	Boris Becker	I. Lendl	76 16 63 76
1927	Rene Lacoste	B. Tilden	11-9 63 11-9	1990	Pete Sampras	A. Agassi	64 63 62
1928	Henri Cochet	F. Hunter	46 64 36 75 63	1991	Stefan Edberg	J. Courier	62 64 60
1929	Bill Tilden	F. Hunter	36 63 46 62 64	1992	Stefan Edberg	P. Sampras	36 64 76 62
1930	John Doeg	F. Shields	10-8 16 64 16-14	1993	Pete Sampras	C. Pioline	64 64 63
1931	Ellsworth Vines	G. Lott Jr.	79 63 97 75	1994	Andre Agassi	M. Stich	61 76 75
1932	Ellsworth Vines	H. Cochet	64 64 64	1995	Pete Sampras	A. Agassi	64 63 46 75
1933	Fred Perry	J. Crawford	63 11-13 46 60 61	1996	Pete Sampras	M. Chang	61 64 76
1934	Fred Perry	W. Allison	64 63 16 86	1997	Patrick Rafter	G. Rusedski	63 62 46 75
1935	Wilmer Allison	S. Wood	62 62 63	1998	Patrick Rafter	M. Philippoussis	63 36 62 60
1936	Fred Perry	D. Budge	26 62 86 16 10-8	1999	Andre Agassi	T. Martin	64 67 67 63 62
1937	Don Budge	G. von Cramm	61 79 61 36 61	2000	Marat Safin	P. Sampras	64 63 63
1938	Don Budge	G. Mako	63 68 62 61	2001	Lleyton Hewitt	P. Sampras	76 61 61
1939	Bobby Riggs	S.W. van Horn	64 62 64	2002	Pete Sampras	A. Agassi	63 64 57 64
1940	Don McNeill	B. Riggs	46 68 63 63 75	2003	Andy Roddick	J.C. Ferrero	63 76 63
1941	Bobby Riggs	F. Kovacs	57 61 63 63	2004	Roger Federer	L. Hewitt	60 76 60
1942	Fred Schroeder	F. Parker	86 75 36 46 62	2005	Roger Federer	A. Agassi	63 26 76 61
1943	Joe Hunt	J. Kramer	63 68 10-8 60	2006	Roger Federer	A. Roddick	62 46 75 61
1944	Frank Parker	B. Talbert	64 36 63 63	2007	Roger Federer	N. Djokovic	76 76 64
1945	Frank Parker	B. Talbert	14-12 61 62	2008	Roger Federer	A. Murray	62 75 62

WOMEN

Challenge round system used from 1887-1918. Five set final played from 1887 to 1901. Amateur and Open Championships held in 1968 and '69. Became an exclusively Open Championship in 1970.

Multiple winners: Molla Bjurstedt Mallory (8); Helen Wills Moody (7); Chris Evert Lloyd (6); Margaret Smith Court and Steffi Graf (5); Pauline Betz, Maria Bueno, Helen Jacobs, Billie Jean King, Alice Marble, Elisabeth Moore, Martina Navratilova and Hazel Hotchkiss Wightman (4); Juliette Atkinson, Mary Browne, Maureen Connolly, Margaret Osborne du Pont and Serena Williams (3); Tracy Austin, Mabel Cahill, Sarah Palfrey Cooke, Althea Gibson, Darlene Hard, Doris Hart, Justine Henin, Marion Jones, Monica Seles, Bertha Townsend and Venus Williams (2).

Year	Winner	Loser	Score	Year	Winner	Loser	Score
1887	Ellen Hansell	L. Knight	61 60	1949	Margaret du Pont	D. Hart	64 61
1888	Bertha Townsend	E. Hansell	63 65	1950	Margaret du Pont	D. Hart	64 63
1889	Bertha Townsend	L. Voorhes	75 62	1951	Maureen Connolly	S. Fry	63 16 64
1890	Ellen Roosevelt	B. Townsend	62 62	1952	Maureen Connolly	D. Hart	63 75
1891	Mabel Cahill	E. Roosevelt	64 61 46 63	1953	Maureen Connolly	D. Hart	62 64
1892	Mabel Cahill	E. Moore	57 63 64 46 62	1954	Doris Hart	L. Brough	68 61 86
1893	Aline Terry	A. Schultz	61 63	1955	Doris Hart	P. Ward	64 62
1894	Helen Hellwig	A. Terry	75 36 60 36 63	1956	Shirley Fry	A. Gibson	63 64
1895	Juliette Atkinson	H. Hellwig	64 62 61	1957	Althea Gibson	L. Brough	63 62
1896	Elisabeth Moore	J. Atkinson	64 46 62 62	1958	Althea Gibson	D. Hard	36 61 62
1897	Juliette Atkinson	E. Moore	63 63 46 36 63	1959	Maria Bueno	C. Truman	61 64
1898	Juliette Atkinson	M. Jones	63 57 64 26 75	1960	Darlene Hard	M. Bueno	64 10-12 64
1899	Marion Jones	M. Banks	61 61 75	1961	Darlene Hard	A. Haydon	63 64
1900	Myrtle McAteer	E. Parker	62 62 60	1962	Margaret Smith	D. Hard	97 64
1901	Elisabeth Moore	M. McAteer	64 36 75 26 62	1963	Maria Bueno	M. Smith	75 64
1902	Marion Jones	E. Moore	61 10(ret)	1964	Maria Bueno	C. Graebner	61 60
1903	Elisabeth Moore	M. Jones	75 86	1965	Margaret Smith	B.J. Moffitt	86 75
1904	May Sutton	E. Moore	61 62	1966	Maria Bueno	N. Richey	63 61
1905	Elisabeth Moore	H. Homans	64 57 61	1967	Billie Jean King	A. Jones	11-9 64
1906	Helen Homans	M. Barger-Wallach	64 63	1968	Am-Margaret Court	M. Bueno	62 62
1907	Evelyn Sears	C. Neely	63 62		Op-Virginia Wade	B.J. King	64 62
1908	Maud B. Wallach	Ev. Sears	63 16 63	1969	Am-Margaret Court	V. Wade	46 63 60
1909	Hazel Hotchkiss	M. Barger-Wallach	60 61		Op-Margaret Court	N. Richey	62 62
1910	Hazel Hotchkiss	L. Hammond	64 62	1970	Margaret Court	R. Casals	62 26 61
1911	Hazel Hotchkiss	F. Sutton	8-10 61 97	1971	Billie Jean King	R. Casals	64 76
1912	Mary Browne	E. Sears	64 62	1972	Billie Jean King	K. Melville	63 75
1913	Mary Browne	D. Green	62 75	1973	Margaret Court	E. Goolagong	76 57 62
1914	Mary Browne	M. Wagner	62 16 61	1974	Billie Jean King	E. Goolagong	36 63 75
1915	Molla Bjurstedt	H. Wightman	46 62 60	1975	Chris Evert	E. Cawley	57 64 62
1916	Molla Bjurstedt	L. Raymond	60 61	1976	Chris Evert	E. Cawley	63 60
1917	Molla Bjurstedt	M. Vanderhoef	46 60 62	1977	Chris Evert	W. Turnbull	76 62
1918	Molla Bjurstedt	E. Goss	64 63	1978	Chris Evert	P. Shriver	75 64
1919	Hazel Wightman	M. Zinderstein	61 62	1979	Tracy Austin	C. Evert Lloyd	64 63
1920	Molla Mallory	M. Zinderstein	63 61	1980	Chris Evert Lloyd	H. Mandlikova	57 61 61
1921	Molla Mallory	M. Browne	46 64 62	1981	Tracy Austin	M. Navratilova	16 76 76
1922	Molla Mallory	H. Wills	63 61	1982	Chris Evert Lloyd	H. Mandlikova	63 61
1923	Helen Wills	M. Mallory	62 61	1983	Martina Navratilova	C. Evert Lloyd	61 63
1924	Helen Wills	M. Mallory	61 63	1984	Martina Navratilova	C. Evert Lloyd	46 64 64
1925	Helen Wills	K. McKane	36 60 62	1985	Hana Mandlikova	M. Navratilova	76 16 76
1926	Molla Mallory	E. Ryan	46 64 97	1986	Martina Navratilova	H. Sukova	63 62
1927	Helen Wills	B. Nuthall	61 64	1987	Martina Navratilova	S. Graf	76 61
1928	Helen Wills	H. Jacobs	62 61	1988	Steffi Graf	G. Sabatini	63 36 61
1929	Helen Wills	P. Watson	64 62	1989	Steffi Graf	M. Navratilova	36 75 61
1930	Betty Nuthall	A. Harper	61 64	1990	Gabriela Sabatini	S. Graf	62 76
1931	Helen Moody	E. Whittingstall	64 61	1991	Monica Seles	M. Navratilova	76 61
1932	Helen Jacobs	C. Babcock	62 62	1992	Monica Seles	A.S. Vicario	63 63
1933	Helen Jacobs	H. Moody	86 36 30(ret)	1993	Steffi Graf	H. Sukova	63 63
1934	Helen Jacobs	S. Palfrey	61 64	1994	A. Sanchez Vicario	S. Graf	16 76 64
1935	Helen Jacobs	S. Fabyan	62 64	1995	Steffi Graf	M. Seles	76 06 63
1936	Alice Marble	H. Jacobs	46 63 62	1996	Steffi Graf	M. Seles	75 64
1937	Anita Lizana	J. Jedrzejowska	64 62	1997	Martina Hingis	V. Williams	60 64
1938	Alice Marble	N. Wynne	60 63	1998	Lindsay Davenport	M. Hingis	63 75
1939	Alice Marble	H. Jacobs	60 8-10 64	1999	Serena Williams	M. Hingis	63 76
1940	Alice Marble	H. Jacobs	62 63	2000	Venus Williams	L. Davenport	64 75
1941	Sarah Cooke	P. Betz	75 62	2001	Venus Williams	S. Williams	64 62
1942	Pauline Betz	L. Brough	46 61 64	2002	Serena Williams	V. Williams	64 63
1943	Pauline Betz	L. Brough	63 57 63	2003	J. Henin-Hardenne	K. Clijsters	75 61
1944	Pauline Betz	M. Osborne	63 86	2004	Svetlana Kuznetsova	E. Dementieva	63 75
1945	Sarah Cooke	P. Betz	36 86 64	2005	Kim Clijsters	M. Pierce	63 61
1946	Pauline Betz	P. Canning	11-9 63	2006	Maria Sharapova	J. Henin-Hardenne	64 64
1947	Louise Brough	M. Osborne	86 46 61	2007	Justine Henin	S. Kuznetsova	61 63
1948	Margaret du Pont	L. Brough	46 64 15-13	2008	Serena Williams	J. Jankovic	64 75

Grand Slam Summary

Singles winners of the four Grand Slam tournaments—Australian, French, Wimbledon and United States—since the French was opened to all comers in 1925. Note that there were two Australian Opens in 1977 and none in 1986.

MEN

Three wins in one year: Jack Crawford (1933); Fred Perry (1934); Tony Trabert (1955); Lew Hoad (1956); Ashley Cooper (1958); Roy Emerson (1964); Jimmy Connors (1974); Mats Wilander (1988); Roger Federer (2004, 2006-07).

Two wins in one year: Roy Emerson and Pete Sampras (4 times); Bjorn Borg (3 times); Rene Lacoste, Ivan Lendl, John Newcombe and Fred Perry (twice); Andre Agassi, Boris Becker, Don Budge, Henri Cochet, Jimmy Connors, Jim Courier, Roger Federer, Neale Fraser, Jack Kramer, John McEnroe, Rafael Nadal, Alex Olmedo, Budge Patty, Bobby Riggs, Ken Rosewall, Dick Savitt, Frank Sedgman and Guillermo Vilas (once).

Year	Australian	French	Wimbledon	U.S.	Year	Australian	French	Wimbledon	U.S.
1925	Anderson	Lacoste	Lacoste	Tilden	1968	Bowrey	Rosewall	Laver	Ashe
1926	Hawkes	Cochet	Borotra	Lacoste	1969	**Laver**	**Laver**	**Laver**	**Laver**
1927	Patterson	Lacoste	Cochet	Lacoste	1970	Ashe	Kodes	Newcombe	Rosewall
1928	Borotra	Cochet	Lacoste	Cochet	1971	Rosewall	Kodes	Newcombe	Smith
1929	Gregory	Lacoste	Cochet	Tilden	1972	Rosewall	Gimeno	Smith	Nastase
1930	Moon	Cochet	Tilden	Doeg	1973	Newcombe	Nastase	Kodes	Newcombe
1931	Crawford	Borotra	Wood	Vines	1974	Connors	Borg	Connors	Connors
1932	Crawford	Cochet	Vines	Vines	1975	Newcombe	Borg	Ashe	Orantes
1933	Crawford	Crawford	Crawford	Perry	1976	Edmondson	Panatta	Borg	Connors
1934	Perry	von Cramm	Perry	Perry	1977	Tanner	Vilas	Borg	Vilas
1935	Crawford	Perry	Perry	Allison		& Gerulaitis			
1936	Quist	von Cramm	Perry	Perry	1978	Vilas	Borg	Borg	Connors
1937	McGrath	Henkel	Budge	Budge	1979	Vilas	Borg	Borg	McEnroe
1938	**Budge**	**Budge**	**Budge**	**Budge**	1980	Teacher	Borg	Borg	McEnroe
1939	Bromwich	McNeill	Riggs	Riggs	1981	Kriek	Borg	McEnroe	McEnroe
1940	Quist	—	—	McNeill	1982	Kriek	Wilander	Connors	Connors
1941	—	—	—	Riggs	1983	Wilander	Noah	McEnroe	Connors
1942	—	—	—	Schroeder	1984	Wilander	Lendl	McEnroe	McEnroe
1943	—	—	—	Hunt	1985	Edberg	Wilander	Becker	Lendl
1944	—	—	—	Parker	1986	—	Lendl	Becker	Lendl
1945	—	—	—	Parker	1987	Edberg	Lendl	Cash	Lendl
1946	Bromwich	Bernard	Petra	Kramer	1988	Wilander	Wilander	Edberg	Wilander
1947	Pails	Asboth	Kramer	Kramer	1989	Lendl	Chang	Becker	Becker
1948	Quist	Parker	Falkenburg	Gonzales	1990	Lendl	Gomez	Edberg	Sampras
1949	Sedgman	Parker	Schroeder	Gonzales	1991	Becker	Courier	Stich	Edberg
1950	Sedgman	Patty	Patty	Larsen	1992	Courier	Courier	Agassi	Edberg
1951	Savitt	Drobny	Savitt	Sedgman	1993	Courier	Bruguera	Sampras	Sampras
1952	McGregor	Drobny	Sedgman	Sedgman	1994	Sampras	Bruguera	Sampras	Agassi
1953	Rosewall	Rosewall	Seixas	Trabert	1995	Agassi	Muster	Sampras	Sampras
1954	Rose	Trabert	Drobny	Seixas	1996	Becker	Kafelnikov	Krajicek	Sampras
1955	Rosewall	Trabert	Trabert	Trabert	1997	Sampras	Kuerten	Sampras	Rafter
1956	Hoad	Hoad	Hoad	Rosewall	1998	Korda	Moya	Sampras	Rafter
1957	Cooper	Davidson	Hoad	Anderson	1999	Kafelnikov	Agassi	Sampras	Agassi
1958	Cooper	Rose	Cooper	Cooper	2000	Agassi	Kuerten	Sampras	Safin
1959	Olmedo	Pietrangeli	Olmedo	Fraser	2001	Agassi	Kuerten	Ivanisevic	Hewitt
1960	Laver	Pietrangeli	Fraser	Fraser	2002	Johansson	Costa	Hewitt	Sampras
1961	Emerson	Santana	Laver	Emerson	2003	Agassi	Ferrero	Federer	Roddick
1962	**Laver**	**Laver**	**Laver**	**Laver**	2004	Federer	Gaudio	Federer	Federer
1963	Emerson	Emerson	McKinley	Osuna	2005	Safin	Nadal	Federer	Federer
1964	Emerson	Santana	Emerson	Emerson	2006	Federer	Nadal	Federer	Federer
1965	Emerson	Stolle	Emerson	Santana	2007	Federer	Nadal	Federer	Federer
1966	Emerson	Roche	Santana	Stolle	2008	Djokovic	Nadal	Nadal	Federer
1967	Emerson	Emerson	Newcombe	Newcombe					

Men's, Women's & Mixed Doubles Grand Slam

The tennis Grand Slam has only been accomplished in doubles competition six times in the same calendar year. Here are the doubles teams to accomplish the feat. The two men and three women to win the singles Grand Slam are noted in the Grand Slam Summary tables.

Men's Doubles

1951 . . . . .Frank Sedgman, Australia
& Ken McGregor, Australia

Mixed Doubles

1963 . . . . .Ken Fletcher, Australia
& Margaret Smith, Australia
1967 . . . . .Owen Davidson and two partners*

*Davidson's partners: AUS—Lesley Turner; FR, WIM, U.S.—Billie Jean King.

Women's Doubles

1960 . . . . .Maria Bueno, Brazil & two partners†
1984 . . . . .Martina Navratilova, USA
& Pam Shriver, USA
1998 . . . .Martina Hingis, Switzerland & two partners#

†Bueno's partners: AUS—Christine Truman; FR, WIM, U.S.—Darlene Hard.

#Hingis' partners: AUS—Mirjana Lucic; FR, WIM, U.S.—Jana Novotna.

WOMEN

Three in one year: Helen Wills Moody (1928 and '29); Margaret Smith Court (1962, '65, '69 and '73); Billie Jean King (1972); Martina Navratilova (1983 and '84); Steffi Graf (1989, '93, '95 and '96); Monica Seles (1991 and '92); Martina Hingis (1997) and Serena Williams (2002).

Two in one year: Chris Evert Lloyd (5 times); Helen Wills Moody and Martina Navratilova (3 times); Maria Bueno, Maureen Connolly, Margaret Smith Court, Althea Gibson, Justine Henin, Billie Jean King and Venus Williams (twice); Cilly Aussem, Pauline Betz, Louise Brough, Jennifer Capriati, Evonne Goolagong Cawley, Margaret Osborne du Pont, Shirley Fry, Darlene Hard, Suzanne Lenglen, Alice Marble, Amelie Mauresmo, Arantxa Sanchez Vicario and Serena Williams (once).

Year	Australian	French	Wimbledon	U.S.
1925	Akhurst	Lenglen	Lenglen	Wills
1926	Akhurst	Lenglen	Godfree	Mallory
1927	Boyd	Bouman	Wills	Wills
1928	Akhurst	Wills	Wills	Wills
1929	Akhurst	Wills	Wills	Wills
1930	Akhurst	Moody	Moody	Nuthall
1931	Buttsworth	Aussem	Aussem	Moody
1932	Buttsworth	Moody	Moody	Jacobs
1933	Hartigan	Scriven	Moody	Jacobs
1934	Hartigan	Scriven	Round	Jacobs
1935	Round	Sperling	Moody	Jacobs
1936	Hartigan	Sperling	Jacobs	Marble
1937	Wynne	Sperling	Round	Lizana
1938	Bundy	Mathieu	Moody	Marble
1939	Westacott	Mathieu	Marble	Marble
1940	Wynne	—	—	Marble
1941	—	—	—	Cooke
1942	—	—	—	Betz
1943	—	—	—	Betz
1944	—	—	—	Betz
1945	—	—	—	Cooke
1946	Bolton	Osborne	Betz	Betz
1947	Bolton	Todd	Osborne	Brough
1948	Bolton	Landry	Brough	du Pont
1949	Hart	du Pont	Brough	du Pont
1950	Brough	Hart	Brough	du Pont
1951	Bolton	Fry	Hart	Connolly
1952	Long	Hart	Connolly	Connolly
1953	**Connolly**	**Connolly**	**Connolly**	**Connolly**
1954	Long	Connolly	Connolly	Hart
1955	Penrose	Mortimer	Brough	Hart
1956	Carter	Gibson	Fry	Fry
1957	Fry	Bloomer	Gibson	Gibson
1958	Mortimer	Kormoczi	Gibson	Gibson
1959	Reitano	Truman	Bueno	Bueno
1960	Smith	Hard	Bueno	Hard
1961	Smith	Haydon	Mortimer	Hard
1962	Smith	Smith	Susman	Smith
1963	Smith	Turner	Smith	Bueno
1964	Smith	Smith	Bueno	Bueno
1965	Smith	Turner	Smith	Smith
1966	Smith	Jones	King	Bueno
1967	Richey	Durr	King	King
1968	King	Richey	King	Wade
1969	Court	Court	Jones	Court
1970	**Court**	**Court**	**Court**	**Court**
1971	Court	Goolagong	Goolagong	King
1972	Wade	King	King	King
1973	Court	Court	King	Court
1974	Goolagong	Evert	Evert	King
1975	Goolagong	Evert	King	Evert
1976	Cawley	Barker	Evert	Evert
1977	Reid & Cawley	Jausovec	Wade	Evert
1978	O'Neil	Ruzici	Navratilova	Evert
1979	Jordan	Evert Lloyd	Navratilova	Austin
1980	Mandlikova	Evert Lloyd	Cawley	Evert Lloyd
1981	Navratilova	Mandlikova	Evert Lloyd	Austin
1982	Evert Lloyd	Navratilova	Navratilova	Evert Lloyd
1983	Navratilova	Evert Lloyd	Navratilova	Navratilova
1984	Evert Lloyd	Navratilova	Navratilova	Navratilova
1985	Navratilova	Evert Lloyd	Navratilova	Mandlikova
1986	–	Evert Lloyd	Navratilova	Navratilova
1987	Mandlikova	Graf	Navratilova	Navratilova
1988	**Graf**	**Graf**	**Graf**	**Graf**
1989	Graf	Vicario	Graf	Graf
1990	Graf	Seles	Navratilova	Sabatini
1991	Seles	Seles	Graf	Seles
1992	Seles	Seles	Graf	Seles
1993	Seles	Graf	Graf	Graf
1994	Graf	Vicario	Martinez	Vicario
1995	Pierce	Graf	Graf	Graf
1996	Graf	Graf	Graf	Graf
1997	Hingis	Majoli	Hingis	Hingis
1998	Hingis	Vicario	Novotna	Davenport
1999	Hingis	Graf	Davenport	S. Williams
2000	Davenport	Pierce	V. Williams	V. Williams
2001	Capriati	Capriati	V. Williams	V. Williams
2002	Capriati	S. Williams	S. Williams	S. Williams
2003	S. Williams	H-Hardenne	S. Williams	H-Hardenne
2004	H-Hardenne	Myskina	Sharapova	Kuznetsova
2005	S. Williams	H-Hardenne	V. Williams	Clijsters
2006	Mauresmo	H-Hardenne	Mauresmo	Sharapova
2007	S. Williams	Henin	V. Williams	Henin
2008	Sharapova	Ivanovic	V. Williams	S. Williams

Overall Leaders

All-Time Grand Slam titlests including all singles and doubles championships at the four major tournaments. Titles listed under each heading are singles, doubles and mixed doubles.

MEN

		Career	Australian	French	Wimbledon	U.S.	S-D-M	Total Titles
1	Roy Emerson	1959-71	6-3-0	2-6-0	2-3-0	2-4-0	12-16-0	28
2	John Newcombe	1965-76	2-5-0	0-3-0	3-6-0	2-3-1	7-17-1	25
3	Frank Sedgman	1949-52	2-2-2	0-2-2	1-3-2	2-2-2	5-9-8	22
	Todd Woodbridge	1988-2005	0-3-1	0-1-1	0-9-1	0-3-3	0-16-6	22
5	Bill Tilden	1913-30	*	0-0-1	3-1-0	7-5-4	10-6-5	21
6	Rod Laver	1959-71	3-4-0	2-1-1	4-1-2	2-0-0	11-6-3	20
7	Jack Bromwich	1938-50	2-8-1	0-0-0	0-2-2	0-3-1	2-13-4	19
	Neale Fraser	1957-62	0-3-1	0-3-0	1-2-1	2-3-3	3-11-5	19
9	Ken Rosewall	1953-72	4-3-0	2-2-0	0-2-0	2-2-1	8-9-1	18
	Jean Borotra	1925-36	1-1-1	1-5-2	2-3-1	0-0-1	4-9-5	18
	Fred Stolle	1962-69	0-3-1	1-2-0	0-2-3	1-3-2	2-10-6	18
12	Four tied with 17 total titles each.							

Grand Slam Overall Leaders (Cont.)
WOMEN

		Career	Australian	French	Wimbledon	U.S.	S-D-M	Total Titles
1	Margaret Smith Court	1960-75	11-8-2	5-4-4	3-2-5	5-5-8	24-19-19	62
2	Martina Navratilova	1974-95, 2000-06	3-8-1	2-7-2	9-7-4	4-9-3	18-31-10	59
3	Billie Jean King	1961-81	1-0-1	1-1-2	6-10-4	4-5-4	12-16-11	39
4	Margaret du Pont	1941-62	*	2-3-0	1-5-1	3-13-9	6-21-10	37
5	Louise Brough	1942-57	1-1-0	0-3-0	4-5-4	1-12-4	6-21-8	35
	Doris Hart	1948-55	1-1-2	2-5-3	1-4-5	2-4-5	6-14-15	35
7	Helen Wills Moody	1923-38	*	4-2-0	8-3-1	7-4-2	19-9-3	31
8	Elizabeth Ryan	1914-34	*	0-4-0	0-12-7	0-1-2	0-17-9	26
9	Suzanne Lenglen	1919-26	*	6-2-2	6-6-3	0-0-0	12-8-5	25
10	Steffi Graf	1982-99	4-0-0	6-0-0	7-1-0	5-0-0	22-1-0	23
11	Pam Shriver	1981-97	0-7-0	0-4-1	0-5-0	0-5-0	0-21-1	22
12	Chris Evert	1974-89	2-0-0	7-2-0	3-1-0	6-0-0	18-3-0	21
	Darlene Hard	1958-69	*	1-3-2	0-4-3	2-6-0	3-13-5	21
14	Natasha Zvereva	1989-2002	0-3-2	0-6-0	0-5-0	0-4-0	0-18-2	20
	Nancye Wynne Bolton	1935-52	6-10-4	0-0-0	0-0-0	0-0-0	6-10-4	20
	Maria Bueno	1958-68	0-1-0	0-1-1	3-5-0	4-5-0	7-12-1	20

All-Time Grand Slam Singles Titles

Men and women with the most singles championships in the Australian, French, Wimbledon and U.S. championships, through 2008. Note that (*) indicates player never played in that particular Grand Slam event; and players active in singles play in 2008 are in **bold** type.

Top 10 Men

		Aus	Fre	Wim	US	Total
1	Pete Sampras	2	0	7	5	14
2	**Roger Federer**	3	0	5	5	13
3	Roy Emerson	6	2	2	2	12
4	Bjorn Borg	0	6	5	0	11
	Rod Laver	3	2	4	2	11
6	Bill Tilden	*	0	3	7	10
7	Andre Agassi	4	1	1	2	8
	Jimmy Connors	1	0	2	5	8
	Ivan Lendl	2	3	0	3	8
	Fred Perry	1	1	3	3	8
	Ken Rosewall	4	2	0	2	8

Top 10 Women

		Aus	Fre	Wim	US	Total
1	Margaret Smith Court	11	5	3	5	24
2	Steffi Graf	4	6	7	5	22
3	Helen Wills Moody	*	4	8	7	19
4	Chris Evert	2	7	3	6	18
	Martina Navratilova	3	2	9	4	18
6	Billie Jean King	1	1	6	4	12
	Suzanne Lenglen	*	6	6	0	12
8	Maureen Connolly	1	2	3	3	9
	Monica Seles	4	3	0	2	9
	Serena Williams	3	1	2	3	9

Annual Number One Players

Unofficial world rankings for men and women determined by the *London Daily Telegraph* from 1914-72. Since then, official world rankings computed by men's and women's tours. Rankings included only amateur players from 1914 until the arrival of open (professional) tennis in 1968. No rankings were released during World Wars I and II.

MEN

Multiple winners: Pete Sampras and Bill Tilden (6); Jimmy Connors (5); Henri Cochet, Roger Federer, Rod Laver, Ivan Lendl and John McEnroe (4); John Newcombe and Fred Perry (3); Bjorn Borg, Don Budge, Ashley Cooper, Stefan Edberg, Roy Emerson, Neale Fraser, Lleyton Hewitt, Jack Kramer, Rene Lacoste, Ilie Nastase, Frank Sedgman and Tony Trabert (2).

Year		Year		Year		Year	
1914	Maurice McLoughlin	1939	Bobby Riggs	1966	Manuel Santana	1988	Mats Wilander
1915-18	No rankings	1940-45	No rankings	1967	John Newcombe	1989	Ivan Lendl
1919	Gerald Patterson	1946	Jack Kramer	1968	Rod Laver	1990	Stefan Edberg
1920	Bill Tilden	1947	Jack Kramer	1969	Rod Laver	1991	Stefan Edberg
1921	Bill Tilden	1948	Frank Parker	1970	John Newcombe	1992	Jim Courier
1922	Bill Tilden	1949	Pancho Gonzales	1971	John Newcombe	1993	Pete Sampras
1923	Bill Tilden	1950	Budge Patty	1972	Ilie Nastase	1994	Pete Sampras
1924	Bill Tilden	1951	Frank Sedgman	1973	Ilie Nastase	1995	Pete Sampras
1925	Bill Tilden	1952	Frank Sedgman	1974	Jimmy Connors	1996	Pete Sampras
1926	Rene Lacoste	1953	Tony Trabert	1975	Jimmy Connors	1997	Pete Sampras
1927	Rene Lacoste	1954	Jaroslav Drobny	1976	Jimmy Connors	1998	Pete Sampras
1928	Henri Cochet	1955	Tony Trabert	1977	Jimmy Connors	1999	Andre Agassi
1929	Henri Cochet	1956	Lew Hoad	1978	Jimmy Connors	2000	Gustavo Kuerten
1930	Henri Cochet	1957	Ashley Cooper	1979	Bjorn Borg	2001	Lleyton Hewitt
1931	Henri Cochet	1958	Ashley Cooper	1980	Bjorn Borg	2002	Lleyton Hewitt
1932	Ellsworth Vines	1959	Neale Fraser	1981	John McEnroe	2003	Andy Roddick
1933	Jack Crawford	1960	Neale Fraser	1982	John McEnroe	2004	Roger Federer
1934	Fred Perry	1961	Rod Laver	1983	John McEnroe	2005	Roger Federer
1935	Fred Perry	1962	Rod Laver	1984	John McEnroe	2006	Roger Federer
1936	Fred Perry	1963	Rafael Osuna	1985	Ivan Lendl	2007	Roger Federer
1937	Don Budge	1964	Roy Emerson	1986	Ivan Lendl		
1938	Don Budge	1965	Roy Emerson	1987	Ivan Lendl		

WOMEN

Multiple winners: Helen Wills Moody (9); Steffi Graf (8); Margaret Smith Court and Martina Navratilova (7); Chris Evert Lloyd and Billie Jean King (5); Lindsay Davenport and Margaret Osborne du Pont (4); Maureen Connolly, Justine Henin, Martina Hingis and Monica Seles (3); Maria Bueno, Althea Gibson and Suzanne Lenglen (2).

Year		Year		Year		Year	
1925	Suzanne Lenglen	1950	Margaret du Pont	1970	Margaret Court	1990	Steffi Graf
1926	Suzanne Lenglen	1951	Doris Hart	1971	Evonne Goolagong	1991	Monica Seles
1927	Helen Wills	1952	Maureen Connolly	1972	Billie Jean King	1992	Monica Seles
1928	Helen Wills	1953	Maureen Connolly	1973	Margaret Court	1993	Steffi Graf
1929	Helen Wills Moody	1954	Maureen Connolly	1974	Billie Jean King	1994	Steffi Graf
1930	Helen Wills Moody	1955	Louise Brough	1975	Chris Evert	1995	Steffi Graf
1931	Helen Wills Moody	1956	Shirley Fry	1976	Chris Evert		& Monica Seles*
1932	Helen Wills Moody	1957	Althea Gibson	1977	Chris Evert	1996	Steffi Graf
1933	Helen Wills Moody	1958	Althea Gibson	1978	Martina Navratilova	1997	Martina Hingis
1934	Dorothy Round	1959	Maria Bueno	1979	Martina Navratilova	1998	Lindsay Davenport
1935	Helen Wills Moody					1999	Martina Hingis
1936	Helen Jacobs	1960	Maria Bueno	1980	Chris Evert Lloyd		
1937	Anita Lizana	1961	Angela Mortimer	1981	Chris Evert Lloyd	2000	Martina Hingis
1938	Helen Wills Moody	1962	Margaret Smith	1982	Martina Navratilova	2001	Lindsay Davenport
1939	Alice Marble	1963	Margaret Smith	1983	Martina Navratilova	2002	Serena Williams
		1964	Margaret Smith	1984	Martina Navratilova	2003	Justine Henin-Hardenne
1940-45	No rankings	1965	Margaret Smith	1985	Martina Navratilova	2004	Lindsay Davenport
1946	Pauline Betz	1966	Billie Jean King	1986	Martina Navratilova	2005	Lindsay Davenport
1947	Margaret Osborne	1967	Billie Jean King	1987	Steffi Graf	2006	Justine Henin
1948	Margaret du Pont	1968	Billie Jean King	1988	Steffi Graf	2007	Justine Henin
1949	Margaret du Pont	1969	Margaret Court	1989	Steffi Graf		

*Upon her return to the WTA Tour on Aug. 15, 1995, Seles retained her #1 ranking and was co-ranked at #1 through her first six tournaments (August '95–May '96). Seles was on leave since April 1993 when she was stabbed by a fan during a match.

Annual Top 10 World Rankings (since 1968)

Year by year Top 10 world computer rankings for men (ATP Tour) and women (WTA Tour) since the arrival of open tennis in 1968. Rankings from 1968-72 made by Lance Tingay of the *London Daily Telegraph*. Since 1973 the WTA Tour and ATP tour had compiled its own computer rankings. Since 2000, the men's rankings reflect the final standings of the ATP Champions Race.

MEN

1968
1 Rod Laver
2 Arthur Ashe
3 Ken Rosewall
4 Tom Okker
5 Tony Roche
6 John Newcombe
7 Clark Graebner
8 Dennis Ralston
9 Cliff Drysdale
10 Pancho Gonzales

1969
1 Rod Laver
2 Tony Roche
3 John Newcombe
4 Tom Okker
5 Ken Rosewall
6 Arthur Ashe
7 Cliff Drysdale
8 Pancho Gonzales
9 Andres Gimeno
10 Fred Stolle

1970
1 John Newcombe
2 Ken Rosewall
3 Tony Roche
4 Rod Laver
5 Arthur Ashe
6 Ilie Nastase
7 Tom Okker
8 Roger Taylor
9 Jan Kodes
10 Cliff Richey

1971
1 John Newcombe
2 Stan Smith
3 Rod Laver
4 Ken Rosewall
5 Jan Kodes
6 Arthur Ashe
7 Tom Okker
8 Marty Riessen
9 Cliff Drysdale
10 Ilie Nastase

1972
1 Stan Smith
2 Ken Rosewall
3 Ilie Nastase
4 Rod Laver
5 Arthur Ashe
6 John Newcombe
7 Bob Lutz
8 Tom Okker
9 Marty Riessen
10 Andres Gimeno

1973
1 Ilie Nastase
2 John Newcombe
3 Jimmy Connors
4 Tom Okker
5 Stan Smith
6 Ken Rosewall
7 Manuel Orantes
8 Rod Laver
9 Jan Kodes
10 Arthur Ashe

1974
1 Jimmy Connors
2 John Newcombe
3 Bjorn Borg
4 Rod Laver
5 Guillermo Vilas
6 Tom Okker
7 Arthur Ashe
8 Ken Rosewall
9 Stan Smith
10 Ilie Nastase

1975
1 Jimmy Connors
2 Guillermo Vilas
3 Bjorn Borg
4 Arthur Ashe
5 Manuel Orantes
6 Ken Rosewall
7 Ilie Nastase
8 John Alexander
9 Roscoe Tanner
10 Rod Laver

1976
1 Jimmy Connors
2 Bjorn Borg
3 Ilie Nastase
4 Manuel Orantes
5 Raul Ramirez
6 Guillermo Vilas
7 Adriano Panatta
8 Harold Solomon
9 Eddie Dibbs
10 Brian Gottfried

1977
1 Jimmy Connors
2 Guillermo Vilas
3 Bjorn Borg
4 Vitas Gerulaitis
5 Brian Gottfried
6 Eddie Dibbs
7 Manuel Orantes
8 Raul Ramirez
9 Ilie Nastase
10 Dick Stockton

1978
1 Jimmy Connors
2 Bjorn Borg
3 Guillermo Vilas
4 John McEnroe
5 Vitas Gerulaitis
6 Eddie Dibbs
7 Brian Gottfried
8 Raul Ramirez
9 Harold Solomon
10 Corrado Barazzutti

1979
1 Bjorn Borg
2 Jimmy Connors
3 John McEnroe
4 Vitas Gerulaitis
5 Roscoe Tanner
6 Guillermo Vilas
7 Arthur Ashe
8 Harold Solomon
9 Jose Higueras
10 Eddie Dibbs

1980
1 Bjorn Borg
2 John McEnroe
3 Jimmy Connors
4 Gene Mayer
5 Guillermo Vilas
6 Ivan Lendl
7 Harold Solomon
8 Jose-Luis Clerc
9 Vitas Gerulaitis
10 Eliot Teltscher

1981
1 John McEnroe
2 Ivan Lendl
3 Jimmy Connors
4 Bjorn Borg
5 Jose-Luis Clerc
6 Guillermo Vilas
7 Gene Mayer
8 Eliot Teltscher
9 Vitas Gerulaitis
10 Peter McNamara

1982
1 John McEnroe
2 Jimmy Connors
3 Ivan Lendl
4 Guillermo Vilas
5 Vitas Gerulaitis
6 Jose-Luis Clerc
7 Mats Wilander
8 Gene Mayer
9 Yannick Noah
10 Peter McNamara

Men's Top 10 World Rankings (since 1968) (Cont.)

1983
1 John McEnroe
2 Ivan Lendl
3 Jimmy Connors
4 Mats Wilander
5 Yannick Noah
6 Jimmy Arias
7 Jose Higueras
8 Jose-Luis Clerc
9 Kevin Curren
10 Gene Mayer

1984
1 John McEnroe
2 Jimmy Connors
3 Ivan Lendl
4 Mats Wilander
5 Andres Gomez
6 Anders Jarryd
7 Henrik Sundstrom
8 Pat Cash
9 Eliot Teltscher
10 Yannick Noah

1985
1 Ivan Lendl
2 John McEnroe
3 Mats Wilander
4 Jimmy Connors
5 Stefan Edberg
6 Boris Becker
7 Yannick Noah
8 Anders Jarryd
9 Miloslav Mecir
10 Kevin Curren

1986
1 Ivan Lendl
2 Boris Becker
3 Mats Wilander
4 Yannick Noah
5 Stefan Edberg
6 Henri Leconte
7 Joakim Nystrom
8 Jimmy Connors
9 Miloslav Mecir
10 Andres Gomez

1987
1 Ivan Lendl
2 Stefan Edberg
3 Mats Wilander
4 Jimmy Connors
5 Boris Becker
6 Miloslav Mecir
7 Pat Cash
8 Yannick Noah
9 Tim Mayotte
10 John McEnroe

1988
1 Mats Wilander
2 Ivan Lendl
3 Andre Agassi
4 Boris Becker
5 Stefan Edberg
6 Kent Carlsson
7 Jimmy Connors
8 Jakob Hlasek
9 Henri Leconte
10 Tim Mayotte

1989
1 Ivan Lendl
2 Boris Becker
3 Stefan Edberg
4 John McEnroe
5 Michael Chang
6 Brad Gilbert
7 Andre Agassi
8 Aaron Krickstein
9 Alberto Mancini
10 Jay Berger

1990
1 Stefan Edberg
2 Boris Becker
3 Ivan Lendl
4 Andre Agassi
5 Pete Sampras
6 Andres Gomez
7 Thomas Muster
8 Emilio Sanchez
9 Goran Ivanisevic
10 Brad Gilbert

1991
1 Stefan Edberg
2 Jim Courier
3 Boris Becker
4 Michael Stich
5 Ivan Lendl
6 Pete Sampras
7 Guy Forget
8 Karel Novacek
9 Petr Korda
10 Andre Agassi

1992
1 Jim Courier
2 Stefan Edberg
3 Pete Sampras
4 Goran Ivanisevic
5 Boris Becker
6 Michael Chang
7 Petr Korda
8 Ivan Lendl
9 Andre Agassi
10 Richard Krajicek

1993
1 Pete Sampras
2 Michael Stich
3 Jim Courier
4 Sergi Bruguera
5 Stefan Edberg
6 Andrei Medvedev
7 Goran Ivanisevic
8 Michael Chang
9 Thomas Muster
10 Cedric Pioline

1994
1 Pete Sampras
2 Andre Agassi
3 Boris Becker
4 Sergi Bruguera
5 Goran Ivanisevic
6 Michael Chang
7 Stefan Edberg
8 Alberto Berasategui
9 Michael Stich
10 Todd Martin

1995
1 Pete Sampras
2 Andre Agassi
3 Thomas Muster
4 Boris Becker
5 Michael Chang
6 Yevgeny Kafelnikov
7 Thomas Enqvist
8 Jim Courier
9 Wayne Ferreira
10 Goran Ivanisevic

1996
1 Pete Sampras
2 Michael Chang
3 Yevgeny Kafelnikov
4 Goran Ivanisevic
5 Thomas Muster
6 Boris Becker
7 Richard Krajicek
8 Andre Agassi
9 Thomas Enqvist
10 Wayne Ferreira

1997
1 Pete Sampras
2 Patrick Rafter
3 Michael Chang
4 Jonas Bjorkman
5 Yevgeny Kafelnikov
6 Greg Rusedski
7 Carlos Moya
8 Sergi Bruguera
9 Thomas Muster
10 Marcelo Rios

1998
1 Pete Sampras
2 Marcelo Rios
3 Alex Corretja
4 Patrick Rafter
5 Carlos Moya
6 Andre Agassi
7 Tim Henman
8 Karol Kucera
9 Greg Rusedski
10 Richard Krajicek

1999
1 Andre Agassi
2 Yevgeny Kafelnikov
3 Pete Sampras
4 Thomas Enqvist
5 Gustavo Kuerten
6 Nicolas Kiefer
7 Todd Martin
8 Nicolas Lapentti
9 Marcelo Rios
10 Richard Krajicek

2000
1 Gustavo Kuerten
2 Marat Safin
3 Pete Sampras
4 Magnus Norman
5 Yevgeny Kafelnikov
6 Andre Agassi
7 Lleyton Hewitt
8 Alex Corretja
9 Thomas Enqvist
10 Tim Henman

2001
1 Lleyton Hewitt
2 Gustavo Kuerten
3 Andre Agassi
4 Yevgeny Kafelnikov
5 Juan Carlos Ferrero
6 Sebastien Grosjean
7 Patrick Rafter
8 Tommy Haas
9 Tim Henman
10 Pete Sampras

2002
1 Lleyton Hewitt
2 Andre Agassi
3 Marat Safin
4 Juan Carlos Ferrero
5 Carlos Moya
6 Roger Federer
7 Jiri Novak
8 Tim Henman
9 Albert Costa
10 Andy Roddick

2003
1 Andy Roddick
2 Roger Federer
3 Juan Carlos Ferrero
4 Andre Agassi
5 Guillermo Coria
6 Rainer Schuettler
7 Carlos Moya
8 David Nalbandian
9 Mark Philippoussis
10 Sebastien Grosjean

2004
1 Roger Federer
2 Andy Roddick
3 Lleyton Hewitt
4 Marat Safin
5 Carlos Moya
6 Tim Henman
7 Guillermo Coria
8 Andre Agassi
9 David Nalbandian
10 Gaston Gaudio

2005
1 Roger Federer
2 Rafael Nadal
3 Andy Roddick
4 Lleyton Hewitt
5 Nikolay Davydenko
6 David Nalbandian
7 Andre Agassi
8 Guillermo Coria
9 Ivan Ljubicic
10 Gaston Gaudio

2006
1 Roger Federer
2 Rafael Nadal
3 Nikolay Davydenko
4 James Blake
5 Ivan Ljubicic
6 Andy Roddick
7 Tommy Robredo
8 David Nalbandian
9 Mario Ancic
10 Fernando Gonzalez

2007
1 Roger Federer
2 Rafael Nadal
3 Novak Djokovic
4 Nikolay Davydenko
5 David Ferrer
6 Andy Roddick
7 Fernando Gonzalez
8 Richard Gasquet
9 David Nalbandian
10 Tommy Robredo

WOMEN

1968
1 Billie Jean King
2 Virginia Wade
3 Nancy Richey
4 Maria Bueno
5 Margaret Court
6 Ann Jones
7 Judy Tegart
8 Annette du Plooy
9 Leslie Bowrey
10 Rosie Casals

1969
1 Margaret Court
2 Ann Jones
3 Billie Jean King
4 Nancy Richey
5 Julie Heldman
6 Rosie Casals
7 Kerry Melville
8 Peaches Bartkowicz
9 Virginia Wade
10 Leslie Bowrey

1970
1 Margaret Court
2 Billie Jean King
3 Rosie Casals
4 Virginia Wade
5 Helga Niessen
6 Kerry Melville
7 Julie Heldman
8 Karen Krantzcke
9 Francoise Durr
10 Nancy R. Gunter

1971
1 Evonne Goolagong
2 Billie Jean King
3 Margaret Court
4 Rosie Casals
5 Kerry Melville
6 Virginia Wade
7 Judy Tegart
8 Francoise Durr
9 Helga N. Masthoff
10 Chris Evert

1972
1 Billie Jean King
2 Evonne Goolagong
3 Chris Evert
4 Margaret Court
5 Kerry Melville
6 Virginia Wade
7 Rosie Casals
8 Nancy R. Gunter
9 Francoise Durr
10 Linda Tuero

1973
1 Margaret S. Court
2 Billie Jean King
3 Evonne G. Cawley
4 Chris Evert
5 Rosie Casals
6 Virginia Wade
7 Kerry Reid
8 Nancy Richey
9 Julie Heldman
10 Helga Masthoff

1974
1 Billie Jean King
2 Evonne G. Cawley
3 Chris Evert
4 Virginia Wade
5 Julie Heldman
6 Rosie Casals
7 Kerry Reid
8 Olga Morozova
9 Lesley Hunt
10 Francoise Durr

1975
1 Chris Evert
2 Billie Jean King
3 Evonne G. Cawley
4 Martina Navratilova
5 Virginia Wade
6 Margaret S. Court
7 Olga Morozova
8 Nancy Richey
9 Francoise Durr
10 Rosie Casals

1976
1 Chris Evert
2 Evonne G. Cawley
3 Virginia Wade
4 Martina Navratilova
5 Sue Barker
6 Betty Stove
7 Dianne Balestrat
8 Mima Jausovec
9 Rosie Casals
10 Francoise Durr

1977
1 Chris Evert
2 Billie Jean King
3 Martina Navratilova
4 Virginia Wade
5 Sue Barker
6 Rosie Casals
7 Betty Stove
8 Dianne Balestrat
9 Wendy Turnbull
10 Kerry Reid

1978
1 Martina Navratilova
2 Chris Evert Lloyd
3 Evonne G. Cawley
4 Virginia Wade
5 Billie Jean King
6 Tracy Austin
7 Wendy Turnbull
8 Kerry Reid
9 Betty Stove
10 Dianne Balestrat

1979
1 Martina Navratilova
2 Chris Evert Lloyd
3 Tracy Austin
4 Evonne G. Cawley
5 Billie Jean King
6 Dianne Balestrat
7 Wendy Turnbull
8 Virginia Wade
9 Kerry Reid
10 Sue Barker

1980
1 Chris Evert Lloyd
2 Tracy Austin
3 Martina Navratilova
4 Hana Mandlikova
5 Evonne G. Cawley
6 Billie Jean King
7 Andrea Jaeger
8 Wendy Turnbull
9 Pam Shriver
10 Greer Stevens

1981
1 Chris Evert Lloyd
2 Tracy Austin
3 Martina Navratilova
4 Andrea Jaeger
5 Hana Mandlikova
6 Sylvia Hanika
7 Pam Shriver
8 Wendy Turnbull
9 Bettina Bunge
10 Barbara Potter

1982
1 Martina Navratilova
2 Chris Evert Lloyd
3 Andrea Jaeger
4 Tracy Austin
5 Wendy Turnbull
6 Pam Shriver
7 Hana Mandlikova
8 Barbara Potter
9 Bettina Bunge
10 Sylvia Hanika

1983
1 Martina Navratilova
2 Chris Evert Lloyd
3 Andrea Jaeger
4 Pam Shriver
5 Sylvia Hanika
6 Jo Durie
7 Bettina Bunge
8 Wendy Turnbull
9 Tracy Austin
10 Zina Garrison

1984
1 Martina Navratilova
2 Chris Evert Lloyd
3 Hana Mandlikova
4 Pam Shriver
5 Wendy Turnbull
6 Manuela Maleeva
7 Helena Sukova
8 Claudia Kohde-Kilsch
9 Zina Garrison
10 Kathy Jordan

1985
1 Martina Navratilova
2 Chris Evert Lloyd
3 Hana Mandlikova
4 Pam Shriver
5 Claudia Kohde-Kilsch
6 Steffi Graf
7 Manuela Maleeva
8 Zina Garrison
9 Helena Sukova
10 Bonnie Gadusek

1986
1 Martina Navratilova
2 Chris Evert Lloyd
3 Steffi Graf
4 Hana Mandlikova
5 Helena Sukova
6 Pam Shriver
7 Claudia Kohde-Kilsch
8 M. Maleeva-Fragniere
9 Zina Garrison
10 Gabriela Sabatini

1987
1 Steffi Graf
2 Martina Navratilova
3 Chris Evert
4 Pam Shriver
5 Hana Mandlikova
6 Gabriela Sabatini
7 Helena Sukova
8 M. Maleeva-Fragniere
9 Zina Garrison
10 Claudia Kohde-Kilsch

1988
1 Steffi Graf
2 Martina Navratilova
3 Chris Evert
4 Gabriela Sabatini
5 Pam Shriver
6 M. Maleeva-Fragniere
7 Natalia Zvereva
8 Helena Sukova
9 Zina Garrison
10 Barbara Potter

1989
1 Steffi Graf
2 Martina Navratilova
3 Gabriela Sabatini
4 Z. Garrison-Jackson
5 A. Sanchez Vicario
6 Monica Seles
7 Conchita Martinez
8 Helena Sukova
9 M. Maleeva-Fragniere
10 Chris Evert

1990
1 Steffi Graf
2 Monica Seles
3 Martina Navratilova
4 Mary Joe Fernandez
5 Gabriela Sabatini
6 Katerina Maleeva
7 A. Sanchez Vicario
8 Jennifer Capriati
9 M. Maleeva-Fragniere
10 Z. Garrison-Jackson

1991
1 Monica Seles
2 Steffi Graf
3 Gabriela Sabatini
4 Martina Navratilova
5 A. Sanchez Vicario
6 Jennifer Capriati
7 Jana Novotna
8 Mary Joe Fernandez
9 Conchita Martinez
10 M. Maleeva-Fragniere

1992
1 Monica Seles
2 Steffi Graf
3 Gabriela Sabatini
4 A. Sanchez Vicario
5 Martina Navratilova
6 Mary Joe Fernandez
7 Jennifer Capriati
8 Conchita Martinez
9 M. Maleeva-Fragniere
10 Jana Novotna

1993
1 Steffi Graf
2 A. Sanchez Vicario
3 Martina Navratilova
4 Conchita Martinez
5 Gabriela Sabatini
6 Jana Novotna
7 Mary Joe Fernandez
8 Monica Seles
9 Jennifer Capriati
10 Anke Huber

1994
1 Steffi Graf
2 A. Sanchez Vicario
3 Conchita Martinez
4 Jana Novotna
5 Mary Pierce
6 Lindsay Davenport
7 Gabriela Sabatini
8 Martina Navratilova
9 Kimiko Date
10 Natasha Zvereva

1995
1 Steffi Graf
  Monica Seles*
2 Conchita Martinez
3 A. Sanchez Vicario
4 Kimiko Date
5 Mary Pierce
6 M. Maleeva
7 Gabriela Sabatini
8 Mary Joe Fernandez
9 Iva Majoli
10 Anke Huber

1996
1 Steffi Graf
2 Monica Seles†
  A. Sanchez Vicario
3 Jana Novotna
4 Martina Hingis
5 Conchita Martinez
6 Anke Huber
7 Iva Majoli
8 Kimiko Date
9 Lindsay Davenport
10 Barbara Paulus

1997
1 Martina Hingis
2 Jana Novotna
3 Lindsay Davenport
4 Amanda Coetzer
5 Monica Seles
6 Iva Majoli
7 Mary Pierce
8 Irina Spirlea
9 A. Sanchez Vicario
10 Mary Joe Fernandez

Annual Top 10 World Rankings (since 1968) (Cont.)

WOMEN

1998	2000	2002	2004	2006
1 Lindsay Davenport	1 Martina Hingis	1 Serena Williams	1 Lindsay Davenport	1 J. Henin-Hardenne
2 Martina Hingis	2 Lindsay Davenport	2 Venus Williams	2 Amelie Mauresmo	2 Maria Sharapova
3 Jana Novotna	3 Venus Williams	3 Jennifer Capriati	3 Anastasia Myskina	3 Amelie Mauresmo
4 A. Sanchez Vicario	4 Monica Seles	4 Kim Clijsters	4 Maria Sharapova	4 Svetlana Kuznetsova
5 Venus Williams	5 Conchita Martinez	5 J. Henin-Hardenne	5 Svetlana Kuznetsova	5 Kim Clijsters
6 Monica Seles	6 Serena Williams	6 Amelie Mauresmo	6 Elena Dementieva	6 Nadia Petrova
7 Mary Pierce	7 Mary Pierce	7 Monica Seles	7 Serena Williams	7 Martina Hingis
8 Conchita Martinez	8 Anna Kournikova	8 Daniela Hantuchova	8 J. Henin-Hardenne	8 Elena Dementieva
9 Steffi Graf	9 A. Sanchez Vicario	9 Jelena Dokic	9 Venus Williams	9 Patty Schnyder
10 Nathalie Tauziat	10 Nathalie Tauziat	10 Martina Hingis	10 Jennifer Capriati	10 Nicole Vaidisova

1999	2001	2003	2005	2007
1 Martina Hingis	1 Lindsay Davenport	1 J. Henin-Hardenne	1 Lindsay Davenport	1 Justine Henin
2 Lindsay Davenport	2 Jennifer Capriati	2 Kim Clijsters	2 Kim Clijsters	2 Svetlana Kuznetsova
3 Venus Williams	3 Venus Williams	3 Serena Williams	3 Amelie Mauresmo	3 Jelena Jankovic
4 Serena Williams	4 Martina Hingis	4 Amelie Mauresmo	4 Maria Sharapova	4 Ana Ivanovic
5 Mary Pierce	5 Kim Clijsters	5 Lindsay Davenport	5 Mary Pierce	5 Maria Sharapova
6 Monica Seles	6 Serena Williams	6 Jennifer Capriati	6 J. Henin-Hardenne	6 Anna Chakvetadze
7 Nathalie Tauziat	7 Justine Henin	7 Anastasia Myskina	7 Patty Schnyder	7 Serena Williams
8 Barbara Schett	8 Jelena Dokic	8 Elena Dementieva	8 Elena Dementieva	8 Venus Williams
9 Julie Halard-Decugis	9 Amelie Mauresmo	9 Chanda Rubin	9 Nadia Petrova	9 Daniela Hantuchova
10 Amelie Mauresmo	10 Monica Seles	10 Ai Sugiyama	10 Venus Williams	10 Marion Bartoli

*Returning to the WTA Tour on Aug. 15, 1995, Seles was co-ranked #1 for her first six tournaments. Seles had been absent from the Tour since April 1993 when she was stabbed by a fan during a match. She was ranked #1 at the time of the stabbing.
†Seles' ranking was revised in May 1996. The revision stipulated that her new modified ranking would be calculated using a divisor of the actual number of tournaments she had played (13), and she would be co-ranked with the player whose average is immediately below her average (Sanchez Vicario).

All-Time Leaders

Tournaments Won (singles)

All-time tournament wins from the arrival of open tennis in 1968 through 2008 (through Sept. 29). Men's totals include ATP Tour, Grand Prix and WCT tournaments. Players active in singles play in 2008 are in **bold** type.

MEN

		Total			Total			Total
1	Jimmy Connors	109	11	Rod Laver	47	21	Tom Okker	31
2	Ivan Lendl	94	12	Thomas Muster	44		**Rafael Nadal**	31
3	John McEnroe	77	13	Stefan Edberg	41	23	Vitas Gerulaitis	27
4	Pete Sampras	64	14	Stan Smith	39	24	Yevgeny Kafelnikov	26
5	Bjorn Borg	62	15	Michael Chang	34		**Lleyton Hewitt**	26
	Guillermo Vilas	62	16	Arthur Ashe	33		**Andy Roddick**	26
6	Andre Agassi	60		Mats Wilander	33	27	Jose-Luis Clerc	25
7	Ilie Nastase	57	18	John Newcombe	32		Brian Gottfried	25
9	**Roger Federer**	56		Manuel Orantes	32	29	Jim Courier	23
10	Boris Becker	49		Ken Rosewall	32		Yannick Noah	23

WOMEN

		Total			Total			Total
1	Martina Navratilova	167	11	**Justine Henin**	41	21	Nancy Richey	25
2	Chris Evert	154	12	**Venus Williams**	37	22	Jana Novotna	24
3	Steffi Graf	107	13	Kim Clijsters	34		**Amelie Mauresmo**	24
4	Margaret Smith Court	92	14	Conchita Martinez	33	24	Kerry Melville Reid	22
5	E. Goolagong Cawley	68	15	**Serena Williams**	32	25	Pam Shriver	21
6	Billie Jean King	67	16	Olga Morozova	31	26	Julie Heldman	20
7	Virginia Wade	55	17	Tracy Austin	30	27	M. Maleeva-Fragniere	19
	Lindsay Davenport	55	18	Arantxa Sanchez-Vicario	29		Nancy Richey	19
9	Monica Seles	53	19	Hana Mandlikova	27		**Maria Sharapova**	19
10	Martina Hingis	43		Gabriela Sabatini	27	30	Mary Pierce	18

Money Won

All-time money winners from the arrival of open tennis in 1968 through 2008 (through Sept. 29). Totals include doubles earnings.

MEN

		Earnings			Earnings			Earnings
1	Pete Sampras	$43,280,489	8	Rafael Nadal	$20,566,948	15	Jim Courier	$14,034,132
2	Roger Federer	43,268,419	9	Goran Ivanisevic	19,876,579	16	Marat Safin	13,797,162
3	Andre Agassi	31,152,975	10	Michael Chang	19,145,632	17	Carlos Moya	13,295,263
4	Boris Becker	25,080,956	11	Lleyton Hewitt	17,629,088	18	Michael Stich	12,592,483
5	Yevgeny Kafelnikov	23,883,797	12	Gustavo Kuerten	14,807,000	19	John McEnroe	12,552,132
6	Ivan Lendl	21,262,417	13	Jonas Bjorkman	14,430,344	20	Thomas Muster	12,225,910
7	Stefan Edberg	20,630,941	14	Andy Roddick	14,424,713			

WOMEN

		Earnings			Earnings			Earnings
1	Lindsay Davenport	$22,144,735	8	A. Sanchez-Vicario	$16,942,640	15	Jennifer Capriati	$10,206,639
2	Steffi Graf	21,895,277	9	Monica Seles	14,891,762	16	Elena Dementieva	10,189,441
3	Serena Williams	21,750,782	10	Kim Clijsters	14,764,296	17	Mary Pierce	9,793,119
4	Mart. Navratilova	21,626,089	11	Amelie Mauresmo	14,143,445	18	Svetlana Kuznetsova	9,685,183
5	Venus Williams	20,445,911	12	Maria Sharapova	12,169,281	19	Chris Evert	8,896,195
6	Martina Hingis	20,130,657	13	Conchita Martinez	11,527,977	20	Gabriela Sabatini	8,785,850
7	Justine Henin	19,461,375	14	Jana Novotna	11,249,284			

Year-end Tournaments

MEN

Tennis Masters Cup

The year-end championship featuring the top eight players in the Tennis Masters Series rankings. Originally called the Masters in 1970, the tournament followed a round-robin format, but was revised in 1972 to include a round-robin to decide the four semifinalists when a single elimination format after that. Replaced by ATP Tour World Championship from 1990 through 1999.

Multiple Winners: Ivan Lendl and Pete Sampras (5); Roger Federer and Ilie Nastase (4); Boris Becker and John McEnroe (3); Bjorn Borg and Lleyton Hewitt (2).

Year	Winner	Runner-Up
1970	Stan Smith (4-1) *	Rod Laver (4-1)
1971	Ilie Nastase (6-0)	Stan Smith (4-2)

Year	Winner	Loser	Score
1972	Ilie Nastase	S. Smith	63 62 36 26 63
1973	Ilie Nastase	T. Okker	63 75 46 63
1974	Guillermo Vilas	I. Nastase	76 62 36 36 64
1975	Ilie Nastase	B. Borg	62 62 61
1976	Manuel Orantes	W. Fibak	57 62 06 76 61
1978	Jimmy Connors	B. Borg	64 16 64
1979	John McEnroe	A. Ashe	67 63 75
1980	Bjorn Borg	V. Gerulaitis	62 62
1981	Bjorn Borg	I. Lendl	64 62 62
1982	Ivan Lendl	V. Gerulaitis	67 26 76 62 64
1983	Ivan Lendl	J. McEnroe	64 64 62
1984	John McEnroe	I. Lendl	63 64 64
1985	John McEnroe	I. Lendl	75 60 64
1986	Ivan Lendl	B. Becker	62 76 63
1986	Ivan Lendl	B. Becker	64 64 64
1987	Ivan Lendl	M. Wilander	62 62 63
1988	Boris Becker	I. Lendl	57 76 36 62 76

Year	Winner	Loser	Score
1989	Stefan Edberg	B. Becker	46 76 63 61
1990	Andre Agassi	S. Edberg	57 76 75 62
1991	Pete Sampras	J. Courier	36 76 63 64
1992	Boris Becker	J. Courier	64 63 75
1993	Michael Stich	P. Sampras	76 26 76 62
1994	Pete Sampras	B. Becker	46 63 75 64
1995	Boris Becker	M. Chang	76 60 76
1996	Pete Sampras	B. Becker	36 76 76 67 64
1997	Pete Sampras	Y. Kafelnikov	63 62 62
1998	Alex Corretja	C. Moya	36 36 75 63 75
1999	Pete Sampras	A. Agassi	61 75 64
2000	Gustavo Kuerten	A. Agassi	64 64 64
2001	Lleyton Hewitt	S. Grosjean	63 63 64
2002	Lleyton Hewitt	J.C. Ferrero	75 75 26 26 64
2003	Roger Federer	A. Agassi	63 60 64
2004	Roger Federer	L. Hewitt	63 62 (rain)
2005	David Nalbandian	R. Federer	67 67 62 61 76
2006	Roger Federer	J. Blake	60 63 64
2007	Roger Federer	D. Ferrer	62 63 62

*Smith was declared the winner because he beat Laver in their round-robin match (4-6, 6-3, 6-4).
Note: The tournament switched from December to January in 1977-78, then back to December in 1986.

WCT Championship (1971-89)

World Championship Tennis was established in 1967 to promote professional tennis and led the way into the open era. Its major singles and doubles championships were held every May among the top eight regular season finishers on the circuit from 1971 until the WCT folded in 1989.

Multiple winners: John McEnroe (5), Jimmy Connors, Ivan Lendl and Ken Rosewall (2).

Year	Winner	Loser	Score
1971	Ken Rosewall	R. Laver	64 16 76 76
1972	Ken Rosewall	R. Laver	46 60 63 67 76
1973	Stan Smith	A. Ashe	63 63 46 64
1974	John Newcombe	B. Borg	46 63 63 62
1975	Arthur Ashe	B. Borg	36 64 64 60
1976	Bjorn Borg	G. Vilas	16 61 75 61
1977	Jimmy Connors	D. Stockton	67 61 64 63
1978	Vitas Gerulaitis	E. Dibbs	60 63 63
1979	John McEnroe	B. Borg	75 46 62 76
1980	Jimmy Connors	J. McEnroe	26 76 61 62

Year	Winner	Loser	Score
1981	John McEnroe	J. Kriek	61 62 64
1982	Ivan Lendl	J. McEnroe	62 36 63 63
1983	John McEnroe	I. Lendl	62 46 63 67 76
1984	John McEnroe	J. Connors	61 62 63
1985	Ivan Lendl	T. Mayotte	76 64 61
1986	Anders Jarryd	B. Becker	67 61 61 64
1987	Miloslav Mecir	J. McEnroe	60 36 62 62
1988	Boris Becker	S. Edberg	64 16 75 62
1989	John McEnroe	B. Gilbert	63 63 76

Year-end Tournaments (Cont.)
WOMEN
WTA Championships

The WTA Tour's year-end tournament took place in March from 1972 until 1986 when the WTA decided to adopt a January-to-November playing season. Given the changeover, two championships were held in 1986. Held in Boca Raton (1972-73), Los Angeles (1974-76, 2002-05), New York (1977, 1979-2000), Oakland (1978), Munich (2001), Madrid (2006-07).

Multiple winners: Martina Navratilova (8); Steffi Graf (5); Chris Evert (4); Monica Seles (3); Kim Clijsters, Evonne Goolagong, Martina Hingis, Justine Henin and Gabriela Sabatini (2).

Year	Winner	Loser	Score	Year	Winner	Loser	Score
1972	Chris Evert	K. Reid	75 64	1990	Monica Seles	G. Sabatini	64 57 36 64 62
1973	Chris Evert	N. Richey	63 63	1991	Monica Seles	M. Navratilova	64 36 75 60
1974	Evonne Goolagong	C. Evert	63 64	1992	Monica Seles	M. Navratilova	75 63 61
1975	Chris Evert	M. Navratilova	64 62	1993	Steffi Graf	A. S. Vicario	61 64 36 61
1976	Evonne Goolagong	C. Evert	63 57 63	1994	Gabriela Sabatini	L. Davenport	63 62 64
1977	Chris Evert	S. Barker	26 61 61	1995	Steffi Graf	A. Huber	61 26 61 46 63
1978	M. Navratilova	E. Goolagong	76 64	1996	Steffi Graf	M. Hingis	63 46 60 46 60
1979	M. Navratilova	T. Austin	63 36 62	1997	Jana Novotna	M. Pierce	76 62 63
1980	Tracy Austin	M. Navratilova	62 26 62	1998	Martina Hingis	L. Davenport	75 64 46 62
1981	M. Navratilova	A. Jaeger	63 76	1999	Lindsay Davenport	M. Hingis	64 62
1982	Sylvia Hanika	M. Navratilova	16 63 64	2000	Martina Hingis	M. Seles	67 64 64
1983	M. Navratilova	C. Evert	62 60	2001	Serena Williams	L. Davenport	walkover
1984	M. Navratilova	C. Evert	63 75 61	2002	Kim Clijsters	S. Williams	75 63
1985	M. Navratilova	H. Sukova	63 75 64	2003	Kim Clijsters	A. Mauresmo	62 60
1986	M. Navratilova	H. Mandlikova	62 60 36 61	2004	Maria Sharapova	S. Williams	46 62 64
1986	M. Navratilova	S. Graf	76 63 62	2005	Amelie Mauresmo	M. Pierce	57 76 64
1987	Steffi Graf	G. Sabatini	46 64 60 64	2006	J. Henin-Hardenne	A. Mauresmo	64 63
1988	Gabriela Sabatini	P. Shriver	75 62 62	2007	Justine Henin	M. Sharapova	57 75 63
1989	Steffi Graf	M. Navratilova	64 75 26 62				

Note: The final was best-of-five sets from 1984-98 and best-of-three sets from 1972-83 and since 1999.

National Team Tournaments
Davis Cup

Established in 1900 as an annual international tournament by American player Dwight Davis. Originally called the International Lawn Tennis Challenge Trophy. Challenge round system until 1972. Since 1981, the top 16 nations in the world have played a straight knockout tournament over the course of a year. The format is a best-of-five match of two singles, one doubles and two singles over three days. Note that from 1900-24 Australia and New Zealand competed together as Australasia.

Multiple winners: USA (32); Australia (22); France (9); Sweden (7); Australasia (6); British Isles (5); Britain (4); Germany (3); Russia and Spain (2).

Challenge Rounds

Year	Winner	Loser	Score	Site	Year	Winner	Loser	Score	Site
1900	USA	British Isles	3-0	Boston	1931	France	Britain	3-2	Paris
1901	Not held				1932	France	USA	3-2	Paris
1902	USA	British Isles	3-2	New York	1933	Britain	France	3-2	Paris
1903	British Isles	USA	4-1	Boston	1934	Britain	USA	4-1	Wimbledon
1904	British Isles	Belgium	5-0	Wimbledon	1935	Britain	USA	5-0	Wimbledon
1905	British Isles	USA	5-0	Wimbledon	1936	Britain	Australia	3-2	Wimbledon
1906	British Isles	USA	5-0	Wimbledon	1937	USA	Britain	4-1	Wimbledon
1907	Australasia	British Isles	3-2	Wimbledon	1938	USA	Australia	3-2	Philadelphia
1908	Australasia	USA	3-2	Melbourne	1939	Australia	USA	3-2	Philadelphia
1909	Australasia	USA	5-0	Sydney	1940-45	Not held World War II			
1910	Not held				1946	USA	Australia	5-0	Melbourne
1911	Australasia	USA	5-0	Christchurch, NZ	1947	USA	Australia	4-1	New York
1912	British Isles	Australasia	3-2	Melbourne	1948	USA	Australia	5-0	New York
1913	USA	British Isles	3-2	Wimbledon	1949	USA	Australia	4-1	New York
1914	Australasia	USA	3-2	New York	1950	Australia	USA	4-1	New York
1915-18	Not held World War I				1951	Australia	USA	3-2	Sydney
1919	Australasia	British Isles	4-1	Sydney	1952	Australia	USA	4-1	Adelaide
1920	USA	Australasia	5-0	Auckland, NZ	1953	Australia	USA	3-2	Melbourne
1921	USA	Japan	5-0	New York	1954	USA	Australia	3-2	Sydney
1922	USA	Australasia	4-1	New York	1955	Australia	USA	5-0	New York
1923	USA	Australasia	4-1	New York	1956	Australia	USA	5-0	Adelaide
1924	USA	Australia	5-0	Philadelphia	1957	Australia	USA	3-2	Melbourne
1925	USA	France	5-0	Philadelphia	1958	USA	Australia	3-2	Brisbane
1926	USA	France	4-1	Philadelphia	1959	Australia	USA	3-2	New York
1927	France	USA	3-2	Philadelphia	1960	Australia	Italy	4-1	Sydney
1928	France	USA	4-1	Paris	1961	Australia	Italy	5-0	Melbourne
1929	France	USA	3-2	Paris	1962	Australia	Mexico	5-0	Brisbane
1930	France	USA	4-1	Paris	1963	USA	Australia	3-2	Adelaide

Year	Winner	Loser	Score	Site	Year	Winner	Loser	Score	Site
1964	Australia	USA	3-2	Cleveland	1966	Australia	India	4-1	Melbourne
1965	Australia	Spain	4-1	Sydney	1967	Australia	Spain	4-1	Brisbane

Final Rounds

Year	Winner	Loser	Score	Site	Year	Winner	Loser	Score	Site
1968	USA	Australia	4-1	Adelaide	1988	W. Germany	Sweden	4-1	Göteborg
1969	USA	Romania	5-0	Cleveland	1989	W. Germany	Sweden	3-2	Stuttgart
1970	USA	W. Germany	5-0	Cleveland	1990	USA	Australia	3-2	St. Petersburg
1971	USA	Romania	3-2	Charlotte	1991	France	USA	3-1	Lyon
1972	USA	Romania	3-2	Bucharest	1992	USA	Switzerland	3-1	Ft. Worth
1973	Australia	USA	5-0	Cleveland	1993	Germany	Australia	4-1	Dusseldorf
1974	So. Africa	India	walkover	Not held	1994	Sweden	Russia	4-1	Moscow
1975	Sweden	Czech.	3-2	Stockholm	1995	USA	Russia	3-2	Moscow
1976	Italy	Chile	4-1	Santiago	1996	France	Sweden	3-2	Malmo
1977	Australia	Italy	3-1	Sydney	1997	Sweden	USA	5-0	Göteborg
1978	USA	Britain	4-1	Palm Springs	1998	Sweden	Italy	4-1	Milan
1979	USA	Italy	5-0	San Francisco	1999	Australia	France	3-2	Nice
1980	Czech.	Italy	4-1	Prague	2000	Spain	Australia	3-1	Barcelona
1981	USA	Argentina	3-1	Cincinnati	2001	France	Australia	3-2	Melbourne
1982	USA	France	4-1	Grenoble	2002	Russia	France	3-2	Paris
1983	Australia	Sweden	3-2	Melbourne	2003	Australia	Spain	3-1	Melbourne
1984	Sweden	USA	4-1	Göteborg	2004	Spain	USA	3-2	Seville
1985	Sweden	W. Germany	3-2	Munich	2005	Croatia	Slovakia	3-2	Bratislava
1986	Australia	Sweden	3-2	Melbourne	2006	Russia	Argentina	3-2	Moscow
1987	Sweden	India	5-0	Göteborg	2007	USA	Russia	4-1	Portland, Ore.

Note: In 1974, India refused to play the final as a protest against the South African government's policies of apartheid.

Fed Cup

Originally the Federation Cup started by the International Tennis Federation as the Davis Cup of women's tennis. Played by 32 teams over one week at one site from 1963-94. Tournament changed to Davis Cup-style format of four rounds and home site in 1995. Currently 16 teams compete in a knockout format, with winners advancing to the quarterfinals, semifinals and finals.

Multiple winners: USA (17); Australia (7); Czechoslovakia and Spain (5); Russia (4); France and Germany (2).

Year	Winner	Loser	Score	Site	Year	Winner	Loser	Score	Site
1963	USA	Australia	2-1	London	1986	USA	Czech.	3-0	Prague
1964	Australia	USA	2-1	Philadelphia	1987	W. Germany	USA	2-1	Vancouver
1965	Australia	USA	2-1	Melbourne	1988	Czech.	USSR	2-1	Melbourne
1966	USA	W. Germany	3-0	Italy	1989	USA	Spain	3-0	Tokyo
1967	USA	Britain	2-0	W. Germany	1990	USA	USSR	2-1	Atlanta
1968	Australia	Holland	3-0	Paris	1991	Spain	USA	2-1	Nottingham
1969	USA	Australia	2-1	Athens	1992	Germany	Spain	2-1	Frankfurt
1970	Australia	Britain	3-0	W. Germany	1993	Spain	Australia	3-0	Frankfurt
1971	Australia	Britain	3-0	Perth	1994	Spain	USA	3-0	Frankfurt
1972	So. Africa	Britain	2-1	So. Africa	1995	Spain	USA	3-2	Valencia
1973	Australia	So. Africa	3-0	W. Germany	1996	USA	Spain	5-0	Atlantic City
1974	Australia	USA	2-1	Italy	1997	France	Netherlands	4-1	Netherlands
1975	Czech.	Australia	3-0	France	1998	Spain	Switzerland	3-2	Geneva
1976	USA	Australia	2-1	Philadelphia	1999	USA	Russia	4-1	Palo Alto
1977	USA	Australia	2-1	Eastbourne	2000	USA	Spain	5-0	Las Vegas
1978	USA	Australia	2-1	Melbourne	2001	Belgium	Russia	2-1	Madrid
1979	USA	Australia	3-0	Spain	2002	Slovakia	Spain	3-1	Canary Islands
1980	USA	Australia	3-0	W. Germany	2003	France	USA	4-1	Moscow
1981	USA	Britain	3-0	Tokyo	2004	Russia	France	3-2	Moscow
1982	USA	W. Germany	3-0	Santa Clara	2005	Russia	France	3-2	Paris
1983	Czech.	W. Germany	2-1	Zurich	2006	Italy	Belgium	3-2	Charleroi
1984	Czech.	Australia	2-1	Brazil	2007	Russia	Italy	4-0	Moscow
1985	Czech.	USA	2-1	Japan	2008	Russia	Spain	4-0	Madrid

COLLEGES

NCAA team titles were not sanctioned until 1946. NCAA women's individual and team championships started in 1982.

Men's NCAA Individual Champions (1883-1945)

Multiple winners: Malcolm Chace and Pancho Segura (3); Edward Chandler, George Church, E.B. Dewhurst, Fred Hovey, Frank Guernsey, W.P. Knapp, Robert LeRoy, P.S. Sears, Cliff Sutter, Ernest Sutter and Richard Williams (2).

Year		Year		Year	
1883	J. Clark, Harvard (spring)	1889	R.P. Huntington Jr., Yale	1896	Malcolm Whitman, Harvard
	H. Taylor, Harvard (fall)	1890	Fred Hovey, Harvard	1897	S.G. Thompson, Princeton
1884	W.P. Knapp, Yale	1891	Fred Hovey, Harvard	1898	Leo Ware, Harvard
1885	W.P. Knapp, Yale	1892	William Larned, Cornell	1899	Dwight Davis, Harvard
1886	G.M. Brinley, Trinity, CT	1893	Malcolm Chace, Brown	1900	Ray Little, Princeton
1887	P.S. Sears, Harvard	1894	Malcolm Chace, Yale	1901	Fred Alexander, Princeton
1888	P.S. Sears, Harvard	1895	Malcolm Chace, Yale	1902	William Clothier, Harvard

Colleges (Cont.)

Year		Year		Year	
1903	E.B. Dewhurst, Penn	1917-1918	Not held	1932	Cliff Sutter, Tulane
1904	Robert LeRoy, Columbia	1919	Charles Garland, Yale	1933	Jack Tidball, UCLA
1905	E.B. Dewhurst, Penn	1920	Lascelles Banks, Yale	1934	Gene Mako, USC
1906	Robert LeRoy, Columbia	1921	Philip Neer, Stanford	1935	Wilbur Hess, Rice
1907	G.P. Gardner Jr., Harvard	1922	Lucien Williams, Yale	1936	Ernest Sutter, Tulane
1908	Nat Niles, Harvard	1923	Carl Fischer, Phi. Osteo.	1937	Ernest Sutter, Tulane
1909	Wallace Johnson, Penn	1924	Wallace Scott, Wash.	1938	Frank Guernsey, Rice
1910	R.A. Holden Jr., Yale	1925	Edward Chandler, Calif.	1939	Frank Guernsey, Rice
1911	E.H. Whitney, Harvard	1926	Edward Chandler, Calif.	1940	Don McNeill, Kenyon
1912	George Church, Princeton	1927	Wilmer Allison, Texas	1941	Joseph Hunt, Navy
1913	Richard Williams, Harv.	1928	Julius Seligson, Lehigh	1942	Ted Schroeder, Stanford
1914	George Church, Princeton	1929	Berkeley Bell, Texas	1943	Pancho Segura, Miami-FL
1915	Richard Williams, Harv.	1930	Cliff Sutter, Tulane	1944	Pancho Segura, Miami-FL
1916	G.C. Caner, Harvard	1931	Keith Gledhill, Stanford	1945	Pancho Segura, Miami-FL

NCAA Men's Division I Champions

Multiple winners (Teams): Stanford (17); UCLA and USC (16); Georgia (6); William & Mary (2). (Players): Matias Boeker, Somdev Devvarman, Alex Olmedo, Mikael Pernfors, Dennis Ralston and Ham Richardson (2).

Year	Team winner	Individual Champion	Year	Team winner	Individual Champion
1946	USC	Bob Falkenburg, USC	1978	Stanford	John McEnroe, Stanford
1947	Wm. & Mary	Gardner Larned, Wm.& Mary	1979	UCLA	Kevin Curren, Texas
1948	Wm. & Mary	Harry Likas, San Francisco	1980	Stanford	Robert Van't Hof, USC
1949	San Francisco	Jack Tuero, Tulane	1981	Stanford	Tim Mayotte, Stanford
1950	UCLA	Herbert Flam, UCLA	1982	UCLA	Mike Leach, Michigan
1951	USC	Tony Trabert, Cincinnati	1983	Stanford	Greg Holmes, Utah
1952	UCLA	Hugh Stewart, USC	1984	UCLA	Mikael Pernfors, Georgia
1953	UCLA	Ham Richardson, Tulane	1985	Georgia	Mikael Pernfors, Georgia
1954	UCLA	Ham Richardson, Tulane	1986	Stanford	Dan Goldie, Stanford
1955	USC	Jose Aguero, Tulane	1987	Georgia	Andrew Burrow, Miami-FL
1956	UCLA	Alex Olmedo, USC	1988	Stanford	Robby Weiss, Pepperdine
1957	Michigan	Barry MacKay, Michigan	1989	Stanford	Donni Leaycraft, LSU
1958	USC	Alex Olmedo, USC	1990	Stanford	Steve Bryan, Texas
1959	Tulane & Notre Dame	Whitney Reed, San Jose St.	1991	USC	Jared Palmer, Stanford
1960	UCLA	Larry Nagler, UCLA	1992	USC	Alex O'Brien Stanford
1961	UCLA	Allen Fox, UCLA	1993	USC	Chris Woodruff, Tennessee
1962	USC	Rafael Osuna, USC	1994	USC	Mark Merklein, Florida
1963	USC	Dennis Ralston, USC	1995	Stanford	Sargis Sargsian, Ariz. St.
1964	USC	Dennis Ralston, USC	1996	Stanford	Cecil Mamiit, USC
1965	UCLA	Arthur Ashe, UCLA	1997	Stanford	Luke Smith, UNLV
1966	USC	Charlie Pasarell, UCLA	1998	Stanford	Bob Bryan, Stanford
1967	USC	Bob Lutz, USC	1999	Georgia	Jeff Morrison, Florida
1968	USC	Stan Smith, USC	2000	Stanford	Alex Kim, Stanford
1969	USC	Joaquin Loyo-Mayo, USC	2001	Georgia	Matias Boeker, Georgia
1970	UCLA	Jeff Borowiak, UCLA	2002	USC	Matias Boeker, Georgia
1971	UCLA	Jimmy Connors, UCLA	2003	Illinois	Amer Delic, Illinois
1972	Trinity-TX	Dick Stockton, Trinity-TX	2004	Baylor	Benjamin Becker, Baylor
1973	Stanford	Alex Mayer, Stanford	2005	UCLA	Benedikt Dorsch, Baylor
1974	Stanford	John Whitlinger, Stanford	2006	Pepperdine	Benjamin Kohlleoffel, UCLA
1975	UCLA	Bill Martin, UCLA	2007	Georgia	Somdev Devvarman, Virginia
1976	USC & UCLA	Bill Scanlon, Trinity-TX	2008	Georgia	Somdev Devvarman, Virginia
1977	Stanford	Matt Mitchell, Stanford			

NCAA Women's Division I Champions

Multiple winners (Teams): Stanford (15); Florida (4); Georgia, Texas and USC (2). (Players): Sandra Birch, Patty Fendick, Laura Granville, Amber Liu and Lisa Raymond (2).

Year	Team winner	Individual Champion	Year	Team winner	Individual Champion
1982	Stanford	Alycia Moulton, Stanford	1996	Florida	Jill Craybas, Florida
1983	USC	Beth Herr, USC	1997	Stanford	Lilia Osterloh, Stanford
1984	Stanford	Lisa Spain, Georgia	1998	Florida	Vanessa Webb, Duke
1985	USC	Linda Gates, Stanford	1999	Stanford	Zuzana Lesenarova, S. Diego
1986	Stanford	Patty Fendick, Stanford	2000	Georgia	Laura Granville, Stanford
1987	Stanford	Patty Fendick, Stanford	2001	Stanford	Laura Granville, Stanford
1988	Stanford	Shaun Stafford, Florida	2002	Stanford	Bea Bielik, Wake Forest
1989	Stanford	Sandra Birch, Stanford	2003	Florida	Amber Liu, Stanford
1990	Stanford	Debbie Graham, Stanford	2004	Stanford	Amber Liu, Stanford
1991	Stanford	Sandra Birch, Stanford	2005	Stanford	Zuzana Zemenova, Baylor
1992	Florida	Lisa Raymond, Florida	2006	Stanford	Suzi Babos, California
1993	Texas	Lisa Raymond, Florida	2007	Georgia Tech	Audra Cohen, Miami-FL
1994	Georgia	Angela Lettiere, Georgia	2008	UCLA	Amanda McDowell, Ga. Tech
1995	Texas	Keri Phoebus, UCLA			

GOLF

2007 / 2008 YEAR IN REVIEW

Padraig Harrington held the Claret Jug for the second straight year after successfully defending his British Open title. He would later add another major win at the PGA Championship.

TORREY STORY:

Tiger Woods' win was the greatest U.S. Open ever.

by
Pat Forde

LET'S START BY THANKING THE SCOTS.

If they hadn't come up with the odd idea of smacking rocks with sticks more than 500 years ago, we wouldn't have golf. And if we didn't have golf, Tiger Woods probably would have become something other than the greatest athlete on the planet. And if we didn't have Woods and his special Torrey Pines guest star, Rocco Mediate, we would not have had the greatest U.S. Open ever.

And arguably the greatest golf tournament ever.

It finally ended Monday afternoon, when Mediate at last submitted to the unbreakable will of Woods. It took five rounds plus a sixth tour of the seventh hole. When Mediate pushed his par putt past the cup, we were 91 and done.

But the memories of this Torrey story will remain for decades to come. Someday, it will be talked about the way misty-eyed historians recall the 1950 and 1960 U.S. Opens, or the '86 Masters.

They'll talk about the staggering upset Mediate almost perpetrated in his bid to become the oldest Open champion. They'll talk about the back-nine drama that saw Woods go from 3 up to 1 down to all square against a 45-year-old chatterbox with a bad back who wouldn't go away. They'll talk about the successive layers of tension that just kept building as the tournament just kept going.

Ultimately, they'll talk about the tourney Tiger won on one leg. How he defied doctors' orders to drag himself through four painful days on an injured left knee, then endured 19

 Pat Forde is a senior writer for ESPN.com

Rocco Mediate, left, jokes with **Tiger Woods** following Woods' thrilling, sudden-death victory at the U.S. Open at Torrey Pines.

extra holes Monday to finish the thing off. How he had to make do-or-die birdie putts on the 18th hole on successive days, with defeat staring him in the eyes. How he had two eagles and a chip-in birdie in one celestial six-hole stretch Saturday, something that just isn't done in a U.S. Open. How he nearly drained his bottomless reservoirs of mental and physical toughness to earn his 14th major title.

"I think this is probably the best ever," Woods said. "All things considered, I don't know how I ended up in this position, to be honest with you."

Then they'll talk about the lovable loser, too. They'll talk about how Mediate went from being a guy most people wouldn't recognize in the aisles at Target to a guy who had fans whistling the theme to "Rocky" as he walked the 15th fairway.

How the galleries started the day cheering more for Tiger but ended it cheering more for "Roc-co!"

How Mediate had the cheek to show up for the playoff wearing Tiger colors — red and black — and the pluck to come back from a 3-stroke deficit with eight holes to play.

"It was an honor being out there,"

Mediate said. "And I'm sure that I scared him. I did good today.

"I *just* about got him."

The golf world is full of guys who *just* about got Tiger. Nobody has gotten him once he has taken the lead in a major into Sunday — but Mediate has now come closest.

Bob May pushed Tiger to the brink in the PGA at Valhalla in 2000, forcing Woods to make a birdie on the 72nd hole. Mediate did it *twice*, pushing Tiger to the wall before he responded with birdies putts of 12 feet on the 72nd hole and four feet on the 90th.

"It wasn't a walk in the park," Mediate said. "I didn't want it to be a walk in the park. It could have been.

"He's got me by 14 years. He's got me by a thousand yards off the tee. And I kept hanging in there, hanging in there, hanging in there.

"When he needed that drive on 18 to go about 340, he got it. ... It's like I told Matt [Achatz, his caddie], 'This guy is impossible.'"

Before the round started, the impossible dream seemed to be a riveting playoff. Woods is 10-1 lifetime in playoffs and as predictably overpowering as the waves that crash unremittingly on the shore below the cliffs here.

On paper, this looked like an anticlimax, a slow-motion rout.

That's one reason why the Open's traditional 18-hole Monday playoff was ridiculed by some. It was called an anachronism by the microwave society that demands resolution of all issues much more quickly. Better, they said, to have a sudden-death playoff like the Masters or a four-hole aggregate playoff like the British Open and the PGA.

But this was the perfect way to spend a June Monday.

On a dreamy California morning, the fans were treated to one more day of brilliant theater by a pair of divergent but complementary personalities.

If you sat next to Mediate on a flight from San Diego to New York, you'd probably know his life story by the time you were over Omaha, Neb. He'd be doing card tricks, telling jokes, showing you pictures from his vacation.

If you sat next to Woods on a flight — well, forget it. He'd be on his private jet.

The thinking going into Monday

Which is the greatest major victory of Tiger Woods' career?

43.8% — *2008 U.S. Open*
36.1% — *1997 Masters*
14.3% — *2000 U.S. Open*
4.2% — *2006 British Open*
1.7% — *Other*

How impressive was Woods' showing given his bothersome knee?

57.1% — *Legendary; put this in the same company as Michael Jordan (flu), Kirk Gibson (hamstring), etc.*
35.5% — *Impressive; it shows Woods can play through pain*
7.4% — *Overblown; the media made more out of it than it deserved*

When Woods was four shots out of the lead after the opening round, did you believe he would win?

76.1% — *Yes*
23.9% — *No*

Total Votes: 85,232

Rank 'Em: Playing Through Pain

Rank		Points
1	Tiger at U.S. Open	132,966
2	Michael Jordan, flu in Finals	122,717
3	Kirk Gibson, '88 series	120,235
4	Keri Strug, gymnastics gold	111,890
5	Jack Youngblood, broken leg	102,764
6	Willis Reed, finals comeback	98,092
7	Steve Yzerman, '02 finals knee	95,625
8	Emmitt Smith, '94 sep. shoulder	93,457
9	Pete Sampras, U.S. Open flu	71,846
10	Terrell Owens, ankle SB 39	69,104

Total Votes: 19,061

was that Mediate's only chance to win this playoff was to yap Tiger to death. Talk from the first tee to the 18th green. Jabber his way into Woods' head and try to crack that formidable focus shield.

But the two are friends, and Mediate respected Tiger's need for alone time on the course. They talked some, but not much. If Rocco felt the need to converse, he talked to Achatz.

As it turned out, Mediate didn't need any psych jobs to stay in this duel. He just needed to weather some nerves, make some putts and wait for Woods to give him a chance.

With Woods at even par and Mediate 3 over after 10, that chance looked as if it would never come. But then The Closer surprisingly bogeyed Nos. 11 and 12, and Mediate even more surprisingly birdied Nos. 13, 14 and 15 to take the lead.

After matching pars on 16 and 17, it was high noon in the Torrey Pines corral. Again.

We'd all sell an organ to be inside Tiger Woods' skin at a time like that — when the stakes are highest and you somehow perform at your best. That was Woods on the par-5 18th tee, where he crushed a drive that split the fairway and gave him a perfect shot at the green in two.

"It's pressure, there's no doubt," Woods said. "I was nervous, and that's a good thing. That means you care. You can try and use that energy as best you can to heighten your focus."

Focus fully heightened, Woods fired a 4-iron more than 200 yards over the pond and onto the green. His eagle putt rolled four feet past, then he buried that for birdie.

Unlike the explosive response after the birdie at 18 on Sunday, Woods left the fist pumping to caddie Steve Williams and instead merely lifted his cap to acknowledge the roar.

One hole later, Mediate finally cracked. His bogey at No. 7 ended the marathon test. As a golf cart took him to the trophy presentation at the 18th hole, grateful fans spilled into the seventh fairway to cheer the vanquished.

"This was probably the best week of his life," said Mediate's teary-eyed college roommate, Steve Puertas.

It wasn't far behind that for Woods, who turned painful perseverance into an art form.

"You keep playing," Woods said. "Whatever it is, you just keep going, keep going forward.

All my buddies and I used to, when we were working out, used to always say 'Four.' How many more reps do you have? Four. Four-ever. And that's the idea. You just keep going, and there's no finish line, and you just keep pushing and pushing."

He kept pushing until the tourney was won, and now the apotheosis of Tiger Woods is complete. He somehow has managed to top himself, with the assistance of Mediate, in the greatest U.S. Open ever.

LIFE OF REILLY

**There's going to be a miracle in Louisville.
I guarantee it.**

by
Rick Reilly

Prediction columns are like Velveeta recipes — too easy and too cheesy. But what's going to happen in Louisville at the Ryder Cup starting Friday will go down as the greatest shocker since Lyle Lovett married Julia Roberts, so here goes:

The Americans, playing without Tiger Woods, hopelessly out-manned, with their worst on-paper team since Europe was added to the mix, will pull the Cupset of the Century. They'll need 14½ points to win, which is weird, because that's exactly how many reasons there are that they will.

1. For the first time in 12 years, Tiger's out. This will work for the

Yanks! Tiger doesn't like this thing. Can you blame him? Does the executioner play on the prison softball team? No. So that Tiger buzzkill is gone. American players are free to care about it, hard.

Plus, without Tiger, they're *The Little Team That Could*. Best of all, the Euros, who usually go bat-guano-crazy whenever they beat Tiger, have no Goliath to slay. Buzzkill back at you.

2. Europe captain Nick Faldo screwed the pooch by not picking Colin Montgomerie. It doesn't matter how bad Monty's playing,

Note: This column originally ran on ESPN.com on Sept. 16 — three days before the start of the 2008 Ryder Cup.

Rick Reilly is a columnist for ESPN.com and *ESPN The Magazine*. He has been voted Sportswriter of the Year 11 times.

Well, Reilly called it. The plucky **U.S. team**, playing without the injured Tiger Woods, took it to the Europeans at the Ryder Cup in September.

AP Images

when he comes to the Ryder Cup, he becomes Jack Nicklaus on beta blockers. He makes everything. This is a mistake the size of New Coke.

3. There is a man on the Euro team named Oliver Wilson. It was unclear at press time whether Wilson was a member of Parliament or the team haberdasher. It may have been a misprint. He is the first Euro to make the team without ever winning a pro tournament. Perhaps he is Faldo's butler.

4. Word is USA captain Paul Azinger is setting up Valhalla like

a $19 muni, so the Euros' fancy punches and miracle gunch shots won't help. It'll be: bomb the driver, float the wedge, bury the putt. Hell, J.B. Holmes may even skip the wedge part. This USA team is longer than Tolstoy.

5. Euros like hard courses and nasty weather. Louisville forecast: sunny, 80 degrees, fairways as open as new 7-Elevens.

6. Faldo, a great announcer, was icy as a player and he'll be icy as a coach. He usually eats dinner in his room, where — no joke — he'll practice his drops. No Euro will fall on a grenade to win for him. I'm not sure they'd fall on a pillow mint.

Bonus Half Point Reason: More about Faldo the Fridge. He's such a loner he only has one assistant coach. Zinger has three. So when those morning matches end and Faldo's got 20 mad minutes to figure out who's hot, who's not, who wants to play again right away, who needs a blow and who needs a new partner, he'll need information. He'll need a pair of smart eyes on all four matches. Can't do it with only two sets. Duh.

7. Every Ryder Cup mints a new star. This time it will be Anthony Kim, a bad ass and a huge talent who's too young to know how big this is. He's about to get very rich.

8. There's a grittiness to this team I haven't seen since the Corey Pavin teams in the early '90s. Holmes is tougher than a Costco steak. He went iris-to-iris with Tiger for most of the Accenture Match Play. Justin Leonard is the Hero of Brookline — the last American win, back in 1999 — and still has glorious bloodstains on him. Steve Stricker won the

AP Images

European assistant captain **Jose Maria Olazabal**, left, and team captain **Nick Faldo** were left scratching their heads after their loss to the Americans at the Ryder Cup.

Accenture, which is about as close to a Ryder Cup Starter Kit as you can get. Jim Furyk and Stewart Cink have steel sacks. And Boo Weekley once said, "It isn't that I don't give a s***, I just don't give a s*** about golf." You think he'll be scared?

9. Zinger has a new strategy. He doesn't give a deceased rodent how comfy the team-room couches are. Last time out, Tom Lehman gave the players the best experience ever and still got fricasseed. "I don't want them happy and comfortable," Zinger says. "I want them nervous and a little tense from the start. Because otherwise, when you get to that first tee Friday morning, you're gonna be shocked at the pressure." Smart.

> "NO EURO IS GOING TO FALL ON A GRENADE TO WIN FOR NICK FALDO. I'M NOT SURE THEY'D FALL ON A PILLOW MINT."

10. Silence is intimidating. Well, Chad Campbell is quieter than a one-man funeral. Ben Curtis doesn't say 10 words in a round. Furyk and Cink can make you think your hearing has gone. You need to lean in to hear Stricker. This squad would make excellent mimes...

11. ...Except for Weekley. Finally, America has somebody who can say how a lot of people feel about Europe and lettuce sandwiches and $9 cups of Starbucks. The Alligator Hunter once came to the British Open and, when asked about the food, declared he didn't like it one bit. Why? "Ain't got no sweet tea and ain't got no fried chicken." Team spokesman!

12. The USA has six rookies who don't know the Euros usually whip the Americans like Rachael Ray whips eggs. They don't know about losing five of the last six, two of 'em Little Bighorns. Ignorance is bliss.

13. Faldo violated the time-honored *Too Many Swedes* theory. Swedes are the sweetest people on earth. Wouldn't hurt a kipper. No Swede has ever won a major. Faldo's got two on his team.

14. Azinger has always had Faldo's number. In four matches over three Ryder Cups, Faldo never got better than a tie against him. He won't even get that this time.

That's my prediction. If I'm wrong, I'll tongue bathe Windsor Castle.

2007-2008 Season In Review

ESPN SPORTS ALMANAC

Tournament Results

Schedules and results of PGA, LPGA, Champions and European PGA tournaments from Nov. 4, 2007 through Oct. 19, 2008.

PGA Tour
Late 2007

Last Rd	Tournament	Winner	Earnings	Runner-Up
Nov. 4	Children's Miracle Network Classic . . .	Stephen Ames (271)	$828,000	T. Clark (272)
Nov. 24@	Omega Mission Hills World Cup	Scotland—Montgomerie/ Warren (263)*	800,000 (each)	USA—H. Slocum/ B. Weekley (263)
Nov. 25@	LG Skins Game	Stephen Ames (9 skins)	675,000	F. Couples (9 skins)
Dec. 9@	Merrill Lynch Shootout	Mark Calcavecchia/ Woody Austin (187)	350,000 (each)	G. Norman/ B. Watson (188)
Dec. 16@	Target World Challenge	Tiger Woods (266)	1,350,000	Z. Johnson (273)

@ Unofficial PGA Tour money event.

*Playoffs: World Cup—Montgomerie/Warren won on 3rd hole.

2008 (through Oct. 19)

Last Rd	Tournament	Winner	Earnings	Runner-Up
Jan. 6	Mercedes-Benz Championships	Daniel Chopra (274)*	$1,100,000	S. Stricker (274)
Jan. 13	Sony Open in Hawaii	K.J. Choi (266)	954,000	R. Sabbatini (269)
Jan. 20	Bob Hope Chrysler Classic	D.J. Trahan (334)	918,000	J. Leonard (337)
Jan. 27	Buick Invitational	Tiger Woods (269)	936,000	R. Imada (277)
Feb. 3	FBR Open	J.B. Holmes (270)*	1,080,000	P. Mickelson (270)
Feb. 10	AT&T Pebble Beach Pro-Am	Steve Lowery (278)*	1,080,000	V. Singh (278)
Feb. 17	Northern Trust Open	Phil Mickelson (272)	1,116,000	J. Quinney (274)
Feb. 24	WGC: Accenture Match Play Championship	Tiger Woods (8&7)	1,350,000	S. Cink
Feb. 24	Mayakoba Classic	Brian Gay (264)	630,000	S. Marino (266)
Mar. 2	Honda Classic	Ernie Els (274)	990,000	L. Donald (275)
Mar. 9	PODS Championship	Sean O'Hair (280)	954,000	6-way tie (282)#
Mar. 16	Arnold Palmer Invitational	Tiger Woods (270)	1,044,000	B. Bryant (271)
Mar. 23	WGC: CA Championship	Geoff Ogilvy (271)	1,350,000	3-way tie (272)#
Mar. 23	Puerto Rico Open	Greg Kraft (274)	630,000	J. Kelly & B. Van Pelt (275)
Mar. 30	Zurich Classic of New Orleans	Andres Romero (275)	1,116,000	P. Lonard (276)
Apr. 6	Shell Houston Open	Johnson Wagner (272)	1,008,000	C. Campbell & G. Ogilvy (274)
Apr. 13	**The Masters** (Augusta, Ga.)	Trevor Immelman (280)	1,350,000	T. Woods (283)
Apr. 20	Verizon Heritage	Boo Weekley (269)	990,000	A. Baddeley & A. Kim (272)
Apr. 27	EDS Byron Nelson Championship	Adam Scott (273)*	1,152,000	R. Moore (273)
May 4	Wachovia Championship	Anthony Kim (272)	1,152,000	B. Curtis (277)
May 11	The Players Championship	Sergio Garcia (283)*	1,710,000	P. Goydos (283)
May 18	AT&T Classic	Ryuji Imada (273)*	990,000	K. Perry (273)
May 25	Crowne Plaza Invitational	Phil Mickelson (266)	1,098,000	T. Clark & R. Pampling (267)
June 1	The Memorial Tournament	Kenny Perry (280)	1,080,000	4-way tie (282)#
June 8	Stanford St. Jude Championship	Justin Leonard (276)*	1,080,000	R. Allenby & T. Immelman (276)
June 15	**U.S. Open** (La Jolla, Calif.)	Tiger Woods (283)*	1,350,000	R. Mediate (283)
June 22	Travelers Championship	Stewart Cink (262)	1,080,000	T. Armour III & H. Mahan (263)
June 29	Buick Open	Kenny Perry (269)	900,000	W. Austin & B. Watson (270)
July 6	AT&T National	Anthony Kim (268)	1,080,000	F. Jacobson (270)
July 13	John Deere Classic	Kenny Perry (268)*	756,000	J. Williamson & B. Adamonis (268)
July 20	U.S. Bank Championship	Richard S. Johnson (264)	720,000	K. Duke (265)
July 20	**British Open** (Royal Birkdale)	Padraig Harrington (283)	1,498,875	I. Poulter (287)
July 27	RBC Canadian Open	Chez Reavie (267)	900,000	B. Mayfair (270)
Aug. 3	Reno-Tahoe Open	Parker McLachlin (270)	540,000	J. Rollins & B. Davis (277)
Aug. 3	WGC: Bridgestone Invitational	Vijay Singh (270)	1,350,000	S. Appleby & L. Westwood (271)
Aug. 10	**PGA Championship** (Bloomfield Township, Mich.)	Padraig Harrington (277)	1,350,000	S. Garcia & B. Curtis (279)
Aug. 17	Wyndham Championship	Carl Pettersson (259)	918,000	S. McCarron (261)
Aug. 24	The Barclays†	Vijay Singh (276)*	1,260,000	S. Garcia & K. Sutherland (276)

PGA Tour Results (Cont.)

Last Rd	Tournament	Winner	Earnings	Runner-Up
Sept. 1	Deutsche Bank Championship†	Vijay Singh (262)	$1,260,000	M. Weir (267)
Sept. 7	BMW Championship†	Camilo Villegas (265)	1,260,000	D. Hart (267)
Sept. 21	Viking Classic	Will MacKenzie (269)*	648,000	B. Gay & M. Turnesa (269)
Sept. 21	The Ryder Cup (Louisville, Ky.)	United States (16½)	—	Europe (11½)
Sept. 28	The Tour Championship†	Camilo Villegas (273)*	1,260,000	S. Garcia (273)
Oct. 5	Turning Stone Resort Championship	Dustin Johnson (279)	1,080,000	R. Allenby (280)
Oct. 12	Valero Texas Open	Zach Johnson (261)	810,000	3-way tie (263)#
Oct. 19	Shriners Hospital for Children Open	Marc Turnesa (263)	738,000	M. Kuchar (264)

† FedExCup Playoff event.

*Playoffs: Mercedes Benz—Chopra won on 4th hole; **FBR**—Holmes won on 1st hole; **Pebble Beach**—Lowery won on 1st hole; **EDS Byron Nelson**—Scott won on 3rd hole; **Players**—Garcia won on 1st hole; **AT&T Classic**—Imada won on 1st hole; **St. Jude**—Leonard won on 2nd hole; **U.S. Open**—Woods won the 1st hole of sudden-death after an 18-hole play off round; **John Deere**—Perry won on 1st hole; **Barclays**—Singh won on 2nd hole; **Viking**—MacKenzie won on 2nd hole; **Tour Championship**—Villegas won on 1st hole.

#Second place ties (3 players or more): 3-WAY—**WGC-CA** (J. Furyk, R. Goosen, V. Singh); **Texas** (C. Wi, T. Wilkinson, M. Wilson); 4-WAY—**Memorial** (J. Kelly, M. Weir, M. Goggin, J. Rose); 6-WAY—**PODS** (S. Cink, B. Mayfair, J. Senden, R. Imada, G. McNeill, T. Matteson).

PGA Majors

The Masters

Edition: 72nd   **Dates:** April 10–13
Site: Augusta National GC, Augusta, Ga.
Par: 36-36—72 (7445 yards)   **Purse:** $7,500,000

		1 2 3 4	Tot	Earnings
1	Trevor Immelman	68-68-69-75	280	$1,350,000
2	Tiger Woods	72-71-68-72	283	810,000
3	Stewart Cink	72-69-71-72	284	435,000
	Brandt Snedeker	69-68-70-77	284	435,000
5	Steve Flesch	72-67-69-78	286	273,750
	Phil Mickelson	71-68-75-72	286	273,750
	Padraig Harrington	74-71-69-72	286	273,750
8	Miguel Angel Jimenez	77-70-72-68	287	217,500
	Robert Karlsson	70-73-71-73	287	217,500
	Andres Romero	72-72-70-73	287	217,500

Early round leaders: 1st—Immelman & Justin Rose (68); 2nd—Immelman (136); 3rd—Immelman (205).

Top amateur: none.

British Open

Edition: 137th   **Dates:** July 17–20
Site: Royal Birkdale Golf Club, Southport, England
Par: 34-36—70 (7173 yards)   **Purse:** $8,600,000

		1 2 3 4	Tot	Earnings
1	Padraig Harrington	74-68-72-69	283	$1,498,875
2	Ian Poulter	72-71-75-69	287	899,325
3	Greg Norman	70-70-72-77	289	509,618
	Henrik Stenson	76-72-70-71	289	509,618
5	Jim Furyk	71-71-77-71	290	359,730
	a-Chris Wood	75-70-73-72	290	—
7	Nine tied at 292.			

Early round leaders: 1st—Robert Allenby, Rocco Mediate & Graeme McDowell (69); 2nd—K.J. Choi (139); 3rd—Norman (212).

a-amateur

U.S. Open

Edition: 108th   **Dates:** June 12–15
Site: Torrey Pines Golf Course (South), La Jolla, Calif.
Par: 35-36—71 (7643 yards)   **Purse:** $7,500,000

		1 2 3 4	Tot	Earnings
1	Tiger Woods*	72-68-70-73	283	$1,350,000
2	Rocco Mediate*	69-71-72-71	283	810,000
3	Lee Westwood	70-71-70-73	284	491,995
4	Robert Karlsson	70-70-75-71	286	307,303
	D.J. Trahan	72-69-73-72	286	307,303
6	Miguel Angel Jimenez	75-66-74-72	287	220,686
	Carl Petterson	71-71-77-68	287	220,686
	John Merrick	73-72-71-71	287	220,686
9	Five tied at 288.			

Early round leaders: 1st—Kevin Streelman & Justin Hicks (68); 2nd—Stuart Appleby (139); 3rd—Woods (210).

Top amateur: Michael Thompson (292, tied for 29th).

*Woods and Mediate remained tied after an 18-hole playoff each shooting a 71 (par). Woods (4) defeated Mediate (5) on the first hole of a sudden death playoff.

PGA Championship

Edition: 90th   **Dates:** Aug. 7–10
Site: Oakland Hills Country Club (South), Bloomfield Township, Mich.
Par: 35-35—70 (7395 yards)   **Purse:** $7,500,000

		1 2 3 4	Tot	Earnings
1	Padraig Harrington	71-74-66-66	277	$1,350,000
2	Sergio Garcia	69-73-69-68	279	660,000
	Ben Curtis	73-67-68-71	279	660,000
4	Henrik Stenson	71-70-68-72	281	330,000
	Camilo Villegas	74-72-67-68	281	330,000
6	Steve Flesch	73-70-70-69	282	270,000
7	Phil Mickelson	70-73-71-70	284	231,250
	Andres Romero	69-78-65-72	284	231,250
9	Four tied at 285.			

Early round leaders: 1st—Robert Karlsson & Jeev Milkha Singh (68); 2nd—J.B. Holmes (139); 3rd—Curtis (208).

Top amateur: none.

FedExCup

The top 144 players in the FedExCup Point Standings (as of the Wyndham Championship on Aug. 17) played a four-week "playoff" for a shot at the FedExCup trophy and its accompanying $10 million bonus. The field narrowed during the first three playoff weeks until 30 were remaining for The Tour Championship on Sept. 28.

2008 Top 3	Events	Points
1 Vijay Singh	4	125,101
2 Camilo Villegas	4	124,550
3 Sergio Garcia	4	119,400

LPGA Tour
Late 2007

Last Rd	Tournament	Winner	Earnings	Runner-Up
Nov. 4	Mizuno Classic	Momoko Ueda (203)	$210,000	M. Hjorth & R. Rankin (205)
Nov. 11	The Mitchell Company TOC	Paula Creamer (268)	150,000	B. Kim (276)
Nov. 18	ADT Tour Championship	Lorena Ochoa (68)†	1,000,000	N. Gulbis (70)
Dec. 9	Lexus Cup	Team Asia (15)	50,000/member	Team International (9)

† At the ADT Tour Championship, the top 8 players after 54 holes participate in a final-day shootout.

2008 (through Oct. 19)

Last Rd	Tournament	Winner	Earnings	Runner-Up
Jan 20	Women's World Cup of Golf	Philippines (198)	$280,000	South Korea (200)
Feb. 16	SBS Open at Turtle Bay	Annika Sorenstam (206)	165,000	3-way tie (208)#
Feb. 23	Fields Open in Hawaii	Paula Creamer (200)	195,000	J. Jang (201)
Mar. 2	HSBC Women's Champions	Lorena Ochoa (268)	300,000	A. Sorenstam (279)
Mar. 16	MasterCard Classic	Louise Friberg (210)	195,000	Y. Tseng (211)
Mar. 30	Safeway International	Lorena Ochoa (266)	225,000	J Y Lee (273)
Apr. 6	**Kraft Nabisco Championship** (Rancho Mirage, Calif.)	Lorena Ochoa (277)	300,000	A. Sorenstam & S. Pettersen (282)
Apr. 13	Corona Championship	Lorena Ochoa (267)	195,000	S-H Kim (278)
Apr. 20	Ginn Open	Lorena Ochoa (269)	390,000	T. Tseng (272)
Apr. 27	Stanford International Pro-Am	Annika Sorenstam (275)*	300,000	P. Creamer (275)
May 4	SemGroup Championship	Paula Creamer (282)*	270,000	J. Inkster (282)
May 11	Michelob Ultra Open	Annika Sorenstam (265)	330,000	4-way tie (272)#
May 18	Sybase Classic	Lorena Ochoa (206)%	300,000	5-way tie (207)
May 25	Corning Classic	Leta Lindley (277)*	225,000	J. Jang (277)
June 1	Ginn Tribute	Seon Hwa Lee (274)*	390,000	K. Webb (274)
June 8	**McDonald's LPGA Championship** (Havre de Grace, Md.)	Yani Tseng (276)*	300,000	M. Hjorth (276)
June 22	Wegmen's Rochester	Eun-Hee Ji (272)	300,000	S. Pettersen (274)
June 29	**U.S. Women's Open** (Edina, Minn.)	Inbee Park (283)	585,000	H. Alfredsson (287)
July 6	NW Arkansas Championship	Seon Hwa Lee (201)	255,000	J. Park & M. Lee (202)
July 13	Jamie Farr Owens Corning Classic	Paula Creamer (270)	195,000	N. Castrale (270)
July 20	State Farm Classic	Ji Young Oh (270)*	255,000	Y. Tseng (270)
July 27	Evian Masters	Helen Alfredsson (273)*	487,500	N Y Choi & A. Park (273)
Aug. 3	**Ricoh Women's British Open** (Berkshire, England)	Ji-Yai Shin (270)	314,464	Y. Tseng (273)
Aug. 17	CN Canadian Women's Open	Katherine Hull (277)	337,500	S.R. Pak (278)
Aug. 24	Safeway Classic	Cristie Kerr (203)*	255,000	H. Alfredsson & S. Gustafson (203)
Sept. 14	Bell Micro Classic	Angela Stafford (277)	210,000	S. Feng (278)
Sept. 28	Navistar LPGA Classic	Lorena Ochoa (273)*	210,000	C. Kerr & C. Kung (273)
Oct. 5	Samsung World Championship	Paula Creamer (279)	250,000	S-H Kim (280)
Oct. 12	Longs Drugs Challenge	In-Kyung Kim (278)	180,000	A. Stanford (281)
Oct. 19	Kapalua LPGA Classic	Morgan Pressel (280)	225,000	S. Pettersen (281)

% Rain-shortened.

*Playoffs: Stanford Int'l—Sorenstam won on 1st hole; **SemGroup**—Creamer won on 2nd hole; **Corning**—Lindley won on 1st hole; **Ginn Tribute**—Lee won on 1st hole; **McDonald's**—Tseng won on 4th hole; **State Farm**—Oh won on 1st hole; **Evian Masters**—Alfredsson won on 3rd hole; **Safeway**—Kerr won on 1st hole; **Navistar**—Ochoa won on 2nd hole.

#Second place ties (3 players or more): 3-WAY—**SBS Open** (R. Gulyanamitta, L. Diaz, J. Park); 4-WAY—**Michelob Ultra** (A. Fouch, K. Stupples, J. Jang, C. Kim); 5-WAY—**Sybase** (M. Pressel, C. Matthew, N Y Choi, B. Lang, S. Gustafson).

LPGA Majors

Kraft Nabisco Championship

Edition: 37th   **Dates:** April 3-6
Site: Mission Hills CC, Rancho Mirage, Calif.
Par: 36-36—72 (6673 yards)   **Purse:** $2,000,000

		1 2 3 4	Tot	Earnings
1	Lorena Ochoa	68-71-71-67	277	$300,000
2	Annika Sorenstam	71-70-73-68	282	160,369
	Suzann Pettersen	74-75-65-68	282	160,369
4	Maria Hjorth	70-70-72-71	283	104,317
5	Seaon Hwa Lee	73-71-68-72	284	83,963
6	Mi Hyn Kim	70-70-76-69	285	58,859
	Na Yeon Choi	74-72-69-70	285	58,859
	Hee-Won Han	72-69-74-70	285	58,859
9	Inbee Park	73-70-70-73	286	45,289
10	Two tied at 287.			

Early round leaders: 1st—Karen Stupples (67); 2nd—Ochoa & Heather Young (139); 3rd—Ochoa (210).
Top amateur: Amanda Blumenherst (293, 30th place).

McDonald's LPGA Championship

Edition: 54th   **Dates:** June 5-8
Site: Bulle Rock Golf Course, Havre de Grace, Md.
Par: 36-36—72 (6641 yards)   **Purse:** $2,000,000

		1 2 3 4	Tot	Earnings
1	Yani Tseng*	73-70-65-68	276	$300,000
2	Maria Hjorth*	68-72-65-71	276	180,180
3	Lorena Ochoa	69-65-72-71	277	115,911
	Annika Sorenstam	70-68-68-71	277	115,911
5	Laura Diaz	71-68-69-70	278	81,385
6	Morgan Pressel	73-69-70-68	280	53,763
	Shi Hyun Ahn	73-69-69-69	280	53,763
	Kelli Kuehne	69-70-71-70	280	53,763
	Irene Cho	72-68-69-71	280	53,763
10	Eight tied at 281.			

Early round leaders: 1st—Lorie Kane & Emily Bastel (66); 2nd—Ochoa (134); 3rd—Jee Young Lee (204).
* Tseng defeated Hjorth on the 4th hole of sudden death.

LPGA Majors (Cont.)

U.S. Women's Open

Edition: 63rd · **Dates:** June 26-29
Site: Interlachen Country Club, Edina, Minn.
Par: 36-37—73 (6789 yds) · **Purse:** $3,250,000

	1 2 3 4	Tot	Earnings
1 Inbee Park	72-69-71-71	283	$585,000
2 Helen Alfredsson	70-71-71-75	287	350,000
3 Angela Park	73-67-75-73	288	162,487
In-Kyung Kim	71-73-69-75	288	162,487
Stacy Lewis	73-70-67-78	288	162,487
6 Giulia Sergas	73-74-72-70	289	94,117
Nicole Castrale	74-70-74-71	289	94,117
Mi Hyun Kim	72-72-70-75	289	94,117
Paula Creamer	70-72-69-78	289	94,117
10 Teresa Lu	71-72-73-74	290	75,734
a-Maria Jose Uribe	69-74-72-75	290	—

Early round leaders: 1st—Ji Young Oh & Pat Hurst (67); 2nd—A. Park (140); 3rd—Lewis (210).
a-amateur

Ricoh Women's British Open

Edition: 15th · **Dates:** July 31-Aug. 3
Site: Sunningdale Golf Club, Berkshire, England
Par: 36-36—72 (6408 yards) · **Purse:** $2,100,000

	1 2 3 4	Tot	Earnings
1 Ji-Yai Shin	66-68-70-66	270	$314,464
2 Yani Tseng	70-69-68-66	273	196,540
3 Eun-Hee Ji	68-70-69-67	274	122,838
Yuri Fudoh	66-68-69-71	274	122,838
5 Ai Miyazato	68-69-68-70	275	88,443
6 Cristie Kerr	71-65-70-70	276	76,651
7 Lorena Ochoa	69-68-71-69	277	65,841
Momoko Ueda	66-72-70-69	277	65,841
9 In-Kyung Kim	71-68-72-67	278	47,563
Hee-Won Han	71-69-71-67	278	47,563
Paula Creamer	72-69-70-67	278	47,563
Karrie Webb	72-69-69-68	278	47,563
Natalie Gulbis	69-68-70-71	278	47,563

Early round leaders: 1st—Juli Inkster (65); 2nd—Shin & Fudoh (134); 3rd—Fudoh (203).

Top amateur: Anna Nordqvist (285, t-42nd place)

Champions Tour
(formerly Senior PGA Tour)

Late 2007

Last Rd	Tournament	Winner	Earnings	Runner-Up
Dec. 2@	Del Webb Father/Son Challenge	Larry & Josh Nelson (120)	$200,000	Bob & Kevin Tway (122)

2008 (through Oct. 19)

Last Rd	Tournament	Winner	Earnings	Runner-Up
Jan. 20	MasterCard Championship	Fred Funk (195)	$300,000	A. Doyle (197)
Jan. 27	Turtle Bay Championship	Jerry Pate (211)	240,000	F. Allem & J. Thorpe (213)
Feb. 10	Allianz Championship	Scott Hoch (202)	247,500	B. Bryant & B. Lietzke (203)
Feb. 17	ACE Group Classic	Scott Hoch (202)*	240,000	3-way tie (202)#
Feb. 24@	Wendy's Champions Skins Game	Fuzzy Zoeller & Peter Jacobsen (6 skins)*	$320,000	J. Nicklaus & & T. Watson (8)
Mar. 9	Toshiba Classic	Bernhard Langer (199)*	255,000	J. Haas (199)
Mar. 16	AT&T Champions Classic	Denis Watson (209)	240,000	B. Bryant & L. Roberts (209)
Mar. 30	Ginn Championship	Bernhard Langer (204)	375,000	L. Nielsen & T. Simpson (212)
April 6	The Cap Cana Championship	Mark Wiebe (202)	300,000	V. Fernandez (206)
April 20	Outback Steakhouse Pro-Am	Tom Watson (204)	255,000	J. Haas & S. Hoch (205)
April 27	Liberty Mutual Legends of Golf	Andy North & Tom Watson (185)	$225,000 (each)	J. Sluman & & C. Stadler (186)
May 4	FedEx Kinko's Classic	Denis Watson (206)	240,000	3-way tie (207)#
May 18	Regions Charity Classic	Andy Bean (203)	255,000	L. Roberts (204)
May 25	**Senior PGA Championship** (Rochester, N.Y.)	Jay Haas (287)	360,000	B. Langer (288)
June 1	The Principal Charity Classic	Jay Haas (203)	258,750	A. Bean (204)
June 22	Bank of America Championship	Jeff Sluman (199)	247,500	L. Roberts (201)
June 29	Commerce Bank Championship	Loren Roberts (201)	240,000	L. Nielsen & N. Price (202)
July 6	Dick's Sporting Goods Open	Eduardo Romero (199)	240,000	F. Allem & G. Koch (200)
July 20	3M Championship	R.W. Eaks (193)	262,500	G. Hallberg & B. Langer (199)
July 27	**Senior British Open** (Ayrshire, Scotland)	Bruce Vaughan (278)*	315,600	J. Cook (278)
Aug. 3	**U.S. Senior Open** (Colorado Springs, Colo.)	Eduardo Romero (274)	470,000	F. Funk (278)
Aug. 17	**JELD-WEN Tradition** (Sunriver, Ore.)	Fred Funk (269)	392,000	M. Goodes (272)
Aug. 24	Boeing Classic	Tom Kite (202)	255,000	S. Simpson (204)
Aug. 31	Wal-Mart First Tee Open	Jeff Sluman (202)	315,000	C. Stadler & F. Zoeller (207)
Sept. 14	Greater Hickory Classic	R.W. Eaks (204)	255,000	T. Jenkins & T. Kite (204)
Sept. 28	SAS Championship	Eduardo Romero (201)	315,000	T. Kite (204)
Oct. 12	**Senior Players Championship** (Baltimore, Md.)	D.A. Weibring (271)	390,000	F. Funk (272)
Oct. 19	Administaff Small Business Classic	Bernhard Langer (204)	255,000	L. Nielsen (206)

@Unofficial Champions Tour money event.

*Playoffs: ACE Group—Hoch won on 1st hole; **Wendy's Champions Skins**—Zoeller/Jacobsen won on 1st hole; **Toshiba**—Langer won on 7th hole; **AT&T Champions**—Watson won on 3rd hole; **Senior British**—Vaughan won on 1st hole.

#Second place tie (3 players or more): 3-WAY—**ACE Group** (T. Kite, B. Bryant, T. Jenkins); **FedEx Kinko's** (S. Hoch, N. Price, T. Simpson).

Champions Tour Majors

Senior PGA Championship

Edition: 69th   **Dates:** May 22-25
Site: Oakland Hill Country Club, Rochester, N.Y.
Par: 35-35—70 (7001 yards)   **Purse:** $2,000,000

	1 2 3 4	Tot	Earnings
1 Jay Haas	69-72-72-74	287	$360,000
2 Bernhard Langer	71-71-70-76	288	216,000
3 Scott Hoch	71-74-72-72	289	102,667
Joey Sindelar	76-69-72-72	289	102,667
Scott Simpson	76-71-69-73	289	102,667
6 Don Pooley	75-73-72-70	290	62,000
Ron Streck	76-71-72-71	290	62,000
Greg Norman	72-73-72-73	290	62,000
9 Vicente Fernandez	74-75-73-69	291	50,000
Gene Jones	76-74-72-69	291	50,000
Jeff Sluman	70-73-70-78	291	50,000

Early round leaders: 1st—Haas (69); 2nd—Tom Purtzer (140); 3rd—Langer (212).

Top amateur: none.

U.S. Senior Open

Edition: 29th   **Dates:** July 28-Aug. 3
Site: The Broadmoor Resort (East), Colorado Springs, Colo.
Par: 36-34—70 (7254 yards)   **Purse:** $2,600,000

	1 2 3 4	Tot	Earnings
1 Eduardo Romero	67-69-65-73	274	$470,000
2 Fred Funk	65-69-69-75	278	280,000
3 Mark McNulty	68-70-73-68	279	177,650
4 Greg Norman	70-72-68-70	280	123,794
5 John Cook	66-72-66-77	281	100,238
6 David Edwards	72-70-73-67	282	80,895
Bernhard Langer	72-70-74-66	282	80,895
Joey Sindelar	73-72-68-69	282	80,895
9 Jay Haas	72-70-70-71	283	62,814
Scott Hoch	76-70-68-69	283	62,814
Jeff Klein	73-73-64-73	283	62,814

Early round leaders: 1st—Funk (65); 2nd—Funk (134); 3rd—Romero (201).

Top amateur: Danny Green (292, tied for 37th).

Senior British Open

Edition: 22nd (6th as major)   **Dates:** July 24-27
Site: Royal Troon Golf Club (Old), Ayshire, Scotland
Par: 36-5—71 (7064 yards)   **Purse:** $2,000,000

	1 2 3 4	Tot	Earnings
1 Bruce Vaughan*	68-71-69-70	278	$315,600
2 John Cook*	69-71-67-71	278	210,500
3 Eduardo Romero	68-73-68-70	279	118,500
4 Bernhard Langer	70-71-71-68	280	94,700
5 Gene Jones	70-76-68-68	282	67,773
Greg Norman	75-72-67-68	282	67,773
Tom Watson	70-71-71-70	282	67,773
8 Phil Blackmar	74-72-71-68	285	44,870
Costantino Rocca	73-73-72-67	285	44,870
10 Andy Bean	69-75-73-69	286	37,820

Early round leaders: 1st—Vaughn & Romero (68); 2nd—Vaughan (139); 3rd—Cook (207).

Top amateur: none.

* Vaughan defeated Cook on the 1st hole of sudden death.

JELD-WEN Tradition

Edition: 19th   **Dates:** Aug. 14-17
Site: Crosswater Golf Club, Sunriver, Oregon
Par: 36-36—72 (7683 yards)   **Purse:** $2,600,000

	1 2 3 4	Tot	Earnings
1 Fred Funk	69-66-65-69	269	$392,000
2 Mike Goodes	68-67-69-68	272	231,000
3 Jay Haas	67-68-66-73	274	174,000
Tom Watson	72-64-68-70	274	174,000
5 Scott Hoch	72-66-66-71	275	126,600
6 Scott Simpson	73-66-67-70	276	106,000
7 Tom Jenkins	71-68-70-68	277	70,600
Gene Jones	67-70-70-70	277	70,600
Bernhard Langer	68-66-72-71	277	70,600
Lonnie Nielsen	70-71-66-70	277	70,600
Loren Roberts	70-69-69-69	277	70,600
D.A. Weibring	68-72-70-67	277	70,600
Fuzzy Zoeller	74-66-69-68	277	70,600

Early round leaders: 1st—7-player tie (67); 2nd—Langer & Tim Simpson (134); 3rd—Funk (200).

Top amateur: none.

Senior Players Championship

Edition: 26th   **Dates:** Oct. 9-12
Site: Baltimore Country Club, Timonium, Md.
Par: 35-35—70 (7037 yards)   **Purse:** $2,600,000

	1 2 3 4	Tot	Earnings		1 2 3 4	Tot	Earnings
1 D.A. Weibring	67-70-66-68	271	$390,000	6 Jay Haas	67-70-69-68	274	$104,000
2 Fred Funk	66-68-72-66	272	228,800	7 Brad Bryant	70-71-67-67	275	79,300
3 Ben Crenshaw	67-66-74-66	273	156,000	John Cook	69-69-70-67	275	79,300
Nick Price	70-66-66-71	273	156,000	Bernhard Langer	66-70-71-68	275	79,300
Jeff Sluman	70-70-64-69	273	156,000	Eduardo Romero	66-72-67-70	275	79,300

Early round leaders:
1st—Des Smyth, Bruce Fleisher and Phil Blackmar (65); 2nd—Crenshaw (133); 3rd—Price (202).

Top amateur: none.

European PGA Tour

Official money won on the European Tour is presented in euros (E).

Late 2007

Last Rd	Tournament	Winner	Earnings	Runner-Up
Nov. 4	Volvo Masters	Justin Rose (283)*	E666,660	S. Dyson & S. Kjeldsen (283)
Nov. 11	HSBC Champions Tournament	Phil Mickelson (278)*	575,445	R. Fisher & L. Westwood (278)
Nov. 18	UBS Hong Kong Open	Miguel Angel Jimenez (266)	255,710	3-way tie (266)#
Nov. 24	MasterCard Masters	Aaron Baddeley (275)*	172,811	D. Chopra (275)
Dec. 2	Michael Hill New Zealand Open	Richard Finch (274)	144,895	S. Bowditch & P. Sheehan (277)
Dec. 9	Alfred Dunhill Championship	John Bickerton (275)	158,500	E. Els & L. Slattery (276)
Dec. 16	South African Airways Open	James Kingston (284)	158,500	O. Wilson (285)

*Playoffs: Volvo—Rose won on 2nd hole; **HSBC**—Mickelson won on 2nd hole; **MasterCard**—Baddeley won on 4th hole.
#Second place ties (3 players or more): 3-WAY—**UBS Hong Kong** (K.J. Choi, T. Jaidee, R. Karlsson).

2008 (through Oct. 19)

Last Rd	Tournament	Winner	Earnings	Runner-Up
Jan. 13	Joburg Open	Richard Sterne (271)*	E174,350	M. Carlsson & G. Mulroy (271)
Jan. 20	Abu Dhabi Championship	Martin Kaymer (273)	225,421	H. Stenson & L. Westwood (277)
Jan. 27	Commercialbank Qatar Masters	Adam Scott (268)	285,071	H. Stenson (271)
Feb. 3	Dubai Desert Classic	Tiger Woods (274)	283,965	M. Kaymer (275)
Feb. 10	Emaar-MGF Indian Masters	SSP Chowrasia (279)	280,561	D. McGrane (281)
Feb. 17	Astro Indonesia Open	Felipe Aguilar (262)	137,883	J M Singh (263)
Feb. 24	WGC: Accenture Match Play Championship	Tiger Woods (8&7)	919,993	S. Cink
Mar. 2	Johnnie Walker Classic	Mark Brown (270)	276,387	3-way tie (273)#
Mar. 9	Maybank Malaysian Open	Arjun Atwal (270)*	219,483	P. Hedblom (270)
Mar. 16	Ballantine's Championship	Graeme McDowell (264)*	333,330	J M Singh (264)
Mar. 23	WGC: CA Championship	Geoff Ogilvy (271)	865,150	3-way tie (272)#
Mar. 23	Madeira Island Open	Alastair Forsyth (273)*	116,660	H. Otto (273)
Mar. 30	Andalucia Open	Thomas Levet (272)*	116,660	O. Fisher (272)
Apr. 6	Estoril Portugal Open	Gregory Bourdy (266)*	208,330	A. Forsyth & D. Howell (266)
Apr. 13	The Masters Tournament	Trevor Immelman (280)	857,957	T. Woods (283)
Apr. 20	Volvo China Open	Damien McGrane (280)	232,121	3-way tie (287)#
Apr. 27	BMW Asian Open	Darren Clarke (280)	243,507	R-J Derksen (281)
May 4	Spanish Open	Peter Lawrie (273)*	333,330	I. Garrido (273)
May 11	Italian Open	Hennie Otto (263)	283,330	O. Wilson (264)
May 18	Irish Open	Richard Finch (278)	416,660	F. Aguilar (280)
May 25	BMW PGA Championship	Miguel Angel Jimenez (277)*	750,000	O. Wilson (277)
June 1	Celtic Manor Wales Open	Scott Strange (262)	376,671	R. Karlsson (266)
June 8	Bank Austria Golf Open	Jeev Milkha Singh (198)%	216,660	S. Wakefield (199)
June 15	Saint-Omer Open	David Dixon (279)	100,000	C. Nilsson (280)
June 16	U.S. Open	Tiger Woods (283)*	858,180	R. Mediate (283)
June 22	BMW International Championship	Martin Kaymer (273)*	333,330	A. Hansen (273)
June 29	French Open	Pablo Larrazabal (269)	666,660	C. Montgomerie (273)
July 6	European Open	Ross Fisher (268)	506,392	S. Garcia (275)
July 13	The Barclays Scottish Open	Graeme McDowell (271)	631,044	J. Kingston (273)
July 20	British Open (Royal Birkdale)	Padraig Harrington (283)	938,565	I. Poulter (287)
July 27	Russian Open	Mikael Lundberg (267)	210,237	J M Lara (269)
Aug. 3	WGC: Bridgestone Invitational	Vijay Singh (270)	860,584	S. Appleby & L. Westwood (271)
Aug. 10	PGA Championship	Padraig Harrington (277)	867,219	B. Curtis & S. Garcia (279)
Aug. 17	SAS Masters	Peter Hanson (271)	266,660	N. Dougherty & P. Edberg (272)
Aug. 24	The KLM Open	Darren Clarke (264)	300,000	P. McGinley (268)
Aug. 31	Johnnie Walker Championship	Gregory Havret (278)	292,355	G. Storm (279)
Sept. 7	Omega European Masters	Jean-Francois Lucquin (271)*	333,330	R. McIlroy (271)
Sept. 14	Mercedes-Benz Championship	Robert Karlsson (275)	320,000	F. Molinari (277)
Sept. 21	The Ryder Cup	United States (16½)	—	Europe (11½)
Sept. 28	The Quinn Insurance British Masters	G. Fernandez-Castano (276)*	381,612	L. Westwood (276)
Oct. 5	Alfred Dunhill Links Championship	Robert Karlsson (278)*	545,811	R. Fisher & M. Kaymer (278)
Oct. 12	Madrid Masters	Charl Schwartzel (265)	166,660	R. Gonzalez (268)
Oct. 19	Portugal Masters	Alvaro Quiros (269)	500,000	P. Lawrie (272)

% Weather-shortened.

*Playoffs: Joburg—Sterne won on 2nd hole; **Malaysian**—Atwal won on 2nd hole; **Ballantine's**—McDowell won on 3rd hole; **Madeira Island**—Forsyth won on 1st hole; **Andalucia**—Level won on 1st hole; **Portugal**—Bourdy won on 3rd hole; **Spanish**—Lawrie won on 2nd hole; **BMW-PGA**—Jimenez won on 2nd hole; **U.S. Open**—Woods won the 1st hole of sudden-death after an 18-hole playoff round; **BMW Int'l**—Kaymer won on 1st hole; **Omega**—Lucquin won on 2nd hole; **Quinn Insurance**—Fernandez-Castano won on 2nd hole; **Alfred Dunhill**—Karlsson won on 1st hole.

#Second place ties (3 players or more): 3-WAY—**Johnnie Walker Classic** (G. Chalmers, T. Kiyota, S. Strange); **WGC: CA** (J. Furyk, R. Goosen, V. Singh); **Volvo China** (S. Griffiths, M. Lorenzo-Vera, O. Wilson).

The Official World Golf Ranking

Begun in 1986, the Official World Golf Ranking (formerly the Sony World Ranking) combines the best golfers on the world's six leading professional tours (U.S. PGA Tour, European Tour, Japan Golf Tour, South African PGA Tour, Asian PGA Tour and the PGA Tour of Australasia) in conjunction with the Canadian, Nationwide and Challenge Tours. Rankings are based on a rolling two-year period and weighted in favor of more recent results. Points are awarded after each worldwide tournament according to finish. Final points-per-tournament averages are determined by dividing a player's total points by the number of tournaments played over that two-year period (through Oct. 19, 2008).

		Avg			Avg			Avg
1	Tiger Woods, USA	15.05	6	Robert Karlsson, SWE	5.34	11	Jim Furyk, USA	4.95
2	Phil Mickelson, USA	8.61	7	Camilo Villegas, COL	5.30	12	Lee Westwood, ENG	4.86
3	Vijay Singh, FIJ	7.58	8	Anthony Kim, USA	5.18	13	Steve Stricker, USA	4.81
4	Padraig Harrington, IRE	7.41	9	Ernie Els, RSA	4.99	14	Stewart Cink, USA	4.54
5	Sergio Garcia, ESP	7.09	10	Henrik Stenson, SWE	4.98	15	Justin Rose, ENG	4.45

2008 Tour Statistics (through Oct. 19)

Statistical leaders on the PGA, LPGA, Champions and European PGA tours.

PGA

	Scoring	Avg		Putting	Avg		Driving Distance	Avg
1	Sergio Garcia	69.12	1	Bob Tway	1.720	1	Bubba Watson	315.4
2	Phil Mickelson	69.17	2	Daniel Chopra	1.724	2	Robert Garrigus	312.0
3	Padraig Harrington	69.28	3	Ryan Palmer	1.728	3	J.B. Holmes	310.9
	Anthony Kim	69.28	4	Padraig Harrington	1.742	4	Dustin Johnson	309.9
5	Camilo Villegas	69.49	5	Nathan Green	1.743	5	Steve Allan	303.8
6	Vijay Singh	69.58	6	Brian Gay	1.745	6	Tag Ridings	303.3
7	Robert Allenby	69.66	7	Shane Bertsch	1.746	7	Nick Watney	302.4
8	Jim Furyk	69.69	8	Chad Collins	1.747	8	Adam Scott	302.1
9	Stuart Appleby	69.73		Justin Leonard	1.747	9	Harrison Frazar	301.7
10	Justin Leonard	69.77	10	Corey Pavin	1.749	10	Charles Warren	301.6

LPGA

	Scoring	Avg		Putting	Avg		Driving Distance	Avg
1	Lorena Ochoa	69.51	1	Inbee Park	1.736	1	Lorena Ochoa	269.5
2	Annika Sorenstam	70.44	2	Cristie Kerr	1.743	2	Sophie Gustafson	268.8
3	Paula Creamer	70.47	3	Paula Creamer	1.769	3	Brittany Lincicome	268.5
4	Yani Tseng	70.55	4	Lorena Ochoa	1.774	4	Jee Young Lee	268.0
5	Suzann Pettersen	70.66	5	Eun-Hee Ji	1.775	5	Becky Lucidi	267.7
6	Cristie Kerr	70.81	6	Suzann Pettersen	1.778	6	Yani Tseng	266.4
7	Na Yeon Choi	70.93	7	Gloria Park	1.778	7	Maria Hjorth	266.2
8	Song-Hee Kim	70.96	8	Hee-Won Han	1.778	8	Suzann Pettersen	265.8
9	Jeong Jang	71.06	9	Jeong Jang	1.780	9	Hee Young Park	263.6
10	Karrie Webb	71.07	10	Shi Hyun Ahn	1.780	10	Wendy Doolan	262.5

Champions

	Scoring	Avg		Putting	Avg		Driving Distance	Avg
1	Fred Funk	69.54	1	Fred Funk	1.727	1	Tom Purtzer	295.3
2	Bernhard Langer	69.54	2	Nick Price	1.727	2	Eduardo Romero	294.1
3	Eduardo Romero	69.64	3	Gary Hallberg	1.740	3	Joey Sindelar	289.1
4	Nick Price	69.68	4	Gene Jones	1.742	4	Sandy Lyle	288.9
5	Loren Roberts	69.70	5	Phil Blackmar	1.744	5	Lonnie Nielsen	287.5

European PGA

	Scoring	Avg		Putting	Avg		Driving Distance	Avg
1	Robert Karlsson	69.93	1	David Howell	1.719	1	Alvaro Quiros	310.2
2	Jeev Milkha Singh	70.44	2	Danny Willett	1.719	2	Rafael Cabrera Bello	303.2
3	Lee Westwood	70.46	3	SSP Chowrasia	1.730	3	Christian Nilsson	302.9
4	Paul McGinley	70.69	4	Robert Karlsson	1.735	4	Emanuele Canonica	302.3
5	Sergio Garcia	70.69	5	Rafa Echenique	1.735	5	Joakim Backstrom	301.3

Key: Scoring—average strokes per round adjusted to the average score of the field each week. If the field is under par, each player's score is adjusted upward a corresponding amount and vice-versa if the field is over par. This keeps a player from receiving an advantage for playing easier-than-average courses. **Putting**—average number of putts taken on greens hit in regulation; **Driving Distance**—average computed by charting exact distances of two tee shots on the most open par-4 or par-5 holes on both front and back nine.

Money Leaders

Official money leaders of PGA, LPGA, Champions and European PGA tours for 2007 and unofficial money leaders for 2008, through Oct. 19, as compiled by the PGA, LPGA and European PGA. Listed are tournaments played (TP), cuts made (CM), 1st, 2nd and 3rd place finishes and earnings for the year.

PGA

Arnold Palmer Award standings

FINAL 2007

		TP	CM	Finish 1-2-3	Earnings
1	Tiger Woods	16	16	7-3-0	$10,867,052
2	Phil Mickelson	22	16	3-1-2	5,819,988
3	Vijay Singh	27	25	2-1-0	4,728,376
4	Steve Stricker	23	19	1-2-1	4,663,077
5	K.J. Choi	25	21	2-1-0	4,587,859
6	Rory Sabbatini	23	18	1-2-3	4,550,040
7	Jim Furyk	23	20	1-2-2	4,154,046
8	Zach Johnson	23	18	2-1-0	3,922,338
9	Sergio Garcia	19	17	0-2-1	3,721,185
10	Aaron Baddeley	23	19	1-1-0	3,441,119

2008 (through Oct. 19)

		TP	CM	Finish 1-2-3	Earnings
1	Vijay Singh	23	18	3-2-1	$6,601,094
2	Tiger Woods	6	6	4-1-0	5,775,000
3	Phil Mickelson	21	20	2-1-1	5,188,875
4	Sergio Garcia	19	18	1-3-0	4,858,224
5	Kenny Perry	26	24	3-1-1	4,663,794
6	Anthony Kim	22	19	2-1-3	4,656,265
7	Camilo Villegas	22	19	2-0-2	4,422,641
8	Padraig Harrington	15	12	2-0-1	4,313,551
9	Stewart Cink	22	19	1-2-2	3,963,661
10	Justin Leonard	25	24	1-1-0	3,943,542

LPGA

FINAL 2007

		TP	CM	Finish 1-2-3	Earnings
1	Lorena Ochoa	25	25	8-5-2	$4,364,994
2	Suzann Pettersen	24	21	5-2-0	1,802,400
3	Paula Creamer	24	22	2-2-2	1,384,798
4	Mi Hyun Kim	27	25	1-2-2	1,273,848
5	Seon Hwa Lee	29	26	1-0-1	1,100,198
6	Cristie Kerr	23	19	1-0-1	1,098,921
7	Jeong Jang	28	24	0-1-3	1,038,598
8	Angela Park	29	27	0-1-3	983,922
9	Morgan Pressel	25	23	1-1-1	972,452
10	Jee Young Lee	24	23	0-3-0	966,256

2008 (through Oct. 19)

		TP	CM	Finish 1-2-3	Earnings
1	Lorena Ochoa	20	20	7-0-2	$2,738,888
2	Paula Creamer	23	23	4-1-1	1,756,199
3	Yani Tseng	23	23	1-5-2	1,726,916
4	Annika Sorenstam	20	20	3-1-1	1,639,561
5	Helen Alfredsson	23	17	2-1-0	1,398,256
6	Seon Hwa Lee	27	24	2-0-0	1,142,051
7	Suzann Pettersen	21	21	0-3-2	1,141,835
8	Inbee Park	23	19	1-0-1	1,115,289
9	Cristie Kerr	24	24	1-1-0	1,080,744
10	Na Yeon Choi	23	23	0-2-1	1,051,418

Champions Tour

FINAL 2007

		TP	CM	Finish 1-2-3	Earnings
1	Jay Haas	27	27	4-4-0	$2,581,001
2	Loren Roberts	23	23	2-3-3	2,170,627
3	Brad Bryant	24	24	2-2-2	1,812,099
4	Denis Watson	25	25	2-2-1	1,636,123
5	D.A. Weibring	27	27	1-1-1	1,557,622
6	R.W. Eaks	26	23	2-4-1	1,534,098
7	Tom Kite	28	28	0-3-3	1,451,941
8	Tom Putzer	27	27	1-1-1	1,382,436
9	Tom Watson	12	12	2-1-1	1,365,365
10	Hale Irwin	21	20	1-2-0	1,269,513

2008 (through Oct. 19)

		TP	CM	Finish 1-2-3	Earnings
1	Bernhard Langer	19	19	3-2-1	$1,992,573
2	Jay Haas	20	20	2-2-4	1,943,226
3	Fred Funk	17	17	2-2-1	1,797,931
4	John Cook	25	24	1-1-1	1,661,538
5	Jeff Sluman	25	25	2-1-2	1,625,276
6	Eduardo Romero	17	17	3-0-1	1,581,099
7	Loren Roberts	24	24	1-3-0	1,497,939
8	Scott Hoch	24	24	2-2-1	1,429,530
9	Tom Kite	27	27	1-3-0	1,230,092
10	Lonnie Nielsen	26	26	0-3-0	1,190,012

European PGA

Order of Merit standings. All amounts are listed in Euros (E).

FINAL 2007

		TP	CM	Finish 1-2-3	Earnings
1	Justin Rose	12	12	2-3-0	E2,944,945
2	Ernie Els	18	17	2-1-3	2,496,237
3	Padraig Harrington	15	14	2-0-0	2,463,742
4	Henrik Stenson	17	13	2-0-1	2,014,841
5	Niclas Fasth	23	21	1-1-1	1,919,339
6	Angel Cabrera	13	12	1-1-0	1,753,024
7	Andres Romero	23	16	1-0-1	1,741,707
8	Søren Hansen	26	19	1-2-1	1,692,054
9	Retief Goosen	21	16	1-1-1	1,478,245
10	Lee Westwood	25	24	2-0-2	1,420,327

2008 (through Oct. 19)

		TP	CM	Finish 1-2-3	Earnings
1	Robert Karlsson	22	21	2-2-4	E2,695,248
2	Padraig Harrington	13	12	2-0-0	2,397,823
3	Lee Westwood	20	18	0-4-3	2,228,642
4	Miguel Angel Jimenez	25	20	2-0-3	2,018,596
5	Henrik Stenson	18	16	0-2-3	1,773,617
6	Ross Fisher	26	22	1-2-2	1,760,180
7	Graeme McDowell	27	21	2-0-1	1,758,846
8	Martin Kaymer	24	19	2-2-0	1,425,500
9	Sergio Garcia	12	11	1-1-0	1,395,917
10	Oliver Wilson	25	18	0-4-0	1,246,705

National Team Competition
2008 Ryder Cup

The 37th Ryder Cup tournament, Sept. 19-21, at Valhalla Golf Club, Louisville, Kentucky.

Rosters

The 2008 U.S. Team was chosen on the basis of points accumulated at official PGA events from Aug. 27, 2006 through the 2008 PGA Championship, which concluded on Aug. 11. The top eight finishers on the points list automatically qualified for the 12-member team, and U.S. Captain Paul Azinger selected the final four players.

The 2008 European Team was chosen as follows: the top five players on The Ryder Cup World Points list as of Aug. 31, 2008, as well as the top five players on the European Ryder Cup points list as of Aug. 31, 2008 were automatic qualifiers for the 12-member team. European Team captain Nick Faldo selected the final two players.

United States: Qualifiers—Phil Mickelson, Stewart Cink, Kenny Perry, Jim Furyk, Anthony Kim, Justin Leonard, Ben Curtis, and Boo Weekley; Captain's selections—Chad Campbell, J.B. Holmes, Hunter Mahan and Steve Stricker.

Europe: Qualifiers—Sergio Garcia (Spain), Søren Hansen (Denmark), Padraig Harrington (Ireland), Miguel Angel Jimenez (Spain), Robert Karlsson (Sweden), Graeme McDowell (Northern Ireland), Justin Rose (England), Henrik Stenson (Sweden), Lee Westwood (England) and Oliver Wilson (England); Captain's selections—Paul Casey (England) and Ian Poulter (England).

First Day

Foursome Match Results

Winner	Score	Loser
Mickelson/Kim	halved	Harrington/Karlsson
Leonard/Mahan	3&2	Stenson/Casey
Cink/Campbell	1-up	Rose/Poulter
Perry/Furyk	halved	Westwood/Garcia

USA wins morning, 3-1

Four-Ball Match Results

Winner	Score	Loser
Mickelson/Kim	2-up	Harrington/McDowell
Poulter/Rose	4&2	Stricker/Curtis
Leonard/Mahan	4&3	Garcia/Jimenez
Holmes/Weekley	halved	Westwood/Hansen

USA wins afternoon, 2½-1½ (USA leads, 5½-2½)

Second Day

Foursome Match Results

Winner	Score	Loser
Poulter/Rose	4&3	Cink/Campbell
Leonard/Mahan	halved	Jimenez/McDowell
Stenson/Wilson	2&1	Mickelson/Kim
Furyk/Perry	3&1	Harrington/Karlsson

Europe wins afternoon, 2½-1½ (USA leads, 7-5)

Four-Ball Match Results

Winner	Score	Loser
Weekley/Holmes	2&1	Westwood/Hansen
Curtis/Stricker	halved	Garcia/Casey
Poulter/McDowell	1-up	Perry/Furyk
Mickelson/Mahan	halved	Stenson/Karlsson

Afternoon tied, 2-2 (USA leads, 9-7)

Third Day
Singles Match Results

Winner	Score	Loser	Winner	Score	Loser
Kim	5&4	Garcia	Holmes	2&1	Hansen
Mahan	halved	Casey	Furyk	2&1	Jimenez
Karlsson	5&3	Leonard	McDowell	2&1	Cink
Rose	3&2	Mickelson	Poulter	3&2	Stricker
Perry	3&2	Stenson	Curtis	2&1	Westwood
Weekley	4&2	Wilson	Campbell	2&1	Harrington

USA wins day, 7½-4½

USA wins Ryder Cup, 16½-11½

Overall Records
One point is awarded for a win. One-half point is awarded for a half.

United States	W	L	H	Pts	Europe	W	L	H	Pts
Hunter Mahan	2	0	3	3½	Ian Poulter	4	1	0	4
Kenny Perry	2	1	1	2½	Justin Rose	3	1	0	3
Jim Furyk	2	1	1	2½	Graeme McDowell	2	1	1	2½
Anthony Kim	2	1	1	2½	Robert Karlsson	1	1	2	2
Justin Leonard	2	1	1	2½	Henrik Stenson	1	2	1	1½
Boo Weekley	2	0	1	2½	Paul Casey	0	1	2	1
J.B. Holmes	2	0	1	2½	Sergio Garcia	0	2	2	1
Chad Campbell	2	1	0	2	Lee Westwood	0	2	2	1
Phil Mickelson	1	2	2	2	Oliver Wilson	1	1	0	1
Ben Curtis	1	1	1	1½	Søren Hansen	0	2	1	½
Stewart Cink	1	2	0	1	Padraig Harrington	0	2	1	½
Steve Stricker	0	2	1	½	Miguel Angel Jimenez	0	2	1	½

1860-2008
Through the Years

SPORTS ALMANAC

Major Golf Championships
MEN
The Masters

The Masters has been played every year (except during World War II) since 1934 at the Augusta National Golf Club in Augusta, Ga. Both the course and the tournament were created by Bobby Jones; (*) indicates playoff winner.

Multiple winners: Jack Nicklaus (6); Arnold Palmer and Tiger Woods (4); Jimmy Demaret, Nick Faldo, Gary Player and Sam Snead (3); Seve Ballesteros, Ben Crenshaw, Ben Hogan, Bernhard Langer, Phil Mickelson, Byron Nelson, Jose Maria Olazabal, Horton Smith and Tom Watson (2).

Year	Winner	Score	Runner-up
1934	Horton Smith	284	Craig Wood (285)
1935	Gene Sarazen*	282	Craig Wood (282)
1936	Horton Smith	285	Harry Cooper (286)
1937	Byron Nelson	283	Ralph Guldahl (285)
1938	Henry Picard	285	Ralph Guldahl & Harry Cooper (287)
1939	Ralph Guldahl	279	Sam Snead (280)
1940	Jimmy Demaret	280	Lloyd Mangrum (284)
1941	Craig Wood	280	Byron Nelson (283)
1942	Byron Nelson*	280	Ben Hogan (280)
1943-45	Not held		World War II
1946	Herman Keiser	282	Ben Hogan (283)
1947	Jimmy Demaret	281	Frank Stranahan & Byron Nelson (283)
1948	Claude Harmon	279	Cary Middlecoff (284)
1949	Sam Snead	282	Lloyd Mangrum & Johnny Bulla (285)
1950	Jimmy Demaret	283	Jim Ferrier (285)
1951	Ben Hogan	280	Skee Riegel (282)
1952	Sam Snead	286	Jack Burke Jr. (290)
1953	Ben Hogan	274	Porky Oliver (279)
1954	Sam Snead*	289	Ben Hogan (289)
1955	Cary Middlecoff	279	Ben Hogan (286)
1956	Jack Burke Jr.	289	Ken Venturi (290)
1957	Doug Ford	283	Sam Snead (286)
1958	Arnold Palmer	284	Doug Ford & Fred Hawkins (285)
1959	Art Wall Jr.	284	Cary Middlecoff (285)
1960	Arnold Palmer	282	Ken Venturi (283)
1961	Gary Player	280	Arnold Palmer & Charles R. Coe (281)
1962	Arnold Palmer*	280	Dow Finsterwald & Gary Player (280)
1963	Jack Nicklaus	286	Tony Lema (287)
1964	Arnold Palmer	276	Jack Nicklaus & Dave Marr (282)
1965	Jack Nicklaus	271	Arnold Palmer & Gary Player (280)
1966	Jack Nicklaus*	288	Gay Brewer Jr. & Tommy Jacobs (288)
1967	Gay Brewer Jr.	280	Bobby Nichols (281)
1968	Bob Goalby	277	Roberto DeVicenzo (278)
1969	George Archer	281	Billy Casper, George Knudson & Tom Weiskopf (282)
1970	Billy Casper*	279	Gene Littler (279)
1971	Charles Coody	279	Jack Nicklaus & Johnny Miller (281)
1972	Jack Nicklaus	286	Bruce Crampton, Bobby Mitchell & Tom Weiskopf (289)
1973	Tommy Aaron	283	J.C. Snead (284)
1974	Gary Player	278	Tom Weiskopf, & Dave Stockton (280)
1975	Jack Nicklaus	276	Johnny Miller & Tom Weiskopf (277)
1976	Ray Floyd	271	Ben Crenshaw (279)
1977	Tom Watson	276	Jack Nicklaus (278)
1978	Gary Player	277	Hubert Green, Rod Funseth & Tom Watson (278)
1979	Fuzzy Zoeller*	280	Ed Sneed & Tom Watson (280)
1980	Seve Ballesteros	275	Gibby Gilbert & Jack Newton (279)
1981	Tom Watson	280	Jack Nicklaus & Johnny Miller (282)
1982	Craig Stadler*	284	Dan Pohl (284)
1983	Seve Ballesteros	280	Ben Crenshaw & Tom Kite (284)
1984	Ben Crenshaw	277	Tom Watson (279)
1985	Bernhard Langer	282	Curtis Strange, Seve Ballesteros & Ray Floyd (284)
1986	Jack Nicklaus	279	Greg Norman & Tom Kite (280)
1987	Larry Mize*	285	Seve Ballesteros & Greg Norman (285)
1988	Sandy Lyle	281	Mark Calcavecchia (282)
1989	Nick Faldo*	283	Scott Hoch (283)
1990	Nick Faldo*	278	Ray Floyd (278)
1991	Ian Woosnam	277	J.M. Olazabal (278)
1992	Fred Couples	275	Ray Floyd (277)
1993	Bernhard Langer	277	Chip Beck (281)
1994	J.M. Olazabal	279	Tom Lehman (281)
1995	Ben Crenshaw	274	Davis Love III (275)
1996	Nick Faldo	276	Greg Norman (281)
1997	Tiger Woods	270	Tom Kite (282)
1998	Mark O'Meara	279	Fred Couples & David Duval (280)
1999	J.M. Olazabal	280	Davis Love III (282)
2000	Vijay Singh	278	Ernie Els (281)
2001	Tiger Woods	272	David Duval (274)
2002	Tiger Woods	276	Retief Goosen (279)
2003	Mike Weir*	281	Len Mattiace (281)
2004	Phil Mickelson	279	Ernie Els (280)
2005	Tiger Woods*	276	Chris DiMarco (276)
2006	Phil Mickelson	281	Tim Clark (283)
2007	Zach Johnson	289	Tiger Woods, Retief Goosen & Rory Sabbatini (291)
2008	Trevor Immelman	280	Tiger Woods (283)

*PLAYOFFS:
1935: Gene Sarazen (144) def. Craig Wood (149) in 36 holes. **1942:** Byron Nelson (69) def. Ben Hogan (70) in 18 holes. **1954:** Sam Snead (70) def. Ben Hogan (71) in 18 holes. **1962:** Arnold Palmer (68) def. Gary Player (71) and Dow Finsterwald (77) in 18 holes. **1966:** Jack Nicklaus (70) def. Tommy Jacobs (72) and Gay Brewer Jr. (78) in 18 holes. **1970:** Billy Casper (69) def. Gene Littler (74) in 18 holes. **1979:** Fuzzy Zoeller (4-3) def. Ed Sneed (4-4) and Tom Watson (4-4) on 2nd hole of sudden death. **1982:** Craig Stadler (4) def. Dan Pohl (5) on 1st hole of sudden death. **1987:** Larry Mize (4-3) def. Greg Norman (4-4) and Seve Ballesteros (5) on 2nd hole of sudden death. **1989:** Nick Faldo (5-3) def. Scott Hoch (5-4) on 2nd hole of sudden death. **1990:** Nick Faldo (4-4) def. Raymond Floyd (4) on 2nd hole of sudden death. **2003:** Mike Weir (5) def. Len Mattiace (6) on 1st hole of sudden death. **2005:** Tiger Woods (3) def. Chris DiMarco (4) on 1st hole of sudden death.

U.S. Open

Played at a different course each year, the U.S. Open was launched by the new U.S. Golf Association in 1895. The Open was a 36-hole event from 1895-97 and has been 72 holes since then. It switched from a 3-day, 36-hole Saturday finish to 4 days of play in 1965. Note that (*) indicates playoff winner and (a) indicates amateur.

Multiple winners: Willie Anderson, Ben Hogan, Bobby Jones and Jack Nicklaus (4); Hale Irwin and Tiger Woods (3); Julius Boros, Billy Casper, Ernie Els, Retief Goosen, Ralph Guldahl, Walter Hagen, Lee Janzen, John McDermott, Cary Middlecoff, Andy North, Gene Sarazen, Alex Smith, Payne Stewart, Curtis Strange and Lee Trevino (2).

Year	Winner	Score	Runner-up	Course	Location
1895	Horace Rawlins	173	Willie Dunn (175)	Newport GC	Newport, R.I.
1896	James Foulis	152	Horace Rawlins (155)	Shinnecock Hills GC	Southampton, N.Y.
1897	Joe Lloyd	162	Willie Anderson (163)	Chicago GC	Wheaton, Ill.
1898	Fred Herd	328	Alex Smith (335)	Myopia Hunt Club	Hamilton, Mass.
1899	Willie Smith	315	George Low, W.H. Way & Val Fitzjohn (326)	Baltimore CC	Baltimore
1900	Harry Vardon	313	J.H. Taylor (315)	Chicago GC	Wheaton, Ill.
1901	Willie Anderson*	331	Alex Smith (331)	Myopia Hunt Club	Hamilton, Mass.
1902	Laurie Auchterlonie	307	Stewart Gardner (313)	Garden City GC	Garden City, N.Y.
1903	Willie Anderson*	307	David Brown (307)	Baltusrol GC	Springfield, N.J.
1904	Willie Anderson	303	Gil Nicholls (308)	Glen View Club	Golf, Ill.
1905	Willie Anderson	314	Alex Smith (316)	Myopia Hunt Club	Hamilton, Mass.
1906	Alex Smith	295	Willie Smith (302)	Onwentsia Club	Lake Forest, Ill.
1907	Alec Ross	302	Gil Nicholls (304)	Phila. Cricket Club	Chestnut Hill, Pa.
1908	Fred McLeod*	322	Willie Smith (322)	Myopia Hunt Club	Hamilton, Mass.
1909	George Sargent	290	Tom McNamara (294)	Englewood GC	Englewood, N.J.
1910	Alex Smith*	298	Macdonald Smith & John McDermott (298)	Phila. Cricket Club	Chestnut Hill, Pa.
1911	John McDermott*	307	George Simpson & Mike Brady (307)	Chicago GC	Wheaton, Ill.
1912	John McDermott	294	Tom McNamara (296)	CC of Buffalo	Buffalo
1913	a-Francis Ouimet*	304	Harry Vardon & Ted Ray (304)	The Country Club	Brookline, Mass.
1914	Walter Hagen	290	a-Chick Evans (291)	Midlothian CC	Blue Island, Ill.
1915	a-John Travers	297	Tom McNamara (298)	Baltusrol GC	Springfield, N.J.
1916	a-Chick Evans	286	Jock Hutchinson (288)	Minikahda Club	Minneapolis
1917-18	Not held		World War I		
1919	Walter Hagen*	301	Mike Brady (301)	Brae Burn CC	West Newton, Mass.
1920	Ted Ray	295	Jock Hutchinson, Jack Burke, Leo Diegel & Harry Vardon (296)	Inverness Club	Toledo, Ohio
1921	Jim Barnes	289	Walter Hagen & Fred McLeod (298)	Columbia CC	Chevy Chase, Md.
1922	Gene Sarazen	288	a-Bobby Jones & John Black (289)	Skokie CC	Glencoe, Ill.
1923	a-Bobby Jones*	296	Bobby Cruickshank (296)	Inwood CC	Inwood, N.Y.
1924	Cyril Walker	297	a-Bobby Jones (300)	Oakland Hills CC	Birmingham, Mich.
1925	Willie Macfarlane*	291	a-Bobby Jones (291)	Worcester CC	Worcester, Mass.
1926	a-Bobby Jones	293	Joe Turnesa (294)	Scioto CC	Columbus, Ohio
1927	Tommy Armour*	301	Harry Cooper (301)	Oakmont CC	Oakmont, Pa.
1928	Johnny Farrell*	294	a-Bobby Jones (294)	Olympia Fields CC	Matteson, Ill.
1929	a-Bobby Jones*	294	Al Espinosa (294)	Winged Foot CC	Mamaroneck, N.Y.
1930	a-Bobby Jones	287	Macdonald Smith (289)	Interlachen CC	Hopkins, Minn.
1931	Billy Burke*	292	George Von Elm (292)	Inverness Club	Toledo, Ohio
1932	Gene Sarazen	286	Bobby Cruickshank & Phil Perkins (289)	Fresh Meadow CC	Flushing, N.Y.
1933	a-Johnny Goodman	287	Ralph Guldahl (288)	North Shore GC	Glenview, Ill.
1934	Olin Dutra	293	Gene Sarazen (294)	Merion Cricket Club	Ardmore, Pa.
1935	Sam Parks Jr.	299	Jimmy Thomson (301)	Oakmont CC	Oakmont, Pa.
1936	Tony Manero	282	Harry E. Cooper (284)	Baltusrol GC	Springfield, N.J.
1937	Ralph Guldahl	281	Sam Snead (283)	Oakland Hills CC	Birmingham, Mich.
1938	Ralph Guldahl	284	Dick Metz (290)	Cherry Hills CC	Denver
1939	Byron Nelson*	284	Craig Wood & Denny Shute (284)	Philadelphia CC	Philadelphia
1940	Lawson Little*	287	Gene Sarazen (287)	Canterbury GC	Cleveland

U.S. Open (Cont.)

Year	Winner	Score	Runner-up	Course	Location
1941	Craig Wood	284	Denny Shute (287)	Colonial Club	Ft. Worth
1942-45	Not held		World War II		
1946	Lloyd Mangrum*	284	Byron Nelson & Vic Ghezzi (284)	Canterbury CC	Cleveland
1947	Lew Worsham*	282	Sam Snead (282)	St. Louis CC	Clayton, Mo.
1948	Ben Hogan	276	Jimmy Demaret (278)	Riviera CC	Los Angeles
1949	Cary Middlecoff	286	Clayton Heafner & Sam Snead (287)	Medinah CC	Medinah, Ill.
1950	Ben Hogan*	287	Lloyd Mangrum & George Fazio (287)	Merion Golf Club	Ardmore, Pa.
1951	Ben Hogan	287	Clayton Heafner (289)	Oakland Hills CC	Birmingham, Mich.
1952	Julius Boros	281	Porky Oliver (285)	Northwood Club	Dallas
1953	Ben Hogan	283	Sam Snead (289)	Oakmont GC	Oakmont, Pa.
1954	Ed Furgol	284	Gene Littler (285)	Baltusrol GC	Springfield, N.J.
1955	Jack Fleck*	287	Ben Hogan (287)	Olympic CC	San Francisco
1956	Cary Middlecoff	281	Ben Hogan & Julius Boros (282)	Oak Hill CC	Rochester, N.Y.
1957	Dick Mayer*	282	Cary Middlecoff (282)	Inverness Club	Toledo, Ohio
1958	Tommy Bolt	283	Gary Player (285)	Southern Hills CC	Tulsa
1959	Billy Casper	282	Bob Rosburg (283)	Winged Foot GC	Mamaroneck, N.Y.
1960	Arnold Palmer	280	Jack Nicklaus (282)	Cherry Hills CC	Denver
1961	Gene Littler	281	Doug Sanders & Bob Goalby (282)	Oakland Hills CC	Birmingham, Mich.
1962	Jack Nicklaus*	283	Arnold Palmer (283)	Oakmont CC	Oakmont, Pa.
1963	Julius Boros*	293	Arnold Palmer & Jacky Cupit (293)	The Country Club	Brookline, Mass.
1964	Ken Venturi	278	Tommy Jacobs (282)	Congressional CC	Bethesda, Md.
1965	Gary Player*	282	Kel Nagle (282)	Bellerive CC	St. Louis
1966	Billy Casper*	278	Arnold Palmer (278)	Olympic CC	San Francisco
1967	Jack Nicklaus	275	Arnold Palmer (279)	Baltusrol GC	Springfield, N.J.
1968	Lee Trevino	275	Jack Nicklaus (279)	Oak Hill CC	Rochester, N.Y.
1969	Orville Moody	281	Al Geiberger, Deane Beman & Bob Rosburg (282)	Champions GC	Houston
1970	Tony Jacklin	281	Dave Hill (288)	Hazeltine National GC	Chaska, Minn.
1971	Lee Trevino*	280	Jack Nicklaus (280)	Merion GC	Ardmore, Pa.
1972	Jack Nicklaus	290	Bruce Crampton (293)	Pebble Beach GL	Pebble Beach, Calif.
1973	Johnny Miller	279	John Schlee (280)	Oakmont CC	Oakmont, Pa.
1974	Hale Irwin	287	Forest Fezler (289)	Winged Foot GC	Mamaroneck, N.Y.
1975	Lou Graham*	287	John Mahaffey (287)	Medinah CC	Medinah, Ill.
1976	Jerry Pate	277	Al Geiberger & Tom Weiskopf (279)	Atlanta AC	Duluth, Ga.
1977	Hubert Green	278	Lou Graham (279)	Southern Hills CC	Tulsa
1978	Andy North	285	Dave Stockton & J.C. Snead (286)	Cherry Hills CC	Denver
1979	Hale Irwin	284	Gary Player & Jerry Pate (286)	Inverness Club	Toledo, Ohio
1980	Jack Nicklaus	272	Isao Aoki (274)	Baltusrol GC	Springfield, N.J.
1981	David Graham	273	George Burns & Bill Rogers (276)	Merion GC	Ardmore, Pa.
1982	Tom Watson	282	Jack Nicklaus (284)	Pebble Beach GL	Pebble Beach, Calif.
1983	Larry Nelson	280	Tom Watson (281)	Oakmont CC	Oakmont, Pa.
1984	Fuzzy Zoeller*	276	Greg Norman (276)	Winged Foot GC	Mamaroneck, N.Y.
1985	Andy North	279	Dave Barr, T.C. Chen & Denis Watson (280)	Oakland Hills CC	Birmingham, Mich.
1986	Ray Floyd	279	Lanny Wadkins & Chip Beck (281)	Shinnecock Hills GC	Southampton, N.Y.
1987	Scott Simpson	277	Tom Watson (278)	Olympic Club	San Francisco
1988	Curtis Strange*	278	Nick Faldo (278)	The Country Club	Brookline, Mass.
1989	Curtis Strange	278	Chip Beck, Ian Woosnam & Mark McCumber (279)	Oak Hill CC	Rochester, N.Y.
1990	Hale Irwin*	280	Mike Donald (280)	Medinah CC	Medinah, Ill.
1991	Payne Stewart*	282	Scott Simpson (282)	Hazeltine National GC	Chaska, Minn.
1992	Tom Kite	285	Jeff Sluman (287)	Pebble Beach GL	Pebble Beach, Calif.
1993	Lee Janzen	272	Payne Stewart (274)	Baltusrol GC	Springfield, N.J.
1994	Ernie Els*	279	Colin Montgomerie (279) & Loren Roberts (279)	Oakmont CC	Oakmont, Pa.
1995	Corey Pavin	280	Greg Norman (282)	Shinnecock Hills GC	Southampton, N.Y.
1996	Steve Jones	278	Davis Love III & Tom Lehman (279)	Oakland Hills CC	Bloomfield Hills, Mich.
1997	Ernie Els	276	Colin Montgomerie (277)	Congressional CC	Bethesda, Md.

Year	Winner	Score	Runner-up	Course	Location
1998	Lee Janzen	280	Payne Stewart (281)	Olympic Club	San Francisco
1999	Payne Stewart	279	Phil Mickelson (280)	Pinehurst CC	Pinehurst, N.C.
2000	Tiger Woods	272	Miguel Angel Jimenez & Ernie Els (287)	Pebble Beach GL	Pebble Beach, Calif.
2001	Retief Goosen*	276	Mark Brooks (276)	Southern Hills CC	Tulsa
2002	Tiger Woods	277	Phil Mickelson (280)	Bethpage Black	Farmingdale, N.Y.
2003	Jim Furyk	272	Stephen Leaney (275)	Olympia Fields CC	Olympia Fields, Ill.
2004	Retief Goosen	276	Phil Mickelson (278)	Shinnecock Hills GC	Southampton, N.Y.
2005	Michael Campbell	280	Tiger Woods (282)	Pinehurst CC	Pinehurst, N.C.
2006	Geoff Ogilvy	285	Jim Furyk, Colin Montgomerie & Phil Mickelson (286)	Winged Foot GC	Mamaroneck, N.Y.
2007	Angel Cabrera	285	Jim Furyk & Tiger Woods (286)	Oakmont CC	Oakmont, Pa.
2008	Tiger Woods*	283	Rocco Mediate (283)	Torrey Pines GC	La Jolla, Calif.

*PLAYOFFS:

1901: Willie Anderson (85) def. Alex Smith (86) in 18 holes. **1903:** Willie Anderson (82) def. David Brown (84) in 18 holes. **1908:** Fred McLeod (77) def. Willie Smith (83) in 18 holes. **1910:** Alex Smith (71) def. John McDermott (75) & Macdonald Smith (77) in 18 holes. **1911:** John McDermott (80) def. Mike Brady (82) & George Simpson (85) in 18 holes. **1913:** Francis Ouimet (72) def. Harry Vardon (77) & Edward Ray (78) in 18 holes. **1919:** Walter Hagen (77) def. Mike Brady (78) in 18 holes. **1923:** Bobby Jones (76) def. Bobby Cruickshank (78) in 18 holes. **1925:** Willie Macfarlane (75-72—147) def. Bobby Jones (75-73—148) in 36 holes. **1927:** Tommy Armour (76) def. Harry Cooper (79) in 18 holes. **1928:** Johnny Farrell (70-73—143) def. Bobby Jones (73-71—144) in 36 holes. **1929:** Bobby Jones (141) def. Al Espinosa (164) in 36 holes. **1931:** Billy Burke (149-148) def. George Von Elm (149-149) in 72 holes. **1939:** Byron Nelson (68-70) def. Craig Wood (68-73) and Denny Shute (76) in 36 holes. **1940:** Lawson Little (70) def. Gene Sarazen (73) in 18 holes. **1946:** Lloyd Mangrum (72-72—144) def. Byron Nelson (72-73—145) and Vic Ghezzi (72-73—145) in 36 holes. **1947:** Lew Worsham (69) def. Sam Snead (70) in 18 holes.

1950: Ben Hogan (69) def. Lloyd Mangrum (73) & George Fazio (75) in 18 holes. **1955:** Jack Fleck (69) def. Ben Hogan (72) in 18 holes. **1957:** Dick Mayer (72) def. Cary Middlecoff (79) in 18 holes. **1962:** Jack Nicklaus (71) def. Arnold Palmer (74) in 18 holes. **1963:** Julius Boros (70) def. Jacky Cupit (73) & Arnold Palmer (76) in 18 holes. **1965:** Gary Player (71) def. Kel Nagle (74) in 18 holes. **1966:** Billy Casper (69) def. Arnold Palmer (73) in 18 holes. **1971:** Lee Trevino (68) def. Jack Nicklaus (71) in 18 holes. **1975:** Lou Graham (71) def. John Mahaffey (73) in 18 holes. **1984:** Fuzzy Zoeller (67) def. Greg Norman (75) in 18 holes. **1988:** Curtis Strange (71) def. Nick Faldo (75) in 18 holes. **1990:** Hale Irwin (74-3) def. Mike Donald (74-4) on 1st hole of sudden death after 18 holes. **1991:** Payne Stewart (75) def. Scott Simpson (77) in 18 holes. **1994:** Ernie Els (74-4-4) def. Loren Roberts (74-4-5) and Colin Montgomerie (78) on 2nd hole of sudden death after 18 holes; **2001:** Goosen (70) def. Brooks (72) in 18 holes; **2008:** Tiger Woods (71-4) def. Rocco Mediate (71-5) on 1st hole of sudden death after 18 holes.

Vardon Trophy

Awarded since 1937 by the PGA of America to the PGA Tour regular with the lowest adjusted scoring average, based on a minimum of 60 rounds. The award is named after Harry Vardon, the six-time British Open champion who also won the U.S. Open in 1900. A point system was used from 1937-41.

Multiple winners: Tiger Woods (7); Billy Casper and Lee Trevino (5); Arnold Palmer and Sam Snead (4); Ben Hogan, Greg Norman and Tom Watson (3); Fred Couples, Bruce Crampton, Tom Kite, Lloyd Mangrum and Nick Price (2).

Year		Pts	Year		Avg	Year		Avg
1937	Harry Cooper	500	1963	Billy Casper	70.58	1986	Scott Hoch	70.08
1938	Sam Snead	520	1964	Arnold Palmer	70.01	1987	Dan Pohl	70.25
1939	Byron Nelson	473	1965	Billy Casper	70.85	1988	Chip Beck	69.46
1940	Ben Hogan	423	1966	Billy Casper	70.27	1989	Greg Norman	69.49
1941	Ben Hogan	494	1967	Arnold Palmer	70.18	1990	Greg Norman	69.10
1942-46	No award		1968	Billy Casper	69.82	1991	Fred Couples	69.59
Year		**Avg**	1969	Dave Hill	70.34	1992	Fred Couples	69.38
1947	Jimmy Demaret	69.90	1970	Lee Trevino	70.64	1993	Nick Price	69.11
1948	Ben Hogan	69.30	1971	Lee Trevino	70.27	1994	Greg Norman	68.81
1949	Sam Snead	69.37	1972	Lee Trevino	70.89	1995	Steve Elkington	69.62
1950	Sam Snead	69.23	1973	Bruce Crampton	70.57	1996	Tom Lehman	69.32
1951	Lloyd Mangrum	70.05	1974	Lee Trevino	70.53	1997	Nick Price	68.98
1952	Jack Burke	70.54	1975	Bruce Crampton	70.51	1998	David Duval	69.13
1953	Lloyd Mangrum	70.22	1976	Don January	70.56	1999	Tiger Woods	68.43
1954	E.J. Harrison	70.41	1977	Tom Watson	70.32	2000	Tiger Woods	67.79
1955	Sam Snead	69.86	1978	Tom Watson	70.16	2001	Tiger Woods	68.81
1956	Cary Middlecoff	70.35	1979	Tom Watson	70.27	2002	Tiger Woods	68.56
1957	Dow Finsterwald	70.30	1980	Lee Trevino	69.73	2003	Tiger Woods	68.41
1958	Bob Rosburg	70.11	1981	Tom Kite	69.80	2004	Vijay Singh	68.84
1959	Art Wall	70.35	1982	Tom Kite	70.21	2005	Tiger Woods	68.66
1960	Billy Casper	69.95	1983	Ray Floyd	70.61	2006	Jim Furyk	68.86
1961	Arnold Palmer	69.85	1984	Calvin Peete	70.56	2007	Tiger Woods	67.79
1962	Arnold Palmer	70.27	1985	Don Pooley	70.36			

British Open

The oldest of the Majors, the Open began in 1860 to determine "the champion golfer of the world." While only professional golfers participated in the first year of the tournament, amateurs have been invited ever since. Competition was extended from 36 to 72 holes in 1892. Conducted by the Royal and Ancient Golf Club of St. Andrews, the Open is rotated among select golf courses in England and Scotland. Note that (*) indicates playoff winner and (a) indicates amateur winner.

Multiple winners: Harry Vardon (6); James Braid, J.H. Taylor, Peter Thomson and Tom Watson (5); Walter Hagen, Bobby Locke, Tom Morris Sr., Tom Morris Jr. and Willie Park (4); Jamie Anderson, Seve Ballesteros, Henry Cotton, Nick Faldo, Bob Ferguson, Bobby Jones, Jack Nicklaus, Gary Player and Tiger Woods (3); Padraig Harrington, Harold Hilton, Bob Martin, Greg Norman, Arnold Palmer, Willie Park Jr. and Lee Trevino (2).

Year	Winner	Score	Runner-up	Course	Location
1860	Willie Park	174	Tom Morris Sr. (176)	Prestwick Club	Ayrshire, Scotland
1861	Tom Morris Sr.	163	Willie Park (167)	Prestwick Club	Ayrshire, Scotland
1862	Tom Morris Sr.	163	Willie Park (176)	Prestwick Club	Ayrshire, Scotland
1863	Willie Park	168	Tom Morris Sr. (170)	Prestwick Club	Ayrshire, Scotland
1864	Tom Morris Sr.	167	Andrew Strath (169)	Prestwick Club	Ayrshire, Scotland
1865	Andrew Strath	162	Willie Park (164)	Prestwick Club	Ayrshire, Scotland
1866	Willie Park	169	David Park (171)	Prestwick Club	Ayrshire, Scotland
1867	Tom Morris Sr.	170	Willie Park (172)	Prestwick Club	Ayrshire, Scotland
1868	Tom Morris Jr.	157	Robert Andrew (159)	Prestwick Club	Ayrshire, Scotland
1869	Tom Morris Jr.	154	Tom Morris Sr. (157)	Prestwick Club	Ayrshire, Scotland
1870	Tom Morris Jr.	149	Bob Kirk (161)	Prestwick Club	Ayrshire, Scotland
1871	Not held				
1872	Tom Morris Jr.	166	David Strath (169)	Prestwick Club	Ayrshire, Scotland
1873	Tom Kidd	179	Jamie Anderson (180)	St. Andrews	St. Andrews, Scotland
1874	Mungo Park	159	Tom Morris Jr. (161)	Musselburgh	Musselburgh, Scotland
1875	Willie Park	166	Bob Martin (168)	Prestwick Club	Ayrshire, Scotland
1876	Bob Martin*	176	David Strath (176)	St. Andrews	St. Andrews, Scotland
1877	Jamie Anderson	160	Bob Pringle (162)	Musselburgh	Musselburgh, Scotland
1878	Jamie Anderson	157	Bob Kirk (159)	Prestwick Club	Ayrshire, Scotland
1879	Jamie Anderson	169	Andrew Kirkaldy & James Allan (172)	St. Andrews	St. Andrews, Scotland
1880	Bob Ferguson	162	Peter Paxton (167)	Musselburgh	Musselburgh, Scotland
1881	Bob Ferguson	170	Jamie Anderson (173)	Prestwick Club	Ayrshire, Scotland
1882	Bob Ferguson	171	Willie Fernie (174)	St. Andrews	St. Andrews, Scotland
1883	Willie Fernie*	159	Bob Ferguson (159)	Musselburgh	Musselburgh, Scotland
1884	Jack Simpson	160	Douglas Rolland & Willie Fernie (164)	Prestwick Club	Ayrshire, Scotland
1885	Bob Martin	171	Archie Simpson (172)	St. Andrews	St. Andrews, Scotland
1886	David Brown	157	Willie Campbell (159)	Musselburgh	Musselburgh, Scotland
1887	Willie Park Jr.	161	Bob Martin (162)	Prestwick Club	Ayrshire, Scotland
1888	Jack Burns	171	David Anderson & Ben Sayers (172)	St. Andrews	St. Andrews, Scotland
1889	Willie Park Jr.*	155	Andrew Kirkaldy (155)	Musselburgh	Musselburgh, Scotland
1890	a-John Ball	164	Willie Fernie (167) & A. Simpson (167)	Prestwick Club	Ayrshire, Scotland
1891	Hugh Kirkaldy	166	Andrew Kirkaldy & Willie Fernie (168)	St. Andrews	St. Andrews, Scotland
1892	a-Harold Hilton	305	John Ball, Sandy Herd & Hugh Kirkaldy (308)	Muirfield	Gullane, Scotland
1893	Willie Auchterlonie	322	Johnny Laidley (324)	Prestwick Club	Ayrshire, Scotland
1894	J.H. Taylor	326	Douglas Rolland (331)	Royal St. George's	Sandwich, England
1895	J.H. Taylor	322	Sandy Herd (326)	St. Andrews	St. Andrews, Scotland
1896	Harry Vardon*	316	J.H. Taylor (316)	Muirfield	Gullane, Scotland
1897	a-Harold Hilton	314	James Braid (315)	Hoylake	Hoylake, England
1898	Harry Vardon	307	Willie Park Jr. (308)	Prestwick Club	Ayrshire, Scotland
1899	Harry Vardon	310	Jack White (315)	Royal St. George's	Sandwich, England
1900	J.H. Taylor	309	Harry Vardon (317)	St. Andrews	St. Andrews, Scotland
1901	James Braid	309	Harry Vardon (312)	Muirfield	Gullane, Scotland
1902	Sandy Herd	307	Harry Vardon (308)	Hoylake	Hoylake, England
1903	Harry Vardon	300	Tom Vardon (306)	Prestwick Club	Ayrshire, Scotland
1904	Jack White	296	James Braid (297)	Royal St. George's	Sandwich, England
1905	James Braid	318	J.H. Taylor (323) & Rowland Jones (323)	St. Andrews	St. Andrews, Scotland
1906	James Braid	300	J.H. Taylor (304)	Muirfield	Gullane, Scotland
1907	Arnaud Massy	312	J.H. Taylor (314)	Hoylake	Hoylake, England
1908	James Braid	291	Tom Ball (299)	Prestwick Club	Ayrshire, Scotland
1909	J.H. Taylor	295	James Braid (299)	Deal	Deal, England
1910	James Braid	299	Sandy Herd (303)	St. Andrews	St. Andrews, Scotland
1911	Harry Vardon*	303	Arnaud Massy (303)	Royal St. George's	Sandwich, England
1912	Ted Ray	295	Harry Vardon (299)	Muirfield	Gullane, Scotland
1913	J.H. Taylor	304	Ted Ray (312)	Hoylake	Hoylake, England
1914	Harry Vardon	306	J.H. Taylor (309)	Prestwick Club	Ayrshire, Scotland

Year	Winner	Score	Runner-up	Course	Location
1915-19	Not held		World War I		
1920	George Duncan	303	Sandy Herd (305)	Deal	Deal, England
1921	Jock Hutchison*	296	Roger Wethered (296)	St. Andrews	St. Andrews, Scotland
1922	Walter Hagen	300	George Duncan & Jim Barnes (301)	Royal St. George's	Sandwich, England
1923	Arthur Havers	295	Walter Hagen (296)	Royal Troon	Troon, Scotland
1924	Walter Hagen	301	Ernest Whitcombe (302)	Hoylake	Hoylake, England
1925	Jim Barnes	300	Archie Compston & Ted Ray (301)	Prestwick Club	Ayrshire, Scotland
1926	a-Bobby Jones	291	Al Watrous (293)	Royal Lytham	Lytham, England
1927	a-Bobby Jones	285	Aubrey Boomer (291)	St. Andrews	St. Andrews, Scotland
1928	Walter Hagen	292	Gene Sarazen (294)	Royal St. George's	Sandwich, England
1929	Walter Hagen	292	Johnny Farrell (298)	Muirfield	Gullane, Scotland
1930	a-Bobby Jones	291	Macdonald Smith & Leo Diegel (293)	Hoylake	Hoylake, England
1931	Tommy Armour	296	Jose Jurado (297)	Carnoustie	Carnoustie, Scotland
1932	Gene Sarazen	283	Macdonald Smith (288)	Prince's	Prince's, England
1933	Denny Shute*	292	Craig Wood (292)	St. Andrews	St. Andrews, Scotland
1934	Henry Cotton	283	Sid Brews (288)	Royal St. George's	Sandwich, England
1935	Alf Perry	283	Alf Padgham (287)	Muirfield	Gullane, Scotland
1936	Alf Padgham	287	Jimmy Adams (288)	Hoylake	Hoylake, England
1937	Henry Cotton	290	Reg Whitcombe (292)	Carnoustie	Carnoustie, Scotland
1938	Reg Whitcombe	295	Jimmy Adams (297)	Royal St. George's	Sandwich, England
1939	Dick Burton	290	Johnny Bulla (292)	St. Andrews	St. Andrews, Scotland
1940-45	Not held		World War II		
1946	Sam Snead	290	Bobby Locke (294) & Johnny Bulla (294)	St. Andrews	St. Andrews, Scotland
1947	Fred Daly	293	Frank Stranahan & Reg Horne (294)	Hoylake	Hoylake, England
1948	Henry Cotton	284	Fred Daly (289)	Muirfield	Gullane, Scotland
1949	Bobby Locke*	283	Harry Bradshaw (283)	Royal St. George's	Sandwich, England
1950	Bobby Locke	279	Roberto de Vicenzo (281)	Royal Troon	Troon, Scotland
1951	Max Faulkner	285	Tony Cerda (287)	Royal Portrush	Portrush, Ireland
1952	Bobby Locke	287	Peter Thomson (288)	Royal Lytham	Lytham, England
1953	Ben Hogan	282	Frank Stranahan, Dai Rees, Tony Cerda & Peter Thomson (286)	Carnoustie	Carnoustie, Scotland
1954	Peter Thomson	283	Sid Scott, Dai Rees & Bobby Locke (284)	Royal Birkdale	Southport, England
1955	Peter Thomson	281	Johny Fallon (283)	St. Andrews	St. Andrews, Scotland
1956	Peter Thomson	286	Flory Van Donck (289)	Hoylake	Hoylake, England
1957	Bobby Locke	279	Peter Thomson (282)	St. Andrews	St. Andrews, Scotland
1958	Peter Thomson*	278	Dave Thomas (278)	Royal Lytham	Lytham, England
1959	Gary Player	284	Flory Van Donck & Fred Bullock (286)	Muirfield	Gullane, Scotland
1960	Kel Nagle	278	Arnold Palmer (279)	St. Andrews	St. Andrews, Scotland
1961	Arnold Palmer	284	Dai Rees (285)	Royal Birkdale	Southport, England
1962	Arnold Palmer	276	Kel Nagle (282)	Royal Troon	Troon, Scotland
1963	Bob Charles*	277	Phil Rodgers (277)	Royal Lytham	Lytham, England
1964	Tony Lema	279	Jack Nicklaus (284)	St. Andrews	St. Andrews, Scotland
1965	Peter Thomson	285	Christy O'Connor & Brian Huggett (287)	Royal Birkdale	Southport, England
1966	Jack Nicklaus	282	Doug Sanders & Dave Thomas (283)	Muirfield	Gullane, Scotland
1967	Roberto de Vicenzo	278	Jack Nicklaus (280)	Hoylake	Hoylake, England
1968	Gary Player	289	Jack Nicklaus & Bob Charles (291)	Carnoustie	Carnoustie, Scotland
1969	Tony Jacklin	280	Bob Charles (282)	Royal Lytham	Lytham, England
1970	Jack Nicklaus*	283	Doug Sanders (283)	St. Andrews	St. Andrews, Scotland
1971	Lee Trevino	278	Lu Liang Huan (279)	Royal Birkdale	Southport, England
1972	Lee Trevino	278	Jack Nicklaus (279)	Muirfield	Gullane, Scotland
1973	Tom Weiskopf	276	Johnny Miller & Neil Coles (279)	Royal Troon	Troon, Scotland
1974	Gary Player	282	Peter Oosterhuis (286)	Royal Lytham	Lytham, England
1975	Tom Watson*	279	Jack Newton (279)	Carnoustie	Carnoustie, Scotland
1976	Johnny Miller	279	Seve Ballesteros & Jack Nicklaus (285)	Royal Birkdale	Southport, England
1977	Tom Watson	268	Jack Nicklaus (269)	Turnberry	Turnberry, Scotland
1978	Jack Nicklaus	281	Tom Kite, Ray Floyd, Ben Crenshaw & Simon Owen (283)	St. Andrews	St. Andrews, Scotland
1979	Seve Ballesteros	283	Jack Nicklaus & Ben Crenshaw (286)	Royal Lytham	Lytham, England

British Open (Cont.)

Year	Winner	Score	Runner-up	Course	Location
1980	Tom Watson	271	Lee Trevino (275)	Muirfield	Gullane, Scotland
1981	Bill Rogers	276	Bernhard Langer (280)	Royal St. George's	Sandwich, England
1982	Tom Watson	284	Peter Oosterhuis & Nick Price (285)	Royal Troon	Troon, Scotland
1983	Tom Watson	275	Hale Irwin & Andy Bean (276)	Royal Birkdale	Southport, England
1984	Seve Ballesteros	276	Bernhard Langer & Tom Watson (278)	St. Andrews	St. Andrews, Scotland
1985	Sandy Lyle	282	Payne Stewart (283)	Royal St. George's	Sandwich, England
1986	Greg Norman	280	Gordon J. Brand (285)	Turnberry	Turnberry, Scotland
1987	Nick Faldo	279	Paul Azinger & Rodger Davis (280)	Muirfield	Gullane, Scotland
1988	Seve Ballesteros	273	Nick Price (275)	Royal Lytham	Lytham, England
1989	Mark Calcavecchia*	275	Greg Norman & Wayne Grady (275)	Royal Troon	Troon, Scotland
1990	Nick Faldo	270	Payne Stewart & Mark McNulty (275)	St. Andrews	St. Andrews, Scotland
1991	Ian Baker-Finch	272	Mike Harwood (274)	Royal Birkdale	Southport, England
1992	Nick Faldo	272	John Cook (273)	Muirfield	Gullane, Scotland
1993	Greg Norman	267	Nick Faldo (269)	Royal St. George's	Sandwich, England
1994	Nick Price	268	Jesper Parnevik (269)	Turnberry	Turnberry, Scotland
1995	John Daly*	282	Costantino Rocca (282)	St. Andrews	St. Andrews, Scotland
1996	Tom Lehman	271	Mark McCumber & Ernie Els (273)	Royal Lytham	Lytham, England
1997	Justin Leonard	272	Jesper Parnevik & Darren Clarke (275)	Royal Troon	Troon, Scotland
1998	Mark O'Meara*	280	Brian Watts (280)	Royal Birkdale	Southport, England
1999	Paul Lawrie*	290	Justin Leonard & Jean Van de Velde (290)	Carnoustie	Carnoustie, Scotland
2000	Tiger Woods	269	Thomas Bjorn & Ernie Els (277)	St. Andrews	St. Andrews, Scotland
2001	David Duval	274	Niclas Fasth (277)	Royal Lytham	Lytham, England
2002	Ernie Els*	278	Thomas Levet, Stuart Appleby & Steve Elkington (278)	Muirfield	Gullane, Scotland
2003	Ben Curtis	283	Vijay Singh & Thomas Bjorn (284)	Royal St. George's	Sandwich, England
2004	Todd Hamilton*	274	Ernie Els (274)	Royal Troon	Troon, Scotland
2005	Tiger Woods	274	Colin Montgomerie (279)	St. Andrews	St. Andrews, Scotland
2006	Tiger Woods	270	Chris DiMarco (272)	Royal Liverpool	Hoylake, England
2007	Padraig Harrington*	277	Sergio Garcia (277)	Carnoustie	Carnoustie, Scotland
2008	Padraig Harrington	283	Ian Poulter (287)	Royal Birkdale	Southport, England

*PLAYOFFS:

1876: Bob Martin awarded title when David Strath refused playoff. **1883:** Willie Fernie (158) def. Robert Ferguson (159) in 36 holes. **1889:** Willie Park Jr. (158) def. Andrew Kirkaldy (163) in 36 holes. **1896:** Harry Vardon (157) def. John H. Taylor (161) in 36 holes. **1911:** Harry Vardon won when Arnaud Massy conceded at 35th hole. **1921:** Jock Hutchison (150) def. Roger Wethered (159) in 36 holes. **1933:** Denny Shute (149) def. Craig Wood (154) in 36 holes. **1949:** Bobby Locke (135) def. Harry Bradshaw (147) in 36 holes. **1958:** Peter Thomson (139) def. Dave Thomas (143) in 36 holes. **1963:** Bob Charles (140) def. Phil Rodgers (148) in 36 holes. **1970:** Jack Nicklaus (72) def. Doug Sanders (73) in 18 holes. **1975:** Tom Watson (71) def. Jack Newton (72) in 18 holes. **1989:** Mark Calcavecchia (4-3-3-3—13) def. Wayne Grady (4-4-4-4—16) and Greg Norman (3-3-4) in 4 holes. **1995:** John Daly (3-4-4-4—15) def. Costantino Rocca (4-5-7-3—19) in 4 holes. **1998:** Mark O'Meara (4-4-5-4—17) def. Brian Watts (4-5-5-5—19) in 4 holes. **1999:** Paul Lawrie (5-4-3-3—15) def. Justin Leonard (5-4-4-5—18) and Jean Van de Velde (6-4-3-5—18) in 4 holes. **2002:** Els (4-3-5-4—16) and Levet (4-2-5-5—16) remained tied after a four-hole playoff that also included Appleby (4-4-4-5—17) and Elkington (5-3-4-5—17). The pair moved on to sudden death, where Els (4) def. Levet (5) on the 1st hole. **2004:** Todd Hamilton (4-4-3-4—15) def. Ernie Els (4-4-4-4—16) in 4 holes. **2007:** Padraig Harrington (3-3-4-5—15) def. Sergio Garcia (5-3-4-4—16) in 4 holes.

PGA Championship

The PGA Championship began in 1916 as a professional golfers match play tournament, but switched to stroke play in 1958. Conducted by the PGA of America, the tournament is played on a different course each year.

Multiple winners: Walter Hagen and Jack Nicklaus (5); Tiger Woods (4); Gene Sarazen and Sam Snead (3); Jim Barnes, Leo Diegel, Ray Floyd, Ben Hogan, Byron Nelson, Larry Nelson, Gary Player, Nick Price, Paul Runyan, Denny Shute, Vijay Singh, Dave Stockton and Lee Trevino (2).

Year	Winner	Score	Runner-up	Course	Location
1916	Jim Barnes	1-up	Jock Hutchison	Siwanoy CC	Bronxville, N.Y.
1917-18	Not held		World War I		
1919	Jim Barnes	6 & 5	Fred McLeod	Engineers CC	Roslyn, N.Y.
1920	Jock Hutchison	1-up	J. Douglas Edgar	Flossmoor CC	Flossmoor, Ill.
1921	Walter Hagen	3 & 2	Jim Barnes	Inwood CC	Inwood, N.Y.
1922	Gene Sarazen	4 & 3	Emmet French	Oakmont CC	Oakmont, Pa.
1923	Gene Sarazen*	1-up/38	Walter Hagen	Pelham CC	Pelham, N.Y.

Year	Winner	Score	Runner-up	Course	Location
1924	Walter Hagen	2-up	Jim Barnes	French Lick CC	French Lick, Ind.
1925	Walter Hagen	6 & 5	Bill Mehlhorn	Olympia Fields CC	Matteson, Ill.
1926	Walter Hagen	5 & 3	Leo Diegel	Salisbury CC	Westbury, N.Y.
1927	Walter Hagen	1-up	Joe Turnesa	Cedar Crest CC	Dallas
1928	Leo Diegel	6 & 5	Al Espinosa	Five Farms CC	Baltimore
1929	Leo Diegel	6 & 4	John Farrell	Hillcrest CC	Los Angeles
1930	Tommy Armour	1-up	Gene Sarazen	Fresh Meadow CC	Flushing, N.Y.
1931	Tom Creavy	2 & 1	Denny Shute	Wannamoisett CC	Rumford, R.I.
1932	Olin Dutra	4 & 3	Frank Walsh	Keller GC	St. Paul, Minn.
1933	Gene Sarazen	5 & 4	Willie Goggin	Blue Mound CC	Milwaukee
1934	Paul Runyan*	1-up/38	Craig Wood	Park CC	Williamsville, N.Y.
1935	Johnny Revolta	5 & 4	Tommy Armour	Twin Hills CC	Oklahoma City
1936	Denny Shute	3 & 2	Jimmy Thomson	Pinehurst CC	Pinehurst, N.C.
1937	Denny Shute*	1-up/37	Harold McSpaden	Pittsburgh FC	Aspinwall, Pa.
1938	Paul Runyan	8 & 7	Sam Snead	Shawnee CC	Shawnee-on-Del, Pa.
1939	Henry Picard*	1-up/37	Byron Nelson	Pomonok CC	Flushing, N.Y.
1940	Byron Nelson	1-up	Sam Snead	Hershey CC	Hershey, Pa.
1941	Vic Ghezzi*	1-up/38	Byron Nelson	Cherry Hills CC	Denver
1942	Sam Snead	2 & 1	Jim Turnesa	Seaview CC	Atlantic City, N.J.
1943	Not held		World War II		
1944	Bob Hamilton	1-up	Byron Nelson	Manito G & CC	Spokane, Wash.
1945	Byron Nelson	4 & 3	Sam Byrd	Morraine CC	Dayton, Ohio
1946	Ben Hogan	6 & 4	Porky Oliver	Portland GC	Portland, Ore.
1947	Jim Ferrier	2 & 1	Chick Harbert	Plum Hollow CC	Detroit
1948	Ben Hogan	7 & 6	Mike Turnesa	Norwood Hills CC	St. Louis
1949	Sam Snead	3 & 2	John Palmer	Hermitage CC	Richmond, Va.
1950	Chandler Harper	4 & 3	Henry Williams Jr.	Scioto CC	Columbus, Ohio
1951	Sam Snead	7 & 6	Walter Burkemo	Oakmont CC	Oakmont, Pa.
1952	Jim Turnesa	1-up	Chick Harbert	Big Spring CC	Louisville
1953	Walter Burkemo	2 & 1	Felice Torza	Birmingham CC	Birmingham, Mich.
1954	Chick Harbert	4 & 3	Walter Burkemo	Keller GC	St. Paul, Minn.
1955	Doug Ford	4 & 3	Cary Middlecoff	Meadowbrook CC	Detroit
1956	Jack Burke	3 & 2	Ted Kroll	Blue Hill CC	Boston
1957	Lionel Hebert	2 & 1	Dow Finsterwald	Miami Valley GC	Dayton, Ohio
1958	Dow Finsterwald	276	Billy Casper (278)	Llanerch CC	Havertown, Pa.
1959	Bob Rosburg	277	Jerry Barber & Doug Sanders (278)	Minneapolis GC	St. Louis Park, Minn.
1960	Jay Hebert	281	Jim Ferrier (282)	Firestone CC	Akron, Ohio
1961	Jerry Barber**	277	Don January (277)	Olympia Fields CC	Matteson, Ill.
1962	Gary Player	278	Bob Goalby (279)	Aronimink GC	Newtown Square, Pa.
1963	Jack Nicklaus	279	Dave Ragan (281)	Dallas AC	Dallas
1964	Bobby Nichols	271	Jack Nicklaus & Arnold Palmer (274)	Columbus CC	Columbus, Ohio
1965	Dave Marr	280	Jack Nicklaus & Billy Casper (282)	Laurel Valley GC	Ligonier, Pa.
1966	Al Geiberger	280	Dudley Wysong (284)	Firestone CC	Akron, Ohio
1967	Don January**	281	Don Massengale (281)	Columbine CC	Littleton, Colo.
1968	Julius Boros	281	Arnold Palmer & Bob Charles (282)	Pecan Valley CC	San Antonio
1969	Ray Floyd	276	Gary Player (277)	NCR GC	Dayton, Ohio
1970	Dave Stockton	279	Arnold Palmer & Bob Murphy (281)	Southern Hills CC	Tulsa
1971	Jack Nicklaus	281	Billy Casper (283)	PGA National GC	Palm Beach Gardens, Fla.
1972	Gary Player	281	Jim Jamieson & Tommy Aaron (283)	Oakland Hills GC	Birmingham, Mich.
1973	Jack Nicklaus	277	Bruce Crampton (281)	Canterbury GC	Cleveland
1974	Lee Trevino	276	Jack Nicklaus (277)	Tanglewood GC	Winston-Salem, N.C.
1975	Jack Nicklaus	276	Bruce Crampton (278)	Firestone CC	Akron, Ohio
1976	Dave Stockton	281	Don January & Ray Floyd (282)	Congressional CC	Bethesda, Md.
1977	Lanny Wadkins**	282	Gene Littler (282)	Pebble Beach GL	Pebble Beach, Calif.
1978	John Mahaffey**	276	Jerry Pate & Tom Watson (276)	Oakmont CC	Oakmont, Pa.
1979	David Graham**	272	Ben Crenshaw (272)	Oakland Hills CC	Birmingham, Mich.
1980	Jack Nicklaus	274	Andy Bean (281)	Oak Hill CC	Rochester, N.Y.
1981	Larry Nelson	273	Fuzzy Zoeller (277)	Atlanta AC	Duluth, Ga.
1982	Ray Floyd	272	Lanny Wadkins (275)	Southern Hills CC	Tulsa
1983	Hal Sutton	274	Jack Nicklaus (275)	Riviera CC	Los Angeles
1984	Lee Trevino	273	Lanny Wadkins & Gary Player (277)	Shoal Creek	Birmingham, Ala.
1985	Hubert Green	278	Lee Trevino (280)	Cherry Hills CC	Denver
1986	Bob Tway	276	Greg Norman (278)	Inverness Club	Toledo, Ohio

PGA Championship (Cont.)

Year	Winner	Score	Runner-up	Course	Location
1987	Larry Nelson**	287	Lanny Wadkins (287)	PGA National	Palm Beach Gardens, Fla.
1988	Jeff Sluman	272	Paul Azinger 275)	Oak Tree GC	Edmond, Okla.
1989	Payne Stewart	276	Andy Bean, Mike Reid & Curtis Strange (277)	Kemper Lakes GC	Hawthorn Woods, Ill.
1990	Wayne Grady	282	Fred Couples (285)	Shoal Creek	Birmingham, Ala.
1991	John Daly	276	Bruce Lietzke (279)	Crooked Stick GC	Carmel, Ind.
1992	Nick Price	278	Nick Faldo, John Cook, Jim Gallagher & Gene Sauers (281)	Bellerive CC	St. Louis
1993	Paul Azinger**	272	Greg Norman (272)	Inverness Club	Toledo, Ohio
1994	Nick Price	269	Corey Pavin (275)	Southern Hills CC	Tulsa
1995	Steve Elkington**	267	Colin Montgomerie (267)	Riviera CC	Pacific Palisades, Calif.
1996	Mark Brooks**	277	Kenny Perry (277)	Valhalla GC	Louisville, Ky.
1997	Davis Love III	269	Justin Leonard (274)	Winged Foot GC	Mamaroneck, N.Y.
1998	Vijay Singh	271	Steve Stricker (273)	Sahalee CC	Redmond, Wash.
1999	Tiger Woods	277	Sergio Garcia (278)	Medinah CC	Medinah, Ill.
2000	Tiger Woods**	270	Bob May (270)	Valhalla GC	Louisville, Ky.
2001	David Toms	265	Phil Mickelson (266)	Atlanta AC	Duluth, Ga.
2002	Rich Beem	278	Tiger Woods (279)	Hazeltine National GC	Chaska, Minn.
2003	Shaun Micheel	276	Chad Campbell (278)	Oak Hill CC	Rochester, N.Y.
2004	Vijay Singh**	280	Chris DiMarco & Justin Leonard (280)	Whistling Straits	Kohler, Wis.
2005	Phil Mickelson	276	Steve Elkington & Thomas Bjorn (277)	Baltusrol GC	Springfield, N.J.
2006	Tiger Woods	270	Shaun Micheel (275)	Medinah CC	Medinah, Ill.
2007	Tiger Woods	272	Woody Austin (274)	Southern Hills CC	Tulsa
2008	Padraig Harrington	277	Sergio Garcia & Ben Curtis (279)	Oakland Hills CC	Bloomfield Hills, Mich.

*While the PGA Championship was a match play tournament from 1916-57, the two finalists played 36 holes for the title. In the five years that a playoff was necessary, the match was decided on the 37th or 38th hole.

PLAYOFFS

1961: Jerry Barber (67) def. Don January (68) in 18 holes. **1967:** Don January (69) def. Don Massengale (71) in 18 holes. **1977:** Lanny Wadkins (4-4-4) def. Gene Littler (4-4-5) on 3rd hole of sudden death. **1978:** John Mahaffey (4-3) def. Jerry Pate (4-4) and Tom Watson (4-5) on 2nd hole of sudden death. **1979:** David Graham (4-4-2) def. Ben Crenshaw (4-4-4) on 3rd hole of sudden death. **1987:** Larry Nelson (4) def. Lanny Wadkins (5) on 1st hole of sudden death. **1993:** Paul Azinger (4-4) def. Greg Norman (4-5) on 2nd hole of sudden death. **1995:** Steve Elkington (3) def. Colin Montgomerie (4) on 1st hole of sudden death. **1996:** Mark Brooks (4) def. Kenny Perry (5) on 1st hole of sudden death. **2000:** Tiger Woods (3-4-5—12) won a three-hole playoff over Bob May (4-4-5—13). **2004:** Vijay Singh (3-3-4—10) won a three-hole playoff over Chris DiMarco (4-3-DNF) and Justin Leonard (4-3-DNF).

Grand Slam Summary

The only golfer ever to win a recognized Grand Slam—four major championships in a single season—was Bobby Jones in 1930. That year, Jones won the U.S. and British Opens as well as the U.S. and British Amateurs.

The men's professional Grand Slam—the Masters, U.S. Open, British Open and PGA Championship—did not gain acceptance until 30 years later when Arnold Palmer won the 1960 Masters and U.S. Open. The media wrote that the popular Palmer was chasing the "new" Grand Slam and would have to win the British Open and the PGA to claim it. He did not, but then nobody has before or since.

Three wins in one year (2): Ben Hogan (1953) and Tiger Woods (2000). **Two wins in one year** (21): Jack Nicklaus (5 times); Tiger Woods (4 times); Ben Hogan, Arnold Palmer and Tom Watson (twice); Nick Faldo, Padraig Harrington, Mark O'Meara, Gary Player, Nick Price, Sam Snead, Lee Trevino and Craig Wood (once).

Year	Masters	US Open	Brit. Open	PGA	Year	Masters	US Open	Brit. Open	PGA
1934	H. Smith	Dutra	Cotton	Runyan	1952	Snead	Boros	Locke	Turnesa
1935	Sarazen	Parks	Perry	Revolta	1953	Hogan	Hogan	Hogan	Burkemo
1936	H. Smith	Manero	Padgham	Shute	1954	Snead	Furgol	Thomson	Harbert
1937	B. Nelson	Guldahl	Cotton	Shute	1955	Middlecoff	Fleck	Thomson	Ford
1938	Picard	Guldahl	Whitcombe	Runyan	1956	Burke	Middlecoff	Thomson	Burke
1939	Guldahl	B. Nelson	Burton	Picard	1957	Ford	Mayer	Locke	L. Hebert
1940	Demaret	Little	—	B. Nelson	1958	Palmer	Bolt	Thomson	Finsterwald
1941	Wood	Wood	—	Ghezzi	1959	Wall	Casper	Player	Rosburg
1942	B. Nelson	—	—	Snead	1960	Palmer	Palmer	Nagle	J. Hebert
1943	—	—	—	—	1961	Player	Littler	Palmer	J. Barber
1944	—	—	—	Hamilton	1962	Palmer	Nicklaus	Palmer	Player
1945	—	—	—	B. Nelson	1963	Nicklaus	Boros	Charles	Nicklaus
1946	Keiser	Mangrum	Snead	Hogan	1964	Palmer	Venturi	Lema	Nichols
1947	Demaret	Worsham	F. Daly	Ferrier	1965	Nicklaus	Player	Thomson	Marr
1948	Harmon	Hogan	Cotton	Hogan	1966	Nicklaus	Casper	Nicklaus	Geiberger
1949	Snead	Middlecoff	Locke	Snead	1967	Brewer Jr.	Nicklaus	De Vicenzo	January
1950	Demaret	Hogan	Locke	Harper	1968	Goalby	Trevino	Player	Boros
1951	Hogan	Hogan	Faulkner	Snead	1969	Archer	Moody	Jacklin	Floyd

Year	Masters	US Open	Brit. Open	PGA	Year	Masters	US Open	Brit. Open	PGA
1970	Casper	Jacklin	Nicklaus	Stockton	1990	Faldo	Irwin	Faldo	Grady
1971	Coody	Trevino	Trevino	Nicklaus	1991	Woosnam	Stewart	Baker-Finch	J. Daly
1972	Nicklaus	Nicklaus	Trevino	Player	1992	Couples	Kite	Faldo	Price
1973	Aaron	J. Miller	Weiskopf	Nicklaus	1993	Langer	Janzen	Norman	Azinger
1974	Player	Irwin	Player	Trevino	1994	Olazabal	Els	Price	Price
1975	Nicklaus	L. Graham	T. Watson	Nicklaus	1995	Crenshaw	Pavin	Daly	Elkington
1976	Floyd	J. Pate	Miller	Stockton	1996	Faldo	S. Jones	Lehman	Brooks
1977	T. Watson	H. Green	T. Watson	L. Wadkins	1997	Woods	Els	Leonard	Love
1978	Player	North	Nicklaus	Mahaffey	1998	O'Meara	Janzen	O'Meara	Singh
1979	Zoeller	Irwin	Ballesteros	D. Graham	1999	Olazabal	Stewart	Lawrie	Woods
1980	Ballesteros	Nicklaus	T. Watson	Nicklaus	2000	Singh	Woods	Woods	Woods
1981	T. Watson	D. Graham	Rogers	L. Nelson	2001	Woods	Goosen	Duval	Toms
1982	Stadler	T. Watson	T. Watson	Floyd	2002	Woods	Woods	Els	Beem
1983	Ballesteros	L. Nelson	T. Watson	Sutton	2003	Weir	Furyk	Curtis	Micheel
1984	Crenshaw	Zoeller	Ballesteros	Trevino	2004	Mickelson	Goosen	Hamilton	Singh
1985	Langer	North	Lyle	H. Green	2005	Woods	Campbell	Woods	Mickelson
1986	Nicklaus	Floyd	Norman	Tway	2006	Mickelson	Ogilvy	Woods	Woods
1987	Mize	S. Simpson	Faldo	L. Nelson	2007	Johnson	Cabrera	Harrington	Woods
1988	Lyle	Strange	Ballesteros	Sluman	2008	Immelman	Woods	Harrington	Harrington
1989	Faldo	Strange	Calcavecchia	Stewart					

U.S. Amateur

Match play from 1895-64, stroke play from 1965-72, match play 1973-79, 36-hole stroke-play qualifying before match play since 1979.

Multiple winners: Bobby Jones (5); Jerry Travers (4); Walter Travis and Tiger Woods (3); Deane Beman, Charles Coe, Gary Cowan, H. Chandler Egan, Chick Evans, Lawson Little, Jack Nicklaus, Francis Ouimet, Jay Sigel, William Turnesa, Bud Ward, Harvie Ward, and H.J. Whigham (2).

Year		Year		Year		Year	
1895	Charles Macdonald	1924	Bobby Jones	1955	Harvie Ward	1983	Jay Sigel
1896	H.J. Whigham	1925	Bobby Jones	1956	Harvie Ward	1984	Scott Verplank
1897	H.J. Whigham	1926	George Von Elm	1957	Hillman Robbins	1985	Sam Randolph
1898	Findlay Douglas	1927	Bobby Jones	1958	Charles Coe	1986	Buddy Alexander
1899	H.M. Harriman	1928	Bobby Jones	1959	Jack Nicklaus	1987	Billy Mayfair
1900	Walter Travis	1929	Harrison Johnston	1960	Deane Beman	1988	Eric Meeks
1901	Walter Travis	1930	Bobby Jones	1961	Jack Nicklaus	1989	Chris Patton
1902	Louis James	1931	Francis Ouimet	1962	Labron Harris	1990	Phil Mickelson
1903	Walter Travis	1932	Ross Somerville	1963	Deane Beman	1991	Mitch Voges
1904	H. Chandler Egan	1933	George Dunlap	1964	Bill Campbell	1992	Justin Leonard
1905	H. Chandler Egan	1934	Lawson Little	1965	Bob Murphy	1993	John Harris
1906	Eben Byers	1935	Lawson Little	1966	Gary Cowan	1994	Tiger Woods
1907	Jerry Travers	1936	John Fischer	1967	Bob Dickson	1995	Tiger Woods
1908	Jerry Travers	1937	John Goodman	1968	Bruce Fleisher	1996	Tiger Woods
1909	Robert Gardner	1938	William Turnesa	1969	Steve Melnyk	1997	Matt Kuchar
1910	W.C. Fownes Jr.	1939	Bud Ward	1970	Lanny Wadkins	1998	Hank Kuehne
1911	Harold Hilton	1940	Richard Chapman	1971	Gary Cowan	1999	David Gossett
1912	Jerry Travers	1941	Bud Ward	1972	Vinny Giles	2000	Jeff Quinney
1913	Jerry Travers	1942-45	Not held	1973	Craig Stadler	2001	Bubba Dickerson
1914	Francis Ouimet	1946	Ted Bishop	1974	Jerry Pate	2002	Ricky Barnes
1915	Robert Gardner	1947	Skee Riegel	1975	Fred Ridley	2003	Nick Flanagan
1916	Chick Evans	1948	William Turnesa	1976	Bill Sander	2004	Ryan Moore
1917-18	Not held	1949	Charles Coe	1977	John Fought	2005	Edoardo Molinari
1919	Davidson Herron	1950	Sam Urzetta	1978	John Cook	2006	Richie Ramsay
1920	Chick Evans	1951	Billy Maxwell	1979	Mark O'Meara	2007	Colt Knost
1921	Jesse Guilford	1952	Jack Westland	1980	Hal Sutton	2008	Danny Lee
1922	Jess Sweetser	1953	Gene Littler	1981	Nathaniel Crosby		
1923	Max Marston	1954	Arnold Palmer	1982	Jay Sigel		

Major Championship Leaders

Through 2008; active PGA players in **bold** type.

	US Open	British Open	PGA	Masters	US Am	British Am	Total
Jack Nicklaus	4	3	5	6	2	0	20
Tiger Woods	3	3	4	4	3	0	17
Bobby Jones	4	3	0	0	5	1	13
Walter Hagen	2	4	5	0	0	0	11
Ben Hogan	4	1	2	2	0	0	9
Gary Player	1	3	2	3	0	0	9
John Ball	0	1	0	0	0	8	9
Arnold Palmer	1	2	0	4	1	0	8
Tom Watson	1	5	0	2	0	0	8

Four tied with 7 wins each.

British Amateur

Match play since 1885. **Multiple winners:** John Ball (8); Michael Bonallack (5); Harold Hilton (4); Joe Carr (3); Horace Hutchinson, Ernest Holderness, Trevor Homer, Johnny Laidley, Lawson Little, Peter McEvoy, Dick Siderowf, Frank Stranahan, Freddie Tait, Cyril Tolley and Gary Wolstenholme (2).

Year		Year		Year		Year	
1885	Allen MacFie	1914	J.L.C. Jenkins	1952	Harvie Ward	1981	Phillipe Ploujoux
1886	Horace Hutchinson	1915-19	Not held	1953	Joe Carr	1982	Martin Thompson
1887	Horace Hutchinson	1920	Cyril Tolley	1954	Douglas Bachli	1983	Philip Parkin
1888	John Ball	1921	William Hunter	1955	Joe Conrad	1984	Jose-Maria Olazabal
1889	Johnny Laidley	1922	Ernest Holderness	1956	John Beharrell	1985	Garth McGimpsey
1890	John Ball	1923	Roger Wethered	1957	Reid Jack	1986	David Curry
1891	Johnny Laidley	1924	Ernest Holderness	1958	Joe Carr	1987	Paul Mayo
1892	John Ball	1925	Robert Harris	1959	Deane Beman	1988	Christian Hardin
1893	Peter Anderson	1926	Jess Sweetser	1960	Joe Carr	1989	Stephen Dodd
1894	John Ball	1927	William Tweddell	1961	Michael Bonallack	1990	Rolf Muntz
1895	Leslie Balfour-Melville	1928	Thomas Perkins	1962	Richard Davies	1991	Gary Wolstenholme
1896	Freddie Tait	1929	Cyril Tolley	1963	Michael Lunt	1992	Stephen Dundas
1897	Jack Allan	1930	Bobby Jones	1964	Gordon Clark	1993	Ian Pyman
1898	Freddie Tait	1931	Eric Smith	1965	Michael Bonallack	1994	Lee James
1899	John Ball	1932	John deForest	1966	Bobby Cole	1995	Gordon Sherry
1900	Harold Hilton	1933	Michael Scott	1967	Bob Dickson	1996	Warren Bledon
1901	Harold Hilton	1934	Lawson Little	1968	Michael Bonallack	1997	Craig Watson
1902	Charles Hutchings	1935	Lawson Little	1969	Michael Bonallack	1998	Sergio Garcia
1903	Robert Maxwell	1936	Hector Thomson	1970	Michael Bonallack	1999	Graeme Storm
1904	Walter Travis	1937	Robert Sweeny Jr.	1971	Steve Melnyk	2000	Mikko Ilonen
1905	Arthur Barry	1938	Charles Yates	1972	Trevor Homer	2001	Michael Hoey
1906	James Robb	1939	Alexander Kyle	1973	Dick Siderowf	2002	Alejandro Larrazabal
1907	John Ball	1940-45	Not held	1974	Trevor Homer	2003	Gary Wolstenholme
1908	E.A. Lassen	1946	James Bruen	1975	Vinny Giles	2004	Stuart Wilson
1909	Robert Maxwell	1947	William Turnesa	1976	Dick Siderowf	2005	Brian McElhinney
1910	John Ball	1948	Frank Stranahan	1977	Peter McEvoy	2006	Julien Guerrier
1911	Harold Hilton	1949	Samuel McCready	1978	Peter McEvoy	2007	Drew Weaver
1912	John Ball	1950	Frank Stranahan	1979	Jay Sigel	2008	Reinier Saxton
1913	Harold Hilton	1951	Richard Chapman	1980	Duncan Evans		

WOMEN
Kraft Nabisco Championship

Formerly known as the Colgate Dinah Shore (1972-81) and the Nabisco Dinah Shore (1982-99), the tournament became the LPGA's fourth designated major championship in 1983. Shore's name, which was dropped from the tournament in 2000, is preserved with the Nabisco Dinah Shore Trophy, which is awarded to the winner. The tourney has been played at Mission Hills CC in Rancho Mirage, Calif., since it began; (*) indicates playoff winner.

Multiple winners: (as a major): Amy Alcott, Betsy King and Annika Sorenstam (3); Juli Inkster, Dottie Pepper and Karrie Webb (2).

Year	Winner	Score	Runner-up	Year	Winner	Score	Runner-up
1972	Jane Blalock	213	Carol Mann & Judy Rankin (216)	1991	Amy Alcott	273	Dottie Pepper (281)
1973	Mickey Wright	284	Joyce Kazmierski (286)	1992	Dottie Pepper*	279	Juli Inkster (279)
1974	Jo Anne Prentice*	289	Jane Blalock & Sandra Haynie (289)	1993	Helen Alfredsson	284	Amy Benz & Tina Barrett (286)
1975	Sandra Palmer	283	Kathy McMullen (284)	1994	Donna Andrews	276	Laura Davies (277)
1976	Judy Rankin	285	Betty Burfeindt (288)	1995	Nanci Bowen	285	Susie Redman (286)
1977	Kathy Whitworth	289	JoAnne Carner & Sally Little (290)	1996	Patty Sheehan	281	Kelly Robbins, Meg Mallon & Annika Sorenstam (276)
1978	Sandra Post*	283	Penny Pulz (283)	1997	Betsy King	276	Kris Tschetter (278)
1979	Sandra Post	276	Nancy Lopez (277)	1998	Pat Hurst	281	Helen Dobson (282)
1980	Donna Caponi	275	Amy Alcott (277)	1999	Dottie Pepper	269	Meg Mallon (275)
1981	Nancy Lopez	277	Carolyn Hill (279)	2000	Karrie Webb	274	Dottie Pepper (284)
1982	Sally Little	278	Hollis Stacy & Sandra Haynie (281)	2001	Annika Sorenstam	281	Akiko Fukushima, Janice Moodie, Dottie Pepper, Rachel Teske & Karrie Webb (284)
1983	Amy Alcott	282	Beth Daniel & Kathy Whitworth (284)	2002	Annika Sorenstam	280	Liselotte Neumann (281)
1984	Juli Inkster*	280	Pat Bradley (280)	2003	P. Meunier-Lebouc	281	Annika Sorenstam (282)
1985	Alice Miller	275	Jan Stephenson (278)	2004	Grace Park	277	Aree Song (278)
1986	Pat Bradley	280	Val Skinner (282)	2005	Annika Sorenstam	273	Rosie Jones (281)
1987	Betsy King*	283	Patty Sheehan (283)	2006	Karrie Webb*	279	Lorena Ochoa (279)
1988	Amy Alcott	274	Colleen Walker (276)	2007	Morgan Pressel	285	Catriona Matthew, Brittany Lincicome & Suzann Pettersen (286)
1989	Juli Inkster	279	Tammie Green & JoAnne Carner (284)				
1990	Betsy King	283	Kathy Postlewait & Shirley Furlong (285)	2008	Lorena Ochoa	277	Annika Sorenstam & Suzann Pettersen (282)

*PLAYOFFS: 1974: Jo Ann Prentice def. Jane Blalock in sudden death. **1978:** Sandra Post def. Penny Pulz in sudden death. **1984:** Juli Inkster def. Pat Bradley in sudden death. **1987:** Betsy King def. Patty Sheehan in sudden death. **1992:** Dottie Pepper def. Juli Inkster in sudden death. **2006:** Karrie Webb def. Lorena Ochoa in sudden death.

U.S. Women's Open

The U.S. Women's Open began under the direction of the defunct Women's Professional Golfers Assn. in 1946, passed to the LPGA in 1949 and to the USGA in 1953. The tournament used a match play format its first year then switched to stroke play; (*) indicates playoff winner and (a) indicates amateur.

Multiple winners: Betsy Rawls and Mickey Wright (4); Susie Maxwell Berning, Annika Sorenstam, Hollis Stacy and Babe Zaharias (3); JoAnne Carner, Donna Caponi, Juli Inkster, Betsy King, Meg Mallon, Patty Sheehan, Louise Suggs and Karrie Webb (2).

Year	Winner	Score	Runner-up	Course	Location
1946	Patty Berg	5&4	Betty Jameson	Spokane CC	Spokane, Wash.
1947	Betty Jameson	295	a-Sally Sessions & a-Polly Riley (301)	Starmount Forest CC	Greensboro, N.C.
1948	Babe Zaharias	300	Betty Hicks (308)	Atlantic City CC	Northfield, N.J.
1949	Louise Suggs	291	Babe Zaharias (305)	Prince Georges CC	Landover, Md.
1950	Babe Zaharias	291	a-Betsy Rawls (300)	Rolling Hills CC	Wichita, Kan.
1951	Betsy Rawls	293	Louise Suggs (298)	Druid Hills GC	Atlanta, Ga.
1952	Louise Suggs	284	Marlene Hagge (291)	Bala GC	Philadelphia, Penn.
1953	Betsy Rawls*	302	Jackie Pung (302)	CC of Rochester	Rochester, N.Y.
1954	Babe Zaharias	291	Betty Hicks (303)	Salem CC	Peabody, Mass.
1955	Fay Crocker	299	Mary Lena Faulk (303)	Wichita CC	Wichita, Kan.
1956	Kathy Cornelius*	302	Barbara McIntire (302)	Northland CC	Duluth, Minn.
1957	Betsy Rawls	299	Patty Berg (305)	Winged Foot GC	Mamaroneck, N.Y.
1958	Mickey Wright	290	Louise Suggs (295)	Forest Lake CC	Detroit, Mich.
1959	Mickey Wright	287	Louise Suggs (289)	Churchill Valley CC	Pittsburgh, Penn.
1960	Betsy Rawls	292	Joyce Ziske (293)	Worcester CC	Worcester, Mass.
1961	Mickey Wright	293	Betsy Rawls (299)	Baltusrol GC	Springfield, N.J.
1962	Murle Breer	301	Jo Anne Prentice & Ruth Jessen (303)	Dunes GC	Myrtle Beach, S.C.
1963	Mary Mills	289	Sandra Haynie & Louise Suggs (292)	Kenwood CC	Cincinnati, Ohio
1964	Mickey Wright*	290	Ruth Jessen (290)	San Diego CC	Chula Vista, Calif.
1965	Carol Mann	290	Kathy Cornelius (292)	Atlantic City CC	Northfield, N.J.
1966	Sandra Spuzich	297	Carol Mann (298)	Hazeltine National GC	Chaska, Minn.
1967	a-Catherine LaCoste	294	Susie Berning & Beth Stone (296)	Hot Springs GC	Hot Springs, Va.
1968	Susie Berning	289	Mickey Wright (292)	Moselem Springs GC	Fleetwood, Penn.
1969	Donna Caponi	294	Peggy Wilson (295)	Scenic Hills CC	Pensacola, Fla.
1970	Donna Caponi	287	Sandra Haynie (288)	Muskogee CC	Muskogee, Okla.
1971	JoAnne Carner	288	Kathy Whitworth (295)	Kahkwa CC	Erie, Penn.
1972	Susie Berning	299	Kathy Ahern, Pam Barnett & Judy Rankin (300)	Winged Foot GC	Mamaroneck, N.Y.
1973	Susie Berning	290	Gloria Ehret (295)	CC of Rochester	Rochester, N.Y.
1974	Sandra Haynie	295	Carol Mann & Beth Stone (296)	La Grange CC	La Grange, Ill.
1975	Sandra Palmer	295	JoAnne Carner, a-Nancy Lopez & Sandra Post (299)	Atlantic City CC	Northfield, N.J.
1976	JoAnne Carner*	292	Sandra Palmer (292)	Rolling Green CC	Springfield, Penn.
1977	Hollis Stacy	292	Nancy Lopez (294)	Hazeltine National GC	Chaska, Minn.
1978	Hollis Stacy	289	JoAnne Carner & Sally Little (290)	CC of Indianapolis	Indianapolis, Ind.
1979	Jerilyn Britz	284	Debbie Massey & Sandra Palmer (286)	Brooklawn CC	Fairfield, Conn.
1980	Amy Alcott	280	Hollis Stacy (289)	Richland CC	Nashville, Tenn.
1981	Pat Bradley	279	Beth Daniel (280)	La Grange CC	La Grange, Ill.
1982	Janet Anderson	283	Beth Daniel, Sandra Haynie & Donna White (289)	Del Paso CC	Sacramento, Calif.
1983	Jan Stephenson	290	JoAnne Carner (291)	Cedar Ridge CC	Tulsa, Okla.
1984	Hollis Stacy	290	Rosie Jones (291)	Salem CC	Peabody, Mass.
1985	Kathy Baker	280	Judy Dickenson (283)	Baltusrol GC	Springfield, N.J.
1986	Jane Geddes*	287	Sally Little (287)	NCR GC	Dayton, Ohio
1987	Laura Davies*	285	Ayako Okamoto & JoAnne Carner (285)	Plainfield CC	Plainfield, N.J.
1988	Liselotte Neumann	277	Patty Sheehan (280)	Baltimore CC	Baltimore, Md.
1989	Betsy King	278	Nancy Lopez (282)	Indianwood GC	Lake Orion, Mich.
1990	Betsy King	284	Patty Sheehan (285)	Atlanta Athletic Club	Duluth, Ga.
1991	Meg Mallon	283	Pat Bradley (285)	Colonial CC	Ft. Worth, Texas
1992	Patty Sheehan*	280	Juli Inkster (280)	Oakmont CC	Oakmont, Penn.
1993	Lauri Merten	280	Donna Andrews & Helen Alfredsson (281)	Crooked Stick GC	Carmel, Ind.
1994	Patty Sheehan	277	Tammie Green (278)	Indianwood CC	Lake Orion, Mich.
1995	Annika Sorenstam	278	Meg Mallon (279)	The Broadmoor	Colorado Springs, Colo.
1996	Annika Sorenstam	272	Kris Tschetter (278)	Pine Needles Lodge & GC	Southern Pines, N.C.
1997	Alison Nicholas	274	Nancy Lopez (275)	Pumpkin Ridge GC	Cornelius, Ore.
1998	Se Ri Pak*	290	a-Jenny Chuasiriporn (290)	Blackwolf Run GC	Kohler, Wis.

U.S. Women's Open (Cont.)

Year	Winner	Score	Runner-up	Course	Location
1999	Juli Inkster	272	Sherri Turner (277)	Old Waverly GC	West Point, Miss.
2000	Karrie Webb	282	Cristie Kerr & Meg Mallon (287)	Merit Club	Libertyville, Ill.
2001	Karrie Webb	273	Se Ri Pak (281)	Pine Needles Lodge & GC	Southern Pines, N.C.
2002	Juli Inkster	276	Annika Sorenstam (278)	Prairie Dunes CC	Hutchinson, Kan.
2003	Hilary Lunke*	283	Angela Stanford & Kelly Robbins (283)	Pumpkin Ridge GC	North Plains, Ore.
2004	Meg Mallon	274	Annika Sorenstam (276)	Orchards GC	South Hadley, Mass.
2005	Birdie Kim	287	a-Brittany Lang & a-Morgan Pressel (289)	Cherry Hills CC	Cherry Hills Vill., Colo.
2006	Annika Sorenstam*	284	Pat Hurst (284)	Newport CC	Newport, R.I.
2007	Cristie Kerr	279	Angela Park & Lorena Ochoa (281)	Pine Needles Lodge & GC	Southern Pines, N.C.
2008	Inbee Park	283	Helen Alfredsson (287)	Interlachen CC	Edina, Minn.

*PLAYOFFS:

1953: Betsy Rawls (70) def. Jackie Pung (77) in 18 holes. **1956:** Kathy Cornelius (75) def. Barbara McIntire (82) in 18 holes. **1964:** Mickey Wright (70) def. Ruth Jessen (72) in 18 holes. **1976:** JoAnne Carner (76) def. Sandra Palmer (78) in 18 holes. **1986:** Jane Geddes (71) def. Sally Little (73) in 18 holes. **1987:** Laura Davies (71) def. Ayako Okamoto (73) and JoAnne Carner (74) in 18 holes. **1992:** Patty Sheehan (72) def. Juli Inkster (74) in 18 holes. **1998:** Se Ri Pak def. Jenny Chuasiriporn on the second sudden death hole after both players were tied after an 18-hole playoff. **2003:** Hilary Lunke (70) def. Angela Stanford (71) and Kelly Robbins (73) in 18 holes. **2006:** Annika Sorenstam (70) def. Pat Hurst (74) in 18 holes.

LPGA Championship

Officially the McDonald's LPGA Championship since 1994 (Mazda was the title sponsor from 1987-93), the tournament began in 1955 and has had extended stays at the Stardust CC in Las Vegas (1961-66), Pleasant Valley CC in Sutton, Mass. (1967-68, 70-74), the Jack Nicklaus Sports Center at Kings Island, Ohio (1978-89), Bethesda CC in Maryland (1990-93), DuPont CC in Wilmington, Del. (1994-2004) and Bulle Rock GC in Havre de Grace, Md. (2005–); (*) indicates playoff winner, (a) amateur and (#) weather-shortened.

Multiple winners: Mickey Wright (4); Nancy Lopez, Se Ri Pak, Patty Sheehan, Annika Sorenstam and Kathy Whitworth (3); Donna Caponi, Laura Davies, Sandra Haynie, Juli Inkster, Mary Mills and Betsy Rawls (2).

Year	Winner	Score	Runner-up	Year	Winner	Score	Runner-up
1955	Beverly Hanson	220	Louise Suggs (223)	1983	Patty Sheehan	279	Sandra Haynie (281)
1956	Marlene Hagge*	291	Patty Berg (291)	1984	Patty Sheehan	272	Beth Daniel & Pat Bradley (282)
1957	Louise Suggs	285	Wiffi Smith (288)				
1958	Mickey Wright	288	Fay Crocker (294)	1985	Nancy Lopez	273	Alice Miller (281)
1959	Betsy Rawls	288	Patty Berg (289)	1986	Pat Bradley	277	Patty Sheehan (278)
1960	Mickey Wright	292	Louise Suggs (295)	1987	Jane Geddes	275	Betsy King (275)
1961	Mickey Wright	287	Louise Suggs (296)	1988	Sherri Turner	281	Amy Alcott (282)
1962	Judy Kimball	282	Shirley Spork (286)	1989	Nancy Lopez	274	Ayako Okamoto (277)
1963	Mickey Wright	294	Mary Lena Faulk & Mary Mills (296)	1990	Beth Daniel	280	Rosie Jones (281)
1964	Mary Mills	278	Mickey Wright (280)	1991	Meg Mallon	274	Pat Bradley & Ayako Okamoto (275)
1965	Sandra Haynie	279	Clifford A. Creed (280)				
1966	Gloria Ehret	282	Mickey Wright (285)	1992	Betsy King	267	JoAnne Carner, Karen Noble & Liselotte Neumann (278)
1967	Kathy Whitworth	284	Shirley Englehorn (285)				
1968	Sandra Post	294	Kathy Whitworth (294)	1993	Patty Sheehan	275	Lauri Merten (276)
1969	Betsy Rawls	293	Susie Berning & Carol Mann (297)	1994	Laura Davies	279	Alice Ritzman (280)
				1995	Kelly Robbins	274	Laura Davies (275)
1970	Shirley Englehorn	285	Kathy Whitworth (285)	1996	Laura Davies#	213	Julie Piers (214)
1971	Kathy Whitworth	288	Kathy Ahern (292)	1997	Chris Johnson*	281	Leta Lindley (281)
1972	Kathy Ahern	293	Jane Blalock (299)	1998	Se Ri Pak	273	Donna Andrews & Lisa Hackney (276)
1973	Mary Mills	288	Betty Burfeindt (289)				
1974	Sandra Haynie	288	JoAnne Carner (290)	1999	Juli Inkster	268	Liselotte Neumann (272)
1975	Kathy Whitworth	288	Sandra Haynie (289)	2000	Juli Inkster*	281	Stefania Croce (281)
1976	Betty Burfeindt	287	Judy Rankin (288)	2001	Karrie Webb	270	Laura Diaz (272)
1977	Chako Higuchi	279	Pat Bradley, Sandra Post & Judy Rankin (282)	2002	Se Ri Pak	279	Beth Daniel (282)
				2003	Annika Sorenstam*	278	Grace Park (278)
1978	Nancy Lopez	275	Amy Alcott (281)	2004	Annika Sorenstam	271	Shi Hyun Ahn (274)
1979	Donna Caponi	279	Jerilyn Britz (282)	2005	Annika Sorenstam	277	a-Michelle Wie (280)
1980	Sally Little	285	Jane Blalock (288)	2006	Se Ri Pak*	280	Karrie Webb (280)
1981	Donna Caponi	280	Jerilyn Britz & Pat Meyers (281)	2007	Suzann Pettersen	274	Karrie Webb (275)
				2008	Yani Tseng*	276	Maria Hjorth (276)
1982	Jan Stephenson	279	JoAnne Carner (281)				

*PLAYOFFS:

1956: Marlene Hagge def. Patti Berg in sudden death. **1968:** Sandra Post (68) def. Kathy Whitworth (75) in 18 holes. **1970:** Shirley Englehorn def. Kathy Whitworth in sudden death. **1997:** Chris Johnson def. Leta Lindley in sudden death. **2000:** Juli Inkster def. Stefania Croce in sudden death. **2003:** Annika Sorenstam def. Grace Park in sudden death. **2006:** Se Ri Pak def. Karrie Webb in sudden death; **2008:** Yani Tseng def. Maria Hjorth in sudden death..

Women's British Open

Sponsored by Ricoh (Weetabix was title sponsor until 2007), this has been an official stop on the LPGA Tour since 1994, and it became the fourth designated major championship in 2001 when it replaced the du Maurier Classic.

Multiple winners Karrie Webb and Sherri Steinhauer (3); (as a major): none.

Year	Winner	Score	Runner-up	Course	Location
1994	Liselotte Neumann	280	Dottie Mochrie & Annika Sorenstam (283)	Woburn G&CC	Milton Keynes, England
1995	Karrie Webb	278	Annika Sorenstam & Jill McGill (284)	Woburn G&CC	Milton Keynes, England
1996	Emilee Klein	277	Penny Hammel & Amy Alcott (284)	Woburn G&CC	Milton Keynes, England
1997	Karrie Webb	269	Rosie Jones (277)	Sunningdale GC	Berkshire, England
1998	Sherri Steinhauer	292	Sophie Gustafson & Brandie Burton (293)	Royal Lytham	Lytham, England
1999	Sherri Steinhauer	283	Annika Sorenstam (284)	Woburn G&CC	Milton Keynes, England
2000	Sophie Gustafson	282	Kirsty Taylor, Liselotte Neumann, Becky Iverson & Meg Mallon (284)	Royal Birkdale	Southport, England
2001	Se Ri Pak	277	Mi Hyun Kim (279)	Sunningdale GC	Berkshire, England
2002	Karrie Webb	273	Michelle Ellis & Paula Marti (275)	Turnberry GC	Turnberry, Scotland
2003	Annika Sorenstam	278	Se Ri Pak (279)	Royal Lytham	Lytham, England
2004	Karen Stupples	269	Rachel Teske (274)	Sunningdale GC	Berkshire, England
2005	Jeong Jang	272	Sophie Gustafson (276)	Royal Birkdale GC	Merseyside, England
2006	Sherri Steinhauer	281	Cristie Kerr & Sophie Gustafson (284)	Royal Lytham	Lytham, England
2007	Lorena Ochoa	287	Jee Young Lee & Maria Hjorth (291)	St. Andrews	St. Andrews, Scotland
2008	Ji-Yai Shin	270	Yani Tseng (273)	Sunningdale GC	Berkshire, England

du Maurier Classic (1979-2000)

The du Maurier Classic was considered a major title on the women's tour from 1979 until it was discontinued in 2000; (*) indicates playoff winner. **Multiple winners** (as a major): Pat Bradley (3); Brandie Burton (2).

Year		Year		Year		Year	
1973	Jocelyne Bourassa	1980	Pat Bradley	1987	Jody Rosenthal	1994	Martha Nause
1974	Carole Jo Skala	1981	Jan Stephenson	1988	Sally Little	1995	Jenny Lidback
1975	JoAnne Carner	1982	Sandra Haynie	1989	Tammie Green	1996	Laura Davies
1976	Donna Caponi	1983	Hollis Stacy	1990	Cathy Johnston	1997	Colleen Walker
1977	Judy Rankin	1984	Juli Inkster	1991	Nancy Scranton	1998	Brandie Burton
1978	JoAnne Carner	1985	Pat Bradley	1992	Sherri Steinhauer	1999	Karrie Webb
1979	Amy Alcott	1986	Pat Bradley*	1993	Brandie Burton*	2000	Meg Mallon

Titleholders Championship (1937-72)

The Titleholders was considered a major title on the women's tour until it was discontinued after the 1972 tournament.

Multiple winners: Patty Berg (7); Louise Suggs (4); Babe Zaharias (3); Dorothy Kirby, Marilynn Smith, Kathy Whitworth and Mickey Wright (2).

Year		Year		Year		Year	
1937	Patty Berg	1947	Babe Zaharias	1955	Patty Berg	1963	Marilynn Smith
1938	Patty Berg	1948	Patty Berg	1956	Louise Suggs	1964	Marilynn Smith
1939	Patty Berg	1949	Peggy Kirk	1957	Patty Berg	1965	Kathy Whitworth
1940	Betty Hicks	1950	Babe Zaharias	1958	Beverly Hanson	1966	Kathy Whitworth
1941	Dorothy Kirby	1951	Pat O'Sullivan	1959	Louise Suggs	1967-71	Not held
1942	Dorothy Kirby	1952	Babe Zaharias	1960	Fay Crocker	1972	Sandra Palmer
1943-45	Not held	1953	Patty Berg	1961	Mickey Wright		
1946	Louise Suggs	1954	Louise Suggs	1962	Mickey Wright		

Western Open (1930-67)

The Western Open was considered a major title on the women's tour until it was discontinued after the 1967 tournament.

Multiple winners: Patty Berg (7); Louise Suggs and Babe Zaharias (4); Mickey Wright (3); June Beebe, Opal Hill, Betty Jameson and Betsy Rawls (2).

Year		Year		Year		Year	
1930	Mrs. Lee Mida	1940	Babe Zaharias	1950	Babe Zaharias	1960	Joyce Ziske
1931	June Beebe	1941	Patty Berg	1951	Patty Berg	1961	Mary Lena Faulk
1932	Jane Weiller	1942	Betty Jameson	1952	Betsy Rawls	1962	Mickey Wright
1933	June Beebe	1943	Patty Berg	1953	Louise Suggs	1963	Mickey Wright
1934	Marian McDougall	1944	Babe Zaharias	1954	Betty Jameson	1964	Carol Mann
1935	Opal Hill	1945	Babe Zaharias	1955	Patty Berg	1965	Susie Maxwell
1936	Opal Hill	1946	Louise Suggs	1956	Beverly Hanson	1966	Mickey Wright
1937	Betty Hicks	1947	Louise Suggs	1957	Patty Berg	1967	Kathy Whitworth
1938	Bea Barrett	1948	Patty Berg	1958	Patty Berg		
1939	Helen Dettweiler	1949	Louise Suggs	1959	Betsy Rawls		

Grand Slam Summary

From 1955-66, the U.S. Open, LPGA Championship, Western Open and Titleholders tournaments served as the Women's Grand Slam. From 1983-2000 the U.S. Open, LPGA, du Maurier Classic and Nabisco Championship were the major events. In 2001, the Weetabix Women's British Open replaced the du Maurier Classic as the tour's fourth major. No one has won a four-event Grand Slam on the women's tour.

Three wins in one year (3): Babe Zaharias (1950), Mickey Wright (1961) and Pat Bradley (1986).

Two wins in one year (19): Patty Berg and Mickey Wright (3 times); Juli Inkster, Annika Sorenstam, Louise Suggs and Karrie Webb (twice); Laura Davies, Sandra Haynie, Betsy King, Meg Mallon, Se Ri Pak, Betsy Rawls and Kathy Whitworth (once).

Year	LPGA	US Open	T'holders	Western
1937	—	—	Berg	Hicks
1938	—	—	Berg	Barrett
1939	—	—	Berg	Dettweiler
1940	—	—	Hicks	Zaharias
1941	—	—	Kirby	Berg
1942	—	—	Kirby	Jameson
1943	—	—	—	Berg
1944	—	—	—	Zaharias
1945	—	—	—	Zaharias
1946	—	Berg	Suggs	Suggs
1947	—	Jameson	Zaharias	Suggs
1948	—	Zaharias	Berg	Suggs
1949	—	Suggs	Kirk	Suggs
1950	—	Zaharias	Zaharias	Zaharias
1951	—	Rawls	O'Sullivan	Berg
1952	—	Suggs	Zaharias	Rawls
1953	—	Rawls	Berg	Suggs
1954	—	Zaharias	Suggs	Jameson
1955	Hanson	Crocker	Berg	Berg
1956	Hagge	Cornelius	Suggs	Hanson
1957	Suggs	Rawls	Berg	Berg
1958	Wright	Wright	Hanson	Berg
1959	Rawls	Wright	Suggs	Rawls
1960	Wright	Rawls	Crocker	Ziske
1961	Wright	Wright	Wright	Faulk
1962	Kimball	Lindstrom	Wright	Wright
1963	Wright	Mills	M. Smith	Wright
1964	Mills	Wright	M. Smith	Mann
1965	Haynie	Mann	Whitworth	Maxwell
1966	Ehret	Spuzich	Whitworth	Wright
1967	Whitworth	a-LaCoste	—	Whitworth
1968	Post	Berning	—	—
1969	Rawls	Caponi	—	—
1970	Englehorn	Caponi	—	—
1971	Whitworth	Carner	—	—
1972	Ahern	Berning	Palmer	—
1973	Mills	Berning	—	—
1974	Haynie	Haynie	—	—

Year	LPGA	US Open	T'holders	Western
1975	Whitworth	Palmer	—	—
1976	Burfeindt	Carner	—	—
1977	Higuchi	Stacy	—	—
1978	Lopez	Stacy	—	—

Year	LPGA	US Open	duMaurier	Nabisco
1979	Caponi	Britz	Alcott	—
1980	Little	Alcott	Bradley	—
1981	Caponi	Bradley	Stephenson	—
1982	Stephenson	Anderson	Haynie	—
1983	Sheehan	Stephenson	Stacy	Alcott
1984	Sheehan	Stacy	Inkster	Inkster
1985	Lopez	Baker	Bradley	Miller
1986	Bradley	Geddes	Bradley	Bradley
1987	Geddes	Davies	Rosenthal	King
1988	Turner	Neumann	Little	Alcott
1989	Lopez	King	Green	Inkster
1990	Daniel	King	Johnston	King
1991	Mallon	Mallon	Scranton	Pepper
1992	King	Sheehan	Steinhauer	Pepper
1993	Sheehan	Merten	Burton	Alfredsson
1994	Davies	Sheehan	Nause	Andrews
1995	Robbins	Sorenstam	Lidback	Bowen
1996	Davies	Sorenstam	Davies	Sheehan
1997	Johnson	Nicholas	Walker	King
1998	Pak	Pak	Burton	Hurst
1999	Inkster	Inkster	Webb	Pepper
2000	Inkster	Webb	Mallon	Webb

Year	LPGA	US Open	Brit. Open	Nabisco
2001	Webb	Webb	Pak	Sorenstam
2002	Pak	Inkster	Webb	Sorenstam
2003	Sorenstam	Lunke	Sorenstam	Meunier-Lebouc
2004	Sorenstam	Mallon	Stupples	G. Park
2005	Sorenstam	Kim	Jang	Sorenstam
2006	Pak	Sorenstam	Steinhauer	Webb
2007	Pettersen	Kerr	Ochoa	Pressel
2008	Tseng	I. Park	J-Y Shin	Othoa

Major Championship Leaders

Through 2008; active LPGA players in **bold** type.

	US Open	LPGA	Nabisco	British Open	duM	Title	Western	US Am	Brit Am	Total
Patty Berg	1	0	0	0	0	7	7	1	0	16
Mickey Wright	4	4	0	0	0	2	3	0	0	13
Louise Suggs	2	1	0	0	0	4	4	1	1	13
Babe Didrikson Zaharias	3	0	0	0	0	3	4	1	1	12
Juli Inkster	2	2	2	0	1	0	0	3	0	10
Annika Sorenstam	3	3	3	1	0	0	0	0	0	10
Betsy Rawls	4	2	0	0	0	2	0	0	0	8
JoAnne Carner	2	0	0	0	0	0	0	5	0	7
Karrie Webb	2	1	2	1	1	0	0	0	0	7
Kathy Whitworth	0	3	0	0	0	2	1	0	0	6
Pat Bradley	1	1	1	0	3	0	0	0	0	6
Betsy King	2	1	3	0	0	0	0	0	0	6
Patty Sheehan	2	3	1	0	0	0	0	0	0	6
Glenna C. Vare	0	0	0	0	0	0	0	6	0	6

Tournaments: U.S. Open, LPGA Championship, Nabisco Championship, British Open, du Maurier Classic (1979-2000), Titleholders (1930-72), Western Open (1937-67), U.S. Amateur and British Amateur.

U.S. Women's Amateur

Stroke play in 1895, match play since 1896.

Multiple winners: Glenna Collett Vare (6); JoAnne Gunderson Carner (5); Margaret Curtis, Beatrix Hoyt, Dorothy Campbell Hurd, Juli Inkster, Alexa Stirling, Virginia Van Wie, Anne Quast Decker Welts (3); Kay Cockerill, Beth Daniel, Vicki Goetze, Katherine Harley, Genevieve Hecker, Betty Jameson, Kelli Kuehne and Barbara McIntire (2).

Year		Year		Year		Year	
1895	Mrs. C.S. Brown	1924	Dorothy C. Hurd	1955	Patricia Lesser	1983	Joanne Pacillo
1896	Beatrix Hoyt	1925	Glenna Collett	1956	Marlene Stewart	1984	Deb Richard
1897	Beatrix Hoyt	1926	Helen Stetson	1957	JoAnne Gunderson	1985	Michiko Hattori
1898	Beatrix Hoyt	1927	Miriam Burns Horn	1958	Anne Quast	1986	Kay Cockerill
1899	Ruth Underhill	1928	Glenna Collett	1959	Barbara McIntire	1987	Kay Cockerill
		1929	Glenna Collett			1988	Pearl Sinn
1900	Frances Griscom			1960	JoAnne Gunderson	1989	Vicki Goetze
1901	Genevieve Hecker	1930	Glenna Collett	1961	Anne Quast Decker		
1902	Genevieve Hecker	1931	Helen Hicks	1962	JoAnne Gunderson	1990	Pat Hurst
1903	Bessie Anthony	1932	Virginia Van Wie	1963	Anne Quast Welts	1991	Amy Fruhwirth
1904	Georgianna Bishop	1933	Virginia Van Wie	1964	Barbara McIntire	1992	Vicki Goetze
1905	Pauline Mackay	1934	Virginia Van Wie	1965	Jean Ashley	1993	Jill McGill
1906	Harriot Curtis	1935	Glenna Collett Vare	1966	JoAnne G. Carner	1994	Wendy Ward
1907	Margaret Curtis	1936	Pamela Barton	1967	Mary Lou Dill	1995	Kelli Kuehne
1908	Katherine Harley	1937	Estelle Lawson	1968	JoAnne G. Carner	1996	Kelli Kuehne
1909	Dorothy Campbell	1938	Patty Berg	1969	Catherine Lacoste	1997	Silvia Cavalleri
		1939	Betty Jameson			1998	Grace Park
1910	Dorothy Campbell			1970	Martha Wilkinson	1999	Dorothy Delasin
1911	Margaret Curtis	1940	Betty Jameson	1971	Laura Baugh		
1912	Margaret Curtis	1941	Elizabeth Hicks	1972	Mary Budke	2000	Marcy Newton
1913	Gladys Ravenscroft	1942-45	Not held	1973	Carol Semple	2001	Meredith Duncan
1914	Katherine Harley	1946	Babe D. Zaharias	1974	Cynthia Hill	2002	Becky Lucidi
1915	Florence Vanderbeck	1947	Louise Suggs	1975	Beth Daniel	2003	V. Nirapathpongporn
1916	Alexa Stirling	1948	Grace Lenczyk	1976	Donna Horton	2004	Jane Park
1917-18	Not held	1949	Dorothy Porter	1977	Beth Daniel	2005	Morgan Pressel
1919	Alexa Stirling			1978	Cathy Sherk	2006	Kimberly Kim
		1950	Beverly Hanson	1979	Carolyn Hill	2007	Maria Jose Uribe
1920	Alexa Stirling	1951	Dorothy Kirby	1980	Juli Inkster	2008	Amanda Blumenherst
1921	Marion Hollins	1952	Jacqueline Pung	1981	Juli Inkster		
1922	Glenna Collett	1953	Mary Lena Faulk	1982	Juli Inkster		
1923	Edith Cummings	1954	Barbara Romack				

British Women's Amateur

Match play since 1893.

Multiple winners: Cecil Leitch and Joyce Wethered (4); May Hezlet, Lady Margaret Scott, Jessie Anderson Valentine, Brigitte Varangot and Enid Wilson (3); Rhona Adair, Pam Barton, Dorothy Campbell, Elizabeth Chadwick, Helen Holm, Rebecca Hudson, Marley Spearman, Louise Stahle, Frances Stephens and Michelle Walker (2).

Year		Year		Year		Year	
1893	Lady Margaret Scott	1924	Joyce Wethered	1956	Wiffi Smith	1983	Jill Thornhill
1894	Lady Margaret Scott	1925	Joyce Wethered	1957	Philomena Garvey	1984	Jody Rosenthal
1895	Lady Margaret Scott	1926	Cecil Leitch	1958	Jessie Valentine	1985	Lillian Behan
1896	Amy Pascoe	1927	Simone de la Chaume	1959	Elizabeth Price	1986	Marnie McGuire
1897	Edith Orr	1928	Nanette le Blan			1987	Janet Collingham
1898	Lena Thomson	1929	Joyce Wethered	1960	Barbara McIntire	1988	Joanne Furby
1899	May Hezlet			1961	Marley Spearman	1989	Helen Dobson
		1930	Diana Fishwick	1962	Marley Spearman		
1900	Rhona Adair	1931	Enid Wilson	1963	Brigitte Varangot	1990	Julie Wade Hall
1901	Mary Graham	1932	Enid Wilson	1964	Carol Sorenson	1991	Valerie Michaud
1902	May Hezlet	1933	Enid Wilson	1965	Brigitte Varangot	1992	Bernille Pedersen
1903	Rhona Adair	1934	Helen Holm	1966	Elizabeth Chadwick	1993	Catriona Lambert
1904	Lottie Dod	1935	Wanda Morgan	1967	Elizabeth Chadwick	1994	Emma Duggleby
1905	Bertha Thompson	1936	Pam Barton	1968	Brigitte Varangot	1995	Julie Wade Hall
1906	Mrs. W. Kennion	1937	Jessie Anderson	1969	Catherine Lacoste	1996	Kelli Kuehne
1907	May Hezlet	1938	Helen Holm			1997	Alison Rose
1908	Maud Titterton	1939	Pam Barton	1970	Dinah Oxley	1998	Kim Rostron
1909	Dorothy Campbell			1971	Michelle Walker	1999	Marine Monnet
		1940-45	Not held	1972	Michelle Walker		
1910	Elsie Grant-Suttie	1946	Jean Hetherington	1973	Ann Irvin	2000	Rebecca Hudson
1911	Dorothy Campbell	1947	Babe Zaharias	1974	Carol Semple	2001	Marta Prieto
1912	Gladys Ravenscroft	1948	Louise Suggs	1975	Nancy Roth Syms	2002	Rebecca Hudson
1913	Muriel Dodd	1949	Frances Stephens	1976	Cathy Panton	2003	Elisa Serramia
1914	Cecil Leitch			1977	Angela Uzielli	2004	Louise Stahle
1915-19	Not held	1950	Lally de St. Sauveur	1978	Edwina Kennedy	2005	Louise Stahle
		1951	Catherine MacCann	1979	Maureen Madill	2006	Belen Mozo
1920	Cecil Leitch	1952	Moira Paterson	1980	Anne Quast Sander	2007	Carlota Ciganda
1921	Cecil Leitch	1953	Marlene Stewart	1981	Belle Robertson	2008	Anna Nordqvist
1922	Joyce Wethered	1954	Frances Stephens	1982	Kitrina Douglas		
1923	Doris Chambers	1955	Jessie Valentine				

Vare Trophy

The Vare Trophy for best scoring average by a player on the LPGA Tour has been awarded since 1953 by the LPGA. The award is named after Glenna Collett Vare, winner of six U.S. women's amateur titles from 1922-35.

Multiple winners: Kathy Whitworth (7); Annika Sorenstam (6); JoAnne Carner and Mickey Wright (5); Patty Berg, Beth Daniel, Nancy Lopez, Judy Rankin and Karrie Webb (3); Pat Bradley, Betsy King and Lorena Ochoa (2).

Year		Avg	Year		Avg	Year		Avg
1953	Patty Berg	75.00	1972	Kathy Whitworth	72.38	1991	Pat Bradley	70.66
1954	Babe Zaharias	75.48	1973	Judy Rankin	73.08	1992	Dottie Pepper	70.80
1955	Patty Berg	74.47	1974	JoAnne Carner	72.87	1993	Betsy King	70.85
1956	Patty Berg	74.57	1975	JoAnne Carner	72.40	1994	Beth Daniel	70.90
1957	Louise Suggs	74.64	1976	Judy Rankin	72.25	1995	Annika Sorenstam	71.00
1958	Beverly Hanson	74.92	1977	Judy Rankin	72.16	1996	Annika Sorenstam	70.47
1959	Betsy Rawls	74.03	1978	Nancy Lopez	71.76	1997	Karrie Webb	70.00
1960	Mickey Wright	73.25	1979	Nancy Lopez	71.20	1998	Annika Sorenstam	69.99
1961	Mickey Wright	73.55	1980	Amy Alcott	71.51	1999	Karrie Webb	69.43
1962	Mickey Wright	73.67	1981	JoAnne Carner	71.75	2000	Karrie Webb	70.05
1963	Mickey Wright	72.81	1982	JoAnne Carner	71.49	2001	Annika Sorenstam	69.42
1964	Mickey Wright	72.46	1983	JoAnne Carner	71.41	2002	Annika Sorenstam	68.70
1965	Kathy Whitworth	72.61	1984	Patty Sheehan	71.40	2003	Se Ri Pak	70.03
1966	Kathy Whitworth	72.60	1985	Nancy Lopez	70.73	2004	Grace Park	69.99
1967	Kathy Whitworth	72.74	1986	Pat Bradley	71.10	2005	Annika Sorenstam	69.25
1968	Carol Mann	72.04	1987	Betsy King	71.14	2006	Lorena Ochoa	69.24
1969	Kathy Whitworth	72.38	1988	Colleen Walker	71.26	2007	Lorena Ochoa	69.69
1970	Kathy Whitworth	72.26	1989	Beth Daniel	70.38			
1971	Kathy Whitworth	72.88	1990	Beth Daniel	70.54			

Champions Tour
Senior PGA Championship

First played in 1937. Two championships played in 1979 and 1984.

Multiple winners: Sam Snead (6); Hale Irwin (4); Gary Player, Al Watrous and Eddie Williams (3); Julius Boros, Jay Haas, Jock Hutchison, Don January, Arnold Palmer, Paul Runyan, Gene Sarazen and Lee Trevino (2).

Year		Year		Year		Year	
1937	Jock Hutchison	1957	Al Watrous	1976	Pete Cooper	1993	Tom Wargo*
1938	Fred McLeod*	1958	Gene Sarazen	1977	Julius Boros	1994	Lee Trevino
1939	Not held	1959	Willie Goggin	1978	Joe Jiminez*	1995	Ray Floyd
1940	Otto Hackbarth*	1960	Dick Metz	1979	Jack Fleck*	1996	Hale Irwin
1941	Jack Burke	1961	Paul Runyan	1979	Don January	1997	Hale Irwin
1942	Eddie Williams	1962	Paul Runyan	1980	Arnold Palmer*	1998	Hale Irwin
1943-44	Not held	1963	Herman Barron	1981	Miller Barber	1999	Allen Doyle
1945	Eddie Williams	1964	Sam Snead	1982	Don January	2000	Doug Tewell
1946	Eddie Williams*	1965	Sam Snead	1983	Not held	2001	Tom Watson
1947	Jock Hutchison	1966	Fred Haas	1984	Arnold Palmer	2002	Fuzzy Zoeller
1948	Charles McKenna	1967	Sam Snead	1984	Peter Thomson	2003	John Jacobs
1949	Marshall Crichton	1968	Chandler Harper	1985	Not held	2004	Hale Irwin
1950	Al Watrous	1969	Tommy Bolt	1986	Gary Player	2005	Mike Reid*
1951	Al Watrous*	1970	Sam Snead	1987	Chi Chi Rodriguez	2006	Jay Haas*
1952	Ernest Newnham	1971	Julius Boros	1988	Gary Player	2007	Denis Watson
1953	Harry Schwab	1972	Sam Snead	1989	Larry Mowry	2008	Jay Haas
1954	Gene Sarazen	1973	Sam Snead	1990	Gary Player		
1955	Mortie Dutra	1974	Roberto De Vicenzo	1991	Jack Nicklaus		
1956	Pete Burke	1975	Charlie Sifford*	1992	Lee Trevino		

*PLAYOFFS:

1938: Fred McLeod def. Otto Hackbarth in 18 holes. **1940:** Otto Hackbarth def. Jock Hutchison in 36 holes. **1946:** Eddie Williams def. Jock Hutchison in 18 holes. **1951:** Al Watrous def. Jock Hutchison in 18 holes. **1975:** Charlie Sifford def. Fred Wampler on 1st extra hole **1978:** Joe Jiminez def. Paul Harney on 1st extra hole. **1979:** Jack Fleck def. Bill Johnston on 1st extra hole. **1980:** Arnold Palmer def. Paul Harney on 1st extra hole. **1993:** Tom Wargo def. Bruce Crampton on 2nd extra hole. **2005:** Mike Reid def. Dana Quigley and Jerry Pate on 1st extra hole. **2006:** Jay Haas def. Brad Bryant on 3rd extra hole.

Major Senior Championship Leaders

Through 2007. All players are still active. **Note:** The Senior British Open became the Champions Tour's fifth major in 2003.

		Sr. PGA	US Open	Sr. Play	Trad	Br. Open	Tot			Sr. PGA	US Open	Sr. Play	Trad	Br. Open	Tot
1	Jack Nicklaus	1	2	1	4	0	8	5	Allen Doyle	2	2	0	0	0	4
2	Hale Irwin	4	2	1	0	0	7		Ray Floyd	1	0	2	1	0	4
3	Gary Player	3	2	1	0	0	6		Lee Trevino	2	1	0	1	0	4
4	Tom Watson	1	0	0	1	3	5								

U.S. Senior Open

Established in 1980 for senior players 55 years old and over, the minimum age was dropped to 50 (the Champions Tour entry age) in 1981. Arnold Palmer, Billy Casper, Hale Irwin, Orville Moody, Jack Nicklaus and Lee Trevino are the only golfers who have won both the U.S. Open and U.S. Senior Open.

Multiple winners: Miller Barber (3); Allen Doyle, Hale Irwin, Jack Nicklaus and Gary Player (2).

Year		Year		Year		Year	
1980	Roberto De Vicenzo	1988	Gary Player*	1996	Dave Stockton	2004	Peter Jacobsen
1981	Arnold Palmer*	1989	Orville Moody	1997	Graham Marsh	2005	Allen Doyle
1982	Miller Barber	1990	Lee Trevino	1998	Hale Irwin	2006	Allen Doyle
1983	Bill Casper*	1991	Jack Nicklaus*	1999	Dave Eichelberger	2007	Brad Bryant
1984	Miller Barber	1992	Larry Laoretti	2000	Hale Irwin	2008	Eduardo Romero
1985	Miller Barber	1993	Jack Nicklaus	2001	Bruce Fleisher		
1986	Dale Douglass	1994	Simon Hobday	2002	Don Pooley*		
1987	Gary Player	1995	Tom Weiskopf	2003	Bruce Lietzke		

*PLAYOFFS:

1981: Arnold Palmer (70) def. Bob Stone (74) and Billy Casper (77) in 18 holes. **1983:** Tied at 75 after 18-hole playoff, Casper def. Rod Funseth with a birdie on the 1st extra hole. **1988:** Gary Player (68) def. Bob Charles (70) in 18 holes. **1991:** Jack Nicklaus (65) def. Chi Chi Rodriguez (69) in 18 holes. **2002:** Don Pooley and Tom Watson remained tied after a three hole playoff and Pooley won on the second hole of sudden death.

Senior Players Championship

Sponsored by Ford since 1993. First played in 1983 and contested in Cleveland (1983-86), Ponte Vedra, Fla. (1987-89), Dearborn, Mich. (1990-2006), Baltimore, Md. (2007—).

Multiple winners: Ray Floyd, Arnold Palmer and Dave Stockton (2).

Year		Year		Year		Year	
1983	Miller Barber	1990	Jack Nicklaus	1997	Larry Gilbert	2004	Mark James
1984	Arnold Palmer	1991	Jim Albus	1998	Gil Morgan	2005	Peter Jacobsen
1985	Arnold Palmer	1992	Dave Stockton	1999	Hale Irwin	2006	Bobby Wadkins
1986	Chi Chi Rodriguez	1993	Jim Colbert	2000	Ray Floyd	2007	Loren Roberts
1987	Gary Player	1994	Dave Stockton	2001	Allen Doyle*	2008	D.A. Weibring
1988	Billy Casper	1995	J.C. Snead*	2002	Stewart Ginn		
1989	Orville Moody	1996	Ray Floyd	2003	Craig Stadler		

*PLAYOFFS:

1995: J.C. Snead def. Jack Nicklaus on 1st extra hole. **2001:** Allen Doyle def. Doug Tewell on 1st extra hole.

The Tradition

Sponsored by window and door manufacturer JELD-WEN since 2003, it was formerly called The Tradition at Desert Mountain (1989-91), The Tradition (1992-99) and The Countrywide Tradition (2000-02). Held at GC at Desert Mountain in Scottsdale, Ariz. (1989-2001), Superstition Mountain (Ariz.) G & CC (2002), The Reserve Vineyards & GC in Aloha, Ore. (2003-06) and Crosswater GC in Sunriver, Ore. (2007—).

Multiple winners: Jack Nicklaus (4); Gil Morgan (2).

Year		Year		Year		Year	
1989	Don Bies	1994	Ray Floyd*	1999	Graham Marsh	2004	Craig Stadler
1990	Jack Nicklaus	1995	Jack Nicklaus*	2000	Tom Kite	2005	Loren Roberts*
1991	Jack Nicklaus	1996	Jack Nicklaus	2001	Doug Tewell	2006	Eduardo Romero*
1992	Lee Trevino	1997	Gil Morgan	2002	Jim Thorpe*	2007	Mark McNulty
1993	Tom Shaw	1998	Gil Morgan	2003	Tom Watson	2008	Fred Funk

*PLAYOFFS:

1994: Ray Floyd def. Dale Douglass on 1st extra hole. **1995:** Jack Nicklaus def. Isao Aoki on 3rd extra hole. **2002:** Jim Thorpe def. John Jacobs on 1st extra hole. **2005:** Loren Roberts def. Dana Quigley on 2nd extra hole. **2006:** Eduardo Romero def. Lonnie Nielsen on 1st extra hole.

Senior British Open

First played in 1987 and contested in Turnberry, Scotland (1987-90, 2003), Lytham, England (1991-94), Portrush, Ireland (1995-99, 2004), Newcastle, Ireland (2000-02). Royal Aberdeen, Scotland (2005), Muirfield, Scotland (2007) and Royal Troon, Scotland (2008). In 2003 it became the fifth designated major championship on the Champions Tour.

Multiple winners: Gary Player and Tom Watson (3); Brian Barnes, Bob Charles and Christy O'Connor Jr. (2). (as a major): Watson (3).

Year		Year		Year		Year	
1987	Neil Coles	1993	Bob Charles	1999	Christy O'Connor Jr.	2005	Tom Watson*
1988	Gary Player	1994	Tom Wargo	2000	Christy O'Connor Jr.	2006	Loren Roberts
1989	Bob Charles	1995	Brian Barnes	2001	Ian Stanley	2007	Tom Watson
1990	Gary Player	1996	Brian Barnes	2002	Noboru Sugai	2008	Bruce Vaughan*
1991	Bobby Verwey	1997	Gary Player	2003	Tom Watson*		
1992	John Fourie	1998	Brian Huggett	2004	Pete Oakley		

*PLAYOFFS (as a Major):

2003: Watson def. Mason on 2nd extra hole. **2005:** Watson def. Smyth on 3rd extra hole. **2008:** Vaughan def. Cook on 1st extra hole.

Champions Tour Grand Slam Summary

The Senior Grand Slam had officially consisted of The Tradition, the Senior PGA Championship, the Senior Players Championship and the U.S. Senior Open from 1990-2002. In 2003, the Senior British Open was added. Jack Nicklaus won three of the four events in 1991, but no one has won all four (or now five) in one season.

Three wins in one year: Jack Nicklaus (1991). **Two wins in one year** (8): Gary Player (twice); Hale Irwin, Gil Morgan, Orville Moody, Jack Nicklaus, Arnold Palmer, Lee Trevino and Tom Watson (once).

Year	Tradition	Sr. PGA	Players	US Open	Year	Tradition	Sr. PGA	Players	US Open
1983	—	—	M. Barber	Casper	1993	Shaw	Wargo	Colbert	Nicklaus
1984	—	Palmer	Palmer	M. Barber	1994	Floyd	Trevino	Stockton	Hobday
1985	—	Thomson	Palmer	M. Barber	1995	Nicklaus	Floyd	Snead	Weiskopf
1986	—	Player	Rodriguez	Douglass	1996	Nicklaus	Irwin	Floyd	Stockton
1987	—	Rodriguez	Player	Player	1997	Morgan	Irwin	Gilbert	Marsh
1988	—	Player	Casper	Player	1998	Morgan	Irwin	Morgan	Irwin
1989	Bies	Mowry	Moody	Moody	1999	Marsh	Doyle	Irwin	Eichelberger
1990	Nicklaus	Player	Nicklaus	Trevino	2000	Kite	Tewell	Floyd	Irwin
1991	Nicklaus	Nicklaus	Albus	Nicklaus	2001	Tewell	T. Watson	Doyle	Fleisher
1992	Trevino	Trevino	Stockton	Laoretti	2002	Thorpe	Zoeller	Ginn	Pooley

Year	Tradition	Sr. PGA	Players	US Open	Sr. Brit. Open
2003	T. Watson	Jacobs	Stadler	Lietzke	T. Watson
2004	Stadler	Irwin	James	Jacobsen	Oakley
2005	Roberts	Reid	Jacobsen	Doyle	T. Watson
2006	Romero	Haas	Wadkins	Doyle	Roberts
2007	McNulty	D. Watson	Roberts	Bryant	T. Watson
2008	Funk	Haas	Weibring	Romero	Vaughan

Annual Money Leaders

Official annual money leaders on the PGA, European PGA, Champions and LPGA tours.

PGA

Multiple leaders: Jack Nicklaus and Tiger Woods (8); Ben Hogan and Tom Watson (5); Arnold Palmer (4); Greg Norman, Sam Snead and Curtis Strange (3); Julius Boros, Billy Casper, Tom Kite, Byron Nelson, Nick Price and Vijay Singh (2).

Year		Earnings	Year		Earnings	Year		Earnings
1934	Paul Runyan	$6,767	1959	Art Wall	$53,168	1984	Tom Watson	$476,260
1935	Johnny Revolta	9,543	1960	Arnold Palmer	75,263	1985	Curtis Strange	542,321
1936	Horton Smith	7,682	1961	Gary Player	64,540	1986	Greg Norman	653,296
1937	Harry Cooper	14,139	1962	Arnold Palmer	81,448	1987	Curtis Strange	925,941
1938	Sam Snead	19,534	1963	Arnold Palmer	128,230	1988	Curtis Strange	1,147,644
1939	Henry Picard	10,303	1964	Jack Nicklaus	113,285	1989	Tom Kite	1,395,278
1940	Ben Hogan	10,655	1965	Jack Nicklaus	140,752	1990	Greg Norman	1,165,477
1941	Ben Hogan	18,358	1966	Billy Casper	121,945	1991	Corey Pavin	979,430
1942	Ben Hogan	13,143	1967	Jack Nicklaus	188,998	1992	Fred Couples	1,344,188
1943	No records kept		1968	Billy Casper	205,169	1993	Nick Price	1,478,557
1944	Byron Nelson	37,968	1969	Frank Beard	164,707	1994	Nick Price	1,499,927
1945	Byron Nelson	63,336	1970	Lee Trevino	157,037	1995	Greg Norman	1,654,959
1946	Ben Hogan	42,556	1971	Jack Nicklaus	244,491	1996	Tom Lehman	1,780,159
1947	Jimmy Demaret	27,937	1972	Jack Nicklaus	320,542	1997	Tiger Woods	2,066,833
1948	Ben Hogan	32,112	1973	Jack Nicklaus	308,362	1998	David Duval	2,591,031
1949	Sam Snead	31,594	1974	Johnny Miller	353,022	1999	Tiger Woods	6,616,585
1950	Sam Snead	35,759	1975	Jack Nicklaus	298,149	2000	Tiger Woods	9,188,321
1951	Lloyd Mangrum	26,089	1976	Jack Nicklaus	266,439	2001	Tiger Woods	5,687,777
1952	Julius Boros	37,033	1977	Tom Watson	310,653	2002	Tiger Woods	6,912,625
1953	Lew Worsham	34,002	1978	Tom Watson	362,429	2003	Vijay Singh	7,573,907
1954	Bob Toski	65,820	1979	Tom Watson	462,636	2004	Vijay Singh	10,905,166
1955	Julius Boros	63,122	1980	Tom Watson	530,808	2005	Tiger Woods	10,628,024
1956	Ted Kroll	72,836	1981	Tom Kite	375,699	2006	Tiger Woods	9,941,563
1957	Dick Mayer	65,835	1982	Craig Stadler	446,462	2007	Tiger Woods	10,867,052
1958	Arnold Palmer	42,608	1983	Hal Sutton	426,668			

Note: In 1944-45, Nelson's winnings were in War Bonds.

Champions Tour

Multiple leaders: Hale Irwin and Don January (3); Miller Barber, Bob Charles, Jim Colbert, Jay Haas, Dave Stockton and Lee Trevino (2).

Year		Earnings	Year		Earnings	Year		Earnings
1980	Don January	$44,100	1990	Lee Trevino	$1,190,518	2000	Larry Nelson	$2,708,005
1981	Miller Barber	83,136	1991	Mike Hill	1,065,657	2001	Allen Doyle	2,553,582
1982	Miller Barber	106,890	1992	Lee Trevino	1,027,002	2002	Hale Irwin	3,028,304
1983	Don January	237,571	1993	Dave Stockton	1,175,944	2003	Tom Watson	1,853,108
1984	Don January	328,597	1994	Dave Stockton	1,402,519	2004	Craig Stadler	2,306,066
1985	Peter Thomson	386,724	1995	Jim Colbert	1,444,386	2005	Dana Quigley	2,170,258
1986	Bruce Crampton	454,299	1996	Jim Colbert	1,627,890	2006	Jay Haas	2,420,227
1987	Chi Chi Rodriguez	509,145	1997	Hale Irwin	2,343,364	2007	Jay Haas	2,581,001
1988	Bob Charles	533,929	1998	Hale Irwin	2,861,945			
1989	Bob Charles	725,887	1999	Bruce Fleisher	2,515,705			

European PGA

Official money in the Volvo Order of Merit was awarded in British pounds from 1961-98 and euros (€) since 1999.

Multiple leaders: Colin Montgomerie (8); Seve Ballesteros (6); Sandy Lyle (3); Gay Brewer Jr., Ernie Els, Nick Faldo, Retief Goosen, Bernard Hunt, Bernhard Langer, Peter Thomson and Ian Woosnam (2).

Year		Earnings	Year		Earnings	Year		Earnings
1961	Bernard Hunt	£4,492	1977	Seve Ballesteros	£46,436	1993	Colin Montgomerie	£798,145
1962	Peter Thomson	5,764	1978	Seve Ballesteros	54,348	1994	Colin Montgomerie	920,647
1963	Bernard Hunt	7,209	1979	Sandy Lyle	49,233	1995	Colin Montgomerie	1,038,718
1964	Neil Coles	7,890	1980	Greg Norman	74,829	1996	Colin Montgomerie	1,034,752
1965	Peter Thomson	7,011	1981	Bernhard Langer	95,991	1997	Colin Montgomerie	1,583,904
1966	Bruce Devlin	13,205	1982	Sandy Lyle	86,141	1998	Colin Montgomerie	1,082,833
1967	Gay Brewer Jr.	20,235	1983	Nick Faldo	140,761	1999	C. Montgomerie	€2,066,885
1968	Gay Brewer Jr.	23,107	1984	Bernhard Langer	160,883	2000	Lee Westwood	3,125,147
1969	Billy Casper	23,483	1985	Sandy Lyle	254,711	2001	Retief Goosen	2,862,806
1970	Christy O'Connor	31,532	1986	Seve Ballesteros	259,275	2002	Retief Goosen	2,360,128
1971	Gary Player	11,281	1987	Ian Woosnam	439,075	2003	Ernie Els	2,975,374
1972	Bob Charles	18,538	1988	Seve Ballesteros	502,000	2004	Ernie Els	4,061,905
1973	Tony Jacklin	24,839	1989	Ronan Rafferty	465,981	2005	Colin Montgomerie	2,794,223
1974	Peter Oosterhuis	32,127	1990	Ian Woosnam	737,977	2006	Padraig Harrington	2,489,337
1975	Dale Hayes	20,507	1991	Seve Ballesteros	790,811	2007	Justin Rose	2,944,945
1976	Seve Ballesteros	39,504	1992	Nick Faldo	1,220,540			

LPGA

Multiple leaders: Annika Sorenstam and Kathy Whitworth (8); Mickey Wright (4); Patty Berg, JoAnne Carner, Beth Daniel, Betsy King, Nancy Lopez and Karrie Webb (3); Pat Bradley, Lorena Ochoa, Judy Rankin, Betsy Rawls, Louise Suggs and Babe Zaharias (2).

Year		Earnings	Year		Earnings	Year		Earnings
1950	Babe Zaharias	$14,800	1970	Kathy Whitworth	$30,235	1990	Beth Daniel	863,578
1951	Babe Zaharias	15,087	1971	Kathy Whitworth	41,181	1991	Pat Bradley	763,118
1952	Betsy Rawls	14,505	1972	Kathy Whitworth	65,063	1992	Dottie Pepper	693,335
1953	Louise Suggs	19,816	1973	Kathy Whitworth	82,864	1993	Betsy King	595,992
1954	Patty Berg	16,011	1974	JoAnne Carner	87,094	1994	Laura Davies	687,201
1955	Patty Berg	16,492	1975	Sandra Palmer	76,374	1995	Annika Sorenstam	666,533
1956	Marlene Hagge	20,235	1976	Judy Rankin	150,734	1996	Karrie Webb	1,002,000
1957	Patty Berg	16,272	1977	Judy Rankin	122,890	1997	Annika Sorenstam	1,236,789
1958	Beverly Hanson	12,639	1978	Nancy Lopez	189,814	1998	Annika Sorenstam	1,092,748
1959	Betsy Rawls	26,774	1979	Nancy Lopez	197,489	1999	Karrie Webb	1,591,959
1960	Louise Suggs	16,892	1980	Beth Daniel	231,000	2000	Karrie Webb	1,876,853
1961	Mickey Wright	22,236	1981	Beth Daniel	206,998	2001	Annika Sorenstam	2,105,868
1962	Mickey Wright	21,641	1982	JoAnne Carner	310,400	2002	Annika Sorenstam	2,863,904
1963	Mickey Wright	31,269	1983	JoAnne Carner	291,404	2003	Annika Sorenstam	2,029,506
1964	Mickey Wright	29,800	1984	Betsy King	266,771	2004	Annika Sorenstam	2,544,707
1965	Kathy Whitworth	28,658	1985	Nancy Lopez	416,472	2005	Annika Sorenstam	2,588,240
1966	Kathy Whitworth	33,517	1986	Pat Bradley	492,021	2006	Lorena Ochoa	2,592,872
1967	Kathy Whitworth	32,937	1987	Ayako Okamoto	466,034	2007	Lorena Ochoa	4,364,994
1968	Kathy Whitworth	48,379	1988	Sherri Turner	350,851			
1969	Carol Mann	49,152	1989	Betsy King	654,132			

All-Time Leaders

PGA, Champions Tour and LPGA leaders through Oct. 19, 2008.

Tournaments Won

	PGA	No		Champions	No		LPGA	No
1	Sam Snead	82	1	Hale Irwin	45	1	Kathy Whitworth	88
2	Jack Nicklaus	73	2	Lee Trevino	29	2	Mickey Wright	82
3	Tiger Woods	65	3	Gil Morgan	25	3	Annika Sorenstam	72
4	Ben Hogan	64	4	Miller Barber	24	4	Patty Berg	60
5	Arnold Palmer	62	5	Bob Charles	23	5	Louise Suggs	58
6	Byron Nelson	52	6	Don January	22	6	Betsy Rawls	55
7	Billy Casper	51		Chi Chi Rodriguez	22	7	Nancy Lopez	48
8	Walter Hagen	44	8	Bruce Crampton	20	8	JoAnne Carner	43
9	Cary Middlecoff	40		Jim Colbert	20	9	Sandra Haynie	42
10	Gene Sarazen	39	10	George Archer	19	10	Babe Zaharias	41
	Tom Watson	39		Larry Nelson	19	11	Carol Mann	38
12	Lloyd Mangrum	36		Gary Player	19	12	Patty Sheehan	35
13	Phil Mickelson	34	13	Mike Hill	18		Karrie Webb	35
	Vijay Singh	34		Bruce Fleisher	18	14	Betsy King	34
15	Horton Smith	32	15	Dave Stockton	14	15	Beth Daniel	33
16	Harry Cooper	31		Raymond Floyd	14	16	Pat Bradley	31
	Jimmy Demaret	31	17	Jim Thorpe	13		Juli Inkster	31
18	Leo Diegel	30	18	Jim Dent	12	18	Amy Alcott	29
19	Three tied with 29 wins.			Jay Haas	12	19	Jane Blalock	27
				Tom Watson	12	20	Judy Rankin	26

All-Time Leaders (Cont.)
Money Won
All-time earnings through Oct. 19, 2008.

PGA

		Earnings			Earnings			Earnings
1	Tiger Woods	$82,354,376	10	Stewart Cink	$25,040,354	19	Chris DiMarco	$20,228,878
2	Vijay Singh	60,709,312	11	Sergio Garcia	24,399,000	20	Fred Couples	20,121,480
3	Phil Mickelson	50,522,901	12	Mike Weir	23,860,124	21	Retief Goosen	19,707,369
4	Jim Furyk	38,809,826	13	Stuart Appleby	23,194,485	22	Robert Allenby	19,125,214
5	Davis Love III	36,497,550	14	Mark Calcavecchia	23,081,228	23	K.J. Choi	18,801,639
6	Ernie Els	33,663,401	15	Scott Verplank	22,163,492	24	Scott Hoch	18,498,499
7	David Toms	28,711,065	16	Fred Funk	20,925,849	25	Adam Scott	18,369,560
8	Justin Leonard	27,109,459	17	Nick Price	20,563,108			
9	Kenny Perry	26,196,442	18	Tom Lehman	20,378,513			

European PGA
Official earnings in Euros (E).

		Earnings			Earnings			Earnings
1	C. Montgomerie	E23,507,329	10	Bernhard Langer	E12,523,713	19	Ian Woosnam	E9,570,678
2	Ernie Els	21,798,220	11	Sergio Garcia	11,863,205	20	Paul Casey	9,118,527
3	Padraig Harrington	19,354,267	12	Angel Cabrera	11,691,431	21	Niclas Fasth	8,844,321
4	Retief Goosen	18,391,752	13	J.M. Olazabal	11,506,939	22	Henrik Stenson	8,640,659
5	Darren Clarke	16,619,132	14	Michael Campbell	11,384,644	23	Nick Faldo	7,996,254
6	Lee Westwood	16,250,892	15	Robert Karlsson	10,881,455	24	Paul Lawrie	7,524,376
7	M. Angel Jimenez	14,101,788	16	Paul McGinley	10,073,949	25	Eduardo Romero	7,518,085
8	Vijay Singh	13,299,221	17	David Howell	9,892,447			
9	Thomas Bjorn	12,582,672	18	Ian Poulter	9,572,177			

Champions Tour

		Earnings			Earnings			Earnings
1	Hale Irwin	$24,920,665	10	Jim Colbert	$11,684,239	19	Bob Charles	$9,044,003
2	Gil Morgan	18,964,040	11	Dave Stockton	11,159,503	20	Jim Dent	8,992,119
3	Dana Quigley	14,406,269	12	Tom Watson	11,023,827	21	Bruce Summerhays	8,943,420
4	Bruce Fleisher	13,990,356	13	Lee Trevino	9,853,603	22	Vicente Fernandez	8,694,146
5	Larry Nelson	13,262,808	14	Raymond Floyd	9,472,853	23	John Jacobs	8,489,965
6	Allen Doyle	13,031,711	15	Bob Gilder	9,400,793	24	Jay Haas	8,485,027
7	Jim Thorpe	12,985,193	16	Jay Sigel	9,392,812	25	Mike Hill	8,383,104
8	Tom Kite	12,824,002	17	Isao Aoki	9,343,160			
9	Tom Jenkins	12,023,131	18	Graham Marsh	9,149,600			

LPGA

		Earnings			Earnings			Earnings
1	Annika Sorenstam	$22,476,840	10	Rosie Jones	$8,355,068	19	Pat Bradley	$5,755,951
2	Karrie Webb	14,208,493	11	Mi Hyun Kim	8,260,080	20	Paula Creamer	5,748,940
3	Lorena Ochoa	13,173,104	12	Betsy King	7,637,621	21	Kelly Robbins	5,738,599
4	Juli Inkster	12,433,674	13	Dottie Pepper	6,827,284	22	Rachel Hetherington	5,589,548
5	Se Ri Pak	10,133,300	14	Lorie Kane	6,697,214	23	Hee-Won Han	5,537,147
6	Meg Mallon	9,019,694	15	Pat Hurst	6,163,586	24	Patty Sheehan	5,513,409
7	Cristie Kerr	8,910,795	16	Jeong Jang	5,974,024	25	Catriona Matthew	5,466,598
8	Beth Daniel	8,755,733	17	Sherrie Steinhauer	5,929,838			
9	Laura Davies	8,521,650	18	Liselotte Neumann	5,833,099			

Official World Golf Ranking

Begun in 1986, the Official World Golf Ranking (formerly the Sony World Ranking) combines the best golfers on the six pro men's tours which make up the International Federation of PGA Tours. Rankings are based on a rolling two-year period and weighed in favor of more recent results. While annual winners are not announced, certain players reaching No. 1 have dominated each year.

Multiple winners (at year's end): Tiger Woods (10); Greg Norman (6); Nick Faldo (3); Seve Ballesteros (2).

Year		Year		Year		Year	
1986	Seve Ballesteros	1991	Ian Woosnam	1997	Tiger Woods	2004	Vijay Singh
1987	Greg Norman	1992	Fred Couples	1998	Tiger Woods	2005	Tiger Woods
1988	Greg Norman		& Nick Faldo	1999	Tiger Woods	2006	Tiger Woods
1989	Seve Ballesteros	1993	Nick Faldo	2000	Tiger Woods	2007	Tiger Woods
	& Greg Norman	1994	Nick Price	2001	Tiger Woods		
1990	Nick Faldo	1995	Greg Norman	2002	Tiger Woods		
	& Greg Norman	1996	Greg Norman	2003	Tiger Woods		

Annual Awards
PGA of America Player of the Year

Awarded by the PGA of America; based on points scale that weighs performance in major tournaments, regular events, money earned and scoring average.

Multiple winners: Tiger Woods (9); Tom Watson (6); Jack Nicklaus (5); Ben Hogan (4); Julius Boros, Billy Casper, Arnold Palmer and Nick Price.

Year		Year		Year		Year	
1948	Ben Hogan	1963	Julius Boros	1978	Tom Watson	1993	Nick Price
1949	Sam Snead	1964	Ken Venturi	1979	Tom Watson	1994	Nick Price
1950	Ben Hogan	1965	Dave Marr	1980	Tom Watson	1995	Greg Norman
1951	Ben Hogan	1966	Billy Casper	1981	Bill Rogers	1996	Tom Lehman
1952	Julius Boros	1967	Jack Nicklaus	1982	Tom Watson	1997	Tiger Woods
1953	Ben Hogan	1968	No award	1983	Hal Sutton	1998	Mark O'Meara
1954	Ed Furgol	1969	Orville Moody	1984	Tom Watson	1999	Tiger Woods
1955	Doug Ford	1970	Billy Casper	1985	Lanny Wadkins	2000	Tiger Woods
1956	Jack Burke	1971	Lee Trevino	1986	Bob Tway	2001	Tiger Woods
1957	Dick Mayer	1972	Jack Nicklaus	1987	Paul Azinger	2002	Tiger Woods
1958	Dow Finsterwald	1973	Jack Nicklaus	1988	Curtis Strange	2003	Tiger Woods
1959	Art Wall Jr.	1974	Johnny Miller	1989	Tom Kite	2004	Vijay Singh
1960	Arnold Palmer	1975	Jack Nicklaus	1990	Nick Faldo	2005	Tiger Woods
1961	Jerry Barber	1976	Jack Nicklaus	1991	Corey Pavin	2006	Tiger Woods
1962	Arnold Palmer	1977	Tom Watson	1992	Fred Couples	2007	Tiger Woods

PGA Tour Player of the Year

Award by the PGA Tour starting in 1990. Winner voted on by tour members from list of nominees. Winner receives the Jack Nicklaus Trophy, which originated in 1997.

Multiple winners: Tiger Woods (9); Fred Couples and Nick Price (2).

Year		Year		Year		Year	
1990	Wayne Levi	1995	Greg Norman	2000	Tiger Woods	2005	Tiger Woods
1991	Fred Couples	1996	Tom Lehman	2001	Tiger Woods	2006	Tiger Woods
1992	Fred Couples	1997	Tiger Woods	2002	Tiger Woods	2007	Tiger Woods
1993	Nick Price	1998	Mark O'Meara	2003	Tiger Woods		
1994	Nick Price	1999	Tiger Woods	2004	Vijay Singh		

PGA Tour Rookie of the Year

Awarded by the PGA Tour in 1990. Winner voted on by tour members from list of first-year nominees.

Year		Year		Year		Year	
1990	Robert Gamez	1995	Woody Austin	2000	Michael Clark II	2005	Sean O'Hair
1991	John Daly	1996	Tiger Woods	2001	Charles Howell III	2006	Trevor Immelman
1992	Mark Carnevale	1997	Stewart Cink	2002	Jonathan Byrd	2007	Brandt Snedeker
1993	Vijay Singh	1998	Steve Flesch	2003	Ben Curtis		
1994	Ernie Els	1999	Carlos Franco	2004	Todd Hamilton		

Champions Tour Player of the Year

Awarded by the Champions Tour starting in 1990. Winner voted on by tour members from list of nominees.

Multiple winner: Hale Irwin and Lee Trevino (3); Jim Colbert and Jay Haas (2).

Year		Year		Year		Year	
1990	Lee Trevino	1994	Lee Trevino	1999	Bruce Fleisher	2004	Craig Stadler
1991	George Archer & Mike Hill	1995	Jim Colbert	2000	Larry Nelson	2005	Dana Quigley
		1996	Jim Colbert	2001	Allen Doyle	2006	Jay Haas
1992	Lee Trevino	1997	Hale Irwin	2002	Hale Irwin	2007	Jay Haas
1993	Dave Stockton	1998	Hale Irwin	2003	Tom Watson		

European Tour Golfer of the Year

Formerly the Ritz Club Trophy (1985-92), Johnnie Walker Trophy (1993-97) and Asprey Golfer of the Year (1998-2004); voting done by panel of European golf writers and tour members.

Multiple winners: Colin Montgomerie (4); Seve Ballesteros, Ernie Els, and Nick Faldo (3); Bernhard Langer and Lee Westwood (2).

Year		Year		Year		Year	
1985	Bernhard Langer	1991	Seve Ballesteros	1997	Colin Montgomerie	2003	Ernie Els
1986	Seve Ballesteros	1992	Nick Faldo	1998	Lee Westwood	2004	Vijay Singh
1987	Ian Woosnam	1993	Bernhard Langer	1999	Colin Montgomerie	2005	Michael Campbell
1988	Seve Ballesteros	1994	Ernie Els	2000	Lee Westwood	2006	Paul Casey
1989	Nick Faldo	1995	Colin Montgomerie	2001	Retief Goosen	2007	Padraig Harrington
1990	Nick Faldo	1996	Colin Montgomerie	2002	Ernie Els		

LPGA Player of the Year

Sponsored by Rolex and awarded by the LPGA; based on performance points accumulated during the year.
Multiple winners: Annika Sorenstam (8); Kathy Whitworth (7); Nancy Lopez (4); JoAnne Carner, Beth Daniel and Betsy King (3); Pat Bradley, Lorena Ochoa, Judy Rankin and Karrie Webb (2).

Year		Year		Year		Year	
1966	Kathy Whitworth	1977	Judy Rankin	1988	Nancy Lopez	1999	Karrie Webb
1967	Kathy Whitworth	1978	Nancy Lopez	1989	Betsy King	2000	Karrie Webb
1968	Kathy Whitworth	1979	Nancy Lopez	1990	Beth Daniel	2001	Annika Sorenstam
1969	Kathy Whitworth	1980	Beth Daniel	1991	Pat Bradley	2002	Annika Sorenstam
1970	Sandra Haynie	1981	JoAnne Carner	1992	Dottie Mochrie	2003	Annika Sorenstam
1971	Kathy Whitworth	1982	JoAnne Carner	1993	Betsy King	2004	Annika Sorenstam
1972	Kathy Whitworth	1983	Patty Sheehan	1994	Beth Daniel	2005	Annika Sorenstam
1973	Kathy Whitworth	1984	Betsy King	1995	Annika Sorenstam	2006	Lorena Ochoa
1974	JoAnne Carner	1985	Nancy Lopez	1996	Laura Davies	2007	Lorena Ochoa
1975	Sandra Palmer	1986	Pat Bradley	1997	Annika Sorenstam		
1976	Judy Rankin	1987	Ayako Okamoto	1998	Annika Sorenstam		

LPGA Rookie of the Year

Sponsored by Rolex and awarded by the LPGA; based on performance points accumulated during the year. Winner receives Louise Suggs Trophy, which originated in 2000. Officially the Louise Suggs Rolex Rookie of the Year.

Year		Year		Year		Year	
1962	Mary Mills	1974	Jan Stephenson	1986	Jody Rosenthal	1998	Se Ri Pak
1963	Clifford Ann Creed	1975	Amy Alcott	1987	Tammie Green	1999	Mi Hyun Kim
1964	Susie Berning	1976	Bonnie Lauer	1988	Liselotte Neumann	2000	Dorothy Delasin
1965	Margie Masters	1977	Debbie Massey	1989	Pamela Wright	2001	Hee-Won Han
1966	Jan Ferraris	1978	Nancy Lopez	1990	Hiromi Kobayashi	2002	Beth Bauer
1967	Sharron Moran	1979	Beth Daniel	1991	Brandie Burton	2003	Lorena Ochoa
1968	Sandra Post	1980	Myra Van Hoose	1992	Helen Alfredsson	2004	Shi Hyun Ahn
1969	Jane Blalock	1981	Patty Sheehan	1993	Suzanne Strudwick	2005	Paula Creamer
1970	JoAnne Carner	1982	Patti Rizzo	1994	Annika Sorenstam	2006	Seon-Hwa Lee
1971	Sally Little	1983	Stephanie Farwig	1995	Pat Hurst	2007	Angela Park
1972	Jocelyne Bourassa	1984	Juli Inkster	1996	Karrie Webb		
1973	Laura Baugh	1985	Penny Hammel	1997	Lisa Hackney		

National Team Competition
MEN
Ryder Cup

The Ryder Cup was presented by British seed merchant and businessman Samuel Ryder in 1927 for competition between professional golfers from Great Britain and the United States. The British team was expanded to include Irish players in 1973 and the rest of Europe in 1979. The 2001 event was postponed due to the attacks on America, causing the event to switch from an odd- to even-year schedule. The United States leads the series 25-10-2 after 37 matches.

Year		Year		Year		Year	
1927	USA, 9½-2½	1953	USA, 6½-5½	1973	USA, 19-13	1993	USA, 15-13
1929	Britain-Ireland, 7-5	1955	USA, 8-4	1975	USA, 21-11	1995	Europe, 14½-13½
1931	USA, 9-3	1957	Britain-Ireland, 7½-4½	1977	USA, 12½-13½	1997	Europe, 14½-13½
1933	Great Britain, 6½-5½	1959	USA, 8½-3½	1979	USA, 17-11	1999	USA, 14½-13½
1935	USA, 9-3	1961	USA, 14½-9½	1981	USA, 18½-9½	2002	Europe, 15½-12½
1937	USA, 8-4	1963	USA, 23-9	1983	USA, 14½-13½	2004	Europe, 18½-9½
1939-45 Not held		1965	USA, 19½-12½	1985	Europe, 16½-11½	2006	Europe, 18½-9½
1947	USA, 11-1	1967	USA, 23½-8½	1987	Europe, 15-13	2008	USA, 16½-11½
1949	USA, 7-5	1969	Draw, 16-16	1989	Draw, 14-14		
1951	USA, 9½-2½	1971	USA, 18½-13½	1992	USA, 14½-13½		

Playing Sites

1927—Worcester CC (Mass.); **1929**—Moortown, England; **1931**—Scioto CC (Ohio); **1933**—Southport & Ainsdale, England; **1935**—Ridgewood CC (N.J.); **1937**—Southport & Ainsdale, England; **1939-45**—Not held. **1947**—Portland CC (Ore.); **1949**—Ganton GC, England; **1951**—Pinehurst CC (N.C.); **1953**—Wentworth, England; **1955**—Thunderbird Ranch & CC (Calif.); **1957**—Lindrick GC, England; **1959**—Eldorado CC (Calif.); **1961**—Royal Lytham & St. Annes, England; **1963**—East Lake CC (Ga.); **1965**—Royal Birkdale, England; **1967**—Champions GC (Tex.); **1969**—Royal Birkdale, England; **1971**—Old Warson CC (Mo.); **1973**—Muirfield, Scotland; **1975**—Laurel Valley GC (Pa.); **1977**—Royal Lytham & St. Annes, England; **1979**—The Greenbrier (W.Va.); **1981**—Walton Heath GC, England; **1983**—PGA National GC (Fla.); **1985**—The Belfry, England; **1987**—Muirfield Village GC (Ohio); **1989**—The Belfry, England; **1991**—Ocean Course (S.C.); **1993**—The Belfry, England; **1995**—Oak Hill CC (N.Y.); **1997**—Valderrama, Costa del Sol, Spain; **1999**—The Country Club (Mass.); **2002**— The Belfry, England; **2004**— Oakland Hills CC (Mich.); **2006**— Kildare Hotel & CC, Ireland; **2008**—Valhalla GC (Ky.); **2010**— Celtic Manor, Wales; **2012**— Medinah CC (Ill.); **2014**— Gleneagles, Scotland; **2016**—Hazeltine National GC (Minn); **2018**—TBA (Europe); **2020**—Whistling Straits (Wisc.).

Presidents Cup

The Presidents Cup is a biennial event played in non-Ryder Cup years in which the world's best non-European players compete against players from the United States. The U.S. leads the series, 5-1-1. In 2003 the match was called off due to darkness after three sudden-death playoff holes. It was deemed a tie with both teams sharing the Cup until 2005.

Year		Year		Year		Year	
1994	USA, 20-12	1998	Internat'l, 20½-11½	2003	Tie, 17-17	2007	USA, 19½-14½
1996	USA, 16½-15½	2000	USA, 21½-10½	2005	USA, 18½-15½		

Walker Cup

The Walker Cup was presented by American businessman George Herbert Walker in 1922 for competition between amateur golfers from Great Britain, Ireland and the United States. The U.S. leads the series against the combined Great Britain-Ireland team, 33-7-1, after 41 matches.

Year		Year		Year		Year	
1922	USA, 8-4	1949	USA, 10-2	1973	USA, 14-10	1995	Britain-Ireland, 14-10
1923	USA, 6½-5½	1951	USA, 7½-4½	1975	USA, 15½-8½	1997	USA, 18-6
1924	USA, 9-3	1953	USA, 9-3	1977	USA, 16-8	1999	Britain-Ireland, 15-9
1926	USA, 6½-5½	1955	USA, 10-2	1979	USA, 15½-8½	2001	Britain-Ireland, 15-9
1928	USA, 11-1	1957	USA, 8½-3½	1981	USA, 15-9	2003	Britain-Ireland,
1930	USA, 10-2	1959	USA, 9-3	1983	USA, 13½-10½		12½-11½
1932	USA, 9½-2½	1961	USA, 11-1	1985	USA, 13-11	2005	USA, 12½-11½
1934	USA, 9½-2½	1963	USA, 14-10	1987	USA, 16½-7½	2007	USA, 12½-11½
1936	USA, 10½-1½	1965	Draw, 12-12	1989	Britain-Ireland,		
1938	Britain-Ireland, 7½-4½	1967	USA, 15-9		12½-11½		
1940-46	Not held	1969	USA, 13-11	1991	USA, 14-10		
1947	USA, 8-4	1971	Britain-Ireland, 13-11	1993	USA, 19-5		

WOMEN

Solheim Cup

The Solheim Cup was presented by the Karsten Manufacturing Co. in 1990 for competition between women professional golfers from Europe and the United States. The event was switched from even- to odd-numbered years after 2002 so it would not conflict with the men's Ryder Cup event. The U.S. leads the series, 7-3.

Year		Year		Year		Year	
1990	USA, 11½-4½	1996	USA, 17-11	2002	USA, 15½-12½	2007	USA, 16-12
1992	Europe, 11½-6½	1998	USA, 16-12	2003	Europe, 17½-10½		
1994	USA, 13-7	2000	Europe, 14½-11½	2005	USA, 15½-12½		

Playing Sites

1990—Lake Nona CC (Fla.); **1992**—Dalmahoy CC, Scotland; **1994**—The Greenbrier (W. Va.); **1996**—Marriott St. Pierre Hotel G&CC, Wales; **1998**—Muirfield Village GC (Ohio); **2000**—Loch Lomond GC, Scotland; **2002**—Interlachen CC (Minn.); **2003**—Barseback G&CC, Sweden; **2005**—Crooked Stick GC (Ind.); **2007**—Halmstad GC (Sweden); **2009**—Rich Harvest Farms (Ill.).

Curtis Cup

Named after British golfing sisters Harriot and Margaret Curtis, the Curtis Cup was first contested in 1932 between teams of women amateurs from the United States and the British Isles.

Competed for every other year since 1932 (except during WWII). The U.S. leads the series, 26-6-3, after 35 matches.

Year		Year		Year		Year	
1932	USA, 5½-3½	1956	British Isles, 5-4	1974	USA, 13-5	1992	British Isles, 10-8
1934	USA, 6½-2½	1958	Draw, 4½-4½	1976	USA, 11½-6½	1994	Draw, 9-9
1936	Draw, 4½-4½	1960	USA, 6½-2½	1978	USA, 12-6	1996	British Isles, 11½-6½
1938	USA, 5½-3½	1962	USA, 8-1	1980	USA, 13-5	1998	USA, 10-8
1940-46	Not held	1964	USA, 10½-7½	1982	USA, 14½-3½	2000	USA, 10-8
1948	USA, 6½-2½	1966	USA, 13-5	1984	USA, 9½-8½	2002	USA, 11-7
1950	USA, 7½-1½	1968	USA, 10½-7½	1986	British Isles, 13-5	2004	USA, 10-8
1952	British Isles, 5-4	1970	USA, 11½-6½	1988	British Isles, 11-7	2006	USA, 11½-6½
1954	USA, 6-3	1972	USA, 10-8	1990	USA, 14-4	2008	USA, 13-7

COLLEGES

Men's NCAA Division I Champions

College championships decided by match play from 1897-1964 and stroke play since 1965.

Multiple winners (Teams): Yale (21); Houston (16); Oklahoma St. (10); Stanford (8); Harvard (6); Florida, LSU and North Texas (4); Wake Forest (3); Arizona St., Georgia, Michigan, Ohio St., Texas and UCLA (2).

Multiple winners (Individuals): Ben Crenshaw and Phil Mickelson (3); Dick Crawford, Dexter Cummings, G.T. Dunlop, Fred Lamprecht and Scott Simpson (2).

Year	Team winner	Individual champion	Year	Team winner	Individual champion
1897	Yale	Louis Bayard, Princeton	1905	Yale	Robert Abbott, Yale
1898	Harvard (spring)	John Reid, Yale	1906	Yale	W.E. Clow Jr., Yale
1898	Yale (fall)	James Curtis, Harvard	1907	Yale	Ellis Knowles, Yale
1899	Harvard	Percy Pyne, Princeton	1908	Yale	H.H. Wilder, Harvard
1900	Not held		1909	Yale	Albert Seckel, Princeton
1901	Harvard	H. Lindsley, Harvard	1910	Yale	Robert Hunter, Yale
1902	Yale (spring)	Chas. Hitchcock Jr., Yale	1911	Yale	George Stanley, Yale
1902	Harvard (fall)	Chandler Egan, Harvard	1912	Yale	F.C. Davison, Harvard
1903	Harvard	F.O. Reinhart, Princeton	1913	Yale	Nathaniel Wheeler, Yale
1904	Harvard	A.L. White, Harvard	1914	Princeton	Edward Allis, Harvard

Colleges (Cont.)

Year	Team winner	Individual champion	Year	Team winner	Individual champion
1915	Yale	Francis Blossom, Yale	1963	Oklahoma St.	R.H. Sikes, Arkansas
1916	Princeton	J.W. Hubbell, Harvard	1964	Houston	Terry Small, San Jose St.
1917-18	Not held		1965	Houston	Marty Fleckman, Houston
1919	Princeton	A.L. Walker Jr., Columbia	1966	Houston	Bob Murphy, Florida
1920	Princeton	Jess Sweetser, Yale	1967	Houston	Hale Irwin, Colorado
1921	Dartmouth	Simpson Dean, Princeton	1968	Florida	Grier Jones, Oklahoma St.
1922	Princeton	Pollack Boyd, Dartmouth	1969	Houston	Bob Clark, Cal St.-LA
1923	Princeton	Dexter Cummings, Yale	1970	Houston	John Mahaffey, Houston
1924	Yale	Dexter Cummings, Yale	1971	Texas	Ben Crenshaw, Texas
1925	Yale	Fred Lamprecht, Tulane	1972	Texas	Ben Crenshaw, Texas
1926	Yale	Fred Lamprecht, Tulane			& Tom Kite, Texas
1927	Princeton	Watts Gunn, Georgia Tech	1973	Florida	Ben Crenshaw, Texas
1928	Princeton	Maurice McCarthy, G'town	1974	Wake Forest	Curtis Strange, W.Forest
1929	Princeton	Tom Aycock, Yale	1975	Wake Forest	Jay Haas, Wake Forest
1930	Princeton	G.T. Dunlap Jr., Princeton	1976	Oklahoma St.	Scott Simpson, USC
1931	Yale	G.T. Dunlap Jr., Princeton	1977	Houston	Scott Simpson, USC
1932	Yale	J.W. Fischer, Michigan	1978	Oklahoma St.	David Edwards, Okla. St.
1933	Yale	Walter Emery, Oklahoma	1979	Ohio St.	Gary Hallberg, Wake Forest
1934	Michigan	Charles Yates, Ga.Tech	1980	Oklahoma St.	Jay Don Blake, Utah St.
1935	Michigan	Ed White, Texas	1981	Brigham Young	Ron Commans, USC
1936	Yale	Charles Kocsis, Michigan	1982	Houston	Billy Ray Brown, Houston
1937	Princeton	Fred Haas Jr., LSU	1983	Oklahoma St.	Jim Carter, Arizona St.
1938	Stanford	John Burke, Georgetown	1984	Houston	John Inman, N.Carolina
1939	Stanford	Vincent D'Antoni, Tulane	1985	Houston	Clark Burroughs, Ohio St.
1940	Princeton & LSU	Dixon Brooke, Virginia	1986	Wake Forest	Scott Verplank, Okla. St.
1941	Stanford	Earl Stewart, LSU	1987	Oklahoma St.	Brian Watts, Oklahoma St.
1942	LSU & Stanford	Frank Tatum Jr., Stanford	1988	UCLA	E.J. Pfister, Oklahoma St.
1943	Yale	Wallace Ulrich, Carleton	1989	Oklahoma	Phil Mickelson, Ariz. St.
1944	Notre Dame	Louis Lick, Minnesota	1990	Arizona St.	Phil Mickelson, Ariz. St.
1945	Ohio State	John Lorms, Ohio St.	1991	Oklahoma St.	Warren Schuette, UNLV
1946	Stanford	George Hamer, Georgia	1992	Arizona	Phil Mickelson, Ariz. St.
1947	LSU	Dave Barclay, Michigan	1993	Florida	Todd Demsey, Ariz. St.
1948	San Jose St.	Bob Harris, San Jose St.	1994	Stanford	Justin Leonard, Texas
1949	North Texas	Harvie Ward, N.Carolina	1995	Oklahoma St.	Chip Spratlin, Auburn
1950	North Texas	Fred Wampler, Purdue	1996	Arizona St.	Tiger Woods, Stanford
1951	North Texas	Tom Nieporte, Ohio St.	1997	Pepperdine	Charles Warren, Clemson
1952	North Texas	Jim Vickers, Oklahoma	1998	UNLV	James McLean, Minnesota
1953	Stanford	Earl Moeller, Oklahoma St.	1999	Georgia	Luke Donald, Northwestern
1954	SMU	Hillman Robbins, Memphis St.	2000	Oklahoma St.	Charles Howell, Oklahoma St.
1955	LSU	Joe Campbell, Purdue	2001	Florida	Nick Gilliam, Florida
1956	Houston	Rick Jones, Ohio St.	2002	Minnesota	Troy Matteson, Georgia Tech
1957	Houston	Rex Baxter Jr., Houston	2003	Clemson	Alejandro Canizares, Ariz. St.
1958	Houston	Phil Rodgers, Houston	2004	California	Ryan Moore, UNLV
1959	Houston	Dick Crawford, Houston	2005	Georgia	James Lepp, Washington
1960	Houston	Dick Crawford, Houston	2006	Oklahoma St.	Jonathan Moore, Oklahoma St.
1961	Purdue	Jack Nicklaus, Ohio St.	2007	Stanford	Jamie Lovemark, USC
1962	Houston	Kermit Zarley, Houston	2008	UCLA	Kevin Chappell, UCLA

Women's NCAA Division I Champions

College championships decided by stroke play since 1982.

Multiple winners (teams): Arizona St. (6); Duke (5); Arizona, Florida, San Jose St., Tulsa, UCLA and USC (2).

Year	Team winner	Individual champion	Year	Team winner	Individual champion
1982	Tulsa	Kathy Baker, Tulsa	1996	Arizona	Marisa Baena, Arizona
1983	TCU	Penny Hammel, Miami	1997	Arizona St.	Heather Bowie, Texas
1984	Miami-FL	Cindy Schreyer, Georgia	1998	Arizona St.	Jennifer Rosales, USC
1985	Florida	Danielle Ammaccapane, Ariz.St.	1999	Duke	Grace Park, Arizona St.
1986	Florida	Page Dunlap, Florida	2000	Arizona	Jenna Daniels, Arizona
1987	San Jose St.	Caroline Keggi, New Mexico	2001	Georgia	Candy Hannemann, Duke
1988	Tulsa	Melissa McNamara, Tulsa	2002	Duke	Virada Nirapathpongporn, Duke
1989	San Jose St.	Pat Hurst, San Jose St.	2003	USC	Mikaela Parmlid, USC
1990	Arizona St.	Susan Slaughter, Arizona	2004	UCLA	Sarah Huarte, California
1991	UCLA	Annika Sorenstam, Arizona	2005	Duke	Anna Grzebien, Duke
1992	San Jose St.	Vicki Goetze, Georgia	2006	Duke	Dewi Schreefel, USC
1993	Arizona St.	Charlotta Sorenstam, Ariz. St.	2007	Duke	Stacy Lewis, Arkansas
1994	Arizona St.	Emilee Klein, Ariz. St.	2008	USC	Azahara Munoz, Arizona St.
1995	Arizona St.	K. Mourgue d'Algue, Ariz. St.			

With seven Sprint Cup wins through October, **Carl Edwards** spent lots of time upside-down in 2008.

ALL SYSTEMS GO

The Chase isn't perfect...
but other sports leagues are taking note.

by
Ed Hinton

BECAUSE THE CHASE SEEMS STATUS QUO IN THIS, ITS FIFTH YEAR, A LOOK AT HOW PLAYOFFS HAVE CHANGED NASCAR MUST BEGIN WITH PRE-CHASE NASCAR.

Lest we forget, about this time of year the doldrums used to set in and the grousing would begin. For example, would Matt Kenseth really win the 2003 Winston Cup with only one race victory?

He would. But was that fair, when Kenseth merely drove consistently while Ryan Newman won eight races but finished sixth in points?

Last year's Chase took a media beating because the Homestead-Miami finale came down to only two drivers, teammates at that, Jimmie Johnson and Jeff Gordon.

But consider that the last of the late Dale Earnhardt's seven season titles,

in 1994, was locked up in the backwater outpost of Rockingham, N.C., with two races left. That didn't do much for ratings and ticket sales in Phoenix and Atlanta.

In years like that, the end of the NASCAR season droned on as little more than background noise to baseball's playoffs and the World Series, the crescendo of the college football season, the meat of the NFL schedule, the startup of the NBA and NHL …

"The fall is a busy, busy time," says John Skipper, ESPN's executive vice president, content. "So NASCAR needed to figure out a way to make sure they sustained interest, and I think they've done that."

 Ed Hinton is a Senior Writer at ESPN.com.

Doug Pensinger/Getty Images

Jimmie Johnson, shown here battling for position with Jeff Gordon and Carl Edwards, has thrived perhaps more than anyone since the inception of the Chase in 2004.

Enough interest that Skipper estimates that ABC/ESPN paid perhaps "10 to 20" percent more for eight years of telecast rights to the second half of the Cup season than it would have under the old points system. That's a difference of up to $400 million in the estimated $2.1 billion rights package.

"In the old days, nobody would have looked at our fall as some kind of nice property to have," says NASCAR chairman Brian France, who birthed and pushed the idea of the Chase past even his own ruling family.

"ABC and ESPN bought it in part because they got exclusive rights to the playoffs."

The success of the Chase in sustaining public interest and enhancing TV money has been enough to influence other sports organizations — the NHRA, the PGA and the LPGA — to create their own autumn playoff systems.

"Our structure in many ways is very similar to NASCAR," says Steve Dennis, director of communications strategy for the PGA Tour, which began its playoff system in 2007. "The two key pieces are that they are individual sports, and finishing position beyond win or lose matters. And it matters a whole lot, in both sports."

The PGA had been considering stimulating autumn interest in the Tour for years, but critical mass for action

Chairman **Brian France**, creator of NASCAR's playoff system, isn't afraid to tinker with the system when needed. And it's paying dividends.

Scott A. Schneider/Getty Images for NASCAR

came in 2005 and 2006. "And the fact that NASCAR's Chase, implemented in 2004, was doing well gave us some level of confidence that we could put [a playoff system] together that would also do well," Dennis says.

The LPGA was weighing traditionalism versus spicing up the end of its season, and "when NASCAR broke ranks, so to speak, and created this thing called the Chase, we thought, 'That's interesting that they would step outside their roots and go do this,'" says Chris Higgs, the LPGA's senior vice president and chief operations officer. "I think that probably helped us along in the process."

The NHRA would have gone to playoffs regardless of what NASCAR did — but for the same reasons, says Gary Darcy, the drag racing organization's senior vice president of sales and marketing.

"A lot of the time, through the course of a long season, championships are locked up early and you lose a little excitement down the stretch," Darcy says. "We looked at what they [NASCAR] were doing, but that wasn't a driving force for us."

There is no other real purpose of playoffs, in any sport, than to stimulate interest and television ratings.

Lest we forget that the World Series used to be played between the champions of the National League regular season and the American League regular season. The old NFL championship games were between the regular-season champions of the East and West divisions.

History lost?

Jeff Gordon is perhaps the Chase's biggest victim. Under the old system, he arguably would have six championships by now and would be gunning for Earnhardt and Richard Petty's shared record of seven. The two he theoretically lost under the new system were in 2004 and '07.

"The only issue I have with [the Chase]," Gordon says, "is that we build our sport on history, and you can't compare the history of the old point system to the new point system. You can't compare a champion [the old way], even myself, to any champion today. It's just done totally different."

So has the Chase fractured NASCAR history — drawn a line through it?

"It did when it comes to championships," Gordon says. "It doesn't change race wins any. [He is the leader among active drivers with 81.] But as far as championships, it has completely changed it."

Yet even Gordon acknowledges that the Chase has been a change for the better.

"It's made it extremely exciting, and it gives teams that have a rough first half and a strong second half [a chance] to win the championship," he says. "Where in the past if you had a really strong first half, you could ride it out in the second half and just not make mistakes, and the championship was yours. It's totally different now — different in a positive way for the fans, for the sponsors.

"It doesn't always work out for every competitor out there," Gordon acknowledges, "but I still think when it comes down to it, the best teams and drivers still win the championship."

Chase takes off

No sooner had Brian France ascended the throne of NASCAR in 2003 than he set to work on a play-off system. Most of all, he had to sell the idea to his father, Bill France Jr., who'd been NASCAR's cautious, methodical czar from 1972 through the growth-spurt period of the late 1990s and into its current level of popularity early this millennium.

The aging czar, who died in 2007, said in 2004 that he finally decided to go along with the Chase "because if it doesn't work, we can always change it."

But his son felt that once the plunge was taken, it couldn't be easily revoked.

"I thought you needed to be in for at least a number of years, unless there was some fiasco that eroded the credibility of the sport," France says now. "Absent something we weren't seeing, we had to be committed for a long period of time. And it was a big deal."

Yet there was no knot in his stomach, no anxiety, as the third-generation France got his way — and all the responsibility for it.

"I didn't really feel like it was risky. If you look at it compared to the old system, it just had so many more easy-to-understand benefits that frankly I couldn't understand why we wouldn't have thought about it before."

The younger France makes no pretense that the Chase has worked ideally every year.

"We've really had the true full benefits of it only maybe one or two years," he says.

The first year, 2004, came down to a cavalry charge into Homestead-Miami Speedway for the finale, with Kurt Busch winning out over Gordon and Jimmie Johnson. But since then, there's been a relative lull in drama.

By full benefits, "I mean where it comes down to Homestead-Miami and they're really, really, really tight, three or more cars, say inside of 30 points or so — that would be the ultimate scenario," France says. "And it's no different from what the Super Bowl wants to be. They'd like it to be like last year, where it comes down to the last play of the game. That's the goal.

"The reality in sports is, that doesn't always happen. No matter what playoff format you have, it can't guarantee [drama down to the wire].

"You ask yourself, 'Have we given ourselves the best opportunity?'" And I think we have. And time will tell, over many years, how great it can become."

France admits, "I would have thought we would have had more 'down to the last lap of the last race'" than the Chase. But that doesn't mean the next three won't be.

"And I can assure you that under the old format, you were never going to have that."

France remains open to tweaking and last year made the biggest changes yet, expanding the playoff field from 10 to 12 drivers and —

even more importantly — seeding the playoffs according to the number of race wins in the regular season.

"When we did that, people said, 'You didn't do enough [to reward winning]. That's only 10 points in the seed.' Well, as it turns out, with what Kyle Busch [eight wins through Oct.] and Carl Edwards [seven] have done this year...I would have hated to have 30 points [as a bonus for a race win]. So that's the balance."

Most of all, the Chase in its current format has come to reward winning races — which purists consider the point of this entire exercise of racing — more than at any time since the season championship became the overriding goal in NASCAR in the 1980s.

"We will do anything to strike the right balance between winning individual races and being good enough to win the championship," France says. "That's our goal."

"Frankly, the old system was one of the worst at that."

2007-2008 Season in Review

ESPN SPORTS ALMANAC

NASCAR RESULTS

Sprint Cup Series

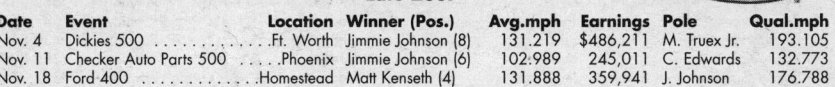

Results of NASCAR Sprint Cup races from Nov. 4, 2007 through Oct. 26, 2008.
Note: Earnings include bonus money.

Late 2007

Date	Event	Location	Winner (Pos.)	Avg.mph	Earnings	Pole	Qual.mph
Nov. 4	Dickies 500	Ft. Worth	Jimmie Johnson (8)	131.219	$486,211	M. Truex Jr.	193.105
Nov. 11	Checker Auto Parts 500	Phoenix	Jimmie Johnson (6)	102.989	245,011	C. Edwards	132.773
Nov. 18	Ford 400	Homestead	Matt Kenseth (4)	131.888	359,941	J. Johnson	176.788

Winning cars (entire 2007 season): CHEVROLET (26)—Johnson 10, J. Gordon 6, Stewart 3, Bowyer, Ky. Busch, Burton, Hamlin, Harvick, Mears and Truex Jr.; FORD (7)—Edwards 3, Kenseth 2, Biffle and McMurray; DODGE (3)—Ku. Busch 2 and Montoya.

2008 Season (through Oct. 26)

Date	Event	Location	Winner (Pos.)	Avg.mph	Earnings	Pole	Qual.mph
Feb. 17	**Daytona 500**	Daytona	Ryan Newman (7)	152.675	$1,506,040	J. Johnson	187.075
Feb. 24	Auto Club 500	Los Angeles	Carl Edwards (9)	132.704	340,500	J. Johnson	—**
Mar. 2	UAW-Dodge 400	Las Vegas	Carl Edwards (2)	127.729	425,675	Ky. Busch	182.352
Mar. 9	Kobalt Tools 500	Atlanta	Kyle Busch (6)	140.975	194,175	J. Gordon	185.251
Mar. 16	Food City 500	Bristol	Jeff Burton (8)	89.775	209,558	J. Johnson	—**
Mar. 30	Goody's Cool Orange 500	Martinsville	Denny Hamlin (2)	73.163	201,391	J. Gordon	96.288
Apr. 6	Samsung 500	Ft. Worth	Carl Edwards (2)	144.814	541.150	D. Earnhardt Jr.	190.907
Apr. 12	Subway Fresh Fit 500	Phoenix	Jimmie Johnson (7)	103.292	262,111	R. Newman	133.457
Apr. 27	Aaron's 499	Talladega	Kyle Busch (5)	157.409	321,400	J. Nemechek	187.386
May 3	Crown Royal/Dan Lowery 400	Richmond	Clint Bowyer (31)	95.786	226,550	D. Hamlin	126.198
May 10	Dodge Challenger 500	Darlington	Kyle Busch (6)	140.350	313,700	G. Biffle	179.442
May 17@	Sprint All-Star Race	Charlotte	Kasey Kahne (24)	131.132	1,012,975	Ky. Busch	132.835
May 25	**Coca-Cola 600**	Charlotte	Kasey Kahne (2)	135.772	422,766	Ky. Busch	185.433
June 1	Best Buy 400	Dover	Kyle Busch (3)	121.171	302,550	G. Biffle	155.214
June 8	Pocono 500	Pocono	Kasey Kahne (1)	125.209	260,866	K. Kahne	170.219
June 15	LifeLock 400	Michigan	Dale Earnhardt Jr. (3)	145.375	173,550	Ky. Busch	—**
June 22	Toyota/Save Mart 350	Sonoma	Kyle Busch (30)	76.445	309,925	K. Kahne	92.153
June 29	Lenox Industrial Tools 301	Loudon	Kurt Busch (26)	106.719	204,950	P. Carpentier	129.776
July 5	Coke Zero 400	Daytona	Kyle Busch (9)	138.554	315,950	P. Menard	185.916
July 12	LifeLock.com 400	Chicago	Kyle Busch (1)	133.996	331,175	Ky. Busch	—**
July 27	**Allstate 400/Brickyard**	Indianapolis	Jimmie Johnson (1)	115.117	509,236	J. Johnson	181.763
Aug. 3	Pennsylvania 500	Pocono	Carl Edwards (15)	130.567	241,875	J. Johnson	168.215
Aug. 10	Centurion Boats at the Glen	Watkins Glen	Kyle Busch (1)	97.148	227,000	Ky. Busch	—**
Aug. 17	3M Performance 400	Michigan	Carl Edwards (27)	140.351	226,075	B. Vickers	188.536
Aug. 23	Sharpie 500	Bristol	Carl Edwards (1)	91.581	344,625	C. Edwards	121.860
Aug. 31	Pepsi 500	Los Angeles	Jimmie Johnson (1)	138.857	314,611	J. Johnson	180.397
Sept. 7	Chevy Rock & Roll 400	Richmond	Jimmie Johnson (3)	92.680	256,836	Ky. Busch	—**

— Chase for the Sprint Cup —

Date	Event	Location	Winner (Pos.)	Avg.mph	Earnings	Pole	Qual.mph
Sept. 14	Sylvania 300	Loudon	Greg Biffle (9)	105.468	233,575	Ky. Busch	—**
Sept. 21	Camping World RV 400	Dover	Greg Biffle (5)	114.168	218,450	J. Gordon	157.061
Sept. 28	Camping World RV 400	Kansas City	Jimmie Johnson (1)	133.549	364,411	J. Johnson	172.007
Oct. 5	**Amp Energy 500**	Talladega	Tony Stewart (34)	140.281	270,136	T. Kvapil	187.364
Oct. 11	Bank of America 500	Charlotte	Jeff Burton (4)	133.699	286,208	J. Johnson	—**
Oct. 19	Tums QuikPak 500	Martinsville	Jimmie Johnson (1)	75.931	219,161	J. Johnson	—**
Oct. 26	Pep Boys Auto 500	Atlanta	Carl Edwards (4)	134.272	357,800	J. Johnson	—**

@ A non-points exhibition event, formerly known as The Winston and the Nextel All-Star Challenge.
**Qualifying was canceled due to weather and the pole was awarded based on Owner points.

Winning Cars: TOYOTA (10)—Ky. Busch 8, Hamlin, Stewart; CHEVROLET (10)—Johnson 6, Burton 2, Bowyer, Earnhardt Jr.; FORD (9)—Edwards 7, Biffle 2; DODGE (4)—Kahne 2, Ku. Busch, Newman.

Remaining Races (3): Dickies 500 in Fort Worth (Nov. 2); Checker O'Reilly Auto Parts 500 in Phoenix (Nov. 9); Ford 400 in Homestead (Nov. 16).

2008 Daytona 500

Date—Sunday, Feb. 17, 2008, at Daytona International Speedway. **Distance**—500 miles; **Course**—2.5 miles; **Field**—43 cars; **Average speed**—152.672 mph; **Margin of victory**—0.092 seconds; **Time of race**—3 hours, 16 minutes, 30 seconds.

Caution flags—7 for 23 laps; **Lead changes**—42 among 16 drivers; **Lap leaders**—Ky. Busch (86); Hamlin (32); Stewart (16); Earnhardt Jr. (12); Burton and Ku. Busch (9); Newman (8); Biffle (7); J. Gordon and Sorenson (5); Bowyer (4); Waltrip (3); Blaney, Johnson, Kahne and Kenseth (1).

Pole sitter—Jimmie Johnson at 187.075 mph.

Attendance—185,000 (estimated). **Rating**—10.2/20 share (FOX).

(r) indicates rookie driver.

	Driver	Start	Sponsor	Car	Laps	Ended	Earnings
1	Ryan Newman	7	Alltel	Dodge	200	Running	$1,506,045
2	Kurt Busch	43	Miller Lite	Dodge	200	Running	1,063,870
3	Tony Stewart	6	Home Depot	Toyota	200	Running	871,049
4	Kyle Busch	24	M&M's	Toyota	200	Running	652,938
5	Reed Sorenson	5	Target	Dodge	200	Running	547,159
6	Elliott Sadler	35	Best Buy	Dodge	200	Running	430,815
7	Kasey Kahne	10	Budweiser	Dodge	200	Running	389,804
8	Robby Gordon	26	Jim Beam	Dodge	200	Running	352,921
9	Dale Earnhardt Jr.	3	AMP Energy/Nat'l Guard	Chevrolet	200	Running	352,920
10	Greg Biffle	18	3M	Ford	200	Running	313,763
11	Bobby Labonte	13	Cheerios/Betty Crocker	Dodge	200	Running	329,756
12	Brian Vickers	23	Red Bull	Toyota	200	Running	285,245
13	Jeff Burton	36	AT&T Mobility	Chevrolet	200	Running	323,496
14	Kevin Harvick	16	Shell/Pennzoil	Chevrolet	200	Running	322,224
15	r-Sam Hornish Jr.	19	Mobil 1	Dodge	200	Running	319,845
16	Dale Jarrett	20	UPS	Toyota	200	Running	277,213
17	Denny Hamlin	4	FedEx Express	Toyota	200	Running	341,416
18	David Reutimann	42	Aaron's Dream Machine	Toyota	200	Running	291,221
19	Carl Edwards	11	Office Depot	Ford	200	Running	321,520
20	Martin Truex Jr.	25	Bass Pro Shops	Chevrolet	200	Running	303,978
21	Scott Riggs	27	State Water Heaters	Chevrolet	200	Running	287,928
22	Paul Menard	21	Menards/Peak	Chevrolet	200	Running	279,295
23	Jeremy Mayfield	33	Junior Johnson's Midnight Moon	Chevrolet	200	Running	271,220
24	Clint Bowyer	31	Jack Daniel's	Chevrolet	200	Running	284,545
25	J.J. Yeley	37	DLP HDTV	Toyota	200	Running	277,095
26	Jamie McMurray	38	Crown Royal Cask No. 16	Ford	200	Running	276,888
27	Jimmie Johnson	1	Lowe's	Chevrolet	200	Running	329,606
28	David Gilliland	32	freecreditreport.com	Ford	200	Running	278,746
29	Michael Waltrip	2	NAPA Auto Parts	Toyota	200	Running	275,135
30	Travis Kvapil	30	K&N Filters	Ford	200	Running	291,202
31	Mark Martin	12	U.S. Army	Chevrolet	200	Running	301,846
32	Juan Pablo Montoya	15	Texaco/Havoline	Dodge	200	Running	290,753
33	r-Dario Franchitti	40	Dodge Journey	Dodge	199	Running	270,613
34	Kyle Petty	39	Wells Fargo	Dodge	197	Running	260,320
35	Casey Mears	9	Kellogg's/Carquest	Chevrolet	194	Accident	284,945
36	Matt Kenseth	28	DeWalt	Ford	194	Running	308,129
37	r-Regan Smith	29	The Principal Financial Group	Chevrolet	194	Running	267,095
38	Dave Blaney	34	Caterpillar	Toyota	189	Accident	259,563
39	Jeff Gordon	8	DuPont	Chevrolet	186	Suspension	319,599
40	John Andretti	22	Makoto	Chevrolet	184	Running	258,613
41	Joe Nemechek	41	Furniture Row Racing	Chevrolet	171	Running	258,470
42	David Ragan	14	AAA	Ford	161	Accident	267,763
43	Kenny Wallace	17	Furniture Row Racing	Chevrolet	141	Engine	256,735

Top 5 Finishing Order + Pole

2008 SPRINT CUP SEASON (through Oct. 26)

No.	Event	Winner	2nd	3rd	4th	5th	Pole
1	Daytona 500	R. Newman	Ku. Busch	T. Stewart	Ky. Busch	R. Sorenseon	J. Johnson
2	Auto Club 500	C. Edwards	J. Johnson	J. Gordon	Ky. Busch	M. Kenseth	J. Johnson
3	UAW-Dodge 400	C. Edwards	D. Earnhardt Jr.	G. Biffle	K. Harvick	J. Burton	Ky. Busch
4	Kobalt Tools 500	Ky. Busch	T. Stewart	D. Earnhardt Jr.	G. Biffle	J. Gordon	J. Gordon
5	Food City 500	J. Burton	K. Harvick	C. Bowyer	G. Biffle	D. Earnhardt Jr.	J. Johnson
6	Goody's Cool Orange 500	D. Hamlin	J. Gordon	J. Burton	J. Johnson	T. Stewart	J. Gordon
7	Samsung 500	C. Edwards	J. Johnson	Ky. Busch	R. Newman	D. Hamlin	D. Earnhardt Jr.
8	Subway Fresh Fit 500	J. Johnson	C. Bowyer	D. Hamlin	C. Edwards	M. Martin	R. Newman

No.	Event	Winner	2nd	3rd	4th	5th	Pole
9	Aaron's 499	Ky. Busch	J P Montoya	D. Hamlin	D. Ragan	B. Vickers	J. Nemechek
10	Crown Royal 400	C. Bowyer	Ky. Busch	M. Martin	T. Stewart	M. Truex Jr.	D. Hamlin
11	Dodge Challenger 500 . .	Ky. Busch	C. Edwards	J. Gordon	D. Earnhardt Jr.	D. Ragan	G. Biffle
12	Coca-Cola 600	K. Kahne	G. Biffle	Ky. Busch	J. Gordon	D. Earnhardt Jr.	Ky. Busch
13	Best Buy 400	Ky. Busch	C. Edwards	G. Biffle	M. Kenseth	J. Gordon	G. Biffle
14	Pocono 500	K. Kahne	B. Vickers	D. Hamlin	D. Earnhardt Jr.	J. Burton	K. Kahne
15	LifeLock 400	D. Earnhardt Jr.	K. Kahne	M. Kenseth	B. Vickers	T. Stewart	Ky. Busch
16	Toyota/Save Mart 350 . .	Ky. Busch	D. Gilliland	J. Gordon	C. Bowyer	C. Mears	K. Kahne
17	Lenox Industrial Tools 301	Ku. Busch	M. Waltrip	J.J. Yeley	M. Truex Jr.	E. Sadler	P. Carpentier
18	Coke Zero 400	Ky. Busch	C. Edwards	M. Kenseth	Ku. Busch	D. Ragan	P. Menard
19	LifeLock.com 400	Ky. Busch	J. Johnson	K. Harvick	G. Biffle	T. Stewart	Ky. Busch
20	Allstate 400 @ Brickyard	J. Johnson	C. Edwards	D. Hamlin	E. Sadler	J. Gordon	J. Johnson
21	Pennsylvania 500	C. Edwards	T. Stewart	J. Johnson	K. Harvick	D. Ragan	J. Johnson
22	Cent. Boats at The Glen .	Ky. Busch	T. Stewart	M. Ambrose	J P Montoya	M. Truex Jr.	Ky. Busch
23	3M Performance 400 . . .	C. Edwards	Ky. Busch	D. Ragan	G. Biffle	M. Kenseth	B. Vickers
24	Sharpie 500	C. Edwards	Ky. Busch	D. Hamlin	K. Harvick	J. Gordon	C. Edwards
25	Pepsi 500	J. Johnson	G. Biffle	D. Hamlin	K. Harvick	M. Kenseth	Ky. Busch
26	Chevy Rock & Roll 400 . .	J. Johnson	T. Stewart	D. Hamlin	D. Earnhardt Jr.	M. Martin	Ky. Busch
		— Chase for the Sprint Cup —					
27	Sylvania 300	G. Biffle	J. Johnson	C. Edwards	J. Burton	D. Earnhardt Jr.	Ky. Busch
28	Camping World RV 400 .	G. Biffle	M. Kenseth	C. Edwards	M. Martin	J. Johnson	J. Gordon
29	Camping World RV 400 .	J. Johnson	C. Edwards	G. Biffle	J. Gordon	M. Kenseth	J. Johnson
30	Amp Energy 500	T. Stewart	P. Menard	D. Ragan	J. Burton	C. Bowyer	T. Kvapil
31	Bank of America 500 . . .	J. Burton	K. Kahne	Ku. Busch	Ky. Busch	J. McMurray	J. Johnson
32	Tums Quikpak 500 . . .	J. Johnson	D. Earnhardt Jr.	C. Edwards	J. Gordon	D. Hamlin	J. Johnson
33	Pep Boys Auto 500	C. Edwards	J. Johnson	D. Hamlin	M. Kenseth	Ky. Busch	J. Johnson

Chase for the Sprint Cup Standings

Official NASCAR Chase for the Sprint Cup standings for 2007 and unofficial standings for 2008 as of Oct. 26 (with three races remaining). Points are awarded for all qualifying drivers (winner received 185) and lap leaders. Earnings include in-season bonuses. Listed are starts (Sts), top-5 finishes (1-2-3-4-5), poles won (PW) and points (Pts).

NASCAR's "Chase for the Sprint Cup" was implemented in 2004 to involve more drivers in the championship hunt, and intensify fan interest and drama during the season's stretch run. After the first 26 official races, the top 12 drivers in the point standings (was top 10 from 2004-06) are eligible for the "chase" over the final ten races of the season. All drivers will begin with 5,000 points; each will then receive a 10-point bonus for each victory during the first 26 events. Drivers not in the top 12 still participate in the final ten races, but are not eligible for the championship.

FINAL 2007

		Sts	Finishes 1-2-3-4-5	PW	Pts
1	Jimmie Johnson	36	10-2-5-1-2	4	6723
2	Jeff Gordon	36	6-5-3-5-2	7	6646
3	Clint Bowyer	36	1-2-1-1-0	2	6377
4	Matt Kenseth	36	2-3-2-3-3	0	6298
5	Kyle Busch	36	1-2-2-5-1	0	6293
6	Tony Stewart	36	3-3-2-2-1	0	6242
7	Kurt Busch	36	2-1-2-0-1	1	6231
8	Jeff Burton	36	1-1-2-4-1	0	6231
9	Carl Edwards	36	3-2-2-1-3	1	6222
10	Kevin Harvick	36	1-1-0-2-0	0	6199
11	Martin Truex Jr. . .	36	1-2-3-0-1	1	6164
12	Denny Hamlin	36	1-2-6-2-1	1	6143

2008 (through Race 33, Oct. 26)

		Sts	Finishes 1-2-3-4-5	PW	Pts
1	Jimmie Johnson	33	6-5-1-1-1	5	6248
2	Carl Edwards	33	7-5-3-1-0	1	6065
3	Greg Biffle	33	2-1-4-4-0	2	6063
4	Jeff Burton	33	2-0-3-2-0	0	6030
5	Kevin Harvick	33	0-1-1-4-0	0	5941
6	Jeff Gordon	33	0-1-3-3-4	3	5936
7	Clint Bowyer	33	1-1-1-1-0	0	5934
8	Tony Stewart	33	1-4-1-1-3	0	5847
9	Matt Kenseth	33	0-1-2-2-4	0	5835
10	Dale Earnhardt Jr. . .	33	1-2-1-3-3	1	5829
11	Denny Hamlin	33	1-0-8-0-2	1	5823
12	Kyle Busch	33	8-3-2-3-1	2	5783

Note: Poles listed do not include those awarded for being points leader when qualification was canceled.

Jimmie Johnson

Carl Edwards

Greg Biffle

Jeff Burton

Sprint Cup Series (Cont.)
Money Leaders

FINAL 2007	Earnings		2008 (through Oct. 26)	Earnings
1 Jimmie Johnson	$15,313,920		1 Carl Edwards	$7,068,675
2 Jeff Gordon	10,926,687		2 Jimmie Johnson	6,807,278
3 Kevin Harvick	8,861,128		3 Kyle Busch	6,269,645
4 Matt Kenseth	8,624,816		4 Kasey Kahne	5,901,011
5 Tony Stewart	8,023,584		5 Tony Stewart	5,880,549
6 Jeff Burton	7,447,288		6 Ryan Newman	5,823,561
7 Kurt Busch	6,852,008		7 Jeff Gordon	5,249,232
8 Clint Bowyer	6,574,793		8 Jeff Burton	5,153,607
9 Kyle Busch	6,475,098		9 Matt Kenseth	5,120,296
10 Carl Edwards	6,011,044		10 Denny Hamlin	5,105,441

Nationwide Series

Results of NASCAR Nationwide Series races from Nov. 3, 2007 through Oct. 25, 2008.
Note: Earnings include bonus money.

Late 2007

Date	Event	Location	Winner (Pos.)	Avg.mph	Earnings	Pole	Qual.mph
Nov. 3	O'Reilly Challenge 300	Ft. Worth	Kevin Harvick (4)	144.212	$73,275	D. Reutimann	191.646
Nov. 10	Arizona.Travel 200	Phoenix	Kyle Busch (4)	89.111	53,575	C. Bowyer	132.954
Nov. 17	Ford 300	Homestead	Jeff Burton (30)	112.512	92,400	D. Ragan	173.472

Winning cars (entire 2007 season): CHEVROLET (22)—Harvick 6, Burton 5, Ky. Busch 4, Hamlin 3, Bowyer 2, Almirola, Labonte; FORD (7)—Edwards 4, Kenseth 2, Leicht; DODGE (4)—Kahne 2, Montoya, Sorenson; TOYOTA (2)—Leffler, Reutimann.

2008 Season (through Oct. 25)

Date	Event	Location	Winner (Pos.)	Avg.mph	Earnings	Pole	Qual.mph
Feb. 17	Camping World 300	Daytona	Tony Stewart (1)	154.154	$118,120	T. Stewart	180.937
Feb. 25	Stater Bros. 300	Los Angeles	Tony Stewart (2)	141.769	77,245	J. Burton	—**
Mar. 1	Sam's Town 300	Las Vegas	Mark Martin (3)	108.118	95,945	B. Vickers	181.708
Mar. 8	Nicorette 300	Atlanta	Matt Kenseth (10)	131.290	56,000	J. Burton	—**
Mar. 15	Sharpie Mini 300	Bristol	Clint Bowyer (4)	78.874	54,695	Scott Wimmer	—**
Mar. 22	Pepsi 300	Nashville	Scott Wimmer (14)	134.095	57,313	Ky. Busch	163.726
Apr. 5	O'Reilly 300	Ft. Worth	Kyle Busch (31)	151.707	76,820	K. Harvick	—**
Apr. 11	Bashas' Supermarkets 200	Phoenix	Kyle Busch (1)	98.764	77,045	Ky. Busch	132.582
Apr. 20	Corona Mexico 200	Mexico	Kyle Busch (6)	68.124	113,345	C. Braun	102.756
Apr. 26	Aaron's 312	Talladega	Tony Stewart (1)	133.111	59,320	T. Stewart	185.308
May 2	Lipton Tea 250	Richmond	Denny Hamlin (3)	96.238	45,595	K. Kahne	125.127
May 9	Diamond Hill Plywood 200	Darlington	Tony Stewart (3)	107.139	47,420	C. Edwards	176.994
May 24	Carquest Auto Parts 300	Charlotte	Kyle Busch (6)	120.331	66,020	B. Vickers	179.904
May 31	Heluva Good! 200	Dover	Denny Hamlin (2)	112.395	47,595	C. Edwards	154.387
June 7	Federated Auto Parts 300	Nashville	Brad Keselowski (2)	117.643	56,913	J. Logano	159.944
June 14	Meijer 300	Kentucky	Joey Logano (1)	135.508	107,488	J. Logano	175.558
June 21	Camping World RV 250	Milwaukee	Carl Edwards (11)	91.678	50,945	B. Keselowski	121.298
June 28	Camping World RV 200	Loudon	Tony Stewart (8)	109.025	49,745	L. Cassill	127.799
July 4	Winn-Dixie 250	Daytona	Denny Hamlin (17)	155.761	93,620	B. Clauson	180.610
July 11	Dollar General 300	Chicago	Kyle Busch (10)	144.443	84,845	D. Reutimann	176.436
July 19	Dodge Dealers 250	Gateway	Carl Edwards (3)	108.095	64,545	J. McMurray	133.101
July 26	Kroger 200	Indianapolis	Kyle Busch (2)	80.522	48,770	C. Braun	108.140
Aug. 2	NAPA Auto Parts 200	Montreal	Ron Fellows (6)	50.149	109,963	S. Pruett	95.082
Aug. 9	Zippo 200	Watkins Glen	Marcos Ambrose (12)	85.957	57,763	D. Franchitti	121.327
Aug. 16	Carfax 250	Michigan	Carl Edwards (1)	136.571	55,895	C. Edwards	186.104
Aug. 22	Food City 250	Bristol	Brad Keselowski (37)	93.509	57,438	C. Gale	122.007
Aug. 30	Camping World 300	Los Angeles	Kyle Busch (1)	144.212	99,195	Ky. Busch	177.401
Sept. 7	Emerson Radio 250	Richmond	Carl Edwards (5)	90.787	45,770	J. Logano	—**
Sept. 20	Camping World RV 200	Dover	Kyle Busch (1)	107.084	50,595	Ky. Busch	155.246
Sept. 27	Kansas Lottery 300	Kansas City	Denny Hamlin (19)	122.296	84,845	K. Harvick	172.227
Oct. 10	Dollar General 300	Charlotte	Kyle Busch (16)	103.647	73,295	J. McMurray	184.508
Oct. 25	Kroger On Track For Cure 250	Memphis	Carl Edwards (34)	88.783	60,345	J. Buescher	117.591

**Qualifying was canceled due to weather and the pole was awarded based on Owner points.

Winning Cars: TOYOTA (19)—Ky. Busch 9, Stewart 5, Hamlin 4, Logano; FORD (7)—Edwards 5, Ambrose, Kenseth; CHEVROLET (7)—Keselowski 2, Bowyer, Fellows, Martin, Wimmer.

Remaining Races (3): O'Reilly Challenge in Fort Worth (Nov. 1); Heft Odor Block 200 in Phoenix (Nov. 8); Ford 300 in Homestead (Nov. 15).

Top 5 Finishing Order + Pole

2008 NATIONWIDE SERIES SEASON (through Oct. 25)

No.	Event	Winner	2nd	3rd	4th	5th	Pole
1	Camping World 300	T. Stewart	Ky. Busch	D. Earnhardt Jr.	B. Vickers	M. Kenseth	T. Stewart
2	Stater Bros. 300	T. Stewart	Ky. Busch	K. Harvick	D. Reutimann	C. Edwards	J. Burton
3	Sam's Town 300	M. Martin	G. Biffle	C. Bowyer	K. Harvick	D. Stremme	B. Vickers
4	Nicorette 300	M. Kenseth	K. Harvick	J. Burton	C. Edwards	B. Labonte	J. Burton
5	Sharpie Mini 300	C. Bowyer	K. Kahne	D. Reutimann	B. Keselowski	M. Bliss	S. Wimmer
6	Pepsi 300	S. Wimmer	C. Bowyer	C. Edwards	B. Keselowski	K. Bires	Ky. Busch
7	O'Reilly 300	Ky. Busch	J. Burton	C. Bowyer	B. Labonte	J. McMurray	K. Harvick
8	Bashas' Supermarkets 200	Ky. Busch	C. Edwards	D. Hamlin	K. Harvick	D. Ragan	K. Busch
9	Corona Mexico 200	Ky. Busch	M. Ambrose	S. Pruett	C. Edwards	P. Carpentier	C. Braun
10	Aaron's 312	T. Stewart	D. Stremme	B. Hamilton Jr.	J. Leffler	M. Green	T. Stewart
11	Lipton Tea 250	D. Hamlin	K. Harvick	Ky. Busch	D. Ragan	S. Wallace	K. Kahne
12	Diamond Hill Plywood 200	T. Stewart	C. Bowyer	D. Reutimann	T. Bodine	S. Wallace	C. Edwards
13	Carquest Auto Parts 300	Ky. Busch	D. Hamlin	B. Keselowski	D. Earnhardt Jr.	B. Vickers	B. Vickers
14	Heluva Good! 200	D. Hamlin	C. Edwards	D. Stremme	D. Reutimann	G. Biffle	C. Edwards
15	Federated Auto Parts 300	B. Keselowski	D. Stremme	D. Reutimann	C. Bowyer	D. Ragan	J. Logano
16	Meijer 300	J. Logano	S. Wimmer	M. Wallace	B. Keselowski	B. Clauson	J. Logano
17	Camping World RV 250	C. Edwards	J. Logano	C. Bowyer	D. Ragan	D. Reutimann	B. Keselowski
18	Camping World RV 200	T. Stewart	D. Hamlin	Ky. Busch	K. Harvick	C. Edwards	L. Cassill
19	Winn-Dixie 250	D. Hamlin	Ky. Busch	D. Earnhardt Jr.	C. Bowyer	B. Keselowski	B. Clauson
20	Dollar General 300	Ky. Busch	D. Hamlin	B. Keselowski	B. Vickers	D. Reutimann	D. Reutimann
21	Dodge Dealers 250	C. Edwards	J. Logano	J. Keller	J. Leffler	B. Keselowski	J. McMurray
22	Kroger 200	Ky. Busch	C. Braun	M. Bliss	S. Wimmer	J. Wise	C. Braun
23	NAPA Auto Parts 200	R. Fellows	P. Carpentier	M. Ambrose	R. Hornaday Jr.	B. Said	S. Pruett
24	Zippo 200	M. Ambrose	Ky. Busch	M. Kenseth	K. Harvick	D. Franchitti	D. Franchitti
25	Carfax 250	C. Edwards	B. Vickers	T. Stewart	M. Martin	G. Biffle	C. Edwards
26	Food City 250	B. Keselowski	C. Bowyer	G. Biffle	C. Gale	D. Stremme	C. Gale
27	Camping World RV 300	Ky. Busch	C. Edwards	B. Vickers	J. Burton	J. McMurray	Ky. Busch
28	Emerson Radio 250	C. Edwards	S. Wimmer	C. Bowyer	D. Hamlin	D. Ragan	J. Logano
29	Camping World RV 200	Ky. Busch	M. Bliss	B. Keselowski	S. Wimmer	C. Edwards	Ky. Busch
30	Kansas Lottery 300	D. Hamlin	C. Bowyer	D. Ragan	C. Edwards	M. Kenseth	K. Harvick
31	Dollar General 300	Ky. Busch	J. Burton	B. Vickers	C. Bowyer	C. Edwards	J. McMurray
32	Kroger 250	C. Edwards	D. Reutimann	K. Wallace	A. Dillon	J. Logano	J. Buescher

Nationwide Series Standings

Official Top 10 NASCAR Nationwide Series point leaders for 2007 and unofficial leaders for 2008 as of Oct. 25 (with three races remaining). Points are awarded for all qualifying drivers (winner received 180) and lap leaders. Earnings include in-season bonuses. Listed are starts (Sts), top-5 finishes (1-2-3-4-5), poles won (PW) and points (Pts).

	FINAL 2007		Finishes				2008 (through Oct. 25)		Finishes		
		Sts	1-2-3-4-5	PW	Pts			Sts	1-2-3-4-5	PW	Pts
1	Carl Edwards	35	4-2-3-5-1	0	4805	1	Clint Bowyer	32	1-4-4-3-0	0	4667
2	David Reutimann	35	1-1-3-0-0	1	4187	2	Carl Edwards	32	5-3-1-3-4	3	4551
3	Jason Leffler	35	1-1-2-2-1	2	3996	3	Brad Keselowski	32	2-0-3-3-2	1	4378
4	Kevin Harvick	26	6-2-1-1-1	1	3993	4	Mike Bliss	32	0-1-1-0-1	0	4168
5	David Ragan	35	0-0-1-1-2	2	3739	5	David Ragan	32	0-0-1-2-3	0	4155
6	Bobby Hamilton Jr.	35	0-0-0-0-0	0	3667	6	David Reutimann	32	0-1-3-2-2	1	4052
7	Stephen Leicht	35	1-0-0-0-2	0	3603	7	Kyle Busch	27	9-4-2-0-0	4	3931
8	Marcos Ambrose	35	0-0-0-1-0	1	3477	8	Mike Wallace	32	0-0-1-0-0	0	3754
9	Greg Biffle	31	0-1-0-0-2	3	3466	9	Jason Leffler	32	0-0-0-2-0	0	3726
10	Matt Kenseth	24	2-7-3-1-2	2	3451	10	Marcos Ambrose	32	1-1-1-0-0	0	3692

Money Leaders

	FINAL 2007	Earnings		2008 (through Oct. 25)	Earnings
1	Carl Edwards	$1,241,985	1	Kyle Busch	$1,218,425
2	Jason Leffler	1,144,831	2	Carl Edwards	1,091,670
3	David Reutimann	1,130,097	3	Brad Keselowski	1,084,281
4	Kevin Harvick	1,123,130	4	Marcos Ambrose	998,816
5	Stephn Leicht	1,076,536	5	Mike Bliss	989,886
6	Marcos Ambrose	986,780	6	Clint Bowyer	949,145
7	Mike Wallace	963,570	7	Mike Wallace	933,716
8	Bobby Hamilton Jr.	940,480	8	Jason Leffler	925,966
9	Scott Wimmer	937,146	9	Kelly Bires	911,296
10	Matt Kenseth	904,380	10	Jason Keller	904,506

Craftsman Truck Series

Results of NASCAR Craftsman Truck Series races from Nov. 2, 2007 through Oct. 25, 2008.
Note: Earnings include bonus money.

Late 2007

Date	Event	Location	Winner (Pos.)	Avg.mph	Earnings	Pole	Qual.mph
Nov. 2	Silverado 350	Ft. Worth	Ted Musgrave (3)	131.363	$71,575	M. Skinner	184.137
Nov. 9	Casino Arizona 150	Phoenix	Kyle Busch (8)	83.218	50,700	M. Skinner	131.301
Nov. 16	Ford 200	Homestead	Johnny Benson (2)	134.513	60,975	J. Wood	173.188

Winning Trucks (entire 2007 season): TOYOTA (13)—Skinner 5, Benson 4, Bodine 2, Musgrave, Sprague; CHEVROLET (7)—Hornaday 4, Ky. Busch 2, Setzer; FORD (5)—Kvapil 4, Darnell.

2008 Season (through Oct. 25)

Date	Event	Location	Winner (Pos.)	Avg.mph	Earnings	Pole	Qual.mph
Feb. 15	Chevy Silverado 250	Daytona	Todd Bodine (12)	127.551	$96,850	E. Darnell	176.529
Feb. 23	San Bernardino County 200	Los Angeles	Kyle Busch (20)	146.341	62,300	R. Hornaday Jr.	—**
Mar. 7	Amer. Commercial Lines 200	Atlanta	Kyle Busch (3)	127.561	55,050	R. Hornaday Jr.	175.571
Mar. 29	Kroger 250	Martinsville	Dennis Setzer (10)	61.311	55,025	J. Sprague	96.327
Apr. 26	O'Reilly Auto Parts 250	Kansas City	Ron Hornaday Jr. (1)	105.820	61,475	R. Hornaday Jr.	170.460
May 16	NC Education Lottery 200	Charlotte	Matt Crafton (18)	111.490	61,800	Ky. Busch	179.045
May 24	Ohio 250	Mansfield	Donny Lia (28)	62.517	45,500	J. Benson	110.004
May 30	AAA Insurance 200	Dover	Scott Speed (4)	100.279	67,525	M. Skinner	155.407
June 6	Sam's Town 400	Ft. Worth	Ron Hornaday Jr. (3)	109.988	74,275	J. Marks	176.951
June 14	Cool City Customs 200	Michigan	Erik Darnell (11)	140.433	58,375	M. Skinner	174.944
June 20	Camping World RV 200	Milwaukee	Johnny Benson (1)	89.686	64,450	J. Benson	121.082
June 28	O'Reilly 200	Memphis	Ron Hornaday Jr. (3)	86.617	57,100	J. Benson	118.229
July 19	Built Ford Tough 225	Kentucky	Johnny Benson (4)	114.592	89,650	M. Skinner	171.499
July 25	Power Stroke Diesel 200	Indianapolis	Johnny Benson (8)	74.859	58,125	B. East	108.602
Aug. 9	Toyota Tundra 200	Nashville	Johnny Benson (16)	115.300	57,200	T. Bodine	158.669
Aug. 20	O'Reilly 200	Bristol	Kyle Busch (3)	65.388	50,075	S. Speed	123.865
Sept. 6	Camping World 200	Gateway	Ron Hornaday Jr. (2)	93.860	64,650	D. Setzer	132.638
Sept. 13	Camping World RV Rental 200	Loudon	Ron Hornaday Jr. (3)	98.279	61,750	J. Benson	—**
Sept. 20	Qwik Liner Las Vegas 350	Las Vegas	Mike Skinner (3)	101.070	57,450	R. Hornaday Jr.	170.428
Oct. 4	Mountain Dew 250	Talladega	Todd Bodine (5)	145.513	78,700	E. Darnell	181.753
Oct. 18	Kroger 200	Martinsville	Johnny Benson (6)	68.213	52,725	R. Hornaday Jr.	95.554
Oct. 25	E-Z-Go 200	Atlanta	Ryan Newman (10)	137.437	52,325	J. Benson	—**

**Qualifying was canceled due to weather and the pole was awarded based on Owner points.

Winning Trucks: TOYOTA (12)—Benson 4, Ky. Busch 3, Bodine 3, Skinner, Speed; CHEVROLET (8)—Hornaday Jr. 5, Crafton, Lia, Newman; DODGE (1)—Setzer; FORD (1)—Darnell.

Remaining Races (3): Chevy Silverado 350 in Ft. Worth (Oct. 31); Lucas Oil 150 in Phoenix (Nov. 7); Ford 200 in Homestead (Nov. 14).

Top 5 Finishing Order + Pole

2008 CRAFTSMAN TRUCK SERIES SEASON (through Oct. 25)

No.	Event	Winner	2nd	3rd	4th	5th	Pole
1	Chevy Silverado 250	T. Bodine	Ky. Busch	J. Benson	D. Starr	R. Crawford	E. Darnell
2	San Bernardino Cty 200	Ky. Busch	T. Bodine	J. Benson	T. Cook	R. Hornaday Jr.	R. Hornaday Jr.
3	Amer. Commer. Lines 200	Ky. Busch	R. Hornaday Jr.	M. Skinner	M. Crafton	C. McCumbee	R. Hornaday Jr.
4	Kroger 250	D. Setzer	M. Crafton	R. Crawford	K. Schrader	E. Darnell	J. Sprague
5	O'Reilly Auto Parts 250	R. Hornaday Jr.	J. Sprague	C. Braun	J. Benson	M. Skinner	R. Hornaday Jr.
6	NC Education Lottery 200	M. Crafton	C. McCumbee	B. Gaughan	E. Darnell	R. Crawford	Ky. Busch
7	Ohio 250	D. Lia	D. Starr	T. Bodine	T. Cook	M. Skinner	J. Benson
8	AAA Insurance 200	S. Speed	J. Sprague	R. Hornaday Jr.	T. Kvapil	M. Crafton	M. Skinner
9	Sam's Town 400	R. Hornaday Jr.	Ky. Busch	J. Benson	J. Sprague	T. Bodine	J. Marks
10	Cool City Customs 200	E. Darnell	J. Benson	S. Speed	T. Bodine	B. Gaughan	M. Skinner
11	Camping World RV 200	J. Benson	M. Crafton	L. Cassill	E. Darnell	T. Bodine	J. Benson
12	O'Reilly 200, Memphis	R. Hornaday Jr.	E. Darnell	M. Crafton	R. Crawford	D. Starr	J. Benson
13	Built Ford Tough 225	J. Benson	M. Annett	M. Crafton	D. Setzer	D. Starr	M. Skinner
14	Power Stroke Diesel 200	J. Benson	R. Hornaday Jr.	E. Darnell	M. Crafton	S. Howard	B. East
15	Toyota Tundra 200	J. Benson	E. Darnell	T. Bodine	J. Sprague	R. Hornaday Jr.	T. Bodine
16	O'Reilly 200, Bristol	Ky. Busch	T. Bodine	S. Speed	J. Benson	R. Crawford	S. Speed
17	Camping World 200	R. Hornaday Jr.	D. Setzer	J. Benson	T. Bodine	J. Sprague	D. Setzer
18	Camping World RV 200	R. Hornaday Jr.	J. Benson	T. Kvapil	E. Darnell	R. Crawford	J. Benson
19	Qwik Liner Las Vegas 350	M. Skinner	E. Darnell	M. Crafton	J. Andretti	R. Hornaday Jr.	R. Hornaday Jr.
20	Mountain Dew 250	T. Bodine	R. Hornaday Jr.	Ky. Busch	C. Braun	M. Wallace	E. Darnell
21	Kroger 200	J. Benson	D. Setzer	R. Crawford	Ky. Busch	T. Bodine	R. Hornaday Jr.
22	E-Z-Go 200	R. Newman	R. Hornaday Jr.	D. Hamlin	T. Bodine	S. Speed	J. Benson

Johnny Benson (23) and Ron Hornaday Jr. (33) were neck and neck all season long on the Craftsman Truck circuit.

John Harrelson/Getty Images for NASCAR

Craftsman Truck Series Standings

Official Top 10 NASCAR Craftsman Truck Series point leaders for 2007 and unofficial leaders for 2008 as of Oct. 25 (with three races remaining). Points are awarded for all qualifying drivers (winner received 180) and lap leaders. Earnings include in-season bonuses. Listed are starts (Sts), top-5 finishes (1-2-3-4-5), poles won (PW) and points (Pts).

FINAL 2007

		Sts	Finishes 1-2-3-4-5	PW	Pts
1	Ron Hornaday Jr.	25	4-6-2-1-0	1	3982
2	Mike Skinner	25	5-1-3-7-1	11	3928
3	Johnny Benson	25	4-3-2-2-1	0	3557
4	Todd Bodine	25	2-2-2-2-2	2	3525
5	Rick Crawford	25	0-2-3-2-4	0	3523
6	Travis Kvapil	25	4-1-3-0-0	3	3511
7	Ted Musgrave	24	1-0-2-0-4	0	3183
8	Matt Crafton	25	0-0-1-0-0	0	3060
9	Jack Sprague	25	1-3-2-0-0	2	3001
10	David Starr	25	0-0-0-2-1	0	2921

2008 (through Oct. 25)

		Sts	Finishes 1-2-3-4-5	PW	Pts
1	Johnny Benson	22	5-2-4-2-0	3	3324
2	Ron Hornaday Jr.	22	5-4-1-0-3	4	3293
3	Todd Bodine	22	2-2-2-3-3	1	3106
4	Erik Darnell	22	1-3-1-3-1	2	3027
5	Matt Crafton	22	1-2-3-2-1	0	3027
6	Rick Crawford	22	0-0-2-1-4	0	2983
7	Mike Skinner	22	1-0-1-0-2	3	2981
8	Dennis Setzer	22	1-2-0-1-0	1	2800
9	Jack Sprague	22	0-2-0-2-1	1	2792
10	Chad McCumbee	22	0-1-0-0-1	0	2654

Money Leaders

FINAL 2007

		Earnings
1	Mike Skinner	$737,520
2	Ron Hornaday Jr.	681,875
3	Johnny Benson	636,160
4	Travis Kvapil	583,025
5	Todd Bodine	569,125
6	Jack Sprague	464,210
7	Rick Crawford	446,800
8	Ted Musgrave	419,475
9	Erik Darnell	368,450
10	Brendan Gaughan	356,767

2008 (through Oct. 25)

		Earnings
1	Johnny Benson	$695,340
2	Ron Hornaday Jr.	680,315
3	Todd Bodine	529,365
4	Matt Crafton	439,970
5	Erik Darnell	433,115
6	Kyle Busch	415,135
7	Dennis Setzer	379,940
8	Mike Skinner	360,645
9	Rick Crawford	333,665
10	Jack Sprague	325,775

On Oct. 23, 2008, NASCAR announced that **Camping World** will be the title sponsor for the NASCAR Truck Series beginning in 2009. Camping World replaces Craftsman, which had been the sole title sponsor since the inception of the NASCAR Truck Series in 1995. Camping World is America's largest direct marketer and specialty retailer of recreational vehicles and outdoor camping accessories and services. **Source:** NASCAR Media.

INDY RACING LEAGUE RESULTS

IndyCar Series

Schedule and results of IndyCar Series events during the 2008 season.

2008 Season

Date	Event	Location	Winner (Pos.)	Time	Avg.mph	Pole	Qual.mph
Mar. 29	Gainsco Auto Ins. 300	Homestead	Scott Dixon (1)	1:44:03.5914	171.248	S. Dixon	213.341
Apr. 6	Honda GP	St. Petersburg	Graham Rahal (9)	2:00:43.5562	74.251	T. Kanaan	103.627
Apr. 20	Japan 300	Motegi	Danica Patrick (6)	1:51:02.6739	164.258	H. Castroneves	—**
Apr. 20	Toyota GP	Long Beach	Will Power (4)	1:45:25.4150	92.964	J. Wilson	105.898
Apr. 27	Road Runner 300	Kansas City	Dan Wheldon (2)	1:52:44.9806	161.774	S. Dixon	213.341
May 25	**Indianapolis 500**	Indianapolis	Scott Dixon (1)	3:28:57:6792	143.567	S. Dixon	226.366
June 1	A.J. Foyt 225	Milwaukee	Ryan Briscoe (11)	1:42:41.7387	133.428	M. Andretti	168.079
June 7	Bombardier Learjet 550k	Ft. Worth	Scott Dixon (1)	2:04:36.3153	159.740	S. Dixon	214.878
June 22	Iowa Corn 250	Iowa	Dan Wheldon (3)	1:38:35.8923	136.007	S. Dixon	—**
June 28	SunTrust Challenge	Richmond	Tony Kanaan (1)	2:04:05.5111	108.790	T. Kanaan	167.876
July 6	Camping World GP	Watkins Glen	Ryan Hunter-Reay (3)	1:54:01.1795	106.403	R. Briscoe	135.787
July 12	Firestone 200	Nashville	Scott Dixon (5)	1:30:04.6499	148.072	H. Castroneves	204.519
July 20	Honda 200	Ohio	Ryan Briscoe (2)	2:01:22.8496	84.873	H. Castroneves	120.878
July 26	Rexall Edmonton Indy	Edmonton	Scott Dixon (4)	1:51:05.7039	96.967	R. Briscoe	116.955
Aug. 9	Meijer 300	Kentucky	Scott Dixon (1)	1:36:42.3467	183.650	S. Dixon	218.968
Aug. 24	Peak Antifreeze GP	Infineon	Helio Castroneves (1)	1:50:15.8282	100.254	H. Castroneves	107.809
Aug. 31	Detroit Grand Prix	Belle Isle	Justin Wilson (4)	2:00:10.7618	89.911	S. Dixon	103.090
Sept. 7	Peak Antifreeze 300	Chicago	Helio Castroneves (28)	2:01:04.5907	150.648	R. Briscoe	215.818
Oct. 26	Nikon Indy 300	Surfers Paradise	Ryan Briscoe (3)	1:45:50.3868	95.068	W. Power	105.977

**Qualifying was canceled due to inclement weather and the pole was awarded to the season points leader.

Note: All IndyCar Series cars use DALLARA chassis, HONDA engines and FIRESTONE tires.

Top 5 Finishing Order + Pole
2008 Season

No.	Event	Winner	2nd	3rd	4th	5th	Pole
1	Gainsco Auto Ins. 300	S. Dixon	M. Andretti	D. Wheldon	H. Castroneves	E. Carpenter	S. Dixon
2	Honda GP of St. Pete	G. Rahal	H. Castroneves	T. Kanaan	E. Viso	E. Bernoldi	T. Kanaan
3	Japan 300	D. Patrick	H. Castroneves	S. Dixon	D. Wheldon	T. Kanaan	H. Castroneves
4	Toyota GP, Long Beach	W. Power	F. Montagny	M. Dominguez	E. Bernoldi	O. Servia	J. Wilson
5	Road Runner 300	D. Wheldon	T. Kanaan	S. Dixon	H. Castroneves	M. Andretti	S. Dixon
6	Indianapolis 500	S. Dixon	V. Meira	M. Andretti	H. Castroneves	E. Carpenter	S. Dixon
7	AJ Foyt 225	R. Briscoe	S. Dixon	T. Kanaan	D. Wheldon	H. Castroneves	M. Andretti
8	Bombardier Learjet 500	S. Dixon	H. Castroneves	R. Briscoe	D. Wheldon	T. Kanaan	S. Dixon
9	Iowa Corn 250	D. Wheldon	H. Mutoh	M. Andretti	S. Dixon	A.J. Foyt IV	S. Dixon
10	SunTrust Challenge	T. Kanaan	H. Castroneves	S. Dixon	D. Wheldon	O. Servia	T. Kanaan
11	Camping World GP	R. Hunter-Reay	D. Manning	T. Kanaan	B. Rice	M. Andretti	R. Briscoe
12	Firestone 200	S. Dixon	D. Wheldon	H. Castroneves	T. Kanaan	D. Patrick	H. Castroneves
13	Honda 200	R. Briscoe	H. Castroneves	S. Dixon	W. Power	O. Servia	H. Castroneves
14	Rexall Edmonton	S. Dixon	H. Castroneves	J. Wilson	P. Tracy	O. Servia	R. Briscoe
15	Meijer 300	S. Dixon	H. Castroneves	M. Andretti	V. Meira	D. Wheldon	S. Dixon
16	Peak Antifreeze GP	H. Castroneves	R. Briscoe	T. Kanaan	D. Wheldon	D. Patrick	H. Castroneves
17	Detroit GP	J. Wilson	H. Castroneves	T. Kanaan	O. Servia	S. Dixon	S. Dixon
18	Peak Antifreeze 300	H. Castroneves	S. Dixon	R. Briscoe	T. Kanaan	W. Power	R. Briscoe
19	Nikon Indy 300	R. Briscoe	S. Dixon	R. Hunter-Reay	A. Tagliani	O. Servia	W. Power

Champ Car World Series and IndyCar Series Merge

After 12 years apart and a myriad of rumors and discussions, major American open-wheel racing finally unified in 2008 as the Champ Car World Series essentially dissolved into IndyCar. Indy Racing League founder and CEO Tony George and owners of the Champ Car World Series completed the agreement on February 28, and the Champ Car owners filed for bankruptcy in March.

92nd Indianapolis 500

Date—Sunday, May 25, 2008, at Indianapolis Motor Speedway. **Distance**—500 miles; **Course**—2.5 mile oval; **Field**—33 cars; **Winner's average speed**—143.567 mph; **Margin of victory**—1.7498 seconds; **Time of race**—3 hours, 28 minutes, 57.6792 seconds; **Caution flags**—8 for 69 laps; **Lead changes**—18 by 9 drivers; **Lap leaders**—Dixon (115), Wheldon (30), M. Andretti (15), Meira (12), Kanaan (12), Rice (8), Moraes (3), Carpentier (3), Junqueira (2); **Pole Sitter**—Scott Dixon at 226.366 mph; **Attendance**—400,000 (est.); **TV Rating**—4.6 (ABC). Note that (r) indicates rookie driver.

	Driver	Start	Country	Car	Laps	Ended	Earnings
1	Scott Dixon	1	New Zealand	D/H/F	200	Running	$2,988,065
2	Vitor Meira	8	Brazil	D/H/F	200	Running	1,273,215
3	Marco Andretti	7	United States	D/H/F	200	Running	782,065
4	Helio Castroneves	4	Brazil	D/H/F	200	Running	482,815
5	Ed Carpenter	10	United States	D/H/F	200	Running	399,665
6	r-Ryan Hunter-Reay	20	United States	D/H/F	200	Running	328,065
7	r-Hideki Mutoh	9	Japan	D/H/F	200	Running	307,115
8	Buddy Rice	17	United States	D/H/F	200	Running	311,415
9	Darren Manning	14	England	D/H/F	200	Running	301,815
10	Townsend Bell	12	United States	D/H/F	200	Running	275,315
11	r-Oriol Servia	25	Spain	D/H/F	200	Running	302,065
12	Dan Wheldon	2	England	D/H/F	200	Running	366,815
13	r-Will Power	23	Australia	D/H/F	200	Running	300,565
14	Davey Hamilton	18	United States	D/H/F	200	Running	270,315
15	r-Enrique Bernoldi	29	Brazil	D/H/F	200	Running	300,565
16	John Andretti	21	United States	D/H/F	199	Running	300,315
17	Buddy Lazier	32	United States	D/H/F	195	Running	327,015
18	r-Mario Moraes	28	Brazil	D/H/F	194	Running	303,415
19	Milka Duno	27	Venezuela	D/H/F	185	Running	300,315
20	Bruno Junqueira	15	Brazil	D/H/F	184	Running	301,215
21	A.J. Foyt IV	31	United States	D/H/F	180	Running	311,815
22	Danica Patrick	5	United States	D/H/F	171	Contact	301,915
23	Ryan Briscoe	3	Australia	D/H/F	171	Contact	312,315
24	Tomas Scheckter	11	South Africa	D/H/F	156	Mechanical	270,315
25	r-Alex Lloyd	19	England	D/H/F	151	Contact	272,065
26	r-E.J. Viso	26	Venezuela	D/H/F	139	Mechanical	301,565
27	r-Justin Wilson	16	England	D/H/F	132	Contact	302,065
28	Jeff Simmons	24	United States	D/H/F	112	Contact	270,000
29	Tony Kanaan	6	Brazil	D/H/F	105	Contact	331,215
30	Sarah Fisher	22	United States	D/H/F	103	Contact	277,215
31	r-Jaime Camara	30	Brazil	D/H/F	79	Contact	300,565
32	Marty Roth	33	Canada	D/H/F	59	Contact	300,315
33	r-Graham Rahal	13	United States	D/H/F	36	Contact	312,065

Car Legend: Chassis/Engine/Tires. D—Dallara (chassis); H—Honda (engine); F—Firestone (tires).

Indy Racing League Point Standings

Final top-10 Indy Racing League driver points leaders for 2007 and 2008. Points are awarded for places 1 to 33 (winner receives 50) and overall lap leader. Listed are starts (Sts), top-5 finishes, poles won (PW) and points (Pts).

FINAL 2007

			Finishes		
		Sts	1-2-3-4-5	PW	Pts
1	Dario Franchitti	17	4-4-3-1-1	4	637
2	Scott Dixon	17	4-6-0-3-0	2	624
3	Tony Kanaan	17	5-1-1-4-1	2	576
4	Dan Wheldon	17	2-1-3-0-0	1	466
5	Sam Hornish Jr.	17	1-1-2-2-2	0	465
6	Helio Castroneves	17	1-1-3-1-0	7	446
7	Danica Patrick	17	0-1-2-0-1	0	424
8	Scott Sharp	17	0-0-2-0-1	1	412
9	Buddy Rice	17	0-0-0-1-2	0	360
10	Tomas Scheckter	17	0-0-0-0-2	0	357

FINAL 2008

			Finishes		
		Sts	1-2-3-4-5	PW	Pts
1	Scott Dixon	17	6-2-4-1-1	6	646
2	Helio Castroneves	17	2-8-1-3-1	3	629
3	Tony Kanaan	17	1-1-5-2-2	2	513
4	Dan Wheldon	17	2-1-1-5-1	0	492
5	Ryan Briscoe	17	2-1-2-0-0	3	447
6	Danica Patrick	17	1-0-0-0-2	0	379
7	Marco Andretti	17	0-1-3-0-2	1	363
8	Ryan Hunter-Reay	17	1-0-0-0-0	0	360
9	Oriol Servia	17	0-0-0-1-4	0	358
10	Hideki Mutoh	17	0-1-0-0-0	0	346

Photo by Shawn Payne, IndyCar

Danica Patrick stands on the podium with Helio Castroneves, left, and Scott Dixon, right, after winning the Indy Japan 300 and becoming the first woman to win a major auto racing event.

FORMULA ONE RESULTS

Results of Formula One Grand Prix races in 2008, through October 19.

2008 Season (through Oct. 19)

Date	Grand Prix	Location	Winner (Pos.)	Time	Avg.mph	Pole
Mar. 16	Australian	Melbourne	Lewis Hamilton (1)	1:34:50.616	120.905	L. Hamilton
Mar. 23	Malaysian	Kuala Lumpur	Kimi Raikkonen (2)	1:31:18.555	126.742	F. Massa
Apr. 6	Bahrain	Bahrain	Felipe Massa (2)	1:31:06.970	126.122	R. Kubica
Apr. 27	Spanish	Catalunya	Kimi Raikkonen (1)	1:38:19.051	116.454	K. Raikkonen
May 11	Turkish	Istanbul	Felipe Massa (1)	1:26:49.451	132.854	F. Massa
May 25	Monaco	Monte Carlo	Lewis Hamilton (3)	2:00:42.742	78.398	F. Massa
June 8	Canadian	Montreal	Robert Kubica (2)	1:36:24.447	118.052	L. Hamilton
June 22	French	Magny-Cours	Felipe Massa (2)	1:31:50.245	125.273	K. Raikkonen
July 6	British	Silverstone	Lewis Hamilton (4)	1:39:09.440	115.939	H. Kovalainen
July 20	German	Hockenheim	Lewis Hamilton (1)	1:31:20.874	125.076	L. Hamilton
Aug. 3	Hungarian	Budapest	Heikki Kovalainen (2)	1:37:27.067	117.309	L. Hamilton
Aug. 24	European	Valencia	Felipe Massa (1)	1:35:32.339	120.535	F. Massa
Sept. 7	Belgian	Spa-Francorchamps	Felipe Massa (2)	1:22:59.394	138.389	L. Hamilton
Sept. 14	Italian	Monza	Sebastian Vettel (1)	1:26:47.494	131.755	S. Vettel
Sept. 28	Singapore	Singapore	Fernando Alonso (15)	1:57:16.304	98.219	F. Massa
Oct. 12	Japanese	Fuji	Fernando Alonso (4)	1:30:21.892	126.007	K. Raikkonen
Oct. 19	Chinese	Shanghai	Lewis Hamilton (22)	1:31:57.403	123.683	K. Raikkonen

Winning Constructors: FERRARI (8)—Massa 5, Raikkonen 2, Vettel; McLAREN-MERCEDES (6)—Hamilton 5, Kovalainen; RENAULT (2)—Alonso 2; BMW SAUBER (1)—Kubica.
Remaining Race (1): Brazil GP in Sao Paulo (Nov. 2).

Top 5 Finishing Order + Pole
2008 Season

No. Event	Winner	2nd	3rd	4th	5th	Pole
1 Australian	L. Hamilton	N. Heidfeld	N. Rosberg	F. Alonso	H. Kovalainen	L. Hamilton
2 Malaysian	K. Raikkonen	R. Kubica	H. Kovalainen	J. Trulli	L. Hamilton	F. Massa
3 Bahrain	F. Massa	K. Raikkonen	R. Kubica	N. Heidfeld	H. Kovalainen	R. Kubica
4 Spanish	K. Raikkonen	F. Massa	L. Hamilton	R. Kubica	M. Webber	K. Raikkonen
5 Turkish	F. Massa	L. Hamilton	K. Raikkonen	R. Kubica	N. Heidfeld	F. Massa
6 Monaco	L. Hamilton	R. Kubica	F. Massa	M. Webber	S. Vettel	F. Massa
7 Canadian	R. Kubica	N. Heidfeld	D. Coulthard	T. Glock	F. Massa	L. Hamilton
8 French	F. Massa	K. Raikkonen	J. Trulli	H. Kovalainen	R. Kubica	K. Raikkonen
9 British	L. Hamilton	N. Heidfeld	R. Barrichello	K. Raikkonen	H. Kovalainen	H. Kovalainen
10 German	L. Hamilton	N. Piquet	F. Massa	N. Heidfeld	H. Kovalainen	L. Hamilton
11 Hungarian	H. Kovalainen	T. Glock	K. Raikkonen	F. Alonso	L. Hamilton	L. Hamilton
12 European	F. Massa	L. Hamilton	R. Kubica	H. Kovalainen	J. Trulli	F. Massa
13 Belgian	F. Massa	N. Heidfeld	L. Hamilton	F. Alonso	S. Vettel	L. Hamilton
14 Italian	S. Vettel	H. Kovalainen	R. Kubica	R. Kubica	N. Heidfeld	S. Vettel
15 Singapore	F. Alonso	N. Rosberg	L. Hamilton	T. Glock	S. Vettel	F. Massa
16 Japanese	F. Alonso	R. Kubica	K. Raikkonen	N. Piquet	J. Trulli	K. Raikkonen
17 Chinese	L. Hamilton	F. Massa	K. Raikkonen	F. Alonso	N. Heidfeld	K. Raikkonen

2008 Formula One Point Standings

Top-10 Formula One World Drivers and Constructors Championship point leaders for 2008 (through Oct. 19, with one race remaining). Points are awarded for places 1 through 8 only (i.e., 10-8-6-5-4-3-2-1). Listed are starts (Sts), top-8 finishes, poles won (PW) and points (Pts). **Note:** Formula One does not keep money leader standings.

Drivers

		Finishes			
	Sts	1-2-3-4-5-6-7-8	PW	Pts	
1 Lewis Hamilton	17	5-2-3-0-2-0-1-0	5	94	
2 Felipe Massa	17	5-2-2-0-1-1-1-0	5	87	
3 Robert Kubica	17	1-3-3-2-1-2-1-1	1	75	
4 Kimi Raikkonen	17	2-2-4-1-0-1-0-1	4	69	
5 Nick Heidfeld	17	0-4-0-2-3-2-0-0	0	60	
6 Fernando Alonso	17	2-0-0-5-0-2-0-2	0	53	
7 Heikki Kovalainen	17	1-1-1-2-4-0-0-1	1	51	
8 Sebastian Vettel	17	1-0-0-0-3-2-0-2	1	30	
9 Jarno Trulli	17	0-0-1-1-2-2-2-1	0	30	
10 Timo Glock	17	0-1-0-1-1-0-2-0	0	22	

Constructors

	Pts
1 Scuderia Ferrari Marlboro	156
2 Vodafone McLaren-Mercedes	145
3 BMW Sauber	135
4 ING Renault	72
5 Panasonic Toyota	52
6 Scuderia Toro Rosso	34
7 Red Bull Racing	29
8 AT&T Williams	26
9 Honda Racing	14
10 Force India	0
11 Super Aguri	0

Major 2008 Endurance Races

24 Hours of Daytona

Jan. 26-27, at Daytona Beach, Fla.

Officially the Rolex 24 at Daytona and first held in 1962 (as a 3-hour race). An IMSA Camel GT race for exotic prototype sports cars and contested over a 3.56-mile road course at Daytona International Speedway. Listed are qualifying position, drivers, chassis and laps completed.

1 (6) Scott Pruett, Memo Rojas, Juan Pablo Montoya and Dario Franchitti; LEXUS RILEY; 695 laps (2,474 miles) at 103.057 mph; margin of victory—2 laps.

2 (11) Jon Fogarty, Alex Gurney, Jimmy Vasser and Jimmie Johnson; PONTIAC RILEY, 693 laps.

3 (13) Ryan Briscoe, Helio Castroneves and Kurt Busch; PONTIAC RILEY, 689 laps.

4 (15) Nic Jonsson, Ricardo Zonta and Darren Turner; PONTIAC RILEY, 688 laps.

5 (4) Wayne Taylor, Max Angelelli, Michael Valiante and Ricky Taylor; PONTIAC RILEY; 687 laps.

Top qualifier: Oswaldo Negri Jr, FORD RILEY, 127.151 mph.

24 Hours of Le Mans

June 14-15, at Le Mans, France

Officially the Le Mans Grand Prix d'Endurance and first held in 1923. Contested over the 8.468-mile Circuit de la Sarthe in Le Mans, France. Listed are qualifying position, drivers, car, and laps completed.

1 (4) Tom Kristensen, Rinaldo Capello and Allan McNish; AUDI R10; 381 laps (3,227 miles) at 134.402 mph; margin of victory—4 minutes, 31.094 seconds.

2 (3) Jacques Villeneuve, Marc Gene and Nicolas Minassian; PEUGEOT 908; 381 laps.

3 (2) Franck Montagny, Christian Klien, Ricardo Zonta; PEUGEOT 908; 379 laps.

4 (5) Lucas Luhr, Mike Rockenfeller and Alexandre Premat; AUDI R10; 374 laps.

5 (1) Pedro Lamy, Stephane Sarrazin, Alexander Wurz; PEUGEOT 908; 368 laps.

Top qualifier: Stephane Sarrazin, PEUGEOT 908, 3:18.513 (153.578 mph).

NHRA RESULTS

Winners of National Hot Rod Association's POWERade Drag Racing events in the Top Fuel, Funny Car, Pro Stock and Pro Stock Motorcycle divisions through Oct. 12, 2008. All times are based on two cars/motorcycles racing head-to-head from a standing start over a straight line, quarter-mile course. Differences in reaction time account for apparently faster losing times.

2008 Season (through Oct. 12)

Top Fuel

Date	Event	Winner	Time	MPH	2nd Place	Time	MPH
Feb. 10	Carquest Winternationals	Tony Schumacher	4.499	331.28	C. McClenathan	4.536	329.26
Feb. 24	Kragen Nationals	Larry Dixon	4.532	327.19	D. Grubnic	5.002	259.26
Mar. 16	ACDelco Gatornationals	Tony Schumacher	4.603	325.37	B. Bernstein	4.665	323.27
Mar. 30	O'Reilly Spring Nationals	Antron Brown	4.605	320.28	L. Dixon	4.621	309.06
Apr. 13	SummitRacing.com Nationals	Cory McClenathan	4.654	315.86	A. Brown	4.703	315.93
Apr. 27	Southern Nationals	Antron Brown	4.537	325.14	T. Schumacher	4.521	329.58
May 4	O'Reilly Midwest Nationals	Rod Fuller	4.525	328.70	T. Schumacher	4.583	325.45
May 18	O'Reilly Thunder Valley Nationals	Tony Schumacher	4.555	306.81	L. Dixon	4.958	253.37
June 1	O'Reilly Summer Nationals	Hillary Will	4.744	304.53	L. Dixon	4.960	281.42
June 8	Torco Racing Fuels Rt. 66 Nationals	Tony Schumacher	4.499	329.83	R. Fuller	5.529	223.14
June 22	Lucas Oil SuperNationals	Tony Schumacher	4.589	325.06	B. Bernstein	4.562	323.04
June 29	Summit Racing Equipment Nationals	Doug Herbert	4.636	311.70	B. Bernstein	4.611	313.58
July 13	Mopar Mile-High Nationals	Tony Schumacher	4.007	304.05	A. Brown	4.173	276.97
July 20	Schuck's Auto Supply Nationals	Tony Schumacher	3.902	309.98	B. Bernstein	4.056	291.19
July 27	Fram-Autolite Nationals	Tony Schumacher	3.886	307.93	H. Will	3.988	306.19
Aug. 10	Lucas Oil Nationals	Tony Schumacher	3.865	310.05	C. McClenathan	3.900	306.74
Aug. 17	Toyo Tires Nationals	Tony Schumacher	3.845	313.88	L. Dixon	3.891	302.35
Sept. 1	Mac Tools U.S. Nationals	Tony Schumacher	3.916	309.13	D. Kalitta	4.036	299.86
Sept. 14	Carolinas Nationals	Tony Schumacher	3.882	317.64	A. Brown	3.923	309.42
Sept. 21	O'Reilly Fall Nationals	J.R. Todd	3.912	309.84	T. Schumacher	3.910	310.63
Sept. 28	O'Reilly Mid-South Nationals	Tony Schumacher	3.880	309.91	D. Herbert	3.979	295.85
Oct. 12	Virginia Nationals	Tony Schumacher	3.811	316.08	H. Will	3.847	307.09

Funny Car

Date	Event	Winner	Time	MPH	2nd Place	Time	MPH
Feb. 10	Carquest Winternationals	Robert Hight	4.861	284.39	C. Pedregon	4.879	322.50
Feb. 24	Kragen Nationals	Jack Beckman	4.868	320.20	R. Hight	8.030	105.28
Mar. 16	ACDelco Gatornationals	Tony Pedregon	4.921	315.27	G. Densham	4.924	309.13
Mar. 30	O'Reilly Spring Nationals	Del Worsham	4.933	316.60	A. Force	4.971	302.62
Apr. 13	SummitRacing.com Nationals	Tim Wilkerson	4.962	292.58	A. Force	4.993	313.95
Apr. 27	Southern Nationals	Ashley Force	4.837	320.36	J. Force	11.223	85.97
May 4	O'Reilly Midwest Nationals	Tim Wilkerson	4.874	317.27	M. Neff	4.886	321.58
May 18	O'Reilly Thunder Valley Nationals	Melanie Troxel	5.066	310.27	M. Neff	6.471	146.21
June 1	O'Reilly Summer Nationals	John Force	4.996	299.66	T. Wilkerson	6.183	152.61
June 8	Torco Racing Fuels Rt. 66 Nationals	Tony Pedregon	4.818	319.75	S. Kalitta	4.957	308.92
June 22	Lucas Oil SuperNationals	Tim Wilkerson	4.877	319.29	M. Neff	4.883	316.75
June 29	Summit Racing Equipment Nationals	Tony Pedregon	4.882	306.26	R. Hight	4.903	304.74
July 13	Mopar Mile-High Nationals	Tim Wilkerson	4.398	262.23	J. Beckman	4.661	205.41
July 20	Schuck's Auto Supply Nationals	Tony Bartone	4.454	238.17	R. Capps	4.708	227.46
July 27	Fram-Autolite Nationals	Robert Hight	4.163	296.50	G. Densham	4.222	289.14
Aug. 10	Lucas Oil Nationals	Tony Pedregon	4.238	288.89	J. Beckman	4.216	293.28
Aug. 17	Toyo Tires Nationals	Jack Beckman	4.183	291.57	F. Hawley	6.967	95.08
Sept. 1	Mac Tools U.S. Nationals	Robert Hight	4.312	283.85	J. Beckman	4.438	254.04
Sept. 14	Carolinas Nationals	Jack Beckman	4.130	302.82	C. Pedregon	4.162	302.08
Sept. 21	O'Reilly Fall Nationals	Tim Wilkerson	4.172	297.55	T. Pedregon	4.206	295.98
Sept. 28	O'Reilly Mid-South Nationals	Tim Wilkerson	4.166	298.47	A. Force	4.183	294.18
Oct. 12	Virginia Nationals	Cruz Pedregon	4.113	296.44	J. Beckman	7.503	88.14

Pro Stock Car

Date	Event	Winner	Time	MPH	2nd Place	Time	MPH
Feb. 10	Carquest Winternationals	Greg Anderson	6.616	209.23	J. Coughlin	6.638	208.42
Feb. 24	Kragen Nationals	V. Gaines	6.702	205.38	J. Line	20.239	39.18
Mar. 16	ACDelco Gatornationals	Jeg Coughlin	6.652	208.07	J. Line	6.656	209.10
Mar. 30	O'Reilly Spring Nationals	Greg Anderson	6.692	207.37	K. Johnson	13.425	64.01
Apr. 13	SummitRacing.com Nationals	Jason Line	6.782	203.83	G. Stanfield	6.816	203.16
Apr. 27	Southern Nationals	Mike Edwards	6.680	206.20	J. Line	6.680	206.92
May 4	O'Reilly Midwest Nationals	Kurt Johnson	6.631	209.30	D. Connolly	6.651	208.78
May 18	O'Reilly Thunder Valley Nationals	Dave Connolly	6.731	204.70	G. Stanfield	6.717	204.42
June 1	O'Reilly Summer Nationals	Ron Krisher	6.758	204.70	L. Morgan	12.144	62.96
June 8	Torco Racing Fuels Rt. 66 Nationals	Kurt Johnson	6.733	205.22	J. Coughlin	19.755	72.78
June 22	Lucas Oil SuperNationals	Greg Anderson	7.578	200.23	D. Connolly	20.285	36.59
June 29	Summit Racing Equipment Nationals	Greg Anderson	6.704	206.04	L. Morgan	6.789	204.57

Date	Event	Winner	Time	MPH	2nd Place	Time	MPH
July 13	Mopar Mile-High Nationals	Greg Anderson	7.024	196.39	A. Johnson	7.028	195.79
July 20	Schuck's Auto Supply Nationals . .	Jason Line	6.659	208.10	A. Johnson	6.664	207.78
July 27	Fram-Autolite Nationals	Dave Connolly	6.628	207.69	J. Coughlin	6.627	207.24
Aug. 10	Lucas Oil Nationals	Kurt Johnson	6.671	207.05	D. Connolly	6.696	206.29
Aug. 17	Toyo Tires Nationals	Jeg Coughlin	6.650	206.39	D. Connolly	12.142	71.55
Sept. 1	Mac Tools U.S. Nationals	Dave Connolly	6.743	206.04	L. Morgan	6.797	204.70
Sept. 14	Carolinas Nationals	Justin Humphreys	19.849	42.40	K. Johnson	broke	—
Sept. 21	O'Reilly Fall Nationals	Jeg Coughlin	6.686	205.51	G. Stanfield	6.678	206.35
Sept. 28	O'Reilly Mid-South Nationals	Mike Edwards	6.702	207.27	J. Line	16.481	48.20
Oct. 12	Virginia Nationals	Dave Connolly	6.574	209.33	J. Coughlin	6.611	206.86

Pro Stock Motorcycles

Date	Event	Winner	Time	MPH	2nd Place	Time	MPH
Mar. 16	ACDelco Gatornationals	Matt Guidera	6.949	191.54	A. Hines	6.985	189.55
Mar. 30	O'Reilly Spring Nationals	Matt Smith	7.060	187.76	M. Guidera	7.140	185.03
Apr. 27	Southern Nationals	Andrew Hines	6.946	191.40	C. Ellis	6.958	190.70
May 4	O'Reilly Midwest Nationals	Andrew Hines	6.882	194.13	M. Smith	8.098	114.02
June 8	Torco Racing Fuels Rt. 66 Nationals	Chris Rivas	7.051	185.43	C. Treble	7.134	185.38
June 22	Lucas Oil SuperNationals	Chip Ellis	7.040	187.21	C. Rivas	7.104	183.52
June 29	Summit Racing Equipment Nationals	Hector Arana	7.027	187.60	C. Treble	7.061	187.83
July 13	Mopar Mile-High Nationals	Matt Smith	7.326	180.74	S. Johnson	7.340	180.81
July 27	Fram-Autolite Nationals	Matt Guidera	7.054	185.74	A. Hines	7.026	187.34
Aug. 10	Lucas Oil Nationals	Matt Smith	6.973	188.60	A. Sampey	broke	—
Aug. 17	Toyo Tires Nationals	Matt Smith	6.957	188.81	A. Sampey	7.061	186.28
Sept. 1	Mac Tools U.S. Nationals	Steve Johnson	7.034	189.79	A. Hines	7.063	187.63
Sept. 14	Carolinas Nationals	Steve Johnson	7.029	191.46	E. Krawiec	6.974	192.91
Sept. 21	O'Reilly Fall Nationals	Chris Rivas	7.024	183.97	M. Smith	7.098	187.00
Sept. 28	O'Reilly Mid-South Nationals	Craig Treble	6.985	188.57	E. Krawiec	broke	—

Remaining Races (2): ACDelco Las Vegas Nationals (Nov. 2); Automobile Club of Southern California Finals (Nov. 16).

2008 NHRA POWERade Point Standings (through Oct. 12)

Top Fuel

		Points
1	Tony Schumacher	2527
2	Hillary Will	2315
3	Antron Brown	2283
4	Cory McClenathan	2278
5	Larry Dixon	2253
6	Doug Herbert	2245
7	Brandon Bernstein	2240
8	Rod Fuller	2179
9	Doug Kalitta	2145
10	David Grubnic	2110

Funny Car

		Points
1	Tim Wilkerson	2404
2	Jack Beckman	2353
3	Cruz Pedregon	2335
4	Tony Pedregon	2313
5	Robert Hight	2312
6	Ashley Force	2274
7	Ron Capps	2177
8	John Force	2171
9	Mike Neff	2154
10	Gary Densham	2135

Pro Stock Car

		Points
1	Jeg Coughlin	2374
2	Kurt Johnson	2300
3	Dave Connolly	2297
4	Greg Anderson	2292
5	Jason Line	2275
6	Mike Edwards	2261
7	Allen Johnson	2233
8	Greg Stanfield	2185
9	V. Gaines	2168
10	Ron Krisher	2073

Pro Stock Motorcycle

		Points				Points
1	Matt Smith	2319	6	Andrew Hines		2187
2	Ed Krawiec	2277	7	Chip Ellis		2176
3	Chris Rivas	2240	8	Craig Treble		2167
4	Angelle Sampey	2217	9	Matt Guidera		2114
5	Steve Johnson	2200	10	Karen Stoffer		2080

2008 AMA Motocross/Supercross
Final Championship Point Standings

Motocross

		Points
1	James Stewart	600
2	Timmy Ferry	414
3	Andrew Short	392
4	Michael Byrne	377
5	Cody Cooper	266

Motocross Lites

		Points
1	Ryan Villopoto	540
2	Ryan Dungey	468
3	Brett Metcalfe	382
4	Jake Weimer	321
5	Nico Izzi	292

Supercross

		Points
1	Chad Reed	365
2	Kevin Windham	352
3	Andrew Short	281
4	Davi Millsaps	278
5	Josh Hill	228

1909-2008
Through the Years

SPORTS ALMANAC

NASCAR CIRCUIT

Daytona 500

Held over 200 laps on 2.5-mile oval at Daytona International Speedway in Daytona Beach, Fla. First race in 1959, although stock car racing at Daytona dates back to 1936. Winners who started from pole position are in **bold** type.

Multiple winners: Richard Petty (7); Cale Yarborough (4); Bobby Allison, Jeff Gordon and Dale Jarrett (3); Bill Elliott, Sterling Marlin and Michael Waltrip (2). **Multiple poles:** Buddy Baker and Cale Yarborough (4); Bill Elliott, Dale Jarrett, Fireball Roberts and Ken Schrader (3); Donnie Allison (2).

Year	Winner	Car	Owner	MPH	Pole Sitter	MPH
1959	Lee Petty	Oldsmobile	Petty Enterprises	135.521	Bob Welborn	140.121
1960	Junior Johnson	Chevrolet	Ray Fox	124.740	Cotton Owens	149.892
1961	Marvin Panch	Pontiac	Smokey Yunick	149.601	Fireball Roberts	155.709
1962	**Fireball Roberts**	Pontiac	Smokey Yunick	152.529	Fireball Roberts	156.999
1963	Tiny Lund	Ford	Wood Brothers	151.566	Fireball Roberts	160.943
1964	Richard Petty	Plymouth	Petty Enterprises	154.334	Paul Goldsmith	174.910
1965-a	Fred Lorenzen	Ford	Holman-Moody	141.539	Darel Dieringer	171.151
1966-b	**Richard Petty**	Plymouth	Petty Enterprises	160.627	Richard Petty	175.165
1967	Mario Andretti	Ford	Holman-Moody	149.926	Curtis Turner	180.831
1968	**Cale Yarborough**	Mercury	Wood Brothers	143.251	Cale Yarborough	189.222
1969	Lee Roy Yarbrough	Ford	Junior Johnson	157.950	Buddy Baker	188.901
1970	Pete Hamilton	Plymouth	Petty Enterprises	149.601	Cale Yarborough	194.015
1971	Richard Petty	Plymouth	Petty Enterprises	144.462	A.J. Foyt	182.744
1972	A.J. Foyt	Mercury	Wood Brothers	161.550	Bobby Isaac	186.632
1973	Richard Petty	Dodge	Petty Enterprises	157.205	Buddy Baker	185.662
1974-c	Richard Petty	Dodge	Petty Enterprises	140.894	David Pearson	185.017
1975	Benny Parsons	Chevrolet	L.G. DeWitt	153.649	Donnie Allison	185.827
1976	David Pearson	Mercury	Wood Brothers	152.181	Ramo Stott	183.456
1977	Cale Yarborough	Chevrolet	Junior Johnson	153.218	Donnie Allison	188.048
1978	Bobby Allison	Ford	Bud Moore	159.730	Cale Yarborough	187.536
1979	Richard Petty	Oldsmobile	Petty Enterprises	143.977	Buddy Baker	196.049
1980	**Buddy Baker**	Oldsmobile	Ranier Racing	177.602*	Buddy Baker	194.099
1981	Richard Petty	Buick	Petty Enterprises	169.651	Bobby Allison	194.624
1982	Bobby Allison	Buick	DiGard Racing	153.991	Benny Parsons	196.317
1983	Cale Yarborough	Pontiac	Ranier Racing	155.979	Ricky Rudd	198.864
1984	**Cale Yarborough**	Chevrolet	Ranier Racing	150.994	Cale Yarborough	201.848
1985	**Bill Elliott**	Ford	Melling Racing	172.265	Bill Elliott	205.114
1986	Geoff Bodine	Chevrolet	Hendrick Motorsports	148.124	Bill Elliott	205.039
1987	**Bill Elliott**	Ford	Melling Racing	176.263	Bill Elliott	210.364†
1988	Bobby Allison	Buick	Stavola Brothers	137.531	Ken Schrader	198.823
1989	Darrell Waltrip	Chevrolet	Hendrick Motorsports	148.466	Ken Schrader	196.996
1990	Derrike Cope	Chevrolet	Bob Whitcomb	165.761	Ken Schrader	196.515
1991	Ernie Irvan	Chevrolet	Morgan-McClure	148.148	Davey Allison	195.955
1992	Davey Allison	Ford	Robert Yates	160.256	Sterling Marlin	192.213
1993	Dale Jarrett	Chevrolet	Joe Gibbs Racing	154.972	Kyle Petty	189.426
1994	Sterling Marlin	Chevrolet	Morgan-McClure	156.931	Loy Allen	190.158
1995	Sterling Marlin	Chevrolet	Morgan-McClure	141.710	Dale Jarrett	193.498
1996	Dale Jarrett	Ford	Robert Yates	154.308	Dale Earnhardt	189.510
1997	Jeff Gordon	Chevrolet	Hendrick Motorsports	148.295	Mike Skinner	189.813
1998	Dale Earnhardt	Chevrolet	Richard Childress	172.712	Bobby Labonte	192.415
1999	**Jeff Gordon**	Chevrolet	Hendrick Motorsports	161.551	Jeff Gordon	195.067
2000	**Dale Jarrett**	Ford	Robert Yates	155.669	Dale Jarrett	191.091
2001	Michael Waltrip	Chevrolet	Dale Earnhardt, Inc.	161.783	Bill Elliott	183.565
2002	Ward Burton	Dodge	Bill Davis	142.971	Jimmie Johnson	185.831
2003-d	Michael Waltrip	Chevrolet	Dale Earnhardt, Inc.	133.870	Jeff Green	186.606
2004	Dale Earnhardt Jr.	Chevrolet	Dale Earnhardt, Inc.	156.345	Greg Biffle	188.387
2005	Jeff Gordon	Chevrolet	Hendrick Motorsports	135.173	Dale Jarrett	188.312
2006	Jimmie Johnson	Chevrolet	Hendrick Motorsports	142.667	Jeff Burton	189.151
2007	Kevin Harvick	Chevrolet	Richard Childress	142.667	David Gilliland	186.320
2008	Ryan Newman	Dodge	Roger Penske	152.672	Jimmie Johnson	187.075

*Track and race record for winning speed. †Track and race record for qualifying speed.
Notes: a—rain shortened 1965 race to 332.5 miles; b—rain shortened 1966 race to 495 miles; c—in 1974, race shortened 50 miles due to energy crisis; d—rain shortened 2003 race to 272.5 miles. **Also:** Pole sitters determined by pole qualifying race (1959-65); by two-lap average (1966-68); by fastest single lap (since 1969).

Amp Energy 500

Held over 188 laps on 2.66-mile tri-oval at Talladega Superspeedway in Talladega, Ala.

Previously known as Winston 500 (1970-93, 1997-2000), Winston Select 500 (1994-96), EA Sports 500 (2001-04) and UAW-Ford 500 (2005-07). Winners who started from pole position are in **bold** type.

Multiple winners: Dale Earnhardt (4); Bobby Allison, Davey Allison, Buddy Baker, Dale Earnhardt Jr. and David Pearson (3); Dale Jarrett, Mark Martin, Darrell Waltrip and Cale Yarborough (2).

Year		Year		Year		Year	
1970	Pete Hamilton	1980	Buddy Baker	1990	**Dale Earnhardt**	2000	Dale Earnhardt
1971	**Donnie Allison**	1981	**Bobby Allison**	1991	Harry Gant	2001	Dale Earnhardt Jr.
1972	David Pearson	1982	Darrell Waltrip	1992	Davey Allison	2002	Dale Earnhardt Jr.
1973	David Pearson	1983	Richard Petty	1993	Ernie Irvan	2003	Michael Waltrip
1974	**David Pearson**	1984	**Cale Yarborough**	1994	Dale Earnhardt	2004	Dale Earnhardt Jr.
1975	**Buddy Baker**	1985	Bill Elliott	1995	**Mark Martin**	2005	Dale Jarrett
1976	Buddy Baker	1986	Bobby Allison	1996	Sterling Marlin	2006	Brian Vickers
1977	Darrell Waltrip	1987	Davey Allison	1997	Mark Martin	2007	Jeff Gordon
1978	**Cale Yarborough**	1988	Phil Parsons	1998	Dale Jarrett	2008	Tony Stewart
1979	Bobby Allison	1989	Davey Allison	1999	Dale Earnhardt		

Coca-Cola 600

Held over 400 laps on 1.5-mile oval at Lowe's Motor Speedway in Concord, N.C.

Previously known as World 600 (1960-85). It has been Coca-Cola 600 since 1986 (in 2002, sponsors announced a one-time-only name change to The Coca-Cola Racing Family 600). Winners who started from pole position are in **bold** type.

Multiple winners: Darrell Waltrip (5); Bobby Allison, Buddy Baker, Dale Earnhardt, Jeff Gordon, Jimmie Johnson and David Pearson (3); Neil Bonnett, Jeff Burton, Kasey Kahne, Fred Lorenzen, Jim Paschal and Richard Petty (2).

Year		Year		Year		Year	
1960	Joe Lee Johnson	1973	**Buddy Baker**	1986	Dale Earnhardt	1999	Jeff Burton
1961	David Pearson	1974	**David Pearson**	1987	Kyle Petty	2000	Matt Kenseth
1962	Nelson Stacy	1975	Richard Petty	1988	Darrell Waltrip	2001	Jeff Burton
1963	Fred Lorenzen	1976	**David Pearson**	1989	Darrell Waltrip	2002	Mark Martin
1964	Jim Paschal	1977	Richard Petty	1990	Rusty Wallace	2003	Jimmie Johnson*
1965	**Fred Lorenzen**	1978	Darrell Waltrip	1991	Davey Allison	2004	**Jimmie Johnson**
1966	Marvin Panch	1979	Darrell Waltrip	1992	Dale Earnhardt	2005	Jimmie Johnson
1967	Jim Paschal	1980	Benny Parsons	1993	Dale Earnhardt	2006	Kasey Kahne
1968	Buddy Baker*	1981	Bobby Allison	1994	**Jeff Gordon**	2007	Casey Mears
1969	Lee Roy Yarbrough	1982	Neil Bonnett	1995	Bobby Labonte	2008	Kasey Kahne
1970	Donnie Allison	1983	Neil Bonnett	1996	Dale Jarrett		* rain-shortened.
1971	Bobby Allison	1984	Bobby Allison	1997	**Jeff Gordon***		
1972	Buddy Baker	1985	Darrell Waltrip	1998	**Jeff Gordon**		

Allstate 400 at the Brickyard

Held over 160 laps at 2.5-mile Indianapolis Motor Speedway in Indianapolis, Ind.

Previously known as Brickyard 400 (1994-2004). Winners who started from pole position are in **bold** type.

Multiple winners: Jeff Gordon (4); Dale Jarrett, Jimmie Johnson and Tony Stewart (2).

Year		Year		Year		Year		Year	
1994	Jeff Gordon	1997	Ricky Rudd	2000	Bobby Labonte	2003	**Kevin Harvick**	2006	Jimmie Johnson
1995	Dale Earnhardt	1998	Jeff Gordon	2001	Jeff Gordon	2004	Jeff Gordon	2007	Tony Stewart
1996	Dale Jarrett	1999	Dale Jarrett	2002	Bill Elliott	2005	Tony Stewart	2008	**J. Johnson**

Mountain Dew Southern 500

Final race held in 2004. Held over 367 laps on 1.366-mile oval at Darlington International Raceway in Darlington, S.C.

Previously known as Southern 500 (1950-88); Heinz 500 (1989-91); and Pepsi Southern 500 (1998-2000). It was the Mountain Dew Southern 500 from 1992-97, and 2001-04. Winners who started from pole position are in **bold** type.

Multiple winners: Jeff Gordon and Cale Yarborough (5); Bobby Allison (4); Buck Baker, Dale Earnhardt, Bill Elliott, David Pearson and Herb Thomas (3); Harry Gant and Fireball Roberts (2).

Year		Year		Year		Year	
1950	Johnny Mantz	1964	Buck Baker	1978	Cale Yarborough	1992	Darrell Waltrip*
1951	Herb Thomas	1965	Ned Jarrett	1979	David Pearson	1993	Mark Martin*
1952	**Fonty Flock**	1966	Darel Dieringer	1980	Terry Labonte	1994	Bill Elliott
1953	Buck Baker	1967	**Richard Petty**	1981	Neil Bonnett	1995	Jeff Gordon
1954	Herb Thomas	1968	Cale Yarborough	1982	Cale Yarborough	1996	Jeff Gordon
1955	Herb Thomas	1969	Lee Roy Yarbrough*	1983	Bobby Allison	1997	Jeff Gordon*
1956	Curtis Turner	1970	Buddy Baker	1984	**Harry Gant**	1998	Jeff Gordon
1957	Speedy Thompson	1971	**Bobby Allison**	1985	**Bill Elliott**	1999	Jeff Burton*
1958	Fireball Roberts	1972	**Bobby Allison**	1986	**Tim Richmond**	2000	Bobby Labonte*
1959	Jim Reed	1973	Cale Yarborough	1987	Dale Earnhardt*	2001	Ward Burton
1960	Buck Baker	1974	Cale Yarborough	1988	**Bill Elliott**	2002	Jeff Gordon
1961	Nelson Stacy	1975	Bobby Allison	1989	Dale Earnhardt	2003	Terry Labonte
1962	Larry Frank	1976	**David Pearson**	1990	**Dale Earnhardt**	2004	Jimmie Johnson
1963	Fireball Roberts	1977	David Pearson	1991	Harry Gant		* rain shortened

NASCAR Circuit (Cont.)
Sprint Cup Series Champions

Originally the Grand National Championship (1949-70), then Winston Cup Series Championship (1971-2003), then Nextel Cup Series Championship (2004-07), and based on official NASCAR records. Drivers listed since 2004 are winners of the Chase for the Nextel Cup, NASCAR's first playoff series run over the final ten races of the season.

Multiple winners: (drivers) Dale Earnhardt and Richard Petty (7); Jeff Gordon (4); David Pearson, Lee Petty, Darrell Waltrip and Cale Yarborough (3); Buck Baker, Tim Flock, Ned Jarrett, Jimmie Johnson, Terry Labonte, Tony Stewart, Herb Thomas and Joe Weatherly (2).

Multiple winners: (cars) Chevrolet (25); Ford (7); Plymouth (5); Dodge, Oldsmobile and Pontiac (4); Buick and Hudson (3); and Chrysler (2).

Year	Car #	Driver	Car	Owner	Sts	Wins	Poles	Earnings
1949	22	**Red Byron**	Oldsmobile	Raymond Parks	5	2	1	$5,800
1950	60	**Bill Rexford**	Oldsmobile	Julian Buesink	17	1	0	6,175
1951	92	**Herb Thomas**	Hudson	Herb Thomas	34	7	4	18,200
1952	91	**Tim Flock**	Hudson	Ted Chester	33	8	4	20,210
1953	92	**Herb Thomas**	Hudson	Herb Thomas	37	11	10	27,300
1954	42	**Lee Petty**	Chrysler	Herb Thomas	34	7	3	26,706
1955	300	**Tim Flock**	Chrysler	Carl Kiekhaefer	38	18	19	33,750
1956	300B	**Buck Baker**	Chevrolet	Carl Kiekhaefer	48	14	12	29,790
1957	87	**Buck Baker**	Chevrolet	Buck Baker	40	10	5	24,712
1958	42	**Lee Petty**	Oldsmobile	Petty Enterprises	49	7	4	20,600
1959	42	**Lee Petty**	Plymouth	Petty Enterprises	42	10	2	45,570
1960	4	**Rex White**	Chevrolet	White-Clements	40	6	3	45,260
1961	11	**Ned Jarrett**	Chevrolet	W.G. Holloway Jr.	46	1	4	27,285
1962	8	**Joe Weatherly**	Pontiac	Bud Moore	52	9	6	56,110
1963	8	**Joe Weatherly**	Mercury	Wood Brothers	53	3	6	58,110
1964	43	**Richard Petty**	Plymouth	Petty Enterprises	61	9	8	98,810
1965	11	**Ned Jarrett**	Ford	Bondy Long	54	13	9	77,960
1966	6	**David Pearson**	Dodge	Cotton Owens	42	14	7	59,205
1967	43	**Richard Petty**	Plymouth	Petty Enterprises	48	27	18	130,275
1968	17	**David Pearson**	Ford	Holman-Moody	48	16	12	118,842
1969	17	**David Pearson**	Ford	Holman-Moody	51	11	14	183,700
1970	71	**Bobby Isaac**	Dodge	Nord Krauskopf	47	11	13	121,470
1971	43	**Richard Petty**	Plymouth	Petty Enterprises	46	21	9	309,225
1972	43	**Richard Petty**	Plymouth	Petty Enterprises	31	8	3	227,015
1973	72	**Benny Parsons**	Chevrolet	L.G. DeWitt	28	1	0	114,345
1974	43	**Richard Petty**	Dodge	Petty Enterprises	30	10	7	299,175
1975	43	**Richard Petty**	Dodge	Petty Enterprises	30	13	3	378,865
1976	11	**Cale Yarborough**	Chevrolet	Junior Johnson	30	9	2	387,173
1977	11	**Cale Yarborough**	Chevrolet	Junior Johnson	30	9	3	477,499
1978	11	**Cale Yarborough**	Oldsmobile	Junior Johnson	30	10	8	530,751
1979	43	**Richard Petty**	Chevrolet	Petty Enterprises	31	5	1	531,292
1980	2	**Dale Earnhardt**	Chevrolet	Rod Osterlund	31	5	0	588,926
1981	11	**Darrell Waltrip**	Buick	Junior Johnson	31	12	11	693,342
1982	11	**Darrell Waltrip**	Buick	Junior Johnson	30	12	7	873,118
1983	22	**Bobby Allison**	Buick	Bill Gardner	30	6	0	828,355
1984	44	**Terry Labonte**	Chevrolet	Billy Hagan	30	2	2	713,010
1985	11	**Darrell Waltrip**	Chevrolet	Junior Johnson	28	3	4	1,318,735
1986	3	**Dale Earnhardt**	Chevrolet	Richard Childress	29	5	1	1,783,880
1987	3	**Dale Earnhardt**	Chevrolet	Richard Childress	29	11	1	2,099,243
1988	9	**Bill Elliott**	Ford	Harry Meling	29	6	6	1,574,639
1989	27	**Rusty Wallace**	Pontiac	Raymond Beadle	29	6	4	2,247,950
1990	3	**Dale Earnhardt**	Chevrolet	Richard Childress	29	9	4	3,083,056
1991	3	**Dale Earnhardt**	Chevrolet	Richard Childress	29	4	0	2,396,685
1992	7	**Alan Kulwicki**	Ford	Alan Kulwicki	29	2	6	2,322,561
1993	3	**Dale Earnhardt**	Chevrolet	Richard Childress	30	6	2	3,353,789
1994	3	**Dale Earnhardt**	Chevrolet	Richard Childress	31	4	2	3,400,733
1995	24	**Jeff Gordon**	Chevrolet	Rick Hendrick	31	7	8	4,347,343
1996	5	**Terry Labonte**	Chevrolet	Rick Hendrick	31	2	4	4,030,648
1997	24	**Jeff Gordon**	Chevrolet	Rick Hendrick	32	10	1	6,375,658
1998	24	**Jeff Gordon**	Chevrolet	Rick Hendrick	33	13	7	9,306,584
1999	88	**Dale Jarrett**	Ford	Robert Yates	34	4	0	6,649,596
2000	18	**Bobby Labonte**	Pontiac	Joe Gibbs	34	4	2	7,361,387
2001	24	**Jeff Gordon**	Chevrolet	Rick Hendrick	36	6	6	10,879,757
2002	20	**Tony Stewart**	Pontiac	Joe Gibbs	36	3	2	9,163,761
2003	17	**Matt Kenseth**	Ford	Mark Martin	36	1	0	9,422,764
2004	97	**Kurt Busch**	Ford	Roush Racing	36	3	1	9,661,513
2005	20	**Tony Stewart**	Chevrolet	Joe Gibbs	36	5	3	13,578,168
2006	48	**Jimmie Johnson**	Chevrolet	Rick Hendrick	36	5	1	15,952,125
2007	48	**Jimmie Johnson**	Chevrolet	Rick Hendrick	36	10	4	15,313,920

Sprint Cup Rookie of the Year

Sponsored by Raybestos, the official brake of NASCAR, and presented to rookie driver who accumulates the most Sprint Cup Series Raybestos Rookie of the Year points based on their best 17 finishes.

Year	Year	Year	Year
1957 Ken Rush	1970 Bill Dennis	1983 Sterling Marlin	1996 Johnny Benson
1958 Shorty Rollins	1971 Walter Ballard	1984 Rusty Wallace	1997 Mike Skinner
1959 Richard Petty	1972 Larry Smith	1985 Ken Schrader	1998 Kenny Irwin
1960 David Pearson	1973 Lennie Pond	1986 Alan Kulwicki	1999 Tony Stewart
1961 Woodie Wilson	1974 Earl Ross	1987 Davey Allison	2000 Matt Kenseth
1962 Tom Cox	1975 Bruce Hill	1988 Ken Bouchard	2001 Kevin Harvick
1963 Billy Wade	1976 Skip Manning	1989 Dick Trickle	2002 Ryan Newman
1964 Doug Cooper	1977 Ricky Rudd	1990 Rob Moroso	2003 Jamie McMurray
1965 Sam McQuagg	1978 Ronnie Thomas	1991 Bobby Hamilton	2004 Kasey Kahne
1966 James Hylton	1979 Dale Earnhardt	1992 Jimmy Hensley	2005 Kyle Busch
1967 Donnie Allison	1980 Jody Ridley	1993 Jeff Gordon	2006 Denny Hamlin
1968 Pete Hamilton	1981 Ron Bouchard	1994 Jeff Burton	2007 Juan Pablo Montoya
1969 Dick Brooks	1982 Geoff Bodine	1995 Ricky Craven	

Manufacturers' Championship

Awarded to the most successful car manufacturer in the Sprint Cup Series since 1949. Manufacturers whose cars finish in the top six in each race are awarded points based on the following format: 9-6-4-3-2-1.

Multiple winners: Chevrolet (30); Ford (16); Oldsmobile (4); Dodge and Hudson (3); Buick and Pontiac (2).

Year	Year	Year	Year	Year
1949 Oldsmobile	1961 Chevrolet	1973 Chevrolet	1985 Chevrolet	1996 Chevrolet
1950 Oldsmobile	1962 Pontiac	1974 Chevrolet	1986 Chevrolet	1997 Ford
1951 Oldsmobile	1963 Ford	1975 Dodge	1987 Chevrolet	1998 Chevrolet
1952 Hudson	1964 Ford	1976 Chevrolet	1988 Pontiac	1999 Ford
1953 Hudson	1965 Ford	1977 Chevrolet	1989 Chevrolet	2000 Ford
1954 Hudson	1966 Ford	1978 Chevrolet	1990 Chevrolet	2001 Chevrolet
1955 Oldsmobile	1967 Ford	1979 Chevrolet	& Ford	2002 Ford
1956 Ford	1968 Ford	1980 Chevrolet	1991 Chevrolet	2003 Chevrolet
1957 Ford	1969 Ford	1981 Buick	1992 Ford	2004 Chevrolet
1958 Chevrolet	1970 Dodge	1982 Buick	1993 Chevrolet	2005 Chevrolet
1959 Chevrolet	1971 Dodge	1983 Chevrolet	1994 Ford	2006 Chevrolet
1960 Chevrolet	1972 Chevrolet	1984 Chevrolet	1995 Chevrolet	2007 Chevrolet

Champion Crew Chiefs

Crew chiefs of Sprint Cup Series champions since 1949.

Multiple winners: Dale Inman (8); Kirk Shelmerdine (4); Ray Evernham and Lee Petty (3); Tim Brewer, Travis Carter, Jake Elder, Jeff Hammond, Chad Knaus, Bud Moore, Herb Nab, Andy Petree, Smokey Yunick and Greg Zipadelli (2).

Year	Year	Year	Year
1949 Red Vogt	1964 Dale Inman	1979 Dale Inman	1994 Andy Petree
1950 Julian Buesink	1965 John Ervin	1980 Doug Richert	1995 Ray Evernham
1951 Smokey Yunick	1966 Cotton Owens	1981 Tim Brewer	1996 Gary DeHart
1952 B.B. Blackburn	1967 Dale Inman	1982 Jeff Hammond	1997 Ray Evernham
1953 Smokey Yunick	1968 Jake Elder	1983 Gary Nelson	1998 Ray Evernham
1954 Lee Petty	1969 Jake Elder	1984 Dale Inman	1999 Todd Parrott
1955 Carl Kiekhafer	1970 Harry Hyde	1985 Jeff Hammond	2000 Jimmy Makar
1956 Carl Kiekhafer	1971 Dale Inman	1986 Kirk Shelmerdine	2001 Robbie Loomis
1957 Bud Moore	1972 Dale Inman	1987 Kirk Shelmerdine	2002 Greg Zipadelli
1958 Lee Petty	1973 Travis Carter	1988 Ernie Elliott	2003 Robbie Reiser
1959 Lee Petty	1974 Dale Inman	1989 Barry Dodson	2004 Jimmy Fennig
1960 Louis Clements	1975 Dale Inman	1990 Kirk Shelmerdine	2005 Greg Zipadelli
1961 Bud Allman	1976 Herb Nab	1991 Kirk Shelmerdine	2006 Chad Knaus
1962 Bud Moore	1977 Herb Nab	1992 Paul Andrews	2007 Chad Knaus
1963 Bud Moore	1978 T Brewer/T. Carter	1993 Andy Petree	

Sprint All-Star Race

The NASCAR Sprint All-Star Race is a non-points event held each May at Lowe's Motor Speedway in Concord, N.C. It is open to race winners from the previous and current season, the winner of the Sprint Showdown qualifying race, former All-Star winners, former Sprint Cup champions and one driver chosen by fan vote. The Challenge winner earns $1 million.

Multiple winners: Dale Earnhardt and Jeff Gordon (3); Davey Allison, Jimmie Johnson, Terry Labonte and Mark Martin (2).

Year	Year	Year	Year
1985 Darrell Waltrip	1991 Davey Allison	1997 Jeff Gordon	2003 Jimmie Johnson
1986 Bill Elliott	1992 Davey Allison	1998 Mark Martin	2004 Matt Kenseth
1987 Dale Earnhardt	1993 Dale Earnhardt	1999 Terry Labonte	2005 Mark Martin
1988 Terry Labonte	1994 Geoff Bodine	2000 Dale Earnhardt Jr.	2006 Jimmie Johnson
1989 Rusty Wallace	1995 Jeff Gordon	2001 Jeff Gordon	2007 Kevin Harvick
1990 Dale Earnhardt	1996 Michael Waltrip	2002 Ryan Newman	2008 Kasey Kahne

NASCAR Circuit (Cont.)
Sprint Cup All-Time Leaders

NASCAR Sprint Cup's all-time Top 20 drivers in victories and pole positions through Oct. 26, 2008, and earnings through 2007. Drivers active in 2008 are in **bold** type.

Career

#	Victories		#	Pole Positions		#	Earnings	
1	Richard Petty	200	1	Richard Petty	126	1	**Jeff Gordon**	$93,300,213
2	David Pearson	105	2	David Pearson	113	2	**Tony Stewart**	65,240,202
3	Bobby Allison	84	3	Cale Yarborough	70	3	**Mark Martin**	63,829,009
	Darrell Waltrip	84	4	**Jeff Gordon**	66	4	**Jimmie Johnson**	59,531,336
5	Cale Yarborough	83	5	Darrell Waltrip	59	5	**Dale Jarrett**	59,100,821
6	**Jeff Gordon**	81	6	Bobby Allison	57	6	**Bobby Labonte**	55,860,859
7	Dale Earnhardt	76	7	**Bill Elliott**	55	7	**Jeff Burton**	54,345,624
8	Lee Petty	55	8	Bobby Isaac	51	8	**Matt Kenseth**	51,726,470
	Rusty Wallace	55	9	Junior Johnson	47	9	Rusty Wallace	49,741,326
10	Ned Jarrett	50	10	Buck Baker	44	10	**Dale Earnhardt Jr.**	48,903,000
	Junior Johnson	50	11	**Ryan Newman**	43	11	Ricky Rudd	44,400,533
12	Herb Thomas	48	12	**Mark Martin**	41	12	**Kurt Busch**	43,046,288
13	Buck Baker	46	13	Buddy Baker	40	13	**Kevin Harvick**	42,432,766
14	**Bill Elliott**	44	14	Tim Flock	39	14	**Sterling Marlin**	42,356,204
15	Tim Flock	40		Herb Thomas	39	15	Dale Earnhardt	41,742,384
16	**Jimmie Johnson**	39	16	Geoff Bodine	37	16	**Bill Elliott**	40,917,292
17	Bobby Isaac	37	17	Rusty Wallace	36	17	Terry Labonte	40,867,147
18	**Mark Martin**	35	18	Ned Jarrett	35	18	**Ryan Newman**	37,340,232
19	**Tony Stewart**	33		Fireball Roberts	35	19	Michael Waltrip	36,654,526
20	Fireball Roberts	32		Rex White	35	20	**Elliott Sadler**	34,184,869
	Dale Jarrett	32						

Single Season (through 2007)

#	Victories		#	Pole Positions		#	Earnings	
1	Richard Petty, '67	27	1	Bobby Isaac, '69	20	1	Jimmie Johnson, '06	$15,952,125
2	Richard Petty, '71	21	2	Richard Petty, '67	19	2	Jimmie Johnson, '07	15,313,920
3	Tim Flock, '55	18	3	Tim Flock, '55	18	3	Tony Stewart, '05	13,578,168
	Richard Petty, '70	18	4	Richard Petty, '66	16	4	Jeff Gordon, '07	10,926,687
5	Bobby Isaac, '69	17	5	Cale Yarborough, '80	14	5	Jeff Gordon, '01	10,879,757
6	David Pearson, '68	16	6	David Pearson, '69	13	6	Kurt Busch, '04	9,677,543
	Richard Petty, '68	16		Bobby Isaac, '70	13	7	Matt Kenseth, '06	9,544,966
8	Ned Jarrett, '64	15	7	Fonty Flock, '51	12	8	Matt Kenseth, '03	9,422,764
	David Pearson, '66	15		David Pearson, '64	12	9	Jeff Gordon, '98	9,306,584
10	Buck Baker, '56	14		David Pearson, '68	12	10	Tony Stewart, '02	9,163,761
	Richard Petty, '63	14		Richard Petty, '68	12	11	D. Earnhardt Jr., '04	8,913,510
						12	Kevin Harvick, '07	8,861,128
	Modern Era (since 1972)			**Modern Era** (since 1972)		13	Tony Stewart '06	8,749,169
1	Richard Petty, '75	13	1	Cale Yarborough, '80	14	14	Matt Kenseth, '07	8,624,816
	Jeff Gordon, '98	13	2	Bobby Allison, '72	11	15	Jeff Gordon, '04	8,439,382
3	Darrell Waltrip, '81	12		David Pearson, '74	11	16	Greg Biffle, '05	8,354,052
	Darrell Waltrip, '82	12		Darrell Waltrip, '81	11	17	Jimmie Johnson, '05	8,336,712
5	David Pearson, '73	11		Bill Elliott, 85	11	18	Jimmie Johnson, '04	8,275,721
	Bill Elliott, '85	11		Ryan Newman, '03	11	19	Kevin Harvick, '06	8,231,406
	Dale Earnhardt, '87	11	7	Geoff Bodine, '86	9	20	Tony Stewart, '07	8,023,584
8	Nine tied with 10 wins each, including twice by Cale Yarborough and Jeff Gordon.			Rusty Wallace, '00	9			
				Ryan Newman, '04	9			
			10	Eight tied with 8 poles each.				

Richard Petty speeds through qualifying at the 1968 Daytona 500. Petty won 16 races in 1968, tied for 6th on the all-time single-season list and 11 behind his record of 27 set in 1967.

AP Images

Nationwide Series Champions

The Nationwide Series was founded in 1982 as the Budweiser Late Model Sportsman Series, and has since grown into the No. 2 motorsports series in the United States. The series emerged from NASCAR's old Sportsman Division, which was formed in 1950 as NASCAR's short track race division. The series switched sponsorship to the Busch brand in 1984 and became the Busch Grand National Series. Grand National was dumped from the series' title in 2003. Nationwide Insurance took over sponsorship in 2008. Note that earnings totals include bonus awards.

Multiple winners: (drivers) Sam Ard, Dale Earnhardt Jr., Kevin Harvick, Jack Ingram, Randy LaJoie, Larry Pearson and Martin Truex Jr. (2). **Multiple winners:** (cars) Chevrolet (15); Oldsmobile (5); Pontiac (4); Ford (2).

Year	Car #	Driver	Car	Owner	Sts	Wins	Poles	Earnings
1982	11	Jack Ingram	Olds/Pontiac	Aline Ingram	29	7	1	$122,100
1983	00	Sam Ard	Oldsmobile	Howard Thomas	35	10	10	192,362
1984	00	Sam Ard	Oldsmobile	Howard Thomas	28	8	7	217,531
1985	11	Jack Ingram	Pontiac	Aline Ingram	27	5	2	164,710
1986	21	Larry Pearson	Pontiac	David Pearson	31	1	1	184,344
1987	21	Larry Pearson	Chevrolet	David Pearson	27	6	3	256,372
1988	99	Tommy Ellis	Buick	John Jackson	30	3	5	200,003
1989	25	Rob Moroso	Oldsmobile	Dick Moroso	29	4	6	346,739
1990	63	Chuck Brown	Pontiac	Hubert Hensley	31	6	4	323,399
1991	44	Bobby Labonte	Oldsmobile	Bobby Labonte	31	2	2	246,368
1992	87	Joe Nemechek	Chevrolet	Joe Nemechek	31	2	1	285,008
1993	31	Steve Grissom	Chevrolet	Wayne Grissom	28	2	0	336,432
1994	44	David Green	Chevrolet	Bobby Labonte	28	1	9	391,670
1995	74	Johnny Benson	Chevrolet	William Baumgardner	26	2	0	469,129
1996	74	Randy LaJoie	Chevrolet	William Baumgardner	26	5	2	532,823
1997	74	Randy LaJoie	Chevrolet	William Baumgardner	30	5	2	1,105,201
1998	3	Dale Earnhardt Jr.	Chevrolet	Dale Earnhardt	31	5	3	1,332,701
1999	3	Dale Earnhardt Jr.	Chevrolet	Dale Earnhardt	32	6	3	1,680,549
2000	10	Jeff Green	Chevrolet	Greg Pollex	32	6	7	1,929,937
2001	2	Kevin Harvick	Chevrolet	Richard Childress	33	5	5	1,833,570
2002	60	Greg Biffle	Ford	Jack Roush	34	4	5	2,337,255
2003	5	Brian Vickers	Chevrolet	Ricky Hendrick	34	3	1	1,987,255
2004	8	Martin Truex Jr.	Chevrolet	T. Earnhardt/D. Earnhardt. Jr.	34	6	7	2,537,171
2005	8	Martin Truex Jr.	Chevrolet	T. Earnhardt/D. Earnhardt. Jr.	35	6	3	3,143,692
2006	21	Kevin Harvick	Chevrolet	Richard Childress	35	9	1	2,850,864
2007	60	Carl Edwards	Ford	Jack Roush	35	4	0	2,485,582

Nationwide Series Rookie of the Year

Sponsored by Raybestos, the official brake of NASCAR, and presented to rookie driver who accumulates the most Nationwide Series Raybestos Rookie of the Year points based on their best 16 finishes.

Year		Year		Year		Year	
1989	Kenny Wallace	1994	Johnny Benson	1999	Tony Raines	2004	Kyle Busch
1990	Joe Nemechek	1995	Jeff Fuller	2000	Kevin Harvick	2005	Carl Edwards
1991	Jeff Gordon	1996	Glenn Allen	2001	Greg Biffle	2006	Danny O'Quinn Jr.
1992	Ricky Craven	1997	Steve Park	2002	Scott Riggs	2007	David Ragan
1993	Hermie Sadler	1998	Andy Santerre	2003	David Stremme		

Manufacturers' Championship

Officially the Bill France Performance Cup and awarded to the most successful car manufacturer in the Nationwide Series. Manufacturers whose cars finish in the top four in each race are awarded points based on the following format: 9-6-4-3.

Multiple winners: Chevrolet (14); Ford (2).

Year		Year		Year		Year		Year	
1991	Oldsmobile	1995	Ford	1999	Chevrolet	2002	Ford	2005	Chevrolet
1992	Chevrolet	1996	Chevrolet	2000	Chevrolet	2003	Chevrolet	2006	Chevrolet
1993	Chevrolet	1997	Chevrolet	2001	Chevrolet	2004	Chevrolet	2007	Chevrolet
1994	Chevrolet	1998	Chevrolet						

Nationwide Series All-Time Leaders

NASCAR Nationwide Series all-time Top 10 drivers in victories and pole positions through Oct. 25, 2008, and earnings through 2007.

Victories

1. Mark Martin 48
2. Kevin Harvick 32
3. Jack Ingram 31
4. Jeff Burton 27
5. Tommy Houston 24
6. Matt Kenseth 23
7. Sam Ard 22
   Dale Earnhardt Jr. 22
   Tommy Ellis 22
10. Dale Earnhardt 21
   Harry Gant 21

Pole Positions

1. Mark Martin 30
2. Tommy Ellis 28
3. Sam Ard 24
4. Jeff Green 23
5. David Green 22
6. Tommy Houston 18
   Joe Nemechek 18
8. Kevin Harvick 17
9. Brett Bodine 16
10. Three tied at 15.

Earnings

1. Jason Keller $11,295,558
2. Kevin Harvick 10,274,818
3. Greg Biffle 9,065,529
4. David Green 8,954,715
5. Randy LaJoie 7,702,143
6. Matt Kenseth 7,221,405
7. Jeff Green 6,915,833
8. Kenny Wallace 6,758,071
9. Mike McLaughlin 6,257,873
10. Martin Truex Jr. 6,169,757

NASCAR Circuit (Cont.)

Craftsman Truck Series Champions

The NASCAR Craftsman Truck Series features modified pickup trucks. The idea for the Series originated in 1993, when a group of off-road racers created a prototype for a NASCAR-style pickup truck. The trucks proved extremely popular and were first displayed during the 1994 Daytona 500. NASCAR created the series, first called the "SuperTruck Series," in 1995. The series became known as the Craftsman Truck Series in 1996. Beginning in 2009, Camping World will take over as title sponsor. Note that earnings totals include bonus awards.

Multiple winners: (drivers) Ron Hornaday Jr. and Jack Sprague (3).
Multiple winners: (cars) Chevrolet (9); Dodge (2).

Year	Truck #	Driver	Car	Owner	Sts	Wins	Poles	Earnings
1995	3	Mike Skinner	Chevrolet	Richard Childress	20	8	10	$428,096
1996	16	Ron Hornaday Jr.	Chevrolet	Teresa Earnhardt	24	4	2	625,634
1997	24	Jack Sprague	Chevrolet	Rick Hendrick	26	3	5	880,835
1998	16	Ron Hornaday Jr.	Chevrolet	Teresa Earnhardt	27	6	2	915,407
1999	24	Jack Sprague	Chevrolet	Rick Hendrick	25	3	1	834,016
2000	50	Greg Biffle	Ford	Jack Roush	24	5	4	1,002,510
2001	24	Jack Sprague	Chevrolet	Rick Hendrick	24	4	7	967,493
2002	16	Mike Bliss	Chevrolet	Steve Coulter	22	5	4	894,388
2003	16	Travis Kvapil	Chevrolet	Steve Coulter	25	1	0	872,395
2004	4	Bobby Hamilton	Dodge	Debbie Hamilton	25	4	0	973,428
2005	1	Ted Musgrave	Dodge	Jim Smith	25	1	1	880,553
2006	30	Todd Bodine	Toyota	Stephen Germain	25	3	1	1,046,680
2007	33	Ron Hornaday Jr.	Chevrolet	DeLana Harvick	25	4	1	1,137,044

Craftsman Truck Series Rookie of the Year

Sponsored by Raybestos, the official brake of NASCAR, and presented to rookie driver who accumulates the most Craftsman Truck Series Raybestos Rookie of the Year points based on their best 14 finishes.

Year		Year		Year		Year	
1996	Bryan Reffner	1999	Mike Stefanik	2002	Brendan Gaughan	2005	Todd Kluever
1997	Kenny Irwin	2000	Kurt Busch	2003	Carl Edwards	2006	Erik Darnell
1998	Greg Biffle	2001	Travis Kvapil	2004	David Reutimann	2007	Willie Allen

Manufacturers' Championship

Awarded each year to the most successful car manufacturer in the Craftsman Truck Series. Manufacturers whose cars finish in the top four in each race are awarded points based on the following format: 9-6-4-3.

Multiple winners: Chevrolet (6); Dodge (3); Ford and Toyota (2).

Year		Year		Year		Year	
1995	Chevrolet	1999	Ford	2003	Dodge	2007	Toyota
1996	Chevrolet	2000	Ford	2004	Dodge		
1997	Chevrolet	2001	Dodge	2005	Chevrolet		
1998	Chevrolet	2002	Chevrolet	2006	Toyota		

Craftsman Truck Series All-Time Leaders

NASCAR Craftsman Truck Series all-time Top 10 drivers in victories and pole positions through Oct. 25, 2008, and earnings through 2007.

Victories

1	Ron Hornaday Jr.	38
2	Jack Sprague	28
3	Mike Skinner	25
4	Dennis Setzer	17
	Ted Musgrave	17
6	Greg Biffle	16
7	Todd Bodine	14
	Johnny Benson	14
9	Joe Ruttman	13
	Mike Bliss	13

Pole Positions

1	Mike Skinner	46
2	Jack Sprague	31
3	Mike Bliss	18
	Ron Hornaday Jr.	18
5	Joe Ruttman	17
6	Greg Biffle	12
	Ted Musgrave	12
8	Jason Leffler	10
9	Stacy Compton	9
10	Terry Cook	8

Earnings

1	Jack Sprague	$6,846,738
2	Ron Hornaday Jr.	5,297,266
3	Dennis Setzer	5,063,448
4	Ted Musgrave	4,843,621
5	Rick Crawford	4,502,429
6	Terry Cook	3,671,280
7	Mike Skinner	3,646,812
8	Mike Bliss	3,425,745
9	Joe Ruttman	3,172,902
10	Travis Kvapil	3,063,502

Auto Racing Royalty

There must be something about auto racing that gets into a family's bloodstream. Generations of racers follow in each other's footsteps, working their way up the rungs of the ladder, starting in go-karts and graduating to the big time circuits. Is the need for speed in the genes? It certainly looks like it when you check out these fast-driving families, considered auto racing royalty in NASCAR and open-wheel racing.

The Allisons

Bobby (b. 12/3/1937): Collected 84 wins in 718 starts; won only Winston Cup title in 1983 at age 45; inducted into IMHOF in 1993; raced 1961-1988.

Donnie, Bobby's brother (b. 9/7/1939): Won 10 Grand National/Winston Cup races in 239 starts; raced from 1966 to 1988 on part-time basis.

Davey, Bobby's son (b. 2/25/1961, d. 7/13/1993): Won 19 Winston Cup races; killed in a 1993 helicopter accident at Talladega Superspeedway at age 32; inducted into IMHOF in 1998; raced from 1985-93.

Clifford, Bobby's son (b. 10/20/1964, d. 8/13/1992): Ran Busch Series from 1990-1992; killed in practice for a Busch Series race at Michigan in 1992 at age 27.

The Andrettis

Mario (b. 2/28/1940): Accumulated 111 career wins racing from 1961-2000; won four Champ Car titles, the 1978 Formula 1 title and the 1979 IROC crown; A.P. named him "Driver of the Century" along with A.J. Foyt.

Aldo, Mario's twin brother (b. 2/28/1940): After his second severe car crash, he retired from racing in 1969.

Michael, Mario's son (b. 10/5/1962): Raced from 1980-2003, won first Champ Car race in 1986 and joined his father's team in 1989; won only Champ Car crown in 1991; totaled 42 Champ Car wins.

Jeff, Mario's son (b. 4/14/1964): Joined father and brother in Champ Car in 1990; was 1991 Indy 500 and CART Rookie of the Year; raced from 1990-2000.

John, Aldo's son (b. 3/12/1963): Started racing in Champ Car in 1987, transitioned into NASCAR in 90's; won two Winston Cup races.

Marco, Michael's son (b. 3/13/1987) Third-generation racer debuted as rookie in Indy in 2006; surprised watchers with second place finish at Indy 500; raced Indy 500 with father, who came out of retirement to join son.

The Earnhardts

Ralph (b. 2/23/1928, d. 9/26/1973): "Mr. Consistency" in Grand National; was inducted into IMHOF in 1997; raced from 1956-1964.

Dale, Ralph's son (b. 4/29/1951, d. 2/18/2001): "The Intimidator" won ROY in 1979, seven Winston Cup titles and 76 races; more than $27 million; career was cut short by fatal crash at the 2001 Daytona 500; raced from 1975-2001.

Dale Jr., Dale's son (b. 10/10/1974): "Little E" had won 18 races and won more than $50 million midway through his eighth full season. First full season in Sprint Cup was 2000.

The Jarretts

Ned (b. 10/12/1932): won two Grand National titles; won 50 races in 352 starts; nicknamed "Gentleman Ned"; inducted into IMHOF in 1991; raced from 1953-1966.

Dale, Ned's son (b. 11/26/1956): Started full-time in Winston Cup in 1987; won title in 1999; has 32 wins; with his Cup title, the Jarretts became the second father/son duo after the Pettys to grab titles; began racing in 1984.

The Labontes

Terry (b. 11/16/1956): First NASCAR start came in 1978; won Winston Cup crowns in 1984, 1996; broke Richard Petty's streak of 513 straight starts in 1996 (his eventual record of 655 consecutive starts was broken by Ricky Rudd in 2002).

Bobby, Terry's brother (b. 5/8/1964): Won the 2000 Winston Cup title; win gave the brothers the honor of being the first sibling tandem to win the title. He is the only driver to win both a Busch Series (now Nationwide) and Cup Series championship; began racing in 1991.

The Pettys

Lee (b. 3/14/1914, d. 4/5/2000): Won 54 strictly Stock/Grand National races, three titles; photo-finish winner of the first Daytona 500 in 1959; inducted into IMHOF in 1990; raced from 1953-1966.

Richard, Lee's son (b. 7/2/1937): "The King" was a seven-time Grand National/Winston Cup champ; 200 wins; seven-time winner of the Daytona 500; won single-season record 27 races in 1967; inducted into IMHOF in 1997; raced from 1958-1992.

Kyle, Richard's son (b. 6/2/1960): More than $24M in career earnings; more than 170 top-10 finishes; began racing in 1979.

Adam, Kyle's son (b. 7/10/1980, d. 5/12/2000): Killed at New Hampshire International Speedway in preparation for only his second Winston Cup start.

The Unsers

The Unser family tree continues to sprout branches of racing addicts. Eight Unsers (Jerry Jr., Louie, Bobby Sr., Al Sr., Johnny, Bobby Jr., Robby and Al Jr.) have spent time in the pits, while third-generation motorsports converts Jason Tanner and Al Unser III are trying their hand at advancing the Unser legacy.

Bobby (b. 2/20/1934): Three-time winner of the Indy 500 (1968, 1975, 1981); 1981 win was controversial, as Mario Andretti was declared winner because Unser passed cars during yellow flag, but Unser appealed and victory was restored; 35 CART wins; raced from 1949-1982.

Al Sr., Bobby's brother (b. 5/29/1939) "Big Al" won Indy 500 four times (1970, 1971, 1978, 1987); won 1987 Indy 500 at 47 years old, the oldest winner in history; posted 39 Indy wins; raced from 1957-1994.

Al Jr., Al's son (b. 4/19/1962): "Little Al" won the Indy 500 in 1992 and 1994; lost CART points title to his father by a single point in 1985; raced from 1982 to 2004.

The Waltrips

Darrell (b. 2/5/1947): Three-time Winston Cup champ, won 1989 Daytona 500; accumulated 84 Cup victories and 59 poles; inducted into IMHOF in 2005; raced 1972-2000.

Michael, Darrell's brother (b. 4/30/1963): two-time Daytona 500 winner; has earned more than $36 million; began racing in 1985.

INDY RACING LEAGUE CIRCUIT
Indianapolis 500

Held every Memorial Day weekend; 200 laps around a 2.5-mile oval at Indianapolis Motor Speedway. First race was held in 1911. The Indy Racing League began in 1996 and made the Indianapolis 500 its cornerstone event. Winning drivers are listed with starting positions. Winners who started from pole position are in **bold** type.

Multiple wins: A.J. Foyt, Rick Mears and Al Unser (4); Louis Meyer, Mauri Rose, Johnny Rutherford, Wilbur Shaw and Bobby Unser (3); Helio Castroneves, Emerson Fittipaldi, Gordon Johncock, Arie Luyendyk, Tommy Milton, Al Unser Jr., Bill Vukovich and Rodger Ward (2).

Multiple poles: Rick Mears (6); A.J. Foyt and Rex Mays (4); Mario Andretti, Arie Luyendyk, Johnny Rutherford and Tom Sneva (3); Scott Brayton, Helio Castroneves, Bill Cummings, Ralph DePalma, Leon Duray, Parnelli Jones, Jimmy Murphy, Duke Nalon, Eddie Sachs and Bobby Unser (2).

Year	Winner (Pos.)	Car	MPH	Pole Sitter	MPH
1911	Ray Harroun (28)	Marmon Wasp	74.602	Lewis Strang	–
1912	Joe Dawson (7)	National	78.719	Gil Anderson	–
1913	Jules Goux (7)	Peugeot	75.933	Caleb Bragg	–
1914	Rene Thomas (15)	Delage	82.474	Jean Chassagne	–
1915	Ralph DePalma (2)	Mercedes	89.840	Howard Wilcox	98.90
1916-a	Dario Resta (4)	Peugeot	84.001	John Aitken	96.69
1917-18	Not held	World War I			
1919	Howdy Wilcox (2)	Peugeot	88.050	Rene Thomas	104.78
1920	Gaston Chevrolet (6)	Monroe	88.618	Ralph DePalma	99.15
1921	Tommy Milton (20)	Frontenac	89.621	Ralph DePalma	100.75
1922	**Jimmy Murphy (1)**	Murphy Special	94.484	Jimmy Murphy	100.50
1923	**Tommy Milton (1)**	H.C.S. Special	90.954	Tommy Milton	108.17
1924	L.L. Corum & Joe Boyer (21)	Duesenberg Special	98.234	Jimmy Murphy	108.037
1925	Peter DePaolo (2)	Duesenberg Special	101.127	Leon Duray	113.196
1926-b	Frank Lockhart (20)	Miller Special	95.904	Earl Cooper	111.735
1927	George Souders (22)	Duesenberg	97.545	Frank Lockhart	120.100
1928	Louie Meyer (13)	Miller Special	99.482	Leon Duray	122.391
1929	Ray Keech (6)	Simplex Piston Ring Special	97.585	Cliff Woodbury	120.599
1930	**Billy Arnold (1)**	Miller-Hartz Special	100.448	Billy Arnold	113.268
1931	Louis Schneider (13)	Bowes Seal Fast Special	96.629	Russ Snowberger	112.796
1932	Fred Frame (27)	Miller-Hartz Special	104.144	Lou Moore	117.363
1933	Louie Meyer (6)	Tydol Special	104.162	Bill Cummings	118.530
1934	Bill Cummings (10)	Boyle Products Special	104.863	Kelly Petillo	119.329
1935	Kelly Petillo (22)	Gilmore Speedway Special	106.240	Rex Mays	120.736
1936	Louie Meyer (28)	Ring Free Special	109.069	Rex Mays	119.644
1937	Wilbur Shaw (2)	Shaw-Gilmore Special	113.580	Bill Cummings	123.343
1938	**Floyd Roberts (1)**	Burd Piston Ring Special	117.200	Floyd Roberts	125.681
1939	Wilbur Shaw (3)	Boyle Special	115.035	Jimmy Snyder	130.138
1940	Wilbur Shaw (2)	Boyle Special	114.277	Rex Mays	127.850
1941	Floyd Davis & Mauri Rose (17)	Noc-Out Hose Clamp Special	115.117	Mauri Rose	128.691
1942-45	Not held	World War II			
1946	George Robson (15)	Thorne Engineering Special	114.820	Cliff Bergere	126.471
1947	Mauri Rose (3)	Blue Crown Spark Plug Special	116.338	Ted Horn	126.564
1948	Mauri Rose (3)	Blue Crown Spark Plug Special	119.814	Rex Mays	130.577
1949	Bill Holland (4)	Blue Crown Spark Plug Special	121.327	Duke Nalon	132.939
1950-c	Johnnie Parsons (5)	Wynn's Friction Proofing	124.002	Walt Faulkner	134.343
1951	Lee Wallard (2)	Belanger Special	126.244	Duke Nalon	136.498
1952	Troy Ruttman (7)	Agajanian Special	128.922	Fred Agabashian	138.010
1953	**Bill Vukovich (1)**	Fuel Injection Special	128.740	Bill Vukovich	138.392
1954	Bill Vukovich (19)	Fuel Injection Special	130.840	Jack McGrath	141.033
1955	Bob Sweikert (14)	John Zink Special	128.213	Jerry Hoyt	140.045
1956	**Pat Flaherty (1)**	John Zink Special	128.490	Pat Flaherty	145.596
1957	Sam Hanks (13)	Belond Exhaust Special	135.601	Pat O'Connor	143.948
1958	Jimmy Bryan (7)	Belond AP Parts Special	133.791	Dick Rathmann	145.974
1959	Rodger Ward (6)	Leader Card 500 Roadster	135.857	Johnny Thomson	145.908
1960	Jim Rathmann (2)	Ken-Paul Special	138.767	Eddie Sachs	146.592
1961	A.J. Foyt (7)	Bowes Seal Fast Special	139.130	Eddie Sachs	147.481
1962	Rodger Ward (2)	Leader Card 500 Roadster	140.293	Parnelli Jones	150.370
1963	**Parnelli Jones (1)**	Agajanian-Willard Special	143.137	Parnelli Jones	151.153
1964	A.J. Foyt (5)	Sheraton-Thompson Special	147.350	Jim Clark	158.828
1965	Jim Clark (2)	Lotus Ford	150.686	A.J. Foyt	161.233
1966	Graham Hill (15)	American Red Ball Special	144.317	Mario Andretti	165.899
1967-d	A.J. Foyt (4)	Sheraton-Thompson Special	151.207	Mario Andretti	168.982
1968	Bobby Unser (3)	Rislone Special	152.882	Joe Leonard	171.559
1969	Mario Andretti (2)	STP Oil Treatment Special	156.867	A.J. Foyt	170.568
1970	**Al Unser (1)**	Johnny Lightning Special	155.749	Al Unser	170.221
1971	Al Unser (5)	Johnny Lightning Special	157.735	Peter Revson	178.696
1972	Mark Donohue (3)	Sunoco McLaren	162.962	Bobby Unser	195.940
1973-e	Gordon Johncock (11)	STP Double Oil Filters	159.036	Johnny Rutherford	198.413

Year	Winner (Pos.)	Car	MPH	Pole Sitter	MPH
1974	Johnny Rutherford (25)	McLaren	158.589	A.J. Foyt	191.632
1975-f	Bobby Unser (3)	Jorgensen Eagle	149.213	A.J. Foyt	193.976
1976-g	**Johnny Rutherford** (1)	Hy-Gain McLaren/Goodyear	148.725	Johnny Rutherford	188.957
1977	A.J. Foyt (4)	Gilmore Racing Team	161.331	Tom Sneva	198.884
1978	Al Unser (5)	FNCTC Chaparral Lola	161.363	Tom Sneva	202.156
1979	**Rick Mears** (1)	The Gould Charge	158.899	Rick Mears	193.736
1980	**Johnny Rutherford** (1)	Pennzoil Chaparral	142.862	Johnny Rutherford	192.256
1981-h	**Bobby Unser** (1)	Norton Spirit Penske PC-9B	139.084	Bobby Unser	200.546
1982	Gordon Johncock (5)	STP Oil Treatment	162.029	Rick Mears	207.004
1983	Tom Sneva (4)	Texaco Star	162.117	Teo Fabi	207.395
1984	Rick Mears (3)	Pennzoil Z-7	163.612	Tom Sneva	210.029
1985	Danny Sullivan (8)	Miller American Special	152.982	Pancho Carter	212.583
1986	Bobby Rahal (4)	Budweiser/Truesports/March	170.722	Rick Mears	216.828
1987	Al Unser (20)	Cummins Holset Turbo	162.175	Mario Andretti	215.390
1988	**Rick Mears** (1)	Pennzoil Z-7/Penske Chevy V-8	144.809	Rick Mears	219.198
1989	Emerson Fittipaldi (3)	Marlboro/Penske Chevy V-8	167.581	Rick Mears	223.885
1990	Arie Luyendyk (3)	Domino's Pizza Chevrolet	185.981*	Emerson Fittipaldi	225.301
1991	**Rick Mears** (1)	Marlboro Penske Chevy	176.457	Rick Mears	224.113
1992	Al Unser Jr. (12)	Valvoline Galmer '92	134.477	Roberto Guerrero	232.482
1993	Emerson Fittipaldi (9)	Marlboro Penske Chevy	157.207	Arie Luyendyk	223.967
1994	**Al Unser Jr.** (1)	Marlboro Penske Mercedes	160.872	Al Unser Jr.	228.011
1995	Jacques Villeneuve (5)	Player's Ltd. Reynard Ford	153.616	Scott Brayton	231.604
1996	Buddy Lazier (5)	Reynard Ford	147.956	Tony Stewart	233.100&
1997	**Arie Luyendyk** (1)	G-Force Olds Aurora	145.827	Arie Luyendyk	218.263
1998	Eddie Cheever Jr. (17)	Dallara Olds Aurora	145.155	Billy Boat	223.503
1999	Kenny Brack (8)	Dallara Olds Aurora	153.176	Arie Luyendyk	225.179
2000	Juan Montoya (2)	G-Force Olds Aurora	167.607	Greg Ray	223.471
2001	Helio Castroneves (11)	Dallara Olds Aurora	153.601	Scott Sharp	226.037
2002-i	Helio Castroneves (13)	Dallara Chevrolet	166.499	Bruno Junqueira	231.342
2003	Gil de Ferran (10)	G-Force Toyota	156.291	Helio Castroneves	231.725
2004-j	**Buddy Rice** (1)	G-Force Honda	138.518	Buddy Rice	222.024
2005	Dan Wheldon (16)	Dallara Honda	157.603	Tony Kanaan	227.566
2006	**Sam Hornish Jr.** (1)	Dallara Honda	157.085	Sam Hornish Jr.	228.985
2007-k	Dario Franchitti (3)	Dallara Honda	151.774	Helio Castroneves	225.817
2008	**Scott Dixon** (1)	Dallara Honda	143.567	Scott Dixon	226.366

*Track record for winning time.

& Scott Brayton won the pole position with an avg. mph of 233.718 but was killed in a practice run. Stewart was awarded pole position with the next fastest speed.

Notes: a—1916 race scheduled for 300 miles; **b**—rain shortened 1926 race to 400 miles; **c**—rain shortened 1950 race to 345 miles; **d**—1967 race postponed due to rain after 18 laps (May 30), resumed next day (May 31); **e**—rain shortened 1973 race to 332.5 miles; **f**—rain shortened 1975 race to 435 miles; **g**—rain shortened 1976 race to 255 miles; **h**—in 1981, runner-up Mario Andretti was awarded 1st place when winner Bobby Unser was penalized a lap after the race was completed for passing cars illegally under the caution flag. Unser and car-owner Roger Penske appealed the race stewards' decision to the U.S. Auto Club. Four months later, USAC overturned the ruling, saying that the penalty was too harsh and Unser should be fined $40,000 rather than stripped of his championship; **i**—Team Green, runner-up Paul Tracy's team, appealed Castroneves' victory, citing video evidence and driver testimonials that proved Tracy passed Castroneves moments before the caution flag on lap 199. The IRL denied the appeal the following day; **j**—rain shortened 2004 race to 450 miles; **k**—rain shortened 2007 race to 415 miles.

Indy 500 Rookie of the Year

Officially the Chase Rookie of the Year Award and voted on by a panel of auto racing media. Award does not necessarily go to highest-finishing first-year driver. Graham Hill won the race on his first try in 1966, but the rookie award went to Jackie Stewart, who led with 10 laps to go only to lose oil pressure and finish 6th.

Father and son winners: Mario and Michael Andretti (1965 and 1984); Michael and Marco Andretti (1984 and 2006); Bill and Billy Vukovich III (1968 and 1988).

Year		Year		Year		Year	
1952	Art Cross	1967	Denis Hulme	1982	Jim Hickman	1996	Tony Stewart
1953	Jimmy Daywalt	1968	Bill Vukovich	1983	Teo Fabi	1997	Jeff Ward
1954	Larry Crockett	1969	Mark Donohue	1984	Michael Andretti	1998	Steve Knapp
1955	Al Herman	1970	Donnie Allison		& Roberto Guerrero	1999	Robby McGehee
1956	Bob Veith	1971	Denny Zimmerman	1985	Arie Luyendyk	2000	Juan Montoya
1957	Don Edmunds	1972	Mike Hiss	1986	Randy Lanier	2001	Helio Castroneves
1958	George Amick	1973	Graham McRae	1987	Fabrizio Barbazza	2002	Alex Barron
1959	Bobby Grim	1974	Pancho Carter	1988	Billy Vukovich III		& Tomas Scheckter
1960	Jim Hurtubise	1975	Bill Puterbaugh	1989	Bernard Jourdain	2003	Tora Takagi
1961	Parnelli Jones	1976	Vern Schuppan		& Scott Pruett	2004	Kosuke Matsuura
	& Bobby Marshman	1977	Jerry Sneva	1990	Eddie Cheever	2005	Danica Patrick
1962	Jimmy McElreath	1978	Rick Mears	1991	Jeff Andretti	2006	Marco Andretti
1963	Jim Clark		& Larry Rice	1992	Lyn St. James	2007	Phil Giebler
1964	Johnny White	1979	Howdy Holmes	1993	Nigel Mansell	2008	Ryan Hunter-Reay
1965	Mario Andretti	1980	Tim Richmond	1994	Jacques Villeneuve		
1966	Jackie Stewart	1981	Josele Garza	1995	Christian Fittipaldi		

Indy Racing League Circuit (Cont.)

IRL IndyCar Series Champions

The Indy Racing League (IRL) split from the open-wheel CART series in 1994, then re-unified with what became the Champ Car World Series in 2008. Past series' sponsors include Pep Boys (1998-99) and Northern Light Technology, Inc., an Internet search engine (2000-01). **Multiple winners:** Sam Hornish Jr. (3); Scott Dixon (2).

Year	Driver	Car	Team	Sts	Wins	Poles	Earnings
1996	**Buzz Calkins**	Reynard Ford	A.J. Foyt Enterprises	3	1	0	$345,553
	Scott Sharp	Lola Ford	A.J. Foyt Enterprises	3	0	0	330,303
1997	**Tony Stewart**	Dallara Oldsmobile	Team Menard	10	1	4	1,142,450
1998	**Kenny Brack**	Dallara Oldsmobile	A.J. Foyt Enterprises	11	3	0	2,106,700
1999	**Greg Ray**	Dallara Oldsmobile	Team Menard	10	3	4	2,061,800
2000	**Buddy Lazier**	Dallara Oldsmobile	Hemelgarn Racing	9	2	1	2,176,200
2001	**Sam Hornish Jr.**	Dallara Oldsmobile	Panther Racing	13	3	0	2,477,025
2002	**Sam Hornish Jr.**	Dallara Oldsmobile	Panther Racing	15	5	2	2,470,615
2003	**Scott Dixon**	G-Force Toyota	Target Chip Ganassi	16	3	5	1,481,265
2004	**Tony Kanaan**	Dallara Honda	Andretti Green Racing	16	3	2	1,912,990
2005	**Dan Wheldon**	Dallara Honda	Andretti Green Racing	17	6	0	2,711,005
2006	**Sam Hornish Jr.**	Dallara Honda	Marlboro Team Penske	14	4	4	2,775,205
2007	**Dario Franchitti**	Dallara Honda	Andretti Green Racing	17	4	4	4,017,583
2008	**Scott Dixon**	Dallara Honda	Target Chip Ganassi	17	6	6	not available

Note: In 1996, Calkins and Sharp were named co-champions after finishing the series tied in drivers' points (246).

IRL Rookie of the Year

Officially the Bombardier Rookie of the Year Award, presented to rookie driver who accumulates the most points in the IRL standings.

Year		Year		Year		Year	
1996	None	2000	Airton Dare	2004	Kosuke Matsuura	2008	Hideki Mutoh
1997	Jim Guthrie	2001	Felipe Giaffone	2005	Danica Patrick		
1998	Robby Unser	2002	Laurent Redon	2006	Marco Andretti		
1999	Scott Harrington	2003	Dan Wheldon	2007	Ryan Hunter-Reay		

All-Time IRL Leaders

IRL IndyCar Series all-time Top 10 drivers in victories and pole positions through 2008, and unofficial earnings through 2007. Earnings totals include season-ending contingency awards.

Victories

1 Sam Hornish Jr. 19
2 Scott Dixon 16
3 Dan Wheldon 15
4 Helio Castroneves 14
5 Tony Kanaan 13
6 Scott Sharp 9
7 Buddy Lazier 8
   Dario Franchitti 8
9 Eddie Cheever Jr. 5
   Greg Ray 5
   Gil de Ferran 5

Pole Positions

1 Helio Castroneves 26
2 Scott Dixon 14
3 Greg Ray 13
4 Sam Hornish Jr. 10
   Tony Kanaan 10
6 Billy Boat 9
7 Tomas Scheckter 7
8 Tony Stewart 7
9 Dario Franchitti 6
   Scott Sharp 6

Earnings

1 Sam Hornish Jr. . . .$14,466,094
2 Helio Castroneves . .11,109,108
3 Buddy Lazier 10,405,514
4 Scott Sharp 10,321,563
5 Dan Wheldon 9,233,420
6 Tony Kanaan 9,153,319
7 Scott Dixon 7,948,982
8 Dario Franchitti 7,720,798
9 Eddie Cheever Jr. . . .6,763,298
10 Buddy Rice 6,258,215

CHAMP CAR CIRCUIT

Champ Car Series Champions

Formerly, AAA (American Automobile Assn., 1909-55), USAC (U.S. Auto Club, 1956-78), CART (Championship Auto Racing Teams, 1979-91). CART was renamed IndyCar in 1992 and then lost use of the name in 1997. It was known as the FedEx Championship Series from 1998-2002 and the "Bridgestone Presents The Champ Car World Series Powered by Ford" from 2003-06. **Merged with IndyCar Series beginning in 2008.**

Multiple titles: A.J. Foyt (7); Mario Andretti and Sebastien Bourdais (4); Jimmy Bryan, Earl Cooper, Ted Horn, Rick Mears, Louie Meyer, Bobby Rahal, Al Unser (3); Tony Bettenhausen, Gil de Ferran, Ralph DePalma, Peter DePaolo, Joe Leonard, Rex Mays, Tommy Milton, Ralph Mulford, Jimmy Murphy, Wilbur Shaw, Al Unser Jr., Bobby Unser, Rodger Ward and Alex Zanardi (2).

AAA

Year		Year		Year		Year	
1909	George Robertson	1920	Tommy Milton	1931	Louis Schneider	1942-45	No racing
1910	Ray Harroun	1921	Tommy Milton	1932	Bob Carey	1946	Ted Horn
1911	Ralph Mulford	1922	Jimmy Murphy	1933	Louie Meyer	1947	Ted Horn
1912	Ralph DePalma	1923	Eddie Hearne	1934	Bill Cummings	1948	Ted Horn
1913	Earl Cooper	1924	Jimmy Murphy	1935	Kelly Petillo	1949	Johnnie Parsons
1914	Ralph DePalma	1925	Peter DePaolo	1936	Mauri Rose	1950	Henry Banks
1915	Earl Cooper	1926	Harry Hartz	1937	Wilbur Shaw	1951	Tony Bettenhausen
1916	Dario Resta	1927	Peter DePaolo	1938	Floyd Roberts	1952	Chuck Stevenson
1917	Earl Cooper	1928	Louie Meyer	1939	Wilbur Shaw	1953	Sam Hanks
1918	Ralph Mulford	1929	Louie Meyer	1940	Rex Mays	1954	Jimmy Bryan
1919	Howard Wilcox	1930	Billy Arnold	1941	Rex Mays	1955	Bob Sweikert

USAC

Champ Car World Series (formerly CART)

Year	Driver	Car	Team	Sts	Wins	Poles	Earnings
1979	Rick Mears	Penske Ford	Penske	14	3	2	$408,078
1980	Johnny Rutherford	Chaparral Ford	Chaparral	12	5	3	503,595
1981	Rick Mears	Penske Ford	Penske	11	6	2	323,670
1982	Rick Mears	Penske Ford	Penske	11	4	8	306,454
1983	Al Unser	Penske Ford	Penske	13	1	0	500,109
1984	Mario Andretti	Lola Ford	Newman/Haas	16	6	8	931,929
1985	Al Unser	March Ford	Penske	14	1	1	843,885
1986	Bobby Rahal	March Ford	TrueSports	17	6	2	1,488,049
1987	Bobby Rahal	Lola Ford	TrueSports	15	3	1	1,261,098
1988	Danny Sullivan	Penske Chevrolet	Penske	15	4	9	1,222,791
1989	Emerson Fittipaldi	Penske Chevrolet	Patrick	15	5	4	2,166,078
1990	Al Unser Jr.	Lola Chevrolet	Galles-Kraco	16	6	1	1,946,833
1991	Michael Andretti	Lola Chevrolet	Newman/Haas	17	8	8	2,461,734
1992	Bobby Rahal	Lola Chevrolet	Rahal-Hogan	16	4	3	2,235,298
1993	Nigel Mansell	Lola Ford	Newman/Haas	15	5	7	2,526,953
1994	Al Unser Jr.	Penske Ilmor	Marlboro Team Penske	16	8	4	3,535,813
1995	Jacques Villeneuve	Reynard Ford	Team Green	17	4	6	2,996,269
1996	Jimmy Vasser	Reynard Honda	Target Chip Ganassi	16	4	4	3,071,500
1997	Alex Zanardi	Reynard Honda	Target Chip Ganassi	16	5	4	2,096,250
1998	Alex Zanardi	Reynard Honda	Target Chip Ganassi	19	7	0	2,229,250
1999	Juan Montoya	Reynard Honda	Target Chip Ganassi	20	7	7	1,973,000
2000	Gil de Ferran	Reynard Honda	Marlboro Team Penske	20	2	5	1,677,000
2001	Gil de Ferran	Reynard Honda	Marlboro Team Penske	20	2	5	1,761,500
2002	Cristiano da Matta	Lola Toyota	Newman/Haas	19	7	7	2,053,000
2003	Paul Tracy	Lola Ford-Cosworth	Player's/Forsythe	18	7	6	1,007,000
2004	Sebastien Bourdais	Lola Ford-Cosworth	Newman/Haas	14	7	8	843,500
2005	Sebastien Bourdais	Lola Ford-Cosworth	Newman/Haas	13	6	5	668,500
2006	Sebastien Bourdais	DP01-Cosworth	Newman/Haas/Lanigan	14	7	7	757,500
2007	Sebastien Bourdais	DP01-Cosworth	Newman/Haas/Lanigan	14	8	6	761,000
2008	Merged with IndyCar Series						

Champ Car Rookie of the Year

Officially the Roshfrans Rookie of the Year Award and presented to the rookie who accumulates the most Champ Car Series points among first year drivers. Roshfrans is the official lubricant of Champ Car.

All-Time Champ Car Leaders

Champ Car's all-time Top 10 drivers in victories, pole positions and earnings, based on records through 2007. Totals include victories, poles and earnings before Champ Car (then CART) was established in 1979. Earnings totals include year-end performance awards. Note that Champ Car merged with IndyCar in 2008.

Victories

1. A.J. Foyt 67
2. Mario Andretti 52
3. Michael Andretti 42
4. Al Unser 39
5. Bobby Unser 35
6. Al Unser Jr. 31
   Paul Tracy 31
8. Sebastien Bourdais 30
9. Rick Mears 29
10. Johnny Rutherford 27

Pole Positions

1. Mario Andretti 67
2. A.J. Foyt 53
3. Bobby Unser 49
4. Rick Mears 40
5. Michael Andretti 32
6. Sebastien Bourdais 31
7. Al Unser 27
8. Paul Tracy 25
9. Johnny Rutherford 23
10. Gordon Johncock 20

Earnings (unofficial)

1. Al Unser Jr. $18,828,406
2. Michael Andretti . .18,228,119
3. Bobby Rahal 16,344,008
4. Emerson Fittipaldi .14,293,625
5. Jimmy Vasser 12,125,726
6. Mario Andretti . . .11,552,154
7. Paul Tracy 11,497,270
8. Rick Mears 11,050,807
9. Danny Sullivan 8,884,126
10. Arie Luyendyk 7,732,188

FORMULA ONE CIRCUIT
United States Grand Prix

Federation Internationale Sportive Automobile (FISA) sanctioned two annual U.S. Grand Prix–USA/East and USA/West–from 1976-80 and 1983-84. Phoenix was the site of the U.S. Grand Prix from 1989-91. Indianapolis Motor Speedway has hosted the U.S. Grand Prix since 2000.

Indianapolis 500
Officially sanctioned as Grand Prix race from 1950-60 only. See page 904 for details.

U.S. Grand Prix—East

Held from 1959-80 and 1981-88 at the following locations: Sebring, Fla. (1959); Riverside, Calif. (1960); Watkins Glen, N.Y. (1961-80); and Detroit (1982-88). There was no race in 1981. Race discontinued in 1989.

Multiple winners: Jim Clark, Graham Hill and Ayrton Senna (3); James Hunt, Carlos Reutemann and Jackie Stewart (2).

Year	Driver	Car	Year	Driver	Car
1959	Bruce McLaren, NZE	Cooper Climax	1974	Carlos Reutemann, ARG	Brabham Ford
1960	Stirling Moss, GBR	Lotus Climax	1975	Niki Lauda, AUT	Ferrari
1961	Innes Ireland, GBR	Lotus Climax	1976	James Hunt, GBR	McLaren Ford
1962	Jim Clark, GBR	Lotus Climax	1977	James Hunt, GBR	McLaren Ford
1963	Graham Hill, GBR	BRM	1978	Carlos Reutemann, ARG	Ferrari
1964	Graham Hill, GBR	BRM	1979	Gilles Villeneuve, CAN	Ferrari
1965	Graham Hill, GBR	BRM	1980	Alan Jones, AUS	Williams Ford
1966	Jim Clark, GBR	Lotus BRM	1981	Not held	
1967	Jim Clark, GBR	Lotus Ford	1982	John Watson, GBR	McLaren Ford
1968	Jackie Stewart, GBR	Matra Ford	1983	Michele Alboreto, ITA	Tyrrell Ford
1969	Jochen Rindt, AUT	Lotus Ford	1984	Nelson Piquet, BRA	Brabham BMW Turbo
1970	Emerson Fittipaldi, BRA	Lotus Ford	1985	Keke Rosberg, FIN	Williams Honda Turbo
1971	Francois Cevert, FRA	Tyrrell Ford	1986	Ayrton Senna, BRA	Lotus Renault Turbo
1972	Jackie Stewart, GBR	Tyrrell Ford	1987	Ayrton Senna, BRA	Lotus Honda Turbo
1973	Ronnie Peterson, SWE	Lotus Ford	1988	Ayrton Senna, BRA	McLaren Honda Turbo

U.S. Grand Prix—West

Held from 1976-83 at Long Beach, Calif. Races also held in Las Vegas (1981-82), Dallas (1984) and Phoenix (1989-91). Race discontinued in 1992.

Multiple winners: Alan Jones and Ayrton Senna (2).

Year	Driver	Car	Year	Driver	Car
1976	Clay Regazzoni, SWI	Ferrari	1983	John Watson, GBR	McLaren Ford
1977	Mario Andretti, USA	Lotus Ford	1984	Keke Rosberg, FIN	Williams Honda Turbo
1978	Carlos Reutemann, ARG	Ferrari	1985-88	Not held	
1979	Gilles Villeneuve, CAN	Ferrari	1989	Alain Prost, FRA	McLaren Honda
1980	Nelson Piquet, BRA	Brabham Ford	1990	Ayrton Senna, BRA	McLaren Honda
1981	Alan Jones, AUS	Williams Ford	1991	Ayrton Senna, BRA	McLaren Honda
1982	Niki Lauda, AUT	McLaren Ford			

U.S. Grand Prix
Held from 2000-07 at Indianapolis Motor Speedway.

Multiple winner: Michael Schumacher (4).

Year	Driver	Car	Year	Driver	Car
2000	Michael Schumacher, GER	Ferrari	2004	Michael Schumacher, GER	Ferrari
2001	Mika Hakkinen, FIN	McLaren Mercedes	2005	Michael Schumacher, GER	Ferrari
2002	Rubens Barrichello, BRA	Ferrari	2006	Michael Schumacher, GER	Ferrari
2003	Michael Schumacher, GER	Ferrari	2007	Lewis Hamilton, GBR	McLaren-Mercedes

World Champions

Officially called the World Championship of Drivers and based on Formula One (Grand Prix) records through the 2007 season.

Multiple winners: Michael Schumacher (7); Juan-Manuel Fangio (5); Alain Prost (4); Jack Brabham, Niki Lauda, Nelson Piquet, Ayrton Senna and Jackie Stewart (3); Fernando Alonso, Alberto Ascari, Jim Clark, Emerson Fittipaldi, Mika Hakkinen and Graham Hill (2).

Year	Driver	Country	Car	Sts	Wins	Poles	Runner(s)-up
1950	**Guiseppe Farina**	Italy	Alfa Romeo	7	3	2	J.M. Fangio, ARG
1951	**Juan-Manuel Fangio**	Argentina	Alfa Romeo	8	3	4	A. Ascari, ITA
1952	**Alberto Ascari**	Italy	Ferrari	8	6	5	G. Farina, ITA
1953	**Alberto Ascari**	Italy	Ferrari	9	5	6	J.M. Fangio, ARG
1954	**Juan-Manuel Fangio**	Argentina	Maserati/Mercedes	9	6	5	F. Gonzalez, ARG
1955	**Juan-Manuel Fangio**	Argentina	Mercedes	7	4	3	S. Moss, GBR
1956	**Juan-Manuel Fangio**	Argentina	Lancia/Ferrari	8	3	5	S. Moss, GBR
1957	**Juan-Manuel Fangio**	Argentina	Maserati	8	4	4	S. Moss, GBR
1958	**Mike Hawthorn**	Great Britain	Ferrari	11	1	4	S. Moss, GBR
1959	**Jack Brabham**	Australia	Cooper Climax	9	2	1	T. Brooks, GBR
1960	**Jack Brabham**	Australia	Cooper Climax	10	5	3	B. McLaren, NZE

Year	Driver	Country	Car	Sts	Wins	Poles	Runner(s)-up
1961	Phil Hill	United States	Ferrari	8	2	5	W. von Trips, GER
1962	Graham Hill	Great Britain	BRM	9	4	1	J. Clark, GBR
1963	Jim Clark	Great Britain	Lotus Climax	10	7	7	G. Hill, GBR
							& R. Ginther, USA
1964	John Surtees	Great Britain	Ferrari	10	2	2	G. Hill, GBR
1965	Jim Clark	Great Britain	Lotus Climax	10	6	6	G. Hill, GBR
1966	Jack Brabham	Australia	Brabham Repco	9	4	3	J. Surtees, GBR
1967	Denis Hulme	New Zealand	Brabham Repco	11	2	0	J. Brabham, AUS
1968	Graham Hill	Great Britain	Lotus Ford	12	3	2	J. Stewart, GBR
1969	Jackie Stewart	Great Britain	Matra Ford	11	6	2	J. Ickx, BEL
1970	Jochen Rindt	Austria	Lotus Ford	13	5	3	J. Ickx, BEL
1971	Jackie Stewart	Great Britain	Tyrrell Ford	11	6	6	R. Peterson, SWE
1972	Emerson Fittipaldi	Brazil	Lotus Ford	12	5	3	J. Stewart, GBR
1973	Jackie Stewart	Great Britain	Tyrrell Ford	15	5	3	E. Fittipaldi, BRA
1974	Emerson Fittipaldi	Brazil	McLaren Ford	15	3	2	C. Regazzoni, SWI
1975	Niki Lauda	Austria	Ferrari	14	5	9	E. Fittipaldi, BRA
1976	James Hunt	Great Britain	McLaren Ford	16	6	8	N. Lauda, AUT
1977	Niki Lauda	Austria	Ferrari	17	3	2	J. Scheckter, RSA
1978	Mario Andretti	United States	Lotus Ford	16	6	8	R. Peterson, SWE
1979	Jody Scheckter	South Africa	Ferrari	15	3	1	G. Villeneuve, CAN
1980	Alan Jones	Australia	Williams Ford	14	5	3	N. Piquet, BRA
1981	Nelson Piquet	Brazil	Brabham Ford	15	3	4	C. Reutemann, ARG
1982	Keke Rosberg	Finland	Williams Ford	16	1	1	D. Pironi, FRA
							& J. Watson, GBR
1983	Nelson Piquet	Brazil	Brabham BMW Turbo	15	3	1	A. Prost, FRA
1984	Niki Lauda	Austria	McL. TAG Turbo	16	5	0	A. Prost, FRA
1985	Alain Prost	France	McL. TAG Turbo	16	5	2	M. Alboreto, ITA
1986	Alain Prost	France	McL. TAG Turbo	16	4	1	N. Mansell, GBR
1987	Nelson Piquet	Brazil	Williams Honda Turbo	16	3	4	N. Mansell, GBR
1988	Ayrton Senna	Brazil	McLaren Honda Turbo	16	8	13	A. Prost, FRA
1989	Alain Prost	France	McLaren Honda	16	4	2	A. Senna, BRA
1990	Ayrton Senna	Brazil	McLaren Honda	16	6	10	A. Prost, FRA
1991	Ayrton Senna	Brazil	McLaren Honda	16	7	8	N. Mansell, GBR
1992	Nigel Mansell	Great Britain	Williams Renault	16	9	14	R. Patrese, ITA
1993	Alain Prost	France	Williams Renault	16	7	13	A. Senna, BRA
1994	Michael Schumacher	Germany	Benetton Ford	14	8	6	D. Hill, GBR
1995	Michael Schumacher	Germany	Benetton Renault	17	9	4	D. Hill, GBR
1996	Damon Hill	Great Britain	Williams Renault	16	8	9	J. Villeneuve, CAN
1997	Jacques Villeneuve	Canada	Williams Renault	17	7	10	H.H. Frentzen, GER
1998	Mika Hakkinen	Finland	McLaren Mercedes	16	8	9	M. Schumacher, GER
1999	Mika Hakkinen	Finland	McLaren Mercedes	16	5	11	E. Irvine, GBR
2000	Michael Schumacher	Germany	Ferrari	17	9	9	M. Hakkinen, FIN
2001	Michael Schumacher	Germany	Ferrari	17	9	11	D. Coulthard, GBR
2002	Michael Schumacher	Germany	Ferrari	17	11	7	R. Barrichello, BRA
2003	Michael Schumacher	Germany	Ferrari	16	6	5	K. Raikkonen, FIN
2004	Michael Schumacher	Germany	Ferrari	18	13	8	R. Barrichello, BRA
2005	Fernando Alonso	Spain	Renault	19	7	6	K. Raikkonen, FIN
2006	Fernando Alonso	Spain	Renault	18	7	6	M. Schumacher, GER
2007	Kimi Raikkonen	Finland	Ferrari	17	6	3	F. Alonso, SPA
							& L. Hamilton, GBR

All-Time Leaders

The all-time Top 15 Grand Prix winning drivers, based on records through 2008. Listed are starts (Sts), poles won (Pole), wins (1st), second place finishes (2nd), and third (3rd). Drivers active in 2008 and career victories in **bold** type.

		Sts	Pole	1st	2nd	3rd			Sts	Pole	1st	2nd	3rd
1	Michael Schumacher	.249	68	**91**	43	20	10	Damon Hill	.99	20	**22**	15	5
2	Alain Prost	.199	33	**51**	35	20	11	**Fernando Alonso**	.122	17	**21**	18	12
3	Ayrton Senna	.161	65	**41**	23	16	12	Mika Hakkinen	.163	27	**20**	14	17
4	Nigel Mansell	.187	32	**31**	17	11	13	**Kimi Raikkonen**	.105	18	**17**	18	17
5	Jackie Stewart	.99	17	**27**	11	5	14	Stirling Moss	.66	16	**16**	5	3
6	Jim Clark	.72	33	**25**	1	6	15	Jack Brabham	.126	13	**14**	10	7
	Niki Lauda	.171	24	**25**	20	9		Emerson Fittipaldi	.144	6	**14**	13	8
8	Juan-Manuel Fangio	.51	28	**24**	10	1		Graham Hill	.176	13	**14**	15	7
9	Nelson Piquet	.207	24	**23**	20	17							

ENDURANCE RACES

The 24 Hours of Le Mans

Officially, the Le Mans Grand Prix. First run May 22-23, 1923. All subsequent races have been held in June, except in 1956 (July) and 1968 (September). Originally contested on a 10.73-mile track, the circuit was shortened to 8.383 miles in 1932 and has fluxuated around 8.5 miles ever since.

Multiple winners: Tom Kristensen (8); Jacky Ickx (6); Derek Bell, Frank Biela and Emanuele Pirro (5); Yannick Dalmas, Oliver Gendebien and Henri Pescarolo (4); Woolf Barnato, Rinaldo Capello, Luigi Chinetti, Hurley Haywood, Phil Hill, Al Holbert, Klaus Ludwig and Marco Werner (3); Sir Henry Birkin, Ivoe Bueb, Ron Flockhart, Jean-Pierre Jaussaud, Gerard Larrousse, JJ Lehto, Allan McNish, Andre Rossignol, Raymond Sommer, Hans Stuck, Gijs van Lennep, and Jean-Pierre Wimille (2).

Year	Drivers	Car	MPH
1923	Andre Lagache & Rene Leonard	Chenard & Walcker	57.21
1924	John Duff & Francis Clement	Bentley	53.78
1925	Gerard de Courcelles & Andre Rossignol	La Lorraine	57.84
1926	Robert Bloch & Andre Rossignol	La Lorraine	66.08
1927	J.D. Benjafield & Sammy Davis	Bentley	61.35
1928	Woolf Barnato & Bernard Rubin	Bentley	69.11
1929	Woolf Barnato & Sir Henry Birkin	Bentley Speed 6	73.63
1930	Woolf Barnato & Glen Kidston	Bentley Speed 6	75.88
1931	Earl Howe & Sir Henry Birkin	Alfa Romeo	78.13
1932	Raymond Sommer & Luigi Chinetti	Alfa Romeo	76.48
1933	Raymond Sommer & Tazio Nuvolari	Alfa Romeo	81.40
1934	Luigi Chinetti & Philippe Etancelin	Alfa Romeo	74.74
1935	John Hindmarsh & Louis Fontes	Lagonda	77.85
1936	Not held		
1937	Jean-Pierre Wimille & Robert Benoist	Bugatti 57G	85.13
1938	Eugene Chaboud & Jean Tremoulet	Delahaye	82.36
1939	Jean-Pierre Wimille & Pierre Veyron	Bugatti 57G	86.86
1940-48	Not held		
1949	Luigi Chinetti & Lord Selsdon	Ferrari	82.28
1950	Louis Rosier & Jean-Louis Rosier	Talbot-Lago	89.71
1951	Peter Walker & Peter Whitehead	Jaguar C	93.50
1952	Hermann Lang & Fritz Reiss	Mercedes-Benz	96.67
1953	Tony Rolt & Duncan Hamilton	Jaguar C	98.65
1954	Froilan Gonzalez & Maurice Trintignant	Ferrari 375	105.13
1955	Mike Hawthorn & Ivor Bueb	Jaguar D	107.05
1956	Ron Flockhart & Ninian Sanderson	Jaguar D	104.47
1957	Ron Flockhart & Ivor Bueb	Jaguar D	113.83
1958	Oliver Gendebien & Phil Hill	Ferrari 250	106.18
1959	Roy Salvadori & Carroll Shelby	Aston Martin	112.55
1960	Oliver Gendebien & Paul Fräre	Ferrari 250	109.17
1961	Oliver Gendebien & Phil Hill	Ferrari 250	115.88
1962	Oliver Gendebien & Phil Hill	Ferrari 250	115.22
1963	Lodovico Scarfiotti & Lorenzo Bandini	Ferrari 250	118.08
1964	Jean Guichel & Nino Vaccarella	Ferrari 275	121.54
1965	Masten Gregory & Jochen Rindt	Ferrari 250	121.07
1966	Bruce McLaren & Chris Amon	Ford Mk. II	125.37
1967	A.J. Foyt & Dan Gurney	Ford Mk. IV	135.46
1968	Pedro Rodriguez & Lucien Bianchi	Ford GT40	115.27
1969	Jacky Ickx & Jackie Oliver	Ford GT40	129.38
1970	Hans Herrmann & Richard Attwood	Porsche 917	119.28
1971	Gijs van Lennep & Helmut Marko	Porsche 917	138.13
1972	Graham Hill & Henri Pescarolo	Matra-Simca	121.45
1973	Henri Pescarolo & Gerard Larrousse	Matra-Simca	125.67
1974	Henri Pescarolo & Gerard Larrousse	Matra-Simca	119.27
1975	Derek Bell & Jacky Ickx	Mirage-Ford	118.98
1976	Jacky Ickx & Gijs van Lennep	Porsche 936	123.49
1977	Jacky Ickx, Jurgen Barth & Hurley Haywood	Porsche 936	120.95
1978	Jean-Pierre Jaussaud & Didier Pironi	Renault-Alpine	130.60
1979	Klaus Ludwig, Bill Wittington & Don Whittington	Porsche 935	108.10
1980	Jean-Pierre Jaussaud & Jean Rondeau	Rondeau-Cosworth	119.23
1981	Jacky Ickx & Derek Bell	Porsche 936	124.94
1982	Jacky Ickx & Derek Bell	Porsche 956	126.85
1983	Vern Schuppan, Hurley Haywood & Al Holbert	Porsche 956	130.70
1984	Klaus Ludwig & Henri Pescarolo	Porsche 956	126.88
1985	Klaus Ludwig, Paolo Barilla & John Winter	Porsche 956	131.75
1986	Derek Bell, Hans Stuck & Al Holbert	Porsche 962	128.75
1987	Derek Bell, Hans Stuck & Al Holbert	Porsche 962	124.06
1988	Jan Lammers, Johnny Dumfries & Andy Wallace	Jaguar XJR	137.75
1989	Jochen Mass, Manuel Reuter & Stanley Dickens	Sauber-Mercedes	136.39
1990	John Nielsen, Price Cobb & Martin Brundle	Jaguar XJR-12	126.71
1991	Volker Weider, Johnny Herbert & Bertrand Gachof	Mazda 787B	127.31

Year	Drivers Car	MPH
1992	Derek Warwick, Yannick Dalmas & Mark Blundell ..... Peugeot 905B	123.89
1993	Geoff Brabham, Christophe Bouchut & Eric Helary ...... Peugeot 905	132.58
1994	Yannick Dalmas, Hurley Haywood & Mauro Baldi .... Porsche 962LM	129.82
1995	Yannick Dalmas, JJ Lehto & Masanori Sekiya ... McLaren BMW	105.00
1996	Davy Jones, Manuel Reuter & Alexander Wurz ...TWR Porsche	124.65
1997	Michele Alberto, Stefan Johansson & Tom Kristensen ...TWR Porsche	126.88
1998	Laurent Aiello, Allan McNish & Stephane Ortelli ...Porsche 911 GT1	123.86
1999	Yannick Dalmas, Joachim Winkelhock & Pierluigi Martini ....BMW V-12 LMR	129.38
2000	Frank Biela, Tom Kristensen & Emanuele Pirro ... Audi R8	128.34
2001	Frank Biela, Tom Kristensen & Emanuele Pirro ....Audi R8	129.66
2002	Frank Biela, Tom Kristensen & Emanuele Pirro ....Audi R8	131.89
2003	Tom Kristensen, Rinaldo Capello & Guy Smith ....Bentley Speed 8	143.43
2004	Tom Kristensen, Rinaldo Capello & Seiji Ara .....Audi R8	133.86
2005	Tom Kristensen, JJ Lehto & Marco Werner .....Audi R8	130.73
2006	Frank Biela, Emanuele Pirro & Marco Werner .....Audi R10	133.85
2007	Frank Biela, Emanuele Pirro & Marco Werner ....Audi R10	129.96
2008	Tom Kristensen, Rinaldo Capello & Allan McNish .....Audi R10	134.40

The 24 Hours of Daytona

Officially, the Rolex 24 at Daytona. First run in 1962 as a three-hour race and won by Dan Gurney in a Lotus 19 Ford. Contested over a 3.56-mile course at Daytona (Fla.) International Speedway. There have been several distance changes since 1962: the event was a three-hour race (1962-63); a 2,000-kilometer race (1964-65); a 24-hour race (1966-71); a six-hour race (1972) and a 24-hour race again since 1973. The race was canceled in 1974 due to a national energy crisis.

Multiple winners: Hurley Haywood (5); Peter Gregg, Pedro Rodriguez and Bob Wollek (4); Derek Bell, Butch Leitzinger, Scott Pruett, Rolf Stommelen and Andy Wallace (3); Mauro Baldi, A.J. Foyt, Al Holbert, Ken Miles, John Paul Jr., Brian Redman, Elliott Forbes-Robinson, Juan Pablo Montoya, Lloyd Ruby, Wayne Taylor, Didier Theys and Al Unser Jr. (2).

Year	Drivers Car	MPH
1962	Dan Gurney .... Lotus 19 Ford	104.101
1963	Pedro Rodriguez ..... Ferrari GTO	102.074
1964	Pedro Rodriguez & Phil Hill .... Ferrari GTO	98.230
1965	Ken Miles & Lloyd Ruby ...... Ford GT	99.944
1966	Ken Miles & Lloyd Ruby ...... Ford Mk. II	108.020
1967	Lorenzo Bandini & Chris Amon ...... Ferrari 330	105.688
1968	Vic Elford & Jochen Neerpasch . Porsche 907	106.697
1969	Mark Donohue & Chuck Parsons ..... Lola Chevrolet	99.268
1970	Pedro Rodriguez & Leo Kinnunen ...... Porsche 917	114.866
1971	Pedro Rodriguez & Jackie Oliver ..... Porsche 917K	109.203
1972	Mario Andretti & Jacky Ickx .... Ferrari 312P	122.573
1973	Peter Gregg & Hurley Haywood ... Porsche Carrera	106.225
1974	Not held	
1975	Peter Gregg & Hurley Haywood ... Porsche Carrera	108.531
1976	Peter Gregg, Brian Redman & John Fitzpatrick .... BMW CSL	104.040
1977	Hurley Haywood, John Graves & Dave Helmick ... Porsche Carrera	108.801
1978	Peter Gregg, Rolf Stommelen & Antoine Hezemans . Porsche Turbo	108.743
1979	Hurley Haywood, Ted Field & Danny Ongais ..... Porsche Turbo	109.249
1980	Rolf Stommelen, Volkert Merl & Reinhold Joest .... Porsche Turbo	114.303
1981	Bobby Rahal, Brian Redman & Bob Garretson .... Porsche Turbo	113.153
1982	John Paul Sr., John Paul Jr. & Rolf Stommelen ..... Porsche Turbo	114.794
1983	A.J. Foyt, Preston Henn, Bob Wollek & Claude Ballot-Lena . Porsche Turbo	98.781
1984	Sarel van der Merwe, Tony Martin & Graham Duxbury .. March Porsche	103.119
1985	A.J. Foyt, Bob Wollek, Al Unser Sr. & Thierry Boutsen ... Porsche 962	104.162
1986	Al Holbert, Derek Bell & Al Unser Jr ...... Porsche 962	105.484
1987	Al Holbert, Derek Bell, Chip Robinson & Al Unser Jr ...... Porsche 962	111.599
1988	Raul Boesel, Martin Brundle & John Nielsen .... Jaguar XJR-9	107.943
1989	John Andretti, Derek Bell & Bob Wollek .... Porsche 962	92.009
1990	Davy Jones, Jan Lammers & Andy Wallace .... Jaguar XJR-12	112.857
1991	Hurley Haywood, John Winter, Frank Jelinski, Henri Pescarolo & Bob Wollek ...... Porsche 962-C	106.633
1992	Masahiro Hasemi, Kazuyoshi Hoshino & Toshio Suzuki .... Nissan R-91	112.897
1993	P.J. Jones, Mark Dismore & Rocky Moran ...... Toyota Eagle	103.537
1994	Paul Gentilozzi, Scott Pruett, Butch Leitzinger & Steve Millen .... Nissan 300 ZXT	104.80
1995	Jurgen Lassig, Christophe Bouchut, Giovanni Lavaggi & Marco Werner ..... Porsche Spyder	102.280
1996	Wayne Taylor, Scott Sharp & Jim Pace .... Olds Arness MK-III	103.32
1997	Rob Dyson, James Weaver, Butch Leitzinger, Andy Wallace, John Paul Jr., Eliot Forbes-Robinson & John Schneider .... Ford R&S MK-III	102.29
1998	Mauro Baldi, Arie Luyendyk, Gianpiero Moretti & Didier Theys .... Ferrari 333	105.40
1999	Elliot Forbes-Robinson, Butch Leitzinger & Andy Wallace ..... Riley & Scott Ford	104.957
2000	Olivier Beretta, Dominique Dupuy & Karl Wendlinger ... Dodge Viper	107.207
2001	Ron Fellows, Franck Freon, Chris Kneifel & Johnny O'Connell .. Chevy Corvette	97.293

The 24 Hours of Daytona (Cont.)

Year	Drivers	Car	MPH
2002	Mauro Baldi, Fredy Lienhard, Max Papis & Didier Theys	Dallara LMP900	106.143
2003	Kevin Buckler, Michael Schrom, Timo Bernhard & Jorg Bergmeister	Porsche GT3 RS	115.969
2004	Terry Borcheller, Forest Barber, Andy Pilgrim & Christian Fittipaldi	Pontiac Doran	77.927
2005	Wayne Taylor, Max Angelelli & Emmanuel Collard	Pontiac Riley	105.204
2006	Scott Dixon, Dan Wheldon & Casey Mears	Lexus Riley	108.826
2007	Scott Pruett, Juan Pablo Montoya & Salvador Duran	Lexus Riley	99.020
2008	Scott Pruett, Memo Rojas, Juan Pablo Montoya & Dario Franchitti	Lexus Riley	103.057

NHRA DRAG RACING

NHRA Champions

Based on points earned during the NHRA POWERade Drag Racing series. The series, originally sponsored by the R.J. Reynolds Tobacco Company's Winston brand, began for Top Fuel, Funny Car and Pro Stock in 1975. The Coca-Cola Company's POWERade brand soft drink began a sponsorship deal with the series in 2002.

Top Fuel

Multiple winners: Joe Amato and Tony Schumacher (5); Don Garlits, Shirley Muldowney and Gary Scelzi (3); Kenny Bernstein, Larry Dixon and Scott Kalitta (2).

Year		Year		Year		Year	
1975	Don Garlits	1984	Joe Amato	1993	Eddie Hill	2002	Larry Dixon
1976	Richard Tharp	1985	Don Garlits	1994	Scott Kalitta	2003	Larry Dixon
1977	Shirley Muldowney	1986	Don Garlits	1995	Scott Kalitta	2004	Tony Schumacher
1978	Kelly Brown	1987	Dick LaHaie	1996	Kenny Bernstein	2005	Tony Schumacher
1979	Rob Bruins	1988	Joe Amato	1997	Gary Scelzi	2006	Tony Schumacher
1980	Shirley Muldowney	1989	Gary Ormsby	1998	Gary Scelzi	2007	Tony Schumacher
1981	Jeb Allen	1990	Joe Amato	1999	Tony Schumacher		
1982	Shirley Muldowney	1991	Joe Amato	2000	Gary Scelzi		
1983	Gary Beck	1992	Joe Amato	2001	Kenny Bernstein		

Funny Car

Multiple winners: John Force (14); Don Prudhomme, Kenny Bernstein (4); Raymond Beadle (3); Frank Hawley and Tony Pedregon (2).

Year		Year		Year		Year	
1975	Don Prudhomme	1984	Mark Oswald	1993	John Force	2002	John Force
1976	Don Prudhomme	1985	Kenny Bernstein	1994	John Force	2003	Tony Pedregon
1977	Don Prudhomme	1986	Kenny Bernstein	1995	John Force	2004	John Force
1978	Don Prudhomme	1987	Kenny Bernstein	1996	John Force	2005	Gary Scelzi
1979	Raymond Beadle	1988	Kenny Bernstein	1997	John Force	2006	John Force
1980	Raymond Beadle	1989	Bruce Larson	1998	John Force	2007	Tony Pedregon
1981	Raymond Beadle	1990	John Force	1999	John Force		
1982	Frank Hawley	1991	John Force	2000	John Force		
1983	Frank Hawley	1992	Cruz Pedregon	2001	John Force		

Pro Stock

Multiple winners: Bob Glidden (9); Warren Johnson (6); Lee Shepherd (4); Greg Anderson and Jeg Coughlin (3); Darrell Alderman and Jim Yates (2).

Year		Year		Year		Year	
1975	Bob Glidden	1984	Lee Shepherd	1993	Warren Johnson	2002	Jeg Coughlin
1976	Larry Lombardo	1985	Bob Glidden	1994	Darrell Alderman	2003	Greg Anderson
1977	Don Nicholson	1986	Bob Glidden	1995	Warren Johnson	2004	Greg Anderson
1978	Bob Glidden	1987	Bob Glidden	1996	Jim Yates	2005	Greg Anderson
1979	Bob Glidden	1988	Bob Glidden	1997	Jim Yates	2006	Jason Line
1980	Bob Glidden	1989	Bob Glidden	1998	Warren Johnson	2007	Jeg Coughlin
1981	Lee Shepherd	1990	John Myers	1999	Warren Johnson		
1982	Lee Shepherd	1991	Darrell Alderman	2000	Jeg Coughlin		
1983	Lee Shepherd	1992	Warren Johnson	2001	Warren Johnson		

All-Time Leaders
Career Victories

All-time leaders through Oct. 12, 2008. Drivers active in 2008 are in **bold**.

Top Fuel		Funny Car		Pro Stock	
1 **Tony Schumacher**	55	1 **John Force**	126	1 **Warren Johnson**	96
2 Joe Amato	52	2 **Tony Pedregon**	40	2 Bob Glidden	85
3 **Larry Dixon**	42	3 Don Prudhomme	35	3 **Greg Anderson**	56
4 Kenny Bernstein	39	4 Kenny Bernstein	30	4 **Jeg Coughlin**	40
5 Don Garlits	35	5 Two tied with 24.		5 Kurt Johnson	39

BOXING

Welshman **Joe Calzaghe** had reasons to smile in 2008. A win over Bernard Hopkins in April was a big one.

OLD SCHOOL

Aged veteran Bernard Hopkins taught undefeated middleweight champion Kelly Pavlik some things about the sweet science.

by Dan Rafael

Bernard Hopkins has defied the odds his whole life.

He'll tell you that he defied the odds just by not going back to prison after serving a 4½-year stint for armed robbery.

He became middleweight champion and held his title through 20 defenses, another odds-defying accomplishment, especially when as a huge underdog he knocked out Felix Trinidad to become undisputed champion in 2001.

On and on it went for Hopkins, who fought the system throughout his career and later beat the odds again when he jumped up 15 pounds to the 175-pound light heavyweight division and toppled Antonio Tarver in a virtuoso performance to lay claim to that throne in 2006.

And now Hopkins, his legend beyond established, did it once again. He didn't just beat middleweight champion Kelly Pavlik. He laid waste to him in a stunning, one-sided unanimous decision Saturday at Boardwalk Hall, where he broke the hearts of most of the 11,332 fans who were overwhelmingly rooting for the Youngstown, Ohio, hero.

And don't forget this fact: Pavlik is 26 and in his prime. Hopkins is 43.

It was supposed to be the other way around.

But Hopkins, still the master against the student Pavlik, dominated from Round 1 through Round 12 and stamped himself as perhaps the greatest 40-plus fighter in boxing history. At the very least, he's in the conversation with light heavyweight great Archie Moore and heavyweight icon George Foreman.

The history of what Hopkins had just done was not lost on the hardened tough guy.

After the fight, but before the scores everyone knew were coming were actually read, Hopkins walked

 **Dan Rafael** covers boxing for ESPN.com.

AP Images

Despite his advanced age **Bernard Hopkins** showed he still had some fight left in him in 2008. Will a rematch against Roy Jones Jr. be next?

to the ropes facing the press section, looked down on the assembled media, many of whom have been covering Hopkins for many years, and said, "I'm tired of proving myself."

His lips were quivering and he was on the verge of tears, overcome by the emotion of what he had just done.

"I could box another two to three years," Hopkins said. "I think this was my best performance – better than Tarver, better than Trinidad, better than Oscar [De La Hoya]. I am extremely happy tonight. Ninety percent of the media picked Pavlik. I always appreciate naysayers. That is what motivates me – when people are against me. I don't wish I was like

that, but that's the way it is."

Pavlik had no answers in the fight and none afterward either.

"I just couldn't get off," he said. "I don't know why. It was not his slickness. I just couldn't throw a jab, a double jab. I couldn't do what I was used to doing. We'll go back to the drawing board. It just wasn't me tonight. I will be more comfortable going back to 160."

For years, Hopkins had entered the ring wearing an executioner's mask, but he left it behind for the past few years. But Saturday, he returned to it, perhaps a sign of the execution that was to come.

In recent fights, Hopkins (49-5-1, 32 KOs) had started oh, so slowly.

who won 119-106, 118-108 and 117-109. ESPN.com had it 119-107 for Hopkins.

"He's a great fighter, but I knew my style and quickness were underrated and I was going give him problems," Hopkins said. "I wanted him to lead so I could do what I love to do — counterpunch. He kept coming forward, which was an advantage to me. He was really heavy-handed. I could feel his power, but he never hurt me. I didn't get hit flush."

Round after round, Hopkins took it to Pavlik, whose middleweight championship was not on the line because they met at contract weight of 170 pounds, five below the light heavyweight limit.

Hopkins landed combinations, gave Pavlik a mouse under his right eye and answered every time Pavlik mustered any kind of offense.

Before the eighth round, when it was already clear that Pavlik (34-1, 30 KOs) had virtually no chance to win, his manager, Cameron Dunkin, who was seated at the end of one of the media rows, acknowledged that Pavlik had nothing.

After both fighters had a point deducted by referee Benjy Esteves, Pavlik for hitting behind the head in

Undefeated Light Heavyweight **Chad Dawson** made the leap this year with a decisive win over former champ Antonio Tarver.

But against Pavlik, he started fast, outlanding and outthrowing Pavlik 34-26 in the first round. He never let up.

Hopkins threw more punches than Pavlik in nine of the 12 rounds, and outlanded him in 10 rounds. In the end, Hopkins landed 172 of 530 blows (32 percent), according to CompuBox. Pavlik connected on just 108 of 463 (23 percent).

It was an extraordinary performance for boxing's elder statesman,

the eighth and Hopkins for holding in the ninth, Hopkins closed the show as strong as he started.

In the 12th, he wobbled Pavlik with a booming right hand and had him on the verge of going down. All the way to the final bell, Hopkins was firing hard shots, trying to stop his man.

"I wanted to stop him because I had been playing it safe [in other fights] because of my age," he said. "I wanted to pick it up, step it up, and I really wanted to stop him. I was definitely going for the knockout, but he's tough.

"I want anyone I fight next to know I am going for the knockout. That's what I was trying to do tonight."

Hopkins, who like Pavlik earned at least $3 million, has designs on facing old nemesis Roy Jones, who beat him in a 1993 middleweight title bout.

"I would fight Roy in a heartbeat. I would even go to England and fight [Joe] Calzaghe if he beats Roy [on Nov. 8]," said Hopkins, who lost a close decision to Calzaghe in April. "But wouldn't the fight against Roy be huge?"

Although Hopkins was thinking of Jones, he was also aware of what Pavlik was going through.

After the fight, Hopkins went over to speak to Pavlik.

"Don't let this fight destroy you,"

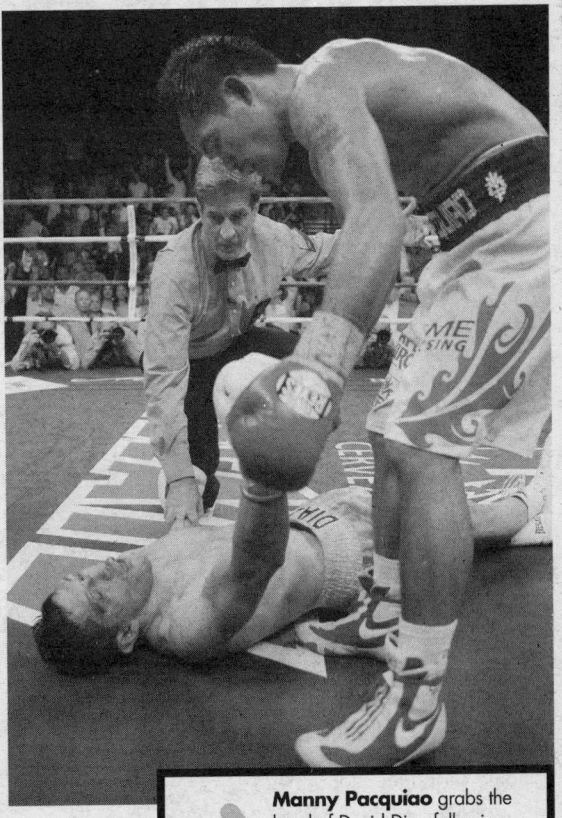

Manny Pacquiao grabs the hand of David Diaz following their WBC lightweight fight on June 28 in Las Vegas.

Hopkins told him. "You're a great middleweight champion. You have a great heart. Keep your head up. Keep fighting. You have to learn one thing. You have to learn that slickness that black fighters have and then you'll really be a great champion. I don't want you to quit. If I have to go to your house and take you to the gym, I will."

It was classic Hopkins, the master, still schooling his pupil even after the fight.

OH BROTHER

Vitali Klitschko's return begs questions

Almost four years since his last fight – Dec. 11, 2004 against Danny Williams – Klitschko came out of retirement and destroyed Peter in stunningly one-sided fashion. It was an incredible performance considering the length of the layoff and all of the injuries that forced Klitschko to vacate his title back then and retire. It literally didn't look like he had missed a day, much less four years; that's how good he was. From the opening bell, Peter had no idea what to do. He was inept and looked like a rank amateur. He wasn't in the fight for one moment, as Klitschko, with his superior size, reach, thudding jab and powerful right, slammed home shot after shot on a nearly defenseless Peter, who showed only the ability not to go down. Klitschko rocked Peter several times in the first round and never let up. It was as dominant a performance as there has been in recent years in such a high-profile fight. Think Winky Wright-Felix Trinidad, Joe Calzaghe-Jeff Lacy or Bernard Hopkins-Antonio Tarver, except this one ended with a stoppage. By the time the eighth round was over, Peter had zero chance to win. He had not landed a single telling blow and because of the WBC's horrible open scoring system, he knew officially that he was losing via shutout on two scorecards and 7-1 in rounds on the third (the judge that gave Peter, 28, even one round, Thailand's

The **Klitschko brothers** have long maintained they will never fight each other.

Anek Hongtongkam, should be ashamed of himself). Whether that influenced his decision to quit is not known, but Peter refused to come out for the ninth round, instead meekly quitting on his stool and yielding his heavyweight title belt in his first defense.

Klitschko, the mandatory challenger because of the WBC's wacky "champion emeritus" status he was granted when he retired – meaning if he ever decided to unretire he would immediately be the mandatory challenger – won back the belt he vacated after his lone defense against Williams. Aside from the historical nature of winning a title in his first fight back after such a long layoff, Klitschko, 37, joined his younger brother Wladimir Klitschko, the world's No. 1 heavyweight who holds two of the four alphabet belts, as a simultaneous heavyweight champion. For years, the brothers' stated goal was to hold titles at the same time. Mission accomplished. But because they have said over and over that they will never fight each other, the division is held hostage with no chance for a unification or for the two best heavyweights to fight each other. It's a difficult but interesting situation for heavyweight boxing.

--Dan Rafael, ESPN.com

2007-2008
Year in Review

SPORTS ALMANAC

Current Champions

WBA, WBC and IBF Titleholders (through Oct. 31, 2008)

The champions of professional boxing's 17 principal weight divisions, as recognized by the Word Boxing Association (WBA), World Boxing Council (WBC), International Boxing Federation (IBF) and World Boxing Organization (WBO). Where applicable, records listed below fighters' names indicate wins-losses-draws-no contest (knockouts).

Weight Class (limit)	WBA	WBC	IBF
Heavyweight	Nikolay Valuev 49-1 (34)	Vitali Klitschko 36-2 (35)	Wladimir Klitschko 51-3 (45)
Cruiserweight (190 lbs)	Guillermo Jones 36-3-2 (28)	Giacobbe Fragomeni 26-1 (11)	Steve Cunningham 21-1 (11)
Light Heavyweight (175)	Hugo Hernan Garay 30-3 (17)	Adrian Diaconu 25-0 (15)	Chad Dawson 27-0 (17)
Super Middleweight (168)	Mikkel Kessler 41-1 (31)	Vacant	Lucian Bute 23-0 (18)
Middleweight (160)	Felix Sturm 30-2-1 (12)	Kelly Pavlik 34-1 (30)	Arthur Abraham 27-0 (22)
Jr. Middleweight (154)	Daniel Santos 32-3-1 (23)	Vernon Forrest* 41-3 (29)	Verno Phillips 42-10-1 (21)
Welterweight (147)	Antonio Margarito* 37-5 (27)	Andre Berto 23-0 (19)	Joshua Clottey 35-2 (20)
Jr. Welterweight (140)	Andreas Kotelnik 30-2-1 (13)	Timothy Bradley 23-0 (11)	Vacant
Lightweight (135)	Nate Campbell 23-2-1 (12)	Manny Pacquiao* 47-3-2 (36)	Nate Campbell 32-5-1 (25)
Jr. Lightweight (130)	Edwin Valero 24-0 (22)	Humberto Soto 45-7-2 (29)	Cassius Baloyi 36-3-1 (19)
Featherweight (126)	Chris John 42-0-1 (22)	Oscar Larios 63-6-1 (39)	Cristobal Cruz 37-11-1 (23)
Jr. Featherweight (122)	Celestino Caballero* 30-2 (21)	Israel Vazquez* 43-4 (31)	Steve Molitor 28-0 (11)
Bantamweight (118)	Anselmo Morena 23-1-1 (8)	Hozumi Hasegawa 25-2 (9)	Joseph Agbeko 25-1 (22)
Jr. Bantamweight (115)	Nobuo Nashiro* 12-1 (7)	Cristian Mijares 36-3-2 (15)	Vic Darchinyan 30-3-1 (24)
Flyweight (112)	Takefumi Sakata 33-4-2 (15)	Daisuke Naito 33-2-3 (21)	Nonito Donaire 19-1 (12)
Jr. Flyweight (108)	Brahim Asloum* 23-2 (9)	Edgar Sosa 33-5 (16)	Ulises Solis 27-1-2 (20)
Minimumweight (105)	Roman Gozalez 21-0 (19)	O. Sithsamerchai* 27-0 (11)	Raul Garcia 24-0-1 (15)

*Sergio Gabriel Martinez is the interim WBC super welterweight champion; Antonio Margarito is the WBA "Super" welterweight champion (Yuriy Nuzhnenko is the WBA welter champ); Antonio Pitalua is the interim WBC lightweight champion; Ricardo Cordoba is the interim WBA super bantamweight champion; Toshiaki Nishioka interim WBC super bantamweight champion; Jorge Arce is the interim WBA super flyweight champion; Cesar Canchila is the interim WBA light flyweight champion; Juan Palacios is the the interim WBC strawweight champion.

Note: The following weight divisions are also known by these names—**Cruiserweight** as Jr. Heavyweight; **Jr. Middleweight** as Super Welterweight; **Jr. Welterweight** as Super Lightweight; **Jr. Lightweight** as Super Featherweight; **Jr. Featherweight** as Super Bantamweight; **Jr. Bantamweight** as Super Flyweight; **Jr. Flyweight** as Light Flyweight; and **Minimumweight** as Strawweight or Mini-Flyweights.

Major Bouts, 2007-08
Division by division, from Nov. 1, 2007 through Oct. 31, 2008.

WBA, WBC and IBF champions are listed in **bold** type. Note the following Result column abbreviations (in alphabetical order): **Disq.** (won by disqualification); **KO** (knockout); **MDraw** (majority draw); **NC** (no contest); **SDraw** (split draw); **TDraw** (technical draw); **TKO** (technical knockout); **TWm** (won by technical majority decision); **TWs** (won by technical split decision); **TWu** (won by technical unanimous decision); **Wm** (won by majority decision); **Ws** (won by split decision) and **Wu** (won by unanimous decision).

Heavyweights

Date	Winner	Loser	Result	Title	Site
Jan. 19	**Ruslan Chagaev**	Matt Skelton	Wu 12	**WBA**	Dusseldorf, Germany
Jan. 26	Alekander Povetkin	Eddie Chambers	Wu 12	—	Berlin, Germany
Feb. 23	**Wladimir Klitschko**	Sultan Ibragimov	Wu 12	**IBF**	New York City
Mar. 8	Samuel Peter	**Oleg Maskaev**	TKO 6	**WBC**	Cancun, Mexico
July 12	**Wladimir Klitschko**	Tony Thompson	KO 11	**IBF**	Hermosillo, Mexico
Aug. 30	Nikolai Valuev	John Ruiz	Wu 12	**WBA***	Berlin, Germany
Oct. 11	Vitali Klitschko	**Samuel Peter**	TKO 8	**WBC**	Berlin, Germany

*Valuev won the title that became vacant when Ruslan Chagaev underwent surgery on a torn achilles tendon and the WBA designated him as its "champion in recess".

Cruiserweights (190 lbs)
(Jr. Heavyweights)

Date	Winner	Loser	Result	Title	Site
Nov. 10	David Haye	**Jean-Marc Mormeck**	KO 7	**WBA/WBC**	Paris
Nov. 24	Firat Arslan	**Virgil Hill**	Wu 12	**WBA**	Dresden, Germany
Dec. 29	**Steve Cunningham**	Marco Huck	TKO 12	**IBF**	Bielefeld, Germany
Mar. 8	**David Haye**	Enzo Maccarinelli	TKO 2	**WBA/WBC**	Greenwich, England
May 3	**Firat Arslan**	Darnell Wilson	Wu 12	**WBA**	Stuttgart, Germany
Sept. 12	Guillermo Jones	**Firat Arslan**	TKO 10	**WBA**	Hamburg, Germany
Oct. 24	Giacobbe Fragomeni	Rudolf Kraj	Twu 12	**WBC***	Milan, Italy

*vacant tile.

Light Heavyweights (175 lbs)

Date	Winner	Loser	Result	Title	Site
Dec. 16	Danny Green	**Stipe Drews**	Wu 12	**WBA**	Perth, Australia
Jan. 19	Roy Jones Jr.	Felix Trinidad	Wu 12^	—	New York City
Apr. 12	**Chad Dawson**	Glen Johnson	Wu 12	**WBC**	Tampa, Fla.
Apr. 12	Antonio Tarver	**Clinton Woods**	Wu 12	**IBF**	Tampa, Fla.
Apr. 19	Joe Calzaghe	Bernard Hopkins	Ws 12	—	Las Vegas
Apr. 19	Adrian Diaconu	Chris Henry	Wu 12	**WBC***	Bucharest, Romania
July 3	Hugo Hernan Garay	Yuri Barashian	Wu 12	**WBA**†	Buenos Aires, Argentina
Oct. 11	Chad Dawson	**Antonio Tarver**	Wu 12	**IBF**	Las Vegas

^The Roy Jones-Felix Trinidad fight was at a 170-pound catchweight.

*Diaconu won the title that was vacated by Chad Dawson when he chose to fight Antonio Tarver rather his mandatory challenger.

†Garay won the belt vacated by Danny Green.

Super Middleweights (168 lbs)

Date	Winner	Loser	Result	Title	Site
Nov. 3	**Joe Calzaghe**	**Mikkel Kessler**	Wu 12	**WBA/WBC**	Cardiff, Wales
Dec. 10	Anthony Mundine	Jose Alberto Clavero	KO 4	WBA	Sydney, Australia
Feb. 27	Anthony Mundine	Nader Haman	Wu 12	WBA	Sydney, Australia
Feb. 29	**Lucian Bute**	William Joppy	TKO 10	**IBF**	Montreal, Canada
May 28	Anthony Mundine	Sam Soliman	Wu 12	WBA	Melbourne, Australia
June 21	Mikkel Kessler	Dmitri Sartison	TKO 12	**WBA***	Copenhagen, Denmark
Oct. 24	**Lucian Bute**	Librado Andrade	Wu 12	**IBF**	Montreal, Canada
Oct. 25	**Mikkel Kessler**	Danilo Haussler	KO 3	**WBA**	Dusseldorf, Germany

*Kessler won the WBA belt that was vacated when Joe Calzaghe agreed to fight Roy Jones Jr. rather than his mandatory challengers.

Note: Mikkel Kessler is the WBA Super Middleweight "super world champion," while Anthony Mundine is just considered the WBA champion a confusing but lesser title.

Middleweights (160 lbs)

Date	Winner	Loser	Result	Title	Site
Dec. 8	**Arthur Abraham**	Wayne Elcock	TKO 5	IBF	Basel, Switzerland
Feb. 16	Kelly Pavlik	Jermain Taylor	Wu 12	—	Las Vegas
Mar. 29	**Arthur Abraham**	Elvin Ayala	KO 12	IBF	Kiel, Germany
Apr. 5	**Felix Sturm**	Jamie Pittman	TKO 7	WBA	Dusseldorf, Germany
June 7	**Kelly Pavlik**	Gary Lockett	TKO 6	WBC	Atlantic City
June 21	**Arthur Abraham**	Edison Miranda	TKO 4	IBF	Hollywood, Florida
July 5	**Felix Sturm**	Randy Griffin	Wu 12	WBA	Halle, Germany

Junior Middleweights (154 lbs)
(Super Welterweights)

Date	Winner	Loser	Result	Title	Site
Dec. 1	**Vernon Forrest**	Michele Piccirillo	TKO 11	WBC	Mashantucket, Conn.
Dec. 7	**Joachim Alcine**	Alfonso Mosquera	TKO 12	WBA	Montreal, Canada
Mar. 27	Verno Phillips	**Cory Spinks**	Ws 12	IBF	St. Louis, Mo.
June 7	Sergio Mora	**Vernon Forrest**	Wm 12	WBC	Uncasville, Conn.
July 11	Daniel Santos	**Joachim Alcine**	KO 6	WBA	Montreal, Canada
Sept. 13	Vernon Forrest	**Sergio Mora**	Wu 12	WBC	Las Vegas
Oct. 4	Sergio Gabriel Martinez	Alex Bunema	TKO 8	WBC*	Temecula, Calif.

*interim belt

Welterweights (147 lbs)

Date	Winner	Loser	Result	Title	Site
Nov. 10	**Miguel Cotto**	Shane Mosley	Wu12	WBA	New York City
Nov. 23	**Kermit Cintron**	Jesse Feliciano	TKO 10	IBF	Los Angeles
Dec. 8	**Floyd Mayweather Jr.**	Ricky Hatton	TKO 10	WBC	Las Vegas
Feb. 9	Carlos Quintana	Paul Williams	Wu 12	—	Temecula, Calif.
Feb. 9	Andre Berto	Michel Trabant	TKO 6	—	Temecula, Calif.
Apr. 12	Antonio Margarito	**Kermit Cintron**	KO 6	IBF	Atlantic City
Apr. 12	**Miguel Cotto**	Alfonso Gomez	TKO 5	WBA	Atlantic City
Apr. 19	Yuriy Nuzhnenko	Irving Garcia	TDraw 12	WBA†	Kiev, Ukraine
June 21	Andre Berto	Miguel Rodriguez	TKO 7	WBC*	Memphis, Tenn.
July 26	Antonio Margarito	**Miguel Cotto**	TKO 11	WBA**	Las Vegas
Aug. 2	Joshua Clottey	Zab Judah	TWu 12‡	IBF	Las Vegas
Sept. 27	Shane Mosley	Ricardo Mayorga	KO 12	—	Las Vegas
Sept. 27	**Andre Berto**	Steve Forbes	Wu 12	WBC	Los Angeles

*Berto won the title vacated by the retirement of Floyd Mayweather Jr.

**Margarito vacated the IBF belt to fight Cotto instead of his mandatory challenger. Joshua Clottey won the vacated belt Aug 2 against Zab Judah .

‡Clottey won a unanimous technical decision after the fight went to the scorecards after an accidental head butt opened a deep cut over Judah's right eye.

†interim title.

Junior Welterweights (140 lbs)
(Super Lightweights)

Date	Winner	Loser	Result	Title	Site
Jan. 3	**Paul Malignaggi**	Herman Ngoudjo	Wu 12	IBF	Atlantic City
Mar. 22	Andreas Kotelnik	**Gavin Rees**	TKO 12	WBA	Cardiff, Wales
May 3	Oscar De La Hoya	Steve Forbes	Wu 12	—	Los Angeles
May 10	Timothy Bradley	**Junior Witter**	Ws 12	WBC	Nottingham, England
May 24	**Paul Malignaggi**	Lovemore N'dou	Ws 12	IBF	Manchester, England
Sept. 13	**Andreas Kotelnik**	Norio Kimura	Wu 12	WBA	Lviv, Ukraine
Sept. 13	**Timothy Bradley**	Edner Cherry	Wu 12	WBC	Biloxi, Miss.

Major Bouts Scheduled for Late 2008

Date	Division	Match-up	Title	Location
Nov. 8	middleweight	Arthur Abraham–Raul Marquez	IBF	Bamberg, Germany
Nov. 8	light heavyweight	Joe Calzaghe–Roy Jones Jr.	—	New York City
Nov. 15	super middleweight	Jermain Taylor–Jeff Lacy	—	Nashville, Tenn.
Nov. 22	junior welterweight	Ricky Hatton–Paulie Malignaggi	—	Las Vegas
Nov. 22	light heavyweight	Hugo Hernan Garay–Juergen Braehmer	—	Rostock, Germany
Dec. 6	super middleweight	Carl Froch–Jean Pascal	WBC	Nottingham, England
Dec. 6	lightweights	Manny Pacquiao–Oscar De La Hoya	—	Las Vegas
Dec. 11	cruiserweight	Steve Cunningham–Tomasz Adamek	IBF	Newark, N.J.
Dec. 13	light flyweight	Ulises Solis–Brian Viloria	IBF	Macau, China

Major Bouts, 2007-08 (Cont.)

Lightweights (135 lbs)

Date	Winner	Loser	Result	Title	Site
Nov 10	**Joel Casamayor**	J.A. Santa Cruz	Ws12	**WBC***	New York City
Dec. 29	Jose Alfaro	**Prawet Singwancha**	Ws 12	**WBA†**	Bielefeld, Germany
Mar. 8	Nate Campbell	**Juan Diaz**	Ws 12	**WBA/IBF**	Cancun, Mexico
Mar. 22	Joel Casamayor	Michael Katsidis	TKO 10	—	Cabazon, Calif.
May 19	Yusuke Kobori	**Jose Alfaro**	TKO 3	**WBA**	Tokyo, Japan
June 28	Manny Pacquiao	**David Diaz**	TKO 9	**WBC**	Las Vegas
Sept. 6	Juan Diaz	Michael Katsidis	Wu 12	—	Houston, Texas
Sept. 13	Juan Manuel Marquez	Joel Casamayor	TKO 11	—	Las Vegas
Sept. 20	Antonio Pitalua	J.A. Santa Cruz	KO 6	**WBC****	Monterrey, Mexico

*interim belt
†vacant title.
**vacant interim belt.

Junior Lightweights (130 lbs)
(Super Featherweights)

Date	Winner	Loser	Result	Title	Site
Nov. 3	**Juan Manuel Marquez**	Rocky Juarez	Wu 12	**WBC**	Tucson, Ariz.
Nov. 17	Joan Guzman	Humberto Soto	Wu 12	—	Atlantic City
Dec. 15	**Edwin Valero**	Zaid Zavaleta	KO 3	**WBA**	Cancun, Mexico
Mar. 15	Manny Pacquiao	**J. Manuel Marquez**	Ws 12	**WBC**	Las Vegas
Apr. 12	Cassius Baloyi	**Mzonke Fana**	Wm 12	**IBF**	Mafiking, S. Africa
June 12	**Edwin Valero**	Takehiro Shimada	TKO 7	**WBA**	Tokyo, Japan
June 28	Humberto Soto	Francisco Lorenzo	NC 4	**WBC***	Las Vegas
Sept. 13	**Cassius Baloyi**	Javier Osvaldo Alvarez	KO 3	**IBF**	Mafiking, S. Africa
Oct. 11	Humberto Soto	Gamaliel Diaz	TKO 10	**WBC†**	Torreon, Mexico

*Soto was disqualified after hitting Lorenzo with a glancing blow when he was still on the mat. Referee Joe Cortez disqualified Soto in a highly controversial decision. Soto has been winning the lop-sided fight and the WBC refused to award the interim belt (that was created when Manny Pacquiao moved up to lightweight) to Lorenzo after the fight.
†vacant title.

Featherweights (126 lbs)

Date	Winner	Loser	Result	Title	Site
Nov. 3	Robert Guerrero	**Martin Honorio**	KO 1	**IBF**	Tucson, Ariz.
Dec. 15	**Jorge Lineres**	Gamaliel Diaz	KO 8	**WBC**	Cancun, Mexico
Jan. 26	**Chris John**	Roinet Caballero	TKO 7	**WBA**	Jakarta, Indonesia
Feb. 29	**Robert Guerrero**	Jason Litzau	KO 8	**IBF**	Lemore, Calif.
May 31	Oscar Larios	Feider Viloria	TKO 5	**WBC***	Chetumal, Mexico
Aug. 2	Oscar Larios	Marlon Aguilar	KO 7	**WBC***	Jalisco, Mexico
Oct. 16	Oscar Larios	Takahiro Aoh	Ws 12	**WBC***	Tokyo, Japan
Oct. 23	Cristobal Cruz	Orlando Salido	Ws 12	**IBF†**	Airway Heights, Wash.
Oct. 24	**Chris John**	Hiroyuki Enoki	Wu 12	**WBA**	Tokyo, Japan

*interim title.
†Cruz won the IBF title vacated by Robert Guerrero when he moved up to 130 pounds

Junior Featherweights (122 lbs)
(Super Bantamweights)

Date	Winner	Loser	Result	Title	Site
Dec. 1	**Celestino Caballero**	Mauricio Pastrana	TKO 8	**WBA**	Panama City, Panama
Jan. 19	**Steve Molitor**	Ricardo Castillo	Wu 12	**IBF**	Ontario, Canada
Mar. 1	**Israel Vazquez**	Rafael Marquez	Ws 12	**WBC**	Carson, Calif.
Apr. 5	**Steve Molitor**	Fernando Beltran Jr.	Wu 12	**IBF**	Rama, Ontario
June 7	**Celestino Caballero**	Lorenzo Parra	TKO 12	**WBA**	San Juan, Venezuela
Aug. 29	**Steve Molitor**	Ceferino Dario Labarda	TKO 10	**IBF**	Rama, Ontario
Sept. 18	Toshiaki Nishioka	N. Kiatisakchokchai	Wu 12	WBC*	Yokohama, Japan
Sept. 18	**Celestino Caballero**	Elvis Meja	TKO 1	**WBA**	Panama City, Panama
Sept. 18	Ricardo Cordoba	Luis Alberto Perez	Wu 12	**WBA†**	Panama City, Panama

*interim belt.
†vacant interim belt

Bantamweights (118 lbs)

Date	Winner	Loser	Result	Title	Site
Jan. 10	**Wladimir Sidorenko**	Nobuto Ikehara	Wu 12	**WBA**	Osaka, Japan
Jan. 10	**Hozumi Hasegawa**	Simone Maludrottu	Wu 12	**WBC**	Osaka, Japan
May 31	Anselmo Moreno	**Wladimir Sidorenko**	Wu 12	**WBA**	Dusseldorf, Germany
June 12	**Hozumi Hasegawa**	Cristian Faccio	TKO 2	**WBC**	Tokyo, Japan
Sept. 18	**Anselmo Moreno**	Cecilio Santos	TWu 7	**WBA**	Panama City, Panama
Oct. 16	**Hozumi Hasegawa**	Alejandro Valdez	TKO 2	**WBC**	Tokyo

Junior Bantamweights (115 lbs)
(Super Flyweights)

Date	Winner	Loser	Result	Title	Site
Jan. 14	**Alexander Munoz**	Katsushige Kawashima	Wu 12	WBA	Yokohama, Japan
Feb. 16	**Cristian Mijares**	Jose Navarro	Ws 12	WBC	Las Vegas
Feb. 28	**Dimitri Kirilov**	Cecilio Santos	Wm 12	IBF	New York City
May 17	**Cristian Mijares**	**Alexander Munoz**	Ws 12	WBC/WBA	Gomez Palacio, Mexico
July 26	Rafael Concepcion	AJ Banal	KO 10	WBA*	Cebu City, Phillipines
Aug. 2	Vic Darchinyan	**Dmitri Kirilov**	KO 5	IBF	Tacoma, Wash.
Aug. 30	**Cristian Mijares**	Chatchai Saskul	TKO 3	WBA/WBC	Monterrey, Mexico
Sept. 15	Nobuo Nashiro	Kohei Kono	Ws 12	WBA†	Yokohama
Sept. 15	Jorge Arce	**Rafael Concepcion**	TKO 9	WBA*	Mexico City

*interim title
†vacant title.

Flyweights (112 lbs)

Date	Winner	Loser	Result	Title	Site
Nov. 4	**Takefumi Sakata**	Denkaosen Singwacha	Draw 12	WBA	Saitama, Japan
Dec. 1	Nonito Donaire	Luis Maldonado	TKO 8	IBF	Mashantucket, Conn.
Mar. 8	**Daisuke Naito**	Pongsaklek Wonjongkam	Draw 12	WBC	Tokyo, Japan
Mar. 29	**Takefumi Sakata**	Shingo Yamaguchi	Wu 12	WBA	Chiba, Japan
July 30	**Daisuke Naito**	Tomonobu Shimizu	KO 10	WBC	Tokyo, Japan
July 30	**Takefumi Sakata**	Hiroyuki Hisataka	Wu 12	WBA	Tokyo, Japan

Junior Flyweights (108 lbs)
(Light Flyweights)

Date	Winner	Loser	Result	Title	Site
Dec. 8	Brahim Asloum	**Juan Carlos Reveco**	Wu 12	WBA	Alpes-Maritimes, France
Dec. 15	**Ulises Solis**	Bert Batawang	TKO 10	IBF	Guadalajara, Mexico
Feb. 9	**Edgar Sosa**	Jesus Iribe	Wu 12	WBC	Guanajuanto, Mexico
June 14	**Edgar Sosa**	Takashi Kunishige	KO 8	WBC	Mexico City
July 12	**Ulises Solis**	Glenn Donaire	Wu 12	IBF	Hermosillo, Mexico
July 26	Cesar Canchila	Giovanni Segura	Wu 12	WBA*	Las Vegas
Sept. 27	**Edgar Sosa**	Sonny Boy Jaro	Wu 12	WBC	Mexico City

*interim title.

Minimumweights (105 lbs)
(Strawweights or Mini-Flyweights)

Date	Winner	Loser	Result	Title	Site
Nov. 29	Oleydong Sithsamerchai	**Eagle Kyowa**	Wu 12	WBC	Bangkok, Thailand
Mar. 1	**Yutaka Niida**	Jose Luis Varela	KO 6	WBA	Tokyo, Japan
June 14	Raul Garcia	**Florante Condes**	Ws 12	IBF	La Paz, Mexico
June 18	**Oleydong Sithsamerchai**	Junichi Ebisuoka	KO 9	WBC	Phuket, Thailand
Aug. 2	Juan Palacios	**Omar Soto**	KO 10	WBC*	Ponce, Puerto Rico
Sept. 13	**Raul Garcia**	Jose Varela	Wu 12	IBF	La Paz, Mexico
Sept. 15	Roman Gonzalez	**Yutaka Niida**	TKO 4	WBA	Yokohama, Japan

*interim title.

The Ring Magazine Champions

The Ring in an effort to clear up the mess created by the questionable practices by boxing's governing organizations, created The Ring champions in 2002. Championship vacancies can be filled by winning a bout between The Ring's #1 and #2 contenders or, in certain instances, a bout between their #1 and #3 contenders. The only ways a fighter can lose his championship are if he retires, moves to another weight division, or is beaten in a championship bout. *Source: thering-online.com*

Current Ring Champions (as of Oct. 31, 2008)

Heavyweight: vacant	**Welterweight:** vacant	**Bantamweight:** vacant
Crusierweight: vacant	**Jr. Welterweight:** Ricky Hatton	**Jr. Bantamweight:** vacant
Lt. Heavyweight: Joe Cazalghe	**Lightweight:** Juan Manuel Marquez	**Flyweight:** vacant
Super Middleweight: vacant	**Jr. Lightweight:** vacant	**Jr. Flyweight:** Ivan Calderon
Middleweight: Kelly Pavlik	**Featherweight:** vacant	**Strawweight:** vacant
Jr. Middleweight: vacant	**Jr. Featherweight:** Israel Vazquez	

1892-2008
Through the Years

World Heavyweight Championship Fights

Widely accepted world champions in **bold** type. Note following result abbreviations: KO (knockout), TKO (technical knock out), Wu (unanimous decision), Wm (majority decision), Ws (split decision), Ref (referee's decision), ND (no decision), Disq (won on disqualification).

Year	Date	Winner	Age	Wgt	Loser	Wgt	Result	Location
1892	Sept. 7	James J. Corbett	26	178	John L. Sullivan	212	KO 21	New Orleans
1894	Jan. 25	**James J. Corbett**	27	184	Charley Mitchell	158	KO 3	Jacksonville, Fla.
1897	Mar. 17	Bob Fitzsimmons	34	167	**James J. Corbett**	183	KO 14	Carson City, Nev.
1899	June 9	James J. Jeffries	24	206	**Bob Fitzsimmons**	167	KO 11	Coney Island, N.Y.
1899	Nov. 3	**James J. Jeffries**	24	215	Tom Sharkey	183	Ref 25	Coney Island, N.Y.
1900	Apr. 6	**James J. Jeffries**	24	NA	Jack Finnegan	NA	KO 1	Detroit
1900	May 11	**James J. Jeffries**	25	218	James J. Corbett	188	KO 23	Coney Island, N.Y.
1901	Nov. 15	**James J. Jeffries**	26	211	Gus Ruhlin	194	TKO 6	San Francisco
1902	July 25	**James J. Jeffries**	27	219	Bob Fitzsimmons	172	KO 8	San Francisco
1903	Aug. 14	**James J. Jeffries**	28	220	James J. Corbett	190	KO 10	San Francisco
1904	Aug. 25	**James J. Jeffries***	29	219	Jack Munroe	186	TKO 2	San Francisco
1905	July 3	Marvin Hart	28	190	Jack Root	171	KO 12	Reno, Nev.
1906	Feb. 23	Tommy Burns	24	180	**Marvin Hart**	188	Ref 20	Los Angeles
1906	Oct. 2	**Tommy Burns**	25	NA	Jim Flynn	NA	KO 15	Los Angeles
1906	Nov. 28	**Tommy Burns**	25	172	Phila. Jack O'Brien	163½	Draw 20	Los Angeles
1907	May 8	**Tommy Burns**	25	180	Phila. Jack O'Brien	167	Ref 20	Los Angeles
1907	July 4	**Tommy Burns**	26	181	Bill Squires	180	KO 1	Colma, Calif.
1907	Dec. 2	**Tommy Burns**	26	177	Gunner Moir	204	KO 10	London
1908	Feb. 10	**Tommy Burns**	26	NA	Jack Palmer	NA	KO 4	London
1908	Mar. 17	**Tommy Burns**	26	NA	Jem Roche	NA	KO 1	Dublin
1908	Apr. 18	**Tommy Burns**	26	NA	Jewey Smith	NA	KO 5	Paris
1908	June 13	**Tommy Burns**	26	184	Bill Squires	183	KO 8	Paris
1908	Aug. 24	**Tommy Burns**	27	181	Bill Squires	184	KO 13	Sydney
1908	Sept. 2	**Tommy Burns**	27	183	Bill Lang	187	KO 6	Melbourne
1908	Dec. 26	Jack Johnson	30	192	**Tommy Burns**	168	TKO 14	Sydney
1909	Mar. 10	**Jack Johnson**	30	NA	Victor McLaglen	NA	ND 6	Vancouver
1909	May 19	**Jack Johnson**	31	205	Phila. Jack O'Brien	161	ND 6	Philadelphia
1909	June 30	**Jack Johnson**	31	207	Tony Ross	214	ND 6	Pittsburgh
1909	Sept. 9	**Jack Johnson**	31	209	Al Kaufman	191	ND 10	San Francisco
1909	Oct. 16	**Jack Johnson**	31	205½	Stanley Ketchel	170¼	KO 12	Colma, Calif.
1910	July 4	**Jack Johnson**	32	208	James J. Jeffries	227	KO 15	Reno, Nev.
1912	July 4	**Jack Johnson**	34	195½	Jim Flynn	175	TKO 9	Las Vegas, Nev.
1913	Dec. 19	**Jack Johnson**	35	NA	Jim Johnson	NA	Draw 10	Paris
1914	June 27	**Jack Johnson**	36	221	Frank Moran	203	Ref 20	Paris
1915	Apr. 5	Jess Willard	33	230	**Jack Johnson**	205½	KO 26	Havana
1916	Mar. 25	**Jess Willard**	34	225	Frank Moran	203	ND 10	NYC (Mad.Sq. Garden)
1919	July 4	Jack Dempsey	24	187	**Jess Willard**	245	TKO 4	Toledo, Ohio
1920	Sept. 6	**Jack Dempsey**	25	185	Billy Miske	187	KO 3	Benton Harbor, Mich.
1920	Dec. 14	**Jack Dempsey**	25	188¼	Bill Brennan	197	KO 12	NYC (Mad. Sq. Garden)
1921	July 2	**Jack Dempsey**	26	188	Georges Carpentier	172	KO 4	Jersey City, N.J.
1923	July 4	**Jack Dempsey**	28	188	Tommy Gibbons	175½	Ref 15	Shelby, Mont.
1923	Sept. 14	**Jack Dempsey**	28	192½	Luis Firpo	216½	KO 2	NYC (Polo Grounds)
1926	Sept. 23	Gene Tunney	29	189½	**Jack Dempsey**	190	Wu 10	Philadelphia
1927	Sept. 22	**Gene Tunney**	30	189½	Jack Dempsey	192½	Wu 10	Chicago
1928	July 26	**Gene Tunney****	31	192	Tom Heeney	203	TKO 11	NYC (Yankee Stadium)
1930	June 12	Max Schmeling	24	188	Jack Sharkey	197	Disq. 4	NYC (Yankee Stadium)
1931	July 3	**Max Schmeling**	25	189	Young Stribling	186½	TKO 15	Cleveland

*James J. Jeffries retired as champion on May 13, 1905, then came out of retirement to fight Jack Johnson for the title in 1910.
**Gene Tunney retired as champion in 1928.

Year	Date	Winner	Age	Wgt	Loser	Wgt	Result	Location
1932	June 21	Jack Sharkey	29	205	**Max Schmeling**	188	Ws 15	Long Island City, N.Y.
1933	June 29	Primo Carnera	26	260½	**Jack Sharkey**	201	KO 6	Long Island City, N.Y.
1933	Oct. 22	**Primo Carnera**	26	259½	Paulino Uzcudun	229¼	Wu 15	Rome
1934	Mar. 1	**Primo Carnera**	27	270	Tommy Loughran	184	Wu 15	Miami
1934	June 14	Max Baer	25	209½	**Primo Carnera**	263¼	TKO 11	Long Island City, N.Y.
1935	June 13	James J. Braddock	29	193¾	**Max Baer**	209	Wu 15	Long Island City, N.Y.
1937	June 22	Joe Louis	23	197¼	**James J. Braddock**	197	KO 8	Chicago
1937	Aug. 30	**Joe Louis**	23	197	Tommy Farr	204¼	Wu 15	NYC (Yankee Stadium)
1938	Feb. 23	**Joe Louis**	23	200	Nathan Mann	193½	KO 3	NYC (Mad. Sq. Garden)
1938	Apr. 1	**Joe Louis**	23	202½	Harry Thomas	196	KO 5	Chicago
1938	June 22	**Joe Louis**	24	198¾	Max Schmeling	193	KO 1	NYC (Yankee Stadium)
1939	Jan. 25	**Joe Louis**	24	200¼	John Henry Lewis	180¾	KO 1	NYC (Mad. Sq. Garden)
1939	Apr. 17	**Joe Louis**	24	201¼	Jack Roper	204¾	KO 1	Los Angeles
1939	June 28	**Joe Louis**	25	200¾	Tony Galento	233¾	TKO 4	NYC (Yankee Stadium)
1939	Sept. 20	**Joe Louis**	25	200	Bob Pastor	183	KO 11	Detroit
1940	Feb. 9	**Joe Louis**	25	203	Arturo Godoy	202	Ws 15	NYC (Mad. Sq. Garden)
1940	Mar. 29	**Joe Louis**	25	201½	Johnny Paychek	187½	KO 2	NYC (Mad. Sq. Garden)
1940	June 20	**Joe Louis**	26	199	Arturo Godoy	201¼	TKO 8	NYC (Yankee Stadium)
1940	Dec. 16	**Joe Louis**	26	202¼	Al McCoy	180¾	TKO 6	Boston
1941	Jan. 31	**Joe Louis**	26	202½	Red Burman	188	KO 5	NYC (Mad. Sq. Garden)
1941	Feb. 17	**Joe Louis**	26	203½	Gus Dorazio	193½	KO 2	Philadelphia
1941	Mar. 21	**Joe Louis**	26	202	Abe Simon	254½	TKO 13	Detroit
1941	Apr. 8	**Joe Louis**	26	203½	Tony Musto	199½	TKO 9	St. Louis
1941	May 23	**Joe Louis**	27	201½	Buddy Baer	237½	Disq. 7	Washington, D.C.
1941	June 18	**Joe Louis**	27	199½	Billy Conn	174	KO 13	NYC (Polo Grounds)
1941	Sept. 29	**Joe Louis**	27	202¼	Lou Nova	202½	TKO 6	NYC (Polo Grounds)
1942	Jan. 9	**Joe Louis**	27	206¾	Buddy Baer	250	KO 1	NYC (Mad. Sq. Garden)
1942	Mar. 27	**Joe Louis**	27	207½	Abe Simon	255½	KO 6	NYC (Mad. Sq. Garden)
1942-45 World War II								
1946	June 9	**Joe Louis**	32	207	Billy Conn	187	KO 8	NYC (Yankee Stadium)
1946	Sept. 18	**Joe Louis**	32	211	Tami Mauriello	198½	KO 1	NYC (Yankee Stadium)
1947	Dec. 5	**Joe Louis**	33	211½	Jersey Joe Walcott	194½	Ws 15	NYC (Mad. Sq. Garden)
1948	June 25	**Joe Louis***	34	213½	Jersey Joe Walcott	194¾	KO 11	NYC (Yankee Stadium)
1949	June 22	**Ezzard Charles**	27	181¾	Jersey Joe Walcott	195½	Wu 15	Chicago
1949	Aug. 10	**Ezzard Charles**	28	180	Gus Lesnevich	182	TKO 8	NYC (Yankee Stadium)
1949	Oct. 14	**Ezzard Charles**	28	182	Pat Valentino	188½	KO 8	San Francisco
1950	Aug. 15	**Ezzard Charles**	29	183¼	Freddie Beshore	184½	TKO 14	Buffalo
1950	Sept. 27	**Ezzard Charles**	29	184½	Joe Louis	218	Wu 15	NYC (Yankee Stadium)
1950	Dec. 5	**Ezzard Charles**	29	185	Nick Barone	178½	KO 11	Cincinnati
1951	Jan. 12	**Ezzard Charles**	29	185	Lee Oma	193	TKO 10	NYC (Mad. Sq. Garden)
1951	Mar. 7	**Ezzard Charles**	29	186	Jersey Joe Walcott	193	Wu 15	Detroit
1951	May 30	**Ezzard Charles**	29	182	Joey Maxim	181½	Wu 15	Chicago
1951	July 18	Jersey Joe Walcott	37	194	**Ezzard Charles**	182	KO 7	Pittsburgh
1952	June 5	**Jersey Joe Walcott**	38	196	Ezzard Charles	191½	Wu 15	Philadelphia
1952	Sept. 23	Rocky Marciano	29	184	**Jersey Joe Walcott**	196	KO 13	Philadelphia
1953	May 15	**Rocky Marciano**	29	184½	Jersey Joe Walcott	197¾	KO 1	Chicago
1953	Sept. 24	**Rocky Marciano**	30	185	Roland LaStarza	184¾	TKO 11	NYC (Polo Grounds)
1954	June 17	**Rocky Marciano**	30	187½	Ezzard Charles	185½	Wu 15	NYC (Yankee Stadium)
1954	Sept. 17	**Rocky Marciano**	31	187	Ezzard Charles	192½	KO 8	NYC (Yankee Stadium)
1955	May 16	**Rocky Marciano**	31	189	Don Cockell	205	TKO 9	San Francisco
1955	Sept. 21	**Rocky Marciano****	32	188¼	Archie Moore	188	KO 9	NYC (Yankee Stadium)
1956	Nov. 30	Floyd Patterson	21	182¼	Archie Moore	187¾	KO 5	Chicago
1957	July 29	**Floyd Patterson**	22	184	Tommy Jackson	192½	TKO 10	NYC (Polo Grounds)
1957	Aug. 22	**Floyd Patterson**	22	187¼	Pete Rademacher	202	KO 6	Seattle
1958	Aug. 18	**Floyd Patterson**	23	184½	Roy Harris	194	TKO 13	Los Angeles
1959	May 1	**Floyd Patterson**	24	182½	Brian London	206	KO 11	Indianapolis
1959	June 26	Ingemar Johansson	26	196	**Floyd Patterson**	182	TKO 3	NYC (Yankee Stadium)
1960	June 20	Floyd Patterson	25	190	**Ingemar Johansson**	194¾	KO 5	NYC (Polo Grounds)
1961	Mar. 13	**Floyd Patterson**	26	194¾	Ingemar Johansson	206½	KO 6	Miami Beach
1961	Dec. 4	**Floyd Patterson**	26	188½	Tom McNeeley	197	KO 4	Toronto
1962	Sept. 25	Sonny Liston	30	214	**Floyd Patterson**	189	KO 1	Chicago
1963	July 22	**Sonny Liston**	31	215	Floyd Patterson	194½	KO 1	Las Vegas
1964	Feb. 25	Cassius Clay**	22	210½	**Sonny Liston**	218	TKO 7	Miami Beach

*Joe Louis retired as champion on Mar. 1, 1949, then came out of retirement to fight Ezzard Charles for the title in 1950.

**Rocky Marciano retired as undefeated champion on Apr. 27, 1956.

World Heavyweight Championship Fights (Cont.)

Year	Date	Winner	Age	Wgt	Loser	Wgt	Result	Location
1965	Mar. 5	Ernie Terrell WBA	25	199	Eddie Machen	192	Wu 15	Chicago
1965	May 25	**Muhammad Ali**	23	206	Sonny Liston	215¼	KO 1	Lewiston, Maine
1965	Nov. 1	Ernie Terrell WBA	26	206	George Chuvalo	209	Wu 15	Toronto
1965	Nov. 22	**Muhammad Ali**	23	210	Floyd Patterson	196¾	TKO 12	Las Vegas
1966	Mar. 29	**Muhammad Ali**	24	214½	George Chuvalo	216	Wu 15	Toronto
1966	May 21	**Muhammad Ali**	24	201½	Henry Cooper	188	TKO 6	London
1966	June 28	Ernie Terrell WBA	27	209½	Doug Jones	187½	Wu 15	Houston
1966	Aug. 6	**Muhammad Ali**	24	209½	Brian London	201½	KO 3	London
1966	Sept. 10	**Muhammad Ali**	24	203½	Karl Mildenberger	194¼	TKO 12	Frankfurt, W. Ger.
1966	Nov. 14	**Muhammad Ali**	24	212¾	Cleveland Williams	210½	TKO 3	Houston
1967	Feb. 6	**Muhammad Ali**	25	212¼	Ernie Terrell WBA	212¼	Wu 15	Houston
1967	Mar. 22	**Muhammad Ali**	25	211½	Zora Folley	202½	KO 7	NYC (Mad. Sq. Garden)
1968	Mar. 4	Joe Frazier	24	204½	Buster Mathis	243½	TKO 11	NYC (Mad. Sq. Garden)
1968	Apr. 27	Jimmy Ellis	28	197	Jerry Quarry	195	Wm 15	Oakland
1968	June 24	Joe Frazier NY	24	203½	Manuel Ramos	208	TKO 2	NYC (Mad. Sq. Garden)
1968	Aug. 14	Jimmy Ellis WBA	28	198	Floyd Patterson	188	Ref 15	Stockholm
1968	Dec. 10	Joe Frazier NY	24	203	Oscar Bonavena	207	Wu 15	Philadelphia
1969	Apr. 22	Joe Frazier NY	25	204½	Dave Zyglewicz	190½	KO 1	Houston
1969	June 23	Joe Frazier NY	25	203½	Jerry Quarry	198½	TKO 8	NYC (Mad. Sq. Garden)
1970	Feb. 16	Joe Frazier NY	26	205	Jimmy Ellis WBA	201	TKO 5	NYC (Mad. Sq. Garden)
1970	Nov. 18	**Joe Frazier**	26	209	Bob Foster	188	KO 2	Detroit
1971	Mar. 8	**Joe Frazier**	27	205½	Muhammad Ali	215	Wu 15	NYC (Mad. Sq. Garden)
1972	Jan. 15	**Joe Frazier**	28	215½	Terry Daniels	195	TKO 4	New Orleans
1972	May 26	**Joe Frazier**	28	217½	Ron Stander	218	TKO 5	Omaha, Neb.
1973	Jan. 22	George Foreman	24	217½	**Joe Frazier**	214	TKO 2	Kingston, Jamaica
1973	Sept. 1	**George Foreman**	24	219½	Jose (King) Roman	196½	KO 1	Tokyo
1974	Mar. 26	**George Foreman**	25	224¾	Ken Norton	212¾	TKO 2	Caracas, Venezuela
1974	Oct. 30	Muhammad Ali	32	216½	**George Foreman**	220	KO 8	Kinshasa, Zaire
1975	Mar. 24	**Muhammad Ali**	33	223½	Chuck Wepner	225	TKO 15	Cleveland
1975	May 16	**Muhammad Ali**	33	224½	Ron Lyle	219	TKO 11	Las Vegas
1975	June 30	**Muhammad Ali**	33	224½	Joe Bugner	230	Wu 15	Kuala Lumpur, Malaysia
1975	Oct. 1	**Muhammad Ali**	33	224½	Joe Frazier	215	TKO 14	Manila, Philippines
1976	Feb. 20	**Muhammad Ali**	34	226	Jean Pierre Coopman	206	KO 5	San Juan, P.R.
1976	Apr. 30	**Muhammad Ali**	34	230	Jimmy Young	209	Wu 15	Landover, Md.
1976	May 24	**Muhammad Ali**	34	220	Richard Dunn	206½	TKO 5	Munich, W. Ger.
1976	Sept. 28	**Muhammad Ali**	34	221	Ken Norton	217½	Wu 15	NYC (Yankee Stadium)
1977	May 16	**Muhammad Ali**	35	221¼	Alfredo Evangelista	209¼	Wu 15	Landover, Md.
1977	Sept. 29	**Muhammad Ali**	35	225	Earnie Shavers	211¼	Wu 15	NYC (Mad. Sq. Garden)
1978	Feb. 15	Leon Spinks	24	197¼	**Muhammad Ali**	224¼	Ws 15	Las Vegas
1978	June 9	Larry Holmes	28	209	Ken Norton WBC††	220	Ws 15	Las Vegas
1978	Sept. 15	Muhammad Ali†	36	221	**Leon Spinks**	201	Wu 15	New Orleans
1978	Nov. 10	Larry Holmes WBC	29	214	Alfredo Evangelista	208¼	KO 7	Las Vegas
1979	Mar. 23	Larry Holmes WBC	29	214	Osvaldo Ocasio	207	TKO 7	Las Vegas
1979	June 22	Larry Holmes WBC	29	215	Mike Weaver	202	TKO 12	NYC (Mad. Sq. Garden)
1979	Sept. 28	Larry Holmes WBC	29	210	Earnie Shavers	211	TKO 11	Las Vegas
1979	Oct. 20	John Tate	24	240	Gerrie Coetzee	222	Wu 15	Pretoria, S. Africa
1980	Feb. 3	Larry Holmes WBC	30	213½	Lorenzo Zanon	215	TKO 6	Las Vegas
1980	Mar. 31	Mike Weaver	27	232	John Tate WBA	232	KO 15	Knoxville, Tenn.
1980	Mar. 31	Larry Holmes WBC	30	211	Leroy Jones	254½	TKO 8	Las Vegas
1980	July 7	Larry Holmes WBC	30	214¼	Scott LeDoux	226	TKO 7	Minneapolis
1980	Oct. 2	Larry Holmes WBC	30	211½	Muhammad Ali	217½	TKO 11	Las Vegas
1980	Oct. 25	Mike Weaver WBA	28	210	Gerrie Coetzee	226½	KO 13	Sun City, S. Africa
1981	Apr. 11	**Larry Holmes**	31	215	Trevor Berbick	215½	Wu 15	Las Vegas
1981	June 12	**Larry Holmes**	31	212½	Leon Spinks	200¼	TKO 3	Detroit
1981	Oct. 3	Mike Weaver WBA	29	215	James (Quick) Tillis	209	Wu 15	Rosemont, Ill.
1981	Nov. 6	**Larry Holmes**	32	213¼	Renaldo Snipes	215¾	TKO 11	Pittsburgh
1982	June 11	**Larry Holmes**	32	212½	Gerry Cooney	225½	TKO 13	Las Vegas
1982	Nov. 26	**Larry Holmes**	33	217½	Randall (Tex) Cobb	234¼	Wu 15	Houston
1982	Dec. 10	Michael Dokes	24	216	Mike Weaver WBA	209¾	TKO 1	Las Vegas

*.*After defeating Liston, Cassius Clay announced that he had changed his name to Muhammad Ali. He was later stripped of his title by the WBA and most state boxing commissions after refusing induction into the U.S. Army on Apr. 28, 1967.

† Muhammad Ali retired as champion on June 27, 1979, then came out of retirement to fight Larry Holmes for the title in 1980.

†† WBC recognized Ken Norton as world champion when Leon Spinks refused to meet Norton before Spinks' rematch with Muhammad Ali. Norton had scored a 15-round split decision over Jimmy Young on Nov. 5, 1977 in Las Vegas.

Year	Date	Winner	Age	Wgt	Loser	Wgt	Result	Location
1983	Mar. 27	**Larry Holmes**	33	221	Lucien Rodriguez	209	Wu 12	Scranton, Pa.
1983	May 20	Michael Dokes WBA	24	223	Mike Weaver	218½	Draw 15	Las Vegas
1983	May 20	**Larry Holmes**	33	213	Tim Witherspoon	219½	Ws 12	Las Vegas
1983	Sept. 10	**Larry Holmes**	33	223	Scott Frank	211¼	TKO 5	Atlantic City
1983	Sept. 23	Gerrie Coetzee	28	215	Michael Dokes WBA	217	KO 10	Richfield, Ohio
1983	Nov. 25	**Larry Holmes**	34	219	Marvis Frazier	200	TKO 1	Las Vegas
1984	Mar. 9	Tim Witherspoon*	26	220¼	Greg Page	239½	Wm 12	Las Vegas
1984	Aug. 31	Pinklon Thomas	26	216	Tim Witherspoon	217	Wm 12	Las Vegas
1984	Nov. 9	**Larry Holmes** IBF	35	221½	Bonecrusher Smith	227	TKO 12	Las Vegas
1984	Dec. 1	Greg Page	26	236½	Gerrie Coetzee WBA	218	KO 8	Sun City, S. Africa
1985	Mar. 15	**Larry Holmes** IBF	35	223½	David Bey	233¼	TKO 10	Las Vegas
1985	Apr. 29	Tony Tubbs	26	229	Greg Page WBA	239½	Wu 15	Buffalo
1985	May 20	**Larry Holmes** IBF	35	224¼	Carl Williams	215	Wu 15	Las Vegas
1985	June 15	Pinklon Thomas WBC	27	220¼	Mike Weaver	221¼	KO 8	Las Vegas
1985	Sept. 21	Michael Spinks	29	200	**Larry Holmes** IBF	221½	Wu 15	Las Vegas
1986	Jan. 17	Tim Witherspoon	28	227	Tony Tubbs WBA	229	Wm 15	Atlanta
1986	Mar. 22	Trevor Berbick	33	218½	Pinklon Thomas WBC	222¾	Ws 15	Las Vegas
1986	Apr. 19	**Michael Spinks** IBF	29	205	Larry Holmes	223	Ws 15	Las Vegas
1986	July 19	Tim Witherspoon WBA	28	234¾	Frank Bruno	228	TKO 11	Wembley, England
1986	Sept. 6	**Michael Spinks** IBF	30	201	Steffen Tangstad	214¾	TKO 4	Las Vegas
1986	Nov. 22	Mike Tyson	20	221¼	Trevor Berbick WBC	218½	TKO 2	Las Vegas
1986	Dec. 12	Bonecrusher Smith	33	228½	Tim Witherspoon WBA	233½	TKO 1	NYC (Mad. Sq. Garden)
1987	Mar. 7	Mike Tyson WBC	20	219	Bonecrusher Smith WBA	233	Wu 12	Las Vegas
1987	May 30	Mike Tyson	20	218¾	Pinklon Thomas	217¾	TKO 6	Las Vegas
1987	May 30	Tony Tucker**	28	222¼	Buster Douglas	227¼	TKO 10	Las Vegas
1987	June 15	**Michael Spinks**†	30	208¾	Gerry Cooney	238	TKO 5	Atlantic City
1987	Aug. 1	Mike Tyson	21	221	Tony Tucker IBF	221	Wu 12	Las Vegas
1987	Oct. 16	Mike Tyson	21	216	Tyrell Biggs	228¾	TKO 7	Atlantic City
1988	Jan. 22	Mike Tyson	21	215¾	Larry Holmes	225¾	TKO 4	Atlantic City
1988	Mar. 20	Mike Tyson	21	216¼	Tony Tubbs	238¼	KO 2	Tokyo
1988	June 27	Mike Tyson	21	218¼	**Michael Spinks**	212¼	KO 1	Atlantic City
1989	Feb. 25	**Mike Tyson**	22	218	Frank Bruno	228	TKO 5	Las Vegas
1989	July 21	**Mike Tyson**	23	219¼	Carl Williams	218	TKO 1	Atlantic City
1990	Feb. 10	Buster Douglas	29	231½	**Mike Tyson**	220½	KO 10	Tokyo
1990	Oct. 25	Evander Holyfield	28	208	**Buster Douglas**	246	KO 3	Las Vegas
1991	Apr. 19	**Evander Holyfield**	28	208	George Foreman	257	Wu 12	Atlantic City
1991	Nov. 23	**Evander Holyfield**	29	210	Bert Cooper	215	TKO 7	Atlanta
1992	June 19	**Evander Holyfield**	29	210	Larry Holmes	233	Wu 12	Las Vegas
1992	Nov. 13	Riddick Bowe	25	235	**Evander Holyfield**	205	Wu 12	Las Vegas
1993	Feb. 6	**Riddick Bowe**	25	243	Michael Dokes	244	TKO 1	NYC (Mad. Sq. Garden)
1993	May 8	Lennox Lewis WBC‡	27	235	Tony Tucker	235	Wu 12	Las Vegas
1993	May 22	**Riddick Bowe**	25	244	Jesse Ferguson	224	TKO 2	Washington, D.C.
1993	Oct. 1	Lennox Lewis WBC	28	233	Frank Bruno	238	TKO 7	Cardiff, Wales
1993	Nov. 6	Evander Holyfield	31	217	**Riddick Bowe** WBA/IBF	246	Wm 12	Las Vegas
1994	Apr. 22	Michael Moorer	26	214	**Evander Holyfield**	214	Wm 12	Las Vegas
1994	May 6	Lennox Lewis WBC	28	235	Phil Jackson	218	TKO 8	Atlantic City
1994	Sept. 25	Oliver McCall	29	231¼	**Lennox Lewis** WBC	238	TKO 2	London
1994	Nov. 5	George Foreman!	45	250	**Michael Moorer**	222	KO 10	Las Vegas
1995	Apr. 8	Oliver McCall WBC	29	231	Larry Holmes	236	Wu 12	Las Vegas
1995	Apr. 8	Bruce Seldon!	28	236	Tony Tucker	240	TKO 7	Las Vegas
1995	Apr. 22	**George Foreman**!	46	256	Axel Schulz	221	Ws 12	Las Vegas
1995	Aug. 19	Bruce Seldon WBA	28	234	Joe Hipp	223	TKO 10	Las Vegas
1995	Sept. 2	Frank Bruno	33	248	Oliver McCall WBC	235	Wu 12	London
1995	Dec. 9	Frans Botha*	27	237	Axel Schulz	222	Wu 12	Stuttgart, GER
1996	Mar. 16	Mike Tyson	29	220	Frank Bruno WBC	247	TKO 3	Las Vegas

*WBC recognized winner of Mar. 9, 1984 fight between Tim Witherspoon and Greg Page as world champion after Larry Holmes relinquished title in dispute. IBF then recognized Holmes.

**IBF recognized winner of May 30, 1987 fight between Tony Tucker and James (Buster) Douglas as world champion after Michael Spinks relinquished the title in dispute.

†The July 15, 1987 Spinks-Cooney fight was not an official championship bout because it was not sanctioned by any boxing associations, councils or federations.

‡WBC recognized Lennox Lewis as world champion when Riddick Bowe gave up that portion of his title on Dec. 14, 1992, rather than fight Lewis, the WBC's mandatory challenger.

!George Foreman won WBA and IBF championships when he beat Michael Moorer on Nov. 5, 1994. He was stripped of WBA title on Mar. 4, 1995, when he refused to fight No. 1 contender Tony Tucker, and he relinquished IBF title on June 29, 1995, rather than give Axel Schulz a rematch. Tucker lost to Bruce Seldon in their April 8, 2001 fight for vacant WBA title.

World Heavyweight Championship Fights (Cont.)

Year	Date	Winner	Age	Wgt	Loser	Wgt	Result	Location
1996	June 22	Michael Moorer*	28	222	Axel Schulz	223	Ws 12	Dortmund, GER
1996	Sept. 7	Mike Tyson WBC†	30	219	Bruce Seldon WBA	229	TKO 1	Las Vegas
1996	Nov. 9	Evander Holyfield	34	215	**Mike Tyson** WBA	222	TKO 11	Las Vegas
1997	Feb. 7	Lennox Lewis†	31	251	Oliver McCall	237	TKO 5	Las Vegas
1997	Mar. 29	Michael Moorer IBF	29	212	Vaughn Bean	212	Wm 12	Las Vegas
1997	June 28	**Evander Holyfield** WBA‡	34	218	Mike Tyson	218	Disq. 3	Las Vegas
1997	July 12	Lennox Lewis WBC	31	242	Henry Akinwande	237½	Disq. 5	Stateline, Nev.
1997	Oct. 4	Lennox Lewis WBC	32	244	Andrew Golota	244	TKO 1	Atlantic City
1997	Nov. 8	Evander Holyfield WBA	35	214	Michael Moorer IBF	223	TKO 8	Las Vegas
1998	Mar. 28	Lennox Lewis WBC	32	243	Shannon Briggs	228	TKO 5	Atlantic City
1998	Sept. 19	**Evander Holyfield** WBA/IBF	35	217	Vaughn Bean	231	Wu 12	Atlanta
1998	Sept. 26	Lennox Lewis WBC	33	250	Zeljko Mavrovic	220	Wu 12	Uncasville, Conn.
1999	Mar. 13	Lennox Lewis WBC	33	246	**Evander Holyfield** WBA/IBF	215	Draw 12	NYC (Mad. Sq. Garden)
1999	Nov. 13	Lennox Lewis WBC	34	240	**Evander Holyfield** WBA/IBF	218	Wu 12	Las Vegas
2000	Apr. 29	**Lennox Lewis** WBC/IBF!	34	247	Michael Grant	250	KO 2	NYC (Mad. Sq. Garden)
2000	July 15	**Lennox Lewis** WBC/IBF	34	250	Frans Botha	237	TKO 2	London
2000	Aug. 12	Evander Holyfield	37	221	John Ruiz	224	Wu 12	Las Vegas
2000	Nov. 11	**Lennox Lewis** WBC/IBF	35	249	David Tua	245	Wu 12	Las Vegas
2001	Mar. 3	John Ruiz	29	227	Evander Holyfield	217	Wu 12	Las Vegas
2001	Apr. 22	Hasim Rahman	28	237	**Lennox Lewis** WBC/IBF	253	KO 5	Johannesburg, S. Africa
2001	Nov. 17	Lennox Lewis	36	247	**Hasim Rahman** WBC/IBF	236	KO 4	Las Vegas
2001	Dec. 15	**John Ruiz** WBA	29	232	Evander Holyfield	219	Draw 12	Mashantucket, Conn.
2002	June 8	**Lennox Lewis** WBC/IBF@	36	249	Mike Tyson	235	KO 8	Memphis, Tenn.
2002	July 27	**John Ruiz** WBA	30	233	Kirk Johnson	238	Disq. 10	Las Vegas
2002	Dec. 14	Chris Byrd	32	214	Evander Holyfield	220	Wu 12	Atlantic City
2003	Mar. 1	Roy Jones Jr.	34	193	**John Ruiz** WBA	226	Wu 12	Las Vegas
2003	June 21	**Lennox Lewis** WBC	37	257	Vitali Klitschko	248	TKO 6	Los Angeles
2003	Sept. 20	**Chris Byrd** IBF	33	212	Fres Oquendo	224	Wu 12	Uncasville, Conn.
2003	Dec. 13	John Ruiz WBA%	31	241	Hasim Rahman	246	Wu 12	Atlantic City
2004	Apr. 17	**John Ruiz** WBA	32	240	Fres Oquendo	222	TKO 11	NYC (Mad. Sq. Garden)
2004	Apr. 17	**Chris Byrd** IBF	33	210	Andrew Golota	237	Draw 12	NYC (Mad. Sq. Garden)
2004	Apr. 24	Vitali Klitschko WBC^	32	245	Corrie Sanders	236	TKO 8	Los Angeles
2004	Nov. 13	**John Ruiz** WBA	32	226	Andrew Golota	240	Wu 12	NYC (Mad. Sq. Garden)
2004	Nov. 13	**Chris Byrd** IBF	34	214	Jameel McCline	270	Wu 12	NYC (Mad. Sq. Garden)
2004	Dec. 11	**Vitali Klitschko** WBC	33	250	Danny Williams	270	TKO 8	Las Vegas
2005	Apr. 30	James Toney$	36	233	**John Ruiz** WBA	241	NC 12	NYC (Mad. Sq. Garden)
2005	Oct. 1	**Chris Byrd** IBF	35	213	DaVarryl Williamson	225	Wu 12	Reno, Nev.

*Frans Botha won the vacant IBF title with a controversial 12-round decision over Axel Schulz on Dec. 9, 1995, but after legal sparring, was eventually stripped of the IBF belt for using anabolic steroids. Moorer then claimed the revacated title with his June 22, 1996 win over Schulz.

†Mike Tyson won the WBC belt from Frank Bruno on Mar. 16, 1996 and still held it at the time of his Sept. 7, 1996 win over Bruce Seldon (although it was not at risk for that fight) but was forced to relinquish the title after the bout for not fighting mandatory challenge Lennox Lewis. Tyson also paid Lewis $4 million to step aside and allow the Tyson-Seldon bout to take place. Lewis then fought Oliver McCall for the vacant WBC belt. The fight was stopped 55 seconds into round 5 because, inexplicably, McCall was visibly distraught and stopped throwing punches.

‡Holyfield won the bout by disqualification and retained the WBA belt after Tyson spit out his mouthpiece and bit off a piece of Holyfield's ear. Tyson had received a two-point deduction from referee Mills Lane and after a stern warning and a short delay the fight was allowed to continue. Later in round 3, he bit Holyfield's other ear and Tyson was disqualified.

!Lewis was stripped of the WBA title for choosing to fight Michael Grant instead of John Ruiz, the WBA's #1 challenger. The WBA sanctioned the Evander Holyfield-John Ruiz bout August 12 bout for its vacant heavyweight belt.

@Lewis effectively sold his IBF title to promoter Don King for $1 million and a Range Rover in September 2002. Lewis stepped aside (in exchange for the car and substantial fee), relinquishing his IBF belt by declining to fight Chris Byrd the mandatory challenger. The IBF sanctioned the Dec. 14, 2002 fight between Byrd and Holyfield for its vacant heavyweight belt.

%Ruiz won the interim WBA title after Roy Jones Jr. declined to defend the title he won from Ruiz on Mar. 1, 2003. The interim tag was later dropped when Jones returned to the light heavyweight division.

^Klitschko won the WBC title vacated by the retirement of Lennox Lewis.

$Toney won a uanimous 12-round decision but tested positive for steroids in a post-fight drug test.

Year	Date	Winner	Age	Wgt	Loser	Wgt	Result	Location
2005	Dec. 17	Nikolai Valuev	32	324	**John Ruiz** WBA	238	Wm 12	Berlin
2006	Mar. 18	**Hasim Rahman** WBC*	33	238	James Toney	237	MDraw 12	Atlantic City
2006	Apr. 22	Wladimir Klitschko	30	241	**Chris Byrd** IBF	231	TKO 7	Mannheim, Germany
2006	June 3	**Nikolai Valuev** WBA	32	321	Owen Beck	243	TKO 3	Hannover, Germany
2006	Aug. 12	Oleg Maskaev	37	238	**Hasim Rahman** WBC	235	TKO 12	Las Vegas
2006	Oct. 7	**Nikolai Valuev** WBA	33	330	Monte Barrett	229	TKO 11	Rosemont, Ill.
2006	Nov. 11	**W. Klitschko** IBF	30	241	Calvin Brock	224½	TKO 7	New York City
2006	Dec. 10	Oleg Maskaev WBC	37	240	Peter Okhello	255½	Wu 12	Moscow
2007	Jan. 20	**Nikolai Valuev** WBA	33	322⅓	Jameel McCline	268⅓	TKO 3	Basel, Switzerland
2007	Mar. 10	**W. Klitschko** IBF	30	246½	Ray Austin	247	TKO 2	Mannheim, Germany
2007	Apr. 14	Ruslan Chagaev	28	228	**Nikolai Valuev**	319	Wm 12	Stuttgart, Germany
2007	July 7	**W. Klitschko** IBF	31	243	Lamon Brewster	227	TKO 6	Cologne, Germany
2008	Jan. 19	**R. Chagaev** WBA	29	229	Matt Skelton	245	Wu 12	Dusseldorf, Germany
2008	Feb. 23	**W. Klitschko** IBF	31	238	Sultan Ibragimov	219	Wu 12	New York City
2008	Mar. 8	Samuel Peter	27	250	Oleg Maskaev	243	TKO 6	Cancun, Mexico
2008	July 12	**W. Klitschko** IBF	32	240	Tony Thompson	247	KO 11	Hermosillo, Mexico
2008	Aug. 30	Nikolay Valuev	35	318	John Ruiz	239	Wu 12	Berlin, Germany
2008	Oct. 11	Vitali Klitschko	37	246	**Samuel Peter** WBC	253	TKO 8	Berlin, Germany

*The WBC voted to award interim champ Rahman its heavyweight belt on Nov. 10, 2005 in the wake of the retirement of titleholder Vitali Klitschko who had previously postponed his scheduled rematch with Rahman four times.

All-Time Heavyweight Upsets

Buster Douglas was a 42-1 underdog when he defeated previously unbeaten heavyweight champion Mike Tyson on Feb. 10, 1990. That 10th-round knockout ranks as the biggest upset in boxing history. By comparison, 45-year-old George Foreman was only a 3-1 underdog before he unexpectedly won the title from Michael Moorer on Nov. 5, 1994.

Here are the best-known upsets in the annals of the heavyweight division. All fights were for the world championship except the Max Schmeling-Joe Louis bout.

Date	Winner	Loser	Result	KO Time	Location
9/7/1892	James J. Corbett	John L. Sullivan	KO 21	1:30	Olympic Club, New Orleans
4/5/1915	Jess Willard	Jack Johnson	KO 26	1:26	Mariano Race Track, Havana
9/23/26	Gene Tunney	Jack Dempsey	Wu 10	–	Sesquicentennial Stadium, Phila.
6/13/35	James J. Braddock	Max Baer	Wu 15	–	Mad. Sq.Garden Bowl, L.I. City
6/19/36	Max Schmeling	Joe Louis	KO 12	2:29	Yankee Stadium, New York
7/18/51	Jersey Joe Walcott	Ezzard Charles	KO 7	0:55	Forbes Field, Pittsburgh
6/26/59	Ingemar Johansson	Floyd Patterson	TKO 3	2:03	Yankee Stadium, New York
2/25/64	Cassius Clay	Sonny Liston	TKO 7	*	Convention Hall, Miami Beach
10/30/74	Muhammad Ali	George Foreman	KO 8	2:58	20th of May Stadium, Zaire
2/15/78	Leon Spinks	Muhammad Ali	Ws 15	–	Hilton Pavilion, Las Vegas
9/21/85	Michael Spinks	Larry Holmes	Wu 15	–	Riviera Hotel, Las Vegas
2/10/90	Buster Douglas	Mike Tyson	KO 10	1:23	Tokyo Dome, Tokyo
11/5/94	George Foreman	Michael Moorer	KO 10	2:03	MGM Grand, Las Vegas
11/9/96	Evander Holyfield	Mike Tyson	TKO 11	0:37	MGM Grand, Las Vegas
4/22/2001	Hasim Rahman	Lennox Lewis	KO 5	2:32	Johannesburg, South Africa

*Liston failed to answer bell for Round 7.

Major Titleholders

Note the following sanctioning body abbreviations: NBA (National Boxing Association), WBA (World Boxing Association), WBC (World Boxing Council), GBR (Great Britain), IBF (International Boxing Federation), plus other national and state commissions. Fighters who retired as champion are indicated by (*) and champions who abandoned or relinquished their titles are indicated by (†).

Heavyweights

Widely accepted champions in CAPITAL letters. Current champions in **bold** type (as of Oct. 31, 2008).

Note: Muhammad Ali was stripped of his world title in 1967 after refusing induction into the Army (see Muhammad Ali's Career Pro Record). George Foreman was stripped of his WBA and IBF titles in 1995, but remained active as linear champion.

Champion	Held Title
JOHN L. SULLIVAN	1885–92
JAMES J. CORBETT	1892–97
BOB FITZSIMMONS	1897–99
JAMES J. JEFFRIES	1899–1905*
MARVIN HART	1905–06
TOMMY BURNS	1906–08
JACK JOHNSON	1908–15
JESS WILLARD	1915–19
JACK DEMPSEY	1919–26
GENE TUNNEY	1926–28*
MAX SCHMELING	1930–32
JACK SHARKEY	1932–33
PRIMO CARNERA	1933–34
MAX BAER	1934–35
JAMES J. BRADDOCK	1935–37
JOE LOUIS	1937–49*
EZZARD CHARLES	1949–51
JERSEY JOE WALCOTT	1951–52
ROCKY MARCIANO	1952–56*
FLOYD PATTERSON	1956–59
INGEMAR JOHANSSON	1959–60
FLOYD PATTERSON	1960–62
SONNY LISTON	1962–64
CASSIUS CLAY (MUHAMMAD ALI)	1964–67
Ernie Terrell (WBA)	1965–67
Joe Frazier (NY)	1968–70
Jimmy Ellis (WBA)	1968–70
JOE FRAZIER	1970–73
GEORGE FOREMAN	1973–74
MUHAMMAD ALI	1974–78
LEON SPINKS	1978
Ken Norton (WBC)	1978
Larry Holmes (WBC)	1978–80
MUHAMMAD ALI	1978–79*
John Tate (WBA)	1979–80
Mike Weaver (WBA)	1980–82
LARRY HOLMES	1980–85
Michael Dokes (WBA)	1982–83
Gerrie Coetzee (WBA)	1983–84
Tim Witherspoon (WBC)	1984
Pinklon Thomas (WBC)	1984–86
Greg Page (WBA)	1984–85
MICHAEL SPINKS	1985–87

Champion	Held Title
Trevor Berbick (WBC)	1986
Tim Witherspoon (WBA)	1986
Mike Tyson (WBC)	1986–87
James (Bonecrusher) Smith (WBA)	1986–87
Tony Tucker (IBF)	1987
MIKE TYSON (WBC, WBA, IBF)	1987–90
BUSTER DOUGLAS (WBC, WBA, IBF)	1990
EVANDER HOLYFIELD (WBC, WBA, IBF)	1990–92
RIDDICK BOWE (WBA, IBF)	1992–93
Lennox Lewis (WBC)	1992–94
EVANDER HOLYFIELD (WBA, IBF)	1993–94
MICHAEL MOORER (WBA, IBF)	1994
Oliver McCall (WBC)	1994–95
GEORGE FOREMAN (WBA, IBF)	1994–95
Bruce Seldon (WBA)	1995–96
GEORGE FOREMAN	1995–96
Frank Bruno (WBC)	1995–96
Mike Tyson (WBC)	1996†
Mike Tyson (WBC)	1996
Michael Moorer (IBF)	1996–1997
Evander Holyfield (WBA, IBF)	1996–2000
Lennox Lewis (WBC)	1997–2000
LENNOX LEWIS (WBA, WBC, IBF)	2000
Evander Holyfield (WBA)	2000–01
LENNOX LEWIS (WBC, IBF)	2000–01
John Ruiz (WBA)	2001-03
Hasim Rahman (WBC, IBF)	2001
LENNOX LEWIS (WBC, IBF)	2001–02†
LENNOX LEWIS (WBC)	2001–04*
Roy Jones Jr. (WBA)	2003–04
Chris Byrd (IBF)	2003–06
John Ruiz (WBA)	2004–05
Vitali Klitschko (WBC)	2004–05*
Hasim Rahman (WBC)	2005–06
Nikolai Valuev (WBA)	2005–07
Wladimir Klitschko (IBF)	2006—
Oleg Maskaev (WBC)	2006–08
Ruslan Chagaev (WBA)	2007–08
Samuel Peter (WBC)	2008
Nikolai Valuev (WBA)	2008—
Vitali Klitschko (WBC)	2008—

Note: John L. Sullivan held the Bare Knuckle championship from 1882-85.

Cruiserweights

Current champions in **bold** type.

Champion	Held Title
Marvin Camel (WBC)	1980
Carlos De Leon (WBC)	1980–82
Ossie Ocasio (WBA)	1982–84
S.T. Gordon (WBC)	1982–83
Carlos De Leon (WBC)	1983–85
Marvin Camel (IBF)	1983–84
Lee Roy Murphy (IBF)	1984–86
Piet Crous (WBA)	1984–85
Alfonso Ratliff (WBC)	1985
Dwight Braxton (WBA)	1985–86
Bernard Benton (WBC)	1985–86
Carlos De Leon (WBC)	1986–88
Evander Holyfield (WBA)	1986–88
Ricky Parkey (IBF)	1986–87
Evander Holyfield (WBA/IBF)	1987–88
Evander Holyfield	1988†

Champion	Held Title
Toufik Belbouli (WBA)	1989
Robert Daniels (WBA)	1989–91
Carlos De Leon (WBC)	1989–90
Glenn McCrory (IBF)	1989–90
Jeff Lampkin (IBF)	1990
Massimiliano Duran (WBC)	1990–91
Bobby Czyz (WBA)	1991–92†
Anaclet Wamba (WBC)	1991–95
James Pritchard (IBF)	1991
James Warring (IBF)	1991–92
Alfred Cole (IBF)	1992–96
Orlin Norris (WBA)	1993–95
Nate Miller (WBA)	1995–97
Marcelo Dominguez (WBC)	1996–98
Adolpho Washington (IBF)	1996–97
Uriah Grant (IBF)	1997

Champion	Held Title
Imamu Mayfield (IBF)	1997–98
Arthur Williams (IBF)	1998–99
Fabrice Tiozzo (WBA)	1997–2000
Juan Carlos Gomez (WBC)	1998–2002†
Vassiliy Jirov (IBF)	1999–2003
Virgil Hill (WBA)	2000–02
Jean-Marc Mormeck (WBA)	2002–06
Wayne Braithwaite (WBC)	2002–05
James Toney (IBF)	2003†
Kelvin Davis (IBF)	2004–05

Champion	Held Title
Jean-Marc Mormeck (WBA/WBC)	2005–06
O'Neil Bell (IBF)	2005–07
O'NEIL BELL (IBF/WBA/WBC)	2006–07
JEAN-MARC MORMECK (WBA/WBC)	2007
Steve Cunningham (IBF)	2007–
David Haye (WBA/WBC)	2007–08
Firat Arslan (WBA)	2008
Guillermo Jones (WBA)	2008–
Giacobbe Fragomeni (WBC)	2008–

Light Heavyweights

Widely accepted champions in CAPITAL letters. Current champions in **bold** type.

Champion	Held Title
JACK ROOT	1903
GEORGE GARDNER	1903
BOB FITZSIMMONS	1903–05
PHILADELPHIA JACK O'BRIEN	1905–12*
JACK DILLON	1914–16
BATTLING LEVINSKY	1916–20
GEORGES CARPENTIER	1920–22
BATTLING SIKI	1922–23
MIKE McTIGUE	1923–25
PAUL BERLENBACH	1925–26
JACK DELANEY	1926–27†
Jimmy Slattery (NBA)	1927
TOMMY LOUGHRAN	1927-29
JIMMY SLATTERY	1930
MAXIE ROSENBLOOM	1930–34
George Nichols (NBA)	1932
Bob Godwin (NBA)	1933
BOB OLIN	1934–35
JOHN HENRY LEWIS	1935–38
MELIO BETTINA (NY)	1939
Len Harvey (GBR)	1939–42
BILLY CONN	1939–40†
ANTON CHRISTOFORIDIS (NBA)	1941
GUS LESNEVICH	1941–48
Freddie Mills (GBR)	1942–46
FREDDIE MILLS	1948–50
JOEY MAXIM	1950–52
ARCHIE MOORE	1952–62
Harold Johnson (NBA)	1961
HAROLD JOHNSON	1962–63
WILLIE PASTRANO	1963–65
Eddie Cotton (Mich.)	1963–64
JOSE TORRES	1965–66
DICK TIGER	1966–68
BOB FOSTER	1968–74*
Vicente Rondon (WBA)	1971–72
John Conteh (WBC)	1974–77
Victor Galindez (WBA)	1974–78
Miguel A. Cuello (WBC)	1977–78
Mate Parlov (WBC)	1978
Mike Rossman (WBA)	1978–79
Marvin Johnson (WBC)	1978–79
Matthew (Franklin) Saad Muhammad (WBC)	1979–81
Marvin Johnson (WBA)	1979–80
Eddie (Gregory) Mustapha Muhammad (WBA)	1980–81
Michael Spinks (WBA)	1981–83
Dwight (Braxton) Muhammad Qawi (WBC)	1981–83

Champion	Held Title
MICHAEL SPINKS	1983–85†
J.B.Williamson (WBC)	1985–86
Slobodan Kacar (IBF)	1985–86
Marvin Johnson (WBA)	1986–87
Dennis Andries (WBC)	1986–87
Bobby Czyz (IBF)	1986–87
Leslie Stewart (WBA)	1987
Virgil Hill (WBA)	1987–91
Prince Charles Williams (IBF)	1987–93
Thomas Hearns (WBC)	1987
Donny Lalonde (WBC)	1987–88
Sugar Ray Leonard (WBC)	1988
Dennis Andries (WBC)	1989
Jeff Harding (WBC)	1989–90
Dennis Andries (WBC)	1990–91
Jeff Harding (WBC)	1991–94
Thomas Hearns (WBA)	1991–92
Iran Barkley (WBA)	1992†
Virgil Hill (WBA)	1992–97
Henry Maske (IBF)	1993–96
Virgil Hill (WBA/IBF)	1996–97
Mike McCallum (WBC)	1994–95
Fabrice Tiozzo (WBC)	1995–96
Roy Jones Jr. (WBC)	1996
Montell Griffin (WBC)	1996
D. Michaelczewski (WBA/IBF)	1997†
William Guthrie (IBF)	1997–98
Lou Del Valle (WBA)	1997–98
ROY JONES JR. (WBA/WBC)	1997–2003†
Reggie Johnson (IBF)	1998–99
ROY JONES JR. (WBA/WBC/IBF)	1999–2003†
Antonio Tarver (WBC/IBF)	2003
Mehdi Sahnoune (WBA)	2003
ROY JONES JR. (WBC)	2003–04
Silvio Branco (WBA)	2003–04
Antonio Tarver (WBC)	2003–04†
Glen Johnson (IBF)	2004†
Fabrice Tiozzo (WBA)	2004–06*
ANTONIO TARVER	2005–06†
Clinton Woods (IBF)	2006–08
Tomasz Adamek (WBC)	2006–07
Silvio Branco (WBA)	2007
Chad Dawson (WBC)	2007–08†
Stipe Drews (WBA)	2007
Danny Green (WBA)	2007–08†
Antonio Tarver (WBA)	2008
Adrian Dianonu (WBC)	2008–
Hugo Hernan Garay (WBA)	2008–
Chad Dawson (IBF)	2008–

Super Middleweights

Current champions in **bold** type.

Champion	Held Title
Murray Sutherland (IBF)	1984
Chong-Pal Park (IBF)	1984–87
Chong-Pal Park (WBA)	1987–88
Graziano Rocchigiani (IBF)	1988–89
Fugencio Obelmejias (WBA)	1988–89
Ray Leonard (WBC)	1988–90†
In-Chut Baek (WBA)	1989–90

Champion	Held Title
Lindell Holmes (IBF)	1990–91
Christophe Tiozzo (WBA)	1990–91
Mauro Galvano (WBC)	1990–92
Victor Cordova (WBA)	1991
Darrin Van Horn (IBF)	1991–92
Iran Barkley (WBA)	1992
Nigel Benn (WBC)	1992–96

Major Titleholders (Cont.)
Super Middleweights (Cont.)

Champion	Held Title
James Toney (IBF)	1992–94
Michael Nunn (WBA)	1992–94
Steve Little (WBA)	1994
Frank Liles (WBA)	1994–99
Roy Jones (IBF)	1994–96
Thulane Malinga (WBC)	1996
Vincenzo Nardiello (WBC)	1996
Robin Reid (WBC)	1996–97
Charles Brewer (IBF)	1997–98
Sven Ottke (IBF)	1998–2004*
Thulane Malinga (WBC)	1997–98
Richie Woodhall (WBC)	1998–99
Byron Mitchell (WBA)	1999–2000
Markus Beyer (WBC)	1999–2000
Glenn Gatley (WBC)	2000
Dingaan Thobela (WBC)	2000
Bruno Girard (WBA)	2000–01†

Champion	Held Title
Dave Hilton (WBC)	2000†
Byron Mitchell (WBA)	2001–03
Eric Lucas (WBC)	2001–03
Sven Ottke (IBF/WBA)	2003–04*
Markus Beyer (WBC)	2003–04
Anthony Mundine (WBA)	2004
Manny Siaca (WBA)	2004
Cristian Sanavia (WBC)	2004
Jeff Lacy (IBF)	2004–06
Markus Beyer (WBC)	2004–06
Mikkel Kessler (WBA)	2004–
Joe Calzaghe (IBF)	2006–07†
Mikkel Kessler (WBA/WBC)	2006–07
Joe Calzaghe (WBA/WBC)	2007–08†
Lucian Bute (IBF)	2008–
Mikkel Kessler (WBA)	2008–

Middleweights

Widely accepted champions in CAPITAL letters. Current champions in **bold** type.

Champion	Held Title
JACK (NONPAREIL) DEMPSEY	1884–91
BOB FITZSIMMONS	1891–97
CHARLES (KID) McCOY	1897–98
TOMMY RYAN	1898–1907
STANLEY KETCHEL	1908
BILLY PAPKE	1908
STANLEY KETCHEL	1908–10
FRANK KLAUS	1913
GEORGE CHIP	1913–14
AL McCOY	1914–17
Jeff Smith (AUS)	1914
Mick King (AUS)	1914
Jeff Smith (AUS)	1914–15
Lee Darcy (AUS)	1915–17
MIKE O'DOWD	1917–20
JOHNNY WILSON	1920–23
Wm. Bryan Downey (Ohio)	1921–22
Dave Rosenberg (NY)	1922
Jock Malone (Ohio)	1922–23
Mike O'Dowd (NY)	1922
Lou Bogash (NY)	1923
HARRY GREB	1923–26
TIGER FLOWERS	1926
MICKEY WALKER	1926–31†
GORILLA JONES	1931–32
MARCEL THIL	1932–37
Ben Jeby (NY)	1932–33
Lou Brouillard (NBA, NY)	1933
Vince Dundee (NBA, NY)	1933–34
Teddy Yarosz (NBA, NY)	1934–35
Babe Risko (NBA, NY)	1935–36
Freddie Steele (NBA, NY)	1936–38
FRED APOSTOLI	1937–39
Al Hostak (NBA)	1938
Solly Krieger (NBA)	1938–39
Al Hostak (NBA)	1939–40
CEFERINO GARCIA	1939–40
KEN OVERLIN	1940–41
Tony Zale (NBA)	1940–41
BILLY SOOSE	1941
TONY ZALE	1941–47
ROCKY GRAZIANO	1947–48
TONY ZALE	1948
MARCEL CERDAN	1948–49
JAKE La MOTTA	1949–51
SUGAR RAY ROBINSON	1951
RANDY TURPIN	1951
SUGAR RAY ROBINSON	1951–52*
CARL (BOBO) OLSON	1953–55

Champion	Held Title
SUGAR RAY ROBINSON	1955–57
GENE FULLMER	1957
SUGAR RAY ROBINSON	1957
CARMEN BASILIO	1957–58
SUGAR RAY ROBINSON	1958–60
Gene Fullmer (NBA)	1959–62
PAUL PENDER	1960–61
TERRY DOWNES	1961–62
PAUL PENDER	1962–63
Dick Tiger (WBA)	1962–63
DICK TIGER	1963
JOEY GIARDELLO	1963–65
DICK TIGER	1965–66
EMILE GRIFFITH	1966–67
NINO BENVENUTI	1967
EMILE GRIFFITH	1967–68
NINO BENVENUTI	1968–70
CARLOS MONZON	1970–77*
Rodrigo Valdez (WBC)	1974–76
RODRIGO VALDEZ	1977–78
HUGO CORRO	1978–79
VITO ANTUOFERMO	1979–80
ALAN MINTER	1980
MARVELOUS MARVIN HAGLER	1980–87
SUGAR RAY LEONARD	1987
Frank Tate (IBF)	1987–88
Sumbu Kalambay (WBA)	1987–89
Thomas Hearns (WBC)	1987–88
Iran Barkley (WBC)	1988–89
Michael Nunn (IBF)	1988–91
Roberto Duran (WBC)	1989–90*
Mike McCallum (WBA)	1989–91
Julian Jackson (WBC)	1990–93
James Toney (IBF)	1991–93†
Reggie Johnson (WBA)	1992–93
Roy Jones Jr. (IBF)	1993–94†
Gerald McClellan (WBC)	1993–95†
John David Jackson (WBA)	1993–94
Jorge Castro (WBA)	1994–97
Julian Jackson (WBC)	1995
Bernard Hopkins (IBF)	1995–
Quincy Taylor (WBC)	1995–96
Shinji Takehara (WBA)	1995–96
William Joppy (WBA)	1996–97
Keith Holmes (WBC)	1996–98
Julio Cesar Green (WBA)	1997–98
William Joppy (WBA)	1998–2001
Hassine Cherifi (WBC)	1998–99
Keith Holmes (WBC)	1999–2001

Champion	Held Title
Bernard Hopkins (IBF/WBC)	2001–05
Felix Trinidad (WBA)	2001
BERNARD HOPKINS (IBF/WBA/WBC)	2001–05
JERMAIN TAYLOR (IBF/WBA/WBC)	2005–06†
JERMAIN TAYLOR (WBA/WBC)	2005–07†

Champion	Held Title
JERMAIN TAYLOR (WBC)	2005–07
Arthur Abraham (IBF)	2006–
Javier Castillejo (WBA)	2006–07
Felix Sturm (WBA)	2007–
Kelly Pavlik (WBC)	2007–

Junior Middleweights

Widely accepted champions in CAPITAL letters. Current champions in **bold** type.

Champion	Held Title
ERNIE GRIFFITH (EBU)	1962–63
DENNIS MOYER	1962–63
RALPH DUPAS	1963
SANDRO MAZZINGHI	1963–65
NINO BENVENUTI	1965–66
KI-SOO KIM	1966–68
SANDRO MAZZINGHI	1968
FREDDIE LITTLE	1969–70
CARMELO BOSSI	1970–71
KOICHI WAJIMA	1971–74
OSCAR ALBARADO	1974–75
KOICHI WAJIMA	1975
Miguel de Oliveira (WBC)	1975–76
JAE-DO YUH	1975–76
Elisha Obed (WBC)	1975–76
KOICHI WAJIMA	1976
JOSE DURAN	1976
Eckhard Dagge (WBC)†	1976–77
MIGUEL ANGEL CASTELLINI	1976–77
EDDIE GAZO	1977–78
Rocky Mattioli (WBC)	1977–79
MASASHI KUDO	1978–79
Maurice Hope (WBC)	1979–81
AYUB KALULE	1979–81
Wilfred Benitez (WBC)	1981–82
SUGAR RAY LEONARD	1981–82
Tadashi Mihara (WBA)	1981–82
Davey Moore (WBA)	1982–83
Thomas Hearns (WBC)	1982–84
Roberto Duran (WBA)	1983–84
Mark Medal (IBF)	1984
THOMAS HEARNS	1984–86
Mike McCallum (WBA)	1984–87
Carlos Santos (IBF)	1984–86
Buster Drayton (IBF)	1986–87
Duane Thomas (WBC)	1986–87
Matthew Hilton (IBF)	1987–88
Lupe Aquino (WBC)	1987
Gianfranco Rosi (WBC)	1987–88
Julian Jackson (WBA)	1987–90
Donald Curry (WBC)	1988–89
Robert Hines (IBF)	1988–89
Darrin Van Horn (IBF)	1989
Rene Jacquote (WBC)	1989

Champion	Held Title
John Mugabi (WBC)	1989–90
Gianfranco Rosi (IBF)	1989–94
Terry Norris (WBC)	1990–94
Gilbert Dele (WBA)	1991
Vinny Pazienza (WBA)	1991–92
Julio Cesar Vasquez (WBA)	1992–95
Simon Brown (WBC)	1994
Terry Norris (WBC)	1994–
Vincent Pettway (IBF)	1994–95
Paul Vaden (IBF)	1995
Carl Daniels (WBA)	1995
Terry Norris (WBC)	1995–97
Terry Norris (IBF)	1995–96
Laurent Boudouani (WBA)	1996–99
Raul Marquez (IBF)	1997
Keith Mullings (WBC)	1997–99
Yori Boy Campas (IBF)	1997–98
Fernando Vargas (IBF)	1998–2000
Javier Castillejo (WBC)	1999–2001
David Reid (WBA)	1999–00
Felix Trinidad (WBA/IBF)	2000–01†
Oscar De La Hoya (WBC)	2001–03
Fernando Vargas (WBA)	2001–02
Winky Wright (IBF)	2001–
Oscar De La Hoya (WBA/WBC)	2002-03
Shane Mosley (WBA/WBC)	2003–04
WINKY WRIGHT (IBF/WBA/WBC)	2004
WINKY WRIGHT (WBA/WBC)	2004–05†
Kassim Ouma (IBF)	2004–05
Javier Castillejo (WBC)	2005
Roman Karmazin (IBF)	2005–06
Alejandro Garcia (WBA)	2005–06
Ricardo Mayorga (WBC)	2005–06
Jose Antonio Rivera (WBA)	2006–07
Oscar De La Hoya (WBC)	2006–07
Cory Spinks (IBF)	2006–08
Travis Simms (WBA)	2007
Floyd Mayweather Jr. (WBC)	2007†
Vernon Forrest (WBA)	2007–08
Joachim Alcine (WBA)	2007–08
Verno Phillips (IBF)	2008–
Sergio Mora (WBC)	2008
Vernon Forrest (WBC)	2008–
Daniel Santos (WBA)	2008–

Welterweights

Widely accepted champions in CAPITAL letters. Current champions in **bold** type.

Champion	Held Title
PADDY DUFFY	1888–90
MYSTERIOUS BILLY SMITH	1892–94
TOMMY RYAN	1894–98
MYSTERIOUS BILLY SMITH	1898–1900
MATTY MATTHEWS	1900
EDDIE CONNOLLY	1900
JAMES (RUBE) FERNS	1900
MATTY MATHEWS	1900–01
JAMES (RUBE) FERNS	1901
JOE WALCOTT	1901–04
THE DIXIE KID	1904–05
HONEY MELLODY	1906–07
Mike (Twin) Sullivan	1907–08†
Harry Lewis	1908–11
Jimmy Gardner	1908
Jimmy Clabby	1910–11

Champion	Held Title
WALDEMAR HOLBERG	1914
TOM McCORMICK	1914
MATT WELLS	1914–15
MIKE GLOVER	1915
JACK BRITTON	1915
TED (KID) LEWIS	1915–16
JACK BRITTON	1916–17
TED (KID) LEWIS	1917–19
JACK BRITTON	1919–22
MICKEY WALKER	1922–26
PETE LATZO	1926–27
JOE DUNDEE	1927–29
JACKIE FIELDS	1929–30
YOUNG JACK THOMPSON	1930
TOMMY FREEMAN	1930–31
YOUNG JACK THOMPSON	1931

Major Titleholders (Cont.)
Welterweights (Cont.)

Champion	Held Title	Champion	Held Title
LOU BROUILLARD	1931–32	LLOYD HONEYGHAN	1986–87
JACKIE FIELDS	1932–33	JORGE VACA (WBC)	1987–88
YOUNG CORBETT III	1933	LLOYD HONEYGHAN (WBC)	1988–89
JIMMY McLARNIN	1933–34	Mark Breland (WBA)	1987
BARNEY ROSS	1934	Marlon Starling (WBA)	1987–88
JIMMY McLARNIN	1934–35	Tomas Molinares (WBA)	1988–89
BARNEY ROSS	1935–38	Simon Brown (IBF)	1988–91
HENRY ARMSTRONG	1938–40	Mark Breland (WBA)	1989–90
FRITZIE ZIVIC	1940–41	MARLON STARLING (WBC)	1989–90
Izzy Jannazzo (Md.)	1940–41	Aaron Davis (WBA)	1990–91
Freddie (Red) Cochrane	1941–46	Maurice Blocker (WBC)	1990–91
MARTY SERVO	1946*	Meldrick Taylor (WBA)	1991–92
SUGAR RAY ROBINSON	1946–51†	Simon Brown (WBC)	1991
Johnny Bratton	1951	Maurice Blocker (IBF)	1991–93
KID GAVILAN	1951–54	Buddy McGirt (WBC)	1991–93
JOHNNY SAXTON	1954–55	Crisanto Espana (WBA)	1992–94
TONY DeMARCO	1955	Pernell Whitaker (WBC)	1993–97
CARMEN BASILIO	1955–56	Felix Trinidad (IBF)	1993–99
JOHNNY SAXTON	1956	Ike Quartey (WBA)	1994–98†
CARMEN BASILIO	1956–57†	James Page (WBA)	1998–2000†
VIRGIL AKINS	1958	Oscar De La Hoya (WBC)	1997–99
DON JORDAN	1958–60	Felix Trinidad (WBC/IBF)	1999–2000†
BENNY (KID) PARET	1960–61	Oscar De La Hoya (WBC)	2000
EMILE GRIFFITH	1961	Shane Mosley (WBC)	2000–00
BENNY (KID) PARET	1961–62	Andrew Lewis (WBA)	2001–02
EMILE GRIFFITH	1962–63	Vernon Forrest (IBF)	2001–02†
LUIS RODRIGUEZ	1963	Vernon Forrest (WBC)	2002–03
EMILE GRIFFITH	1963–66†	Richard Mayorga (WBA)	2002–03
Charlie Shipes (Calif.)	1966–67	Michele Piccirillo (IBF)	2002–03
CURTIS COKES	1966–69	Richard Mayorga (WBA/WBC)	2003
JOSE NAPOLES	1969–70	Cory Spinks (IBF)	2003–05
BILLY BACKUS	1970–71	CORY SPINKS (IBF/WBA/WBC)	2003–05
JOSE NAPOLES	1971–75	ZAB JUDAH (IBF/WBA/WBC)	2005–06
Hedgemon Lewis (NY)	1972–73	Zab Judah (IBF)	2006
Angel Espada (WBA)	1975–76	Carlos Baldomir (WBC)	2006
JOHN H. STRACEY	1975–76	Floyd Mayweather (IBF)	2006†
CARLOS PALOMINO	1976–79	Ricky Hatton (WBA)	2006†
Pipino Cuevas (WBA)	1976–80	Floyd Mayweather (WBC)	2006–08†
WILFREDO BENITEZ	1979	Miguel Cotto (WBA)	2006–08
SUGAR RAY LEONARD	1979–80	Kermit Cintron (IBF)	2006–08
ROBERTO DURAN	1980	Antonio Margarito (IBF)	2008†
Thomas Hearns (WBA)	1980–81	**Andre Berto** (WBC)	2008—
SUGAR RAY LEONARD	1980–82	**Antonio Margarito** (WBA)	2008—
Donald Curry (WBA)	1983–85	**Josh Clottey** (IBF)	2008—
Milton McCrory (WBC)	1983–85		
DONALD CURRY	1985–86		

Junior Welterweights

Widely accepted champions in CAPITAL letters. Current champions in **bold** type.

Champion	Held Title	Champion	Held Title
PINKEY MITCHELL	1922–25	PAUL FUJII	1967–68
RED HERRING	1925	NICOLINO LOCHE	1968–72
MUSHY CALLAHAN	1926–30	Pedro Adigue (WBC)	1968–70
JACK (KID) BERG	1930–31	Bruno Arcari (WBC)	1970–74
TONY CANZONERI	1931–32	ALFONSO FRAZER	1972
JOHNNY JADICK	1932–33	ANTONIO CERVANTES	1972–76
Sammy Fuller	1932–33	Perico Fernandez (WBC)	1974–75
BATTLING SHAW	1933	Saensak Muangsurin (WBC)	1975–76
TONY CANZONERI	1933	WILFRED BENITEZ	1976–79
BARNEY ROSS	1933–35	Miguel Velasquez (WBC)	1976
TIPPY LARKIN	1946	Saensak Muangsurin (WBC)	1976–78
CARLOS ORTIZ	1959–60	Antonio Cervantes (WBA)	1977–80
DUILIO LOI	1960–62	Sang-Hyun Kim (WBC)	1978–80
EDDIE PERKINS	1962	Saoul Mamby (WBC)	1980–82
DUILIO LOI	1962–63	Aaron Pryor (WBA)	1980–83
Roberto Cruz	1963	Leroy Haley (WBC)	1982–83
EDDIE PERKINS	1963–65	Aaron Pryor (IBF)	1983–85
CARLOS HERNANDEZ	1965–66	Bruce Curry (WBC)	1983–84
SANDRO LOPOPOLO	1966–67	Johnny Bumphus (WBA)	1984

Champion	Held Title
Bill Costello (WBC)	1984–85
Gene Hatcher (WBA)	1984–85
Ubaldo Sacco (WBA)	1985–86
Lonnie Smith (WBC)	1985–86
Patrizio Oliva (WBA)	1986–87
Gary Hinton (IBF)	1986
Rene Arredondo (WBC)	1986
Tsuyoshi Hamada (WBC)	1986–87
Joe Louis Manley (IBF)	1986–87
Terry Marsh (IBF)	1987
Juan Coggi (WBA)	1987–90
Rene Arredondo (WBC)	1987
Roger Mayweather (WBC)	1987–89
James McGirt (IBF)	1988
Meldrick Taylor (IBF)	1988–90
Julio Cesar Chavez (WBC)	1989–94
Julio Cesar Chavez (IBF)	1990–91
Loreto Garza (WBA)	1990–91
Juan Coggi (WBA)	1991
Edwin Rosario (WBA)	1991–92
Rafael Pineda (IBF)	1991–92
Akinobu Hiranaka (WBA)	1992
Pernell Whitaker (IBF)	1992–93†
Charles Murray (IBF)	1993–94
Jake Rodriguez (IBF)	1994–95
Juan Coggi (WBA)	1993–94
Frankie Randall (WBC)	1994

Champion	Held Title
Frankie Randall (WBA)	1994–96
Juan Coggi (WBA)	1996
Julio Cesar Chavez (WBC)	1994–96
Kostya Tszyu (IBF)	1995–97
Frankie Randall (WBA)	1996–97
Oscar De La Hoya (WBC)	1996–97†
Khalid Rahilou (WBA)	1997–98
Sharmba Mitchell (WBA)	1998–2001
Vincent Phillips (IBF)	1997–99
Terronn Millet (IBF)	1999–00†
Kostya Tszyu (WBC)	1999–2005
Zab Judah (IBF)	2000–01
Kostya Tszyu (WBA/WBC)	2001–04†
KOSTYA TSZYU (IBF/WBA/WBC)	2001–04†
KOSTYA TSZYU (IBF/WBC)	2004–05
Vivian Harris (WBA)	2004–05
Arturo Gatti (WBC)	2005
Ricky Hatton (IBF)	2005–07†
Ricky Hatton (IBF/WBA)	2005–06†
Carlos Maussa (WBA)	2005–06
Floyd Mayweather Jr. (WBC)	2005–06†
Junior Witter (WBC)	2006–08
Souleymane M'baye (WBA)	2007
Gavin Rees (WBA)	2007–08
Paul Malignaggi (IBF)	2007–08†
Andreas Kotelnik (WBA)	2008—
Timothy Bradley (WBC)	2008—

Lightweights

Widely accepted champions in CAPITAL letters. Current champions in **bold** type.

Champion	Held Title
JACK McAULIFFE	1886–94
GEORGE (KID) LAVIGNE	1896–99
FRANK ERNE	1899–02
JOE GANS	1902–04
JIMMY BRITT	1904–05 *
BATTLING NELSON	1905–06
JOE GANS	1906–08
BATTLING NELSON	1908–10
AD WOLGAST	1910–12
WILLIE RITCHIE	1912–14
FREDDIE WELSH	1915–17
BENNY LEONARD	1917–25*
JIMMY GOODRICH	1925
ROCKY KANSAS	1925–26
SAMMY MANDELL	1926–30
AL SINGER	1930
TONY CANZONERI	1930–33
BARNEY ROSS	1933–35†
TONY CANZONERI	1935–36
LOU AMBERS	1936–38
HENRY ARMSTRONG	1938–39
LOU AMBERS	1939–40
Sammy Angott (NBA)	1940–41
LEW JENKINS	1940–41
SAMMY ANGOTT	1941–42
Beau Jack (NY)	1942–43
Slugger White (Md.)	1943
Bob Montgomery (NY)	1943
Sammy Angott (NBA)	1943–44
Beau Jack (NY)	1943–44
Bob Montgomery (NY)	1944–47
Juan Zurita (NBA)	1944–45
IKE WILLIAMS	1947–51
JAMES CARTER	1951–52
LAURO SALAS	1952
JAMES CARTER	1952–54
PADDY DeMARCO	1954
JAMES CARTER	1954–55
WALLACE (BUD) SMITH	1955–56
JOE BROWN	1956–62
CARLOS ORTIZ	1962–65
Kenny Lane (Mich.)	1963–64

Champion	Held Title
ISMAEL LAGUNA	1965
CARLOS ORTIZ	1965–68
CARLOS TEO CRUZ	1968–69
MANDO RAMOS	1969–70
ISMAEL LAGUNA	1970
KEN BUCHANAN	1970–72
Pedro Carrasco (WBC)	1971–72
Mando Ramos (WBC)	1972
ROBERTO DURAN	1972–79†
Chango Carmona (WBC)	1972
Rodolfo Gonzalez (WBC)	1972–74
Ishimatsu Suzuki (WBC)	1974–76
Esteban De Jesus (WBC)	1976–78
Jim Watt (WBC)	1979–81
Ernesto Espana (WBA)	1979–80
Hilmer Kenty (WBA)	1980–81
Sean O'Grady (WBA, WAA)	1981
Alexis Arguello (WBC)	1981–82
Claude Noel (WBA)	1981
Andrew Ganigan (WAA)	1981–82
Arturo Frias (WBA)	1981–82
Ray Mancini (WBA)	1982–84
ALEXIS ARGUELLO	1982–83
Edwin Rosario (WBC)	1983–84
Choo Choo Brown (IBF)	1984
Livingstone Bramble (WBA)	1984–86
Harry Arroyo (IBF)	1984–85
Jose Luis Ramirez (WBC)	1984–85
Jimmy Paul (IBF)	1985–86
Hector Camacho (WBC)	1985–86
Edwin Rosario (WBA)	1986–87
Greg Haugen (IBF)	1986–87
Julio Cesar Chavez (WBA)	1987–88
Jose Luis Ramirez (WBC)	1987–88
JULIO CESAR CHAVEZ (WBC, WBA)	1988–89
Vinny Pazienza (WBA)	1987–88
Greg Haugen (IBF)	1988–89
Pernell Whitaker (IBF, WBC)	1989–90
Edwin Rosario (WBA)	1989–90
Juan Nazario (WBA)	1990
PERNELL WHITAKER (IBF, WBC, WBA)	1990–92†
Joey Gamache (WBA)	1992

Major Titleholders (Cont.)
Lightweights (Cont.)

Champion	Held Title
Miguel A. Gonzalez (WBC)	1992–96
Tony Lopez (WBA)	1992–93
Dingaan Thobela (WBA)	1993
Fred Pendleton (IBF)	1993–94
Orzubek Nazarov (WBA)	1993–98
Rafael Ruelas (IBF)	1994–95
Oscar De La Hoya (IBF)	1995†
Phillip Holiday (IBF)	1995–97
Jean-Baptiste Mendy (WBC)	1996–97
Stevie Johnston (WBC)	1997–98
Shane Mosley (IBF)	1997–99†
Cesar Bazan (WBC)	1998–99
Jean-Baptiste Mendy (WBA)	1998–99
Julien Lorcy (WBA)	1999
Stevie Johnston (WBC)	1999–00
Stefano Zoff (WBA)	1999
Israel Cardona (IBF)	1999
Paul Spadafora (IBF)	1999–2004†
Gilberto Serrano (WBA)	1999–00
Takanori Hatakeyama (WBA)	2000–01

Champion	Held Title
Jose Luis Castillo (WBC)	2000–02
Julien Lorcy (WBA)	2001
Raul Balbi (WBA)	2001–02
Leonard Dorin (WBA)	2002–03
Floyd Mayweather Jr. (WBC)	2002–04†
Javier Jauregui (IBF)	2003-04
Lakva Sim (WBA)	2004
Juan Diaz (WBA)	2004–08
Jose Luis Castillo (WBC)	2004–05
Julio Diaz (IBF)	2004–05
Diego Corrales (WBC)	2005–
Leavander Johnson (IBF)	2005
Jesus Chavez (IBF)	2005–07
Joel Casamayor (WBC)	2006–07†
Julio Diaz (IBF)	2007
Juan Diaz (WBA/IBF)	2007–08
David Diaz (WBC)	2007–08
Nate Campbell (WBA/IBF)	2008–
Manny Pacquiao (WBC)	2008–

Junior Lightweights
Widely accepted champions in CAPITAL letters. Current champions in **bold** type.

Champion	Held Title
JOHNNY DUNDEE	1921–23
JACK BERNSTEIN	1923
JOHNNY DUNDEE	1923–24
STEVE (KID) SULLIVAN	1924–25
MIKE BALLERINO	1925
TOD MORGAN	1925–29
BENNY BASS	1929–31
KID CHOCOLATE	1931–33
FRANKIE KLICK	1933–34
SANDY SADDLER	1949–50
HAROLD GOMES	1959–60
GABRIEL (FLASH) ELORDE	1960–67
YOSHIAKI NUMATA	1967
HIROSHI KOBAYASHI	1967–71
Rene Barrientos (WBC)	1969–70
Yoshiaki Numata (WBC)	1970–71
ALFREDO MARCANO	1971–72
Ricardo Arredondo (WBC)	1971–74
BEN VILLAFLOR	1972–73
KUNIAKI SHIBATA	1973
BEN VILLAFLOR	1973–76
Kuniaki Shibata (WBC)	1974–75
Alfredo Escalera (WBC)	1975–78
SAMUEL SERRANO	1976–80
Alexis Arguello (WBC)	1978–80
YASUTSUNE UEHARA	1980–81
Rafael Limon (WBC)	1980–81
Cornelius Boza-Edwards (WBC)	1981
SAMUEL SERRANO	1981–83
Rolando Navarrete (WBC)	1981–82
Rafael Limon (WBC)	1982
Bobby Chacon (WBC)	1982–83
ROGER MAYWEATHER	1983–84
Hector Camacho (WBC)	1983–84
ROCKY LOCKRIDGE	1984–85
Hwan-Kil Yuh (IBF)	1984–85
Julio Cesar Chavez (WBC)	1984–87
Lester Ellis (IBF)	1985
WILFREDO GOMEZ	1985–86
Barry Michael (IBF)	1985–87
ALFREDO LAYNE	1986
BRIAN MITCHELL	1986–91
Rocky Lockridge (IBF)	1987–88

Champion	Held Title
Azumah Nelson (WBC)	1988–94
Tony Lopez (IBF)	1988–89
Juan Molina (IBF)	1989–90
Tony Lopez (IBF)	1990–91
Joey Gamache (WBA)	1991
Brian Mitchell (IBF)	1991
Genaro Hernandez (WBA)	1991–95
James Leija (WBC)	1994
Juan Molina (IBF)	1991–95
Gabriel Ruelas (WBC)	1994–95
Eddie Hopson (IBF)	1995
Tracy Patterson (IBF)	1995
Azumah Nelson (WBC)	1995–97
Choi Yong-Soo (WBA)	1995–98
Arturo Gatti (IBF)	1995–98†
Genaro Hernandez (WBC)	1997–98
Floyd Mayweather Jr. (WBC)	1998–2002†
Takanori Hatakeyama (WBA)	1998–99
Roberto Garcia (IBF)	1998–99
Lavka Sim (WBA)	1999
Diego Corrales (IBF)	1999–2001
Baek Jong-Kwon (WBA)	1999–2000
Joel Casamayor (WBA)	2000–02
Steve Forbes (IBF)	2001-02†
Acelino Freitas (WBA)	2002–04†
Sirimongkol Singmanassak (WBC)	2002–03
Jesus Chavez (WBC)	2003–04
Carlos Hernandez (IBF)	2003–04
Erik Morales (WBC)	2004
Erik Morales (IBF/WBC)	2004
Marco Antonio Barrera (WBC)	2004–07
Marco Antonio Barrera (IBF/WBC)	2005–06
Vicente Mosquera (WBA)	2005–06
Cassius Baloyi (IBF)	2006
Gairy St. Clair (IBF)	2006
Edwin Valero (WBA)	2006–
Malcolm Klassen (IBF)	2006-07
Juan Manuel Marquez (WBC)	2007–08
Mzonke Fana (IBF)	2007–08
Cassius Baloyi (IBF)	2008–
Humberto Soto (WBC)	2008–

Featherweights

Widely accepted champions in CAPITAL letters. Current champions in **bold** type.

Champion	Held Title
TORPEDO BILLY MURPHY	1890
YOUNG GRIFFO	1890–92
GEORGE DIXON	1892–97
SOLLY SMITH	1897–98
Ben Jordan (GBR)	1898–99
Eddie Santry (GBR)	1899–1900
DAVE SULLIVAN	1898
GEORGE DIXON	1898–1900
TERRY McGOVERN	1900–01
YOUNG CORBETT II	1901–04
JIMMY BRITT	1904
ABE ATTELL	1904
BROOKLYN TOMMY SULLIVAN	1904–05
ABE ATTELL	1906–12
JOHNNY KILBANE	1912–23
Jem Driscoll (GBR)	1912–13
EUGENE CRIQUI	1923
JOHNNY DUNDEE	1923–24†
LOUIS (KID) KAPLAN	1925–26†
Dick Finnegan (Mass.)	1926–27
BENNY BASS	1927–28
TONY CANZONERI	1928
ANDRE ROUTIS	1928–29
BATTLING BATTALINO	1929–32†
Tommy Paul (NBA)	1932–33
Kid Chocolate (NY)	1932–33
Freddie Miller (NBA)	1933–36
Baby Arizmendi (MEX)	1935–36
Mike Belloise (NY)	1936–37
Petey Sarron (NBA)	1936–37
HENRY ARMSTRONG	1937–38†
Joey Archibald (NY)	1938–39
Leo Rodak (NBA)	1938–39
JOEY ARCHIBALD	1939–40
Petey Scalzo (NBA)	1940–41
Jimmy Perrin (La.)	1940–41
HARRY JEFFRA	1940–41
JOEY ARCHIBALD	1941
Richie Lemos (NBA)	1941
CHALKY WRIGHT	1941–42
Jackie Wilson (NBA)	1941–43
WILLIE PEP	1942–48
Jackie Callura (NBA)	1943
Phil Terranova (NBA)	1943–44
Sal Bartolo (NBA)	1944–46
SANDY SADDLER	1948–49
WILLIE PEP	1949–50
SANDY SADDLER	1950–57*
HOGAN (KID) BASSEY	1957–59
DAVEY MOORE	1959–63
ULTIMINIO (SUGAR) RAMOS	1963–64
VICENTE SALDIVAR	1964–67*
Howard Winstone (GBR)	1968
Raul Rojas (WBA)	1968
Jose Legra (WBC)	1968–69
Shozo Saijyo (WBA)	1968–71
JOHNNY FAMECHON (WBC)	1969–70
VICENTE SALDIVAR (WBC)	1970
KUNIAKI SHIBATA (WBC)	1970–72
Antonio Gomez (WBA)	1971–72
CLEMENTE SANCHEZ (WBC)	1972
Ernesto Marcel (WBA)	1972–74
JOSE LEGRA (WBC)	1972–73
EDER JOFRE (WBC)	1973–74
Ruben Olivares (WBA)	1974
Bobby Chacon (WBC)	1974–75
ALEXIS ARGUELLO (WBA)	1974–76†
Ruben Olivares (WBC)	1975
David (Poison) Kotey (WBC)	1975–76
DANNY (LITTLE RED) LOPEZ (WBC)	1976–80
Rafael Ortega (WBA)	1977
Cecilio Lastra (WBA)	1977–78
Eusebio Pedroza (WBA)	1978–85
SALVADOR SANCHEZ (WBC)	1980–82
Juan LaPorte (WBC)	1982–84
Wilfredo Gomez (WBC)	1984
Min-Keun Oh (IBF)	1984–85
Azumah Nelson (WBC)	1984–88
Barry McGuigan (WBA)	1985–86
Ki-Young Chung (IBF)	1985–86
Steve Cruz (WBA)	1986–87
Antonio Rivera (IBF)	1986–88
Antonio Esparragoza (WBA)	1987–91
Calvin Grove (IBF)	1988
Jorge Paez (IBF)	1988–91†
Jeff Fenech (WBC)	1988–90†
Marcos Villasana (WBC)	1990–91
Yung-Kyun Park (WBA)	1991–93
Troy Dorsey (IBF)	1991
Manuel Medina (IBF)	1991–93
Paul Hodkinson (WBC)	1991–93
Tom Johnson (IBF)	1993–97
Goyo Vargas (WBC)	1993
Kevin Kelley (WBC)	1993–95
Eloy Rojas (WBA)	1993–96
Alejandro Gonzalez (WBC)	1995
Manuel Medina (WBC)	1995–96
Wilfredo Vasquez (WBA)	1996–98†
Luisito Espinosa (WBC)	1995–99
Naseem Hamed (IBF)	1997†
Hector Lizarraga (IBF)	1997–98
Freddie Norwood (WBA)	1998
Manuel Medina (IBF)	1998–99
Antonio Cermeno (WBA)	1998–99
Cesar Soto (WBC)	1999–00
Paul Ingle (IBF)	1999–2000
Mbuelo Botile (IBF)	2000–01
Guty Espadas (WBC)	2000–01
Freddie Norwood (WBA)	1999–00
Derrick Gainer (WBA)	2000–03
Erik Morales (WBC)	2001–02
Frankie Toledo (IBF)	2001
Manuel Medina (IBF)	2001–02
Johnny Tapia (IBF)	2002†
Erik Morales (WBC)	2002–03†
Juan Manuel Marquez (IBF)	2003–05†
Juan Manuel Marquez (WBA)	2003–06†
Chi In-jin (WBC)	2004–06
Chris John (WBA)	2006—
Takashi Koshimoto (WBC)	2006
Rudy Lopez (WBC)	2006
Robert Guerrero (IBF)	2006–08†
In Jin Chi (WBC)	2006–07†
Jorge Linares (WBC)	2007—
Cristobal Cruz (IBF)	2008—

Junior Featherweights

Current champions in **bold** type.

Champion	Held Title	Champion	Held Title
Jack (Kid) Wolfe	1922–23	Royal Kobayashi (WBC)	1976
Carl Duane	1923–24	Dong-Kyun Yum (WBC)	1976–77
Rigoberto Riasco (WBC)	1976	Wilfredo Gomez (WBC)	1977–83

Major Titleholders (Cont.)

Junior Featherweights (Cont.)

Champion	Held Title
Soo-Hwan Hong (WBA)	1977–78
Ricardo Cardona (WBA)	1978–80
Leo Randolph (WBA)	1980
Sergio Palma (WBA)	1980–82
Leonardo Cruz (WBA)	1982–84
Jaime Garza (WBC)	1983
Bobby Berna (IBF)	1983–84
Loris Stecca (WBA)	1984
Seung-Il Suh (IBF)	1984–85
Victor Callejas (WBA)	1984–85
Juan (Kid) Meza (WBC)	1984–85
Ji-Woo Kim (IBF)	1985–86
Lupe Pintor (WBC)	1985–86
Samart Payakaroon (WBC)	1986–87
Seung-Hoon Lee (IBF)	1987–88
Louie Espinoza (WBA)	1987
Jeff French (WBC)	1987
Julio Gervacio (WBA)	1987–88
Daniel Zaragoza (WBC)	1988–90
Jose Sanabria (IBF)	1988–90
Bernardo Pinango (WBA)	1988
Juan Jose Estrada (WBA)	1988–89
Fabrice Benichou (IBF)	1989–90
Jesus Salud (WBA)	1989–90
Welcome Ncita (IBF)	1990–92
Paul Banke (WBC)	1990
Luis Mendoza (WBA)	1990–91
Raul Perez (WBA)	1992
Pedro Decima (WBC)	1990–91
Kiyoshi Hatanaka (WBC)	1991

Champion	Held Title
Daniel Zaragoza (WBC)	1991–92
Tracy Patterson (WBC)	1992–94
Kennedy McKinney (IBF)	1993–94
Wilfredo Vasquez (WBA)	1992–95
Vuyani Bungu (IBF)	1994–99†
Hector Acero Sanchez (WBC)	1994–95
Antonio Cermeno (WBA)	1995–98†
Daniel Zaragoza (WBC)	1995–97
Erik Morales (WBC)	1997–00†
Enrique Sanchez (WBA)	1998
Nestor Garza (WBA)	1998–00
Lehlohonolo Ledwaba (IBF)	1999–2001
Clarence Adams (WBA)	2000–01†
Willie Jorrin (WBC)	2000–02
Manny Pacquiao (IBF)	2001–04†
Yorber Ortega (WBA)	2001–02
Yoddamrong Sithyodthong (WBA)	2002
Osamu Sato (WBA)	2002
Salim Medjkoune (WBA)	2002–03
Oscar Larios (WBC)	2002–05
Mahyar Monshipour (WBA)	2003–06
Israel Vazquez (IBF)	2004–06
Israel Vazquez (IBF/WBC)	2005†
Israel Vazquez (WBC)	2005–07
Somsak Sithchatchawal (WBA)	2006
Celestino Caballero (WBA)	2006–
Rafael Marquez (WBC)	2007
Steve Molitor (IBF)	2007–
Israel Vazquez (WBC)	2007–

Bantamweights

Widely accepted champions in CAPITAL letters. Current champions in **bold** type.

Champion	Held Title
TOMMY (SPIDER) KELLY	1887
HUGHEY BOYLE	1887–88
TOMMY (SPIDER) KELLY	1889
CHAPPIE MORAN	1889–90
Tommy (Spider) Kelly	1890–92
GEORGE DIXON	1890–91
Billy Plummer	1892–95
JIMMY BARRY	1894–99
Pedlar Palmer	1895–99
TERRY McGOVERN	1899–1900
HARRY HARRIS	1901–02
DANNY DOUGHERTY	1900–01
HARRY FORBES	1901–03
FRANKIE NEIL	1903–04
JOE BOWKER	1904–05
JIMMY WALSH	1905–06†
OWEN MORAN	1907–08
MONTE ATTELL	1909–10
FRANKIE CONLEY	1910–11
JOHNNY COULON	1911–14
Digger Stanley (GBR)	1910–12
Charles Ledoux (GBR)	1912–13
Eddie Campi (GBR)	1913–14
KID WILLIAMS	1914–17
Johnny Ertle	1915–18
PETE HERMAN	1917–20
Memphis Pal Moore	1918–19
JOE LYNCH	1920–21
PETE HERMAN	1921
JOHNNY BUFF	1921–22
JOE LYNCH	1922–24
ABE GOLDSTEIN	1924
CANNONBALL EDDIE MARTIN	1924–25
PHIL ROSENBERG	1925–27
Teddy Baldock (GBR)	1927
BUD TAYLOR (NBA)	1927–28†

Champion	Held Title
Willie Smith (GBR)	1927–28
Bushy Graham (NY)	1928–29
PANAMA AL BROWN	1929–35
Sixto Escobar (NBA)	1934–35
BALTAZAR SANGCHILLI	1935–36
Lou Salica (NBA)	1935
Sixto Escobar (NBA)	1935–36
TONY MARINO	1936
SIXTO ESCOBAR	1936–37
HARRY JEFFRA	1937–38
SIXTO ESCOBAR	1938–39*
Georgie Pace (NBA)	1939–40
LOU SALICA	1940–42
MANUEL ORTIZ	1942–47
HAROLD DADE	1947
MANUEL ORTIZ	1947–50
VIC TOWEEL	1950–52
JIMMY CARRUTHERS	1952–54*
ROBERT COHEN	1954–56
Raul Macias (NBA)	1955–57
MARIO D'AGATA	1956–57
ALPHONSE HALIMI	1957–59
JOE BECERRA	1959–60*
Johnny Caldwell (EBU)	1961–62
EDER JOFRE	1961–65
MASAHIKO FIGHTING HARADA	1965–68
LIONEL ROSE	1968–69
RUBEN OLIVARES	1969–70
CHUCHO CASTILLO	1970–71
RUBEN OLIVARES	1971–72
RAFAEL HERRERA	1972
ENRIQUE PINDER	1972–73
ROMEO ANAYA	1973
Rafael Herrera (WBC)	1973–74
ARNOLD TAYLOR	1973–74
SOO-HWAN HONG	1974–75

Champion	Held Title
Rodolfo Martinez (WBC)	1974–76
ALFONSO ZAMORA	1975–77
Carlos Zarate (WBC)	1976–79
JORGE LUJAN	1977–80
Lupe Pintor (WBC)	1979–83
JULIAN SOLIS	1980
JEFF CHANDLER	1980–84
Albert Davila (WBC)	1983–85
RICHARD SANDOVAL	1984–86
Satoshi Shingaki (IBF)	1984–85
Jeff Fenech (IBF)	1985
Daniel Zaragoza (WBC)	1985
Miguel (Happy) Lora (WBC)	1985–88
GABY CANIZALES	1986
BERNARDO PINANGO	1986–87
Wilfredo Vasquez (WBA)	1987–88
Kevin Seabrooks (IBF)	1987–88
Kaokor Galaxy (WBA)	1988
Moon Sung-Kil (WBA)	1988–89
Kaokor Galaxy (WBA)	1989
Raul Perez (WBC)	1988–91
Orlando Canizales (IBF)	1988–94†
Luisito Espinosa (WBA)	1989–91
Greg Richardson	1991
Joichiro Tatsuyoshi (WBC)	1991–92
Israel Contreras (WBA)	1991–92
Eddie Cook (WBA)	1992
Victor Rabanales (WBC)	1992–93

Champion	Held Title
Jorge Julio (WBA)	1992–93
Jung-Il Byun (WBC)	1993
Junior Jones (WBA)	1993–94
Yasuei Yakushiji (WBC)	1993–95
John M. Johnson (WBA)	1994
Daorung Chuvatana (WBA)	1994–95
Harold Mestre (IBF)	1995
Mbuelo Botile (IBF)	1995–97
Wayne McCullough (WBC)	1995–96
Veeraphol Sahaprom (WBA)	1995–96
Nana Yaw Konadu (WBA)	1996
Daorung Chuvatana (WBA)	1996–97
Nana Yaw Konadu (WBA)	1997–98
Sirimongkol Singmanassak (WBC)	1996–97
Tim Austin (IBF)	1997–2003
Joichiro Tatsuyoshi (WBC)	1997–98
Johnny Tapia (WBA)	1998–99
Veerapol Sahaprom (WBC)	1998–2005
Paulie Ayala (WBA)	1999–2001
Eidy Moya (WBA)	2001–02
Johnny Bredahl (WBA)	2002–04†
Rafael Marquez (IBF)	2003–07†
Wladimir Sidorenko (WBA)	2005–08
Hozumi Hasegawa (WBC)	2005–
Luis Alberto Perez (IBF)	2007
Joseph Agbeko (IBF)	2007–
Anselmo Morena (WBA)	2008–

Junior Bantamweights

Widely accepted champions in CAPITAL letters. Current champions in **bold** type.

Champion	Held Title
Rafael Orono (WBC)	1980–81
Chul-Ho Kim (WBC)	1981–82
Gustavo Ballas (WBA)	1981
Rafael Pedroza (WBA)	1981–82
Jiro Watanabe (WBA)	1982–84
Rafael Orono (WBC)	1982–83
Payao Poontarat (WBC)	1983–84
Joo-Do Chun (IBF)	1983–85
JIRO WATANABE	1984–86
Kaosai Galaxy (WBA)	1984
Ellyas Pical (IBF)	1985–86
Cesar Polanco (WBA)	1986
GILBERTO ROMAN	1986–87
Ellyas Pical (IBF)	1986
Santos Laciar (WBC)	1987
Tae-Il Chang (IBF)	1987
Sugar Rojas (WBC)	1987–88
Ellyas Pical (IBF)	1987–89
Gilberto Roman (WBC)	1988–89
Juan Polo Perez (IBF)	1989–90
Nana Konadu (WBC)	1989–90
Sung-Kil Moon (WBC)	1990–93
Robert Quiroga (IBF)	1990–93
Julio Borboa (IBF)	1993–94
Katsuya Onizuka (WBA)	1993–94
Lee Hyung-Chul (WBA)	1994–95
Jose Luis Bueno (WBC)	1993–94
Hiroshi Kawashima (WBC)	1994–97

Champion	Held Title
Harold Grey (IBF)	1994–95
Alimi Goitia (WBA)	1995–96
Yokthai Sith-Oar (WBA)	1996–97
Carlos Salazar (IBF)	1995–96
Harold Grey (IBF)	1996
Danny Romero (IBF)	1996–97
Gerry Penalosa (WBC)	1997–98
Johnny Tapia (IBF)	1997–98†
Satoshi Iida (WBA)	1997–98
Cho In-Joo (WBC)	1998–00
Jesus Rojas (WBA)	1998–99
Mark Johnson (IBF)	1999–00†
Hideki Todaka (WBA)	1999–2000
Masanori Tokuyama (WBC)	2000–04
Felix Machado (IBF)	2000–03
Leo Gamez (WBA)	2000–01
Celes Kobayashi (WBA)	2001–02
Alexander Munoz (WBA)	2002–04
Luis Perez (IBF)	2003–06†
Katsushige Kawashima (WBC)	2004–05
Martin Castillo (WBA)	2004–06
Masmori Tokuyama (WBC)	2005–06
Nobuo Nashiro (WBA)	2006–07
Alexander Munoz (WBA)	2007–08
Cristian Mijares (WBC)	2006–
Dmitri Kirilov (IBF)	2007–08
Vic Darchinyan (IBF)	2008–
Nobuo Nashiro (WBA)	2008–

Flyweights

Widely accepted champions in CAPITAL letters. Current champions in **bold** type.

Champion	Held Title
Sid Smith (GBR)	1913
Bill Ladbury (GBR)	1913–14
Percy Jones (GBR)	1914
Joe Symonds (GBR)	1914–16
JIMMY WILDE	1916–23
PANCHO VILLA	1923–25
FIDEL LaBARBA	1925–27*

Champion	Held Title
FRENCHY BELANGER (NBA,IBU)	1927–28
Izzy Schwartz (NY)	1927–29
Johnny McCoy (Calif.)	1927–28
Newsboy Brown (Calif.)	1928
FRANKIE GENARO (NBA,IBU)	1928–29
Johnny Hill (GBR)	1928–29
SPIDER PLADNER (NBA,IBU)	1929

Major Titleholders (Cont.)
Flyweights (Cont.)

Champion	Held Title	Champion	Held Title
FRANKIE GENARO (NBA,IBU)	1929–31	Santos Laciar (WBA)	1982–85
Willie LaMorte (NY)	1929–30	Freddie Castillo (WBC)	1982
Midget Wolgast (NY)	1930–35	Eleoncio Mercedes (WBC)	1982–83
YOUNG PEREZ (NBA,IBU)	1931–32	Charlie Magri (WBC)	1983
JACKIE BROWN (NBA,IBU)	1932–35	Frank Cedeno (WBC)	1983–84
BENNY LYNCH	1935–38†	Soon-Chun Kwon (IBF)	1983–85
Small Montana (NY,Calif.)	1935–37	Koji Kobayashi (WBC)	1984
PETER KANE	1938–43	Gabriel Bernal (WBC)	1984
Little Dado (NBA,Calif.)	1938–40	Sot Chitalada (WBC)	1984–88
JACKIE PATERSON	1943–48	Hilario Zapate (WBA)	1985–87
RINTY MONAGHAN	1948–50*	Chong-Kwan Chung (IBF)	1985–86
TERRY ALLEN	1950	Bi-Won Chung (IBF)	1986
SALVADOR (DADO) MARINO	1950–52	Hi-Sup Shin (IBF)	1986–87
YOSHIO SHIRAI	1953–54	Dodie Penalosa (IBF)	1987
PASCUAL PEREZ	1954–60	Fidel Bassa (WBA)	1987–89
PONE KINGPETCH	1960–62	Choi Chang-Ho (WBC)	1987–88
MASAHIKO (FIGHTING) HARADA	1962–63	Rolando Bohol (IBF)	1988
PONE KINGPETCH	1963	Yong-Kang Kim (WBC)	1988–89
HIROYUKI EBIHARA	1963–64	Duke McKenzie (IBF)	1988–89
PONE KINGPETCH	1964–65	Dave McAuley (IBF)	1989–92
SALVATORE BURRINI	1965–66	Sot Chitalada (WBC)	1989–91
Horacio Accavallo (WBA)	1966–68	Jesus Rojas (WBA)	1989–90
WALTER McGOWAN	1966	Yul-Woo Lee (WBA)	1990
CHARTCHAI CHIONOI	1966–69	Leopard Tamakuma (WBA)	1990–91
EFREN TORRES	1969–70	Muangchai Kittikasem (WBC)	1991–92
Hiroyuki Ebihara (WBA)	1969	Yong-Kang Kim (WBA)	1991–92
Bernabe Villacampo (WBA)	1969–70	Rodolfo Blanco (IBF)	1992
CHARTCHAI CHIONOI	1970	Yuri Arbachakov (WBC)	1992–97
Berkrerk Chartvanchai (WBA)	1970	Aquiles Guzman (WBA)	1992
Masao Ohba (WBA)	1970–73	Phichit Sithbangprachan (IBF)	1992–94†
ERBITO SALAVARRIA	1970–73	David Griman (WBA)	1992–94
Betulio Gonzalez (WBC)	1972	Saen Sor Ploenchit (WBA)	1994–96
Venice Borkorsor (WBC)	1972–73	Francisco Tejedor (IBF)	1995
VENICE BORKORSOR	1973	Danny Romero (IBF)	1995–96
Chartchai Chionoi (WBA)	1973–74	Mark Johnson (IBF)	1996–99†
Betulio Gonzalez (WBA)	1973–74	Jose Bonilla (WBA)	1996–97
Shoji Oguma (WBC)	1974–75	Chatchai Sasakul (WBC)	1997–98
Susumu Hanagata (WBA)	1974–75	Hugo Soto (WBA)	1998–99
Miguel Canto (WBC)	1975–79	Manny Pacquiao (WBC)	1998–99
Erbito Salavarria (WBA)	1975–76	Irene Pacheco (IBF)	1999–2005
Alfonso Lopez (WBA)	1976	Leo Gamez (WBA)	1999
Guty Espadas (WBA)	1976–78	Medgoen Lukchaopormasak (WBC)	1999–00
Betulio Gonzalez (WBA)	1978–79	Sornpichai Kratindaenggym (WBA)	1999–00
Chan-Hee Park (WBC)	1979–80	Eric Morel (WBA)	2000–03
Luis Ibarra (WBA)	1979–80	Malcolm Tunacao (WBC)	2000–01
Tae-Shik Kim (WBA)	1980	Pongsaklek Wonjongkam (WBC)	2001–07
Shoji Oguma (WBC)	1980–81	Lorenzo Parra (WBA)	2003–07
Peter Mathebula (WBA)	1980–81	Vic Darchinyan (IBF)	2004–07
Santos Laciar (WBA)	1981	**Takefumi Sakata** (WBA)	2007–
Antonio Avelar (WBC)	1981–82	**Nonito Donaire** (IBF)	2007–
Luis Ibarra (WBA)	1981	**Daisuke Naito** (WBC)	2007–
Juan Herrera (WBA)	1981–82		
Prudencio Cardona (WBC)	1982		

Junior Flyweights
Current champions in **bold** type.

Champion	Held Title	Champion	Held Title
Franco Udella (WBC)	1975	Katsuo Tokashiki (WBA)	1981–83
Jaime Rios (WBA)	1975–76	Amado Urzua (WBC)	1982
Luis Estaba (WBC)	1975–78	Tadashi Tomori (WBC)	1982
Juan Guzman (WBA)	1976	Hilario Zapata (WBC)	1982–83
Yoko Gushiken (WBA)	1976–81	Jung-Koo Chang (WBC)	1983–88
Freddy Castillo (WBC)	1978	Lupe Madera (WBA)	1983–84
Netrnoi Vorasingh (WBC)	1978	Dodie Penalosa (IBF)	1983–86
Sung-Jun Kim (WBC)	1978–80	Francisco Quiroz (WBA)	1984–85
Shigeo Nakajima (WBC)	1980	Joey Olivo (WBA)	1985
Hilario Zapata (WBC)	1980–82	Myung-Woo Yuh (WBA)	1985–91
Pedro Flores (WBA)	1981	Jum-Hwan Choi (IBF)	1986–88
Hwan-Jin Kim (WBA)	1981	Tacy Macalos (IBF)	1988–89

Champion	Held Title
German Torres (WBC)	1988–89
Yul-Woo Lee (WBC)	1989
Muangchai Kittikasem (IBF)	1989–90
Humberto Gonzalez (WBC)	1989–90
Michael Carbajal (IBF)	1990–94
Rolando Pascua (WBC)	1990
Melchor Cob Castro (WBC)	1991
Humberto Gonzalez (WBC)	1991–93
Hirokia Ioka (WBA)	1991–92
Michael Carbajal (WBC)	1993–94
Myung-Woo Yuh (WBA)	1993
Leo Gamez (WBA)	1993–95
Humberto Gonzalez (WBC/IBF)	1994–95
Choi Hi-Yong (WBA)	1995–96
Saman Sor Jaturong (WBC/IBF)	1995–96
Carlos Murillo (WBA)	1996
Keiji Yamaguchi (WBA)	1996
Michael Carbajal (IBF)	1996–97
Saman Sor Jaturong (WBC)	1995–99

Champion	Held Title
Phichit Chor Siriwat (WBA)	1996–00†
Mauricio Pastrana (IBF)	1997–98†
Will Grigsby (IBF)	1999
Choi Yo-Sam (WBC)	1999–2002
Ricardo Lopez (IBF)	1999–2003*
Beibis Mendoza (WBA)	2000–01
Rosendo Alvarez (WBA)	2001–04†
Jorge Arce (WBC)	2002–05†
Jose Victor Burgos (IBF)	2003–05
Eric Ortiz (WBC)	2005
Roberto Vasquez (WBA)	2005–06
Brian Viloria (WBC)	2005–06
Will Grigsby (IBF)	2005–06
Ulises Solis (IBF)	2006–
Koki Kameda (WBA)	2006–07†
Edgar Sosa (WBC)	2007–
Juan Carlos Reveco (WBA)	2007
Brahim Asloum (WBA)	2007–.

Strawweights

Current champions in **bold** type.

Champion	Held Title
Franco Udella (WBC)	1975
Jaime Rios (WBA)	1975–76
Luis Estraba (WBC)	1975–78
Juan Guzman (WBA)	1976
Yoko Gushiken (WBA)	1976–81
Freddy Castillo (WBC)	1978
Netrnoi Vorasingh (WBC)	1978
Sung-Jun Kim (WBC)	1978–80
Shigeo Nakajima (WBC)	1980
Hilario Zapata (WBA)	1980–82
Pedro Flores (WBA)	1981
Hwan-Jin Kim (WBA)	1981
Katsuo Tokashiki (WBA)	1981–83
Amado Urzua (WBC)	1982
Tadashi Tomori (WBC)	1982
Hilario Zapata (WBC)	1982–83
Jung-Koo Chang (WBC)	1983–88
Lupe Madera (WBA)	1983–84
Dodie Penalosa (WBA)	1983–86
Francisco Quiroz (WBA)	1984–85
Joey Olivo (WBA)	1985
Myung-Woo Yuh (WBA)	1985–93
Jum-Hwan Choi (IBF)	1986–88
Tacy Macalos (IBF)	1988–89
German Torres (WBC)	1988–89
Yul-Woo Lee (WBC)	1989
Muangchai Kittikasem (IBF)	1989–90
Humberto Gonzalez (WBC)	1989–90
Michael Carbajal (IBF)	1990
Rolando Pascua (WBC)	1990

Champion	Held Title
Melchor Cob Castro (WBC)	1991
Ricardo Lopez (WBC)	1990–98
Ratanapol Voraphin (IBF)	1992–97
Chana Porpaoin (WBA)	1993–95
Rosendo Alvarez (WBA)	1995–98
Ricardo Lopez (WBA/WBC)	1998–99†
Zolani Petelo (IBF)	1997–2001†
Wandee Chor Chareon (WBC)	1999–00
Noel Arambulet (WBA)	1999–00†
Joma Gamboa (WBA)	2000
Keitaro Hoshino (WBA)	2000–01
Jose Antonio Aguirre (WBC)	2000–04
Chana Porpaoin (WBA)	2001
Robert Leyva (IBF)	2001–02
Yutaka Niida (WBA)	2001*
Keitaro Hoshino (WBA)	2002
Noel Arambulent (WBA)	2002–04
Miguel Barrera (IBF)	2002–03
Edgar Cardenas (IBF)	2003
Daniel Reyes (IBF)	2003–04
Eagle Kyowa (WBC)	2004
Yutaka Niida (WBA)	2004–08
Muhammad Rachman (IBF)	2004–07
Isaac Bustos (WBC)	2004–05
Katsunari Takayama (WBC)	2005
Eagle Kyowa (WBC)	2005–07
Florante Condes (IBF)	2007–08
Oleydong Sithsamerchai (WBC)	2007–
Raul Garcia (IBF)	2008–
Roman Gonzalez (WBA)	2008–

Annual Awards

Ring Magazine Fight of the Year

First presented in 1945 by Nat Fleischer, who started *The Ring* magazine in 1922.

Multiple matchups: Muhammad Ali vs. Joe Frazier, Marco Antonio Barrera vs. Erik Morales; Carmen Basilio vs. Sugar Ray Robinson, Arturo Gatti vs. Micky Ward and Rocky Graziano vs. Tony Zale (2).

Multiple fights: Muhammad Ali (6); Carmen Basilio (5); George Foreman, Arturo Gatti and Joe Frazier (4); Rocky Graziano, Rocky Marciano, Micky Ward and Tony Zale (3); Marco Antonio Barrera, Nino Benvenuti, Bobby Chacon, Ezzard Charles, Marvin Hagler, Thomas Hearns, Evander Holyfield, Sugar Ray Leonard, Erik Morales, Floyd Patterson, Sugar Ray Robinson, Jersey Joe Walcott (2).

Year	Winner	Loser	Result
1945	Rocky Graziano	Red Cochrane	KO 10
1946	Tony Zale	Rocky Graziano	KO 6
1947	Rocky Graziano	Tony Zale	KO 6
1948	Marcel Cerdan	Tony Zale	KO 12
1949	Willie Pep	Sandy Saddler	W 15
1950	Jake LaMotta	Laurent Dauthuille	KO 15
1951	Jersey Joe Walcott	Ezzard Charles	KO 7
1952	Rocky Marciano	Jersey Joe Walcott	KO 13
1953	Rocky Marciano	Roland LaStarza	KO 11

Annual Awards (Cont.)
Ring Magazine Fight of the Year (Cont.)

Year	Winner	Loser	Result	Year	Winner	Loser	Result
1954	Rocky Marciano	Ezzard Charles	KO 8	1982	Bobby Chacon	Rafael Limon	W 15
1955	Carmen Basilio	Tony DeMarco	KO 12	1983	Bobby Chacon	C. Boza-Edwards	W 12
1956	Carmen Basilio	Johnny Saxton	KO 9	1984	Jose Luis Ramirez	Edwin Rosario	KO 4
1957	Carmen Basilio	Sugar Ray Robinson	W 15	1985	Marvin Hagler	Thomas Hearns	KO 3
1958	Sugar Ray Robinson	Carmen Basilio	W 15	1986	Stevie Cruz	Barry McGuigan	W 15
1959	Gene Fullmer	Carmen Basilio	KO 14	1987	Sugar Ray Leonard	Marvin Hagler	W 12
1960	Floyd Patterson	Ingemar Johansson	KO 5	1988	Tony Lopez	Rocky Lockridge	W 12
1961	Joe Brown	Dave Charnley	W 15	1989	Roberto Duran	Iran Barkley	W 12
1962	Joey Giardello	Henry Hank	W 10	1990	Julio Cesar Chavez	Meldrick Taylor	KO 12
1963	Cassius Clay	Doug Jones	W 10	1991	Robert Quiroga	Akeem Anifowoshe	W 12
1964	Cassius Clay	Sonny Liston	KO 7	1992	Riddick Bowe	Evander Holyfield	W 12
1965	Floyd Patterson	George Chuvalo	W 12	1993	Michael Carbajal	Humberto Gonzalez	KO 7
1966	Jose Torres	Eddie Cotton	W 15	1994	Jorge Castro	John David Jackson	TKO 9
1967	Nino Benvenuti	Emile Griffith	W 15	1995	Saman Sorjaturong	Chiquita Gonzalez	KO 7
1968	Dick Tiger	Frank DePaula	W 10	1996	Evander Holyfield	Mike Tyson	TKO 11
1969	Joe Frazier	Jerry Quarry	KO 7	1997	Arturo Gatti	Gabriel Ruelas	KO 5
1970	Carlos Monzon	Nino Benvenuti	KO 12	1998	Ivan Robinson	Arturo Gatti	W 10
1971	Joe Frazier	Muhammad Ali	W 15	1999	Paulie Ayala	Johnny Tapia	W 12
1972	Bob Foster	Chris Finnegan	KO 14	2000	Erik Morales	Marco Antonio Barrera	W 12
1973	George Foreman	Joe Frazier	KO 2	2001	Micky Ward	Emanuel Burton	W 10
1974	Muhammad Ali	George Foreman	KO 8	2002	Micky Ward	Arturo Gatti	W 10
1975	Muhammad Ali	Joe Frazier	KO 14	2003	Arturo Gatti	Micky Ward	W 10
1976	George Foreman	Ron Lyle	KO 4	2004	Marco Antonio Barrera	Erik Morales	W 12
1977	Jimmy Young	George Foreman	W 12	2005	Diego Corrales	Jose Luis Castillo	KO 10
1978	Leon Spinks	Muhammad Ali	W 15	2006	Somsak Sithchatchawai	Mahyar Monshipour	TKO 10
1979	Danny Lopez	Mike Ayala	KO 15	2007	Israel Vazquez	Rafael Marquez	KO 6
1980	Saad Muhammad	Yaqui Lopez	KO 14				
1981	Sugar Ray Leonard	Thomas Hearns	KO 14				

Ring Magazine Fighter of the Year

First presented in 1928 by Nat Fleischer, who started *The Ring* magazine in 1922.

Multiple winners: Muhammad Ali (5); Joe Louis (4); Joe Frazier, Evander Holyfield and Rocky Marciano (3); Ezzard Charles, George Foreman, Marvin Hagler, Thomas Hearns, Ingemar Johansson, Sugar Ray Leonard, Tommy Loughran, Floyd Mayweather Jr., Floyd Patterson, Sugar Ray Robinson, Barney Ross, Dick Tiger, James Toney and Mike Tyson (2).

Year		Year		Year	
1928	Gene Tunney	1956	Floyd Patterson	1983	Marvin Hagler
1929	Tommy Loughran	1957	Carmen Basilio	1984	Thomas Hearns
1930	Max Schmeling	1958	Ingemar Johansson	1985	Donald Curry
1931	Tommy Loughran	1959	Ingemar Johansson		& Marvin Hagler
1932	Jack Sharkey	1960	Floyd Patterson	1986	Mike Tyson
1933	No award	1961	Joe Brown	1987	Evander Holyfield
1934	Tony Canzoneri	1962	Dick Tiger	1988	Mike Tyson
	& Barney Ross	1963	Cassius Clay	1989	Pernell Whitaker
1935	Barney Ross	1964	Emile Griffith	1990	Julio Cesar Chavez
1936	Joe Louis	1965	Dick Tiger	1991	James Toney
1937	Henry Armstrong	1966	No award	1992	Riddick Bowe
1938	Joe Louis	1967	Joe Frazier	1993	Michael Carbajal
1939	Joe Louis	1968	Nino Benvenuti	1994	Roy Jones Jr.
1940	Billy Conn	1969	Jose Napoles	1995	Oscar De La Hoya
1941	Joe Louis	1970	Joe Frazier	1996	Evander Holyfield
1942	Sugar Ray Robinson	1971	Joe Frazier	1997	Evander Holyfield
1943	Fred Apostoli	1972	Muhammad Ali	1998	Floyd Mayweather Jr.
1944	Beau Jack		& Carlos Monzon	1999	Paulie Ayala
1945	Willie Pep	1973	George Foreman	2000	Felix Trinidad
1946	Tony Zale	1974	Muhammad Ali	2001	Bernard Hopkins
1947	Gus Lesnevich	1975	Muhammad Ali	2002	Vernon Forrest
1948	Ike Williams	1976	George Foreman	2003	James Toney
1949	Ezzard Charles	1977	Carlos Zarate	2004	Glen Johnson
1950	Ezzard Charles	1978	Muhammad Ali	2005	Ricky Hatton
1951	Sugar Ray Robinson	1979	Sugar Ray Leonard	2006	Manny Pacquiao
1952	Rocky Marciano	1980	Thomas Hearns	2007	Floyd Mayweather Jr.
1953	Carl (Bobo) Olson	1981	Sugar Ray Leonard		
1954	Rocky Marciano		& Salvador Sanchez		
1955	Rocky Marciano	1982	Larry Holmes		

Note: Cassius Clay changed his name to Muhammad Ali after winning the heavyweight title in 1964.

All-Time Leaders

Based on rankings compiled by *The Ring Record Book and Encyclopedia.*

Knockouts

		Division	Career	No
1	Archie Moore	Lt. Heavy	1936–63	130
2	Young Stribling	Heavy	1921–33	126
3	Billy Bird	Welter	1920–48	125
4	George Odwel	Welter	1930–45	114
5	Sugar Ray Robinson	Middle	1940–65	110

Total Bouts

		Division	Career	No
1	Len Wickwar	Lt. Heavy	1928–47	463
2	Reggie Strickland	Lt. Heavy	1987–05	363
3	Jack Britton	Welter	1905–30	350
4	Johnny Dundee	Feather	1910–32	333
5	Billy Bird	Welter	1920–48	318

Triple Champions

Fighters who have won widely-accepted world titles in more than two divisions. Henry Armstrong is the only fighter listed to hold three titles simultaneously. Note that (*) indicates title claimant.

Sugar Ray Leonard (5) WBC Welterweight (1979-80,80-82); WBA Jr. Middleweight (1981); WBC Middleweight (1987); WBC Super Middleweight (1988-90); WBC Light Heavyweight (1988).

Floyd Mayweather Jr. (5) WBC Jr. Lighweight (1998-2002); WBC Lightweight (2002-04); WBC Jr. Welterweight (2005-06); WBC Welterweight (2006–); WBC Jr. Middleweight (2007).

Roy Jones Jr. (4) IBF Middleweight (1993-94); IBF Super Middleweight (1994-96); WBC Light Heavyweight (1996, 1997-2003); WBA Light Heavyweight (1998–); IBF Light Heavyweight (1999-2003); WBA Heavyweight (2003-04).

Oscar De La Hoya (4) IBF Lightweight (1995-96); WBC Super Lightweight (1996-97); WBC Welterweight (1997-99); WBC Jr. Middleweight (2001-03); WBA Jr. Middleweight (2002-03); WBC Jr. Middleweight (2006).

Roberto Duran (4) Lightweight (1972-79); WBC Welterweight (1980); WBA Jr. Middleweight (1983-84); WBC Middleweight (1989-90).

Leo Gamez (4) WBA Strawweight (1988-90); WBA Jr. Flyweight (1993-95); WBA Flyweight (1999); WBA Junior Bantamweight (2000-01).

Thomas Hearns (4) WBA Welterweight (1980-81); WBC Jr. Middleweight (1982-84); WBC Light Heavyweight (1987); WBC Middleweight (1987-88); WBA Light Heavyweight (1991).

James Toney (4) IBF Middleweight (1991-93); IBF Super Middleweight (1992-94); IBF Cruiserweight (2003); WBA Heavyweight† (2005).

Pernell Whitaker (4) IBF/WBC/WBA Lightweight (1989-92); IBF Jr. Welterweight (1992-93); WBC Welterweight (1993-97); WBC Jr. Middleweight (1995).

Manny Pacquio (4) WBC Flyweight (1998-99); WBC Lightweight (2008—); WBC Super Featherweight (2008); IBF Super Bantamweight (2001-03)

Alexis Arguello (3) WBA Featherweight (1974-77); WBC Jr. Lightweight (1978-80); WBC Lightweight (1981-83).

Henry Armstrong (3) Featherweight (1937-38); Welterweight (1938-40); Lightweight (1938-39).

Iran Barkley (3) WBC Middleweight (1988-89); IBF Super Middleweight (1992-93); WBA Light Heavyweight (1992).

Wilfredo Benitez (3) Jr. Welterweight (1976-79); Welterweight (1979); WBC Jr. Middleweight (1981-82).

Tony Canzoneri (3) Featherweight (1928); Lightweight (1930-33); Jr. Welterweight (1931-32,33).

Julio Cesar Chavez (3) WBC Jr. Lightweight (1984-87); WBA/WBC Lightweight (1987-89); WBC/IBF Jr. Welterweight (1989-91); WBC Jr. Welterweight (1991-94, 1994).

Jeff Fenech (3) IBF Bantamweight (1985); WBC Jr. Featherweight (1986-88); WBC Featherweight (1988-90).

Bob Fitzsimmons (3) Middleweight (1891-97); Light Heavyweight (1903-05); Heavyweight (1897-99).

Wilfredo Gomez (3) WBC Super Bantamweight (1977-83); WBC Featherweight (1984); WBA Jr. Lightweight (1985-86).

Emile Griffith (3) Welterweight (1961,62-63,63-66); Jr. Middleweight (1962-63); Middleweight (1966-67,67-68).

Mike McCallum (3) WBA Jr. Middleweight (1984-88); WBA Middleweight (1989-91); WBC Light Heavyweight (1994-95).

Terry McGovern (3) Bantamweight (1889-1900); Featherweight (1900-01); Lightweight* (1900-01).

Erik Morales (3) WBC Jr. Featherweight (1997-2000); WBC Featherweight (2001-02); IBF/WBC Jr. Lightweight (2004)

Barney Ross (3) Lightweight (1933-35); Jr. Welterweight (1933-35); Welterweight (1934, 35-38).

Johnny Tapia (3) IBF Jr. Bantamweight (1997-98); WBA Bantamweight (1998-99); IBF Featherweight (2002).

Felix Trinidad (3) IBF/WBC Welterweight (1993-2000); WBA/IBF Jr. Middleweight (2000-01); WBA Middleweight (2001).

Wilfredo Vazquez (3) WBA Bantamweight (1987-88); WBA Jr. Featherweight (1992-95); WBC Featherweight (1996-98).

†Toney won a uaninmous 12-round decision over WBA champion John Ruiz but tested positive for steroids in a post-fight drug test and the fight was ruled a no-contest.

Muhammad Ali's Career Pro Record

Born Cassius Marcellus Clay, Jr. on Jan. 17, 1942, in Louisville; Amateur record of 100-5; won light-heavyweight gold medal at 1960 Olympic Games; Pro record of 56-5 with 37 KOs in 61 fights.

1960

Date	Opponent (location)	Result
Oct. 29	Tunney Hunsaker, Louisville	Wu 6
Dec. 27	Herb Siler, Miami Beach	TKO 4

1961

Date	Opponent (location)	Result
Jan. 17	Tony Esperti, Miami Beach	TKO 3
Feb. 7	Jim Robinson, Miami Beach	TKO 1
Feb. 21	Donnie Fleeman, Miami Beach	TKO 7
Apr. 19	Lamar Clark, Louisville	KO 2
June 26	Duke Sabedong, Las Vegas	Wu 10
July 22	Alonzo Johnson, Louisville	Wu 10
Oct. 7	Alex Miteff, Louisville	TKO 6
Nov. 29	Willi Besmanoff, Louisville	TKO 7

1962

Date	Opponent (location)	Result
Feb. 10	Sonny Banks, New York	TKO 4
Feb. 28	Don Warner, Miami Beach	TKO 4
Apr. 23	George Logan, Los Angeles	TKO 4
May 19	Billy Daniels, Los Angeles	TKO 7
July 20	Alejandro Lavorante, Los Angeles	KO 5
Nov. 15	Archie Moore, Los Angeles	KO 4

1963

Date	Opponent (location)	Result
Jan. 24	Charlie Powell, Pittsburgh	KO 3
Mar. 13	Doug Jones, New York	Wu 10
June 18	Henry Cooper, London	TKO 5

1964

Date	Opponent (location)	Result
Feb. 25	Sonny Liston, Miami Beach	TKO 7

(won World Heavyweight title)

After the fight, Clay announces he is a member of the Black Muslim religious sect and has changed his name to Muhammad Ali.

1965

Date	Opponent (location)	Result
May 25	Sonny Liston, Lewiston, Me	KO 1
Nov. 22	Floyd Patterson, Las Vegas	TKO 12

1966

Date	Opponent (location)	Result
Mar. 29	George Chuvalo, Toronto	Wu 15
May 21	Henry Cooper, London	TKO 6
Aug. 6	Brian London, London	KO 3
Sept. 10	Karl Mildenberger, Frankfurt	TKO 12
Nov. 14	Cleveland Williams, Houston	TKO 3

1967

Date	Opponent (location)	Result
Feb. 6	Ernie Terrell, Houston	Wu 15
Mar. 22	Zora Folley, New York	KO 7
Apr. 28	Refuses induction into U.S. Army and is stripped of world title by WBA and most state commissions the next day.	
June 20	Found guilty of draft evasion in Houston; fined $10,000 and sentenced to 5 years; remains free pending appeals, but is barred from the ring.	

1968-69 (Inactive)

1970

Date	Opponent (location)	Result
Feb. 3	Announces retirement.	
Oct. 26	Jerry Quarry, Atlanta	TKO 3
Dec. 7	Oscar Bonavena, New York	TKO 15

1971

Date	Opponent (location)	Result
Mar. 8	Joe Frazier, New York	Lu 15

(for World Heavyweight title)

June 28	U.S. Supreme Court reverses Ali's 1967 conviction saying he had been drafted improperly.	
July 26	Jimmy Ellis, Houston	TKO 12

(won vacant NABF Heavyweight title)

Nov. 17	Buster Mathis, Houston	Wu 12
Dec. 26	Jurgen Blin, Zurich	KO 7

1972

Date	Opponent (location)	Result
Apr. 1	Mac Foster, Tokyo	Wu 15
May 1	George Chuvalo, Vancouver	Wu 12
June 27	Jerry Quarry, Las Vegas	TKO 7
July 19	Al (Blue) Lewis, Dublin, Ire	TKO 11
Sept. 20	Floyd Patterson, New York	TKO 7
Nov. 21	Bob Foster, Stateline, Nev	TKO 8

1973

Date	Opponent (location)	Result
Feb. 14	Joe Bugner, Las Vegas	Wu 12
Mar. 31	Ken Norton, San Diego	Ls 12

(lost NABF Heavyweight title)

Sept. 10	Ken Norton, Inglewood, Calif	Ws 12

(regained NABF Heavyweight title)

Oct. 20	Rudi Lubbers, Jakarta, Indonesia	Wu 12

1974

Date	Opponent (location)	Result
Jan. 28	Joe Frazier, New York	Wu 12
Oct. 30	George Foreman, Kinshasa, Zaire	KO 8

(regained World Heavyweight title)

1975

Date	Opponent (location)	Result
Mar. 24	Chuck Wepner, Cleveland	TKO 15
May 16	Ron Lyle, Las Vegas	TKO 11
June 30	Joe Bugner, Kuala Lumpur, Malaysia	Wu 15
Oct. 1	Joe Frazier, Manila, Philippines	TKO 14

1976

Date	Opponent (location)	Result
Feb. 20	Jean Pierre Coopman, San Juan	KO 5
Apr. 30	Jimmy Young, Landover, Md	Wu 15
May 24	Richard Dunn, Munich	TKO 5
Sept. 28	Ken Norton, New York	Wu 15

1977

Date	Opponent (location)	Result
May 16	Alfredo Evangelista, Landover	Wu 15
Sept. 29	Earnie Shavers, New York	Wu 15

1978

Date	Opponent (location)	Result
Feb. 15	Leon Spinks, Las Vegas	Ls 15

(lost World Heavyweight title)

Sept. 15	Leon Spinks, New Orleans	Wu 15

(regained World Heavyweight title)

1979

June 27	Announces retirement.	

1980

Date	Opponent (location)	Result
Oct. 2	Larry Holmes, Las Vegas	TKO by 11

1981

Date	Opponent (location)	Result
Dec. 11	Trevor Berbick, Nassau	Lu 10

(retires after fight)

MISCELLANEOUS SPORTS

Lance Mackey won his second straight Iditarod race with a little help from lead dog **Handsome**.

BOWLING

Major Championships
MEN
U.S. Open

Started in 1941 by the Bowling Proprietors' Association of America, 18 years before the founding of the Professional Bowlers Association. Originally the BPAA All-Star Tournament, it became the U.S. Open in 1971.

Multiple winners: Don Carter, Dick Weber and Pete Weber (4); Dave Husted (3); Del Ballard Jr., Marshall Holman, Junie McMahon, Connie Schwoegler, Andy Varipapa and Walter Ray Williams Jr. (2).

Year		Year		Year		Year	
1942	John Crimmins	1959	Billy Welu	1976	Paul Moser	1993	Del Ballard Jr.
1943	Connie Schwoegler	1960	Harry Smith	1977	Johnny Petraglia	1994	Justin Hromek
1944	Ned Day	1961	Bill Tucker	1978	Nelson Burton Jr.	1995	Dave Husted
1945	Buddy Bomar	1962	Dick Weber	1979	Joe Berardi	1996	Dave Husted
1946	Joe Wilman	1963	Dick Weber	1980	Steve Martin	1997	Not held
1947	Andy Varipapa	1964	Bob Strampe	1981	Marshall Holman	1998	Walter Ray Williams Jr.
1948	Andy Varipapa	1965	Dick Weber	1982	Dave Husted	1999	Bob Learn Jr.
1949	Connie Schwoegler	1966	Dick Weber	1983	Gary Dickinson	2000	Robert Smith
1950	Junie McMahon	1967	Les Schissler	1984	Mark Roth	2001	Miko Koivuniemi
1951	Dick Hoover	1968	Jim Stefanich	1985	Marshall Holman	2003	Walter Ray Williams Jr.
1952	Junie McMahon	1969	Billy Hardwick	1986	Steve Cook	2004	Pete Weber
1953	Don Carter	1970	Bobby Cooper	1987	Del Ballard Jr.	2005	Chris Barnes
1954	Don Carter	1971	Mike Limongello	1988	Pete Weber	2006	Tommy Jones
1955	Steve Nagy	1972	Don Johnson	1989	Mike Aulby	2007	Pete Weber
1956	Bill Lillard	1973	Mike McGrath	1990	Ron Palombi Jr.	2008	Norm Duke
1957	Don Carter	1974	Larry Laub	1991	Pete Weber		
1958	Don Carter	1975	Steve Neff	1992	Robert Lawrence		

PBA World Championship

The Professional Bowlers Association was formed in 1958 and its first national championship tournament was held in Memphis in 1960. Formerly known as the PBA National Championship, the name was changed in 2002. The tournament was held in various locations (1960-80), Toledo, Ohio (1981-2002), Taylor, Mich. (2003-06) and Wyoming, Mich. (2007).

Multiple winners: Earl Anthony (6); Walter Ray Williams Jr. (3); Mike Aulby, Dave Davis, Norm Duke, Mike McGrath, Pete Weber and Wayne Zahn (2).

Year		Year		Year		Year	
1960	Don Carter	1973	Earl Anthony	1986	Tom Crites	1999	Tim Criss
1961	Dave Soutar	1974	Earl Anthony	1987	Randy Pedersen	2000	Norm Duke
1962	Carmen Salvino	1975	Earl Anthony	1988	Brian Voss	2001	Walter Ray Williams Jr.
1963	Billy Hardwick	1976	Paul Colwell	1989	Pete Weber	2002	Doug Kent
1964	Bob Strampe	1977	Tommy Hudson	1990	Jim Pencak	2003	Walter Ray Williams Jr.
1965	Dave Davis	1978	Warren Nelson	1991	Mike Miller	2004	Tom Baker
1966	Wayne Zahn	1979	Mike Aulby	1992	Eric Forkel	2005	Patrick Allen
1967	Dave Davis	1980	Johnny Petraglia	1993	Ron Palombi Jr.	2006	Walter Ray Williams Jr.
1968	Wayne Zahn	1981	Earl Anthony	1994	David Traber	2007	Doug Kent
1969	Mike McGrath	1982	Earl Anthony	1995	Scott Alexander	2008	Norm Duke
1970	Mike McGrath	1983	Earl Anthony	1996	Butch Soper		
1971	Mike Limongello	1984	Bob Chamberlain	1997	Rick Steelsmith		
1972	Johnny Guenther	1985	Mike Aulby	1998	Pete Weber		

Tournament of Champions

Originally the Firestone Tournament of Champions (1965-93), the tournament has also been sponsored by General Tire (1994), Brunswick Corp. (1995-2000) and Dexter (2002-). Held in Akron, Ohio in 1965, then Fairlawn, Ohio (1966-94), Lake Zurich, Ill. (1995-96, 2000), Reno, N.V. (1997), Overland Park, Kan. (1998-99) and Uncasville, Conn. (2002-).

Multiple winners: Jason Couch and Mike Durbin (3); Earl Anthony, Dave Davis, Jim Godman, Marshall Holman and Mark Williams (2).

Year		Year		Year		Year	
1965	Billy Hardwick	1976	Marshall Holman	1987	Pete Weber	1998	Bryan Goebel
1966	Wayne Zahn	1977	Mike Berlin	1988	Mark Williams	1999	Jason Couch
1967	Jim Stefanich	1978	Earl Anthony	1989	Del Ballard Jr.	2000	Jason Couch
1968	Dave Davis	1979	George Pappas	1990	Dave Ferraro	2001	Not held
1969	Jim Godman	1980	Wayne Webb	1991	David Ozio	2002	Jason Couch
1970	Don Johnson	1981	Steve Cook	1992	Marc McDowell	2003	Patrick Healey Jr.
1971	Johnny Petraglia	1982	Mike Durbin	1993	George Branham III	2005	Steve Jaros
1972	Mike Durbin	1983	Joe Berardi	1994	Norm Duke	2006	Chris Barnes
1973	Jim Godman	1984	Mike Durbin	1995	Mike Aulby	2007	Tommy Jones
1974	Earl Anthony	1985	Mark Williams	1996	Dave D'Entremont	2008	Michael Haugen Jr.
1975	Dave Davis	1986	Marshall Holman	1997	John Gant		

USBC Masters Tournament

Sponsored by the United States Bowling Congress, the Masters became an official PBA Tour, title event in 1998. It is open to qualified pros and amateurs. The tournament was formerly known as the American Bowling Congress Masters.

Multiple winners: Mike Aulby (3); Earl Anthony, Billy Golembiewski, Dick Hoover and Billy Welu (2).

Year		Year		Year		Year	
1951	Lee Jouglard	1966	Bob Strampe	1981	Randy Lightfoot	1996	Ernie Schlegel
1952	Willard Taylor	1967	Lou Scalia	1982	Joe Berardi	1997	Jason Queen
1953	Rudy Habetler	1968	Pete Tountas	1983	Mike Lastowski	1998	Mike Aulby
1954	Red Elkins	1969	Jim Chestney	1984	Earl Anthony	1999	Brian Boghosian
1955	Buzz Fazio	1970	Don Glover	1985	Steve Wunderlich	2000	Mika Koivuniemi
1956	Dick Hoover	1971	Jim Godman	1986	Mark Fahy	2001	Parker Bohn III
1957	Dick Hoover	1972	Bill Beach	1987	Rick Steelsmith	2002	Brett Wolfe
1958	Tom Hennessey	1973	Dave Soutar	1988	Del Ballard Jr.	2003	Bryon Smith
1959	Ray Bluth	1974	Paul Colwell	1989	Mike Aulby	2004*	Walter Ray Williams Jr.
1960	Billy Golembiewski	1975	Eddie Ressler Jr.	1990	Chris Warren	2004*	Danny Wiseman
1961	Don Carter	1976	Nelson Burton Jr.	1991	Doug Kent	2005	Mike Scroggins
1962	Billy Golembiewski	1977	Earl Anthony	1992	Ken Johnson	2006	Doug Kent
1963	Harry Smith	1978	Frank Ellenburg	1993	Norm Duke	2007	Sean Rash
1964	Billy Welu	1979	Doug Myers	1994	Steve Fehr		*held Jan. and Oct., 2004
1965	Billy Welu	1980	Neil Burton	1995	Mike Aulby		

WOMEN
U.S. Open

Started by the Bowling Proprietors' Association of America in 1949. Originally the BPAA Women's All-Star Tournament (1949-70); and U.S. Open from 1971-2003. There were two BPAA All-Star tournaments in 1955, in January and December.

Multiple winners: Marion Ladewig (8); Donna Adamek, Paula Sperber Carter, Pat Costello, Dotty Fothergill, Liz Johnson, Dana Miller-Mackie, Aleta Sill, Kim Terrell-Kearney and Sylvia Wene (2).

Year		Year		Year		Year	
1949	Marion Ladewig	1963	Marion Ladewig	1978	Donna Adamek	1993	Dede Davidson
1950	Marion Ladewig	1964	LaVerne Carter	1979	Diana Silva	1994	Aleta Sill
1951	Marion Ladewig	1965	Ann Slattery	1980	Patty Costello	1995	Cheryl Daniels
1952	Marion Ladewig	1966	Joy Abel	1981	Donna Adamek	1996	Liz Johnson
1953	Not held	1967	Gloria Simon	1982	Shinobu Saitoh	1997	Not held
1954	Marion Ladewig	1968	Dotty Fothergill	1983	Dana Miller	1998	Aleta Sill
1955	Sylvia Wene	1969	Dotty Fothergill	1984	Karen Ellingsworth	1999	Kim Adler
1955	Anita Cantaline	1970	Mary Baker	1985	Pat Mercatanti	2000	Tennelle Grijalva
1956	Marion Ladewig	1971	Paula Sperber	1986	Wendy Macpherson	2001	Kim Terrell
1957	Not held	1972	Lorrie Koch	1987	Carol Norman	2002	Not held
1958	Merle Matthews	1973	Millie Martorella	1988	Lisa Wagner	2003	Kelly Kulick
1959	Marion Ladewig	1974	Patty Costello	1989	Robin Romeo	2004-06	Not held
1960	Sylvia Wene	1975	Paula Sperber Carter	1990	Dana Miller-Mackie	2007	Liz Johnson
1961	Phyllis Notaro	1976	Patty Costello	1991	Anne Marie Duggan	2008	Kim Terrell-Kearney
1962	Shirley Garms	1977	Betty Morris	1992	Tish Johnson		

USBC Queens

Originally, sponsored by the Women's International Bowling Congress, the Queens is open to qualified pros and amateurs. Beginning in 2006, the tournament was renamed the USBC Queens, sponsored by the United States Bowling Congress.

Multiple winners: Wendy Macpherson and Millie Martorella (3); Donna Adamek, Lynda (Norry) Barnes, Dotty Fothergill, Aleta Sill and Katsuko Sugimoto (2).

Year		Year		Year		Year	
1961	Janet Harman	1973	Dotty Fothergill	1985	Aleta Sill	1997	Sandra Jo Odom
1962	Dorothy Wilkinson	1974	Judy Soutar	1986	Cora Fiebig	1998	Lynda Norry
1963	Irene Monterosso	1975	Cindy Powell	1987	Cathy Almeida	1999	Leanne Barrette
1964	D.D. Jacobson	1976	Pam Rutherford	1988	Wendy Macpherson	2000	Wendy Macpherson
1965	Betty Kuczynski	1977	Dana Stewart	1989	Carol Gianotti	2001	Carolyn Dorin-Ballard
1966	Judy Lee	1978	Loa Boxberger	1990	Patty Ann	2002	Kim Terrell
1967	Millie Martorella	1979	Donna Adamek	1991	Dede Davidson	2003	Wendy Macpherson
1968	Phyllis Massey	1980	Donna Adamek	1992	Cindy Coburn-Carroll	2004	Marianne DiRupo
1969	Ann Feigel	1981	Katsuko Sugimoto	1993	Jan Schmidt	2005	Tennelle Milligan
1970	Millie Martorella	1982	Katsuko Sugimoto	1994	Anne Marie Duggan	2006	Shannon Pluhowsky
1971	Millie Martorella	1983	Aleta Sill	1995	Sandra Postma	2007	Kelly Kulick
1972	Dotty Fothergill	1984	Kazue Inahashi	1996	Lisa Wagner	2008	Lynda Barnes

Annual Leaders
Average
PBA Tour

The George Young Memorial Award, named after the late ABC Hall of Fame bowler. Based on at least 16 national PBA tournaments from 1959-78, and at least 400 games of tour competition since 1979.

Multiple winners: Walter Ray Williams Jr. (7); Mark Roth (6); Earl Anthony (5); Norm Duke and Marshall Holman (3); Parker Bohn III, Billy Hardwick, Don Johnson and Wayne Zahn (2).

Year	Avg	Year	Avg	Year	Avg
1962 Don Carter	212.84	1978 Mark Roth	219.83	1994 Norm Duke	222.83
1963 Billy Hardwick	210.35	1979 Mark Roth	221.66	1995 Mike Aulby	225.49
1964 Ray Bluth	210.51	1980 Earl Anthony	218.54	1996 Walter Ray Williams Jr.	225.37
1965 Dick Weber	211.90	1981 Mark Roth	216.70	1997 Walter Ray Williams Jr.	222.00
1966 Wayne Zahn	208.63	1982 Marshall Holman	216.15	1998 Walter Ray Williams Jr.	226.13
1967 Wayne Zahn	212.14	1983 Earl Anthony	216.65	1999 Parker Bohn III	228.04
1968 Jim Stefanich	211.90	1984 Marshall Holman	213.91	2000 Chris Barnes	220.93
1969 Billy Hardwick	212.96	1985 Mark Baker	213.72	2002 Parker Bohn III	221.54
1970 Nelson Burton Jr.	214.91	1986 John Gant	214.38	2003 Walter Ray Williams Jr.	224.94
1971 Don Johnson	213.98	1987 Marshall Holman	216.80	2004 Mika Koivuniemi	222.73
1972 Don Johnson	215.29	1988 Mark Roth	218.04	2005 Walter Ray Williams Jr.	227.00
1973 Earl Anthony	215.80	1989 Pete Weber	215.43	2006 Norm Duke	228.98
1974 Earl Anthony	219.34	1990 Amleto Monacelli	218.16	2007 Walter Ray Williams Jr.	228.34
1975 Earl Anthony	219.06	1991 Norm Duke	218.21		
1976 Mark Roth	215.97	1992 Dave Ferraro	219.70		
1977 Mark Roth	218.17	1993 Walter Ray Williams Jr.	222.98		

Note: After its first nine events of 2001, the PBA instituted a new September-to-March schedule with the statistics for those first nine tournaments rolled over into players' final 2001-02 statistics.

PWBA Tour

The Professional Women's Bowling Association (PWBA) went by the name Ladies Professional Bowling Tour (LPBT) from 1981-97 and the Women's Professional Bowling Association prior to that. This table is based on at least 282 games of tour competition, with the expection of 2003 when the minimum was 122 games. In 2003 the fall season was unexpectedly cancelled, shortening the year to eight tournaments. There was no PWBA Tour in 2004, 2005 or 2006.

Multiple winners: Leanne Barrette (4); Nikki Gianulias, Wendy Macpherson and Lisa Rathgeber Wagner (3); Carolyn Dorin-Ballard, Anne Marie Duggan and Aleta Sill (2).

Year	Avg	Year	Avg	Year	Avg
1981 Nikki Gianulias	213.71	1989 Lisa Wagner	211.87	1997 Wendy Macpherson	214.68
1982 Nikki Gianulias	210.63	1990 Leanne Barrette	211.53	1998 Dede Davidson	217.25
1983 Lisa Rathgeber	208.50	1991 Leanne Barrette	211.48	1999 Wendy Macpherson	218.85
1984 Aleta Sill	210.68	1992 Leanne Barrette	211.36	2000 Cara Honeychurch	215.18
1985 Aleta Sill	211.10	1993 Tish Johnson	215.39	2001 Carolyn Dorin-Ballard	214.73
1986 Nikki Gianulias	213.89	1994 Anne Marie Duggan	213.47	2002 Leanne Barrette	216.45
1987 Wendy Macpherson	211.11	1995 Anne Marie Duggan	215.79	2003 Carolyn Dorin-Ballard	215.22
1988 Lisa Wagner	213.02	1996 Tammy Turner	215.23		

Money Won
PBA Tour

Multiple winners: Earl Anthony and Walter Ray Williams Jr. (6); Mark Roth and Dick Weber (4); Mike Aulby (3); Parker Bohn III, Don Carter and Norm Duke (2).

Year	Earnings	Year	Earnings	Year	Earnings
1959 Dick Weber	$7,672	1975 Earl Anthony	$107,585	1991 David Ozio	$225,585
1960 Don Carter	22,525	1976 Earl Anthony	110,833	1992 Marc McDowell	176,215
1961 Dick Weber	26,280	1977 Mark Roth	105,583	1993 Walter Ray Williams Jr.	296,370
1962 Don Carter	49,972	1978 Mark Roth	134,500	1994 Norm Duke	273,752
1963 Dick Weber	46,333	1979 Mark Roth	124,517	1995 Mike Aulby	219,792
1964 Bob Strampe	33,592	1980 Wayne Webb	116,700	1996 Walter Ray Williams Jr.	244,630
1965 Dick Weber	47,675	1981 Earl Anthony	164,735	1997 Walter Ray Williams Jr.	240,544
1966 Wayne Zahn	54,720	1982 Earl Anthony	134,760	1998 Walter Ray Williams Jr.	238,225
1967 Dave Davis	54,165	1983 Earl Anthony	135,605	1999 Parker Bohn III	232,595
1968 Jim Stefanich	67,375	1984 Mark Roth	158,712	2000 Norm Duke	136,900
1969 Billy Hardwick	64,160	1985 Mike Aulby	201,200	2002 Parker Bohn III	245,200
1970 Mike McGrath	52,049	1986 Walter Ray Williams Jr.	145,550	2003 Walter Ray Williams Jr.	419,700
1971 Johnny Petraglia	85,065	1987 Pete Weber	179,516	2004 Mika Koivuniemi	238,590
1972 Don Johnson	56,648	1988 Brian Voss	225,485	2005 Patrick Allen	350,740
1973 Don McCune	69,000	1989 Mike Aulby	298,237	2006 Doug Kent	200,530
1974 Earl Anthony	99,585	1990 Amleto Monacelli	204,775	2007 Norm Duke	176,855

Note: After its first nine events of 2001, the PBA instituted a new September-to-March schedule with the statistics for those first nine tournaments rolled over into players' final 2001-02 statistics.

All-Time Leaders

All-time leading tournament winners on the PBA Tour, through Mar. 30, 2008. PBA figures date back to 1959.

PBA Top 20 Tournaments Won

		Titles				Titles
1	Walter Ray Williams Jr.	44	11	Marshall Holman		22
2	Earl Anthony	43	12	Dick Ritger		20
3	Mark Roth	34		Wayne Webb		20
	Pete Weber	34	14	Amleto Monacelli		19
5	Parker Bohn III	31	15	Dave Davis		18
6	Dick Weber	30	16	Nelson Burton Jr.		18
7	Mike Aulby	29		Billy Hardwick		18
	Norm Duke	29		Dave Soutar		18
9	Don Johnson	26	19	Carmen Salvino		17
10	Brian Voss	24	20	Steve Cook		15
				Jason Couch		15

Note: In 2008 the PBA revised its records to include ABC Masters and BPAA All-Star titles.

Annual Awards

MEN

BWAA Bowler of the Year

Winners selected by Bowling Writers Association of America.

Multiple winners: Walter Ray Williams Jr. (8); Earl Anthony and Don Carter (6); Mark Roth (4); Mike Aulby and Dick Weber (3); Patrick Allen, Parker Bohn III, Buddy Bomar, Ned Day, Norm Duke, Billy Hardwick, Don Johnson and Steve Nagy (2).

Year		Year		Year		Year	
1942	John Crimmins	1959	Ed Lubanski	1976	Earl Anthony	1993	Walter Ray Williams Jr.
1943	Ned Day	1960	Don Carter	1977	Mark Roth	1994	Norm Duke
1944	Ned Day	1961	Dick Weber	1978	Mark Roth	1995	Mike Aulby
1945	Buddy Bomar	1962	Don Carter	1979	Mark Roth	1996	Walter Ray Williams Jr.
1946	Joe Wilman	1963	Dick Weber	1980	Wayne Webb	1997	Walter Ray Williams Jr.
1947	Buddy Bomar	1964	Billy Hardwick	1981	Earl Anthony	1998	Walter Ray Williams Jr.
1948	Andy Varipapa	1965	Dick Weber	1982	Earl Anthony	1999	Parker Bohn III
1949	Connie Schwoegler	1966	Wayne Zahn	1983	Earl Anthony	2000	Norm Duke
1950	Junie McMahon	1967	Dave Davis	1984	Mark Roth	2001	Parker Bohn III
1951	Lee Jouglard	1968	Jim Stefanich	1985	Mike Aulby	2002	Walter Ray Williams Jr.
1952	Steve Nagy	1969	Billy Hardwick	1986	Walter Ray Williams Jr.	2003	Walter Ray Williams Jr.
1953	Don Carter	1970	Nelson Burton Jr.	1987	Marshall Holman	2004	Walter Ray Williams Jr.
1954	Don Carter	1971	Don Johnson	1988	Brian Voss	2005	Patrick Allen
1955	Steve Nagy	1972	Don Johnson	1989	Mike Aulby	2006	Tommy Jones
1956	Bill Lillard	1973	Don McCune	1990	Amleto Monacelli	2007	Patrick Allen
1957	Don Carter	1974	Earl Anthony	1991	David Ozio		
1958	Don Carter	1975	Earl Anthony	1992	Marc McDowell		

PBA Player of the Year

Named after longtime broadcaster Chris Schenkel, winners are selected by members of Professional Bowlers Association. The PBA Player of the Year has differed from the BWAA Bowler of the Year four times—in 1963, '64, '89 and '92.

Multiple winners: Earl Anthony and Walter Ray Williams Jr. (6); Mark Roth (4); Mike Aulby, Parker Bohn III, Norm Duke, Billy Hardwick, Don Johnson and Amleto Monacelli (2).

Year		Year		Year		Year	
1963	Billy Hardwick	1975	Earl Anthony	1987	Marshall Holman	1999	Parker Bohn III
1964	Bob Strampe	1976	Earl Anthony	1988	Brian Voss	2000	Norm Duke
1965	Dick Weber	1977	Mark Roth	1989	Amleto Monacelli	2002	Parker Bohn III
1966	Wayne Zahn	1978	Mark Roth	1990	Amleto Monacelli	2003	Walter Ray Williams Jr.
1967	Dave Davis	1979	Mark Roth	1991	David Ozio	2004	Mika Koivuniemi
1968	Jim Stefanich	1980	Wayne Webb	1992	Dave Ferraro	2005	Patrick Allen
1969	Billy Hardwick	1981	Earl Anthony	1993	Walter Ray Williams Jr.	2006	Tommy Jones
1970	Nelson Burton Jr.	1982	Earl Anthony	1994	Norm Duke	2007	Doug Kent
1971	Don Johnson	1983	Earl Anthony	1995	Mike Aulby	2008	Chris Barnes
1972	Don Johnson	1984	Mark Roth	1996	Walter Ray Williams Jr.		
1973	Don McCune	1985	Mike Aulby	1997	Walter Ray Williams Jr.		
1974	Earl Anthony	1986	Walter Ray Williams Jr.	1998	Walter Ray Williams Jr.		

Note: After its first nine events of 2001, the PBA instituted a new September-to-March schedule with the statistics for those first nine tournaments rolled over into players' final 2001-02 statistics. Individual awards were handed out in 2002.

CHESS

World Champions

Garry Kasparov became the youngest man to win the world chess championship when he beat fellow Russian Anatoly Karpov in 1985 at age 22. In 1993, Kasparov and then-#1 challenger Nigel Short of England broke away from the established International Chess Federation (FIDE) to form the Professional Chess Association (the PCA was disbanded in 1998). FIDE retaliated by stripping Kasparov of the world title and arranging a playoff that was won by Karpov, the former title-holder. Karpov successfully defended the FIDE title several times before failing to show up for the 1999 FIDE World Championship Tournament that was won by Alexander Khalifman. Indian Viswanathan Anand won the 2000 FIDE World Championship.

In his first title defense in five years, Kasparov faced world #2 Vladimir Kramnik for 16 matches in the unofficial (though more widely recognized) world championship from Oct. 8-Nov. 4, 2000 in London. The 25-year-old Kramnik defeated the longtime world champion 8½-6½ in a stunning result. Kasparov failed to win a single game, but despite the loss was still the top-ranked player in the world. Ruslan Ponomariov of Ukraine won the 2002 FIDE title and a plan, known as the Prague Agreement, to unify the world chess championship was hatched. FIDE hosted a knockout tournament in 2003 which was won by the 18-year-old Ponomariov. Ponomariov was supposed to then play world No. 1 Kasparov. But Ponomariov could not agree to the terms set for his match with Kasparov and was stripped of his title. .

Uzbekistan's Rustam Kasimdzhanov won the FIDE title in 2004 (however many of the world's top players didn't compete) and was scheduled to play Kasparov in 2005. The winner of that match was supposed to play the winner of the Kramnik-Peter Leko match (Kramnik retained his title in a 7-7 draw) but Kasparov withdrew from the Kasimdzhanov match in a financial dispute, effectively ending the Prague Agreement. In 2005, the FIDE championship was won by 30-year-old Bulgarian Veselin Topalov. The tournament included eight of the world's top players; each played two games against the others in a round-robin format. However, Kramnik, the linear world champion, did not compete.

Meanwhile, Kasparov stunned many when he announced his retirement from professional chess in March 2005 after winning the prestigious Linares tournament in Spain, claiming there are no real challenges on the horizon.

The 2006 FIDE Championship, designed to crown a unified champion, took place in Russia from Sept. 23-Oct. 13. Linear champ Vladimir Kramnik defeated the world's top-rated player, Veselin Topalov, 2½-1½ in a series of rapid tie-break games following a disputed 6-6 tie in the 12 games series. In a strange twist, the bathroom arrangements had an impact on the match when Topalov complained about Kramnik's frequent in-match bathroom breaks, seeming to imply Kramnik may be getting help from outside sources. Outraged at the accusations, Kramnik balked at playing game 5 and FIDE ruled it a forfeit. Despite that Kramnik prevailed in the tie-break. **Viswanathan Anand** of India won the 2007 FIDE World Championship tournament in Mexico City. Anand successfully defended his title in a 12-game match against Vladimir Kramnik in Bonn, Germany in 2008.

Years		Years		Years	
1866-94	Wilhelm Steinitz, Austria	1957-58	Vassily Smyslov, USSR	1975-85	Anatoly Karpov, USSR
1894-1921	Emanuel Lasker, Germany	1958-59	Mikhail Botvinnik, USSR	1985-2000	Garry Kasparov, RUS
1921-27	Jose Capablanca, Cuba	1960-61	Mikhail Tal, USSR	2000-07	Vladimir Kramnik, RUS
1927-35	Alexander Alekhine, France	1961-63	Mikhail Botvinnik, USSR	2002-03	Ruslan Ponomariov, UKR
1935-37	Max Euwe, Holland	1963-69	Tigran Petrosian, USSR	2004-05	Rustam Kasimdzhanov, UZB
1937-46	Alexander Alekhine, France	1969-72	Boris Spassky, USSR	2005-06	Veselin Topalov, BUL
1948-57	Mikhail Botvinnik, USSR	1972-75	Bobby Fischer, USA*	2007—	Viswanathan Anand, IND

*Fischer defaulted the championship in 1975.

DOGS

Iditarod Trail Sled Dog Race

Lance Mackey, 37, won his second straight Iditarod in 2008. The previous year Mackey made history as the first musher to win both the 1,000-mile Yukon Quest International Sled Dog Race and the Iditarod back-to-back. He repeated the same feat in 2008. The Fairbanks resident won the $69,000 prize for first place and a 2008 Dodge Ram truck valued at $45,000.

In even-numbered years the trail follows the 1,151-mile Northern Route, while in odd-numbered years, it takes a slightly different 1,161-mile Southern Route. The Iditarod, the longest sled dog race in the world, commemorates a 674-mile relay race from Nenana to Nome in 1925 when mushers and dog teams successfully delivered serum to stave off an outbreak of diphtheria among children.

Multiple winners: Rick Swenson (5); Martin Buser, Susan Butcher, Jeff King and Doug Swingley (4); Lance Mackey and Robert Sorlie (2).

Year		Elapsed Time	Year		Elapsed Time
1973	Dick Wilmarth	20 days, 00:49:41	1991	Rick Swenson	12 days, 16:34:39
1974	Carl Huntington	20 days, 15:02:07	1992	Martin Buser	10 days, 19:17:00
1975	Emmitt Peters	14 days, 14:43:45	1993	Jeff King	10 days, 15:38:15
1976	Gerald Riley	18 days, 22:58:17	1994	Martin Buser	10 days, 13:02:39
1977	Rick Swenson	16 days, 16:27:13	1995	Doug Swingley	9 days, 02:42:19
1978	Dick Mackey	14 days, 18:52:24	1996	Jeff King	9 days, 05:43:13
1979	Rick Swenson	15 days, 10:37:47	1997	Martin Buser	9 days, 08:31:45
1980	Joe May	14 days, 07:11:51	1998	Jeff King	9 days, 05:52:26
1981	Rick Swenson	12 days, 08:45:02	1999	Doug Swingley	9 days, 14:31:07
1982	Rick Swenson	16 days, 04:40:10	2000	Doug Swingley	9 days, 00:58:06
1983	Rick Mackey	12 days, 14:10:44	2001	Doug Swingley	9 days, 19:55:50
1984	Dean Osmar	12 days, 15:07:33	2002	Martin Buser	8 days, 22:46:02*
1985	Libby Riddles	18 days, 00:20:17	2003	Robert Sorlie	9 days, 15:47:36
1986	Susan Butcher	11 days, 15:06:00	2004	Mitch Seavey	9 days, 12:20:22
1987	Susan Butcher	11 days, 02:05:13	2005	Robert Sorlie	9 days, 18:39:31
1988	Susan Butcher	11 days, 11:41:40	2006	Jeff King	9 days, 11:11:36
1989	Joe Runyan	11 days, 05:24:34	2007	Lance Mackey	9 days, 05:08:41
1990	Susan Butcher	11 days, 01:53:23	2008	Lance Mackey	9 days, 11:46:48

*Race record.

Westminster Kennel Club

Best in Show

The Best in Show prize at the 132nd annual All-Breed Dog Show of the Westminster Kennel Club, held Feb. 11-12, 2008 at Madison Square Garden, went to Ch. K-Run's Park Me In First. It was the first time that a beagle won Best in Show, in fact a beagle hadn't even won the hound group in nearly 70 years. The 3-year-old male who answers to the name Uno, barked loudly in agreement and the crowd gave a standing ovation when he was selected from more than 2,627 dogs in 169 breeds and varieties.

The Westminster show is the most prestigious dog show in the country, and one of America's oldest annual sporting events.

Multiple winners: Ch. Warren Remedy (3); Ch. Chinoe's Adamant James, Ch. Comejo Wycollar Boy, Ch. Flornell Spicy Piece of Halleston; Ch. Matford Vic, Ch. My Own Brucie, Ch. Pendley Calling of Blarney, Ch. Rancho Dobe's Storm (2).

Year		Breed
1907	Warren Remedy	Fox Terrier
1908	Warren Remedy	Fox Terrier
1909	Warren Remedy	Fox Terrier
1910	Sabine Rarebit	Fox Terrier
1911	Tickle Em Jock	Scottish Terrier
1912	Kenmore Sorceress	Airedale
1913	Strathway Prince Albert	Bulldog
1914	Brentwood Hero	Old English Sheepdog
1915	Matford Vic	Old English Sheepdog
1916	Matford Vic	Old English Sheepdog
1917	Comejo Wycollar Boy	Fox Terrier
1918	Haymarket Faultless	Bull Terrier
1919	Briergate Bright Beauty	Airedale
1920	Comejo Wycollar Boy	Fox Terrier
1921	Midkiff Seductive	Cocker Spaniel
1922	Boxwood Barkentine	Airedale
1923	No best-in-show award	
1924	Barberryhill Bootlegger	Sealyham
1925	Governor Moscow	Pointer
1926	Signal Circuit	Fox Terrier
1927	Pinegrade Perfection	Sealyham
1928	Talavera Margaret	Fox Terrier
1929	Land Loyalty of Bellhaven	Collie
1930	Pendley Calling of Blarney	Fox Terrier
1931	Pendley Calling of Blarney	Fox Terrier
1932	Nancolleth Markable	Pointer
1933	Warland Protector of Shelterock	Airedale
1934	Flornell Spicy Bit of Halleston	Fox Terrier
1935	Nunsoe Duc de la Terrace of Blakeen	Stan. Poodle
1936	St. Margaret Magnificent of Clairedale	Sealyham
1937	Flornell Spicy Bit of Halleston	Fox Terrier
1938	Daro of Maridor	English Setter
1939	Ferry v.Rauhfelsen of Giralda	Doberman
1940	My Own Brucie	Cocker Spaniel
1941	My Own Brucie	Cocker Spaniel
1942	Wolvey Pattern of Edgerstoune	W. Highland Terrier
1943	Pitter Patter of Piperscroft	Miniature Poodle
1944	Flornell Rarebit of Twin Ponds	Welsh Terrier
1945	Shieling's Signature	Scottish Terrier
1946	Hetherington Model Rhythm	Fox Terrier
1947	Warlord of Mazelaine	Boxer
1948	Rock Ridge Night Rocket	Bedling. Terrier
1949	Mazelaine's Zazarac Brandy	Boxer
1950	Walsing Winning Trick of Edgerstoune	Scot. Terrier
1951	Bang Away of Sirrah Crest	Boxer
1952	Rancho Dobe's Storm	Doberman
1953	Rancho Dobe's Storm	Doberman
1954	Carmor's Rise and Shine	Cocker Spaniel
1955	Kippax Fearnought	Bulldog
1956	Wilber White Swan	Toy Poodle
1957	Shirkhan of Grandeur	Afghan Hound
1958	Puttencove Promise	Standard Poodle
1959	Fontclair Festoon	Miniature Poodle

Year		Breed
1960	Chick T'Sun of Caversham	Pekingese
1961	Cappoquin Little Sister	Toy Poodle
1962	Elfinbrook Simon	W. Highland Terrier
1963	Wakefield's Black Knight	English Springer Spaniel
1964	Courtenay Fleetfoot of Pennyworth	Whippet
1965	Carmichaels Fanfare	Scottish Terrier
1966	Zeloy Mooremaides Magic	Fox Terrier
1967	Bardene Bingo	Scottish Terrier
1968	Stingray of Derryabah	Lakeland Terrier
1969	Glamoor Good News	Skye Terrier
1970	Arriba's Prima Donna	Boxer
1971	Chinoe's Adamant James	E.S. Spaniel
1972	Chinoe's Adamant James	E.S. Spaniel
1973	Acadia Command Performance	Standard Poodle
1974	Gretchenhof Columbia River	German SH Pointer
1975	Sir Lancelot of Barvan	Old Eng. Sheepdog
1976	Jo Ni's Red Baron of Crofton	Lakeland Terrier
1977	Dersade Bobby's Girl	Sealyham
1978	Cede Higgens	Yorkshire Terrier
1979	Oak Tree's Irishtocrat	Irish Water Spaniel
1980	Sierra Cinnar	Siberian Husky
1981	Dhandy Favorite Woodchuck	Pug
1982	St. Aubrey Dragonora of Elsdon	Pekingese
1983	Kabik's The Challenger	Afghan Hound
1984	Seaward's Blackbeard	Newfoundland
1985	Braeburn's Close Encounter	Scottish Terrier
1986	Marjetta National Acclaim	Pointer
1987	Covy Tucker Hill's Manhattan	German Shepherd
1988	Great Elms Prince Charming II	Pomeranian
1989	Royal Tudor's Wild As The Wind	Doberman
1990	Wendessa Crown Prince	Pekingese
1991	Whisperwind on a Carousel	Stan. Poodle
1992	Lonesome Dove	Fox Terrier
1993	Salilyn's Condor	E.S. Spaniel
1994	Chidley Willum	Norwich Terrier
1995	Gaelforce Post Script	Scottish Terrier
1996	Clussex Country Sunrise	Clumber Spaniel
1997	Parsifal di Casa Netzer	Standard Schnauzer
1998	Fairewood Frolic	Norwich Terrier
1999	Loteki's Supernatural Being	Papillon
2000	Salilyn 'N Erin's Shameless	E.S. Spaniel
2001	Special Times Just Right	Bichon Frise
2002	Surrey Spice Girl	Miniature Poodle
2003	Torums Scarf Michael	Kerry Blue Terrier
2004	Darbydale's All Rise Pouchcove	Newfoundland
2005	Kan-Point's VJK Autumn Roses	German SH Pointer
2006	Rocky Top's Sundance Kid ROM	Colored Bull Terrier
2007	Felicity's Diamond Jim	English Springer Spaniel
2008	K-Run's Park Me In First	Beagle, 15 in.

FISHING

IGFA All-Tackle World Records

All-tackle records are maintained for the heaviest fish of any species caught on any line up to 130-lb (60 kg) class and certified by the International Game Fish Association. Records logged through Jan. 1, 2008. Selected species included below. **Address:** 300 Gulf Stream Way, Dania Beach, Fla. 33004. **Telephone:** (954) 927-2628. **Web:** www.igfa.org

FRESHWATER FISH

Species	Lbs-Oz	Where Caught	Date	Angler
Barramundi	83-7	N. Queensland, Australia	Sept. 23, 1999	David Powell
Bass, Guadalupe	3-11	Lake Travis, TX	Sept. 25, 1983	Allen Christenson Jr.
Bass, largemouth	22-4	Montgomery Lake, GA	June 2, 1932	George W. Perry
Bass, Roanoke	1-5	Nottoway River, VA	Nov. 11, 1991	Tom Elkins
Bass, rock	3-0	York River, Ontario	Aug. 1, 1974	Peter Gulgin
	3-0	Lake Erie, PA	June 18, 1998	Herbert G. Ratner Jr.
Bass, shoal	8-12	Apalachicola River, FL	Jan. 28, 1995	Carl W. Davis
Bass, smallmouth	11-15	Dale Hollow, TN	July 9, 1955	David Hayes
Bass, spotted	10-4	Pine Flat Lake, CA	Apr. 21, 2001	Bryan Shishido
Bass, striped (landlocked)	67-8	O'Neill Forebay, San Luis, CA	May 7, 1992	Hank Ferguson
Bass, Suwannee	3-14	Suwannee River, FL	Mar. 2, 1985	Ronnie Everett
Bass, white	6-13	Lake Orange, VA	July 31, 1989	Ronald L. Sprouse
Bass, whiterock	27-5	Greers Ferry Lake, AR	Apr. 24, 1997	Jerald C. Shaum
Bass, yellow	2-9	Duck River, TN	Feb. 27, 1998	John T. Chappell
Bass, yellow (hybrid)	4-0	Lake Fork, TX	Mar. 26, 2003	C. Runyan
Bluegill	4-12	Ketona Lake, AL	Apr. 9, 1950	T.S. Hudson
Bowfin	21-8	Florence, SC	Jan. 29, 1980	Robert L. Harmon
Buffalo, bigmouth	70-5	Bussey Brake, Bastrop, LA	Apr. 21, 1980	Delbert Sisk
Buffalo, black	63-6	Mississippi River, IA	Aug. 14, 1999	Jim Winters
Buffalo, smallmouth	82-3	Athens Lake, AL	June 6, 1993	Randy Collins
Bullhead, black	7-7	Mill Pond, NY	Aug. 25, 1993	Kevin Kelly
Bullhead, brown	6-5	Lake Mahopac, NY	Sept. 8, 2002	Ray Lawrence
Bullhead, yellow	6-6	Drevel, MO	May 27, 2006	John R. Irvin
Burbot	18-11	Angenmanelren, Sweden	Oct. 22, 1996	Margit Agren
Carp, bighead	90-0	Guntersville Lake, TN	June 2, 2005	Jeffrey J. Rorex
Carp, black	40-12	Chiba, Japan	Apr. 1, 2000	Kenichi Hosoi
Carp, common	75-11	St. Cassien, France	May 21, 1987	Leo van der Gugten
Carp, crucian	8-2	Seeland, Denmark	Sept. 20, 2005	Brian Jensen
Catfish, blue	124-0	Mississippi River, IL	May 21, 2005	Tim Pruitt
Catfish, channel	58-0	Santee-Cooper Res., SC	July 7, 1964	W.B. Whaley
Catfish, flathead	123-0	Elk City Reservoir, KS	May 19, 1998	Ken Paulie
Catfish, flatwhiskered	16-15	Xingu River, Brazil	Aug. 7, 2001	Ian-Arthur de Sulocki
Catfish, gilded	85-8	Amazon River, Brazil	Nov. 15, 1986	Gilberto Fernandes
Catfish, redtail	113-9	Rio Negro, Brazil	Oct. 6, 2007	J. Masullo de Aguiar
Catfish, sharptoothed	79-5	Orange River, South Africa	Dec. 5, 1992	Hennie Moller
Catfish, white	19-5	Oakdale, CA	May 7, 2005	Russell D. Price
Char, Arctic	32-9	Tree River, Canada	July 30, 1981	Jeffery Ward
Crappie, black	5-0	Private Lake, MO	Apr. 21, 2006	John R. Horstman
Crappie, white	5-3	Enid Dam, MS	July 31, 1957	Fred L. Bright
Dolly Varden	20-14	Wulik River, AK	July 7, 2001	Raz Reid
Dorado	55-11	Uruguay River, Argentina	Jan. 1, 2006	Andre L. S. de Botton
Drum, freshwater	54-8	Nickajack Lake, TN	Apr. 20, 1972	Benny E. Hull
Gar, alligator	279-0	Rio Grande, TX	Dec. 2, 1951	Bill Valverde
Gar, Florida	10-0	The Everglades, FL	Jan. 28, 2002	Herbert G. Ratner Jr.
Gar, longnose	50-5	Trinity River, TX	July 30, 1954	Townsend Miller
Gar, shortnose	5-12	Rend Lake, IL	July 16, 1995	Donna K. Willmart
Gar, spotted	9-12	Lake Mexia, TX	Apr. 7, 1994	Rick Rivard
Goldfish	9-6	Lindo Lakes, CA	Nov. 29, 2002	Matthew Servant
Grayling, Arctic	5-15	Katseyedie River, N.W.T.	Aug. 16, 1967	Jeanne P. Branson
Inconnu	53-0	Pah River, AK	Aug. 20, 1986	Lawrence E. Hudnall
Kokanee	9-6	Okanagan Lake, Brit. Columbia	June 18, 1988	Norm Kuhn
Muskellunge	67-8	Hayward, WI	July 24, 1949	Cal Johnson
Muskellunge, tiger	51-3	Lac Vieux-Desert, WI-MI	July 16, 1919	John A. Knobla
Peacock, butterfly	12-9	Chiguao River, Venezuela	Jan. 6, 2000	Antonio Campa G.
Peacock, speckled	27-0	Rio Negro, Brazil	Dec. 4, 1994	Gerald (Doc) Lawson
Perch, Nile	230-0	Lake Nasser, Egypt	Dec. 20, 2000	William Toth
Perch, white	3-1	Forest Hill Park, NJ	May 6, 1989	Edward Tango
Perch, yellow	4-3	Bordentown, NJ	May, 1865	Dr. C.C. Abbot
Pickerel, chain	9-6	Homerville, GA	Feb. 17, 1961	Baxley McQuaig Jr.
Pickerel, grass	1-0	Dewart Lake, IN	June 9, 1990	Mike Berg
Pickerel, redfin	2-4	Gall Berry Swamp, NC	June 27, 1997	Edward C. Davis
Pike, northern	55-1	Lake of Grefeern, Germany	Oct. 16, 1986	Lothar Louis
Redhorse, greater	9-3	Salmon River, Pulaski, NY	May 11, 1985	Jason Wilson

Species	Lbs-Oz	Where Caught	Date	Angler
Redhorse, silver	11-7	Plum Creek, WI	May 29, 1985	Neal D.G. Long
Salmon, Atlantic	79-2	Tana River, Norway	1928	Henrik Henriksen
Salmon, chinook	97-4	Kenai River, AK	May 17, 1985	Les Anderson
Salmon, chum	35-0	Edye Pass, Brit. Columbia	July 11, 1995	Todd Johansson
Salmon, coho	33-4	Salmon River, Pulaski, NY	Sept. 27, 1989	Jerry Lifton
Salmon, pink	14-13	Monroe, WA	Sept. 30, 2001	Alexander Minerich
Salmon, sockeye	15-3	Kenai River, AK	Aug. 9, 1987	Stan Roach
Sauger	8-12	Lake Sakakawea, ND	Oct. 6, 1971	Mike Fischer
Shad, American	11-4	Conn. River, S. Hadley, MA	May 19, 1986	Bob Thibodo
Shad, gizzard	4-6	Lake Michigan, IN	Mar. 2, 1996	Mike Berg
Sturgeon, lake	168-0	Georgian Bay, Canada	May 29, 1982	Edward Paszkowski
Sturgeon, white	468-0	Benicia, CA	July 9, 1983	Joey Pallotta III
Tigerfish, giant	97-0	Zaire River, Kinshasa, Zaire	July 9, 1988	Raymond Houtmans
Tilapia, spotted	4-0	Plantation, FL	June 6, 2005	Reed McLane
Trout, Apache	5-3	White Mountain, AZ	May 29, 1991	John Baldwin
Trout, brook	14-8	Nipigon River, Ontario	July, 1916	Dr. W.J. Cook
Trout, brown	40-4	Little Red River, AR	May 9, 1992	Rip Collins
Trout, bull	32-0	Lake Pend Orielle, ID	Oct. 27, 1949	N.L. Higgins
Trout, cutthroat	41-0	Pyramid Lake, NV	Dec., 1925	John Skimmerhorn
Trout, golden	11-0	Cooks Lake, WY	Aug. 5, 1948	Charles S. Reed
Trout, lake	72-0	Great Bear Lake, N.W.T.	Aug. 19, 1995	Lloyd E. Bull
Trout, rainbow	43-10	Lake Deinfenbaker, Canada	June 5, 2007	Adam Konrad
Trout, tiger	20-13	Lake Michigan, WI	Aug. 12, 1978	Peter M. Friedland
Walleye	25-0	Old Hickory Lake, TN	Aug. 2, 1960	Mabry Harper
Warmouth	2-7	Guess Lake, Holt, FL	Oct. 19, 1985	Tony D. Dempsey
Whitefish, lake	14-6	Meaford, Ontario	May 21, 1984	Dennis M. Laycock
Whitefish, round	6-0	Putahow River, Manitoba	June 14, 1984	Allan J. Ristori
Zander	25-2	Trosa, Sweden	June 12, 1986	Harry Lee Tennison

SALTWATER FISH

Species	Lbs-Oz	Where Caught	Date	Angler
Albacore	88-2	Gran Canaria, Canary Islands	Nov. 19, 1977	Siegfried Dickemann
Amberjack, greater	155-12	Challenger Bank, Bermuda	Aug. 16, 1992	Larry Trott
Angelfish, gray	4-0	S.Beach Jetty, Miami, FL	July 12, 1999	Rene G. de Dios
Barracuda, great	85-0	Christmas Is., Rep. of Kiribati	Apr. 11, 1992	John W. Helfrich
Barracuda, Mexican	22-8	Pinas Bay, Panama	Nov. 11, 2005	Frank Ibarra
Barracuda, pickhandle	29-12	Malindi, Kenya	Nov. 7, 2002	Paul Gerritsen
Bass, barred sand	13-3	Huntington Beach, CA	Aug. 29, 1988	Robert Halal
Bass, black sea	10-4	Virginia Beach, VA	Jan. 1, 2000	Allan P. Paschall
Bass, European	20-14	Cap d'Agde, France	Sept. 8, 1999	Robert Mari
Bass, giant sea	563-8	Anacapa Island, CA	Aug. 20, 1968	J.D. McAdam Jr.
Bass, striped	78-8	Atlantic City, NJ	Sept. 21, 1982	Albert R. McReynolds
Bluefish	31-12	Hatteras, NC	Jan. 30, 1972	James M. Hussey
Bonefish	19-0	Zululand, South Africa	May 26, 1962	Brian W. Batchelor
Bonito, Atlantic	18-4	Faial Island, Azores	July 8, 1953	D. Gama Higgs
Bonito, Pacific	21-5	181 Spot, CA	Oct. 19, 2003	Kim Larson
Cabezon	23-0	Juan de Fuca Strait, WA	Aug. 4, 1990	Wesley Hunter
Cobia	135-9	Shark Bay, W. Australia	July 9, 1985	Peter W. Goulding
Cod, Atlantic	98-12	Isle of Shoals, NH	June 8, 1969	Alphonse Bielevich
Cod, Pacific	38-9	Kamoenia, Japan	Jan. 16, 2005	Atsunori Takahira
Conger	133-4	South Devon, England	June 5, 1995	Vic Evans
Dolphinfish	88-0	Highbourne Cay, Bahamas	May 5, 1998	Richard D. Evans
Drum, black	113-1	Lewes, DE	Sept. 15, 1975	Gerald M. Townsend
Drum, red	94-2	Avon, NC	Nov. 7, 1984	David G. Deuel
Eel, American	9-4	Cape May, NJ	Nov. 9, 1995	Jeff Pennick
Eel, marbled	36-1	Durban, South Africa	June 10, 1984	Ferdie van Nooten
Flounder, southern	20-9	Nassau Sound, FL	Dec. 23, 1983	Larenza Mungin
Flounder, summer	22-7	Montauk, NY	Sept. 15, 1975	Charles Nappi
Grouper, goliath	680-0	Fernandina Beach, FL	May 20, 1961	Lynn Joyner
Grouper, Warsaw	436-12	Gulf of Mexico, Destin, FL	Dec. 22, 1985	Steve Haeusler
Haddock	14-15	Saltraumen, Germany	Aug. 15, 1997	Heike Neblinger
Halibut, Atlantic	418-13	Vannaya Troms, Norway	July 28, 2004	Thomas Nielsen
Halibut, California	58-9	Santa Rosa Island, CA	June 26, 1999	Roger W. Borrell
Halibut, Pacific	459-0	Dutch Harbor, AK	June 11, 1996	Jack Tragis
Jack, almaco (Pacific)	132-0	La Paz, Baja Calif., Mexico	July 21, 1964	Howard H. Hahn
Jack, crevalle	58-6	Barra do Kwanza, Angola	Dec. 10, 2000	Nuno A.P. da Silva
Jack, horse-eye	29-8	Ascencion Island, South Atlantic	May 28, 1993	Mike Hanson
Kawakawa	29-0	Clarion Island, Mexico	Dec. 17, 1986	Ronald Nakamura
Lingcod	77-3	Homer, Alaska	July 5, 2006	Kindal Murry
Mackerel, cero	17-2	Islamorada, FL	Apr. 5, 1986	G. Michael Mills

FISHING (Cont.)

Species	Lbs-Oz	Where Caught	Date	Angler
Mackerel, king	.93-0	San Juan, Puerto Rico	Apr. 18, 1999	Steve Perez Graulau
Mackerel, Spanish	.13-0	Ocracoke Inlet, NC	Nov. 4, 1987	Robert Cranton
Marlin, Atlantic blue	1402-2	Vitoria, Brazil	Feb. 29, 1992	Paulo R.A. Amorim
Marlin, black	1560-0	Cabo Blanco, Peru	Aug. 4, 1953	A.C. Glassell Jr.
Marlin, Pacific blue	1376-0	Kaaiwi Point, Kona, HI	May 31, 1982	Jay W. deBeaubien
Marlin, striped	.494-0	Tutakaka, New Zealand	Jan. 16, 1986	Bill Boniface
Marlin, white	.181-14	Vitoria, Brazil	Dec. 8, 1979	Evandro Luiz Coser
Permit	.60-0	Paranagua, Brazil	Dec. 14, 2002	Renato Fiedler
Pollack, European	.27-6	Salcombe, Devon, England	Jan. 16, 1986	Robert S. Milkins
Pollock	.50-0	Salstraumen, Norway	Nov. 30, 1996	Thor-Magnus Lekang
Pompano, African	.50-8	Daytona Beach, FL	Apr. 21, 1990	Tom Sargent
Roosterfish	.114-0	La Paz, Baja Calif., Mexico	June 1, 1960	Abe Sackheim
Runner, blue	.11-2	Dauphin Island, AL	June 28, 1997	Stacey M. Moiren
Runner, rainbow	.37-9	Clarion Island, Mexico	Nov. 21, 1991	Tom Pfleger
Sailfish, Atlantic	.141-1	Luanda, Angola	Feb. 19, 1994	Alfredo de Sousa Neves
Sailfish, Pacific	.221-0	Santa Cruz Is., Ecuador	Feb. 12, 1947	C.W. Stewart
Seabass, white	.83-12	San Felipe, Mexico	Mar. 31, 1953	L.C. Baumgardner
Seatrout, spotted	.17-7	Ft. Pierce, FL	May 11, 1995	Craig F. Carson
Shark, blue	.528-0	Montauk Point, NY	Aug. 9, 2001	Joe Seidel
Shark, great white	.2664-0	Ceduna, S. Australia	Apr. 21, 1959	Alfred Dean
Shark, Greenland	.1708-9	Trondheimsfjord, Norway	Oct. 18, 1987	Terje Nordtvedt
Shark, hammerhead	.1280-0	Boca Grande, FL	May 23, 2006	Bucky Grande
Shark, shortfin mako	.1221-0	Chatham, MA	July 21, 2001	Luke Sweeney
Shark, porbeagle	.507-0	Pentland Firth, Scotland	Mar. 9, 1993	Christopher Bennet
Shark, bigeye thresher	.802-0	Tutakaka, New Zealand	Feb. 8, 1981	Dianne North
Shark, tiger	.1785-11	Ulladulla, Australia	Mar. 28, 2004	Kevin James Clapson
Snapper, cubera	.124-12	Garden Bank, LA	June 23, 2007	Marion Rose
Snapper, red	.50-4	Gulf of Mexico, LA	June 23, 1996	Capt. Doc Kennedy
Snook, Pacific black	.57-12	Rio Naranjo, Quepos, Costa Rica	Aug. 23, 1991	George Beck
Spearfish, Mediterranean	.90-13	Madeira Island, Portugal	June 2, 1980	Joseph Larkin
Swordfish	.1182-0	Iquique, Chile	May 7, 1953	Louis Marron
Tarpon	.283-4	Sherbro Is., Sierra Leone	Apr. 16, 1991	Yvon Victor Sebag
Tautog	.25-0	Ocean City, NJ	Jan. 20, 1998	Anthony R. Monica
Tuna, Atlantic bigeye	.392-6	Gran Canaria, Puerto Rico	July 25, 1996	Dieter Vogel
Tuna, blackfin	.49-6	Marathon, FL	April 6, 2006	Matthew E. Pullen
Tuna, bluefin	.1496-0	Aulds Cove, Nova Scotia	Oct. 26, 1979	Ken Fraser
Tuna, longtail	.79-2	Montague Is., NSW, Australia	Apr. 12, 1982	Tim Simpson
Tuna, Pacific bigeye	.435-0	Cabo Blanco, Peru	Apr. 17, 1957	Dr. Russell Lee
Tuna, skipjack	.45-4	Flathead Bank, Mexico	Nov. 16, 1996	Brian Evans
Tuna, southern bluefin	.348-5	Whakatane, New Zealand	Jan. 16, 1981	Rex Wood
Tuna, yellowfin	.388-12	San Benedicto Island, Mexico	Apr. 1, 1977	Curt Wiesenhutter
Tunny, little	.36-0	Washington Canyon, NJ	Nov. 5, 2006	Jess Lubert
Wahoo	.184-0	Cab San Lucas, Mexico	July 29, 2005	Sara Hayward
Weakfish	.19-2	Jones Beach, Long Island, NY	Oct. 11, 1984	Dennis R. Rooney
	19-2	Delaware Bay, DE	May 20, 1989	William E. Thomas

Bassmasters Classic

Waco, Texas native Alton Jones won the 38th Bassmaster Classic, held on South Carolina's Lake Hartwell, his 15 bass limit weighed 49 pounds, 7 ounces, more than 5 pounds ahead of runner-up Cliff Pace (44-5). Kevin VanDam finished third with 43-8 for his fifth Top 5 Classic finish in the last five years. The 44-year-old Jones held a slim lead after the second day of the three day event but scored big on Day 3 to take home the $500,000 check for first place.

The 2009 Bassmasters Classic will be held Feb. 20-22 on the Red River in Bossier City, Louisiana and for the first time the 51-angler field will include a woman. Kim Bain won the inagural Women's Bassmaster Tour Angler of the Year Race and the first become the first female angler to compete in the 39-year history of fishing's marquee event.

The Bassmasters Classic, hosted by B.A.S.S. (Bass Anglers Sportsman Society), is professional bass fishing's world championship. Anglers may weigh only five bass per day and each bass must be at least 12 inches long. Only artificial lures are permitted. The first Classic, held at Lake Mead, Nev. in 1971, was a $10,000 winner-take-all event.

Multiple winners: Rick Clunn (4); George Cochran, Bobby Murray, Hank Parker and Kevin VanDam (2).

Year		Weight	Year		Weight
1971	Bobby Murray, Hot Springs, Ark	43-11	1979	Hank Parker, Clover, S.C	31-0
1972	Don Butler, Tulsa, Okla	38-11	1980	Bo Dowden, Natchitoches, La	54-10
1973	Rayo Breckenridge, Paragould, Ark	52-8	1981	Stanley Mitchell, Fitzgerald, Ga	35-2
1974	Tommy Martin, Hemphill, Tex	33-7	1982	Paul Elias, Laurel, Miss	32-8
1975	Jack Hains, Rayne, La	45-4	1983	Larry Nixon, Hemphill, Tex	18-1
1976	Rick Clunn, Montgomery, Tex	59-15	1984	Rick Clunn, Montgomery, Tex	75-9
1977	Rick Clunn, Montgomery, Tex	27-7	1985	Jack Chancellor, Phenix City, Ala	45-0
1978	Bobby Murray, Nashville, Tenn	37-9	1986	Charlie Reed, Broken Bow, Okla	23-9

Year		Weight
1987	George Cochran, N. Little Rock, Ark	15-5
1988	Guido Hibdon, Gravois Mills, Mo	28-8
1989	Hank Parker, Denver, N.C.	31-6
1990	Rick Clunn, Montgomery, Tex	34-5
1991	Ken Cook, Meers, Okla	33-2
1992	Robert Hamilton Jr., Brandon, Miss	59-6
1993	David Fritts, Lexington, N.C.	48-6
1994	Bryan Kerchal, Newtown, Conn	36-7
1995	Mark Davis, Mount Ida, Ark.	47-14
1996	George Cochran, Hot Springs, Ark.	31-14
1997	Dion Hibdon, Stover, Mo.	34-13

Year		Weight
1998	Denny Brauer, Camdenton, Mo.	46-3
1999	Davy Hite, Prosperity, S.C.	55-10
2000	Woo Daves, Spring Grove, Va.	27-13
2001	Kevin VanDam, Kalamazoo, Mich.	32-5
2002	Jay Yelas, Tyler, Texas	45-13
2003	Michael Iaconelli, Woodbury Heights, N.J.	37-14
2004	Takahiro Omori, Emory, Texas	39-2
2005	Kevin VanDam, Kalamazoo, Mich.	12-15
2006	Luke Clausen, Spokane Valley, Wash.	56-2
2007	Boyd Duckett, Demopolis, Ala.	48-10
2008	Alton Jones, Waco, Texas	49-7

LITTLE LEAGUE BASEBALL

World Series

Waipahu, Hawaii crushed Mexico, 12-3 and gave the United States it's fourth straight Little League World Series title. It was only the second time in LLWS history that a team scored in every inning of the title game. The boys from Kao Hsiung, Taiwan did the same in 1974. Tanner Tokunaga hit two home runs in the win. It was the first appearance for Mexico in the final since Guadalupe won it all in 1997. Tokyo, Japan beat Lake Charles, La., 4-3, in the third-place game.

Played annually in late August in Williamsport, Penn. at Original Field in Williamsport, Penn. from 1947-1958 and at Howard J. Lamade Stadium since 1959 and also at newly constructed Volunteer Stadium starting in 2001.

In order to be invited to the World Series, teams must first win their regional tournaments. There are eight regions from the U.S. (Great Lakes, Midwest, Mid-Atlantic, New England, Northwest, Southeast, Southwest and West) and eight outside of the U.S. (Asia, Canada, Caribbean, European, Latin America, Mexico, Pacific and Trans-Atlantic). The eight U.S. regions then play each other and the the eight international regions play each other and the two winners from each meet in the championship game. This ensures that a team from the U.S. will always participate in the final game.

Multiple winners: Taiwan (16); Japan (6); California (5); Connecticut, New Jersey and Pennsylvania (4); Georgia and Mexico (3); Hawaii, New York, South Korea, Texas and Venezuela (2).

Year	Winner	Score	Loser
1947	Williamsport, PA	16-7	Lock Haven, PA
1948	Lock Haven, PA	6-5	St. Petersburg, FL
1949	Hammonton, NJ	5-0	Pensacola, FL
1950	Houston, TX	2-1	Bridgeport, CT
1951	Stamford, CT	3-0	Austin, TX
1952	Norwalk, CT	4-3	Monongahela, PA
1953	Birmingham, AL	1-0	Schenectady, NY
1954	Schenectady, NY	7-5	Colton, CA
1955	Morrisville, PA	4-3†	Merchantville, NJ
1956	Roswell, NM	3-1	Merchantville, NJ
1957	Monterrey, Mexico	4-0	La Mesa, CA
1958	Monterrey, Mexico	10-1	Kankakee, IL
1959	Hamtramck, MI	12-0	Auburn, CA
1960	Levittown, PA	5-0	Ft. Worth, TX
1961	El Cajon, CA	4-2	El Campo, TX
1962	San Jose, CA	3-0	Kankakee, IL
1963	Granada Hills, CA	2-1	Stratford, CT
1964	Staten Island, NY	4-0	Monterrey, Mex.
1965	Windsor Locks, CT	3-1	Stoney Creek, Can.
1966	Houston, TX	8-2	W. New York, NJ
1967	West Tokyo, Japan	4-1	Chicago, IL
1968	Osaka, Japan	1-0	Richmond, VA
1969	Taipei, Taiwan	5-0	Santa Clara, CA
1970	Wayne, NJ	2-0	Campbell, CA
1971	Tainan, Taiwan	12-3†	Gary, IN
1972	Taipei, Taiwan	6-0	Hammond, IN
1973	Tainan City, Taiwan	12-0	Tucson, AZ
1974	Kao Hsiung, Taiwan	12-1	Red Bluff, CA
1975	Lakewood, NJ	4-3*	Tampa, FL
1976	Tokyo, Japan	10-3	Campbell, CA
1977	Li-Teh, Taiwan	7-2	El Cajon, CA
1978	Pin-Tung, Taiwan	11-1	Danville, CA

Year	Winner	Score	Loser
1979	Hsien, Taiwan	2-1†	Campbell, CA
1980	Hua Lian, Taiwan	4-3	Tampa, FL
1981	Tai-Chung, Taiwan	4-2	Tampa, FL
1982	Kirkland, WA	6-0	Hsien, Taiwan
1983	Marietta, GA	3-1	Barahona, D. Rep.
1984	Seoul, S. Korea	6-2	Altamonte, FL
1985	Seoul, S. Korea	7-1	Mexicali, Mex.
1986	Tainan Park, Taiwan	12-0	Tucson, AZ
1987	Hua Lian, Taiwan	21-1	Irvine, CA
1988	Tai Ping, Taiwan	10-0	Pearl City, HI
1989	Trumbull, CT	5-2	Kaohsiung, Taiwan
1990	Taipei, Taiwan	9-0	Shippensburg, PA
1991	Taichung, Taiwan	11-0	Danville, CA
1992	Long Beach, CA	6-0	Zamboanga, Phil.
1993	Long Beach, CA	3-2	Panama
1994	Maracaibo, Venezuela	4-3	Northridge, CA
1995	Tainan, Taiwan	17-3	Spring, TX
1996	Taipei, Taiwan	13-3	Cranston, RI (called after 5th inn.)
1997	Guadalupe, Mexico	5-4	Mission Viejo, CA
1998	Toms River, NJ	12-9	Kashima, Japan
1999	Osaka, Japan	5-0	Phenix City, AL
2000	Maracaibo, Venezuela	3-2	Bellaire, TX
2001	Tokyo, Japan	2-1	Apopka, FL
2002	Louisville, KY	1-0	Sendai, Japan
2003	Tokyo, Japan	10-1	Boynton Beach, FL
2004	Willemstad, Curacao	5-2	Thousand Oaks, CA
2005	Ewa Beach, HI	7-6†	Willemstad, Curacao
2006	Columbus, GA	2-1	Kawaguchi City, Jap.
2007	Warner Robbins, GA	3-2†	Tokyo, Japan
2008	Waipahu, HI	12-3	Matamoros, Mexico

† extra innings.
* Foreign teams were banned from the tournament in 1975, but allowed back in the following year.

Note: In 1992, Zamboanga City of the Philippines beat Long Beach, 15-4, but was stripped of the title a month later when it was discovered that the team had used several players from outside the city limits. Long Beach was then awarded the title by forfeit, 6-0 (one run for each inning of the game).

POKER

World Series of Poker

Created by Benny Binion in 1970, the World Series of Poker brings together the world's greatest poker players. It was held each year at Binion's Horseshoe Casino in Las Vegas, Nev. until 2005 when it moved to the Rio All-Suite Casino. The marquee event is the no-limit Texas hold-'em tournament. The first World Series was a seven-player tournament in which the champion Johnny Moss was chosen by a vote of his peers.

The 2007 World Champion was California psychologist Jerry Yang, who beat out 6,358 entrants over 12 days and won a first prize of $8.25 million—a larger payday than the winner of the Kentucky Derby, Wimbledon, Indianapolis 500 and the Masters combined. The 39-year-old Laotian immigrant and father of six entered the final table eighth in chips but quickly leap-frogged to first and proceeded to personally knock out seven of the other eight players at the table. In the end only Yang and Tuan Lam, a fellow South Asian refugee, were left. Yang caught a straight on the river to beat the queens that Lam flopped.

In a departure from the traditional WSOP schedule, once the field of 6,844 entrants at the 2008 tournament was narrowed down to a nine-player final table in July, the tournament was put on hold until November when the players were scheduled to reconvene to decide the winner of the bracelet and the first prize of $9.1 million. Nicknamed the "November Nine" the final table was comprised of the following folks (listed in order of chips): Dennis Phillips ($26,295,000), Ivan Demidov ($24,400,000), Scott Montgomery ($19,690,000), Peter Eastgate ($18,375,000), Ylon Schwarts (12,525,000), Darus Suharto ($12,520,000), David Rheem ($10,230,000), Craig Marquis ($10,210,000) and Kelly Kim ($2,620,000).

Anyone that's over 21 years old and can pay the $10,000 entry fee can compete. The field at the 2008 tournament includ-ed celebrities from the world of sports and entertainment including former MLB stars Orel Hershiser, David Wells and Jose Canseco, the UFC's Chuck Liddell and Forrest Griffin, actors Jason Alexander, Ray Ramano, Mekhi Phifer, Shannon Elizabeth and Jennifer Tilly, and 2008 Ryder Cup Team USA captain Paul Azinger.

No-Limit Texas Hold-'em Champions

Multiple winners: Johnny Moss and Stu Ungar (3); Doyle Brunson and Johnny Chan (2).

Year	Champion	Prize Money	Year	Champion	Prize Money
1970	Johnny Moss	n/a	1989	Phil Hellmuth Jr.	$ 755,000
1971	Johnny Moss	$ 30,000	1990	Mansour Matloubi	895,000
1972	"Amarillo Slim" Preston	80,000	1991	Brad Daugherty	1,000,000
1973	Puggy Pearson	130,000	1992	Hamid Datsmalchi	1,000,000
1974	Johnny Moss	160,000	1993	Jim Bechtel	1,000,000
1975	Sailor Roberts	210,000	1994	Russ Hamilton	1,000,000
1976	Doyle Brunson	220,000	1995	Dan Harrington	1,000,000
1977	Doyle Brunson	340,000	1996	Huck Seed	1,000,000
1978	Bobby Baldwin	210,000	1997	Stu Ungar	1,000,000
1979	Hal Fowler	270,000	1998	Scotty Nguyen	1,000,000
1980	Stu Ungar	385,000	1999	Noel Furlong	1,000,000
1981	Stu Ungar	375,000	2000	Chris Ferguson	1,500,000
1982	Jack Strauss	520,000	2001	Carlos Mortensen	1,500,000
1983	Tom McEvoy	580,000	2002	Robert Varkyoni	2,000,000
1984	Jack Keller	660,000	2003	Chris Moneymaker	2,500,000
1985	Bill Smith	700,000	2004	Greg Raymer	5,000,000
1986	Berry Johnston	570,000	2005	Joseph Hachem	7,500,000
1987	Johnny Chan	625,000	2006	Jamie Gold	12,000,000
1988	Johnny Chan	700,000	2007	Jerry Yang	8,250,000

Selected 2008 WSOP results

Buy-in	Event	Bracelet winner	Prize Money
$10,000	World Championship Pot-Limit Hold'em (Event 1)	Nenad Medic	$794,112
$10,000	World Championship Mixed Event (Event 8)	Anthony Rivera	$483,688
$2,500	Omaha/Seven Card Stud Hi-Low-8 or Better (Event 10)	Farzad Rouhani	$232,911
$5,000	No-Limit Hold'em Shootout (Event 11)	Phillip Tom	$477,990
$10,000	World Championship Seven Card Stud (Event 14)	Eric Brooks	$415,856
$5,000	No-Limit 2-7 Draw Lowball w/ReBuys (Event 18)	Mike Matusow	$537,862
$2,000	Limit Hold'em (Event 20)	Daniel Negreanu	$204,874
$5,000	No-Limit Hold'em (Event 21)	Scott Seiver	$755,891
$3,000	H.O.R.S.E. (Event 22)	Jens Voertmann	$298,253
$10,000	World Championship Heads Up No-Limit Hold'em (Event 25)	Kenny Tran	$539,056
$5,000	Pot-Limit Omaha W/Rebuys (Event 28)	Philip Galfond	$817,781
$3,000	No-Limit Hold'em (Event 29)	John "Razor" Phan	$434,789
$10,000	World Championship Limit Hold'em (Event 30)	Rob Hollink	$496,931
$1,500	Pot-Limit Omaha W/ReBuys (Event 34)	Layne Flack	$577,725
$10,000	World Championship Omaha Hi-Low Split-8 or Better (Event 37)	David Benyamine	$535,687
$2,500	2-7 Triple Draw Lowball - Limit (Event 40)	John "Razor" Phan	$151,911
$50,000	World Championship H.O.R.S.E. (Event 45)	Scotty Nguyen	$1,989,120
$5,000	No-Limit Hold'em / Six Handed (Event 46)	Joe Commisso	$911,855
$1,500	Seven Card Stud Hi-Low-8 or Better (Event 47)	Ryan Hughes	$183,368
$2,000	No-Limit Hold'em (Event 48)	Alexandre Gomes	$770,540
$10,000	World Championship Pot Limit Omaha (Event 50)	Marty Smyth	$859,549
$1,500	Limit Hold'em Shootout (Event 53)	Matthew Graham	$278,180

All-Around Champion Cowboy

Trevor Brazile of Decatur, Tex., won his fifth career all-around world title, earning a PRCA-record $425,115 during the 2007 season. Brazile also became the first PRCA cowboy since Roy Cooper in 1983 to win a Triple Crown taking the tie-down roping, steer roping and all-around world titles.

The Professional Rodeo Cowboys Association (PRCA) title of all-around world champion cowboy goes to the rodeo athlete who wins the most prize money in a single year in two or more events, earning a minimum of $3,000 in each event. Only prize money earned in sanctioned PRCA rodeos is counted. From 1929-44, all-around champions were named by the Rodeo Association of America (earnings for those years are not available).

Multiple winners: Ty Murray (7); Tom Ferguson and Larry Mahan (6); Trevor Brazile and Jim Shoulders (5); Joe Beaver, Lewis Feild and Dean Oliver (3); Everett Bowman, Louis Brooks, Clay Carr, Bill Linderman, Phil Lyne, Gerald Roberts, Casey Tibbs and Harry Tompkins (2).

Year		Year		Year		Year	
1929	Earl Thode	1934	Leonard Ward	1939	Paul Carney	1944	Louis Brooks
1930	Clay Carr	1935	Everett Bowman	1940	Fritz Truan	1945	No award
1931	John Schneider	1936	John Bowman	1941	Homer Pettigrew	1946	No award
1932	Donald Nesbit	1937	Everett Bowman	1942	Gerald Roberts		
1933	Clay Carr	1938	Burel Mulkey	1943	Louis Brooks		

Year		Earnings	Year		Earnings	Year		Earnings
1947	Todd Whatley	$18,642	1968	Larry Mahan	$ 49,129	1989	Ty Murray	$ 134,806
1948	Gerald Roberts	21,766	1969	Larry Mahan	57,726	1990	Ty Murray	213,772
1949	Jim Shoulders	21,495	1970	Larry Mahan	41,493	1991	Ty Murray	244,231
1950	Bill Linderman	30,715	1971	Phil Lyne	49,245	1992	Ty Murray	225,992
1951	Casey Tibbs	29,104	1972	Phil Lyne	60,852	1993	Ty Murray	297,896
1952	Harry Tompkins	30,934	1973	Larry Mahan	64,447	1994	Ty Murray	246,170
1953	Bill Linderman	33,674	1974	Tom Ferguson	66,929	1995	Joe Beaver	141,753
1954	Buck Rutherford	40,404	1975	Tom Ferguson	50,300	1996	Joe Beaver	166,103
1955	Casey Tibbs	42,065	1976	Tom Ferguson	87,908	1997	Dan Mortensen	184,559
1956	Jim Shoulders	43,381	1977	Tom Ferguson	65,981	1998	Ty Murray	264,673
1957	Jim Shoulders	33,299	1978	Tom Ferguson	83,734	1999	Fred Whitfield	217,819
1958	Jim Shoulders	32,212	1979	Tom Ferguson	96,272	2000	Joe Beaver	225,396
1959	Jim Shoulders	32,905	1980	Paul Tierney	105,568	2001	Cody Ohl	296,419
1960	Harry Tompkins	32,522	1981	Jimmie Cooper	105,861	2002	Trevor Brazile	273,998
1961	Benny Reynolds	31,309	1982	Chris Lybbert	123,709	2003	Trevor Brazile	294,839
1962	Tom Nesmith	32,611	1983	Roy Cooper	153,391	2004	Trevor Brazile	253,170
1963	Dean Oliver	31,329	1984	Dee Pickett	122,618	2005	Ryan Jarrett	263,665
1964	Dean Oliver	31,150	1985	Lewis Feild	130,347	2006	Trevor Brazile	329,924
1965	Dean Oliver	33,163	1986	Lewis Feild	166,042	2007	Trevor Brazile	425,115
1966	Larry Mahan	40,358	1987	Lewis Feild	144,335			
1967	Larry Mahan	51,996	1988	Dave Appleton	121,546			

All-American Soap Box Derby

The 71st annual All-American Soap Box Derby was held on July 26, 2008 in Akron, Ohio. A record 606 finalists from 160 cities and six nations competed

The AASBD is a coasting race for small gravity-powered cars built by their drivers and assembled within strict guidelines on size, weight and cost. The Derby was started by Dayton, Ohio newsman Myron Scott after he witnessed several boys racing handmade carts down a hill while on a photographic assignment in 1933. Scott decided to start an organized race for kids and the first All-American Soap Box Derby was held in Dayton in 1934. The race got its name because early on most cars were built from wooden soap boxes. The following year, the race was moved to Akron because of its central location and hilly terrain. In 1936, town leaders saw the need for a permanent site for the growing event and with the help of the Works Progress Administration, Derby Downs was constructed.

Held every summer at Derby Downs in Akron, Ohio, the Soap Box Derby is open to all boys and girls from 8 to 17 years old who qualify. There are three competitive divisions: 1. Stock (ages 8-17)— made up of generic, prefab racers that come from Derby-approved kits, can be assembled in four hours and don't exceed 200 pounds when driver, car and wheels are weighed together; 2. Super Stock (ages 10-17)— the same as Stock only with a weight limit of 220 pounds; 3. Masters (ages 11-17)— made up of racers designed by the drivers, but constructed with Derby-approved hardware. The racing ramp at Derby Downs is 989 feet, four inches with an 11 percent grade.

One champion reigned at the All-American Soap Box Derby each year from 1934-75; Junior and Senior division champions from 1976-87; Kit and Masters champions from 1988-91; Stock, Kit and Masters champions from 1992-94; Stock, Super Stock and Masters champions starting in 1995.

Year		Hometown	Age	Year		Hometown	Age
1934	Robert Turner	Muncie, IN	11	1941	Claude Smith	Akron, OH	14
1935	Maurice Bale Jr.	Anderson, IN	13	1942-45	Not held		
1936	Herbert Muench Jr.	St. Louis	14	1946	Gilbert Klecan	San Diego	14
1937	Robert Ballard	White Plains, NY	12	1947	Kenneth Holmboe	Charleston, WV	14
1938	Robert Berger	Omaha, NE	14	1948	Donald Strub	Akron, OH	13
1939	Clifton Hardesty	White Plains, NY	11	1949	Fred Derks	Akron, OH	15
1940	Thomas Fisher	Detroit	12				

All-American Soap Box Derby (Cont.)

Year		Hometown	Age	Year		Hometown	Age
1950	Harold Williamson	Charleston, WV	15	1990	MAS: Sami Jones	Salem, OR	13
1951	Darwin Cooper	Williamsport, PA	15		KIT: Mark Mihal	Valparaiso, IN	12
1952	Joe Lunn	Columbus, GA	11	1991	MAS: Danny Garland	San Diego, CA	14
1953	Fred Mohler	Muncie, IN	14		KIT: Paul Greenwald	Saginaw, MI	13
1954	Richard Kemp	Los Angeles	14	1992	MAS: Bonnie Thornton	Redding, CA	12
1955	Richard Rohrer	Rochester, NY	14		KIT: Carolyn Fox	Sublimity, OR	11
1956	Norman Westfall	Rochester, NY	14		STK: Loren Hurst	Hudson, OH	10
1957	Terry Townsend	Anderson, IN	14	1993	MAS: Dean Lutton	Delta, OH	14
1958	James Miley	Muncie, IN	15		KIT: D.M. Del Ferraro	Stow, OH	12
1959	Barney Townsend	Anderson, IN	13		STK: Owen Yuda	Boiling Springs, PA	10
1960	Fredric Lake	South Bend, IN	11	1994	MAS: D.M. Del Ferraro	Akron, OH	13
1961	Dick Dawson	Wichita, KS	13		KIT: Joel Endres	Akron, OH	14
1962	David Mann	Gary, IN	14		STK: Kristina Damond	Jamestown, NY	13
1963	Harold Conrad	Duluth, MN	12	1995	MAS: J. Fensterbush	Kingman, AZ	11
1964	Gregory Schumacher	Tacoma, WA	14		SS: Darcie Davisson	Kingman, AZ	11
1965	Robert Logan	Santa Ana, CA	12		STK: Karen Thomas	Jamestown, NY	11
1966	David Krussow	Tacoma, WA	12	1996	MAS: Tim Scrofano	Conneaut, OH	12
1967	Kenneth Cline	Lincoln, NE	13		SS: Jeremy Phillips	Charlestown, WV	14
1968	Branch Lew	Muncie, IN	11		STK: Matt Perez	No. Canton, OH	12
1969	Steve Souter	Midland, TX	12	1997	MAS: Wade Wallace	Elk Hart, IN	11
1970	Samuel Gupton	Durham, NC	13		SS: Dolline Vance	Salem, OR	13
1971	Larry Blair	Oroville, CA	13		STK: Mark Stephens	Waynesboro, VA	13
1972	Robert Lange Jr.	Boulder, CO	14	1998	MAS: James Marsh	Cleveland, OH	12
1973	Bret Yarborough	Elk Grove, CA	11		SS: Stacy Sharp	Kingman, AZ	14
1974	Curt Yarborough	Elk Grove, CA	11		STK: Hailey Simpson	Salem, OR	10
1975	Karren Stead	Lower Bucks, PA	11	1999	MAS: Allan Endres	Barberton, OH	14
1976	JR: Phil Raber	Sugarcreek, OH	11		SS: Alisha Ebner	Salem, OR	13
	SR: Joan Ferdinand	Canton, OH	14		STK: Justin Pillow	Deland, FL	12
1977	JR: Mark Ferdinand	Canton, OH	10	2000	MAS: Cody Butler	Anderson, IN	12
	SR: Steve Washburn	Bristol, CT	15		SS: Derek Etherington	Anderson, IN	11
1978	JR: Darren Hart	Salem, OR	11		STK: Rachel Curran	Medina, OH	13
	SR: Greg Cardinal	Flint, MI	13	2001	MAS: Michael Flynn	Harrison Township, MI	12
1979	JR: Russell Yurk	Flint, MI	10		SS: James Rogers	Hilton, NY	15
	SR: Craig Kitchen	Akron, OH	14		STK: Chad Eyerly	Alta Loma, CA	11
1980	JR: Chris Fulton	Indianapolis	11	2002	MAS: Evan Griffin	Winter Park, FL	15
	SR: Dan Porul	Sherman Oaks, CA	12		SS: Roger Youmans Jr.	Spencerport, NY	13
1981	JR: Howie Fraley	Portsmouth, OH	11		STK: Cameron Vannatta	Anderson, IN	12
	SR: Tonia Schlegel	Hamilton, OH	13	2003	MAS: Anthony Marulli	Rochester, NY	14
1982	JR: Carol A. Sullivan	Rochester, NH	10		SS: Corey Harkins	Chicago	14
	SR: Matt Wolfgang	Lehigh Val., PA	12		STK: Nicholas Sibeto	New Castle, PA	12
1983	JR: Tony Carlini	Del Mar, CA	10	2004	MAS: Hilary Pearson	Kansas City, MO	14
	SR: Mike Burdgick	Flint, MI	14		SS: RickiLea Murphy	Mantua, OH	12
1984	JR: Chris Hess	Hamilton, OH	11		STK: Perrin Norris	Tullahoma, TN	10
	SR: Anita Jackson	St. Louis	15	2005	MAS: Stephanie Inglezakis	Stow, OH	16
1985	JR: Michael Gallo	Danbury, CT	12		SS: Tyler Gallagher	Mantua, OH	14
	SR: Matt Sheffer	York, PA	14		STK: Nick Hoffaman	Lancaster, OH	9
1986	JR: Marc Behan	Dover, NH	9	2006	MAS: Garrett Kysar	Martinsburg, WV	14
	SR: Tami Jo Sullivan	Lancaster, OH	13		SS: Sally Sue Thornton	Vallejo, CA	14
1987	JR: Matt Margules	Danbury, CT	11		STK: Michael Neely	North Canton, OH	14
	SR: Brian Drinkwater	Bristol, CT	14	2007	MAS: Kacie Rader	Washington, DC	16
1988	KIT: Jason Lamb	Des Moines, IA	10		SS: Andrew Feldpausch	Saginaw, MI	15
	MAS: David Duffield	Kansas City	13		STK: Tyler Shoff	Akron, OH	13
1989	KIT: David Schiller	Dayton, OH	12	2008	MAS: Courtney Rayle	Washington, DC	16
	MAS: Faith Chavarria	Ventura, CA	12		SS: Hayley Beitel	Tullahoma, TN	11
					STK: Johanna Barnowski	Akron, OH	13

SOFTBALL

Men's national champions since 1933 in Major Fast Pitch and Major Slow Pitch. Sanctioned by the Amateur Softball Association of America.

MEN
Major Fast Pitch

Multiple winners: Clearwater Bombers (10); Raybestos Cardinals (5); Sealmasters (4); Briggs Beautyware, Decatur Pride, Pay'n Pak and Zollner Pistons (3); Billard Barbell, Farm Tavern, Frontier Players Casino, Hammer Air Field, Kodak Park, Meierhoffer, National Health Care, Penn Corp, Peterbilt Western and Tampa Bay Smokers (2).

Year	Year	Year
1933 J.L. Gill Boosters, Chicago	1961 Sealmasters	1987 Pay'n Pak
1934 Ke-Nash-A, Kenosha, WI	1962 Clearwater Bombers	1988 TransAire, Elkhart, IN
1935 Crimson Coaches, Toledo, OH	1963 Clearwater Bombers	1989 Penn Corp, Sioux City, IA
1936 Kodak Park, Rochester, NY	1964 Burch Tool, Detroit	1990 Penn Corp
1937 Briggs Body Team, Detroit	1965 Sealmasters	1991 Gianella Bros., Rohnert Park, CA
1938 The Pohlers, Cincinnati	1966 Clearwater Bombers	1992 National Health Care,
1939 Carr's Boosters, Covington, KY	1967 Sealmasters	Sioux City, IA
1940 Kodak Park	1968 Clearwater Bombers	1993 National Health Care
1941 Bendix Brakes, South Bend, IN	1969 Raybestos Cardinals	1994 Decatur (IL) Pride
1942 Deep Rock Oilers, Tulsa, OK	1970 Raybestos Cardinals	1995 Decatur Pride
1943 Hammer Air Field, Fresno, CA	1971 Welty Way, Cedar Rapids, IA	1996 Green Bay All-Car,
1944 Hammer Air Field	1972 Raybestos Cardinals	Green Bay, WI
1945 Zollner Pistons, Ft. Wayne, IN	1973 Clearwater Bombers	1997 Tampa Bay Smokers,
1946 Zollner Pistons	1974 Gianella Bros., Santa Rosa, CA	Tampa Bay, FL
1947 Zollner Pistons	1975 Rising Sun Hotel, Reading, PA	1998 Meierhoffer-Fleeman,
1948 Briggs Beautyware, Detroit	1976 Raybestos Cardinals	St. Joseph, MO
1949 Tip Top Tailors, Toronto	1977 Billard Barbell, Reading, PA	1999 Decatur Pride
1950 Clearwater (FL) Bombers	1978 Billard Barbell	2000 Meierhoffer
1951 Dow Chemical, Midland, MI	1979 McArdle Pontiac/Cadillac,	2001 Frontier Players Casino,
1952 Briggs Beautyware	Midland, MI	St. Joseph, MO
1953 Briggs Beautyware	1980 Peterbilt Western, Seattle	2002 Frontier Players Casino
1954 Clearwater Bombers	1981 Archer Daniels Midland,	2003 Farm Tavern, Madison, WI
1955 Raybestos Cardinals,	Decatur, IL	2004 Farm Tavern
1956 Clearwater Bombers	1982 Peterbilt Western	2005 Tampa Bay Smokers,
1957 Clearwater Bombers	1983 Franklin Cardinals,	Tampa Bay, FL
1958 Raybestos Cardinals	Stratford, CA	2006 Circle Tap, Denmark, WI
1959 Sealmasters, Aurora, IL	1984 California Kings, Merced, CA	2007 Patsy's, New York, NY
1960 Clearwater Bombers	1985 Pay'n Pak, Seattle	
	1986 Pay'n Pak	

Major Slow Pitch

Multiple winners: Gatliff Auto Sales, Riverside Paving and Skip Hogan A.C. (3); Campbell Carpets, Hamilton Tailoring, Howard's Furniture, Long Haul TPS and New Construction (2).

Year	Year	Year
1953 Shields Construction,	1973 Howard's Furniture,	1992 Vernon's, Jacksonville, FL
Newport, KY	Denver, NC	1993 Back Porch/Destin (FL) Roofing
1954 Waldneck's Tavern, Cincinnati	1974 Howard's Furniture	1994 Riverside Paving, Louisville
1955 Lang Pet Shop, Covington, KY	1975 Pyramid Cafe, Lakewood, OH	1995 Riverside Paving
1956 Gatliff Auto Sales, Newport, KY	1976 Warren Motors, J'ville, FL	1996 Bell II, Orlando, FL
1957 Gatliff Auto Sales	1977 Nelson Painting, Okla. City	1997 Long Haul TPS, Albertville, MN
1958 East Side Sports, Detroit	1978 Campbell Carpets,	1998 Chase Mortgage/Easton,
1959 Yorkshire Restaurant,	Concord, CA	Wilmington, NC
Newport, KY	1979 Nelco Mfg. Co., Okla. City	1999 Gasoline Heaven/Worth,
1960 Hamilton Tailoring, Cincinnati	1980 Campbell Carpets	Commack, NY
1961 Hamilton Tailoring	1981 Elite Coating, Gordon, CA	2000 Long Haul TPS
1962 Skip Hogan A.C., Pittsburgh	1982 Triangle Sports, Minneapolis	2001 New Construction
1963 Gatliff Auto Sales	1983 No.1 Electric & Heating,	2002 Twin States/Worth,
1964 Skip Hogan A.C.	Gastonia, NC	Montgomery, AL
1965 Skip Hogan A.C.	1984 Lilly Air Systems, Chicago	2003 New Construction/B&J/
1966 Michael's Lounge, Detroit	1985 Blanton's Fayetteville, NC	Snap-On, Metamora, IL
1967 Jim's Sport Shop, Pittsburgh	1986 Non-Ferrous Metals, Cleveland	2004 U.S. Vinyl, Houston, TX
1968 County Sports, Levittown, NY	1987 Stapath, Monticello, KY	2005 AM/Las Vegas/Benfield,
1969 Copper Hearth, Milwaukee	1988 Bell Corp/FAF, Tampa, FL	Bowling Green, KY
1970 Little Caesar's, Southgate, MI	1989 Ritch's Salvage, Harrisburg, NC	2006 discontinued
1971 Pile Drivers, Va. Beach, VA	1990 New Construction,	
1972 Jiffy Club, Louisville, KY	Shelbyville, IN	
	1991 Riverside Paving, Louisville	

EATING

Nathan's Famous Hot Dog Eating Contest

Contested since 1916, The Nathan's International July 4th Hot Dog Eating Contest brings some of the world's top competitive eaters together each July fourth at the world famous hot dog restaurant at Coney Island in Brooklyn, New York. Winner receives the Mustard Yellow Belt.

At the 93rd annual event in 2008 which was shortened from 12 minutes to 10, American Joey Chestnut and Japan's Takeru Kobayashi finished tied at 59 dogs apiece and five-hot dog eat off was won by Chestnut. Tim "Eater X" Janus finised third with 42.

Note that **HDBs** in the list below refers to hot dogs and buns.

Recent Champions

Year		HDBs	Year		HDBs
1999	Steve Keinter	20¼	2004	Takeru Kobayashi	53½
2000	Kazutoyo Arai	25⅛	2005	Takeru Kobayashi	49
2001	Takeru Kobayashi	50	2006	Takeru Kobayashi	53¾
2002	Takeru Kobayashi	50½	2007	Joey Chestnut	66
2003	Takeru Kobayashi	44½	2008	Joey Chestnut	59

OTHER NOTABLE EATING RECORDS:

Baked Beans
Don Lerman, 6 pounds; 1:48

Birthday Cake
Richard LeFevre, 5 pounds; 11:26

Butter
Don Lerman, 7 quarter-pound sticks (salted); 5:00

Cow Brains
Takeru Kobayashi
17.7 pounds; 15:00

Doughnuts
Eric Booker, 49 (glazed); 8:00

Hard-boiled Eggs
Sonya Thomas, 65; 6:40.

Mayonnaise
Oleg Zhornitskiy, Four 32-ounce bowls; 8:00

Meat Pies
Boyd Bulot, 16 six-ounce pies; 10:00

Pasta
Cookie Jarvis
6⅔ pounds (linguine); 10:00

SPAM
Richard LeFevre, 6 pounds; 12:00

Sweet Corn
Joe LaRue, 34 ears; 12:00

Watermelon
Jim Reeves, 13.22 pounds; 15:00

Source: 23 Ways to Get to First Base, The ESPN Uncyclopedia

TRIATHLON

World Championship

Contested since 1989, the Triathlon World Championship consists of a 1.5-kilometer swim, a 40-kilometer bike ride and a 10-kilometer run. The 2008 championship was held June 5 in Vancouver, Canada.

Multiple winners: MEN—Simon Lessing (4); Peter Robertson (3); Spencer Smith (2). WOMEN—Emma Snowsill (3); Emma Carney, Michellie Jones and Karen Smyers (2).

MEN

Year		Time	Year		Time
1989	Mark Allen, United States	1:58:46	1999	Dimitry Gaag, Kazahkstan	1:45:25
1990	Greg Welch, Australia	1:51:37	2000	Oliver Marceau, France	1:51:41
1991	Miles Stewart, Australia	1:48:20	2001	Peter Robertson, Australia	1:48:01
1992	Simon Lessing, Great Britain	1:49:04	2002	Iván Raña, Spain	1:50:41
1993	Spencer Smith, Great Britain	1:51:20	2003	Peter Robertson, Australia	1:54:13
1994	Spencer Smith, Great Britain	1:51:04	2004	Bevan Docherty, New Zealand	1:41:04
1995	Simon Lessing, Great Britain	1:48:29	2005	Peter Robertston, Austrlia	1:49:31
1996	Simon Lessing, Great Britain	1:39:50	2006	Tim Don, Great Britain	1:51:32
1997	Chris McCormack, Australia	1:48:29	2007	Daniel Unger, Germany	1:43:18
1998	Simon Lessing, Great Britain	1:55:31	2008	Javier Gomez, Spain	1:49:48

WOMEN

Year		Time	Year		Time
1989	Erin Baker, New Zealand	2:10:01	1999	Loretta Harrop, Australia	1:55:28
1990	Karen Smyers, United States	2:03:33	2000	Nicole Hackett, Australia	1:54:43
1991	Joanne Ritchie, Canada	2:02:04	2001	Siri Lindley, United States	1:58:51
1992	Michellie Jones, Australia	2:02:08	2002	Leanda Cave, Wales	2:01:31
1993	Michellie Jones, Australia	2:07:41	2003	Emma Snowsill, Australia	2:06:40
1994	Emma Carney, Australia	2:03:19	2004	Sheila Taormina, United States	1:52:17
1995	Karen Smyers, USA	2:04:58	2005	Emma Snowsill, Australia	1:58:03
1996	Jackie Gallagher, Australia	1:50:52	2006	Emma Snowsill, Australia	2:04:03
1997	Emma Carney, Australia	1:59:22	2007	Vanessa Fernandes, Portugal	1:53:27
1998	Joanne King, Australia	2:07:25	2008	Helen Tucker, Great Britain	2:01:37

Ironman Championship

Contested in Hawaii since 1978, the Ironman Triathlon Championship consists of a 2.4-mile swim, a 112-mile bike ride and 26.2-mile run. The race begins at 7 A.M. and continues all day until the course is closed at midnight.

MEN

Multiple winners: Mark Allen and Dave Scott (6); Peter Reid (3); Tim DeBoom, Luc Van Lierde, Normann Stadler and Scott Tinley (2).

Year	Date	Winner	Time	Runner-up	Margin	Start	Finish	Location
I	2/18/78	Gordon Haller	11:46	John Dunbar	34:00	15	12	Waikiki Beach
II	1/14/79	Tom Warren	11:15:56	John Dunbar	48:00	15	12	Waikiki Beach
III	1/10/80	Dave Scott	9:24:33	Chuck Neumann	1:08	108	95	Ala Moana Park
IV	2/14/81	John Howard	9:38:29	Tom Warren	26:00	326	299	Kailua-Kona
V	2/6/82	Scott Tinley	9:19:41	Dave Scott	17:16	580	541	Kailua-Kona
VI	10/9/82	Dave Scott	9:08:23	Scott Tinley	20:05	850	775	Kailua-Kona
VII	10/22/83	Dave Scott	9:05:57	Scott Tinley	0:33	964	835	Kailua-Kona
VIII	10/6/84	Dave Scott	8:54:20	Scott Tinley	24:25	1036	903	Kailua-Kona
IX	10/25/85	Scott Tinley	8:50:54	Chris Hinshaw	25:46	1018	965	Kailua-Kona
X	10/18/86	Dave Scott	8:28:37	Mark Allen	9:47	1039	951	Kailua-Kona
XI	10/10/87	Dave Scott	8:34:13	Mark Allen	11:06	1380	1284	Kailua-Kona
XII	10/22/88	Scott Molina	8:31:00	Mike Pigg	2:11	1277	1189	Kailua-Kona
XIII	10/15/89	Mark Allen	8:09:15	Dave Scott	0:58	1285	1231	Kailua-Kona
XIV	10/6/90	Mark Allen	8:28:17	Scott Tinley	9:23	1386	1255	Kailua-Kona
XV	10/19/91	Mark Allen	8:18:32	Greg Welch	6:01	1386	1235	Kailua-Kona
XVI	10/10/92	Mark Allen	8:09:08	Cristian Bustos	7:21	1364	1298	Kailua-Kona
XVII	10/30/93	Mark Allen	8:07:45	Paulli Kiuru	6:37	1438	1353	Kailua-Kona
XVIII	10/15/94	Greg Welch	8:20:27	Dave Scott	4:05	1405	1290	Kailua-Kona
XIX	10/7/95	Mark Allen	8:20:34	Thomas Hellriegel	2:25	1487	1323	Kailua-Kona
XX	10/26/96	Luc Van Lierde	8:04:08	Thomas Hellriegel	1:59	1420	1288	Kailua-Kona
XXI	10/18/97	Thomas Hellriegel	8:33:01	Jurgen Zack	6:17	1534	1365	Kailua-Kona
XXII	10/3/98	Peter Reid	8:24:20	Luc Van Lierde	7:37	1487	1379	Kailua-Kona
XXIII	10/23/99	Luc Van Lierde	8:17:17	Peter Reid	5:37	1471	1419	Kailua-Kona
XXIV	10/14/00	Peter Reid	8:21:01	Tim DeBoom	2:09	1525	1426	Kailua-Kona
XXV	10/6/01	Tim DeBoom	8:31:18	Cameron Brown	14:52	1558	1364	Kailua-Kona
XXVI	10/19/02	Tim DeBoom	8:29:56	Peter Reid	3:10	1540	1457	Kailua-Kona
XXVII	10/18/03	Peter Reid	8:22:35	Rutger Beke	5:51	1647	1569	Kailua-Kona
XXVIII	10/16/04	Normann Stadler	8:33:29	Peter Reid	10:11	1728	1579	Kailua-Kona
XXIX	10/15/05	Faris Al-Sultan	8:14:17	Cameron Brown	5:19	1743	1688	Kailua-Kona
XXX	10/21/06	Normann Stadler	8:11:56	Chris McCormack	1:11	1689	1627	Kailua-Kona
XXXI	10/13/07	Chris McCormack	8:15:34	Craig Alexander	3:30	1787	1685	Kailua-Kona
XXXII	10/11/08	Craig Alexander	8:17:45	E. Llanos Burguera	3:05	1731	1636	Kailua-Kona

WOMEN

Multiple winners: Paula Newby-Fraser (8); Natascha Badmann (6); Erin Baker, Lori Bowden, Sylviane Puntous and Chrissie Wellington (2).

Year	Winner	Time	Runner-up	Year	Winner	Time	Runner-up
1978	No finishers			1993	Paula Newby-Fraser	8:58:23	Erin Baker
1979	Lyn Lemaire	12:55.00	None	1994	Paula Newby-Fraser	9:20:14	Karen Smyers
1980	Robin Beck	11:21:24	Eve Anderson	1995	Karen Smyers	9:16:46	Isabelle Mouthon
1981	Linda Sweeney	12:00:32	Sally Edwards	1996	Paula Newby-Fraser	9:06:49	Natascha Badmann
1982	Kathleen McCartney	11:09:40	Julie Moss	1997	Heather Fuhr	9:31:43	Lori Bowden
1982	Julie Leach	10:54:08	Joann Dahlkoetter	1998	Natascha Badmann	9:24:16	Lori Bowden
1983	Sylviane Puntous	10:43:36	Patricia Puntous	1999	Lori Bowden	9:13:02	Karen Smyers
1984	Sylviane Puntous	10:25:13	Patricia Puntous	2000	Natascha Badmann	9:26:17	Lori Bowden
1985	Joanne Ernst	10:25:22	Liz Bulman	2001	Natascha Badmann	9:28:37	Lori Bowden
1986	Paula Newby-Fraser	9:49:14	Sylviane Puntous	2002	Natascha Badmann	9:07:54	Nina Kraft
1987	Erin Baker	9:35:25	Sylviane Puntous	2003	Lori Bowden	9:11:55	Natascha Badmann
1988	Paula Newby-Fraser	9:01:01	Erin Baker	2004	Natascha Badmann*	9:50:04	Heather Fuhr
1989	Paula Newby-Fraser	9:00:56	Sylviane Puntous	2005	Natascha Badmann	9:09:30	Michellie Jones
1990	Erin Baker	9:13:42	P. Newby-Fraser	2006	Michellie Jones	9:18:31	Desiree Ficker
1991	Paula Newby-Fraser	9:07:52	Erin Baker	2007	Chrissie Wellington	9:08:45	Samantha McGlone
1992	Paula Newby-Fraser	8:55:28	Julie Anne White	2008	Chrissie Wellington	9:06:23	Yvonne Van Vlerken

*Nina Kraft of Germany was the first woman to cross the finish line in 2004 with her time of 9:33:25 but she was disqualified after failing a post-race drug test by testing positive for EPO. Badmann finished second but was awarded the title (and Canada's Heather Fuhr became runner-up) following the test.

MIXED MARTIAL ARTS

Ultimate Fighting Championship
Major Fights Results

Results Key: KO (knockout), TKO (technical knockout), Wu (Win by unanimous decision), Ws (win by split decision), Sub (win by submission).

Late 2007

Date	Event	Weight	Winner	Loser	Result (Rd.)	Site
Nov. 14	**UFC 78**	205	Rashad Evans	Michael Bisping	Ws 3	E. Rutherford, N.J.
		205	Thiago Silva	Houston Alexander	TKO 1	
		185	Ed Herman	Joe Doerksen	KO 3	
		170	Karo Parisyan	Ryo Chonan	Wu 3	
Dec. 29	**UFC 79**	170	Georges St.-Pierre	Matt Hughes	Sub 2	Las Vegas
		205	Chuck Liddell	Wanderlei Silva	Wu 3	
		205	Lyoto Machida	Rameau Sokoudjou	Sub 2	
		155	Rich Clementi	Melvin Guillard	Sub 1	

2008

Date	Event	Weight	Winner	Loser	Result (Rd.)	Site
Jan. 19	**UFC 80**	155	B.J. Penn	Joe Stevenson	Sub 2	Newcastle, ENG
		Hvy	Fabricio Werdum	Gabriel Gonzaga	KO 1	
		185	Wilson Gouveia	Jason Lambert	KO 2	
		185	Jorde Rivera	Kendall Grove	TKO 1	
Jan. 23	UFC Fight Night	170	Mike Swick	Josh Burkman	Wm 3	Las Vegas
		185	Patrick Cote	Drew McFedries	TKO 1	
		155	Nate Diaz	Alvin Robinson	Sub 1	
Feb. 2	**UFC 81**	Hvy	Antonio Nogueira	Tim Sylvia	Sub 3	Las Vegas
		Hvy	Frank Mir	Brock Lesnar	Sub 1	
		185	Nate Marquardt	Jeremy Horn	Sub 1	
		185	Ricardo Almeida	Rob Yundt	Sub 1	
Mar. 1	**UFC 82**	185	Anderson Silva	Dan Henderson	Sub 2	Columbus, Ohio
		Hvy	Heath Herring	Cheick Kongo	Ws 3	
		185	Chris Leben	Alessio Sakara	TKO 1	
		185	Yushin Okami	Evan Tanner	KO 2	
Apr. 2	UFC Fight Night	155	Kenny Florian	Joe Lauzon	TKO 2	Broomfield, Colo.
		170	Thiago Alves	Karo Parisyan	TKO 2	
		205	Matt Hamill	Tim Boetsch	TKO 2	
		155	Nate Diaz	Kurt Pellegrino	Sub 2	
Apr. 19	**UFC 83**	170	Georges St. Pierre	Matt Serra	TKO 2	Montreal, CAN
		185	Rich Franklin	Travis Lutter	TKO 2	
		185	Michael Bisping	Charles McCarthy	TKO 1	
		155	Mac Danzig	Mark Bocek	Sub 3	
May 24	**UFC 84**	155	B.J. Penn	Sean Sherk	TKO 3	Las Vegas
		205	Wanderlai Silva	Keith Jardine	KO 1	
		185	Goran Reljic	Wilson Gouveia	TKO 2	
		205	Lyoto Machida	Tito Ortiz	Wu 3	
June 7	**UFC 85**	170	Thiago Alves	Matt Hughes	TKO 2	London, ENG
		185	Michael Bisping	Jason Day	TKO 1	
		185	Thales Leites	Nate Marquardt	Ws 3	
		Hvy	Fabricio Werdum	Brandon Vera	TKO 1	
July 5	**UFC 86**	205	Forrest Griffin	Quinton Jackson	Wu 3	Las Vegas
		185	Patrick Cote	Gleison Tibau	Sub 2	
		170	Josh Koscheck	Chris Lytle	Wu 3	
		155	Tyson Griffin	Marcus Aurelio	Wu 3	
Jul 19	UFC Fight Night	185	Anderson Silva	James Irvin	KO 1	Las Vegas
		205	Brandon Vera	Reese Andy	Wu 3	
		155	Frank Edgar	Hermes Franca	Wu 3	
		Hvy	Cain Velasquez	Jake O'Brien	TKO 1	
Aug. 9	**UFC 87**	170	Georges St.-Pierre	Jon Fitch	Wu 3	Minneapolis, Minn.
		Hvy	Brock Lesnar	Heath Herring	Wu 3	
		155	Kenny Florian	Roger Huerta	Wu 3	
		155	Rob Emerson	Manny Gamburyan	TKO 1	

Date	Event	Weight	Winner	Loser	Result (Rd.)	Site
Sept. 6	**UFC 88**	205	Rashad Evans	Chuck Liddell	KO 2	Atlanta, Ga.
		205	Rich Franklin	Matt Hammill	TKO 3	
		205	Dan Henderson	Rousimar Palhares	Wu 3	
		185	Nate Marquardt	Martin Kampmann	TKO 1	
Oct. 18	**UFC 89**	185	Michael Bisping	Chris Leben	Wu 3	Birmingham, ENG
		205	Keith Jardine	Brandon Vera	Ws 3	
		205	Luis Cane	Rameau Sokoudjou	TKO 2	
		170	Chris Lytle	Paul Taylor	Wu 3	
Oct. 25	**UFC 90**	185	Anderson Silva	Patrick Cote	TKO 3	Chicago, Ill.
		170	Thiago Alves	Josh Koscheck	Wu 3	
		155	Gray Maynard	Rich Clementi	Wu 3	
		Hvy	Junior Dos Santos	Fabricio Werdum	KO 1	
		155	Sean Sherk	Tyson Griffin	Wu 3	

Sherdog Official Mixed Martial Arts Rankings
(as of Oct. 31, 2008)

Heavyweights
1. Fedor Emelianenko (28-1-0, 1 NC)
2. Antonio Rodrigo Nogueria (31-4-1, 1 NC)
3. Andrei Arlovski (14-5-0)
4. Josh Barnett (23-5-0)
5. Tim Sylvia (24-5-0)
6. Ben Rothwell (29-6-0)
7. Alistair Overeem (28-11-0, 1 NC)
8. Junior dos Santos (7-1-0)
9. Fabricio Wedrum (11-4-1)
10. Gabriel Gonzaga (9-3-0)

Light Heavweights
1. Forrest Grffin (16-4-0)
2. Quinton Jackson (28-7-0)
3. Rashad Evans (12-0-1)
4. Lyoto Machida (13-0-0)
5. Chuck Liddell (21-6-0)
6. Wanderleì Silva (32-8-1, 1 NC)
7. Keith Jardine (14-4-1)
8. Thiago Silva (13-0-0)
9. Luis Arthur Cane (9-1-0)
10. Vladimir Matyushenko (21-3-0)

Middleweights
1. Anderson Silva (23-4-0)
2. Paulo Filho (16-0-0)
3. Rich Franklin (24-3-0, 1 NC)
4. Robbie Lawler (16-4-0, 1 NC)
5. Yushin Okami (22-4-0)
6. Gegard Mousasi (24-2-1)
7. Nate Marquardt (27-8-2)
8. Dan Henderson (23-7-0)
9. Thales Leites (14-1-0)
10. Frank Trigg (18-6-0)

Welterweights
1. Georges St. Pierre (17-2)
2. Thiago Alves (16-3)
3. Jon Fitch (17-3, 1 NC)
4. Josh Koscheck (11-3)
5. Diego Sanchez (19-2)
6. Jake Shields (22-4-1)
7. Matt Hughes (42-7)
8. Matt Serra (9-5)
9. Karo Parisyan (18-5)
10. Carlos Condit (23-4)

Lightweights
1. B.J. Penn (13-4-1)
2. Eddie Alvarez (15-1)
3. Joachim Hansen (19-7-1)
4. Takanori Gomi (29-3, 1 NC)
5. Shinya Aoki (18-3, 1 NC)
6. Gesias Cavalcante (14-2-1, 1 NC)
7. Sean Sherk (33-3-1)
8. Josh Thomson (16-2, 1 NC)
9. Gilbert Melendez (14-2)
10. Tatsuya Kawajirl (22-5-2)

Featherweights
1. Urijah Faber (21-1)
2. Mike Thomas Brown (!7-4)
3. Leonard Garcia (11-3)
4. Dokonjonosuke Mishima (18-6-2)
5. Jeff Curran (30-10-1)
6. Masakazu Imanari (15-6-1)
7. Hatsu Hioki (16-3-2)
8. Hiroyuki Takaya (9-5-1)
9. Takeshi Inoue (14-3)
10. Wagnney Fabiano (10-1)

Bantamweights
1. Miguel Torres (33-1)
2. Masakatsu Ueda (8-0-2)
3. Brian Bowles (6-0)
4. Koetsu Okazaki (5-1-1)
5. Atsushi Yamamota (12-5-1)

Flyweights
1. Shinichi Kojima (9-3-4)
2. Mamoru Yamaguchi (20-5-3)
3. Yuki Shoujou (8-4-2)
4. Yasuhiro Urushitani (14-4-6)
5. Ryuichi Miki (7-2-3)

Source: Sherdog.com

LACROSSE

Major League Lacrosse

2008 Regular Season Standings

(*) denotes team advanced to playoffs.

Western Conference	W	L	GB	Pct	GF	2Pt GF	GA	2PtGA
*Denver	8	4	—	.667	173	7	160	4
*Los Angeles	7	5	1	.583	173	2	157	8
San Francisco	4	8	4	.333	149	8	173	7
Chicago	3	9	5	.250	158	4	168	6

Eastern Conference	W	L	GB	Pct	GF	2Pt GF	GA	2PtGA
*Rochester	9	3	—	.750	202	5	161	4
*Philadelphia	7	5	2	.583	166	6	173	5
Boston	7	5	2	.583	182	7	166	8
New Jersey	6	6	3	.500	171	4	179	3
Long Island	5	7	4	.417	188	6	194	8
Washington	4	8	5	.333	156	7	187	3

MLL Playoffs

Semifinals (Aug. 23)

Rochester 16 . . . . OT . . . . Philadelphia 15

Denver 13 . . . . Los Angeles 12

Finals (Aug. 24)

Rochester 16 . . . . Denver 6

Individual Leaders

Scoring Leaders

	Gm	G	2G	A	Pts
John Grant Jr., Roc	12	47	4	13	64
Merrick Thomson, NJ	12	42	0	10	52
Kevin Leveille, Chi	12	35	0	12	47
Brian Langtry, Den	12	24	3	20	47
Jeff Zywicki, Roc	11	31	0	14	45
Joe Walters, Roc	12	32	0	12	44
Brendan Mundorf, Den	12	30	0	14	44
Ryan Boyle, Phi	12	21	1	22	44
Matt Striebel, Phi	12	31	0	11	42
Casey Powell, Roc	12	15	1	26	42

Defense Scoring Leaders

	Gm	G	2G	A	Pts
Brodie Merrill, Roc	10	6	0	12	18
Kyle Sweeney, Phi	11	5	0	4	9
Jake Deane, Chi	12	7	0	1	8
Eric Martin, SF	12	3	0	3	6
John Gagliardi, LI	11	3	0	2	5
Ray Megill, Bos	12	2	1	2	5
Steve Holmes, SF	11	2	0	3	5

Team Leaders

Team	GP	GB	Shots	SPCT	SOG	SOGPCT	FO	FOPCT
Philadelphia	12	362	557	.298	366	.657	180-386	.466
Boston	12	419	617	.295	421	.682	176-393	.448
Chicago	12	417	498	.317	339	.681	177-372	.476
Denver	12	393	528	.328	359	.680	186-385	.483
Long Island	12	493	604	.311	383	.634	259-429	.583
Los Angeles	12	415	617	.280	386	.626	184-376	.489
New Jersey	12	403	528	.324	332	.629	168-397	.423
Rochester	12	487	548	.369	401	.732	250-399	.627
San Francisco	12	376	522	.285	342	.655	199-368	.541
Washington	12	372	543	.287	362	.667	174-387	.450

YACHTING

The America's Cup

International yacht racing was launched in 1851 when England's Royal Yacht Squadron staged a 60-mile regatta around the Isle of Wight and offered a silver trophy to the winner. The 101-foot schooner *America*, sent over by the New York Yacht Club, won the race and the prize. Originally called the Hundred-Guinea Cup, the trophy was renamed The America's Cup after the winning boat's owners deeded it to the NYYC with instructions to defend it whenever challenged.

From 1870-1980, the NYYC successfully defended the Cup 25 straight times; first in large schooners and J-class boats that measured up to 140 feet in overall length, then in 12-meter boats. A foreign yacht finally won the Cup in 1983 when *Australia II* beat defender *Liberty* in the seventh and deciding race off Newport, R.I. Four years later, the San Diego Yacht Club's *Stars & Stripes* won the Cup back, sweeping the four races of the final series off Fremantle, Australia.

Then in 1988, New Zealand's Mercury Bay Boating Club, unwilling to wait the usual three- to four-year period between Cup defenses, challenged the SDYC to a match race, citing the Cup's 102-year-old Deed of Gift, which clearly stated that every challenge had to be honored. Mercury Bay announced it would race a 133-foot monohull. San Diego countered with a 60-foot catamaran. The resulting best-of-three series (Sept. 7-8) was a mismatch as the SDYC's catamaran *Stars & Stripes* won two straight by margins of better than 18 and 21 minutes. Mercury Bay syndicate leader Michael Fay protested the outcome and took the SDYC to court in New York State (where the Deed of Gift was first filed) claiming San Diego had violated the spirit of the deed by racing a catamaran instead of a monohull. N.Y. State Supreme Court judge Carmen Ciparick agreed and on March 28, 1989, ordered the SDYC to hand the Cup over to Mercury Bay. The SDYC refused, but did consent to the court's appointment of the New York Yacht Club as custodian of the Cup until an appeal was ruled on.

On Sept. 19, 1989, the Appellate Division of the N.Y. Supreme Court overturned Ciparick's decision and awarded the Cup back to the SDYC. An appeal by Mercury Bay was denied by the N.Y. Court of Appeals on April 26, 1990, ending three years of legal wrangling. To avoid the chaos of 1988-90, a new class of boat—75-foot monohulls with 110-foot masts—has been used by all competing countries since 1992. Note that (*) indicates skipper was also owner of the boat.

The America's Cup moved to Europe for the first time when the Swiss Alinghi Team beat Team New Zealand, 5-0, in the best-of-nine series in February and March 2003. Alinghi, under new skipper Brad Butterworth, successfully defended the title on Mediterranean waters off the Spanish city of Valencia in 2007. The next defense is currently scheduled for May 2009.

Schooners And J-Class Boats

Year	Winner	Skipper	Series	Loser	Skipper
1851	America	Richard Brown	—	—	—
1870	Magic	Andrew Comstock	1-0	Cambria, GBR	J. Tannock
1871	Columbia (2-1) & Sappho (2-0)	Nelson Comstock Sam Greenwood	4-0	Livonia, GBR	J.R. Woods
1876	Madeleine	Josephus Williams	2-0	Countess of Dufferin, CAN	J.E. Ellsworth
1881	Mischief	Nathanael Clock	2-0	Atalanta, CAN	Alexander Cuthbert*
1885	Puritan	Aubrey Crocker	2-0	Genesta, GBR	John Carter
1886	Mayflower	Martin Stone	2-0	Galatea, GBR	Dan Bradford
1887	Volunteer	Henry Haff	2-0	Thistle, GBR	John Barr
1893	Vigilant	William Hansen	3-0	Valkyrie II, GBR	Wm. Granfield
1895	Defender	Henry Haff	3-0	Valkyrie III, GBR	Wm. Granfield
1899	Columbia	Charles Barr	3-0	Shamrock I, GBR	Archie Hogarth
1901	Columbia	Charles Barr	3-0	Shamrock II, GBR	E.A. Sycamore
1903	Reliance	Charles Barr	3-0	Shamrock III, GBR	Bob Wringe
1920	Resolute	Charles F. Adams	3-2	Shamrock IV, GBR	William Burton
1930	Enterprise	Harold Vanderbilt*	4-0	Shamrock V, GBR	Ned Heard
1934	Rainbow	Harold Vanderbilt*	4-2	Endeavour, GBR	T.O.M. Sopwith
1937	Ranger	Harold Vanderbilt*	4-0	Endeavour II, GBR	T.O.M. Sopwith

12-Meter Boats

Year	Winner	Skipper	Series	Loser	Skipper
1958	Columbia	Briggs Cunningham	4-0	Sceptre, GBR	Graham Mann
1962	Weatherly	Bus Mosbacher	4-1	Gretel, AUS	Jock Sturrock
1964	Constellation	Bob Bavier & Eric Ridder	4-0	Sovereign, AUS	Peter Scott
1967	Intrepid	Bus Mosbacher	4-0	Dame Pattie, AUS	Jock Sturrock
1970	Intrepid	Bill Ficker	4-1	Gretel II, AUS	Jim Hardy
1974	Courageous	Ted Hood	4-0	Southern Cross, AUS	John Cuneo
1977	Courageous	Ted Turner	4-0	Australia	Noel Robins
1980	Freedom	Dennis Conner	4-1	Australia	Jim Hardy
1983	Australia II	John Bertrand	4-3	Liberty, USA	Dennis Conner
1987	Stars & Stripes	Dennis Conner	4-0	Kookaburra III, AUS	Iain Murray

60-ft Catamaran vs 133-ft Monohull

Year	Winner	Skipper	Series	Loser	Skipper
1988	Stars & Stripes	Dennis Conner	2-0	New Zealand, NZE	David Barnes

75-ft International America's Cup Class

Year	Winner	Skipper	Series	Loser	Skipper
1992	America [3]	Bill Koch* & Buddy Melges	4-1	Il Moro di Venezia, ITA	Paul Cayard
1995	Black Magic, NZE	Russell Coutts	5-0	Young America, USA	Dennis Conner & Paul Cayard
2000	Black Magic, NZE	Russell Coutts & Dean Barker	5-0	Luna Rossa, ITA	Francesco de Angelis
2003	Alinghi, SUI	Russell Coutts	5-0	New Zealand, NZE	Dean Barker
2007	Alinghi, SUI	Brad Butterworth	5-2	Emirates New Zealand, NZE	Dean Barker

Great Outdoor Games

Sites: Lake Placíd, N.Y. (2000-02); Reno-Tahoe, Nev. (2003); Madison, Wis. (2004); Orlando, Fla. (2005).

Sporting Dogs

Year	Retriever Trials	Year	Agility (large dogs)	Year	Superweave (small)
2000	Barry Lyons & Skeet	2000	D. Bommarito & Lacey	2003	Jean LaValley & Taz
2001	Jerry Day & Super Sue	2001	Julie Daniels & Spring	2004	Not held
2002	A. Washburn & Ticket	2002	Olga Chaiko & Luz	**Year**	**Disc Drive**
2003	Chris Akin & Boomer	2003	S. Kluever & Ransom	2004	Tim Gelb &
2004	J.P. Jackson & Achilles	2004	Marcus Topps & Juice		Lock-Eye Razzle
Year	**Big Air**	2005	Marcus Topps & Juice	**Year**	**Launch**
2000	Beth Gutteridge & Heidi	**Year**	**Superweave** (large)	2005	Angela Jones & Nestle
2001	Mike Wallace & Jerry	2003	Ken Fairchild & Echo	**Year**	**Hot Zone**
2002	Mike Jackson &	2004	S. Kluever & Ransom	2005	Ron Watson & Split
	Little Morgan	2005	Marcus Topps & Juice		
2003	Terry Casey & Skeeter	**Year**	**Agility** (small dogs)		**ATV**
2004	Mike Jackson &	2001	Jean LaValley & Taz	**Year**	**Terracross**
	Little Morgan	2002	Erin Schaefer & Jag	2005	Marty Hart
2005	Chris Piacun & Beau	2003	C. Frank & Kimie	**Year**	**Four Wheel Frenzy**
		2004	Renee King & Hamlet	2005	John Natalie
		2005	Susan Garrett & DeCaff		

Fishing

Year	Flyfishing	Year	Flycasting	Year	Bass Fishing
2000	Tom Rowland	2002	Carter Andrews	2000	Peter Thliveros
2001	Chuck Farneth	2003	Mike McFarland	2001	Peter Thliveros
2002	Peter Erickson	2004	John Wilson	2002	Shaw Grigsby
2003	Lance Egan			2003	S. Grigsby & G. Klein
2004	Lance Egan			2004	M. Gofron & D. Brauer

Target Sports

Year	Rifle	Year	Shotgun	Year	Archery
2000	Bob Mastroianni	2000	Doug Fuller	2000	Jackie Caudle
2001	Jerry Miculek	2001	Dustin Long	2001	Randy Hendrix
2002	Jerry Miculek	2002	Robbie Purser	2002	Randy Hendrix
2003	Doug Koenig	2003	Scott Robertson	2003	Darren Collins
2004	Mike Cumming	2004	Travis Mears	2004	Randy Hendrix
				2005	Keith Brown

Timber Events

Year	Endurance (women)	Year	Boom Run (men)	Year	Log Rolling (women)
2000	Sheree Taylor	2000	J.R. Salzman	2000	Tina Salzman
2001	Penny Halvorson	2001	J.R. Salzman	2001	Tina Salzman
2002	Sheree Taylor	2002	Jamie Fischer	2002	Tina Bosworth
2003	Peg Engasser	2003	Jamie Fischer	2003	Tina Bosworth
2004	Sheree Taylor	2004	J.R. Salzman	2004	Tina Bosworth
2005	Sheree Taylor	2005	Jamie Fischer	2005	Lizzie Hoeschler
Year	**Endurance** (men)	**Year**	**Boom Run** (women)	**Year**	**Speed Climbing**
2000	Jason Wynyard	2000	Tina Salzman	2000	Wade Stewart
2001	Jason Wynyard	2001	Mandy Erdmann	2001	Brian Bartow
2002	Matt Bush	2002	Mandy Erdmann	2002	Brian Bartow
2003	Jason Wynyard	2003	Abby Hosechler	2003	Brian Bartow
2004	Jason Wynyard	2004	Mandy Erdmann	2004	Wade Stewart
2005	Dion Lane	2005	Mandy Erdmann	2005	Brian Bartow
Year	**Hot Saw**	**Year**	**Boom Run** (mixed)	**Year**	**Tree Topping**
2000	Harry Burnsworth	2003	Jamie Fischer &	2000	Mick Lee
2001	Mel Lentz		Tanya Fischer	2001	Gregg Hart
2002	Mike Sullivan	2004	J.R. Salzman &	2002	Wade Stewart
2003	Mike Sullivan		Shana Martin	2003	Greg Hart
2004	Matt Bush	**Year**	**Log Rolling** (men)	2004	Brian Bartow
2005	Harry Burnsworth	2000	J.R. Salzman	**Year**	**Team Relay**
Year	**Springboard**	2001	J.R. Salzman	2001	Team Halvorson
2000	Mitch Hewitt	2002	Darren Hudson	2002	Team Clarke
2001	Mitch Hewitt	2003	Jamie Fischer	2003	Team Wynard
2002	Mitch Hewitt	2004	J.R. Salzman	2004	Team Zalewski
2003	Dave Bolstad	2005	J.R. Salzman	2005	Team USA East
2004	Dale Ryan			**Year**	**SuperJack**
				2005	Cassidy Scheer

DEATHS

↑ Daredevil **Evel Knievel** cheated death many times in his career but finally paid up all debts in Dec., 2007.

AP/Wide World Photos

Notable deaths in the world of sports from Nov. 1, 2007-Oct. 31, 2008.

Luc Bourdon, 21; promising rookie defenseman for the Vancouver Canucks; 1st round pick (10th overall) by Vancouver in the 2005 NHL draft; part of the Canadian team that won gold at the 2007 world junior championships; in a motorcycle accident; near Shippagan, New Brunswick, Canada; May 29.

Christopher Bowman, 40; Two-time U.S. figure skating champion (1989 and 1992); nicknamed "Bowman the Showman" because of his natural charisma and ability to thrill a crowd; won a silver medal at the 1989 World Championships and a bronze at the 1990 Worlds; was also runner-up in 1987 and 1991 U.S. Championships; made two Olympic teams (1988 and 1992); of an accidental drug overdose; in Los Angeles, Calif.; Jan. 10.

Skip Caray, 68; longtime radio and television voice of the Atlanta Braves whose 33-year career spanned last-place finishes and a World Series championship with Atlanta; son of legendary Cubs announcer Harry Caray and father of Chip; after collapsing; in Atlanta, Ga.; Aug. 4.

Myron Cope, 79; legendary Pittsburgh Steelers' radio announcer; created the now familiar "Terrible Towel" which Steelers fans have waved for good luck at games since the mid-1970's; known for his screechy voice as the color analyst from 1970-2004; of heart failure; in Mount Lebanon, Penn.; Feb. 27.

Eight Belles, 3; filly who was a runner up to Big Brown at the 2008 Kentucky Derby; suffered a breakdown at the finish and was euthanized on the track; in Louisville, Ky.; May 3, 2008.

Genuine Risk, 31; filly who at 13-1 won the 1980 Kentucky Derby then finished second at the Preakness and Belmont and becoming the only filly in history to finish in the money in all three Triple Crown races; won 10 of 15 career races; in Upperville, Va.; Aug. 19.

Geremi Gonzalez, 33; former major league pitcher who played for five MLB teams (Cubs, Red Sox, Devil Rays, Brewers and Mets) from 1997-2006; right-hander who appeared in 131 games and had 83 starts finishing with a W-L record of 30-35; killed when he was struck by lightning; in Caracas, Venezuela; May 25.

Don Haskins, 78; Hall of Fame college basketball coach who helped break down color barriers when in 1966 he played five black starters and won an NCAA championship with Texas Western; his decision to go against the prevailing attitudes in much of the country has been credited with helping to greatly improve opportunities for African-American players in the sport; Haskins and his team were the subject of the 2006 film "Glory Road"; had retired in 1999 after 38 at seasons at the school that would later become known as UTEP; finished with a career record of 719-353; in El Paso, Texas; Sept. 7.

Sir Edmund Hilary, 88; New Zealand beekeeper who at 33 years old became one of the first two men to reach the summit of Mount Everest, the world's highest peak, when he did so along with Sherpa mountaineer Tenzing Norgay of Nepal on May 29, 1953; became a worldwide celebrity and a renowned explorer who led numerous other expeditions in the Himalayas in the years following his historic feat; of natural causes; in Auckland, New Zealand; Jan. 11.

Scott Kalitta, 46; drag racer; was the 1994 and 1995 NHRA Top Fuel season champion; 18 career wins (17 in Top Fuel, 1 in Funny Car) in a fiery wreck at the Lucas Oil NHRA SuperNationals at Old Bridge Township Raceway Park in Englishtown, N.J.; June 21.

Terrence Kiel, 27; former San Diego Chargers safety; 2nd round pick out of Texas A&M in the 2003 NFL Draft; played four seasons in NFL (2003-06) before being released by the team; in a single car accident; July 4.

Bobby Murcer, 62; five-time All-Star outfielder who spent most of his career with the New York Yankees; hit .277 with 252 homers 1,043 RBIs in 17 seasons with the Yankees, San Francisco Giants and Chicago Cubs; made his major league debut in 1965 at 19 years old; the only player that spanned the Mantle and Mattingly eras in New York, he had a career with the Yankees as an executive and announcer following his playing days; of complications from a brain tumor; July 12.

Madison "Buzz" Nutter, 77; starting center on the Baltimore Colts 1958 and 1959 NFL Championship teams; an unsung member of an offensive line that featured three All-Pros; played college football at Va. Tech; was a 12th round draft choice of the Washington Redskins in 1953; of complications from a heart illness; in La Plata, Md.; Apr. 12.

Johnny Podres, 75; young left-hander who pitched the Brooklyn Dodgers to their only championship at the 1955 World Series against the New York Yankees; won Game 3 and pitched an 8-hit shutout in Game 7 and was named MVP of the 1955 Series; pitched 15 MLB seasons with several teams finishing his career with a 148-116 record; in Glens Falls, N.Y.; Jan. 14, 2008.

Mando Ramos, 59; two-time former lightweight boxing champion; turned pro in 1965; finished with a career record of 37-11-1; first won lightweight title in 1969 when he beat Carlos Teo Cruz; battled drug and alcohol abuse in the years after his fighting career; in San Pedro, Calif.; July 6.

Ryan Shay, 28; elite distance runner; collapsed at the U.S. men's marathon Olympic trials in New York City and later died; Nov. 3, 2007.

George Ratterman, 80; Notre Dame quarterback who later led the AAFC with 22 TD passes as a rookie with the Buffalo Bills 1947 also played with New York and Cleveland in the NFL, serving as a backup to Otto Graham on two league cham-

Jim McKay, 86

When ABC was able to confirm that the German attempt to rescue the Israeli Olympic hostages in Munich had failed and all the hostages were dead, Jim McKay wasn't thinking about the tens of millions of viewers who were waiting for him to communicate what had happened. He was thinking only about two of them: David Berger's parents, sitting at home in suburban Cleveland. He knew that in all likelihood, his would be the voice – the first – telling them that their son, a 28-year-old Olympic weightlifter, was dead.

Sad and visibly tired, but composed, McKay gathered himself and said, "They're all gone." The Bergers, whose hopes had been raised by false reports that the hostages had been freed, then knew the truth.

That was 36 years ago, and McKay's reporting during the Olympic hostage crisis will endure as the standard by which all such reporting is judged. Not sports reporting. Just reporting. Of all the news, bad and good, terrifying and uplifting, that television hosts have delivered to the American people, perhaps the only moment that compares was nine years earlier, when Walter Cronkite removed his glasses, dried his eyes and told the nation that John F. Kennedy had died.

Shortly after McKay delivered the tragic news in Munich, he received a telegram. "Dear Jim," it read. "Today you honored yourself, your network and your industry. – Walter Cronkite."

McKay was special not just because he was a solid reporter in a field dominated by men who had been trained to call games. He was special because he was a reporter with the soul of a poet, his twin talents perfectly matched to his assignments.

In the hands of someone less sincere, it might have seemed maudlin to recite several lines from A.E. Housman's poem "To An Athlete Dying Young," even in the Munich aftermath. But when McKay memorialized the slain Israelis by saying, "Now you will not swell the rout/Of lads that wore their honors out/Runners whom renown outran/And the name died before the man," it could not have been more poignant or more fitting. Of course, long before Munich, the American people had come to trust McKay.

As the host of "ABC's Wide World of Sports," McKay spent the 1960s and 1970s spanning the globe, calling everything from mainstream events, such as the Indianapolis 500, to the most obscure and seemingly silly sports, such as barrel jumping. Unfailingly, he treated the barrel jumpers and cliff divers and bicycle polo players with the same respect he afforded Mario Andretti and Mark Spitz and Bill Shoemaker. If there was a defining McKay characteristic, that was it. He respected his subjects. He never stripped them of their dignity. It would have been all too easy to play the small sports for laughs. McKay didn't. Sure, he would have fun – he was by no means a stick in the mud – but not at the expense of the athletes or their families.

Case in point: the 1965 world barrel jumping championship. (Barrel jumping, long a staple of Wide World, is simply long jumping on ice skates, over uniformly sized barrels). A young man from Lake Placid, N.Y., named Ken Lebel

AP Images

was attempting to break the world record by clearing 17 barrels, and when he succeeded, McKay was almost overcome with emotion. "Nobody in the history of the sport ever did it before," he said. "There's Kenny's wife, just as tearfully excited as if her husband had just won the World Series." Looking now at the grainy footage, it's clear that McKay was just as excited as Mrs. Lebel.

And it was McKay who was the primary voice at the Olympics for a quarter-century – the quarter-century when the Olympics mattered most, when the games were all but defined by the tensions between the United States and the Soviet Union, when for two separate fortnights every four years little else seemed to matter. With McKay setting the tone for Olympics coverage, first on CBS and then on ABC, the athletes from behind the Iron Curtain were never demonized, even if it was clear that the system that nurtured them was morally reprehensible. McKay and his boss, Roone Arledge, did not resort to Hollywood tactics. They never made Olga Korbut or Sergei Makarov or Nadia Comaneci into Ivan Dragos. In his heart, McKay might have preferred to see the American pixies defeat the Red pixies and our amateurs defeat their pros, but it never showed.

In the end, McKay will stay with us because of all the ways in which he exemplified journalistic professionalism, informed by true grace, a poet's touch and simple humanity. Unlike Housman's athlete, he lived long – 86 years – but not long enough to see his renown outrun. It's unlikely that it ever will be.

— Jeremy Schaap, Special to ESPN.com

pionship teams (1954-55); of Alzheimer's disease; in Centennial, Ohio; Nov. 3, 2007.

Dick Nolan, 75; former coach of the San Francisco 49ers; went 71-85-3 in 11 NFL seasons with San Francisco and New Orleans; also played 9 years in NFL as 4th round pick out of Maryland; father of Niners coach Mike Nolan; of Alzheimer's disease; Nov. 11, 2007.

Robert Taylor, 59; sprinter who won gold (4x100-meter relay) and silver medal (100 meters) at the 1972 Munich Summer Games; of heart disease; in Missouri City, Texas; Nov. 13, 2007.

Joe Nuxhall, 79; youngest player in major league history; at 15 years, 10 months, 11 days old pitched in relief for the Cincinnati Reds on June 10, 1944; later became a radio broadcaster with Reds; in Cincinnati; from complication from pneumonia; Nov. 16, 2007.

Jim Ringo, 75; Hall of Fame center who played 15 seasons for the Green Bay Packers and Philadelphia Eagles; 10-time Pro Bowler; named to the NFL's All-Decade Team of the 1960's; started 182 consecutive games from 1954-67; taken in the 7th round of the 1953 draft out of Syracuse; after a short illness; in Chesapeake, Va.; Nov. 19, 2007.

Tom Johnson, 79; Hall of Fame defenseman with Montreal, helping the Canadiens win six Stanley Cups including five straight from 1956-60; won the 1958-59 Norris Trophy; later coached the Boston Bruins to the Stanley Cup in 1972; of congestive heart failure; in Falmouth, Mass.; Nov. 21, 2007.

Joe Kennedy, 28; a journeyman left-hander who was 43-61 in seven big league seasons with Tampa Bay, Colorado, Oakland, Arizona and Toronto; compiled a 43-61 record with a 4.79 ERA in 222 career appearances; of heart disease; in Tampa, Fla.; Nov. 23, 2007.

Herb McKenley, 85; Jamaican sprinter; won 3 Olympic silver medals (1948 400m, 1952 100m and 400m) and a gold (1952 4x400m); set the world record in the 400 meters in 1948; of complications from pneumonia; in Kingston, Jamaica; Nov. 26, 2007

Bill Hartack, 74; Hall of Fame jockey and one of only two people (Eddie Arcaro) to win the Kentucky Derby 5 times; won his first Derby with Iron Liege in 1957; won Ky Derby with Venetian Way in 1960, Decidedly in 1962, Northern Dancer in 1964 and Majestic Prince in 1969; won the Preakness aboard Fabius in 1956, Northern Dancer in 1964 and Majestic Prince in 1969; won the 1960 Belmont Stakes with Celtic Ash; 4,272 career wins; from complications of heart disease; in Webb County, Texas; Nov. 26, 2007.

Sean Taylor, 24; hard-hitting Washington Redskins safety; drafted fifth overall out of Miami in the 2004 NFL draft; 12 interceptions in four NFL seasons; 2-time Pro Bowler; from injuries sustained when he was shot in his home by an intruder; in Palmetto Bay, Fla.; Nov. 27, 2007

Dr. J. Robert Cade, 80; invented the sports drink Gatorade that launched a multibillion-dollar sports beverage industry and is now a staple of sidelines around the world; first used by the Univ. of Florida Gators in a football game against LSU in 1965; in Gainesville, Fla.; Nov. 27, 2007

Bill Willis, 86; Hall of Fame guard with the Cleveland Browns (1946-53) who helped integrate pro football in the years after WWII; also Ohio State's first black football All-American (1943, 1944); from a stroke; in Columbus, Ohio; Nov. 27, 2007.

Ralph Beard, 79; 3-time All-American guard for Kentucky in the 1940's; won 2 national titles with the Adolph Rupp-coached Wildcats (1948, 49); also a key figure in one of college basketball's biggest betting scandals when prior to the 1952 season, he and teammate Alex Groza were among others involved in a point-shaving scandal; banned for life from the NBA; played in the NBA's first All-Star game in 1951; after a series of illnesses; in Louisville, Ky.; Nov. 29, 2007.

Ken McGregor, 78; Australian Open singles champion in 1952 and was part of a Grand Slam-winning doubles team with Frank Sedgman in 1951; won 7 straight Grand Slam doubles titles (1951-52); played on three winning Davis Cup teams for Australia; inducted into the International Tennis Hall of Fame in 1999; of stomach cancer; in Adelaide, Australia; Dec. 1, 2007.

George Morris, 76; linebacker on Georgia Tech's 1952 perfect team and a member of the College Football Hall of Fame; played briefly in the NFL and later was an SEC football official from 1960-89; of an apparent heart attack; in Highlands, N.C.; Dec. 10, 2007.

Will Robinson, 96; became the first black head coach at an NCAA Div. 1 school when he was hired at Illinois State in 1970; also was a part-time scout for the NBA's Detroit Pistons and NFL's Detroit Lions; of complications of pneumonia; in Detroit, Mich.; Apr. 28.

Other notable sports deaths
Nov. 1, 2007-Oct. 31, 2008

Tommy Byrne, 87	Charlie Jones, 77
Alexei Cherepanov, 19	Evel Knievel, 69
Milt Davis, 79	Tommy Kron, 64
Don Freeland, 82	John Marzano, 45
Mitch Frerotte, 43	Chris Mims, 38
Georgia Frontiere, 80	Paul Newman, 83
Darrell Garretson, 76	Evan Tanner, 37
Jake Gaudaur, 87	Hansel Tookes, 86
Tommy Holmes, 91	Dwight White, 58
Gene Hickerson, 73	John Woodruff, 92

Gene Upshaw, 63

Nearly 26 years ago, shortly after Gene Upshaw was elected president of the NFL Players Association, he walked into his first bargaining session with NFL owners, and everything changed.

At the time, despite valiant and imaginative attempts to gain leverage for NFL players, the union had accomplished little and was struggling for survival. It was up against a group of owners who operated a cartel that was the most powerful engine of commerce in all of sports. The owners were tough, they enjoyed splendid leadership, and they were unanimous in their resistance to any attempt by players to gain a measure of respect.

Seated beside Ed Garvey, the union's founder and executive director, Upshaw and the union suggested that the players were entitled to a percentage of the NFL's gross revenues. Although it is now the foundation of a partnership that has been a bonanza for both players and owners, that was a radical idea in 1982. It had never been suggested anywhere in sports.

AP Images

The owners' negotiators reacted in disbelief and fury. Their macho posturing turned ugly when Vince Lombardi Jr., one of the negotiators for the owners, shook a fist at Garvey and shouted, "I ought to come across the table and take a shot at you."

Without raising his voice, Upshaw told Lombardi, "I'm here. Why don't you take a shot at me?"

In an instant, the posturing came to an end. Upshaw's presence set the tone in the room, and there were no more threats or macho antics. Serious talks about a serious idea began. The discussions were not easy. Upshaw and Garvey remained firm, led the players through a nasty strike and obtained a breakthrough contract.

Garvey later cracked that "If Lombardi actually hit Gene and Gene found out about it, Junior would have been in real trouble."

As player president, Upshaw came after John Mackey and Kermit Alexander, and he soon succeeded Garvey as executive director, as well, inaugurating a quarter-century of leadership that transformed the world of NFL players and gave them bonuses, salaries and benefits that seemed beyond reach in those first negotiations in 1982.

The centerpiece of Upshaw's success for NFL players was his leadership of the battle for free agency that began with a disastrous strike in 1987 and continued through a series of antitrust cases into the early '90s. It was an achievement that rivals, at least, the successes of Marvin Miller for baseball players in the '60s and '70s; and in important ways, it was even more impressive than Miller's accomplishments. Miller outsmarted a group of owners who underestimated him, who were incapable of making a good decision, who could not find lawyers who knew how to help them and who were surprised at what a union could accomplish under American laws.

By the time Upshaw began his battle for free agency, NFL owners knew what Miller had done to their brethren in baseball. They knew the importance of good decisions on labor issues. They knew what a union could accomplish under American law. And, perhaps most important, they enjoyed great leadership under commissioner Pete Rozelle and brilliant legal representation from the firm of Covington and Burling.

Upshaw and the players did not face a clubby group of uninformed and bumbling owners; they faced a tightly organized and brilliantly led group that knew how to make – and keep – money.

When the 1987 strike collapsed, Upshaw could easily have made an agreement with the owners with the hope that he could do better in a few years. But knowing that only free agency would compensate NFL players fairly, Upshaw turned in a vastly more difficult direction: He decertified the union to allow the players to seek free agency in antitrust litigation.

It was a strategy of extraordinary risk. Most labor experts would have recommended against it. Too complicated. Too risky. Too expensive.

And too dangerous.

If you lose, you literally face the end of your union.

By decertifying, Upshaw gave up all the legal protections that had been so beneficial to baseball players. In antitrust litigation, he knew he would be up against Covington lawyers who were brilliant and who specialized in scorched-earth wars of attrition.

There is no field of law or litigation where

intellectual firepower is more important than it is in antitrust litigation. It involves a complex intersection of antitrust and labor laws, and it relies on concepts of economics that can baffle people with doctorates in economics. Unlike the players' union and Upshaw, who was not a lawyer, the Covington attorneys had been demonstrating their mastery of these issues for decades, and they had represented the NFL since its earliest days.

It took extraordinary vision and fortitude for Upshaw to undertake the battle, and even more to push it through to triumph.

I have been around courts and lawyers on a daily basis for more than 40 years, and I have not seen a more impressive performance than I watched as Upshaw led his players to free agency. As expected, the Covington firm and the NFL played hard. Upshaw and his lawyers, Jeff Kessler and Jim Quinn, played just as hard, fighting off attacks both petty and important. The legal papers quickly filled entire file cabinets as the NFL tried to drive the union out of existence.

The NFL was splitting the legal bills among 32 owners. It was not a big expense to an individual owner. The union was paying for everything. The NFL lawyers outnumbered the union lawyers on any given day by two or three to one. The issues grew more and more complex. Upshaw found himself explaining the Sherman Act, the nation's basic antitrust law, and its years-long litigation process to a group of football players with an average playing career of fewer than four years. At one point in the corridor of the federal court in Minneapolis, he was explaining the differences between monopoly and monopsony to me, and how that difference led to free agency.

I am a graduate of the University of Chicago Law School. I studied this stuff. And I could barely keep up with him.

Watching Upshaw and his lawyers work, I often wondered when they would give up the fight and try to settle. Things went wrong again and again. The NFL seemed to spring a surprise legal maneuver at least twice each week, all of them brilliant. But through it all, Upshaw sat in the second row of Judge David Doty's courtroom without a glimmer of doubt on his face, somehow knowing that the facts and the law were on his side.

AP Images

Somehow, a group of Upshaw's players convinced a jury of six women that the NFL was a monopoly, that the league had violated American antitrust laws by trying to restrict player salaries and that it was liable to all players for triple the salaries they had been unable to earn. It was a stunning and breathtaking victory.

Although Upshaw and his lawyers clearly were pleased with their triumph, it was also clear in the moments after the jury verdict that they were ready, under Upshaw's leadership, to take the next step.

The next step was a series of lawsuits and negotiating sessions that ultimately led to a whole new system for the NFL and its players, a collective bargaining agreement that has led to incredible benefits for players and has pushed the owners to the point that they already have stated officially that they want to end it at the earliest opportunity and try for a better deal. After 25 years of Upshaw's leadership, the owners – rather than the players – find themselves pleading for more.

In addition to what he gained for active players, Upshaw also established pension and disability benefits that rank with the best in all of American industry. Although Mike Ditka and other older players continue to complain about the plan, the facts are that most older players have benefited enormously from Upshaw's leadership in that area.

Secure in the knowledge that he had established benefits for older players that Ditka and others had never been able to extract from owners, Upshaw did not offer much resistance to the shots that came his way. Most players, both retired and active, understand what Upshaw accomplished for them.

It will be a difficult adjustment for them now to know that when they next face a bargaining session with owners who are demanding concessions, they will have to walk into the room without the leader who changed everything.

— **Lester Munson**, a Chicago lawyer and journalist who reports on investigative and legal issues in the sports industry, is a senior writer for ESPN.com.

2007 / 2008 YEAR IN REVIEW

Zenyatta won the $2 million Ladies Breeders' Cup Ladies Classic on October 24.

AP /Wide World Photos

GOLF

Late 2008 Tournament Results
PGA Tour

Last Rd Tournament	Winner	Earnings	Runner-Up
Oct. 26 Frys.com Open . . . . Cameron Beckman (262)		$900,000	K. Sutherland (262)*

*Beckman won on the second playoff hole.

Remaining Events (8): Ginn sur Mer Classic (Oct. 30-Nov. 2); Children's Miracle Network Classic (Nov. 6-9); ADT Skills Challenge (Nov. 3); Wendy's 3 Tour Challenge (Nov. 11); LG Skins Game (Nov. 30); Del Webb Father/Son Challenge (Dec. 6); Merrill Lynch Shootout (Dec. 14); Chevron World Challenge (Dec. 21).

European PGA Tour

Last Rd Tournament	Winner	Earnings	Runner-Up
Oct. 26 Castello Masters . . . . Sergio Garcia (264)		E 333,330	P. Hedblom (267)

Remaining Events (5): Volvo Masters (Nov. 2); UBS Hong Kong Open (Nov. 15-18); MasterCard Masters (Nov. 22-25); Michael Hill New Zealand Open (Nov. 29-Dec. 2); Dunhill Championship (Dec. 6-9).

Champions Tour

Last Rd Tournament	Winner	Earnings	Runner-Up
Oct. 26 AT&T Championship . . . . John Cook (197)		$247,500	K. Fergus (200)

Remaining Events (3): Charles Schwab Cup (Oct. 30-Nov. 2); Champions Tour Q-School (Nov. 12-15); Del Webb Father-Son Challenge (Dec. 1-7); Wendy's 3 Tour Challenge (Dec 2).

LPGA Tour

Last Rd Tournament	Winner	Earnings	Runner-Up
Oct. 26 Grand China Air . . . . Helen Alfredsson (204)		$270,000	Y. Tseng (207)

Remaining Events (5): Hana Bank-KOLON Championship (Oct. 31-Nov. 2); Mizuno Classic (Nov. 7-9); Lorena Ochoa Invitational (Nov. 13-16); ADT Championship (Nov. 20-23); Lexus Cup 2008 (Nov. 28-30); Wendy's 3 Tour Challenge (Dec. 13-14).

SOCCER

MLS Cup 2008

Scheduled for Nov. 23 at the Home Depot Center in Carson, Calif.

TENNIS

Late 2008 Tournament Results
Men's Tour

Finals	Tournament	Winner	Earnings	Loser	Score
Oct. 5	AIG Japan Open (Tokyo)	Tomas Berdych	E 135,000	M. Del Potro	61 64
Oct. 5	Open de Moselle (Metz)	Dmitry Tursunov	59,100	P-H Mathieu	76 16 64
Oct. 12	ATP Bank Austria Tennis Trophy (Vienna)	Philipp Petzschner	139,000	G. Monfils	64 64
Oct. 12	Stockholm Open.................	David Nalbandian	115,500	R. Soderling	62 57 63
Oct. 12	Kremlin Cup (Moscow)	Igor Kunitsyn	171,000	M. Safin	76 67 63
Oct. 19	TMS—Madrid	Andy Murray	360,000	G. Simon	64 76
Oct. 26	St. Petersburg Open	Andy Murray	171,000	A. Golubev	61 61
Oct. 26	Swiss Indoors (Basel).............	Roger Federer	145,200	D. Nalbandian	63 64
Oct. 26	Grand Prix of Tennis (Lyon)	Robin Soderling	115,500	J. Benneteau	63 67 61

Remaining Events (3): BNP Paribas Paris Masters (Nov. 9); Tennis Masters Cup Shanghai (Nov. 16); .

Women's Tour

Finals	Tournament	Winner	Earnings	Loser	Score
Oct. 12	Kremlin Cup (Moscow)	Jelena Jankovic	$196,900	V. Zvonareva	62 64
Oct. 19	Zurich Open	Venus Williams	95,500	F. Penetta	76 62
Oct. 26	Generali Open (Linz).............	Ana Ivanovic	95,500	V. Zvonareva	62 61

Remaining Events (2): Bell Challenge (Nov. 2); WTA Tour Championships (Nov. 9).

THOROUGHBRED RACING

Breeders' Cup World Championships

Date	Race	Location	Miles	Winner	Jockey	Purse
Oct. 24	Breeders' Cup F & M Sprint	Santa Anita	7 F	Ventura	Garrett Gomez	$1,000,000
Oct. 24	Breeders' Cup Juvenile Turf	Santa Anita	1	Maram	Jose Lezcano	1,000,000
Oct. 24	Breeders' Cup Juvenile F	Santa Anita	1 1/16	Stardom Bound	Mike Smith	2,000,000
Oct. 24	Breeders' Cup F & M Turf	Santa Anita	1 3/8	Forever Together	Julien R. Leparoux	2,000,000
Oct. 24	Breeders' Cup Ladies Classic	Santa Anita	1 1/8	Zenyatta	Mike E. Smith	2,000,000
Oct. 25	Breeders' Cup Marathon	Santa Anita	1 1/2	Muhannak	Patrick J. Smullen	500,000
Oct. 25	Breeders' Cup Turf Sprint	Santa Anita	6 1/2 F	Desert Code	Richard Migliore	1,000,000
Oct. 25	Breeders' Cup Dirt Mile	Santa Anita	1	Albert Maximus	Garrett Gomez	1,000,000
Oct. 25	Breeders' Cup Mile	Santa Anita	1	Goldikova	Olivier Peslier	2,000,000
Oct. 25	Breeders' Cup Juvenile	Santa Anita	1 1/16	Midshipman	Garrett Gomez	2,000,000
Oct. 25	Breeders' Cup Juvenile Turf	Santa Anita	1	Donativum	Lanfranco Dettori	1,000,000
Oct. 25	Breeders' Cup Sprint	Santa Anita	6 F	Midnight Lute	Garrett Gomez	2,000,000
Oct. 25	Breeders' Cup Turf	Santa Anita	1 1/2	Conduit	Ryan L. Moore	3,000,000
Oct. 25	Breeders' Cup Classic	Santa Anita	1 1/4	Raven's Pass	Lanfranco Dettori	5,000,000

Sidebar navigation:

BUSINESS

INTER-NATIONAL SPORTS

OLYMPIC GAMES

SOCCER

ACTION SPORTS

HORSE RACING

TENNIS

GOLF

MOTOR SPORTS

BOXING

MISC.

Olympics

Winter Games

Year	No.	Host City	Dates
2010	XXI	Vancouver, Canada	Feb. 12-28
2014	XXII	Sochi, Russia	Feb. 7-23

Summer Games

Year	No.	Host City	Dates
2012	XXX	London, England	July 27-Aug. 12

All-Star Games

Baseball

Year	Site	Date
2009	Busch Stadium, St. Louis	July 14
2010	Angel Stadium, Anaheim	July 13

NBA Basketball

Year	Site	Date
2009	U.S. Airways Center, Phoenix	Feb. 15
2010	New Cowboys Stadium, Dallas	Feb. 14

NFL Pro Bowl

Year	Site	Date
2009	Aloha Stadium, Honolulu	Feb. 8
2010	Aloha Stadium, Honolulu	Feb. 7

NHL Hockey

Year	Site	Date
2009	Bell Centre, Montreal	Jan. 25
2010	no game due to Winter Olympics	

Auto Racing

The Daytona 500 stock car race is usually held on the Sunday before the third Monday in February, while the Indianapolis 500 is usually held on the Sunday of Memorial Day weekend in May. The following dates are tentative.

Year	Daytona 500	Indy 500
2009	Feb. 15	May 24
2010	Feb. 14	May 30
2011	Feb. 20	May 29

NCAA Basketball

Men's Final Four

Year	Site	Dates
2009	Ford Field, Detroit	Apr. 4-6
2010	Lucas Oil Stadium, Indianapolis	Apr. 3-5
2011	Reliant Stadium, Houston	Apr. 2-4

Women's Final Four

Year	Site	Dates
2009	Scottrade Center, St. Louis	Apr. 5-7
2010	Alamodome, San Antonio	Apr. 4-6
2011	Lucas Oil Stadium, Indianapolis	Apr. 3-5

Horse Racing

Triple Crown

The Kentucky Derby is always held at Churchill Downs in Louisville on the first Saturday in May, followed two weeks later by the Preakness Stakes at Pimlico Race Course in Baltimore and three weeks after that by the Belmont Stakes at Belmont Park in Elmont, N.Y.

Year	Ky Derby	Preakness	Belmont
2009	May 2	May 16	June 6
2010	May 1	May 15	June 5
2011	May 7	May 21	June 11

NFL Football

Super Bowl

No.	Site	Date
XLIII	Raymond James Stadium, Tampa, Fla	2009
XLIV	Dolphin Stadium, Miami, Fla.	2010
XLV	New Cowboys Stadium, Dallas	2011
XLVI	Lucas Oil Stadium, Indianapolis	2012

Golf

The Masters

Year	Site	Dates
2009	Augusta (Ga.) National GC	April 9-12
2010	Augusta (Ga.) National GC	Apr. 8-11
2011	Augusta (Ga.) National GC	Apr. 7-10

U.S. Open

Year	Site	Dates
2009	Bethpage, Farmingdale, N.Y.	June 18-21
2010	Pebble Beach, Calif.	June 17-20
2011	Congressional, Bethesda, Md.	June 16-19
2012	Olympic Club, San Francisco	June 14-17

U.S. Women's Open

Year	Site	Dates
2009	Saucon Valley, Bethlehem, Pa.	July 9-12
2010	Oakmont CC, Oakmont, Pa.	July 8-11
2011	Broadmoor, Colo. Springs, Colo.	July 7-10

U.S. Senior Open

Year	Site	Dates
2009	Crooked Stick GC, Carmel, Ind.	July 30-Aug. 2
2010	Sahalee, Redmond, Wash.	July 29-Aug. 1

PGA Championship

Year	Site	Dates
2009	Hazeltine, Chaska, Minn.	Aug. 10-16
2010	Sahalee, Redmond, Wash.	TBD
2011	Atlanta Athletic Club, Duluth, Ga.	TBD
2012	The Ocean Course, Kiawah, S.C.	TBD

British Open

Year	Site	Dates
2009	Turnberry, Scotland	July 16-19
2010	St. Andrews, Scotland	July 15-18

Ryder Cup

Year	Site	Date
2010	Celtic Manor, Wales	Oct. 1-3
2012	Medinah, Country Club	TBD

Soccer

World Cup

Year	Site	Dates
2010	South Africa	June 11-July 11
2014	Brazil	

Women's World Cup

Year	Site	Date
2011	Germany	June 26-July 17

Tennis

U.S. Open

Usually held from the last Monday in August through the second Sunday in Sept., with Labor Day weekend the midway point in the tournament.

Year	Site	Dates
2009	Arthur Ashe Stadium, NYC	Aug. 31-Sept. 13
2010	Arthur Ashe Stadium, NYC	Aug. 30-Sept. 12
2011	Arthur Ashe Stadium, NYC	Aug. 29-Sept. 11
2012	Arthur Ashe Stadium, NYC	Aug. 27-Sept. 9